HALSBURY'S
Laws of England

FIFTH EDITION
2013

Volume 75

This is volume 75 of the Fifth Edition of Halsbury's Laws of England, containing the titles MEDICAL PRODUCTS AND DRUGS and MENTAL HEALTH AND CAPACITY.

The title MEDICAL PRODUCTS AND DRUGS replaces the Fourth Edition title MEDICINAL PRODUCTS AND DRUGS, contained in volume 30(2) (Reissue).

The title MENTAL HEALTH AND CAPACITY replaces the Fourth Edition title MENTAL HEALTH, also contained in volume 30(2) (Reissue).

The Fourth Edition volume 30(2) (Reissue) may now be archived.

For a full list of volumes comprised in a current set of Halsbury's Laws of England please see overleaf.

Fifth Edition volumes:

1 (2008), 2 (2008), 3 (2011), 4 (2011), 6 (2011), 7 (2008), 8 (2010), 9 (2012), 10 (2012), 11 (2009), 12 (2009), 13 (2009), 14 (2009), 15 (2009), 16 (2011), 17 (2011), 18 (2009), 19 (2011), 21 (2011), 22 (2012), 23 (2013), 24 (2010), 25 (2010), 26 (2010), 27 (2010), 28 (2010), 30 (2012), 31 (2012), 32 (2012), 34 (2011), 35 (2011), 36 (2011), 39 (2009), 40 (2009), 41 (2009), 42 (2011), 43 (2011), 44 (2011), 45 (2010), 46 (2010), 48 (2008), 49 (2008), 50 (2008), 52 (2009), 53 (2009), 54 (2008), 55 (2012), 56 (2011), 57 (2012), 60 (2011), 61 (2010), 62 (2012), 63 (2012), 64 (2012), 65 (2008), 66 (2009), 67 (2008), 68 (2008), 69 (2009), 70 (2012), 71 (2013), 72 (2009), 73 (2009), 74 (2011), 75 (2013), 77 (2010), 78 (2010), 79 (2008), 81 (2010), 82 (2010), 83 (2010), 85 (2012), 87 (2012), 88 (2012), 89 (2011), 90 (2011), 91 (2012), 92 (2010), 93 (2008), 94 (2008), 96 (2012), 97 (2010), 99 (2012), 100 (2009), 101 (2009), 102 (2010), 103 (2010)

Fourth Edition volumes (bold figures represent reissues):

1(1) (2001 Reissue), **1(2)** (2007 Reissue), **3(2)** (2002 Reissue), **8(1)** (2003 Reissue), **8(2)**, **12(1)**, **13** (2007 Reissue), **15(3)** (2007 Reissue), **15(4)** (2007 Reissue), **16(2)**, **17(2)**, **18(2)**, **23(1)**, **23(2)**, **24**, **26** (2004 Reissue), **31** (2003 Reissue), **35**, **36(1)** (2007 Reissue), **36(2)**, **39(1A)**, **39(1B)**, **44(2)**, **48** (2007 Reissue), **51**, **52**

Additional Materials:

Criminal Law, Evidence and Procedure (*Investigatory Powers*) containing vol **11(1)** (2006 Reissue) paras 390, 394, 395, 407–415, 420–438, 451, 452, 506–526, vol **11(2)** (2006 Reissue) paras 804–818, 851, 852, 856–902, 908–911, 924–940, 945–1041, vol **11(3)** (2006 Reissue) paras 1086–1088, 1090–1093; *Housing* (*Housing Benefit*) containing vol **22** (2006 Reissue) paras 140–186; *Road Traffic* (*Tramways*) containing vol **40(3)** (2007 Reissue) paras 1532–1634; *Specific Performance* containing vol **44(1)** (Reissue) paras 801–1000; *Tort* (*Conversion and Wrongful Interference with Goods*) containing vol **45(2)** (Reissue) paras 542–686

Fourth and Fifth Edition volumes:

2012 Consolidated Index (A–E), 2012 Consolidated Index (F–O), 2012 Consolidated Index (P–Z), 2013 Consolidated Table of Statutes, 2013 Consolidated Table of Statutory Instruments, etc, 2013 Consolidated Table of Cases (A–L), 2013 Consolidated Table of Cases (M–Z, ECJ Cases)

Updating and ancillary materials:

2013 Annual Cumulative Supplement; Monthly Current Service; Annual Abridgments 1974–2011

March 2013

HALSBURY'S
Laws of England

FIFTH EDITION

LORD MACKAY OF CLASHFERN
Lord High Chancellor of Great Britain
1987–97

Volume 75

2013

Members of the LexisNexis Group worldwide

United Kingdom	LexisNexis, a Division of Reed Elsevier (UK) Ltd, Halsbury House, 35 Chancery Lane, LONDON, WC2A 1EL, and London House, 20–22 East London Street, EDINBURGH, EH7 4BQ
Australia	LexisNexis Butterworths, Chatswood, New South Wales
Austria	LexisNexis Verlag ARD Orac GmbH & Co KG, Vienna
Benelux	LexisNexis Benelux, Amsterdam
Canada	LexisNexis Canada, Markham, Ontario
China	LexisNexis China, Beijing and Shanghai
France	LexisNexis SA, Paris
Germany	LexisNexis GmbH, Dusseldorf
Hong Kong	LexisNexis Hong Kong, Hong Kong
India	LexisNexis India, New Delhi
Italy	Giuffrè Editore, Milan
Japan	LexisNexis Japan, Tokyo
Malaysia	Malayan Law Journal Sdn Bhd, Kuala Lumpur
New Zealand	LexisNexis NZ Ltd, Wellington
Poland	Wydawnictwo Prawnicze LexisNexis Sp, Warsaw
Singapore	LexisNexis Singapore, Singapore
South Africa	LexisNexis Butterworths, Durban
USA	LexisNexis, Dayton, Ohio

FIRST EDITION	*Published in 31 volumes between 1907 and 1917*
SECOND EDITION	*Published in 37 volumes between 1931 and 1942*
THIRD EDITION	*Published in 43 volumes between 1952 and 1964*
FOURTH EDITION	*Published in 56 volumes between 1973 and 1987, with reissues between 1988 and 2008*
FIFTH EDITION	*Commenced in 2008*

A CIP Catalogue record for this book is available from the British Library.

ISBN 13 (complete set, standard binding): 9781405734394

ISBN 13: 9781405763745

ISBN 978-1-4057-6374-5

9 781405 763745

Typeset by Letterpart Ltd, Reigate, Surrey
Printed and bound by CPI Group (UK) Ltd, Croydon, CR0 4YY
Visit LexisNexis at www.lexisnexis.co.uk

Editor in Chief

THE RIGHT HONOURABLE

LORD MACKAY OF CLASHFERN

LORD HIGH CHANCELLOR OF GREAT BRITAIN

1987–97

Editors of this Volume

AMANDA WILLIS, LLM

and

MOHINI TULLOCH, LLM

Commissioning Editor

CLAIRE RAMSBOTTOM, LLB, MSc

Indexer

JAMES A. WARD, BA, LLB,
a Solicitor of the Senior Courts of England and Wales

Managing Editor

HELEN HALVEY, LLB

Publisher

SIMON HETHERINGTON, LLB

MEDICAL PRODUCTS AND DRUGS

Consultant Editor
PETER FELDSCHREIBER, MBBS, FFPM, LLB,
of the Middle Temple, Barrister,
Four New Square Chambers;
Fellow of the Faculty of Pharmaceutical Medicine, Royal College of Physicians;
Senior Medical Assessor, Medicines and Healthcare Products Agency,
Department of Health

MENTAL HEALTH AND CAPACITY

Consultant Editors
ASWINI WEERERATNE, LLM,
of Gray's Inn, Barrister

JEANNIE MACKIE, BA,
of the Inner Temple, Barrister

The law stated in this volume is in general that in force on 1 February 2013,
although subsequent changes have been included wherever possible.

Any future updating material will be found in the Current Service and annual
Cumulative Supplement to Halsbury's Laws of England.

TABLE OF CONTENTS

	PAGE
How to use Halsbury's Laws of England	*11*
References and Abbreviations	*13*
Table of Statutes	*19*
Table of Statutory Instruments	*27*
Table of Civil Procedure	*39*
Table of European Union Legislation	*41*
Table of Command Papers	*43*
Table of Non-Statutory Materials	*45*
Table of Cases	*47*

Volume 75

MEDICAL PRODUCTS AND DRUGS

Table of Contents	1
1. Control of Medical Products	7
2. Medicines etc for Human Use	25
3. Veterinary Medicines	314
4. Blood and Blood Products	348
5. Medical Devices	373
6. Controlled Drugs	387
7. Poisons	444

MENTAL HEALTH AND CAPACITY

Table of Contents	463
1. General Scheme of the Legislation	467
2. Mental Health Services	481
3. Mental Capacity	505

PAGE

4. Court of Protection 605

5. The Public Guardian 632

6. Patients with Mental Disorder... 638

7. Applications to Tribunals 850

8. Litigation... 882

9. Offences... 891

Index.. 899

HOW TO USE HALSBURY'S LAWS OF ENGLAND

Volumes

Each text volume of Halsbury's Laws of England contains the law on the titles contained in it as at a date stated at the front of the volume (the operative date).

Information contained in Halsbury's Laws of England may be accessed in several ways.

First, by using the tables of contents.

Each volume contains both a general Table of Contents, and a specific Table of Contents for each title contained in it. From these tables you will be directed to the relevant part of the work.

Readers should note that the current arrangement of titles can be found in the Current Service.

Secondly, by using tables of statutes, statutory instruments, cases or other materials.

If you know the name of the Act, statutory instrument or case with which your research is concerned, you should consult the Consolidated Tables of statutes, cases and so on (published as separate volumes) which will direct you to the relevant volume and paragraph. The Consolidated Tables will indicate if the volume referred to is a Fifth Edition volume.

(Each individual text volume also includes tables of those materials used as authority in that volume.)

Thirdly, by using the indexes.

If you are uncertain of the general subject area of your research, you should go to the Consolidated Index (published as separate volumes) for reference to the relevant volume(s) and paragraph(s). The Consolidated Index will indicate if the volume referred to is a Fifth Edition volume.

(Each individual text volume also includes an index to the material contained therein.)

Additional Materials

The reorganisation of the title scheme of Halsbury's Laws for the Fifth Edition means that from time to time Fourth Edition volumes will be *partially* replaced by Fifth Edition volumes.

In certain instances an Additional Materials softbound book will be issued, in which will be reproduced material which has not yet been replaced by a Fifth Edition title. This will enable users to remove specific Fourth Edition volumes from the shelf and save valuable space pending the replacement of that material in the Fifth Edition. These softbound books are supplied to volumes subscribers free of charge. They continue to form part of the set of Halsbury's Laws Fourth Edition Reissue, and will be updated by the annual Cumulative Supplement and monthly Noter-Up in the usual way.

Updating publications

The text volumes of Halsbury's Laws should be used in conjunction with the annual Cumulative Supplement and the monthly Noter-Up.

The annual Cumulative Supplement

The Supplement gives details of all changes between the operative date of the text volume and the operative date of the Supplement. It is arranged in the same volume, title and paragraph order as the text volumes. Developments affecting particular points of law are noted to the relevant paragraph(s) of the text volumes. As from the commencement of the Fifth Edition, the Supplement will clearly distinguish between Fourth and Fifth Edition titles.

For narrative treatment of material noted in the Cumulative Supplement, go to the Annual Abridgment volume for the relevant year.

Destination Tables

In certain titles in the annual *Cumulative Supplement,* reference is made to Destination Tables showing the destination of consolidated legislation. Those Destination Tables are to be found either at the end of the titles within the annual *Cumulative Supplement,* or in a separate *Destination Tables* booklet provided from time to time with the *Cumulative Supplement.*

The Noter-Up

The Noter-Up is contained in the Current Service Noter-Up booklet, issued monthly and noting changes since the publication of the annual Cumulative Supplement. Also arranged in the same volume, title and paragraph order as the text volumes, the Noter-Up follows the style of the Cumulative Supplement. As from the commencement of the Fifth Edition, the Noter-Up will clearly distinguish between Fourth and Fifth Edition titles.

For narrative treatment of material noted in the Noter-Up, go to the relevant Monthly Review.

REFERENCES AND ABBREVIATIONS

ACT	Australian Capital Territory
A-G	Attorney General
Admin	Administrative Court
Admlty	Admiralty Court
Adv-Gen	Advocate General
affd	affirmed
affg	affirming
Alta	Alberta
App	Appendix
art	article
Aust	Australia
B	Baron
BC	British Columbia
C	Command Paper (of a series published before 1900)
c	chapter number of an Act
CA	Court of Appeal
CAC	Central Arbitration Committee
CA in Ch	Court of Appeal in Chancery
CB	Chief Baron
CCA	Court of Criminal Appeal
CCR	County Court Rules 1981 (SI 1981/1687) as subsequently amended
CCR	Court for Crown Cases Reserved
C-MAC	Courts-Martial Appeal Court
CO	Crown Office
COD	Crown Office Digest
CPR	Civil Procedure Rules 1998 (SI 1998/3132) as subsequently amended (see the Civil Court Practice)
Can	Canada
Cd	Command Paper (of the series published 1900–18)
Cf	compare
Ch	Chancery Division
ch	chapter
cl	clause

Cm	Command Paper (of the series published 1986 to date)
Cmd	Command Paper (of the series published 1919–56)
Cmnd	Command Paper (of the series published 1956–86)
Comm	Commercial Court
Comr	Commissioner
Court Forms (2nd Edn)	Atkin's Encyclopaedia of Court Forms in Civil Proceedings, 2nd Edn. See note 2 post.
Court Funds Rules 1987	Court Funds Rules 1987 (SI 1987/821) as subsequently amended
CrimPR	Criminal Procedure Rules 2010 (SI 2010/60) as subsequently amended
DC	Divisional Court
DPP	Director of Public Prosecutions
EAT	Employment Appeal Tribunal
EC	European Community
ECJ	Court of Justice of the European Community
EComHR	European Commission of Human Rights
ECSC	European Coal and Steel Community
ECtHR Rules of Court	Rules of Court of the European Court of Human Rights
EEC	European Economic Community
EFTA	European Free Trade Association
EWCA Civ	Official neutral citation for judgments of the Court of Appeal (Civil Division)
EWCA Crim	Official neutral citation for judgments of the Court of Appeal (Criminal Division)
EWHC	Official neutral citation for judgments of the High Court
Edn	Edition
Euratom	European Atomic Energy Community
Ex Ch	Court of Exchequer Chamber
ex p	ex parte
Fam	Family Division
Fed	Federal
Forms & Precedents (5th Edn)	Encyclopaedia of Forms and Precedents other than Court Forms, 5th Edn. See note 2 post.
GLC	Greater London Council
HC	High Court
HC	House of Commons
HK	Hong Kong
HL	House of Lords

IAT	Immigration Appeal Tribunal
ILM	International Legal Materials
INLR	Immigration and Nationality Law Reports
IRC	Inland Revenue Commissioners
Ind	India
Int Rels	International Relations
Ir	Ireland
J	Justice
JA	Judge of Appeal
Kan	Kansas
LA	Lord Advocate
LC	Lord Chancellor
LCC	London County Council
LCJ	Lord Chief Justice
LJ	Lord Justice of Appeal
LoN	League of Nations
MR	Master of the Rolls
Man	Manitoba
n	note
NB	New Brunswick
NI	Northern Ireland
NS	Nova Scotia
NSW	New South Wales
NY	New York
NZ	New Zealand
OHIM	Office for Harmonisation in the Internal Market
OJ	The Official Journal of the European Community published by the Office for Official Publications of the European Community
Ont	Ontario
P	President
PC	Judicial Committee of the Privy Council
PEI	Prince Edward Island
Pat	Patents Court
q	question
QB	Queen's Bench Division
QBD	Queen's Bench Division of the High Court
Qld	Queensland
Que	Quebec
r	rule
RDC	Rural District Council
RPC	Restrictive Practices Court

RSC	Rules of the Supreme Court 1965 (SI 1965/1776) as subsequently amended
reg	regulation
Res	Resolution
revsd	reversed
Rly	Railway
s	section
SA	South Africa
S Aust	South Australia
SC	Supreme Court
SI	Statutory Instruments published by authority
SR & O	Statutory Rules and Orders published by authority
SR & O Rev 1904	Revised Edition comprising all Public and General Statutory Rules and Orders in force on 31 December 1903
SR & O Rev 1948	Revised Edition comprising all Public and General Statutory Rules and Orders and Statutory Instruments in force on 31 December 1948
SRNI	Statutory Rules of Northern Ireland
STI	Simon's Tax Intelligence (1973–1995); Simon's Weekly Tax Intelligence (1996-current)
Sask	Saskatchewan
Sch	Schedule
Sess	Session
Sing	Singapore
TCC	Technology and Construction Court
TS	Treaty Series
Tanz	Tanzania
Tas	Tasmania
UDC	Urban District Council
UKHL	Official neutral citation for judgments of the House of Lords
UKPC	Official neutral citation for judgments of the Privy Council
UN	United Nations
V-C	Vice-Chancellor
Vict	Victoria
W Aust	Western Australia
Zimb	Zimbabwe

NOTE 1. A general list of the abbreviations of law reports and other sources used in this work can be found at the beginning of the Consolidated Table of Cases.

NOTE 2. Where references are made to other publications, the volume number precedes and the page number follows the name of the publication; eg the reference '12 Forms & Precedents (5th Edn) 44' refers to volume 12 of the Encyclopaedia of Forms and Precedents, page 44.

NOTE 3. An English statute is cited by short title or, where there is no short title, by regnal year and chapter number together with the name by which it is commonly known or a description of its subject matter and date. In the case of a foreign statute, the mode of citation generally follows the style of citation in use in the country concerned with the addition, where necessary, of the name of the country in parentheses.

NOTE 4. A statutory instrument is cited by short title, if any, followed by the year and number, or, if unnumbered, the date.

TABLE OF STATUTES

PARA

C

Crime (Sentences) Act 1997
s 47 (1)(a) 864
    (b) 863
    (c) 892
    (2)(a) 864
    (b) 892

Criminal Appeal Act 1968
s 6 874
  14 874–875
  16 (3) 879, 894
Sch 3 para 2 894

Criminal Justice Act 1967
s 72 921

Criminal Justice Act 1993
s 73 (1), (2) 480

Criminal Justice Act 2003
s 51A (3)(d) 897

Criminal Procedure (Insanity) Act 1964
s 5 874

H

Health Act 2006
s 17 514
  18 515
  20 516
  21 527
  22 517
  23 518
  24 514

Health and Social Care Act 2008
s 52 (1)–(3) 573
  126
Sch 2 573

Health Services and Public Health Act 1968
s 66 (1) 569

L

Local Authority Social Services Act 1970
s 1 579
  7A 568
  7D, 7E 568

M

Medicines Act 1968
s 10 (1) 52, 150
  (3), (4) 52, 150
  (5) 150
  (6) 52
  (7A)–(7C) 52
  15 (3) 150
  58 (1) 272
  (4) 272
  (7) 272
  58A 273
  60 382

PARA

Medicines Act 1968—*continued*
s 62 (1)–(7) 307
  64 235
  67 (1A), (1B) 272
  (2) 235, 307
  (4) 235, 307
  87 (1)–(3) 314
  88 331
  91 (2) 331
  (3) 314
  104 (1) 28
  105 (1) 28
  108 354
  111 355
  112 356
  (9) 235
  113 356
  114 (1) 355
  (2), (3) 358
  115A 357
  118 359
  119 360
  121 372
  122, 123 373
  124 375
  125 376
  126 377
  128 (5) 354
  129 27
  130 (1) 25
  133 29
Sch 3 para 1–4 357
  8–14 357
  18–27 357
  28 356
  29 .... 235, 356

Medicines Act 1971
s 1 30

Mental Capacity Act 2005
s 2 (1)–(4) 603
  (5), (6) 604
  3 605
  4 606
  4A 648
  4B 650
  5, 6 611
  7 613
  8 611
  9, 10 619
  12 620
  13, 14 621
  15 723
  16 (1) 724, 734
  (2)(a) 724
  (b) 734
  (3)–(8) 734

PARA

Mental Capacity Act 2005—*continued*

s 16A	726
17	726
18	727
19 (1)–(7)	735
(8), (9)	736
20 (1)	737
(2)(a), (b)	738
(3)(a)	738
(b), (c)	736
(4)–(6)	736
(7)–(11)	738
21	745
21A	733
22, 23	622
24	624
25	625
26	626
27	627
28 (1), (1A)	925
(1B)	611
(2)	925
29	629
30	630
31	631
32	632
33	633
34	630
35	635
36	637
37	638
38	639
(7)	577
39	640
39A (1), (2)	640
(4)–(6)	642
39B	642
39C	643
39D, 39E	644
40	645
41	646
42, 43	602
44	1011
45, 46	720
47	721
48	725
49	744
50, 51	740
52	741
53	750
54	746
55	747
56	746–747
57	751
58	752
59	756
60	752
61	748
64 (5), (6)	648
66 (1)(b)	618
(2)–(4)	618
Sch A1 para 1–4	651

PARA

Mental Capacity Act 2005—*continued*

Sch A1 para 6	661
7	658, 663
9	713
12	653
13	654, 658
14	655, 658
15	656
16	657
17	658
20	660
21–23	663
24	661
25, 26	662
27	661
28	661–662
29	666
30	667
31, 32	668
33	669
34	671
35, 36	672
37	673
38–45	674
46	675
48	676
49	670
50	663
51, 52	665
54–56	665
57, 58	677
59	678
60, 61	665
62 (1)(a)	662
(b)	667
(2), (3)	662, 667
63–65	665
66	677
68–73	679
74–77	713
78–81	714
82, 83	715
84–87	716
88–90	714
91–93	680
94–96	681
97	680
98–100	682
101–103	683
104	684
105	685
106	686
107	687
108, 109	688
110	684
111	690
112–114	689
115	691
116	692
117	693
118	694
119	683, 687, 689, 691–692

PARA

Mental Capacity Act 2005—*continued*

Sch A1 para 120, 121	683
122–124	689
127	695
129 (1)–(3)	695
(4)–(6)	696
130	695
131	705
132, 133	706
134–136	705
137	707
138 (1)	707–708
139–142	707
143	708
144 (1)(a)	708
(b)	707
(2)	707–708
145	707
146	708
147	712
149–153	707
155	705
156, 157	670
159	683, 688
160, 161	707
162–168	717
169 ... 665, 677, 680–682, 688, 705–706, 714, 716	
170–173	717
175	577
176–179	652
180–184	664
186, 187	665
1A para 1–5	658
8	658
10, 11	658
12	659
16	658
17 (1)	577
18, 19	660
2 para 1–4	731
5, 6	730
7	728
8, 9	729
10	727

Mental Health Act 1959

s 8	557
131 (1)	584
142	568
152	557

Mental Health Act 1983

s 1	761
2	767
3	768
4	769
5	770
6 (1), (2)	771
(3)	772
(4)	773
7 (1)–(4)	785
(5)	787, 848
8 (1), (2)	787

PARA

Mental Health Act 1983—*continued*

s 8 (3)	788
(4)	789
(5)	787
9	790
10 (1)	794
(3)	796
(4)	890
11	847
(2)	848
(3), (4)	821
(7)	767, 849
12 (1)	849
(2), (2A)	849
(3)	849
12ZA–12ZC	570
12A	825
13 (1)	821
(1A)–1C)	821
(2)–(5)	821
14	582
15 (1)	774
(2)–(4)	775
17	917
17A	797
17B	800
17C	799
17D	798
17E	801
17F	802
17G	803
18 (1)	918
(2A)	918
(3)	793
(4)	918
(4A), (4B)	918
(5)	918
(7)	918
19 (1)	886
(a)	887
(b)	888–889
(2)	890
(3)	887
19A	804
20 (1)	768, 908
(2)	768, 909
(3), (4)	910
(5), (5A)	910
(6)–(8)	910
20A, 20B	799
21 (1)–(4)	911
21A, 21B	911
22	912
23 (1)	913
(1A), (1B)	913
(2)	913
(4)	913
24 (1), (2)	916
25	915
26 (1), (2)	838
(3)	838–839
(4), (5)	839

PARA

Mental Health Act 1983—*continued*

s 26 (6) 838–839
   (7) 838
   27, 28 839
   29 842
   30 (1), (1A) 844
      (2), (2A) 843
      (3) 843–844
      (4) 845
      (4A), (4B) 845
      (5) 843–844
   31 846
   32 .... 766, 784
      (1) 765
      (2)(d) 765
      (3) 766, 784
   33 (1), (2) 786, 847
      (3), (4) 786
   34 (1) 834
      (2) 578
      (3) 791
         (b) 910
   35, 36 862
   37 (1) 864, 877
      (1A) 864
      (2) 864
         (a)(ii) 877
         (b) 877
      (3) 871
      (4) 864
      (5) 868
      (6) 877
      (8) 866
   38 864
      (7) 867
   39 864
   39A 877
   40 867
      (3) 867
      (4) 860, 867, 870, 961
      (5) 867, 878
      (6) 867
   41 869
      (3) 860
      (4) 867, 878
      (5) 860, 870
      (6) 876
   42 (1) 876
      (2) 876, 914
      (3) 876
      (4), (5) 876, 914
      (6) 876
   43 873
   44 873
      (3) 861
   45 880
   45A 863
   45A (3) 864
      (8) 576
   45B 863
   47 892
   48 893

PARA

Mental Health Act 1983—*continued*

s 49 894
   (2) 861
   (3) 876
   50 895
      (2) 894
   51 896
      (7) 873
   52 897
   53 898
   54 865
   54A 864
   55 (4) 861
   56 924
   57 928
   58 930
   59 .... 928, 930
   60 929
   61 933
   62 932
   62A 934
   63 927
   64 (1) 834
      (1A), (1B) 831
      (1C) 766
      (2) 928
      (3) 930
   64A, 64B 935
   64C (1), (2) 938
      (3) 935
      (4) 936
      (4A), (4B) 936
      (5)–(9) 937
   64D 939
   64E 940
   64F 941
   64FA 942
   64G 937
   64G (1)–(4) 943
   64H 944
   64I, 64J 939, 941
   64K (1)–(5) 935
   65 957
   66 (1) 960
      (e) 889
      (2) 960
      (e) 889
      (2A) 960
      (3) 960
      (4) 955
      (5) 960
   67 (1) 965
      (2) 963
   68 (1)–(3) 964
      (5)–(7) 964
      (8) 963
      (9) 964
   68A 964
   69 961
   70 962
   71 (1) 876, 965
      (2) 965

PARA

Mental Health Act 1983—*continued*

s 71 (3), (3A)	965
(4)	965
72 (1)	967
(3)	968
(4)	967
73	969
74	970
75 (1)(a)	965
(b)	962
(2)	962
(3)	971
76	963
77 (1), (2)	959
(3)	972
(4)	962
78	980
78A	958
80 (1)	899
80ZA	899
80A	899
80B	900
80C	901
80D	902
81ZA	903
81, 81A	903
82, 82A	904
83ZA	906
83, 83A	906
84	905
85, 85A	905
86	907
87	920
89	920
91 (1)	903, 907–908
(2)	907
(2A)	903
92 (4)	903, 905–906
(5)	903
114ZA (1), (2)	819
(3)	820
114	815
114A (1), (2)	819
(4)	820
(5)	819
115	820
116	583
117 (1), (2)	945
(2B)–(2G)	945
(3)	945
118 (1), (1A)	762
(2A), (2B)	762
(2D)	762
(3)	762
(7)	762
119 (1), (2)	928
120	806
120A–120C	806
120D (1), (2)	806
(5)	806
122	594, 783
126 (1)–(3)	1008

PARA

Mental Health Act 1983—*continued*

s 126 (4)	1009
(5)	1008
127 (1)–(4)	1010
128 (1), (2)	1013
(3)	1014
(4)	1013
129	1015
130	584
130A	807
130B	808
130C	807
130D	811
130E	807
130F	809
130G	810
130H	812
130I, 130J	807
130K, 130L	811
131 (1)	764
(2)–(5)	765
131A (1)(b)	765
(2)–(4)	765
132	779
132A	805
133	913
134, 134A	780
135 (1)	922
(3A), (3B)	922
(4)	922
136	923
137	776
138	777
(5)	867
(6)	911
139	759
140	576
141	782
142A	833
142B	575
144	557
145 (3)	860
(4)	926
146, 147	557
Sch 1 Pt I	860, 870
I para 2	918
4	918
9	961
II	860
2	957

Mental Health (Amendment) Act 1982

s 34	557
65	557
70	557

Mental Health (Approval Functions) Act 2012 ... 849

Mental Health (Care and Treatment) (Scotland) Act 2003 ... 557

Mental Health (Discrimination) Act 2013

s 1(2)	782

PARA

Mental Health (Wales) Measure 2010

s 1, 2 586
3 589
4 588
5 587
6–8 881
9 883
10 885
13, 14 851
15 852
16 853
17 854
18 855
19–21 950
22, 23 947
24 948
25 949
26 (1) 947
(2), (3) 951
27 953
28 954
29 952
30 947
41 590
42 591
44 (1)–(4) 763
(8) 763
45 586
46 950
47 (1)(a) 883
(b) 853
(2), (3) 853, 883
48 757
49 586
50 587
55 757

Misuse of Drugs Act 1971

s 1 490
2 481
2A, 2B 482
3 491
7 502
7A 503
11 507
12 519
13 520
14 521
15 522
16 (2)–(4) 521–522
17 510
18 504
22 487
23 (1) 523
(3A) 523
(4) 523
25 (1), (2) 520, 523
(4) 525
27 526
29 489
30 (1) 488
31 486
32 480

PARA

Misuse of Drugs Act 1971—*continued*

s 37 (2) 490
39 (3) 480
50 (5) 491
68 (4) 491
170 (4) 491
Sch 1 490
para 1 491
2 Pt I 483
II 484
III 485
3 para 17–20 522
4 .... 520, 523

N

National Health Service Act 2006

s 1H (2), (3) 571
1I (1), (2) 572
3A (1) 572
12A (4), (5) 946
Sch 20 para 2 581

**National Health Service and Community
Care Act 1990**

s 60 480

**National Health Service (Wales)
Act 2006**

Sch 15 para 2 581

P

Poisons Act 1972

s 1 (1) 530
2 530
(3) 533
3 (1)(a) 538
(i)–(iii) 539
(b)(i) 538
(ii) 538, 540
(c) 544
(2) 541
(3) 538
4 546
5 (1), (2) 535
(3)–(5) 536
6 535
(3) 536
(4) 537
7 534
8 (1) 541, 552
(2) 553
(3) 554
(4) 555
9 (4) 548
(5), (5A) 549
(6), (7) 550
(8) 551
(9) 548, 550
10 (2) 530
11 (2) 534
13 (3) 546
Sch 1 530

PARA

S

Social Security Contributions and
   Benefits Act 1992
  s 113 (1)(b) 593

T

Trial of Lunatics Act 1883
  s 2 874

PARA

V

Vaccine Damage Payments Act 1979
  s 1, 2 384
  3, 3A 385
  4 385
  5 (4) 385
  6, 7 386
  7A, 7B 385
  9 (1) 385
  12 (2), (3) 385

TABLE OF STATUTORY INSTRUMENTS

PARA

B

Blood Safety and Quality
  Regulations 2005, SI 2005/50
  reg 2 (2) 449
    (4) 449
    3, 4 453
    5 454
    6 455
    7 456
    8 457
    9, 10 458
    11 459
    12 460
    12A 461
    12B 462
    13 450
    14 463
    15 464
    16 466
    16A 467
    17 465
    18, 19 469
    20 471
    21 470
    22 (1) 452
      (2)(a) 453
      (c) 453
      (3B)–(3D) 458
      (5B), (5C) 452
      (5E), (5F) 452
      (7)(ii)(a), (b) 458
      (8), (9) 452
    23 451
  Schedule Pt 4 458
    7 462

C

Child Benefit and Children's Allowance
  (Administration) Regulations 2003,
  SI 2003/492 593
Children (Secure Accommodation)
  Regulations 1991, SI 1991/1505
  reg 5 765
Controlled Drugs (Supervision of
  Management and Use)
  Regulations 2013, SI 2013/373 ... 514–516
Controlled Drugs (Supervision of
  Management and Use) (Wales)
  Regulations 2008, SI 2008/3239 514–516
Court of Protection Fees Order 2007,
  SI 2007/1745 746
Court of Protection Rules 2007,
  SI 2007/1744
  r 3–5 .... 740, 742
  7, 7A 720

PARA

Court of Protection Rules 2007,
  SI 2007/1744—*continued*
  r 9 742
    10–72 740
    73–76 743
    77–81 740
    82, 82A 740
    83–155 740
    156–168 .... 740, 747
    169–180 .... 740, 750
    181 .... 720, 740, 750
    182 .... 740, 750
    200 .... 735, 740
    202 .... 728, 740
    203 740
Criminal Justice Act 2003
  (Commencement No 9)
  Order 2005, SI 2005/1267
  Schedule Pt 1 para 1 (1)(k) 897
Criminal Justice Act 2003
  (Commencement No 28 and Saving
  Provisions) Order 2012,
  SI 2012/1320
  art 4 (1)(a) 897
    (c) 873
      (iii), (iv) 897
    (2), (3) 873
Criminal Procedure Rules 2011,
  SI 2011/1709
  r 42.9 877

H

Health and Social Care Act 2008 (NHS
  Blood and Transplant Periodic
  Review) Regulations 2009,
  SI 2009/3049
  reg 2 468
Health and Social Care Act 2008
  (Regulated Activities)
  Regulations 2010, SI 2010/781
  Sch 1 para 6 760
    8 478
    9 (1)(a), (b) 468
    15 479
Health and Social Care Act 2012
  (Commencement No 2 and
  Transitional, Savings and Transitory
  Provisions) Order 2012,
  SI 2012/1831
  art 2 (2) 571
Human Medicines Regulations 2012,
  SI 2012/1916
  reg 2 (1), (2) 25
    3 (1) 48
    (2) 49
    (3) 25

PARA

Human Medicines Regulations 2012,
SI 2012/1916—*continued*

reg 3 (4) 48
   (5) 48–49
   (6) 51
   (7) 25
   (8), (9) 48–49
   (10)–(12) 317
   (14) 317
  4 318
   (1) 52, 150
   (2), (3) 318
   (5), (6) 318
  5 26
  6 35
  7 333
  8 (6) 47
  10 (1)–(4) 31
  11 32
  12 (1)–(3) 31–32
  14 33
  17 (1) 45
   (3), (4) 47
   (5), (6) 46
  18 (1)–(3) 77
   (4)–(6) 78
   (7)–(10) 77
  20 50
  21 .... 53, 80
  22 (1) 54
   (2) 81
  23 (1)–(3) 37
   (4), (5) 38
   (6) 39
  24 (1) 61, 66, 68–69, 84, 86–87, 90,
                          94–96
   (2) 61, 66, 68, 84, 86–87, 90, 94,
                                96
  25 37
  26 (1), (2) 40
   (3)(a) 41–42
    (b) 41
    (c) 42
   (4)(a)–(d) 41–42
   (5) 41
   (6) 42
  27 40
  28 43
  29 44
  30 38
  31 55
  32 270
  33 (1) 76
  34 (2), (3) 38
   (4), (5) 45
  35 (1) 38, 76
   (2) 38
  36 (1) 56–57, 62–65, 67
   (2) 56, 62, 67, 69
   (3) 69–75
  37 (1) 62–65
   (2), (3) 62

PARA

Human Medicines Regulations 2012,
SI 2012/1916—*continued*

reg 37 (4) 63
   (5) 64
   (6) 63
  38 (1)–(3) 67
  39, 40 56
  41 57
  42 (1) 82–90
   (2) 82, 85, 87, 89
   (3) 91–94
  43 (1) 82
   (2) 83
   (3), (4) 84
   (5), (6) 85
   (7) 86
   (8) 87
   (9) 88
  44 89
  45 90
  46, 47 141
  48 (1), (2) 155
  49 156
  50–54 157
  56, 57 157
  58 158
  59 160
  60 161
  61 162
  62 163
  63 253
  64 164
  65 165
  66 159
  67 166
  68 167
  69 168
  70 167
  71 169
  72 170
  73 171
  74 172
  75 173
  76 174
  77 175
  78 176
  79 177
  80 178
  81, 82 179
  84–86 179
  87, 88 180
  89, 90 181
  92, 93 182
  94 181
  95 183
  96 184
  97 185
  98 186
  101 (1), (2) 186
   (3), (4) 171, 180, 182–184
  102 187
  103 188

PARA

Human Medicines Regulations 2012,
  SI 2012/1916—*continued*
reg 104 189
    105 191
    106 192
    107 193
    108 190
    109 194
    110 195
    111 (1), (2) 195
    112 196
    113 197
    114 198
    115 199
    116 200
    117 201
    118 202
    119 203
    120 204
    121 205
    122 203–205
    123 203
    124 (1), (2) 205
        (3), (4) 197, 202–204
    125 206
    126 207
    127 208
    128 209
    129 210
    130 211
    131 213
    132 214
    133 212
    134 215
    135 216
    136 217
    137 216–217
    138 218
    139 216
    140 219
    141 220
    142 221
    143 222
    144 223
    145 224
    146 225
    147 226
    148 227
    149 228
    150 229
    152 (2), (3) 231
    153 228–231
    155 (1), (2) 231
        (3), (4) 221, 227, 229–230
    156 232
    157 233
    158 232
    159 151
    160–162 152
    163 153
    164 154
    165 151

PARA

Human Medicines Regulations 2012,
  SI 2012/1916—*continued*
reg 166 154
    167 142
    168 143
    169 144
    170 145
    171 146
    172 147
    173 148
    174 149
    175 (1), (2) 142
        (3) 145
    176 .... 142, 145
    177 (1) 241
        (4) 241
    178 242
    179 243
    180 244
    181 245
    182 246
    183 247
    184 248
    185 249
    186 250
    187 249
    188 251
    189, 190 252
    191 253
    192 254
    193 255
    194 256
    195 257
    196 258
    197 259
    198 260
    199 261
    200 262
    201 263
    202 264
    203 265
    204 266
    205 267
    206 268
    207, 208 269
    211 269
    212 ... 246, 250–251, 254, 260–264, 269
    214 271
    215, 216 274
    217 275
    218 276
    219 (1) 275–276
        (2) 275
        (3) 276
        (4) 275–276
    220 277
    221 278
    222 279
    223 280
    224 281
    225 282
    226 283

PARA

Human Medicines Regulations 2012,
  SI 2012/1916—*continued*

reg 227 284
    228 285
    229 286
    230 287
    231 288
    232 289
    233 290
    234 291
    235 (1), (2) 292
       (4)–(7) 293
    236 294
    237 295
    238 296
    239 297
    240 298
    241 299
    242 300
    243 301
    244 302
    245 303
    246 304
    247 305
    248 306
    249, 250 79
    251, 252 236
    254 (1) 378
    255 (1) 379
       (2)–(4) 380
       (5) 379–380
       (6)–(8) 379
    257, 258 319
    259 320
    260 321
    261 322
    262 323
    263 324
    264 325
    265 326
    266 327
    267 328
    268, 269 329
    270 330
    271 329–330
    273 315
    274 316
    275 332
    276 .... 315, 332
    279, 280 334
    281 335
    282–292 336
    293 337
    294 338
    295 339
    296 .... 336, 338
    297 340
    298 341
    299 342
    300 343
    301 344
    302 345

PARA

Human Medicines Regulations 2012,
  SI 2012/1916—*continued*

reg 303 .... 334–339, 343–345
    304 346
    305–307 347
    308 346–347
    309 348
    310 349
    311 351
    312 352
    313 353
    314 350
    315 .... 346, 350–351
    316 346
    317 237
    318 238
    319 239
    320 (1), (2) 237
       (3) 240
    321 240
    322 361
    323 362
    325 363
    326 364
    327, 328 365
    329 366
    330 367
    331 368
    332 369
    333 370
    334 (1) 363–364
       (2) 364
       (3)–(8) 371
    335 372
    336 373
    337 374
    338 375
    339 376
       (4) 362
       (6) 362
    340 377
    341 35
    342 31
    345 36
    346 34
Sch 1 26
   2 33
   3 para 1, 2 53
       3 80
       4 .... 53, 80
   4 para 1 61
       9 .... 61, 69
      10–14 61
      15–23 66
      24 68–69
      25, 26 68
      27 69
      28 .... 84, 91
      29 84
      30 91
      31 95
      32 .... 87, 96

PARA

Human Medicines Regulations 2012,
SI 2012/1916—*continued*
Sch 4 para 33–36 94
        37 86
        38 94
        39 87
        40 96
        41 87
        44 92
    5 40
    6 para 1 69–75
        2 70
        5 72
        6 73
        7 74
        8 69
        10, 11 69
        12 75
        13 91–94
        14, 15 91
        16 92
        17 93
        18, 19 92
        20 94
    7 para 1–8 59
        9–11 60
        12–15 58
    8, 9 157
    11 .... 195, 211–212, 216–217
    12 209
    13 .... 271, 274
    14 274
    15 278
    16 Pt 1, 2 286
        4 286
    17 Pt 1–3 292
        4, 5 293
    19 296
    20 Pt 1 299
    21 300
    22 79
    23 para 2 281
    25 Pt 1 319
    26 para 1–4 317–318
    28 325
    29 326
    33 .... 246, 254, 260, 262–263
        para 5–8 250
            9, 10 253

I

Ionising Radiation (Medical Exposure)
Regulations 2000, SI 2000/1059
reg 7 (5), (6) 382

Isles of Scilly (Mental Health)
Order 1985, SI 1985/149 557

PARA

L

Lasting Powers of Attorney, Enduring
Powers of Attorney and Public
Guardian Regulations 2007,
SI 2007/1253
reg 30–32 753
    33–37 755
    38–40 736
    41, 42 739
    43, 44 752
    44 749
    45 734
    46, 47 .... 752, 754
    48 754

M

Medical Devices (Consultation
Requirements) (Fees)
Regulations 1995, SI 1995/449 472
Medical Devices Regulations 2002,
SI 2002/618
reg 3 472
    4 (2) 473
    5 (1) 473
    6 (a) 473
    7–18 473
    19, 19A 473
    22–31 474
    33–36 475
    38–44 475
    45–51 476
    53 .... 473, 475
    54, 55 476
    57, 58 .... 473, 475–476
    60 475
    61 477
    65 477

Medicines (Administration of
Radioactive Substances)
Regulations 1978, SI 1978/1006
reg 2 (1), (2) 382
Medicines (Aristolochia and Mu Tong
etc) (Prohibition) Order 2001,
SI 2001/1841 311
Medicines (Bal Jivan Chamcho
Prohibition) (No 2) Order 1977,
SI 1977/670 308
Medicines (Certificates of Analysis)
Regulations 1977, SI 1977/1399 357
Medicines (Chloroform Prohibition)
Order 1979, SI 1979/382 310
Medicines (Control of Substances for
Manufacture) Order 1971,
SI 1971/1200 28
Medicines (Control of Substances for
Manufacture) Order 1985,
SI 1985/1403 28
Medicines (Cyanogenetic Substances)
Order 1984, SI 1984/187 28
Medicines (Dental Filling Substances)
Order 1975, SI 1975/533 28

PARA

Medicines for Human Use (Clinical
  Trials) Regulations 2004,
  SI 2004/1031

reg 3 107
   3A 108
   4 109
   5 110
   6–8 111
   10 110
   12 112
   13 113
   14 114
   15 115
   16 116
   17 117
   18 118
   19 119
   20 120
   21 121
   22 122–123
   23 122
   24 123
   25 124
   26 125
   27 135
   27A 110
   28 126
   29 127
   29A 128
   30 129
   31 130
   31A 131
   32 132
   33 133
   34 133
     (1) 118, 132
   35 134
     (1) 118
   36 (1) 97
     (2) 98
   37 98
     (7) 125
   38 99
   39 100
   40 (1)–(4) 101
     (5) 102
     (6) 101
   41 103
   43 104
   44 105
     (6) 102
   45 106
     (3) 102
   46 136
   47, 48 137
   49 (1)(a) 108
     (aa) 112
     (b) 113
     (c) 135
     (d) 126
     (e) 127
     (ee) 128

PARA

Medicines for Human Use (Clinical Trials)
  Regulations 2004,
  SI 2004/1031—*continued*

reg 49 (1)(f) 129
     (ff) 131
     (g) 132
     (h), (i) 133
     (j) 134
     (k) 97
     (l) 103
     (m) 104
    (2) 113
    (5) 97
    (6) 136
   50 138
    (1)(a) 114
     (b) 117
     (c) 99, 105
    (3) 104
    (4) 114
   51 139
   52 140
  Sch 1 126
    2 para 3–13 111
    3 Pt I 114
    4 para 1–5 116
    5 para 1 125
         2 .... 125, 130
         3 130
    6 99
    8 para 2–6 102
    9 137

Medicines for Human Use (Kava-kava)
  (Prohibition) Order 2002,
  SI 2002/3170 312

Medicines for Human Use (Prohibition)
  (Senecio and Miscellaneous
  Amendments) Order 2008,
  SI 2008/548 313

Medicines (Products for Human Use)
  (Fees) Regulations 2012,
  SI 2012/504 .... 30, 156

Medicines (Prohibition of Non-medicinal
  Antimicrobial Substances)
  Order 1977, SI 1977/2131 309

Medicines (Radioactive Substances)
  Order 1978, SI 1978/1004 .... 28, 381

Medicines (Specified Articles and
  Substances) Order 1976,
  SI 1976/968 28

Medicines (Surgical Materials)
  Order 1971, SI 1971/1267 28

Mental Capacity Act 2005 (Appropriate
  Body) (England) Regulations 2006,
  SI 2006/2810 630

Mental Capacity Act 2005 (Appropriate
  Body) (Wales) Regulations 2007,
  SI 2007/833 630

PARA

Mental Capacity Act 2005 (Independent
  Mental Capacity Advocates)
  (Expansion of Role)
  Regulations 2006, SI 2006/2883
  reg 2, 3 635
      4, 5 641
Mental Capacity Act 2005 (Independent
  Mental Capacity Advocates)
  (General) Regulations 2006,
  SI 2006/1832
  reg 3, 4 638
      5 636
      6 637
      7 647
Mental Capacity Act 2005 (Independent
  Mental Capacity Advocates) (Wales)
  Regulations 2007, SI 2007/852
  reg 3 .... 638, 641
      4 638
      5 636
      6 637
      7 647
      8 635
      9 641
Mental Capacity Act 2005 (Loss of
  Capacity during Research Project)
  (England) Regulations 2007,
  SI 2007/679 630
Mental Capacity Act 2005 (Loss of
  Capacity during Research Project)
  (Wales) Regulations 2007,
  SI 2007/837 630
Mental Capacity Act 2005 (Transfer of
  Proceedings) Order 2007,
  SI 2007/1899
  art 2 745
      4 745
Mental Capacity Act 2005 (Transitional
  and Consequential Provisions)
  Order 2007, SI 2007/1898
  art 4 720
      5 625
Mental Capacity (Deprivation of Liberty:
  Appointment of Relevant Person's
  Representative) Regulations 2008,
  SI 2008/1315
  reg 3 709
      4–6 710
      8 710
      10–15 707
Mental Capacity (Deprivation of Liberty:
  Appointment of Relevant Person's
  Representative) (Wales)
  Regulations 2009, SI 2009/266
  reg 3 719
      4, 5 707
      6 709
      7–9 711
      11 711
      12–14 707
      15 711–712
      16, 17 707

PARA

Mental Capacity (Deprivation of Liberty:
  Assessments, Standard
  Authorisations and Disputes about
  Residence) (Wales)
  Regulations 2009, SI 2009/783
  reg 3 (1)(a) 697
         (b) 698
      (2) 698
      4 699
      5 700
      6 701–702
      7 704
      8 .... 700, 703
      9 .... 669, 703
      10 .... 679, 704
      11 704
      12 .... 675, 702
      13 668
      14–16 664
Mental Capacity (Deprivation of Liberty:
  Monitoring and Reporting; and
  Assessments–Amendment)
  Regulations 2009, SI 2009/827 718
Mental Capacity (Deprivation of Liberty:
  Standard Authorisations,
  Assessments and Ordinary
  Residence) Regulations 2008,
  SI 2008/1858
  reg 3 (1) 697
      (2), (2A) 697
      (3), (4) 698
      4 699
      5 700
      6 701
      7 702
      12 700
      13 669
      14 679
      15 .... 675, 702
      16 668
      17–19 664
Mental Health Act 1983 (Independent
  Mental Health Advocates)
  (England) Regulations 2008,
  SI 2008/3166
  reg 3 813
      6 813
      7 807
Mental Health (Approval of Persons to
  be Approved Mental Health
  Professionals) (Wales)
  Regulations 2008, SI 2008/2436
  reg 3 (1)(b) 815
      (2), (3) 815
      4 815
      6 823
      7 .... 822, 824
      8, 9 815
  Sch 2 817

PARA

Mental Health (Approved Mental Health Professionals) (Approval) (England) Regulations 2008, SI 2008/1206

reg 3 815
　　(2), (3) 816
　4 815
　5 .... 822, 824
　6 823
　8 815
Sch 1 818
　2 815

Mental Health (Assessment of Former Users of Secondary Mental Health Services) (Wales) Regulations 2011, SI 2011/2500

reg 3 (1), (2) 947
　4 951
　5 952
　6 (1), (2) 947

Mental Health (Care and Treatment) (Scotland) Act 2003 (Consequential Provisions) Order 2005, SI 2005/2078 (S 9) 557

art 8 919
　10 (1) 1013–1014
　　(2), (3) 1013
　11 776–777
　12 759

Mental Health (Care Co-ordination and Care and Treatment Planning) (Wales) Regulations 2011, SI 2011/2942

reg 3 852
　4 853
　5 855
　6 856
　7 857
　8, 9 855
　10 858
Sch 2 855

Mental Health (Conflicts of Interest) (England) Regulations 2008, SI 2008/1205

reg 4 826
　5 827
　6 828
　7 829

Mental Health (Conflicts of Interest) (Wales) Regulations 2008, SI 2008/2440

reg 3 828
　4 826
　5 827
　6 829
　7 830

Mental Health (Hospital and Guardianship) (Welsh Forms) Regulations 1971, SI 1971/178

reg 3 785
Schedule 785

PARA

Mental Health (Hospital, Guardianship and Treatment) (England) Regulations 2008, SI 2008/1184

reg 3 850
　　(2) 771
　4 (1)(a) 767, 847
　　(b) 767, 847, 849
　　(c) 768
　　(d) 768, 847, 849
　　(e) 769, 847
　　(f) 769, 849
　　(g), (h) 770
　　(2) 847
　　(4), (5) 769, 847
　5 848
　　(1)(a)–(c) 785
　　(e) 849
　　(5) 849
　6 (1) 797
　　(2) 800
　　(7) 801
　7 887
　8 .... 794, 888
　　(2), (4) 889
　　(6) 889
　9 802
　11, 12 891
　13 (6), (7) 799
　17 804
　18 913
　21 841
　22 792
　23 791
　25 840
　26 (1)(e) 799
　27 (1)(a), (b) 928
　　(2) 930
　　(3)(a), (b) 931
　　(4) 931
　28 (1), (1A) 944
　　(2) 935, 940
　　(3) 936
　29–31 780
Sch 1 ..... 767–770, 785, 847–849, 928, 930

Mental Health (Hospital, Guardianship, Community Treatment and Consent to Treatment) (Wales) Regulations 2008, SI 2008/2439

reg 3 850
　4 (1)(a) 767, 847
　　(b) 767, 847, 849
　　(c) 768
　　(d) 768, 847, 849
　　(e) 769, 847
　　(f) 769, 849
　　(g), (h) 770
　　(3) 769, 847, 849
　　(4) 849
　　(5) 847
　6 800
　7 913
　9 848

PARA

Mental Health (Hospital, Guardianship,
Community Treatment and Consent to
Treatment) (Wales) Regulations 2008,
SI 2008/2439—*continued*

reg 9 (1)(a)–(c) 785
(e) 849
(2), (3) 849
10 791
11 792
14 913
16 797
22 (1) 801
(a) 799
23 887
24 .... 794, 888
(4)–(6) 889
25 804
26 802
27 891
33 841
34 840
38 931
(1) 928
39 (a) 935, 940
(b) 936
40 (1) 928
(2), (3) 931
(4), (5) 944
41, 42 780
Sch 1 .... 767–770, 785, 847–849, 928

Mental Health (Independent Mental
Health Advocates) (Wales)
Regulations 2011, SI 2011/2501

reg 3 814
6 809

Mental Health (Mutual Recognition)
Regulations 2008, SI 2008/1204

reg 2 832
3, 4 833

Mental Health (Nurses) (England)
Order 2008, SI 2008/1207

art 2 770

Mental Health (Nurses) (Wales)
Order 2008, SI 2008/2441

art 2 770

Mental Health (Primary Care Referrals
and Eligibility to Conduct Primary
Mental Health Assessments) (Wales)
Regulations 2012, SI 2012/1305

reg 3 882
4 884
Schedule 884

Mental Health (Regional Provision)
(Wales) Regulations 2012,
SI 2012/1244 .... 586, 950

Mental Health Review Tribunal for
Wales Rules 2008, SI 2008/2705

r 3 980
5, 6 981
7 980
9 982
10 983

PARA

Mental Health Review Tribunal for Wales
Rules 2008, SI 2008/2705—*continued*

r 11 957
12 986
13 987
14–16 988
17 984
18 988
20 989
21 985
22, 23 988
24–27 990
28 991
30 992

Mental Health (Secondary Mental
Health Services) (Wales)
Order 2012, SI 2012/1428 586

Mental Health (Wales) Measure 2010
(Commencement No 1 and
Transitional Provision) Order 2011,
SI 2011/3046 757

Mental Health (Wales) Measure 2010
(Commencement No 2)
Order 2012, SI 2012/1397 757

Misuse of Drugs Act 1971
(Modification) Order 1973,
SI 1973/771 481

Misuse of Drugs Act 1971
(Modification) Order 1975,
SI 1975/421 481

Misuse of Drugs Act 1971
(Modification) Order 1977,
SI 1977/1243 481

Misuse of Drugs Act 1971
(Modification) Order 1979,
SI 1979/299 481

Misuse of Drugs Act 1971
(Modification) Order 1983,
SI 1983/765 481

Misuse of Drugs Act 1971
(Modification) Order 1984,
SI 1984/859 481

Misuse of Drugs Act 1971
(Modification) Order 1985,
SI 1985/1995 481

Misuse of Drugs Act 1971
(Modification) Order 1986,
SI 1986/2230 481

Misuse of Drugs Act 1971
(Modification) Order 1989,
SI 1989/1340 481

Misuse of Drugs Act 1971
(Modification) Order 1990,
SI 1990/2589 481

Misuse of Drugs Act 1971
(Modification) Order 1995,
SI 1995/1966 481

Misuse of Drugs Act 1971
(Modification) Order 1996,
SI 1996/1300 481

PARA

Misuse of Drugs Act 1971
  (Modification) Order 1998,
  SI 1998/750 481
Misuse of Drugs Act 1971
  (Modification) Order 2001,
  SI 2001/3932 481
Misuse of Drugs Act 1971
  (Modification) Order 2003,
  SI 2003/1243 481
Misuse of Drugs Act 1971 (Temporary
  Class Drug) Order 2012,
  SI 2012/980 .... 482, 503
Misuse of Drugs (Designation)
  Order 2001, SI 2001/3997 502
Misuse of Drugs (Licence Fees)
  Regulations 2010, SI 2010/2497 488
Misuse of Drugs Regulations 2001,
  SI 2001/3998 505
  reg 4 (3)–(5) 495
    4A, 4B 495
    5 .... 493–494, 496
    6 492
      (4) 496
      (6), (7) 496
    6A 501
    6B 494, 501
    7 494
    8 (1) 493
      (2) 494
    9 (1) 493
      (2) 494
    10 496
    11 494
    14 508
    15–17 512
    18 511
    20–25 509
    26 510
    27 505
  Sch 1 509
    2 .... 493, 509
    3 493–494
    4, 5 .... 491, 493
    8 .... 492, 494
Misuse of Drugs (Safe Custody)
  Regulations 1973, SI 1973/798 ... 505–506
Misuse of Drugs (Supply to Addicts)
  Regulations 1997, SI 1997/1001 505,
                                        513
Misuse of Drugs Tribunal (England and
  Wales) Rules 1974, SI 1974/85 521

N

National Health Service and Community
  Care Act 1990 (Commencement
  No 1) Order 1990, SI 1990/1329
  Sch 3 480
National Health Service (Direct
  Payments) Regulations 2010,
  SI 2010/1000
  reg 2 946

PARA

National Health Service Pension Scheme
  Regulations 1995, SI 1995/300
  reg R3 837

P

Poisons (Approved Institutions)
  Order 1935, SR & O 1935/1240 546
Poisons List Order 1982, SI 1982/217
  art 2 (a) 532
      (b) 533
  Schedule Pt I 532
           II 533
Poisons Rules 1982, SI 1982/218
  r 3 540
    4 544
    5 proviso (i) 541
    6 541
    7 547
    9 539
    10 (1) 540
       (2) 540
       (a) 547
    11 541
    12, 13 542
    18 544
    21 545
    24 (1), (2) 535
    25 (1)–(3) 541
    26, 27 541
  Sch 4 Group I, II 547
    5 540
    Pt A 547
    8, 9 535
    10, 11 541
    12 Pt I 542
Prescription Only Medicines (Human
  Use) Order 1997, SI 1997/1830
  art 5 272
    10 26
Public Guardian (Fees, etc)
  Regulations 2007, SI 2007/2051 752
  reg 8 (2), (3) 752

S

Social Security and Child Support
  (Decisions and Appeals)
  Regulations 1999, SI 1999/991 385
Social Security (Claims and Payments)
  Regulations 1987, SI 1987/1968
  reg 33 593
Social Security (General Benefit)
  Regulations 1982, SI 1982/1408
  reg 2 (3), (4) 593

T

Transfer of Functions Order 2008,
  SI 2008/2833
  art 6 (1) 958
    (2)(a) 958

PARA

Tribunal Procedure (First-tier Tribunal)
(Health, Education and Social Care
Chamber) Rules 2008,
SI 2008/2699
r 31–33 973
　34 974
　35, 36 975
　38 976
　39 977
　40 978
　41 979

V

Vaccine Damage Payments
Regulations 1979, SI 1979/432
reg 2 385
　4 385
　5, 5A 384
　11, 12 385
Vaccine Damage Payments (Specified
Disease) Order 1990,
SI 1990/623 384
Vaccine Damage Payments (Specified
Disease) Order 1995,
SI 1995/1164 384
Vaccine Damage Payments (Specified
Disease) Order 2001,
SI 2001/1652 384
Vaccine Damage Payments (Specified
Disease) Order 2006,
SI 2006/2066 384
Vaccine Damage Payments (Specified
Disease) Order 2008,
SI 2008/2103 384
Veterinary Medicines Regulations 2011,
SI 2011/2159
reg 3 387
　4 388
　5 (1), (2) 410
　6 .... 388, 448
　7 (2)–(5) 448
　8 422
　9 (1)–(6) 434
　　(7) 431
　10 439
　11 440
　12 441
　13 418
　15 387
　17–24 433
　25 (1) 435
　26, 27 448
　28, 29 442
　30 443
　31 436
　33–35 444
　36 445
　37 446
　38–40 447
　41, 42 444
　43 448

PARA

Veterinary Medicines Regulations 2011,
SI 2011/2159—*continued*
reg 45 387
Sch 1 para 1–3 389
　Pt 2 (para 6–16) 389
　para 17 390
　　19 391
　　20 392
　　21 393
　　22 394
　　24 395
　　25 396
　　26 397
　　27 398
　　28 399
　　29 400
　　30 401
　　31 402
　　32 403
　　33–37 404
　　40 405–406
　　41 407
　　42–44 408
　　45–54 437
　　55–61 430
　　63–67 409
　2 para 1–4 411
　　5 412
　　6, 7 413
　　8 414
　　9–11 415
　　12 416
　　13 417
　3 para 1 431
　　2 432
　　3–10 431
　　12 438
　　13 423
　　14 432
　　16–19 419
　　20 420
　　21 421
　4 para 1–3 423
　　4, 5 424
　　6 425
　　7 426
　　8 427
　　9 428
　6 429
　7 Pt 1 (reg 1–6) 389
　　2 (reg 7–26) 388–389
　para 27–37 410
　　38–41 418
　Pt 6 (reg 45–64) 388

Visiting Forces and International
Headquarters (Application of Law)
Order 1999, SI 1999/1736
art 12 (1) 29
Sch 5 29

TABLE OF CIVIL PROCEDURE

Civil Procedure Rules 1998, SI 1998/3132 (CPR)

PARA

CPR

r 6.13 (2) 999
    (4)–(6) 999
6.25 (1)–(5) 999
14.1 (4) 999
21.2 (1) 995
21.3 (2)–(4) 995
21.4, 21.5 996
21.6, 21.7 997
21.8 997
    (1) 999
21.9 (2)–(6) 995
21.10–21.12 1000
48.5 1001

Practice Directions supplementing CPR

PARA

PD 10A: Applications within proceedings 724
PD 14C: Admissions, Evidence and Depositions 746
PD 20A: Appeals 750
PD 21: Children and Patients
    para 7.1–7.4 1000
    8.1–8.4 1000
    10.2 1000
PD 23B: Where P ceases to lack capacity or dies 728

Other Practice Directions

PARA

Practice Direction (1995) 145 NLJ 1403 994
Practice Direction (First-tier Tribunal: mental health cases) (6 April 2012, unreported) 582, 966
    para 12 583
    16 583
    20 583
    26 583
Practice Note (Official Solicitor, CAFCASS and National Assembly for Wales: urgent and
    out of hours cases in the Family Division of the High Court) [2006] 2 FLR 354 612

TABLE OF EUROPEAN
UNION LEGISLATION

PARA

Commission Directive (EC) 1991/412 (OJ L228, 17.8.1991, p 71)
art 4–6 12
11 12
Commission Directive (EC) 2003/94 (OJ L262, 14.10.2003, p 22–26)
art 4–6 12
11 12
13 12
Commission Directive (EC) 2004/33 (OJ L91, 30.3.2004, p 25–39) 17
Commission Directive (EC) 2005/62 (OJ L56, 10.2005, p 1–48) 17
Commission Regulation (EC) 1234/2008 (OJ L334, 12.12.2008, p 7–24) 11
Commission Regulation (EU) 198/2013 (OJ L65, 7.3.2013, p 17) 21
Council Directive (EC) 1990/385 (OJ L189, 20.7.1990, p 7) 20
Council Directive (EC) 1993/42 (OJ L169, 12.7.1993, p 1) 20
art 16a 19
16c, 16d 19
16f 19
Council Directive (EC) 2002/98 (OJ L33, 8.2.2003, p 30)
art 14 13
24 13
Council Directive (EC) 2004/23 (OJ L102, 7.4.2004, p 48)
art 8 13
14 13
Council Regulation (EC) 726/2004 (OJ L136, 30.4.2004, p 1)
art 2 5
3 (1), (2) 5
4 (1) 5
6 (1) 6
21–23 16
24 .... 14, 16
25 16
26, 27 .... 14, 16
28, 29 16
83 8
Annex 5
European Parliament and Council Directive (EC) 1998/79 (OJ L331, 7.12.1998, p 1) 20
European Parliament and Council Directive (EC) 2001/20 (OJ L121, 1.5.2001, p 34) 18
European Parliament and Council Directive (EC) 2001/82 (OJ L311, 28.11.2001, p 1)
art 5 6
12, 13 6
31 4
32 4
(1) 7
33 .... 4, 7
34–43 4
73 15
74 16
75 (1), (2) 16
(6) 16
European Parliament and Council Directive (EC) 2001/83 (OJ L311, 28.11.2001, p 67) 19
art 5 (2)–(4) 9
6 (1) 4
7, 8 6
10 6
28, 29 .... 4, 7

PARA

European Parliament and Council Directive (EC) 2001/83—*continued*
art 30–39 4
    101 15
    104 16
    126a (1) 10
       (3) 10
European Parliament and Council Directive (EC) 2002/98 (OJ L33, 8.2.2002, p 30–40) 17
European Parliament and Council Regulation (EC) 1394/2007 (OJ L324, 10.12.2007,
    p 121) 5
art 1 22
    2 23
    3 22
    4 (1) 18
    14 22
    15 .... 13, 22
    20 22
    23 22
European Parliament and Council Regulation (EU) 1027/2012 (OJ L316, 25.10.2012,
    p 38) 21

TABLE OF COMMAND PAPERS

PARA

Cmnd 169 (Report of the Royal Commission on the Law relating to Mental Illness and
Mental Deficiency 1954–1957) (1957)
Pt 3 (paras 146–198) 761

TABLE OF
NON-STATUTORY MATERIALS

PARA

C

Code of Practice to Parts 2 and 3 of the
Mental Health (Wales)
Measure 2010 (2012) 763

D

Deprivation of Liberty Safeguards – code
of practice to supplement the main
Mental Capacity Act 2005 code of
practice (2008)
para 2.14, 2.15 649
Pt 3 648
para 4.58–4.76 674
13.51 928

M

Mental Capacity Act 2005 Code of
Practice (2007)
para 4.16–4.25 605
4.32 .... 597, 614, 617
4.33 .... 597, 599, 614, 617
Ch 5 .... 606, 611
para 5.6 606
5.28 606
5.30 606
6.45 611
6.47 611
6.58 613
7.21 619
7.36 619
Ch 8 735
para 8.3, 8.4 724
8.18, 8.19 612
Ch 9 623
para 9.61 624
Ch 10 634
para 10.18, 10.19 636
10.20 637
10.42–10.50 638
10.51–10.58 639–640
10.62–10.88 641
11.2–11.4 630
11.7 631
11.14–11.19 631
11.22–11.28 632
11.29–11.31 633
13.16–13.21 797
Ch 18 734
Mental Health Act 1983 Code of
Practice (2008)
introduction 762
para 1.3 767–768
3–5 761
4.1 767

PARA

Mental Health Act 1983 Code of Practice
(2008)—continued
para 4.9–4.12 764
4.13–4.15 .... 764, 767
4.16–4.23 764
4.24 767
4.25–4.27 767–768
4.28 .... 768, 849
4.33 815
4.48–4.70 821
4.71 849
4.92 771
4.99 771
5.1–5.13 769
Ch 6 768
para 6.16 768
Ch 7 825
para 8.13 842
10 922–923
para 10.53 770
Ch 11 771
para 12.2–12.34 770
13.13 774
13.16–13.21 785
14.2, 14.3 834
Ch 19 .... 569, 781
20 807
para 20.25–20.33 808
Ch 23 924
24 924
para 24.6–24.9 928
24.27 936
24.38, 24.39 928
24.59 930
24.79 928
25.2 797
25.26 797
25.31–25.34 808
25.35 800
25.61 801
25.65–25.70 803
Ch 26 .... 785, 787
para 26. 2 785
4 785
9–26.13 .... 785, 797
32 785
28.7–28.10 797
Ch 30 913
para 30.1 778
30.32 780
Ch 35 768
36 765
para 36.67–36.74 765

PARA

Mental Health Act 1983 Code of
  Practice for Wales (2008)
introduction 762
para 2.1 767
    2.13–2.16 761
    2.27, 2.28 764
    2.29–2.32 767
    2.33 .... 821, 849
    2.34–2.51 821
    2.54 849
    2.74 815
Ch 3 825
    4 767
para 5.1–5.4 767–768
    5.5–5.12 769
Ch 6 .... 785, 787
para 6.2 785
    6.4 785
Ch 7 922–923

PARA

Mental Health Act 1983 Code of Practice for
  Wales (2008)—*continued*
para 8.5 .... 764, 770
    8.8–8.30 770
    10.13 774
Ch 11 913
para 11.1 778
    11.3 780
    12.2, 12.3 834
Ch 17, 18 924
para 18.8, 18.9 928
    18.16 936
    18.27 930
Ch 20 .... 569, 781
    25 807
para 30.3 797
    30.71 801
    30.78–30.82 803
Ch 33 765

TABLE OF CASES

PARA

A

A (a child) (deprivation of liberty), Re [2010] EWHC 978 (Fam), [2010] 2 FLR 1363, [2010] Fam Law 929, [2010] All ER (D) 50 (Aug) 648

A (medical treatment: male sterilisation), Re [2000] 1 FCR 193, [2000] 1 FLR 549, [2000] 02 LS Gaz R 30, CA 606, 612

A v A (a child) [2002] EWHC 2734 (Fam), [2003] Fam 83, [2003] 1 All ER 669, [2003] 2 WLR 1465, [2003] 1 FCR 361, 71 BMLR 61, [2003] NLJR 21, [2002] All ER (D) 263 (Dec) 612

A v Harrow Crown Court [2003] EWHC 2020 (Admin), [2003] All ER (D) 78 (Aug) 864, 869

AB (by his litigation friend NW) v LCC (A local authority) [2011] EWHC 3151 (COP), [2011] NLJR 1744, [2011] All ER (D) 37 (Dec) 733, 740

AG's ref (No 54 of 2011) [2011] EWCA Crim 2276 863

AH v Hertfordshire Partnership NHS Foundation Trust (including costs) [2011] EWHC 276 (COP) 747

AH v West London MH NHS Trust [2010] UKUT 264 (AAC) 976

Aintree University Hospital NHS Trust v David James (by his litigation friend, the Official Solicitor) [2013] EWCA Civ 65, [2013] All ER (D) 09 (Mar) 606

AK, Re (medical treatment: consent) [2001] 2 FCR 35, [2001] 1 FLR 129, [2000] Fam Law 885 .... 601, 605, 623

AVS v NHS Foundation Trust [2010] EWHC 2746 (COP), [2011] 1 FLR 967, [2011] Fam Law 138 740

A child (publication of report of proceedings: restrictions), Re [2011] EWHC 454 (QB), 120 BMLR 59, [2011] EMLR 338, [2011] All ER (D) 56 (Mar) 1000

A County Council v MB, JB and a Residential Home [2010] EWHC 2508 (COP), [2011] PTSR 795, [2011] 1 FLR 790, [2011] Fam Law 32, [2011] All ER (D) 49 (May) ... 650, 665, 713–714, 733

A Local Authority v DL [2012] EWCA Civ 253, [2012] 3 All ER 1064, [2012] 3 WLR 1439, [2012] LGR 757, [2012] 3 FCR 200, 127 BMLR 24, [2012] NLJR 503, (2012) Times, 09 July, 156 Sol Jo (no 13) 31, [2012] All ER (D) 211 (Mar) 563

A Local Authority v E (by her litigation friend, the Official Solicitor) [2012] EWHC 1639 (COP), [2012] 2 FCR 523, 127 BMLR 133, [2012] All ER (D) 96 (Jun) 606, 625

A Local Authority v FG (No 1) [2011] EWHC 3932 (COP) 724

A Local Authority v H [2012] EWHC 49 (COP), [2012] 1 FCR 590, 124 BMLR 98, [2012] NLJR 392, [2012] All ER (D) 34 (Mar) 608–609

A Local Authority v K (by the Official Solicitor) [2012] EWHC 242 (Fam) 605

A Local Authority v Mrs A (by the Official Solicitor) [2010] EWHC 1549 (Fam), [2011] Fam 61, [2011] 3 All ER 706, [2011] 2 WLR 878, [2011] PTSR 435, [2011] 2 FCR 553, [2011] 1 FLR 26, [2010] Fam Law 928, [2011] All ER (D) 205 (Jan) 605

A Local Authority v PB [2011] EWHC 502 (COP) 724

Aerts v Belgium (1998) 29 EHRR 50, 5 BHRC 382, ECtHR 767–768, 892

Affleck v Affleck (1857) 26 LJ Ch 358, 3 Jur NS 326, 3 Sm & G 394, 5 WR 425, 29 LTOS 37 617

Ahsan v University Hospital Leicester NHS Trust [2006] EWHC 2624 (QB), [2007] PIQR P271, [2006] All ER (D) 451 (Jul) 606

Al-Ameri v Kensington and Chelsea Royal London Borough Council [2003] EWCA Civ 235, [2003] 2 All ER 1, [2003] 1 WLR 1289, [2003] LGR 501, [2003] HLR 758, (2003) Times, 19 March, 147 Sol Jo LB 296, [2003] All ER (D) 416 (Feb); affd [2004] UKHL 4, [2004] 2 AC 159, [2004] 1 All ER 1104, [2004] 2 WLR 354, [2004] LGR 161, [2004] HLR 289, [2004] NLJR 225, (2004) Times, 6 February, 148 Sol Jo LB 182, [2004] All ER (D) 64 (Feb) 839

Ali (Nakkuda) v MF De S Jayaratne [1951] AC 66, 94 Sol Jo 516, 66 (pt 2) TLR 214, PC 548

Ames v Parkinson (1847) 2 Ph 388 1002

An NHS Trust v DJ (by his litigation friend, the Official Solicitor) [2012] EWHC 3524 (COP), [2012] All ER (D) 169 (Dec) 606

PARA

An NHS Trust v H [2012] NLJR 1323, [2012] NLJR 1348, [2012] Lexis Citation 82,
  [2012] All ER (D) 110 (Oct) 606
Anderdon v Burrows (1830) 4 C & P 210 759
Anufrijeva v Southwark London Borough Council [2003] EWCA Civ 1406, [2004] QB
  1124, [2004] 1 All ER 833, [2004] 2 WLR 603, [2004] LGR 184, [2003] 3 FCR
  673, [2004] 1 FLR 8, [2004] Fam Law 12, [2003] 44 LS Gaz R 30, (2003) Times,
  17 October, 15 BHRC 526, [2003] All ER (D) 288 (Oct) 969
Ashingdane v Secretary of State for Social Services (Now DHSS) (18 February 1980,
  unreported) 759
Ashingdane v United Kingdom (1985) 7 EHRR 528, [1985] ECHR 8225/78, ECtHR 648, 768,
                                                                              787, 969, 995
Attia v British Gas plc [1988] QB 304, [1987] 3 All ER 455, [1987] 3 WLR 1101,
  [1987] BTLC 394, 131 Sol Jo 1248, [1987] LS Gaz R 2360, [1987] NLJ Rep
  661, CA 761
A-G v Parnther (1792) 3 Bro CC 441 .... 598, 614
A-G v Weeks [1932] 1 Ch 211, 101 LJ Ch 26, 146 LT 59, CA 537
Azam v Secretary of State for the Home Department [1974] AC 18, [1973] 2 All ER
  765, [1973] 2 WLR 1058, 137 JP 626, [1973] Crim LR 512, 117 Sol Jo 546, 123
  NLJ 612, HL 759

B

B (adult: refusal of medical treatment), Re [2002] EWHC 429 (Fam), [2002] 2 All ER
  449, [2002] 2 FCR 1, [2002] 1 FLR 1090, 65 BMLR 149, (2002) Times,
  26 March, [2002] All ER (D) 362 (Mar) 624
B v B [1979] 3 All ER 494, sub nom B (A) v B (L) [1980] 1 WLR 116, 78 LGR 1, 124
  Sol Jo 16, CA 842
B v Croydon Health Authority [1995] Fam 133, [1995] 1 All ER 683, [1995] 2 WLR
  294, [1995] 1 FCR 662, [1995] 1 FLR 470, [1995] Fam Law 244, 22 BMLR 13,
  [1994] NLJR 1696, [1995] PIQR P 145, CA 605, 612, 927, 930, 932
B v Cygnet Healthcare [2008] EWHC 1259 (Admin), [2008] All ER (D) 35 (Mar) 847
B v Forsey. See Black v Forsey
B (a local authority) v RM [2010] EWHC 3802 (Fam), [2011] 1 FLR 1635,
  [2011] Fam Law 459, [2011] All ER (D) 141 (Feb) 745
B Borough Council v S [2006] EWHC 2584 (Fam), [2007] 1 FCR 574, [2007] 1 FLR
  1600, 93 BMLR 1, [2006] All ER (D) 281 (Oct) 842
Bailey v Warren [2006] EWCA Civ 51, (2006) Times, 20 February, [2006] All ER (D) 78
  (Feb) 995
Baker v Ellison [1914] 2 KB 762, 12 LGR 992, 78 JP 244, 83 LJKB 1335, 24 Cox CC
  208, 111 LT 66, 30 TLR 426, DC 1015
Baker v H [2010] 1 WLR 1103 .... 724, 734, 736
Ball v Mannin (1829) 3 Bli NS 1, Dow & Cl 380, HL 617
Banks v Goodfellow (1870) LR 5 QB 549, 39 LJQB 237, [1861–73] All ER Rep 47, 22
  LT 813 615
Barker v Barking, Havering and Brentwood Community Healthcare NHS Trust (Warley
  Hospital) [1999] 1 FLR 106, 47 BMLR 112, CA 768, 909–910
Barlow's Will, Re (1887) 36 Ch D 287, sub nom Re Barlow's Will Trusts, Re Barlow,
  Barton v Spencer 56 LJ Ch 795, 35 WR 737, 57 LT 95, 3 TLR 695, CA 998
Barnet London Borough Council v Robin (1999) 2 CCLR 454, CA 842
Barnsley, ex p (1744) 2 Eq Cas Abr 580, 3 Atk 168 559
Barrow v Barrow (1774) 2 Dick 504 614
Bastin v Davies [1950] 2 KB 579, [1950] 1 All ER 1095, 48 LGR 451, 114 JP 302, 66
  (pt 2) TLR 719, DC 235
Battan Singh v Amirchand [1948] AC 161, [1948] 1 All ER 152, [1948] LJR 827, PC 615
Baxter v Earl of Portsmouth (1826) 5 B & C 170, 2 C & P 178, 7 Dow & Ry KB
  614 614
Beall v Smith (1873) 9 Ch App 85, 38 JP 72, 43 LJ Ch 245, 22 WR 121, 29 LT 625 995
Beaney, Re [1978] 2 All ER 595, [1978] 1 WLR 770, 121 Sol Jo 832 .... 605, 614–615, 617
Beatham v Carlisle Hospitals NHS Trust (1999) Times, 20 May 1000
Beavan v M'Donnell (1854) 9 Exch 309, 2 CLR 474, 22 LTOS 243; affd (1854) 23 LJ
  Ex 326, 10 Exch 184, 2 CLR 1292 614
Beecham and Lunacy Comrs, Re. See Petition for Judicial Separation, Re, ex p Beecham

PARA

Benjamin v United Kingdom (Application 28212/95) (2002) 36 EHRR 1, 13 BHRC 287,
    (2002) Times, 9 October, [2002] ECHR 28212/95, [2002] All ER (D) 160 (Sep),
    ECtHR 894, 969–970
Beverley's Case (1603) 4 Co Rep 123b 559, 614, 617
Birkin v Wing (1890) 63 LT 80 614–615
Black v Forsey 1988 SC (HL) 28, sub nom B v Forsey 1988 SLT 572, HL 758, 769, 908
Black v Yates [1992] QB 526, [1991] 4 All ER 722, [1991] 3 WLR 90, [1991] 1 Lloyd's
    Rep 181 1000
Blouet v Bath and Wansdyke Magistrates Court [2009] EWHC 759 (Admin) 871
Bolam v Friern Hospital Management Committee [1957] 2 All ER 118, [1957] 1 WLR
    582, 101 Sol Jo 357, 1 BMLR 1 612
Bolitho v City and Hackney Health Authority [1998] AC 232, [1997] 4 All ER 771,
    [1997] 3 WLR 1151, [1998] Lloyd's Rep Med 26, 39 BMLR 1,
    [1997] 47 LS Gaz R 30, 141 Sol Jo LB 238, [1998] PNLR 1, HL 612
Borrow v Howland (1896) 60 JP 391, 18 Cox CC 368, 74 LT 787, 12 TLR 414, DC 1015
Boughton v Knight (1873) LR 3 P & D 64, 37 JP 598, 647, 42 LJP & M 25, 41,
    [1861–73] All ER Rep 40, 28 LT 562 .... 609, 614
Brand v Netherlands (Application 9902/99) (2004) 17 BHRC 398, [2004] ECHR
    49902/99, ECtHR 566
Bridges v Griffin [1925] 2 KB 233, 89 JP 122, 94 LJKB 728, 28 Cox CC 7,
    [1925] All ER Rep 224, 69 Sol Jo 558, 133 LT 177, 41 TLR 523, DC 234
Broadmoor Special Health Authority v Robinson [2000] QB 775, [2000] 2 All ER 727,
    [2000] 1 WLR 1590, [2000] 03 LS Gaz R 36, 144 Sol Jo LB 48, CA 759, 780
Brown v Jodrell (1827) 3 C & P 30, Mood & M 105 614
Buck v Nottinghamshire Healthcare NHS Trust [2006] EWCA Civ 1576, 93 BMLR 28,
    (2006) Times, 1 December, 150 Sol Jo LB 1568, [2006] All ER (D) 310 (Nov) 569
Burt v Blackburn (1887) 3 TLR 356, CA 1002
Buxton v Jayne [1960] 2 All ER 688, [1960] 1 WLR 783, 58 LGR 274, 124 JP 380, 104
    Sol Jo 602, CA 559, 922

C

C (a minor) (detention for medical treatment), Re [1997] 3 FCR 49, [1997] 2 FLR 180,
    [1997] Fam Law 474 765
C (adult: refusal of treatment), Re [1994] 1 All ER 819, [1994] 1 WLR 290,
    [1994] 2 FCR 151, [1994] 1 FLR 31, [1994] Fam Law 131, 15 BMLR 77,
    [1993] NLJR 1642 .... 612, 927–928
C (vulnerable adult)(deprivation of liberty), Re [2010] EWHC 978 (Fam), [2010] 2 FLR
    1363, [2010] Fam Law 929, [2010] All ER (D) 50 (Aug) 648
C v Blackburn [2011] EWHC 3321 (COP) 562
C v South London and Maudsley Hospital NHS Trust and Lambeth London Borough
    Council [2001] 1 MHLR 269 759
C v V [2008] EWHC B16 (Fam) 605
C (by his litigation friend, the Official Solicitor) v A Borough Council [2011] EWHC
    3321 (COP), [2011] All ER (D) 203 (Dec) 628, 648, 658, 787
CM v Derbyshire Healthcare NHS Foundation Trust [2011] UKUT 129 (AAC) 761
CVB v MGN Ltd [2012] EWHC 1148 (QB), [2012] All ER (D) 82 (May) 1000
Cambridgeshire County Council v R [1994] 2 FCR 973, [1995] 1 FLR 50,
    [1995] Fam Law 12 612
Campbell v Hooper (1855) 24 LJ Ch 644, 3 Eq Rep 727, 1 Jur NS 670, 3 Sm & G 153,
    3 WR 528, 65 ER 603, 25 LTOS 220 .... 614, 617
Campbell v Secretary of State for the Home Department [1988] AC 120, sub nom
    Secretary of State for the Home Department v Oxford Regional Mental Health
    Review Tribunal [1987] 3 All ER 8, sub nom R v Oxford Regional Mental Health
    Review Tribunal, ex p Secretary of State for the Home Department [1987] 3 WLR
    522, 131 Sol Jo 1086, [1987] LS Gaz R 2690, [1987] NLJ Rep 735, HL 969
Carter v Metropolitan Police Comr [1975] 2 All ER 33, [1975] 1 WLR 507, 119 Sol Jo
    237, CA 759, 923
Cartwright v Cartwright (1793) 1 Phillim 90, 161 ER 923, [1775–1802] All ER Rep
    476; affd [1775–1802] All ER Rep 476n 598
Chatterton v Gerson [1981] QB 432, [1981] 1 All ER 257, [1980] 3 WLR 1003, 124
    Sol Jo 885, 1 BMLR 80 612
Chemische Fabrik Kreussler & Co GmbH: C-308/11 [2012] All ER (D) 79 (Sep), ECJ 25

PARA

Cheshire West and Chester Council v P [2011] EWHC 1330 (Fam), [2011] All ER (D) 155 (Jun); revsd [2011] EWCA Civ 1257, [2012] PTSR 1447, [2012] 1 FLR 693, [2012] Fam Law 137, [2011] NLJR 1670, [2011] All ER (D) 150 (Nov) 648, 740, 747

Clarendon Development Ltd, Re (1965) 50 DLR (2d) 521 234

Clarke, Re [2012] EWHC 2714 (COP), [2012] All ER (D) 19 (Nov) 617

Cleare and Forster v Cleare (1869) LR 1 P & D 655, 38 LJP & M 81, 17 WR 687, 20 LT 497 615

Clerk v Clerk (1700) 2 Vern 412 617

Clunis v Camden and Islington Health Authority [1998] QB 978, [1998] 3 All ER 180, [1998] 2 WLR 902, 40 BMLR 181, [1998] 02 LS Gaz R 23, 142 Sol Jo LB 38, CA 945

Clunis v United Kingdom (Application No 45049/98), unreported 945

Commission of the European Communities v Cambridge Healthcare Supplies: C-471/00 [2001] ECR I-2865, CFI 167

Coombs v Dorset NHS Primary Care Trust [2012] EWHC 521 (QB), [2012] NLJR 543, [2012] All ER (D) 42 (Apr) 945

Coventry City Council v C [2012] EWHC 2190 (Fam), [2013] 1 FCR 54, [2012] Fam Law 1316, [2012] NLJR 1078, 156 Sol Jo (31) 31, [2012] All ER (D) 69 (Aug) 601

Cranmer, ex p (1806) 12 Ves 445 559

Creagh v Blood (1845) 8 I Eq R 434, 2 Jo & Lat 509 .... 598, 614

Cutbush v Cutbush (1893) 37 Sol Jo 685 999

D

D (medical treatment: consent), Re [1998] 2 FCR 178, [1998] 2 FLR 22, 41 BMLR 81, [1997] 48 LS Gaz R 30, 142 Sol Jo LB 30 612

D (mental patient: habeas corpus), Re [2001] 1 FCR 218, [2000] 2 FLR 848, [2000] Fam Law 805, (2000) Times, 19 May, CA 821, 839, 847

D (statutory will), Re [2010] EWHC 2159 (Ch), [2012] Ch 57, [2011] 1 All ER 859, [2011] 3 WLR 1218, [2011] 1 FCR 441, [2010] NLJR 1190, [2010] All ER (D) 102 (Aug) 606, 615, 724, 731

D v An NHS Trust (medical treatment consent: termination) [2003] EWHC 2793 (Fam), [2004] 1 FLR 1110, [2004] Fam Law 415 612

D v R [2010] EWHC 2405 (COP) 601, 605

D v R (the deputy of S) [2010] EWHC 3748 (COP) 747

D v United Kingdom (Application 30240/96) (1997) 24 EHRR 423, [1997] 24 LS Gaz R 33, 2 BHRC 273, ECtHR 907

DCC v KH (Case No 11729380) (11 September 2009, unreported) 649

DD v Durham County Council [2012] EWHC 1053 (QB), [2012] PTSR D35 759

DL-H v Devon Partnership NHS Trust [2010] UKUT 102 (AAC) 761, 768

D Borough Council v AB [2011] EWHC 101 (COP), [2012] Fam 36, [2011] 3 All ER 435, [2011] 3 WLR 1257, [2011] 3 FCR 62, [2011] 2 FLR 72, [2011] Fam Law 473, [2011] NLJR 254, [2011] All ER (D) 71 (Feb) 605, 609

Daily Telegraph Newspaper Co Ltd v McLaughlin [1904] AC 776, 73 LJPC 95, 1 CLR 243, 91 LT 233, 20 TLR 674, PC 600, 617

De Freville v Dill (1927) 96 LJKB 1056, [1927] All ER Rep 205, 138 LT 83, 43 TLR 702 759

De Linden, Re, Re Spurrier's Settlement, De Hayn v Garland [1897] 1 Ch 453, 66 LJ Ch 295, 45 WR 342, 76 LT 180, 13 TLR 258 998

Dearden v Whiteley (1916) 14 LGR 502, 80 JP 215, 85 LJKB 1420, 25 Cox CC 356, 114 LT 702, 32 TLR 260, DC 234

Denison v Hardings [1867] WN 17, 15 WR 346 999

Didisheim v London and Westminster Bank [1900] 2 Ch 15, 69 LJ Ch 443, 48 WR 501, 82 LT 738, 16 TLR 311, CA 995, 998

DPP v Goodchild. See R v Goodchild (No 2)

DPP v P [2007] EWHC 946 (Admin), [2007] 4 All ER 628, [2008] 1 WLR 1005, 171 JP 349, [2008] Crim LR 165, 171 JPN 659, [2007] All ER (D) 244 (Apr) 872

Dlodlo v Mental Health Review Tribunal for South Thames Region (1996) 36 BMLR 145, CA 914

Donaghy v Brennan (1901) 19 NZLR 289, NZ CA 761

Dorset County Council v EH [2009] EWHC 784 (Fam), [2009] All ER (D) 166 (Apr) 606

PARA
Dorset Healthcare NHS Foundation Trust v MH [2009] UKUT 4 (AAC), [2009] PTSR
  1112, 111 BMLR 1 .... 973, 984
Drew v Nunn (1879) 4 QBD 661, 43 JP 541, 48 LJQB 591, 27 WR 810,
  [1874–80] All ER Rep 1144, 40 LT 671, CA 600, 614
Drinkall v Whitwood [2003] EWCA Civ 1547, [2004] 4 All ER 378, [2004] 1 WLR
  462, (2003) Times, 13 November, 147 Sol Jo LB 1308, [2003] All ER (D) 76
  (Nov) 1000
D'souza v DPP [1992] 4 All ER 545, [1992] 1 WLR 1073, 96 Cr App Rep 278, 10
  BMLR 139, [1992] NLJR 1540, HL 922
Dunhill (by her litigation friend) v Burgin [2012] EWCA Civ 397, [2012] All ER (D) 32
  (Apr) 605, 995
Durham v Durham (1885) 10 PD 80, 1 TLR 338 609

E

E, Re [1985] 1 All ER 609, [1985] 1 WLR 245, 129 Sol Jo 67, CA 727
E (Mental Health: Habeas Corpus), Re (a minor) [1991] FCR 771, [1991] 2 FLR 585,
  [1992] Fam Law 15, 7 BMLR 117; on appeal [1993] Fam Law 15, CA 612
E (an alleged patient), Re [2005] Fam Law 279. See Sheffield City Council v E
E, Re (10 December 1966, unreported) 774, 789
E (by her litigation friend the Official Solicitor) v Channel Four, News International Ltd
  and St Helens Borough Council [2005] EWHC 1144 (Fam), [2005] 2 FLR 913,
  [2005] Fam Law 866, sub nom E v Channel Four Television Corpn [2005] EMLR
  709 612
EB v RC [2011] EWHC 3805 (COP) 734
EC Commission v Germany: C-290/90 [1992] ECR I-3317, ECJ 25
EG, Re [1914] 1 Ch 927, 83 LJ Ch 586, 58 Sol Jo 497, 111 LT 95, [1914–15] All ER
  Rep Ext 1486, CA 600
ETK v News Group Newspapers Ltd [2011] EWCA Civ 439, [2011] 1 WLR 1827,
  [2011] 18 LS Gaz R 18, (2011) Times, 22 April, [2011] EMLR 434, [2011] All ER
  (D) 197 (Apr) 1000
Elliot v Ince (1857) 7 De GM & G 475, 26 LJ Ch 821, 3 Jur NS 597, 5 WR 465, 30
  LTOS 92 .... 600, 614, 617
Emmens v Pottle (1885) 16 QBD 354, 50 JP 228, 55 LJQB 51, 34 WR 116, 53 LT 808,
  2 TLR 115, CA 761
Enfield London Borough Council v SA (by her Litigation Friend, the Official Solicitor),
  FA and KA [2010] EWHC 196 (Admin), [2010] 1 FLR 1836, [2010] Fam Law
  457 740
European Commission v Germany: C-141/07 [2008] ECR I-6935, [2008] 3 CMLR
  1479, ECJ 307
Everett v Griffiths [1921] 1 AC 631, 19 LGR 283, 85 JP 149, 90 LJKB 737, 65 Sol Jo
  395, 125 LT 230, 37 TLR 481, HL 759, 849

F

F, Re [1990] 2 AC 1, [1989] 2 WLR 1025, [1989] 2 FLR 376, [1989] Fam Law 390,
  133 Sol Jo 785, [1989] NLJR 789, sub nom F v West Berkshire Health Authority
  (Mental Health Act Commission intervening) [1989] 2 All ER 545, 4 BMLR
  1, HL 612, 619, 927
F (Mental Health Act guardianship), Re [2000] 1 FCR 11, [2000] 1 FLR 192,
  [2000] Fam Law 18, 51 BMLR 128, [1999] 39 LS Gaz R 38, [1999] All ER (D)
  1043, CA 761, 785
F (vulnerable adult) (capacity: jurisdiction to make order on vulnerable adults behalf),
  Re [2009] Lexis Citation 4, [2009] All ER (D) 257 (Nov) 725
F v F. See GF, Re
F v West Berkshire Health Authority (Mental Health Act Commission intervening). See F,
  Re [1990] 2 AC 1
FP v GM and A Health Board [2011] EWHC 2778 (COP) 724
Fabio Caronna: C-7/11 [2012] 36 LS Gaz R 16, [2012] All ER (D) 49 (Sep), ECJ 150
Faulder v Silk (1811) 3 Camp 126 617
Folks v Faizey [2006] EWCA Civ 381, [2006] All ER (D) 83 (Apr) 997
Fore Street Warehouse Co Ltd v Durrant & Co (1883) 10 QBD 471, 52 LJQB 287, 31
  WR 765, 48 LT 531 .... 994, 999
Fowlis v Davidson (1848) 6 Notes of Cases 461 598

PARA

Fox v Stirk [1970] 2 QB 463, [1970] 3 All ER 7, [1970] 3 WLR 147, 68 LGR 644,
[1970] RA 330, 134 JP 576, 114 Sol Jo 397, CA 787
Frank v Mainwaring (1839) 2 Beav 115 598
Freshfield v Reed (1842) 11 LJ Ex 193, 9 M & W 404 598
Frost, Re [1936] 2 All ER 182, 80 Sol Jo 464, CA 759
Furber v Kratter (1988) Times, 21 July 759

G

G, Re (1991) Times, 31 January 612
G, Re (11 October 2001, unreported) 622
G (an adult) (mental capacity: court's jurisdiction), Re [2004] EWHC 2222 (Fam),
[2004] All ER (D) 33 (Oct) 785–786
G (TJ), Re [2010] EWHC 3005 (COP), [2010] All ER (D) 218 (Nov) 606, 724, 727
G v E [2010] EWHC 621 (Fam), [2010] 2 FLR 294, [2010] Fam Law 703, [2010] All
ER (D) 120 (Apr) 740
G v E (by his litigation friend, the Official Solicitor) [2010] EWCA Civ 822, [2012] Fam
78, [2010] 4 All ER 579, [2011] 3 WLR 652, [2011] PTSR 1574, [2010] 2 FCR
601, [2011] 1 FLR 239, [2010] Fam Law 1066, 116 BMLR 162, [2010] All ER (D)
180 (Jul) 605, 674
G v E (by his Litigation Friend, the Official Solicitor) [2010] EWHC 2512 (COP),
[2011] 1 FLR 1652, [2011] Fam Law 141 .... 734, 740
G v E (Costs) [2010] EWHC 3385 (Fam), [2011] 1 FLR 1566, [2011] Fam Law 473 747
GC, Re [2008] EWHC 3402 (Fam) 724
GC v Managers of the Kingwood Centre of Central and North West London NHS
Foundation Trust (CO/7784/2008) (3 October 2008, unreported) 761
GD v Edgware Community Hospital [2008] MHLR 282 847
GD v Hospital Managers of the Edgware Community Hospital [2008] EWHC 3572
(Admin), [2008] All ER (D) 439 (Jun) 821
GF, Re [1991] FCR 786, [1992] 1 FLR 293, [1992] Fam Law 63, [1993] 4 Med LR 77,
sub nom F v F 7 BMLR 135 612
GJ (incapacitated adults), Re [2008] EWHC 1097 (Fam), [2008] 2 FLR 1295,
[2008] Fam Law 997 724
GJ v Foundation Trust [2009] EWHC 2972 (Fam), [2010] Fam 70, [2010] 3 WLR 840,
[2010] Fam Law 139, [2010] 1 FLR 1251 .... 562, 628, 649, 658–659, 733, 787, 821, 927
GM (Patient: Consultation), Re [2000] MMHLR 41 .... 821, 847
Gaumont British Distributors Ltd v Henry [1939] 2 KB 711, [1939] 2 All ER 808, 37
LGR 514, 103 JP 256, 108 LJKB 675, 83 Sol Jo 525, 160 LT 646, 55 TLR
750, DC 1013
George Armstrong & Sons, Re [1896] 1 Ch 536, 65 LJ Ch 258, 44 WR 281, 40 Sol Jo
228, 74 LT 134 600
Gillick v West Norfolk and Wisbech Area Health Authority [1986] AC 112,
[1985] 3 All ER 402, [1985] 3 WLR 830, [1986] 1 FLR 224, [1986] Crim LR 113,
129 Sol Jo 738, 2 BMLR 11, [1985] LS Gaz R 3551, [1985] NLJ Rep 1055, HL 612, 765
Gintec International Import-Export Gmbh v Verband Sozialer Wettbewerb eV: C-374/05
[2007] ECR I-9517, [2008] 1 CMLR 808, [2007] All ER (D) 133 (Nov), ECJ 336
Godfrey v United Kingdom (Application 8542/79) (1982) 27 DR 94, EComHR,
EComHR 384
Grant v Mental Health Review Tribunal (1986) Times, 28 April 969
Green v Moore [1982] QB 1044, [1982] 1 All ER 428, [1982] 2 WLR 671, 74 Cr App
Rep 250, 146 JP 142, [1982] Crim LR 233, 126 Sol Jo 79, DC 1015
Grimani v Draper (1848) 12 Jur 924, 6 Notes of Cases 418 598
Groom v Thomas (1829) 2 Hag Ecc 433 598
Guardian News and Media Ltd, Re [2010] UKSC 1, [2010] 2 AC 697, [2010] 2 All ER
799, [2010] 2 WLR 325, [2010] 06 LS Gaz R 18, (2010) Times, 29 January, (2010)
Times, 28 January, [2010] EMLR 378, [2010] 4 LRC 476, [2010] All ER (D) 178
(Jan) 1000
Guzzardi v Italy (Application 7367/76) (1980) 3 EHRR 333, ECtHR 648, 787, 969

H

H (adult patient) (medical treatment), Re [2006] EWHC 1230 (Fam), [2006] 2 FLR 958,
[2006] Fam Law 842, [2006] All ER (D) 372 (May) 605

PARA

HE v A Hospital NHS Trust [2003] EWHC 1017 (Fam), [2003] 2 FLR 408,
    [2003] Fam Law 733 .... 606, 612, 623, 625
HL v United Kingdom (Application 45508/99) (2004) 40 EHRR 761, 81 BMLR 131,
    (2004) Times, 19 October, 17 BHRC 418, [2004] ECHR 45508/99, [2004] All ER
    (D) 39 (Oct), ECtHR 562, 597, 634, 648, 764, 767
HLH Warenvertriebs GmbH v Germany: C-211/03, C-299/03 and C-316/03 to C-318/03
    [2005] ECR I-5141, [2005] All ER (D) 56 (Jun), ECJ 25
Haines v Roberts [1953] 1 All ER 344, [1953] 1 WLR 309, 51 LGR 177, 117 JP 123,
    97 Sol Jo 117, DC 373
Hall v Semple (1862) 3 F & F 337 759
Hammond v Osborn [2002] EWCA Civ 885, [2002] 2 P & CR D41,
    [2002] 34 LS Gaz R 29, (2001) Times, 18 July, [2002] All ER (D) 232 (Jun) 601
Hanbury v Hanbury (1892) 8 TLR 559, CA 761
Harnett v Bond [1925] AC 669, 89 JP 182, 94 LJKB 569, [1925] All ER Rep 110, 69
    Sol Jo 575, 133 LT 482, 41 TLR 509, HL 759
Harnett v Fisher [1927] AC 573, 25 LGR 454, 91 JP 175, 96 LJKB 856, 71 Sol Jo 470,
    137 LT 602, 43 TLR 567, HL 759, 849
Harris v Harris (22 April 1999, unreported), CA 1002
Harris v Ingledew (1730) 2 Eq Cas Abr 255, 462, 3 P Wms 91 598
Hart v O'Connor [1985] AC 1000, [1985] 2 All ER 880, [1985] 3 WLR 214, 129 Sol Jo
    484, [1985] LS Gaz R 2658, PC 614
Hassard v Smith (1872) IR 6 Eq 429 .... 598, 614
Havering London Borough Council v LD [2010] EWHC 3976 (COP) 601, 740
Haycraft v Creasy (1801) 2 East 92 761
Healing v Healing (1902) 51 WR 221, 47 Sol Jo 110, 19 TLR 90 600
Heaphy's Trusts, Re (1870) 18 WR 1070 564
Herczegfalvy v Austria (Applications 10533/83) (1992) 15 EHRR 437, 18 BMLR 48,
    ECtHR 780, 927
Hill, Re [1900] 1 IR 349 998
Hillingdon London Borough Council v Neary [2011] EWHC 1377 (COP),
    [2011] 4 All ER 584, [2011] 3 FCR 448, [2012] 1 FLR 72, [2011] Fam Law 944,
    122 BMLR 1, [2011] NLJR 849, [2011] All ER (D) 57 (Jun) 663, 674, 724
Hillingdon London Borough Council v Neary [2011] EWHC 3522 (COP), [2012] All ER
    (D) 54 (Jan) 747
Hillingdon London Borough Council v Neary [2011] EWHC 413 (COP),
    [2011] Fam Law 476, [2011] NLJR 404, [2011] WTLR 769, [2011] All ER (D) 26
    (Mar) 740
Hinchcliffe v Sheldon [1955] 3 All ER 406, [1955] 1 WLR 1207, 120 JP 13, 99 Sol Jo
    797, DC 1015
Hirst v United Kingdom (No 2) (Application No 74025/01) (2005) 42 EHRR 849,
    (2005) Times, 10 October, 19 BHRC 546, [2005] ECHR 74025/01, [2005] All ER
    (D) 59 (Oct), ECtHR 565
Hodder v DPP [1990] Crim LR 261, DC 483
Hoff v Atherton [2004] EWCA Civ 1554, [2004] All ER (D) 314 (Nov) 615
Holgate v Lancashire Mental Hospitals Board, Gill and Robertson [1937] 4 All ER 19 759
Horne v Pountain (1889) 23 QBD 264, 54 JP 37, 58 LJQB 413, 38 WR 240, 61 LT
    510, DC 1002
Howard v Earl of Digby (1834) 8 Bli NS 224, 2 Cl & Fin 634, 5 Sim 330, 5 ER 928,
    [1824–34] All ER Rep 130, HL 617
Howell v Lewis (1891) 61 LJ Ch 89, 40 WR 88, 36 Sol Jo 61, 65 LT 672 995
Hoyle v Hitchman (1879) 4 QBD 233, 43 JP 430, 40 LJMC 97, 27 WR 487, 40 LT
    252, DC 235
Hunter v Edney (otherwise Hunter) (1881) 10 PD 93 609
Hutchison Reid v United Kingdom (Application No 50272/99) [2003] ECHR 50272/99,
    37 EHRR 211, 14 BHRC 41, (2003) Times, 26 February 767–768

I

IB v CV [2010] EWHC 3815 (QB) 1000
Imperial Loan Co v Stone [1892] 1 QB 599, 56 JP 436, 61 LJQB 449, [1891–4] All ER
    Rep 412, 66 LT 556, 8 TLR 408, CA 614

PARA

Independent News & Media Ltd v A (by his litigation friend the Official Solicitor) [2010] EWCA Civ 343, [2010] 3 All ER 32, [2010] 1 WLR 2262, [2010] 2 FCR 187, [2010] 2 FLR 1290, [2010] Fam Law 705, 113 BMLR 162, (2010) Times, 30 April, [2010] All ER (D) 03 (Apr) 740
Intended Action, Re, Shoesmith v Lancashire Mental Hospitals Board. See Shoesmith, Re
Irvani v Irvani [2000] 1 Lloyd's Rep 412, [1999] All ER (D) 1405, CA 614

J

J (a minor), Re (1992) Times, 15 July, CA 612, 765
J (a child), Re, R (on the application of S) v Secretary of State for the Home Department [2002] EWHC 18 (Fam), [2002] Fam 213, [2002] 3 WLR 24, [2002] 1 FCR 481, [2002] 1 FLR 845, (2002) Times, 11 March, 146 Sol Jo LB 37, [2002] All ER (D) 187 (Jan) 612
J v S [1894] 3 Ch 72, 63 LJ Ch 615, 8 R 436, 42 WR 617, 38 Sol Jo 531, 70 LT 758, 10 TLR 507 616
J (HD) v J (AM) [1980] 1 All ER 156, [1980] 1 WLR 124, (1981) 2 FLR 78, 10 Fam Law 82 610
J (otherwise B) v J [1953] P 186, [1952] 2 All ER 1129, [1953] 1 WLR 36, 97 Sol Jo 12 994
JIH v News Group Newspapers Ltd [2011] EWCA Civ 42, [2011] 2 All ER 324, [2011] 1 WLR 1645, [2011] 2 FCR 95, [2011] IP & T 453, [2011] NLJR 211, (2011) Times, 07 February, [2011] EMLR 300, [2011] All ER (D) 234 (Jan) 1000
JT (adult: refusal of medical treatment), Re [1998] 2 FCR 662, [1998] 1 FLR 48, [1998] Fam Law 23 612
JT v United Kingdom [2000] 30 EHRR CD 77, [2000] 1 FLR 909, [2000] Fam Law 533, (2000) Times, 5 April, ECtHR 821, 839, 842
JXF (a child, by his mother and litigation friend) v York Hospitals NHS Foundation Trust [2010] EWHC 2800 (QB), 117 BMLR 1, [2010] All ER (D) 59 (Nov) 1000
Jacobs v Porter (1854) 18 Beav 300, 23 LJ Ch 557, 2 Eq Rep 299, 18 Jur 527, 2 WR 174, 23 LTOS 44; on appeal (1854) 5 De GM & G 55 614
Jacobs v Richards (1854) 18 Beav 300, 23 LJ Ch 557, 2 Eq Rep 299, 18 Jur 527, 2 WR 174, 23 LTOS 44; on appeal (1854) 5 De GM & G 55 614
James v Mayor and Burgesses of the Havering London Borough Council (1992) 15 BMLR 1, CA 759
Jenkins v Morris (1880) 14 Ch D 674, 49 LJ Ch 392, 42 LT 817, CA 614
Johnson v Blane (1848) 6 Notes of Cases 442 598
Johnson v United Kingdom (1997) 27 EHRR 296, 40 BMLR 1, ECtHR 566, 767–768, 869, 945, 968–969
Johnston v Chief Constable of Merseyside Police [2009] EWHC 2969 (QB), [2009] All ER (D) 226 (Nov) 759
Jones v Lloyd (1874) LR 18 Eq 265, 43 LJ Ch 826, 22 WR 785, 30 LT 487 616

K

K, Re [1988] Ch 310, [1988] 1 All ER 358, [1988] 2 WLR 781, [1988] 2 FLR 15, [1988] Fam Law 203, 11 LDAB 39, 131 Sol Jo 1488, [1987] NLJ Rep 1039 619
K v A local authority [2012] EWCA Civ 79, [2012] 1 FCR 441, [2012] All ER (D) 61 (Feb) 606, 724
KD and LD v Havering London Borough Council [2010] 1 FLR 1393, [2010] Fam Law 244 742
KGS v JDS (by his litigation friend, the Official Solicitor) [2012] EWHC 302 (COP), [2012] NLJR 1536, [2012] All ER (D) 201 (Jan) 724, 727
Katz v Katz [1972] 3 All ER 219, [1972] 1 WLR 955, 116 Sol Jo 546 610
Kay v United Kingdom (1994) 40 BMLR 20, EComHR 917
Kiernan (Peter) v Harrow Crown Court [2003] EWCA Crim 1052 .... 864, 879
Kimber v Kimber [2001] 1 FLR 383, [2000] Fam Law 317 838
Kinsey v North Mersey Community NHS Trust (21 June 1999, unreported) 915
Kirkwall v Flight (1842) 3 WR 529 614
Knight, Re [1898] 1 Ch 257, 67 LJ Ch 136, 46 WR 289, 77 LT 773, CA 998
Knight v Edonya [2009] EWHC 2181 (Ch), [2009] All ER (D) 207 (Aug) 623
Knox v Anderton (1982) 76 Cr App Rep 156, 147 JP 340, [1983] Crim LR 114, DC 923
Kolanis v United Kingdom (Application 517/02) (2005) 42 EHRR 206, 84 BMLR 102, [2005] ECHR 517/02, [2005] All ER (D) 227 (Jun), ECtHR 566, 767–768, 945, 968–969

PARA

Kynaston v Secretary of State for Home Affairs (1981) 73 Cr App Rep 281,
  [1982] Crim LR 117, CA 759

L

L (WJG), Re [1966] Ch 135, [1965] 3 All ER 865, [1966] 2 WLR 233, 110 Sol Jo 74 727
LBH v GP (Claim No FD08P01058) (8 April 2009, unreported) 649
LBL v RYJ [2010] EWHC 2665 (COP), [2011] 1 FLR 1279, [2011] Fam Law 242,
  [2011] All ER (D) 290 (Feb) 598, 605
LG v DK [2011] EWHC 2453 (COP), [2012] 2 All ER 115, [2012] 1 FCR 476,
  [2011] NLJR 1414, [2011] All ER (D) 31 (Oct) 723
LLBC v TG [2007] EWHC 2640 (Fam), [2009] 2 FCR 428, [2009] 1 FLR 414 724
LT (vulnerable adult) (decision making: capacity), Re. See RT v LT
Labrooy v Hammersmith and Fulham London Borough Council [2006] EWHC 1976
  (QB), [2006] All ER (D) 257 (Apr) 759
Leach v Thompson (1698) Show Parl Cas 150, sub nom Thompson v Leach 2 Vent
  208, HL 617
Lewis v Cox [1985] QB 509, [1984] 3 All ER 672, [1984] 3 WLR 875, 80 Cr App Rep
  1, 148 JP 601, [1984] Crim LR 756, 128 Sol Jo 596, [1984] LS Gaz R 2538, DC 1015
Lewis v Gibson [2005] EWCA Civ 587, [2005] 2 FCR 241, 87 BMLR 93, [2005] All ER
  (D) 292 (May) 761, 787, 842
Lindsay v Wood [2006] EWHC 2895 (QB), (2006) Times, 8 December, [2006] All ER
  (D) 204 (Nov) 598, 603, 605
Litwa v Poland (Application 26629/95) (2000) 33 EHRR 1267, 63 BMLR 199, [2000]
  ECHR 26629/95, ECtHR 767–768
London and Globe Finance Corpn Ltd, Re [1903] 1 Ch 728, 82 JP 447, 72 LJ Ch 368,
  10 Mans 198, 31 WR 651, [1900–3] All ER Rep 891, 88 LT 194, 19 TLR 314 1008
Long v Rodman [2012] EWHC 347 (Ch), [2012] All ER (D) 171 (Feb) 734

M

M, Re [2011] EWHC 3590 (COP) 561
M (adult patient) (minimally conscious state: withdrawal of treatment), Re
  [2011] EWHC 2443 (Fam), [2012] 1 WLR 1653, [2012] PTSR 1040,
  [2011] Fam Law 1330, 122 BMLR 67, [2011] 39 LS Gaz R 18, (2011) Times,
  01 December, [2011] All ER (D) 142 (Sep), sub nom W (by her litigation friend, B)
  v M (by her litigation friend, the Official Solicitor) [2012] 1 All ER 1313,
  [2012] 1 FCR 1, [2012] 1 FLR 495 .... 606, 612, 625
M (vulnerable adult) (testamentary capacity), Re [2009] EWHC 2525 (Fam),
  [2010] 3 All ER 682, [2011] 1 WLR 344, [2009] All ER (D) 314 (Oct) ... 606, 615, 724, 727
M v B [2005] EWHC 1681 (Fam), [2005] Fam Law 860, (2005) Times, 10 August,
  [2005] All ER (D) 449 (Jul) 609
M v South West London and St George's Mental Health NHS Trust, Re [2008] EWCA
  Civ 1112, [2008] All ER (D) 63 (Aug) 821, 930
M (by his litigation friend TM) v Hackney London Borough Council [2011] EWCA Civ
  4. See R (on the application of TTM (by his litigation friend TM)) v Hackney
  London Borough Council
MB (an adult: medical treatment), Re [1997] 2 FCR 541, [1997] 2 FLR 426,
  [1997] Fam Law 542, [1997] 8 Med LR 217, 38 BMLR 175, [1997] NLJR
  600, CA 603, 605, 611–612
MD v Nottinghamshire Health Care NHS Trust [2010] UKUT 59 (AAC) 768
MM, Re, Local Authority X v MM [2007] EWHC 2003 (Fam), [2008] 3 FCR 788,
  [2009] 1 FLR 443, [2008] Fam Law 213, [2007] Fam Law 1132 .... 598–599, 605–606, 609,
                                                                              724
MN, Re [2010] EWHC 1926 (Fam) 561
MS v United Kingdom (Application No 24527/08) (2012) 126 BMLR 168, (2012)
  Times, 14 May, [2012] ECHR 24527/08, [2012] All ER (D) 95 (May), ECtHR 923
McArdle v Egan (1933) 32 LGR 85, 98 JP 103, 30 Cox CC 67, [1933] All ER Rep 611,
  150 LT 412, CA 548
McCarthy v Metropolitan Board of Works (1872) LR 8 CP 191, Ex Ch; affd sub nom
  Metropolitan Board of Works v McCarthy (1874) LR 7 HL 243, 38 JP 820, 43
  LJCP 385, 23 WR 115, 31 LT 182 234
McGee, Re [2008] MHLR 216 770
Mackintosh v Smith and Lowe (1865) 4 Macq 913, HL 772

PARA

McLeod v Metropolitan Police Comr [1994] 4 All ER 553, CA 922
Manches v Trimborn [1946] WN 63, 115 LJKB 305, 90 Sol Jo 223, 174 LT 344 614
Manchester City Council v E (by his litigation friend the Official Solicitor)
    [2011] EWCA Civ 939, [2011] 2 FLR 1297, [2011] Fam Law 1196, [2011] All ER
    (D) 38 (Aug) 747
Manning v Gill (1872) LR 13 Eq 485, 36 JP 436, 41 LJ Ch 736, 12 Cox CC 274, 20
    WR 357, 26 LT 14 617
Marshall, Re, Marshall v Whateley [1920] 1 Ch 284, 89 LJ Ch 204, [1920] All ER Rep
    190, 64 Sol Jo 241, 122 LT 673 617
Mason v Mason [1972] Fam 302, [1972] 3 All ER 315, [1972] 3 WLR 405, 116 Sol Jo
    485 610
Masterman-Lister v Brutton & Co [2003] EWCA Civ 70, [2003] 1 WLR 1511, [2003]
    All ER (D) 59 (Jan) 995
Masterman-Lister v Jewell [2002] EWHC 417 (QB), [2002] All ER (D) 247 (Mar); affd
    [2002] EWCA Civ 1889, [2003] 3 All ER 162, [2003] 1 WLR 1511, 73 BMLR 1,
    (2002) Times, 28 December, 147 Sol Jo LB 60, [2002] All ER (D) 297 (Dec) 601, 605
Matthews v DPP [1990] Crim LR 261, DC 483
Mental Health Review Tribunal v Hempstock (1997) 39 BMLR 123 968
Metropolitan Board of Works v McCarthy. See McCarthy v Metropolitan Board of
Works
Minns v Foster [2002] All ER (D) 225 (Dec) 615
Mischeff v Springett [1942] 2 KB 331, [1942] 2 All ER 349, 40 LGR 264, 106 JP 279,
    111 LJKB 690, 167 LT 402, 58 TLR 385, DC 539
Mohamed v Hammersmith and Fulham London Borough Council [2001] UKHL 57,
    [2002] 1 AC 547, [2002] 1 All ER 176, [2001] 3 WLR 1339, [2002] 1 FCR 183,
    [2001] 45 LS Gaz R 26, [2001] NLJR 1664, (2001) Times, 2 November, 145 Sol Jo
    LB 253, [2001] All ER (D) 11 (Nov) 839
Molton v Camroux (1848) 18 LJ Ex 68, 2 Exch 487, 12 Jur 800, 76 RR 669; affd
    (1849) 18 LJ Ex 356, 4 Exch 17, 80 RR 461, 13 LTOS 305 614
Monteil and Samanni, Re: C-60/89 [1991] ECR I-1547, [1992] 3 CMLR 425, 14 BMLR
    112, 135 Sol Jo LB 13, ECJ 25
Moore v Metropolitan Police Comr [1968] 1 QB 26, [1967] 2 All ER 827,
    [1967] 3 WLR 572, 111 Sol Jo 355, CA 759
Moore v Ray [1951] 1 KB 98, [1950] 2 All ER 561, 49 LGR 187, 114 JP 486, 94 Sol Jo
    596, 66 (pt 2) TLR 721, DC 235
Mooren v Germany (Application No 11364/03) (2009) 50 EHRR 554, [2009] ECHR
    11364/03, ECtHR 771
Mordaunt v Mordaunt, Cole and Johnson (1870) LR 2 P & D 109, 39 LJP & M 57, 18
    WR 845, 23 LT 85; on appeal (1872) LR 2 P & D 382, 41 LJP & M 42, 20 WR
    553, 26 LT 812; revsd sub nom Mordaunt v Moncreiffe (1874) LR 2 Sc & Div
    374, 39 JP 4, 43 LJP & M 49, 23 WR 12, [1874–80] All ER Rep 288, 30 LT
    649, HL 761
Morriss v Marsden [1952] 1 All ER 925, 96 Sol Jo 281, [1952] 1 TLR 947 761
Moss v Tribe (1862) 3 F & F 297 614

N

NHS Trust v D (by his litigation friend, the Official Solicitor) [2012] EWHC 886 (COP),
    [2012] NLJR 1421, [2012] All ER (D) 171 (Apr) 747
NHS Trust v T (adult patient: refusal of medical treatment) [2004] EWHC 1279 (Fam),
    [2005] 1 All ER 387, [2004] 3 FCR 297, 80 BMLR 184, [2004] All ER (D) 188
    (Jun) 612
New York Security and Trust Co v Keyser [1901] 1 Ch 666, 70 LJ Ch 330, 49 WR 371,
    45 Sol Jo 239, 84 LT 43, 17 TLR 207 .... 995, 998
Newham London Borough Council v S (adult: court's jurisdiction) [2003] EWHC 1909
    (Fam), [2003] 2 FLR 1235, [2003] Fam Law 870, 75 BMLR 185, [2003] All ER
    (D) 550 (Jul) 761
Niell v Morley (1804) 9 Ves 478 617
Norfolk and Norwich Healthcare (NHS) Trust v W [1997] 1 FCR 269, [1996] 2 FLR
    613, [1997] Fam Law 17, 34 BMLR 16 .... 612, 765
Nottingham City Council v Unison [2004] EWHC 893 (QB) 821

PARA

O

Optident Ltd v Secretary of State for Trade and Industry [2001] UKHL 32,
[2001] 3 CMLR 1, 61 BMLR 10, (2001) Times, 2 July, [2001] All ER (D) 320
(Jun) 472
Oxford v Sangers Ltd [1965] 1 QB 491, [1965] 1 All ER 96, [1965] 2 WLR 145, 129 JP
98, DC 541

P

P, Re [2009] EWHC 163 (Ch), [2010] Ch 33, [2009] 2 All ER 1198, [2009] All ER (D)
160 (Feb) 606, 615, 724, 727, 731, 734
P (adoption: natural father's rights), Re [1995] 2 FCR 58, [1994] 1 FLR 771,
[1994] Fam Law 310 821
P (vulnerable adult) (capacity: appointment of deputies), Re [2010] EWHC 1592 (Fam),
[2010] 2 FLR 1712, [2010] Fam Law 1073, [2010] All ER (D) 52 (Aug) 734–735
P v Mental Health Review Tribunal [2001] EWHC Admin 876 761
P v P (Contempt of Court: Mental Capacity) [1999] 2 FLR 897, CA 1002
P (by his litigation friend the Official Solicitor) v Independent Print Ltd [2011] EWCA
Civ 756, [2012] 2 FCR 503, [2012] 1 FLR 212, [2011] Fam Law 1081, [2011] All
ER (D) 36 (Jul) 740
P (MIG) and Q (MEG) v Surrey County Council [2011] EWCA Civ 190, [2012] Fam
170, [2012] 2 WLR 1056, [2012] PTSR 727, [2011] 1 FCR 559, [2011] 2 FLR
583, [2011] Fam Law 475, 120 BMLR 44, [2011] All ER (D) 286 (Feb) 606, 648
PH v A Local Authority [2011] EWHC 1704 (Fam) 605, 733
Palmer v Walesby (1868) 3 Ch App 732, 37 LJ Ch 612, 16 WR 924, 19 LT 1 995
Park's Estate, Re, Park v Park [1954] P 89, [1953] 2 All ER 408, [1953] 3 WLR 307, 97
Sol Jo 491; affd [1954] P 112, [1953] 2 All ER 1411, [1953] 3 WLR 1012, 97 Sol
Jo 830, CA 609
Pearce v United Bristol Healthcare NHS Trust (1998) 48 BMLR 118, [1998] CLY 3986,
[1999] PIQR P 53, CA 612
Pélégrin v Coutts & Co [1915] 1 Ch 696, 84 LJ Ch 576, 113 LT 140 998
Pélégrin v L Messel & Co [1915] 1 Ch 696, 84 LJ Ch 576, 113 LT 140 998
Penrice v Brander (1921) 53 SLR 307, 1921 JC 63, HC of Justiciary (Sc) 234
Petition for Judicial Separation, Re, ex p Beecham [1901] P 65, sub nom Re Beecham
and Lunacy Comrs 70 LJP 20, 84 LT 63 916
Pharmaceutical Society of Great Britain v Boots Cash Chemists (Southern) Ltd
[1953] 1 QB 401, [1953] 1 All ER 482, [1953] 2 WLR 427, 117 JP 132, 97 Sol Jo
149, CA 539
Pink v J A Sharwood & Co Ltd [1913] 2 Ch 286, 82 LJ Ch 542, 57 Sol Jo 663, 108 LT
1017 995
Pomery v Pomery [1909] WN 158, 53 Sol Jo 631 994–995
Porter v Porter (1888) 37 Ch D 420, 36 WR 580, 58 LT 688, CA 995
Pountney v Griffiths [1976] AC 314, [1975] 2 All ER 881, [1975] 3 WLR 140,
[1975] Crim LR 702, 119 Sol Jo 493, HL 759
Preston v Albuery [1964] 2 QB 796, [1963] 3 All ER 897, [1964] 2 WLR 218, 107 Sol
Jo 891, DC 539
Pretty v United Kingdom (Application 2346/02) (2002) 35 EHRR 1, [2002] 2 FCR 97,
[2002] 2 FLR 45, 12 BHRC 149, 66 BMLR 147, [2002] ECHR 2346/02, [2002]
All ER (D) 286 (Apr), ECtHR 612
Price v Berrington (1849) 7 Hare 394, 15 LTOS 326; on appeal (1851) 15 Jur 999, 3
Mac & G 486, 87 RR 157, 18 LTOS 56 .... 598, 614, 617
Prinsep and East India Co v Dyce Sombre, Troup and Solaroli (1856) 10 Moo PCC 232,
4 WR 714 598
Procureur de la République v Tissier: 35/85 [1986] ECR 1207, [1987] 1 CMLR 551,
ECJ 25

R

R (a minor), Re [1992] Fam 11, [1991] 4 All ER 177, [1991] 3 WLR 592,
[1992] 2 FCR 229, [1992] 1 FLR 190, [1992] Fam Law 67, [1992] 3 Med LR 342,
7 BMLR 147, [1991] NLJR 1297, CA 612, 765
R v A [2005] EWCA Crim 2077, [2006] 1 Cr App Rep (S) 521, [2006] Crim LR 79,
[2005] All ER (D) 28 (Aug) 864, 869, 969
R v Acharya [2005] EWCA Crim 772, [2005] All ER (D) 225 (Mar) 869

PARA

R v Banks [1916] 2 KB 621, 12 Cr App Rep 74, 80 JP 432, 85 LJKB 1657, 25 Cox CC
535, [1916–17] All ER Rep 356, 115 LT 457, CCA 548
R v Beard [1974] 1 WLR 1549, 118 Sol Jo 848 526
R v Bennett [1968] 2 All ER 753, [1968] 1 WLR 988, 52 Cr App Rep 514, 132 JP 365,
112 Sol Jo 418, CA 864
R v Birch (1989) 90 Cr App Rep 78, 11 Cr App Rep (S) 202, [1989] Crim LR 757,
[1990] 2 Med LR 77, CA 869
R v Birmingham Mental Health Trust, ex p Phillips (CO/1501/95) (25 May 1995,
unreported) 847
R v Blackwood (1974) 59 Cr App Rep 170, [1974] Crim LR 437, CA 869
R v Board of Control, ex p Rutty [1956] 2 QB 109, [1956] 1 All ER 769,
[1956] 2 WLR 822, 54 LGR 276, 120 JP 153, 100 Sol Jo 263, DC 922, 967
R v Board of Control, ex p Winterflood [1938] 1 KB 420, [1937] 4 All ER 163, 107
LJKB 264, DC; revsd [1938] 2 KB 366, [1938] 2 All ER 463, 107 LJKB 409, 82
Sol Jo 373, 159 LT 345, 54 TLR 698, CA 967
R v Bournewood Community and Mental Health NHS Trust, ex p L [1999] 1 AC 458,
[1998] 3 All ER 289, [1998] 3 WLR 107, [1998] 2 FCR 501, [1998] 2 FLR 550,
[1998] Fam Law 592, 44 BMLR 1, [1998] 29 LS Gaz R 27, [1998] NLJR 1014,
142 Sol Jo LB 195, HL 562, 612, 634, 764, 767
R v Broadmoor and Secretary of State for the Home Department, ex p S, H and D
(CO/199/98), unreported, CA 759
R v Broadmoor Special Hospital Authority, ex p S [1998] 08 LS Gaz R 32, 142 Sol Jo
LB 76, CA 776
R v Canons Park Mental Health Review Tribunal, ex p A [1995] QB 60,
[1994] 2 All ER 659, [1994] 3 WLR 630, 18 BMLR 94, [1994] 13 LS Gaz R 35,
138 Sol Jo LB 75, CA 967
R v Central London County Court, ex p London [1999] QB 1260, [1999] 3 All ER 991,
[1999] 3 WLR 1, [1999] 2 FLR 161, [1999] Fam Law 452,
[1999] 15 LS Gaz R 30, CA 771, 842
R v Chalk [2002] EWCA Crim 2434, [2002] All ER (D) 509 (Oct) 869
R v Chippenham Magistrates' Court, ex p Thompson (1996) 32 BMLR 69,
(1995) 160 JP 207, (1995) Times, 6 December 871
R v Chowdhury (Taher Ahmed) [2011] EWCA Crim 936 867
R v Collins, ex p Brady (2000) 58 BMLR 173, 58 MHLR 17 .... 612, 927
R v Collins, ex p S [1999] Fam 26, [1998] 3 All ER 673, [1998] 3 WLR 936,
[1998] 2 FCR 685, [1998] 2 FLR 728, [1998] Fam Law 526, 44 BMLR 160,
[1998] 22 LS Gaz R 29, [1998] NLJR 693, 142 Sol Jo LB 164, [1998] CCL Rep
410, CA 612, 767, 821, 927
R v Cooper [2009] UKHL 42, [2009] 4 All ER 1033, [2009] 1 WLR 1786, [2010] 1 Cr
App Rep 104, [2010] Crim LR 75, (2009) Times, 7 August, 153 Sol Jo (no 31) 30,
[2009] All ER (D) 329 (Jul) 608, 761
R v Coughlan (1994) 16 Cr App Rep (S) 519, (1994) Times, 31 October, CA 491
R v Courtney (1987) 9 Cr App Rep (S) 404, [1988] Crim LR 130, CA 869
R v Couzens and Frankel (1992) 14 Cr App Rep (S) 33, [1992] Crim LR 822, CA 483
R v Cox [1968] 1 All ER 386, [1968] 1 WLR 308, 52 Cr App Rep 130, 132 JP 162,
111 Sol Jo 966, CA 864, 869
R v Cramp (1880) 5 QBD 307, 44 JP 411, 39 LJMC 44, 14 Cox CC 401, 28 WR 701,
42 LT 442, CCR 528
R v Crawley [1982] 3 All ER 969, [1982] 1 WLR 1405, 76 Cr App Rep 29,
[1982] Crim LR 752, 126 Sol Jo 657, 4 Cr App R (S) 298, CA 526
R v Criminal Injuries Compensation Board, ex p Lawton [1972] 3 All ER 582,
[1972] 1 WLR 1589, 136 JP 828, 116 Sol Jo 901 .... 777, 1013
R v Crookes [1999] 1 MHLR 416 869
R v Cunliffe (1987) 9 Cr App Rep (S) 442, [1986] Crim LR 547, CA 483
R v Cuthbertson [1981] AC 470, [1980] 2 All ER 401, [1980] 3 WLR 89, 71 Cr App
Rep 148, 124 Sol Jo 443, HL 480, 526
R v Czarnoti [2002] EWCA Crim 785, [2002]1 MHLR 144 869
R v Davies [1999] All ER (D) 1450, CA 1010
R v Dhaliwal (appeal under s 58 of the Criminal Justice Act 2003) [2006] EWCA Crim
1139, [2006] 2 Cr App Rep 348, [2006] Crim LR 923, [2006] All ER (D) 236
(May) 761

PARA

R v Drew [2003] UKHL 25, [2003] 4 All ER 557, [2003] 1 WLR 1213, [2003] 2 Cr
App Rep 371, [2004] 1 Cr App Rep (S) 65, 75 BMLR 34, [2003] 26 LS Gaz R 35,
[2003] NLJR 749, (2003) Times, 9 May, 147 Sol Jo LB 597, [2003] All ER (D) 100
(May) 892
R v Dunn [2010] EWCA Crim 2935, [2011] 1 Cr App Rep 425, 174 CL&J 766, [2010]
All ER (D) 250 (Nov) 1011
R v Ealing District Health Authority, ex p Fox [1993] 3 All ER 170, [1993] 1 WLR 373,
11 BMLR 59, 136 Sol Jo LB 220 945
R v East London NHS Foundation Trust and Hackney London Borough Council,
ex p M [2009] MHLR 154 821
R v Edwards (1978) 67 Cr App Rep 228, [1978] Crim LR 564, 122 Sol Jo 177, CA 923
R v Ewens [1967] 1 QB 322, [1966] 2 All ER 470, [1966] 2 WLR 1372, 50 Cr App
Rep 171, 110 Sol Jo 483, CCA 491
R v Forde [1923] 2 KB 400, 17 Cr App Rep 99, 87 JP 76, 92 LJKB 501, 27 Cox CC
406, [1923] All ER Rep 477, 67 Sol Jo 539, 128 LT 798, 39 TLR 322, CCA 548
R v Fox (Wayne Anthony) [2011] EWCA Crim 3299 863
R v Galfetti [2002] EWCA Crim 1916, [2002] All ER (D) 521 (Jul) 864
R v Gardiner [1967] 1 All ER 895, [1967] 1 WLR 464, 51 Cr App Rep 187, 131 JP
273, 111 Sol Jo 93, CA 869
R v Gardner, ex p L [1986] QB 1090, [1986] 2 All ER 306, [1986] 2 WLR 883, 130 Sol
Jo 204, [1986] LS Gaz R 786 .... 767–768, 909–910, 917, 967
R v Glover (1974), unreported 526
R v Goodchild [1977] 2 All ER 163, [1977] 1 WLR 473, 64 Cr App Rep 100, 141 JP
295, 121 Sol Jo 103, CA; revsd [1978] 2 All ER 161, [1978] 1 WLR 578, 67 Cr
App Rep 56, 122 Sol Jo 263, DPP v Goodchild, HL 484
R v Goodchild (No 2) [1978] 1 All ER 649, [1977] 1 WLR 1213, 65 Cr App Rep 165,
121 Sol Jo 644, CA; revsd sub nom DPP v Goodchild [1978] 2 All ER 161,
[1978] 1 WLR 578, 67 Cr App Rep 56, 142 JP 338, 122 Sol Jo 263, HL 484
R v Greensmith [1983] 3 All ER 444, [1983] 1 WLR 1124, 77 Cr App Rep 202, 148 JP
270, [1983] Crim LR 798, 127 Sol Jo 578, CA 483
R v Griffiths [2002] EWCA Crim 1762 896
R v Gunnell (1966) 50 Cr App Rep 242, 110 Sol Jo 706, CCA 864
R v Gwent County Council, ex p Harris [1995] 1 FCR 551, [1995] 2 FLR 1021,
[1995] ELR 27 927
R v Hallam [1957] 1 QB 569, [1957] 1 All ER 665, [1957] 2 WLR 521, 41 Cr App Rep
111, 121 JP 254, 101 Sol Jo 268, CCA 1013
R v Hallstrom, ex p W [1985] 3 All ER 775. See Waldron, ex p
R v Hallstrom, ex p W [1986] QB 1090, [1986] 2 All ER 306, [1986] 2 WLR 883, 130
Sol Jo 204, [1986] LS Gaz R 786 .... 767–768, 909–910, 917, 967
R v Harrison [1938] 3 All ER 134, 26 Cr App Rep 166, 31 Cox CC 98, 82 Sol Jo 436,
159 LT 95, CCA 548
R v Higginbotham [1961] 3 All ER 616, [1961] 1 WLR 1277, 45 Cr App Rep 379, 125
JP 642, 105 Sol Jo 726, CCA 869
R v Holmes (1979) 1 Cr App Rep (S) 233, [1979] Crim LR 52, Crown Ct 1010
R v Hopkins [2011] EWCA Crim 1513, 123 BMLR 1 1011
R v Hunt [1986] QB 125, [1986] 1 All ER 184, [1986] 2 WLR 225, 82 Cr App Rep
244, 150 JP 83, [1986] Crim LR 172, 129 Sol Jo 889, [1986] LS Gaz R 38, CA;
revsd [1987] AC 352, [1987] 1 All ER 1, [1986] 3 WLR 1115, 84 Cr App Rep
163, [1987] Crim LR 263, 130 Sol Jo 984, [1987] LS Gaz R 417, [1986] NLJ Rep
1183, HL 491, 502
R v Hurst [2007] EWCA Crim 3436 869
R v Immigration Appeal Tribunal and Secretary of State for the Home Department,
ex p Alghali [1986] Imm AR 376 907
R v IRC, ex p Rossminster Ltd [1980] AC 952, [1979] 3 All ER 385, [1980] 2 WLR 1,
[1977] STC 677, 52 TC 160, [1979] TR 287, 123 Sol Jo 554; revsd [1980] AC
952, [1979] 3 All ER 385, [1980] 2 WLR 1, [1979] STC 677, 52 TC 160, 170,
[1979] TR 309, 123 Sol Jo 586, CA; revsd [1980] AC 952, [1980] 1 All ER 80,
[1980] 2 WLR 1, 70 Cr App Rep 157, [1980] STC 42, 52 TC 160, 191, [1979] TR
309, 124 Sol Jo 18, L(TC) 2753, HL 548
R v JTB. See R v T
R v Kamara [2000] 1 MHLR 9, CA 869
R v Kane [1965] 1 All ER 705, 129 JP 170 923

PARA

R v Kent County Council, ex p Marston (CO/1819/96), unreported 787
R v Khan [1982] 3 All ER 969, [1982] 1 WLR 1405, 76 Cr App Rep 29, 4 Cr App Rep
    (S) 298, [1982] Crim LR 752, 126 Sol Jo 657, CA 526
R v Kirklees Metropolitan Borough Council, ex p C (a minor) [1992] 2 FCR 321,
    [1992] 2 FLR 117, [1992] Fam Law 334, 8 BMLR 110; affd [1993] 2 FCR 381,
    [1993] 2 FLR 187, [1993] Fam Law 455, 15 BMLR 6, CA 765, 767
R v Layton (1849) 4 Cox CC 149 598
R v Licensing Authority established by the Medicines Act 1968 (acting by the Medicines
    Control Agency), ex p Generics (UK) Ltd: C-368/96 [1998] ECR I-7967,
    [1999] 2 CMLR 181, 48 BMLR 161, ECJ 6
R v Lincolnshire (Kesteven) Justices, ex p O'Connor [1983] 1 All ER 901,
    [1983] 1 WLR 335, 147 JP 97, [1983] Crim LR 621, 127 Sol Jo 121 871
R v Liverpool County Council, ex p F (CO/2744/96) (16 April 1997, unreported) 839
R v London South and South West Region Mental Health Review Tribunal, ex p Moyle
    (2000) Times, 10 February, [1999] All ER (D) 1504 .... 967, 969
R v Macauley (1967) 52 Cr App Rep 230, [1967] Crim LR 716, 111 Sol Jo 791, CA 483
R v Macrow [2004] EWCA Crim 1159, [2004] All ER (D) 277 (Apr) 869
R v Mahmood [2002] MHLR 416 869
R v Managers of South Western Hospital, ex p M [1993] QB 683, [1994] 1 All ER 161,
    [1993] 3 WLR 376, [1993] 12 LS Gaz R 32 .... 768, 771, 774, 821, 847
R v Marsden [1968] 2 All ER 341, [1968] 1 WLR 785, 52 Cr App Rep 301, 132 JP
    347, 112 Sol Jo 331, CA 864
R v Martin (6 November 1998, unreported), CA 869
R v Medicines Control Agency, ex p Pharmanord (UK) Ltd [1998] 3 CMLR 109, 44
    BMLR 41, [1998] COD 315, 10 Admin LR 646, CA 25
R v Medicines Control Agency, ex p Rhône-Poulenc Rorer Ltd: C-94/98 [1999] ECR
    I-8789, [2000] All ER (EC) 46, [2000] 1 CMLR 409, 56 BMLR 71, [1999] All ER
    (D) 1449, ECJ 6, 25
R v Melbourne [2000] 1 MHLR 2, CA 869
R v Mental Health Act Commission, ex p Smith (1998) 43 BMLR 174 759
R v Mental Health Commission, ex p W (1988) Times, 27 May 927–928
R v Mental Health Commission, ex p X (1988) 9 BMLR 77 928
R v Mental Health Review Tribunal, ex p Hall [1999] 4 All ER 883, [2000] 1 WLR
    1323, 51 BMLR 117, [1999] 33 LS Gaz R 31, [1999] NLJR 1368, CA 945, 969
R v Mental Health Review Tribunal, ex p P (CO/467/96), unreported 968
R v Mental Health Review Tribunal, ex p Pickering [1986] 1 All ER 99 967
R v Mental Health Review Tribunal for the South Thames Region, ex p Smith
    (1998) 47 BMLR 104 .... 768, 960, 969
R v Merseyside Mental Health Review Tribunal, ex p K [1990] 1 All ER 694, CA 869, 969
R v Mitchell [1977] 2 All ER 168, [1977] 1 WLR 753, 65 Cr App Rep 185, 141 JP 299,
    121 Sol Jo 252, CA 484
R v Mitchell [1997] 1 Cr App Rep (S) 90, [1996] Crim LR 604, CA 869
R v Morrell [2002] EWCA Crim 2547, [2002] All ER (D) 372 (Nov) 1010
R v Morris [1961] 2 QB 237, [1961] 2 All ER 672, [1961] 2 WLR 986, 45 Cr App Rep
    185, 105 Sol Jo 445, CCA 864
R v Newington (1990) 91 Cr App Rep 247, [1990] Crim LR 593, 134 Sol Jo 785, 6
    BMLR 99, CA 1010
R v North West London Mental Health NHS Trust, ex p S [1998] QB 628,
    [1997] 4 All ER 871, [1998] 2 WLR 189, CA 768, 859, 869, 914
R v North West Thames Mental Health Review Tribunal, ex p Cooper (1990) 5 BMLR
    7 969
R v Northampton Juvenile Court, ex p Hammersmith and Fulham London Borough
    Council [1985] FLR 193, [1985] Fam Law 124 765
R v Nottingham Mental Health Review Tribunal, ex p Secretary of State for the Home
    Department (1988) Times, 12 October, CA 969
R v Nwohia [1996] 1 Cr App Rep (S) 170, 26 BMLR 157, CA 869
R v Oliver [1944] KB 68, [1943] 2 All ER 800, 42 LGR 37, 29 Cr App Rep 137, 108 JP
    30, 113 LJKB 119, 170 LT 110, 60 TLR 82, CCA 491
R v Osker (Donna) [2010] EWCA Crim 955 869
R v Oxford Regional Mental Health Review Tribunal, ex p Secretary of State for the
    Home Department. See Campbell v Secretary of State for the Home Department
R v Preston [2003] EWCA Crim 2086 864

PARA

R v Priest [2011] EWCA Crim 1513, 123 BMLR 1 1011
R v Quayle, A-G's Reference (No 2 of 2004) [2005] EWCA Crim 1415, [2006] 1 All ER
    988, [2005] 1 WLR 3642, [2005] 2 Cr App Rep 527, [2006] Crim LR 148, 89
    BMLR 169, (2005) Times, 22 June, 149 Sol Jo LB 712, [2005] All ER (D) 447
    (May) 491
R v Ramsgate Justices, ex p Kazmarek (1984) 80 Cr App Rep 366, 149 JP 16, DC 871
R v Reynolds [2000] All ER (D) 1313, CA 869
R v Ristic [2002] EWCA Crim 165, [2002] All ER (D) 341 (Jan) 869
R v Riverside Mental Health Trust, ex p Huzzey (1998) 43 BMLR 167, [1998] All ER
    (D) 164 .... 771, 910, 913, 915
R v Rosso [2003] EWCA Crim 3242, [2003] All ER (D) 381 (Nov) 776, 922
R v Royse (1981) 3 Cr App Rep (S) 58, CA 869
R v Runighian [1977] Crim LR 361, Crown Ct 759
R v Russell (1991) 94 Cr App Rep 351, CA 483
R v Secretary of State for the Home Department, ex p Arthur H Cox & Co Ltd
    (1998) 46 BMLR 144, [1998] All ER (D) 724 491
R v Secretary of State for the Home Department, ex p Didlick [1993] 16 BMLR 71,
    (1993) Times, 30 March, (1993) Independent, 9 April 914
R v Secretary of State for the Home Department, ex p Gilkes (1999) 1 MHLR 6 892
R v Secretary of State for the Home Department, ex p Hickey [1995] QB 43,
    [1995] 1 All ER 479, [1994] 3 WLR 1110, 22 BMLR 32, CA 895
R v Secretary of State for the Home Department, ex p K [1991] 1 QB 270,
    [1990] 3 All ER 562, [1990] 3 WLR 755, 134 Sol Jo 1106, CA 869, 914
R v Secretary of State for the Home Department, ex p S (1992) Times, 19 August 895
R v Secretary of State for the Home Department, ex p T (1993) Times, 29 July, CA 894
R v Secretary of State for the Home Department, ex p Talmasani [1987] Imm AR
    32, CA 907
R v Secretary of State for the Home Department, ex p Turgut [2001] 1 All ER 719,
    [2000] Imm AR 306, [2000] 07 LS Gaz R 40, [2000] NLJR 131, [2000] INLR
    292, [2000] HRLR 337, [2000] All ER (D) 87, CA 907
R v Senior [1899] 1 QB 283, 63 JP 8, 68 LJQB 175, 19 Cox CC 219, 47 WR 367,
    [1895-9] All ER Rep 511, 43 Sol Jo 114, 79 LT 562, 15 TLR 102, CCR 551
R v Sheppard [1981] AC 394, [1980] 3 All ER 899, [1980] 3 WLR 960, 72 Cr App Rep
    82, 145 JP 65, [1981] Crim LR 171, 124 Sol Jo 864, HL 1010
R v Spencer [1987] AC 128, [1986] 2 All ER 928, [1986] 3 WLR 348, 83 Cr App Rep
    277, 151 JP 177, 130 Sol Jo 572, [1986] NLJ Rep 733, HL 1005
R v Staincross Justices, ex p Teasdale [1961] 1 QB 170, [1960] 3 All ER 572,
    [1960] 3 WLR 827, 124 JP 511, 104 Sol Jo 913 551
R v Stevens [1981] Crim LR 568, CA 483
R v Sweeney [2010] EWCA Crim 2355 859
R v T [2008] EWCA Crim 815, [2008] 3 WLR 923, [2008] 2 Cr App Rep 235, 172 JP
    335, (2008) Times, 5 May, [2008] All ER (D) 215 (Apr); affd sub nom R v JTB
    [2009] UKHL 20, [2009] AC 1310, [2009] 3 All ER 1, [2009] 2 WLR 1088,
    [2009] 2 Cr App Rep 189, 173 JP 289, [2009] Crim LR 581, [2009] NLJR 672,
    153 Sol Jo (no 18) 27, [2009] 5 LRC 431, [2009] All ER (D) 211 (Apr) 872
R v Thames Magistrates' Court, ex p Ramadan [1999] 1 Cr App Rep 386, 163 JP 428,
    [1999] Crim LR 498, DC 864
R v Trent Health Authority, ex p Somarante (1996) 31 BMLR 140, CA 849
R v Trent Mental Health Review Tribunal, ex p Ryan [1992] COD 157 761
R v Trent Mental Health Review Tribunal, ex p Secretary of State for the Home
    Department (1988) Times, 12 October, CA 969
R v Uxbridge County Council, ex p Binns [2000] MHLR 179 842
R v Walker [1987] Crim LR 565, CA 483
R v Watts [1984] 2 All ER 380, [1984] 1 WLR 757, 79 Cr App Rep 127, 128 Sol Jo
    363, [1984] LS Gaz R 1838, CA 484
R v Welsh [2011] EWCA Crim 73, [2011] 2 Cr App Rep (S) 399, [2011] Crim LR 421,
    119 BMLR 21, [2011] All ER (D) 03 (Feb) 859, 864
R v Wessex Mental Health Review Tribunal, ex p Wiltshire County Council (1989)
    Times, 29 August, CA 967
R v Wilson, ex p Williamson [1996] COD 42 .... 767, 769-770
R v Wood [2009] EWCA Crim 651, [2010] 1 Cr App Rep (S) 6, [2009] Crim LR 543,
    (2009) Times, 8 April, [2009] All ER (D) 49 (Apr) 859

PARA

R v Wright [2007] EWCA Crim 1744, [2007] All ER (D) 315 (Jul) 151

R v Yalman [1998] 2 Cr App Rep 269, [1998] Crim LR 569, CA 491

R (on the application Generics (UK) Ltd) v Licensing Authority: C-527/07 [2009] ECR
I-5259, 111 BMLR 46, [2009] All ER (D) 182 (Jun), ECJ 6

R (on the application of A) v Mental Health Review Tribunal [2004] EWHC 1999
(Admin), [2004] All ER (D) 78 (Aug) 970

R (on the application of A) v Partnerships in Care Ltd [2002] EWHC 529 (Admin),
[2002] 1 WLR 2610, (2002) Times, 23 April, [2002] All ER (D) 23 (Apr) 566, 778, 834,
945

R (on the application of A) v Secretary of State for the Home Department
[2002] EWHC 1618 (Admin), [2003] 1 WLR 330, (2002) Times, 5 September,
[2002] All ER (D) 457 (Jul) 869, 917

R (on the application of A) v Secretary of State for the Home Department [2003] EWCA
Civ 2846 759

R (on the application of AN) v Mental Health Review Tribunal (Northern Region)
[2005] EWHC 587 (Admin), (2005) Times, 18 April, [2005] All ER (D) 71 (Apr);
affd on other grounds [2005] EWCA Civ 1605, [2006] QB 468, [2006] 4 All ER
194, [2006] 2 WLR 850, 88 BMLR 59, [2005] All ER (D) 360 (Dec) 967, 969

R (on the application of Anderson) v Inner North Greater London Coroner
[2004] EWHC 2729 (Admin), [2004] All ER (D) 410 (Nov) 923

R (on the application of Armstrong) v Redcar and Cleveland Borough Council
[2002] UKHL 34, [2002] 2 AC 1127, [2002] 4 All ER 124, [2002] 3 WLR 584,
[2002] LGR 557, 68 BMLR 247, (2002) Times, 29 August, [2002] All ER (D) 366
(Jul) 945

R (on the application of AS (Lebanon) v Secretary of State for Home Department
[2012] EWHC 1349 (Admin), [2012] All ER (D) 198 (May) 893

R (on the application of Ashworth Hospital Authority) v Mental Health Review
Tribunal for West Midlands and Northwest Region [2002] EWCA Civ 923,
[2003] 1 WLR 127, 70 BMLR 40, [2002] 34 LS Gaz R 29, (2002) Times, 10 July,
[2002] All ER (D) 252 (Jun) 768, 918

R (on the application of Association of the British Pharmaceutical Industry) v Medicines
and Healthcare Products Regulatory Agency: C-62/09 [2010] ECR I-3603, [2011]
All ER (EC) 102, [2011] PTSR 391, 115 BMLR 26, [2010] NLJR 620, (2010)
Times, 7 May, [2010] All ER (D) 142 (Apr), ECJ 343

R (on the application of B) v Ashworth Hospital Authority [2005] UKHL 20,
[2005] 2 AC 278, [2005] 2 All ER 289, [2005] 2 WLR 695, 83 BMLR 160,
[2005] NLJR 546, (2005) Times, 18 March, 149 Sol Jo LB 359, [2005] All ER (D)
279 (Mar) 930

R (on the application of B) v Camden London Borough Council [2005] EWHC 1366
(Admin), [2006] LGR 19, 85 BMLR 28, [2005] All ER (D) 43 (Jul) 574, 945

R (on the application of B) v Haddock [2005] EWHC 921 (Admin), 85 BMLR 57,
[2005] All ER (D) 309 (May); affd [2006] EWCA Civ 961, 93 BMLR 52, [2006]
All ER (D) 137 (Jul) 928, 930

R (on the application of B) v Lambeth London Borough Council [2006] EWHC 2362
(Admin) 945

R (on the application of B) v Mental Health Review Tribunal [2003] EWHC 815
(Admin) 967

R (on the application of B) v S [2005] EWHC 1936 (Admin), [2005] All ER (D) 38
(Sep); affd [2006] EWCA Civ 28, [2006] 1 WLR 810, 90 BMLR 1,
[2006] 07 LS Gaz R 24, (2006) Times, 2 February, 150 Sol Jo LB 163, [2006] All
ER (D) 200 (Jan) 928, 930

R (on the application of Bartram) v Southend Magistrates' Court [2004] EWHC 2691
(Admin), [2004] All ER (D) 326 (Oct) 871

R (on the application of Biggs) v Secretary of State for the Home Department
[2002] EWHC 1012 (Admin), [2002] All ER (D) 292 (May) 914

R (on the application of Bitcon) v West Allderdale Magistrates' Court [2003] EWHC
2460 (Admin), 147 Sol Jo LB 1028, [2003] All ER (D) 33 (Sep) 862

R (on the application of Burke) v General Medical Council [2005] EWCA Civ 1003,
[2006] QB 273, [2005] 3 WLR 1132, [2005] 3 FCR 169, [2005] 2 FLR 1223,
[2005] Fam Law 776, 85 BMLR 1, [2005] NLJR 1457, (2005) Times, 2 August,
[2005] All ER (D) 445 (Jul) 623

PARA

R (on the application of C) v A Local Authority [2011] EWHC 1539 (Admin), [2011]
All ER (D) 171 (Jun) 601, 724, 763
R (on the application of C) v London Maudsley NHS Trust and the Mental Health
Review Tribunal [2003] EWHC 3467 (Admin) 849
R (on the application of C) v Secretary of State for the Home Department
[2001] EWHC 501 (Admin) 965
R (on the application of C) v Secretary of State for the Home Department [2002] EWCA
Civ 647, (2002) Times, 24 May, [2002] All ER (D) 220 (May) 965, 969
R (on the application of C) v South London and Maudsley NHS Trust [2001] EWHC
Admin 1025 .... 821, 847
R (on the application of Care Principles Ltd) v Mental Health Review Tribunal
[2006] EWHC 3194 (Admin), 94 BMLR 145 .... 768, 772
R (on the application of Cobham) v Harrow London Borough Council [2002] UKHL
34, [2002] 2 AC 1127, [2002] 4 All ER 124, [2002] 3 WLR 584, [2002] LGR 557,
68 BMLR 247, (2002) Times, 29 August, [2002] All ER (D) 366 (Jul) 945
R (on the application of Craven) v Secretary of State for the Home Department
[2001] EWHC Admin 850, [2001] All ER (D) 74 (Oct) 914
R (on the application of D) v Secretary of State for the Home Department
[2002] EWHC 2805 (Admin), [2003] 1 WLR 1315, (2002) Times, 31 December,
[2002] All ER (D) 312 (Dec) 894–895, 970
R (on the application of D) v Secretary of State for the Home Department
[2004] EWHC 2857 (Admin), [2004] All ER (D) 250 (Dec) 892
R (on the application of D) v West Midlands and North West Mental Health Review
Tribunal [2004] EWCA Civ 311, 148 Sol Jo LB 384, [2004] All ER (D) 339
(Mar) 850
R (on the application of DB) v Nottinghamshire Healthcare NHS Trust [2008] EWCA
Civ 1354, [2009] 2 All ER 792, [2009] PTSR 547, [2008] All ER (D) 33 (Dec) 867
R (on the application of DJ) v Mental Health Review Tribunal [2005] EWHC 587
(Admin), (2005) Times, 18 April, [2005] All ER (D) 71 (Apr); affd on other
grounds [2005] EWCA Civ 1605, [2006] QB 468, [2006] 4 All ER 194,
[2006] 2 WLR 850, 88 BMLR 59, [2005] All ER (D) 360 (Dec) 969
R (on the application of DR) v Mersey Care NHS Trust [2002] MHLR 386 801
R (on the application of DR) v Merseycare NHS Trust [2002] EWHC 1810 (Admin),
(2002) Times, 11 October, [2002] All ER (D) 28 (Aug) 768, 770, 910
R (on the application of E) v Ashworth Hospital Authority [2001] EWHC Admin 1089,
(2002) Times, 17 January, [2001] All ER (D) 295 (Dec) 759
R (on the application of E) v Bristol City Council [2005] EWHC 74 (Admin), [2005] All
ER (D) 57 (Jan) 779, 821, 839, 842, 847
R (on the application of East London and the City Mental Health NHS Trust) v Mental
Health Review Tribunal [2005] EWHC 2329 (Admin), [2005] All ER (D) 107
(Aug) 969
R (on the application of Epsom and St Helier NHS Trust) v Mental Health Review
Tribunal [2001] EWHC101 (Admin), [2001] 1 MHLR 8, [2001] All ER (D) 194
(Feb) 910, 967
R (on the application of F) v Oxfordshire Mental Healthcare NHS Trust [2001] EWHC
Admin 535, [2001] All ER (D) 19 (Jul) 834
R (on the application of G) v Mental Health Review Tribunal [2004] EWHC 2193
(Admin), [2004] All ER (D) 86 (Oct) 864, 869, 914
R (on the application of Ganatra) v Ealing London Borough Council [2002] EWHC
1112 (Admin), [2002] All ER (D) 294 (Apr) 821, 847
R (on the application of GP) v Derby City Council and Derbyshire Mental Health NHS
Foundation Trust [2012] EWHC 1451 (Admin) 821
R (on the application of Greenwich London Borough Council) v Secretary of State for
Health [2006] EWHC 2576 (Admin), [2006] All ER (D) 178 (Jul) 839
R (on the application of H) v London North and East Region Mental Health Review
Tribunal (Secretary of State for Health intervening) [2001] EWCA Civ 415,
[2002] QB 1, [2001] 3 WLR 512, 61 BMLR 163, [2001] 21 LS Gaz R 40, [2001]
All ER (D) 328 (Mar) 768, 967
R (on the application of H) v Mental Health Review Tribunal [2002] EWHC 1522
(Admin), [2002] All ER (D) 542 (Jul) 968
R (on the application of H) v Oxfordshire Mental Healthcare NHS Trust [2002] EWHC
465 (Admin), [2002] All ER (D) 63 (Mar) 849

PARA

R (on the application of H) v Secretary of State for Health [2004] EWCA Civ 1609,
    [2005] 3 All ER 468, [2005] 1 WLR 1209, 82 BMLR 168, (2004) Times,
    8 December, 148 Sol Jo LB 1437, [2004] All ER (D) 64 (Dec); revsd [2005] UKHL
    60, [2006] 1 AC 441, [2005] 4 All ER 1311, [2005] 3 WLR 867, 86 BMLR 71,
    (2005) Times, 25 October, [2005] All ER (D) 218 (Oct) 767, 842, 960
R (on the application of HA (Nigeria)) v Secretary of State for the Home Department
    [2012] EWHC 979 (Admin), [2012] All ER (D) 76 (Apr) 893
R (on the application of Hertfordshire County Council) v Hammersmith and Fulham
    London Borough Council [2011] EWCA Civ 77, [2011] LGR 536, 119 BMLR 27,
    [2011] All ER (D) 164 (Feb) 945
R (on the application of Holloway) v Oxfordshire County Council [2007] EWHC 776
    (Admin), [2007] LGR 891, [2007] All ER (D) 39 (Apr) 842
R (on the application of HP) v Islington London Borough Council [2004] EWHC 7
    (Admin), 82 BMLR 113, [2004] All ER (D) 71 (Jan) 574, 945
R (on the application of Hurlock) v Page and Secretary of State for the Home
    Department [2001] EWHC 380 (Admin) 869
R (on the application of IH) v Secretary of State for the Home Department
    [2002] EWCA Civ 646, [2003] QB 320, [2002] 3 WLR 967,
    [2002] 25 LS Gaz R 35, (2002) Times, 24 May, 146 Sol Jo LB 146, [2002] All ER
    (D) 219 (May); affd sub nom R (on the application of H) v Secretary of State for
    the Home Department [2003] UKHL 59, [2004] 2 AC 253, [2004] 1 All ER 412,
    [2003] 3 WLR 1278, 76 BMLR 179, [2004] 02 LS Gaz R 30, (2003) Times,
    14 November, 147 Sol Jo LB 1365, 15 BHRC 571, [2003] All ER (D) 192 (Nov) ... 566, 945,
                                                                                        965, 969
R (on the application of Jones) v Isleworth Crown Court [2005] EWHC 662 (Admin),
    [2005] All ER (D) 33 (Mar) 869
R (on the application of K) v Camden and Islington Health Authority [2001] EWCA Civ
    240, [2002] QB 198, [2001] 3 WLR 553, 61 BMLR 173, [2001] 16 LS Gaz R 34,
    145 Sol Jo LB 69, [2001] All ER (D) 250 (Feb) 945, 969
R (on the application of K) v West London Mental Health NHS Trust [2006] EWCA
    Civ 118, [2006] 1 WLR 1865, 90 BMLR 214, [2006] 11 LS Gaz R 26, (2006)
    Times, 16 March, [2006] All ER (D) 298 (Feb) 568, 834, 917
R (on the application of Keating) v Cardiff Local Health Board (Secretary of State for
    Health, intervening) [2005] EWCA Civ 847, [2005] 3 All ER 1000, [2006] 1 WLR
    158, 85 BMLR 190, (2005) Times, 6 September, [2005] All ER (D) 67 (Jul) 568
R (on the application of Kenneally) v Rampton Hospital Authority [2001] EWHC
    Admin 968, [2002] QB 1169, [2002] 2 WLR 1430, (2001) Times, 17 December,
    [2001] All ER (D) 390 (Nov) 896
R (on the application of Kenneally) v Snaresbrook Crown Court [2001] EWHC Admin
    968, [2002] QB 1169, [2002] 2 WLR 1430, (2001) Times, 17 December, [2001] All
    ER (D) 390 (Nov) 896
R (on the application of L) v Secretary of State for Health [2001] 1 FCR 326,
    [2001] 1 FLR 406, [2001] Fam Law 101, 58 BMLR 101, (2000) Times,
    26 October, [2000] All ER (D) 1349 .... 569, 781
R (on the application of L) v Secretary of State for the Home Department [2005] EWCA
    Civ 02, [2006] 1 WLR 88, [2005] NLJR 140, (2005) Times, 27 January, 149 Sol Jo
    LB 144, [2005] All ER (D) 142 (Jan) 914
R (on the application of Li) v Mental Health Review Tribunal [2004] EWHC 51
    (Admin), [2004] All ER (D) 173 (Jan) 967
R (on the application of M) v Hammersmith and Fulham London Borough Council
    [2010] EWHC 562 (Admin), [2010] LGR 678, 116 BMLR 46, [2010] All ER (D)
    218 (Mar) 945
R (on the application of M) v Homerton University Hospital NHS Trust [2008] EWCA
    Civ 197 842
R (on the application of M) v Hospital Managers of Queen Mary's Hospital
    [2008] EWHC 1959 (Admin) 773, 849
R (on the application of M) v Secretary of State for Health [2003] EWHC 1094
    (Admin), [2003] 3 All ER 672n, (2003) Times, 25 April, [2003] All ER (D) 307
    (Apr) 839, 842

PARA

R (on the application of M) v Secretary of State for the Home Department
[2003] EWCA Civ 1406, [2004] QB 1124, [2004] 1 All ER 833, [2004] 2 WLR
603, [2004] LGR 184, [2003] 3 FCR 673, [2004] 1 FLR 8, [2004] Fam Law 12,
[2003] 44 LS Gaz R 30, (2003) Times, 17 October, 15 BHRC 526, [2003] All ER
(D) 288 (Oct) 969
R (on the application of M) v Secretary of State for the Home Department
[2007] EWCA Civ 687, 98 BMLR 130, [2007] All ER (D) 99 (Jul) 864
R (on the application of Merck Sharp & Dohme Ltd) v Licensing Authority
[2005] EWHC 710 (Admin), [2005] All ER (D) 401 (Apr) 6
R (on the application of Miah) v Secretary of State for the Home Department
[2004] EWHC 2569 (Admin), (2004) Times, 10 September, [2005] All ER (D) 22
(Jan) 892
R (on the application of Modaresi) v Secretary of State for Health [2011] EWCA Civ
1359, [2012] PTSR 999 767–768
R (on the application of Morley) v Nottinghamshire Health Care NHS Trust
[2002] EWCA Civ 1728, [2003] 1 All ER 784, [2002] All ER (D) 414 (Nov) 895
R (on the application of Munjaz) v Mersey Care NHS Trust [2005] UKHL 58,
[2006] 2 AC 148, [2006] 4 All ER 736, [2005] 3 WLR 793, 86 BMLR 84, (2005)
Times, 18 October, [2005] All ER (D) 139 (Oct) 602, 757–759, 763, 924, 927
R (on the application of Mwanza) v Greenwich London Borough Council [2010] EWHC
1462 (Admin), [2010] LGR 868, [2011] PTSR 965, [2010] NLJR 905, [2010] All
ER (D) 124 (Jun) 945
R (on the application of N) v Ashworth Special Hospital (11 May 2001, unreported) 781
R (on the application of N) v M [2002] EWCA Civ 1789, [2003] 1 WLR 562,
[2003] 1 FCR 124, [2003] 1 FLR 667, [2003] Fam Law 160, 72 BMLR 81,
[2003] 08 LS Gaz R 29, (2002) Times, 12 December, [2002] All ER (D) 75 (Dec) ... 612, 930
R (on the application of N) v Secretary of State for the Home Department
[2003] EWCA Civ 1406, [2004] QB 1124, [2004] 1 All ER 833, [2004] 2 WLR
603, [2004] LGR 184, [2003] 3 FCR 673, [2004] 1 FLR 8, [2004] Fam Law 12,
[2003] 44 LS Gaz R 30, (2003) Times, 17 October, 15 BHRC 526, [2003] All ER
(D) 288 (Oct) 969
R (on the application of National Association of Health Stores) v Secretary of State for
Health [2005] EWCA Civ 154, (2005) Times, 9 March, [2005] All ER (D) 324
(Feb) 27, 307, 314, 331
R (on the application of Novartis Pharmaceuticals UK Ltd) v Medicines Control Agency:
C-106/01 [2004] ECR I-4403, [2005] All ER (EC) 192, [2004] 2 CMLR 565, 81
BMLR 200, [2004] All ER (D) 357 (Apr), ECJ 6
R (on the application of O) v Mental Health Review Tribunal [2006] EWHC 2659
(Admin), 93 BMLR 110, [2006] All ER (D) 190 (Oct) 968
R (on the application of P) v Barking Youth Court [2002] EWHC 734 (Admin),
[2002] 2 Cr App Rep 294, 166 JP 641, [2002] All ER (D) 93 (Apr) 871–872
R (on the application of P) v Secretary of State for the Home Department [2003] EWHC
2953 (Admin), (2003) Times, 29 December, [2003] All ER (D) 205 (Dec) 969–970
R (on the application of PS) v Responsible Medical Officer [2003] EWHC 2335
(Admin), [2003] All ER (D) 178 (Oct) 612, 930
R (on the application of R) v Responsible Medical Officer [2003] EWHC 3022 (Admin),
[2003] All ER (D) 165 (Dec) 895–896
R (on the application of R) v Responsible Medical Officer [2003] EWHC 3152 (Admin),
[2003] All ER (D) 243 (Dec), sub nom R (on the application of R) v Secretary of
State for the Home Department (2004) Times, 9 January 864, 894
R (on the application of R) v Secretary of State for the Home Department. See R (on the
application of R) v Responsible Medical Officer
R (on the application of Rayner) v Secretary of State for the Home Department
[2008] EWCA Civ 176, [2009] 1 WLR 310, 101 BMLR 83 965
R (on the application of RD) v Secretary of State for Work and Pensions [2008] EWHC
2635 (Admin), [2008] All ER (D) 317 (Oct) 593
R (on the application of Robinson) v The Hospital Managers of Park Royal Hospital
(26 November 2007, unreported) 838
R (on the application of S) v Mental Health Review Tribunal [2004] EWHC 2958
(Admin), [2004] All ER (D) 87 (Dec) 917, 967
R (on the application of SC) v Mental Health Review Tribunal [2005] EWHC 17
(Admin), (2005) Times, 24 January, [2005] All ER (D) 90 (Jan) 969, 971

PARA

R (on the application of Sessay) v South London and Maudsley NHS Foundation Trust
[2011] EWHC 2617 (QB), [2012] QB 760, [2012] 2 WLR 1071, [2012] PTSR 742,
[2011] All ER (D) 159 (Oct) 611, 769–771

R (on the application of Singh) v Stratford Magistrates' Court [2007] EWHC 1582
(Admin), [2007] 4 All ER 407, [2007] 1 WLR 3119, [2008] 1 Cr App Rep 36, 171
JP 557, 172 JPN 69, (2007) Times, 13 August, [2007] All ER (D) 30 (Jul) 871

R (on the application of South West London and St George's Mental Health NHS Trust)
v W [2002] All ER (D) 62 (Aug) 913

R (on the application of SR by her Litigation Friend the Official Solicitor) v
Huntercombe Maidenhead Hospital [2005] EWHC 2361 (Admin), [2005] All ER
(D) 115 (Sep) 913, 915

R (on the application of Stennett) v Manchester City Council [2002] UKHL 34,
[2002] 2 AC 1127, [2002] 4 All ER 124, [2002] 3 WLR 584, [2002] LGR 557, 68
BMLR 247, (2002) Times, 29 August, [2002] All ER (D) 366 (Jul) 574, 945

R (on the application of Stevens) v Plymouth City Council [2002] EWCA Civ 388,
[2002] 1 WLR 2583, [2002] LGR 565, [2002] 1 FLR 1177, [2002] All ER (D) 414
(Mar) 839, 842

R (on the application of Sunderland City Council) v South Tyneside Council
[2012] EWCA Civ 1232, [2012] NLJR 1323, [2012] All ER (D) 97 (Oct) 945

R (on the application of T) v Secretary of State for Justice [2008] EWHC 1707 (Admin),
[2008] All ER (D) 259 (Jul) 914

R (on the application of T) v Secretary of State for the Home Department [2003] EWHC
538 (Admin) 894

R (on the application of Tagoe-Thompson) v Central and North West London Mental
Health NHS Trust [2003] EWCA Civ 330, [2003] 1 WLR 1272, (2003) Times,
18 April, [2003] All ER (D) 153 (Mar) 913

R (on the application of Taylor) v Haydn-Smith [2005] EWHC 1668 (Admin), [2005]
All ER (D) 460 (May) 930

R (on the application of TF) v Secretary of State for Justice [2008] EWCA Civ 1457,
106 BMLR 54, [2008] All ER (D) 211 (Dec) 892

R (on the application of the Secretary of State for the Home Department) v Mental
Health Review Tribunal [2001] EWHC 849 (Admin) 969

R (on the application of the Secretary of State for the Home Department) v Mental
Health Tribunal [2002] EWCA Civ 1868, [2002] All ER (D) 307 (Dec) 969

R (on the application of the Secretary of State for the Home Department) v Mental
Health Review Tribunal [2004] EWHC 1029 (Admin), [2004] All ER (D) 127
(Apr) 967, 969

R (on the application of the Secretary of State for the Home Department) v Mental
Health Review Tribunal [2004] EWHC 2194 (Admin), [2004] All ER (D) 87
(Oct) 864, 869, 914, 969

R (on the application of the Secretary of State for the Home Department) v Mental
Health Review Tribunal for the North East Thames Region (2000) 63 BMLR 181,
[2000] All ER (D) 2308 968

R (on the application of TTM (by his litigation friend TM)) v Hackney London Borough
Council [2010] EWHC 1349 (Admin), [2010] All ER (D) 88 (Jun); revsd sub nom
M (by his litigation friend TM) v Hackney London Borough Council [2011] EWCA
Civ 4, [2011] 3 All ER 529, [2011] 1 WLR 2873, [2011] PTSR 1419, (2011)
Times, 17 February, [2011] All ER (D) 76 (Jan) 759, 768, 772, 820–821, 847, 849

R (on the application of V) v South London and Maudsley NHS Foundation Trust
[2010] EWHC 742 (Admin) 847

R (on the application of Von Brandenburg (aka Hanley)) v East London and the City
Mental Health NHS Trust [2003] UKHL 58, [2004] 2 AC 280, [2004] 1 All ER
400, [2003] 3 WLR 1265, 76 BMLR 168, [2004] 05 LS Gaz R 28, (2003) Times,
14 November, 147 Sol Jo LB 1366, [2003] All ER (D) 174 (Nov) ... 767–768, 821, 914, 967,
                                                                                    969

R (on the application of W) v Croydon Borough Council [2011] All ER (D) 93 (Mar) 606

R (on the application of W) v Doncaster Metropolitan Borough Council. See W v
Doncaster Metropolitan Borough Council

R (on the application of WC) v South London and Maudsley NHS Trust and Orekeye
[2001] 1 MHLR 187 821

PARA

R (on the application of Wilkinson) v Responsible Medical Officer Broadmoor Hospital
    [2001] EWCA Civ 1545, [2002] 1 WLR 419, 65 BMLR 15,
    [2001] 44 LS Gaz R 36, (2001) Times, 2 November, 145 Sol Jo LB 247, [2001] All
    ER (D) 294 (Oct) 611, 820, 849, 928, 930
R (on the application of Wooder) v Feggetter [2002] EWCA Civ 554, [2003] QB 219,
    [2002] 3 WLR 591, [2002] 22 LS Gaz R 33, (2002) Times, 28 May, 146 Sol Jo LB
    125, [2002] All ER (D) 243 (Apr) 779, 928, 930
R (on the application of X) v An NHS Trust [2008] EWCA Civ 1354, [2009] 2 All ER
    792, [2009] PTSR 547, [2008] All ER (D) 33 (Dec) 867
RC (dec'd), Re, SC v Hackney London Borough Council [2010] EWHC B29 (COP),
    [2011] 1 FLR 1447, [2011] Fam Law 345 747
RT v LT [2010] EWHC 1910 (Fam), sub nom LT (vulnerable adult) (decision making:
    capacity), Re [2011] 1 FLR 594, [2010] Fam Law 1283, [2010] All ER (D) 02
    (Aug) 605
Rabone v Pennine Care NHS Foundation Trust [2012] UKSC 2, [2012] 2 AC 72,
    [2012] 2 All ER 381, [2012] 2 WLR 381, [2012] PTSR 497, 156 Sol Jo (no 6) 31,
    124 BMLR 148, [2012] 08 LS Gaz R 19, [2012] NLJR 261, (2012) Times,
    20 February, 33 BHRC 208, [2012] All ER (D) 59 (Feb) 764
Raine v Wilson (1873) LR 16 Eq 576, 43 LJ Ch 469, 29 LT 51 999
Rao v Wyles [1949] 2 All ER 685, 47 LGR 720, 113 JP 516, 93 Sol Jo 679, 65 TLR
    659 506
Reed v Bronglais Hospital Pembrokeshire and Derwen NHS Trust [2001] EWHC 792
    (Admin) 849
Registrar of Restrictive Trading Agreements v WH Smith & Son Ltd (1969) LR 7 RP
    122, [1969] 3 All ER 1065, [1969] 1 WLR 1460, 113 Sol Jo 636, CA 548
Reid v Secretary of State for Scotland [1999] 2 AC 512, [1999] 1 All ER 481,
    [1999] 2 WLR 28, 1999 SC (HL) 17, 1999 SLT 279, HL 768, 967
Rhodes, Re, Rhodes v Rhodes (1890) 44 Ch D 94, 59 LJ Ch 298, 38 WR 385,
    [1886–90] All ER Rep 871, 62 LT 342, CA 614
Rice v Connolly [1966] 2 QB 414, [1966] 2 All ER 649, [1966] 3 WLR 17, 130 JP 322,
    110 Sol Jo 371, DC 1015
Richards v Richards [1972] 3 All ER 695, [1972] 1 WLR 1073, 116 Sol Jo 599 610
Richardson v LCC [1957] 2 All ER 330, [1957] 1 WLR 751, 55 LGR 270, 121 JP 355,
    101 Sol Jo 429, CA 759, 922
Richmond v Branson & Son [1914] 1 Ch 968, 83 LJ Ch 749, 58 Sol Jo 455, 110 LT
    763 .... 600, 994
Richmond v Richmond (1914) 58 Sol Jo 784, 111 LT 273 599
Ricketts v Registration Officer for the City of Cambridge [1970] 2 QB 463,
    [1970] 3 All ER 7, [1970] 3 WLR 147, 68 LGR 644, [1970] RA 330, 134 JP 576,
    114 Sol Jo 397, CA 787
Roberts, Re, Roberts v Roberts [1978] 3 All ER 225, [1978] 1 WLR 653; affd
    [1978] 3 All ER 225, [1978] 1 WLR 653, 122 Sol Jo 264, CA 609
Roberts v Gwyrfai District Council [1899] 1 Ch 583, 63 JP 181, 68 LJ Ch 233, 47 WR
    376, 80 LT 107, 15 TLR 165; affd [1899] 2 Ch 608, 64 JP 52, 68 LJ Ch 757, 48
    WR 51, 44 Sol Jo 10, 81 LT 465, 16 TLR 2, [1895–9] All ER Rep Ext 1345, CA 234
Roberts v Littlewood's Mail Order Stores Ltd [1943] 1 KB 269, [1943] 1 All ER 271, 41
    LGR 74, 107 JP 81, 112 LJKB 221, 87 Sol Jo 121, 168 LT 253, 59 TLR
    158, DC 539
Robinson v Galland (1889) 5 TLR 504 999
Robinson v Robinson (by his guardian) [1965] P 192, [1964] 3 All ER 232,
    [1964] 3 WLR 935, 108 Sol Jo 505 559
Roper v Taylor's Central Garages (Exeter) Ltd. See Taylor's Central Garages (Exeter) Ltd
    v Roper

S

S (adult patient: sterilisation), Re [2001] Fam 15, [2000] 3 WLR 1288, [2000] 2 FCR
    452, [2000] Fam Law 711, [2000] All ER (D) 683, CA 612
S (adult: sterilisation), Re [1999] 1 FCR 277, [1998] 1 FLR 944, [1998] Fam Law 325 612
S (hospital patient: court's jurisdiction), Re [1996] Fam 1, [1995] 3 All ER 290,
    [1995] 3 WLR 78, [1995] 3 FCR 496, [1995] 1 FLR 1075, [1995] Fam Law 412,
    24 BMLR 52, [1995] 15 LS Gaz R 40, 139 Sol Jo LB 87, CA 612

PARA

S (hospital patient: foreign curator), Re [1996] Fam 23, [1995] 4 All ER 30,
  [1995] 3 WLR 596, [1996] 1 FCR 128, [1996] 1 FLR 167, [1996] Fam Law 27, 30
  BMLR 179 998
S (protected persons), Re [2010] 1 WLR 1082 606
SA (vulnerable adult with capacity: marriage), Re [2005] EWHC 2942 (Fam),
  [2007] 2 FCR 563, [2006] 1 FLR 867, [2006] Fam Law 268 .... 563, 601
SBC v PBA [2011] EWHC 2580 (Fam) 734
SK, Re [2012] EWHC 1990 (Fam), [2012] All ER (D) 80 (Aug) 743
SK (an adult) (forced marriage: appropriate relief), Re [2004] EWHC 3202 (Fam),
  [2005] 3 All ER 421, [2006] 1 WLR 81, [2005] 2 FCR 459, [2005] All ER (D) 130
  (Feb) 609
SK (vulnerable adult: capacity), Re [2008] EWHC 636 (Fam), [2008] 2 FLR 720,
  [2008] Fam Law 633, [2008] All ER (D) 395 (Jun) 606
St George's Healthcare NHS Trust v S [1999] Fam 26, [1998] 3 All ER 673,
  [1998] 3 WLR 936, [1998] 2 FCR 685, [1998] 2 FLR 728, [1998] Fam Law 526,
  44 BMLR 160, [1998] 22 LS Gaz R 29, [1998] NLJR 693, 142 Sol Jo LB 164,
  [1998] CCL Rep 410, CA 612, 761, 767, 821, 927
Saulle v Nouvet [2007] EWHC 2902 (QB), [2007] All ER (D) 08 (Dec) 601, 995
Sayer v Bennet (1784) 1 Cox Eq Cas 107 616
S-C (mental patient: habeas corpus), Re [1996] QB 599, [1996] 1 All ER 532,
  [1996] 2 WLR 146, [1996] 2 FCR 692, [1996] 1 FLR 548, [1996] Fam Law
  210, CA 768, 771, 774
Scott v Bentley (1855) 1 K & J 281, 24 LJ Ch 244, 3 Eq Rep 428, 1 Jur NS 394, 3 WR
  280, 25 LTOS 114 998
Scott v Wakem (1862) 3 F & F 328 759
Seal v Chief Constable of South Wales Police [2007] UKHL 31, [2007] 4 All ER 177,
  [2007] 1 WLR 1910, 97 BMLR 172, (2007) Times, 5 July, 22 BHRC 769, [2007]
  All ER (D) 49 (Jul) 759
Secretary of State for Justice v RB [2011] EWCA Civ 1608, [2012] 1 WLR 2043, 124
  BMLR 13, [2012] NLJR 137, (2012) Times, 19 January, [2012] All ER (D) 92
  (Jan) 969
Secretary of State for the Home Department v Mental Health Review Tribunal for the
  Mersey Regional Health Authority [1986] 3 All ER 233, [1986] 1 WLR 1170, 130
  Sol Jo 697, [1986] LS Gaz R 3001 .... 914, 967, 969
Secretary of State for the Home Department v Mental Health Review Tribunal for Wales
  [1986] 3 All ER 233, [1986] 1 WLR 1170, 130 Sol Jo 697,
  [1986] LS Gaz R 3001 .... 914, 969
Secretary of State for the Home Department v Oxford Regional Mental Health Review
  Tribunal. See Campbell v Secretary of State for the Home Department
Selby v Jackson (1844) 6 Beav 192, 13 LJ Ch 249, 49 ER 799, 2 LTOS 366 .... 614, 617
Sentance v Poole (1827) 3 C & P 1 617
Shah v Barnet London Borough Council [1983] 2 AC 309, [1983] 1 All ER 226,
  [1983] 2 WLR 16, 81 LGR 305, 127 Sol Jo 36, HL... 839
Sheffield City Council v E [2004] EWHC 2808 (Fam), [2005] Fam 326, [2005] 2 WLR
  953, [2005] Times, 20 January, [2005] All ER (D) 192 (Jan), sub nom E (an alleged
  patient), Re [2005] Fam Law 279 609
Sheffield City Council v S (an adult patient) [2002] EWHC 2278 (Fam) 724
Shoesmith, Re [1938] 2 KB 637, 107 LJKB 582, sub nom Intended Action, Re,
  Shoesmith v Lancashire Mental Hospitals Board [1938] 3 All ER 186, 36 LGR
  617, 102 JP 415, 82 Sol Jo 476, 159 LT 155, 54 TLR 940, CA 759
Sidaway v Board of Governors of the Bethlem Royal Hospital and the Maudsley
  Hospital [1985] AC 871, [1985] 1 All ER 643, [1985] 2 WLR 480, 129 Sol Jo
  154, 1 BMLR 132, [1985] LS Gaz R 1256, HL 612
Simms v Simms [2002] EWHC 2734 (Fam), [2003] Fam 83, [2003] 1 All ER 669,
  [2003] 2 WLR 1465, [2003] 1 FCR 361, 71 BMLR 61, [2003] NLJR 21, [2002]
  All ER (D) 263 (Dec) 612
Simpson-Cleghorn v Lancashire County Council (5 July 1999, unreported), CA 759
Small v Bickley (1875) 40 JP 119, 32 LT 726, DC 548
Smirek v Williamson [2000] EWCA Civ 3025, [2000] MHLR 38 768
Smith v Tebbitt (1867) LR 1 P & D 398, 36 LJP & M 97, 16 WR 18, 16 LT 841 598
Smith (by her mother and next friend) v Secretary of State for Health [2002] EWHC 200
  (QB), 67 BMLR 34, (2002) Times, 11 March, [2002] All ER (D) 196 (Feb) 29, 31

PARA

Smith Kline & French Laboratories Ltd, Re [1990] 1 AC 64, [1989] 2 WLR 397,
[1989] 17 LS Gaz R 42, sub nom Smith Kline & French Laboratories Ltd v
Licensing Authority (Generics (UK) Ltd intervening) [1989] 1 All ER 578, 133 Sol
Jo 263, HL 35, 53, 80
Snook v Watts (1848) 11 Beav 105, 12 Jur 444, 12 LTOS 1 .... 598, 614
South Glamorgan County Council v W and B [1993] 1 FCR 626, [1993] 1 FLR 574,
[1993] Fam Law 398, 11 BMLR 162 765
South West Hertfordshire Health Authority v KB [1994] 2 FCR 1051 927
Sparrow, Re (1870) 5 Ch App 662, 18 WR 1185 564
Steed v Calley (1836) 1 Keen 620 598
Stewart-Brady v United Kingdom (1997) 24 EHRR CD 38 995
Storck v Germany (Application no 61603/00) (2005) 43 EHRR 96, [2005] ECHR
61603/00, ECtHR 648
Surrey County Council Social Services v McMurray (11 November 1994,
unreported), CA 842
Swallow v LCC [1916] 1 KB 224, 14 LGR 301, 80 JP 164, 85 LJKB 234, 25 Cox CC
295, [1914–15] All ER Rep 403, 114 LT 368, 32 TLR 181, DC 1015
Symm v Fraser (1863) 3 F & F 859 759

T

T (adult: refusal of treatment), Re [1993] Fam 95, [1992] 4 All ER 649, [1992] 3 WLR
782, [1992] 2 FCR 861, [1992] 2 FLR 458, [1993] Fam Law 27, 9 BMLR 46,
[1992] NLJR 1125, CA 601, 603, 605, 612
T v T [1988] Fam 52, [1988] 1 All ER 613, [1988] 2 WLR 189, [1988] 1 FLR 400, 131
Sol Jo 1286, [1987] LS Gaz R 2456 927
Tameside and Glossop Acute Services Trust v CH [1996] 1 FCR 753, [1996] 1 FLR 762,
[1996] Fam Law 353, 31 BMLR 93 927
Taylor's Central Garages (Exeter) Ltd v Roper [1951] WN 383, 115 JP 445, sub nom
Roper v Taylor's Central Garages (Exeter) Ltd [1951] 2 TLR 284, DC 1013
Ter Voort, Re: C-219/91 [1992] ECR I-5485, [1995] 2 CMLR 591, 30 BMLR 165,
ECJ 25
Thiery v Chalmers, Guthrie & Co [1900] 1 Ch 80, 69 LJ Ch 122, 48 WR 148, 44 Sol
Jo 59, 81 LT 511 998
Thompson v Leach. See Leach v Thompson
Thurlow v Thurlow [1976] Fam 32, [1975] 2 All ER 979, [1975] 3 WLR 161, 119 Sol
Jo 406 610
Towart v Sellars (1817) 5 Dow 231, HL 598, 617

U

Upjohn Co and Upjohn NV v Farzoo Inc and Kortmann: C-112/89 [1991] ECR I-1703,
[1993] 1 CMLR 657, 14 BMLR 79, ECJ 25
Upjohn Ltd v Licensing Authority established under the Medicines Act 1968: C-120/97
[1999] ECR I-223, [1999] 1 WLR 927, [1999] 1 CMLR 825, 51 BMLR 206,
[1999] 19 LS Gaz R 30, [1999] All ER (D) 40, ECJ 167

V

V v South London and Maudsley NHS Foundation Trust [2010] All ER (D) 76 (Feb) 821
Van Bennekom: 227/82 [1983] ECR 3883, [1985] 2 CMLR 692, ECJ 25
Varbanov v Bulgaria (Application 31365/96) (5 October 2000, unreported) 849
Vitamin Supplements, Re, European Commission v Germany: C-387/99 [2004] ECR
I-3751, [2006] 3 CMLR 491, [2004] All ER (D) 192 (Jul), ECJ 25

W

W, Re [1993] 2 FCR 187, [1993] 1 FLR 381, [1993] Fam Law 208 612
W (adult: refusal of medical treatment), Re [2002] EWHC 901 (Fam), [2002] All ER (D)
223 (Apr) 605
W (an infant), Re [1971] AC 682, [1971] 2 All ER 49, [1971] 2 WLR 1011, 135 JP
259, 115 Sol Jo 286, HL 842
W (by her litigation friend, B) v M (by her litigation friend, the Official Solicitor)
[2012] 1 All ER 1313. See M (adult patient) (minimally conscious state: withdrawal
of treatment), Re [2011] EWHC 2443 (Fam)

PARA

W (Enduring Power of Attorney), Re [2001] Ch 609, [2001] 4 All ER 88,
  [2001] 2 WLR 957, [2003] 3 FCR 662, [2001] 1 FLR 832, [2001] Fam Law 262,
  [2001] 04 LS Gaz R 50, (2001) Times, 10 January, 145 Sol Jo LB 16, [2000] All
  ER (D) 2230, CA 619
W v Doncaster Metropolitan Borough Council [2004] EWCA Civ 378, [2004] LGR 743,
  148 Sol Jo LB 572, [2004] All ER (D) 49 (May), sub nom R (on the application of
  W) v Doncaster Metropolitan Borough Council [2004] 22 LS Gaz R 32, (2004)
  Times, 13 May 945, 969
W v Egdell [1990] Ch 359, [1989] 1 All ER 1089, [1989] 2 WLR 689, 133 Sol Jo 570;
  affd [1990] Ch 359, [1990] 1 All ER 835, [1990] 2 WLR 471, 134 Sol Jo 286, 4
  BMLR 96, [1990] 12 LS Gaz R 41, CA 963
W v L [1974] QB 711, [1973] 3 All ER 884, [1973] 3 WLR 859, 117 Sol Jo 775, CA 842
W (by her litigation friend, B) v M (by her litigation friend, the Official Solicitor)
  [2011] EWHC 1197 (COP), [2011] NLJR 811, [2011] All ER (D) 08 (Jun), sub
  nom W (by her litigation friend, B) v M (an adult patient by the Official Solicitor),
  S, NHS Primary Care Trus and TImes Newspaper Ltd, Re [2011] 4 All ER 1295,
  [2012] 1 WLR 287, [2012] 1 FCR 237, [2011] 2 FLR 1143, [2011] Fam Law
  811 740
WCC v GS [2011] EWHC 2244 (Admin) 724
WM (Petition of) [2002] MHLR 367 930
W Healthcare NHS Trust v H [2004] EWCA Civ 1324, (2004) Times, 9 December,
  [2005] All ER (D) 94 (Jan) 624
W Primary Care Trust v TB [2009] EWHC 1737 (Fam), [2010] 2 All ER 331,
  [2010] 1 WLR 2662, [2011] PTSR 135, [2010] 1 FLR 682, [2009] Fam Law 1032,
  110 BMLR 45, [2009] All ER (D) 150 (Dec) 577, 658
Waldron, ex p [1986] QB 824, [1985] 3 WLR 1090, 129 Sol Jo 892,
  [1986] LS Gaz R 199, sub nom R v Hallstrom, ex p W [1985] 3 All ER 775, CA ... 759, 967
Walker, Re [1905] 1 Ch 160, 74 LJ Ch 86, 91 LT 713, CA 617
Ward v Metropolitan Police Comr [2005] UKHL 32, [2006] 1 AC 23, [2005] 3 All ER
  1013, [2005] 2 WLR 1114, 84 BMLR 185, (2005) Times, 9 May, 149 Sol Jo LB
  581, [2005] All ER (D) 65 (May) 922
Waring v Waring (1848) 6 Moo PCC 341, 12 Jur 947, 6 Notes of Cases 388 598
Waterhouse v Worsnop (1888) 59 LT 140 995
Watson v Coupland [1945] 1 All ER 217, 43 LGR 60, 109 JP 90, 175 LT 92n, DC 539
Weaver v Ward (1616) Hob 134, Moore KB 864 761
Welham v DPP [1961] AC 103, [1960] 1 All ER 805, [1960] 2 WLR 669, 44 Cr App
  Rep 124, 124 JP 280, 104 Sol Jo 308, HL 1008
Wellcome Foundation Ltd v Secretary of State for Social Services [1988] 2 All ER 684,
  [1988] 1 WLR 635, 132 Sol Jo 821, HL 37
Westminster Social and Community Services Department v C [2008] EWCA Civ 198,
  [2009] Fam 11, [2009] 2 WLR 185, [2008] 2 FCR 146, [2008] 2 FLR 267,
  [2008] Fam Law 517, [2008] NLJR 479, (2008) Times, 3 April, 152 Sol Jo (no 13)
  29, [2008] All ER (D) 276 (Mar) 609
Whitbread (mental patient: habeas corpus), Re (1997) 39 BMLR 94, 141 Sol Jo LB
  152, CA 821, 847
White v Driver (1809) 1 Phillim 84 598
White v Wilson (1806) 13 Ves 87 598
Whitehouse v Board of Control [1960] 3 All ER 182n, [1960] 1 WLR 1093, 104 Sol Jo
  824, HL 759
Whysall v Whysall [1960] P 52, [1959] 3 All ER 389, [1959] 3 WLR 592, 103 Sol Jo
  835 559
Wilkinson, Re (1919) 83 JP Jo 422 922
Williams v Williams [1964] AC 698, [1963] 2 All ER 994, [1963] 3 WLR 215, 107 Sol
  Jo 533, HL 610
Williams v Williams [2003] EWHC 742 (Ch), [2003] All ER (D) 403 (Feb) 614
Winch v Hayward [1986] QB 296, [1985] 3 All ER 97, [1985] 3 WLR 729, 129 Sol Jo
  669, CA 759
Winch v Jones [1986] QB 296, [1985] 3 All ER 97, [1985] 3 WLR 729, 129 Sol Jo
  669, CA 759
Winterwerp v Netherlands (Application 6301/73) (1979) 2 EHRR 387, ECtHR; on
  appeal sub nom Winterwerp v Netherlands (Art 50) (1981) 4 EHRR 228, ECtHR 761,
  767–770, 914, 969

PARA

Wood v Allan 1988 SLT 341, HC of Justiciary (Sc) 491
Wookey v Wookey; Re S (a child) (injunction) [1991] Fam 121, [1991] 3 All ER 365,
    [1991] 3 WLR 135, [1991] FCR 811, [1991] 2 FLR 319, CA 1002
Wychavon District Council v EM (HB) [2012] UKUT 12 (AAC) 613

X

X (adult sterilisation), Re [1999] 3 FCR 426, [1998] 2 FLR 1124, [1998] Fam Law
    737 612
X v A, B and C and Mental Health Act Commission (1991) 9 BMLR 91 .... 759, 928
X v Secretary of State for the Home Department [2001] 1 WLR 740, [2000] All ER (D)
    2162, CA 907
X v United Kingdom (Application 7215/75) (1981) 4 EHRR 188, ECtHR 965, 969
XCC v AA [2012] EWHC 2183 (COP), [2012] All ER (D) 38 (Aug) 609

Y

Y (mental incapacity: bone marrow transplant) Re, [1997] Fam 110, [1997] 2 WLR 556,
    [1997] 2 FCR 172, [1996] 2 FLR 787, [1997] Fam Law 91, 35 BMLR 111 .... 606, 612
YA (F) v A local authority [2010] EWHC 2770 (Fam), [2011] 1 WLR 1505,
    [2011] 1 FLR 2007, [2011] Fam Law 143, [2011] All ER (D) 112 (Jan) 721–722
YL v Birmingham City Council [2007] UKHL 27, [2008] 1 AC 95, [2007] 3 All ER 957,
    [2007] 3 WLR 112, [2008] LGR 273, [2007] HLR 651, 96 BMLR 1, [2007] NLJR
    938, 151 Sol Jo LB 860, [2007] All ER (D) 207 (Jun) 566, 945
Yates v Boen (1738) 2 Stra 1104 617
Yonge v Toynbee [1910] 1 KB 215, 79 LJKB 208, [1908–10] All ER Rep 204, 102 LT
    57, 26 TLR 211, CA 600, 994
York Glass Co Ltd v Jubb [1925] All ER Rep 285, 134 LT 36, 42 TLR 1, CA 614, 617

Z

Z (medical treatment: hysterectomy), Re [2000] 1 FCR 274 612
ZH (by his litigation friend) v Metropolitan Police Commissioner [2012] EWHC 604
    (Admin), 176 CL&J 241, [2012] All ER (D) 134 (Mar) 611
Zoan v Rouamba [2000] 2 All ER 620, [2000] 1 WLR 1509, [2000] NLJR 99, [2000]
    All ER (D) 47, CA 774

Decisions of the European Court of Justice are listed below numerically. These decisions
are also included in the preceding alphabetical list.

227/82: Van Bennekom [1983] ECR 3883, [1985] 2 CMLR 692, ECJ 25
35/85: Procureur de la République v Tissier [1986] ECR 1207, [1987] 1 CMLR 551,
    ECJ 25
C-60/89: Monteil and Samanni, Re [1991] ECR I-1547, [1992] 3 CMLR 425, 14 BMLR
    112, 135 Sol Jo LB 13, ECJ 25
C-112/89: Upjohn Co and Upjohn NV v Farzoo Inc and Kortmann [1991] ECR I-1703,
    [1993] 1 CMLR 657, 14 BMLR 79, ECJ 25
C-290/90: EC Commission v Germany [1992] ECR I-3317, ECJ 25
C-219/91: Ter Voort, Re [1992] ECR I-5485, [1995] 2 CMLR 591, 30 BMLR 165,
    ECJ 25
C-368/96: R v Licensing Authority established by the Medicines Act 1968 (acting by the
    Medicines Control Agency), ex p Generics (UK) Ltd [1998] ECR I-7967,
    [1999] 2 CMLR 181, 48 BMLR 161, ECJ 6
C-120/97: Upjohn Ltd v Licensing Authority established under the Medicines Act 1968
    [1999] ECR I-223, [1999] 1 WLR 927, [1999] 1 CMLR 825, 51 BMLR 206,
    [1999] 19 LS Gaz R 30, [1999] All ER (D) 40, ECJ 167
C-94/98: R v Medicines Control Agency, ex p Rhône-Poulenc Rorer Ltd [1999] ECR
    I-8789, [2000] All ER (EC) 46, [2000] 1 CMLR 409, 56 BMLR 71, [1999] All ER
    (D) 1449, ECJ 6, 25
C-387/99: Vitamin Supplements, Re, European Commission v Germany [2004] ECR
    I-3751, [2006] 3 CMLR 491, [2004] All ER (D) 192 (Jul), ECJ 25
C-471/00: Commission of the European Communities v Cambridge Healthcare Supplies
    [2001] ECR I-2865, CFI 167

C-106/01: R (on the application of Novartis Pharmaceuticals UK Ltd) v Medicines
  Control Agency [2004] ECR I-4403, [2005] All ER (EC) 192, [2004] 2 CMLR 565,
  81 BMLR 200, [2004] All ER (D) 357 (Apr), ECJ 6
C-211/03, C-299/03 and C-316/03 to C-318/03: HLH Warenvertriebs GmbH v Germany
  [2005] ECR I-5141, [2005] All ER (D) 56 (Jun), ECJ 25
C-374/05: Gintec International Import-Export Gmbh v Verband Sozialer Wettbewerb eV
  [2007] ECR I-9517, [2008] 1 CMLR 808, [2007] All ER (D) 133 (Nov), ECJ 336
C-141/07: European Commission v Germany [2008] ECR I-6935, [2008] 3 CMLR
  1479, ECJ 307
C-527/07: R (on the application Generics (UK) Ltd) v Licensing Authority [2009] ECR
  I-5259, 111 BMLR 46, [2009] All ER (D) 182 (Jun), ECJ 6
C-62/09: R (on the application of Association of the British Pharmaceutical Industry) v
  Medicines and Healthcare Products Regulatory Agency [2010] ECR I-3603, [2011]
  All ER (EC) 102, [2011] PTSR 391, 115 BMLR 26, [2010] NLJR 620, (2010)
  Times, 7 May, [2010] All ER (D) 142 (Apr), ECJ 343
C-7/11: Fabio Caronna [2012] 36 LS Gaz R 16, [2012] All ER (D) 49 (Sep), ECJ 150
C-308/11: Chemische Fabrik Kreussler & Co GmbH [2012] All ER (D) 79 (Sep), ECJ 25

MEDICAL PRODUCTS AND DRUGS

PARA

1.	CONTROL OF MEDICAL PRODUCTS		1
(1)	Introduction		1
(2)	European Law		4
	(i)	European Systems for Authorisations	4
	(ii)	Manufacturing of Products	12
	(iii)	Traceability	13
	(iv)	Pharmacovigilance	14
	(v)	Blood and Blood Products	17
	(vi)	Clinical Trials	18
	(vii)	Traditional Herbal Medicinal Products for Human Use	19
	(viii)	Medical Devices	20
	(ix)	Recent Developments	21
(3)	Advanced Therapy Medicinal Products		22
2.	MEDICINES ETC FOR HUMAN USE		25
(1)	Introduction		25
(2)	Administration		31
(3)	Manufacturing and Wholesale Dealing		35
	(i)	The Licensing Authority	35
	(ii)	Manufacturer's Licence	45
		A. Requirement and Exemptions	45
		B. Application	53
		C. Certification	55
		D. Licence Conditions	56
		(A) In general	56
		(B) Licence relating to the Manufacture or Assembly of Medicinal Products	61
		(C) Licences relating to the Import of Medicinal Products from a Non-EEA State	66
		(D) Licences relating to Exempt Advanced Therapy Medicinal Products	68
	(iii)	Wholesale Dealing Licence	77
		A. Requirement and Exemptions	77
		B. Application	80

PARA

     C.   Licence Conditions 82

  (iv)   Manufacture and Importation of Investigational Medicinal Products 97

     A.   Requirement and Exemptions 97

     B.   Application 99

(4)   Clinical Trials 107

  (i)   In general 107

  (ii)   Ethics Committees 110

  (iii)   Ethics Committee Opinion and Authorisation for Clinical Trials 112

     A.   In general 112

     B.   Ethics Committee Opinion 114

     C.   Authorisation for Clinical Trials 117

  (iv)   Conduct of Clinical Trials 126

  (v)   Labelling 136

  (vi)   Enforcement 137

(5)   Authorisations 141

  (i)   Requirement for Authorisation and Exceptions 141

  (ii)   Borderline Products 151

  (iii)   Marketing Authorisation 155

     A.   Applications 155

     B.   Conditions 160

     C.   Duties of Licensing Authority 164

     D.   Validity of UK Marketing Authorisation 165

     E.   Revocation, Suspension or Variation and Ceasing of Authorisation 166

     F.   Obligations of Holders of Marketing Authorisations 171

     G.   Offences 177

  (iv)   Certification of Homoeopathic Medicinal Products 187

     A.   Applications 187

     B.   Conditions 191

     C.   Validity of Certificate of Registration 193

     D.   Revocation, Suspension or Variation and Ceasing of Authorisation 194

     E.   Obligations of Holder of Certificate of Registration 197

                                                                        PARA
                F.   Offences 203
        (v)   Traditional Herbal Registration 206
                A.   Applications 206
                B.   Conditions 213
                C.   Validity of Certificate of Registration 214
                D.   Revocation, Suspension or Variation and Ceasing of
                        Authorisation 215
                E.   Obligations of Holder of Traditional Herbal
                        Registration 221
                F.   Offences 228
        (vi)   Article 126a Authorisation 232
(6)   Quality and Standards; Compendia 234
        (i)   Quality and Compliance with Standards 234
        (ii)   The British Pharmacopoeia and other Compendia 237
(7)   Pharmacovigilance 241
        (i)   Application 241
        (ii)   Obligations on Licensing Authority in relation to
                Pharmacovigilance 242
        (iii)   Obligations on Holders in relation to Pharmacovigilance 246
        (iv)   Reporting, Recording and Assessment of
                Pharmacovigilance Data 249
        (v)   Signal Detection 252
        (vi)   Periodic Safety Update Records 253
        (vii)   Urgent Action 258
        (viii) Post-authorisation Safety Studies 260
        (ix)   Transparency and Communications 265
        (x)   Enforcement 268
(8)   Prohibited Sales etc 270
        (i)   Starting Materials 270
        (ii)   Sale and Supply of Medicines 271
        (iii)   Exemptions 280
        (iv)   Specified Products 307
(9)   Packaging, Leaflets and Colours etc 314
        (i)   Containers 314
        (ii)   Packaging and Leaflets 317
        (iii)   Colours, Marking etc of Medicinal Products 331

PARA

(10) Advertising 333

    (i)   In general 333

    (ii)   Advertising to the Public 336

    (iii)   Promotional Purposes 337

    (iv)   Advertising to Persons Qualified to Prescribe or Supply 338

    (v)   Homoeopathic Medicinal Products and Herbal Medicinal
          Products 344

    (vi)   Scrutiny by Ministers 346

    (vii)   Complaints 348

    (viii) Injunctions 351

(11) Enforcement, Sampling and Forfeiture 354

    (i)   Medicines Act 1968 354

    (ii)   Human Medicines Regulations 2012 361

    (iii)   Offences and Proceedings 372

(12) Radioactive Materials 381

(13) Liability for Vaccine Damage 384

3.   VETERINARY MEDICINES 387

(1) Introduction 387

(2) Authorisations 388

    (i)   Introduction 388

    (ii)   Marketing Authorisations 389

    (iii)   Manufacturing Authorisations 410

    (iv)   Wholesale Dealer Authorisations 418

    (v)   Exemptions 422

(3) Pharmacovigilance 430

(4) Classification and Supply 431

(5) Records 433

(6) Imports and Exports 434

(7) Labelling, Marking and Leaflets 437

(8) Advertising 439

(9) Enforcement 442

(10) Offences 448

4.   BLOOD AND BLOOD PRODUCTS 449

(1) In general 449

(2) Blood Establishments and Blood Banks 453

PARA

(3) Management of Blood Products etc 468

(4) Offences 469

5. MEDICAL DEVICES 472

6. CONTROLLED DRUGS 480

(1) Introduction 480

(2) The Advisory Council on the Misuse of Drugs 490

(3) The Control of Drugs 491

     (i) Prohibitions and Offences 491

     (ii) Prevention of Misuse of Controlled Drugs 505

     (iii) Supervising of Management and Use of Controlled Drugs 514

(4) Directions to Practitioners and Pharmacists 519

(5) Enforcement and Offences 523

7. POISONS 528

(1) The Control of Poisons 528

(2) Sale, Storage and Transport of Poisons 535

     (i) Local Authorities' Lists 535

     (ii) Restrictions 538

     (iii) Labelling, Packaging, Storage and Transport 544

     (iv) Exemptions 546

(3) Enforcement, Penalties and Proceedings 548

     (i) Enforcement 548

     (ii) Penalties and Proceedings 552

1. CONTROL OF MEDICAL PRODUCTS

(1) INTRODUCTION

1. The scope of control. The Human Medicines Regulations 2012[1] consolidate the law concerning medicinal products[2] for human use[3]. In general, the manufacture, import and export and wholesale dealing of a medicinal product in the course of a business is prohibited except under licence[4] and a medicinal product can only be sold, supplied, or offered for sale or supply, if it has the necessary authorisation[5]. The ministers[6] act as the licensing authority[7], and may grant, refuse, suspend or renew such licences[8] and authorisations[9]. The licensing authority and the holder of an authorisation are under certain obligations to monitor the safety of medicines subject to an authorsation[10]. Certain medicines may not be sold, supplied or imported[11] or may only be sold or supplied by prescription[12] or subject to specified conditions[13]. Provision is also made regarding advertising and packaging and leaflets[14].

Legislation also exists that places restrictions on poisons[15] and drugs considered dangerous or otherwise harmful[16].

There is also significant control of medicinal products by way of European Union legislation[17], and regulations have been made under the European Communities Act 1972 implementing this legislation in respect of veterinary medicinal products[18]; clinical trials[19]; blood safety and quality[20]; and medical devices[21].

1 Ie the Human Medicines Regulations 2012, SI 2012/1916.
2 As to the meaning of 'medicinal product' see PARA 25.
3 See PARA 25 et seq.
4 See PARA 35 et seq. There are a number of exemptions from these provisions see PARAS 46–52, 78.
5 See PARA 141 et seq.
6 As to the meaning of 'the ministers' see PARA 35 note 1.
7 As to the licensing authority see PARA 35 note 1.
8 See PARA 37 et seq.
9 See PARA 155 et seq.
10 See PARA 242 et seq.
11 See PARAS 307–313.
12 See PARA 271 et seq.
13 See PARA 278.
14 See PARAS 314 et seq, 333 et seq.
15 See PARAS 528–555.
16 See PARA 480 et seq.
17 As to special provisions relating to the patenting of medicinal products see PATENTS AND REGISTERED DESIGNS vol 79 (2008) PARA 341 et seq. As to the provisions relating to the imposition of customs tariffs see CUSTOMS AND EXCISE vol 30 (2012) PARA 2 et seq. As to provisions relating to the use of medicinal products in animal feeding stuffs see AGRICULTURAL PRODUCTION AND MARKETING vol 1 (2008) PARA 996 et seq.
18 See the Marketing Authorisations for Veterinary Medicines Regulations 2011, SI 2011/2159; and PARA 388 et seq.
19 See the Medicines for Human Use (Clinical Trials) Regulations 2004, SI 2004/1031; and PARA 107 et seq.
20 See the Blood Safety and Quality Regulations 2005, SI 2005/50; and PARA 449 et seq.
21 See the Medical Devices Regulations 2002, SI 2002/618; and PARA 472 et seq.

2. Price control. The Secretary of State[1] may by order provide for the control of maximum prices to be charged for any medical supplies[2], other than health service medicines, required for the purposes of the National Health Service Act 2006[3].

Provision also exists for the Secretary of State to make statutory or voluntary schemes limiting the prices which may be charged by a manufacturer or supplier for the supply of any health service medicines or limiting the profits which may accrue to them in connection with the manufacture or supply of any health service medicines[4]. Where a voluntary scheme does not apply, the Secretary of State has the power to limit any price which may be charged by any manufacturer or supplier for the supply of any health service medicine and to provide for any amount representing sums charged by that person for that medicine in excess of the limit to be paid to the Secretary of State within a specified period[5]. Regulations have been made which control the price of presentations[6] of medicines which are supplied for health service purposes[7].

A person who breaches the above provisions may be liable to pay a penalty[8].

1   In any enactment, 'Secretary of State' means one of Her Majesty's principal Secretaries of State: see the Interpretation Act 1978 s 5, Sch 1. As to the office of Secretary of State see CONSTITUTIONAL LAW AND HUMAN RIGHTS vol 8(2) (Reissue) PARA 355.

2   'Medical supplies' includes surgical, dental and optical materials and equipment: National Health Service Act 2006 s 260(5).

3   See the National Health Service Act 2006 s 260(1); and HEALTH SERVICES vol 54 (2008) PARA 27. At the date at which this volume states the law no such orders had been made.

4   See the National Health Service Act 2006 ss 261, 263; and HEALTH SERVICES vol 54 (2008) PARAS 30, 31. The voluntary scheme may require certain sales information to be provided to the Secretary of State: see s 261(7); the Health Service Medicines (Information Relating to Sales of Branded Medicines etc) Regulations 2007, SI 2007/1320; and HEALTH SERVICES vol 54 (2008) PARA 29.

5   See the National Health Service Act 2006 s 262; and HEALTH SERVICES vol 54 (2008) PARA 29.

6   'Presentation' means a particular form of a relevant medicine which may be distinguished from other forms of the medicine by reference to its active ingredients and excipients, pack size, type of packaging, clinical indications or indicated method of administration for use in clinical practice: Health Service Branded Medicines (Control of Prices and Supply of Information) (No 2) Regulations 2008, SI 2008/3258, reg 1(2).

7   See the Health Service Branded Medicines (Control of Prices and Supply of Information) (No 2) Regulations 2008, SI 2008/3258; and HEALTH SERVICES vol 54 (2008) PARA 29.

8   See the National Health Service Act 2006 s 265; the Health Service Medicines (Information Relating to Sales of Branded Medicines etc) Regulations 2007, SI 2007/1320, reg 4; the Health Service Branded Medicines (Control of Prices and Supply of Information) (No 2) Regulations 2008, SI 2008/3258, reg 7; and HEALTH SERVICES vol 54 (2008) PARA 32.

3.   Pharmaceutical services.   Each Primary Care Trust must prepare, maintain and publish two lists of persons, other than medical practitioners or dental practitioners, who undertake to provide pharmaceutical services from premises in the area of the Primary Care Trust[1]. These lists ('pharmaceutical lists') are a list of persons who undertake to provide pharmaceutical services in particular by way of the provision of drugs and a list of persons who undertake to provide pharmaceutical services only by way of the provision of appliances[2].

Each Primary Care Trust must assess the needs for pharmaceutical services in its area, and publish a statement of its first assessment and of any revised assessment ('pharmaceutical needs assessment')[3]. The pharmaceutical services to which each pharmaceutical needs assessment must relate are all the pharmaceutical services that may be provided under arrangements made by a Primary Care Trust for the provision of pharmaceutical services (including directed services) by a person on a pharmaceutical list, the provision of local pharmaceutical services under certain local pharmaceutical schemes or the dispensing of drugs and appliances by a person on a dispensing doctors list (but not other NHS services that may be provided under arrangements made by a Primary Care Trust with a dispensing doctor)[4].

1   See the National Health Service (Pharmaceutical Services) Regulations 2012, SI 2012/1909, reg 10(1); and HEALTH SERVICES. As from 1 April 2013 Primary Care Trusts are abolished: see the Health and Social Care Act 2012 s 34; and the Health and Social Care Act 2012 (Commencement No 4, Transitional, Savings and Transitory Provisions) Order 2013, SI 2013/160. From that date pharmaceutical needs assessments will be carried out by Health and Wellbeing Boards and pharmaceutical lists will be the responsibility of National Health Service Commissioning Boards: see the National Health Service Act 2006 s 128A(1) (amended by the Health and Social Care Act 2012 s 206); and the National Health Service (Pharmaceutical and Local Pharmaceutical Services) Regulations 2013, SI 2013/349, regs 3, 10. See also the National Health Service Act 2006 ss 147A, 275(1) (s 147A added and s 275(1) amended by the Health and Social Care Act 2012 s 208(2), Sch 4 para 138).

2   See the National Health Service (Pharmaceutical Services) Regulations 2012, SI 2012/1909, reg 10(2); and HEALTH SERVICES.

3   See the National Health Service Act 2006 s 128A(1); the National Health Service (Pharmaceutical Services) Regulations 2012, SI 2012/1909, reg 3(1); and HEALTH SERVICES. See note 1.

4   See the National Health Service (Pharmaceutical Services) Regulations 2012, SI 2012/1909, reg 3(2); and HEALTH SERVICES.

(2) EUROPEAN LAW

(i) European Systems for Authorisations

4.   Requirement for authorisation. A medicinal product[1], whether for human or veterinary use, may not generally be placed on the market without a marketing authorisation[2].

The European system for the authorisation of medicinal products for human and animal use offers several routes for authorisation:

(1)   the centralised procedure[3];

(2)   the mutual recognition procedure[4]; and

(3)   the decentralised procedure[5].

1   As to the meaning of 'medicinal product' see PARA 25.

2   See PARA 6. As to an exception to this rule see PARA 8.

3   See Council Regulation (EC) 726/2004 (OJ L136, 30.4.2004, p 1) laying down Community procedures for the authorisation and supervision of medicinal products for human and veterinary use and establishing a European Medicines Agency; and PARA 5. The centralised procedure allows applicants to obtain an authorisation that is valid throughout the European Union.

4   See European Parliament and Council Directive (EC) 2001/82 (OJ L311, 28.11.2001, p 1) on the Community code relating to veterinary medicinal products, arts 31–43 (amended by European Parliament and Council Directive (EC) 2004/28 (OJ L136, 30.4.2004, p 58)); European Parliament and Council Directive (EC) 2001/83 (OJ L311, 28.11.2001, p 67) on the Community code relating to medicinal products for human use, arts 28–39.

5   See European Parliament and Council Directive (EC) 2001/82 (OJ L311, 28.11.2001, p 1), arts 31–43 (as amended: see note 3); European Parliament and Council Directive (EC) 2001/83 (OJ L311, 28.11.2001, p 67), arts 28–39.

5.   Centralised procedure. The following products must not be placed on the market within the European Union unless a marketing authorisation[1] has been granted[2]:

(1)   medicinal products developed by means of one of the following biotechnological processes: (a) recombinant DNA technology; (b) controlled expression of genes coding for biologically active proteins in prokaryotes and eukaryotes including transformed mammalian cells; (c) hybridoma and monoclonal antibody methods[3];

(2)   advanced therapy medicinal products[4];

(3)   medicinal products for veterinary use intended primarily for use as

performance enhancers in order to promote the growth of treated animals or to increase yields from treated animals[5];

(4)	medicinal products for human use containing a new active substance, which was not authorised before 20 May 2004[6], for which the therapeutic indication is the treatment of any of the following diseases: (a) acquired immune deficiency syndrome; (b) cancer; (c) neurodegenerative disorder; (d) diabetes; (e) auto-immune diseases and other immune dysfunctions; (f) viral diseases[7].

(5)	orphan medicinal products[8].

Any medicinal product not appearing in heads (1) to (5) above may be granted a marketing authorisation if:

(i)	it contains a new active substance which before 20 May 2004[9] was not authorised in the EU[10]; or

(ii)	the applicant shows that the medicinal product constitutes a significant therapeutic, scientific or technical innovation or that the granting of authorisation is in the interests of patients or animal health at EU level[11].

Immunological veterinary medicinal products for the treatment of animal diseases that are subject to European Union prophylactic measures may also be granted such authorisation[12].

Applications for a marketing authorisation must be submitted to the European Medicines Agency[13].

1	Ie a marketing authorisation referred to in Council Regulation (EC) 726/2004 (OJ L136, 30.4.2004, p 1) laying down Community procedures for the authorisation and supervision of medicinal products for human and veterinary use and establishing a European Medicines Agency, art 3.
2	Council Regulation (EC) 726/2004 (OJ L136, 30.4.2004, p 1), art 3(1).
3	Council Regulation (EC) 726/2004 (OJ L136, 30.4.2004, p 1), Annex.
4	Council Regulation (EC) 726/2004 (OJ L136, 30.4.2004, p 1), Annex (amended by Council Regulation (EC) 1394/2007 (OJ L324, 10.1.2007, p 121)). As to the meaning of 'advanced therapy medicinal products' see European Parliament and Council Regulation (EC) 1394/2007 (OJ L324, 10.12.2007, p 121–137) on advanced therapy medicinal products; and PARA 23.
5	Council Regulation (EC) 726/2004 (OJ L136, 30.4.2004, p 1), Annex.
6	Ie the date on which Council Regulation (EC) 726/2004 (OJ L136, 30.4.2004, p 1) came into force.
7	Council Regulation (EC) 726/2004 (OJ L136, 30.4.2004, p 1), Annex.
8	See Council Regulation (EC) 726/2004 (OJ L136, 30.4.2004, p 1), Annex. As to orphan medicinal products see European Parliament and Council Regulation (EC) 141/2000 (OJ L18, 22.1.2000, p 1) on orphan medical products.
9	See note 6.
10	Council Regulation (EC) 726/2004 (OJ L136, 30.4.2004, p 1), art 3(2)(a).
11	Council Regulation (EC) 726/2004 (OJ L136, 30.4.2004, p 1), art 3(2)(b).
12	Council Regulation (EC) 726/2004 (OJ L136, 30.4.2004, p 1), art 2.
13	Council Regulation (EC) 726/2004 (OJ L136, 30.4.2004, p 1), art 4(1). As to the European Medicines Agency see PARA 14.

**6.	Marketing authorisation.**	No medicinal product[1] or veterinary medicinal product[2] may be placed on the market of a member state unless a marketing authorisation has been issued[3] by the competent authorities of that member state or an authorisation has been granted[4] in accordance with the centralised procedure[5].

1	As to the meaning of 'medicinal product' see PARA 25. European Parliament and Council Directive (EC) 2001/83 (OJ L311, 28.11.2001, p 67) on the Community code relating to medicinal products for human use applies to medicinal products for human use intended to be placed on the market in member states and either prepared industrially or manufactured by a method involving an industrial process: art 2(1). A marketing authorisation is not required for certain radiopharmaceuticals: see art 7 (amended by European Parliament and Council Directive (EC) 2004/27 (OJ L136, 30.4.2004, p 34)).

2 As to the meaning of 'veterinary medicinal product' see PARA 387.

3 Ie issued in accordance with European Parliament and Council Directive (EC) 2001/82 (OJ L311, 28.11.2007, p 1) or, as appropriate, European Parliament and Council Directive (EC) 2001/83 (OJ L311, 28.11.2001, p 67).

4 Ie in accordance with Council Regulation (EC) 726/2004 (OJ L136, 30.4.2004, p 1) laying down Community procedures for the authorisation and supervision of medicinal products for human and veterinary use and establishing a European Medicines Agency (see PARA 14).

5 See European Parliament and Council Directive (EC) 2001/82 (OJ L311, 28.11.2001, p 1), art 5(1) (amended by European Parliament and Council Directive (EC) 2004/28 (OJ L136, 30.4.2004, p 58)); European Parliament and Council Directive (EC) 2001/83 (OJ L311, 28.11.2001, p 67), art 6(1) (amended by European Parliament and Council Regulation (EC) 1901/2006 (OJ L378, 27.12.2007, p 1); and European Parliament and Council Regulation (EC) 1394/2007 (OJ L324, 10.12.2007, p 121)). As to the documentation to be submitted along with an application see European Parliament and Council Directive (EC) 2001/82 (OJ L311, 28.11.2001, p 1), art 12 (amended by European Parliament and Council Directive (EC) 2004/28 (OJ L136, 30.4.2004, p 58)); European Parliament and Council Directive (EC) 2001/83 (OJ L311, 28.11.2001, p 67), art 8 (amended by European Parliament and Council Directive (EC) 2004/27 (OJ L136, 30.4.2004, p 34); European Parliament and Council Directive (EU) 2012/84 (OJ L348, 31.12.2010, p 74) and European Parliament and Council Directive (EU) 2011/62 (OJ L174, 1.7.2011, p 74)). See also Council Regulation (EC) 726/2004 (OJ L136, 30.4.2004, p 1), art 6(1); and PARA 179. Such documentation includes the results of certain tests and clinical trials (see European Parliament and Council Directive (EC) 2001/82 (OJ L311, 28.11.2001, p 1), art 12(3)(j) (amended by European Parliament and Council Directive (EC) 2004/28 (OJ L136, 30.4.2004, p 58)); and European Parliament and Council Directive (EC) 2001/83 (OJ L311, 28.11.2001, p 67), art 8(3)(i) (amended by European Parliament and Council Directive (EC) 2004/27 (OJ L136, 30.4.2004, p 34))) but these are not required if the medicinal product is essentially similar to a medicinal product previously authorised (see European Parliament and Council Directive (EC) 2001/82 (OJ L311, 28.11.2001, p 1), art 13 (amended by European Parliament and Council Directive (EC) 2004/28 (OJ L136, 30.4.2004, p 58)); and European Parliament and Council Directive (EC) 2001/83 (OJ L311, 28.11.2001, p 67), art 10 (amended by European Parliament and Council Directive (EC) 2004/27 (OJ L136, 30.4.2004, p 34))). As to what constitutes an essentially similar product and the grant of marketing authorisations in respect thereof see Case C-368/96 *R v Licensing Authority established by the Medicines Act 1968, ex p Generics (UK) Ltd (ER Squibb & Sons Ltd, intervener)* [1998] ECR I-7967, 48 BMLR 161, ECJ; Case C-106/01 *R (on the application of Novartis Pharmaceuticals UK Ltd) v Licensing Authority* [2004] ECT I-4403, 81 BMLR 200, ECJ; *R (on the application of Merck Sharp & Dohme Ltd) v Licensing Authority* [2005] EWHC 710 (Admin), [2005] All ER (D) 401 (Apr); Case C-527/07 *R (on the application Generics (UK) Ltd) v Licensing Authority* [2009] ECR I-5259, 111 BMLR 46, ECJ. As to applications relating to parallel imports see Case C-94/98 *R v Medicines Control Agency, ex p Rhone-Poulenc Rorer Ltd* [1999] ECR I-8789, 56 BMLR 71, ECJ.

7. Mutual recognition and decentralised procedure. With a view to the granting of a marketing authorisation for a medicinal product or veterinary medicinal product[1] in more than one member state, an applicant must submit an application based on an identical dossier in these member states[2]. The applicant must request one member state to act as 'reference member state' and to prepare an assessment report on the medicinal product[3].

Where the medicinal product has already received a marketing authorisation at the time of application, the concerned member states must recognise the marketing authorisation granted by the reference member state[4].

In cases where the medicinal product has not received a marketing authorisation at the time of application, the applicant must request the reference member state to prepare a draft assessment report, a draft summary of product characteristics and a draft of the labelling and package leaflet[5] which must be approved by the member states[6]. Otherwise if a member state cannot approve the assessment report, the summary of product characteristics, the labelling and the package leaflet on the grounds of potential serious risk to public health, it must give a detailed exposition of the reasons for its position to the reference member state, to the other member states concerned and to the applicant and refer the points of disagreement to the coordination group[7]. Within the coordination group the member states must use their best endeavours to reach an agreement on the action to be taken[8]. If they fail to reach a decision the matter is referred to the European Medicines Agency[9] but member states that have approved the assessment report, the draft summary of product characteristics and the labelling and package leaflet, may, at the request of the applicant, authorise the medicinal product[10].

1   As to the meaning of 'medicinal product' see PARA 25. As to the meaning of 'veterinary medicinal product' see PARA 387.

2   European Parliament and Council Directive (EC) 2001/82 (OJ L311, 28.11.2001, p 1) on the Community code relating to veterinary medicinal products, art 32(1); European Parliament and Council Directive (EC) 2001/83 (OJ L311, 28.11.2001, p 67), on the Community code relating to medicinal products for human use, art 28(1).

3   European Parliament and Council Directive (EC) 2001/82 (OJ L311, 28.11.2001, p 1), art 35(1); European Parliament and Council Directive (EC) 2001/83 (OJ L311, 28.11.2001, p 67), art 28(1).

4   European Parliament and Council Directive (EC) 2001/82 (OJ L311, 28.11.2001, p 1), art 35(2); European Parliament and Council Directive (EC) 2001/83 (OJ L311, 28.11.2001, p 67), art 28(2).

5   European Parliament and Council Directive (EC) 2001/82 (OJ L311, 28.11.2001, p 1), art 35(3); European Parliament and Council Directive (EC) 2001/83 (OJ L311, 28.11.2001, p 67), art 28(3).

6   See European Parliament and Council Directive (EC) 2001/82 (OJ L311, 28.11.2001, p 1), art 35(4); and European Parliament and Council Directive (EC) 2001/83 (OJ L311, 28.11.2001, p 67), art 28(4).

7   See European Parliament and Council Directive (EC) 2001/82 (OJ L311, 28.11.2001, p 1), art 33(1); and European Parliament and Council Directive (EC) 2001/83 (OJ L311, 28.11.2001, p 67), art 29(1).

8   European Parliament and Council Directive (EC) 2001/82 (OJ L311, 28.11.2001, p 1), art 33(3); European Parliament and Council Directive (EC) 2001/83 (OJ L311, 28.11.2001, p 67), art 29(3).

9   See PARA 5.

10 European Parliament and Council Directive (EC) 2001/82 (OJ L311, 28.11.2001, p 1), art 33(6); European Parliament and Council Directive (EC) 2001/83 (OJ L311, 28.11.2001, p 67), art 29(6).

8.   Compassionate use exemption.   By way of an exemption to the rule requiring a marketing authorisation[1] member states may make a medicinal product for human use[2] available for compassionate use to a group of patients with a chronically or seriously debilitating disease or whose disease is considered to be life-threatening, and who cannot be treated satisfactorily by an authorised medicinal product[3]. The medicinal product concerned must either be the subject of an application for a marketing authorisation[4] or must be undergoing clinical trials[5].

When compassionate use is envisaged, the Committee for Medicinal Products for Human Use[6], after consulting the manufacturer or the applicant[7], may adopt opinions[8] on the conditions for use, the conditions for distribution and the patients targeted[9]. Member states must take account of any available opinions[10].

Where a compassionate use programme has been set up, the applicant must ensure that patients taking part also have access to the new medicinal product during the period between authorisation and placing on the market[11].

1   Ie the rule set out in European Parliament and Council Directive (EC) 2001/83 (OJ L311, 28.11.2001, p 67) on the Community code relating to medicinal products for human use, art 6 (see PARA 4).
2   Ie a medicinal product belonging to one of the categories referred to in European Parliament and Council Regulation (EC) 726/2004 (OJ L136, 30.04.2004, p 1) laying down Community procedures for the authorisation and supervision of medicinal products for human and veterinary use and establishing a European Medicines Agency, art 3(1), (2). As to the meaning of 'medicinal product' see PARA 25.
3   See European Parliament and Council Regulation (EC) 726/2004 (OJ L136, 30.04.2004, p 1), art 83(1), (2). When a member state makes use of this provision it must notify the European Medicines Agency (see PARA 14): art 83(3).
4   Ie in accordance with European Parliament and Council Regulation (EC) 726/2004 (OJ L136, 30.04.2004, p 1), art 6 (see PARA 6).
5   European Parliament and Council Regulation (EC) 726/2004 (OJ L136, 30.04.2004, p 1), art 83(2). As to clinical trials see PARA 107 et seq.
6   As to the Committee for Medicinal Products for Human Use see PARA 14 note 1.
7   Such opinions do not affect the civil or criminal liability of the manufacturer or of the applicant for marketing authorisation: European Parliament and Council Regulation (EC) 726/2004 (OJ L136, 30.04.2004, p 1) art 83(7).
8   The opinions must be updated on a regular basis and kept on the Agency's website: see European Parliament and Council Regulation (EC) 726/2004 (OJ L136, 30.04.2004, p 1) art 83(4), (6) (art 83(6) amended by European Parliament and Council Regulation (EU) 1235/2010 (L348, 31.12.2010, p 1)).
9   European Parliament and Council Regulation (EC) 726/2004 (OJ L136, 30.04.2004, p 1) art 83(4).
10 European Parliament and Council Regulation (EC) 726/2004 (OJ L136, 30.04.2004, p 1) art 83(5).
11 European Parliament and Council Regulation (EC) 726/2004 (OJ L136, 30.04.2004, p 1) art 83(8).

9.   Temporary use exemption.   Member states may temporarily authorise the distribution of an unauthorised medicinal product for human use in response to the suspected or confirmed spread of pathogenic agents, toxins, chemical agents or nuclear radiation any of which could cause harm[1].

1   European Parliament and Council Directive (EC) 2001/83 (OJ L311, 28.11.2001, p 67), on the Community code relating to medicinal products for human use, art 5(2) (art 5 substituted by Council Directive (EC) 2004/27 (OJ L136, 30.4.2006, p 34)). As to protection from liability from consequences from use of such products, unless such product is defective, see European Parliament and Council Directive (EC) 2001/83 (OJ L311, 28.11.2001, p 67), art 5(3), (4) (as so substituted).

10.   Article 126a authorisation.   In the absence of a marketing authorisation or a pending application for a medicinal product[1] authorised in another member state[2] a member state may for justified public health reasons authorise the placing on the market of the said medicinal product[3].

Before granting the authorisation the member state must notify the holder of the marketing authorisation of the proposal to grant it and may request copies of the assessment report[4] and of the marketing authorisation in force in respect of the medicinal product concerned[5].

1   As to the meaning of 'medicinal product' see PARA 25.
2   Ie in accordance with European Parliament and Council Directive (EC) 2001/83 (OJ L311, 28.11.2001, p 67), on the Community code relating to medicinal products for human use.
3   European Parliament and Council Directive (EC) 2001/83 (OJ L311, 28.11.2001, p 67), art 126a(1) (added by European Parliament and Council Directive (EC) 2004/27 (OJ L136, 30.4.2004, p 34)). As to the granting of an Article 12a Authorisation see PARA 232 et seq.
4   Ie the assessment report referred to in European Parliament and Council Directive (EC) 2001/83 (OJ L311, 28.11.2001, p 67), art 21(4).

5 European Parliament and Council Directive (EC) 2001/83 (OJ L311, 28.11.2001, p 67), art 126a(3) (added by European Parliament and Council Directive (EU) 2010/4 (OJ L348, 31.12.2010, p 74)).

11. Variations of licences in relation to mutual recognition or centralised procedures. The Variations Regulation[1] lays down provisions concerning the examination of variations to the terms of certain marketing authorisations for human use and veterinary medicinal products[2]. Variations are classified, depending on their impact on the medicinal product, into one of the following categories: minor variation of type 1A[3], major variation of type II[4], minor variation of type IB[5], extension of marketing authorisation[6]. The Variations Regulation sets out the procedure to be followed for each category with exceptions for human influenza vaccines[7].

In the event of a risk to public health in the case of medicinal products for human use or, in the case of veterinary medicinal products, in the event of a risk to human or animal health or to the environment, relevant authorities or, in the case of centralised marketing authorisations, the Commission may impose urgent safety restrictions on the holder[8]. If the holder takes urgent safety restrictions on his own initiative, he must inform all relevant authorities and, in the case of a centralised marketing authorisation, the Commission[9].

1 Commission Regulation (EC) 1234/2008 (OJ L334, 12.12.2008. p 7–24) concerning the examination of variations to the terms of marketing authorisations for medicinal products for human use and veterinary medicinal products. This regulation took effect on 1 January 2010 and although it applies to variation in marketing authorisations covered by European procedures, it has also been applied in the UK to purely national variation applications since that date.

2 Commission Regulation (EC) 1234/2008 (OJ L334, 12.12.2008. p 7–24) art 1(1).

3 'Minor variation of type 1A' means a variation which has only minimal impact, or no impact at all, on the quality, safety or efficacy of the medicinal product: Commission Regulation (EC) 1234/2008 (OJ L334, 12.12.2008. p 7–24), art 2(2).

4 'Major variation of type II' means a variation which is not an extension and which may have a significant impact on the quality, safety or efficacy of the medicinal product concerned: Commission Regulation (EC) 1234/2008 (OJ L334, 12.12.2008. p 7–24), art 2(3).

5 'Minor variation of type IB' means a variation which is neither a minor variation of type IA nor a major variation of type II nor an extension: Commission Regulation (EC) 1234/2008 (OJ L334, 12.12.2008. p 7–24), art 2(5).

6 'Extension of marketing authorisation' or 'extension' means a variation listed in Commission Regulation (EC) 1234/2008 (OJ L334, 12.12.2008. p 7–24), Annex I and fulfils the conditions laid down therein: art 2(4).

7 See Commission Regulation (EC) 1234/2008 (OJ L334, 12.12.2008. p 7–24) arts 12, 18, 21.

8 See Commission Regulation (EC) 1234/2008 (OJ L334, 12.12.2008. p 7–24) art 22(2). The holder must submit the corresponding application for variation within 15 days following the initiation of that restriction: art 22(3). As to offences committed for failing to comply with such provisions see PARA 178.

9 See Commission Regulation (EC) 1234/2008 (OJ L334, 12.12.2008. p 7–24) art 22(1) (amended by Commission Regulation (EU) 712/2012 (OJ L209, 4.8.2012, p 4). If the relevant authority or, in the case of a centralised marketing authorisation, the Commission has not raised objections within 24 hours following receipt of such information from the holder, the urgent safety restrictions are deemed accepted: Commission Regulation (EC) 1234/2008 (OJ L334, 12.12.2008. p 7–24), art 22(1) (as so amended). See note 8.

(ii) Manufacturing of Products

12. Manufacturing of products. The Good Manufacturing Practice Directive[1] lays down the principles and guidelines of good manufacturing practice in respect of medicinal products[2] for human use and investigational medicinal products for human use[3]. The principles and guidelines of good manufacturing practice for veterinary medicinal products are set out in a further directive[4].

Certain obligations are placed on the manufacturer such as ensuring that manufacturing operations are carried out in accordance with good manufacturing practice[5] and the manufacturing authorisation[6] and establishing an effective pharmaceutical quality assurance system[7], quality control system[8], a system for recording and reviewing complaints together with an effective system for recalling, promptly and at any time, products in the distribution network[9].

1   Ie Commission Directive (EC) 2003/94 (OJ L262, 14.10.2003, p 22–26) laying down the principles and guidelines of good manufacturing practice in respect of medicinal products for human use and investigational medicinal products for human use ('the Good Manufacturing Practice Directive').

2   As to the meaning of 'medicinal product' see PARA 25.

3   Commission Directive (EC) 2003/94 (OJ L262, 14.10.2003, p 22–26) art 1.

4   See Commission Directive (EC) 1991/412 (OJ L228, 17.8.1991, p 71) laying down the principles and guidelines of good manufacturing practice for veterinary medicinal products.

5   'Good manufacturing practice' means the part of quality assurance which ensures that products are consistently produced and controlled in accordance with the quality standards appropriate to their intended use: Commission Directive (EC) 1991/412 (OJ L228, 17.8.1991, p 71) art 2; Commission Directive (EC) 2003/94 (OJ L262, 14.10.2003, p 22–26) art 2(6).

6   See Commission Directive (EC) 1991/412 (OJ L228, 17.8.1991, p 71) arts 4, 5; and Commission Directive (EC) 2003/94 (OJ L262, 14.10.2003, p 22–26) arts 4, 5.

7   See Commission Directive (EC) 1991/412 (OJ L228, 17.8.1991, p 71) art 6; and Commission Directive (EC) 2003/94 (OJ L262, 14.10.2003, p 22–26) art 6. 'Pharmaceutical quality assurance' means the total sum of the organised arrangements made with the object of ensuring that medicinal products or investigational medicinal products are of the quality required for their intended use: Commission Directive (EC) 1991/412 (OJ L228, 17.8.1991, p 71) art 2; Commission Directive (EC) 2003/94 (OJ L262, 14.10.2003, p 22–26) art 2(5).

8   See Commission Directive (EC) 1991/412 (OJ L228, 17.8.1991, p 71) art 11; and Commission Directive (EC) 2003/94 (OJ L262, 14.10.2003, p 22–26) art 11.

9   See Commission Directive (EC) 2003/94 (OJ L262, 14.10.2003, p 22–26) art 13; and Commission Directive (EC) 2003/94 (OJ L262, 14.10.2003, p 22–26) art 13.

(iii) Traceability

13. Traceability. A traceability system must be established in relation to human cells and tissues[1], in relation to blood and blood components[2] and in relation to advanced therapy medicinal products[3]. Such data must be kept in a manner that meets certain standards relating to confidentiality and data protection[4].

1   See Council Directive (EC) 2004/23 (OJ L102, 7.4.2004, p 48) on setting standards of quality and safety for the donation, procurement, testing, processing, preservation, storage and distribution of human tissues and cells, art 8 (amended by Council Regulation (EC) 596/2009 (OJ L188, 18.7.2009, p 14)). For this purpose 'cells' means individual human cells or a collection of human cells when not bound by any form of connective tissue; and 'tissue' means all constituent parts of the human body formed by cells: Council Directive (EC) 2004/23 (OJ L102, 7.4.2004, p 48) art 3.

2   See Council Directive (EC) 2002/98 (OJ L33, 8.2.2003, p 30) setting standards of quality and safety for the collection, testing, processing, storage and distribution of human blood and blood components, art 14. For this purpose 'blood' mean whole blood collected from a donor and processed either for transfusion or for further manufacturing; and 'blood component' means a therapeutic constituent of blood (red cells, white cells, platelets, plasma) that can be prepared by various methods: art 3.

3   See European Parliament and Council Regulation (EC) 1394/2007 (OJ L324, 10.12.2007, p 121) on advanced therapy medicinal products, art 15.

4   See Council Directive (EC) 2004/23 (OJ L102, 7.4.2004, p 48) art 14; and Council Directive (EC) 2002/98 (OJ L33, 8.2.2003, p 30) art 24.

(iv) Pharmacovigilance

14.   European Medicines Agency. The European Medicines Agency is responsible for coordinating the existing scientific resources put at its disposal by member states for the evaluation, supervision and pharmacovigilance of medicinal products[1].

It must provide the member states with the best possible scientific advice on any question relating to the evaluation of the quality, safety and efficacy of medicinal products for human or veterinary use which is referred to it in accordance with the provisions of EU legislation relating to medicinal products[2].

The Agency may give a scientific opinion, in the context of cooperation with the World Health Organisation, for the evaluation of certain medicinal products for human use intended exclusively for markets outside the European Union[3].

The Agency must take care to ensure early identification of potential sources of conflict between its scientific opinions and those of other bodies established under EU law carrying out a similar task in relation to issues of common concern[4].

At the request of the Commission, the Agency must, in respect of authorised medicinal products, collect any available information on methods that member states' competent authorities use to determine the added therapeutic value that any new medicinal product provides[5]. The Agency must set up and maintain a database (known as the 'Eudravigilance database') containing information on suspected adverse drug reactions[6]. It is also responsible for setting up and maintaining a European medicines web-portal for the dissemination of information on medicinal products authorised in the European Union[7].

The Agency must monitor selected medical literature for reports of suspected adverse reactions to medicinal products containing certain active substances and publish the list of active substances being monitored and the medical literature subject to this monitoring[8].

An offence may be committed for failing to provide the Agency with specified information[9].

1   Council Regulation (EC) 726/2004 (OJ L136, 30.4.2004, p 1) laying down Community procedures for the authorisation and supervision of medicinal products for human and veterinary use and establishing a European Medicines Agency, art 55. The Committee for Medicinal Products for Human Use is responsible for drawing up the opinion of the Agency in relation to applications for medicinal products for human use and the Committee for Medicinal Products for Veterinary Use is responsible for drawing up the opinion of the Agency in relation to application for medicinal products for veterinary medicinal products: see arts 5, 30.
2   Council Regulation (EC) 726/2004 (OJ L136, 30.4.2004, p 1), art 57(1).
3   Council Regulation (EC) 726/2004 (OJ L136, 30.4.2004, p 1), art 58(1).
4   See Council Regulation (EC) 726/2004 (OJ L136, 30.4.2004, p 1), art 59.
5   Council Regulation (EC) 726/2004 (OJ L136, 30.4.2004, p 1), art 60.
6   See Council Regulation (EC) 726/2004 (OJ L136, 30.4.2004, p 1) art 24 (substituted by European and Parliament Regulation (EU) 1235/2010 (OJ L348, 31.12.2010, p 1).
7   See Council Regulation (EC) 726/2004 (OJ L136, 30.4.2004, p 1) art 26 (substituted by European and Parliament Regulation (EU) 1235/2010 (OJ L348, 31.12.2010, p 1).
8   See Council Regulation (EC) 726/2004 (OJ L136, 30.4.2004, p 1) art 27 (substituted by European and Parliament Regulation (EU) 1235/2010 (OJ L348, 31.12.2010, p 1).
9   See the Human Medicines Regulations 2012, SI 2012/1916, regs 81, 82, 84; and PARA 179.

15.   Duty on member states. Member states must operate a pharmacovigilance system[1].

In relation to medicinal products for human use[2] the pharmacovigilance system must be used to collect information on the risks of those products as regards patients' or public health and that information must in particular refer to adverse reactions[3] in human beings, arising from use of the medicinal product within the terms of the marketing authorisation as well as from use outside the terms of the marketing authorisation, and to adverse reactions associated with occupational exposure[4]. Member states must, by means of this pharmacovigilance system, evaluate all information scientifically, consider options for risk minimisation and prevention and take regulatory action concerning the marketing authorisation as necessary[5].

In relation to veterinary medicinal products, the system must be used to collect information useful in the surveillance of veterinary medicinal products, with particular reference to adverse reactions in animals and in human beings relating to the use of veterinary medicinal products, and to evaluate such information scientifically[6].

1 European Parliament and Council Directive (EC) 2001/82 (OJ L311, 28.11.2001, p 1) on the Community code relating to veterinary medicinal products, art 73 (amended by European Parliament and Council Directive (EC) 2004/28 (OJ L136, 30.4.2004, p 58)); European Parliament and Council Directive (EC) 2001/83 (OJ L311, 28.11.2001, p 67) on the Community code relating to medicinal products for human use, art 101(1) (added by European Parliament and Council Directive (EU) 2010/84 (OJ L343, 31.12.2010, p 74). In relation to products for human use, 'pharmacovigilance system' means a system used by the marketing authorisation holder and by member states to fulfil the tasks and responsibilities listed in European Parliament and Council Directive (EC) 2001/83 (OJ L311, 28.11.2001, p 67) Title IX and designed to monitor the safety of authorised medicinal products and detect any change to their risk-benefit balance: art 28d (added by European Parliament and Council Directive (EU) 2010/84 (OJ L343, 31.12.2010, p 74)).
2 As to the meaning of 'medicinal product' see PARA 25.
3 As to the meaning of 'adverse reaction' see PARA 70 note 6.
4 European Parliament and Council Directive (EC) 2001/83 (OJ L311, 28.11.2001, p 67), art 101(1) (as added: see note 1).
5 European Parliament and Council Directive (EC) 2001/83 (OJ L311, 28.11.2001, p 67), art 101(2) (as added: see note 1).
6 European Parliament and Council Directive (EC) 2001/82 (OJ L311, 28.11.2001, p 1) art 73 (as added see note 1).

16. Duty on marketing authorisation holder. In relation to medicinal products for human use, the marketing authorisation holder must operate a pharmacovigilance system[1] for the fulfilment of his pharmacovigilance tasks equivalent to the relevant member state's pharmacovigilance system[2] and, by means of this system, he must evaluate all information scientifically, consider options for risk minimisation and prevention and take appropriate measures as necessary[3].

As part of the pharmacovigilance system, the marketing authorisation holder must:

(1) have permanently and continuously at his disposal an appropriately qualified person responsible for pharmacovigilance;

(2) maintain and make available on request a pharmacovigilance system master file[4];

(3) operate a risk management system[5] for each medicinal product[6];

(4) monitor the outcome of risk minimisation measures which are contained in the risk management plan[7] or which are laid down as conditions[8] of the marketing authorisation;

(5) update the risk management system and monitor pharmacovigilance data to determine whether there are new risks or whether risks have changed or whether there are changes to the benefit-risk balance of medicinal products[9].

In relation to veterinary medicinal products the marketing authorisation holder must maintain detailed records of suspected adverse reactions and report any serious adverse reactions or human adverse reactions to the competent authority of the member state in whose territory the incident occurred[10]. The marketing authorisation holder must also have permanently and continuously at his disposal an appropriately qualified person responsible for pharmacovigilance with certain responsibilities[11].

1   As to the meaning of 'pharmacovigilance system' see PARA 15 note 1.
2   European Parliament and Council Directive (EC) 2001/83 (OJ L311, 28.11.2001, p 67) on the Community code relating to medicinal products for human use, art 104(1). As to the member state's pharmacovigilance system see PARA 15. As to obligations relating to pharmacovigilance see also Council Regulation (EC) 726/2004 (OJ L136, 30.4.2004, p 1) laying down Community procedures for the authorisation and supervision of medicinal products for human and veterinary use and establishing a European Medicines Agency, arts 21–29.
3   European Parliament and Council Directive (EC) 2001/83 (OJ L311, 28.11.2001, p 67), art 104(2) (added by European Parliament and Council Directive (EU) 2010/84 (OJ L343, 31.12.2010, p 74)). He must also carry out a regular audit: see European Parliament and Council Directive (EC) 2001/83 (OJ L311, 28.11.2001, p 67), art 104(2).
4   As to the meaning of 'pharmacovigilance system master file' see PARA 246 note 3.
5   As to the meaning of 'risk management system' see PARA 74 note 6.
6   'As to the meaning of 'medicinal product' see PARA 25.
7   'Risk management plan' means a detailed description of the risk management system: European Parliament and Council Directive (EC) 2001/83 (OJ L311, 28.11.2001, p 67), art 1(28c) (definition added by European Parliament and Council Directive (EU) 2010/84 (OJ L343, 31.12.2010, p 74)).
8   Ie pursuant to European Parliament and Council Directive (EC) 2001/83 (OJ L311, 28.11.2001, p 67), art 21a, 22 or 22a.
9   European Parliament and Council Directive (EC) 2001/83 (OJ L311, 28.11.2001, p 67), art 104(3) (as added: see note 3).
10 See European Parliament and Council Directive (EC) 2001/82 (OJ L311, 28.11.2001, p 1) on the Community code relating to veterinary medicinal products, art 75(1), (2) (substituted by European and Parliament Directive (EC) 2004/28 (L136, 30.4.2004, p 58). Reports of all adverse reactions must be submitted to the competent authority in the form of a period safety report including a scientific evaluation of the risk-benefit balance of the veterinary medicinal product: see European Parliament and Council Directive (EC) 2001/82 (OJ L311, 28.11.2001, p 1) art 75(5) (substituted by European and Parliament Directive (EC) 2004/28 (L136, 30.4.2004, p 58).
11 See European Parliament and Council Directive (EC) 2001/82 (OJ L311, 28.11.2001, p 1), art 74 (amended by European and Parliament Directive (EC) 2004/28 (L136, 30.4.2004, p 58).

(v) Blood and Blood Products

17. Blood and blood products. Provision is made for the standards of quality and safety for the collection, testing, processing, storage and distribution of human blood and blood components[1] and for the establishment of specific technical requirements to prevent the transmission of diseases by blood and blood products[2].

1   See European Parliament and Council Directive (EC) 2002/98 (OJ L33, 8.2.2002, p 30–40) setting standards of quality and safety for the collection, testing, processing, storage and distribution of human blood and blood components.
2   See Commission Directive (EC) 2004/33 (OJ L91, 30.3.2004, p 25–39) implementing European Parliament and Council Directive (EC) 2002/98 (OJ L33, 8.2.2002, p 30–40) as regards certain technical requirements for blood and blood products; and Commission Directive (EC) 2005/62 (OJ L56, 10.2005, p 1–48) as regards Community standards and specifications relating to a quality system for blood establishments.

(vi) Clinical Trials

18. Clinical trials. Clinical trials are regulated by European Parliament and Council Directive on the approximation of the laws, regulations and administrative provisions of the member states relating to the implementation of good clinical practice in the conduct of clinical trials on medicinal products for human use[1]. A clinical trial may only be undertaken subject to certain conditions[2]. The Ethics Committee must give its opinion, before a clinical trial commences, on any issue requested[3]. A clinical trial must follow certain procedures[4] including entering information regarding the trial in a European database[5]. Member states must take all appropriate measures to ensure that the manufacture or importation of investigational medicinal products[6] is subject to the holding of authorisation and the Commission must lay down the minimum requirements which the applicant and, subsequently, the holder of the authorisation must meet in order to obtain the authorisation[7]. Provision is also made regarding labelling the packaging of the investigational medicinal product[8], the verification of compliance with the provisions on good clinical and manufacturing practice[9] and the notification of adverse events and serious adverse reactions[10].

1   See European Parliament and Council Directive (EC) 2001/20 (OJ L121, 1.5.2001, p 34) on the approximation of the laws, regulations and administrative provisions of the Member States relating to the implementation of good clinical practice in the conduct of clinical trials on medicinal products for human use. Articles 6(7), 9(4), (6) in respect of gene therapy and somatic cell therapy medicinal products also apply to tissue engineered products: European Parliament and Council Regulation (EC) 1394/2007 (OJ L324, 10.12.2007, p 121) on advanced therapy medicinal products, art 4(1). 'Clinical trial' means any investigation in human subjects intended to discover or verify the clinical, pharmacological and/or other pharmacodynamics effects of one or more investigational medicinal product(s), and/or to identify any adverse reactions to one or more investigational medicinal product(s) and/or to study absorption, distribution, metabolism and excretion of one or more investigational medicinal product(s) with the object of ascertaining its (their) safety and/or efficacy; this includes clinical trials carried out in either one site or multiple sites, whether in one or more than one member state: European Parliament and Council Directive (EC) 2001/20 (OJ L121, 1.5.2001, p 34), art 2(a).

2   See European Parliament and Council Directive (EC) 2001/20 (OJ L121, 1.5.2001, p 34), arts 3–5.

3   See European Parliament and Council Directive (EC) 2001/20 (OJ L121, 1.5.2001, p 34), art 6.

4   See European Parliament and Council Directive (EC) 2001/20 (OJ L121, 1.5.2001, p 34), arts 9, 10.

5   See European Parliament and Council Directive (EC) 2001/20 (OJ L121, 1.5.2001, p 34), art 11.

6   'Investigational medicinal product' means a pharmaceutical form of an active substance or placebo being tested or used as a reference in a clinical trial, including products already with a marketing authorisation but used or assembled (formulated or packaged) in a way different from the authorised form, or when used for an unauthorised indication, or when used to gain further information about the authorised form: European Parliament and Council Directive (EC) 2001/20 (OJ L121, 1.5.2001, p 34), art 2(d).

7   See European Parliament and Council Directive (EC) 2001/20 (OJ L121, 1.5.2001, p 34), art 13(1) (amended by European Parliament and Council Directive (EC) 1901/2006 (OJ L378, 27.12.2006, p 1)). As to measures to be taken by the member state see European Parliament and Council Directive (EC) 2001/20 (OJ L121, 1.5.2001, p 34), art 13(2), (3).

8   See European Parliament and Council Directive (EC) 2001/20 (OJ L121, 1.5.2001, p 34), art 14.

9   See European Parliament and Council Directive (EC) 2001/20 (OJ L121, 1.5.2001, p 34), art 15.

10   See European Parliament and Council Directive (EC) 2001/20 (OJ L121, 1.5.2001, p 34), arts 16, 17.

(vii) Traditional Herbal Medicinal Products for Human Use

19.   Traditional herbal medicinal products for human use. European legislation makes provision for a simplified registration procedure in relation to herbal medicinal products[1] that satisfy certain criteria[2]. An application must be accompanied by certain documentation[3] including the results of specific pharmaceutical tests[4] and bibliographical or expert evidence that the product in question, or a corresponding product, has been in medicinal use throughout a period of at least 30 years preceding the date of the application, including at least 15 years within the Community[5]. However, if the application for registration relates to a product on the list of herbal substances, preparations and combinations for use in traditional herbal medicinal products established by the Committee for Herbal Medicinal Products[6], certain information does not need to be provided[7].

The mutual recognition and centralised procedures[8] apply to registrations granted in accordance with the above provisions provided that a Community herbal monograph has been established[9] or the herbal medicinal product consists of herbal substances, preparations or combinations thereof contained in the list mentioned above[10].

1   See Council Directive (EC) 2001/83 (OJ L311, 28.11.2001, p 67), on the Community code relating to medicinal products for human use, Chapter 2a (added by European Parliament and Council Directive (EC) 2004/24 (OJ L136, 30.4.2004, p 85)).
2   See Council Directive (EC) 2001/83 (OJ L311, 28.11.2001, p 67), art 16a (as added: see note 1).
3   See Council Directive (EC) 2001/83 (OJ L311, 28.11.2001, p 67), art 16c (as added: see note 1).
4   See Council Directive (EC) 2001/83 (OJ L311, 28.11.2001, p 67), art 16c(1)(a)(ii) (as added: see note 1).
5   See Council Directive (EC) 2001/83 (OJ L311, 28.11.2001, p 67), art 16c(1)(c) (as added: see note 1). Where a product does not fulfil this criterion but is otherwise eligible for the simplified registration procedure, the member state where the application has been submitted must refer the product to the Committee for Herbal Medicinal Products: see art 16(4) (as so added). The Committee for Herbal Medicinal Products is established under art 16h (as so added).
6   The list must contain, with regard to each herbal substance, the indication, the specified strength and the posology, the route of administration and any other information necessary for the safe use of the herbal substance as a traditional medicinal product: Council Directive (EC) 2001/83 (OJ L311, 28.11.2001, p 67), art 16f(1) (as added: see note 1).
7   See Council Directive (EC) 2001/83 (OJ L311, 28.11.2001, p 67), art 16f(2) (as added: see note 1).
8   Ie Council Directive (EC) 2001/83 (OJ L311, 28.11.2001, p 67) Title III, Chapter 4.
9   The Committee for Herbal Medicinal Products must establish Community herbal monographs for herbal medicinal products with regard to the application of art 10(1)(a)(ii) as well as traditional herbal medicinal products: see art 16h(3).
10   See Council Directive (EC) 2001/83 (OJ L311, 28.11.2001, p 67), art 16d(1) (as added: see note 1). For other herbal medicinal products as referred to in art 16a, each member state must, when evaluating an application for traditional use registration, take due account of registrations granted by another member state: see art 16d(2).

(viii) Medical Devices

20.   Medical devices. European law regulates a wide range of medical devices and their accessories[1], including in vitro diagnostic devices[2] and active implantable devices[3], and has been implemented in the United Kingdom[4].

1   See Council Directive (EC) 1993/42 (OJ L169, 12.7.1993, p 1) concerning medical devices. As to the definition of 'medical devices' see PARA 472. As to determinations relating to borderline products see PARAS 151–154.
2   See European Parliament and Council Directive (EC) 1998/79 (OJ L331, 7.12.1998, p 1) on in vitro diagnostic medical devices.

3 See Council Directive (EC) 1990/385 (OJ L189, 20.7.1990, p 7) on the approximation of the laws of the member states relating to implantable medical devices.

4 As to implementation see the Medical Devices Regulations 2002, SI 2002/618; and PARA 472 et seq. 'United Kingdom' means Great Britain and Northern Ireland: Interpretation Act 1978 s 5, Sch 1. 'Great Britain' means England, Scotland and Wales: Union with Scotland Act 1706 preamble art I; Interpretation Act 1978 s 22(1), Sch 2 para 5(a). Neither the Channel Islands nor the Isle of Man is within the United Kingdom. See further CONSTITUTIONAL LAW AND HUMAN RIGHTS vol 8(2) (Reissue) PARA 3.

(ix) Recent Developments

21. Falsified Medicines Directive and Pharmacovigilance Directive. The European Union has recently adopted a directive aimed at tackling the issue of falsified medicines[1]. This directive:

(1) introduces the concept of brokering for finished medicinal products;

(2) introduces a requirement that brokers have to register with the competent authority of the member state in which they are established;

(3) extends the requirement for a wholesale dealer's licence for export of medicines to third countries;

(4) extends existing obligations for wholesale dealers and provides new obligations, in particular reporting any suspected falsified medicines;

(5) formalises current regulatory expectations for the manufacturer of the medicinal product to have audited their suppliers of active substances for compliance with the relevant Good Manufacturing Practice and provides a solid legal basis in the Directive for the written confirmation of audit;

(6) introduces a formal requirement for manufacturers of medicinal products (or a third party acting under contract) to audit their suppliers of active substances for compliance with the requirements of Good Distribution Practice particular to active substances;

(7) formalises the regulatory expectation that manufacturers of the medicinal product will verify the authenticity and quality of the active substances and excipients they use;

(8) introduces a new obligation on product manufacturers to inform the competent authority and marketing authorisation holder should the manufacturer obtain information that products (manufactured under the scope of the manufacturing authorisation) may be falsified, whether those products are being distributed through the legitimate supply chain, or by illegal means;

(9) makes a number of significant changes to the controls on active substances and excipients intended for use in the manufacture of a medicinal product for human use, and in particular introduces two new definitions for active substances and excipients;

(10) introduces a new requirement for manufacturers, importers and distributors of active substances to be registered with the competent authority of the member state in which they are established;

(11) introduces a new requirement for companies selling medicines at a distance to members of the public to be registered and a requirement for a common internet logo on their website.

Further legislation introduces changes relating to pharmacovigilance[3], which include:

(a) placing a duty on the marketing authorisation holder to notify the relevant member state if a product ceases to be placed on the market and to give the reasons for its withdrawal;

(b) the ability for member states or the Commission to suspend a marketing authorisation and prohibit the use of the medicinal product concerned at any stage of proceedings where urgent action is required to protect public health; and

(c) the introduction of a list of medicinal products subject to additional monitoring[4].

To ensure transparency, medicinal products subject to the additional monitoring mentioned in head (c) must be labelled with an inverted equilateral black triangle[5].

1 Ie European Parliament Directive (EU) 2011/62 (OJ L174, 1.7.2011, p 74–87) on the Community code relating to medicinal products for human use, as regards the prevention of the entry into the legal supply chain of falsified medicinal products (which amends European Parliament and Council Directive (EC) 2001/83 (OJ L311, 28.11.2001, p 67) on the Community code relating to medicinal products for human use).

2 The directive has yet to be implemented in the United Kingdom. As to the date of implementation of European Parliament and Council Directive (EC) 2001/83 (OJ L311, 28.11.2001, p 67) see art 2. At the date at which this volume states the law a draft statutory instrument amending the Human Medicines Regulations 2012, SI 2012/1916, had yet to be laid before Parliament.

3 As to European law relating to pharmacovigilance see PARAS 14–16.

4 See European Parliament and Council Directive (EU) 2012/26 (OJ L299, 27.10.2012, p 1–4) amending European Parliament and Council Directive (EC) 2001/83 (OJ L311, 28.11.2001, p 67) as regards pharmacovigilance (which must be complied with by 28 October 2013 at the latest: see art 2(1)); and European Parliament and Council Regulation (EU) 1027/2012 (OJ L316, 25.10.2012, p 38) amending Council Regulation (EC) 726/2004 (OJ L136, 30.4.2004, p 1) as regards pharmacovigilance (which applies from 5 June 2013).

5 See Commission implementing Regulation (EU) 198/2013 (OJ L65, 7.3.2013, p 17) on the selection of a symbol for the purpose of identifying medicinal products for human use that are subject to additional monitoring.

(3) ADVANCED THERAPY MEDICINAL PRODUCTS

22. European Regulation. European Parliament and Council Regulation on advanced therapy medicinal products[1] lays down specific rules concerning the authorisation[2], labelling, and packaging[3], supervision[4] and pharmacovigilance of advanced therapy medicinal products[5].

There is a Committee for Advanced Therapies[6] which has certain tasks including formulating a draft opinion on the quality, safety and efficacy of an advanced therapy medicinal product for final approval by the Committee for Medicinal Products for Human Use and to advise the latter on any data generated in the development of such a product; providing advice on certain matters and providing scientific expertise[7].

1 Ie European Parliament and Council Regulation (EC) 1394/2007 (OJ L324, 10.12.2007, p 121) on advanced therapy medicinal products (amended by European Parliament and Council Regulation (EU) 1235/2010 (OJ L348, 31.12.2010)).

2 Where an advanced therapy medicinal product contains human cells or tissues, the donation, procurement and testing of those cells or tissues must be made in accordance with Council Directive (EC) 2004/23 (OJ L102, 7.4.2004, p 48) on setting standards of quality and safety for the donation, procurement, testing, processing, preservation, storage and distribution of human tissues and cells (see PARA 22): European Parliament and Council Regulation (EC) 1394/2007 (OJ L324, 10.12.2007, p 121) art 3. As to the marketing authorisation requirements see European Parliament and Council Regulation (EC) 1394/2007 (OJ L324, 10.12.2007, p 121) arts 3–9.

3   As to labelling and packaging requirements see European Parliament and Council Regulation
    (EC) 1394/2007 (OJ L324, 10.12.2007, p 121) arts 10–13.
4   In addition to the requirements for pharmacovigilance in Council Regulation (EC) 726/2004
    (OJ L136, 30.4.2004, p 1) laying down Community procedures for the authorisation and
    supervision of medicinal products for human and veterinary use and establishing a European
    Medicines Agency, arts 21–29 there are certain post-authorisation follow-up requirements
    relating to efficacy and adverse reactions and risk management see European Parliament and
    Council Regulation (EC) 1394/2007 (OJ L324, 10.12.2007, p 121) on advanced therapy
    medicinal products, art 14. Failure to comply may be an offence see the Human Medicines
    Regulations 2012, SI 2012/1916, reg 87; and PARA 180. A system of traceability is also required
    see European Parliament and Council Regulation (EC) 1394/2007 (OJ L324, 10.12.2007,
    p 121), art 15.
5   European Parliament and Council Regulation (EC) 1394/2007 (OJ L324, 10.12.2007, p 121)
    art 1. As to the meaning of 'advanced medicinal product' see PARA 23.
6   See European Parliament and Council Regulation (EC) 1394/2007 (OJ L324, 10.12.2007,
    p 121) art 20.
7   See European Parliament and Council Regulation (EC) 1394/2007 (OJ L324, 10.12.2007,
    p 121) art 23.

23.   Definition 'advanced therapy medicinal product'. 'Advanced therapy
medicinal product' means any of the following medicinal products for human
use:

(1)   a gene therapy medicinal product[1];

(2)   a somatic cell therapy medicinal product[2];

(3)   a tissue engineered product[3].

'Tissue engineered product' means a product that contains or consists of
engineered cells or tissues[4] and is presented as having properties for, or is used in
or administered to human beings with a view to regenerating, repairing or
replacing a human tissue[5]. A tissue engineered product may contain cells or
tissues of human or animal origin, or both[6]. The cells or tissues may be viable or
non-viable[7]. It may also contain additional substances, such as cellular products,
bio-molecules, bio-materials, chemical substances, scaffolds or matrices[8].

1   'Gene therapy medicinal product' means a biological medicinal product which has the following
    characteristics: (1) it contains an active substance which contains or consists of a recombinant
    nucleic acid used in or administered to human beings with a view to regulating, repairing,
    replacing, adding or deleting a genetic sequence; (2) its therapeutic, prophylactic or diagnostic
    effect relates directly to the recombinant nucleic acid sequence it contains, or to the product of
    genetic expression of this sequence. Gene therapy medicinal products do not include vaccines
    against infectious diseases: Council Directive (EC) 2001/83 (OJ L311, 28.11.2001, p 67) on the
    Community code relating to medicinal products for human use, Annex 1 Part IV.
2   'Somatic cell therapy medicinal product' means a biological medicinal product which has the
    following characteristics: (1) contains or consists of cells or tissues that have been subject to
    substantial manipulation so that biological characteristics, physiological functions or structural
    properties relevant for the intended clinical use have been altered, or of cells or tissues that are
    not intended to be used for the same essential function or functions in the recipient and the
    donor; (2) is presented as having properties for, or is used in or administered to human beings
    with a view to treating, preventing or diagnosing a disease through the pharmacological,
    immunological or metabolic action of its cells or tissues: Council Directive (EC) 2001/83
    (OJ L311, 28.11.2001, p 67) Annex 1 Part IV.
3   European Parliament and Council Regulation (EC) 1394/2007 (OJ L324, 10.12.2007, p 121) on
    advanced therapy medicinal products, art 2(1)(a).
4   Cells or tissues are considered 'engineered' if they fulfil at least one of the following conditions:
    (1)   the cells or tissues have been subject to substantial manipulation, so that biological
          characteristics, physiological functions or structural properties relevant for the intended
          regeneration, repair or replacement are achieved;
    (2)   the cells or tissues are not intended to be used for the same essential function or
          functions in the recipient as in the donor: European Parliament and Council Regulation
          (EC) 1394/2007 (OJ L324, 10.12.2007, p 121), art 2(1)(c).

The manipulations listed in Annex I, in particular, are not considered as substantial manipulations.

5   European Parliament and Council Regulation (EC) 1394/2007 (OJ L324, 10.12.2007, p 121) art 2(1)(d).

6   European Parliament and Council Regulation (EC) 1394/2007 (OJ L324, 10.12.2007, p 121) art 2(1)(d).

7   European Parliament and Council Regulation (EC) 1394/2007 (OJ L324, 10.12.2007, p 121) art 2(1)(d). Products containing or consisting exclusively of non-viable human or animal cells and/or tissues, which do not contain any viable cells or tissues and which do not act principally by pharmacological, immunological or metabolic action, are excluded from the definition of 'tissue engineered product': see art 2(1)(d).

8   European Parliament and Council Regulation (EC) 1394/2007 (OJ L324, 10.12.2007, p 121) art 2(1)(d).

24.   UK regulation.   Activities involving material, other than gametes, which consists of or includes human cells[1] are regulated by the Human Tissue Authority[2] and may require a licence[3] whilst the Human Fertilisation and Embryology Authority regulate and licence treatment and research involving embryos and gametes[4].

1   See the Human Tissue Act 2004 s 53(1); and MEDICAL PROFESSIONS vol 74 (2011) PARA 57. This does not include embryos outside the human body or hair and nail from the body of a living person: see s 53(2); and MEDICAL PROFESSIONS vol 74 (2011) PARA 57.

2   See the Human Tissue Act 2004; and MEDICAL PROFESSIONS vol 74 (2011) PARA 54 et seq. As to the activities within the remit of the Authority see MEDICAL PROFESSIONS vol 74 (2011) PARA 57.

3   See the Human Tissue Act 2004 s 16; and MEDICAL PROFESSIONS vol 74 (2011) PARA 83. Appropriate consent may also be required; see s 1 and MEDICAL PROFESSIONS vol 74 (2011) PARA 61 et seq.

4   See the Human Fertilisation and Embryology Act 1990; and MEDICAL PROFESSIONS vol 74 (2011) PARA 119 et seq.

2. MEDICINES ETC FOR HUMAN USE

(1) INTRODUCTION

25. Introduction. The Human Medicines Regulations 2012[1] consolidate the law concerning medicinal products for human use.

A 'medicinal product' is (1) any substance[2] or combination of substances presented as having properties of preventing or treating disease[3] in human beings; or (2) any substance or combination of substances that may be used by or administered[4] to human beings with a view to restoring, correcting or modifying a physiological function by exerting a pharmacological, immunological or metabolic action or making a medical diagnosis[5].

A similar definition is adopted by Council Directive on the Community code relating to medicinal products for human use and the Good Manufacturing Practice Directive[6].

The Human Medicines Regulations 2012 do not apply to whole human blood or any human blood component[7], other than plasma prepared by a method involving an industrial process[8]. Nor do they apply where the product is a radionuclide[9] that is in the form of a sealed source[10].

1 Ie the Human Medicines Regulations 2012, SI 2012/1916.
2 'Substance' means any matter regardless of its origins and includes:
    (1)   human substances (such as human blood and human blood products) (Human Medicines Regulations 2012, SI 2012/1916, reg 8(1));
    (2)   animal substances (such as micro-organisms, whole animals, parts of organs, animal secretions, toxins, extracts and blood products) (reg 8(1));
    (3)   vegetable substances (such as micro-organisms, plants, parts of plants, vegetable secretions and extracts) (reg 8(1));
    (4)   chemical substances (such as elements, naturally occurring chemical materials and chemical products obtained by chemical change or synthesis) (reg 8(1)); and
    (5)   gases and vapours (reg 8(1)).
3 'Disease' includes any injury, ailment or adverse condition, whether of body or mind: Human Medicines Regulations 2012, SI 2012/1916, reg 8(1).
4 'Administer' means administer to a human being orally, by injection, or by introduction into the body in any other way or by external application (whether or not by direct application to the body), and any reference in the Human Medicines Regulations 2012, SI 2012/1916 to administering anything is to administering it in its existing state or after it has been dissolved or dispersed in, or diluted or mixed with, a substance used as a vehicle: reg 8(1).
5 Human Medicines Regulations 2012, SI 2012/1916, reg 2(1). This definition also applies for the purposes of the Medicines Act 1968: see s 130(1) (substituted by SI 2012/1916).
6 See Council Directive (EC) 2001/83 (OJ L311, 28.11.2001, p 67) on the Community code relating to medicinal products for human use, art 1(2) (amended by Directive (EC) 2004/27 (OJ L136, 30.4.2004, p 34)); and Commission Directive (EC) 2003/94 (OJ L262, 14.10.2003, p 22–26) laying down the principles and guidelines of good manufacturing practice in respect of medicinal products for human use and investigational medicinal products for human use ('the Good Manufacturing Practice Directive'), art 2(1). For cases relating to the classification of medicinal products see: Case C-227/82 *Van Bennekom* [1983] ECR 3883, [1985] 2 CMLR 692, ECJ; Case C-35/85 *Procureur de la Republique v Tissier* [1986] ECR 1207, [1987] 1 CMLR 551, ECJ; Case C-60/89 *Re Monteil and Samanni* [1991] ECR I-1547, 14 BMLR 112, ECJ; Case C-112/89 *Upjohn Co and Upjohn NV v Farzoo Inc and Kortmann* [1991] ECR I-1703, 14 BMLR 79, ECJ; Case C-290/90 *EC Commission v Germany* [1992] ECR I-3317, ECJ; Case C-219/91 *Re Ter Voort* [1992] ECR I-5485, 30 BMLR 165, ECJ; *R v Medicines Control Agency, ex p Pharma Nord (UK) Ltd* [1998] 3 CMLR 109, 44 BMLR 41, CA; Case C-94/98 *R v Medicines Control Agency, ex p Rhone-Poulenc Rorer Ltd* [1999] ECR I-8789, 56 BMLR 71, ECJ; Joined Cases C-211/03, C-299/03 and C-316/03–C-318/03 *HLH Warenvertriebs GmbH v Germany* [2005] ECR I-5141, ECJ; Case C-387/99 *Re Vitamin Supplements: EC Commission v Germany* [2004] ECR I-3751, [2006] 3 CMLR 491, ECJ; Case C-308/11 *Chemische Fabrik Kreussler & Co GmbH* [2012] All ER (D) 79 (Sep).

7   'Blood component' means any of the following: (1) red cells; (2) white cells; (3) platelets and; (4) plasma: Human Medicines Regulations 2012, SI 2012/1916, reg 8(1).
8   Human Medicines Regulations 2012, SI 2012/1916, reg 2(2). As to the regulation of blood products see PARAS 449–471.
9   'Radionuclide' means a radioactive isotope: Human Medicines Regulations 2012, SI 2012/1916, reg 8(1).
10   See the Human Medicines Regulations 2012, SI 2012/1916, reg 3(3), (7).

26.   Classification of medicinal products. For the purposes of the Human Medicines Regulations 2012[1] references to a medicinal product[2] subject to general sale are to a product that is not a prescription only medicine or a pharmacy medicine but is:

(1)   a product that is covered by an authorisation[3] of which it is a term that the product is to be available on general sale[4]; or

(2)   a product that is covered by: (a) an EU marketing authorisation[5]; and (b) is not classified in the authorisation as a prescription only medicine; and (c) the licensing authority[6] has determined should be available on general sale[7].

References to a prescription only medicine are to any of the following:

(i)   a medicinal product that is covered by an authorisation[8] of which it is a term that the product is to be available only on prescription[9];

(ii) a medicinal product that is covered by an EU marketing authorisation and is classified in the authorisation as a prescription only medicine[10];

(iii) a medicinal product that is a specified as a prescription only medicine[11]; or

(iv) a medicinal product that is the result of the assembly[12], or the reformulation (including the combining with other substances), of a medicinal product that is a prescription only medicine by virtue of heads (i) or (ii)[13].

References to a pharmacy medicine are to a medicinal product that is not a prescription only medicinal product or a medicinal product subject to general sale but is:

(A)   covered by an authorisation of which it is a term that the product is to be available only from a pharmacy[14];

(B)   a product that is covered by an EU marketing authorisation, and is not classified in the authorisation as a prescription only medicine, other than a product to which head (2)(c) above applies[15];

(C)   specified medicinal products available only from a pharmacy[16] or the result of the assembly or the reformulation (including the combining with other substances), of a medicinal product that is a pharmacy medicine by virtue of head (A) or (B)[17].

1   Ie the Human Medicines Regulations 2012, SI 2012/1916.
2   As to the meaning of 'medicinal product' see PARA 25.
3   For the purposes of the Human Medicines Regulations 2012, SI 2012/1916, reg 5(1)(a), (5)(a), 'authorisation' means a UK marketing authorisation, a certificate of registration, a traditional herbal registration or an Article 126a authorisation: reg 5(2). As to the meanings of 'UK marketing authorisation', 'certificate of registration', 'traditional herbal registration' and 'Article 126a authorisation' see PARA 141 notes 2–6.
4   Human Medicines Regulations 2012, SI 2012/1916, reg 5(1)(a). As to the exemption of medicinal products at high dilutions see Prescriptions Only Medicines (Human Use) Order 1997, SI 1997/1830, art 10 (amended by SI 2003/696, SI 2006/915, SI 2012/1916).
5   As to the meaning of 'EU marketing authorisation' see PARA 141 note 3.
6   As to the meaning of 'licensing authority' see PARA 35 note 1.
7   Human Medicines Regulations 2012, SI 2012/1916, reg 5(1)(b).

8　For this purpose 'authorisation' means a UK marketing authorisation or an Article 126a authorisation: Human Medicines Regulations 2012, SI 2012/1916, reg 5(4).

9　Human Medicines Regulations 2012, SI 2012/1916, reg 5(3)(a).

10　Human Medicines Regulations 2012, SI 2012/1916, reg 5(3)(b).

11　Human Medicines Regulations 2012, SI 2012/1916, reg 5(3)(c). The following medicinal products are available only on prescription:

(1)　a product for parenteral administration (Sch 1 para 1(a));

(2)　a product that is a controlled drug, unless it is covered by a marketing authorisation in which the product is classified as a pharmacy medicine or as a medicinal product subject to general sale (Sch 1 para 1(b));

(3)　cyanogenic substances, other than preparations for external use (Sch 1 para 1(c));

(4)　medicinal substances that on administration emit radiation, or contain or generate any substance which emits radiation, in order that radiation may be used (Sch 1 para 1(d));

(5)　a product that is covered by a marketing authorisation in which the product is classified as a pharmacy medicine or as a medicinal product subject to general sale, and consists of or contains aloxiprin, aspirin or paracetamol in the form of non-effervescent tablets or capsules (Sch 1 para 1(e));

(6)　a product that is covered by a marketing authorisation in which the product is classified as a pharmacy medicine or as a medicinal product subject to general sale, and consists of or contains (in any pharmaceutical form) pseudoephedrine salts or ephedrine base or salts (Sch 1 para 1(f)); and

(7)　a product that is not covered by a marketing authorisation and is a prescription only medicine by virtue of the Prescription Only Medicines (Human Use) Order 1997, SI 1997/1830, arts 5, 10, Schs 1, 2 (Human Medicines Regulations 2012, SI 2012/1916, Sch 1 para (1)(g)).

For the purposes of heads (1)–(7) above 'cyanogenic substances' means preparations which are presented for sale or supply under the name of, or as containing, amygdalin, laetrile or vitamin B17 or contain more than 0.1 per cent by weight of any substance having the formula either alpha-Cyanobenzyl -6-O-Beta-d-glucopyranosyl -Beta-d-glucopyranoside, or alpha-Cyanobenzyl -Beta-d-glucopyranosiduronic acid: Sch 1 para 2. As to orders prescribing prescription only medicines see PARA 272.

12　As to the meaning of 'assemble' see PARA 141 note 8.

13　Human Medicines Regulations 2012, SI 2012/1916, reg 5(3)(d).

14　Human Medicines Regulations 2012, SI 2012/1916, reg 5(5)(a).

15　Human Medicines Regulations 2012, SI 2012/1916, reg 5(5)(b).

16　Human Medicines Regulations 2012, SI 2012/1916, reg 5(5)(c). The specified medicinal products mentioned in the text are those set out in Sch 1 Pt 2 as follows. The following medicinal products are available only from a pharmacy: a product comprising eye ointment, a product that contains Vitamin A, Vitamin A acetate or Vitamin A palmitate, in each case with a maximum daily dose equivalent to more than 7500 international units of Vitamin A or 2250 micrograms of retinol, and a product that contains Vitamin D with a maximum daily dose of more than 400 units of antirachitic activity: Sch 1 para 3. The following medicinal products are available only from a pharmacy unless they are the subject of a marketing authorisation or traditional herbal registration that classifies them as medicinal products subject to general sale: (1) a product that is for use as an anthelmintic; (2) a product that is for parenteral administration; (3) a product that is for use as an enema; (4) a product that is for use wholly or mainly for irrigation of wounds or the bladder, vagina or rectum; (5) a product that is for administration wholly or mainly to children being a preparation of aloxiprin or aspirin: Sch 1 para 4. A medicinal product is available only from a pharmacy if it is a medicinal product of a kind specified in Sch 15 (see PARA 278) but is not presented for sale in accordance with the requirements specified in that Schedule for a product of that kind to be subject to general sale: Sch 1 para 5.

17　Human Medicines Regulations 2012, SI 2012/1916, reg 5(5)(d).

27.　Orders and regulations. Where the Medicines Act 1968 authorises or requires regulations to be made for any purpose, the regulations are to be made by the ministers[1], unless the specific provision states otherwise[2]. Any power to make orders[3] or regulations[4] under the Act is exercisable by statutory instrument[5]. Any power to make regulations or orders may be exercised so as to make different provision for different areas or in relation to different cases or different circumstances, and to make any such provision subject to any exceptions, limitations or conditions which may be considered necessary or expedient[6]. Before making any regulations or order[7] under the Act, the ministers proposing to make the order or regulations must consult such organisations as appear to them to be representative of interests likely to be substantially affected by the regulations or order[8].

1 As to the meaning of 'the ministers' see the Human Medicines Regulations 2012, SI 2012/1916, reg 6(6)–(8); and PARA 35 (definition applied by the Medicines Act 1968 s 1 (substituted by SI 2012/1916)).

2 Medicines Act 1968 s 129(1). In relation to the making of regulations and orders, the knowledge of civil servants cannot be imputed to ministers, and ministers must know or be told enough to ensure that nothing that it is necessary, because legally relevant, for them to know is left out of account, although this does not mean that they must know everything that is relevant; what it is relevant for them to know is enough to enable them to make an informed judgment: *R (on the application of National Association of Health Stores) v Secretary of State for Health* [2005] EWCA Civ 154, (2005) Times, 9 March. In the absence of any public interest in non-disclosure, a briefing to a minister in respect of a proposed regulation or order should be disclosed in litigation contesting the regulation or order: *R (on the application of National Association of Health Stores) v Secretary of State for Health* at [49] per Sedley LJ. As to disclosure of documents see CIVIL PROCEDURE vol 11 (2009) PARA 749 et seq.

3 Ie other than an order made by a court or judge, or certain orders relating to Northern Ireland: Medicines Act 1968 s 129(2).

4 Ie other than certain regulations relating to Northern Ireland: see the Medicines Act 1968 s 129(2).

5 Medicines Act 1968 s 129(2). Any power to make an order under any provision of the Medicines Act 1968 includes power to revoke or vary the order by a subsequent order: s 129(4) (amended by SI 2012/1916).

6 Medicines Act 1968 s 129(5) (amended by the Health Act 2006 s 32).

7 Ie except an order made in accordance with any provision of the Medicines Act 1968 under which, in case of urgency, an order can be made with immediate effect: s 129(6).

8 Medicines Act 1968 s 129(6).

28. Application of provisions to non-medicinal products. The ministers[1], may specify by order any description or class of articles or substances[2] appearing to them to be articles or substances which are not medicinal products[3] but are manufactured, sold, supplied, imported or exported[4] for use wholly or partly for a medicinal purpose, and may direct that, subject to such exceptions and modifications as may be specified in the order, specified provisions of the Human Medicines Regulations 2012[5] or the clinical trials regulations[6], including provisions which relate to offences or penalties, are to have effect in relation to articles or substances of that description or class as they have effect in relation to medicinal products[7].

The ministers may also specify by order any substance appearing to them to be a substance which is not itself a medicinal product but which is used as an ingredient in the manufacture[8] of medicinal products[9], or which if used without proper safeguards is capable of causing danger to the health of the community and direct that, subject to such exceptions and modifications as may be specified in the order, specified provisions of the Medicines Act 1968 or the clinical trials regulations are to have effect in relation to that substance as they have effect in relation to medicinal products[10]. This power may be exercised in relation to a class of substances if it appears to the ministers that the conditions[11] are fulfilled in relation to all substances falling within the class[12].

1 As to the meaning of 'the ministers' see PARA 35 note 1 (definition applied by the Medicines Act 1968 s 1 (substituted by SI 2012/1916)).

2 As to the meaning of 'substance' see PARA 25 note 2 (definition applied by the Medicines Act 1968 s 132(1) (substituted by SI 2012/1916)).

3   As to the meaning of 'medicinal product' see PARA 25 (definition applied by the Medicines
    Act 1968 s 132(1) (as substituted: see note 2)).
4   As to the meanings of 'import' and 'export' see PARA 55 note 5 (definition applied by the
    Medicines Act 1968 s 132(1) (as substituted: see note 2)).
5   Ie the Human Medicines Regulations 2012, SI 2012/1916.
6   'The clinical trials regulations' means the Medicines for Human Use (Clinical Trials)
    Regulations 2004, SI 2004/1031: Human Medicines Regulations 2012, SI 2012/1916, reg 8(1).
7   Medicines Act 1968 s 104(1) (amended by SI 2004/1031; SI 2006/2407; SI 2012/1916). For
    orders made under the Medicines Act 1968 s 104 see the Medicines (Surgical Materials)
    Order 1971, SI 1971/1267 (amended by SI 1994/3119; SI 2004/1031; SI 2006/2407) (specified
    surgical ligatures or sutures or absorbable materials); the Medicines (Dental Filling Substances)
    Order 1975, SI 1975/533 (amended by SI 1994/3119l; SI 2004/1031); the Medicines (Specified
    Articles and Substances) Order 1976, SI 1976/968 (amended by SI 2012/1916) (contact lenses,
    contact lens fluids and associated substances and intra-uterine contraceptive devices); the
    Medicines (Radioactive Substances) Order 1978, SI 1978/1004 (radioactive substances for
    insertion into or contact with the body, and administration for tests); and the Medicines
    (Cyanogenetic Substances) Order 1984, SI 1984/187 (amended by SI 2006/2407) (preparations
    of or containing amygdalin, laetrile, vitamin B17, or containing specified cyanide-producing
    substances).
8   As to the meaning of 'manufacture' see PARA 141 note 7 (definition applied by the Medicines
    Act 1968 s 132(1) (as substituted: see note 2)).
9   Medicines Act 1968 s 105(1)(a).
10 Medicines Act 1968 s 105(1) (amended by SI 2004/1031; SI 2006/2407; SI 2012/1916). For
    orders under the Medicines Act 1968 s 105(1) see the Medicines (Control of Substances for
    Manufacture) Order 1971, SI 1971/1200 (amended by SI 1994/787); and the Medicines
    (Control of Substances for Manufacture) Order 1985, SI 1985/1403 (amended by SI 1994/787).
11 Ie the conditions specified in the Medicines Act 1968 s 105(1)(a) or (b).
12 Medicines Act 1968 s 105(2).

29.   The operation and effect of the Medicines Act 1968. The provisions of
the Medicines Act 1968 and of any regulations or order made under it[1] operate
cumulatively, and any exemption or exception from any of those provisions is
not to be construed as conferring any exemption or exception in relation to any
other of those provisions[2]. Except in so far as the Act expressly provides
otherwise, and subject to the statutory provisions[3] relating to offences under two
or more laws, the provisions of the Act do not confer any right of action in any
civil proceedings (other than proceedings for recovery of a fine) in respect of any
contravention[4] of the Act or of any regulations or order made under it[5], or affect
any restrictions[6] imposed by or under any other enactment[7], or derogate from
any right of action or other remedy, civil or criminal, in proceedings instituted
otherwise than under the Act[8]. No exemption conferred by or under any
provision of the Act derogates from any exemption or immunity of the Crown[9].

1   As to the making of regulations and orders see PARA 27.
2   Medicines Act 1968 s 133(1).
3   Ie the Interpretation Act 1978 s 18: see STATUTES AND LEGISLATIVE PROCESS vol 96 (2012) PARA
    1147.
4   As to the meaning of 'contravention' see PARA 41 note 8 (definition applied by the Medicines
    Act 1968 s 132(1) (substituted by SI 2012/1916)).
5   Medicines Act 1968 s 133(2)(a). As to the effect of s 133(2) in respect of claims in tort see *Smith
    v Secretary of State for Health* [2002] EWHC 200 (QB), (2005) Times, 11 March.
6   Ie whether contained in a public general Act or in a local or private Act: Medicines Act 1968
    s 133(2)(b).
7   Medicines Act 1968 s 133(2)(b).
8   Medicines Act 1968 s 133(2)(c). See note 5.
9   Medicines Act 1968 s 133(3). As to Crown immunity see CONSTITUTIONAL LAW AND HUMAN
    RIGHTS vol 8(2) (Reissue) PARA 382 et seq; CROWN AND ROYAL FAMILY vol 12(1) (Reissue)
    PARAS 47–48, 52 et seq; CROWN PROCEEDINGS AND CROWN PRACTICE vol 12(1) (Reissue) PARA
    101 et seq; STATUTES AND LEGISLATIVE PROCESS vol 96 (2012) PARA 720. A visiting force or
    headquarters, members of such a force or headquarters, persons employed in the service of such

a force, and property used for the purposes of such a force or headquarters, are exempt from the operation of the Medicines Act 1968 to the extent that, by virtue of the rule of law whereby enactments do not bind the Crown, such a force or headquarters, such members, such persons, or such property, would be so exempt if the force or headquarters were a part of any of the home forces: Visiting Forces and International Headquarters (Application of Law) Order 1999, SI 1999/1736, art 12(1), Sch 5. As to the forces and headquarters to which the order applies see art 3, Schs 1, 2.

30. Fees. With the consent of the Treasury[1], the ministers may make regulations[2] providing for:

(1)　the payment and recovery of prescribed fees: (a) in connection with applications under the Medicines Act 1968 for a licence, certificate or direction[3] or the variation or renewal of a licence or certificate[4]; or (b) in respect of inspections made in connection with applications for licences or during the currency of any such licence[5];

(2)　the payment and recovery of: (a) prescribed annual or periodic fees (in addition to inspection fees) in connection with the holding of a licence; or (b) penalty for failure to pay such a fee in time[6];

(3)　the calculation of any such annual or periodic fee by reference to the United Kingdom turnover[7] of the medicinal products[8] to which the licence relates or of all such products to which licences held by the holder relate, or the fees received by the holder in respect of the medicinal product or products to which the licence relates or in respect of all the medicinal products to which licences held by the holder relate[9];

(4)　the calculation of any such annual or periodic fee in a manner specified, where no or insufficient evidence is submitted to enable the calculation set out in head (3) above to be made[10];

(5)　the payment of any fee by instalments, and the refund, adjustment, set-off, waiver or reduction of fees[11]; and

(6)　the suspension of any licence or certificate while the fee remains unpaid[12].

1　As to the Treasury see CONSTITUTIONAL LAW AND HUMAN RIGHTS vol 8(2) (Reissue) PARAS 512–517.

2　As to the regulations that have been made see the Medicines (Products for Human Use) (Fees) Regulations 2012, SI 2012/504. As to the meaning of 'the ministers' see PARA 35 note 1 (definition applied by the Medicines Act 1968 s 1 (substituted by SI 2012/1916)).

3　Ie under the Medicines Act 1968 Pt II (ss 6–50). In the Medicines Act 1971 s 1(1), (2)(b) any reference to a licence under the Medicines Act 1968 Pt II includes a reference to a manufacturing authorisation under the Medicines for Human Use (Clinical Trials) Regulations 2004, SI 2004/1031: Medicines Act 1971 s 1(2A) (added by SI 2004/1031). As to authorisations in respect of clinical trials see PARA 112 et seq.

4　Medicines Act 1971 s 1(1)(a). See note 3.

5　Medicines Act 1971 s 1(1)(aa) (s 1(1)(aa)–(ad), (1A) added, and s 1(1)(b) amended, by the Health and Medicines Act 1988 s 21). See note 3.

6　See the Medicines Act 1971 s 1(1)(ab) (as added: see note 5). See also note 3.

7　'United Kingdom turnover' means the value, determined under the regulations, of the aggregate of all quantities of a medicinal product (see note 8) other than quantities excluded by the regulations, which, during a specified period: (1) in the case of a product licence, are sold or supplied in the United Kingdom by the holder of a licence or other prescribed person; (2) in the case of a manufacturer's licence (see PARA 45 et seq), are manufactured or assembled in the United Kingdom by the holder; (3) in the case of a wholesale dealer's licence (see PARA 77 et seq), are sold by way of wholesale dealing in the United Kingdom: Medicines Act 1971 s 1(1A) (as added: see note 5). As to the meaning of 'manufacture' and 'assemble' see PARA 141 notes 7, 8 (definitions applied by the Medicines Act 1968 s 132(1) (as substituted: see note 2)). As to the meaning of 'United Kingdom' see PARA 20 note 4.

8   For these purposes, 'medicinal product' includes: (1) substances or articles to which provisions of the Medicines Act 1968 Pt II have been extended under s 104 or s 105 (see PARA 28): Medicines Act 1971 s 1(1A) (as added (see note 5); amended by SI 2006/2407). As to the meaning of 'medicinal product' for the purposes of the Medicines Act 1968 see PARA 25.

9   Medicines Act 1971 s 1(1)(ac) (as added: see note 5).

10   Medicines Act 1971 s 1(1)(ad) (as added: see note 5).

11   Medicines Act 1971 s 1(1)(b) (as amended: see note 5).

12   Medicines Act 1971 s 1(2)(b). See note 3.

(2) ADMINISTRATION

31. Commission on Human Medicines. The Commission on Human Medicines[1] performs the functions assigned to it by or under the Human Medicines Regulations 2012[2].

The Commission[3], where either it considers it appropriate or it is requested by the minister or ministers in question to do so, must give advice on matters relating to the execution of any duty imposed by, or the exercise of any power conferred by the Human Medicines Regulations 2012[4], the Medicines for Human Use (Clinical Trials) Regulations 2004[5] or otherwise relating to medicinal products[6]. Without prejudice to this duty, and to any other functions conferred on the Commission[7], the Commission must give advice with respect to safety, quality or efficacy of medicinal products[8] and promote the collection and investigation of information relating to adverse reactions[9], for the purposes of enabling such advice to be given[10].

Under certain cicumstances[11] the Commission must also advise the licensing authority[12].

The Commission must give a report to the ministers[13] each year, at a time specified by the ministers, about the performance of its functions and the performance of the functions of any expert advisory group appointed[14] by it[15].

1   In the Medicines Act 1968 and the Human Medicines Regulations 2012, SI 2012/1916, the Commission on Human Medicines is referred to as 'the Commission': reg 8(1); Medicines Act 1968 s 132(1) (substituted by SI 2012/1916). The Commission replaced the Medicines Commission established under the Medicines Act 1968 s 2 (repealed) which was abolished on 30 October 2005: see the Medicines (Advisory Bodies) Regulations 2005, SI 2005/1094, reg 2 (revoked). As to the constitution of the Commission on Human Medicine see the Human Medicines Regulations 2012, SI 2012/1916, reg 9(3)–(6). The Commission may co-opt one or more additional members for the purposes of a meeting and a person so co-opted ceases to be a member at the end of the meeting: see reg 13.

2   Ie under the Human Medicines Regulations 2012, SI 2012/1916: see reg 9(1). As to delegation of functions see PARA 33.

3   As to the possibility of bringing a claim in negligence against the Commission in respect of the exercise of its functions see _Smith v Secretary of State for Health_ [2002] EWHC 200 (QB), (2005) Times, 11 March.

4   Ie the Human Medicines Regulations 2012, SI 2012/1916.

5   Ie the Medicines for Human Use (Clinical Trials) Regulations 2004, SI 2004/1031 (see PARA 107 et seq).

6   See the Human Medicines Regulations 2012, SI 2012/1916, reg 10(1), (2).

7   Ie by or under the Human Medicines Regulations 2012, SI 2012/1916.

8   Human Medicines Regulations 2012, SI 2012/1916, reg 10(3)(a).

9   As to the meaning of 'adverse reaction' see PARA 70 note 6.

10   Human Medicines Regulations 2012, SI 2012/1916, reg 10(3)(b).

11   Ie if:
      (1)   the licensing authority is required under the Human Medicines Regulations 2012, SI 2012/1916, Sch 11 (advice and representations) or the Medicines for Human Use (Clinical Trials) Regulations 2004, SI 2004/1031, (see PARA 107 et seq) to consult the Commission about any matter arising under those provisions (Human Medicines Regulations 2012, SI 2012/1916, reg 10(4)(a)); or

(2)   the licensing authority consults the Commission about any matter arising under the provisions mentioned in head (1) above (reg 10(4)(b)).

12 See the Human Medicines Regulations 2012, SI 2012/1916, reg 10(4). As to the meaning of 'the licensing authority' see PARA 35 note 1.

13 As to the meaning of 'the ministers' see the Human Medicines Regulations 2012, SI 2012/1916, reg 6(6)–(8); and PARA 35: reg 8(1). If, by any provision of the Human Medicines Regulations 2012, SI 2012/1916 a person is required to provide any information or document to the licensing authority or to the ministers, or any assistance to the licensing authority or to the ministers, and no time is specified in that provision within which the obligation must be performed, the obligation must be performed within such time as may be specified in a written notice given to the person by the licensing authority or the ministers (as the case may be): reg 342.

14 Ie appointed under the Human Medicines Regulations 2012, SI 2012/1916, reg 14 (see PARA 33).

15 See the Human Medicines Regulations 2012, SI 2012/1916, reg 12(1)–(3).

32.   British Pharmacopoeia Commission.   The British Pharmacopoeia Commission ('BPC') has the following functions[1]:

(1)   the preparation[2] of editions of the British Pharmacopoeia[3];

(2)   the preparation[4] of compendia[5];

(3)   the preparation[6] of lists of suitable names to be used in the compendia[7]; and

(4)   the preparation[8] of any other relevant document[9].

The BPC must give a report to the ministers[10] each year, at a time specified by the ministers, about the performance of its functions and the performance of the functions of any expert advisory group appointed[11] by it[12].

1   As to the constitution of the British Pharmacopoeia Commission see the Human Medicines Regulations 2012, SI 2012/1916, reg 11(3)–(6). As to delegation of functions see PARA 33.

2   Ie preparation under the Human Medicines Regulations 2012, SI 2012/1916, reg 317(1) (see PARA 237). For these purposes a reference to preparation includes revision or amendment: reg 11(7).

3   Human Medicines Regulations 2012, SI 2012/1916, reg 11(1), (2)(a). 'British Pharmacopoeia' means the British Pharmacopoeia referred to in reg 317 (see PARA 237).

4   Ie the preparation under the Human Medicines Regulations 2012, SI 2012/1916, reg 317(3) (see PARA 237).

5   Human Medicines Regulations 2012, SI 2012/1916, reg 11(2)(b).

6   Ie preparation under the Human Medicines Regulations 2012, SI 2012/1916, reg 318 (see PARA 238).

7   Human Medicines Regulations 2012, SI 2012/1916, reg 11(2)(c).

8   Ie the preparation of any document under the Human Medicines Regulations 2012, SI 2012/1916, reg 319.

9   Human Medicines Regulations 2012, SI 2012/1916, reg 11(2)(d).

10   As to the meaning of 'the ministers' see the Human Medicines Regulations 2012, SI 2012/1916, reg 6(6)–(8); and PARA 35 note 1: reg 8(1).

11   Ie appointed under the Human Medicines Regulations 2012, SI 2012/1916, reg 14 (see PARA 33).

12   See the Human Medicines Regulations 2012, SI 2012/1916, reg 12(1)–(3).

33.   Expert advisory groups.   An advisory body[1], or the advisory bodies acting jointly, may, subject to the approval of the licensing authority[2], appoint sub-committees to be known as expert advisory groups[3]. The licensing authority may direct an advisory body to appoint an expert advisory group to advise on such matters as may be specified in the direction[4].

With the exception of certain advisory functions[5], an advisory body may delegate to an expert advisory group any of its functions[6]. However, an advisory body may arrange for an expert advisory group to provide advice in relation to the performance of any of the excepted functions[7].

1   'Advisory body' means the Commission on Human Medicine (see PARA 31) or the British Pharmacopoeia Commission (see PARA 32): Human Medicines Regulations 2012, SI 2012/1916, reg 12(1). As to the constitution of an advisory group see reg 14(3)–(7), Sch 2.

2   As to the meaning of 'licensing authority' see PARA 35 note 1.

3   Human Medicines Regulations 2012, SI 2012/1916, reg 14(1). For the purposes of the Human Medicines Regulations 2012, SI 2012/1916 an 'expert advisory group' means an expert advisory group established under reg 14(1): reg 8(1).

4   Human Medicines Regulations 2012, SI 2012/1916, reg 14(2).

5   Ie in any case where the licencing authority is required to consult the advisory body under the Human Medicines Regulations 2012, SI 2012/1916, Sch 11 and the Medicines for Human Use (Clinical Trials) Regulations 2004, SI 2004/1031 (see PARA 107 et seq).

6   Human Medicines Regulations 2012, SI 2012/1916, reg 15(1), (2).

7   Human Medicines Regulations 2012, SI 2012/1916, reg 15(3). As to the excepted functions see note 5.

34. Review by Secretary of State. The Secretary of State[1] must from time to time carry out a review of certain provisions[2] of the Human Medicines Regulations 2012[3].

The Secretary of State must set out, and publish, the conclusions of the review in a report[4].

1   As to the Secretary of State see PARA 2 note 1.

2   Those provisions are the Human Medicines Regulations 2012, SI 2012/1916, regs 59, 60(3)(b), (9), (10), 61, 63, 64(4)(b), (d), (e), (5)(a), (6)(c), 65(2), 66(5), (6), 68(2)(a), (b), (5), 69(2)(a), (b), (5), (10), 75(2)(b), (c), 76, 79, 85, 86, 97, 105(3)(b), 107(2), 108(5), 115(2)(b), (c), 132(2), 133(5), (6), 177–212, 266(4), (5), 327(2)(g), 331, and reg 349 insofar as it repeals the Medicines Act 1968 s 10(7); and the Human Medicines Regulations 2012, SI 2012/1916, Sch 8 paras 12, 13, 19, 23, Sch 12 para 21, and Sch 27 paras 14, 15: reg 346(2).

3   Human Medicines Regulations 2012, SI 2012/1916, reg 346(1). In carrying out the review the Secretary of State must, so far as is reasonable, have regard to how Council Directive (EC) 2001/83 (OJ L311, 28.11.2001, p 67) on the Community code relating to medicinal products for human use and European Parliament and Council Directive (EU) 2010/84 (OJ L343, 31.12.2010, p 74) of the European Parliament and of the Council amending, as regards pharmacovigilance, Council Directive 2001/83/EC on the Community Code relating to medicinal products for human use are implemented in other member States in relation to the subject matter of the provisions mentioned in the Human Medicines Regulations 2012, SI 2012/1916, reg 346(2): reg 346(4).

4   See the Human Medicines Regulations 2012, SI 2012/1916, reg 346(3). The report must in particular:

    (1)   set out the objectives intended to be achieved by the regulatory system established by the provisions of the Human Medicines Regulations 2012, SI 2012/1916 that implement the Directives mentioned in reg 346(4) (see note 3) in relation to the subject matter of the regs 59, 60(3)(b), (9), (10), 61, 63, 64(4)(b), (d), (e), (5)(a), (6)(c), 65(2), 66(5), (6), 68(2)(a), (b), (5), 69(2)(a), (b), (5), (10), 75(2)(b), (c), 76, 79, 85, 86, 97, 105(3)(b), 107(2), 108(5), 115(2)(b), (c), 132(2), 133(5), (6), 177–212, 266(4), (5), 327(2)(g), 331, Sch 8 paras 12, 13, 19, 23, Sch 12 para 21, and Sch 27 paras 14, 15 (see reg 346(5)(a));

    (2)   assess the extent to which those objectives are achieved (reg 346(5)(b)); and

    (3)   assess whether those objectives remain appropriate and, if so, the extent to which they could be achieved with a system that imposes less regulation (reg 346(5)(c)).

The first report must be published before the end of the period of 5 years beginning with the day on which the Human Medicines Regulations 2012, SI 2012/1916 came into force and are to be published thereafter at intervals not exceeding five years: reg 346(6), (7).

(3) MANUFACTURING AND WHOLESALE DEALING

(i) The Licensing Authority

35. Responsibilities. The licensing authority[1] is responsible for the grant[2], renewal, variation, suspension and revocation[3] of licences, authorisations, certificates[4] and registrations[5]. The functions of a member state, or of the competent authority of a member state, under any of the relevant EU provisions are to be exercised by the licensing authority if they relate to medicinal products[6] and they are to be exercised by, or by any authority of, the United Kingdom[7].

1   For the purposes of the Human Medicines Regulations 2012, SI 2012/1916 'licensing authority' means either or both of the ministers and 'the ministers' means the Secretary of State and the Minister for Health, Social Services and Public Safety: reg 6(2), (6). Any functions conferred on the ministers by the Human Medicines Regulations 2012, SI 2012/1916 is to be exercised by the ministers acting jointly, except where the regulations provide for a function to be exercised by either of them acting alone or both of them acting jointly: see reg 6(7), (8).
2   As to the grant of licences see PARA 37.
3   As to the variation, suspension and revocation of licences see PARA 40.
4   As to certificates see PARA 55.
5   Human Medicines Regulations 2012, SI 2012/1916, reg 6(1). The duty of the licensing authority is to safeguard the health of the nation and it must act fairly and equally between applicants; it cannot fulfil those obligations without having recourse to all the information available to it, confidential or otherwise: *Re Smith Kline & French Laboratories Ltd* [1990] 1 AC 64, sub nom *Smith Kline & French Laboratories Ltd v Licensing Authority (Generics (UK) Ltd intervening)* [1990] 1 AC 64, [1989] 1 All ER 578, HL. Where the licensing authority notifies a person of a decision under the Human Medicines Regulations 2012, SI 2012/1916, it must state its reasons for the decision and inform the person of any action the person may take to challenge that decision and of the time for taking that action: see reg 341(1). This is without prejudice to any other provision of the Human Medicines Regulations 2012, SI 2012/1916 concerning notification by the licensing authority: reg 341(2). The licensing authority must publicise any decision to grant or revoke a marketing authorisation, grant or revoke a certificate of registration or grant or revoke a traditional herbal registration in such manner as it thinks fit: see reg 341(3), (4). As to the meanings of 'marketing authorisation', 'certificate of registration' and 'traditional herbal registration' see PARA 141 notes 3–5.
6   As to the meaning of 'medicinal product' see PARA 25.
7   Human Medicines Regulations 2012, SI 2012/1916, reg 6(4). This does not apply to any function that is conferred by the Human Medicines Regulations 2012, SI 2012/1916 on a person or body other than the licensing authority: reg 6(5).

36.   Immunity from civil liability.   The following applies where the licensing authority[1] makes a recommendation or requirement for the use of a medicinal product[2] without an authorisation[3], or for the use of a medicinal product with an authorisation but for a therapeutic indication that is not permitted under the authorisation, in response to the suspected or confirmed spread of pathogenic agents, toxins, chemical agents or nuclear radiation, which may cause harm to human beings[4].

None of the following are to be subject to any civil liability for any loss or damage resulting from the use of the product in accordance with that recommendation or requirement:

(1)   any holder of an authorisation for the product[5];

(2)   any manufacturer of the product[6];

(3)   any officer, servant, employee or agent of a person within head (1) or (2) above[7]; or

(4)   any health care professional[8].

1   As to the meaning of 'licensing authority' see PARA 35 note 1.
2   As to the meaning of 'medicinal product' see PARA 25.

3   For these purposes 'authorisation' means a marketing authorisation, certificate of registration, traditional herbal registration or Article 126a authorisation: Human Medicines Regulations 2012, SI 2012/1916, reg 345(5). As to the meanings of 'marketing authorisation', 'Article 126a authorisation', 'certificate of registration' and 'traditional herbal registration' see PARA 141 notes 3–5.

4   Human Medicines Regulations 2012, SI 2012/1916, reg 345(1), (2). Regulation 345 does not apply in relation to liability under the Consumer Protection Act 1987 s 2 (liability for defective products: see CONSUMER PROTECTION vol 21 (2011) PARA 645): Human Medicines Regulations 2012, SI 2012/1916, reg 345(4).
5   Human Medicines Regulations 2012, SI 2012/1916, reg 345(3)(a).
6   Human Medicines Regulations 2012, SI 2012/1916, reg 345(3)(b).
7   Human Medicines Regulations 2012, SI 2012/1916, reg 345(3)(c).
8   Human Medicines Regulations 2012, SI 2012/1916, reg 345(3)(d). 'Health care professional' means a doctor, a dentist, a pharmacist, a pharmacy technician registered in Part 2 or 5 of the register of pharmacists and pharmacy technicians established and maintained under the Pharmacy Order 2010, SI 2010/231, art 19(2) (see MEDICAL PROFESSIONS vol 74 (2011) PARA 821), a registered nurse, a registered midwife, a registered optometrist, a registered osteopath as defined in the Osteopaths Act 1993 s 41 (see MEDICAL PROFESSIONS vol 74 (2011) PARA 525), a registered chiropractor as defined in the Chiropractors Act 1994 s 43 (see MEDICAL PROFESSIONS vol 74 (2011) PARA 603), a person registered as a member of a relevant profession within the meaning of the Health and Social Work Professions Order 2001, SI 2002/254, art 2, Sch 3 para 1, other than a social worker, in the Health and Care Professions Council register or a person registered in the dental care professionals register established and maintained under the Dentists Act 1984 s 36B (see MEDICAL PROFESSIONS vol 74 (2011) PARA 474) as a member of a profession complementary to dentistry specified by the European Qualifications (Professions Complementary to Dentistry) Regulations 2006, SI 2006/1718, reg 2: Human Medicines Regulations 2012, SI 2012/1916, reg 8(1). 'Registered optometrist' means a person whose name is entered in the register of optometrists maintained under the Opticians Act 1989 s 7(1) (see MEDICAL PROFESSIONS vol 74 (2011) PARA 344) or the register of visiting optometrists from relevant European states maintained under s 8B(1)(a): Human Medicines Regulations 2012, SI 2012/1916, reg 8(1). 'Relevant European state' means an EEA state or Switzerland: reg 8(1). As to the meanings of 'registered nurse' and 'registered midwife' see PARA 48 note 3. As to the meanings of 'doctor' and 'dentist' see PARA 48 note 6. 'The Health and Care Professions Council register' means the register established and maintained by the Health and Care Professions Council under article 5 of the Health and Social Work Professions Order 2001, SI 2002/254, art 5 (see MEDICAL PROFESSIONS): Human Medicines Regulations 2012, SI 2012/1916, reg 8(1).

37. Grant or refusal of licence. On any application to the licensing authority[1] for a licence, the authority may grant a licence containing such provisions[2] as it considers appropriate[3], or may refuse to grant a licence if, having regard to the provisions of the Human Medicines Regulations 2012[4] and any European Union obligation, it considers it necessary or appropriate to do so[5].

The licence stays in force until it is revoked by the licensing authority or it is surrendered by the holder[6].

1   As to the meaning of 'the licensing authority' see PARA 35 note 1. As to applications for licences see PARAS 53–54.
2   As to the incorporation of standard provisions in licences see PARA 61.
3   Human Medicines Regulations 2012, SI 2012/1916, reg 23(1)(a). As to the grant or refusal of marketing authorisations for medicines for human use see PARA 158.
4   Ie the Human Medicines Regulations 2012, SI 2012/1916.
5   Human Medicines Regulations 2012, SI 2012/1916, reg 23(1)(b). See *Wellcome Foundation Ltd v Secretary of State for Social Services* [1988] 2 All ER 684, [1988] 1 WLR 635, HL (trade mark issues irrelevant to such consideration). As to the principles governing the exercise by public bodies of their statutory powers and judicial control thereof see ADMINISTRATIVE LAW vol 1(1) (2001 Reissue) PARAS 16 et seq; JUDICIAL REVIEW. Providing the requirements of the Human Medicines Regulations 2012, SI 2012/1916, Sch 3 are met, the licensing authority must grant or refuse an application for a licence under Pt 3 (regs 17–45: see PARA 53) within the period of 90 days beginning immediately after the day on which it receives the application: see reg 23(2), (3).
6   Human Medicines Regulations 2012, SI 2012/1916, reg 25.

38. Provision of further information. Where an application has been made to the licensing authority[1] for a licence[2], the authority, before determining the application, may request the applicant to furnish such information relating to the application as it thinks necessary[3].

The licensing authority may give a notice to the holder of a licence requiring the holder to provide information of a kind specified in the notice within the period specified in the notice[4]. Such a notice may not be given to the holder of a licence unless it appears to the licensing authority, or representations are made to the licensing authority by the Commission of Human Medicines[5], an expert advisory group of the Commission[6], or an expert committee appointed by the licensing authority, that it is necessary for the licensing authority to consider whether the licence should be varied, suspended or revoked[7].

The notice may specify information which the licensing authority, or the Commission, an expert advisory group of the Commission, or an expert committee appointed by the licensing authority, thinks necessary for considering whether the notice should be varied, suspended or revoked[8].

1 As to the meaning of 'the licensing authority' see PARA 35 note 1.
2 Ie a licence under the Human Medicines Regulations 2012, SI 2012/1916, Pt 3 (reg 17–45: see PARA 53).
3 Human Medicines Regulations 2012, SI 2012/1916, reg 30(1). If a notice under reg 30 requires the applicant to provide the licensing authority with information, the information period is not to be counted for the purposes of reg 23(2) (see PARA 37): reg 23(4). For this purpose the 'information period' means the period beginning with the day on which the notice is given and ending with the day on which the licensing authority receives the information or the applicant shows to the licensing authority's satisfaction that the applicant is unable to provide it: reg 23(5). A person is guilty of an offence if he knowingly gives false information in response to a notice under reg 30(1): reg 34(2). A person guilty of an offence under reg 34(2) is liable, on summary conviction, to a fine not exceeding the statutory maximum or, on conviction on indictment, to a fine, to imprisonment for a term not exceeding two years, or to both: reg 35(1). As to the statutory maximum see SENTENCING AND DISPOSITION OF OFFENDERS vol 92 (2010) PARA 140.
4 Human Medicines Regulations 2012, SI 2012/1916, reg 30(2). A person is guilty of an offence if, without reasonable excuse, he fails to comply with a notice under reg 30(2): reg 34(3). A person guilty of an offence under reg 34(3) is liable on summary conviction to a fine not exceeding level 3 on the standard scale: reg 35(2). As to the standard scale see SENTENCING AND DISPOSITION OF OFFENDERS vol 92 (2010) PARA 142.
5 As to the Commission of Human Medicines see PARA 31.
6 As to expert advisory groups see PARA 33.
7 Human Medicines Regulations 2012, SI 2012/1916, reg 30(3).
8 Human Medicines Regulations 2012, SI 2012/1916, reg 30(4).

39. Reasons for decisions. Where on an application for a licence[1] the licensing authority[2] refuses to grant a licence, or grants a licence otherwise than in accordance with the application, and the applicant requests it to state its reasons, the authority must give the applicant a notice stating the reasons for its decision[3].

1 Ie a licence under the Human Medicines Regulations 2012, SI 2012/1916, Pt 3 (regs 17–45: see PARA 54).
2 As to the meaning of 'the licensing authority' see PARA 35 note 1.
3 See the Human Medicines Regulations 2012, SI 2012/1916, reg 23(6).

40. Power to suspend, revoke or vary licences. On certain grounds[1] the licensing authority[2] may suspend a licence[3] for such period as it thinks fit, or may revoke or vary the provisions of any such licence[4]. The suspension or revocation may be total or may be limited to medicinal products[5] of one or more descriptions or to medicinal products manufactured[6], assembled[7] or stored on any particular premises or in a particular part of any premises[8].

Except in cases of urgency[9], where the authority proposes to suspend, vary or revoke a licence, it must notify the licence holder in writing of its proposal, the reasons for it and the date (which must be no earlier than 28 days from the notice given by the licensing authority) on which it is proposed that the suspension, revocation or variation should take effect[10].

The licence holder may before the date specified in the notice make written representations to the licensing authority with respect to the proposal[11] or notify the licensing authority that the holder wishes the licensing authority to submit the proposal to review upon oral representations[12].

If the licensing authority proceeds to suspend, revoke or vary a licence in accordance with these provisions it must give a notice[13] to the licence holder[14].

1   In relation to manufacturer's licence see PARA 41 and for wholesale dealer's licences see PARA 42.
2   As the meaning of 'the licensing authority' see PARA 35 note 1.
3   Ie a licence granted under the Human Medicines Regulations 2012, SI 2012/1916, Pt 3 (regs 17–45). As to the grant of licences see PARA 37.
4   Human Medicines Regulations 2012, SI 2012/1916, reg 26(1). As to information that may be required see PARA 38.
5   As to the meaning of 'medicinal product' see PARA 25.
6   As to the meaning of 'manufacture' see PARA 141 note 7.
7   As to the meaning of 'assemble' see PARA 141 note 8.
8   Human Medicines Regulations 2012, SI 2012/1916, reg 26(2).
9   Ie except in cases where the Human Medicines Regulations 2012, SI 2012/1916, reg 28 applies (see PARA 43).
10 See the Human Medicines Regulations 2012, SI 2012/1916, reg 27(1), (2).
11 If the licence holder makes such written representations the licensing authority must take those representations into account before making a decision in the matter: Human Medicines Regulations 2012, SI 2012/1906, reg 27(3).
12 Human Medicines Regulations 2012, SI 2012/1916, reg 27(5). If the licence holder notifies the licensing authority that the holder wishes the licensing authority to submit the proposal to review upon oral representations Sch 5 has effect: reg 27(6). As to the procedure for the review upon oral representations see Sch 5.
13 The notice must give particulars of the suspension, revocation or variation and give reasons for the decision to suspend, revoke or vary the licence: Human Medicines Regulations 2012, SI 2012/1916, reg 27(7). Regulation 27(6), (7) is without prejudice to any requirement of Sch 5 as to notification: reg 27(8).
14 Human Medicines Regulations 2012, SI 2012/1916, reg 27(6).

41.   Grounds for suspension of manufacturer's licence. The powers[1] of the licensing authority[2] to suspend, revoke or vary licences are not exercisable by the authority in relation to a manufacturer's licence[3] except on one or more of the following grounds[4]:

(1)   that the matters stated in the application[5] on which the licence was granted were false or incomplete in a material particular[6];

(2)   a material change of circumstances has occurred in relation to any of the matters stated in the application[7];

(3)   the holder of the licence has materially contravened a provision of it[8];

(4)   that the holder has failed without reasonable excuse to comply with a requirement[9] to furnish information with respect to medicinal products[10] of any such description[11];

(5)   that the holder has manufactured[12] or assembled[13] medicinal products to the order of another person[14] who is the holder of a marketing authorisation, Article 126a authorisation, certificate of registration or traditional herbal registration (an 'authorisation')[15], and has habitually failed to comply with the provisions of that product licence[16];

(6)   that the holder of the manufacturer's licence does not have appropriate facilities to carry out processes of manufacture or assembly authorised by the licence[17].

1   Ie the powers conferred by the Human Medicines Regulations 2012, SI 2012/1916, reg 26 (see PARA 40).
2   As to the meaning of 'the licensing authority' see PARA 35 note 1.
3   As the meaning of 'manufacturer's licence' see PARA 45.
4   Human Medicines Regulations 2012, SI 2012/1916, reg 26(3)(a).
5   As to applications see PARA 53.
6   Human Medicines Regulations 2012, SI 2012/1916, reg 26(3)(b), (4)(a).
7   Human Medicines Regulations 2012, SI 2012/1916, reg 26(4)(b).
8   Human Medicines Regulations 2012, SI 2012/1916, reg 26(4)(c). 'Contravention' includes failure to comply (and 'contravene' has a corresponding meaning): reg 8(1).
9   Ie a requirement imposed on him under the Human Medicines Regulations 2012, SI 2012/1916, reg 30(2): see PARA 38.
10 As to the meaning of 'medicinal product' see PARA 25.
11 Human Medicines Regulations 2012, SI 2012/1916, reg 26(4)(d).
12 As to the meaning of 'manufacture' see PARA 141 note 7.
13 As to the meaning of 'assemble' see PARA 141 note 8.
14 As to the meaning of 'person' see PARA 45 note 2.
15 As to the meanings of 'marketing authorisation', 'Article 126a authorisation', 'certificate of registration' and 'traditional herbal registration' see PARA 141 notes 3–5.
16 Human Medicines Regulations 2012, SI 2012/1916, reg 26(5)(a).
17 Human Medicines Regulations 2012, SI 2012/1916, reg 26(5)(b).

42.   Grounds for suspension of wholesale dealer's licence. The powers[1] of the licensing authority[2] to suspend, revoke or vary licences are not exercisable in relation to a wholesale dealer's licence[3] except on one or more of the following grounds[4]:

(1)   that the matters stated in the application[5] on which the licence was granted were false or incomplete in a material particular[6];

(2)   a material change of circumstances has occurred in relation to any of the matters stated in the application[7];

(3)   the holder of the licence has materially contravened a provision of it[8];

(4)   that the holder has failed without reasonable excuse to comply with a requirement[9] to furnish information with respect to medicinal products[10] of any such description[11];

(5)   that the equipment and facilities for storing or distributing medicinal products which are available to the holder of the licence are inadequate to maintain the quality of medicinal products of one or more descriptions to which the application for the licence related[12].

1   Ie the powers conferred by the Human Medicines Regulations 2012, SI 2012/1916, reg 26 see PARA 40.
2   As to the meaning of 'the licensing authority' see PARA 35 note 1.
3   As the meaning of 'wholesaler dealer's licence' see PARA 77.
4   Human Medicines Regulations 2012, SI 2012/1916, reg 26(3)(a).
5   As to applications see PARA 80.
6   Human Medicines Regulations 2012, SI 2012/1916, reg 26(3)(c), (4)(a).
7   Human Medicines Regulations 2012, SI 2012/1916, reg 26(4)(b).
8   Human Medicines Regulations 2012, SI 2012/1916, reg 26(4)(c).
9   Ie a requirement imposed on him under the Human Medicines Regulations 2012, SI 2012/1916, reg 30(2): see PARA 270.
10 As to the meaning of 'medicinal product' see PARA 25.
11 Human Medicines Regulations 2012, SI 2012/1916, reg 26(4)(d).
12 Human Medicines Regulations 2012, SI 2012/1916, reg 26(6).

43.   Procedure in cases of urgency. Where it appears to the licensing authority[1] that in the interests of safety it is necessary to suspend a licence[2] with immediate effect, the licensing authority may do so for a period not exceeding three months[3].

Where a licence has been so suspended and it appears to the licensing authority that it is necessary to consider whether the licence ought to be further suspended, or ought to be revoked or varied, the licensing authority must proceed in accordance with such of the appropriate provisions[4] as are applicable in the circumstances[5]. However, if any such proceedings relating to a further suspension of the licence have not been finally disposed of before the end of the period for which the licence was originally[6] suspended[7], or for which it has been further suspended[8], the licensing authority may, if it appears to it to be necessary in the interests of safety to do so, further suspend the licence for a period which, in the case of each such further suspension, must not exceed three months[9].

1   As to the meaning of 'the licensing authority' see PARA 35 note 1.
2   Ie a licence under the Human Medicines Regulations 2012, SI 2012/1916, Pt 3 (regs 17–45). As to such licences see PARA 45 et seq. As to applications for licences see PARA 53.
3   Human Medicines Regulations 2012, SI 2012/1916, reg 28(1). This is notwithstanding anything in regs 17–45. 'Month' means calendar month: Interpretation Act 1978 s 5, Sch 1.
4   Ie the provisions of the Human Medicines Regulations 2012, SI 2012/1916, reg 27 (see PARA 40). In the event that any challenge against a decision under reg 27 to suspend, vary or revoke the licence is made on an application to the High Court under reg 322(4),(5) (see PARA 361) reg 28(5) (see text to note 9) applies, but this is without prejudice to reg 322(6)(a) (see PARA 361): reg 28(6).
5   Human Medicines Regulations 2012, SI 2012/1916, reg 28(2).
6   Ie under the Human Medicines Regulations 2012, SI 2012/1916, reg 28(1).
7   Human Medicines Regulations 2012, SI 2012/1916, reg 28(4).
8   Ie under the Human Medicines Regulations 2012, SI 2012/1916, reg 28(5).
9   Human Medicines Regulations 2012, SI 2012/1916, reg 28(5).

44. Variation of licence on holder's application. If the holder of a licence[1] applies to the licensing authority[2] for the variation of the provisions of the licence, the licensing authority must consider that request[3]. Where the variation would have the effect of altering the types of medicinal product in respect of which the licence was granted, any operation carried out under the licence or any premises, equipment or facilities in respect of which the licence was granted, the licensing authority must vary the licence or refuse to vary it before the end of the period allowed for considering the application[4].

The period allowed for consideration of an application under these provisions is:

(1)   in a case where the licensing authority considers that it is necessary to inspect premises to which the licence relates, 90 days beginning with the day after the date when the licensing authority receives the application[5]; and

(2)   in any other case 30 days beginning with that day[6].

The licensing authority may give a notice to the applicant requiring the applicant to supply further information in connection with the application[7].

1   Ie a licence granted under the Human Medicines Regulations 2012, SI 2012/1916, Pt 3 (regs 17–45).
2   As to the meaning of 'the licensing authority' see PARA 35 note 1. The application must be in writing, specify the variation requested, be signed by or on behalf of the applicant, be accompanied by such information as may be required to enable the licensing authority to consider the application and be accompanied by the required fee (if any): Human Medicines Regulations 2012, SI 2012/1916, reg 29(2). Nothing in reg 29(1) affects the power conferred by reg 26: reg 29(10). As to fees see PARA 30.
3   See the Human Medicines Regulations 2012, SI 2012/1916, reg 29(1), (3).
4   See the Human Medicines Regulations 2012, SI 2012/1916, reg 29(4), (5).
5   Human Medicines Regulations 2012, SI 2012/1916, reg 29(6)(a).
6   Human Medicines Regulations 2012, SI 2012/1916, reg 29(6)(b).

7 Human Medicines Regulations 2012, SI 2012/1916, reg 29(7). If a notice under reg 29(7) requires the applicant to provide the licensing authority with information, the information period is not to be counted for the purposes of reg 29(6): reg 29(8). For this purpose the 'information period means the period beginning with the day on which the notice is given and ending with the day on which the licensing authority receives the information or the applicant shows to the licensing authority's satisfaction that the applicant is unable to provide it: reg 29(9).

(ii) Manufacturer's Licence

A. REQUIREMENT AND EXEMPTIONS

45.   Requirement for a manufacturer's licence.   Subject to certain exceptions[1], a person[2] may not, except in accordance with a licence (a 'manufacturer's licence'), manufacture, assemble or import[3] from a state other than an EEA state any medicinal product[4]. Nor may a person possess a medicinal product for the purpose of any such activity[5].

1 Ie the exemptions conferred by or under the Human Medicines Regulations 2012, SI 2012/1916, reg 17(3)–(5) (see PARAS 46, 47): see reg 17(2). See also reg 3 (see PARAS 48, 49, 51) and reg 4 (see PARA 52).
2 'Person' includes a body of persons corporate or unincorporate: Interpretation Act 1978 s 5, Sch 1. As to bodies corporate and unincorporate see COMPANIES; CORPORATIONS vol 24 (2010) PARA 301 et seq.
3 As to the meanings of 'manufacture' and 'assemble' see PARA 141 notes 7, 8. As to the meaning of 'import' see PARA 55 note 5.
4 Human Medicines Regulations 2012, SI 2012/1916, reg 17(1)(a). As to the meaning of 'medicinal product' see PARA 25. A person is guilty of an offence if he contravenes the provisions of reg 17(1): reg 34(1). The defence in reg 34(5) applies to a person who is charged under reg 34(1) with an offence of contravening reg 17(1) (prohibition on manufacturing a medicinal product except in accordance with a licence) by virtue of a breach of reg 37(2)(b) (see PARA 62) (requirement that active substances used as starting materials are manufactured or assembled in accordance with the Good Manufacturing Practice Directive): reg 34(4). It is a defence for the person to show that the person could not, by taking all reasonable precautions and exercising all due diligence, have discovered that an active substance was not manufactured in accordance with regulation 37(2)(b): reg 34(5). As to the meaning of 'contravene' see PARA 41 note 8. As to the meaning of 'Good Manufacturing Practice Directive' see PARA 62 note 3.
5 Human Medicines Regulations 2012, SI 2012/1916, reg 17(1)(b).

46.   Import exemptions.   The general requirement for a manufacturer's licence[1] does not apply to a person[2] who, in connection with the importation of a medicinal product[3] from a state other than an EEA state, provides facilities solely for transporting the product, or is acting as an import agent and imports the medicinal product solely to the order of another person who holds a manufacturer's licence authorising the importation of the product[4].

Nor does the general requirement for a manufacturer's licence apply to a person who imports a medicinal product for administration[5] to himself or herself or to any other person who is a member of that person's household[6].

1 Ie the requirement set out in the Human Medicines Regulations 2012, SI 2012/1916, reg 17(1) (see PARA 45). As to the meaning of 'manufacturer's licence' see PARA 45.
2 As to the meaning of 'person' see PARA 45 note 2.
3 As to the meaning of 'medicinal product' see PARA 25. As to the meaning of 'import' see PARA 55 note 5.
4 Human Medicines Regulations 2012, SI 2012/1916, reg 17(5).
5 As to the meaning of 'administer' see PARA 25 note 4.
6 Human Medicines Regulations 2012, SI 2012/1916, reg 17(6).

47. Exemption in relation to investigational medicinal products. The general requirement for a manufacturer's licence[1] applies in relation to an investigational medicinal product[2] only:

> (1) if the product has a marketing authorisation[3], Article 126a authorisation[4], certificate of registration[5] or traditional herbal registration[6]; and
>
> (2) to the extent that the manufacture or assembly[7] of the product is in accordance with the terms and conditions of that authorisation, certificate or registration[8].

1 Ie the requirement set out in the Human Medicines Regulations 2012, SI 2012/1916, reg 17(1) (see PARA 45). As to the meaning of 'manufacturer's licence' see PARA 45.
2 As to the meaning of 'investigational medicinal product' see the Medicines for Human Use (Clinical Trials) Regulations 2004, SI 2004/1031, reg 2(1); and PARA 107 note 1 (definition applied by the Human Medicines Regulations 2012, SI 2012/1916, reg 8(1)).
3 For this purpose 'marketing authorisation' means a marketing authorisation issued by a competent authority in accordance with Council Directive (EC) 2001/83 (OJ L311, 28.11.2001, p 67) on the Community code relating to medicinal products for human use (see PARA 6) or an EU marketing authorisation: Human Medicines Regulations 2012, SI 2012/1916, reg 17(4). As to the meaning of 'EU marketing authorisation' see PARA 141 note 3.
4 As to the meaning of 'Article 126a authorisation' see PARA 141 note 6.
5 As to the meaning of 'certificate of registration' see PARA 141 note 4.
6 Human Medicines Regulations 2012, SI 2012/1916, reg 17(3)(a). As to the meaning of 'traditional herbal registration' see PARA 141 note 5.
7 As to the meanings of 'manufacture' and 'assembly' see PARA 141 notes 7, 8.
8 Human Medicines Regulations 2012, SI 2012/1916, reg 17(3)(b). As to references to the terms of a marketing authorisation, a certificate of registration and a traditional herbal registration see PARA 141 notes 10–12. References in the Human Medicines Regulations 2012, SI 2012/1916 to a condition of a marketing authorisation is to a condition to which the authorisation is subject by virtue of reg 59(1) or 60(1) (see PARA 161) and a certificate of registration is to a condition to which the certificate is subject by virtue of reg 105(1) (see PARA 191): reg 8(6).

48. Exemption in relation to registered nurses and midwives. The general requirement for a manufacturer's licence[1] does not apply where a medicinal product[2] is assembled by a registered nurse or a registered midwife[3] if the nurse or midwife is acting in the course of his profession and the following conditions are met[4].

The first condition is that the medicinal product is supplied to a patient in the course of the treatment of that patient or, where the product is manufactured or assembled[5] by a doctor or dentist[6], to a patient of another doctor or dentist who is a member of the same medical or dental practice[7]. The second condition is that the medicinal product is not manufactured or, as the case may be, assembled on a large scale or by an industrial process[8].

1 Ie the requirement set out in the Human Medicines Regulations 2012, SI 2012/1916, reg 17(1) (see PARA 45). As to the meaning of 'manufacturer's licence' see PARA 45.
2 As to the meaning of 'medicinal product' see PARA 25.
3 'Registered nurse' means a person registered in the Nurses Part or the Specialist Community Public Health Nurses Part of the register maintained by the Nursing and Midwifery Council under the Nursing and Midwifery Order 2001, SI 2002/253, art 5 (see MEDICAL PROFESSIONS vol 74 (2011) PARA 714) and 'registered midwife' means a person registered in the Midwives Part of that register: see the Human Medicines Regulations 2012, SI 2012/1916, reg 8(1).
4 See the Human Medicines Regulations 2012, SI 2012/1916, reg 3(1), (4).
5 As to the meaning of 'manufactured' and 'assembled' see PARA 141 notes 7, 8.
6 For the purposes of the Human Medicines Regulations 2012, SI 2012/1916 and the Medicines for Human Use (Clinical Trials) Regulations 2004, SI 2004/1031 'doctor' means a registered medical practitioner and 'dentist' means a person registered in the dentists register under the Dentists Act 1984 s 14 (see MEDICAL PROFESSIONS vol 74 (2011) PARA 442): Human Medicines Regulations 2012, SI 2012/1916, reg 8(1); Medicines for Human Use (Clinical Trials)

Regulations 2004, SI 2004/1031, reg 2(1) (definition of 'dentist' amended by SI 2007/3101). As to the meaning of 'registered medical practitioner' see MEDICAL PROFESSIONS vol 74 (2011) PARA 176.

7   See the Human Medicines Regulations 2012, SI 2012/1916, reg 3(5), (8).
8   See the Human Medicines Regulations 2012, SI 2012/1916, reg 3(9).

49.   Exemption in relation to doctors and dentists. The general requirement for a manufacturer's licence[1] does not apply where a medicinal product[2] is manufactured or assembled[3] by a doctor or dentist[4] and the following conditions are met[5].

The first condition is that the medicinal product is supplied to a patient in the course of the treatment of that patient or to a patient of another doctor or dentist who is a member of the same medical or dental practice[6]. The second condition is that the medicinal product is not manufactured or, as the case may be, assembled on a large scale or by an industrial process[7].

1   Ie the requirement set out in the Human Medicines Regulations 2012, SI 2012/1916, reg 17(1) (see PARA 45). As to the meaning of 'manufacturer's licence' see PARA 45.
2   As to the meaning of 'medicinal product' see PARA 25.
3   As to the meaning of 'manufactured' and 'assembled' see PARA 141 notes 7, 8.
4   As to the meanings of 'doctor' and 'dentist' see PARA 48 note 6.
5   See the Human Medicines Regulations 2012, SI 2012/1916, reg 3(2), (5).
6   See the Human Medicines Regulations 2012, SI 2012/1916, reg 3(8).
7   Human Medicines Regulations 2012, SI 2012/1916, reg 3(9).

50.   Exemption in relation to mixing of medicines. The general requirement for a manufacturer's licence[1] does not apply to the mixing of medicines[2] by:

(1)   a nurse independent prescriber[3];

(2)   a pharmacist independent prescriber[4];

(3)   a supplementary prescriber[5], if the mixing of medicines forms part of the clinical management plan for an individual patient[6];

(4)   a person acting in accordance with the written directions of a doctor, dentist, nurse independent prescriber or pharmacist independent prescriber[7]; or

(5)   a person acting in accordance with the written directions of a supplementary prescriber, if the mixing of medicines forms part of the clinical management plan for an individual patient[8].

1   Ie the requirement set out in the Human Medicines Regulations 2012, SI 2012/1916, reg 17(1) (see PARA 45). As to the meaning of 'manufacturer's licence' see PARA 45.
2   For this purpose 'mixing of medicines' means the combining of two or more medicinal products together for the purposes of administering them to meet the needs of an individual patient: Human Medicines Regulations 2012, SI 2012/1916, reg 20(2). As to the meaning of 'administer' see PARA 25 note 4.
3   Human Medicines Regulations 2012, SI 2012/1916, reg 20(1)(a). For the purposes of the Human Medicines Regulations 2012, SI 2012/1916 and the Prescription Only Medicines (Human Use) Order 1997, SI 1997/1830 'nurse independent prescriber' means a person who is a registered nurse or registered midwife and is noted in the professional register as qualified to order drugs, medicines and appliances as a nurse independent prescriber or a nurse independent/ supplementary prescriber: Human Medicines Regulations 2012, SI 2012/1916, reg 8(1); Prescription Only Medicines (Human Use) Order 1997, SI 1997/1830, art 1(2) (definition added by SI 2006/915). As to the meanings of 'registered nurse' and 'registered midwife' see PARA 48 note 3. 'The professional register' means the register maintained by the Nursing and Midwifery Council under the Nursing and Midwifery Order 2001, SI 2002/253, art 5 (see MEDICAL PROFESSIONS): Human Medicines Regulations 2012, SI 2012/1916, reg 8(1).
4   Human Medicines Regulations 2012, SI 2012/1916, reg 20(1)(b). 'Pharmacist independent prescriber' means a person who is a pharmacist and is noted in the relevant register as qualified to order drugs, medicines and appliances as a pharmacist independent prescriber: reg 8(1). As to the meaning of 'pharmacist' see PARA 52 note 5.

5 'Supplementary prescriber' means a person who is noted in the relevant register as qualified to order drugs, medicines and appliances as a supplementary prescriber (or, in the case of a registered nurse or registered midwife, as a nurse independent/supplementary prescriber) and is a pharmacist, a registered midwife, a registered nurse, a chiropodist, podiatrist, physiotherapist or radiographer or a registered optometrist: Human Medicines Regulations 2012, SI 2012/1916, reg 8(1). As to the meaning of 'registered optometrist' see PARA 36 note 8.

6 Human Medicines Regulations 2012, SI 2012/1916, reg 20(1)(c). As to the meaning of 'clinical management plan' see PARA 274 note 6.

7 Human Medicines Regulations 2012, SI 2012/1916, reg 20(1)(d).

8 Human Medicines Regulations 2012, SI 2012/1916, reg 20(1)(e).

51. Exemption in relation to herbal medicines. The general requirement for a manufacturer's licence[1] does not apply where a herbal medicinal product[2] is manufactured or assembled[3] by a person ('A') if:

(1)   the manufacture or assembly takes place on premises occupied by A and from which A can exclude the public[4];

(2)   the product is for administration to a person ('B') and A has been requested by or on behalf of B, and in B's presence, to use A's judgment as to the treatment required[5];

(3)   the product does not contain Apocynum cannabinum[6], Areca catechu[7], Artemisia cina[8], Brayera anthelmintica[9], Catha edulis[10], Chenopodium ambrosioides var anthelminticum[11], Crotalaria berberoana[12], Crotalaria spectabilis[13], Cucurbita maxima[14], Delphinium staphisagria[15], Dryopteris filix-mas[16], Duboisia leichardtii[17], Duboisia myoporoides, Ecballium elaterium[18], Embelia ribes[19], Embelia robusta, Erysimum canescens[20], Holarrhena antidysenterica[21], Juniperus Sabina[22], Mallotus philippinensis[23], Pausinystalia yohimbe[24], Punica granatum[25], Rhus radicans[26], Scopolia carniolica[27], Scopolia japonica, Strophanthus courmonti[28], Strophanthus emini, Strophanthus gratus, Strophanthus hispidus, Strophanthus kombe, Strophanthus nicholsoni, Strophanthus sarmentosus, Ulmus fulva[29], Ulmus rubra, Viscum album[30];

(4)   the product does not contain: (a) Aconitum balfourni, Aconitum chasmanthum Aconitum deinorrhizum, Aconitum lycoctonum Aconitum napellus, Aconitum spicatum, Aconitum stoerkianum Aconitum uncinatum var japonicum[31]; (b) Adonis vernalis[32]; (c) Aspidosperma quebrachoblanco[33]; (d) Atropa acuminate, Atropa belladonna[34]; (e) Chelidonium majus[35]; (f) Cinchona calisaya, Cinchona ledgerana Cinchona micrantha, Cinchona officinalis, Cinchona succirubra[36]; (g) Colchicum autumnale[37]; (h) Conium maculatum[38]; (i) Convallaria majalis[39];(j) Datura innoxia, Datura stramonium[40]; (k) Ephedra distachya, Ephedra equisetina, Ephedra gerardiana, Ephedra intermedia, Ephedra sinica[41]; (l) Gelsemium sempervirens[42]; (m) Hyoscyamus albus, Hyoscyamus muticus, Hyoscyamus niger[43]; (n) Lobelia inflate[44]; (o) Pilocarpus jaborandi, Pilocarpus microphyllus[45]; (p) Rhus toxicodendron[46]; or (q) Senecio jacobaea[47], unless the product is sold or supplied: (i) in or from containers or packages[48] labelled to show a dose not exceeding the maximum dose or maximum daily dose permitted[49]; or (ii) in the case of a product for external use only, with a percentage of the substance in the product that does not exceed a specified[50] percentage[51]; and

(5)   the medicinal product is not manufactured or, as the case may be, assembled on a large scale or by an industrial process[52].

1 Ie the requirement set out in the Human Medicines Regulations 2012, SI 2012/1916, reg 17(1) (see PARA 45). As to the meaning of 'manufacturer's licence' see PARA 45.

2 'Herbal medicinal product' means a medicinal product whose only active ingredients are herbal substances or herbal preparations (or both): Human Medicines Regulations 2012, SI 2012/1916, reg 8(1). As to the meaning of 'medicinal product' see PARA 25. 'Herbal preparation' means a preparation obtained by subjecting herbal substances to processes such as extraction, distillation, expression, fractionation, purification, concentration or fermentation, and includes a comminuted or powdered herbal substance, a tincture, an extract, an essential oil, an expressed juice or a processed exudate: art 8(1). 'Herbal substance' means a plant or part of a plant, algae, fungi or lichen, or an unprocessed exudate of a plant, defined by the plant part used and the botanical name of the plant, either fresh or dried, but otherwise unprocessed: art 8(1).

3 As to the meaning of 'manufactured' and 'assembled' see PARA 141 notes 7, 8.

4 Human Medicines Regulations 2012, SI 2012/1916, reg 3(6)(a).

5 Human Medicines Regulations 2012, SI 2012/1916, reg 3(6)(b).

6 Common name: Canadian hemp. The 'common name' in relation to a medicinal product, active substance or excipient means its international non-proprietary name recommended by the World Health Organisation or, if such a name does not exist, its usual common name: Human Medicines Regulations 2012, SI 2012/1916, reg 8(1).

7 Common name: Areca.

8 Common name: Santonica.

9 Common name: Kousso.

10 Common name: Catha.

11 Common name: Chenopodium.

12 Common name: Crotalaria fulva.

13 Common name: Crotalaria spect.

14 Common name: Cucurbita.

15 Common name: Stavesacre seeds.

16 Common name: Male fern.

17 Common name: Duboisia.

18 Common name: Elaterium.

19 Common name: Embelia.

20 Common name: Erysimum.

21 Common name: Holarrhena.

22 Common name: Savin.

23 Common name: Kamala.

24 Common name: Yohimbe bark.

25 Common name: Pomegranate bark.

26 Common name: Poison ivy.

27 Common name: Scopolia.

28 Common name: Strophanthus.

29 Common name: Slippery elm bark (whole or unpowdered).

30 See the Human Medicines Regulations 2012, SI 2012/1916, reg 3(6)(c), Sch 20 Pt 1. The common name for Viscum album is Mistletoe berry.

31 Common name: Aconite.

32 Common name: Adonis vernalis.

33 Common name: Quebracho.

34 Common name: Belladonna herb, belladonna root.

35 Common name: Celandine.

36 Common name: Cinchona bark.

37 Common name: Colchicum corm.

38 Common name: Conium fruits, conium leaf.

39 Common name: Convallaria.

40 Common name: Stramonium.

41 Common name: Ephedra.

42 Common name: Gelsemium.

43 Common name: Hyoscyamus.

44 Common name: Lobelia.

45 Common name: Jarorandi.

46 Common name: Poison oak.

47 Ie a substance listed in the Human Medicines Regulations 2012, SI 2012/1916, Sch 20 Pt 2. The common name for Senecio jacobaea is Ragwort.

48 'Package' in relation to a medicinal product, includes: (1) a container of the product; (2) any box, packet or other article in which one or more containers of the product are or are to be enclosed; and (3) any box, packet or other article in which a box, packet or other article mentioned in head (2) or head (3) or is to be enclosed: Human Medicines Regulations 2012, SI 2012/1916, reg 8(1).

49 In relation to head (b) in the text the daily dose is 100 mg and the maximum daily dose is 300 mg, in relation to head (c) in the text the daily dose is 50 mg and the maximum daily dose is 150 mg, in relation to head (d) in the text the daily dose for the belladonna herb is 50mg and the maximum daily dose is 150 mg, and for the belladonna root the daily dose is 30 mg and the maximum daily dose is 90 mg; in relation to head (e) in the text the daily dose is 2 g and the maximum daily dose is 6 g, in relation to head (f) in the text the daily dose is 250 mg and the maximum daily dose is 750 mg, in relation to head (g) in the text the daily dose is 100 mg and the maximum daily dose 300 mg, in relation to head (i) in the text the daily dose is 150 mg and the maximum daily dose 450 mg, in relation (j) in the text the daily dose is 50 mg and the maximum daily dose is 150 mg, in relation to head (k) the daily dose is 600 mg and the maximum daily dose is 1800 mg, in relation to head (l) in the text the daily dose is 25 mg and the maximum daily dose is 75 mg, in relation to head (m) in the text the daily dose is 100 mg and the maximum daily dose is 300 mg, in relation to head (n) in the text the daily dose is 200 mg and the maximum daily dose is 600 mg: see the Human Medicines Regulations 2012, SI 2012/1916, Sch 20, Pt 2, column 2.

50 The specified percentage is, in relation to head (a) in the text, 1.3%, in relation to head (h) in the text, 7%, in relation to head (o) in the text, 5%, in relation to head (p) in the text, 10%, in relation to head (q) in the text, 10%: see the Human Medicines Regulations 2012, SI 2012/1916, Sch 20, Pt 2, column 3.

51 Human Medicines Regulations 2012, SI 2012/1916, reg 3(6)(d).

52 Human Medicines Regulations 2012, SI 2012/1916, reg 3(6)(e).

52. Exemptions for pharmacists. The general requirement for a manufacturer's licence[1] does not apply to anything done in a registered pharmacy[2], a hospital[3] or a health centre[4] and is done there by or under the supervision of a pharmacist[5] and consists of[6]:

(1) preparing or dispensing a medicinal product[7] in accordance with a prescription given by an appropriate practitioner[8]; or

(2) assembling[9] a medicinal product, providing that where the assembly takes place in a registered pharmacy: (a) the business[10] in medicinal products carried on there must be restricted to retail sale or supply in circumstances corresponding to retail sale[11] and the assembling must be done with a view to such sale or supply either there or at another such pharmacy forming part of the same retail pharmacy business[12]; (b) the medicinal product must not have been the subject of an advertisement[13].

Nor does the general requirement for a manufacturer's licence apply to anything done by or under the supervision of a pharmacist which consists of procuring the preparation or dispensing of a medicinal product in accordance with a prescription given by a practitioner, or of procuring the assembly of a medicinal product[14].

The general requirement for a manufacturer's licence does not apply to the preparation or dispensing in a registered pharmacy of a medicinal product by or under the supervision of a pharmacist in accordance with a specification furnished by the person to whom the product is to be sold or supplied where the product is prepared or dispensed for administration to that person or to a person under his care[15].

Without prejudice to the preceding provisions, the general requirement to have a manufacturer's licence does not apply to anything which is done in a registered pharmacy by or under the supervision of a pharmacist and consists of:

(i) preparing or dispensing a medicinal product for administration to a person where the pharmacist is requested by or on behalf of that person to do so in accordance with the pharmacist's own judgment as to the treatment required, and that person is present in the pharmacy at the time of the request in pursuance of which that product is prepared or dispensed[16];

(ii)   preparing a stock of medicinal products with a view to dispensing them as mentioned above[17] provided that such stock is prepared with a view to retail sale or to supply in circumstances corresponding to retail sale and the preparation is done with a view to such sale or supply either at that registered pharmacy or at any other registered pharmacy forming part of the same retail pharmacy business[18],

and the general requirement for a manufacturer's licence does not apply to anything which is done in a hospital or a health centre by or under the supervision of a pharmacist and consists of preparing a stock of medicinal products with a view to dispensing them as mentioned in head (1) above[19].

Without prejudice to the preceding provisions the requirement for a manufacturer's licence[20] do not apply to anything with is done in a registered pharmacy by or under the supervision of a pharmacist and consists of preparing a medicinal product with a view to retail sale or supply in circumstances corresponding to retail sale at that registered pharmacy[21].

1   Ie the requirement set out in the Human Medicines Regulations 2012, SI 2012/1916, reg 17(1) (see PARA 45). As to the meaning of 'manufacturer's licence' see PARA 45.

2   'Registered pharmacy' means, in relation to Great Britain, premises entered in the register required to be kept under the Pharmacy Order 2010, SI 2010/231, art 19 (see MEDICAL PROFESSIONS vol 74 (2011) PARA 821) for the purposes of the Medicines Act 1968 ss 74A, 74J (see MEDICAL PROFESSIONS vol 74 (2011) PARAS 836, 840) and, in relation to Northern Ireland, premises entered in the register required to be kept under s 75 (see MEDICAL PROFESSIONS vol 74 (2011) PARA 784): Human Medicines Regulations 2012, SI 2012/1916, reg 8(1); Medicines Act 1968 s 132(1) (substituted by SI 2012/1916).

3   'Hospital' includes a clinic, nursing home or similar institution: Human Medicines Regulations 2012, SI 2012/1916, reg 8(1); Medicines Act 1968 s 132(1) (as substituted: see note 2).

4   'Health centre' means a health centre maintained under the National Health Service Act 2006 s 2 or s 3 (see HEALTH SERVICES vol 54 (2008) PARAS 11, 12), the National Health Service (Wales) Act 2006 s 2 or s 3, the National Health Service (Scotland) Act 1978 s 36(1)(b) or the Health and Personal Social Services (Northern Ireland) Order 1972, SI 1972/1265, art 5: Human Medicines Regulations 2012, SI 2012/1916, reg 8(1); Medicines Act 1968 s 132(1) (as substituted: see note 2).

5   'Pharmacist' means, in relation to Great Britain, a person registered in Part 1 or 4 of the register of pharmacists and pharmacy technicians maintained under the Pharmacy Order 2010, SI 2010/231, art 19(2) (see HEALTH SERVICES vol 54 (2008) PARA 821) and, in relation to Northern Ireland, a person registered in the register of pharmaceutical chemists for Northern Ireland or the register of visiting pharmaceutical chemists from a relevant European State maintained under the Pharmacy (Northern Ireland) Order 1976, SI 1976/1265, arts 6 and 9: Human Medicines Regulations 2012, SI 2012/1916, reg 8(1); Medicines Act 1968 s 132(1) (as substituted: see note 2). The ministers may make regulations prescribing conditions which must be complied with if a thing is to be considered for the purposes of s 10 as done under the supervision of a pharmacist: s 10(7A) (s 10(7A)–(7C) added by the Health Act 2006 s 26(1); the Medicines Act 1968 s 10(7A) amended by SI 2006/2407)). Conditions so prescribed may relate to supervision in the case where the pharmacist is not at the place where the thing is being done and, in that case, the thing is not to be so considered: Medicines Act 1968 s 10(7B) (as so added). In any case, compliance with any applicable conditions is sufficient for the thing to be so considered: s 10(7C) (as so added). As to the meaning of 'the ministers' see PARA 2 note 1 (definition applied by s 1 (substituted by SI 2012/1916)).

6   Medicines Act 1968 s 10(1) (amended by SI 2006/2407, SI 2012/1916).

7   As to the meaning of 'medicinal product' see PARA 25.

8   Medicines Act 1968 s 10(1)(a) (amended by SI 2012/1916); Human Medicines Regulations 2012, SI 2012/1916, reg 4(1). As to the meaning of 'appropriate practitioner' see the Human Medicines Regulations 2012, SI 2012/1916, reg 214; PARA 271. Furthermore the

general requirements for a manufacture's licence does not apply to anything done by or under the supervision of a pharmacist which consists of procuring the preparation or dispensing of a medicinal product in accordance with a prescription given by a practitioner: see the Medicines Act 1968 s 10(1).

9   As to the meaning of 'assembly' see PARA 141 note 8.

10 'Business' includes a professional practice, any activity carried on by a body of persons whether corporate or unincorporated and the provision of services by or on behalf of the Secretary of State, the Minister for Health, Social Services and Public Safety or the Welsh Ministers as the case may be under the National Health Service Act 2006, the Health and Personal Social Services (Northern Ireland) Order 1972, SI 1972/1265, the Health and Social Care (Reform) Act (Northern Ireland) 2009, and the National Health Service (Wales) Act 2006: Human Medicines Regulations 2012, SI 2012/1916, reg 8(1); Medicines Act 1968 s 132(1) (as substituted: see note 2).

11 For the purposes of the Human Medicines Regulations 2012, SI 2012/1916, references to selling by retail, or to retail sale, are references to selling a product to a person who buys it otherwise than for a purpose specified in reg 18(8) (see PARA 77) and references to supplying anything in circumstances corresponding to retail sale are references to supplying it, otherwise than by way of sale, to a person who receives it otherwise than for a purpose specified in regulation 18(8): reg 8(3).

12 Medicines Act 1968 s 10(1)(b)(i) (s 10(1)(b), (4)(b) amended, and s 10(1)(b)(i), (ii), (5), (6) added, by SI 1971/1445). As to references to retail sale see PARA 52 note 11. 'Retail pharmacy business' means a business (other than a professional practice carried on by a doctor or dentist) which consists of or includes the retail sale of medicinal products that are not subject to general sale: Human Medicines Regulations 2012, SI 2012/1916, reg 8(1); Medicines Act 1968 s 132(1) (as substituted: see note 2).

13 Medicines Act 1968 s 10(1)(b)(ii) (as added: see note 12). As to the meaning of 'advertisement' see the Human Medicines Regulations 2012, SI 2012/1916, reg 7; and PARA 333 (definition applied by the Medicines Act 1968 s 10(8) (as so added; amended by SI 2012/1916)).

14 Medicines Act 1968 s 10(1).

15 Medicines Act 1968 s 10(3) (amended by SI 2006/2407).

16 Medicines Act 1968 s 10(4)(a) (amended by SI 2012/1916).

17 Ie as mentioned in the Medicines Act 1968 s 10(1)(a), (3), (4)(a).

18 Medicines Act 1968 s 10(4)(b) (amended by SI 1971/1445).

19 Medicines Act 1968 s 10(4).

20 Ie the restrictions imposed by the Human Medicines Regulations 2012, SI 2012/1916, reg 17(1) (see PARA 45).

21 Medicines Act 1968 s 10(6) (added by SI 1971/1445; amended by SI 2012/1916).

B. APPLICATION

53.   Application for licence.   An application for a grant of a manufacturer's licence[1] must be made to the licensing authority[2] and must indicate the descriptions of medicinal products[3] in respect of which the licence is required, either by specifying the descriptions of medicinal products in question or by way of an appropriate general classification[4].

1   As to the meaning of 'manufacturer's licence' see PARA 45.

2   Human Medicines Regulations 2012, SI 2012/1916, reg 21(1)(a). The application must be made in the way and form specified in the Human Medicines Regulations 2012, SI 2012/1916, Sch 3 paras 1, 2, 4 and contain or be accompanied by the information, documents, samples and other material so specified: reg 21(1)(b), (c). Information supplied by the original manufacturer of a drug may be considered on a subsequent application by a manufacturer of a generic version of a drug: *Re Smith Kline & French Laboratories Ltd* [1990] 1 AC 64, sub nom *Smith Kline & French Laboratories Ltd v Licensing Authority (Generics (UK) Ltd intervening)* [1990] 1 AC 64, [1989] 1 All ER 578, HL.

3   As to the meaning of 'medicinal product' see PARA 25.

4   Human Medicines Regulations 2012, SI 2012/1916, reg 21(2).

54.   Factors relevant to determination of licence application.   In dealing with an application for a manufacturer's licence[1] the licensing authority[2] must in particular take into consideration[3] the operations proposed to be carried out under the licence, the premises in which those operations are to be carried out, the equipment which is or will be available on those premises for carrying out those operations, the qualifications of the persons under whose supervision the operations will be carried out and the arrangements made or to be made for securing the safekeeping of, and the maintenance of adequate records in respect of, medicinal products[4] manufactured or assembled[5] in pursuance of the licence[6].

1   As to the meaning of 'manufacturer's licence' see PARA 45.
2   As to the meaning of 'the licensing authority' see PARA 35 note 1.
3   As to the principles governing the exercise by public bodies of their statutory powers and judicial control thereof see ADMINISTRATIVE LAW vol 1(1) (2001 Reissue) PARAS 16 et seq; JUDICIAL REVIEW.
4   As to the meaning of 'medicinal product' see PARA 25.
5   As to the meanings of 'manufacture' and 'assemble' see PARA 141 notes 7, 8.
6   Human Medicines Regulations 2012, SI 2012/1916, reg 22(1).

C. CERTIFICATION

55. Certification of manufacturer's licence. The licensing authority[1] must issue a certificate in accordance with the following provisions in relation to a manufacturer's licence[2] relating to the manufacture or assembly of medicinal products[3] if requested to do so by:

(1)   the holder of the licence[4];

(2)   a person who intends to export[5] a medicinal product manufactured or assembled by the holder under the licence[6]; or

(3)   the competent authorities of a country other than an EEA state into which a medicinal product manufactured or assembled under the licence is, or is proposed to be, imported[7].

The certificate must contain information sufficient to identify the holder of the manufacturer's licence[8], details of the medicinal products that may be manufactured or assembled under the licence[9] and any other information concerning the holder, the product or the licence that the licensing authority thinks it appropriate to include, including information relating to clinical trials[10].

If a request is made under head (1) above in relation to the export or the proposed export of a product, or under head (2) or (3) above, and there is a marketing authorisation or a traditional herbal registration in force for any product to which the licence relates, the certificate must be accompanied by the summary of the product characteristics[11] relating to that product[12].

The licensing authority must have regard to the prevailing administrative arrangements of the World Health Organisation when issuing the certificate[13].

1   As to the meaning of 'the licensing authority' see PARA 35 note 1.
2   As to the meaning of 'manufacturer's licence' see PARA 45.
3   As to the meanings of 'manufacture' and 'assembly' see PARA 141 notes 7, 8. As to the meaning of 'medicinal product' see PARA 25.
4   Human Medicines Regulations 2012, SI 2012/1916, reg 31(1)(a). A licence holder who makes such a request must produce to the licensing authority a marketing authorisation, certificate of registration or traditional herbal registration in relation to any product to which the certificate is to relate or make a declaration to the licensing authority explaining why no marketing authorisation, certificate of registration or traditional herbal registration is available: reg 31(5). As to the meaning of 'marketing authorisation', 'certificate of registration' and 'traditional herbal registration' see PARA 141 notes 3–5.
5   'Export' means export, or attempt to export, from the United Kingdom, whether by land, sea or air, and 'import' has a corresponding meaning: Human Medicines Regulations 2012, SI 2012/1916, reg 8(1).

6 Human Medicines Regulations 2012, SI 2012/1916, reg 31(1)(b).
7 Human Medicines Regulations 2012, SI 2012/1916, reg 31(1)(c).
8 Human Medicines Regulations 2012, SI 2012/1916, reg 31(2)(a). The licensing authority may restrict the information provided under reg 31(2)(a), (b), (3) to information relating to the specific medicinal products mentioned in the request made under reg 31(1): reg 31(4).
9 Human Medicines Regulations 2012, SI 2012/1916, reg 31(2)(b).
10 Human Medicines Regulations 2012, SI 2012/1916, reg 31(2)(c).
11 'The summary of the product characteristics' in relation to a medicinal product means: (1) where the product has a UK marketing authorisation or traditional herbal registration, the summary of the product characteristics as approved by the licensing authority in granting the authorisation or registration or where the summary has been varied since that approval, as so amended; or (2) where the product has an EU marketing authorisation, the summary of the product characteristics as approved by the European Commission in granting the authorisation or, where the summary has been varied since that approval, as so amended: Human Medicines Regulations 2012, SI 2012/1916, reg 8(1).
12 Human Medicines Regulations 2012, SI 2012/1916, reg 31(3).
13 Human Medicines Regulations 2012, SI 2012/1916, reg 31(6).

D. LICENCE CONDITIONS

(A) In general

56.   General conditions applicable to any manufacturer's licence.   The following apply in relation to any manufacturer's licence[1] and have effect as if they were provisions of the licence[2].

The licence holder must maintain such staff, premises, equipment and facilities for the handling, control, storage and distribution of medicinal products[3] under the licence as are appropriate in order to maintain the quality of the medicinal products[4].

The licence holder must ensure that any arrangements made for the handling, control, storage and distribution of medicinal products are adequate to maintain the quality of the products[5].

The licence holder must not handle, control, store or distribute medicinal products on any premises other than those specified in the licence as approved by the licensing authority for the purpose[6].

The licence holder must inform the licensing authority before making a material alteration to the premises or facilities used under the licence, or to the purposes for which those premises or facilities are used[7]. The licence holder must also inform the licensing authority of any proposed change to the qualified person[8] and any person named in the licence as having responsibility for quality control[9].

For the purposes of enabling the licensing authority to determine whether there are grounds for suspending, revoking or varying the licence, the licence holder must permit a person authorised in writing by the licensing authority to do anything that the licensing authority could have done for the purposes of verifying a statement made in an application for a licence[10].

In distributing a medicinal product by way of wholesale dealing, the licence holder must comply with certain provisions[11] as if the licence holder were the holder of a wholesale dealer's licence[12].

1 As to the meaning of 'manufacturer's licence' see PARA 45.
2 Human Medicines Regulations 2012, SI 2012/1916, regs 36(1), 39(1).
3 As to the meaning of 'medicinal products' see PARA 25.
4 Human Medicines Regulations 2012, SI 2012/1916, reg 39(2).
5 Human Medicines Regulations 2012, SI 2012/1916, reg 39(3). Except in relation to the holder of a manufacturer's licence insofar as the licence relates to the manufacture or assembly of

exempt advanced therapy medicinal products, the licensing authority may require the licence holder to provide the authority with proof of the control methods employed by the holder in relation to a medicinal product: see regs 36(2), 40. As to the meanings of 'manufacture' and 'assemble' see PARA 141 notes 7, 8. As to the meaning of 'the licensing authority' see PARA 35 note 1. As to the meaning of 'exempt advanced therapy medicinal products' see the Human Medicines Regulations 2012, SI 2012/1916, reg 171; and PARA 146: reg 8(1).

6   Human Medicines Regulations 2012, SI 2012/1916, reg 39(4).

7   Human Medicines Regulations 2012, SI 2012/1916, reg 39(5).

8   This does not apply to the holder of a manufacturer's licence insofar as the licence relates to the manufacture or assembly of exempt advanced therapy medicinal products: see the Human Medicines Regulations 2012, SI 2012/1916, reg 36(2).

9   Human Medicines Regulations 2012, SI 2012/1916, reg 39(6).

10   Human Medicines Regulations 2012, SI 2012/1916, reg 39(7).

11   Ie with the Human Medicines Regulations 2012, SI 2012/1916, regs 43(1), (2), (5), 44(2), (3) (see PARAS 64, 67).

12   Human Medicines Regulations 2012, SI 2012/1916, reg 39(8). This does not apply to the holder of a manufacturer's licence insofar as the licence relates to the manufacture or assembly of exempt advanced therapy medicinal products: see reg 36(2). See further the Department of Health *Trading Medicines for Human Use: Shortages and Supply Chain Obligations* (updated January 2013); and the Department of Health *Notification and Management of Medicines Shortages: Best Practice Guidelines* (2006).

57.   Requirements as to qualified persons.   Except in relation to the holder of a manufacturer's licence[1] insofar as the licence relates to the manufacture or assembly[2] of exempt advanced therapy medicinal products[3], the following apply in relation to any manufacturer's licence and have effect as if they were provisions of the licence[4].

The licence holder must ensure that there is at the disposal of the holder at all times at least one qualified person[5] who is responsible for carrying out, in relation to medicinal products manufactured, assembled or imported[6] under the licence, certain specified[7] duties[8].

If the licence holder satisfies certain specified requirements[9] the licence holder may act as a qualified person[10].

A qualified person may be treated by the licence holder as satisfying such requirements if that person produces evidence that he or she is a member of a specified body[11] and is regarded by that body as satisfying those requirements[12].

Where the qualified person changes, the licence holder must give the licensing authority advance notification of that change and the name, address and qualifications of the new qualified person[13].

Under certain circumstances[14] the licensing authority must notify the licence holder in writing that the person is not permitted to act as a qualified person[15].

The licence holder must at all times provide and maintain such staff, premises and equipment as are necessary to enable the qualified person to carry out his duties[16].

The licence holder is not obliged to meet the above requirements of this regulation in relation to any activity under the licence which relates to special medicinal products[17] or to products authorised[18] on a temporary basis[19].

1   As to the meaning of 'manufacturer's licence' see PARA 45.

2   As to the meanings of 'manufacture' and 'assembly' see PARA 141 notes 7, 8.

3   As to the meaning of 'exempt advanced therapy medicinal products' see the Human Medicines Regulations 2012, SI 2012/1916, reg 171; and PARA 146: reg 8(1).

4   Human Medicines Regulations 2012, SI 2012/1916, regs 36(1), 41(1).

5   A 'qualified person', except in relation to the expression 'appropriately qualified person', means a person who satisfies the requirements specified in the Human Medicines Regulations 2012, SI 2012/1916, Sch 7 Pt 1 or 2 (see PARAS 59, 60) or, where an application for a licence is made before 30th April 2013, in so far as the application relates to activities in respect of traditional

herbal medicinal products, a person who has been engaged in activities in respect of traditional herbal medicinal products equivalent to those in Sch 7 Pt 3 (see PARA 58) on or before 30th April 2011 and continues to be so engaged at the time when the application is made: reg 8(1).

6   As to the meaning of 'import' see PARA 55 note 5.

7   Ie the duties specified in the Human Medicines Regulations 2012, SI 2012/1916, Sch 7 Pt 3 (see PARA 58).

8   Human Medicines Regulations 2012, SI 2012/1916, reg 41(2).

9   Ie the requirements specified in the Human Medicines Regulations 2012, SI 2012/1916, Sch 7 Pts 1, 2 (see PARAS 59, 60).

10 Human Medicines Regulations 2012, SI 2012/1916, reg 41(3).

11 Ie the Society of Biology, the Royal Pharmaceutical Society, the Pharmaceutical Society of Northern Ireland, the Royal Society of Chemistry or such other body as may be specified by the licensing authority for this purpose: see the Human Medicines Regulations 2012, SI 2012/1916, reg 41(5). As to the Royal Pharmaceutical Society of Great Britain see MEDICAL PROFESSIONS vol 74 (2011) PARA 785 et seq.

12 Human Medicines Regulations 2012, SI 2012/1916, reg 41(4).

13 Human Medicines Regulations 2012, SI 2012/1916, reg 41(6). The licence holder must not permit any person to act as a qualified person other than the person named in the licence or another person notified to the licensing authority under reg 41(6): reg 41(7).

14 Ie if the licensing authority thinks, after giving the licence holder and a person acting as a qualified person the opportunity to make representations (orally or in writing), that the person: (1) does not satisfy the requirements of the Human Medicines Regulations 2012, SI 2012/1916, Sch 7 Pt 1 or 2 (see PARAS 59, 60) in relation to qualifications or experience; (2) does not satisfy reg 8(b) of the definition of 'qualified person' (see note 5); or (3) is failing to carry out the duties referred to in head (2) adequately or at all: reg 41(8). As to the meaning of 'licensing authority' see PARA 35 note 1.

15 See the Human Medicines Regulations 2012, SI 2012/1916, reg 41(9).

16 See the Human Medicines Regulations 2012, SI 2012/1916, reg 41(10).

17 As to the meaning of 'special medicinal products' see PARA 142.

18 Ie under the Human Medicines Regulations 2012, SI 2012/1916, reg 174 (supply in response to spread of pathogenic agents etc: see PARA 149).

19 Human Medicines Regulations 2012, SI 2012/1916, reg 41(11).

58.   Obligations of qualified persons. The qualified person[1] is responsible for securing:

(1)   that each batch of medicinal products[2] manufactured[3] in the United Kingdom has been manufactured and checked in accordance with the Human Medicines Regulations 2012[4] and the requirements of the marketing authorisation, Article 126a authorisation, certificate of registration or traditional herbal registration[5] relating to those products[6]; and

(2)   in the case of medicinal products imported[7] from a non-EEA state, irrespective of whether the products have been manufactured in an EEA state, that each batch has undergone a full qualitative analysis, a quantitative analysis of all the active substances and all other tests or checks necessary to ensure the quality of medicinal products in accordance with the requirements of the marketing authorisation, Article 126a authorisation, certificate of registration or traditional herbal registration relating to those products[8].

However, the qualified person is not responsible for carrying out the controls referred to above[9] where a medicinal product imported to the United Kingdom has already undergone such controls in another member state and each batch of the product is accompanied by control reports signed by another qualified person in respect of the medicinal product[10].

Nor is the qualified person responsible for carrying out the above mentioned controls[11] where medicinal products are imported from a country other than an EEA state and appropriate arrangements have been made by the European Union with that country to ensure that the manufacturer of the medicinal products applies standards of good manufacturing practice[12] at least equivalent to those laid down by the European Union and the controls referred to in head (1) have been carried out in that country[13].

1   As to the meaning of 'qualified person' see PARA 57 note 5.
2   As to the meaning of 'medicinal products' see PARA 25. The qualified person is responsible for ensuring, in relation to a medicinal product, that documentary evidence is produced that each batch of the product satisfies the requirements of the Human Medicines Regulations 2012, SI 2012/1916, Sch 7 para 12: Sch 7 para 15(1). Such documentary evidence must be kept up to date and must be available for inspection by the licensing authority for a period of at least 5 years: Sch 7 para 15(2).
3   As to the meaning of 'manufacture' see PARA 141 note 7.
4   Ie the Human Medicines Regulations 2012, SI 2012/1916.
5   As to the meaning of 'marketing authorisation', 'certificate of registration', 'Article 126a authorisation' and 'traditional herbal registration' see PARA 141 notes 3–5.
6   Human Medicines Regulations 2012, SI 2012/1916, Sch 7 para 12(a).
7   As to the meaning of 'import' see PARA 55 note 5.
8   Human Medicines Regulations 2012, SI 2012/1916, Sch 7 para 12(b).
9   Ie the controls referred to in the Human Medicines Regulations 2012, SI 2012/1916, Sch 7 para 12.
10 See the Human Medicines Regulations 2012, SI 2012/1916, Sch 7 para 13.
11 Ie the controls referred to in the Human Medicines Regulations 2012, SI 2012/1916, Sch 7 para 12.
12 As to the standards of good manufacturing practice laid down by the European Union see PARA 12.
13 See the Human Medicines Regulations 2012, SI 2012/1916, Sch 7 para 14.

59.   Qualification requirements of qualified persons.   Before acting as a qualified person[1] a person must satisfy the following requirements[2]:

(1)   the person must have a degree, diploma or other formal qualification which satisfies the necessary requirements[3], in pharmacy, medicine, veterinary medicine, chemistry, pharmaceutical chemistry and technology or biology[4] and have at least two years' practical experience[5] in an undertaking authorised to manufacture medicinal products of qualitative analysis of medicinal products, quantitative analysis of active substances and the testing and checking necessary to ensure the quality of medicinal products[6]; or

(2)   if the person's formal qualifications do not satisfy the necessary requirements, the person may act as a qualified person if the licensing authority is satisfied, on the production of evidence, that the person has adequate knowledge of the specified core subjects[7] and has at least two years' practical experience[8] in an undertaking authorised to manufacture medicinal products of qualitative analysis of medicinal products, quantitative analysis of active substances and the testing and checking necessary to ensure the quality of medicinal products[9].

1   As to the meaning of 'qualified person' see PARA 57 note 5.
2   Human Medicines Regulations 2012, SI 2012/1916, Sch 7 para 1. This is subject to Sch 7 Pt 2 (paras 9–11) (see PARA 60).
3   A qualification satisfies the necessary requirements if it is awarded on completion of a university course of study, or a course recognised as equivalent by the member state in which it is studied, which satisfies the minimum core subject requirements; and extends over a period of at least 4 years of theoretical and practical study of a subject specified in head (1) in the text (but this is subject to the Human Medicines Regulations 2012, SI 2012/1916, Sch 7 paras 5 and 6): see Sch 7 para 3. The core subjects that must be included in a course are experimental physics, general and inorganic chemistry, organic chemistry, analytical chemistry, pharmaceutical chemistry, including analysis of medicinal products, general and applied medical biochemistry,

physiology, microbiology, pharmacology, pharmaceutical technology, toxicology and pharmacognosy: Sch 7 para 4(1). These subjects should be balanced in such a way as to enable the person to fulfil the obligations specified in Sch 7 Pt 3 (paras 12–15) (see PARA 58): Sch 7 para 4(2).

If the course referred to in Sch 7 para 3 is followed by a period of theoretical and practical training of at least one year, including a training period of at least 6 months in a pharmacy open to the public and a final examination at university level, the minimum duration of the course is three and a half years: Sch 7 para 5. If two university courses, or courses recognised as of university equivalent standard, co-exist, one of which extends over four years and the other over three years, the three-year course is to be treated as fulfilling the condition as to the duration of the course in Sch 7 para 3, provided that the member State in which the courses take place recognises the formal qualifications gained from each course as being equivalent: Sch 7 para 6. As to the meaning of 'month' see PARA 43 note 3.

4 Human Medicines Regulations 2012, SI 2012/1916, Sch 7 para 2.
5 However, if the person has completed a university course lasting at least five years, the minimum period of practical experience under this provision is one year and, if the person has completed a university course lasting at least six years, the minimum period of practical experience under this provision is 6 months: Human Medicines Regulations 2012, SI 2012/1916, Sch 7 para 8(2).
6 Human Medicines Regulations 2012, SI 2012/1916, Sch 7 para 8(1).
7 Human Medicines Regulations 2012, SI 2012/1916, Sch 7 para 7. See note 3.
8 See note 5.
9 Human Medicines Regulations 2012, SI 2012/1916, Sch 7 para 8(1).

60. Qualified persons with long experience. A person who has acted as a qualified person since 20 May 1975[1] may continue to act as a qualified person[2].

A person who holds a degree, diploma or other formal qualification in a scientific discipline awarded on completion of a university course or course recognised as equivalent and began the course before 21 May 1975[3], may act as a qualified person provided that if, for at least two years before 21 May 1985, the person has carried out one of the following activities in an undertaking authorised to manufacture medicinal products[4]:

(1) production supervision;
(2) qualitative and quantitative analysis of active substances; or
(3) testing and checking, under the direct supervision of the qualified person in respect of the undertaking, to ensure the quality of the medicinal products[5].

1 Ie since the coming into force of Second Council Directive (EC) 75/319 (OJ L147, 9.6.1975, p 13–22) on the approximation of provisions laid down by Law, Regulation or Administrative Action relating to proprietary medicinal products.
2 Human Medicines Regulations 2012, SI 2012/1916, Sch 7 para 9.
3 If a person to whom the Human Medicines Regulations 2012, SI 2012/1916, Sch 7 para 10 applies acquired the practical experience mentioned in Sch 7 para 10(3) before 21 May 1965, the person must complete a further one year's practical experience of the kind specified in that provision immediately before the person may act as a qualified person: Sch 7 para 11.
4 As to the meaning of 'manufacture' see PARA 141 note 7. As to the meaning of 'medicinal product' see PARA 25.
5 Human Medicines Regulations 2012, SI 2012/1916, Sch 7 para 10.

(B) Licence relating to the Manufacture or Assembly of Medicinal Products

61. Standard provisions. The licensing authority[1] may incorporate the following standard provisions in a manufacturer's licence[2] relating to the manufacture or assembly of medicinal products[3].

The licence holder must place the quality control system[4] under the authority of the person notified to the licensing authority[5] to have responsibility for quality control[6].

The licence holder may use a contract laboratory[7] if the laboratory is operated by a person approved by the licensing authority[8].

The licence holder must provide such information as may be requested by the licensing authority about the products currently being manufactured or assembled by the licence holder and about the operations being carried out in relation to such manufacture or assembly[9].

The licence holder must inform the licensing authority of any change that the licence holder proposes to make to a person named in the licence as (1) the person whose duty it is to supervise the manufacturing or assembling operations; (2) in charge of the animals from which are derived substances used in the production of the medicinal products being manufactured or assembled; or (3) responsible for the culture of living tissues used in the manufacture of the medicinal products being manufactured or assembled[10].

The licence holder must keep readily available for inspection by a person authorised by the licensing authority the batch documentation[11] and permit the authorised person to take copies or make extracts from such documentation[12].

The licence holder must keep readily available for examination the samples in each batch of finished medicinal product[13] by a person authorised by the licensing authority[14].

Where the licence holder has been informed by the licensing authority that the strength, quality or purity of a batch of a medicinal product to which the licence relates has been found not to conform with the specification for the finished product or the provisions of the Human Medicines Regulations 2012[15] applicable to the medicinal product, the holder must, if so directed, withhold the batch from distribution, so far as reasonably practicable, for a period (not exceeding six weeks) specified by the licensing authority[16].

The licence holder must ensure that tests for determining conformity with the standards and specifications applying to a product used in the manufacture of a medicinal product must, except so far as the conditions of the product specification for that product otherwise provide, be applied to samples taken from the medicinal product after all manufacturing processes have been completed, or at such earlier stage of the manufacture as may be approved by the licensing authority[17].

Where the manufacturer's licence relates to the assembly of a medicinal product or class of product, and the licence holder supplies the product at such a stage of assembly that does not fully comply with the provisions of the product specification which relate to labelling, the licence holder must communicate the particulars of those provisions to the person to whom that product has been supplied[18].

Where the manufacturer's licence relates to the assembly of a medicinal product, the medicinal product is not manufactured by the licence holder and particulars of the name and address of the manufacturer of the product, or the person who imports the product, have been given by the licence holder to the licensing authority, the licence holder must immediately notify the licensing authority in writing of any changes in the particulars[19].

The licence holder must keep readily available for examination by a person authorised by the licensing authority durable records of the details of the manufacture of intermediate products held by the licence holder for use in the manufacture of biological medicinal products[20], and the records must:

(a)   be in such form as to ensure that the licence holder has a comprehensive record of all matters that are relevant to an evaluation of the safety, quality and efficacy of a finished biological medicinal product manufactured using those intermediate products[21]; and

(b) not be destroyed without the consent of the licensing authority until the records of the details of manufacture of finished medicinal products which were or may be manufactured using those intermediate products may be destroyed in accordance with the requirements of the Human Medicines Regulations 2012[22].

Where animals are used in the production of medicinal products, and a marketing authorisation, Article 126a authorisation, certificate of registration or traditional herbal registration[23] contains provisions relating to them, the manufacturer's licence holder must arrange for the animals to be housed in such premises, and managed in such a manner, as facilitates compliance with those provisions[24].

The licence holder must take all reasonable precautions and exercise all due diligence to ensure that any information provided to the licensing authority is not false or misleading in any material particular if it relates to a medicinal product which the licence holder manufactures or assembles or it relates to any starting materials or intermediate products held by the licence holder which are for use in the manufacture of medicinal products[25].

1 As to the meaning of 'the licensing authority' see PARA 35 note 1.
2 As to the meaning of 'manufacturer's licence' see PARA 45.
3 See the Human Medicines Regulations 2012, SI 2012/1916, reg 24(1), Sch 4 para 1. The standard provisions may be incorporated in a licence with or without modifications and either generally or in relation to medicinal products of a particular class: reg 24(2). As to the meanings of 'manufacture' and 'assembly' see PARA 141 notes 7, 8. As to the meaning of 'medicinal product' see PARA 25.
4 Ie the quality control system referred to in Commission Directive (EC) 2003/94 (OJ L262, 14.10.2003, p 22–26) laying down the principles and guidelines of good manufacturing practice in respect of medicinal products for human use and investigational medicinal products for human use ('the Good Manufacturing Practice Directive'), art 11(2) (see PARA 12).
5 Ie in accordance with the Human Medicines Regulations 2012, SI 2012/1916, Sch 3 para 1(2)(g).
6 See the Human Medicines Regulations 2012, SI 2012/1916, Sch 4 para 2.
7 Ie pursuant to Commission Directive (EC) 2003/94 (OJ L262, 14.10.2003, p 22–26) art 11(2) (see PARA 12).
8 Human Medicines Regulations 2012, SI 2012/1916, Sch 4 para 3.
9 Human Medicines Regulations 2012, SI 2012/1916, Sch 4 para 4.
10 Human Medicines Regulations 2012, SI 2012/1916, Sch 4 para 5.
11 Ie the batch documentation referred to in Commission Directive (EC) 2003/94 (OJ L262, 14.10.2003, p 22–26) art 9(1).
12 Human Medicines Regulations 2012, SI 2012/1916, Sch 4 para 6.
13 Ie the samples referred to in Commission Directive (EC) 2003/94 (OJ L262, 14.10.2003, p 22–26) art 11(4) (see PARA 12).
14 See the Human Medicines Regulations 2012, SI 2012/1916, Sch 4 para 7.
15 Ie the Human Medicines Regulations 2012, SI 2012/1916.
16 Human Medicines Regulations 2012, SI 2012/1916, Sch 4 para 8.
17 Human Medicines Regulations 2012, SI 2012/1916, Sch 4 para 9.
18 Human Medicines Regulations 2012, SI 2012/1916, Sch 4 para 10.
19 Human Medicines Regulations 2012, SI 2012/1916, Sch 4 para 11.
20 As to the meaning of 'biological medicinal product' see Council Directive (EC) 2001/83 (OJ L311, 28.11.2001, p 67) on the Community code relating to medicinal products for human use, Annex I, para 3.2.1.1(b): Human Medicines Regulations 2012, SI 2012/1916, reg 8(1).
21 Human Medicines Regulations 2012, SI 2012/1916, Sch 4 para 12(a).
22 Human Medicines Regulations 2012, SI 2012/1916, Sch 4 para 12(b).
23 As to the meaning of 'marketing authorisation', 'Article 126a authorisation', 'certificate of registration' and 'traditional herbal registration' see PARA 141 notes 3–5.
24 Human Medicines Regulations 2012, SI 2012/1916, Sch 4 para 13.
25 Human Medicines Regulations 2012, SI 2012/1916, Sch 4 para 14.

62.   Good manufacturing practice. The following apply in relation to the holder of a manufacturer's licence relating to the manufacture or assembly of medicinal products ('the licence holder')[1] and have effect as if they were provisions of the licence[2].

The licence holder must comply with the principles and guidelines for good manufacturing practice set out in the Good Manufacturing Practice Directive[3].

Except in relation to the manufacture or assembly of exempt advanced therapy medicinal products or special medicinal products[4], the licence holder must use active substances as starting materials only if those substances have been manufactured or assembled in accordance with the above principles and guidelines in so far as those principles and guidelines relate to starting materials[5].

1   As to the meaning of 'manufacturer's licence' see PARA 45. As to the meaning of 'medicinal product' see PARA 25. As to the meanings of 'manufacture' and 'assembly' see PARA 141 notes 7, 8.
2   See the Human Medicines Regulations 2012, SI 2012/1916, regs 36(1), 37(1).
3   Human Medicines Regulations 2012, SI 2012/196, reg 37(2)(a). The Good Manufacturing Directive referred to in the text is Commission Directive (EC) 2003/94 (OJ L262, 14.10.2003, p 22–26) laying down the principles and guidelines of good manufacturing practice in respect of medicinal products for human use and investigational medicinal products for human use (see PARA 12): Human Medicines Regulations 2012, SI 2012/1916, reg 8(1).
4   As to the meaning of 'exempt advanced therapy medicinal products' see the Human Medicines Regulations 2012, SI 2012/1916, reg 171; and PARA 146: reg 8(1). As to the meaning of 'special medicinal products' see PARA 142.
5   See the Human Medicines Regulations 2012, SI 2012/1916, regs 36(2), 37(2), (3).

63.   Staff and premises conditions. The following apply in relation to the holder of a manufacturer's licence relating to the manufacture or assembly of medicinal products ('the licence holder')[1] and have effect as if they were provisions of the licence[2].

The licence holder must maintain such staff, premises and equipment as are necessary for the stages of manufacture and assembly of medicinal products undertaken by the licence holder in accordance with the manufacturer's licence and in accordance with the marketing authorisations, Article 126a authorisations, certificates of registration or traditional herbal registrations[3] applying to the medicinal products[4].

The licence holder must not manufacture or assemble medicinal products on premises other than those specified in the licence as approved by the licensing authority for the purpose[5].

1   As to the meaning of 'manufacturer's licence' see PARA 45. As to the meaning of 'medicinal product' see PARA 25. As to the meanings of 'manufacture' and 'assembly' see PARA 141 notes 7, 8.
2   See the Human Medicines Regulations 2012, SI 2012/1916, regs 36(1), 37(1).
3   As to the meaning of 'marketing authorisation', 'Article 126a authorisation', 'certificate of registration' and 'traditional herbal registration' see PARA 141 notes 3–5.
4   Human Medicines Regulations 2012, SI 2012/1916, reg 37(4).
5   Human Medicines Regulations 2012, SI 2012/1916, reg 37(6).

64.   Condition to only manufacture or assemble products covered by the licence. The following applies in relation to the holder of a manufacturer's licence relating to the manufacture or assembly of medicinal products ('the licence holder')[1] and have effect as if they were provisions of the licence[2]. The licence holder must not manufacture or assemble medicinal products, or classes of medicinal products, other than those specified in the licence[3].

1   As to the meaning of 'manufacturer's licence' see PARA 45. As to the meaning of 'medicinal
    product' see PARA 25. As to the meanings of 'manufacture' and 'assembly' see PARA 141
    notes 7, 8.
2   See the Human Medicines Regulations 2012, SI 2012/1916, regs 36(1), 37(1).
3   Human Medicines Regulations 2012, SI 2012/1916, reg 37(5).

65.   Imported blood or blood products.   The following applies in relation to
the holder of a manufacturer's licence relating to the manufacture or assembly of
medicinal products ('the licence holder')[1] and have effect as if they were
provisions of the licence[2].

The licence holder must ensure that blood, or blood components[3], imported
into the United Kingdom and used as a starting material or raw material in the
manufacture of a medicinal product meet the specified standards of quality and
safety[4] or equivalent standards[5].

1   As to the meaning of 'manufacturer's licence' see PARA 45. As to the meaning of 'medicinal
    product' see PARA 25. As to the meanings of 'manufacture' and 'assembly' see PARA 141
    notes 7, 8.
2   See the Human Medicines Regulations 2012, SI 2012/1916, regs 36(1), 37(1).
3   As to the meaning of 'blood component' see PARA 25 note 7.
4   Ie the standards and safety specified in Commission Directive (EC) 2004/33 (OJ L91, 22.3.2004,
    p 25) as regards certain technical requirements for blood and blood products (see PARA 17). As
    to blood and blood products see PARA 449 et seq.
5   Human Medicines Regulations 2012, SI 2012/1916, reg 37(7).

(C)   *Licences relating to the Import of Medicinal Products from a Non-EEA State*

66.   Standard provisions.   The licensing authority[1] may incorporate the
following standard provisions in a manufacturer's licence relating to the import
of medicinal products[2] from a state other than an EEA State[3].

The licence holder must place the quality control system[4] under the authority
of the person[5] notified[6].

The licence holder may use a contract laboratory[7] if operated by a person
approved by the licensing authority[8].

The licence holder must provide such information as may be requested by the
licensing authority concerning the type and quantity of any medicinal products
which the licence holder imports[9] and must keep readily available for inspection
by a person authorised by the licensing authority the batch documentation[10] and
permit the person authorised to take copies or make extracts from such
documentation[11].

Where the licence holder has been informed by the licensing authority that the
strength, quality or purity of a batch of a medicinal product to which the licence
relates has been found not to conform with the specification of the medicinal
product in question or those provisions of the Human Medicines
Regulations 2012[12] that are applicable to the medicinal product, the licence
holder must, if so directed, withhold the batch from distribution, so far as
reasonably practicable, for such a period (not exceeding six weeks) as may be
specified by the licensing authority[13].

The licence holder must ensure that any tests for determining conformity with
the standards and specifications applying to any ingredient used in the
manufacture of a medicinal product must, except so far as the conditions of the
product specification for that ingredient otherwise provide, be applied to samples

taken from the medicinal product after all manufacturing processes have been completed, or at such earlier stage in the manufacture as may be approved by the licensing authority[14].

The licence holder must take all reasonable precautions and exercise due diligence to ensure that any information provided to the licensing authority which is relevant to an evaluation of the safety, quality or efficacy of a medicinal product for human use which is imported from a state other than an EEA State, handled, stored or distributed under the licence is not false or misleading in a material particular[15].

Where and in so far as the licence relates to special medicinal products, the licence holder may only import such products from a state other than an EEA State in response to an order which satisfies the requirements provisions relating to a supply to fulfil special patient needs[16] and where certain conditions are complied with[17]. No later than 28 days before the day on which each importation of a special medicinal product takes place[18], the licence holder must give written notice to the licensing authority stating the intention to import the product and stating the following particulars:

(1)   the brand name, common name or scientific name of the medicinal product and (if different) any name under which the medicinal product is to be sold or supplied in the United Kingdom[19];

(2)   any trademark or the name of the manufacturer of the medicinal product[20];

(3)   in respect of each active constituent of the medicinal product, any international non-proprietary name or the British approved name or the monograph name[21], or where that constituent does not have any of those, the accepted scientific name or any other name descriptive of the true nature of the constituent[22];

(4)   the quantity of medicinal product to be imported, which must not exceed the specified[23] quantity[24]; and

(5)   the name and address of the manufacturer or assembler of the medicinal product in the form in which it is to be imported and, if the person who will supply the medicinal product for importation is not the manufacturer or assembler, the name and address of the supplier[25].

Where the licence holder sells or supplies special medicinal products, the licence holder must, in addition to any other records which are required by the provisions of the licence, make and maintain written records relating to the batch number of the batch of the product from which the sale or supply was made and details of any adverse reaction to the product sold or supplied of which the licence holder becomes aware[26].

The licence holder must not publish any advertisement, catalogue or circular relating to a special medicinal product or make any representations in respect of that product[27].

The licence holder must inform the licensing authority immediately of any matter coming to the licence holder's attention which might reasonably cause the licensing authority to believe that a special medicinal product imported in accordance with this provision can no longer be regarded as a product which can safely be administered to human beings or as a product which is of satisfactory quality for such administration[28].

The licence holder must cease importing or supplying a special medicinal product if the licence holder receives a notice in writing from the licensing authority directing that, from a date specified in the notice, a particular product or class of products may no longer be imported or supplied[29].

1   As to the meaning of 'the licensing authority' see PARA 35 note 1.
2   As to the meaning of 'medicinal product' see PARA 25; and as to the meaning of 'manufacturer's licence' see PARA 45.
3   See the Human Medicines Regulations 2012, SI 2012/1916, reg 24(1), Sch 4 para 15. The standard provisions may be incorporated in a licence with or without modifications and either generally or in relation to medicinal products of a particular class: reg 24(2).
4   Ie the quality control system referred to in Commission Directive (EC) 2003/94 (OJ L262, 14.10.2003, p 22–26) laying down the principles and guidelines of good manufacturing practice in respect of medicinal products for human use and investigational medicinal products for human use ('the Good Manufacturing Practice Directive') art 11(1) (see PARA 12).
5   Ie the person notified under the Human Medicines Regulations 2012, SI 2012/1916, Sch 3 para 2(2)(h).
6   Human Medicines Regulations 2012, SI 2012/1916, Sch 4 para 16.
7   Ie a contract laboratory pursuant to Commission Directive (EC) 2003/94 (OJ L262, 14.10.2003, p 22–26) art 11(2) (see PARA 12).
8   Human Medicines Regulations 2012, SI 2012/1916, Sch 4 para 17.
9   Human Medicines Regulations 2012, SI 2012/1916, Sch 4 para 18.
10 Ie the documentation referred to in Commission Directive (EC) 2003/94 (OJ L262, 14.10.2003, p 22–26) art 9(1).
11 Human Medicines Regulations 2012, SI 2012/1916, Sch 4 para 19.
12 Ie the Human Medicines Regulations 2012, SI 2012/1916.
13 Human Medicines Regulations 2012, SI 2012/1916, Sch 4 para 20.
14 Human Medicines Regulations 2012, SI 2012/1916, Sch 4 para 21.
15 Human Medicines Regulations 2012, SI 2012/1916, Sch 4 para 23.
16 Ie the requirement of the Human Medicines Regulations 2012, SI 2012/1916, reg 167 (see PARA 142).
17 Human Medicines Regulations 2012, SI 2012/1916, Sch 4 para 22(1).
18 The licence holder may not import the special medicinal product if, before the end of 28 days beginning immediately after the date on which the licensing authority sends or gives the licence holder an acknowledgement in writing by the licensing authority that it has received the notice referred to in the text, the licensing authority has notified the licence holder in writing that the product should not be imported: Sch 4 para 22(3). As to the meaning of 'special medicinal product' see PARA 142.
19 Human Medicines Regulations 2012, SI 2012/1916, Sch 4 para 22(2)(a).
20 Human Medicines Regulations 2012, SI 2012/1916, Sch 4 para 22(2)(b).
21 'British approved name' means the name which appears in the current edition of the list prepared by the British Pharmacopoeia Commission under the Human Medicines Regulations 2012, SI 2012/1916, reg 318 (British Pharmacopoeia: lists of names: see PARA 238); 'international non-proprietary name' means a name which has been selected by the World Health Organisation as a recommended international non-proprietary name and in respect of which the Director-General of the World Health Organisation has given notice to that effect in the World Health Organisation Chronicle; and 'monograph name' means the name or approved synonym which appears at the head of a monograph in the current edition of the British Pharmacopoeia, the European Pharmacopoeia or a foreign or international compendium of standards and 'current' in this definition means current at the time the notice is sent to the licensing authority: Human Medicines Regulations 2012, SI 2012/1916, Sch 4 para 22(10). 'The European Pharmacopoeia' means the European Pharmacopoeia published by the European Directorate for the Quality of Medicines: reg 8(1).
22 Human Medicines Regulations 2012, SI 2012/1916, Sch 4 para 22(2)(c).
23 Ie specified in the Human Medicines Regulations 2012, SI 2012/1916, Sch 4 para 2(6) whereby the licence holder must not, on any one occasion, import more than such amount as is sufficient for 25 single administrations, or for 25 courses of treatment where the amount imported is sufficient for a maximum of 3 months' treatment, and must not, on any one occasion, import more than the quantity notified to the licensing authority under head (3) in the text: Sch 4 para 2(3). The licence holder may import the special medicinal product referred to in the notice where the licence holder has been notified in writing by the licensing authority, before the end of the 28-day period referred to in Sch 4 para 22(3) that the product may be imported: Sch 4 para 22(4). As to the meaning of 'month' see PARA 43 note 3.
24 Human Medicines Regulations 2012, SI 2012/1916, Sch 4 para 22(2)(d).

25 Human Medicines Regulations 2012, SI 2012/1916, Sch 4 para 22(2)(e).
26 Human Medicines Regulations 2012, SI 2012/1916, Sch 4 para 22(5).
27 Human Medicines Regulations 2012, SI 2012/1916, Sch 4 para 22(7).
28 Human Medicines Regulations 2012, SI 2012/1916, Sch 4 para 22(8).
29 Human Medicines Regulations 2012, SI 2012/1916, Sch 4 para 22(9).

67. Good manufacturing practice. The following apply in relation to the holder of a manufacturer's licence relating to the import of medicinal products from a state other than an EEA State ('the licence holder')[1] and have effect as if they were provisions of the licence[2].

Except in relation to the manufacture or assembly of exempt advanced therapy medicinal products[3], the licence holder must comply with the principles and guidelines on good manufacturing practice in the Good Manufacturing Practice Directive[4] in so far as they are relevant to the import of medicinal products[5] and ensure that active substances have been used as starting materials in the manufacture of medicinal products, other than special medicinal products[6], imported from a state other than an EEA State only if those substances have been manufactured or assembled[7] in accordance with such principles and guidelines, in so far as those principles and guidelines relate to starting materials[8].

1   As to the meaning of 'manufacturer's licence' see PARA 45. As to the meaning of 'medicinal product' see PARA 25. As to the meanings of 'manufacture' and 'assembly' see PARA 141 notes 7, 8.
2   See the Human Medicines Regulations 2012, SI 2012/1916, regs 36(1), 38(1), (2).
3   As to the meaning of 'exempt advanced therapy medicinal products' see the Human Medicines Regulations 2012, SI 2012/1916, reg 171; and PARA 146: reg 8(1).
4   Ie Commission Directive (EC) 2003/94 (OJ L262, 14.10.2003, p 22–26) laying down the principles and guidelines of good manufacturing practice in respect of medicinal products for human use and investigational medicinal products for human use: Human Medicines Regulations 2012, SI 2012/1916, reg 8(1).
5   Human Medicines Regulations 2012, SI 2012/1916, regs 36(2), 38(3)(a).
6   As to the meaning of 'special medicinal products' see PARA 142.
7   As to the meanings of 'manufacture' and 'assembly' see PARA 141 notes 7, 8.
8   Human Medicines Regulations 2012, SI 2012/1916, reg 38(3)(b).

(D) Licences relating to Exempt Advanced Therapy Medicinal Products

68. Packaging. The licensing authority[1] may incorporate a standard provision[2] in a manufacturer's licence relating to the manufacture and assembly[3] of exempt advanced therapy medicinal products[4] that the licence holder must ensure that the immediate packaging of an exempt advanced therapy medicinal product and the package leaflet[5] show certain particulars[6].

1   As to the meaning of 'the licensing authority' see PARA 35 note 1.
2   The standard provisions may be incorporated in a licence with or without modifications and either generally or in relation to medicinal products of a particular class: Human Medicines Regulations 2012, SI 2012/1916, reg 24(2). As to the meaning of 'medicinal product' see PARA 25.
3   As to the meanings of 'manufacture' and 'assembly' see PARA 141 notes 7, 8.
4   See the Human Medicines Regulations 2012, SI 2012/1916, reg 24(1), Sch 4 para 24. The standard provisions may be incorporated in a licence with or without modifications and either generally or in relation to medicinal products of a particular class: reg 24(2). As to the meaning of 'exempt advanced therapy medicinal product' see PARA 146: reg 8(1).
5   'Package leaflet' in relation to a medicinal product, means a leaflet that accompanies the product and contains information for the user of the product: Human Medicines Regulations 2012, SI 2012/1916, reg 8(1).
6   See the Human Medicines Regulations 2012, SI 2012/1916, Sch 4 paras 25, 26.

69. Tracing data. The following apply to a manufacturer's licence[1] insofar as it relates to the manufacture and assembly[2] of exempt advanced therapy medicinal products[3] and have effect as if they were provisions of the licence[4].

The licence holder must establish and maintain a system ('traceability system') ensuring that the exempt advanced therapy medicinal product and its starting and raw materials, including all substances[5] coming into contact with the cells or tissues it may contain, can be traced through the sourcing, manufacturing, packaging, storage, transport and delivery to the establishment where the product is used[6].

The licence holder must, where an exempt advanced therapy medicinal product contains human cells or tissues, ensure that the traceability system is complementary to and compatible with EU requirements[7].

The traceability system must be kept by the licence holder for a minimum of 30 years after the expiry date of the exempt advanced therapy medicinal product[8] although a standard provision[9] may be incorporated in the licence that the data is kept for such period, being a period longer than 30 years, as may be specified by the licensing authority[10].

The licence holder must secure that the data will, in the event that the licence is suspended, revoked or withdrawn, or the licence holder becomes bankrupt or insolvent, be held available to the licensing authority by the holder of a manufacturer's licence for the period described above[11].

1 As to the meaning of 'manufacturer's licence' see PARA 45.
2 As to the meanings of 'manufacture' and 'assembly' see PARA 141 notes 7, 8.
3 As to the meaning of 'exempt advanced therapy medicinal products' see the Human Medicines Regulations 2012, SI 2012/1916, reg 171; and PARA 146: reg 8(1).
4 See the Human Medicines Regulations 2012, SI 2012/1916, reg 36(3), Sch 6 para 1.
5 As to the meaning of 'substances' see PARA 25 note 2.
6 Human Medicines Regulations 2012, SI 2012/1916, Sch 6 para 8.
7 See the Human Medicines Regulations 2012, SI 2012/1916, Sch 6 para 11. The EU requirements mentioned in the text are those laid down, as regards human cells and tissues other than blood cells, in Council Directive (EC) 2004/23 (OJ L102, 7.4.2004, p 48) on setting standards of quality and safety for the donation, procurement, testing, processing, preservation, storage and distribution of human tissues and cells, arts 8, 14 and, as regards human blood cells, in Council Directive (EC) 2002/98 (OJ L33, 8.2.2003, p 30) setting standards of quality and safety for the collection, testing, processing, storage and distribution of human blood and blood components, arts 14, 24 (see PARA 13).
8 Human Medicines Regulations 2012, SI 2012/1916, Sch 4 para 9.
9 See the Human Medicines Regulations 2012, SI 2012/1916, reg 24(1), Sch 4 para 24. The standard provisions may be incorporated in a licence with or without modifications and either generally or in relation to medicinal products of a particular class: reg 24(2).
10 See the Human Medicines Regulations 2012, SI 2012/1916, Sch 4 para 27. As to the meaning of 'the licensing authority' see PARA 35 note 1.
11 See the Human Medicines Regulations 2012, SI 2012/1916, Sch 6 para 10.

70. Adverse reaction. The following applies to a manufacturer's licence[1] insofar as it relates to the manufacture and assembly[2] of exempt advanced therapy medicinal products[3] and has effect as if it was a provision of the licence[4].

The licence holder must inform the licensing authority[5] of any adverse reaction[6] or suspected[7] adverse reaction of which the holder is aware within the period of 15 days beginning on the day following the first day on which the holder knew about the reaction[8].

1 As to the meaning of 'manufacturer's licence' see PARA 45.
2 As to the meanings of 'manufacture' and 'assembly' see PARA 141 notes 7, 8.
3 As to the meaning of 'exempt advanced therapy medicinal products' see the Human Medicines Regulations 2012, SI 2012/1916, reg 171; and PARA 146: reg 8(1).

4   See the Human Medicines Regulations 2012, SI 2012/1916, reg 36(3), Sch 6 para 1.
5   As to the meaning of 'the licensing authority' see PARA 35 note 1.
6   'Adverse reaction' means a response to a medicinal product that is noxious and unintended:
     Human Medicines Regulations 2012, SI 2012/1916, reg 8(1). A similar definition applies to the
     European Parliament and Council Directive (EC) 2001/83 (OJ L311, 28.11.2001, p 67): see
     art 1(11).
7   'Suspected' in relation to an adverse reaction means that there is at least a reasonable possibility
     of there being a causal relationship between a medicinal product and an adverse event: Human
     Medicines Regulations 2012, SI 2012/1916, reg 8(1).
8   Human Medicines Regulations 2012, SI 2012/1916, Sch 6 para 2.

71.   Human cells or tissues.   The following apply to a manufacturer's licence[1] insofar as it relates to the manufacture and assembly[2] of exempt advanced therapy medicinal products[3] and have effect as if they were provisions of the licence[4].

The licence holder must ensure, if using human cells or tissues in an exempt advanced therapy medicinal product, that the donation, procurement and testing of those cells or tissues is in accordance with EU requirements[5].

The licence holder must also ensure that any human tissue or cell component imported[6] into the United Kingdom and used by the holder as a starting material or raw material in the manufacture of an exempt advanced therapy medicinal product meets equivalent EU standards[7] of quality and safety and traceability requirements, notification of serious adverse reactions[8] and events and certain technical requirements for the coding, processing, preservation, storage and distribution of human tissues and cells[9].

1   As to the meaning of 'manufacturer's licence' see PARA 45.
2   As to the meanings of 'manufacture' and 'assembly' see PARA 141 notes 7, 8.
3   As to the meaning of 'exempt advanced therapy medicinal products' see the Human Medicines
     Regulations 2012, SI 2012/1916, reg 171; and PARA 146: reg 8(1).
4   See the Human Medicines Regulations 2012, SI 2012/1916, reg 36(3), Sch 6 para 1.
5   See the Human Medicines Regulations 2012, SI 2012/1916, Sch 6 para 3. As to the EU
     requirements referred to in the text see Council Directive (EC) 2004/23 (OJ L102, 7.4.2004,
     p 48) on setting standards of quality and safety for the donation, procurement, testing,
     processing, preservation, storage and distribution of human tissues and cells (see PARA 22).
6   As to the meaning of 'import' see PARA 55 note 5.
7   Ie those laid down in Commission Directive (EC) 2006/17 (OJ L38, 9.2.2006, p 162–174) and
     in Commission Directive (EC) 2006/86 (OJ L294, 24.10.2006, p 32–50) both implementing
     Council Directive (EC) 2004/23 (OJ L102, 7.4.2004, p 48).
8   'Serious adverse reaction' means an adverse reaction that results in a person's death, threatens a
     person's life, results in a person being hospitalised as an inpatient or prolongs a person's existing
     stay in hospital, results in a person's persistent or significant disability or incapacity or results in
     a congenital anomaly or birth defect: Human Medicines Regulations 2012, SI 2012/1916,
     reg 8(1).
9   See the Human Medicines Regulations 2012, SI 2012/1916, Sch 6 para 4.

72.   Blood or blood products.   The following applies to a manufacturer's licence[1] insofar as it relates to the manufacture and assembly[2] of exempt advanced therapy medicinal products[3] and has effect as if it was a provision of the licence[4].

The licence holder must ensure that any blood or blood component[5] imported into the United Kingdom and used by the manufacturer's licence holder as a starting material or raw material in the manufacture of an exempt advanced therapy medicinal product meets equivalent EU standards[6] of quality and safety as regards certain technical requirements for blood and blood components[7].

1   As to the meaning of 'manufacturer's licence' see PARA 45.
2   As to the meanings of 'manufacture' and 'assembly' see PARA 141 notes 7, 8.

3   As to the meaning of 'exempt advanced therapy medicinal products' see the Human Medicines Regulations 2012, SI 2012/1916, reg 171; and PARA 146: reg 8(1).
4   See the Human Medicines Regulations 2012, SI 2012/1916, reg 36(3), Sch 6 para 1.
5   As to the meaning of 'blood component' see PARA 25 note 7.
6   Ie those laid down in Commission Directive (EC) 2004/33 (OJ L91, 30.3.2004, p 25–39) implementing Council Directive (EC) 2002/98 (OJ L33, 8.2.2003, p 30) setting standards of quality and safety for the collection, testing, processing, storage and distribution of human blood and blood components (see PARA 17).
7   See the Human Medicines Regulations 2012, SI 2012/1916, Sch 6 para 5.

73.   Distribution by way of wholesale dealing.   The following applies to a manufacturer's licence[1] insofar as it relates to the manufacture and assembly[2] of exempt advanced therapy medicinal products[3] and has effect as if it was a provision of the licence[4].

Where the holder of a manufacturer's licence distributes by way of wholesale dealing any exempt advanced therapy medicinal product manufactured or assembled pursuant to the licence that person must comply with certain licence conditions[5] for wholesale dealer's licences and the guidelines on good distribution practice published by the European Commission[6], as if that person were the holder of a wholesale dealer's licence[7].

1   As to the meaning of 'manufacturer's licence' see PARA 45.
2   As to the meanings of 'manufacture' and 'assembly' see PARA 141 notes 7, 8.
3   As to the meaning of 'exempt advanced therapy medicinal products' see the Human Medicines Regulations 2012, SI 2012/1916, reg 171; and PARA 146: reg 8(1).
4   See the Human Medicines Regulations 2012, SI 2012/1916, reg 36(3), Sch 6 para 1.
5   Ie the requirements of the Human Medicines Regulations 2012, SI 2012/1916, Sch 6 paras 15, 16, 18, 19.
6   Ie published in accordance with Council Regulation (EC) 726/2004 (OJ L136, 30.4.2004, p 1) laying down Community procedures for the authorisation and supervision of medicinal products for human and veterinary use and establishing a European Medicines Agency, art 84.
7   Human Medicines Regulations 2012, SI 2012/1916, Sch 6 para 6.

74.   Risk management system.   The following applies to a manufacturer's licence[1] insofar as it relates to the manufacture and assembly[2] of exempt advanced therapy medicinal products[3] and has effect as if it was a provision of the licence[4].

The licence holder must, at the written request of the licensing authority[5], set up a risk management system[6] designed to identify, characterise, prevent or minimise risks related to the exempt advanced therapy medicinal product[7].

1   As to the meaning of 'manufacturer's licence' see PARA 45.
2   As to the meanings of 'manufacture' and 'assembly' see PARA 141 notes 7, 8.
3   As to the meaning of 'exempt advanced therapy medicinal products' see the Human Medicines Regulations 2012, SI 2012/1916, reg 171; and PARA 146: reg 8(1).
4   See the Human Medicines Regulations 2012, SI 2012/1916, reg 36(3), Sch 6 para 1.
5   As to the meaning of 'the licensing authority' see PARA 35 note 1.
6   'Risk management system' means a set of pharmacovigilance activities and interventions designed to identify, characterise, prevent or minimise risks relating to a medicinal product, including an assessment of the effectiveness of those activities and interventions: Human Medicines Regulations 2012, SI 2012/1916, reg 8(1). A similar definition applies to the European Parliament and Council Directive (EC) 2001/83 (OJ L311, 28.11.2001, p 67): see art 1(28b) (definition added by European Parliament and Council Directive (EU) 2010/84 (OJ L343, 31.12.2010, p 74)). As to the meaning of 'medicinal product' see PARA 25.
7   Human Medicines Regulations 2012, SI 2012/1916, Sch 6 para 7.

75.   Import and export.   The following applies to a manufacturer's licence[1] insofar as it relates to the manufacture and assembly[2] of exempt advanced therapy medicinal products[3] and has effect as if it was a provision of the licence[4].

The licence holder must not import or export[5] any exempt advanced therapy medicinal product[6].

1　As to the meaning of 'manufacturer's licence' see PARA 45.
2　As to the meanings of 'manufacture' and 'assemble' see PARA 141 notes 7, 8.
3　As to the meaning of 'exempt advanced therapy medicinal products' see the Human Medicines Regulations 2012, SI 2012/1916, reg 171; and PARA 146: reg 8(1).
4　See the Human Medicines Regulations 2012, SI 2012/1916, reg 36(3), Sch 6 para 1.
5　As to the meanings of 'import' and 'export' see PARA 55 note 5.
6　Human Medicines Regulations 2012, SI 2012/1916, Sch 6 para 12.

76.　Offence. A person who is, or immediately before its revocation or suspension was, the holder of a manufacturer's licence[1] relating to an advanced therapy medicinal product[2] is guilty of an offence if he fails to keep the required data[3] or transfer the data[4] to the licensing authority[5] in the event of that person's bankruptcy or liquidation[6].

It is a defence for a person charged with such an offence to prove that he took all reasonable precautions and exercised all due diligence to avoid commission of the offence[7].

Where evidence is adduced that is sufficient to raise an issue with respect to this defence, the court or jury must presume that the defence is satisfied unless the prosecution proves beyond reasonable doubt that it is not[8].

1　As to the meaning of 'manufacturer's licence' see PARA 45.
2　'Advanced therapy medicinal product' means a medicinal product described in European Parliament and Council Regulation (EC) 1394/2007 (OJ L324, 10.12.2007, p 121) on advanced therapy medicinal products, art 2(1)(a); and PARA 23: Human Medicines Regulations 2012, SI 2012/1916, reg 8(1).
3　Ie the data referred to in European Parliament and Council Regulation (EC) 1394/2007 (OJ L324, 10.12.2007, p 121) on advanced therapy medicinal products, art 15(1) (see PARA 22) in accordance with the requirements of art 15(4).
4　This does not apply if the person is bankrupt or in liquidation and has transferred the data to another person or the period for which the person was required to keep the data in accordance with the requirements of European Parliament and Council Regulation (EC) 1394/2007 (OJ L324, 10.12.2007, p 121), art 15(4) has expired: see the Human Medicines Regulations 2012, SI 2012/1916, reg 33(2).
5　As to the meaning of 'licensing authority' see PARA 35 note 1.
6　Human Medicines Regulations 2012, SI 2012/1916, reg 33(1). A person guilty of an offence under reg 33(1) is liable on summary conviction to a fine not exceeding the statutory maximum or, on conviction on indictment to a fine, to imprisonment for a term not exceeding two years, or to both: reg 35(1). As to the statutory maximum see SENTENCING AND DISPOSITION OF OFFENDERS vol 92 (2010) PARA 140.
7　Human Medicines Regulations 2012, SI 2012/1916, reg 33(3).
8　Human Medicines Regulations 2012, SI 2012/1916, reg 33(4).

(iii)　Wholesale Dealing Licence

A.　REQUIREMENT AND EXEMPTIONS

77.　Requirement for a wholesaler dealer's licence. Subject to certain exceptions[1], a person[2] may not, except in accordance with a licence (a 'wholesale dealer's licence'), distribute a medicinal product[3] by way of wholesale dealing[4] or possess a medicinal product for the purpose of such distribution[5].

A wholesale dealer's licence does not authorise the distribution of a medicinal product by way of wholesale dealing, or possession for the purpose of such distribution, unless a marketing authorisation[6], Article 126a authorisation, certificate of registration or traditional herbal registration is in force in respect of the product[7].

1   Ie the exemptions conferred by or under the Human Medicines Regulations 2012, SI 2012/1916, reg 18(3)–(6) (see PARA 78) and reg 19 (see PARA 78): see reg 18(2).
2   As to the meaning of 'person' see PARA 45 note 2.
3   As to the meaning of 'medicinal product' see PARA 25.
4   A reference to distributing a product by way of wholesale dealing is a reference to selling or supplying it or procuring or holding it or exporting it to another EEA state for the purposes of sale or supply, to a person who receives it for the purpose of selling or supplying the product or administering it or causing it to be administered to one or more human beings, in the course of a business carried on by that person: Human Medicines Regulations 2012, SI 2012/1916, reg 18(7), (8). Distribution of a medicinal product by way of wholesale dealing, or possession for the purpose of such distribution, is not to be taken to be in accordance with a wholesale dealer's licence unless the distribution is carried on, or as the case may be the product held, at premises specified in the licence: reg 18(3). As to the meaning of 'export' see PARA 55 note 5.
5   Human Medicines Regulations 2012, SI 2012/1916, reg 18(1). For the purposes of the Human Medicines Regulations 2012, SI 2012/1916, 'wholesaler dealer's licence' has the meaning in reg 18(1): reg 8(1).
6   For this purpose 'marketing authorisation' means a marketing authorisation issued by a competent authority in accordance with Council Directive (EC) 2001/83 (OJ L311, 28.11.2001, p 67) on the Community code relating to medicinal products for human use (see PARA 6) or an EU marketing authorisation: Human Medicines Regulations 2012, SI 2012/1916, reg 18(10). As to the meaning of 'EU marketing authorisation' see PARA 141 note 3.
7   Human Medicines Regulations 2012, SI 2012/1916, reg 18(9). This is subject to the exceptions in reg 43(6) (see PARA 85). As to the meanings of 'Article 126a authorisation', 'certificate of registration' and 'traditional herbal registration' see PARA 141 notes 4–6.

78. Exemptions. The requirement for a wholesaler dealer's licence[1] does not apply:

(1)   to anything done in relation to a medicinal product[2] by the holder of a manufacturer's licence[3] in respect of that product[4];

(2)   where the product concerned is an investigational medicinal product[5];

(3)   if the product is a radiopharmaceutical in which the radionuclide[6] is in the form of a sealed source[7];

(4)   to a person who, in connection with the importation of a medicinal product, provides facilities solely for transporting the product[8];

(5)   to a person who in connection with the importation of a medicinal product acting as an import agent, handles the product where the product is imported solely to the order of another person who intends to sell the product or offer it for sale by way of wholesale dealing or to distribute it in any other way[9];

(6)   to the distribution of a medicinal product by way of wholesale dealing, or to the possession of a medicinal product for the purpose of such distribution, if the distribution or possession is solely for the purpose of exporting the product to states other than EEA States[10].

Nor does the requirement for a wholesaler dealer's licence apply to the sale or offer for sale of a medicinal product by way of wholesale dealing, or possession for the purpose of such sale or offer, where:

(a)   until the sale, the medicinal product has been kept on the premises ('authorised premises')[11] of the person who manufactured or assembled[12] the product; and those premises are premises authorised for use for manufacture or assembly by that person's manufacturer's licence[13]; and

(b)   the person selling or offering the product for sale is:

(i)   the holder of a marketing authorisation, Article 126a authorisation, certificate of registration or traditional herbal registration[14], (an 'authorisation') which relates to the product, including a holder of an authorisation who manufactured or assembled the product[15]; or

(ii) a person who is not the holder of an authorisation in relation to the product but manufactured or assembled the product to the order of a person who is the holder of an authorisation relating to the product[16].

1   Ie the requirement under the Human Medicines Regulations 2012, SI 2012/1916, reg 18(1) (see PARA 77).
2   As to the meaning of 'medicinal product' see PARA 25.
3   As to the meaning of 'manufacturer's licence' see PARA 45.
4   Human Medicines Regulations 2012, SI 2012/1916, reg 18(4).
5   Human Medicines Regulations 2012, SI 2012/1916, reg 18(5). As to the meaning of 'investigational medicinal product' see the Medicines for Human Use (Clinical Trials) Regulations 2004, SI 2004/1031, reg 2(1); and PARA 107 note 1 (definition applied by the Human Medicines Regulations 2012, SI 2012/1916, reg 8(1)).
6   As to the meaning of 'radiopharmaceutical' see PARA 148 note 2. As to the meaning of 'radionuclide' see PARA 25 note 9.
7   Human Medicines Regulations 2012, SI 2012/1916, reg 18(6).
8   Human Medicines Regulations 2012, SI 2012/1916, reg 19(4)(a). As to the meaning of 'import' see PARA 55 note 5.
9   Human Medicines Regulations 2012, SI 2012/1916, reg 19(4)(b).
10 Human Medicines Regulations 2012, SI 2012/1916, reg 19(5). As to the meaning of 'export' see PARA 55 note 5.
11 For the purposes of the Human Medicines Regulations 2012, SI 2012/1916, a medicinal product is regarded as having been kept on authorised premises at a time when it was being moved from one set of authorised premises to another, or from one part of authorised premises to another part or it was being moved from authorised premises by way of delivery to a purchaser: reg 19(3).
12 As to the meanings of 'manufacture' and 'assembly' see PARA 141 notes 7, 8.
13 Human Medicines Regulations 2012, SI 2012/1916, reg 19(2).
14 As to the meanings of 'Article 126a authorisation', 'certificate of registration' and 'traditional herbal registration' see PARA 141 notes 4–6.
15 Human Medicines Regulations 2012, SI 2012/1916, reg 19(1)(a).
16 Human Medicines Regulations 2012, SI 2012/1916, reg 19(1)(b).

79.   Restrictions on persons to be supplied with medicinal products. The holder of an authorisation[1] may not sell a prescription only medicine[2] or a pharmacy medicine[3] by way of wholesale dealing to a person who does not fall within a specified class[4].

Nor may a person, in the course of a business[5] consisting (wholly or partly) of manufacturing medicinal products[6] or of selling medicinal products by way of wholesale dealing, sell a prescription only medicine or a pharmacy medicine by way of wholesale dealing to a person who does not fall within that specified class[7].

Breach of the above restrictions[8] is an offence[9].

However the restrictions are subject to the following exceptions[10].

A person may sell by way of wholesale dealing a pharmacy medicine which is for the purpose of being administered[11] to human beings in the course of a business to any person carrying on such a business[12].

A person may also sell by way of wholesale dealing a pharmacy medicine to which a general sale exemption[13] applies to any person who by virtue of that exemption may sell the pharmacy medicine by retail, or supply it in circumstances corresponding to retail sale, otherwise than by or under the supervision of a pharmacist[14].

A person may sell by way of wholesale dealing to a specified person a prescription only medicine specified[15] in relation to that person[16].

A person may sell by way of wholesale dealing to a registered optometrist[17] a product that is a prescription only medicine by reason only that it contains one or more of the following substances: (1) amethocaine hydrochloride; (2) lidocaine hydrochloride; (3) oxybuprocaine hydrochloride; or (4) proxymetacaine hydrochloride[18].

A person may sell by way of wholesale dealing to an additional supply optometrist[19] a product that is a prescription only medicine by reason only that it contains thymoxamine hydrochloride[20].

A person may sell by way of wholesale dealing to a registered dispensing optician[21] a prescription only medicine that is required for use by a registered optometrist or doctor[22] attending the optician's practice and that contains one or more of the following substances: (a) amethocaine hydrochloride; (b) chloramphenicol; (c) cyclopentolate hydrochloride; (d) fusidic acid; (e) lidocaine hydrochloride; (f) oxybuprocaine hydrochloride; (g) proxymetacaine hydrochloride; and (h) tropicamide[23].

A person may sell by way of wholesale dealing to a registered dispensing optician a prescription only medicine that is required for use by the optician in the course of a professional practice as a contact lens specialist[24] and contains one or more of the following substances: (i) lidocaine hydrochloride; (ii) oxybuprocaine hydrochloride; and (iii) proxymetacaine hydrochloride[25].

1   Ie a marketing authorisation, a certificate of registration, a traditional herbal registration or an Article 126a authorisation: see Human Medicines Regulations 2012, SI 2012/1916, reg 249(2). As to the meanings of 'marketing authorisation', 'Article 126a authorisation', 'certificate of registration' and 'traditional herbal registration' see PARA 141 notes 3–6.

2   As to the meaning of 'prescription only medicine' see the Human Medicines Regulations 2012, SI 2012/1916, reg 5(3); and PARA 26: reg 8(1).

3   As to the meaning of 'pharmacy medicine' see the Human Medicines Regulations 2012, SI 2012/1916, reg 5(5); and PARA 26: reg 8(1).

4   Human Medicines Regulations 2012, SI 2012/1916, reg 249(1). The specified class mentioned in the text is a class specified under Sch 22.

5   As to the meaning of 'business' see PARA 52 note 10.

6   As to the meaning of 'medicinal products' see PARA 25.

7   Human Medicines Regulations 2012, SI 2012/1916, reg 249(3).

8   Ie breach of the Human Medicines Regulations 2012, SI 2012/1916, reg 249.

9   Human Medicines Regulations 2012, SI 2012/1916, reg 255(1)(d); and see PARA 388.

10 See the Human Medicines Regulations 2012, SI 2012/1916, regs 249(4), 250(1).

11 As to the meaning of 'administer' see PARA 25 note 4.

12 Human Medicines Regulations 2012, SI 2012/1916, reg 250(2).

13 For this purpose 'general sale exemption' means an exemption from the Human Medicines Regulations 2012, SI 2012/1916, reg 220 (see PARA 277) conferred by a provision of Chapter 3: reg 250(4).

14 Human Medicines Regulations 2012, SI 2012/1916, reg 250(3). As to the meaning of 'pharmacist' see PARA 52 note 5.

15 Ie a person specified in column 1 of the Human Medicines Regulations 2012, SI 2012/1916, Sch 17 Pts 1–3 may sell a prescription only medicines specified in relation to that person in column 2 of Sch 17 Pts 1–3.

16 Human Medicines Regulations 2012, SI 2012/1916, reg 250(5).

17 As to the meaning of 'registered optometrist' see PARA 36 note 8.

18 Human Medicines Regulations 2012, SI 2012/1916, reg 250(6).

19 For this purpose 'additional supply optometrist' means a person who is registered as an optometrist, and against whose name particulars of the additional supply speciality have been entered in the relevant register: Human Medicines Regulations 2012, SI 2012/1916, reg 250(10).

20 Human Medicines Regulations 2012, SI 2012/1916, reg 250(7).

21 For the purposes of the Human Medicines Regulations 2012, SI 2012/1916, Pt 12, 'registered dispensing optician' means a person whose name is entered in the register of dispensing opticians maintained under the Opticians Act 1989 s 7(b) of or the register of visiting dispensing opticians from relevant European States maintained under s 8B(1)(b): Human Medicines Regulations 2012, SI 2012/1916, reg 213(1).

22 As to the meaning of 'doctor' see PARA 48 note 6.

23 Human Medicines Regulations 2012, SI 2012/1916, reg 250(8).

24 For this purpose 'contact lens specialist' means a person who is a registered dispensing optician and against whose name particulars of the contact lens speciality have been entered in the register of dispensing opticians maintained under the Opticians Act 1989 s 7(b) (see MEDICAL PROFESSIONS vol 74 (2011) PARA 344) or the register of visiting dispensing opticians from relevant European States maintained under s 8B(1)(b) MEDICAL PROFESSIONS vol 74 (2011) PARA 346): Human Medicines Regulations 2012, SI 2012/1916, reg 250(10). As to the meaning of 'relevant European state' see PARA 36 note 8.

25 Human Medicines Regulations 2012, SI 2012/1916, reg 250(9).

B. APPLICATION

80.   Application for licence. An application for a grant of a wholesaler dealer's licence[1] must be made to the licensing authority[2] and must indicate the descriptions of medicinal products[3] in respect of which the licence is required, either by specifying the descriptions of medicinal products in question or by way of an appropriate general classification[4].

1 As to the meaning of 'wholesale dealer's licence' see PARA 77.

2 Human Medicines Regulations 2012, SI 2012/1916, reg 21(1)(a). The application must be made in the way and form specified in the Human Medicines Regulations 2012, SI 2012/1916, Sch 3 paras 3, 4 and contain or be accompanied by the information, documents, samples and other material specified in that provision: reg 21(1)(b), (c). Information supplied by the original manufacturer of a drug may be considered on a subsequent application by a manufacturer of a generic version of a drug: *Re Smith Kline & French Laboratories Ltd* [1990] 1 AC 64, sub nom *Smith Kline & French Laboratories Ltd v Licensing Authority (Generics (UK) Ltd intervening)* [1990] 1 AC 64, [1989] 1 All ER 578, HL.

3 As to the meaning of 'medicinal products' see PARA 25.

4 Human Medicines Regulations 2012, SI 2012/1916, reg 21(2).

81.   Factors relevant to determination of wholesale dealer's licence application. In dealing with an application for a wholesale dealer's licence[1], the licensing authority[2] must in particular take into consideration[3] the premises on which medicinal products[4] of the descriptions to which the application relates will be stored[5], the equipment which is or will be available for storing medicinal products on those premises[6], the equipment and facilities which are or will be available for distributing medicinal products from those premises[7], and the arrangements made or to be made for securing the safekeeping of, and the maintenance of adequate records in respect of, medicinal products stored on or distributed from those premises[8].

1 As to the meaning of 'wholesale dealer's licence' see PARA 77.

2 As to the meaning of 'the licensing authority' see PARA 35 note 1.

3 As to the principles governing the exercise by public bodies of their statutory powers and judicial control thereof see ADMINISTRATIVE LAW vol 1(1) (2001 Reissue) PARAS 16 et seq; JUDICIAL REVIEW.

4 As to the meaning of 'medicinal product' see PARA 25.

5 Human Medicines Regulations 2012, SI 2012/1916, reg 22(2)(a).

6   Human Medicines Regulations 2012, SI 2012/1916, reg 22(2)(b).
7   Human Medicines Regulations 2012, SI 2012/1916, reg 22(2)(c).
8   Human Medicines Regulations 2012, SI 2012/1916, reg 22(2)(d).

C. LICENCE CONDITIONS

82.   Good distribution practice. The following applies to the holder of a wholesaler dealer's licence[1] (the 'licence holder') and has effect as if it was a provision of the licence[2].

The licence holder must comply with the guidelines on good distribution practice published[3] by the European Commission[4].

1   As to the meaning of 'wholesale dealer's licence' see PARA 77.
2   Human Medicines Regulations 2012, SI 2012/1916, reg 42(1).
3   Ie published in accordance with Council Regulation (EC) 726/2004 (OJ L136, 30.4.2004, p 1) laying down Community procedures for the authorisation and supervision of medicinal products for human and veterinary use and establishing a European Medicines Agency, art 84.
4   Human Medicines Regulations 2012, SI 2012, reg 43(1).

83.   Continued supply to pharmacies and others. The following applies to the holder of a wholesaler dealer's licence[1] and has effect as if it was a provision of the licence[2] except insofar as the licence relates to exempt advanced therapy medicinal products[3].

The licence holder[4] must ensure, within the limits of the holder's responsibility, the continued supply of medicinal products[5] to pharmacies, and other persons who may lawfully sell medicinal products by retail[6] or supply them in circumstances corresponding to retail sale, so that the needs of patients in the United Kingdom are met[7].

1   As to the meaning of 'wholesale dealer's licence' see PARA 77.
2   Human Medicines Regulations 2012, SI 2012/1916, reg 42(1).
3   See the Human Medicines Regulations 2012, SI 2012/1916, reg 42(2). As to the meaning of 'exempt advanced therapy medicinal products' see the Human Medicines Regulations 2012, SI 2012/1916, reg 171; and PARA 146: reg 8(1).
4   As to the meaning of 'licence holder' see PARA 82.
5   As to the meaning of 'medicinal product' see PARA 25.
6   As to the meaning of 'selling by retail' see PARA 52 note 11.
7   Human Medicines Regulations 2012, SI 2012/1916, reg 43(2). See further the Department of Health *Trading Medicines for Human Use: Shortages and Supply Chain Obligations* (2012).

84.   Staff, premises and equipment. The following apply to the holder of a wholesaler dealer's licence[1] and have effect as if they were provisions of the licence[2].

The licence holder[3] must provide and maintain such staff, premises, equipment and facilities for the handling, storage and distribution of medicinal products[4] under the licence as are necessary to maintain the quality of the products and to ensure their proper distribution[5].

The licence holder must inform the licensing authority[6] of any proposed structural alteration to, or discontinuance of use of, premises to which the licence relates or which have otherwise been approved by the licensing authority[7].

A standard provision may be incorporated[8] into the licence by the licensing authority that the licence holder must not use any premises for the handling, storage or distribution of medicinal products other than those specified in the licence or notified to the licensing authority from time to time and approved by the licensing authority[9].

1   As to the meaning of 'wholesale dealer's licence' see PARA 77.
2   Human Medicines Regulations 2012, SI 2012/1916, reg 42(1).
3   As to the meaning of 'licence holder' see PARA 82.
4   As to the meaning of 'medicinal product' see PARA 25.
5   Human Medicines Regulations 2012, SI 2012/1916, reg 43(3).
6   As to the meaning of 'licensing authority' see PARA 35 note 1.
7   Human Medicines Regulations 2012, SI 2012/1916, reg 43(4).
8   The standard provisions may be incorporated in a licence with or without modifications and either generally or in relation to medicinal products of a particular class: Human Medicines Regulations 2012, SI 2012/1916, reg 24(2).
9   See the Human Medicines Regulations 2012, SI 2012/1916, s 24(1), Sch 4 paras 28, 29.

85.   Authorisation requirement.   The following apply to the holder of a wholesaler dealer's licence[1], except insofar as the licence relates to exempt advanced therapy medicinal products[2], and have effect as if they were provisions of the licence[3].

The licence holder[4] must not sell or supply a medicinal product[5], or offer it for sale or supply, unless there is a marketing authorisation[6], Article 126a authorisation, certificate of registration or traditional herbal registration[7] (an 'authorisation') in force in relation to the product and the sale or supply, or offer for sale or supply, is in accordance with the authorisation[8].

This does not apply to:

(1)   the sale or supply, or offer for sale or supply, of a special medicinal product[9];

(2)   the export[10] to an EEA state, or supply for the purposes of such export, of a medicinal product which may be placed on the market in that state without a marketing authorisation, Article 126a authorisation, certificate of registration or traditional herbal registration by virtue of legislation by that state under EU provisions[11] for a temporary authorisation[12] or

(3)   the sale or supply, or offer for sale or supply, of an unauthorised medicinal product where the Secretary of State has temporarily authorised[13] the distribution of the product[14].

1   As to the meaning of 'wholesale dealer's licence' see PARA 77.
2   See the Human Medicines Regulations 2012, SI 2012/1916, reg 42(2). As to the meaning of 'exempt advanced therapy medicinal products' see the Human Medicines Regulations 2012, SI 2012/1916, reg 171; and PARA 146: reg 8(1).
3   Human Medicines Regulations 2012, SI 2012/1916, reg 42(1).
4   As to the meaning of 'licence holder' see PARA 82.
5   As to the meaning of 'medicinal product' see PARA 25.
6   For this purpose 'marketing authorisation' means a marketing authorisation issued by a competent authority in accordance with Council Directive (EC) 2001/83 (OJ L311, 28.11.2001, p 67) on the Community code relating to medicinal products for human use or an EU marketing authorisation: Human Medicines Regulations 2012, SI 2012/1916, reg 43(10).
7   As to the meanings of 'Article 126a authorisation', 'certificate of registration' and 'traditional herbal registration' see PARA 141 notes 4–6.
8   Human Medicines Regulations 2012, SI 2012/1916, reg 43(5).
9   Human Medicines Regulations 2012, SI 2012/1916, reg 43(6)(a). As to the meaning of 'special medicinal product' see PARA 269 note 6.
10   As to the meaning of 'export' see PARA 55 note 5.
11   Ie by virtue of legislation adopted by that state under Council Directive (EC) 2001/83 (OJ L311, 28.11.2001, p 67) art 5(1).
12   Human Medicines Regulations 2012, SI 2012/1916, reg 43(6)(b).
13   Ie temporarily authorised distribution under the Human Medicines Regulations 2012, SI 2012/1916, reg 174 (see PARA 149).
14   Human Medicines Regulations 2012, SI 2012/1916, reg 43(6)(c).

86.   Keeping of documents.   The following apply to the holder of a wholesaler dealer's licence[1] and have effect as if they were provisions of the licence[2].

The licence holder[3] must:

(1)   keep documents relating to the sale or supply of medicinal products[4] under the licence which may facilitate the withdrawal or recall from sale of medicinal products in accordance with head (2) below[5];

(2)   maintain an emergency plan to ensure effective implementation of the recall from the market of a medicinal product where recall is ordered by the licensing authority[6] or by the competent authority of any EEA state or carried out in co-operation with the manufacturer[7] of, or the holder of the marketing authorisation[8], Article 126a authorisation, certificate of registration or traditional herbal registration[9] for, the product[10]; and

(3)   keep records, in relation to the receipt and dispatch of medicinal products, of the date of receipt, the date of despatch, the name of the medicinal product, the quantity of the product received or dispatched and the name and address of the person from whom the products were received or to whom they are dispatched[11].

Where a licence relates to special medicinal products[12] standard provisions may be incorporated[13] by the licensing authority in a licence as follows[14].

Where the licence holder sells or supplies special medicinal products, the licence holder must, in addition to any other records which are required by the provisions of the licence, make and maintain written records relating to the batch number of the batch of the product from which the sale or supply was made and details of any adverse reaction to the product sold or supplied of which the licence holder becomes aware[15].

1   As to the meaning of 'wholesale dealer's licence' see PARA 77.
2   Human Medicines Regulations 2012, SI 2012/1916, reg 42(1).
3   As to the meaning of 'licence holder' see PARA 82.
4   As to the meaning of 'medicinal product' see PARA 25.
5   Human Medicines Regulations 2012, SI 2012/1916, reg 43(7)(a).
6   As to the meaning of 'licensing authority' see PARA 35 note 1.
7   As to the meaning of 'manufacturer' see PARA 141 note 7.
8   For this purpose 'marketing authorisation' means a marketing authorisation issued by a competent authority in accordance with the Council Directive (EC) 2001/83 (OJ L311, 28.11.2001, p 67) on the Community code relating to medicinal products for human use or an EU marketing authorisation or an EU marketing authorisation: Human Medicines Regulations 2012, SI 2012/1916, reg 43(10).
9   As to the meanings of 'Article 126a authorisation', 'certificate of registration' and 'traditional herbal registration' see PARA 141 notes 4–6.
10 Human Medicines Regulations 2012, SI 2012/1916, reg 43(7)(b).
11 Human Medicines Regulations 2012, SI 2012/1916, reg 43(7)(c).
12 As to the meaning of 'special medicinal product' see PARA 269 note 6.
13 The standard provisions may be incorporated in a licence with or without modifications and either generally or in relation to medicinal products of a particular class: Human Medicines Regulations 2012, SI 2012/1916, reg 24(2).
14 See the Human Medicines Regulations 2012, SI 2012/1916, reg 24(1), Sch 4 para 32.
15 Human Medicines Regulations 2012, SI 2012/1916, Sch 4 para 37.

87.   Importing.   The following apply to the holder of a wholesaler dealer's licence[1], except insofar as the licence relates to exempt advanced therapy medicinal products[2], and have effect as if they were provisions of the licence[3].

The licence holder[4] must notify the licensing authority and the holder of a marketing authorisation, Article 126a authorisation, certificate of registration or traditional herbal registration[5] (an 'authorisation') in relation to a medicinal product if the licence holder intends to import the product from another EEA state and is neither the holder of an authorisation in relation to the product nor acting on behalf of the holder of an authorisation[6].

Where a licence relates to special medicinal products[7] a standard provision may be incorporated[8] by the licensing authority in a licence that the licence holder must cease importing or supplying a special medicinal product if the licence holder receives a notice in writing from the licensing authority directing that, from a date specified in the notice, a particular product or class of products may no longer be imported or supplied[9]. A standard provision may also be incorporated that the licence holder must inform the licensing authority immediately of any matter coming to the licence holder's attention which might reasonably cause the licensing authority to believe that a special medicinal product imported in accordance with this provision can no longer be regarded as a product which can safely be administered to human beings or as a product which is of satisfactory quality for such administration[10].

1   As to the meaning of 'wholesale dealer's licence' see PARA 77.
2   See the Human Medicines Regulations 2012, SI 2012/1916, reg 42(2). As to the meaning of 'exempt advanced therapy medicinal products' see the Human Medicines Regulations 2012, SI 2012/1916, reg 171; and PARA 146: reg 8(1).
3   Human Medicines Regulations 2012, SI 2012/1916, reg 42(1).
4   As to the meaning of 'licence holder' see PARA 82.
5   As to the meanings of 'Article 126a authorisation', 'certificate of registration' and 'traditional herbal registration' see PARA 141 notes 4–6. As to the meaning of 'marketing authorisation' see PARA 86 note 8.
6   Human Medicines Regulations 2012, SI 2012/1916, reg 43(8).
7   As to the meaning of 'special medicinal product' see PARA 269 note 6.
8   The standard provisions may be incorporated in a licence with or without modifications and either generally or in relation to medicinal products of a particular class: Human Medicines Regulations 2012, SI 2012/1916, reg 24(2).
9   See the Human Medicines Regulations 2012, SI 2012/1916, reg 24(1), Sch 4 paras 32, 41.
10 Human Medicines Regulations 2012, SI 2012/1916, Sch 4 para 39.

88. Inspections. The following apply to the holder of a wholesaler dealer's licence[1] and have effect as if they were provisions of the licence[2].

For the purposes of enabling the licensing authority[3] to determine whether there are grounds for suspending, revoking or varying the licence, the licence holder[4] must permit a person authorised in writing by the licensing authority, on production of identification, to carry out any inspection, or to take any samples or copies, which an inspector could carry out or take under the enforcement provisions[5].

1   As to the meaning of 'wholesale dealer's licence' see PARA 77.
2   Human Medicines Regulations 2012, SI 2012/1916, reg 42(1).
3   As to the meaning of 'licensing authority' see PARA 35 note 1.
4   As to the meaning of 'licence holder' see PARA 82.
5   Human Medicines Regulations 2012, SI 2012/1916, reg 43(9). The enforcement provisions mentioned in the text are those under Pt 16 (see regs 322–334).

89. Requirement to deal with only specified persons. The following apply to the holder of a wholesaler dealer's licence[1], except insofar as the licence relates to exempt advanced therapy medicinal products[2], and have effect as if they were provisions of the licence[3].

The licence holder[4] may not obtain supplies of medicinal products[5] from anyone except the holder of a manufacturer's licence or wholesale dealer's licence in relation to products of that description[6] or from a person who holds an authorisation granted by another EEA state authorising the manufacture of products of that description or their distribution by way of wholesale dealing[7].

The licence holder may distribute medicinal products by way of wholesale dealing only to:

(1) the holder of a wholesale dealer's licence relating to those products[8];

(2) the holder of an authorisation granted by the competent authority of another EEA state authorising the supply of those products by way of wholesale dealing[9];

(3) a person who may lawfully sell those products by retail or may lawfully supply them in circumstances corresponding to retail sale[10]; or

(4) a person who may lawfully administer those products[11].

Where a medicinal product is supplied to a person pursuant to head (3) above, the licence holder must enclose with the product a document stating the date on which the supply took place, the name and pharmaceutical form of the product supplied, the quantity of product supplied and the name and address of the licence holder[12].

The licence holder must keep a record of such information for at least five years beginning immediately after the date on which the information is supplied and ensure that the record is available to the licensing authority for inspection[13].

1 As to the meaning of 'wholesale dealer's licence' see PARA 77.
2 See the Human Medicines Regulations 2012, SI 2012/1916, reg 42(2). As to the meaning of 'exempt advanced therapy medicinal products' see the Human Medicines Regulations 2012, SI 2012/1916, reg 171; and PARA 146: reg 8(1).
3 Human Medicines Regulations 2012, SI 2012/1916, reg 42(1).
4 As to the meaning of 'licence holder' see PARA 82.
5 As to the meaning of 'medicinal product' see PARA 25.
6 Human Medicines Regulations 2012, SI 2012/1916, reg 44(1)(a).
7 Human Medicines Regulations 2012, SI 2012/1916, reg 44(1)(b). See further the Department of Health *Trading Medicines for Human Use: Shortages and Supply Chain Obligations* (2012).
8 Human Medicines Regulations 2012, SI 2012/1916, reg 44(2)(a).
9 Human Medicines Regulations 2012, SI 2012/1916, reg 44(2)(c).
10 Human Medicines Regulations 2012, SI 2012/1916, reg 44(2)(d).
11 Human Medicines Regulations 2012, SI 2012/1916, reg 44(2)(e).
12 Human Medicines Regulations 2012, SI 2012/1916, reg 44(3).
13 Human Medicines Regulations 2012, SI 2012/1916, reg 44(4).

90. Requirement as to responsible persons. The following apply to the holder of a wholesaler dealer's licence[1] and have effect as if they were provisions of the licence[2].

The licence holder[3] must ensure that there is available at all times at least one person (the 'responsible person') who in the opinion of the licensing authority[4]:

(1) has knowledge of the activities to be carried out and of the procedures to be performed under the licence which is adequate to carry out the functions of: (a) ensuring that the conditions under which the licence was granted have been, and are being, complied with; and (b) ensuring that the quality of medicinal products[5] handled by the licence holder is being maintained in accordance with the requirements of the marketing authorisations, Article 126a authorisations, certificates of registration or traditional herbal registrations[6] applicable to those products[7]; and

(2) has adequate experience relating to those activities and procedures[8].

The licence holder must not permit any person to act as a responsible person other than the person named in the licence unless a change to the responsible person has been notified to them[9].

If, after giving the licence holder and a person acting as a responsible person the opportunity to make representations (orally or in writing), the licensing authority thinks that the person does not satisfy the requirements in relation to qualifications or experience[10] or that he is failing to carry out his functions[11] adequately or at all, the licensing authority must notify the licence holder in writing that the person is not permitted to act as a responsible person[12].

1 As to the meaning of 'wholesale dealer's licence' see PARA 77.
2 Human Medicines Regulations 2012, SI 2012/1916, reg 42(1).
3 As to the meaning of 'licence holder' see PARA 82.
4 As to the meaning of 'licensing authority' see PARA 35 note 1.
5 As to the meaning of 'medicinal product' see PARA 25.
6 As to the meanings of 'marketing authorisation', 'Article 126a authorisation', 'certificate of registration' and 'traditional herbal registration' see PARA 141 notes 3–6.
7 Human Medicines Regulations 2012, SI 2012/1916, reg 45(1)(a), (2).
8 Human Medicines Regulations 2012, SI 2012/1916, reg 45(1)(b).
9 See the Human Medicines Regulations 2012, SI 2012/1916, reg 45(3), (4). The licence holder must notify the licensing authority of the name, address, qualifications and experience of the responsible person: see reg 45(3).
10 Ie the requirements of the Human Medicines Regulations 2012, SI 2012/1916, reg 45(1).
11 Ie the functions referred to in the Human Medicines Regulations 2012, SI 2012/1916, reg 45(2).
12 See the Human Medicines Regulations 2012, SI 2012/1916, reg 45(5), (6).

91. Obtaining and distributing products. The following applies to a wholesaler dealer's licence[1] insofar as it relates to exempt advanced therapy medicinal products[2] and has effect as if it was a provision of the licence[3].

The licence holder must obtain supplies of exempt advanced therapy medicinal products only from the holder of a manufacturer's licence in respect of those products or the holder of a wholesale dealer's licence in respect of those products[4].

The licence holder must distribute an exempt advanced therapy medicinal product by way of wholesale dealing only to the holder of a wholesale dealer's licence in respect of those products or a person who may lawfully administer those products and solicited the product for an individual patient[5].

A standard provision may be incorporated[6] in a licence by the licensing authority providing that the licence holder must provide such information as may be requested by the licensing authority concerning the type and quantity of medicinal products which the licence holder handles, stores or distributes[7].

1 As to the meaning of 'wholesale dealer's licence' see PARA 77.
2 As to the meaning of 'exempt advanced therapy medicinal products' see the Human Medicines Regulations 2012, SI 2012/1916, reg 171; and PARA 146: reg 8(1).
3 Human Medicines Regulations 2012, SI 2012/1916, reg 42(3), Sch 6 para 13.
4 Human Medicines Regulations 2012, SI 2012/1916, Sch 6 para 14.
5 Human Medicines Regulations 2012, SI 2012/1916, Sch 6 para 15.
6 The standard provisions may be incorporated in a licence with or without modifications and either generally or in relation to medicinal products of a particular class: Human Medicines Regulations 2012, SI 2012/1916, reg 24(2).
7 See the Human Medicines Regulations 2012, SI 2012/1916, reg 24(1), Sch 4 paras 28, 30.

92. Tracing data. The following apply to a wholesaler dealer's licence[1] insofar as it relates to exempt advanced therapy medicinal products[2] and have effect as if they were provisions of the licence[3].

The licence holder must establish and maintain a system ensuring that the exempt advanced therapy medicinal product and its starting and raw materials, including all substances[4] coming into contact with the cells or tissues it may contain, can be traced through the sourcing, manufacturing[5], packaging, storage, transport and delivery to the establishment where the product is used[6].

Such information must be kept by the licence holder minimum of 30 years after the expiry date of the exempt advanced therapy medicinal product[7] although a standard provision may be incorporated in the licence that the data is kept for a longer period as specified by the licence authority[8]. The licence holder must secure that the data will, in the event that the licence is suspended, revoked or withdrawn or the licence holder becomes bankrupt or insolvent, be held available to the licensing authority by the holder of a wholesale dealer's licence for this period[9].

1   As to the meaning of 'wholesale dealer's licence' see PARA 77.
2   As to the meaning of 'exempt advanced therapy medicinal products' see the Human Medicines Regulations 2012, SI 2012/1916, reg 171; and PARA 146: reg 8(1).
3   Human Medicines Regulations 2012, SI 2012/1916, reg 42(3), Sch 6 para 13.
4   As to the meaning of 'substances' see PARA 25 note 2.
5   As to the meaning of 'manufacture' see PARA 141 note 7.
6   Human Medicines Regulations 2012, SI 2012/1916, Sch 6 para 16.
7   Human Medicines Regulations 2012, SI 2012/1916, Sch 6 para 18. This is subject to Sch 4 para 44.
8   Human Medicines Regulations 2012, SI 2012/1916, Sch 6 para 19.
9   See the Human Medicines Regulations 2012, SI 2012/1916, Sch 4 para 44.

93.   Adverse reactions. The following applies to a wholesaler dealer's licence[1] insofar as it relates to exempt advanced therapy medicinal products[2] and has effect as if it was a provision of the licence[3].

The licence holder must inform the licensing authority[4] of any adverse reaction[5] to any exempt advanced therapy medicinal product supplied by the holder of the wholesale dealer's licence of which the holder is aware[6].

1   As to the meaning of 'wholesale dealer's licence' see PARA 77.
2   As to the meaning of 'exempt advanced therapy medicinal products' see the Human Medicines Regulations 2012, SI 2012/1916, reg 171; and PARA 146: reg 8(1).
3   Human Medicines Regulations 2012, SI 2012/1916, reg 42(3), Sch 6 para 13.
4   As to the meaning of 'licensing authority' see PARA 35 note 1.
5   As to the meaning of 'adverse reaction' see PARA 70 note 6.
6   Human Medicines Regulations 2012, SI 2012/1916, Sch 6 para 17.

94.   Import and export. A licence holder must not import or export any exempt advanced therapy medicinal product[1] under a wholesaler dealer's licence[2] and this has effect as if it was a provision of the licence[3].

Where a licence relates to special medicinal products[4] standard provisions may be incorporated[5] by the licensing authority[6] in a licence as follows[7].

The licence holder may only import such products from another EEA state in response to an order which satisfies the requirements of certain provisions relating to special patient needs[8] and where certain conditions[9] are complied with[10]. The licence holder must not, on any one occasion, import more than such amount as is sufficient for 25 single administrations, or for 25 courses of treatment where the amount imported is sufficient for a maximum of three months' treatment, and must not, on any one occasion, import more than the quantity notified to the licensing authority under the provisions below[11].

No later than 28 days prior to each importation of a special medicinal product, the licence holder must give written notice to the licensing authority stating the intention to import the product and stating the following particulars:

(1)   the brand name, common name or scientific name of the medicinal

product and (if different) any name under which the medicinal product is to be sold or supplied in the United Kingdom[12];

(2)   any trademark or the name of the manufacturer of the medicinal product[13];

(3)   in respect of each active constituent of the medicinal product, any international non-proprietary name[14] or the British approved name or the monograph name[15], or where that constituent does not have any of those, the accepted scientific name or any other name descriptive of the true nature of the constituent[16];

(4)   the quantity[17] of medicinal product to be imported[18]; and

(5)   the name and address of the manufacturer or assembler of the medicinal product in the form in which it is to be imported and, if the person who will supply the medicinal product for importation is not the manufacturer or assembler, the name and address of the supplier[19].

The licence holder may not import the special medicinal product if, before the end of 28 days beginning immediately after the date on which the licensing authority sends or gives the licence holder an acknowledgement in writing by the licensing authority that it has received the notice referred to above, the licensing authority has notified the licence holder in writing that the product should not be imported[20]. The licence holder may import the special medicinal product referred to in the notice where the licence holder has been notified in writing by the licensing authority, before the end of the 28-day period, that the product may be imported[21].

1   As to the meanings of 'import' and 'export' see PARA 55 note 5. As to the meaning of 'exempt advanced therapy medicinal products' see the Human Medicines Regulations 2012, SI 2012/1916, reg 171; and PARA 146: reg 8(1).

2   As to the meaning of 'wholesale dealer's licence' see PARA 77.

3   See the Human Medicines Regulations 2012, SI 2012/1916, reg 42(3), Sch 6 paras 13, 20.

4   As to the meaning of 'special medicinal product' see PARA 269 note 6.

5   The standard provisions may be incorporated in a licence with or without modifications and either generally or in relation to medicinal products of a particular class: Human Medicines Regulations 2012, SI 2012/1916, reg 24(2).

6   As to the meaning of 'licensing authority' see PARA 35 note 1.

7   See the Human Medicines Regulations 2012, SI 2012/1916, reg 24(1), Sch 4 para 32.

8   Ie which satisfy the requirements of the Human Medicines Regulations 2012, SI 2012/1916, reg 167 (see PARA 142).

9   Ie the conditions set out in the Human Medicines Regulations 2012, SI 2012/1916, Sch 6 paras 34–41.

10   Human Medicines Regulations 2012, SI 2012/1916, Sch 4 para 33.

11   Human Medicines Regulations 2012, SI 2012/1916, Sch 4 para 38. As to the meaning of 'month' see PARA 43 note 3.

12   Human Medicines Regulations 2012, SI 2012/1916, Sch 4 para 34(a).

13   Human Medicines Regulations 2012, SI 2012/1916, Sch 4 para 34(b).

14   'International non-proprietary name' means a name which has been selected by the World Health Organisation as a recommended international non-proprietary name and in respect of which the Director-General of the World Health Organisation has given notice to that effect in the World Health Organisation Chronicle: Human Medicines Regulations 2012, SI 2012/1916, Sch 4 para 42.

15   'British approved name' means the name which appears in the current edition of the list prepared by the British Pharmacopoeia Commission under the Human Medicines Regulations 2012, SI 2012/1916, reg 318 (British Pharmacopoeia- lists of names: see PARAS 237–240): Sch 4 para 42. 'Monograph name' means the name or approved synonym which appears at the head of a monograph in the current edition of the British Pharmacopoeia, the European Pharmacopoeia or a foreign or international compendium of standards, and 'current' in this definition means current at the time the notice is sent to the licensing authority: Sch 4 para 42. As to the meaning of 'European Pharmacopoeia' see PARA 66 note 21.

16   Human Medicines Regulations 2012, SI 2012/1916, Sch 4 para 34(c).

17 This must not exceed the quantity specified in the Human Medicines Regulations 2012, SI 2012/1916, Sch 4 para 38.
18 Human Medicines Regulations 2012, SI 2012/1916, Sch 4 para 34(d).
19 Human Medicines Regulations 2012, SI 2012/1916, Sch 4 para 34(e).
20 Human Medicines Regulations 2012, SI 2012/1916, Sch 4 para 35.
21 Human Medicines Regulations 2012, SI 2012/1916, Sch 4 para 36.

95.   Due diligence. A provision may be incorporated[1] by the licencing authority[2] in a wholesaler dealer's licence[3] that the licence holder must take all reasonable precautions and exercise all due diligence to ensure that any information provided by the licence holder to the licensing authority which is relevant to an evaluation of the safety, quality or efficacy of a medicinal product which the licence holder handles, stores or distributes is not false or misleading[4].

1 The standard provisions may be incorporated in a licence with or without modifications and either generally or in relation to medicinal products of a particular class: Human Medicines Regulations 2012, SI 2012/1916, reg 24(2). As to the meaning of 'medicinal product' see PARA 25.
2 As to the meaning of 'licensing authority' see PARA 35 note 1.
3 As to the meaning of 'wholesale dealer's licence' see PARA 77.
4 See the Human Medicines Regulations 2012, SI 2012/1916, reg 24(1), Sch 4 para 31.

96.   Advertising. Where a licence relates to special medicinal products[1] standard provisions may be incorporated[2] by the licensing authority[3] in a licence that licence holder must not publish any advertisement, catalogue, or circular relating to a special medicinal product or make any representations in respect of that product[4].

1 As to the meaning of 'special medicinal product' see PARA 269 note 6; and as to the meaning of 'medicinal product' see PARA 25.
2 The standard provisions may be incorporated in a licence with or without modifications and either generally or in relation to medicinal products of a particular class: Human Medicines Regulations 2012, SI 2012/1916, reg 24(2).
3 As to the meaning of 'licensing authority' see PARA 35 note 1.
4 See the Human Medicines Regulations 2012, SI 2012/1916, reg 24(1), Sch 4 paras 32, 40.

(iv) Manufacture and Importation of Investigational Medicinal Products

A. REQUIREMENT AND EXEMPTIONS

97.   Requirement for authorisation. Subject to certain exceptions[1], a person[2] may not manufacture[3], assemble[4] or import[5] any investigational medicinal product except in accordance with an authorisation granted by the licensing authority ('a manufacturing authorisation')[6].

Any person who contravenes the restriction on the manufacture, assembly or importation of investigational medicinal products[7] is guilty of an offence[8]. Similarly, where an investigational medicinal product is manufactured, assembled or imported in contravention of that restriction, any person who sells or supplies the product for the purposes of a clinical trial knowing or having reasonable cause to suspect that it was so manufactured, assembled or imported is guilty of offence[9]; and, where an investigational medicinal product is imported in contravention of that restriction, any person who, otherwise than for the purpose of performing or exercising a duty or power[10], is in possession of the product knowing or having reasonable cause to suspect that it was so imported is guilty of offence[11].

1 Ie subject to the Medicines for Human Use (Clinical Trials) Regulations 2004, SI 2004/1031, regs 36(2), 37: see PARA 98.

2 As to the meaning of 'person' see PARA 45 note 2.

3 'Manufacture', in relation to an investigational medicinal product, includes any process carried out in the course of making the product, but does not include dissolving or dispersing the product in, or diluting it or mixing it with, some other substance used as a vehicle for the purposes of administering it: Medicines for Human Use (Clinical Trials) Regulations 2004, SI 2004/1031, reg 2(1). As to the meaning of 'investigational medicinal product' see PARA 107 note 1.

4 'Assemble', in relation to an investigational medicinal product, means: (1) enclosing the product (with or without other medicinal products of the same description) in a container which is labelled before the product is sold or supplied or used in a clinical trial; or (2) where the product (with or without other medicinal products of the same description) is already contained in the container in which it is to be sold or supplied or used in a clinical trial, labelling the container before the product is sold or supplied or used in a clinical trial in that container; and 'assembly' has a corresponding meaning: Medicines for Human Use (Clinical Trials) Regulations 2004, SI 2004/1031, reg 2(1). 'Container', in relation to an investigational medicinal product, means the bottle, jar, box, packet or other receptacle which contains or is to contain it, not being a capsule, cachet or other article in which the product is or is to be administered, and where any such receptacle is or is to be contained in another such receptacle, includes the former but does not include the latter receptacle: reg 2(1). 'Labelling', in relation to an investigational medicinal product, means affixing to or otherwise displaying on it a notice describing or otherwise relating to the contents; and 'label' has a corresponding meaning: reg 2(1). As to the meaning of 'medicinal product' see the Human Medicines Regulations 2012, SI 2012/1916, reg 2(1); and PARA 25 (definition applied by the Medicines for Human Use (Clinical Trials) Regulations 2004, SI 2004/1031, reg 2(1) (amended by SI 2012/1916)). As to the meaning of 'clinical trial' see PARA 107.

5 'Import' means import into the United Kingdom from a third country, whether by land, sea or air: Medicines for Human Use (Clinical Trials) Regulations 2004, SI 2004/1031, reg 2(1). As to the meaning of 'United Kingdom' see PARA 20 note 4. As to the meaning of 'third country' see PARA 121 note 5.

6 Medicines for Human Use (Clinical Trials) Regulations 2004, SI 2004/1031, reg 36(1). Such an authorisation is known as a 'manufacturing authorisation': regs 2(1), 36(1). As to the meaning of 'the licensing authority' see the Human Medicines Regulations 2012, SI 2012/1916, reg 6; PARA 35 note 1; definition applied by the Medicines for Human Use (Clinical Trials) Regulations 2004, SI 2004/1031, reg 2(1) (amended by SI 2012/1916).

7 Ie the restriction in the Medicines for Human Use (Clinical Trials) Regulations 2004, SI 2004/1031, reg 36(1).

8 Medicines for Human Use (Clinical Trials) Regulations 2004, SI 2004/1031, reg 49(1)(k). As to offences generally, defences and penalties see PARAS 138–140.

9 Medicines for Human Use (Clinical Trials) Regulations 2004, SI 2004/1031, reg 49(4).

10 Ie a duty or power imposed or conferred by or under the Medicines for Human Use (Clinical Trials) Regulations 2004, SI 2004/1031, the Human Medicines Regulations 2012, SI 2012/1916 or any other enactment.

11 Medicines for Human Use (Clinical Trials) Regulations 2004, SI 2004/1031, reg 49(5) (amended by SI 2012/1916).

98. Exemptions. The restriction[1] on the manufacturing, importing or the assembly of investigational medicinal products[2] does not apply: (1) to the manufacture or assembly of a medicinal product to the extent that such manufacture or assembly is in accordance with the terms and conditions of a marketing authorisation[3] relating to that product[4]; (2) to the assembly of an investigational medicinal product where certain conditions are satisfied[5]. The conditions are that the assembly is carried out in a hospital[6] or health centre[7] by a doctor[8], a pharmacist[9] or a person acting under the supervision of a pharmacist[10], and the investigational medicinal products are assembled exclusively for use in that hospital or health centre[11], or any other hospital or health centre which is a trial site[12] for the clinical trial in which the product is to be used[13].

1　Ie the restriction under the Medicines for Human Use (Clinical Trials) Regulations 2004, SI 2004/1031, reg 36(1) (see PARA 97).
2　As to the meanings of 'manufacture' and 'assemble' see PARA 97 notes 3, 4. As to the meaning of 'investigational medicinal product' see PARA 107 note 1.
3　As to the meaning of 'marketing authorisation' see PARA 107 note 1.
4　Medicines for Human Use (Clinical Trials) Regulations 2004, SI 2004/1031, reg 36(2).
5　Medicines for Human Use (Clinical Trials) Regulations 2004, SI 2004/1031, reg 37(1).
6　As to the meaning of 'hospital' see PARA 113 note 23.
7　Medicines for Human Use (Clinical Trials) Regulations 2004, SI 2004/1031, reg 37(2)(a)(i). As to the meaning of 'health centre' see PARA 113 note 23.
8　As to the meaning of 'doctor' see PARA 48 note 6.
9　'Pharmacist' means, in relation to Great Britain, a person registered in Part 1 or 4 of the register of pharmacists and pharmacy technicians maintained under the Pharmacy Order 2010, SI 2010/231, art 19(2) (see HEALTH SERVICES vol 54 (2008) PARA 821) and, in relation to Northern Ireland, a person registered in the register of pharmaceutical chemists for Northern Ireland or the register of visiting pharmaceutical chemists from a relevant European State maintained under the Pharmacy (Northern Ireland) Order 1976, SI 1976/1265, arts 6 and 9: Medicines for Human Use (Clinical Trials) Regulations 2004, SI 2004/1031, reg 2(1) (definition amended by SI 2010/231).
10　Medicines for Human Use (Clinical Trials) Regulations 2004, SI 2004/1031, reg 37(2)(a)(ii).
11　Medicines for Human Use (Clinical Trials) Regulations 2004, SI 2004/1031, reg 37(2)(b)(i).
12　As to the meaning of 'trial site' see PARA 113 note 4.
13　Medicines for Human Use (Clinical Trials) Regulations 2004, SI 2004/1031, reg 37(2)(b)(ii). As to the meaning of 'clinical trial' see PARA 107.

B. APPLICATION

99. Application for manufacturing authorisation. An application for the grant of a manufacturing authorisation[1] must be made to the licensing authority[2] in writing[3] and signed by or on behalf of the applicant[4]. Every application for the grant of a manufacturing authorisation must specify which, if any, of the standard provisions[5] it is desired be excluded or modified in relation to the grant of the authorisation[6], and must be accompanied by the specified particulars[7] and any fee which may be payable[8] in connection with that application[9]. The application and any accompanying material must be supplied to the licensing authority in the English language[10].

Any person[11] who, in the course of making an application for the grant of a manufacturing authorisation, provides to the licensing authority any relevant information[12] which is false or misleading in a material particular is guilty of an offence[13].

1　As to the meaning of 'manufacturing authorisation' see PARA 97.
2　Medicines for Human Use (Clinical Trials) Regulations 2004, SI 2004/1031, reg 38(1)(a). As to the meaning of 'the licensing authority' see the Human Medicines Regulations 2012, SI 2012/1916, reg 6; PARA 35 note 1; definition applied by the Medicines for Human Use (Clinical Trials) Regulations 2004, SI 2004/1031, reg 2(1) (amended by SI 2012/1916).
3　Medicines for Human Use (Clinical Trials) Regulations 2004, SI 2004/1031, reg 38(1)(b).
4　Medicines for Human Use (Clinical Trials) Regulations 2004, SI 2004/1031, reg 38(1)(c). As to references to 'signed' see PARA 114 note 11.
5　Ie referred to in the Medicines for Human Use (Clinical Trials) Regulations 2004, SI 2004/1031, reg 40(4): see PARA 101.
6　Medicines for Human Use (Clinical Trials) Regulations 2004, SI 2004/1031, reg 38(2).
7　Medicines for Human Use (Clinical Trials) Regulations 2004, SI 2004/1031, reg 38(3)(a). As to the specified particulars see Sch 6 (amended by SI 2006/1928)
8　Ie under the Medicines (Products for Human Use—Fees) Regulations 2012, SI 2012/504: see PARA 30. No fee need accompany an application for the grant of a manufacturing authorisation where arrangements have been made with the licensing authority for the payment of the fee referred to in the Medicines for Human Use (Clinical Trials) Regulations 2004, SI 2004/1031, reg 38(3)(b) other than at the time of the application: reg 38(3A) (added by SI 2006/1928).

9   Medicines for Human Use (Clinical Trials) Regulations 2004, SI 2004/1031, reg 38(3)(b) (amended by SI 2012/504).
10 Medicines for Human Use (Clinical Trials) Regulations 2004, SI 2004/1031, reg 38(4).
11 As to the meaning of 'person' see PARA 45 note 2.
12 As to the meaning of 'relevant information' see PARA 114 note 15.
13 Medicines for Human Use (Clinical Trials) Regulations 2004, SI 2004/1031, reg 50(1)(c). As to offences generally, defences and penalties see PARAS 138–140.

100. Consideration of application for manufacturing authorisation. The licensing authority[1] must[2] consider a valid application[3] for a manufacturing authorisation[4] and must grant, or refuse to grant, an authorisation within a period not exceeding 90 days from the date the application is received[5]. Following receipt of an application, the licensing authority may give a notice in writing to the applicant requesting him to provide further information relating to the specified[6] particulars[7] or the qualified person[8].

If the application for a manufacturing authorisation relates, wholly or partially, to the importation[9] of investigational medicinal products[10], the licensing authority may, if it thinks fit, require the production by the applicant of an undertaking, given by the manufacturer[11] of any such products, to permit the premises where they are or are to be manufactured[12], and the operations carried on or to be carried on in the course of manufacturing them[13], to be inspected by or on behalf of the licensing authority[14].

1   As to the meaning of 'the licensing authority' see the Human Medicines Regulations 2012, SI 2012/1916, reg 6; PARA 35 note 1; definition applied by the Medicines for Human Use (Clinical Trials) Regulations 2004, SI 2004/1031, reg 2(1) (amended by SI 2012/1916).
2   Ie subject to the Medicines for Human Use (Clinical Trials) Regulations 2004, SI 2004/1031, reg 39(3) (see note 5), reg 40 (see PARA 101).
3   'Valid application' means an application which complies with the provisions of the Medicines for Human Use (Clinical Trials) Regulations 2004, SI 2004/1031, reg 38 (see PARA 99): reg 39(5).
4   As to the meaning of 'manufacturing authorisation' see PARA 97.
5   Medicines for Human Use (Clinical Trials) Regulations 2004, SI 2004/1031, reg 39(1). Where the licensing authority gives a notice pursuant to reg 39(2) (see the text to notes 6–8), the period for granting or refusing to grant an authorisation is suspended from the date the notice is given and recommences only on receipt of the information requested: reg 39(3).
6   Ie specified in the Medicines for Human Use (Clinical Trials) Regulations 2004, SI 2004/1031, reg 38(3): see PARA 99.
7   Medicines for Human Use (Clinical Trials) Regulations 2004, SI 2004/1031, reg 39(2)(a). See also note 5.
8   Medicines for Human Use (Clinical Trials) Regulations 2004, SI 2004/1031, reg 39(2)(b). See also note 5. As to the meaning of 'qualified person' see PARA 104 note 2. It is an offence for a person to provide false or misleading information in response to such a notice: see reg 50(1)(c); and PARA 99.
9   As to the meaning of 'import' see PARA 97 note 5.
10 As to the meaning of 'investigational medicinal product' see PARA 107 note 1.
11 As to the meaning of 'manufacture' see PARA 97 note 3.
12 Medicines for Human Use (Clinical Trials) Regulations 2004, SI 2004/1031, reg 39(4)(a).
13 Medicines for Human Use (Clinical Trials) Regulations 2004, SI 2004/1031, reg 39(4)(b).
14 Medicines for Human Use (Clinical Trials) Regulations 2004, SI 2004/1031, reg 39(4).

101. Grant or refusal of manufacturing authorisation. The licensing authority[1] must grant a manufacturing authorisation[2] only if:
(1)   the applicant: (a) has complied with the requirements[3] relating to applications[4]; (b) has at his disposal the services of staff and suitable and sufficient premises, technical equipment and control facilities complying with specified requirements[5], as regards the manufacture[6] or import[7], and control, of the products to which the authorisation relates

and the storage of such products[8]; (c) has at his disposal the services of at least one qualified person[9]; and (d) if a notice has been given[10] requesting further information, has provided the information requested by the licensing authority[11]; and

(2)   it has established that the particulars supplied[12] with the application are accurate[13].

Subject to these provisions, the licensing authority may grant a manufacturing authorisation in respect of any or all of the descriptions of investigational medicinal products[14], the manufacturing, assembling[15] or importation operations[16], or the premises[17], specified in the application[18]. The licensing authority may grant a manufacturing authorisation containing any of the specified provisions[19] to be incorporated in the authorisation[20], or such other provisions as the licensing authority considers appropriate[21].

Where the licensing authority refuses to grant a manufacturing authorisation[22], or grants a manufacturing authorisation otherwise than in accordance with the application[23], and the applicant requests the authority to state its reasons, the authority must give the applicant a notice in writing stating the reasons for its decision[24].

1   As to the meaning of 'the licensing authority' see the Human Medicines Regulations 2012, SI 2012/1916, reg 6; PARA 35 note 1; definition applied by the Medicines for Human Use (Clinical Trials) Regulations 2004, SI 2004/1031, reg 2(1) (amended by SI 2012/1916).
2   As to the meaning of 'manufacturing authorisation' see PARA 97. As to the consideration, grant or refusal of such authorisations see PARAS 100–101. As to the requirement for such authorisations see PARA 97.
3   Ie the requirements of the Medicines for Human Use (Clinical Trials) Regulations 2004, SI 2004/1031, reg 38: see PARA 99.
4   Medicines for Human Use (Clinical Trials) Regulations 2004, SI 2004/1031, reg 40(1)(a)(i).
5   Ie the requirements of Commission Directive (EC) 2003/94 (OJ L262, 14.10.2003, p 22) laying down the principles and guidelines of good manufacturing practice for medicinal products for human use and for investigational medicinal products for human use.
6   As to the meaning of 'manufacture' see PARA 97 note 3.
7   As to the meaning of 'import' see PARA 97 note 5.
8   Medicines for Human Use (Clinical Trials) Regulations 2004, SI 2004/1031, reg 40(1)(a)(ii) (substituted by SI 2006/1928).
9   Medicines for Human Use (Clinical Trials) Regulations 2004, SI 2004/1031, reg 40(1)(a)(iii). As to the meaning of 'qualified person' see PARA 104 note 2.
10 Ie under the Medicines for Human Use (Clinical Trials) Regulations 2004, SI 2004/1031, reg 39(2): see PARA 100.
11 Medicines for Human Use (Clinical Trials) Regulations 2004, SI 2004/1031, reg 40(1)(a)(iv).
12 Ie pursuant to the Medicines for Human Use (Clinical Trials) Regulations 2004, SI 2004/1031, reg 38(3): see PARA 99.
13 Medicines for Human Use (Clinical Trials) Regulations 2004, SI 2004/1031, reg 40(1)(b).
14 Medicines for Human Use (Clinical Trials) Regulations 2004, SI 2004/1031, reg 40(2)(a). As to the meaning of 'investigational medicinal product' see PARA 107 note 1.
15 As to the meaning of 'assemble' see PARA 97 note 4.
16 Medicines for Human Use (Clinical Trials) Regulations 2004, SI 2004/1031, reg 40(2)(b).
17 Medicines for Human Use (Clinical Trials) Regulations 2004, SI 2004/1031, reg 40(2)(c).
18 Medicines for Human Use (Clinical Trials) Regulations 2004, SI 2004/1031, reg 40(2).
19 The provisions specified:
    (1)   in the case of a manufacturing authorisation relating to the manufacture or assembly of investigational medicinal products, in the Medicines for Human Use (Clinical Trials) Regulations 2004, SI 2004/1031, Sch 7 Pt 2 (reg 40(4)(a)); and
    (2)   in the case of a manufacturing authorisation relating to the importation of investigational medicinal products, in Sch 7 Pt 3 (reg 40(4)(b)),
    may be incorporated by the licensing authority in any manufacturing authorisation, with or without modifications, and either generally or in relation to investigational medicinal products of any particular class (reg 40(4)).
20 Medicines for Human Use (Clinical Trials) Regulations 2004, SI 2004/1031, reg 40(3)(a).

21 Medicines for Human Use (Clinical Trials) Regulations 2004, SI 2004/1031, reg 40(3)(b).
22 Medicines for Human Use (Clinical Trials) Regulations 2004, SI 2004/1031, reg 40(6)(a).
23 Medicines for Human Use (Clinical Trials) Regulations 2004, SI 2004/1031, reg 40(6)(b).
24 Medicines for Human Use (Clinical Trials) Regulations 2004, SI 2004/1031, reg 40(6). As to the procedure where the licensing authority refuses to grant a manufacturing authorisation or grants a manufacturing authorisation otherwise than in accordance with the application see PARA 102.

102. Procedural provisions. If the licensing authority[1] proposes:

(1) not to grant a manufacturing authorisation[2];

(2) to grant an authorisation other than in accordance with the application[3]; or

(3) to revoke, vary or suspend an authorisation[4],

the authority must notify the applicant or holder[5] accordingly[6].

The applicant or holder to whom notice is given may, within the time allowed[7] after the notification was given, notify the licensing authority that he wishes to appear before and be heard by a person appointed by the licensing authority with respect to the decision[8], or make representations in writing to the licensing authority with respect to the decision referred to in the notice[9]. If the applicant or holder makes written representations, the licensing authority must take those representations into account before deciding whether to grant the authorisation[10], revoke, vary or suspend the authorisation[11], or confirm or alter its decision[12], as the case may be[13].

If the applicant or holder gives notice of his wish to appear before or be heard by a person appointed by the licensing authority, the authority must make that appointment[14] and arrange for the applicant or holder who gave notice to have an opportunity of appearing before the person appointed[15]. The applicant or holder must, before the end of the period of three months beginning with the date of his notice[16], provide the person appointed with a written summary of the oral representations he intends to make[17] and any documents on which he wishes to rely in support of those representations[18]. If the applicant or holder fails to comply with the time limit, or any extended time limit, he may not appear before or be heard by the person appointed[19] and the licensing authority must decide whether to grant the authorisation, revoke, vary or suspend the authorisation, or confirm or alter its decision, as the case may be[20].

At the hearing before the person appointed, both the applicant or holder and the licensing authority may make representations[21] and, if the applicant or holder so requests, the hearing must be in public[22]. After the hearing, the person appointed must provide a report to the licensing authority[23], and the licensing authority must take this report into account and decide whether to grant the authorisation, revoke, vary or suspend the authorisation, or confirm or alter its decision, as the case may be[24]. The licensing authority must then notify the applicant or holder of its decision[25] and, if the applicant or holder so requests, provide him with a copy of the report of the person appointed[26].

1 As to the meaning of 'the licensing authority' see the Human Medicines Regulations 2012, SI 2012/1916, reg 6; PARA 35 note 1; definition applied by the Medicines for Human Use (Clinical Trials) Regulations 2004, SI 2004/1031, reg 2(1) (amended by SI 2012/1916).

2 Medicines for Human Use (Clinical Trials) Regulations 2004, SI 2004/1031, reg 40(5), Sch 8 para 2(a). As to the meaning of 'manufacturing authorisation' see PARA 97. As to the requirement for such authorisations see PARA 97. As to applications for such authorisations and the determination of applications see PARAS 99–101.

3 Medicines for Human Use (Clinical Trials) Regulations 2004, SI 2004/1031, Sch 8 para 2(b).

4 Medicines for Human Use (Clinical Trials) Regulations 2004, SI 2004/1031, regs 44(6), 45(3), Sch 8 para 2(c). Schedule 8 para 2 does not apply to the suspension of an authorisation where it appears to the licensing authority that, in the interests of safety, it is necessary to suspend the

authorisation with immediate effect for a period not exceeding 3 months: Sch 8 para 6(1). If, after the suspension has taken effect, it appears to the licensing authority that the authorisation should be further suspended or revoked, the licensing authority must proceed in accordance with Sch 8 paras 2–5: Sch 8 para 6(2). As to the variation of an authorisation see PARA 105; and as to the suspension and revocation of authorisations see PARA 106. As to the meaning of 'month' see PARA 43 note 3.

5 Any reference to the holder of a manufacturing authorisation must be construed as a reference to the holder of such an authorisation which is for the time being in force: Medicines for Human Use (Clinical Trials) Regulations 2004, SI 2004/1031, reg 2(2).

6 Medicines for Human Use (Clinical Trials) Regulations 2004, SI 2004/1031, Sch 8 para 2. Any such notification must include a statement of the proposals of the licensing authority and of the reasons for them: Sch 8 para 3.

7 'Time allowed' means the period of 28 days or such extended period as the licensing authority may in any particular case allow: Medicines for Human Use (Clinical Trials) Regulations 2004, SI 2004/1031, Sch 8 para 1.

8 Medicines for Human Use (Clinical Trials) Regulations 2004, SI 2004/1031, Sch 8 para 4(1)(a) (Sch 8 paras 4, 5 substituted by SI 2005/2754).

9 Medicines for Human Use (Clinical Trials) Regulations 2004, SI 2004/1031, Sch 8 para 4(1)(b) (as substituted: see note 8).

10 Medicines for Human Use (Clinical Trials) Regulations 2004, SI 2004/1031, Sch 8 para 4(2)(a) (as substituted: see note 8).

11 Medicines for Human Use (Clinical Trials) Regulations 2004, SI 2004/1031, Sch 8 para 4(2)(b) (as substituted: see note 8).

12 Medicines for Human Use (Clinical Trials) Regulations 2004, SI 2004/1031, Sch 8 para 4(2)(c) (as substituted: see note 8).

13 Medicines for Human Use (Clinical Trials) Regulations 2004, SI 2004/1031, Sch 8 para 4(2) (as substituted: see note 8).

14 Medicines for Human Use (Clinical Trials) Regulations 2004, SI 2004/1031, Sch 8 para 5(1)(a) (as substituted: see note 8). The person appointed must not be, or at any time have been, a member of the Commission on Human Medicines, an expert committee appointed by the licensing authority, an expert advisory group within the meaning of the Human Medicines Regulations 2012, SI 2012/1916, reg 14, the British Pharmacopoeia Commission or any of its sub-committees, the Medicines Commission formerly established under the Medicines Act 1968 s 2 or any of its committees, the Advisory Board on the Registration of Homoeopathic Products formerly established under s 4 or any of its committees or the Herbal Medicines Advisory Committee formerly established under s 4 or any of its sub-committees or any of its expert advisory groups, the former Medicines Commission or any of its committees; and must not be an officer or servant of a Minister of the Crown, the Scottish minister, the Welsh ministers or a Northern Ireland minster (Medicines for Human Use (Clinical Trials) Regulations 2004, SI 2004/1031, Sch 8 para 5(2) (as so substituted; amended by SI 2012/1916)).

15 Medicines for Human Use (Clinical Trials) Regulations 2004, SI 2004/1031, Sch 8 para 5(1)(b) (as substituted: see note 8).

16 If the applicant or holder so requests, the person appointed may, after consulting the licensing authority, extend the time limit up to a maximum period of 6 months beginning with the date of the notice: Medicines for Human Use (Clinical Trials) Regulations 2004, SI 2004/1031, Sch 8 para 5(4) (as substituted: see note 8). The applicant or holder may not submit any additional written representations or documents once the time limit has expired, except with the permission of the person appointed: Sch 8 para 5(6) (as so substituted). As to the meaning of 'month' see PARA 43 note 3.

17 Medicines for Human Use (Clinical Trials) Regulations 2004, SI 2004/1031, Sch 8 para 5(3)(a) (as substituted: see note 8).

18 Medicines for Human Use (Clinical Trials) Regulations 2004, SI 2004/1031, Sch 8 para 5(3)(b) (as substituted: see note 8).

19 Medicines for Human Use (Clinical Trials) Regulations 2004, SI 2004/1031, Sch 8 para 5(5)(a) (as substituted: see note 8).

20 Medicines for Human Use (Clinical Trials) Regulations 2004, SI 2004/1031, Sch 8 para 5(5)(b) (as substituted: see note 8).

21 Medicines for Human Use (Clinical Trials) Regulations 2004, SI 2004/1031, Sch 8 para 5(7) (as substituted: see note 8).

22 Medicines for Human Use (Clinical Trials) Regulations 2004, SI 2004/1031, Sch 8 para 5(8) (as substituted: see note 8).

23 Medicines for Human Use (Clinical Trials) Regulations 2004, SI 2004/1031, Sch 8 para 5(9)(a) (as substituted: see note 8).

24 Medicines for Human Use (Clinical Trials) Regulations 2004, SI 2004/1031, Sch 8 para 5(9)(b) (as substituted: see note 8).
25 Medicines for Human Use (Clinical Trials) Regulations 2004, SI 2004/1031, Sch 8 para 5(10)(a) (as substituted: see note 8).
26 Medicines for Human Use (Clinical Trials) Regulations 2004, SI 2004/1031, Sch 8 para 5(10)(b) (as substituted: see note 8).

103.   Application and effect of manufacturing authorisation. A manufacturing authorisation[1] applies only in relation to the descriptions of investigational medicinal products[2], the manufacturing[3], assembling[4] or importation[5] operations[6], in the case of an authorisation relating to the inactivation of viral or non-conventional agents, the manufacturing process[7], and the premises[8], specified in the application[9] and in respect of which the authorisation is granted[10]. The holder of a manufacturing authorisation[11] must comply with the principles and guidelines of good manufacturing practice[12], the provisions[13] subject to which the authorisation is granted[14], allow the licensing authority access to his premises at any reasonable time[15] and put and keep in place arrangements which enable the qualified person to carry out his duties, including placing at his disposal all the necessary facilities[16]. Any person[17] who contravenes these provisions is guilty of an offence[18].

1 As to the meaning of 'manufacturing authorisation' see PARA 97.
2 Medicines for Human Use (Clinical Trials) Regulations 2004, SI 2004/1031, reg 41(a). As to the meaning of 'investigational medicinal product' see PARA 107 note 1.
3 As to the meaning of 'manufacture' see PARA 97 note 3.
4 As to the meaning of 'assemble' see PARA 97 note 4.
5 As to the meaning of 'import' see PARA 97 note 5.
6 Medicines for Human Use (Clinical Trials) Regulations 2004, SI 2004/1031, reg 41(b).
7 Medicines for Human Use (Clinical Trials) Regulations 2004, SI 2004/1031, reg 41(bb) (added by SI 2006/1928).
8 Medicines for Human Use (Clinical Trials) Regulations 2004, SI 2004/1031, reg 41(c).
9 Ie the application made pursuant to the Medicines for Human Use (Clinical Trials) Regulations 2004, SI 2004/1031, reg 38: see PARA 99.
10 Medicines for Human Use (Clinical Trials) Regulations 2004, SI 2004/1031, reg 41. As to the requirement for such authorisations see PARA 97. As to the determination of applications see PARAS 100–102.
11 As to references to 'the holder of a manufacturing authorisation' see PARA 102 note 5.
12 Medicines for Human Use (Clinical Trials) Regulations 2004, SI 2004/1031, reg 42(a) (substituted by SI 2006/1928). 'The principles and guidelines of good manufacturing practice' means the principles and guidelines of good manufacturing practice set out in Commission Directive (EC) 2003/94 (OJ L262, 14.10.2003, p 22): Medicines for Human Use (Clinical Trials) Regulations 2004, SI 2004/1031, reg 2(1).
13 Ie the provisions referred to in the Medicines for Human Use (Clinical Trials) Regulations 2004, SI 2004/1031, reg 40(3): see PARA 101.
14 Medicines for Human Use (Clinical Trials) Regulations 2004, SI 2004/1031, reg 42(b) (as substituted: see note 12).
15 Medicines for Human Use (Clinical Trials) Regulations 2004, SI 2004/1031, reg 42(c) (as substituted: see note 12).
16 Medicines for Human Use (Clinical Trials) Regulations 2004, SI 2004/1031, reg 42(d) (as substituted: see note 12).
17 As to the meaning of 'person' see PARA 45 note 2.
18 Medicines for Human Use (Clinical Trials) Regulations 2004, SI 2004/1031, reg 49(1)(l). As to offences generally, defences and penalties see PARAS 138–140.

104.   Qualified persons. The holder of a manufacturing authorisation[1] must have at his disposal the services of at least one qualified person[2] who is responsible for carrying out the specified duties[3] in respect of the investigational medicinal products manufactured[4], assembled[5] or imported[6] in accordance with the authorisation in question[7]. If the holder of the authorisation satisfies the requirements as to qualifications and experience[8], he may act as the qualified person for the purposes of that authorisation[9]. A qualified person must perform his functions in accordance with the Code of Practice for Qualified Persons in the Pharmaceutical Industry, published jointly by the Institute of Biology, the Royal Pharmaceutical Society of Great Britain and the Royal Society of Chemistry in March 2004[10].

Where, after giving the holder of the authorisation and the person acting as a qualified person the opportunity of making representations to it, orally or in writing, the licensing authority is of the opinion that:

(1)   the person so acting does not satisfy the provisions[11] or requirements[12] as respects qualifications and experience[13]; or

(2)   he is failing to carry out the duties[14] of a qualified person adequately or at all[15],

and has notified the holder of the authorisation accordingly in writing, the holder of the authorisation must not permit that person to act as a qualified person[16].

Any person[17] who contravenes the requirement to have at his disposal the services of a qualified person[18] or not to permit a person to act as a qualified person[19] commits an offence[20]; and any person who, for the purpose of being engaged as a qualified person, provides to the licensing authority or to the holder of a manufacturing authorisation any information which is false or misleading in a material particular is guilty of an offence[21].

1   As to references to 'the holder of a manufacturing authorisation' see PARA 102 note 5.
2   'Qualified person' means:
    (1)   a person who as respects qualifications and experience satisfies the requirements of Council Directive (EC) 2001/83 (OJ L311, 28.11.2001, p 67) on the Community code relating to medicinal products for human use, art 49 or 50 (Medicines for Human Use (Clinical Trials) Regulations 2004, SI 2004/1031, reg 2(1)); or
    (2)   a person who, without satisfying those requirements:
        (a)   has been engaged in activities equivalent to those to be performed in accordance with the Medicines for Human Use (Clinical Trials) Regulations 2004, SI 2004/1031, reg 43(2) (see the text to notes 4–7) in respect of investigational medicinal products for a period of at least 6 months prior to 1 May 2004 (reg 2(1));
        (b)   has, in accordance with Sch 6 para 6(1) (see PARA 99), been named as a qualified person in a valid application for a manufacturing authorisation made prior to 1 May 2006 (reg 2(1)); and
        (c)   is a member of the Institute of Biology, the Pharmaceutical Society, the Royal Society of Chemistry, or such other body as may appear to the licensing authority to be an appropriate body for these purposes, or is the holder of a diploma, certificate or other evidence of formal qualifications awarded on completion of a university or other higher education course of study in pharmacy, chemistry, medicine, biology or a related life science, which the licensing authority has stated in a notice in writing to that person to be qualifications sufficient for the purpose of performing the functions of a qualified person (reg 2(1)).
    The holder of the authorisation may regard a person as satisfying the provisions of Council Directive (EC) 2001/83 (OJ L311, 28.11.2001, p 67) art 49 or 50 as respects formal qualifications if he produces evidence that he is a member of the Institute of Biology, the Pharmaceutical Society, the Royal Society of Chemistry, or such other body as may appear to the licensing authority to be an appropriate body for these purposes, and he is regarded by the body of which he is a member as satisfying those provisions: Medicines for Human Use (Clinical Trials) Regulations 2004, SI 2004/1031, reg 43(5). This provision is expressed to be without prejudice to reg 43(6): see the text to notes 11–16. As to the meaning of 'month' see PARA 43 note 3.
    As to the meaning of 'investigational medicinal product' see PARA 107 note 1. As to the meaning of 'manufacturing authorisation' see PARA 97. 'Pharmaceutical Society' in relation to Great Britain means the Royal Pharmaceutical Society of Great Britain, and in relation to

Northern Ireland means the Pharmaceutical Society of Northern Ireland: reg 2(1). As to the Royal Pharmaceutical Society of Great Britain see MEDICAL PROFESSIONS vol 74 (2011) PARA 785 et seq. As to the meaning of 'the licensing authority' see the Human Medicines Regulations 2012, SI 2012/1916, reg 6; PARA 35 note 1; definition applied by the Medicines for Human Use (Clinical Trials) Regulations 2004, SI 2004/1031, reg 2(1) (amended by SI 2012/1916).

3 Medicines for Human Use (Clinical Trials) Regulations 2004, SI 2004/1031, reg 43(1). The specified duties are those specified in European Parliament and Council Directive (EC) 2001/20 (OJ L121, 1.5.2001, p 34) on the approximation of the laws, regulations and administrative provisions of the Member States relating to the implementation of good clinical practice in the conduct of clinical trials on medicinal products for human use, art 13(3), (4), carried out in accordance with that article: Medicines for Human Use (Clinical Trials) Regulations 2004, SI 2004/1031, reg 43(2).

4 As to the meaning of 'manufacture' see PARA 97 note 3.

5 As to the meaning of 'assemble' see PARA 97 note 4.

6 As to the meaning of 'import' see PARA 97 note 5.

7 Medicines for Human Use (Clinical Trials) Regulations 2004, SI 2004/1031, reg 43(2). As to the requirement for such authorisations see PARA 97; and as to the determination of applications for authorisations see PARAS 100–102. As to the application and effect of authorisations see PARA 103.

8 Ie as specified in head (1) or head (2) of the definition of 'qualified person': see note 2.

9 Medicines for Human Use (Clinical Trials) Regulations 2004, SI 2004/1031, reg 43(4).

10 Medicines for Human Use (Clinical Trials) Regulations 2004, SI 2004/1031, reg 43(3). A copy of the Code of Practice may be obtained by writing to the Institute of Biology, 20 Queensbury Place, London SW7 2DZ; the Royal Pharmaceutical Society of Great Britain, 1 Lambeth High Street, London SE1 7JN; or the Royal Society of Chemistry, Burlington House, Piccadilly, London W1V 0BN.

11 Ie the provisions of Council Directive (EC) 2001/83 (OJ L311, 28.11.2001, p 67) arts 49, 50.

12 Ie as specified in head (2) of the definition of 'qualified person': see note 2.

13 Medicines for Human Use (Clinical Trials) Regulations 2004, SI 2004/1031, reg 43(6)(a)(i), (ii).

14 Ie referred to in the Medicines for Human Use (Clinical Trials) Regulations 2004, SI 2004/1031, reg 43(2): see the text to notes 4–7.

15 Medicines for Human Use (Clinical Trials) Regulations 2004, SI 2004/1031, reg 43(6)(b).

16 Medicines for Human Use (Clinical Trials) Regulations 2004, SI 2004/1031, reg 43(6).

17 As to the meaning of 'person' see PARA 45 note 2.

18 Ie under the Medicines for Human Use (Clinical Trials) Regulations 2004, SI 2004/1031, reg 43(1): see the text to notes 1–3.

19 Ie under the Medicines for Human Use (Clinical Trials) Regulations 2004, SI 2004/1031, reg 43(6): see the text to notes 11–16.

20 Medicines for Human Use (Clinical Trials) Regulations 2004, SI 2004/1031, reg 49(1)(m). As to offences generally, defences and penalties see PARAS 138–140.

21 Medicines for Human Use (Clinical Trials) Regulations 2004, SI 2004/1031, reg 50(3). See note 20.

105. Variation of manufacturing authorisation. The licensing authority[1] may vary a manufacturing authorisation[2], whether on the application of the holder of the authorisation[3] or otherwise[4]. If the holder of a manufacturing authorisation makes a valid application[5] to vary the manufacturing authorisation, the licensing authority must consider the application and, in a case where the effect of the variation would be to change[6] the types of investigational medicinal products[7], the manufacturing[8], assembling[9] or importation[10] operations[11], the manufacturing process[12], the premises[13], the technical equipment and control facilities[14] or the staff, including the qualified person[15], in respect of which the authorisation has been granted, may vary or refuse to vary the authorisation within a period not exceeding 30 days from the date the application is received[16]. In any other case, the authority may vary or refuse to vary the authorisation within such period as it considers appropriate[17]. Following receipt of a valid application to vary a manufacturing authorisation, the licensing authority may give a notice in writing to the applicant requesting him to provide further information relating to the contents of the application or any particulars relevant to the application[18]. Where the licensing authority varies a manufacturing authorisation otherwise than in accordance with a valid application by the holder of the authorisation[19] or, after consideration of such an application, refuses to vary a manufacturing authorisation[20], the licensing authority must notify the holder of that authorisation in writing, stating the reasons for its decision[21].

Any person[22] who in the course of making an application for the variation of a manufacturing authorisation provides to the licensing authority any relevant information[23] which is false or misleading in a material particular is guilty of an offence[24].

1   As to the meaning of 'the licensing authority' see the Human Medicines Regulations 2012, SI 2012/1916, reg 6; PARA 35 note 1; definition applied by the Medicines for Human Use (Clinical Trials) Regulations 2004, SI 2004/1031, reg 2(1) (amended by SI 2012/1916).

2   As to the meaning of 'manufacturing authorisation' see PARA 97. As to the requirement for manufacturing authorisations see PARA 97; and as to the application and effect of authorisations see PARA 103. As to applications for authorisations and their determination see PARAS 99–102.

3   As to references to 'the holder of a manufacturing authorisation' see PARA 102 note 5.

4   Medicines for Human Use (Clinical Trials) Regulations 2004, SI 2004/1031, reg 44(1). The provisions of Sch 8 (see PARA 102) have effect where the licensing authority proposes to vary a manufacturing authorisation otherwise than on the application of the holder of the authorisation: reg 44(6).

5   'Valid application' means an application made to the licensing authority, in writing and signed by or on behalf of the applicant, specifying the variation requested by the applicant, accompanied by such particulars as are necessary to enable the licensing authority to consider the application, and unless arrangements have been made with the licensing authority for the payment of any relevant fee other than at the time of the application, any such fee; and the application and any accompanying material must be in the English language: Medicines for Human Use (Clinical Trials) Regulations 2004, SI 2004/1031, reg 44(8) (substituted by SI 2006/1928). 'Any relevant fee' means, in relation to an application to vary a manufacturing authorisation, any fee which may be payable in connection with that application under the Medicines (Products for Human Use) (Fees) Regulations 2012, SI 2012/1916: Medicines for Human Use (Clinical Trials) Regulations 2004, SI 2004/1031, reg 44(8) (as so substituted; definition amended by SI 2012/1916). As to references to 'signed' see PARA 114 note 11.

6   Medicines for Human Use (Clinical Trials) Regulations 2004, SI 2004/1031, reg 44(2) (amended by SI 2006/1928).

7   Medicines for Human Use (Clinical Trials) Regulations 2004, SI 2004/1031, reg 44(2)(a)(i). As to the meaning of 'investigational medicinal product' see PARA 107 note 1.

8   As to the meaning of 'manufacture' see PARA 97 note 3.

9   As to the meaning of 'assemble' see PARA 97 note 4.

10   As to the meaning of 'import' see PARA 97 note 5.

11   Medicines for Human Use (Clinical Trials) Regulations 2004, SI 2004/1031, reg 44(2)(a)(ii).

12   Medicines for Human Use (Clinical Trials) Regulations 2004, SI 2004/1031, reg 44(2)(a)(iia) (added by SI 2006/1928).

13   Medicines for Human Use (Clinical Trials) Regulations 2004, SI 2004/1031, reg 44(2)(a)(iii).

14   Medicines for Human Use (Clinical Trials) Regulations 2004, SI 2004/1031, reg 44(2)(a)(iv).

15   Medicines for Human Use (Clinical Trials) Regulations 2004, SI 2004/1031, reg 44(2)(a)(v) (added by SI 2006/1928). As to the meaning of 'qualified person' see PARA 104 note 2.

16   Medicines for Human Use (Clinical Trials) Regulations 2004, SI 2004/1031, reg 44(2)(a). If the application falls within reg 44(2)(a), but it appears to the licensing authority to be necessary to conduct an inspection of any premises to which the variation relates, the authority may vary or refuse to vary the authorisation within a period not exceeding 90 days from the date the application is received: reg 44(3).

17   Medicines for Human Use (Clinical Trials) Regulations 2004, SI 2004/1031, reg 44(2)(b).

18   Medicines for Human Use (Clinical Trials) Regulations 2004, SI 2004/1031, reg 44(4). Where the licensing authority gives such a notice, and a period specified in reg 44(2)(a), (3) applies, that period is suspended from the date the notice is given and recommences only on receipt of the information requested: reg 44(5).

19   Medicines for Human Use (Clinical Trials) Regulations 2004, SI 2004/1031, reg 44(7)(a).

20 Medicines for Human Use (Clinical Trials) Regulations 2004, SI 2004/1031, reg 44(7)(b).

21 Medicines for Human Use (Clinical Trials) Regulations 2004, SI 2004/1031, reg 44(7).

22 As to the meaning of 'person' see PARA 45 note 2.

23 As to the meaning of 'relevant information' see PARA 114 note 15.

24 Medicines for Human Use (Clinical Trials) Regulations 2004, SI 2004/1031, reg 50(1)(c). As to offences generally, defences and penalties see PARAS 138–140.

106. Suspension and revocation of manufacturing authorisation. The licensing authority[1] may by a notice in writing to the holder of a manufacturing authorisation[2], forthwith or from a date specified in the notice, suspend the authorisation for such period as the authority may determine, or revoke the authorisation, on one or more of the following grounds[3]:

(1) the holder is not carrying out, or has indicated by a notice in writing that he is no longer to carry out, the manufacturing[4], assembly[5] or importation[6] operations to which the authorisation relates[7];

(2) the particulars accompanying the application[8] were false or incomplete in a material particular[9];

(3) a material change of circumstances has occurred in relation to any of those matters or particulars[10];

(4) the holder of the authorisation has failed to any material extent to comply with his obligations in relation to the authorisation[11] or the availability of the services of a qualified person[12];

(5) the holder has manufactured, assembled or, as the case may be, imported investigational medicinal products[13] otherwise than in accordance with the terms of the authorisation[14];

(6) the holder has manufactured or assembled investigational medicinal products otherwise than in accordance with:

  (a) in the case of products manufactured before a request for authorisation to conduct the clinical trial[15] involving those products has been made[16], the specification for the product provided by the person[17] who is to act as the sponsor[18] of the proposed clinical trial[19];

  (b) in the case of products manufactured for the purpose of export[20], the specification for the product provided by the person to whose order the products are manufactured[21]; or

  (c) in any other case, the specification for the product contained in the investigational medicinal product dossier[22] for that product[23];

(7) the qualified person[24] has failed to carry out his duties[25] adequately or at all[26]; and

(8) the holder of the authorisation does not have the staff, premises, equipment or facilities necessary for carrying out properly:

  (a) the manufacture or assembly operations to which the authorisation relates[27]; or

  (b) the importation operations to which the authorisation relates[28],

  including any handling, storage or distribution activities relating to those operations[29].

The suspension or revocation of an authorisation may be total[30], or limited to investigational medicinal products of one or more descriptions[31] or manufactured, assembled or stored on any particular premises or in a particular part of any premises[32]. Where the licensing authority suspends or revokes a manufacturing authorisation, it must notify the holder of that authorisation in writing, stating the reasons for its decision to suspend or revoke the authorisation[33].

1   As to the meaning of 'the licensing authority' see the Human Medicines Regulations 2012, SI 2012/1916, reg 6; PARA 35 note 1; definition applied by the Medicines for Human Use (Clinical Trials) Regulations 2004, SI 2004/1031, reg 2(1) (amended by SI 2012/1916).

2   As to the meaning of 'manufacturing authorisation' see PARA 97. As to references to 'the holder of a manufacturing authorisation' see PARA 102 note 5. As to the requirement for manufacturing authorisations see PARA 97; and as to the application and effect of authorisations see PARA 103. As to applications for authorisations and their determination see PARAS 99–102.

3   Medicines for Human Use (Clinical Trials) Regulations 2004, SI 2004/1031, reg 45(1). The provisions of Sch 8 (see PARA 102) have effect where the licensing authority proposes to suspend or revoke a manufacturing authorisation: reg 45(3).

4   As to the meaning of 'manufacture' see PARA 97 note 3.

5   As to the meaning of 'assembly' see PARA 97 note 4.

6   As to the meaning of 'import' see PARA 97 note 5.

7   Medicines for Human Use (Clinical Trials) Regulations 2004, SI 2004/1031, reg 45(1)(a).

8   Ie in accordance with the Medicines for Human Use (Clinical Trials) Regulations 2004, SI 2004/1031, reg 38(3): see PARA 99.

9   Medicines for Human Use (Clinical Trials) Regulations 2004, SI 2004/1031, reg 45(1)(b). As to the offence of providing false or misleading information in relation to an application see PARA 99.

10 Medicines for Human Use (Clinical Trials) Regulations 2004, SI 2004/1031, reg 45(1)(c).

11 Ie under the Medicines for Human Use (Clinical Trials) Regulations 2004, SI 2004/1031, reg 42: see PARA 103.

12 Medicines for Human Use (Clinical Trials) Regulations 2004, SI 2004/1031, reg 45(1)(d). The obligations in relation to a qualified person are those under reg 43(1): see PARA 104.

13 As to the meaning of 'investigational medicinal product' see PARA 107 note 1.

14 Medicines for Human Use (Clinical Trials) Regulations 2004, SI 2004/1031, reg 45(1)(e).

15 As to the meaning of 'clinical trial' see PARA 107.

16 Ie in accordance with the Medicines for Human Use (Clinical Trials) Regulations 2004, SI 2004/1031, reg 17 (see PARA 117) or any equivalent provisions in any EEA state other than the United Kingdom: reg 45(1)(f)(i). As to the meaning of 'EEA state' see PARA 107 note 1. As to the meaning of 'United Kingdom' see PARA 20 note 4.

17 As to the meaning of 'person' see PARA 45 note 2.

18 As to the meaning of 'sponsor' see PARA 107.

19 Medicines for Human Use (Clinical Trials) Regulations 2004, SI 2004/1031, reg 45(1)(f)(i).

20 'Export' means export to a third country from an EEA state, whether by land, sea or air: Medicines for Human Use (Clinical Trials) Regulations 2004, SI 2004/1031, reg 2(1). As to the meaning of 'third country' see PARA 121 note 5.

21 Medicines for Human Use (Clinical Trials) Regulations 2004, SI 2004/1031, reg 45(1)(f)(ii).

22 'Investigational medicinal product dossier' means, in relation to an investigational medicinal product, the dossier relating to that product which accompanies a request for authorisation to conduct a trial in which that product is or is to be used, in accordance with the Medicines for Human Use (Clinical Trials) Regulations 2004, SI 2004/1031, reg 17(2), Sch 3 para 11: reg 2(1).

23 Medicines for Human Use (Clinical Trials) Regulations 2004, SI 2004/1031, reg 45(1)(f)(iii).

24 As to the meaning of 'qualified person' see PARA 104 note 2.

25 Ie as referred to in the Medicines for Human Use (Clinical Trials) Regulations 2004, SI 2004/1031, reg 43(2): see PARA 104.

26 Medicines for Human Use (Clinical Trials) Regulations 2004, SI 2004/1031, reg 45(1)(g).

27 Medicines for Human Use (Clinical Trials) Regulations 2004, SI 2004/1031, reg 45(1)(h)(i).

28 Medicines for Human Use (Clinical Trials) Regulations 2004, SI 2004/1031, reg 45(1)(h)(ii).

29 Medicines for Human Use (Clinical Trials) Regulations 2004, SI 2004/1031, reg 45(1)(h).

30 Medicines for Human Use (Clinical Trials) Regulations 2004, SI 2004/1031, reg 45(2)(a).

31 Medicines for Human Use (Clinical Trials) Regulations 2004, SI 2004/1031, reg 45(2)(b)(i).

32 Medicines for Human Use (Clinical Trials) Regulations 2004, SI 2004/1031, reg 45(2)(b)(ii).

33 Medicines for Human Use (Clinical Trials) Regulations 2004, SI 2004/1031, reg 45(4).

(4) CLINICAL TRIALS

(i) In general

107. Meanings of 'clinical trial' and 'sponsor'. 'Clinical trial' means any investigation in human subjects[1], other than a non-interventional trial[2], intended:

(1) to discover or verify the clinical, pharmacological or other pharmacodynamic effects of one or more medicinal products;

(2) to identify any adverse reactions[3] to one or more such products; or

(3) to study absorption, distribution, metabolism and excretion of one or more such products,

with the object of ascertaining the safety or efficacy of those products[4].

'Sponsor' means, in relation to a clinical trial, the person[5] who takes responsibility for the initiation, management and financing, or for arranging the financing, of that trial[6]. If two or more persons take responsibility for those matters in relation to a clinical trial, those persons may take joint responsibility for carrying out the functions of the sponsor of that trial[7] or allocate responsibility for carrying out the functions of the sponsor of that trial[8].

In cases where responsibility is so allocated, one of those persons must be responsible for carrying out the functions of a sponsor in relation to authorisation for clinical trials and ethics committee opinion[9] and must make the request[10] for authorisation to conduct the trial[11]. After the clinical trial has been authorised by the licensing authority[12], a different person may be specified as responsible for carrying out the functions of the sponsor[13] by making a substantial amendment[14] to the terms of a clinical trial authorisation[15].

A person who is a sponsor of a clinical trial must be established in an EEA state[16], or have a legal representative who is so established[17].

1   'Subject' means, in relation to a clinical trial, an individual, whether a patient or not, who participates in a clinical trial as a recipient of an investigational medicinal product or of some other treatment or product, or, without receiving any treatment or product, as a control: Medicines for Human Use (Clinical Trials) Regulations 2004, SI 2004/1031, reg 2(1). 'Investigational medicinal product' means a pharmaceutical form of an active substance or placebo being tested, or to be tested, or used, or to be used, as a reference in a clinical trial, and includes a medicinal product which has a marketing authorisation but is, for the purposes of the trial: (1) used or assembled (formulated or packaged) in a way different from the form of the product authorised under the authorisation; (2) used for an indication not included in the summary of product characteristics under the authorisation for that product; or (3) used to gain further information about the form of that product as authorised under the authorisation: reg 2(1). 'Pharmaceutical form of an active substance' includes any substance or article in relation to which the Medicines for Human Use (Clinical Trials) Regulations 2004, SI 2004/1031 have effect by virtue of an order under the Medicines Act 1968 ss 104, 105 (which relate to the application of the Act to certain articles and substances which are not medicinal products: see PARA 28): Medicines for Human Use (Clinical Trials) Regulations 2004, SI 2004/1031, reg 2(1). As to the meaning of 'medicinal product' see the Human Medicines Regulations 2012, SI 2012/1916, reg 2(1); and PARA 25 (definition applied by the Medicines for Human Use (Clinical Trials) Regulations 2004, SI 2004/1031, reg 2(1) (amended by SI 2012/1916)). 'Marketing authorisation' means: (a) a marketing authorisation granted by the licensing authority under the Human Medicines Regulations 2012, SI 2012/1916 (see PARA 141 et seq); (b) a marketing authorisation issued by the competent authority of an EEA state, other than the United Kingdom, in accordance with Council Directive (EC) 2001/83 (OJ L311, 28.11.2001, p 67) on the Community code relating to medicinal products for human use; (c) a marketing authorisation granted by the European Commission under Council Regulation (EC) 2309/93 (OJ L214, 24.8.1993, p 1) or Parliament and Council Regulation (EC) 726/2004 (OJ L136, 30.4.2004, p 1); or (d) a product licence granted by the licensing authority for the purposes of the Medicines Act 1968 s 7 (repealed): Medicines for Human Use (Clinical Trials) Regulations 2004, SI 2004/1031, reg 2(1) (definition amended by SI 2005/2759; SI 2012/1916).

'EEA state' means a member state, Norway, Iceland or Liechtenstein: Medicines for Human Use (Clinical Trials) Regulations 2004, SI 2004/1031, reg 2(1) (definition substituted by SI 2006/1928). As to the meaning of 'the licensing authority' see the Human Medicines Regulations 2012, SI 2012/1916, reg 6; PARA 35 note 1; definition applied by the Medicines for Human Use (Clinical Trials) Regulations 2004, SI 2004/1031, reg 2(1) (amended by SI 2012/1916). As to the meaning of 'assemble' see PARA 97 note 4. As to the meaning of 'United Kingdom' see PARA 20 note 4.

2   'Non-interventional trial' means a study of one or more medicinal products which have a marketing authorisation, where the following conditions are met: (1) the products are prescribed in the usual manner in accordance with the terms of that authorisation; (2) the assignment of any patient involved in the study to a particular therapeutic strategy is not decided in advance by a protocol but falls within current practice; (3) the decision to prescribe a particular medicinal product is clearly separated from the decision to include the patient in the study; (4) no diagnostic or monitoring procedures are applied to the patients included in the study, other than those which are ordinarily applied in the course of the particular therapeutic strategy in question; and (5) epidemiological methods are to be used for the analysis of the data arising from the study: Medicines for Human Use (Clinical Trials) Regulations 2004, SI 2004/1031, reg 2(1). 'Protocol' means a document that describes the objectives, design, methodology, statistical considerations and organisation of a clinical trial: reg 2(1).

3   As to the meaning of 'adverse reaction' see PARA 132 note 3.

4   Medicines for Human Use (Clinical Trials) Regulations 2004, SI 2004/1031, reg 2(1).

5   As to the meaning of 'person' see PARA 45 note 2.

6   Medicines for Human Use (Clinical Trials) Regulations 2004, SI 2004/1031, regs 2(1), 3(1). A person who is a sponsor of a clinical trial in accordance with the Medicines for Human Use (Clinical Trials) Regulations 2004, SI 2004/1031 may delegate any or all of his functions under those regulations to any person but any such arrangement must not affect the responsibility of the sponsor: reg 3(12) (added by SI 2006/1928).

7   Medicines for Human Use (Clinical Trials) Regulations 2004, SI 2004/1031, reg 3(2)(a). If two or more persons take joint responsibility in accordance with reg 3(2)(a), any reference to the sponsor must, in relation to that trial, be construed as a reference to those persons (reg 3(3)(a)); and the provisions of reg 3(4)–(10) do not apply (reg 3(3)(b)).

8   Medicines for Human Use (Clinical Trials) Regulations 2004, SI 2004/1031, reg 3(2)(b). Such allocation must be in accordance with the provisions of reg 3(4)–(10): reg 3(3)(b).

9   Ie under the Medicines for Human Use (Clinical Trials) Regulations 2004, SI 2004/1031, Pt 3 (regs 11–27): see PARA 112 et seq.

10   Ie in accordance with the Medicines for Human Use (Clinical Trials) Regulations 2004, SI 2004/1031, reg 17: see PARA 117.

11   Medicines for Human Use (Clinical Trials) Regulations 2004, SI 2004/1031, reg 3(4). The request for authorisation must specify: (1) who is responsible for carrying out the functions of the sponsor under Pt 3 (ie authorisation for clinical trials and ethics committee opinion) (reg 3(5)(a)); (2) who is to be responsible for carrying out the functions of the sponsor under Pt 4 (regs 28–31) (ie goods clinical practice and the conduct of clinical trials: see PARA 126 et seq) (reg 3(5)(b)); and (3) who is to be responsible for carrying out the functions of the sponsor under Pt 5 (regs 32–35) (ie pharmacovigilance: see PARA 132 et seq) (reg 3(5)(c)).

Where a person is responsible for carrying out the functions of the sponsor under Pt 3 by virtue of reg 3(5), or is specified in accordance with reg 3(6) (see the text to notes 12–15) as responsible for those functions, any reference to the sponsor in that Part (except reg 15) (see PARA 115), Sch 3 Pts 2–4, Sch 5 in so far as it relates to decisions of the licensing authority under Pt 3, and Sch 12 (transitional provisions), must, in relation to the trial, be construed as a reference to that person: reg 3(7). Where a person is specified in accordance with reg 3(5) or reg 3(6) as responsible for carrying out the functions of the sponsor under Pt 4, any reference to the sponsor in that Part (except reg 28(1)) (see PARA 126), or Sch 5 in so far as it relates to notices under reg 31(1) (see PARA 130), must, in relation to the trial, be construed as a reference to that person: reg 3(8). Where a person is specified in accordance with reg 3(5) or reg 3(6) as responsible for carrying out the functions of the sponsor under Pt 5, any reference to the sponsor in that Part must, in relation to the trial, be construed as a reference to that person: reg 3(9). Any reference to the sponsor in reg 15, reg 28(1), Pts 2, 6–9 (regs 36–56) (see PARA 97 et seq), Sch 1 (see PARA 126), Sch 3 Pt 1, and Sch 7, must, in relation to the trial, include a reference to a person specified in accordance with reg 3(5) or reg 3(6): reg 3(10).

12   Ie in accordance with the Medicines for Human Use (Clinical Trials) Regulations 2004, SI 2004/1031, regs 18–20: see PARAS 118–120. As to the meaning of 'clinical trial' see PARA 107.

13   Ie under the Medicines for Human Use (Clinical Trials) Regulations 2004, SI 2004/1031, Pt 3, 4 or 5.

14 Ie in accordance with the Medicines for Human Use (Clinical Trials) Regulations 2004, SI 2004/1031, regs 24–26: see PARAS 123–125.
15 Medicines for Human Use (Clinical Trials) Regulations 2004, SI 2004/1031, reg 3(6). See also note 11.
16 Medicines for Human Use (Clinical Trials) Regulations 2004, SI 2004/1031, reg 3(11)(a) (amended by SI 2006/1928).
17 Medicines for Human Use (Clinical Trials) Regulations 2004, SI 2004/1031, reg 3(11)(b).

108.   Sponsor's responsibility for the investigator's brochure. The sponsor of a clinical trial[1] must:

(1)   ensure that the investigator's brochure[2] for that trial, and any update of that brochure, presents the information it contains in a concise, simple, objective, balanced and non-promotional form that enables a clinician or potential investigator to understand it and make an unbiased risk-benefit assessment of the appropriateness of the proposed clinical trial[3]; and

(2)   validate and update the investigator's brochure at least once a year[4].

It is an offence to contravene this provision[5].

1   As to the meaning of 'sponsor' and 'clinical trial' see PARA 107.
2   'Investigator's brochure' means a document containing a summary of the clinical and non-clinical data relating to an investigational medicinal product which are relevant to the study of the product in human subjects: Medicines for Human Use (Clinical Trials) Regulations 2004, SI 2004/1031, reg 2(1). As to the meaning of 'investigational medicinal product' see PARA 107 note 1.
3   Medicines for Human Use (Clinical Trials) Regulations 2004, SI 2004/1031, reg 3A(a) (added by SI 2006/1928).
4   Medicines for Human Use (Clinical Trials) Regulations 2004, SI 2004/1031, reg 3A(b) (as added: see note 3).
5   See the Medicines for Human Use (Clinical Trials) Regulations 2004, SI 2004/1031, reg 49(1)(a) (added by SI 2006/1928). As to offences generally, defences and penalties see PARAS 138–140.

109.   Competent authority. The competent authority[1] of the United Kingdom[2] is the licensing authority[3]. Except where any functions fall to be performed by the exercise of any powers or duties conferred[4] on a person or body other than the licensing authority[5], the licensing authority must perform, as respects the United Kingdom, the functions[6] of the member state[7].

1   Ie for the purposes of Parliament and Council Directive (EC) 2001/20 (OJ L121, 1.5.2001, p 34) on the approximation of the laws, regulations and administrative provisions of the member states relating to the implementation of good clinical practice in the conduct of clinical trials on medicinal products for human use and the purposes of Commission Directive (EC) 2005/28 (OJ L91, 9.4.2006, p 309–315) laying down principles and detailed guidelines for good clinical practice as regards investigational medicinal products for human use, as well as the requirements for authorisation of the manufacturing or importation of such products: Medicines for Human Use (Clinical Trials) Regulations 2004, SI 2004/1031, reg 2(1), 4(1) (both amended by SI 2006/1928).
2   As to the meaning of 'United Kingdom' see PARA 20 note 4.
3   Medicines for Human Use (Clinical Trials) Regulations 2004, SI 2004/1031, reg 4(1) (as amended: see note 1).
4   Ie by any provision of the Medicines for Human Use (Clinical Trials) Regulations 2004, SI 2004/1031, or by any provision of the Human Medicines Regulations 2012, SI 2012/1916 as applied by the Medicines for Human Use (Clinical Trials) Regulations 2004, SI 2004/1031: reg 4(3) (amended by SI 2012/1916).
5   Medicines for Human Use (Clinical Trials) Regulations 2004, SI 2004/1031, reg 4(3).
6   Ie under Parliament and Council Directive (EC) 2001/20 (OJ L121, 1.5.2001, p 34) and Commission Directive (EC) 2005/28 (OJ L91, 9.4.2006, p 309–315).
7   Medicines for Human Use (Clinical Trials) Regulations 2004, SI 2004/1031, reg 4(2).

(ii) Ethics Committees

110. United Kingdom Ethics Committees Authority. The body responsible for establishing, recognising and monitoring ethics committees[1] in the United Kingdom[2] is the United Kingdom Ethics Committees Authority[3]. The Authority consists of the Secretary of State for Health, the Welsh Ministers, the Scottish Ministers, and the Department for Health, Social Services and Public Safety for Northern Ireland[4]. The Authority must monitor the extent to which ethics committees adequately perform their functions[5], and may provide advice and assistance to ethics committees with respect to the performance of their functions[6].

The Authority may appoint such persons as it thinks necessary for the proper discharge by it of its functions; and those persons may be appointed on such terms and conditions, including conditions as to remuneration, benefits, allowances and reimbursement for expenses, as the Authority think fit[7]. Arrangements may be made between the Authority and any relevant authority[8] for any functions of the Authority to be exercised by, or by members of staff of, the relevant authority[9], or for the provision of staff, premises or administrative services by the relevant authority to the Authority[10].

The licensing authority and an ethics committee may disclose to each other any information acquired in carrying out their respective functions under the Medicines for Human Use (Clinical Trials) Regulations 2004[11] where disclosing such information may assist the other body in carrying out its functions[12].

1 As to the meaning of 'ethics committee' see PARA 111 note 2.
2 As to the meaning of 'United Kingdom' see PARA 20 note 4.
3 Medicines for Human Use (Clinical Trials) Regulations 2004, SI 2004/1031, reg 5(1). As to the establishment and recognition of ethics committees see PARA 111.
4 Medicines for Human Use (Clinical Trials) Regulations 2004, SI 2004/1031, reg 5(1)(a)–(d). As to the Secretary of State for Health see CONSTITUTIONAL LAW AND HUMAN RIGHTS vol 8(2) (Reissue) PARA 464.
    The functions of the Authority: (1) may, by agreement between them, be performed by any one of the Secretary of State for Health, the Welsh Ministers, the Scottish Ministers and the Department for Health, Social Services and Public Safety for Northern Ireland acting alone, or any two or more of them acting jointly (reg 5(2)(a)); and (2) may be performed by any one of the Secretary of State for Health, the Welsh Ministers, the Scottish Ministers and the Department for Health, Social Services and Public Safety for Northern Ireland acting alone solely in relation to a part of the United Kingdom with respect to which the Secretary of State, the Assembly, the Ministers or the Department, as the case may be, have responsibilities (reg 5(2)(b)). In the Medicines for Human Use (Clinical Trials) Regulations 2004, SI 2004/1031, the United Kingdom Ethics Committees Authority is referred to as 'the Authority', which means any one or more of the Secretary of State for Health, the Welsh Ministers, the Scottish Ministers and the Department for Health, Social Services and Public Safety for Northern Ireland, and, in the case of anything falling to be done by the Authority, means any one or more of them acting as mentioned in reg 5(2): reg 5(3).
5 Medicines for Human Use (Clinical Trials) Regulations 2004, SI 2004/1031, reg 10(1).
6 Medicines for Human Use (Clinical Trials) Regulations 2004, SI 2004/1031, reg 10(2).
7 Medicines for Human Use (Clinical Trials) Regulations 2004, SI 2004/1031, reg 5(4).
8 'Relevant authority' means any government department, local or public authority or holder of public office: Medicines for Human Use (Clinical Trials) Regulations 2004, SI 2004/1031, reg 5(7).
9 Medicines for Human Use (Clinical Trials) Regulations 2004, SI 2004/1031, reg 5(5)(a). Any such arrangements for the exercise of any functions of the Authority do not affect the responsibility of the Authority: reg 5(6).
10 Medicines for Human Use (Clinical Trials) Regulations 2004, SI 2004/1031, reg 5(5)(b).
11 Ie the Medicines for Human Use (Clinical Trials) Regulations 2004, SI 2004/1031.
12 Medicines for Human Use (Clinical Trials) Regulations 2004, SI 2004/1031, reg 27A (added by SI 2006/1928).

111.   Establishment and recognition of ethics committees. The United Kingdom Ethics Committees Authority[1] may establish ethics committees[2] to act for the entire United Kingdom[3] or for such areas of the United Kingdom[4], and in relation to such descriptions or classes of clinical trials[5], as the Authority considers appropriate[6]. The Authority may vary the area for which any committee it has established acts or, as the case may be, the descriptions or classes of clinical trials in relation to which such a committee acts[7], and may abolish any such committee[8].

The Authority may, by a notice in writing, recognise a committee as an ethics committee if an application in relation to that committee has been made[9] and it is satisfied that the proposed arrangements for the membership and operation of that ethics committee would enable that committee to perform the functions of an ethics committee adequately[10], and comply with other provisions[11] relating to such committees[12]. When recognising a committee, the Authority must specify whether the committee may act for the entire United Kingdom or only for a particular area of the United Kingdom[13], the description or class of clinical trial in relation to which it may act as an ethics committee[14], and any other conditions or limitations that apply to that committee[15]. The Authority may, where it considers it necessary or appropriate to do so, vary the area for which a recognised committee acts[16], vary the description or class of clinical trial in relation to which it may act as an ethics committee[17], or vary or revoke any conditions or limitations so imposed[18]. The Authority may revoke a recognition of an ethics committee if it is satisfied that specified provisions[19] are not complied with in relation to that committee[20], the committee is failing to perform its functions adequately or at all[21], or it is otherwise necessary or expedient to do so[22].

Where recognition of an ethics committee is revoked[23], abolished or ceases operation[24], if the person[25] who was the appointing authority[26] before revocation, abolition or the ceasing of operation of the committee (known as 'the old committee') is the Authority, that person may nominate another ethics committee as responsible for the work of the committee[27], and if the person was not the Authority, that person may only nominate an ethics committee with the approval of the Authority[28]. Where an ethics committee is nominated, that committee must consider any applications made[29] to the old committee, if the old committee had not given an opinion before the date of revocation, abolition or ceasing of operation[30]; and it is the relevant ethics committee for any clinical trial in relation to which the old committee had given[31] a favourable opinion[32].

1   As to the United Kingdom Ethics Committees Authority see PARA 110.
2   'Ethics committee' means: (1) a committee established or recognised in accordance with the Medicines for Human Use (Clinical Trials) Regulations 2004, SI 2004/1031, Pt 2 (regs 5–10); (2) the ethics committee constituted by regulations made by the Scottish Ministers under the Adults with Incapacity (Scotland) Act 2000 s 51(6); or (3) the gene therapy advisory committee: Medicines for Human Use (Clinical Trials) Regulations 2004, SI 2004/1031, reg 2(1). 'The gene therapy advisory committee' means the gene therapy advisory committee appointed by the Secretary of State: reg 2(1) (amended by SI 2008/941). As to the Secretary of State see PARA 2 note 1. As to the Scottish Ministers see CONSTITUTIONAL LAW AND HUMAN RIGHTS. As to the constitution of the ethics committee see Sch 2 paras 3–11. As to the duty to produce an annual report see Sch 2 para 12.
3   As to the meaning of 'United Kingdom' see PARA 20 note 4.
4   Medicines for Human Use (Clinical Trials) Regulations 2004, SI 2004/1031, reg 6(1)(a).
5   Medicines for Human Use (Clinical Trials) Regulations 2004, SI 2004/1031, reg 6(1)(b). As to the meaning of 'clinical trial' see PARA 107.
6   Medicines for Human Use (Clinical Trials) Regulations 2004, SI 2004/1031, reg 6(1).
7   Medicines for Human Use (Clinical Trials) Regulations 2004, SI 2004/1031, reg 6(2)(a).

8   Medicines for Human Use (Clinical Trials) Regulations 2004, SI 2004/1031, reg 6(2)(b).

9   Medicines for Human Use (Clinical Trials) Regulations 2004, SI 2004/1031, reg 7(1)(a). An
     application for recognition of an ethics committee must be made in writing to the Authority
     (reg 7(2)(a)), and accompanied by such information, documents and particulars as are necessary
     to enable the Authority to determine the application (reg 7(2)(b)). If any committee was
     established or recognised by the Secretary of State, the Scottish Ministers, the Welsh Ministers,
     the Department of Health, Social Services and Public Safety, or by a strategic health authority,
     health board or health and social services board, for the purpose of advising on the ethics of
     research investigations on human beings (reg 7(3)(a)), and was in existence on 30 April 2004
     (reg 7(3)(b)), the Authority may recognise that committee without an application for recognition
     being submitted (reg 7(3)). 'Strategic health authority' means a strategic health authority
     established under the National Health Service Act 1977 (see HEALTH SERVICES vol 54 (2008)
     PARA 94 et seq); 'health board' means a health board established under the National Health
     Service (Scotland) Act 1978; and 'health and social services board' means a health and social
     services board established under the Health and Personal Social Services (Northern Ireland)
     Order 1972, SI 1972/1265 (NI 14): Medicines for Human Use (Clinical Trials)
     Regulations 2004, SI 2004/1031, reg 2(1). As from 1 April 2013, strategic health authorities are
     abolished: see the Health and Social Care Act 2012 s 33.

10   Medicines for Human Use (Clinical Trials) Regulations 2004, SI 2004/1031, reg 7(1)(b)(i).

11   Ie the provisions of the Medicines for Human Use (Clinical Trials) Regulations 2004,
     SI 2004/1031, reg 9, Sch 2.

12   Medicines for Human Use (Clinical Trials) Regulations 2004, SI 2004/1031, reg 7(1)(b)(ii).

13   Medicines for Human Use (Clinical Trials) Regulations 2004, SI 2004/1031, reg 7(4)(a).

14   Medicines for Human Use (Clinical Trials) Regulations 2004, SI 2004/1031, reg 7(4)(b).

15   Medicines for Human Use (Clinical Trials) Regulations 2004, SI 2004/1031, reg 7(4)(c).

16   Medicines for Human Use (Clinical Trials) Regulations 2004, SI 2004/1031, reg 7(5)(a).

17   Medicines for Human Use (Clinical Trials) Regulations 2004, SI 2004/1031, reg 7(5)(b).

18   Medicines for Human Use (Clinical Trials) Regulations 2004, SI 2004/1031, reg 7(5)(c)
     (amended by SI 2006/1928).

19   Ie the provisions of the Medicines for Human Use (Clinical Trials) Regulations 2004,
     SI 2004/1031, Sch 2.

20   Medicines for Human Use (Clinical Trials) Regulations 2004, SI 2004/1031, reg 8(a).

21   Medicines for Human Use (Clinical Trials) Regulations 2004, SI 2004/1031, reg 8(b).

22   Medicines for Human Use (Clinical Trials) Regulations 2004, SI 2004/1031, reg 8(c).

23   Medicines for Human Use (Clinical Trials) Regulations 2004, SI 2004/1031, reg 9, Sch 2
     para 13(1)(a).

24   Medicines for Human Use (Clinical Trials) Regulations 2004, SI 2004/1031, Sch 2
     para 13(1)(b).

25   As to the meaning of 'person' see PARA 45 note 2.

26   If the person no longer exists or if that person fails to nominate another ethics committee, the
     Authority must nominate such a committee: Medicines for Human Use (Clinical Trials)
     Regulations 2004, SI 2004/1031, Sch 2 para 13(4). 'Appointing authority' means in relation to
     an ethics committee established under reg 6 (see the text to notes 1–8), the Authority; in relation
     to an ethics committee recognised by the Authority after an application in accordance with
     reg 7(1) (see the text to notes 10–14), the person who applied for recognition; in relation to an
     ethics committee recognised without an application for recognition being submitted in
     accordance with reg 7(3), the Authority, or, in relation to the Gene Therapy Advisory
     Committee, the Secretary of State: Sch 2 para 1 (amended by SI 2006/1928).

27   Medicines for Human Use (Clinical Trials) Regulations 2004, SI 2004/1031, Sch 2 para 13(2).

28   Medicines for Human Use (Clinical Trials) Regulations 2004, SI 2004/1031, Sch 2 para 13(3).

29   Ie in accordance with the Medicines for Human Use (Clinical Trials) Regulations 2004,
     SI 2004/1031, reg 14: see PARA 114.

30   Medicines for Human Use (Clinical Trials) Regulations 2004, SI 2004/1031, Sch 2
     para 13(5)(a).

31   Ie in accordance with the Medicines for Human Use (Clinical Trials) Regulations 2004,
     SI 2004/1031, reg 15: see PARA 115.

32   Medicines for Human Use (Clinical Trials) Regulations 2004, SI 2004/1031, Sch 2
     para 13(5)(b).

(iii) Ethics Committee Opinion and Authorisation for Clinical Trials

A. IN GENERAL

112. Requirement for authorisation and ethics committee opinion. No person[1] may start a clinical trial[2] or cause a clinical trial to be started[3], or conduct a clinical trial[4], unless the following conditions are satisfied[5]: (1) an ethics committee[6] to which an application in relation to the trial may be made[7] or an appeal panel[8] has given a favourable opinion in relation to the clinical trial[9]; and (2) the clinical trial has been authorised by the licensing authority[10].

No person may recruit an individual to be a subject[11] in a trial[12], or issue an advertisement for the purpose of recruiting individuals to be subjects in a trial[13], unless condition (1) above has been satisfied[14].

It is an offence to contravene these provisions[15].

1   As to the meaning of 'person' see PARA 45 note 2.
2   As to the meaning of 'clinical trial' see PARA 107.
3   Medicines for Human Use (Clinical Trials) Regulations 2004, SI 2004/1031, reg 12(1)(a).
4   Medicines for Human Use (Clinical Trials) Regulations 2004, SI 2004/1031, reg 12(1)(b). 'Conducting a clinical trial' includes:
   (1)   administering, or giving directions for the administration of, an investigational medicinal product to a subject for the purposes of that trial;
   (2)   giving a prescription for an investigational medicinal product for the purposes of that trial;
   (3)   carrying out any other medical or nursing procedure in relation to that trial; and
   (4)   carrying out any test or analysis to discover or verify the clinical, pharmacological or other pharmacodynamic effects of the investigational medicinal products administered in the course of the trial, to identify any adverse reactions to those products, or to study absorption, distribution, metabolism and excretion of those products,
   but does not include any activity undertaken prior to the commencement of the trial which consists of making such preparations for the trial as are necessary or expedient: reg 2(1).
5   Medicines for Human Use (Clinical Trials) Regulations 2004, SI 2004/1031, reg 12(1).
6   As to the meaning of 'ethics committee' see PARA 111 note 2.
7   Ie in accordance with the Medicines for Human Use (Clinical Trials) Regulations 2004, SI 2004/1031, reg 14 (see PARA 114).
8   Ie appointed under the Medicines for Human Use (Clinical Trials) Regulations 2004, SI 2004/1031, reg 16(6), Sch 4: see PARA 116.
9   Medicines for Human Use (Clinical Trials) Regulations 2004, SI 2004/1031, reg 12(3)(a) (amended by SI 2006/1928). As to ethics committee opinions see PARA 114 et seq.
10 Medicines for Human Use (Clinical Trials) Regulations 2004, SI 2004/1031, reg 12(3)(b). As to the meaning of 'the licensing authority' see the Human Medicines Regulations 2012, SI 2012/1916, reg 6; PARA 35 note 1; definition applied by the Medicines for Human Use (Clinical Trials) Regulations 2004, SI 2004/1031, reg 2(1) (amended by SI 2012/1916). For these purposes, a clinical trial has been authorised by the licensing authority if:
   (1)   in the case of a trial to which reg 18 (see PARA 118) relates:
      (a)   the trial is to be treated as authorised by virtue of reg 18 (reg 12(4)(a)(i)); or
      (b)   the authority has accepted the request for authorisation in accordance with the procedure specified in Sch 5 (see PARA 125) (reg 12(4)(a)(ii)); or
   (2)   in the case of a clinical trial to which reg 19 (see PARA 119) or reg 20 (see PARA 120) applies:
      (a)   the authority has given a notice of authorisation in accordance with those regulations (reg 12(4)(b)(i)); or
      (b)   the authority has accepted the request for authorisation in accordance with the procedure specified in Sch 5 (reg 12(4)(b)(ii)).
11 As to the meaning of 'subject' see PARA 107 note 1.
12 Medicines for Human Use (Clinical Trials) Regulations 2004, SI 2004/1031, reg 12(2)(a).
13 Medicines for Human Use (Clinical Trials) Regulations 2004, SI 2004/1031, reg 12(2)(b).
14 Medicines for Human Use (Clinical Trials) Regulations 2004, SI 2004/1031, reg 12(2).

15 Medicines for Human Use (Clinical Trials) Regulations 2004, SI 2004/1031, reg 49(1)(aa)
    (renumbered as such by SI 2006/1928). As to offences generally, defences and penalties see
    PARAS 138–140.

113. Supply of investigational medicinal products for clinical trials. No
person[1] may, in the course of a business[2] carried on by him, sell or supply any
investigational medicinal product[3] to an investigator[4], a health care professional[5]
who is a member of an investigator's team[6], a person who provides or is to
provide health care[7] under the direction or control of an investigator or such a
health care professional[8], or a subject[9], for the purpose of administering that
product in a clinical trial[10], unless certain conditions are satisfied[11]. The
conditions are that:

(1)   the licensing authority[12] has authorised the clinical trial[13] for the
        purposes of which the product is sold or supplied[14];

(2)   in the case of an investigational medicinal product manufactured[15] or
        assembled[16] in an EEA state[17], other than in accordance with the terms
        of a marketing authorisation[18] relating to that product, or imported into
        an EEA state:

        (a)   the product has been manufactured, assembled or imported in
                accordance with the terms of a manufacturing authorisation[19], an
                authorisation[20] granted by a competent authority of an EEA state
                other than the United Kingdom[21], or in the case of assembly only,
                under the exemption[22] for hospitals and health centres[23]; and

        (b)   the production batch of investigational medicinal products of
                which the product is a part has been checked and certified[24] by a
                qualified person[25].

The restriction on the sale or supply of investigational medicinal products
does not apply to the sale or supply of a medicinal product[26] in accordance with
the terms of a marketing authorisation relating to that product, other than a
marketing authorisation issued by the competent authority of an EEA state other
than the United Kingdom[27].

It is an offence to contravene this restriction[28]; and any person who has in his
possession a medicinal product for the purpose of selling or supplying it in
contravention of the restriction is also guilty of an offence[29].

1   As to the meaning of 'person' see PARA 45 note 2.

2   'Business' includes a professional practice and includes any activity carried on by a body of
    persons, whether corporate or unincorporate: Medicines for Human Use (Clinical Trials)
    Regulations 2004, SI 2004/1031, reg 2(1). As to bodies corporate see COMPANIES;
    CORPORATIONS.

3   As to the meaning of 'investigational medicinal product' see PARA 107 note 1.

4   Medicines for Human Use (Clinical Trials) Regulations 2004, SI 2004/1031, reg 13(1)(a).
    'Investigator' means, in relation to a clinical trial, the authorised health professional responsible
    for the conduct of that trial at a trial site, and if the trial is conducted by a team of authorised
    health professionals at a trial site, the investigator is the leader responsible for that team:
    reg 2(1). 'Trial site' means a hospital, health centre, surgery or other establishment or facility at
    or from which a clinical trial, or any part of such a trial, is conducted: reg 2(1).

5   'Health care professional' means a doctor, a dentist, a nurse, a pharmacist, a person registered in
    the register of optometrists maintained under the Opticians Act 1989 s 7(a) (see MEDICAL
    PROFESSIONS vol 74 (2011) PARA 344), or in the register of visiting optometrists from relevant
    European States maintained under s 8B(1)(a) (see MEDICAL PROFESSIONS vol 74 (2011) PARA
    346), a person registered in a register established and maintained under the Health and Social
    Work Professions Order 2001, SI 2002/254, art 5 (MEDICAL PROFESSIONS) other than a social
    worker registered in Pt 16, a registered osteopath as defined in the Osteopaths Act 1993 s 41
    (see MEDICAL PROFESSIONS vol 74 (2011) PARA 525) or a registered chiropractor as defined by

the Chiropractors Act 1994 s 43 (see MEDICAL PROFESSIONS vol 74 (2011) PARA 603): Medicines for Human Use (Clinical Trials) Regulations 2004, SI 2004/1031, reg 2(1) (amended by SI 2007/3101, SI 2012/1479).

6   Medicines for Human Use (Clinical Trials) Regulations 2004, SI 2004/1031, reg 13(1)(b).

7   'Health care' means services for or in connection with the prevention, diagnosis or treatment of illness: Medicines for Human Use (Clinical Trials) Regulations 2004, SI 2004/1031, reg 2(1).

8   Medicines for Human Use (Clinical Trials) Regulations 2004, SI 2004/1031, reg 13(1)(c).

9   Medicines for Human Use (Clinical Trials) Regulations 2004, SI 2004/1031, reg 13(1)(d). As to the meaning of 'subject' see PARA 107 note 1.

10   As to the meaning of 'clinical trial' see PARA 107.

11   Medicines for Human Use (Clinical Trials) Regulations 2004, SI 2004/1031, reg 13(1).

12   As to the meaning of 'the licensing authority' see the Human Medicines Regulations 2012, SI 2012/1916, reg 6; PARA 35 note 1; definition applied by the Medicines for Human Use (Clinical Trials) Regulations 2004, SI 2004/1031, reg 2(1) (amended by SI 2012/1916).

13   As to the authorisation of clinical trials see PARA 117 et seq.

14   Medicines for Human Use (Clinical Trials) Regulations 2004, SI 2004/1031, reg 13(2)(a).

15   As to the meaning of 'manufacture' see PARA 97 note 3.

16   As to the meaning of 'assemble' see PARA 97 note 4.

17   As to the meaning of 'EEA state' see PARA 107 note 1.

18   As to the meaning of 'marketing authorisation' see PARA 107 note 1.

19   Medicines for Human Use (Clinical Trials) Regulations 2004, SI 2004/1031, reg 13(2)(b)(i)(aa) (reg 13(2)(b)(i) substituted by SI 2006/1928). As to the meaning of 'manufacturing authorisation' see PARA 97 note 6. If an investigational medicinal product has been manufactured or imported prior to 1 May 2004: (1) the condition specified in the Medicines for Human Use (Clinical Trials) Regulations 2004, SI 2004/1031, reg 13(2)(b)(i) applies only in relation to any assembly of that product which takes place on or after that date (reg 13(3)(a)); and (2) the conditions specified in reg 13(2)(b)(ii) (see the text to notes 24–25) do not apply (reg 13(3)(b)).

20   Ie referred to in European Parliament and Council Directive (EC) 2001/20 (OJ L121, 1.5.2001, p 34) on the approximation of the laws, regulations and administrative provisions of the Member States relating to the implementation of good clinical practice in the conduct of clinical trials on medicinal products for human use, art 13.

21   Medicines for Human Use (Clinical Trials) Regulations 2004, SI 2004/1031, reg 13(2)(b)(i)(bb) (as substituted: see note 19). See also note 19. As to the meaning of 'United Kingdom' see PARA 20 note 4.

22   Ie the exemption under the Medicines for Human Use (Clinical Trials) Regulations 2004, SI 2004/1031, reg 37 (see PARA 98).

23   Medicines for Human Use (Clinical Trials) Regulations 2004, SI 2004/1031, reg 13(2)(b)(i)(cc) (as substituted: see note 19). 'Hospital' includes a clinic, nursing home or similar institution; and 'health centre' means a health centre maintained under the National Health Service Act 1977 s 2 or s 3 or the Health and Personal Social Services (Northern Ireland) Order 1972, SI 1972/1262 (NI 14), art 5: Medicines for Human Use (Clinical Trials) Regulations 2004, SI 2004/1031, reg 2(1).

24   Ie pursuant to European Parliament and Council Directive (EC) 2001/20 (OJ L121, 1.5.2001, p 34) art 13(3), (4).

25   Medicines for Human Use (Clinical Trials) Regulations 2004, SI 2004/1031, reg 13(2)(b)(ii). See also note 19. As to the meaning of 'qualified person' see PARA 104 note 2.

26   As to the meaning of 'medicinal product' see the Human Medicines Regulations 2012, SI 2012/1916, reg 2(1); and PARA 25 (definition applied by the Medicines for Human Use (Clinical Trials) Regulations 2004, SI 2004/1031, reg 2(1) (amended by SI 2012/1916)).

27   Medicines for Human Use (Clinical Trials) Regulations 2004, SI 2004/1031, reg 13(4).

28   Medicines for Human Use (Clinical Trials) Regulations 2004, SI 2004/1031, reg 49(1)(b). As to offences generally, defences and penalties see PARAS 138–140.

29   Medicines for Human Use (Clinical Trials) Regulations 2004, SI 2004/1031, reg 49(2).

B.   ETHICS COMMITTEE OPINION

114.   Application for ethics committee opinion.   An application for an ethics committee[1] opinion in relation to a clinical trial[2] must be made by the chief investigator[3] for that trial[4]. A chief investigator for a trial must make an application for an ethics committee opinion in relation to that trial to one ethics committee only, regardless of the number of trial sites at which the trial is to be conducted[5]. The application must be made to an ethics committee established or recognised[6] for the entire United Kingdom[7], or in relation to an area of the United Kingdom in which the chief investigator is professionally based[8], and in relation to a description or class of clinical trial into which the proposed trial falls[9]. An application must be in writing[10], signed by the chief investigator making the application[11], and accompanied by the specified particulars and documents[12]. The application and any accompanying material must be supplied in the English language[13].

Any person[14] who in the course of making an application for an ethics committee opinion provides to an ethics committee any relevant information[15] which is false or misleading in a material particular is guilty of an offence[16].

1 As to the meaning of 'ethics committee' see PARA 111 note 2.
2 As to the meaning of 'clinical trial' see PARA 107.
3 'Chief investigator' means, in relation to a clinical trial conducted at a single trial site, the investigator for that site or, in relation to a clinical trial conducted at more than one trial site, the authorised health professional, whether or not he is an investigator at any particular site, who takes primary responsibility for the conduct of the trial: Medicines for Human Use (Clinical Trials) Regulations 2004, SI 2004/1031, reg 2(1) (amended by SI 2006/1928). As to the meanings of 'trial site', 'investigator', 'health care professional' see PARA 113 notes 4, 5, and as to the meaning of 'conducting a clinical trial', see PARA 112 note 4.
4 Medicines for Human Use (Clinical Trials) Regulations 2004, SI 2004/1031, reg 14(1).
5 Medicines for Human Use (Clinical Trials) Regulations 2004, SI 2004/1031, reg 14(2).
6 As to the establishment and recognition of ethics committees see PARA 111.
7 Medicines for Human Use (Clinical Trials) Regulations 2004, SI 2004/1031, reg 14(3)(a)(i). As to the meaning of 'United Kingdom' see PARA 20 note 4.
8 Medicines for Human Use (Clinical Trials) Regulations 2004, SI 2004/1031, reg 14(3)(a)(ii). A chief investigator is professionally based at the hospital, health centre, surgery or other establishment or facility at or from which he primarily conducts his professional practice: reg 14(8). As to the meanings of 'hospital' and 'health centre' see PARA 113 note 23.
9 Medicines for Human Use (Clinical Trials) Regulations 2004, SI 2004/1031, reg 14(3)(b). An application for an ethics committee opinion in relation to a clinical trial involving medicinal products for gene therapy must be made to the gene therapy advisory committee: reg 14(5). As to the meaning of 'the gene therapy advisory committee' see PARA 111 note 2.
10 Medicines for Human Use (Clinical Trials) Regulations 2004, SI 2004/1031, reg 14(6)(a).
11 Medicines for Human Use (Clinical Trials) Regulations 2004, SI 2004/1031, reg 14(6)(b). Any reference to an application, request or other document that is signed includes a reference to an application, request or other document that is signed with an electronic signature: reg 2(3). 'Electronic signature' means data in electronic form which are attached to or logically associated with other electronic data and which serve as a method of authentication: reg 2(1).
12 Medicines for Human Use (Clinical Trials) Regulations 2004, SI 2004/1031, reg 14(6)(c). The specified particulars and documents are those specified in Sch 3 Pt 1 (amended by SI 2008/941).
13 Medicines for Human Use (Clinical Trials) Regulations 2004, SI 2004/1031, reg 14(7).
14 As to the meaning of 'person' see PARA 45 note 2.
15 'Relevant information' means any information which is relevant to an evaluation of: (1) the safety, quality or efficacy of an investigational medicinal product (Medicines for Human Use (Clinical Trials) Regulations 2004, SI 2004/1031, reg 50(4)(a)); (2) the safety or scientific validity of a clinical trial (reg 50(4)(b)); or (3) whether, with regard to a clinical trial, the conditions and principles of good clinical practice are being satisfied or adhered to (reg 50(4)(c)). As to the meaning of 'investigational medicinal product' see PARA 107 note 1. As to the meaning of 'the conditions and principles of good clinical practice' see PARA 126 note 5.
16 Medicines for Human Use (Clinical Trials) Regulations 2004, SI 2004/1031, reg 50(1)(a). As to offences generally, defences and penalties see PARAS 138–140.

115. Ethics committee opinion. An ethics committee[1] must, within the specified period[2] following receipt of a valid application[3], give an opinion in relation to the clinical trial to which the application relates[4]. Where, following receipt of a valid application, it appears to the committee that further information is required in order to give an opinion on a trial, the committee may, within the specified period and before giving its opinion, send a notice in writing to the applicant requesting that he furnishes the committee with that information[5]. An ethics committee may give a favourable opinion subject to conditions specified in writing in relation to a clinical trial[6] in which case the ethics committee is treated as having given a favourable opinion in relation to the clinical trial only if the specified conditions are satisfied[7].

The chairman, vice-chairman or alternate vice-chairman of the Gene Therapy Advisory Committee[8] may notify the United Kingdom Ethics Committees Authority (instead of giving an opinion) within the specified period beginning with the date of the Committee's receipt of an application that the clinical trial to which that application relates does not merit an opinion from the Gene Therapy Advisory Committee[9]. Where this occurs:

(1)   the Gene Therapy Advisory Committee must not give an opinion in relation to the clinical trial to which the application subject to that notification relates[10];

(2)   the Authority must direct that the application be considered by another ethics committee specified in the direction[11];

(3)   the Gene Therapy Advisory Committee must send the application to the ethics committee specified in the direction immediately following the direction being given[12]; and

(4)   the ethics committee specified in the direction must, subject to the application being valid, give an opinion in relation to the clinical trial to which that application relates within the specified period beginning with the date of the Gene Therapy Advisory Committee's receipt of the application[13].

In preparing its opinion, the committee must consider, in particular, the following matters: (a) the relevance of the clinical trial and its design[14]; (b) whether the evaluation of the anticipated benefits and risks[15] is satisfactory and whether the conclusions are justified[16]; (c) the protocol[17]; (d) the suitability of the investigator and supporting staff[18]; (e) the investigator's brochure or, where the investigational medicinal product has a marketing authorisation and the product is to be used in accordance with the terms of that authorisation, the summary of product characteristics relating to that product[19]; (f) the quality of the facilities for the trial[20]; (g) the adequacy and completeness of the written information to be given, and the procedure to be followed, for the purpose of obtaining informed consent[21] to the subjects' participation in the trial[22]; (h) if the subjects are to include minors or persons incapable of giving informed consent, whether the research is justified having regard to the specified[23] conditions and principles[24]; (i) provision for indemnity or compensation in the event of injury or death attributable to the clinical trial[25]; (j) any insurance or indemnity[26] to cover the liability of the investigator or sponsor[27]; (k) the amounts, and, where appropriate, the arrangements, for rewarding or compensating investigators and subjects[28]; (l) the terms of any agreement between the sponsor and the owner or occupier of the trial site[29] which are relevant to the arrangements referred to in head (k) above[30]; and (l) the arrangements for the recruitment of subjects[31]. The ethics committee must consider, and give an opinion on, any other issue relating to the clinical trial, if the committee has been asked by the applicant to consider the issue[32] or it is, in the committee's opinion, relevant to the other matters considered[33] by the committee[34].

Where an ethics committee gives an opinion it must publish a summary of that opinion[35].

1   As to the meaning of 'ethics committee' see PARA 111 note 2.

2   'The specified period' means: (1) in the case of a clinical trial involving a medicinal product for gene therapy or somatic cell therapy or a medicinal product containing a genetically modified organism or a tissue engineered product where a specialist group or committee is consulted, 180 days, or where there is no such consultation, 90 days; or (2) in any other case, 60 days: Medicines for Human Use (Clinical Trials) Regulations 2004, SI 2004/1031, reg 15(10) (amended by SI 2006/1928). 'Specialist group or committee' means a group or committee whose functions include the provision of advice on ethical or scientific issues in relation to: (1) tissue engineered products; (2) in the case of medicinal products for gene therapy or somatic cell therapy, the use of such therapies in the treatment of humans; or (3) in the case of medicinal products containing genetically modified organisms, the administration of such products to humans: Medicines for Human Use (Clinical Trials) Regulations 2004, SI 2004/1031, reg 15(10) (definition substituted by SI 2010/1882). As to the meaning of 'clinical trial' see PARA 107. As to the meaning of 'medicinal product' see the Human Medicines Regulations 2012, SI 2012/1916, reg 2(1); and PARA 25 (definition applied by the Medicines for Human Use (Clinical Trials) Regulations 2004, SI 2004/1031, reg 2(1) (amended by SI 2012/1916)).

3   'Valid application' means an application for an ethics committee opinion which complies with the provisions of the Medicines for Human Use (Clinical Trials) Regulations 2004, SI 2004/1031, reg 14 (see PARA 114): reg 11.

4   Medicines for Human Use (Clinical Trials) Regulations 2004, SI 2004/1031, reg 15(1) (substituted by SI 2008/941). If the clinical trial involves a medicinal product for xenogenic cell therapy, the time limits referred to in the Medicines for Human Use (Clinical Trials) Regulations 2004, SI 2004/1031, reg 15(1)–(3) do not apply and the ethics committee may give an opinion in relation to that trial or send a notice under reg 15(2) (see the text to note 5) at any time after receipt of the valid application: reg 15(4).

5   Medicines for Human Use (Clinical Trials) Regulations 2004, SI 2004/1031, reg 15(2). Where the committee sends such a request, the specified period is suspended pending receipt of the information requested: reg 15(3).

6   Medicines for Human Use (Clinical Trials) Regulations 2004, SI 2004/1031, reg 15(3A) (reg 15(3A), (3B), (4A), (4B) added by SI 2008/941).

7   Medicines for Human Use (Clinical Trials) Regulations 2004, SI 2004/1031, reg 15(3B) (as added: see note 6).

8   As to the meaning of 'the Gene Therapy Advisory Committee' see PARA 111 note 2.

9   Medicines for Human Use (Clinical Trials) Regulations 2004, SI 2004/1031, reg 15(4B) (as added: see note 6).

10   Medicines for Human Use (Clinical Trials) Regulations 2004, SI 2004/1031, reg 15(4A)(a) (as added: see note 6).

11   Medicines for Human Use (Clinical Trials) Regulations 2004, SI 2004/1031, reg 15(4A)(b) (as added: see note 6).

12   Medicines for Human Use (Clinical Trials) Regulations 2004, SI 2004/1031, reg 15(4A)(c) (as added: see note 6).

13   Medicines for Human Use (Clinical Trials) Regulations 2004, SI 2004/1031, reg 15(4A)(d) (as added: see note 6).

14   Medicines for Human Use (Clinical Trials) Regulations 2004, SI 2004/1031, reg 15(5)(a).

15   Ie as required under the Medicines for Human Use (Clinical Trials) Regulations 2004, SI 2004/1031, reg 2(1), Sch 1 Pt 2 para 10.

16   Medicines for Human Use (Clinical Trials) Regulations 2004, SI 2004/1031, reg 15(5)(b) (amended by SI 2006/1928).

17   Medicines for Human Use (Clinical Trials) Regulations 2004, SI 2004/1031, reg 15(5)(c). As to the meaning of 'protocol' see PARA 107 note 2.

18   Medicines for Human Use (Clinical Trials) Regulations 2004, SI 2004/1031, reg 15(5)(d). As to the meaning of 'investigator' see PARA 113 note 4.

19   Medicines for Human Use (Clinical Trials) Regulations 2004, SI 2004/1031, reg 15(5)(e) (amended SI 2006/1928). 'Investigator's brochure' means a document containing a summary of the clinical and non-clinical data relating to an investigational medicinal product which are relevant to the study of the product in human subjects: Medicines for Human Use (Clinical Trials) Regulations 2004, SI 2004/1031, reg 2(1). As to the meanings of 'investigational medicinal product' and 'subject' see PARA 107 note 1.

20   Medicines for Human Use (Clinical Trials) Regulations 2004, SI 2004/1031, reg 15(5)(f).

21 A person gives informed consent to take part, or that a subject is to take part, in a clinical trial only if his decision is given freely after that person is informed of the nature, significance, implications and risks of the trial, and either is evidenced in writing, dated and signed, or otherwise marked, by that person so as to indicate his consent, or if the person is unable to sign or to mark a document so as to indicate his consent, is given orally in the presence of at least one witness and recorded in writing; and references to 'informed consent' are to be construed accordingly and include references to informed consent given or refused by an adult unable by virtue of physical or mental incapacity to give informed consent, prior to the onset of that incapacity: Medicines for Human Use (Clinical Trials) Regulations 2004, SI 2004/1031, reg 2(1), Sch 1 para 3. As to references to 'signed' see PARA 114 note 11. For these purposes, 'adult' means a person who has attained the age of 16 years: reg 2(1).

22 Medicines for Human Use (Clinical Trials) Regulations 2004, SI 2004/1031, reg 15(5)(g).

23 Ie specified in the Medicines for Human Use (Clinical Trials) Regulations 2004, SI 2004/1031, Sch 1 Pt 4 or 5. 'Minor' means a person under the age of 16 years: reg 2(1).

24 Medicines for Human Use (Clinical Trials) Regulations 2004, SI 2004/1031, reg 15(5)(h) (amended by SI 2006/1928). If any subject of the clinical trial is to be a minor (Medicines for Human Use (Clinical Trials) Regulations 2004, SI 2004/1031, reg 15(6)(a)) and the committee does not have a member with professional expertise in paediatric care (reg 15(6)(b)), it must, before giving its opinion, obtain advice on the clinical, ethical and psychosocial problems in the field of paediatric care which may arise in relation to that trial (reg 15(6)). If any subject of the clinical trial is to be an adult incapable by reason of physical and mental incapacity to give informed consent to participation in the trial (reg 15(7)(a)) and the committee does not have a member with professional expertise in the treatment of the disease to which the trial relates (reg 15(7)(b)(i)) and the patient population suffering that disease (reg 15(7)(b)(ii)), it must, before giving its opinion, obtain advice on the clinical, ethical and psychosocial problems in the field of that disease and patient population which may arise in relation to that trial (reg 15(7)).

25 Medicines for Human Use (Clinical Trials) Regulations 2004, SI 2004/1031, reg 15(5)(i).

26 'Insurance or indemnity' includes provision for meeting losses or liabilities: (1) under a scheme established under the National Health Service and Community Care Act 1990 s 21 (schemes for meeting losses and liabilities etc of certain health service bodies in England and Wales), the National Health Service (Scotland) Act 1978 s 85B (schemes for meeting losses and liabilities etc of certain health service bodies in Scotland), or the Health and Personal Social Services (Northern Ireland) Order 1991, SI 1991/194 (NI 1) art 24 (schemes for meeting losses and liabilities etc of certain health service bodies in Northern Ireland); or (2) in accordance with guidance issued by the Secretary of State, the Scottish Ministers, the National Assembly for Wales, or the Department for Health, Social Services and Public Safety, as to the arrangements to be adopted by health service bodies for meeting the costs arising from clinical negligence (known as NHS Indemnity): Medicines for Human Use (Clinical Trials) Regulations 2004, SI 2004/1031, reg 2(1). As to the Secretary of State see PARA 2 note 1. As to the Scottish Ministers and the National Assembly for Wales see CONSTITUTIONAL LAW AND HUMAN RIGHTS.

27 Medicines for Human Use (Clinical Trials) Regulations 2004, SI 2004/1031, reg 15(5)(j). As to the meaning of 'sponsor' see PARA 107.

28 Medicines for Human Use (Clinical Trials) Regulations 2004, SI 2004/1031, reg 15(5)(k).

29 As to the meaning of 'trial site' see PARA 113 note 4.

30 Medicines for Human Use (Clinical Trials) Regulations 2004, SI 2004/1031, reg 15(5)(l).

31 Medicines for Human Use (Clinical Trials) Regulations 2004, SI 2004/1031, reg 15(5)(m).

32 Medicines for Human Use (Clinical Trials) Regulations 2004, SI 2004/1031, reg 15(8)(a).

33 Ie in accordance with the Medicines for Human Use (Clinical Trials) Regulations 2004, SI 2004/1031, reg 15.

34 Medicines for Human Use (Clinical Trials) Regulations 2004, SI 2004/1031, reg 15(8)(b).

35 Medicines for Human Use (Clinical Trials) Regulations 2004, SI 2004/1031, reg 15(9).

116.   Review and appeal relating to ethics committee opinion. Where a chief investigator[1] for a trial has been notified by the ethics committee[2] to which he made an application[3] that the committee's opinion in relation to that trial is not favourable[4], except where the opinion was given by the gene therapy advisory committee[5], the chief investigator may within 90 days of being notified that the committee's opinion is not favourable, give a notice to the United Kingdom Ethics Committees Authority stating his wish to appeal against the opinion[6] and setting out his representations with respect to that opinion[7]. Where the Authority receives a notice[8] that a chief investigator wishes to appeal against an ethics committee opinion which is not favourable, it must direct that the application for that opinion may be considered by another ethics committee specified in the direction[9], or appoint an appeal panel[10] and refer the opinion to that panel[11]. However, except where the opinion was given by the gene therapy advisory committee[12], the Authority may refuse to give a direction or appoint a panel where it considers that the grounds for appealing against the opinion are unfounded[13].

Where a direction is given that the application be considered by another ethics committee, the ethics committee which gave the unfavourable opinion must send to the ethics committee specified in the direction the application for that opinion[14], and any additional information provided by the chief investigator[15], and the committee specified in the direction must consider[16] the application[17].

An appeal panel must consider an ethics committee opinion referred to it[18] by considering the opinion[19], the application for that opinion[20], the particulars and documents accompanying that application[21], specified matters[22], any representations set out in the notice to the Authority[23], and, in a case where the opinion has been confirmed by the gene therapy advisory committee on a review[24], the reasons given by the committee for that confirmation[25]. The panel may, if the chief investigator so requests, hold a hearing to consider the opinion, at which the chief investigator may make oral representations[26]. The panel must within 30 days of the opinion being referred to it, or such extended period as the Authority may in any particular case allow, either confirm the opinion or give a favourable opinion[27].

1   As to the meaning of 'chief investigator' see PARA 114 note 3.
2   The Medicines for Human Use (Clinical Trials) Regulations 2004, SI 2004/1031, reg 16 does not apply in relation to an opinion given by an ethics committee asked to review an opinion pursuant to reg 16(8), Sch 4 para 2 (see the text to notes 14–17): reg 16(2)(b). As to the meaning of 'ethics committee' see PARA 111 note 2.
3   Ie in accordance with the Medicines for Human Use (Clinical Trials) Regulations 2004, SI 2004/1031, reg 14: see PARA 114.
4   Medicines for Human Use (Clinical Trials) Regulations 2004, SI 2004/1031, reg 16(1) (amended by SI 2006/1928). As to ethics committee opinions see PARA 115.
5   Where the opinion was given by the gene therapy advisory committee, the chief investigator may, within 14 days of being notified of that opinion give a notice in writing to the committee requiring the committee to review its opinion (Medicines for Human Use (Clinical Trials) Regulations 2004, SI 2004/1031, reg 16(4)(a)), or give a notice in writing to the United Kingdom Ethics Committee Authority stating his wish to appeal against the opinion (reg 16(4)(b)(i)) and setting out his representations with respect to that opinion (reg 16(4)(b)(ii)). Where the gene therapy advisory committee is required by a notice to review its opinion, it must do so within 60 days of receipt of the notice: reg 16(5). On a such review the committee may vary or confirm its opinion and must give notice in writing to the chief investigator of the variation or confirmation: reg 16(6). If the committee confirms its opinion, a chief investigator may within 14 days of being notified of the confirmation give notice in writing to the Authority stating his wish to appeal against the committee's opinion (reg 16(7)(a)) and setting out his representations with respect to that opinion (reg 16(7)(b)). As to the meaning of 'the gene therapy advisory committee' see PARA 111 note 2. As to the United Kingdom Ethics Committee Authority see PARA 110.
6   Medicines for Human Use (Clinical Trials) Regulations 2004, SI 2004/1031, reg 16(3)(a).
7   Medicines for Human Use (Clinical Trials) Regulations 2004, SI 2004/1031, reg 16(3)(b).
8   Ie pursuant to the Medicines for Human Use (Clinical Trials) Regulations 2004, SI 2004/1031, reg 16(3), (4)(b), (7): see the text to notes 5–7.
9   Medicines for Human Use (Clinical Trials) Regulations 2004, SI 2004/1031, Sch 4 para 1(1)(a) (amended by SI 2006/1928).
10 An appeal panel must consist of a chairman and at least six other members: Medicines for Human Use (Clinical Trials) Regulations 2004, SI 2004/1031, Sch 4 para 3(1). One of the members must be a person who is not a health care professional (Sch 4 para 3(2)(a)); a person having professional qualifications or experience relating to the conduct of, or use of statistics in,

clinical trials, unless those professional qualifications or experience relate only to the ethics of clinical research or medical treatment (Sch 4 para 3(2)(b)); or a person who, although not a health care professional, has been a registered medical practitioner or a person registered in the dentists register under the Dentists Act 1984 (Medicines for Human Use (Clinical Trials) Regulations 2004, SI 2004/1031, Sch 4 para 3(2)(c)). The Authority may pay to members of an appeal panel such travelling and other allowances as the Authority may determine: Sch 4 para 6. As to the meaning of 'health care professional' see PARA 113 note 5. As to the meaning of 'clinical trial' see PARA 107. As to the meaning of 'registered medical practitioner' see MEDICAL PROFESSIONS vol 74 (2011) PARA 176; and as to the register under the Dentists Act 1984 see MEDICAL PROFESSIONS vol 74 (2011) PARA 442 et seq.

11 Medicines for Human Use (Clinical Trials) Regulations 2004, SI 2004/1031, Sch 4 para 1(1)(b).
12 Where the opinion was given by the gene therapy advisory committee, the Authority must appoint an appeal panel and refer the opinion to that panel: Medicines for Human Use (Clinical Trials) Regulations 2004, SI 2004/1031, Sch 4 para 1(4).
13 Medicines for Human Use (Clinical Trials) Regulations 2004, SI 2004/1031, Sch 4 para 1(2). Where the Authority refuses to give a direction or appoint a panel, it must send a notice to the chief investigator setting out its reasons for refusal: Sch 4 para 1(3).
14 Medicines for Human Use (Clinical Trials) Regulations 2004, SI 2004/1031, Sch 4 para 2(a)(i).
15 Medicines for Human Use (Clinical Trials) Regulations 2004, SI 2004/1031, Sch 4 para 2(a)(ii).
16 Ie in accordance with the Medicines for Human Use (Clinical Trials) Regulations 2004, SI 2004/1031, reg 15: see PARA 115.
17 Medicines for Human Use (Clinical Trials) Regulations 2004, SI 2004/1031, Sch 4 para 2(b).
18 Medicines for Human Use (Clinical Trials) Regulations 2004, SI 2004/1031, Sch 4 para 4(1).
19 Medicines for Human Use (Clinical Trials) Regulations 2004, SI 2004/1031, Sch 4 para 4(2)(a).
20 Medicines for Human Use (Clinical Trials) Regulations 2004, SI 2004/1031, Sch 4 para 4(2)(b).
21 Medicines for Human Use (Clinical Trials) Regulations 2004, SI 2004/1031, Sch 4 para 4(2)(c).
22 Medicines for Human Use (Clinical Trials) Regulations 2004, SI 2004/1031, Sch 4 para 4(2)(d) (amended by SI 2006/1928). Schedule 4 para 4(2)(d) refers to the matters specified in reg 15(5) (see PARA 115); however, it is submitted that this should be a reference to reg 15(5) (see PARA 115).
23 Medicines for Human Use (Clinical Trials) Regulations 2004, SI 2004/1031, Sch 4 para 4(2)(e).
24 Ie pursuant to the Medicines for Human Use (Clinical Trials) Regulations 2004, SI 2004/1031, reg 16(5): see note 5.
25 Medicines for Human Use (Clinical Trials) Regulations 2004, SI 2004/1031, Sch 4 para 4(2)(f) (amended by SI 2006/1928).
26 Medicines for Human Use (Clinical Trials) Regulations 2004, SI 2004/1031, Sch 4 para 4(3).
27 Medicines for Human Use (Clinical Trials) Regulations 2004, SI 2004/1031, Sch 4 para 4(4). If an appeal panel gives a favourable opinion, the condition specified in reg 12(3)(a) (see PARA 112) is deemed to have been satisfied: Sch 4 para 5 (amended by SI 2006/1928).

C. AUTHORISATION FOR CLINICAL TRIALS

117. Request for authorisation to conduct a clinical trial. A request for authorisation to conduct a clinical trial[1] must be made to the licensing authority[2] by the sponsor[3] of the trial[4]. A request must be in writing and signed[5] by or on behalf of the sponsor[6], and be accompanied by the specified particulars and documents[7] and any fee which may be payable[8] in connection with that application[9]. The request and any accompanying material must be supplied in the English language[10].

Any person[11] who in the course of making a request for authorisation to conduct a clinical trial provides to the licensing authority any relevant information[12] which is false or misleading in a material particular is guilty of an offence[13].

1 As to the meaning of 'conducting a clinical trial' see PARA 112 note 4. As to the meaning of 'clinical trial' see PARA 107.
2 As to the meaning of 'the licensing authority' see the Human Medicines Regulations 2012, SI 2012/1916, reg 6; PARA 35 note 1; definition applied by the Medicines for Human Use (Clinical Trials) Regulations 2004, SI 2004/1031, reg 2(1) (amended by SI 2012/1916).
3 As to the meaning of 'sponsor' see PARA 107.

4   Medicines for Human Use (Clinical Trials) Regulations 2004, SI 2004/1031, reg 17(1).

5   As to references to 'signed' see PARA 114 note 11.

6   Medicines for Human Use (Clinical Trials) Regulations 2004, SI 2004/1031, reg 17(2)(a).

7   Medicines for Human Use (Clinical Trials) Regulations 2004, SI 2004/1031, reg 17(2)(b)(i). As to the specified particulars and documents see Sch 3 Pt 2.

8   Ie under the Medicines (Products for Human Use) (Fees) Regulations 2012, SI 2012/504: see PARA 30.

9   Medicines for Human Use (Clinical Trials) Regulations 2004, SI 2004/1031, reg 17(2)(b)(ii) (amended by SI 2012/504).

10   Medicines for Human Use (Clinical Trials) Regulations 2004, SI 2004/1031, reg 17(3).

11   As to the meaning of 'person' see PARA 45 note 2.

12   As to the meaning of 'relevant information' see PARA 114 note 15.

13   Medicines for Human Use (Clinical Trials) Regulations 2004, SI 2004/1031, reg 50(1)(b). As to offences generally, defences and penalties see PARAS 138–140.

118.   Authorisation procedure for clinical trials involving general medicinal products. The provisions described below apply to clinical trials[1] involving medicinal products[2] other than medicinal products for gene therapy[3] or medicinal products with special characteristics[4].

The licensing authority[5] may, within the period of 30 days from the date of receipt of a valid request for authorisation[6] of a clinical trial, give written notice to the sponsor[7] setting out the licensing authority's grounds for not accepting the request[8], or stating that the licensing authority accepts the request for authorisation[9], or stating that the licensing authority accepts the request for authorisation subject to the conditions specified in the notice[10]. If a notice is given stating that the licensing authority accepts the request for authorisation[11], or the licensing authority gives no notice[12], the clinical trial is to be treated as authorised[13]. If a notice is given accepting the request for authorisation subject to conditions, the clinical trial is to be treated as authorised only if the conditions specified in the notice are satisfied[14].

If the sponsor is given a notice not accepting the request or accepting it subject to conditions, he may, within the period of 14 days, or such extended period as the licensing authority may in any particular case allow, from the date on which the notice was received, send an amended request to the licensing authority for further consideration[15]. The licensing authority must consider a valid amended request and may, within the period of 60 days from the date on which the original request was received, give a written notice to the sponsor setting out the licensing authority's grounds for not accepting the amended request[16], or stating that the licensing authority accepts the amended request[17], or stating that the licensing authority accepts the amended request subject to the conditions specified in the notice[18]. If a valid amended request has been received and a notice is given accepting the amended request[19], or no notice is given[20], the clinical trial is to be treated as authorised[21]. If a valid amended request has been received and a notice is given accepting the request subject to conditions, the clinical trial is to be treated as authorised only if the conditions specified in the notice are satisfied[22].

If the licensing authority gives written notice to the sponsor of grounds for non-acceptance of a request for authorisation[23] and the sponsor does not submit an amended request[24], or the sponsor has submitted an amended request but the licensing authority gives written notice[25] to the sponsor of grounds for non-acceptance[26], the request is to be treated as rejected and the authority must not consider any further amendments to the request[27].

1   As to the meaning of 'clinical trial' see PARA 107.

2 As to the meaning of 'medicinal product' see the Human Medicines Regulations 2012, SI 2012/1916, reg 2(1); and PARA 25 (definition applied by the Medicines for Human Use (Clinical Trials) Regulations 2004, SI 2004/1031, reg 2(1) (amended by SI 2012/1916)).

3 As to applications in respect of clinical trials involving such medicinal products see PARA 119.

4 Medicines for Human Use (Clinical Trials) Regulations 2004, SI 2004/1031, reg 18(1). As to applications in respect of clinical trials involving medicinal products with special characteristics see PARA 120. A person is guilty of an offence if he contravenes reg 18(1): reg 34(1). A person guilty of an offence under reg 34(1) is liable on summary conviction to a fine not exceeding the statutory maximum or, on conviction on indictment to a fine, to imprisonment for a term not exceeding two years, or to both: reg 35(1). As to the statutory maximum see SENTENCING AND DISPOSITION OF OFFENDERS vol 92 (2010) PARA 140.

5 As to the meaning of 'the licensing authority' see the Human Medicines Regulations 2012, SI 2012/1916, reg 6; PARA 35 note 1; definition applied by the Medicines for Human Use (Clinical Trials) Regulations 2004, SI 2004/1031, reg 2(1) (amended by SI 2012/1916).

6 'Valid request for authorisation' means a request to the licensing authority for authorisation to conduct a clinical trial which complies with the provisions of the Medicines for Human Use (Clinical Trials) Regulations 2004, SI 2004/1031, reg 17 (see PARA 117); and 'valid amended request' must be construed accordingly: reg 11.

7 As to the meaning of 'sponsor' see PARA 107.

8 Medicines for Human Use (Clinical Trials) Regulations 2004, SI 2004/1031, reg 18(2)(a). As to appeals against decisions not to accept a request for authorisation or to grant an authorisation subject to conditions see PARA 125.

9 Medicines for Human Use (Clinical Trials) Regulations 2004, SI 2004/1031, reg 18(2)(b).

10 Medicines for Human Use (Clinical Trials) Regulations 2004, SI 2004/1031, reg 18(2)(c). See also note 8.

11 Medicines for Human Use (Clinical Trials) Regulations 2004, SI 2004/1031, reg 18(3)(a).

12 Medicines for Human Use (Clinical Trials) Regulations 2004, SI 2004/1031, reg 18(3)(b).

13 Medicines for Human Use (Clinical Trials) Regulations 2004, SI 2004/1031, reg 18(3).

14 Medicines for Human Use (Clinical Trials) Regulations 2004, SI 2004/1031, reg 18(4).

15 Medicines for Human Use (Clinical Trials) Regulations 2004, SI 2004/1031, reg 18(5).

16 Medicines for Human Use (Clinical Trials) Regulations 2004, SI 2004/1031, reg 18(6)(a).

17 Medicines for Human Use (Clinical Trials) Regulations 2004, SI 2004/1031, reg 18(6)(b).

18 Medicines for Human Use (Clinical Trials) Regulations 2004, SI 2004/1031, reg 18(6)(c).

19 Medicines for Human Use (Clinical Trials) Regulations 2004, SI 2004/1031, reg 18(7)(a).

20 Medicines for Human Use (Clinical Trials) Regulations 2004, SI 2004/1031, reg 18(7)(b).

21 Medicines for Human Use (Clinical Trials) Regulations 2004, SI 2004/1031, reg 18(7).

22 Medicines for Human Use (Clinical Trials) Regulations 2004, SI 2004/1031, reg 18(8).

23 Ie in accordance with the Medicines for Human Use (Clinical Trials) Regulations 2004, SI 2004/1031, reg 18(2)(a): see the text to note 8.

24 Medicines for Human Use (Clinical Trials) Regulations 2004, SI 2004/1031, reg 18(9)(a).

25 Ie in accordance with the Medicines for Human Use (Clinical Trials) Regulations 2004, SI 2004/1031, reg 18(6)(a): see the text to note 16.

26 Medicines for Human Use (Clinical Trials) Regulations 2004, SI 2004/1031, reg 18(9)(b).

27 Medicines for Human Use (Clinical Trials) Regulations 2004, SI 2004/1031, reg 18(9).

119. Authorisation procedure for clinical trials involving medicinal products for gene therapy. The provisions described below apply to clinical trials[1] involving medicinal products[2] for gene therapy and somatic cell therapy, including xenogenic cell therapy[3], medicinal products containing genetically modified organisms[4] or tissue engineered products[5].

The licensing authority[6] may, within the period of 30 days from the date of receipt of a valid request for authorisation[7] of a clinical trial, issue a written authorisation to the sponsor[8], or give a notice in writing to the sponsor setting out the grounds for not accepting the request[9]. The licensing authority must not authorise a clinical trial involving products for gene therapy if the use of those products in that trial would result in modifications to any subject's[10] germ line genetic identity[11]. If the licensing authority considers that it is appropriate to do so, it may consult the relevant committee[12] before deciding whether to authorise a clinical trial[13].

Where a sponsor is given a notice setting out the grounds for not accepting the request, he may, within the period of 30 days, or such extended period as the licensing authority may in any particular case allow, from the date on which the notice was received, send an amended request to the licensing authority for further consideration[14]. The licensing authority must consider a valid amended request[15] and, not later than 90 days[16] from the date on which the original request was received, issue a written authorisation to the sponsor[17] or give a notice in writing to the sponsor setting out the grounds for not accepting the request[18].

A written authorisation issued under these provisions may contain such conditions as the licensing authority considers appropriate[19].

1   As to the meaning of 'clinical trial' see PARA 107.
2   As to the meaning of 'medicinal product' see the Human Medicines Regulations 2012, SI 2012/1916, reg 2(1); and PARA 25 (definition applied by the Medicines for Human Use (Clinical Trials) Regulations 2004, SI 2004/1031, reg 2(1) (amended by SI 2012/1916)).
3   Medicines for Human Use (Clinical Trials) Regulations 2004, SI 2004/1031, reg 19(1)(a) (reg 19(1) substituted by SI 2010/1882).
4   Medicines for Human Use (Clinical Trials) Regulations 2004, SI 2004/1031, reg 19(1)(b).
5   Medicines for Human Use (Clinical Trials) Regulations 2004, SI 2004/1031, reg 19(1)(c).
6   As to the meaning of 'the licensing authority' see the Human Medicines Regulations 2012, SI 2012/1916, reg 6; PARA 35 note 1; definition applied by the Medicines for Human Use (Clinical Trials) Regulations 2004, SI 2004/1031, reg 2(1) (amended by SI 2012/1916).
7   As to the meaning of 'valid request for authorisation' see PARA 118 note 6.
8   Medicines for Human Use (Clinical Trials) Regulations 2004, SI 2004/1031, reg 19(2)(a). As to the extension of time where the authority consults the relevant committee see note 13. As to the meaning of 'sponsor' see PARA 107. If the clinical trial involves a medicinal product for xenogenic cell therapy, the time limits set out in reg 19(2), (5) (see note 13) and reg 19(7) (see the text to note 16) do not apply and the authority may issue an authorisation or notice under those provisions at any time after receipt of the request: reg 19(9).
9   Medicines for Human Use (Clinical Trials) Regulations 2004, SI 2004/1031, reg 19(2)(b).
10 As to the meaning of 'subject' see PARA 107 note 1.
11 Medicines for Human Use (Clinical Trials) Regulations 2004, SI 2004/1031, reg 19(3).
12 'The relevant committee' means the Commission on Human Medicines or such other body or committee as the licensing authority may consider appropriate in relation to the application under consideration: Medicines for Human Use (Clinical Trials) Regulations 2004, SI 2004/1031, reg 19(10) (amended by SI 2005/2754; SI 2012/1916). As to the Commission on Human Medicines see PARA 31.
13 Medicines for Human Use (Clinical Trials) Regulations 2004, SI 2004/1031, reg 19(4). Where the authority consults the relevant committee, the period specified in reg 19(2) (see the text to note 8) is extended by a further 90 days: reg 19(5). See also note 8.
14 Medicines for Human Use (Clinical Trials) Regulations 2004, SI 2004/1031, reg 19(6).
15 As to the meaning of 'valid amended request' see PARA 118 note 6.
16 Or 180 days, in a case where the authority consults the relevant committee (see the text to note 12): Medicines for Human Use (Clinical Trials) Regulations 2004, SI 2004/1031, reg 19(7). See also note 8.
17 Medicines for Human Use (Clinical Trials) Regulations 2004, SI 2004/1031, reg 19(7)(a).
18 Medicines for Human Use (Clinical Trials) Regulations 2004, SI 2004/1031, reg 19(7)(b).
19 Medicines for Human Use (Clinical Trials) Regulations 2004, SI 2004/1031, reg 19(8). As to appeals against decisions not to accept a request for authorisation or to grant an authorisation subject to conditions see PARA 125.

120. Authorisation procedure for clinical trials involving medicinal products with special characteristics. The provisions described below apply to clinical trials[1] involving medicinal products[2] which do not have a marketing authorisation[3] and are of a particular type[4]; or which have a specified active ingredient[5]; or where the licensing authority[6], within seven days from the date of receipt of a valid request for authorisation[7] of the trial, issues a notice to the sponsor[8] specifying that by virtue of the special characteristics of the medicinal product to which the trial relates, written authorisation for that trial is required[9].

The licensing authority may, within the period of 30 days from the date of receipt of a valid request for authorisation of a clinical trial, issue a written authorisation to the sponsor[10], or give a notice in writing to the sponsor setting out the grounds for not authorising the trial[11]. Where a sponsor is given a notice setting out the grounds for not authorising the trial, he may, within the period of 14 days, or such extended period as the licensing authority may in any particular case allow, from the date on which the notice was received, send an amended request to the licensing authority for further consideration[12]. The licensing authority must consider a valid amended request[13] and, not later than 60 days from the date on which the original request was received, issue a written authorisation to the sponsor[14], or give a notice in writing to the sponsor setting out the grounds for not accepting the request[15].

A written authorisation issued under these provisions may contain such conditions as the licensing authority considers appropriate[16].

1   As to the meaning of 'clinical trial' see PARA 107.
2   As to the meaning of 'medicinal product' see the Human Medicines Regulations 2012, SI 2012/1916, reg 2(1); and PARA 25 (definition applied by the Medicines for Human Use (Clinical Trials) Regulations 2004, SI 2004/1031, reg 2(1) (amended by SI 2012/1916)).
3   As to the meaning of 'marketing authorisation' see PARA 107 note 1.
4   Medicines for Human Use (Clinical Trials) Regulations 2004, SI 2004/1031, reg 20(1)(a)(i). The medicinal products must be of a type referred to in Council Regulation (EC) 2309/93 (OJ L214, 24.8.1993, p 1) Annex Pt A.
5   Medicines for Human Use (Clinical Trials) Regulations 2004, SI 2004/1031, reg 20(1)(a)(ii). This provision refers to medicinal products which have an active ingredient:
    (1)   that is a biological product of human or animal origin (reg 20(1)(a)(ii)(aa));
    (2)   containing biological components of human or animal origin (reg 20(1)(a)(ii)(bb)); or
    (3)   the manufacturing of which requires such components (reg 20(1)(a)(ii)(cc)),
    other than products falling within reg 19 (see PARA 119) (reg 20(1)(a)(ii)).
6   As to the meaning of 'the licensing authority' see the Human Medicines Regulations 2012, SI 2012/1916, reg 6; PARA 35 note 1; definition applied by the Medicines for Human Use (Clinical Trials) Regulations 2004, SI 2004/1031, reg 2(1) (amended by SI 2012/1916).
7   As to the meaning of 'valid request for authorisation' see PARA 118 note 6.
8   As to the meaning of 'sponsor' see PARA 107.
9   Medicines for Human Use (Clinical Trials) Regulations 2004, SI 2004/1031, reg 20(1)(b).
10 Medicines for Human Use (Clinical Trials) Regulations 2004, SI 2004/1031, reg 20(2)(a).
11 Medicines for Human Use (Clinical Trials) Regulations 2004, SI 2004/1031, reg 20(2)(b). As to appeals against decisions not to accept a request for authorisation or to grant an authorisation subject to conditions see PARA 125.
12 Medicines for Human Use (Clinical Trials) Regulations 2004, SI 2004/1031, reg 20(3).
13 As to the meaning of 'valid amended request' see PARA 118 note 6.
14 Medicines for Human Use (Clinical Trials) Regulations 2004, SI 2004/1031, reg 20(4)(a).
15 Medicines for Human Use (Clinical Trials) Regulations 2004, SI 2004/1031, reg 20(4)(b).
16 Medicines for Human Use (Clinical Trials) Regulations 2004, SI 2004/1031, reg 20(5). See also note 11.

121.   Clinical trials conducted in third countries. If the licensing authority[1] receives a valid request for authorisation[2] relating to a clinical trial[3] which is or is to be conducted[4] in a third country[5] as well as the United Kingdom[6], the licensing authority may, if it thinks fit, require the production by the sponsor[7] of any one or more of the following:

(1)   an undertaking, given by the sponsor, to permit its premises in that country to be inspected by or on behalf of the licensing authority for the purpose of establishing whether the conditions and principles of good clinical practice[8] are satisfied or adhered to in relation to that trial[9]; or

(2)   an undertaking, given by the owner or occupier of any premises in that country at which the clinical trial is or is to be conducted, to permit those premises to be inspected by or on behalf of the licensing authority for the purpose of establishing whether the conditions and principles of good clinical practice are satisfied or adhered to in relation to that trial[10].

If a sponsor fails to produce an undertaking required by the licensing authority, that failure constitutes[11] a ground for not accepting the request for authorisation[12].

1   As to the meaning of 'the licensing authority' see the Human Medicines Regulations 2012, SI 2012/1916, reg 6; PARA 35 note 1; definition applied by the Medicines for Human Use (Clinical Trials) Regulations 2004, SI 2004/1031, reg 2(1) (amended by SI 2012/1916).
2   As to the meaning of 'valid request for authorisation' see PARA 118 note 6.
3   As to the meaning of 'clinical trial' see PARA 107.
4   As to the meaning of 'conducting a clinical trial' see PARA 112 note 4.
5   'Third country' means a country or territory outside the European Economic Area: Medicines for Human Use (Clinical Trials) Regulations 2004, SI 2004/1031, reg 2(1). As to the meaning of 'European Economic Area' see PARA 107 note 1.
6   As to the meaning of 'United Kingdom' see PARA 20 note 4.
7   As to the meaning of 'sponsor' see PARA 107.
8   As to the meaning of 'the conditions and principles of good clinical practice' see PARA 126 note 5.
9   Medicines for Human Use (Clinical Trials) Regulations 2004, SI 2004/1031, reg 21(1)(a).
10 Medicines for Human Use (Clinical Trials) Regulations 2004, SI 2004/1031, reg 21(1)(b).
11 Ie for the purposes of the Medicines for Human Use (Clinical Trials) Regulations 2004, SI 2004/1031, regs 18–20: see PARAS 118–120.
12 Medicines for Human Use (Clinical Trials) Regulations 2004, SI 2004/1031, reg 21(2).

122.   Amendments to clinical trial authorisation by the licensing authority.
Subject to the provisions relating to urgent safety measures[1], an amendment to a clinical trial authorisation[2] may be made by the licensing authority[3], or by the sponsor[4].

The licensing authority may make amendments[5] to a clinical trial authorisation if it appears to the authority to be necessary to ensure the safety or scientific validity of the clinical trial[6], or that the conditions and principles of good clinical practice[7] are satisfied or adhered to in relation to the clinical trial[8]. Where the licensing authority proposes to make an amendment, it must, at least 14 days before the date on which it is proposed the amendment should take effect, serve a notice on the sponsor stating its proposal and the reasons for it[9]. If, within 14 days of the date such a notice is served, the sponsor makes representations in writing to the licensing authority, the authority must take those representations into account before deciding whether to make the amendment[10], and may delay the date the proposed amendment is to take effect in order to allow time for it to consider those representations[11].

1   Ie the Medicines for Human Use (Clinical Trials) Regulations 2004, SI 2004/1031, reg 30: see PARA 129.
2   'Amendment to the clinical trial authorisation' means an amendment to: (1) the terms of the request for authorisation to conduct that trial or the application for an ethics committee opinion in relation to that trial; (2) the protocol for that trial; or (3) the other particulars or documents accompanying that request for authorisation or application for ethics committee approval: Medicines for Human Use (Clinical Trials) Regulations 2004, SI 2004/1031, reg 11. As to the meaning of 'clinical trial' see PARA 107. As to requests for clinical trial authorisations see PARA 117; and as to authorisations see PARAS 118–121. As to applications for ethics committee opinions see PARA 114. As to the meaning of 'protocol' see PARA 107 note 2.
3   Medicines for Human Use (Clinical Trials) Regulations 2004, SI 2004/1031, reg 22(a). As to the meaning of 'the licensing authority' see the Human Medicines Regulations 2012, SI 2012/1916,

reg 6; PARA 35 note 1; definition applied by the Medicines for Human Use (Clinical Trials) Regulations 2004, SI 2004/1031, reg 2(1) (amended by SI 2012/1916).

4	Medicines for Human Use (Clinical Trials) Regulations 2004, SI 2004/1031, reg 22(b). As to such applications see regs 24–25; and PARAS 123–124. As to the meaning of 'sponsor' see PARA 107.

5	This is subject to the Medicines for Human Use (Clinical Trials) Regulations 2004, SI 2004/1031, reg 23(2), (3): reg 23(1) (amended by SI 2006/1928).

6	Medicines for Human Use (Clinical Trials) Regulations 2004, SI 2004/1031, reg 23(1)(a). As to appeals against amendments see reg 26; and PARA 125.

7	As to the meaning of 'the conditions and principles of good clinical practice' see PARA 126 note 5.

8	Medicines for Human Use (Clinical Trials) Regulations 2004, SI 2004/1031, reg 23(1)(b).

9	Medicines for Human Use (Clinical Trials) Regulations 2004, SI 2004/1031, reg 23(2).

10	Medicines for Human Use (Clinical Trials) Regulations 2004, SI 2004/1031, reg 23(3)(a).

11	Medicines for Human Use (Clinical Trials) Regulations 2004, SI 2004/1031, reg 23(3)(b).

123. Amendments to clinical trial authorisation by the sponsor. Subject to the provisions relating to urgent safety measures[1], a sponsor[2] may make an amendment to a clinical trial authorisation[3], other than a substantial amendment[4], at any time[5]. A sponsor must keep records of the amendments made[6] and send those records, or copies of such records, to the licensing authority[7] where the authority sends him a notice in writing requiring him to provide those records, or copies of such records[8].

If the sponsor proposes to make a substantial amendment to a clinical trial authorisation which consists of, or includes, an amendment to the terms of the request for authorisation of the clinical trial[9], or the particulars or documents that accompanied that request[10], he must send a valid notice of amendment[11] to the licensing authority[12]. The licensing authority may, within the period of 35 days from the date of receipt of a valid notice of amendment, give written notice to the sponsor setting out the licensing authority's grounds for not accepting the proposed amendment[13], or stating that the licensing authority accepts the application for amendment, subject to any conditions which may be specified in the notice[14]. If the sponsor has sent a notice[15], he may make the amendment only if the licensing authority has given him a notice stating that it accepts the application for amendment[16], or no notice has been given by the licensing authority[17].

If the sponsor proposes to make a substantial amendment to a clinical trial authorisation which consists of, or includes, an amendment to the terms of the application for an ethics committee opinion in relation to the clinical trial[18], or the particulars or documents that accompanied that application[19], he must send a valid notice of amendment to the relevant ethics committee[20]. A relevant ethics committee must, within the period of 35 days from the date of receipt of a valid notice of amendment, give an opinion to the sponsor[21]. If the sponsor has sent a notice[22] to the relevant ethics committee, he may make the amendment only if the relevant ethics committee has given a favourable opinion[23].

1	Ie the Medicines for Human Use (Clinical Trials) Regulations 2004, SI 2004/1031, reg 30: see PARA 129.

2	As to the meaning of 'sponsor' see PARA 107.

3	See the Medicines for Human Use (Clinical Trials) Regulations 2004, SI 2004/1031, reg 22(b). As to the meaning of 'amendment to the clinical trial authorisation' see PARA 122 note 2. As to clinical trial authorisations see PARA 117 et seq. As to the meaning of 'clinical trial' see PARA 107. As to infringement notices see PARA 137.

4	'Substantial amendment to the clinical trial authorisation' means an amendment to the clinical trial authorisation which is likely to affect to a significant degree: (1) the safety or physical or mental integrity of the subjects of the trial; (2) the scientific value of the trial; (3) the conduct or management of the trial; or (4) the quality or safety of any investigational medicinal product used in the trial: Medicines for Human Use (Clinical Trials) Regulations 2004, SI 2004/1031, reg 11. As to the meanings of 'subject' and 'investigational medicinal product' see PARA 107 note 1.

5   Medicines for Human Use (Clinical Trials) Regulations 2004, SI 2004/1031, reg 24(1).

6   Medicines for Human Use (Clinical Trials) Regulations 2004, SI 2004/1031, reg 24(2)(a).

7   As to the meaning of 'the licensing authority' see the Human Medicines Regulations 2012, SI 2012/1916, reg 6; PARA 35 note 1; definition applied by the Medicines for Human Use (Clinical Trials) Regulations 2004, SI 2004/1031, reg 2(1) (amended by SI 2012/1916).

8   Medicines for Human Use (Clinical Trials) Regulations 2004, SI 2004/1031, reg 24(2)(b).

9   Medicines for Human Use (Clinical Trials) Regulations 2004, SI 2004/1031, reg 24(3)(a).

10 Medicines for Human Use (Clinical Trials) Regulations 2004, SI 2004/1031, reg 24(3)(b).

11 'Valid notice of amendment' means a notice that is in writing and accompanied by the specified particulars and unless arrangements have been made with the licensing authority for the payment of any relevant fee other than at the time of the request, any such fee: Medicines for Human Use (Clinical Trials) Regulations 2004, SI 2004/1031, reg 24(10) (definition substituted by SI 2006/1928) As to the specified particulars see the Medicines for Human Use (Clinical Trials) Regulations 2004, SI 2004/1031, Sch 3 Pt 3. 'Any relevant fee' means, in relation to a notice of amendment, any fee which may be payable in connection with that notice under the Medicines (Products for Human Use) (Fees) Regulations 2012, SI 2012/504: Medicines for Human Use (Clinical Trials) Regulations 2004, SI 2004/1031, reg 24(10) (definition added by SI 2006/1928).

12 Medicines for Human Use (Clinical Trials) Regulations 2004, SI 2004/1031, reg 24(3). The sponsor must send such notice whether or not he is also required to send a notice in accordance with reg 24(4) (see the text to notes 18–20): reg 24(3).

13 Medicines for Human Use (Clinical Trials) Regulations 2004, SI 2004/1031, reg 24(5)(a). As to modifying or adapting rejected proposals for amendment see PARA 124. As to appeals against rejected proposals see PARA 125.

14 Medicines for Human Use (Clinical Trials) Regulations 2004, SI 2004/1031, reg 24(5)(b).

15 Ie in accordance with the Medicines for Human Use (Clinical Trials) Regulations 2004, SI 2004/1031, reg 24(3): see the text to notes 9–12.

16 Medicines for Human Use (Clinical Trials) Regulations 2004, SI 2004/1031, reg 24(7)(a). If the sponsor has been given a notice stating that the licensing authority accepts the application for amendment, he may make the amendment subject to the conditions, if any, specified in the notice: reg 24(8).

17 Medicines for Human Use (Clinical Trials) Regulations 2004, SI 2004/1031, reg 24(7)(b).

18 Medicines for Human Use (Clinical Trials) Regulations 2004, SI 2004/1031, reg 24(4)(a). As to applications for ethics committee opinions see PARA 114.

19 Medicines for Human Use (Clinical Trials) Regulations 2004, SI 2004/1031, reg 24(4)(b).

20 Medicines for Human Use (Clinical Trials) Regulations 2004, SI 2004/1031, reg 24(4). The sponsor must send such a notice whether or not he is also required to send a notice in accordance with reg 24(3) (see the text to notes 9–12): reg 24(4). 'Relevant ethics committee', in relation to a clinical trial, means: (1) in a case where an ethics committee has given a favourable opinion in relation to that trial and Sch 2 para 13 (see PARA 111) applies, the ethics committee which is the relevant ethics committee for that trial by virtue of Sch 2 para 13(5); (2) in a case where an ethics committee has given an unfavourable opinion in relation to that trial but a favourable opinion has been given by an appeal panel in accordance with Sch 4 para 4(4) (see PARA 116), that committee; or (3) in any other case, the ethics committee which has given a favourable opinion in relation to that trial in accordance with reg 15 (see PARA 115): reg 2(1).

21 Medicines for Human Use (Clinical Trials) Regulations 2004, SI 2004/1031, reg 24(6). As to modifying or adapting rejected proposals for amendment see PARA 124.

22 Ie in accordance with the Medicines for Human Use (Clinical Trials) Regulations 2004, SI 2004/1031, reg 24(4): see the text to notes 18–20.

23 Medicines for Human Use (Clinical Trials) Regulations 2004, SI 2004/1031, reg 24(9).

124.   Modifying or adapting rejected proposals for amendment. If the ethics committee[1] opinion on a proposed amendment[2] to the protocol[3] is not favourable[4], or the sponsor[5] has been notified by the licensing authority[6] of any grounds for non-acceptance of a proposed amendment to the protocol[7], and it is possible to modify or adapt the proposed amendment in order to meet the concerns of the ethics committee or the licensing authority as set out in the opinion or, as the case may be, the grounds for non-acceptance, the sponsor may amend the protocol accordingly[8]. If a sponsor proposes to so amend the protocol, he must, at least 14 days before the amendment is to be made, give a notice in writing to the licensing authority and the relevant ethics committee[9]. The licensing authority may, within the period of 14 days from the date of receipt of such a notice, give written notice to the sponsor setting out the licensing authority's further grounds for not accepting the modified or adapted amendment[10]; and the relevant ethics committee may, within the period of 14 days from the date of receipt of such a notice, give a written notice to the sponsor stating that its opinion of the modified or adapted amendment is unfavourable[11]. If the sponsor receives such a written notice from the licensing authority or the relevant ethics committee, he may not make the amendment[12]; and if he receives no such notice he may make the modified or adapted amendment[13].

1   As to the meaning of 'ethics committee' see PARA 111 note 2.
2   As to ethics committee opinions on proposed amendments see PARA 123.
3   As to the meaning of 'protocol' see PARA 107 note 2.
4   Medicines for Human Use (Clinical Trials) Regulations 2004, SI 2004/1031, reg 25(1)(a).
5   As to the meaning of 'sponsor' see PARA 107.
6   As to such notifications see PARA 123. As to the meaning of 'the licensing authority' see the Human Medicines Regulations 2012, SI 2012/1916, reg 6; PARA 35 note 1; definition applied by the Medicines for Human Use (Clinical Trials) Regulations 2004, SI 2004/1031, reg 2(1) (amended by SI 2012/1916).
7   Medicines for Human Use (Clinical Trials) Regulations 2004, SI 2004/1031, reg 25(1)(b).
8   Medicines for Human Use (Clinical Trials) Regulations 2004, SI 2004/1031, reg 25(1).
9   Medicines for Human Use (Clinical Trials) Regulations 2004, SI 2004/1031, reg 25(2). As to the meaning of 'relevant ethics committee' see PARA 123 note 20.
10 Medicines for Human Use (Clinical Trials) Regulations 2004, SI 2004/1031, reg 25(3). As to appeals against such decisions see PARA 125.
11 Medicines for Human Use (Clinical Trials) Regulations 2004, SI 2004/1031, reg 25(4).
12 Medicines for Human Use (Clinical Trials) Regulations 2004, SI 2004/1031, reg 25(5)(a).
13 Medicines for Human Use (Clinical Trials) Regulations 2004, SI 2004/1031, reg 25(5)(b).

125.   Reference to the appropriate committee or the Commission on Human Medicines.   If:

(1)   a sponsor[1] has been notified by the licensing authority[2] that there are grounds for not accepting a request for authorisation[3], or the trial is authorised[4] subject to specified conditions[5];

(2)   the licensing authority has amended[6] a clinical trial authorisation[7]; or

(3)   the sponsor has been notified[8] by the licensing authority that the authority does not accept a proposed, modified or adapted amendment to the clinical trial authorisation[9], or the authority accepts such an amendment subject to conditions[10],

the sponsor may, within 28 days, or such extended period as the licensing authority may in any particular case allow, of the notice being given, give notice in writing to the licensing authority of his wish to make written or oral representations to the appropriate committee[11].

If a sponsor or investigator[12] has been served a notice[13] by the licensing authority requiring that a trial, or the conduct of the trial at a particular site, be suspended or terminated, he may give notice of his wish to make written or oral representations to the appropriate committee[14].

Where the licensing authority is notified[15] of the wish of a sponsor or investigator to make representations, the authority must inform the appropriate committee and the committee must give the sponsor or investigator an opportunity to make such representations[16]. The sponsor or investigator must provide the appropriate committee with his written representations or a written summary of the oral representations he intends to make[17] and any documents on which he wishes to rely in support of those representations[18], before the end of the period of six months beginning with the date of the notice or within such shorter period as the licensing authority may specify in its notification[19]. If the sponsor or investigator gave notice of his wish to make oral representations, the appropriate committee must, after receiving a written summary and any other documents, arrange for the sponsor or investigator to make such representations at a hearing before the committee[20]. The appropriate committee must take into account such representations as are made[21] and report its findings and advice to the licensing authority, together with the reasons for its advice[22].

In the case of a decision not to accept a request for authorisation to conduct a clinical trial or an amendment to the clinical trial authorisation, the licensing authority must, after considering the report of the appropriate committee confirm that it has grounds for not accepting the request or amendment[23], or accept the request for authorisation or amendment to the clinical trial authorisation subject to such conditions as the licensing authority may consider appropriate[24]. In the case of a decision to impose a condition following a request for authorisation to conduct a clinical trial or a notice of amendment to a clinical trial authorisation, the licensing authority must, after considering the report of the appropriate committee, confirm its decision[25] or remove or alter the condition in question[26].

1 As to the meaning of 'sponsor' see PARA 107.

2 As to the meaning of 'the licensing authority' see the Human Medicines Regulations 2012, SI 2012/1916, reg 6; PARA 35 note 1; definition applied by the Medicines for Human Use (Clinical Trials) Regulations 2004, SI 2004/1031, reg 2(1) (amended by SI 2012/1916).

3 Medicines for Human Use (Clinical Trials) Regulations 2004, SI 2004/1031, reg 26(1)(a)(i). As to requests for authorisation see PARA 117.

4 Ie in accordance with the Medicines for Human Use (Clinical Trials) Regulations 2004, SI 2004/1031, reg 18(2), (6) (see PARA 118), reg 19(8) (see PARA 119), reg 20(5) (see PARA 120).

5 Medicines for Human Use (Clinical Trials) Regulations 2004, SI 2004/1031, reg 26(1)(a)(ii).

6 Ie under the Medicines for Human Use (Clinical Trials) Regulations 2004, SI 2004/1031, reg 23: see PARA 122.

7 Medicines for Human Use (Clinical Trials) Regulations 2004, SI 2004/1031, reg 26(1)(b). As to the meaning of 'clinical trial' see PARA 107.

8 Ie in accordance with the Medicines for Human Use (Clinical Trials) Regulations 2004, SI 2004/1031, reg 24(5) (see PARA 123) or reg 25(3) (see PARA 124).

9 Medicines for Human Use (Clinical Trials) Regulations 2004, SI 2004/1031, reg 26(1)(c)(i) (amended by SI 2005/2754).

10 Medicines for Human Use (Clinical Trials) Regulations 2004, SI 2004/1031, reg 26(1)(c)(ii).

11 Medicines for Human Use (Clinical Trials) Regulations 2004, SI 2004/1031, reg 26(1) (amended by SI 2005/2754). 'Appropriate committee', for the purposes of any provision of the Medicines for Human Use (Clinical Trials) Regulations 2004, SI 2004/1031 under which a function falls to be performed, means whichever the licensing authority consider to be appropriate of the Commission on Human Medicines or an expert committee appointed by the licensing authority: Medicines for Human Use (Clinical Trials) Regulations 2004, SI 2004/1031, reg 2(1) (definition substituted by SI 2012/1916). As to the Commission on Human Medicines see PARA 31.

12 As to the meaning of 'investigator' see PARA 113 note 4.

13 Ie in accordance with the Medicines for Human Use (Clinical Trials) Regulations 2004, SI 2004/1031, reg 37(1), (2) (see PARA 98).

14 See the Medicines for Human Use (Clinical Trials) Regulations 2004, SI 2004/1031, reg 37(7) (amended by SI 2005/2754).

15 Ie in accordance with the Medicines for Human Use (Clinical Trials) Regulations 2004, SI 2004/1031, reg 26(1) (see the text and notes 1–12) or reg 31(7) (see PARA 130).

16 Medicines for Human Use (Clinical Trials) Regulations 2004, SI 2004/1031, regs 26(2), 31(8), Sch 5 para 1(1) (regs 26(2), 31(8) amended, and Sch 5 substituted, by SI 2005/2754).

17 Medicines for Human Use (Clinical Trials) Regulations 2004, SI 2004/1031, Sch 5 para 1(2)(a) (as substituted: see note 14).
18 Medicines for Human Use (Clinical Trials) Regulations 2004, SI 2004/1031, Sch 5 para 1(2)(b) (as substituted: see note 14).
19 Medicines for Human Use (Clinical Trials) Regulations 2004, SI 2004/1031, Sch 5 para 1(2) (as substituted: see note 14). If the sponsor or investigator so requests, the appropriate committee may extend the time limit up to a maximum period of 12 months beginning with the date of the notice: Sch 5 para 1(3) (as so substituted). The sponsor or investigator may not submit any additional written representations or documents once the time limit or time limit as extended has expired except with the permission of the appropriate committee: Sch 5 para 1(4) (as so substituted). As to the meaning of 'month' see PARA 43 note 3.
20 Medicines for Human Use (Clinical Trials) Regulations 2004, SI 2004/1031, Sch 5 para 1(5) (as substituted: see note 14).
21 Medicines for Human Use (Clinical Trials) Regulations 2004, SI 2004/1031, Sch 5 para 1(6)(a) (as substituted: see note 14).
22 Medicines for Human Use (Clinical Trials) Regulations 2004, SI 2004/1031, Sch 5 para 1(6)(b) (as substituted: see note 14).
23 Medicines for Human Use (Clinical Trials) Regulations 2004, SI 2004/1031, Sch 5 para 2(1)(a) (as substituted: see note 14).
24 Medicines for Human Use (Clinical Trials) Regulations 2004, SI 2004/1031, Sch 5 para 2(1)(b) (as substituted: see note 14).
25 Medicines for Human Use (Clinical Trials) Regulations 2004, SI 2004/1031, Sch 5 para 2(2)(a) (as substituted: see note 14).
26 Medicines for Human Use (Clinical Trials) Regulations 2004, SI 2004/1031, Sch 5 para 2(2)(b) (as substituted: see note 14).

(iv) Conduct of Clinical Trials

126. Good clinical practice and protection of clinical trial subjects. No person[1] may conduct a clinical trial[2], or perform the functions of the sponsor[3] of a clinical trial[4], otherwise than in accordance with the conditions and principles of good clinical practice[5]. The sponsor of a clinical trial must put and keep in place arrangements for the purpose of ensuring that with regard to that trial the conditions and principles of good clinical practice are satisfied or adhered to[6]. The sponsor of a clinical trial must ensure that the investigational medicinal products[7] used in the trial[8], and any devices used for the administration of such products[9], are made available to the subjects[10] of the trial free of charge[11].

Any person who contravenes these provisions[12] is guilty of an offence[13].

The sponsor is required to notify the licensing authority of serious breaches, and is required to keep a trial master file for a clinical trial[14].

1 As to the meaning of 'person' see PARA 45 note 2.
2 Medicines for Human Use (Clinical Trials) Regulations 2004, SI 2004/1031, reg 28(1)(a). As to the meaning of 'conducting a clinical trial' see PARA 112 note 4. As to the meaning of 'clinical trial' see PARA 107.
3 As to the meaning of 'sponsor' see PARA 107.
4 Medicines for Human Use (Clinical Trials) Regulations 2004, SI 2004/1031, reg 28(1)(b). This restriction applies whether that person is the sponsor or is acting under arrangements made with that sponsor: reg 28(1)(b).
5 Medicines for Human Use (Clinical Trials) Regulations 2004, SI 2004/1031, reg 28(1). 'Conditions and principles of good clinical practice' means the conditions and principles specified in the Medicines for Human Use (Clinical Trials) Regulations 2004, SI 2004/1031: reg 2(1). As to such conditions and principles see Sch 1 (amended by SI 2006/1928; SI 2008/941). As to infringement notices see PARA 137.
6 Medicines for Human Use (Clinical Trials) Regulations 2004, SI 2004/1031, reg 28(2). If a clinical trial is conducted at more than one trial site, and the request for authorisation to conduct that trial specifies that in relation to one or more trial sites the duties of the sponsor under reg 28(2), (3) (see the text to notes 7–11) are to be performed by a person other than the sponsor, those duties must, in relation to that site or those sites, be performed by the person so specified: reg 28(5).

7   As to the meaning of 'investigational medicinal product' see PARA 107 note 1.
8   Medicines for Human Use (Clinical Trials) Regulations 2004, SI 2004/1031, reg 28(3)(a).
9   Medicines for Human Use (Clinical Trials) Regulations 2004, SI 2004/1031, reg 28(3)(b).
10 As to the meaning of 'subject' see PARA 107 note 1.
11 Medicines for Human Use (Clinical Trials) Regulations 2004, SI 2004/1031, reg 28(3). This
    restriction does not apply in relation to any charge payable by a subject under regulations made
    under the National Health Service Act 1977, the National Health Service (Scotland) Act 1978,
    or the Health and Personal Social Services (Northern Ireland) Order 1972, SI 1972/1265
    (NI 14), in respect of any medicinal products or devices provided in pursuance of those Acts or
    that order: Medicines for Human Use (Clinical Trials) Regulations 2004, SI 2004/1031,
    reg 28(4). See also note 6.
12 Ie the provisions of the Medicines for Human Use (Clinical Trials) Regulations 2004,
    SI 2004/1031, reg 28(1)–(3).
13 Medicines for Human Use (Clinical Trials) Regulations 2004, SI 2004/1031, reg 49(1)(d). As to
    offences generally, defences and penalties see PARAS 138–140.
14 Medicines for Human Use (Clinical Trials) Regulations 2004, SI 2004/1031, regs 29A, 31A; and
    PARAS 128, 131.

127.   Conduct of trial in accordance with clinical trial authorisation. Subject
to the provisions relating to urgent safety measures[1], no person[2] may conduct a
clinical trial[3] otherwise than in accordance with: (1) the protocol[4] relating to that
trial, as amended[5] from time to time[6]; (2) the terms, as amended from time to
time[7], of the request for authorisation to conduct that trial[8], the application for
an ethics committee[9] opinion in relation to that trial[10], and any particulars or
documents, other than the protocol, accompanying that request or that
application[11]; (3) any conditions imposed by the licensing authority[12] on an
authorisation[13].
    Any person who contravenes these provisions is guilty of an offence[14].

1   Ie the Medicines for Human Use (Clinical Trials) Regulations 2004, SI 2004/1031, reg 30: see
    PARA 129.
2   As to the meaning of 'person' see PARA 45 note 2.
3   As to the meaning of 'conducting a clinical trial' see PARA 112 note 4. As to the meaning of
    'clinical trial' see PARA 107. As to infringement notices see PARA 137.
4   As to the meaning of 'protocol' see PARA 107 note 2.
5   Ie in accordance with the Medicines for Human Use (Clinical Trials) Regulations 2004,
    SI 2004/1031, regs 22–25: see PARAS 122–124.
6   Medicines for Human Use (Clinical Trials) Regulations 2004, SI 2004/1031, reg 29(a).
7   Ie in accordance with the Medicines for Human Use (Clinical Trials) Regulations 2004,
    SI 2004/1031, regs 22–25: see PARAS 122–124.
8   Medicines for Human Use (Clinical Trials) Regulations 2004, SI 2004/1031, reg 29(b)(i). As to
    requests for authorisation see PARA 117.
9   As to the meaning of 'ethics committee' see PARA 111 note 2.
10 Medicines for Human Use (Clinical Trials) Regulations 2004, SI 2004/1031, reg 29(b)(ii). As to
    applications for ethics committee opinions see PARA 114.
11 Medicines for Human Use (Clinical Trials) Regulations 2004, SI 2004/1031, reg 29(b)(iii).
12 Ie under the Medicines for Human Use (Clinical Trials) Regulations 2004, SI 2004/1031,
    reg 18(2), (6) (see PARA 118), reg 19(8) (see PARA 119), reg 20(5) (see PARA 120), reg 24(5) (see
    PARA 123), reg 26, Sch 5 (see PARA 125). As to the meaning of 'the licensing authority' see the
    Human Medicines Regulations 2012, SI 2012/1916, reg 6; PARA 35 note 1; definition applied by
    the Medicines for Human Use (Clinical Trials) Regulations 2004, SI 2004/1031, reg 2(1)
    (amended by SI 2012/1916).
13 Medicines for Human Use (Clinical Trials) Regulations 2004, SI 2004/1031, reg 29(c) (amended
    by SI 2006/1928).
14 Medicines for Human Use (Clinical Trials) Regulations 2004, SI 2004/1031, reg 49(1)(e). As to
    offences generally, defences and penalties see PARAS 138–140.

128.   Notification of serious breaches. The sponsor[1] of a clinical trial[2] must
notify the licensing authority[3] in writing of any serious breach[4] of the conditions
and principles of good clinical practice in connection with that trial, or any

serious breach of the protocol[5] relating to that trial within seven days of becoming aware of that breach[6]. Breach of these provisions is an offence[7].

1   As to the meaning of 'sponsor' see PARA 107.
2   As to the meaning of 'clinical trial' see PARA 107.
3   As to the meaning of 'the licensing authority' see the Human Medicines Regulations 2012, SI 2012/1916, reg 6; PARA 35 note 1; definition applied by the Medicines for Human Use (Clinical Trials) Regulations 2004, SI 2004/1031, reg 2(1) (amended by SI 2012/1916).
4   A 'serious breach' is a breach which is likely to effect to a significant degree the safety or physical or mental integrity of the subjects of the trial or the scientific value of the trial: Medicines for Human Use (Clinical Trials) Regulations 2004, SI 2004/1031, reg 29A (reg 29A added by SI 2006/1928). As to the meaning of 'subject' see PARA 107 note 1.
5   Ie the protocol as amended from time to time in accordance with SI 2004/1031 regs 22–25 (see PARAS 122–124). As to the meaning of 'protocol' see PARA 107 note 2.
6   Medicines for Human Use (Clinical Trials) Regulations 2004, SI 2004/1031, reg 29A(1).
7   Medicines for Human Use (Clinical Trials) Regulations 2004, SI 2004/1031, reg 49(1)(ee) (added by SI 2006/1928). As to offences generally, defences and penalties see PARAS 138–140.

129.   Urgent safety measures.   The sponsor[1] and investigator[2] may take appropriate urgent safety measures in order to protect the subjects[3] of a clinical trial[4] against any immediate hazard to their health or safety[5]. During a period in which a disease is pandemic and is a serious or potentially serious risk to human health, the sponsor must, as soon as possible, give written notice to the licensing authority[6] and the relevant ethics committee[7] of the measures taken and the circumstances giving rise to those measures[8]. In any other case the written notice must be given immediately, and in any event no later than 3 days from the date the measures are taken[9].

Any person[10] who contravenes this provision relating to the giving of notice[11] is guilty of an offence[12].

1   As to the meaning of 'sponsor' see PARA 107.
2   As to the meaning of 'investigator' see PARA 113 note 4.
3   As to the meaning of 'subject' see PARA 107 note 1.
4   As to the meaning of 'clinical trial' see PARA 107.
5   Medicines for Human Use (Clinical Trials) Regulations 2004, SI 2004/1031, reg 30(1).
6   As to the meaning of 'the licensing authority' see the Human Medicines Regulations 2012, SI 2012/1916, reg 6; PARA 35 note 1; definition applied by the Medicines for Human Use (Clinical Trials) Regulations 2004, SI 2004/1031, reg 2(1) (amended by SI 2012/1916).
7   As to the meaning of 'relevant ethics committee' see PARA 123 note 20.
8   Medicines for Human Use (Clinical Trials) Regulations 2001, SI 2004/1031, reg 30(2).
9   Medicines for Human Use (Clinical Trials) Regulations 2001, SI 2004/1031, reg 30(2).
10 As to the meaning of 'person' see PARA 45 note 2.
11 Ie the Medicines for Human Use (Clinical Trials) Regulations 2004, SI 2004/1031, reg 30(2): see the text to notes 6–8.
12 Medicines for Human Use (Clinical Trials) Regulations 2004, SI 2004/1031, reg 49(1)(f). As to offences generally, defences and penalties see PARAS 138–140.

130.   Suspension or termination of clinical trial.   If, in relation to a clinical trial[1]: (1) the licensing authority[2] has objective grounds for considering that any condition, restriction or limitation which applies to the conduct of the trial[3] and is set out in the request for authorisation[4] or the particulars or documents accompanying that request[5], or any condition imposed[6] by the licensing authority[7], is no longer satisfied, either generally or at a particular trial site[8]; or (2) the licensing authority has information raising doubts about the safety or scientific validity of the trial, or the conduct of the trial at a particular trial site[9], then the licensing authority may, by a notice[10], require that the trial, or the conduct of the trial at a particular trial site, be suspended or terminated[11]. Except where it appears to the licensing authority that there is an imminent risk to the health or safety of any of the subjects[12] of the clinical trial[13], at least one week before issuing such a notice the licensing authority must, by a notice in writing to the sponsor or the investigator, inform him that the authority is minded to issue a notice suspending or terminating the trial, or the conduct of a trial at a particular site, and of the reasons why it is so minded[14], and advise him that he may, within one week of the date of the notice, furnish the authority with written representations as to whether the trial, or the conduct of the trial at the particular site, should be so suspended or terminated[15].

A person[16] on whom a notice has been served may, within 28 days, or such extended period as the licensing authority may in any particular case allow, of the notice being given, give notice of his wish to make written or oral representations to the appropriate committee[17]. The licensing authority must, after considering the report of the appropriate committee, confirm or revoke the notice[18], and give notice to the sponsor or investigator of its decision[19]. Where the notice of suspension or termination is referred to an appropriate committee, it remains in force unless revoked in accordance with the provisions relating to such referral[20].

Any person who fails to comply with a notice of suspension or termination served on him, unless that notice has been withdrawn or revoked by the licensing authority, is guilty of an offence[21].

1 As to the meaning of 'clinical trial' see PARA 107.
2 As to the meaning of 'the licensing authority' see the Human Medicines Regulations 2012, SI 2012/1916, reg 6; PARA 35 note 1; definition applied by the Medicines for Human Use (Clinical Trials) Regulations 2004, SI 2004/1031, reg 2(1) (amended by SI 2012/1916).
3 As to the meaning of 'conducting a clinical trial' see PARA 112 note 4.
4 As to requests for authorisation see PARA 117.
5 Medicines for Human Use (Clinical Trials) Regulations 2004, SI 2004/1031, reg 31(1)(a)(i).
6 Ie under the Medicines for Human Use (Clinical Trials) Regulations 2004, SI 2004/1031, reg 18(2), (6) (see PARA 118), reg 19(8) (see PARA 119), reg 20(5) (see PARA 120), reg 24(5) (see PARA 123), reg 26, Sch 5 (see PARA 125).
7 Medicines for Human Use (Clinical Trials) Regulations 2004, SI 2004/1031, reg 31(1)(a)(ii) (amended by SI 2006/1928).
8 Medicines for Human Use (Clinical Trials) Regulations 2004, SI 2004/1031, reg 31(1)(a). As to the meaning of 'trial site' see PARA 113 note 4.
9 Medicines for Human Use (Clinical Trials) Regulations 2004, SI 2004/1031, reg 31(1)(b).
10 A notice must be served: (1) in a case where the suspension or termination applies to the trial generally, on the sponsor (Medicines for Human Use (Clinical Trials) Regulations 2004, SI 2004/1031, reg 31(2)(a)(i)) or the investigator at each trial site (reg 31(2)(a)(ii)); (2) in a case where the suspension or termination applies to the conduct of a trial at a particular trial site, on the sponsor (reg 31(2)(b)(i)) or the investigator at that trial site (reg 31(2)(b)(ii)). As to the meaning of 'sponsor' see PARA 107. As to the meaning of 'investigator' see PARA 113 note 4. The notice must specify whether the notice applies to the trial generally or to one or more of the trial sites (reg 31(3)(a)); whether the notice requires suspension or termination of the trial (reg 31(3)(b)); if the notice requires suspension of the trial, whether the suspension applies until further notice from the licensing authority or for such period as may be specified in the notice (reg 31(3)(c)(i)), and any conditions which are to be satisfied before the trial or, as the case may be, the conduct of the trial at a particular site, may be recommenced (reg 31(3)(c)(ii)); and whether suspension or termination is to take effect immediately on receipt of the notice or on such date as may be specified in the notice (reg 31(3)(d)).
11 Medicines for Human Use (Clinical Trials) Regulations 2004, SI 2004/1031, reg 31(1). If the licensing authority issues such a notice, it must forthwith inform: (1) where the notice has not been served on the sponsor, the sponsor (reg 31(4)(a)); (2) competent authorities of each EEA state, other than the United Kingdom (reg 31(4)(b)); (3) the relevant ethics committee (reg 31(4)(c)); (4) the European Medicines Agency (reg 31(4)(d)); and (5) the European Commission (reg 31(4)(e)). As to the meaning of 'EEA state' see PARA 107 note 1. As to the meaning of 'United Kingdom' see PARA 20 note 4. As to the meaning of 'relevant ethics committee' see PARA 123 note 20. 'The European Medicines Agency' means the European Medicines Agency established by Parliament and Council Regulation (EC) 726/2004 (OJ L137,

30.4.2004, p 1) laying down Community procedures for the authorisation and supervision of medicinal products for human and veterinary use and establishing a European Medicines Agency: Medicines for Human Use (Clinical Trials) Regulations 2004, SI 2004/1031, reg 2(1) (definition substituted by SI 2004/3224). As to the European Medicines Agency see PARA 14.

12 As to the meaning of 'subject' see PARA 107 note 1.

13 Medicines for Human Use (Clinical Trials) Regulations 2004, SI 2004/1031, reg 31(6).

14 Medicines for Human Use (Clinical Trials) Regulations 2004, SI 2004/1031, reg 31(5)(a).

15 Medicines for Human Use (Clinical Trials) Regulations 2004, SI 2004/1031, reg 31(5)(b).

16 As to the meaning of 'person' see PARA 45 note 2.

17 Medicines for Human Use (Clinical Trials) Regulations 2004, SI 2004/1031, reg 31(7) (reg 31(7)–(9) amended by SI 2005/2754). As to the meaning of 'the appropriate committee' see PARA 125 note 12.

    The Medicines for Human Use (Clinical Trials) Regulations 2004, SI 2004/1031, Sch 5 has effect to regulate the procedure for reference to the appropriate committee: reg 31(8) (as so amended). See the text and notes 18–19; and PARA 125.

18 Medicines for Human Use (Clinical Trials) Regulations 2004, SI 2004/1031, Sch 5 para 2(3) (Sch 5 substituted by SI 2005/2754).

19 Medicines for Human Use (Clinical Trials) Regulations 2004, SI 2004/1031, Sch 5 para 2(4)(b) (as substituted: see note 18). The notice must also give details of the findings and advice of the appropriate committee and the reasons for it: Sch 5 para 2(4)(a) (as so substituted). If a sponsor or investigator to whom such a notice is given is dissatisfied, he may within 28 days of the notice being given, or such longer period as the licensing authority may in any particular case allow, notify the licensing authority that he wishes to appear before and be heard by a person appointed by the licensing authority with respect to the decision (Sch 5 para 3(1)(a) (as so substituted)), or make representations in writing to the licensing authority with respect to the decision referred to in the notice (Sch 5 para 3(1)(b) (as so substituted)). However, Sch 5 para 3(1)(a) does not apply where the sponsor or investigator had not made any representations in accordance with Sch 5 para 1(2)–(5) (Sch 5 para 3(2)(a) (as so substituted)) and the decision of the licensing authority was in accordance with the advice of the appropriate committee (Sch 5 para 3(2)(b) (as so substituted)). If the sponsor or investigator makes written representations in accordance with Sch 5 para 3(2)(b), the licensing authority must take those representations into account before deciding whether to confirm or alter its decision: Sch 5 para 3(3) (as so substituted). As to the procedure in cases to be heard before a person appointed after the giving of a notice under Sch 5 para 3(1)(a) see Sch 5 para 4 (as so substituted).

20 Medicines for Human Use (Clinical Trials) Regulations 2004, SI 2004/1031, reg 31(9) (as amended: see note 17).

21 Medicines for Human Use (Clinical Trials) Regulations 2004, SI 2004/1031, reg 49(3). As to offences generally, defences and penalties see PARAS 138–140.

131. Trial master file. The sponsor[1] must keep a trial master file for a clinical trial[2], and must ensure that it is readily available at all reasonable times for inspection by the licensing authority[3] or by any person appointed by the sponsor to audit the arrangements for the trial[4]. The master file must at all times contain the essential documents[5] relating to that clinical trial[6], which are to contain information specific to each phase of the trial[7]. The sponsor is also required to ensure the traceability of any alteration to a document contained, or which has been contained, in the trial master file[8]. It is an offence to contravene these provisions[9].

1 As to the meaning of 'sponsor' see PARA 107.

2 Medicines for Human Use (Clinical Trials) Regulations 2004, SI 2004/1031, reg 31A(1) (reg 31A added by SI 2006/1928). As to the meaning of 'clinical trial' see PARA 107. The sponsor must appoint named individuals in his organisation to be responsible for archiving the documents which are, or have been, contained in the trial master file and, subject to the Medicines for Human Use (Clinical Trials) Regulations 2004, SI 2004/1031, reg 31A(2), access to those documents must be restricted to those appointed individuals: reg 31A(9). For the purposes of reg 31A, an individual is an individual in the sponsor's organisation where (1) he is employed or engaged by the sponsor; (2) he is acting under arrangements made with the sponsor for the purposes of managing or conducting the clinical trial; (3) where the sponsor is an individual, he is the sponsor; or (4) where the sponsor is a body of persons, he is a member of the body or employed or engaged by such a member: reg 31A(10).

3   As to the meaning of 'the licensing authority' see the Human Medicines Regulations 2012, SI 2012/1916, reg 6; PARA 35 note 1; definition applied by the Medicines for Human Use (Clinical Trials) Regulations 2004, SI 2004/1031, reg 2(1) (amended by SI 2012/1916).

4   Medicines for Human Use (Clinical Trials) Regulations 2004, SI 2004/1031, reg 31A(2).

5   The essential documents relating to a clinical trial are those which enable both the conduct of the clinical trial and the quality of the data produced to be evaluated and show whether the trial is, or has been, conducted in accordance with the applicable requirements of Council Directive (EC) 2001/83 (OJ L311, 28.11.2001, p 67) on the Community code relating to medicinal products for human use, European Parliament and Council Directive (EC) 2001/20 (OJ L121, 1.5.2001, p 34) on the approximation of the laws, regulations and administrative provisions of the Member States relating to the implementation of good clinical practice in the conduct of clinical trials on medicinal products for human use, Commission Directive (EC) 2005/28 (OJ L91, 9.4.2005, p 13–15) laying down principles and detailed guidelines for good clinical practice as regards investigational medicinal products for human use, as well as the requirements for authorisation of the manufacturing or importation of such products and Commission Directive (EC) 2003/94 (OJ L262, 14.10.2003, p 22–26) laying down the principles and guidelines of good manufacturing practice in respect of medicinal products for human use and investigational medicinal products for human use (see PARA 12): Medicines for Human Use (Clinical Trials) Regulations 2004, SI 2004/1031, reg 31A(4).

6   Medicines for Human Use (Clinical Trials) Regulations 2004, SI 2004/1031, reg 31A(3).

7   Medicines for Human Use (Clinical Trials) Regulations 2004, SI 2004/1031, reg 31A(5).

8   Medicines for Human Use (Clinical Trials) Regulations 2004, SI 2004/1031, reg 31A(6). The sponsor and the chief investigator must ensure that the documents contained, or which have been contained, in the trial master file are retained for at least five years after the conclusion of the trial and that during that period are readily available to the licensing authority on request, and are complete and legible: reg 31A(7) (as so added). As to the meaning of 'chief investigator' see PARA 114 note 3. The sponsor and chief investigator must ensure that the medical files of trial subjects are retained for at least five years after the conclusion of the trial: reg 31A(8). As to the meaning of 'subject' see PARA 107 note 1. If there is transfer of ownership of data or documents connected with the clinical trial, the sponsor must record the transfer and the new owner is to be responsible for data retention and archiving in accordance with reg 31A(2), (7) and (8): reg 31A(9).

9   Medicines for Human Use (Clinical Trials) Regulations 2004, SI 2004/1031, reg 49(1)(ff) (added by SI 2006/1928). As to offences, defences and penalties generally see PARAS 138–140.

132. Notification of adverse events. An investigator[1] must report[2] any serious adverse event[3] which occurs in a subject at a trial site at which he is responsible for the conduct of a clinical trial[4] immediately to the sponsor[5]. Following the immediate report of a serious adverse event, the investigator must make a detailed written report on the event[6]. Where the event reported[7] consists of, or results in, the death of a subject, the investigator must supply the sponsor[8] and, in any case where the death has been reported to the relevant ethics committee[9], that committee[10], with any additional information requested by the sponsor or, as the case may be, the committee[11]. The sponsor must keep detailed records of all adverse events relating to a clinical trial which are reported to him by the investigators for that trial[12]. The licensing authority[13] may, by sending a notice in writing to the sponsor, require him to send the records, or copies of such records, to the authority[14].

Any person[15] who contravenes these provisions[16] commits an offence[17].

1   As to the meaning of 'investigator' see PARA 113 note 4.

2   The reports made under the Medicines for Human Use (Clinical Trials) Regulations 2004, SI 2004/1031, reg 32(1), (3) (see the text to note 6), and reg 32(5) (see note 3) must identify each subject referred to in the report by a number assigned to that subject in accordance with the protocol for the trial: reg 32(6). The number assigned to a subject in accordance with the protocol must be different from the number of any other subject in that trial, including any subject at a trial site outside the United Kingdom: reg 32(7). As to the meaning of 'subject' see PARA 107 note 1. As to the meaning of 'protocol' see PARA 107 note 2. As to the meaning of 'trial site' see PARA 113 note 4. As to the meaning of 'United Kingdom' see PARA 20 note 4.

3   The provisions of the Medicines for Human Use (Clinical Trials) Regulations 2004, SI 2004/1031, reg 32(1)–(3) do not apply to serious adverse events specified in the protocol or the investigator's brochure as not requiring immediate reporting: reg 32(4). As to the meaning of 'investigator's brochure' see PARA 115 note 19. Adverse events, other than those to which the provisions of reg 32(1)–(3) apply, that are identified in the protocol as critical to evaluations of the safety of the trial must be reported to the sponsor in accordance with the reporting requirements, including the time periods for such reporting, specified in that protocol: reg 32(5). See also note 2. As to the meaning of 'sponsor' see PARA 107.

'Serious adverse event', 'serious adverse reaction' or 'unexpected serious adverse reaction' means any adverse event, adverse reaction or unexpected adverse reaction, respectively, that results in death, is life-threatening, requires hospitalisation or prolongation of existing hospitalisation, results in persistent or significant disability or incapacity, or consists of a congenital anomaly or birth defect; 'adverse event' means any untoward medical occurrence in a subject to whom a medicinal product has been administered, including occurrences which are not necessarily caused by or related to that product; 'adverse reaction' means any untoward and unintended response in a subject to an investigational medicinal product which is related to any dose administered to that subject; and 'unexpected adverse reaction' means an adverse reaction the nature and severity of which is not consistent with the information about the medicinal product in question set out, in the case of a product with a marketing authorisation, in the summary of product characteristics for that product or, in the case of any other investigational medicinal product, in the investigator's brochure relating to the trial in question: Medicines for Human Use (Clinical Trials) Regulations 2004, SI 2004/1031, reg 2(1). As to the meaning of 'medicinal product' see the Human Medicines Regulations 2012, SI 2012/1916, reg 2(1); and PARA 25 (definition applied by the Medicines for Human Use (Clinical Trials) Regulations 2004, SI 2004/1031, reg 2(1) (amended by SI 2012/1916)). As to the meanings of 'investigational medicinal product' and 'marketing authorisation' see PARA 107 note 1.

4   As to the meaning of 'conducting a clinical trial' see PARA 112 note 4. As to the meaning of 'clinical trial' see PARA 107.

5   Medicines for Human Use (Clinical Trials) Regulations 2004, SI 2004/1031, reg 32(1). Such an immediate report may be made orally or in writing: reg 32(2). See also notes 2, 3. As to infringement notices see PARA 137. A person is guilty of an offence if he contravenes reg 32: reg 34(1).

6   Medicines for Human Use (Clinical Trials) Regulations 2004, SI 2004/1031, reg 32(3). See also notes 2, 3.

7   Ie under the Medicines for Human Use (Clinical Trials) Regulations 2004, SI 2004/1031, reg 32(1) (see the text to notes 1–5), reg 32(5) (see note 3).

8   Medicines for Human Use (Clinical Trials) Regulations 2004, SI 2004/1031, reg 32(8)(a).

9   As to the meaning of 'relevant ethics committee' see PARA 123 note 20.

10 Medicines for Human Use (Clinical Trials) Regulations 2004, SI 2004/1031, reg 32(8)(b).

11 Medicines for Human Use (Clinical Trials) Regulations 2004, SI 2004/1031, reg 32(8).

12 Medicines for Human Use (Clinical Trials) Regulations 2004, SI 2004/1031, reg 32(9).

13 As to the meaning of 'the licensing authority' see the Human Medicines Regulations 2012, SI 2012/1916, reg 6; PARA 35 note 1; definition applied by the Medicines for Human Use (Clinical Trials) Regulations 2004, SI 2004/1031, reg 2(1) (amended by SI 2012/1916).

14 Medicines for Human Use (Clinical Trials) Regulations 2004, SI 2004/1031, reg 32(10).

15 As to the meaning of 'person' see PARA 45 note 2.

16 Ie the Medicines for Human Use (Clinical Trials) Regulations 2004, SI 2004/1031, reg 32(1), (3), (5)–(9): see the text and notes 1–12.

17 Medicines for Human Use (Clinical Trials) Regulations 2004, SI 2004/1031, reg 49(1)(g). As to offences generally, defences and penalties see PARAS 138–140.

133.   Notification of suspected unexpected serious adverse reactions.   A sponsor[1] must ensure that all relevant information about a suspected unexpected serious adverse reaction[2] which occurs during the course of a clinical trial[3] in the United Kingdom[4] and is fatal or life-threatening is recorded[5], and reported as soon as possible to the licensing authority[6], the competent authorities of any EEA state[7], other than the United Kingdom, in which the trial is being conducted[8], and the relevant ethics committee[9], and in any event not later that seven days after the sponsor was first aware of the reaction[10]. A sponsor must ensure that a suspected unexpected serious adverse reaction which occurs during

the course of a clinical trial in the United Kingdom, other than those referred to above, is reported as soon as possible to the same bodies, and in any event not later than 15 days after the sponsor is first aware of the reaction[11]. A sponsor must ensure that, in relation to each clinical trial in the United Kingdom for which he is the sponsor, the investigators[12] responsible for the conduct of a trial are informed of any suspected unexpected serious adverse reaction which occurs in relation to an investigational medicinal product used in that trial, whether that reaction occurs during the course of that trial or another trial for which the sponsor is responsible[13].

If a clinical trial is being conducted at a trial site[14] in a third country[15] in addition to sites in the United Kingdom, the sponsor of that trial must ensure that all suspected unexpected serious adverse reactions occurring at that site are entered into the European database[16].

Any person[17] who contravenes any of these provisions[18] is guilty of an offence[19].

1 As to the meaning of 'sponsor' see PARA 107.
2 As to the meaning of 'unexpected serious adverse reaction' see PARA 132 note 3. As to the meaning of 'suspected' see PARA 70 note 7.
3 As to the meaning of 'clinical trial' see PARA 107.
4 As to the meaning of 'United Kingdom' see PARA 20 note 4.
5 Medicines for Human Use (Clinical Trials) Regulations 2004, SI 2004/1031, reg 33(1)(a).
6 Medicines for Human Use (Clinical Trials) Regulations 2004, SI 2004/1031, reg 33(1)(b)(i). As to the meaning of 'the licensing authority' see the Human Medicines Regulations 2012, SI 2012/1916, reg 6; PARA 35 note 1; definition applied by the Medicines for Human Use (Clinical Trials) Regulations 2004, SI 2004/1031, reg 2(1) (amended by SI 2012/1916).
7 As to the meaning of 'EEA state' see PARA 107 note 1.
8 Medicines for Human Use (Clinical Trials) Regulations 2004, SI 2004/1031, reg 33(1)(b)(ii). As to the meaning of 'conducting a clinical trial' see PARA 112 note 4.
9 Medicines for Human Use (Clinical Trials) Regulations 2004, SI 2004/1031, reg 33(1)(b)(iii). As to the meaning of 'relevant ethics committee' see PARA 123 note 20.
10 Medicines for Human Use (Clinical Trials) Regulations 2004, SI 2004/1031, reg 33(1). A sponsor must ensure that within eight days of such a report, any additional relevant information is sent to the persons or bodies listed in reg 33(1): reg 33(2). For the purposes of reg 33(1)–(3) (see the text to note 11), the sponsor may fulfil his obligations to report or provide information to the licensing authority and the competent authorities of any EEA state, other than the United Kingdom, by entering the report or information in the European database established in accordance with European Parliament and Council Directive (EC) 2001/20 (OJ L121, 1.5.2001, p 34) on the approximation of the laws, regulations and administrative provisions of the Member States relating to the implementation of good clinical practice in the conduct of clinical trials on medicinal products for human use, art 11: Medicines for Human Use (Clinical Trials) Regulations 2004, SI 2004/1031, reg 33(4). The licensing authority must keep a record of all suspected unexpected serious adverse reactions relating to an investigational medicinal product which are brought to its attention, whether pursuant to reg 33(1), (3) or otherwise (reg 33(6)(a)); and ensure that the details of those reactions are entered in the European database established in accordance with European Parliament and Council Directive (EC) 2001/20 (OJ L121, 1.5.2001, p 34) art 11, whether by the sponsor or the authority (Medicines for Human Use (Clinical Trials) Regulations 2004, SI 2004/1031, reg 33(6)(b)). As to the meaning of 'investigational medicinal product' see PARA 107 note 1. As to infringement notices see PARA 137.
11 Medicines for Human Use (Clinical Trials) Regulations 2004, SI 2004/1031, reg 33(3). See also note 10.
12 As to the meaning of 'investigator' see PARA 113 note 4.
13 Medicines for Human Use (Clinical Trials) Regulations 2004, SI 2004/1031, reg 33(5). As to the authorisation of clinical trials see PARA 117 et seq.
14 As to the meaning of 'trial site' see PARA 113 note 4.
15 As to the meaning of 'third country' see PARA 121 note 5.
16 Medicines for Human Use (Clinical Trials) Regulations 2004, SI 2004/1031, reg 34. The European database is that established in accordance with European Parliament and Council

Directive (EC) 2001/20 (OJ L121, 1.5.2001, p 34) art 11: Medicines for Human Use (Clinical Trials) Regulations 2004, SI 2004/1031, reg 34.
17 As to the meaning of 'person' see PARA 45 note 2.
18 Ie the Medicines for Human Use (Clinical Trials) Regulations 2004, SI 2004/1031, regs 33(1)–(5), 34: see the text and notes 1–16.
19 Medicines for Human Use (Clinical Trials) Regulations 2004, SI 2004/1031, reg 49(1)(h), (i). As to offences generally, defences and penalties see PARAS 138–140.

134. Annual list of suspected serious adverse reactions and safety report. As soon as practicable after the end of the reporting year[1], a sponsor must, in relation to each investigational medicinal product tested in clinical trials in the United Kingdom for which he is the sponsor, furnish the licensing authority and the relevant ethics committees[2] with: (1) a list of all the suspected serious adverse reactions[3] which have occurred during that year in relation to those trials, whether at trial sites[4] in the United Kingdom or elsewhere[5], or any other trials relating to that product which are conducted outside the United Kingdom and for which he is the sponsor[6], including those reactions relating to any investigational medicinal product used as a placebo or as a reference in those trials[7]; and (2) a report on the safety of the subjects[8] of those trials[9]. Any person who contravenes any of these provisions is guilty of an offence[10].

1 'Reporting year', in relation to an investigational medicinal product, means the year ending on the anniversary of: (1) in the case of a product which has a marketing authorisation, the earliest date on which any such authorisation relating to that product was granted or issued (Medicines for Human Use (Clinical Trials) Regulations 2004, SI 2004/1031, reg 35(2)(a)); or (2) in any other case, the earliest date on which any clinical trial relating to that product, and for which the person responsible for making the report was the sponsor, was authorised in an EEA state (reg 35(2)(b)). For these purposes, the date on which a clinical trial was authorised in an EEA state is: (a) in the case of the United Kingdom, the date on which the trial was authorised by the licensing authority in accordance with the Medicines for Human Use (Clinical Trials) Regulations 2004, SI 2004/1031 (reg 35(3)(a)); or (b) in the case of any other EEA state, the date on which the trial was authorised by the competent authority of that EEA state in accordance with European Parliament and Council Directive (EC) 2001/20 (OJ L121, 1.5.2001, p 34) on the approximation of the laws, regulations and administrative provisions of the Member States relating to the implementation of good clinical practice in the conduct of clinical trials on medicinal products for human use (Medicines for Human Use (Clinical Trials) Regulations 2004, SI 2004/1031, reg 35(3)(b)). As to the meanings of 'investigational medicinal product', 'marketing authorisation' and 'EEA state' see PARA 107 note 1. As to the meanings of 'clinical trial' and 'sponsor' see PARA 107. As to the meaning of 'person' see PARA 45 note 2. As to the meaning of 'United Kingdom' see PARA 20 note 4. As to the meaning of 'the licensing authority' see the Human Medicines Regulations 2012, SI 2012/1916, reg 6; PARA 35 note 1; definition applied by the Medicines for Human Use (Clinical Trials) Regulations 2004, SI 2004/1031, reg 2(1) (amended by SI 2012/1916). As to the authorisation of clinical trials see PARA 117 et seq.
2 As to the meaning of 'relevant ethics committee' see PARA 123 note 20.
3 As to the meaning of 'serious adverse reaction' see PARA 132 note 3. As to the meaning of 'suspected' see PARA 70 note 7.
4 As to the meaning of 'trial site' see PARA 113 note 4.
5 Medicines for Human Use (Clinical Trials) Regulations 2004, SI 2004/1031, reg 35(1)(a)(i).
6 Medicines for Human Use (Clinical Trials) Regulations 2004, SI 2004/1031, reg 35(1)(a)(ii).
7 Medicines for Human Use (Clinical Trials) Regulations 2004, SI 2004/1031, reg 35(1)(a). As to infringement notices see PARA 137.
8 As to the meaning of 'subject' see PARA 107 note 1.
9 Medicines for Human Use (Clinical Trials) Regulations 2004, SI 2004/1031, reg 35(1)(b).
10 Medicines for Human Use (Clinical Trials) Regulations 2004, SI 2004/1031, reg 49(1)(j). As to offences generally, defences and penalties see PARAS 138–140.

135. Conclusion of clinical trial. Within 90 days of the conclusion of a clinical trial[1], the sponsor[2] must notify the licensing authority[3] and the relevant ethics committee[4] in writing that the trial has ended[5]. However, if a trial is terminated[6] before the date for the conclusion of the trial specified in the protocol[7] for that trial[8], or before the event specified in the protocol as the event which indicates the end of the trial has occurred[9], the sponsor must notify the licensing authority and the relevant ethics committee in writing of the termination of the trial within 15 days of the date of termination[10]. A notification[11] must contain the specified particulars[12].

A person[13] who contravenes these provisions is guilty of an offence[14].

1 As to the meaning of 'clinical trial' see PARA 107.
2 As to the meaning of 'sponsor' see PARA 107.
3 As to the meaning of 'the licensing authority' see the Human Medicines Regulations 2012, SI 2012/1916, reg 6; PARA 35 note 1; definition applied by the Medicines for Human Use (Clinical Trials) Regulations 2004, SI 2004/1031, reg 2(1) (amended by SI 2012/1916).
4 As to the meaning of 'relevant ethics committee' see PARA 123 note 20.
5 Medicines for Human Use (Clinical Trials) Regulations 2004, SI 2004/1031, reg 27(1). As to infringement notices see PARA 137.
6 As to the termination of clinical trials by the licensing authority see PARA 130.
7 As to the meaning of 'protocol' see PARA 107 note 2.
8 Medicines for Human Use (Clinical Trials) Regulations 2004, SI 2004/1031, reg 27(2)(a).
9 Medicines for Human Use (Clinical Trials) Regulations 2004, SI 2004/1031, reg 27(2)(b).
10 Medicines for Human Use (Clinical Trials) Regulations 2004, SI 2004/1031, reg 27(2).
11 Ie made in accordance with the Medicines for Human Use (Clinical Trials) Regulations 2004, SI 2004/1031, reg 27(1), (2): see the text and notes 1–10.
12 Medicines for Human Use (Clinical Trials) Regulations 2004, SI 2004/1031, reg 27(3). As to the specified particulars see Sch 3 Pt 4.
13 As to the meaning of 'person' see PARA 45 note 2.
14 Medicines for Human Use (Clinical Trials) Regulations 2004, SI 2004/1031, reg 49(1)(c). As to offences generally, defences and penalties see PARAS 138–140.

(v) Labelling

136. Labelling. An investigational medicinal product[1] must be labelled[2] in accordance with specified provisions[3]. However, this does not apply where the investigational medicinal product is for use in a clinical trial[4] with specified characteristics[5], dispensed to a subject[6] in accordance with a prescription given by a health care professional[7], and labelled as per the requirements[8] that apply in relation to medicinal products sold or supplied in accordance with a prescription given by a person who is an appropriate practitioner[9].

Any sponsor[10] who sells or supplies, or procures the sale or supply, of an investigational medicinal product to a subject for the purposes of a clinical trial[11], or to a person for the purpose of administering the product to such a subject[12], the labelling of which does not comply with these provisions, is guilty of an offence[13]. Any person[14] who sells or supplies an investigational medicinal product to a subject for the purposes of a clinical trial[15], or to a person for the purpose of administering the product to such a subject[16], the labelling of which does not comply with these provisions, knowing, or having reasonable cause to believe, that the labelling does not so comply, is also guilty of an offence[17].

1 As to the meaning of 'investigational medicinal product' see PARA 107 note 1.
2 As to the meaning of 'label' see PARA 97 note 4.
3 Medicines for Human Use (Clinical Trials) Regulations 2004, SI 2004/1031, reg 46(1). The specified provisions are those of Commission Directive (EC) 2003/94 (OJ L262, 14.10.2003, p 22) art 15: Medicines for Human Use (Clinical Trials) Regulations 2004, SI 2004/1031, reg 46(1).
4 As to the meaning of 'clinical trial' see PARA 107.
5 Medicines for Human Use (Clinical Trials) Regulations 2004, SI 2004/1031, reg 46(2)(a). The characteristics are those specified in European Parliament and Council Directive (EC) 2001/20 (OJ L121, 1.5.2001, p 34) on the approximation of the laws, regulations and administrative

provisions of the member states relating to the implementation of good clinical practice in the conduct of clinical trials on medicinal products for human use. art 14 (second paragraph): Medicines for Human Use (Clinical Trials) Regulations 2004, SI 2004/1031, reg 46(2)(a).

6 As to the meaning of 'subject' see PARA 107 note 1.

7 Medicines for Human Use (Clinical Trials) Regulations 2004, SI 2004/1031, reg 46(2)(b) (amended by SI 1996/1928). As to the meaning of 'health care professional' see PARA 113 note 5.

8 Ie the requirements of the Human Medicines Regulations 2012, SI 2012/1916, Pt 3: see PARA 158.

9 Medicines for Human Use (Clinical Trials) Regulations 2004, SI 2004/1031, reg 46(2)(c) (amended by SI 2012/1916). As to the meaning of 'appropriate practitioner' see reg 214(3)–(6); and PARA 271.

10 As to the meaning of 'sponsor' see PARA 107.

11 Medicines for Human Use (Clinical Trials) Regulations 2004, SI 2004/1031, reg 49(6)(a).

12 Medicines for Human Use (Clinical Trials) Regulations 2004, SI 2004/1031, reg 49(6)(b).

13 Medicines for Human Use (Clinical Trials) Regulations 2004, SI 2004/1031, reg 49(6). As to offences generally, defences and penalties see PARAS 138–140.

14 As to the meaning of 'person' see PARA 45 note 2.

15 Medicines for Human Use (Clinical Trials) Regulations 2004, SI 2004/1031, reg 49(7)(a).

16 Medicines for Human Use (Clinical Trials) Regulations 2004, SI 2004/1031, reg 49(7)(b).

17 Medicines for Human Use (Clinical Trials) Regulations 2004, SI 2004/1031, reg 49(7). See note 13.

(vi) Enforcement

137. Enforcement. The enforcement provisions of the Human Medicines Regulations 2012[1] apply for the purposes of the clinical trials regulations[2], with modifications[3].

If an enforcement authority[4] has objective grounds for considering that any person[5] has contravened any of the provisions relating to the sponsor's responsibility for the investigator's brochure[6], the restriction on starting or conducting a trial without authorisation[7], the amendment of a clinical trial authorisation[8], the notification of the conclusion of a clinical trial[9], the conduct of a trial[10], serious breaches[11], urgent safety measures[12], the requirement to keep a master file for a clinical trial[13], or the notification of adverse events[14], it may serve upon that person a notice in writing, known as an 'infringement notice'[15]. The notice must inform the person of the authority's grounds for considering that he has contravened one or more of those provisions[16]; specify the relevant provision[17] and the measures which he must take in order to ensure that the contravention does not continue or, as the case may be, does not recur[18]; require him to take those measures within such period as may be specified in the notice[19]; and warn him that unless those requirements are met further action may be taken in respect of the contravention[20].

If an enforcement authority serves an infringement notice, it must forthwith inform the competent authorities of each EEA state[21] other than the United Kingdom[22], the relevant ethics committee[23] and the European Commission[24].

1 Ie the Human Medicines Regulations 2012, SI 2012/1916, regs 2, 8(1), 322, 323(1), 325–330, 332–339, 343, Sch 31.

2 Ie the Medicines for Human Use (Clinical Trials) Regulations 2004, SI 2004/1031.

3 Medicines for Human Use (Clinical Trials) Regulations 2004, SI 2004/1031, reg 47(1) (substituted by SI 2012/1916). As to the modifications see the Medicines for Human Use (Clinical Trials) Regulations 2004, SI 2004/1031, Sch 9. In those provisions as applying by virtue of reg 47(1), a reference to any part of those provisions or a part of any of them is a reference to the provision or part as so applying: reg 47(2). Also in those provisions as applying by virtue of reg 47(1), any reference to, or relating to, a requirement, a power, a function, a

right, a duty, an entitlement, or a protections is read as a reference to, or relating to, that requirement, power, function, right, duty, entitlement, or protection as so applying: see reg 47(3) (added by SI 2012/1916).

4   'Enforcement authority' means any minister or body on whom a duty or power to enforce any provisions of the Medicines for Human Use (Clinical Trials) Regulations 2004, SI 2004/1031 is imposed or conferred by or under the Human Medicines Regulations 2012, SI 2012/1916 as applied by the Medicines for Human Use (Clinical Trials) Regulations 2004, SI 2004/1031, reg 47 (see the text to notes 1–3): reg 48(5) (amended by SI 2012/1916).

5   As to the meaning of 'person' see PARA 45 note 2.

6   Ie under the Medicines for Human Use (Clinical Trials) Regulations 2004, SI 2004/1031, reg 3A: see PARA 108.

7   Ie under the Medicines for Human Use (Clinical Trials) Regulations 2004, SI 2004/1031, reg 12(1): see PARA 112.

8   Ie under the Medicines for Human Use (Clinical Trials) Regulations 2004, SI 2004/1031, reg 22(b): see PARA 123.

9   Ie under the Medicines for Human Use (Clinical Trials) Regulations 2004, SI 2004/1031, reg 27: see PARA 135.

10   Ie under the Medicines for Human Use (Clinical Trials) Regulations 2004, SI 2004/1031, regs 28(1)–(3), 29: see PARAS 126–127.

11   Ie under the Medicines for Human Use (Clinical Trials) Regulations 2004, SI 2004/1031, reg 29A: see PARA 128.

12   Ie under the Medicines for Human Use (Clinical Trials) Regulations 2004, SI 2004/1031, reg 30(2): see PARA 129.

13   Ie under the Medicines for Human Use (Clinical Trials) Regulations 2004, SI 2004/1031, reg 31A: see PARA 131.

14   Ie under the Medicines for Human Use (Clinical Trials) Regulations 2004, SI 2004/1031, regs 32–35: see PARAS 132–134.

15   Medicines for Human Use (Clinical Trials) Regulations 2004, SI 2004/1031, reg 48(1), (4) (s 48(4) amended by SI 2006/1928, SI 2012/1916).

16   Medicines for Human Use (Clinical Trials) Regulations 2004, SI 2004/1031, reg 48(1)(a).

17   Medicines for Human Use (Clinical Trials) Regulations 2004, SI 2004/1031, reg 48(1)(b).

18   Medicines for Human Use (Clinical Trials) Regulations 2004, SI 2004/1031, reg 48(1)(c). An infringement notice may include directions as to the measures to be taken by the person on whom the notice is served to ensure that the contravention does not continue or, as the case may be, does not recur, including the different ways of securing compliance: reg 48(2).

19   Medicines for Human Use (Clinical Trials) Regulations 2004, SI 2004/1031, reg 48(1)(d).

20   Medicines for Human Use (Clinical Trials) Regulations 2004, SI 2004/1031, reg 48(1)(e).

21   As to the meaning of 'EEA state' see PARA 107 note 1.

22   Medicines for Human Use (Clinical Trials) Regulations 2004, SI 2004/1031, reg 48(3)(a). As to the meaning of 'United Kingdom' see PARA 20 note 4.

23   Medicines for Human Use (Clinical Trials) Regulations 2004, SI 2004/1031, reg 48(3)(b). As to the meaning of 'relevant ethics committee' see PARA 123 note 20.

24   Medicines for Human Use (Clinical Trials) Regulations 2004, SI 2004/1031, reg 48(3)(c).

138. False or misleading information.   Any person[1] who:

(1)   is conducting an authorised[2] clinical trial[3];

(2)   is a sponsor[4] of such a clinical trial[5];

(3)   while acting under arrangements made with a sponsor of such a clinical trial, performs the functions of that sponsor[6]; or

(4)   holds a manufacturing authorisation[7],

and who[8] provides to the licensing authority[9] or an ethics committee[10] any relevant information[11] which is false or misleading in a material particular is guilty of an offence[12].

1   As to the meaning of 'person' see PARA 45 note 2.

2   Ie authorised in accordance with the Medicines for Human Use (Clinical Trials) Regulations 2004, SI 2004/1031. As to authorisations for clinical trials see PARA 117 et seq.

3   Medicines for Human Use (Clinical Trials) Regulations 2004, SI 2004/1031, reg 50(2)(a). As to the meaning of 'conducting a clinical trial' see PARA 112 note 4. As to the meaning of 'clinical trial' see PARA 107.

4   As to the meaning of 'sponsor' see PARA 107.

5   Medicines for Human Use (Clinical Trials) Regulations 2004, SI 2004/1031, reg 50(2)(b).
6   Medicines for Human Use (Clinical Trials) Regulations 2004, SI 2004/1031, reg 50(2)(c).
7   Medicines for Human Use (Clinical Trials) Regulations 2004, SI 2004/1031, reg 50(2)(d). As to references to 'the holder of a manufacturing authorisation' see PARA 102 note 5. As to the meaning of 'manufacturing authorisation' see PARA 97 note 6.
8   Ie for the purposes of the Medicines for Human Use (Clinical Trials) Regulations 2004, SI 2004/1031.
9   As to the meaning of 'the licensing authority' see the Human Medicines Regulations 2012, SI 2012/1916, reg 6; PARA 35 note 1; definition applied by the Medicines for Human Use (Clinical Trials) Regulations 2004, SI 2004/1031, reg 2(1) (amended by SI 2012/1916).
10 As to the meaning of 'ethics committee' see PARA 111 note 2.
11 As to the meaning of 'relevant information' see PARA 114 note 15.
12 Medicines for Human Use (Clinical Trials) Regulations 2004, SI 2004/1031, reg 50(2). As to defences and penalties see PARAS 139–140.

139.   Defence of due diligence.   A person[1] does not commit an offence under the clinical trials regulations[2] if he took all reasonable precautions and exercised all due diligence to avoid the commission of that offence[3]. Where evidence is adduced which is sufficient to raise an issue with respect to that defence, the court or jury must assume that the defence is satisfied unless the prosecution proves beyond reasonable doubt that it is not[4].

1   As to the meaning of 'person' see PARA 45 note 2.
2   Ie the Medicines for Human Use (Clinical Trials) Regulations 2004, SI 2004/1031. For offences under the regulations see reg 43.
3   Medicines for Human Use (Clinical Trials) Regulations 2004, SI 2004/1031, reg 51(1).
4   Medicines for Human Use (Clinical Trials) Regulations 2004, SI 2004/1031, reg 51(2). As to the burden and standard of proof in criminal trials generally see CRIMINAL PROCEDURE vol 28 (2010) PARA 464 et seq.

140.   Penalties.   A person[1] guilty of an offence under the clinical trials regulations[2] is liable on conviction to a fine or to imprisonment, or to both[3].

1   As to the meaning of 'person' see PARA 45 note 2.
2   Ie the Medicines for Human Use (Clinical Trials) Regulations 2004, SI 2004/1031. For offences under the regulations see reg 43.
3   Medicines for Human Use (Clinical Trials) Regulations 2004, SI 2004/1031, reg 52. The penalty on summary conviction is a fine not exceeding the statutory maximum or imprisonment for a term not exceeding 3 months or both, and on conviction on indictment is a fine or imprisonment for a term not exceeding two years or both: see reg 52(a), (b). As to the statutory maximum see SENTENCING AND DISPOSITION OF OFFENDERS vol 92 (2010) PARA 140.

(5) AUTHORISATIONS

(i) Requirement for Authorisation and Exceptions

141.   Requirement for authorisation.   A person may not sell or supply, or offer to sell or supply[1], an unauthorised medicinal product[2]. A medicinal product is unauthorised if none of the following is in force for the product:

(1)   a marketing authorisation[3];
(2)   a certificate of registration[4];
(3)   a traditional herbal registration[5]; or
(4)   an Article 126a authorisation[6].

Nor may a person manufacture[7] or assemble[8] a medicinal product or procure the sale, supply, manufacture or assembly of a medicinal product, where he knows or has reasonable cause to believe that the medicinal product has been, or is intended to be, sold or supplied contrary to the above provisions[9].

A person may not sell or supply, or offer to sell or supply, a medicinal product otherwise than in accordance with the terms of a marketing authorisation[10], a certificate of registration[11], a traditional herbal registration[12] or an Article 126a authorisation[13].

A person may not possess an unauthorised medicinal product if he knows or has reasonable cause to believe that the product is intended to be sold or supplied to another person within the European Economic Area[14].

A person who breaches the above requirement for an authorisation[15] is guilty of an offence[16].

If the holder of a marketing authorisation, certificate of registration, traditional herbal registration or Article 126a authorisation is charged with an offence under these provisions in respect of anything that:

(a) has been manufactured or assembled to the holder's order by another person; and

(b) has been so manufactured or assembled as not to comply with the terms of the authorisation, certificate or registration,

it is a defence for him to prove that the holder communicated the terms of the authorisation, certificate or registration to the other person and that the holder did not know and could not by the exercise of reasonable care have known that those terms had not been complied with[17].

1 The Human Medicines Regulations 2012, SI 2012/1916, reg 46(1), (2) do not apply to the sale of a medicinal product outside the European Economic Area: reg 46(9). Nor do they apply to the sale, supply, or offer for sale or supply, of an investigational medicinal product to a person specified in the Medicines for Human Use (Clinical Trials) Regulations 2004, SI 2004/1031, reg 13(1) (see PARA 113) for the purposes of administering that product in a clinical trial, provided that the conditions specified in reg 13(2) are satisfied: Human Medicines Regulations 2012, SI 2012/1916, reg 46(10). As to the meaning of 'investigational medicinal product' see the Medicines for Human Use (Clinical Trials) Regulations 2004, SI 2004/1031, reg 2(1); and PARA 107 note 1 (definition applied by the Human Medicines Regulations 2012, SI 2012/1916, reg 8(1)). 'European Economic Area' or 'EEA' means the European Economic Area created by the EEA agreement: reg 8(1). As to the meaning of 'medicinal product' see PARA 25.

2 Human Medicines Regulations 2012, SI 2012/1916, reg 46(1). A medicinal product is not unauthorised for the purposes of reg 46 if it is sold or supplied, or offered for sale or supply, for export to an EEA state and the product may lawfully be sold or supplied in that state by virtue of legislation adopted by that state in compliance with Council Directive (EC) 2001/83 (OJ L311, 28.11.2001, p 67) on the Community code relating to medicinal products for human use: Human Medicines Regulations 2012, SI 2012/1916, reg 46(8). This is subject to certain exceptions: see reg 46(7). As to such exceptions see Pt 10 (regs 167–176: see PARAS 142–149) and Council Regulation (EC) 726/2004 (OJ L136, 30.4.2004, p 1), art 83 (authorisation of placing on the market of medicinal product for compassionate reasons: see PARA 8).

3 Human Medicines Regulations 2012, SI 2012/1916, reg 46(6)(a). 'Marketing authorisation' means a UK marketing authorisation or an EU marketing authorisation: reg 8(1). 'UK marketing authorisation' means a marketing authorisation granted by the licensing authority under Pt 5 (regs 48–101: see PARAS 155–186) or by Council Directive (EC) 2001/83 (OJ L311, 28.11.2001, p 67) arts 28–39 (mutual recognition and decentralised procedure: see PARA 7): Human Medicines Regulations 2012, SI 2012/1916, reg 8(1). 'EU marketing authorisation' means a marketing authorisation granted or renewed by Council Regulation (EC) 726/2004 (OJ L136, 30.4.2004, p 1) laying down Community procedures for the authorisation and supervision of medicinal products for human and veterinary use and establishing a European Medicines Agency (see PARA 6): Human Medicines Regulations 2012, SI 2012/1916, reg 8(1). As to the meaning of 'licensing authority' see reg 6(2); and PARA 35 note 1.

4 Human Medicines Regulations 2012, SI 2012/1916, reg 46(6)(b). 'Certificate of registration' means a certificate of registration granted by the licensing authority under Pt 6 (regs 102–124: see PARAS 187–205): reg 8(1).

5 Human Medicines Regulations 2012, SI 2012/1916, reg 46(6)(c). 'Traditional herbal registration' means a traditional herbal registration granted by the licensing authority under the Human Medicines Regulations 2012, SI 2012/1916: reg 8(1).

6   Human Medicines Regulations 2012, SI 2012/1916, reg 46(6)(d). 'Article 126a authorisation' means an authorisation granted by the licensing authority under Pt 8 (regs 156–158): reg 8(1).

7   'Manufacture', in relation to a medicinal product, includes any process carried out in the course of making the product, but does not include dissolving or dispersing the product in, or diluting or mixing it with, a substance used as a vehicle for the purpose of administering it: Human Medicines Regulations 2012, SI 2012/1916, reg 8(1). As to the meaning of 'administer' see PARA 25 note 4.

8   'Assemble' in relation to a medicinal product includes the various processes of dividing up, packaging and presentation of the product, and 'assembly' has a corresponding meaning: Human Medicines Regulations 2012, SI 2012/1916, reg 8(1).

9   See the Human Medicines Regulations 2012, SI 2012/1916, reg 8(4), (5).

10 References in the Human Medicines Regulations 2012, SI 2012/1916 to the terms of a marketing authorisation include the information supplied in relation to the authorisation in accordance with reg 50 and Sch 8 (see PARA 157) and, if appropriate, Sch 10 (national homoeopathic products), as updated in accordance with reg 57 (see PARA 157), as approved upon grant under reg 49 (see PARA 156) and as varied under reg 68 (see PARA 167): reg 8(5)(a).

11 References in the Human Medicines Regulations 2012, SI 2012/1916 to the terms of a certificate of registration include the information supplied in relation to the certificate in accordance with reg 103 (see PARA 188), as approved upon grant under reg 103 (see PARA 188) and as varied under reg 110 (see PARA 195): reg 8(5)(b).

12 References in the Human Medicines Regulations 2012, SI 2012/1916 to the terms of a traditional herbal registration include the information supplied in relation to the registration in accordance with reg 128 and Sch 12 (see PARA 209), as updated in accordance with reg 129 (see PARA 210), as approved upon grant under reg 127 (see PARA 208) and as varied under reg 135 (see PARA 216): reg 8(5)(c).

13 Human Medicines Regulations 2012, SI 2012/1916, reg 46(2). See note 1.

14 Human Medicines Regulations 2012, SI 2012/1916, reg 46(3). This does not apply to possession of an investigational medicinal product by a person who knows or has reasonable cause to believe that the investigational medicinal product is intended to be sold or supplied within the European Economic Area and that reg 46(10) will apply to the sale or supply: reg 46(11). It is to be presumed for the purposes of reg 46(3) that, if a person ('P') knows or has reasonable cause to believe that a medicinal product is intended to be sold or supplied to another person, P knows or has reasonable cause to believe that the other person is within the European Economic Area: reg 47(3). This does not apply if P proves that P did not know or have reasonable cause to believe that the person was within the European Economic Area: reg 47(4). Where evidence is adduced that is sufficient to raise an issue with respect to the defence in reg 47(4), the court or jury must assume that the defence is satisfied unless the prosecution proves beyond reasonable doubt that it is not: reg 47(5).

15 Ie a person who breaches the Human Medicines Regulations 2012, SI 2012/1916, reg 46.

16 Human Medicines Regulations 2012, SI 2012/1916, reg 47(1). A person guilty of such an offence under this regulation is liable on summary conviction to a fine not exceeding the statutory maximum or on conviction on indictment to a fine, to imprisonment not exceeding two years or to both: reg 47(2). As to the statutory maximum see SENTENCING AND DISPOSITION OF OFFENDERS vol 92 (2010) PARA 140.

17 See the Human Medicines Regulations 2012, SI 2012/1916, regs 47(6), (7).

142.   Special patient needs.   The requirement for authorisation[1] does not apply in relation to a medicinal product[2] (a 'special medicinal product') if:

(1)   the medicinal product is supplied in response to an unsolicited order[3];

(2)   the medicinal product is manufactured and assembled[4] in accordance with the specification of a person who is a doctor, dentist[5], nurse independent prescriber, pharmacist independent prescriber[6] or supplementary prescriber[7];

(3)   the medicinal product is for use by a patient for whose treatment that person is directly responsible in order to fulfil the special needs of that patient[8]; and

(4)   certain conditions are met[9].

The conditions are:

(a)   that the medicinal product is supplied to a doctor, dentist, nurse independent prescriber, pharmacist independent prescriber or supplementary prescriber or that it is supplied for use under the supervision of a pharmacist in a registered pharmacy, a hospital or a health centre[10];

(b) that no advertisement relating to the medicinal product is published by any person[11];

(c) that the manufacture and assembly of the medicinal product are carried out under such supervision and that such precautions are taken, as are adequate to ensure that the medicinal product meets the specification of the doctor, dentist, nurse independent prescriber, pharmacist independent prescriber or supplementary prescriber who requires it[12];

(d) that written records of the manufacture or assembly of the medicinal product in accordance with head (c) above are maintained and are available to the licensing authority or to the enforcement authority[13] on request[14];

(e) that if the medicinal product is manufactured or assembled in the United Kingdom or imported into the United Kingdom from a country other than an EEA state[15]:
    (i) it is manufactured, assembled or imported by the holder of a manufacturer's licence that relates specifically to the manufacture, assembly or importation of special medicinal products[16]; or
    (ii) it is manufactured, assembled or imported as an investigational medicinal product by the holder of a manufacturing authorisation granted by the licensing authority for the purposes of certain provisions[17] of the Medicines for Human Use (Clinical Trials) Regulations 2004[18];

(f) that if the product is imported from an EEA state:
    (i) it is manufactured or assembled in that state by a person who is the holder of an authorisation in relation to its manufacture or assembly in accordance with certain EU provisions[19] as implemented in that state[20]; or
    (ii) it is manufactured or assembled as an investigational medicinal product[21] in that State by the holder of an authorisation in relation to its manufacture or assembly in accordance with certain EU provisions[22] as implemented in that state[23];

(g) that if the product is distributed by way of wholesale dealing[24] by a person ('P'), who has not, as the case may be, manufactured, assembled[25] or imported the product in accordance with heads (e)(i) or (f)(i) above, P must be the holder of a wholesale dealer's licence[26] in relation to the product in question[27].

A person, who for the above purposes[28], sells or supplies a product or provides a specification for that product, is guilty of an offence if he provides to the licensing authority any information that is relevant to the evaluation of the safety, quality or efficacy of a medicinal product that is false or misleading in a material particular[29].

1   Ie the requirement due to the prohibition under the Human Medicines Regulations 2012, SI 2012/1916, reg 46 (see PARA 141).
2   As to the meaning of 'medicinal product' see PARA 25.
3   Human Medicines Regulations 2012, SI 2012/1916, reg 164(1)(a).
4   As to the meanings of 'manufacture' and 'assemble' see PARA 141 notes 7, 8.
5   As to the meanings of 'doctor' and 'dentist' see PARA 48 note 6.

6   As to the meanings of 'nurse independent prescriber' and 'pharmacist independent prescriber' see PARA 50 note 3.

7   Human Medicines Regulations 2012, SI 2012/1916, reg 167(1)(b). As to the meaning of 'supplementary prescriber' see PARA 50 note 5.

8   Human Medicines Regulations 2012, SI 2012/1916, reg 167(1)(c).

9   Human Medicines Regulations 2012, SI 2012/1916, reg 167(1)(d).

10 Human Medicines Regulations 2012, SI 2012/1916, reg 167(2). As to the meanings of 'pharmacist', 'registered pharmacy', 'hospital' and 'health centre' see PARA 52 notes 2–5.

11 Human Medicines Regulations 2012, SI 2012/1916, reg 167(3). As to the meaning of 'publish' see reg 277(1) and PARA 334 note 5: reg 167(9).

12 Human Medicines Regulations 2012, SI 2012/1916, reg 167(4).

13 As to the meaning of 'licensing authority' see PARA 35 note 1. 'Enforcement authority' means the Secretary of State, the Minister for Health, Social Services and Public Safety or a person on whom a function of enforcing a provision of these Regulations has been conferred by virtue of the Human Medicines Regulations 2012, SI 2012/1916, regs 323–324 (see PARA 362): reg 8(1).

14 Human Medicines Regulations 2012, SI 2012/1916, reg 167(5).

15 Human Medicines Regulations 2012, SI 2012/1916, reg 167(6).

16 Human Medicines Regulations 2012, SI 2012/1916, reg 167(6)(a).

17 Ie for the purposes of the Medicines for Human Use (Clinical Trials) Regulations 2004, SI 2004/1031, reg 36 (see PARA 97).

18 Human Medicines Regulations 2012, SI 2012/1916, reg 167(6)(b).

19 Ie in accordance with provisions of Council Directive (EC) 2001/83 (OJ L311, 28.11.2001, p 67) on the Community code relating to medicinal products for human use: see art 1 (amended by Directive (EC) 2004/27 (OJ L136, 30.4.2004, p 34).

20 Human Medicines Regulations 2012, SI 2012/1916, reg 167(7)(a).

21 As to the meaning of 'investigational medicinal product' see the Medicines for Human Use (Clinical Trials) Regulations 2004, SI 2004/1031, reg 2(1); and PARA 107 note 1 (definition applied by the Human Medicines Regulations 2012, SI 2012/1916, reg 8(1)).

22 Ie in accordance with European Parliament and Council Directive (EC) 2001/20 (OJ L121, 1.5.2001, p 34) on the approximation of the laws, regulations and administrative provisions of the Member States relating to the implementation of good clinical practice in the conduct of clinical trials on medicinal products for human use, art 13 (see PARA 6).

23 Human Medicines Regulations 2012, SI 2012/1916, reg 167(7)(b).

24 As to references to the distribution of a product by way of wholesale dealing see the Human Medicines Regulations 2012, SI 2012/1916, reg 18(7), (8); and PARA 77 note 4.

25 As to the meanings of 'manufacture' and 'assemble' see PARA 141 notes 7, 8.

26 As to the meaning of 'wholesaler dealer's licence' see PARA 77.

27 Human Medicines Regulations 2012, SI 2012/1916, reg 167(8).

28 Ie for the purposes of the Human Medicines Regulations 2012, SI 2012/1916, reg 167.

29 See the Human Medicines Regulations 2012, SI 2012/1916, reg 175(1), (2). A person guilty of such an offence is liable, on summary conviction, to a fine not exceeding the statutory maximum or, on conviction on indictment, to a fine, to imprisonment for a term not exceeding two years or to both: reg 176(1). It is a defence for a person charged with such an offence to prove that the person took all reasonable precautions and exercised all due diligence to avoid commission of that offence: reg 176(2). Where evidence is adduced that is sufficient to raise an issue with respect to this defence, the court or jury must presume that the defence is satisfied unless the prosecution proves beyond reasonable doubt that it is not: reg 176(3). As to the statutory maximum see SENTENCING AND DISPOSITION OF OFFENDERS vol 92 (2010) PARA 140.

143.   Use of non-prescription medicines in the course of a business. The requirement for authorisation[1] does not apply to anything done in relation to a medicinal product[2] if the following conditions are met[3]:

(1)   that the medicinal product is not a prescription only medicine[4];

(2)   that the medicinal product is sold or supplied to a person who is a health care professional ('P') exclusively for use by P in the course of a business carried on by P and for the purposes of administering it or causing it to be administered otherwise than by selling it[5];

(3)   that the medicinal product is manufactured and assembled[6] in

accordance with the specification of P and is for use by a patient for whose treatment P is directly responsible in order to fulfil the special needs of that patient[7];

(4)   that if sold or supplied through the holder of a wholesale dealer's licence[8] the medicinal product is sold or supplied to such a person and for such use as mentioned in head (2) above[9];

(5)   that no advertisement relating to the medicinal product is published[10] by any person[11];

(6)   that the sale or supply of the medicinal product is in response to an unsolicited order[12];

(7)   that if the medicinal product is:

      (a)   manufactured or assembled in the United Kingdom or imported into the United Kingdom from a country other than an EEA state, it is manufactured, assembled or imported by the holder of a manufacturer's licence[13] that relates specifically to the manufacture, assembly or importation of special medicinal products[14]; or

      (b)   imported from an EEA state, it is manufactured or assembled in that state by a person who is the holder of an authorisation in relation to its manufacture or assembly in accordance with certain EU provisions[15] as implemented in that state[16].

1   Ie the requirement due to the prohibition under the Human Medicines Regulations 2012, SI 2012/1916, reg 46 (see PARA 141).
2   As to the meaning of 'medicinal product' see PARA 25.
3   Human Medicines Regulations 2012, SI 2012/1916, reg 168(1).
4   Human Medicines Regulations 2012, SI 2012/1916, reg 168(2). As to the meaning of 'prescription only medicine' see reg 5(3); PARA 26: reg 8(1).
5   Human Medicines Regulations 2012, SI 2012/1916, reg 168(3).
6   As to the meanings of 'manufacture' and 'assemble' see PARA 141 notes 7, 8.
7   Human Medicines Regulations 2012, SI 2012/1916, reg 168(4).
8   As to the meaning of 'wholesaler dealer's licence' see PARA 77.
9   Human Medicines Regulations 2012, SI 2012/1916, reg 168(5).
10   As to the meaning of 'publish' see the Human Medicines Regulations 2012, SI 2012/1916, reg 277(1); and PARA 334 note 5.
11   Human Medicines Regulations 2012, SI 2012/1916, reg 168(6).
12   Human Medicines Regulations 2012, SI 2012/1916, reg 168(7).
13   As to the meaning of 'manufacturer's licence' see PARA 45.
14   Human Medicines Regulations 2012, SI 2012/1916, reg 168(8)(a).
15   Ie in accordance with Council Directive (EC) 2001/83 (OJ L311, 28.11.2001, p 67) on the Community code relating to medicinal products for human use.
16   Human Medicines Regulations 2012, SI 2012/1916, reg 168(8)(b).

144. Mixing of general sale medicinal products. The requirement for authorisation[1] does not apply to a medicinal product[2] ('the product') in respect of which the following conditions are met[3]:

(1)   that the product is manufactured[4] by the mixing of authorised medicinal products[5] with other authorised medicinal products, or with substances that are not medicinal products[6];

(2)   that any authorised medicinal product that is so mixed is subject to general sale[7];

(3)   that the product is manufactured by a person ('H') who is the holder of a manufacturer's licence[8] that:

      (i)   relates specifically to the manufacture of medicinal products in accordance with this provision[9]; and

      (ii)   was granted or renewed not more than five years before the date on which the product is sold or supplied in accordance with heads (4) and (5) below, and that the product is manufactured in accordance with the terms of that licence[10];

(4)   that the product is sold or supplied by H to a person ('P') for administration to P or to a member of P's household[11];

(5)   that P is present and asks H to use H's judgment as to the treatment required[12];

(6)   that no advertisement relating to the product is published by any person[13];

(7)   that written records of the manufacture of the product and of the sale or supply of the product are maintained and are made available to the licensing authority or to the enforcement authority on request[14].

1   Ie the requirement due to the prohibition under the Human Medicines Regulations 2012, SI 2012/1916, reg 46 (see PARA 141).
2   As to the meaning of 'medicinal product' see PARA 25.
3   Human Medicines Regulations 2012, SI 2012/1916, reg 169(1).
4   As to the meaning of 'manufacture' see PARA 141 note 7.
5   For these purposes 'authorised medicinal product' means a medicinal product that is the subject of a marketing authorisation, a certificate of registration or a traditional herbal registration: Human Medicines Regulations 2012, SI 2012/1916, reg 169(9). As to the meanings of 'marketing authorisation', 'certificate of registration' and 'traditional herbal registration' see PARA 141 notes 3–5.
6   Human Medicines Regulations 2012, SI 2012/1916, reg 169(2). As to the meaning of 'substances' see PARA 25 note 2.
7   Human Medicines Regulations 2012, SI 2012/1916, reg 169(3).
8   As to the meaning of 'manufacturer's licence' see PARA 45.
9   Human Medicines Regulations 2012, SI 2012/1916, reg 169(4)(a).
10   Human Medicines Regulations 2012, SI 2012/1916, reg 169(4)(b).
11   Human Medicines Regulations 2012, SI 2012/1916, reg 169(5).
12   Human Medicines Regulations 2012, SI 2012/1916, reg 169(6).
13   Human Medicines Regulations 2012, SI 2012/1916, reg 169(7).
14   Human Medicines Regulations 2012, SI 2012/1916, reg 169(8). As to the meaning of 'enforcement authority' see PARA 142 note 13.

145.   Record-keeping requirements. Where the sale or supply of a medicinal product[1] relies on the exemptions relating to a supply to fulfil special patient needs[2], the use of non-prescription medicines in the course of a business[3], or mixing of general sale medicinal products[4], the person who sells or supplies the product must maintain for at least five years a record showing:

(1)   the source from which and the date on which the person obtained the product[5];

(2)   the person to whom and the date on which the sale or supply was made[6];

(3)   the quantity of the sale or supply[7];

(4)   the batch number of the batch of that product from which the sale or supply was made[8]; and

(5)   details of any suspected adverse reaction[9] to the product so sold or supplied of which the person is aware or subsequently becomes aware[10].

The person must make the records available for inspection by the licensing authority[11] on request[12].

The person must notify the licensing authority of any suspected adverse reaction to the medicinal product which is a serious adverse reaction[13].

A person is guilty of an offence if he fails to maintain any record or make any record available or notify the licensing authority of any suspected serious adverse reaction as required by the above provisions[14].

1   As to the meaning of 'medicinal product' see PARA 25.
2   Ie the exemption under the Human Medicines Regulations 2012, SI 2012/1916, reg 167 (see PARA 142).
3   Ie the exemption under the Human Medicines Regulations 2012, SI 2012/1916, reg 168 (see PARA 143). As to the meaning of 'business' see PARA 52 note 10.
4   Ie the exemption under the Human Medicines Regulations 2012, SI 2012/1916, reg 169 (see PARA 144). In the case of a medicinal product that is sold or supplied in reliance on the exemption in reg 169 the reference in reg 170(1)(a) to 'the product' means all the medicinal products that were mixed in the course of the manufacture of the product; and reg 170(1)(d) does not apply: reg 170(4).
5   Human Medicines Regulations 2012, SI 2012/1916, reg 170(1)(a).
6   Human Medicines Regulations 2012, SI 2012/1916, reg 170(1)(b).
7   Human Medicines Regulations 2012, SI 2012/1916, reg 170(1)(c).
8   Human Medicines Regulations 2012, SI 2012/1916, reg 170(1)(d).
9   As to the meaning of 'adverse reaction' see PARA 70 note 6. As to the meaning of 'suspected' see PARA 70 note 7.
10   Human Medicines Regulations 2012, SI 2012/1916, reg 170(1)(e).
11   As to the meaning of 'licensing authority' see PARA 35 note 1.
12   Human Medicines Regulations 2012, SI 2012/1916, reg 170(2).
13   Human Medicines Regulations 2012, SI 2012/1916, reg 170(3). As to the meaning of 'serious adverse reaction' see PARA 71 note 8.
14   See the Human Medicines Regulations 2012, SI 2012/1916, reg 175(3). A person guilty of such an offence is liable, on summary conviction, to a fine not exceeding the statutory maximum or, on conviction on indictment, to a fine, to imprisonment for a term not exceeding two years or to both: reg 176(1). It is a defence for a person charged with such an offence to prove that the person took all reasonable precautions and exercised all due diligence to avoid commission of that offence: reg 176(2). Where evidence is adduced that is sufficient to raise an issue with respect to this defence, the court or jury must presume that the defence is satisfied unless the prosecution proves beyond reasonable doubt that it is not: reg 176(3). As to the statutory maximum see SENTENCING AND DISPOSITION OF OFFENDERS vol 92 (2010) PARA 140.

146. Exempt advanced therapy medicinal products. The requirement for authorisation[1] does not apply in relation to an advanced therapy medicinal product[2] (an 'exempt advanced therapy medicinal product') if the following conditions are met[3]:

(1)   that the product is prepared on a non-routine basis in the United Kingdom and according to specific quality standards[4] equivalent to those provided for advanced therapy medicinal products[5];

(2)   that the product is used in a hospital[6] in the United Kingdom, under the exclusive professional responsibility of a doctor[7] and in order to comply with an individual medical prescription for a product made to order for an individual patient[8];

(3)   that no advertisement relating to the medicinal product is published[9] by any person[10];

(4)   that the sale or supply of the medicinal product is in response to an unsolicited order[11].

1   Ie the requirement due to the prohibition under the Human Medicines Regulations 2012, SI 2012/1916, reg 46 (see PARA 141).
2   'Advanced therapy medicinal product' means a medicinal product described in European Parliament and Council Regulation (EC) 1394/2007 (OJ L324, 10.12.2007, p 121) on advanced therapy medicinal products, art 2(1)(a) (see PARA 23): Human Medicines Regulations 2012, SI 2012/1916, reg 8(1).
3   Human Medicines Regulations 2012, SI 2012/1916, reg 171(1).
4   Ie specific quality standards equivalent to those provided for advanced medicinal products authorised under Council Regulation (EC) 726/2004 (OJ L136, 30.4.2004, p 1) laying down Community procedures for the authorisation and supervision of medicinal products for human and veterinary use and establishing a European Medicines Agency.
5   Human Medicines Regulations 2012, SI 2012/1916, reg 171(2).

6 As to the meaning of 'hospital' see PARA 52 note 3.
7 As to the meaning of 'doctor' see PARA 48 note 6.
8 Human Medicines Regulations 2012, SI 2012/1916, reg 171(3).
9 As to the meaning of 'publish' see the Human Medicines Regulations 2012, SI 2012/1916, reg 277(1); and PARA 334 note 5: reg 171(6).
10 Human Medicines Regulations 2012, SI 2012/1916, reg 171(4).
11 Human Medicines Regulations 2012, SI 2012/1916, reg 171(5).

147.   Parallel import licence.   The requirement for authorisation[1] does not prevent the holder of a parallel import licence[2] from placing the medicinal product to which the licence relates on the market[3]. Nor does it prevent the sale or supply, or offer for sale or supply, of a medicinal product to which a parallel import licence relates, in accordance with the terms of that licence[4].

1 Ie the requirement due to the prohibition under the Human Medicines Regulations 2012, SI 2012/1916, reg 46 (see PARA 141).
2 For this purpose 'parallel import licence' means a licence that is granted by the licensing authority in compliance with the rules of European Union law relating to parallel imports and that authorises the holder to place on the market a medicinal product imported into the United Kingdom from another EEA state: Human Medicines Regulations 2012, SI 2012/1916, reg 172(2). As to the meaning of 'medicinal product' see PARA 25. As to the meaning of 'licensing authority' see PARA 35 note 1.
3 Human Medicines Regulations 2012, SI 2012/1916, reg 172(1)(a).
4 Human Medicines Regulations 2012, SI 2012/1916, reg 172(1)(b).

148.   Exemption for certain radiopharmaceuticals.   The requirement for authorisation[1] does not apply where a radiopharmaceutical[2] is prepared:
(1)   at the time when it is intended to be administered[3];
(2)   in accordance with the manufacturer's instructions and by the person by whom it is to be administered[4];
(3)   from radionuclide generators[5], radionuclide kits[6] and radionuclide precursors[7] in respect of which a marketing authorisation is in force[8]; and
(4)   for administration in accordance with certain provisions[9].

1 Ie the requirement due to the prohibition under the Human Medicines Regulations 2012, SI 2012/1916, reg 46 (see PARA 141).
2 'Radiopharmaceutical' means a medicinal product which, when ready for use, contains one or more radionuclides included for a medicinal purpose: Human Medicines Regulations 2012, SI 2012/1916, reg 8(1). As to the meaning of 'radionuclide' see PARA 25 note 9.
3 Human Medicines Regulations 2012, SI 2012/1916, reg 173(a).
4 Human Medicines Regulations 2012, SI 2012/1916, reg 173(b).
5 'Radionuclide generator' means any system incorporating a fixed parent radionuclide from which is produced a daughter radionuclide which is to be removed by elution or by any other method and is to be used in a radiopharmaceutical: Human Medicines Regulations 2012, SI 2012/1916, reg 8(1).
6 'Radionuclide kit' means any preparation to be reconstituted or combined with radionuclides in the final radiopharmaceutical, usually prior to its administration: Human Medicines Regulations 2012, SI 2012/1916, reg 8(1).
7 'Radionuclide precursor' means any radionuclide produced for the radio-labelling of another substance prior to administration, other than a radionuclide that is incorporated in or produced from a generator or is included in a radiopharmaceutical: Human Medicines Regulations 2012, SI 2012/1916, reg 8(1).
8 Human Medicines Regulations 2012, SI 2012/1916, reg 173(c).
9 Human Medicines Regulations 2012, SI 2012/1916, reg 173(d). The provisions mentioned in the text are the Medicines (Administration of Radioactive Substances) Regulations 1978, SI 1978/1006, reg 2 (see PARA 382).

149.   Supply in response to certain pathogenic agents, etc.   The requirement for authorisation[1] does not apply where the sale or supply of a medicinal product[2] is authorised by the licensing authority[3] on a temporary basis in response to the suspected or confirmed spread of pathogenic agents, toxins, chemical agents or nuclear radiation, which may cause harm to human beings[4].

1 Ie the requirement due to the prohibition under the Human Medicines Regulations 2012, SI 2012/1916, reg 46 (see PARA 141).
2 As to the meaning of 'medicinal product' see PARA 25.
3 As to the meaning of 'licensing authority' see PARA 35 note 1.
4 Human Medicines Regulations 2012, SI 2012/1916, reg 174.

150.   Exemptions for pharmacists.   The general requirement for a licence[1] does not apply to anything done in a registered pharmacy[2], a hospital[3] or a health centre[4] and is done there by or under the supervision of a pharmacist[5] and consists of[6]:

(1)   preparing or dispensing a medicinal product[7] in accordance with a prescription given by an appropriate practitioner[8]; or

(2)   assembling[9] a medicinal product, providing that where the assembly takes place in a registered pharmacy: (a) the business[10] in medicinal products carried on there must be restricted to retail sale[11] or supply in circumstances corresponding to retail sale and the assembling must be done with a view to such sale or supply either there or at another such pharmacy forming part of the same retail pharmacy business[12]; (b) the medicinal product must not have been the subject of an advertisement[13].

Nor does the general requirement for a licence apply to anything done by or under the supervision of a pharmacist which consists of procuring the preparation or dispensing of a medicinal product in accordance with a prescription given by a practitioner, or of procuring the assembly of a medicinal product[14].

The general requirement for a licence does not apply to the preparation or dispensing in a registered pharmacy of a medicinal product by or under the supervision of a pharmacist in accordance with a specification furnished by the person to whom the product is to be sold or supplied where the product is prepared or dispensed for administration to that person or to a person under his care[15].

Without prejudice to the preceding provisions, the general requirement to have a licence does not apply to anything which is done in a registered pharmacy by or under the supervision of a pharmacist and consists of:

(a)   preparing or dispensing a medicinal product for administration to a person where the pharmacist is requested by or on behalf of that person to do so in accordance with the pharmacist's own judgment as to the treatment required, and that person is present in the pharmacy at the time of the request in pursuance of which that product is prepared or dispensed[16];

(b)   preparing a stock of medicinal products with a view to dispensing them as mentioned above[17] provided that such stock is prepared with a view to retail sale or to supply in circumstances corresponding to retail sale and the preparation is done with a view to such sale or supply either at that registered pharmacy or at any other registered pharmacy forming part of the same retail pharmacy business[18],

and the general requirement for a licence does not apply to anything which is done in a hospital or a health centre by or under the supervision of a pharmacist and consists of preparing a stock of medicinal products with a view to dispensing them as mentioned in head (1) above[19].

In similar circumstances[20] the general requirement for a licence[21] does not apply to the preparation or dispensing of a medicinal product which has not been ordered by another person[22], or subject to an advertisement[23], where it is prepared for retail sale or supply in circumstances corresponding to retail sale at the pharmacy at which it is prepared[24].

1   Ie the requirement due to the prohibition under the Human Medicines Regulations 2012, SI 2012/1916, reg 46 (see PARA 141).
2   As to the meaning of 'registered pharmacy' see PARA 52 note 2.
3   As to the meaning of 'hospital' see PARA 52 note 3.
4   As to the meaning of 'health centre' see PARA 52 note 4.
5   As to the meaning of 'pharmacist' see PARA 52 note 5. The ministers may make regulations prescribing conditions which must be complied with if a thing is to be considered for the purposes of s 10 as done under the supervision of a pharmacist: s 10(7A) (s 10(7A)–(7C) added by the Health Act 2006 s 26(1); the Medicines Act 1968 s 10(7A) amended by SI 2006/2407)). Conditions so prescribed may relate to supervision in the case where the pharmacist is not at the place where the thing is being done and, in that case, the thing is not to be so considered: Medicines Act 1968 s 10(7B) (as so added). In any case, compliance with any applicable conditions is sufficient for the thing to be so considered: s 10(7C) (as so added). The requirement to obtain authorisation for the wholesale distribution of medicinal products is applicable to a pharmacist: see Case C-7/11 *Fabio Caronna* [2012] 35 LS Gaz R 16. The ministers may by order provide that any of the provisions of the Medicines Act 1968 s 10 specified in the order cease to have effect, or have effect subject to such exceptions or modifications as may be so specified: s 15(3) (amended by SI 2006/2407). As to the meaning of 'the ministers' see the Human Medicines Regulations 2012, SI 2012/1916, reg 6(6)–(8); and PARA 35 (definition applied by the Medicines Act 1968 s 1 (substituted by SI 2012/1916)).
6   Medicines Act 1968 s 10(1) (amended by SI 2006/2407, SI 2012/1916).
7   As to the meaning of 'medicinal product' see PARA 25.
8   Medicines Act 1968 s 10(1)(a) (amended by SI 2012/1916); Human Medicines Regulations 2012, SI 2012/1916, reg 4(1). As to the meaning of 'appropriate practitioner' see the Human Medicines Regulations 2012, SI 2012/1916, reg 214; PARA 271. Furthermore the general requirements for a manufacture's licence does not apply to anything done by or under the supervision of a pharmacist which consists of procuring the preparation or dispensing of a medicinal product in accordance with a prescription given by a practitioner: see the Medicines Act 1968 s 10(1).
9   As to the meaning of 'assembly' see PARA 141 note 8.
10 As to the meaning of 'business' see PARA 52 note 10.
11 For the purposes of the Human Medicines Regulations 2012, SI 2012/1916, references to selling by retail, or to retail sale, are references to selling a product to a person who buys it otherwise than for a purpose specified in reg 18(8) (see PARA 77): reg 8(3).
12 Medicines Act 1968 s 10(1)(b)(i) (s 10(1)(b), (4)(b) amended, and s 10(1)(b)(i), (ii), (5), (6) added, by SI 1971/1445). As to references to retail sale see PARA 52 note 11. 'Retail pharmacy business' means a business (other than a professional practice carried on by a doctor or dentist) which consists of or includes the retail sale of medicinal products that are not subject to general sale: Human Medicines Regulations 2012, SI 2012/1916, reg 8(1); Medicines Act 1968 s 132(1) (substituted by SI 2012/1916).
13 Medicines Act 1968 s 10(1)(b)(ii) (as added: see note 12). As to the meaning of 'advertisement' see the Human Medicines Regulations 2012, SI 2012/1916, reg 7; and PARA 333 (definition applied by the Medicines Act 1968 s 10(8) (as so added; amended by SI 2012/1916)).
14 Medicines Act 1968 s 10(1).
15 Medicines Act 1968 s 10(3) (amended by SI 2006/2407).
16 Medicines Act 1968 s 10(4)(a) (amended by SI 2012/1916).
17 Ie as mentioned in the Medicines Act 1968 s 10(1)(a), (3), (4)(a).
18 Medicines Act 1968 s 10(4)(b) (amended by SI 1971/1445).
19 Medicines Act 1968 s 10(4).
20 Ie where anything is done by or under the supervision of a pharmacist in a registered pharmacy: Medicines Act 1968 s 10(5), (6) (as added: see note 12).
21 Ie the requirement set out in the Human Medicines Regulations 2012, SI 2012/1916, reg 17(1) (see PARA 45).
22 Medicines Act 1968 s 10(5)(a) (as added: see note 12).
23 Medicines Act 1968 s 10(5)(c) (as added: see note 12).
24 Medicines Act 1968 s 10(5)(b) (as added: see note 12).

(ii) Borderline Products

151.   Provisional determination.   Where the licensing authority[1] is of the opinion that a product without a marketing authorisation[2], traditional herbal registration[3], certificate of registration[4] or Article 126a authorisation[5] is a medicinal product[6], it may[7] give a notice in writing (a 'provisional determination notice') to any person[8] ('the recipient') who has sold or supplied the product, or has offered to sell or supply it or who in the opinion of the licensing authority may sell or supply it[9].

The provisional determination notice must: (1) advise the recipient that the licensing authority has made a provisional determination that the product is a medicinal product; (2) give reasons for the provisional determination; (3) advise the recipient of the recipient's rights to challenge the provisional determination[10]; and (4) specify a period of at least six weeks beginning immediately after the date on which the provisional determination notice is given to the recipient ('the determination date') within which any written representations[11] must be made to the licensing authority[12].

1   As to the meaning of 'the licensing authority' see PARA 35 note 1.
2   As to the meaning of 'marketing authorisation' see PARA 141 note 3.
3   As to the meaning of 'traditional herbal registration' see PARA 141 note 5.
4   As to the meaning of 'certificate of registration' see PARA 141 note 4.
5   As to the meaning of 'Article 126a authorisation' see PARA 141 note 6.
6   As to the meaning of 'medicinal product' see PARA 25.
7   The use of the word 'may' indicates that SI 1994/3144 reg 3A is not the sole mandatory machinery for determining whether a product is a relevant medicinal product: *R v Wright* [2007] EWCA Crim 1744, [2007] All ER (D) 315 (Jul). Nothing in the Human Medicines Regulations 2012, SI 2012/1916, Pt 9 prevents the licensing authority from determining that a product is a medicinal product without following the procedures in this Part when it thinks it appropriate: reg 165.
8   As to the meaning of 'person' see PARA 45 note 2.
9   Human Medicines Regulations 2012, SI 2012/1916, reg 159(1), (2).
10 Ie in accordance with the Human Medicines Regulations 2012, SI 2012/1916, reg 160 (see PARA 152).
11 Ie in accordance with the Human Medicines Regulations 2012, SI 2012/1916, reg 160(2)(a) (see PARA 152).
12 Human Medicines Regulations 2012, SI 2012/1916, reg 159(3). As to challenges to the provisions determination see reg 160; and PARA 152.

152.   Challenge to provisional determination.   A recipient of a provisional determination notice[1] may, within four weeks beginning immediately after the determination date[2], give notice in writing to the licensing authority[3] requesting the authority to submit the provisional determination to review[4].

If the recipient gives such notice the recipient must:

(1)   within the period specified in the provisional determination notice, make written representations to the licensing authority explaining why the recipient thinks the product is not a medicinal product[5]; or

(2)   within the period of four weeks beginning immediately after the determination date, inform the licensing authority in writing that the recipient wants to make oral representations explaining why the recipient thinks the product is not a medicinal product[6].

1   As to the meaning of 'provisional determination notice' see PARA 151.
2   If the recipient has informed the licensing authority that the recipient wants to make written representations in accordance with the Human Medicines Regulations 2012, SI 2012/1916, reg 160(2)(a) and the licensing authority thinks that, because of exceptional circumstances or the nature or complexity of the issues involved, additional time is needed for the preparation of

written representations, the licensing authority may alter the period for making written representations: reg 160(3). The licensing authority must inform the recipient of in writing of such an alteration in the date and the reasons for it: reg 160(4).

3   As to the meaning of 'the licensing authority' see PARA 35 note 1.
4   Human Medicines Regulations 2012, SI 2012/1916, reg 160(1).
5   Human Medicines Regulations 2012, SI 2012/1916, reg 160(2)(a). As to the meaning of 'medicinal product' see PARA 25. As to the procedure for written representations see reg 161.
6   Human Medicines Regulations 2012, SI 2012/1916, reg 160(2)(b). As to the procedure for oral representations see reg 162.

153.   Final determination without representation. The following applies if the recipient:

(1)   does not give notification to the licensing authority[1] that he wishes to challenge its provisional determination within the period of four weeks beginning immediately after the determination date[2];

(2)   gives such notification, but fails to make written representations to the licensing authority within the period for making those representations[3]; or

(3)   gives such notification, but fails to make oral representations at a hearing before the reviewers appointed for the purposes of advising on the provisional determination[4],

the licensing authority must make a final determination as to whether the product is a medicinal product and inform the recipient in writing of its final determination and of the reasons for it[5].

1   As to the meaning of 'the licensing authority' see PARA 35 note 1.
2   Human Medicines Regulations 2012, SI 2012/1916, reg 163(1)(a).
3   Human Medicines Regulations 2012, SI 2012/1916, reg 163(1)(b).
4   Human Medicines Regulations 2012, SI 2012/1916, reg 163(1)(c).
5   Human Medicines Regulations 2012, SI 2012/1916, reg 163(2).

154.   Effect of final determination. If the licensing authority[1] makes a final determination that a product is a medicinal product[2], it may give a notice to any person who has sold or supplied the product, or has offered to sell or supply it or to whom the licensing authority thinks may sell or supply the product[3].

The notice must require the person:

(1)   to cease to sell, supply or offer to sell or supply the product from the date specified in the notice until a marketing authorisation[4], traditional herbal registration[5], certificate of registration[6] or Article 126a authorisation[7] is granted in respect of the product[8]; or

(2)   not to sell, supply or offer to sell or supply the product unless a marketing authorisation, traditional herbal registration, certificate of registration or Article 126a authorisation is granted in respect of the product[9].

A person is guilty of an offence if that person sells or supplies, or offers to sell or supply a product in breach of such a notice imposing a requirement under head (1) or (2) above[10].

1   As to the meaning of 'the licensing authority' see PARA 35 note 1.
2   As to the meaning of 'medicinal product' see PARA 25.
3   Human Medicines Regulations 2012, SI 2012/1916, reg 164(1).
4   As to the meaning of 'marketing authorisation' see PARA 141 note 3.
5   As to the meaning of 'traditional herbal registration' see PARA 141 note 5.
6   As to the meaning of 'certificate of registration' see PARA 141 note 4.
7   As to the meaning of 'Article 126a authorisation' see PARA 141 note 6.
8   Human Medicines Regulations 2012, SI 2012/1916, reg 164(2)(a).

9   Human Medicines Regulations 2012, SI 2012/1916, reg 164(2)(b).
10   Human Medicines Regulations 2012, SI 2012/1916, reg 166(1). A person guilty of such an offence is liable on summary conviction to a fine not exceeding the statutory maximum or, on conviction on indictment, to a fine, to imprisonment for a term not exceeding two years or to both: reg 166(2). As to the statutory maximum see SENTENCING AND DISPOSITION OF OFFENDERS vol 92 (2010) PARA 140.

(iii) Marketing Authorisation

A. APPLICATIONS

155. Applicable products. The provisions relating to marketing authorisations[1] under the Human Medicines Regulations 2012[2] only apply to relevant medicinal products[3]. 'Relevant medicinal product' means a medicinal product[4] that is not a registrable homoeopathic medicinal product[5] or a traditional herbal medicinal product[6].

1   As to the meaning of 'marketing authorisation' see PARA 141 note 3.
2   Ie the Human Medicines Regulations 2012, SI 2012/1916, Pt 5 (regs 48–101).
3   Human Medicines Regulations 2012, SI 2012/1916, reg 48(1).
4   As to the meaning of 'medicinal product' see PARA 25.
5   As to the meaning of 'registrable homoeopathic medicinal product' and 'homoeopathic medicinal product' see PARA 187 notes 1, 2.
6   Human Medicines Regulations 2012, SI 2012/1916, reg 48(2). 'Traditional herbal medicinal product' means a herbal medicinal product to which reg 125 (see PARA 141 note 5) applies: reg 8(1).

156. Applications for the grant of a United Kingdom marketing authorisation. The licensing authority[1] may[2] grant a UK marketing authorisation[3] for a relevant medicinal product[4] in response to an application made in accordance with the relevant provisions[5]. A marketing authorisation so granted must contain terms approved by the licensing authority[6].

The applicant must be established in the European Union[7] and the application must be made in writing, signed by or on behalf of the applicant[8] and, unless the licensing authority directs otherwise, accompanied by any fee payable in connection with the application[9].

The application must include a statement indicating whether the product to which the application relates should be available only on prescription, only from a pharmacy or on general sale[10].

The application must include a statement indicating whether any terms of the authorisation are proposed relating to the method of sale or supply of the product (including, in particular, any proposed restrictions affecting the circumstances of the use or promotion of the product) and, if so, what terms are proposed[11].

1   As to the meaning of 'the licensing authority' see PARA 35 note 1.
2   This is subject to the Human Medicines Regulations 2012, SI 2012/1916, reg 58 (see PARA 158).
3   As to the meaning of 'UK marketing authorisation' see PARA 141 note 3.
4   As to the meaning of 'relevant medicinal product' see PARA 155.
5   Human Medicines Regulations 2012, SI 2012/1916, reg 49(1).
6   Human Medicines Regulations 2012, SI 2012/1916, reg 49(2).
7   Human Medicines Regulations 2012, SI 2012/1916, reg 49(3). The application and any accompanying material must be in English: reg 49(6).
8   An application is treated as signed for this purposes if it is signed with an electronic signature: Human Medicines Regulations 2012, SI 2012/1916, reg 49(5).
9   Human Medicines Regulations 2012, SI 2012/1916, reg 49(4). As to the fees see the Medicines (Products for Human Use) (Fees) Regulations 2012, SI 2012/504 (amended by SI 2012/2546). As to the accompanying material see PARA 157.

10 Human Medicines Regulations 2012, SI 2012/1916, reg 49(7).
11 Human Medicines Regulations 2012, SI 2012/1916, reg 49(8).

157. Accompanying material. An applicant for the grant of a UK marketing authorisation[1] for a relevant medicinal product[2] must provide specified material[3] in relation to the product[4].

The applicant must also, if requested by the licensing authority to do so, provide the licensing authority with material or information that the licensing authority[5] reasonably considers necessary for dealing with the application[6]. This may include an undertaking from the manufacturer to comply with certain matters[7] where any of the medicinal products to which the application relates is liable to be imported from a country other than an EEA state[8].

These provisions are subject to provisions relating to the following applications[9]:

(1)   applications relating to generic medicinal products[10];
(2)   applications relating to certain medicinal products that do not qualify as generic etc[11];
(3)   applications relating to similar biological medicinal products[12];
(4)   applications relating to products in well-established medicinal use[13];
(5)   applications relating to new combinations of active substances[14];
(6)   applications containing information supplied in relation to another product with consent[15].

1   As to the meaning of 'UK marketing authorisation' see PARA 141 note 3.
2   As to the meaning of 'relevant medicinal product' see PARA 155.
3   Ie material specified in the Human Medicines Regulations 2012, SI 2012/1916, Sch 8. The applicant for a UK marketing authorisation must update information supplied in accordance with Sch 8 paras 18–21 (material to accompany an application for a UK marketing authorisation) in connection with the application: reg 57(1). The applicant must update information supplied in connection with the application to include any further information that is relevant to the evaluation of the safety, quality or efficacy of the product concerned: reg 57(2). Updated information within reg 57(1) or (2) must be provided as soon as is reasonably practicable after the applicant becomes aware of it: reg 57(3). Additional material is required in relation to a radionuclide generator: see reg 50(2): reg 57(3). Material that is submitted under reg 50 must be submitted in accordance with the applicable provisions of Council Directive (EC) 2001/83 (OJ L311, 28.11.2001, p 67) on the Community code relating to medicinal products for human use, Annex I: Human Medicines Regulations 2012, SI 2012/1916, reg 50(5).
4   Human Medicines Regulations 2012, SI 2012/1916, reg 50(1).
5   As to the meaning of 'the licensing authority' see PARA 35 note 1.
6   Human Medicines Regulations 2012, SI 2012/1916, reg 50(3).
7   Ie matters set out in the Human Medicines Regulations 2012, SI 2012/1916, Sch 9.
8   See the Human Medicines Regulations 2012, SI 2012/1916, reg 50(4).
9   Ie subject to the Human Medicines Regulations 2012, SI 2012/1916, regs 51–56 (see notes 10–15) reg 50(6)(a)–(f). Regulation 56 is subject to Sch 10 (see PARA 141): see reg 50(6)(g).
10 An applicant for a UK marketing authorisation for a relevant medicinal product that is a generic medicinal product may provide information in relation to the application in accordance with Council Directive (EC) 2001/83 (OJ L311, 28.11.2001, p 67), art 10(1), (5), (6): see the Human Medicines Regulations 2012, SI 2012/1916, reg 51(1). If the licensing authority grants a UK marketing authorisation for the generic medicinal product in accordance with reg 51(1), it is a term of the authorisation that the product must not be sold or supplied, or offered for sale or supply, in the United Kingdom before the time at which it may be placed on the market in accordance with Council Directive (EC) 2001/83 (OJ L311, 28.11.2001, p 67) art 10(1) or, in a case where the application for the marketing authorisation for the reference medicinal product referred to in the application was submitted on or before 30th October 2005, art 10(1) as it stood before it was amended: see the Human Medicines Regulations 2012, SI 2012/1916, reg 51(2).
11 Where an application is made for a UK marketing authorisation in respect of a product by reference to another medicinal product as reference medicinal product, and one or more of the circumstances listed in Council Directive (EC) 2001/83 (OJ L311, 28.11.2001, p 67) art 10(3)

applies in respect of the application, the applicant must provide information in accordance with art 10(3), (6): see the Human Medicine Regulations 2012, SI 2012/1916, reg 52(1), (2). Regulation 51(2) applies to the application as it applies in relation to an application made in accordance with reg 51(1): reg 52(2).

12 If an applicant for a UK marketing authorisation for a biological medicinal product is not able to show that it meets a condition for its being a generic version of a similar medicinal product because of any of the reasons described in Council Directive (EC) 2001/83 (OJ L311, 28.11.2001, p 67) art 10(4), he must provide information in accordance with art 10(4), (6): Human Medicines Regulations 2012, SI 2012/1916, reg 53(1), (2). Regulation 51(2) applies to the application as it applies in relation to an application made in accordance with reg 51(1); reg 53(3). As to the meaning of 'biological medicinal product' see Council Directive (EC) 2001/83 (OJ L311, 28.11.2001, p 67), Annex I, para 3.2.1.1(b): Human Medicines Regulations 2012, SI 2012/1916, reg 8(1).

13 If an applicant for a UK marketing authorisation for a relevant medicinal product is able to demonstrate that the active substances of the product have been in well-established medicinal use within the European Union for at least 10 years, with recognised efficacy and an acceptable level of safety in terms of the conditions set out in Council Directive (EC) 2001/83 (OJ L311, 28.11.2001, p 67) Annex I, the applicant must provide information in accordance with art 10a: Human Medicines Regulations 2012, SI 2012/1916, reg 54(1), (2).

14 In relation to an application for a UK marketing authorisation for a relevant medicinal product that contains active substances that have been used in medicinal products that have been the subject of a marketing authorisation under the Human Medicines Regulations 2012, SI 2012/1916, Council Directive (EC) 2001/83 (OJ L311, 28.11.2001, p 67) or Council Regulation (EC) 726/2004 (OJ L136, 30.4.2004, p 1) laying down Community procedures for the authorisation and supervision of medicinal products for human and veterinary use and establishing a European Medicines Agency; but have not been used in that combination for therapeutic purposes, the applicant must provide information in accordance with Council Directive (EC) 2001/83 (OJ L311, 28.11.2001, p 67) art 10b: Human Medicines Regulations 2012, SI 2012/1916, reg 55(1), (2).

15 In respect of an application for a UK marketing authorisation for a relevant medicinal product where:
   (1)   the product that is the subject of the application ('product A') has the same qualitative and quantitative composition in terms of active substances and the same pharmaceutical form as a product ('product B');
   (2)   product B is the subject of a UK marketing authorisation; and
   (3)   the holder of the marketing authorisation for product B has allowed use to be made of the pharmaceutical, pre-clinical and clinical documentation contained in the file on product B with a view to examining subsequent applications relating to other medicinal products possessing the same qualitative and quantitative composition in terms of active substances and the same pharmaceutical form,
   the documentation referred to in head (3) above in relation to product B may be used in relation to the application in relation to product A, in accordance with Council Directive (EC) 2001/83 (OJ L311, 28.11.2001, p 67) art 10c: Human Medicines Regulations 2012, SI 2012/1916, reg 56(1) (2).

158.   Consideration of applications.   The licensing authority[1] must take all reasonable steps to ensure that it makes a decision to grant or refuse a UK marketing authorisation[2] before the end of 210 days beginning immediately after the day on which the application for the authorisation is submitted[3].

If the licensing authority requests the applicant to provide any further information or material, the period referred to above is suspended for the period beginning with the date on which the request is made and ending with the date on which the information or material is provided[4].

If the licensing authority requests the applicant to give an oral or written explanation of the application, the period is also suspended for the period beginning with the date on which the request is made and ending with the date on which the explanation is provided[5].

The licensing authority may grant the application only if, having considered the application and the accompanying material, the authority thinks that:

(1)   the applicant has established the therapeutic efficacy of the product to which the application relates[6];

(2)   the positive therapeutic effects of the product outweigh the risks to the health of patients or of the public associated with the product[7];

(3)   the application and the accompanying material complies with certain provisions[8]; and

(4)   the product's qualitative and quantitative composition is as described in the application and the accompanying material[9].

1   As to the meaning of 'the licensing authority' see PARA 35 note 1.
2   As to the meaning of 'UK marketing authorisation' see PARA 141 note 3.
3   Human Medicines Regulations 2012, SI 2012/1916, reg 58(1). As to the submission of applications see regs 49–55; and PARAS 156, 157.
4   Human Medicines Regulations 2012, SI 2012/1916, reg 58(2). Sch 11 (see PARA 241 et seq) makes provision about advice and representations in relation to an application for the grant of a UK marketing authorisation: reg 58(5). Regulation 58 does not apply to an application that has been submitted to the licensing authority in accordance with Council Directive (EC) 2001/83 (OJ L311, 28.11.2001, p 67) on the Community code relating to medicinal products for human use or that has been referred to the Committee for Medicinal Products for Human Use established under Council Regulation (EC) 726/2004 (OJ L136, 30.4.2004, p 1) laying down Community procedures for the authorisation and supervision of medicinal products for human and veterinary use and establishing a European Medicines Agency for the application of the procedure laid down in Council Directive (EC) 2001/83 (OJ L311, 28.11.2001, p 67) arts 32–34: Human Medicines Regulations 2012, SI 2012/1916, reg 58(6). An application to which reg 58(6) applies is to be determined by the licensing authority in accordance with Council Directive (EC) 2001/83 (OJ L311, 28.11.2001, p 67) Title III, Chapter 4: Human Medicines Regulations 2012, SI 2012/1916, reg 58(7).
5   Human Medicines Regulations 2012, SI 2012/1916, reg 58(3).
6   Human Medicines Regulations 2012, SI 2012/1916, reg 58(4)(a).
7   Human Medicines Regulations 2012, SI 2012/1916, reg 58(4)(b).
8   Human Medicines Regulations 2012, SI 2012/1916, reg 58(4)(c). The provisions mentioned in the text are regs 49–55 (see PARAS 156, 157).
9   Human Medicines Regulations 2012, SI 2012/1916, reg 58(4)(d).

159.   Renewal of applications.   The licensing authority[1] may renew a UK marketing authorisation[2] in response to an application made in accordance with the following[3]. The applicant must be established in the European Union[4] and the application must be made in writing, signed by or on behalf of the applicant[5] and, unless the licensing authority directs otherwise, accompanied by any fee payable in connection with the application[6].

The holder must provide a consolidated version of the file in respect of quality, safety and efficacy, including the evaluation of data contained in suspected adverse reaction reports and periodic safety update reports submitted[7] and all amendments made since the authorisation was granted[8].

The licensing authority may renew a UK marketing authorisation only if, having considered the application and the material accompanying it, the authority thinks that the positive therapeutic effects of the product to which the authorisation relates outweigh the risks of the product to the health of patients or of the public[9].

1   As to the meaning of 'the licensing authority' see PARA 35 note 1.
2   As to the meaning of 'UK marketing authorisation' see PARA 141 note 3.
3   Human Medicines Regulations 2012, SI 2012/1916, reg 66(1). Sch 11 (see PARA 241 et seq) makes provision about advice and representations in relation to an application for the renewal of a UK marketing authorisation: reg 66(8).
4   Human Medicines Regulations 2012, SI 2012/1916, reg 66(2).
5   An application is treated as signed for the purposes of the Human Medicines Regulations 2012, SI 2012/1916, reg 66(3)(b) if it is signed with an electronic signature: reg 66(4).

6 Human Medicines Regulations 2012, SI 2012/1916, reg 66(3). The application must be made so that it is received by the licensing authority before the beginning of the period of 9 months ending with the expiry of the period mentioned in reg 66(1)(a) or (as the case may be) 66(3)(a) of reg 65 (initial and further period of validity): 66(5). As to fees see PARA 30. As to the meaning of 'month' see PARA 43 note 3.
7 Ie in accordance with the Human Medicines Regulations 2012, SI 2012/1916, Pt 11 (regs 177–212).
8 Human Medicines Regulations 2012, SI 2012/1916, reg 66(6).
9 Human Medicines Regulations 2012, SI 2012/1916, reg 66(7).

B. CONDITIONS

160. In general. The licensing authority[1] may grant a UK marketing authorisation[2] subject to one or more of the conditions given below or may vary or remove such a condition to which the UK marketing authorisation is subject[3].

Those conditions are:

(1) to take certain measures for ensuring the safe use of the medicinal product[4] and include them in the risk management plan[5];

(2) to conduct post-authorisation safety studies[6];

(3) to comply with obligations on the recording or reporting of suspected adverse reactions[7] which are stricter than the provisions[8] relating to pharmcovigilance[9];

(4) any other conditions or restrictions with regard to the safe and effective use of the medicinal product[10];

(5) the existence of an adequate pharmacovigilance system[11]; and

(6) to conduct post-authorisation efficacy studies where concerns relating to some aspects of the efficacy of the medicinal product are identified and can be resolved only after the medicinal product has been marketed[12].

The marketing authorisation must lay down deadlines for the fulfilment of the above conditions where necessary[13].

The licensing authority must notify the European Medicines Agency[14] of any marketing authorisation that it has granted subject to a condition included in accordance with this regulation[15].

The holder of the authorisation must incorporate any condition included in a marketing authorisation in accordance with this regulation into the risk management system[16] for the product[17].

Failure to comply with a condition under these provisions is an offence[18].

1 As to the meaning of 'the licensing authority' see PARA 35 note 1.
2 As to the meaning of 'UK marketing authorisation' see PARA 141 note 3.
3 Human Medicines Regulations 2012, SI 2012/1916, reg 59(1). Schedule 11 makes provision about advice and representations in relation to proposals to vary or remove a condition to which a UK marketing authorisation is subject: reg 59(7).
4 As to the meaning 'medicinal product' see PARA 25.
5 Human Medicines Regulations 2012, SI 2012/1916, reg 59(2)(a). 'Risk management plan' means a detailed description of the risk management system: reg 8(1). As to the meaning of 'risk management system' see PARA 74 note 6.
6 Human Medicines Regulations 2012, SI 2012/1916, reg 59(2)(b).
7 As to the meaning of 'suspected' see PARA 70 note 7. As to the meaning of 'adverse reaction' see PARA 70 note 6.
8 Ie those referred to in the Human Medicines Regulations 2012, SI 2012/1916 Pt 11 (regs 177–212: see PARA 241 et seq).
9 Human Medicines Regulations 2012, SI 2012/1916, reg 59(2)(c).
10 Human Medicines Regulations 2012, SI 2012/1916, reg 59(2)(d).
11 Human Medicines Regulations 2012, SI 2012/1916, reg 59(2)(e). As to the meaning of 'pharmacovigilance system' see PARA 243 note 2.

12 Human Medicines Regulations 2012, SI 2012/1916, reg 59(2)(f). An obligation to conduct such studies as are referred to in head (6) must be based on the delegated acts adopted pursuant to Council Directive (EC) 2001/83 (OJ L311, 28.11.2001, p 67) on the Community code relating to medicinal products for human use, art 22b, while taking into account the scientific guidance referred to in art 108a: Human Medicines Regulations 2012, SI 2012/1916, reg 59(3).
13 Human Medicines Regulations 2012, SI 2012/1916, reg 59(4).
14 As to the European Medicines Agency see PARA 14.
15 Human Medicines Regulations 2012, SI 2012/1916, reg 59(5).
16 As to the meaning of 'risk management system' see PARA 74 note 6.
17 Human Medicines Regulations 2012, SI 2012/1916, reg 59(6).
18 See the Human Medicines Regulations 2012, SI 2012/1916, reg 97; and PARA 185.

161. Exceptional circumstances. The licensing authority[1] may grant a UK marketing authorisation[2] subject to conditions[3] or vary or remove such a condition to which the UK marketing authorisation is subject[4].

This power may be exercised only after consultation with the applicant for the authorisation or (as the case may be) its holder[5].

The power to grant an authorisation subject to conditions may be exercised only in exceptional circumstances and when the applicant can show that he is unable to provide comprehensive data on the efficacy and safety of the medicinal product under normal conditions of use[6].

The conditions may, in particular, relate to the safety of the product to which the authorisation relates[7] and may require that, where there is a serious adverse reaction[8] relating to the use of the product the reaction must be reported to the licensing authority and such other action as may be specified in the conditions must be taken[9].

The licensing authority must keep under review the conditions under these provisions to which a UK marketing authorisation is subject and the holder's compliance with those conditions[10]. The licensing authority must consider those matters no less frequently than at the end of the period of one year beginning with the date on which the authorisation was granted and at the end of each subsequent period of one year[11].

The holder of the authorisation must incorporate any condition included in a marketing authorisation in accordance with these provisions into the risk management system[12] for the product[13].

Failure to comply with a condition imposed under the above provisions is an offence[14].

1   As to the meaning of 'the licensing authority' see PARA 35 note 1.
2   As to the meaning of 'UK marketing authorisation' see PARA 141 note 3.
3   Ie conditions in accordance with the Human Medicines Regulations 2012, SI 2012/1916, reg 60(2)–(11). The conditions must relate to a matter addressed by Council Directive (EC) 2001/83 (OJ L311, 28.11.2001, p 67) on the Community code relating to medicinal products for human use, Annex I: Human Medicines Regulations 2012, SI 2012/1916, reg 60(4). The licensing authority must notify the European Medicines Agency of any marketing authorisation that it has granted subject to a condition included in accordance with these provisions: reg 60(9). As to the European Medicines Agency see PARA 14. Schedule 11 makes provision about advice and representations in relation to proposals to vary or remove a condition to which a UK marketing authorisation is subject: reg 60(11). As to the European Medicines Agency see PARA 14.
4   Human Medicines Regulations 2012, SI 2012/1916, reg 60(1).
5   Human Medicines Regulations 2012, SI 2012/1916, reg 60(2).
6   Human Medicines Regulations 2012, SI 2012/1916, reg 60(3).
7   Human Medicines Regulations 2012, SI 2012/1916, reg 60(5).
8   As to the meaning of 'serious adverse reaction' see PARA 71 note 8.
9   Human Medicines Regulations 2012, SI 2012/1916, reg 60(6).
10 Human Medicines Regulations 2012, SI 2012/1916, reg 60(7).

11 Human Medicines Regulations 2012, SI 2012/1916, reg 60(8).
12 As to the meaning of 'risk management system' see PARA 74 note 6.
13 Human Medicines Regulations 2012, SI 2012/1916, reg 60(10).
14 See the Human Medicines Regulations 2012, SI 2012/1916, reg 97; and PARA 185.

162. New obligations post-authorisation. After the granting of a UK marketing authorisation[1], the licensing authority[2] may impose certain obligations on the holder of the authorisation[3]. If there are concerns about the risks of a medicinal product[4] that is the subject of a marketing authorisation the licensing authority may impose an obligation on the holder of the authorisation to conduct a post-authorisation safety study[5]. If the understanding of the disease or the clinical methodology indicate that previous efficacy evaluations might have to be revised significantly, the licensing authority may impose an obligation on the holder of the authorisation to conduct a post-authorisation efficacy study[6].

Where the licensing authority imposes such an obligation, it must without delay give written notice to the holder of the imposition of the obligation, the justification for the imposition, the objectives and timeframe for submission and conduct of the study and the opportunity to present written observations[7] along with the time limit specified for doing so[8].

Where the holder presents such written observations the licensing authority must withdraw or confirm the imposition of the obligation on the basis of the written observations as soon as is reasonably practicable[9].

Where the licensing authority imposes an obligation and the holder does not present written representations, or the licensing authority has confirmed the imposition of an obligation, the licensing authority must vary the marketing authorisation to include the obligation as a condition[10] of the marketing authorisation[11].

The holder of the authorisation must incorporate any condition so included in a marketing authorisation into the risk management system[12] for the product[13].

Failure to comply with a condition imposed under the above provisions is an offence[14].

1 As to the meaning of 'UK marketing authorisation' see PARA 141 note 3.
2 As to the meaning of 'the licensing authority' see PARA 35 note 1.
3 See the Human Medicines Regulations 2012, SI 2012/1916, reg 61(1).
4 As to the meaning of 'medicinal product' see PARA 25. If concerns as described in the Human Medicines Regulations 2012, SI 2012/1916, reg 61(2) apply to more than one medicinal product, the licensing authority must, following consultation with the Pharmacovigilance Risk Assessment Committee, encourage the marketing authorisation holders concerned to conduct a joint post-authorisation safety study: reg 61(6). 'Post-authorisation safety study' means any study relating to a medicinal product to which a marketing authorisation, traditional herbal registration or Article 126a authorisation relates that is conducted with the aim of identifying, characterising or quantifying a safety hazard, confirming the safety profile of the medicinal product or measuring the effectiveness of risk management measures: reg 8(1). As to the meanings of 'marketing authorisation', 'traditional herbal registration' and 'Article 126a authorisation' see PARA 141 notes 3, 5, 6. The 'Pharmacovigilance Risk Assessment Committee' means the committee of the European Medicines Agency established by Council Regulation (EC) 726/2004 (OJ L136, 30.4.2004, p 1) laying down Community procedures for the authorisation and supervision of medicinal products for human and veterinary use and establishing a European Medicines Agency, art 56(1)(aa): Human Medicines Regulations 2012, SI 2012/1916, reg 8(1).
5 See the Human Medicines Regulations 2012, SI 2012/1916, reg 61(1)(a), (2), (4).
6 See the Human Medicines Regulations 2012, SI 2012/1916, reg 61(1)(b), (3), (5). The obligation under the Human Medicines Regulations 2012, SI 2012/1916, reg 61(5) must be based on the delegated acts adopted pursuant to Council Directive (EC) 2001/83 (OJ L311, 28.11.2001, p 67) on the Community code relating to medicinal products for human use, art 22b while

taking account of the scientific guidance referred to in art 108a: Human Medicines Regulations 2012, SI 2012/1916, reg 61(7). 'Post-authorisation efficacy study' means any study relating to a medicinal product to which a marketing authorisation relates that is conducted with the aim of considering the efficacy of that product: reg 8(1).

7   Where the holder so requests within the period of thirty days beginning on the day after the receipt by the holder of the notice referred to in the Human Medicines Regulations 2012, SI 2012/1916, reg 61(8), the licensing authority must provide the holder of the authorisation with an opportunity to present written observations in response to the imposition of the obligation within the time limit specified by the licensing authority in the notice: reg 61(9).

8   Human Medicines Regulations 2012, SI 2012/1916, reg 61(8).

9   See the Human Medicines Regulations 2012, SI 2012/1916, reg 61(9).

10 Ie as if it were a condition imposed under the Human Medicines Regulations 2012, SI 2012/1916, reg 59 (see PARA 160).

11 See the Human Medicines Regulations 2012, SI 2012/1916, reg 61(11), (12). The licensing authority must notify the European Medicines Agency that the marketing authorisation is subject to a condition included in accordance with reg 61(12): reg 61(13). Schedule 11, which makes provision about advice and representations in relation to proposals to vary or remove a condition to which a UK marketing authorisation is subject, applies in relation to the variation or removal of a condition included in a marketing authorisation in accordance with reg 61(12): reg 61(15). As to the European Medicines Agency see PARA 14.

12 As to the meaning of 'risk management system' see PARA 74 note 6.

13 Human Medicines Regulations 2012, SI 2012/1916, reg 61(14).

14 See the Human Medicines Regulations 2012, SI 2012/1916, reg 97; and PARA 185.

163. Classification of UK marketing authorisations. A UK marketing authorisation[1] must include a term that the product to which the authorisation relates is to be available only on prescription, only from a pharmacy or on general sale[2].

In making such a determination, the licensing authority[3] must have regard, in relation to the product, the maximum single dose, the maximum daily dose, the strength of the product, its pharmaceutical form, its packaging and such other circumstances relating to its use as the licensing authority considers relevant[4].

A UK marketing authorisation must be granted subject to a condition that the product to which the authorisation relates is to be available only on prescription if the licensing authority considers[5] that the product:

(1)   is likely to present a direct or indirect danger to human health, even when used correctly, if used without the supervision of a doctor or dentist[6];

(2)   is frequently and to a very wide extent used incorrectly, and as a result is likely to present a direct or indirect danger to human health[7];

(3)   contains substances, or preparations of substances, of which the activity requires, or the side effects require, further investigation[8]; or

(4)   is normally prescribed by a doctor or dentist for parenteral administration[9].

A UK marketing authorisation may include a term that the product to which the authorisation relates is to be available on general sale only if the licensing authority considers that the product can with reasonable safety be sold or supplied otherwise than by, or under the supervision of, a pharmacist[10].

1   As to the meaning of 'UK marketing authorisation' see PARA 141 note 3.

2   Human Medicines Regulations 2012, SI 2012/1916, reg 62(1).

3   As to the meaning of 'the licensing authority' see PARA 35 note 1.

4   Human Medicines Regulations 2012, SI 2012/1916, reg 62(2).

5   In deciding whether the Human Medicines Regulations 2012, SI 2012/1916, reg 62(3) applies to a product, the licensing authority must take into account whether the product:

(1)   contains a substance listed in the Narcotics Drugs Convention Schs I, II or IV (where the product is not a preparation listed in Sch III to that Convention) (Human Medicines Regulations 2012, SI 2012/1916, reg 62(4)(a));

(2)   contains a substance listed in any of the Psychotropic Substances Convention Schs I–IV of (where the product is not a preparation which may be exempted from measures of control in accordance with art 3(2), (3) (Human Medicines Regulations 2012, SI 2012/1916, reg 62(4)(b));

(3)   is likely, if incorrectly used to present a substantial risk of medicinal abuse, to lead to addiction or to be used for illegal purposes (reg 62(4)(c));

(4)   contains a substance that, by reason of its novelty or properties, might fall within head (3), but as to which there is insufficient information available to determine whether it does so fall (reg 62(4)(d));

(5)   by reason of its pharmaceutical characteristics or novelty, or in the interests of public health, is reserved for treatments that can only be followed in a hospital (reg 62(4)(e));

(6)   is used in the treatment of conditions that must be diagnosed in a hospital or in an institution with special diagnostic facilities (although administration and subsequent supervision may be carried out elsewhere) (reg 62(4)(f)); or

(7)   is intended for outpatients but may produce very serious side effects which would require a prescription drawn up as required by a specialist and special supervision throughout the treatment (reg 62(4)(g)).

The 'Narcotics Drugs Convention' means the Single Convention on Narcotic Drugs (New York 30 March to 1 August 1961; TS 34 (1965); Cmnd 2631) as amended by the Protocol Amending the Single Convention on Narcotic Drugs (Geneva, 25 March to 31 December 1972; TS 23 (1979); Cmd 7466); and 'the Psychotropic Substances Convention' means the Convention on Psychotropic Substances (Vienna, 21 February 1971; TS 51 (1993); Cmnd 2307): Human Medicines Regulations 2012, SI 2012/1916, reg 8(1).

6   Human Medicines Regulations 2012, SI 2012/1916, reg 62(3)(a). As to the meanings of 'doctor' and 'dentist' see PARA 48 note 6.
7   Human Medicines Regulations 2012, SI 2012/1916, reg 62(3)(b).
8   Human Medicines Regulations 2012, SI 2012/1916, reg 62(3)(c).
9   Human Medicines Regulations 2012, SI 2012/1916, reg 62(3)(d).
10   Human Medicines Regulations 2012, SI 2012/1916, reg 62(5).

C. DUTIES OF LICENSING AUTHORITY

164. Duties of licensing authority in connection with determination. If the licensing authority[1] grants a UK marketing authorisation[2], the licensing authority must inform the holder of the authorisation of the summary of the product characteristics as approved by the authority[3].

The licensing authority must ensure that the summary of the product characteristics continues to match the version it has approved, subject to any changes it approves and, as soon as is reasonably practicable after granting the marketing authorisation, it must make available publicly the marketing authorisation, the package leaflet[4], the summary of the product characteristics, any conditions[5] and any deadlines for the fulfilment of those conditions[6].

The licensing authority must draw up an assessment report and make comments[7] on the file[8]. It must:

(1)   revise the assessment report whenever new information becomes available that is of importance for the evaluation of the quality, safety or efficacy of the medicinal product[9];

(2)   make the assessment report publicly available (with the omission of information of a commercially confidential nature) as soon as is reasonably practicable after it has been prepared or revised[10]; and

(3)   include in the assessment report a summary, written in a manner that is understandable to the public, that contains, in particular, a section relating to the conditions of use of the medicinal product[11].

The assessment must be provided separately for each indication that is authorised[12].

1   As to the meaning of 'the licensing authority' see PARA 35 note 1.

2   As to the meaning of 'UK marketing authorisation' see PARA 141 note 3.

3   Human Medicines Regulations 2012, SI 2012/1916, reg 64(1), (2). As to the meaning of 'the summary of the product characteristics' see PARA 55 note 11.

4   As to the meaning of 'package leaflet' see PARA 68 note 5.

5   Ie conditions established in accordance with Council Directive (EC) 2001/83 (OJ L311, 28.11.2001, p 67) on the Community code relating to medicinal products for human use, arts 21a, 22 and 22a.

6   Human Medicines Regulations 2012, SI 2012/1916, reg 64(3), (4).

7   Ie as regards the results of the pharmaceutical and pre-clinical tests, the clinical trials, the risk management system and the pharmacovigilance system of the product to which the authorisation relates or, in the case of a national homoeopathic medicinal product within the meaning of the Human Medicines Regulations 2012, SI 2012/1916, Sch 10 (see PARA 141), the information submitted under Sch 10 paras 3–5: reg 64(5)(a), (b). As to the meaning of 'risk management system' see PARA 74 note 6.

8   Human Medicines Regulations 2012, SI 2012/1916, reg 64(5).

9   Human Medicines Regulations 2012, SI 2012/1916, reg 64(6)(a).

10 Human Medicines Regulations 2012, SI 2012/1916, reg 64(6)(b).

11 Human Medicines Regulations 2012, SI 2012/1916, reg 64(6)(c).

12 Human Medicines Regulations 2012, SI 2012/1916, reg 64(7).

D. VALIDITY OF UK MARKETING AUTHORISATION

165.   Validity of UK marketing authorisations.   A UK marketing authorisation[1] remains in force for an initial period of five years beginning with the date on which it is granted and, if the authorisation is renewed[2], for an unlimited period after its renewal[3].

The licensing authority may, on the first application for renewal of an authorisation, determine on grounds relating to pharmacovigilance, including exposure of an insufficient number of patients to the medicinal product[4] concerned, that it should be necessary for the holder to make one further application for renewal[5]. In that event the authorisation remains in force for a further period of five years beginning with the date on which it is first renewed and, if the authorisation is further renewed[6], for an unlimited period after its further renewal[7].

If an application for the renewal or further renewal[8] of an authorisation is made the authorisation remains in force until the licensing authority notifies the applicant of its decision on the application[9].

1   As to the meaning of 'UK marketing authorisation' see PARA 141 note 3.

2   Ie in accordance with the Human Medicines Regulations 2012, SI 2012/1916, reg 66 (see PARA 159).

3   Human Medicines Regulations 2012, SI 2012/1916, reg 65(1). Regulation 65 is subject to regs 67, 68 (see PARAS 166, 167): reg 65(5).

4   As to the meaning of 'medicinal product' see PARA 25.

5   Human Medicines Regulations 2012, SI 2012/1916, reg 65(2).

6   See note 2.

7   Human Medicines Regulations 2012, SI 2012/1916, reg 65(3).

8   See note 2.

9   Human Medicines Regulations 2012, SI 2012/1916, reg 65(4).

E. REVOCATION, SUSPENSION OR VARIATION AND CEASING OF AUTHORISATION

166.   Ceasing of UK marketing authorisation.   Unless the licensing authority[1] grants an exemption[2] from its operation a UK marketing authorisation[3] ceases to be in force in the following circumstances[4].

A UK marketing authorisation ceases to be in force if the product to which it relates is not placed on the market in the United Kingdom during the period of three years beginning immediately after the day on which it was granted[5].

A UK marketing authorisation for a product which has been placed on the market ceases to be in force if the product to which it relates is not sold or supplied in the United Kingdom for a period of three years[6].

1   As to the meaning of 'the licensing authority' see PARA 35 note 1.
2   An exemption may be granted in response to an application in writing by the holder of the UK marketing authorisation or by the licensing authority of its own motion: Human Medicines Regulations 2012, SI 2012/1916, reg 67(4). An exemption may be granted only in exceptional circumstances and on public health grounds: reg 67(5). An exemption has effect for the period determined by the licensing authority, which may not exceed three years beginning with the day on which it is granted and may be renewed or further renewed: reg 67(6).
3   As to the meaning of 'UK marketing authorisation' see PARA 141 note 3.
4   Human Medicines Regulations 2012, SI 2012/1916, reg 67(3).
5   Human Medicines Regulations 2012, SI 2012/1916, reg 67(1).
6   Human Medicines Regulations 2012, SI 2012/1916, reg 67(2).

167. Revocation, suspension or variation of UK marketing authorisations.
The licensing authority[1] may revoke, suspend or vary a UK marketing authorisation[2] if any of the following conditions are met[3].

Condition A is that the licensing authority thinks that:

(1)   the product to which the authorisation relates is harmful[4];

(2)   the positive therapeutic effects of the product do not outweigh the risks of the product to the health of patients or of the public[5];

(3)   the product lacks therapeutic efficacy, in that therapeutic results cannot be obtained from the product[6]; or

(4)   the product's qualitative or quantitative composition is not as described in the application for the authorisation or the material supplied with it[7].

Condition B is that the licensing authority thinks that the application or the material supplied with it is incorrect[8].

Condition C is that the licensing authority thinks that there has been a breach of a term of the authorisation or a requirement imposed by certain provisions[9] relating to packaging and leaflets[10].

Condition D is that the licensing authority thinks that a condition to which the authorisation is subject[11] by has not been fulfilled[12].

Condition E is that the licensing authority thinks that the holder of the authorisation has not complied with requirements[13] to provide information[14].

Condition F is that the holder of the authorisation has ceased to be established in the European Union[15].

Condition G is that the product to which the authorisation relates is manufactured in the United Kingdom and the licensing authority thinks that the holder of the manufacturer's licence[16] for the product has failed to comply in relation to the product with provisions relating to manufacturing and assembly[17], importing from states other than EEA states[18], further requirements for manufacturer's licence[19], obligations to provide information relating to control methods[20] or requirements[21] as to qualified persons[22].

Condition H is that the product to which the authorisation relates is manufactured in a member state other than the United Kingdom and the licensing authority thinks that the licensee under the manufacturer's licence for the product has failed to comply in relation to the product with EU requirements relating to manufacturing authorisations[23] in that member state[24].

Condition I is that the licensing authority thinks that urgent action to protect public health is necessary, in which case it may suspend the authorisation and it must notify the suspension to the European Medicines Agency[25], the European Commission, and all other member states by the end of the next working day following the day on which the suspension comes into force[26].

Condition J is that the holder applies to vary the authorisation and that the licensing authority thinks that the application should be granted[27].

1 As to the meaning of 'the licensing authority' see PARA 35 note 1.
2 As to the meaning of 'UK marketing authorisation' see PARA 141 note 3.
3 Human Medicines Regulations 2012, SI 2012/1916, reg 68(1). For cases relevant to the revocation, suspension or variation of authorisations see: Case C-120/97 *Upjohn Ltd v Licensing Authority established under the Medicines Act 1968* [1999] ECR 1–223, 51 BMLR 206, ECJ; Case C-471/00 *Commission of the European Communities v Cambridge Healthcare Supplies Ltd* [2001] ECR 1–2865, CFI. The Human Medicines Regulations 2012, SI 2012/1916, Sch 11 makes provision about advice and representations in relation to a proposal to revoke, vary or suspend a UK marketing authorisation, other than a proposal to vary an authorisation on the application of its holder: reg 68(12). Regulations 68, 69 are subject to reg 70 (see regs 68(13), 69(10)) and do not apply in relation to a UK marketing authorisation that: (1) was granted in accordance with the mutual recognition procedure and decentralised procedure (see Council Directive (EC) 2001/83 (OJ L311, 28.11.2001, p 67) on the Community code relating to medicinal products for human use, Title III, Chapter 4); (2) was granted before 1 January 1995 in accordance with Council Directive (EEC) 87/22 (OJ L15, 17.1.1987, p 37–41 on the approximation of national measures relating to the placing on the market of high-technology medicinal products, particularly those derived from biotechnology, art 4; or (3) was subject to the procedure laid down in Council Directive (EC) 2001/83 (OJ L311, 28.11.2001, p 67) arts 32–34 following a referral under art 30 or 31, unless the procedure was limited to certain specific parts of the authorisation: Human Medicines Regulations 2012, SI 2012/1916, reg 70(1). A proposal by the licensing authority to vary, suspend or revoke a marketing authorisation within reg 70(1), or an application by the holder of such an authorisation to vary or revoke it, is to be determined in accordance with Council Directive (EC) 2001/83 (OJ L311, 28.11.2001, p 67), Title III, Chapter 4: Human Medicines Regulations 2012, SI 2012/1916, reg 70(2).
4 Human Medicines Regulations 2012, SI 2012/1916, reg 68(2)(a).
5 Human Medicines Regulations 2012, SI 2012/1916, reg 68(2)(b).
6 Human Medicines Regulations 2012, SI 2012/1916, reg 68(2)(c).
7 Human Medicines Regulations 2012, SI 2012/1916, reg 68(2)(d).
8 Human Medicines Regulations 2012, SI 2012/1916, reg 68(3).
9 Ie the Human Medicines Regulations 2012, SI 2012/1916, Pt 13 (regs 257–276).
10 Human Medicines Regulations 2012, SI 2012/1916, reg 68(4).
11 Ie by virtue of the Human Medicines Regulations 2012, SI 2012/1916, reg 59 (conditions of UK marketing authorisations: general: see PARA 160), 60 (conditions of UK marketing authorisations: exceptional circumstances: see PARA 161) or 61 (conditions of UK marketing authorisations: new obligations post-authorisation: see PARA 162).
12 Human Medicines Regulations 2012, SI 2012/1916, reg 68(5).
13 Ie the requirements under the Human Medicines Regulations 2012, SI 2012/1916, reg 75(1)–(3) (see PARA 173).
14 Human Medicines Regulations 2012, SI 2012/1916, reg 68(6).
15 Human Medicines Regulations 2012, SI 2012/1916, reg 68(7).
16 As to the meaning of 'manufacturer's licence' see PARA 45.
17 Ie the Human Medicines Regulations 2012, SI 2012/1916, reg 37 (see PARA 62).
18 Ie the Human Medicines Regulations 2012, SI 2012/1916, reg 38 (see PARA 67).
19 Ie the Human Medicines Regulations 2012, SI 2012/1916, reg 39 (see PARA 56).
20 Ie the Human Medicines Regulations 2012, SI 2012/1916, reg 40 (see PARA 56).
21 Ie the Human Medicines Regulations 2012, SI 2012/1916, reg 41 (see PARA 57).
22 Human Medicines Regulations 2012, SI 2012/1916, reg 68(8).
23 Ie Council Directive (EC) 2001/83 (OJ L311, 28.11.2001, p 67), art 41.
24 Human Medicines Regulations 2012, SI 2012/1916, reg 68(9).
25 As to the European Medicines Agency see PARA 14.
26 Human Medicines Regulations 2012, SI 2012/1916, reg 68(10).
27 Human Medicines Regulations 2012, SI 2012/1916, reg 68(11).

168.   Suspension of use etc of relevant medicinal product.   The licensing authority[1] may, if any of the following conditions are met, suspend the use, sale, supply or offer for sale or supply within the United Kingdom of a product to which a UK marketing authorisation[2] relates[3].

Condition A is that the licensing authority thinks that the product to which the authorisation relates is harmful, the positive therapeutic effects of the product do not outweigh the risks of the product to the health of patients or of the public, the product lacks therapeutic efficacy, in that therapeutic results cannot be obtained from the product or the product's qualitative or quantitative composition is not as described in the application for the authorisation or the material supplied with it[4].

Condition B is that the licensing authority thinks that the holder of the authorisation has not complied with requirements[5] to provide proof of controls on manufacturing process[6].

Condition C is that the licensing authority thinks that there has been a breach of a term of the authorisation or a requirement[7] relating to packaging and leaflets[8].

Condition D is that the licensing authority thinks that the power to revoke, suspend or vary manufacturers' licences[9] applies in relation to the manufacturer's licence for the product to which the authorisation relates[10].

A suspension under these provisions may relate to batches of the product[11].

The licensing authority must give notice in writing of a suspension under these provisions to the holder of the UK marketing authorisation and the notice must provide that the suspension is to take effect immediately or from a date specified in the notice and is to apply for the period specified in the notice[12].

Where a medicinal product is the subject of a suspension under these provisions, the licensing authority may, in exceptional circumstances and for such a transitional period as the licensing authority may determine, allow the supply of the medicinal product[13] to patients who are already being treated with the medicinal product[14].

1   As to the meaning of 'the licensing authority' see PARA 35 note 1.
2   As to the meaning of 'UK marketing authorisation' see PARA 141 note 3.
3   Human Medicines Regulations 2012, SI 2012/1916, reg 69(1). Regulation 69 is subject to reg 70 (see PARA 167 note 3): reg 69(10).
4   Human Medicines Regulations 2012, SI 2012/1916, reg 69(2).
5   Ie the requirements under the Human Medicines Regulations 2012, SI 2012/1916, reg 75(7) (see PARA 173).
6   Human Medicines Regulations 2012, SI 2012/1916, reg 69(3).
7   Ie a requirement imposed by the Human Medicines Regulations 2012, SI 2012/1916, Pt 13 (regs 257–276).
8   Human Medicines Regulations 2012, SI 2012/1916, reg 69(4).
9   Ie the power under the Human Medicines Regulations 2012, SI 2012/1916, reg 26(4) or (5) (see PARA 41).
10   Human Medicines Regulations 2012, SI 2012/1916, reg 69(5).
11   Human Medicines Regulations 2012, SI 2012/1916, reg 69(6).
12   Human Medicines Regulations 2012, SI 2012/1916, reg 69(7), (8).
13   As to the meaning of 'medicinal product' see PARA 25.
14   Human Medicines Regulations 2012, SI 2012/1916, reg 69(9).

169.   Withdrawal of medicinal product from the market.   If the European Commission revokes or suspends a marketing authorisation[1] or the licensing authority[2] suspends the use, sale, supply or offer for sale or supply[3] within the United Kingdom of a product to which a marketing authorisation relates[4], the licensing authority may give written notice to the person who is, or immediately before its revocation was, the holder of the authorisation requiring that person to comply with both of the following requirements[5].

Requirement A is to take all reasonably practicable steps to inform wholesalers, retailers, medical practitioners, patients and others who may be in possession of the product to which the authorisation relates of the revocation or suspension, the reasons for the revocation or suspension and any action to be taken to restrict or prevent further use, sale, supply or offer for sale or supply of the product[6].

Requirement B is to take all reasonably practicable steps to withdraw from the market in the United Kingdom and recover possession of the product or the batches of the product specified in the notice, within the time and for the period specified in the notice[7].

1   Ie under the Human Medicines Regulations 2012, SI 2012/1916, regs 68, 70(2) (see PARA 167), Council Directive (EC) 2001/83 (OJ L311, 28.11.2001, p 67) on the Community code relating to medicinal products for human use or Council Regulation (EC) 726/2004 (OJ L136, 30.4.2004, p 1) laying down Community procedures for the authorisation and supervision of medicinal products for human and veterinary use and establishing a European Medicines Agency.
2   As to the meaning of 'the licensing authority' see PARA 35 note 1.
3   Ie under the Human Medicines Regulations 2012, SI 2012/1916, reg 69 (see PARA 168) or Council Regulation (EC) 726/2004 (OJ L136, 30.4.2004, p 1), art 20(4).
4   Human Medicines Regulations 2012, SI 2012/1916, reg 71(1).
5   Human Medicines Regulations 2012, SI 2012/1916, reg 71(2).
6   Human Medicines Regulations 2012, SI 2012/1916, reg 71(3).
7   Human Medicines Regulations 2012, SI 2012/1916, reg 71(4).

170.   Sale etc of suspended medicinal product. If the use, sale, supply or offer for sale or supply of a medicinal product[1] is suspended[2], a person must not sell, supply or offer to sell or supply the product or procure the sale, supply or offer for sale or supply of the product, knowing, or having reasonable cause to believe, that such use, sale, supply or offer for sale or supply is suspended[3].

1   As to the meaning of 'medicinal products' see PARA 25.
2   Ie in accordance with the Human Medicines Regulations 2012, SI 2012/1916, reg 69 or 70(2) (see PARAS 167, 168) or Council Regulation (EC) 726/2004 (OJ L136, 30.4.2004, p 1) laying down Community procedures for the authorisation and supervision of medicinal products for human and veterinary use and establishing a European Medicines Agency, art 20(4).
3   Human Medicines Regulations 2012, SI 2012/1916, reg 72(1), (2).

F.   OBLIGATIONS OF HOLDERS OF MARKETING AUTHORISATIONS

171.   To notify placing on the market etc. The holder of a UK marketing authorisation[1] must notify the licensing authority[2] of the date on which the product to which the authorisation relates is placed on the market in the United Kingdom, taking account of the various presentations authorised[3].

The holder of a UK marketing authorisation must also notify the licensing authority if the product to which the authorisation relates is to be withdrawn from the market in the United Kingdom (whether temporarily or permanently)[4].

The licensing authority may require the holder of a UK marketing authorisation to provide information relating to the volume of sales in the United Kingdom of the product to which the authorisation relates or to provide information of which the holder is aware relating to the volume of prescriptions in the United Kingdom for the product[5].

The holder of a UK marketing authorisation must provide the licensing authority with such information where the period within which the information must be provided is specified in a written notice given to the holder by the licensing authority, before the end of that period or, otherwise, as soon as is reasonably practicable after receipt of the request[6].

1   As to the meaning of 'UK marketing authorisation' see PARA 141 note 3.
2   As to the meaning of 'the licensing authority' see PARA 35 note 1.
3   Human Medicines Regulations 2012, SI 2012/1916, reg 73(1). Such a notification must be given before the end of the period of 2 months beginning with the date on which the product is placed on the market: reg 73(2). As to the meaning of 'month' see PARA 43 note 3.
4   Human Medicines Regulations 2012, SI 2012/1916, reg 73(3). Such a notification must be given before the beginning of the period of 2 months ending with the date on which the product is to be withdrawn from the market unless it is not reasonably practicable to do so: reg 73(4). In that event, the notification must be given as far as is reasonably practicable in advance of the date on which the product is withdrawn from the market: reg 73(5). It is a defence for a person charged with an offence consisting of a breach of reg 73(3) to prove that he took all reasonable precautions and exercised all due diligence to avoid commission of that offence: reg 101(3). Where evidence is adduced that is sufficient to raise an issue with respect to this defence, the court or jury must presume that the defence is satisfied unless the prosecution proves beyond reasonable doubt that it is not: reg 101(4).
5   Human Medicines Regulations 2012, SI 2012/1916, reg 73(6).
6   Human Medicines Regulations 2012, SI 2012/1916, reg 73(7).

172.   To take account of scientific and technical progress. The holder of a UK marketing authorisation[1] must keep under review the methods of manufacture and control of the product to which the authorisation relates, taking account of scientific and technical progress[2]. As soon as is reasonably practicable after becoming aware of the need to do so, the holder must apply to vary the marketing authorisation to make any changes to those methods that are required to ensure they are generally accepted scientific methods[3].

1   As to the meaning of 'UK marketing authorisation' see PARA 141 note 3.
2   Human Medicines Regulations 2012, SI 2012/1916, reg 74(1).
3   Human Medicines Regulations 2012, SI 2012/1916, reg 74(2).

173.   Obligation to provide information relating to safety, etc. The holder of a UK marketing authorisation[1] must provide the licensing authority[2] with any new information that might entail the variation of the authorisation[3] and, in particular, the following information:

(1)   information about any prohibition or restriction imposed in relation to the product to which the authorisation relates by the competent authority of any country in which the product is on the market[4];

(2)   positive and negative results of clinical trials or other studies in all indications and populations, whether or not included in the marketing authorisation[5];

(3)   data on the use of the medicinal product[6] where such use is outside the terms of the marketing authorisation[7]; and

(4)   any other information that the holder considers might influence the evaluation of the benefits and risks of the product[8].

Such information must be provided as soon as is reasonably practicable after the holder becomes aware of it[9].

The licensing authority may require the holder of a UK marketing authorisation to provide the authority with information that is specified by the licensing authority and that demonstrates that the positive therapeutic effects of the product to which the authorisation relates continue to outweigh the risks of the product to the health of patients or of the public[10]. Such information includes information arising from use of the product in a country which is not an EEA state or outside the terms of the marketing authorisation, including use in clinical trials[11].

If the information supplied under the above provisions[12] entails the variation of the UK marketing authorisation, the holder must make an application to the licensing authority to that effect as soon as is reasonably practicable after becoming aware of the information[13].

The licensing authority may require the holder of a UK marketing authorisation to provide the authority with proof of the control methods employed by the manufacturer of the product to which the authorisation relates[14].

1   As to the meaning of 'UK marketing authorisation' see PARA 141 note 3.
2   As to the meaning of 'the licensing authority' see PARA 35 note 1.
3   Human Medicines Regulations 2012, SI 2012/1916, reg 75(1).
4   Human Medicines Regulations 2012, SI 2012/1916, reg 75(2)(a).
5   Human Medicines Regulations 2012, SI 2012/1916, reg 75(2)(b).
6   As to the meaning of 'medicinal products' see PARA 25.
7   Human Medicines Regulations 2012, SI 2012/1916, reg 75(2)(c).
8   Human Medicines Regulations 2012, SI 2012/1916, reg 75(2)(d).
9   Human Medicines Regulations 2012, SI 2012/1916, reg 75(3).
10 Human Medicines Regulations 2012, SI 2012/1916, reg 75(4). The holder of a UK marketing authorisation must provide the licensing authority with information it requests under reg 75(4) or (7), where the period within which the information must be provided is specified in a written notice given to the holder by the licensing authority, before the end of that period or, otherwise, as soon as is reasonably practicable after receipt of the request: reg 75(8).
11 Human Medicines Regulations 2012, SI 2012/1916, reg 75(5).
12 Ie under the Human Medicines Regulations 2012, SI 2012/1916, reg 75(1), (2) or (4).
13 Human Medicines Regulations 2012, SI 2012/1916, reg 75(6).
14 Human Medicines Regulations 2012, SI 2012/1916, reg 75(7). See note 10.

174.   In relation to product information.   The holder of a UK marketing authorisation[1] for a medicinal product[2] must ensure that the product information[3] relating to the product is kept up to date with current scientific knowledge[4].

1   As to the meaning of 'UK marketing authorisation' see PARA 141 note 3.
2   As to the meaning of 'medicinal products' see PARA 25.
3   'Product information', in relation to a medicinal product, means the summary of the product characteristics, the immediate and outer packaging and the package leaflet: Human Medicines Regulations 2012, SI 2012/1916, reg 8(1). As to the meaning of 'summary of the product characteristics' see PARA 55 note 11. As to the meanings of 'immediate packaging' and 'outer packaging' see PARA 278 note 5. As to the meaning of 'package leaflet' see PARA 68 note 5.
4   Human Medicines Regulations 2012, SI 2012/1916, reg 76(1). For this purpose 'current scientific knowledge' includes the conclusions of the assessment and recommendations made public by means of the European medicines web-portal established in accordance with Council Regulation (EC) 726/2004 (OJ L136, 30.4.2004, p 1) laying down Community procedures for the authorisation and supervision of medicinal products for human and veterinary use and establishing a European Medicines Agency, art 26: Human Medicines Regulations 2012, SI 2012/1916, reg 76(2).

175.   Record-keeping.   The holder of a marketing authorisation[1] must keep any documents or information that will facilitate the withdrawal or recall from sale or supply of any product to which the authorisation relates[2].

1   As to the meaning of 'UK marketing authorisation' see PARA 141 note 3.
2   Human Medicines Regulations 2012, SI 2012/1916, reg 77.

176. Ensuring appropriate and continued supplies. The holder of a marketing authorisation[1] must take all reasonable steps to ensure appropriate and continued supplies of the product to which the authorisation relates to pharmacies and persons authorised to supply the product so that the needs of patients in the United Kingdom are met[2].

1   As to the meaning of 'UK marketing authorisation' see PARA 141 note 3.
2   Human Medicines Regulations 2012, SI 2012/1916, reg 78. It is a defence for a person charged with an offence consisting of a breach of reg 78 to prove that he took all reasonable precautions and exercised all due diligence to avoid commission of that offence: reg 101(3). Where evidence is adduced that is sufficient to raise an issue with respect to this defence, the court or jury must presume that the defence is satisfied unless the prosecution proves beyond reasonable doubt that it is not: reg 101(4).

G.   OFFENCES

177. Failure to provide information on marketing authorisations to European Medicines Authority. The holder of a marketing authorisation[1] is guilty of an offence if the holder has not submitted information to the European Medicines Authority[2] as required by EU provisions[3] in relation to any medicinal product that is the subject of a marketing authorisation granted before 2 July 2012 and fails to do so as soon as is reasonably practicable after the coming into force of the Human Medicines Regulations 2012[4].

The holder of a marketing authorisation is guilty of an offence if the holder fails to submit information to the European Medicines Authority as required by EU provisons[5] in relation to any medicinal product that is the subject of a marketing authorisation granted on or after 2 July 2012 as soon as is reasonably practicable after the grant of the authorisation[6].

1   As to the meaning of 'marketing authorisation' see PARA 141 note 3.
2   As to the European Medicines Authority see PARA 14.
3   Ie as required by Council Regulation (EC) 726/2004 (OJ L136, 30.4.2004, p 1) laying down Community procedures for the authorisation and supervision of medicinal products for human and veterinary use and establishing a European Medicines Agency, art 57(2)(b).
4   Human Medicines Regulations 2012, SI 2012/1916, reg 79(1). These regulations came into force on 14 August 2012: reg 1(2). A person guilty of an offence under this provision is liable, on summary conviction, to a fine not exceeding the statutory maximum or, on conviction on indictment, to a fine: reg 99(2). As to the statutory maximum see SENTENCING AND DISPOSITION OF OFFENDERS vol 92 (2010) PARA 140.
5   Ie as required by Council Regulation (EC) 726/2004 (OJ L136, 30.4.2004, p 1) art 57(2)(c).
6   Human Medicines Regulations 2012, SI 2012/1916, reg 79(2).

178. Urgent safety restrictions. The holder of a marketing authorisation is guilty of an offence[1] if the holder:

(1)   fails to inform the licensing authority[2] or the European Commission[3] that the holder has taken urgent safety restrictions on the holder's own initiative[4];

(2)   fails to implement an urgent safety restriction imposed[5] on the holder by the licensing authority or the European Commission[6]; or

(3)   fails to submit an application for variation of the marketing authorisation to the licensing authority or the European Commission before the end of a period of fifteen days beginning on the day after the taking, as the case may be, the imposition, of such an urgent safety restriction[7].

1   As to the meaning of 'marketing authorisation' see PARA 141 note 3. A person guilty of such an offence is liable, on summary conviction, to a fine not exceeding the statutory maximum or, on

conviction on indictment, to a fine, to imprisonment for a term not exceeding two years or to both: Human Medicines Regulations 2012, SI 2012/1916, reg 99(1). As to the statutory maximum see SENTENCING AND DISPOSITION OF OFFENDERS vol 92 (2010) PARA 140.

2   As to the meaning of 'the licensing authority' see PARA 35 note 1.

3   Ie in accordance with Commission Regulation (EC) 1234/2008 (OJ L334, 12.12.2008, p 7–24) concerning the examination of variations to the terms of marketing authorisations for medicinal products for human use and veterinary medicinal products, art 22(1) (see PARA 11).

4   Human Medicines Regulations 2012, SI 2012/1916, reg 80(a).

5   Ie imposed under Commission Regulation (EC) 1234/2008 (OJ L334, 12.12.2008, p 7–24) art 22(2) (see PARA 11).

6   Human Medicines Regulations 2012, SI 2012/1916, reg 80(b).

7   See the Human Medicines Regulations 2012, SI 2012/1916, reg 80(c).

179.   Offences relating to EU marketing authorisations.   An applicant for an EU marketing authorisation is guilty of an offence[1] if he fails to supply specified updated information[2] to the European Medicines Agency ('the Agency')[3].

If the holder of an EU marketing authorisation fails to inform the Agency of the dates of actual marketing the medicinal product for human use in the member states or that a product has ceased to be placed on the market, either temporarily or permanently[4], he is guilty of an offence[5]. He is also guilty of an offence of he fails to provide the Agency with information it has requested relating to the volume of sales of the medicinal product at Community level, broken down by member state, and any data in the holder's possession relating to the volume of prescriptions[6]:

(1)   where the period within which the information must be provided is specified in a written notice given to the holder by the Agency, before the end of that period[7]; or

(2)   otherwise, as soon as is reasonably practicable after receipt of the request[8].

The holder of an EU marketing authorisation is guilty of an offence if he fails to provide new information which might entail amendment of particulars or documents[9] to the Agency, the Commission or the licensing authority as soon as is reasonably practicable after becoming aware of the information[10]. The holder of an EU marketing authorisation is also guilty of an offence if he fails to provide the Agency with information that it requests[11] relating to data on risk-benefit balance[12].

The holder of an EU marketing authorisation has an obligation to take into account scientific and technical progress and introduce any changes that may be required[13]. Failure to vary the marketing authorisation accordingly is an offence[14].

The holder of an EU marketing authorisation for a medicinal product is guilty of an offence if he fails to ensure[15] that the product information[16] relating to the product is kept up to date with current scientific knowledge[17].

If the holder of an EU marketing authorisation fails to comply with any obligation to which the marketing authorisation is subject[18], or any condition to which the authorisation is subject[19], he is guilty of an offence[20].

The holder of an EU marketing authorisation is guilty of an offence he fails to incorporate into the risk management system[21] for the product a recommendation[22], obligation[23] or condition[24] as required[25].

1   As to the meaning of 'EU marketing authorisation' see PARA 141 note 3. A person guilty of an offence under these provisions is liable, on summary conviction, to a fine not exceeding the statutory maximum or, on conviction on indictment, to a fine, to imprisonment for a term not

exceeding two years or to both: Human Medicines Regulations 2012, SI 2012/1916, reg 99(1). As to the statutory maximum see SENTENCING AND DISPOSITION OF OFFENDERS vol 92 (2010) PARA 140.

2   Ie in accordance with Council Directive (EC) 2001/83 (OJ L311, 28.11.2001, p 67) on the Community code relating to medicinal products for human use, art 8(3) as applied by Council Regulation (EC) 726/2004 (OJ L136, 30.4.2004, p 1) laying down Community procedures for the authorisation and supervision of medicinal products for human and veterinary use and establishing a European Medicines Agency, art 6(1).

3   Human Medicines Regulations 2012, SI 2012/1916, reg 81. As to the European Medicines Agency see PARA 14.

4   Ie he fails to notify the Agency in accordance with Council Regulation (EC) 726/2004 (OJ L136, 30.4.2004, p 1), art 13(4).

5   See the Human Medicines Regulations 2012, SI 2012/1916, reg 82(1).

6   Ie information that the Agency requires under Council Regulation (EC) 726/2004 (OJ L136, 30.4.2004, p 1), art 13(4).

7   See the Human Medicines Regulations 2012, SI 2012/1916, reg 82(2)(a).

8   See the Human Medicines Regulations 2012, SI 2012/1916, reg 82(2)(b).

9   Ie information required to be provided under Council Regulation (EC) 726/2004 (OJ L136, 30.4.2004, p 1), art 16(2).

10   See the Human Medicines Regulations 2012, SI 2012/1916, reg 84(1).

11   Ie that it requests under the Council Regulation (EC) 726/2004 (OJ L136, 30.4.2004, p 1), art 16(4).

12   See the Human Medicines Regulations 2012, SI 2012/1916, reg 84(2).

13   See the Council Regulation (EC) 726/2004 (OJ L136, 30.4.2004, p 1), art 16(1).

14   See the Human Medicines Regulations 2012, SI 2012/1916, reg 83.

15   Ie as required by Council Regulation (EC) 726/2004 (OJ L136, 30.4.2004, p 1), art 16(3).

16   As to the meaning of 'product information' see PARA 174 note 3.

17   Human Medicines Regulations 2012, SI 2012/1916, reg 85(1). For this purpose 'current scientific knowledge' includes the conclusions of the assessment and recommendations made public by means of the European medicines web-portal established in accordance with Council Regulation (EC) 726/2004 (OJ L136, 30.4.2004, p 1), art 26: Human Medicines Regulations 2012, SI 2012/1916, reg 85(2).

18   Ie by virtue of the Council Regulation (EC) 726/2004 (OJ L136, 30.4.2004, p 1), art 10a(1) or 14(7).

19   Ie by virtue of the Council Regulation (EC) 726/2004 (OJ L136, 30.4.2004, p 1), art 14(8).

20   See the Human Medicines Regulations 2012, SI 2012/1916, reg 86(1).

21   As to the meaning of 'risk management system' see PARA 74 note 6.

22   Ie any recommendation referred to in Council Regulation (EC) 726/2004 (OJ L136, 30.4.2004, p 1), art 9(4)(c), (ca), (cb) or (cc).

23   Ie any obligation to which the authorisation is subject by virtue of Council Regulation (EC) 726/2004 (OJ L136, 30.4.2004, p 1), art 10a(1) or 14(7).

24   Ie any condition to which the marketing authorisation is subject by virtue of Council Regulation (EC) 726/2004 (OJ L136, 30.4.2004, p 1), art 14(8).

25   Human Medicines Regulations 2012, SI 2012/1916, reg 86(2).

180.   Offences relating to advanced therapy medicinal products.   The holder of an EU marketing authorisation[1] for an advanced therapy medicinal product[2] who fails to:

(1)   submit an additional report evaluating the effectiveness of a risk management system[3] and the results of studies within the period of 21 days beginning on the day following receipt of a request made[4] or such longer period as the European Medicines Agency[5] may specify; or

(2)   include in any periodic safety update report[6] an evaluation of the effectiveness of a risk management system or of the results of any study[7],

is guilty of an offence[8].

A person who is, or who immediately before its revocation or withdrawal was, the holder of an EU marketing authorisation for an advanced therapy medicinal product is guilty of an offence if he fails to: (a) establish and maintain a traceability system[9]; (b) where the product contains human cells or tissues, to ensure that the traceability system is complementary to and compatible with the EU requirements[10]; or (c) to keep the data to which the traceability system relates in accordance with the EU requirements[11].

A person who is, or immediately before its revocation or suspension was, the holder of an EU marketing authorisation relating to an advanced therapy medicinal product is guilty of an offence if he fails to the keep specified data[12] as required[13] or fails to transfer that data to the European Medicines Agency[14] in the event of that person's bankruptcy or liquidation[15].

1   As to the meaning of 'EU marketing authorisation' see PARA 141 note 3.
2   'Advanced therapy medicinal product' means a medicinal product described in European Parliament and Council Regulation (EC) 1394/2007 (OJ L324, 10.12.2007, p 121) on advanced therapy medicinal products, art 2(1)(a) (see PARA 23): Human Medicines Regulations 2012, SI 2012/1916, reg 8(1).
3   As to the meaning of 'risk management system' see PARA 74 note 6.
4   Ie made under European Parliament and Council Regulation (EC) 1394/2007 (OJ L324, 10.12.2007, p 121) on advanced therapy medicinal products, art 14(2).
5   As to the European Medicines Agency see PARA 14.
6   Ie as referred to in Council Regulation (EC) 726/2004 (OJ L136, 30.4.2004, p 1) laying down Community procedures for the authorisation and supervision of medicinal products for human and veterinary use and establishing a European Medicines Agency, art 28(2).
7   Ie any study performed pursuant to European Parliament and Council Regulation (EC) 1394/2007 (OJ L324, 10.12.2007, p 121) the first sub-paragraph of art 14(2) as required by the third sub-paragraph of art 14(2) (see PARA 22).
8   See the Human Medicines Regulations 2012, SI 2012/1916, reg 87(1). A person guilty of an offence under these provisions is liable, on summary conviction, to a fine not exceeding the statutory maximum or, on conviction on indictment, to a fine, to imprisonment for a term not exceeding two years or to both: reg 99(1). As to the statutory maximum see SENTENCING AND DISPOSITION OF OFFENDERS vol 92 (2010) PARA 140.
9   Ie in accordance with the requirements set out in European Parliament and Council Regulation (EC) 1394/2007 (OJ L324, 10.12.2007, p 121) on advanced therapy medicinal products, art 15 (see PARA 13).
10 Ie the requirements laid down in Council Directive (EC) 2004/23 (OJ L102, 7.4.2004, p 48) on setting standards of quality and safety for the donation, procurement, testing, processing, preservation, storage and distribution of human tissues and cells, arts 8, 14, as regards human cells and tissues other than blood cells and Council Directive (EC) 2002/98 (OJ L33, 8.2.2003, p 30) setting standards of quality and safety for the collection, testing, processing, storage and distribution of human blood and blood components, arts 14, 24 (see PARA 13).
11 Human Medicine Regulations 2012, SI 2012/1916, reg 87(2). The EU requirements mentioned in head (c) in the text is European Parliament and Council Regulation (EC) 1394/2007 (OJ L324, 10.12.2007, p 121) on advanced therapy medicinal products, art 15(4) (see PARA 13).
12 Ie he fails to keep the data referred to in European Parliament and Council Regulation (EC) 1394/2007 (OJ L324, 10.12.2007, p 121) on advanced therapy medicinal products art 15(1) in accordance with the requirements of art 15(4).
13 Human Medicines Regulations 2012, SI 2012/1916, reg 88(1)(a). It is a defence for a person charged with an offence under reg 88 to prove that he took all reasonable precautions and exercised all due diligence to avoid commission of that offence: reg 101(3). Where evidence is adduced that is sufficient to raise an issue with respect to this defence, the court or jury must presume that the defence is satisfied unless the prosecution proves beyond reasonable doubt that it is not: reg 101(4).
14 Ie in accordance with European Parliament and Council Regulation (EC) 1394/2007 (OJ L324, 10.12.2007, p 121), art 15(5). As to the European Medicines Agency see PARA 14.
15 Human Medicines Regulations 2012, SI 2012/1916, reg 88(1)(b). This does not apply if the person is bankrupt or in liquidation and has transferred the data to another person or the period for which the person was required to keep the data in accordance with the requirements of European Parliament and Council Regulation (EC) 1394/2007 (OJ L324, 10.12.2007, p 121), art 15(4) mentioned in the Human Medicines Regulations 2012, SI 2012/1916, reg 88(1)(a) has expired: reg 88(2).

181. Offences by the holder of a UK marketing authorisation relating to the Paediatric Regulation. If a person is the holder of a UK marketing authorisation[1] who has benefited from one or more rewards or incentives under the Paediatric Regulation[2] in relation to the product to which the authorisation relates, and all of the periods of protection provided[3] have expired in relation to him[4], he is guilty of an offence if he ceases to supply the product:

(1) without previously[5] transferring the UK marketing authorisation to another person who has declared an intention to continue to supply the product or allowing such a person to use the pharmaceutical, pre-clinical and clinical documentation contained in the file[6] on that product[7];

(2) if he ceases to supply the product and does not[8] inform the European Medicines Agency ('the Agency')[9] of his intention to do so before the beginning of the period of six months ending immediately before the day on which he does so[10].

A person is guilty of an offence if he is the holder of a UK marketing authorisation who obtained a paediatric indication[11] in respect of the product to which the authorisation relates following completion of an agreed paediatric investigation plan, the product was placed on the market for other indications before that person obtained that paediatric indication and the person failed to place the product on the market taking account of the paediatric indication[12] before the end of the period of two years beginning immediately after the day on which the paediatric indication is authorised[13].

If a decision by the Agency in respect of a paediatric investigation plan is addressed to a person who is established in the United Kingdom and the plan refers to clinical trials carried out in third countries ('third country clinical trials'), that person is guilty of an offence if he does not enter the relevant details into the specified database[14] within the specified period[15]. That person is also guilty of an offence if he does not submit the results of those clinical trials to the Agency[16] within the specified period[17].

The holder of a marketing authorisation is guilty of an offence if the holder fails to submit the required[18] annual report to the Agency[19].

1 As to the meaning of 'UK marketing authorisation' see PARA 141 note 3.
2 Ie under the Paediatric Regulation arts 36, 37 or 38. 'The Paediatric Regulation' means European Parliament and Council Regulation (EC) 1901/2006 (OJ L378, 27.12.2006, p 1) on medicinal products for paediatric use.
3 Ie provided pursuant to European Parliament and of the Council Regulation (EC) 1901/2006 (OJ L378, 27.12.2006, p 1), arts 36, 37, 38.
4 Human Medicines Regulations 2012, SI 2012/1916, reg 89(1).
5 Ie in accordance with European Parliament and of the Council Regulation (EC) 1901/2006 (OJ L378, 27.12.2006, p 1), art 35.
6 Ie as provided for in the Human Medicines Regulations 2012, SI 2012/1916, reg 56 (see PARA 157).
7 Human Medicines Regulations 2012, SI 2012/1916, reg 89(2).
8 Ie in accordance with European Parliament and of the Council Regulation (EC) 1901/2006 (OJ L378, 27.12.2006, p 1), art 35.
9 As to the European Medicines Agency see PARA 14.
10 Human Medicines Regulations 2012, SI 2012/1916, reg 89(3). A person guilty of an offence under these provisions is liable, on summary conviction, to a fine not exceeding the statutory maximum or, on conviction on indictment, to a fine, to imprisonment for a term not exceeding two years or to both: reg 99(1). As to the statutory maximum see SENTENCING AND DISPOSITION OF OFFENDERS vol 92 (2010) PARA 140. It is a defence for a person charged with an offence under regs 89, 90 to prove that he took all reasonable precautions and exercised all due diligence to avoid commission of that offence: reg 101(3). Where evidence is adduced that is sufficient to raise an issue with respect to this defence, the court or jury must presume that the

defence is satisfied unless the prosecution proves beyond reasonable doubt that it is not: reg 101(4). As to the meaning of 'month' see PARA 43 note 3.

11 For these purposes 'paediatric indication' means a term of the marketing authorisation enabling the product to which it relates to be used by or administered to persons under the age of 18 years: Human Medicines Regulations 2012, SI 2012/1916, reg 90(2).

12 Ie in accordance with European Parliament and of the Council Regulation (EC) 1901/2006 (OJ L378, 27.12.2006, p 1), art 33.

13 Human Medicines Regulations 2012, SI 2012/1916, reg 90(1).

14 Ie the database referred to in European Parliament and Council Directive (EC) 2001/20 (OJ L121, 1.5.2001, p 34) on the approximation of the laws, regulations and administrative provisions of the Member States relating to the implementation of good clinical practice in the conduct of clinical trials on medicinal products for human use, art 11 the details set out in art 11 in relation to the third country clinical trials in accordance with European Parliament and of the Council Regulation (EC) 1901/2006 (OJ L378, 27.12.2006, p 1), art 41(1).

15 See the Human Medicines Regulations 2012, SI 2012/1916, reg 91(1), (2). The specified period mentioned in the text is whichever is the later of the period of one month beginning after the day on which the decision was received; or the period of one month beginning after the day on which the necessary permission to conduct the clinical trial was received from the competent authorities in the country where the clinical trial is to take place: reg 91(2)(a), (b).

16 Ie in accordance with European Parliament and of the Council Regulation (EC) 1901/2006 (OJ L378, 27.12.2006, p 1), art 41(2).

17 See the Human Medicines Regulations 2012, SI 2012/1916, reg 91(3). The specified period mentioned in the text is 6 months, if the person mentioned in the text is the holder of a marketing authorisation for the medicinal product concerned; or otherwise 12 months beginning with the day on which the last of those trials ended: see reg 91(3). Regulations 91(3) does not apply, and reg 93(3) applies, in the case of a clinical trial that forms part of a paediatric study to which reg 93 applies: reg 91(4).

18 Ie as required by European Parliament and of the Council Regulation (EC) 1901/2006 (OJ L378, 27.12.2006, p 1), art 34(4).

19 Human Medicines Regulations 2012, SI 2012/1916, reg 94.

182.   Offences by the sponsor of a UK paediatric trial or study.   The following applies to the sponsor of a paediatric clinical trial in the United Kingdom in respect of a medicinal product[1] if the product has a UK marketing authorisation[2] but that person is not the holder of the authorisation or the product does not have a marketing authorisation[3]. That person is guilty of an offence if he does not submit the results of the clinical trial to the European Medicines Agency ('the Agency')[4] within the period of twelve months beginning with the day on which the trial ended[5].

The following applies to a person who is the holder of a UK marketing authorisation and sponsors a paediatric study in respect of the product to which the authorisation relates[6].

Such a person is guilty of an offence if he does not submit the results of the study to the licensing authority[7] within the period of six months beginning with the day on which the study ended[8]. He is also guilty of an offence if he does not submit the results of any clinical trial that forms part of that study to the Agency[9] within the period of six months beginning with the day on which the trial ended[10].

1   As to the meaning of 'medicinal product' see PARA 25. 'Paediatric clinical trial' means a clinical trial conducted in whole or in part on persons under the age of 18 years: Human Medicines Regulations 2012, SI 2012/1916, reg 8(1).

2   As to the meaning of 'UK marketing authorisation' see PARA 141 note 3.

3   Human Medicines Regulations 2012, SI 2012/1916, reg 92(1).

4   Ie in accordance with European Parliament and of the Council Regulation (EC) 1901/2006 (OJ L378, 27.12.2006, p 1) on medicinal products for paediatric use. As to the European Medicines Agency see PARA 14.

5   Human Medicines Regulations 2012, SI 2012/1916, reg 92(2). A person guilty of an offence under these provisions is liable, on summary conviction, to a fine not exceeding the statutory

maximum or, on conviction on indictment, to a fine, to imprisonment for a term not exceeding two years or to both: reg 99(1). As to the statutory maximum see SENTENCING AND DISPOSITION OF OFFENDERS vol 92 (2010) PARA 140. It is a defence for a person charged with an offence under regs 92, 93 to prove that he took all reasonable precautions and exercised all due diligence to avoid commission of that offence: reg 101(3). Where evidence is adduced that is sufficient to raise an issue with respect to this defence, the court or jury must presume that the defence is satisfied unless the prosecution proves beyond reasonable doubt that it is not: reg 101(4). As to the meaning of 'month' see PARA 43 note 3.

6 Human Medicines Regulations 2012, SI 2012/1916, reg 93(1).
7 Ie accordance with European Parliament and of the Council Regulation (EC) 1901/2006 (OJ L378, 27.12.2006, p 1), art 46(1).
8 Human Medicines Regulations 2012, SI 2012/1916, reg 93(2).
9 Ie in accordance with European Parliament and of the Council Regulation (EC) 1901/2006 (OJ L378, 27.12.2006, p 1), art 41(2).
10 Human Medicines Regulations 2012, SI 2012/1916, reg 93(3).

183.   Offences in connection with application. A person is guilty of an offence[1] if, in the course of an application for the grant, renewal or variation of a marketing authorisation[2] for a relevant medicinal product[3], the person:

(1) fails to provide the licensing authority[4] with any information that is relevant to the evaluation of the safety, quality or efficacy of the product[5];

(2) provides to the licensing authority any information that is relevant to the evaluation of the safety, quality or efficacy of the product but that is false or misleading in a material particular[6];

(3) fails to provide the European Medicines Agency ('the Agency')[7] with any information[8] that is relevant to the evaluation of the safety, quality or efficacy of the product[9]; or

(4) provides to the Agency any information of the kind described in head (3) that is false or misleading in a material particular[10].

1 If a breach of this provision is committed by a person acting as employee or agent, the employer or principal of that person is guilty of the same offence and is liable to be proceeded against and punished accordingly: Human Medicines Regulations 2012, SI 2012/1916, reg 100. It is a defence for a person charged with an offence under reg 95 to prove that he took all reasonable precautions and exercised all due diligence to avoid commission of that offence: reg 101(3). Where evidence is adduced that is sufficient to raise an issue with respect to this defence, the court or jury must presume that the defence is satisfied unless the prosecution proves beyond reasonable doubt that it is not: reg 101(4).
2 As to the meaning of 'marketing authorisation' see PARA 141 note 3.
3 As to the meaning of 'relevant medicinal product' see PARA 155.
4 As to the meaning of 'licensing authority' see PARA 35 note 1.
5 Human Medicines Regulations 2012, SI 2012/1916, reg 95(a).
6 Human Medicines Regulations 2012, SI 2012/1916, reg 95(b). A person guilty of an offence under these provisions is liable, on summary conviction, to a fine not exceeding the statutory maximum or, on conviction on indictment, to a fine, to imprisonment for a term not exceeding two years or to both: reg 99(1). As to the statutory maximum see SENTENCING AND DISPOSITION OF OFFENDERS vol 92 (2010) PARA 140.
7 As to the European Medicines Agency see PARA 14.
8 Ie as required by European Parliament and Council Directive (EC) 2001/83 (OJ L311, 28.11.2001, p 67) on the Community code relating to medicinal products for human use, Annex 1 as applied by Council Regulation (EC) 726/2004 (OJ L136, 30.4.2004, p 1) laying down Community procedures for the authorisation and supervision of medicinal products for human and veterinary use and establishing a European Medicines Agency, art 6(1).
9 Human Medicines Regulations 2012, SI 2012/1916, reg 95(c).
10 Human Medicines Regulations 2012, SI 2012/1916, reg 95(d).

184.   Provision of false or misleading information. The holder of a marketing authorisation[1] is guilty of an offence if the holder provides certain information[2] that is relevant to the evaluation of the safety, quality or efficacy of a medicinal product but that is false or misleading in a material particular to the licensing authority³, the European Medicines Agency⁴ or the competent authorities of other EEA states⁵.

1 As to the meaning of 'marketing authorisation' see PARA 141 note 3.
2 Ie information about the product that is supplied pursuant to the obligations in the Human Medicines Regulations 2012, SI 2012/1916, or Council Regulation (EC) 726/2004 (OJ L136, 30.4.2004, p 1) laying down Community procedures for the authorisation and supervision of medicinal products for human and veterinary use and establishing a European Medicines Agency.
3 As to the meaning of 'licensing authority' see PARA 35 note 1.
4 As to the European Medicines Agency see PARA 14.
5 Human Medicines Regulations 2012, SI 2012/1916, reg 96(1). This is without prejudice to the operation of reg 95 (see PARA 183): reg 96(3). A person guilty of an offence under this provision is liable, on summary conviction, to a fine not exceeding the statutory maximum or, on conviction on indictment, to a fine, to imprisonment for a term not exceeding two years or to both: reg 99(1). As to the statutory maximum see SENTENCING AND DISPOSITION OF OFFENDERS vol 92 (2010) PARA 140. It is a defence for a person charged with an offence under reg 96 to prove that he took all reasonable precautions and exercised all due diligence to avoid commission of that offence: reg 101(3). Where evidence is adduced that is sufficient to raise an issue with respect to this defence, the court or jury must presume that the defence is satisfied unless the prosecution proves beyond reasonable doubt that it is not: reg 101(4).

185.   Breach of pharmacovigilance condition.   The holder of a marketing authorisation¹ is guilty of an offence if the holder fails to comply with a condition² to which the marketing authorisation is subject³.

1 As to the meaning of 'marketing authorisation' see PARA 141 note 3.
2 Ie by virtue of the Human Medicines Regulations 2012, SI 2012/1916, reg 59 (conditions of UK marketing authorisation: general: see PARA 160), 60 (conditions of UK marketing authorisation: exceptional circumstances: see PARA 161) or 61 (conditions of UK marketing authorisation: new obligations post-authorisation: see PARA 162).
3 Human Medicines Regulations 2012, SI 2012/1916, reg 97. A person guilty of an offence under this provision is liable, on summary conviction, to a fine not exceeding the statutory maximum or, on conviction on indictment, to a fine, to imprisonment for a term not exceeding two years or to both: reg 99(1). As to the statutory maximum see SENTENCING AND DISPOSITION OF OFFENDERS vol 92 (2010) PARA 140.

186.   General offence and general defence.   A person is guilty of an offence if that person commits a breach¹ of a provision in Part 5² of the Human Medicines Regulations 2012³.

If the holder of a marketing authorisation is charged with an offence under Part 5 in respect of anything that has been manufactured or assembled to the holder's order by another person and has been so manufactured or assembled as not to comply with the terms of the authorisation, it is a defence for him to prove that:

(1)   he communicated the terms of the authorisation to the other person⁴; and

(2)   he did not know and could not by the exercise of reasonable care have known that those terms had not been complied with⁵.

1 A breach of a provision in the Human Medicines Regulations 2012, SI 2012/1916, Pt 5 includes any failure by the holder of a marketing authorisation to comply with any requirement or obligation in Pt 5, contravention by any person of any prohibition in Pt 5 or failure to comply with any requirement imposed on a person by the licensing authority pursuant to Pt 5: reg 98(2). As to the meaning of 'contravene' see PARA 41 note 8.
2 Ie the Human Medicines Regulations 2012, SI 2012/1916, regs 48–101.
3 Human Medicines Regulations 2012, SI 2012/1916, reg 98(1). This provision is without prejudice to any offence established by any other provision in Pt 5: reg 98(3). A person guilty of

such an offence is liable, on summary conviction, to a fine not exceeding the statutory maximum or, on conviction on indictment, to a fine, to imprisonment for a term not exceeding two years or to both: reg 99(1). As to the statutory maximum see SENTENCING AND DISPOSITION OF OFFENDERS vol 92 (2010) PARA 140.

4　Human Medicines Regulations 2012, SI 2012/1916, reg 101(1), (2)(a).
5　Human Medicines Regulations 2012, SI 2012/1916, reg 101(1), (2)(b).

(iv)　Certification of Homoeopathic Medicinal Products

A.　APPLICATIONS

187.　Applicable products. The provisions relating to the certification of homoeopathic medicinal products[1] apply to a homoeopathic medicinal product (a 'registrable homoeopathic medicinal product') that meets the following conditions[2]:

(1)　that the product is administered orally or externally[3];
(2)　that no specific therapeutic indication appears on the labelling of the product or in any information supplied with the product[4];
(3)　that the product contains no more than one part per 10,000 of the mother tincture and, in a case where the product's active substance is a relevant allopathic substance[5], the product contains no more than 1/100th of the smallest concentration of that substance used in allopathy[6].

1　Ie the Human Medicines Regulations 2012, SI 2012/1916, Pt 6 (regs 102–124). 'Homoeopathic medicinal product' means a medicinal product prepared from homoeopathic stocks in accordance with a homoeopathic manufacturing procedure described by the European Pharmacopoeia or, in the absence of such a description in the European Pharmacopoeia, in any pharmacopoeia used officially in an EEA state: reg 8(1). As to the meaning of 'European Pharmacopoeia' see PARA 66 note 21. As to the meaning of 'medicinal product' see PARA 25.
2　Human Medicines Regulations 2012, SI 2012/1916, reg 102(1). For the purposes of the Human Medicines Regulations 2012, SI 2012/1916 a 'registrable homoeopathic medicinal product' means a homoeopathic medicinal product to which reg 102 applies: reg 8(1).
3　Human Medicines Regulations 2012, SI 2012/1916, reg 102(2).
4　Human Medicines Regulations 2012, SI 2012/1916, reg 102(3).
5　For these purposes 'relevant allopathic substance' means an active substance whose presence in an allopathic medicinal product means that the product is only available on prescription and 'allopathic medicinal product' means a medicinal product other than a homoeopathic medicinal product: Human Medicines Regulations 2012, SI 2012/1916, reg 102(5), (6)(a).
6　Human Medicines Regulations 2012, SI 2012/1916, reg 102(4). For these purposes 'allopathy' means treatment using an allopathic medicinal product: reg 102(6)(b).

188.　Application for certification of registration. The licensing authority[1] may[2] grant an application for a certificate of registration[3] for a registrable homoeopathic medicinal product[4] in response to an application made in accordance with Part 6[5] of the Human Medicines Regulations 2012[6].

A certificate so granted must contain terms approved by the licensing authority[7].

The application may relate to two or more homoeopathic medicinal products derived from the same homoeopathic stock or the same combination of homoeopathic stocks[8].

The applicant must be established in the European Union[9] and the application must be made in writing, signed by or on behalf of the applicant[10] and, unless the licensing authority directs otherwise, accompanied by any fee payable in connection with the application[11].

The applicant must provide each of the following for each product to which the application relates:

(1) a statement of the scientific name, or other name given in a pharmacopoeia, of the homoeopathic stock or stocks from which the product is derived[12];

(2) a statement of the routes of administration, pharmaceutical forms and degree of dilution of the product[13];

(3) a dossier describing how the homoeopathic stock or stocks are obtained and controlled and justifying their homoeopathic use on the basis of an adequate bibliography[14];

(4) a manufacturing and control file for each pharmaceutical form and a description of the method of dilution and potentisation of the product[15];

(5) evidence that each manufacturer of the medicinal product is authorised to manufacture it (which, in the case of a product manufactured in the United Kingdom or another EEA state, means the manufacturer's licence[16] or (as the case may be) its equivalent in that EEA State)[17];

(6) where an authorisation to place the product on the market has been granted by another member state, a copy of the authorisation[18];

(7) a mock-up of the outer and immediate packaging of the product[19]; and

(8) data concerning the stability of the product[20].

This material, taken as a whole, must be such as to demonstrate the pharmaceutical quality and batch to batch homogeneity of each product to which the application relates[21].

The applicant must also, if requested by the licensing authority to do so, provide the licensing authority with material or information that the licensing authority reasonably considers necessary for considering the application[22].

1 As to the meaning of 'licensing authority' see PARA 35 note 1.
2 This is subject to the Human Medicines Regulations 2012, SI 2012/1916, reg 104 (see PARA 189).
3 As to the meaning of 'certificate of registration' see PARA 141 note 4.
4 As to the meaning of 'registrable homoeopathic medicinal product' see PARA 187 note 2.
5 Ie the Human Medicines Regulations 2012, SI 2012/1916, regs 102–124.
6 Human Medicines Regulations 2012, SI 2012/1916, reg 103(1).
7 Human Medicines Regulations 2012, SI 2012/1916, reg 103(2). As to terms and conditions see PARAS 191, 192.
8 Human Medicines Regulations 2012, SI 2012/1916, reg 103(3).
9 Human Medicines Regulations 2012, SI 2012/1916, reg 103(4).
10 An application is treated as signed for this purpose if it is signed with an electronic signature: Human Medicines Regulations 2012, SI 2012/1916, reg 103(6).
11 Human Medicines Regulations 2012, SI 2012/1916, reg 103(4). The application and any accompanying material must be in English: reg 103(7). As to fees see PARA 30.
12 Human Medicines Regulations 2012, SI 2012/1916, reg 103(8)(a).
13 Human Medicines Regulations 2012, SI 2012/1916, reg 103(8)(b).
14 Human Medicines Regulations 2012, SI 2012/1916, reg 103(8)(c).
15 Human Medicines Regulations 2012, SI 2012/1916, reg 103(8)(d).
16 As to the meaning of 'manufacturer's licence' see PARA 45.
17 Human Medicines Regulations 2012, SI 2012/1916, reg 103(8)(e).
18 Human Medicines Regulations 2012, SI 2012/1916, reg 103(8)(f).
19 Human Medicines Regulations 2012, SI 2012/1916, reg 103(8)(g).
20 Human Medicines Regulations 2012, SI 2012/1916, reg 103(8)(h).
21 Human Medicines Regulations 2012, SI 2012/1916, reg 103(9).
22 Human Medicines Regulations 2012, SI 2012/1916, reg 103(10).

189. Consideration of application. The licensing authority[1] must take all reasonable steps to ensure that it makes a decision to grant or refuse a certificate of registration[2] before the end of the period of 210 days beginning immediately after the day on which an application for the certificate is submitted[3].

If the licensing authority requests the applicant to provide any further information or material, this period[4] is suspended for the period beginning with the date on which the request is made and ending with the date on which the information or material is provided[5].

The licensing authority may grant a certificate only if, having considered the application and the accompanying material, the authority thinks that:

(1)   the risks to the health of patients or of the public associated with the product do not outweigh any beneficial effects of the homoeopathic medicinal product[6] in question[7];

(2)   the application and the accompanying material complies with the relevant provisions[8]; and

(3)   the product's qualitative or quantitative composition is as described in the application and the accompanying material[9].

1   As to the meaning of 'licensing authority' see PARA 35 note 1.
2   As to the meaning of 'certificate of registration' see PARA 141 note 4.
3   Human Medicines Regulations 2012, SI 2012/1916, reg 104(1). As to the submission of the certificate see PARA 188. Schedule 11 makes provision about advice and representations in relation to an application for the grant of a certificate of registration: reg 104(4). Regulation 104 does not apply to an application that has been submitted to the licensing authority in accordance with Article 28 of the 2001 Directive; or has been referred to the Committee for Medicinal Products for Human Use for the application of the procedure laid down in Council Directive (EC) 2001/83 (OJ L311, 28.11.2001, p 67) on the Community code relating to medicinal products for human use, arts 32–34: Human Medicines Regulations 2012, SI 2012/1916, reg 104(5). An application to which reg 104(5) applies is to be determined by the licensing authority in accordance with Council Directive (EC) 2001/83 (OJ L311, 28.11.2001, p 67), Title III, Chapter 4: Human Medicines Regulations 2012, SI 2012/1916, reg 104(5).
4   Ie the period referred to in the Human Medicines Regulations 2012, SI 2012/1916, reg 104(1).
5   Human Medicines Regulations 2012, SI 2012/1916, reg 104(2).
6   As to the meaning of 'homoeopathic medicinal product' see PARA 187 note 1.
7   Human Medicines Regulations 2012, SI 2012/1916, reg 104(3)(a).
8   Human Medicines Regulations 2012, SI 2012/1916, reg 104(3)(b). The 'relevant provisions' mentioned in the text are reg 103.
9   Human Medicines Regulations 2012, SI 2012/1916, reg 104(3)(c).

190.   Renewal of applications.   An application for the renewal of a certificate of registration[1] must be made to the licensing authority[2]. The applicant must be established in the European Union[3] and the application must be made in writing, signed by or on behalf of the applicant[4] and, unless the licensing authority directs otherwise, accompanied by any fee payable in connection with the application[5].

The holder must provide a consolidated version of the file in respect of quality, safety and efficacy (including all amendments made since the authorisation was granted)[6].

The licensing authority may renew a certificate only if, having considered the application and the material accompanying it, the authority thinks that the risks to the health of patients or of the public associated with the homoeopathic medicinal product[7] to which the certificate relates do not outweigh any beneficial effects of the product[8].

1   As to the meaning of 'certificate of registration' see PARA 141 note 4.
2   Human Medicines Regulations 2012, SI 2012/1916, reg 108(1). As to the meaning of 'licensing authority' see PARA 35 note 1. Schedule 11 makes provision about advice and representations in relation to an application for the renewal of a certificate of registration: reg 108(8).
3   Human Medicines Regulations 2012, SI 2012/1916, reg 108(2).

4   An application is treated as signed for these purposes if it is signed with an electronic signature: Human Medicines Regulations 2012, SI 2012/1916, reg 108(4).

5   Human Medicines Regulations 2012, SI 2012/1916, reg 108(3). The application must be made so that it is received by the licensing authority before the beginning of the period of 9 months ending with the expiry of the period mentioned in reg 107(1)(a) or (as the case may be) reg 107(3)(a) (initial and further period of validity): reg 108(5). As to fees see PARA 30. As to the meaning of 'month' see PARA 43 note 3.

6   Human Medicines Regulations 2012, SI 2012/1916, reg 108(6).

7   As to the meaning of 'homoeopathic medicinal product' see PARA 187 note 1.

8   Human Medicines Regulations 2012, SI 2012/1916, reg 108(7).

B. CONDITIONS

191.   Conditions of certificate of registration.   The licensing authority[1] may grant a certificate of registration[2] subject to conditions or vary or remove a condition to which the certificate of registration is subject[3].

This powers may be exercised only after consultation with the applicant for the certificate or (as the case may be) its holder[4].

The power to grant an authorisation subject to conditions[5] may be exercised only in exceptional circumstances and when the applicant can show that the applicant is unable to provide comprehensive data on the safety of the medicinal product[6] under normal conditions of use[7].

The conditions may, in particular, relate to the safety of the product to which the certificate relates[8] and may require that, where there is an incident relating to the use of the product, the incident must be reported to the licensing authority and such other action as may be specified in the conditions must be taken[9].

The licensing authority must keep under review the conditions to which a certificate of registration is subject and the holder's compliance with those conditions[10]. The licensing authority must consider those matters no less frequently than at the end of the period of one year beginning with the date on which the certificate was granted and at the end of each subsequent period of one year[11].

1   As to the meaning of 'licensing authority' see PARA 35 note 1.

2   As to the meaning of 'certificate of registration' see PARA 141 note 4.

3   Human Medicines Regulations 2012, SI 2012/1916, reg 105(1). The conditions must relate to a matter addressed by Council Directive (EC) 2001/83 (OJ L311, 28.11.2001, p 67) on the Community code relating to medicinal products for human use, Annex I: Human Medicines Regulations 2012, SI 2012/1916, reg 105(4). Schedule 11 makes provision about advice and representations in relation to proposals to vary or remove a condition to which a certificate of registration is subject: reg 105(9).

4   Human Medicines Regulations 2012, SI 2012/1916, reg 105(2).

5   Ie the power in the Human Medicines Regulations 2012, SI 2012/1916, reg 105(1)(a).

6   As to the meaning of 'medical product' see PARA 25.

7   Human Medicines Regulations 2012, SI 2012/1916, reg 105(3).

8   Human Medicines Regulations 2012, SI 2012/1916, reg 105(5).

9   Human Medicines Regulations 2012, SI 2012/1916, reg 105(6).

10 Human Medicines Regulations 2012, SI 2012/1916, reg 105(7).

11 Human Medicines Regulations 2012, SI 2012/1916, reg 105(8).

192.   Classification of certificate of registration.   A certificate of registration[1] must include a term that the product to which the certificate relates is to be available only from a pharmacy or on general sale[2].

A certificate of registration may include a term that the product to which the certificate relates is to be available on general sale only if the licensing authority[3] considers that the product can with reasonable safety be sold or supplied otherwise than by, or under the supervision of, a pharmacist[4].

1 As to the meaning of 'certificate of registration' see PARA 141 note 4.
2 Human Medicines Regulations 2012, SI 2012/1916, reg 106(1).
3 As to the meaning of 'licensing authority' see PARA 35 note 1.
4 Human Medicines Regulations 2012, SI 2012/1916, reg 106(2). As to the meaning of 'pharmacist' see PARA 52 note 5.

C. VALIDITY OF CERTIFICATE OF REGISTRATION

193. Validity of certificate of registration. Subject to the following, a certificate of registration[1] remains in force for an initial period of five years beginning with the date on which it is granted and if the authorisation is renewed[2] for an unlimited period after its renewal[3].

The licensing authority[4] may, on the first application for renewal of a certificate, determine on grounds relating to pharmacovigilance, including exposure of an insufficient number of patients to the medicinal product concerned, that it should be necessary for the holder to make one further application for renewal[5]. In that event, the certificate remains in force for a further period of five years beginning with the date on which it is first renewed and if the authorisation is further renewed[6] for an unlimited period after its further renewal[7].

If an application for the renewal or further renewal of a certificate is made[8] the certificate remains in force until the licensing authority notifies the applicant of its decision on the application[9].

1 As to the meaning of 'certificate of registration' see PARA 141 note 4.
2 Ie renewed under the Human Medicines Regulations 2012, SI 2012/1916, reg 108 (see PARA 190).
3 Human Medicines Regulations 2012, SI 2012/1916, reg 107(1). Regulation 107 is subject to reg 109 (see PARA 194) and reg 110 (see PARA 195): reg 107(5).
4 As to the meaning of 'licensing authority' see PARA 35 note 1.
5 Human Medicines Regulations 2012, SI 2012/1916, reg 107(2).
6 Ie under the Human Medicines Regulations 2012, SI 2012/1916, reg 108 (see PARA 190).
7 Human Medicines Regulations 2012, SI 2012/1916, reg 107(3).
8 Ie in accordance with the Human Medicines Regulations 2012, SI 2012/1916, reg 108 (see PARA 190).
9 Human Medicines Regulations 2012, SI 2012/1916, reg 107(4).

D. REVOCATION, SUSPENSION OR VARIATION AND CEASING OF AUTHORISATION

194. Failure to place on market, etc. A certificate of registration[1] ceases to be in force if the product to which it relates is not placed on the market in the United Kingdom during the period of three years beginning immediately after the day on which it was granted[2].

A certificate of registration for a product which has been placed on the market ceases to be in force if the product to which it relates is not sold or supplied in the United Kingdom for a period of three years[3].

The above provisions do not apply if the licensing authority grants an exemption from their operation[4]. An exemption may be granted in response to an application in writing by the holder of the certificate of registration or by the licensing authority[5] of its own motion[6]. An exemption may be granted only in exceptional circumstances and on public health grounds[7].

An exemption has effect for the period determined by the licensing authority, which may not exceed three years beginning with the day on which it is granted and may be renewed or further renewed[8].

1 As to the meaning of 'certificate of registration' see PARA 141 note 4.
2 Human Medicines Regulations 2012, SI 2012/1916, reg 109(1).
3 Human Medicines Regulations 2012, SI 2012/1916, reg 109(2).
4 Human Medicines Regulations 2012, SI 2012/1916, reg 109(3).
5 As to the meaning of 'licensing authority' see PARA 35 note 1.
6 Human Medicines Regulations 2012, SI 2012/1916, reg 109(4).
7 Human Medicines Regulations 2012, SI 2012/1916, reg 109(5).
8 Human Medicines Regulations 2012, SI 2012/1916, reg 109(6).

195. Revocation, variation and suspension of certificate of registration. The licensing authority[1] may revoke, vary or suspend a certificate of registration[2] if any of the following conditions are met[3]:

Condition A is that the licensing authority thinks that the product to which the certificate relates is harmful, the risks of the product to the health of patients or of the public outweigh any beneficial effects of the product or the product's qualitative or quantitative composition is not as described in the application for the certificate or the material supplied with it[4].

Condition B is that the licensing authority thinks that the application or the material accompanying it is incorrect[5].

Condition C is that the licensing authority thinks that there has been a breach of a term of the certificate or a requirement imposed[6] in relation to packaging and leaflets[7].

Condition D is that the licensing authority thinks that a condition to which the certificate is subject[8] has not been fulfilled[9].

Condition E is that the licensing authority thinks that the holder of the certificate has not complied[10] with certain requirements to provide information[11].

Condition F is that the holder of the certificate has ceased to be established in the European Union[12].

Condition G is that the holder applies to vary the certificate and that the licensing authority thinks that the application should be granted[13].

1 As to the meaning of 'licensing authority' see PARA 35 note 1.
2 As to the meaning of 'certificate of registration' see PARA 141 note 4.
3 Human Medicines Regulations 2012, SI 2012/1916, reg 110(1). Regulation 110 does not apply in relation to a certificate of registration that was granted in accordance with the provisions of Council Directive (EC) 2001/83 (OJ L311, 28.11.2001, p 67) on the Community code relating to medicinal products for human use, Title III, Chapter 4 (mutual recognition procedure and decentralised procedure): Human Medicines Regulations 2012, SI 2012/1916, regs 110(10), 111(1). A proposal by the licensing authority to vary, suspend or revoke a certificate of registration within the Human Medicines Regulations 2012, SI 2012/1916, reg 111(1), or an application by the holder of such a certificate to vary or revoke it, is to be determined in accordance with Council Directive (EC) 2001/83 (OJ L311, 28.11.2001, p 67), Chapter 4 of Title III: Human Medicines Regulations 2012, SI 2012/1916, reg 111(2). Schedule 11 makes provision about advice and representations in relation to a proposal to revoke, vary or suspend a certificate of registration, other than a proposal to vary a certificate on the application of its holder: reg 110(9).
4 Human Medicines Regulations 2012, SI 2012/1916, reg 110(2).
5 Human Medicines Regulations 2012, SI 2012/1916, reg 110(3).
6 Ie imposed by the Human Medicines Regulations 2012, SI 2012/1916, Pt 13, Chapter 1 (regs 257–271).
7 Human Medicines Regulations 2012, SI 2012/1916, reg 110(4).
8 Ie by virtue of the Human Medicines Regulations 2012, SI 2012/1916, reg 105 (see PARA 191).
9 Human Medicines Regulations 2012, SI 2012/1916, reg 110(5).

10 Ie not complied with the Human Medicines Regulations 2012, SI 2012/1916, reg 115(1)–(3) (see PARA 199).
11 Human Medicines Regulations 2012, SI 2012/1916, reg 110(6).
12 Human Medicines Regulations 2012, SI 2012/1916, reg 110(7).
13 Human Medicines Regulations 2012, SI 2012/1916, reg 110(8).

196. Withdrawal of homoeopathic medicinal product from the market. If the licensing authority[1] revokes or suspends[2] a certificate of registration[3] it may give written notice to the person who is, or immediately before its revocation was, the holder of the certificate requiring the holder to comply with the following requirement[4].

That requirement is to take all reasonably practicable steps to withdraw from the market in the United Kingdom and recover possession of the product to which the certificate relates, or the batches of the product specified in the notice, within the time and for the period specified in the notice[5].

The notice must specify the grounds for giving the notice[6].

1 As to the meaning of 'licensing authority' see PARA 35 note 1.
2 Ie revokes or suspends the certificate of registration under the Human Medicines Regulations 2012, SI 2012/1916, reg 110 or 111(2) (see PARA 195).
3 Human Medicines Regulations 2012, SI 2012/1916, reg 112(1). As to the meaning of 'certificate of registration' see PARA 141 note 4.
4 Human Medicines Regulations 2012, SI 2012/1916, reg 112(2).
5 Human Medicines Regulations 2012, SI 2012/1916, reg 112(3).
6 Human Medicines Regulations 2012, SI 2012/1916, reg 112(4).

E. OBLIGATIONS OF HOLDER OF CERTIFICATE OF REGISTRATION

197. To notify placing on the market etc. The holder of a certificate of registration[1] must notify the licensing authority[2] of the date on which the product to which the certificate relates is placed on the market in the United Kingdom taking account of the various presentations authorised[3]. A notification under these provisions must be given before the end of the period of two months beginning with the date on which the product is placed on the market[4].

The holder of a certificate of registration must notify the licensing authority if the product to which the certificate relates is to be withdrawn from the market in the United Kingdom (whether temporarily or permanently)[5]. The notification must be given before the beginning of the period of two months ending with the date on which the product is to be withdrawn from the market unless it is not reasonably practicable to do so[6]. In that event, the notification must be given as far as is reasonably practicable in advance of the date on which the product is withdrawn from the market[7].

The licensing authority may require the holder of a certificate of registration to provide information relating to the volume of sales in the United Kingdom of the product to which the certificate relates[8].

The holder of a certificate of registration must provide the licensing authority with such information where the period within which the information must be provided is specified in a written notice given to the holder by the licensing authority, before the end of that period or, otherwise, as soon as is reasonably practicable after receipt of the request[9].

1 As to the meaning of 'certificate of registration' see PARA 141 note 4.
2 As to the meaning of 'licensing authority' see PARA 35 note 1.
3 Human Medicines Regulations 2012, SI 2012/1916, reg 113(1). It is a defence for a person charged with an offence consisting of a breach of reg 113(3) (see reg 121; and PARA 205) to

prove that the person took all reasonable precautions and exercised all due diligence to avoid commission of that offence: reg 124(3). Where evidence is adduced that is sufficient to raise an issue with respect to the defence in reg 124(3), the court or jury must presume that the defence is satisfied unless the prosecution proves beyond reasonable doubt that it is not: reg 124(4).

4   Human Medicines Regulations 2012, SI 2012/1916, reg 113(2). As to the meaning of 'month' see PARA 43 note 3.
5   Human Medicines Regulations 2012, SI 2012/1916, reg 113(3).
6   Human Medicines Regulations 2012, SI 2012/1916, reg 113(4).
7   Human Medicines Regulations 2012, SI 2012/1916, reg 113(5).
8   Human Medicines Regulations 2012, SI 2012/1916, reg 113(6).
9   Human Medicines Regulations 2012, SI 2012/1916, reg 113(7).

198.   To take account of scientific and technical progress. The holder of a certificate of registration[1] must keep under review the methods of manufacture[2] and control of the product to which the certificate relates, taking account of scientific and technical progress[3].

As soon as is reasonably practicable after becoming aware of the need to do so, the holder must apply to vary the certificate of registration to make any changes to those methods that are required to ensure they are generally accepted scientific methods[4].

1   As to the meaning of 'certificate of registration' see PARA 141 note 4.
2   As to the meaning of 'manufacture' see PARA 141 note 7.
3   Human Medicines Regulations 2012, SI 2012/1916, reg 114(1).
4   Human Medicines Regulations 2012, SI 2012/1916, reg 114(2).

199.   To provide information relating to safety etc. The holder of a certificate of registration[1] must provide the licensing authority[2] with any new information that might entail the variation of the certificate[3].

The holder must, in particular, provide the licensing authority with the following information:

(1)   information about any prohibition or restriction imposed in relation to the product to which the certificate relates by the competent authority of any country in which the product is on the market[4];

(2)   positive and negative results of clinical trials or other studies in all indications and populations, whether or not included in the certificate of registration[5];

(3)   data on the use of the product where such use is outside the terms of the certificate of registration[6]; and

(4)   any other information that the holder considers might influence the evaluation of the benefits and risks of the product[7].

Information referred to above[8] must be provided as soon as is reasonably practicable after the holder becomes aware of it[9].

The licensing authority may require the holder of a certificate of registration to provide the authority with information that is specified by the licensing authority and demonstrates that the risks of the product to the health of patients or of the public do not outweigh any beneficial effects of the product to which the certificate relates[10]. Such information includes information arising from use of the product in a country which is not an EEA state or outside the terms of the certificate of registration[11].

The licensing authority may require the holder of a certificate of registration to provide the authority with proof of the control methods employed by the manufacturer of the product to which the certificate relates[12].

The licensing authority may notify the holder of a certificate of registration that it requires the holder to provide to the licensing authority information of any description specified in the notice, within the period specified in the notice[13].

1   As to the meaning of 'certificate of registration' see PARA 141 note 4.
2   As to the meaning of 'licensing authority' see PARA 35 note 1.
3   Human Medicines Regulations 2012, SI 2012/1916, reg 115(1). If the information supplied under reg 115(1), (2) or (4) entails the variation of the certificate of registration, the holder must make an application to the licensing authority to that effect as soon as is reasonably practicable after becoming aware of the information: reg 115(6).
4   Human Medicines Regulations 2012, SI 2012/1916, reg 115(2)(a).
5   Human Medicines Regulations 2012, SI 2012/1916, reg 115(2)(b).
6   Human Medicines Regulations 2012, SI 2012/1916, reg 115(2)(c).
7   Human Medicines Regulations 2012, SI 2012/1916, reg 115(2)(d).
8   Ie within the Human Medicines Regulations 2012, SI 2012/1916, reg 115(1) or (2).
9   Human Medicines Regulations 2012, SI 2012/1916, reg 115(3).
10 Human Medicines Regulations 2012, SI 2012/1916, reg 115(4). The holder of a certificate of registration must provide the licensing authority with information that it requires under reg 115(4) or (7) where the period within which the information must be provided is specified in a written notice given to the holder by the licensing authority, before the end of that period or, otherwise, as soon as is reasonably practicable after receipt of the request: reg 115(10).
11 Human Medicines Regulations 2012, SI 2012/1916, reg 115(5).
12 Human Medicines Regulations 2012, SI 2012/1916, reg 115(7).
13 Human Medicines Regulations 2012, SI 2012/1916, reg 115(8). A notice under reg 115(8) must not be served unless it appears to the licensing authority, or it is represented to the licensing authority by the Commission or by an expert committee appointed by the licensing authority: (a) that circumstances exist by reason of which it is necessary to consider whether the certificate of registration should be varied, suspended or revoked; and (b) that the information required by the notice is needed to consider that question: reg 115(9).

200.   In relation to product information.   The holder of the certificate of registration[1] for a medicinal product[2] must ensure that the product information relating to the product is kept up to date with current scientific knowledge[3].

1   As to the meaning of 'certificate of registration' see PARA 141 note 4.
2   As to the meaning of 'medicinal product' see PARA 25.
3   Human Medicines Regulations 2012, SI 2012/1916, reg 116(1). For this purpose 'current scientific knowledge' includes the conclusions of the assessment and recommendations made public by means of the European medicines web-portal established in accordance with Council Regulation (EC) 726/2004 (OJ L136, 30.4.2004, p 1) laying down Community procedures for the authorisation and supervision of medicinal products for human and veterinary use and establishing a European Medicines Agency, art 26: Human Medicines Regulations 2012, SI 2012/1916, reg 116(2).

201.   Record-keeping obligation.   The holder of a certificate of registration[1] must keep any documents or information that will facilitate the withdrawal or recall from sale or supply of the product to which the certificate relates[2].

1   As to the meaning of 'certificate of registration' see PARA 141 note 4.
2   Human Medicines Regulations 2012, SI 2012/1916, reg 117.

202.   To ensure appropriate and continued supplies.   The holder of a certificate of registration[1] must take all reasonable steps to ensure appropriate and continued supplies of the product to which the certificate relates to pharmacies and persons authorised to supply the product so that the needs of patients in the United Kingdom are met[2].

1   As to the meaning of 'certificate of registration' see PARA 141 note 4.
2   Human Medicines Regulations 2012, SI 2012/1916, reg 118. It is a defence for a person charged with an offence consisting of a breach of reg 118 to prove that the person took all reasonable

precautions and exercised all due diligence to avoid commission of that offence: reg 124(3). Where evidence is adduced that is sufficient to raise an issue with respect to the defence in reg 124(3), the court or jury must presume that the defence is satisfied unless the prosecution proves beyond reasonable doubt that it is not: reg 124(4).

F. OFFENCES

203. In connection with applications. A person is guilty of an offence if, in the course of an application for the grant, renewal or variation of a certificate of registration[1] for a registrable homoeopathic medicinal product[2], he fails to provide the licensing authority[3] with any information that is relevant to an evaluation of the quality of the product or he provides to the licensing authority any information that is relevant to an evaluation of the quality of the product that is false or misleading in a material particular[4].

1 As to the meaning of 'certificate of registration' see PARA 141 note 4.
2 As to the meaning of 'registrable homoeopathic medicinal product' see PARA 187 note 2.
3 As to the meaning of 'licensing authority' see PARA 35 note 1.
4 Human Medicines Regulations 2012, SI 2012/1916, reg 119. If an offence under reg 119 (offences in connection with applications) is committed by a person acting as employee or agent, the employer or principal of that person is guilty of the same offence and is liable to be proceeded against and punished accordingly: reg 123. A person guilty of an offence under Pt 6 is liable, on summary conviction to a fine not exceeding the statutory maximum or, on conviction on indictment, to a fine, to imprisonment for a term not exceeding two years or to both: reg 122. It is a defence for a person charged with an offence under reg 119 to prove that the person took all reasonable precautions and exercised all due diligence to avoid commission of that offence: reg 124(3). Where evidence is adduced that is sufficient to raise an issue with respect to the defence in reg 124(3), the court or jury must presume that the defence is satisfied unless the prosecution proves beyond reasonable doubt that it is not: reg 124(4). As to the statutory maximum see SENTENCING AND DISPOSITION OF OFFENDERS vol 92 (2010) PARA 140.

204. Provision of false or misleading information. The holder of a certificate of registration[1] for a medicinal product[2] is guilty of an offence if the person provides the licensing authority with any information that is relevant to the quality of the product but that is false or misleading in a material particular[3].

1 As to the meaning of 'certificate of registration' see PARA 141 note 4.
2 As to the meaning of 'medicinal product' see PARA 25.
3 Human Medicines Regulations 2012, SI 2012/1916, reg 120(1). This is without prejudice to the operation of reg 119 (see PARA 203): reg 120(2). A person guilty of an offence under Pt 6 is liable, on summary conviction to a fine not exceeding the statutory maximum or, on conviction on indictment, to a fine, to imprisonment for a term not exceeding two years or to both: reg 122. It is a defence for a person charged with an offence under reg 120 to prove that the person took all reasonable precautions and exercised all due diligence to avoid commission of that offence: reg 124(3). Where evidence is adduced that is sufficient to raise an issue with respect to the defence in reg 124(3), the court or jury must presume that the defence is satisfied unless the prosecution proves beyond reasonable doubt that it is not: reg 124(4). As to the statutory maximum see SENTENCING AND DISPOSITION OF OFFENDERS vol 92 (2010) PARA 140.

205. General offence and defence. A person is guilty of an offence if that person commits a breach of a provision[1] relating to the certification of homoeopathic medicinal products[2].

A breach of such a provision includes any:

(1) failure by the holder of a certificate of registration to comply with any necessary[3] requirement or obligation[4];

(2) contravention by any person of any necessary[5] prohibition[6]; or

(3) failure to comply with any requirement imposed[7] on a person by the licensing authority[8].

If the holder of a certificate of registration is charged with an offence under the Human Medicines Regulations 2012, Part 6[9] in respect of anything that has been manufactured or assembled[10] to the holder's order by another person and has been so manufactured or assembled as not to comply with the terms of the certificate[11], it is a defence for the holder to prove that he communicated the terms of the certificate to the other person and the holder did not know and could not by the exercise of reasonable care have known that those terms had not been complied with[12].

1   Ie a breach of the Human Medicines Regulations 2012, SI 2012/1916, Pt 6 (regs 102–124).
2   Human Medicines Regulations 2012, SI 2012/1916, reg 121(1). A person guilty of an offence under Pt 6 is liable, on summary conviction to a fine not exceeding the statutory maximum or, on conviction on indictment, to a fine, to imprisonment for a term not exceeding two years or to both: reg 122. As to the statutory maximum see SENTENCING AND DISPOSITION OF OFFENDERS vol 92 (2010) PARA 140. Regulation 121(1) is without prejudice to any offence established by any other provision in Pt 6: reg 121(3).
3   Ie any requirement or obligation in the Human Medicines Regulations 2012, SI 2012/1916, Pt 6 (regs 102–124). As to the meaning of 'certificate of registration' see PARA 141 note 4.
4   Human Medicines Regulations 2012, SI 2012/1916, reg 124(1)(a).
5   Ie any necessary prohibition in the Human Medicines Regulations 2012, SI 2012/1916, Pt 6 (regs 102–124). As to the meaning of 'contravene' see PARA 41 note 8.
6   Human Medicines Regulations 2012, SI 2012/1916, reg 124(1)(b).
7   Ie imposed pursuant to the Human Medicines Regulations 2012, SI 2012/1916, Pt 6 (regs 102–124).
8   Human Medicines Regulations 2012, SI 2012/1916, reg 124(1)(c).
9   Human Medicines Regulations 2012, SI 2012/1916, regs 102–124.
10 As to the meaning of 'manufacture' and 'assemble' see PARA 141 notes 7, 8.
11 Human Medicines Regulations 2012, SI 2012/1916, reg 124(1)(d).
12 Human Medicines Regulations 2012, SI 2012/1916, reg 124(2).

(v) Traditional Herbal Registration

A. APPLICATIONS

206.   Applicable products. The following applies to a herbal medicinal product[1] (a 'traditional herbal medicinal product') if the following conditions are met[2].

Condition A is met if by virtue of its composition and indications the product is appropriate for use without the need for a medical practitioner to diagnose the condition to be treated by the product, prescribe the product or monitor the product's use[3].

Condition B is met if the product is intended to be administered at a particular strength and in accordance with a particular posology[4].

Condition C is met if the product is intended to be administered externally, orally or by inhalation[5].

Condition D is met if the product has been in medicinal use for a continuous period of at least 30 years and the product has been in medicinal use in the European Union for a continuous period of at least 15 years[6].

Condition E is met if there is sufficient information about the use of the product as mentioned in condition D (referred to as its 'traditional use'), so that (in particular) it has been established that the traditional use of the product is not harmful and the pharmacological effects or efficacy of the product are plausible on the basis of long-standing use and experience[7].

1   As to the meaning of 'herbal medicinal product' see PARA 51 note 2.
2   Human Medicines Regulations 2012, SI 2012/1916, reg 125(1).

3   Human Medicines Regulations 2012, SI 2012/1916, reg 125(2).
4   Human Medicines Regulations 2012, SI 2012/1916, reg 125(3).
5   Human Medicines Regulations 2012, SI 2012/1916, reg 125(4).
6   Human Medicines Regulations 2012, SI 2012/1916, reg 125(5). It is immaterial for the purposes
    of condition D whether or not during a period mentioned in that condition the sale or supply of
    the product has been based on a specific authorisation or the number or quantity of the
    ingredients (or any of them) has been reduced: reg 125(6).
7   Human Medicines Regulations 2012, SI 2012/1916, reg 125(7).

207. Addition of vitamins or minerals. The addition to a traditional herbal
medicinal product[1] of a vitamin or mineral does not prevent a traditional herbal
registration from being granted for the product if there is well-documented
evidence of the safety of the vitamin or mineral and the action of the vitamin or
mineral is ancillary to the action of the product's active herbal ingredients in
connection with the use authorised by the traditional herbal registration[2].

1   As to the meaning of 'traditional herbal medicinal product' see PARA 141 note 5.
2   Human Medicines Regulations 2012, SI 2012/1916, reg 126.

208. Application for grant of traditional herbal registration. The licensing
authority[1] may[2] grant an application for a traditional herbal registration for a
traditional herbal medicinal product in response to an application made in
accordance with the Human Medicines Regulations 2012[3], Part 7[4].

A registration so granted must contain terms approved by the licensing
authority[5].

The applicant must be established in the European Union[6] and the application
must be made in writing, signed by or on behalf of the applicant[7] and, unless the
licensing authority directs otherwise, accompanied by any fee payable in
connection with the application[8].

The application must include a statement indicating whether the product to
which the application relates should be available only from a pharmacy or on
general sale[9].

The application must also include a statement indicating whether any terms of
the registration are proposed relating to the method of sale or supply of the
product (including, in particular, any proposed restrictions affecting the
circumstances of the use or promotion of the product) and, if so, what terms are
proposed[10].

1   As to the meaning of 'licensing authority' see PARA 35 note 1.
2   This is subject to the Human Medicines Regulations 2012, SI 2012/1916, reg 130 (see PARA
    211).
3   Ie the Human Medicines Regulations 2012, SI 2012/1916, regs 125–155.
4   Human Medicines Regulations 2012, SI 2012/1916, reg 127(1).
5   Human Medicines Regulations 2012, SI 2012/1916, reg 127(2).
6   Human Medicines Regulations 2012, SI 2012/1916, reg 127(3).
7   An application is treated as signed for this purpose if it is signed with an electronic signature:
    Human Medicines Regulations 2012, SI 2012/1916, reg 127(5).
8   Human Medicines Regulations 2012, SI 2012/1916, reg 127(4). The application and any
    accompanying material must be in English: reg 127(6). As to fees see PARA 30.
9   Human Medicines Regulations 2012, SI 2012/1916, reg 127(6). As to the meaning of 'medicinal
    product subject to general sale' see reg 5(1); and PARA 26: reg 8(1).
10 Human Medicines Regulations 2012, SI 2012/1916, reg 127(8).

209. Accompanying material. The applicant for the grant of a traditional
herbal registration[1] must provide specified material[2] in relation to the product[3].

The applicant must also, if requested by the licensing authority[4] to do so, provide the licensing authority with material or information that the licensing authority reasonably considers necessary for considering the application[5].

1   As to the meaning of 'traditional herbal registration' see PARA 141 note 5.
2   Ie material specified in the Human Medicines Regulations 2012, SI 2012/1916, Sch 12.
3   Human Medicines Regulations 2012, SI 2012/1916, reg 128(1). If the application relates to a product that is contained in the list referred to in Council Directive (EC) 2001/83 (OJ L311, 28.11.2001, p 67) on the Community code relating to medicinal products for human use, art 16f(1) the applicant does not need to provide the material referred to in the Human Medicines Regulations 2012, SI 2012/1916, Sch 12, paras 16–20 and reg 128(2) does not apply: reg 128(3). Material that is submitted under the Human Medicines Regulations 2012, SI 2012/1916, reg 128 must be submitted in accordance with Council Directive (EC) 2001/83 (OJ L311, 28.11.2001, p 67), Annex I, so far as applicable to traditional herbal medicinal products: Human Medicines Regulations 2012, SI 2012/1916, reg 128(4).
4   As to the meaning of 'licensing authority' see PARA 35 note 1.
5   Human Medicines Regulations 2012, SI 2012/1916, reg 128(2).

210.   Obligation to update information supplied in connection with application.   The applicant for a traditional herbal registration[1] must update information[2] supplied in connection with the application to include any further information that is relevant to the evaluation of the safety, quality or efficacy of the product concerned[3].

1   As to the meaning of 'traditional herbal registration' see PARA 141 note 5.
2   Such updated information must be provided as soon as is reasonably practicable after the applicant becomes aware of it: Human Medicines Regulations 2012, SI 2012/1916, reg 129(2).
3   Human Medicines Regulations 2012, SI 2012/1916, reg 129(1).

211.   Consideration of application.   The licensing authority[1] must take all reasonable steps to ensure that it makes a decision to grant or refuse a traditional herbal registration[2] before the end of the period of 210 days beginning immediately after the day on which an application for the registration is submitted in accordance with the relevant provision[3].

If the licensing authority requests the applicant to provide any further information or material, this period is suspended for the period beginning with the date on which the request is made and ending with the date on which the information or material is provided[4].

If the licensing authority requests the applicant to give an oral or written explanation of the application, the period referred to above[5] is suspended for the period beginning with the date on which the request is made and ending with the date on which the explanation is provided[6].

The licensing authority may grant the application only if, having considered the application and the accompanying material, the authority thinks that:

(1)   the product complies with the conditions[7] for a product to be a traditional herbal medicinal product[8];

(2)   the product to which the application relates is not harmful under normal conditions of use[9];

(3)   the application and the accompanying material complies with the requirements of Part 7[10] of the Human Medicines Regulations 2012[11];

(4)   the product's qualitative and quantitative composition is as described in the application and the accompanying material[12]; and

(5)   the product's pharmaceutical quality has been satisfactorily demonstrated[13].

The licensing authority may refuse the application on the ground that it is more appropriate to consider whether to authorise the placing of the product on the market in response to an application for a marketing authorisation or certificate of registration for the product[14].

The licensing authority must take into account a relevant herbal monograph[15] that the authority thinks relevant to the application or if no such relevant monograph has been established, such other monographs, publications or data as the authority thinks relevant[16].

1 As to the meaning of 'licensing authority' see PARA 35 note 1.

2 As to the meaning of 'traditional herbal registration' see PARA 141 note 5.

3 Human Medicines Regulations 2012, SI 2012/1916, reg 130(1). The relevant provision mentioned in the text is reg 128 (see PARA 209). Schedule 11 makes provision about advice and representations in relation to an application for the grant of a traditional herbal registration: reg 130(11). Regulation 130 does not apply where Council Directive (EC) 2001/83 (OJ L311, 28.11.2001, p 67) on the Community code relating to medicinal products for human use, art 16d(1) applies to the product and the application has been submitted to the licensing authority in accordance with art 28 or has been referred to the Committee for Herbal Medicinal Products for the application of the procedure laid down in arts 32–34: Human Medicines Regulations 2012, SI 2012/1916, reg 130(12). An application to which reg 130(12) applies is to be determined by the licensing authority in accordance with Council Directive (EC) 2001/83 (OJ L311, 28.11.2001, p 67) Title III, Chapter 4: Human Medicines Regulations 2012, SI 2012/1916, reg 130(13).

4 Human Medicines Regulations 2012, SI 2012/1916, reg 130(2). The licensing authority need not take into account any updated information supplied in connection with the application under reg 129 (obligation to update information supplied in connection with application: see PARA 210), unless it thinks that the information is unfavourable in respect of the safety, quality or efficacy of the product concerned: reg 130(5).

5 Ie the period referred to in Human Medicines Regulations 2012, SI 2012/1916, reg 130(1).

6 Human Medicines Regulations 2012, SI 2012/1916, reg 130(3).

7 Ie the conditions A to E in the Human Medicines Regulations 2012, SI 2012/1916, reg 125 (see PARA 206).

8 Human Medicines Regulations 2012, SI 2012/1916, reg 130(4)(a). This is subject to Council Directive (EC) 2001/83 (OJ L311, 28.11.2001, p 67), reg 16c(4): Human Medicines Regulations 2012, SI 2012/1916, reg 130(7). If the application relates to a herbal medicinal product that is contained in the list in Council Directive (EC) 2001/83 (OJ L311, 28.11.2001, p 67) art 16f(1) then the Human Medicines Regulations 2012, SI 2012/1916, reg 130(4)(a) applies as if it referred to conditions A–D in reg 125 and reg 130(4)(b) does not apply: reg 130(8). Where Council Directive (EC) 2001/83 (OJ L311, 28.11.2001, p 67), art 16d(1) does not apply to the product, the licensing authority must, in considering the application, take into account any registrations granted by other member States in accordance with Chapter 2a of Title III: Human Medicines Regulations 2012, SI 2012/1916, reg 134(9).

9 Human Medicines Regulations 2012, SI 2012/1916, reg 130(4)(b). See note 8.

10 Ie the Human Medicines Regulations 2012, SI 2012/1916, Pt 7 (regs 125–155).

11 Human Medicines Regulations 2012, SI 2012/1916, reg 130(4)(c).

12 Human Medicines Regulations 2012, SI 2012/1916, reg 130(4)(d).

13 Human Medicines Regulations 2012, SI 2012/1916, reg 134(4)(e).

14 Human Medicines Regulations 2012, SI 2012/1916, reg 134(6).

15 Ie of the kind mentioned in Council Directive (EC) 2001/83 (OJ L311, 28.11.2001, p 67), art 16h(3).

16 Human Medicines Regulations 2012, SI 2012/1916, reg 134(10).

212. Renewal of registration. An application for the renewal of a traditional herbal registration[1] must be made to the licensing authority[2]. The applicant must be established in the European Union[3] and the application must be made in writing, signed by or on behalf of the applicant[4] and, unless the licensing authority directs otherwise, accompanied by any fee payable in connection with the application[5].

The holder must provide a consolidated version of the file in respect of quality, safety and efficacy including the evaluation of data contained in suspected adverse reaction reports[6] and periodic safety update reports[7] and all variations introduced since the traditional herbal registration was granted[8].

The licensing authority may renew a traditional herbal registration only if, having considered the application and the material accompanying it, the authority thinks that the positive therapeutic effects of the product to which the registration relates outweigh the risks of the product to the health of patients or of the public[9].

1 As to the meaning of 'traditional herbal registration' see PARA 141 note 5.
2 Human Medicines Regulations 2012, SI 2012/1916, reg 133(1). As to the meaning of 'licensing authority' see PARA 35 note 1. The application must be made so that it is received by the licensing authority before the beginning of the period of 9 months ending with the expiry of the period mentioned in reg 132(1)(a) or (3)(a) (initial and further period of validity: see PARA 214), as the case may be: reg 133(5). Schedule 11 makes provision about advice and representations in relation to an application for the renewal of a traditional herbal registration: reg 133(8). As to the meaning of 'month' see PARA 43 note 3.
3 Human Medicines Regulations 2012, SI 2012/1916, reg 133(2).
4 An application is treated as signed for this purpose if it is signed with an electronic signature: Human Medicines Regulations 2012, SI 2012/1916, reg 133(4).
5 Human Medicines Regulations 2012, SI 2012/1916, reg 133(3). As to fees see PARA 30.
6 As to the meaning of 'adverse reaction ' see PARA 70 note 6. As to the meaning of 'suspected' see PARA 70 note 7.
7 Ie as submitted in accordance with the Human Medicines Regulations 2012, SI 2012/1916 Pt 11 (regs 177–212).
8 Human Medicines Regulations 2012, SI 2012/1916, reg 133(6).
9 Human Medicines Regulations 2012, SI 2012/1916, reg 133(7).

B. CONDITIONS

213. Classification of traditional herbal registration. A traditional herbal registration[1] must include a term that the product to which the registration relates is to be available only from a pharmacy or on general sale[2].

A traditional herbal registration may include a term that the product to which the registration relates is to be available on general sale only if the licensing authority considers that the product can with reasonable safety be sold or supplied otherwise than by, or under the supervision of, a pharmacist[3].

1 As to the meaning of 'traditional herbal registration' see PARA 141 note 5.
2 Human Medicines Regulations 2012, SI 2012/1916, reg 131(1)
3 Human Medicines Regulations 2012, SI 2012/1916, reg 131(2). As to the meaning of 'pharmacist' see PARA 52 note 5.

C. VALIDITY OF CERTIFICATE OF REGISTRATION

214. Validity of traditional herbal registration. Subject to the following provisions, a traditional herbal registration[1] remains in force for an initial period of five years beginning with the date on which it is granted and, if the registration is renewed[2] for an unlimited period after its renewal[3].

The licensing authority[4] may on the first application for renewal of a registration determine on grounds relating to pharmacovigilance[5], including exposure of an insufficient number of patients to the medicinal product concerned, that it should be necessary for the holder to make one further application for renewal[6]. In that event, the registration remains in force for a further period of five years beginning with the date on which it is first renewed and if the registration is further renewed[7] for an unlimited period after its further renewal[8].

If an application for the renewal or further renewal of a registration is made[9] the certificate remains in force until the licensing authority notifies the applicant of its decision on the application[10].

1　As to the meaning of 'traditional herbal registration' see PARA 141 note 5.
2　Ie renewed under the Human Medicines Regulations 2012, SI 2012/1916, reg 133 (see PARA 212).
3　Human Medicines Regulations 2012, SI 2012/1916, reg 132(1). Regulation 132 is subject to reg 134 (see PARA 211) and reg 135 (see PARA 216): reg 132(5).
4　As to the meaning of 'licensing authority' see PARA 35 note 1.
5　As to pharmacovigilance see PARA 241 et seq.
6　Human Medicines Regulations 2012, SI 2012/1916, reg 132(2).
7　Ie under the Human Medicines Regulations 2012, SI 2012/1916, reg 133 (see PARA 212).
8　Human Medicines Regulations 2012, SI 2012/1916, reg 132(3).
9　Ie in accordance with the Human Medicines Regulations 2012, SI 2012/1916, reg 133 (see PARA 212).
10　Human Medicines Regulations 2012, SI 2012/1916, reg 132(4).

D.　REVOCATION, SUSPENSION OR VARIATION AND CEASING OF AUTHORISATION

215.　Failure to place on the market etc.　A traditional herbal registration[1] ceases to be in force if the product to which it relates is not placed on the market in the United Kingdom during the period of three years beginning immediately after the day on which it was granted[2].

A traditional herbal registration for a product which has been placed on the market ceases to be in force if the product to which it relates is not sold or supplied in the United Kingdom for a period of three years[3].

These provisions do not apply if the licensing authority[4] grants an exemption from its operation[5]. An exemption may be granted in response to an application in writing by the holder of the traditional herbal registration or by the licensing authority of its own motion[6].

An exemption may only be granted only in exceptional circumstances and on public health grounds[7].

An exemption has effect for the period determined by the licensing authority, which may not exceed three years beginning with the day on which it is granted and may be renewed or further renewed[8].

1　As to the meaning of 'traditional herbal registration' see PARA 141 note 5.
2　Human Medicines Regulations 2012, SI 2012/1916, reg 134(1).
3　Human Medicines Regulations 2012, SI 2012/1916, reg 134(2).
4　As to the meaning of 'licensing authority' see PARA 35 note 1.
5　Human Medicines Regulations 2012, SI 2012/1916, reg 134(3).
6　Human Medicines Regulations 2012, SI 2012/1916, reg 134(4).
7　Human Medicines Regulations 2012, SI 2012/1916, reg 134(5).
8　Human Medicines Regulations 2012, SI 2012/1916, reg 134(6).

216.　Revocation, variation and suspension of traditional herbal registration. The licensing authority[1] may revoke, vary or suspend a traditional herbal registration[2] if any of the following conditions are met[3].

Condition A is that the licensing authority thinks that the product to which the registration relates is harmful, the pharmacological effects or efficacy of the product are no longer plausible or the product's qualitative or quantitative composition is not as described in the application for the registration or the material accompanying it[4].

Condition B is that the licensing authority thinks that the application or the material supplied with it is incorrect[5].

Condition C is that the licensing authority thinks that there has been a breach of a term of the registration or a requirement imposed[6] in relation to packaging and leaflets[7].

Condition D is that the licensing authority thinks that the holder of the registration has not complied with a requirement[8] to provide information that may entail amendment of authorisation[9].

Condition E is that the holder of the registration has ceased to be established in the United Kingdom[10].

Condition F is that the product to which the registration relates is manufactured[11] in the United Kingdom and the licensing authority thinks that the holder of the manufacturer's licence for the product has failed to comply in relation to the product with provisions relating to manufacturing and assembly[12], imports from states other than EEA States[13], further requirements for manufacturer's licence[14], obligation to provide information relating to control methods[15] or requirements[16] as to qualified persons[17].

Condition G is that the product to which the registration relates is manufactured in an EEA state other than the United Kingdom and the licensing authority thinks that the holder of the manufacturer's licence[18] for the product has failed to comply in relation to the product with provision giving effect to EU requirements relating to manufacturing authorisations[19] in that member state[20].

Condition H is that the licensing authority thinks that urgent action to protect public health is necessary, in which case it may suspend the registration and it must notify the suspension to the European Medicines Agency[21], the European Commission, and all other member states by the end of the next working day following the day on which the suspension comes into force[22].

Condition I is that the holder applies to vary the registration and that the licensing authority thinks that the application should be granted[23].

1   As to the meaning of 'licensing authority' see PARA 35 note 1.
2   As to the meaning of 'traditional herbal registration' see PARA 141 note 5.
3   Human Medicines Regulations 2012, SI 2012/1916, reg 135(1). Schedule 11 makes provision about advice and representations in relation to a proposal to revoke, vary or suspend a traditional herbal registration, other than a proposal to vary a registration on the application of its holder: reg 137. Regulations 135 to 138 do not apply in relation to a traditional herbal registration that was granted in accordance with the provisions of Council Directive (EC) 2001/83 (OJ L311, 28.11.2001, p 67) on the Community code relating to medicinal products for human use Chapter 4 of Title III (mutual recognition procedure and decentralised procedure) or was subject to the procedure laid down in arts 32–34 following a referral under art 30 or 31, unless the procedure was limited to certain specific parts of the registration: Human Medicines Regulations 2012, SI 2012/1916, reg 139(1). A proposal by the licensing authority to vary, suspend or revoke a traditional herbal registration within the Human Medicines Regulations 2012, SI 2012/1916, reg 139(1), or an application by the holder of such a registration to vary or revoke it, is to be determined in accordance with Council Directive (EC) 2001/83 (OJ L311, 28.11.2001, p 67), Chapter 4 of Title III: Human Medicines Regulations 2012, SI 2012/1916, reg 139(2).
4   Human Medicines Regulations 2012, SI 2012/1916, reg 135(2).
5   Human Medicines Regulations 2012, SI 2012/1916, reg 135(3).
6   Ie imposed by the Human Medicines Regulations 2012, SI 2012/1916, regs 257–271.
7   Human Medicines Regulations 2012, SI 2012/1916, reg 135(4).
8   Ie complied with the Human Medicines Regulations 2012, SI 2012/1916, reg 145(1)–(3) (see PARA 224).

9   Human Medicines Regulations 2012, SI 2012/1916, reg 135(5).
10 Human Medicines Regulations 2012, SI 2012/1916, reg 135(6).
11 As to the meaning of 'manufacture' see PARA 141 note 7.
12 Ie the Human Medicines Regulations 2012, SI 2012/1916, reg 37 (see PARA 62).
13 Ie the Human Medicines Regulations 2012, SI 2012/1916, reg 38 (see PARA 67).
14 Ie the Human Medicines Regulations 2012, SI 2012/1916, reg 39 (see PARA 56).
15 Ie the Human Medicines Regulations 2012, SI 2012/1916, reg 40 (see PARA 56).
16 Ie the Human Medicines Regulations 2012, SI 2012/1916, reg 41 (see PARA 57).
17 Human Medicines Regulations 2012, SI 2012/1916, reg 135(7).
18 As to the meaning of 'manufacturer's licence' see PARA 45.
19 Ie giving effect to Council Directive (EC) 2001/83 (OJ L311, 28.11.2001, p 67), art 41.
20 Human Medicines Regulations 2012, SI 2012/1916, reg 135(8).
21 As to the European Medicines Agency see PARA 14.
22 Human Medicines Regulations 2012, SI 2012/1916, reg 135(9).
23 Human Medicines Regulations 2012, SI 2012/1916, reg 135(10).

217.   Revocation by licensing authority.   The licensing authority[1] must revoke a traditional herbal registration[2] if the application for the registration was submitted[3] on the basis that the herbal medicinal product to which it relates was contained in the list of herbal substances[4] and the product ceases to be contained in that list[5].

1   As to the meaning of 'licensing authority' see PARA 35 note 1.
2   As to the meaning of 'traditional herbal registration' see PARA 141 note 5.
3   Ie submitted in accordance with the Human Medicines Regulations 2012, SI 2012/1916, reg 128(3) (see PARA 209).
4   Ie the list referred to in Council Directive (EC) 2001/83 (OJ L311, 28.11.2001, p 67) on the Community code relating to medicinal products for human use, art 16F(1) (see PARA 19). As to the meaning of 'herbal substances' see PARA 51 note 2.
5   Human Medicines Regulations 2012, SI 2012/1916, reg 136(1). Regulation 136(1) does not apply if within the period of 3 months beginning immediately after the day on which product ceases to be contained on the list the holder submits to the licensing authority the material specified in Sch 12 (see PARA 209) in relation to the product and provides the licensing authority with any material or information that the licensing authority reasonably considers necessary for considering the application and requests the holder to provide: reg 136(2). Regulation 136 is subject to reg 139 (see PARA 216): reg 136(3). Schedule 11 makes provision about advice and representations in relation to a proposal to revoke, vary or suspend a traditional herbal registration, other than a proposal to vary a registration on the application of its holder: reg 137. As to the meaning of 'month' see PARA 43 note 3.

218.   Suspension of use etc of traditional herbal medicinal product.   The licensing authority[1] may suspend the use, sale, supply or offer for sale or supply within the United Kingdom of a product to which a traditional herbal registration[2] relates if any of the following conditions are met[3].

Condition A is that the licensing authority thinks that the product is harmful, the pharmacological effects or efficacy of the product are no longer plausible or the product's qualitative or quantitative composition is not as described in the application for the registration or the material accompanying it[4].

Condition B is that the licensing authority thinks that the holder has not complied with the requirements[5] to provide proof of controls on the manufacturing process[6].

Condition C is that the licensing authority thinks that there has been a breach of a term of the registration or a requirement imposed[7] in relation to packaging and leaflets[8].

Condition D is that the licensing authority thinks that the power to revoke, suspend or vary manufacturers' licences[9] applies in relation to the manufacturer's licence for the product[10].

The licensing authority must give notice in writing of such a suspension to the holder of the registration[11] and must provide in the notice that the suspension is to take effect immediately or from a date specified in the notice and that it is to apply for the period specified in the notice[12].

Where a medicinal product is the subject of a suspension, the licensing authority may, in exceptional circumstances, and for such a transitional period as the licensing authority may determine, allow the supply of the medicinal product to patients who are already being treated with the medicinal product[13].

1   As to the meaning of 'licensing authority' see PARA 35 note 1.
2   As to the meaning of 'traditional herbal registration' see PARA 141 note 5.
3   Human Medicines Regulations 2012, SI 2012/1916, reg 138(1). A suspension under reg 137 may relate to batches of the product: reg 138(6). Regulation 138 is subject to reg 139 (see PARA 216): reg 138(10).
4   Human Medicines Regulations 2012, SI 2012/1916, reg 138(2).
5   Ie the requirements under the Human Medicines Regulations 2012, SI 2012/1916, reg 145(7) (see PARA 224).
6   Human Medicines Regulations 2012, SI 2012/1916, reg 138(3).
7   Ie imposed by the Human Medicines Regulations 2012, SI 2012/1916, regs 257–271.
8   Human Medicines Regulations 2012, SI 2012/1916, reg 138(4).
9   Ie the power under the Human Medicines Regulations 2012, SI 2012/1916, reg 23(4) or (5). As to the meaning of 'manufacturer's licence' see PARA 45.
10 Human Medicines Regulations 2012, SI 2012/1916, reg 138(5).
11 Human Medicines Regulations 2012, SI 2012/1916, reg 138(7).
12 Human Medicines Regulations 2012, SI 2012/1916, reg 138(8).
13 Human Medicines Regulations 2012, SI 2012/1916, reg 138(9). As to the meaning of 'medicinal product' see PARA 25.

219.   Withdrawal of traditional herbal medicinal product from the market.   If the licensing authority[1] revokes or suspends[2] a traditional herbal registration[3] or it suspends the use, sale, supply or offer for sale or supply within the United Kingdom of a product[4] to which a traditional herbal registration relates[5], it may give written notice to the person who is, or immediately before its revocation was, the holder of the registration requiring the holder to comply with both of the following requirements[6].

Requirement A is to take all reasonably practicable steps to inform wholesalers, retailers, medical practitioners, patients and others who may be in possession of the product to which the registration relates of the revocation or suspension, the reasons for the revocation or suspension and any action to be taken to restrict or prevent further use, sale, supply or offer for sale or supply of the product[7].

Requirement B is to take all reasonably practicable steps to withdraw from the market in the United Kingdom and recover possession of the product or the batches of the product specified in the notice, within the time and for the period specified in the notice[8].

1   As to the meaning of 'licensing authority' see PARA 35 note 1.
2   Ie under the Human Medicines Regulations 2012, SI 2012/1916, reg 135 (see PARA 216), 136 (see PARA 217), 139(2) (see PARA 216) or Council Directive (EC) 2001/83 (OJ L311, 28.11.2001, p 67) on the Community code relating to medicinal products for human use, art 34(3).
3   As to the meaning of 'traditional herbal registration' see PARA 141 note 5.
4   Ie under the Human Medicines Regulations 2012, SI 2012/1916, reg 138 (see PARA 218).
5   Human Medicines Regulations 2012, SI 2012/1916, reg 140(1).
6   Human Medicines Regulations 2012, SI 2012/1916, reg 140(2).
7   Human Medicines Regulations 2012, SI 2012/1916, reg 140(3).
8   Human Medicines Regulations 2012, SI 2012/1916, reg 140(4).

220.   Sale etc of suspended medicinal product. If the use, sale, supply or offer for sale or supply of a traditional herbal medicinal product[1] is suspended[2] a person must not sell, supply or offer to sell or supply the product or procure the sale, supply or offer for sale or supply of the product, knowing, or having reasonable cause to believe, that such use, sale, supply or offer for sale or supply is suspended[3].

1   As to the meaning of 'traditional herbal medicinal product' see PARA 141 note 5.
2   Ie in accordance with the Human Medicines Regulations 2012, SI 2012/1916, reg 138, 139(2) (see PARAS 216, 218).
3   Human Medicines Regulations 2012, SI 2012/1916, reg 141.

E.   OBLIGATIONS OF HOLDER OF TRADITIONAL HERBAL REGISTRATION

221.   To notify placing on the market etc. The holder of a traditional herbal registration[1] must notify the licensing authority[2] of the date on which the product to which the registration relates is placed on the market in the United Kingdom taking account of the various presentations authorised[3].

The holder of a traditional herbal registration must also notify the licensing authority if the product to which the registration relates is to be withdrawn from the market in the United Kingdom (whether temporarily or permanently)[4].

The licensing authority may require the holder of a traditional herbal registration to provide information relating to the volume of sales in the United Kingdom of the product to which the registration relates[5].

1   As to the meaning of 'traditional herbal registration' see PARA 141 note 5.
2   As to the meaning of 'licensing authority' see PARA 35 note 1. The notification must be given before the end of the period of 2 months beginning with the date on which the product is placed on the market: Human Medicines Regulations 2012, SI 2012/1916, reg 142(2). As to the meaning of 'month' see PARA 43 note 3.
3   Human Medicines Regulations 2012, SI 2012/1916, reg 142(1). It is a defence for a person charged with an offence consisting of a breach of reg 142(3) to prove that the person took all reasonable precautions and exercised all due diligence to avoid commission of that offence: reg 155(3). Where evidence is adduced that is sufficient to raise an issue with respect to the defence in reg 155(3), the court or jury must presume that the defence is satisfied unless the prosecution proves beyond reasonable doubt that it is not: reg 155(4).
4   Human Medicines Regulations 2012, SI 2012/1916, reg 142(3). The notification must be given before the beginning of the period of 2 months ending with the date on which the product is to be withdrawn from the market unless it is not reasonably practicable to do so: reg 142(4). In that event, the notification must be given as far as is reasonably practicable in advance of the date on which the product is withdrawn from the market: reg 142(5).
5   Human Medicines Regulations 2012, SI 2012/1916, reg 142(6). The holder of a traditional herbal registration must provide the licensing authority with such information where the period within which the information must be provided is specified in a written notice given to the holder by the licensing authority, before the end of that period or, otherwise, as soon as is reasonably practicable after receipt of the request: reg 142(7).

222.   To take account of scientific and technical progress. The holder of a traditional herbal registration[1] must keep under review the methods of manufacture[2] and control of the product to which the registration relates, taking account of scientific and technical progress[3].

As soon as is reasonably practicable after becoming aware of the need to do so, the holder must apply to vary the traditional herbal registration to make any changes to those methods that are required to ensure they are generally accepted scientific methods[4].

1   As to the meaning of 'traditional herbal registration' see PARA 141 note 5.
2   As to the meaning of 'manufacture' see PARA 141 note 7.

3   Human Medicines Regulations 2012, SI 2012/1916, reg 143(1).
4   Human Medicines Regulations 2012, SI 2012/1916, reg 143(2).

223.   Following new herbal monograph.   Where a new herbal monograph[1] is established the holder of a traditional herbal registration[2] for a product to which the monograph relates must as soon as is reasonably practicable consider whether to modify the registration dossier and notify any modification to the licensing authority[3].

1   Ie of the kind referred to in Council Directive (EC) 2001/83 (OJ L311, 28.11.2001, p 67) on the Community code relating to medicinal products for human use, art 16h(3) (see PARA 19).
2   As to the meaning of 'traditional herbal registration' see PARA 141 note 5.
3   Human Medicines Regulations 2012, SI 2012/1916, reg 144. As to the meaning of 'licensing authority' see PARA 35 note 1.

224.   To provide information relating to safety etc.   The holder of a traditional herbal registration[1] must provide the licensing authority[2] with any new information[3] that might entail the variation of the registration[4].

The holder must, in particular, provide the licensing authority with the following information:

(1)   information about any prohibition or restriction imposed in relation to the product to which the registration relates by the competent authority of any country in which the product is on the market[5];

(2)   positive and negative results of clinical trials or other studies in all indications and populations, whether or not included in the traditional herbal registration[6];

(3)   data on the use of the product where such use is outside the terms of the traditional herbal registration[7]; and

(4)   any other information that the holder considers might influence the evaluation of the benefits and risks of the product[8].

The licensing authority may require the holder of a traditional herbal registration to provide the authority with information[9] that is specified by the licensing authority and demonstrates that the positive therapeutic effects of the product to which the registration relates outweigh the risks of the product to the health of patients or of the public[10].

If the information supplied under the above provisions entails the variation of the traditional herbal registration, the holder must make an application to the licensing authority to that effect as soon as is reasonably practicable after becoming aware of the information[11].

The licensing authority may require the holder of a traditional herbal registration to provide the authority with proof of the control methods employed by the manufacturer of the product to which the registration relates[12].

1   As to the meaning of 'traditional herbal registration' see PARA 141 note 5.
2   As to the meaning of 'licensing authority' see PARA 35 note 1.
3   Information within the Human Medicines Regulations 2012, SI 2012/1916, reg 145(1) or (2) must be provided as soon as is reasonably practicable after the holder becomes aware of it: reg 145(3).
4   Human Medicines Regulations 2012, SI 2012/1916, reg 145(1).
5   Human Medicines Regulations 2012, SI 2012/1916, reg 145(2)(a).
6   Human Medicines Regulations 2012, SI 2012/1916, reg 145(2)(b).
7   Human Medicines Regulations 2012, SI 2012/1916, reg 145(2)(c).
8   Human Medicines Regulations 2012, SI 2012/1916, reg 145(2)(d).

9   The information that may be required under the Human Medicines Regulations 2012, SI 2012/1916, reg 145(4) includes information arising from use of the product in a country which is not an EEA state, or outside the terms of the traditional herbal registration, including use in clinical trials: reg 145(5).

10 Human Medicines Regulations 2012, SI 2012/1916, reg 145(4). The holder of a traditional herbal registration must provide the licensing authority with information that it requires under reg 145(4) or (7) where the period within which the information must be provided is specified in a written notice given to the holder by the licensing authority, before the end of that period or otherwise, as soon as is reasonably practicable after receipt of the request: reg 145(8).

11 Human Medicines Regulations 2012, SI 2012/1916, reg 145(6).

12 Human Medicines Regulations 2012, SI 2012/1916, reg 145(7).

225.   In relation to product information. The holder of the traditional herbal registration[1] for a medicinal product[2] must ensure that the product information[3] relating to the product is kept up to date with current scientific knowledge[4].

1   As to the meaning of 'traditional herbal registration' see PARA 141 note 5.

2   As to the meaning of 'medicinal product' see PARA 25.

3   As to the meaning of 'product information' see PARA 174 note 3.

4   Human Medicines Regulations 2012, SI 2012/1916, reg 146(1). For this purpose 'current scientific knowledge' includes the conclusions of the assessment and recommendations made public by means of the European medicines web-portal established in accordance with Council Regulation (EC) 726/2004 (OJ L136, 30.4.2004, p 1) laying down Community procedures for the authorisation and supervision of medicinal products for human and veterinary use and establishing a European Medicines Agency, art 26 (see PARA 14): Human Medicines Regulations 2012, SI 2012/1916, reg 146(2).

226.   Record-keeping obligations. The holder of a traditional herbal registration[1] must keep any documents or information that will facilitate the withdrawal or recall from sale or supply of any product to which the registration relates[2].

1   As to the meaning of 'traditional herbal registration' see PARA 141 note 5.

2   Human Medicines Regulations 2012, SI 2012/1916, reg 147.

227.   Ensuring appropriate and continued supplies. The holder of a traditional herbal registration[1] must take all reasonable steps to ensure appropriate and continued supplies of the product to which the registration relates to pharmacies and persons authorised to supply the product so that the needs of patients in the United Kingdom are met[2].

1   As to the meaning of 'traditional herbal registration' see PARA 141 note 5.

2   Human Medicines Regulations 2012, SI 2012/1916, reg 148. It is a defence for a person charged with an offence consisting of a breach of reg 148 to prove that the person took all reasonable precautions and exercised all due diligence to avoid commission of that offence: reg 155(3). Where evidence is adduced that is sufficient to raise an issue with respect to the defence in reg 155(3), the court or jury must presume that the defence is satisfied unless the prosecution proves beyond reasonable doubt that it is not: reg 155(4).

F.   OFFENCES

228.   Urgent safety restrictions. The holder of a traditional herbal registration[1] is guilty of an offence[2] if he:

(1)   fails to inform the licensing authority[3] or the European Commission[4] that he has taken urgent safety restrictions on the holder's own initiative[5];

(2)   fails to implement an urgent safety restriction imposed on the holder[6] by the licensing authority[7]; or

(3)   fails to submit an application for variation of the traditional herbal
       registration to the licensing authority or the European Commission[8]
       before the end of a period of fifteen days beginning on the day after the
       taking under head (1) or, as the case may be, the imposition in head (2)
       of an urgent safety restriction[9].

1   As to the meaning of 'traditional herbal registration' see PARA 141 note 5.
2   A person guilty of an offence under Pt 7 (regs 125–155) is liable on summary conviction, to a
     fine not exceeding the statutory maximum or, on conviction on indictment, to a fine, to
     imprisonment for a term not exceeding two years or to both: reg 153. As to the statutory
     maximum see SENTENCING AND DISPOSITION OF OFFENDERS vol 92 (2010) PARA 140.
3   As to the meaning of 'licensing authority' see PARA 35 note 1.
4   Ie in accordance with Commission Regulation (EC) 1234/2008 (OJ L334, 12.12.2008. p 7–24)
     concerning the examination of variations to the terms of marketing authorisations for medicinal
     products for human use and veterinary medicinal products, art 22(1) (see PARA 19).
5   Human Medicines Regulations 2012, SI 2012/1916, reg 149(1)(a).
6   Ie under Commission Regulation (EC) 1234/2008 (OJ L334, 12.12.2008. p 7–24), art 22(2) (see
     PARA 19).
7   Human Medicines Regulations 2012, SI 2012/1916, reg 149(1)(b).
8   Ie in accordance with Commission Regulation (EC) 1234/2008 (OJ L334, 12.12.2008. p 7–24),
     art 22(3) (see PARA 19).
9   See the Human Medicines Regulations 2012, SI 2012/1916, reg 149(1)(c).

229.   Offences in connection with applications.   A person is guilty of an
offence[1] if in the course of an application for the grant, renewal or variation of a
traditional herbal registration[2] for a traditional herbal medicinal product he fails
to provide the licensing authority[3] with any information that is relevant to the
evaluation of the safety, quality or efficacy of the product or he provides to the
licensing authority any information that is relevant to the evaluation of the
safety, quality or efficacy of the product that is false or misleading in a material
particular[4].

1   A person guilty of an offence under the Human Medicines Regulations 2012, SI 2012/1916, Pt 7
     (regs 125–155) is liable on summary conviction, to a fine not exceeding the statutory maximum
     or, on conviction on indictment, to a fine, to imprisonment for a term not exceeding two years
     or to both: reg 153. As to the statutory maximum see SENTENCING AND DISPOSITION OF
     OFFENDERS vol 92 (2010) PARA 140. It is a defence for a person charged with an offence under
     reg 150 to prove that the person took all reasonable precautions and exercised all due diligence
     to avoid commission of that offence: reg 155(3). Where evidence is adduced that is sufficient to
     raise an issue with respect to the defence in reg 155(3), the court or jury must presume that the
     defence is satisfied unless the prosecution proves beyond reasonable doubt that it is not:
     reg 155(4).
2   As to the meaning of 'traditional herbal registration' see PARA 141 note 5.
3   As to the meaning of 'licensing authority' see PARA 35 note 1.
4   Human Medicines Regulations 2012, SI 2012/1916, reg 150.

230.   Provision of false or misleading information.   The holder of a traditional
herbal registration[1] is guilty of an offence[2] if the holder provides to the licensing
authority[3] any information that is relevant to the evaluation of the safety, quality
or efficacy of a traditional herbal medicinal product but that is false or
misleading in a material particular[4].

1   As to the meaning of 'traditional herbal registration' see PARA 141 note 5.
2   A person guilty of an offence under the Human Medicines Regulations 2012, SI 2012/1916, Pt 7
     (regs 125–155) is liable on summary conviction, to a fine not exceeding the statutory maximum
     or, on conviction on indictment, to a fine, to imprisonment for a term not exceeding two years
     or to both: reg 153. As to the statutory maximum see SENTENCING AND DISPOSITION OF
     OFFENDERS vol 92 (2010) PARA 140. It is a defence for a person charged with an offence under
     reg 151 to prove that the person took all reasonable precautions and exercised all due diligence

to avoid commission of that offence: reg 155(3). Where evidence is adduced that is sufficient to raise an issue with respect to the defence in reg 155(3), the court or jury must presume that the defence is satisfied unless the prosecution proves beyond reasonable doubt that it is not: reg 155(4).

3   As to the meaning of 'licensing authority' see PARA 35 note 1.

4   Human Medicines Regulations 2012, SI 2012/1916, reg 151(1). Regulation 151 is without prejudice to reg 150 (see PARA 229): reg 151(2).

231.   General offence and general defence.   A person is guilty of an offence[1] if that person commits a breach[2] of a provision of Part 7[3] of the Human Medicines Regulations 2012[4].

If the holder of a traditional herbal registration is charged with an offence under Part 7 in respect of anything that has been manufactured or assembled[5] to the holder's order by another person and has been so manufactured or assembled as not to comply with the terms of the authorisation, it is a defence for the holder to prove that the holder communicated the terms of the registration to the other person and that the holder did not know, and could not by the exercise of reasonable care have known, that those terms had not been complied with[6].

1   A person guilty of an offence under the Human Medicines Regulations 2012, SI 2012/1916, Pt 7 (regs 125–155) is liable on summary conviction, to a fine not exceeding the statutory maximum or, on conviction on indictment, to a fine, to imprisonment for a term not exceeding two years or to both: reg 153. As to the statutory maximum see SENTENCING AND DISPOSITION OF OFFENDERS vol 92 (2010) PARA 140.

2   A breach of a provision in the Human Medicines Regulations 2012, SI 2012/1916, Pt 7 (regs 125–155) includes any failure by the holder of a traditional herbal registration to comply with any requirement or obligation in that Part, contravention by any person of any prohibition in Pt 7 or failure to comply with any requirement imposed on a person by the licensing authority pursuant to that Part: see reg 152(2). This is without prejudice to any offence established by any other provision in Pt 7: reg 152(3). As to the meaning of 'traditional herbal registration' see PARA 141 note 5. As to the meaning of 'licensing authority' see PARA 35 note 1. As to the meaning of 'contravene' see PARA 41 note 8.

3   Ie the Human Medicines Regulations 2012, SI 2012/1916, Pt 7 (regs 125–155).

4   Human Medicines Regulations 2012, SI 2012/1916, reg 152(1).

5   As to the meanings of 'assemble' and 'manufacture' see PARA 141 notes 7, 8.

6   See the Human Medicines Regulations 2012, SI 2012/1916, reg 155(1), (2).

(vi)   Article 126a Authorisation

232.   Granting of an Article 126a authorisation.   The licensing authority[1] may grant an Article 126a authorisation[2] for a medicinal product[3] if the following conditions are met[4].

Condition A is that no United Kingdom marketing authorisation, certificate of registration or traditional herbal registration[5] is in force for the product[6].

Condition B is that no application is pending in the United Kingdom for a marketing authorisation, certificate of registration or traditional herbal registration for the product[7].

Condition C is that the licensing authority considers that the placing of the product on the market in the United Kingdom is justified for public health reasons[8].

Condition D is that the product is imported from another member state that has[9] authorised the placing on the market of the product in that member state[10].

Condition E is that the person to whom the authorisation is granted is established in the European Union[11].

Before granting an Article 126a authorisation, the licensing authority must notify the authorisation holder in the member state mentioned in Condition D of the proposal to grant the Article 126a authorisation and it may request the competent authority in that member state to provide[12] a copy of the assessment report for that product[13] and the authorisation in force for that product[14].

An Article 126a authorisation remains in force for the period specified in it unless revoked before the end of that period which may be specified by reference to the occurrence or non-occurrence of a particular event or events[15].

1   As to the meaning of 'licensing authority' see PARA 35 note 1.
2   As to the meaning of 'Article 126a authorisation' see PARA 141 note 6.
3   As to the meaning of 'medicinal product' see PARA 25.
4   Human Medicines Regulations 2012, SI 2012/1916, reg 156(1). The following provisions that apply to marketing authorisations also apply to an Article 126a authorisation as they apply to a marketing authorisation: regs 62 (classification of marketing authorisation: see PARA 163), 63 (frequency of periodic safety update reports: see PARA 253), 68 (revocation etc of marketing authorisation: see PARA 167) (and Sch 11 far as it relates to reg 68), 69 (suspension of use etc of medicinal product: see PARA 168), 71 (withdrawal of medicinal products from the market: see PARA 169), 72 (sale etc of suspended medicinal product: see PARA 170), 80 (urgent safety restrictions: see PARA 178) and regs 98 (general offence: see PARA 186), 99 (penalties) and 101(1) and (2) (defences), so far as they relate to regs 62, 71, 72: see reg 158.
5   As to the meanings of 'UK marketing authorisation', 'certificate of registration' and 'traditional herbal registration' see PARA 141 notes 3–5.
6   Human Medicines Regulations 2012, SI 2012/1916, reg 156(2).
7   Human Medicines Regulations 2012, SI 2012/1916, reg 156(3).
8   Human Medicines Regulations 2012, SI 2012/1916, reg 156(4).
9   Ie in accordance with Council Directive (EC) 2001/83 (OJ L311, 28.11.2001, p 67), on the Community code relating to medicinal products for human use.
10   Human Medicines Regulations 2012, SI 2012/1916, reg 156(5).
11   Human Medicines Regulations 2012, SI 2012/1916, reg 156(6).
12   Ie in accordance with Council Directive (EC) 2001/83 (OJ L311, 28.11.20, p 67).
13   Ie as mentioned in Council Directive (EC) 2001/83 (OJ L311, 28.11.2001, p 67), art 21(4).
14   See the Human Medicines Regulations 2012, SI 2012/1916, reg 156(7), (8).
15   Human Medicines Regulations 2012, SI 2012/1916, reg 156(9), (10).

233. Requests from other member states. Where the licensing authority[1] is requested by the competent authority of another member state to provide[2] a copy of the assessment report for a medicinal product[3] and the marketing authorisation[4] in force for that product, the licensing authority must supply those documents to the competent authority before the end of the period of thirty days beginning on the day after the request is received[5].

1   As to the meaning of 'licensing authority' see PARA 35 note 1.
2   Ie to provide in accordance with Council Directive (EC) 2001/83 (OJ L311, 28.11.2001, p 67) on the Community code relating to medicinal products for human use, art 126a(3)(b) (see PARA 10).
3   Ie the assessment report mentioned in the Human Medicines Regulations 2012, SI 2012/1916, reg 64(5) (see PARA 164). As to the meaning of 'medicinal product' see PARA 25.
4   As to the meaning of 'marketing authorisation' see PARA 141 note 3.
5   See the Human Medicines Regulations 2012, SI 2012/1916, reg 157.

(6) QUALITY AND STANDARDS; COMPENDIA

(i) Quality and Compliance with Standards

234. Adulteration of medicinal products. No one may add any substance[1] to, or abstract[2] any substance from, a medicinal product[3] so as to affect injuriously[4] the composition of the product, with intent that the product is to be sold or supplied in that state[5], or sell or supply, or offer or expose for sale or supply, or have in his possession for the purpose of sale or supply, any medicinal product whose composition has been injuriously affected by the addition or abstraction of any substance[6].

Anyone who contravenes[7] this provision is guilty of an offence[8].

1 As to the meaning of 'substance' see PARA 25 note 2.
2 As to the meaning of 'abstract' see *Penrice v Brander* 1921 JC 63; *Bridges v Griffin* [1925] 2 KB 233; *Dearden v Whiteley* (1916) 85 LJKB 1420, DC.
3 As to the meaning of 'medicinal product' see PARA 25.
4 This phrase is not defined for the purposes of the Medicines Act 1968. It would seem that, since it is the composition of the product which is, or is not, injuriously affected, the likelihood of actual injury to the eventual consumer is irrelevant. However, it is not clear how the ingredients, proportions, degrees of strength, quality and purity of a medicinal product can themselves be injured. In relation to the phrase 'injuriously affected by the execution of the works' in the Lands Clauses Consolidation Act 1845, Bramwell B explained the meaning as follows: 'The word 'injuriously' does not mean 'wrongfully' affected ... It means hurtfully or 'damnously' affected. As when we say of a man that he fell and injured his leg. We do not mean that his leg was wronged, but that it was hurt. We mean he fell, and his leg was injuriously, that is to say, hurtfully affected': *McCarthy v Metropolitan Board of Works* (1872) LR 8 CP 191 at 208–209, Ex Ch. Cf, however, *Roberts v Gwyrfai District Council* [1899] 1 Ch 583, where Kekewich J held that the Lands Clauses Consolidation Act 1845 decisions on the meaning of the phrase were irrelevant in a great measure to the construction of a similar phrase in the Public Health Act 1875 s 332 (repealed), referring to injuriously affecting any reservoir, canal, river or stream; affd [1899] 2 Ch 608, CA. The Food and Drugs Act 1955 s 1(2) (repealed), which contained provision similar to that in the Medicines Act 1968 s 63, referred to affecting injuriously the quality, constitution or potency of the drug. See also *Re Clarendon Development Ltd* (1965) 50 DLR (2d) 521, Nova Scotia SC (a Canadian planning decision).
5 Medicines Act 1968 s 63(a).
6 Medicines Act 1968 s 63(b). A person charged with contravening s 63(b) may in certain circumstances raise the defence that he purchased the article to which the charge relates under a warranty as to its quality: see s 122; and PARA 373. Certain presumptions apply to such an offence: see PARA 377.
7 As to the meaning of 'contravene' see PARA 41 note 8 (definition applied by the Medicines Act 1968 s 132(1) (substituted by SI 2012/1916)).
8 Medicines Act 1968 s 67(2) (amended by SI 2012/1916). Such a person is liable on summary conviction to a fine not exceeding the prescribed sum (Medicines Act 1968 s 67(4)(a) (amended by virtue of the Magistrates' Courts Act 1980 s 32(2) and SI 2012/1916), or on conviction on indictment to a fine or to imprisonment for a term not exceeding two years or to both (Medicines Act 1968 s 67(4)(b)). As to the prescribed sum see SENTENCING AND DISPOSITION OF OFFENDERS vol 92 (2010) PARA 141.

235. Protection of purchasers of medicinal products. No one may, to the prejudice of the purchaser[1], sell any medicinal product[2] which is not of the nature or quality demanded[3] by the purchaser[4]. Where a medicinal product is sold or supplied in pursuance of a prescription given by an appropriate practitioner[5], no person may sell or supply, to the prejudice of the purchaser or the person for whom the product was prescribed by the practitioner, any medicinal product which is not of the nature or quality specified in the prescription[6].

These provisions must not be taken to be contravened[7] by reason only that: (1) a medicinal product contains some extraneous matter, if it is proved that the presence of the matter was an inevitable consequence of the process of manufacture[8] of the product[9]; or (2) a substance[10] has been added to, or abstracted[11] from, the medicinal product, if it is proved that: (a) the addition or abstraction was not carried out fraudulently, and did not injuriously affect[12] the composition of the product[13]; and (b) the product was sold having attached to it, or to a container or package[14] in which it was sold, a conspicuous notice of adequate size and legibly printed specifying the substance added or abstracted[15].

Anyone who contravenes these provisions is guilty of an offence[16].

1   For the purposes of the Medicines Act 1968 s 64, the sale of a medicinal product is not to be taken to be otherwise than to the prejudice of the purchaser by reason only that he buys it for the purpose of analysis or examination: s 64(2). As to the meaning of 'to the prejudice of the purchaser' see the Food Safety Act 1990 s 14; and FOOD vol 18(2) (Reissue) PARAS 360–362. It seems that 'prejudice' is wider than 'injury' or 'damage', and that it is not necessary to prove actual harm done to the purchaser: see *Hoyle v Hitchman* (1879) 4 QBD 233, DC.
2   As to the meaning of 'medicinal product' see PARA 25 (definition applied by the Medicines Act 1968 s 132(1) (substituted by SI 2012/1916)).
3   As to the meaning given to this expression under the food and drugs legislation (from which it is derived) see the Food Safety Act 1990 s 14; and FOOD vol 18(2) (Reissue) PARAS 360–362.
4   Medicines Act 1968 s 64(1). By analogy with cases under the similar provisions in the food and drugs legislation, it would seem that, whereas a deficiency either in nature or in quality is sufficient, an information alleging the sale of an article 'which was not of the nature or not of the quality' demanded would be bad for duplicity: see *Bastin v Davies* [1950] 2 KB 579, [1950] 1 All ER 1095, DC; and cf *Moore v Ray* [1951] 1 KB 98, [1950] 2 All ER 561, DC. See FOOD vol 18(2) (Reissue) PARA 360. A person charged with contravening the Medicines Act 1968 s 64 may in certain circumstances raise the defence that he purchased the article to which the charge relates under a warranty as to its quality: see s 122; and PARA 373.
5   As to the meaning of 'appropriate practitioner' see PARA 271.
6   Medicines Act 1968 s 64(1), (5) (s 64(5) amended by SI 2012/1916). The provisions of the Medicines Act 1968 s 64(1)–(4) apply to samples taken by a sampling officer in the exercise of his powers under s 112 (see PARA 356) as if the taking of the sample were a sale to him: s 112(9), Sch 3 para 29.
7   As to the meaning of 'contravene' see PARA 41 note 8 (definition applied by the Medicines Act 1968 s 132(1) (substituted by SI 2012/1916)).
8   As to the meaning of 'manufacture' see PARA 141 note 7.
9   Medicines Act 1968 s 64(3). See also note 6.
10 As to the meaning of 'substance' see PARA 25 note 2.
11 As to the meaning of 'abstract' see PARA 234 note 2.
12 See PARA 234 note 4.
13 Medicines Act 1968 s 64(4)(a).
14 As to the meaning of 'package' see PARA 51 note 48.
15 Medicines Act 1968 s 64(4)(b). See also note 6. Cf the Food Safety Act 1990 s 14; and FOOD vol 18(2) (Reissue) PARA 360.
16 Medicines Act 1968 s 67(2) (amended by SI 2012/1916). Such a person is liable on summary conviction to a fine not exceeding the prescribed sum (Medicine Act 1968 s 67(4)(a) (amended by virtue of the Magistrates' Courts Act 1980 s 32(2) and SI 2012/1916), or on conviction on indictment to a fine or to imprisonment for a term not exceeding two years or to both (Medicines Act 1968 s 67(4)(b)). As to the prescribed sum see SENTENCING AND DISPOSITION OF OFFENDERS vol 92 (2010) PARA 141.

236.   Compliance with standards specified in certain publications. A person may not sell a medicinal product[1] that has been demanded by the purchaser by, or by express reference to, a particular name[2] if the name is a name at the head of the relevant monograph[3] and the product does not comply with the standard specified in that monograph[4].

A person may not sell or supply a medicinal product in pursuance of a prescription given by a doctor or dentist[5] in which the product required is described by, or by express reference to, a particular name if the name is a name at the head of the relevant monograph and the product does not comply with the standard specified in that monograph[6].

A person may not sell or supply a medicinal product that has been offered or exposed for sale by, or by express reference to, a particular name if the name is a name at the head of the relevant monograph and the product does not comply with the standard specified in that monograph[7].

Breach of the above provisions[8] is an offence[9].

1   As to the meaning of 'medicinal product' see PARA 25.

2   If the particular name referred to in the Human Medicines Regulations 2012, SI 2012/1916, reg 251(1), (2) or (3) is that of an active ingredient of the product, the product does not comply with the standard specified in the relevant monograph if, in so far as it consists of that ingredient, it does not comply with that standard: reg 252(4).

3   Where, together with the particular name specified as described in the Human Medicines Regulations 2012, SI 2012/1916, reg 251(1), (2) or (3) there was specified a particular edition of a particular publication, 'the relevant monograph' means the monograph (if any) headed by the name in that edition or, if there is no such monograph, the appropriate current monograph (if any) headed by that name: reg 252(1). Where, together with the particular name specified as described in reg 251(1), (2) or (3), there was specified a particular publication, but not an edition of that publication, 'the relevant monograph' means the monograph (if any) headed by the name in the current edition or, if there is no such monograph, the appropriate current monograph (if any) headed by that name or, if there is no such monograph of either kind, the monograph headed by that name in the latest edition of the specified publication that contained a monograph headed by that name: reg 252(2). Where no publication was specified with the particular name specified as described in reg 251(1), (2) or (3), 'the relevant monograph' means the appropriate current monograph (if any): reg 252(3). For these purposes 'publication means the British Pharmacopoeia or a compendium published under Pt 15 (British Pharmacopoeia): reg 252(4). For these purposes 'current' means current at the time when the medicinal product is demanded, described in a prescription or offered or exposed for sale (as the case may be) (reg 252(5)) and 'the appropriate current monograph', in relation to a particular name, means the monograph (if any) headed by that name in the current edition of the British Pharmacopoeia or, if there is no such monograph, the monograph (if any) headed by that name in the current edition of a compendium published under Pt 15 (British Pharmacopoeia) (reg 252(6)). For the purposes of regs 251, 252, any monograph in an edition of a publication must be construed in accordance with any general monograph or notice, or any appendix, note or other explanatory material, that is contained in that edition and applies to that monograph: reg 252(7).

4   Human Medicines Regulations 2012, SI 2012/1916, reg 251(1).

5   As to the meanings of 'doctor' and 'dentist' see PARA 48 note 6.

6   Human Medicines Regulations 2012, SI 2012/1916, reg 251(2).

7   Human Medicines Regulations 2012, SI 2012/1916, reg 251(3).

8   Ie breach of the Human Medicines Regulations 2012, SI 2012/1916, reg 251.

9   See the Human Medicines Regulations 2012, SI 2012/1916: reg 255(1)(e); and PARA 379.

(ii) The British Pharmacopoeia and other Compendia

237.   The British Pharmacopoeia and other publications.   The British Pharmacopoeia Commission[1] ('the BPC') must, at such intervals as it thinks appropriate, prepare or cause to be prepared[2] editions of the British Pharmacopoeia, containing such relevant information relating to the following substances[3], combinations of substances and articles as the BPC thinks appropriate[4].

The substances, combinations of substances, and articles are:

(1)   substances, combinations of substances and articles (whether medicinal products[5] or not) which are or may be used in the practice of medicine or surgery (other than veterinary medicine or veterinary surgery), dentistry or midwifery[6]; and

(2)   substances, combinations of substances and articles used in the manufacture of anything falling within head (1) above[7].

The BPC may also, at such intervals as it thinks appropriate, prepare or cause to be prepared:

(a)   a compendium (other than the British Pharmacopoeia) containing such relevant information[8] relating to substances, combinations of substances and articles within heads (1) and (2) above as it thinks appropriate[9]; and

(b)   a compendium containing such relevant information as the BPC thinks appropriate in relation to: (i) substances, combinations of substances and articles (whether veterinary medicinal products or not) which are or may be used in the practice of veterinary medicine or veterinary surgery; and (ii) substances, combinations of substances and articles used in the manufacture of anything falling within head (i)[10].

The ministers[11] must arrange for the publication[12] of anything prepared or caused to be prepared by the BPC under this provision[13].

1   As to the British Pharmacopoeia Commission see PARA 32.
2   For the purposes of the Human Medicines Regulations 2012, SI 2012/1916, Pt 15 (regs 317–321) a reference to preparing a thing or causing it to be prepared includes amending it, or causing it to be amended: reg 317(5)(a).
3   As to the meaning of 'substance' see PARA 25 note 2.
4   Human Medicines Regulations 2012, SI 2012/1916, reg 317(1).
5   As to the meaning of 'medicinal product' see PARA 25.
6   Human Medicines Regulations 2012, SI 2012/1916, reg 317(2)(a).
7   Human Medicines Regulations 2012, SI 2012/1916, reg 317(2)(b).
8   As to the meaning of 'relevant information' see PARA 239 note 4.
9   Human Medicines Regulations 2012, SI 2012/1916, reg 317(3)(a).
10 Human Medicines Regulations 2012, SI 2012/1916, reg 317(3)(b).
11 As to the meaning of 'the ministers' see the Human Medicines Regulations 2012, SI 2012/1916, reg 6(6)–(8); and PARA 35: reg 8(1).
12 For the purposes of the Human Medicines Regulations 2012, SI 2012/1916, Pt 15 (regs 317–321) a reference to publication includes publication by electronic means: reg 317(5)(b). Anything published in accordance with a provision of Pt 15 (other than reg 319 (see PARA 239)) must specify the date on which it is to take effect: reg 320(1). The ministers must give notice of this date by notices published in the London, Edinburgh and Belfast Gazettes not less than 21 days before that date: reg 320(2).
13 Human Medicines Regulations 2012, SI 2012/1916, reg 317(4).

238.   Lists of names of substances and articles. The British Pharmacopoeia Commission[1] ('the BPC') must, at such intervals as it thinks appropriate, prepare or cause to be prepared[2] a list of names which appear to it to be suitable to be used as the names of the specified substances[3], combinations of substances or articles and to be placed at the head of monographs relating to those substances, combinations of substances or articles in any edition of the British Pharmacopoeia or edition of a compendium[4].

Where a list has been so prepared the ministers must cause it to be published[5].

1   As to the British Pharmacopoeia Commission see PARA 32.
2   As to references to preparing a thing or causing it to be prepared see PARA 237 note 2.
3   Ie the substances and articles to which the Human Medicines Regulations 2012, SI 2012/1916, reg 317(2) or (3)(b) apply (see PARA 237). As to the meaning of 'substances' see PARA 25 note 2.
4   Human Medicines Regulations 2012, SI 2012/1916, reg 318(1). As to the preparation of the British Pharmacopoeia and other compendia see PARA 237.
5   Human Medicines Regulations 2012, SI 2012/1916, reg 318(2). As to the meaning of 'the ministers' see reg 6(6)–(8); and PARA 35: reg 8(1). As to the publication of this list see PARA 237 note 12.

239.   Publication of other documents containing relevant information relating to substances etc. The British Pharmacopoeia Commission[1] ('the BPC') must, at such intervals as it thinks appropriate, prepare or cause to be prepared[2] documents, other than the British Pharmacopoeia, other compendia and the list of names and substances and articles for those publications[3], containing such relevant information[4] relating to specified substances, combinations of substances or articles[5] as the BPC thinks appropriate[6].

Where a document has been so prepared the ministers may cause it to be published[7].

1   As to the British Pharmacopoeia Commission see PARA 32.

2 As to references to preparing a thing or causing it to be prepared see PARA 237 note 2.
3 Ie in addition to those falling within the Human Medicines Regulations 2012, SI 2012/1916, reg 317 (see PARA 237) or reg 318 (see PARA 238).
4 For the purposes of the Human Medicines Regulations 2012, SI 2012/1916, Pt 15 (regs 317–321) 'relevant information', in relation to a substance, combination of substances or article, means information consisting of descriptions of, standards for, or notes or other matter relating to the substance, combination of substances or article: reg 317(5)(c).
5 Ie substances, combinations of substances or articles falling within the Human Medicines Regulations 2012, SI 2012/1916, reg 317(2) or (3)(b) (see PARA 237).
6 Human Medicines Regulations 2012, SI 2012/1916, reg 319(1).
7 Human Medicines Regulations 2012, SI 2012/1916, reg 319(2). As to the meaning of 'the ministers' see reg 6(6)–(8); and PARA 35: reg 8(1).

240. Presumption of current edition. Where an authorisation[1] refers to a specified publication[2], but not to a particular edition of it, then, for the purpose of determining whether anything done is done in accordance with the authorisation, the reference is to be construed, unless the authorisation otherwise expressly provides, as a reference to the edition of the specified publication in force[3] at that time[4].

Where in any proceedings an enforcement authority[5] produces a copy of a publication[6], it is presumed that the copy is a true copy of the edition of that publication that was in force at the time when the events that are the subject of the proceedings took place, unless evidence is adduced to the contrary[7].

1 For these purposes 'authorisation' means a manufacturer's licence, (see PARA 45), a wholesale dealer's licence (see PARA 77), a marketing authorisation, an Article 126a authorisation (see PARA 141), a certificate of registration (see PARA 141) or a traditional herbal registration (see PARA 141): Human Medicines Regulations 2012, SI 2012/1916, reg 321(5).
2 'Specified publication' means the European Pharmacopoeia, the British Pharmacopoeia, the Cumulative List of Recommended International Non-proprietary Names, any compendium prepared and published under the Human Medicines Regulations 2012, SI 2012/1916, reg 317 (see PARA 237), and any list of names prepared and published under reg 318 (see PARA 238): reg 321(1).
3 This reference to the edition of a specified publication in force at a particular time is a reference to the edition of that publication in force, under whatever title, at that time: Human Medicines Regulations 2012, SI 2012/1916, reg 321(4).
4 See the Human Medicines Regulations 2012, SI 2012/1916, reg 321(2), (3).
5 As to the meaning of 'enforcement authority' see PARA 142 note 13.
6 Ie anything published in accordance with a provision of the Human Medicines Regulations 2012, SI 2012/1916, Pt 15 (regs 317–321): see reg 320(1).
7 Human Medicines Regulations 2012, SI 2012/1916, reg 320(3).

(7) PHARMACOVIGILANCE

(i) Application

241. Application of pharmacovigilance. Provisions in the Human Medicines Regulations 2012 that relate to pharmacovigilance[1] apply in relation to medicinal products[2] that are the subject of a UK marketing authorisation, a traditional herbal registration or an Article 126a authorisation[3]. Some provisions[4] apply in relation to medicinal products that are the subject of an EU marketing authorisation[5].

1 Ie the Human Medicines Regulations 2012, SI 2012/1916, regs 177–212 and Sch 33 (except to the extent set out in Sch 33 para 4(b)).
2 As to the meaning of 'medicinal product' see PARA 25.
3 Human Medicines Regulations 2012, SI 2012/1916, reg 177(1). For transitional arrangements see reg 212, Sch 33. As to the meanings of 'UK marketing authorisation', 'traditional herbal registration' and 'Article 126a authorisation' see PARA 141 notes 3, 5, 6.

4 Ie the Human Medicines Regulations 2012, SI 2012/1916, reg 206 (see PARA 268), reg 210 (see PARA 269) and Sch 33 paras 2–4.
5 Human Medicines Regulations 2012, SI 2012/1916, reg 177(4). Regulation 210 and Sch 33 paras 2–4 do not apply to the medicinal products specified in reg 177(1): see reg 177(4).

(ii) Obligations on Licensing Authority in relation to Pharmacovigilance

242. General obligations. The licensing authority[1] must:

(1) take all appropriate measures to encourage the reporting to it of suspected adverse reactions[2];

(2) facilitate reporting through the provision of alternative reporting formats in addition to web-based formats[3];

(3) take all appropriate measures to obtain accurate and verifiable data for the scientific evaluation of suspected adverse reaction reports[4];

(4) ensure that the public is given important information on pharmacovigilance concerns relating to the use of a medicinal product[5] in a timely manner, through publication on the UK web-portal[6], and through other means of publicly available information as necessary[7]; and

(5) ensure that all appropriate measures are taken to identify any biological medicinal product[8] (including name and batch number) prescribed, dispensed or sold in the United Kingdom which is the subject of a suspected adverse reaction report through the methods for collecting data and, where necessary, the follow up of suspected adverse reaction reports[9].

1 As to the meaning of 'licensing authority' see PARA 35 note 1.
2 Human Medicines Regulations 2012, SI 2012/1916, reg 178(a). As to the meaning of 'adverse reaction' see PARA 70 note 6. As to the meaning of 'suspected' see PARA 70 note 7.
3 Human Medicines Regulations 2012, SI 2012/1916, reg 178(b).
4 Human Medicines Regulations 2012, SI 2012/1916, reg 178(c).
5 As to the meaning of 'medicinal product' see PARA 25.
6 As to the meaning of 'UK web-portal' see the Human Medicines Regulations 2012, SI 2012/1916, reg 203 (obligations on licensing authority in relation to national medicines web-portal: see PARA 265): reg 177(5).
7 Human Medicines Regulations 2012, SI 2012/1916, reg 178(d).
8 As to the meaning of 'biological medicinal product' see Council Directive (EC) 2001/83 (OJ L311, 28.11.2001, p 67) on the Community code relating to medicinal products for human use, Annex I, para 3.2.1.1(b): Human Medicines Regulations 2012, SI 2012/1916, reg 8(1).
9 Human Medicines Regulations 2012, SI 2012/1916, reg 178(e).

243. Obligation on licensing authority to operate pharmacovigilance system. The licensing authority[1] must operate a pharmacovigilance system[2].

The pharmacovigilance system must in particular enable the collection of information on the risks that medicinal products present to patients' health or public health, including information on adverse reactions[3] in humans arising from use of a medicinal product (irrespective of whether the use was within the terms of an authorisation or registration) and adverse reactions associated with occupational exposure[4].

The licensing authority must on an on-going basis evaluate scientifically the information collected under the pharmacovigilance system, consider options for minimising and preventing risks presented by medicinal products and take appropriate regulatory action, if any[5].

1 As to the meaning of 'licensing authority' see PARA 35 note 1.

2   Human Medicines Regulations 2012, SI 2012/1916, reg 179(1). 'Pharmacovigilance system' means a system used by the holder of a marketing authorisation, traditional herbal registration or article 126a authorisation, or by the licensing authority, to fulfil the tasks and responsibilities set out in Pt 11 (regs 177–212) and designed to monitor the safety of authorised or registered medicinal products and detect any change to their risk-benefit balance: reg 8(1). As to the meanings of 'marketing authorisation', 'traditional herbal registration' and 'article 126a authorisation' see PARA 141 notes 3, 5, 6. As to the meaning of 'medicinal product' see PARA 25.
3   As to the meaning of 'adverse reaction' see PARA 70 note 6.
4   Human Medicines Regulations 2012, SI 2012/1916, reg 179(2).
5   Human Medicines Regulations 2012, SI 2012/1916, reg 179(3).

244.   Obligation on licensing authority to audit pharmacovigilance system. The licensing authority[1] must perform a regular audit of its pharmacovigilance system[2] and report the results of that audit to the European Commission[3].

1   As to the meaning of 'licensing authority' see PARA 35 note 1.
2   As to the meaning of 'pharmacovigilance system' see PARA 243 note 2.
3   Human Medicines Regulations 2012, SI 2012/1916, reg 180(1). The results of the audit must be reported to the European Commission on the first occasion no later than 21st September 2013 and every two years after the first occasion: reg 180(2).

245.   Delegation of obligations. The licensing authority[1] may delegate any of its obligations relating to pharmacovigilance[2] to another EEA state where the following conditions are met[3]. The conditions are that the EEA state to whom the obligations are to be delegated has given its written agreement to the delegation and that it is not performing delegated obligations[4] on behalf of another EEA state[5].

Where the licensing authority has delegated any of its obligations[6] it must inform the European Commission, the European Medicines Agency[7] and all other EEA states in writing of the delegation as soon as is reasonably practicable and make the delegation public as soon as is reasonably practicable[8].

1   As to the meaning of 'licensing authority' see PARA 35 note 1.
2   Ie its obligations under the Human Medicines Regulations 2012, SI 2012/1916, Pt 11 (regs 177–212).
3   Human Medicines Regulations 2012, SI 2012/1916, reg 181(1). The licensing authority may agree to carry out any of the obligations of another EEA state under Council Directive (EC) 2001/83 (OJ L311, 28.11.2001, p 67) on the Community code relating to medicinal products for human use, Title IX on a delegated basis, but may carry out obligations under that Title only for one EEA state at any time: Human Medicines Regulations 2012, SI 2012/1916, reg 181(4).
4   Ie obligations delegated under the Human Medicines Regulations 2012, SI 2012/1916, Pt 11.
5   Human Medicines Regulations 2012, SI 2012/1916, reg 181(2).
6   Ie under the Human Medicines Regulations 2012, SI 2012/1916, reg 181(1).
7   As to the European Medicines Agency see PARA 14.
8   Human Medicines Regulations 2012, SI 2012/1916, reg 181(3).

(iii)   Obligations on Holders in relation to Pharmacovigilance

246.   To operate pharmacovigilance system. The holder[1] must operate a pharmacovigilance system[2] and, as part of its pharmacovigilance system, the holder must:

(1)   have permanently and continuously at its disposal an appropriately qualified person responsible for pharmacovigilance who resides and operates in the EU and is responsible for the establishment and maintenance of the pharmacovigilance system[3];

(2)   maintain and make available on the request of the licensing authority[4] a pharmacovigilance system master file[5];

(3)   operate a risk management system[6] for the product in accordance with the risk management plan[7] (if any) for the product[8];

(4)   monitor the outcome of the risk minimisation measures which are contained in the risk management plan (if any) for the product or which are laid down as conditions of the authorisation of the product[9]; and

(5)   update the risk management system for the product and monitor pharmacovigilance data to determine whether in relation to the product there are new risks, the risks have changed or if there are changes to the risk-benefit balance[10].

The holder must keep the licensing authority and the European Medicines Agency[11] informed of the name and contact details of the appropriately qualified person mentioned in head (1) above at all times[12].

The holder must use its pharmacovigilance system to:

(a)   evaluate scientifically all information relevant to the product[13];

(b)   consider options for minimising and preventing the risk presented by the use of the product[14]; and

(c)   take appropriate measures as soon as is reasonably practicable to investigate the potential risks of the product, communicate the risks and implement actions for minimising and preventing the risks, including updating the risk management system for the product[15].

1   References in the Human Medicines Regulations 2012, SI 2012/1916, regs 177–212 to a 'holder' are to the holder of a UK marketing authorisation, a traditional herbal registration or an Article 126a authorisation, and, in relation to such references, 'product' means the product to which the authorisation or registration relates: reg 177(2). As to the meanings of 'UK marketing authorisation', Article 126a authorisation', 'certificate of registration' and 'traditional herbal registration' see PARA 141 notes 3–6.

2   Human Medicines Regulations 2012, SI 2012/1916, reg 182(1). Reg 182 is subject to transitional provisions see Sch 33: reg 182(6), 212. As to the meaning of 'pharmacovigilance system' see PARA 243 note 2.

3   Human Medicines Regulations 2012, SI 2012/1916, reg 182(2)(a). 'Pharmacovigilance system master file' means a detailed description of the pharmacovigilance system used by the holder of a marketing authorisation, traditional herbal registration or Article 126a authorisation with respect to one or more authorised or registered medicinal products: reg 8(1). A similar definition applies to the European Parliament and Council Directive (EC) 2001/83 (OJ L311, 28.11.2001, p 67) on the Community code relating to medicinal products for human use: see art 1(28e) (added by European Parliament and Council Directive (EU) 2010/84 (OJ L343, 31.12.2010, p 74). As to the meaning of 'marketing authorisation' see PARA 141 note 3.

4   As to the meaning of 'licensing authority' see PARA 35 note 1.

5   Human Medicines Regulations 2012, SI 2012/1916, reg 182(2)(b). Where the licensing authority requests that the pharmacovigilance system master file is made available under reg 182(2)(b), the holder must submit a copy of the pharmacovigilance system master file to the licensing authority before the end of the period of 7 days beginning on the day after the day when the request was made: reg 182(5).

6   As to the meaning of 'risk management system' see PARA 74 note 6.

7   As to the meaning of 'risk management plan' see PARA 160 note 5.

8   Human Medicines Regulations 2012, SI 2012/1916, reg 182(2)(c). This is subject to reg 183 (see PARA 247).

9   Human Medicines Regulations 2012, SI 2012/1916, reg 182(2)(d). As to the conditions see regs 59–61; and PARAS 160–162.

10   Human Medicines Regulations 2012, SI 2012/1916, reg 182(2)(e).

11   As to the European Medicines Agency see PARA 14.

12   Human Medicines Regulations 2012, SI 2012/1916, reg 182(3).

13   Human Medicines Regulations 2012, SI 2012/1916, reg 182(4)(a).

14   Human Medicines Regulations 2012, SI 2012/1916, reg 182(4)(b).

15   Human Medicines Regulations 2012, SI 2012/1916, reg 182(4)(c).

247.   Exception to operate risk management system.   The holder[1] is not required to operate a risk management system[2] in relation to a medicinal product[3] which has an authorisation or registration[4] that was granted before 21 July 2012[5].

The licensing authority[6] may impose an obligation on the holder to operate a risk management system in relation to a medicinal product referred to above if there are concerns about new or changed risks affecting the risk-benefit balance of that product[7] and the following apply where such an obligation is imposed[8].

The licensing authority must without delay notify the holder in writing of the imposition of the obligation, the justification for the obligation, the timeframe for submission of the detailed description of the risk management system[9] and the opportunity to present written observations[10].

Where the licensing authority imposes an obligation[11] and the holder does not present written observations[12] or confirms the imposition of the obligation[13] the holder must submit to the licensing authority in writing a detailed description of the risk management system which it intends to introduce for the product in accordance with the timeframe set out in the notification[14] and comply with the obligation to operate a risk management system[15].

1   As to the meaning of 'holder' see PARA 246 note 1.
2   Ie under the Human Medicines Regulations 2012, SI 2012/1916, reg 182(2)(c) (see PARA 246). As to the meaning of 'risk management system' see PARA 74 note 6.
3   As to the meaning of 'medicinal product' see PARA 25.
4   References to an 'authorisation or registration' in the Human Medicines Regulations 2012, SI 2012/1916, Pt 11 and Sch 33 are references to a UK marketing authorisation, a traditional herbal registration or an Article 126a authorisation, and 'authorised or registered' is to be read accordingly: reg 177(3). As to the meanings of 'UK marketing authorisation', 'traditional herbal registration' and 'Article 126a authorisation' see PARA 141 notes 3, 5, 6.
5   Human Medicines Regulations 2012, SI 2012/1916, reg 183(1).
6   As to the meaning of 'licensing authority' see PARA 35 note 1.
7   Human Medicines Regulations 2012, SI 2012/1916, reg 183(2).
8   See the Human Medicines Regulations 2012, SI 2012/1916, reg 183(3).
9   Ie as required under the Human Medicines Regulations 2012, SI 2012/1916, reg 183(8)(a).
10 Human Medicines Regulations 2012, SI 2012/1916, reg 183(4). Where the holder so requests before the end of the period of thirty days beginning on the day after the receipt by the holder of the notice referred to in reg 183(4), the licensing authority must provide the holder with an opportunity to present written observations in response to the imposition of the obligation within such a time limit as the licensing authority may specify: reg 183(5). Where a holder presents written observations under reg 183(5), the licensing authority must withdraw or confirm the imposition of the obligation under reg 183(2), having regard to the written observations, as soon as is reasonably practicable: reg 183(6).
11 Ie under the Human Medicines Regulations 2012, SI 2012/1916, reg 183(2). Where the imposition relates to a product with a UK marketing authorisation, the licensing authority must vary the authorisation to include the measures to be taken as part of the risk management system as conditions of the authorisation as if they were conditions imposed under reg 59 (conditions of UK marketing authorisations: general: see PARA 160): reg 183(9).
12 Ie under the Human Medicines Regulations 2012, SI 2012/1916, reg 183(5). The word 'obligations' is used in the Queen's Printer copy. It is submitted that this is in error and should refer to 'observations'.
13 Ie under the Human Medicines Regulations 2012, SI 2012/1916, reg 183(2) pursuant to reg 183(6).
14 Ie under the Human Medicines Regulations 2012, SI 2012/1916, reg 183(4).
15 Human Medicines Regulations 2012, SI 2012/1916, reg 183(7), (8).

248.   Obligation on holder to audit pharmacovigilance system.   The holder[1] must:

(1)   perform a regular audit of its pharmacovigilance system[2];

(2)   place a note concerning the main findings of each audit on the pharmacovigilance system master file[3] on completion of each audit[4]; and

(3)   ensure that an appropriate corrective action plan is prepared and implemented as soon as is reasonably practicable after completion of each audit[5].

1   As to the meaning of 'holder' see PARA 246 note 1.
2   Human Medicines Regulations 2012, SI 2012/1916, reg 184(1)(a). As to the meaning of 'pharmacovigilance system' see PARA 243 note 2.
3   As to the meaning of 'pharmacovigilance system master file' see PARA 246 note 3.
4   Human Medicines Regulations 2012, SI 2012/1916, reg 184(1)(b). The holder may remove this note when all the measures in the corrective action plan under reg 184(1)(c) have been fully implemented: reg 184(2).
5   Human Medicines Regulations 2012, SI 2012/1916, reg 184(1)(c).

(iv) Reporting, Recording and Assessment of Pharmacovigilance Data

249.   Recording obligations.   The licensing authority[1] must record all suspected adverse reactions[2] to medicinal products[3] that occur in the United Kingdom and are reported to it by a patient or a patient's carer, a health care professional[4], a coroner or a procurator fiscal[5].

The holder[6] must record all suspected adverse reactions to the product occurring in the EEA or in third countries which are brought to its attention irrespective of whether the reaction is reported spontaneously by patients or health care professionals or whether the reaction occurred in the context of a post-authorisation study[7]. However, this does not apply where the suspected adverse reaction occurred in the context of a clinical trial[8].

The holder must not refuse to consider reports of suspected adverse reactions to the product received electronically or by any other appropriate means from patients or from health care professionals[9].

The holder must ensure that reports recorded are accessible (electronically or physically) at a single point within the EEA[10].

1   As to the meaning of 'licensing authority' see PARA 35 note 1.
2   As to the meaning of 'adverse reaction' see PARA 70 note 6. As to the meaning of 'suspected' see PARA 70 note 7.
3   As to the meaning of 'medicinal product' see PARA 25.
4   As to the meaning of 'health care professional' see PARA 36 note 8.
5   Human Medicines Regulations 2012, SI 2012/1916, reg 185.
6   As to the meaning of 'holder' see PARA 246 note 1.
7   Human Medicines Regulations 2012, SI 2012/1916, reg 187(1).
8   Human Medicines Regulations 2012, SI 2012/1916, reg 187(2). As to the meaning of 'clinical trial' see the Medicines for Human Use (Clinical Trials) Regulations 2004, SI 2004/1031, reg 2(1); and PARA 107: Human Medicines Regulations 2012, SI 2012/1916, reg 8(1).
9   Human Medicines Regulations 2012, SI 2012/1916, reg 187(3).
10 Human Medicines Regulations 2012, SI 2012/1916, reg 187(4).

250.   Reporting obligations of licensing authority.   The licensing authority[1] must:

(1)   when it receives a suspected adverse reaction[2] report from a patient or a patient's carer, a health care professional, a coroner or a procurator fiscal[3], follow up that report with that person as appropriate[4];

(2)   ensure that reports of suspected adverse reactions in the United Kingdom may be submitted to it, whether by the UK web-portal[5] or by other means[6];

(3)   collaborate with the European Medicines Agency[7] and the holders of authorisations or registrations[8] in the detection of duplicates of suspected adverse reaction reports[9];

(4)   submit reports of serious suspected adverse reactions that it has recorded[10] electronically to the Eudravigilance database[11] before the end of the period of 15 days beginning on the day following the day on which the report was received[12]; and

(5)   submit reports of non-serious suspected adverse reactions it has recorded[13] electronically to the Eudravigilance database before the end of the period of 90 days beginning on the day following the day on which the report was received[14].

In addition to the above requirements, where the licensing authority has received a report of a suspected adverse reaction arising from an error associated with the use of a medicinal product[15], it must ensure that the report is made available to any statutory body with functions in relation to patient safety within the United Kingdom[16].

1   As to the meaning of 'licensing authority' see PARA 35 note 1.
2   As to the meaning of 'adverse reaction' see PARA 70 note 6. As to the meaning of 'suspected' see PARA 70 note 7.
3   Ie from a person mentioned in the Human Medicines Regulations 2012, SI 2012/1916, reg 185(b) (see PARA 249). As to the meaning of 'health care professionals' see PARA 36 note 8.
4   Human Medicines Regulations 2012, SI 2012/1916, reg 186(1)(a). Regulation 186 is subject to transitional provisions see Sch 33 paras 5–8: regs 186(4), 212.
5   As to the meaning of 'UK web-portal' see the Human Medicines Regulations 2012, SI 2012/1916, reg 203 (obligations on licensing authority in relation to national medicines web-portal: see PARA 265): reg 177(5).
6   Human Medicines Regulations 2012, SI 2012/1916, reg 186(1)(b).
7   As to the European Medicines Agency see PARA 14.
8   As to the meaning of 'holder' see PARA 246 note 1. As to the meanings of 'authorisation' and 'registration' see PARA 247 note 4.
9   Human Medicines Regulations 2012, SI 2012/1916, reg 186(1)(c).
10   Ie under the Human Medicines Regulations 2012, SI 2012/1916, reg 185 (see PARA 249).
11   'Eudravigilance database' means the database and data-processing network set up and maintained by the European Medicines Agency under Council Regulation (EC) 726/2004 (OJ L136, 30.4.2004, p 1) laying down Community procedures for the authorisation and supervision of medicinal products for human and veterinary use and establishing a European Medicines Agency, art 24 (see PARA 14): Human Medicines Regulations 2012, SI 2012/1916, reg 177(5).
12   Human Medicines Regulations 2012, SI 2012/1916, reg 186(1)(d).
13   Ie it has recorded under the Human Medicines Regulations 2012, SI 2012/1916, reg 185 (see PARA 249).
14   Human Medicines Regulations 2012, SI 2012/1916, reg 186(1)(e).
15   As to the meaning of 'medicinal product' see PARA 25.
16   Human Medicines Regulations 2012, SI 2012/1916, reg 186(2), (3).

251.   Reporting obligations of holder. The holder[1] must in relation to the product[2]:

(1)   submit electronically to the Eudravigilance database[3] a report on all serious suspected adverse reactions[4] that occur in the EEA and third countries before the end of the period of 15 days beginning on the day following the day on which the holder gained knowledge of the reaction[5];

(2)   submit electronically to the Eudravigilance database a report on all non-serious suspected adverse reactions that occur in the EEA before the end of the period of 90 days beginning on the day following the day on which the holder gained knowledge of the reaction[6];

(3) establish procedures in order to obtain accurate and verifiable data for the scientific evaluation of suspected adverse reaction reports[7];

(4) collect follow-up information on reports submitted under heads (1) or (2) above and submit it electronically to the Eudravigilance database by way of an update to the original report within the specified time period[8]; and

(5) collaborate with the European Medicines Agency[9] and the competent authorities of the EEA states in the detection of duplicates of suspected adverse reaction reports[10].

The holder is not required to submit a report of a suspected adverse reaction to the product under heads (1) or (2) above, or to provide follow-up information under head (4) above, where the suspected adverse reaction relates to a medicinal product[11] which contains a monitored active substance[12] and the suspected adverse reaction is recorded in a monitored publication[13].

Where a medicinal product contains a monitored active substance, the holder must monitor medical literature, other than the monitored publications, for reports of suspected adverse reactions to the product and report suspected adverse reactions so identified in accordance with heads (1) to (5) above[14].

1 As to the meaning of 'holder' see PARA 246 note 1.
2 As to the meaning of 'product' see PARA 246 note 1.
3 As to the meaning of 'Eudravigilance database' see PARA 250 note 11.
4 As to the meaning of 'adverse reaction' see PARA 70 note 6. As to the meaning of 'suspected' see PARA 70 note 7.
5 Human Medicines Regulations 2012, SI 2012/1916, reg 188(1)(a).
6 Human Medicines Regulations 2012, SI 2012/1916, reg 188(1)(b).
7 Human Medicines Regulations 2012, SI 2012/1916, reg 188(1)(c).
8 Human Medicines Regulations 2012, SI 2012/1916, reg 188(1)(d). For the purposes of reg 188 'specified time period' means, in the case of serious adverse reactions, the period of 15 days beginning on the day following the day on which the follow up information became known to the holder and, in the case of non-serious adverse reactions, the period of 90 days beginning on the day following the day on which the follow up information became known to the holder: reg 188(5).
9 As to the European Medicines Agency see PARA 14.
10 Human Medicines Regulations 2012, SI 2012/1916, reg 188(1)(e).
11 As to the meaning of 'medicinal product' see PARA 25.
12 For these purposes 'monitored active substance' means an active substance on the list of active substances being monitored by the European Medicines Agency published under European Medicines Agency under Council Regulation (EC) 726/2004 (OJ L136, 30.4.2004, p 1) laying down Community procedures for the authorisation and supervision of medicinal products for human and veterinary use and establishing a European Medicines Agency, art 27 (see PARA 14): Human Medicines Regulations 2012, SI 2012/1916, reg 188(5).
13 Human Medicines Regulations 2012, SI 2012/1916, reg 188(2). For these purposes 'monitored publication' means a publication on the list of publications being monitored by the European Medicines Agency published under Council Regulation (EC) 726/2004 (OJ L136, 30.4.2004, p 1), art 27 (see PARA 14): Human Medicines Regulations 2012, SI 2012/1916, reg 188(5).
14 See the Human Medicines Regulations 2012, SI 2012/1916, reg 188(3), (4).

(v) Signal Detection

252. Obligations. The licensing authority[1] must in relation to each medicinal product[2]:

(1) monitor the data in the Eudravigilance database[3] to determine whether there are any relevant changes[4];

(2) assess updates to the risk management system[5] for the product[6];

(3) monitor the outcome of risk minimisation measures contained in the risk management plan[7], if any[8]; and

(4)   monitor the outcome of conditions imposed[9], if any[10].

The licensing authority must collaborate with the European Medicines Agency[11] in carrying out the above functions[12].

The licensing authority must inform the European Medicines Agency and the relevant competent authorities[13] without delay if it detects any relevant changes in relation to a medicinal product[14].

Likewise, the holder[15] must inform the European Medicines Agency and the licensing authority without delay if it detects any relevant changes[16] in relation to the product[17].

1   As to the meaning of 'licensing authority' see PARA 35 note 1.
2   As to the meaning of 'medicinal product' see PARA 25.
3   As to the meaning of 'Eudravigilance database' see PARA 250 note 11.
4   Human Medicines Regulations 2012, SI 2012/1916, reg 189(1)(a). For these purposes 'relevant changes' in relation to a medicinal product means new risks, risks that have changed or changes to the risk-benefit balance: reg 189(5).
5   As to the meaning of 'risk management system' see PARA 74 note 6.
6   Human Medicines Regulations 2012, SI 2012/1916, reg 189(1)(b). As to the meaning of 'product' see PARA 246 note 1.
7   As to the meaning of 'risk management plan' see PARA 160 note 5.
8   Human Medicines Regulations 2012, SI 2012/1916, reg 186(1)(c).
9   Ie conditions imposed under the Human Medicines Regulations 2012, SI 2012/1916, regs 59–61 (see PARAS 160–162).
10   Human Medicines Regulations 2012, SI 2012/1916, reg 186(1)(d).
11   As to the European Medicines Agency see PARA 14.
12   See the Human Medicines Regulations 2012, SI 2012/1916, reg 186(2).
13   Ie the European Medicines Agency and the relevant competent authorities: Human Medicines Regulations 2012, SI 2012/1916, reg 186(4). 'Relevant competent authorities' means the competent authority of each EEA state other than the United Kingdom which has granted in relation to a medicinal product an authorisation in accordance with Council Directive (EC) 2001/83 (OJ L311, 28.11.2001, p 67) on the Community code relating to medicinal products for human use, Title III, Chapter 1 (marketing authorisation: see PARA 6), an authorisation in accordance with Title III, Chapter 4 (mutual recognition and decentralised procedure: see PARA 7), a registration in accordance with Title III Chapter 2a (traditional use registration for herbal medicinal products: see PARA 19) or an authorisation in accordance with art 126a (see PARA 10): Human Medicines Regulations 2012, SI 2012/1916, reg 177(5).
14   Human Medicines Regulations 2012, SI 2012/1916, reg 186(3).
15   As to the meaning of 'holder' see PARA 246 note 1.
16   See note 4.
17   Human Medicines Regulations 2012, SI 2012/1916, reg 190(2). As to the meaning of 'product' see PARA 246 note 1.

(vi) Periodic Safety Update Records

253.   General requirement to submit periodic safety update reports.   The holder[1] must submit reports known as periodic safety update reports ('PSURs') in relation to the product to the European Medicines Agency[2] as follows[3].

Each PSUR must contain:

(1)   summaries of data relevant to the benefits and risks of the product[4], including results of all studies, with a consideration of their potential impact on the authorisation[5] for the product[6];

(2)   a scientific evaluation of the risk-benefit balance of the product[7]; and

(3)   all data relating to the volume of sales of the product and any data the holder has relating to the volume of prescriptions, including an estimate of the population exposed to the product[8].

Each PSUR must be submitted electronically to the European Medicines Agency[9].

However different provisions apply[10] where a medicinal product[11] is granted a UK marketing authorisation relating to generic medicinal products[12] or relating to products in well-established medicinal use[13] or a traditional herbal registration[14].

1 For these purposes 'the holder' means the holder of a UK marketing authorisation or an Article 126a authorisation: Human Medicines Regulations 2012, SI 2012/1916, reg 191(3). As to the meanings of 'UK marketing authorisation' and 'Article 126a authorisation' see PARA 141 notes 3, 6.
2 As to the European Medicines Agency see PARA 14.
3 See the Human Medicines Regulations 2012, SI 2012/1916, reg 191(1). Regulation 191 is subject to transitional provisions in Sch 33 paras 9, 10: see regs 191(11), 212.
4 For these purposes 'product' means a product to which a UK marketing authorisation or Article 126a authorisation relates: Human Medicines Regulations 2012, SI 2012/1916, reg 191(3).
5 For these purposes 'authorisation' means a UK marketing authorisation or an Article 126a authorisation: Human Medicines Regulations 2012, SI 2012/1916, reg 191(3).
6 Human Medicines Regulations 2012, SI 2012/1916, reg 191(4)(a).
7 Human Medicines Regulations 2012, SI 2012/1916, reg 191(4)(b). For the purposes of reg 191(4)(b), the scientific evaluation must be based on all available data, including data from clinical trials conducted outside the terms of the authorisation for the product: reg 191(5).
8 Human Medicines Regulations 2012, SI 2012/1916, reg 191(4)(c).
9 See the Human Medicines Regulations 2012, SI 2012/1916, reg 191(5), (6). In the case of an authorisation granted on or after 21st July 2012, the holder must submit PSURs with the frequency as specified in the authorisation for the product, with the dates of submission being calculated from the date of authorisation: reg 191(7). In the case of an authorisation granted before 21st July 2012 which specifies the frequency and dates of submission of PSURs, the holder must submit PSURs with the frequency and on the dates as specified in the authorisation for the product: reg 191(8). In the case of an authorisation granted before 21st July 2012, which does not specify the frequency and dates of submission of PSURs, the holder must submit a PSUR immediately upon the request of the licensing authority, where the product has not yet been placed on the market within the EEA, at least every six months following authorisation until the placing on the market within the EEA and where the product has been placed on the market within the EEA at least every six months during the first two years following the initial placing on the market, once a year for the following two years and every three years after that: reg 191(10). Where reg 191(8) applies by virtue of reg 191(1) the licensing authority must include in a UK marketing authorisation a term that specifies the frequency, calculated from the date on which the authorisation is granted, with which the holder of the authorisation must submit periodic safety update reports in accordance with reg 191(8): see reg 63. As to the meaning of 'licensing authority' see PARA 35 note 1.
10 Ie the Human Medicines Regulations 2012, SI 2012/1916, reg 192 applies.
11 As to the meaning of 'medicinal product' see PARA 25.
12 Ie in accordance with the Human Medicines Regulations 2012, SI 2012/1916, reg 51 (see PARA 157).
13 Ie in accordance with the Human Medicines Regulations 2012, SI 2012/1916, reg 54 (see PARA 157).
14 See the Human Medicines Regulations 2012, SI 2012/1916, reg 191(1), (2). As to the meaning of 'traditional herbal registration' see PARA 141 note 5.

254. Derogation from general requirements. The following apply in relation to medicinal products[1] granted (1) a marketing authorisation relating to generic medicinal products[2] or relating to products in well-established medicinal use[3]; or (2) a traditional herbal registration[4].

The licensing authority[5] may request the holder[6] to submit periodic safety update reports ('PSURs') where it has concerns relating to the product's[7] pharmacovigilance data or it considers there is a lack of PSUR data relating to an active substance[8] of the product after the authorisation or registration[9] is granted[10]. In such a case the holder must submit the PSURs to the European Medicines Agency[11] in accordance with the request[12]. The holder must also submit a PSUR in the case of a product to which head (1) above applies where it is a condition to which the marketing authorisation for the product is subject[13] to do so[14].

Each PSUR must contain:

(a)   summaries of data relevant to the benefits and risks of the product, including results of all studies, with a consideration of their potential impact on the authorisation or registration for the product[15];

(b)   a scientific evaluation of the risk-benefit balance of the product[16]; and

(c)   all data relating to the volume of sales of the product and any data the holder has relating to the volume of prescriptions, including an estimate of the population exposed to the product[17].

1   As to the meaning of 'medicinal product' see PARA 25.
2   Ie in accordance with the Human Medicines Regulations 2012, SI 2012/1916, reg 51 (see PARA 157).
3   Ie in accordance with the Human Medicines Regulations 2012, SI 2012/1916, reg 54 (see PARA 157).
4   Human Medicines Regulations 2012, SI 2012/1916, reg 192(1). As to the meaning of 'traditional herbal registration' see PARA 141 note 5. Each PSUR must be submitted electronically: reg 192(8). Regulation 192 is subject to transitional provisions in Sch 33: see regs 192(11), 212.
5   As to the meaning of 'licensing authority' see PARA 35 note 1.
6   For these purposes 'the holder' means the holder of a marketing authorisation to which head (1) in the text applies or of a traditional herbal registration: Human Medicines Regulations 2012, SI 2012/1916, reg 192(2).
7   For these purposes 'product' means a product to which a marketing authorisation referred to in head (1) in the text or a traditional herbal registration relates: Human Medicines Regulations 2012, SI 2012/1916, reg 192(2).
8   As to the meaning of 'substance' see PARA 25 note 2.
9   For these purposes 'authorisation or registration' means a marketing authorisation to which head (1) in the text applies or a traditional herbal registration: Human Medicines Regulations 2012, SI 2012/1916, reg 192(2).
10   See the Human Medicines Regulations 2012, SI 2012/1916, reg 192(4).
11   As to the European Medicines Agency see PARA 14.
12   See the Human Medicines Regulations 2012, SI 2012/1916, reg 192(3)(a), (5)(a). Where the licensing authority requests submission of PSURs under reg 192(3)(a), it must communicate a PSUR assessment report to the EMA as soon as is reasonably practicable after each report is received: reg 192(9). For this purpose 'PSUR assessment report' means a report which evaluates the information provided in a PSUR: reg 192(10).
13   Ie subject by virtue of the Human Medicines Regulations 2012, SI 2012/1916, reg 59 or 60 (see PARA 161).
14   See the Human Medicines Regulations 2012, SI 2012/1916, reg 192(3)(b). The report must be submitted in accordance with the terms of the condition: reg 192(5)(b).
15   Human Medicines Regulations 2012, SI 2012/1916, reg 192(6)(a).
16   Human Medicines Regulations 2012, SI 2012/1916, reg 192(6)(b). For the purposes of reg 192(6)(b), the scientific evaluation must be based on all available data, including data from clinical trials conducted outside the terms of the authorisation or registration for the product: reg 192(7).
17   Human Medicines Regulations 2012, SI 2012/1916, reg 192(6)(c).

255.   Harmonisation of PSUR frequency or date of submission. Where products[1] that are subject to different authorisations or registrations[2] contain the same active substance[3] or the same combination of active substances, the frequency and dates of submission of periodic safety update reports ('PSURs') may be amended and harmonised in accordance specified EU provisions[4] or the following provisions[5].

The holder[6] may, where one or more of specified grounds is met[7], submit a request in relation to the product to the European Medicines Agency to determine an EU reference date[8] or to change the frequency of submission of the PSUR[9].

1 As to the meaning of 'product' see PARA 246 note 1.
2 As to the meanings of 'authorisation' and 'registration' see PARA 247 note 4.
3 As to the meaning of 'substance' see PARA 25 note 2.
4 Ie in accordance with Council Directive (EC) 2001/83 (OJ L311, 28.11.2001, p 67) on the Community code relating to medicinal products for human use, art 107c(4). The second paragraph of art 107c(6) has effect in relation to the submission and determination of a request under reg 193(2): reg 193(4). Where the frequency or dates of submission of a PSUR are changed in accordance with Council Directive (EC) 2001/83 (OJ L311, 28.11.2001, p 67), art 107c(4) or art 107c(6), the holder must apply to vary the product's authorisation or registration to reflect the new frequency or date of submission before the end of the period of 6 months beginning on the day after the change is made public by the European Medicines Agency: reg 193(5). As to the European Medicines Agency see PARA 14.
5 Human Medicines Regulations 2012, SI 2012/1916, reg 193(1).
6 As to the meaning of 'holder' see PARA 246 note 1.
7 The grounds are reasons relating to public health, in order to avoid duplication of the assessment or in order to achieve international harmonisation: Human Medicines Regulations 2012, SI 2012/1916, reg 193(3).
8 For these purposes 'EU reference date' in relation to a product means:
   (1) the date of the first marketing authorisation in the EEA of a medicinal product containing the same active substance or the same combination of active substances as that product (Human Medicines Regulations 2012, SI 2012/1916, reg 193(6)); or
   (2) if the date referred to in head (1) cannot be ascertained, the earliest of the known dates of the marketing authorisations in the EEA for a medicinal product containing the same active substance or the same combination of active substances as that product (reg 193(6)).
As to the meaning of 'medicinal product' see PARA 25.
9 Human Medicines Regulations 2012, SI 2012/1916, reg 193(2).

256. Responding to single assessment of PSUR. Where periodic safety update reports ('PSURs') relating to a medicinal product[1] have been assessed under the EU single assessment procedure[2] the licensing authority[3] must implement:

   (1) the necessary measures that are consequent upon any agreement reached[4] as part of the EU single assessment process, in accordance with the implementation timetable determined in the agreement[5]; or

   (2) any decision adopted[6] before the end of the period of 30 days beginning on the day after the day on which the licensing authority received notification of the decision[7].

1 As to the meaning of 'medicinal product' see PARA 25.
2 For these purposes 'EU single assessment procedure' means the single assessment procedure laid down in Council Directive (EC) 2001/83 (OJ L311, 28.11.2001, p 67), on the Community code relating to medicinal products for human use, art 107c(4), which covers medicinal products that are authorised in more than one member state and medicinal products that contain the same active substance or the same combination of active substances and for which a harmonised EU reference date and frequency of submission of PSURs have been established under art 107c: Human Medicines Regulations 2012, SI 2012/1916, reg 194(5).
3 As to the meaning of 'licensing authority' see PARA 35 note 1.
4 Ie under Council Directive (EC) 2001/83 (OJ L311, 28.11.2001, p 67), art 107g(2). Where an agreement reached under art 107g(2) requires a variation to be made to an authorisation or registration and the terms of the agreement are known to the holder of that authorisation or registration, that holder must submit to the licensing authority in accordance with the implementation timetable determined in the agreement an appropriate application for a variation, including an updated summary of the product characteristics and an updated package leaflet: Human Medicines Regulations 2012, SI 2012/1916, reg 194(4). As to the meaning of

'holder' see PARA 246 note 1. As to the meaning of 'package leaflet' see PARA 68 note 5. As to the meaning of 'the summary of the product characteristics' see PARA 55 note 11.
5 Human Medicines Regulations 2012, SI 2012/1916, reg 194(1), (2)(a).
6 Ie under Council Directive (EC) 2001/83 (OJ L311, 28.11.2001, p 67), art 107g(4)(a).
7 Human Medicines Regulations 2012, SI 2012/1916, reg 194(1), (2)(b).

257. Obligation on licensing authority to assess PSUR's where EU single assessment procedure does not apply. Where periodic safety update reports ('PSURs') relating to a medicinal product[1] have not been assessed under the EU single assessment procedure[2] because:

(1) the medicinal product to which the PSUR relates has not been authorised to be placed on the market[3] in an EEA state other than the United Kingdom[4]; and

(2) a harmonised EU reference date[5] and frequency of submission of PSURs have not been established[6] for that product[7],

the licensing authority[8] must assess the PSURs to determine whether there are any relevant changes[9].

Where the licensing authority has assessed a PSUR under the above provisions it must consider whether any action concerning the authorisation or registration of the product[10] to which the PSUR relates is necessary and it must vary, suspend, or revoke the authorisation or registration as appropriate[11].

1 As to the meaning of 'medicinal product' see PARA 25.
2 As to the meaning of 'EU single assessment procedure' see the Human Medicines Regulations 2012, SI 2012/1916, reg 194(5); and PARA 256: reg 195(4).
3 Ie in accordance with Council Directive (EC) 2001/83 (OJ L311, 28.11.2001, p 67) on the Community code relating to medicinal products for human use.
4 Human Medicines Regulations 2012, SI 2012/1916, reg 195(1)(a).
5 As to the meaning of 'EU reference date' see the Human Medicines Regulations 2012, SI 2012/1916, reg 193(6); and PARA 255: reg 195(4).
6 Ie under Council Directive (EC) 2001/83 (OJ L311, 28.11.2001, p 67), art 107c.
7 Human Medicines Regulations 2012, SI 2012/1916, reg 195(1)(b).
8 As to the meaning of 'licensing authority' see PARA 35 note 1.
9 Human Medicines Regulations 2012, SI 2012/1916, reg 195(2). For these purposes 'relevant changes', in relation to a medicinal product' means new risks, risks that have changed or changes to the risk-benefit analysis: reg 195(4).
10 As to the meanings of 'authorisation' and 'registration' see PARA 247 note 4. As to the meaning of 'product' see PARA 246 note 1.
11 Human Medicines Regulations 2012, SI 2012/1916, reg 195(3).

(vii) Urgent Action

258. Urgent action. The following applies where the licensing authority[1] forms the view that as a result of the evaluation of data resulting from pharmacovigilance activities urgent action is necessary in connection with:

(1) suspending or revoking an authorisation or registration[2] of a medicinal product[3] or class of medicinal products[4];

(2) prohibiting the supply of a medicinal product or class of medicinal products[5];

(3) refusing the renewal of an authorisation or registration of a medicinal product[6];

(4) receiving information from the holder that, on the basis of safety concerns, the holder[7] has interrupted the sale or supply, or offer for sale or supply, of the product[8] or that the holder has taken action to have the product's authorisation or registration cancelled or that the holder intends to do so[9]; or

(5)   considering whether the terms of the authorisation or registration of a medicinal product or class of medicinal products should be varied to include a new contra-indication, an alteration of a recommended dose or a restriction to the therapeutic indications[10].

The licensing authority must provide information about the urgent action it considers necessary by the end of the day following the day on which the view under the above provisions was formed to the competent authorities of the EEA states (other than the United Kingdom), the European Medicines Agency[11] and the European Commission[12].

Where the EU urgent action procedure[13] does not apply in relation to the medicinal product or class of medicinal products referred to above[14], the licensing authority must inform the holder that it has taken such action[15] and it may take such steps as it sees fit to address the safety concerns[16].

Where the EU urgent action procedure does apply in relation to the medicinal product or class of medicinal products[17], the licensing authority may where certain conditions[18] are met suspend the authorisation or registration of the medicinal product or the authorisations and registrations for the class of medicinal products[19] (as the case may be) or prohibit its or their use within the United Kingdom[20].

Where the licensing authority takes such action, it must by the end of the next working day after the day on which the action is taken, inform of the reasons for the action the European Commission, the European Medicines Agency and the competent authority of each EEA state other than the United Kingdom[21].

1   As to the meaning of 'licensing authority' see PARA 35 note 1.
2   As to the meanings of 'authorisation' and 'registration' see PARA 247 note 4.
3   As to the meaning of 'medicinal product' see PARA 25.
4   Human Medicines Regulations 2012, SI 2012/1916, reg 196(1)(a).
5   Human Medicines Regulations 2012, SI 2012/1916, reg 196(1)(b).
6   Human Medicines Regulations 2012, SI 2012/1916, reg 196(1)(c).
7   As to the meaning of 'holder' see PARA 246 note 1.
8   As to the meaning of 'product' see PARA 246 note 1.
9   Human Medicines Regulations 2012, SI 2012/1916, reg 196(1)(d).
10 Human Medicines Regulations 2012, SI 2012/1916, reg 196(1)(e).
11 As to the European Medicines Agency see PARA 14. When informing the European Medicines Agency, the licensing authority must make available to the Agency in relation to the medicinal product or class of medicinal products all relevant scientific information at its disposal and any assessment it has carried out: Human Medicines Regulations 2012, SI 2012/1916, reg 196(3).
12 Human Medicines Regulations 2012, SI 2012/1916, reg 196(2).
13 For these purposes 'the EU urgent action procedure' means the procedure under Council Directive (EC) 2001/83 (OJ L311, 28.11.2001, p 67) on the Community code relating to medicinal products for human use, arts 107j and 107k: Human Medicines Regulations 2012, SI 2012/1916, reg 196(8).
14 Ie referred to in the Human Medicines Regulations 2012, SI 2012/1916, reg 196(1).
15 Ie the action under the Human Medicines Regulations 2012, SI 2012/1916, reg 196(2).
16 Human Medicines Regulations 2012, SI 2012/1916, reg 196(4).
17 Ie referred to in the Human Medicines Regulations 2012, SI 2012/1916, reg 196(1).
18 The conditions are that urgent action is necessary to protect public health and an agreement under Council Directive (EC) 2001/83 (OJ L311, 28.11.2001, p 67), art 107k in respect of the medicinal product or class of medicinal products has not been reached: Human Medicines Regulations 2012, SI 2012/1916, reg 196(6).
19 Ie as referred to in the Human Medicines Regulations 2012, SI 2012/1916, reg 196(1).
20 Human Medicines Regulations 2012, SI 2012/1916, reg 196(5).
21 Human Medicines Regulations 2012, SI 2012/1916, reg 196(7).

259.   EU urgent action procedure.   Where the EU urgent action procedure[1] is initiated in relation to a medicinal product[2], or class of medicinal products, the licensing authority[3] may publicly announce the initiation of the EU urgent action procedure on the UK web-portal[4]. It must also implement the measures set out in any agreement reached[5] in relation to the medicinal product or class of medicinal products in accordance with the implementation timetable determined in the agreement[6].

Where an agreement[7] in relation to a medicinal product or class of medicinal products requires a variation to be made to one or more authorisation or registration[8], each holder of an authorisation or registration covered by the agreement must submit to the licensing authority in accordance with the terms of the agreement (including its implementation timetable) an application for a variation in respect of the authorisation or registration including an updated summary of the product characteristics[9] and an updated package leaflet[10].

1 As to the meaning of 'EU urgent action procedure' see the Human Medicines Regulations 2012, SI 2012/1916, reg 196(8); and PARA 258: reg 197(4).
2 As to the meaning of 'medicinal product' see PARA 25.
3 As to the meaning of 'licensing authority' see PARA 35 note 1.
4 Human Medicines Regulations 2012, SI 2012/1916, reg 197(1)(a). As to the meaning of 'UK web-portal' see reg 203 (obligations on licensing authority in relation to national medicines web-portal: see PARA 265): reg 177(5).
5 Ie any agreement reached under Council Directive (EC) 2001/83 (OJ L311, 28.11.2001, p 67) on the Community code relating to medicinal products for human use, art 107k.
6 Human Medicines Regulations 2012, SI 2012/1916, reg 197(1)(b).
7 See note 5.
8 As to the meanings of 'authorisation' and 'registration' see PARA 247 note 4.
9 As to the meaning of 'the summary of the product characteristics' see PARA 55 note 11.
10 Human Medicines Regulations 2012, SI 2012/1916, reg 197(2), (3). As to the meaning of 'package leaflet' see PARA 68 note 5.

(viii) Post-authorisation Safety Studies

260. Post-authorisation safety studies: general provisions. A relevant post-authorisation safety study[1] may not be conducted where the act of conducting the study promotes the use of a medicinal product[2]. Nor may it provide for payments to health care professionals for participating in the study except in compensation for time and expenses incurred[3].

The licensing authority[4] may require the holder for the product[5] which is the subject of a relevant post-authorisation safety study to submit the protocol and progress reports for the study to the competent authorities of the EEA states in which the study is conducted[6].

The holder for the product which is the subject of a relevant post-authorisation safety study must:

(1) comply with a requirement imposed by the licensing authority[7] (if any)[8];

(2) while the study is being conducted monitor the data generated and consider its implications for the risk-benefit balance of the product which is the subject of the study[9];

(3) communicate to the relevant competent authorities[10] any new information that arises at any point during the study which might influence the evaluation of the risk-benefit balance for that product as soon as is reasonably practicable after it becomes known to the holder[11]; and

(4) send the final report on the study to the competent authorities of the EEA states in which the study was conducted before the end of the period of 12 months beginning on the day after the day on which data collection for the study ended[12].

1 'Relevant post-authorisation safety study' means a post-authorisation safety study which is (1) non-interventional; (2) is initiated, managed or financed by the holder voluntarily or pursuant to conditions imposed under the Human Medicines Regulations 2012, SI 2012/1916, reg 59 (conditions of a UK marketing authorisation: general: see PARA 160) or 61 (conditions of a UK marketing authorisation: new obligations post-authorisation: see PARA 162); and (3) involves the collection of safety data from patients or health care professionals: reg 177(5). As to the meaning of 'health care professionals' see PARA 113 note 5.

2 Human Medicines Regulations 2012, SI 2012/1916, reg 198(1)(a). As to the meaning of 'medicinal product' see PARA 25. Regulation 198 is subject to transitional provisions in Sch 33: regs 198(4), 212.

3 Human Medicines Regulations 2012, SI 2012/1916, reg 198(1)(b).

4 As to the meaning of 'licensing authority' see PARA 35 note 1.

5 As to the meanings of 'holder' and 'product' see PARA 246 note 1.

6 Human Medicines Regulations 2012, SI 2012/1916, reg 198(2).

7 Ie a requirement imposed under the Human Medicines Regulations 2012, SI 2012/1916, reg 198(2).

8 Human Medicines Regulations 2012, SI 2012/1916, reg 198(3)(a).

9 Human Medicines Regulations 2012, SI 2012/1916, reg 198(3)(b).

10 As to the meaning of 'relevant competent authorities' see PARA 252 note 13.

11 Human Medicines Regulations 2012, SI 2012/1916, reg 198(3)(c).

12 Human Medicines Regulations 2012, SI 2012/1916, reg 198(3)(d).

261. Submission of draft study protocols for required studies. The following applies to a relevant post-authorisation safety study[1] that is to be conducted pursuant to a condition[2] of a UK marketing authorisation[3].

The holder for the product[4] which is the intended subject of the study must submit a draft protocol for the study to the specified body[5] before the study is commenced[6].

Where a draft protocol is submitted[7] to the licensing authority[8], the licensing authority, before the end of the period of 60 days beginning on the day after the day on which the draft protocol is submitted, must issue a letter[9] endorsing the draft protocol[10], a letter objecting to the draft protocol on the grounds that it considers that the conduct of the study promotes the use of a medicinal product[11] or that it considers that the design of the study does not fulfil the study objectives, or a letter notifying the holder for the product which is the intended subject of the study that the study is a clinical trial[12].

1 As to the meaning of 'relevant post authorisation study' see PARA 260 note 1.

2 Ie pursuant to a condition imposed under the Human Medicines Regulations 2012, SI 2012/1916, reg 59 (see PARA 160) or reg 61(see PARA 162).

3 Human Medicines Regulations 2012, SI 2012/1916, reg 199(1). Regulation 199 is subject to transitional provisions in Sch 33: see regs 199(10), 212. As to the meaning of 'UK marketing authorisation' see PARA 141 note 3.

4 As to the meanings of 'holder' and 'product' see PARA 246 note 1.

5 The specified body is, where the study is to be conducted in the United Kingdom only, the licensing authority or, in all other cases, the Pharmacovigilance Risk Assessment Committee: Human Medicines Regulations 2012, SI 2012/1916, reg 199(3). As to the meaning of 'Pharmacovigilance Risk Assessment Committee' see PARA 162 note 4.

6 Human Medicines Regulations 2012, SI 2012/1916, reg 199(2).

7 Ie under the Human Medicines Regulations 2012, SI 2012/1916, reg 199(2) and (3)(a).

8 As to the meaning of 'licensing authority' see PARA 35 note 1.

9 For the purposes of the Human Medicines Regulations 2012, SI 2012/1916, reg 199 'letter' includes email correspondence: reg 199(9).

10 A study may not commence unless a letter endorsing the draft protocol has been so issued by the licensing authority or the Pharmacovigilance Risk Assessment Committee under Council Directive (EC) 2001/83 (OJ L311, 28.11.2001, p 67) on the Community code relating to medicinal products for human use, art 107n(2): Human Medicines Regulations 2012, SI 2012/1916, reg 199(6). Where a letter endorsing the draft protocol has been issued by the Pharmacovigilance Risk Assessment Committee under Council Directive (EC) 2001/83 (OJ L311, 28.11.2001, p 67), art 107n(2) the holder for the product which is the intended

subject of the study must forward the protocol to the competent authorities of the EEA States in which the study is to be conducted before commencing the study: Human Medicines Regulations 2012, SI 2012/1916, reg 199(7), (8).

11 As to the meaning of 'medicinal product' see PARA 25.

12 Human Medicines Regulations 2012, SI 2012/1916, reg 199(4). As to the meaning of 'clinical trial' see the Medicines for Human Use (Clinical Trials) Regulations 2004, SI 2004/1031, reg 2(1); and PARA 107: Human Medicines Regulations 2012, SI 2012/1916, reg 8(1).

262.   Amendment to study protocols for required studies. Where a relevant post-authorisation safety study[1] has been commenced, the holder for the product[2] which is the subject of the study must submit any substantial amendments to the study protocol to the specified body[3] before their implementation[4].

Where a proposed amendment to a study protocol is submitted to the licensing authority[5], the licensing authority must as soon as is reasonably practicable assess the amendment and inform the holder of its endorsement of, or objection to, the proposed amendment[6].

Where the proposed amendment to a study protocol is submitted to the Pharmacovigilance Risk Assessment Committee[7], the holder who submitted the amendment must inform the competent authorities of the EEA states in which the study is being conducted of any amendment to the study protocol approved by the Pharmacovigilance Risk Assessment Committee as soon as is reasonably practicable[8].

1   Ie a study to which the Human Medicines Regulations 2012, SI 2012/1916, reg 199 applies (see PARA 261).

2   As to the meanings of 'holder' and 'product' see PARA 246 note 1.

3   The specified body is where the study is being conducted in the United Kingdom only, the licensing authority or, in all other cases, the Pharmacovigilance Risk Assessment Committee: Human Medicines Regulations 2012, SI 2012/1916, reg 200(3).

4   Human Medicines Regulations 2012, SI 2012/1916, reg 200(1). Regulation 200 is subject to transitional provisions in Sch 33: regs 200(8), 212.

5   Ie submitted under the Human Medicines Regulations 2012, SI 2012/1916, reg 200(2) and (3)(a). As to the meaning of 'licensing authority' see PARA 35 note 1.

6   See the Human Medicines Regulations 2012, SI 2012/1916, reg 200(3), (4).

7   Ie submitted under the Human Medicines Regulations 2012, SI 2012/1916, reg 200(2) and (3)(b). As to the meaning of 'Pharmacovigilance Risk Assessment Committee' see PARA 162 note 4.

8   See the Human Medicines Regulations 2012, SI 2012/1916, reg 200(5), (6).

263.   Submission and evaluation of final study reports for required studies. Where a relevant post-authorisation safety study[1] has been completed, the holder for the product[2] which is the subject of the study must submit electronically, before the end of the period of 12 months beginning on the day after the day on which data collection for the study ended, to the specified body[3] a final study report and an abstract of the study results[4].

The holder must without delay evaluate whether the results of the final study report have an impact on the authorisation or registration[5] of the medicinal product[6] to which the report relates and, if necessary, submit an application to vary the authorisation or registration for the product[7].

1   Ie a study to which the Human Medicines Regulations 2012, SI 2012/1916, reg 199 applies (see PARA 261).

2   As to the meanings of 'holder' and 'product' see PARA 246 note 1.

3   The specified body is where the study was conducted in the United Kingdom only, the licensing authority or, in all other cases, the Pharmacovigilance Risk Assessment Committee: Human Medicines Regulations 2012, SI 2012/1916, reg 201(3).

4 Human Medicines Regulations 2012, SI 2012/1916, reg 201(1), (2). This does not apply where a written waiver has been granted by either the licensing authority or by the Pharmacovigilance Risk Assessment Committee in relation to the applicable report: see reg 201(4). Regulation 201 is subject to transitional provisions see Sch 33: regs 201(6), 212. As to the meaning of 'licensing authority' see PARA 35 note 1. As to the meaning of 'Pharmacovigilance Risk Assessment Committee' see PARA 162 note 4.
5 As to the meanings of 'authorisation' and 'registration' see PARA 247 note 4.
6 As to the meaning of 'medicinal product' see PARA 25.
7 Human Medicines Regulations 2012, SI 2012/1916, reg 201(5).

264. Follow-up of final study reports. The following applies where the Pharmacovigilance Risk Assessment Committee[1] has made recommendations concerning an authorisation or registration[2] or a class of authorisations or registrations based on a final study report[3] and an agreement on the action to be taken in respect of the authorisation or registration or the class of authorisations or registrations has been reached by the co-ordination group[4] under the specified procedure[5] ('the agreement')[6].

The licensing authority[7] must implement the measures set out in the agreement in accordance with the implementation timetable determined in the agreement[8].

Where the agreement requires a variation to be made to one or more authorisation or registration and the terms of the agreement are known to the holder or holders for the product or products[9] which is, or which are, the subject of the agreement, each holder must submit to the licensing authority in accordance with the terms of the agreement (including its implementation timetable) an application for a variation including an updated summary of the product characteristics[10] and an updated package leaflet[11].

1 As to the meaning of 'Pharmacovigilance Risk Assessment Committee' see PARA 162 note 4.
2 As to the meanings of 'authorisation' and 'registration' see PARA 247 note 4.
3 Ie a final study report under Council Directive (EC) 2001/83 (OJ L311, 28.11.2001, p 67) on the Community code relating to medicinal products for human use, art 107q(1).
4 'Co-ordination group' means the group of that name established under Council Directive (EC) 2001/83 (OJ L311, 28.11.2001, p 67), art 27: Human Medicines Regulations 2012, SI 2012/1916, reg 177(5).
5 Ie the one laid out in Council Directive (EC) 2001/83 (OJ L311, 28.11.2001, p 67), art 107q(2).
6 Human Medicines Regulations 2012, SI 2012/1916, reg 202(1). Regulation 202 is subject to transitional provisions in Sch 33: see regs 202(5), 212.
7 As to the meaning of 'licensing authority' see PARA 35 note 1.
8 Human Medicines Regulations 2012, SI 2012/1916, reg 202(2).
9 As to the meanings of 'holder' and 'product' see PARA 246 note 1.
10 As to the meaning of 'the summary of the product characteristics' see PARA 55 note 11.
11 Human Medicines Regulations 2012, SI 2012/1916, reg 202(3), (4). As to the meaning of 'package leaflet' see PARA 68 note 5.

(ix) Transparency and Communications

265. Obligations on licensing authority in relation to national medicines web-portal. The licensing authority[1] must set up and maintain a national medicines web-portal ('the UK web-portal') linked to the EU web-portal[2].

The licensing authority must make available publicly by means of the UK web-portal the following (at a minimum):

(1) the assessment reports prepared or revised by the licensing authority under its duties in connection with determination[3], each with a summary[4];

(2)   the summary of the product characteristics for the medicinal products[5] concerned[6];

(3)   the package leaflet for the medicinal products concerned[7];

(4)   a summary of the risk management plan[8] (if any) for the medicinal products concerned[9];

(5)   the list of medicinal products that are subject to additional monitoring[10]; and

(6)   information on the different ways of reporting suspected adverse reactions[11] to medicinal products to the licensing authority by patients or their carers, health care professionals[12], coroners or procurators fiscal[13].

1   As to the meaning of 'licensing authority' see PARA 35 note 1.
2   Human Medicines Regulations 2012, SI 2012/1916, reg 203(1). The EU web-portal mentioned in the text is the European Medicines web-portal established in accordance with Council Regulation (EC) 726/2004 (OJ L136, 30.4.2004, p 1) laying down Community procedures for the authorisation and supervision of medicinal products for human and veterinary use and establishing a European Medicines Agency, art 26.
3   Ie under the Human Medicines Regulations 2012, SI 2012/1916, reg 64(5), (6) (see PARA 164).
4   Human Medicines Regulations 2012, SI 2012/1916, reg 203(2)(a).
5   As to the meaning of 'medicinal product' see PARA 25. As to the meaning of 'the summary of the product characteristics' see PARA 55 note 11.
6   Human Medicines Regulations 2012, SI 2012/1916, reg 203(2)(b).
7   Human Medicines Regulations 2012, SI 2012/1916, reg 203(2)(c). As to the meaning of 'package leaflet' see PARA 68 note 5.
8   As to the meaning of 'risk management plan' see PARA 160 note 5.
9   Human Medicines Regulations 2012, SI 2012/1916, reg 203(2)(d).
10 Human Medicines Regulations 2012, SI 2012/1916, reg 203(2)(e). The list of medicinal products mentioned in the text is the one referred to in Council Regulation (EC) 726/2004 (OJ L136, 30.4.2004, p 1) art 23.
11 As to the meaning of 'adverse reaction' see PARA 70 note 6. As to the meaning of 'suspected' see PARA 70 note 7.
12 As to the meaning of 'health care professionals' see PARA 113 note 5.
13 Human Medicines Regulations 2012, SI 2012/1916, reg 203(2)(f). This includes by way of the web-based structured forms referred to in Council Regulation (EC) 726/2004 (OJ L136, 30.4.2004, p 1), art 25.

266.   Obligations in licensing authority in relation to public announcements. Where the licensing authority[1] intends to make a public announcement relating to information on pharmacovigilance concerns it must inform the European Medicines Agency[2], the European Commission and the competent authority of each EEA state other than the United Kingdom not less than 24 hours prior to making the public announcement[3].

This does not apply if the information in the announcement needs to be made public urgently for the protection of public health[4].

1   As to the meaning of 'licensing authority' see PARA 35 note 1.
2   As to the European Medicines Agency see PARA 14.
3   See the Human Medicines Regulations 2012, SI 2012/1916, reg 204(1)–(3).
4   Human Medicines Regulations 2012, SI 2012/1916, reg 204(4).

267.   Obligations on holders in relation to public announcements. Where the holder[1] intends to make a public announcement relating to information on pharmacovigilance concerns in relation to the use of a medicinal product[2], the holder must inform the licensing authority[3], the European Medicines Agency[4] and the European Commission of its intention to make the public announcement, as soon as is practicable once it forms that intention and in any event no later than at the same time as, or before, the public announcement is made[5].

The holder must ensure that the information in the public announcement is presented objectively and is not misleading[6].

1　As to the meaning of 'holder' see PARA 246 note 1.
2　As to the meaning of 'medicinal product' see PARA 25.
3　As to the meaning of 'licensing authority' see PARA 35 note 1.
4　As to the European Medicines Agency see PARA 14.
5　See the Human Medicines Regulations 2012, SI 2012/1916, reg 205(1), (2).
6　Human Medicines Regulations 2012, SI 2012/1916, reg 205(4).

(x) Enforcement

268. Infringement notices. If an enforcement authority[1] has objective grounds for considering that a person has contravened[2] a provision relating to pharmovigilance[3], it may serve upon him a notice in writing (an 'infringement notice')[4]:

(1)　informing him of the authority's grounds for considering that he has contravened one or more of the relevant provisions[5];

(2)　specifying the relevant provision[6];

(3)　specifying the measures which the person must take in order to ensure that the contravention does not continue or, as the case may be, does not recur[7];

(4)　requiring the person to take those measures, within such period as may be specified in the notice[8];

(5)　specifying the further action (if any) that the enforcement authority may take[9].

An infringement notice may include directions as to the measures to be taken by the person to ensure that the contravention does not continue or, as the case may be, does not recur, including the different ways of securing compliance[10].

1　As to the meaning of 'enforcement authority' see PARA 142 note 13.
2　As to the meaning of 'contravene' see PARA 41 note 8.
3　Ie a provision of the Human Medicines Regulations 2012, SI 2012/1916, Pt 11 (regs 177–212) or European Medicines web-portal established in accordance with Council Regulation (EC) 726/2004 (OJ L136, 30.4.2004, p 1) laying down Community procedures for the authorisation and supervision of medicinal products for human and veterinary use and establishing a European Medicines Agency, Title II, Chapter 3.
4　If an enforcement authority serves an infringement notice in accordance with the Human Medicines Regulations 2012, SI 2012/1916, reg 206(1), it must as soon as is reasonably practicable inform the European Medicines Agency and the European Commission: reg 206(3). As to the European Medicines Agency see PARA 14.
5　See the Human Medicines Regulations 2012, SI 2012/1916, reg 206(1)(a).
6　Human Medicines Regulations 2012, SI 2012/1916, reg 206(1)(b).
7　Human Medicines Regulations 2012, SI 2012/1916, reg 206(1)(c).
8　Human Medicines Regulations 2012, SI 2012/1916, reg 206(1)(d).
9　Human Medicines Regulations 2012, SI 2012/1916, reg 206(1)(e).
10　Human Medicines Regulations 2012, SI 2012/1916, reg 206(2).

269. Offences. A person[1] is guilty of an offence if he commits a breach of a certain provisions[2] relating to pharmcovigilance[3]. Such a breach includes any failure by a holder[4] to comply with any requirement or obligation[5] or a contravention by any person of those provisions[6].

A person is guilty of an offence if the person provides information to the licensing authority[7] or the European Medicines Agency[8], pursuant to an obligation[9], but that information is false or misleading in a material particular[10].

A person[11] is guilty of an offence[12] if he breaches[13] certain EU provisions relating to pharmacovigilance[14] or he provides information which is false or misleading in a material particular to the licensing authority or the European Medicines Agency pursuant to an obligation under certain EU provisons[15].

1   If an offence under the Human Medicines Regulations 2012, SI 2012/1916, reg 207(1) or reg 210(1)(a) is committed by a person acting as employee or agent, the employer or principal of that person is guilty of the same offence and is liable to be proceeded against and punished accordingly: reg 211.

2   Ie the Human Medicines Regulations 2012, SI 2012/1916, Pt 11 (regs 177–212), other than reg 199(2) or (6) (see PARA 261).

3   See the Human Medicines Regulations 2012, SI 2012/1916, reg 207(1). Subject to reg 209(2), a person guilty of such an offence is liable, on summary conviction, to a fine not exceeding the statutory maximum or, on conviction on indictment, to imprisonment for a term not exceeding 2 years or to both: reg 209(1). However a person guilty of an offence under reg 207 which relates to a breach of regs 182(2)(a), (b), (3), (5) (see PARA 246), 183(8)(a) (see PARA 247), 184(1)(a), (b) (see PARA 248), 187(4) (see PARA 249), 188(1)(c), (e) (see PARA 251), 193(5) (see PARA 255), 198(1), (3)(a), (d) (see PARA 260), 199(8) (see PARA 261), or 200(7) (see PARA 262), is liable, on summary conviction to a fine not exceeding the statutory maximum or, on conviction on indictment, to a fine: reg 209(2), (3). As to the statutory maximum see SENTENCING AND DISPOSITION OF OFFENDERS vol 92 (2010) PARA 140.

4   As to the meaning of 'holder' see PARA 246 note 1.

5   Ie any requirement or obligation under the Human Medicines Regulations 2012, SI 2012/1916, Pt 11 (regs 177–212).

6   See the Human Medicines Regulations 2012, SI 2012/1916, reg 207(2). As to the meaning of 'contravene' see PARA 41 note 8.

7   As to the meaning of 'licensing authority' see PARA 35 note 1.

8   As to the European Medicines Agency see PARA 14.

9   Ie under the Human Medicines Regulations 2012, SI 2012/1916, Pt 11 (regs 177–212).

10 Human Medicines Regulations 2012, SI 2012/1916, reg 208.

11 See note 1.

12 Subject to the Human Medicines Regulations 2012, SI 2012/1916, reg 210(5), a person guilty of an offence under reg 210 is liable, on summary conviction, to a fine not exceeding the statutory maximum or, on conviction on indictment, to a fine, to imprisonment for a term not exceeding two years or to both: reg 210(4). A person guilty of an offence under reg 210 in relation to a provision of Council Regulation (EC) 726/2004 (OJ L136, 30.4.2004, p 1) laying down Community procedures for the authorisation and supervision of medicinal products for human and veterinary use and establishing a European Medicines Agency as listed in reg 210(6) (see note 15) is liable, on summary conviction, to a fine not exceeding the statutory maximum or, on conviction on indictment, to a fine: reg 210(5).

13 A breach of a provision listed in the Human Medicines Regulations 2012, SI 2012/1916, reg 210(3) (see note 14) includes any failure to comply with any requirement or obligation contained in any of those provisions, contravention of any prohibition contained in any of those provisions or failure to comply with any requirement imposed by the licensing authority or the European Medicines Agency pursuant to any of those provisions: reg 210(2).

14 Ie Council Regulation (EC) 726/2004 (OJ L136, 30.4.2004, p 1) the second paragraph of art 16(4), art 20(8), 21(1), (2), art 22, art 28(1), (2), (5), art 28a(3) and art 28b(1) (except insofar as it imposes an obligation under Council Directive (EC) 2001/83 (OJ L311, 28.11.2001, p 67) on the Community code relating to medicinal products for human use, art 107n(1) or the first paragraph of art 107n(3)): Human Medicines Regulations 2012, SI 2012/1916, reg 210(3).

15 Human Medicines Regulations 2012, SI 2012/1916, reg 210(1). The EU provisions mentioned in the text refers to Council Regulation (EC) 726/2004 (OJ L136, 30.4.2004, p 1) Title II Chapter 3. Regulation 210 is subject to transitional provisions in Sch 33: see reg 210(7), 212. Subject to reg 210(5), a person guilty of an offence under reg 210 is liable, on summary conviction to a fine not exceeding the statutory maximum or, on conviction on indictment, to a fine, to imprisonment for a term not exceeding two years or to both: reg 210(4). A person guilty of an offence in relation to (1) Council Regulation (EC) 726/2004 (OJ L136, 30.4.2004, p 1),

the second paragraph of art 16(4); (2) art 21(1) (insofar as it relates to obligations set out in the second paragraph of Council Directive (EC) 2001/83 (OJ L311, 28.11.2001, p 67) art 104(2) save the obligation regarding preparing and implementing a corrective action plan), Directive EC 2001/83 (OJ L311, 28.11.2001, p 67), arts 104(3)(a), (b) or the second paragraph of art 104(3)); (3) Council Regulation (EC) 726/2004 (OJ L136, 30.4.2004, p 1), art 21(2) (insofar as it relates to the obligation to submit a detailed description of a risk management system); (4) art 28(1) (insofar as it relates to obligations set out in Council Directive (EC) 2001/83 (OJ L311, 28.11.2001, p 67), the second paragraph of art 107(1), the first sentence of art 107(4) or art 107(5)); (5) Council Regulation (EC) 726/2004 (OJ L136, 30.4.2004, p 1), art 28(2) (insofar as it relates to the obligation set out in Council Directive (EC) 2001/83 (OJ L311, 28.11.2001, p 67), the third paragraph of art 107c(4)); and (6) Council Regulation (EC) 726/2004 (OJ L136, 30.4.2004, p 1), art 28b(1) (insofar as it relates to prohibitions or obligations set out in Council Directive (EC) 2001/83 (OJ L311, 28.11.2001, p 67), art 107m(3)–(6), the second paragraph of art 107n(3) or the last sentence of art 107o: Human Medicines Regulations 2012, SI 2012/1916, reg 210(6).

(8) PROHIBITED SALES ETC

(i) Starting Materials

270. Sale and supply of starting materials. A person must not sell or supply an active substance[1] if the active substance has not been manufactured or assembled[2] in accordance with the principles and guidelines for good manufacturing practice[3] applicable to starting materials[4] and is sold or supplied to a person for use in the manufacture of a medicinal product[5], except where the product is a special medicinal product[6] or the requirement for a manufacturer's licence[7] does not apply to the manufacture of the product by virtue of provisons[8] exempting pharmacists[9].

1　As to the meaning of 'substance' see PARA 25 note 2.
2　As to the meaning of 'manufacture' and 'assemble' see PARA 141 notes 7, 8.
3　Ie the principles set out in Commission Directive (EC) 2003/94 (OJ L262, 14.10.2003, p 22–26) laying down the principles and guidelines of good manufacturing practice in respect of medicinal products for human use and investigational medicinal products for human use ('the Good Manufacturing Practice Directive') (see PARA 12).
4　Human Medicines Regulations 2012, SI 2012/1916, reg 32(1)(a).
5　As to the meaning of 'medicinal product' see PARA 25.
6　'Special medicinal product' means a product within the meaning of the Human Medicines Regulations 2012, SI 2012/1916, reg 167 (see PARA 142) or any equivalent legislation in an EEA state other than the United Kingdom: reg 8(1).
7　Ie the Human Medicines Regulations 2012, SI 2012/1916, reg 17(1) (see PARA 45).
8　Ie by virtue of the Medicines Act 1968 s 10 (see PARA 150).
9　See the Human Medicines Regulations 2012, SI 2012/1916, reg 32(1)(b).

(ii) Sale and Supply of Medicines

271. Sale or supply of prescription only medicines. A person may not sell[1] or supply a prescription only medicine[2] except in accordance with a prescription given by an appropriate practitioner[3].

A person may not parenterally administer (otherwise than to himself or herself) a prescription only medicine unless the person is an appropriate practitioner other than an EEA health professional or he is acting in accordance with the directions of such an appropriate practitioner[4].

Breach of the above[5] provisions is an offence[6].

The following are appropriate practitioners in relation to any prescription only medicine[7]:

(1)　a doctor[8];

(2)   a dentist[9];

(3)   a supplementary prescriber[10];

(4)   a nurse independent prescriber[11]; and

(5)   a pharmacist independent prescriber[12].

An optometrist independent prescriber[13] is an appropriate practitioner in relation to any prescription only medicine other than a medicinal product[14] that is a controlled drug or a medicinal product that is for parenteral administration[15].

An EEA health professional[16] is an appropriate practitioner in relation to any prescription only medicine other than a controlled drug[17].

1   For the purposes of the Human Medicines Regulations 2012, SI 2012/1916, Pt 12 (regs 213–256) 'sell' means sell by retail (and 'sale' has a corresponding meaning: reg 213(1)). 'Supply' means supply in circumstances corresponding to retail sale: reg 213(1).

2   As to the meaning of 'prescription only medicine' see the Human Medicines Regulations 2012, SI 2012/1916, reg 5(3); and PARA 26: reg 8(1).

3   Human Medicines Regulations 2012, SI 2012/1916, reg 214(1). Regulation 214 is subject to regs 223–248 (exemptions: see PARAS 280–306): reg 214(7).

4   Human Medicines Regulations 2012, SI 2012/1916, reg 214(2).

5   Ie breach of the Human Medicines Regulations 2012, SI 2012/1916, reg 214(1), (2).

6   See the Human Medicines Regulations 2012, SI 2012/1916: reg 255(1)(a), (b); and PARA 379.

7   If an appropriate practitioner gives a prescription or directions in respect of a medicinal product in relation to which he is not an appropriate practitioner, he is guilty of an offence: see the Human Medicines Regulations 2012, SI 2012/1916, reg 255(2); and PARA 379.

8   Human Medicines Regulations 2012, SI 2012/1916, reg 214(3)(a). As to the meaning of 'doctor' see PARA 48 note 6.

9   Human Medicines Regulations 2012, SI 2012/1916, reg 214(3)(b). As to the meaning of 'dentist' see PARA 48 note 6.

10   Human Medicines Regulations 2012, SI 2012/1916, reg 214(3)(a). As to the meaning of 'supplementary prescriber' see PARA 50 note 5.

11   Human Medicines Regulations 2012, SI 2012/1916, reg 214(3)(a). As to the meaning of 'nurse independent prescriber' see PARA 50 note 3. A community practitioner nurse prescriber is an appropriate practitioner in relation to a prescription only medicine specified in Sch 13: reg 214(4). 'Community practitioner nurse prescriber' means a person who is a registered nurse or a registered midwife and against whose name is recorded in the professional register an annotation signifying that the person is qualified to order drugs, medicines and appliances from the Nurse Prescribers' Formulary for Community Practitioners in the current edition of the British National Formulary: reg 8(1). As to the meaning of 'professional register' see PARA 50 note 3.

12   Human Medicines Regulations 2012, SI 2012/1916, reg 214(3)(a). As to the meaning of 'pharmacist independent prescriber' see PARA 50 note 4.

13   'Optometrist independent prescriber' means a person who is a registered optometrist and against whose name is recorded in the relevant register an annotation signifying that the person is qualified to order drugs, medicines and appliances as an optometrist independent prescriber: Human Medicines Regulations 2012, SI 2012/1916, reg 8(1). As to the meaning of 'registered optometrist' see PARA 36 note 8.

14   As to the meaning of 'medicinal product' see PARA 25.

15   Human Medicines Regulations 2012, SI 2012/1916, reg 214(5).

16   'EEA health professional' means a doctor who is lawfully engaged in medical practice in an EEA state other than the United Kingdom or in Switzerland or a dentist who is lawfully engaged in dental practice in an EEA state other than the United Kingdom or in Switzerland (including a person whose formal qualifications as a doctor are recognised for the purposes of the pursuit of the professional activities of a dental practitioner under European Parliament and Council Directive (EC) 2005/36 (OJ L255, 30.9.2005, p 22–145) on the recognition of professional qualifications), art 37 and who is not otherwise a doctor or a dentist for the purpose of the Human Medicines Regulations 2012, SI 2012/1916: reg 213(1).

17   Human Medicines Regulations 2012, SI 2012/1916, reg 214(6).

272.   Prescription only medicines. The ministers[1] may by order specify descriptions or classes of medicinal products[2] as prescription only medicines[3].

Any order made by the ministers may provide that the restrictions[4] are to have effect subject to such exemptions as may be specified in the order or, in the case of an appropriate practitioner[5], other than a doctor or dentist, such modifications as may be so specified[6]; or that, for the purpose of the restriction on sale or supply[7], a medicinal product must not be taken to be sold or supplied in accordance with a prescription given by an appropriate practitioner unless such conditions as are prescribed by the order are fulfilled[8].

An order may provide, in relation to a person who is an appropriate practitioner, other than a doctor or dentist, that such a person may[9]:

(1)   give a prescription for a medicinal product falling within a description or class specified in the order[10];

(2)   administer any such medicinal product[11]; or

(3)   give directions for the administration of any such medicinal product[12],

only where he complies with such conditions as may be specified in the order in respect of the cases or circumstances in which he may do so[13].

An order may provide, in relation to any such condition, for the condition to have effect subject to such exemptions as may be specified in the order[14].

Any person who gives a prescription or directions or administers a medicinal product in contravention of a condition imposed[15] by an order is guilty of an offence[16]; and any person who is an appropriate practitioner[17] and gives a prescription or directions in respect of a medicinal product of a description or class in relation to which he is not an appropriate practitioner is guilty of an offence[18].

1   As to the meaning of 'the ministers' see the Human Medicines Regulations 2012, SI 2012/1916, reg 6(6)–(8); and PARA 35 (definition applied by the Medicines Act 1968 s 132(1) (substituted by SI 2012/1916)).

2   As to the meaning of 'medicinal products' see PARA 25.

3   Medicines Act 1968 s 58(1) (amended by SI 2006/2407, SI 2012/1916). Any order made by the ministers for the purposes of the Medicines Act 1967 s 58 may provide (1) that the Human Medicines Regulations 2012, SI 2012/1916, reg 214(1) or (2) (see PARA 271) has effect subject to such exemptions as may be specified in the order or, in the case of an appropriate practitioner, other than a doctor or dentist, such modifications as may be so specified; (2) that, for the purpose of reg 214(1), a medicinal product must not be taken to be sold or supplied in accordance with a prescription given by an appropriate practitioner unless such conditions as are prescribed by the order are fulfilled: Medicines Act 1968 s 58(4) (amended by SI 2006/2407, SI 2012/1916). As to the meanings of 'doctor' and 'dentist' see PARA 48 note 6 (definitions applied by the Medicines Act 1968 s 132(1) (substituted by SI 2012/1916)). Before making an order the ministers must consult the appropriate committee: see the Medicines Act 1968 s 58(6) (amended by SI 2005/1094, SI 2006/2407). For this purpose 'the appropriate committee' means whichever the ministers consider appropriate of the Commission on Human Medicines or an expert committee appointed by the ministers, or by one of them acting alone: Medicines Act 1968 s 58(7) (added by SI 2012/1916). The advice of the committee must be taken into account: see the Medicines Act 1968 s 129(7). As to the meaning of 'prescription only medicine' see the Human Medicines Regulations 2012, SI 2012/1916, reg 5(3); PARA 26: reg 8(1); Medicines Act 1968 s 132(1) (as substituted: see note 1).

    As to the orders that have been made under the Medicines Act 1968 s 58 see the Prescription Only Medicines (Human Use) Order 1997, SI 1997/1830, reg 5 (amended by SI 2012/1916).

4   Ie the restrictions under the Human Medicines Regulations 2012, SI 2012/1916, reg 214(1) or (2) (see PARA 271).

5   As to the meaning of 'appropriate practitioner' see PARA 271.

6   Medicines Act 1968 s 58(4)(a) (amended by SI 2006/2407, SI 2012/1916).

7   Ie the restrictions under the Human Medicines Regulations 2012, SI 2012/1916, reg 214(1) (see PARA 271).

8   Medicines Act 1968 s 58(4)(b) (amended by SI 2012/1916).

9   Medicines Act 1968 s 58(4A) (s 58(4A)–(4C) added by the Health and Social Care Act 2001 s 63(1), (5); amended by SI 2012/1916).

10 Medicines Act 1968 s 58(4A)(a) (as added: see note 9).

11 Medicines Act 1968 s 58(4A)(b) (as added: see note 9).

12 Medicines Act 1968 s 58(4A)(c) (as added: see note 9).

13 Medicines Act 1968 s 58(4A) (as added: see note 9). Where a condition is specified by virtue of s 58(4A), any prescription or direction given by a person in contravention of the condition is not (subject to such exemptions or modifications as may be specified in the order by virtue of s 58(4)(a)) given by an appropriate practitioner for the purposes of the Human Medicines Regulations 2012, SI 2012/1916, reg 214(1) or (2): Medicines Act 1968 s 58(4C) (as so added; amended by SI 2012/1916). Any exemption conferred or modification made by an order in accordance with the Medicines Act 1968 s 58(4)(a) or 58(4B) may be conferred or made subject to such conditions or limitations as may be specified in the order: s 58(5) (amended by the Medicinal Products: Prescription by Nurses etc Act 1992 s 1; and the Health and Social Care Act 2001 s 63(1), (6)). As to the meaning of 'contravene' see PARA 41 note 8 (definition applied by the Medicines Act 1968 s 132(1) (substituted by SI 2012/1916)).

14 Medicines Act 1968 s 58(4B) (as added: see note 9).

15 Ie under the Medicines Act 1968 s 58(4A).

16 Medicines Act 1968 s 67(1A) (s 67(1A), (1B) added by the Health and Social Care Act 2001 s 63(1), (7)(a)). For the penalty for such an offence see the Medicines Act 1968 s 67(4).

17 Ie within the meaning of the Human Medicines Regulations 2012, SI 2012/1916, reg 214.

18 Medicines Act 1968 s 67(1B) (as added (see note 16); amended by SI 2012/1916). For the penalty for such an offence see the Medicines Act 1968 s 67(4).

273. Requirement to specify certain products as prescription only products. The ministers[1] must exercise their powers to make orders in respect of prescription only medicinal products[2] as to secure that every product which:

(1) is likely to present a direct or indirect danger to human health, even when used correctly, if used without the supervision of a doctor or dentist[3]; or

(2) is frequently and to a very wide extent used incorrectly, and as a result is likely to present a direct or indirect danger to human health[4]; or

(3) contains substances or preparations of substances of which the activity requires, or the side-effects require, further investigation[5]; or

(4) is normally prescribed by a doctor or dentist for parenteral administration[6],

is specified as a prescription only medicine[7].

1 As to the meaning of 'the ministers' see the Human Medicines Regulations 2012, SI 2012/1916, reg 6(6)–(8); and PARA 35 (definition applied by the Medicines Act 1968 s 132(1) (substituted by SI 2012/1916)).

2 Ie their power under the Medicines Act 1968 s 58(1): see PARA 272.

3 Medicines Act 1968 s 58A(2)(a) (s 58A added by SI 1992/3271). As to the meanings of 'doctor' and 'dentist' see PARA 48 note 6 (definitions applied by the Medicines Act 1968 s 132(1) (substituted by SI 2012/1916)). In considering whether conditions under s 58A(2) apply to a product, the ministers must take into account whether the product: (1) contains a substance which is listed in any of Schedules I, II or IV to the Narcotic Drugs Convention (where the product is not a preparation listed in Schedule III to that Convention) (Medicines Act 1968 s 58A(3)(a) (as so added)); or (2) contains a substance which is listed in any of Schedules I to IV of the Psychotropic Substances Convention (where the product is not a preparation which may be exempted from measures of control in accordance with article 3(2), (3)) (Medicines Act 1968 s 58A(3)(b) (as so added)); or (3) is likely, if incorrectly used, to present a substantial risk of medicinal abuse, or to lead to addiction, or to be used for illegal purposes (s 58A(3)(c) (as so added)); or (4) contains a substance which, by reason of its novelty or properties, might fall within head (3), but as to which there is insufficient information available to determine whether it does so fall (s 58A(3)(d) (as so added)); or (5) by reason of its pharmaceutical characteristics or novelty, or in the interests of public health, is reserved for treatments which can only be followed in a hospital (s 58A(3)(e) (as so added)); or (6) is used in the treatment of conditions which must be diagnosed in a hospital or in an institution with special diagnostic facilities (although administration and subsequent supervision may be carried out elsewhere) (s 58A(3)(f) (as so added)); or (7) is intended for outpatients but may produce very serious side-effects which would require a prescription drawn up as required by a specialist and special supervision throughout the treatment (s 58A(3)(g) (as so added)). For these purposes, 'the Narcotic Drugs

Convention' means the Single Convention on Narcotic Drugs signed by the United Kingdom on 30 March 1961 (New York 30 March to 1 August 1961; TS 34 (1965); Cmnd 2631) as amended by the Protocol Amending the Single Convention on Narcotic Drugs signed by the United Kingdom on 25 March 1972 (Geneva, 25 March to 31 December 1972; TS 23 (1979); Cmd 7466); and 'the Psychotropic Substances Convention' means the Convention on Psychotropic Substances (Vienna, 21 February 1971; TS 51 (1993); Cmnd 2307): Medicines Act 1968 s 58A(5) (as so added). As to the meaning of 'substance' see PARA 25 note 2; as to the meaning of 'hospital' see PARA 52 note 3; and as to the meaning of 'administer' see PARA 25 note 4: Human Medicines Regulations 2012, SI 2012/1916, reg 8(1) (definition applied by the Medicines Act 1968 s 132(1) (substituted by SI 2012/1916)).

4   Medicines Act 1968 s 58A(2)(b) (as added: see note 3). See also note 3.
5   Medicines Act 1968 s 58A(2)(c) (as added: see note 3). See also note 3.
6   Medicines Act 1968 s 58A(2)(d) (as added: see note 3). See also note 3.
7   See the Medicines Act 1968 s 58A(1) (amended by SI 2006/2407; SI 2012/1916). As to the meaning of 'prescription only medicine' see the Human Medicines Regulations 2012, SI 2012/1916, reg 5(3); PARA 26: reg 8(1): Medicines Act 1968 s 132(1) (as substituted: see note 1).

274. Prescribing and administration by supplementary prescribers. A supplementary prescriber[1] may not give a prescription for a prescription only medicine[2] unless he meets conditions A and C below[3].

A supplementary prescriber may not parenterally administer[4] a prescription only medicine, or give directions for the parenteral administration of a prescription only medicine, unless he meets conditions B and C below[5].

Condition A is that the supplementary prescriber is acting in accordance with the terms of a clinical management plan[6] that relates to the patient to whom the product is prescribed, that has effect when the prescription is given and that includes specified particulars[7].

Condition B is that the supplementary prescriber is acting in accordance with the terms of a clinical management plan that relates to the patient to whom the product is, or is to be, administered, that has effect when the product is administered or (as the case may be) the direction is given and that includes specified particulars[8].

Condition C is that the supplementary prescriber has access to health records[9] that are the health records of the patient to whom the plan relates and that are used by any doctor or dentist who is a party to the plan[10].

1   As to the meaning of 'supplementary prescriber' see para 50 note 5. The Human Medicines Regulations, SI 2012/1916, reg 215 does not apply if the supplementary prescriber is a community practitioner nurse prescriber and the prescription only medicine prescribed or administered, or in respect of which the supplementary prescriber gives directions for administration, is specified in Sch 13: reg 216(1).
2   As to the meaning of 'prescription only medicine' see the Human Medicines Regulations 2012, SI 2012/1916, reg 5(3); and PARA 26: reg 8(1).
3   Human Medicines Regulations 2012, SI 2012/1916, reg 215(1). Regulation 215 is subject to reg 216: reg 215(6).
4   'Parenteral administration' means administration by break of the skin or mucous membrane: Human Medicines Regulations 2012, SI 2012/1916, reg 213(1).
5   Human Medicines Regulations 2012, SI 2012/1916, reg 215(2). Regulation 215(2) does not apply if the supplementary prescriber is acting in accordance with the directions of another person who is an appropriate practitioner (other than a supplementary prescriber or an EEA health professional) in relation to the prescription only medicine in question: reg 216(2).
6   'Clinical management plan' means a written plan (which may be amended from time to time) relating to the treatment of an individual patient and agreed by the patient, the doctor or dentist who is a party to the plan and any supplementary prescriber who is to prescribe, give directions for administration or administer under the plan: Human Medicines Regulations 2012, SI 2012/1916, regs 8(1), 215(7). As to the meanings of 'doctor' and 'dentist' see PARA 48 note 6.
7   Human Medicines Regulations 2012, SI 2012/1916, reg 215(3). As to the specified particulars see Sch 14.

8 Human Medicines Regulations 2012, SI 2012/1916, reg 215(4). As to the specified particulars see Sch 14.
9 For these purposes 'health record' has the meaning given by the Data Protection Act 1998 s 68(2) (see CONFIDENCE AND INFORMATIONAL PRIVACY vol 19 (2011) PARA 97): Human Medicines Regulations 2012, SI 2012/1916, reg 215(7).
10 Human Medicines Regulations 2012, SI 2012/1916, reg 215(5).

275. Requirements for prescriptions: general. For the purposes of the sale and supply of prescription only medicines[1], a prescription only medicine is not sold or supplied in accordance with a prescription given by an appropriate practitioner[2] unless the following conditions are met[3].

Condition A is that the prescription is signed in ink by the appropriate practitioner giving it[4].

Condition B is that the prescription is written in ink or otherwise so as to be indelible or, in the case of a health prescription which is not for a controlled drug[5], is written as described in head (1) or by means of carbon paper or similar material[6].

Condition C is that the prescription contains the following particulars:

(a)   the address of the appropriate practitioner giving it[7];
(b)   the appropriate date[8];
(c)   an indication of the kind of appropriate practitioner giving it[9];
(d)   the name and address of the person for whose treatment it is given[10]; and
(e)   if that person is under 12, that person's age[11].

Condition D is that the prescription is not dispensed after the end of the period of six months beginning with the appropriate date or, in the case of a repeatable prescription, it is not dispensed for the first time after the end of that period and it is dispensed in accordance with the directions contained in the prescription[12].

Condition E is that, in the case of a repeatable prescription that does not specify the number of times it may be dispensed it is not dispensed on more than two occasions or in the case of a prescription for an oral contraceptive, it is not dispensed on more than six occasions or after the end of the period of six months beginning with the appropriate date[13].

The following applies to a prescription that is not a health prescription[14] for a controlled drug[15]. A prescription only medicine[16] is also sold or supplied in accordance with a prescription given by an appropriate practitioner other than an EEA health professional[17] if conditions A and B above are not met; but the prescription is created in electronic form, signed with an advanced electronic signature[18], sent to the person by whom it is dispensed as an electronic communication[19] (whether or not through one or more intermediaries) and conditions C to E above are met[20].

1 Ie for the purposes of the Human Medicines Regulations 2012, SI 2012/1916, regs 214–222. As to the meaning of 'prescription only medicine' see the Human Medicines Regulations 2012, SI 2012/1916, reg 5(3); and PARA 26: reg 8(1). As to the meanings of 'sale' and 'supply' see PARA 271 note 1.
2 As to the meaning of 'appropriate practitioner' see PARA 271.
3 Human Medicines Regulations 2012, SI 2012/1916, reg 217(1). Regulation 217 does not apply to a prescription given by an EEA health professional (as to which see reg 218); and is subject to reg 219 (electronic prescriptions: see PARA 276): reg 217(8).
4 Human Medicines Regulations 2012, SI 2012/1916, reg 217(2).
5 'Controlled drug' means any substance or product for the time being specified in the Misuse of Drugs Regulations 2001, SI 2001/3998, Sch 1, 2 or 3 except where the context requires otherwise: Human Medicines Regulations 2012, SI 2012/1916, reg 213(1).

6   Human Medicines Regulations 2012, SI 2012/1916, reg 217(3).

7   Human Medicines Regulations 2012, SI 2012/1916, reg 217(4)(a).

8   Human Medicines Regulations 2012, SI 2012/1916, reg 217(4)(b). In reg 217 'appropriate date' means, subject to reg 217(8), in the case of a health prescription, whichever is the later of the date on which it was signed by the appropriate practitioner giving it or, a date indicated by the appropriate practitioner as the date before which it should not be dispensed and, otherwise, the date on which the prescription was signed by the appropriate practitioner giving it: reg 217(7).

9   Human Medicines Regulations 2012, SI 2012/1916, reg 217(4)(c).

10   Human Medicines Regulations 2012, SI 2012/1916, reg 217(4)(d).

11   Human Medicines Regulations 2012, SI 2012/1916, reg 217(4)(e).

12   Human Medicines Regulations 2012, SI 2012/1916, reg 217(5).

13   Human Medicines Regulations 2012, SI 2012/1916, reg 217(6).

14   'Health prescription' means a prescription issued by a doctor, dentist, supplementary prescriber, nurse independent prescriber, optometrist independent prescriber, pharmacist independent prescriber or community practitioner nurse prescriber under, in England, the National Health Service Act 2006 and, in Wales, the National Health Service (Wales) Act 2006: Human Medicines Regulations 2012, SI 2012/1916, reg 213(1). As to the meanings of 'doctor' and 'dentist' see PARA 48 note 6. As to the meaning of 'supplementary prescriber' see PARA 50 note 5. As to the meaning of 'nurse independent prescriber' see PARA 50 note 3. As to the meaning of 'optometrist independent prescriber' see PARA 271 note 13. As to the meaning of 'pharmacist independent prescriber' see PARA 50 note 4. As to the meaning of 'community practitioner nurse prescriber' see PARA 271 note 11.

15   Human Medicines Regulations 2012, SI 2012/1916, reg 219(1).

16   As to the meaning of 'prescription only medicine' see the Human Medicines Regulations 2012, SI 2012/1916, reg 5(3); and PARA 26: reg 8(1).

17   As to the meaning of 'EEA health professional' see PARA 271 note 16.

18   For this purpose 'advanced electronic signature' means an electronic signature that is uniquely linked to the person ('P') giving the prescription, capable of identifying P, created using means that P can maintain under P's sole control and linked to the data to which it relates in such a manner that any subsequent change of data is detectable: Human Medicines Regulations 2012, SI 2012/1916, reg 219(5).

19   'Electronic communication' means a communication transmitted (whether from one person to another, from one device to another or from a person to a device or vice versa) by means of an electronic communications network within the meaning of the Communications Act 2003 s 32(1) (see TELECOMMUNICATIONS vol 97 (2010) PARA 60); or by other means but while in an electronic form: Human Medicines Regulations 2012, SI 2012/1916, reg 8(1).

20   Human Medicines Regulations 2012, SI 2012/1916, reg 219(2), (4).

276. Requirements for prescriptions: EEA health professionals. For the purposes of the sale and supply of prescription only medicines[1], a prescription only medicine is not sold or supplied in accordance with a prescription given by an appropriate practitioner[2] who is an EEA health professional[3] unless the following conditions are met[4].

Condition A is that it is an EEA prescription[5].

Condition B is that the prescription is signed in ink by the EEA health professional giving it[6].

Condition C is that the prescription is written in ink or otherwise so as to be indelible[7].

Condition D is that the prescription contains the address of the EEA health professional giving it, the date on which it is signed by the EEA health professional, an indication of whether the EEA health professional is a doctor or dentist[8] and the name of the person for whose treatment it is given[9].

Condition E is that the prescription is not dispensed after the end of the period of six months beginning with the date on which it is signed by the EEA health professional or, in the case of a repeatable prescription, it is not dispensed for the first time after the end of that period and it is dispensed in accordance with the directions contained in the prescription[10].

Condition F is that, in the case of a repeatable prescription that does not specify the number of times it may be dispensed it is not dispensed on more than two occasions or, in the case of a prescription for an oral contraceptive, it is not dispensed on more than six occasions or after the end of the period of six months beginning with the date on which it is signed by the EEA health professional[11].

The following applies to a prescription that is not a health prescription[12] for a controlled drug[13]. A prescription only medicine[14] is also sold or supplied in accordance with a prescription is also sold or supplied in accordance with a prescription given by an EEA health professional if conditions B and C above are not met, but the prescription is created in electronic form, signed with an advanced electronic signature[15], sent to the person by whom it is dispensed as an electronic communication[16] (whether or not through one or more intermediaries) and conditions A and D to F above are met[17].

1 Ie for the purposes of the Human Medicines Regulations 2012, SI 2012/1916, regs 214–222. As to the meaning of 'prescription only medicine' see the Human Medicines Regulations 2012, SI 2012/1916, reg 5(3); and PARA 26: reg 8(1). As to the meanings of 'sale' and 'supply' see PARA 271 note 1.
2 As to the meaning of 'appropriate practitioner' see PARA 271.
3 As to the meaning of 'EEA health professional' see PARA 271 note 16.
4 Human Medicines Regulations 2012, SI 2012/1916, reg 218(1). Regulations 218 is subject to reg 219 (see text and notes 12–17): reg 218(8).
5 Human Medicines Regulations 2012, SI 2012/1916, reg 218(2). 'EEA prescription' means a prescription given in an EEA state other than the United Kingdom or in Switzerland: reg 213(1).
6 Human Medicines Regulations 2012, SI 2012/1916, reg 218(3).
7 Human Medicines Regulations 2012, SI 2012/1916, reg 218(4).
8 As to the meanings of 'doctor' and 'dentist' see PARA 48 note 6.
9 Human Medicines Regulations 2012, SI 2012/1916, reg 218(5).
10 Human Medicines Regulations 2012, SI 2012/1916, reg 218(6).
11 Human Medicines Regulations 2012, SI 2012/1916, reg 218(7).
12 As to the meaning of 'health prescription' see PARA 275 note 13.
13 Human Medicines Regulations 2012, SI 2012/1916, reg 219(1). As to the meaning of 'controlled drug' see PARA 275 note 5.
14 As to the meaning of 'prescription only medicine' see the Human Medicines Regulations 2012, SI 2012/1916, reg 5(3); and PARA 26: reg 8(1).
15 As to the meaning of 'advanced electronic signature' PARA 275 note 18.
16 As to the meaning of 'electronic communication' see PARA 275 note 19.
17 Human Medicines Regulations 2012, SI 2012/1916, reg 219(3), (4).

277. Sale or supply of medicinal products not subject to general sale. A person ('P') may not sell or supply[1], or offer for sale or supply, a medicinal product[2] that is not subject to general sale unless:

(1)   P is a person lawfully conducting a retail pharmacy business[3];
(2)   the product is sold, supplied, or offered for sale or supply, on premises that are a registered pharmacy[4]; and
(3)   P or, if the transaction is carried out on P's behalf by another person, that other person is, or acts under the supervision of, a pharmacist[5].

Breach of the above provisions[6] is an offence[7].

1 As to the meanings of 'sell' or 'supply' see PARA 271 note 1.
2 As to the meaning of 'medicinal product' see PARA 25.
3 Human Medicines Regulations 2012, SI 2012/1916, reg 220(1), (2)(a). Regulation 220 is subject to Chapter 3 (regs 223–235); reg 220(3).
4 Human Medicines Regulations 2012, SI 2012/1916, reg 220(1), (2)(b).
5 Human Medicines Regulations 2012, SI 2012/1916, reg 220(1), (2)(c).
6 Ie breach of the Human Medicines Regulations 2012, SI 2012/1916, reg 220.
7 See the Human Medicines Regulations 2012, SI 2012/1916, reg 255(1)(c); and PARA 379.

278. Sale or supply of medicinal products subject to general sale. A person ('P') may not sell or supply, or offer for sale or supply, a medicinal product[1] that is subject to general sale elsewhere than at a registered pharmacy[2] unless the following conditions are met[3].

Condition A is that the place at which the medicinal product is sold, supplied, or offered for sale or supply, consists of premises of which P is the occupier and which P is able to close so as to exclude the public[4].

Condition B is that:

(1) the medicinal product was made up for sale in its immediate and outer packaging[5] elsewhere than at the place at which it is sold, supplied, or offered for sale or supply[6]; and

(2) the immediate and outer packaging has not been opened since the product was made up for sale in it[7].

Condition C is that, if the medicinal product is of a specified kind[8] it is presented for sale in accordance with the appropriate specified requirements[9] for a product of that kind[10].

Breach of the above provisions[11] is an offence[12].

1 As to the meaning of 'medicinal product' see PARA 25. As to the meanings of 'sale', 'sell' and 'supply' see PARA 271 note 1.

2 As to the meaning of 'registered pharmacy' see PARA 52 note 2.

3 Human Medicines Regulations 2012, SI 2012/1916, reg 221(1). Regulation 221 is subject to Chapter 3 (regs 223–248): reg 221(5).

4 Human Medicines Regulations 2012, SI 2012/1916, reg 221(2).

5 'Immediate packaging' in relation to a medicinal product means the container or other form of packaging immediately in contact with the medicinal product: Human Medicines Regulations 2012, SI 2012/1916, reg 8(1). 'Outer packaging' in relation to a medicinal product means any packaging into which the immediate packaging of the medicinal product is placed; reg 8(1).

6 Human Medicines Regulations 2012, SI 2012/1916, reg 221(3)(a).

7 Human Medicines Regulations 2012, SI 2012/1916, reg 221(3)(b).

8 Ie a kind specified in the Human Medicines Regulations 2012, SI 2012/1916, Sch 15. A medicinal product that contains aloxiprin, aspirin or paracetamol (or, where appropriate, any combination of those substances) and that is in a specified form must be presented for sale in a separate and individual package containing not more than the specified limited amount of the product: see Sch 15. Similarly a medicinal product that contains tablets, capsules, powder, granules or liquid preparations of ibuprofen must be presented for sale in a separate and individual package containing not more than a specified limited amount of the product: see Sch 15.

9 Ie the requirements specified in the Human Medicines Regulations 2012, SI 2012/1916, Sch 15.

10 Human Medicines Regulations 2012, SI 2012/1916, reg 221(4).

11 Ie breach of the Human Medicines Regulations 2012, SI 2012/1916, reg 221.

12 See the Human Medicines Regulations 2012, SI 2012/1916, reg 255(6)(a); and PARA 379.

279. Sale of medicinal products from automatic machines. A person may not sell or offer for sale a medicinal product[1] by means of an automatic machine if the product is not subject to general sale[2]. Breach of this provision[3] is an offence[4].

1 As to the meaning of 'medicinal product' see PARA 25. As to the meanings of 'sell' and 'sale' see PARA 271 note 1.

2 Human Medicines Regulations 2012, SI 2012/1916, reg 222.

3 Ie breach of the Human Medicines Regulations 2012, SI 2012/1916, reg 222.

4 See the Human Medicines Regulations 2012, SI 2012/1916, reg 255(6)(b); and PARA 379.

(iii) Exemptions

280. Exemptions for doctors and dentists etc. The restriction relating to the sale or supply of prescription only medicines[1] does not apply to the sale or supply of a prescription only medicine by a doctor or dentist[2] to a patient of that doctor or dentist[3].

The restrictions relating to the sale or supply of a medicinal product[4] do not apply to the sale, offer for sale, or supply of a medicinal product by a doctor or dentist to a patient of the doctor or dentist or to a person under whose care such a patient is[5]. Nor do those provisions apply to the sale, offer for sale or supply of a medicinal product in the course of the business of a hospital or health centre[6], where:

(1) the product is sold, offered for sale or supplied for the purposes of being administered to a person (whether in the hospital or health centre or elsewhere) in accordance with directions relating to that person[7]; and

(2) those directions have been given by a doctor, a dentist, a supplementary prescriber[8], a pharmacist independent prescriber[9], an optometrist independent prescriber[10], a nurse independent prescriber[11] or a community practitioner nurse prescriber[12].

The restrictions relating to the sale or supply of a medicinal product[13] do not apply to the sale or supply of certain medicinal products[14] where:

(a) the product is sold or supplied by a registered midwife[15] in the course of the registered midwife's professional practice[16]; or

(b) the product is delivered or administered by a registered midwife on being supplied the product under arrangements made by the Secretary of State or the Minister for Health, Social Services and Public Safety[17].

1 Ie the Human Medicines Regulations 2012, SI 2012/1916, reg 214(1) (see PARA 271). As to the meanings of 'sale' and 'supply' see PARA 271 note 1. As to the meaning of 'prescription only medicine' see the Human Medicines Regulations 2012, SI 2012/1916, reg 5(3); and PARA 26: reg 8(1).
2 As to the meanings of 'doctor' and 'dentist' see PARA 48 note 6.
3 Human Medicines Regulations 2012, SI 2012/1916, reg 223(1).
4 Ie the Human Medicines Regulations 2012, SI 2012/1916, reg 220, 221 (see PARAS 277, 278). As to the meaning of 'medicinal product' see PARA 25.
5 Human Medicines Regulations 2012, SI 2012/1916, reg 223(2).
6 As to the meaning of 'hospital' and 'health centre' see PARA 52 notes 3, 4.
7 Human Medicines Regulations 2012, SI 2012/1916, reg 223(3)(a).
8 As to the meaning of 'supplementary prescriber' see PARA 50 note 5.
9 As to the meaning of 'pharmacist independent prescriber' see PARA 50 note 4.
10 As to the meaning of 'optometrist independent prescriber' see PARA 271 note 13.
11 As to the meaning of 'nurse independent prescriber' see PARA 50 note 3.
12 Human Medicines Regulations 2012, SI 2012/1916, reg 223(3)(b). As to the meaning of 'community practitioner nurse prescriber' see PARA 271 note 11.
13 See note 4.
14 The products to which the Human Medicines Regulations 2012, SI 2012/1916, reg 223 applies are:
    (1) medicinal products that are not prescription only medicines (reg 223(5)(a));
    (2) prescription only medicines which by virtue of an exemption conferred under reg 235(1) and 235(3) and Sch 17 Pt 1 may be sold or supplied by a registered midwife otherwise than in accordance with a prescription given by a doctor or a dentist (reg 223(5)(b)); and
    (3) prescription only medicines which by virtue of an exemption conferred under reg 235(3) and Sch 17 Pt 3 may be administered by a registered midwife or a student midwife otherwise than in accordance with a prescription given by a doctor or a dentist (reg 223(5)(c)).
15 As to the meaning of 'registered midwife' see PARA 48 note 3.

16 Human Medicines Regulations 2012, SI 2012/1916, reg 223(4)(a).
17 Human Medicines Regulations 2012, SI 2012/1916, reg 223(4)(b).

281.   Emergency sale by pharmacist where prescriber unable to provide prescription. The restriction relating to the sale or supply of prescription only medicines[1] does not apply to the sale or supply of a prescription only medicine by a person lawfully conducting a retail pharmacy business[2] if conditions A to E are met[3].

Condition A is that the pharmacist[4] by or under whose supervision the prescription only medicine is to be sold or supplied is satisfied that the sale or supply has been requested by a relevant prescriber[5] who by reason of an emergency is unable to provide a prescription immediately[6].

Condition B is that the relevant prescriber has undertaken to provide the person lawfully conducting the retail pharmacy business with a prescription within the period of 72 hours beginning with the sale or supply[7].

Condition C is that the prescription only medicine is sold or supplied in accordance with the directions of the relevant prescriber[8].

Condition D is that the prescription only medicine is not a controlled drug[9], other than a prescription only medicine that consists of or contains phenobarbital or phenobarbital sodium and is sold or supplied for use in the treatment of epilepsy[10].

Condition E is that an entry is made in the pharmacy record[11] kept within the specified time[12] stating the particulars required[13].

1   Ie the Human Medicines Regulations 2012, SI 2012/1916, reg 214(1) (see PARA 271). As to the meanings of 'sale' and 'supply' see PARA 271 note 1. As to the meaning of 'prescription only medicine' see the Human Medicines Regulations 2012, SI 2012/1916, reg 5(3); and PARA 26: reg 8(1).
2   As to the meaning of 'retail pharmacy business' see PARA 52 note 12.
3   Human Medicines Regulations 2012, SI 2012/1916, reg 224(1).
4   As to the meaning of 'pharmacist' see PARA 52 note 5.
5   'Relevant prescriber' means any of the following a doctor, a dentist, a supplementary prescriber, a nurse independent prescriber, a pharmacist independent prescriber, a community practitioner nurse prescriber, an optometrist independent prescriber and an EEA health professional: Human Medicines Regulations 2012, SI 2012/1916, reg 213(1). As to the meanings of 'doctor' and 'dentist' see PARA 48 note 6. As to the meanings of 'supplementary prescriber', 'pharmacist independent prescriber' and 'nurse independent prescriber' see PARA 50 notes 3–5. As to the meanings of 'community practitioner nurse prescriber', 'optometrist independent prescriber' and 'EEA health professional' see PARA 271 notes 11, 13, 16.
6   Human Medicines Regulations 2012, SI 2012/1916, reg 224(2).
7   Human Medicines Regulations 2012, SI 2012/1916, reg 224(3).
8   Human Medicines Regulations 2012, SI 2012/1916, reg 224(4).
9   As to the meaning of 'controlled drug' see PARA 275 note 5.
10 Human Medicines Regulations 2012, SI 2012/1916, reg 224(5).
11 Ie the record kept under the Human Medicines Regulations 2012, SI 2012/1916, reg 253 (see MEDICAL PROFESSIONS).
12 Ie the time specified in the Human Medicines Regulations 2012, SI 2012/1916, reg 253 (see MEDICAL PROFESSIONS).
13 Human Medicines Regulations 2012, SI 2012/1916, reg 224(6). As to the particulars that are required see Sch 23 para 2.

282.   Emergency sale by pharmacist at patient's request. The restriction relating to the sale or supply of prescription only medicines[1] does not apply to the sale or supply of a prescription only medicine by a person lawfully conducting a retail pharmacy business[2] if conditions A to E are met[3].

Condition A is that the pharmacist[4] by or under whose supervision the prescription only medicine is to be sold or supplied has interviewed the person requesting it and is satisfied:

(1)   that there is an immediate need for the prescription only medicine to be sold or supplied and that it is impracticable in the circumstances to obtain a prescription without undue delay[5];

(2)   that treatment with the prescription only medicine has on a previous occasion been prescribed by a relevant prescriber[6] for the person requesting it[7]; and

(3)   as to the dose which in the circumstances it would be appropriate for that person to take[8].

Condition B is that for a specified prescription only medicine, the quantity of the product that is sold or supplied does not exceed a set amount[9] for that prescription only medicine[10].

Condition C is that the prescription only medicine does not consist of or contain a specified substance[11] and is not a controlled drug, other than a prescription only medicine that consists of or contains phenobarbital or phenobarbital sodium and is sold or supplied for use in the treatment of epilepsy[12].

Condition D is that an entry is made in the pharmacy records[13] within the time specified in that regulation stating the certain particulars[14].

Condition E is that the inner or outer packaging[15] of the prescription only medicine is labelled to show the date on which the prescription only medicine is sold or supplied, the name, quantity and (unless apparent from the name) the pharmaceutical strength of the prescription only medicine, the name of the person requesting the prescription only medicine, the name and address of the registered pharmacy from which the prescription only medicine is sold or supplied and the words 'Emergency Supply'[16].

1   Ie the Human Medicines Regulations 2012, SI 2012/1916, reg 214(1) (see PARA 271). As to the meanings of 'sale' and 'supply' see PARA 271 note 1. As to the meaning of 'prescription only medicine' see the Human Medicines Regulations 2012, SI 2012/1916, reg 5(3); and PARA 26: reg 8(1).

2   As to the meaning of 'retail pharmacy business' see PARA 52 note 12.

3   Human Medicines Regulations 2012, SI 2012/1916, reg 225(1).

4   As to the meaning of 'pharmacist' see PARA 52 note 5.

5   Human Medicines Regulations 2012, SI 2012/1916, reg 225(2)(a).

6   As to the meaning of 'relevant prescriber' see PARA 281 note 5.

7   Human Medicines Regulations 2012, SI 2012/1916, reg 225(2)(b).

8   Human Medicines Regulations 2012, SI 2012/1916, reg 225(2)(c).

9   Ie (1) a prescription only medicine that is a preparation of insulin, an aerosol for the relief of asthma, an ointment or cream and has been made up for sale in a package elsewhere than at the place of sale or supply that does not exceed the smallest pack that the pharmacist has available for sale or supply; (2) an oral contraceptive that does not exceed the quantity sufficient for a full treatment cycle; (3) an antibiotic for oral administration in liquid form does not exceed the smallest quantity that will provide a full course of treatment; (4) a controlled drug within the meaning of the Misuse of Drugs Regulations 2011, SI 2001/3998, Sch 4 or 5 does not exceed 5 days' treatment; (5) any other prescription only medicine does not exceed 30 days' treatment: Human Medicines Regulations 2012, SI 2012/1916, reg 225(3). As to the meaning of 'controlled drug' see PARA 275 note 5. 'Aerosol' means a product that is dispersed from its container by a propellant gas or liquid: Human Medicines Regulations 2012, SI 2012/1916, reg 225(7).

10   Human Medicines Regulations 2012, SI 2012/1916, reg 225(3).

11   Human Medicines Regulations 2012, SI 2012/1916, reg 225(4)(a). The specified substances are ammonium bromide, calcium bromide, calcium bromidolactobionate, embutramide, fencamfamin hydrochloride, fluanisone, hexobarbitone, hexobarbitone sodium, hydrobromic

acid, meclofenoxate hydrochloride, methohexitone sodium, pemoline, piracetam, potassium bromide, prolintane hydrochloride, sodium bromide, strychnine hydrochloride, tacrine hydrochloride, thiopentone sodium: Sch 18.

12 Human Medicines Regulations 2012, SI 2012/1916, reg 225(4)(b).
13 Ie the records kept under the Human Medicines Regulations 2012, SI 2012/1916, reg 253.
14 Human Medicines Regulations 2012, SI 2012/1916, reg 225(5). The particulars mentioned in the text are the ones set out in the Human Medicines Regulations 2012, SI 2012/1916, Sch 23 para 4.
15 As to the meanings of 'immediate packaging' and 'outer packaging' see PARA 278 note 5.
16 Human Medicines Regulations 2012, SI 2012/1916, reg 225(6).

283.   Emergency sale by pharmacist in pandemic. The restriction relating to the sale or supply of prescription only medicines[1] does not apply to the sale or supply of a prescription only medicine by a person lawfully conducting a retail pharmacy business[2] if conditions A and B are met[3].

Condition A is that the supply is made whilst a disease is, or in anticipation of a disease being imminently, pandemic and a serious risk, or potentially a serious risk, to human health[4].

Condition B is that the pharmacist[5] by or under whose supervision the prescription only medicine is to be sold or supplied is satisfied:

(1)   that treatment with the prescription only medicine has on a previous occasion been prescribed by a relevant prescriber[6] for the person to be treated with it[7]; and

(2)   as to the dose which in the circumstances it would be appropriate for that person to take[8].

1 Ie the Human Medicines Regulations 2012, SI 2012/1916, reg 214(1) (see PARA 271). As to the meanings of 'sale' and 'supply' see PARA 271 note 1. As to the meaning of 'prescription only medicine' see the Human Medicines Regulations 2012, SI 2012/1916, reg 5(3); and PARA 26: reg 8(1).
2 As to the meaning of 'retail pharmacy business' see PARA 52 note 12.
3 Human Medicines Regulations 2012, SI 2012/1916, reg 226(1).
4 Human Medicines Regulations 2012, SI 2012/1916, reg 226(2).
5 As to the meaning of 'pharmacist' see PARA 52 note 5.
6 As to the meaning of 'relevant prescriber' see PARA 281 note 5.
7 Human Medicines Regulations 2012, SI 2012/1916, reg 226(3)(a).
8 Human Medicines Regulations 2012, SI 2012/1916, reg 226(3)(b).

284.   Sale or supply in hospitals. The restriction relating to the sale or supply of prescription only medicines[1] does not apply to the sale or supply of a prescription only medicine in the course of the business of a hospital[2] and for the purpose of being administered[3] (in the hospital or elsewhere) to a particular person in accordance with directions that meet the following conditions[4].

Those conditions are that the directions are in writing, relate to the particular person to whom the prescription only medicine is to be administered and are given by a person who is an appropriate practitioner[5] in relation to that prescription only medicine[6].

However, such directions may be given by a supplementary prescriber only where he complies with the relevant prescribing and administration provisions[7] or the exceptions to those provisions[8] in relation to the directions as if they were a prescription[9].

1 Ie the Human Medicines Regulations 2012, SI 2012/1916, reg 214(1) (see PARA 271). As to the meanings of 'sale' and 'supply' see PARA 271 note 1. As to the meaning of 'prescription only medicine' see the Human Medicines Regulations 2012, SI 2012/1916, reg 5(3); and PARA 26: reg 8(1).
2 As to the meaning of 'hospital' see PARA 52 note 3.

3   As to the meaning of 'administer' see PARA 25 note 4.
4   Human Medicines Regulations 2012, SI 2012/1916, reg 227(1). Regulation 227 applies regardless of whether the directions comply with reg 217 (see PARA 275): reg 227(4).
5   As to the meaning of 'appropriate practitioner' see PARA 271.
6   Human Medicines Regulations 2012, SI 2012/1916, reg 227(2).
7   Ie the Human Medicines Regulations 2012, SI 2012/1916, reg 215 (see PARA 274).
8   Ie the Human Medicines Regulations 2012, SI 2012/1916, reg 216 (see PARA 274).
9   Human Medicines Regulations 2012, SI 2012/1916, reg 227(3).

285.   Prescriptions given by certain health professionals.   The restriction relating to the sale or supply of prescription only medicines[1] does not apply to the sale or supply of a prescription only medicine by a pharmacist[2] where:

(1)   the sale or supply is in accordance with a prescription given by another pharmacist, a registered nurse[3], a registered midwife[4], a registered optometrist[5] or a person whose name is entered in the part of the Health and Care Professions Council register relating to chiropodists and podiatrists, physiotherapists or diagnostic or therapeutic radiographers[6], who is not an appropriate practitioner[7] in relation to that prescription only medicine[8]; but

(2)   the pharmacist, having exercised all due diligence, believes on reasonable grounds that the person is such a practitioner[9].

Nor does the restriction relating to the sale or supply of prescription only medicines[10] apply to the sale or supply of a prescription only medicine by a pharmacist where the sale or supply is in accordance with a prescription given by a supplementary prescriber[11] and the pharmacist, having exercised all due diligence, believes on reasonable grounds that the supplementary prescriber has complied with the prescribing and administration provisions[12].

1   Ie the Human Medicines Regulations 2012, SI 2012/1916, reg 214(1) (see PARA 271). As to the meanings of 'sale' and 'supply' see PARA 271 note 1. As to the meaning of 'prescription only medicine' see the Human Medicines Regulations 2012, SI 2012/1916, reg 5(3); and PARA 26: reg 8(1).
2   As to the meaning of 'pharmacist' see PARA 52 note 5.
3   As to the meaning of 'registered nurse' see PARA 48 note 3.
4   As to the meaning of 'registered midwife' see PARA 48 note 3.
5   As to the meaning of 'registered optometrist' see PARA 36 note 8.
6   See MEDICAL PROFESSIONS.
7   As to the meaning of 'appropriate practitioner' see PARA 271.
8   See the Human Medicines Regulations 2012, SI 2012/1916, reg 228(1), (2)(a).
9   Human Medicines Regulations 2012, SI 2012/1916, reg 228(2)(b).
10 See note 1.
11 As to the meaning of 'supplementary prescriber' see PARA 50 note 5.
12 Human Medicines Regulations 2012, SI 2012/1916, reg 228(3). The prescribing and administration provisions mentioned in the text refers to reg 215 (see PARA 274).

286.   Supply by national health service bodies.   Restrictions relating to the sale or supply of prescription only medicines[1], medicines not subject to general sale[2] and medicines subject to general sale[3] do not apply to the supply of a medicinal product[4] in accordance with condition A or B below by the Common Services Agency[5], a health authority[6] or special health authority[7], an NHS trust[8], an NHS foundation trust[9], a Primary Care Trust[10] or a person who is not a doctor, dentist[11] or person lawfully conducting a retail pharmacy business[12], where the person supplies the product pursuant to an arrangement with one of the persons previously mentioned[13].

Condition A is that the product is supplied for the purpose of being administered[14] to a person in accordance with the written directions of a doctor, dentist, nurse independent prescriber[15], optometrist independent prescriber[16] or pharmacist independent prescriber[17] relating to that person, regardless of whether the directions comply with the general requirements[18] for prescriptions[19].

Condition B is that:

(1) the product is supplied for the purpose of being administered to a person in accordance with a patient group direction ('PGD')[20];

(2) the PGD relates to the supply of a description or class of medicinal product by the person by whom the medicinal product is supplied and has effect at the time at which it is supplied[21];

(3) the PGD contains specified particulars[22];

(4) the PGD is signed on behalf of a specified person[23];

(5) the individual who supplies the product belongs to one of the specified classes of individual[24] and is designated in writing, on behalf of the authorising person, for the purpose of the supply or administration of products under the PGD[25]; and

(6) when the product is supplied, a marketing authorisation, Article 126a authorisation, certificate of registration or traditional herbal registration[26] is in force in relation to it[27].

1 Ie the Human Medicines Regulations 2012, SI 2012/1916, reg 214(1) (see PARA 271). As to the meanings of 'sale' and 'supply' see PARA 271 note 1. As to the meaning of 'prescription only medicine' see the Human Medicines Regulations 2012, SI 2012/1916, reg 5(3); and PARA 26: reg 8(1).

2 Ie the Human Medicines Regulations 2012, SI 2012/1916, reg 220 (see PARA 277).

3 Ie the Human Medicines Regulations 2012, SI 2012/1916, reg 221 (see PARA 278).

4 As to the meaning of 'medicinal product' see PARA 25.

5 'The Common Services Agency' means the Common Services Agency for the Scottish Health Service established under the National Health Service (Scotland) Act 1978 s 10: Human Medicines Regulations 2012, SI 2012/1916, reg 213(1).

6 'Health authority' means, in relation to England, a strategic health authority established or continued under the National Health Service Act 2006 s 13 and, in relation to Wales, a local health board established under the National Health Service (Wales) Act 2006 s 11: Human Medicines Regulations 2012, SI 2012/1916, reg 213(1). As from 1 April 2013, strategic health authorities are abolished: see PARA 111 note 9.

7 'Special health authority' means, in relation to England, a Special Health Authority established under the National Health Service Act 2006 s 28 and, in relation to Wales, a Special Health Authority established under the National Health Service (Wales) Act 2006 s 22: Human Medicines Regulations 2012, SI 2012/1916, reg 213(1).

8 'NHS trust', in relation to England, means an NHS trust established under the National Health Service Act 2006 s 25(1) and, in relation to Wales, means an NHS trust established under the National Health Service (Wales) Act 2006 s 18(1): Human Medicines Regulations 2012, SI 2012/1916, reg 213(1). As from a day to be appointed, NHS trusts are abolished: see the Health and Social Care Act 2012 s 179.

9 'NHS foundation trust' has the meaning given by the National Health Service Act 2006 s 30(1): Human Medicines Regulations 2012, SI 2012/1916, reg 213(1).

10 'Primary Care Trust' means a Primary Care Trust established or continued under the National Health Service Act 2006 s 18 (see HEALTH SERVICES vol 54 (2008) PARA 111): Human Medicines Regulations 2012, SI 2012/1916, reg 213(1). As from 1 April 2013, Primary Care Trusts are abolished: see PARA 3 note 1.

11 As to the meanings of 'doctor' and 'dentist' see PARA 48 note 6.

12 As to the meaning of 'retail pharmacy business' see PARA 52 note 12.

13 Human Medicines Regulations 2012, SI 2012/1916, reg 229(1).

14 As to the meaning of 'administer' see PARA 25 note 4.

15 As to the meaning of 'nurse independent prescriber' see PARA 50 note 3.

16 As to the meaning of 'optometrist independent prescriber' see PARA 271 note 13.

17 As to the meaning of 'pharmacist independent prescriber' see PARA 50 note 4.

18 Ie the Human Medicines Regulations 2012, SI 2012/1916, reg 217 (see PARA 275).

19 Human Medicines Regulations 2012, SI 2012/1916, reg 229(2).

20 Human Medicines Regulations 2012, SI 2012/1916, reg 229(3)(a). 'Patient group direction' or 'PGD' means a written direction that relates to the sale or supply and to the administration of a description or class of medicinal product and that is signed by a doctor or dentist and by a pharmacist and by any other person who may be required to sign it in the circumstances specified for its use in any provision of Pt 12 (regs 213–256) and that relates to sale or supply and to administration to persons generally (subject to any exclusions that may be specified in the PGD): reg 213(1).

21 Human Medicines Regulations 2012, SI 2012/1916, reg 229(3)(b).

22 Human Medicines Regulations 2012, SI 2012/1916, reg 229(3)(c). The specified particulars mentioned in the text refers to the particulars specified in Sch 16 Pt 1.

23 Human Medicines Regulations 2012, SI 2012/1916, reg 229(3)(d). The specified person mentioned in the text is a person specified in Sch 16 Pt 2 column 2 who is to sign against the entry in column 1 for the class of person by whom the product is supplied.

24 Ie pharmacists, registered chiropodists and podiatrists, registered dental hygienist, registered dental therapist, registered dietitians, registered midwives, registered nurses, registered occupational therapists, registered optometrists, registered orthoptists, registered orthotists and prosthetists, registered paramedics, registered physiotherapists, registered radiographers, registered speech and language therapists: Human Medicines Regulations 2012, SI 2012/1916, Sch 16 Pt 4. 'Registered chiropodist' and 'registered podiatrist' means a person who is registered in the Health and Care Professions Council register Part 2, 'registered dietitian' means a person who is registered in Part 4, 'registered occupational therapist' means a person who is registered in Part 6, 'registered orthoptist' means a person who is registered in Part 7, 'registered paramedic' means a person who is registered in Part 8, 'registered physiotherapist' means a person who is registered in Part 9, 'registered orthotist and prosthetist' means a person who is registered in Part 10, 'registered radiographer' means a person who is registered in Part 11, 'registered speech and language therapist' means a person who is registered in Part 12, 'registered dental hygienist' and 'registered dental therapist' means a person registered under those titles in the dental care professionals register: Human Medicines Regulations 2012, SI 2012/1916, reg 213(1). As to the meanings of 'registered midwife' and 'registered nurse' see PARA 48 note 3. As to the meaning of 'registered optometrist' see PARA 36 note 8. See also MEDICAL PROFESSIONS.

25 Human Medicines Regulations 2012, SI 2012/1916, reg 229(3)(e).

26 As to the meanings of 'marketing authorisation', 'Article 126a authorisation', 'certificate of registration' and 'traditional herbal registration' see PARA 141 notes 3–6.

27 Human Medicines Regulations 2012, SI 2012/1916, reg 229(3)(f).

287. Supply under a patient group direction to assist doctors or dentists. Restrictions relating to the sale or supply of prescription only medicines[1], medicines not subject to general sale[2] and medicines subject to general sale[3] do not apply to the supply or administration of a medicinal product[4] by an individual belonging to one of the specified classes[5] where:

(1) the individual supplies or (as the case may be) administers the product to assist a doctor[6] in the provision of NHS primary medical services[7] or a dentist[8] in the provision of NHS primary dental services[9];

(2) the product is supplied for the purpose of being administered to a person in accordance with a patient group direction ('PGD')[10]; and

(3) the following conditions are met[11].

Condition A is that the PGD relates to the supply or (as the case may be) administration of a description or class of medicinal product in order to assist the doctor or dentist in providing the services (whether or not it relates to such supply in order to assist any other doctor or dentist)[12].

Condition B is that the PGD has effect at the time at which the product is supplied or (as the case may be) administered[13].

Condition C is that the PGD contains specified particulars[14].

Condition D is that the PGD is signed by the doctor or dentist or, where it also relates to supply or administration to assist one or more other doctors or dentists, by one of those doctors or dentists[15].

Condition E is that the PGD is signed in the case of NHS primary medical services or NHS primary dental services in England or Wales, on behalf of the health authority or Primary Care Trust[16] with which a contract or agreement for the provision of those services has been made or which provides those services[17].

Condition F is that the individual supplying the product is designated in writing for the purpose of the supply or (as the case may be) administration of medicinal products under the PGD by the doctor or dentist or, where it also relates to supply to assist one or more other doctors or dentists, by one of those doctors or dentists[18].

Condition G is that when the product is supplied or (as the case may be) administered, a marketing authorisation, Article 126a authorisation, certificate of registration or traditional herbal registration[19] is in force in relation to it[20].

1   Ie the Human Medicines Regulations 2012, SI 2012/1916, reg 214(1) (see PARA 271). As to the meanings of 'sale' and 'supply' see PARA 271 note 1. As to the meaning of 'prescription only medicine' see the Human Medicines Regulations 2012, SI 2012/1916, reg 5(3); and PARA 26: reg 8(1).

2   Ie the Human Medicines Regulations 2012, SI 2012/1916, reg 220 (see PARA 277).

3   Ie the Human Medicines Regulations 2012, SI 2012/1916, reg 221 (see PARA 278).

4   As to the meaning of 'medicinal product' see PARA 25. As to the meaning of 'administer' see PARA 25 note 4.

5   Ie specified under the Human Medicines Regulations 2012, SI 2012/1916, Sch 16 Pt 4 (see PARA 286 note 24).

6   As to the meaning of 'doctor' see PARA 48 note 6.

7   'NHS primary medical services' means, in relation to England, primary medical services under the National Health Service Act 2006 and, in relation to Wales, primary medical services under the National Health Service (Wales) Act 2006: Human Medicines Regulations 2012, SI 2012/1916, reg 8(1).

8   As to the meaning of 'dentist' see PARA 48 note 6.

9   Human Medicines Regulations 2012, SI 2012/1916, reg 230(1)(a). 'NHS primary dental services' means, in relation to England, primary dental services under the National Health Service Act 2006 and, in relation to Wales, primary dental services under the National Health Service (Wales) Act 2006: Human Medicines Regulations 2012, SI 2012/1916, reg 8(1).

10   Human Medicines Regulations 2012, SI 2012/1916, reg 230(1)(b). As to the meaning of 'patient group direction' see PARA 286 note 20.

11   Human Medicines Regulations 2012, SI 2012/1916, reg 230(1)(c).

12   Human Medicines Regulations 2012, SI 2012/1916, reg 230(2).

13   Human Medicines Regulations 2012, SI 2012/1916, reg 230(3).

14   Human Medicines Regulations 2012, SI 2012/1916, reg 230(4). The specified particulars mentioned in the text are the particulars specified in the Human Medicines Regulations 2012, SI 2012/1916, Sch 16 Pt 1 (but with the omission of Sch 16 para 4 in the case of a PGD relating to administration only).

15   Human Medicines Regulations 2012, SI 2012/1916, reg 230(5).

16   As to the meaning of 'Primary Care Trust' see PARA 286 note 10. As from 1 April 2013, Primary Care Trusts are abolished: see PARA 3 note 1.

17   Human Medicines Regulations 2012, SI 2012/1916, reg 230(6)(a).

18   Human Medicines Regulations 2012, SI 2012/1916, reg 230(7).

19   As to the meanings of 'marketing authorisation', 'Article 126a authorisation', 'certificate of registration' and 'traditional herbal registration' see PARA 141 notes 3–6.

20   Human Medicines Regulations 2012, SI 2012/1916, reg 230(8).

288. Supply under a patient group direction by independent hospitals. Restrictions relating to the sale or supply of prescription only medicines[1], medicines not subject to general sale[2] and medicines subject to general sale[3] do not apply to the sale or supply, or administration[4], of a medicinal product[5] in accordance with the following conditions by an independent hospital[6], an independent clinic[7], an independent medical agency[8] or a nursing home (in Northern Ireland)[9].

Condition A, which applies only to England, is that the registered provider[10] at the hospital, clinic or agency is registered[11] in respect of one or more of the following regulated activities:

(1)   treatment of disease, disorder or injury[12];

(2)   assessment or medical treatment of persons detained under the Mental Health Act 1983[13];

(3)   surgical procedures[14];

(4)   diagnostic and screening procedures[15];

(5)   maternity and midwifery services[16]; and

(6)   family planning[17].

Condition B is that the product is sold or supplied for the purpose of being administered to a person in accordance with a patient group direction ('PGD')[18].

Condition C is that the PGD relates to the sale or supply or (as the case may be) administration of a description or class of medicinal product by the person by whom the medicinal product is sold or supplied or administered and that is has effect at the time at which it is sold or supplied[19].

Condition D is that the PGD contains specified particulars[20].

Condition E is that the PGD is signed by or on behalf of the registered provider[21] and, if there is a relevant manager[22] for the independent hospital, clinic or medical agency, or nursing home, by that manager[23].

Condition F is that the individual who sells or supplies or (as the case may be) administers the product belongs to one of the specified classes of individual[24] and is designated in writing for the purpose of the sale or supply or (as the case may be) administration of products under the PGD by or on behalf of the registered provider or if there is a relevant manager for the independent hospital, clinic or medical agency, or nursing home, by that manager[25].

Condition G is that when the product is supplied, a marketing authorisation, Article 126a authorisation, certificate of registration or traditional herbal registration[26] is in force in relation to it[27].

1   Ie the Human Medicines Regulations 2012, SI 2012/1916, reg 214(1) (see PARA 271). As to the meanings of 'sale' and 'supply' see PARA 271 note 1. As to the meaning of 'prescription only medicine' see the Human Medicines Regulations 2012, SI 2012/1916, reg 5(3); and PARA 26: reg 8(1).

2   Ie the Human Medicines Regulations 2012, SI 2012/1916, reg 220 (see PARA 277).

3   Ie the Human Medicines Regulations 2012, SI 2012/1916, reg 221 (see PARA 278).

4   As to the meaning of 'administer' see PARA 25 note 4.

5   As to the meaning of 'medicinal product' see PARA 25.

6   'Independent hospital', in relation to England, means a hospital as defined by the National Health Service Act 2006 s 275 that is not a health service hospital as defined by that provision and, in relation to Wales, has the meaning given by the Care Standards Act 2000 s 2(2): Human Medicines Regulations 2012, SI 2012/1916, reg 213(1).

7   'Independent clinic':

   (1)   in relation to England, means an establishment of either of the following kinds:

      (a)   a walk-in centre, in which one or more medical practitioners provides services of a kind which, if provided in pursuance of the National Health Services Act 2006, would be provided as primary medical services under Part 4 of that Act (Human Medicines Regulations 2012, SI 2012/1916, reg 213(1)); or

      (b)   a surgery or consulting room in which a medical practitioner who provides no services in pursuance of the National Health Services Act 2006 provides medical services of any kind (including psychiatric treatment), except where such medical services are provided only under arrangements made on behalf of the patients by their employer, a government department or any executive agency of any government department, a prison or other establishment in which patients are held under custody, other than pursuant to any provision under the Mental Health Act 1983 or an insurance provider with whom the patients hold an insurance policy, other than an insurance policy which is solely or primarily intended to provide benefits in connection with the diagnosis or treatment of physical or mental illness, disability or infirmity, and where two or more medical practitioners use different parts of the same premises as a surgery or consulting room, or use the same surgery or consulting room at different times, each of the medical practitioners are regarded as carrying on a separate independent clinic unless they practise together (Human Medicines Regulations 2012, SI 2012/1916, reg 213(1));

    (2)   in relation to Wales, has the meaning given by the Care Standards Act 2000 s 2(4) (Human Medicines Regulations 2012, SI 2012/1916, reg 213(1)).

8   'Independent medical agency':

    (1)   in relation to England, means an undertaking (not being an independent hospital) which consists of or includes the provision of services by medical practitioners, and the term 'undertaking' in this definition includes any business or profession and in relation to a public or local authority includes the exercise of any functions of that authority and, in relation to any other body of persons, whether corporate or unincorporated, includes any of the activities of that body (Human Medicines Regulations 2012, SI 2012/1916, reg 213(1));

    (2)   in relation to Wales, has the meaning given by the Care Standards Act 2000 s 2(5) (Human Medicines Regulations 2012, SI 2012/1916, reg 213(1)).

9   Human Medicines Regulations 2012, SI 2012/1916, reg 231(1).

10   'Registered provider':

    (1)   in England, in relation to an independent hospital, independent clinic, an independent medical agency, a dental clinic or a dental practice means the person who is registered as a service provider under the Health and Social Care Act 2008 Pt 1 Chapter 2 in respect of regulated activities (within the meaning of that Part) carried on in that hospital, clinic, agency, dental clinic or dental practice (Human Medicines Regulations 2012, SI 2012/1916, reg 213(1));

    (2)   in Wales, in relation to an independent hospital, an independent clinic or an independent medical agency, means the person who is registered under the Care Standards Act 2000 Pt 2 as the person who carries on the hospital, clinic or agency (Human Medicines Regulations 2012, SI 2012/1916, reg 213(1)).

11   Ie in compliance with the Health and Social Care Act 2008 s 10 (see SOCIAL SERVICES AND COMMUNITY CARE).

12   Human Medicines Regulations 2012, SI 2012/1916, reg 231(2)(a).

13   Human Medicines Regulations 2012, SI 2012/1916, reg 231(2)(b).

14   Human Medicines Regulations 2012, SI 2012/1916, reg 231(2)(c).

15   Human Medicines Regulations 2012, SI 2012/1916, reg 231(2)(d).

16   Human Medicines Regulations 2012, SI 2012/1916, reg 231(2)(e).

17   Human Medicines Regulations 2012, SI 2012/1916, reg 231(2)(f).

18   Human Medicines Regulations 2012, SI 2012/1916, reg 231(3). As to the meaning of 'patient group direction' see PARA 286 note 20.

19   Human Medicines Regulations 2012, SI 2012/1916, reg 231(4).

20   Human Medicines Regulations 2012, SI 2012/1916, reg 231(5). The specified particulars mentioned in the text refers to the particulars specified in Sch 16 Pt 1 (but with the omission of Sch 16 para 4 in the case of a PGD relating to administration only).

21   As to the meaning of 'registered provider' see PARA 288 note 10.

22   'Relevant manager':

    (1)   in England, means a person, other than the registered provider, who is registered under the Health and Social Care Act 2008 Pt 1 Chapter 2 as the manager of an independent hospital, independent clinic, an independent medical agency, a dental clinic or a dental practice or, if there is no such person, but the registered provider has appointed a person to manage the hospital, clinic, agency, dental clinic or dental practice, that person (Human Medicines Regulations 2012, SI 2012/1916, reg 213(1));

    (2)   in Wales, means a person, other than the registered provider, who is registered under the Care Standards Act 2000 Pt 2 as the manager of an independent hospital, an independent clinic or an independent medical agency or, if there is no such person, but the registered provider has appointed a person to manage the hospital, clinic or agency, that person (Human Medicines Regulations 2012, SI 2012/1916, reg 213(1)).

23   Human Medicines Regulations 2012, SI 2012/1916, reg 231(6).

24   Ie the individual specified by the Human Medicines Regulations 2012, SI 2012/1916, Sch 16 Pt 4 (see PARA 286 note 24).

25   Human Medicines Regulations 2012, SI 2012/1916, reg 231(7).

26 As to the meanings of 'marketing authorisation', 'Article 126a authorisation', 'certificate of registration' and 'traditional herbal registration' see PARA 141 notes 3–6.

27 Human Medicines Regulations 2012, SI 2012/1916, reg 213(8).

289. Supply under a patient group direction by dental practices and clinics. Restrictions relating to the sale or supply of prescription only medicines[1], medicines not subject to general sale[2] and medicines subject to general sale[3] do not apply to the sale or supply, or administration[4], of a medicinal product[5] by a dental practice or dental clinic in England[6] and Wales[7] in accordance with the following conditions[8].

Condition A is that the product is sold or supplied for the purpose of being administered to a person in accordance with a patient group direction ('PGD')[9].

Condition B is that the PGD relates to the sale or supply or (as the case may be) administration of a description or class of medicinal product by the person by whom the medicinal product is sold or supplied or administered and has effect at the time at which it is sold or supplied[10].

Condition C is that the PGD contains specified particulars[11].

Condition D is that the PGD is signed, in England, by or on behalf of the registered provider[12] and, if there is a relevant manager[13] for the practice or clinic, by that manager and, in Wales, by the private dentist who is treating the person and, if there is a manager for the practice or clinic, by that manager[14].

Condition E is that the individual who sells or supplies or (as the case may be) administers the product belongs to one of the specified classes of individual[15] and is designated in writing for the purpose of the sale or supply or (as the case may be) administration of products under the PGD, in England, by or on behalf of the registered provider or, if there is a relevant manager for the practice or clinic, by that manager or, in Wales, by the private dentist who is treating the person[16].

Condition F is that when the product is supplied, a marketing authorisation, Article 126a authorisation, certificate of registration or traditional herbal registration[17] is in force in relation to it[18].

1 Ie the Human Medicines Regulations 2012, SI 2012/1916, reg 214(1) (see PARA 271). As to the meanings of 'sale' and 'supply' see PARA 271 note 1. As to the meaning of 'prescription only medicine' see the Human Medicines Regulations 2012, SI 2012/1916, reg 5(3); and PARA 26: reg 8(1).

2 Ie the Human Medicines Regulations 2012, SI 2012/1916, reg 220 (see PARA 277).

3 Ie the Human Medicines Regulations 2012, SI 2012/1916, reg 221 (see PARA 278).

4 As to the meaning of 'administer' see PARA 25 note 4.

5 As to the meaning of 'medicinal product' see PARA 25.

6 Ie a dental practice or dental clinic in respect of which the registered provider is registered in compliance with the Health and Social Care Act 2008 s 10 in respect of one or both of the following regulated activities: (1) treatment of disease, disorder or injury; or (2) diagnostic and screening procedures: Human Medicines Regulations 2012, SI 2012/1916, reg 232(2)(a).

7 Ie a dental practice or dental clinic in which dental services are provided by private dentists and those dentists are registered with Healthcare Inspectorate Wales in accordance with the Private Dentistry (Wales) Regulations 2008, SI 2008/1976, in relation to the services provided by those dentists: Human Medicines Regulations 2012, SI 2012/1916, reg 232(2)(b).

8 See the Human Medicines Regulations 2012, SI 2012/1916, reg 232(1).

9 Human Medicines Regulations 2012, SI 2012/1916, reg 232(3). As to the meaning of 'patient group direction' see PARA 286 note 20.

10 Human Medicines Regulations 2012, SI 2012/1916, reg 232(4).

11 Human Medicines Regulations 2012, SI 2012/1916, reg 232(5). The specified particulars mentioned in the text refers to the particulars specified in Sch 16 Pt 1 (but with the omission of Sch 16 para 4 in the case of a PGD relating to administration only).

12 As to the meaning of 'registered provider' see PARA 288 note 10.

13 As to the meaning of 'relevant manager' see PARA 288 note 22.

14   Human Medicines Regulations 2012, SI 2012/1916, reg 232(6). For these purposes, in relation to Wales, 'manager' means a person who carries on the dental practice or dental clinic or, if there is no such person, a person who manages the practice or clinic: reg 232(9).
15   Ie as specified by the Human Medicines Regulations 2012, SI 2012/1916, Sch 16 Pt 4 (see PARA 286 note 24).
16   Human Medicines Regulations 2012, SI 2012/1916, reg 232(7).
17   As to the meanings of 'marketing authorisation', 'Article 126a authorisation', 'certificate of registration' and 'traditional herbal registration' see PARA 141 notes 3–6.
18   Human Medicines Regulations 2012, SI 2012/1916, reg 232(8).

290.   Supply under a patient group direction by person conducting a retail pharmacy business.   The restriction relating to the sale or supply of prescription only medicines[1] does not apply to the sale or supply, or administration, of a prescription only medicine by a person lawfully conducting a retail pharmacy business[2] where:

(1)   the person sells, supplies or (as the case may be) administers the prescription only medicine pursuant to an arrangement for the supply or administration of prescription only medicines with the Common Services Agency[3], a health authority or special health authority[4], an NHS trust, an NHS foundation trust[5], a Primary Care Trust[6], a police force, a prison service[7], Her Majesty's Forces or an authority or person carrying on the business of an independent hospital, an independent clinic or an independent medical agency[8];

(2)   the prescription only medicine is sold or supplied for the purpose of being supplied or (as the case may be) is administered to a person in accordance with a patient group direction ('PGD')[9]; and

(3)   the following conditions are met[10].

Condition A is that the PGD relates to the sale or supply or (as the case may be) administration of a description or class of medicinal product[11] by the person lawfully conducting a retail pharmacy business who sells or supplies or (as the case may be) administers the prescription only medicine[12].

Condition B is that the PGD has effect at the time at which the prescription only medicine is sold or supplied or (as the case may be) administered[13].

Condition C is that the PGD contains specified particulars[14].

Condition D is that the PGD is signed[15].

Condition E is that, where the prescription only medicine is administered by the person lawfully conducting a retail pharmacy business, the person belongs to one of the specified classes of individual[16] and is designated in writing for the purpose of the administration of medicinal products under the PGD on behalf of the relevant body[17].

Condition F is that when the prescription only medicine is supplied or (as the case may be) administered, a marketing authorisation, Article 126a authorisation, certificate of registration or traditional herbal registration[18] is in force in relation to it[19].

1   Ie the Human Medicines Regulations 2012, SI 2012/1916, reg 214(1) (see PARA 271). As to the meanings of 'sale' and 'supply' see PARA 271 note 1. As to the meaning of 'prescription only medicine' see the Human Medicines Regulations 2012, SI 2012/1916, reg 5(3); and PARA 26: reg 8(1).
2   As to the meaning of 'retail pharmacy business' see PARA 52 note 12.
3   As to the meaning of 'the Common Services Agency' see PARA 286 note 5.
4   As to the meanings of 'health authority' and 'special health authority' see PARA 286 notes 6, 7.
5   As to the meanings of 'NHS trust' and 'NHS foundation trust', and the abolition of NHS trusts, see PARA 286 notes 8, 9.

6 As to the meaning of 'Primary Care Trust' see PARA 286 note 10. As from 1 April 2013, Primary Care Trusts are abolished: see PARA 3 note 1.

7 'Prison service' means, in relation to England and Wales, a Minister of the Crown exercising functions in relation to prisons (within the meaning of the Prison Act 1952): Human Medicines Regulations 2012, SI 2012/1916, reg 213(1).

8 Human Medicines Regulations 2012, SI 2012/1916, reg 233(1)(a). As to the meanings of 'independent clinic', 'independent hospital' and 'independent medical agency' see PARA 288 notes 6, 7, 8.

9 Human Medicines Regulations 2012, SI 2012/1916, reg 233(1)(b). As to the meaning of 'patient group direction' see PARA 286 note 20.

10 Human Medicines Regulations 2012, SI 2012/1916, reg 233(1)(c).

11 As to the meaning of 'medicinal product' see PARA 25.

12 Human Medicines Regulations 2012, SI 2012/1916, reg 233(2).

13 Human Medicines Regulations 2012, SI 2012/1916, reg 233(3).

14 Human Medicines Regulations 2012, SI 2012/1916, reg 233(4). The specified particulars mentioned in the text are the particulars specified in Sch 16 Pt 1 (but with the omission of Sch 16 para 4 in the case of a PGD relating to administration only).

15 Human Medicines Regulations 2012, SI 2012/1916, reg 233(5). As to the person it should be signed on behalf of see reg 233(5)(a)-(e).

16 Ie a classes of individuals specified in the Human Medicines Regulations 2012, SI 2012/1916, Sch 16 Pt 4.

17 Human Medicines Regulations 2012, SI 2012/1916, reg 233(6). As to the relevant body see reg 233(6)(a)-(c).

18 As to the meanings of 'marketing authorisation', 'Article 126a authorisation', 'certificate of registration' and 'traditional herbal registration' see PARA 141 notes 3-6.

19 Human Medicines Regulations 2012, SI 2012/1916, reg 233(7).

291. Supply under a patient group direction to assist the police. Restrictions relating to the sale or supply of prescription only medicines[1], medicines not subject to general sale[2] and medicines subject to general sale[3] do not apply to the supply or administration[4] of a medicinal product by an individual belonging to one of a specified class[5] in accordance with the following conditions[6].

Condition A is that the individual supplies or (as the case may be) administers the product to assist the provision of health care[7] by, on behalf of, or under arrangements made by, one of the following bodies ('the relevant body') a police force in England and Wales or in Scotland, the Police Service of Northern Ireland, a prison service[8] or Her Majesty's Forces[9].

Condition B is that the product is supplied for the purpose of being administered to a person in accordance with a patient group direction ('PGD')[10].

Condition C is that the PGD relates to the supply or (as the case may be) the administration of a description or class of medicinal product[11] to assist the provision of health care by, on behalf of, or under arrangements made by, the relevant body[12].

Condition D is that the PGD has effect at the time at which the product is supplied or (as the case may be) administered[13].

Condition E is that the PGD contains specified particulars[14].

Condition F is that the PGD is signed by or on behalf of the appropriate person[15].

Condition G is that the individual who supplies the product is designated in writing by or on behalf of the relevant body for the purpose of the supply or (as the case may be) the administration of medicinal products under the PGD[16].

Condition H is that when the product is supplied, a marketing authorisation, Article 126a authorisation, certificate of registration or traditional herbal registration[17] is in force in relation to it[18].

1   Ie the Human Medicines Regulations 2012, SI 2012/1916, reg 214(1) (see PARA 271). As to the meanings of 'sale' and 'supply' see PARA 271 note 1. As to the meaning of 'prescription only medicine' see the Human Medicines Regulations 2012, SI 2012/1916, reg 5(3); and PARA 26: reg 8(1).
2   Ie the Human Medicines Regulations 2012, SI 2012/1916, reg 220 (see PARA 277).
3   Ie the Human Medicines Regulations 2012, SI 2012/1916, reg 221 (see PARA 278).
4   As to the meaning of 'administer' see PARA 25 note 4.
5   Ie belonging to one the classes specified in the Human Medicines Regulations 2012, SI 2012/1916, Sch 16 Pt 4.
6   Human Medicines Regulations 2012, SI 2012/1916, reg 234(1).
7   'Health care' means services for or in connection with the prevention, diagnosis or treatment of disease: Human Medicines Regulations 2012, SI 2012/1916, reg 213(1).
8   As to the meaning of 'prison service' see PARA 290 note 7.
9   Human Medicines Regulations 2012, SI 2012/1916, reg 234(2).
10 Human Medicines Regulations 2012, SI 2012/1916, reg 234(3). As to the meaning of 'patient group direction' see PARA 286 note 20.
11 As to the meaning of 'medicinal product' see PARA 25.
12 Human Medicines Regulations 2012, SI 2012/1916, reg 234(4).
13 Human Medicines Regulations 2012, SI 2012/1916, reg 234(5).
14 Human Medicines Regulations 2012, SI 2012/1916, reg 234(6). The specified particulars mentioned in the text are the particulars specified in Sch 16 Pt 1 (but with the omission of Sch 16 pararaph 4 in the case of a PGD relating to administration only).
15 See the Human Medicines Regulations 2012, SI 2012/1916, reg 234(7). The appropriate person mentioned in the text is a person specified in column 2 of Part 3 of Sch 16 against the entry in column 1 for the relevant body.
16 Human Medicines Regulations 2012, SI 2012/1916, reg 234(8).
17 As to the meanings of 'marketing authorisation', 'Article 126a authorisation', 'certificate of registration' and 'traditional herbal registration' see PARA 141 notes 3–6.
18 Human Medicines Regulations 2012, SI 2012/1916, reg 234(9).

292.   Sale or supply of prescription only medicines by certain persons. The restriction relating to the sale or supply of prescription only medicines[1] does not apply in the following situations[2]:

(1)   the sale or supply of all prescription only medicines by persons selling or supplying prescription only medicines to universities, other institutions concerned with higher education or institutions concerned with research, subject to certain conditions[3];

(2)   the sale or supply of all prescription only medicines by persons selling or supplying prescription only medicines to a public analyst[4], an authorised officer[5], an inspector[6], a sampling officer[7], subject to certain conditions[8];

(3)   the sale or supply of all prescription only medicines by persons selling or supplying prescription only medicines to any person employed or engaged in connection with a scheme for testing the quality and checking the amount of the drugs and appliances supplied under the National Health Service Act 2006 or under any subordinate legislation made under those Acts, subject to certain conditions[9];

(4)   supply of all prescription only medicines, subject to certain conditions, by the Royal National Lifeboat Institution and certified first aiders of the Institution and the owner or master of a ship which does not carry a doctor on board as part of the ship's complement[10];

(5)   the supply by person, authorised by licence[11] to supply a controlled drug, of such prescription only medicines being controlled drugs as are specified in the licence, subject to conditions[12];

(6)   the supply of ampoules of sterile water for injection that contain no more than 2ml of water each, by persons employed or engaged in the provision of lawful drug treatment services, subject to conditions[13];

(7)   the supply by persons requiring prescription only medicines for the purpose of enabling them, in the course of any business carried on by them, to comply with any requirements made by or in pursuance of any enactment with respect to the medical treatment of their employees, of such prescription only medicines as may be specified in the relevant enactment, subject to conditions[14];

(8)   the supply by persons operating an occupational health scheme, of prescription only medicines sold or supplied to a person operating an occupational health scheme in response to an order in writing signed by a doctor or a registered nurse, subject to conditions[15];

(9)   the supply by the operator or commander of an aircraft of prescription only medicines which are not for parenteral administration[16] and which have been sold or supplied to an operator or commander of an aircraft in response to an order in writing signed by a doctor, subject to conditions[17];

(10)   the supply of all prescription only medicines, by persons employed as qualified first-aid personnel on off-shore installations, subject to conditions[18];

(11)   the supply by persons who hold a certificate in first aid from the Mountain Rescue Council of England and Wales, or from the Northern Ireland Mountain Rescue Co-ordinating Committee, of prescription only medicines supplied to that person in response to an order in writing by a doctor, subject to conditions[19];

(12)   the supply by persons who are members of Her Majesty's armed forces of all prescription only medicines, subject to conditions[20];

(13)   the administration of certain prescription only medicines, subject to conditions, by registered chiropodists or podiatrists[21], against whose names are recorded in the relevant register annotations signifying that they are qualified to use such medicines, registered midwives and student nurses, and registered paramedics[22];

(14)   the administration, by persons who are authorised as members of a group by a group authority[23] to supply a controlled drug by way of administration only, of prescription only medicines that are specified in the group authority, subject to conditions[24];

(15)   the administration, by the owner or master of a ship which does not carry a doctor on board as part of the ship's complement, of all prescription only medicines that are for parenteral administration, subject to conditions[25];

(16)   the administration, by persons operating an occupational health scheme, of prescription only medicines that are for parenteral administration sold or supplied to the person operating an occupational health scheme in response to an order in writing signed by a doctor or a registered nurse, subject to conditions[26];

(17)   the administration, by the operator or commander of an aircraft, of prescription only medicines for parenteral administration which have been sold or supplied to the operator or commander of the aircraft in response to an order in writing signed by a doctor, subject to conditions[27];

(18)   the administration, of all prescription only medicines that are for parenteral administration, by persons employed as qualified first-aid personnel on off-shore installations, subject to conditions[28];

(19) the administration of certain prescription only medicines for parenteral administration by persons who hold the advanced life support provider certificate issued by the Resuscitation Council (UK), subject to conditions[29].

1   Ie the Human Medicines Regulations 2012, SI 2012/1916, reg 214(1) (see PARA 271). As to the meanings of 'sale' and 'supply' see PARA 271 note 1. As to the meaning of 'prescription only medicine' see the Human Medicines Regulations 2012, SI 2012/1916, reg 5(3); and PARA 26: reg 8(1).
2   See the Human Medicines Regulations 2012, SI 2012/1916, reg 235(1), (2).
3   See the Human Medicines Regulations 2012, SI 2012/1916, Sch 17 Pt 1.
4   Ie a public analyst appointed under the Food Safety Act 1990 s 27 (see FOOD vol 18(2) (Reissue) PARA 268).
5   Ie an authorised officer within the meaning of the Food Safety Act 1990 s 5(6) (see FOOD vol 18(2) (Reissue) PARA 253).
6   Ie an inspector acting under the Human Medicines Regulations 2012, SI 2012/1916, regs 325–328 (see PARAS 363–365).
7   Ie a sampling officer within the meaning of the Human Medicines Regulations 2012, SI 2012/1916, Sch 31.
8   See the Human Medicines Regulations 2012, SI 2012/1916, Sch 17 Pt 1.
9   See the Human Medicines Regulations 2012, SI 2012/1916, Sch 17 Pt 1.
10 See the Human Medicines Regulations 2012, SI 2012/1916, Sch 17 Pt 2.
11 Ie authorised under the Misuse of Drugs Regulations 2001, SI 2001/3998, reg 5 (see PARA 494).
12 See the Human Medicines Regulations 2012, SI 2012/1916, Sch 17 Pt 2.
13 See the Human Medicines Regulations 2012, SI 2012/1916, Sch 17 Pt 2.
14 See the Human Medicines Regulations 2012, SI 2012/1916, Sch 17 Pt 2.
15 See the Human Medicines Regulations 2012, SI 2012/1916, Sch 17 Pt 2.
16 As to the meaning of 'parenteral administration' see PARA 274 note 4.
17 See the Human Medicines Regulations 2012, SI 2012/1916, Sch 17 Pt 2.
18 See the Human Medicines Regulations 2012, SI 2012/1916, Sch 17 Pt 2.
19 See the Human Medicines Regulations 2012, SI 2012/1916, Sch 17 Pt 2.
20 See the Human Medicines Regulations 2012, SI 2012/1916, Sch 17 Pt 2.
21 As to the meanings of 'registered chiropodist' and 'registered podiatrist' see PARA 286 note 24.
22 See the Human Medicines Regulations 2012, SI 2012/1916, Sch 17, Pt 3.
23 Ie granted under the Misuse of Drugs Regulations 2001, SI 2001/3998, regs 8(3) or 9(3) (see PARA 494).
24 See the Human Medicines Regulations 2012, SI 2012/1916, Sch 17 Pt 3.
25 See the Human Medicines Regulations 2012, SI 2012/1916, Sch 17 Pt 3.
26 See the Human Medicines Regulations 2012, SI 2012/1916, Sch 17 Pt 3.
27 See the Human Medicines Regulations 2012, SI 2012/1916, Sch 17 Pt 3.
28 See the Human Medicines Regulations 2012, SI 2012/1916, Sch 17 Pt 3.
29 See the Human Medicines Regulations 2012, SI 2012/1916, Sch 17 Pt 3.

293. Sale or supply by certain persons of medicinal products not subject to general sale. The restrictions relating to the sale and supply, and offer for sale or supply, of medicines subject, and not subject, to general sale[1] do not apply to the sale, supply or offer for sale or supply by registered chiropodists and podiatrists[2] in relation to certain medicinal products[3] on a general sale list which are for external use and are not veterinary drugs[4].

Furthermore those restrictions are also exempt in relation to the supply of certain prescription only medicines or pharmacy medicines[5], and the sale, supply, or offer for sale or supply, of certain medicinal products subject to general sale in the following circumstances, subject to conditions[6]:

(1)   the Royal National Lifeboat Institution and certificated first aiders of the institution, in relation to all medicinal products;

(2)   the British Red Cross Society, St Andrew's Ambulance Association, the Order of Malta Ambulance Corps and relevant certificated first aid and

certificated nursing members, in relation to pharmacy medicines and all medicinal products on a general sale list;

(3) persons authorised by licences[7], in relation to such prescription only medicines and such pharmacy medicines as are specified in the licence;

(4) persons employed or engaged in the provision of lawful drug treatment services, in relation to ampoules of sterile water for injection that contain no more than 5ml of water each;

(5) persons requiring medicinal products for the purpose of enabling them, in the course of any business carried on by them, to comply with any requirements made by or in pursuance of any enactment with respect to the medical treatment of their employees, in relation to such prescription only medicines and such pharmacy medicines as may be specified in the relevant enactment and medicinal products on a general sale list;

(6) the owner or master of a ship which does not carry a doctor on board as part of the ship's complement, persons employed as qualified first-aid personnel on offshore installations, and Her Majesty's armed forces, in relation to all medicinal products;

(7) persons operating an occupational health scheme, in relation to all pharmacy medicines, all medicinal products on a general sale list and such prescription only medicines as are sold or supplied to a person operating an occupational health scheme in response to an order signed by a doctor or a registered nurse;

(8) persons carrying on the business of a school providing full-time education, in relation to pharmacy medicines that are for use in the prevention of dental caries and consist of or contain Sodium Fluoride;

(9) health authorities or Primary Health Trusts, in relation to pharmacy medicines that are for use in the prevention of dental caries and consist of or contain Sodium Fluoride;

(10) the operator or commander of an aircraft, in relation to all pharmacy medicines, all medicinal products on a general sale list and such prescription only medicines which are not for parenteral administration and which have been sold or supplied to the operator or commander of an aircraft in response to an order in writing signed by a doctor;

(11) a prison officer, in relation to all medicinal products on the general sale list;

(12) persons who hold a certificate in first aid from the Mountain Rescue Council of England and Wales, in relation to all pharmacy medicines, all medicinal products on a general sale list and such prescription only medicines which are sold or supplied to such a person in response to an order in writing signed by a doctor[8].

1 Ie the Human Medicines Regulations 2012, SI 2012/1916, reg 220 (see PARA 277) and reg 221 (see PARA 278). As to the meanings of 'sale' and 'supply' see PARA 271 note 1.
2 As to the meaning of 'registered chiropodist' and 'registered podiatrist' see PARA 286 note 24.
3 As to the meaning of 'medicinal products' see PARA 25.
4 See the Human Medicines Regulations 2012, SI 2012/1916, reg 235(4), (6), Sch 17, Pt 4.
5 As to the meaning of 'pharmacy medicine' see the Human Medicines Regulations 2012, SI 2012/1916, reg 5(5); and PARA 26: reg 8(1).
6 See the Human Medicines Regulations 2012, SI 2012/1916, reg 235(5), (7), Sch 17, Pt 5.
7 Ie by licences granted under the Misuse of Drugs Regulations 2001, SI 2001/3998.
8 See the Human Medicines Regulations 2012, SI 2012/1916, Sch 17 Pt 5.

294. Products containing paracetamol, aspirin or aloxiprin. The restriction relating to the sale or supply of prescription only medicines[1] does not apply to a product that is covered by a marketing authorisation in which the product is classified as a pharmacy medicine[2] or as a medicinal product subject to general sale and that consists of or contains aloxiprin, aspirin or paracetamol in the form of non-effervescent tablets or capsules[3] if the quantity of the product sold or supplied to a person at any one time does not exceed 100 tablets or capsules[4].

1   Ie the Human Medicines Regulations 2012, SI 2012/1916, reg 214(1) (see PARA 271). As to the meanings of 'sale' and 'supply' see PARA 271 note 1. As to the meaning of 'prescription only medicine' see the Human Medicines Regulations 2012, SI 2012/1916, reg 5(3); and PARA 26: reg 8(1).
2   As to the meaning of 'pharmacy medicine' see the Human Medicines Regulations 2012, SI 2012/1916, reg 5(5); and PARA 26: reg 8(1).
3   Ie a medicinal product that is a prescription only medicine by virtue of the Human Medicines Regulations 2012, SI 2012/1916, Sch 1 para 1(e). As to the meaning of 'medicinal product' see PARA 25.
4   See the Human Medicines Regulations 2012, SI 2012/1916, reg 236.

295. Products containing pseudoephedrine salts or ephedrine base or salts. The restriction relating to the sale or supply of prescription only medicines[1] does not apply to a product that is covered by a marketing authorisation[2] in which the product is classified as a pharmacy medicine[3] or as a medicinal product subject to general sale and which consists of or contains (in any pharmaceutical form) pseudoephedrine salts or ephedrine base or salts[4] if conditions A and B are met[5].

Condition A is that the product is not sold or supplied at the same time as another medicinal product that consists of or contains in the case of pseudoephedrine salts, ephedrine base or salts or, in the case of ephedrine base or salts, pseudoephedrine salts[6].

Condition B is that the medicinal products sold or supplied to a person at any one time do not in total contain more than, in the case of pseudoephedrine salts, 720mg pseudoephedrine salts, or, in the case of ephedrine base or salts, 180mg ephedrine base or salts[7].

1   Ie the Human Medicines Regulations 2012, SI 2012/1916, reg 214(1) (see PARA 271). As to the meanings of 'sale' and 'supply' see PARA 271 note 1. As to the meaning of 'prescription only medicine' see the Human Medicines Regulations 2012, SI 2012/1916, reg 5(3); and PARA 26: reg 8(1).
2   As to the meaning of 'marketing authorisation' see PARA 141 note 3.
3   As to the meaning of 'pharmacy medicine' see the Human Medicines Regulations 2012, SI 2012/1916, reg 5(5); and PARA 26: reg 8(1).
4   Ie a medicinal product that is a prescription only medicine by virtue of the Human Medicines Regulations 2012, SI 2012/1916, Sch 1 para 1(f). As to the meaning of 'medicinal product' see PARA 25.
5   Human Medicines Regulations 2012, SI 2012/1916, reg 237(1).
6   Human Medicines Regulations 2012, SI 2012/1916, reg 237(2).
7   Human Medicines Regulations 2012, SI 2012/1916, reg 237(3).

296. Administration of certain medicines in an emergency. The restriction relating to parenteral administration of prescription only medicines[1] does not apply to the administration of certain prescription only medicines[2] where this is for the purpose of saving life in an emergency[3].

1   Ie the Human Medicines Regulations 2012, SI 2012/1916, reg 214(2) (see PARA 271). As to the meaning of 'parenteral administration' see PARA 274 note 4. As to the meaning of 'prescription only medicine' see the Human Medicines Regulations 2012, SI 2012/1916, reg 5(3); and PARA 26: reg 8(1).

2   Ie the prescription only medicines specified in the Human Medicines Regulations 2012, SI 2012/1916, Sch 19.

3   See the Human Medicines Regulations 2012, SI 2012/1916, reg 238.

297.   Administration of smallpox vaccine.   The restriction relating to parenteral administration of prescription only medicines[1] does not apply to the administration of smallpox vaccine[2] if condition A or B is met[3].

Condition A is that the vaccine has been supplied by, on behalf of, or under arrangements made by, the Secretary of State, the Welsh Ministers, the Department of Health, Social Services and Public Safety or an NHS body[4] and the vaccine is administered for the purpose of providing protection against smallpox virus in the event of a suspected or confirmed case of smallpox in the United Kingdom[5].

Condition B is that the vaccine has been supplied by, on behalf of, or under arrangements made by, Her Majesty's Forces and that it is administered for the purpose of providing protection against smallpox virus to members of Her Majesty's Forces or other persons employed or engaged by them[6].

1   Ie the Human Medicines Regulations 2012, SI 2012/1916, reg 214(2) (see PARA 271). As to the meaning of 'parenteral administration' see PARA 274 note 4. As to the meaning of 'prescription only medicine' see the Human Medicines Regulations 2012, SI 2012/1916, reg 5(3); and PARA 26: reg 8(1).

2   'Vaccine' means an antigenic substance which consists wholly or partly of any micro-organisms, viruses or other organisms in any state, any toxins of microbial origin which have been detoxified (toxoids) or any extracts or derivatives of any micro-organisms or of any viruses, being substances which, when administered to human beings, are used for the prevention of specific diseases: Human Medicines Regulations 2012, SI 2012/1916, reg 8(1).

3   Human Medicines Regulations 2012, SI 2012/1916, reg 239(1).

4   As to the Secretary of State see PARA 2 note 1. 'NHS body' means the Common Services Agency, a health authority, a special health authority, a Primary Care Trust, an NHS trust or an NHS foundation trust: Human Medicines Regulations 2012, SI 2012/1916, reg 213(1). As to the meanings of 'Common Services Agency', 'health authority', 'special health authority', 'Primary Care Trust', 'NHS trust' and 'NHS foundation trust' see PARA 286 notes 5–10. As from 1 April 2013, Primary Care Trusts and NHS trusts are abolished: see PARAS 3 note 1, 268 note 8.

5   Human Medicines Regulations 2012, SI 2012/1916, reg 239(2).

6   Human Medicines Regulations 2012, SI 2012/1916, reg 239(3).

298.   Radioactive medicinal products.   The restriction relating to parenteral administration of prescription only medicines[1] does not apply to a radioactive medicinal product[2], administration of which results in a medical exposure[3], or any other prescription only medicine if it is being administered in connection with a medical exposure, if the following conditions are met[4].

Condition A is that the prescription only medicine is administered by an operator acting in accordance with prescribed[5] procedures and protocols which apply to the exposure[6].

Condition B is that the medical exposure has been authorised by an IRME practitioner[7] or, where it is not practical for an IRME practitioner to authorise the exposure, by an operator acting in accordance with written guidelines issued by an IRME practitioner[8].

Condition C is that the IRME practitioner mentioned above is the holder of a specified[9] certificate[10].

Condition D is that the prescription only medicine is not a controlled drug[11].

Condition E is that, in the case of a prescription only medicine that is not a radioactive medicinal product, it is specified in the protocols referred to in condition A above[12].

1   Ie the Human Medicines Regulations 2012, SI 2012/1916, reg 214(2) (see PARA 271). As to the meaning of 'parenteral administration' see PARA 274 note 4. As to the meaning of 'prescription only medicine' see the Human Medicines Regulations 2012, SI 2012/1916, reg 5(3); and PARA 26: reg 8(1).

2   For these purposes, 'radioactive medicinal product' means a medicinal product which consists of, contains or generates a radioactive substance so that, when the product is administered, the radiation it emits may be used: Human Medicines Regulations 2012, SI 2012/1916, reg 240(7). As to the meaning of 'medicinal product' see PARA 25.

3   For these purposes, 'medical exposure' has the same meaning as in the Ionising Radiation (Medical Exposure) Regulations 2000, SI 2000/1059: Human Medicines Regulations 2012, SI 2012/1916, reg 240(7).

4   Human Medicines Regulations 2012, SI 2012/1916, reg 240(1).

5   Ie the procedures and protocols referred to in the Ionising Radiation (Medical Exposure) Regulations 2000, SI 2000/1059, reg 4(1), (2) (see PARA 382).

6   Human Medicines Regulations 2012, SI 2012/1916, reg 240(2).

7   For these purposes 'IRME practitioner' means, in relation to a medical exposure, a practitioner for the purposes of the Ionising Radiation (Medical Exposure) Regulations 2000, SI 2000/1059: Human Medicines Regulations 2012, SI 2012/1916, reg 240(7).

8   Human Medicines Regulations 2012, SI 2012/1916, reg 240(3).

9   Ie a certificate granted pursuant to the Medicines (Administration of Radioactive Substances) Regulations 1978, SI 1978/1006 (see PARA 382).

10   Human Medicines Regulations 2012, SI 2012/1916, reg 240(4).

11   Human Medicines Regulations 2012, SI 2012/1916, reg 240(5). As to the meaning of 'controlled drug' see PARA 275 note 5.

12   Human Medicines Regulations 2012, SI 2012/1916, reg 240(6).

299. Certain herbal remedies. Restrictions relating to the sale or supply, or offer for sale or supply, of a medicinal product that is, and is not, subject to general sale[1], do not apply to the sale or supply, or offer for sale or supply by a person ('A') of a herbal medicinal product[2] if:

(1)   the product does not contain certain specified substances[3];

(2)   the product does not contain a specified substance[4] unless the product is sold or supplied, in relation to certain products, in or from containers or packages[5] labelled to show a dose not exceeding a specified maximum dose or maximum daily dose or, in the case of other specified products, with the percentage of the substance in the product not exceeding a specified amount[6];

(3)   the sale or supply, or offer for sale or supply, takes place on premises occupied by A and from which A can exclude the public[7]; and

(4)   the product is for administration to a person ('B') and A has been requested by or on behalf of B and in B's presence to use A's judgment as to the treatment required[8].

1   Ie the Human Medicines Regulations 2012, SI 2012/1916, regs 220, 221 (see PARAS 277, 278). As to the meanings of 'sale' and 'supply' see PARA 271 note 1. As to the meaning of 'medicinal product' see PARA 25.

2   As to the meaning of 'herbal medicinal product' see PARA 51 note 2.

3   Human Medicines Regulations 2012, SI 2012/1916, reg 241(1)(a). As to the specified substances see Sch 20 Pt 1.

4   Ie a substance listed in the Human Medicines Regulations 2012, SI 2012/1916, Sch 20 Pt 2 column 1.

5   As to the meaning of 'package' see PARA 51 note 48.

6   See the Human Medicines Regulations 2012, SI 2012/1916, reg 241(1)(b), Sch 20 Pt 2.

7   Human Medicines Regulations 2012, SI 2012/1916, reg 241(1)(c).

8   Human Medicines Regulations 2012, SI 2012/1916, reg 241(1)(d).

300. Medicinal products at high dilution. Restrictions relating to the sale or supply, or offer for sale or supply, of a medicinal product that is, and is not, subject to general sale[1], do not apply to the sale or supply, or offer for sale or supply by a person ('P') of a medicinal product if:

(1)   the medicinal product is neither for parenteral administration nor a controlled drug[2];

(2)   the medicinal product consists solely of one or more unit preparations of: (a) any substance where the unit preparation has been diluted to at least one part in a million (6x); (b) a specified substance[3] where the unit preparation has been diluted to at least one part in a thousand (3x); or (c) any substance that is the active substance of a medicine that is subject to general sale, is of a specified type[4] or, in the case of a medicinal product for external use[5] only, is of a specified type[6], where the unit preparation has been diluted to at least one part in ten (1x)[7]; and

(3)   P has been requested by or on behalf of a particular person and in that person's presence to use P's own judgment as to the treatment required[8].

The restriction relating to the sale or supply of medicinal products not subject to general sale[9], does not apply to the sale, supply, or offer for sale or supply, by a person of a medicinal product if:

(i)   the medicinal product is neither for parenteral administration nor a controlled drug[10];

(ii)   the medicinal product consists solely of one or more unit preparations of: (A) any substance where the unit preparation has been diluted to at least one part in a million million (6c)[11]; (B) a specified substance[12] where the unit preparation has been diluted to at least one part in a million (6x)[13]; or (C) any substance that is the active substance of a medicine that is subject to general sale, is a specified substance[14] or, in the case of a medicinal product for external use only, is a specified product[15], where the unit preparation has been diluted to at least one part in ten (1x)[16];

(iii)   certain conditions are met[17].

1   Ie the Human Medicines Regulations 2012, SI 2012/1916, regs 220, 221 (see PARAS 277, 278). As to the meanings of 'sale' and 'supply' see PARA 271 note 1. As to the meaning of 'medicinal product' see PARA 25.

2   Human Medicines Regulations 2012, SI 2012/1916, reg 242(1)(a). As to the meaning of 'parenteral administration' see PARA 274 note 4. As to the meaning of 'controlled drug' see PARA 275 note 5.

3   Ie specified in the Human Medicines Regulations 2012, SI 2012/1916, Sch 21 Pt 1.

4   Ie is listed in the Human Medicines Regulations 2012, SI 2012/1916, Sch 21 Pt 3.

5   'External use' in relation to a medicinal product means its use by application to the skin, teeth, mucosa of the mouth, throat, nose, ear, eye, vagina or anal canal in circumstances where local action only is necessary and systematic absorption is unlikely to occur; but it does not include its use by means of a throat spray, nasal spray, nasal inhalation or teething preparation or by means of throat pastilles, throat lozenges, throat tablets or nasal drops: Human Medicines Regulations 2012, SI 2012/1916, reg 213(1).

6   Ie is listed in the Human Medicines Regulations 2012, SI 2012/1916, Sch 21 Pt 4.

7   Human Medicines Regulations 2012, SI 2012/1916, reg 242(1)(b), (2).

8   Human Medicines Regulations 2012, SI 2012/1916, reg 242(1)(c).

9   Ie the Human Medicines Regulations 2012, SI 2012/1916, reg 220 (see PARA 277).

10 Human Medicines Regulations 2012, SI 2012/1916, reg 242(3)(a).

11 Human Medicines Regulations 2012, SI 2012/1916, reg 242(4)(a).

12 Ie a substance that is listed in the Human Medicines Regulations 2012, SI 2012/1916, Sch 21 Pt 2.

13 Human Medicines Regulations 2012, SI 2012/1916, reg 242(4)(b).

14 Ie a substance that is listed in the Human Medicines Regulations 2012, SI 2012/1916, Sch 21 Pt 3.

15 Ie a substance that is listed in the Human Medicines Regulations 2012, SI 2012/1916, Sch 21 Pt 4.

16 Human Medicines Regulations 2012, SI 2012/1916, reg 242(3), (b), (4)(c).

17 Human Medicines Regulations 2012, SI 2012/1916, reg 242(3)(c). The conditions mentioned in the text are the conditions in reg 221 (see PARA 278).

301.   Certain homoeopathic medicinal products. Restrictions relating to the sale or supply, or offer for sale or supply, of a medicinal product that is, and is not, subject to general sale[1], do not apply to the sale or supply, or offer for sale or supply by a person ('P') of a medicinal product if a certificate of registration[2] is in force in relation to the product, the product is not an excluded product[3] and that P has been requested by or on behalf of a particular person and in that person's presence to use P's own judgment as to the treatment required[4].

The restriction relating to the sale or supply of medicinal products not subject to general sale[5] do not apply to the sale or supply, or offer for sale or supply by a person ('P') of a medicinal product if a certificate of registration is in force in relation to the product, the product is not an excluded product and certain conditions[6] are met[7].

1 Ie the Human Medicines Regulations 2012, SI 2012/1916, regs 220, 221 (see PARAS 277, 278). As to the meanings of 'sale' and 'supply' see PARA 271 note 1. As to the meaning of 'medicinal product' see PARA 25.

2 As to the meaning of 'certificate of registration' see PARA 141 note 4.

3 For these purposes, 'excluded product' means a product that is promoted, recommended or marketed for use as an anthelmintic, for parenteral administration, for use as eye drops, for use as an eye ointment, for use as an enema, for use wholly or mainly for irrigation of wounds or of the bladder, vagina or rectum or for administration wholly or mainly to children being a preparation of aloxiprin or aspirin: Human Medicines Regulations 2012, SI 2012/1916, reg 243(3).

4 Human Medicines Regulations 2012, SI 2012/1916, reg 243(1).

5 Ie the Human Medicines Regulations 2012, SI 2012/1916, reg 220 (see PARA 277).

6 Ie under the Human Medicines Regulations 2012, SI 2012/1916, reg 221 (see PARA 278).

7 Human Medicines Regulations 2012, SI 2012/1916, reg 243(2).

302.   In cases involving another's default. The restriction relating to the sale or supply of a prescription only medicine[1] does not apply to the sale or supply of a prescription only medicine by a person if the person, having exercised all due diligence, believes on reasonable grounds that the product is not a prescription only medicine[2].

The restriction relating to the sale or supply of medicinal products not subject to general sale[3] does not apply to the sale or supply, or offer for sale or supply of a medicinal product by a person if the person, having exercised all due diligence, believes on reasonable grounds that the product is subject to general sale, that belief is due to the act or default of another person and certain conditions[4] are met in relation to the sale or supply, or offer for sale or supply of the product[5].

1 Ie the Human Medicines Regulations 2012, SI 2012/1916, reg 214(1) (see PARA 271). As to the meanings of 'sale' and 'supply' see PARA 271 note 1. As to the meaning of 'prescription only medicine' see the Human Medicines Regulations 2012, SI 2012/1916, reg 5(3); and PARA 26: reg 8(1).

2 Human Medicines Regulations 2012, SI 2012/1916, reg 244(1).

3 Ie the Human Medicines Regulations 2012, SI 2012/1916, reg 220 (see PARA 277). As to the meaning of 'medicinal product' see PARA 25.

4 Ie the conditions in the Human Medicines Regulations 2012, SI 2012/1916, reg 221 (see PARA 278).

5 Human Medicines Regulations 2012, SI 2012/1916, reg 244(2).

303.   In case of forged prescription.   The restriction relating to the sale or supply of a prescription only medicine[1] does not apply to the sale or supply of a prescription only medicine by a pharmacist[2] in accordance with a forged prescription if the pharmacist, having exercised all due diligence, believes on reasonable grounds that the prescription is genuine[3].

1   Ie the Human Medicines Regulations 2012, SI 2012/1916, reg 214(1) (see PARA 271). As to the meanings of 'sale' and 'supply' see PARA 271 note 1. As to the meaning of 'prescription only medicine' see the Human Medicines Regulations 2012, SI 2012/1916, reg 5(3); and PARA 26: reg 8(1).
2   As to the meaning of 'pharmacist' see PARA 52 note 5.
3   Human Medicines Regulations 2012, SI 2012/1916, reg 245.

304.   Requirements for prescription not met.   The restriction relating to the sale or supply of a prescription only medicine[1] does not apply to the sale or supply of a prescription only medicine otherwise than in accordance with a prescription given by an appropriate practitioner[2] if the sale or supply is otherwise than in accordance with such a prescription because a specified condition[3] is not met and the person selling or supplying the prescription only medicine, having exercised all due diligence, believes on reasonable grounds that the condition is met[4].

1   Ie the Human Medicines Regulations 2012, SI 2012/1916, reg 214(1) (see PARA 271). As to the meanings of 'sale' and 'supply' see PARA 271 note 1. As to the meaning of 'prescription only medicine' see the Human Medicines Regulations 2012, SI 2012/1916, reg 5(3); and PARA 26: reg 8(1).
2   As to the meaning of 'appropriate practitioner' see PARA 271.
3   Ie a condition in the Human Medicines Regulations 2012, SI 2012/1916, reg 217, 218 or 219 (see PARAS 275–276).
4   Human Medicines Regulations 2012, SI 2012/1916, reg 246.

305.   Supply in the event or anticipation of pandemic disease.   Restrictions relating to the sale or supply of prescription only medicines[1], medicines not subject to general sale[2] and medicines subject to general sale[3], do not apply to the supply of a medicinal product that meets the following conditions[4].

Condition A is that the supply is made whilst a disease is, or in anticipation of a disease being imminently, pandemic and a serious risk, or potentially a serious risk, to human health[5].

Condition B is that the supply is in accordance with a protocol that is approved by the ministers[6], an NHS body[7] or the Health Protection Agency[8], that is specifies the symptoms of and treatment for the disease and that it contains requirements as to the recording of the name of the person who supplies the product to the person to be treated ('the patient') or to a person acting on the patient's behalf and evidence that the product was supplied to the patient or to a person acting on the patient's behalf[9].

1   Ie the Human Medicines Regulations 2012, SI 2012/1916, reg 214(1) (see PARA 271). As to the meanings of 'sale' and 'supply' see PARA 271 note 1. As to the meaning of 'prescription only medicine' see the Human Medicines Regulations 2012, SI 2012/1916, reg 5(3); and PARA 26: reg 8(1).
2   Ie the Human Medicines Regulations 2012, SI 2012/1916, reg 220 (see PARA 277).
3   Ie the Human Medicines Regulations 2012, SI 2012/1916, reg 221 (see PARA 278).
4   Human Medicines Regulations 2012, SI 2012/1916, reg 247(1).
5   Human Medicines Regulations 2012, SI 2012/1916, reg 247(2).
6   As to the meaning of 'the ministers' see the Human Medicines Regulations 2012, SI 2012/1916, reg 6(6)–(8); and PARA 35: reg 8(1).
7   As to the meaning of 'NHS body' see PARA 297 note 4.

8 'Health Protection Agency' means the body of that name established under the Health Protection Agency Act 2004 s 1 (see HEALTH SERVICES vol 54 (2008) PARAS 213–227): Human Medicines Regulations 2012, SI 2012/1916, reg 213(1).

9 Human Medicines Regulations 2012, SI 2012/1916, reg 247(3).

306. Certain collection and delivery arrangements. Restrictions relating to the sale or supply, or offer for sale or supply, of a medicinal product that is, and is not, subject to general sale[1], do not apply to the supply of a medicinal product on premises that are not a registered pharmacy[2] where the supply:

(1)   is in accordance with a prescription issued by a doctor, dentist, nurse independent prescriber, pharmacist independent prescriber or optometrist independent prescriber[3]; and

(2)   forms part of a collection and delivery arrangement[4] used by a person who lawfully conducts a retail pharmacy business[5].

1   Ie the Human Medicines Regulations 2012, SI 2012/1916, regs 220, 221 (see PARAS 277, 278). As to the meanings of 'sale' and 'supply' see PARA 271 note 1. As to the meaning of 'medicinal product' see PARA 25.

2   As to the meaning of 'registered pharmacy' see PARA 52 note 2.

3   Human Medicines Regulations 2012, SI 2012/1916, reg 248(1)(a). As to the meanings of 'doctor' and 'dentist' see PARA 48 note 6. As to the meanings of 'nurse independent prescriber' and 'pharmacist independent prescriber' see PARA 50 notes 3, 4. As to the meaning of 'optometrist independent prescriber' see PARA 271 note 13.

4   For these purposes, 'collection and delivery arrangement' means an arrangement whereby a person may:

(1)   take or send a prescription given by a doctor, dentist, nurse independent prescriber, pharmacist independent prescriber or optometrist independent prescriber to premises other than a registered pharmacy and which are capable of being closed by the occupier to exclude the public (Human Medicines Regulations 2012, SI 2012/1916, reg 248(2)(a)); and

(2)   collect or have collected on his or her behalf from such premises a medicinal product prepared or dispensed in accordance with such a prescription at a registered pharmacy by or under the supervision of a pharmacist (reg 248(2)(b)).

5   Human Medicines Regulations 2012, SI 2012/1916, reg 248(1)(b). As to the meaning of 'retail pharmacy business' see PARA 52 note 12.

(iv) Specified Products

307. Prohibitions as to specified medicinal products. Where it appears to them to be necessary to do so in the interests of safety[1], the ministers[2] may by order[3] prohibit the sale, supply or importation of medicinal products[4] of any description, or falling within any class, specified in the order, or designate[5] particular medicinal products and prohibit their sale, supply or importation[6]. Unless in their opinion it is essential to make such an order with immediate effect to avoid serious danger to health the ministers must, before making an order, consult the appropriate committee[7].

Any person who contravenes such an order is guilty of an offence[8] and is liable to a penalty[9]. Where a medicinal product is sold, supplied or imported in contravention of such an order, any person who, otherwise than for the purpose of performing or exercising a duty or power imposed or conferred by or under the Medicines Act 1968, is in possession of it, knowing or having reasonable cause to suspect that it was sold, supplied or imported in contravention of the order, is guilty of an offence[10] and is liable to a penalty[11].

1   As to pharmacovigilance relating to certain medicinal products see PARA 241 et seq.

2   As to the meaning of 'the ministers' see the Human Medicines Regulations 2012, SI 2012/1916, reg 6(6)–(8); and PARA 35: Medicines Act 1968 s 132(1) (substituted by SI 2012/1916).

3 In relation to the making of regulations and orders, the knowledge of civil servants cannot be imputed to ministers, and ministers must know or be told enough to ensure that nothing that it is necessary, because legally relevant, for them to know is left out of account, although this does not mean that they must know everything that is relevant; what it is relevant for them to know is enough to enable them to make an informed judgment: *R (on the application of National Association of Health Stores) v Secretary of State for Health* [2005] EWCA Civ 154, (2005) Times, 9 March. In the absence of any public interest in non-disclosure, a briefing to a minister in respect of a proposed order should be disclosed in litigation contesting the order: *R (on the application of National Association of Health Stores) v Secretary of State for Health* at [49] per Sedley LJ. As to disclosure of documents see CIVIL PROCEDURE vol 11 (2009) PARA 749 et seq. See Case C-141/07 Re Supply of Medicines by Pharmacies to Nearby Hospitals: *EC Commission v Germany* [2008] ECR I-6935, [2008] 3 CMLR 1479, ECJ (geographical restriction on supply of medicinal products to hospitals justified on grounds of protection of public health).

4 As to the meaning of 'medicinal product' see the Human Medicines Regulations 2012, SI 2012/1916, reg 2(1); and PARA 25 (definition applied by the Medicines Act 1968 s 132(1) (substituted by SI 2012/1916)).

5 Ie in such manner as appears to the ministers sufficient to identify the products in question.

6 Medicines Act 1968 s 62(1) (amended by SI 2006/2407). The prohibition may be total, or subject to specified exceptions: see the Medicines Act 1968 s 62(2).

7 Medicines Act 1968 s 62(3) (amended by SI 2005/1094, SI 2006/2407). For this purpose 'the appropriate committee' means whichever the ministers consider appropriate of the Commission on Human Medicines or an expert committee appointed by the ministers, or by one of them acting alone: Medicines Act 1968 s 62(8) (added by SI 2012/1916). Where an order is made without such prior consultation it does not have effect after the end of a specified period not exceeding three months, although a further order may be made: see the Medicines Act 1968 s 62(4) (amended by SI 2005/1094). As to the meaning of 'month' see PARA 43 note 3. Unless an immediate order is essential, the ministers must also consult organisations representing interests likely to be affected substantially (see s 129(6); and PARA 27); these organisations may then give notice of their desire to be heard by or make written representations to the appropriate committee (see s 62(5), (6) (s 62(5) (amended by SI 2005/1094, SI 2006/2407)). The ministers must take into account the advice of the appropriate committee: see the Medicines Act 1968 s 62(5), s 129(7) (s 62(5) as so amended). If an order is made and either the appropriate committee has not considered the proposal to make the order, or the order is made contrary to the advice of the appropriate committee, the order must include a statement of the fact that it has been so made: s 62(7) (substituted by SI 2005/1094).

As to the orders that have been made under the Medicines Act 1968 s 62 see PARAS 308–313.

8 Medicines Act 1968 s 67(2). As to the meaning of 'contravene' see PARA 41 note 8 (definition applied by s 132(1) (substituted by SI 2012/1916)).

9 See the Medicines Act 1968 s 67(4) (amended by virtue of the Magistrates' Courts Act 1980 s 32(2); SI 2012/1916). The penalty on summary conviction is a fine not exceeding the prescribed sum, or on conviction on indictment is a fine or imprisonment for a term not exceeding two years or both: Medicines Act 1968 s 67(4)(a), (b) (as so amended). As to the prescribed sum see SENTENCING AND DISPOSITION OF OFFENDERS vol 92 (2010) PARA 141.

10 Medicines Act 1968 s 67(3).

11 Medicines Act 1968 s 67(4) (as amended: see note 9). The penalty on summary conviction is a fine not exceeding the prescribed sum, and on conviction on indictment is a fine or imprisonment for a term not exceeding two years or both: s 67(4)(a), (b) (as so amended).

308. Bal Jivan Chamcho. The sale, supply and importation of the baby tonic under the name of Bal Jivan Chamcho[1] is prohibited[2].

This prohibition does not apply to the sale or supply of that product where the sale or supply is to any of the following persons:

(1) a public analyst[3];

(2) an authorised officer of a drugs authority[4];

(3) a sampling officer[5];

(4) a person duly authorised[6] by an enforcement authority[7];

(5) an inspector appointed[8] by the General Pharmaceutical Council[9].

Nor does the prohibition apply where the medicinal product is imported from an EEA state, if the product originates in an EEA state or originates outside the

European Economic Area, but is in free circulation in member states[10], and is being, or is to be, exported to a third country[11] or an EEA state other than the United Kingdom[12].

1   Ie the baby tonic under the name of BAL JIVAN CHAMCHO consisting of a dark brown aromatic solid substance affixed to a spoon-shaped metal appliance which is contained in a cardboard container measuring approximately 12 x 4 x 2 centimetres and labelled in pink type in three languages, that is to say English, Gujarati and Hindi, with directions in English as follows: 'CHILDREN DISEASES VIZ VARADH-CAPILLARY, BRONCHITIES, GREENISH DIARRHOEA, RICKETS, COUGH, CONVULSIONS ETC. RUBBING THE MEDICINE WITH WATER OR MILK TILL IT GETS COLOUR TO BE TAKEN TWICE A DAY.': see the Medicines (Bal Jivan Chamcho Prohibition) (No 2) Order 1977, SI 1977/670, art 2(2).

2   See the Medicines (Bal Jivan Chamcho Prohibition) (No 2) Order 1977, SI 1977/670, art 2(1).

3   Medicines (Bal Jivan Chamcho Prohibition) (No 2) Order 1977, SI 1977/670, art 2(3)(a) (substituted by SI 1990/2487). The public analyst mentioned in the text is one appointed under the Food Safety Act 1990 s 27 (see FOOD vol 18(2) (Reissue) PARA 268).

4   Medicines (Bal Jivan Chamcho Prohibition) (No 2) Order 1977, SI 1977/670, art 2(3)(b) (added by SI 1997/856).

5   Medicines (Bal Jivan Chamcho Prohibition) (No 2) Order 1977, SI 1977/670, art 2(3)(c). As to the meaning of sampling officer see the Medicines Act 1968 Sch 3; PARA 357.

6   Ie authorised under the Medicines Act 1968 ss 111, 112 (see PARAS 355, 356).

7   Medicines (Bal Jivan Chamcho Prohibition) (No 2) Order 1977, SI 1977/670, art 2(3)(d).

8   Ie an inspector appointed under the Pharmacy Order 2010, SI 2010/231, art 8(1) (see MEDICAL PROFESSIONS vol 74 (2011) PARA 815).

9   Medicines (Bal Jivan Chamcho Prohibition) (No 2) Order 1977, SI 1977/670, art 2(3)(e) (substituted by SI 2010/231). As to the General Pharmaceutical Council see MEDICAL PROFESSIONS vol 74 (2011) PARA 784 et seq.

10   For this purpose 'free circulation in member states' has the same meaning as in the Treaty on the Functioning of the European Union (Rome, 25 March 1957; TS 1 (1973); Cmnd 5179) ('TFEU'), art 28(2), as read with art 29 (formerly arts 14, 15 of the Treaty Establishing the European Community (Rome, 25 March 1957; TS 1 (1973); Cmnd 5179)), which was renamed and renumbered by the Treaty of Lisbon Amending the Treaty on European Union and the Treaty Establishing the European Community (Lisbon, 13 December 2007; ECS 13 (2007); Cm 7294) (OJ C306, 17.12.2007, p 1): Medicines (Bal Jivan Chamcho Prohibition) (No 2) Order 1977, SI 1977/670, art 2(5) (added by SI 2008/548)

11   For this purpose 'third country' means any country other than an EEA state: Medicines (Bal Jivan Chamcho Prohibition) (No 2) Order 1977, SI 1977/670, art 2(5) (as added: see note 10).

12   Medicines (Bal Jivan Chamcho Prohibition) (No 2) Order 1977, SI 1977/670, art 2(4) (added by SI 1997/856).

309. Non-medicinal antimicrobial substances. The sale or supply of certain antimicrobial substances[1] is prohibited[2] and this applies whether or not the substance is contained in any other substance or article unless that other substance or article is either a medicinal product[3] or an animal feeding stuff[4]. The antimicrobial substances are:

(1)   Amphomycin, Bacitracin, Candicidin, Capreomycin, Chloramphenicol, Cycloserine, Erythromycin, Framycetin, Furaltadone, Furazolidone, Fusidic Acid, Griseofulvin, Hachimycin, Nalidixic Acid, Nitrofurantoin, Nitrofurazone, Novobiocin, Nystatin, Oleandomycin, Paromomycin, Spectinomycin, Spiramycin, Tylosin, Vancomycin, Viomycin, Virginiamycina[5];

(2)   a substance falling within the following class of substances[6]: (a) Amphotericins[7]; (b) Cephalosporins[8]; (c) Gentamicins[9]; (d) Kanamycins[10]; (e) Lincomycins[11]; (f) Neomycins[12]; (g) Pencillins[13]; (h) Polymixins[14]; (i) Rifamycins[15]; (j) Ristocetins[16]; (k) Streptomycins[17]; (l) Sulphanilamide[18]; (m) Tetracyclines[19];

(3)   a salt or derivative of the substances specified in head (1) or (2) above or a salt of a derivative of the said substances[20]; or

(4)   a substance the chemical and biological properties of which are identical
       with or similar to a substance or a class of substances listed in head (1)
       or (2) above which is produced by means other than the growth of
       specific organisms[21].

The above prohibition does not apply to certain agricultural, horticultural or
forestry purposes in relation to Sulphanilamide, Griseofulvin, Streptomycins,
Amphotericins, Gentamicins, Kanamycins, Lincomycins, Nystatin, Penicillins,
Spectinomycin and Tylosin[22].

Nor does the prohibition apply where the sale is to a person who buys it for
one or more of the purposes of selling or supplying it or administering it or
causing it to be administered to one or more human beings[23] and such sale is to
a veterinary surgeon or veterinary practitioner, a person lawfully conducting a
retail pharmacy business, a holder of a manufacturer's licence[24] or a person
carrying on the business of selling by way of wholesale dealing[25]. Furthermore
the prohibition does not apply where the sale or supply is to a public analyst[26],
an agricultural analyst[27], a person duly authorised by an enforcement
authority[28], a sampling officer[29] or universities, other institutions concerned with
higher education or institutions concerned with research[30].

1   See heads (1) to (4) in the text.
2   Medicines (Prohibition of Non-medicinal Antimicrobial Substances) Order 1977, SI 1977/2131,
    art 2(1). This order does not apply to veterinary medicinal products: art 1A (added by
    SI 2005/2745). As to veterinary medicinal products see PARA 387 et seq.
3   As to the meaning of 'medicinal product' see PARA 25: Medicines (Prohibition of Non-medicinal
    Antimicrobial Substances) Order 1977, SI 1977/2131, art 1(2)(b); Medicines Act 1968 s 132(1)
    (substituted by SI 2012/1916); Human Medicines Regulations 2012, SI 2012/1916, art 2(1).
4   Medicines (Prohibition of Non-medicinal Antimicrobial Substances) Order 1977, SI 1977/2131,
    art 2(3).
5   Medicines (Prohibition of Non-medicinal Antimicrobial Substances) Order 1977, SI 1977/2131,
    art 2(1)(a), Sch 1, Pt 1.
6   Ie substances falling within the Medicines (Prohibition of Non-medicinal Antimicrobial
    Substances) Order 1977, SI 1977/2131, art 2(1)(b), Sch 1, Pt 2.
7   Ie antimicrobial substances or mixtures of such substances produced by Streptomyces nodosus.
8   Ie antimicrobial substances containing in their chemical structure a fused dihydrothiazine
    Beta-lactam nucleus.
9   Any antimicrobial basic substance or mixture of such substances produced by the strain
    Micromonospora purpurea which on 1 September 1967 was numbered NRRL 2953 in the
    culture collection of the Northern Utilisation Research and Development Branch of the United
    States Department of Agriculture.
10 Ie any antimicrobial substance or mixture of such substances produced by Streptomyces
    Kanamyceticus.
11 Ie antimicrobial substances produced by Streptomyces linocolnensis (var. lincolnensis). These
    substances are the basic amides of hygric acid or of a substituted hygric acid with 6-amino-6,
    8-dideoxy-l-thiogalacto-octopyranose   or   with   substituted   6-amino-6,
    8-dideoxy-l-thiogalacto-octopyranose.
12 Ie antimicrobial substances or mixtures of such substances produced by Streptomyces fradiae
    which are complex organic bases and which yield on hydrolysis with mineral acids the base
    neamine.
13 Ie any antimicrobial acid which contains in its structure a fused thiazolidine Beta-lactam
    nucleus.
14 Ie any antimicrobial substance produced by any strain of Badillus polymyxa.
15 Ie a group of related antimicrobial macrolactams produced by the growth of Streptomyces
    mediterranei   and   containing   the   chemical   structure   of   11-acetoxy-7,9,
    15-trihydroxy-13-methoxy-2,6,8,10,   12-pentamethylpentadeca-2,4,   14-trienoic   acid   amide
    attached by the nitrogen atom and by the oxygen atom in the 15-position respectively to the 7-
    and 2-positions of a 5,6, 9-trioxygenated 2, 4-dimethyl-l-oxo-naptho (2, l-b) furan.
16 Ie antimicrobial substances produced by a strain of a Nocardia species referred to as Nocardia
    lurida.

17 Ie any antimicrobial complex organic base or mixture of such bases produced by Streptomyces griseus which: (1) yields on hydrolysis with mineral acids the base streptidine (meso-l 3-diguanidocyclohexane-2,4,5,6-tetraol); and (2) yields on hydrolysis by a 4 per cent solution of sodium hydroxide the substance maltol (3-hydroxy-2-methyl-8-pyrone).

18 Sulphanilamide being p-aminobenzenesulphonamide, having any of the hydrogen atoms of either or both nitrogen atoms substituted by an equal number of univalent atoms or radicals.

19 Ie antimicrobial bases which contain the chemical structure naphthacene-2-carboxamide, hydrogenated to any extent and having each of the positions 1,3,10,11,12 and 12a substituted by a hydroxyl or an oxo group.

20 Medicines (Prohibition of Non-medicinal Antimicrobial Substances) Order 1977, SI 1977/2131, art 2(1)(c).

21 Medicines (Prohibition of Non-medicinal Antimicrobial Substances) Order 1977, SI 1977/2131, art 2(1)(d).

22 Medicines (Prohibition of Non-medicinal Antimicrobial Substances) Order 1977, SI 1977/2131, art 2(4)(a), Sch 2.

23 Ie the purposes specified in the Medicines Act 1968 s 131(2).

24 As to a manufacturer's licence see PARA 45 et seq.

25 Medicines (Prohibition of Non-medicinal Antimicrobial Substances) Order 1977, SI 1977/2131, art 2(4)(b).

26 Ie appointed under the Food Safety Act 1990 s 27 (see FOOD vol 18(2) (Reissue) PARA 268).

27 Ie appointed under the Agriculture Act 1970 s 67 (see AGRICULTURAL PRODUCTION AND MARKETING vol 1 (2008) PARA 958).

28 Ie under the Medicines Act 1968 ss 111, 112 (see PARAS 355, 356).

29 As to the meaning of 'sampling officer' see the Medicines Act 1968 Sch 3; and PARA 357.

30 Medicines (Prohibition of Non-medicinal Antimicrobial Substances) Order 1977, SI 1977/2131, art 2(4)(c).

310. Chloroform. The sale or supply of any medicinal product[1] consisting of or containing chloroform, not being a veterinary drug, is prohibited[2]. This does not apply where such sale or supply is:

    (1)   by a doctor or dentist to a patient of his and the medicinal product has been specially prepared by that doctor or dentist for administration to that particular patient[3]; or

    (2)   by a doctor or dentist who has specially prepared the medicinal product at the request of another doctor or dentist for administration to a particular patient of that other doctor or dentist[4]; or

    (3)   from a registered pharmacy or a hospital or by a doctor or dentist and the medicinal product has been specially prepared, in accordance with a prescription given by a doctor or dentist for a particular patient of his in a registered pharmacy, in a hospital or by a doctor or dentist[5].

Nor does the prohibition apply where such sale or supply is:

    (a)   to a hospital or to a doctor or to a dentist for either or both of the following purposes, namely: (i) solely for use by administration to human beings for the purpose of inducing anaesthesia; or (ii) solely for use as an ingredient in the preparation of a substance or article to be administered to human beings for the purpose of inducing anaesthesia[6]; or

    (b)   to a person who buys or obtains it for purpose of selling or supplying it to a hospital or to a doctor or to a dentist for either or both of the purposes described in head (a)[7].

The prohibition is also subject to the additional exceptions that the sale or supply or any such medicinal product is not prohibited in any one or more of the following circumstances, namely:

    (A)   where such product contains chloroform in a proportion of not more than 0.5 per cent calculated in terms of weight in weight (w/w) or volume in volume (v/v) as appropriate[8]; or

(B)   where such product is solely for use in dental surgery[9]; or

(C)   without prejudice to head (B) where such product is for sale or supply solely for use by being applied to the external surface of the body[10].

The prohibition does not apply where the sale or supply involves, or is for the purpose of, exporting the medicinal product[11]. Nor does it apply where the medicinal product is for use as an ingredient in the preparation of any substance or article in a registered pharmacy, in a hospital, by a doctor or by a dentist[12].

1   As to the meaning of 'medicinal product' see PARA 25.
2   Medicines (Chloroform Prohibition) Order 1979, SI 1979/382, art 2. As to transitional provisions see arts 4, 5 (art 5 added by SI 1980/263).
3   Medicines (Chloroform Prohibition) Order 1979, SI 1979/382, art 3(1)(a).
4   Medicines (Chloroform Prohibition) Order 1979, SI 1979/382, art 3(1)(b).
5   Medicines (Chloroform Prohibition) Order 1979, SI 1979/382, art 3(1)(c) (amended by SI 1989/1184).
6   Medicines (Chloroform Prohibition) Order 1979, SI 1979/382, art 3(2)(a).
7   Medicines (Chloroform Prohibition) Order 1979, SI 1979/382, art 3(2)(b).
8   Medicines (Chloroform Prohibition) Order 1979, SI 1979/382, art 3(3)(a).
9   Medicines (Chloroform Prohibition) Order 1979, SI 1979/382, art 3(3)(b).
10 Medicines (Chloroform Prohibition) Order 1979, SI 1979/382, art 3(3)(c). For this purpose the external surface of the body does not include the mouth or any part of the mouth (including teeth) or the mucous membranes: art 3(6).
11 See the Medicines (Chloroform Prohibition) Order 1979, SI 1979/382, art 3(4).
12 Medicines (Chloroform Prohibition) Order 1979, SI 1979/382, art 3(5).

311.   Products containing certain plants.   The sale, supply and importation of any medicinal product[1] consisting of or containing a plant belonging to a species of the genus Aristolochia or belonging to any of the species Akebia quinata, Akebia trifoliata, Clematis armandii, Clematis montana, Cocculus laurifolius, Cocculus orbiculatus, Cocculus trilobus, Stephania tetrandra, or consisting of or containing an extract from such a plant, is prohibited[2].

The sale, supply and importation of any medicinal product is prohibited where, at the time of the sale, supply or importation the label on the product's container or package or any document accompanying the product, indicates in any language that the product consists of or contains Mu Tong or Fangji, or any term derived from either of those terms or that the product consists of or contains a plant mentioned above[3] or an extract from such a plant[4].

The above prohibitions do not apply where a medicinal product as referred to above is sold or supplied to, or, in the case of importation, is imported by or on behalf of, any of the following persons:

(1)   a food analyst or food examiner[5];

(2)   an authorised officer[6];

(3)   a person duly authorised[7] by an enforcement authority[8];

(4)   a sampling officer[9].

The prohibitions do not apply where the medicinal product is imported from an EEA state, if the product originates in an EEA state or originates outside the European Economic Area, but is in free circulation in member states[10], and is being, or is to be, exported to a third country[11] or an EEA State other than the United Kingdom[12].

Nor do the prohibitions not apply where a medicinal product as referred to the above prohibitions is the subject of a product licence, a marketing authorisation, certificate of registration, traditional herbal registration or Article 126a authorisation[13].

1   This does not include a medicinal product that is a veterinary drug: Medicines (Aristolochia and Mu Tong etc) (Prohibition) Order 2001, SI 2001/1841, art 1(1).
2   Medicines (Aristolochia and Mu Tong etc) (Prohibition) Order 2001, SI 2001/1841, art 2.
3   Ie mentioned in the Medicines (Aristolochia and Mu Tong etc) (Prohibition) Order 2001, SI 2001/1841, art 2.
4   Medicines (Aristolochia and Mu Tong etc) (Prohibition) Order 2001, SI 2001/1841, art 3.
5   Medicines (Aristolochia and Mu Tong etc) (Prohibition) Order 2001, SI 2001/1841, art 4(1), (2)(a), (b). As to the meaning of 'food analyst or examiner' see the Food Safety Act 1990 s 30; FOOD vol 18(2) (Reissue) PARA 267; and the Food Safety (Northern Ireland) Order 1991, SI 1991/672 (NI 7) arts 30, 31.
6   Medicines (Aristolochia and Mu Tong etc) (Prohibition) Order 2001, SI 2001/1841, art 4(2)(c). As to the meaning of 'an authorised officer' see the Food Safety Act 1990 s 5(6); FOOD vol 18(2) (Reissue) PARA 253; and the Food Safety (Northern Ireland) Order 1991, SI 1991/672 (NI 7) art 2(2).
7   Ie duly authorised under the Medicines Act 1968 ss 111, 112 (see PARAS 355, 356).
8   Medicines (Aristolochia and Mu Tong etc) (Prohibition) Order 2001, SI 2001/1841, art 4(2)(d).
9   Medicines (Aristolochia and Mu Tong etc) (Prohibition) Order 2001, SI 2001/1841, art 4(2)(e). As to the meaning of 'sampling officer' see the Medicines Act 1968 Sch 3; and PARA 357.
10 'Free circulation in member states' has the same meaning as in the Treaty on the Functioning of the European Union (Rome, 25 March 1957; TS 1 (1973); Cmnd 5179) ('TFEU'), art 28(2), as read with art 29 (formerly arts 14, 15 of the Treaty Establishing the European Community (Rome, 25 March 1957; TS 1 (1973); Cmnd 5179), which was renamed and renumbered (see PARA 308 note 10): Medicines (Aristolochia and Mu Tong etc) (Prohibition) Order 2001, SI 2001/1841, art 1(2) (definition added by SI 2008/548; amended by SI 2012/1809).
11 'Third country' means any country other than an EEA state: Medicines (Aristolochia and Mu Tong etc) (Prohibition) Order 2001, SI 2001/1841, art 2(2) (definition added by SI 2008/548).
12 Medicines (Aristolochia and Mu Tong etc) (Prohibition) Order 2001, SI 2001/1841, art 4(3) (substituted by SI 2008/548).
13 Medicines (Aristolochia and Mu Tong etc) (Prohibition) Order 2001, SI 2001/1841, art 4(4) (amended by SI 2012/1916). As to the meaning of a 'marketing authorisation' 'certificate of registration', 'traditional herbal registration' and 'Article 126a authorisation' see PARA 141 notes 3–6.

312.   Products containing Kava-kava.   The sale, supply or importation of any medicinal product[1] consisting of or containing a plant belonging to the species Piper methysticum (known as Kava-kava) or an extract from such a plant is prohibited[2].

This prohibition does not apply where the medicinal product is:

(1)   for external use only[3];

(2)   sold or supplied to, or is imported by or on behalf of an authorised officer[4]; a food analyst or food examiner[5], a person duly authorised by an enforcement authority[6] or a sampling officer[7];

(3)   imported from an EEA state, if the product originates in an EEA State or originates outside the European Economic Area, but is in free circulation in member states[8], and is being, or is to be, exported to a third country[9] or an EEA State other than the United Kingdom[10]; or

(4)   the subject of a marketing authorisation, certificate of registration, traditional herbal registration or Article 126a authorisation[11].

1   This does not include a medicinal product which is a veterinary drug: Medicines for Human Use (Kava-kava) (Prohibition) Order 2002, SI 2002/3170, art 1(2).
2   Medicines for Human Use (Kava-kava) (Prohibition) Order 2002, SI 2002/3170, art 2.
3   Medicines for Human Use (Kava-kava) (Prohibition) Order 2002, SI 2002/3170, art 3(a). 'External use' means application to the skin, hair, teeth, mucosa of the mouth, throat, nose, ear, eye, vagina or anal canal when a local action only is intended and extensive systemic absorption is unlikely to occur, and references to medicinal products being 'for external use' are to be read accordingly, except that such references do not include throat sprays, throat pastilles, throat lozenges, throat tablets, nasal drops, nasal sprays, nasal inhalations or teething preparations: art 1(2).

4 Ie within the meaning of the Food Safety Act 1990 s 5(6) (see FOOD vol 18(2) (Reissue) PARA 253) or the Food Safety (Northern Ireland) Order 1991, SI 1991/672 (NI 7) art 2(2).
5 Ie within the meaning of the Food Safety Act 1990 s 30(see FOOD vol 18(2) (Reissue) PARA 267); or the Food Safety (Northern Ireland) Order 1991, SI 1991/672 (NI 7) arts 30, 31.
6 Ie duly authorised under the Medicines Act 1968 ss 111, 112 (see PARAS 355, 356).
7 Medicines for Human Use (Kava-kava) (Prohibition) Order 2002, SI 2002/3170, art 3(b). As to a sampling officer see the Medicines Act 1968 Sch 3; and PARA 357.
8 'Free circulation in member states' has the same meaning as in the Treaty on the Functioning of the European Union (Rome, 25 March 1957; TS 1 (1973); Cmnd 5179) ('TFEU'), art 23.2 as read with art 28(2), as read with art 29 (formerly arts 14, 15 of the Treaty Establishing the European Community (Rome, 25 March 1957; TS 1 (1973); Cmnd 5179), which was renamed and renumbered (see PARA 308 note 10): Medicines for Human Use (Kava-kava) (Prohibition) Order 2002, SI 2002/3170, art 1(2) (definition amended by SI 2012/1809).
9 'Third country' means any country other than an EEA state: Medicines for Human Use (Kava-kava) (Prohibition) Order 2002, SI 2002/3170, art 1(2) (definition added by SI 2008/548).
10 Medicines for Human Use (Kava-kava) (Prohibition) Order 2002, SI 2002/3170, art 3(c) (substituted by SI 2008/548).
11 Medicines for Human Use (Kava-kava) (Prohibition) Order 2002, SI 2002/3170, art 3(d) (amended by SI 2012/1916). As to the meanings of a 'marketing authorisation', 'certificate of registration', 'traditional herbal registration' and 'Article 126a authorisation' see PARA 141 notes 3–6.

313. Products containing Senecio. The sale, supply or importation of any medicinal product consisting of or containing a plant belonging to the species Senecio or an extract from such a plant is prohibited[1].

This prohibition does not apply where the medicinal product is for external use only[2] and is not a teething preparation, throat spray, throat pastille, throat lozenge, throat tablet, nasal spray or nasal inhalation or nasal drops[3]. The prohibition does not apply where the medicinal product is sold or supplied to, or imported by or on behalf of, an authorised officer[4], a food analyst or food examiner[5], a person duly authorised by an enforcement authority[6] or a sampling officer[7].

The prohibition does not apply where the medicinal product is imported from an EEA state, if the product originates in an EEA State or originates outside the European Economic Area, but is in free circulation in member states[8], and is being, or is to be, exported to a third country[9] or an EEA state other than the United Kingdom[10].

Nor does the prohibition apply where the medicinal product is the subject of a product licence, a marketing authorisation, a certificate of registration or a traditional herbal registration[11].

1 Medicines for Human Use (Prohibition) (Senecio and Miscellaneous Amendments) Order 2008, SI 2008/548, art 2.
2 'External use' means application to the skin, hair, teeth, mucosa of the mouth, throat, nose, ear, eye, vagina or anal canal when a local action only is intended and extensive systemic absorption is unlikely to occur: Medicines for Human Use (Prohibition) (Senecio and Miscellaneous Amendments) Order 2008, SI 2008/548, art 1(2).
3 Medicines for Human Use (Prohibition) (Senecio and Miscellaneous Amendments) Order 2008, SI 2008/548, art 3(a).
4 Ie within the meaning of the Food Safety Act 1990 s 5(6) (see FOOD vol 18(2) (Reissue) PARA 253) or the Food Safety (Northern Ireland) Order 1991, SI 1991/672 (NI 7) art 2(2).
5 Ie within the meaning of the Food Safety Act 1990 s 30(see FOOD vol 18(2) (Reissue) PARA 267); or the Food Safety (Northern Ireland) Order 1991, SI 1991/672 (NI 7) arts 30, 31.
6 Ie duly authorised under the Medicines Act 1968 ss 111, 112 (see PARAs 355, 356).
7 Medicines for Human Use (Prohibition) (Senecio and Miscellaneous Amendments) Order 2008, SI 2008/548, art 3(b). As to a sampling officer see the Medicines Act 1968 Sch 3; and PARA 357.
8 'Free circulation in member states' has the same meaning as in the Treaty on the Functioning of the European Union (Rome, 25 March 1957; TS 1 (1973); Cmnd 5179) ('TFEU'), art 28(2), as

read with art 29 (formerly arts 14, 15 of the Treaty Establishing the European Community (Rome, 25 March 1957; TS 1 (1973); Cmnd 5179), which was renamed and renumbered (see PARA 308 note 10): Medicines for Human Use (Prohibition) (Senecio and Miscellaneous Amendments) Order 2008, SI 2008/548, art 1(2) (definition amended by SI 2012/1916).

9 'Third country' means any country other than an EEA state: Medicines for Human Use (Prohibition) (Senecio and Miscellaneous Amendments) Order 2008, SI 2008/548, art 1(2).

10 Medicines for Human Use (Prohibition) (Senecio and Miscellaneous Amendments) Order 2008, SI 2008/548, art 3(c).

11 Medicines for Human Use (Prohibition) (Senecio and Miscellaneous Amendments) Order 2008, SI 2008/548, art 3(d) (amended by SI 2012/1916). As to the meanings of a 'marketing authorisation', 'certificate of registration', 'traditional herbal registration' and 'Article 126a authorisation' see PARA 141 notes 3–6.

(9) PACKAGING, LEAFLETS AND COLOURS ETC

(i) Containers

314. Containers. The ministers[1] may make regulations[2] prohibiting the sale or supply of medicinal products otherwise than in containers which comply with such requirements as the ministers consider necessary or expedient for certain purposes[3] or for the purpose of preserving the quality of the products, and, in particular, may by the regulations require such containers to be of such strength, to be made of such materials, and to be of such shapes or patterns, as may be prescribed[4].

No person[5], in the course of a business[6] carried on by him, may sell or supply, or have in his possession for the purpose of sale or supply, any medicinal product in such circumstances as to contravene[7] any requirements imposed by regulations which are applicable to that product[8]. Regulations may provide that any person who contravenes this provision or the regulations is guilty of an offence[9].

1 As to the meaning of 'the ministers' see the Human Medicines Regulations 2012, SI 2012/1916, reg 6(6)–(8); and PARA 35 (definition applied by the Medicines Act 1968 s 132(1) (substituted by SI 2012/1916)).

2 Without prejudice to the application of the Medicines Act 1968 s 129(5) (see PARA 27), any such power to make regulations conferred by s 87 may be exercised so as to impose requirements either in relation to medicinal products generally or in relation to medicinal products of a particular description, or falling within a particular class, specified in the regulations: s 91(3) (amended by SI 2006/2407, SI 2012/1916). As to the meaning of 'medicinal product' see the Human Medicines Regulations 2012, SI 2012/1916, reg 2(1); and PARA 25 (definition applied by the Medicines Act 1968 s 132(1) (substituted by SI 2012/1916)). Before making any such regulations the ministers must consult appropriate organisations: see s 129(6); and PARA 27. As to the information to be made available to ministers before they make regulations see *R (on the application of National Association of Health Stores) v Secretary of State for Health* [2005] EWCA Civ 154, (2005) Times, 9 March.

3 These purposes are:
   (1)   securing that medicinal products are correctly described and readily identifiable (Medicines Act 1968 s 87(3)(a) (added by SI 2012/1916));
   (2)   securing that any appropriate warning or other appropriate instruction or information is given, and that false or misleading information is not given, with respect to medicinal products (Medicines Act 1968 s 87(3)(b) (as so added));
   (3)   promoting safety in relation to medicinal products (s 87(3)(c) (as so added)).

4 Medicines Act 1968 s 87(1) (amended by SI 2006/2407 and SI 2012/1916). As to the regulations that have been made see the Human Medicines Regulations 2012, SI 2012/1916.

5 As to the meaning of 'person' see PARA 45 note 2.

6 As to the meaning of 'business' see PARA 52 note 10 (definition applied by the Medicines Act 1968 s 132(1) (substituted by SI 2012/1916)).

7 As to the meaning of 'contravene' see PARA 41 note 8 (definition applied by the Medicines Act 1968 s 132(1) (substituted by SI 2012/1916)).

8 Medicines Act 1968 s 87(2). In relation to this offence, certain presumptions apply in respect of a person having a medicinal product in his possession for the purpose of sale or supply: see s 126(2), (3); and PARA 377.

9 See the Medicines Act 1968 s 91(2) (amended by SI 2006/2407, SI 2012/1916). See also the regulations mentioned in note 4. Such a person is liable on summary conviction to a fine not exceeding the prescribed sum or such lesser sum as may be specified in the regulations (Medicines Act 1968 s 91(2)(a) (amended by virtue of the Magistrates' Courts Act 1980 s 32(2))) or, if the regulations so provide, on conviction on indictment to a fine or to imprisonment for a term not exceeding two years or to both (Medicines Act 1968 s 91(2)(b)). As to the prescribed sum see SENTENCING AND DISPOSITION OF OFFENDERS vol 92 (2010) PARA 141.

315. Child resistant containers. Regulated medicinal products[1], sold or supplied otherwise than in accordance with exemptions to this provision[2], may be sold only in containers which are opaque or dark tinted and child resistant[3].

A person is guilty of an offence if, in the course of a business, he sells or supplies, or possesses for the purposes of sale or supply a regulated medicinal product in a container which does not comply with the above requirements[4] unless the sale or supply is or would be exempt[5] from those requirements[6].

1 'Regulated medicinal product' means a medicinal product containing aspirin, paracetamol or more than 24mg of elemental iron, in the form of tablets, capsules, pills, lozenges, pastilles, suppositories or oral liquids, but does not include: (1) effervescent tablets containing not more than 25% of aspirin or paracetamol by weight; (2) medicinal products in sachets or other sealed containers which hold only one dose; (3) medicinal products which are not intended for retail sale or for supply in circumstances corresponding to retail sale; or (4) medicinal products which are for export only: Human Medicines Regulations 2012, SI 2012/1916, reg 272. As to the meaning of 'medicinal product' see PARA 25. 'Effervescent', in relation to a tablet or capsule, means containing not less than 75 per cent, by weight of the tablet or capsule, of ingredients included wholly or mainly for the purpose of releasing carbon dioxide when the tablet or capsule is dissolved or dispersed in water: reg 8(1).

2 Ie otherwise that in accordance with the Human Medicines Regulations 2012, SI 2012/1916, reg 274 (see PARA 316).

3 Human Medicines Regulations 2012, SI 2012/1916, reg 273(1). Containers which are not reclosable are child resistant if they have been evaluated in accordance with, and comply with the requirements of British Standard EN 14375:2003 published by the British Standards Institution on 18th April 2005 or any equivalent or higher technical specification for non-reclosable child resistant packaging recognised for use in the European Economic Area: reg 273(2). Containers which are reclosable are child resistant if they have been evaluated in accordance with, and comply with the requirements of British Standard EN ISO 8317:2004 published by the British Standards Institution on 11th May 2005 or any equivalent or higher technical specification for reclosable child resistant packaging recognised for use in the European Economic Area: reg 273(3).

4 Ie the requirements of the Human Medicines Regulations 2012, SI 2012/1916, reg 273.

5 Ie exempt under the Human Medicines Regulations 2012, SI 2012/1916, reg 274 (see PARA 316).

6 Human Medicines Regulations 2012, SI 2012/1916, reg 276(1). A person guilty of such an offence is liable, on summary conviction, to a fine not exceeding the statutory maximum or, on conviction on indictment, to a fine, to imprisonment for a term not exceeding 2 years, or to both: reg 276(2). As to the statutory maximum see SENTENCING AND DISPOSITION OF OFFENDERS vol 92 (2010) PARA 140.

316. Exemptions from child resistant containers. The requirement to sell regulated medicinal products in child resistant containers[1] does not apply to the retail sale, or supply in circumstances corresponding to retail sale[2], of regulated medicinal products where the sale or supply is carried out by or under the supervision of a pharmacist[3], on premises which are a registered pharmacy[4] and either:

(1) in accordance with a prescription given by an appropriate practitioner

where it is not reasonably practicable to provide the regulated medicinal products in containers that are both opaque or dark tinted and child resistant[5]; or

(2)   at the request of a person who is aged 16 or over and specifically requests that the regulated medicinal products not be contained in a child resistant container[6].

Nor does the requirement to sell regulated medicinal products in child resistant containers[7] apply to the sale or supply of regulated medicinal products:

(a)   by a doctor or dentist[8] to a patient, or the patient's carer, for the patient's use[9];

(b)   by a doctor or dentist to a person who is an appropriate practitioner[10], at the request of that person, for administration[11] to a patient of that person[12]; or

(c)   in the course of the business of a hospital or health centre[13], where the sale or supply is for the purposes of administration, whether in the hospital or health centre or elsewhere, in accordance with the directions of an appropriate practitioner[14].

1   Ie the Human Medicines Regulations 2012, SI 2012/1916, reg 273 (see PARA 315). As to the meaning of 'regulated medicinal product' see PARA 315 note 1.
2   As to the meaning of 'retail sale' and 'circumstances corresponding to retail sale' see PARA 52 note 11.
3   As to the meaning of 'pharmacist' see PARA 52 note 5.
4   As to the meaning of 'registered pharmacy' see PARA 52 note 2.
5   Human Medicines Regulations 2012, SI 2012/1916, reg 274(1)(a).
6   Human Medicines Regulations 2012, SI 2012/1916, reg 274(1)(b).
7   See note 1.
8   As to the meanings of 'doctor' and 'dentist' see PARA 48 note 6.
9   Human Medicines Regulations 2012, SI 2012/1916, reg 274(3)(a).
10   As to the meaning of 'appropriate practitioner' see PARA 271.
11   As to the meaning of 'administer' see PARA 25 note 4.
12   Human Medicines Regulations 2012, SI 2012/1916, reg 274(3)(b).
13   As to the meaning of 'hospital' and 'health centre' see PARA 52 notes 3, 4.
14   Human Medicines Regulations 2012, SI 2012/1916, reg 274(3)(c).

(ii) Packaging and Leaflets

317. Scope of provisions. The requirements for packaging and package leaflets relating to medicinal products[1] do not apply to medicinal products that are sold or supplied in the following circumstances[2].

The provisions do not apply where the product is the result of a process of manufacture[3] which does not require a manufacturing licence[4] because either[5] the medicinal product is manufactured or assembled by a doctor or dentist, or it is a herbal medicinal product manufactured and assembled by a person, and certain provisions apply[6].

Nor do the provisions apply where: (1) the product is the result of a process of assembly of an authorised medicinal product[7]; (2) the requirement for a manufacturing licence[8] does not apply to the process of assembly[9] because the product is assembled by a registered nurse or registered midwife[10], or it is manufactured or assembled by a doctor or dentist, and certain conditions are met[11]; (3) the process of assembly results in a change in the presentation of the authorised medicinal product; and (4) by reason of that change the product so assembled is not sold or supplied in accordance with the terms of the marketing authorisation, the certificate of registration, the traditional herbal registration, or the Article 126a authorisation, that relates to the authorised medicinal product[12].

However, certain information[13] must appear on the outer packaging, or, if there is no outer packaging, on the immediate packaging[14] of medicinal product that is sold or supplied[15].

1 Ie Human Medicines Regulations 2012, SI 2012/1916, Pt 13 Chapter 1 (regs 257–271). As to the meaning of 'medicinal product' see PARA 25. Regulations 269 (offences relating to packaging and package leaflets: other persons) and 271 (offences: penalties) still have effect in relation to reg 3(13) as if reg 3(13) were a requirement of Part 13: reg 3(14). As to the meaning of 'package leaflet' see PARA 68 note 5.

2 See the Human Medicines Regulations 2012, SI 2012/1916, reg 3(10).

3 As to the meaning of 'manufacture' see PARA 141 note 7.

4 Ie to which the Human Medicines Regulations 2012, SI 2012/1916, reg 17(1) (see PARA 45) does not apply.

5 Ie the Human Medicines Regulations 2012, SI 2012/1916, reg 17(1) does not apply by virtue of reg 3(5) or (6) (see PARAS 48, 49).

6 See the Human Medicines Regulations 2012, SI 2012/1916, reg 3(11).

7 For the purposes of the Human Medicines Regulations 2012, SI 2012/1916, regs 3, 4 (special provisions for pharmacies etc), a medicinal product is authorised if there is in force for the product a marketing authorisation, a certificate of registration, a traditional herbal registration or an Article 126a authorisation: reg 3(15). As to the meanings of 'marketing authorisation', 'certificate of registration', 'traditional herbal registration' and 'Article 126a authorisation' see PARA 141 notes 3–6.

8 Ie the Human Medicines Regulations 2012, SI 2012/1916, reg 17(1) does not apply.

9 As to the meaning of 'assemble' see PARA 141 note 8.

10 As to the meanings of 'registered nurse' and 'registered midwife' see PARA 48 note 3.

11 Ie the Human Medicines Regulations 2012, SI 2012/1916, reg 17(1) does not apply to the process of assembly by virtue of reg 3(4) or (5) (see PARAS 47, 48).

12 See the Human Medicines Regulations 2012, SI 2012/1916, reg 3(12).

13 The information specified in the Human Medicines Regulations 2012, SI 2012/1916, Sch 26 paras 1–4 must appear on the outer packaging, or, if there is no outer packaging, on the immediate packaging of medicinal product that is sold or supplied in circumstances: (1) where reg 3(11) applies to the product, except in the case of a product manufactured in accordance with reg 3(6) (see PARA 51); or (2) where reg 3(12) applies in relation to the product: reg 3(13). Regulations 269 (offences relating to packaging and package leaflets: other persons: see PARA 329) and 271 (offences: penalties: see PARA 329) have effect in relation to reg 3(13) as if it were a requirement of Part 13: reg 3(14).

14 As to the meanings of 'immediate packaging' and 'outer packaging' see PARA 278 note 5.

15 See the Human Medicines Regulations 2012, SI 2012/1916, reg 3(13).

318. Special provision for pharmacies. The requirements for packaging and package leaflets[1] relating to medicinal products[2] do not apply to a medicinal product that is sold or supplied in the following circumstances[3].

The requirements do not apply where a medicinal product is the result of a process of manufacture[4] which does not require a manufacturing licence[5] by virtue of the exemptions[6] relating to pharmacists under the Medicines Act 1968[7].

Nor do the requirements apply in the case of a medicinal product where:

(1) the product is the result of a process of assembly[8] of a medicinal product that is an authorised medicinal product[9];

(2) the requirement for a manufacturing licence[10] does not apply to the process of assembly by virtue of the exemptions[11] relating to pharmacists under the Medicines Act 1968[12];

(3) the process of assembly results in a change in the presentation of the authorised medicinal product[13]; and

(4) by reason of that change the product so assembled is not sold or supplied in accordance with the terms of the marketing authorisation,

the certificate of registration, the traditional herbal registration or the Article 126a authorisation[14], that relates to the authorised medicinal product[15].

Certain information[16] must appear on the outer packaging, or, if there is no outer packaging, on the immediate packaging[17] of a medicinal product that is sold or supplied in circumstances where the above provisions[18] apply in relation to the product[19].

1 As to the meaning of 'package leaflet' see PARA 68 note 5.
2 Ie the Human Medicines Regulations 2012, SI 2012/1916, Pt 13, Chapter 1 (regs 257–271). As to the meaning of 'medicinal product' see PARA 25.
3 See the Human Medicines Regulations 2012, SI 2012/1916, reg 4(2).
4 As to the meaning of 'manufacture' see PARA 141 note 7.
5 Ie to which the Human Medicines Regulations 2012, SI 2012/1916, reg 17(1) (see PARA 45) does not apply.
6 Ie by virtue of the Medicines Act 1968 s 10 (see PARA 52).
7 See the Human Medicines Regulations 2012, SI 2012/1916, reg 4(3).
8 As to the meaning of 'assemble' see PARA 141 note 8.
9 Human Medicines Regulations 2012, SI 2012/1916, reg 4(4)(a). As to the meaning of 'authorised medicinal product' see PARA 144 note 5.
10 Ie the Human Medicines Regulations 2012, SI 2012/1916, reg 17(1) (see PARA 45).
11 See note 6.
12 See the Human Medicines Regulations 2012, SI 2012/1916, reg 4(4)(b).
13 Human Medicines Regulations 2012, SI 2012/1916, reg 4(4)(c).
14 As to the meanings of 'marketing authorisation', 'Article 126a authorisation', 'certificate of registration' and 'traditional herbal registration' see PARA 141 notes 3–6.
15 Human Medicines Regulations 2012, SI 2012/1916, reg 4(4)(d).
16 Ie the information specified in the Human Medicines Regulations 2012, SI 2012/1916, Sch 26 paras 1–4.
17 As to the meanings of 'immediate packaging' and 'outer packaging' see PARA 278 note 5.
18 Ie where the Human Medicines Regulations 2012, SI 2012/1916, reg 4(3) or (4) apply.
19 Human Medicines Regulations 2012, SI 2012/1916, reg 4(5). Regulations 269 (offences relating to packaging and package leaflets: other persons: see PARA 329) and 271 (offences: penalties: see PARA 329) have effect in relation to reg 4(5) as if that provision were a requirement of Part 13: reg 4(6).

319. General and specific packaging requirements. Specified information[1] must appear on the outer packaging of a medicinal product[2] and, except under specified circumstances[3], on the immediate packaging[4] of the product[5].

In addition[6], the specified information referred to above[7], must appear on the outer packaging, or, if there is no outer packaging, on the immediate packaging of a medicinal product sold or supplied in accordance with a prescription given by a person who is an appropriate practitioner[8], whether or not the medicinal product in question is a prescription only medicine[9].

Specified information[10] must appear on a package[11] which contains a number of packages of medicinal products of the same description, other than special medicinal products[12], for the purpose of transport, delivery or storage[13].

Such provisions[14] do not require information to appear on:

(1)   a package containing a medicinal product where part of the package is transparent or open, provided that the information required[15] is clearly visible through the transparent or open part of the package[16];

(2)   a paper bag or similar wrapping in which a package that contains a medicinal product and bears information in accordance with the requirements of the relevant provisions[17] is placed at the time of sale or supply[18];

(3)   a package enclosing a package of a medicinal product for export[19];

(4)   an ampoule or other container of not more than 10 millilitres' nominal

capacity which is enclosed in a package on which information appears in accordance with the specified requirements[20]; or

(5)   a blister pack or similar packaging enclosed in a package on which specified information[21] appears[22].

Nor do such provisions[23] apply to a medicinal product:

(a)   which is an anti-viral medicine in the form of a solution to be used for the treatment of a child under the age of one year[24];

(b)   on the container of which appears the name of the person to whom the product is to be administered, the date on which the product is sold or supplied and the necessary instructions for proper use[25]; and

(c)   which is sold or supplied for the purpose of treating a disease which is a serious risk to human health, or potentially a serious risk to human health and which is pandemic or imminently pandemic[26].

1   Ie the information specified in the Human Medicines Regulations 2012, SI 2012/1916, Sch 25 Pt 1. Information included on the packaging of a product in accordance with regs 257, 261 and Sch 24 must be easily legible, comprehensible and indelible: reg 257(6). Nothing in reg 257 or Sch 24 applies to a registrable homoeopathic medicinal product: reg 257(7). As to the meaning of 'registrable homoeopathic medicinal product' see PARA 187.

2   As to the meaning of 'medicinal product' see PARA 25; and as to the meaning of 'outer packaging' see PARA 278 note 5.

3   Ie where the Human Medicines Regulations 2012, SI 2012/1916, reg 257(2) or (3) applies. Regulation 257(2) applies to immediate packaging if the packaging is in the form of a blister pack and is placed in outer packaging which complies with the requirements of Sch 24 Pt 1: reg 257(2). In such a case the information specified in Sch 25 Pt 1 must appear on the immediate packaging: see reg 257(4). Regulation 257(3) applies to immediate packaging if the packaging is too small to display the information required by Sch 24 Pt 1: reg 257(3). In such a case the information specified in Sch 24 Pt 3 must appear on immediate packaging: see reg 257(5).

4   As to the meaning of 'immediate packaging' see PARA 278 note 5.

5   Human Medicines Regulations 2012, SI 2012/1916, reg 257(1).

6   Ie in addition to other information required by the Human Medicines Regulations 2012, SI 2012/1916, regs 257–276.

7   Ie the information specified in the Human Medicines Regulations 2012, SI 2012/1916, Sch 25 Pt 1. The requirements of Sch 25 para 4 or 6, as the case may be, are satisfied in relation to a package containing a number of packages of medicinal products of the same description if the information specified in Sch 25 para 4 or 6 is shown on one or more of those packages: reg 258(2).

8   Ie for the purposes of the Human Medicines Regulations 2012, SI 2012/1916, reg 214(3)–(6) (see PARA 271).

9   Human Medicines Regulations 2012, SI 2012/1916, reg 258(1). As to the meaning of 'prescription only medicine' see the Human Medicines Regulations 2012, SI 2012/1916, reg 5(3); and PARA 26: reg 8(1). Nothing in reg 258 or Sch 25 applies to a traditional herbal medicinal product or a registrable homoeopathic medicinal product: reg 258(8).

10 Ie the information specified in the Human Medicines Regulations 2012, SI 2012/1916, Sch 25 Pt 2.

11 As to the meaning of 'package' see PARA 51 note 48.

12 As to the meaning of 'special medicinal product' see PARA 269 note 6.

13 Human Medicines Regulations 2012, SI 2012/1916, reg 258(3). This does not apply to a packing case, crate or other covering used solely for the purposes of transport or delivery of packages of medicinal products, each of which is labelled in accordance with the other requirements of Pt 13 (regs 257–276). In addition to the other information required by Pt 13, the information specified in Sch 25 Pts 3 and 4 must appear on the outer packaging and the immediate packaging of products of the kind specified in those provisions: see reg 258(5).

14 Ie the Human Medicines Regulations 2012, SI 2012/1916, reg 258 and Sch 25.

15 Ie by the Human Medicines Regulations 2012, SI 2012/1916, reg 258 and Sch 25.

16 Human Medicines Regulations 2012, SI 2012/1916, reg 258(6)(a).

17 Ie with the Human Medicines Regulations 2012, SI 2012/1916, reg 258 and Sch 25.

18 Human Medicines Regulations 2012, SI 2012/1916, reg 258(6)(b).

19 Human Medicines Regulations 2012, SI 2012/1916, reg 258(6)(c). As to the meaning of 'export' see PARA 55 note 5.

20 Human Medicines Regulations 2012, SI 2012/1916, reg 258(6)(d). The specified requirements mentioned in the text are reg 258 and Sch 25.
21 Ie the information specified in accordance with the requirements of the Human Medicines Regulations 2012, SI 2012/1916, Sch 25 Pts 3, 4.
22 Human Medicines Regulations 2012, SI 2012/1916, reg 258(6)(e).
23 Ie the Human Medicines Regulations 2012, SI 2012/1916, reg 258 and Sch 25.
24 Human Medicines Regulations 2012, SI 2012/1916, reg 286(7)(a).
25 Human Medicines Regulations 2012, SI 2012/1916, reg 286(7)(b).
26 Human Medicines Regulations 2012, SI 2012/1916, reg 286(7)(c).

320. Information for blind and partially sighted people. The name of a medicinal product[1] must also be expressed in Braille format on the outer packaging of the product (or, if there is no outer packaging, on the immediate packaging of the product)[2].

The holder of a marketing authorisation, Article 126a authorisation or traditional herbal registration for a medicinal product[3] must ensure that the package leaflet[4] is made available on request in formats suitable for blind and partially-sighted persons[5].

1 As to the meaning of 'medicinal product' see PARA 25.
2 Human Medicines Regulations 2012, SI 2012/1916, reg 259(1). Nothing in reg 259 applies to a registrable homoeopathic medicinal product: reg 259(3). As to the meaning of 'registrable homoeopathic medicinal product' see PARA 187.
3 As to the meanings of 'marketing authorisation', 'Article 126a authorisation' and 'traditional herbal registration' see PARA 141 notes 3, 5, 6.
4 As to the meaning of 'package leaflet' see PARA 68 note 5.
5 Human Medicines Regulations 2012, SI 2012/1916, reg 259(2).

321. Package leaflet. A package leaflet[1] for a medicinal product[2] must be drawn up in accordance with the summary of the product characteristics and contain specified information[3].

A package leaflet must be included in the packaging of a medicinal product unless all the required information[4] is conveyed on the outer packaging or the immediate packaging of the product[5].

A package leaflet relating to a medicinal product must be legible, clear and easy to use, and the applicant for, or holder of, a marketing authorisation, Article 126a authorisation or traditional herbal registration[6] relating to the product must ensure that target patient groups are consulted in order to achieve this[7].

1 As to the meaning of 'package leaflet' see PARA 68 note 5.
2 As to the meaning of 'medicinal product' see PARA 25.
3 Human Medicines Regulations 2012, SI 2012/1916, reg 260(1). The specified information mentioned in the text refers to information specified in Sch 27 in the order specified in that provision. Nothing in reg 260 or Sch 27 applies to a registrable homoeopathic medicinal product: reg 260(6). As to the meaning of 'registrable homoeopathic medicinal product' see PARA 187. As to the meaning of 'the summary of the product characteristics' see PARA 55 note 11.
4 Ie the information required by the Human Medicines Regulations 2012, SI 2012/1916, Sch 27 Pt 1 (and, where the product contains paracetamol, the information required by Sch 27 Pt 2).
5 Human Medicines Regulations 2012, SI 2012/1916, reg 260(2). Where a package leaflet is not provided under reg 260(2) because all the information required by Sch 27 is conveyed on the outer packaging or the immediate packaging of the product, any requirement of these provisions that is expressed by reference to a package leaflet is taken to refer to the outer packaging or, as the case may be, the immediate packaging of the product: see reg 260(4), (5). As to the meaning of 'immediate packaging' and 'outer packaging' see PARA 278 note 5.
6 As to the meanings of 'marketing authorisation', 'Article 126a authorisation' and 'traditional herbal registration' see PARA 141 notes 3, 5, 6.
7 Human Medicines Regulations 2012, SI 2012/1916, reg 260(3).

322. Use of pictures and symbols. The outer packaging and the package leaflet of a medicinal product[1] may include symbols, diagrams or pictures designed to clarify certain information[2] and other information, compatible with the summary of the product characteristics[3], which is useful to the patient[4].

Symbols, diagrams, pictures or additional information included in accordance with this regulation must not include any element of a promotional nature[5].

1   As to the meaning of 'outer packaging' see PARA 278 note 5; as to the meaning of 'package leaflet' see PARA 68 note 5; and as to the meaning of 'medicinal product' see PARA 25.
2   Ie the information mentioned in the Human Medicines Regulations 2012, SI 2012/1916, Sch 24 Pt 1 or Sch 27.
3   As to the meaning of 'the summary of the product characteristics' see PARA 55 note 11.
4   Human Medicines Regulations 2012, SI 2012/1916, reg 261(1). Nothing in reg 261 applies to a registrable homoeopathic product: reg 261(3). As to the meaning of 'registrable homoeopathic medicinal product' see PARA 187.
5   Human Medicines Regulations 2012, SI 2012/1916, reg 261(2).

323. Labelling requirements for radionuclides. Where a medicinal product contains radionuclides[1]:

(1)   the carton and the container of the product must be labelled in accordance with the regulations for the safe transport of radioactive materials laid down by the International Atomic Energy Agency[2]; and

(2)   the labelling on the shielding and the vial must comply with the specified provisions[3].

1   As to the meaning of 'medicinal product' see PARA 25 and as to the meaning of 'radionuclide' see PARA 25 note 8.
2   Human Medicines Regulations 2012, SI 2012/1916, reg 262(1)(a).
3   Human Medicines Regulations 2012, SI 2012/1916, reg 262(1)(b). The label on the shielding must include the information specified in Sch 24 Pt 1, explain in full the codings used on the vial, indicate, where necessary, for a given time and date, the amount of radioactivity per dose or per vial and indicate the number of capsules or, for liquids, the number of millilitres per container: reg 262(2). The label on the vial must include the name or code of the medicinal product, including the name or chemical symbol of the radionuclide, the batch identification and expiry date of the product, the international symbol for radioactivity, the name and address of the manufacturer and the amount of radioactivity; as mentioned in reg 262(2): reg 262(3).

324. Leaflets relating to radionuclides. The licensing authority[1] must ensure that a detailed instruction leaflet[2] is enclosed with radiopharmaceuticals, radionuclide generators, radionuclide kits or radionuclide precursors[3].

1   As to the meaning of 'licensing authority' see PARA 35 note 1.
2   The leaflet must include the information specified in the Human Medicines Regulations 2012, SI 2012/1916, Sch 27: reg 262(2). It must also include any precautions to be taken by the user and the patient during the preparation and administration of the medicinal product and any special precautions for the disposal of the packaging and its unused contents: reg 262(3).
3   Human Medicines Regulations 2012, SI 2012/1916, reg 263(1). As to the meanings of 'radiopharmaceuticals', 'radionuclide generators', 'radionuclide kits' and 'radionuclide precursors' see PARA 148 notes 2, 5–7.

325. Homoeopathic medicines. The outer packaging and immediate packaging[1] and, where a package leaflet[2] is included, the package leaflet of a homoeopathic medicinal product[3] must clearly include the words 'homoeopathic medicinal product'[4] and must also include specified information[5].

1   As to the meanings of 'immediate packaging' and 'outer packaging' see PARA 278 note 5.
2   As to the meaning of 'package leaflet' see PARA 68 note 5. Where a package leaflet is not included with a registrable homoeopathic medicinal product, unless the context requires otherwise, any requirement of the Human Medicines Regulations 2012, SI 2012/1916, reg 264

that is expressed by reference to a package leaflet is taken to refer to the outer packaging or the immediate packaging of the product or, in a case to which reg 264(5) or reg 264(6) applies, the outer packaging of the product: reg 264(4).
3 As to the meaning of 'registrable homoeopathic medicinal product' see PARA 187.
4 Human Medicines Regulations 2012, SI 2012/1916, reg 264(1).
5 Human Medicines Regulations 2012, SI 2012/1916, reg 264(2). The specified information referred to in the text is information specified in reg 26(1) and Sch 28 Pt 1 and other information unless reg 264(5) or (6) applies: see reg 264(2). Where the immediate packaging of a registrable homoeopathic medicinal product is in the form of a blister pack and is placed in outer packaging which complies with the requirements of reg 264 and Sch 28 Pt 1, the immediate packaging must include the information specified in reg 264 and Sch 28 Pt 2: reg 264(5). Where the immediate packaging of a registrable homoeopathic medicinal product is too small to display the information required by Sch 28 Pt 1, the immediate packaging must include the information specified in reg 264 and Sch 28 Pt 3: reg 264(6).

326. Additional requirements for traditional herbal medicinal products. Additional information is required in relation to traditional herbal medicinal products[1] but this does not require information to appear on:
(1) a package[2] containing a traditional herbal medicinal product where part of the package is transparent or open, provided that the required additional information[3] is clearly visible through the transparent or open part of the package[4];
(2) a paper bag or similar wrapping in which a package that contains a traditional herbal medicinal product and bears the required additional information[5] is placed at the time of sale or supply[6];
(3) a package enclosing a package of a traditional herbal medicinal product for export[7];
(4) an ampoule or other container of not more than 10 millilitres' nominal capacity which is enclosed in a package on which the required additional information[8] appears[9]; or
(5) a blister pack or similar packaging, enclosed in a package labelled in accordance with the requirements of provisions[10] relating to the additional information[11].

1 Human Medicines Regulations 2012, SI 2012/1916, reg 265(1). As to the meaning of 'traditional herbal medicinal product' see PARA 155 note 6. As to the information required see Sch 29.
2 As to the meaning of 'package' see PARA 51 note 48.
3 Ie the information required by the Human Medicines Regulations 2012, SI 2012/1916, reg 265 and Sch 29.
4 Human Medicines Regulations 2012, SI 2012/1916, reg 265(2)(a).
5 See note 3.
6 See the Human Medicines Regulations 2012, SI 2012/1916, reg 265(2)(b).
7 Human Medicines Regulations 2012, SI 2012/1916, reg 265(2)(c). As to the meaning of 'export' see PARA 55 note 5.
8 See note 3.
9 Human Medicines Regulations 2012, SI 2012/1916, reg 265(2)(d).
10 See note 3.
11 Human Medicines Regulations 2012, SI 2012/1916, reg 265(2)(e).

327. Language requirements. Information given in accordance with provisions relating to packaging and leaflets[1] must be given in English[2] unless either or both of the following applies[3]:
(1) in the case of a medicinal product[4] that has been designated as an orphan medicinal product[5], such information[6] is given in a language of an EEA state other than English and the licensing authority[7] accedes to a reasoned request that the information need not be given in English[8];

(2)   in the case of a product for which the licensing authority grants an
        Article 126a authorisation[9] where the licensing authority decides that
        the information need not be given in English[10].

When a medicinal product is not intended to be delivered directly to the patient
or where there are severe problems in respect of the availability of the medicinal
product[11], the licensing authority may grant[12] either or both of:

(a)   an exemption from the obligation that certain particulars should appear
        on the outer and immediate packaging[13] and in the package leaflet[14] of
        the medicinal product[15]; and

(b)   a full or partial exemption from the obligation that the information
        included on the outer and immediate packaging and in the package
        leaflet for the product must be given in English in accordance with the
        above provision[16].

1   Ie in accordance with the Human Medicines Regulations 2012, SI 2012/1916, Pt 13
    (regs 257–276).
2   Information given in English in accordance with the Human Medicines Regulations 2012,
    SI 2012/1916, reg 266 may be given in several languages in addition to English, provided that
    the same particulars appear in all the languages used: reg 266(7).
3   Human Medicines Regulations 2012, SI 2012/1916, reg 266(1).
4   As to the meaning of 'medicinal product' see PARA 25.
5   Ie designated under European Parliament and of the Council Regulation (EC) 141/2000
    (OJ L18, 22.1.2000, p 1–15) on orphan medicinal products.
6   Ie the information specified in the Human Medicines Regulations 2012, SI 2012/1916, Pt 13
    (regs 257–276).
7   As to the meaning of 'licensing authority' see PARA 35 note 1.
8   Human Medicines Regulations 2012, SI 2012/1916, reg 266(2).
9   As to the meaning of 'Article 126a authorisation' see PARA 141 note 6.
10 Human Medicines Regulations 2012, SI 2012/1916, reg 266(3).
11 See the Human Medicines Regulations 2012, SI 2012/1916, reg 266(5).
12 The licensing authority may make the grant of an exemption in accordance with the Human
    Medicines Regulations 2012, SI 2012/1916, reg 266(4) subject to measures that it considers
    necessary to safeguard human health: reg 266(6).
13 As to the meanings of 'immediate packaging' and 'outer packaging' see PARA 278 note 5.
14 As to the meaning of 'package leaflet' see PARA 68 note 5.
15 Ie in accordance with the Human Medicines Regulations 2012, SI 2012/1916, Pt 13
    (regs 257–276).
16 See the Human Medicines Regulations 2012, SI 2012/1916, reg 266(4).

328.   Submission of mock-ups of packaging and leaflets to licensing authority.
At the time when a person applies for a marketing authorisation, Article 126a
authorisation, certificate of registration or traditional herbal registration for a
medicinal product[1], the person must submit to the licensing authority[2] one or
more mock-ups of the outer packaging and immediate packaging[3] proposed for
the product and a draft package leaflet[4].

    If the application is for a marketing authorisation, Article 126a authorisation
or traditional herbal registration, the person must also provide to the licensing
authority the results of assessments of the packaging and package leaflet[5] carried
out in co-operation with target patient groups[6].

    The licensing authority must refuse the application for a marketing
authorisation, Article 126a authorisation, certificate of registration or traditional
herbal registration if the packaging or the package leaflet does not comply with
the packaging and leaflet requirements[7] or, in relation to an application for a
marketing authorisation, Article 126a authorisation or traditional herbal
registration, the information on the packaging or the package leaflet does not
accord with the particulars listed in the summary of the product characteristics[8].

If the holder of a marketing authorisation, Article 126a authorisation, certificate of registration or traditional herbal registration for a product wishes to make changes to the packaging or the package leaflet (other than a change connected with the summary of the product characteristics), the proposed change must submit to the licensing authority such of the following as are affected by the proposed change[9]:

(1)   one or more mock-ups of the outer packaging and immediate packaging of the product showing the proposed change[10]; and

(2)   a draft package leaflet showing the proposed change[11].

If the licensing authority has not refused a proposed change within the period of 90 days beginning with the date of the submission, the applicant may make the change[12].

1   As to the meanings of 'marketing authorisation', 'Article 126a authorisation', 'certificate of registration' and 'traditional herbal registration' see PARA 141 notes 3–6. As to the meaning of 'medicinal product' see PARA 25.
2   As to the meaning of 'licensing authority' see PARA 35 note 1.
3   As to the meanings of 'immediate packaging' and 'outer packaging' see PARA 278 note 5.
4   Human Medicines Regulations 2012, SI 2012/1916, reg 267(1).
5   As to the meaning of 'package leaflet' see PARA 68 note 5.
6   Human Medicines Regulations 2012, SI 2012/1916, reg 267(2).
7   Ie the requirements of the Human Medicines Regulations 2012, SI 2012/1916, Pt 13 (regs 257–276).
8   Human Medicines Regulations 2012, SI 2012/1916, reg 267(3). As to the meaning of 'the summary of the product characteristics' see PARA 55 note 11.
9   See the Human Medicines Regulations 2012, SI 2012/1916, reg 267(4).
10 Human Medicines Regulations 2012, SI 2012/1916, reg 267(4)(a).
11 Human Medicines Regulations 2012, SI 2012/1916, reg 267(4)(b).
12 Human Medicines Regulations 2012, SI 2012/1916, reg 267(6).

329.   Offence relating to packaging and package leaflets. The holder of a marketing authorisation, Article 126a authorisation, certificate of registration or traditional herbal registration[1] for a medicinal product[2] who sells or supplies, offers to sell or supply, or possesses for the purpose of sale or supply, a medicinal product to which the authorisation, certificate or registration relates[3], is guilty of an offence[4] if a package or package leaflet[5] relating to the product does not comply with the applicable requirements[6] or the product is not accompanied by a package leaflet[7] when one is required[8].

A person, other than the holder of a marketing authorisation, Article 126a authorisation, certificate of registration or traditional herbal registration for a medicinal product, who, in the course of a business sells or supplies, or offers to sell or supply the product, or possesses the product for the purpose of sale or supply is guilty of an offence[9], if he sells or supplies, or offers to sell or supply, the product, or possesses the product for the purpose of sale or supply, knowing or having reasonable cause to believe that a package or package leaflet relating to the medicinal product does not comply with the applicable requirements[10] or that the product is not accompanied by a package leaflet[11] when one is required[12].

1   As to the meanings of 'marketing authorisation', 'Article 126a authorisation', 'certificate of registration' and 'traditional herbal registration' see PARA 141 notes 3–6.
2   As to the meaning of 'medicinal product' see PARA 25.
3   Human Medicines Regulations 2012, SI 2012/1916, reg 268(1).
4   Such a person is liable, on summary conviction, to a fine not exceeding the statutory maximum or, on conviction on indictment, to a fine, to imprisonment for a term not exceeding two years, or to both: Human Medicines Regulations 2012, SI 2012/1916, reg 271. As to the statutory maximum see SENTENCING AND DISPOSITION OF OFFENDERS vol 92 (2010) PARA 140.

5   As to the meaning of 'package' see PARA 51 note 48. As to the meaning of 'package leaflet' see PARA 68 note 5.
6   Ie the applicable requirements of the Human Medicines Regulations 2012, SI 2012/1916, Pt 13 (regs 257–276) or European Parliament and of the Council Regulation (EC) 1901/2006 (OJ L378, 27.12.2006) on medicinal products for paediatric use, art 28 or 32.
7   Ie a package leaflet as required by virtue of the Human Medicines Regulations 2012, SI 2012/1916, Pt 13 (regs 257–276).
8   See the Human Medicines Regulations 2012, SI 2012/1916, reg 268(2).
9   See the Human Medicines Regulations 2012, SI 2012/1916, reg 269(1). Such a person is liable, on summary conviction, to a fine not exceeding the statutory maximum or, on conviction on indictment, to a fine, to imprisonment for a term not exceeding two years, or to both: reg 271.
10   See note 6.
11   See note 7.
12   See the Human Medicines Regulations 2012, SI 2012/1916, reg 269(2).

330.   Non-compliance with regulations.   If the holder of a marketing authorisation, Article 126a authorisation, certificate of registration or traditional herbal registration[1] fails to comply with a packaging and packet leaflet requirement[2] in relation to a medicinal product[3], the licensing authority[4] may give a notice to the holder requiring compliance within three months or such other period (which may be less than three months) as may be specified in the notice[5].

If the holder fails to comply with the notice, the licensing authority may suspend the marketing authorisation, Article 126a authorisation, certificate of registration or traditional herbal registration until the holder complies with the requirements[6].

A person who fails to comply with such a notice is guilty of an offence[7].

1   As to the meanings of 'marketing authorisation', 'Article 126a authorisation', 'certificate of registration' and 'traditional herbal registration' see PARA 141 notes 3–6.
2   Ie a requirement imposed by the Human Medicines Regulations 2012, SI 2012/1916, Pt 13 (regs 257–276).
3   As to the meaning of 'medicinal product' see PARA 25.
4   As to the meaning of 'licensing authority' see PARA 35 note 1.
5   Human Medicines Regulations 2012, SI 2012/1916, reg 270(1).
6   See the Human Medicines Regulations 2012, SI 2012/1916, reg 270(2).
7   See the Human Medicines Regulations 2012, SI 2012/1916, reg 270(3). A person who is guilty of such an offence is liable, on summary conviction to a fine not exceeding the statutory maximum or, on conviction on indictment, to a fine, to imprisonment for a term not exceeding two years, or to both: reg 271. As to the statutory maximum see SENTENCING AND DISPOSITION OF OFFENDERS vol 92 (2010) PARA 140.

(iii)   Colours, Marking etc of Medicinal Products

331.   Distinctive colours, shapes and markings.   Regulations[1] made by the ministers[2] may impose such requirements as they consider necessary or expedient for any of the purposes specified in the provisions concerned with containers[3] with respect to the colour of the products, the shape of the products and distinctive marks to be displayed on the products[4]. Such regulations may provide that medicinal products of any such description[5], or falling within any such class, as may be specified must not, except in such circumstances (if any) as may be specified, be of any such colour or shape, or display any such mark, as may be specified[6].

No person, in the course of a business[7] carried on by him, may sell or supply, or have in his possession for the purpose of sale or supply, any medicinal product which contravenes[8] any requirements imposed by such regulations[9]. The regulations may provide that any person who contravenes the regulations is guilty of an offence[10].

1 Before making any such regulations the appropriate organisations must be consulted: see the Medicines Act 1968 s 129(6); and PARA 27. As to the information to be made available to ministers before they make regulations see *R (on the application of National Association of Health Stores) v Secretary of State for Health* [2005] EWCA Civ 154, (2005) Times, 9 March.
2 As to the meaning of 'the ministers' see reg 6(6)–(8); and PARA 35 (definition applied by Medicines Act 1968 s 132(1) (substituted by SI 2012/1916)).
3 Ie the purposes specified in the Medicines Act 1968 s 88(3).
4 Medicines Act 1968 s 88(1) (amended by SI 2006/2407, SI 2012/1916). As to the regulations that have been made see the Human Medicines Regulations 2012, SI 2012/1916.
5 As to the meaning of 'medicinal product' see the Human Medicines Regulations 2012, SI 2012/1916, reg 2(1); and PARA 25 (definition applied by the Medicines Act 1968 s 132(1) (substituted by SI 2012/1916)).
6 Medicines Act 1968 s 88(2).
7 As to the meaning of 'business' see PARA 52 note 10.
8 As to the meaning of 'contravene' see PARA 41 note 8 (definition applied by the Medicines Act 1968 s 132(1) (substituted by SI 2012/1916)).
9 Medicines Act 1968 s 88(3). In relation to this offence, certain presumptions apply in respect of a person having a medicinal product in his possession for the purpose of sale or supply: see s 126(2), (3); and PARA 184.
10 See the Medicines Act 1968 s 91(2) (amended by SI 2012/1916). Such a person is liable on summary conviction to a fine not exceeding the prescribed sum or such lesser sum as may be specified in the regulations (Medicines Act 1968 s 91(2)(a) (amended by virtue of the Magistrates' Courts Act 1980 s 32(2))) or, if the regulations so provide, on conviction on indictment to a fine or to imprisonment for a term not exceeding two years or to both (Medicines Act 1968 s 91(2)(b)). As to the prescribed sum see SENTENCING AND DISPOSITION OF OFFENDERS vol 92 (2010) PARA 141.

332. Colouring of aspirin and paracetamol for children. The sale or supply of a medicinal product[1] containing aspirin or paracetamol of any colour other than white is prohibited if it is a product for children aged twelve or under and, in the case of paracetamol, it is in a solid form (including tablets, capsules, pills, lozenges, pastilles or suppositories)[2].

A person is guilty of an offence if, in the course of a business, the person sells or supplies, or possesses for the purposes of sale or supply a medicinal product containing aspirin or paracetamol the sale or supply of which is prohibited under the above provisions[3].

1 As to the meaning of 'medicinal product' see PARA 25.
2 Human Medicines Regulations 2012, SI 2012/1916, reg 275.
3 Human Medicines Regulations 2012, SI 2012/1916, reg 276(1). A person guilty of such an offence is liable, on summary conviction, to a fine not exceeding the statutory maximum or, on conviction on indictment to a fine, to imprisonment for a term not exceeding 2 years, or to both: reg 276(2). As to the statutory maximum see SENTENCING AND DISPOSITION OF OFFENDERS vol 92 (2010) PARA 140.

(10) ADVERTISING

(i) In general

333. Meaning of 'advertisement'. In the Human Medicines Regulations 2012[1] 'advertisement', in relation to a medicinal product[2], includes anything designed to promote the prescription, supply, sale or use of that product[3]. This includes, in particular, the following activities[4]:

(1) door-to-door canvassing[5];

(2)   visits by medical sales representatives to persons qualified to prescribe or supply medicinal products[6];

(3)   the supply of samples[7];

(4)   the provision of inducements to prescribe or supply medicinal products by the gift, offer or promise of any benefit or bonus, whether in money or in kind, except where the intrinsic value of such inducements is minimal[8];

(5)   the sponsorship of promotional meetings attended by persons qualified to prescribe or supply medicinal products[9]; and

(6)   the sponsorship of scientific congresses attended by persons qualified to prescribe or supply medicinal products[10], including the payment of their travelling and accommodation expenses in that connection[11].

But references in the Human Medicines Regulations 2012[12] to an 'advertisement' do not include any of the following:

(a)   a medicinal product's package or package leaflet[13];

(b)   reference material and announcements of a factual and informative nature, including material relating to changes to a medicinal product's package or package leaflet, adverse reaction warnings, trade catalogues and price lists, provided that no product claim is made[14]; or

(c)   correspondence, which may be accompanied by material of a non-promotional nature, answering a specific question about a medicinal product[15].

1   Ie the Human Medicines Regulations 2012, SI 2012/1916.
2   As to the meaning of 'medicinal product' see PARA 25.
3   Human Medicines Regulations 2012, SI 2012/1916, reg 7(1).
4   Human Medicines Regulations 2012, SI 2012/1916, reg 7(2).
5   Human Medicines Regulations 2012, SI 2012/1916, reg 7(2)(a).
6   Human Medicines Regulations 2012, SI 2012/1916, reg 7(2)(b).
7   Human Medicines Regulations 2012, SI 2012/1916, reg 7(2)(c).
8   Human Medicines Regulations 2012, SI 2012/1916, reg 7(2)(d).
9   Human Medicines Regulations 2012, SI 2012/1916, reg 7(2)(e).
10 A 'person qualified to prescribe or supply medicinal products' includes persons who, in the course of their profession or in the course of a business, may lawfully prescribe medicinal products, sell medicinal products by retail or supply medicinal products in circumstances corresponding to retail sale and employees of such persons: Human Medicines Regulations 2012, SI 2012/1916, reg 277(1); and PARA 334 (applied by reg 7(3)(d)). As to the meaning of 'business' see PARA 52 note 10.
11 Human Medicines Regulations 2012, SI 2012/1916, reg 7(2)(f).
12 See note 1.
13 Human Medicines Regulations 2012, SI 2012/1916, reg 7(3)(a). As to the meaning of 'package' see PARA 51 note 48. As to the meaning of 'package leaflet' see PARA 68 note 5.
14 Human Medicines Regulations 2012, SI 2012/1916, reg 7(3)(b).
15 Human Medicines Regulations 2012, SI 2012/1916, reg 7(3)(c).

334.   General principles.   A person may not publish an advertisement[1] for a medicinal product[2] unless a marketing authorisation, a certificate of registration, a traditional herbal registration or an Article 126a authorisation[3], is in force for the product[4].

A person may not publish[5] an advertisement for a medicinal product with a marketing authorisation, traditional herbal registration or Article 126a authorisation unless the advertisement complies with the particulars listed in the summary of the product characteristics[6].

A person may not publish an advertisement for a medicinal product unless the advertisement encourages the rational use of the product by presenting it objectively and without exaggerating its properties[7].

A person may not publish an advertisement for a medicinal product that is misleading[8].

Breach[9] of the above provisions[10] is an offence[11].

1   As to the meaning of 'advertisement' see PARA 333.
2   As to the meaning of 'medicinal product' see PARA 25.
3   As to the meanings of 'marketing authorisation', 'Article 126a authorisation', 'certificate of registration' and 'traditional herbal registration' see PARA 141 notes 3–6.
4   See the Human Medicines Regulations 2012, SI 2012/1916, reg 279.
5   'Publication', in relation to an advertisement, means the dissemination or issue of that advertisement orally, in writing, by means of an electronic communications network within the meaning of the Communications Act 2003 (see TELECOMMUNICATIONS vol 97 (2010) PARA 60) or in any other way, and includes causing or procuring such publication by or on behalf of another person, and 'publish' has a corresponding meaning: Human Medicines Regulations 2012, SI 2012/1916, reg 277(1).
6   Human Medicines Regulations 2012, SI 2012/1916, reg 280(1). As to the meaning of 'the summary of the product characteristics' see PARA 55 note 11.
7   Human Medicines Regulations 2012, SI 2012/1916, reg 280(2).
8   Human Medicines Regulations 2012, SI 2012/1916, reg 280(3).
9   A person is guilty of an offence if that person commits a breach of a provision in the Human Medicines Regulations 2012, SI 2012/1916, Pt 14, Chapter 2 (regs 279–303): reg 303(1). A breach of a provision in the Human Medicines Regulations 2012, SI 2012/1916, Pt 14, Chapter 2 includes any contravention by any person of any prohibition in that Chapter and failure by any person to comply with any requirement or obligation in that Chapter: reg 303(2).
10 Ie the Human Medicines Regulations 2012, SI 2012/1916, regs 279, 280.
11 Human Medicines Regulations 2012, SI 2012/1916, reg 303(1). A person guilty of such an offence is liable, on summary conviction, to a fine not exceeding the statutory maximum or, on conviction on indictment to a fine, to imprisonment for a term not exceeding two years or to both: reg 303(3). As to the statutory maximum see SENTENCING AND DISPOSITION OF OFFENDERS vol 92 (2010) PARA 140.

335.   Duties of authorisation holders and registration holders.   The following applies to a person who holds a marketing authorisation for a medicinal product, a certificate of registration for a medicinal product, a traditional herbal registration for a medicinal product or an Article 126a authorisation for a medicinal product[1].

The person must establish a scientific service to compile and collate all information relating to the product (whether received from medical sales representatives employed by that person or from any other source)[2].

The person must ensure that any medical sales representative who promotes the product is given sufficient training, and has sufficient scientific knowledge, to enable the representative to provide information about the product that is as precise and complete as possible[3].

The person must retain a sample of any advertisement[4] for which the person is responsible relating to the product[5] and a statement indicating the persons to whom the advertisement is addressed, the method of its publication and the date when it was first published[6].

The person must, if required to do so by notice given to the person by the ministers[7], within the period specified in that notice provide a copy of the sample and statement mentioned above to the ministers, supply such other information as the ministers may request for the purposes of their functions[8] or provide such assistance as the ministers may request for those purposes[9].

Breach[10] of the above provision[11] is an offence[12].

1   Human Medicines Regulations 2012, SI 2012/1916, reg 281(1). As to the meanings of 'marketing authorisation', 'Article 126a authorisation', 'certificate of registration' and 'traditional herbal registration' see PARA 141 notes 3–6. As to the meaning of 'medicinal product' see PARA 25.

2   Human Medicines Regulations 2012, SI 2012/1916, reg 281(2).
3   Human Medicines Regulations 2012, SI 2012/1916, reg 281(3).
4   As to the meaning of 'advertisement' see PARA 333.
5   Human Medicines Regulations 2012, SI 2012/1916, reg 281(4)(a).
6   Human Medicines Regulations 2012, SI 2012/1916, reg 281(4)(b).
7   As to the meaning of 'the ministers' see the Human Medicines Regulations 2012, SI 2012/1916, reg 6(6)–(8); and PARA 35: reg 8(1).
8   Ie their functions under the Human Medicines Regulations 2012, SI 2012/1916, Pt 14 (regs 277–316).
9   Human Medicines Regulations 2012, SI 2012/1916, reg 281(5).
10 As to what constitutes 'breach' see PARA 334 note 9.
11 Ie breach of the Human Medicines Regulations 2012, SI 2012/1916, reg 281.
12 Human Medicines Regulations 2012, SI 2012/1916: reg 303(1). A person guilty of such an offence is liable, on summary conviction, to a fine not exceeding the statutory maximum or, on conviction on indictment to a fine, to imprisonment for a term not exceeding two years or to both: reg 303(3). As to the statutory maximum see SENTENCING AND DISPOSITION OF OFFENDERS vol 92 (2010) PARA 140.

(ii) Advertising to the Public

336. Advertising to the public. The following apply to advertisements[1] wholly or mainly directed at members of the public[2].

A person[3] may not publish an advertisement that is likely to lead to the use of a medicinal product[4] for the purpose of inducing an abortion[5]. Nor may a person publish an advertisement that is likely to lead to the use of a prescription only medicine[6].

A person may not publish an advertisement relating to a medicinal product that contains certain controlled narcotic substances[7] or certain[8] controlled psychotropic substances[9].

A person may not publish an advertisement relating to a medicinal product that states, or implies, that a medical consultation or surgical operation is unnecessary[10] or that offers to provide a diagnosis or suggest a treatment by post or by means of an electronic communications network[11]. Nor may a person publish an advertisement relating to a medicinal product that might, by a description or detailed representation of a case history, lead to erroneous self-diagnosis[12].

A person may not publish an advertisement relating to a medicinal product that suggests that the effects of taking the medicinal product are guaranteed, are better than or equivalent to those of another identifiable treatment or medicinal product or are not accompanied by any adverse reaction[13].

A person may not publish an advertisement relating to a medicinal product that uses in terms that are misleading or likely to cause alarm pictorial representations of changes in the human body caused by disease or injury or the action of the medicinal product on the human body[14].

A person may not publish an advertisement relating to a medicinal product that refers in terms that are misleading or likely to cause alarm to claims of recovery[15]. A person may not publish an advertisement relating to a medicinal product that suggests that the health of a person who is not suffering from any disease or injury could be enhanced by taking the medicinal product[16] or that the health of a person could be affected by not taking the medicinal product[17].

A person may not publish an advertisement relating to a medicinal product that suggests that it is a foodstuff, cosmetic or other consumer product that is not a medicinal product or that its safety or efficacy is due to the fact that it is natural[18].

A person may not publish an advertisement relating to a medicinal product that refers to a recommendation by scientists, health care professionals or persons who because of their celebrity could encourage use of the medicinal product[19].

A person may not publish an advertisement relating to a medicinal product that contains any material that is directed principally at children[20].

A person may not publish an advertisement relating to a medicinal product unless it is presented so that it is clear that it is an advertisement and that the product is clearly identified as a medicinal product[21]. Nor may a person publish an advertisement relating to a medicinal product unless it includes the name of the medicinal product, if the medicinal product contains only one active ingredient, the common name of the active ingredient, the information necessary for the correct use of the medicinal product and an express and clear invitation to read carefully the instructions on the package or in the package leaflet (as the case may be)[22].

Breach[23] of any of the above[24] is an offence[25].

1   As to the meaning of 'advertisement' see PARA 333.
2   Human Medicines Regulations 2012, SI 2012/1916, reg 282. Regulations 283–292 (exception for approved vaccination campaigns) apply to advertisements wholly or mainly directed at members of the public: reg 292.
3   As to the meaning of 'person' see PARA 45 note 2.
4   As to the meaning of 'medicinal product' see PARA 25.
5   Human Medicines Regulations 2012, SI 2012/1916, reg 283.
6   Human Medicines Regulations 2012, SI 2012/1916, reg 284(1). Regulations 284, 285 and 287(4)(b) do not apply to an advertisement as part of a vaccination campaign that relates to a medicinal product that is a vaccine or serum and has been approved by the ministers. regs 284(2), 285(2), 287(5), 292. As to the meaning of 'prescription only medicine' see PARA 26. As to the meaning of 'vaccine' see PARA 297 note 2.
7   Ie a substance listed in the Single Convention on Narcotic Drugs (New York, 30 March 1961 to 1 August 1961; TS 34 (1965); Cmnd 2631), Sch I, II or IV.
8   Ie a substance listed in the Convention on Psychotropic Substances (Vienna, 21 February 1971; TS 51 (1993); Cmnd 2307), Sch I, II, III or IV.
9   Human Medicines Regulations 2012, SI 2012/1916, reg 285(1). See note 6.
10   Human Medicines Regulations 2012, SI 2012/1916, reg 286(1).
11   Human Medicines Regulations 2012, SI 2012/1916, reg 286(2). As to the meaning of 'electronic communications network' see the Communications Act 2003; and TELECOMMUNICATIONS vol 97 (2010) PARA 60.
12   Human Medicines Regulations 2012, SI 2012/1916, reg 286(3).
13   Human Medicines Regulations 2012, SI 2012/1916, reg 287(1). As to the meaning of 'adverse reaction' see PARA 70 note 6.
14   Human Medicines Regulations 2012, SI 2012/1916, reg 287(2).
15   Human Medicines Regulations 2012, SI 2012/1916, reg 287(3). The term 'claims of recovery' does not include references to the reinforcement of a person's well-being where the therapeutic efficacy of the medicinal product in terms of the elimination of a particular illness is not referred to: see Case C-374/05 *Gintec International Import-Export GMBH v Verband Sozialer Wettbewerb EV* [2007] ECR I-9517, [2008] 1 CMLR 808, ECJ.
16   Human Medicines Regulations 2012, SI 2012/1916, reg 287(4)(a).
17   Human Medicines Regulations 2012, SI 2012/1916, reg 287(4)(b). See note 6.
18   Human Medicines Regulations 2012, SI 2012/1916, reg 288. 'Cosmetic' means any substance or preparation intended to be applied to the surfaces of the human body (including the epidermis, pilary system and hair, nails, lips and external genital organs), or the teeth or buccal mucosa, wholly or mainly for the purpose of perfuming them, cleansing them, protecting them, caring for them or keeping them in condition, modifying their appearance (for aesthetic purposes or otherwise) or combating body odours or normal body perspiration: reg 8(1).
19   Human Medicines Regulations 2012, SI 2012/1916, reg 289.
20   Human Medicines Regulations 2012, SI 2012/1916, reg 290.
21   Human Medicines Regulations 2012, SI 2012/1916, reg 291(1). Regulation 291 is subject to reg 296: reg 291(3). Regulations 291 does not apply to an advertisement relating to a medicinal

product if the advertisement is intended solely as a reminder of the product and consists solely of, in the case of a product other than a homoeopathic medicinal product to which a certificate of registration relates, its name, international non-proprietary name or trademark and, in the case of a homoeopathic medicinal product to which a certificate of registration relates, its name, international non-proprietary name, invented name or trademark or the scientific name of the stock or stocks from which it is derived: reg 296. As to the meaning of 'homoeopathic medicinal product' see PARA 187 note 1.

22 Human Medicines Regulations 2012, SI 2012/1916, reg 291(2). This is subject to reg 301 (see PARA 344): reg 291(4).

23 As to what constitutes 'breach' see PARA 334 note 5.

24 Ie breach of the Human Medicines Regulations 2012, SI 2012/1916, regs 282–291.

25 Human Medicines Regulations 2012, SI 2012/1916: reg 303(1). A person guilty of such an offence is liable, on summary conviction, to a fine not exceeding the statutory maximum or, on conviction on indictment to a fine, to imprisonment for a term not exceeding two years or to both: reg 303(3). As to the statutory maximum see SENTENCING AND DISPOSITION OF OFFENDERS vol 92 (2010) PARA 140.

(iii) Promotional Purposes

337. Prohibition of supply to the public for promotional purposes. The holder of a marketing authorisation, certificate of registration, traditional herbal registration or Article 126a authorisation[1] may not sell or supply a medicinal product[2] for a promotional purpose to a person who is not qualified to prescribe medicinal products[3].

A person who carries on a medicines business[4] may not sell or supply a medicinal product for a promotional purpose to a person[5] who is not qualified to prescribe medicinal products[6].

Breach[7] of the above provisions[8] is an offence[9].

1 As to the meanings of 'marketing authorisation', 'Article 126a authorisation', 'certificate of registration' and 'traditional herbal registration' see PARA 141 notes 3–6.

2 As to the meaning of 'medicinal product' see PARA 25.

3 Human Medicines Regulations 2012, SI 2012/1916, reg 293(1).

4 For this purpose 'medicines business' means a business that consists in whole or in part of manufacturing, selling or supplying medicinal products: Human Medicines Regulations 2012, SI 2012/1916, reg 293(3).

5 The Human Medicines Regulations 2012, SI 2012/1916 apply regardless of whether the promotional purpose is that of the seller or supplier or of a third party: reg 293(3).

6 Human Medicines Regulations 2012, SI 2012/1916, reg 293(2).

7 As to what constitutes 'breach' see PARA 334 note 5.

8 Ie breach of the Human Medicines Regulations 2012, SI 2012/1916, reg 293.

9 Human Medicines Regulations 2012, SI 2012/1916: reg 303(1). A person guilty of such an offence is liable, on summary conviction, to a fine not exceeding the statutory maximum or, on conviction on indictment to a fine, to imprisonment for a term not exceeding two years or to both: reg 303(3). As to the statutory maximum see SENTENCING AND DISPOSITION OF OFFENDERS vol 92 (2010) PARA 140.

(iv) Advertising to Persons Qualified to Prescribe or Supply

338. General provisions relating to advertising to persons qualified to prescribe etc. A person may not publish an advertisement[1] that relates to a medicinal product[2] and is wholly or mainly directed at persons qualified to prescribe or supply such products unless it contains specified particulars[3] and, in the case of a written advertisement, it contains certain particulars[4].

In the case of an advertisement that is not a written advertisement, those particulars may alternatively be made available in written form to all persons to whom the advertisement is made available[5].

Breach[6] of the above[7] is an offence[8].

1   As to the meaning of 'advertisement' see PARA 333.
2   As to the meaning of 'medicinal product' see PARA 25.
3   Ie the particulars set out in the Human Medicines Regulations 2012, SI 2012/1916, Sch 30 para 1–8.
4   See the Human Medicines Regulations 2012, SI 2012/1916, reg 294(1), (2). The particulars mentioned in the text are those in Sch 30 para 9. Regulation 294 does not apply to an advertisement to which reg 295 (see PARA 339) applies or to oral representations made by medical sales representatives to which reg 299 (see PARA 343) applies: reg 294(4)(a), (b). Nor does it apply to an advertisement relating to a medicinal product if the advertisement is intended solely as a reminder of the product and consists solely of, in the case of a product other than a homoeopathic medicinal product to which a certificate of registration relates, its name, international non-proprietary name or trademark and, in the case of a homoeopathic medicinal product to which a certificate of registration relates, its name, international non-proprietary name, invented name or trademark or the scientific name of the stock or stocks from which it is derived: reg 294(4)(c), 296. As to the meaning of 'homoeopathic medicinal product' see PARA 187 note 1.
5   Human Medicines Regulations 2012, SI 2012/1916, reg 294(3).
6   As to what constitutes 'breach' see PARA 334 note 5.
7   Ie breach of the Human Medicines Regulations 2012, SI 2012/1916, reg 294.
8   Human Medicines Regulations 2012, SI 2012/1916: reg 303(1). A person guilty of such an offence is liable, on summary conviction, to a fine not exceeding the statutory maximum or, on conviction on indictment to a fine, to imprisonment for a term not exceeding two years or to both: reg 303(3). As to the statutory maximum see SENTENCING AND DISPOSITION OF OFFENDERS vol 92 (2010) PARA 140.

339. Abbreviated advertisement. A person may not issue an abbreviated advertisement[1] that relates to a medicinal product[2] and is wholly or mainly directed at persons qualified to prescribe or supply such products, unless it contains specified particulars[3], the statement 'Information about this product, including adverse reactions[4], precautions, contra-indications, and method of use can be found at:' accompanied by a web site address[5] that corresponds to that statement and the name and address of the holder of the marketing authorisation, certificate of registration, traditional herbal registration or Article 126a authorisation[6] for the medicinal product, or the business name and address of the part of the holder's business that is responsible for its sale or supply[7].

Breach[8] of the above[9] is an offence[10].

1   As to the meaning of 'advertisement' see PARA 333. For these purposes, 'abbreviated advertisement' means an advertisement, other than a loose insert, that does not exceed 420 square centimetres in size; and appears in a publication sent or delivered wholly or mainly to persons qualified to prescribe or supply medicinal products: Human Medicines Regulations 2012, SI 2012/1916, reg 295(4).
2   As to the meaning of 'medicinal product' see PARA 25.
3   Ie the particulars set out in the Human Medicines Regulations 2012, SI 2012/1916, Sch 30 paras 2–6.
4   As to the meaning of 'adverse reaction' see PARA 132 note 3.
5   The web site at the address must make available the particulars set out in the Human Medicines Regulations 2012, SI 2012/1916, Sch 30; or a copy of the summary of the product characteristics: reg 295(3). As to the meaning of 'the summary of the product characteristics' see PARA 55 note 11.
6   As to the meanings of 'marketing authorisation', 'Article 126a authorisation', 'certificate of registration' and 'traditional herbal registration' see PARA 141 notes 3–6.
7   Human Medicines Regulations 2012, SI 2012/1916, reg 295(1), (2). Regulation 295 is subject to reg 301 (see PARA 344): reg 295(5).
8   As to what constitutes 'breach' see PARA 334 note 5.
9   Ie breach of the Human Medicines Regulations 2012, SI 2012/1916, reg 295.
10   Human Medicines Regulations 2012, SI 2012/1916: reg 303(1). A person guilty of such an offence is liable, on summary conviction, to a fine not exceeding the statutory maximum or, on

conviction on indictment to a fine, to imprisonment for a term not exceeding two years or to both: reg 303(3). As to the statutory maximum see SENTENCING AND DISPOSITION OF OFFENDERS vol 92 (2010) PARA 140.

340. Written material accompanying promotions. A person may not, as part of the promotion of a medicinal product[1], send or deliver any written material to a person qualified to prescribe or supply medicinal products unless the material contains specified particulars[2] and states the date on which it was drawn up or last revised[3].

A person may not include any information in written material to which this provision applies unless it is accurate, is up-to-date, can be verified and is sufficiently complete to enable the recipient to form an opinion of the therapeutic value of the product to which it relates[4].

A person may not include any illustrative material[5] in written material to which this provision applies unless the illustrative material is accurately reproduced and the written material indicates the precise source of the illustrative material[6].

Breach[7] of the above provisions[8] is an offence[9].

1   As to the meaning of 'medicinal product' see PARA 25.
2   Ie in accordance with the Human Medicines Regulations 2012, SI 2012/1916, Sch 30.
3   Human Medicines Regulations 2012, SI 2012/1916, reg 297(1).
4   Human Medicines Regulations 2012, SI 2012/1916, reg 297(2).
5   For this purpose 'illustrative material' means quotation, table or any other illustrative material taken from a medical journal or other scientific work: Human Medicines Regulations 2012, SI 2012/1916, reg 297(4),
6   Human Medicines Regulations 2012, SI 2012/1916, reg 297(3).
7   As to what constitutes 'breach' see PARA 334 note 5.
8   Ie breach of the Human Medicines Regulations 2012, SI 2012/1916, reg 297.
9   Human Medicines Regulations 2012, SI 2012/1916: reg 303(1). A person guilty of such an offence is liable, on summary conviction, to a fine not exceeding the statutory maximum or, on conviction on indictment to a fine, to imprisonment for a term not exceeding two years or to both: reg 303(3). As to the statutory maximum see SENTENCING AND DISPOSITION OF OFFENDERS vol 92 (2010) PARA 140.

341. Free samples. A person ('the supplier') may not supply a free sample of a medicinal product[1] to another person ('the recipient') unless the following conditions are met[2].

Condition A is that the recipient is qualified to prescribe medicinal products and receives the sample for the purpose of acquiring experience in dealing with the product in question[3].

Condition B is that the sample is supplied to the recipient on an exceptional basis and in response to a request from, and signed and dated by, the recipient[4].

Condition C is that, taking the year in which the sample is supplied as a whole, only a limited number of samples of the product in question are supplied to the recipient in that year[5].

Condition D is that the sample is no larger than the smallest presentation of the product that is available for sale in the United Kingdom, is marked 'free medical sample—not for resale' or bears a similar description and is accompanied by a copy of the summary of the product characteristics[6].

Condition E is that the sample does not contain a specified substance[7].

Condition F is that the supplier maintains an adequate system of control and accountability in relation to the supply of free samples[8].

Breach[9] of the above[10] is an offence[11].

1   As to the meaning of 'medicinal product' see PARA 25.

2 Human Medicines Regulations 2012, SI 2012/1916, reg 298(1).
3 Human Medicines Regulations 2012, SI 2012/1916, reg 298(2).
4 Human Medicines Regulations 2012, SI 2012/1916, reg 298(3).
5 Human Medicines Regulations 2012, SI 2012/1916, reg 298(4).
6 Human Medicines Regulations 2012, SI 2012/1916, reg 298(5). As to the meaning of 'the summary of the product characteristics' see PARA 55 note 11.
7 Human Medicines Regulations 2012, SI 2012/1916, reg 298(6). The specified substance mentioned in the text is a substance listed in the Narcotics Drugs Convention Schs I, II, IV (where the product is not a preparation listed in Sch III) or a substance which is listed in the Psychotropic Substances Convention Sch 1–IV (where the product is not a preparation which may be exempted from measures of control in accordance with art 3(2), (3)). As to the meanings of 'Narcotics Drugs Convention' and 'Psychotropic Substances Convention' see PARA 163 note 5.
8 Human Medicines Regulations 2012, SI 2012/1916, reg 298(7).
9 As to what constitutes 'breach' see PARA 334 note 5.
10 Ie breach of the Human Medicines Regulations 2012, SI 2012/1916, reg 298.
11 Human Medicines Regulations 2012, SI 2012/1916: reg 303(1). A person guilty of such an offence is liable on summary conviction to a fine not exceeding level 5 on the standard scale: reg 303(4)(a), (5). As to the standard scale see SENTENCING AND DISPOSITION OF OFFENDERS vol 92 (2010) PARA 142.

342. Medical sales representatives. The following applies in relation to the promotion by a medical sales representative of medicinal products[1] to persons qualified to prescribe or supply such products[2].

During each visit for promotional purposes the representative must give to, or have available for, each person visited a copy of the summary of the product characteristics for each product promoted[3].

The representative must report all information, with particular reference to any adverse reactions[4], that is received from persons visited for promotional purposes and relates to the use of a product promoted, to the scientific service[5] by the holder of the marketing authorisation, certificate of registration, traditional herbal registration or Article 126a authorisation for the product[6].

Breach[7] of the above[8] is an offence[9].

1 As to the meaning of 'medicinal product' see PARA 25.
2 Human Medicines Regulations 2012, SI 2012/1916, reg 299(1).
3 Human Medicines Regulations 2012, SI 2012/1916, reg 299(2). As to the meaning of 'the summary of the product characteristics' see PARA 55 note 11.
4 As to the meaning of 'adverse reaction' see PARA 70 note 6.
5 Ie the scientific service established in accordance with the Human Medicines Regulations 2012, SI 2012/1916, reg 281(2) (see PARA 335).
6 Human Medicines Regulations 2012, SI 2012/1916, reg 299(3). As to the meanings of 'marketing authorisation', 'Article 126a authorisation', 'certificate of registration' and 'traditional herbal registration' see PARA 141 notes 3–6.
7 As to what constitutes 'breach' see PARA 334 note 5.
8 Ie breach of the Human Medicines Regulations 2012, SI 2012/1916, reg 299(2), (3).
9 Human Medicines Regulations 2012, SI 2012/1916: reg 303(1). A person guilty of such an offence is liable on summary conviction to a fine not exceeding level 5 on the standard scale: reg 303(4)(b), (5). As to the standard scale see SENTENCING AND DISPOSITION OF OFFENDERS vol 92 (2010) PARA 142.

343. Inducements and hospitality. A person may not, in connection with the promotion of medicinal products[1] to persons qualified to prescribe or supply them, supply, offer, or promise any gift, pecuniary advantage or benefit[2] unless it is inexpensive and relevant to the practice of medicine or pharmacy[3].

A person may not provide hospitality[4] at a meeting or event held for the purposes of the promotion of a medicinal product unless the hospitality is strictly limited to the main purposes of the meeting or event and the person to whom it is provided or offered is a health care professional[5].

Nothing in these provisions prevents any person providing hospitality at an event held for purely professional or scientific purposes provided that the hospitality is strictly limited to the main scientific objective of the event and the person to whom it is provided or offered is a health care professional[6].

A person qualified to prescribe or supply medicinal products may not solicit or accept any gift, pecuniary advantage, benefit or hospitality that is prohibited by these provisions[7].

Breach[8] of the above[9] is an offence[10].

1   As to the meaning of 'medicinal product' see PARA 25.
2   National public health authorities of member states may lawfully offer financial incentives to doctors to prescribe certain medicines in preference to others: Case C-62/09 *R (on the application of Association of the British Pharmaceutical Industry) v Medicines and Healthcare Products Regulatory Agency (the NHS Confederation (Employers) Co Ltd intervening)* [2010] ECR I-3603, 115 BMLR 26, ECJ.
3   Human Medicines Regulations 2012, SI 2012/1916, reg 300(1). Regulation 300 does not apply in relation to measures or trade practices relating to prices, margins or discounts that were in existence on 1 January 1993: reg 300(6).
4   For these purposes, 'hospitality' includes sponsorship of a person's attendance at a meeting or event and the payment of travelling or accommodation expenses: Human Medicines Regulations 2012, SI 2012/1916, reg 300(5).
5   Human Medicines Regulations 2012, SI 2012/1916, reg 300(2). As to the meaning of 'health care professional' see PARA 36 note 8.
6   Human Medicines Regulations 2012, SI 2012/1916, reg 300(3).
7   Human Medicines Regulations 2012, SI 2012/1916, reg 300(4).
8   As to what constitutes 'breach' see PARA 334 note 5.
9   Ie breach of the Human Medicines Regulations 2012, SI 2012/1916, reg 300.
10 Human Medicines Regulations 2012, SI 2012/1916: reg 303(1). A person guilty of an offence under reg 300(1), (2) is liable, on summary conviction, to a fine not exceeding the statutory maximum or, on conviction on indictment to a fine, to imprisonment for a term not exceeding two years or to both: reg 303(3). A person guilty of an offence under reg 300(4) is liable on summary conviction to a fine not exceeding level 5 on the standard scale: reg 303(4)(c), (5). As to the statutory maximum see SENTENCING AND DISPOSITION OF OFFENDERS vol 92 (2010) PARA 140 and as to the standard scale see SENTENCING AND DISPOSITION OF OFFENDERS vol 92 (2010) PARA 142.

(v) Homoeopathic Medicinal Products and Herbal Medicinal Products

344.   Advertisements for registered homoeopathic medicinal products.   A person may not publish an advertisement[1] relating to a homoeopathic medicinal product[2] to which a certificate of registration[3] relates unless the advertisement meets the following conditions[4].

Condition A is that the advertisement does not mention any specific therapeutic indications[5].

Condition B is that the advertisement does not contain any details other than[6] the labelling requirements for registrable homoeopathic medicinal products[7].

Breach[8] of the above[9] is an offence[10].

1   As to the meaning of 'advertisement' see PARA 333.
2   As to the meaning of 'homoeopathic medicinal product' see PARA 36 note 8.
3   As to the meaning of 'certificate of registration' see PARA 141 note 4.
4   Human Medicines Regulations 2012, SI 2012/1916, reg 301(1). Nothing in reg 291(2) (form and content of advertisement: see PARA 336), 294 (general requirements: see PARA 338) or 295 (abbreviated advertisements: see PARA 339) requires an advertisement relating to a homoeopathic medicinal product to which a certificate of registration relates to contain any detail not specified in Sch 28: reg 301(4).
5   Human Medicines Regulations 2012, SI 2012/1916, reg 301(2).

6   Ie other than those mentioned in the Human Medicines Regulations 2012, SI 2012/1916, Sch 28.
7   Human Medicines Regulations 2012, SI 2012/1916, reg 301(3). As to the meaning of 'registrable homoeopathic medicinal products' see PARA 187 note 1.
8   As to what constitutes 'breach' see PARA 334 note 5.
9   Ie breach of the Human Medicines Regulations 2012, SI 2012/1916, reg 301.
10 Human Medicines Regulations 2012, SI 2012/1916: reg 303(1). A person guilty of such an offence is liable, on summary conviction, to a fine not exceeding the statutory maximum or, on conviction on indictment to a fine, to imprisonment for a term not exceeding two years or to both: reg 303(3). As to the statutory maximum see SENTENCING AND DISPOSITION OF OFFENDERS vol 92 (2010) PARA 140.

345.   Advertisements for traditional herbal medicinal products.   A person may not publish an advertisement[1] relating to a herbal medicinal product[2] to which a traditional herbal registration[3] relates unless it contains the words 'Traditional herbal medicinal product for use in' followed by a statement of one or more therapeutic indications for the product consistent with the terms of the registration followed by the words 'exclusively based on long standing use'[4].

Breach[5] of the above[6] is an offence[7].

1   As to the meaning of 'advertisement' see PARA 333.
2   As to the meaning of 'herbal medicinal product' see PARA 51 note 2.
3   As to the meaning of 'traditional herbal registration' see PARA 141 note 5.
4   Human Medicines Regulations 2012, SI 2012/1916, reg 302.
5   As to what constitutes 'breach' see PARA 334 note 5.
6   Ie breach of the Human Medicines Regulations 2012, SI 2012/1916, reg 302.
7   Human Medicines Regulations 2012, SI 2012/1916: reg 303(1). A person guilty of such an offence is liable, on summary conviction, to a fine not exceeding the statutory maximum or, on conviction on indictment to a fine, to imprisonment for a term not exceeding two years or to both: reg 303(3). As to the statutory maximum see SENTENCING AND DISPOSITION OF OFFENDERS vol 92 (2010) PARA 140.

(vi)   Scrutiny by Ministers

346.   Requirement to provide copy of advertisement.   The ministers[1] may give, to any person appearing to them to be concerned or likely to be concerned with the publication of advertisements[2] relating to medicinal products[3], a notice[4] that requires the person to whom it is given to provide the ministers within a specified[5] period with a copy of any advertisement that, as at the date of service of the notice, the person has published or proposes to publish and that relates to a specified medicinal product or medicinal products of a specified class or description[6].

The ministers may also give, to any person appearing to them to be concerned or likely to be concerned with the publication of advertisements relating to medicinal products, a notice[7] that requires the person to whom it is given to provide the ministers with a copy of any advertisement that the person proposes to publish during a specified period[8] and that relates to a specified medicinal product or medicinal products of a specified class or description[9].

1   As to the meaning of 'the ministers' see the Human Medicines Regulations 2012, SI 2012/1916, reg 6(6)–(8); and PARA 35: reg 8(1). In exercising the functions conferred on them by Chapter 3 (regs 304–316), the ministers must have regard, in particular, to the public interest: reg 315.
2   As to the meaning of 'advertisement' see PARA 333.
3   As to the meaning of 'medicinal product' see PARA 25.
4   A notice under the Human Medicines Regulations 2012, SI 2012/1916, reg 304(2) or (3) may require the person to whom it is given not to publish, or further publish, during a specified period any advertisement a copy of which the person is required by the notice to provide to the

ministers: reg 304(7). A notice under reg 304(2) or (3) must give the ministers' reasons for giving the notice and (if appropriate) for imposing a requirement under reg 304(7): reg 304(8).

5   For this purpose 'specified' means specified in the notice; Human Medicines Regulations 2012, SI 2012/1916, reg 304(9).

6   See the Human Medicines Regulations 2012, SI 2012/1916, reg 304(1), (2). A person is guilty of an offence if he fails to comply with a requirement imposed by a notice given to that person under reg 304(2) or (3): reg 308(1). A person guilty of such an offence is liable, on summary conviction, to a fine not exceeding the statutory maximum or, on conviction on indictment to a fine, to imprisonment for a term not exceeding two years or to both: reg 308(2). In exercising the functions conferred on them by regs 277–316, the ministers may institute civil proceedings in their own name: reg 316. As to the statutory maximum see SENTENCING AND DISPOSITION OF OFFENDERS vol 92 (2010) PARA 140.

7   A notice under the Human Medicines Regulations 2012, SI 2012/1916, reg 304(3) must specify the number of days before the proposed publication date of any advertisement by which a copy of the advertisement must be provided to the ministers: reg 304(5). A notice under reg 304(3) may be withdrawn by the Ministers before the expiry of the specified period: reg 304(6).

8   This period must not exceed 12 months: see the Human Medicines Regulations 2012, SI 2012/1916, reg 304(4).

9   Human Medicines Regulations 2012, SI 2012/1916, reg 304(8).

347.   Compatibility. If, having considered an advertisement[1], the ministers[2] are minded to make a determination[3] that the advertisement is incompatible with the prohibitions relating to advertising imposed by the Human Medicines Regulations 2012[4], they may give a notice in writing[5] to any person appearing to them to be concerned or likely to be concerned with the publication of the advertisement[6]. Such a notice may require the person to whom it is given not to publish, or to cease to publish, the advertisement[7].

If the ministers have given a notice under the above provisions ('the original notice') to a person, after the end of the specified period[8], the ministers must give a further notice in writing ('the new notice') to that person of their determination whether the advertisement is compatible with the prohibitions relating to advertising imposed[9] by the Human Medicines Regulations 2012[10]. If the ministers make such determination and the original notice imposed a requirement[11], the new notice must provide that the requirement no longer applies[12].

If the ministers make a determination that the advertisement is incompatible with the prohibitions[13] the new notice must give the ministers' reasons for the determination[14].

If the original notice imposed a requirement[15], the new notice may provide that the requirement is to continue to apply or that the requirement no longer applies[16].

If the original notice did not impose a requirement[17], the new notice may require the person to whom it is given not to publish, or to cease to publish, the advertisement[18].

If the new notice maintains the application of an imposed requirement[19] to cease to publish the advertisement that is the subject of the notice, or imposes a requirement to cease to publish that advertisement[20], the new notice may require the person to whom it is given to publish the ministers' reasons for making the determination that the advertisement was incompatible with the prohibitions relating to advertising[21], either in full or in part and publish a corrective statement concerning the advertisement[22].

1   As to the meaning of 'advertisement' see PARA 333. As to obtaining a copy of the advertisement see PARA 346.

2   As to the meaning of 'the ministers' see the Human Medicines Regulations 2012, SI 2012/1916, reg 6(6)–(8); and PARA 35: reg 8(1).

3 Ie a determination under the Human Medicines Regulations 2012, SI 2012/1916, reg 306 (see notes 8–18).
4 Human Medicines Regulations 2012, SI 2012/1916, reg 305(1). As to the prohibitions see Chapter 2 (regs 279–303).
5 Ie under the Human Medicines Regulations 2012, SI 2012/1916, reg 305. A notice under reg 305 must:
   (1) state that the ministers are minded to make a determination under reg 306 (see notes 8–18) that the advertisement is incompatible with the prohibitions imposed by Chapter 2 (reg 305(4)(a));
   (2) give the reasons why they are minded to make the determination (reg 305(4)(b));
   (3) state that the person to whom it is given may make written representations to the Ministers within the period of 21 days beginning immediately after the date of the notice as to why the advertisement is compatible with the prohibitions imposed by Chapter 2 (reg 305(4)(c)); and
   (4) refer to the action that may be taken by the Ministers under reg 306 (reg 305(4)(d)).
6 Human Medicines Regulations 2012, SI 2012/1916, reg 305(2). A person is guilty of an offence if that person fails to comply with a requirement imposed by a notice given to that person under reg 305(4) (including such a notice as maintained under reg 306(7)): reg 308(1). A person guilty of such an offence is liable, on summary conviction, to a fine not exceeding the statutory maximum or on conviction on indictment to a fine, to imprisonment for a term not exceeding two years or to both: reg 308(2). As to the statutory maximum see SENTENCING AND DISPOSITION OF OFFENDERS vol 92 (2010) PARA 140.
7 Human Medicines Regulations 2012, SI 2012/1916, reg 305(4).
8 Ie the period of 21 days referred to in the Human Medicines Regulations 2012, SI 2012/1916, reg 305.
9 Ie the provisions imposed under the Human Medicines Regulations 2012, SI 2012/1916, Chapter 2 (regs 279–303).
10 Human Medicines Regulations 2012, SI 2012/1916, reg 306(1), (2). In making that determination, the Ministers must take account of any representations made in accordance with reg 305: see reg 306(3).
11 Ie under the Human Medicines Regulations 2012, SI 2012/1916, reg 305(4).
12 Human Medicines Regulations 2012, SI 2012/1916, reg 306(4).
13 Ie the provisions imposed under the Human Medicines Regulations 2012, SI 2012/1916, Chapter 2 (regs 279–303).
14 Human Medicines Regulations 2012, SI 2012/1916, reg 306(4).
15 Ie under the Human Medicines Regulations 2012, SI 2012/1916, reg 305(4).
16 Human Medicines Regulations 2012, SI 2012/1916, reg 306(7).
17 See note 15.
18 Human Medicines Regulations 2012, SI 2012/1916, reg 306(8). A person is guilty of an offence if that person fails to comply with a requirement imposed by a notice given to that person under reg 306(8): reg 308(1). A person guilty of such an offence is liable, on summary conviction, to a fine not exceeding the statutory maximum or on conviction on indictment to a fine, to imprisonment for a term not exceeding two years or to both: reg 308(2).
19 Ie a requirement imposed under the Human Medicines Regulations 2012, SI 2012/1916, reg 305(4).
20 See the Human Medicines Regulations 2012, SI 2012/1916, reg 307(2). A requirement under reg 307(2) must specify the time within which publication must take place and may specify the form of publication: reg 307(3).
21 See note 13.
22 Human Medicines Regulations 2012, SI 2012/1916, reg 307(1). A person is guilty of an offence if that person fails to comply with a requirement imposed on that person under reg 307(2): reg 308(3). A person guilty of such an offence is liable on summary conviction to a fine not exceeding level 5 on the standard scale: reg 308(4). As to the standard scale see SENTENCING AND DISPOSITION OF OFFENDERS vol 92 (2010) PARA 142.

(vii) Complaints

348. Duty to consider complaints to ministers. If a person makes a complaint to the ministers[1] that an advertisement[2] that has been published, or that is proposed to be published, is incompatible with the prohibitions relating to advertising imposed by the Human Medicines Regulations 2012[3], subject to certain exceptions[4], the ministers must consider the complaint unless it appears to them to be frivolous or vexatious[5].

The ministers are not under any duty to consider a complaint if either OFCOM[6] or a body that appears to the ministers to be a self-regulatory body that deals with complaints about advertisements of the type in question is already dealing with the same complaint[7].

If the ministers have served a notice in respect of the advertisement[8] they may consider the complaint but are not under any duty to do so[9].

If the complaint is one that OFCOM would be under a duty to consider if it had been made to OFCOM[10] the ministers must investigate the complaint or seek the agreement of the complainant to the complaint being referred to OFCOM[11].

If, within a reasonable time of being approached by the ministers, the complainant agrees to the complaint being referred to OFCOM the ministers must refer the complaint to OFCOM[12].

If, within a reasonable time of being approached by the ministers, the complainant does not agree to the referral of the complaint, the ministers must consider the complaint[13].

The Ministers must also consider the complaint if, having referred it to OFCOM, OFCOM decides not to consider the complaint because it appears to OFCOM to be frivolous or vexatious or fails to deal adequately with the complaint within a reasonable time of the referral being made[14].

1   As to the meaning of 'the ministers' see the Human Medicines Regulations 2012, SI 2012/1916, reg 6(6)–(8); and PARA 35: reg 8(1).
2   As to the meaning of 'advertisement' see PARA 333.
3   Ie the prohibitions imposed by the Human Medicines Regulations 2012, SI 2012/1916, Chapter 2 (regs 279–303).
4   Ie subject to the Human Medicines Regulations 2012, SI 2012/1916, regs 309, 310 (see PARA 349).
5   Human Medicines Regulations 2012, SI 2012/1916, reg 309(1), (2).
6   As to OFCOM see TELECOMMUNICATIONS vol 97 (2010) PARA 2 et seq.
7   Human Medicines Regulations 2012, SI 2012/1916, reg 309(3).
8   Ie under the Human Medicines Regulations 2012, SI 2012/1916, reg 305 (whether or not they have taken action in respect of it under reg 306).
9   Human Medicines Regulations 2012, SI 2012/1916, reg 309(4).
10 As to complaints to OFCOM see the Human Medicines Regulations 2012, SI 2012/1916, reg 314; and PARA 350.
11 Human Medicines Regulations 2012, SI 2012/1916, reg 309(5).
12 Human Medicines Regulations 2012, SI 2012/1916, reg 309(6).
13 Human Medicines Regulations 2012, SI 2012/1916, reg 309(7).
14 Human Medicines Regulations 2012, SI 2012/1916, reg 309(8).

349.   Power to refer.   If a person ('the complainant') makes a complaint[1] to the ministers[2] that an advertisement[3] that has been published, or that it is proposed be published, is incompatible with the prohibitions relating to advertisements in the Human Medicines Regulations 2012[4], and the complaint does not appear to the ministers to be frivolous or vexatious[5], the ministers may:

(1)   select a body that appears to them to be a self-regulatory body that deals with complaints about advertisements of the type in question ('the appropriate body')[6]; and

(2)   seek the agreement of the complainant to the complaint being referred to the appropriate body[7].

If within a reasonable time of being approached by the ministers the complainant agrees to the complaint being referred to the appropriate body, the ministers must refer the complaint to that body[8]. However, if within a reasonable time of being approached, the complainant does not agree to the referral of the complaint, the ministers must consider the complaint[9].

The Ministers must also consider the complaint if, having referred it to the appropriate body, the appropriate body decides not to consider the complaint because it appears to the body to be frivolous or vexatious or the Ministers think that the appropriate body has failed to deal adequately with the complaint within a reasonable time of the referral being made[10].

1 Ie a complaint that the advertisement contains material prohibited by any of the Human Medicines Regulations 2012, SI 2012/1916, regs 286–290 (see PARA 336), but is not a complaint that OFCOM would be under a duty to consider if it had been made to OFCOM (see reg 314: see PARA 350) or it is a complaint that the advertisement is incompatible with any of the prohibitions imposed by regs 294–300: reg 310(2). As to OFCOM see TELECOMMUNICATIONS vol 97 (2010) PARA 2 et seq.
2 As to the meaning of 'the ministers' see the Human Medicines Regulations 2012, SI 2012/1916, reg 6(6)–(8); and PARA 35: reg 8(1).
3 As to the meaning of 'advertisement' see PARA 333.
4 Ie the prohibitions imposed by the Human Medicines Regulations 2012, SI 2012/1916, Chapter 2 (regs 279–303).
5 Human Medicines Regulations 2012, SI 2012/1916, reg 310(1).
6 Human Medicines Regulations 2012, SI 2012/1916, reg 310(3)(a).
7 Human Medicines Regulations 2012, SI 2012/1916, reg 310(3)(b).
8 Human Medicines Regulations 2012, SI 2012/1916, reg 310(4).
9 Human Medicines Regulations 2012, SI 2012/1916, reg 310(5).
10 Human Medicines Regulations 2012, SI 2012/1916, reg 310(6). But if the ministers have served a notice in respect of the advertisement under reg 305 (whether or not they have taken action in respect of it under reg 306) the duties in reg 310(4)–(6) do not apply but has effect as if it conferred a power on the ministers to act as mentioned in that provision: reg 310(7).

350. Complaints to OFCOM. If OFCOM[1] receives from a person a complaint that an advertisement[2] containing prohibited material[3] has been included in a licensed service[4] or S4C Digital[5] or a service provided by the Welsh Authority[6] or has such a complaint referred to it[7] by the ministers[8], it must consider the complaint unless the complaint appears to it to be frivolous or vexatious or the following applies[9].

If the ministers have served a notice in respect of the advertisement[10] OFCOM may consider the complaint but is not subject to any duty to do so[11].

If, having considered the complaint, OFCOM considers that the advertisement contains prohibited material it may:

(1)   in the case of an advertisement that has been included in a licensed service, give to the person who is the holder of the licence in respect of that service a direction[12] to exclude the advertisement from the licensed service[13]; and

(2)   in the case of an advertisement that has been included in S4C Digital or a service provided by the Welsh Authority[14], give to the Welsh Authority a direction to exclude the advertisement from S4C Digital or the service provided by the Welsh Authority[15].

If OFCOM gives such a direction, it must inform the licence holder or (as the case may be) the Welsh Authority in writing of its reasons for doing so[16].

1 As to OFCOM see TELECOMMUNICATIONS vol 97 (2010) PARA 2 et seq. In exercising the functions conferred on them by the Human Medicines Regulations 2012, SI 2012/1916, Chapter 3 (regs 304–314) OFCOM must have regard, in particular, to the public interest: reg 315.

2 As to the meaning of 'advertisement' see PARA 333.
3 Ie material prohibited by the Human Medicines Regulations 2012, SI 2012/1916, regs 286–290 (see PARA 336).
4 For these purposes 'licensed service' means a service in respect of which OFCOM has granted a licence under the Broadcasting Act 1990 Pt 1 or 3 or the Broadcasting Act 1996 Pt 1 or 2 (see BROADCASTING): Human Medicines Regulations 2012, SI 2012/1916, reg 314(10).
5 For these purposes 'S4C Digital' means the television service provided in digital form and known as S4C Digital: Human Medicines Regulations 2012, SI 2012/1916, reg 314(10).
6 Ie a service provided under the Communications Act 2003 s 205 (see BROADCASTING vol 4 (2011) PARA 644). For these purposes 'Welsh Authority' means the authority whose name is, by virtue of the Broadcasting Act 1990 s 56(1), Sianel Pedwar Cymru (see BROADCASTING vol 4 (2011) PARA 645): Human Medicines Regulations 2012, SI 2012/1916, reg 314(10).
7 Ie referred to it under the Human Medicines Regulations 2012, SI 2012/1916, reg 309(5), (6) (see PARA 348).
8 See the Human Medicines Regulations 2012, SI 2012/1916, reg 314(1). As to the meaning of 'the ministers' see the Human Medicines Regulations 2012, SI 2012/1916, reg 6(6)–(8); and PARA 35: reg 8(1).
9 Human Medicines Regulations 2012, SI 2012/1916, reg 314(2).
10 Ie under the Human Medicines Regulations 2012, SI 2012/1916, reg 305 (whether or not they have taken action in respect of it under reg 306).
11 Human Medicines Regulations 2012, SI 2012/1916, reg 314(3).
12 If OFCOM gives a direction under the Human Medicines Regulations 2012, SI 2012/1916, reg 314(4), it may also give a direction to the licence holder or (as the case may be) the Welsh Authority to exclude from the service any advertisement in similar terms or likely to convey a similar impression: reg 314(5). A direction given under reg 314 to a licence holder is to be treated for the purposes of the Communications Act 2003 as a direction with respect to a matter mentioned in s 325(5): Human Medicines Regulations 2012, SI 2012/1916, reg 314(7). In deciding whether or not to exercise its power to give a direction under heads (1) and (2) in the text, OFCOM must disregard any lack of evidence that the publication of the advertisement has given rise to loss or damage to any person or that the person responsible for the advertisement intended it to be incompatible with the prohibitions imposed by Chapter 2 (regs 279–303) or failed to exercise proper care to prevent it from being so incompatible: reg 314(6).
13 Human Medicines Regulations 2012, SI 2012/1916, reg 314(4)(a).
14 Ie under the Communications Act 2003 s 205 (see BROADCASTING vol 4 (2011) PARA 644). A direction given under the Human Medicines Regulations 2012, SI 2012/1916, reg 314 to the Welsh Authority is to be treated for the purposes of the Communications Act 2003 as a direction with respect to a matter mentioned in Sch 12 para 14(2) (see BROADCASTING vol 4 (2011) PARA 661): Human Medicines Regulations 2012, SI 2012/1916, reg 314(8).
15 Human Medicines Regulations 2012, SI 2012/1916, reg 314(4)(b).
16 Human Medicines Regulations 2012, SI 2012/1916, reg 314(9).

(viii) Injunctions

351. Application. If the ministers[1] consider that an advertisement[2] that has been published, or that is proposed to be published, is incompatible with the prohibitions relating to advertisements[3], whether or not a complaint has been made to the ministers or to any other person, the ministers may apply to the court for an injunction against any person appearing to them to be concerned or likely to be concerned with the publication of the advertisement[4].

On the making of such an application, the court may grant an injunction prohibiting the publication, or further publication, of the advertisement[5].

The injunction may also prohibit the publication, or further publication, of any advertisement in similar terms or likely to convey a similar impression[6].

The court may not refuse to grant an injunction for lack of evidence that (1) the publication, or proposed publication, of the advertisement has given rise to loss or damage to any person; or (2) the person responsible for the advertisement intended it to be incompatible with the prohibitions imposed[7] or failed to exercise proper care to prevent it from being so incompatible[8].

The court must give its detailed reasons in writing for its decision to grant or refuse an injunction[9].

Where the court grants an injunction, the ministers must as soon as is reasonably practicable provide the following in writing to each person against whom the injunction has been granted: the court's reasons for granting the injunction; any remedy available in the court; and the time limit to be met for any remedy to be available[10].

1   As to the meaning of 'the ministers' see the Human Medicines Regulations 2012, SI 2012/1916, reg 6(6)–(8); and PARA 35: reg 8(1).
2   As to the meaning of 'advertisement' see PARA 333.
3   Ie the prohibitions imposed by the Human Medicines Regulations 2012, SI 2012/1916, Chapter 2 (regs 279–303).
4   Human Medicines Regulations 2012, SI 2012/1916, reg 311(1), (2). In exercising the functions conferred on them by this Chapter, the ministers and the court must have regard, in particular, to the public interest: reg 315.
5   Human Medicines Regulations 2012, SI 2012/1916, reg 311(3).
6   Human Medicines Regulations 2012, SI 2012/1916, reg 311(4).
7   See note 3.
8   Human Medicines Regulations 2012, SI 2012/1916, reg 311(5).
9   Human Medicines Regulations 2012, SI 2012/1916, reg 311(6).
10   Human Medicines Regulations 2012, SI 2012/1916, reg 311(7).

352. Accuracy of factual claim. If an application for an injunction is made[1], and the advertisement[2] in question makes a factual claim about the medicinal product[3] to which it relates, the court may require any person appearing to it to be responsible for the advertisement to provide evidence as to the accuracy of the factual claim[4].

The court may impose such a requirement on the application of any party to the proceedings for the injunction or of its own motion[5] and, in deciding whether or not to impose a requirement, the court must have regard to the interests of any person who would be subject to, or affected by, the requirement[6].

If the person on whom a requirement is imposed fails to comply with it the court may infer that the factual claim is inaccurate[7].

1   Ie under the Human Medicines Regulations 2012, SI 2012/1916, reg 311 (see PARA 351).
2   As to the meaning of 'advertisement' see PARA 333.
3   As to the meaning of 'medicinal product' see PARA 25.
4   Human Medicines Regulations 2012, SI 2012/1916, reg 312(1), (2). A requirement imposed under reg 312(2) must specify the time within which the evidence must be provided: reg 312(5).
5   Human Medicines Regulations 2012, SI 2012/1916, reg 312(3).
6   Human Medicines Regulations 2012, SI 2012/1916, reg 312(4).
7   Human Medicines Regulations 2012, SI 2012/1916, reg 312(6). A person may fail to comply with a requirement under reg 312(2) by not providing any evidence; or providing evidence that the court considers inadequate: reg 312(7).

353. Publication. If the court grants an injunction[1], other than an interim injunction, in respect of an advertisement[2] that has been published, the ministers[3] may by notice in writing require[4] any person against whom the injunction has been granted to publish all or part of the court's decision and a corrective statement concerning the advertisement in respect of which the application for the injunction was made[5].

If a person ('P') fails to comply with such a requirement the ministers may certify that failure to the court and the court may enquire into the matter[6].

If the court enquires into the matter it must as part of its enquiry, hear any witnesses produced against or on behalf of P and consider any statement offered in P's defence[7] and, if having conducted its enquiry, the court is satisfied that P failed without reasonable excuse to comply with a requirement imposed it may deal with P as if P were in contempt of court[8].

1 Ie under the Human Medicines Regulations 2012, SI 2012/1916, reg 311 (see PARA 351).
2 As to the meaning of 'advertisement' see PARA 333.
3 As to the meaning of 'the ministers' see the Human Medicines Regulations 2012, SI 2012/1916, reg 6(6)–(8); and PARA 35: reg 8(1).
4 Such a requirement must specify the time within which publication must take place and may specify the form of publication: Human Medicines Regulations 2012, SI 2012/1916, reg 313(3).
5 Human Medicines Regulations 2012, SI 2012/1916, reg 313(1), (2).
6 Human Medicines Regulations 2012, SI 2012/1916, reg 313(4).
7 Human Medicines Regulations 2012, SI 2012/1916, reg 313(5).
8 Human Medicines Regulations 2012, SI 2012/1916, reg 315(6).

(11) ENFORCEMENT, SAMPLING AND FORFEITURE

(i) Medicines Act 1968

354. Enforcement authorities. It is the duty of the appropriate minister[1] to enforce or to secure the enforcement of the provisions of the Medicines Act 1968 and any regulations or orders made under it[2]. For the purpose of performing that duty in relation to certain statutory provisions and regulations[3], he must, in respect of each area for which there is a drugs authority[4], make arrangements or give directions by which the General Pharmaceutical Council[5] or the drugs authority for that area or both have power or are under a duty concurrently with him to enforce those provisions and regulations to such extent as the arrangements or directions may provide[6].

The General Pharmaceutical Council is under a duty to enforce certain provisions[7].

However, no duty or power conferred or imposed by or under any of these provisions[8] on any body other than the appropriate minister may be performed or is exercisable in relation to any hospital (except in relation to so much of the hospital premises as is a registered pharmacy)[9], so much of any premises as is used by a practitioner for carrying on his practice[10], or so much of any other premises as is used for veterinary medicine or veterinary surgery for the purposes of any institution[11].

If the appropriate minister is satisfied, after making such inquiry as he thinks fit, that the General Pharmaceutical Council has in relation to any matter failed to perform a duty imposed on it as mentioned above[12] and that the public interest requires that the provisions in question should be enforced, he may determine that he will himself enforce those provisions in relation to that matter[13].

1 'The appropriate minister' means the Secretary of State and the Welsh Ministers: see the Medicines Act 1968 s 108(11) (amended by SI 2006/2407); National Assembly for Wales (Transfer of Functions) Order 1999, SI 1999/672, art 2, Sch 1. However the appropriate minister is under no duty to enforce those other provisions, or any regulations made under them, in their application to England and Wales: Medicines Act 1968 s 18(6C) (s 18(6A)–(6D) added by the Health Act 2006 s 31(1)(b)).
2 Medicines Act 1968 s 108(1) (amended by Health Act 2006 s 31(1)(a)).
3 Ie the provisions of any order made under the Medicines Act 1968 s 62(1)(a) (prohibiting, in the interests of safety, the sale or supply of specified medicinal products: see PARA 307) and s 63(b) (prohibiting the sale or supply of adulterated medicinal products: see PARA 234), s 64, (prohibiting the sale or supply of medicinal products not of the required quality or which do not comply with specified standards: see PARA 235), s 87(2) (prohibiting the possession, sale or supply of medicinal products not complying with the requirements as to containers: see PARA

314) and s 88(3), in the application of any of these provisions to the retail sale, offer or exposure for retail sale, or possession for the purpose of retail sale, of medicinal products, and to the supply, offer or exposure for supply or possession for the purpose of supply, of medicinal products in circumstances corresponding to retail sale: s 108(2)(a) (amended by SI 2012/1916)). As to references to retail sale and selling by retail see PARA 26. As to references to supplying anything in circumstances corresponding to retail sale see PARA 52 note 11 and as to the meaning of 'medicinal product' see PARA 25 (definitions applied by s 132(1) (substituted by SI 2012/1916)).

4 'Drugs authority' means, in relation to an area in England other than the City of London, the council of a non-metropolitan county, metropolitan district or London Borough, in relation to the City of London (including Inner Temple and Middle Temple), the Common Council of the City of London and, in relation to an area of Wales, the council of a county or county borough: Medicines Act 1968 s 108(12) (added by the Food Safety Act 1990 s 59(1), Sch 3 para 8; and amended by the Local Government (Wales) Act 1994 s 66(6), Sch 16 para 33(b); SI 2012/1916). As to local government areas and authorities in England and Wales see LOCAL GOVERNMENT vol 69 (2009) PARA 22 et seq. As to the London boroughs and their councils see LONDON GOVERNMENT vol 71 (2013) PARAS 15, 20–22, 55 et seq. As to the Common Council of the City of London see LONDON GOVERNMENT vol 71 (2013) PARA 34 et seq.

5 As to the General Pharmaceutical Council see MEDICAL PROFESSIONS vol 74 (2011) PARA 785.

6 Medicines Act 1968 s 108(2) (amended by the Food Safety Act 1990 Sch 3 para 8, SI 2012/1916). As to restrictions on the power of such bodies to bring prosecutions see the Medicines Act 1968 s 125(4); and PARA 183.

7 Medicines Act 1968 s 108(6) (amended by SI 2010/1621, SI 2012/1916). The provisions referred to in the text are (1) the regulations made under the Medicines Act 1968 s 60 (restricting the sale of certain medicinal products: see PARA 382), in their application to premises in England and Wales at which medicinal products are sold by retail or are supplied in circumstances corresponding to retail sale (s 108(6)(b), (c) (as so amended)); (2) s 78 and any regulations made under s 79(2), in their application to England and Wales (s 108(6)(c) (as so amended)); and (3) s 72A(4), (5) (see MEDICAL PROFESSIONS vol 74 (2011) PARA 806) in their application to England and Wales (s 108(6A) (added by the Health Act 1999 s 31(1)(b), amended by SI 2012/1916)). Such provisions are to be enforced concurrently with the appropriate minister: see the Medicines Act 1968 s 108(6)(b), (c), (6A) (as so added and amended). The General Pharmaceutical Council is also under a duty to enforce the other provisions of the Medicines Act 1968 s 72A, and any regulations made under them, in their application to England and Wales (s 108(6B) (added by the Health Act 1999 s 31(1)(b); and amended by SI 2012/1916) but the appropriate ministers are under no such duty (see the Medicines Act 1968 s 108(6C) (added by the Health Act 1999 s 31(1)(b)). Notwithstanding the Medicines Act 1968 s 108(6C) the appropriate minister is to be treated for the purposes of ss 111–114 (1) as empowered by s 108 to enforce those other provisions, or any regulations made under them, in their application to England and Wales and; (2) to that extent as an enforcement authority in relation to those other provisions or those regulations in their application to England and Wales: s 108(6D) (added by the Health Act 1999 s 31(1)(b)). As to the meaning of 'enforcement authority' see PARA 142 note 13 (definition applied by the Medicines Act 1968 s 132(1) (substituted by SI 2012/1916)).

8 Ie the Medicines Act 1968 s 108(2)–(6D).

9 Medicines Act 1968 s 108(9)(a) (amended by SI 2006/2407, SI 2012/1916). As to the meanings of 'hospital' and 'registered pharmacy' see PARA 52 notes 2, 3 (definitions applied by the Medicines Act 1968 s 132(1) (substituted by SI 2012/1916)).

10 Medicines Act 1968 s 108(9)(b).

11 Medicines Act 1968 s 108(9)(c).

12 Ie imposed on it by the Medicines Act 1968 s 108(6A) or (6B) to enforce any provisions mentioned therein.

13 Medicines Act 1968 s 108(10) (amended by SI 2012/1916). Where under this provision either of the ministers makes a determination in respect of the enforcement of any provision in relation to a particular matter, he is entitled to recover from the General Pharmaceutical Council or as the case may be the Pharmaceutical Society of Northern Ireland or other body which was under a duty to enforce that provision in relation to that matter any expenses reasonably incurred by that minister in taking steps to enforce that provision in relation to that matter: Medicines Act 1968 s 128(5) (amended by SI 2012/1916). As to financial matters generally see PARA 30.

355. Rights of entry. Any person duly authorised in writing[1] by an enforcement authority[2] has a right at any reasonable time, on production, if required, of his credentials: (1) to enter any premises[3] for the purpose of ascertaining whether there is or has been, on or in connection with those premises, any contravention[4] of any provisions of the Medicines Act 1968 or of any regulations or order made under the Act which that authority is required or empowered[5] to enforce[6], or generally for the purposes of the performance by the authority of its functions under the Act or under any such regulations or order[7]; (2) to enter any vehicle other than a hover vehicle, any stall or place other than premises, or any home-going ship[8], for any purpose for which under head (1) above the person so authorised would have a right to enter any premises[9]. A justice of the peace[10] may, in certain circumstances[11], by warrant[12] authorise the enforcement authority, or any person duly authorised by it, to enter any premises, if need be by force[13].

Any person entering any property[14] by virtue of any of these provisions[15] may take with him such other persons and such equipment as may appear to him to be necessary[16]. On leaving any such property which he has entered in pursuance of a warrant, he must leave it, if the property is unoccupied or the occupier or other person in charge[17] is temporarily absent, as effectively secured against trespass as he found it[18].

1   As to the meaning of 'writing' see PARA 507 note 2.
2   As to the meaning of 'enforcement authority' see PARA 142 note 13 (definition applied by the Medicines Act 1968 s 132(1) (substituted by SI 2012/1916)).
3   Admission to any premises used only as a private dwelling house may not be demanded as of right by virtue of the Medicines Act 1968 s 111(1)–(3), unless 24 hours' notice of the intended entry has been given to the occupier: s 111(4).
4   As to the meaning of 'contravention' see PARA 41 note 8 (definition applied by the Medicines Act 1968 s 132(1) (as substituted by SI 2012/1916)).
5   Ie by or under the Medicines Act 1968 s 108: see PARA 354.
6   Medicines Act 1968 s 111(1)(a).
7   Medicines Act 1968 s 111(1)(b).
8   'Home-going ship' means a ship plying exclusively in inland waters or engaged exclusively in coastal voyages; 'inland waters' means any canal, river, lake, loch, navigation or estuary; and 'coastal voyage' means a voyage which starts and ends in the United Kingdom and does not involve calling at any place outside the United Kingdom: Medicines Act 1968 s 111(8). As to the meaning of 'United Kingdom' see PARA 20 note 4.
9   Medicines Act 1968 s 111(2)(b).
10 For this purpose a justice of the peace includes a reference to a district judge (magistrates' courts): Medicines Act 1968 s 111(9)(a) (substituted by SI 2012/1916).
11 Ie where the justice is satisfied, on sworn information in writing, that there are reasonable grounds for entering any premises for any purpose for which a person authorised by an enforcement authority has a right to enter them under the Medicines Act 1968 s 111(1)–(4) (s 111(5)) and: (1) that admission has been refused or that refusal is apprehended, and that notice of intention to apply for a warrant has been given to the occupier (s 111(5)(a)); or (2) that an application for admission or the giving of such a notice would defeat the object of the entry (s 111(5)(b)); or (3) that the case is one of urgency (s 111(5)(c)); or (4) that the premises are unoccupied or the occupier is temporarily absent (s 111(5)(d)). In the case of a ship, vehicle, stall or place, references to the occupier should be read as references to the master or other person in charge: s 111(6) (amended by SI 2012/1916).
12 Any such warrant continues in force for one month: Medicines Act 1968 s 111(7). As to the meaning of 'month' see PARA 43 note 3.
13 Medicines Act 1968 s 111(5). This provision also has effect in relation to entering any ship, aircraft, vehicle, stall or place which may be entered under s 111(2): s 111(6) (amended by SI 2012/1916).
14 Ie any premises, ship, vehicle, stall or place: Medicines Act 1968 s 114(1) (amended by SI 2012/1916).
15 Ie by virtue of the Medicines Act 1968 s 111, whether in pursuance of a warrant or not: s 114(1).

16 Medicines Act 1968 s 114(1) (amended by SI 2012/1916). For restrictions on the disclosure of information obtained by entry see PARA 359; and as to the protection of officers see PARA 360. It is an offence to obstruct a person exercising a right of entry: see s 114(2)(a); and PARA 358.

17 Ie in the case of a ship, aircraft, vehicle, stall or place: Medicines Act 1968 s 114(1).

18 Medicines Act 1968 s 114(1).

356. Power to inspect, take samples and seize goods and documents. For the purpose of ascertaining whether there is or has been a contravention[1] of the Medicines Act 1968 or of any regulations or order made under the Act which an enforcement authority[2] is required or empowered to enforce[3], any person duly authorised in writing[4] by that authority has a right to inspect: (1) any substance[5] or article appearing to him to be a medicinal product[6]; (2) any article appearing to him to be a container or package[7] used or intended to be used to contain any medicinal product or to be a label or leaflet used or intended to be used in connection with a medicinal product[8]; or (3) any plant or equipment appearing to him to be used or intended to be used in connection with the manufacture[9] or assembly[10] of medicinal products, and any process of manufacture or assembly of any medicinal products and the means employed, at any stage in the processes of manufacture or assembly, for testing the materials after they have been subjected to these processes[11].

Where for these purposes a person so authorised requires a sample of any substance or article appearing to him to be a medicinal product sold or supplied or intended to be sold or supplied[12], or a substance or article used or intended to be used in the manufacture of a medicinal product[13], if he does not obtain the sample by purchase, he has a right to take a sample[14]. He may also for the specified[15] purposes require the production of books and documents and take copies of them[16].

Any person so authorised has a right to seize and detain any substance or article which he has reasonable cause to believe to be a substance or article in relation to which, or by means of which, an offence under the Medicines Act 1968[17] is being or has been committed, and any document which he has reasonable cause to believe to be a document which may be required as evidence in proceedings under the Act[18]. He must inform the person from whom the substance or article, including any document, is seized[19]; and he must, if requested by that person at the time of seizure or at any subsequent time not later than 21 days afterwards, set aside a sample or treat the substance or article as a sample, whichever he considers more appropriate having regard to the nature of the substance or article[20], unless the nature of the substance or article is such that it is not reasonably practicable to do either of those things[21].

Any person duly authorised in writing by the licensing authority[22] has the rights conferred by these provisions in relation to things belonging to, or any business carried on by, an applicant for a licence or certificate[23], and may exercise those rights for the purpose of verifying any statement contained in the application[24].

Where a person claiming to exercise a right by virtue of these provisions is required to produce his credentials, the right is not exercisable by him except on production of those credentials[25].

1 As to the meaning of 'contravention' see PARA 41 note 8 (definition applied by the Medicines Act 1968 s 132(1) (substituted by SI 2012/1916)).

2 As to the meaning of 'enforcement authority' see PARA 142 note 13 (definition applied by the Medicines Act 1968 s 132(1) (as substituted: see note 1)).

3 Ie by or under the Medicines Act 1968 s 108: see PARA 354.

4 As to the meaning of 'writing' see PARA 507 note 2.

5 As to the meaning of 'substance' see PARA 25 note 2 (definition applied by the Medicines Act 1968 s 132(1) (as substituted: see note 1)).

6 Medicines Act 1968 s 112(1)(a). As to the meaning of 'medicinal product' see PARA 25 (definition applied by the Medicines Act 1968 s 132(1) (as substituted: see note 1)).

7 As to the meaning of 'package' see PARA 51 note 48 (definition applied by the Medicines Act 1968 s 132(1) (as substituted: see note 1)).

8 Medicines Act 1968 s 112(1)(b).

9 As to the meaning of 'manufacture' see PARA 141 note 7 (definition applied by the Medicines Act 1968 s 132(1) (as substituted: see note 1)).

10 As to the meaning of 'assembly' see PARA 141 note 8 (definition applied by the Medicines Act 1968 s 132(1) (as substituted: see note 1)).

11 Medicines Act 1968 s 112(1)(c).

12 Medicines Act 1968 s 112(2)(a).

13 Medicines Act 1968 s 112(2)(b).

14 Medicines Act 1968 s 112(2). As to the procedure to be followed where a sample is obtained for these purposes see PARA 357. If payment is demanded, a sample obtained under s 112 must be paid for: s 112(9), Sch 3 para 28(1). There is procedure for arbitration in default of agreement as to the value of the sample: see Sch 3 para 28(2). The taking of a sample is deemed to be a sale for the purposes of s 64(1)–(4) (see PARA 235): Sch 3 para 29.

15 Ie the purposes specified by the Medicines Act 1968 s 112(1): see the text to notes 1–14.

16 See the Medicines Act 1968 s 112(3). Thus he may require any person carrying on a business which consists of or includes the manufacture, assembly, sale or supply of medicinal products, and any person employed in connection with such a business, to produce any books or documents relating to the business which are in his possession or under his control (s 112(3)(a)), and he may take copies of, or of any entry in, any book or document so produced (s 112(3)(b)). As to the meaning of 'person' see PARA 45 note 2. As to the meaning of 'business' see PARA 52 note 10 (definition applied by the Medicines Act 1968 s 132(1) (as substituted: see note 1)).

17 'Offence under the Medicines Act 1968' includes an offence under any regulations or order made under the Act: s 132(1).

18 Medicines Act 1968 s 112(4). For the purpose of exercising this right, the person having the right may, so far as is reasonably necessary to secure the due observance of the Act and any regulations and order made under it, require any person having authority to do so to break open any container or package or open any vending machine, or to permit him to do so: s 112(5).

19 Medicines Act 1968 s 112(6). In the case of anything seized from a vending machine, he must inform the person whose name and address are stated on the machine as being those of its owner or, if no name and address are stated, the occupier of the premises on which the machine stands or to which it is affixed: s 112(6).

20 Medicines Act 1968 s 113(1), (2) (s 113(1) amended by SI 2012/1916).

21 Medicines Act 1968 s 113(1), (3). Where such a sample is set aside, or where a substance or article is treated as a sample, the authorised person must divide it into three parts, each part being marked and sealed or fastened up in such manner as its nature will permit, and one such part must be supplied to the person making the request for sampling: s 113(1), (4). The procedure laid down in Sch 3 paras 10–12, 15–27 (see PARA 357) must then be followed in respect of the remaining two parts of the sample, substance or article: see s 113(5).

22 As to the meaning of 'licensing authority' see PARA 35 note 1.

23 Ie a licence or certificate under the Medicines Act 1968 Pt II (ss 6–50).

24 Medicines Act 1968 s 112(7). Where by virtue of s 112(7) a person exercises any right specified in s 112(4), he is subject to the duty imposed by s 112(6): s 112(7).

25 Medicines Act 1968 s 112(8). It is an offence wilfully to obstruct an authorised person acting in pursuance of s 112: see PARA 358. As to the protection of officers see PARA 360.

357. Sampling and analysis. Where either by purchase or in the exercise of certain powers[1] a person, referred to as a 'sampling officer', authorised by an enforcement authority[2] obtains a sample of any substance[3] or article for the purpose of ascertaining whether there is or has been, in connection with that substance or article, any contravention[4] of the provisions of the Medicines Act 1968 or of any regulations or order made under the Act which the authority is required or empowered[5] to enforce[6], or otherwise for any purpose connected with the authority's performance of its functions under the Act, any regulations or order[7], he must deal with that sample in accordance with a specified procedure[8].

The sampling officer must forthwith divide the sample into three parts, each to be marked and sealed or fastened up in such manner as its nature permits[9]. One part must be supplied to the seller[10] or owner[11] of the substance or article from which the sample was taken[12], who must be informed that the sample has been obtained for the purpose of analysis or other appropriate examination[13]. Where it appears to the sampling officer that any such person is not the manufacturer[14] or assembler[15] named on the container of the substance or article, that manufacturer or assembler must also, within three days, be notified that the sample has been obtained and informed from whom it was purchased or from where it was obtained[16]. Unless the sampling officer decides not to submit the sample for analysis or examination, one of the remaining parts of the sample must be retained for future comparison[17], and the third part must be submitted to the public analyst[18] for the area, or in certain circumstances to other specified persons, for analysis[19].

The analyst must send to the sampling officer a certificate in the prescribed form[20], specifying the results of the analysis[21]. On payment of the prescribed fee[22] to the relevant enforcement authority, the person to whom a part of the sample is required to be supplied is entitled to be supplied with a copy of the certificate as to the result of the analysis or examination[23]. In any proceedings for an offence under the Act, this certificate is sufficient evidence[24] of the facts stated in it, unless the other party requires the person who issued the certificate to be called as a witness[25]. In any such proceedings, the court may cause the part of the sample retained for future comparison[26] to be sent for analysis to the government chemist or to be sent for other appropriate examination to the person having the management or control of a laboratory specified by the court[27].

A person, other than a person so authorised by an enforcement authority, who has purchased a medicinal product may submit a sample of it for analysis to the public analyst for the area in which the product was purchased, or, if for the time being there is no such public analyst, to the public analyst for another area[28].

The ministers may by order modify the sampling provisions[29].

A drugs authority[30] or a non-metropolitan district council[31] may provide facilities for the microbiological examination of drugs[32].

1   Ie conferred by the Medicines Act 1968 s 112: see PARA 356.
2   As to the meaning of 'enforcement authority' see PARA 142 note 13 (definition applied by the Medicines Act 1968 s 132(1) (substituted by SI 2012/1916)).
3   As to the meaning of 'substance' see PARA 25 note 2 (definition applied by the Medicines Act 1968 s 132(1) (as substituted: see note 2)).
4   As to the meaning of 'contravention' see PARA 41 note 8 (definition applied by the Medicines Act 1968 s 132(1) (as substituted: see note 2)).
5   Ie under the Medicines Act 1968 s 108: see PARA 354.
6   Medicines Act 1968 s 112(9), Sch 3 para 1(1)(a).
7   Medicines Act 1968 Sch 3 para 1(1)(b).
8   Medicines Act 1968 Sch 3 para 1.
9   Medicines Act 1968 Sch 3 para 2. Where a sample consists of substances or articles enclosed in unopened containers, and to open them and divide the contents is impracticable or might affect the composition of the contents or impede the analysis or examination, the sampling officer may divide the sample into parts by dividing the unopened containers into three lots: Sch 3 para 11.
10 Medicines Act 1968 Sch 3 para 3. This applies where the sample was purchased otherwise than from an automatic machine: Sch 3 para 3.

11 Medicines Act 1968 Sch 3 paras 4, 8. This applies if the sample was obtained from an automatic machine and a person's name and an address in the United Kingdom are stated on the machine as being those of the owner of the machine: Sch 3 para 4(a). As to the meaning of 'United Kingdom' see PARA 20 note 4. In any other case where the sample is so obtained, one part of the sample must be supplied to the occupier of the premises on which the machine stands or to which it is affixed: Sch 3 para 4(b). Further, in any case not falling within Sch 3 paras 3 or 4, one part of the sample must be supplied to the person appearing to the sampling officer to be the owner of the substance or article from which the sample was taken: Sch 3 para 8 (amended by SI 2012/1916).

12 See the Medicines Act 1968 Sch 3 paras 3, 4, 8. The provisions of s 127 apply to the supply of parts of samples as they apply to the service of documents: Sch 3 para 12.

13 Medicines Act 1968 Sch 3 para 9 (amended by SI 2012/1916). If after reasonable inquiry the sampling officer is unable to ascertain the name of a person to whom or the address at which this part of the sample ought to be supplied, he may retain it: Medicines Act 1968 Sch 3 para 13. As to the meaning of 'person' see PARA 45 note 2.

14 As to the meaning of 'manufacturer' see PARA 141 note 7 (definition applied by the Medicines Act 1968 s 132(1) (as substituted: see note 2)).

15 As to the meaning of 'assembler' cf PARA 141 note 8.

16 Medicines Act 1968 Sch 3 para 14.

17 Medicines Act 1968 Sch 3 para 10(a).

18 'Public analyst' has the meaning set out in the Food Safety Act 1990 s 27 (see FOOD vol 18(2) (Reissue) PARA 268): Medicines Act 1968 Sch 3 para 1(2) (amended by the Food Safety Act 1990 s 59(1), Sch 3 para 12).

19 See the Medicines Act 1968 Sch 3 paras 10(b), 15–17 (Sch 3 para 17 amended by SI 2006/2407, SI 2012/1916). The person to whom the sample is submitted must analyse or examine it, or have it analysed or examined under his direction, as soon as practicable: Medicines Act 1968 Sch 3 para 18(1). If he is a public analyst and he determines that for any reason an effective analysis cannot be performed by him or under his direction, he must send it to the public analyst for some other area for analysis by him or under his direction as soon as practicable: Sch 3 para 18(2).

20 Ie in the form prescribed by the ministers: Medicines Act 1968 Sch 3 para 19(3). As to the meaning of 'the ministers' see the Human Medicines Regulations 2012, SI 2012/1916, reg 6(6)–(8); and PARA 35 (definition applied by the Medicines Act 1968 s 132(1) (as substituted: see note 2)). As to the regulations that have been made see the Medicines (Certificates of Analysis) Regulations 1977, SI 1977/1399 (amended by SI 2005/2745).

21 See the Medicines Act 1968 Sch 3 para 19(1), (2).

22 Any regulations prescribing a fee must be made by the ministers: Medicines Act 1968 Sch 3 para 20(2). As to the regulations that have been made see the Medicines (Certificates of Analysis) Regulations 1977, SI 1977/1399. As to fees see PARA 30.

23 Medicines Act 1968 Sch 3 para 20(1).

24 As to what is sufficient evidence see CIVIL PROCEDURE vol 11 (2009) PARA 767.

25 Medicines Act 1968 Sch 3 para 21. A document produced by one of the parties to the proceedings which has been supplied to him by the other party as being a copy of such a certificate is also sufficient evidence of the facts stated: Sch 3 para 22. If, in proceedings before a magistrates' court, a defendant intends to produce such a certificate, or to require the person who issued the certificate to be called as a witness, he must give the other party to the proceedings a notice of his intention, and where he intends to produce such a certificate, a copy of the certificate, at least three clear days before the day on which the summons is returnable: Sch 3 para 23(1). If this provision is not complied with, the court may, if it thinks fit, adjourn the hearing on such terms as it thinks proper: Sch 3 para 23(2). The provisions of Sch 3 paras 21, 22, 24 have effect in respect of such certificates and documents, instead of the similar provisions of the Criminal Justice Act 1967 s 9: Medicines Act 1968 Sch 3 para 26. As to magistrates courts see MAGISTRATES.

26 Where either party to the proceedings so requests, the court must cause the sample to be sent for analysis or examination and, in the absence of any such request, it may do so if it thinks fit: Medicines Act 1968 Sch 3 para 24(1).

27 Medicines Act 1968 Sch 3 para 24(1). The cost of the analysis or examination must be paid by the prosecutor or defendant, as the court may order: Sch 3 para 25.

28 Medicines Act 1968 s 115(1). The provisions of Sch 3 paras 2–13 apply to such a sample as if the person submitting the sample were the sampling officer: s 115(2).

29 Medicines Act 1968 Sch 3 para 27. The sampling provisions are contained in Sch 3 paras 1–26.

30 As to the meaning of 'drugs authority' see PARA 354 note 4.

31 As to non-metropolitan district councils see LOCAL GOVERNMENT vol 69 (2009) PARA 130.
32 Medicines Act 1968 s 115A (added by the Food Safety Act 1990 s 59 (1), Sch 3 para 10).

358. Offences related to enforcement. Any person who wilfully obstructs a person acting in pursuance of the Medicines Act 1968 and duly authorised so to act by an enforcement authority[1], or who wilfully fails to comply with any requirement properly made to him by a person so acting under the provisions[2] relating to inspection, the taking of samples and the seizing of goods and documents[3], or who without reasonable cause fails to give to a person so acting any other assistance or information which that person may reasonably require of him for the performance of his functions under the Act[4], is guilty of an offence[5]. If any person in giving such information makes any statement which he knows to be false he is guilty of an offence[6].

1 Medicines Act 1968 s 114(2)(a). As to the meaning of 'enforcement authority' see PARA 142 note 13 (definition applied by s 132(1) (substituted by SI 2012/1916)).
2 Ie under the Medicines Act 1968 s 112: see PARA 356.
3 Medicines Act 1968 s 114(2)(b).
4 Medicines Act 1968 s 114(2)(c). Nothing in s 114 is to be construed as requiring a person to answer any question or give any information if to do so might incriminate that person or (where that person is married or a civil partner) the spouse or civil partner of that person: s 114(4) (amended by the Civil Partnership Act 2004 s 261(1), Sch 27 para 32).
5 Medicines Act 1968 s 114(2) (amended by virtue of the Criminal Justice Act 1982 ss 37, 46). Such a person is liable on summary conviction to a fine not exceeding level 3 on the standard scale: Medicines Act 1968 s 114(2) (as so amended). As to the standard scale see SENTENCING AND DISPOSITION OF OFFENDERS vol 92 (2010) PARA 142.
6 Medicines Act 1968 s 114(3). See also note 4. Such a person is liable on summary conviction to a fine not exceeding the prescribed sum (s 114(3)(a) (amended by virtue of the Magistrates' Courts Act 1980 s 32(2))), or on conviction on indictment to a fine or to imprisonment for a term not exceeding two years or to both (Medicines Act 1968 s 114(3)(b)). As to the prescribed sum see SENTENCING AND DISPOSITION OF OFFENDERS vol 92 (2010) PARA 141.

359. Disclosure of information. If any person discloses to any other person any information with respect to any manufacturing process or trade secret obtained by him in premises which he has entered under his powers of entry[1] or any information obtained by or furnished to him in pursuance of the Medicines Act 1968[2], then, unless the disclosure was made in the performance of his duty, he is guilty of an offence[3].

1 Medicines Act 1968 s 118(1)(a). The powers of entry referred to are the powers under s 111: see PARA 355.
2 Medicines Act 1968 s 118(1)(b).
3 Medicines Act 1968 s 118(1). Such a person is liable on summary conviction to a fine not exceeding the prescribed sum (s 118(2)(a) (amended by virtue of the Magistrates' Courts Act 1980 s 32(2))), or on conviction on indictment to a fine or to imprisonment for a term not exceeding two years or to both (Medicines Act 1968 s 118(2)(b)). As to the prescribed sum see SENTENCING AND DISPOSITION OF OFFENDERS vol 92 (2010) PARA 141. Section 118(1) does not apply if the person making the disclosure referred to is, or is acting on behalf of a person who is a public authority for the purposes of the Freedom of Information Act 2000 (see CONFIDENCE AND DATA PROTECTION vol 8(1) (2003 Reissue) PARA 583), and the information is not held by the authority on behalf of another person: Medicines Act 1968 s 118(1A) (added by SI 2004/3363). As to the prosecution of offences see PARA 376.

360. Protection of officers. An officer of an enforcement authority[1] is not personally liable in respect of any act done by him in the execution or purported execution of the Medicines Act 1968 and within the scope of his employment[2] if he did it in the honest belief that his duty under the Act required or entitled him to do it[3]. Where an action has been brought against an officer of an enforcement authority in respect of an act done by him in the execution or purported execution of the Act, and the circumstances are such that he is not legally entitled to require the enforcement authority to indemnify him, the authority may nevertheless indemnify him against the whole or part of the damages and costs or expenses which he may have been ordered to pay or may have incurred, if it is satisfied that he honestly believed that his duty under the Act required or entitled him to do it[4].

1   As to the meaning of 'enforcement authority' see PARA 142 note 13 (definition applied by the Medicines Act 1968 s 132(1) (substituted by SI 2012/1916)). Any reference to an officer of such an authority includes a reference to any person who, not being such an officer, is authorised to act in pursuance of the Medicines Act 1968 by such an authority: s 119(3).

2   In the case of a person who is not an officer (see note 1), the reference to the scope of his employment is a reference to the scope of the authorisation under which he acts: Medicines Act 1968 s 119(3).

3   Medicines Act 1968 s 119(1).

4   Medicines Act 1968 s 119(2). See also note 1.

(ii) Human Medicines Regulations 2012

361.   Validity of decisions and proceedings.   The validity of a decision of the licensing authority[1] in relation to manufacturing and wholesale dealing[2], UK marketing authorisations[3], certification of homoeopathic medicinal products[4], traditional herbal medicinal products[5] or Article 126a authorisations[6] is not to be questioned in any legal proceedings[7].

The validity of a licence, authorisation, certificate or registration granted or issued, or other thing done, in pursuance of such a decision is not to be questioned in any legal proceedings[8].

A person to whom notice of the decision is given may make an application to the High Court to challenge the validity of the decision on the grounds that the decision is not within the powers conferred on the licensing authority or a requirement of the Human Medicines Regulations 2012[9] in connection with the matter to which the decision relates has not been complied with[10].

On such an application the High Court may make an interim order suspending the operation of the decision to which the application relates until the final determination of proceedings or quash the decision[11].

If a decision to grant a licence, authorisation, certificate or registration is quashed under these provisions, a licence, authorisation, certificate or registration granted in pursuance of the decision is void and the application process for the grant of the licence, authorisation, certificate or registration may be continued as if the decision had not been made[12].

1   As to the meaning of 'licensing authority' see PARA 35 note 1.

2   Ie under the Human Medicines Regulations 2012, SI 2012/1916, Pt 3 (regs 17–45): see PARA 45 et seq.

3   Ie under the Human Medicines Regulations 2012, SI 2012/1916, Pt 5 (regs 48–101): see PARA 141 et seq. As to the meaning of 'UK marketing authorisations' see PARA 141 note 3.

4   Ie under the Human Medicines Regulations 2012, SI 2012/1916, Pt 6 (regs 102–124): see PARA 187 et seq. As to the meaning of 'homoeopathic medicinal products' see PARA 187 note 1.

5   Ie under the Human Medicines Regulations 2012, SI 2012/1916, Pt 7 (regs 125–155): see PARA 206 et seq. As to the meaning of 'traditional herbal medicinal products' see PARA 155 note 6.

6   Ie under the Human Medicines Regulations 2012, SI 2012/1916, Pt 8 (regs 156–158): see PARAS 232, 233. As to the meaning of 'Article 126a authorisation' see PARA 141 note 6.

7   Human Medicines Regulations 2012, SI 2012/1916, reg 322(1). Regulation 322(1), (2) are subject to the other provisions of reg 322: reg 322(3).

8   Human Medicines Regulations 2012, SI 2012/1916, reg 322(2).

9   Human Medicines Regulations 2012, SI 2012/1916.

10 Human Medicines Regulations 2012, SI 2012/1916, reg 322(4). An application under reg 322(4) must be made within the period of three months beginning immediately after the day on which notice of the decision is given to the applicant: reg 322(5).

11 Human Medicines Regulations 2012, SI 2012/1916, reg 322(6). It may quash the decision if satisfied that the decision is not within the powers of the Human Medicines Regulations 2012, SI 2012/1916 or the interests of the applicant have been substantially prejudiced by a failure to comply with a requirement under the Human Medicines Regulations 2012, SI 2012/1916: reg 322(6)(b).

12 Human Medicines Regulations 2012, SI 2012/1916, reg 322(7).

362. Enforcement authorities. The Secretary of State must enforce or secure the enforcement of the Human Medicines Regulations 2012[1] and the relevant EU provisions in England, Wales and Scotland[2].

The Secretary of State may make arrangements for either or both[3] of the General Pharmaceutical Council[4] or, in respect of each area for which there is a drugs authority[5], the drugs authority for the area, to enforce certain provisions of the Human Medicines Regulations 2012[6] to the extent specified in the arrangements[7].

1 Ie under the Human Medicines Regulations 2012, SI 2012/1916.

2 Human Medicines Regulations 2012, SI 2012/1916, reg 323(1). Nothing in reg 323 confers a function on a person in relation to a hospital (except so much of the hospital as is a registered pharmacy) or so much of any premises as is used as a doctor's or dentist's practice: reg 323(9). For the purposes of Pt 16 (regs 322–334) 'premises' includes any place and a ship, aircraft, hovercraft or vehicle: reg 323(11). As to the meaning of 'registered pharmacy' see PARA 52 note 2.

3 Functions conferred by virtue of the Human Medicines Regulations 2012, SI 2012/1916, reg 323(2), (5) and (6) are to be exercised concurrently with the Secretary of State: reg 323(8).

4 As to the General Pharmaceutical Council see MEDICAL PROFESSIONS vol 74 (2011) PARA 785. The General Pharmaceutical Council must continue to enforce regs 214, 220 (see PARAS 271, 277), and, in their application to or in relation to premises that are registered pharmacies, regs 221, 222 (see PARAS 278, 279): reg 323(3), (7).

5 In each area for which there is a drugs authority, that drugs authority must continue to enforce the Human Medicines Regulations 2012, SI 2012/1916, regs 221, 222 (see PARAS 278, 279) in their application to or in relation to premises that are not registered pharmacies: reg 323(6), (7). For these purposes 'drugs authority' means, in England, in relation to a non-metropolitan county, metropolitan district or London borough, the council of that county, district or borough and, in relation to the City of London (including the Inner Temple and the Middle Temple), the Common Council of the City of London and, in Wales, the council of a county or county borough: reg 323(10)(a), (b).

6 Ie the Human Medicines Regulations 2012, SI 2012/1916, regs 251 (compliance with standards specified in certain publications: see PARA 236) and 255(1)(e) (offences relating to dealings with medicinal products: compliance with standards specified in certain publications: see PARA 379), Pt 13 (packaging and leaflets: see PARA 319 et seq); and Pt 14 Chapter 2 (requirements relating to advertising: see PARA 333 et seq): reg 323(3). A body referred to in reg 323(2) (enforcement in England, Wales and Scotland) may not institute proceedings for an offence under the Human Medicines Regulations 2012, SI 2012/1916 in relation to a contravention of a provision which it may or must enforce by virtue of arrangements made under that regulation unless it has given no less than 28 days' notice of its intention to do so, together with a summary of the facts on which the charges are founded, to the Secretary of State: reg 339(4). A certificate of the Secretary of State that the requirements of reg 339(4) have been complied with is to be conclusive evidence that the requirements have been complied with, and a document purporting to be such a certificate is to be presumed to be such a certificate unless the contrary is proved: reg 339(6).

7 Human Medicines Regulations 2012, SI 2012/1916, reg 323(2). Arrangements made with the General Pharmaceutical Council under reg 323(2)(a) in relation to Part 14 Chapter 2 are to be limited to the enforcement of those provisions in respect of advertisements displayed or representations made on or in any premises where medicinal products are sold by retail or supplied in circumstances corresponding to retail sale, advertisements displayed on any web site associated with such premises and advertisements displayed on, or in close proximity to, a

vending machine in which medicinal products are offered or exposed for sale: reg 323(4). As to the meaning of 'advertisement' see PARA 333. As to the meaning of 'medicinal products' see PARA 25.

363.   Rights of entry.   An inspector[1] may at any reasonable time enter premises:

(1)   in order to determine whether there has been a contravention of a provision of the Human Medicines Regulations 2012[2] which the enforcement authority[3] is required or empowered to enforce[4];

(2)   in order to verify whether the data submitted in respect of an active substance used as a starting material in order to obtain a conformity certificate issued by the European Directorate for the Quality of Medicines and Healthcare ('EDQM') comply with the monographs of the European Pharmacopoeia[5], if the EDQM asks the enforcement authority to do so[6]; and

(3)   for the purposes of any other function of the enforcement authority under the Human Medicines Regulations 2012[7].

A person may not exercise a right of entry under these provisions in relation to premises used only as a private dwelling unless 24 hours' notice has been given to the occupier[8].

A person exercising, or attempting to exercise, a right of entry under these provisions must produce identification on request[9].

An inspector entering any premises by virtue of the above provisions may be accompanied by such persons, and take such equipment, as the inspector thinks appropriate[10].

1   'Inspector' means a person authorised in writing by an enforcement authority for the purposes of the Human Medicines Regulations 2012, SI 2012/1916, Part 16 (enforcement) (and references to 'the enforcement authority', in relation to an inspector, are to the enforcement authority by whom the inspector is so authorised): reg 8(1).
2   Ie the Human Medicines Regulations 2012, SI 2012/1916, reg 323 (see PARA 362).
3   As to the meaning of 'enforcement authority' see PARA 142 note 13.
4   Human Medicines Regulations 2012, SI 2012/1916, reg 325(1)(a).
5   As to the meaning of 'European Pharmacopoeia' see PARA 66 note 21.
6   Human Medicines Regulations 2012, SI 2012/1916, reg 325(1)(b).
7   Human Medicines Regulations 2012, SI 2012/1916, reg 325(1)(c).
8   Human Medicines Regulations 2012, SI 2012/1916, reg 325(2).
9   Human Medicines Regulations 2012, SI 2012/1916, reg 325(3).
10 Human Medicines Regulations 2012, SI 2012/1916, reg 334(1).

·364.   Application for warrant.   A justice of the peace[1] may issue a warrant[2] authorising an inspector to enter premises, by force if necessary if, on sworn information in writing, he is satisfied that[3]:

(1)   there are reasonable grounds for entering the premises by virtue of the enforcement authority's functions under these provisions[4];

(2)   an inspector has a right[5] to enter them[6]; and

(3)   a specified condition is satisfied[7].

The conditions mentioned in head (3) above are that:

(a)   admission to the premises has been refused or is expected to be refused and that notice of the intention to apply for a warrant has been given to the occupier[8];

(b)   that a request for admission, or the giving of notice, would defeat the object of the entry[9];

(c)   that the case is one of urgency[10]; or

(d)   that the premises are unoccupied or the occupier is temporarily absent[11].

An inspector entering any premises by virtue of a warrant under the above provisions may be accompanied by such persons, and take such equipment, as the inspector thinks appropriate[12] and where an inspector enters premises in pursuance of such a warrant he must, if the property is unoccupied or the occupier[13] is temporarily absent, leave the premises as effectively secured against trespass as they were before the inspector entered[14].

1   In relation to England, this includes a district judge (magistrates' courts): Human Medicines Regulations 2012, SI 2012/1916, reg 326(6).
2   A warrant granted under the Human Medicines Regulations 2012, SI 2012/1916, reg 326 continues in force for a period of 30 days beginning with the day on which the warrant is granted: reg 326(5).
3   See the Human Medicines Regulations 2012, SI 2012/1916, reg 326(1), (2).
4   Human Medicines Regulations 2012, SI 2012/1916, reg 326(2)(a).
5   Ie a right to enter by virtue of the Human Medicines Regulations 2012, SI 2012/1916, reg 325 (see PARA 363).
6   Human Medicines Regulations 2012, SI 2012/1916, reg 326(2)(b).
7   Human Medicines Regulations 2012, SI 2012/1916, reg 326(2)(c).
8   Human Medicines Regulations 2012, SI 2012/1916, reg 326(3)(a). In relation to a ship, aircraft, hovercraft or vehicle, references in Pt 16 (regs 322–334) to the occupier of premises are to be read as references to the master, commander or other person in charge of the ship, aircraft, hovercraft or vehicle: reg 326(4).
9   Human Medicines Regulations 2012, SI 2012/1916, reg 326(3)(b).
10 Human Medicines Regulations 2012, SI 2012/1916, reg 326(3)(c).
11 Human Medicines Regulations 2012, SI 2012/1916, reg 326(3)(d).
12 Human Medicines Regulations 2012, SI 2012/1916, reg 334(1).
13 For this purpose 'occupier', in relation to a ship, aircraft, or vehicle, is to be read in accordance with the Human Medicines Regulations 2012, SI 2012/1916, reg 326(4) (see note 8): reg 334(9).
14 Human Medicines Regulations 2012, SI 2012/1916, reg 334(2).

365.   Powers of inspection, sampling and seizure. For certain purposes[1], an inspector[2] may inspect[3]:

(1)   a substance[4] or article appearing to the inspector to be a medicinal product[5];

(2)   an article appearing to the inspector to be a container or package[6] used or intended to be used to contain a medicinal product or a label or leaflet used or intended to be used in connection with a medicinal product[7];

(3)   plant or equipment, including computer equipment, appearing to the inspector to be used or intended to be used in connection with the manufacture, assembly[8], importation[9], sale, supply or advertising of, or wholesale dealing[10] in, medicinal products[11];

(4)   any process of manufacture or assembly of medicinal products[12];

(5)   the way in which medicinal products, or the materials used in the manufacture of medicinal products, are tested at any stage in the process of manufacture or assembly[13];

(6)   information and documents[14] relating to the manufacture, assembly, importation, sale, supply or advertising of, or wholesale dealing in, medicinal products[15]; and

(7)   information and documents relating to the safety of medicinal products, including information and documents relating to compliance with certain conditions[16].

For these purposes the inspector may take or purchase a sample[17] of a substance or article which appears to the inspector to be a medicinal product which is, or is intended to be, sold or supplied; or a substance or article used, or intended to be used, in the manufacture of a medicinal product[18]. The inspector may also require a person carrying on a business which consists of or includes the manufacture, assembly, importation, sale, supply or advertising of, or wholesale dealing in, medicinal products, or a person employed in connection with such a business[19], to produce information or documents relating to the business which are in the person's possession or under the person's control[20].

The inspector may seize and retain a substance or article appearing to the inspector to be a medicinal product if the inspector reasonably believes that an offence under these provisions is being or has been committed in relation to, or by means of, that substance or article[21]. The inspector may, if the inspector reasonably believes that it may be required as evidence in proceedings, seize and retain any document or anything inspected, or discovered in the course of an inspection, under the above provisions[22]. For the purpose of enabling the inspector to seize a substance, article, document or other thing under these provisions, the inspector may, if necessary, require a person who has the authority to do so, to open a container or package, to open a vending machine or to allow the inspector to open a container, package or vending machine[23].

1　Ie:
　　(1)　in order to determine whether there has been a contravention of any provision of the Human Medicines Regulations 2012, SI 2012/1916 which the enforcement authority must or may enforce by virtue of reg 323 (see PARA 362) (reg 327(1)(a));
　　(2)　for the purpose described in reg 325(1)(b) (verification of data at the request of the European Directorate for the Quality of Medicines and Healthcare: see PARA 363) (reg 327(1)(b)); or
　　(3)　in order to verify any statement made by an applicant for a manufacturer's or wholesale dealer's licence, marketing authorisation, certificate of registration, traditional herbal registration or Article 126a authorisation in an application under Parts 3 or 5 to 8 (reg 327(1)(c)).
　　As to the meaning of 'contravention' see PARA 41 note 8. As to the meaning of 'enforcement authority' see PARA 142 note 13. As the meaning of 'manufacturer's licence' see PARA 45. As to the meaning of 'wholesale dealer's licence' see PARA 77. As to the meanings of 'marketing authorisation', 'Article 126a authorisation', 'certificate of registration' and 'traditional herbal registration' see PARA 141 notes 3–6.
2　As to the meaning of 'inspector' see PARA 363 note 1. An inspector exercising, or attempting to exercise, a right under the Human Medicines Regulations 2012, SI 2012/1916, reg 327 must produce identification on request: reg 328(2).
3　See the Human Medicines Regulations 2012, SI 2012/1916, reg 327(1).
4　As to the meaning of 'substance' see PARA 25 note 2.
5　Human Medicines Regulations 2012, SI 2012/1916, reg 327(2)(a). As to the meaning of 'medicinal product' see PARA 25.
6　As to the meaning of 'package' see PARA 51 note 48.
7　Human Medicines Regulations 2012, SI 2012/1916, reg 327(2)(b).
8　As to the meanings of 'manufacture' and 'assemble' see PARA 141 notes 7, 8.
9　As to the meaning of 'import' see PARA 55 note 5.
10　As to wholesale dealing see PARA 77 et seq.
11　Human Medicines Regulations 2012, SI 2012/1916, reg 327(2)(c).
12　Human Medicines Regulations 2012, SI 2012/1916, reg 327(2)(d).
13　Human Medicines Regulations 2012, SI 2012/1916, reg 327(2)(e).
14　The information and documents referred to in the Human Medicines Regulations 2012, SI 2012/1916, reg 327 include any that are stored electronically: reg 327(9).
15　Human Medicines Regulations 2012, SI 2012/1916, reg 327(2)(f). The inspector may take copies of information or documents inspected under reg 327(2)(f) or (g) or produced under reg 327(4): reg 327(5).
16　Human Medicines Regulations 2012, SI 2012/1916, reg 327(2)(g). The conditions mentioned in the text are (1) conditions imposed under any of regs 59 (conditions of UK marketing authorisation: general: see PARA 160), 60 (conditions of UK marketing authorisation: exceptional circumstances: see PARA 161), 61 (conditions of UK marketing authorisation: new

obligations post-authorisation: see PARA 162) or 105 (conditions of certificate of registration: see PARA 191); (2) the requirements of Pt 11 (pharmacovigilance: see PARAS 242–269); (3) obligations and conditions under Council Regulation (EC) 726/2004 (OJ L136, 30.4.2004, p 1) laying down Community procedures for the authorisation and supervision of medicinal products for human and veterinary use and establishing a European Medicines Agency, arts 10a(1), 14(7) or 14(8); and (4) the requirements of Chapter 3 (pharmacovigilance) of Title II: Human Medicines Regulations 2012, SI 2012/1916, reg 327(2).

17 The provisions of the Human Medicines Regulations 2012, SI 2012/1916, Sch 31 have effect in relation to samples obtained by inspectors on behalf of enforcement authorities: reg 328(3).

18 Human Medicines Regulations 2012, SI 2012/1916, reg 327(3).

19 As to the meaning of 'business' see PARA 52 note 10.

20 Human Medicines Regulations 2012, SI 2012/1916, reg 327(4).

21 Human Medicines Regulations 2012, SI 2012/1916, reg 327(6). Where an inspector seizes a substance, article, document or other thing under reg 327(6) or (7) (powers of inspection, sampling and seizure) he must, where practicable, inform the person, if any, from whom it was seized and the occupier of the premises from which it was seized; or, in relation to anything seized from a vending machine, he must inform the person whose name and address are stated on the machine to be those of the machine's owner or, if no name and address are stated, the occupier of the premises on which the machine stands or to which it is affixed: reg 328(1).

22 Human Medicines Regulations 2012, SI 2012/1916, reg 327(7).

23 See the Human Medicines Regulations 2012, SI 2012/1916, reg 327(8).

366. Application of sampling procedure to substance or article seized. Where an inspector[1] seizes a substance[2] or article under his powers of inspection, sampling and seizure[3], on request[4], he must either set aside a sample[5] of the substance or article seized or treat the substance or article as a sample, whichever seems more appropriate having regard to the nature of the substance or article[6].

1 As to the meaning of 'inspector' see PARA 363 note 1.

2 As to the meaning of 'substance' see PARA 25 note 2.

3 Ie his powers under the Human Medicines Regulations 2012, SI 2012/1916, reg 327 (see PARA 365).

4 A request is made if it is made by a person ('P') who is entitled to be informed of the seizure under the Human Medicines Regulations 2012, SI 2012/1916, reg 328 and it is made either at the time of the seizure or within the period of 21 days beginning with the day immediately after the day on which P is informed of the seizure: reg 329(3).

5 An inspector is not required by the Human Medicines Regulations 2012, SI 2012/1916, reg 329(2) to set aside a sample, or to treat a substance or article as a sample, if the nature of the substance or article is such that it is not reasonably practicable to do either of those things: reg 329(4). An inspector must divide a sample under reg 329(2) into three parts, mark each part, seal or fasten each part and supply one part to P: reg 329(5).

6 Human Medicines Regulations 2012, SI 2012/1916, reg 329(1), (2). Schedule 31 paras 10–12 apply to a sample under reg 329 as they apply to a sample obtained as mentioned in Sch 31 para 1, but as if references to the preceding provisions of Sch 31 were references to the preceding provisions of reg 329, references to a sampling officer were references to an inspector who seized a substance or article under reg 327 (powers of inspection, sampling and seizure) and a reference to the relevant enforcement authority were a reference to the authority by which the inspector is authorised: reg 329(6).

367. Analysis of samples: other cases. Where a person other than an inspector[1] or a person authorised by an enforcement authority[2] has purchased a medicinal product[3], he may submit a sample of the medicinal product for analysis to the public analyst[4] for the area in which the product was purchased or, if for the time being there is no public analyst for the area, to the public analyst for another area[5].

A public analyst to whom such a sample is submitted must analyse the sample, or cause it to be analysed, as soon as practicable, but this is subject to the following provisions[6].

If the public analyst to whom a sample is submitted thinks that a proper analysis cannot be carried out for any reason, he must send it to the public analyst for some other area, who must as soon as practicable analyse the sample, or cause it to be analysed[7].

A public analyst to whom a sample is submitted or sent under these provisions may demand payment in advance of the required fee, and if payment in advance is demanded may refuse to carry out the analysis until the fee is paid[8].

1 As to the meaning of 'inspector' see PARA 363 note 1.
2 As to the meaning of 'enforcement authority' see PARA 142 note 13.
3 Human Medicines Regulations 2012, SI 2012/1916, reg 330(1). As to the meaning of 'medicinal product' see PARA 25. Schedule 31 paras 21–23 have effect in relation to a certificate issued under this regulation as they have effect in relation to a certificate issued under Sch 31 para 19: reg 330(8).
4 As to the meaning of 'public analyst' for these purposes see the Food Safety Act 1990 s 27; and FOOD vol 18(2) (Reissue) PARA 268: Human Medicines Regulations 2012, SI 2012/1916, reg 330(9).
5 Human Medicines Regulations 2012, SI 2012/1916, reg 330(2). Schedule 31 paras 2–13 have effect, in relation to a person proposing to submit a sample in pursuance of reg 330(2), as if in that Sch 31 references to the sampling officer were references to that person: reg 330(3). A public analyst who has analysed a sample or caused it to be analysed must issue a certificate specifying the result of the analysis to the person by whom the sample was submitted under reg 330(2): reg 330(7).
6 Human Medicines Regulations 2012, SI 2012/1916, reg 330(4).
7 Human Medicines Regulations 2012, SI 2012/1916, reg 330(5).
8 Human Medicines Regulations 2012, SI 2012/1916, reg 330(6).

368. Findings and reports of inspections. If the outcome of the inspection of information and documents relating to safety[1] is that the holder of a marketing authorisation or traditional herbal registration[2] does not comply with the pharmacovigilance system[3] as described in the pharmacovigilance system master file[4], or other provisions relating to pharmacovigilance[5], the enforcement authority[6] must bring the deficiencies to the attention of the holder, give the holder the opportunity to submit comments and inform the other EEA states, the European Medicines Agency[7] and the European Commission[8].

After every inspection carried out in accordance with provisions relating to rights of entry[9] and the powers of inspection, sampling and seizure[10] in connection with medicinal products[11] other than registrable homoeopathic medicinal products[12], the enforcement authority must report on whether the activities to which the inspection relates comply with such of specified provisions[13] as apply to those activities[14].

The enforcement authority must, before adopting the report, communicate the content of the report to the person to whose activities the inspection relates and give that person the opportunity to submit comments[15].

1 Ie as referred to in the Human Medicines Regulations 2012, SI 2012/1916, reg 327(2)(g) (see PARA 365).
2 As to the meaning of 'marketing authorisation' see PARA 141 note 3. As to the meaning of 'traditional herbal registration' see PARA 141 note 5.
3 As to the meaning of 'pharmacovigilance system' see PARA 243 note 2.
4 As to the meaning of 'pharmacovigilance system master file' see PARA 246 note 3.
5 Ie any provision of the Human Medicines Regulations 2012, SI 2012/1916, Pt 11 (regs 177–212).
6 As to the meaning of 'enforcement authority' see PARA 142 note 13.
7 As to the European Medicines Agency see PARA 14.
8 Human Medicines Regulations 2012, SI 2012/1916, reg 331(1). Regulation 331(1) is without prejudice to reg 331(3) and (5); reg 331(2).

9 Ie in accordance with the Human Medicines Regulations 2012, SI 2012/1916, reg 325 (see PARA 363).
10 Ie in accordance with the Human Medicines Regulations 2012, SI 2012/1916, reg 327 (see PARA 365).
11 As to the meaning of 'medicinal product' see PARA 25.
12 As to the meaning of 'registrable homoeopathic medicinal products' see PARA 187 note 1.
13 Those provisions are: (1) Commission Directive (EC) 2003/94 (OJ L262, 14.10.2003, p 22–26) laying down the principles and guidelines of good manufacturing practice in respect of medicinal products for human use and investigational medicinal products for human use ('the Good Manufacturing Practice Directive') (see PARA 12) and any principles or guidelines of good manufacturing practice referred to in Council Directive (EC) 2001/83 (OJ L311, 28.11.2001, p 67) on the Community code relating to medicinal products for human use, art 47; (2) the guidelines on good distribution practice referred to in art 84; and (3) in the case of the holder of a marketing authorisation or traditional herbal registration Council Regulation (EC) 726/2004 (OJ L136, 30.4.2004, p 1) laying down Community procedures for the authorisation and supervision of medicinal products for human and veterinary use and establishing a European Medicines Agency, Pt 11 (pharmacovigilance) and Chapter 3 (pharmacovigilance) of Title II (authorisation and supervision of medicinal products for human use): Human Medicines Regulations 2012, SI 2012/1916, reg 331(4).
14 Human Medicines Regulations 2012, SI 2012/1916, reg 331(3).
15 Human Medicines Regulations 2012, SI 2012/1916, reg 331(5).

369. Restrictions on disclosure of information. A person ('P') must not disclose to another person, otherwise than in the performance of P's functions: (1) any information relating to a manufacturing process or trade secret obtained by P on premises which P has entered[1] by virtue of provisions giving him the right of entry or of a warrant; or (2) any information obtained by P or given to P in pursuance of the Human Medicines Regulations 2012[2].

This does not apply if P is, or is acting on behalf of, a public authority for the purposes of the Freedom of Information Act 2000 and the information is not held by the authority on behalf of another person[3].

1 Ie by virtue of the Human Medicines Regulations 2012, SI 2012/1916, reg 325 (see PARA 363) or a warrant under reg 326 (see PARA 364).
2 Human Medicines Regulations 2012, SI 2012/1916, reg 332(1). It is an offence to breach reg 332(1) see PARA 371.
3 Human Medicines Regulations 2012, SI 2012/1916, reg 332(2).

370. Protection for inspectors. An inspector[1] is not personally liable in respect of any act done in the execution, or purported execution, of a function under the Human Medicines Regulations 2012[2] and within the scope of the inspector's employment by an enforcement authority[3] (or, where the inspector is not employed by the authority, the scope of the inspector's authorisation), provided that the act was done in the honest belief that the Human Medicines Regulations 2012[4] required or permitted it[5].

Where an action is brought against an inspector in respect of an act falling within the above provisions the enforcement authority may indemnify the inspector against any damages, costs or expenses incurred, if the authority is satisfied that the inspector honestly believed that the Human Medicines Regulations 2012[6] required or permitted the act[7].

1 As to the meaning of 'inspector' see PARA 363 note 1. For these purposes a reference to an inspector includes a reference to an employee of the licensing authority who accompanies an inspector pursuant to the Human Medicines Regulations 2012, SI 2012/1916, reg 334(1) (see PARA 363): reg 333(4). As to the meaning of 'licensing authority' see PARA 35 note 1.
2 Ie the Human Medicines Regulations 2012, SI 2012/1916.
3 As to the meaning of 'enforcement authority' see PARA 142 note 13.
4 See note 2.

5   Human Medicines Regulations 2012, SI 2012/1916, reg 333(1).
6   See note 2.
7   Human Medicines Regulations 2012, SI 2012/1916, reg 333(2). This applies in a case where the person is not legally entitled to require an indemnity from the enforcement authority: reg 333(3).

371. Offences related to enforcement. It is an offence[1] for a person:

(1)   intentionally to obstruct an inspector[2];

(2)   intentionally to fail to comply with a requirement properly made[3] by an inspector under his powers of inspection, sampling and seizure[4]; or

(3)   without reasonable cause, to fail to give an inspector any other assistance or information which the inspector may reasonably require in order to perform a function under the Human Medicines Regulations 2012[5].

A person who breaches the prohibition[6] on disclosure of information is guilty of an offence[7].

1   A person guilty of an offence under the Human Medicines Regulations 2012, SI 2012/1916, reg 334(3) is liable on summary conviction to a fine not exceeding level 3 on the standard scale: reg 334(4). As to the standard scale see SENTENCING AND DISPOSITION OF OFFENDERS vol 92 (2010) PARA 142.
2   Human Medicines Regulations 2012, SI 2012/1916, reg 334(3)(a). As to the meaning of 'inspector' see PARA 363 note 1.
3   Ie made under the Human Medicines Regulations 2012, SI 2012/1916, reg 327 (see PARA 365). Nothing in reg 334 is to be read as requiring a person to answer a question or to give information if doing so might incriminate that person or the spouse or civil partner of that person: reg 334(8).
4   Human Medicines Regulations 2012, SI 2012/1916, reg 334(3)(b).
5   Human Medicines Regulations 2012, SI 2012/1916, reg 334(3)(c). A person who knowingly makes a false statement in giving information as mentioned in head (3) in the text is guilty of an offence: reg 334(5). A person who is guilty of such an offence under is liable, on summary conviction, to a fine not exceeding the statutory maximum or, on conviction on indictment, to a fine or to imprisonment for a term not exceeding two years, or to both: reg 334(7). As to the statutory maximum see SENTENCING AND DISPOSITION OF OFFENDERS vol 92 (2010) PARA 140.
6   Ie the prohibition in the Human Medicines Regulations 2012, SI 2012/1916, reg 332(1) (see PARA 369).
7   Human Medicines Regulations 2012, SI 2012/1916, erg 334(6). A person who is guilty of such an offence under is liable, on summary conviction, to a fine not exceeding the statutory maximum or, on conviction on indictment, to a fine or to imprisonment for a term not exceeding two years, or to both: reg 334(7).

(iii) Offences and Proceedings

372. Contravention due to another's default. Where a contravention[1] by any person[2] of certain provisions of the Medicines Act 1968[3] constitutes an offence under the Act and is due to an act or default of another person, then, whether proceedings are taken against the first-mentioned person or not, that other person may be charged with and convicted of that offence and is liable on conviction to the same punishment as might have been imposed on the first-mentioned person if he had been convicted of the offence[4].

Where a person charged with an offence under the Act in respect of a contravention of any of those provisions proves[5] to the satisfaction of the court that he exercised all due diligence to secure that the provision in question would not be contravened[6], and that contravention was due to the act or default of another person[7], the first-mentioned person, if he has given the required notice or obtained the leave of the court[8], must be acquitted of the offence[9].

Where a contravention of certain provisions under the Human Medicines Regulations 2012[10] constitutes an offence and a person ('A') contravenes the provision by reason of the act or omission of another person ('B'), B may be charged with and convicted of the offence, whether or not proceedings are also brought against A[11]. If B is convicted B is liable to the same punishment as would have been imposed on A if A had been convicted of the offence[12].

If A is charged with the offence it is a defence for A to prove on the balance of probabilities that A exercised all due diligence to avoid contravening the provision and the contravention was due to the act or omission of B[13].

1   As to the meaning of 'contravention' see PARA 41 note 8 (definition applied by the Medicines Act 1968 s 132(1) (substituted by SI 2012/1916)).
2   As to the meaning of 'person' see PARA 45 note 2.
3   Ie the Medicines Act 1968 ss 63, 64 (see PARAS 234–235), ss 87–88 (see PARAS 314, 331) and the provisions of any regulations made under any of those provisions: s 121(4) (amended by SI 2012/1916).
4   Medicines Act 1968 s 121(1).
5   As to the standard of proof on the accused see CRIMINAL PROCEDURE vol 28 (2010) PARA 469.
6   Medicines Act 1968 s 121(2)(a).
7   Medicines Act 1968 s 121(2)(b).
8   A person is not entitled, without the leave of the court, to rely on this defence unless, not later than seven clear days before the date of the hearing, he has served on the prosecutor written notice giving such information, identifying or assisting in the identification of the other person in question, as was then in his possession: Medicines Act 1968 s 121(3).
9   Medicines Act 1968 s 121(2).
10   Ie the Human Medicines Regulations 2012, SI 2012/1916, reg 251 (compliance with standards specified in certain publications: see PARA 236), regs 268 and 269 (offences relating to packaging and package leaflets: see PARA 329), reg 273 (child resistant containers for regulated medicinal products: see PARA 315), reg 275 (colouring of aspirin and paracetamol products for children: see PARA 332), any prohibition or requirement in Pt 14 Chapter 2 (advertising: see PARA 333 et seq) and regs 305(4) and 306(7), (8) (notices not to publish, or to cease to publish, an advertisement: see PARA 347): reg 335(6).
11   Human Medicines Regulations 2012, SI 2012/1916, reg 335(1), (2).
12   Human Medicines Regulations 2012, SI 2012/1916, reg 335(3).
13   Human Medicines Regulations 2012, SI 2012/1916, reg 335(4). A may not rely on the defence in reg 335(4) unless not later than seven clear days before the date of the hearing A serves on the prosecutor a notice in writing of any information held by A which identifies, or assists in identifying, B: reg 335(5).

373. Warranty as a defence. In any proceedings for an offence under the Medicines Act 1968[1] in respect of a contravention[2] of certain provisions[3], it is a defence for the defendant to prove[4]: (1) that he purchased the substance[5] or article to which the contravention relates in the United Kingdom[6] as being a substance or article which could be lawfully sold, supplied or offered or exposed for sale, or could be lawfully sold, supplied or offered or exposed for sale under the name or description or for the purpose under or for which he sold, supplied or offered or exposed it for sale, and with a written[7] warranty[8] to that effect[9]; (2) that at the time of the commission of the alleged offence he had no reason to believe that it was otherwise[10]; and (3) that the substance or article was then in the same state as when he purchased it[11].

A defendant may not rely on this defence unless, not later than three clear days before the date of the hearing, he has sent to the prosecutor a copy of the warranty with a notice stating that he intends to rely on it and specifying the name and address of the person[12] from whom he received it, and has also sent a like notice to that person[13]. The person by whom the warranty is alleged to have been given is entitled to appear at the hearing and give evidence[14].

If a defendant in any such proceedings for an offence wilfully applies to any substance or article a warranty given in relation to a different substance or article[15], or a certificate of analysis[16] which relates to a sample of a different substance or article[17], he is guilty of an offence[18]. A person who, in respect of any substance or article sold by him in respect of which a warranty might be pleaded[19], gives to the purchaser a false warranty in writing is guilty of an offence unless he proves that when he gave the warranty he had reason to believe that the statement or description contained in it was accurate[20]. Any person guilty of either such offence is liable to a penalty[21].

If proceedings are brought against a person ('the defendant')[22] for an offence under the Human Medicines Regulations 2012[23] in respect of a contravention of certain provisions[24], it is a defence for the defendant to prove that: (a) the substance or article to which the contravention relates (the 'relevant substance or article') was sold to the defendant in the United Kingdom as a substance or article which could be lawfully sold, supplied or offered for sale or supply or a substance or article which could be lawfully sold, supplied or offered for sale or supply under the name or description or for the purpose under or for which it was sold[25]; (b) the relevant substance or article was sold with a written warranty[26] certifying a matter specified in head (a), and that if the warranty were true the alleged offence would not have been committed[27]; (c) at the time of the commission of the alleged offence the defendant had no reason to believe that the matter certified in the warranty was otherwise[28]; and (d) at the time of the commission of the alleged offence the relevant substance or article was in the same state as when the defendant purchased it[29].

The person by whom the warranty is alleged to have been given is entitled to appear at the hearing and to give evidence[30].

1 As to the meaning of 'offence under the Medicines Act 1968' see PARA 356 note 17.
2 As to the meaning of 'contravention' see PARA 41 note 8 (definition applied by the Medicines Act 1968 s 132(1) (substituted by SI 2012/1916)).
3 Ie the Medicines Act 1968 ss 63(b), 64 (see PARA 234) and s 88 (see PARA 331) and the provisions of any regulations made under any of those provisions: s 122(1), (2) (amended by SI 2006/2407, SI 2012/1916).
4 As to the standard of proof see CRIMINAL PROCEDURE vol 28 (2010) PARA 469.
5 As to the meaning of 'substance' see PARA 25 note 2 (definition applied by the Medicines Act 1968 s 132(1) (as substituted: see note 2)).
6 As to the meaning of 'United Kingdom' see PARA 20 note 4.
7 As to the meaning of 'written' see PARA 507 note 2.
8 A name or description entered in an invoice is deemed to be a written warranty that the article or substance to which the name or description applies can be sold, supplied, or offered or exposed for sale under that name or description by any person without contravening the provisions mentioned in note 3: Medicines Act 1968 s 122(6).
9 Medicines Act 1968 s 122(1)(a).
10 Medicines Act 1968 s 122(1)(b).
11 Medicines Act 1968 s 122(1)(c). Where the defendant is an employee of the person who purchased the substance or article under the warranty, he is entitled to rely upon s 122 in the same way as his employer would have been entitled to do if he had been the defendant: s 122(4).
12 As to the meaning of 'person' see PARA 45 note 2.
13 Medicines Act 1968 s 122(3).
14 Medicines Act 1968 s 122(5). The court may, if it thinks fit, adjourn the hearing to enable him to do so: s 122(5).
15 Medicines Act 1968 s 123(1)(a).
16 Ie a certificate given under the Medicines Act 1968 s 115 or Sch 3 para 19: see PARA 357.
17 Medicines Act 1968 s 123(1)(b) (amended by SI 2012/1916).
18 Medicines Act 1968 s 123(1).
19 Ie under the Medicines Act 1968 s 122.

20   Medicines Act 1968 s 123(2). Where in any such proceedings as are mentioned in s 122(1) (see the text and notes 1–11) the defendant successfully relies on a warranty given to him or to his employer, proceedings for an offence under s 123(2) in respect of the warranty may, at the prosecutor's option, be taken either before a court having jurisdiction in the place where a sample of the substance or article in question was procured or before a court having jurisdiction in the place where the warranty was given: s 123(3).

21   Such a person is liable on summary conviction to a fine not exceeding the prescribed sum (Medicines Act 1968 s 123(4)(a) (amended by virtue of the Magistrates' Courts Act 1980 s 32(2))), or on conviction on indictment to a fine or to imprisonment for a term not exceeding two years or to both (Medicines Act 1968 s 123(4)(b)). As to the prescribed sum see SENTENCING AND DISPOSITION OF OFFENDERS vol 92 (2010) PARA 141.

22   Where the defendant is an employee of the person who purchased the substance or article under the warranty, the defendant is entitled to rely on the provisions of this regulation in the same way as the employer: Human Medicines Regulations 2012, SI 2012/1916, reg 336(5).

23   Ie under the Human Medicines Regulations 2012, SI 2012/1916.

24   Ie the Human Medicines Regulations 2012, SI 2012/1916, reg 251 (compliance with standards specified in certain publications: see PARA 236), regs 268 and 269 (offences relating to packaging and package leaflets: see PARA 329), reg 273 (child resistant containers for regulated medicinal products: see PARA 315) and reg 275 (colouring of aspirin and paracetamol products for children: see PARA 332): reg 336(3).

25   Human Medicines Regulations 2012, SI 2012/1916, reg 336(1), (2)(a). A person who intentionally or recklessly gives a purchaser a false warranty certifying a matter specified in reg 336(2)(a) is guilty of an offence see PARA 374.

26   A warranty is not to be a defence under the Human Medicines Regulations 2012, SI 2012/1916 unless, no later than 3 clear days before the date of the hearing, the defendant sends to the prosecutor, and to the person who gave the warranty to the defendant a copy of the warranty, a notice stating that the defendant intends to rely on it and the name and address of the person from whom the defendant received the warranty: reg 336(4). For the purposes of reg 336, a name or description entered in an invoice is to be deemed to be a written warranty that the article or substance to which the name or description applies can be sold, supplied, or offered or exposed for sale under that name or description without contravening a provision mentioned in reg 336(3): reg 336(8).

27   Human Medicines Regulations 2012, SI 2012/1916, reg 336(2)(b).

28   Human Medicines Regulations 2012, SI 2012/1916, reg 336(2)(c).

29   Human Medicines Regulations 2012, SI 2012/1916, reg 336(2)(d).

30   Human Medicines Regulations 2012, SI 2012/1916, reg 336(6). The court may adjourn the hearing in order to enable a person to appear and give evidence in accordance with reg 336(6): reg 336(7).

374.   Offences relating to warranties and certificates. It is an offence[1] for a defendant in proceedings for an offence under the Human Medicines Regulations 2012[2] in respect of a contravention[3] of certain provisions[4]:

(1)   intentionally to apply a warranty given in relation to one substance or article to a different substance or article[5]; or

(2)   intentionally to apply to one substance or article a certificate[6] in relation to a sample of a different substance or article[7].

A person who intentionally or recklessly gives a purchaser a false warranty certifying a specified matter[8] is guilty of an offence[9].

1   A person guilty of an offence under the Human Medicines Regulations 2012, SI 2012/1916, reg 337 is liable, on summary conviction, to a fine not exceeding the statutory maximum or, on conviction on indictment, to a fine or to imprisonment for a term not exceeding two years, or to both: reg 337(5). As to the statutory maximum see SENTENCING AND DISPOSITION OF OFFENDERS vol 92 (2010) PARA 140.

2   Ie under the Human Medicines Regulations 2012, SI 2012/1916.

3   As to the meaning of 'contravention' see PARA 41 note 8.

4   Ie the provisions mentioned in the Human Medicines Regulations 2012, SI 2012/1916, reg 336(3) (see PARA 373 note 24).

5   Human Medicines Regulations 2012, SI 2012/1916, reg 337(1)(a).

6   Ie a certificate issued under the Human Medicines Regulations 2012, SI 2012/1916, reg 330 (see PARA 367) or Sch 31 para 19.

7   Human Medicines Regulations 2012, SI 2012/1916, reg 337(1)(b).

8   Ie a matter specified under the Human Medicines Regulations 2012, SI 2012/1916, reg 336(2) (see PARA 373).

9   Human Medicines Regulations 2012, SI 2012/1916, reg 337(2). If the defendant in proceedings for an offence under the Human Medicines Regulations 2012, SI 2012/1916 in respect of a contravention of a provision mentioned in reg 336(3) (see PARA 373 note 24) relies successfully on a warranty given to the defendant or to the defendant's employer, proceedings for an offence under reg 337(2) may be brought in accordance with reg 336(4): reg 337(3). Such proceedings may be brought, as the prosecutor chooses before a court which has jurisdiction in the place where a sample of the substance or article to which the warranty relates was taken or before a court which has jurisdiction in the place where the warranty was given: reg 337(4).

375.   Offences by bodies corporate.   Where an offence under the Medicines Act 1968[1] committed by a body corporate[2] is proved to have been committed with the consent and connivance of, or to be attributable to any neglect on the part of, any director[3], manager, secretary or other similar officer[4] of the body corporate, or any person who was purporting to act in such capacity, he as well as the body corporate is liable to be proceeded against and punished accordingly[5].

If an offence under the Human Medicines Regulations 2012[6] committed by a body corporate is proved to have been committed with the consent or connivance of, or to be attributable to neglect on the part of, an officer[7] of the body corporate[8], or a person purporting to act as an officer of the body corporate, that officer or person (as well as the body corporate) is guilty of the offence and is liable to be proceeded against and punished accordingly[9].

1   As to the meaning of 'offence under the Medicines Act 1968' see PARA 356 note 17.

2   As to bodies corporate see COMPANIES; CORPORATIONS.

3   'Director', in relation to a body corporate whose affairs are managed by its members and which was established by or under any enactment for the purpose of carrying on under national ownership any industry or part of an industry or undertaking, means a member of that body corporate: Medicines Act 1968 s 124(3).

4   In relation to a body corporate carrying on a retail pharmacy business as mentioned in the Medicines Act 1968 s 71(1) (see MEDICAL PROFESSIONS vol 74 (2011) PARA 801), s 124(1) has effect in relation to a person who (not being such an officer mentioned as is mentioned in s 124(1)) is the superintendent referred to in s 124(1) or, at any premises where the business is carried on, is the pharmacist referred to in s 124(4)(b) who acts under the directions of the superintendent: s 124(2) (amended by the Health Act 2006 s 28(2)). As to the meaning of 'pharmacist' see PARA 52 note 5 (definition applied by the Medicines Act 1968 s 132(1) (substituted by SI 2012/1916)).

5   Human Medicines Act 1968 s 124(1).

6   Ie the Human Medicines Regulations 2012, SI 2012/1916.

7   For this purpose 'officer' in relation to a body corporate means a director, secretary or other similar officer of the body corporate: Human Medicines Regulations 2012, SI 2012/1916, reg 338(4).

8   If the affairs of a body corporate are managed by its members, the Human Medicines Regulations 2012, SI 2012/1916, reg 338(1) applies in relation to the acts and omissions of a member in connection with the member's functions of management as it applies to an officer of the body corporate: reg 338(2).

9   Human Medicines Regulations 2012, SI 2012/1916, reg 338(1).

376.   Prosecutions.   Neither the General Pharmaceutical Council[1] nor any of certain bodies[2] may institute proceedings in respect of a contravention[3] of any provisions which it has a power or duty to enforce[4] unless it has given to the appropriate minister[5] not less than 28 days' notice of its intention to institute proceedings together with a summary of the facts upon which the charges are founded[6].

A magistrates' court may try an information for an offence under the Medicines Act 1968[7] if the information was laid at any time within 12 months[8] from the commission of the offence[9].

A magistrates' court in England or Wales may try an information for an offence under the Human Medicines Regulations 2012[10] that is triable only summarily if the information was laid at any time within the period of 12 months beginning with the commission of the offence[11].

1   As to the General Pharmaceutical Council see MEDICAL PROFESSIONS vol 74 (2011) PARA 784 et seq.
2   Ie the bodies specified in the Medicines Act 1968 s 108(2) (see PARA 354).
3   As to the meaning of 'contravention' see PARA 41 note 8 (definition applied by the Medicines Act 1968 s 132(1) (substituted by SI 2012/1916)).
4   Ie provisions which by virtue of the Medicines Act 1968 s 108(2), the Council or body has a power or duty to enforce: see PARA 354.
5   'The appropriate minister' means the minister who in accordance with the Medicines Act 1968 s 108 (see PARA 354), has a concurrent duty to enforce the provision: s 125(5).
6   Medicines Act 1968 s 125(4) (amended by SI 2006/2407, SI 2012/1916). A certificate of the appropriate minister is conclusive evidence that these provisions have been complied with: Medicines Act 1968 s 125(7). Any document purporting to be such a certificate and to be signed by or on behalf of the minister is presumed to be such a certificate unless the contrary is proved: s 125(7).
7   As to the meaning of 'offence under the Medicines Act 1968' see PARA 356 note 17.
8   As to the meaning of 'month' see PARA 43 note 3.
9   Medicines Act 1968 s 125(1). This is so notwithstanding the provisions of the Magistrates' Courts Act 1980 s 127(1) (see MAGISTRATES vol 71 (2013) PARA 526): Medicines Act 1968 s 125(1) (amended by the Magistrates' Courts Act 1980 s 154, Sch 7 para 77).
10 Ie the Human Medicines Regulations 2012, SI 2012/1916.
11 Human Medicines Regulations 2012, SI 2012/1916, reg 339(1).

377. Presumptions.   Certain presumptions arise for the purposes of any proceedings under the Medicines Act 1968 for an offence consisting of offering[1] an adulterated medicinal product for sale[2]. Where it is proved that the medicinal product[3] in question was found on a vehicle from which medicinal products are sold, it must be presumed, unless the contrary is proved[4], that the person in charge of the vehicle[5] offered that medicinal product for sale[6].

For the purposes of any proceedings for an offence consisting of a contravention[7] of certain provisions[8] so far as they relate to a person's having any medicinal product in his possession for the purpose of sale or supply, where it is proved that the product was found on premises at which the person charged carries on a business[9] consisting of or including the sale or supply of medicinal products, it must be presumed, unless the contrary is proved, that he had that medicinal product in his possession for the purpose of sale or supply[10].

Certain presumptions apply for the purposes of proceedings under the Human Medicines Regulations 2012[11] for an offence[12] consisting of offering a medicinal product for sale by retail[13]. If it is proved that the medicinal product in question was found on a vehicle from which medicinal products are sold, it is to be presumed, unless the contrary is proved, that the person in charge of the vehicle offered the medicinal product for sale[14].

For the purposes of proceedings under the Human Medicines Regulations 2012[15] for an offence consisting of a contravention of certain provisions[16], where it is proved that the medicinal product in question was found on premises at which the person charged with the offence carries on a business consisting of or including the sale or supply of medicinal products, it is to be presumed, unless the contrary is proved, that the person charged possessed the medicinal product for the purpose of sale or supply[17].

1   Ie in contravention of the Medicines Act 1968 s 63(b): see PARA 234.
2   Medicines Act 1968 s 126(1)(c).
3   As to the meaning of 'medicinal product' see the Human Medicines Regulations 2012, SI 2012/1916, reg 2(1); and PARA 25 (definition applied by the Medicines Act 1968 s 132(1) (substituted by SI 2012/1916)).
4   As to the standard of proof see CRIMINAL PROCEDURE vol 28 (2010) PARA 469.
5   In general, a person who takes a motor vehicle on a road remains in charge of it until he puts it into the charge of some other person: *Haines v Roberts* [1953] 1 All ER 344, [1953] 1 WLR 309, DC.
6   Medicines Act 1968 s 126(1) (amended by SI 2006/2407, SI 2012/1916).
7   As to the meaning of 'contravention' see PARA 41 note 8.
8   Ie the Medicines Act 1968 s 63(b) (see PARA 234), s 87(2), 88(3) (see PARAS 314, 331): s 126(3) (amended by SI 2006/2407, SI 2012/1916).
9   As to the meaning of 'business' see PARA 52 note 10.
10 Medicines Act 1968 s 126(2) (amended by SI 2006/2407).
11 Ie the Human Medicines Regulations 2012, SI 2012/1916.
12 Ie in contravention of the Human Medicines Regulations 2012, SI 2012/1916, reg 220 (see PARA 277) or reg 221 (see PARA 278).
13 Human Medicines Regulations 2012, SI 2012/1916, reg 340(1).
14 Human Medicines Regulations 2012, SI 2012/1916, reg 340(2).
15 See note 11.
16 The provisions referred to in the text are the Human Medicines Regulations 2012, SI 2012/1916, reg 268 (offences relating to packaging and package leaflets: authorisation holders: see PARA 329), 269 (offences relating to packaging and package leaflets: other persons: see PARA 329) and 276 (offences: requirements relating to child safety: see PARAS 315, 332) to the extent that they establish an offence based on possession of a medicinal product for the purpose of sale or supply: reg 340(5).
17 See the Human Medicines Regulations 2012, SI 2012/1916, reg 340(4), (5).

378.   Prohibitions concerning traceability of treatment with advanced therapy medicinal products.   A person may not treat a patient with an advanced therapy medicinal product[1] if there is not a system in place for patient and product traceability in relation to such treatment containing sufficient detail to enable the linking of the product to the patient who received it and vice versa[2].

Nor may a person treat a patient with an advanced therapy medicinal product if the treatment involves a product which contains human cells or tissues and such a traceability system is not complementary to, and compatible with, certain requirements[3].

Breach of these provisions[4] is an offence[5] but it is a defence if the person who treats a patient was assured in writing before the treatment was given that a system of traceability as described above was in place in relation to the treatment given by that person[6].

A person may not give an assurance in writing to a person ('P') who treats a patient with an advanced therapy medicinal product that a system of traceability as described above is in place in relation to treatment with an advanced therapy medicinal product given by P if no such system is in place[7].

Breach of the above provisions[8] is an offence[9].

1   'Advanced therapy medicinal product' means a medicinal product described in European Parliament and Council Regulation (EC) 1394/2007 (OJ L324, 10.12.2007, p 121) on advanced therapy medicinal products, art 2(1)(a) (see PARA 23): Human Medicines Regulations 2012, SI 2012/1916, reg 8(1).
2   Human Medicines Regulations 2012, SI 2012/1916, reg 254(1).
3   Human Medicines Regulations 2012, SI 2012/1916, reg 254(2). The requirements mentioned in the text are Council Directive (EC) 2004/23 (OJ L102, 7.4.2004, p 48) on setting standards of quality and safety for the donation, procurement, testing, processing, preservation, storage and distribution of human tissues and cells, arts 8, 14 as regards human cells and tissues other than blood cells and Council Directive (EC) 2002/98 (OJ L33, 8.2.2003, p 30) setting standards of

quality and safety for the collection, testing, processing, storage and distribution of human blood and blood components, arts 14, 24 (see PARA 13).
4   Ie breach of the Human Medicines Regulations 2012, SI 2012/1916, reg 254.
5   See PARA 379.
6   See the Human Medicines Regulations 2012, SI 2012/1916, reg 254(3).
7   Human Medicines Regulations 2012, SI 2012/1916, reg 254(4).
8   Ie breach of the Human Medicines Regulations 2012, SI 2012/1916, reg 254.
9   Human Medicines Regulations 2012, SI 2012/1916: reg 255(1)(f); and PARA 379.

379. Offences relating to prohibited uses of medicinal products and breach of certain provisions.   A person is guilty of an offence[1] if he breaches certain provisions[2] relating to:

(1)   the prohibition[3] on the sale etc of prescription only medicine otherwise than in accordance with a prescription from an appropriate practitioner[4];

(2)   the prohibition[5] on parenteral administration of prescription only medicine otherwise than by or under directions of an appropriate practitioner[6];

(3)   the prohibition[7] on the sale etc of medicinal product[8] not subject to general sale otherwise than by or under supervision of a pharmacist[9];

(4)   the prohibition[10] on the sale of prescription only medicine or pharmacy medicine[11] by way of wholesale dealing to a person who is not within the specified permitted class of person[12];

(5)   prohibitions[13] concerning traceability of treatment with advanced therapy medicinal products[14];

(6)   the prohibition[15] on the sale or supply of medicinal products subject to general sale except in accordance with specified exceptions[16];

(7)   the prohibition[17] on the sale by automatic machine of medicinal product not subject to general sale[18].

A person is guilty of an offence[19] if he breaches (a) provisions[20] relating to the sale or supply of a medicinal product that does not comply with standards specified in certain publications[21]; (b) provisions relating to the record-keeping requirements[22] for persons carrying on a retail pharmacy business[23].

1   A person guilty of an offence under any of the Human Medicines Regulations 2012, SI 2012/1916, reg 255(1) is liable, on summary conviction, to a fine not exceeding the statutory maximum or, on conviction on indictment, to a fine, to imprisonment for a term not exceeding two years, or to both: reg 255(5). A person guilty of an offence under reg 255(6) is liable on summary conviction to a fine not exceeding level 3 on the standard scale: reg 255(7). As to the statutory maximum and the standard scale see SENTENCING AND DISPOSITION OF OFFENDERS vol 92 (2010) PARAS 140, 142.
2   See the Human Medicines Regulations 2012, SI 2012/1916, reg 255(1).
3   Ie the prohibition in the Human Medicines Regulations 2012, SI 2012/1916, reg 214(1) (see PARA 271).
4   See the Human Medicines Regulations 2012, SI 2012/1916, reg 255(1)(a).
5   Ie the prohibition in the Human Medicines Regulations 2012, SI 2012/1916, reg 214(2) (see PARA 271).
6   See the Human Medicines Regulations 2012, SI 2012/1916, reg 255(1)(b).
7   Ie the prohibition in the Human Medicines Regulations 2012, SI 2012/1916, reg 220 (see PARA 277).
8   As to the meaning of 'medicinal product' see PARA 25.
9   See the Human Medicines Regulations 2012, SI 2012/1916, reg 255(1)(c).
10   Ie the prohibition in the Human Medicines Regulations 2012, SI 2012/1916, reg 249 (see PARA 79).
11   As to the meaning of 'pharmacy medicine' see the Human Medicines Regulations 2012, SI 2012/1916, reg 5(5); and PARA 26: reg 8(1).
12   See the Human Medicines Regulations 2012, SI 2012/1916, reg 255(1)(d).

13 Ie the prohibitions in the Human Medicines Regulations 2012, SI 2012/1916, reg 254 (see PARA 378).
14 See the Human Medicines Regulations 2012, SI 2012/1916, reg 255(1)(f).
15 Ie the prohibition in the Human Medicines Regulations 2012, SI 2012/1916, reg 221 (see PARA 278).
16 See the Human Medicines Regulations 2012, SI 2012/1916, reg 255(6)(a).
17 Ie the prohibition in the Human Medicines Regulations 2012, SI 2012/1916, reg 222 (see PARA 279).
18 See the Human Medicines Regulations 2012, SI 2012/1916, reg 255(6)(b).
19 See note 1.
20 Ie the Human Medicines Regulations 2012, SI 2012/1916, reg 251 (see PARA 236).
21 See the Human Medicines Regulations 2012, SI 2012/1916, reg 255(1)(e).
22 Ie the requirements under the Human Medicines Regulations 2012, SI 2012/1916, reg 253 (see MEDICAL PROFESSIONS).
23 Human Medicines Regulations 2012, SI 2012/1916, reg 255(8).

380. Offences relating to prescribing medicinal products. A person is guilty of an offence[1] if he is an appropriate practitioner[2] and he gives a prescription or directions in respect of a medicinal product[3] in relation to which the person is not an appropriate practitioner[4].

A person is also guilty of an offence if he gives a prescription or directions or administers[5] a medicinal product without meeting the conditions[6] for doing so that apply to that person[7].

A person is guilty of an offence if he has in his possession a prescription only medicine[8] and he intends to supply it otherwise than in accordance with a prescription of an appropriate practitioner[9].

1 A person guilty of an offence under any of the Human Medicines Regulations 2012, SI 2012/1916, reg 255(2)–(4) is liable, on summary conviction, to a fine not exceeding the statutory maximum or, on conviction on indictment, to a fine, to imprisonment for a term not exceeding two years, or to both: reg 255(5). As to the statutory maximum see SENTENCING AND DISPOSITION OF OFFENDERS vol 92 (2010) PARA 140.
2 Ie by virtue of the Human Medicines Regulations 2012, SI 2012/1916, reg 214 (see PARA 271).
3 As to the meaning of 'medicinal product' see PARA 25.
4 Human Medicines Regulations 2012, SI 2012/1916, reg 255(2).
5 As to the meaning of 'administer' see PARA 25 note 4.
6 Ie the conditions that apply by virtue of the Human Medicines Regulations 2012, SI 2012/1916, reg 215 (see PARA 274).
7 Human Medicines Regulations 2012, SI 2012/1916, reg 255(3).
8 Ie a medicinal product to which the Human Medicines Regulations 2012, SI 2012/1916, reg 214(1) (see PARA 271) applies.
9 Human Medicines Regulations 2012, SI 2012/1916, reg 255(4).

(12) RADIOACTIVE MATERIALS

381. Application of provisions to radioactive substances. Certain provisions of the Human Medicines Regulations 2012[1] and the Clinical Trials Regulations[2] have effect in relation to the following[3]:

(1) interstitial and intracavitary appliances (other than nuclear powered cardiac pacemakers) which contain or are to contain a radioactive substance sealed in a container (otherwise than solely for the purpose of storage, transport or disposal) or bonded solely within material and including the immediate container or bonding that are designed to be inserted into the human body or body cavities[4];

(2) surface applicators, that is to say plates, plaques and ophthalmic applicators which contain or are to contain a radioactive substance sealed in a container (otherwise than solely for the purpose of storage,

transport or disposal) or bonded solely within material and including the immediate container or bonding that are designed to be brought into contact with the human body[5];

(3) any apparatus capable of administering neutrons to human beings when the neutrons are administered in order to generate a radioactive substance in the person to whom they are administered for the purpose of diagnosis or research[6];

(4) other substances or articles (not being an instrument, apparatus or appliance) which consist of or contain or generate a radioactive substance and which consist of or contain or generate that substance in order, when administered, to utilise the radiation emitted therefrom, and are manufactured, sold or supplied for use wholly or mainly by being administered to one or more human beings solely by way of a test for ascertaining what effects it has when so administered[7].

1   Ie the Human Medicines Regulations 2012, SI 2012/1916.
2   Ie the Medicines for Human Use (Clinical Trials) Regulations 2004, SI 2004/1031.
3   See the Medicines (Radioactive Substances) Order 1978, SI 1978/1004, art 2(1) (amended by SI 2006/2407).
4   Medicines (Radioactive Substances) Order 1978, SI 1978/1004, Schedule para 1.
5   Medicines (Radioactive Substances) Order 1978, SI 1978/1004, Schedule para 2.
6   Medicines (Radioactive Substances) Order 1978, SI 1978/1004, Schedule para 3.
7   Medicines (Radioactive Substances) Order 1978, SI 1978/1004, Schedule para 4.

382. Administration of radioactive substances. Regulations impose duties on those responsible for administering ionising radiation[1] to protect persons undergoing medical exposure whether as part of their own medical diagnosis or treatment or as part of occupational health surveillance, health screening, voluntary participation in research or medico-legal procedures[2]. Written procedures for medical exposures must be in place[3] which, in the case of patients undergoing treatment or diagnosis with radioactive medicinal products[4], must include the provision of certain information and instructions[5].

Regulations have also been made prohibiting the administration of a radioactive medicinal product[6] unless it is being administered by a doctor or a dentist holding an appropriate certificate[7] or a person acting in accordance with the directions of such a doctor or dentist[8]. This prohibition does not apply where the administration would result in a medical exposure and certain conditions[9] are satisfied[10].

1   'Ionising radiation' means the transfer of energy in the form of particles or electromagnetic waves of a wavelength of 100 nanometres or less or a frequency of 3×1015 hertz or more capable of producing ions directly or indirectly: Ionising Radiation (Medical Exposure) Regulations 2000, SI 2000/1059, reg 2(1).
2   See the Ionising Radiation (Medical Exposure) Regulations 2000, SI 2000/1059; and MEDICAL PROFESSIONS vol 74 (2011) PARA 913.
3   See the Ionising Radiation (Medical Exposure) Regulations 2000, SI 2000/1059, reg 4(1).
4   'Radioactive medicinal product' means a medicinal product which is, which contains or which generates a radioactive substance and which is, contains or generates that substance in order, when administered, to utilize, the radiation emitted therefrom: Medicines (Administration of Radioactive Substances) Regulations 1978, SI 1978/1006, reg 1(2) (definition applied by the Ionising Radiation (Medical Exposure) Regulations 2000, SI 2000/1059, reg 2(1)). 'Radioactive substance' means any substance that contains one or more radionuclides of which the activity or the concentration cannot be disregarded as far as radiation protection is concerned: Medicines (Administration of Radioactive Substances) Regulations 1978, SI 1978/1006, reg 1(2).
5   See the Ionising Radiation (Medical Exposure) Regulations 2000, SI 2000/1059, reg 7(5), (6) (reg 7(5) amended by SI 2007/1898).
6   See note 4.

7	Ie a certificate made under the Medicines Act 1968 s 60. Section 60 has been repealed by the Human Medicines Regulations 2012, SI 2012/1916, subject to transitional provisions and savings in Sch 32 para 7 which provides that the Medicines Act 1968 s 60 is to continue to have effect insofar as it relates to the making of, and continued operation of, the Medicines (Administration of Radioactive Substances) Regulations 1978, SI 1978/1006. The Human Medicines Regulations 2012, SI 2012/1916, Sch 32 para 7 also provides that certain provisions of the Medicines Act 1968 mentioned in the Medicines (Administration of Radioactive Substances) Regulations 1978, SI 1978/1006 continue to have effect as they did immediately before the coming into force of the Human Medicines Regulations 2012, SI 2012/1916.

8	See the Medicines (Administration of Radioactive Substances) Regulations 1978, SI 1978/1006, reg 2(1) (reg 2 substituted by SI 2006/2806).

9	The conditions are that (1) the medicinal product is administered by an operator acting in accordance with the procedures and protocols referred to in the Ionising Radiation (Medical Exposure) Regulations 2000, SI 2000/1059, reg 4(1), (2) which apply to the exposure referred to in Medicines (Administration of Radioactive Substances) Regulations 1978, SI 1978/1006, reg 2(1), (2) that medical exposure has been authorised by a practitioner or, where it is not practicable for a practitioner to authorise the exposure, an operator acting in accordance with written guidelines issued by a practitioner; (3) the practitioner is the holder of a certificate; and (4) the medicinal product is not a controlled drug: reg 2(3) (as substituted: see note 8).

10	Medicines (Administration of Radioactive Substances) Regulations 1978, SI 1978/1006, reg 2(2) (as substituted: see note 8).

383. Protection against radiation. Provision has been made prohibiting the carrying out of types or classes of practice involving exposure to ionising radiation unless they have been justified by the appropriate national authority[1].

Certain duties are imposed on employers to protect employees and other persons against ionising radiation arising from work with radioactive substances and other sources of ionising radiation[2]. Certain duties are also imposed on employees[3].

1	See the Justification of Practices Involving Ionising Radiation Regulations 2004, SI 2004/1769; and HEALTH AND SAFETY AT WORK vol 53 (2009) PARA 647.

2	See the Ionising Radiation Regulations 1999, SI 1999/3232, regs 5–33; and HEALTH AND SAFETY AT WORK vol 53 (2009) PARAS 647–652.

3	See the Ionising Radiation Regulations 1999, SI 1999/3232, reg 34; and HEALTH AND SAFETY AT WORK vol 53 (2009) PARA 653.

(13) LIABILITY FOR VACCINE DAMAGE

384. Payments to persons severely disabled by vaccination. If, on consideration of a claim[1], the Secretary of State[2] is satisfied that a person is, or was immediately before his death, severely disabled[3] as a result of vaccination against any one of certain diseases[4], and that the conditions of entitlement are fulfilled[5], he must make a payment of the relevant statutory sum[6] to or for the benefit of that person or to his personal representatives[7]. These provisions have effect with respect to a person who is severely disabled as a result of a vaccination given to his mother before he was born as if the vaccination had been given directly to him, and in certain circumstances[8] also have effect with respect to a person who is severely disabled as a result of contracting a disease through contact with a third person who was vaccinated against it as if the vaccination had been given to him and the disablement resulted from it[9].

The conditions of entitlement to such a payment are:

(1)	that the vaccination in question was carried out in the United Kingdom[10] or the Isle of Man[11] on or after 5 July 1948[12] and, in the case of vaccination against smallpox, before 1 August 1971[13];

(2)	except in the case of vaccination against poliomyelitis or rubella, that the vaccination was carried out either at a time when the person to whom it was given[14] was under the age of 18[15] or at the time of an outbreak within the United Kingdom or the Isle of Man of the disease against which the vaccination was given[16]; and

(3)   that the disabled person was over the age of two on the date when the claim was made or, if he died before that date, that he died after 9 May 1978 and was over the age of two when he died[17].

With respect to claims made after such date as may be specified in the order and relating to vaccination against such disease as may be so specified, the Secretary of State may by order made by statutory instrument provide that, in such circumstances as may be specified in the order, one or more of the conditions of entitlement appropriate to vaccination against that disease need not be fulfilled[18]; or add to the conditions of entitlement which are appropriate to vaccination against that disease, either generally or in such circumstances as may be specified in the order[19].

1   Ie a claim under the Vaccine Damage Payments Act 1979. As to the making of a claim see PARA 385.

2   As to the Secretary of State see PARA 2 note 1.

3   For these purposes a person is severely disabled if he suffers disablement to the extent of 60% or more, assessed as for the purposes of the Social Security Contributions and Benefits Act 1992 s 103 (see SOCIAL SECURITY AND PENSIONS vol 44(2) (Reissue) PARA 142) or equivalent Northern Ireland provisions: Vaccine Damage Payments Act 1979 s 1(4) (amended by the Social Security (Consequential Provisions) Act 1992 Sch 2 para 53; SI 2002/1592).

4   Vaccine Damage Payments Act 1979 s 1(1)(a). The diseases to which the Vaccine Damage Payments Act 1979 applies are: diphtheria, tetanus, whooping cough, poliomyelitis, measles, rubella, tuberculosis and smallpox, together with any other disease specified by the Secretary of State for the purpose by order made by statutory instrument: s 1(2)(a)–(i). Diseases which have been so specified by order are: mumps, with effect from 9 April 1990 (see the Vaccine Damage Payments (Specified Disease) Order 1990, SI 1990/623, arts 1, 2); haemophilus influenzae type b, with effect from 31 May 1995 (see the Vaccine Damage Payments (Specified Disease) Order 1995, SI 1995/1164, arts 1, 2); meningococcal group C, with effect from 30 May 2001 (see the Vaccine Damage Payments (Specified Disease) Order 2001, SI 2001/1652, arts 1(a), 2); pneumococcal infection, with effect from 4 September 2006 (see the Vaccine Damage Payments (Specified Disease) Order 2006, SI 2006/2066, arts 1, 2); human papillomavirus, with effect from 1 September 2008 (Vaccine Damage Payments (Specified Disease) Order 2008, SI 2008/2103, arts 1, 2). Such an order specifying a disease may make appropriate modifications to the conditions of entitlement: Vaccine Damage Payments Act 1979 s 2(2).

5   Vaccine Damage Payments Act 1979 s 1(1)(b).

6   'Relevant statutory sum' means £120,000 or such other sum as is specified by the Secretary of State for the purposes by order made by statutory instrument with the consent of the Treasury; and the relevant statutory sum is the statutory sum at the time when a claim for payment is first made: Vaccine Damage Payments Act 1979 s 1(1A) (added by the Social Security Act 1985 s 23; and amended by SI 2007/1931). As to the Treasury see CONSTITUTIONAL LAW AND HUMAN RIGHTS vol 8(2) (Reissue) PARAS 512–517.

7   Vaccine Damage Payments Act 1979 s 1(1) (amended by the Social Security Act 1985 s 23). As to personal representatives see WILLS AND INTESTACY vol 103 (2010) PARA 605 et seq. Where vaccination is not compulsory a compensation scheme is a social security measure outside the scope of the European Convention on Human Rights: *Godfrey v United Kingdom* Application 8542/79 (1982) 27 DR 94, EComHR. As to that Convention see CONSTITUTIONAL LAW AND HUMAN RIGHTS vol 8(2) (Reissue) PARAS 122–181.

8   Ie in such circumstances as may be prescribed by regulations: Vaccine Damage Payments Act 1979 s 1(3). The prescribed circumstances are that: (1) the disabled person has been in close physical contact with a person who has been vaccinated against poliomyelitis with orally administered vaccine; (2) that contact occurred within a period of 60 days beginning with the fourth day immediately following that vaccination; and (3) the disabled person was, within that period, either looking after the vaccinated person or himself being looked after together with the vaccinated person: Vaccine Damage Payments Regulations 1979, SI 1979/432, reg 5A (added by SI 1979/1441). As to the making of regulations under the Vaccine Damage Payments Act 1979 see generally s 8 (amended by the Welfare Reform Act 2007 Sch 7 para 1(5)–(7), Sch 8, Sch 11 para 3(2)–(4); Social Security Act 1998 Sch 7 para 9).

9   Vaccine Damage Payments Act 1979 s 1(3).

10   As to the meaning of 'United Kingdom' see PARA 20 note 4.

11   Vaccine Damage Payments Act 1979 s 2(1)(a)(i). Regulations must specify the cases in which vaccinations given outside the United Kingdom and the Isle of Man to persons defined in the regulations as serving members of Her Majesty's forces or members of their families are to be treated as carried out in England: Vaccine Damage Payments Act 1979 s 2(5). As from a day to be appointed s 2(5) is repealed and replaced by the following: The Secretary of State may by order made by statutory instrument provide that, in such circumstances as may be specified in the order, the condition in s 2(1)(a)(i) need not be fulfilled in the case of vaccinations of persons of a description so specified which are given under arrangements made by or on behalf of Her Majesty's forces, a government department so specified, or any other body so specified: s 2(5A) (s 2(5A), (5B) prospectively added by the Welfare Reform Act 2007 s 56(1), (2)). Orders under the Vaccine Damage Payments Act 1979 s 2(5A) may make different provision in relation to different cases: s 2(5B) (as so prospectively added).

Vaccinations given outside the United Kingdom and the Isle of Man to serving members of Her Majesty's forces or members of their families are to be treated as carried out in England where the vaccination in question has been given as part of medical facilities provided under arrangements made by or on behalf of the service authorities: Vaccine Damage Payments Regulations 1979, SI 1979/432, reg 5(1). 'Serving members of Her Majesty's forces' means a member of the naval, military or air forces of the Crown or of any women's service administered by the Defence Council (reg 5(2)(a)); and a person is a member of the family of a serving member of Her Majesty's forces if he is the spouse or civil partner of that serving member, he and that serving member live together as husband and wife or as if they were civil partners, or he is a child whose requirements are provided by that serving member (reg 5(2)(b) (substituted by SI 2005/3070)). As to the Defence Council see CONSTITUTIONAL LAW AND HUMAN RIGHTS vol 8(2) (Reissue) PARAS 443–447. As to civil partnerships see MATRIMONIAL AND CIVIL PARTNERSHIP LAW.

12   Vaccine Damage Payments Act 1979 s 2(1)(a)(ii).

13   Vaccine Damage Payments Act 1979 s 2(1)(a)(iii).

14   In a case where the Vaccine Damage Payments Act 1979 has effect by virtue of s 1(3) (see the text to notes 8–9), the reference to the person to whom a vaccination was given is a reference to the person to whom it was actually given and not to the disabled person: s 2(3).

15   The time at which a person attains a particular age expressed in years is the commencement of the relevant anniversary of the date of his birth: see the Family Law Reform Act 1969 s 9.

16   Vaccine Damage Payments Act 1979 s 2(1)(b). The condition of entitlement in s 2(1)(b) is omitted in relation to vaccination against meningococcal group C and the human papillomavirus: Vaccine Damage Payments (Specified Disease) Order 2001, SI 2001/1652, art 3; Vaccine Damage Payments (Specified Disease) Order 2008, SI 2008/2103, art 3.

17   Vaccine Damage Payments Act 1979 s 2(1)(c).

18   Vaccine Damage Payments Act 1979 s 2(4)(a).

19   Vaccine Damage Payments Act 1979 s 2(4)(b). As to the orders that have been made see note 16.

385.   Determination of claims.   A claim for a payment in respect of vaccine damage[1] must be made to the Secretary of State[2] by or on behalf of the disabled person concerned or, as the case may be, by his personal representatives[3], in the prescribed manner[4], on or before whichever is the later of: (1) the date on which the disabled person attains the age of 21[5], or where he has died, the date on which he would have attained the age of 21[6], and (2) the end of the period of six years beginning with the date of the vaccination to which the claim relates[7]. As soon as practicable after he has received a claim, the Secretary of State must give notice in writing to the claimant of his determination whether he is satisfied that a payment is due to or for the benefit of the disabled person or to his personal representatives[8]. If the Secretary of State is satisfied that the conditions of entitlement are fulfilled[9], but is not satisfied that the disabled person is or, where he has died, was immediately before his death severely disabled as a result of the vaccination[10], the notice must inform the claimant of his right of appeal[11].

Any decision of the Secretary of State[12], and any decision of an appeal tribunal[13], may be reversed by a decision made by the Secretary of State either within the prescribed period or in prescribed cases or circumstances[14], and either on an application made for the purpose or on his own initiative[15]. In making such a decision, the Secretary of State need not consider any issue that is not raised by the application or, as the case may be, did not cause him to act on his own initiative[16]. Except as provided[17], no payment is recoverable by virtue of such a decision[18].

The claimant may appeal to a First-tier Tribunal[19] against any decision of the Secretary of State under the above provisions[20]. In deciding an appeal, an appeal tribunal must consider all the circumstances of the case (including any not obtaining at the time when the decision appealed against was made)[21].

If, whether fraudulently or otherwise, any person misrepresents or fails to disclose any material fact and in consequence of the misrepresentation or failure a payment is made, the person to whom the payment was made is liable to repay the amount of that payment to the Secretary of State unless he can show that the misrepresentation or failure occurred without his connivance or consent[22]. Any person who, for the purpose of obtaining any payment, whether for himself or some other person, knowingly makes any false statement or representation[23], or produces or furnishes or causes or knowingly allows to be produced or furnished any document or information which he knows to be false in a material particular[24], commits an offence[25].

Any decision made in accordance with the provisions of the Vaccine Damage Payments Act 1979 is final[26]. Regulations[27] may make provision with respect to the correction of accidental errors in any decision or record of a decision made by the Secretary of State or appeals tribunal under the above provisions, and the setting aside of any such decision in a case where it appears just to set the decision aside on certain grounds[28].

1   Ie a payment under the Vaccine Damage Payments Act 1979 s 1(1): see PARA 384.

2   As to the Secretary of State see PARA 2 note 1.

3   See the Vaccine Damage Payments Act 1979 s 3(1)(a). As to personal representatives see WILLS AND INTESTACY vol 103 (2010) PARA 605 et seq.

4   See the Vaccine Damage Payments Act 1979 s 3(1)(b). Every claim for payment must be made in writing to the Secretary of State on the form approved by him, or in such other manner, being in writing, as he may accept as sufficient in the circumstances of any particular case or class of cases: Vaccine Damage Payments Regulations 1979, SI 1979/432, reg 2(1). Any person who has made a claim may amend his claim, at any time before a decision has been given thereon: see reg 2(2). Every person who makes a claim must furnish such certificates, documents, information and evidence for the purpose of determining the claim as may be required by the Secretary of State: reg 3. As to the meaning of 'writing' see PARA 507 note 2.

5   As to the time at which a person attains a particular age see PARA 384 note 15.

6   Vaccine Damage Payments Act 1979 s 3(1)(c)(i) (reg 3(1)(c) substituted by SI 2002/1592).

7   Vaccine Damage Payments Act 1979 s 3(1)(c)(ii) (as substituted: see note 6).

8   Vaccine Damage Payments Act 1979 s 3(2). If the Secretary of State is not satisfied that a payment is due, the notice in writing must state the grounds on which he is not so satisfied: s 3(3).

9   Vaccine Damage Payments Act 1979 s 3(4)(a). As to the conditions of entitlement see PARA 384.

10 Vaccine Damage Payments Act 1979 s 3(4)(b). If in any case a person is severely disabled, the question whether his severe disablement results from vaccination against any of the diseases to which the Vaccine Damage Payments Act 1979 applies (see PARA 384) must be determined on the balance of probability: s 3(5). Every disabled person in respect of whom a claim has been made must comply with every notice given to him or, where he is not the claimant, to the claimant by the Secretary of State which requires such disabled person to submit himself to a medical examination either by a medical practitioner appointed by the Secretary of State or by an appeal tribunal for the purpose of determining whether he is severely disabled as a result of vaccination against any of the diseases to which the Act applies: Vaccine Damage Payments Regulations 1979, SI 1979/432, reg 4(1) (amended by SI 1999/2677). Every such notice must be in writing and must specify the time and place of examination and must not require the disabled person to submit himself to examination before the expiration of the period of 14 days

beginning with the date of the notice or such shorter period as may be reasonable in the circumstances: Vaccine Damage Payments Regulations 1979, SI 1979/432, reg 4(2). Travelling and other allowances for this purpose, and medical practitioners' fees, are payable by the Secretary of State: see the Vaccine Damage Payments Act 1979 s 12(2), (3) (s 12(2) amended by the Social Security (Consequential Provisions) Act 1992 Sch 2 para 54).

11 Vaccine Damage Payments Act 1979 s 3(4) (amended by the Social Security Act 1998 Sch 7 para 5; SI 2008/2833).

12 Ie under the Vaccine Damage Payments Act 1979 s 3 (see the text to notes 1–11) or s 3A.

13 Ie under the Vaccine Damage Payments Act 1979 s 4: see the text to notes 19–20. Until a day to be appointed, 'appeal tribunal' means an appeal tribunal constituted under the Social Security Act 1998 Pt I Ch 1 (ss 1–7) (see SOCIAL SECURITY AND PENSIONS): Vaccine Damage Payments Act 1979 s 3A(6) (s 3A added by the Social Security Act 1998 s 45; Vaccine Damage Payments Act 1979 s 3A(6) prospectively repealed by the Welfare Reform Act 2007 Sch 7 para 1(1), (8), Sch 8). At the date at which this volume states the law no such days had been appointed.

14 Vaccine Damage Payments Act 1979 s 3A(1)(a) (as added: see note 13). Regulations may prescribe the procedure by which a decision may be made: s 3A(3) (as so added). Such notice as may be prescribed by regulations must be given of a decision: s 3A(4) (as so added). As to the prescribed provisions see the Vaccine Damage Payments Regulations 1979, SI 1979/432, regs 11, 12 (reg 11 substituted, reg 12 added, by SI 1999/2677).

15 Vaccine Damage Payments Act 1979 s 3A(1)(b) (as added: see note 13).

16 Vaccine Damage Payments Act 1979 s 3A(2) (as added: see note 13).

17 Ie by the Vaccine Damage Payments Act 1979 s 5(4): see the text to note 22.

18 Vaccine Damage Payments Act 1979 s 3A(5) (as added: see note 13).

19 As from a day to be appointed this right of appeal is to an appropriate appeal tribunal (ie if the claimant's address is in Northern Ireland, to an appeal tribunal constituted under the Social Security (Northern Ireland) Order 1998, SI 1998/1506, Pt 2, Chapter 1 (arts 3–8) and, otherwise, to the First-tier Tribunal): see the Vaccine Damage Payments Act 1979 s 4(1), (1A) (s 4 as substituted (see note 20); s 4(1A) prospectively added by the Welfare Reform Act 2007 s 57(2); the Vaccine Damage Payments Act 1979 s 4(1), (1A) both prospectively amended by SI 2008/2833).

20 Vaccine Damage Payments Act 1979 s 4(1) (s 4 substituted by the Social Security Act 1998 s 46; SI 2008/2833). Regulations may make provision as to the making and conduct of appeals: see s 4(2), (3) (as so substituted). As to the regulations made see the Social Security and Child Support (Decisions and Appeals) Regulations 1999, SI 1999/991 (amended by SI 1999/2677; SI 2002/1379; SI 2004/3368; SI 2005/337). The Secretary of State must pay such travelling and other allowances as he may determine to persons required to attend before a tribunal and, in circumstances where he considers it appropriate, to any person who accompanies a disabled person to a tribunal: see the Vaccine Damage Payments Act 1979 s 12(3). As from a day to be appointed, in relation to payments of travelling allowances etc in Northern Ireland see s 12(3A) (prospectively added by the Welfare Reform Act 2007 s 57(2)). At the date at which this volume states the law no such day had been appointed.

21 Vaccine Damage Payments Act 1979 s 4(4) (as substituted: see note 20).

22 Vaccine Damage Payments Act 1979 s 5(4).

23 Vaccine Damage Payments Act 1979 s 9(1)(a).

24 Vaccine Damage Payments Act 1979 s 9(1)(b).

25 See the Vaccine Damage Payments Act 1979 s 9(1). The penalty for such offence is, on summary conviction, a fine not exceeding level 5 on the standard scale: see s 9(1) (amended by virtue of the Criminal Justice Act 1982 s 46). As to the standard scale see SENTENCING AND DISPOSITION OF OFFENDERS vol 92 (2010) PARA 142. As to the penalty on conviction in the Isle of Man see the Vaccine Damage Payments Act 1979 s 9(2).

26 Vaccine Damage Payments Act 1979 s 7B(1) (s 7B added by the Social Security Act 1998 Sch 7 para 8). This provision is expressed to be subject to the provisions of the Vaccine Damage Payments Act 1979 and the Regulatory Reform (Vaccine Damage Payments Act 1979) Order 2002, SI 2002/1592, art 4, Schedule (modifications of the Act in relation to transitional claims): Vaccine Damage Payments Act 1979 s 7B(1) (as so added; and amended by SI 2002/1592). If and to the extent that regulations so provide, any finding of fact or other determination embodied in or necessary to such a decision, or on which such a decision is based, is conclusive for the purposes of further such decisions and decisions under certain other statutory provisions: see the Vaccine Damage Payments Act 1979 s 7B(2) (as so added). At the date at which this volume states the law no such regulations had been made. As to judicial review of decisions expressed to be final see JUDICIAL REVIEW vol 61 (2010) PARA 655.

27 As to the making of regulations see the Vaccine Damage Payments Act 1979 s 8 (amended by the Social Security Act 1998 Sch 7 para 9).

28 See the Vaccine Damage Payments Act 1979 s 7A (added by the Social Security Act 1998 s 47).
    As to the provision made see the Social Security and Child Support (Decisions and Appeals)
    Regulations 1999, SI 1999/991 (as amended: see note 20).

386. Making of payments; claims prior to the Act. Where a payment in
respect of vaccine damage[1] falls to be made in respect of a disabled person who
is over 18[2] and capable of managing his own affairs, the payment must be made
to him[3]; or where a payment falls to be made in respect of a disabled person who
has died, the payment must be made to his personal representatives[4]. Where such
a payment falls to be made in respect of any other disabled person, the payment
must be made for his benefit by paying it to such trustees as the Secretary of
State[5] may appoint to be held by them upon such trusts as may be declared by
the Secretary of State[6].

The making of a claim for, or the receipt of a payment does not prejudice the
right of any person to institute or carry on proceedings in respect of disablement
suffered as a result of vaccination against any disease to which the Vaccine
Damage Payments Act 1979 applies[7].

Special provision is made in relation to payments of £10,000 made by the
Secretary of State to or in respect of a disabled person after 9 May 1978 and
before 22 March 1979[8] pursuant to a non-statutory scheme of payments for
severe vaccine damage and their effect on claims made for payment under the
Vaccine Damage Payments Act 1979[9].

1 Ie a payment under the Vaccine Damage Payments Act 1979 s 1(1): see PARA 384.
2 As to the time at which a person attains a particular age see PARA 384 note 15.
3 Vaccine Damage Payments Act 1979 s 6(1).
4 Vaccine Damage Payments Act 1979 s 6(2). As to personal representatives see WILLS AND
   INTESTACY vol 103 (2010) PARA 605 et seq.
5 As to the Secretary of State see PARA 2 note 1.
6 Vaccine Damage Payments Act 1979 s 6(3).
7 Vaccine Damage Payments Act 1979 s 6(4). However, in any civil proceedings brought in respect
   of disablement resulting from vaccination against such a disease, the court must treat a payment
   made to or in respect of the disabled person concerned under s 1(1) (see PARA 384) as paid on
   account of any damages which the court awards in respect of such disablement: s 6(4). As to the
   diseases to which the Vaccine Damage Payments Act 1979 applies see PARA 384.
8 Ie the date of the passing of the Vaccine Damage Payments Act 1979.
9 See the Vaccine Damage Payments Act 1979 s 7 (amended by the Social Security Act 1998 Sch 7
   para 7, Sch 8).

3. VETERINARY MEDICINES

(1) INTRODUCTION

387. Overview. The law relating to veterinary medicine is mainly contained in the Veterinary Medicines Regulations 2011[1]. The regulations apply to a veterinary medicinal product which is defined as (1) any substance or combination of substances presented as having properties for treating or preventing disease in animals[2]; or (2) any substance or combination of substances that may be used in, or administered to, animals with a view either to restoring, correcting or modifying physiological functions by exerting a pharmacological, immunological or metabolic action, or to making a medical diagnosis[3].

The regulations do not apply to a veterinary medicinal product based on radio-active isotopes[4]. Nor do they apply in relation to a product intended for administration in the course of a licensed procedure[5], except that, if the animals are to be put into the human food chain, the only products that may be administered to the animals are (a) authorised veterinary medicinal products administered in accordance with their marketing authorisation, or (b) products administered in accordance with an animal test certificate[6]. Further, the provisions do not apply to an inactivated autogenous vaccine that is manufactured, on the instructions of a veterinary surgeon, from pathogens or antigens obtained from an animal and used for the treatment of that animal[7].

Provisions also exist prohibiting the use of certain poisons from being used for destroying animals[8].

1   Ie the Veterinary Medicines Regulations 2011, SI 2011/2159 (see PARA 388 et seq). As to the law relating to medicated feedingstuffs and specified feed additives see AGRICULTURAL PRODUCTION AND MARKETING. There is a duty on the Secretary of State to review the Veterinary Medicines Regulations 2011, SI 2011/2159 five years beginning with the day on which the regulations came into force, and, subject to reg 45(6), each successive period of five years thereafter: see reg 45(1), (5). If a report under this regulation is published before the last day of the review period to which it relates, the following review period is to begin with the day on which that report is published: reg 45(6). In carrying out the review the Secretary of State must, so far as is reasonable, have regard to how the EU instruments, or provisions of EU instruments, to which this regulation applies are implemented in other member states: see reg 45(2). As to the EU instruments see reg 45(3). The Secretary of State must set out the conclusion of the review in a report which he must publish: see reg 45(1)(b), (c). As to the meaning of 'member state' see PARA 389 note 4.

2   'Animal' means all animals other than man and includes birds, reptiles, fish, molluscs, crustacea and bees: Veterinary Medicines Regulations 2011, SI 2011/2159, reg 2(1).

3   Veterinary Medicines Regulations 2011, SI 2011/2159, reg 2(1). This definition also applies to European Parliament and Council Directive (EC) 2001/82 (OJ L311, 28.11.2001, p 1) on the Community code relating to veterinary medicinal products: see art 1(2) (amended by European Parliament and Council Directive (EC) 2004/28 (OJ L136, 30.4.2004, p 58)).

4   Veterinary Medicines Regulations 2011, SI 2011/2159 reg 3(1).

5   Ie licensed under the Animals (Scientific Procedure) Act 1986: see ANIMALS vol 2 (2008) PARA 875 et seq.

6   Ie granted under Veterinary Medicines Regulations 2011, SI 2011/2159 Sch 4 para 9 (see PARA 428): reg 3(2).

7   Veterinary Medicines Regulations 2011, SI 2011/2159 reg 15(1). Further, Sch 1 and Sch 2 Pt 1 do not apply in relation to an inactivated autogenous vaccine that is (1) manufactured by a person and in premises authorised in accordance with Sch 2 Pt 2, on the instructions of a veterinary surgeon, from pathogens or antigens obtained from an animal; and (2) used for the treatment of other animals on the same site, animals intended to be sent to those premises, or animals on a site that receives animals from those premises: reg 15(2).

8   See the Animals (Cruel Poisons) Act 1962; the Animal (Cruel Poisons) Regulations 1963, SI 1963/1278; and ANIMALS vol 2 (2008) PARA 864.

(2) AUTHORISATIONS

(i) Introduction

388. Requirement for an authorisation. It is an offence to place a veterinary medicinal product[1] on the market unless that product has been granted a marketing authorisation by the Secretary of State or the European Medicines Agency[2]. Any person who certifies data in relation to an application for a marketing authorisation or in relation to an existing marketing authorisation and who knows that those data are false, or does not believe that they are accurate, is guilty of an offence[3]. Further, the holder of a marketing authorisation for a veterinary medicinal product is guilty of an offence if the finished product supplied by the holder or the manufacturer is not completely in accordance with the marketing authorisation[4].

1   As to the meaning of 'veterinary medicinal product' see PARA 387.
2   Veterinary Medicines Regulations 2011, SI 2011/2159, reg 4(1). As to the European Medicines Agency see PARA 14. As to fees relating to marketing authorisations see Sch 7 Pt 2 (paras 7–26). See generally Sch 7 Pt 6 (paras 45–64). As to the Secretary of State see PARA 2 note 1.
3   Veterinary Medicines Regulations 2011, SI 2011/2159, reg 4(2).
4   Veterinary Medicines Regulations 2011, SI 2011/2159, reg 6.

(ii) Marketing Authorisations

389. Applications. An application for a marketing authorisation for a veterinary medicinal product[1] must be made to the Secretary of State[2], and must include specified information about the product[3]. A marketing authorisation may be granted only to an applicant established in a member state[4].

1   As to the meaning of 'veterinary medicinal product' see PARA 387.
2   Veterinary Medicines Regulations 2011, SI 2011/2159, Sch 1 para 1. As to time limits applicable in the case of a veterinary medicinal product for food-producing animals: see Sch 1 para 5. As to the Secretary of State see PARA 2 note 1. As to the meaning of 'animal' see PARA 387 note 2.
3   Veterinary Medicines Regulations 2011, SI 2011/2159, Sch 1 paras 2, 3. As to derogations from certain of the requirements to provide information, see Sch 1 Pt 2 (paras 6–16). As to fees relating to marketing authorisations see Sch 7 Pts 1, 2 (paras 1–26).
4   Veterinary Medicines Regulations 2011, SI 2011/2159, Sch 1 para 18. For the purposes of the Veterinary Medicines Regulations 2011, SI 2011/2159, a reference to a member state is a reference to a member state of the European Union and Norway, Iceland and Liechtenstein: reg 2(4). As to the mutual recognition of marketing authorisations between member states, and applications for a marketing authorisation in more than one member state, see Sch 1 Pt 6; and PARA 408.

390. Time for authorisation. The Secretary of State[1] must ensure that the procedure for granting an authorisation for a veterinary medicinal product[2] is completed within a maximum of 210 days after the submission of the application[3].

1   As to the Secretary of State see PARA 2 note 1.
2   As to the meaning of 'veterinary medicinal product' see PARA 387.
3   Veterinary Medicines Regulations 2011, SI 2011/2159, Sch 1 para 17.

391. Additional information. The Secretary of State[1] may require the applicant to provide additional information or to generate additional data, including laboratory testing, or may require the applicant to provide samples of any medicinal product, its starting materials and intermediate products or other constituent materials for testing in a laboratory[2].

1 As to the Secretary of State see PARA 2 note 1.
2 Veterinary Medicines Regulations 2011, SI 2011/2159, Sch 1 para 19.

392. Products authorised in another member state. Where the Secretary of State[1] is informed or discovers that another member state[2] has authorised a veterinary medicinal product[3] that is the subject of an application for authorisation by the Secretary of State, the Secretary of State must reject the application unless it was submitted in accordance with the mutual recognition procedure or the decentralised procedure[4].

1 As to the Secretary of State see PARA 2 note 1.
2 As to the meaning of 'member state' see PARA 389 note 4.
3 As to the meaning of 'veterinary medicinal product' see PARA 387.
4 Veterinary Medicines Regulations 2011, SI 2011/2159, Sch 1 para 20. As to the mutual recognition procedure and the decentralised procedure see Sch 1 Pt 6; and PARA 408.

393. Assessment reports. The Secretary of State[1] must produce an assessment of the dossier[2], consisting of an evaluation of the results of the pharmaceutical, safety and residue tests and the pre-clinical and clinical trials of the veterinary medicinal product[3] concerned, and any additional related information[4].

1 As to the Secretary of State see PARA 2 note 1.
2 In any provision in the Veterinary Medicines Regulations 2011, SI 2011/2159 requiring the Secretary of State to issue an authorisation within a set time, the clock does not start until the Secretary of State has checked that the application dossier is in accordance with these Regulations and has validated the application: reg 32(1). The clock is stopped during any period that the Secretary of State requires an applicant to provide further data until all the further data required have been provided: reg 32(2). The clock is also stopped during any period that the applicant is given to provide oral or written explanations: reg 32(3). The Secretary of State may stop the clock pending payment of outstanding fees: reg 32(4).
3 As to the meaning of 'veterinary medicinal product' see PARA 387.
4 Veterinary Medicines Regulations 2011, SI 2011/2159, Sch 1 para 21.

394. Grant of a marketing authorisation. When granting a marketing authorisation, the Secretary of State[1] must inform the applicant of the summary of product characteristics that has been approved, and the distribution category of the product[2].

The Secretary of State may not grant a marketing authorisation for a veterinary medicinal product[3] for food-producing species unless the pharmacologically active substances comply with certain requirements[4].

1 As to the Secretary of State see PARA 2 note 1.
2 Veterinary Medicines Regulations 2011, SI 2011/2159, Sch 1 para 22.
3 As to the meaning of 'veterinary medicinal product' see PARA 387.
4 See the Veterinary Medicines Regulations 2011, SI 2011/2159, Sch 1 para 23.

395. Refusal of a marketing authorisation. The Secretary of State[1] must refuse to grant a marketing authorisation if the application does not comply with the Veterinary Medicines Regulations 2011[2]. In addition, the Secretary of State must refuse to grant it if:

(1) the data submitted with the application are inadequate[3];
(2) the risk-benefit balance of the veterinary medicinal product is unfavourable[4];

(3) the product has insufficient therapeutic effect[5];

(4) the withdrawal period proposed by the applicant is not long enough to ensure that EU requirements[6] are complied with, or insufficiently substantiated[7];

(5) the veterinary medicinal product is for a prohibited use[8];

(6) the way that the product will be used will have an unnecessarily undesirable effect on the environment[9].

The Secretary of State may refuse to grant a marketing authorisation if there is Community legislation pending that is incompatible with the requested authorisation or if additional data have been requested and those data are not provided within such time limit as may be stipulated[10].

If the Secretary of State, on the grounds of safety, quality or efficacy intends to refuse an application, or proposes to grant a marketing authorisation that is different from the one applied for, the Secretary of State must notify the applicant accordingly, and the applicant may appeal to the Veterinary Products Committee[11].

1 As to the Secretary of State see PARA 2 note 1.
2 Veterinary Medicines Regulations 2011, SI 2011/2159, Sch 1 para 24(1). The Veterinary Medicines Regulations 2011 mentioned in the text are the Veterinary Medicines Regulations 2011, SI 2011/2159.
3 Veterinary Medicines Regulations 2011, SI 2011/2159, Sch 1 para 24(2)(a).
4 Veterinary Medicines Regulations 2011, SI 2011/2159, Sch 1 para 24(2)(b). 'Risk-benefit balance' means an evaluation of the positive therapeutic effects of the veterinary medicinal product in relation to any risk to human or animal health relating to the quality, safety or efficacy of the veterinary medicinal product or any risk of undesirable effects on the environment: art 2(2). As to the meaning of 'animal' see PARA 387 note 2.
5 Veterinary Medicines Regulations 2011, SI 2011/2159, Sch 1 para 24(2)(c).
6 Ie the requirements under the European Parliament and Council Regulation (EC) 470/2009 (OJ L152, 16.6.2009, p 11–22) laying down Community procedures for the establishment of residue limits of pharmacologically active substances in foodstuffs of animal origin.
7 Veterinary Medicines Regulations 2011, SI 2011/2159, Sch 1 para 24(2)(d).
8 Veterinary Medicines Regulations 2011, SI 2011/2159, Sch 1 para 24(2)(e).
9 Veterinary Medicines Regulations 2011, SI 2011/2159, Sch 1 para 24(2)(f).
10 Veterinary Medicines Regulations 2011, SI 2011/2159, Sch 1 para 24(3).
11 Veterinary Medicines Regulations 2011, SI 2011/2159, Sch 1 para 24(4). As to the Veterinary Products Committee see PARA 442.

396. Publication following the grant of a marketing authorisation. On granting a marketing authorisation the Secretary of State[1] must publish the notice granting the marketing authorisation, the summary of the product characteristics and the assessment report that has already been prepared but with any commercially confidential or personal information deleted[2].

The Secretary of State must update the assessment report whenever new information that is of importance and relates to the quality, safety or efficacy of the veterinary medicinal product[3] becomes available[4].

The Secretary of State must send a copy of the assessment report, and any update, to the holder of the marketing authorisation before publication to enable the holder to make representations concerning any confidential or personal information that may be in it, and may specify a date by which representations must be made[5].

1 As to the Secretary of State see PARA 2 note 1.
2 Veterinary Medicines Regulations 2011, SI 2011/2159, Sch 1 para 25(1).
3 As to the meaning of 'veterinary medicinal product' see PARA 387.
4 Veterinary Medicines Regulations 2011, SI 2011/2159, Sch 1 para 25(2).
5 Veterinary Medicines Regulations 2011, SI 2011/2159, Sch 1 para 25(3).

397.   Marketing authorisations in exceptional circumstances. In exceptional circumstances, and if there is no other product with a full marketing authorisation for the indicated condition in the target species, the Secretary of State[1] may grant an exceptional marketing authorisation consisting of a provisional marketing authorisation subject to a requirement for the applicant to provide further data or a limited marketing authorisation for a product with a limited market[2].

The Secretary of State must reassess each provisional or limited marketing authorisation annually[3].

1   As to the Secretary of State see PARA 2 note 1.
2   Veterinary Medicines Regulations 2011, SI 2011/2159, Sch 1 para 26(1).
3   Veterinary Medicines Regulations 2011, SI 2011/2159, Sch 1 para 26(2).

398.   Provisions of samples and expertise. The Secretary of State[1] may require a marketing authorisation holder to provide, at any time and at any stage of the manufacturing process, samples of starting materials or the veterinary medicinal product[2] for testing[3]. At the request of the Secretary of State, the marketing authorisation holder must provide technical expertise to facilitate any analysis of the product[4]. Failure to comply with these provisions is an offence[5].

1   As to the Secretary of State see PARA 2 note 1.
2   As to the meaning of 'veterinary medicinal product' see PARA 387.
3   Veterinary Medicines Regulations 2011, SI 2011/2159, Sch 1 para 27(1).
4   Veterinary Medicines Regulations 2011, SI 2011/2159, Sch 1 para 27(2).
5   See the Veterinary Medicines Regulations 2011, SI 2011/2159, Sch 1 para 27(3).

399.   Supply of information. A marketing authorisation holder must immediately inform the Secretary of State[1] on receipt of any new information that might adversely affect the risk-benefit balance of the veterinary medicinal product[2].

The holder must immediately inform the Secretary of State of any prohibition or restriction imposed by the competent authorities of any country in which the veterinary medicinal product is authorised[3].

The Secretary of State may at any time require the marketing authorisation holder to provide data relating to the risk-benefit balance[4].

It is an offence to fail to comply with the above provisions or a requirement under them[5].

1   As to the Secretary of State see PARA 2 note 1.
2   Veterinary Medicines Regulations 2011, SI 2011/2159, Sch 1 para 28(1). As to the meaning of 'veterinary medicinal product' see PARA 387. As to the meaning of 'risk-benefit balance' see PARA 395 note 4.
3   Veterinary Medicines Regulations 2011, SI 2011/2159, Sch 1 para 28(2).
4   Veterinary Medicines Regulations 2011, SI 2011/2159, Sch 1 para 28(3).
5   Veterinary Medicines Regulations 2011, SI 2011/2159, Sch 1 para 28(4).

400.   Duties on the holder of a marketing authorisation relating to an immunological product. Before placing an immunological product[1] on the market the holder of the marketing authorisation must either notify the Secretary of State[2] asking for written approval to do so or, if the holder has already received written approval from another member state[3] permitting the release of the product, send a copy of that approval to the Secretary of State[4].

If so notified the Secretary of State must give or refuse a written approval as soon as is reasonably practicable[5].

It is an offence to place an immunological product on the market without a written approval issued by the Secretary of State or (if the approval was issued by another member state) without sending a copy of that approval to the Secretary of State[6].

1   'Immunological veterinary medicinal product' means a veterinary medicinal product administered to animals in order to produce active or passive immunity or to diagnose the state of immunity: Veterinary Medicines Regulations 2011, SI 2011/2159, reg 2(1). As to the meaning of 'veterinary medicinal product' see PARA 387. As to the meaning of 'animal' see PARA 387 note 2.
2   As to the Secretary of State see PARA 2 note 1.
3   As to the meaning of 'member state' see PARA 389 note 4.
4   Veterinary Medicines Regulations 2011, SI 2011/2159, Sch 1 para 29(1).
5   Veterinary Medicines Regulations 2011, SI 2011/2159, Sch 1 para 29(2).
6   Veterinary Medicines Regulations 2011, SI 2011/2159, Sch 1 para 29(3).

401. Control tests. The holder of a marketing authorisation must give to the Secretary of State[1] on demand evidence that the holder has carried out all control tests required under the marketing authorisation, and the results of those tests, and failure to do so is an offence[2].

1   As to the Secretary of State see PARA 2 note 1.
2   Veterinary Medicines Regulations 2011, SI 2011/2159, Sch 1 para 30.

402. Placing on the market. A holder of a marketing authorisation must notify the Secretary of State[1] when the veterinary medicinal product[2] is first placed on the market in the United Kingdom[3], and the date on which it was placed on the market[4].

A holder of a marketing authorisation who removes the veterinary medicinal product from the market in the United Kingdom must notify the Secretary of State at least two months (or a shorter period in exceptional circumstances) before doing so[5].

Upon request by the Secretary of State, the marketing authorisation holder must provide all data relating to the volume of sales of the veterinary medicinal product by the holder and any data in the holder's possession relating to the number of prescriptions written for the product and the total volume supplied under those prescriptions[6].

It is an offence to fail to comply with the above provisions[7].

1   As to the Secretary of State see PARA 2 note 1.
2   As to the meaning of 'veterinary medicinal product' see PARA 387.
3   As to the meaning of 'United Kingdom' see PARA 20 note 4.
4   Veterinary Medicines Regulations 2011, SI 2011/2159, Sch 1 para 31(1).
5   Veterinary Medicines Regulations 2011, SI 2011/2159, Sch 1 para 31(2).
6   Veterinary Medicines Regulations 2011, SI 2011/2159, Sch 1 para 31(3).
7   Veterinary Medicines Regulations 2011, SI 2011/2159, Sch 1 para 31(4).

403. Duration and validity of a marketing authorisation. A marketing authorisation is initially valid for five years but may be renewed after that time on the basis of a re-evaluation of the risk-benefit balance[1].

Once renewed, the marketing authorisation is valid indefinitely unless, within five years of the renewal, the Secretary of State[2] notifies the holder, on justified grounds relating to pharmacovigilance, that the authorisation will cease to be valid five years from the first renewal unless the holder applies for a further renewal[3]. The further renewal is not time-limited[4].

Any marketing authorisation granted under the Veterinary Medicines Regulations 2011[5] that is not followed within three years of its granting by the actual placing on the market of the authorised veterinary medicinal product[6] in the United Kingdom[7] ceases to be valid[8].

When a veterinary medicinal product authorised under the Veterinary Medicines Regulations 2011[9] and previously placed on the market in the United Kingdom is not present on the market in the United Kingdom for a period of three consecutive years, its marketing authorisation ceases to be valid[10].

1 Veterinary Medicines Regulations 2011, SI 2011/2159, Sch 1 para 32(1). An application for renewal must be made at least six months, and not more than nine months, before the marketing authorisation ceases to be valid and an applicant who applies for the renewal of the marketing authorisation must enclose a list of all documents concerning the product that the applicant has submitted to the Secretary of State since the marketing authorisation was granted: Sch 1 para 32(2), (3). The Secretary of State may require the applicant to provide a copy of any of the listed documents at any time: Sch 1 para 32(4). As to the meaning of 'risk-benefit balance' see PARA 395 note 4.

2 As to the Secretary of State see PARA 2 note 1.

3 Veterinary Medicines Regulations 2011, SI 2011/2159, Sch 1 para 32(6).

4 Veterinary Medicines Regulations 2011, SI 2011/2159, Sch 1 para 32(7).

5 Ie the Veterinary Medicines Regulations 2011, SI 2011/2159.

6 As to the meaning of 'veterinary medicinal product' see PARA 387.

7 As to the meaning of 'United Kingdom' see PARA 20 note 4.

8 Veterinary Medicines Regulations 2011, SI 2011/2159, Sch 1 para 32(8). The Secretary of State may, on human or animal health grounds, grant exemptions from Sch 1 para 32(8) and (9): Sch 1 para 32(10). As to the meaning of 'animal' see PARA 387 note 2.

9 See note 5.

10 Veterinary Medicines Regulations 2011, SI 2011/2159, Sch 1 para 32(9). See note 8.

404. Variation of a marketing authorisation. The holder of a marketing authorisation may apply to the Secretary of State[1] for a variation of that marketing authorisation[2]. The Secretary of State, when granting a variation of a veterinary medicinal product may[3] (unless there are exceptional circumstances necessary to protect human or animal health or the environment) specify transitional measures to enable products produced in accordance with the previous authorisation to continue to be marketed for the transitional period[4].

The Secretary of State must give written reasons for refusing to grant a variation[5]; and if those reasons are on the grounds of safety, quality or efficacy and the variation is Type II or an extension application[6] (whether or not in each case as part of an application for a worksharing or grouped application), the applicant may appeal to the Veterinary Products Committee[7].

The holder of a marketing authorisation may apply for a minor change in a marketing authorisation to be made without the Secretary of State considering any scientific data (an 'administrative variation')[8]. If the Secretary of State grants an administrative variation, and subsequently establishes that this should have been a variation requiring consideration of scientific data, the Secretary of State may notify the marketing authorisation holder, require the holder to submit an application for a variation enabling data to be assessed and revoke the administrative variation[9].

After a marketing authorisation has been issued, the holder must take account of scientific and technical progress in manufacturing and control methods, and apply to the Secretary of State for any variation in the marketing authorisation that may be required to enable that veterinary medicinal product to be manufactured and checked by means of generally accepted scientific methods[10].

If the Secretary of State decides, for any of the reasons for suspending a marketing authorisation[11], or because the classification of a veterinary medicinal product should be changed, that a variation to a marketing authorisation is necessary, the Secretary of State must by a notification in writing to the holder of the marketing authorisation require that person to apply for a variation of the marketing authorisation[12], giving reasons for requiring the application to be made[13].

1   As to the Secretary of State see PARA 2 note 1.

2   Veterinary Medicines Regulations 2011, SI 2011/2159, Sch 1 para 33(2). The Secretary of State is the competent authority for the purposes of Commission Regulation (EC) 1234/2008 (OJ L334, 12.12.2008. p 7–24) concerning the examination of variations to the terms of marketing authorisations for medicinal products for human use and veterinary medicinal products (see PARA 11): Veterinary Medicines Regulations 2011, SI 2011/2159, Sch 1 para 33(1). An application for a variation under Sch 1 para 33(2) may only relate to a 'single variation' unless the application is submitted in accordance with Commission Regulation (EC) 1234/2008 (OJ L334, 12.12.2008. p 7–24), art 7 or art 20: Veterinary Medicines Regulations 2011, SI 2011/2159, Sch 1 para 33(3).

3   As to the meaning of 'veterinary medicinal product' see PARA 387.

4   Veterinary Medicines Regulations 2011, SI 2011/2159, Sch 1 para 33(4). As to the meaning of 'animal' see PARA 387 note 2.

5   The grounds on which the Secretary of State may refuse an application for a variation of a marketing authorisation are those set out in the Veterinary Medicines Regulations 2011, SI 2011/2159, Sch 1 para 24 (refusal of a marketing authorisation: see PARA 395): Sch 1 para 34(2).

6   As to the meaning of 'extension variation' see the definition 'extension of a marketing authorisation' in Commission Regulation (EC) 1234/2008 (OJ L334, 12.12.2008. p 7–24), art 2. For the purposes of the Veterinary Medicines Regulations 2011, SI 2011/2159 references to Types of variation are to those specified in Commission Regulation (EC) 1234/2008 (OJ L334, 12.12.2008. p 7–24): Veterinary Medicines Regulations 2011, SI 2011/2159, reg 2(3).

7   Veterinary Medicines Regulations 2011, SI 2011/2159, Sch 1 para 34(3). Schedule 1 para 33 applies in relation to the refusal by the Secretary of State of an application for a variation unless the procedure following the refusal of a variation is one of those set out in Commission Regulation (EC) 1234/2008 (OJ L334, 12.12.2008. p 7–24), art 13 (see PARA 11): Veterinary Medicines Regulations 2011, SI 2011/2159, Sch 1 para 34(1). As to the Veterinary Products Committee see PARA 442.

8   Veterinary Medicines Regulations 2011, SI 2011/2159, Sch 1 para 35(1).

9   Veterinary Medicines Regulations 2011, SI 2011/2159, Sch 1 para 35(2).

10   Veterinary Medicines Regulations 2011, SI 2011/2159, Sch 1 para 36.

11   Ie the grounds specified in the Veterinary Medicines Regulations 2011, SI 2011/2159, Sch 1 para 38 (see PARA 405).

12   The notification may specify a time limit within which the marketing authorisation holder must apply for the variation: Veterinary Medicines Regulations 2011, SI 2011/2159, Sch 1 para 37(2). If the marketing authorisation holder fails to apply for the variation within that time limit the Secretary of State may suspend or revoke the marketing authorisation: Sch 1 para 37(4).

13   Veterinary Medicines Regulations 2011, SI 2011/2159, Sch 1 para 37(1). If the variation is on the grounds of safety, quality or efficacy, the applicant may, within 28 days of the notification, appeal to the Veterinary Products Committee: Sch 1 para 37(3).

405. Suspension of marketing authorisation. The Secretary of State[1] may suspend a marketing authorisation at any time on being satisfied that this is necessary for the protection of animal or public health or the environment, the terms of the marketing authorisation have not been complied with or the veterinary medicinal product[2] has insufficient therapeutic effect[3].

The Secretary of State may also suspend a marketing authorisation on being satisfied that a marketing authorisation holder has failed to make an application for a variation to take account of scientific and technical progress in manufacturing and control methods to enable the veterinary medicinal product to be manufactured and checked by means of generally accepted scientific methods[4].

The Secretary of State must suspend a marketing authorisation on being satisfied that:

(1) the risk-benefit balance is unfavourable[5];

(2) the withdrawal period does not ensure that residues in foodstuffs obtained from the treated animal comply with the necessary EU requirements[6];

(3) information given in the application documents is incorrect[7];

(4) any control tests required have not been carried out[8];

(5) changes have been made to the manufacturing process without the authority of the Secretary of State[9]; or

(6) any information required to be supplied to the Secretary of State has not been so supplied[10].

If a marketing authorisation is suspended the Secretary of State must notify the holder immediately, and, unless the Secretary of State directs otherwise, the suspension has immediate effect, and continues in effect unless the marketing authorisation is reinstated[11].

If the suspension is on the grounds of safety, quality or efficacy, the holder may, within 28 days of the notification, appeal to the Veterinary Products Committee[12].

If the veterinary medicinal product is authorised in more than one member state[13], the Secretary of State: (a) must immediately refer the matter to the European Medicines Agency, and must comply with a decision of the Commission within 30 days of the decision; and (b) may suspend the marketing and the use of the veterinary medicinal product in the United Kingdom pending a decision of the Agency, but must inform the Commission and the other member states no later than the following working day of the reasons for the action[14].

When a marketing authorisation is suspended, the Secretary of State may in addition prohibit the supply of the veterinary medicinal product, and if necessary require the marketing authorisation holder to recall the product; and failure to comply with a requirement or prohibition under this sub-paragraph is an offence[15].

1 As to the Secretary of State see PARA 2 note 1.

2 As to the meaning of 'veterinary medicinal product' see PARA 387.

3 Veterinary Medicines Regulations 2011, SI 2011/2159, Sch 1 para 40(1). As to the meaning of 'animal' see PARA 387 note 2.

4 Veterinary Medicines Regulations 2011, SI 2011/2159, Sch 1 para 38(2).

5 Veterinary Medicines Regulations 2011, SI 2011/2159, Sch 1 para 38(3)(a). As to the meaning of 'risk-benefit balance' see PARA 395 note 4.

6 Veterinary Medicines Regulations 2011, SI 2011/2159, Sch 1 para 38(3)(b). The EU requirements mentioned in the text are those under European Parliament and Council Directive (EC) 470/2009 laying down Community procedures for the establishment of residue limits of pharmacologically active substances in foodstuffs of animal origin.

7 Veterinary Medicines Regulations 2011, SI 2011/2159, Sch 1 para 38(3)(c).

8 Veterinary Medicines Regulations 2011, SI 2011/2159, Sch 1 para 38(3)(d).

9 Veterinary Medicines Regulations 2011, SI 2011/2159, Sch 1 para 38(3)(e).

10 Veterinary Medicines Regulations 2011, SI 2011/2159, Sch 1 para 38(3)(f).

11 Veterinary Medicines Regulations 2011, SI 2011/2159, Sch 1 para 39(1).

12 Veterinary Medicines Regulations 2011, SI 2011/2159, Sch 1 para 39(2). As to the Veterinary Products Committee see PARA 442.

13 As to the meaning of 'member state' see PARA 389 note 4.

14 Veterinary Medicines Regulations 2011, SI 2011/2159, Sch 1 para 39(3).

15 Veterinary Medicines Regulations 2011, SI 2011/2159, Sch 1 para 39(4).

406. Revocation of marketing authorisation. The Secretary of State[1] may revoke any marketing authorisation that has been suspended for more than 28 days unless there is a current appeal to the Veterinary Products Committee[2], and may publicise a revocation in such manner as the Secretary of State sees fit[3].

1   As to the Secretary of State see PARA 2 note 1.
2   As to the Veterinary Products Committee see PARA 442.
3   Veterinary Medicines Regulations 2011, SI 2011/2159, Sch 1 para 40.

407.   Prohibiting the supply of veterinary medicinal products.   In addition to the powers to suspend a marketing authorisation[1], the Secretary of State[2], on being satisfied that a product has not been manufactured in accordance with the marketing authorisation, may prohibit the supply of a veterinary medicinal product[3], and if necessary require the marketing authorisation holder to recall it, and failure to comply with a requirement or prohibition under provision an offence[4].

The prohibition on supply and the requirement for recall may be confined to specific production batches[5].

In the case of an immunological veterinary medicinal product[6] manufactured outside the United Kingdom, if a batch has had all the tests that were originally carried out by the manufacturer repeated by the competent authority of another member state[7], the Secretary of State may not prohibit the release of that batch if all the results have been submitted to the Secretary of State and the results demonstrate that the product is within the terms of the authorisation[8].

1   See PARA 405.
2   As to the Secretary of State see PARA 2 note 1.
3   As to the meaning of 'veterinary medicinal product' see PARA 387.
4   Veterinary Medicines Regulations 2011, SI 2011/2159, Sch 1 para 41(1).
5   Veterinary Medicines Regulations 2011, SI 2011/2159, Sch 1 para 41(2).
6   As to the meaning of 'immunological veterinary product' see PARA 400 note 1.
7   As to the meaning of 'member state' see PARA 389 note 4.
8   Veterinary Medicines Regulations 2011, SI 2011/2159, Sch 1 para 41(3).

408.   Mutual recognition and multiple applications.   If a veterinary medicinal product[1] has already received a marketing authorisation in another member state at the time of application, and the holder of the marketing authorisation applies for a marketing authorisation in the United Kingdom[2], the mutual recognition procedure applies[3].

The Secretary of State[4] may grant the marketing authorisation even though not all member states have agreed to grant it, but must revoke or vary the authorisation if this is necessary to comply with the decision of the Commission when it is received[5].

If an applicant wishes to apply for a marketing authorisation in more than one member state, and a marketing authorisation does not exist in any member state for the product ('the decentralised procedure'), the applicant must (1) apply simultaneously in all the relevant member states[6]; (2) submit a dossier to the Secretary of State that is identical to the dossier being submitted to all the other member states[7]; (3) include a list of all member states in which applications have been made[8]; and (4) nominate one of them to act as the reference member state[9] to prepare a draft assessment report and drafts of the summary of product characteristics, labelling and package leaflet for consideration by the other member states ('the concerned member states')[10]. The Secretary of State may only refuse an application on the grounds of serious risk to human or animal health or the environment[11].

1   As to the meaning of 'veterinary medicinal product' see PARA 387.

2 As to the meaning of 'United Kingdom' see PARA 20 note 4.
3 Veterinary Medicines Regulations 2011, SI 2011/2159, Sch 1 para 42(1). As to the mutual recognition procedure see Sch 1 para 42(3)–(9). As to the procedure for an application in another member state see Sch 1 para 43. As to the meaning of 'member state' see PARA 389 note 4.
4 As to the Secretary of State see PARA 2 note 1.
5 Veterinary Medicines Regulations 2011, SI 2011/2159, Sch 1 para 42(10).
6 Veterinary Medicines Regulations 2011, SI 2011/2159, Sch 1 para 44(1)(a). As to the procedure see further Sch 1 para 44(5)–(8).
7 Veterinary Medicines Regulations 2011, SI 2011/2159, Sch 1 para 44(1)(b).
8 Veterinary Medicines Regulations 2011, SI 2011/2159, Sch 1 para 44(1)(c).
9 If the United Kingdom is the reference member state, the Secretary of State must prepare a draft assessment report and drafts of the summary of product characteristics, labelling and package leaflet within 120 days of the receipt of a valid application and must send them to the other concerned member states and to the applicant: Veterinary Medicines Regulations 2011, SI 2011/2159, Sch 1 para 44(2). If the United Kingdom is not the reference member state, within 90 days after receipt of the assessment report and drafts of the summary of product characteristics, labelling and package leaflet from the reference member state, the Secretary of State must, subject to the following provisions, either approve the assessment report, the summary of product characteristics, the labelling and the package leaflet, and inform the reference member state accordingly or notify the reference member state that the Secretary of State will not approve it, and provide the reference member state with a detailed statement of the reasons: Sch 1 para 44(3).
10 Veterinary Medicines Regulations 2011, SI 2011/2159, Sch 1 para 44(1)(d).
11 Veterinary Medicines Regulations 2011, SI 2011/2159, Sch 1 para 44(4). As to the meaning of 'animal' see PARA 387 note 2.

409. Homoeopathic veterinary medicinal products. A homoeopathic remedy[1] may be placed on the market in accordance with a registration by the Secretary of State[2] instead of in accordance with a marketing authorisation if it complies with the following[3]. It must not be an immunological product[4]. The route of administration must be as described in the European Pharmacopoeia or, if it is not described there, by a pharmacopoeia currently used officially in any member state[5]. There must be a sufficient degree of dilution to guarantee the safety of the product, and in any event it must not contain more than one part in 10,000 of the mother tincture[6]. All other provisions relating to marketing authorisations apply in the same way to registrations of a homoeopathic remedy[7].

1 For these purposes, a homoeopathic remedy is a veterinary medicinal product (which may contain a number of principles) prepared from homoeopathic stocks in accordance with a homoeopathic manufacturing procedure described in the European Pharmacopoeia or, if it is not described there, in a pharmacopoeia published by the British Pharmacopoeia Commission or by the competent authority of any member state: Veterinary Medicines Regulations 2011, SI 2011/2159, Sch 1 para 62. As to the meaning of 'member state' see PARA 389 note 4.
2 As to the Secretary of State see PARA 2 note 1.
3 Veterinary Medicines Regulations 2011, SI 2011/2159, Sch 1 para 63(1). This is by way of derogation from the provisions of the Veterinary Medicines Regulations 2011, SI 2011/2159, requiring a marketing authorisation for a veterinary medicinal product: Sch 1 para 63(1). As to the application and procedure for registration see Sch 1 paras 64, 65. As to special provisions for products on the market before 1994 see Sch 1 para 66. The registration must specify the classification of the homoeopathic remedy, which must be one of the classifications specified for a veterinary medicinal product in Sch 3: Sch 1 para 67.
4 Veterinary Medicines Regulations 2011, SI 2011/2159, Sch 1 para 63(2).
5 Veterinary Medicines Regulations 2011, SI 2011/2159, Sch 1 para 63(3).
6 Veterinary Medicines Regulations 2011, SI 2011/2159, Sch 1 para 63(4).
7 Veterinary Medicines Regulations 2011, SI 2011/2159, Sch 1 para 63(5).

(iii) Manufacturing Authorisations

410. Manufacture of veterinary medicinal products. The holder of a marketing authorisation must ensure that every stage in the manufacture of the veterinary medicinal product[1] is carried out by the manufacturer specified in the marketing authorisation (who must, if the manufacture is carried out in the United Kingdom[2], hold a manufacturing authorisation for that type of product granted by the Secretary of State[3]) and failure to do so is an offence[4].

1   'Manufacture' includes any part of the manufacture of a veterinary medicinal product until the finished product is ready for sale in its final form as specified in the marketing authorisation but does not include the manufacture of an ingredient or breaking open the package of a veterinary medicinal product: Veterinary Medicines Regulations 2011, SI 2011/2159, reg 5(2). As to the meaning of 'veterinary medicinal product' see PARA 387.
2   As to the meaning of 'United Kingdom' see PARA 20 note 4.
3   As to the Secretary of State see PARA 2 note 1.
4   Veterinary Medicines Regulations 2011, SI 2011/2159, reg 5(1). As to the fees payable by manufacturers see Sch 7 paras 27–37.

411.   Granting an authorisation.   An application for a manufacturing authorisation must be made to the Secretary of State[1].

The Secretary of State must grant a manufacturing authorisation on being satisfied that the applicant has suitable and sufficient premises, staff, technical equipment and facilities for the manufacture, control and storage of the products, and will comply with the Veterinary Medicines Regulations 2011[2].

The holder of a manufacturing authorisation must notify the Secretary of State, and if necessary apply for a variation of the authorisation, before making a material alteration to the premises or facilities used under the authorisation, or to the operations for which they are used, and failure to do so is an offence[3].

1   Veterinary Medicines Regulations 2011, SI 2011/2159, Sch 2 para 1. As to the Secretary of State see PARA 2 note 1. The application must be processed within a specified time limit see Sch 2 para 2.
2   Veterinary Medicines Regulations 2011, SI 2011/2159, Sch 2 para 3. As to the information to be specified in the authorisation see Sch 2 para 4(1), (2).
3   Veterinary Medicines Regulations 2011, SI 2011/2159, Sch 2 para 4(3).

412.   Suspension, variation or revocation.   The Secretary of State[1] may suspend, vary or revoke a manufacturing authorisation if the holder has not complied with the Veterinary Medicines Regulations 2011[2], has manufactured a veterinary medicinal product[3] not authorised by the manufacturing authorisation, has produced a veterinary medicinal product outside the terms of a marketing authorisation or no longer has suitable premises or equipment[4]. The Secretary of State may also suspend, vary or revoke it on being satisfied that the qualified person (manufacture)[5] is not fulfilling their duties under the Veterinary Medicines Regulations 2011[6].

1   As to the Secretary of State see PARA 2 note 1.
2   Ie the Veterinary Medicines Regulations 2011, SI 2011/2159.
3   As to the meaning of 'veterinary medicinal product' see PARA 387.
4   Veterinary Medicines Regulations 2011, SI 2011/2159, Sch 2 para 5(1).
5   See the Veterinary Medicines Regulations 2011, SI 2011/2159, Sch 2 para 9; and PARA 415.
6   Veterinary Medicines Regulations 2011, SI 2011/2159, Sch 2 para 5(2).

413.   Inspection of premises.   The Secretary of State must inspect the premises relating to a manufacturing authorisation on a regular basis to ensure compliance with good manufacturing practice[2]. If the inspection complies with the specified principles[3] then the Secretary of State must issue a certificate of good manufacturing practice[4]. If an inspection is carried out at the request of the

European Pharmacopoeia to establish compliance with a monograph, the Secretary of State must issue a certificate of compliance with the monograph, if appropriate[5].

The Secretary of State must provide details of each certificate of good manufacturing practice issued to the European Medicines Agency for entry into a database[6]. If the outcome of the inspection is that the manufacturer does not comply with the principles and guidelines of good manufacturing practice, the Secretary of State must provide details to the Agency for entry into the database[7].

After each inspection of manufacturing premises, the inspector must make a written report to the Secretary of State on whether the principles and guidelines on good manufacturing practice and the conditions[8] are being complied with[9].

1　As to the Secretary of State see PARA 2 note 1.
2　Veterinary Medicines Regulations 2011, SI 2011/2159, Sch 2 para 6(1).
3　Ie with the Commission Directive (EC) 1991/412 (OJ L228, 17.8.1991, p 71) principles and guidelines of good manufacturing practice for veterinary medicinal products (see PARA 12).
4　See the Veterinary Medicines Regulations 2011, SI 2011/2159, Sch 2 para 6(2).
5　Veterinary Medicines Regulations 2011, SI 2011/2159, Sch 2 para 6(3).
6　Veterinary Medicines Regulations 2011, SI 2011/2159, Sch 2 para 6(4).
7　Veterinary Medicines Regulations 2011, SI 2011/2159, Sch 2 para 6(5).
8　Ie the conditions of the Veterinary Medicines Regulations 2011, SI 2011/2159.
9　Veterinary Medicines Regulations 2011, SI 2011/2159, Sch 2 para 7(1). The Secretary of State must inform the inspected manufacturer of the content of such reports: Sch 2 para 7(2).

414. Duties on the holder of a manufacturing authorisation. A holder of a manufacturing authorisation must ensure that the veterinary medicinal product[1] is manufactured in accordance with the marketing authorisation[2].

The holder must have permanently at their disposal the services of at least one qualified person (manufacture) who is on the register of qualified persons (manufacture) maintained by the Secretary of State[3] and must place all necessary facilities at the qualified person's disposal[4].

The holder must have a current Certificate of Good Manufacturing Practice[5], have in place a system of Quality Assurance and Quality Control; and give to the Secretary of State on request proof of all control tests carried out on the veterinary medicinal product or the constituents and intermediate products of the manufacturing process in accordance with the data submitted in support of the application for the marketing authorisation[6].

A holder who makes up a bulk package of veterinary medicinal products must ensure that the package is labelled, in a way that the label is clearly visible and legible, with specified information[7].

A holder must keep an adequate number of representative samples of each batch of a veterinary medicinal product in stock at least until the expiry date of the batch, and must submit any such sample to the Secretary of State if required in writing to do so[8].

1　As to the meaning of 'veterinary medicinal product' see PARA 387.
2　Veterinary Medicines Regulations 2011, SI 2011/2159, Sch 2 para 8(1).
3　As to the Secretary of State see PARA 2 note 1.
4　Veterinary Medicines Regulations 2011, SI 2011/2159, Sch 2 para 8(2).
5　As to the issuing of a Certificate of Good Manufacturing Practice see PARA 413.
6　Veterinary Medicines Regulations 2011, SI 2011/2159, Sch 2 para 8(3).
7　Veterinary Medicines Regulations 2011, SI 2011/2159, Sch 2 para 8(4). As to the specified information see Sch 2 para 8(4)(a)–(e).
8　Veterinary Medicines Regulations 2011, SI 2011/2159, Sch 2 para 8(5).

415. Qualified persons for manufacture. The Secretary of State[1] may appoint as a qualified person (manufacture) any person who is registered as a pharmaceutical chemist with the General Pharmaceutical Council or with the Pharmaceutical Society of Northern Ireland, a Chartered Chemist or a Fellow, Member or Associate Member of the Royal Society of Chemistry or a Chartered Biologist or a Fellow, Member or Associate Member of the Society of Biology, who qualified on the basis of a formal course of study lasting not less than three years full-time or equivalent and who has sufficient practical experience to carry out the specified duties[2].

The Secretary of State may refuse or revoke an appointment if the Secretary of State is not satisfied that a person has fulfilled or will fulfil his duties[3].

The qualified person (manufacture) must[4] ensure that each batch of veterinary medicinal product[5] manufactured under that person's responsibility is manufactured and checked in compliance with the Veterinary Medicines Regulations 2011[6] and in accordance with the data submitted in support of the application for the marketing authorisation[7].

If a manufacturer imports a veterinary medicinal product from a third country, including a product manufactured in a member state[8], the qualified person (manufacture) must ensure that, following importation, each production batch imported is fully tested in a member state, including a full qualitative analysis, a quantitative analysis of at least all the active substances and all the other tests or controls necessary to ensure the quality of a veterinary medicinal product is in accordance with the requirements of the marketing authorisation[9].

At each stage of manufacture, including release for sale, the qualified person (manufacture) must certify in writing that all control tests required under the marketing authorisation have been carried out, and that the production batch complies with the marketing authorisation[10].

1   As to the Secretary of State see PARA 2 note 1.
2   Veterinary Medicines Regulations 2011, SI 2011/2159, Sch 2 para 9(1). The specified duties mentioned in the text refers to the duties under Sch 2. The Secretary of State may exceptionally appoint a person who is not a member of one of the institutions mentioned in the text to act as a qualified person (manufacture) on being satisfied that that person has the educational qualifications or practical experience to carry out the duties under Sch 2: Sch 2 para 9(2).
3   Veterinary Medicines Regulations 2011, SI 2011/2159, Sch 2 para 10.
4   It is an offence to fail to comply with the Veterinary Medicines Regulations 2011, SI 2011/2159, Sch 2 para 11: Sch 2 para 11(5).
5   As to the meaning of 'veterinary medicinal product' see PARA 387.
6   Ie in accordance with the Veterinary Medicines Regulations 2011, SI 2011/2159.
7   Veterinary Medicines Regulations 2011, SI 2011/2159, Sch 2 para 11(1).
8   As to the meaning of 'member state' see PARA 389 note 4.
9   Veterinary Medicines Regulations 2011, SI 2011/2159, Sch 2 para 11(2). This does not apply where appropriate arrangements have been made by the European Community with the exporting country to ensure that the manufacturer of the veterinary medicinal product applies standards of good manufacturing practice at least equivalent to those laid down in Commission Directive (EC) 1991/412 (OJ L228, 17.8.1991, p 71) principles and guidelines of good manufacturing practice for veterinary medicinal products (see PARA 12) and to ensure that the controls in the Veterinary Medicines Regulations 2011, SI 2011/2159, Sch 2 para 11(2) have been carried out in the exporting country: Sch 2 para 11(3).
10   Veterinary Medicines Regulations 2011, SI 2011/2159, Sch 2 para 11(4).

416. Register. The Secretary of State[1] must maintain and publish a register of holders of manufacturing authorisations and qualified persons (manufacture)[2].

1   As to the Secretary of State see PARA 2 note 1.
2   Veterinary Medicines Regulations 2011, SI 2011/2159, Sch 2 para 12.

417.   Test sites.   The Secretary of State[1] may authorise premises to act as a test site to carry out contract testing for a holder of a manufacturing authorisation[2]. The premises must have a current certificate of good manufacturing practice[3]. Authorisation and inspection of the premises are the same as for a manufacturing authorisation[4].

1   As to the Secretary of State see PARA 2 note 1.
2   Veterinary Medicines Regulations 2011, SI 2011/2159, Sch 2 para 13(1).
3   Veterinary Medicines Regulations 2011, SI 2011/2159, Sch 2 para 13(2). As to the issuing of a certificate of good manufacturing practice see PARA 413.
4   Veterinary Medicines Regulations 2011, SI 2011/2159, Sch 2 para 13(3).

(iv) Wholesale Dealer Authorisations

418.   Wholesale dealing.   It is an offence to buy a veterinary medicinal product[1], other than by retail or for the purposes of retail supply[2], unless the buyer has a wholesale dealer's authorisation granted[3] by the Secretary of State[4].

1   As to the meaning of 'veterinary medicinal product' see PARA 387.
2   Ie in accordance with the Veterinary Medicines Regulations 2011, SI 2011/2159, Sch 3.
3   Ie granted under the Veterinary Medicines Regulations 2011, SI 2011/2159, reg 13 and Sch 3. As to the Secretary of State see PARA 2 note 1.
4   Veterinary Medicines Regulations 2011, SI 2011/2159, reg 13. As to the fees relating to a wholesale dealer's authorisation see Sch 7 paras 38–41.

419.   Granting a wholesale dealer's authorisation.   An application for a wholesale dealer's authorisation must be made to the Secretary of State[1].

The Secretary of State must grant a wholesale dealer's authorisation[2] on being satisfied that the following are complied with[3]:

(1)   the authorised site must be weatherproof, secure and lockable, clean and free from contaminants[4];

(2)   if the veterinary medicinal products covered by the authorisation are subject to specific storage conditions, the site must be capable of fulfilling those requirements[5];

(3)   the authorisation holder must have the services of technically competent staff and have an effective emergency recall plan[6].

The authorisation may cover more than one site and lapses if the holder does not deal in veterinary medicinal products for five years[7].

The holder of a wholesale dealer's authorisation must notify the Secretary of State, and if necessary apply for a variation of the authorisation, before making a material alteration to the premises or facilities used under the authorisation, or in the operations for which they are used, and failure to do so is an offence[8].

1   Veterinary Medicines Regulations 2011, SI 2011/2159, Sch 3 para 16. As to the Secretary of State see PARA 2 note 1. The Secretary of State must process an application for a wholesale dealer's authorisation within 90 days of receiving it: Sch 3 para 17.
2   As to the information to be contained in the authorisation see the Veterinary Medicines Regulations 2011, SI 2011/2159, Sch 3 para 19(1).
3   Veterinary Medicines Regulations 2011, SI 2011/2159, Sch 3 para 18(1).
4   Veterinary Medicines Regulations 2011, SI 2011/2159, Sch 3 para 18(2).
5   Veterinary Medicines Regulations 2011, SI 2011/2159, Sch 3 para 18(3).
6   Veterinary Medicines Regulations 2011, SI 2011/2159, Sch 3 para 18(4).
7   Veterinary Medicines Regulations 2011, SI 2011/2159, Sch 3 para 19(2).
8   Veterinary Medicines Regulations 2011, SI 2011/2159, Sch 3 para 19(3).

420.   Suspension, variation or revocation of the authorisation.   The Secretary of State[1] may suspend, vary or revoke a wholesale dealer's authorisation if the holder has not complied with the Veterinary Medicines Regulations 2011[2] or no longer has suitable premises or equipment[3].

1   As to the Secretary of State see PARA 2 note 1.
2   Ie the Veterinary Medicines Regulations 2011, SI 2011/2159.
3   Veterinary Medicines Regulations 2011, SI 2011/2159, Sch 3 para 20.

421. Duties on the holder of a wholesale dealer's authorisation. The holder of a wholesale dealer's authorisation must[1]:

(1)   store veterinary medicinal products[2] in accordance with the terms of the marketing authorisation for each product[3];

(2)   comply with the Guidelines on Good Distribution Practice of Medicinal Products for Human Use as if the veterinary medicinal products were authorised human medicinal products[4];

(3)   carry out a detailed stock audit at least once a year[5]; and

(4)   supply information and samples to the Secretary of State on demand[6].

1   It is an offence to fail to comply with the Veterinary Medicines Regulations 2011, SI 2011/2159, Sch 3 para 21: Sch 3 para 21(3).
2   As to the meaning of 'veterinary medicinal product' see PARA 387.
3   Veterinary Medicines Regulations 2011, SI 2011/2159, Sch 3 para 21(1)(a).
4   Veterinary Medicines Regulations 2011, SI 2011/2159, Sch 3 para 21(1)(b). As to human medicinal products see PARA 25 et seq.
5   Veterinary Medicines Regulations 2011, SI 2011/2159, Sch 3 para 21(1)(c).
6   Veterinary Medicines Regulations 2011, SI 2011/2159, Sch 3 para 21(1)(d).

(v) Exemptions

422. Administration of a product. It is an offence to administer a veterinary medicinal product to an animal[1] unless the product has a marketing authorisation authorising its administration in the United Kingdom[2], and the administration is in accordance with that marketing authorisation or it is administered in accordance with provisions[3] relating to the administration of a veterinary medicinal product outside the terms of a marketing authorisation or exemptions for small pet animals[4].

1   As to the meaning of 'veterinary medicinal product' and 'animal' see PARA 387.
2   As to the meaning of 'United Kingdom' see PARA 20 note 4.
3   As to such provision see the Veterinary Medicines Regulations 2011, SI 2011/2159, Schs 4, 6; and PARAS 423–429.
4   Veterinary Medicines Regulations 2011, SI 2011/2159, reg 8.

423. Administration outside the terms of a marketing authorisation. If there is no authorised veterinary medicinal product in the United Kingdom[1] for a condition the veterinary surgeon responsible for an animal[2] may, in particular to avoid unacceptable suffering, treat the animal concerned[3] with the following ('the cascade'), cascaded in the following order:

(1)   a veterinary medicinal product authorised in the United Kingdom for use with another animal species, or for another condition in the same species[4]; or

(2)   if there is no such product that is suitable, either a human medicinal product authorised in the United Kingdom or a veterinary medicinal product not authorised in the United Kingdom but authorised in another member state for use with any animal species (in the case of a food-producing animal, it must be a food-producing species)[5]; or

(3)   if there is no such product that is suitable, a veterinary medicinal

product prepared extemporaneously by a pharmacist, a veterinary surgeon or a person holding a manufacturing authorisation authorising the manufacture of that type of product[6].

1   As to the meaning of 'veterinary medicinal product' see PARA 387. As to the meaning of 'United Kingdom' see PARA 20 note 4.
2   As to the meaning of 'animal' see PARA 387 note 2.
3   A veterinary surgeon acting under the Veterinary Medicines Regulations 2011, SI 2011/2159, Sch 4 para 1 who prescribes a veterinary medicinal product may either administer it personally or may direct another person to do so under the responsibility of the veterinary surgeon: Sch 4 para 1(1).
4   Veterinary Medicines Regulations 2011, SI 2011/2159, Sch 4 para 1(2)(a). Any pharmacologically active substances included in a medicinal product administered to a food-producing animal under the cascade must be listed in Commission Regulation (EU) 37/2010 (OJ L15, 20.1.2010, p 1–72) on pharmacologically active substances and their classification regarding maximum residue limits in foodstuffs of animal origin, Annex Table 1: Veterinary Medicines Regulations 2011, SI 2011/2159, Sch 4 para 1(4). A veterinary surgeon prescribing or administering a veterinary medicinal product to a food-producing animal under the cascade must specify an appropriate withdrawal period: Sch 4 para 2(1). As to the withdrawal periods see Sch 4 para 2(2), (3). As to administration to food-producing horses see Sch 4 para 3. A veterinary medicinal product supplied for administration under the cascade may only be supplied in accordance with a prescription from a veterinary surgeon: Sch 3 para 13(1). As to the labelling of the product see Sch 3 para 13(2). It is an offence to fail to comply with Sch 3 para 13: Sch 3 para 13(3).
5   Veterinary Medicines Regulations 2011, SI 2011/2159, Sch 4 para 1(2)(b). In the case of a veterinary medicinal product imported from another member state, if the veterinary surgeon has not obtained a certificate from the Secretary of State under reg 25(5) (see PARA 435) permitting importation, the veterinary surgeon must obtain a certificate from the Secretary of State before administration: Sch 4 para 1(3). As to the meaning of 'member state' see PARA 389 note 4.
6   Veterinary Medicines Regulations 2011, SI 2011/2159, Sch 4 para 1(2)(c).

424. Immunological products. In the event of serious epizootic diseases, the Secretary of State[1] may permit in writing the administration of immunological veterinary medicinal products[2] without a marketing authorisation, in the absence of a suitable medicinal product and after informing the Commission of the detailed conditions of use and may publicise any permit as the Secretary of State sees fit[3].

If an animal is imported from, or exported to, a third country, the Secretary of State may permit the administration to that animal of an immunological veterinary medicinal product that is not covered by a marketing authorisation in the United Kingdom[4] but is authorised under the legislation of the third country[5].

1   As to the Secretary of State see PARA 2 note 1.
2   As to the meaning of 'immunological veterinary medicinal product' see PARA 400 note 1.
3   Veterinary Medicines Regulations 2011, SI 2011/2159, Sch 4 para 4.
4   As to the meaning of 'United Kingdom' see PARA 20 note 4.
5   Veterinary Medicines Regulations 2011, SI 2011/2159, Sch 4 para 5.

425. Administration by veterinary surgeons from other member states. Veterinary surgeons practising in another member state may bring into the United Kingdom[1] and administer to animals small quantities of veterinary medicinal products[2] that are not authorised for use in the United Kingdom if:

(1)   the quantity does not exceed the requirements for the treatment of specific animals[3];

(2)   the product is authorised in the member state in which the veterinary surgeon is established[4];

(3)   the product is transported by the veterinary surgeon in the original manufacturer's packaging[5];

(4)   in the case of administration to food-producing animals, there is a veterinary medicinal product authorised in the United Kingdom that has the same qualitative and quantitative composition in terms of active substances[6];

(5)   the veterinary surgeon is acquainted with the Guide to Professional Conduct issued by the Royal College of Veterinary Surgeons[7].

The veterinary surgeon must only supply to the owner or keeper enough veterinary medicinal product to complete the treatment of the animals concerned[8].

The veterinary surgeon must[9]:

(a)   ensure that the withdrawal period specified on the label of the product is complied with, or the United Kingdom withdrawal period for the equivalent product authorised in the United Kingdom if this is longer than the one on the label[10]; and

(b)   keep detailed records of the animals treated, the diagnosis or clinical assessment, the products administered, the dosage administered, the duration of treatment and the withdrawal period applied, and must keep them in the United Kingdom for at least three years[11].

The overall range and quantity of veterinary medicinal products carried by the veterinary surgeon must not exceed that generally required for the daily needs of good veterinary practice[12].

1   As to the meaning of 'United Kingdom' see PARA 20 note 4. As to the meaning of 'member state' see PARA 389 note 4.
2   As to the meaning of 'veterinary medicinal product' see PARA 387. The Veterinary Medicines Regulations 2011, SI 2011/2159, Sch 4 para 6 does not apply in relation to immunological veterinary medicinal products: Sch 4 para 6(5). As to the meaning of 'immunological veterinary medicinal product' see PARA 400 note 1.
3   Veterinary Medicines Regulations 2011, SI 2011/2159, Sch 4 para 6(1)(a). As to the meaning of 'animal' see PARA 387 note 2.
4   Veterinary Medicines Regulations 2011, SI 2011/2159, Sch 4 para 6(1)(b).
5   Veterinary Medicines Regulations 2011, SI 2011/2159, Sch 4 para 6(1)(c).
6   Veterinary Medicines Regulations 2011, SI 2011/2159, Sch 4 para 6(1)(d).
7   Veterinary Medicines Regulations 2011, SI 2011/2159, Sch 4 para 6(1)(e).
8   Veterinary Medicines Regulations 2011, SI 2011/2159, Sch 4 para 6(2).
9   Failure to comply with these provisions is an offence: Veterinary Medicines Regulations 2011, SI 2011/2159, Sch 4 para 6(3).
10   Veterinary Medicines Regulations 2011, SI 2011/2159, Sch 4 para 6(3)(a).
11   Veterinary Medicines Regulations 2011, SI 2011/2159, Sch 4 para 6(3)(b).
12   Veterinary Medicines Regulations 2011, SI 2011/2159, Sch 4 para 6(4).

426.   Treatment in exceptional circumstances. Where the health situation so requires, and where there is no suitable veterinary medicinal product available either as an authorised product or under the cascade[1], a veterinary surgeon may treat an animal with a medicinal product authorised in a third country; but a veterinary surgeon who has not obtained a certificate from the Secretary of State[2] permitting importation must obtain a certificate from the Secretary of State before treating the animal[3].

1   As to the meaning of 'veterinary medicinal product' see PARA 387. As to the meaning of 'cascade' see PARA 423.
2   Ie under the Veterinary Medicines Regulations 2011, SI 2011/2159, reg 25(5) (see PARA 435). As to the Secretary of State see PARA 2 note 1. The certificate may be granted subject to any condition the Secretary of State thinks fit: Veterinary Medicines Regulations 2011, SI 2011/2159, Sch 4 para 7(2).

3   Veterinary Medicines Regulations 2011, SI 2011/2159, Sch 4 para 7(1). As to the meaning of 'animal' see PARA 387 note 2.

427.   Administration of a homoeopathic remedy.   A registered homoeopathic remedy or a homoeopathic remedy prepared and supplied by a pharmacist[1] may be administered to an animal[2] by anyone, subject to any restrictions specified in its registration[3].

A veterinary surgeon may administer, either personally or under the veterinary surgeon's responsibility a homoeopathic remedy authorised for human use or a homoeopathic remedy prepared extemporaneously by a veterinary surgeon, a pharmacist or a person holding a manufacturing authorisation authorising the manufacture of that type of product[4].

1   Ie under the Veterinary Medicines Regulations 2011, SI 2011/2159, Sch 3 para 10 (see PARA 431).
2   As to the meaning of 'animal' see PARA 387 note 2.
3   Veterinary Medicines Regulations 2011, SI 2011/2159, Sch 4 para 8(1). A homoeopathic remedy that was on the market before 1st January 1994 may be administered by anyone: Sch 4 para 8(2).
4   Veterinary Medicines Regulations 2011, SI 2011/2159, Sch 4 para 8(2).

428.   Administration under an animal test certificate.   A medicinal product may be administered in accordance with an animal test certificate granted for research purposes by the Secretary of State[1].

An application for an animal test certificate may be refused if this is necessary for the protection of animal[2] or public health or the environment, and the animal test certificate may be varied, suspended or revoked in the same way as a marketing authorisation[3].

The holder of an animal test certificate who supplies a product for administration that is not within the terms of the animal test certificate is guilty of an offence[4].

The holder of an animal test certificate test who becomes aware of any serious adverse reaction[5] following the administration of a product under an animal test certificate must report the reaction to the Secretary of State within 15 days of learning of it[6].

1   Veterinary Medicines Regulations 2011, SI 2011/2159, Sch 4 para 9(1). As to the Secretary of State see PARA 2 note 1.
2   As to the meaning of 'animal' see PARA 387 note 2.
3   Veterinary Medicines Regulations 2011, SI 2011/2159, Sch 4 para 9(2). As to the variation, suspension or revocation of a marketing authorisation see PARAS 404–406.
4   Veterinary Medicines Regulations 2011, SI 2011/2159, Sch 4 para 9(3).
5   As to the meaning of 'serious adverse reaction' see PARA 430 note 8.
6   Veterinary Medicines Regulations 2011, SI 2011/2159, Sch 4 para 9(4).

429.   Small pets.   A veterinary medicinal product[1] intended solely for an animal to which these provisions apply[2] may be placed on the market, imported or administered without a marketing authorisation if it complies with certain conditions[3] relating to its manufacture[4] and the active substance in the veterinary product must be approved by the Secretary of State[5]. The veterinary medicinal product must not be an antibiotic[6]. Nor must it contain any narcotic or psychotropic substance[7] or be intended for treatments or pathological processes that require a precise prior diagnosis or the use of which may cause effects that impede or interfere with subsequent diagnostic or therapeutic measures[8].

The product must be clearly labelled[9] as being exempt from the requirements of the Veterinary Medicines Regulations 2011[10] in relation to a marketing authorisation[11].

The method of administration must be oral or topical or (in the case of a product for fish) by addition to the water[12].

The pack size must only be sufficient for a single course of treatment or, in the case of a veterinary medicinal product for aquarium fish, sufficient for a single course of treatment of no more than 7 administrations to an aquarium of 25,000 litres[13].

The manufacturer, importer or retailer of a veterinary medicinal product must notify the Secretary of State within 15 days of learning of any serious adverse reactions[14] and make a record of each adverse reaction and serious adverse reaction on becoming aware of it and keep it for three years[15].

1   As to the meaning of 'veterinary medicinal product' see PARA 387.

2   Ie aquarium animals, cage birds, ferrets, homing pigeons, rabbits, small rodents; and terrarium animals kept exclusively as a pet: see the Veterinary Medicines Regulations 2011, SI 2011/2159, Sch 6 para 1.

3   See the Veterinary Medicines Regulations 2011, SI 2011/2159, Sch 6 para 2.

4   The product must have been manufactured by (1) the holder of a manufacturing authorisation, if manufactured in the United Kingdom; (2) the holder of a manufacturing authorisation issued under European Parliament and Council Directive (EC) 2001/82 (OJ L311, 28.11.2001, p 1) on the Community code relating to veterinary medicinal products, if manufactured in another member state; (3) in the case of Australia, Canada, New Zealand, or Switzerland, the holder of an authorisation from the competent authority permitting the manufacture of medicinal products; (4) in the case of any other country, a manufacturer whose premises have been inspected and approved by an officer of the Secretary of State: Veterinary Medicines Regulations 2011, SI 2011/2159, Sch 6 para 3. As to the meaning of 'United Kingdom' see PARA 20 note 4. As to the meaning of 'member state' see PARA 389 note 4.

5   See the Veterinary Medicines Regulations 2011, SI 2011/2159, Sch 6 para 5(1). The Secretary of State may approve an active substance for use in a veterinary medicinal product manufactured under Sch 6: Sch 6 para 6(1). The Secretary of State may not grant an approval if the active substance requires veterinary control: Sch 6 para 6(2). The approval must specify the species of animals for which it is approved, and may specify how the active substance or a product containing it is to be administered: Sch 6 para 6(3). The Secretary of State may suspend or revoke the approval (or limit it to a smaller number of species) if: (1) it is demonstrated that the substance requires veterinary control; (2) serious adverse reactions are reported making suspension or revocation necessary; or (3) it is demonstrated that the substance is carcinogenic, is genotoxic or shows developmental toxicity (including teratogenicity): Sch 6 para 6(4). The procedure for the refusal, suspension or revocation of an approval under Sch 6 para 6 is the same as the procedure for a marketing authorisation: Sch 6 para 6(4). As to marketing authorisations see PARA 389 et seq.

6   Veterinary Medicines Regulations 2011, SI 2011/2159, Sch 6 para 5(2).

7   Veterinary Medicines Regulations 2011, SI 2011/2159, Sch 6 para 5(3).

8   Veterinary Medicines Regulations 2011, SI 2011/2159, Sch 6 para 5(4).

9   As to information to be shown on the label see the Veterinary Medicines Regulations 2011, SI 2011/2159, Sch 6 para 6(2). If there is insufficient room on the label, the information may instead be in a package leaflet see Sch 6 para 6(3).

10   Ie the Veterinary Medicines Regulations 2011, SI 2011/2159.

11   Veterinary Medicines Regulations 2011, SI 2011/2159, Sch 6 para 6(1).

12   Veterinary Medicines Regulations 2011, SI 2011/2159, Sch 6 para 7.

13   Veterinary Medicines Regulations 2011, SI 2011/2159, Sch 6 para 8.

14   Ie as defined in the Veterinary Medicines Regulations 2011, SI 2011/2159, Sch 1 para 57 (see PARA 430 note 8).

15   Veterinary Medicines Regulations 2011, SI 2011/2159, Sch 6 para 9(1). It is an offence to fail to comply with Sch 6 para 9: Sch 6 para 9(2).

(3) PHARMACOVIGILANCE

430. Pharmacovigilance. A marketing authorisation holder must have permanently and continuously the services of an appropriately qualified person responsible for pharmacovigilance ('a qualified person (pharmacovigilance)') who resides in a member state[1].

The marketing authorisation holder must ensure that the qualified person (pharmacovigilance)[2]:

(1)   establishes and maintains a system that ensures that information about all suspected adverse reactions reported to the marketing authorisation holder is collected and collated in order to be accessible at least at one point in a member state[3];

(2)   answers any request from the Secretary of State[4] for the provision of additional information necessary for the evaluation of the benefits and risks afforded by a veterinary medicinal product[5] fully and within any time limit imposed by the Secretary of State when the information was requested, including the volume of sales of the veterinary medicinal product concerned and, if available, details of prescriptions[6];

(3)   provides to the Secretary of State any other information relevant to the evaluation of the benefits and risks afforded by a veterinary medicinal product, including appropriate information on post-marketing surveillance studies[7].

Where a marketing authorisation holder learns of any suspected serious adverse reaction[8], human adverse reaction[9] or unintended transmission of an infectious agent through a veterinary medicinal product, following the administration of the product in the United Kingdom, he must[10] make a record of what happened, report it (electronically if this is practicable) to the Secretary of State[11] and supply to the Secretary of State all relevant veterinary pharmacovigilance information that the holder possesses relating to the reaction, giving a full description of the incident and a list of all the symptoms using internationally recognised veterinary and medical terminology, either with the report or, if the information becomes available after the report has been sent, as soon after it becomes available as is reasonably practicable[12].

Where a marketing authorisation holder for a veterinary medicinal product authorised in the United Kingdom learns of any suspected serious, unexpected adverse reaction[13], human adverse reaction or unintended transmission of an infectious agent through a veterinary medicinal product, following the administration of the product in a third country, the holder must make a record of what happened, report the suspected reaction or transmission[14] (electronically if this is practicable) to the Secretary of State, the competent authorities of all member states in which the product is authorised, and the European Medicines Agency[15] and the holder must[16] supply to the Secretary of State, the competent authorities of all other member states where the product is authorised and the Agency, all relevant veterinary pharmacovigilance information in the holder's possession relating to the reaction[17].

The marketing authorisation holder must[18] submit to the Secretary of State records of all adverse reactions (including nil reports) in the form of a periodic safety update report for each marketing authorisation[19], including a summary of each incident and a list of all the symptoms using internationally recognised veterinary and medical terminology[20]. The periodic safety update report must include a scientific evaluation of the risk-benefit balance[21] of the veterinary medicinal product[22].

A marketing authorisation holder must not communicate information relating to pharmacovigilance concerns to the general public in relation to its authorised veterinary medicinal product without giving prior or simultaneous notification to the Secretary of State[23]. The marketing authorisation holder must ensure that such information is presented objectively and is not misleading[24].

Where, as a result of the evaluation of veterinary pharmacovigilance data, the Secretary of State considers that a marketing authorisation should be suspended, revoked or varied[25], the Secretary of State must forthwith inform the Agency, all other member states (irrespective of whether the product is authorised in another member state) and the marketing authorisation holder[26]. If urgent action is necessary for protecting human or animal health, the Secretary of State may suspend the marketing authorisation of a veterinary medicinal product, but must inform the Agency, the European Commission and the other member states within one working day[27].

If, following the opinion of the Agency, the Commission requests the Secretary of State to suspend, withdraw or vary the marketing authorisation, the Secretary of State must comply with that request immediately on a temporary basis[28]. The Secretary of State must take final measures in accordance with the decision of the Commission[29].

1   Veterinary Medicines Regulations 2011, SI 2011/2159, Sch 1 para 55(1). It is an offence to fail to comply with Sch 1 para 55: Sch 1 para 55(2). As to the meaning of 'member state' see PARA 389 note 4.
2   It is an offence to fail to comply with the Veterinary Medicines Regulations 2011, SI 2011/2159, Sch 1 para 56: Sch 1 para 56(2).
3   Veterinary Medicines Regulations 2011, SI 2011/2159, Sch 1 para 56(1)(a).
4   As to the Secretary of State see PARA 2 note 1.
5   As to the meaning of 'veterinary medicinal product' see PARA 387.
6   Veterinary Medicines Regulations 2011, SI 2011/2159, Sch 1 para 56(1)(b).
7   Veterinary Medicines Regulations 2011, SI 2011/2159, Sch 1 para 56(1)(c). 'Post-marketing surveillance studies' means a pharmacoepidemiological study or a clinical trial carried out in accordance with the terms of the marketing authorisation, conducted with the aim of identifying and investigating a safety hazard relating to an authorised veterinary medicinal product: Sch 1 para 56(1)(c).
8   'Serious adverse reaction' means an adverse reaction that results in death, is life-threatening, results in significant disability or incapacity, is a congenital anomaly or birth defect, or that results in permanent or prolonged signs in the animals treated: Veterinary Medicines Regulations 2011, SI 2011/2159, Sch 1 para 57(5).
9   'Human adverse reaction' means a reaction that is noxious and unintended and that occurs in a human being following exposure to a veterinary medicine: Veterinary Medicines Regulations 2011, SI 2011/2159, Sch 1 para 57(5).
10 It is an offence to fail to comply with the Veterinary Medicines Regulations 2011, SI 2011/2159, Sch 1 para 57: Sch 1 para 57(6).
11 See the Veterinary Medicines Regulations 2011, SI 2011/2159, Sch 1 para 57(1)–(3). This must be without delay and in any event within 15 days: Veterinary Medicines Regulations 2011, SI 2011/2159, Sch 1 para 57(3).
12 Veterinary Medicines Regulations 2011, SI 2011/2159, Sch 1 para 57(4).
13 For these purposes a reaction is unexpected if its nature, severity or outcome is not consistent with the summary of the product characteristics: Veterinary Medicines Regulations 2011, SI 2011/2159, Sch 1 para 58(1).
14 This must be reported without delay and in any event within 15 days: Veterinary Medicines Regulations 2011, SI 2011/2159, Sch 1 para 58(3).
15 See the Veterinary Medicines Regulations 2011, SI 2011/2159, Sch 1 para 58(1)–(3).
16 It is an offence to fail to comply with the Veterinary Medicines Regulations 2011, SI 2011/2159, Sch 1 para 58: Sch 1 para 58(5).

17 See the Veterinary Medicines Regulations 2011, SI 2011/2159, Sch 1 para 58(4).
18 It is an offence to fail to comply with the Veterinary Medicines Regulations 2011, SI 2011/2159, Sch 1 para 59: Sch 1 para 59(9).
19 As to when the report must be provided see the Veterinary Medicines Regulations 2011, SI 2011/2159, Sch 1 para 59(2)–(4).
20 Veterinary Medicines Regulations 2011, SI 2011/2159, Sch 1 para 59(1).
21 As to the meaning of 'risk-benefit balance' see PARA 395 note 4.
22 Veterinary Medicines Regulations 2011, SI 2011/2159, Sch 1 para 59(5). As to other information to be included in the report see Sch 1 para 59(6)–(8).
23 Veterinary Medicines Regulations 2011, SI 2011/2159, Sch 1 para 60(1). It is an offence to fail to comply with Sch 1 para 60(3).
24 Veterinary Medicines Regulations 2011, SI 2011/2159, Sch 1 para 60(2). See note 23.
25 Ie so as to restrict the indications, change the distribution category, amend the dose, add a contraindication or add a new precautionary measure.
26 Veterinary Medicines Regulations 2011, SI 2011/2159, Sch 1 para 61(1).
27 Veterinary Medicines Regulations 2011, SI 2011/2159, Sch 1 para 61(2).
28 Veterinary Medicines Regulations 2011, SI 2011/2159, Sch 1 para 61(3).
29 Veterinary Medicines Regulations 2011, SI 2011/2159, Sch 1 para 61(4).

(4) CLASSIFICATION AND SUPPLY

431. Retail supply. Veterinary Medicinal products[1] are classified according to how they may be supplied and the Secretary of State[2] must specify the classification when granting the initial marketing authorisation[3]. The categories of authorised veterinary medicinal products are (1) Prescription Only Medicine—Veterinarian[4]; (2) Prescription Only Medicine—Veterinarian, Pharmacist, Suitably Qualified Person[5]; (3) Non-Food Animal—Veterinarian, Pharmacist, Suitably Qualified Person; (4) Authorised Veterinary Medicine—General Sales List[6].

A person who prescribes a product under heads (1), (2) or (3) is under certain duties in relation to the safe administration of the product[7].

At least once a year every person entitled to supply a veterinary medicinal product on prescription must carry out a detailed audit, and incoming and outgoing veterinary medicinal products must be reconciled with products currently held in stock, any discrepancies being recorded[8].

1 As to the meaning of 'veterinary medicinal product' see PARA 387.
2 As to the Secretary of State see PARA 2 note 1.
3 Veterinary Medicines Regulations 2011, SI 2011/2159, Sch 3 para 1(2). The Secretary of State may change the classification after the marketing authorisation has been granted: see Sch 3 para 1(3).
4 Such a product may only be supplied by a veterinary surgeon or a pharmacist and must be supplied in accordance with a prescription from a veterinary surgeon after he has carried out an assessment of the animal (unless the animal is a wild animal and administration is authorised by the Secretary of State): see the Veterinary Medicines Regulations 2011, SI 2011/2159, Sch 3 paras 3(2), 4. Specified products must be classified as Prescription Only Medicine—Veterinarian, and others must be classified as Prescription Only Medicine—Veterinarian or Prescription Only Medicine—Veterinarian, Pharmacist, Suitably Qualified Person: see Sch 3 para 1(4), (5). As to the provision of prescriptions see Sch 3 paras 5, 6.
5 Such a product may only be supplied by a veterinary surgeon, a pharmacist or a suitably qualified person, and must be in accordance with a prescription from one of those persons: Veterinary Medicines Regulations 2011, SI 2011/2159, Sch 3 para 3(3). As to suitably qualified persons see Sch 3 para 14. See also note 4.
6 Veterinary Medicines Regulations 2011, SI 2011/2159, Sch 3 para 1(1). There are no restrictions on the importation or supply of these products: see reg 9(7), Sch 3 para 3(5).
7 See the Veterinary Medicines Regulations 2011, SI 2011/2159, Sch 3 paras 7–10.
8 Veterinary Medicines Regulations 2011, SI 2011/2159, Sch 3 para 15(1). It is an offence to fail to comply with this provision: Sch 3 para 15(2).

432. Wholesale supply. Only a holder of a marketing authorisation, the holder of a manufacturing authorisation or the holder of a wholesale dealer's authorisation granted by the Secretary of State[1] may supply a veterinary medicinal product[2] wholesale, or be in possession of it for that purpose[3].

Such a person may only supply a veterinary medicinal product if the authorisation in question relates to that product and the supply is to another person who is entitled to supply that product under the Veterinary Medicines Regulations 2011[4], either wholesale or retail[5].

It is immaterial whether or not the supply is for profit[6].

A wholesale dealer may break open any package (other than the immediate packaging) of a veterinary medicinal product[7].

It is an offence to fail to comply with these provisions[8].

1   As to the Secretary of State see PARA 2 note 1.
2   As to the meaning of 'veterinary medicinal product' see PARA 387.
3   Veterinary Medicines Regulations 2011, SI 2011/2159, Sch 3 para 2(1). Schedule 3 para 2 does not apply in relation to a retailer of veterinary medicinal products who supplies another retailer with such products for the purpose of alleviating a temporary supply shortage that could be detrimental to animal welfare: Sch 3 para 2(5).
4   Ie the Veterinary Medicines Regulations 2011, SI 2011/2159.
5   Veterinary Medicines Regulations 2011, SI 2011/2159, Sch 3 para 2(2). If the supply is to a suitably qualified person, it must be to the premises approved in accordance with Sch 3 para 14: Sch 3 para 2(3). As to the supply to a suitably qualified person see Sch 3 para 14.
6   Veterinary Medicines Regulations 2011, SI 2011/2159, Sch 3 para 2(4).
7   Veterinary Medicines Regulations 2011, SI 2011/2159, Sch 3 para 2(6).
8   Veterinary Medicines Regulations 2011, SI 2011/2159, Sch 3 para 2(7).

(5) RECORDS

433. Records. The keeper of a food-producing animal must keep proof of purchase of all veterinary medicinal products acquired for the animal[1] (or, if they were not bought, documentary evidence of how they were acquired)[2].

A veterinary surgeon who administers a veterinary medicinal product to a food-producing animal must enter certain information[3] personally in the keeper's records or give it to the keeper in writing in which case the keeper must enter the information[4].

The keeper of a food-producing animal must record certain information[5] in relation to the purchase, or otherwise acquisition, administration or destruction of a veterinary medicinal product[6].

A holder of a manufacturing authorisation must, as soon as is reasonably practicable, record certain information relating to each batch of veterinary medicinal product manufactured, assembled or supplied[7].

A holder of a wholesale dealer's authorisation must record certain information as soon as is reasonably practicable after each incoming or outgoing transaction (including disposal) relating to a veterinary medicinal product[8].

Certain records must be kept in relation to the receipt or supply of specified prescription products[9].

A veterinary surgeon administering a veterinary medicinal product to food-producing animals under the cascade[11], or permitting another person to administer it under that veterinary surgeon's responsibility, must, as soon as is reasonably practicable, record certain information[10].

It is an offence to fail to comply with the above provisions[11].

1   As to the meanings of 'veterinary medicinal product' and 'animal' see PARA 387.

2   Veterinary Medicines Regulations 2011, SI 2011/2159, reg 17(1). The keeper of a food-producing animal must keep the documentation on the acquisition of a veterinary medicinal product and the records relating to the product for at least five years following the administration or other disposal of the product, irrespective of whether or not the animal concerned is no longer in that keeper's possession or has been slaughtered or has died during that period: reg 20(1). It is an offence to fail to comply with this provision: reg 20(2).
3   As to the information see the Veterinary Medicines Regulations 2011, SI 2011/2159, reg 18(1)(a)–(f).
4   See the Veterinary Medicines Regulations 2011, SI 2011/2159, reg 18(1).
5   As to the information see the Veterinary Medicines Regulations 2011, SI 2011/2159, reg 19(1)(a)–(d), (2)(a)–(e), (3)(a)–(c).
6   See the Veterinary Medicines Regulations 2011, SI 2011/2159, reg 19(1)–(3).
7   See the Veterinary Medicines Regulations 2011, SI 2011/2159, reg 21(1). As to the information see reg 21(1)(a)–(e). The holder must keep with the record all certification provided by the qualified person (manufacture) in relation to that batch: reg 21(2) The holder must keep all records and certificates for at least five years from the date the veterinary medicinal product is placed on the market: reg 21(3).
8   See the Veterinary Medicines Regulations 2011, SI 2011/2159, reg 22(1). As to the information see reg 21(1)(a)–(f). The records must be kept for 5 years: reg 22(1).
9   See the Veterinary Medicines Regulations 2011, SI 2011/2159, reg 23(1). As to the specified products see Sch 3 para 1(1)(a), (b); and PARA 431 heads (1) and (2). As to the information see reg 23(1)(a)–(f). If the documents do not include this information that person must make a record of the missing information as soon as is reasonably practicable following the transaction: reg 23(2). As an alternative to reg 23(1), (2) the person may make a record of all the information required there provided that this is done as soon as is reasonably practicable following the transaction: reg 23(3). The documentation and records must be kept for 5 years: reg 23(4).
10 See the Veterinary Medicines Regulations 2011, SI 2011/2159, reg 24(1). As to the information see reg 24(1)(a)–(j). The records must be kept for 5 years: reg 24(1).
11 As to the meaning of 'cascade' see PARA 423.
12 Veterinary Medicines Regulations 2011, SI 2011/2159, regs 17(2), 18(2), 19(4), 21(4), 22(2), 23(5), 24(2).

(6) IMPORTS AND EXPORTS

434.   Importation of authorised veterinary medicinal products. It is an offence to import a veterinary medicinal product[1] authorised for use in the United Kingdom except in accordance with the following[2].

A holder of a marketing authorisation for a veterinary medicinal product may import that veterinary medicinal product[3]. A holder of a manufacturing authorisation may import a veterinary medicinal product to which that authorisation relates[4].

An authorised wholesale dealer may import a veterinary medicinal product if the authorisation covers the product and the dealer has notified the holder of the marketing authorisation in writing before importation[5].

A veterinary surgeon or a pharmacist may import any authorised veterinary medicinal product[6].

A suitably qualified person[7] may import any authorised veterinary medicinal product that that person is permitted to supply[8].

1   As to the meaning of 'veterinary medicinal product' see PARA 387.
2   Veterinary Medicines Regulations 2011, SI 2011/2159, reg 9(1).
3   Veterinary Medicines Regulations 2011, SI 2011/2159, reg 9(2).
4   Veterinary Medicines Regulations 2011, SI 2011/2159, reg 9(3).
5   Veterinary Medicines Regulations 2011, SI 2011/2159, reg 9(4).
6   Veterinary Medicines Regulations 2011, SI 2011/2159, reg 9(5).
7   Ie a person registered in accordance with the Veterinary Medicines Regulations 2011, SI 2011/2159, Sch 3 para 14.
8   Veterinary Medicines Regulations 2011, SI 2011/2159, reg 9(6).

435. Importation of an unauthorised veterinary medicinal product. It is an offence to import an unauthorised veterinary medicinal product[1] except in accordance with the following[2].

A holder of a marketing authorisation may import an unauthorised veterinary medicinal product if it is for the purpose of the manufacture of a veterinary medicinal product for which the importer holds the marketing authorisation[3].

A holder of a manufacturing authorisation may import an unauthorised veterinary medicinal product if it is for the manufacture of a veterinary medicinal product that the importer is permitted to manufacture[4].

A holder of a wholesale dealer's authorisation may import an unauthorised veterinary medicinal product for the purposes of re-export[5].

A veterinary surgeon may import an unauthorised veterinary medicinal product that is authorised in another member state[6] if it is for the purpose of administration by that veterinary surgeon or under that veterinary surgeon's responsibility under the cascade[7] or administration in exceptional circumstances[8]; the import must be in accordance with the appropriate certificate granted by the Secretary of State[9], and the product may be imported by the veterinary surgeon personally or by using a wholesale dealer or pharmacist as an agent[10].

A wholesale dealer or a pharmacist may import an unauthorised veterinary medicinal product for the purpose of storing it pending administration by a veterinary surgeon under the cascade or administration in exceptional circumstances[11] if:

(1)　the veterinary medicinal product is authorised in another member State or a third country[12];

(2)　the Secretary of State has issued a certificate certifying that:

(a)　the disease or condition is such that the veterinary medicinal product is likely to be needed as a matter of urgency for the treatment of an animal[13];

(b)　delay in administering the product will seriously affect the health or welfare of the animal[14]; and

(c)　there is no suitable veterinary medicinal product authorised in the United Kingdom[15]; and

(3)　in the case of a wholesale dealer, the product is within the terms of the authorisation[16].

The holder of an animal test certificate[17] may import anything specified in the animal test certificate in accordance with the conditions in that certificate[18].

The Secretary of State may authorise in writing the importation of any product or substance for use under a licence granted under the Animals (Scientific Procedures) Act 1986[19].

1　As to the meaning of 'veterinary medicinal product' see PARA 387.
2　Veterinary Medicines Regulations 2011, SI 2011/2159, reg 25(1).
3　Veterinary Medicines Regulations 2011, SI 2011/2159, reg 25(2).
4　Veterinary Medicines Regulations 2011, SI 2011/2159, reg 25(3).
5　Veterinary Medicines Regulations 2011, SI 2011/2159, reg 25(4).
6　As to the meaning of 'member state' see PARA 389 note 4.
7　As to the meaning of 'cascade' see PARA 423.
8　Ie in accordance with the Veterinary Medicines Regulations 2011, SI 2011/2159, Sch 4.
9　As to the Secretary of State see PARA 2 note 1.
10　Veterinary Medicines Regulations 2011, SI 2011/2159, reg 25(5).
11　See note 6.
12　Veterinary Medicines Regulations 2011, SI 2011/2159, reg 25(6)(a).
13　Veterinary Medicines Regulations 2011, SI 2011/2159, reg 25(6)(b)(i).

14 Veterinary Medicines Regulations 2011, SI 2011/2159, reg 25(6)(b)(ii).
15 Veterinary Medicines Regulations 2011, SI 2011/2159, reg 25(6)(b)(iii).
16 Veterinary Medicines Regulations 2011, SI 2011/2159, reg 25(6)(c).
17 Ie granted under the Veterinary Medicines Regulations 2011, SI 2011/2159, Sch 4 para 9.
18 Veterinary Medicines Regulations 2011, SI 2011/2159, reg 25(7).
19 Veterinary Medicines Regulations 2011, SI 2011/2159, reg 25(8). As to the Animals (Scientific Procedures) Act 1986 see ANIMALS vol 2 (2008) PARA 875.

436.   Exports. It is an offence to export a veterinary medicinal product for use in another member state[1] unless the veterinary medicinal product may be lawfully supplied or administered in that member state[2].

If a veterinary medicinal product has been manufactured in accordance with a marketing authorisation, or if a product without a marketing authorisation has been manufactured under a manufacturing authorisation, and the product is intended for export outside the European Union, the Secretary of State must, at the request of the exporter or the competent authorities of the country to which it is being exported, provide a certificate to that effect[3].

When issuing the certificate the Secretary of State[4] must take account of the model certificates issued by the World Health Organization[5].

If the veterinary medicinal product is authorised in the United Kingdom[6] the Secretary of State must ensure that the exporter or the competent authorities of the third country has access to the summary of product characteristics[7].

1 As to the meaning of 'veterinary medicinal product' see PARA 387. As to the meaning of 'member state' see PARA 389 note 4.
2 Veterinary Medicines Regulations 2011, SI 2011/2159, reg 31(1).
3 Veterinary Medicines Regulations 2011, SI 2011/2159, reg 31(2).
4 As to the Secretary of State see PARA 2 note 1.
5 Veterinary Medicines Regulations 2011, SI 2011/2159, reg 31(3).
6 As to the meaning of 'United Kingdom' see PARA 20 note 4.
7 Veterinary Medicines Regulations 2011, SI 2011/2159, reg 31(4).

(7) LABELLING, MARKING AND LEAFLETS

437.   Labelling and package leaflets. The Secretary of State[1], when issuing a marketing authorisation, must approve all containers, packaging, labels and package leaflets[2]. The label and package leaflet must contain specified information[3] and be in English, but may contain other languages provided that the information given is identical in all the languages[4]. Special provision is made for homoeopathic remedies[5].

The Secretary of State may permit variations in the above in any individual marketing authorisation if this is necessary for public or animal health purposes or the protection of the environment[6].

1 As to the Secretary of State see PARA 2 note 1.
2 Veterinary Medicines Regulations 2011, SI 2011/2159, Sch 1 para 45.
3 See the Veterinary Medicines Regulations 2011, SI 2011/2159, Sch 1 paras 46, 48–50, 52. As to ampoules or other unit dose forms see Sch 1 para 51.
4 Veterinary Medicines Regulations 2011, SI 2011/2159, Sch 1 para 47(1). This requirement does not apply in the case of a product imported by a veterinary surgeon and administered by or under the responsibility of that same veterinary surgeon: Sch 1 para 47(2).
5 See the Veterinary Medicines Regulations 2011, SI 2011/2159, Sch 1 para 53.
6 Veterinary Medicines Regulations 2011, SI 2011/2159, Sch 1 para 54.

438.   Labelling at the time of retail supply. If a veterinary medicinal product[1] is supplied in a container specified in the marketing authorisation, it is an offence to supply it if any information on the outer packaging (or, if there is no outer packaging, the immediate packaging) is not clearly visible at the time of supply or has been changed in any way[2].

If a veterinary medicinal product is supplied in a container other than that specified in the marketing authorisation, the person supplying the veterinary medicinal product must ensure that the container is suitably labelled and must supply sufficient written information (which may include a copy of the summary of product characteristics or the package leaflet) to enable the product to be used safely, and failure to do so is an offence[3].

1 As to the meaning of 'veterinary medicinal product' see PARA 387.
2 Veterinary Medicines Regulations 2011, SI 2011/2159, Sch 3 para 12(1). This provision does not apply to a veterinary surgeon who amends a label, or a pharmacist who amends it in accordance with a prescription from a veterinary surgeon, provided that the unamended information remains clearly visible: Sch 3 para 12(2).
3 Veterinary Medicines Regulations 2011, SI 2011/2159, Sch 3 para 12(3).

(8) ADVERTISING

439. Advertising the product. It is an offence to advertise a veterinary medicinal product[1] if the advertisement is misleading or contains any medicinal claim that is not in the summary of product characteristics[2].

It is an offence to advertise an authorised human medicinal product for administration to animals (including sending a price list of or including authorised human medicinal products to a veterinary surgeon or veterinary practice)[3].

1 As to the meaning of 'veterinary medicinal product' see PARA 387.
2 Veterinary Medicines Regulations 2011, SI 2011/2159, reg 10(1).
3 Veterinary Medicines Regulations 2011, SI 2011/2159, reg 10(2). This does not apply to the holder of a wholesale dealer's authorisation who supplies a list of authorised human medicinal products, together with prices, to a veterinary surgeon for use under the cascade provided that the list is sent following a request from the veterinary surgeon to whom it is sent; and the list states clearly that the product does not have a marketing authorisation as a veterinary medicinal product, and may only be prescribed and administered under the cascade: reg 10(3). As to the meaning of 'cascade' see PARA 423.

440. Advertising of prescription products and products containing psychotropic drugs or narcotics. It is an offence to advertise a veterinary medicinal product[1] that is available on veterinary prescription only or contains psychotropic drugs or narcotics[2].

In the case of a product containing psychotropic drugs or narcotics, this does not apply to advertisements aimed at veterinary surgeons or pharmacists[3].

In the case of Prescription Only Medicine—Veterinarian medicines, this does not apply to price lists, or to advertisements aimed at veterinary surgeons, veterinary nurses, pharmacists or professional keepers of animals[4].

In the case of Prescription Only Medicine—Veterinarian, Pharmacist, Suitably Qualified Person medicines, this does not apply to price lists, or to advertisements aimed at veterinary surgeons, pharmacists, suitably qualified persons[5], other veterinary health care professionals, professional keepers of animals or owners or keepers of horses[6].

1 As to the meaning of 'veterinary medicinal product' see PARA 387.
2 Veterinary Medicines Regulations 2011, SI 2011/2159, reg 11(1).
3 Veterinary Medicines Regulations 2011, SI 2011/2159, reg 11(2).
4 Veterinary Medicines Regulations 2011, SI 2011/2159, reg 11(3).

5　Ie registered in accordance with the Veterinary Medicines Regulations 2011, SI 2011/2159, Sch 3 para 14.
6　Veterinary Medicines Regulations 2011, SI 2011/2159, reg 11(4).

441.　Defence of publication in the course of business. In proceedings for an offence under the Veterinary Medicines Regulations 2011[1] relating to advertising, it is a defence for the person charged to prove (1) that that person's business is to publish or arrange for the publication of advertisements; and (2) that the advertisement was received in the ordinary course of business and the person charged did not know and had no reason to suspect that its publication would amount to an offence under the Veterinary Medicines Regulations 2011[2].

1　Ie under the Veterinary Medicines Regulations 2011, SI 2011/2159.
2　Veterinary Medicines Regulations 2011, SI 2011/2159, reg 12.

(9) ENFORCEMENT

442.　Veterinary products committee. There is a Veterinary Products Committee[1] with the function of providing scientific advice on any aspect of veterinary medicinal products[2] asked for by the Secretary of State[3] and to carry out any functions specified in the Veterinary Medicines Regulations 2011[4].

Certain provisions of the Veterinary Medicines Regulations 2011[5] provide for a right appeal to the Committee[6]. An appellant must notify the Secretary of State of an intention to appeal[7]. The Committee must consider the appeal and any representations made by the Secretary of State, and report its findings in writing to the Secretary of State together with its recommendations[8]. The Secretary of State must consider the report and form a provisional decision which he must notify to the appellant, together with the reasons for it[9]. The appellant may then appeal against the Secretary of State's provisional decision to a person appointed for the purpose by the Secretary of State[10].

1　Veterinary Medicines Regulations 2011, SI 2011/2159, reg 28(1). The Secretary of State may appoint members of the Committee from professional people who are eminent in their field, and any lay members as the Secretary of State sees fit: reg 28(2). As to the Secretary of State see PARA 2 note 1. The Secretary of State may pay members of the Committee such amounts as the Secretary of State may decide: reg 28(4).
2　As to the meaning of 'veterinary medicinal product' see PARA 387.
3　The Secretary of State may consult the Committee at any time: Veterinary Medicines Regulations 2011, SI 2011/2159, reg 28(5).
4　Veterinary Medicines Regulations 2011, SI 2011/2159, reg 28(3).
5　Ie the Veterinary Medicines Regulations 2011, SI 2011/2159.
6　See the Veterinary Medicines Regulations 2011, SI 2011/2159, reg 24 (see PARA 395), Sch 1 paras 34(3), 37(3), 39(2), 40 (see PARAS 404–406).
7　See the Veterinary Medicines Regulations 2011, SI 2011/2159, reg 29(2). As to the appeals procedure to the Veterinary Products Committee see reg 29.
8　Veterinary Medicines Regulations 2011, SI 2011/2159, reg 29(5).
9　See the Veterinary Medicines Regulations 2011, SI 2011/2159, reg 29(7), (8).
10　Veterinary Medicines Regulations 2011, SI 2011/2159, reg 29(9). As to appeals to an appointed person see PARA 443.

443.　Appeals to an appointed person. A person aggrieved by a provisional decision of the Secretary of State[1] may appeal against the decision to a person appointed for the purpose by the Secretary of State in accordance with this provision[2]. So may an applicant for:

(1)　a manufacturing authorisation[3];

(2)   appointment as a qualified person for the purposes of a manufacturing authorisation[4];
(3)   authorisation for a person or premises to manufacture autogenous vaccines[5];
(4)   an authorisation of a blood bank[6];
(5)   authorisation of a person and premises to manufacture an unauthorised veterinary medicinal product[7] for administration under the cascade[8];
(6)   authorisation of an equine stem cell centre[9];
(7)   a wholesale dealer's authorisation[10];
(8)   the approval of premises for the supply of Prescription Only Medicine—Veterinarian, Pharmacist, Suitably Qualified Person or Non-Food Animal—Veterinarian, Pharmacist, Suitably Qualified Person veterinary medicinal products by a suitably qualified person[11],

if such an application is refused[12].

A holder of any of the above authorisations, appointment or approvals may appeal against a suspension or compulsory variation in the same way[13].

The appointed person must consider the appeal (but may not consider any new data not available to the Secretary of State at the time of the original decision) and any representations made by the Secretary of State and report in writing, with a recommended course of action, to the Secretary of State[14].

The Secretary of State must then reach a final decision and notify the appellant, together with the reasons for it[15].

1   Ie a decision under the Veterinary Medicines Regulations 2011, SI 2011/2159, reg 29 (see PARA 442).
2   Veterinary Medicines Regulations 2011, SI 2011/2159, reg 30(1).
3   Veterinary Medicines Regulations 2011, SI 2011/2159, reg 30(2)(a).
4   Veterinary Medicines Regulations 2011, SI 2011/2159, reg 30(2)(b).
5   Veterinary Medicines Regulations 2011, SI 2011/2159, reg 30(2)(c).
6   Veterinary Medicines Regulations 2011, SI 2011/2159, reg 30(2)(d).
7   As to the meaning of 'veterinary medicinal product' see PARA 387.
8   Veterinary Medicines Regulations 2011, SI 2011/2159, reg 30(2)(e).
9   Veterinary Medicines Regulations 2011, SI 2011/2159, reg 30(2)(f).
10   Veterinary Medicines Regulations 2011, SI 2011/2159, reg 30(2)(g).
11   Veterinary Medicines Regulations 2011, SI 2011/2159, reg 30(2)(h).
12   Veterinary Medicines Regulations 2011, SI 2011/2159, reg 30(2).
13   Veterinary Medicines Regulations 2011, SI 2011/2159, reg 30(3).
14   Veterinary Medicines Regulations 2011, SI 2011/2159, reg 30(4).
15   Veterinary Medicines Regulations 2011, SI 2011/2159, reg 30(5).

444.   Inspectors. An inspector[1] may, on giving reasonable notice, and on producing a duly authenticated authorisation if required, enter any premises[2] at any reasonable hour for the purpose of ensuring that the provisions of the Veterinary Medicines Regulations 2011[3] are being complied with[4].

The requirement to give notice does not apply:
(1)   where the entry is pursuant to any provision of an EU instrument which requires inspection without notice[5];
(2)   where the requirement has been waived[6];
(3)   where reasonable efforts to agree an appointment have failed[7];
(4)   where an inspector has reasonable suspicion of a failure to comply with the Veterinary Medicines Regulations 2011[8]; or
(5)   in an emergency[9].

The inspector may be accompanied by such other persons as he considers necessary and any representative of the European Commission acting for the purpose of the enforcement of a Community obligation[10].

If a justice of the peace, on sworn information in writing, is satisfied that there are reasonable grounds for entry into any premises for the purposes of the enforcement of these provisions, and either:

(a)   admission has been refused, or a refusal is expected, and (in either case) that notice to apply for a warrant has been given to the occupier[11];

(b)   asking for admission, or the giving of such a notice, would defeat the object of the entry[12];

(c)   the case is one of urgency[13]; or

(d)   the premises are unoccupied or the occupier is temporarily absent[14],

the justice may, by signed warrant, authorise the inspector to enter the premises, if need be by reasonable force[15].

An inspector who enters any unoccupied premises must leave them as effectively secured against unauthorised entry as they were before entry[16].

An inspector may enter the premises of manufacturers of active substances used as starting materials for veterinary medicinal products[17], and the premises of the marketing authorisation holder[18]. An inspector may carry out an inspection at the request of another member state, the European Commission or the European Medicines Agency[19].

An inspector entering premises under the above provisions has certain powers[20].

1   The Secretary of State must appoint inspectors for the purposes of the enforcement of the Veterinary Medicines Regulations 2011, SI 2011/2159, and 'inspector' means an inspector appointed under reg 34 or a veterinary inspector appointed under the Animal Health Act 1981: Veterinary Medicines Regulations 2011, SI 2011/2159, reg 33.

2   For these purposes 'premises' includes any place, vehicle, trailer, container, stall, moveable structure, ship or aircraft: Veterinary Medicines Regulations 2011, SI 2011/2159, reg 34(1). Regulations 34(1) does not apply in relation to any premises which are used wholly or mainly as a private dwelling, unless those premises are approved, registered or authorised for the sale of veterinary medicines under Sch 3 paras 8, 10, 14(4) or 18, or any part of those premises is so approved, registered or authorised for that purpose: Veterinary Medicines Regulations 2011, SI 2011/2159, reg 34(3). Regulation 34(1) and (3) do not affect any right of entry conferred by a warrant issued by a justice of the peace: reg 34(4).

3   Ie the Veterinary Medicines Regulations 2011, SI 2011/2159.

4   Veterinary Medicines Regulations 2011, SI 2011/2159, reg 34(1).

5   Veterinary Medicines Regulations 2011, SI 2011/2159, reg 34(2)(a).

6   Veterinary Medicines Regulations 2011, SI 2011/2159, reg 34(2)(b).

7   Veterinary Medicines Regulations 2011, SI 2011/2159, reg 34(2)(c).

8   Veterinary Medicines Regulations 2011, SI 2011/2159, reg 34(2)(d).

9   Veterinary Medicines Regulations 2011, SI 2011/2159, reg 34(2)(e).

10   Veterinary Medicines Regulations 2011, SI 2011/2159, reg 34(5).

11   Veterinary Medicines Regulations 2011, SI 2011/2159, reg 34(6)(a).

12   Veterinary Medicines Regulations 2011, SI 2011/2159, reg 34(6)(b).

13   Veterinary Medicines Regulations 2011, SI 2011/2159, reg 34(6)(c).

14   Veterinary Medicines Regulations 2011, SI 2011/2159, reg 34(6)(d).

15   Veterinary Medicines Regulations 2011, SI 2011/2159, reg 34(6). The warrant is valid for one month: reg 36(7).

16   Veterinary Medicines Regulations 2011, SI 2011/2159, reg 34(8).

17   As to the meaning of 'veterinary medicinal product' see PARA 387.

18   Veterinary Medicines Regulations 2011, SI 2011/2159, reg 34(9).

19   Veterinary Medicines Regulations 2011, SI 2011/2159, reg 34(10). As to the meaning of 'member state' see PARA 389 note 4.

20   The inspector may:

(1)   inspect the premises, and any plant, machinery or equipment (Veterinary Medicines Regulations 2011, SI 2011/2159, reg 35(1)(a));

(2)   search the premises (reg 35(1)(b));

(3)   take samples (reg 35(1)(c));

(4)   seize any computers and associated equipment (reg 35(1)(d));

(5)   seize any veterinary medicinal product, anything purporting to be a veterinary medicinal product, or any additive to which Sch 5 applies (see AGRICULTURAL PRODUCTION AND MARKETING), if it is not authorised in the United Kingdom (reg 35(1)(e));

(6)   seize any premixture or feedingstuff that contains a veterinary medicinal product or additive to which Sch 5 applies that is not authorised in the United Kingdom (reg 35(1)(f));

(7)   seize any veterinary medicinal product, anything purporting to be a veterinary medicinal product, any additive to which Sch 5 applies, any premixture or any feedingstuff if: (a) it has not been lawfully supplied in accordance with the Veterinary Medicines Regulations 2011, SI 2011/2159; (b) it has been stored in a way that affects its safety, quality or efficacy; (c) it is sold or offered for sale by a person not permitted to supply it under the Veterinary Medicines Regulations 2011, SI 2011/2159 (reg 35(1)(g));

(8)   carry out any inquiries, examinations and tests (reg 35(1)(h));

(9)   have access to, and inspect and copy or seize any documents or records (in whatever form they are held) relating to the Veterinary Medicines Regulations 2011, SI 2011/2159 (reg 35(1)(i)); and

(10)   have access to, inspect and check the operation of any computer and any associated apparatus or material that is or has been in use in connection with the records; and for this purpose may require any person having charge of, or otherwise concerned with the operation of, the computer, apparatus or material to afford such assistance as may reasonably be required and, where a record is kept by means of a computer, may require the records to be produced in a form in which they may be taken away (reg 35(1)(j)).

An officer of any local authority who has entered premises exercising any statutory power of entry for the purposes of enforcing any legislation relating to food hygiene, feed hygiene or animal health, may inspect any records made under the Veterinary Medicines Regulations 2011, SI 2011/2159 (in whatever form they are held) relating to food-producing animals, and may remove them to enable them to be copied: reg 35(2).

Where an inspector has entered any premises and it is not reasonably practicable to determine at the time whether documents on those premises are relevant to the Veterinary Medicines Regulations 2011, SI 2011/2159, the inspector may seize them to ascertain whether or not they are relevant: reg 35(3).

When seizing anything under the Veterinary Medicines Regulations 2011, SI 2011/2159 an inspector must follow a specified procedure including serving a seizure notice see reg 41. The Secretary of State must publicise all improvement notices and seizure notices issued under the Veterinary Medicines Regulations 2011, SI 2011/2159 and the suspension or revocation of anything issued under the Veterinary Medicines Regulations 2011, SI 2011/2159, and may do so in such manner as the Secretary of State sees fit: reg 42(1). This does not apply in relation to a seizure notice issued to a common carrier who does not own the seized goods: reg 42(2).

445.   Inspection of pharmacies.   In relation to a pharmacy, all the powers of an inspector to enforce the Veterinary Medicines Regulations 2011[1] may also be exercised by an officer of the General Pharmaceutical Council appointed for the purpose[2].

1   Veterinary Medicines Regulations 2011, SI 2011/2159.
2   Veterinary Medicines Regulations 2011, SI 2011/2159, reg 36.

446.   Obstruction.   Any person who: (1) intentionally obstructs any person acting in the execution of the Veterinary Medicines Regulations 2011[1]; (2) without reasonable cause, fails to give to any person acting in the execution of the Veterinary Medicines Regulations 2011 any assistance or information that that person may reasonably require under the Veterinary Medicines Regulations 2011; (3) furnishes to any person acting in the execution of the Veterinary Medicines Regulations 2011 any information knowing it to be false or misleading; or (4) fails to produce a record when required to do so to any person acting in the execution of the Veterinary Medicines Regulations 2011, is guilty of an offence[2].

1 Ie the Veterinary Medicines Regulations 2011, SI 2011/2159.
2 Veterinary Medicines Regulations 2011, SI 2011/2159, reg 37.

447. Improvement notices. An inspector who has reasonable grounds for believing that any person is failing to comply with the Veterinary Medicines Regulations 2011[1] may serve a notice on that person (an 'improvement notice') that:

(1)   states the inspector's grounds for believing this[2];

(2)   specifies the matters that constitute the failure to comply[3];

(3)   specifies the measures that, in the inspector's opinion, the person must take in order to secure compliance[4]; and

(4)   requires the person to take those measures, or measures at least equivalent to them, within the period (being not less than 14 days) specified in the notice[5].

It is an offence to fail to comply with an improvement notice[6].

Any person who is aggrieved by an improvement notice may appeal to a magistrates' court[7]. A court may suspend an improvement notice pending an appeal[8].

On an appeal against an improvement notice, the court may either cancel the notice or confirm it, with or without modification[9].

1 Veterinary Medicines Regulations 2011, SI 2011/2159.
2 Veterinary Medicines Regulations 2011, SI 2011/2159, reg 38(1)(a).
3 Veterinary Medicines Regulations 2011, SI 2011/2159, reg 38(1)(b).
4 Veterinary Medicines Regulations 2011, SI 2011/2159, reg 38(1)(c).
5 Veterinary Medicines Regulations 2011, SI 2011/2159, reg 38(1)(d). An improvement notice must state the right of appeal to a magistrates' court and the period within which such an appeal may be brought: reg 39(5).
6 Veterinary Medicines Regulations 2011, SI 2011/2159, reg 38(2).
7 Veterinary Medicines Regulations 2011, SI 2011/2159, reg 39(1). The procedure is by way of a complaint and the Magistrates' Courts Act 1980 applies to the proceedings: reg 39(2). The period within which an appeal may be brought is 28 days or the period specified in the improvement notice, whichever ends the earlier: reg 39(4).
8 Veterinary Medicines Regulations 2011, SI 2011/2159, reg 39(6).
9 Veterinary Medicines Regulations 2011, SI 2011/2159, reg 40.

(10) OFFENCES

448. The finished product. The holder of a marketing authorisation for a veterinary medicinal product[1] is guilty of an offence if either the holder or the manufacturer supplies a product that is not completely in accordance with the marketing authorisation[2].

Any person who supplies a veterinary medicinal product that has passed its expiry date is guilty of an offence[3].

Any person who opens the package (including the outer package) of a veterinary medicinal product before it has been supplied to the final user, other than as permitted[4], is guilty of an offence[5].

Any person who supplies an authorised human medicinal product for administration to an animal[6] is guilty of an offence[7].

Any person in possession of a veterinary medicinal product that was supplied to that person other than as permitted[8] is guilty of an offence[9].

It is an offence to be in possession of an unauthorised veterinary medicinal product[10]. It is also an offence to supply an unauthorised veterinary medicinal product[11].

It is an offence to import a veterinary medicinal product authorised for use in the United Kingdom or an unauthorised veterinary medicinal product except as permitted[12]. It is an offence to export a veterinary medicinal product for use in another member state unless the veterinary medicinal product may be lawfully supplied or administered in that member state[13].

Wholesale dealing without an appropriate licence is an offence[14].

1   As to the meaning of 'veterinary medicinal product' see PARA 387.
2   Veterinary Medicines Regulations 2011, SI 2011/2159, reg 6. A person guilty of an offence under the Veterinary Medicines Regulations 2011, SI 2011/2159 liable on summary conviction, to a fine not exceeding the statutory maximum or to imprisonment for a term not exceeding three months or both or, on conviction on indictment, to a fine or to imprisonment for a term not exceeding two years or both: reg 43(1). Where a body corporate is guilty of an offence under the Veterinary Medicines Regulations 2011, SI 2011/2159, and that offence is proved to have been committed with the consent or connivance of, or to have been attributable to any neglect on the part of a qualified person appointed as such for the purposes of the Veterinary Medicines Regulations 2011, SI 2011/2159, any director, manager, secretary or other similar person of the body corporate or any person who was purporting to act in any such capacity, that person is guilty of the offence as well as the body corporate: reg 43(2). For these purposes 'director', in relation to a body corporate whose affairs are managed by its members, means a member of the body corporate: reg 43(3).
3   Veterinary Medicines Regulations 2011, SI 2011/2159, reg 7(2).
4   Ie permitted under the Veterinary Medicines Regulations 2011, SI 2011/2159, Sch 3 (see PARA 418 et seq).
5   Veterinary Medicines Regulations 2011, SI 2011/2159, reg 7(3).
6   This does not include a product supplied by a veterinary surgeon or in accordance with a written prescription from a veterinary surgeon that includes all the information specified in Sch 3 para 6. As to the meaning of 'animal' see PARA 387 note 2.
7   Veterinary Medicines Regulations 2011, SI 2011/2159, reg 7(4).
8   Ie other than in accordance with the Veterinary Medicines Regulations 2011, SI 2011/2159, Sch 3.
9   Veterinary Medicines Regulations 2011, SI 2011/2159, reg 7(5).
10 Veterinary Medicines Regulations 2011, SI 2011/2159, reg 26(1). This does not apply to (1) a veterinary medicinal product imported in accordance with a certificate granted by the Secretary of State under the Veterinary Medicines Regulations 2011, SI 2011/2159; (2) a product prescribed by a veterinary surgeon under the cascade; (3) a holder of a manufacturing authorisation if the possession is for export; (4) a holder of a wholesale dealer's authorisation if the possession is for export or re-export; or (5) a holder of a manufacturer's authorisation or marketing authorisation if the intention is to manufacture a veterinary medicinal product: reg 26(2). A veterinary surgeon who practises in both the United Kingdom and another member state may hold veterinary medicinal products authorised in the other member state provided that the amount held does not exceed the amount expected to be used in that member state: reg 26(3). It is a defence for a person charged under reg 26(1) to prove that the product was for the purposes of research or development of a veterinary medicinal product: reg 26(4). A veterinary surgeon may have possession of an authorised human medicinal product intended for administration to animals under the cascade, but commits an offence if the amount possessed exceeds the amount expected to be used under the cascade: reg 26(5). As to the meaning of 'member state' see PARA 389 note 4. As to the meaning of 'cascade' see PARA 423.
11 Veterinary Medicines Regulations 2011, SI 2011/2159, reg 27(1). This does not apply to a veterinary medicinal product prescribed by a veterinary surgeon under the cascade or to a product supplied in accordance with a certificate granted by the Secretary of State under the Veterinary Medicines Regulations 2011, SI 2011/2159: reg 27(2). It is a defence for a person charged under reg 27(1) to prove that the supply was for the purposes of research or development of a veterinary medicinal product: reg 27(3).
12 See the Veterinary Medicines Regulations 2011, SI 2011/2159, regs 9(1), 25; and PARAS 434, 435.
13 See the Veterinary Medicines Regulations 2011, SI 2011/2159, reg 31(1); and PARA 436.
14 See the Veterinary Medicines Regulations 2011, SI 2011/2159, reg 13; and PARA 418.

4. BLOOD AND BLOOD PRODUCTS

(1) IN GENERAL

449. Scope of regulation. The requirements relating to blood safety and quality[1] apply to the collection and testing of blood[2] and blood components[3], whatever their intended purpose, and to their processing, storage, and distribution[4] when they are intended to be used for transfusion[5]. The requirements do not apply to blood stem cells[6].

The Secretary of State[7] is designated[8] as the competent authority[9].

Provision is made for the Secretary of State to authorise blood banks for non-food producing animals[10].

The management of blood and blood products is an activity regulated by the Care Quality Commission[11].

1 Ie the requirements of the Blood Safety and Quality Regulations 2005, SI 2005/50.

2 'Blood' means whole human blood collected from a donor and processed either for transfusion or for further manufacturing: Blood Safety and Quality Regulations 2005, SI 2005/50, reg 1(3).

3 'Blood component' means a therapeutic constituent of human blood (red cells, white cells, platelets and plasma) that can be prepared by various methods: Blood Safety and Quality Regulations 2005, SI 2005/50, reg 1(3).

4 'Distribution' means the act of delivery of blood and blood components to other blood establishments, hospital blood banks and manufacturers of blood products, other than the issuing of blood or blood components for transfusion: Blood Safety and Quality Regulations 2005, SI 2005/50, reg 1(3). As to the meaning of 'blood establishment' see PARA 453 note 4. As to the meaning of 'hospital blood bank' see PARA 458 note 1. 'Blood product' means any therapeutic product derived from human blood or plasma: reg 1(3). As to the regulation of imported blood or blood products used as a starting material or raw material see PARA 65. 'Manufacturer' means a person who: (1) holds a licence under the Medicines Act 1968 s 8(2) to manufacture medicinal products; (2) holds an authorisation to manufacture an investigational medicinal product granted pursuant to the Medicines for Human Use (Clinical Trials) Regulations 2004, SI 2004/1031, reg 36 (see PARA 97); or (3) falls within the definition of 'manufacturer' in the Medical Devices Regulations 2002, SI 2002/618, reg 2(1) (see PARA 472 note 1): Blood Safety and Quality Regulations 2005, SI 2005/50, reg 1(3) (definition added by SI 2006/2013). The Medicines Act 1968 s 8 has been repealed. As to licences to manufacture medicinal products see PARA 45 et seq.

5 Blood Safety and Quality Regulations 2005, SI 2005/50, reg 2(2). The Blood Safety and Quality Regulations 2005, SI 2005/50 apply without prejudice to the Medical Devices Regulations 2002, SI 2002/618: Blood Safety and Quality Regulations 2005, SI 2005/50, reg 2(3). As to the Medical Devices Regulations 2002, SI 2002/618 see PARA 472 et seq. As to the NHS Blood and Transplant (Gwaed a Thrawsblaniadau'r GIG) which has functions with regard to blood and blood components in the national health service see HEALTH SERVICES vol 54 (2008) PARA 147.

6 Blood Safety and Quality Regulations 2005, SI 2005/50, reg 2(4).

7 As to the Secretary of State see PARA 2 note 1.

8 Ie for the purpose of Parliament and Council Directive (EC) 2002/98 (OJ L033, 8.2.2003, p 30) setting standards of quality and safety for the collection, testing, processing, storage and distribution of human blood and blood components.

9 Blood Safety and Quality Regulations 2005, SI 2005/50, regs 1(3), 2(1). As to the establishment of the medicines and healthcare products regulatory agency trading fund in connection with certain operations of the Department of Health in relation to blood safety and quality see the Medicines and Healthcare Products Regulatory Agency Trading Fund Order 2003, SI 2003/1076 (amended by SI 2005/2061). As to government trading funds generally see CONSTITUTIONAL LAW AND HUMAN RIGHTS vol 8(2) (Reissue) PARA 743 et seq.

10 See the Veterinary Medicines Regulations 2011, SI 2011/2159 Sch 2 paras 20–24; and PARAS 392–395.

11 See the Health and Social Care Act 2008 (Regulated Activities) Regulations 2010, SI 2010/781, Sch 1 para 9; and PARA 468.

450. Import of blood and blood components. Any person[1] who imports into the United Kingdom[2] any blood[3] or blood components[4], from a third country must ensure that each unit of blood and each blood component which he imports has been prepared in accordance with the specified standards[5] and meets the required standards of quality and safety[6].

1   As to the meaning of 'person' see PARA 45 note 2.
2   As to the meaning of 'United Kingdom' see PARA 20 note 4.
3   As to the meaning of 'blood' see PARA 449 note 2.
4   As to the meaning of 'blood component' see PARA 449 note 3.
5   Ie prepared in accordance with standards equivalent to the Community standards and requirements set out in the Commission Directive (EC) 2005/62(OJ L56, 10.2005, p 1–48) as regards Community standards and specifications relating to a quality system for blood establishments, Annex.
6   Blood Safety and Quality Regulations 2005, SI 2005/50, reg 13 (substituted by SI 2006/2013). The specified standards of quality and safety are standards equivalent to those laid down in Schedule Pt 5: reg 13. It is an offence to contravene reg 13: see reg 18(1)(d); and PARA 201.

451. Specific epidemiological situations. Where the Secretary of State[1] is aware of a specific epidemiological situation, such as an outbreak of a disease, which may affect the safety of blood[2] donations, and as a result of which he considers that specific deferral[3] criteria for the collection of blood donations should be adopted, he must notify blood establishments[4] that those criteria must be adopted[5], and notify the European Commission[6] of the epidemiological situation[7] and the additional deferral criteria which blood establishments are required[8] to adopt in relation to it[9].

A blood establishment must adopt and comply with any criteria for additional tests notified[10] to it by the Secretary of State[11].

1   As to the Secretary of State see PARA 2 note 1.
2   As to the meaning of 'blood' see PARA 449 note 2.
3   'Deferral' means suspension of the eligibility of an individual to donate blood or blood components, such suspension being either permanent or temporary: Blood Safety and Quality Regulations 2005, SI 2005/50, reg 1(3). As to the meaning of 'blood component' see PARA 449 note 3.
4   As to the meaning of 'blood establishment' see PARA 453 note 4.
5   Blood Safety and Quality Regulations 2005, SI 2005/50, reg 23(1)(a).
6   See the Blood Safety and Quality Regulations 2005, SI 2005/50, reg 1(3).
7   Blood Safety and Quality Regulations 2005, SI 2005/50, reg 23(1)(b)(i).
8   Ie pursuant to the Blood Safety and Quality Regulations 2005, SI 2005/50, reg 23(1)(a): see the text to notes 1–5.
9   Blood Safety and Quality Regulations 2005, SI 2005/50, reg 23(1)(b)(ii).
10   Ie pursuant to the Blood Safety and Quality Regulations 2005, SI 2005/50, reg 23(1): see the text and notes 1–9.
11   Blood Safety and Quality Regulations 2005, SI 2005/50, reg 23(2). It is an offence to contravene this provision: see reg 18(1)(e); and PARA 469.

452. Fees. Fees are payable by blood establishments[1] to the Secretary of State[2] in relation to authorisation[3], where the Secretary of State carries out an inspection[4] at a site[5] of a blood establishment[6], and in respect of the assessment by the Secretary of State of serious adverse events and serious adverse reactions notified by such establishments[7]. Fees are payable by the person responsible for management of the hospital blood bank[8] where the Secretary of State carries out an inspection of a hospital blood bank[9], in respect of each year in which a hospital blood bank has operated[10], and in respect of the assessment by the Secretary of State of serious adverse events and serious adverse reactions notified by such persons[11]. Where the Secretary of State carries out an inspection of a contract laboratory[12], he may charge the person having control of that laboratory a fee[13].

The Secretary of State may in exceptional circumstances, where it appears to him to be in the interests of safety or otherwise appropriate to do so, waive any fee or reduce any fee or part of a fee otherwise payable[14], or refund the whole or part of any fee paid[15]. All unpaid sums due by way of, or on account of, any fees payable are recoverable as debts due to the Crown[16].

1   As to the meaning of 'blood establishment' see PARA 453 note 4.
2   See the Blood Safety and Quality Regulations 2005, SI 2005/50, reg 22(1). As to the Secretary of State see PARA 2 note 1.
3   See the Blood Safety and Quality Regulations 2005, SI 2005/50, reg 22(2); and PARA 453.
4   As to the meaning of 'inspection' see PARA 464 note 2.
5   As to the meaning of 'site' see PARA 453 note 8.
6   See the Blood Safety and Quality Regulations 2005, SI 2005/50, reg 22(3); and PARA 464.
7   See the Blood Safety and Quality Regulations 2005, SI 2005/50, reg 22(2)(bb); and PARA 192. 'Serious adverse reaction' means an unintended response in a donor or in a patient associated with the collection or transfusion of blood or blood components that is fatal, life-threatening, disabling or incapacitating, or which results in or prolongs hospitalisation or morbidity: reg 1(3). 'Serious adverse event' means any untoward occurrence associated with the collection, testing, processing, storage and distribution of blood or blood components that might lead to death or life-threatening, disabling or incapacitating conditions for patients or which results in, or prolongs, hospitalisation or morbidity: reg 1(3).
8   As to the meaning of 'person responsible for management of the hospital blood bank' see PARA 458 note 1.
9   See the Blood Safety and Quality Regulations 2005, SI 2005/50, reg 22(4), (5); and PARA 464. As to the meaning of 'hospital blood bank' see PARA 458 note 1.
10 See the Blood Safety and Quality Regulations 2005, SI 2005/50, reg 22(3A); and PARA 458.
11 See the Blood Safety and Quality Regulations 2005, SI 2005/50, reg 22(3B); and PARA 458.
12 'Contract laboratory' means a laboratory carrying out testing of blood or blood components on behalf of, and pursuant to a contractual arrangement with a blood establishment authorised under the Blood Safety and Quality Regulations 2005, SI 2005/50 or a person responsible for management of a hospital blood bank: reg 22(6) (definition added by SI 2005/2898). As to the meaning of 'blood' see PARA 449 note 2; and as to the meaning of 'blood component' see PARA 449 note 3.
13 See the Blood Safety and Quality Regulations 2005, SI 2005/50, reg 22(5A) (reg 22(5A)–(5C) added by SI 2005/2898). As to the amount of such fees see the Blood Safety and Quality Regulations 2005, SI 2005/50, reg 22(5B)–(5C), (5E), (5F) (as so added; fee amounts amended and reg 22(5E), (5F) added by SI 2010/554).
14 Blood Safety and Quality Regulations 2005, SI 2005/50, reg 22(9)(a). This does not apply in the case of reg 22(5E): reg 22(9) (amended by SI 2010/554).
15 Blood Safety and Quality Regulations 2005, SI 2005/50, reg 22(9)(b).
16 Blood Safety and Quality Regulations 2005, SI 2005/50, reg 22(8). As to the enforcement of court orders in respect of debts due to the Crown see CIVIL PROCEDURE vol 12 (2009) PARA 1239; CONTEMPT OF COURT vol 22 (2012) PARA 90.

(2) BLOOD ESTABLISHMENTS AND BLOOD BANKS

453.   Authorisation of blood establishments. No person[1] may carry on any of the specified activities otherwise than in accordance with an authorisation[2]. The specified activities are: (1) the collection and testing of blood or blood components, whatever their intended purpose[3]; (2) the processing, storage and distribution of blood and blood components when they are intended to be used for transfusion[4]; and (3) the import of blood or blood components from a third country[5].

The Secretary of State[6] may grant an authorisation to a blood establishment to carry out any of the specified activities[7] following an application for authorisation made to him[8]. An application must include the prescribed information[9] and be accompanied by the prescribed fee[10]. Where the Secretary of State grants an application for authorisation, he must give notice in writing to the blood establishment specifying the activities which the blood establishment may undertake at each site in respect of which authorisation is granted[11], and the conditions which apply to the undertaking of those activities[12]. The Secretary of State may at any time remove or vary any of the conditions subject to which the authorisation is granted, or may impose additional conditions[13]. A blood establishment may not make any substantial change in the activities which it undertakes[14] without the prior written approval of the Secretary of State[15].

1   As to the meaning of 'person' see PARA 45 note 2.
2   Blood Safety and Quality Regulations 2005, SI 2005/50, reg 3(1). This restriction does not apply to:

    (1)   the storage and distribution of, and the performance of compatibility tests on, blood and blood components exclusively for use within hospital facilities, including transfusion activities where such activities are performed by a hospital blood bank (reg 3(3)(a));

    (2)   any person carrying out any of the specified activities, where that person carries out that activity on behalf of, and pursuant to a contractual arrangement with a blood establishment which is authorised under these provisions to carry out the activity in question or a person responsible for management of a hospital blood bank (reg 3(3)(b));

    (3)   the import of blood and blood components from a third country when undertaken by a manufacturer or a person acting on behalf of and pursuant to a contractual arrangement with a manufacturer, for the purposes of manufacturing a medicinal product within the meaning of the Medicines Act 1968 or the Medical Devices Regulations 2002, SI 2002/618 (Blood Safety and Quality Regulations 2005, SI 2005/50, reg 3(3)(c) (added by SI 2006/2013)).

   As to the meaning of 'distribution' see PARA 449 note 4; as to the meaning of 'blood' see PARA 449 note 2; and as to the meaning of 'blood component' see PARA 449 note 3. As to the meanings of 'hospital', 'hospital blood bank' and 'person responsible for management of a hospital blood bank' see PARA 458 note 1. As to offences relating to the contravention of reg 3(1) see PARA 469. As to the meaning of 'manufacturer' see PARA 449 note 4.

3   Blood Safety and Quality Regulations 2005, SI 2005/50, reg 3(2)(a).
4   Blood Safety and Quality Regulations 2005, SI 2005/50, reg 3(2)(b). 'Blood establishment' means any person who carries out any of the activities specified in reg 3(2) (see heads (1), (2), (3) in the text) which require an authorisation by virtue of that regulation: reg 1(3) (definition amended by SI 2005/2898).
5   Blood Safety and Quality Regulations 2005, SI 2005/50, reg 3(2)(c) (added by SI 2006/2013).
6   As to the Secretary of State see PARA 2 note 1.
7   Blood Safety and Quality Regulations 2005, SI 2005/50, reg 4(1).
8   Blood Safety and Quality Regulations 2005, SI 2005/50, reg 4(2). The Secretary of State may grant or refuse any application for authorisation made to him (reg 4(5)(a)); and he may grant such an application in respect of particular sites or activities only (reg 4(5)(b)(i)), and subject to conditions (reg 4(5)(b)(ii)). 'Site', in relation to a blood establishment, means any premises at which the blood establishment carries out any of the activities listed in reg 3(2) (see heads (1), (2) in the text), but does not include any premises not owned or managed by the blood establishment at which blood is collected, or any mobile blood collection unit: reg 1(3). As to objections to the refusal of authorisation or the imposition of conditions see PARA 460.
9   Blood Safety and Quality Regulations 2005, SI 2005/50, reg 4(3)(a). As to the prescribed information see reg 4(4) (amended by SI 2005/1098).
10 Blood Safety and Quality Regulations 2005, SI 2005/50, reg 4(3)(b). The fee payable in respect of an application is the sum of £3,074 (reg 22(2)(a) (amended by SI 2010/554)) and it is payable at the time the application is made (Blood Safety and Quality Regulations 2005, SI 2005/50, reg 22(7)(i)). As to fees generally see PARA 452.
11 Blood Safety and Quality Regulations 2005, SI 2005/50, reg 4(6)(a).
12 Blood Safety and Quality Regulations 2005, SI 2005/50, reg 4(6)(b). An annual fee of the sum of £463 is payable in connection with the holding of an authorisation: reg 22(2)(c) (amended by SI 2010/554). As to when such fee is payable see the Blood Safety and Quality Regulations 2005, SI 2005/50, reg 22(7)(ii), (7A) (reg 22(7) amended, (7A) added, by SI 2005/2898).

13 Blood Safety and Quality Regulations 2005, SI 2005/50 reg 4(7). Where the Secretary of State removes or varies any condition or imposes any additional condition, he must serve a notice on the blood establishment in question which must: (1) give details of the conditions which he proposes to remove, or of the variation which he proposes to make to any existing conditions, or of any additional condition which he proposes to impose (reg 4(8)(a)); (2) give the reasons for his decision (reg 4(8)(b)); and (3) specify the date, which must be not less than 14 days from the date on which the notice is served, from which the removal or variation of any condition, or the imposition of any additional condition, applies (reg 4(8)(c)). As to objections to suspensions or revocations, and as to objections to any such notice, see PARA 460.

14 A substantial change in a blood establishment's activities is any change: (1) to the sites from which the blood establishment operates or to the activities to be carried out at each site (Blood Safety and Quality Regulations 2005, SI 2005/50, reg 4(11)(a)); (2) which would result in breach of the Blood Safety and Quality Regulations 2005, SI 2005/50 or of any condition to an authorisation specified by the Secretary of State (reg 4(11)(b)); or (3) to the quality system which is likely to have a substantial impact on the conduct of, or might compromise the safety of, any of the activities which the blood establishment has been authorised to undertake (reg 4(11)(c)).

15 Blood Safety and Quality Regulations 2005, SI 2005/50, reg 4(9). Any application for approval to make a substantial change in its activities must be made in writing to the Secretary of State, and be accompanied by the prescribed fee: reg 4(10). The fee payable is the sum of £400 (reg 22(2)(b)) and it is payable at the time the application is made (reg 22(7)(i)). It is an offence to contravene reg 4(9): see PARA 469.

454. Suspension or revocation of authorisation. The Secretary of State[1] may suspend or revoke the authorisation of a blood establishment[2] on one or more of the following grounds: (1) that the blood establishment has failed, in any material respect, to comply with the appropriate requirements[3]; (2) that the collection, testing, processing, storage or distribution[4] of blood or blood components[5] by the establishment cannot be carried out safely[6]; (3) that any blood or blood components cannot be supplied to hospital blood banks[7] in such a state that they could be safely administered for transfusion[8]; or (4) that the information given[9] by the blood establishment in its application for authorisation was false or incomplete in any material respect[10]. Before suspending or revoking the authorisation of a blood establishment, the Secretary of State must serve a notice on the blood establishment stating that he intends to suspend or revoke its authorisation with effect from the date specified in the notice[11]; except that, where the Secretary of State considers that it is necessary in the interests of safety, he may, by a notice served on a blood establishment, suspend or revoke its authorisation with immediate effect[12].

However, where the blood establishment is in contravention of head (1) or head (4) above[13] and the Secretary of State considers that the failure in question is not sufficiently serious to warrant suspension or revocation of the authorisation of the blood establishment in the first instance, he may serve a notice on the responsible person of the blood establishment[14] identifying the requirements of which the blood establishment is in breach or, in the case of false and incomplete information, the further information which is required[15], identifying the action which the blood establishment is required to take[16], and giving the timescale within which the blood establishment must take such action[17]. If the blood establishment fails to comply with the requirements set out in the notice within the specified timescale, the Secretary of State may, by a notice served on the blood establishment, suspend or revoke the authorisation[18].

Any suspension pursuant to these provisions is for such period as the Secretary of State considers necessary having regard to the reasons for the suspension[19], and may be total, or may be limited to a particular activity or to one or more activities carried out at a particular site[20] or sites, or to a particular blood component[21].

1   As to the Secretary of State see PARA 2 note 1.
2   As to the meaning of 'blood establishment' see PARA 453 note 4. As to authorisations see PARA 453.
3   Blood Safety and Quality Regulations 2005, SI 2005/50, reg 5(1)(a). The appropriate requirements are those of the Blood Safety and Quality Regulations 2005, SI 2005/50.
4   As to the meaning of 'distribution' see PARA 449 note 4.
5   As to the meaning of 'blood' see PARA 449 note 2; and as to the meaning of 'blood component' see PARA 449 note 3.
6   Blood Safety and Quality Regulations 2005, SI 2005/50, reg 5(1)(b).
7   As to the meaning of 'hospital blood bank' see PARA 458 note 1.
8   Blood Safety and Quality Regulations 2005, SI 2005/50, reg 5(1)(c).
9   Ie pursuant to the Blood Safety and Quality Regulations 2005, SI 2005/50, reg 4(3): see PARA 453.
10   Blood Safety and Quality Regulations 2005, SI 2005/50, reg 5(1)(d).
11   Blood Safety and Quality Regulations 2005, SI 2005/50, reg 5(2). Such date must be not less than seven days from the date on which the notice is served: reg 5(2). As to objections to any notice served under reg 5 or to any suspension or revocation of authorisation see PARA 460.
12   Blood Safety and Quality Regulations 2005, SI 2005/50, reg 5(3). See also note 11.
13   Blood Safety and Quality Regulations 2005, SI 2005/50, reg 5(4)(a), (b) (amended by SI 2005/1098).
14   Blood Safety and Quality Regulations 2005, SI 2005/50, reg 5(4). As to the meaning of 'responsible person' see PARA 455 note 2.
15   Blood Safety and Quality Regulations 2005, SI 2005/50, reg 5(5)(a).
16   Blood Safety and Quality Regulations 2005, SI 2005/50, reg 5(5)(b).
17   Blood Safety and Quality Regulations 2005, SI 2005/50, reg 5(5)(c). See also note 11.
18   Blood Safety and Quality Regulations 2005, SI 2005/50, reg 5(6). Such a suspension or revocation takes effect, in a case where the Secretary of State considers that it is necessary in the interests of safety, immediately (reg 5(7)(a)); or, in all other cases, from a date specified in the notice (reg 5(7)(b)). See also note 11.
19   Blood Safety and Quality Regulations 2005, SI 2005/50, reg 5(8).
20   As to the meaning of 'site' see PARA 453 note 8.
21   Blood Safety and Quality Regulations 2005, SI 2005/50, reg 5(9). It is an offence to fail to comply with a notice of suspension or revocation served pursuant to reg 5: see reg 18(3); and PARA 469.

455. The responsible person for a blood establishment. A blood establishment[1] must designate a person[2] who is responsible for the following tasks: (1) ensuring that every unit of blood or blood component that has been collected or tested for any purpose has been collected and tested in accordance with the specified requirements[3]; (2) ensuring that every unit of blood or blood components intended for transfusion has been processed, stored and distributed in accordance with those requirements[4]; (3) providing[5] information to the Secretary of State relating to the authorisation of the blood establishment[6]; and (4) the implementation in the blood establishment of the blood establishment requirements[7], and the requirements as to labelling of blood and blood components and traceability[8], and as to disclosure of information[9]. The responsible person may delegate any of these tasks to other persons who are qualified by training and experience to perform them[10].

If the Secretary of State considers that the responsible person does not meet the requirements as to qualification[11] or that he is failing to carry out the tasks specified in heads (1) to (4) above adequately or at all, he may serve a notice to that effect on the blood establishment[12]. If, within 14 days of receiving such a notice, a blood establishment is not able to demonstrate to the reasonable satisfaction of the Secretary of State that the responsible person does meet those requirements or that he is carrying out those tasks adequately, it must, without delay relieve him of the duties of responsible person in respect of the establishment[13], appoint a new responsible person in his place[14], and notify the

Secretary of State that it has appointed a new responsible person and provide details of the name and qualifications of the person appointed[15].

1   As to the meaning of 'blood establishment' see PARA 453 note 4.

2   A blood establishment must not designate a person unless that person has: (1) a diploma, certificate or other evidence of formal qualification in the field of medical or biological sciences awarded on completion of a university course of study (Blood Safety and Quality Regulations 2005, SI 2005/50, reg 6(2)(a)(i)), or a course recognised as an equivalent course by the Secretary of State (reg 6(2)(a)(ii)); and (2) practical post-graduate experience in areas of work relevant to the responsibilities of the responsible person for at least two years, in an establishment (or more than one establishment) authorised in any member state to undertake activities related to the collection or testing (or both) of blood and blood components, or to their preparation, storage and distribution (reg 6(2)(b)). The Secretary of State must from time to time publish details of courses recognised by him for the purpose of reg 6(2)(a)(ii): reg 6(3). 'Responsible person' in relation to a blood establishment means the person who has been designated pursuant to reg 6 as the responsible person for that blood establishment: reg 1(3). As to the Secretary of State see PARA 2 note 1. As to the meaning of 'member state' see the European Communities Act 1972 s 1(2), Sch 1 Pt II; and the Interpretation Act 1978 s 5, Sch 1. As to the meaning of 'blood' see PARA 449 note 2; and as to the meaning of 'blood component' see PARA 449 note 3. As to the meaning of 'distribution' see PARA 449 note 4.

3   Blood Safety and Quality Regulations 2005, SI 2005/50, reg 6(1)(a). The specified requirements are those of the Blood Safety and Quality Regulations 2005, SI 2005/50.

4   Blood Safety and Quality Regulations 2005, SI 2005/50, reg 6(1)(b).

5   Ie for the purpose of the Blood Safety and Quality Regulations 2005, SI 2005/50, reg 4: see PARA 453.

6   Blood Safety and Quality Regulations 2005, SI 2005/50, reg 6(1)(c). As to offences relating to the contravention of reg 6 (other than reg 6(3)) see reg 18(2)(b); and PARA 469.

7   Ie under the Blood Safety and Quality Regulations 2005, SI 2005/50, reg 7: see PARA 456.

8   Ie under the Blood Safety and Quality Regulations 2005, SI 2005/50, reg 8: see PARA 457.

9   Blood Safety and Quality Regulations 2005, SI 2005/50, reg 6(1)(d). The requirements as to disclosure of information are those under reg 14: see PARA 463.

10   Blood Safety and Quality Regulations 2005, SI 2005/50, reg 6(4). Blood establishments must notify the Secretary of State of the name of any persons to whom tasks have been delegated by the responsible person, and the specific tasks which have been delegated to such persons: reg 6(5). Where the responsible person or a person to whom tasks have been delegated is permanently or temporarily replaced, the blood establishment must without delay provide the Secretary of State with the name of the replacement, details of his qualifications and the date on which the replacement began his duties: reg 6(6).

11   Ie the requirements of the Blood Safety and Quality Regulations 2005, SI 2005/50, reg 6(2): see note 2.

12   Blood Safety and Quality Regulations 2005, SI 2005/50, reg 6(7) (reg 6(7), (8) amended by SI 2005/2898).

13   Blood Safety and Quality Regulations 2005, SI 2005/50, reg 6(8)(a) (as amended: see note 12).

14   Blood Safety and Quality Regulations 2005, SI 2005/50, reg 6(8)(b).

15   Blood Safety and Quality Regulations 2005, SI 2005/50, reg 6(8)(c).

456. Blood establishment requirements. A blood establishment[1] must: (1) ensure that the personnel directly involved in the collection, testing, processing, storage and distribution[2] of human blood and blood components[3] for the blood establishment are qualified to perform those tasks and are provided with timely, relevant and regularly updated training[4]; (2) establish and maintain a quality system for blood establishments based on the principles of good practice, which complies with the Community standards and requirements[5]; (3) ensure that all testing and processes[6] of the blood establishment are validated[7]; (4) maintain documentation on operational procedures, guidelines, training and reference manuals and reporting forms so that they are readily available for inspection[8]; (5) establish and maintain a procedure, which is accurate, efficient and verifiable, for the withdrawal from distribution of blood or blood components associated with any such notification[9]; and (6) retain, for a period of at least 15 years, a record of any serious adverse events[10] which may affect the quality or safety of blood and blood components[11].

In relation to the donation of blood, a blood establishment must: (a) give all prospective donors of blood or blood components the required information[12]; (b) obtain the required information[13] from all persons who are willing to provide blood or blood components[14]; (c) put and keep in place procedures for the evaluation of donors[15]; (d) apply eligibility criteria[16] for all donors of blood and blood components[17]; (e) maintain records of the results of donor evaluations and report to donors any relevant abnormal findings from the evaluations[18]; (f) ensure that an examination of the donor, including an interview, is carried out before any donation of blood or blood components[19], that a qualified health professional[20] is responsible for giving to and gathering from donors the information which is necessary to assess their eligibility to donate[21], and that, on the basis of that information, a qualified health professional assesses the eligibility of all donors to donate[22]; and (g) encourage voluntary and unpaid blood donations with a view to ensuring that blood and blood components are, in so far as possible, provided from such donations, in particular, by disseminating information about blood donation[23] and advertising for blood donors[24].

A blood establishment must ensure that, in relation to the blood and blood components which it collects, processes, stores or distributes: (i) each donation of blood and blood components, including blood and blood components which are imported into the European Union, is tested in conformity with the basic testing requirements for whole blood and apheresis donations[25], and any additional tests which may be necessary for specific components, types of donors or epidemiological situations[26]; (ii) the storage, transport and distribution conditions of blood and blood components comply with the specified requirements[27]; and (iii) quality and safety requirements for blood and blood components meet the specified standards[28].

A blood establishment must, in relation to the activities[29] for which it is responsible, maintain records for a minimum period of 15 years[30]. As soon as practicable after the end of the reporting year[31], each blood establishment must provide to the Secretary of State a report specifying the information[32] relating to the blood and blood components which it collects, processes, stores or distributes for that year[33], and details of the steps it has taken during that year to comply with its obligation[34] to encourage donations[35].

1   As to the meaning of 'blood establishment' see PARA 453 note 4.
2   As to the meaning of 'distribution' see PARA 449 note 4.
3   As to the meaning of 'blood' see PARA 449 note 2; and as to the meaning of 'blood component' see PARA 449 note 3.
4   Blood Safety and Quality Regulations 2005, SI 2005/50, reg 7(1)(a). As to offences relating to the contravention of reg 7 see reg 18(1)(b); and PARA 469.
5   Blood Safety and Quality Regulations 2005, SI 2005/50, reg 7(1)(b) (amended by SI 2006/2013). The Community standards and requirements mentioned in the text are those set out in Commission Directive (EC) 2005/62) (OJ L256, 1.10.2006, p 41–48) as regards Community standards and specifications relating to quality system for blood establishments, Annex.
6   As to such testing and processes see the Blood Safety and Quality Regulations 2005, SI 2005/50, Schedule Pts 2–5.
7   Blood Safety and Quality Regulations 2005, SI 2005/50, reg 7(1)(c). 'Validation' means the establishment of documented and objective evidence that the particular requirements for a specific intended use can be consistently fulfilled: reg 1(3).

8 Blood Safety and Quality Regulations 2005, SI 2005/50, reg 7(1)(d). As to inspection see reg 15; and PARA 464.
9 Blood Safety and Quality Regulations 2005, SI 2005/50, reg 7(1)(f).
10 As to the meaning of 'serious adverse event' see PARA 452 note 7.
11 Blood Safety and Quality Regulations 2005, SI 2005/50, reg 7(1)(g) (added by SI 2006/2013).
12 Blood Safety and Quality Regulations 2005, SI 2005/50, reg 7(2)(a). As to the required information see Schedule Pt 2 Pt A.
13 As to the required information see the Blood Safety and Quality Regulations 2005, SI 2005/50, Schedule Pt 2 Pt B.
14 Blood Safety and Quality Regulations 2005, SI 2005/50, reg 7(2)(b).
15 Blood Safety and Quality Regulations 2005, SI 2005/50, reg 7(2)(c).
16 As to such criteria see the Blood Safety and Quality Regulations 2005, SI 2005/50, Schedule Pt 3.
17 Blood Safety and Quality Regulations 2005, SI 2005/50, reg 7(2)(d).
18 Blood Safety and Quality Regulations 2005, SI 2005/50, reg 7(2)(e).
19 Blood Safety and Quality Regulations 2005, SI 2005/50, reg 7(2)(f)(i).
20 'Qualified health professional' means a doctor, a nurse, or a donor carer: Blood Safety and Quality Regulations 2005, SI 2005/50, reg 1(3). 'Doctor' means a registered medical practitioner (see MEDICAL PROFESSIONS vol 74 (2011) PARA 176); and 'nurse' means a registered nurse or registered midwife (see MEDICAL PROFESSIONS vol 74 (2011) PARA 712 et seq): reg 1(3). 'Donor carer' means a person who has passed both the written and practical examinations of the NHS Blood and Transplant (Gwaed a Thrawsblaniadau'r GIG) (see HEALTH SERVICES vol 54 (2008) PARA 147), the Scottish National Blood Transfusion Service, the Northern Ireland Blood Transfusion Service or the Welsh Blood Service in the care of blood donors and who holds a current certificate of competence, awarded by that body, in the care of blood donors: reg 1(3) (amended by SI 2005/2532).
21 Blood Safety and Quality Regulations 2005, SI 2005/50, reg 7(2)(f)(ii).
22 Blood Safety and Quality Regulations 2005, SI 2005/50, reg 7(2)(f)(iii).
23 Blood Safety and Quality Regulations 2005, SI 2005/50, reg 7(2)(g)(i).
24 Blood Safety and Quality Regulations 2005, SI 2005/50, reg 7(2)(g)(ii).
25 As to such requirements see the Blood Safety and Quality Regulations 2005, SI 2005/50, reg 7(7).
26 Blood Safety and Quality Regulations 2005, SI 2005/50, reg 7(3)(a) (amended by SI 2011/1043). The Secretary of State may issue guidance as to the additional tests which are necessary in relation to specific components, types of donor or epidemiological situations; and blood establishments must have regard to such guidance: Blood Safety and Quality Regulations 2005, SI 2005/50, reg 7(8).
27 Blood Safety and Quality Regulations 2005, SI 2005/50, reg 7(3)(b). As to the specified requirements see Schedule Pt 4.
28 Blood Safety and Quality Regulations 2005, SI 2005/50, reg 7(3)(c). As to the specified standards see Schedule Pt 5.
29 Ie specified in the Blood Safety and Quality Regulations 2005, SI 2005/50, reg 3(2): see PARA 453.
30 Blood Safety and Quality Regulations 2005, SI 2005/50, reg 7(4). The records are to be records of the specified information (reg 7(4)(a)) and the conduct of the tests referred to in reg 7(3)(a) (see the text to notes 25, 26) (reg 7(4)(b)). The specified information is: the total number of donors who give blood and blood components (reg 7(5)(a)); the total number of donations (reg 7(5)(b)); an updated list of the hospital blood banks which it supplies (reg 7(5)(c)); the total number of whole donations not used (reg 7(5)(d)); the number of each component produced and distributed (reg 7(5)(e)); the incidence and prevalence of transfusion transmissible infectious markers in donors of blood and blood components (reg 7(5)(f)); the number of product recalls (reg 7(5)(g)); the number of serious adverse events and serious reactions reported (reg 7(5)(h)); the information provided to donors by the blood establishment in accordance with reg 7(2)(a) (see the text to note 12) (reg 7(6)(a)); the information obtained from donors by the blood establishment in accordance with reg 7(2)(b) (see the text to notes 13–14) (reg 7(6)(b)); and the information relating to the suitability of blood and plasma donors in accordance with the eligibility criteria specified in Schedule Pt 3 (reg 7(6)(c)). As to the meaning of 'hospital blood bank' see PARA 458 note 1.
31 'Reporting year' means the period of 12 months ending on 31 March: Blood Safety and Quality Regulations 2005, SI 2005/50, reg 1(3). As to the meaning of 'month' see PARA 43 note 3.
32 Ie the information referred to in the Blood Safety and Quality Regulations 2005, SI 2005/50, reg 7(3).
33 Blood Safety and Quality Regulations 2005, SI 2005/50, reg 7(9)(a).

34 Ie under the Blood Safety and Quality Regulations 2005, SI 2005/50, reg 7(2)(g).
35 Blood Safety and Quality Regulations 2005, SI 2005/50, reg 7(9)(b).

457. Labelling of blood and blood components, and traceability. A blood establishment[1] must ensure that the label on each unit of blood or blood component[2] supplied by it, or imported by it from outside the European Union, contains the specified information[3]. A blood establishment must maintain in relation to all blood and blood components collected or prepared by it (including blood and blood components which are imported by it into the European Union) specified records[4] and such other records as are necessary to ensure full traceability of blood and blood components and identification of each single donation, unit and component[5].

A blood establishment must ensure that the traceability system in place in the blood establishment enables the tracing of blood and blood components to their location and processing stage[6].

A blood establishment must have in place a system to uniquely identify each donor, each blood unit collected and each blood component prepared, whatever its intended purpose, and the facilities to which a given unit of blood or blood component has been delivered[7].

A blood establishment must ensure, when it issues[8] a unit of blood or blood components for transfusion, that the facility to which the unit of blood is issued has in place a procedure to verify that each unit of blood issued has been transfused to the intended recipient or, if not transfused, to verify its subsequent disposition[9].

1   As to the meaning of 'blood establishment' see PARA 453 note 4.
2   As to the meaning of 'blood' see PARA 449 note 2; and as to the meaning of 'blood component' see PARA 449 note 3.
3   Blood Safety and Quality Regulations 2005, SI 2005/50, reg 8(1) (amended by SI 2011/1043). As to the specified information see the Blood Safety and Quality Regulations 2005, SI 2005/50, reg 8(1)(a)–(i). As to offences relating to the contravention of reg 8 see reg 18(2)(c); and PARA 469. These records must be maintained in an appropriate and readable storage medium for a period of not less than 30 years: reg 8(3) (reg 8(3)–(6) added by SI 2006/2013).
4   Ie records of the information referred to in the Blood Safety and Quality Regulations 2005, SI 2005/50, reg 8(1) and records referred to in Schedule, Pt 6, Part A.
5   Blood Safety and Quality Regulations 2005, SI 2005/50, reg 8(2) (amended by SI 2006/1043, SI 2011/1043). As to the meaning of 'hospital' see PARA 458 note 1.
6   Blood Safety and Quality Regulations 2005, SI 2005/50, reg 8(4) (as added: see note 3).
7   Blood Safety and Quality Regulations 2005, SI 2005/50, reg 8(5) (as added: see note 3).
8   'Issue' means the provision of blood or blood components by a blood establishment or a hospital bank for transfusion to a recipient: reg 1(3) (definition added by SI 2006/2013).
9   Blood Safety and Quality Regulations 2005, SI 2005/50, reg 8(6) (as added: see note 3).

458. Hospital blood bank requirements. The person responsible for the management of a hospital blood bank[1] must: (1) ensure that personnel directly involved in the testing, storage and distribution of human blood and blood components for the hospital blood bank are qualified to perform those tasks and are provided with timely, relevant and regularly updated training[2]; (2) establish and maintain a quality system for the hospital blood bank which is based on the principles of good practice which complies with the Community standards and EU requirements[3] insofar as these are applicable to hospital blood banks[4]; (3) ensure that all processes[5] which are applicable to activities carried out by the hospital blood bank are validated[6]; (4) maintain documentation on operational procedures, guidelines, training and reference manuals and reporting forms so that they are readily available for inspection[7]; (5) maintain in an appropriate and readable storage medium and for a period of not less than 30 years the data on traceability[8] (insofar as those data are applicable to the activities carried out by the hospital blood bank) and such other data as are needed to ensure full traceability of blood and blood components and the unique identification of each unit of blood and each blood component from the point of receipt of the blood or blood components by the hospital blood bank[9]; (6) retain, for a period of at least 15 years, a record of any serious adverse events[10] which may affect the quality or safety of blood and blood components[11]; (7) establish and maintain a procedure, which is accurate, efficient and verifiable, for the withdrawal from distribution of blood or blood components associated with any such notification[12]; (8) ensure that the storage, transport and distribution conditions of blood and blood components by the hospital blood bank comply with the specified requirements[13]; and (9) ensure that the traceability system in place in the hospital blood bank enables the tracing of blood components to their final destination[14]; and (10) where it delivers blood or blood components for transfusion at another facility, have in place a system to uniquely identify the facility to which a given unit of blood or blood component has been delivered[15].

A person responsible for management of a hospital blood bank must ensure that when a hospital blood bank issues a unit of blood for transfusion, that it has in place a procedure to verify that each unit of blood issued has been transfused to the intended recipient, or if not transfused, to verify its subsequent disposition[16].

On or before the specified date[17], the person responsible for management of a hospital blood bank must submit a report to the Secretary of State, which must include a declaration that the hospital blood bank has in place appropriate systems to ensure compliance with the specified requirements[18], and provide details of the systems which it has in place to ensure such compliance[19].

1 'Person responsible for management of a hospital blood bank' means in the case of a hospital blood bank located in a hospital managed by a health service body, that body; and in the case of an independent hospital, the registered person: Blood Safety and Quality Regulations 2005, SI 2005/50, reg 1(3). 'Hospital blood bank' means any unit within a hospital which stores and distributes, and may perform compatibility tests on, blood and blood components exclusively for use within hospital facilities, including hospital based transfusion activities: reg 1(3). 'Hospital' means a health service hospital or an independent hospital; 'health service hospital' has the same meaning as in the National Health Service Act 1977 s 128 (see HEALTH SERVICES vol 54 (2008) PARA 21); and 'independent hospital' in England, means a hospital as defined in the National Health Service Act 2006 s 275 (see HEALTH SERVICES) that is not a health service hospital as so defined and in Wales has the same meaning as in the Care Standards Act 2000 s 2 (see CHILDREN AND YOUNG PERSONS vol 10 (2012) PARA 992): Blood Safety and Quality Regulations 2005, SI 2005/50, reg 1(3) (definition substituted by SI 2006/2013; and amended by SI 2010/1881). As to the meaning of 'blood' see PARA 449 note 2; and as to the meaning of 'blood component' see PARA 449 note 3. As to the meaning of 'distribution' see PARA 449 note 4. 'Health service body' means a strategic health authority, special health authority, primary care trust or local health board established under the National Health Service Act 1977; a national health service trust established under the National Health Service and Community Care Act 1990; or an NHS foundation trust within the meaning of the Health and Social Care (Community Health and Standards) Act 2003 s 1(1): Blood Safety and Quality Regulations 2005, SI 2005/50, reg 1(3). As to all such bodies see HEALTH SERVICES vol 54 (2008) PARA 75 et seq. As from 1 April 2013, primary care trusts and strategic health authorities are abolished: see PARAS 3 note 1, 111 note 9. 'Registered person' means, in England, the person registered as manager under the Health and Social Care Act 2008 Pt 1 Chapter 2 in respect of regulated activities (within the meaning of that Part) carried on in an independent hospital, a care home or an independent clinic and, in relation to Wales, means the person registered as the manager of an independent hospital following an application to be registered as such pursuant to the Care Standards Act 2000 s 12(3) (see SOCIAL SERVICES AND COMMUNITY CARE): Blood Safety and Quality Regulations 2005, SI 2005/50, reg 1(3) (definition substituted by

SI 2010/1881). As to the meaning of 'person' see PARA 45 note 2. 'Independent clinic', in Wales, has the same meaning as in the Care Standards Act 2000 s 2 and, in England, means an establishment of the following kind: (1) a walk-in centre, in which one or more medical practitioners provide services of a kind which, if provided in pursuance of the National Health Service Act 2006, would be provided as primary medical services under Part 4 of that Act; or (2) a surgery or consulting room in which a medical practitioner who provides no services in pursuance of the National Health Service Act 2006 provides medical services of any kind (including psychiatric treatment), except where such medical services are provided only under arrangements made on behalf of the patients by their employer, a government department or any executive agency of a government department, a prison or other establishment in which patients are held in custody, other than pursuant to any provision of the Mental Health Act 1983 or an insurance provider with whom the patients hold an insurance policy, other than an insurance policy which is solely or primarily intended to provide benefits in connection with the diagnosis or treatment of physical or mental illness, disability or infirmity, and where two or more medical practitioners use different parts of the same premises as a surgery or consulting room, or use the same surgery or consulting room at different times, each of the medical practitioners must be regarded as carrying on a separate independent clinic unless they are in practice together: Blood Safety and Quality Regulations 2005, SI 2005/50, reg 1(3) (definition added by SI 2011/2581). 'Care home', in England and Wales, has the same meaning as in the Care Standards Act 2000 s 3 (see CHILDREN AND YOUNG PERSONS vol 10 (2012) PARA 994): Blood Safety and Quality Regulations 2005, SI 2005/50, reg 1(3) (definition added by SI 2006/2013).

2   Blood Safety and Quality Regulations 2005, SI 2005/50, reg 9(1)(a). As to offences relating to the contravention of reg 9 see reg 18(1)(c); and PARA 469.

3   Ie the requirements set out in Commission Directive (EC) 2005/62(OJ L56, 10.2005, p 1–48) as regards Community standards and specifications relating to a quality system for blood establishments, Annex.

4   Blood Safety and Quality Regulations 2005, SI 2005/50, reg 9(1)(b) (amended by SI 2006/2013).

5   As to such processes see the Blood Safety and Quality Regulations 2005, SI 2005/50, Schedule Pt 4.

6   Blood Safety and Quality Regulations 2005, SI 2005/50, reg 9(1)(c). As to the meaning of 'validation' see PARA 456 note 7.

7   Blood Safety and Quality Regulations 2005, SI 2005/50, reg 9(1)(d). As to inspection see reg 15; and PARA 464.

8   Ie the data set out in the Blood Safety and Quality Regulations 2005, SI 2005/50, Schedule Pt 6. 'Traceability' means the ability to trace each individual unit of blood or blood component from the donor to its final destination (whether this is a recipient, a manufacturer of medicinal products or disposal) and from its final destination back to the donor: reg 1(3) (definition added by SI 2006/2013). As to the meaning of 'manufacturer' see PARA 449 note 4.

9   Blood Safety and Quality Regulations 2005, SI 2005/50, reg 9(1)(e) (substituted by SI 2006/2013).

10 As to the meaning of 'serious adverse event' see PARA 452 note 7.

11 Blood Safety and Quality Regulations 2005, SI 2005/50, reg 9(1)(f) (substituted by SI 2006/2013). In respect of the assessment by the Secretary of State of serious adverse events and serious adverse reactions notified by hospital blood banks an annual haemovigilance fee is payable: see reg 22(3B)–(3D), (7)(iia), (iib) (all added by SI 2005/2898; amended by SI 2006/2013, SI 2010/554).

12 Blood Safety and Quality Regulations 2005, SI 2005/50, reg 9(1)(g).

13 Blood Safety and Quality Regulations 2005, SI 2005/50, reg 9(1)(h). As to the specified requirements see Schedule Pt 4.

14 Blood Safety and Quality Regulations 2005, SI 2005/50, reg 9(1)(i) (added by SI 2006/2013).

15 Blood Safety and Quality Regulations 2005, SI 2005/50, reg 9(1)(ii) (added by SI 2006/2013).

16 Blood Safety and Quality Regulations 2005, SI 2005/50, reg 9(2) (added by SI 2006/2013).

17 The specified date is, in relation to the reporting year ending on 31 March 2006, 31 December 2005; and in relation to each subsequent reporting year, 30 April following the end of that year: Blood Safety and Quality Regulations 2005, SI 2005/50, reg 10(1A) (reg 10(1) amended, (1A) added, by SI 2005/2898). As to the meaning of 'reporting year' see PARA 456 note 31.

18 Blood Safety and Quality Regulations 2005, SI 2005/50, reg 10(1)(a) (as amended: see note 17). The specified requirements are those of the Blood Safety and Quality Regulations 2005, SI 2005/50 (as so amended). The person responsible for management of a hospital blood bank must without delay notify the Secretary of State of any changes to the matters in respect of

which evidence has been supplied pursuant to reg 10(1) which might affect compliance with those requirements: reg 10(2). As to offences relating to the contravention of reg 10 see reg 18(2)(d); and PARA 469.

19 Blood Safety and Quality Regulations 2005, SI 2005/50, reg 10(1)(b). A fee is payable to the Secretary of State in respect of each reporting year in which a hospital blood bank has operated: see reg 22(3A) (added by SI 2005/2898; amended by SI 2010/554).

459. Notices relating to hospital blood banks. If the Secretary of State[1] is of the opinion that the person responsible for management of a hospital blood bank[2] has failed, in any material respect, to comply with the specified requirements[3], or that the testing, storage or distribution[4] of blood or blood components[5] by the hospital blood bank is such that any blood or blood components cannot be safely administered for transfusion[6], or that the information given[7] by the person responsible for management of a hospital blood bank was false or incomplete in any material respect[8], he may serve a notice on the person responsible for management of the hospital blood bank requiring the hospital to cease to conduct any of the activities specified in the notice, or to refrain from administering to patients any blood or blood components specified in the notice, until certain requirements are met[9]. The requirements are, as may be applicable in each case, that: (1) the person responsible for management of the hospital blood bank is no longer in breach of the specified requirements[10]; (2) the hospital blood bank is able to show that the activity or product referred to in the notice[11] may be safely carried out or, as the case may be, administered[12]; or (3) that all necessary information has been supplied to the Secretary of State[13].

Any notice served by the Secretary of State must specify the date from which the prohibition specified in the notice takes effect, which must be not less than seven days from the date on which the notice is served[14]. However, where the Secretary of State considers that it is necessary in the interests of safety, he may specify in the notice that the prohibition is to take immediate effect[15].

1 As to the Secretary of State see PARA 2 note 1.
2 As to the meanings of 'person responsible for management of a hospital blood bank' and 'hospital blood bank' see PARA 458 note 1.
3 Blood Safety and Quality Regulations 2005, SI 2005/50, reg 11(1)(a). The specified requirements are those of the Blood Safety and Quality Regulations 2005, SI 2005/50.
4 As to the meaning of 'distribution' see PARA 449 note 4.
5 As to the meaning of 'blood' see PARA 449 note 2; and as to the meaning of 'blood component' see PARA 449 note 3.
6 Blood Safety and Quality Regulations 2005, SI 2005/50, reg 11(1)(b).
7 Ie pursuant to the Blood Safety and Quality Regulations 2005, SI 2005/50, reg 10: see PARA 458.
8 Blood Safety and Quality Regulations 2005, SI 2005/50, reg 11(1)(c).
9 Blood Safety and Quality Regulations 2005, SI 2005/50, reg 11(1). As to objections to such notices see reg 12; and PARA 460. It is an offence to contravene the requirements of a notice under reg 11(1): see reg 18(5); and PARA 469.
10 Blood Safety and Quality Regulations 2005, SI 2005/50, reg 11(4)(a).
11 Ie the notice given pursuant to the Blood Safety and Quality Regulations 2005, SI 2005/50, reg 11(1)(b): see the text to notes 4–6.
12 Blood Safety and Quality Regulations 2005, SI 2005/50, reg 11(4)(b).
13 Blood Safety and Quality Regulations 2005, SI 2005/50, reg 11(4)(c).
14 Blood Safety and Quality Regulations 2005, SI 2005/50, reg 11(2).
15 Blood Safety and Quality Regulations 2005, SI 2005/50, reg 11(3).

460. Objections to suspensions, revocations and notices. A blood establishment[1] or a person responsible for the management of a hospital blood bank[2] who objects to any suspension or revocation of authorisation[3] or to any notice served[4] on it[5], or objects to the refusal of authorisation or the imposition of any condition[6] on an authorisation[7], may notify the Secretary of State[8] of its or his desire to make written representations to, or to appear before and be heard by, a person appointed by the Secretary of State for that purpose[9]. Where the Secretary of State receives such a notification, he must appoint a person to consider the matter[10]. The person appointed must determine the procedure to be followed with respect to the consideration of any objection[11], and must consider any written or oral representations made by the blood establishment or the person responsible for management of the hospital blood bank in support of the objection, and make a recommendation to the Secretary of State[12]. The Secretary of State must take into account any recommendation made by the person appointed[13] and, within 14 days of receipt thereof, must inform the blood establishment or the person responsible for the management of the hospital blood bank whether he accepts the recommendation and, if he does not accept it, of the reasons for his decision[14].

Where the Secretary of State is notified of an objection[15] before the date upon which the suspension or revocation or the notice is due to take effect, the suspension or revocation or notice in respect of which the objection is made does not take effect until the person appointed has considered the matter and made a recommendation[16], and the Secretary of State has informed the blood establishment or the person responsible for the management of the hospital blood bank concerned of his decision with regard to the recommendation[17]. Where the Secretary of State is notified of an objection[18], within the period specified[19], to a suspension, revocation or other notice which has already taken effect on the date the notification was made, the suspension, revocation or notice in respect of which the objection is made ceases to have effect until the person appointed has considered the matter and made a recommendation[20], and the Secretary of State has informed the blood establishment or the person responsible for the management of the hospital blood bank concerned of his decision with regard to the recommendation[21]. However, these provisions[22] do not apply in relation to a suspension or revocation, or a notice served[23] on the person responsible for management of a hospital blood bank, which takes[24] immediate effect[25], or, in any other case, where the Secretary of State determines that it is necessary in the interests of public safety for the suspension, revocation or notice to take effect on the date originally specified, and serves a notice in writing to that effect on the blood establishment or person responsible for management of the hospital blood bank concerned[26].

1   As to the meaning of 'blood establishment' see PARA 453 note 4.
2   As to the meanings of 'person responsible for management of a hospital blood bank' and 'hospital blood bank' see PARA 458 note 1.
3   As to the suspension or revocation of authorisation see PARA 454.
4   Ie pursuant to the Blood Safety and Quality Regulations 2005, SI 2005/50, regs 4(8), 5, 11: see PARAS 453, 454, 459.
5   Blood Safety and Quality Regulations 2005, SI 2005/50, reg 12(1)(a).
6   Ie pursuant to the Blood Safety and Quality Regulations 2005, SI 2005/50, reg 4(5): see PARA 453 note 8.
7   Blood Safety and Quality Regulations 2005, SI 2005/50, reg 12(1)(b).
8   As to the Secretary of State see PARA 2 note 1.
9   Blood Safety and Quality Regulations 2005, SI 2005/50, reg 12(1) (amended by SI 2005/1098). Any such notification of an objection must be made within 14 days of service on the blood establishment or the person responsible for the management of the hospital blood bank of the notice to which the notification relates: Blood Safety and Quality Regulations 2005, SI 2005/50, reg 12(2).
10 Blood Safety and Quality Regulations 2005, SI 2005/50, reg 12(3).
11 Blood Safety and Quality Regulations 2005, SI 2005/50, reg 12(4).

12 Blood Safety and Quality Regulations 2005, SI 2005/50, reg 12(5). Such a recommendation must be made in writing to the Secretary of State, and a copy of it must be sent to the blood establishment or the person responsible for the management of the hospital blood bank concerned, or to its nominated representative: reg 12(6).

13 Blood Safety and Quality Regulations 2005, SI 2005/50, reg 12(7).

14 Blood Safety and Quality Regulations 2005, SI 2005/50, reg 12(8).

15 Ie pursuant to the Blood Safety and Quality Regulations 2005, SI 2005/50, reg 12(1)(a): see the text to notes 1–5.

16 Blood Safety and Quality Regulations 2005, SI 2005/50,reg 12(9)(a) (amended by SI 2005/1098).

17 Blood Safety and Quality Regulations 2005, SI 2005/50, reg 12(9)(b) (as amended: see note 16).

18 Ie pursuant to the Blood Safety and Quality Regulations 2005, SI 2005/50, reg 12(1)(a): see the text to notes 1–5.

19 Ie specified in the Blood Safety and Quality Regulations 2005, SI 2005/50, reg 12(2): see note 9.

20 Blood Safety and Quality Regulations 2005, SI 2005/50, reg 12(10)(a).

21 Blood Safety and Quality Regulations 2005, SI 2005/50, reg 12(10)(b).

22 Ie the Blood Safety and Quality Regulations 2005, SI 2005/50, reg 12(9), (10): see the text to notes 15–21.

23 Ie pursuant to the Blood Safety and Quality Regulations 2005, SI 2005/50, reg 11: see PARA 459.

24 Ie in accordance with the Blood Safety and Quality Regulations 2005, SI 2005/50, regs 5(3), 11(3): see PARAS 454, 459.

25 Blood Safety and Quality Regulations 2005, SI 2005/50, reg 12(11)(a) (amended by SI 2005/1098).

26 Blood Safety and Quality Regulations 2005, SI 2005/50, reg 12(11)(b) (as amended: see note 25).

461. Retention of certain data. A person responsible for management of a facility must ensure that the facility:

(1) retains specified data[1], in an appropriate and readable storage medium, for a period of at least 30 years[2]; and

(2) has in place a system in place to record each unit of blood or blood component[3] received, whether or not locally used, and the final destination of that received unit whether transfused, used in the manufacture of medicinal products, discarded or returned to the blood establishment or hospital blood bank[4].

1 Ie the data set out in the Blood Safety and Quality Regulations 2005, SI 2005/50, Schedule Pt 6 Section B (added by SI 2006/2013).

2 Blood Safety and Quality Regulations 2005, SI 2005/50, reg 12A(a) (added by SI 2006/2013).

3 As to the meanings of 'blood' and 'blood component' see PARA 449 notes 2, 3.

4 Blood Safety and Quality Regulations 2005, SI 2005/50, reg 12A(b) (as added: see note 2). As to the meaning of 'hospital blood bank' see PARA 458 note 1. Contravention of reg 12A is an offence: see reg 18(1)(f); and PARA 469.

462. Requirement to report serious adverse reactions and events. A person responsible for management of a reporting establishment[1] must ensure that the reporting establishment:

(1) has in place procedures to retain the record of transfusions for a period of at least 30 years[2];

(2) notifies blood establishments[3] without delay of any serious adverse reactions[4] observed in recipients during or after transfusion which may be attributable to the quality or safety of blood or blood components[5]; and

(3) notifies the Secretary of State[6] as soon as is known all relevant information about suspected serious adverse reactions[7] using the specified[8] notification formats[9].

A person responsible for management of a reporting establishment must ensure that the reporting establishment:

(a)　notifies the Secretary of State of all relevant information about serious adverse reactions of imputability level 2 and 3[10], which may be attributable to the quality and safety of blood or blood components[11];

(b)　notifies the Secretary of State, as soon as is known, of any case of transmission of infectious agents by blood or blood components[12];

(c)　as part of the notification referred to in head (a), describes the actions taken with respect to other implicated blood or blood components that have been distributed for transfusion or for plasma fractionation[13];

(d)　as soon as is reasonably practicable after each suspected serious adverse reaction, evaluates that reaction according to the specified[14] imputability levels[15];

(e)　completes the serious adverse reaction notification, upon conclusion of the investigation, using the specified format[16]; and

(f)　submits a complete report to the Secretary of State on serious adverse reactions in any calendar year by no later than 1st April in the following calendar year, using the specified format[17].

A person responsible for management of a reporting establishment must ensure that the reporting establishment notifies the Secretary of State as soon as is known, using the specified notification formats[18], of all relevant information about serious adverse events which may put in danger donors or recipients other than those directly involved in the event concerned[19].

A person responsible for management of a reporting establishment must ensure that the reporting establishment:

(i)　as soon as is reasonably practicable after each serious adverse event, evaluates that serious adverse event to identify preventable causes within the process[20];

(ii)　upon completion of the investigation, completes the serious adverse event notification, using the specified format[21]; and

(iii)　submits a complete report to the Secretary of State on serious adverse events in any calendar year by no later than 1st April in the following calendar year, using the specified format[22].

1　As to the meanings of 'person responsible for management of a hospital blood bank' and 'hospital blood bank' see PARA 458 note 1. 'Reporting establishment' means the blood establishment, the hospital blood bank or the facility where the transfusion takes place: Blood Safety and Quality Regulations 2005, SI 2005/50, reg1(3) (definition added by SI 2006/2013).

2　Blood Safety and Quality Regulations 2005, SI 2005/50, reg 12B(1)(a) (reg 12B and Schedule Pts 7, 8 added by SI 2006/2013). Contravention of the Blood Safety and Quality Regulations 2005, SI 2005/50, reg 12B is an offence see reg 18(1)(g); and PARA 469.

3　As to the meaning of 'blood establishment' see PARA 452 note 4.

4　As to the meaning of 'serious adverse reaction' see PARA 452 note 7.

5　Blood Safety and Quality Regulations 2005, SI 2005/50, reg 12B(1)(b) (as added: see note 2). As to the meanings of 'blood' and 'blood component' see PARA 449 notes 2, 3. A facility may make arrangements with a hospital blood bank for the hospital blood bank to submit to the Secretary of State or the blood establishment the reports required by reg 12B(1)(b), (c), (2)(a), (b), (e), (f), (4)(b), (c) on the facility's behalf provided that:

　(1)　the person responsible for management of the hospital blood bank is the same person as the person responsible for management of the facility with which the arrangement is made; or

　(2)　the arrangements referred to above are evidenced by a written agreement and made with the person responsible for management of the hospital blood bank who supplied the blood or blood components to the facility for transfusion and that the facility will supply the information necessary to enable the hospital blood bank to make the reports within the timescale specified by this regulation in relation to that report: reg 12B(5), (6) (as so added; reg 12B(5) amended by SI 2008/941).

6　As to the Secretary of State see PARA 2 note 1.

7 As to the meaning of 'serious adverse reaction' see PARA 452 note 7.

8 Ie the notification formats set out in the Blood Safety and Quality Regulations 2005, SI 2005/50, Schedule Pt 7 sections A, C (as added: see note 2).

9 Blood Safety and Quality Regulations 2005, SI 2005/50, reg 12B(1)(c) (as added: see note 2). See note 5.

10 Ie as referred to in the Blood Safety and Quality Regulations 2005, SI 2005/50, Schedule Pt 7 section B (as added: see note 2). 'Imputability' means the likelihood that a serious adverse reaction in a recipient can be attributed to the blood or blood component transfused, or that a serious adverse reaction in a donor can be attributed to the donation process: reg 1(3) (definition added by SI 2006/2013).

11 Blood Safety and Quality Regulations 2005, SI 2005/50, reg 12B(2)(a) (as added: see note 2). As to the meanings of 'blood' and 'blood component' see PARA 449 notes 2, 3. See note 5.

12 Blood Safety and Quality Regulations 2005, SI 2005/50, reg 12B(2)(b) (as added: see note 2). See note 5.

13 Blood Safety and Quality Regulations 2005, SI 2005/50, reg 12B(2)(c) (as added: see note 2).

14 Ie the imputability levels set out in the Blood Safety and Quality Regulations 2005, SI 2005/50, Schedule Pt 7 section B (as added: see note 2).

15 Blood Safety and Quality Regulations 2005, SI 2005/50, reg 12B(2)(d) (as added: see note 2).

16 Blood Safety and Quality Regulations 2005, SI 2005/50, reg 12B(2)(e) (as added: see note 2). The specified format mentioned in the text is the format set out in Schedule Pt 7 section C. See note 5.

17 Blood Safety and Quality Regulations 2005, SI 2005/50, reg 12B(2)(f) (as added: see note 2). The specified format mentioned in the text is the format set out in Schedule Pt 7 section D. See note 5.

18 Ie the notification formats set out in the Blood Safety and Quality Regulations 2005, SI 2005/50, Schedule Pt 8 section A (as added: see note 2).

19 Blood Safety and Quality Regulations 2005, SI 2005/50, reg 12B(3) (as added: see note 2).

20 Blood Safety and Quality Regulations 2005, SI 2005/50, reg 12B(4)(a) (as added: see note 2).

21 Blood Safety and Quality Regulations 2005, SI 2005/50, reg 12B(4)(b) (as added: see note 2). The specified format mentioned in the text is the format set out in Schedule Pt 8 section B (as added: see note 2). See note 5.

22 Blood Safety and Quality Regulations 2005, SI 2005/50, reg 12B(4)(c) (as added (see note 2); substituted by SI 2007/604). The specified format mentioned in the text is the format set out in the Blood Safety and Quality Regulations 2005, SI 2005/50, Schedule Pt 8 section C (as added: see note 2). See note 5.

463. Disclosure of information. A blood establishment[1] and the person responsible for management of a hospital blood bank[2] must ensure that all information which is collected[3] with regard to blood[4] safety and quality is held securely so that it is available for the purpose of tracing donations[5], is not disclosed except in accordance with one or more of the specified requirements[6] or where they have been rendered anonymous so that donors are no longer identifiable[7], and is subject to safeguards against unauthorised additions, deletions or modifications[8].

The responsible person[9] of the blood establishment and the person responsible for management of the hospital blood bank must ensure that they put in place a procedure to ensure that any discrepancies relating to data which are brought to their attention are resolved without delay[10].

1 As to the meaning of 'blood establishment' see PARA 453 note 4.

2 As to the meanings of 'person responsible for management of a hospital blood bank' and 'hospital blood bank' see PARA 458 note 1.

3 Ie for the purposes of the Blood Safety and Quality Regulations 2005, SI 2005/50.

4 As to the meaning of 'blood' see PARA 449 note 2.

5 Blood Safety and Quality Regulations 2005, SI 2005/50, reg 14(1)(a).

6 Blood Safety and Quality Regulations 2005, SI 2005/50, reg 14(1)(b)(i). The specified requirements are: (1) the disclosure is made in accordance with an order of a court or is otherwise required by law (reg 14(2)(a)); (2) the disclosure is to an inspector appointed by the Secretary of State in accordance with reg 15(10) (see PARA 464) (reg 14(2)(b)); or (3) the disclosure is for the purpose of tracing a donation from donor to recipient or recipient to donor

(reg 14(2)(c)). Where a disclosure is made to an inspector pursuant to reg 14(2)(b), the inspector must not further disclose the information received unless the disclosure is made in accordance with an order of a court or is otherwise required by law (reg 14(3)(a)), the disclosure is to another officer of the Secretary of State where this is necessary for the proper performance of the inspector or officer's duties (reg 14(3)(b)), or the information has been rendered anonymous so that that donors are no longer identifiable (reg 14(3)(c)). Where a disclosure is so made by an inspector to another officer of the Secretary of State, that person must not further disclose the information he receives other than in accordance with the requirements of reg 14(3): reg 14(4). As to the Secretary of State see PARA 2 note 1.

7　Blood Safety and Quality Regulations 2005, SI 2005/50, reg 14(1)(b)(ii).

8　Blood Safety and Quality Regulations 2005, SI 2005/50, reg 14(1)(c). As to offences relating to the contravention of reg 14 see reg 18(6); and PARA 469.

9　As to the meaning of 'responsible person' see PARA 455 note 2.

10　Blood Safety and Quality Regulations 2005, SI 2005/50, reg 14(5).

464. Inspections. The Secretary of State[1] must conduct a regular inspection[2] of each site[3] of a blood establishment, not less than once every two years, for the purpose of ensuring that blood establishments comply with the specified requirements[4] and problems relating to compliance with those requirements are identified[5]. The Secretary of State may conduct such additional inspections of blood establishments sites as he considers necessary for the purpose of ensuring compliance with the specified requirements[6]. The Secretary of State may also serve a notice on a blood establishment requiring that it furnish him with such information concerning its compliance with the specified requirements as are specified in the notice within such period as is so specified[7].

The Secretary of State may inspect hospital blood banks and facilities[8] with a view to ensuring that they and persons responsible for the management of such blood banks and facilities comply with the specified requirements[9] and problems relating to compliance with those requirements are identified[10]. The Secretary of State may also serve a notice on the person responsible for managing a hospital blood bank or a facility requiring that he furnish him with such information concerning the compliance of the blood bank with the specified requirements as is specified in the notice within such period as is so specified[11].

In the event of any serious adverse event[12] or any serious adverse reaction[13] or suspicion thereof, the Secretary of State must request such information or conduct such inspections in accordance with these provisions as he considers appropriate[14].

The Secretary of State may appoint such persons to be inspectors as he thinks necessary for the proper discharge by them of his functions[15]; and he may appoint such persons upon such terms and conditions, including conditions as to remuneration, benefits, allowances and reimbursement for expenses, as he thinks fit[16].

1　As to the Secretary of State see PARA 2 note 1.

2　'Inspection' means formal and objective control to identify problems in accordance with standards adopted to assess compliance with the Blood Safety and Quality Regulations 2005, SI 2005/50: reg 1(3).

3　Any reference to an inspection of a site which the Secretary of State is required or empowered to conduct by virtue of the Blood Safety and Quality Regulations 2005, SI 2005/50, reg 15 must be construed so as to include an inspection of premises within the United Kingdom at which any of the activities listed in reg 3(2) (see PARA 453) are carried out by any person on behalf of, and pursuant to a contractual arrangement with, a blood establishment or, as the case may be, a person responsible for management of a hospital blood bank: reg 15(9). As to the meaning of 'site' see PARA 453 note 8; and as to the meaning of 'blood establishment' see PARA 453 note 4. As to the meanings of 'person responsible for management of a hospital blood bank' and 'hospital blood bank' see PARA 458 note 1.

4 Blood Safety and Quality Regulations 2005, SI 2005/50, reg 15(1)(a). The specified requirements are those of the Blood Safety and Quality Regulations 2005, SI 2005/50.

5 Blood Safety and Quality Regulations 2005, SI 2005/50, reg 15(1)(b). Where the Secretary of State carries out an inspection at a site of a blood establishment he may charge the establishment and that establishment must, if so charged, pay to the Secretary of State a fee: reg 22(3). As to the amounts of such fees see reg 22(3)(a), (b) (substituted by SI 2010/554). Any such fee is payable within 14 days following written notice from the Secretary of State requiring payment of the fee: Blood Safety and Quality Regulations 2005, SI 2005/50, reg 22(7)(iii). As to fees generally see PARA 452.

6 Blood Safety and Quality Regulations 2005, SI 2005/50, reg 15(2). See also note 5.

7 Blood Safety and Quality Regulations 2005, SI 2005/50, reg 15(3). Any blood establishment which receives such a request for information must provide the information requested within the period specified in the notice: reg 15(4). It is an offence to contravene reg 15(4): see reg 18(2)(e); and PARA 469.

8 'Facility' means a hospital, any other facility or service owned or managed by a health service body, a care home, an independent clinic, a manufacturer or a biomedical research institute: Blood Safety and Quality Regulations 2005, SI 2005/50, reg 1(3) (definition added by SI 2006/2013). As to the meanings of 'hospital', 'health service body', 'care home' and 'independent clinic' see PARA 458 note 1. As to the meaning of 'manufacturer' see PARA 449 note 4. 'Biomedical research institution' means any body which carries out biomedical research: Blood Safety and Quality Regulations 2005, SI 2005/50, reg 1(3) (definition added by SI 2006/2013).

9 Blood Safety and Quality Regulations 2005, SI 2005/50, reg 15(5)(a) (amended by SI 2006/2013).

10 Blood Safety and Quality Regulations 2005, SI 2005/50, reg 15(5)(b). Where the Secretary of State carries out an inspection of a hospital blood bank or a facility he may charge the person responsible for management of the hospital blood bank or facility and that person must, if so charged, pay to the Secretary of State a fee: reg 22(4) (amended by SI 2006/2013). As to the amount of such fees see Blood Safety and Quality Regulations 2005, SI 2005/50, reg 22(5) (amended by SI 2006/2013). Any such fee is payable within 14 days following written notice from the Secretary of State requiring payment of the fee: Blood Safety and Quality Regulations 2005, SI 2005/50, reg 22(7)(iii).

11 Blood Safety and Quality Regulations 2005, SI 2005/50, reg 15(6) (amended by SI 2006/2013). Any person responsible for management of a hospital blood bank or a facility who receives such a request for information must provide the information requested within the period specified in the notice: Blood Safety and Quality Regulations 2005, SI 2005/50, reg 15(7) (amended by SI 2006/2013). It is an offence to contravene Blood Safety and Quality Regulations 2005, SI 2005/50, reg 15(7): see reg 18(2)(e); and PARA 469.

12 As to the meaning of 'serious adverse event' see PARA 452 note.7.

13 As to the meaning of 'serious adverse reaction' see PARA 452 note 7.

14 Blood Safety and Quality Regulations 2005, SI 2005/50, reg 15(8). See also notes 5, 9.

15 Ie set out in the Blood Safety and Quality Regulations 2005, SI 2005/50.

16 Blood Safety and Quality Regulations 2005, SI 2005/50, reg 15(10). 'Inspector' means a person appointed by the Secretary of State to carry out inspections pursuant to reg 15(10): reg 1(3).

465. Inspector's powers. For the purposes of enforcing compliance with the specified requirements[1] or conducting inspections[2], and upon production of evidence that he is so authorised, an inspector[3] has the right[4]:

(1)   at any reasonable hour to enter any premises, other than premises used only as a private dwelling house, which he has reason to believe it is necessary for him to visit, including:

(a)   any premises owned or managed by a blood establishment[5] or person responsible for management of a hospital blood bank[6], or at which the blood establishment or person responsible for management of a hospital blood bank carries out any of the activities[7] requiring authorisation[8];

(b)   any premises of any person who carries out any such activities on behalf of, or pursuant to a contractual arrangement with, a blood establishment or a person responsible for management of a hospital blood bank[9];

(c) where any facilities for donor evaluation and testing are in the premises of any person[10] other than a blood establishment or hospital blood bank, those facilities in that person's premises[11]; and

(d) any premises where transfusion of blood or blood components[12] takes place, or which are owned or managed by a person responsible for management of a facility to which blood or blood components have been delivered[13];

(2) to carry out at those premises during that visit inspections, examinations, tests and analyses as he considers necessary[14];

(3) to require the production of, and inspect, any article or substance at the premises[15];

(4) to require the production of, inspect and take copies of, or extracts from, any book, document, data or record, in whatever form it is held, at, or in the case of computer data or records accessible at, the premises[16];

(5) to take possession of any samples for examination and analysis and any other article, substance, book, document, data or record, in whatever form they are held, at, or in the case of computer data or records accessible at, the premises[17];

(6) to question any person whom he finds at the premises and whom he has reasonable cause to believe is able to give him relevant information[18];

(7) to require any person to afford him such assistance as he considers necessary with respect to any matter within that person's control, or in relation to which that person has responsibilities[19];

(8) to require, as he considers necessary, any person to afford him such facilities as he may reasonably require that person to afford him[20].

If a justice of the peace[21] is satisfied by any written information on oath[22] that there are reasonable grounds for entry into any premises, other than premises used only as a private dwelling house, for any purpose mentioned in heads (1) to (8) above, and certain conditions are met[23], the justice may by warrant signed by him authorise an inspector to enter the premises, if need be by force[24].

An inspector entering premises by virtue of his powers of entry under heads (1) to (8) above or of a warrant may take with him when he enters those premises such equipment as may appear to him necessary and any person who is authorised by the Secretary of State[25] to accompany him on that visit[26].

On leaving any premises which an inspector is authorised to enter by a warrant, he must, if the premises are unoccupied or the occupier is temporarily absent, leave the premises as effectively secured against trespassers as he found them[27]. Where, pursuant to head (5) above, an inspector takes possession of any article, substance, book, document, data or record, he must leave at the premises with a responsible person, or if there is no such person present on the premises, leave in the premises in a prominent position, a statement giving particulars of the article, substance, book, document, data or record sufficient to identify it and stating that he has taken possession of it[28]; and where, pursuant to head (5) above, an inspector takes a sample for analysis, the Secretary of State may make such arrangements for analysis of that sample as he considers appropriate[29].

1 Ie the Blood Safety and Quality Regulations 2005, SI 2005/50.

2	Ie pursuant to the Blood Safety and Quality Regulations 2005, SI 2005/50, reg 15: see PARA 464. As to the meaning of 'inspection' see PARA 464 note 2.
3	As to the meaning of 'inspector' see PARA 464 note 16.
4	Blood Safety and Quality Regulations 2005, SI 2005/50, reg 17(1). Nothing in reg 17(1) may be taken to compel the production by any person of a document of which he would on grounds of legal professional privilege be entitled to withhold production on an order for disclosure in an action in the High Court: reg 17(1). As to legal professional privilege see CIVIL PROCEDURE vol 11 (2009) PARAS 558 et seq, 972. It is an offence to obstruct an inspector, to fail to comply with any requirements made by an inspector or to give false or misleading information in purported compliance with such a requirement: see reg 18(7), (8); and PARA 469.
5	As to the meaning of 'blood establishment' see PARA 453 note 4.
6	As to the meanings of 'person responsible for management of a hospital blood bank' and 'hospital blood bank' see PARA 458 note 1.
7	Ie referred to in the Blood Safety and Quality Regulations 2005, SI 2005/50, reg 3: see PARA 453.
8	Blood Safety and Quality Regulations 2005, SI 2005/50, reg 17(1)(a)(i).
9	Blood Safety and Quality Regulations 2005, SI 2005/50, reg 17(1)(a)(ii) (amended by SI 2006/2013).
10	As to the meaning of 'person' see PARA 45 note 2.
11	Blood Safety and Quality Regulations 2005, SI 2005/50, reg 17(1)(a)(iii).
12	As to the meanings of 'blood' and 'blood components' see PARA 449 note 2, 3.
13	Blood Safety and Quality Regulations 2005, SI 2005/50, reg 17(1)(iv) (added by SI 2006/2013).
14	Blood Safety and Quality Regulations 2005, SI 2005/50, reg 17(1)(b).
15	Blood Safety and Quality Regulations 2005, SI 2005/50, reg 17(1)(c).
16	Blood Safety and Quality Regulations 2005, SI 2005/50, reg 17(1)(d). See also note 4.
17	Blood Safety and Quality Regulations 2005, SI 2005/50, reg 17(1)(e) (amended by SI 2005/1098). See also note 4, and the text to notes 26–27.
18	Blood Safety and Quality Regulations 2005, SI 2005/50, reg 17(1)(f).
19	Blood Safety and Quality Regulations 2005, SI 2005/50, reg 17(1)(g). See also note 4.
20	Blood Safety and Quality Regulations 2005, SI 2005/50, reg 17(1)(h).
21	As to justices of the peace see MAGISTRATES vol 71 (2013) PARA 404 et seq.
22	As to oaths, affirmations and declarations see CIVIL PROCEDURE vol 11 (2009) PARA 1021 et seq.
23	The conditions are that: (1) admission to the premises has been refused or is likely to be refused and notice of intention to apply for a warrant has been given to the occupier (Blood Safety and Quality Regulations 2005, SI 2005/50, reg 17(2)(a)); (2) an application for admission, or the giving of such notice, would defeat the object of the entry (reg 17(2)(b)); or (3) the premises are unoccupied or the occupier is temporarily absent and it might defeat the object of the entry to await his return (reg 17(2)(c)).
24	Blood Safety and Quality Regulations 2005, SI 2005/50, reg 17(2). Such a warrant continues in force for a period of one month: reg 17(2). As to the meaning of 'month' see PARA 43 note 3.
25	As to the Secretary of State see PARA 2 note 1.
26	Blood Safety and Quality Regulations 2005, SI 2005/50, reg 17(3).
27	Blood Safety and Quality Regulations 2005, SI 2005/50, reg 17(4).
28	Blood Safety and Quality Regulations 2005, SI 2005/50, reg 17(5).
29	Blood Safety and Quality Regulations 2005, SI 2005/50, reg 17(6). In such a case, the Secretary of State must inform the responsible person of the blood establishment or person responsible for the management of the hospital blood bank from which the sample was taken that he intends to make arrangements for analysis of the sample, and of the tests which he intends should be made (reg 17(7)(a)); and if the responsible person or person responsible for the management of the hospital blood bank so requests, the Secretary of State must divide the sample of which an analysis is to be made into three equal parts (reg 17(7)(b)). If the sample is so divided, the parts must be dealt with as follows: (1) the Secretary of State must make arrangements for the testing of one part of the sample (reg 17(8)(a)); (2) one part of the sample must be sent to the responsible person of the blood establishment or person responsible for the management of the hospital blood bank (reg 17(8)(b)); and (3) one part of the sample must be retained by the Secretary of State for a reasonable period in case of dispute (reg 17(8)(c)). As to the meaning of 'responsible person' see PARA 455 note 2.

466. Records to be kept by the Secretary of State. The Secretary of State[1] must keep such records of information which he receives from, or relating to, blood establishments[2] as he considers appropriate and must, in particular, keep records relating to authorisations[3], the designation[4] of responsible persons[5], notification[6] of serious adverse events[7] and serious adverse reactions[8] by such establishments[9], and inspections or requests for information[10].

The Secretary of State must also keep such records of information which he receives from persons responsible for management of hospital blood banks and facilities[11], or otherwise relating to hospital blood banks or facilities, as he considers appropriate and must, in particular, keep records relating to[12] notification[13] of serious adverse events and serious adverse reactions[14], the information supplied[15] by hospital blood banks in annual reports[16], and inspections or requests for information[17].

1 As to the Secretary of State see PARA 2 note 1.
2 As to the meaning of 'blood establishment' see PARA 453 note 4.
3 Blood Safety and Quality Regulations 2005, SI 2005/50, reg 16(1)(a). As to authorisations see reg 4; and PARA 453.
4 Ie under the Blood Safety and Quality Regulations 2005, SI 2005/50, reg 6: see PARA 455.
5 Blood Safety and Quality Regulations 2005, SI 2005/50, reg 16(1)(b).
6 Ie pursuant to the Blood Safety and Quality Regulations 2005, SI 2005/50, reg 12B: see PARA 462.
7 As to the meaning of 'serious adverse event' see PARA 452 note 7.
8 As to the meaning of 'serious adverse reaction' see PARA 452 note 7.
9 Blood Safety and Quality Regulations 2005, SI 2005/50, reg 16(1)(c) (amended by SI 2007/604).
10 Blood Safety and Quality Regulations 2005, SI 2005/50, reg 16(1)(d). As to inspections and requests for information see reg 15; and PARA 464. Records must also be kept of the operation, during the period from 8 February 2005 to 7 November 2005, of blood establishments licensed under the Medicines Act 1968 s 8 (repealed): Blood Safety and Quality Regulations 2005, SI 2005/50, reg 16(1)(e) (amended by SI 2005/1098).
11 As to the meanings of 'person responsible for management of a hospital blood bank' and 'hospital blood bank' see PARA 458 note 1. As to the meaning of 'facility' see PARA 464 note 8.
12 Blood Safety and Quality Regulations 2005, SI 2005/50, reg 16(2) (amended by SI 2006/2013).
13 Ie pursuant to the Blood Safety and Quality Regulations 2005, SI 2005/50, reg 12B: see PARA 462.
14 Blood Safety and Quality Regulations 2005, SI 2005/50, reg 16(2)(a) (amended by SI 2007/604).
15 Ie pursuant to the Blood Safety and Quality Regulations 2005, SI 2005/50, reg 10: see PARA 458.
16 Blood Safety and Quality Regulations 2005, SI 2005/50, reg 16(2)(b).
17 Blood Safety and Quality Regulations 2005, SI 2005/50, reg 16(2)(c). As to inspections and requests for information see reg 15; and PARA 464.

467. Communication of certain information by the Secretary of State. The Secretary of State[1] must communicate to the competent authorities of other member states such information as is appropriate with regard to serious adverse reactions and events[2] in order to guarantee that blood or blood components[3] known or suspected to be defective are withdrawn from use and discarded[4].

1 As to the Secretary of State see PARA 2 note 1.
2 As to the meaning of 'serious adverse event' and 'serious adverse reaction' see PARA 452 note 7.
3 As to the meanings of 'blood' and 'blood components' see PARA 449 note 2, 3.
4 Blood Safety and Quality Regulations 2005, SI 2005/50, reg 16A (added by SI 2006/2013).

(3) MANAGEMENT OF BLOOD PRODUCTS ETC

468. Management of supply of blood and blood derived products etc. The management of:

(1) the supply of blood, blood components and blood derived products intended for transfusion[1];

(2) the supply of tissues and tissue derived products intended for transplant, grafting or use in a surgical procedure[2]; and

(3)   the matching and allocation of donor organs intended for transplant, and of stem cells and bone marrow intended for transfusion[3],

is an activity regulated by the Health and Social Care Act 2008[4]. As such a person is guilty of an offence if he carries out such an activity without being registered[5]. The Care Quality Commission[6] is required to carry out periodic reviews of this activity, assessing the performance of NHS Blood and Transplant following each such review and publishing a report of its assessment[7].

1   See the Health and Social Care Act 2008 (Regulated Activities) Regulations 2010, SI 2010/781, Sch 1 para 9(1)(a) (Sch 1 para 9(1) amended and Sch 1 para 9(2), (3) added by SI 2012/1916). These provisions do not apply to the management of the supply of blood, blood components, tissues and products mentioned in head (1) and (2) in the text where that management does not involve direct physical contact with patients or donors: Health and Social Care Act 2008 (Regulated Activities) Regulations 2010, SI 2010/781, Sch 1 para 9(2) (as so added). 'Donor' means a person from whom anything mentioned in head (1) or (2) in the text is derived, and 'patient' means a person to whom anything mentioned in head (1) or (2) in the text is administered: Sch 1 para 9(3) (as so added).
2   Health and Social Care Act 2008 (Regulated Activities) Regulations 2010, SI 2010/781, Sch 1 para 9(1)(b).
3   Health and Social Care Act 2008 (Regulated Activities) Regulations 2010, SI 2010/781, Sch 1 para 9(1)(c).
4   See the Health and Social Care Act 2008 (Regulated Activities) Regulations 2010, SI 2010/781, reg 3(1).
5   See the Health and Social Care Act 2008 s 10; and SOCIAL SERVICES AND COMMUNITY CARE.
6   As to the Care Quality Commission see SOCIAL SERVICES AND COMMUNITY CARE.
7   See the Health and Social Care Act 2008 (NHS Blood and Transplant Periodic Review) Regulations 2009, SI 2009/3049, reg 2.

(4) OFFENCES

469.   Offences. A person[1] is guilty of an offence if he contravenes any of the provisions relating to[2]:
(1)   the requirement[3] for authorisation[4];
(2)   the blood establishment[5] requirements[6];
(3)   the hospital blood bank[7] requirements[8];
(4)   the importation of blood and blood components[9];
(5)   specific epidemiological situations[10];
(6)   making any substantial change in the activities of a blood establishment[11];
(7)   the responsible person for a blood establishment[12];
(8)   the labelling of blood and blood components and traceability[13];
(9)   the provision of information by hospital blood banks to the Secretary of State[14];
(10)   the provision of other information to the Secretary of State[15];
(11)   the requirement that facilities retain certain data[16];
(12)   the requirement to report serious adverse reactions and events[17].
A person is guilty of an offence[18] if he is a person who:
(a)   fails to comply with a notice[19] of suspension or revocation of his authorisation, save where the operation of that notice has been suspended[20], or has been withdrawn or revoked by the Secretary of State[21];
(b)   knowingly sells or supplies blood or any blood component which is not labelled[22] in accordance with the appropriate requirements[23];
(c)   contravenes the requirements of any notice served[24] by the Secretary of State in relation to hospital blood banks[25];

(d)   contravenes the provisions[26] relating to the disclosure of information by blood establishments and hospital blood banks[27], or discloses any information[28] to which he has access[29] otherwise than in accordance with one or more of the permitted requirements[30];

(e)   intentionally obstructs an inspector[31]; or without reasonable cause fails to comply with any requirements made of him by an inspector, in circumstances where that inspector is acting in pursuance of any of his permitted functions[32]; or, in purported compliance with any such requirement, intentionally or recklessly furnishes information which is false or misleading in a material respect[33].

A person guilty of any such offence is liable to a penalty[34].

1   As to the meaning of 'person' see PARA 45 note 2.
2   Blood Safety and Quality Regulations 2005, SI 2005/50, reg 18(1), (2). As to defences to these offences see PARA 471; and as to offences by bodies corporate see PARA 470.
3   Ie under the Blood Safety and Quality Regulations 2005, SI 2005/50, reg 3(1): see PARA 453.
4   Blood Safety and Quality Regulations 2005, SI 2005/50, reg 18(1)(a).
5   As to the meaning of 'blood establishment' see PARA 453 note 4.
6   Blood Safety and Quality Regulations 2005, SI 2005/50, reg 18(1)(b). The blood establishment requirements are those of reg 7: see PARA 456.
7   As to the meaning of 'hospital blood bank' see PARA 458 note 1.
8   Blood Safety and Quality Regulations 2005, SI 2005/50, reg 18(1)(c). The hospital blood bank requirements are those of reg 9: see PARA 458.
9   Blood Safety and Quality Regulations 2005, SI 2005/50, reg 18(1)(d). The provisions referred to in the text are those of reg 13: see PARA 450. As to the meaning of 'blood' see PARA 449 note 2; and as to the meaning of 'blood component' see PARA 449 note 3.
10   Blood Safety and Quality Regulations 2005, SI 2005/50, reg 18(1)(e). The provisions referred to in the text are those of reg 23(2): see PARA 451.
11   Blood Safety and Quality Regulations 2005, SI 2005/50, reg 18(2)(a). The provisions referred to in the text are those of reg 4(9): see PARA 453.
12   Blood Safety and Quality Regulations 2005, SI 2005/50, reg 18(2)(b). The provisions referred to in the text are those of reg 6 (other than reg 6(3)): see PARA 455.
13   Blood Safety and Quality Regulations 2005, SI 2005/50, reg 18(2)(c). The provisions referred to in the text are those of reg 8: see PARA 457.
14   Blood Safety and Quality Regulations 2005, SI 2005/50, reg 18(2)(d). The provisions referred to in the text are those of reg 10: see PARA 458. As to the Secretary of State see PARA 2 note 1.
15   Blood Safety and Quality Regulations 2005, SI 2005/50, reg 18(2)(e). The provisions referred to in the text are those of reg 15(4), (7): see PARA 464.
16   Blood Safety and Quality Regulations 2005, SI 2005/50, reg 18(2)(f) (reg 18(2)(f), (g) added by SI 2006/2013). The provisions referred to in the text are those of the Blood Safety and Quality Regulations 2005, SI 2005/50, reg 12A: see PARA 461.
17   Blood Safety and Quality Regulations 2005, SI 2005/50, reg 18(2)(g) (as added: see note 16). The provisions referred to in the text are reg 12B: see PARA 462.
18   As to defences to these offences see PARA 471; and as to offences by bodies corporate see PARA 470.
19   Ie served pursuant to the Blood Safety and Quality Regulations 2005, SI 2005/50, reg 5: see PARA 454.
20   Ie pursuant to the Blood Safety and Quality Regulations 2005, SI 2005/50, reg 12: see PARA 460.
21   Blood Safety and Quality Regulations 2005, SI 2005/50, reg 18(3).
22   Ie in accordance with the requirements of the Blood Safety and Quality Regulations 2005, SI 2005/50, reg 8: see PARA 457.
23   Blood Safety and Quality Regulations 2005, SI 2005/50, reg 18(4).
24   Ie under the Blood Safety and Quality Regulations 2005, SI 2005/50, reg 11(1): see PARA 459.
25   Blood Safety and Quality Regulations 2005, SI 2005/50, reg 18(5).
26   Ie the Blood Safety and Quality Regulations 2005, SI 2005/50, reg 14: see PARA 463.
27   Blood Safety and Quality Regulations 2005, SI 2005/50, reg 18(6)(a).
28   Ie referred to in the Blood Safety and Quality Regulations 2005, SI 2005/50, reg 14(1): see PARA 463.
29   Ie by virtue of the Blood Safety and Quality Regulations 2005, SI 2005/50.

30 Blood Safety and Quality Regulations 2005, SI 2005/50, reg 18(6)(b). The permitted requirements are those specified in reg 14(2), (3): see PARA 463.

31 Blood Safety and Quality Regulations 2005, SI 2005/50, reg 18(7)(a)(i). As to the meaning of 'inspector' see PARA 464 note 16.

32 Blood Safety and Quality Regulations 2005, SI 2005/50, reg 18(7)(a)(ii) (amended by SI 2005/2898). An inspector's permitted functions are those under the Blood Safety and Quality Regulations 2005, SI 2005/50. Nothing in reg 18(7)(a)(ii) may be construed as requiring any person to answer any question or give any information if to do so might incriminate him or, in the case of a person who is married or a civil partner, his spouse or civil partner: reg 18(8) (amended by SI 2005/2898).

33 Blood Safety and Quality Regulations 2005, SI 2005/50, reg 18(7)(a)(iii).

34 A person guilty of an offence under heads (1)–(5), (a), (c) or (e) in the text is liable on summary conviction to a fine not exceeding the statutory maximum or to imprisonment for a term not exceeding three months or to both (Blood Safety and Quality Regulations 2005, SI 2005/50, reg 19(1)(a) (amended by SI 2005/1098)), or on conviction on indictment to a fine or to imprisonment for a term not exceeding two years or to both (Blood Safety and Quality Regulations 2005, SI 2005/50, reg 19(1)(b)). A person guilty of an offence under heads (6)–(10), (b) or (d) in the text is liable on summary conviction to a fine not exceeding level 5 on the standard scale, or to imprisonment for a term not exceeding three months or to both: reg 19(2) (amended by SI 2005/1098). As to the standard scale see SENTENCING AND DISPOSITION OF OFFENDERS vol 92 (2010) PARA 142.

470. Offences by bodies corporate. Where an offence under the regulations relating to blood safety and quality[1] is committed by a body corporate[2] and is proved to have been committed with the consent or connivance of, or to be attributable to any neglect on the part of, any director, manager, secretary[3], or any person who was purporting to act in any such capacity[4], he, as well as the body corporate, is deemed to be guilty of that offence and is liable to be proceeded against and punished accordingly[5].

1 As to offences under the Blood Safety and Quality Regulations 2005, SI 2005/50 see PARA 469.
2 As to bodies corporate see COMPANIES; CORPORATIONS.
3 Blood Safety and Quality Regulations 2005, SI 2005/50, reg 21(a).
4 Blood Safety and Quality Regulations 2005, SI 2005/50, reg 21(b).
5 Blood Safety and Quality Regulations 2005, SI 2005/50, reg 21.

471. Defence of due diligence. In any proceedings for an offence under the regulations relating to blood safety and quality[1], it is a defence for the person[2] charged to prove that he took all reasonable precautions and exercised all due diligence to avoid commission of the offence[3]. Where evidence is adduced which is sufficient to raise an issue with respect to that defence, the court or jury must assume that the defence is satisfied unless the prosecution proves beyond all reasonable doubt that it is not[4].

1 As to offences under the Blood Safety and Quality Regulations 2005, SI 2005/50 see PARA 469.
2 As to the meaning of 'person' see PARA 45 note 2.
3 Blood Safety and Quality Regulations 2005, SI 2005/50, reg 20(1). As to the standard of proof on the accused see CRIMINAL PROCEDURE vol 28 (2010) PARA 469.
4 Blood Safety and Quality Regulations 2005, SI 2005/50, reg 20(2).

5. MEDICAL DEVICES

472. Meaning of 'medical device'. 'Medical device' means any instrument, apparatus, appliance, software, material or other article, whether used alone or in combination, together with any accessories, including the software intended by its manufacturer to be used specifically for diagnosis or therapeutic purposes or both and necessary for its proper application, which:

(1) is intended by the manufacturer[1] to be used for human beings for the purpose of:

    (a) diagnosis, prevention, monitoring, treatment or alleviation of disease;

    (b) diagnosis, monitoring, treatment, alleviation of or compensation for an injury or handicap;

    (c) investigation, replacement or modification of the anatomy or of a physiological process; or

    (d) control of conception; and

(2) does not achieve its principal intended action in or on the human body by pharmacological, immunological or metabolic means, even if it is assisted in its function by such means,

and includes devices intended to administer a medicinal product[2] or which incorporate as an integral part a substance which, if used separately, would be a medicinal product and which is liable to act upon the body with action ancillary to that of the device[3].

However, the regulations[4] regulating medical devices do not apply to: (i) medicinal products[5] for human use[6]; (ii) human blood, human blood products, plasma or blood cells of human origin[7]; (iii) devices that incorporate, at the time of placing on the market, human blood, blood products, plasma or blood cells of human origin, except for stable derivatives devices[8], active implantable medical devices and accessories to such devices and in vitro diagnostic medical devices and accessories to such devices[9]; and (iv) transplants or tissues[10] or cells of human origin or products incorporating or derived from tissues or cells of human origin, except for in vitro diagnostic medical devices and accessories to such devices save where medicinal products are incorporated as ancillary to the device[11]; (v) transplants or tissues or cells of animal origin, unless a device is manufactured utilising animal tissue which is rendered non-viable[12] or non-viable products derived from animal tissue or a product is an in vitro diagnostic medical device, or an accessory to such a device[13]; or (vi) cosmetic products[14].

1   'Manufacturer' means: (1) the person with responsibility for the design, manufacture, packaging and labelling of a device before it is placed on the market under his own name, regardless of whether these operations are carried out by that person himself or on his behalf by a third party; or (2) any other person who assembles, packages, processes, fully refurbishes or labels one or more ready-made products or assigns to them their intended purpose as a device with a view to their being placed on the market under his own name, apart from a person who assembles or adapts devices already on the market to their intended purpose for an individual patient: Medical Devices Regulations 2002, SI 2002/618, reg 2(1). As to the meaning of 'person' see PARA 45 note 2. 'Placing on the market' means, in relation to a medical device, the first making available in return for payment or free of charge of a new or fully refurbished device, other than a device intended for clinical investigation, with a view to distribution, use, or both, on the Community market: reg 2(1). 'Intended purpose' means, in relation to an active implantable medical device, the use for which it is intended and for which it is suited according to the data supplied by the manufacturer in the instructions relating to it; and, in relation to any other medical device, the use to which the device is intended according to the data supplied by the manufacturer on the labelling, the instructions for use and/or the promotional materials:

reg 2(1). As to the meaning of 'active implantable medical device' see PARA 474 note 4. 'Intended for clinical investigation' means, intended for use by a registered medical practitioner when conducting investigations of that device in an adequate human clinical environment or intended for use by any other person in a member state who, by virtue of their professional qualification, is authorised to carry out investigations of that device in an adequate human clinical environment: reg 2(1) (definition substituted by SI 2008/2936). For these purposes, 'the Community' means, in the context of any requirement relating to an in vitro diagnostic medical device, the European Union and, in the context of any requirement relating to any other medical device, the European Economic Area; and 'European Economic Area' means the European Economic Area created by the Agreement on the European Economic Area (Oporto, 2 May 1992; EC 7 (1992); Cm 2183) as adjusted by the Protocol (Brussels, 17 March 1993; EC 2 (1993); Cm 2183) ('the EEA Agreement'): Medical Devices Regulations 2002, SI 2002/618, reg 2(1) (definition 'the Community' amended by SI 2011/1043). As to the meaning of 'in vitro diagnostic medical device' see PARA 475 note 4.

2 'Medicinal product' has the meaning given in European Parliament and Council Directive (EC) 2001/83 (OJ L311, 28.11.2001, p 67) on the Community code relating to medicinal products for human use, art 1.2: see the Medical Devices Regulations 2002, SI 2002/618, reg 2(1).

3 Medical Devices Regulations 2002, SI 2002/618, reg 2(1) (amended by SI 2008/2936). In certain circumstances a fee is payable in connection with consultations with the competent body in relation to the safety, quality and usefulness of a medicinal substance incorporated in a medical device: see the Medical Devices (Consultation Requirements) (Fees) Regulations 1995, SI 1995/449 (amended by SI 2002/236, SI 2005/2759, SI 2007/803, SI 2010/557, SI 2012/1916). A similar definition also applies to Council Directive (EC) 1993/42 (OJ L169, 12.7.1993, p 1) concerning medical devices (see art 1(2)); Council Directive (EC) 90/385 (OJ L189, 20.7.1990, p 7) on the approximation of the laws of the member states relating to implantable medical devices (see art 1(2)(a)) (both amended by Council Directive (EC) 2007/47 (OJ L247, 21.9.2007, p 21)); and Council Directive (EC) (OJ L331, 7.12.1998, p 1) on in vitro diagnostic medical devices, art 2(a). See PARA 20.

4 Ie the Medical Devices Regulations 2002, SI 2002/618.

5 Ie governed by Parliament and Council Directive (EC) 2001/83 (OJ L311, 28.11.2001, p 67), including medicinal products derived from human blood or human plasma governed by Parliament and Council Directive (EC) 2001/83 (OJ L311, 28.11.2001, p 67) Title X.

6 Medical Devices Regulations 2002, SI 2002/618, reg 3(a).

7 Medical Devices Regulations 2002, SI 2002/618, reg 3(b).

8 'Stable derivatives device' means a medical device that contains human blood, blood products, plasma or blood cells of human origin, and which incorporates, as an integral part, a substance which, if used separately, may be considered to be a medicinal product constituent or a medicinal product derived from human blood or human plasma within the meaning of Parliament and Council Directive (EC) 2001/83 (OJ L311, 28.11.2001, p 67) art 1.10 and which is liable to act upon the human body with action ancillary to that of the device: Medical Devices Regulations 2002, SI 2002/618, reg 2(1).

9 Medical Devices Regulations 2002, SI 2002/618, reg 3(c) (amended by SI 2007/400).

10 'Tissue' means an organisation of cells and/or extra-cellular constituents: Medical Devices Regulations 2002, SI 2002/618, reg 2(1) (definition added by SI 2003/1697).

11 Medical Devices Regulations 2002, SI 2002/618, reg 3(d) (amended SI 2007/400, SI 2008/2936).

12 'Non-viable' means having no potential for metabolism or multiplication: Medical Devices Regulations 2002, SI 2002/618, reg 2(1) (definition added by SI 2003/1697).

13 Medical Devices Regulations 2002, SI 2002/618. reg 3(e) (amended by SI 2007/400).

14 Medical Devices Regulations 2002, SI 2002/618, reg 3(f). The cosmetic products referred to in the text are those governed by Council Directive (EC) 76/768 (OJ L262, 27.9.1976, p 169): Medical Devices Regulations 2002, SI 2002/618, reg 3(f). See *Optident Ltd v Secretary of State for Trade and Industry* [2001] UKHL 32, [2001] CMLR 1, 61 BMLR 10, (whether product should be classified as a cosmetic or a medical device).

473. General medical devices. No person[1] may place on the market[2] or put into service[3] a relevant device[4] unless that device meets those essential requirements[5] which apply to it[6]; and no person may supply[7] a relevant device if that supply is also a placing on the market or putting into service of that device[8], or in circumstances where that device has been placed on the market or put into service[9], unless that device meets those essential requirements[10] which apply to it[11].

Where a hazard exists, devices which are also machinery must also meet the essential health and safety requirements[12].

Restrictions are imposed on the placing on the market, putting into service, and supply of general medical devices unless the device, packaging or instructions for use bear a CE marking[13]; and there are restrictions on the affixing of a CE marking to general medical devices[14]. Restrictions are also placed on the supply of custom-made devices[15], and on the supply of general medical devices for the purposes of a clinical investigation in the United Kingdom[16]. Manufacturers of general medical devices must follow certain procedures[17], and provision is made for conformity assessments of such devices[18]. Persons placing general medical devices on the market must provide the Secretary of State with prescribed information[19].

1   As to the meaning of 'person' see PARA 45 note 2.

2   As to the meaning of 'placing on the market' see PARA 472 note 1.

3   'Putting into service' means: (1) in relation to an active implantable medical device, the making available of the device to a registered medical practitioner for implantation; (2) in relation to any other medical device, the first making available of the device in the Community to a final user, including where a device is used in a professional context for the purposes of medical analysis without being marketed: Medical Devices Regulations 2002, SI 2002/618, reg 2(1). As to the meaning of 'active implantable medical device' see PARA 474 note 4. As to the meaning of 'medical device' see PARA 472. As to the meaning of 'registered medical practitioner' see MEDICAL PROFESSIONS vol 74 (2011) PARA 176. As to the meaning of 'the Community' see PARA 472 note 1.

4   'Relevant device' means medical devices (including stable derivatives devices), accessories to such devices, single-use combination products, and systems and procedure packs, other than:
    (1)   active implantable medical devices and accessories to such devices (Medical Devices Regulations 2002, SI 2002/618, regs 5(1), 6(a));
    (2)   in vitro diagnostic medical devices and accessories to such devices (regs 5(1), 6(b)); and
    (3)   devices that come within the scope of Council Directive (EC) 1993/42 (OJ L169, 12.7.1993, p 1) of 14 June 1993 concerning medical devices and another Directive ('the other Directive') issued by one or more of the institutions of the Community, if: (a) the other Directive includes a provision allowing the manufacturer of the device to choose, during a transitional period that has not ended, which set of arrangements applies to it; and (b) the manufacturer chooses to follow the set of arrangements in the other Directive (Medical Devices Regulations 2002, SI 2002/618, regs 2(1), 5(1), 6(c)(i), (ii)).
As to the meaning of 'stable derivatives device' see PARA 472 note 8; and as to the meaning of 'manufacturer' see PARA 472 note 1. As to the meaning of 'in vitro diagnostic medical device' see PARA 475 note 4. 'Accessory' means an article which, whilst not being a medical device, is intended specifically by its manufacturer to be used together with a medical device to enable it to be used in accordance with the use of the medical device intended by its manufacturer; 'single-use combination product' means a product which comprises a medical device and medicinal product forming a single integral product which is intended exclusively for use in the given combination and which is not reusable; and 'system or procedure pack' has the same meaning as in Council Directive (EC) 1993/42 (OJ L169, 12.7.1993, p 1) art 12: Medical Devices Regulations 2002, SI 2002/618, reg 5(1). As to the meaning of 'medicinal product' see PARA 472 note 2.
    The Medical Devices Regulations 2002, SI 2002/618, Pt II (regs 5–19A) must not be applied: (i) before 10 January 2007 in respect of a stable derivatives device placed on the market without a CE marking, if the device satisfies the requirements of the laws of that part of the United Kingdom in which it is placed on the market as in force on 10 January 2002 (reg 4(2)(a)); or (ii) before 10 January 2009 in respect of a stable derivatives device put into service without a CE marking, if the device satisfies the requirements of the laws of that part of the United Kingdom in which it is placed on the market as in force on 10 January 2002 (reg 4(2)(b)). 'CE marking' means a conformity marking consisting of the initials 'CE': reg 2(1). As to the meaning of 'United Kingdom' see PARA 20 note 4.

5 Ie set out in Council Directive (EC) 1993/42 (OJ L169, 12.7.1993, p 1) Annex I: Medical Devices Regulations 2002, SI 2002/618, regs 5(2), 8(1). As to the determination of the compliance of general medical devices with essential requirements see reg 9.

6 Medical Devices Regulations 2002, SI 2002/618, reg 8(1). There are additional requirements relating to the use of animal tissues: see reg 19A (added by SI 2003/1697). For the purpose of the Medical Devices Regulations 2002, SI 2002/618, reg 13, 17, 19A and 47 'animal' means any animal from a bovine, ovine or caprine species, as well as deer, elk, mink and cats: 2(1). As to the meaning of 'tissue' see PARA 472 note 10. As to the classification of general medical devices see the Medical Devices Regulations 2002, SI 2002/618, reg 7 (amended by SI 2003/1697, SI 2007/400). A relevant device or a single use combination product being shown at a trade fair, exhibition, demonstration or similar gathering is not being placed on the market or put into service if a visible sign clearly indicates that the device or product cannot be marketed or put into service until it complies with the requirements of Council Directive (EC) 1993/42 (OJ L169, 12.7.1993, p 1) or the Medical Devices Regulations 2002, SI 2002/618: reg 12(1). Regulation 8 does not apply where, following a duly justified request and in the interests of the protection of health, the Secretary of State has authorised, where appropriate for a specified period, the placing on the market or putting into service of a particular relevant device or relevant devices of a particular class or description without a CE marking, where appropriate subject to conditions (which are complied with), and has not withdrawn that authorisation: reg 12(5). As to the Secretary of State see PARA 2 note 1.

7 'Supply', in relation to a medical device, means the supply of, or the offer or agreement to supply, the device, or the exposure or possession for supply of the device: Medical Devices Regulations 2002, SI 2002/618, reg 2(1).

8 Medical Devices Regulations 2002, SI 2002/618, reg 8(2)(a).

9 Medical Devices Regulations 2002, SI 2002/618, reg 8(2)(b).

10 Ie set out in Council Directive (EC) 1993/42 (OJ L169, 12.7.1993, p 1) Annex I: Medical Devices Regulations 2002, SI 2002/618, regs 5(2), 8(2). See also note 5.

11 Medical Devices Regulations 2002, SI 2002/618, reg 8(2). This provision is expressed to be subject to reg 12: see note 6.

12 Medical Devices Regulations 2002, SI 2002/618, reg 8(3) (added by SI 2008/2936). The health and safety requirements mentioned in the text are the ones set out in European Parliament and Council Directive (EC) 2006/42 (OJ L157, 9.6.2006, p 35–35) on machinery, Annex I, to the extent to which those essential health and safety requirements are more specific than the essential requirements to Council Directive (EC) 1993/42 (OJ L169, 12.7.1993, p 1–43) concerning medical devices. 'Hazard' means a potential source of injury or damage to health: Medical Devices Regulations 2002, SI 2002/618, reg 2(1) (definition added by SI 2008/2936).

13 See the Medical Devices Regulations 2002, SI 2002/618, regs 10, 12, 14 (reg 14 amended by SI 2008/2936).

14 See the Medical Devices Regulations 2002, SI 2002/618, reg 11 (amended by SI 2011/1043). As to procedures for affixing a CE marking to general medical devices see Medical Devices Regulations 2002, SI 2002/618, reg 13 (amended by SI 2008/1697).

15 See the Medical Devices Regulations 2002, SI 2002/618, reg 15 (amended by SI 2008/2936). For these purposes, 'custom-made device' means a relevant device that is:
   (1)   manufactured specifically in accordance with a written prescription of a registered medical practitioner, or other person authorised to write such a prescription by virtue of his professional qualification, which gives, under his responsibility, specific characteristics as to its design; and
   (2)   intended for the sole use of a particular patient,
but does not include a mass-produced product which needs to be adapted to meet the specific requirements of the medical practitioner or professional user: reg 5(1) (amended by SI 2008/2936).

16 See the Medical Devices Regulations 2002, SI 2002/618, reg 16 (amended by SI 2008/2936). As to the meaning of 'United Kingdom' see PARA 20 note 4. As to the fees payable in respect of such matters see the Medical Devices Regulations 2002, SI 2002/618, regs 56–58 (reg 56 amended by SI 2013/525).

17 See the Medical Devices Regulations 2002, SI 2002/618, reg 17 (amended by SI 2003/1697).

18 See the Medical Devices Regulations 2002, SI 2002/618, reg 18 (amended by SI 2003/1697, SI 2008/2936).

19 See the Medical Devices Regulations 2002, SI 2002/618, reg 19 (amended by SI 2008/2936). As to the fee payable in respect of the provision of such information see the Medical Devices Regulations 2002, SI 2002/618, regs 53, 57, 58.

474. Active implantable medical devices. No person[1] may place on the market[2] or put into service[3] a relevant device[4] unless that device meets those essential requirements[5] which apply to it[6]; and no person may supply[7] a relevant device if that supply is also a placing on the market or putting into service of that device[8], or in circumstances where that device has also been placed on the market or put into service[9], unless that device meets those essential requirements[10] which apply to it[11].

Restrictions are imposed: (1) on the placing on the market, putting into service, and supply of active implantable medical devices unless the device, packaging or instructions for use bear a CE marking[12]; (2) on the use of misleading markings[13]; and (3) on the affixing of a CE marking to such devices[14]. Restrictions are also placed on the supply of custom-made devices[15], and on the supply of active implantable medical devices for the purposes of a clinical investigation in the United Kingdom[16]. Manufacturers of active implantable medical devices must follow certain procedures[17], and provision is made for conformity assessments of such devices[18].

1 As to the meaning of 'person' see PARA 45 note 2.
2 As to the meaning of 'placing on the market' see PARA 472 note 1.
3 As to the meaning of 'putting into service' see PARA 473 note 3.
4 'Relevant device' means active implantable medical devices and accessories to such devices, except for devices that come within the scope of Council Directive (EC) 1990/385 (OJ L189, 20.7.1990, p 17) on the approximation of the laws of the member states relating to active implantable medical devices and another Directive ('the other Directive') issued by one or more of the institutions of the Community, if: (1) the other Directive includes a provision allowing the manufacturer of the device to choose, during a transitional period that has not ended, which set of arrangements applies to it; and (2) the manufacturer chooses to follow the set of arrangements in the other Directive: Medical Devices Regulations 2002, SI 2002/618, regs 2(1), 20(1), 21(1) (reg 21(1) numbered as such by SI 2008/2936). Where a hazard exists, devices which are also machinery must also meet the essential health and safety requirements set out in Annex I to that Directive (it is submitted that the phrase 'that Directive' refers to Council Directive (EC) 2006/42) to the extent to which those requirements are more specific than the essential requirements in Council Directive (EC) 1990/385 Annex I: Medical Devices Regulations 2002, SI 2002/618, SI 2002/618, reg 21(2) (added by SI 2008/2936). As to the meaning of 'hazard' see PARA 473. Where an active implantable medical device is intended to administer a medicinal product, that device is governed by Council Directive (EC) 1990/385 without prejudice to the provisions of European Parliament and Council Directive (EC) 2001/83 (OJ L311, 28.11.2001, p 67) on the Community code relating to medicinal products for human use: Medical Devices Regulations 2002, SI 2002/618, reg 21(3) (added by SI 2008/2936). 'Active implantable medical device' means a medical device which:
    (a) relies for its functioning on a source of electrical energy or a source of power other than that generated directly by the human body or by gravity; and
    (b) is intended to be totally or partially introduced into the human body (whether surgically or medically, including being introduced into a natural orifice) and which is intended to remain in the human body after completion of the surgical or medical procedure during which it is introduced,
    even if it is intended to administer a medicinal product or incorporates as an integral part a substance which, if used separately, would be a medicinal product: reg 2(1). As to the meanings of 'the Community' and 'manufacturer' see PARA 472 note 1; as to the meaning of 'medical device' see PARA 472; and as to the meaning of 'medicinal product' see PARA 472 note 2.
5 Ie set out in Council Directive (EC) 1990/385 (OJ L189, 20.7.1990, p 17) Annex 1: Medical Devices Regulations 2002, SI 2002/618, regs 20(2), 22(1) (reg 20(2) amended by SI 2003/1697). As to the determination of the compliance of active implantable medical devices with relevant essential requirements see the Medical Devices Regulations 2002, SI 2002/618, reg 23.
6 Medical Devices Regulations 2002, SI 2002/618, reg 22(1). A relevant device being shown at a trade fair, exhibition, demonstration or similar gathering is not being placed on the market or put into service if a visible sign clearly indicates that the device or product cannot be marketed or put into service until it complies with the requirements of Council Directive (EC) 1990/385 (OJ L189, 20.7.1990, p 17) or the Medical Devices Regulations 2002, SI 2002/618: reg 26(1).

Regulation 22 does not apply where, following a duly justified request and in the interests of the protection of health, the Secretary of State has authorised, where appropriate for a specified period, the placing on the market or putting into service of a particular relevant device or relevant devices of a particular class or description without a CE marking, where appropriate subject to conditions (which are complied with), and has not withdrawn that authorisation: reg 26(3). As to the meaning of 'CE marking' see PARA 473 note 4. As to the Secretary of State see PARA 2 note 1.

7   As to the meaning of 'supply' see PARA 473 note 7.
8   Medical Devices Regulations 2002, SI 2002/618, reg 22(2)(a).
9   Medical Devices Regulations 2002, SI 2002/618, reg 22(2)(b).
10 Ie set out in Council Directive (EC) 1990/385 (OJ L189, 20.7.1990, p 17) Annex 1: Medical Devices Regulations 2002, SI 2002/618, regs 20(2), 22(2) (reg 20(2) as amended: see note 5). See also note 5.
11 Medical Devices Regulations 2002, SI 2002/618, reg 22(2). This provision is expressed to be subject to reg 26: see note 6.
12 See the Medical Devices Regulations 2002, SI 2002/618, regs 24(1)–(4), 26.
13 See the Medical Devices Regulations 2002, SI 2002/618, regs 24(5), 26.
14 See the Medical Devices Regulations 2002, SI 2002/618, reg 25 (amended by SI 2011/1043). As to procedures for affixing a CE marking to active implantable medical devices see the Medical Devices Regulations 2002, SI 2002/618, reg 27.
15 See the Medical Devices Regulations 2002, SI 2002/618, reg 28. For these purposes, 'custom-made device' means an active implantable medical device that is manufactured specifically in accordance with a medical specialist's written prescription which gives, under his responsibility, specific characteristics as to its design, and which is intended to be used only for a particular patient: reg 20(1).
16 See the Medical Devices Regulations 2002, SI 2002/618, reg 29 (amended by SI 2008/2936). As to the fees payable in respect of such matters see regs 56–58 (reg 56 amended by SI 2013/525).
17 See the Medical Devices Regulations 2002, SI 2002/618, reg 30 (amended by SI 2008/2936).
18 See the Medical Devices Regulations 2002, SI 2002/618, reg 31 (amended by SI 2008/2936).

475.   In vitro diagnostic medical devices. No person[1] may place on the market[2] or put into service[3] a relevant device[4] unless that device meets those essential requirements[5] which apply to it[6]; and no person may supply[7] a relevant device if that supply is also a placing on the market or putting into service of that device[8], or in circumstances where that device has been placed on the market or put into service[9], unless that device meets those essential requirements[10] which apply to it[11]. Nor may any person:

(1)   put into service a relevant device[12];
(2)   supply a relevant device if that supply is also a putting into service of that device[13], or in circumstances where that device has been placed on the market or put into service[14],

which is not ready for use[15]. No person may supply a device for performance evaluation[16], if that supply is also a making available of the device, unless certain conditions are met[17].

Restrictions are imposed: (a) on the placing on the market, putting into service, and supply of in vitro diagnostic medical devices unless the device, packaging or instructions for use bear a CE marking[18]; (b) on the use of misleading markings[19]; and (c) on the affixing of a CE marking to such devices[20]. Manufacturers of in vitro diagnostic medical devices must follow certain procedures[21], and provision is made for conformity assessments of such devices[22]. Persons placing in vitro diagnostic medical devices on the market must provide the Secretary of State with prescribed information[23].

1   As to the meaning of 'person' see PARA 45 note 2.
2   As to the meaning of 'placing on the market' see PARA 472 note 1.
3   As to the meaning of 'putting into service' see PARA 473 note 3.
4   'Relevant device' means in vitro diagnostic medical devices and accessories to such devices, except for: (1) products manufactured and used within the same health institution and either on

the premises of their manufacture or on premises in the immediate vicinity without having been transferred to another legal entity (Medical Devices Regulations 2002, SI 2002/618, reg 33(1)(a)); and (2) devices that come within the scope of Parliament and Council Directive (EC) 1998/79 (OJ L331, 7.12.1998, p 1) on in vitro diagnostic medical devices and another Directive ('the other Directive') issued by one or more of the institutions of the Community, if the other Directive includes a provision allowing the manufacturer of the device to choose, during a transitional period that has not ended, which set of arrangements applies to it, and the manufacturer chooses to follow the set of arrangements in the other Directive (Medical Devices Regulations 2002, SI 2002/618, regs 2(1), 33(1)(b)). 'In vitro diagnostic medical device' means a medical device which:

(a)   is a reagent, reagent product, calibrator, control material, kit, instrument, apparatus, equipment or system, whether used alone or in combination; and

(b)   is intended by the manufacturer to be used in vitro for the examination of specimens, including blood and tissue donations, derived from the human body, solely or principally for the purpose of providing information:

(i)   concerning a physiological or pathological state;

(ii)   concerning a congenital abnormality;

(iii) to determine the safety and compatibility of donations, including blood and tissue donations, with potential recipients; or

(iv)   to monitor therapeutic measures,

and includes a specimen receptacle but not a product for general laboratory use, unless that product, in view of its characteristics, is specifically intended by its manufacturer to be used for in vitro diagnostic examination: reg 2(1). 'Accessory' means an article intended specifically by its manufacturer to be used together with an in vitro diagnostic medical device to enable that device to be used in accordance with its intended purpose, which is not itself an in vitro diagnostic medical device, an invasive sampling medical device, or a medical device which is directly applied to the human body for the purpose of obtaining a specimen: reg 32(1). As to the meanings of 'the Community' and 'manufacturer' see PARA 472 note 1. As to the meaning of 'medical device' see PARA 472. As to the meaning of 'tissue' see PARA 472 note 10. 'Specimen receptacle' means a medical device which (whether vacuum-type or not) is specifically intended by its manufacturer to be used for the primary containment and preservation of specimens derived from the human body for the purpose of in vitro diagnostic examination: reg 2(1).

Part IV (regs 32–44) does not apply before 7 December 2005 in respect of a device put into service which is:

(A)   an in vitro diagnostic medical device without a CE marking; or

(B)   a device for performance evaluation (see note 16) and the manufacturer or his authorised representative does not indicate, directly or indirectly, that it is a device which is subject to the provisions of the regulations,

if the device satisfies the requirements of the laws of that part of the United Kingdom in which it is put into service as in force on 7 December 1998: reg 4(4). As to the meaning of 'CE marking' see PARA 473 note 4. As to the meaning of 'United Kingdom' see PARA 20 note 4. 'Authorised representative' means a person established within the Community or in a state which is a party to an association agreement who, explicitly designated by the manufacturer, acts for the manufacturer and may be addressed by authorities and bodies in the Community instead of the manufacturer with regard to the latter's obligation under Council Directive (EC) 1990/385 (OJ L7, 11.1.1994, p 20) on the approximation of the laws of the Member States relating to active implantable medical devices, Council Directive (EC) 1993/42 (OJ L169, 12.7.1993, p 1–43) concerning medical devices and Council Directive (EC) 1998/79 (OJ L331, 7.12.1998, p1–37) on in vitro diagnostic medical devices; and 'association agreement' means an agreement, listed in the Medical Devices Regulations 2002, SI 2002/618, Sch 1, establishing an association between the European Communities and their member states, on the one part, and another state on the other part (a 'state which is a party to an association agreement') on conformity assessment and acceptance of industrial products: reg 2(1). As to the meaning of 'member state' see the European Communities Act 1972 s 1(2), Sch 1 Pt II; and the Interpretation Act 1978 s 5, Sch 1. As to provisions relating to the designation of authorised representatives see the Medical Devices Regulations 2002, SI 2002/618, reg 60 (amended by SI 2008/2936).

5   Ie set out in Parliament and Council Directive (EC) 1998/79 (OJ L331, 7.12.1998, p 1) Annex I: Medical Devices Regulations 2002, SI 2002/618, regs 32(2), 34(1) (reg 32(2) amended by SI 2003/1697). As to the determination of the compliance of in vitro diagnostic medical devices with relevant essential requirements see the Medical Devices Regulations 2002, SI 2002/618, reg 35.

6 Medical Devices Regulations 2002, SI 2002/618, reg 34(1). A relevant device being shown at a trade fair, exhibition, scientific gathering or technical gathering is not being placed on the market or put into service if the device is not used on any specimen taken from the participants, and a visible sign clearly indicates that the device cannot be marketed or put into service until it complies with the requirements of Parliament and Council Directive (EC) 1998/79 (OJ L331, 7.12.1998, p 1) or the Medical Devices Regulations 2002, SI 2002/618: reg 39(1). Regulations 34, 36, 38 (see the text to notes 12–15, 18–19) do not apply where, following a duly justified request and in the interests of the protection of health, the Secretary of State has authorised, where appropriate for a specified period, the placing on the market or putting into service of a particular relevant device or relevant devices of a particular class or description without a CE marking, where appropriate subject to conditions (which are complied with), and has not withdrawn that authorisation: reg 39(2). As to the Secretary of State see PARA 2 note 1.

7 As to the meaning of 'supply' see PARA 473 note 7.

8 Medical Devices Regulations 2002, SI 2002/618, reg 34(2)(a).

9 Medical Devices Regulations 2002, SI 2002/618, reg 34(2)(b).

10 Ie set out in Parliament and Council Directive (EC) 1998/79 (OJ L331, 7.12.1998, p 1) Annex I: Medical Devices Regulations 2002, SI 2002/618, regs 32(2), 34(2) (reg 32(2) as amended: see note 5). See also note 5.

11 Medical Devices Regulations 2002, SI 2002/618, reg 34(2). This provision is expressed to be subject to reg 39: see note 6.

12 Medical Devices Regulations 2002, SI 2002/618, reg 38(a).

13 Medical Devices Regulations 2002, SI 2002/618, reg 38(b)(i).

14 Medical Devices Regulations 2002, SI 2002/618, reg 38(b)(ii).

15 Medical Devices Regulations 2002, SI 2002/618, reg 38. This provision is expressed to be subject to reg 39: see note 6.

16 'Device for performance evaluation' means a product which is intended by its manufacturer to be subject to one or more performance evaluation studies in laboratories for medical analysis or in other appropriate environments outside his own premises: Medical Devices Regulations 2002, SI 2002/618, reg 2(1).

17 Medical Devices Regulations 2002, SI 2002/618, reg 43. As to the conditions see reg 43(a)–(c). The requirements of Pt IV in respect of devices for performance evaluation do not apply in respect of: (1) products manufactured and used only within the same health institution and either on the premises of their manufacture or on premises in the immediate vicinity without having been transferred to another legal entity (reg 33(2)(a)); and (2) devices that come within the scope of Parliament and Council Directive (EC) 1998/79 (OJ L331, 7.12.1998, p 1) and another Directive ('the other Directive') issued by one or more of the institutions of the Community, if the other Directive includes a provision allowing the manufacturer of the device to choose, during a transitional period that has not ended, which set of arrangements applies to it, and the manufacturer chooses to follow the set of arrangements in the other Directive (Medical Devices Regulations 2002, SI 2002/618, reg 33(2)(b)).

18 See the Medical Devices Regulations 2002, SI 2002/618, reg 36(1)–(4), 37. Regulation 36 is expressed to be subject to reg 39: see note 6.

19 See the Medical Devices Regulations 2002, SI 2002/618, reg 36(5). This provision is expressed to be subject to reg 39: see note 6.

20 See the Medical Devices Regulations 2002, SI 2002/618, reg 40.

21 See the Medical Devices Regulations 2002, SI 2002/618, reg 41.

22 See the Medical Devices Regulations 2002, SI 2002/618, reg 42.

23 See the Medical Devices Regulations 2002, SI 2002/618, reg 44. As to the fee payable in respect of the provision of such information see regs 53, 57, 58.

476. Notified bodies and conformity assessment bodies. The Secretary of State[1] may designate[2] any corporate or other body as a body which is to carry out any of the tasks of a notified body[3], and, if he so designates a body, he must designate the tasks which it is to carry out[4]. The Secretary of State may designate for the purposes of the mutual recognition agreements any corporate or other body as a body which is to carry out any of the tasks of a European Community conformity assessment body, and, if he so designates a body, he must designate the tasks which it is to carry out[5].

Restrictions are placed on the affixing of a notified body or conformity assessment body number to a medical device[6], to the supply[7] of a medical device which has affixed to it a notified body or conformity assessment body number[8], and to the provision of information comprising a notified body or conformity assessment body number on a medical device[9]. Restrictions are also placed on the affixing of the CE marking[10] for a medical device to a product which is not a medical device[11], the supply of a product so marked[12], and the provision of information comprising a CE marking for a medical device if the product is not a medical device[13].

1   As to the Secretary of State see PARA 2 note 1.
2   Ie for the purposes of Council Directive (EC) 1990/385 (OJ L189, 20.7.1990, p 17) art 11, Council Directive (EC) 1993/42 (OJ L169, 12.7.1993, p 1) art 16 or Parliament and Council Directive (EC) 1998/79 (OJ L331, 7.12.1998, p 1) art 15.
3   'Notified body' means a body authorised in accordance with the Medical Devices Regulations 2002, SI 2002/618, Pt V (regs 44A–51), or the Medical Devices Directives to carry out tasks of a notified body or the importing party under the Medical Devices Directives or the mutual recognition agreements in respect of a conformity assessment procedure: reg 2(1) (definition amended by SI 2003/1697). 'The Medical Devices Directives' means Council Directive (EC) 1990/385 (OJ L189, 20.7.1990, p 17), Council Directive (EC) 1993/42 (OJ L169, 12.7.1993, p 1) read with Commission Directive (EC) 2003/32 (OJ L105, 26.4.2003, p 18), and Parliament and Council Directive (EC) 1998/79 (OJ L331, 7.12.1998, p 1): Medical Devices Regulations 2002, SI 2002/618, reg 2(1) (definition amended by SI 2003/1697). 'Mutual recognition agreements' means the agreements, listed in the Medical Devices Regulations 2002, SI 2002/618, Sch 2, concluded between the European Union and states which are not part of the European Union on matters including the conditions under which each party will accept or recognise the results of the conformity assessment procedures undertaken by the other party's designated bodies: reg 2 (amended by SI 2011/1043).
4   Medical Devices Regulations 2002, SI 2002/618, reg 45(1). As to the conditions relating to the appointment of such bodies see reg 45(2)–(8) (amended by SI 2003/1697). As to general matters relating to UK notified bodies see the Medical Devices Regulations 2002, SI 2002/618, reg 47 (amended by SI 2003/1697, SI 2008/2936). As to the choice by a manufacturer of a notified body see the Medical Devices Regulations 2002, SI 2002/618, reg 46. As to the meaning of 'manufacturer' see PARA 472 note 1. As to fees chargeable by notified bodies see reg 49. As to the fees payable in connection with the designation of notified bodies and certain other matters relating to such bodies see regs 54, 57, 58 (reg 54 amended by SI 2003/1697, SI 2007/803, SI 2010/557).
5   Medical Devices Regulations 2002, SI 2002/618, reg 48. As to the fees payable in connection with the designation of such bodies and certain other matters relating to such bodies see regs 55, 57, 58 (reg 55 amended by SI 2007/803, SI 2010/557).
6   See the Medical Devices Regulations 2002, SI 2002/618, reg 50(1)(a). As to the meaning of 'medical device' see PARA 472.
7   As to the meaning of 'supply' see PARA 473 note 7.
8   See the Medical Devices Regulations 2002, SI 2002/618, regs 50(1)(b), (3).
9   See the Medical Devices Regulations 2002, SI 2002/618, reg 50(2).
10 As to the meaning of 'CE marking' see PARA 473 note 4.
11 Medical Devices Regulations 2002, SI 2002/618, reg 51(1)(a).
12 See the Medical Devices Regulations 2002, SI 2002/618, reg 51(1)(b).
13 See the Medical Devices Regulations 2002, SI 2002/618, reg 51(2).

477.   Enforcement.   The regulations[1] relating to medical devices[2] are to be regarded for all purposes relating to enforcement, whether by criminal proceedings, notices or otherwise, as safety regulations[3] made under the Consumer Protection Act 1987[4]. The Secretary of State[5] is responsible for the enforcement of the safety provisions[6] relating to relevant devices[7] or devices for performance evaluation[8]; but, in relation to devices which are consumer goods[9], each weights and measures authority in Great Britain[10] must, concurrently with the Secretary of State, enforce the provisions in relation to such devices[11].

Except in the case of a device which in the opinion of an enforcement authority[12] is likely to compromise the health or safety of any person, where an enforcement authority has reasonable grounds for suspecting that a relevant device or a device for performance evaluation is a device in respect of which there is a failure to comply with the regulations, that authority may serve upon the manufacturer or his authorised representative a notice[13] requiring him to secure that the device conforms to specified provisions within a specified period[14], or to provide evidence within that period to the satisfaction of the enforcement authority that all the provisions have been complied with in so far as they relate to that device[15], and warning the person[16] on whom the notice is served that unless the requirements of the notice are met, further action may be taken[17].

Where an enforcement authority is of the opinion that, in order to protect the health or safety of any individual or of individuals of any class or description, it is necessary to restrict the availability of a particular medical device, a particular accessory to such a device or a particular device for performance evaluation[18], or medical devices, accessories to such devices or devices for performance evaluation of a particular class or description[19], it may serve on any person a restriction notice including such directions restricting the availability of that device or those devices as appear to it to be necessary in order to protect the health or safety of that individual or individuals of that class or description[20].

Any decision taken by a UK notified body[21], the Secretary of State or any other enforcement authority to withdraw a device from the market, or to prevent or restrict a device being placed on the market[22], put into service[23] or made available, must be notified without delay to the person responsible for marketing the device, placing it on the market, putting it into service or making it available[24]. Except in cases where urgent action is justified, in particular by public health requirements, if a notified body, the Secretary of State or any other enforcement authority is considering making such a decision, it or he must give the manufacturer or his authorised representative an opportunity to make representations to it or him before the decision is taken[25].

In respect of an offence relating to a contravention of the regulations[26], a magistrates' court may try any information laid within three years from the time when the offence was committed[27].

1   Ie the Medical Devices Regulations 2002, SI 2002/618.
2   As to the meaning of 'medical device' see PARA 472.
3   Ie as defined in the Consumer Protection Act 1987: see CONSUMER PROTECTION vol 21 (2011) PARA 676.

4   See the Medical Devices Regulations 2002, SI 2002/618, reg 61(1) (amended by SI 2003/1400).
5   As to the Secretary of State see PARA 2 note 1. The Secretary of State must perform, as respects the United Kingdom, the functions of the member state under Council Directive (EC) 1990/385 (OJ L189, 20.7.1990, p 17) art 8, Council Directive (EC) 1993/42 (OJ L169, 12.7.1993, p 1) art 10 and Parliament and Council Directive (EC) 1998/79 (OJ L331, 7.12.1998, p 1) art 11(1)–(3): Medical Devices Regulations 2002, SI 2002/618, reg 65. As to the meaning of 'United Kingdom' see PARA 20 note 4. As to the meaning of 'member state' see the European Communities Act 1972 s 1(2), Sch 1 Pt II; and the Interpretation Act 1978 s 5, Sch 1. As to the establishment of the medicines and healthcare products regulatory agency trading fund in connection with certain operations of the Department of Health in relation to medical devices see the Medicines and Healthcare Products Regulatory Agency Trading Fund Order 2003, SI 2003/1076 (amended by SI 2005/2061). As to government trading funds generally see CONSTITUTIONAL LAW AND HUMAN RIGHTS vol 8(2) (Reissue) PARA 743 et seq.
6   Ie the duty imposed by the Consumer Protection Act 1987 s 27(1) (see CONSUMER PROTECTION vol 21 (2011) PARA 679) is transferred to the Secretary of State: see the Medical Devices Regulations 2002, SI 2002/618, reg 61(2).

7   'Relevant device' means a device that is a relevant device for the purposes of the Medical Devices Regulations 2002, SI 2002/618, Pt II, III or IV (see PARAS 473 note 4, 474 note 4, 475 note 4): reg 59.

8   See the Medical Devices Regulations 2002, SI 2002/618, reg 61(2). As to the meaning of 'device for performance evaluation' see PARA 475 note 16. The powers conferred by the Consumer Protection Act 1987 s 13 to serve prohibition notices and notices to warn (see CONSUMER PROTECTION vol 21 (2011) PARA 681) are exercisable in relation to non-conforming devices as they are exercisable in relation to relevant goods which the Secretary of State considers are unsafe (as well as being exercisable in relation to goods considered unsafe by the Secretary of State); and, in relation to non-conforming devices, the Consumer Protection Act 1987 Sch 2 (see CONSUMER PROTECTION vol 21 (2011) PARA 682) has effect as if references to goods being unsafe or safe were references to relevant devices being or not being non-conforming devices: Medical Devices Regulations 2002, SI 2002/618, reg 61(7). 'Non-conforming devices' means:
   (1)   relevant devices which, whether or not the Secretary of State considers them unsafe, are devices with or that require a CE marking which he considers to be devices:
      (a)   which do not conform as respects a relevant essential requirement (reg 61(8)(a)(i)); or
      (b)   to which a CE marking has or should have been applied following a conformity assessment procedure set out in the Medical Devices Directives, and the manufacturer or his authorised representative has failed to comply with his obligations under that procedure, or they do not conform to the design or type described in any certificate granted as a result of that procedure (reg 61(8)(a)(ii)); or
   (2)   devices for performance evaluation which, whether or not the Secretary of State considers them unsafe, are devices in respect of which there is a failure to comply with the Medical Devices Regulations 2002, SI 2002/618 (reg 61(8)(b)).
   As to the meaning of 'CE marking' see PARA 473 note 4. As to the meaning of 'Medical Devices Directives' see PARA 476 note 3. As to the meaning of 'manufacturer' see PARA 472 note 1. As to the meaning of 'authorised representative' see PARA 475 note 4.
9   'Consumer goods' means any goods which are ordinarily intended for private use or consumption: Medical Devices Regulations 2002, SI 2002/618, reg 61(7A) (added by SI 2005/2909).
10   As to weights and measures authorities see CONSUMER PROTECTION vol 21 (2011) PARA 752; WEIGHTS AND MEASURES vol 99 (2012) PARA 519. As to the meaning of 'Great Britain' see PARA 20 note 4.
11   See the Medical Devices Regulations 2002, SI 2002/618, reg 61(3) (amended by SI 2005/2909). However, the powers of an enforcement authority to serve restriction notices under the Medical Devices Regulations 2002, SI 2002/618, reg 63 (see the text to notes 18–20) are only exercisable by the Secretary of State: reg 61(4). Each weights and measures authority must give immediate notice to the Secretary of State of certain actions taken by it: see reg 61(5).
12   As to the meaning of 'enforcement authority' see the Consumer Protection Act 1987 s 45(1); and CONSUMER PROTECTION vol 21 (2011) PARA 679.
13   As to the matters to be stated in the notice see the Medical Devices Regulations 2002, SI 2002/618, reg 62(1)(a)–(c), (3). As to the effect of the notice see reg 62(2).
14   Medical Devices Regulations 2002, SI 2002/618, reg 62(1)(d)(i).
15   Medical Devices Regulations 2002, SI 2002/618, reg 62(1)(d)(ii).
16   As to the meaning of 'person' see PARA 45 note 2.
17   See the Medical Devices Regulations 2002, SI 2002/618, reg 62(1)(e).
18   Medical Devices Regulations 2002, SI 2002/618 reg 63(1)(a) (amended by SI 2008/2936).
19   Medical Devices Regulations 2002, SI 2002/618 reg 63(1)(b).
20   Medical Devices Regulations 2002, SI 2002/618, reg 63(1). See also note 11. The enforcement authority responsible for serving a restriction notice may, in appropriate circumstances, withdraw the notice: reg 63(3). A direction in a restriction notice that has not been withdrawn by an enforcement authority or set aside by court order is a safety provision for the purposes of the Consumer Protection Act 1987 ss 14–17 (suspension notices and forfeiture: see CONSUMER PROTECTION vol 21 (2011) PARA 681 et seq): Medical Devices Regulations 2002, SI 2002/618, reg 63(4). As to orders setting aside restriction notices see reg 63(5), (6).
21   'UK notified body' is to be construed in accordance with the Medical Devices Regulations 2002, SI 2002/618, reg 45 (see PARA 476): reg 2(1).
22   As to the meaning of 'placing on the market' see PARA 472 note 1.
23   As to the meaning of 'putting into service' see PARA 473 note 3.
24   Medical Devices Regulations 2002, SI 2002/618, reg 64(1). As to the information to be included in such a notice see reg 64(1)(a)–(c).
25   Medical Devices Regulations 2002, SI 2002/618, reg 64(2).
26   Ie an offence committed under the Consumer Protection Act 1987 s 12: see CONSUMER PROTECTION vol 21 (2011) PARA 678.

27 See the Medical Devices Regulations 2002, SI 2002/618, reg 61(6)(a) (substituted by SI 2007/400). As to magistrates courts see MAGISTRATES.

478. Diagnostic and screening. Diagnostic and screening procedures, and reporting the results of such procedures, involving[1]:

(1)   the use of X-rays and other methods in order to examine the body by the use of radiation, ultrasound or magnetic resonance imaging[2];

(2)   the use of instruments or equipment which are inserted into the body to view its internal parts or to gather physiological data[3];

(3)   the removal of tissues, cells or fluids from the body for the purposes of discovering the presence, cause or extent of disease, disorder or injury[4];

(4)   the use of equipment in order to examine cells, tissues and other bodily fluids for the purposes of obtaining information on the causes and extent of a disease, disorder or injury[5]; and

(5)   the use of equipment to measure or monitor physiological data in relation to the audio-vestibular system, vision system, neurological system, cardiovascular system, respiratory system, gastro-intestinal system or urinary system[6],

for the purposes of obtaining information on the causes and extent of a disease, disorder or injury, or the response to a therapeutic intervention, where such information is needed for the purposes of the planning and delivery of care or treatment[7], are activities regulated by the Health and Social Care Act 2008[8].

The following procedures, and the analysis and reporting of the results of those procedures, are excepted from the above provisions[9]:

(a)   the taking of blood samples where the procedure is carried out by means of a pin prick or from a vein, and it is not necessary to send such samples for analysis to a place which is established for the purposes of carrying out tests or research in relation to samples of bodily cells, tissues or fluids[10];

(b)   the taking and analysis of samples of bodily tissues, cells or fluids in order to ascertain the existence of a genetically inherited disease or disorder, or the influence of an individual's genetic variation on drug response, where such procedures are part of neither the planning and delivery of care or treatment nor a national screening programme, other than for cancer[11];

(c)   the carrying out of procedures as part of a national cancer screening programme by a body established solely for the purpose of such a programme[12];

(d)   fitness screening procedures carried out in a gymnasium in order to ascertain that a person is sufficiently healthy to use fitness equipment or take part in fitness routines safely[13];

(e)   the taking of X-rays by chiropractors[14];

(f)   the use of ultrasound equipment by physiotherapists[15]; and

(g)   the carrying out of a hearing needs assessment or the supply and fitting of a hearing aid carried out by a hearing aid dispenser[16] or a person acting under the direction or supervision of a hearing aid dispenser where the patient is aged 19 or over or the patient is under 19 years old and the procedure is carried out in, or arranged by, a school or 16 to 19 Academy[17];

(h)   the taking of urine samples where it is not necessary to send such samples for analysis to a place which is established for the purposes of carrying out tests or research in relation to samples of bodily cells, tissues or fluids[18];

(i) the taking and analysing of wound swabs, hair samples or nail clippings[19];

(j) the non-ambulatory recording of blood pressure[20];

(k) the use of 12-lead electrocardiography[21];

(l) the use of a peak flow meter to measure peak expiratory flow[22];

(m) pulse oximetry when used for the purpose of spot recording[23];

(n) spirometry when carried out for screening, non-diagnostic or monitoring purposes[24]; and

(o) diagnostic and screening procedures carried out by a person in connection with specified[25] activities[26].

1   Where a service provider is registered in respect of an activity listed in any other provision of the Health and Social Care Act 2008 (Regulated Activities) Regulations 2010, SI 2010/781, Sch 1, the procedures specified in Sch 1 para 8(4B) and the analysis and reporting of the results of those procedures, are excepted from Sch 1 para 8(1), (2): Sch 1 para 8(4A) (Sch 1 para 8(4A)–(4C) added by SI 2012/513). The procedures are the taking of blood or urine samples, the analysis of urine or stool samples by means of dip stick or other reagent and the taking of tissue samples by means of a swab specimen from any external part of the body or from the mouth, ear, nose or throat, or by skin scrapings: Health and Social Care Act 2008 (Regulated Activities) Regulations 2010, SI 2010/781, Sch 1 para 8(4B)(a) (as so added). The carrying out of diagnostic and screening procedures mentioned Sch 1 para 8(1) or analysis and reporting of such procedures for research is excepted from Sch 1 para 8(1), (2) where those procedures, or that analysis and reporting, do not form any part of an individual's care or treatment: Sch 1 para 8(4C) (as so added).

2   Health and Social Care Act 2008 (Regulated Activities) Regulations 2010, SI 2010/781, Sch 1 para 8(1)(a).

3   Health and Social Care Act 2008 (Regulated Activities) Regulations 2010, SI 2010/781, Sch 1 para 8(1)(b).

4   Health and Social Care Act 2008 (Regulated Activities) Regulations 2010, SI 2010/781, Sch 1 para 8(1)(c).

5   Health and Social Care Act 2008 (Regulated Activities) Regulations 2010, SI 2010/781, Sch 1 para 8(1)(d).

6   Health and Social Care Act 2008 (Regulated Activities) Regulations 2010, SI 2010/781, Sch 1 para 8(1)(e).

7   Health and Social Care Act 2008 (Regulated Activities) Regulations 2010, SI 2010/781, Sch 1 para 8(1), (2) (both amended by SI 2012/513).

8   See the Health and Social Care Act 2008 (Regulated Activities) Regulations 2010, SI 2010/781, reg 3(1); and SOCIAL SERVICES AND COMMUNITY CARE.

9   Ie are excepted from the Health and Social Care Act 2008 (Regulated Activities) Regulations 2010, SI 2010/781, Sch 1 para 8(1), (2).

10 Health and Social Care Act 2008 (Regulated Activities) Regulations 2010, SI 2010/781, Sch 1 para 8((3), (4)(a) (amended by SI 2012/513).

11 Health and Social Care Act 2008 (Regulated Activities) Regulations 2010, SI 2010/781, Sch 1 para 8(4)(b).

12 Health and Social Care Act 2008 (Regulated Activities) Regulations 2010, SI 2010/781, Sch 1 para 8(4)(c).

13 Health and Social Care Act 2008 (Regulated Activities) Regulations 2010, SI 2010/781, Sch 1 para 8(4)(d).

14 Health and Social Care Act 2008 (Regulated Activities) Regulations 2010, SI 2010/781, Sch 1 para 8(4)(e). 'Chiropractor' means a person registered with the General Chiropractic Council pursuant to the Chiropractors Act 1994 s 3, 4, 5 or 5A (see MEDICAL PROFESSIONS): Health and Social Care Act 2008 (Regulated Activities) Regulations 2010, SI 2010/781, Sch 1 para 8(5)(a).

15 Health and Social Care Act 2008 (Regulated Activities) Regulations 2010, SI 2010/781, Sch 1 para 8(4)(f). 'Physiotherapist' means a person registered as such with the Health Professions Council pursuant to the Health and Social Work Professions Order 2001, SI 2002/254, art 5: (see MEDICAL PROFESSIONS vol 74 (2011) PARA 928): Health and Social Care Act 2008 (Regulated Activities) Regulations 2010, SI 2010/781, Sch 1 para 8(5)(b).

16 'Hearing aid dispenser' means a person registered as such with the Health Professions Council pursuant to the Health and Social Work Professions Order 2001, SI 2002/254, art 5: (see MEDICAL PROFESSIONS vol 74 (2011) PARA 928): Health and Social Care Act 2008 (Regulated Activities) Regulations 2010, SI 2010/781, Sch 1 para 8(5)(aa) (added by SI 2012/513).

17 Health and Social Care Act 2008 (Regulated Activities) Regulations 2010, SI 2010/781, Sch 1 para 8(4)(g) (Sch 1 para 8(4)(g) substituted and Sch 1 para (h)–(o) added by SI 2012/513). As to the meaning of '16 to 19 Academy' see the Academies Act 2010 s 1B; and EDUCATION: Health and Social Care Act 2008 (Regulated Activities) Regulations 2010, SI 2010/781, Sch 1 para 8(5)(za) (added by SI 2012/513).

18 Health and Social Care Act 2008 (Regulated Activities) Regulations 2010, SI 2010/781, Sch 1 para 8(4)(h) (as added: see note 17).

19 Health and Social Care Act 2008 (Regulated Activities) Regulations 2010, SI 2010/781, Sch 1 para 8(4)(i) (as added: see note 17).

20 Health and Social Care Act 2008 (Regulated Activities) Regulations 2010, SI 2010/781, Sch 1 para 8(4)(j) (as added: see note 17).

21 Health and Social Care Act 2008 (Regulated Activities) Regulations 2010, SI 2010/781, Sch 1 para 8(4)(k) (as added: see note 17).

22 Health and Social Care Act 2008 (Regulated Activities) Regulations 2010, SI 2010/781, Sch 1 para 8(4)(l) (as added: see note 17).

23 Health and Social Care Act 2008 (Regulated Activities) Regulations 2010, SI 2010/781, Sch 1 para 8(4)(m) (as added: see note 17).

24 Health and Social Care Act 2008 (Regulated Activities) Regulations 2010, SI 2010/781, Sch 1 para 8(4)(n) (as added: see note 17).

25 Ie activities listed in the Human Fertilisation and Embryology Act 1990 Sch 2 (activities for which licences may be granted) for which a licence has been granted to that person under s 16 (grant of licence) (see MEDICAL PROFESSIONS).

26 Health and Social Care Act 2008 (Regulated Activities) Regulations 2010, SI 2010/781, Sch 1 para 8(4)(o) (as added: see note 17).

479. Intrauterine contraceptive device. The insertion or removal of an intrauterine contraceptive device carried out by, or under the supervision of, a health care professional is an activity regulated by the Health and Social Care Act 2008[1].

1 See the Health and Social Care Act 2008 (Regulated Activities) Regulations 2010, SI 2010/781, Sch 1 para 15.

6. CONTROLLED DRUGS

(1) INTRODUCTION

480. Control of drugs. The principal statute which is concerned with the control of drugs which are dangerous or otherwise harmful is the Misuse of Drugs Act 1971[1]. These drugs are listed as controlled drugs and are classified according to their relative harmfulness[2]. The Act imposes restrictions on the importation, exportation, production, supply and possession of controlled drugs[3], and makes the cultivation of the cannabis plant an offence[4]. An occupier of premises is prohibited from allowing them to be used for such purposes as producing or supplying a controlled drug and smoking cannabis or opium[5]. The smoking of opium and other activities relating to opium are prohibited[6].

The Secretary of State[7] is given powers to prevent the misuse of controlled drugs. He may make regulations to prevent misuse[8], direct special precautions to be taken for safe custody[9], and restrict prescribing and supply by persons who have been convicted of offences or have contravened regulations or licences or have otherwise acted irresponsibly[10]. He may obtain information from doctors and pharmacists[11]. Regulations may exclude in prescribed cases the application of a provision creating an offence, may extend the investigation procedure to other cases, and may apply the provisions of the Act and regulations to servants or agents of the Crown[12].

The Secretary of State may by order repeal or amend any provision in any local Act[13], and may conduct or assist in conducting research into any matter relating to the misuse of dangerous or otherwise harmful drugs[14]. The Secretary of State may also, with the consent of the Treasury[15], pay such grants to such persons[16] as he considers appropriate in connection with measures intended to combat or deal with drug trafficking or the misuse of drugs[17] or to deal with consequences of the misuse of drugs[18].

The Health Act 2006[19] contains provisions relating to the supervision of management and use of controlled drugs[20].

The Proceeds of Crime Act 2002[21] makes provision for the recovery of the proceeds of crime, including drug trafficking[22], introducing a range of orders designed to facilitate this task, including confiscation orders, restraint orders and property freezing orders[23]. The Act also creates offences relating to money laundering[24]. The Criminal Justice (International Co-operation) Act 1990 contains measures designed to facilitate the detection of drug traffickers and the confiscation of the proceeds of drug trafficking[25]. The Crime (International Co-operation) Act 2003 makes provision for international assistance in criminal matters[26]. Under the Drugs Act 2005 the police are given powers in respect of the assessment of persons suspected of offences relating to the use of Class A controlled drugs[27]; and by the Anti-Social Behaviour Act 2003 the police are given powers to apply to the magistrates' court for an order for the closure of premises they believe to be used in connection with the unlawful use, production or supply of a Class A controlled drug, where the use of the premises is associated with the occurrence of disorder or serious nuisance to members of the public[28].

1   The Misuse of Drugs Act 1971, which repealed the Drugs (Prevention of Misuse) Act 1964 and the Dangerous Drugs Acts 1965 and 1967 (see the Misuse of Drugs Act 1971 s 39(2), Sch 6), is based, in part, upon the Single Convention on Narcotic Drugs (New York, 30 March to

1 August 1961; TS 34 (1965); Cmnd 2631), amended by Protocol (Geneva, 25 March to 31 December 1972; TS 23 (1979); Cmnd 7466).

2 See the Misuse of Drugs Act 1971 s 2, Sch 2; and PARAS 481–485. As to the meaning of 'controlled drug' see PARA 481. Any substance or product may be specified by order as a drug subject to control see s 2A; and PARA 482.

3 See the Misuse of Drugs Act 1971 ss 3–5; and PARAS 491–495.

4 See the Misuse of Drugs Act 1971 s 6; and PARA 497. As to offences committed by bodies corporate see s 21; and CRIMINAL LAW vol 26 (2010) PARA 723.

5 See the Misuse of Drugs Act 1971 s 8; and PARA 498.

6 See the Misuse of Drugs Act 1971 s 9; and PARA 500.

7 As to the Secretary of State see PARA 2 note 1.

8 See the Misuse of Drugs Act 1971 s 10; and PARA 505.

9 See the Misuse of Drugs Act 1971 s 11; and PARA 507.

10 See the Misuse of Drugs Act 1971 ss 12, 13; and PARAS 519–520.

11 See the Misuse of Drugs Act 1971 s 17; and PARA 510.

12 See the Misuse of Drugs Act 1971 ss 22, 31; and PARAS 486–487. Crown immunity from the effect of the Misuse of Drugs Act 1971 in respect of the national health service was removed as from 1 April 1991: see the National Health Service and Community Care Act 1990 s 60; and the National Health Service and Community Care Act 1990 (Commencement No 1) Order 1990, SI 1990/1329, Sch 3. A visiting force or headquarters, members of such a force or headquarters, persons employed in the service of such a force, and property used for the purposes of such a force or headquarters are exempt from the operation of the Misuse of Drugs Act 1971 to the extent that Crown immunity exempts home forces from it: see the Visiting Forces and International Headquarters (Application of Law) Order 1999, SI 1999/1736, art 12(1), Sch 5; and ARMED FORCES vol 3 (2011) PARA 412.

13 Misuse of Drugs Act 1971 s 39(3). This includes an Act confirming a provisional order, or a provision in any instrument in the nature of a local enactment under any Act, where it appears to the Secretary of State that such a provision is inconsistent with, or has become unnecessary or requires modification in consequence of, any provision of the Misuse of Drugs Act 1971: s 39(3). At the date at which this volume states the law, no such order had been made.

14 Misuse of Drugs Act 1971 s 32.

15 As to the Treasury see CONSTITUTIONAL LAW AND HUMAN RIGHTS vol 8(2) (Reissue) PARAS 512–517.

16 As to the meaning of 'person' see PARA 45 note 2.

17 Criminal Justice Act 1993 s 73(1)(a).

18 Criminal Justice Act 1993 s 73(1)(b). Any such grant may be made subject to such conditions as the Secretary of State may, with the agreement of the Treasury, see fit to impose: s 73(2).

19 Ie the Health Act 2006 Pt 3 Ch 1 (ss 17–25).

20 See PARA 527.

21 As to the Proceeds of Crime Act 2002 generally see CRIMINAL LAW vol 26 (2010) PARA 742 et seq; and SENTENCING AND DISPOSITION OF OFFENDERS vol 92 (2010) PARAS 390 et seq.

22 See the Proceeds of Crime Act 2002 s 75, Sch 2.

23 See the Proceeds of Crime Act 2002 Pt 2 (ss 6–91), Pt 5 (ss 240–316). The confiscation procedures of the Drug Trafficking Offences Act 1986 from which those under the Proceeds of Crime Act 2002 derive were enacted in response to the decision of the House of Lords in *R v Cuthbertson* [1981] AC 470, [1980] 2 All ER 401, HL (conspiracy to produce and supply a controlled drug, contrary to the Misuse of Drugs Act 1971 s 4; the appellants successfully argued in the House of Lords that the forfeiture order under the Act applied only to tangible things, not to choses or things in action and other intangibles).

24 See the Proceeds of Crime Act 2002 Pt 7 (ss 327–340).

25 See the Criminal Justice (International Co-operation) Act 1990 Pt II (ss 12–24); and CRIMINAL LAW vol 26 (2010) PARAS 725–726, 733.

26 As to the Crime (International Co-operation) Act 2003 see CRIMINAL LAW vol 25 (2010) PARA 421 et seq; CRIMINAL PROCEDURE vol 28 (2010) PARAS 518, 522–524.

27 See the Drugs Act 2005 Pt 3 (ss 9–19); CRIMINAL LAW, EVIDENCE AND PROCEDURE vol 11(2) (2006 Reissue) PARA 1031 et seq.

28 See the Anti-Social Behaviour Act 2003 Pt 1 (ss 1–9); and PARA 499.

481. Controlled drugs. 'Controlled drug' means any substance or product for the time being specified in Part I, Part II or Part III of Schedule 2 to the Misuse of Drugs Act 1971 or in a temporary class drug order[1] as a drug subject to temporary control[2]. 'Class A drug'[3], 'Class B drug'[4] and 'Class C drug'[5] mean any of the substances and products for the time being specified respectively in Part I, Part II and Part III of that Schedule[6]. 'Temporary class drug' means any substance or product which is for the time being a controlled drug by virtue of a temporary class drug order[7].

Her Majesty may by Order in Council[8] make such amendments to that Schedule[9] as may be requisite for the purpose of adding any substance or product to, or removing any substance or product from, any of those Parts[10].

1   This is subject to the Misuse of Drugs Act 1971 s 2A(6): see PARA 482.
2   Misuse of Drugs Act 1971 s 2(1)(a) (amended by the Police Reform and Social Responsibility Act 2011 Sch 17 para 2(a)).
3   As to Class A drugs see PARA 483.
4   As to Class B drugs see PARA 484.
5   As to Class C drugs see PARA 485.
6   Misuse of Drugs Act 1971 s 2(1)(b).
7   Misuse of Drugs Act 1971 s 2(1)(c) (added by the Police Reform and Social Responsibility Act 2011 Sch 17 para 2(b)). As to temporary class drug orders see PARA 482.
8   Any such order may amend the Misuse of Drugs Act 1971 Sch 2 Pt IV (definitions), whether or not it amends any other Part (s 2(3)); and may be varied or revoked by a subsequent order (s 2(4)). As to the meaning of 'the Advisory Council' see PARA 490. As to the Secretary of State see PARA 2 note 1.
9   Such amendments may include amendments for securing that no substance or product is for the time being specified in a particular Part or for inserting one into any of those Parts in which no substance or product is for the time being specified: Misuse of Drugs Act 1971 s 2(2).
10 Misuse of Drugs Act 1971 s 2(2). The following orders have been made: the Misuse of Drugs Act 1971 (Modification) Order 1973, SI 1973/771; the Misuse of Drugs Act 1971 (Modification) Order 1975, SI 1975/421; the Misuse of Drugs Act 1971 (Modification) Order 1977, SI 1977/1243; the Misuse of Drugs Act 1971 (Modification) Order 1979, SI 1979/299; the Misuse of Drugs Act 1971 (Modification) Order 1983, SI 1983/765; the Misuse of Drugs Act 1971 (Modification) Order 1984, SI 1984/859; the Misuse of Drugs Act 1971 (Modification) Order 1985, SI 1985/1995; the Misuse of Drugs Act 1971 (Modification) Order 1986, SI 1986/2230 (amended by SI 1995/1966); the Misuse of Drugs Act 1971 (Modification) Order 1989, SI 1989/1340; the Misuse of Drugs Act 1971 (Modification) Order 1990, SI 1990/2589; the Misuse of Drugs Act 1971 (Modification) Order 1995, SI 1995/1966; the Misuse of Drugs Act 1971 (Modification) Order 1996, SI 1996/1300; the Misuse of Drugs Act 1971 (Modification) Order 1998, SI 1998/750; the Misuse of Drugs Act 1971 (Modification) Order 2001, SI 2001/3932; and the Misuse of Drugs Act 1971 (Modification) Order 2003, SI 2003/1243.

482.   Temporary class drug orders. The Secretary of State[1] may make a 'temporary class drug order', specifying any substance or product as a drug subject to temporary control if the following two conditions are met[2]. The first condition is that the substance or product is not a Class A drug, a Class B drug or a Class C drug[3]. The second condition is that (1) the Secretary of State has consulted[4] and has determined that the order should be made[5]; or (2) the Secretary of State has received a recommendation[6] that the order should be made[7].

The Secretary of State may make the determination mentioned in head (1) above only if it appears to the Secretary of State that the substance or product is a drug that is being, or is likely to be, misused, and that misuse is having, or is capable of having, harmful effects[8].

A substance or product may be specified in a temporary class drug order by reference to the name of the substance or product, or a description of the substance or product, which may take such form as the Secretary of State thinks appropriate for the purposes of the specification[9].

In exercise of the above powers[10] certain drugs are subject to temporary control[11].

1 As to the Secretary of State see PARA 2 note 1.
2 Misuse of Drugs Act 1971 s 2A(1) (ss 2A, 2B added by the Police Reform and Social Responsibility Act 2011 Sch 17 para 3).
3 Misuse of Drugs Act 1971 s 2A(2) (as added: see note 2). As to the meaning of 'Class A drug', 'Class B drug', 'Class C drug' see PARA 481.
4 The power of the Secretary of State to make an order under the Misuse of Drugs Act 1971 s 2A is subject to s 2B: s 2A(8) (as added: see note 2). Before making an order under s 2A the Secretary of State must consult as mentioned in s 2A(2) or must have received a recommendation from the Advisory Council to make the order: s 2B(1) (as so added). The Secretary of State must consult (1) the Advisory Council; or (2) if the order is to be made under s 2A(1) and the urgency condition applies, the person mentioned in s 2B(3): s 2B(2) (as so added). The person referred to in head (2) is the person who is for the time being the chairman of the Advisory Council appointed under Sch 1 para 1(3) or, if that person has delegated the function of responding to consultation under s 2B(1)(a) to another member of the Advisory Council, that other member: s 2B(3) (as so added). The 'urgency condition' applies if it appears to the Secretary of State that the misuse of the substance or product to be specified in the order as a drug subject to temporary control, or the likelihood of its misuse, poses an urgent and significant threat to public safety or health: s 2B(4) (as so added). The duty of the Advisory Council or any other person consulted under s 2B(1)(a) is limited to giving to the Secretary of State that person's opinion as to whether the order in question should be made: s 2B(5) (as so added). A recommendation under s 2B(1)(b) that a temporary class drug order should be made may be given by the Advisory Council only if it appears to the Council that the substance or product is a drug that is being, or is likely to be, misused and that misuse is having, or is capable of having, harmful effects: s 2B(6) (as so added).
5 Misuse of Drugs Act 1971 s 2A(3)(a) (as added: see note 2).
6 Ie a recommendation under the Misuse of Drugs Act 1971 s 2B.
7 Misuse of Drugs Act 1971 s 2A(3)(b) (as added: see note 2).
8 Misuse of Drugs Act 1971 s 2A(4) (as added: see note 2).
9 Misuse of Drugs Act 1971 s 2A(5) (as added: see note 2). A substance or product specified in a temporary class drug order as a drug subject to temporary control ceases to be a controlled drug by virtue of the order at the end of one year beginning with the day on which the order comes into force, or if earlier, on the coming into force of an Order in Council under s 2(2) by virtue of which the substance or product is specified in Sch 2 Pt I, II or III: s 2A(6) (as so added). Section 2A(6) is subject to s 2A(10) and is without prejudice to the power of the Secretary of State to vary or revoke a temporary class drug order by a further order: s 2A(7) (as so added).
10 Ie the powers under the Misuse of Drugs Act 1971 s 2A(1), (5).
11 See the Misuse of Drugs Act 1971 (Temporary Class Drug) Order 2012, SI 2012/980; and PARA 503.

483. Class A drugs. The controlled drugs[1] which are Class A drugs[2] are:
  (1)   the following substances and products:
         (a)   acetorphine;
                alfentanil;
                allylprodine;
                alphacetylmethadol;
                alphameprodine;
                alphamethadol;
                alphaprodine;
                anileridine;
                benzethidine;
                benzylmorphine (3-benzylmorphine);
                betacetylmethadol;
                betameprodine;
                betamethadol;
                betaprodine;
                bezitramide;
                bufotenine;
                carfentanil;

clonitazene;
coca leaf[3];
cocaine[4];
desomorphine;
dextromoramide;
diamorphine;
diampromide;
diethylthiambutene;
difenoxin
(1–(3-cyano-3,3-diphenylpropyl)-4-phenylpiperidine-4-carboxylic
acid);
dihydrocodeinone O-carboxymethyloxime;
dihydroetorphine;
dihydromorphine;
dimenoxadole;
dimepheptanol;
dimethylthiambutene;
dioxaphetyl butyrate;
diphenoxylate;
dipipanone;
drotebanol (3, 4-dimethoxy-17-methylmorphinan-6ß,14-diol);
ecgonine and any derivative thereof which is convertible to
ecgonine or to cocaine;
ethylmethylthiambutene;
eticyclidine;
etonitazene;
etorphine;
etoxeridine;
etryptamine;
fentanyl;
fungus (of any kind) which contains psilocin or an ester of
psilocin;
furethidine;
hydrocodone;
hydromorphinol;
hydromorphone;
hydroxypethidine;
N-hydroxy-tenamphetamine;
isomethadone;
ketobemidone;
levomethorphan;
levomoramide;
levophenacylmorphan;
levorphanol;
lofentanil;
lysergamide;
lysergide and other N-alkyl derivatives of lysergamide;
mescaline;
metazocine;
methadone;
methadyl acetate;

methylamphetamine;
methyldesorphine;
methyldihydromorphine (6-methyldihydromorphine);
metopon;
morpheridine;
morphine;
morphine methobromide, morphine *N*-oxide and other pentavalent nitrogen morphine derivatives;
myrophine;
nicomorphine (3,6-dinicotinoyl-morphine);
noracymethadol;
norlevorphanol;
normethadone;
normorphine;
norpipanone;
opium, whether raw[5], prepared or medicinal[6];
oxycodone;
oxymorphone;
pethidine;
phenadoxone;
phenampromide;
phenazocine;
phencyclidine;
phenomorphan;
phenoperidine;
piminodine;
piritramide;
poppy-straw[7] and concentrate of poppy-straw[8];
proheptazine;
properidine (1-methyl-4-phenyl-piperidine-4-carboxylic acid isopropyl ester);
psilocin;
racemethorphan;
racemoramide;
racemorphan;
remifentanil;
rolicyclidine;
sufentanil;
tapentadol;
tenocyclidine;
thebacon;
thebaine;
tilidate;
trimeperidine;
4-bromo-2,5-dimethoxy-α-methylphenethylamine;
4-cyano-2-dimethylamino-4,4-diphenylbutane;
4-cyano-1-methyl-phenyl-piperidine;
N,N-diethyltryptamine;
N,N-dimethyltryptamine;
2,5-dimethoxy-α-4-dimethylphenethylamine;
N-hydroxy-tenamphetamine;

1-methyl-4-phenyl-piperidine-4-carboxylic acid;
2-methyl-3-morpholino-1,1-diphenyl-propanecarboxylic acid;
4-methl-aminorex;
4-phenylpiperidine-4-carboxylic acid ethyl ester[9];

(b)   any compound (not being a compound for the time being specified in head (1)(a) above) structurally derived from[10] tryptamine or from a ring-hydroxy tryptamine by substitution at the nitrogen atom of the sidechain with one or more alkyl substituents but no other substituent[11];

(c)   the following phenethylamine derivatives:
allyl(α-methyl-3,4-methylenedioxyphenethyl)amine;
2-amino-1-(2,5-dimethoxy-4-methylphenyl)ethanol;
2-amino-1-(3,4-dimethoxyphenyl)ethanol;
benzyl(α-methyl-3,4-methylenedioxyphenethyl)amine;
4-bromo-β,2,5-trimethoxyphenethylamine;
N-(4-*sec*-butylthio-2,5-dimethoxyphenethyl)hydroxylamine;
cyclopropylmethyl(α-methyl-3,4-methylenedioxyphenethyl)amine;
2-(4,7-dimethoxy-2,3-dihydro-1*H*-indan-5-yl)ethylamine;
2-(4,7-dimethoxy-2,3-dihydro-1*H*-indan-5-yl)-1-methylethylamine;
2-(2,5-dimethoxy-4-methylphenyl)cyclopropylamine;
2-(1,4-dimethoxy-2-naphthyl)ethylamine;
2-(1,4-dimethoxy-2-naphthyl)-1-methylethylamine;
N-(2,5-dimethoxy-4-propylthiophenethyl)hydroxylamine;
2-(1,4-dimethoxy-5,6,7,8-tetrahydro-2-naphthyl)ethylamine;
2-(1,4-dimethoxy-5,6,7,8-tetrahydro-2-naphthyl)-1-methylethylamine;
α,α-dimethyl-3,4-methylenedioxyphenethylamine;
α,α-dimethyl-3,4-methylenedioxyphenethyl(methyl)amine;
dimethyl(α-methyl-3,4-methylenedioxyphenethyl)amine;
N-(4-ethylthio-2,5-dimethoxyphenethyl)hydroxylamine;
4-iodo-2,5-dimethoxy-α-methylphenethyl(dimethyl)amine;
2-(1,4-methano-5,8-dimethoxy-1,2,3,4-tetrahydro-6-naphthyl)ethylamine;
2-(1,4-methano-5,8-dimethoxy-1,2,3,4-tetrahydro-6-naphthyl)-1-methylet
2-(5-methoxy-2,2-dimethyl-2,3-dihydrobenzo[*b*]furan-6-yl)-1-methylethyl
2-methoxyethyl(*a*-methyl-3,4-methylenedioxyphenethyl)amine;
2-(5-methoxy-2-methyl-2,3-dihydrobenzo[*b*]furan-6-yl)-1-methylethylami
β-methoxy-3,4-methylenedioxyphenethylamine;
1-(3,4-methylenedioxybenzyl)butyl(ethyl)amine;
1-(3,4-methylenedioxybenzyl)butyl(methyl)amine;
2-(α-methyl-3,4-methylenedioxyphenethylamino)ethanol;
α-methyl-3,4-methylenedioxyphenethyl(prop-2-ynyl)amine;
N-methyl-N-(α-methyl-3,4-methylenedioxyphenethyl)hydroxylamine;
O-methyl-N-(α-methyl-3,4-methylenedioxyphenethyl)hydroxylamine;
α-methyl-4-(methylthio)phenethylamine;
β,3,4,5-tetramethoxyphenethylamine;
β,2,5-trimethoxy-4-methylphenethylamine[12];

(d)   any compound (not being methoxyphenamine or a compound for the time being specified in head (1)(a) above) structurally derived from: phenethylamine,
an N-alkylphenethylamine,
α-methylphenethylamine,
an N-alkyl-α-methylphenethylamine,

α-ethylphenethylamine, or

N-alkyl-α-ethylphenethylamine,

by substitution in the ring to any extent with alkyl, alkoxy, alkylenedioxy or halide substituents, whether or not further substituted in the ring by one or more other univalent substituents[13];

(e)   any compound (not being a compound for the time being specified in head (1)(a) above) structurally derived from fentanyl by modification in any of the following ways: (i) replacement of the phenyl portion of the phenethyl group by any heteromonocycle whether or not further substituted in the heterocycle; (ii) substitution in the phenethyl group with alkyl, alkenyl, alkoxy, hydroxy, halogeno, haloalkyl, amino or nitro groups; (iii) substitution in the piperidine ring with alkyl or alkenyl groups; (iv) substitution in the aniline ring with alkyl, alkoxy, alkylenedioxy, halogeno or haloalkyl groups; (v) substitution at the 4-position of the piperidine ring with any alkoxycarbonyl or alkoxyalkyl or acyloxy group; (vi) replacement of the N-propionyl group by another acyl group[14];

(f)   any compound (not being a compound for the time being specified in head (1)(a) above) structurally derived from pethidine by modification in any of the following ways: (i) replacement of the 1-methyl group of an acyl, alkyl whether or not unsaturated, benzyl or phenethyl group, whether or not further substituted; (ii) substitution in the piperidine ring with alkyl or alkenyl groups or with a propano bridge, whether or not further substituted; (iii) substitution in the 4-phenyl ring with alkyl, alkoxy, aryloxy, halogeno or haloalkyl groups; (iv) replacement of the 4-ethoxycarbonyl by any other alkoxycarbonyl or any alkoxyalkyl or acyloxy group; (v) formation of an N-oxide or of a quaternary base[15];

(2)   any stereoisomeric form of a substance for the time being specified in head (1) above, not being dextromethorphan or dextrorphan[16];

(3)   any ester or ether of a substance for the time being specified in head (1) or head (2) above, not being a substance for the time being specified as a Class B drug[17];

(4)   any salt of a substance for the time being specified in any of heads (1) to (3) above[18];

(5)   any preparation or other product containing a substance or product for the time being specified in any of heads (1) to (4) above[19];

(6)   any preparation designed for administration by injection which includes any of certain substances or products[20] for the time being specified as Class B drugs[21].

Since 'heroin' is not listed as such, an indictment in respect of heroin should refer to 'diamorphine (commonly known as 'heroin')'[22].

1   As to the meaning of 'controlled drug' see PARA 481.
2   As to Class A drugs see PARA 483. As to the power to make orders amending the list of controlled drugs see the Misuse of Drugs Act 1971 s 2(2)–(5); and PARA 481.
3   'Coca leaf' means the leaf of any plant of the genus *Erythroxylon* from whose leaves cocaine can be extracted either directly or by chemical transformation: Misuse of Drugs Act 1971 Sch 2 Pt IV.

4   To establish possession of cocaine, it is sufficient to prove that the substance is either cocaine or
    a stereoisomeric form or a salt within the Misuse of Drugs Act 1971, Sch 2 Pt 1 paras 2–5: see
    R v Greensmith [1983] 3 All ER 444, [1983] 1 WLR 1124, CA. The conversion of cocaine
    hydrochloride, a substance falling within the Misuse of Drugs Act 1971 Sch 2 Pt I para 4, into
    free base cocaine, a substance falling within Sch 2 Pt I para 1, may however amount to
    'production' of a controlled drug by means other than manufacture or cultivation: *R v Russell*
    (1991) 94 Cr App Rep 351, CA; and see the Misuse of Drugs Act 1971 ss 4(2), 37(1), Sch 2 Pt I.
5   'Raw opium' includes powdered or granulated opium but does not include medicinal opium:
    Misuse of Drugs Act 1971 Sch 2 Pt IV.
6   'Medicinal opium' means raw opium (see note 5) which has undergone the process necessary to
    adapt it for medicinal use in accordance with the requirements of the British Pharmacopoeia (see
    PARA 237 et seq), whether it is in the form of powder or is granulated or is in any other form,
    and whether it is or is not mixed with neutral substances: Misuse of Drugs Act 1971 Sch 2 Pt IV.
7   'Poppy-straw' means all parts, except the seeds, of the opium poppy after mowing, and 'opium
    poppy' means the plant of the species *Papaver somniferum L*: Misuse of Drugs Act 1971 Sch 2
    Pt IV.
8   'Concentrate of poppy-straw' means the material produced when poppy-straw (see note 7) has
    entered into a process for the concentration of its alkaloids: Misuse of Drugs Act 1971 Sch 2
    Pt IV.
9   Misuse of Drugs Act 1971 Sch 2 Pt I para 1(a) (so designated by the Misuse of Drugs Act 1971
    (Modification) Order 1977, SI 1977/1243; and amended by SI 1973/771; SI 1975/421;
    SI 1979/299; SI 1983/765; SI 1984/859; SI 1986/2230; SI 1990/2589; SI 1998/750;
    SI 2003/1243; SI 2003/3201; the Drugs Act 2005 s 21; SI 2006/3331; SI 2011/744).
10 As to the interpretation of 'structurally derived from' see *R v Couzens and Frankel* (1992) 14 Cr
    App Rep (S) 33, [1992] Crim LR 822, CA.
11 Misuse of Drugs Act 1971 Sch 2 Pt I para 1(b) (added by the Misuse of Drugs Act 1971
    (Modification) Order 1977, SI 1977/1243).
12 Misuse of Drugs Act 1971 Sch 2 Pt I para 1(ba) (added by the Misuse of Drugs Act 1971
    (Modification) Order 2001, SI 2001/3932).
13 Misuse of Drugs Act 1971 Sch 2 Pt I para 1(c) (added by the Misuse of Drugs Act 1971
    (Modification) Order 1977, SI 1977/1243). See also note 10.
14 Misuse of Drugs Act 1971 Sch 2 Pt I para 1(d) (added by the Misuse of Drugs Act 1971
    (Modification) Order 1986, SI 1986/2230). See also note 10.
15 Misuse of Drugs Act 1971 Sch 2 Pt I para 1(e) (added by the Misuse of Drugs Act 1971
    (Modification) Order 1986, SI 1986/2230). See also note 10.
16 Misuse of Drugs Act 1971 Sch 2 Pt I para 2.
17 Misuse of Drugs Act 1971 Sch 2 Pt I para 3 (amended by SI 1973/771). As to the meaning of
    'Class B drug' see PARA 481; and as to such drugs see PARA 484.
18 Misuse of Drugs Act 1971 Sch 2 Pt I para 4.
19 Misuse of Drugs Act 1971 Sch 2 Pt I para 5. 'Preparation' should be given its ordinary and
    natural meaning: *R v Stevens* [1981] Crim LR 568, CA (psilocybin-containing mushrooms were
    prepared by merely ceasing to be in their natural growing state and being in some way altered by
    the hand of man to make them into a condition in which they could be used). In *R v Cunliffe*
    (1987) 9 Cr App Rep (S) 442, [1986] Crim LR 547, CA, it was held that it was open to the jury
    to find that the defendants' picking a quantity of mushrooms and subjecting them to a drying
    process involved an act of preparation for future use. See also *R v Walker* [1987] Crim LR
    565, CA. In *Hodder v DPP, Matthews v DPP* [1990] Crim LR 261, CA, it was held that
    picking, packaging and freezing mushrooms did not constitute 'preparation', although the
    mushrooms did constitute a 'product'.
20 Ie any substance or product for the time being specified in the Misuse of Drugs Act 1971 Sch 2
    Pt II paras 1–3: see PARA 484.
21 Misuse of Drugs Act 1971 Sch 2 Pt I para 6. See also note 19.
22 See *R v Macauley* (1967) 52 Cr App Rep 230, [1967] Crim LR 716, CA.

484.   Class B drugs. The controlled drugs[1] which are Class B drugs[2] are:
  (1)   the following substances and products:
         (a)   acetyldihydrocodeine;
                amphetamine[3];
                cannabinol;
                cannabinol derivatives[4];
                cannabis[5] and cannabis resin[6];

codeine;

dihydrocodeine;

ethylmorphine (3-ethylmorphine);

glutethimide;

lefetamine;

mecloqualone;

methaqualone;

methcathinone;

a-methylphenethylhydroxylamine;

methylphenidate;

methylphenobarbitone;

nicocodine;

nicodicodine (6-nicotinoyldihydrocodeine);

norcodeine;

pentazocine;

phenmetrazine;

pholcodine;

propiram;

zipeprol;

2-((Dimethylamino)methyl)-1-(3-hydroxyphenyl)cyclohexanol[7];

(b)   Any compound (not being bupropion, cathinone, diethylpropion, pyrovalerone or a compound for the time being specified in head (1)(a) above) structurally derived from 2-amino-1-phenyl-1-propanone by modification in any of the following ways, that is to say: (i) by substitution in the phenyl ring to any extent with alkyl, alkoxy, alkylenedioxy, haloalkyl or halide substituents, whether or not further substituted in the phenyl ring by one or more other univalent substituents; (ii) by substitution at the 3-position with an alkyl substituent; (iii) by substitution at the nitrogen atom with alkyl or dialkyl groups, or by inclusion of the nitrogen atom in a cyclic structure[8];

(c)   any compound structurally derived from 2-aminopropan-1-one by substitution at the 1-position with any monocyclic, or fused-polycyclic ring system (not being a phenyl ring or alkylenedioxyphenyl ring system), whether or not the compound is further modified in any of the following ways, that is to say: (i) by substitution in the ring system to any extent with alkyl, alkoxy, haloalkyl or halide substituents, whether or not further substituted in the ring system by one or more other univalent substituents; (ii) by substitution at the 3-position with an alkyl substituent; (iii) by substitution at the 2-amino nitrogen atom with alkyl or dialkyl groups, or by inclusion of the 2-amino nitrogen atom in a cyclic structure[9];

(d)   any compound (not being pipradrol) structurally derived from piperidine, pyrrolidine, azepane, morpholine or pyridine by substitution at a ring carbon atom with a diphenylmethyl group, whether or not the compound is further modified in any of the following ways, that is to say: (i) by substitution in any of the phenyl rings to any extent with alkyl, alkoxy, haloalkyl or halide groups; (ii) by substitution at the methyl carbon atom with an alkyl, hydroxyalkyl or hydroxy group; (iii) by substitution at the ring nitrogen atom with an alkyl, alkenyl, haloalkyl or hydroxyalkyl group[10];

(e) any 5,5 disubstituted barbituric acid[11];

(f) [2,3–Dihydro–5–methyl–3–(4–morpholinylmethyl)pyrrolo[1, 2, 3–de]–1,4–benzoxazin–6–yl]–1–naphthalenylmethanone;
3–Dimethylheptyl–11–hydroxyhexahydrocannabinol;
[9–Hydroxy–6–methyl–3–[5–phenylpentan–2–yl] oxy–5, 6, 6a, 7, 8, 9, 10, 10a–octahydrophenanthridin–1–yl] acetate;
9-(Hydroxymethyl)–6, 6–dimethyl–3–(2–methyloctan–2–yl)–6a, 7, 10, 10a–tetrahydrobenzo[c]chromen–1–ol;
nabilone;
any compound structurally derived from 3–(1–naphthoyl)indole, 3-(2-naphthoyl) indole, 1H–indol–3–yl–(1–naphthyl)methane or 1H-indol-3-yl-(2-naphthyl)methane by substitution at the nitrogen atom of the indole ring by alkyl, haloalkyl, alkenyl, cyanoalkyl, hydroxyalkyl, cycloalkylmethyl, cycloalkylethyl, (N-methylpiperidin-2-yl)methyl or 2–(4–morpholinyl)ethyl, whether or not further substituted in the indole ring to any extent and whether or not substituted in the naphthyl ring to any extent;
any compound structurally derived from 3–(1–naphthoyl)pyrrole or 3-(2-naphthoyl)pyrrole by substitution at the nitrogen atom of the pyrrole ring by alkyl, haloalkyl, alkenyl, cyanoalkyl, hydroxyalkyl, cycloalkylmethyl, cycloalkylethyl, (N-methylpiperidin-2-yl)methyl or 2–(4–morpholinyl)ethyl, whether or not further substituted in the pyrrole ring to any extent and whether or not substituted in the naphthyl ring to any extent;
any compound structurally derived from 1–(1–naphthylmethylene)indene or 1-(2-naphthylmethylene)indene by substitution at the 3–position of the indene ring by alkyl, haloalkyl, alkenyl, cyanoalkyl, hydroxyalkyl, cycloalkylmethyl, cycloalkylethyl, (N-methylpiperidin-2-yl)methyl or 2–(4–morpholinyl)ethyl, whether or not further substituted in the indene ring to any extent and whether or not substituted in the naphthyl ring to any extent;
any compound structurally derived from 3–phenylacetylindole by substitution at the nitrogen atom of the indole ring by alkyl, haloalkyl, alkenyl, cyanoalkyl, hydroxyalkyl, cycloalkylmethyl, cycloalkylethyl, (N-methylpiperidin-2-yl)methyl or 2-(4-morpholinyl)ethyl, whether or not further substituted in the indole ring to any extent and whether or not substituted in the phenyl ring to any extent;
any compound structurally derived from 2–(3–hydroxycyclohexyl)phenol by substitution at the 5–position of the phenolic ring by alkyl, alkenyl, cycloalkylmethyl, cycloalkylethyl or 2–(4–morpholinyl)ethyl, whether or not further substituted in the cyclohexyl ring to any extent;
any compound structurally derived from 3-benzoylindole by substitution at the nitrogen atom of the indole ring by alkyl, haloalkyl, alkenyl, cyanoalkyl, hydroxyalkyl, cycloalkylmethyl,

cycloalkylethyl,   (N-methylpiperidin-2-yl)methyl   or
2-(4–morpholinyl)ethyl, whether or not further substituted in the
indole ring to any extent and whether or not substituted in the
phenyl ring to any extent;

any compound structurally derived from 3-(1-adamantoyl)indole
or 3-(2-adamantoyl)indole by substitution at the nitrogen atom of
the indole ring by alkyl, haloalkyl, alkenyl, cyanoalkyl,
hydroxyalkyl,   cycloalkylmethyl,   cycloalkylethyl,
(N-methylpiperidin-2-yl)methyl   or   2-(4–morpholinyl)ethyl,
whether or not further substituted in the indole ring to any extent
and whether or not substituted in the adamantyl ring to any
extent;

any   compound   structurally   derived   from
3-(2,2,3,3-tetramethylcyclopropylcarbonyl)indole by substitution
at the nitrogen atom of the indole ring by alkyl, haloalkyl,
alkenyl, cyanoalkyl, hydroxyalkyl, cycloalkylmethyl,
cycloalkylethyl,   (N-methylpiperidin-2-yl)methyl   or
2-(4–morpholinyl)ethyl, whether or not further substituted in the
indole ring to any extent[12];

(g)   1-Phenylcyclohexylamine or any compound (not being ketamine,
tiletamine or a specified compound[13]) structurally derived from
1-phenylcyclohexylamine or 2-amino-2-phenylcyclohexanone by
modification in any of the following ways, that is to say: (i) by
substitution at the nitrogen atom to any extent by alkyl, alkenyl
or hydroxyalkyl groups, or replacement of the amino group with
a 1-piperidyl, 1–3 pyrrolidyl or 1-azepyl group, whether or not
the nitrogen containing ring is further substituted by one or more
alkyl groups; (ii) by substitution in the phenyl ring to any extent
by amino, alkyl, hydroxy, alkoxy or halide substituents, whether
or not further substituted in the phenyl ring to any extent; (iii) by
substitution in the cyclohexyl or cyclohexanone ring by one or
more alkyl substituents; (iv) by replacement of the phenyl ring
with a thienyl ring[14];

(2)   any stereoisomeric form of a substance for the time being specified in
head (1) above[15];

(3)   any ester or ether of cannabinol or of a cannabinol derivative or of a
substance for the time being specified in head (1)(d), (1)(f) or (1)(g)
above[16];

(4)   any salt of a substance for the time being specified in head (1) or head
(2) above[17];

(5)   any preparation or other product containing a substance or product for
the time being specified in any of heads (1) to (3) above, not being any
of certain preparations[13] specified as Class A drugs[18].

1   As to the meaning of 'controlled drug' see PARA 481.
2   As to the meaning of 'Class B drug' see PARA 481. As to the power to make orders amending the
     list of controlled drugs see the Misuse of Drugs Act 1971 s 2(2)–(5); and PARA 481.
3   The word 'amphetamine' is generic and embraces all of its stereoisomers; accordingly, pure
     dexamphetamine and pure levoamphetamine are both 'amphetamine' for the purposes of the
     Act: *R v Watts* [1984] 2 All ER 380, [1984] 1 WLR 757, CA.
4   'Cannabinol derivatives' means the following substances (except where contained in cannabis or
     cannabis resin: see notes 5–6): tetrahydro derivatives of cannabinol and 3-alkyl homologues of
     cannabinol or of its tetrahydro derivatives: Misuse of Drugs Act 1971 s 2(1), Sch 2 Pt IV.

Possession of a cannabinol derivative is not established by proof of possession of naturally occurring material, namely the leaf and stalk of the plant *Cannabis sativa*, of which a cannabinol derivative is an unseparated constituent: *DPP v Goodchild* [1978] 2 All ER 161, [1978] 1 WLR 578, HL (reversing in this regard [1978] 1 All ER 649, [1977] 1 WLR 1213, CA (Criminal Division)).

5   'Cannabis' (except in the expression 'cannabis resin': see note 6) means any plant of the genus *Cannabis* or any part of any such plant (by whatever name designated) except that it does not include cannabis resin or any of the following products after separation from the rest of the plant, namely, mature stalk of any such plant, fibre produced from such mature stalk, and seed of any such plant: Misuse of Drugs Act 1971 s 37(1) (definition substituted by the Criminal Law Act 1977 s 52).The substitution of this definition followed the decisions in *R v Goodchild* [1977] 2 All ER 163, [1977] 1 WLR 473, CA, and *R v Mitchell* [1977] 2 All ER 168, [1977] 1 WLR 753, CA, to the effect that the original definition did not include the leaves and stalk or cleaned seeds. See also note 4.

6   'Cannabis resin' means the separated resin, whether crude or purified, obtained from any plant of the genus *Cannabis:* Misuse of Drugs Act 1971 s 37(1). The mere possession of leaves and stalk of a cannabis plant which contain resin does not amount to the unlawful possession of cannabis resin. To constitute 'separated resin', there has to be a deliberate removal by some process of the resin of the plant: *R v Goodchild (No 2), A-G's Reference (No 1 of 1977)* [1978] 1 All ER 649, [1977] 1 WLR 1213, CA; affd sub nom *DPP v Goodchild* [1978] 2 All ER 161, [1978] 1 WLR 578, HL. See also note 4.

7   Misuse of Drugs Act 1971 s 2(1), Sch 2 Pt II para 1(a) (so designated by the Misuse of Drugs Act 1971 (Modification) Order 1984, SI 1984/859; and amended by SI 1973/771; SI 1984/859; SI 1985/1995; SI 1998/750; SI 2001/3932; SI 2003/3201; SI 2006/3331; SI 2008/3130; SI 2010/1207; SI 2011/744; SI 2013/239).

8   Misuse of Drugs Act 1971 Sch 2 Pt II para 1(aa) (added by SI 2010/1207).

9   Misuse of Drugs Act 1971 Sch 2 Pt II para 1(ab) (added by SI 2010/1833).

10   Misuse of Drugs Act 1971 Sch 2 Pt II para 1(ac) (added by SI 2012/1390).

11   Misuse of Drugs Act 1971 Sch 2 Pt II para 1(b) (added by SI 1984/859).

12   Misuse of Drugs Act 1971 Sch 2 Pt II para 1(c) (added by SI 2009/3209; substituted SI 2013/239).

13   Ie a compound for the time being specified in the Misuse of Drugs Act 1971 Sch 2 Pt 1.

14   Misuse of Drugs Act 1971 Sch 2 Pt II para 1(d) (added by SI 2013/239).

15   Misuse of Drugs Act 1971 Sch 2 Pt II para 2. See *R v Watts* [1984] 2 All ER 380, [1984] 1 WLR 757, CA; and note 3.

16   Misuse of Drugs Act 1971 Sch 2 Pt II para 2A (added by SI 2008/3130; and amended by SI 2009/3209; SI 2012/1390; SI 2013/239).

17   Misuse of Drugs Act 1971 Sch 2 Pt II para 3.

18   Ie a preparation falling within the Misuse of Drugs Act 1971 Sch 2 Pt I para 6: see PARA 483.

14   Misuse of Drugs Act 1971 Sch 2 Pt II para 4. As to the meaning of 'Class A drug' see PARA 481.

485.   Class C drugs. The controlled drugs[1] which are Class C drugs[2] are:
    (1)   the following substances:
         (a)   alprazolam;
                amineptine;
                aminorex;
                benzphetamine;
                bromazepam;
                7-bromo-5-(2-chlorophenyl)-1,3-dihydro-2*H*-1,4-benzodiazepin-2-one;
                brotizolam;
                buprenorphine;
                camazepam;
                cathine;
                cathinone;
                chlordiazepoxide;
                chlorphentermine;
                clobazam;
                clonazepam;
                clorazepic acid;

clotiazepam;
cloxazolam;
delorazepam;
dextropropoxyphene;
diazepam;
diethylpropion;
estazolam;
ethchlorvynol;
ethinamate;
ethyl loflazepate;
fencamfamin;
fenethylline;
fenproporex;
fludiazepam;
flunitrazepam;
flurazepam;
gamma-butyrolactone;
halazepam;
haloxazolam;
4-hydroxy-n-butyric acid;
Ketamine;
ketazolam;
loprazolam;
lorazepam;
lormetazepam;
mazindol;
medazepam;
mefenorex;
mephentermine;
mesocarb;
methyprylone;
midazolam;
nimetazepam;
nitrazepam;
nordazepam;
oxazepam;
oxazolam;
pemoline;
phentermine;
pinazepam;
pyrovalerone;
temazepam;
tetrazepam;
triazolam;
N-ethylamphetamine;
zolpidem[3];

(b)   5α-androstane-3,17-diol;
androst-4-ene-3,17-diol;
1-androstenediol;
1-androstenedione;
4-androstene-3, 17-dione;

5-androstenedione;
5-androstene-3, 17-diol;
atamestane;
bolandiol;
bolasterone;
bolazine;
boldenone;
boldione;
bolenol;
bolmantalate;
1,4-butanediol;
calusterone;
4-chloromethandienone;
clostebol;
danazol;
desoxymethyltestosterone;
drostanolone;
enestebol;
epitiostanol;
ethyloestrenol;
fluoxymesterone;
formebolone;
furazabol;
gestrinone;
3-hydroxy-5α-androstan-17-one;
mebolazine;
mepitiostane;
mesabolone;
mestanolone;
mesterolone;
methandienone;
methandriol;
methenolone;
methyltestosterone;
metribolone;
mibolerone;
nandrolone;
19-norandrostenedione;
19-nor-4-androstene-3, 17-dione;
19-nor-5-androstene-3, 17-diol;
19-norandrosterone;
norboletone;
norclostebol;
norethandrolone;
19-noretiocholanolone;
oripavine;
ovandrotone;
oxabolone;
oxandrolone;
oxymesterone;
oxymetholone;

pipradrol;

prasterone;

propetandrol;

prostanozol;

quinbolone;

roxibolone;

silandrone;

stanolone;

stanozolol;

stenbolone;

testosterone;

tetrahydrogestrinone;

thiomesterone;

trenbolone[4];

(c)   any compound (not being trilostane or a compound for the time being specified in head (1)(b) above) structurally derived from 17-hydroxyandrostan-3-one or from 17-hydroxyestran-3-one by modification in any of the following ways, that is to say: (i) by further substitution at position 17 by a methyl or ethyl group; (ii) by substitution to any extent at one or more of positions 1, 2, 4, 6, 7, 9, 11 or 16, but at no other position; (iii) by unsaturation in the carbocyclic ring system to any extent, provided that there are no more than two ethylenic bonds in any one carbocyclic ring; (iv) by fusion of ring A with a heterocyclic system[5];

(d)   1-benzylpiperazine or any compound structurally derived from 1-benzylpiperazine or 1-phenylpiperazine by modification in any of the following ways: (i) by substitution at the second nitrogen atom of the piperazine ring with alkyl, benzyl, haloalkyl or phenyl groups; (ii) by substitution in the aromatic ring to any extent with alkyl, alkoxy, alkylenedioxy, halide or haloalkyl groups[6];

(e)   any substance which is an ester or ether (or, where more than one hydroxyl function is available, both an ester and an ether) of a substance specified in head (1)(b) or described in head (1)(c) above[7];

(f)   chorionic gonadotrophin (HCG); clenbuterol; non-human chorionic gonadotrophin; somatotropin; somatrem; somatropin; zeranol; zilpaterol[8];

(2)   any stereoisomeric form of a substance for the time being specified in head (1) above not being phenylpropanolamine[9];

(3)   any salt of a substance for the time being specified in head (1) or head (2) above[10];

(4)   any preparation or other product containing a substance for the time being specified in any of heads (1) to (3) above[11].

1   As to the meaning of 'controlled drug' see PARA 481.

2   As to the meaning of 'Class C drug' see PARA 481. As to the power to make orders amending the list of controlled drugs see the Misuse of Drugs Act 1971 s 2(2)–(5); and PARA 481.

3   Misuse of Drugs Act 1971 Sch 2 Pt III para 1(a) (so designated by the Misuse of Drugs Act 1971 (Modification) Order 1996, SI 1996/1300; and amended by SI 1973/771; SI 1983/765; SI 1984/859; SI 1985/1995; SI 1986/2230; SI 1989/1340; SI 1990/2589; SI 1995/1966; SI 1998/750; SI 2003/1243; SI 2003/3201; SI 2005/3178; SI 2008/3130; SI 2009/3209; SI 2011/744; SI 2012/1390).

4   Misuse of Drugs Act 1971 Sch 2 Pt III para 1(b) (Sch 2 Pt III para 1(b)–(e) added by SI 1996/1300; and the Misuse of Drugs Act 1971 Sch 2 Pt III para 1(b) amended by SI 2003/1243; SI 2009/3209; SI 2012/1390).

5   Misuse of Drugs Act 1971 Sch 2 Pt III para 1(c) (as added: see note 4).

6   Misuse of Drugs Act 1971 Sch 2 Pt III para 1(ca) (added by SI 2009/3209).

7   Misuse of Drugs Act 1971 Sch 2 Pt III para 1(d) (as added (see note 4); and amended by SI 2003/3201; SI 2008/3130).

8   Misuse of Drugs Act 1971 Sch 2 Pt III para 1(e) (as added (see note 4); amended by SI 2009/3209).

9   Misuse of Drugs Act 1971 Sch 2 Pt III para 2 (amended by SI 1986/2230).

10   Misuse of Drugs Act 1971 Sch 2 Pt III para 3.

11   Misuse of Drugs Act 1971 Sch 2 Pt III para 4.

486.   Regulations generally. Regulations made by the Secretary of State[1] under any provision of the Misuse of Drugs Act 1971 may: (1) make different provision in relation to different controlled drugs[2], different classes of persons[3], different provisions of that Act or other different cases or circumstances[4]; (2) make the opinion, consent or approval of a prescribed[5] authority or of any person authorised in a prescribed manner material for purposes of any provision of the regulations[6]; and (3) contain such supplementary, incidental and transitional provisions as appear expedient to the Secretary of State[7].

The Secretary of State may not make any regulations under the Misuse of Drugs Act 1971 except after consultation with the Advisory Council[8].

1   As to the Secretary of State see PARA 2 note 1.

2   As to the meaning of 'controlled drug' see PARA 481.

3   As to the meaning of 'person' see PARA 45 note 2.

4   Misuse of Drugs Act 1971 s 31(1)(a).

5   'Prescribed' means prescribed by regulations made by the Secretary of State under the Misuse of Drugs Act 1971: s 37(1).

6   Misuse of Drugs Act 1971 s 31(1)(b).

7   Misuse of Drugs Act 1971 s 31(1)(c).

8   Misuse of Drugs Act 1971 s 31(3). As to the meaning of 'the Advisory Council' see PARA 490.

487.   Variation of the Misuse of Drugs Act 1971 by regulation. The Secretary of State[1] may by regulations[2] make provision for:

(1)   excluding in such cases as may be prescribed[3] the application of any provision of the Misuse of Drugs Act 1971 which creates an offence[4] or the application of any of certain provisions of the Customs and Excise Management Act 1979[5] in so far as they apply in relation to a prohibition or restriction on importation or exportation of a controlled drug[6];

(2)   applying any of the provisions of the Misuse of Drugs Act 1971[7] relating to investigation of cases by tribunals, advisory bodies or professional panels, with such modifications, if any, as may be prescribed, in relation to any proposal by the Secretary of State to give a direction[8] prohibiting a practitioner[9] or pharmacist[10] convicted of the specified offences from being concerned with controlled drugs[11], or for such purposes of regulations under that Act as may be prescribed[12]; and

(3)   the application of any of the provisions of the Misuse of Drugs Act 1971or regulations or orders made under it to servants or agents of the Crown, subject to such exceptions, adaptations and modifications as may be prescribed[13].

1   As to the Secretary of State see PARA 2 note 1.

2   As to regulations made under this provision see the Misuse of Drugs Regulations 2001, SI 2001/3998 (amended by SI 2003/1432; SI 2003/1653; SI 2003/2429; SI 2004/1031;

SI 2004/1771; SI 2005/271; SI 2005/1653; SI 2005/3372; Commissioners for Revenue and Customs Act 2005 s 50(2), (7); SI 2006/986; SI 2006/1450; SI 2006/2178; SI 2007/2154; SI 2009/3136; SI 2010/231; SI 2010/1144; SI 2010/1799; SI 2011/448; SI 2011/2085; SI 2011/2581; SI 2012/973; SI 2012/1311; SI 2012/1479; SI 2012/1916; SI 2013/176); and the Misuse of Drugs (Supply to Addicts) Regulations 1997, SI 1997/1001 (amended by SI 2005/2864). The power to make regulations under the Misuse of Drugs Act 1971 s 22 does not apply in relation to temporary class drugs (see instead s 7A: see PARA 503): s 22(2) (added by the Police Reform and Social Responsibility Act 2011 Sch 17 para 14(b)).

3 As to the meaning of 'prescribed' see PARA 486 note 5.
4 Misuse of Drugs Act 1971 s 22(1)(a)(i) (renumbered by the Police Reform and Social Responsibility 2011 Sch 17 para 14(a)).
5 Ie the Customs and Excise Management Act 1979 ss 50(1)–(4), 68(2), (3), 170: see PARA 491 note 3.
6 Misuse of Drugs Act 1971 s 22(1)(a)(ii) (as renumbered (see note 4); and amended by the Customs and Excise Management Act 1979 s 177(1), Sch 4 para 12 Table Pt I). As to the meaning of 'controlled drug' see PARA 481.
7 Ie the Misuse of Drugs Act 1971 ss 14–16, Sch 3: see PARA 521 et seq.
8 Ie under the Misuse of Drugs Act 1971 s 12(2): see PARA 519.
9 'Practitioner' means a doctor, dentist, veterinary practitioner or veterinary surgeon: Misuse of Drugs Act 1971 s 37(1). 'Doctor' means a registered medical practitioner within the meaning of the Interpretation Act 1978 Sch 1 (see MEDICAL PROFESSIONS vol 74 (2011) PARA 176): Misuse of Drugs Act 1971 s 37(1) (definition substituted by the Medical Act 1983 s 56(1), Sch 5 para 9). 'Dentist' means a person registered in the dentists register under the Dentists Act 1984: Misuse of Drugs Regulations 2001, SI 2001/3998, reg 37(1) (definition amended by the Dentists Act 1984 Sch 5 para 3; SI 2007/3101). As to the registration of dentists see MEDICAL PROFESSIONS vol 74 (2011) PARA 442 et seq. 'Veterinary practitioner' means a person registered in the supplementary veterinary register kept under the Veterinary Surgeons Act 1966 s 8 (see ANIMALS vol 2 (2008) PARA 1134); and 'veterinary surgeon' means a person registered in the register of veterinary surgeons kept under s 2 (see ANIMALS vol 2 (2008) PARA 1133): Misuse of Drugs Act 1971 s 37(1).
10 As to the meaning of 'pharmacist' see PARA 52 note 5; definition applied by the Misuse of Drugs Act 1971 s 37(1).
11 Misuse of Drugs Act 1971 s 22(1)(b)(i) (as renumbered: see note 4). For the specified offences see s 12(1); and PARA 519.
12 Misuse of Drugs Act 1971 s 22(1)(b)(ii) (as renumbered: see note 4).
13 Misuse of Drugs Act 1971 s 22(1)(c) (as renumbered: see note 4). See also PARA 480 note 12.

488. Licences and authorities generally. A licence or other authority issued by the Secretary of State[1] for purposes of the Misuse of Drugs Act 1971[2] or of regulations or orders[3] made under that Act may be issued, to any general or specific degree, on such terms and subject to such conditions including, in the case of a licence, the payment of a prescribed[4] fee, as the Secretary of State thinks proper, and may be modified or revoked by him at any time[5].

1 As to the Secretary of State see PARA 2 note 1.
2 As to licences and authorities see the Misuse of Drugs Act 1971 s 3 (see PARA 491) and s 7 (see PARA 502).
3 As to the regulations that have been made see the Misuse of Drugs (Licence Fees) Regulations 2010, SI 2010/2497 (amended by SI 2011/2199).
4 As to the meaning of 'prescribed' see PARA 486 note 5.
5 Misuse of Drugs Act 1971 s 30(1) (renumbered by the Scotland Act 2012 s 19(6)(a)).

489. Service of notices and documents. Any notice or other document required or authorised by any provision of the Misuse of Drugs Act 1971 to be served on any person[1] may be served on him either by delivering it to him or by leaving it at his proper address or by sending it by post[2]. Any notice or other document so required or authorised to be served on a body corporate is duly served if it is served on the secretary or clerk of that body[3]. For these purposes[4], the proper address of any person, in the case of the secretary or clerk of the body corporate, is that of the registered or principal office of that body and, in any other case, is the last address of the person to be served which is known to the Secretary of State[5].

1   As to the meaning of 'person' see PARA 45 note 2.
2   Misuse of Drugs Act 1971 s 29(1). Where an Act authorises or requires any document to be served by post (whether the expression 'serve' or the expression 'give' or 'send' or any other expression is used) then, unless the contrary intention appears, the service is deemed to be effected by properly addressing, pre-paying and posting a letter containing the document and, unless the contrary is proved, to have been effected at the time at which the letter would be delivered in the ordinary course of post: Interpretation Act 1978 s 7. If a notice under the Misuse of Drugs Act 1971 s 11(1) (see PARA 507) or s 15(6) (see PARA 522 note 15) or, if a copy of a direction given under s 12(2), s 13(1) or (2) or s 16(3) (see PARAS 519–522) is served by sending it by registered post or by the recorded delivery service, service is deemed to have been effected at the time when the letter containing it would be delivered in the ordinary course of post; and so much of the Interpretation Act 1978 s 7 as relates to the time when service by post is deemed to have been effected does not apply to such a document if it is served by so sending it: see the Misuse of Drugs Act 1971 s 29(4).
3   Misuse of Drugs Act 1971 s 29(2). As to bodies corporate see COMPANIES; CORPORATIONS.
4   Ie for the purposes of the Misuse of Drugs Act 1971 s 29, and of the Interpretation Act 1978 s 7 (see note 2) in its application to the Misuse of Drugs Act 1971 s 29.
5   Misuse of Drugs Act 1971 s 29(3). As to the registered office of a company see COMPANIES vol 14 (2009) PARA 129.

(2) THE ADVISORY COUNCIL ON THE MISUSE OF DRUGS

490.   The Advisory Council.   An advisory body known as the Advisory Council on the Misuse of Drugs has been established[1].

It is the duty of the Advisory Council to keep under review the situation in the United Kingdom[2] with respect to drugs which are being or appear to it likely to be misused[3] and of which the misuse is having or appears to it capable of having harmful effects sufficient to constitute a social problem, and to give to any one or more of the ministers[4], where either the Advisory Council considers it expedient to do so or it is consulted by the minister or ministers in question, advice on measures, whether or not involving alteration of the law, which in the Advisory Council's opinion ought to be taken for preventing the misuse of such drugs or dealing with social problems connected with their misuse[5], and in particular on measures which in its opinion ought to be taken: (1) for restricting the availability of such drugs or supervising the arrangements for their supply[6]; (2) for enabling persons affected by the misuse of such drugs to obtain proper advice, and for securing the provision of proper facilities and services for their treatment, rehabilitation and after-care[7]; (3) for promoting co-operation between the various professional and community services which in the Advisory Council's opinion have a part to play in dealing with social problems connected with the misuse of such drugs[8]; (4) for educating the public, particularly the young, in the dangers of misusing such drugs, and for giving publicity to those dangers[9]; and (5) for promoting research into, or otherwise obtaining information about, any matter which in the Advisory Council's opinion is of relevance for the purpose of preventing the misuse of such drugs or dealing with any social problem connected with their misuse[10].

It is also the Advisory Council's duty to consider any matter relating to drug dependence or the misuse of drugs which may be referred to it by any one or more of the ministers and to advise the minister or ministers in question thereon, and in particular to consider and advise the Secretary of State[11] with respect to any communication referred by him to the Advisory Council, being a communication relating to the control of any dangerous or otherwise harmful drug made to the government by any organisation or authority established by or under any treaty, convention or other agreement or arrangement to which the government is for the time being a party[12].

1 Misuse of Drugs Act 1971 s 1(1). 'The Advisory Council' means the Advisory Council on the Misuse of Drugs so established: s 37(1). As to the constitution of the Advisory Council see Sch 1 (amended by the Police Reform and Social Responsibility Act 2011 s 152).
2 As to the meaning of 'United Kingdom' see PARA 20 note 4.
3 References in the Misuse of Drugs Act 1971 s 1 to misusing a drug are references to misusing it by taking it; and the reference in the foregoing provision to the taking of a drug is a reference to the taking of it by a human being by way of any form of self-administration, whether or not involving assistance by another: s 37(2).
4 As to the meaning of 'the ministers' for these purposes see the Misuse of Drugs Act 1971 s 1(4); Northern Ireland Act 1998 s 95(5), Sch 12 para 10.
5 Misuse of Drugs Act 1971 s 1(2).
6 Misuse of Drugs Act 1971 s 1(2)(a).
7 Misuse of Drugs Act 1971 s 1(2)(b).
8 Misuse of Drugs Act 1971 s 1(2)(c).
9 Misuse of Drugs Act 1971 s 1(2)(d).
10 Misuse of Drugs Act 1971 s 1(2)(e).
11 As to the Secretary of State see PARA 2 note 1.
12 Misuse of Drugs Act 1971 s 1(3).

(3) THE CONTROL OF DRUGS

(i) Prohibitions and Offences

491. Restrictions on importation and exportation. The importation of a controlled drug[1] and the exportation of a controlled drug[2] are both prohibited[3]. This does not, however, apply to the importation or exportation of a controlled drug which is excepted from the prohibition by regulations[4] or by provision made in a temporary class drug order[5] or to the importation or exportation under and in accordance with the terms of a licence issued by the Secretary of State and in compliance with any conditions attached to the licence[6].

1 Misuse of Drugs Act 1971 s 3(1)(a). As to the meaning of 'controlled drug' see PARA 481.
2 Misuse of Drugs Act 1971 s 3(1)(b).
3 Misuse of Drugs Act 1971 s 3(1). Goods imported contrary to any prohibition are subject to forfeiture under the Customs and Excise Management Act 1979 s 49(1)(b) (see CUSTOMS AND EXCISE vol 31 (2012) PARA 991); and goods exported or brought to any place in the United Kingdom for the purpose of being exported contrary to any prohibition are subject to forfeiture under s 68(1) (see CUSTOMS AND EXCISE vol 31 (2012) PARA 1027). As to the meaning of 'United Kingdom' see PARA 20 note 4. The penalties for these offences set out in s 50 (importation) (see CUSTOMS AND EXCISE vol 31 (2012) PARA 992), s 68 (exportation) (see CUSTOMS AND EXCISE vol 31 (2012) PARA 1027) and s 170 (fraudulent evasion of duty) (see CUSTOMS AND EXCISE vol 31 (2012) PARA 1175) are modified in respect of controlled drugs as follows: where such offences are concerned with Class A, Class B or a temporary class drugs (see PARAS 481–484), a person is liable on conviction on indictment, where the goods are a Class A drug, to a penalty of any amount or to imprisonment for life or to both and, where the goods are a Class B drug, to a penalty of any amount or to imprisonment for a term not exceeding 14 years or to both, and on summary conviction to a penalty of the prescribed sum or of three times the value of the goods, whichever is greater, or to imprisonment for a term not exceeding six months or to both: ss 50(5), 68(4), 170(4), Sch 1 para 1 (amended by the Controlled Drugs (Penalties) Act 1985 s 1(2); and the Police Reform and Social Responsibility Act 2011 Sch 17 para 21(a)). In a case concerning a Class C drug (see PARAS 481, 485), a person is liable on conviction on indictment to imprisonment for a term not exceeding 14 years or to a penalty of any amount or to both, or on summary conviction to a penalty of three times the value of the goods or level 5 on the standard scale, whichever is greater, or to imprisonment for a term not exceeding three months or to both: Customs and Excise Management Act 1979 Sch 1 para 2

(amended by virtue of the Criminal Justice Act 1982 s 46; and the Criminal Justice Act 2003 s 284, Sch 28 para 2). As to the standard scale and the prescribed sum see SENTENCING AND DISPOSITION OF OFFENDERS vol 92 (2010) PARA 141, 142. It is not a defence to such an offence that the importation of the drug was for the purpose of its use for the alleviation of pain in seriously ill persons: *R v Quayle; A-G's Reference (No 2 of 2004)* [2005] EWCA Crim 1415, [2006] 1 All ER 988, BMLR 169. As to sentence see *R v Coughlan* (1994) 16 Cr App Rep (S) 519, (1994) Times, 31 October, CA. See also *R v Yalman* [1998] 2 Cr App Rep 269, [1998] Crim LR 569, CA (evidence of past drug use relevant to rebut defendant's claim of innocence in respect of importation). As to incitement to commit offences under the Misuse of Drugs Act 1971 and as to persons assisting in or inducing the commission of offences under comparable foreign legislation see PARA 504. As to the power of the Secretary of State to exclude the application of the Customs and Excise Management Act 1979 s 50(1)–(4), s 68(2), (3), s 170 in prescribed cases see the Misuse of Drugs Act 1971 s 22; and PARA 487. As to the Secretary of State see PARA 2 note 1.

An offence under the Customs and Excise Management Act 1979 s 50(2), (3), s 68(2), s 170, in connection with a prohibition or restriction on importation or exportation having effect by virtue of the Misuse of Drugs Act 1971 s 3, is a 'lifestyle offence' for the purposes of the Proceeds of Crime Act 2002 ss 75, 223: see SENTENCING AND DISPOSITION OF OFFENDERS vol 92 (2010) PARA 393. For the power of the court to impose a travel banning order on an individual convicted of such an offence in connection with a prohibition or restriction on importation or exportation having effect by virtue of the Misuse of Drugs Act 1971 s 3 see the Criminal Justice and Police Act 2001 ss 33–37; and SENTENCING AND DISPOSITION OF OFFENDERS vol 92 (2010) PARAS 372–374. Such offences, in connection with a prohibition or restriction on importation or exportation having effect by virtue of the Misuse of Drugs Act 1971 s 3, are excluded offences for the purposes of the Criminal Justice Act 1982 s 32 (early release of prisoners): see s 32(2)(c), Sch 1 Pt III; and PRISONS vol 36(2) (Reissue) PARA 613.

4	The regulations referred to in the text are any made under the Misuse of Drugs Act 1971 s 7: see PARA 502. The restrictions on importation and exportation of controlled drugs are not to have effect in relation to the controlled drugs specified in the Misuse of Drugs Regulations 2001, SI 2001/3998, Schs 4, 5 (Sch 4 amended by SI 2003/1432; SI 2005/3372; SI 2007/2154; SI 2009/3136; SI 2012/973; SI 2001/3998; and the Misuse of Drugs Regulations 2001, SI 2001/3998, Sch 5 amended by SI 2005/2864). See *R v Hunt* [1987] AC 352, [1987] 1 All ER 1, HL; and PARA 259.

5	Misuse of Drugs Act 1971 s 3(2)(a) (amended by the Police Reform and Social Responsibility Act 2011 Sch 17 para 4). 'Temporary class drug order' means an order made under the Misuse of Drugs Act 1971 s 2A(1) (see PARA 482) (s 31(1) (definition added by the Police Reform and Social Responsibility Act 2011 Sch 17 para 9)) and the provision made in a temporary class drug order referred to in the text is one made by virtue of the Misuse of Drugs Act 1971 s 7A (see PARA 503).

6	Misuse of Drugs Act 1971 s 3(2)(b). As to the issue of licences see s 7(2); and PARA 502. See *R v Secretary of State for the Home Department, ex p Arthur H Cox & Co Ltd* (1998) 46 BMLR 144 (refusal to grant licence for importation from more than one country justified). The Misuse of Drugs Act 1971 provides for an offence of contravening a term or condition of a licence (see PARA 504), and places the onus of proving that the defendant had a licence on the defendant. It would appear that he discharges this burden by proof on a balance of probabilities: *R v Ewens* [1967] 1 QB 322, [1966] 2 All ER 470, CCA. See also *Wood v Allan* 1988 SLT 341; *R v Oliver* [1944] KB 68, [1943] 2 All ER 800, CCA; and CRIMINAL PROCEDURE vol 28 (2010) PARA 469.

492. Restrictions on production and supply. The production and supply or offer to supply of a controlled drug is restricted[1] and it is generally an offence to produce, or to be concerned in the production by another, or supply or offer to supply, a controlled drug[2].

However: (1) any person who is lawfully in possession of a controlled drug may supply that drug to the person from whom he obtained it[3]; (2) any person who has in his possession a specified drug[4] which has been supplied by or on the prescription of a practitioner[5], a registered nurse[6], a pharmacist independent prescriber[7], a supplementary prescriber[8] or a specified person[9], acting in accordance with a patient group direction[10], for the treatment of that person, or of a person whom he represents, may supply that drug to any doctor, dentist or pharmacist for the purpose of destruction[11]; (3) any person who is lawfully in possession of a specified drug[12] which has been supplied by or on the prescription of a veterinary practitioner or veterinary surgeon[13] for the treatment of animals may supply that drug to any veterinary practitioner, veterinary surgeon or pharmacist for the purpose of destruction[14]; (4) any of the following persons, namely, a constable when acting in the course of his duty as such, a person engaged in the business of a carrier when acting in the course of that business, a person engaged in the business of a postal operator[15] when acting in the course of that business, an officer of customs and excise when acting in the course of his duty as such, a person engaged in the work of any laboratory to which the drug has been sent for forensic examination when acting in the course of his duty as a person so engaged, or a person engaged in conveying the drug to a person who may lawfully have that drug in his possession, may supply any controlled drug to any person who may lawfully have that drug in his possession[16].

1 See the Misuse of Drugs Act 1971 s 4(1); and CRIMINAL LAW vol 26 (2010) PARA 725.

2 See the Misuse of Drugs Act 1971 s 4(2), (3); and CRIMINAL LAW vol 26 (2010) PARA 725. As to the aggravation of an offence under s 4 see s 4A; and CRIMINAL LAW vol 26 (2010) PARA 725. As to the defence of lack of knowledge in relation to an offence under s 4(2), (3) see s 28; and CRIMINAL LAW vol 26 (2010) PARA 731.

3 Misuse of Drugs Regulations 2001, SI 2001/3998, reg 6(1).

4 Ie a drug specified under the Misuse of Drugs Regulations 2001, SI 2001/3998, Schs 2–5.

5 As to the meaning of 'practitioner' see PARA 487 note 9.

6 As to the meaning of 'registered nurse' see the Human Medicines Regulations 2012, SI 2012/1916; and PARA 48 note 3: definition applied by the Misuse of Drugs Regulations 2001, SI 2001/3998, reg 2(1) (amended by SI 2012/1916).

7 'Pharmacist independent prescriber' has the same meaning as in the Human Medicines Regulations 2012 (see PARA 50 note 4), and such a person may only prescribe controlled drugs in accordance with the Misuse of Drugs Regulations 2001, SI 2001/3998, reg 6B (see PARA 494): Misuse of Drugs Regulations 2001, SI 2001/3998, reg 2(1) (definition added by SI 2012/973 and amended by SI 2012/1916). As to the meaning of 'pharmacist' see the Human Medicines Regulations 2012, SI 2012/1916; and PARA 52 note 5; definition applied by the Misuse of Drugs Regulations 2001, SI 2001/3998, reg 2(1) (definition added by SI 2006/1450; and amended by SI 2012/1916).

8 As to the meaning of 'supplementary prescriber' see the Human Medicines Regulations 2012, SI 2012/1916, and PARA 50 note 5: Misuse of Drugs Regulations 2001, SI 2001/3998, reg 2(1) (definition added by SI 2005/271; and amended by SI 2012/1916). As to the meanings of 'registered midwife' and 'registered optometrist' see the Human Medicines Regulations 2012, SI 2012/1916; and PARAS 36 note 8, 48 note 3: Misuse of Drugs Regulations 2001, SI 2001/3998, reg 2(1) (amended by SI 2012/1916). 'Nurse independent prescriber' has the same meaning as in the Human Medicines Regulations 2012, SI 2012/1916 (see PARA 50 note 3), and such a person may only prescribe controlled drugs in accordance with the Misuse of Drugs Regulations 2001, SI 2001/3998, reg 6B (see PARA 494): reg 2(1) (definition added by SI 2006/986; amended by SI 2012/1916).

9 Ie a person specified in the Misuse of Drugs Regulations 2001, SI 2001/3998, Sch 8 (amended by SI 2003/2429; SI 2004/1771; SI 2006/1450; SI 2007/2154; SI 2012/973).

10 As to the meaning of 'Patient Group Direction' see the Human Medicines Regulations 2012, SI 2012/1916; and PARA 286 note 20: Misuse of Drugs Regulations 2001, SI 2001/3998, reg 2(1) (definition added by SI 2003/2429; amended by SI 2012/1916).

11 Misuse of Drugs Regulations 2001, SI 2001/3998, reg 6(2) (amended by SI 2003/2429; SI 2004/1771; SI 2005/271; SI 2012/973).

12 Ie a drug specified in the Misuse of Drugs Regulations 2001, SI 2001/3998, Schs 2–5.

13 As to the meanings of 'veterinary practitioner' and 'veterinary surgeon' see PARA 487 note 9.

14 Misuse of Drugs Regulations 2001, SI 2001/3998, reg 6(3).

15 Ie within the meaning of the Postal Services Act 2011 Pt 3: see POSTAL SERVICES.

16 Misuse of Drugs Regulations 2001, SI 2001/3998, reg 6(5), (7) (amended by SI 2003/1653; SI 2011/2085).

493.   Persons authorised to produce controlled drugs. Notwithstanding the general prohibition[1] on the production of controlled drugs[2], a practitioner[3] or pharmacist[4] acting in his capacity as such[5] and a person lawfully conducting a retail pharmacy business[6] and acting in his capacity as such and at the registered pharmacy[7] at which he carries on that business[8] may manufacture or compound any specified drug[9]; a person who is authorised by a written authority issued[10] by the Secretary of State[11] and for the time being in force may, at the premises specified in that authority and in compliance with any conditions so specified, produce any specified drug[12]; and a nurse independent prescriber[13] acting in her capacity as such, or a supplementary prescriber[14] acting under and in accordance with the terms of a clinical management plan[15] and any person acting in accordance with the written directions of a doctor, a dentist[16], a nurse independent prescriber, a pharmacist independent prescriber[17], or a supplementary prescriber acting under and in accordance with the terms of a clinical management plan[18] may compound any specified drug[19] the purposes of administration[20].

Where any person is authorised by a licence[21] of the Secretary of State for the time being in force to produce any controlled drug, it is not[22] unlawful for that person to produce that drug in accordance with the terms of the licence and in compliance with any conditions attached to the licence[23].

1   Ie under the Misuse of Drugs Act 1971 s 4(1)(a): see PARA 492.
2   As to the meaning of 'controlled drug' see PARA 481.
3   As to the meaning of 'practitioner' see PARA 487 note 9.
4   As to the meaning of 'pharmacist' see PARA 52 note 5; definition applied by the Misuse of Drugs Regulations 2001, SI 2001/3998, reg 2(1) (as amended by SI 2006/1450; and amended by SI 2012/1916).
5   Misuse of Drugs Regulations 2001, SI 2001/3998, regs 8(1)(a), 9(1)(a).
6   'Person lawfully conducting a retail pharmacy business' means a person lawfully conducting such a business in accordance with the Medicines Act 1968 s 69 (see MEDICAL PROFESSIONS vol 74 (2011) PARA 799): Misuse of Drugs Act 1971 s 37(1) (definition amended by the Statute Law (Repeals) Act 2004).
7   As to the meaning of 'registered pharmacy' see PARA 52 note 2; definition applied by the Misuse of Drugs Regulations 2001, SI 2001/3998, reg 2(1) (amended by SI 2012/1916).
8   Misuse of Drugs Regulations 2001, SI 2001/3998, regs 8(1)(b), 9(1)(b).
9   Misuse of Drugs Regulations 2001, SI 2001/3998, regs 8(1)(a), (b), 9(1)(a), (b). As to the specified drugs see Schs 2–5 (Sch 2 amended by SI 2003/1432; SI 2009/3136; SI 2011/448; the Misuse of Drugs Regulations 2001, SI 2001/3998 Sch 3 amended by SI 2007/2154; SI 2012/1311; the Misuse of Drugs Regulations 2011, SI 2011/3998 Sch 4 amended by SI 2003/1432; SI 2005/3372; SI 2009/3136).
10   Ie under and for the purposes of Misuse of Drugs Regulations 2001, SI 2001/3998, reg 9(1)(c).
11   As to the Secretary of State see PARA 2 note 1.
12   Misuse of Drugs Regulations 2001, SI 2001/3998, reg 9(1)(c). As to the specified drugs see Schs 3, 4 (Sch 4 amended by SI 2003/1432). Such a person may also supply or offer to supply certain controlled drugs: see PARA 494 head (g).
13   'Nurse independent prescriber' has the same meaning as in the Human Medicines Regulations 2012, SI 2012/1916 (see PARA 50 note 3), and such a person may only prescribe controlled drugs in accordance with the Misuse of Drugs Regulations 2001, SI 2001/3998, reg 6B (see PARA 494): reg 2(1) (definition added by SI 2006/986; amended by SI 2012/1916).
14   As to the meanings of 'supplementary prescriber' and 'registered nurse' see PARA 492 note 6.
15   Misuse of Drugs Regulations 2001, SI 2001/3998, regs 8(1)(c), 9(1)(d) (added by SI 2012/973). A 'clinical management plan' means a written plan (which may be amended from time to time) relating to the treatment of an individual patient agreed by (1) the patient to whom the plan relates, (2) the doctor or dentist who is a party to the plan, and (3) any supplementary prescriber who is to prescribe, give directions for administration or administer under the plan: Prescription Only Medicines (Human Use) Order 1997, SI 1997/1830, art 1(2) (definition added by SI 2003/696).
16   As to the meanings of 'doctor' and 'dentist' see PARA 48 note 6.
17   As to the meaning of 'pharmacist independent prescriber' see PARA 50 note 4.

18 Misuse of Drugs Regulations 2001, SI 2001/3998, regs 8(1)(d), 9(1)(e) (added by SI 2012/973).
19 Ie a drug specified in the Misuse of Drugs Regulations 2001, SI 2001/3998, Sch 2 or 5.
20 Misuse of Drugs Regulations 2001, SI 2001/3998, regs 8(1)(c), (d), 9(1)(d), (e) (as added: see note 8). The purposes of administration mentioned in the text are the purposes of administration in accordance with reg 7 (see PARA 494).
21 Ie issued under the Misuse of Drugs Regulations 2001, SI 2001/3998, reg 5.
22 Ie by virtue of the Misuse of Drugs Act 1971 s 4(1): see PARA 492.
23 Misuse of Drugs Regulations 2001, SI 2001/3998, reg 5. As to licences generally see PARA 488. As to the offence of contravening a term of a licence see the Misuse of Drugs Act 1971 s 18(2); and PARA 504.

494. Persons authorised to supply controlled drugs. Notwithstanding the general prohibition[1] on the supplying or offering for supply of controlled drugs[2] any of the following persons, namely:

(1)   a practitioner[3];
(2)   a pharmacist[4];
(3)   a person lawfully conducting a retail pharmacy business[5];
(4)   the person in charge or acting person in charge of a hospital or care home[6];
(5)   in the case of such a drug supplied by a person responsible for the dispensing and supply of medicines at the hospital or care home, the senior registered nurse or acting senior registered nurse for the time being in charge of a ward, theatre or other department in such a hospital or care home[7];
(6)   in the case of such a drug supplied to him by a person responsible for the dispensing and supply of medicines at a hospital, an operating department practitioner practising in that hospital[8];
(7)   a person who is in charge of a laboratory the recognised activities of which consist in, or include, the conduct of scientific education or research and which is attached to a university, university college or such a hospital or to any other institution approved for these purposes by the Secretary of State[9];
(8)   a public analyst[10];
(9)   a sampling officer[11];
(10)   a person employed or engaged in connection with a scheme for testing the quality or amount of the drugs, preparations and appliances supplied under the National Health Service Act 1977 and the regulations made thereunder[12];
(11)   a person authorised[13] by the General Pharmaceutical Council[14];
(12)   a supplementary prescriber acting under and in accordance with the terms of a clinical management plan[15],

may, when acting in his capacity as such, supply or offer to supply any specified drug[16] to any person who may lawfully have that drug in his possession[17].

There are also exceptions in respect of the supply or offer to supply of any specified drug to any person who may lawfully have that drug in his possession, in the case of: (a) a person who is authorised as a member of a group who acts under and in accordance with the terms of his group authority and in compliance with any conditions attached thereto[18]; (b) a person who is authorised by a written authority issued[19] by the Secretary of State, and for the time being in force, at the premises specified in that authority and in compliance with any conditions so specified[20]; (c) the owner of a ship, or the master of a ship which does not carry a doctor among the seamen employed in it, or the installation manager of an offshore installation[21]; (d) a nurse independent prescriber, when acting in her capacity as such, who may supply or offer to supply any specified controlled drug to any person who may lawfully have any of those drugs in his possession provided it is supplied or offered in circumstances where she may prescribe[22]; (e) a registered nurse[23]; (f) certain other health professionals[24]; (g) a person who is authorised[25] to produce controlled drugs, in respect of any drug which he may, by virtue of being so authorised, lawfully produce[26]; (h) a person in charge of a laboratory, when acting in his capacity as such, in respect of any specified drug which is required for use as a buffering agent in chemical analysis[27]; (i) a registered midwife[28]; (j) a pharmacist[29].

A nurse independent prescriber or a pharmacist independent prescriber may prescribe any specified controlled drug[30].

Where any person is authorised by a licence[31] of the Secretary of State, for the time being in force, to supply or offer to supply any controlled drug, it is not unlawful for that person to supply or offer to supply that drug in accordance with the terms of the licence and in compliance with any conditions attached to the licence[32].

1 Ie under the Misuse of Drugs Act 1971 s 4(1)(b): see PARA 492.
2 As to the meaning of 'controlled drug' see PARA 481.
3 Misuse of Drugs Regulations 2001, SI 2001/3998, regs 8(2)(a), 9(2)(a). As to the meaning of 'practitioner' see PARA 487 note 9.
4 Misuse of Drugs Regulations 2001, SI 2001/3998, regs 8(2)(b), 9(2)(b). As to the meaning of 'pharmacist' see PARA 52 note 5.
5 Misuse of Drugs Regulations 2001, SI 2001/3998, regs 8(2)(c), 9(2)(c). As to the meaning of 'a person lawfully conducting a retail pharmacy business' see PARA 493 note 6.
6 Misuse of Drugs Regulations 2001, SI 2001/3998, regs 8(2)(d), 9(3)(b) (both amended by SI 2007/2154). 'Care home', in relation to England and Wales, has the same meaning as in the Care Standards Act 2000 (see CHILDREN AND YOUNG PERSONS vol 10 (2012) PARA 994): Misuse of Drugs Regulations 2001, SI 2001/3998, reg 2(1) (definition added by SI 2007/2154). In relation to the Misuse of Drugs Regulations 2001, SI 2001/3998, reg 8(2)(d) the hospital or care home must be wholly or mainly maintained by a public authority out of public funds or by a charity or by voluntary subscriptions: reg 8(2)(d). Nothing in regs 8(2), 9(3) authorises the person in charge or acting person in charge of a hospital or care home, having a pharmacist responsible for the dispensing and supply of medicines, to supply or offer to supply any drug: regs 8(2)(i), 9(3)(i) (both amended by SI 2007/2154).
7 Misuse of Drugs Regulations 2001, SI 2001/3998, regs 8(2)(e), 9(3)(c) (both amended by SI 2007/2154). Nothing in the Misuse of Drugs Regulations 2001, SI 2001/3998, regs 8(2), 9(3) authorises a senior registered nurse or acting senior registered nurse for the time being in charge of a ward, theatre or other department to supply any drug otherwise than for administration to a patient in that ward, theatre or department in accordance with the directions of a doctor, dentist, supplementary prescriber acting under and in accordance with the terms of a clinical management plan or, subject to regs 8(2A), 9(3A) (as appropriate), a nurse independent prescriber or a pharmacist independent prescriber: regs 8(2)(ii), 9(3)(ii) (amended by SI 2007/2154; SI 2012/973). The directions given by a nurse independent prescriber or a pharmacist independent prescriber referred to in the Misuse of Drugs Regulations 2001, SI 2001/3998, regs 8(2)(ii), (iii), 9(3)(ii) and (iii) relate only to a controlled drug which such nurse independent prescriber or such pharmacist independent prescriber respectively may prescribe under reg 6B and a purpose for which it may be prescribed under that provision: regs 8(2A), 9(3A) (both added by SI 2007/2154; and substituted by SI 2012/2154). As to the meanings of 'doctor' and 'dentist' see PARA 48 note 6. As to the meaning of 'supplementary prescriber' see PARA 492 note 8. As to the meaning of 'clinical management plan' see PARA 493 note 15. 'Nurse independent prescriber' has the same meaning as in the Human Medicines Regulations 2012, SI 2012/1916 (see PARA 50 note 3), and such a person may only prescribe controlled drugs in accordance with the Misuse of Drugs Regulations 2001, SI 2001/3998, reg 6B (see PARA 494): reg 2(1) (definition added by SI 2006/986; amended by SI 2012/1916). As to the meaning of 'pharmacist independent prescriber' see PARA 492 note 7.
8 Misuse of Drugs Regulations 2001, SI 2001/3998, regs 8(2)(ea), 9(3)(d) (both added by SI 2007/2154). 'Operating department practitioner' means a person who is registered under the Health and Social Work Professions Order 2001, SI 2002/254 as an operating department

practitioner (see MEDICAL PROFESSIONS vol 74 (2011) PARA 907): Misuse of Drugs Regulations 2001, SI 2001/3998, reg 2(1) (definition added by SI 2007/2154; and amended by SI 2012/1479). Nothing in the Misuse of Drugs Regulations 2001, SI 2001/3998, regs 8(2) 9(3) authorises an operating department practitioner to supply any drug otherwise than for administration to a patient in a ward, theatre or other department in accordance with the directions of a doctor, dentist, supplementary prescriber acting under and in accordance with the terms of a clinical management plan or, subject to regs 8(2A), 9(3A) (see note 7), a nurse independent prescriber or a pharmacist independent prescriber: regs 8(2)(iii), 9(3(iii) (both added by SI 2007/2154; and amended by SI 2012/973).

9   See the Misuse of Drugs Regulations 2001, SI 2001/3998, regs 8(2)(f), 9(2)(d). In the case of reg 9(2)(d) it is not necessary that the laboratory be attached to a university, university college, hospital or any other institution: see reg 9(2)(d). As to the Secretary of State see PARA 2 note 1.

10   Misuse of Drugs Regulations 2001, SI 2001/3998, regs 8(2)(g), 9(2)(e). A public analyst is one appointed under the Food Safety Act 1990 s 27 (see FOOD vol 18(2) (Reissue) PARA 268): Misuse of Drugs Regulations 2001, SI 2001/3998, regs 8(2)(g), 9(2)(e).

11   Misuse of Drugs Regulations 2001, SI 2001/3998, regs 8(2)(h), 9(2)(f). A sampling officer is one within the meaning of the Medicines Act 1968 Sch 3 (see PARA 357): Misuse of Drugs Regulations 2001, SI 2001/3998, regs 8(2)(h), 9(2)(f).

12   Misuse of Drugs Regulations 2001, SI 2001/3998, regs 8(2)(i), 9(2)(g).

13   Ie for the purposes of the Medicines Act 1968 s 108: see PARA 354.

14   Misuse of Drugs Regulations 2001, SI 2001/3998, regs 8(2)(j), 9(2)(h) (both amended by SI 2010/231). As to the General Pharmaceutical Council see MEDICAL PROFESSIONS vol 74 (2011) PARA 785 et seq.

15   Misuse of Drugs Regulations 2001, SI 2001/3998, regs 8(2)(k), 9(2)(i) (both added by SI 2005/271). As to the meaning of 'supplementary prescriber' see PARA 492 note 8. As to the meaning of 'clinical management plan' see PARA 493 note 15.

16   In relation to the Misuse of Drugs Regulations 2001, SI 2001/3998, reg 8, the specified drugs are those set out in Sch 2 or 5 and, in relation to reg 9, the specified drugs are those set out in Sch 3 or 4: see reg 8(2), 9(2).

17   Misuse of Drugs Regulations 2001, SI 2001/3998, regs 8(2), 9(2).

18   See the Misuse of Drugs Regulations 2001, SI 2001/3998, regs 8(3), 9(3)(a).

19   Ie under and for the purposes of the Misuse of Drugs Regulations 2001, SI 2001/3998, regs 8(4), 9(4)(a).

20   Misuse of Drugs Regulations 2001, SI 2001/3998, reg 8(4), 9(4)(a). As to the specified drugs in the case of an authority under reg 8(4) see Sch 5; and as to the specified drugs in the case of an authority under reg 9(4)(a) see Schs 3, 4.

21   See the Misuse of Drugs Regulations 2001, SI 2001/3998, regs 8(5), 9(5) reg 9(5) amended by SI 2012/973). Certain conditions must be met for the supply to be lawful: see the Misuse of Drugs Regulations 2001, SI 2001/3998, regs 8(5), (6), 9(5). As to the specified drugs for the purposes of reg 8(5) see Schs 2, 5; and as to the specified drugs for the purposes of reg 9(5) see Schs 3, 4. 'Master' and 'seamen' have the same meanings as in the Merchant Shipping Act 1995 (see SHIPPING AND MARITIME LAW vol 93 (2008) PARA 424): Misuse of Drugs Regulations 2001, SI 2001/3998, reg 2(1). 'Installation manager' and 'offshore installation' have the same meanings as in the Mineral Workings (Offshore Installations) Act 1971 (see ENERGY AND CLIMATE CHANGE vol 44 (2011) PARA 1081): Misuse of Drugs Regulations 2001, SI 2001/3998, reg 2(1).

22   See the Misuse of Drugs Regulations 2001, SI 2001/3998, regs 8(7), 9(7) (both added by SI 2003/2429; and substituted by SI 2012/973). The specified controlled drugs mentioned in the text are those specified under the Misuse of Drugs Regulations 2001, SI 2001/3998, Sch 2 or 5 in respect of reg 8(7) and Sch 3 or 4 in respect of reg 9(7). The circumstances where the nurse independent prescriber may prescribe such drugs as mentioned in the text is where she may prescribe it under reg 6B. 'Nurse independent prescriber' has the same meaning as in the Prescription Only Medicines (Human Use) Order 1997, SI 1997/1830 (see PARA 50 note 3), and such a person may only prescribe controlled drugs in accordance with the Misuse of Drugs Regulations 2001, SI 2001/3998, reg 6B: reg 2(1) (definition added by SI 2006/986).

23   See the Misuse of Drugs Regulations 2001, SI 2001/3998, regs 8(8)(a), (b), 9(8) (both added by SI 2003/2429; and amended by SI 2012/973). 'Registered nurse' means a person registered in the Nurses' Part of the professional register: Prescription Only Medicines (Human Use) Order 1997, SI 1997/1830, art 1(2) (definition substituted by SI 2004/1771); Misuse of Drugs Regulations 2001, SI 2001/3998, reg 2(1). As to the drugs that the registered nurse may supply or offer to supply see regs 8(8), 9(8) (as so added and amended).

24 See the Misuse of Drugs Regulations 2001, SI 2001/3998, regs 8(8)(b), 9(8), Sch 8 (regs 8(8), 9(8) as added and amended (see note 23); and Sch 8 added by SI 2003/2429; and amended by SI 2004/1771; SI 2006/1450; SI 2007/2154; SI 2012/973).
25 Ie under the Misuse of Drugs Regulations 2001, SI 2001/3998, reg 9(1)(c): see PARA 493.
26 Misuse of Drugs Regulations 2001, SI 2001/3998, reg 9(4)(b).
27 Misuse of Drugs Regulations 2001, SI 2001/3998, reg 9(6), Sch 3.
28 See the Misuse of Drugs Regulations 2001, SI 2001/3998, reg 11 (amended by SI 2004/1771). 'Registered midwife' has the same meaning as in the Prescription Only Medicines (Human Use) Order 1997, SI 1997/1830: Misuse of Drugs Regulations 2001, SI 2001/3998, reg 2(1).
29 See the Misuse of Drugs Regulations 2001, SI 2001/3998, reg 8(8)(a) (amended by SI 2012/973). As to the drugs that the pharmacist may supply or offer to supply see regs 8(8).
30 Misuse of Drugs Regulations 2001, SI 2001/3998, reg 6B(1) (added by SI 2005/2864; and substituted by SI 2012/973). The specified controlled drugs mentioned in the text are those specified in the Misuse of Drugs Regulations 2001, SI 2001/3998, Schs 2–5. The supply of drugs by a nurse independent prescriber or a pharmacist independent prescriber is subject to an exception relating to persons the nurse independent prescriber or pharmacist independent prescriber suspects to be addicted to the drug: see reg 6B(2), (3) (as so added; and substituted). As to further provisions relating to the lawful administration of controlled drugs: see the Misuse of Drugs Regulations 2001, SI 2001/3998, reg 7 (amended by SI 2003/2429; SI 2005/271; SI 2012/973).
31 Ie issued under the Misuse of Drugs Regulations 2001, SI 2001/3998, reg 5.
32 Misuse of Drugs Regulations 2001, SI 2001/3998, reg 5. As to the offence of contravening a term of a licence see the Misuse of Drugs Act 1971 s 18(2); and PARA 260.

495.   Restrictions on possession. It is an offence for a person to have a controlled drug in his possession unlawfully[1]. It is also an offence for a person to have a controlled drug in his possession, whether lawfully or not, with intent to supply it to another[2].

1 See the Misuse of Drugs Act 1971 s 5(1), (2); and CRIMINAL LAW vol 26 (2010) PARA 723. Section 5(1), (2) do not apply in relation to a temporary class drug: s 5(2A) (added by the Police Reform and Social Responsibility Act 2011 Sch 17 para 6). Under certain circumstances Gamma-butyrolactone and 1,4-butanediol are excepted from the Misuse of Drugs Act 1971 s 5(1): see the Misuse of Drugs Regulations 2001, SI 2001/3998, reg 4B (added by SI 2009/3136; and substituted by SI 2011/448).
    The Misuse of Drugs Act 1971 5(1) does not have effect in relation to poppy-straw (see PARA 483 note 7) (Misuse of Drugs Regulations 2001, SI 2001/3998, reg 4(4)); and does not have effect in relation to any exempt product (reg 4(5)). 'Exempt product' means a preparation or other product consisting of one or more component parts, any of which contains a controlled drug, where: (1) the preparation or other product is not designed for administration of the controlled drug to a human being or animal; (2) the controlled drug in any component part is packaged in such a form, or in combination with other active or inert substances in such a manner, that it cannot be recovered by readily applicable means or in a yield which constitutes a risk to health; and (3) no one component part of the product or preparation contains more than one milligram of the controlled drug or one microgram in the case of lysergide or any other N -alkyl derivative of lysergamide: reg 2(1). The Misuse of Drugs Act 1971 s 5(1) does not have effect in relation to any drug specified in the Misuse of Drugs Regulations 2001, SI 2001/3998, Sch 4 Pt II (reg 4(3)(a) (amended by SI 2012/973)); and the drugs specified in the Misuse of Drugs Regulations 2001, SI 2001/3998, Sch 5 (reg 4(3)(b)). The Misuse of Drugs Act 1971 s 5(1) does not have effect in relation to a fungus (of any kind) which contains psilocin or an ester of psilocin where that fungus: (1) is growing uncultivated (Misuse of Drugs Regulations 2001, SI 2001/3998, reg 4A(1)(a) (reg 4A added by SI 2005/1653)); (2) is picked by a person already in lawful possession of it for the purpose of delivering it as soon as is reasonably practicable into the custody of a person lawfully entitled to take custody of it and it remains in that person's possession for and in accordance with that purpose (Misuse of Drugs Regulations 2001, SI 2001/3998, reg 4A(1)(b) (as so added)); (3) is picked for either of the specified purposes and is held for the purpose of destroying the fungus as soon as is reasonably practicable, either by the person who picked it or by another person (reg 4A(1)(c) (as so added)); or (4) is picked for the purpose of destroying the fungus as soon as is reasonably practicable and is held for the purpose of delivering the fungus as soon as is reasonably practicable into the custody of a person lawfully entitled to take custody of it, either by the person who picked it or by another person (reg 4A(1)(d) (as so added)). The specified purposes are: (a) the delivering of

the fungus as soon as is reasonably practicable into the custody of a person lawfully entitled to take custody of it (reg 4A(2)(a) (as so added)); and (b) the destroying of the fungus as soon as is reasonably practicable (reg 4A(2)(b) (as so added)).

2   See the Misuse of Drugs Act 1971 s 5(2); and CRIMINAL LAW vol 26 (2010) PARA 723. As to the defence of lack of knowledge in relation to an offence under s 5(3); see s 28; and CRIMINAL LAW vol 26 (2010) PARA 731.

496. Persons authorised to possess controlled drugs. Notwithstanding the general prohibition[1] on the possession of a controlled drug[2]:

(1)   various of the persons authorised to supply such drugs[3] may have in their possession any specified drug for the purpose of acting in their capacity as such a person[4];

(2)   a person may have in his possession any specified drug for administration for medical, dental or veterinary purposes in accordance with the directions of a practitioner[5], a supplementary prescriber acting under and in accordance with the terms of a clinical management plan[6], a nurse independent prescriber or a pharmacist independent prescriber[7];

(3)   a person who is authorised as a member of a group may, under and in accordance with the terms of his group authority and in compliance with any conditions attached to it, have any specified drug in his possession[8];

(4)   a person who is authorised by a written authority issued[9] by the Secretary of State[10] and for the time being in force, may, at the premises specified in that authority and in compliance with any conditions so specified, have in his possession any specified drug[11];

(5)   a person who is authorised[12] by the Secretary of State may have in his possession any drug which he may, by virtue of being so authorised, lawfully produce[13];

(6)   a person who is authorised[14] by the Secretary of State may have in his possession any drug which he may, by virtue of being so authorised, lawfully supply or offer to supply[15];

(7)   any person may have in his possession any specified drug for the purpose of compliance with any of certain[16] provisions[17];

(8)   the master of a foreign ship which is in a port in Great Britain[18] may have in his possession any specified drug so far as necessary for the equipment of the ship[19];

(9)   any person in respect of whom a licence has been granted which is in force under the Wildlife and Countryside Act 1981[20] may have in his possession any specified drug for the purposes for which that licence was granted[21].

Any of the following persons may also have any controlled drug in his possession[22]: a constable when acting in the course of his duty as such[23]; a person engaged in the business of a carrier when acting in the course of that business[24]; a person engaged in the business of a postal operator[25] when acting in the course of that business[26]; an officer of customs and excise when acting in the course of his duty as such[27]; a person engaged in the work of any laboratory to which the drug has been sent for forensic examination when acting in the course of his duty as a person so engaged[28]; and a person engaged in conveying the drug to a person who may lawfully have that drug in his possession[29].

Where any person is authorised by a licence[30] of the Secretary of State, for the time being in force, to have in his possession any controlled drug, it is not unlawful[31] for that person to have in his possession that drug in accordance with the terms of the licence and in compliance with any conditions attached to the licence[32].

1   Ie under the Misuse of Drugs Act 1971 s 5(1): see PARA 495.

2   The provisions of the Misuse of Drugs Regulations 2001, SI 2001/3998, reg 10 are without prejudice to the provisions of reg 4(3)(a) (see PARA 495 note 1): reg 10(6). As to the meaning of 'controlled drug' see PARA 481.

3   Ie under the Misuse of Drugs Regulations 2001, SI 2001/3998, regs 8, 9: see PARA 494.

4   Misuse of Drugs Regulations 2001, SI 2001/3998, reg 10(1). The persons concerned and the drugs specified are:

    (1)   a person specified in reg 8(2)(a)–(k) (see PARA 494) may have in his possession any drug specified in Sch 2 (Misuse of Drugs Regulations 2001, SI 2001/3998, reg 10(1)(a) (reg 10(1)(a), (b) amended by SI 2005/271));

    (2)   a person specified in the Misuse of Drugs Regulations 2001, SI 2001/3998, reg 9(2)(a)–(i) (see PARA 494) may have in his possession any drug specified in Sch 3, 4 (Misuse of Drugs Regulations 2001, SI 2001/3998, reg 10(1)(b) (as so amended));

    (3)   a person specified in reg 9(3)(b)–(d), (6) (see PARA 494) may have in his possession any drug specified in Sch 3 (reg 10(1)(c) (amended by SI 2007/2154));

    (4)   a person specified in reg 9(3)(b)–(d) (see PARA 494) may have in his possession any drug specified in Sch 4 Pt I which is contained in a medicinal product (reg 10(1)(d) (added by SI 2003/2429; and amended by SI 2007/2154));

    (5)   a person specified in the Misuse of Drugs Regulations 2001, SI 2001/3998, reg 8(7), reg 8(8)(a) (see PARA 494), reg 9(7), or reg 9(8) (see PARA 494) may have in his possession any drug specified in those provisions in accordance with the conditions specified therein (reg 10(1)(e) (added by SI 2003/2429; substituted by SI 2012/973),

except that nothing in these provisions authorises a person specified in the Misuse of Drugs Regulations 2001, SI 2001/3998, reg 8(2)(e) or (ea), reg 9(3)(c) or (d) or reg 9(6), to have in his possession any drug other than such a drug as is mentioned in the head above specifying him: reg 10(1) (amended by SI 2007/2154).

5   As to the meaning of 'practitioner' see PARA 487 note 9.

6   As to the meaning of 'supplementary prescriber' see PARA 492 note 8 and as to the meaning of 'clinical management plan' see PARA 493 note 15.

7   Misuse of Drugs Regulations 2001, SI 2001/3998, reg 10(2) (amended by SI 2003/2429; SI 2005/271; SI 2012/973). This provision is subject to certain conditions: see the Misuse of Drugs Regulations 2001, SI 2001/3998, reg 10(2) (as so amended). 'Nurse independent prescriber' has the same meaning as in the Human Medicines Regulations 2012, SI 2012/1916 (see PARA 50 note 3), and such a person may only prescribe controlled drugs in accordance with the Misuse of Drugs Regulations 2001, SI 2001/3998, reg 6B (see PARA 494): reg 2(1) (definition added by SI 2006/986; amended by SI 2012/1916). As to the meaning of 'pharmacist independent prescriber' see PARA 492 note 7. As to the drugs specified see the Misuse of Drugs Regulations 2001, SI 2001/3998, Schs 2, 3, 4 Pt I.

8   Misuse of Drugs Regulations 2001, SI 2001/3998, reg 10(3). As to the specified drugs see Schs 2, 3, 4 Pt I.

9   Ie under and for the purposes of the Misuse of Drugs Regulations 2001, SI 2001/3998, reg 10(4)(a).

10   As to the Secretary of State see PARA 2 note 1.

11   Misuse of Drugs Regulations 2001, SI 2001/3998, reg 10(4)(a). As to the specified drugs see Schs 3, 4.

12   Ie under the Misuse of Drugs Regulations 2001, SI 2001/3998, reg 9(1)(c): see PARA 494.

13   Misuse of Drugs Regulations 2001, SI 2001/3998, reg 10(4)(b).

14   Ie under the Misuse of Drugs Regulations 2001, SI 2001/3998, reg 9(4)(a): see PARA 494.

15   Misuse of Drugs Regulations 2001, SI 2001/3998, reg 10(4)(c).

16   As to the provisions see the Misuse of Drugs Regulations 2001, SI 2001/3998, reg 8(6).

17   Misuse of Drugs Regulations 2001, SI 2001/3998, reg 10(5)(a). As to the specified drugs see Schs 2, 3, 4 Pt I.

18   As to the meaning of 'Great Britain' see PARA 20 note 4.

19   Misuse of Drugs Regulations 2001, SI 2001/3998, reg 10(5)(b). As to the specified drugs see Schs 2, 3, 4 Pt I. As to the meaning of 'master' see the Merchant Shipping Act 1995; and SHIPPING AND MARITIME LAW vol 93 (2008) PARA 424.

20   Ie the Wildlife and Countryside Act 1981 s 16(1): see ANIMALS vol 2 (2008) PARA 1006.

21 Misuse of Drugs Regulations 2001, SI 2001/3998, reg 6(4). As to the specified drugs see Schs 2, 3.
22 Misuse of Drugs Regulations 2001, SI 2001/3998, reg 6(6).
23 Misuse of Drugs Regulations 2001, SI 2001/3998, reg 6(7)(a). See POLICE.
24 Misuse of Drugs Regulations 2001, SI 2001/3998, reg 6(7)(b). See CARRIAGE AND CARRIERS.
25 Ie within the meaning of the Postal Services Act 2011: see POSTAL SERVICES.
26 Misuse of Drugs Regulations 2001, SI 2001/3998, reg 6(7)(c) (amended by SI 2003/1653; SI 2011/2085).
27 Misuse of Drugs Regulations 2001, SI 2001/3998, reg 6(7)(d). See CUSTOMS AND EXCISE.
28 Misuse of Drugs Regulations 2001, SI 2001/3998, reg 6(7)(e).
29 Misuse of Drugs Regulations 2001, SI 2001/3998, reg 6(7)(f).
30 Ie issued under the Misuse of Drugs Regulations 2001, SI 2001/3998, reg 5.
31 Ie by virtue of the Misuse of Drugs Act 1971 s 5(1): see PARA 495.
32 Misuse of Drugs Regulations 2001, SI 2001/3998, reg 5. As to the offence of contravening a term of a licence see the Misuse of Drugs Act 1971 s 18(2); and PARA 504.

497. Cultivation of cannabis plants. Unless otherwise authorised by licence[1], it is an offence for a person[2] to cultivate any plant of the genus *Cannabis* or to incite another to commit such an offence[3].

1 Ie a licence issued under the Misuse of Drugs Regulations 2001, SI 2001/3998, reg 12.
2 As to the meaning of 'person' see PARA 45 note 2.
3 See the Misuse of Drugs Act 1971 s 6; and CRIMINAL LAW vol 26 (2010) PARA 717. As to the defence of lack of knowledge in relation to an offence under s 6(2) see s 28; and CRIMINAL LAW vol 26 (2010) PARA 731.

498. Offences by occupiers of premises. Unless otherwise authorised the occupier or manager of premises may commit certain offences if he knowingly permits or suffers certain drug related activities to take place on those premises[1].

1 See the Misuse of Drugs Act 1971 s 8; the Misuse of Drugs Regulations 2001, SI 2001/3998, reg 13; and CRIMINAL LAW vol 26 (2010) PARA 730.

499. Closure of premises. If a police officer not below the rank of superintendent has reasonable grounds for believing that premises[1] have been used in connection with the unlawful use, production or supply of a Class A controlled drug[2], and that the use of the premises is associated with the occurrence of disorder or serious nuisance to members of the public[3], he may authorise the issue of a closure notice in respect of premises[4]. If a closure notice has been issued, a constable must apply to a magistrates' court for the making of a closure order[5]. A closure order is an order that the premises in respect of which the order is made are to be closed to all persons for such period, not exceeding three months, as the court decides[6].

1 'Premises' includes any land or other place (whether enclosed or not) and any outbuildings which are, or are used as, part of the premises: Anti-Social Behaviour Act 2003 s 11(3).
2 See the Anti-Social Behaviour Act 2003 s 1(1)(a); and CRIMINAL LAW vol 26 (2010) PARA 735. As to the meanings of 'controlled drug' and 'Class A drug' see PARA 481; definitions applied by s 11(2).
3 Anti-Social Behaviour Act 2003 s 1(1)(b); and CRIMINAL LAW vol 26 (2010) PARA 735.
4 See the Anti-Social Behaviour Act 2003 s 1(2); and CRIMINAL LAW vol 26 (2010) PARA 735.
5 See the Anti-Social Behaviour Act 2003 s 2(1); and CRIMINAL LAW vol 26 (2010) PARA 735.
6 Anti-Social Behaviour Act 2003 s 2(4); and CRIMINAL LAW vol 26 (2010) PARA 735. As to closure orders generally see CRIMINAL LAW vol 26 (2010) PARA 735.

500. Offences relating to opium. Smoking or otherwise using prepared opium is an offence, as is frequenting a place used for the purpose of smoking opium[1]. There are also offences in relation to the possession of pipes or utensils in connection with the smoking or opium[2].

1   See the Misuse of Drugs Act 1971 s 9(a), (b); and CRIMINAL LAW vol 26 (2010) PARA 728. As to the defence of lack of knowledge in relation to an offence under s 49 see s 28; and CRIMINAL LAW vol 26 (2010) PARA 731.
2   See the Misuse of Drugs Act 1971 s 9(c); and CRIMINAL LAW vol 26 (2010) PARA 728.

501. Supply of articles for administration of controlled drugs. Supplying or offering to supply articles which may be used or adapted to be used in the administration by any person of a controlled drug to himself or another is an offence[1]. It is also for a person to supply or offer to supply any article which may be used to prepare a controlled drug for administration by any person to himself or another believing that the article is to be so used in circumstances where the administration is unlawful[2].

Notwithstanding these provisions, any of the following persons may, when acting in their capacity as such, supply or offer to supply specified articles[3]. The persons concerned are a practitioner[4], a pharmacist[5], a person employed or engaged in the lawful provision of drug treatment services[6], a supplementary prescriber[7] acting under and in accordance with the terms of a clinical management plan[8] and a nurse independent prescriber[9].

1   See the Misuse of Drugs Act 1971 s 9A(1); and CRIMINAL LAW vol 26 (2010) PARA 729. This does not apply to hypodermic needles: see s 9A(2); and CRIMINAL LAW vol 26 (2010) PARA 728.
2   See the Misuse of Drugs Act 1971 s 9A(3); and CRIMINAL LAW vol 26 (2010) PARA 729.
3   Misuse of Drugs Regulations 2001, SI 2001/3998, reg 6A(1) (reg 6A added by SI 2003/1653). The specified articles are: a swab; utensils for the preparation of a controlled drug; citric acid; a filter; ampoules of water for injection, but only when supplied or offered for supply in accordance with the Medicines Act 1968 and of any instrument which is in force thereunder; ascorbic acid: Misuse of Drugs Regulations 2001, SI 2001/3998, reg 6A(1)(a)–(f) (as so added; amended by SI 2005/2864).
4   Misuse of Drugs Regulations 2001, SI 2001/3998, reg 6A(2)(a) (as added: see note 8). As to the meaning of 'practitioner' see PARA 487 note 9.
5   Misuse of Drugs Regulations 2001, SI 2001/3998, reg 6A(2)(b) (as added: see note 8). As to the meaning of 'pharmacist' see PARA 52 note 5.
6   Misuse of Drugs Regulations 2001, SI 2001/3998, reg 6A(2)(c) (as added: see note 8).
7   As to the meaning of 'supplementary prescriber' see PARA 492 note 8.
8   Misuse of Drugs Regulations 2001, SI 2001/3998, reg 6A(2)(d) (reg 6A as added (see note 8); and reg 6A(2)(d) added by SI 2005/271). As to the meaning of 'clinical management plan' see PARA 493 note 15.
9   Misuse of Drugs Regulations 2001, SI 2001/3998, reg 6A(2)(e) (added by SI 2012/973). 'Nurse independent prescriber' has the same meaning as in the Human Medicines Regulations 2012, SI 2012/1916 (see PARA 50 note 3), and such a person may only prescribe controlled drugs in accordance with the Misuse of Drugs Regulations 2001, SI 2001/3998, reg 6B (see PARA 494): reg 2(1) (definition added by SI 2006/986; amended by SI 2012/1916).

502. Authorisation of activities otherwise unlawful. The Secretary of State[1] may by regulations[2] except such controlled drugs[3] specified in the regulations from any of the restrictions imposed by the Misuse of Drugs Act 1971 on their importation, exportation[4], production, supply[5] or possession[6], and make such other provision as he thinks fit for the purpose of making it lawful for persons[7] to produce, supply or possess any controlled drug or to cultivate cannabis[8]. In particular, such regulations may provide for the doing[9] of a thing to be lawful if done under and in accordance with the terms of a licence[10] or other authority issued by the Secretary of State and in compliance with any conditions attached to such licence or authority[11] or prescribed in the regulations[12].

The Secretary of State must so exercise his power to make regulations as to secure that it is not unlawful[13] for a doctor, dentist, veterinary practitioner or veterinary surgeon[14] acting in his capacity as such to prescribe, administer, manufacture, compound or supply a controlled drug, or for a pharmacist[15] or person lawfully conducting a retail pharmacy business[16] while acting in his capacity as such to manufacture, compound or supply a controlled drug[17], and that it is not unlawful[18] for any of those persons to have a controlled drug in his possession for the purpose of acting in that capacity[19].

The Secretary of State has additional powers if in the case of any controlled drug he is of the opinion that it is in the public interest for its production, supply and possession to be either wholly unlawful or unlawful except for purposes of research or other special purposes[20], or for it to be unlawful for practitioners[21], pharmacists and persons lawfully conducting retail pharmacy businesses to do in relation to that drug any of the things mentioned above[22] except under a licence or other authority issued by the Secretary of State[23]. In these circumstances he may by order[24] designate that drug as a drug to which this provision[25] applies[26].

1 As to the Secretary of State see PARA 2 note 1.
2 As to the making of regulations see PARA 486. As to the regulations that have been made see the Misuse of Drugs Regulations 2001, SI 2001/3998.
3 As to the meaning of 'controlled drug' see PARA 481. For the purposes of the Misuse of Drugs Act 1971 s 7 a reference to 'controlled drugs' does not include a reference to temporary class drugs (see instead s 7A; and PARA 503): s 7(10) (added by the Police Reform and Social Responsibility Act 2011 Sch 17 para 7).
4 As to restrictions on the importation and exportation of controlled drugs see the Misuse of Drugs Act 1971 s 3(1); and PARA 491.
5 As to restrictions on the production and supply of controlled drugs see the Misuse of Drugs Act 1971 s 4(1); and PARA 492. 'Produce', where the reference is to producing a controlled drug, means producing it by manufacture, cultivation or any other method, and 'production' has a corresponding meaning: s 37(1). As to the meaning of 'supplying' see PARA 519 note 9.
6 Misuse of Drugs Act 1971 s 7(1)(a). As to restrictions on the possession of controlled drugs see s 5(1); and PARA 495. The exceptions specified are general and are not restricted to possession for medical purposes: *R v Hunt* [1986] QB 125, [1986] 1 All ER 184, CA (conviction quashed on appeal: see [1987] AC 352, [1987] 1 All ER 1, HL).
7 As to the meaning of 'person' see PARA 45 note 2.
8 Misuse of Drugs Act 1971 s 7(1)(b). These acts would otherwise be unlawful under ss 4(1), 5(1), 6(1). As to restrictions on the cultivation of cannabis see s 6(1); and PARA 497. As to the meaning of 'cannabis' see PARA 484 note 5.
9 References to a person's 'doing' things include references to his having things in his possession: Misuse of Drugs Act 1971 s 7(8). As to the meaning of 'possession' see CRIMINAL LAW vol 26 (2010) PARA 724.
10 It is an offence to contravene a condition or other term of a licence or other authority granted under the Misuse of Drugs Act 1971: see s 18(2); and PARA 504. As to licences see PARA 488.
11 Misuse of Drugs Act 1971 s 7(2)(a). As to the power of the Secretary of State to modify or revoke a licence or authority see PARA 488.
12 Misuse of Drugs Act 1971 s 7(2)(b).
13 Ie under the Misuse of Drugs Act 1971 s 4(1): see PARA 492.
14 As to the meanings of 'doctor', 'dentist', 'veterinary practitioner' and 'veterinary surgeon' see PARA 487 note 9.
15 As to the meaning of 'pharmacist' see PARA 52 note 5.
16 As to the meaning of 'person lawfully conducting a retail pharmacy business' see PARA 493 note 6.
17 Misuse of Drugs Act 1971 s 7(3)(a).
18 Ie under the Misuse of Drugs Act 1971 s 5(1): see PARA 495.
19 Misuse of Drugs Act 1971 s 7(3)(b).
20 Misuse of Drugs Act 1971 s 7(4)(a).
21 As to the meaning of 'practitioner' see PARA 487 note 9.
22 Ie any of the things mentioned in the Misuse of Drugs Act 1971 s 7(3): see the text to notes 13–19.
23 Misuse of Drugs Act 1971 s 7(4)(b).
24 The Secretary of State may not make such an order except after consultation with or on the recommendation of the Advisory Council: Misuse of Drugs Act 1971 s 7(7). As to the meaning of 'the Advisory Council' see PARA 490. As to the order that has been made see the Misuse of

Drugs (Designation) Order 2001, SI 2001/3997 (amended by SI 2005/1652; SI 2009/3135; SI 2010/1143; SI 2010/1800; SI 2011/447; SI 2012/1310; SI 2013/177).

25   Ie the Misuse of Drugs Act 1971 s 7(4).

26   See the Misuse of Drugs Act 1971 s 7(4). Where such an order is in force designating any drug, s 7(3) (see the text and notes 13–19) does not apply to that drug: see s 7(4).

503.   Temporary class drug order: further provision. The following applies if a temporary class drug order[1] specifies a substance or product as a drug subject to temporary control[2].

The order may: (1) include provision for the exception of the drug from any of the restrictions imposed by the Misuse of Drugs Act 1971 on their importation, exportation[3], production and supply[4]; (2) make such other provision as the Secretary of State thinks fit for the purpose of making it lawful for persons to do things in respect of the drug which the restrictions relating to production and supply[5] it would otherwise be unlawful for them to do[6]; (3) provide for circumstances in which a person's possession of the drug is to be treated as excepted possession for the purposes of the Misuse of Drugs Act 1971[7]; and (4) include any provision in relation to the drug of a kind that could be made under certain regulations[8] if the drug were a Class A drug, a Class B drug or a Class C drug[9].

1   As to temporary class drug orders see PARA 482.

2   Misuse of Drugs Act 1971 s 7A(1) (s 7A added by the Police Reform and Social Responsibility Act 2011 Sch 17 para 8).

3   As to restrictions on the importation and exportation of controlled drugs see the Misuse of Drugs Act 1971 s 3(1); and PARA 491.

4   Misuse of Drugs Act 1971 s 7A(2)(a) (as added: see note 2). As to restrictions on the production and supply of drugs see s 4(1); and PARA 492. As to the meaning of 'produce' see PARA 502 note 5. As to the meaning 'supplying' see PARA 519 note 9. As to orders made see the Misuse of Drugs Act 1971 (Temporary Class Drug) Order 2012, SI 2012/980, made under s 7A(2), (3), (6).

5   Ie the restrictions under the Misuse of Drugs 1971 s 4(1) (see PARA 492).

6   Misuse of Drugs Act 1971 s 7A(2)(b) (as added: see note 2). Provision under head (2) in the text, may, in particular, provide for the doing of something to be lawful if it is done in circumstances mentioned in head (1) in the text, or in compliance with such conditions as may be prescribed by virtue of head (2) in the text: s 7A(4) (as so added).

7   Misuse of Drugs Act 1971 s 7A(2)(c) (as added: see note 2).

8   Ie regulations under the Misuse of Drugs Act 1971 s 10 (see PARA 505) or 22 (see PARA 487). However s 31(3) is ignored (see para MP243): see reg 7A(2)(d) (as added: see note 2).

9   Misuse of Drugs Act 1971 s 7A(2)(d) (as added: see note 2). Provision under s 7A(2) may take the form of applying, with or without modifications, any provision made in regulations under ss 7(1), 10 or s 22: s 7A(3) (as so added). Section 7(8) applies for the purposes of s 7A: s 7A(5) (as so added). Section 31(1) applies in relation to a temporary class drug order that contains provision made by virtue of s 7A as it applies to regulations under the Misuse of Drugs Act 1971: s 7A(6) (as so added).

504.   Miscellaneous offences. It is an offence for a person[1]: (1) to contravene[2] any regulations, other than the addiction regulations[3], made under the Misuse of Drugs Act 1971[4]; (2) to contravene a condition or other term of a licence[5] permitting the importation or exportation of a controlled drug[6] or of a licence or other authority issued under regulations made under the Act, other than a licence[7] issued under the addiction regulations[8]; (3) to give any information[9] which he knows to be false in a material particular or recklessly to give any information which is false in a material particular[10]; (4) for the purpose of obtaining, whether for himself or another, the issue or renewal of a licence or other authority under the Misuse of Drugs Act 1971 or under any regulations made under it, to make any statement or give any information which he knows to be false in a material particular or recklessly to give any information which is false in a material particular[11], or for that purpose to produce or otherwise make use of any book, record or other document which to his knowledge contains any statement or information which he knows to be false in a material particular[12]; (5) to incite another to commit an offence under the Act[13]; (6) in the United Kingdom[14] to assist in or induce the commission in any place outside the United Kingdom of an offence punishable under the provisions of a corresponding law in force in that place[15].

1   As to the meaning of 'person' see PARA 45 note 2.
2   'Contravention' includes failure to comply, and 'contravene' has a corresponding meaning: Misuse of Drugs Act 1971 s 37(1).
3   Ie regulations made in pursuance of the Misuse of Drugs Act 1971 s 10(2)(h) or (i): see PARA 505. As to the consequences of contravening such regulations see PARA 520. For this purpose, a reference in s 18(1) or (2) to regulations made in pursuance of s 10(2)(h) or (i) is a reference to any provision of a temporary class drug order which is made by virtue of s 7A(2)(d) (see PARA 503) and is of a corresponding description to regulations made in pursuance of s 10(2)(h) or (as the case may be) (i): s 18(6) (s 18(5), (6) added by the Police Reform and Social Responsibility Act 2011 Sch 17 para 13).
4   Misuse of Drugs Act 1971 s 18(1). A person committing an offence under s 18 is liable on summary conviction to imprisonment for a term not exceeding six months or to a fine not exceeding the prescribed sum or to both, or on conviction on indictment to imprisonment for a term not exceeding two years or to a fine or to both: s 25(1), (2), Sch 4 (amended by virtue of the Magistrates' Courts Act 1980 s 32(2)). As to the prescribed sum see SENTENCING AND DISPOSITION OF OFFENDERS vol 92 (2010) PARA 141. As to powers of entry, search and seizure see PARAS 523–527. As to the prosecution of offences in the magistrates' court see PARA 525. As to the powers of a court to order forfeiture of anything shown to relate to an offence see PARA 526.
5   Ie a licence issued under the Misuse of Drugs Act 1971 s 3: see PARA 491.
6   As to the meaning of 'controlled drug' see PARA 481. In the Misuse of Drugs Act 1971 s 18 (and in references in Sch 4 that refer to s 18), any reference to regulations made under the Misuse of Drugs Act 1971 is to be taken as including a reference to provision made in a temporary class drug order by virtue of s 7A (see PARA 503): s 18(5) (as added: see note 3).
7   Ie a licence issued under regulations made in pursuance of the Misuse of Drugs Act 1971 s 10(2)(i); and PARA 513.
8   Misuse of Drugs Act 1971 s 18(2). For the penalties see note 4.
9   Ie in purported compliance with any obligation to give information to which he is subject under or by virtue of regulations made under the Misuse of Drugs Act 1971: s 18(3).
10 Misuse of Drugs Act 1971 s 18(3). For the penalties see note 4.
11 Misuse of Drugs Act 1971 s 18(4)(a). For the penalties see note 4.
12 Misuse of Drugs Act 1971 s 18(4)(b). For the penalties see note 4.
13 See the Misuse of Drugs Act 1971 s 19; and CRIMINAL LAW.
14 As to the meaning of 'United Kingdom' see PARA 20 note 4.
15 See the Misuse of Drugs Act 1971 s 20; and CRIMINAL LAW vol 26 (2010) PARA 732.

(ii) Prevention of Misuse of Controlled Drugs

505.   Regulations for preventing misuse.   The Secretary of State[1] has power to make regulations[2] making such provision as appears to him necessary or expedient for preventing the misuse[3] of controlled drugs[4]. Such regulations may in particular make provision:

(1)   for requiring precautions to be taken for the safe custody of controlled drugs[5];

(2)   for requiring the documentation of transactions involving controlled drugs and the furnishing of copies of documents relating to such transactions to the prescribed authority[6];

(3)   for requiring the keeping of records and the furnishing of information[7];

(4)   for providing for the inspection of precautions taken or records kept[8];

(5)   as to packaging and labelling[9];

(6)   for regulating transport and providing for the destruction or disposal of drugs no longer required[10];

(7)   for regulating the issue and supply of prescriptions, and requiring persons issuing prescriptions to furnish information relating thereto[11];

(8)   for requiring a doctor[12] attending a person considered or suspected to be an addict to furnish particulars[13]; and

(9)   for prohibiting a doctor from administering and supplying[14] controlled drugs to addicts and from authorising the administration and supply of, and prescribing, such drugs for addicts except under licence[15].

1   As to the Secretary of State see PARA 2 note 1.
2   As to the making of regulations see PARA 486.
3   As to references to misusing a drug see PARA 490 note 3.
4   Misuse of Drugs Act 1971 s 10(1). In s 10 a reference to 'controlled drugs' does not include a reference to temporary class drugs (see instead s 7A: see PARA 503): s 10(3) (added by the Police Reform and Social Responsibility Act 2011 Sch 17 para 10). As to the meaning of 'controlled drug' see PARA 481. The following regulations have been made: the Misuse of Drugs (Safe Custody) Regulations 1973, SI 1973/798 (amended by SI 1974/1449; SI 1975/294; SI 1986/2332; SI 1999/1403; SI 2001/1149; SI 2007/2154; SI 2011/2085; SI 2011/2581); the Misuse of Drugs (Supply to Addicts) Regulations 1997, SI 1997/1001 (amended by SI 2005/2864; SI 2012/2394); and the Misuse of Drugs Regulations 2001, SI 2001/3998 (amended by SI 2003/1432; SI 2003/1653; SI 2003/2429; SI 2004/1031; SI 2004/1771; SI 2005/271; SI 2005/1653; SI 2005/3372; Commissioners for Revenue and Customs Act 2005 s 50(2), (7); SI 2006/986; SI 2006/1450; SI 2006/2178; SI 2007/2154; SI 2009/3136; SI 2010/231; SI 2010/1144; SI 2010/1799; SI 2011/448; SI 2011/2085; SI 2011/2581; SI 2012/973; SI 2012/1311; SI 2012/1479; SI 2012/1916).
5   Misuse of Drugs Act 1971 s 10(2)(a). See PARA 506. See also s 11; and PARA 507.
6   Misuse of Drugs Act 1971 s 10(2)(b). See PARA 508. 'Prescribed' means prescribed by regulations made by the Secretary of State under the Misuse of Drugs Act 1971: s 37(1).
7   Misuse of Drugs Act 1971 s 10(2)(c). See PARA 509. See also s 17; and PARA 510.
8   Misuse of Drugs Act 1971 s 10(2)(d). See PARA 509.
9   Misuse of Drugs Act 1971 s 10(2)(e). See PARA 511.
10 Misuse of Drugs Act 1971 s 10(2)(f). See PARA 506.
11 Misuse of Drugs Act 1971 s 10(2)(g). See PARA 512.
12 As to the meaning of 'doctor' see PARA 487 note 9.
13 Misuse of Drugs Act 1971 s 10(2)(h). See PARA 513.
14 As to the meaning 'supplying' see PARA 519 note 9.
15 Misuse of Drugs Act 1971 s 10(2)(i). See PARA 513.

506.   Custody of controlled drugs. The occupier and every person concerned in the management of certain premises[1] must ensure that all controlled drugs[2] on the premises are, so far as circumstances permit, kept in a locked safe, cabinet or room which is so constructed and maintained as to prevent unauthorised access to the drugs[3]. Structural requirements are prescribed for safes, cabinets and rooms used for keeping drugs in accordance with this rule[4]. Where any controlled drug is kept otherwise than in a locked safe, cabinet or room which is so constructed and maintained as to prevent unauthorised access to the drug, any person having possession of the drug must ensure that, so far as circumstances permit, it is kept in a locked receptacle[5] which can be opened only by him or by a person authorised by him[6].

Provision is made for the destruction of controlled drugs in certain circumstances in accordance with prescribed conditions[7].

1   The Misuse of Drugs (Safe Custody) Regulations 1973, SI 1973/798, reg 3 applies to those occupied by a retail dealer for the purposes of his business and a care home: reg 3(1) (substituted by SI 2007/2154). 'Care home' in relation to England and Wales, has the same meaning as in the Care Standards Act 2000 (see CHILDREN AND YOUNG PERSONS vol 10 (2012) PARA 994): Misuse

of Drugs (Safe Custody) Regulations 1973, SI 1973/798, reg 2(1) (definition added by SI 2007/2154). 'Retail dealer' means a person lawfully conducting a retail pharmacy business or a pharmacist engaged in supplying drugs to the public at a health centre: Misuse of Drugs (Safe Custody) Regulations 1973, SI 1973/798, reg 2(1). As to the meaning of 'retail pharmacy business' see PARA 52 note 12; as to the meaning of 'pharmacist' see PARA 52 note 5; and as to the meaning of 'health centre' see PARA 52 note 4 (definitions applied by reg 2(1)).

2   Ie other than those specified in the Misuse of Drugs (Safe Custody) Regulations 1973, SI 1973/798, Sch 1 (substituted by SI 1986/2332; and amended by SI 1999/1403; SI 2007/2154). As to the meaning of 'controlled drug' see PARA 481.

3   Misuse of Drugs (Safe Custody) Regulations 1973, SI 1973/798, reg 3(2). These requirements do not apply in certain cases where the controlled drug is for the time being under the direct personal supervision of: (1) in the case of premises occupied by a retail dealer, a pharmacist who is not prohibited from handling the drugs under the Misuse of Drugs Act 1971 s 12(2) (see PARA 519); or (2) in the other cases, the person in charge of the premises or a designated member of that person's staff: Misuse of Drugs (Safe Custody) Regulations 1973, SI 1973/798, reg 3(4).

4   Misuse of Drugs (Safe Custody) Regulations 1973, SI 1973/798, reg 3(3), Sch 2 (amended by SI 1975/294). An exception to these requirements is made in the case of a person lawfully conducting a retail pharmacy business who holds a current certificate issued by the chief officer of police for the police area in which the premises are situated: see the Misuse of Drugs (Safe Custody) Regulations 1973, SI 1973/798, regs 3(4), 4(1). The chief officer of police, on application by the occupier of premises, and after inspection of the premises and particularly of the room, cabinet or safe in which the controlled drugs are to be stored, may grant such a certificate with or without conditions: reg 4(2), (3). The certificate remains in force for one year: reg 4(6). Further inspection may be carried out while the certificate is in force, and the certificate may be cancelled for breach of a condition, change of circumstances, or refusal to admit a police officer to make an inspection: reg 4(4), (5).

5   In *Dhulipala Kameswara Rao v Wyles* [1949] 2 All ER 685, DC, it was held that a motor car was not a receptacle for the purpose of corresponding earlier regulations.

6   Misuse of Drugs (Safe Custody) Regulations 1973, SI 1973/798, reg 5(1). This requirement applies to any person other than: (1) a person to whom the drug has been supplied by or on the prescription of a practitioner for his own treatment or that of another person or an animal (reg 5(2)(a)); (2) a person engaged in the business of a carrier when acting in the course of that business (reg 5(2)(b)); (3) a person engaged in the business of a postal operator (within the meaning of the Postal Services Act 2011: see POSTAL SERVICES) when acting in the course of that business (reg 5(2)(c) (amended by SI 2001/1149; SI 2011/2085)). As to the meaning of 'practitioner' see PARA 487 note 9. As to carriers generally see CARRIAGE AND CARRIERS.

7   See the Misuse of Drugs Regulations 2001, SI 2001/3998, reg 27 (amended by SI 2007/2154).

507.   Notices directing special precautions for safe custody. The Secretary of State[1], by written[2] notice served[3] on the occupier of any premises on which controlled drugs[4] are or are proposed to be kept, may give directions as to the taking of precautions or further precautions for the safe custody of any controlled drugs of a description specified in the notice which are kept there[5]. It is an offence to contravene[6] such a direction[7].

1   As to the Secretary of State see PARA 2 note 1.
2   'Writing' includes typing, printing, lithography, photography and other modes of representing or reproducing words in a visible form; and expressions referring to writing are to be construed accordingly: Interpretation Act 1978 s 5, Sch 1.
3   As to the service of notices see PARA 489.
4   As to the meaning of 'controlled drug' see PARA 481.
5   Misuse of Drugs Act 1971 s 11(1).
6   As to the meaning of 'contravene' see PARA 504 note 2.
7   Misuse of Drugs Act 1971 s 11(2). The penalty on summary conviction is imprisonment for a term not exceeding six months or a fine not exceeding the prescribed sum or both, and on conviction on indictment is imprisonment for a term not exceeding two years or a fine or both: s 25(1), (2), Sch 4 (amended by virtue of the Magistrates' Courts Act 1980 s 32(2)). As to the prescribed sum see SENTENCING AND DISPOSITION OF OFFENDERS vol 92 (2010) PARA 141. The Misuse of Drugs Act 1971 s 11 is without prejudice to any requirement imposed by regulations made in pursuance of s 10(2)(a) (see PARA 505) or by provision made in a temporary class drug order by virtue of s 7A (see PARA 503) that is of a corresponding description to such regulations: s 11(1) (amended by the Police Reform and Social Responsibility Act 2011 Sch 17 para 11).

508. Documents to be obtained by supplier of controlled drugs. Where a person ('the supplier'), not being a practitioner[1], supplies a controlled drug[2] otherwise than on a prescription[3], he must not deliver the drug to a person who purports to be sent by or on behalf of the person to whom it is supplied ('the recipient[4]') and is not authorised[5] to have that drug in his possession[6], unless that person produces to the supplier a statement in writing signed by the recipient to the effect that he is empowered by the recipient to receive that drug on behalf of the recipient, and the supplier is reasonably satisfied that the document is a genuine document[7].

Where a supplier supplies a controlled drug, otherwise than on a prescription or by way of administration, to any of the specified persons[8], the supplier must not deliver the drug until he has obtained a requisition in writing[9] and unless he is reasonably satisfied that the signature is that of the person purporting to have signed the requisition and that that person is engaged in the profession or occupation specified in the requisition[10].

Where the person responsible for the dispensing and supply of medicines at any hospital or care home supplies a controlled drug to the senior registered nurse or acting senior registered nurse[11] for the time being in charge of any ward, theatre or other department in that hospital or care home ('the recipient'), he must obtain a requisition in writing, signed by the recipient, which specifies the total quantity of the drug to be supplied[12] and mark the requisition in such manner as to show that it has been complied with[13].

Nothing in these provisions has effect in relation to specified drugs[14] or any exempt product[15].

1   As to the meaning of 'practitioner' see PARA 487 note 9.
2   As to the meaning of 'controlled drug' see PARA 481.
3   'Prescription' means a prescription issued by a doctor for the medical treatment of a single individual, by a supplementary prescriber for the medical treatment of a single individual, by a nurse independent prescriber for the medical treatment of a single individual, by a pharmacist independent prescriber for the medical treatment of a single individual, by a dentist for the dental treatment of a single individual or by a veterinary surgeon or veterinary practitioner for the purposes of animal treatment: Misuse of Drugs Regulations 2001, SI 2001/3998, reg 2(1) (amended by SI 2003/2429; SI 2006/986; SI 2012/973). As to the meanings of 'doctor', 'dentist', veterinary surgeon' and 'veterinary practitioner' see PARA 487 note 9. As to the meaning of 'supplementary prescriber' see PARA 492 note 8. 'Nurse independent prescriber' has the same meaning as in the Human Medicines Regulations 2012, SI 2012/1916 (see PARA 50 note 3), and such a person may only prescribe controlled drugs in accordance with the Misuse of Drugs Regulations 2001, SI 2001/3998, reg 6B (see PARA 494): reg 2(1) (definition added by SI 2006/986; amended by SI 2012/1916). As to the meaning of 'pharmacist independent prescriber' see PARA 50 note 4.
4   Misuse of Drugs Regulations 2001, SI 2001/3998, reg 14(1)(a).
5   Ie by any provision of the Misuse of Drugs Regulations 2001, SI 2001/3998, other than the provisions of reg 6(6), (7)(f): see PARA 496.
6   Misuse of Drugs Regulations 2001, SI 2001/3998, reg 14(1)(b).
7   Misuse of Drugs Regulations 2001, SI 2001/3998, reg 14(1).
8   The specified persons are: a practitioner; the person in charge or acting person in charge of a hospital or nursing home; a person who is in charge of a laboratory; the owner of a ship, or the master of a ship which does not carry a doctor among the seamen employed in it; the master of a foreign ship in a port in Great Britain; the installation manager of an offshore installation; a supplementary prescriber; a nurse independent prescriber; and a pharmacist independent prescriber: Misuse of Drugs Regulations 2001, SI 2001/3998, reg 14(4)(a)–(g) (reg 14(4)(g) added by SI 2005/271; and the Misuse of Drugs Regulations 2001, SI 2001/3998 reg 14(4)(h), (i) added by SI 2012/973). As to the meanings of 'master', 'seamen', 'installation manager' and 'offshore installation' see PARA 494 note 21. As to the meaning of 'Great Britain' see PARA 20 note 4.
9   Misuse of Drugs Regulations 2001, SI 2001/3998, reg 14(2)(a) (amended by SI 2007/2154). The requisition must be signed by the person to whom the drug is supplied ('the recipient') (Misuse

of Drugs Regulations 2001, SI 2001/3998, reg 14(2)(a)(i)); state the name, address and profession or occupation of the recipient (reg 14(2)(a)(ii)); specify the purpose for which the drug supplied is required and the total quantity to be supplied (reg 14(2)(a)(iii)); and, where appropriate, satisfy additional requirements (reg 14(2)(a)(iv)). The additional requirements are that the requisition must, where furnished by the person in charge or acting person in charge of a hospital or care home, be signed by a doctor or dentist employed or engaged in that hospital or care home (reg 14(5)(a) (amended by SI 2007/2154)); and, where furnished by the master of a foreign ship, contain a statement, signed by the proper officer of the port health authority within whose jurisdiction the ship is, that the quantity of the drug to be supplied is the quantity necessary for the equipment of the ship (Misuse of Drugs Regulations 2001, SI 2001/3998, reg 14(5)(b)). As to port health authorities see ENVIRONMENTAL QUALITY AND PUBLIC HEALTH vol 45 (2010) PARAS 102, 103. Subject to reg 14(5B), on receipt of a requisition (other than a veterinary requisition) mentioned in reg 14(2), the supplier must mark on the requisition in ink or otherwise indelibly his name and address and send the requisition to the relevant National Health Service agency in accordance with arrangements specified by that agency: reg 14(5A) (reg 14(5A), (5B) added by SI 2007/2154). Misuse of Drugs Regulations 2001, SI 2001/3998, reg 14(5A) does not apply where the supplier is a wholesale dealer or a person responsible for the dispensing and supply of medicines at a hospital or care home: reg 14(5B) (as so added). For the purposes of reg 14 'veterinary requisition' means a requisition which states, in accordance with reg 14(2)(ii), that the recipient is a veterinary surgeon or veterinary practitioner: reg 14(8) (added by SI 2007/2154).

10 Misuse of Drugs Regulations 2001, SI 2001/3998, reg 14(2)(b). However, where the recipient is a practitioner and he represents that he urgently requires a controlled drug for the purpose of his profession, the supplier may, if he is reasonably satisfied that the recipient so requires the drug and is, by reason of some emergency, unable before delivery to furnish to the supplier a requisition in writing duly signed, deliver the drug to the recipient on an undertaking by the recipient to furnish such a requisition within the 24 hours next following: reg 14(2). A person who has given such an undertaking must deliver to the person by whom the controlled drug was supplied a signed requisition in accordance with the undertaking: reg 14(3).

11 As to the meaning of 'registered nurse' see PARA 492 note 6.

12 Misuse of Drugs Regulations 2001, SI 2001/3998, reg 14(6)(a) (amended by SI 2007/2154).

13 Misuse of Drugs Regulations 2001, SI 2001/3998, reg 14(6)(b). Any such requisition must be retained in the dispensary at which the drug was supplied and a copy of the requisition or a note of it must be retained or kept by the recipient: reg 14(6).

14 Ie (1) the drugs specified in the Misuse of Drugs Regulations 2001, SI 2001/3998, Schs 4 and 5 or poppy-straw (reg 14(7)(a)); (2) any drug specified in Sch 3 contained in or comprising a preparation which: (a) is required for use as a buffering agent in chemical analysis (reg 14(7)(b)(i)); (b) has present in it both a substance specified in Sch 3 para 1 or 2 and a salt of that substance (reg 14(7)(b)(ii)); and (c) is pre-mixed in a kit (reg 14(7)(b)(iii)). As to the meaning of 'poppy-straw' see PARA 483 note 7.

15 Misuse of Drugs Regulations 2001, SI 2001/3998, reg 14(7)(c). As to the meaning of 'exempt product' see PARA 495 note 1.

509. Registers and records. Every person authorised[1] to supply any specified drug[2] must keep a register[3] and must enter in it in chronological sequence in the form specified[4] particulars of every quantity of such a drug obtained by him and of every quantity of such a drug supplied, whether by way of administration or otherwise, by him whether to persons within or outside Great Britain[5]. In the case of a drug supplied[6] to him for the purpose of destruction, these provisions do not have effect in relation to a practitioner or pharmacist[7], a person licensed[8] to supply any drug (where the licence so directs)[9], or the senior registered nurse or acting senior registered nurse[10] for the time being in charge of a ward, theatre or other department in a hospital or care home[11]. Any person required to keep such a register must comply with the prescribed requirements[12]. All registers and books must be preserved for a period of two years from the date on which the last entry is made in them[13].

Every person who is authorised[14] to produce any specified drug[15] must make a record of each quantity of such a drug produced by him[16]; every person who is authorised by or under any provision of the Misuse of Drugs Act 1971 to import or export any specified drug[17] must make a record of each quantity of such a drug imported or exported by him[18]; and every person who is authorised[19] to supply any specified drug[20] must make a record of each quantity of such a drug imported or exported by him[21]. Every such record must be preserved for a period of two years from the date on which the record was made[22].

A producer of any specified drug[23] and a wholesale dealer[24] in any such drug must keep every invoice or other like record issued in respect of each quantity of such a drug obtained by him and in respect of each quantity of such a drug supplied by him[25]. A person who is authorised[26] to supply any specified drug[27] must keep every invoice or other like record issued in respect of each quantity of such a drug obtained by him and in respect of each quantity of such a drug supplied by him[28]; and a retail dealer[29] in any such drug, a person in charge or acting person in charge of a hospital or care home, and a person in charge of a laboratory, must keep every invoice or other like record issued in respect of each quantity of such a drug obtained by him and in respect of each quantity of such a drug supplied by him[30]. A retail dealer in specified drugs[31] must keep every invoice or other like record issued in respect of each quantity of such a drug obtained by him[32].

Every veterinary prescription on which a controlled drug is supplied[33], and every prescription[34] on which a specified controlled drug[35] is supplied, must be preserved for a period of two years from the date on which the last delivery under it was made[36].

Nothing in these provisions has effect in relation to any exempt product[37].

1 Ie by or under the Misuse of Drugs Regulations 2001, SI 2001/3998, regs 5, 8: see PARA 494.
2 Ie specified in the Misuse of Drugs Regulations 2001, SI 2001/3998, Schs 1, 2 (Sch 1 amended by SI 2005/1653; SI 2009/3136; SI 2010/1144; SI 2010/1799; SI 2011/448; SI 2012/1311; SI 2013/176; and the Misuse of Drugs Regulations 2001, SI 2001/3998, Sch 2 amended by SI 2003/1432; SI 2009/3136; SI 2011/448). Specific requirements apply in respect of drugs in the Misuse of Drugs Regulations 2001, SI 2001/3998, Sch 2 in particular circumstances: see reg 21.
3 He must use a separate register or separate part of the register for entries made in respect of each class of drugs, and each of the drugs specified in the Misuse of Drugs Regulations 2001, SI 2001/3998, Sch 1 paras 1, 3 and Sch 2 paras 1, 3 and 6 together with its salts and any preparation or other product containing it or any of its salts must be treated as a separate class, so however that any stereoisomeric form of a drug or its salts must be classed with that drug: reg 19(1)(b). Entries made in respect of drugs obtained and drugs supplied may be made on the same page or on separate pages in the register: reg 19(2) (substituted by SI 2007/2154). In the case of drugs specified in the Misuse of Drugs Regulations 2001, SI 2001/3998, Sch 2, where the drug was supplied on prescription, he must in addition enter into the register in the form specified in Sch 6 Pt II, whether the person who collected the drug was the patient, the patient's representative or a healthcare professional acting on behalf of the patient and if the person who collected the drug was a healthcare professional acting on behalf of the patient, that person's name and address or if the person who collected the drug was the patient or the patient's representative, whether evidence of identity was requested of that person, and whether evidence of identity was provided by the person collecting the drug: reg 19(1)(c) (added by SI 2006/1450). Subject to the Misuse of Drugs Regulations 2001, SI 2001/3998, reg 20(e), nothing in reg 19(1) prevents the use of a register to record additional information to that required or allowed under those provisions: reg 19(2A) (added by SI 2006/1450).
4 This is subject to the Misuse of Drugs Regulations 2001, SI 2001/3998, reg 19(1)(f), using the headings specified in reg 19(1)(d) and (e). As to the headings see reg 19(1)(d)–(f) (added by SI 2007/2154).
5 Misuse of Drugs Regulations 2001, SI 2001/3998, reg 19(1)(a). As to the meaning of 'Great Britain' see PARA 20 note 4.
6 Ie in pursuance of the Misuse of Drugs Regulations 2001, SI 2001/3998, reg 6(2), (3): see PARA 492.
7 Misuse of Drugs Regulations 2001, SI 2001/3998, reg 19(3)(a). As to the meaning of 'practitioner' see PARA 487 note 9. As to the meaning of 'pharmacist' see PARA 52 note 5.
8 Ie under the Misuse of Drugs Regulations 2001, SI 2001/3998, reg 5: see PARA 494.

9 Misuse of Drugs Regulations 2001, SI 2001/3998, reg 19(3)(b).

10 As to the meaning of 'registered nurse' see PARA 492 note 6.

11 Misuse of Drugs Regulations 2001, SI 2001/3998, reg 19(3)(c) (amended by SI 2007/2154).

12 See the Misuse of Drugs Regulations 2001, SI 2001/3998, reg 20 (amended by SI 2005/2864; SI 2006/1450; SI 2007/2154). As to the prescribed requirements see the Misuse of Drugs Regulations 2001, SI 2001/3998, reg 20(a)–(g) (as so amended).

13 Misuse of Drugs Regulations 2001, SI 2001/3998, reg 23(1).

14 Ie under the Misuse of Drugs Regulations 2001, SI 2001/3998, reg 5 or reg 9(1)(c): see PARA 494.

15 Ie specified in the Misuse of Drugs Regulations 2001, SI 2001/3998, Schs 3, 4.

16 Misuse of Drugs Regulations 2001, SI 2001/3998, reg 22(1).

17 Ie specified in the Misuse of Drugs Regulations 2001, SI 2001/3998, Sch 3.

18 Misuse of Drugs Regulations 2001, SI 2001/3998, reg 22(2). This provision does not have effect in relation to a person licensed under the Misuse of Drugs Act 1971 to import or export any drug where the licence so directs: Misuse of Drugs Regulations 2001, SI 2001/3998, reg 22(4). As to such licenses see PARA 491.

19 Ie under the Misuse of Drugs Regulations 2001, SI 2001/3998, reg 9(4): see PARA 494.

20 Ie specified in the Misuse of Drugs Regulations 2001, SI 2001/3998, Sch 4.

21 Misuse of Drugs Regulations 2001, SI 2001/3998, reg 22(3).

22 Misuse of Drugs Regulations 2001, SI 2001/3998, reg 23(2).

23 Ie specified in the Misuse of Drugs Regulations 2001, SI 2001/3998, Schs 3, 5.

24 'Wholesale dealer' means a person who carries on the business of selling drugs to persons who buy to sell again: Misuse of Drugs Regulations 2001. SI 2001/3998, reg 2(1).

25 Misuse of Drugs Regulations 2001, SI 2001/3998, reg 24(1). Every invoice or other record which is required by reg 24 to be kept in respect of a drug specified in Sch 3 must contain information sufficient to identify the date of the transaction and the person by whom or to whom the drug was supplied: reg 24(5). Every document kept in pursuance of reg 24 (other than a health prescription) must be preserved for a period of two years from the date on which it is issued, except that the keeping of a copy of the document made at any time during the said period of two years is treated for these purposes as if it were the keeping of the original document: reg 24(6). 'Health prescription' means a prescription issued by a doctor or a dentist under the National Health Service Act 1977: Misuse of Drugs Regulations 2001, SI 2001/3998, reg 2(1). As to the meaning of 'prescription' see PARA 508 note 3. As to the meanings of 'doctor' and 'dentist' see PARA 487 note 9.

26 Ie under the Misuse of Drugs Regulations 2001, SI 2001/3998, reg 9(4)(a): see PARA 494.

27 Ie specified in the Misuse of Drugs Regulations 2001, SI 2001/3998, Sch 3.

28 Misuse of Drugs Regulations 2001, SI 2001/3998, reg 24(2). See also note 25.

29 'Retail dealer' means a person lawfully conducting a retail pharmacy business or a pharmacist engaged in supplying drugs to the public at a health centre: Misuse of Drugs Regulations 2001, SI 2001/3998, reg 2(1). As to the meaning of 'person lawfully conducting a retail pharmacy business' see PARA 493 note 6.

30 Misuse of Drugs Regulations 2001, SI 2001/3998, reg 24(3) (amended by SI 2007/2154). See also note 25.

31 Ie specified in the Misuse of Drugs Regulations 2001, SI 2001/3998, Sch 5.

32 Misuse of Drugs Regulations 2001, SI 2001/3998, reg 24(4). See also note 25.

33 Ie on which a controlled drug is supplied in pursuance of the Misuse of Drugs Regulations 2001, SI 2001/3998. As to the meaning of 'controlled drug' see PARA 481.

34 This requirement does not apply to a health prescription: Misuse of Drugs Regulations 2001, SI 2001/3998, reg 23(3). Every prescription (other than a health prescription or a veterinary prescription) on which a controlled drug other than a drug specified in Sch 4 or 5 is supplied must be sent to the relevant National Health Service agency in accordance with arrangements specified by that agency: reg 23(4) (added by SI 2006/1450; and amended by SI 2006/2178; SI 2007/2154).

35 Ie a controlled drug specified under the Misuse of Drugs Regulations 2001, SI 2001/3998, Schs 4 or 5 is so supplied.

36 Misuse of Drugs Regulations 2001, SI 2001/3998, reg 23(3) (amended by SI 2006/2178; SI 2007/2154).

37 Misuse of Drugs Regulations 2001, SI 2001/3998, reg 25. As to the meaning of 'exempt product' see PARA 495 note 1.

510.   Information.   Certain persons[1] must, on demand made by the Secretary of State[2] or by any person authorised in writing by the Secretary of State in that behalf, furnish such particulars as may be requested in respect of the producing, obtaining or supplying by him of any controlled drug or in respect of any stock of such drugs in his possession[3]; for the purpose of confirming any such particulars, produce any stock of such drugs in his possession[4]; and produce any register, book or document required to be kept relating to any dealings in controlled drugs which is in his possession[5]. However, these provisions do not require the furnishing of personal records[6] which a person has acquired or created in the course of his profession or occupation and which he holds in confidence[7].

If it appears to the Secretary of State that there exists in any area in Great Britain[8] a social problem caused by the extensive misuse[9] of dangerous or otherwise harmful drugs in that area, he may by notice in writing served[10] on any doctor[11] or pharmacist[12] practising in or in the vicinity of that area, or on any person[13] carrying on a retail pharmacy business[14] at any premises situated in or in the vicinity of that area, require him to furnish information to the Secretary of State relating to the quantities in which and the number and frequency of the occasions on which the drugs specified in the notice have been prescribed, administered or supplied during the period specified in the notice[15]. Failure to comply with the requirements set out in such a notice without reasonable excuse is an offence[16]. It is also an offence if a person in purported compliance with any such requirement gives any information which he knows to be false in a material particular or if he recklessly gives any information which is false in a material particular[17].

1 The persons are: any person authorised by or under the Misuse of Drugs Regulations 2001, SI 2001/3998 to produce any controlled drug (reg 26(2)(a)); any person authorised by or under any provision of the Misuse of Drugs Act 1971 to import or export any controlled drug (Misuse of Drugs Regulations 2001, SI 2001/3998, reg 26(2)(b)); a wholesale dealer (reg 26(2)(c)); a retail dealer (reg 26(2)(d)); a practitioner (reg 26(2)(e)); the person in charge or acting person in charge of a hospital or care home (reg 26(2)(f) (amended by SI 2007/2154)); a person who is in charge of a laboratory (Misuse of Drugs Regulations 2001, SI 2001/3998, reg 26(2)(g)); a person who is authorised under reg 9(4)(a) (see PARA 494) to supply any controlled drug (reg 26(2)(h)); a supplementary prescriber (reg 26(2)(i) (added by SI 2005/271)); and a nurse independent prescriber (reg 26(2)(j) (added by SI 2012/973)). As to the meaning of 'controlled drug' see PARA 481. As to the meaning of 'wholesale dealer' see PARA 509 note 24; and as to the meaning of 'retail dealer' see PARA 509 note 29. As to the meaning of 'practitioner' see PARA 487 note 9. As to the meaning of 'supplementary prescriber' see PARA 492 note 8. 'Nurse independent prescriber' has the same meaning as in the Human Medicines Regulations 2012, SI 2012/1916 (see PARA 50 note 3), and such a person may only prescribe controlled drugs in accordance with the Misuse of Drugs Regulations 2001, SI 2001/3998, reg 6B (see PARA 494): reg 2(1) (definition added by SI 2006/986; amended by SI 2012/1916).

2 As to the Secretary of State see PARA 2 note 1.

3 Misuse of Drugs Regulations 2001, SI 2001/3998, reg 26(1)(a).

4 Misuse of Drugs Regulations 2001, SI 2001/3998, reg 26(1)(b).

5 Misuse of Drugs Regulations 2001, SI 2001/3998, reg 26(1)(c). As to the requirements relating to registers and records see PARA 509. For the purposes of reg 26(1)(c), the Secretary of State or any person authorised in writing by the Secretary of State in that behalf may request that a register which is kept in computerised form be produced by sending a copy of it, in computerised or other form, to the appropriate person: reg 26(1A) (added by SI 2005/2864).

6 'Personal records' means documentary and other records concerning an individual (whether living or dead) who can be identified from them and relating to his physical or mental health: Misuse of Drugs Regulations 2001, SI 2001/3998, reg 26(3).

7 Misuse of Drugs Regulations 2001, SI 2001/3998, reg 26(3).

8 As to the meaning of 'Great Britain' see PARA 20 note 4.

9 As to references to misusing a drug see PARA 490 note 3.

10 As to the service of notices see PARA 489.

11 As to the meaning of 'doctor' see PARA 487 note 9.

12 As to the meaning of 'pharmacist' see PARA 52 note 5.

13 As to the meaning of 'person' see PARA 45 note 2.

14 As to the meaning of 'retail pharmacy business' see PARA 52 note 12; definition applied by the Misuse of Drugs Act 1971 s 17(1).

15 Misuse of Drugs Act 1971 s 17(1). Such a notice may require the particulars requested to be furnished in a specified manner and within a specified period, and may require a pharmacist or person carrying on a retail pharmacy business to furnish the names and addresses of doctors on whose prescriptions any dangerous or otherwise harmful drugs to which the notice relates were supplied, but must not require any person to furnish particulars relating to the identity of any person for or to whom any such drug has been prescribed, administered or supplied: s 17(2).

16 Misuse of Drugs Act 1971 s 17(3). Proof of reasonable excuse lies on the accused: s 17(3). As to the standard of proof see CRIMINAL PROCEDURE vol 28 (2010) PARA 469. The penalty for this offence on summary conviction is a fine of level 3 on the standard scale: s 25(1), (2), Sch 4 (amended by virtue of the Criminal Justice Act 1982 s 46). As to the standard scale see SENTENCING AND DISPOSITION OF OFFENDERS vol 92 (2010) PARA 142.

17 Misuse of Drugs Act 1971 s 17(4). The penalty for this offence on summary conviction is imprisonment for a term not exceeding six months or a fine not exceeding the prescribed sum or both, and on conviction on indictment is imprisonment for a term not exceeding two years or a fine or both: Sch 4 (amended by virtue of the Magistrates' Courts Act 1980 s 32(2)). As to the prescribed sum see SENTENCING AND DISPOSITION OF OFFENDERS vol 92 (2010) PARA 141.

511. Marking of bottles or other containers. No person may supply a controlled drug[1] otherwise than in a bottle, package or other container which is plainly marked[2]. In the case of a controlled drug other than a preparation, it must be marked with the amount of the drug contained therein[3]. In the case of a controlled drug which is a preparation made up into tablets, capsules or other dosage units, it must be marked with the amount of each component, being a controlled drug, of the preparation in each dosage unit and the number of dosage units in the bottle, package or other container[4]; and in the case of one not so made up, it must be marked with the total amount of the preparation in the bottle, package or other container and the percentage of each of its components which is a controlled drug[5].

1 Nothing in the Misuse of Drugs Regulations 2001, SI 2001/3998, reg 18 has effect in relation to: (1) the drugs specified in Schs 4 and 5 or poppy-straw (reg 18(2)(a)); (2) any drug specified in Sch 3 contained in or comprising a preparation which is required for use as a buffering agent in chemical analysis, has present in it both a substance specified in Sch 3 para 1 or 2 and a salt of that substance, and is pre-mixed in a kit (reg 18(2)(b)); (3) any exempt product; (4) the supply of a controlled drug by or on the prescription of a practitioner, a supplementary prescriber, a nurse independent prescriber or a pharmacist independent prescriber (reg 18(2)(d) (substituted by SI 2012/973)); (5) the supply of a controlled drug for administration in a clinical trial or a medicinal test on animals (Misuse of Drugs Regulations 2001, SI 2001/3998, reg 18(2)(e) (added by SI 2005/271)). As to the meaning of 'poppy-straw' see PARA 483 note 7. As to the meaning of 'exempt product' see PARA 495 note 1. As to the meaning of 'controlled drug' see PARA 481. As to the meaning of 'prescription' see PARA 508 note 3. As to the meaning of 'practitioner' see PARA 487 note 9. As to the meaning of 'supplementary prescriber' see PARA 492 note 8. As to the meaning of 'clinical trial' see PARA 107. 'Nurse independent prescriber' has the same meaning as in the Human Medicines Regulations 2012, SI 2012/1916 (see PARA 50 note 3), and such a person may only prescribe controlled drugs in accordance with the Misuse of Drugs Regulations 2001, SI 2001/3998, reg 6B (see PARA 494): reg 2(1) (definition added by SI 2006/986; amended by SI 2012/1916). As to the meaning of 'pharmacist independent prescriber' see PARA 50 note 4.

2 Misuse of Drugs Regulations 2001, SI 2001/3998, reg 18(1).

3 Misuse of Drugs Regulations 2001, SI 2001/3998, reg 18(1)(a).

4 Misuse of Drugs Regulations 2001, SI 2001/3998, reg 18(1)(b)(i).

5 Misuse of Drugs Regulations 2001, SI 2001/3998, reg 18(1)(b)(ii).

512. Supply of controlled drugs on prescription. A person must not issue a prescription[1] containing a controlled drug[2] unless the prescription complies with the prescribed requirements[3]. A person must not supply a controlled drug[4] on a prescription: (1) unless the prescription complies with those requirements[5]; (2)

unless the address specified in the prescription as the address of the person issuing it is an address within the United Kingdom[6]; (3) unless he either is acquainted with the signature of the person by whom it purports to be issued and has no reason to suppose that it is not genuine, or has taken reasonably sufficient steps to satisfy himself that it is genuine[7]; (4) before the date specified in the prescription[8]; or (5) later than 13 weeks after the date specified in the prescription[9]. A person supplying on prescription a controlled drug[10] must, at the time of the supply, mark on the prescription the date on which the drug is supplied and, unless it is a veterinary prescription[11], must retain the prescription on the premises from which the drug was supplied[12].

A person who is asked to supply on prescription a specified controlled drug[13] must first ascertain whether the person collecting the drug is the patient, the patient's representative[14] or a healthcare professional[15] acting in his professional capacity on behalf of the patient and (a) where that person is the patient or the patient's representative he may request evidence of that person's identity and refuse to supply the drug if he is not satisfied as to the identity of that person[16]; and (b) where that person is a healthcare professional acting in his professional capacity on behalf of the patient, he must obtain that person's name and address, unless he is acquainted with that person, request evidence of that person's identity, but may supply the drug even if he is not satisfied as to the identity of that person[17].

Nothing in these provisions has effect in relation to a prescription issued for the purposes of a scheme for testing the quality or amount of the drugs, preparations and appliances supplied under the National Health Service Act 1977 and the regulations made thereunder or to any prescriptions issued for the purposes of the Medicines Act 1968 to a sampling officer[18].

1   As to the meaning of 'prescription' see PARA 508 note 3.
2   Ie other than a drug specified in the Misuse of Drugs Regulations 2001, SI 2001/3998, Sch 4 or Sch 5 or temazepam: Misuse of Drugs Regulations 2001, SI 2001/3998, reg 15(1). As to the meaning of 'controlled drug' see PARA 481.
3   Misuse of Drugs Regulations 2001, SI 2001/3998, reg 15(1). As to the prescribed requirements see reg 15(1), (3) (reg 15(1) amended by SI 2005/2864; SI 2006/1450; SI 2006/2178; Misuse of Drugs Regulations 2001, SI 2001/3998, reg 15(3) (amended by SI 2007/2154). A person must not issue a prescription other than a health prescription or a veterinary prescription containing temazepam unless it is written on a prescription form provided by a Primary Care Trust or equivalent body for the purposes of private prescribing and it specifies the prescriber identification number and the address of the person issuing it: Misuse of Drugs Regulations 2001, SI 2001/3998, reg 15(1A) (added by SI 2006/1450; and amended by SI 2006/2178). Nothing in the Misuse of Drugs Regulations 2001, SI 2001/3998, reg 15 prevents the issue of a prescription, other than a health prescription, which is not written on a prescription form provided by a Primary Care Trust or equivalent body for the purposes of private prescribing, containing a controlled drug other than a drug specified in Sch 4 or 5, where the person issuing the prescription believes on reasonable grounds that the drug will be supplied by a pharmacist in a hospital: reg 15(1B) (added by SI 2006/2154). As from 1 April 2013, Primary Care Trusts are abolished: see PARA 3 note 1.
4   Ie other than a drug specified in the Misuse of Drugs Regulations 2001, SI 2001/3998, Schs 4, 5. This is subject to reg 16(5) whereby a person must not supply a controlled drug specified in Sch 4 on a prescription later than 28 days after the appropriate date: reg 16(5) (reg 16(5)–(7) added by SI 2006/1450). 'Appropriate date' means later of the date on which it was signed by the person issuing it or the date indicated by him as being the date before which it must not be supplied: SI 2001/3998 reg 16(7) (as so added).
5   Misuse of Drugs Regulations 2001, SI 2001/3998, reg 16(1)(a). This is subject to reg 16(1A), (1C): see reg 16(1)(a) (amended by SI 2006/1450). A pharmacist may supply a controlled drug other than a drug specified in the Misuse of Drugs Regulations 2001, SI 2001/3998, Sch 4 or 5 or temazepam if the prescription contains minor typographical errors or spelling mistakes or if it does not comply with the provisions of reg 15 in the way specified in reg 16(1B), provided that:

(1) having exercised all due diligence, he is satisfied on reasonable grounds that the prescription is genuine; (2) having exercised all due diligence, he is satisfied on reasonable grounds that he is supplying the drug in accordance with the intention of the person issuing the prescription; (3) he amends the prescription in ink or otherwise indelibly to correct the minor typographical errors or spelling mistakes or so that the prescription complies with the requirements of regulation 15 as the case may be; and (4) he marks the prescription so that the amendment he has made under head (3) is attributable to him: reg 16(1A) (reg 16(1A), (1B) added by SI 2006/1450). The way specified in the Misuse of Drugs Regulations 2001, SI 2001/3998, reg 16(1A) is that, in relation to regulation 15(1)(f), the total quantity of the preparation or of the controlled drug or the number of dosage units as the case may be is specified in either words or figures but not both: reg 16(1B) (as so added). A pharmacist may supply a controlled drug other than a drug specified in Sch 4 or 5 on a prescription other than a health prescription in a hospital if it does not comply with regulation 15 in the ways specified in reg 16(1D): reg 16(1C) (reg 16(1C), (1D) (added by SI 2006/1450). The ways specified in reg 16(1C) are (a) the prescription is not written on a prescription form provided by a Primary Care Trust or equivalent body for the purposes of private prescribing; (b) the prescription does not specify the prescriber identification number of the person issuing it: reg 16(1D) (as so added).

6   Misuse of Drugs Regulations 2001, SI 2001/3998, reg 16(1)(b). As to the meaning of 'United Kingdom' see PARA 20 note 4.
7   Misuse of Drugs Regulations 2001, SI 2001/3998, reg 16(1)(c).
8   Misuse of Drugs Regulations 2001, SI 2001/3998, reg 16(1)(d).
9   Misuse of Drugs Regulations 2001, SI 2001/3998, reg 16(1)(e) (amended by SI 2003/1653). In the case of a prescription containing a controlled drug other than a drug specified in the Misuse of Drugs Regulations 2001, SI 2001/3998, Sch 4 or Sch 5, which contains a direction that specified instalments of the total amount may be supplied at stated intervals, the person supplying the drug must not do so otherwise than in accordance with that direction, and reg 16(1) has effect as if for the requirement contained in reg 16(1)(e) there were substituted a requirement that the occasion on which the first instalment is supplied must not be later than 28 days after the appropriate date: reg 16(4)(a) (amended by SI 2006/1450).
10 Ie other than a drug specified in the Misuse of Drugs Regulations 2001, SI 2001/3998, Schs 4, 5.
11 'Veterinary prescription' means a prescription issued by a veterinary surgeon or veterinary practitioner for the purposes of animal treatment: Misuse of Drugs Regulations 2001, SI 2001/3998 (definition added by SI 2006/2178).
12 Misuse of Drugs Regulations 2001, SI 2001/3998, reg 16(2). In the case of a prescription containing a controlled drug other than a drug specified in Sch 4 or Sch 5, which contains a direction that specified instalments of the total amount may be supplied at stated intervals, the person supplying the drug must not do so otherwise than in accordance with that direction, and reg 16(2) has effect as if for the words 'at the time of the supply' there were substituted the words 'on each occasion on which an instalment is supplied': reg 16(4)(b). Specific requirements apply in the case of the supplying temazepam on prescription: see reg 16(3). As to the general requirements relating to the retention of prescriptions and other records see PARA 509.
13 Ie a controlled drug specified in the Misuse of Drugs Regulations 2001, SI 2001/3998, Sch 2.
14 'Patient' means the person named in the prescription as the person to whom the drug is to be supplied, 'patient's representative' means a person sent by or on behalf of the patient (other than a healthcare representative acting in his professional capacity): Misuse of Drugs Regulations 2001, SI 2001/3998, reg 16(7) (s 16(7)–(9) added by SI 2006/1450).
15 'Healthcare professional' has the same meaning as in the National Health Service Act 1977: Misuse of Drugs Regulations 2001, SI 2001/3998, reg 16(7) (as added: see note 4).
16 Misuse of Drugs Regulations 2001, SI 2001/3998, reg 16(6)(a) (as added: see note 4).
17 Misuse of Drugs Regulations 2001, SI 2001/3998, reg 16(6)(b) (as added: see note 4).
18 Misuse of Drugs Regulations 2001, SI 2001/3998, reg 17. As to sampling officers see PARA 357.

513. Addiction regulations. A doctor[1] must not administer or supply to a person who he considers, or has reasonable grounds to suspect, is addicted[2] to any drug[3], or authorise the administration or supply to such a person of any specified substance[4], or prescribe for such a person any such substance, except for the purpose of treating organic disease or injury[5] or under and in accordance with the terms of a licence issued[6] by the appropriate authority[7]. However, these provisions do not apply to the administration or supply by a doctor of a specified substance[8] if the administration or supply is authorised by another doctor under and in accordance with the terms of such a licence issued to him[9].

These regulations[10] relating to the supply of drugs to addicts apply to servants and agents of the Crown[11].

1   As to the meaning of 'doctor' see PARA 487 note 9.

2   A person must be regarded as being addicted to a drug if, and only if, he has as a result of repeated administration become so dependent upon the drug that he has an overpowering desire for the administration of it to be continued: Misuse of Drugs (Supply to Addicts) Regulations 1997, SI 1997/1001, reg 2(2). As to the powers of a police officer to require a person in detention to submit to an assessment to establish whether that person is dependent upon or has a propensity to misuse a Class A drug see the Drugs Act 2005 Pt 3 (ss 9–19); and CRIMINAL LAW, EVIDENCE AND PROCEDURE vol 11(2) (2006 Reissue) PARA 1031 et seq.

3   'Drug' means a controlled drug specified in the Misuse of Drugs (Supply to Addicts) Regulations 1997, SI 1997/1001, Schedule: reg 2(1). As to the meaning of 'controlled drug' see PARA 481.

4   The specified substances are: (1) cocaine, its salts and any preparation or other product containing cocaine or its salts (Misuse of Drugs (Supply to Addicts) Regulations 1997, SI 1997/1001, reg 3(3)(a) (substituted by SI 2005/2864); (2) diamorphine, its salts and any preparation or other product containing diamorphine or its salts (Misuse of Drugs (Supply to Addicts) Regulations 1997, SI 1997/1001, reg 3(3)(b)); (3) dipipanone, its salts and any preparation or other product containing dipipanone or its salts (reg 3(3)(c)).

5   Misuse of Drugs (Supply to Addicts) Regulations 1997, SI 1997/1001, reg 3(1)(a).

6   Ie in pursuance of the Misuse of Drugs (Supply to Addicts) Regulations 1997, SI 1997/1001. Notwithstanding the revocation of the Misuse of Drugs (Notification of and Supply to Addicts) Regulations 1973, SI 1973/799, any licence issued by the Secretary of State in pursuance of those regulations before 1 May 1997 continues in force and is deemed to have been issued in pursuance of the Misuse of Drugs (Supply to Addicts) Regulations 1997, SI 1997/1001: reg 5(2). As to licences generally see PARA 488.

7   Misuse of Drugs (Supply to Addicts) Regulations 1997, SI 1997/1001, reg 3(1)(b). As to prohibitions in respect of practitioners contravening the addiction regulations see PARA 520. Any licence issued by the appropriate authority in pursuance of the Misuse of Drugs (Supply to Addicts) Regulations 1997, SI 1997/1001 may permit a doctor to administer, supply or prescribe a drug, or to authorise the administration or supply of a drug, only while at an address specified in that licence: reg 3(1A) (added by SI 2012/2394).

8   See note 4.

9   Misuse of Drugs (Supply to Addicts) Regulations 1997, SI 1997/1001, reg 3(2).

10   Ie the Misuse of Drugs (Supply to Addicts) Regulations 1997, SI 1997/1001, and, in relation only to the requirements of such regulations, the Misuse of Drugs Act 1971 s 13(1), (3) (see PARA 520), ss 14, 16 (see PARA 521), ss 19, 25, Sch 4 (see PARA 519), which relate to their enforcement.

11   Misuse of Drugs (Supply to Addicts) Regulations 1997, SI 1997/1001, reg 4.

(iii) Supervising of Management and Use of Controlled Drugs

514. Accountable officers and their responsibilities as to controlled drugs. The relevant authority[1] may by regulations make provision for or in connection with requiring designated bodies[2] to nominate or appoint persons who are to have prescribed responsibilities in relation to the safe, appropriate and effective management and use of controlled drugs[3] in connection with (1) activities carried on by or on behalf of the designated bodies; and (2) activities carried on by or on behalf of bodies or persons providing services under arrangements made with the designated bodies[4]. The person who is to be so nominated or appointed by a designated body is to be known as its accountable officer[5]. The descriptions of bodies, or bodies, that may be so prescribed are descriptions of bodies, or bodies, appearing to the relevant authority (a) to be directly or indirectly concerned with the provision of health care[6] (whether or not for the purposes of the health service[7]), or (b) to be otherwise carrying on activities that involve, or may involve, the supply or administration of controlled drugs[8].

Regulations under these provisions may make provision (i) for conditions that must be satisfied in relation to a person if he is to be nominated or appointed by a designated body as the body's accountable officer; (ii) for a single person to be nominated or appointed as the accountable officer for each of two or more designated bodies where those bodies are satisfied as to the prescribed matters; (iii) requiring a designated body that has an accountable officer to provide the officer with funds and other resources necessary for enabling the officer to discharge his responsibilities as accountable officer for the body; (iv) for ensuring that an accountable officer, in discharging his responsibilities, has regard to best practice in relation to the use of controlled drugs; (v) for the persons required to be nominated or appointed[9] to be known by such name as is prescribed; (vi) for making such amendments of any enactment[10] as appear to the relevant authority to be required in connection with any provision made in pursuance of head (v) above; (vii) for creating offences punishable on summary conviction by a fine not exceeding level 5 on the standard scale[11] or for creating other procedures for enforcing any provisions of the regulations[12].

The responsibilities that may be imposed on a designated body's accountable officer by regulations under these provisions include responsibilities as to the establishment and operation of arrangements for (A) securing the safe management and use of controlled drugs; (B) monitoring and auditing the management and use of such drugs; (C) ensuring that relevant individuals receive appropriate training and that their training needs are regularly reviewed; (D) monitoring and assessing the performance of such individuals in connection with the management or use of such drugs; (E) making periodic inspections of premises used in connection with the management or use of such drugs; (F) recording, assessing and investigating concerns expressed about incidents that may have involved improper management or use of such drugs; (G) ensuring that appropriate action is taken for the purpose of protecting patients or members of the public in cases where such concerns appear to be well-founded; (H) where required by regulations[13] the sharing of information[14]. A designated body may confer on its accountable officer such powers as it thinks appropriate to enable him to discharge any of the responsibilities imposed on him as accountable officer for the body by regulations under the above provisions[15].

1   In the Health Act 2006 Pt 3 Ch 1 (ss 17–25) 'relevant authority' is to be read in accordance with s 24: s 25(1). The following provisions apply to functions conferred on the relevant authority by Chapter 1 of Part 3 of the Health Act 2006: s 24(1). Any functions to which these provisions apply are exercisable in relation to England by the Secretary of State: s 24(2). Any functions to which these provisions apply are exercisable in relation to Wales by the Welsh Ministers: s 24(3). Any power of the relevant authority to make regulations under Chapter 1 of Part 3 of the Health Act 2006 is exercisable in relation to cross-border bodies by the Secretary of State after consultation with the Welsh Ministers: s 24(3). A 'cross-border body' is a body which (1) performs (and only performs) functions in respect of England and Wales, and (2) does not perform functions mainly in respect of England or mainly in respect of Wales: s 24(5).

2   In the Health Act 2006 Pt 3 Ch 1 'designated body' means (1) a body falling within any description of bodies prescribed as designated bodies for the purposes of s 17, or (2) a body prescribed as a designated body for those purposes: s 17(3). 'Body' includes an unincorporated association: s 25(1). In s 17 'prescribed' means prescribed by regulations under s 17: s 17(11).

3   In the Health Act 2006 Pt 3 Ch 1 'controlled drug' has the meaning given by the Misuse of Drugs Act 1971 s 2 (see PARA 481): Health Act 2006 s 25(1). Any reference to the management or use of controlled drugs includes (1) the storage, carriage and safe custody of such drugs, (2) the prescribing and supply of such drugs, (3) the administration of such drugs, (4) the recovery of such drugs when no longer needed, and (5) the disposal of such drugs: s 25(2).

4   Health Act 2006 s 17(1). See the Controlled Drugs (Supervision of Management and Use) Regulations 2013, SI 2013/373 (as from 1 April 2013); and the Controlled Drugs (Supervision of Management and Use) (Wales) Regulations 2008, SI 2008/3239 (amended by SI 2009/1824, SI 2010/231, SI 2011/1011). As to regulations under the Health Act 2006 generally see s 79. See further note 14.

5   Health Act 2006 s 17(2). This is subject to any regulations made by virtue of s 17(5)(e) (see head
    (v) in the text): s 17(2).
6   In the Health Act 2006 Pt 3 Ch 1 'health care' means (1) services provided to individuals for or
    in connection with the prevention, diagnosis or treatment of illness, and (2) the promotion and
    protection of public health: s 25(1). 'Illness' in relation to England and Wales has the meaning
    given by the National Health Service Act 2006 s 275: Health Act 2006 s 25(1) (amended by the
    National Health Service (Consequential Provisions) Act 2006 Sch 1 para 282(b)).
7   In the Health Act 2006 'the health service', in relation to England and Wales, has the same
    meaning as in the National Health Service Act 2006: Health Act 2006 s 82(1) (amended by the
    National Health Service (Consequential Provisions) Act 2006 Sch 1 para 290(c)).
8   Health Act 2006 s 17(4).
9   As mentioned in the Health Act 2006 s 17(1).
10 In the Health Act 2006 'enactment' includes any provision of subordinate legislation (within the
    meaning of the Interpretation Act 1978), and references to enactments include enactments
    passed or made after the passing of the Health Act 2006 (ie 19 July 2006): s 82(2). Section 82(2)
    applies except where the context otherwise requires: s 82(3).
11 As to the standard scale see SENTENCING AND DISPOSITION OF OFFENDERS vol 92 (2010)
    PARA 142.
12 Health Act 2006 s 17(5). See further note 14.
13 Ie under the Health Act 2006 s 18 (see PARA 515).
14 Health Act 2006 s 17(6). The arrangements mentioned in s 17(6) may be arrangements
    established (according to the circumstances) (1) by the accountable officer, (2) by the designated
    body (or any of the designated bodies) for which he is the accountable officer, or (3) by a body
    or person acting on behalf of, or providing services under arrangements made with, the
    designated body (or any of the designated bodies): s 17(7). In s 17(6) (a) references to the
    management or use of controlled drugs are to the management or use of drugs in connection
    with activities carried on by a body or person within head (2) or (3), and (b) 'relevant individual'
    means an individual who, whether as (i) a health care professional, or (ii) an employee who is
    not a health care professional, or (iii) otherwise, is engaged in any activity carried on by a body
    or person within head (2) or (3) that involves, or may involve, the management or use of
    controlled drugs: s 17(8). 'Health care professional', in relation to England and Wales, has the
    meaning given by the National Health Service Act 2006 s 91(2)(a): Health Act 2006 s 25(1)
    (amended by the National Health Service (Consequential Provisions) Act 2006 Sch 1
    para 282(a)).
       Nothing in the Health Act 2006 s 17(5)–(7) is to be read as prejudicing the generality of
    s 17(1): s 17(10).
15 Health Act 2006 s 17(9).

515.   Co-operation between health bodies and other organisations. The
relevant authority[1] may by regulations make provision for or in connection with
requiring responsible bodies[2] to co-operate with each other in connection with
(1) the identification of cases in which action may need to be taken in respect of
matters arising in relation to the management or use of controlled drugs by
relevant persons[3]; (2) the consideration of issues relating to the taking of action
in respect of such matters; (3) the taking of action in respect of such matters[4].
Regulations under these provisions may make provision (a) for requiring a
responsible body to disclose information to any other such body or bodies in
prescribed circumstances, or in circumstances where it appears to the responsible
body that the prescribed conditions are satisfied, whether or not the disclosure of
information has been requested; (b) in relation to a responsible body which has
an accountable officer[5], for requiring disclosures to be made by or to that officer
instead of by or to the body; (c) in relation to a responsible body which is a
police force, for imposing duties on the chief officer[6]; (d) for requiring a
responsible body, in prescribed circumstances, to consult the prescribed
accountable officer in connection with any requirement imposed on the body
under the regulations; (e) for imposing duties on accountable officers in relation
to the taking of action for the purpose of protecting the safety of patients or the
general public[7].

1 In the Health Act 2006 Pt 3 Ch 1 (ss 17–25) 'relevant authority' is to be read in accordance with s 24: s 25(1).

2 In the Health Act 2006 Pt 3 Ch 1 'responsible body' means (1) a body falling within any description of bodies prescribed as responsible bodies for the purposes of s 18, or (2) a body prescribed as a responsible body for those purposes: s 18(2). As to the meaning of 'body' see PARA 514 note 2. In s 18 'prescribed' means prescribed by regulations under s 18: s 18(9)(c). The descriptions of bodies, or bodies, that may be so prescribed are (a) descriptions of bodies, or bodies, which fall within s 18(4); and (b) police forces: s 18(3). Descriptions of bodies, or bodies, fall within s 18(4) if they appear to the relevant authority (i) to be directly or indirectly concerned with the provision of health care (whether or not for the purposes of the health service), (ii) to be otherwise carrying on activities that involve, or may involve, the supply or administration of controlled drugs, (iii) to have powers of inspection in relation to the management or use of controlled drugs, (iv) to be public or local authorities with responsibilities in relation to social care, or (v) to be public or local authorities (not within heads (i)–(iv)) whose responsibilities include responsibilities with respect to matters such as are mentioned in s 18(1): s 18(4). As to the meaning of 'health care' and 'health service' see PARA 514. As to the meaning of 'controlled drug' and 'management or use of controlled drugs' see PARA 514. In s 18 'police force' means a police force in England or Wales: s 18(9)(b).

3 In the Health Act 2006 s 18 'relevant person' means (1) a person falling within any description of persons prescribed as relevant persons for the purposes of s 18, or (2) an individual to whom s 19(3) applies: s 19(1). In s 19 'prescribed' means prescribed by regulations under s 18: s 19(4). The descriptions of persons that may be prescribed for the purposes of s 18 are descriptions of persons appearing to the relevant authority to be carrying on, or engaged in, activities that involve, or may involve, the supply or administration of controlled drugs: s 19(2). Section 19(3) applies to an individual who, whether as (a) a health care professional, or (b) an employee who is not a health care professional, or (c) otherwise, is engaged in any activity carried on by a designated body, or by a body or person acting on behalf of, or providing services under arrangements made with, a designated body that involves, or may involve, the management or use of controlled drugs: s 19(3). As to the meaning of 'health care professional' and 'designated body' see PARA 514.

4 Health Act 2006 s 18(1). See the Controlled Drugs (Supervision of Management and Use) Regulations 2013, SI 2013/373 (as from 1 April 2013); and the Controlled Drugs (Supervision of Management and Use) (Wales) Regulations 2008, SI 2008/3239 (amended by SI 2009/1824, SI 2010/231, SI 2011/1011). As to regulations under the Health Act 2006 generally see s 79. See further note 7.

5 In the Health Act 2006 Pt 3 Chapter 1 'accountable officer' is to be read in accordance with s 17(2) (see PARA 514): s 25(1).

6 In the Health Act 2006 s 18 'chief officer' means, in relation to a police force in England and Wales, the chief officer of police: s 18(9)(a).

7 Health Act 2006 s 18(5). The duties that may be imposed on an accountable officer in pursuance of head (e) in the text include a duty to make recommendations to a responsible body as to any action which the officer considers that the body should take for the purpose mentioned in that head: s 18(6). The action that may be so recommended includes action in relation to the institution of disciplinary proceedings: s 18(7).

Nothing in s 18(5)–(7) is to be read as prejudicing the generality of s 18(1): s 18(8).

516. Controlled drugs: power to enter and inspect. A constable or an authorised person[1] may, for the purpose of securing the safe, appropriate and effective management and use of controlled drugs[2] (1) enter any relevant premises[3]; (2) inspect any precautions taken on the premises for the safe custody of controlled drugs; (3) inspect any stocks of controlled drugs kept on the premises; (4) require any relevant records[4] kept on the premises to be produced for his inspection[5].

1 In the Health Act 2006 s 20 'authorised person' means (subject to s 20(6)) (1) a person authorised by the relevant authority, (2) an accountable officer, or (3) where a designated body is required by regulations under s 17 (see PARA 514) to nominate or appoint an accountable officer, a member of the staff of the designated body authorised by it: s 20(5). As to the meaning of 'accountable officer' and 'designated body' see PARA 514. Authorisations given under s 20(5) may be general or specific: s 20(5).

The accountable officer of a designated body specified, or of a description specified, in directions given by the relevant authority is not an authorised person for the purposes of s 20;

and such a designated body may not authorise members of its staff under head (3): s 20(6). Directions under s 20(6) are to be given by regulations or in writing; but any such directions which relate to more than one designated body are to be given by regulations: s 20(10). Directions under s 20(6) given in writing may be varied or revoked by subsequent directions under s 20(6): s 20(11).

2 As to the meaning of 'controlled drug' and 'management or use of controlled drugs' see PARA 514.

3 The relevant authority may by regulations prescribe descriptions of premises which are to be 'relevant premises' for the purposes of the Health Act 2006 s 20 in relation to constables and authorised persons of descriptions prescribed in the regulations: s 20(7). See the Controlled Drugs (Supervision of Management and Use) Regulations 2013, SI 2013/373 (as from 1 April 2013); and the Controlled Drugs (Supervision of Management and Use) (Wales) Regulations 2008, SI 2008/3239 (amended by SI 2009/1824; SI 2010/231; SI 2011/1011). As to regulations under the Health Act 2006 generally see s 79. The descriptions of premises that may be so prescribed are descriptions of premises (or parts thereof) appearing to the relevant authority to be used in connection with (1) the provision of health care (whether or not for the purposes of the health service), or (2) the supply or administration of controlled drugs: s 20(8). As to the meaning of 'health care' and 'health service' see PARA 514.

4 In the Health Act 2006 Pt 3 Ch 1 (ss 17–25) 'relevant records' means records kept with respect to controlled drugs in pursuance of regulations under the Misuse of Drugs Act 1971 s 10 (see PARA 505): Health Act 2006 s 20(9).

5 Health Act 2006 s 20(1). The powers conferred by s 20(1) may be exercised only (1) at a reasonable hour, and (2) on production (if required) of the written authority of the person exercising them: s 20(2). The power conferred by head (1) in the text may be exercised by an authorised person to enter relevant premises which are or form part of a private dwelling only if he is accompanied by a constable: s 20(3). But s 20(3) does not apply in such circumstances as may be prescribed by regulations by the relevant authority: s 20(3). See SI 2006/3148; SI 2008/3239, and note 3. The power conferred by head (4) in the text includes power (a) to take copies of or extracts from relevant records, and (b) to take possession of any relevant records kept on the premises and retain them for so long as the person exercising the power considers necessary: Health Act 2006 s 20(4).

517. Guidance. The relevant authority[1] may issue guidance to designated bodies[2] in connection with (1) determining whether conditions specified in regulations[3] have been satisfied in relation to the nomination or appointment of a person as a designated body's accountable officer[4]; (2) the discharge by a designated body's accountable officer of any responsibilities imposed on him by regulations[5]; (3) the exercise by designated bodies of their powers relating to accountable officers and their responsibilites[6]; (4) the exercise by designated bodies of their powers relating to power to enter and inspect[7]. The relevant authority may issue guidance to responsible bodies[8] in connection with their discharge of any duties imposed on them by regulations[9]. Guidance under these provisions may make different provision for different cases or circumstances[10]. Designated bodies and responsible bodies must have regard to any guidance under these provisions in exercising any functions to which the guidance relates[11].

1 As to 'relevant authorities' see PARA 514.
2 As to the meaning of 'designated body' see PARA 514.
3 Ie under the Health Act 2006 s 17 (see PARA 514).
4 As to the meaning of 'accountable officer' see PARA 514.
5 Ie under the Health Act 2006 s 17.
6 Ie under the Health Act 2006 s 17(9).
7 Ie under the Health Act 2006 s 20(5)(c) (see PARA 516): s 22(1).
8 In the Health Act 2006 Pt 3 Ch 1 (ss 17–25) 'responsible body' has the meaning given by s 18(2) (see PARA 515): s 25(1).
9 Ie under the Health Act 2006 s 18 (see PARA 515): s 22(2).
10 Health Act 2006 s 22(3).
11 Health Act 2006 s 22(4).

518. Crown application. Chapter 1 of Part 3 of the Health Act 2006[1] binds the Crown[2]. No contravention by the Crown of any provision of Chapter 1 of Part 3 of the Health Act 2006 will make the Crown criminally liable; but the High Court may declare unlawful any act or omission of the Crown which constitutes such a contravention[3]. The provisions of Chapter 1 of Part 3 of the Health Act 2006 apply to persons in the public service of the Crown as they apply to other persons[4].

1   Ie the Health Act 2006 ss 17–25.
2   Health Act 2006 s 23(1).
3   Health Act 2006 s 23(2).
4   Health Act 2006 s 23(3).

(4) DIRECTIONS TO PRACTITIONERS AND PHARMACISTS

519. Prohibitions in respect of convicted practitioners and pharmacists. The Secretary of State[1] may give a direction in respect of any practitioner[2] or pharmacist[3] who has after 30 June 1973[4] been convicted of an offence[5] under the Misuse of Drugs Act 1971 or under the Dangerous Drugs Act 1965[6], or of an offence under certain provisions of the customs and excise legislation[7], or of an offence under the Criminal Justice (International Co-operation) Act 1990[8].

In the case of a practitioner, the direction is that he be prohibited from having in his possession, prescribing, administering, manufacturing, compounding and supplying[9] and from authorising the administration and supply of such controlled drugs[10] as may be specified in the direction[11]. In the case of a pharmacist, the direction is that he be prohibited from having in his possession, manufacturing, compounding and supplying and from supervising and controlling the manufacture, compounding and supply of such controlled drugs as may be so specified[12].

Any such direction takes effect when a copy of it is served[13] on the person to whom it applies[14]. In addition to causing a copy to be so served, the Secretary of State must cause notice of the direction to be published in the London, Edinburgh and Belfast Gazettes[15]. He may at any time give a further direction cancelling or suspending the direction, or cancelling any further direction suspending another direction[16].

It is an offence to contravene[17] any such direction[18].

1   As to the Secretary of State see PARA 2 note 1.
2   As to the meaning of 'practitioner' see PARA 487 note 9.
3   As to the meaning of 'pharmacist' see PARA 52 note 5.
4   Ie after the coming into force of the relevant provisions of the Misuse of Drugs Act 1971: Misuse of Drugs Act 1971 (Commencement No 2) Order 1973, SI 1973/795.
5   This reference to an 'offence' includes references to an attempted offence under the Criminal Attempts Act 1981 s 1: s 7(3). As to attempts to commit an offence see CRIMINAL LAW vol 25 (2010) PARA 86.
6   Misuse of Drugs Act 1971 s 12(1)(a). The Dangerous Drugs Act 1965 was repealed by the Misuse of Drugs Act 1971 s 39(2), Sch 6. Section 12 refers also to any enactment repealed by the Dangerous Drugs Act 1965.
7   Ie an offence under the Customs and Excise Act 1952 s 45, s 56 or s 304 (all repealed), or under the Customs and Excise Management Act 1979 s 50, s 68 or s 170, in connection with a prohibition of or restriction on importation or exportation of a controlled drug having effect by virtue of the Misuse of Drugs Act 1971 s 3 (see PARA 491), or which had effect by virtue of any provision contained in or repealed by the Dangerous Drugs Act 1965: Misuse of Drugs Act 1971 s 12(1)(b) (amended by the Customs and Excise Management Act 1979 s 177(1), Sch 4 para 8).

8   Misuse of Drugs Act 1971 s 12(1)(c) (added by the Criminal Justice (International
    Co-operation) Act 1990 s 23(2)). The offence referred to in the text is an offence under the
    Criminal Justice (International Co-operation) Act 1990 ss 12, 13: see CRIMINAL LAW vol 26
    (2010) PARA 726.
9   'Supplying' includes distributing: Misuse of Drugs Act 1971 s 2(1).
10 As to the meaning of 'controlled drug' see PARA 481.
11 Misuse of Drugs Act 1971 s 12(2)(a).
12 Misuse of Drugs Act 1971 s 12(2)(b).
13 As to the service of documents see PARA 489.
14 Misuse of Drugs Act 1971 s 12(5).
15 Misuse of Drugs Act 1971 s 12(4).
16 Misuse of Drugs Act 1971 s 12(3).
17 As to the meaning of 'contravene' see PARA 504 note 2.
18 Misuse of Drugs Act 1971 s 12(6). In cases concerning a Class A or Class B drug (see PARAS
    481–484), a person is liable on summary conviction to imprisonment for a term not exceeding
    six months or to a fine not exceeding the prescribed sum or to both, or on conviction on
    indictment to imprisonment for a term not exceeding 14 years or to a fine or to both:
    s 25(1), (2), Sch 4 (amended by virtue of the Magistrates' Courts Act 1980 ss 31(1)–(3), 32(2)).
    In cases concerning a Class C drug (see PARAS 481, 485), a person is liable on summary
    conviction to imprisonment for a term not exceeding three months or to a fine of £2,500 or
    both, or on conviction on indictment to imprisonment for a term not exceeding 14 years or to a
    fine or both: Misuse of Drugs Act 1971 Sch 4 (amended by the Criminal Law Act 1977 s 28(8),
    Sch 5; the Criminal Justice and Public Order Act 1994 s 157(2), (4), Sch 8 Pt II; and the
    Criminal Justice Act 2003 s 284, Sch 28 para 1).

**520. Prohibitions in respect of practitioners contravening addiction regulations
or acting irresponsibly.** If a doctor[1] contravenes[2] regulations relating to the
treatment of addicts[3] or of corresponding provision made in a temporary class
drug order[4] or if he contravenes the terms of a licence issued under such
regulations, the Secretary of State[5] may give a direction prohibiting that doctor
from prescribing, administering and supplying[6] such controlled drugs[7] as may be
specified in the direction and from authorising the administration and supply of
such drugs[8]. If the Secretary of State is of the opinion that a practitioner is or has
after 1 July 1973[9] been prescribing, administering or supplying or authorising
the administration or supply of any controlled drug in an irresponsible manner,
he may give a similar direction prohibiting that practitioner from prescribing,
administering and supplying the controlled drugs specified in the direction and
from authorising the administration and supply of such drugs[10].
    It is an offence to contravene any such direction[11].

1   As to the meaning of 'doctor' see PARA 487 note 9.
2   As to the meaning of 'contravene' see PARA 504 note 2.
3   Ie regulations made under the Misuse of Drugs Act 1971 s 10(2)(h), (i): see PARA 505. As to such
    regulations see the Misuse of Drugs (Supply to Addicts) Regulations 1997, SI 1997/1001; and
    PARA 513. It is not an offence to contravene such regulations or the terms of such a licence, but
    it is an offence to contravene a direction given by the Secretary of State under the Misuse of
    Drugs Act 1971 s 13(1) or (2): s 13(3).
4   As to the meaning of 'temporary class order' see PARA 481. For the purposes of the Misuse of
    Drugs Act 1971 s 13(1), provision made in a temporary class drug order is 'corresponding
    provision' if it is made by virtue of s 7A(2)(d) (see PARA 503) and is of a corresponding
    description to regulations made in pursuance of s 10(2)(h) or (as the case may be) 10(2)(i) (see
    PARA 505): s 13(1A) (added by the Police Reform and Social Responsibility Act 2011 Sch 17
    para 12(3)).
5   As to the Secretary of State see PARA 2 note 1.
6   As to the meaning 'supplying' see PARA 519 note 9.
7   As to the meaning of 'controlled drug' see PARA 481.
8   Misuse of Drugs Act 1971 s 13(1) (amended by the Police Reform and Social Responsibility
    Act 2011, Sch 17 para 12(2)(a)). The Secretary of State must exercise his powers subject to and
    in accordance with the Misuse of Drugs Act 1971 s 14 (see PARA 521): s 13(1). A direction given

under this power takes effect when a copy of it is served on the person to whom it applies: s 16(4). As to the service of documents see PARA 489.

9 Ie the date on which the Misuse of Drugs Act 1971 s 13(2) came into effect: Misuse of Drugs Act 1971 (Commencement No 2) Order 1973, SI 1973/795.

10 Misuse of Drugs Act 1971 s 13(2). The Secretary of State must exercise his powers subject to and in accordance with ss 14, 15 (see PARAS 521–522): s 13(2). A direction given under this power takes effect when a copy of it is served on the person to whom it applies: s 16(4).

11 Misuse of Drugs Act 1971 s 13(3). In cases concerning a Class A or Class B drug (see PARAS 481–484), a person is liable on summary conviction to imprisonment for a term not exceeding six months or to a fine not exceeding the prescribed sum or to both, or on conviction on indictment to imprisonment for a term not exceeding 14 years or to a fine or to both: s 25(1), (2), Sch 4 (amended by virtue of the Magistrates' Courts Act 1980 ss 31(1)–(3), 32(2)). In cases concerning a Class C drug (see PARAS 481, 485), a person is liable on summary conviction to imprisonment for a term not exceeding three months or to a fine of £2,500 or both, or on conviction on indictment to imprisonment for a term not exceeding 14 years or to a fine or both: Misuse of Drugs Act 1971 Sch 4 (amended by the Criminal Law Act 1977 s 28(8), Sch 5; the Criminal Justice and Public Order Act 1994 s 157(2), (4), Sch 8 Pt II; and the Criminal Justice Act 2003 s 284, Sch 28 para 1).

521. References to tribunals and advisory bodies. If the Secretary of State[1] considers that there are grounds for giving a direction[2] on account of the contravention[3] by a doctor[4] of regulations relating to the treatment of addicts or the terms of a licence issued under such regulations, or for giving a direction[5] on account of a practitioner[6] prescribing, administering or supplying[7] or authorising the administration or supply of any controlled drug[8] in an irresponsible manner, he may refer the case to a tribunal[9] constituted for the purpose; and it is the duty of the tribunal to consider the case and report on it to the Secretary of State[10].

Where the tribunal finds that there has been no such contravention by the doctor in question or where it finds that the practitioner in question has not conducted himself irresponsibly, or it finds that there has been a contravention or irresponsible conduct but does not recommend the giving of a direction[11], the Secretary of State must cause notice to that effect to be served[12] on the respondent[13].

Where, on the other hand, the tribunal finds that there has been a contravention or irresponsible conduct and considers that a direction[14] should be given in respect of the respondent, it must include in its report a recommendation to that effect indicating the controlled drugs which it considers should be specified in the direction or indicating that the direction should specify all controlled drugs[15]. In such a case, the Secretary of State must cause a notice to be served on the respondent stating whether or not he proposes to give a direction pursuant to the tribunal's recommendation[16], and, where he does so propose, the notice must set out the terms of the proposed direction[17] and inform the respondent that consideration will be given to any representations relating to the case made by him in writing[18] to the Secretary of State within the period of 28 days beginning with the date of service of the notice[19]. If any such representations are received within that period, the Secretary of State must refer the case to an advisory body constituted for the purpose[20], which must consider the case and advise the Secretary of State as to the exercise of his powers[21].

After the period of 28 days has expired and, in the case of a reference to an advisory body, after considering the advice of that body, the Secretary of State may: (1) give a direction[22] in respect of the respondent specifying all or any of the controlled drugs indicated in the tribunal's recommendation[23]; or (2) order that the case be referred back to the tribunal or referred to another properly constituted tribunal[24]; or (3) order that no further proceedings be taken in the case[25].

The Secretary of State must cause a copy of any such order or direction[26] to be served on the person to whom it applies and must cause notice of any such direction to be published in the London, Edinburgh and Belfast Gazettes[27]. The Secretary of State may at any time give a direction cancelling or suspending any earlier direction[28] given by him or cancelling any direction by which a direction so given was suspended[29], and in such a case similar provisions as to notice and publication apply[30].

1 As to the Secretary of State see PARA 2 note 1.
2 Ie under the Misuse of Drugs Act 1971 s 13(1): see PARA 520.
3 As to the meaning of 'contravention' see PARA 504 note 2.
4 As to the meaning of 'doctor' see PARA 487 note 9.
5 Ie under the Misuse of Drugs Act 1971 s 13(2): see PARA 520.
6 As to the meaning of 'practitioner' see PARA 487 note 9.
7 As to the meaning 'supplying' see PARA 519 note 9.
8 As to the meaning of 'controlled drug' see PARA 481.
9 As to the constitution and procedure of such tribunal see the Misuse of Drugs Act 1971 Sch 3 Pt 1 (amended by the Senior Courts Act 1981 Sch 5, the Courts and Legal Services Act 1990 Sch 10 para 33, the Judicial Pensions and Retirement Act 1993 Sch 6 para 42(2), the Constitutional Reform Act 2005 Sch 11 para 5, the Tribunals, Courts and Enforcement Act 2007 Sch 10 para 10); and the Misuse of Drugs Tribunal (England and Wales) Rules 1974, SI 1974/85 (modified by SI 1991/2684, SI 2011/2866).
10 Misuse of Drugs Act 1971 s 14(1).
11 Ie under the Misuse of Drugs Act 1971 s 13(1), (2): see PARA 520.
12 As to the service of notices see PARA 489.
13 Misuse of Drugs Act 1971 s 14(3). For these purposes, 'the respondent' means the doctor or practitioner in respect of whom the reference is made: s 14(2).
14 Ie under the Misuse of Drugs Act 1971 s 13(1), (2): see PARA 520.
15 Misuse of Drugs Act 1971 s 14(4).
16 Misuse of Drugs Act 1971 s 14(5).
17 Misuse of Drugs Act 1971 s 14(5)(a).
18 As to the meaning of 'writing' see PARA 507 note 2.
19 Misuse of Drugs Act 1971 s 14(5)(b).
20 As to the constitution and procedure of the 'advisory body' see the Misuse of Drugs Act 1971 Sch 3 paras 13–16 (amended by the Judicial Pensions and Retirement Act 1993 Sch 6 para 42(3)).
21 Misuse of Drugs Act 1971 s 14(6). The powers referred to are those under s 14(7): see the text to notes 22–25.
22 Ie a direction under the Misuse of Drugs Act 1971 s 13(1), (2): see PARA 520.
23 Misuse of Drugs Act 1971 s 14(7)(a).
24 Misuse of Drugs Act 1971 s 14(7)(b). If a case is referred or referred back to a tribunal, the provisions of s 14(2)–(7) apply as if the reference had been under s 14(1); and any finding, recommendation or advice previously made or given must be disregarded: s 14(8).
25 Misuse of Drugs Act 1971 s 14(7)(c).
26 Ie any order or direction under the Misuse of Drugs Act 1971 s 14(7): see the text to notes 22–25.
27 Misuse of Drugs Act 1971 s 16(2).
28 Ie a direction under the Misuse of Drugs Act 1971 s 14(7): see the text to notes 22–25.
29 Misuse of Drugs Act 1971 s 16(3)(a).
30 Misuse of Drugs Act 1971 s 16(3). Any such direction takes effect when a copy of it is served on the person to whom it applies: s 16(4).

522. Temporary directions in urgent cases. If the Secretary of State[1] considers that there are grounds for giving a direction[2] prohibiting a practitioner[3] from prescribing, administering and supplying[4], and from authorising the administration and supply of, controlled drugs[5] on account of his irresponsible conduct, and that the circumstances of the case require such a direction to be given with the minimum of delay, he may give such a direction for a period of six weeks, beginning with the date on which the direction takes effect[6], specifying such controlled drugs as he thinks fit[7].

Where the Secretary of State proposes to give such a temporary direction, he must refer the case to a professional panel[8] constituted for the purpose[9], which, after affording the respondent[10] an opportunity of appearing before it and being heard by it, must consider the circumstances of the case, so far as known to it, and must report to the Secretary of State whether the information before it appears to it to afford reasonable grounds for thinking that there has been irresponsible conduct by the practitioner[11]. The Secretary of State may not give a temporary direction unless the panel reports that the information before it appears to it to afford reasonable grounds for so thinking[12]. Where a temporary direction is given, the Secretary of State must forthwith refer[13] the case to a tribunal, if he has not already done so[14].

Unless previously cancelled[15], such a direction ceases to have effect on the occurrence of any of certain events[16].

1 As to the Secretary of State see PARA 2 note 1.

2 Ie a direction under the Misuse of Drugs Act 1971 s 13(2): see PARA 520.

3 As to the meaning of 'practitioner' see PARA 487 note 9.

4 As to the meaning 'supplying' see PARA 519 note 9.

5 As to the meaning of 'controlled drug' see PARA 481.

6 Misuse of Drugs Act 1971 s 15(5). In certain circumstances the period may be extended: see s 15(6); and note 15. As to when a direction takes effect see note 7.

7 Misuse of Drugs Act 1971 s 15(1). The Secretary of State must cause a copy of the direction to be served on the person to whom it applies and must cause notice of it to be published in the London, Edinburgh and Belfast Gazettes: s 16(2). As to the service of documents see PARA 489. The Secretary of State may at any time by further direction cancel the direction (s 16(3)(b)) and must similarly serve and publish any such direction (s 16(3)). Any direction under s 13(2) (as applied by s 15(1)) or under s 16(3) takes effect when the copy is so served: s 16(4).

8 As to the constitution and procedure of such panels see the Misuse of Drugs Act 1971 Sch 3 paras 17–20.

9 Misuse of Drugs Act 1971 s 15(2).

10 For these purposes, 'the respondent' means the practitioner in respect of whom the reference is made: Misuse of Drugs Act 1971 s 15(3).

11 Misuse of Drugs Act 1971 s 15(2)(a).

12 Misuse of Drugs Act 1971 s 15(2)(b).

13 Ie in accordance with the Misuse of Drugs Act 1971 s 14(1): see PARA 521.

14 Misuse of Drugs Act 1971 s 15(4). In these circumstances the Secretary of State may from time to time by notice in writing served on the person to whom the direction applies extend or further extend the period of operation of the direction for a further 28 days, but may not do so without the consent of the tribunal or, if the case has been referred to another tribunal under s 14(7) (see PARA 521), of that other tribunal: s 15(6). A copy of any such notice must be published in the London, Edinburgh and Belfast Gazettes: s 16(2). As to the meaning of 'writing' see PARA 507 note 2.

15 Ie under the Misuse of Drugs Act 1971 s 16(3): see note 7.

16 Misuse of Drugs Act 1971 s 15(7). The events are: (1) the service on the person concerned of a notice under s 14(3) (see PARA 521) (s 15(7)(a)); (2) the service on him of a notice under s 14(5) (see PARA 521) that the Secretary of State does not propose to give a direction under s 13(2) (see PARA 520) (s 15(7)(b)); (3) the service on him of a copy of a direction given under s 14(7) (see PARA 521) (s 15(7)(c)); (4) the making of an order under s 14(7)(c) (see PARA 521) that no further proceedings are to be taken (s 15(7)(d)); (5) the expiration of the period of operation of the temporary direction (s 15(7)(e)).

(5) ENFORCEMENT AND OFFENCES

523. Powers of entry and inspection. For the purposes of the execution of the Misuse of Drugs Act 1971 and Part II of the Criminal Justice (International Co-operation) Act 1990[1], a constable[2] or other person authorised by a general or special order of the Secretary of State[3] may enter the premises of a person[4] carrying on business as a producer or supplier[5] of any controlled drugs[6] and may demand the production of, and inspect, any books or documents relating to dealings in any such drugs and may inspect stocks of any such drugs[7]. A person commits an offence[8] if he intentionally obstructs a person in the exercise of his powers under these provisions[9], or if he conceals from such a person any such books, documents, stocks or drugs[10], or if without reasonable excuse, he fails to produce any such books or documents where their production is demanded by such a person[11].

1 The powers conferred by the Misuse of Drugs Act 1971 s 23(1) are exercisable also for the purposes of the execution of the Criminal Justice (International Co-operation) Act 1990 Pt II (ss 12–24) (see CRIMINAL LAW vol 26 (2010) PARAS 725–726, 733): Misuse of Drugs Act 1971 s 23(3A) (added by the Criminal Justice (International Co-operation) Act 1990 s 23(1), (4)).
2 As to the office of constable see POLICE vol 36(1) (2007 Reissue) PARA 101 et seq.
3 As to the Secretary of State see PARA 2 note 1.
4 As to the meaning of 'person' see PARA 45 note 2.
5 As to the meaning 'supplying' see PARA 519 note 9.
6 As to the meaning of 'controlled drug' see PARA 481.
7 Misuse of Drugs Act 1971 s 23(1).
8 The penalty for such an offence on summary conviction is imprisonment for a term not exceeding six months or a fine not exceeding the prescribed sum or both, and on conviction on indictment is imprisonment for a term not exceeding two years or a fine or both: Misuse of Drugs Act 1971 s 25(1), (2), Sch 4 (amended by virtue of the Magistrates' Courts Act 1980 s 32(2)). As to the prescribed sum see SENTENCING AND DISPOSITION OF OFFENDERS vol 92 (2010) PARA 141.
9 Misuse of Drugs Act 1971 s 23(4)(a).
10 Misuse of Drugs Act 1971 s 23(4)(b).
11 Misuse of Drugs Act 1971 s 23(4)(c). The burden of proving reasonable excuse rests on the accused: s 23(4)(c). As to the standard of proof see CRIMINAL PROCEDURE vol 28 (2010) PARA 469.

524. Powers of search and seizure. A constable[1] has a power of search and seizure where he has reasonable grounds to suspect that a person is in possession of a controlled drug[2] or a temporary controlled drug[3] in contravention of the Misuse of Drugs Act 1971 or regulations or orders made under it[4].

1 As to the office of constable see POLICE vol 36(1) (2007 Reissue) PARA 101 et seq.
2 As to the meaning of 'controlled drug' see PARA 481.
3 As to the meaning of 'temporary class drug' see PARA 481.
4 See the Misuse of Drugs Act 1971 s 23(2), 23A(1); and CRIMINAL LAW vol 26 (2010) PARA 734.

525. Offences. It is an offence under the Misuse of Drugs Act 1971 unlawfully to produce or be concerned in the production of a controlled drug[1]; to supply or offer to supply such a drug or to be concerned in the doing of either activity by another[2]; to have possession of a controlled drug[3] or to have such possession with intent to supply it to another[4]; to cultivate cannabis plants[5]; to be the occupier of or to be concerned in the management of premises and to permit or suffer certain activities there[6]; to smoke or otherwise use prepared opium, or frequent a place used for that purpose or have possession of utensils used for that purpose[7]; to supply or offer to supply articles which may be used for administering drugs[8]; to contravene regulations[9] or the terms of a licence or authority[10]; to give false information[11]; to assist in or induce the commission abroad of an offence under a corresponding law[12]; to contravene directions as to safe custody[13]; to fail to comply with a notice requiring information as to prescriptions and other matters[14] or to give false information under such a notice[15]; to contravene certain directions[16]; to obstruct powers of entry[17], and search and seizure[18] or to incite another to commit any such offence[19].

A magistrates' court may try an information for any such offence if the information was laid at any time within 12 months from the commission of the offence[20].

1	See the Misuse of Drugs Act 1971 s 4(2); and PARA 492. As to the meaning of 'controlled drug' see PARA 481.

2	See the Misuse of Drugs Act 1971 s 4(3); and PARA 492.

3	See the Misuse of Drugs Act 1971 s 5(2); and PARA 495.

4	See the Misuse of Drugs Act 1971 s 5(3); and PARA 495.

5	See the Misuse of Drugs Act 1971 s 6(2); and PARA 497.

6	See the Misuse of Drugs Act 1971 s 8; and PARA 498.

7	See the Misuse of Drugs Act 1971 s 9; and PARA 500.

8	See the Misuse of Drugs Act 1971 s 9A; and PARA 501.

9	See the Misuse of Drugs Act 1971 s 18(1); and PARA 504.

10	See the Misuse of Drugs Act 1971 s 18(2); and PARA 504.

11	See the Misuse of Drugs Act 1971 s 18(3), (4); and PARA 504.

12	See the Misuse of Drugs Act 1971 s 20; and PARA 504.

13	See the Misuse of Drugs Act 1971 s 11(2); and PARA 507.

14	See the Misuse of Drugs Act 1971 s 17(3); and PARA 510.

15	See the Misuse of Drugs Act 1971 s 17(4); and PARA 510.

16	See the Misuse of Drugs Act 1971 ss 12(6), 13(3); and PARAS 519–520.

17	See the Misuse of Drugs Act 1971 s 23(4); and PARA 523.

18	See the Misuse of Drugs Act 1971 ss 23(4), 23A(6); and CRIMINAL LAW vol 26 (2010) PARA 734.

19	See the Misuse of Drugs Act 1971 s 19; and PARA 504.

20	Misuse of Drugs Act 1971 s 25(4) (amended by the Magistrates' Courts Act 1980 s 154, Sch 7 para 103). This provision is expressed to apply notwithstanding anything in the Magistrates' Courts Act 1980 s 127(1) (general limitation of six months): see MAGISTRATES vol 71 (2013) PARA 526.

**526.	Forfeiture.**	The court by or before which a person[1] is convicted of an offence under the Misuse of Drugs Act 1971, or of a drug trafficking offence[2], may order anything[3] shown to the satisfaction of the court to relate to the offence to be forfeited and either destroyed or dealt with in such other manner as the court may order[4]. However, the court must not order anything to be forfeited where a person claiming to be the owner of or otherwise interested in it applies to be heard by the court, unless an opportunity has been given to him to show cause why the order should not be made[5].

1	As to the meaning of 'person' see PARA 45 note 2.

2	Ie an offence which is specified in the Proceeds of Crime Act 2002 Sch 2 para 1, or so far as it relates to that provision, Sch 2 para 10: Misuse of Drugs Act 1971 s 27(3) (added by the Proceeds of Crime Act 2002 s 456, Sch 11 paras 1, 5(1), (3)). As to such offences see SENTENCING AND DISPOSITION OF OFFENDERS vol 92 (2010) PARA 393.

3	'Anything' refers to tangible things of which physical possession can be taken by a person authorised to do so and which are capable of being physically destroyed by that person or disposed of by him in some other way: *R v Cuthbertson* [1981] AC 470, [1980] 2 All ER 401, HL. It does not include real property: *R v Beard* [1974] 1 WLR 1549, 118 Sol Jo 848; *R v Khan, R v Crawley* [1982] 3 All ER 969, [1982] 1 WLR 1405, CA.

4	Misuse of Drugs Act 1971 s 27(1) (amended by the Criminal Justice Act 1988 s 70; and the Proceeds of Crime Act 2002 s 456 Sch 11 paras 1, 5(1), (2)). The court must adopt a judicial and not a whimsical approach in determining how anything is to be dealt with: *R v Beard* [1974] 1 WLR 1549; *R v Glover* (1974) (unreported). To come within the forfeiture provisions under the Misuse of Drugs Act 1971, the offence has to be one which has been expressly created by the Act: *R v Cuthbertson* [1981] AC 470, [1980] 2 All ER 401, HL (appellants had been convicted of conspiracy to contravene the Misuse of Drugs Act 1971 s 4, but successfully argued that conspiracy to commit an offence under that Act was not an offence expressly created by the Act, and the court therefore had no jurisdiction to order forfeiture under s 27). As to the confiscation of the proceeds of crime see the Proceeds of Crime Act 2002 s 13; and SENTENCING AND DISPOSITION OF OFFENDERS vol 92 (2010) PARA 400.

5   Misuse of Drugs Act 1971 s 27(2). The defendant must also be given an opportunity to call evidence to establish that these requirements have not been met, before a forfeiture order is made: *R v Churcher* (1986) 8 Cr App Rep (S) 94, CA.

527.   Offences in connection with power to enter and inspect. A person commits an offence if he (1) intentionally obstructs a person in the exercise of his powers to enter and inspect[1], (2) conceals from a person[2] anything which that person is entitled to inspect, or (3) without reasonable excuse fails to produce any relevant records[3] which a person[4] requires to be produced[5]. A person guilty of such an offence is liable (a) on conviction on indictment, to imprisonment for a term not exceeding two years or to a fine, or to both; (b) on summary conviction, to imprisonment for a term not exceeding 12 months or to a fine not exceeding the statutory maximum[6], or to both[7].

1   Ie under the Health Act 2006 s 20(1) (see PARA 516).
2   Ie a person acting under the Health Act 2006 s 20(1).
3   In the Health Act 2006 Pt 3 Ch 1 (ss 17–25) 'relevant records' has the meaning given by s 20(9) (see PARA 516): s 25(1).
4   Ie a person acting under the Health Act 2006 s 20(1).
5   Health Act 2006 s 21(1).
6   As to the statutory maximum see SENTENCING AND DISPOSITION OF OFFENDERS vol 92 (2010) PARA 140.
7   Health Act 2006 s 21(2). For transitional modification see s 78(2) (s 78 partly in force: SI 2007/204, SI 2008/3171 (Wales), SI 2008/1147 (England)).
     As to offences committed by bodies corporate, partnerships and other unincorporated associations, see the Health Act 2006 ss 76, 77 (ss 76, 77 partly in force: SI 2007/204, SI 2008/3171 (Wales), SI 2007/1375, SI 2008/1147 (England)).

7. POISONS

(1) THE CONTROL OF POISONS

528. Introduction. The law relating to the control of poisons[1] is contained principally in the Poisons Act 1972[2] and in the Poisons Rules made under that Act[3]. Under this statutory scheme of control the poisons included in the Poisons List are subject to detailed controls covering their sale, supply, labelling, transport, storage and the containers in which they must be sold[4].

1 Ie the poisons included in the Poisons List (see PARAS 531–533). As to the meaning of the word 'poison' in another context see *R v Cramp* (1880) 5 QBD 307 (administration of poisons or noxious substances with intent to procure abortion); and CRIMINAL LAW vol 25 (2010) PARA 120. As to offences relating to the administration of drugs and poisons generally see CRIMINAL LAW vol 25 (2010) PARAS 132–134. As to the sale and use of poisoned grain and bait see ANIMALS vol 2 (2008) PARA 864; and as to the administration of a poisonous or injurious drug to an animal see ANIMALS vol 2 (2008) PARA 864. As to the protection of agricultural workers against risks from hazardous substances see AGRICULTURAL PRODUCTION AND MARKETING vol 1 (2008) PARA 1246. As to the control of hazardous and dangerous substances generally see HEALTH AND SAFETY AT WORK vol 53 (2009) PARA 619 et seq; ENVIRONMENTAL QUALITY AND PUBLIC HEALTH vol 46 (2010) PARA 788 et seq.

2 The principal enactment relating to poisons is the Poisons Act 1972, which came into force on 1 February 1978, ie immediately after all the amendments of the Pharmacy and Poisons Act 1933 made by the Medicines Act 1968 Schs 5, 6, were brought into operation by order under s 136: Poisons Act 1972 s 13(1); Medicines Act 1968 (Commencement No 7) Order 1977, SI 1977/2128. As to the transitional provisions see the Poisons Act 1972 s 13(2)–(6). Dealings in certain narcotic and addictive drugs are controlled by the Misuse of Drugs Act 1971: see PARA 480 et seq. Dealings with medicinal products are controlled by the Medicines Act 1968 and the Human Medicines Regulations 2012, SI 2012/1916: see PARA 1 et seq.

3 Ie the Poisons Rules 1982, SI 1982/218: see PARA 534.

4 See PARA 538 et seq. A visiting force or headquarters, members of such a force or headquarters, persons employed in the service of such a force, and property used for the purposes of such a force or headquarters are exempt from the operation of the Poisons Act 1972 to the extent that Crown immunity exempts home forces from it: see the Visiting Forces and International Headquarters (Application of Law) Order 1999, SI 1999/1736, art 12(1), Sch 5; and ARMED FORCES vol 3 (2011) PARA 412.

529. Cruel poisons. Regulations may be made that prohibit or restrict the use of certain poisons for destroying animals[1]. Such regulations have been made prohibiting the use of phosphorous and red squill for destroying mammals of any description and restricting the use of strychnine except in relation to moles[2].

1 See the Animals (Cruel Poisons) Act 1962 s 2(1); and ANIMALS vol 2 (2008) PARA 864.

2 See the Animal (Cruel Poisons) Regulations 1963, SI 1963/1278, reg 1; and ANIMALS vol 2 (2008) PARA 864.

530. The Poisons Board. The Poisons Board is an advisory committee composed of 16 members[1] representing the government departments specially interested in poisons and the professions of medicine and pharmacy[2]. The Board's principal function is concerned with the preparation and modification from time to time of the Poisons List[3] and any poisons rules[4].

1 Poisons Act 1972 s 1(1), Sch 1 para 1. As to the constitution of the board see Sch 1 paras 3–9 (amended by SI 2002/794)

2 See the Poisons Act 1972 s 1(1), Sch 1. The procedure of the Poisons Board is (subject to any regulations made by the Board) such as the Board may determine: s 1(2). Regulations made by the Board are not statutory instruments and are not noted in this work.

3 See the Poisons Act 1972 s 2; and PARA 531.
4 See the Poisons Act 1972 s 7; and PARA 534.

531.   The Poisons List. There is a list of substances treated as poisons for the purposes of the Poisons Act 1972, which is called 'the Poisons List'[1]. The Secretary of State[2] may from time to time, after consultation with or on the recommendation of the Poisons Board[3], by order amend or vary the Poisons List as he thinks proper[4].

The Poisons List is divided into two parts[5]. In determining the distribution of poisons between Part I and Part II of the Poisons List regard is to be had to the desirability of restricting Part II to articles which are in common use, or likely to come into common use, for purposes other than the treatment of human ailments, and which it is reasonably necessary to include in Part II if the public is to have adequate facilities for obtaining them[6].

1 Poisons Act 1972 s 2(1), (2). The present Poisons List is contained in the Schedule to the Poisons List Order 1982, SI 1982/217 (see PARAS 532–533).
2 As to the Secretary of State see PARA 2 note 1. See also PARA 530 note 1.
3 As to the Poisons Board see PARA 530.
4 Poisons Act 1972 s 2(2). If the Secretary of State by order makes amendments or variations in the Poisons List in which the Board does not concur, he must give a statement of his reasons for making the order: see s 10(2).
5 Poisons Act 1972 s 2(3). As to Part I poisons see PARA 532; and as to Part II poisons see PARA 533.
6 Poisons Act 1972 s 2(4).

532.   Part I poisons. Part I of the Poisons List[1] consists of those substances which, where they are non-medicinal poisons[2], are by virtue of, and subject to the provisions of, the Poisons Act 1972 to be prohibited from being sold except by a person lawfully conducting a retail pharmacy business[3]. The substances are:

(1)   aluminium phosphide;
(2)   arsenic; its compounds, other than those specified in Part II of the Poisons List[4];
(3)   barium, salts of, other than barium sulphate and the salts of barium specified in Part II of the Poisons List;
(4)   bromomethane;
(5)   chloropicrin;
(6)   fluoroacetic acid; its salts; fluoroacetamide;
(7)   hydrogen cyanide; metal cyanides, other than ferrocyanides and ferricyanides;
(8)   lead acetates; compounds of lead with acids from fixed oils;
(9)   magnesium phosphide;
(10) mercury, the following compounds of: nitrates of mercury; oxides of mercury; mercuric cyanide oxides; mercuric thiocyanate; ammonium mercuric chlorides; potassium mercuric iodides; organic compounds of mercury which contain a methyl (CH_3) group directly linked to the mercury atom;
(11) oxalic acid;
(12) phenols (phenol; phenolic isomers of the following: cresols, xylenols, monoethylphenols) except in substances containing less than 60 per cent, weight in weight, of phenols; compounds of phenols with a metal, except in substances containing less than the equivalent of 60 per cent, weight in weight, of phenols;
(13) phosphorus, yellow;

(14)   strychnine; its salts; its quaternary compounds;
(15)   thallium, salts of[5].

1   As to the Poisons List see PARA 531.
2   'Non-medicinal poison' means a substance which is included in Part I or Part II of the Poisons List and is neither: (1) a medicinal product as defined by the Medicines Act 1968 s 130 (see PARA 25); nor (2) a veterinary medicinal product as defined by the Veterinary Medicines Regulations 2006, SI 2006/2407, reg 2 (repealed); nor a substance in relation to which, by virtue of an order under the Medicines Act 1968 s 104 or s 105 (see PARA 28), for the time being in force (and whether referred to in an order under s 104 as a substance or as an article), the provisions of ss 51–54 (repealed) and ss 69–77 (see MEDICAL PROFESSIONS vol 74 (2011) PARA 798 et seq) have effect (whether or not subject to exceptions and modifications) as they have effect in relation to medicinal products so defined: Poisons Act 1972 s 11(1) (amended by SI 2006/2407).
3   Poisons Act 1972 s 2(3). 'Person lawfully conducting a retail pharmacy business' must be construed in accordance with the Medicines Act 1968 s 69 (see MEDICAL PROFESSIONS vol 74 (2011) PARA 799): Poisons Act 1972 s 11(2). As to the meaning of 'retail pharmacy business' see PARA 52 note 12; definition applied by s 11(2). As to the distribution of poisons between Part I and Part II of the Poisons List see s 2(4); and PARA 531.
4   For Part II poisons see PARA 533.
5   Poisons List Order 1982, SI 1982/217, art 2(a), Schedule Pt I (amended by SI 1992/2292).

533.   Part II poisons.   Part II of the Poisons List[1] consists of those substances which, where they are non-medicinal poisons[2], are by virtue of, and subject to the provisions of, the Poisons Act 1972 to be prohibited from being sold except by a person lawfully conducting a retail pharmacy business[3] or by a person[4] whose name is entered in a local authority's list[5]. The substances are:

(1)   aldicarb;
(2)   alpha-chloralose;
(3)   ammonia;
(4)   arsenic, the following compounds of: calcium arsenites; copper acetoarsenite; copper arsenates; copper arsenites; lead arsenates;
(5)   barium, the following salts of: barium carbonate; barium silicofluoride;
(6)   carbofuran;
(7)   cycloheximide;
(8)   dinitrocresols (DNOC); their compounds with a metal or a base;
(9)   dinoseb; its compounds with a metal or a base;
(10)   dinoterb;
(11)   drazoxolon; its salts;
(12)   endosulfan;
(13)   endothal; its salts;
(14)   endrin;
(15)   fentin, compounds of;
(16)   formaldehyde;
(17)   formic acid;
(18)   hydrochloric acid;
(19)   hydrofluoric acid; alkali metal bifluorides; ammonium bifluoride; alkali metal fluorides; ammonium fluoride; sodium silicofluoride;
(20)   mercuric chloride; mercuric iodide; organic compounds of mercury except compounds which contain a methyl (CH_3) group directly linked to the mercury atom;
(21)   metallic oxalates;
(22)   methomyl;
(23)   nicotine; its salts; its quaternary compounds;
(24)   nitric acid;

(25) nitrobenzene;
(26) oxamyl;
(27) paraquat, salts of;
(28) phenols[6] in substances containing less than 60 per cent, weight in weight, of phenols; compounds of phenols with a metal in substances containing less than the equivalent of 60 per cent, weight in weight, of phenols;
(29) phosphoric acid;
(30) phosphorus, the following compounds: azinphos methyl, chlorfenvinphos, demephion, demeton-S-methyl, demeton-S-methyl sulphone, dialifos, dichlorvos, dioxathion, disulfoton, fonofos, mecarbam, mephosfolan, methidathion, mevinphos, omethoate, oxydemeton-methyl, parathion, phenkapton, phorate, phosphamidon, pirimiphos-ethyl, quinalphos, thiometon, thionazin, triazophos, vamidothion;
(31) potassium hydroxide;
(32) sodium hydroxide;
(33) sodium nitrite;
(34) sulphuric acid;
(35) thiofanox;
(36) zinc phosphide[7].

1   As to the Poisons List see PARA 531.
2   As to the meaning of 'non-medicinal poison' see PARA 532 note 2.
3   As to the meaning of 'person lawfully conducting a retail pharmacy business' see PARA 493 note 6, and as to the meaning of 'retail pharmacy business' see PARA 52 note 12; definitions applied by the Poisons Act 1972 s 11(2).
4   As to the meaning of 'person' see PARA 45 note 2.
5   Poisons Act 1972 s 2(3). As to the meaning of 'local authority's list' see PARA 535 note 4. As to the distribution of poisons between Part I and Part II of the Poisons List see s 2(4); and PARA 531.
6   Ie as defined in Part I of the Poisons List (see PARA 532).
7   Poisons List Order 1982, SI 1982/217, art 2(b), Schedule Pt II (amended by SI 1992/2292).

534. Poisons Rules. After consultation with or on the recommendation of the Poisons Board[1], the Secretary of State[2] may make rules, known as 'Poisons Rules'[3], with respect to any of the following matters or for any of the following purposes[4]:

(1)   the sale, whether wholesale or retail, or the supply of non-medicinal poisons, by or to any persons or classes of persons[5], and in particular[6]: (a) for regulating or restricting the sale or supply of non-medicinal poisons by persons whose names are entered in a local authority's list[7] and for prohibiting the sale of any specified non-medicinal poison or class of non-medicinal poisons by any class of such persons[8]; and (b) for dispensing with or relaxing with respect to non-medicinal poisons any of certain provisions of the Poisons Act 1972[9] relating to the sale of non-medicinal poisons[10];
(2)   the storage, transport and labelling of non-medicinal poisons[11];
(3)   the containers in which non-medicinal poisons may be sold or supplied[12];
(4)   the addition to non-medicinal poisons of specified ingredients for the purpose of rendering them readily distinguishable as non-medicinal poisons[13];
(5)   the compounding of non-medicinal poisons, and the supply of

non-medicinal poisons on and in accordance with a prescription duly given by a doctor, a dentist, a veterinary surgeon or a veterinary practitioner[14];

(6) the period for which any books required to be kept for the purposes of the Poisons Act 1972 are to be preserved[15];

(7) the period for which any certificate[16] certifying a person to be a person to whom a Part I poison may properly be sold is to remain in force[17];

(8) for prescribing anything which is required by that the Poisons Act 1972 to be prescribed[18] by rules[19].

The Secretary of State may issue to the Poisons Board a direction that its power to make recommendations as to the making of rules with respect to certain of these matters[20] must not be exercised except after consultation with such body of persons as is specified in the direction, being a body which is, in his opinion, representative of persons engaged in the manufacture of poisons or preparations containing poisons, and the Board must comply with any such direction[21].

1 As to the Poisons Board see PARA 530.

2 As to the Secretary of State see PARA 2 note 1. See also PARA 530 note 1.

3 Poisons Act 1972 s 11(2). As to the rules that have been made see the Poisons Rules 1982, SI 1982/218.

4 Poisons Act 1972 s 7(1). The power to make rules with respect to non-medicinal poisons includes power to make rules with respect to any class of such poisons or any particular such poison: s 7(2). As to the meaning of 'non-medicinal poison' see PARA 532 note 2.

5 As to the meaning of 'person' see PARA 45 note 2.

6 Poisons Act 1972 s 7(1)(a).

7 As to the meaning of 'local authority's list' see PARA 535 note 4.

8 Poisons Act 1972 s 7(1)(a)(i).

9 Ie the Poisons Act 1972 ss 1–6.

10 Poisons Act 1972 s 7(1)(a)(ii). As to such rules see PARA 539 et seq.

11 Poisons Act 1972 s 7(1)(b). As to provisions relating to such matters see PARAS 544–545.

12 Poisons Act 1972 s 7(1)(c). As to provisions relating to such matters see PARA 544.

13 Poisons Act 1972 s 7(1)(d).

14 Poisons Act 1972 s 7(1)(e). 'Doctor' means a registered medical practitioner within the meaning of the Interpretation Act 1978 Sch 1 (see MEDICAL PROFESSIONS vol 74 (2011) PARA 176): Poisons Act 1972 s 11(2) (definition substituted by the Medical Act 1983 s 56(1), Sch 5). 'Dentist' means a person registered in the dentists register kept under the Dentists Act 1984 or a person entered in the list of visiting EEA practitioners under Sch 4: Poisons Act 1972 s 11(2) (definition amended by the Dentists Act 1984 s 54(1), Sch 5 para 4; and SI 1996/1496). As to the registration of dentists see MEDICAL PROFESSIONS vol 74 (2011) PARA 442 et seq. 'Veterinary surgeon' means a person registered in the register of veterinary surgeons kept under the Veterinary Surgeons Act 1966 s 2 (see ANIMALS vol 2 (2008) PARA 1133); and 'veterinary practitioner' means a person registered in the supplementary veterinary register kept under the Veterinary Surgeons Act 1966 s 8 (see ANIMALS vol 2 (2008) PARA 1134): Poisons Act 1972 s 11(2).

15 Poisons Act 1972 s 7(1)(f).

16 Ie a certificate given under the Poisons Act 1972 s 3(2)(a)(i): see PARA 541.

17 Poisons Act 1972 s 7(1)(g).

18 'Prescribed' means prescribed by the Poisons Rules 1982, SI 1982/218: Poisons Act 1972 s 11(2).

19 Poisons Act 1972 s 7(1)(h).

20 Ie those specified in the Poisons Act 1972 s 7(1)(a)(i), (b), (c), (d): see heads (1)(a), (2)–(4) in the text.

21 Poisons Act 1972 s 7(3). The Secretary of State may from time to time revoke or vary any such direction, without prejudice to the issue of a new one: s 7(4).

(2) SALE, STORAGE AND TRANSPORT OF POISONS

(i) Local Authorities' Lists

535. Listed sellers. Every local authority[1] must keep a list of persons[2] who are entitled, on premises in respect of which their names are entered, to sell non-medicinal poisons[3] which are substances included in Part II of the Poisons List[4]; and must enter in the list the name of any person who, having premises in the area of the local authority, makes an application in the prescribed form[5] to have his name entered in the list in respect of those premises[6].

Fees are payable to the local authority in respect of the entry of names in the list[7], the making of alterations in the list in relation to the premises in respect of which a name is entered[8], and the retention of names on the list in years[9] subsequent to the year of entry in the list[10].

1 'Local authority' means, in relation to England, the council of a county, metropolitan district or London borough or the Common Council of the City of London; and, in relation to Wales, the council of a county or county borough: Poisons Act 1972 s 11(2) (definition amended by the Statute Law (Repeals) Act 1978; the Local Government Act 1985 s 16, Sch 8 para 16; and the Local Government (Wales) Act 1994 s 66(6), (8), Sch 16 para 39, Sch 18). As to local government areas and authorities in England and Wales see LOCAL GOVERNMENT vol 69 (2009) PARA 22 et seq. As to the London boroughs and their councils see LONDON GOVERNMENT vol 71 (2013) PARAS 15, 20–22, 55 et seq. As to the Common Council of the City of London see LONDON GOVERNMENT vol 71 (2013) PARA 34 et seq.
2 As to the meaning of 'person' see PARA 45 note 2.
3 As to the meaning of 'non-medicinal poison' see PARA 532 note 2.
4 Poisons Act 1972 s 5(1). As to the Poisons List see PARA 531; and as to Part II poisons see PARA 533. A list kept by a local authority under s 5 is called a 'local authority's list': s 11(2). As to refusal of entry in, and removal from, a list see PARA 536; and as to the use of titles in connection with entries in a list see PARA 537.
5 For the prescribed form see the Poisons Rules 1982, SI 1982/218, r 24(1), Sch 8.
6 Poisons Act 1972 s 5(2). A local authority's list must: (1) include particulars of the premises in respect of which the name of any person is entered in the list (s 6(1)(a)); (2) subject to head (1), be in such form as may be prescribed (s 6(1)(b)); and (3) be open at all reasonable times to the inspection of any person without fee (s 6(1)(c)). For the prescribed form of the list see the Poisons Rules 1982, SI 1982/218, r 24(2), Sch 9.
7 Poisons Act 1972 s 6(2)(a). The fees payable are such reasonable fees as the authority may determine: s 6(2) (amended by the Local Government, Planning and Land Act 1980 s 1 (6), Sch 6 para 13 (2)).
8 Poisons Act 1972 s 6(2)(b). As to the level of fees see note 7.
9 'Year' means a period of 12 months beginning on such date as the local authority may from time to time determine: Poisons Act 1972 s 6(2)(c). As to the meaning of 'month' see PARA 43 note 3.
10 Poisons Act 1972 s 6(2)(c). As to the level of fees see note 7.

536. Refusal of entry in, and removal from, list. A local authority[1] may refuse to enter in, or may remove from, the local authority's list[2] the name of any person[3] who fails to pay the requisite fees[4] or who in the authority's opinion is, for any sufficient reason relating either to him personally[5] or to his premises, not fit to be on the list[6]. Any person aggrieved by the refusal of a local authority to enter his name in the list or by the removal of his name from it may appeal to the Crown Court[7].

If any person whose name is entered in a local authority's list is convicted before any court of any offence which, in the court's opinion, renders him unfit to be on the list, the court may, as part of the sentence, order his name to be removed from the list and direct that he be disqualified for having it entered in any local authority's list for such period as may be specified in the order[8].

1 As to the meaning of 'local authority' see PARA 535 note 1.
2 As to the meaning of 'local authority's list' see PARA 535 note 4.
3 As to the meaning of 'person' see PARA 45 note 2.
4 As to the fees see PARA 535 notes 7, 8, 10.
5 'Relating to him personally' means, in relation to a body corporate, relating personally to the members of the board or to the managers or other officers of the body corporate: Poisons Act 1972 s 5(5). As to whether a reason relating personally to only one member of the board or one manager or other officer is sufficient, see the Interpretation Act 1978 s 6(c), which provides that, unless the contrary intention appears, words denoting the plural include the singular (and vice versa). 'The board', in relation to a body corporate, means the persons controlling that body, by whatever name called: Poisons Act 1972 s 11(2). As to bodies corporate see COMPANIES; CORPORATIONS.
6 Poisons Act 1972 s 5(3) (amended by the Local Government, Planning and Land Act 1980 s 1(6), Sch 6 para 13(1)).
7 Poisons Act 1972 s 5(4). As to the Crown Court see COURTS AND TRIBUNALS vol 24 (2010) PARA 716 et seq.
8 Poisons Act 1972 s 6(3).

537. Use of titles. It is not lawful for any person[1] whose name is entered in a local authority's list[2] to use in connection with his business any title, emblem or description reasonably calculated[3] to suggest that he is entitled to sell any poison which he is not entitled to sell[4]. If any person acts in contravention of this provision, he is liable to a penalty[5].

1 As to the meaning of 'person' see PARA 45 note 2.
2 As to the meaning of 'local authority's list' see PARA 535 note 4.
3 'Reasonably calculated' must mean reasonably calculated to persons who are qualified to exercise reason upon the subject, and that does not exclude, but rather includes and lays emphasis on, those who are instructed and educated persons in touch with and having some knowledge of the profession: *A-G v Weeks* [1932] 1 Ch 211 at 221, CA, per Lord Hanworth MR (a decision in connection with the use of titles and descriptions by registered dentists: see MEDICAL PROFESSIONS vol 74 (2011) PARA 435).
4 Poisons Act 1972 s 6(4).
5 See the Poisons Act 1972 s 6(4) (amended by virtue of the Criminal Justice Act 1982 s 46). Such a person is liable on summary conviction, in respect of each offence, to a fine not exceeding level 2 on the standard scale and, in the case of a continuing offence, to a further fine not exceeding £5 for every day subsequent to the day on which he is convicted of the offence during which the contravention continues: Poisons Act 1972 s 6(4) (as so amended). As to the standard scale see SENTENCING AND DISPOSITION OF OFFENDERS vol 92 (2010) PARA 142.

(ii) Restrictions

538. Restrictions generally. Two classes of persons are entitled to sell non-medicinal poisons[1] by retail, namely persons lawfully conducting a retail pharmacy business[2], who may sell poisons included in both parts of the Poisons List[3], and persons whose names are included in a local authority's list[4], who may sell poisons in Part II of that list[5].

It is not lawful for a non-medicinal poison to be exposed for sale in, or offered for sale by means of, an automatic machine[6]. Detailed requirements are imposed as respects the labelling of poisons and containers for them[7], and as to their storage and transport[8].

1 As to the meaning of 'non-medicinal poison' see PARA 532 note 2.
2 As to the meaning of 'person lawfully conducting a retail pharmacy business' see PARA 493 note 6; definition applied by the Poisons Act 1972 s 11(2).
3 See the Poisons Act 1972 s 3(1)(a), (b)(i); and PARA 539. As to the Poisons List see PARA 531.
4 As to the meaning of 'local authority's list' see PARA 535 note 4.
5 See the Poisons Act 1972 s 3(1)(b)(ii); and PARA 540. As to Part II of the Poisons List see PARA 533.
6 Poisons Act 1972 s 3(3).

7   See PARA 544.
8   See PARA 545.

539.   Sales through retail pharmacy businesses.   Subject to exemptions[1], it is not lawful for a person[2]:

  (1)   to sell[3] any non-medicinal poison[4] included in Part I of the Poisons List[5] unless he is a person lawfully conducting a retail pharmacy business[6], the sale is effected on premises which are a registered pharmacy[7], and the sale is effected by or under the supervision of a pharmacist[8];

  (2)   to sell any non-medicinal poison included in Part II of the Poisons List[9] unless he is a person lawfully conducting a retail pharmacy business and the sale is effected on premises which are a registered pharmacy[10].

It is not lawful for any shopkeeper to sell poisons[11] on any premises used for or in connection with his retail business, notwithstanding that the sale is an exempted sale[12], unless he complies with these provisions[13]. Nor is it lawful for any person lawfully conducting a retail pharmacy business to sell any specified poison[14], notwithstanding that it is a Part II poison, unless the sale is effected by or under the supervision of a pharmacist[15].

1   For exemptions see PARAS 546–547.
2   As to the meaning of 'person' see PARA 45 note 2.
3   An agreement to sell does not of itself constitute a sale, which is incomplete without the passing of property: see eg *Mischeff v Springett* [1942] 2 KB 331, [1942] 2 All ER 349; *Watson v Coupland* [1945] 1 All ER 217, DC. A sale is, however, effected where a person appropriates or transfers goods under an agreement for the sale of unascertained goods: *Preston v Albuery* [1964] 2 QB 796, [1963] 3 All ER 897, DC. See further SALE OF GOODS AND SUPPLY OF SERVICES vol 91 (2012) PARA 1 et seq.
4   As to the meaning of 'non-medicinal poison' see PARA 532 note 2.
5   As to the Poisons List see PARA 531; and as to Part I poisons see PARA 532.
6   Poisons Act 1972 s 3(1)(a)(i). As to the meaning of 'person lawfully conducting a retail pharmacy business' see PARA 493 note 6; definition applied by s 11(2).
7   Poisons Act 1972 s 3(1)(a)(ii). As to the meaning of 'registered pharmacy' see PARA 52 note 2; definition applied by s 11(2).
8   Poisons Act 1972 s 3(1)(a)(iii). 'Pharmacist' means a person registered in Part 1 of the register maintained under the Pharmacy Order 2010, SI 2012/231, art 19 (pharmacists other than visiting practitioners :see MEDICAL PROFESSIONS vol 74 (2011) PARA 821): Poisons Act 1972 s 11(2). It is not sufficient for the registered pharmacist to be in another room on the premises, out of sight and hearing: *Roberts v Littlewood's Mail Order Stores Ltd* [1943] 1 KB 269, [1943] 1 All ER 271, DC. However, the requirement is satisfied where a customer in a self-service store himself takes a poison from the shelf and pays for it at a cash desk supervised by a pharmacist: *Pharmaceutical Society of Great Britain v Boots Cash Chemists (Southern) Ltd* [1953] 1 QB 401, [1953] 1 All ER 482, CA.
9   As to Part II poisons see PARA 533.
10 Poisons Act 1972 s 3(1)(b)(i). Part II poisons may also be sold by persons on a local authority's list: see s 3(1)(b)(ii); and PARA 540.
11 'Poison' means a non-medicinal poison: Poisons Rules 1982, SI 1982/218, r 2(1). The Poisons Rules 1982, SI 1982/218 do not have effect in relation to any poison other than a non-medicinal poison: r 2(3).
12 'Exempted sale' means a sale within any of the provisions of the Poisons Act 1972 s 4(a)–(e) (see PARA 546): Poisons Rules 1982, SI 1982/218, r 2(1).
13 Poisons Rules 1982, SI 1982/218, r 3. The provisions referred to in the text are those of the Poisons Act 1972 s 3(1)(a) or (b): see the text to notes 1–10.
14 Ie any poison included in the Poisons Act 1972 Sch 1 (amended by SI 1985/1077; SI 1986/10). For certain special exemptions see PARA 547. The poisons included in the Poisons Rules 1982, SI 1982/218, Sch 1 are:
    (1)   aldicarb;
    (2)   alpha-chloralose;
    (3)   aluminium phosphide:
    (4)   arsenic; its compounds, except substances containing less than the equivalent of 0.0075% of arsenic (As);

(5)   barium, salts of, other than barium sulphate;
(6)   bromomethane;
(7)   carbofuran;
(8)   chloropicrin;
(9)   cycloheximide;
(10) dinitrocresols (DNOC); their compounds with a metal or a base; except winter washes containing not more than the equivalent of 5% of dinitrocresols;
(11) dinoseb; its compounds with a metal or a base;
(12) dinoterb;
(13) drazoxolon; its salts;
(14) endosulfan;
(15) endothal; its salts;
(16) endrin;
(17) fentin, compounds of;
(18) fluoroacetic acid; its salts; fluoroacetamide;
(19) hydrogen cyanide except substances containing less than 0.15%, weight in weight, of hydrogen cyanide (HCN); metal cyanides, other than ferrocyanides and ferricyanides, except substances containing less than the equivalent of 0.1%, weight in weight, of hydrogen cyanide (HCN);
(20) lead, compounds of, with acids from fixed oils;
(21) magnesium phosphide;
(22) mercuric chloride except substances containing less than 1% of mercuric chloride;
(23) mercuric iodide except substances containing less than 2% of mercuric iodide; nitrates of mercury except substances containing less than the equivalent of 3%, weight in weight, of mercury (Hg); potassio-mercuric iodides except substances containing less than the equivalent of 1% of mercuric iodide; organic compounds of mercury except substances, not being aerosols, containing less than the equivalent of 0.2%, weight in weight, of mercury (Hg);
(24) methomyl;
(25) nicotine; its salts; its quaternary compounds;
(26) oxamyl;
(27) paraquat, salts of;
(28) phosphorus, the following compounds: azinphosmethyl; chlorfen vinphos; demephion; demeton-S-methyl; demeton-S-methyl sulphone; dialifos; dichlorvos; dioxathion; disulfoton; fonofos; mecarbam; mephosfolan; methidathion; mevinphos; omethoate; oxydemetonmethyl; parathion; phenkapton; phorate: phosphamidon; pirimiphos-ethyl; quinalphos; thiometon; thionazin; triazophos; vamidothion;
(29) strychnine; its salts; its quaternary compounds; except substances containing less than 0.2% of strychnine;
(30) thallium, salts of;
(31) thiofanox;
(32) zinc phosphide.

15 Poisons Rules 1982, SI 1982/218, r 9.

540.   Sales by listed sellers.   Subject to certain exemptions[1], it is not lawful for a person[2] (other than a person lawfully conducting a retail pharmacy business[3]) to sell[4] any non-medicinal poison[5] included in Part II of the Poisons List[6] unless his name is entered in a local authority's list[7] in respect of the premises on which the poison is sold[8]. It is not lawful for a shopkeeper to sell poisons[9] on any premises used for or in connection with his retail business, notwithstanding that the sale is an exempted sale[10], unless this provision is complied with[11].

No shopkeeper is entitled, by virtue of being a listed seller of Part II poisons[12], to sell any poison which has, since being obtained by him, been subject to any form of manipulation, treatment or processing as a result of which the poison has been exposed[13], or to sell any specified poisons[14] unless the sale is effected by himself or by a responsible deputy[15]. No person is entitled by virtue of being a listed seller of Part II poisons to sell any of certain poisons[16] unless the purchaser is engaged in the trade or business of agriculture, horticulture or forestry and requires the poison for the purpose of that trade or business[17]; nor to sell certain other poisons[18] except specified articles or substances[19].

1 For exemptions see PARAS 546–547.
2 As to the meaning of 'person' see PARA 45 note 2.
3 As to sales of Part II poisons by such persons see PARA 539. As to the meaning of 'person lawfully conducting a retail pharmacy business' see PARA 493 note 6; definition applied by the Poisons Act 1972 s 11(2).
4 As to what amounts to a sale see PARA 539 note 3.
5 As to the meaning of 'non-medicinal poison' see PARA 532 note 2.
6 As to the Poisons List see PARA 531; and as to Part II poisons see PARA 533.
7 As to the meaning of 'local authority's list' see PARA 535 note 4.
8 Poisons Act 1972 s 3(1)(b)(ii).
9 As to the meaning of 'poison' see PARA 539 note 11.
10 As to the meaning of 'exempted sale' see PARA 539 note 12.
11 Poisons Rules 1982, SI 1982/218, r 3.
12 'Listed seller of Part II poisons' means a person whose name is for the time being entered in a local authority's list: Poisons Rules 1982, SI 1982/218, r 2(1).
13 Poisons Rules 1982, SI 1982/218, r 10(1)(a) (substituted by SI 1985/1077). For general exemptions see PARA 546.
14 Ie any poison included in the Poisons Rules 1982, SI 1982/218, Sch 1: see PARA 539 note 14.
15 Poisons Rules 1982, SI 1982/218 r 10(1)(b). 'Responsible deputy' means a person nominated as a deputy on the seller's form of application under r 24, Sch 8, for entry as a listed seller, or any person substituted, by written notice to the local authority, for a person so nominated and more than two deputies may be nominated at the same time in respect of one set of premises: r 10(1).
16 As to such poisons see the Poisons Rules 1982, SI 1982/218, Sch 5 Pt B.
17 Poisons Rules 1982, SI 1982/218, r 10(2)(b).
18 As to such poisons see the Poisons Rules 1982, SI 1982/218, Sch 5 Pt A col 1.
19 Poisons Rules 1982, SI 1982/218, r 10(2)(a) (amended by SI 1985/1077). As to the specified articles and substances (which include e g preparations for use in agriculture, horticulture or forestry; agricultural, horticultural and forestal insecticides or fungicides; preparations for the destruction of rats or mice; and photographic solutions or materials) see the Poisons Rules 1982, SI 1982/218, Sch 5 Pt A col 2.

541.   Persons to whom certain poisons may be sold. Subject to certain exemptions[1], it is not lawful to sell[2], or supply in the form of commercial sample otherwise than on sale[3], any non-medicinal poison[4] which is a substance included in Part I of the Poisons List[5] to any person[6] unless that person is either: (1) certified, in writing[7] in the prescribed manner[8] by an authorised person[9], to be a person to whom the poison may properly be sold or supplied[10]; or (2) is known, by the seller or supplier or by a registered pharmacist[11] in the employment of the seller or supplier at the premises where the sale or supply is effected, to be such a person[12]. The seller or supplier of any such poison must not deliver it until he has made or caused to be made an entry in a book kept for the purpose[13], stating in the prescribed form[14] particulars of the transaction[15], and the purchaser has signed the entry[16].

These provisions as to the persons to whom poisons may be sold[17] and as to the recording of sales[18] apply to exempted sales[19] other than sales of poisons to be exported to purchasers outside the United Kingdom[20]; they do not, however, apply to the sale or supply of any article by its manufacturer or by a person carrying on a business in the course of which poisons are regularly sold by way of wholesale dealing[21], if the article is sold or supplied to a person carrying on a business in the course of which poisons are regularly sold or are regularly used in the manufacture of other articles[22], and the seller or supplier is reasonably satisfied that the purchaser requires the article for the purpose of that business[23].

1 For exemptions see PARAS 546–547.
2 As to what amounts to a sale see PARA 539 note 3.

3   See the Poisons Rules 1982, SI 1982/218, r 6(1).

4   As to the meaning of 'non-medicinal poison' see PARA 532 note 2.

5   As to the Poisons List see PARA 531; and as to Part I poisons see PARA 532. The provisions of the Poisons Act 1972 s 3(2) apply with respect to all poisons included in the Poisons Rules 1982, SI 1982/218, Sch 1 (see PARA 539 note 14), whether or not the poison sold is a poison included in Part I of the Poisons List, and do not apply with respect to any other poison: r 5. As to the meaning of 'poison' see PARA 539 note 11. Certain substances are, however, exempted: see r 5 proviso (ii).

6   Poisons Act 1972 s 3(2)(a). As to the meaning of 'person' see PARA 45 note 2.

7   As to the meaning of 'writing' see PARA 507 note 2.

8   For the form of the certificate and the particulars which it must contain see the Poisons Rules 1982, SI 1982/218, r 25(1), Sch 10. On the sale, the seller must retain the certificate: r 25(3).

9   All householders are authorised to give certificates, provided that a certificate given by a householder who is not known to the seller or supplier as a responsible person of good character must be endorsed in the manner specified in the Poisons Act 1982, SI 1982/218, Sch 10 by a police officer in charge of a police station: r 25(2).

10 Poisons Act 1972 s 3(2)(a)(i).

11 As to the meaning of 'pharmacist' see PARA 539 note 8.

12 Poisons Act 1972 s 3(2)(a)(ii). In its application to sales by listed sellers of Part II poisons, this provision is deemed to be satisfied if the person to whom the poison is sold or supplied is known by the person in charge of the premises, or of the department of the business, in which the poison is sold or supplied, to be a person to whom it may properly be sold or supplied: Poisons Rules 1982, SI 1982/218, r 5 proviso (i). As to the meaning of 'listed sellers of Part II poisons' see PARA 540 note 12. In its application to sales exempted by the Poisons Act 1972 s 4 (see PARA 546), and to the supply of commercial samples of poisons included in the Poisons Rules 1982, SI 1982/218, Sch 1, it is deemed to be satisfied if the person to whom the poison or sample is sold or supplied is known by the person in charge of the department of the business through which the sale or supply is effected, to be a person to whom it may properly be sold or supplied: r 6(2).

13 Any book kept for the purposes of the Poisons Act 1972 must be preserved for two years after the last entry was made in it: see the Poisons Rules 1982, SI 1982/218, r 27.

14 For the prescribed form see Poisons Rules 1982, SI 1982/218, r 26, Sch 11.

15 Poisons Act 1972 s 3(2)(b)(i). These particulars are the date of sale or supply, the name and address of the person to whom it is sold or supplied and of the person who gave the certificate, if any, under s 3(2)(a)(i) (see the text to note 10), the name and quantity of the article sold or supplied and the purposes for which it was stated by the purchaser to be required: s 3(2)(b)(i).

16 Poisons Act 1972 s 3(2)(b)(ii). The entry need not be so signed where the poison is required for the purposes of the purchaser's trade, business or profession and the following requirements are satisfied: (1) the seller must, before completing the sale, obtain a written order signed by the purchaser stating his name and address, trade, business or profession, the purpose for which the poison is required and the quantity (Poisons Rules 1982, SI 1982/218, r 6(3)(a)); (2) the seller must be reasonably satisfied that the signature is that of the person purporting to sign and that he does carry on the trade, business or profession stated, being one in which that poison is used (r 6(3)(b)); and (3) the seller must insert in the entry in the prescribed book 'signed order' with an identifiable reference number (r 6(3)(c)).

    If the seller is reasonably satisfied that by reason of some emergency no signed order can be given or signed entry made and the poison is urgently required for the purpose of a person's trade, business or profession, the seller may deliver the poison on that person's undertaking to furnish such an order within 72 hours: r 6(3) proviso (amended by SI 1989/112). Any person who breaks such an undertaking, or who knowingly makes a false statement in order to obtain delivery under the Poisons Rules 1982, SI 1982/218, r 6(3) proviso, commits an offence: Poisons Act 1972 s 8(1) (amended by virtue of the Criminal Justice Act 1982 s 46); Poisons Rules 1982, SI 1982/218, r 6(3). As to offences and penalties see PARA 552.

17 Ie the provisions of the Poisons Act 1972 s 3(2)(a) and the Poisons Rules 1982, SI 1982/218, r 5.

18 Ie the provisions of the Poisons Act 1972 s 3(2)(b).

19 As to the meaning of 'exempted sale' see PARA 539 note 12.

20 Poisons Rules 1982, SI 1982/218, r 6(1). As to the meaning of 'United Kingdom' see PARA 20 note 4.

21 'Sale by way of wholesale dealing' means sale to a person who buys for the purpose of selling again: Poisons Act 1972 s 11(2). That the person who buys cannot lawfully sell again is immaterial: see *Oxford v Sangers Ltd* [1965] 1 QB 491, [1965] 1 All ER 96, DC. However, it is not lawful to sell by way of wholesale dealing any Part I poison to a person carrying on the

business of shopkeeping unless the seller: (1) has reasonable grounds for believing that the purchaser is a person lawfully conducting a retail pharmacy business (Poisons Rules 1982, SI 1982/218, r 11(a)); or (2) has received a statement signed by the purchaser or a person authorised by him or on his behalf to the effect that the purchaser does not intend to sell the poison on any premises used for or in connection with his retail business (r 11(b)). As to the meaning of 'person lawfully conducting a retail pharmacy business' see PARA 493 note 6; definition applied by the Poisons Act 1972 s 11(2).

22 Poisons Rules 1982, SI 1982/218, r 6(1) proviso (a).
23 Poisons Rules 1982, SI 1982/218, r 6(1) proviso (b).

542. Sale of strychnine, cyanides and certain other poisons. It is not lawful to sell[1] or supply strychnine, its salts or quaternary compounds[2], fluoroacetic acid, any salt of it or fluoroacetamide[3], salts of thallium[4], zinc phosphide[5], sodium arsenites or potassium arsenites[6] unless the substance is to be exported to purchasers outside the United Kingdom[7], or to a person or institution concerned with scientific education or research or chemical analysis for the purposes of that education, research or analysis[8], or it is to be sold by way of wholesale dealing[9].

However, strychnine, its salts or quaternary compounds may be sold or supplied to a person producing a written authority in the prescribed form[10], as may fluoroacetic acid, any salt of it or fluoroacetamide[11] or thallium sulphate[12]. Salts of thallium may be sold to a local authority[13] or a port health authority[14] for the purpose of the exercise of its statutory powers[15], or to a government department or an officer of the Crown for the purposes of the public service[16]; or, in the case of salts of thallium other than thallium sulphate, to a person, or body of persons, carrying on a business in the course of which salts of thallium are regularly used in the manufacture of other articles, for the purposes of that business[17], or as an ingredient in any article not being an article intended for internal consumption by any person or animal[18]. Zinc phosphide may be sold to a local authority for the purpose of the exercise of its statutory powers[19], or to a government department or an officer of the Crown for the purposes of the public service[20], or to a person, or body of persons, carrying on a trade or business for the purposes of that trade or business[21].

Unless the sale is an exempted sale[22], it is not lawful to sell calcium cyanide, potassium cyanide or sodium cyanide[23].

1   As to what amounts to a sale see PARA 539 note 3.
2   Poisons Rules 1982, SI 1982/218, r 12(1).
3   Poisons Rules 1982, SI 1982/218, r 12(2).
4   Poisons Rules 1982, SI 1982/218, r 12(3).
5   Poisons Rules 1982, SI 1982/218, r 12(4).
6   Poisons Rules 1982, SI 1982/218, r 12(5).
7   Poisons Rules 1982, SI 1982/218, r 12, Sch 12 Pt I para 1. As to the meaning of 'United Kingdom' see PARA 20 note 4.
8   Poisons Rules 1982, SI 1982/218, Sch 12 Pt I para 2.
9   Poisons Rules 1982, SI 1982/218, Sch 12 Pt I para 3. As to the meaning of 'sale by way of wholesale dealing' see PARA 541 note 21.
10 See the Poisons Rules 1982, SI 1982/218, r 12(1), Sch 12 Pt I paras 4, 5, Pts II, III. The authority must be retained by the seller: r 12(6).
11 See the Poisons Rules 1982, SI 1982/218, r 12(2), Sch 12 Pt I para 6(1), Pt IV. The authority must be retained by the seller: r 12(6).
12 See the Poisons Rules 1982, SI 1982/218, r 12(3), Sch 12 Pt I para 7(2), Pt V. The authority must be retained by the seller: r 12(6).
13 For these purposes, 'local authority' in Greater London means the Common Council of the City of London or the council of a London borough; and elsewhere in England or Wales means the council of a county or a district: Poisons Rules 1982, SI 1982/218, Sch 12 Pt I paras 6(2), 7(3). As to local government areas and authorities in England and Wales see LOCAL GOVERNMENT vol 69 (2009) PARA 22 et seq. As to the Common Council of the City of London see LONDON

GOVERNMENT vol 71 (2013) PARA 34 et seq. As to the London boroughs and their councils see LONDON GOVERNMENT vol 71 (2013) PARAS 15, 20–22, 55 et seq.

14 'Port health authority' means the port health authority of the Port of London or a port health authority for the purposes of the Public Health Act 1936: Poisons Rules 1982, SI 1982/218, Sch 12 Pt I paras 6(2), 7(3). The relevant provisions of the Public Health Act 1936 are repealed and replaced by the Public Health (Control of Disease) Act 1984: see ENVIRONMENTAL QUALITY AND PUBLIC HEALTH vol 46 (2010) PARA 884 et seq. As to port health authorities see ENVIRONMENTAL QUALITY AND PUBLIC HEALTH vol 45 (2010) PARAS 102, 103.

15 See the Poisons Rules 1982, SI 1982/218, r 12(3), Sch 12 Pt I para 7(1)(a).
16 See the Poisons Rules 1982, SI 1982/218, r 12(3), Sch 12 Pt I para 7(1)(b).
17 See the Poisons Rules 1982, SI 1982/218, r 12(3), Sch 12 Pt I para 7(1)(c).
18 See the Poisons Rules 1982, SI 1982/218, r 12(3), Sch 12 Pt I para 7(1)(d).
19 See the Poisons Rules 1982, SI 1982/218, r 12(4), Sch 12 Pt I para 8(1)(a).
20 See the Poisons Rules 1982, SI 1982/218, r 12(4), Sch 12 Pt I para 8(1)(b).
21 See the Poisons Rules 1982, SI 1982/218, r 12(4), Sch 12 Pt I para 8(1)(c).
22 As to the meaning of 'exempted sale' see PARA 539 note 12.
23 Poisons Rules 1982, SI 1982/218, r 13.

543. Export of pancuronium bromide. It is an offence to export to the United States of America a human or veterinary medicinal product containing the active ingredient pancuronium bromide in a form suitable for injection or for preparation of an injection[1]. This offence also applies where the destination is not the United States of America but the exporter knows that the final destination of the product is the United States of America[2].

1 See the Export Control Order 2008, SI 2008/3231, reg 4A(1), (2); and TRADE AND INDUSTRY vol 97 (2010) PARA 817.
2 See the Export Control Order 2008, SI 2008/3231, reg 4A(3); and TRADE AND INDUSTRY vol 97 (2010) PARA 817.

(iii) Labelling, Packaging, Storage and Transport

544. Labelling and packaging of poisons. The provisions of the Poisons Act 1972[1] relating to the labelling of containers of non-medicinal poisons do not apply to the sale[2] of any such poison[3]. The regulation of the labelling and packaging of poisons is now governed by provisions relating to dangerous substances generally[4].

It is not lawful to sell or supply any compressed hydrogen cyanide unless the container is labelled with the prescribed words[5], except where the sale or supply is for export to purchasers outside the United Kingdom[6].

1 Ie the provisions which make it unlawful for a person to sell any non-medicinal poison, whether it is a substance included in Part I or in Part II of the Poisons List, unless the container of the poison is labelled in the prescribed manner: see the Poisons Act 1972 s 3(1)(c). As to the meaning of 'non-medicinal poison' see PARA 532 note 2. As to the Poisons List see PARA 531; as to Part I poisons see PARA 532, and as to Part II poisons see PARA 533.
2 As to what amounts to a sale see PARA 539 note 3.
3 Poisons Rules 1982, SI 1982/218, r 4 (substituted by SI 1985/1077).
4 See the Chemicals (Hazard Information and Packaging for Supply) Regulations 2009, SI 2009/716; and HEALTH AND SAFETY AT WORK vol 53 (2009) PARAS 571–572.
5 Poisons Rules 1982, SI 1982/218, r 18(1) (renumbered by SI 1985/1077). The prescribed words are: 'Warning. This container holds poisonous gas and should only be opened and used by persons having expert knowledge of the precautions to be taken in its use': Poisons Rules 1982, SI 1982/218, r 18(1) (as so renumbered).
6 Poisons Rules 1982, SI 1982/218, r 18(2) (substituted by SI 1985/1077). As to the meaning of 'United Kingdom' see PARA 20 note 4.

545. Storage and transport of poisons. It is not lawful to store any of certain poisons[1] in any retail shop or premises used in connection with it unless it is stored in a cupboard or drawer reserved solely for the storage of poisons[2], or in a part of the premises partitioned off or otherwise separated from the remainder and to which customers are not permitted access[3], or on a shelf, directly under which no food[4] is kept, reserved solely for the storage of poisons[5]. Additional notification and marking requirements are imposed on persons in control of sites at which a significant quantity of a dangerous substance is present[6].

The transport of poisons is regulated by provisions relating to dangerous substances generally[7].

1 As to the meaning of 'poison' see PARA 539 note 11. The poisons referred to in the text are those listed in the Poisons Rules 1982, SI 1982/218, Sch 1: see PARA 539 note 14.
2 Poisons Rules 1982, SI 1982/218, r 21(a).
3 Poisons Rules 1982, SI 1982/218, r 21(b).
4 'Food' includes a beverage: Poisons Rules 1982, SI 1982/218, r 2(1).
5 Poisons Rules 1982, SI 1982/218, r 21(c). In the case of any such poison to be used in agriculture, horticulture or forestry, it is not lawful to store it on any shelf, or in any such part of the premises as is referred to in the text if food is kept in that part, or in any cupboard or drawer unless the cupboard or drawer is reserved solely for the storage of poisons to be used for those purposes: r 21 proviso.
6 See the Dangerous Substances (Notification and Marking of Sites) Regulations 1990, SI 1990/304; and HEALTH AND SAFETY AT WORK vol 53 (2009) PARA 629.
7 See the Carriage of Dangerous Goods and Use of Transportable Pressure Equipment Regulations 2009, SI 2009/1348; and CARRIAGE AND CARRIERS vol 7 (2008) PARA 106.

(iv) Exemptions

546. Exemption of certain sales. Except as provided by the Poisons Rules 1982[1], nothing in the statutory provisions imposing restrictions on the sale of non-medicinal poisons[2] extends to or interferes with: (1) the sale of poisons by way of wholesale dealing[3]; (2) the sale of poisons to be exported to purchasers outside the United Kingdom[4]; (3) the sale of an article to a doctor, dentist, veterinary surgeon or veterinary practitioner for the purpose of his profession[5]; (4) the sale of an article for use in or in connection with any hospital, infirmary, dispensary or similar institution approved by an order, whether general or special, of the Secretary of State[6]; or (5) the sale of an article by a person[7] carrying on a business in the course of which poisons are regularly sold either by way of wholesale dealing or for use by the purchasers in their trade or business: (a) to a person who requires the article for the purpose of his trade or business[8]; or (b) to a person who requires the article to enable him to comply with any requirements made by or in pursuance of any enactment[9] with respect to the medical treatment of persons employed by him in any trade or business carried on by him[10]; or (c) to a government department or an officer of the Crown requiring the article for the purposes of the public service or any local authority[11] requiring the article in connection with the exercise by it of any statutory powers[12]; or (d) to a person or institution concerned with scientific education or research if the article is required for the purposes of that education or research[13].

1 Ie the Poisons Rules 1982, SI 1982/218. In particular, see r 3 (see PARAS 539–540); rr 5, 6, 11 (see PARA 541); and rr 12, 13 (see PARA 542).
2 Ie nothing in the Poisons Act 1972 s 3(1), (2): see PARAS 539–541, 544. As to the meaning of 'non-medicinal poison' see PARA 532 note 2.
3 Poisons Act 1972 s 4(a). As to the meaning of 'sale by way of wholesale dealing' see PARA 541 note 21.
4 Poisons Act 1972 s 4(b). As to the meaning of 'United Kingdom' see PARA 20 note 4.
5 Poisons Act 1972 s 4(c). As to the meanings of 'doctor', 'dentist', 'veterinary surgeon' and 'veterinary practitioner' see PARA 534 note 14.

6 Poisons Act 1972 s 4(d). As to the Secretary of State see PARA 2 note 1. See also PARA 530 note 1. The Poisons (Approved Institutions) Order 1935, SR & O 1935/1240, continues to have effect: see the Poisons Act 1972 s 13(3). By this order there are approved for this purpose any hospital, infirmary or dispensary maintained by any public authority or maintained out of any public funds or by a charity or by voluntary subscriptions.

7 As to the meaning of 'person' see PARA 45 note 2.

8 Poisons Act 1972 s 4(e)(i).

9 'Enactment' does not include an enactment comprised in, or in an instrument made under, an Act of the Scottish Parliament: Interpretation Act 1978 s 5, Sch 1.

10 Poisons Act 1972 s 4(e)(ii).

11 Ie any local authority, whether as defined in the Poisons Act 1972 (see PARA 535 note 1), or not: s 4(e)(iii).

12 Poisons Act 1972 s 4(e)(iii).

13 Poisons Act 1972 s 4(e)(iv).

547.   Exemptions with respect to certain articles and substances. Certain prescribed articles and substances[1] are specifically exempted from the restrictions imposed[2] on the sale and supply of poisons[3]; and other prescribed articles[4] are exempted from the special restrictions imposed[5] with respect to certain substances[6].

1 Ie adhesives, anti-fouling compositions, builders' materials, ceramics, cosmetic products, distempers, electrical valves, enamels, explosives, fillers, fireworks, fluorescent lamps, flux in any form used for soldering, glazes, glue, inks, lacquer solvents, loading materials, matches, medicated animal feeding stuffs, motor fuels and lubricants, paints, photographic paper, pigments, plastics, propellants, rubber, varnishes, vascular plants and their seeds: Poisons Rules 1982, SI 1982/218, r 8(a), Sch 4 Group I (amended by SI 1986/1704). 'Medicated animal feeding stuff' means an animal feeding stuff in which a medicinal product has been incorporated or in which a substance other than a medicinal product has been incorporated for a medicinal purpose: Poisons Rules 1982, SI 1982/218, r 2(1). As to the meaning of 'medicinal product' see PARA 25.

2 Ie by the Poisons Act 1972 and by the Poisons Rules 1982, SI 1982/218. In particular, see the Poisons Act 1972 s 3(1), (2) (see PARAS 539–541, 544) and s 6 (see PARAS 535–537).

3 Poisons Rules 1982, SI 1982/218, r 8(a). As to the meaning of 'poison' see PARA 539 note 11. Similar exemption is afforded, so far as any poison specified in Sch 4 Group II col 1, is concerned, with respect to any of the articles or substances specified opposite it in col 2 (amended by SI 1986/10; SI 1992/2293): see the Poisons Rules 1982, SI 1982/218, r 8(b). This exempts eg refrigerators containing ammonia; fire extinguishers containing barium chloride or bromomethane; seed treatments containing drazoxolon, mercuric chloride, mercuric iodide or organic compounds of mercury; batteries containing mercuric chloride; tree paints containing oxides of mercury; tobacco containing nicotine; photographic solutions containing formaldehyde; polishes and cleaners containing not more than 10% of oxalic acid dihydrate; creosotes, liquid disinfectants, antiseptics, soaps and tars containing phenols; toilet and cosmetic preparations containing traces of phenylmercuric salts; and aerosols containing small quantities of phosphorus compounds.

4 Ie articles containing barium carbonate, zinc phosphide or alpha-chloralose where the article is one of the articles to which sale of the poison is restricted by the Poisons Rules 1982, SI 1982/218: see rr 7, 10(2)(a), Sch 5 Pt A (r 7 amended by SI 1985/1077).

5 Ie by the Poisons Rules 1982, SI 1982/218, rr 5, 6 (see PARA 541), r 9 (see PARA 539), and r 10(1) (see PARA 540).

6 Poisons Rules 1982, SI 1982/218, r 7. The substances referred to in the text are the poisons included in Sch 1: see PARA 539 note 14.

(3) ENFORCEMENT, PENALTIES AND PROCEEDINGS

(i) Enforcement

548.   Powers of Pharmaceutical Society inspectors. An inspector appointed by the General Pharmaceutical Council[1] has power[2]:

(1)   for the purpose of securing compliance by pharmacists[3] and persons[4] carrying on a retail pharmacy business[5] at all reasonable times[6] to enter any registered pharmacy[7]; and

(2)   for the purpose of securing compliance by persons other than pharmacists and persons carrying on a retail pharmacy business, so far as they relate to substances included in Part I of the Poisons List[8], to enter any premises in which he has reasonable cause to suspect[9] that a breach of the law has been committed in relation to any such substances, and make such examination and inquiry and to do such other things, including the taking, on payment, of samples, as may be necessary for ascertaining whether those provisions are being complied with[10].

However, this provision does not authorise an inspector to enter or inspect the premises, not being a shop, of a doctor, a dentist, a veterinary surgeon or a veterinary practitioner[11].

1   Ie an inspector appointed under the Pharmacy Order 2010, SI 2010/231, art 8(1). As to the General Pharmaceutical Council see MEDICAL PROFESSIONS vol 74 (2011) PARA 785 et seq.
2   Poisons Act 1972 s 9(4) (amended by SI 2010/231).
3   As to the meaning of 'pharmacist' see PARA 539 note 8.
4   As to the meaning of 'person' see PARA 45 note 2.
5   As to the meaning of 'retail pharmacy business' see PARA 52 note 12; definition applied by the Poisons Act 1972 s 11(2).
6   As to what is a reasonable time see *Small v Bickley* (1875) 32 LT 726, DC (Sunday afternoon might be reasonable).
7   Poisons Act 1972 s 9(4)(a) (substituted by SI 2010/231). As to the meaning of 'registered pharmacy' see PARA 52 note 2; definition applied by the Poisons Act 1972 s 11(2).
8   As to the Poisons List see PARA 531; and as to Part I poisons see PARA 532.
9   As to the meaning of 'reasonable cause to suspect' see *R v Banks* [1916] 2 KB 621, CCA; *R v Forde* [1923] 2 KB 400, CCA; *McArdle v Egan* (1933) 150 LT 412, CA; *R v Harrison* [1938] 3 All ER 134, 26 Cr App Rep 166, CCA; *Ali (Nakkuda) v MF De S Jayaratne* [1951] AC 66, 94 Sol Jo 516, PC; *Registrar of Restrictive Trading Agreements v WH Smith & Son Ltd* [1969] 3 All ER 1065, [1969] 1 WLR 1460, CA; *R v IRC, ex p Rossminster Ltd* [1980] AC 952, sub nom *IRC v Rossminster Ltd* [1980] 1 All ER 80, HL.
10   Poisons Act 1972 s 9(4)(b) (amended by SI 2010/231). It is an offence to obstruct an inspector in the exercise of his powers and to otherwise fail to co-operate with him: see s 9(8); and PARA 551.
11   Poisons Act 1972 s 9(9). As to the meanings of 'doctor', 'dentist', 'veterinary surgeon' and 'veterinary practitioner' see PARA 534 note 14.

549. Enforcement duties of local authorities.

It is the duty of every local authority[1] by means of inspection and otherwise to take all reasonable steps to secure compliance by persons[2] who are not persons lawfully conducting a retail pharmacy business[3] with the statutory provisions relating to poisons[4] so far as those provisions relate to substances included in Part II of the Poisons List[5], and to secure compliance with those provisions by persons lawfully conducting such a business at premises which are not a registered pharmacy[6], and for those purposes to appoint inspectors[7].

1   As to the meaning of 'local authority' see PARA 535 note 1.
2   As to the meaning of 'person' see PARA 45 note 2.
3   As to the meaning of 'person lawfully conducting a retail pharmacy business' see PARA 493 note 6; definition applied by the Poisons Act 1972 s 11(2).
4   Ie the provisions of the Poisons Act 1972 ss 1–8 and of the Poisons Rules 1982, SI 1982/218.
5   Poisons Act 1972 s 9(5)(a). As to the Poisons List see PARA 531; and as to Part II poisons see PARA 533.
6   Poisons Act 1972 s 9(5)(b). As to the meaning of 'registered pharmacy' see PARA 52 note 2; definition applied by s 11(2).

7   Poisons Act 1972 s 9(5) (amended by SI 2010/231). A local authority may, with the consent of
    the General Pharmaceutical Council, appoint an inspector appointed by the General
    Pharmaceutical Council under the Pharmacy Order 2010, SI 2010/231, art 8(1) to be also an
    inspector for the purposes of the Poisons Act 1972 s 9(5): s 9(5A) (added by SI 2010/231).

550.   Powers of local authority inspectors.   An inspector appointed by a local
authority[1] has power, for the purpose of the authority's enforcement duty[2], at all
reasonable times[3] to enter:

(1)   any premises on which any person[4] whose name is entered in a local
       authority's list[5] carries on business; and

(2)   any premises on which the inspector has reasonable cause to suspect[6]
       that a breach of the law has been committed in respect of any
       substances included in Part II of the Poisons List[7],

and in either case he has power to make such examination and inquiry and to do
such other things, including the taking, on payment, of samples as may be
necessary for the purposes of the inspection[8]. This provision does not, however,
authorise an inspector to enter or inspect the premises, not being a shop, of a
doctor, a dentist, a veterinary surgeon or a veterinary practitioner[9].

An inspector appointed by a local authority has power with the consent of the
local authority[10] to institute proceedings under the Poisons Act 1972 before a
magistrates' court[11] in the name of the authority and to conduct any proceedings
so instituted by him[12].

1   As to the meaning of 'local authority' see PARA 535 note 1.
2   Ie the duty under the Poisons Act 1972 s 9(5): see PARA 549.
3   As to what is a reasonable time see PARA 548 note 9.
4   As to the meaning of 'person' see PARA 45 note 2.
5   As to the meaning of 'local authority's list' see PARA 535 note 4.
6   As to the meaning of 'reasonable cause to suspect' see PARA 548 note 9.
7   As to the Poisons List see PARA 531; and as to Part II poisons see PARA 533.
8   Poisons Act 1972 s 9(6). It is an offence to obstruct an inspector in the exercise of his powers
    and to otherwise fail to co-operate with him: see s 9(8); and PARA 551.
9   Poisons Act 1972 s 9(9). As to the meanings of 'doctor', 'dentist', 'veterinary surgeon' and
    'veterinary practitioner' see PARA 534 note 14.
10 As to the power of a local authority to authorise its officers to take proceedings see LOCAL
    GOVERNMENT vol 69 (2009) PARA 573.
11 As to magistrates' courts see MAGISTRATES vol 71 (2013) PARA 470 et seq.
12 Poisons Act 1972 s 9(7) (amended by the Legal Services Act 2007 Sch 21 para 27, Sch 23).

551.   Obstruction etc of inspectors; information.   If a person:

(1)   wilfully[1] delays or obstructs[2] an inspector, whether appointed by the
       Pharmaceutical Society of Great Britain[3] or by a local authority[4], in the
       exercise of his powers[5]; or

(2)   refuses to allow any sample to be taken[6]; or

(3)   fails without reasonable excuse to give any information which he is duly
       required to give[7],

he is in respect of each offence liable to a penalty[8].

1   'Wilfully' means deliberately and intentionally, not accidentally or inadvertently: *R v Senior*
    [1899] 1 QB 283 at 290, CCR, per Lord Russell CJ.
2   As to the meaning of 'obstructs', in the context of obstructing a constable, see CRIMINAL LAW
    vol 26 (2010) PARA 691.
3   Ie under the Poisons Act 1972 s 9.
4   Ie under the Poisons Act 1972 s 9.
5   Poisons Act 1972 s 9(8)(a). The reference in the text is a reference to an inspector's powers
    under s 9: see PARAS 548, 550.
6   Poisons Act 1972 s 9(8)(b). The reference in the text is a reference to the taking of samples
    under s 9: see PARAS 548, 550.

7 Poisons Act 1972 s 9(8)(c). The reference in the text is a reference to information required to be given under s 9: see PARAS 548, 550.
8 Poisons Act 1972 s 9(8) (amended by virtue of the Criminal Justice Act 1982 s 46). Such a person is liable on summary conviction to a fine not exceeding level 2 on the standard scale: see the Poisons Act 1972 s 9(8) (as so amended). As to the standard scale see SENTENCING AND DISPOSITION OF OFFENDERS vol 92 (2010) PARA 142.

(ii) Penalties and Proceedings

552.   Penalties. A person[1] who acts in contravention of or fails to comply[2] with any of the provisions of the Poisons Act 1972[3] or with the Poisons Rules 1982[4] is liable to a fine in respect of each offence[5] and, in the case of a continuing offence, he is liable to a further fine[6] for every day subsequent to the day on which he is convicted of the offence during which the contravention or default continues[7].

1 As to the meaning of 'person' see PARA 45 note 2.
2 The words 'fails to comply' mean a failure to comply with some substantive provision of the Poisons Act 1972 and do not apply to something which is a requirement if exemption is to be obtained: *R v Staincross Justices, ex p Teasdale* [1961] 1 QB 170, [1960] 3 All ER 572, QBD (a case decided in respect of the Pharmacy and Poisons Act 1933).
3 Ie the provisions of the Poisons Act 1972 ss 1–7, other than s 6(4) (which provides its own penalty: see PARA 537): s 8(1).
4 Ie the Poisons Rules 1982, SI 1982/218.
5 The penalty on summary conviction is a fine in respect of each offence not exceeding level 4 on the standard scale: Poisons Act 1972 s 8(1) (amended by virtue of the Criminal Justice Act 1982 s 46). As to the standard scale see SENTENCING AND DISPOSITION OF OFFENDERS vol 92 (2010) PARA 142. As to the time limit for commencing proceedings see PARA 554.
6 Ie not exceeding £10: see the Poisons Act 1972 s 8(1) (as amended: see note 5).
7 Poisons Act 1972 s 8(1) (as amended: see note 5).

553.   Proceedings for default of employees. In the case of proceedings[1] against a person[2] for or in connection with the sale, exposure for sale or supply of a non-medicinal poison[3] effected by an employee, it is not a defence that the employee acted without the authority of the employer[4], and any material fact known to the employee is deemed to have been known to the employer[5].

1 Ie under the Poisons Act 1972 s 8: see PARA 552.
2 As to the meaning of 'person' see PARA 45 note 2.
3 As to the meaning of 'non-medicinal poison' see PARA 532 note 2.
4 Poisons Act 1972 s 8(2)(a).
5 Poisons Act 1972 s 8(2)(b).

554.   Time limit for prosecutions. Notwithstanding any provision in any Act prescribing the period within which summary proceedings may be commenced[1], proceedings for an offence under the Poisons Act 1972 may be commenced at any time within the period of 12 months[2] after the date of the commission of the offence or, in the case of proceedings instituted by, or by the direction of, the Secretary of State[3], either within that period or within the period of three months after the date on which evidence sufficient in his opinion to justify a prosecution for the offence comes to his knowledge[4], whichever period ends on the later date[5].

1 See e g the Magistrates' Courts Act 1980 s 127(1); and MAGISTRATES vol 71 (2013) PARA 526.
2 As to the meaning of 'month' see PARA 43 note 3.
3 As to the Secretary of State see PARA 2 note 1. See also PARA 530 note 1.

4   For this purpose, a certificate purporting to be signed by the Secretary of State as to the date on which such evidence came to his knowledge is conclusive evidence of that date: Poisons Act 1972 s 8(3).

5   Poisons Act 1972 s 8(3).

555.   Analysts' certificates as evidence. A document purporting to be a certificate signed by a public analyst[1] or a person appointed by the Secretary of State[2] to make analyses for the purposes of the Poisons Act 1972[3], stating the result of an analysis made by him, is admissible in any proceedings under the Poisons Act 1972 as evidence of the matters stated in it, but either party may require the person by whom the analysis was made to be called as a witness[4].

1   Poisons Act 1972 s 8(4)(a) (amended by the Food Safety Act 1990 s 59(1), Sch 3 para 16). A public analyst is a public analyst appointed under the Food Safety Act 1990 s 27 (see FOOD vol 18(2) (Reissue) PARA 510): Poisons Act 1972 s 8(4)(a).

2   As to the Secretary of State see PARA 2 note 1. See also PARA 530 note 1.

3   Poisons Act 1972 s 8(4)(b).

4   Poisons Act 1972 s 8(4).

MENTAL HEALTH AND CAPACITY

PARA

1. GENERAL SCHEME OF THE LEGISLATION 556

2. MENTAL HEALTH SERVICES 566
(1) In general 566
(2) Functions of Central Government 567
(3) The National Health Service Commissioning Board and Clinical Commissioning Groups 571
(4) The Care Quality Commission 573
(5) Health and Hospital Services 574
(6) Social Services 579
(7) Local Mental Health Support Services: Wales 586
(8) Education 592
(9) Finances 593
(10) Inquiries 596

3. MENTAL CAPACITY 597
(1) Introduction 597
(2) Persons Lacking Capacity under the Mental Capacity Act 2005 601
    (i) Persons who Lack Capacity 601
    (ii) Lasting Powers of Attorney 618
    (iii) Advance Decisions to Refuse Treatment 623
    (iv) Decisions that Cannot be made on Behalf of a Person 627
    (v) Restrictions on Intrusive Research 630
    (vi) Independent Mental Capacity Advocate Service 634
(3) Deprivation of Liberty under the Mental Capacity Act 2005 648
    (i) Introduction 648
    (ii) Deprivation of Liberty Authorisations under Schedule A1 651
    (iii) Qualifying Requirements 653
    (iv) Standard Authorisations 661
        A. Giving a Standard Authorisation 661
        B. Eligibility Requirement Not Met: Suspension of Standard Authorisation 680
        C. Change in Supervisory Responsibility 682
        D. Review 683

PARA

    E.   Assessments 695

    F.   Relevant Person's Representative 707

(v)   Urgent Authorisations 713

(vi)   Monitoring and Supervisory Powers 717

4.   COURT OF PROTECTION 720

(1)   In general 720

(2)   Powers 723

    (i)   Court of Protection 723

    (ii)   Deputies 734

(3)   Practice and Procedure 740

(4)   Visiting 748

(5)   Right of Appeal 750

5.   THE PUBLIC GUARDIAN 751

6.   PATIENTS WITH MENTAL DISORDER 757

(1)   Introduction 757

(2)   Guidance 762

(3)   Admission 764

    (i)   Voluntary Admission 764

    (ii)   Compulsory Admission 766

(4)   Guardianship 784

(5)   Community Treatment Orders 797

(6)   Protection of Relevant Patients 806

(7)   Independent Mental Health Advocates 807

(8)   Mental Health Professionals 815

    (i)   Approved Mental Health Professionals 815

    (ii)   Conflict of Interest 825

    (iii)   Approved Clinician and Responsible Clinician 831

    (iv)   Medical Practitioners and Mental Health Nurses 835

    (v)   Pensions 837

(9)   Relatives 838

(10)   Applications Procedures 847

(11)   Care Coordinators: Wales 851

(12)   Hospital and Guardianship Orders by Criminal Courts 859

(13)   Primary Mental Health Assessments: Wales 881

			PARA
(14)	Transfer of Patients		886
	(i)	Transfer from Hospital to Hospital or Guardianship	886
	(ii)	Transfer and Removal of Prisoners to Hospital	892
	(iii)	Transfer within United Kingdom etc	899
(15)	Duration, Discharge (other than by Tribunal) and Reclassification		908
(16)	Absence and Escape		917
(17)	Place of Safety Powers		922
(18)	Medical Treatment		924
	(i)	Consent to Treatment	924
	(ii)	Treatment of Community Patients not Recalled to Hospital	935
(19)	Aftercare and Assessments		945
	(i)	Aftercare	945
	(ii)	Assessment of Former Users of Secondary Mental Health Services: Wales	947
7.	APPLICATIONS TO TRIBUNALS		955
(1)	The Tribunals		955
	(i)	The Appropriate Tribunal	955
	(ii)	First-tier Tribunal	956
	(iii)	Mental Health Review Tribunal for Wales	957
	(iv)	Further Appeals	958
(2)	Applications and References		959
(3)	Powers of Tribunals		967
(4)	Procedure		972
	(i)	General Provisions	972
	(ii)	First-tier Tribunal (Health, Education and Social Care Chamber)	973
	(iii)	Mental Health Review Tribunal for Wales	980
8.	LITIGATION		993
(1)	Civil		993
(2)	Criminal		1004
9.	OFFENCES		1008

1. GENERAL SCHEME OF THE LEGISLATION

556. Former statutory law. Before the Mental Health Act 1959, the Lunacy and Mental Treatment Acts 1890 to 1930[1] provided generally for the reception, care and treatment of the mentally ill (apart from criminal lunatics[2]) either as voluntary[3] or temporary[4] patients, or as patients detained under reception orders[5] made by single justices, or orders having the like effect[6]. The Mental Deficiency Acts 1913 to 1938[7] similarly provided for the reception, care and treatment of the mentally defective[8] under orders made by judicial authorities[9], or in certain cases by a court[10], or by the Secretary of State[11], or on the written authority of a parent or guardian[12]. Criminal lunatics were detained in institutions such as Broadmoor or, if suitable, in mental hospitals on the warrant of the Secretary of State[13].

The central authority charged with the provision of hospital and specialist services for the mentally ill and mentally defective was (as in the case of the physically ill) the Minister of Health[14]. The Board of Control[15], an independent corporate body with certain statutory powers of discharge, was responsible for the visitation[16] of all establishments for mental patients, for the examination of copies of the documents authorising the reception and detention of mental patients[17] and for the periodical review of their cases[18]. The board was also the statutory manager of Broadmoor[19] and of the two state institutions for mental defectives of dangerous or violent propensities[20]. The local health authorities were responsible for providing supervision, training or occupation for the mentally defective in the community and for securing their removal to institutions or to guardianship, where appropriate[21].

1   The Acts described by this collective title and in force immediately before the coming into force of the Mental Health Act 1959 were the Lunacy Act 1890, the Lunacy Act 1891 (see s 1), the Lunacy Act 1908 (see s 5), the Lunacy Act 1922 (see s 3) and the Mental Treatment Act 1930 (see s 22(1)), all of which were repealed by the Mental Health Act 1959 ss 1, 149(2), Sch 8 Pt I. The repeal of the Mental Treatment Act 1930 s 20 did not affect any amendment made by s 20 (which related to nomenclature) in any enactment not repealed by the Mental Health Act 1959: see the Mental Health Act 1983 s 148(1), Sch 5 paras 29, 30.

2   These were termed 'Broadmoor patients' by the Criminal Justice Act 1948 s 62(2) (repealed); they had been termed 'criminal lunatics' in the Criminal Lunatics Act 1884 s 16 (repealed). As to the powers under the Mental Health Act 1983 of the Secretary of State to transfer prisoners to hospital see PARA 892 et seq; and as to the power of the courts to order admission to hospital in criminal proceedings see PARA 859 et seq. As to the current prison system see PRISONS AND PRISONERS vol 85 (2012) PARA 401 et seq.

3   Mental Treatment Act 1930 s 1(1) (repealed).

4   Mental Treatment Act 1930 s 5 (repealed).

5   Lunacy Act 1890 ss 4, 6, 16 (repealed).

6   Eg under the Magistrates' Courts Act 1952 s 30(1) (repealed).

7   The Acts described by this collective title were the Mental Deficiency Act 1913, the Mental Deficiency (Amendment) Act 1925, the Mental Deficiency Act 1927 (see s 11) and the Mental Deficiency Act 1938 (see s 2), all of which were repealed by the Mental Health Act 1959 Sch 8 Pt I.

8   As to the meaning of 'defective' see PARA 559 note 7.

9   Mental Deficiency Act 1913 ss 5, 6 (repealed).

10   Mental Deficiency Act 1913 s 8(1)(b) (repealed).

11   Mental Deficiency Act 1913 s 9 (repealed).

12   Mental Deficiency Act 1913 s 3 (repealed).

13   See note 2.

14   National Health Service Act 1946 ss 1, 3(1) (repealed). The minister's functions are now carried out in England by the Secretary of State or the Welsh Ministers: see the National Health Service Act 2006; the National Health Service (Wales) Act 2006; and PARA 568. See further HEALTH SERVICES vol 54 (2008) PARA 10 et seq.

15 As to the establishment and reorganisation of the Board of Control see the Mental Deficiency Act 1913 ss 22, 65 (repealed); and the Mental Treatment Act 1930 s 11 (repealed).

16 Lunacy Act 1890 ss 187, 191, 198–200 (repealed); Mental Deficiency Act 1913 s 25 (repealed).

17 See the Lunacy Act 1890 s 34 (repealed); and the Mental Deficiency Act 1913 ss 20, 41 (repealed).

18 Lunacy Act 1890 s 38 (repealed); Lunacy Act 1891 s 7 (repealed); Mental Deficiency Act 1913 s 11 (repealed).

19 Criminal Justice Act 1948 s 62(3) (repealed). Broadmoor became a special hospital, and is now a hospital providing high security psychiatric services: see PARA 569.

20 National Health Service Act 1946 s 49(4) (repealed). Rampton and Moss Side (now part of Ashworth hospital) became special hospitals, and are now within the regime of hospitals providing high security psychiatric services: see PARA 569.

21 Mental Deficiency Act 1913 s 30 (repealed); Mental Deficiency Act 1927 s 7(2) (repealed); National Health Service Act 1946 ss 50, 51 (repealed).

557. Origin and territorial scope. The Mental Health Act 1959 gave legislative effect to most of the recommendations contained in the report made in 1957 by the Royal Commission appointed to inquire into the then existing law relating to mental illness and mental deficiency[1]. The Mental Health Act 1959 was extensively amended by the Mental Health (Amendment) Act 1982, which implemented the proposals made by the government's review of the Mental Health Act 1959[2]. Most of the provisions of the 1959 and 1982 Acts were consolidated in the Mental Health Act 1983[3].

Generally, the Mental Health Act 1983 applies only to England[4] and Wales[5], and to the Isles of Scilly[6]. However, certain provisions of the Act, relating mainly to the removal and return within the British islands of mentally disordered persons[7] who are liable to detention under the Act, are specifically extended to Northern Ireland[8]; and specific provisions apply to the removal of patients[9] to and from the Channel Islands and the Isle of Man[10] and the removal of alien patients to countries outside the United Kingdom, the Isle of Man and the Channel Islands[11]. Certain provisions of the Act apply also to Scotland[12].

1 See the *Report of the Royal Commission on the Law relating to Mental Illness and Mental Deficiency 1954–1957* (Cmnd 169 (1957)).

2 See the White Paper *Review of the Mental Health Act 1959* (Cmnd 7320), which was published in 1978; the changes made were explained in *Reform of Mental Health Legislation* (Cmnd 8405), published in 1981.

3 The provisions of the Mental Health Act 1959 not repealed by the Mental Health Act 1983 include: the Mental Health Act 1959 s 8 (amended by the Charities Act 1972 s 78(2), Sch 7; the Local Government Act 1972 s 195, Sch 23 para 9(1); the National Health Service Act 1977 s 129, Sch 15 para 24, Sch 6; the National Health Service and Community Care Act 1990 s 66(2), Sch 10 as from a day to be appointed; and the National Health Service (Consequential Provisions) Act 2006 s 2, Sch 1 paras 22, 23) (functions of welfare authorities); the Mental Health Act 1959 s 131(1) (prosecution by local authorities: see PARA 584); s 142 (default powers of minister) (see PARA 568); s 144(1)(a) (expenses); s 145(1) (general provisions as to regulations, orders and rules); s 149(1) (minor and consequential amendments and repeals); s 152 (amended by the Northern Ireland Constitution Act 1973 s 41(1), Sch 6 Pt I; the House of Commons Disqualification Act 1975 s 10(2), Sch 3; the Mental Health (Amendment) Act 1982 s 65(2), Sch 4; and the Mental Health Act 1983 s 148(3), Sch 6) (application to Northern Ireland); and the Mental Health Act 1983 s 154(1) (short title and application to Scilly Isles). The following provisions were not repealed by the Mental Health Act 1983 but have been repealed subsequently: the Mental Health Act 1959 s 9 (repealed) (functions of children authorities); s 128 (repealed) (sexual intercourse with patients) (but see PARA 1012); s 143 (repealed) (inquiries).

The provisions of the Mental Health (Amendment) Act 1982 not repealed by the Mental Health Act 1983 include: the Mental Health (Amendment) Act 1982 s 34 (amended by the Statute Law (Repeals) Act 2004) (amendments to the Bail Act 1976 etc); the Mental Health (Amendment) Act 1982 s 65 (consequential amendments and repeals); s 67 (expenses); s 68(1) (interpretation); s 69(1), (6) (transitional provisions); s 70 (amended by the Mental Health Act 1983 s 148, Sch 4 para 61, Sch 6) (short title etc).

The following enactments were also consolidated in the Mental Health Act 1983: the Mental Health Act (Northern Ireland) 1961 Sch 5 paras 1–5; the Criminal Procedure (Insanity) Act 1964 s 4(7); the Administration of Justice Act 1965 Sch 1 (part); the Courts-Martial (Appeals) Act 1968 Sch 4 (part); the Family Law Reform Act 1969 s 12 (not repealed) and Sch 1 (part); the Children and Young Persons Act 1969 Sch 5 paras 38–40; the Administration of Justice Act 1969 ss 17–19; the Local Authority Social Services Act 1970 Sch 1 (prospectively amended) (part); the Courts Act 1971 Sch 8 para 38(a), (b), Sch 9 (part); the Immigration Act 1971 s 30(2) (part); the Local Government Act 1972 Sch 23 para 9(1) (part), (2) (part), (4)–(6); the Guardianship Act 1973 s 1(8) (part); the Nursing Homes Act 1975 Sch 1 paras 1–3, 147; the Criminal Law Act 1977 s 32 (not repealed), Sch 6 (part); the National Health Service Act 1977 s 105(3) (part), Sch 15 paras 23, 26–28, 30–31, 32 (not repealed), 33; the Child Care Act 1980 Sch 5 paras 13, 14; the Magistrates' Courts Act 1980 s 32(2) (not repealed), Sch 7 paras 31, 32; the Health Services Act 1980 Sch 1 para 13; the Forgery and Counterfeiting Act 1981 s 11(1); the Senior Courts Act 1981 s 144, Sch 5 (part), Sch 6 para 4; and the British Nationality Act 1981 s 39(7) (part).

Provision is made for the repeal or amendment of any local enactment so far as appears to be necessary in consequence of the Mental Health Act 1983: see s 144.

4 'England' means, subject to any alteration of boundaries of local government areas, the area consisting of the counties established by the Local Government Act 1972 s 1 (see LOCAL GOVERNMENT vol 69 (2009) PARA 24), Greater London and the Isles of Scilly: Interpretation Act 1978 s 5, Sch 1. As to local government areas see LOCAL GOVERNMENT vol 69 (2009) PARA 24 et seq; and as to boundary changes see LOCAL GOVERNMENT vol 69 (2009) PARA 56 et seq. As to Greater London see LONDON GOVERNMENT vol 71 (2013) PARA 14.

5 As to the transfer of certain ministerial functions under the Mental Health Act 1959, the Mental Health Act 1983 and other legislation to the Welsh Ministers in so far as they are exercisable in relation to Wales see PARA 567. 'Wales' means the combined area of the counties which were created by the Local Government Act 1972 s 20 (as originally enacted) (see LOCAL GOVERNMENT vol 69 (2009) PARA 37), but subject to any alteration made under s 73 (consequential alteration of boundary following alteration of watercourse) (see LOCAL GOVERNMENT vol 69 (2009) PARA 90): Interpretation Act 1978 Sch 1 (definition substituted by the Local Government (Wales) Act 1994 s 1(3), Sch 2 para 9).

6 See the Mental Health Act 1983 s 149(4). The Isles of Scilly (Mental Health) Order 1985, SI 1985/149, made under the National Health Service Act 1977 s 130(4), extended the Mental Health Act 1983 to the Isles of Scilly from 12 March 1985, with the modification that the expression 'local social services authority' in the Mental Health Act 1983, in relation to the Isles, means the Council of the Isles of Scilly.

7 As to removal and return between Northern Ireland and England and Wales see PARAS 918, 903–904, 920–921. As to the meaning of 'mentally disordered' see PARA 761.

8 See the Mental Health Act 1983 s 147. The relevant provisions are: ss 81–82 (see PARAS 903–904), s 86 (see PARA 907), s 87 (see PARA 920), s 88 (repealed) (and, so far as applied by s 88, s 18 (see PARA 918), s 22 (see PARA 912) and s 138 (see PARA 777), as is applied in relation to Northern Ireland by s 110), s 128 (see PARAS 1013–1014) (except as it relates to patients subject to guardianship), s 137 (see PARA 776), s 139 (see PARA 759), s 141 (see PARA 782), s 142 (repealed), s 143 (so far as applicable to any Order in Council extending to Northern Ireland) and s 144 (see note 3): see s 147 (amended by the Mental Capacity Act 2005 s 167, Sch 6 para 29(1), (9), Sch 7). As from 28 April 2013 the Mental Health Act 1983 s 147 is further amended and the reference to s 141 is repealed: see the Mental Health (Discrimination) Act 2013 s 4(1), Schedule para 1(3). As to the Mental Capacity Act 2005 generally see PARA 597.

9 As to the meaning of 'patient' see PARA 758.

10 See the Mental Health Act 1983 ss 83–85, 89; and PARAS 905–906, 920.

11 See the Mental Health Act 1983 s 86; and PARA 907.

12 See the Mental Health Act 1983 s 146 (amended by the Mental Capacity Act 2005 s 167, Sch 6 para 29(1), (8), Sch 7; Mental Health Act 2007 Sch 11 Pt 7). As from 28 April 2013 the Mental Health Act 1983 s 146 is further amended by the Mental Health (Discrimination) Act 2013: see s 4(1), Schedule para 1(2). As to moving patients from or to Scotland see also the Mental Health (Care and Treatment) (Scotland) Act 2003; and the Mental Health (Care and Treatment) (Scotland) Act 2003 (Consequential Provisions) Order 2005, SI 2005/2078 (S 9).

558. The former jurisdiction in lunacy. Until the coming into force of the Mental Health Act 1959[1], the jurisdiction in lunacy under which a patient's property was administered was partly statutory and partly an inherent jurisdiction under the royal prerogative exercised by the Lord Chancellor[2] and certain of the judges[3] to whom the jurisdiction was entrusted under the sign manual[4].

In theory the royal prerogative still exists, but there is no one to exercise it since no one is now entrusted under the sign manual with the exercise of the inherent jurisdiction under the royal prerogative[5], nor is there any person qualified to hold an inquisition. In effect, therefore, the jurisdiction is now entirely statutory.

1   Ie the Mental Health Act 1959 Pt VIII (ss 100–121) (largely repealed). The Mental Health Act 1983 made changes in relation to the admission, reception and treatment of mentally disordered patients but not to the management of their property and affairs: see the Mental Health Act 1983 Pt VII (ss 93–113) (repealed). The Mental Capacity Act 2005 Pt 2 (ss 45–61) on the management of patients' property and affairs replaced those contained in the Mental Health Act 1983 Pt VII. The replacement provisions deal with a new superior court of record (the Court of Protection), its judges and procedures (see PARA 720 et seq); establish a new statutory official (the Public Guardian) to support the work of the court (see PARA 751 et seq); and also provide for Court of Protection Visitors (see PARA 748). The Court of Protection has an expanded jurisdiction to cover decisions relating to the personal welfare of incapacitated adults in addition to their property and affairs: see PARA 727 et seq. Decisions relating to personal welfare and property and affairs will also be able to be taken by the donee of a lasting power of attorney (see PARAS 618–622) who will be subject to the supervision of the Public Guardian. As to the court's power in relation to lasting powers of attorney see PARA 622.

2   As to the Lord Chancellor see CONSTITUTIONAL LAW AND HUMAN RIGHTS vol 8(2) (Reissue) PARA 477 et seq.

3   See COURTS AND TRIBUNALS vol 24 (2010) PARA 843 et seq.

4   See CONSTITUTIONAL LAW AND HUMAN RIGHTS vol 8(2) (Reissue) PARA 309. It was a condition precedent to the exercise of the inherent jurisdiction that the patient should be found by inquisition to be of unsound mind.

5   The jurisdiction under the prerogative remained at large in those to whom the warrant was addressed until the coming into operation of the Mental Health Act 1959. The last royal warrant, dated 10 April 1956, was revoked by royal warrant dated 1 November 1960.

559. Historical development of legislative terms. Since early times a distinction has been recognised in the law between idiots, that is to say natural fools who were incurable and whose lack of capacity was from birth[1], and lunatics[2], who became insane after birth and whose incapacity was or might be temporary or intermittent[3]. The expression 'non compos mentis' was used in an old statute of limitation[4] as a general term, and was approved by Sir Edward Coke as being 'most sure and legal'[5]. The term 'lunatic' was used in the Lunacy Act 1890, which consolidated the previous legislation relating both to care and treatment and to the management of a person's property and affairs[6]. Separate legislative provision was made for 'mental defectives' in the Mental Deficiency Acts 1913 and 1927[7]. In the Mental Treatment Act 1930, the term 'person of unsound mind' was applied to persons formerly described as lunatics[8]. However, the term 'person of unsound mind' was not statutorily defined, and the courts were loath to attempt to define it[9].

The Mental Health Act 1959 replaced the previous legislation dealing with persons of unsound mind and mental defectives and introduced the general term 'mental disorder' to cover all forms of mental ill-health or disability[10]. That Act was consolidated, with amendments, in the Mental Health Act 1983[11] which effectively created four categories of mental disorder[12]; namely mental illness, mental impairment[13], psychopathic disorder[14] and severe mental impairment[15] and specifically excluded a person from being dealt with under the Act and suffering from any mental disorder, or from any form of mental disorder described in the Act, by reason only of promiscuity or other immoral conduct, sexual deviancy or dependency on alcohol or drugs[16]. The Mental Health Act 1983 has since been amended by the Mental Health Act 2007 which, amongst other things, abolished the four categories of mental disorder and extended the definition of mental disorder to cover 'any disorder or disability of the mind'[17]. Persons with a learning disability[18] are excluded from certain provisions of the Act and dependence on alcohol or drugs is not considered to be a disorder or disability of the mind[19].

The Mental Capacity Act 2005 applies to a person who lacks capacity[20]. Under the Act a person lacks capacity in relation to a matter if at the material time he is unable to make a decision for himself[21] in relation to the matter because of an impairment of, or a disturbance in the functioning of, the mind or brain[22].

1   In ordinary speech 'idiot' means a person so deficient in mind as to be permanently incapable of rational conduct. A distinction between idiots (ie persons permanently incapable from birth) and other persons was recognised in the statute de Praerogativa Regis (temp incert but generally cited as 17 Edward 2) ch 11, 12 (repealed), whereby the Sovereign had the custody of the land of natural fools: see the *Report of the Royal Commission on the Law relating to Mental Illness and Mental Deficiency 1954–1957* (Cmnd 169 (1957)) PARA 146.

2   The term 'lunatic' was first found in the statute book in 33 Hen 8 c 20 (Attainder and Forfeiture for Treason) (1541) (repealed), and was there applied to those who became insane after birth. It was used by Sir Edward Coke and Sir Matthew Hale as applicable to a person whose insanity was temporary or intermittent: see *Beverley's Case* (1603) 4 Co Rep 123b; Co Litt 247a; 1 Hale PC 34. In 2 & 3 Edw 6 c 8 (Inquisitions of Escheator) (1548) (repealed), 'lunatic' and 'idiot' were used indiscriminately; similarly, in the writ de lunatico inquirendo, 'lunatic' was used to cover all forms of insanity. In the Lunacy Act 1890 (repealed), which was a consolidating Act, 'lunatic' (see s 341 as originally enacted) was defined to mean an idiot or person of unsound mind. In ancient times, 'lunatic' ('lunaticus') described a man who 'hath sometimes his understanding and sometimes not': see *Ex p Cranmer* (1806) 12 Ves 445 per Lord Erskine.

3   Sir Matthew Hale distinguishes three sorts of mental defect or incapacity, namely idiocy, madness and lunacy: 1 Hale PC 29. These three were included in the common term 'dementia'. The first was dementia naturalis, the second and third were dementia accidentalis vel adventitia. 'Madness' denoted incapacity of mind that was complete and permanent, and 'lunacy' denoted an incapacity of mind which was intermittent and interpolated with lucid intervals. However, in 33 Hen 8 c 20 (Attainder and Forfeiture for Treason) (1541) (repealed), 'lunacy' was used as an alternative for madness.

4   23 Eliz 1 c 3 (Fines and Recoveries) (1580–81) s 3 (repealed).

5   Co Litt 246b; and see *Ex p Barnsley* (1744) 3 Atk 168 at 173 per Lord Hardwicke LC.

6   Lunacy Act 1890 s 98 (repealed). Cf s 90(1) (repealed). As to the meaning of 'lunatic' in that Act see note 2.

7   Mental defectiveness was defined as 'a condition of arrested or incomplete development of mind existing before the age of 18 years, whether arising from inherent causes or induced by disease or injury'; it consisted of four categories: idiots, imbeciles, feeble-minded persons and moral defectives: Mental Deficiency Act 1913 s 1(2) (repealed); Mental Deficiency Act 1927 s 1 (repealed). See the *Report of the Royal Commission on the Care and Control of the Feeble-minded 1904–1908* (Cd 4202 (1908)); and the *Report of the Royal Commission on Lunacy and Mental Disorders 1924–1926* (Cmd 2700 (1926)).

8   See the Mental Treatment Act 1930 s 20(5) (repealed), whereby 'lunatic' was no longer to be used except eg in the phrase 'criminal lunatic'; and the *Report of the Royal Commission on Lunacy and Mental Disorders 1924–1926* (Cmd 2700 (1926)). Criminal lunatics were subsequently described as 'Broadmoor patients': see the Criminal Justice Act 1948 s 62(2) (repealed). See also *Whysall v Whysall* [1960] P 52 at 62–64, [1959] 3 All ER 389 at 394–395; *Buxton v Jayne* [1960] 2 All ER 688 at 692, 697, [1960] 1 WLR 783 at 788, 795, CA; *Robinson v Robinson (by his guardian)* [1965] P 192, [1964] 3 All ER 232.

9   See eg *Whysall v Whysall* [1960] P 52 at 64–65, [1959] 3 All ER 389 at 395.

10 The Mental Health Act 1959 s 4(1) (repealed) defined 'mental disorder' as 'mental illness, arrested or incomplete development of mind, psychopathic disorder and any other disorder or disability of mind'. See now the Mental Health Act 1983 s 1(2); and PARA 761.

11 There have been numerous changes in this area since the incorporation into English law by the Human Rights Act 1998 of certain provisions of the Convention for the Protection of Human Rights and Fundamental Freedoms (1950) (Rome, 4 November 1950; TS 71 (1953); Cmd 8969) (commonly known as the 'European Convention on Human Rights'): see RIGHTS AND FREEDOMS. Other important relevant regional and international instruments include: the United Nations Principles for the Protection of Persons with Mental Illness and for the Improvement of Mental Health Care (1991); and the Council of Europe Recommendation 2004 (10) concerning the Protection of the Human Rights and Dignity of Persons with Mental Disorder.

12 'Mental disorder' was originally defined as mental illness, arrested or incomplete development of mind, psychopathic disorder and any other disorder or disability of mind: Mental Health Act 1983 s 1(2) (as originally enacted).

13 'Mental impairment' was defined to mean a state of arrested or incomplete development of mind (not amounting to severe mental impairment) which includes significant impairment of intelligence and social functioning and is associated with abnormally aggressive or seriously irresponsible conduct on the part of the person concerned: Mental Health Act 1983 s 1(2) (as originally enacted).

14 'Psychopathic disorder' was defined to mean a persistent disorder or disability of mind (whether or not including significant impairment of intelligence) which results in abnormally aggressive or seriously irresponsible conduct on the part of the person concerned: Mental Health Act 1983 s 1(2) (as originally enacted).

15 'Severe mental impairment' was defined to mean a state of arrested or incomplete development of mind which includes severe impairment of intelligence and social functioning and is associated with abnormally aggressive or seriously irresponsible conduct on the part of the person concerned: Mental Health Act 1983 s 1(2) (as originally enacted).

16 See the Mental Health Act 1983 s 1(3) (as originally enacted).

17 See the Mental Health Act 1983 s 1(2); and PARA 761.

18 As to the meaning of 'learning disability' see PARA 761 note 8.

19 See the Mental Health Act 1983 s 1(2); and PARA 761.

20 The Limitation Act 1980 now uses the term 'lacks capacity': see s 38(2) (amended by the Mental Capacity Act 2005 Sch 6 para 25).

21 As to when a person is unable to make decisions for himself see the Mental Capacity Act 2005 s 3; and PARA 605.

22 See the Mental Capacity Act 2005 s 2(1); and PARA 603.

560. General overview of current legislation. The Mental Health Act 1983[1] prescribes a single code under which patients[2] in need of treatment for mental disorder[3] may be compulsorily admitted to and detained in[4] any hospital[5] or a registered establishment[6] or received into the guardianship[7] of a local social services authority[8] or other person[9]. The Act also provides for courts in criminal proceedings to make orders for admission to hospital or guardianship orders in respect of people suffering from mental disorder[10], for the treatment of patients whilst in the community[11] and for the transfer to hospital of certain prisoners and other persons liable to be detained[12]. Provision is also made, inter alia, for the temporary removal of people suffering or believed to be suffering from mental disorder to a place of safety[13]; for the removal and return of patients within the United Kingdom[14] and abroad[15]. Provision is also made for informal patients[16].

The Mental Health Act 1983 also contains provisions as to the circumstances in which the patient's consent to treatment is or is not necessary[17] and for the after-care of detained patients[18].

The Mental Capacity Act 2005[19] reformed, updated and codified[20] the law under which decisions are to be made on behalf of incapacitated adults in their best interests. It applies where a person loses mental capacity at some point in their lives and where they have been incapacitated since birth. Part 1 of the Act[21] has provisions defining 'persons who lack capacity'[22]. It contains a set of principles[23] and a checklist to be used in ascertaining a person's best interests[24]. There are provisions dealing with liability for actions in connection with the care and treatment of a person who lacks capacity to consent to what is done and for acts of restraint falling short of a deprivation of liberty[25]. A statutory scheme is provided for decision-making. It includes lasting powers of attorney[26], provisions setting out the general powers of the Court of Protection and court appointed deputies where a person lacks capacity[27]. Decisions may extend to personal welfare matters, including health and medical treatment, and the management of property and affairs. Part 1 of the Act also sets out rules on advance decisions to refuse medical treatment[28], the circumstances under which a person may and may not be deprived of his liberty[29], decisions which cannot be made by another person on behalf of the person lacking capacity[30], and research involving people who lack capacity[31]; and a system for providing independent consultees for particularly vulnerable people[32]. Part 2 of the Act[33] deals with the Court of Protection[34]; the Public Guardian, to support the work of the court[35], and Court of Protection Visitors[36]. The Act does not affect the law relating to murder, manslaughter or assisted suicide[37]. It makes provision as to the private international law of England and Wales in relation to persons who cannot protect their interests, governing which jurisdiction should apply when a national of one country is in another state[38].

Under both the Mental Health Act 1983 and the Mental Capacity Act 2005, the effects of the Human Rights Act 1998 and the European Convention on Human Rights must also be considered[39]. The United Nations Convention of the Rights of Persons with Disabilities is also relevant[40].

In relation to Wales, provision is also made in relation to primary mental health support services[41]; the coordination of and planning for secondary mental health services[42]; assessments of the needs of former users of secondary mental health services[43]; independent advocacy for persons detained under the Mental Health Act 1983 and other persons who are receiving in-patient hospital treatment for mental health[44].

1   Significant changes to the Mental Health Act 1983 were made by the Mental Health Act 2007. This Act received Royal Assent on 19 July 2007. Most of the law relating to mental and capacity is to be found in the Mental Health Act 1983 and the Mental Capacity Act 2005. However additional restrictions also exist for example the domicile of a mentally incapacitated person cannot be changed either by his own act or by the person having charge of him (see CONFLICT OF LAWS vol 19 (2011) PARA 357); a firearm certificate may be revoked by the chief officer for police for the area in which the holder resides if he has reason to believe that the holder is of intemperate habits or unsound mind or is otherwise unfit to be trusted with a firearm (see the Firearms Act 1968 s 30A(1), (2)(a); and CRIMINAL LAW vol 26 (2010) PARA 639); and see also PARA 1016.

2   As to the meaning of 'patient' see PARA 758 note 4.

3   As to the meaning of 'mental disorder' see PARA 761.

4   Ie under the Mental Health Act 1983 Pt 2 (ss 2–34): see PARA 767 et seq.

5   As to the meaning of 'hospital' see PARA 577.

6   As to registered establishments see PARA 578; and SOCIAL SERVICES AND COMMUNITY CARE.

7   See the Mental Health Act 1983 ss 7–8; and PARAS 785, 787 et seq.

8   As to the meaning of 'local social services authority' see PARA 579.

9   See the Mental Health Act 1983 Pt 2 (ss 2–34); and PARA 767 et seq.

10   As to the meaning of 'mental disorder' and its various forms see PARA 761.

11   See the Mental Health Act 1983 Pt 4A (ss 64A–64K); and PARAS 935–941.

12   See the Mental Health Act 1983 Pt 3 (ss 35–55); and PARAS 859–880, 892–898.

13   See the Mental Health Act 1983 ss 135–136; and PARAS 922–923.

14   'United Kingdom' means Great Britain and Northern Ireland: Interpretation Act 1978 s 5, Sch 1. 'Great Britain' means England, Scotland and Wales: Union with Scotland Act 1706, preamble

     art I; Interpretation Act 1978 s 22(1), Sch 2 para 5(a). Neither the Channel Islands nor the Isle of Man are within the United Kingdom. See further CONSTITUTIONAL LAW AND HUMAN RIGHTS vol 8(2) (Reissue) PARA 3.

15   See the Mental Health Act 1983 Pt VI (ss 80–92); and PARAS 899–907, 920.

16   See the Mental Health Act 1983 s 131(1); and PARA 764.

17   See the Mental Health Act 1983 Pt 4 (ss 56–64); and PARAS 924–933.

18   See the Mental Health Act 1983 s 117; and PARA 945.

19   The Mental Capacity Act 2005 has its origin in the *Report on Mental Incapacity* (Law Com no 231) (1995). This report was followed by a policy statement 'Making Decisions' (1999), and then the publication of a draft Mental Incapacity Bill and accompanying notes ((Cm 5859-I, II) (2003)). The Bill was subjected to scrutiny by a Joint Committee of both Houses of Parliament which published its report in November 2003 (HL Paper (2002–03) no 189-I; HC Paper (2002–03) no 1083-I), and the government's response to this report was presented to Parliament in February 2004 ((Cm 6121) (2004)). The Bill was renamed and introduced into Parliament as the Mental Capacity Bill in June 2004, and it received Royal Assent on 7 April 2005.

20   The Mental Capacity Act 2005 places on a statutory footing many of the developments of the common law in relation to treatment and welfare of those who are incapacitated and their best interests, and advance decisions refusing medical treatment. As to the broader scheme of the Act and its relationship with the common law and the Mental Health Act 1983 see PARA 597.

21   Ie the Mental Capacity Act 2005 Pt 1 (ss 1–44).

22   See the Mental Capacity Act 2005 ss 2, 3; and PARAS 603, 605.

23   See the Mental Capacity Act 2005 s 1; and PARA 601.

24   See the Mental Capacity Act 2005 s 4; and PARA 606.

25   See the Mental Capacity Act 2005 ss 5–8; and PARAS 611, 613.

26   See the Mental Capacity Act 2005 ss 9–14; and PARAS 618–622. See also AGENCY vol 1 (2008) PARA 217 et seq.

27   See the Mental Capacity Act 2005 ss 15–21; and PARAS 723–735.

28   See the Mental Capacity Act 2005 ss 24–26; and PARAS 623–626.

29   See the Mental Capacity Act 2005 ss 4A, 4B, Schs A1, 1A; and PARA 648.

30   See the Mental Capacity Act 2005 ss 27–29; and PARAS 627–629.

31   See the Mental Capacity Act 2005 ss 30–34; and PARAS 630–633.

32   See the Mental Capacity Act 2005 ss 35–41; and PARAS 634–646.

33   Ie the Mental Capacity Act 2005 Pt 2 (ss 45–61).

34   See the Mental Capacity Act 2005 ss 45–56; and PARA 720 et seq.

35   See the Mental Capacity Act 2005 ss 57–60; and PARAS 751–756.

36   See the Mental Capacity Act 2005 s 61; and PARA 748.

37   See the Mental Capacity Act 2005 s 62; and PARA 932.

38   See the Mental Capacity Act 2005 s 63; and PARA 561.

39   See PARA 559 note 11.

40   Adopted by the UN General Assembly on 13 December 2006 and ratified by the UK on 8 June 2009.

41   See the Mental Health (Wales) Measure 2010 Pt 1 (ss 1–11); and PARAS 586–589, 881 et seq.

42   See the Mental Health (Wales) Measure 2010 Pt 2 (ss 12–18); and PARAS 851–855.

43   See the Mental Health (Wales) Measure 2010 Pt 3 (ss 19–30); and PARAS 947–954.

44   See the Mental Health Act 1983 ss 130A–130H; and PARA 807 et seq.

561. Private international law. Provision is made in the Mental Capacity Act 2005 regarding private international law in relation to persons who cannot protect their interests, governing which jurisdiction should apply when a national of one country is in another state, in particular giving effect in England[1] and Wales[2] to the Convention on the International Protection of Adults[3].

     As well as various preliminary provisions[4], the Mental Capacity Act 2005 provides the grounds[5] on which the Court of Protection[6] will exercise its jurisdiction when dealing with cases with an international element[7]. The court may exercise its jurisdiction in relation to: (1) an adult habitually resident in England and Wales; (2) an adult's property in England and Wales; (3) an adult present in England or Wales or who has property there (if the matter is urgent); or (4) an adult present in England and Wales (if a protective measure which is temporary and limited in its effect to England and Wales is proposed in relation to him)[8]. An adult present in England and Wales is to be treated as habitually resident if his habitual residence cannot be ascertained, he is a refugee or he has been displaced as a result of disturbance in the country of his habitual residence[9]. Once the provisions of the Convention are in force the court will also be able to exercise jurisdiction, in so far as it cannot otherwise do so, in relation to a British citizen with a closer connection with England and Wales than with Scotland or Northern Ireland; the jurisdiction may be exercised provided that the court considers that it is in a better position to assess the interests of the adult, that certain requirements as to notification of other Convention countries are complied with and that other Convention countries which may have jurisdiction on certain grounds have not dealt, or are not dealing, with the matter[10].

The Mental Capacity Act 2005 makes provision as to which law is to apply in various situations[11]. Although the Court of Protection will normally apply the law of England and Wales, and the conditions of implementation of any protective measure taken abroad will be governed by the law of England and Wales if implemented in England and Wales, the court may apply the law of another country if it thinks that a matter has a substantial connection with that country[12]. In addition, the donor of a foreign power like a lasting power of attorney[13] may specify that the law applicable to the existence, extent, modification or extinction of the power is to be the law of a country of which he is a national, in which he is habitually resident, or in which he has property[14]. Protection is provided for a third party who enters into a transaction with a representative on behalf of a person, where that representative was actually not entitled so to act under the law of a country other than England and Wales applicable by virtue of the Mental Capacity Act 2005[15].

The Mental Capacity Act 2005 provides for the recognition and enforcement of protective measures taken in other countries[16]. It provides that: (a) a protective measure is to be recognised in England and Wales if it was taken on the ground that the adult is habitually resident in the other country; (b) a protective measure taken in another Convention country is to be recognised provided that it was taken on a ground provided for in the Convention, although the court may refuse to recognise a protective measure where it thinks that the case in which the measure was taken was not urgent, the adult was not given an opportunity to be heard, and that omission amounted to a breach of natural justice[17].

Provision is made for co-operation between authorities in England and Wales and authorities in other Convention countries[18].

1 As to the meaning of 'England' see PARA 557 note 4.
2 As to the meaning of 'Wales' see PARA 557 note 5.
3 See the Mental Capacity Act 2005 s 63, Sch 3. Schedule 3 gives effect in England and Wales to the Convention on the International Protection of Adults (the Hague, 13 January 2000; Cm 5881) ('the Hague Convention') (in so far as the Mental Capacity Act 2005 does not otherwise do so) and makes related provision as to the private international law of England and Wales: Mental Capacity Act 2005 s 63. For the purposes of the Convention, England and Wales, Scotland and Northern Ireland constitute separate jurisdictions. The Convention only enters into force once ratified by three states but the Mental Capacity Act 2005 Sch 3 provides private international law rules to govern jurisdictional issues between England and Wales on the one hand and Scotland on the other, regardless of whether the Convention is actually in force. See CONFLICT OF LAWS vol 19 (2011) PARA 623 et seq.
   The Mental Capacity Act 2005 Sch 3 contains powers to make further provision as to private international law by Order in Council and regulations; and there are also provisions about certificates of proof, exceptions and commencement: see Sch 3 Pt 6 (paras 30–35). See CONFLICT OF LAWS vol 19 (2011) PARA 627.
   See also *Re MN* [2010] EWHC 1926 (Fam), *Re M* [2011] EWHC 3590 (COP).

4   See the Mental Capacity Act 2005 Sch 3 Pt 1 (paras 1–6); and CONFLICT OF LAWS vol 19 (2011)
    PARAS 623, 626.
5   Ie based on the Hague Convention arts 5–11.
6   As to the Court of Protection under the Mental Capacity Act 2005 see PARA 720.
7   See the Mental Capacity Act 2005 Sch 3 Pt 2 (paras 7–10); and CONFLICT OF LAWS vol 19
    (2011) PARA 623.
8   See the Mental Capacity Act 2005 Sch 3 para 7(1); and CONFLICT OF LAWS vol 19 (2011) PARA
    623.
9   See the Mental Capacity Act 2005 Sch 3 para 7(2); and CONFLICT OF LAWS vol 19 (2011) PARA
    623.
10 See the Mental Capacity Act 2005 Sch 3 para 8; and CONFLICT OF LAWS vol 19 (2011) PARA
    623. As to where jurisdiction is exercisable in connection with a matter involving a Convention
    country other than England and Wales see Sch 3 para 9; and CONFLICT OF LAWS vol 19 (2011)
    PARA 623.
11 See the Mental Capacity Act 2005 Sch 3 Pt 2 (paras 11–18); and CONFLICT OF LAWS vol 19
    (2011) PARA 624.
12 See the Mental Capacity Act 2005 Sch 3 paras 11, 12; and CONFLICT OF LAWS vol 19 (2011)
    PARA 624.
13 As to the meaning of 'lasting power of attorney' under the Mental Capacity Act 2005 see PARA
    606 note 16. See also PARA 618 et seq.
14 See the Mental Capacity Act 2005 Sch 3 paras 13–15; and CONFLICT OF LAWS vol 19 (2011)
    PARA 624.
15 See the Mental Capacity Act 2005 Sch 3 para 16; and CONFLICT OF LAWS vol 19 (2011) PARA
    624. There are also provisions on mandatory provisions of the law of England and Wales where
    the court is exercising jurisdiction and qualifications for public policy: see Sch 3 paras 17, 18;
    and CONFLICT OF LAWS vol 19 (2011) PARA 624.
16 See the Mental Capacity Act 2005 Sch 3 Pt 4 (paras 19–25); and CONFLICT OF LAWS vol 19
    (2011) PARAS 625, 626.
17 See the Mental Capacity Act 2005 Sch 3 para 19; and CONFLICT OF LAWS vol 19 (2011) PARA
    625. The court may also refuse recognition if it would be manifestly contrary to public policy,
    the measure would be inconsistent with a mandatory provision of the law of England and Wales,
    or the measure is inconsistent with one subsequently taken or recognised in relation to the adult:
    see Sch 3 para 19.
18 See the Mental Capacity Act 2005 Sch 3 Pt 5 (paras 26–29); and CONFLICT OF LAWS vol 19
    (2011) PARA 626.

562. Interaction between the Acts. There is no overlap intended between the
Mental Health Act 1983 and the Mental Capacity Act 2005. The Mental Health
Act 1983 provides a statutory basis for the compulsory treatment of people with
mental disorder in hospital[1]. It carries safeguards for the use of treatment
without consent[2] and the requisite review mechanism in the form of the First Tier
Tribunal (formerly the Mental Health Review Tribunal) safeguards[3]. Unlike the
Mental Capacity Act 2005, the Mental Health Act 1983 is concerned only with
the treatment of mental disorder[4].

The purpose of the Mental Capacity Act 2005 is to provide a decision-making
framework for incapacitated persons on different issues, including care and
treatment, health and welfare decisions and the management of finances,
property and affairs in their best interests[5]. If the consequence of a health or
welfare decision is that a person is deprived of their liberty[6], the Mental Capacity
Act 2005 provides safeguards, known as deprivation of liberty safeguards by
which the deprivation of liberty can be authorised and reviewed by a statutory
procedure[7]. Prior to the enactment of the Mental Capacity Act 2005 any
deprivation of liberty flowing from a best interests decision, but falling outside
the scope of the Mental Health Act 1983, was capable of authorisation under the
inherent jurisdiction of the High Court[8]. Patients falling outside the Mental
Health Act 1983 are not protected by the safeguards under that Act, but now
may be safeguarded under the Mental Capacity Act 2005[9]. The eligibility of a
person for deprivation of liberty safeguards under the Mental Capacity Act 2005

is defined by reference to the application of the Mental Health Act 1983 so that a person is ineligible in a number of prescribed circumstances conflicting with the use of the Mental Health Act 1983 or where the treatment is for mental disorder in a hospital or where the person is objecting to treatment for mental disorder in a hospital[10].

Nothing in the Mental Capacity Act 2005 authorises anyone to give a patient medical treatment for mental disorder[11] or to consent to a patient being given medical treatment[12] for mental disorder[13], if, at the time when it is proposed to treat the patient, his treatment is regulated by Part 4 of the Mental Health Act 1983[14].

The two regimes are not, however, mutually exclusive and both may apply in defined situations[15]. In general, where it applies, the Mental Health Act 1983 has primacy over the Mental Capacity Act 2005 and decision makers should take all practical steps to ensure that that primacy is recognised and given effect to[16]. The relevant decision-makers under both the Mental Health Act 1983 and the Mental Capacity Act 2005 should approach the questions they have to answer relating to the application of the Mental Health Act 1983 on the basis of an assumption that an alternative solution is not available under the Mental Capacity Act 2005[17].

1   See PARA 757 et seq.

2   See the Mental Health Act 1983 ss 56–64; and PARA 924 et seq.

3   See PARA 955 et seq.

4   See PARA 761.

5   See PARA 606. See also PARA 925.

6   For the purposes of the Mental Capacity Act 2005 references to deprivation of a person's liberty have the same meaning as in the Convention for the Protection of Human Rights and Fundamental Freedoms (Rome, 4 November 1950; TS 71 (1953); Cmd 8969) art 5 (see RIGHTS AND FREEDOMS): Mental Capacity Act 2005 s 64(5) (added by the Mental Health Act 2007 Sch 9 para 10(4)). As to deprivation of liberty under the Mental Capacity Act 2005 see PARA 648.

7   See the Mental Capacity Act 2005 ss 4, 4A, 16(2)(a), Schs A1, 1A; and see PARAS 606, 648, 651 et seq, 658 et seq, 724.

8   As to the remaining power of the high court in relation to vulnerable adults see PARA 563.

9   Ie see *R v Bournewood Community and Mental Health NHS Trust, ex p L* [1999] 1 AC 458, [1998] 3 All ER 289, HL; Application 45508/99 *HL v United Kingdom* (2004) 40 EHRR 761, 81 BMLR 131, ECtHR; and PARA 597. As to deprivation of liberty see PARA 648. The Mental Capacity Act 2005 was amended by the Mental Health Act 2007 which added the Mental Capacity Act 2005 ss 4A, 4B, 16A and Sch A1 (see PARAS 606, 648, 651 et seq, 658 et seq, 72).

10   See the Mental Capacity Act 2005 Sch 1A para 2 cases A–E; and PARA 658.

11   See the Mental Capacity Act 2005 s 28(1)(a); and PARA 925. As to the meaning of 'mental disorder' and 'patient' see the Mental Health Act 1983; and PARAS 758 note 4, 761 (definitions applied by the Mental Capacity Act 2005 s 28(2)).

12   As to the meaning of 'medical treatment' see the Mental Health Act 1983; and PARA 926 (definition applied by the Mental Capacity Act 2005 s 28(2)). Section 28(1) does not apply in relation to any form of treatment to which the Mental Health Act 1983 s 58A (electro-convulsive therapy, etc: see PARA 931) applies if the patient comes within s 58A(7) (informal patient under 18 who cannot give consent): Mental Capacity Act 2005 s 28(1A) (added by the Mental Health Act 2007 s 28(10)).

13   See the Mental Capacity Act 2005 s 28(1)(b); and PARA 925.

14   See the Mental Capacity Act 2005 s 28(1); and PARA 925. The reference in the text is a reference to the Mental Health Act 1983 Pt 4 (ss 56–64) (see PARA 924 et seq). However certain treatments are excluded from the Mental Capacity Act 2005 s 28; see PARA 925.

15   See the Mental Capacity Act 2005 Sch 1A para 2 cases C and D which relate to community treatment orders and guardianship (see PARA 658).

16   See *GJ v The Foundation Trust* [2009] EWHC 2972 (Fam), [2010] Fam 70, [2010] 3 WLR 840.

17   See *GJ v The Foundation Trust* [2009] EWHC 2972 (Fam), [2010] Fam 70, [2010] 3 WLR 840; *C v Blackburn* [2011] EWHC 3321.

563.   Inherent jurisdiction in relation to vulnerable adults.   The Mental Capacity Act 2005 is limited to those persons lacking mental capacity[1]. It has been held that, in the absence of express reference in that Act to the High Court or to those adults whose ability to make decisions for themselves has been compromised by matters other than those covered by the Mental Capacity Act 2005, the High Court may intervene using its inherent jurisdiction[2] and that there is a sound and strong public policy justification for the continued availability of this jurisdiction for this purpose[3]. The jurisdiction is, in part, aimed at enhancing or liberating the autonomy of a vulnerable adult whose autonomy was compromised by a reason other than mental incapacity because they were: (1) under constraint; or (2) subject to coercion or undue influence; or (3) for some other reason deprived of the capacity to make the relevant decision or disabled from making a free choice, or incapacitated or disabled from giving or expressing a real and genuine consent[4].

1   See PARA 597.

2   See *A local authority v DL* [2012] EWCA Civ 253, [2012] 3 All ER 1064, [2012] 3 WLR 1439 (elderly parents not lacking capacity by reason of impairment or disturbance in functioning of mind or brain but son exercising undue influence and duress over elderly parents; court had jurisdiction).

3   Furthermore, the use of the inherent jurisdiction in such circumstances is compatible with the Convention for the Protection of Human Rights and Fundamental Freedoms (Rome, 4 November 1950; TS 71 (1953) Cmd 8969) art 8 in just the same manner as the Mental Capacity Act 2005 was compatible: see *A local authority v DL* [2012] EWCA Civ 253, [2012] All ER (D) 211 (Mar). The Convention has been incorporated into English law by the Human Rights Act 1998 which came into force on 2 October 2000: see the Human Rights Act 1998 (Commencement No 2) Order 2000, SI 2000/1851; and RIGHTS AND FREEDOMS.

4   See *Re SA (vulnerable adult with capacity: marriage)* [2005] EWHC 2942 (Fam), [2007] 2 FCR 563, [2006] 1 FLR 867; and *A local authority v DL* [2012] EWCA Civ 253, [2012] All ER (D) 211 (Mar).

564.   Positions of responsibility.   Any person who suffers or has suffered from mental disorder[1] and on account of that condition is either resident in a hospital or other similar institution or regularly attends for treatment by a medical practitioner, any person for the time being under guardianship under the Mental Health Act 1983[2], or subject to a community treatment order[3]; or any person who lacks capacity[4], is ineligible for jury service[5].

There is a statutory procedure for vacating the seat of a member of the House of Commons who has been compulsorily detained because of mental disorder for six months or more[6]. There appears to be no similar provision for members of the House of Lords, but a court or authority ordering the imprisonment or restraint of a member of the House of Lords is usually required to give written notice to the Clerk of the Parliaments[7].

Provision is made in relation to certain legal professionals and medical professionals lacking capacity within the meaning of the Mental Capacity Act 2005[8].

Where a trustee[9] is incapable of acting, provision is made for a new trustee to be appointed in his place[10]. However, where a trustee lacks capacity to exercise his functions and is also entitled in possession to some beneficial interest in the trust property, unless the appointment of the new trustee is made by the person or persons nominated by the trust instrument to make such an appointment, no new appointment may be made without leave of the Court of Protection[11].

The court[12] may appoint a new trustee whenever it is found inexpedient, difficult or impracticable to do so without its assistance, and in particular may appoint a new trustee in place of a trustee who lacks capacity to exercise his functions as such[13].

If land subject to a trust of land is vested, either solely or jointly with any other person or persons, in a person who lacks capacity of exercising his functions as trustee, a new trustee must be appointed in his place before the legal estate is dealt with by the trustees[14].

Where a person entitled to a grant of administration of an estate lacks capacity to manage his affairs, a grant of administration may be made to another person during the period of mental incapacity; similarly, if a person becomes so incapable after a grant, a new grant may be made[15].

If any person who would otherwise be protector of a settlement[16] is so incapable, the Court of Protection is to take his place while he lacks capacity[17].

1 Ie within the meaning of the Mental Health Act 1983 (see PARA 761).
2 Ie within the meaning of the Mental Health Act 1983 s 7. As to such guardianship see PARAS 785, 877.
3 Ie under the Mental Health Act 1983 s 17A (see PARA 797).
4 Ie within the meaning of the Mental Capacity Act 2005 (see PARA 603).
5 See the Juries Act 1974 s 1, Sch 1 Pt I paras 1–3; and JURIES vol 61 (2010) PARA 804. As from a day to be appointed the Juries Act 1974 s 1, Sch 1 is amended by the Mental Health (Discrimination) Act 2013 s 2 and no longer excludes from jury service those people voluntarily receiving regular treatment for a mental health disorder but who are not resident in a hospital or similar institution.
6 See the Mental Health Act 1983 s 141; PARA 782; and PARLIAMENT vol 78 (2010) PARAS 900, 1094.
7 There has been an indication that the provisions for mentally disordered persons under the Mental Health Act 1983 ss 2–6 override any privilege of Parliament or peerage: see PARLIAMENT vol 78 (2010) PARA 1085. See also HL Standing Orders (Public Business) (1994) no 79.
8 See LEGAL PROFESSIONS; MEDICAL PROFESSIONS.
9 As to the meaning of 'trustee' see the Trustee Act 1925 s 68(1) PARA (17); and TRUSTS vol 48 (2007 Reissue) PARA 601.
10 See the Trustee Act 1925 s 36(1); and TRUSTS vol 48 (2007 Reissue) PARA 836.
11 See the Trustee Act 1925 s 36(9); and TRUSTS vol 48 (2007 Reissue) PARA 838. As to the Court of Protection see PARA 720.
12 'Court' means the High Court or the county court where those courts respectively have jurisdiction: Trustee Act 1925 s 67(1) (amended by the Courts Act 1971 s 56, Sch 11 Pt II). As to the High Court see COURTS AND TRIBUNALS vol 24 (2010) PARA 695 et seq. As to county courts see COURTS AND TRIBUNALS vol 24 (2010) PARA 758 et seq.
13 See the Trustee Act 1925 s 41(1); and TRUSTS vol 48 (2007 Reissue) PARAS 849, 856; and see *Re Sparrow* (1870) 5 Ch App 662; *Re Heaphy's Trusts* (1870) 18 WR 1070.
   The power does not extend to the appointment of a personal representative: see the Trustee Act 1925 s 41(4). The powers of the High Court include power to authorise the remuneration of a trust corporation (see s 42; and TRUSTS vol 48 (2007 Reissue) PARA 801), to make vesting orders, eg where a trustee is under disability (see ss 44, 51; and TRUSTS vol 48 (2007 Reissue) PARAS 875–876, 884–888), or to appoint a person to convey land (see s 50; and TRUSTS vol 48 (2007 Reissue) PARA 879), and to charge the costs of certain applications on the trust estate (see s 60; and TRUSTS vol 48 (2007 Reissue) PARAS 853, 873).
14 See the Law of Property Act 1925 s 22(2); and TRUSTS vol 48 (2007 Reissue) PARA 838. This does not prevent a legal estate being dealt with without the appointment of a new trustee, or the discharge of the incapable trustee, at a time when the donee of an enduring power of attorney or lasting power of attorney (within the meaning of the Mental Capacity Act 2005) is entitled to act for the incapable trustee in the dealing: see the Law of Property Act 1925 s 22(3); and TRUSTS vol 48 (2007 Reissue) PARA 838.
15 See WILLS AND INTESTACY vol 103 (2010) PARAS 621, 804 et seq, 850.
16 As to the protector of a settlement see REAL PROPERTY AND REGISTRATION vol 87 (2012) PARA 119.
17 See the Fines and Recoveries Act 1833 s 33; and REAL PROPERTY AND REGISTRATION vol 87 (2012) PARA 119.

565.   Voting.   A person in respect of whom certain hospital orders or directions in relation to mental health[1] have been made is legally incapable of voting at any parliamentary or local government election[2]. Where such orders or directions have not been made in respect of a person who is a patient in a mental hospital[3], but he is not a detained offender or a person remanded in custody[4], he is to be regarded[5] as resident at the mental hospital in question if the length of the period which he is likely to spend at the hospital is sufficient for him to be regarded as being resident there for the purposes of electoral registration[6].

Nothing in the Mental Capacity Act 2005 permits a decision on voting at an election for any public office, or at a referendum[7], to be made on behalf of a person[8].

1   Ie an order has been made under the Mental Health Act 1983 ss 37, 38, 44 or 51(5) or a direction has been given under s 45A, 46 or 47 or any person in respect of whom an order has been made under the Criminal Procedure (Insanity) Act 1964 s 5(2)(a) (see SENTENCING AND DISPOSITION OF OFFENDERS vol 92 (2010) PARA 332).

2   See the Representation of the People Act 1983 s 3A; and ELECTIONS AND REFERENDUMS vol 15(3) (2007 Reissue) PARA 122. As to voting see also the Mental Capacity Act 2005 s 29; and PARA 629.

3   'Mental hospital' means any establishment (or part of an establishment) maintained wholly or mainly for the reception and treatment of persons suffering from any form of mental disorder; and for these purposes, 'mental disorder' has the same meaning as in the Mental Health Act 1983 (see PARA 761): Representation of the People Act 1983 s 7(6) (s 7 substituted by the Representation of the People Act 2000 s 4).

4   Ie a person to whom the Representation of the People Act 1983 s 3A or s 7A applies.

5   Ie for the purposes of the Representation of the People Act 1983 s 4 (entitlement to be registered as parliamentary or local government elector).

6   See the Representation of the People Act 1983 s 7(1), (2); and ELECTIONS AND REFERENDUMS vol 15(3) (2007 Reissue) PARA 134. See, however, Application 74025/01 *Hirst v United Kingdom (No 2)* (2005) 42 EHRR 849, (2005) Times, 10 October, ECtHR.

7   As to the meaning of referendum see PARA 629.

8   See the Mental Capacity Act 2005 s 29; and PARA 629.

2. MENTAL HEALTH SERVICES

(1) IN GENERAL

566. Mental health services. Services for mentally disordered[1] people consist, broadly, of: (1) services provided by the health authorities[2], including hospital and specialist services[3]; and (2) social services provided by local social services authorities[4] for people living in the community.

A public authority must act in a way that is compatible with a convention right[5] as must a person who provides accommodation, together with nursing or personal care, in a care home for an individual under statutory arrangements[6].

1   As to the meaning of 'mentally disordered' see PARA 761.
2   See PARA 574 et seq.
3   See PARA 575.
4   See PARA 579 et seq.
5   See the Human Rights Act 1998 s 6(1); and RIGHTS AND FREEDOMS. As to the Convention rights (ie rights under the Convention for the Protection of Human Rights and Fundamental Freedoms (Rome, 4 November 1950; TS 71 (1953); Cmd 8969) (the European Convention on Human Rights)) see RIGHTS AND FREEDOMS. As to what constitutes a public authority see RIGHTS AND FREEDOMS. See also *Johnson v United Kingdom* (1997) 27 EHRR 296, 40 BMLR 1, ECtHR; *R (on the application of A) v Partnerships in Care* [2002] EWHC 529 (Admin), [2002] 1 WLR 2610, (2002) Times, 23 April (the decision of the managers of a private psychiatric hospital to change the focus of one of its wards was an act of a public nature susceptible of judicial review); *R (on the application of IH) v Secretary of State for the Home Department* [2003] UKHL 59, [2004] 2 AC 253, [2004] 1 All ER 412 (duty of the health authority is to use its best endeavours to procure compliance with the conditions laid down by the tribunal; it was not subject to an absolute duty to procure compliance and was not at fault for failing to do so); *Brand v Netherlands* (2004) 17 BHRC 398, [2004] ECHR 49902/99, *YL v Birmingham City Council* [2007] UKHL 27, [2008] 1 AC 95, [2007] 3 All ER 957 (private care home was not exercising functions of a private nature (case over-turned by the Health and Social Care Act 2008 s 145)); Application 517/02 *Kolanis v United Kingdom* (2005) 42 EHRR 206, 84 BMLR 102.
6   See the Health and Social Care Act 2008 s 145; and SOCIAL SERVICES AND COMMUNITY CARE vol 44(2) (Reissue) PARA 1029.

(2) FUNCTIONS OF CENTRAL GOVERNMENT

567. The appropriate national authority. Certain statutory functions relating to mental health and mental capacity are exercisable by the Secretary of State[1] (in relation to England) and the Welsh Ministers (in relation to Wales)[2]. The functions exercisable by the Welsh Ministers are:

(1)   functions originally transferred to the National Assembly for Wales[3] by Order in Council and subsequently transferred to the Welsh Ministers[4];

(2)   functions originally conferred on the National Assembly for Wales by enactments made after the establishment of that body and subsequently transferred[5] to the Welsh Ministers[6];

(3)   functions transferred to the Welsh Ministers by Order in Council[7]; and

(4)   functions conferred on the Welsh Ministers by enactments made after the establishment of the Welsh Assembly Government[8].

Legislation enacted following the establishment of the Welsh Assembly Government which confers functions on the Secretary of State and the Welsh Ministers often refers to those bodies collectively as 'the appropriate national authority'[9], and that expression is used throughout this title to cover any situation where the function in question is exercised in relation to England by the

Secretary of State and in relation to Wales by the Welsh Ministers, and also where functions may be carried out jointly.

1   In any enactment, 'Secretary of State' means one of Her Majesty's principal secretaries of state: see the Interpretation Act 1978 s 5, Sch 1. As to the office of Secretary of State see CONSTITUTIONAL LAW AND HUMAN RIGHTS vol 8(2) (Reissue) PARA 355. Certain functions are only with the Secretary of State (for example specified provisions of the Mental Health Act 1983 (see note 3)). Some functions of the Secretary of State have been transferred to the Care Quality Commission (see PARA 573) and clinical commissioning groups (see PARA 572).

2   Statutory functions relating to mental health and mental capacity, so far as exercisable in relation to Wales, are now almost exclusively the responsibility of the Welsh Ministers following the establishment of the Welsh Assembly Government under the Government of Wales Act 2006. The appropriate national authority in relation to the Mental Health (Wales) Measure 2010 is the Welsh Ministers. As to the Welsh Ministers and the Welsh Assembly Government see Pt 2 (ss 45–92); and CONSTITUTIONAL LAW AND HUMAN RIGHTS. Some functions which were with the Secretary of State and the Welsh Ministers are, or will be, solely with the Welsh Ministers: see the Mental Health Act 1983 s 122 (which is amended as from 1 April 2013 by the Health and Social Care Act 2012 s 41(2)(a) to apply to the Welsh Ministers only: see the Health and Social Care Act 2012 (Commencement No 4, Transitional, Savings and Transitory Provisions) Order 2013, SI 2013/160, art 2(2)).

3   Ie by Order in Council under the Government of Wales Act 1998 s 22 (now repealed): see CONSTITUTIONAL LAW AND HUMAN RIGHTS.

The National Assembly of Wales (Transfer of Functions) Order 1999, SI 1999/672, Sch 2 provides for transfer of functions under the Mental Health Act 1959 (see PARA 557),the Health Services and Public Health Act 1968 (see PARA 569), the Local Authority Act 1970 (see PARA 568), the Local Authorities Social Services Act 1970 (see PARA 568) and the following provisions of the Mental Health Act 1983 (except those under ss 41 (see PARAS 869–870), 42 (see PARAS 876, 914), 45A(10), (11) (see PARA 863), 45B–51 (see PARAS 863, 892–896), 53 (see PARA 898), 71 (see PARA 965), 73–75 (see PARAS 962, 965, 967, 969), 80A (see PARA 899), 81A (see PARA 903), 82A (see PARA 904), 83A (see PARA 906), 84 (see PARA 905), 85A (see PARA 905), 86 (see PARA 907), and Sch 2 (see PARA 957)):

(1)   functions under ss 80 (see PARA 899), 81 (see PARA 903) and 83 (see PARA 906) are transferred except in relation to a patient who is subject to one or more of the following, namely:
   (a)   a restriction order (see PARA 869);
   (b)   a hospital direction (see PARA 863);
   (c)   a limitation direction (see PARA 863); or
   (d)   a restriction direction (see PARA 894 note 8),
made under s 41 (see PARA 869), s 45A (see PARA 863) or, as the case may be, s 49 (see PARAS 876, 894);

(2)   in s 19(3) (see PARA 887) and in the definition of 'the managers' in s 145(1) (see PARA 778), references to a hospital vested in the Secretary of State for the purposes of his functions under the National Health Service Act 1977 have effect as if they included a reference to a hospital vested in the Welsh Ministers for purposes of its functions under that Act;

(3)   s 23(4), (5) (see PARA 913) do not apply to the exercise by the Welsh Ministers of the powers conferred by that provision;

(4)   s 24(3) (see PARA 916) does have effect as if it applied to an application by the Welsh Ministers as well as to an application by the Secretary of State;

(5)   ss 54(1) (see PARA 865) and 117(2A)(a) (repealed) have effect as if references to a registered medical practitioner approved for the purposes of s 12 (see PARA 849) by the Secretary of State (including references to be construed as such) included a reference to such a practitioner approved by the Welsh Ministers;

(6)   s 139(4) (see PARA 759) has effect as if after the words 'the Secretary of State' there were inserted 'the Welsh Ministers';

(7)   s 142(1) has effect as if the reference to a government department included a reference to the Welsh Ministers;

(8)   the Treasury approval requirements under ss 119(1) (see PARA 928), 120(6) (see PARA 806) and 121(6) (repealed) continue in effect so far as they relate to pensions.

For provisions as to the exercise of transferred functions see the Government of Wales Act 2006 Sch 3, Sch 11 paras 33–35; and STATUTES AND LEGISLATIVE PROCESS vol 96 (2012) PARA 1035.

4   Ie by the operation of the Government of Wales Act 2006 Sch 11 paras 26, 30 (see CONSTITUTIONAL LAW AND HUMAN RIGHTS), which provide that instruments transferring functions to the National Assembly for Wales under the Government of Wales Act 1998 s 22 (repealed) (see note 3) continue to have effect following the transfer of the Assembly's executive functions to the Welsh Ministers as conferring those functions on those Ministers.

5   Ie by the operation of the Government of Wales Act 2006 Sch 11 para 30 (see STATUTES AND LEGISLATIVE PROCESS vol 96 (2012) PARA 1035).

6   Functions were conferred on the National Assembly for Wales by the Mental Capacity Act 2005 and these functions have been transferred to the Welsh Ministers by operation of the Government of Wales Act 2006 Sch 11 para 30 (see STATUTES AND LEGISLATIVE PROCESS vol 96 (2012) PARA 1035).

7   Ie by Order in Council under the Government of Wales Act 2006 s 58 (see STATUTES AND LEGISLATIVE PROCESS vol 96 (2012) PARAS 1034, 1036). At the date at which this volume states the law no functions relating to Mental Health and Mental Capacity had been transferred to the Welsh Ministers by Order in Council under s 58.

     For provisions as to the exercise of transferred functions see the Government of Wales Act 2006 Sch 3, Sch 11 paras 33–35; and STATUTES AND LEGISLATIVE PROCESS vol 96 (2012) PARA 1035.

8   Functions have been specifically conferred on the Welsh Ministers by the Mental Health (Wales) Measure 2010 and the National Health Service (Wales) Act 2006 (see HEALTH SERVICES).

9   See the Mental Capacity Act 2005 Sch 1A para 176(2).

568. Duties of the appropriate national authority. By virtue of its duty to continue the promotion of a comprehensive health service under the National Health Service Act 2006 and National Health Service (Wales) Act 2006, the appropriate national authority[1] is ultimately responsible for providing or securing those mental health services which form part of the national health service[2].

The appropriate national authority[3] has a specific duty to provide, inter alia, hospital accommodation to the extent it considers necessary to meet all reasonable requirements[4], and such facilities for the prevention, care and after-care of illness as are appropriate as part of the health service[5]. It also has a duty to provide hospital accommodation and services for persons liable to be detained under the Mental Health Act 1983 that it considers require treatment under conditions of high security[6].

The appropriate national authority supervises and directs local social services authorities[7] in the exercise of their functions in providing social services for people suffering from a mental disorder[8]. The appropriate national authority may make an order declaring a local social services authority to be in default in carrying out its statutory functions in this respect, and such an order may contain such directions for the purpose of ensuring that the duty is complied with within a specified period as appear necessary to the appropriate national authority[9].

The appropriate national authority must prepare, and from time to time revise, a code of practice in relation to the Mental Health Act 1983[10].

The appropriate national authority has power to pay pocket money to patients in hospitals used wholly or mainly for the treatment of people suffering from mental disorder[11]; to pay travelling expenses to visitors to patients in hospitals in which high security psychiatric services are provided[12]; to transfer patients to Scotland, Northern Ireland, the Channel Islands or the Isle of Man[13]; to remove alien patients abroad[14]; and to refer patients to mental health review tribunals[15]. The appropriate national authority approves medical practitioners as having special experience in the diagnosis or treatment of mental disorder for the purpose of making medical recommendations under the Mental Health Act 1983[16].

The appropriate national authority also has a number of powers under the Mental Health Act 1983 which relate to prisoners and patients subject to special restrictions[17]. These powers enable him in prescribed circumstances to direct the transfer to hospital of certain prisoners and to place restrictions on their discharge from hospital[18]; to direct that a patient is no longer to be subject to restrictions[19]; to discharge restricted patients absolutely or conditionally and to recall conditionally discharged patients to hospital[20]; and to withhold consent to the discharge, transfer or grant of leave of absence to such patients[21]. The appropriate national authority also authorises the removal of restricted patients to Scotland, Northern Ireland, the Channel Islands or the Isle of Man[22]. The appropriate national authority can direct the removal to a hospital in England or Wales, and the return, of an offender found to be insane and ordered to be detained during Her Majesty's pleasure by a court in the Channel Islands or the Isle of Man[23].

1   As to the appropriate national authority see PARA 567. As from 1 April 2013, in relation to England, the duty to provide certain health services is transferred from the Secretary of State to the newly created clinical commissioning groups: see the National Health Service Act 2006 ss 1l, 3(1), 3A; the Health and Social Care Act 2012 (Commencement No 4, Transitional, Savings and Transitory Provisions) Order 2013, SI 2013/160, art 2(2); and HEALTH SERVICES. However, the Secretary of State retains ministerial responsibility to Parliament for the provision of the health service in England and has additional duties set out in the National Health Service Act 2006, such as having regard to the NHS constitution, the need to reduce inequalities between people in England and the promotion of autonomy: see the National Health Service Act 2006 ss 1(3), 1B–1D. As to the financing of the national health service see HEALTH SERVICES vol 54 (2008) PARA 503 et seq. As to the financing of local social services see LOCAL GOVERNMENT FINANCE. As to the clinical commissioning groups see PARA 572.

2   See the National Health Service Act 2006 s 1(1), (2); the National Health Service (Wales) Act 2006 s 1(1), (2); and HEALTH SERVICES vol 54 (2008) PARAS 10, 74. As to the health service generally see HEALTH SERVICES vol 54 (2008) PARA 1 et seq. As to inquiries and investigations see PARA 596.

3   See note 1. As to the duty to follow the decision of a responsible medical officer see *R (on the application of K) v West London Mental Health NHS Trust* [2006] EWCA Civ 118, [2006] 1 WLR 1865, 90 BMLR 214.

4   See the National Health Service Act 2006 s 3(1)(a); the National Health Service (Wales) Act 2006 s 3(1)(a); and HEALTH SERVICES vol 54 (2008) PARAS 12, 74. As to hospitals admitting mentally disordered people see PARA 576.

5   See the National Health Service Act 2006 s 3(1)(e); the National Health Service (Wales) Act 2006 s 3(1)(e); and HEALTH SERVICES vol 54 (2008) PARAS 12, 74. As to the meaning of 'facilities' in s 3(1)(e) see *R (on the application of Keating) v Cardiff Local Health Board (Secretary of State for Health intervening)* [2005] EWCA Civ 847, [2005] 3 All ER 1000, [2006] 1 WLR 158.

6   See the National Health Service Act 2006 s 4; the National Health Service (Wales) Act 2006 s 4; and PARA 569.

7   As to the meaning of 'local social services authority' see PARA 579.

8   Local Authority Social Services Act 1970 s 7A (ss 7A–7E added by the National Health Service and Community Care Act 1990 s 50). As to those functions see PARA 580. The appropriate national authority, with the approval of the Treasury, makes grants towards any expenses of local authorities incurred in connection with the exercise of their social services functions in relation to persons suffering from mental illness: see the Local Authority Social Services Act 1970 s 7E (as so added).

9   See the Local Authority Social Services Act 1970 s 7D(1), (2) (s 7D as added (see note 8); and s 7D(1) amended by the Adoption and Children Act 2002 s 139(1), Sch 3 paras 12, 13). A direction is enforceable, on the application of the Secretary of State, by mandatory order (formerly mandamus): Local Authority Social Services Act 1970 s 7D(3) (as so added). See SOCIAL SERVICES AND COMMUNITY CARE vol 44(2) (Reissue) PARA 1011. As to the complaints procedure and inquiries see ss 7B, 7C (as so added).

    The appropriate national authority may also make an order declaring an authority to be in default in carrying out its statutory functions under the Mental Health Act 1959, and apply the provisions of the National Health Service Act 2006 s 68(4) and the National Health Service

(Wales) Act 2006 s 28(4) (see HEALTH SERVICES vol 54 (2008) PARA 79 et seq): see the Mental Health Act 1959 s 142 (amended by the Local Government Act 1972 s 195(6), Sch 23 para 9(2); and the National Health Service (Consequential Provisions) Act 2006 Sch 1 para 24).

10 See the Mental Health Act 1983 s 118; and PARA 762.
11 See the Mental Health Act 1983 s 122; and PARA 594.
12 See the Health Services and Public Health Act 1968 s 66(1); and PARA 569.
13 See the Mental Health Act 1983 ss 80–85A; and PARAS 899–906.
14 See the Mental Health Act 1983 s 86; and PARA 907.
15 See the Mental Health Act 1983 s 67; and PARA 965.
16 See the Mental Health Act 1983 s 12(2); and PARA 849. As to the delegation of this power see PARA 570.
17 These are patients subject to restriction orders under the Mental Health Act 1983 s 41 (see PARA 869), orders for committal to hospital (see PARA 873), admission orders with a restriction direction (see PARA 874) or transfer directions with restrictions under s 49 (see PARA 894), and any other order or direction to the same effect: see s 55(4); and PARA 861. The power to make such orders and directions is generally exercised by the Home Secretary.
18 See the Mental Health Act 1983 ss 47–49; and PARAS 892–894.
19 See the Mental Health Act 1983 s 42(1); and PARA 876.
20 See the Mental Health Act 1893 ss 42(2), (3); and PARA 914.
21 See the Mental Health Act 1983 s 41(3); and PARA 869.
22 See the Mental Health Act 1983 ss 80, 81, 83; and PARAS 899, 903, 906.
23 See the Mental Health Act 1983 s 84; and PARA 905.

569. Duties in relation to high security psychiatric services. The duty imposed on the appropriate national body[1] to provide services for the purposes of the health service includes a duty to provide hospital accommodation and services for persons who are liable to be detained under the Mental Health Act 1983 and in his, or their, opinion require treatment under conditions of high security on account of their dangerous, violent or criminal propensities[2]. Such hospital accommodation and services are referred to as 'high security psychiatric services'[3].

In accordance with arrangements made with Treasury[4] approval, the appropriate national authority may make payments, at such rates as may be determined under those arrangements, to persons of such class or description as may be so determined in respect of travelling expenses necessarily incurred by them in making visits to patients for the time being detained in hospitals at which high security psychiatric services are provided[5].

1 Ie by the National Health Service Act 2006 s 1; and the National Health Service (Wales) Act 2006 s 1: see PARAS 568, 574; and HEALTH SERVICES vol 54 (2008) PARA 10 et seq. As to the appropriate national body see PARA 567.
2 See the National Health Service Act 2006 s 4(1); and the National Health Service (Wales) Act 2006 s 4(1); and HEALTH SERVICES vol 54 (2008) PARA 12.
3 See the National Health Service Act 2006 s 4(2); and the National Health Service (Wales) Act 2006 s 4(2); and HEALTH SERVICES vol 54 (2008) PARA 12. For the purposes of the Mental Health Act 1983, 'high security psychiatric services' has the same meaning as in the National Health Service Act 2006 s 4; and the National Health Service (Wales) Act 2006 s 4: Mental Health 1983 s 145(1) (definition added by the Health Act 1999 Sch 4 para 69(1), (2)(a); and amended by the National Health Service (Consequential Provisions) Act 2006 Sch 1 para 70(b)). High security psychiatric services must be provided only at hospital premises at which services are provided only for the persons mentioned in the National Health Service Act 2006 s 4(1); and the National Health Service (Wales) Act 2006 s 4(1) (see the text and notes 1–2): see the National Health Service Act 2006 s 4(3); and the National Health Service (Wales) Act 2006 s 4(3). 'Hospital premises' means: (1) a hospital; or (2) any part of a hospital which is treated as a separate unit: National Health Service Act 2006 s 4(4); and the National Health Service (Wales) Act 2006 s 4(4). Where high security psychiatric services and other services are provided at a hospital, the part of the hospital at which high security psychiatric services are provided and the other part must be treated as separate hospitals for the purposes of the Mental Health Act 1983: s 145(1AA) (added by the Health Act 1999 Sch 4 para 69(1), (3)). As to the meaning of 'hospital' see PARA 577.

4   As to the Treasury see CONSTITUTIONAL LAW AND HUMAN RIGHTS vol 8(2) (Reissue) PARAS
    512–517.

5   Health Services and Public Health Act 1968 s 66(1) (amended by SI 2000/90). As to visiting
    patients generally see the Department of Health *Mental Health Act 1983 Code of Practice*
    (2008) Chapter 19 and the Welsh Assembly Government *Mental Health Act 1983 Code of
    Practice for Wales* (2008) Chapter 20. As to the Codes of Practice see PARA 762. Following a
    review of security at Ashworth Hospital in 1998 a number of recommendations were carried
    into effect: see *The Safety and Security in Ashworth, Broadmoor and Rampton Hospitals
    Directions 2000*. Although such directions do not impose mandatory rules on a hospital the
    existence and failure to implement them informs the duty of care owed to employees: see *Buck
    v Nottinghamshire Healthcare NHS Trust* [2006] EWCA Civ 1576, 93 BMLR 28, (2006)
    Times, 1 December. The Guidance has since been revised see now the Department of Health
    *Guidance on the High Security Psychiatric Services (Arrangements for Safety and Security at
    Ashworth, Broadmoor and Rampton Hospitals) Directions 2011*. Visits by children are also
    subject to guidance see the Department of Health, Health Service Circular 1999/190, *Visits by
    Children to the Ashworth, Broadmoor and Rampton Hospitals Directions 1999*. These
    directions have been held not to be in breach of the Convention for the Protection of Human
    Rights and Fundamental Freedoms (Rome, 4 November 1950; TS 71 (1953); Cmd 8969), art 8:
    see *R (on the application of L) v Secretary of State for Health* [2001] 1 FCR 326, [2001] 1 FLR
    406.

570.   Delegation of functions of the Secretary of State.   As from 1 April 2013
the following provisions have effect[1]. The Secretary of State[2] may enter into an
agreement with another person for an approval function[3] of the Secretary of
State to be exercisable by the Secretary of State concurrently with that other
person and, if a requirement to exercise such an approval function by the
National Health Service Commissioning Board or a special health authority[4] has
effect, with the other person by whom the function is exercisable under that
requirement[5].

   Such an agreement may, in particular, provide for an approval function to be
exercisable by the other party in all circumstances or only in specified
circumstances or in all areas or only in specified areas[6]. The agreement may also
provide for an approval function to be exercisable by the other party for a period
specified in the agreement or for a period determined in accordance with the
agreement[7].

   The other party to an agreement must comply with such instructions[8] as the
Secretary of State may give with respect to the exercise of the approval function[9].

   The Secretary of State may impose a requirement on the National Health
Service Commissioning Board or a special health authority for an approval
function of the Secretary of State to be exercisable by the Secretary of State
concurrently with the Board or (as the case may be) special health authority and,
if an agreement under the above provisions[10] has effect, with the other person by
whom the function is exercisable under that agreement[11].

   The Secretary of State may, in particular, require the body concerned to
exercise an approval function in all circumstances or only in specified
circumstances and in all areas or only in specified areas[12]. The Secretary of State
may require the body concerned to exercise an approval function for a period
specified in the requirement or for a period determined in accordance with the
requirement[13].

   A relevant person[14] may provide another person with such information[15] as
the relevant person considers necessary or appropriate for or in connection with
the exercise of an approval function or the exercise by the Secretary of State of
the power to enter into an agreement[16] or impose a requirement[17] or give an
instruction[18] under the above provisions[19].

1 The Mental Health Act 1983 ss 12ZA–12ZC are added by the Health and Social Care Act 2012 s 38(1) and come into force on 1 April 2013: see the Health and Social Care Act 2012 (Commencement No 4, Transitional, Savings and Transitory Provisions) Order 2013, SI 2013/160, art 2(2).

2 As to the Secretary of State see PARA 567.

3 For the purposes of the Mental Health Act 1983 ss 12ZA–12ZC 'approval function' means the function under s 12(2) or the function of approving persons as approved clinicians: s 12ZA(2) (as added: see note 1). As to the meaning of 'approved clinicians' see PARA 831.

4 Ie if a requirement under the Mental Health Act 1983 s 12ZB has effect. As to the National Health Service Commissioning Board see PARA 570.

5 Mental Health Act 1983 s 12ZA(1) (as added: see note 1). An agreement under s 12ZA may provide for the Secretary of State to make payments to the other party; and the Secretary of State may make payments to other persons in connection with the exercise of an approval function by virtue of s 12ZA: s 12ZA(10 (as so added).

6 See the Mental Health Act 1983 s 12ZA(3) (as added: see note 1).

7 Mental Health Act 1983 s 12ZA(4) (as added: see note 1).

8 Such an instruction may require the other party to cease to exercise the function to such extent as the instruction specifies: Mental Health Act 1983 s 12ZA(6) (as added: see note 1). The agreement may provide for the Secretary of State to pay compensation to the other party in the event of an instruction such as is mentioned in s 12ZA(6) being given: s 12ZA(7) (as so added). An instruction under s 12ZA(5) may be given in such form as the Secretary of State may determine: s 12ZA(8) (as so added). The Secretary of State must publish instructions under s 12ZA(5) in such form as the Secretary of State may determine; but that does not apply to an instruction such as is mentioned in s 12ZA(6): s 12ZA(9) (as so added).

9 Mental Health Act 1983 s 12ZA(5) (as added: see note 1).

10 Ie under the Mental Health Act 1983 s 12ZA.

11 Mental Health Act 1983 s 12ZB(1) (as added: see note 1). Where a requirement under s 12ZB(1) is imposed, the Board or (as the case may be) special health authority must comply with such instructions as the Secretary of State may give with respect to the exercise of the approval function: s 12ZB(4) (as so added). Such an instruction may be given in such form as the Secretary of State may determine: s 12ZB(5) (as so added). The Secretary of State must publish instructions under s 12ZA(4) in such form as the Secretary of State may determine: s 12ZA(6) (as so added). Where the Board or a special health authority has an approval function by virtue of s 12ZA, the function is to be treated for the purposes of the National Health Service Act 2006 as a function that it has under that Act: Mental Health Act 1983 s 12ZB(7) (as so added). The Secretary of State may make payments in connection with the exercise of an approval function by virtue of s 12ZB: s 12ZB(8) (as so added).

12 Mental Health Act 1983 s 12ZB(2) (as added: see note 1).

13 Mental Health Act 1983 s 12ZB(3) (as added: see note 1).

14 The relevant persons are the Secretary of State, a person who is a party to an agreement under the Mental Health Act 1983 s 12ZA or, if the Secretary of State imposes a requirement under s 12ZB on the National Health Service Commissioning Board or a special health authority, the Board or (as the case may be) Special Health Authority: s 12ZC(2) (as added: see note 1).

15 For these purposes 'information' includes documents and records: Mental Health Act 1983 s 12ZC(4) (as added: see note 1). Section 12ZC, in so far as it authorises the provision of information by one relevant person to another relevant person, has effect notwithstanding any rule of common law which would otherwise prohibit or restrict the provision: s 12ZC(3) (as so added).

16 Ie under the Mental Health Act 1983 s 12ZA.

17 Ie under the Mental Health Act 1983 s 12ZB.

18 Ie under the Mental Health Act 1983 s 12ZA(5) or 12ZB(4).

19 Mental Health Act 1983 s 12ZC(1) (as added: see note 1).

(3) THE NATIONAL HEALTH SERVICE COMMISSIONING BOARD AND CLINICAL COMMISSIONING GROUPS

571. National Health Service Commissioning Board. The National Health Service Commissioning Board[1] is subject to the same duty[2] as the Secretary of State to continue the promotion in England of a comprehensive health service designed to secure improvement in the prevention, diagnosis and treatment of mental illness, except in relation to the part of the health service that is provided in pursuance of the public health functions of the Secretary of State or local authorities[3]. For the purpose of discharging that duty the Board must exercise its functions[4] in relation to clinical commissioning groups[5] so as to secure that services are provided for those purposes in accordance with the National Health Service Act 2006[6]. As from 1 April 2013[7] the National Health Service Commissioning Board also has the function of arranging for the provision of services for the purposes of the health service in England in accordance with the National Health Service Act 2006[8].

1   As to the National Health Service Commissioning Board see the National Health Service Act 2006 s 1H(1), Sch A1; and HEALTH SERVICES.
2   Ie the duty of the Secretary of State under the National Health Service Act 2006 s 1(1) (see HEALTH SERVICES).
3   National Health Service Act 2006 s 1H(2) (s 1H added by the Health and Social Care Act 2012 s 9(1)). At the date at which this volume states the law s 9(1) was in force only insofar as it added the National Health Service Act 2006 s 1H(1), (2), (3)(b), (4): see the Health and Social Care Act 2012 (Commencement No 2 and Transitional, Savings and Transitory Provisions) Order 2012, SI 2012/1831, art 2(2). However the remainder of the Health and Social Care Act 2012 s 9(1) comes into force on 1 April 2013: see the Health and Social Care Act 2012 (Commencement No 4, Transitional, Savings and Transitory Provisions) Order 2013, SI 2013/160, art 2(1). See also HEALTH SERVICES.
4   Ie the functions conferred on it by the National Health Service Act 2006.
5   As to clinical commissioning groups see PARA 572.
6   See the National Health Service Act 2006 s 1H(3)(b) (as added: see note 3). See also HEALTH SERVICES.
7   See note 3.
8   National Health Service Act 2006 s 1H(3)(a) (as added: see note 3).

572.   Clinical Commissioning Groups.   There are corporate bodies known as clinical commissioning groups[1].

As from 1 April 2013[2], each clinical commissioning group has the function of arranging for the provision of services for the purposes of the health service in England in accordance with the National Health Service Act 2006[3] and may arrange for the provision of such services or facilities as it considers appropriate for the purposes of the health service that relate to securing improvement in the mental health of the persons for whom it has responsibility[4].

1   National Health Service Act 2006 s 1I(1) (as added: see note 2). See also HEALTH SERVICES.
2   The National Health Service Act 2006 s 1I is added by the Health and Social Care Act 2012 s 10 and the National Health Service Act 2006 s 3A is added by the Health and Social Care Act 2012 s 14. At the date at which this volume states the law s 10 was in force only insofar as it added the National Health Service Act 2006 s 1I(1): see the Health and Social Care Act 2012 (Commencement No 2 and Transitional, Savings and Transitory Provisions) Order 2012, SI 2012/1831, art 2(2). However the Health Service Act 2012 ss 10, 14 come fully into force on 1 April 2013: see the Health and Social Care Act 2012 (Commencement No 4, Transitional, Savings and Transitory Provisions) Order 2013, SI 2013/160, art 2(1).
3   National Health Service Act 2006 s 1I(2) (as added: see note 2). See also HEALTH SERVICES.
4   National Health Service Act 2006 s 3A(1) (as added: see note 2). See also HEALTH SERVICES.

(4)   THE CARE QUALITY COMMISSION

573.   Care Quality Commission.   The Mental Health Act Commission has been dissolved and a new body corporate known as the Care Quality Commission has been established[1]. Its main objective in performing its functions is to protect and promote the health, safety and welfare of people who use health and social care services[2]. Its functions include those of the Mental Health Act

Commission and certain other public service inspectorates, in particular, specified functions under the Mental Health Act 1983[3]. Certain functions of the Secretary of State[4] under the Mental Health Act 1983 have been transferred to the Care Quality Commission[5].

1 See the Health and Social Care Act 2008 s 1(1), (2); and SOCIAL SERVICES AND COMMUNITY CARE. As to the Care Quality Commission generally see Pt 1 Chapter 1 (ss 1–7), Schs 1, 2; the Care Quality Commission (Membership) Regulations 2008, SI 2008/225; and SOCIAL SERVICES AND COMMUNITY CARE. The functions of the Mental Health Act Commission under the Mental Health Act 1983 are transferred, in relation to England, to the Care Quality Commission and, in relation to Wales, to the Welsh Ministers: Health and Social Care Act 2008 s 52(3). As to the transfer of property, rights and liabilities of the Mental Health Act Commission to the Care Quality Commission or the Welsh Ministers or to the Crown see Sch 2. The Care Quality Commission is the 'regulatory authority' for England for the purposes of the Mental Health Act 1983: see s 145(1) (definition added by the Health and Social Care Act 2008 Sch 3 para 13). In relation to Wales, this is the Welsh Ministers: see the Mental Health Act 1983 s 145(1) (definition as so added).

2 See the Health and Social Care Act 2008 Pt 1 Chapter 1 (ss 1–7), Schs 1, 2; and SOCIAL SERVICES AND COMMUNITY CARE.

3 See the Health and Social Care Act 2008 Pt 1 Chapter 4 (s 52), Sch 3; and SOCIAL SERVICES AND COMMUNITY CARE.

4 As to the Secretary of State see PARA 567 note 1.

5 Ie functions of the Secretary of State under the following provisions of the Mental Health Act 1983 s 57(2)(a) (appointment of registered medical practitioners and other persons for the purposes of Pt 4 and 4A: see PARA 928), s 58(3)(a) (appointment of registered medical practitioners: see PARA 930), s 61(1) (receipt of reports on treatment: see PARA 748), s 61(3) (power to disapply Part 4 certificates: see PARA 748), s 64H(4) (receipt of reports on treatment: see PARA 944), s 64H(5) (power to disapply Pt 4A certificates: see PARA 944), s 118(2) (code of practice: see PARA 762) so far as it relates to the appointment of registered medical practitioners, s 119(1) (power to make provision for payment to practitioners etc: see PARA 928), and s 120 (duty to keep matters under review etc: see PARA 806) are transferred to the Commission: Health and Social Care Act 2008 s 52(1). Registered medical practitioners, and other persons, appointed or authorised by the Care Quality Commission in the exercise of a function under the Mental Health Act 1983 may include members or employees of the Care Quality Commission: Health and Social Care Act 2008 s 52(2). As to registered medical practitioners see MEDICAL PROFESSIONS vol 74 (2011) PARA 176 et seq.

(5) HEALTH AND HOSPITAL SERVICES

574. General responsibilities. The responsibilities of the national health service, so far as mentally disordered persons are concerned, fall into two groups: (1) the provision of hospital and specialist services[1]; and (2) the provision of health services in the community[2]. Since the enactment of the Mental Health Act 1959, both of these have been provided as part of the general health service; they are now provided under the National Health Service Act 2006 and the National Health Service (Wales) Act 2006[3].

There is also a duty to provide aftercare services in co-operation with relevant voluntary agencies for certain people who were formerly detained patients in hospital[4].

1 See the National Health Service Act 2006 s 3(1)(e); the National Health Service (Wales) Act 2006 s 3(1)(e); PARA 575 et seq; and HEALTH SERVICES vol 54 (2008) PARA 10 et seq.

2 This includes the duty, under the National Health Service Act 2006 s 3(1)(e) and the National Health Service (Wales) Act 2006 s 3(1)(e) (see PARA 568), to provide such services for the prevention, care and after-care of illness as are appropriate as part of the health service: see HEALTH SERVICES vol 54 (2008) PARA 12.

The local authority also has a duty to carry out an assessment of needs for community care services: see the National Health Service and Community Care Act 1990 s 47; and SOCIAL SERVICES AND COMMUNITY CARE vol 44(2) (Reissue) PARA 1015 et seq. As to the meaning of 'community care services' see PARA 580 note 3; and SOCIAL SERVICES AND COMMUNITY CARE vol 44(2) (Reissue) PARA 1012. Note that 'community care services' includes services which the authority may provide or arrange to be provided under the Mental Health Act 1983 s 117. As to the entitlement to community care assessment see *R (on the application of HP) v Islington London Borough Council* [2004] EWHC 7 (Admin), 82 BMLR 113. As to when the duties under the National Health Service and Community Care Act 1990 s 47 and the Mental Health Act 1983 s 117(2) arise see *R (on the application of B) v Camden London Borough Council* [2005] EWHC 1366 (Admin), [2006] LGR 19, 85 BMLR 28. See also PARA 945.

3 See HEALTH SERVICES.

4 See the Mental Health Act 1983 s 117; and PARA 945. Local social services authorities are not entitled to charge for after-care services provided under s 117: see *R v Manchester City Council (ex p Stennett)* [2002] UKHL 34, [2002] 2 AC 1127, [2002] 4 All ER 124. As to charging for services see HEALTH SERVICES vol 54 (2008) PARA 469 et seq. See further SOCIAL SERVICES AND COMMUNITY CARE.

575. Hospital and specialist services. Except for hospitals providing high security psychiatric services[1], hospitals and specialist services for the treatment of mental disorder are administered on behalf of the appropriate national authority[2], subject to its directions and to regulations, by health authorities, strategic health authorities[3], special health authorities[4], primary care trusts[5] and local health boards[6] and by NHS foundation trusts[7]. The Welsh Ministers have similar powers in relation to Wales and may arrange for assistance by voluntary organisations, primary care trusts, special health authorities and local health boards[8].

1 As to the duty to provide high security psychiatric services see PARA 569.

2 As to the appropriate national body see PARA 567.

3 For the purposes of the Mental Health Act 1983 'strategic health authority' means a strategic health authority established under the National Health Service Act 2006 s 13 (see HEALTH SERVICES vol 54 (2008) PARA 94): Mental Health Act 1983 s 145(1) (definition added by SI 2002/2469; amended by the National Health Service (Consequential Provisions) Act 2006 Sch 1 para 70(g)). As from 1 April 2013 strategic health authorities are abolished by the Health and Social Care Act 2012 s 33; and the definition in the Mental Health Act 1983 is repealed by the Health and Social Care Act 2012 Sch 5 para 31(1)(a): see Health and Social Care Act 2012 (Commencement No 4, Transitional, Savings and Transitory Provisions) Order 2013, SI 2013/160, art 2(2).

4 For the purposes of the Mental Health Act 1984 'special health authority' means a special health authority established under the National Health Service Act 2006 s 28 or the National Health Service (Wales) Act 2006 s 22 (see HEALTH SERVICES): Mental Health Act 1983 s 145(1) (definition added by the Health Authorities Act 1995 Sch 1 para 107(14); and amended by the National Health Service (Consequential Provisions) Act 2006 Sch 1 para 70(f)).

5 For the purposes of the Mental Health Act 1983 'primary care trust' means a primary care trust established under the National Health Service Act 2006 s 18 (see HEALTH SERVICES vol 54 (2008) PARA 111): Mental Health Act 1983 s 145(1). As from 1 April 2013 primary care trusts are abolished and the National Health Service Act 2006 s 18 is repealed by the Health and Social Care Act 2012 s 306(4); and the definition of 'primary care trust' in the Mental Health Act 1983 s 145(1) is repealed by the Health and Social Care Act 2012 s 45(1)(b): see the Health and Social Care Act 2012 (Commencement No 4, Transitional, Savings and Transitory Provisions) Order 2013, SI 2013/160, art 2(2). As from that date clinical commissioning groups are responsible for commissioning the majority of health services: see the National Health Service Act 2006 s 1L; and HEALTH SERVICES.

6 For the details of local administration see HEALTH SERVICES vol 54 (2008) PARA 74 et seq. For the purposes of the Mental Health Act 1983 and the Mental Health (Wales) Measure 2010 'local health board' means a local health board established under the National Health Services (Wales) Act 2006 s 11 (see HEALTH SERVICES vol 54 (2008) PARA 74): Mental Health Act 1983 s 145(1) (definition added by SI 2007/961); Mental Health (Wales) Measure 2010 s 51(1).

7 The constitution of an NHS foundation trust may not provide for a function under the Mental Health Act 1983 to be delegated otherwise than in accordance with provision made by or under that Act: s 142B(1) (added by the Mental Health Act 2007 s 45(3)). The National Health Service Act 2006 Sch 7 para 15(3) (which provides that the powers of a public benefit corporation may

be delegated to a committee of directors or to an executive director) (see HEALTH SERVICES) has effect subject to the Mental Health Act 2007 s 142B: s 142B(2) (as so added).

8 See HEALTH SERVICES vol 54 (2008) PARA 74.

576. Notification of hospitals having arrangements for special cases. Patients[1] suffering from mental disorder[2] may be admitted, whether as informal patients[3] or compulsorily[4], to any hospital[5]; or they may be admitted as informal patients, or in some cases compulsorily[6], to a registered establishment[7]. It is the duty of every primary care trust[8] and every local health board[9] to notify every social services authority for an area wholly or partly comprised within the area of the primary care trust[10] or local health board specifying the hospital or hospitals administered by or otherwise available to the primary care trust[11] or local health board in which arrangements are for the time being in force for the reception of patients in cases of special urgency and for the provision of accommodation or facilities designed so as to be specially suitable for patients who have not attained the age of 18 years[12]. It is also the duty of a primary care trust[13] or local health board to provide at the request of a court which is minded to make a hospital order such information as it has or can reasonably obtain about hospitals in its own area or elsewhere which might be able to admit the person concerned[14].

1 As to the meaning of 'patient' generally see PARA 758 note 4.
2 As to the meaning of 'mental disorder' see PARA 761.
3 See the Mental Health Act 1983 s 131; and PARA 764.
4 As to compulsory admission see PARA 767 et seq; and as to admission by court order see PARA 859 et seq. As to transfer of prisoners see PARA 892 et seq.
5 As to the meaning of 'hospital' under the Mental Health Act 1983 see PARA 577.
6 See PARA 766 et seq.
7 As to the meaning of 'registered establishment' see PARA 578. See also SOCIAL SERVICES AND COMMUNITY CARE.
8 As to the meaning of 'primary care trust' see PARA 575 note 6. As from 1 April 2013 primary care trusts are abolished and the words 'primary care trust' wherever they appear in the text are repealed by the Health and Social Care Act 2012 s 45(1)(b) and the words 'clinical commissioning group' are added by s 45(1)(a): see Health and Social Care Act 2012 (Commencement No 4, Transitional, Savings and Transitory Provisions) Order, SI 2013/160, art 2(2).
9 As to the meaning of 'local health board' see PARA 575 note 7.
10 See note 8.
11 See note 8.
12 Mental Health Act 1983 s 140 (amended by the National Health Service and Community Care Act 1990 s 66(1), Sch 9 para 24(8); the Health Authorities Act 1995 s 2(1), Sch 1 para 107; the National Health Service Reform and the Health Care Professions Act 2002 s 2(5), Sch 2 paras 42, 48; the Mental Health Act 2007 s 31(4); and SI 2007/961).
13 See note 8.
14 See the Mental Health Act 1983 s 39(1), (2); and PARA 864. The Mental Health Act 1983 s 39 has effect as if any reference to the making of a hospital order included a reference to the giving of a hospital direction and a limitation direction (see PARA 863): s 45A(8) (added by the Crime (Sentences) Act 1997 s 46).

577. Meaning of 'hospital'. In the Mental Health Act 1983, 'hospital' means: (1) any health service hospital within the meaning of the National Health Service Act 2006[1] or the National Health Service (Wales) Act 2006[2]; (2) any accommodation provided by a local authority and used as a hospital by or on behalf of the Secretary of State under the National Health Service Act 2006; (3) any hospital as defined by the National Health Service (Wales) Act 2006[3] which is vested in a local health board[4].

In Parts 2 and 3 of the Mental Health Act 1983[5], relating to compulsory admission and guardianship and patients concerned in criminal proceedings or under sentence, 'hospital' also includes, except where otherwise expressly provided[6], a registered establishment[7]. In Part 4A[8] 'hospital' includes a registered establishment[9].

In the Mental Capacity Act 2005 'hospital' has the following meanings:

(1)   for the purposes of provisions relating to the deprivation of liberty[10] a 'hospital' is an NHS hospital[11] or an independent hospital[12];

(2)   for purposes relating to persons ineligible to be deprived of liberty[13], 'hospital' has the same meaning as in the Mental Health Act 1983 Part 2[14];

(3)   for the purposes of provisions relating to the provision of accommodation by an NHS body[15] 'hospital' means, in relation to England, a hospital as defined by the National Health Service Act 2006[16] and, in relation to Wales, a health service hospital as defined by the National Health Service (Wales) Act 2006[17] or an independent hospital[18] as defined by the Care Standards Act 2000[19].

1   Ie a hospital vested in the Secretary of State for the purposes of his functions under the National Health Service Act 2006 or vested in a Primary Care Trust, an NHS trust or an NHS foundation trust: s 275(1). As from 1 April 2013 Primary Care Trusts are abolished and the words 'primary care trust' are repealed by the Health and Social Care Act 2012 Sch 4 para 138(2)(a): see Health and Social Care Act 2012 (Commencement No 4, Transitional, Savings and Transitory Provisions) Order 2013, SI 2013/160, art 2(2). As from a day to be appointed NHS trusts are also abolished: see the Health and Social Care Act 2012 s 179(1). As to the meaning of 'primary care trust' see PARA 575 note 6. As to NHS trusts and NHS foundation trusts see HEALTH SERVICES vol 54 (2008) PARA 155 et seq.

2   Ie a hospital vested in the Welsh Ministers for the purposes of their functions under National Health Service (Wales) Act 2006 or vested in an NHS trust: s 206(1). As to such accommodation see SOCIAL SERVICES AND COMMUNITY CARE.

3   Ie as defined by the National Health Service (Wales) 2003 s 206 (see HEALTH SERVICES).

4   Mental Health Act 1983 s 145(1) (amended by National Health Service (Consequential Provisions) Act 2006 Sch 1 para 70(c)). See also *W Primary Care Trust v TB* [2009] EWHC 1737 (Fam), [2010] 2 All ER 331, [2010] 1 WLR 2662.

5   Ie the Mental Health Act 1983 Pt 2 (ss 2–34), Pt 3 (ss 35–55).

6   Ie by the Mental Health Act 1983 s 46(1) (persons ordered to be kept in custody during Her Majesty's pleasure), s 47(1) or s 48(1) (transfer of certain prisoners to hospital): see PARAS 892–893.

7   See the Mental Health Act 1983 ss 34(2), 55(5), 145(1) (s 34(2) amended by the Care Standards Act 2000 s 116, Sch 4 para 9(1), (4)(b)). As to the meaning of 'registered establishment' see PARA 578.

8   Ie the Mental Health Act 1983 ss 64A–64K.

9   See the Mental Health Act 1983 s 64K(7) (added by the Mental Health Act 2007 s 35(1)).

10   Ie for the purposes of the Mental Capacity Act 2005 (see PARA 651 et seq).

11   'NHS hospital' means a health service hospital as defined by the National Health Service Act 2006 s 275 or the National Health Service (Wales) Act 2006 s 206, (see HEALTH SERVICES vol 54 (2008) PARA 12) or a hospital as defined by the National Health Service (Wales) Act 2006 s 206 vested in a local health board: Mental Capacity Act 2005 Sch A1 para 175(2) (Sch A1 added by the Mental Health Act 2007 Sch 7).

12   Mental Capacity Act 2005 Sch A1 para 175(1) (as added: see note 11). 'Independent hospital', in relation to England, means a hospital as defined by the National Health Service Act 2006 s 275 that is not an NHS hospital and, in relation to Wales, means a hospital as defined by the Care Standards Act 2000 s 2 that is not an NHS hospital: Mental Capacity Act 2005 Sch A1 para 175(3) (as so added; substituted by SI 2010/813).

13   Ie for the purposes of the Mental Capacity Act 2005 Sch 1A (see PARAS 658–660).

14   Mental Capacity Act 2005 Sch 1A para 17(1) (added by the Mental Health Act 2007 Sch 8).

15   Ie for the purposes of the Mental Capacity Act 2005 s 38 (see PARA 639).

16   Ie as defined by the National Health Service Act 2006 s 275 (see note 1).

17   Ie as defined by the National Health Service (Wales) Act 2006 s 206 (see note 2).

18   Ie as defined by the Care Standards Act 2000 s 2 (see PARA 578 note 7; and SOCIAL SERVICES AND COMMUNITY CARE).

19   Mental Capacity Act 2005 s 38(7) (substituted by SI 2010/813).

578. Meaning of 'registered establishment'. A 'registered establishment' means an establishment which would not, apart from certain provisions[1], be a hospital for the purposes of the Mental Health Act 1983 Part 2[2] and which:

(1) in England, is a hospital as defined by the National Health Service Act 2006[3] that is used for the carrying on of a regulated activity[4] which relates to the assessment or medical treatment of mental disorder and in respect of which a person is registered[5]; and

(2) in Wales, is an establishment in respect of which a person is registered[6] as an independent hospital[7] in which treatment or nursing (or both) are provided for persons liable to be detained under the Mental Health Act 1983[8].

1   Ie apart from the Mental Health Act 1983 s 34(2). Except where otherwise expressly provided, the Mental Health Act 1983 Pt 2 (ss 2–34) applies in relation to a registered establishment, as it applies in relation to a hospital, and references in Pt 2 to a hospital, and any reference in the Mental Health Act 1983 to a hospital to which Pt 2 applies, is construed accordingly: s 34(2).

2   Ie the Mental Health Act 1983 Pt 2 (ss 2–34).

3   Ie as defined by the National Health Service Act 2006 s 275 (see PARA 577).

4   Ie within the meaning of the Health and Social Care Act 2008 Pt 1 (see s 8; and SOCIAL SERVICES AND COMMUNITY CARE).

5   Ie registered under the Health and Social Care Act 2006 Pt 2 Chapter 2.

6   Ie registered under the Care Standards Act 2000 Pt 2 (ss 11–42). As to such registration see PARA 585; and SOCIAL SERVICES AND COMMUNITY CARE.

7   'Independent hospital', in relation to England, means a hospital as defined by the National Health Service Act 2006 s 275 that is not a health service hospital as defined by that provision (see HEALTH SERVICES vol 54 (2008) PARA 12) and, in relation to Wales, has the same meaning as in the Care Standards Act 2000 (see HEALTH SERVICES vol 54 (2008) PARA 748): Mental Health Act 1983 s 145(1) (definition substituted by SI 2010/813). As to health service hospitals see HEALTH SERVICES vol 54 (2008) PARA 21.

8   Mental Health Act 1983 ss 34(1), 145(1) (definitions added by the Care Standards Act 2000 Sch 4 para 9(1), (4), (10(d))).

(6) SOCIAL SERVICES

579. Meaning of 'local social services authority'. Under the Mental Health Act 1983, 'local social services authority' means a council which is a local authority for the purposes of the Local Authority Social Services Act 1970[1], that is, the council of a non-metropolitan county, the council of a metropolitan district or a London borough, or the Common Council of the City of London or, in relation to Wales[2], the councils of the counties and county boroughs[3]. A similar definition is also adopted by the National Health Service Act 2006 and the National Health Service (Wales) Act 2006[4].

1   Mental Health Act 1983 s 145(1).

2   As to the meaning of 'Wales' see PARA 557 note 5.

3   See the Local Authority Social Services Act 1970 s 1 (amended by the Local Government Act 1972 s 195(1), (3); and the Local Government (Wales) Act 1994 s 22(4), Sch 10 para 7). See SOCIAL SERVICES AND COMMUNITY CARE vol 44(2) (Reissue) PARA 1005. As to local government areas and authorities in England and Wales see LOCAL GOVERNMENT vol 69 (2009) PARAS 24 et seq, 37 et seq. As to London boroughs and the Common Council of the City of London see LONDON GOVERNMENT vol 71 (2013) PARAS 20 et seq, 34 et seq. In relation to the Isles of Scilly, a local social services authority means the Council of the Isles of Scilly: see PARA 557 note 6; and LOCAL GOVERNMENT vol 69 (2009) PARA 36; SOCIAL SERVICES AND COMMUNITY CARE vol 44(2) (Reissue) PARA 1005.

4   See the National Health Service Act 2006 s 275(1); the National Health Services (Wales) Act 2006 s 206(1); and HEALTH SERVICES.

580. General functions of local social services authorities. The care of mentally disordered people[1] living in the community falls principally upon the local social services authority[2]. Its functions fall into the following broad categories[3]: (1) to provide residential accommodation for those aged 18 or over who need care and attention because of age, illness, disability or any other circumstances[4]; (2) to provide occupational, recreational and other services for persons aged 18 or over suffering from certain disabilities, including mental disorder of any description[5]; (3) to publish information relating to welfare arrangments[6] and provide home adaptations and other facilities[7] for disabled persons[8]; (4) to promote the welfare of old people[9]; (5) to provide services for the prevention, care and after-care of illness, including mental disorder[10]; (6) to perform various functions under the Mental Health Act 1983, including: (a) acting as guardian or approving and supervising the appointment of others to act as guardians of mentally disordered persons[11]; (b) appointing and providing the services of approved mental health professionals[12]; (c) providing after-care for certain formerly detained patients[13]; (d) making social reports to hospitals[14]; (e) visiting certain patients in hospital[15]; and (f) prosecuting certain offences[16].

1 As to the meaning of 'mentally disordered' see PARA 761.

2 Generally this is the local social services authority for the area where the person concerned lives. As to the meaning of 'local social services authority' see PARA 579.

3 As to the provision of accommodation and welfare services by local social services authorities see SOCIAL SERVICES AND COMMUNITY CARE vol 44(2) (Reissue) PARA 1020 et seq. A strategic plan for the provision of community care services must be prepared and published: see the National Health Service and Community Care Act 1990 s 46; and SOCIAL SERVICES AND COMMUNITY CARE vol 44(2) (Reissue) PARA 1013. 'Community care services' consist of services under the National Assistance Act 1948 Pt III (ss 21–35), the Health Service and Public Health Act 1968 s 45, the National Health Service Act 2006 s 254, Sch 20 and the National Health Service (Wales) Act 2006 s 192, Sch 15, and the Mental Health Act 1983 s 117 (see PARA 945): National Health Service and Community Care Act 1990 s 46(3) (amended by the Local Government (Wales) Act 1994 Sch 10 para 14 and the National Health Service (Consequential Provisions) Act 2006 Sch 1 para 129). See SOCIAL SERVICES AND COMMUNITY CARE vol 44(2) (Reissue) PARA 1012.

4 See the National Assistance Act 1948 s 21(1)(a); and SOCIAL SERVICES AND COMMUNITY CARE vol 44(2) (Reissue) PARA 1029. As to the provision of such accommodation see SOCIAL SERVICES AND COMMUNITY CARE vol 44(2) (Reissue) PARA 1029 et seq.

5 See the National Assistance Act 1948 s 29(1); and SOCIAL SERVICES AND COMMUNITY CARE vol 44(2) (Reissue) PARA 1020.

6 See the Chronically Sick and Disabled Persons Act 1970 s 1; and SOCIAL SERVICES AND COMMUNITY CARE vol 44(2) (Reissue) PARA 1017.

7 See the Chronically Sick and Disabled Persons Act 1970 s 2; and SOCIAL SERVICES AND COMMUNITY CARE vol 44(2) (Reissue) PARA 1023.

8 Ie those to whom the National Assistance Act 1948 s 29 applies; and SOCIAL SERVICES AND COMMUNITY CARE vol 44(2) (Reissue) PARA 1020 et seq.

9 See the Health Services and Public Health Act 1968 s 45; and SOCIAL SERVICES AND COMMUNITY CARE vol 44(2) (Reissue) PARA 1024.

10 See the National Health Service Act 2006 s 254, Sch 20 para 2; the National Health Service (Wales) Act 2006 s 192, Sch 15 para 2; PARA 581; and SOCIAL SERVICES AND COMMUNITY CARE vol 44(2) (Reissue) PARA 1026.

11 See the Mental Health Act 1983 ss 7(5), 8–10, 37(1), (6); and PARAS 785 et seq, 877. As to the duty of the local social services authority, on request, to inform a court which is minded to make a guardianship order whether the authority or any other person is willing to receive the offender into guardianship, and if so how the guardian could be expected to exercise the statutory powers, see s 39A; and PARA 877.

12 See the Mental Health Act 1983 s 114; and PARA 815. As to the appointment and functions of approved mental health professionals see PARAS 815–821.

13 See the Mental Health Act 1983 s 117; and PARA 945.

14 See the Mental Health Act 1983 s 14; and PARA 582.

15 See the Mental Health Act 1983 s 116; and PARA 583.
16 See PARA 584.

581. Functions in relation to the prevention of illness, care and after-care. A local social services authority[1] may, with the approval of the appropriate national authority[2], and must, to such extent as he may direct, make arrangements for the purpose of the prevention of illness, for the care of persons[3] suffering from illness, and for the after-care of persons who have been suffering from illness[4]. In particular, this includes arrangements for: (1) the provision of centres or other facilities for training and suitable occupation, the equipment and maintenance of such centres[5], and the provision of ancillary and supplemental services for people using them[6]; and (2) the exercise of the functions of the authority in respect of persons suffering from mental disorder[7] who are received into guardianship[8] (whether that of the local social services authority or of other persons)[9].

The appropriate national authority may make regulations as to the conduct of premises in which facilities[10], in pursuance of the above arrangements, are provided, for persons who are or have been suffering from mental disorder within the meaning of the Mental Health Act 1983 or whose care is undertaken with a view to preventing them from becoming sufferers from mental disorder[11].

1 As to the meaning of 'local social services authority' see PARA 579.
2 As to the appropriate national authority see PARA 567.
3 This power does not apply to persons under 18: see the National Health Service Act 2006 Sch 20 para 2(10); and the National Health Service (Wales) Act 2006 Sch 15 para 2(10).
4 National Health Service Act 2006 Sch 20 para 2(1); National Health Service (Wales) Act 2006 Sch 15 para 2(1). No authority is authorised or may be required under these provisions to provide residential accommodation for any person: National Health Service Act 2006 Sch 20 para 2(11); National Health Service (Wales) Act 2006 Sch 15 para 2(11).
5 See the National Health Service Act 2006 Sch 20 para 2(2)(a); and the National Health Service (Wales) Act 2006 Sch 15 para 2(2)(a). Such an authority neither has the power nor is subject to a duty to make arrangements to provide facilities for any of the purposes mentioned in the Disabled Persons (Employment) Act 1944 s 15(1) (see EMPLOYMENT vol 39 (2009) PARAS 538–539): National Health Service Act 2006 Sch 20 para 2(3); National Health Service (Wales) Act 2006 Sch 15 para 2(3). Nor may such arrangements provide for the payment of money to persons for whose benefit they are made except in so far as they may provide for the remuneration of such persons engaged in suitable work in accordance with the arrangements of such amounts as the local social services authority think fit in respect of their occasional personal expenses where it appears to that authority that no such payment would otherwise be made: National Health Service Act 2006 Sch 20 para 2(4), (5); National Health Service (Wales) Act 2006 Sch 15 para 2(4), (5).
   No such arrangements may be given effect in relation to a person to whom the Immigration and Asylum Act 1999 s 115 (see IMMIGRATION AND ASYLUM vol 57 (2012) PARA 335) applies solely because he is destitute or because of the physical effects, or anticipated physical effects, of his being destitute: National Health Service Act 2006 Sch 20 para 2(6); National Health Service (Wales) Act 2006 Sch 15 para 2(6). The provisions of the Immigration and Asylum Act 1999 s 95(2)–(7) (see IMMIGRATION AND ASYLUM vol 57 (2012) PARAS 344–346) apply for the purposes of the National Health Service Act 2006 Sch 20 para 2(6) and the National Health Service (Wales) Act 2006 Sch 15 para 2(6) as they apply for the purposes of the Immigration and Asylum Act 1999 s 95, and for that purpose a reference to the Secretary of State in the Immigration and Asylum Act 1999 s 95(4) or (5) is to be treated as a reference to a local social services authority: National Health Service Act 2006 Sch 20 para 2(7); National Health Service (Wales) Act 2006 Sch 15 para 2(7).
6 See the National Health Service Act 2006 Sch 20 para 2(2)(b); and the National Health Service (Wales) Act 2006 Sch 15 para 2(2)(b).
7 As to the meaning of 'mental disorder' see PARA 761.
8 Ie received into guardianship under the Mental Health Act 1983 Pt 2 (ss 2–34) or Pt 3 (ss 35–55): see PARAS 784–796, 877–878.

9   See the National Health Service Act 2006 Sch 20 para 2(2)(c); and the National Health Service (Wales) Act 2006 Sch 15 para 2(2)(c).

10 'Facilities' means facilities for training such persons or keeping them suitably occupied: National Health Service Act 2006 Sch 20 para 2(9); the National Health Service (Wales) Act 2006 Sch 15 para 2(9).

11 National Health Service Act 2006 Sch 20 para 2(8); the National Health Service (Wales) Act 2006 Sch 15 para 2(8).

582.   Social circumstances reports.   Where a patient[1] is admitted to hospital[2] in pursuance of an application[3] made under Part 2 of the Mental Health Act 1983[4] by his nearest relative[5], the managers[6] of the hospital must as soon as practicable give notice of that fact to the local social services authority[7] for the area in which the patient resided immediately before his admission; and that authority must arrange for an approved mental health professional[8] to interview the patient and provide the managers with a report on his social circumstances[9].

1   As to the meaning of 'patient' see PARA 758 note 4.
2   As to the meaning of 'hospital' see PARA 577.
3   Ie except an emergency application: see PARA 769.
4   Ie the Mental Health Act 1983 Pt 2 (ss 2–34).
5   As to the meaning of 'nearest relative' see PARA 839.
6   As to the meaning of 'managers' see PARA 778.
7   As to the meaning of 'local social services authority' see PARA 579.
8   As to the meaning of 'approved mental health professional' see PARA 815 note 2.
9   Mental Health Act 1983 s 14 (amended by the Children Act 2004 s 65, Sch 5 Pt 4; and the Mental Health Act 2007 Sch 2 para 6). As to the details to be contained in the social services report see *Practice Direction (First-tier Tribunal: mental health cases)* (6 April 2012, unreported) paras 12, 16, 20, 26.

583.   Visiting patients in hospital.   Where a local social services authority[1] is the guardian[2] or nearest relative[3] of a mentally disordered person[4], and that person is admitted to a hospital[5], independent hospital[6] or care home[7] in England[8] and Wales[9], whether for treatment for mental disorder or otherwise, the authority is required to arrange for visits to be made to the patient[10] and to take such steps as would be expected to be taken by his parents[11].

1   As to the meaning of 'local social services authority' see PARA 579.
2   Ie under the Mental Health Act 1983 (see PARAS 784–796, 877–878): Mental Health Act 1983 s 116(2)(b) (amended by the Mental Health (Scotland) Act 1984 s 127(1), Sch 3 para 55; and SI 2005/2078). The Mental Health Act 1983 s 116 extends to Scotland: see s 146; and PARA 557.
3   Ie where the functions of the nearest relative are for the time being transferred to the authority under the Mental Health Act 1983 (see PARA 842): s 116(2)(c) (amended by the Mental Health (Scotland) Act 1984 Sch 3 para 55; and SI 2005/2078). As to the meaning of 'nearest relative' see PARA 839.
4   As to the meaning of 'mentally disordered person' see PARA 761. This duty also applies in respect of a mentally disordered child who is in the care of a local authority by virtue of a care order within the meaning of the Children Act 1989 (see CHILDREN AND YOUNG PERSONS vol 9 (2012) PARA 313): see the Mental Health Act 1983 s 116(2)(a) (substituted by the Courts and Legal Services Act 1990 s 116, Sch 16 para 42).
5   As to the meaning of 'hospital' see PARA 577.
6   As to the meaning of 'independent hospital' see PARA 578 note 7.
7   As to the meaning of 'care home' see the Care Standards Act 2000 s 3; and CHILDREN AND YOUNG PERSONS vol 10 (2012) PARA 994; applied by the Mental Health Act 1983 s 145(1) (definition added by the Care Standards Act 2000 s 116, Sch 4 para 9(1), (10)(a)).
8   As to the meaning of 'England' see PARA 557 note 4.
9   As to the meaning of 'Wales' see PARA 557 note 5.
10 As to the meaning of 'patient' see PARA 758 note 4.

11 Mental Health Act 1983 s 116(1) (amended by the Care Standards Act 2000 s 116, Sch 4 para 9(1), (5)). This provision extends to Scotland: see the Mental Health Act 1983 s 146; and PARA 557.

584. Prosecution of offences. Local social services authorities[1] may institute proceedings for the following offences[2]:

    (1)   the forgery of or the making of false statements in applications, recommendations or other documents required or authorised for the purposes of the Mental Health Act 1983[3];

    (2)   ill-treatment or wilful neglect of patients receiving treatment for mental disorder who are in-patients or out-patients, or who are subject to guardianship or otherwise in the custody or care of an individual, or who are subject to after-care under supervision[4];

    (3)   assisting patients to absent themselves without leave or to escape[5]; and

    (4)   obstruction of authorised persons in the exercise of their functions under the Mental Health Act 1983[6].

1 As to the meaning of 'local social services authority' see PARA 579.
2 A local social services authority may institute proceedings for any offence under the Mental Health Act 1959 Pt IX (ss 131–154) or the Mental Health Act 1983 Pt 9 (ss 126–130), but without prejudice to any provision requiring the consent of the Director of Public Prosecutions for the institution of such proceedings: Mental Health Act 1959 s 131(1) (amended by the Local Government Act 1972 s 195(6), Sch 23 para 9(2)); Mental Health Act 1983 s 130. As to the Director of Public Prosecutions see CRIMINAL PROCEDURE vol 27 (2010) PARAS 23, 33 et seq.
3 See the Mental Health Act 1983 s 126; and PARAS 1008–1009.
4 See the Mental Health Act 1983 s 127; and PARA 1010.
5 See the Mental Health Act 1983 s 128; and PARAS 1013–1014.
6 See the Mental Health Act 1983 s 129; and PARA 1015.

585. Registration of establishments and agencies under the Care Standards Act 2000. Managing an establishment[1] or agency of any description without the necessary registration under Part II of the Care Standards Act 2000[2] is an offence[3]. The Act, amongst other things, makes provision for the registration and regulation of independent hospitals[4] and care homes[5].

There are provisions as to the supply of information relating to the establishment or agency and for the inspection of any relevant premises[6]. Regulations impose requirements in relation to the management of staff, the premises, and the conduct of establishments and agencies, and there is provision for the preparation of national minimum standards[7].

1 As to the meaning of 'registered establishment' see PARA 578.
2 Ie the Care Standards Act 2000 Pt II (ss 11–42).
3 See the Care Standards Act 2000 s 11; and CHILDREN AND YOUNG PERSONS vol 10 (2012) PARA 994.
4 As to the meaning of 'independent hospital' see PARA 578 note 7.
5 As to the meaning of 'care home' see PARA 583 note 7.
6 See the Care Standards Act 2000 ss 31–32; and SOCIAL SERVICES AND COMMUNITY CARE.
7 See the Care Standards Act 2000 ss 22, 23; and SOCIAL SERVICES AND COMMUNITY CARE.

(7) LOCAL MENTAL HEALTH SUPPORT SERVICES: WALES

586. Joint schemes for the provision of local primary mental health support services. The local mental health partners for a local authority area[1] must take all reasonable steps to agree a scheme[2] (1) which identifies the treatment[3] which is to be made available for that area for the purposes of local primary mental health treatment[4]; and (2) for securing the provision for that area of the services, including local primary mental health support services[5].

A scheme must identify the extent to which each of the partners is to be responsible for providing local primary mental health support services[6]. The partners may alter a scheme[7] if they agree the alterations and ensure that the alterations are recorded in writing[8].

1   For the purposes of the Mental Health (Wales) Measure 2010, the local mental health partners for a local authority area are the Local Health Board established under the National Health Service (Wales) Act 2006 s 11 (see HEALTH SERVICES vol 54 (2008) PARA 74) for an area which includes the local authority area and the local authority for that area: s 1. 'Local authority' means a county council or a county borough council; and 'local authority area' means a principal area in Wales within the meaning of the Local Government Act 1972 s 20 (see LOCAL GOVERNMENT vol 69 (2009) PARA 37): Mental Health (Wales) Measure 2010 s 51(1). The Welsh Ministers may by regulations make provision for and in connection with (1) disapplying (for so long as the regulations are in force) Pt 1(ie ss 1–11) 1 in relation to two or more local authority areas; and (2) instead applying that Part and, so far as necessary Pt 5 (ie ss 41–48) and Pt 6 (ie ss 49–56), in relation to the combined areas of the authorities referred to in head (1) (that combined area being referred to in this section as a 'region'): s 45(1). The provision made by regulations under s 45(1) must include provision specifying at least one Local Health Board and one local authority as the mental health partners for the region (and it does not matter if no part of the area for which such a Board or authority is constituted falls within the region): s 45(2). The provision that may be made by regulations under s 45(1) includes (but is not limited to) provision (a) specifying more than one such Board or authority amongst the mental health partners for the region; (b) making such modifications of Pt 1 as appear to the Welsh Ministers to be necessary or expedient: s 45(3). As to regional provision of the Mental Health (Wales) Measure 2010 Pt 1 see the Mental Health (Regional Provision) (Wales) Regulations 2012, SI 2012/1244, reg 3, Schs 1, 2. As to regional provision of the Mental Health (Wales) Measure 2010 Pt 3 see the Mental Health (Regional Provision) (Wales) Regulations 2012, SI 2012/1244, reg 4, Schs 1, 2.

2   If a scheme is agreed, the partners must ensure that it is recorded in writing: Mental Health (Wales) Measure 2010 s 2(2).

3   'Treatment' means treatment for mental disorder within the meaning of the Government of Wales Act 2006 Sch 5 Pt 1 field 9 (see HEALTH SERVICES vol 54 (2008) PARA 710): Mental Health (Wales) Measure 2010 s 51(1).

4   Ie for the purposes of the Mental Health (Wales) Measure 2010 Pt 1 (ss 1–11). 'Local primary mental health treatment', in relation to a local authority area, means the treatment referred to in the scheme for the area agreed under s 2 or determined by the Welsh Ministers under s 4(1)(c) or, where there is no scheme, the treatment which a Local Health Board has decided to make available for the area under s 4(1)(a): s 51(1).

5   Mental Health (Wales) Measure 2010 s 2(1). Local primary mental health support services mentioned in the text refers to local primary mental health treatment, described in s 5 (see PARA 587).

6   Mental Health (Wales) Measure 2010 s 2(3). The scheme may provide that: (1) one of the partners is to be responsible for providing all local primary mental health support services for the local authority area; (2) primary mental health assessments are to be made available in respect of all or particular descriptions of the individuals described in s 8(1) (see PARA 881); (3) primary mental health assessments are to be carried out in respect of particular categories of individual who would not otherwise be entitled to an assessment: s 2(4). 'Primary mental health assessment' is an assessment under the Mental Health (Wales) Measure 2010 s 9 (see PARA 883): s 51(1). If a scheme makes provision under head (2), it must also provide for particular descriptions of staff working in secondary mental health services to be able to refer an individual referred to in head (3) for a primary mental health assessment: s 2(5). For the purposes of the Mental Health (Wales) Measure 2010 'secondary mental health services' has the following meaning: see s 51(1). A secondary mental health service is:
   (a)   a service in the form of treatment for an individual's mental disorder which is provided under the National Health Service (Wales) Act 2006 Pt 1 (ss 1–10: see PARA 574 and HEALTH SERVICES vol 54 (2008) PARA 74) (Mental Health (Wales) Measure 2010 s 49(1)(a));
   (b)   a service provided under the Mental Health Act 1983 s 117 (see PARA 574) (Mental Health (Wales) Measure 2010 s 49(1)(b));

(c)   a community care service the main purpose of which is to meet a need related to an adult's mental health (Mental Health (Wales) Measure 2010 s 49(1)(c));

(d)   a service provided for a child under the Children Act 1989 Pt III (ss 17–30A: see CHILDREN AND YOUNG PERSONS) the main purpose of which is to meet a need related to that child's mental health.

For the purposes of heads (a)–(d) above a service is not to be taken as provided under the National Health Service (Wales) Act 2006 Pt 1 (ss 1–11) if it is provided under: (i) s 41 (see PARA 590); (ii) a general medical services contract entered into by a Local Health Board under s 42 (see PARA 591); (iii) arrangements for the provision of primary medical services entered into by a Local Health Board under s 50 (see PARA 587); (iv) Sch 1 (see PARA 807): Mental Health (Wales) Measure 2006 s 49(2). A service in the form of treatment for an individual's mental disorder includes a service that, in the opinion of the person providing or making arrangements for the provision of the service, is intended to treat a mental disorder that the individual receiving the service is suspected to have: s 49(3). The Welsh Ministers may, by order: (A) specify other services that are to be regarded as secondary mental health services for the purpose of any provision of the Mental Health (Wales) Measure 2010; (B) provide that services that would otherwise be regarded as secondary mental health services for the purpose of any provision of the Mental Health (Wales) Measure 2010 are not to be so regarded: s 49(4). Accordingly services and treatments which are made available as local primary mental health support services in a particular local authority area under a scheme are not to be regarded as secondary mental health services for the purposes of the Mental Health (Wales) Measure 2010 Pt 2 and Pt 3 in that local authority area: Mental Health (Secondary Mental Health Services) (Wales) Order 2012, SI 2012/1428, art 3. A service provided in England, Scotland or Northern Ireland which is the equivalent of a secondary mental health service provided in Wales is to be regarded as a secondary mental health service for the purposes of the Mental Health (Wales) Measure 2010 s 22 (see PARA 947) and s 23 (see PARA 947): Mental Health (Secondary Mental Health Services) (Wales) Order 2012, SI 2012/1428, art 4.

7   Including a scheme determined by the Welsh Ministers under the Mental Health (Wales) Measure 2010 s 4 (see PARA 588) and a scheme which has already been altered.

8   Mental Health (Wales) Measure 2010 s 2(7).

587. Meaning of 'local primary mental health support services'. Local primary mental health support services are the following:

(1)   the carrying out[1] of primary mental health assessments[2];

(2)   the provision for an individual, following a primary mental health assessment, of the local primary mental health treatment[3] identified by the assessment as being treatment which might improve or prevent a deterioration in the individual's mental health[4];

(3)   the making of referrals[5], following a primary mental health assessment, concerning other services the provision of which might improve or prevent a deterioration in the assessed individual's mental health[6];

(4)   the provision of information, advice and other assistance to primary care providers[7] to meet the providers' reasonable requirements for such information, advice and other assistance for the purpose of improving the services related to mental health which they provide or arrange[8];

(5)   the provision for patients[9] and their carers of information and advice about the services[10] available to them, to meet their reasonable requirements for such information and advice[11].

1   Ie the carrying out of primary mental health assessments in accordance with the Mental Health (Wales) Measure 2010 ss 6–10 (see PARAS 881–885). As to the meaning of primary mental health assessment see PARA 586 note 6.

2   Mental Health (Wales) Measure 2010 s 5(1)(a).

3   As to the meaning of 'local primary mental health treatment' see PARA 586 note 4.

4   Mental Health (Wales) Measure 2010 s 5(1)(b).

5   Ie the making of referrals as described in the Mental Health (Wales) Measure 2010 s 10 (see PARA 885).

6   Mental Health (Wales) Measure 2010 s 5(1)(c).

7   'Primary care provider' means a contractor under a general medical services contract entered into under the National Health Service (Wales) Act 2006 s 42 (see HEALTH SERVICES vol 54 (2008) PARA 242), a person with whom arrangements have been made under s 50 (see HEALTH SERVICES vol 54 (2008) PARA 267), a registered medical practitioner employed by a Local Health Board for the purposes of s 41 (see HEALTH SERVICES vol 54 (2008) PARA 241), and a registered medical practitioner providing services to prisoners under arrangements made between the registered medical practitioner and a person responsible for the provision or running of a contracted out prison (within the meaning of the Criminal Justice Act 1991 s 84(4) (see PRISONS AND PRISONERS vol 85 (2012) PARA 521)) in Wales: Mental Health (Wales) Measure 2010 s 51(1).

8   Mental Health (Wales) Measure 2010 s 5(1)(d).

9   In head (5) in the text 'patients' means individuals who have, or may have, a mental disorder; and 'carers' means members of the families of patients, and friends of patients, who are involved in their care and in the case of a patient who is a child, includes the child's local authority foster parent (within the meaning of the Children Act 1989 s 22C(12) (see CHILDREN AND YOUNG PERSONS vol 10 (2012) PARA 857)): Mental Health (Wales) Measure 2010 s 5(2). 'Child' means a person who has not attained the age of 18: Mental Health (Wales) Measure 2010 s 51(1). Until the coming into force of the Children and Young Persons Act 2008 s 8(1) (see CHILDREN AND YOUNG PERSONS vol 10 (2012) PARA 857), all references to the Children Act 1989 s 22C(12) are to be read as references to the Children Act 1989 s 23(3): Mental Health (Wales) Measure 2010 s 51(4).

10 'Services' means (1) secondary mental health services; (2) community care services (not being secondary mental health services); (3) services provided under the Children Act 1989 Pt 3 (ss 17–30A) (not being secondary mental health services); (4) housing or well-being services; and (5) education or training which may be beneficial to a patient's mental health: Mental Health (Wales) Measure 2010 s 5(2). As to the meaning of 'secondary mental health services' see PARA 586 note 6. 'Community care services' has the same meaning as in the National Health Service and Community Care Act 1990 s 46 (see SOCIAL SERVICES AND COMMUNITY CARE vol 44(2) (Reissue) PARA 1012): Mental Health (Wales) Measure 2010 s 51(1). 'Housing or well-being services' are construed as follows: see s 51(1). For the purposes of the Mental Health (Wales) Measure 2010 'housing or well-being services' means:

   (i)   the allocation of accommodation by a local housing authority under the Housing Act 1996 Pt 6 (ss 159–174) (allocation of housing accommodation) or the securing of accommodation by such an authority under Pt 7 of that Act (ss 175–218) (homelessness) (Mental Health (Wales) Measure 2010 s 50(1)(a));

   (ii)   any services related to well-being (including housing) which are specified in regulations made by the Welsh Ministers (whether or not provided by or under arrangements made with a public authority) (s 50(1)(b));

   (iii) the provision of information or advice about any service falling within head (i) or (ii) above (whether or not provided by or under arrangements made with a public authority) (s 50(1)(c)).

The reference to services in s 50(1)(b) includes payments, grants and loans: s 50(2).

11 Mental Health (Wales) Measure 2010 s 5(1)(e).

588.   Failure to agree schemes.   If the local mental health partners[1] for an area cannot agree a scheme[2] (1) for so long as there is no agreement, the Local Health Board[3] must decide what local primary mental health treatment[4] is to be made available in the local authority area[5] in question and is responsible for providing local primary mental health support services[6] for that area[7]; (2) the Local Health Board must inform the Welsh Ministers that agreement cannot be reached[8]; (3) the Welsh Ministers may determine a scheme and, if they do, must record it in writing[9]. If one partner wishes to alter a scheme, but the other does not, the scheme may, upon a request being made to the Welsh Ministers by either partner, be altered by the Welsh Ministers to such extent as the Welsh Ministers think fit[10].

1   As to the meaning of 'local mental health partners' see PARA 586 note 1.
2   Ie a scheme under the Mental Health (Wales) Measure 2010 s 2 (see PARA 586).
3   As to the meaning of 'local health board' see PARA 575 note 7.
4   As to the meaning of 'local primary mental health treatment' see PARA 586 note 4.

5   As to the meaning of 'local authority area' see PARA 586 note 1.
6   As to the meaning of 'local primary mental health support services' see PARA 587.
7   Mental Health (Wales) Measure 2010 s 4(1)(a).
8   Mental Health (Wales) Measure 2010 s 4(1)(b).
9   Mental Health (Wales) Measure 2010 s 4(1)(c).
10 Mental Health (Wales) Measure 2010 s 4(2). If the appropriate national authority alter a scheme under s 4(2), they must record the alterations in writing: s 4(3).

589.   Duty to provide local primary mental health support services. Unless the local mental health partners cannot agree a scheme and the Local Health Board is therefore responsible[1], the local mental health partners for a local authority area[2] must provide local primary mental health support services[3] in accordance with a scheme for their area as agreed[4] or a scheme for their area determined[5] by the Welsh Ministers[6].

1   Ie unless the Mental Health (Wales) Measure 2010 s 4(1)(a) (see PARA 588 head (1)) applies. As to the meaning of 'local mental health partners' see PARA 586 note 1. As to the meaning of Local Health Board see PARA 575 note 7.
2   As to the meaning of 'local authority area' see PARA 586 note 1.
3   As to the meaning of 'local primary mental health support services' see PARA 587.
4   Ie as agreed under the Mental Health (Wales) Measure 2010 s 2 (see PARA 586).
5   Ie determined by the Welsh Ministers under the Mental Health (Wales) Measure 2010 s 4 (see PARA 588).
6   Mental Health (Wales) Measure 2010 s 3(1). If a scheme has been altered under s 2(6) or 4(2) the services must be provided in accordance with the altered scheme: s 3(2).

590.   Cooperative and joint working between Local Health Boards and local authorities. Local mental health partners[1] may for the purposes of their functions under Part 1 and 3[2] of the Mental Health (Wales) Measure 2010 provide staff, goods, services, accommodation or other resources to each other and establish and maintain a pooled fund[3]. Local Health Boards and local authorities[4] may for the purposes of their functions under Part 2[5] of the Mental Health (Wales) Measure 2010 provide staff, goods, services, accommodation or other resources to each other and establish and maintain a pooled fund[6].

1   As to the meaning of 'local mental health partners' see PARA 586 note 1.
2   Ie under the Mental Health (Wales) Measure 2010 Pts 1 (ss 1–11) and 3 (ss 19–30). 'Functions' includes powers and duties: s 51(1).
3   Mental Health (Wales) Measure 2010 s 41(1). For the purposes of s 41(1) and (2) a pooled fund is a fund which is made up of contributions by persons mentioned in s 41(1) and (2); and out of which payments may be made towards expenditure incurred in the discharge of functions under Pts 1–3: s 41(3). The local mental health partners may, if they think fit, exercise any of their functions under Pts 1 and 3 jointly: s 41(4).
4   As to the meaning of 'Local Health Board' see PARA 575 note 7. As to the meaning of 'local authority' see PARA 586 note 1.
5   Ie under the Mental Health (Wales) Measure 2010 Pt 2 (ss 12–18).
6   Mental Health (Wales) Measure 2010 s 41(2).

591.   Information sharing. A local mental health partner[1] (partner 1) may supply to the other partner (partner 2) information (1) which partner 1 has obtained in the discharge of its functions[2]; and (2) which relates to an individual for whom local primary mental health support services[3] are being, or might be, provided by partner 2 or an adult[4] in respect of whom partner 2 is exercising functions under Part 3 of the Mental Health (Wales) Measure 2010[5]. Local authorities, local health boards and the Welsh Ministers may supply to each other information (a) which any of them have obtained in the discharge of their functions under Part 2[6] of the Mental Health (Wales) Measure 2010; and (b) which relates to a relevant patient for the purposes of Part 2[7].

1   As to the meaning of 'local mental health partners' see PARA 586 note 1.

2   Ie its functions under the Mental Health (Wales) Measure 2010 Pt 1 (ss 1–11) or Pt 3 (ss 19–30). As to the meaning of 'functions' see PARA 590 note 2.

3   As to the meaning of 'local primary mental health support services' see PARA 587.

4   'Adult' means a person aged 18 or above: Mental Health (Wales) Measure 2010 s 51(1).

5   Mental Health (Wales) Measure 2010 s 42(1). Nothing in s 42(1) or (2) authorises the disclosure of any information in contravention of any provision of, or made under, the Mental Health (Wales) Measure 2010 or any other Measure or any Act of Parliament or Act of the Welsh Assembly (whenever passed or made) which prevents disclosure of the information: s 42(3). Section 42 is without prejudice to any other power of a local authority, local health board or the Welsh Ministers to supply information: s 42(4). As to the meaning of 'local authority' see PARA 586 note 1.

6   Ie the Mental Health (Wales) Measure 2010 Pt 2 (ss 12–18).

7   Mental Health (Wales) Measure 2010 s 42(2).

(8) EDUCATION

592. Special educational needs. A local authority has a duty to identify if a child for whom they are responsible has special educational needs where it is necessary for the authority to determine any special educational provision which any learning difficulty he may have calls for[1].

A child with special educational needs[2] who should be educated in a school is educated in a mainstream school[3] if no statement of the child's special educational needs is maintained by the authority for the child[4]. If such a statement is maintained the child must be educated in a mainstream school unless that is incompatible with either the wishes of his parent or the provision of efficient education for other children[5]. An authority must have regard to guidance about these requirements[6]. In appropriate circumstances the local education authority may arrange for special educational provision to be made otherwise than in schools[7]. Relevant governing bodies and local education authorities also have duties in relation to special educational provision for pupils with special needs[8].

1   See the Education Act 1996 s 321; and EDUCATION vol 36 (2011) PARA 1180.

2   Ie who has a learning difficulty calling for special educational provision to be made for him: see the Education Act 1996 s 312; and EDUCATION vol 36 (2011) PARA 1178.

3   Ie any school other than a special school or certain independent schools: see the Education Act 1996 s 316(4); and EDUCATION vol 36 (2011) PARA 1204.

4   See the Education Act 1996 s 316(2); and EDUCATION vol 36 (2011) PARA 1204. The statement must be in such a form and contain such information as may be prescribed; and it must give details of the authority's assessment of the child's special educational needs and specify the special educational provision to be made to meet the needs: see s 324; and EDUCATION vol 36 (2011) PARA 1192.

5   See the Education Act 1996 s 316(3); and EDUCATION vol 36 (2011) PARA 1204. As to permissible education other than in mainstream schools including education in certain independent schools and approved special schools if the cost is met otherwise than by a local education authority see s 316A; and EDUCATION vol 36 (2011) PARA 1204.

6   Ie the requirements of the Education Act 1996 s 316 and s 316A.

7   See the Education Act 1996 s 319; and EDUCATION vol 36 (2011) PARA 1207. There is also provision for education outside England and Wales for certain children: see s 320; and EDUCATION vol 36 (2011) PARA 1208.

8   See the Education Act 1996 s 318; and EDUCATION vol 36 (2011) PARA 1213.

(9) FINANCES

593.   Social security benefits.   Where a person who is entitled to social security benefits or income support is unable to act, a suitable person may be appointed to receive them on his behalf[1].

Except where regulations otherwise provide, a person may be disqualified for receiving any benefit, and an increase of benefit will not be payable in respect of any person as the beneficiary's wife, husband or civil partner for any period during which the person is in detention in legal custody[2]. Regulations may provide for suspending payment of benefit to a person during any period in which he is undergoing medical or other treatment as an in-patient in a hospital or similar institution[3].

1   See the Social Security (Claims and Payments) Regulations 1987, SI 1987/1968, reg 33 (amended by SI 1991/2741; SI 1999/2572; SI 2002/2441; SI 2005/337l; SI 2007/2470). The Social Security (Claims and Payments) Regulations 1987, SI 1987/1968 have been replaced, in so far as they relate to child benefit or guardian's allowance, by the Child Benefit and Children's Allowance (Administration) Regulations 2003, SI 2003/492 (amended by SI 2003/2107; SI 2003/2155; SI 2004/761; SI 2004/1240; SI 2005/343; SI 2005/2919; Commissioners for Revenue and Customs Act 2005, s 50; SI 2006/203; SI 2008/2683; SI 2009/3268; SI 2010/2459).
2   Social Security Contributions and Benefits Act 1992 s 113(1)(b) (amended by the Civil Partnership Act 2004 Sch 24 para 38). See the Social Security (General Benefit) Regulations 1982, SI 1982/1408, regs 2(6), 3 (reg 2(6) substituted by SI 1996/425); and SOCIAL SECURITY AND PENSIONS vol 44(2) (Reissue) PARA 21. Persons liable to be detained in a hospital or similar institution as persons suffering from mental disorder at the conclusion of criminal proceedings are not disqualified unless, in effect, they are detained under the Mental Health Act 1983 s 45A or 47 (power of higher courts to direct hospital admission; removal to hospital of persons serving sentences of imprisonment etc: see PARA 863, 892) and, in any case where there is in relation to that person a release date within the meaning of s 50(3), P is being detained on or before the day which the Secretary of State certifies to be that release date: see the Social Security (General Benefit) Regulations 1982, SI 1982/1408, reg 2(3), (4) (reg 2(3) amended and reg 2(4) substituted by SI 2010/442).
3   Social Security Contributions and Benefits Act 1992 s 113(2). See SOCIAL SECURITY AND PENSIONS vol 44(2) (Reissue) PARA 21. See also *R (on the application of RD) v Secretary of State for Work and Pensions* [2008] EWHC 2635 (Admin), [2008] All ER (D) 317 (Oct).

594.   Pocket money for in-patients.   The appropriate national authority[1] may pay to persons who are receiving treatment as in-patients, whether liable to be detained or not, in hospitals wholly or mainly used for the treatment of persons suffering from mental disorder[2], such amounts as he thinks fit in respect of their occasional personal expenses where it appears to him that they would otherwise be without resources to meet those expenses[3].

1   As to the appropriate national authority see PARA 567. As from 1 April 2013 the Mental Health Act 1983 s 122 is amended by the Health and Social Care Act 2012 s 41(2)(a) to abolish this power in relation to the Secretary of State: see the Health and Social Care Act 2012 (Commencement No 4, Transitional, Savings and Transitory Provisions) Order 2013, SI 2013/160, art 2(2).
2   As to the meaning of 'mental disorder' see PARA 761.
3   Mental Health Act 1983 s 122(1) (amended by the Health Act 1999 Sch 4 paras 65, 66, Sch 5). The making of such payments to persons for whom hospital and specialist services are provided under the National Health Service Act 2006 and the National Health Service (Wales) Act 2006 are to be treated for the purposes of those Acts as included among those services: Mental Health Act 1983 s 122(2) (amended by the National Health Service (Consequential Provisions) Act 2006 Sch 1 para 67).

595.   Liability to income tax.   A trustee, guardian or receiver having the direction, control or management of the property or concern of any person suffering from mental disorder is assessable and chargeable to income tax and capital gains tax as that person would be if he were not mentally incapacitated[1].

1   See the Taxes Management Act 1970 ss 72, 75, 77; and INCOME TAXATION vol 23(2) (Reissue) PARAS 1243–1247.

(10) INQUIRIES

596.   Inquiries and investigations.   In addition to statutory inquiries[1], non-statutory independent investigations may be held in the area of mental health practice[2].

The relevant strategic health authority[3] determines whether such an investigation is necessary, appoints the investigation team, agrees terms of reference, publishes and distributes the resultant report, and ensures that there is a process for subsequent action to address issues raised[4]. The National Health Service Commissioning Board Authority may also play a role in independent investigations.

Generally an independent investigation is undertaken: (1) when a homicide has been committed by a person who is or has been under the care of special mental health services six months prior to the event; (2) whenever a state agent is or may be responsible for a death; and (3) where the strategic health agency determines that an adverse event warrants such an investigation[5].

1   Eg in accordance with the Inquiries Act 2005. Under s 1 there is a general power for a minister to cause an inquiry to be held in relation to a case where it appears to him that particular events have caused or are capable of causing public concern or there is public concern that particular events have occurred. See ADMINISTRATIVE LAW.
2   See in particular Department of Health guidance HSG (94) 27 paras 33–36 (substituted by Independent investigation of adverse events in mental health services) (June 2005)).
3   As to the meaning of 'strategic health authority' see PARA 575 note 4.
4   See note 2.
5   See note 2.

3. MENTAL CAPACITY

(1) INTRODUCTION

597. Introduction. Questions of capacity, were for the most part, determined by the court or jury under the common law and in light of any relevant presumptions[1].

The Mental Capacity Act 2005 placed on a statutory footing: (1) the developments of the common law in relation to treatment and welfare decisions for those who are incapacitated, and their best interests; (2) the previous lack of procedural and substantive clarity of the High Court under its inherent powers in relation to such matters; and (3) advance decisions refusing medical treatment. Nothing in the Mental Capacity Act 2005 expressly overrules the common law and indeed concepts framed in the common law have been adopted in relation to definitions of 'capacity' and 'best interests'[2]; and the courts may well look to the common law in interpreting the provisions of the Act[3]. When cases come before the court in relation to the capacity to make a will, make a gift, enter into a contract, litigate or marry, judges can adopt the new definition if they think it is appropriate but the Mental Capacity Act 2005 will apply to all other cases relating to financial, healthcare or welfare decisions[4].

Under the Mental Capacity Act 2005, all acts done, or decisions made for or on behalf of an incapacitated person in relation to welfare and property and affairs[5] are to be taken to be in that person's best interests and may specifically also be taken by any donee of a lasting power of attorney[6], the new Court of Protection[7] or a court-appointed deputy[8]. Independent mental capacity advocates may support the decision making of the incapacitated person in certain prescribed situations[9].

1 As to mental disorder and mental incapacity see PARA 599. As to any applicable presumptions see PARA 598. As to capacity see PARA 601 et seq.

2 See PARAS 601–606. The definition of capacity provided by the Mental Capacity Act 2005 (see PARA 603) is in line with the existing common law tests, and the Act does not replace them.

3 See PARA 601 et seq.

4 See the Department for Constitutional Affairs *Mental Capacity Act 2005 Code of Practice* (2007) paras 4.32, 4.33.

5 The management of property and affairs was previously covered by the Mental Health Act 1983 Pt VII (ss 93–113). These provisions have now been repealed and all property and affairs decisions are now made under the Mental Capacity Act 2005: see s 18; and PARA 727.

6 See PARA 618 et seq.

7 As to the powers of the Court of Protection see PARA 720 et seq.

8 See PARA 735.

9 See PARA 634 et seq. The Mental Capacity Act 2005 ss 35–41 created a new scheme designed to provide for the input of an independent consultee where certain decisions need to be taken for particularly vulnerable people who lack capacity, the apparent intention being to address concerns as to deprivation of liberty under the Convention for the Protection of Human Rights and Fundamental Freedoms (Rome, 4 November 1950; TS 71 (1953); Cmd 8969) art 5 which were raised in Application no 45508/99 *HL v United Kingdom* (2004) 40 EHRR 761, 81 BMLR 131, ECtHR. Detention for the treatment of mental disorder, including those with mental incapacity, in general, continues to be governed by the Mental Health Act 1983, subject to the exercise of the powers of the new Court of Protection and the Mental Capacity Act 2005, Schs A1, 1A (see PARAS 651 et seq, 658 et seq). Welfare decisions that amount to a consequential deprivation of liberty under the European Convention on Human Rights, art 5 must be authorised either by the Court of Protection (see ss 4A, 16, 16A; and PARAS 648, 724, 726) or under Sch A1.

598. Common law presumption of capacity. In civil cases every person is presumed to have mental capacity[1] until the contrary is proved[2]. However, it is for the executors or other people seeking to set up a will to show that the testator had capacity at the time[3].

Where a person has been proved or admitted to have been so mentally disordered as to lack the capacity to make a contract or disposition, such a condition is presumed to continue until it is proved to have ceased, and the burden of proving a recovery or a lucid interval lies on the person alleging it[4]. It has been said that the evidence to prove capacity must be as strong as that required to prove incapacity[5].

If a long time has elapsed since the act which it is sought to attack on the ground of mental incapacity, the court will uphold the act in the absence of strong and cogent evidence to the contrary[6]. Similarly, in the absence of evidence to the contrary, it will be presumed that a person who prepared or attested the deed of a person alleged to be mentally disordered and who has since died would, if available as a witness, have given evidence to prove that the person alleged to be incapable did have capacity at the date of the execution of the deed[7].

1　For the principle under the Mental Capacity Act 2005 s 1(2) see PARA 601. 'Capacity' is not a word used yet in criminal law. The presumption in crime is that every person of the age of discretion is unless the contrary is proved presumed by law to be sane, and to be accountable for his actions: see *R v Layton* 1849 4 Cox CC 149.

2　*White v Wilson* (1806) 13 Ves 87 at 88; *Steed v Calley* (1836) 1 Keen 620; *Creagh v Blood* (1845) 8 I Eq R 434; *Snook v Watts* (1848) 11 Beav 105. As to the presumption of unsoundness of mind for limitation purposes only see PARA 993. See also WILLS AND INTESTACY vol 103 (2010) PARA 899. As to capacity see further *Lindsay v Wood* [2006] EWHC 2895 (QB), (2006) Times, 8 December; *Re MM (an adult); A Local Authority v MM* [2007] EWHC 2003 (Fam), [2008] 3 FCR 788, [2009] 1 FLR 443; *LBL v RYJ* [2010] EWHC 2665 (COP), [2011] 1 FLR 1279, [2011] Fam Law 242.

3　See PARA 615.

4　*A-G v Parnther* (1792) 3 Bro CC 441; *Cartwright v Cartwright* (1793) 1 Phillim 90 at 100; *White v Wilson* (1806) 13 Ves 87; *White v Driver* (1809) 1 Phillim 84 at 88; *Groom v Thomas* (1829) 2 Hag Ecc 433; *Frank v Mainwaring* (1839) 2 Beav 115; *Snook v Watts* (1848) 11 Beav 105; *Waring v Waring* (1848) 6 Moo PCC 341; *Grimani v Draper* (1848) 6 Notes of Cases 418; *Johnson v Blane* (1848) 6 Notes of Cases 442; *Fowlis v Davidson* (1848) 6 Notes of Cases 461 at 474; *Prinsep and East India Co v Dyce Sombre, Troup and Solaroli* (1856) 10 Moo PCC 232 at 239, 244; *Smith v Tebbitt* (1867) LR 1 P & D 398; *Hassard v Smith* (1872) IR 6 Eq 429. See also CIVIL PROCEDURE vol 11 (2009) PARAS 1069, 1106.

5　*A-G v Parnther* (1792) 3 Bro CC 441.

6　*Towart v Sellars* (1817) 5 Dow 231 at 236–237, HL; cf *Price v Berrington* (1851) 3 Mac & G 486 at 495.

7　*Towart v Sellars* (1817) 5 Dow 231, HL; cf *Harris v Ingledew* (1730) 3 P Wms 91 at 93; *Freshfield v Reed* (1842) 9 M & W 404. As to presumptions generally see CIVIL PROCEDURE vol 11 (2009) PARA 1096 et seq.

599. Mental disorder and mental incapacity. The definitions of mental disorder and its various forms in the Mental Health Act 1983[1] are provided for the purpose of the provisions of that Act relating to the care and treatment of patients[2]. The same terminology may also be employed for other purposes in other legislation[3]. However, the fact that a person suffers from mental disorder within the meaning of the Mental Health Act 1983, even if he is liable to be detained or subject to guardianship[4] under that Act, does not of itself affect his capacity in civil or criminal law. Criminal[5] and civil[6] capacity are each judged by their own criteria, which differ according to the particular subject matter[7]. The question of capacity is generally to be determined by the court or jury, having regard to any presumptions applicable[8]; and expert evidence does not relieve the court from the obligation of forming its own judgment[9].

1   See the Mental Health Act 1983 s 1(2), (3); and PARA 761.
2   As to the meaning of 'patient' for the purposes of the Mental Health Act 1983, other than in relation to the management of property and affairs, see PARA 758 note 4.
3   Eg in the Matrimonial Causes Act 1973 s 12(d) (grounds on which a marriage is voidable): see PARA 609.
4   As to guardianship see PARA 784 et seq.
5   As to the defence of insanity see CRIMINAL LAW vol 25 (2010) PARAS 30–32. As to the defence of diminished responsibility see CRIMINAL LAW vol 25 (2010) PARA 103. As to findings that an accused is unfit to be tried see CRIMINAL PROCEDURE vol 27 (2010) PARA 370. As to the disposal of mentally disordered offenders generally see PARAS 859–880, 892–898; and SENTENCING AND DISPOSITION OF OFFENDERS.
6   As to civil capacity see PARA 993 et seq.
7   When cases come before a judge in any court the judge can adopt the definition in the Mental Capacity Act 2005 ss 2, 4 (see PARAS 603, 606) if they think it appropriate: see the Department for Constitutional Affairs *Mental Capacity Act 2005 Code of Practice* (2007) para 4.33; and *Re MM (an adult); Local Authority X v MM* [2007] EWHC 2003 (Fam), [2008] 3 FCR 788, [2009] 1 FLR 443.
8   See PARA 598.
9   *Richmond v Richmond* (1914) 111 LT 273.

600. Agency. Mental disorder such as to render a person incapable of acting on his own behalf incapacitates him from appointing an agent[1]; and a power of attorney executed by a person who is incapable of understanding what is to be effected by it is invalid[2]. Further, if mental incapacity supervenes during the currency of the appointment of an agent, it terminates the agency[3] unless there is an agency by estoppel or holding out on which a third person dealing with the agent without knowledge of the supervening mental disorder may rely[4]. A representation by an agent that he is authorised to act as agent may render him liable for breach of warranty of authority if the principal has at the time become mentally incapacitated, even if the agent was unaware of this[5]. However, statute now provides for the creation of lasting powers of attorney which will survive the subsequent mental incapacity of the donor[6].

Acts done on behalf of a person suffering from such mental disorder as incapacitates him from contracting, without the authority of a person able to act for him, are done at the risk of liability if he does not ratify them on recovering his mental health[7].

1   *Elliot v Ince* (1857) 7 De GM & G 475 (power of attorney granted by lunatic so found by inquisition at the date of execution was invalid; it was indicated that the deed might have been valid if executed during a lucid interval); and see AGENCY vol 1 (2008) PARA 6.
2   *Elliot v Ince* (1857) 7 De G M & G 475 (see note 1); *Daily Telegraph Newspaper Co Ltd v McLaughlin* [1904] AC 776, PC (power of attorney granted by person incapable through mental disorder of understanding it, although not a lunatic so found, was invalid, as was the deed executed by the attorney acting under it). However, as to the power to create lasting powers of attorney see the text and note 6.
3   *Drew v Nunn* (1879) 4 QBD 661 at 666, CA, per Brett LJ; and see *Yonge v Toynbee* [1910] 1 KB 215, CA. This is subject to statutory exception where a power of attorney has been given for valuable consideration and is expressed to be irrevocable: see AGENCY vol 1 (2008) PARAS 171, 215. The mental disorder of the claimant is not a defence to a claim, but denies the authority of solicitors to proceed: see *Richmond v Branson & Son* [1914] 1 Ch 968; and PARA 994.
4   *Drew v Nunn* (1879) 4 QBD 661 at 667–669, CA. As to agency by estoppel see generally AGENCY vol 1 (2008) PARA 25.
5   *Yonge v Toynbee* [1910] 1 KB 215, CA. As to liability for breach of warranty of authority see AGENCY vol 1 (2008) PARAS 160–161. In regard to solicitors' liability and their costs see *Re*

George Armstrong & Sons [1896] 1 Ch 536; *Re E G* [1914] 1 Ch 927, CA (receiver of the income not liable personally to solicitor for costs payable out of patient's estate); and LEGAL PROFESSIONS vol 66 (2009) PARA 884.

6	As to lasting powers of attorney under the Mental Capacity Act 2005 see PARA 618.
7	See *Healing v Healing* (1902) 51 WR 221 (sale of business on wife's instructions and proceeds applied in maintenance of children not of tender years).

(2) PERSONS LACKING CAPACITY UNDER THE MENTAL CAPACITY ACT 2005

(i) Persons who Lack Capacity

601. General principles. The following principles apply for the purposes of the Mental Capacity Act 2005[1]:

(1)	a person must be assumed to have capacity unless it is established that he lacks capacity[2];

(2)	a person is not to be treated as unable to make a decision unless all practicable steps to help him to do so have been taken without success[3];

(3)	a person is not to be treated as unable to make a decision merely because he makes an unwise decision[4];

(4)	an act done, or decision made, under the Mental Capacity Act 2005 for or on behalf of a person who lacks capacity must be done, or made, in his best interests[5]; and

(5)	before the act is done, or the decision is made, regard must be had to whether the purpose for which it is needed can be as effectively achieved in a way that is less restrictive of the person's rights and freedom of action[6].

1	Mental Capacity Act 2005 s 1(1). The approach in the Mental Capacity Act 2005 reflects the common law approach (see PARA 560) except for the lack of a requirement that the person believe the information provided (see also note 2). For the general protection for acts connected with care or treatment under this Act see PARA 611. The courts are likely to turn to the existing common law when interpreting and applying these provisions. A person may have capacity to make one decision but not another and may also have capacity at one time to make the very decision in respect of which he lacked capacity previously: see *Coventry City Council v C* [2012] EWHC 2190 (Fam), [2012] NLJR 1078, 156 Sol Jo (31) 31(the fact that the mother could make decisions about surgery and pain relief did not indicate that she could make decisions about the removal of her child). The principles are integral to the definition of capacity in s 2 (see PARA 603) which is imported into the test of capacity in the Civil Procedure Rules 1998, SI 1998/3132, Pt 21 (see CIVIL PROCEDURE): *Saulle v Nouvet* [2007] EWHC 2902 (QB) at [46].
2	Mental Capacity Act 2005 s 1(2). As to when a person lacks capacity see PARA 603. Power over a person who lacks capacity may not be exercised over a person under the age of 16: see s 2(5); and PARA 604.
3	Mental Capacity Act 2005 s 1(3). As to the inability to make decisions see PARA 605. See further *Saulle v Nouvet* [2007] EWHC 2902 (QB) at [48]; *Re AK (medical treatment: consent)* [2001] 2 FCR 35, [2001] 1 FLR 129 (patient able to communicate by slight eyelash movement). Where an adult patient refuses lifesaving treatment but his capacity to make the decision is overborne by others, it is the duty of the doctors to treat that patient in whatever way they consider, in the exercise of their clinical judgment, to be in his best interests: see *Re T (adult: refusal of treatment)* [1993] Fam 95, [1992] 4 All ER 649. As to consent to medical treatment see also PARA 612. With regard to undue influence and the surviving inherent jurisdiction see *Re SA (vulnerable adult with capacity: marriage)* [2005] EWHC 2942 (Fam), [2007] 2 FCR 563, [2006] 1 FLR 867. As to undue influence and gifts see *Hammond v Osborn* [2002] EWCA Civ 885, [2002] 2 P & CR D41, [2002] 34 LS Gaz R 29; and GIFTS vol 52 (2009) PARA 259. See also the Department for Constitutional Affairs *Mental Capacity Act 2005 Code of Practice* (2007), Chapter 3.
4	Mental Capacity Act 2005 s 1(4). See also *Saulle v Nouvet* [2007] EWHC 2902 (QB) at [49]. See also *Masterman-Lister v Brutton & Co* [2002] EWCA Civ 1889, [2003] 3 All ER 162,

[2003] 1 WLR 1511. In relation to medical treatment decisions and the importance of personal autonomy see *Re T (adult: refusal of treatment)* [1993] Fam 95, [1992] 4 All ER 649; and *D v R (the deputy of S)* [2010] EWHC 2405 (COP).

5 Mental Capacity Act 2005 s 1(5). As to 'best interests' see PARA 606.

6 Mental Capacity Act 2005 s 1(6). Best interests take priority: *R (on the application of C) v A Local Authority* [2011] EWHC 1539 (Admin), [2011] All ER (D) 171 (Jun). An intervention that is not the least restrictive may still be in the person's best interests: *Havering London Borough Council v LD* [2010] EWHC 3976 (COP).

602. Codes of practice issued by the Lord Chancellor. The Lord Chancellor must prepare and issue one or more codes of practice[1]:

(1) for the guidance of persons assessing whether a person has capacity[2] in relation to any matter[3];

(2) for the guidance of persons acting in connection with the care or treatment of another person[4];

(3) for the guidance of donees of lasting powers of attorney[5];

(4) for the guidance of deputies[6] appointed by the Court of Protection[7];

(5) for the guidance of persons carrying out research in reliance on any provision made by or under the Mental Capacity Act 2005[8];

(6) for the guidance of independent mental capacity advocates[9];

(7) for the guidance of persons exercising functions under provisions[10] relating to deprivation of liberty[11];

(8) for the guidance of representatives[12];

(9) with respect to the provisions on advance decisions and apparent advance decisions[13]; and

(10) with respect to such other matters concerned with the Mental Capacity Act 2005 as he thinks fit[14].

The Lord Chancellor may from time to time revise a code[15]. He may also delegate the preparation or revision of the whole or any part of a code so far as he considers expedient[16].

It is the duty of a person to have regard to any relevant code if he is acting in relation to a person who lacks capacity[17] and is doing so in one or more of the following ways: (a) as the donee of a lasting power of attorney[18]; (b) as a deputy appointed by the court[19]; (c) as a person carrying out research in reliance on any provision made by or under the Mental Capacity Act 2005[20]; (d) as an independent mental capacity advocate[21]; (e) in the exercise of functions under provisions relating to deprivation of liberty[22]; (f) as a representative[23]; (g) in a professional capacity[24]; (h) for remuneration[25].

If it appears to a court or tribunal conducting any criminal or civil proceedings that a provision of a code or a failure to comply with a code is relevant to a question arising in the proceedings, the provision or failure must be taken into account in deciding the question[26].

1 As to the Lord Chancellor see CONSTITUTIONAL LAW AND HUMAN RIGHTS vol 8(2) (Reissue) PARA 477 et seq. As to the Code of Practice see the Department for Constitutional Affairs *Mental Capacity Act 2005 Code of Practice* (2007). As to the procedure for preparing and revising the Code see the Mental Capacity Act 2005 s 43.

2 As to capacity see PARA 603.

3 Mental Capacity Act 2005 s 42(1)(a). As to the code of practice under the Mental Health Act 1983 see PARA 602.

4 Mental Capacity Act 2005 s 42(1)(b). As to such care and treatment see s 5; and PARA 611.

5 Mental Capacity Act 2005 s 42(1)(c). As to the meaning of 'lasting power of attorney' see PARA 606 note 16. See also PARA 618 et seq.

6 As to the meaning of 'deputy' see PARA 606 note 18.

7 Mental Capacity Act 2005 s 42(1)(d). As to the Court of Protection generally see PARA 720. A code under s 42(1)(d) may contain separate guidance for deputies appointed by virtue of Sch 5 para 1(2) (functions of deputy conferred on receiver appointed under the Mental Health Act 1983): Mental Capacity Act 2005 s 42(6).

8 Mental Capacity Act 2005 s 42(1)(e). As to such research see, in particular, ss 30–34; and PARAS 630–633.

9 Mental Capacity Act 2005 s 42(1)(f). As to independent mental capacity advocates see PARA 635.

10 Ie exercising functions under the Mental Capacity Act 2005 Sch A1 (see PARAS 695–706).

11 Mental Capacity Act 2005 s 42(1)(fa) (added by the Mental Health Act 2007 Sch 9 para 8(2)).

12 Mental Capacity Act 2005 s 42(1)(fb) (added by the Mental Health Act 2007 Sch 9 para 8(2)). The representatives mentioned in the text are representatives appointed under the Mental Capacity Act 2005 Sch A1 Pt 10 (see PARAS 707–712).

13 Mental Capacity Act 2005 s 42(1)(g). As to advance decisions and apparent advance decisions see ss 24–26; and PARAS 623–626.

14 Mental Capacity Act 2005 s 42(1)(h).

15 Mental Capacity Act 2005 s 42(2). For the purposes of ss 42, 43, 'code' means a code prepared or revised under s 42: s 42(7).

16 Mental Capacity Act 2005 s 42(3).

17 As to lack of capacity see PARA 603.

18 Mental Capacity Act 2005 s 42(4)(a).

19 Mental Capacity Act 2005 s 42(4)(b).

20 Mental Capacity Act 2005 s 42(4)(c). As to such provisions see ss 30–34; and PARAS 630–633.

21 Mental Capacity Act 2005 s 42(4)(d).

22 Mental Capacity Act 2005 s 42(4)(da) (s 42(4)(da), (db) added by the Mental Health Act 2007 Sch 9 para 8(3)). The provisions relating to deprivation of liberty mentioned in the text are the Mental Capacity Act 2005 Sch A1 (see PARAS 695–706).

23 Mental Capacity Act 2005 s 42(4)(db) (as added: see note 22). The representative mentioned in the text is a representative appointed under Sch A1 Pt 10 (see PARAS 707–712).

24 Mental Capacity Act 2005 s 42(4)(e).

25 Mental Capacity Act 2005 s 42(4)(f).

26 Mental Capacity Act 2005 s 42(5). It is necessary to take account of such a code unless there are cogent reasons for departing from it (it is guidance and not instruction but it is more than mere advice), especially where a person's human rights are at stake; failure to do so could give rise to remedies including damages in public law: see *R (on the application of Munjaz) v Mersey Care NHS Trust* [2005] UKHL 58, [2006] 2 AC 148, [2006] 4 All ER 736 (a case concerning a code under the Mental Health Act 1983 s 118: see PARA 762).

603. People who lack capacity. For the purposes of the Mental Capacity Act 2005, a person lacks capacity in relation to a matter if at the material time he is unable to make a decision for himself[1] in relation to the matter because of an impairment of, or a disturbance in the functioning of, the mind or brain[2]. It does not matter whether the impairment or disturbance is permanent or temporary[3]. A lack of capacity cannot be established merely by reference to a person's age or appearance, or to a condition of his, or an aspect of his behaviour, which might lead others to make unjustified assumptions about his capacity[4].

1 As to when a person is unable to make a decision for himself see PARA 605.

2 Mental Capacity Act 2005 s 2(1). As to the presumption of capacity see PARA 598. A wide range of conditions can result in loss of capacity to make decisions eg psychiatric illness, learning disability, dementia, brain damage, toxic confusional state: see the Explanatory Notes to the Mental Capacity Act 2005 para 22. Also someone suffering the effects of pain, shock, exhaustion, fear: see *Re T (adult: refusal of treatment)* [1993] Fam 95, [1992] 4 All ER 649; and *Re MB (an adult: medical treatment)* [1997] 2 FCR 541, [1997] 2 FLR 426. In proceedings under the Mental Capacity Act 2005 or any other enactment, any question whether a person lacks capacity within the meaning of that Act must be decided on the balance of probabilities: s 2(4). As to the capacity of children see PARA 604; and CHILDREN AND YOUNG PERSONS vol 9 (2012) PARA 4 et seq.

3 Mental Capacity Act 2005 s 2(2).

4 Mental Capacity Act 2005 s 2(3). When considering the question of capacity, psychiatrists and psychologists would normally wish to take into account all aspects of the personality and

behaviour of the person in question, including vulnerability to exploitation; vulnerability to exploitation does not, however, of itself lead to the conclusion that there is lack of capacity: see *Lindsay v Wood* [2006] EWHC 2895 (QB), (2006) Times, 8 December.

604. Capacity of children. No power which a person ('D') may exercise under the Mental Capacity Act 2005 in relation to a person ('P') who lacks capacity, or where D reasonably thinks that a person lacks capacity, is exercisable in relation to a person under 16[1]. However matters relating to P's property and affairs might be exercised where P is under 16 if the court thinks it likely P will still lack capacity in respect of that matter when he reaches 18[2].

There is no age limit relating to the offence of ill-treatment or neglect of P[3].

The creation of a lasting power of attorney and an advance decision both require P to have capacity and have reached 18[4].

The requirement to have reached the age of 18 is a qualifying requirement for the purpose of the deprivation of liberty provisions[5].

Provision is made for the transfer of proceedings between the Court of Protection and a court having jurisdiction under the Children Act 1989[6].

The Mental Capacity Act 2005 does not affect the legal right of a person with parental responsibility to consent to medical treatment on the child's behalf[7].

1 Mental Capacity Act 2005 s 2(5). This is subject to s 18(3) (see PARA 727): see s 2(6). As to the capacity of children see CHILDREN AND YOUNG PERSONS vol 9 (2012) PARA 4 et seq. As to the general rule regarding when a person lacks capacity see PARA 603.
2 See the Mental Capacity Act 2005 s 18(3); and PARA 727.
3 See the Mental Capacity Act 2005 s 44; and PARA 1011.
4 See the Mental Capacity Act 2005 ss 9(2)(c), 24(1); PARA 624; and AGENCY vol 1 (2008) PARA 218.
5 See the Mental Capacity Act 2005 Sch A1 para 13; and PARA 654.
6 See the Mental Capacity Act 2005 (Transfer of Proceedings) Order 2007, SI 2007/1899; and PARA 745.
7 See MEDICAL PROFESSIONS vol 74 (2011) PARA 22. See also CHILDREN AND YOUNG PERSONS vol 9 (2012) PARA 4.

605. Inability to make decisions. A person is not to be treated as unable to make a decision unless all practicable steps to help him to do so have been taken without success[1] and a person is not to be treated as unable to make a decision merely because he makes an unwise decision[2].

For the purposes of deciding whether a person lacks capacity[3] a person is unable to make a decision for himself if he is unable[4]:

(1) to understand the information relevant to the decision[5];

(2) to retain that information[6];

(3) to use or weigh that information as part of the process of making the decision[7]; or

(4) to communicate his decision (whether by talking, using sign language or any other means)[8].

A person is not to be regarded as unable to understand the information relevant to a decision if he is able to understand an explanation of it given to him in a way that is appropriate to his circumstances (using simple language, visual aids or any other means)[9].

1 See the Mental Capacity Act 2005 s 1(3); and PARA 601.
2 See the Mental Capacity Act 2005 s 1(4); and PARA 601.
3 Ie for the purposes of the Mental Capacity Act 2005 s 2 (see PARA 603).
4 Mental Capacity Act 2005 s 3(1). There is no relevant distinction between the common law test formulated in *Re MB (an adult: medical treatment)* [1997] 2 FCR 541, [1997] 2 FLR 426, CA and the test set out in the Mental Health Act 2005 s 3(1): see *Re MM (an adult); Local*

Authority X v MM [2007] EWHC 2003 (Fam), [2008] 3 FCR 788, [2009] 1 FLR 443. The test is a functional one and as such it relates to each relevant decision to be made so that the same person may have capacity in relation to one decision but not another: see *C v V* [2008] EWHC B16 (Fam). The test must not be set too high: *PH v A Local Authority* [2011] EWHC 1704. The more serious the decision the greater the level of capacity required: *Re Beaney (deceased)* [1978] 2 All ER 595, [1978] 1 WLR 770; *Re T (adult: refusal of medical treatment)* [1993] Fam 95, [1992] 4 All ER 649. As to deciding when a person has capacity see also the Department for Constitutional Affairs *Mental Capacity Act 2005 Code of Practice* (2007) Chapter 4. As to when professional involvement might be needed see para 4.53. A judge is not required to accept the evidence of psychiatrists as to a person's mental capacity: see *Masterman-Lister v Jewell* [2002] EWHC 417 (QB), [2002] All ER (D) 247 (Mar). The evidence on capacity must be 'credible' and need not be that of a psychiatrist: *G v E (by his litigation friend, the Official Solicitor)* [2010] EWCA Civ 822, [2012] Fam 78, [2010] 4 All ER 579. See also *Lindsay v Wood* [2006] EWHC 2895 (QB), (2006) Times, 8 December where a wife's evidence was preferred to medical evidence. As to the capacity to consent to sexual relations see PARA 608. The Court of Protection may make declarations relating to capacity under the Mental Capacity Act 2005 s 15 in the event of a dispute. Sections 2 and 3 appear to be contrary to the UN Convention on the Rights of Persons with Disabilities insofar as legal capacity is linked to mental capacity. The United Kingdom has entered no derogations with regard to this treaty which is binding as a matter of international law.

5 Mental Capacity Act 2005 s 3(1)(a). Identifying the relevant information can be challenging: see *D v R (the deputy of S)* [2010] EWHC 2405. The information relevant to a decision includes information about the reasonably foreseeable consequences of deciding one way or another or failing to make the decision: s 3(4). The test for capacity to be applied to ascertain a woman's ability to understand and weigh up the immediate medical issues surrounding contraceptive treatment includes consideration of: (1) the reason for contraception and what it does (which includes the likelihood of pregnancy if it is not in use during sexual intercourse); (2) the types available and how each is used; (3) the advantages and disadvantages of each type; (4) the possible side-effects of each and how they can be dealt with; (5) how easily each type can be changed; and (6) the generally accepted effectiveness of each: see *A Local Authority v Mrs A (by the Official Solicitor)* [2010] EWHC 1549 (Fam), [2011] Fam 61, [2011] 3 All ER 706 (applied by *A Local Authority v K (by the Official Solicitor)* [2013] EWHC 242 (Fam)). See also *D v AB* [2011] EWHC 101 (COP). As to assessing someone's understanding see the Department for Constitutional Affairs *Mental Capacity Act 2005 Code of Practice* (2007) paras 4.16–4.19.

6 Mental Capacity Act 2005 s 3(1)(b). The fact that a person is able to retain the information relevant to a decision for a short period only does not prevent him from being regarded as able to make the decision: s 3(3). Section 3(3) is intended to deal with people with fluctuating capacity so that a person may make a decision during a period of lucidity. As to assessing a person's ability to retain information see the Department for Constitutional Affairs *Mental Capacity Act 2005 Code of Practice* (2007) para 4.20.

7 Mental Capacity Act 2005 s 3(1)(c). The use of the word 'or' in s 3(1)(c) demonstrates that the individual incapacities set out in s 3(1) are not cumulative; a person lacks capacity if any one of s 3(1)(a) to (d) applies: see *RT v LT* [2010] EWHC 1910 (Fam) sub nom *Re LT (vulnerable adult) (decision making: capacity)* [2011] 1 FLR 594, [2010] Fam Law 1283. As to when a person lacks capacity to litigate see *Dunhill (by her litigation friend, Paul Tasker) v Burgin* [2012] EWCA Civ 397, [2012] All ER (D) 32 (Apr); and PARA 995. As to when a person has the ability to weigh up information and use it to arrive at a decision see the Department for Constitutional Affairs *Mental Capacity Act 2005 Code of Practice* (2007) paras 4.21, 4.22. See generally *LBL v RYJ* [2010] EWHC 2665 (COP), [2011] 1 FLR 1279, [2011] Fam Law 242; *Re MM* [2007] EWHC 2003 (Fam), [2008] 3 FCR 788, [2009] 1 FLR 443; *B v Croydon Health Authority* [1995] Fam 133, [1995] 1 All ER 683, [1995] 2 WLR 294. A compulsive disorder or phobia may prevent the patient's decision from being a true one, particularly if conditioned by some obsessional belief or feeling which so distorts the judgment as to render the decision invalid: *Re H (adult patient) (medical treatment)* [2006] EWHC 1230 (Fam), [2006] 2 FLR 958, [2006] Fam Law 842. A patient who is very tired, in pain or depressed is much less able to resist having his will overborne than one who is rested, free from pain and cheerful: *Re T (adult: refusal of medical treatment)* [1992] 4 All ER 649. See also *W (Adult: Refusal of Medical Treatment)* [2002] EWHC 901.

8 Mental Capacity Act 2005 s 3(1)(d). This is intended to be a residual category and only affect a small number of persons, in particular some of those with 'locked-in syndrome': see Explanatory Notes to the Mental Capacity Act 2005 para 27. In *Re AK (medical treatment: consent)* [2001] 2 FCR 35, [2001] 1 FLR 129 patient who could communicate by blinking an eye was found to

have capacity to refuse life sustaining treatment. As to the inability to communicate see further the Department for Constitutional Affairs *Mental Capacity Act 2005 Code of Practice* (2007) paras 4.23–4.25.
9 Mental Capacity Act 2005 s 3(2). See principle in s 1(3); and PARA 601.

606. Best interests. In determining for the purposes of the Mental Capacity Act 2005 what is in a person's best interests[1], the person making the determination must not make it merely on the basis of the person's age or appearance, or a condition of his, or an aspect of his behaviour, which might lead others to make unjustified assumptions about what might be in his best interests[2].

The person making the determination must consider all the relevant circumstances[3] and, in particular, take the following steps[4]:

(1) he must consider: (a) whether it is likely that the person will at some time have capacity[5] in relation to the matter in question[6]; and (b) if it appears likely that he will, when that is likely to be[7];

(2) he must, so far as reasonably practicable, permit and encourage the person to participate, or to improve his ability to participate, as fully as possible in any act done for him and any decision affecting him[8];

(3) where the determination relates to life-sustaining treatment[9] he must not, in considering whether the treatment is in the best interests of the person concerned, be motivated by a desire to bring about his death[10];

(4) he must consider, so far as is reasonably ascertainable: (a) the person's past and present wishes and feelings (and, in particular, any relevant written statement made by him when he had capacity)[11]; (b) the beliefs and values that would be likely to influence his decision if he had capacity[12]; and (c) the other factors that he would be likely to consider if he were able to do so[13];

(5) he must take into account, if it is practicable and appropriate to consult them, the views of:

   (a) anyone named by the person as someone to be consulted on the matter in question or on matters of that kind[14];

   (b) anyone engaged in caring for the person or interested in his welfare[15];

   (c) any donee of a lasting power of attorney[16] granted by the person[17]; and

   (d) any deputy[18] appointed for the person by the Court of Protection[19],

   as to what would be in the person's best interests and, in particular, as to the matters mentioned in head (4) above[20].

The above duties[21] also apply in relation to the exercise of any powers which: (i) are exercisable under a lasting power of attorney[22]; or (ii) are exercisable by a person under the Mental Capacity Act 2005 where he reasonably believes that another person lacks capacity[23].

In the case of an act done, or a decision made, by a person other than the court, there is sufficient compliance with the above requirements[24] if[25] he reasonably believes that what he does or decides is in the best interests of the person concerned[26].

1 There is no statutory definition of best interests. However, in cases decided prior to the Mental Capacity Act 2005 best interests were not limited to medical interests but applied where there was an emotional, psychological and social benefit (see *Re Y (mental patient: bone marrow donation)* [1997] Fam 110, [1997] 2 WLR 556) and had a wider application encompassing

medical, emotional and all other welfare issues (see *Re A (medical sterilisation: male sterilisation)* [2000] 1 FCR 193, [2000] 1 FLR 549). The word 'interest' in the best interests test does not confine the court to considering the self-interest of the patient: see *Re G(TJ)* [2010] EWHC 3005 (COP), [2010] All ER (D) 218 (Nov). As to the relevant principles relating to best interests see the Mental Capacity Act 2005 s 1(5), (6); and PARA 601. Section 4 provides a checklist of factors to be taken into account and deals with the process of determining best interests rather than providing specific criteria for the same. The overarching principle is that what is determinative is the court's evaluation of 'best interests'. This identifies the courts core substituted decision-making power under s 16 (see PARA 724): *Re M* [2009] EWHC 2525 (Fam), [2010] 3 All ER 682. As to decisions relating to best interests see PARA 608 et seq. Best interests is not a test of 'substituted judgement' (what the person would have wanted), but rather it requires a determination to be made by applying an objective test as to what would be in the person's best interests: see the Explanatory Notes to the Mental Capacity Act 2005 para 28. See also *Re G(TJ)* [2010] EWHC 3005 (COP), [2010] All ER (D) 218 (Nov).The best interests test applies to all decision making under the Act and not just that of the Court of Protection. See further Department for Constitutional Affairs *Mental Capacity Act 2005 Code of Practice* (2007) Chapter 5. The UN Convention on the Rights of Persons with Disabilities art 12 requires 'supported' decision making of those lacking legal capacity to make decisions.

2   Mental Capacity Act 2005 s 4(1). In assessing the best interests of the respondent a 'balance sheet' setting out the 'pros and cons' of the options may provide assistance: see *Dorset County Council v EH* [2009] EWHC 784 (Fam), [2009] All ER (D) 166 (Apr). This practice was originally set out in *Re A (medical sterilisation: male sterilisation)* [2000] 1 FCR 193, [2000] 1 FLR 549 and endorsed in *Re SK (vulnerable adult: capacity)* [2008] EWHC 636 (Fam), [2008] 2 FLR 720, [2008] Fam Law 633. Decision makers must then form an objective value judgment based on the statutory imperative (ie best interests) and must not be overly risk averse: *Re MM (an adult); A Local Authority v MM* [2007] EWHC 2003 (Fam), [2008] 3 FCR 788, [2009] 1 FLR 443. For a summary of the best interests test in relation to withholding medical treatment from a child see *An NHS Trust v H* [2012] NLJR 1323, [2012] Lexis Citation 82.

3   'Relevant circumstances' are those of which the person making the determination is aware, and which it would be reasonable to regard as relevant: Mental Capacity Act 2005 s 4(11). See *Re M* [2009] EWHC 2525 (Fam), [2010] 3 All ER 682.

4   Mental Capacity Act 2005 s 4(2). This checklist is a departure from the common law but builds on it; it is not exhaustive. It has been held that the safe approach of a trial judge in cases involving the Mental Capacity Act 2005 is to ascertain the best interests of the incapacitated adult on the application of the s 4 checklist and then ask whether the resulting conclusion amounts to a violation of the Convention for the Protection of Human Rights and Fundamental Freedoms (Rome, 4 November 1950; TS 71 (1953) Cmd 8969) art 8 and whether that violation is nonetheless necessary and proportionate: see *K v A local authority* [2012] EWCA Civ 79, [2012] 1 FCR 441.

5   As to issues of capacity see PARA 601 et seq.

6   Mental Capacity Act 2005 s 4(3)(a). As to factors which may indicate that a person may regain or develop capacity in the future see the Department for Constitutional Affairs *Mental Capacity Act 2005 Code of Practice* (2007) para 5.28.

7   Mental Capacity Act 2005 s 4(3)(b).

8   Mental Capacity Act 2005 s 4(4).

9   'Life-sustaining treatment' means treatment which in the view of a person providing health care for the person concerned is necessary to sustain life: Mental Capacity Act 2005 ss 4(10), 64(1). As to whether a treatment is life-sustaining see also Department for Constitutional Affairs *Mental Capacity Act 2005 Code of Practice* (2007) para 5.30. For a consideration of the goal of life-sustaining treatment see *Aintree University Hospital NHS Trust v David James (by his litigation friend, the Official Solicitor)* [2013] EWCA Civ 65, [2013] All ER (D) 09 (Mar). 'Treatment' includes a diagnostic or other procedure: Mental Capacity Act 2005 s 64(1). With regard to ambiguous advance decisions or lasting powers of attorney when treatment should be provided see *HE v A Hospital NHS Trust* [2003] EWHC 1017 (Fam), [2003] 2 FLR 408, [2003] Fam Law 733.

10   Mental Capacity Act 2005 s 4(5).

11   Mental Capacity Act 2005 s 4(6)(a). As to the approach to be taken see Department for Constitutional Affairs *Mental Capacity Act 2005 Code of Practice* (2007) para 5.6. As to the weight to be given to a person's wishes and feelings see *Re M (vulnerable adult) (testamentary capacity)* [2009] EWHC 2525 (Fam) at [35], [2010] 3 All ER 682 at [35], [2011] 1 WLR 344 at [35]; and *Re P* [2009] EWHC 163 (Ch), [2010] Ch 33, [2009] 2 All ER 1198. Where the court is exercising its power under s 18(1)(i) (see PARA 731) to execute a will, a previous will written by the testator is a relevant written statement which falls to be taken into account by the

court: *Re D (statutory will)* [2010] EWHC 2159 (Ch), [2012] Ch 57, [2011] 1 All ER 859. Where a person who lacks capacity expresses a wish which is neither irrational, nor impracticable so far as its physical implementation is concerned, nor irresponsible having regard to that person's resources, that effectively gives rise to a presumption in favour of implementing that wish unless outweighed by some sufficiently detrimental effect for the person of so doing: *Re S (protected persons)* [2010] 1 WLR 1082 (sisters appointed joint attorneys by their parents was an almost inescapable inference that the parents wanted relevant decisions either to be joint or to be made by neither appointee and did not want their affairs to be dealt with by the sole decision of one appointee alone). Happiness may be relevant as to whether deprivation of liberty is in a person's best interests, see *P (otherwise known as MIG) (by the Official Solicitor, their litigation friend) v Surrey County Council (Equality and Human Rights Commission intervening)* [2011] EWCA Civ 190, [2012] Fam 170, [2012] 2 WLR 1056. See also *A Local Authority v E (by her litigation friend, the Official Solicitor)* [2012] EWHC 1639 (COP), [2012] 2 FCR 523, 127 BMLR 133 (E suffered from anorexia nervosa and other mental health problems and wished to be allowed to refuse food; court refused her wishes and feelings when well and decided to permit force feeding); *Re W (by her litigation friend, B) v M (by her litigation friend, the Official Solicitor)* [2011] EWHC 2443 (Fam), [2012] 1 All ER 1313, [2012] 1 WLR 1653 (P was in a minimally conscious state and the family and clinicians wanted to withdraw artificial nutrition and hydration; the court found that continued treatment was in P's best interests rejecting evidence from the family as to her likely wishes and feelings).

12 Mental Capacity Act 2005 s 4(6)(b). See *Ahsan v University Hospital Leicester NHS Trust* [2006] EWHC 2624 (QB), [2007] PIQR P271 (claimant in a persistent vegetative state and the family wanted her cared for at home in a Muslim environment; judge relied on the beliefs and values of the family 'so far as can be properly attributed to her, those which she herself would have held had she continued to have the capacity to do so').

13 Mental Capacity Act 2005 s 4(6)(c). See *Re G(TJ)* [2010] EWHC 3005 (COP), [2010] All ER (D) 218 (Nov).

14 Mental Capacity Act 2005 s 4(7)(a). If there is no-one apart from a paid carer to consult then an independent mental capacity advocate must be consulted: see ss 37–39 (see PARAS 638–640).

15 Mental Capacity Act 2005 s 4(7)(b). Where medical matters are concerned the court must have regard to unanimous expert advice, but assessment of best interests encompasses factors of all kinds, and not medical factors alone, and reaches into areas where doctors are not experts: *An NHS Trust v DJ (by his litigation friend, the Official Solicitor)* [2012] EWHC 3524 (COP), [2012] All ER (D) 169 (Dec) (argument in favour of discontinuing medical treatment significantly undervalued the non-medical aspects of his situation; making full allowance for the unpleasant, painful and distressing aspects of treatment, it would not be right to validate, in advance, the withholding of any of the treatments in all circumstances). Where a parent lacks capacity they may still make telling points about welfare: *An NHS Trust v H* [2012] Lexis Citation 82, [2012] All ER (D) 110 (Oct).

16 'Lasting power of attorney' has the meaning given in the Mental Capacity Act 2005 s 9 (see PARA 619): s 64(1).

17 Mental Capacity Act 2005 s 4(7)(c).

18 'Deputy' has the meaning given in the Mental Capacity Act 2005 s 16(2)(b) (see PARA 724): s 64(1).

19 Mental Capacity Act 2005 s 4(7)(d). As to the Court of Protection see PARA 720.

20 Mental Capacity Act 2005 s 4(7). As to the necessity of providing adequate consultation under s 4(7) see *R (on the application of W) v Croydon Borough Council* [2011] All ER (D) 93 (Mar) (inadequate consultation resulted in quashing of decision).

21 Ie the duties imposed by the Mental Capacity Act 2005 s 4(1)–(7).

22 Mental Capacity Act 2005 s 4(8)(a).

23 Mental Capacity Act 2005 s 4(8)(b).

24 Ie with the Mental Capacity Act 2005 s 4.

25 Ie having complied with the requirements of the Mental Capacity Act 2005 s 4(1)–(7).

26 Mental Capacity Act 2005 s 4(9).

607. General powers of the Court of Protection to make decisions and appoint court deputies. The Court of Protection[1] has the power to make decisions in respect of a person's personal welfare and his property and affairs where that person lacks capacity in relation to those matters[2]. The Court also has the power to make declarations as to whether a person has or lacks capacity to make a decision specified in the declaration, whether a person has or lacks capacity to make decisions on such matters as are described in the declaration and the lawfulness or otherwise of any act done, or yet to be done, in relation to that person[3].

When exercising these powers the Court of Protection must consider the principles of the Mental Capacity Act 2005[4] and the provisions[5] requiring the court to act in the person's best interests[6]. Decisions in such matters may be made by the Court of Protection or by a deputy appointed by them[7] and may in particular relate to:

(1) deciding where the person is to live[8];

(2) deciding what contact, if any, the person is to have with any specified persons[9];

(3) making an order prohibiting a named person from having contact with the person[10];

(4) giving or refusing consent to the carrying out or continuation of a treatment by a person providing health care for the person[11];

(5) giving a direction that a person responsible for the person's health care allow a different person to take over that responsibility[12];

(6) the control and management of the person's property[13];

(7) the sale, exchange, charging, gift or other disposition of the person's property[14];

(8) the acquisition of property in the person's name or on his behalf[15];

(9) the carrying on, on the person's behalf, of any profession, trade or business[16];

(10) the taking of a decision which will have the effect of dissolving a partnership of which the person is a member[17];

(11) the carrying out of any contract entered into by the person[18];

(12) the discharge of the person's debts and of any of his obligations, whether legally enforceable or not[19];

(13) the settlement of any of the person's property, whether for his benefit or for the benefit of others[20];

(14) the execution for the person of a will[21];

(15) the exercise of any power (including a power to consent) vested in the person whether beneficially or as trustee or otherwise[22];

(16) the conduct of legal proceedings in the person's name or on his behalf[23].

1   As to the Court of Protection see PARA 720 et seq.
2   See the Mental Capacity Act 2005 s 16(1); and PARA 724.
3   See the Mental Capacity Act 2005 s 15; and PARA 723.
4   Ie the principles set out in the Mental Capacity Act 2005 s 1 (see PARA 601).
5   Ie the Mental Capacity Act 2005 s 4 (see PARA 606).
6   See the Mental Capacity Act 2005 s 16(3); and PARA 724.
7   See the Mental Capacity Act 2005 s 16(1), (2); and PARA 724.
8   See the Mental Capacity Act 2005 s 17(1)(a); and PARA 726.
9   See the Mental Capacity Act 2005 s 17(1)(b); and PARA 726.
10 See the Mental Capacity Act 2005 s 17(1)(c); and PARA 726.
11 See the Mental Capacity Act 2005 s 17(1)(d); and PARA 726.
12 See the Mental Capacity Act 2005 s 17(1)(e); and PARA 726.
13 See the Mental Capacity Act 2005 s 18(1)(a); and PARA 727.
14 See the Mental Capacity Act 2005 s 18(1)(b); and PARA 727.
15 See the Mental Capacity Act 2005 s 18(1)(c); and PARA 727.
16 See the Mental Capacity Act 2005 s 18(1)(d); and PARA 727.
17 See the Mental Capacity Act 2005 s 18(1)(e); and PARA 727.
18 See the Mental Capacity Act 2005 s 18(1)(f); and PARA 727.
19 See the Mental Capacity Act 2005 s 18(1)(g); and PARA 727.
20 See the Mental Capacity Act 2005 s 18(1)(h); and PARA 727.

21   See the Mental Capacity Act 2005 s 18(1)(i); and PARA 727. See further PARAS 615, 731.
22   See the Mental Capacity Act 2005 s 18(1)(j); and PARA 727.
23   See the Mental Capacity Act 2005 s 18(1)(k); and PARA 727.

608.   Capacity to consent to sexual relations. Nothing in the Mental Capacity Act 2005 permits a decision consenting to sexual relations to be made on behalf of a person[1]. However the Court of Protection has the power to make declarations as to whether or not a person has the required capacity[2].

In order to possess capacity to consent to sexual relations, a person must have a basic understanding of the mechanics of the physical act and an understanding that vaginal intercourse might lead to pregnancy; capacity also requires some grasp of issues of sexual health[3].

The question of capacity to consent to sexual relations is both sensitive and difficult as such a finding may have wide ranging implications not only for the patient and those responsible for her care but for any who have dealings and, in particular, sexual relations with her as any expressed consent may be void and the person concerned be at risk of conviction for a serious offence under the Sexual Offences Act 2003[4].

1   See the Mental Capacity Act 2005 s 27(1)(b); and PARA 627.
2   See the Mental Capacity Act 2005 s 15; and PARA 723.
3   *A local authority v H* [2012] EWHC 49 (COP), [2012] 1 FCR 590, 124 BMLR 98.
4   *A local authority v H* [2012] EWHC 49 (COP), [2012] 1 FCR 590, 124 BMLR 98. Inability to communicate under the Sexual Offences Act 2003 s 30(2)(b) includes where the complainant is unable to refuse because of or for a reason related to a mental disorder which could involve either the inability to choose: see *R v Cooper* [2009] UKHL 42, [2009] 4 All ER 1033, [2009] 1 WLR 1786; and CRIMINAL LAW vol 25 (2010) PARA 210.

609.   Marriage and civil partnership. Nothing in the Mental Capacity Act 2005 permits a decision consenting to marriage or a civil partnership to be made on behalf of a person[1]. However the Court of Protection has the power to make declarations as to whether or not a person has the required capacity[2].

The test of capacity to marry is very closely related to the test of capacity to consent to sexual relations and the test for determining whether a person has capacity is whether the person has sufficient rudimentary knowledge of what the act comprises and of its sexual character to enable him to decide whether to give or withhold consent[3].

A marriage celebrated after 31 July 1971 is voidable on the ground that either party did not validly consent to it in consequence of unsoundness of mind[4]. To be capable of giving a valid consent, a person must be able to understand the nature of the marriage contract[5]. This being relatively simple, the degree of understanding required may not be as great as it is for the purpose of making a valid will[6].

A marriage celebrated after 31 July 1971[7] is also voidable on the ground that at the time of the marriage either party, although capable of giving a valid consent, was suffering (whether continuously or intermittently) from mental disorder within the meaning of the Mental Health Act 1983[8] of such a kind or to such an extent as to be unfitted for marriage[9]. Proceedings must be instituted within three years from the date of the marriage, unless leave is obtained to institute them after that date on the ground that the petitioner has at some time during that period suffered from mental disorder within the meaning of the Mental Health Act 1983 and in all the circumstances it would be just to grant leave[10]. A potentially voidable marriage under the above provisions[11] may be declared invalid[12].

Similar provision is made in relation to civil partnerships whereby a civil partnership is voidable on the ground that either party did not validly consent to it in consequence of unsoundness of mind or, where at the time of formation, one of the parties was suffering from mental disorder of such a kind or to such an extent as to be unfitted for civil partnership[13].

Special provision is made to enable the marriage, or civil partnership, of a person who is detained in hospital for treatment[14] to occur at the hospital[15].

The court is not confined to making a decision dictated only by considerations as to best interest[16], but questions of public policy generally as well as those that affected the individual concerned are relevant[17].

1   See the Mental Capacity Act 2005 s 27(1)(a); and PARA 627.

2   See the Mental Capacity Act 2005 s 15; and PARA 723. The test of capacity under the Mental Capacity Act 2005 is in line with the existing common law test and does not replace it; however, judges can adopt the new definition if they think appropriate: see the Department for Constitutional Affairs *Mental Capacity Act 2005 Code of Practice* (2007) paras 4.32, 4.33; and PARA 597.

3   See *D Borough Council v AB* [2011] EWHC 101 (COP), [2012] Fam 36, [2012] 3 All ER 435. Marriage raises more and complex issues than does consent to sexual relations and for so long as marriage requires sexual intercourse for its consummation, it follows that the person who lacks capacity to consent to sexual relations lacks capacity to marry: *A local authority v H* [2012] EWHC 49 (COP), [2012] 1 FCR 590, 124 BMLR 98. As to capacity in relation to marriage see PARA 609.

4   See the Matrimonial Causes Act 1973 s 12(c); and MATRIMONIAL AND CIVIL PARTNERSHIP LAW vol 72 (2009) PARA 331. The date mentioned in the text is the day before that on which the Nullity of Marriage Act 1971 came into force. A marriage celebrated before that date where either party did not validly consent because of unsoundness of mind is void: see *Re Roberts, Roberts v Roberts* [1978] 3 All ER 225 at 226–227, [1978] 1 WLR 653 at 655 per Walton J.

5   See *Durham v Durham* (1885) 10 PD 80; *Hunter v Edney* (1885) 10 PD 93.

6   See *Re Park's Estate, Park v Park* [1954] P 89, [1953] 2 All ER 1411, CA; and see *Boughton v Knight* (1873) LR 3 P & D 64 at 72. See also *Sheffield City Council v E* [2004] EWHC 2808 (Fam), [2005] Fam 326, [2005] 2 WLR 953, which approved the test in *Re Park's Estate, Park v Park*, that the person had to understand the nature of the marriage contract and be mentally capable of understanding the duties and responsibilities that normally attached to marriage. The court has no jurisdiction to determine whether marriage in general or to a particular person is in the person's best interests. The contract is a simple one and does not require a high degree or intelligence to comprehend; it is also relevant that the person understands the nature of sexual intercourse and its foreseeable consequences: *Re MM (an adult); Local Authority X v MM* [2007] EWHC 2003 (Fam), [2008] 3 FCR 788, [2009] 1 FLR 443. *Sheffield City Council v E* was considered in a case dealing with an arranged marriage, where the capacity of a person to enter into a marriage contract was considered and it was held that in appropriate circumstances there is jurisdiction to make an order to restrain those responsible for an adult lacking capacity from entering into a contract of marriage whether formal or informal if it is required to protect the best interests of the adult: *M v B* [2005] EWHC 1681 (Fam), (2005) Times, 10 August. In a case dealing with a forced marriage, the court assumed jurisdiction to grant declaratory relief in respect of competent adults who were deprived of the capacity to make their own decisions: the court could make orders, give directions and injunctive relief designed to ascertain whether the person concerned had been allowed to exercise free will in decisions concerning her civil status and country of residence: *Re SK (An Adult) (Forced Marriage: Appropriate Relief)* [2004] EWHC 3202 (Fam), [2005] 3 All ER 421, [2006] 1 WLR 81.

7   A marriage celebrated before 1 August 1971 was voidable on the ground that either party was of unsound mind, or was suffering from mental disorder within the meaning of the Mental Health Act 1959 of such a kind or to such an extent as to be unfitted for marriage and the procreation of children, or was subject to recurrent attacks of insanity or epilepsy; and a marriage celebrated before 1 November 1960 was voidable on the ground that either party was of unsound mind, or a mental defective within the meaning of the Mental Deficiency Acts 1913 to 1938, or subject to recurrent fits of insanity or epilepsy: see the Matrimonial Causes Act 1973 s 53, Sch 1 para 11(1)(b), (2); and MATRIMONIAL AND CIVIL PARTNERSHIP LAW vol 72 (2009) PARA 345. However, proceedings had to be instituted within a year of the marriage: see Sch 1 para 11(3); and MATRIMONIAL AND CIVIL PARTNERSHIP LAW vol 72 (2009) PARA 345.

8   As to the meaning of 'mental disorder' see PARA 761.

9 See the Matrimonial Causes Act 1973 s 12(d); and MATRIMONIAL AND CIVIL PARTNERSHIP LAW vol 72 (2009) PARA 331.

10 See the Matrimonial Causes Act 1973 s 13(2), (4); and MATRIMONIAL AND CIVIL PARTNERSHIP LAW vol 72 (2009) PARAS 321–322. Applications for leave may be made after the three year period: Matrimonial Causes Act 1973 s 13(5); and MATRIMONIAL AND CIVIL PARTNERSHIP LAW vol 72 (2009) PARA 323.

11 Ie under the Matrimonial Causes Act 1973 s 12.

12 See *Westminster Social and Community Services Department v C* [2008] EWCA Civ 198, [2009] 2 WLR 185, [2008] 2 FCR 146.

13 See the Civil Partnership Act 2004 s 50(1)(a), (b); and MATRIMONIAL AND CIVIL PARTNERSHIP LAW vol 72 (2009) PARAS 331, 332.

14 Ie otherwise than under the Mental Health Act 1983 s 2, s 4, s 5, s 35, s 36 or s 136 (see PARAS 767, 769–770, 862, 923): Marriage Act 1983 s 1(3); Civil Partnership Act 2005 s 19(2)(a).

15 See the Marriage Act 1983 s 1; the Civil Partnership Act 2004 s 19; and MATRIMONIAL AND CIVIL PARTNERSHIP LAW vol 72 (2009) PARAS 171, 175.

16 Ie whether applying the Mental Capacity Act 2005 s 4 (see PARA 769) or more general welfare considerations.

17 See *XCC v AA* [2012] EWHC 2183 (COP), [2012] All ER (D) 38 (Aug).

610.   Divorce and dissolution.   Nothing in the Mental Capacity Act 2005 permits a decision consenting to a decree of divorce being granted on the basis of two years' separation, or consenting to a dissolution order being made in relation to a civil partnership on the basis of two years' separation[1]. However the Court of Protection has the power to make declarations as to whether or not a person has the required capacity[2].

Mental disorder or incapacity does not of itself either dissolve a valid marriage, or civil partnership, or constitute one of the facts of which the petitioner has to satisfy the court in order that it may hold that the marriage, or civil partnership, has irretrievably broken down[3]. However, one of those facts is desertion for two years[4], and the court may treat a period of desertion as continuing at a time when the deserting party was incapable of continuing the necessary intention if the evidence is such that the court would have inferred that his intention would have continued had he not been so incapable[5]. Another such fact is that the respondent has behaved in such a way that the petitioner cannot reasonably be expected to live with him[6], and such behaviour may be the result of mental disorder[7]. A further such fact is that the parties have lived apart for two years and the respondent consents to a decree[8] or dissolution order being made[9]. Finally, if the parties have lived apart for five years[10], a divorce or dissolution may be granted, unless the respondent proves that the dissolution of the marriage or civil partnership will cause him grave financial or other hardship and that in all the circumstances it would be wrong to dissolve it[11].

The fact that one party is incapable through mental disorder of managing his property and affairs does not debar the other party from claiming and obtaining orders for financial provision and property adjustment in the court, even where a receiver has been appointed[12]. Where the court makes an order[13] in favour of a party to a marriage, or civil partnership, and is satisfied that that party lacks capacity[14] then, subject to any order, direction or authority made or given in relation to that party under the Mental Health Act, the court may order the payments to be made, or property transferred, to such persons as the court may direct[15].

1 See the Mental Capacity Act 2005 s 27(1)(c), (d); and PARA 627.
2 See the Mental Capacity Act 2005 s 15; and PARA 723. The test of capacity under the Mental Capacity Act 2005 is in line with the existing common law test and does not replace it; however,

judges can adopt the new definition if they think appropriate: see the Department for Constitutional Affairs *Mental Capacity Act 2005 Code of Practice* (2007) paras 4.32, 4.33; and PARA 597.

3	See the Matrimonial Causes Act 1973 s 1(1), (2); the Civil Partnership Act 2005 s 44(3), (5); and MATRIMONIAL AND CIVIL PARTNERSHIP LAW vol 72 (2009) PARA 347.

4	See the Matrimonial Causes Act 1973 s 1(2)(c); the Civil Partnership Act 2005 s 44(5)(d); and MATRIMONIAL AND CIVIL PARTNERSHIP LAW vol 72 (2009) PARA 347. See note 1.

5	See the Matrimonial Causes Act 1973 s 2(4); the Civil Partnership Act 2005 s 45(5); and MATRIMONIAL AND CIVIL PARTNERSHIP LAW vol 72 (2009) PARA 347. As to the effect of mental disorder on desertion generally see MATRIMONIAL AND CIVIL PARTNERSHIP LAW vol 72 (2009) PARA 389. See note 1.

6	See the Matrimonial Causes Act 1973 s 1(2)(b); the Civil Partnership Act 2005 s 44(5)(a); and MATRIMONIAL AND CIVIL PARTNERSHIP LAW vol 72 (2009) PARA 347. See note 1.

7	*Katz v Katz* [1972] 3 All ER 219, [1972] 1 WLR 955; *Thurlow v Thurlow* [1976] Fam 32, [1975] 2 All ER 979. See also *Williams v Williams* [1964] AC 698, [1963] 2 All ER 994, HL (a case under the former law of cruelty); *J (HD) v J (AM)* [1980] 1 All ER 156, [1980] 1 WLR 124 (applying the same approach to conduct so far as it is relevant to financial provision). However, it may be reasonable to expect the petitioner to be more tolerant of behaviour which is the result of illness: *Richards v Richards* [1972] 3 All ER 695, [1972] 1 WLR 1073. See further MATRIMONIAL AND CIVIL PARTNERSHIP LAW vol 72 (2009) PARA 360.

8	The capacity to give such consent is the same as that required to consent to marriage: *Mason v Mason* [1972] Fam 302 at 306, [1972] 3 All ER 315 at 317–318 (a person may have this capacity even if he is incapable of managing his property and affairs and is therefore represented by the Official Solicitor as his litigation friend (formerly 'guardian ad litem'); however, the consent must be that of the respondent personally and not of his guardian). See further MATRIMONIAL AND CIVIL PARTNERSHIP LAW vol 72 (2009) PARA 408. As to the test of capacity to marry see PARA 609.

9	See the Matrimonial Causes Act 1973 s 1(2)(d); the Civil Partnership Act 2005 s 44(5)(b); and MATRIMONIAL AND CIVIL PARTNERSHIP LAW vol 72 (2009) PARAS 347, 407. See note 1.

10	See the Matrimonial Causes Act 1973 s 1(2)(e); the Civil Partnership Act 2005 s 44(5)(c); and MATRIMONIAL AND CIVIL PARTNERSHIP LAW vol 72 (2009) PARAS 347, 410. See note 1.

11	See the Matrimonial Causes Act 1973 s 5(1); the Civil Partnership Act 2005 s 47(1); and MATRIMONIAL AND CIVIL PARTNERSHIP LAW vol 72 (2009) PARA 411. See note 1.

12	See MATRIMONIAL AND CIVIL PARTNERSHIP LAW vol 73 (2009) PARA 542.

13	Ie under the Matrimonial Causes Act 1973 Pt II (ss 21–40A) or the Civil Partnership Act 2005 Sch 5 (see MATRIMONIAL AND CIVIL PARTNERSHIP LAW vol 72 (2009) PARA 458 et seq).

14	Ie within the meaning of the Mental Capacity Act 2005 (see PARA 603).

15	See the Matrimonial Causes Act 1973 s 40; the Civil Partnership Act 2005 Sch 5 para 78; and MATRIMONIAL AND CIVIL PARTNERSHIP LAW vol 72 (2009) PARA 455.

**611.	Protection for persons acting in connection with care or treatment of another person.** If a person ('D') does an act in connection with the care or treatment[1] of another person ('P'), and: (1) before doing the act, D takes reasonable steps to establish whether P lacks capacity[2] in relation to the matter in question[3]; and (2) when doing the act, D reasonably believes that P lacks capacity in relation to the matter, and that it will be in P's best interests[4] for the act to be done[5], then in those circumstances D does not incur any liability in relation to the act that he would not have incurred if P: (a) had had capacity to consent in relation to the matter[6]; and (b) had consented to D's doing the act[7].

If D does an act that is intended to restrain P[8], it is not an act such as is referred to above[9] unless two further conditions are satisfied[10]:

(i)	D reasonably believes that it is necessary to do the act in order to prevent harm to P[11]; and

(ii)	the act is a proportionate response to the likelihood of P's suffering harm, and the seriousness of that harm[12].

The provisions in heads (1), (2), (a) and (b) above[13] do not authorise a person to do an act which conflicts with a decision made, within the scope of his authority and in accordance with Part 1 of the Mental Capacity Act 2005[14], by a donee of a lasting power of attorney[15] granted by P, or a deputy[16] appointed for P by the Court of Protection[17]. However, this does not stop a person providing life-sustaining treatment[18], or doing any act which he reasonably believes to be necessary to prevent a serious deterioration in P's condition, while a decision as respects any relevant issue is sought from the court[19].

If an act to which heads (1), (2), (a) and (b) above[20] apply involves expenditure, it is lawful for D to pledge P's credit for the purpose of the expenditure, and to apply money in P's possession for meeting the expenditure[21]. If the expenditure is borne for P by D, it is lawful for D to reimburse himself out of money in P's possession, or to be otherwise indemnified by P[22].

1   As to the meaning of 'treatment' see PARA 606 note 9.
2   As to lack of capacity see PARA 603.
3   Mental Capacity Act 2005 s 5(1)(a). This provision offers protection from civil and criminal liability for certain acts done in connection with the care and treatment of a person that would normally require consent (eg brushing teeth). It clarifies and imports the prior common law doctrine of necessity which enables decisions to be taken for those who lack capacity. Nothing in s 5 excludes a person's civil liability for loss or damage, or his criminal liability, resulting from his negligence in doing the act: s 5(3). Nothing in s 5 affects the operation of ss 24–26 (advance decisions to refuse treatment: see PARA 623 et seq): s 5(4). See further Department for Constitutional Affairs *Mental Capacity Act 2005 Code of Practice* (2007) Chapter 5.
4   As to best interests see PARA 606.
5   Mental Capacity Act 2005 s 5(1)(b).
6   Mental Capacity Act 2005 s 5(2)(a).
7   Mental Capacity Act 2005 s 5(2)(b). Section 5 does not apply to an act to which the Mental Health Act 1983 s 64B applies (treatment of community patients not recalled to hospital: see PARA 935): Mental Capacity Act 2005 s 28(1B) (added by the Mental Health Act 2007 s 35(4), (5)).
8   For these purposes, D restrains P if he: (1) uses, or threatens to use, force to secure the doing of an act which P resists; or (2) restricts P's liberty of movement, whether or not P resists: Mental Capacity Act 2005 s 6(4).
9   Ie an act to which the Mental Capacity Act 2005 s 5 applies. Such acts are sometimes referred to as 'section 5 acts'.
10 Mental Capacity Act 2005 s 6(1).
11 Mental Capacity Act 2005 s 6(2). As to examples of 'harm' see the Department for Constitutional Affairs *Mental Capacity Act 2005 Code of Practice* (2007) para 6.45.
12 Mental Capacity Act 2005 s 6(3). This provision cannot be used to take steps amounting to a deprivation of liberty nor to circumvent the powers under the Mental Health Act 1983 by removing a person from their home so that a mental health assessment may be conducted in a hospital: *R (on the application of Sessay) v South London & Maudsley NHS Foundation Trust* [2011] EWHC 2617 (QB), [2012] QB 760, [2012] 2 WLR 1071. Where the provisions of the Mental Capacity Act 2005 apply, the common law defence of necessity has no application: *ZH (by his litigation friend) v Metropolitan Police Commissioner* [2012] EWHC 604 (Admin), 176 CL&J 241. As to 'proportionate response' see the Department for Constitutional Affairs *Mental Capacity Act 2005 Code of Practice* (2007) para 6.47. See also *Re MB (an adult: medical treatment)* [1997] 2 FCR 541, [1997] 2 FLR 426; *R (on the application of Wilkinson) v Responsible Medical Officer Broadmoor Hospital* [2001] EWCA Civ 1545, [2002] 1 WLR 419, 65 BMLR 15.
13 Ie the Mental Capacity Act 2005 s 5.
14 Ie the Mental Capacity Act 2005 Pt 1 (ss 1–44).
15 As to the meaning of 'lasting power of attorney' see PARA 606 note 16. See also PARA 618 et seq.
16 As to the meaning of 'deputy' see PARA 606 note 18.
17 Mental Capacity Act 2005 s 6(6). As to the Court of Protection see PARA 720.
18 As to the meaning of 'life-sustaining treatment' see PARA 606 note 9.
19 Mental Capacity Act 2005 s 6(7).
20 See note 13.
21 Mental Capacity Act 2005 s 8(1). Section 8(1), (2) does not affect any power under which (apart from those provisions) a person: (1) has lawful control of P's money or other property; and (2) has power to spend money for P's benefit: s 8(3).
22 Mental Capacity Act 2005 s 8(2). See note 21.

612. Medical treatment. Capacity and best interests in relation to medical treatment now fall under the Mental Capacity Act 2005[1]. Cases relating to serious healthcare and treatment decisions should be referred to the Court of Protection for a declaration[2].

Although a parent may consent to medical treatment on behalf of a child who is incapable of giving a valid consent[3], there is a considerable body of case law[4] as to when an adult patient is incapable[5] of consenting to being given medical treatment[6].

For consent to medical treatment to be effective as a defence to a claim for battery, it is enough that the patient's consent is 'real' in the sense that he understands in broad terms what is involved[7]. However, a doctor may be liable in negligence[8] if he fails to give the patient proper advice and information about the treatment and to warn him of any significant risks[9]. This duty to give advice and information will normally be discharged if he acts in accordance with a practice accepted as proper by a responsible body of medical opinion skilled and experienced in the specialty concerned[10], unless disclosure of a particular risk is so obviously necessary to an informed choice on the part of the patient that no reasonably prudent doctor would fail to make it[11]. It would appear, therefore, that the degree of capacity required to consent to medical treatment is either the capacity to understand in broad terms the nature and effect of the treatment proposed or the capacity to understand the explanation which in all the circumstances of the case a reasonably prudent doctor would make[12]. However, the more serious the decision, the greater the capacity required[13]. The Mental Capacity Act 2005 now requires that where it is proposed to provide or secure the provision of serious medical treatment for a person lacking the capacity to consent to the treatment an independent mental capacity advocate must be instructed to represent that person[14].

Patients who are liable to be detained under certain provisions of the Mental Health Act 1983[15] may be given treatment for their mental disorder without their consent, save for particular treatments which require either consent or a second opinion and others which require both consent and a second opinion[16]. A bodily sample which the court has directed to be taken for the purpose of establishing paternity[17] may be taken from a person who lacks capacity[18] to give his consent, if consent is given by the court giving the direction[19] or by a donee of an enduring power of attorney or lasting power of attorney or a deputy appointed, or any other person authorised, by the Court of Protection, with power in that respect[20].

1 As to capacity see PARA 603. As to best interests see PARA 606. As to the law relating to advance decisions see PARA 623–626.

2 See the Department for Constitutional Affairs *Mental Capacity Act 2005 Code of Practice* (2007) paras 8.18, 8.19. See also *Re F (Mental Patient: Sterilisation)* [1990] 2 AC 1, sub nom *F v West Berkshire Health Authority (Mental Health Act Commission intervening)* [1989] 2 All ER 545, HL; *Cambridgeshire County Council v R* [1994] 2 FCR 973, [1995] 1 FLR 50; *Re D (Medical Treatment)* [1998] 2 FCR 178, [1998] 2 FLR 22, (1997) 41 BMLR 81; *Re A (Medical Treatment: Male Sterilisation)* [2000] 1 FCR 193, [2000] 1 FLR 549, CA; *Re Z (Medical Treatment: Hysterectomy)* [2000] 1 FCR 274; *Re S (Adult Patient: Sterilisation)* [2001] Fam 15, [2000] 3 WLR 1288, CA. See *Re S (Medical Treatment: Adult Sterilisation)* [1999] 1 FCR 277, [1998] 1 FLR 944; and note 4. All decisions about withholding or withdrawing artificial nutrition and hydration from a person in a persistent vegetative state or minimally conscious state should always be brought to the court: *W (by her litigation friend, B) v M (by her litigation friend, the Official Solicitor)* [2011] EWHC 2443 (Fam), [2012] 1 All ER 1313, [2012] 1 WLR 1653.

   The jurisdiction deriving from *Re F (Mental Patient: Sterilisation)* used the doctrine of necessity to permit incapable patients to be operated on or treated; this is a new jurisdiction and is not restricted to medical interests but expanded to a near unfettered authority to make decisions for incapacitated adults on the ground of best interests: see *Re S (Hospital Patient: Court's Jurisdiction)* [1996] Fam 1, [1995] 3 All ER 290, CA; *Re MB* [1997] 2 FCR 541, [1997] 2 FLR 426, CA; *Re Y (Mental Incapacity: Bone Marrow Transplant)* [1997] Fam 110, [1997] 2 WLR 556; *Re A (Medical Treatment: Male Sterilisation)*. As to Munby J's guidance on the nature of the High Court's declaratory jurisdiction over incapacitated adults and children see *A v A Health Authority, Re J (a child), R (on the application of S) v Secretary of State for the Home Department* [2002] EWHC 18 (Fam/Admin), [2002] Fam 213, [2002] 3 WLR 24. See also *E (by her Litigation Friend the Official Solicitor) v Channel Four, News International Limited and St Helens Borough Council* [2005] EWHC 1144 (Fam), [2005] 2 FLR 913, [2005] Fam Law 866. As to the Convention for the Protection of Human Rights and Fundamental Freedoms (Rome, 4 November 1950; TS 71 (1953); Cmd 8969) arts 3, 8 see RIGHTS AND FREEDOMS. See *R (on the application of PS) v Responsible Medical Officer* [2003] EWHC 2335 (Admin), [2003] All ER (D) 178 (Oct); Application 2346/02 *Pretty v United Kingdom* (2002) 35 EHRR 1, [2002] 2 FCR 97, ECtHR. As to the exercise of the High Court's jurisdiction by the Court of Protection under the Mental Capacity Act 2005 see PARA 720 et seq. See PARA 597.

3   *Gillick v West Norfolk and Wisbech Area Health Authority* [1986] AC 112, [1985] 3 All ER 402, HL; *Re R (A Minor) (Wardship: Consent to Treatment)* [1992] Fam 11, [1991] 4 All ER 177, CA. See also *Re J (A Minor) (Inherent Jurisdiction: Consent to Treatment)* (1992) Times, 15 July, CA. See *Simms v Simms, A v A* [2002] EWHC 2734 (Fam), [2003] Fam 83, [2003] 1 All ER 669 (evidence from parents that their children would probably have chosen to try experimental treatment for the alleviation of suffering if they had had mental capacity to do so).

4   Eg see *Re S (Medical Treatment: Adult Sterilisation)* [1999] 1 FCR 277, [1998] 1 FLR 944 (sterilisation of a woman incapable of giving her own consent; judge must be satisfied that the procedure is in her best interests; there must be an identifiable, rather than speculative, risk of pregnancy to outweigh the risk of fatality; *Norfolk and Norwich Healthcare (NHS) Trust v W* [1997] 1 FCR 269, [1996] 2 FLR 613 (in certain circumstances, the court has power at common law to authorise the use of reasonable force in the course of treatment); *Re Y (Mental Incapacity: Bone Marrow Transplant)* [1997] 2 FCR 172, [1996] 2 FLR 787, (1996) 35 BMLR 111 (bone marrow transplant from mentally incapacitated donor to carer ordered; in donor's best interests that carer's life be preserved); *Re X (Adult Patient: Sterilisation)* [1999] 3 FCR 426, [1998] 2 FLR 1124 (permanent sterilisation, which would protect a severely mentally retarded woman from risk of physical or psychological harm if she became pregnant while indirectly allowing her more freedom, was considered to be in her best interests); *Re S (Adult Patient: Sterilisation)* [2001] Fam 15, [2000] 2 FCR 452, CA (hysterectomy to eliminate heavy menstrual bleeding was in patient's best interests given disadvantages of alternative less intrusive treatment; a patient lacking the mental capacity to consent to surgery has the right not to have it imposed on her unless it is demonstrably in her best interests); *Re Z (Medical Treatment: Hysterectomy)* above (hysterectomy, which would eliminate patient's painful menstrual periods and protect her from catastrophic consequences of pregnancy, was in patient's best interests); cf *Re A (Medical Treatment: Male Sterilisation)* (sterilisation not in best interests of mentally incapacitated man when birth of child unlikely to impinge on him to significant degree). See also *R v Collins, ex p Brady* (2000) 58 BMLR 173 (force feeding patient on hunger strike). The best interests of the patient are not confined to medical interests, there are also emotional and welfare issues: see *Re Y (Mental Incapacity: Bone Marrow Transplant)*; *Re A (Medical Treatment: Male Sterilisation)*.

     A declaration is not required for a sterilisation which is the incidental result of a hysterectomy performed on a woman for therapeutic reasons, provided that two medical practitioners are satisfied that the operation is necessary for therapeutic reasons, that it is in the best interests of the patient, and that there is no practicable less obtrusive means of treatment (*Re GF (Medical Treatment)* [1991] FCR 786, [1992] 1 FLR 293), or for a proposed abortion which complies with the terms of the Abortion Act 1967 (*Re G (Mental Patient: Termination of Pregnancy)* (1991) Times, 31 January); and see MEDICAL PROFESSIONS vol 74 (2011) PARA 33.

     See also *Re W (An Adult: Sterilisation)* [1993] 2 FCR 187, [1993] 1 FLR 381 (notwithstanding the small risk that a young woman, a mentally handicapped epileptic with a mental age of seven, would become pregnant, in the circumstances sterilisation was in her best interests). As to the Court of Appeal guidelines for the obtaining of a declaration, and the correct procedure to be followed, see *St George's Healthcare NHS Trust v S (No 2), R v Collins, ex p S (No 2)* [1999] Fam 26, [1998] 3 All ER 673, CA. See also *Re X (Adult Patient: Sterilisation)*. The fact that there is a responsible body of opinion against the proposed treatment is merely a relevant factor for the court in determining whether such treatment is medically necessary: *R (on the application of N) v M* [2002] EWCA Civ 1789, [2003] 1 WLR 562, [2003] 1 FCR 124. For guidelines as to when it is necessary to seek a declaration in order to terminate the pregnancy of a mentally incapacitated patient see *D v An NHS Trust (Medical Treatment: Consent: Termination)* [2003] EWHC 2793 (Fam), [2004] Fam Law 415.

5 Eg because the patient is unconscious as a result of an accident or otherwise and the treatment cannot be safely delayed until consciousness is recovered, or because the patient cannot by reason of mental disability understand the nature or purpose of the treatment: *Re F (Mental Patient: Sterilisation)* [1990] 2 AC 1 at 55, sub nom *F v West Berkshire Health Authority (Mental Health Act Commission intervening)* [1989] 2 All ER 545 at 551, HL, per Lord Brandon of Oakbrook. In an emergency where a patient declines treatment necessary to save his life or spare irreparable damage being done to his health, doctors should consider whether he has a capacity commensurate with the gravity of the decision. In some cases doctors should consider whether the refusal is vitiated because it arises from others', not the patient's, will: *Re T (Adult: Refusal of Medical Treatment)* [1992] 4 All ER 649, [1992] 2 FCR 861, CA. A patient who is otherwise competent may be rendered temporarily incapable of consenting to or refusing medical treatment by factors such as panic induced by fear: *Re MB* [1997] 2 FCR 541, [1997] 8 Med LR 217, (1997) 38 BMLR 175, CA. For suggested rules in regard to acting without consent when consent is not available and life is threatened see *Re T (Adult: Refusal of Treatment)*. See also *Re C (Adult: Refusal of Treatment)* [1993] Fam 95, [1994] 1 All ER 819; *B v Croydon Health Authority* [1995] Fam 133, [1995] 1 All ER 683. CA; *Re MB; Re JT (Adult: Refusal of Medical Treatment)* [1998] 2 FCR 662, [1998] 1 FLR 48. As to capacity to consent to medical treatment generally see also *HE v A NHS Trust* [2003] EWHC 1017 (Fam), [2003] 2 FLR 408, [2003] Fam Law 733.

6 A competent adult's anticipatory refusal of consent (ie an advance statement or 'living will') remains binding and effective notwithstanding that the patient has subsequently become incompetent: see *HE v A NHS Trust* [2003] EWHC 1017 (Fam), [2003] 2 FLR 408, [2008] Fam Law 733. See also the Mental Capacity Act 2005 ss 24–26 (which seek to codify and clarify these common law rules); and PARAS 623–626.

7 *Chatterton v Gerson* [1981] QB 432, [1981] 1 All ER 257.

8 This test to be applied is the same as that applicable in claims for negligence: *Re F (Mental Patient: Sterilisation)* [1990] 2 AC 1 at 52, sub nom *F v West Berkshire Health Authority (Mental Health Act Commission intervening)* [1989] 2 All ER 545 at 549, HL, per Lord Bridge of Harwich, at 68 and 560 per Lord Brandon of Oakbrook, and at 78 and 567 per Lord Goff of Chieveley.

9 *Sidaway v Board of Governors of the Bethlem Royal Hospital and the Maudsley Hospital* [1985] AC 871, [1985] 1 All ER 643, HL.

10 See *Bolam v Friern Hospital Management Committee* [1957] 2 All ER 118, [1957] 1 WLR 582 (not at that time negligent to give mental patient electro-convulsive therapy without muscle relaxant). See also *Bolitho v City and Hackney Health Authority* [1998] AC 232, [1997] 4 All ER 771, HL, where it was held that a doctor could be liable for negligence in respect of diagnosis and treatment despite a body of professional opinion sanctioning his conduct where it had not been demonstrated to the judge's satisfaction that the body of opinion relied on was reasonable or responsible. See also *Pearce v Bristol Healthcare NHS* (1999) 48 BMLR 118, [1998] CLY 3986, CA.

11 *Sidaway v Board of Governors of the Bethlem Royal Hospital and the Maudsley Hospital* [1985] AC 871 at 900, [1985] 1 All ER 643 at 663, HL.

12 The precise degree of capacity required is not discussed in the leading case on the effect of incapacity: see *Re F (Mental Patient: Sterilisation)* [1990] 2 AC 1, sub nom *F v West Berkshire Health Authority (Mental Health Act Commission intervening)* [1989] 2 All ER 545, HL; and PARAS 612, 927.

As to whether the consent of the court is required where the effect but not the objective of an operation is the sterilisation of a mentally handicapped minor see *Re E (A Minor) (Medical Treatment)* [1991] FCR 771, [1991] 2 FLR 585; *Re C (Mental Patient: Medical Treatment)* [1994] 1 All ER 819, 15 BMLR 77. See also *Re JT (Adult: Refusal of Medical Treatment)* [1998] 2 FCR 662, [1998] 1 FLR 48 (patient with mental disability declined treatment for kidney failure and evidence showed she had the capacity to do so); *NHS Trust v T (Adult Patient: Refusal of Medical Treatment)* [2004] EWHC 1279 (Fam), [2005] 1 All ER 387, [2004] 3 FCR 297 (patient with borderline personality disorder had previously signed directive refusing treatment). A competent adult's anticipatory refusal of consent (ie an advance statement or 'living will') remains binding and effective notwithstanding that the patient has subsequently become incompetent: see *HE v A NHS Trust* [2003] EWHC 1017 (Fam), [2003] 2 FLR 408, [2003] Fam Law 733 (refusal of blood transfusion). See also the Mental Capacity Act 2005 ss 24–26 (which seek to codify and clarify these common law rules); and PARAS 623–626.

13 *Re T (Adult: Refusal of Medical Treatment)* [1992] 4 All ER 649, CA. There is a prima facie presumption of capacity, and detention under the Mental Health Act 1983 does not of itself

rebut this presumption. Irrationality, panic or disorder of mind may have a role as a symptom or evidence of incapacity or of fluctuating or reduced capacity: see *Re C (Adult: Refusal of Treatment)* [1994] 1 All ER 819, [1994] 2 FCR 151 (test whether capacity so reduced that the patient does not understand the nature, purpose and effects of the proffered medical treatment); *B v Croydon Health Authority* [1995] Fam 133, [1995] 1 All ER 683, CA (the patient did not lack consent but could be tube-fed without consent under the Mental Health Act 1983 s 63 (see PARA 927)); *Re MB* [1997] 2 FCR 541, [1997] 8 Med LR 217, 38 BMLR 175, CA (patient needing emergency Caesarean held to be incapable of giving consent as withholding consent irrational in the circumstances and induced by panic); *Re JT (Adult: Refusal of Medical Treatment)* [1998] 2 FCR 662, [1998] 1 FLR 48 (woman competent to refuse treatment on basis of test in *Re C (Adult: Refusal of Treatment)*); *R v Bournewood Community and Mental Health NHS Trust, ex p L* [1999] 1 AC 458, [1998] 3 All ER 289, HL (importance of assessing capacity). As to anticipatory refusals see the Mental Capacity Act 2005; and note 8. Doubts over capacity must be resolved as soon as clinically possible; in the meantime the patient can be treated in accordance with clinical judgment as to best interests (see PARA 606) and if disagreement persists the hospital should make the relevant application to the High Court or seek the advice of the Official Solicitor: *NHS Trust v T (Adult Patient: Refusal of Medical Treatment)* [2004] EWHC 1279 (Fam), [2005] 1 All ER 387, [2004] 3 FCR 297. As to court intervention concerning medical treatment to, or the welfare of, an adult who lacks capacity to make decisions for himself, see *Practice Note (Official Solicitor, CAFCASS and the National Assembly for Wales: Urgent and Out of Hours Cases in the Family Division of the High Court)* [2006] 2 FLR 354.

14 See the Mental Capacity Act 2005 s 37(1), (3); and PARA 638. This provision may not apply if the treatment needs to be provided as a matter of urgency: see s 37(4); and PARA 638.

15 See PARA 924.

16 See PARAS 927–933.

17 Ie under the Family Law Reform Act 1969 s 20: see CHILDREN AND YOUNG PERSONS vol 9 (2012) PARA 101 et seq.

18 Ie within the meaning of the Mental Capacity Act 2005: see PARA 603.

19 Ie the direction under the Family Law Reform Act 1969 s 20.

20 See the Family Law Reform Act 1969 s 21(4); and CHILDREN AND YOUNG PERSONS vol 9 (2012) PARA 142.

613. Payment for necessary goods and services. If necessary[1] goods or services are supplied to a person who lacks capacity[2] to contract for the supply, he must pay a reasonable price for them[3].

1 'Necessary' means suitable to a person's condition in life and to his actual requirements at the time when the goods or services are supplied: Mental Capacity Act 2005 s 7(2). See further Department for Constitutional Affairs *Mental Capacity Act 2005 Code of Practice* (2007) para 6.58.

2 As to lack of capacity see PARA 603.

3 Mental Capacity Act 2005 s 7(1). This effectively revises the rule in the Sale of Goods Act 1979 s 3(2): see SALE OF GOODS AND SUPPLY OF SERVICES vol 91 (2012) PARA 38. See *Wychavon District Council v EM (HB)* (2012) UKUT 12 (AAC).

614. Contract. The Court of Protection has power to make a declaration in relation to a person's property and affairs including in particular the carrying out of any contract entered into by that person[1]. When cases come before a court in relation to the capacity to enter into a contract the judge can adopt the definition of mental capacity[2] under the Mental Capacity Act 2005 if he thinks it is appropriate, however this definition is in line with the existing common law tests and does not replace them[3].

The original rule of law was that a contract with a person of unsound mind was void, because there could be no consensus ad idem. This was later qualified by a rule that a person could not plead his own unsoundness of mind to avoid a contract he had made. This in turn gave way to a further rule that such a plea was permissible if it could be shown that the other contracting party knew of the insanity[4].

The test of contractual capacity is whether or not the person was capable of understanding the nature of the contract he was entering into[5]. This depends upon whether there was understanding of the particular transaction[6]; the degree of capacity required will therefore differ according to the nature of the transaction[7]. Furthermore, contracts made during a lucid interval by a person who is mentally incapable of contracting at other times are valid[8], even if he is liable to be detained at the time[9]. Hence, mental incapacity in relation to contract may be permanent or temporary, general or in relation only to some transactions, or in relation to some transactions some of the time.

The effect of the above common law rules is that a contract made by a person who at the time lacked the capacity to make it is voidable but not void. The contract is binding upon him in every respect, whether it is executory or executed, unless he can show that the other contracting party knew of the incapacity at the time[10] or knew of such facts and circumstances that he must be taken to have known of the incapacity[11]. Unless there is such knowledge, the validity of a contract entered into by a person who is ostensibly sane is to be judged by the same standards as a contract entered into by a person of sound mind; it is not voidable by reason of unfairness unless the unfairness amounts to equitable fraud which would have enabled the complaining party to avoid the contract even if he had been sane[12].

1   See the Mental Capacity Act 2005 s 18(1)(g); and PARA 727.
2   As to capacity see PARA 601 et seq.
3   See the Department for Constitutional Affairs *Mental Capacity Act 2005 Code of Practice* (2007) para 4.32, 4.33.
4   *Hart v O'Connor* [1985] AC 1000 at 1018–1019, [1985] 2 All ER 880 at 888, PC; *Irvani v Irvani* [2000] 1 Lloyd's Rep 412, CA.
5   *Boughton v Knight* (1873) LR 3 P & D 64 at 72 (contrast capacity to enter various types of contract with capacity to make a will: see further PARA 615); *Jenkins v Morris* (1880) 14 Ch D 674 at 681, CA. See also *Re Rhodes, Rhodes v Rhodes* (1890) 44 Ch D 94 at 105, CA. See Department for Constitutional Affairs *Mental Capacity Act 2005 Code of Practice* (2007) para 4.32.
6   *Boughton v Knight* (1873) LR 3 P & D 64 at 72; *Birkin v Wing* (1890) 63 LT 80 (sale of land, where vendor found capable of understanding transaction despite medical evidence).
7   *Manches v Trimborn* (1946) 174 LT 344 (an action on a cheque was unsuccessful, where the drawer was capable of understanding the act of drawing a cheque but not the transactions of which it formed part). See also *Re Beaney* [1978] 2 All ER 595, [1978] 1 WLR 770 (capacity to make a voluntary disposition differs according to scale of transaction). *Re Beaney* above was applied in *Williams v Williams* [2003] EWHC 742 (Ch), [2003] All ER (D) 403 (Feb).
8   *Beverley's Case* (1603) 4 Co Rep 123b at 125a; *A-G v Parnther* (1792) 3 Bro CC 441; *Selby v Jackson* (1844) 6 Beav 192; and see *Birkin v Wing* (1890) 63 LT 80. Cf *Creagh v Blood* (1845) 8 I Eq R 434, where it was held that acts done when the defendant was wholly sane except on certain matters were not done during a lucid interval.
9   See *Selby v Jackson* (1844) 6 Beav 192 (deed of assignment for the benefit of creditors).
10 *Imperial Loan Co Ltd v Stone* [1892] 1 QB 599, CA (signing promissory note as surety); *York Glass Co Ltd v Jubb* (1925) 134 LT 36, CA (purchase of land). See also *Molton v Camroux* (1848) 2 Exch 487 (affd (1849) 4 Exch 17) (purchase of annuities from life assurance society in the ordinary course of business); *Baxter v Earl of Portsmouth* (1826) 5 B & C 170 (goods supplied); *Brown v Jodrell* (1827) 3 C & P 30; *Price v Berrington* (1851) 3 Mac & G 486 (conveyance); *Elliot v Ince* (1857) 7 De GM & G 475 at 487 per Lord Cranworth LC (sale and purchase); *Hassard v Smith* (1872) IR 6 Eq 429; *Beavan v M'Donnell* (1854) 9 Exch 309 (affd 10 Exch 184) (deposit on purchase of real estate); *Moss v Tribe* (1862) 3 F & F 297; *Barrow v Barrow* (1774) 2 Dick 504 (marriage settlement); *Drew v Nunn* (1879) 4 QBD 661, CA (goods supplied). There appears to have been some doubt at one time whether the proposition applied to mortgages by a person so mentally disordered as to lack capacity to enter into a mortgage (*Snook v Watts* (1848) 11 Beav 105; *Jacobs v Richards, Jacobs v Porter* (1854) 18 Beav 300 (on appeal 5 De G M & G 55)), but it is conceived that it would (*Campbell v Hooper* (1855) 3 Sm & G 153; and see *Kirkwall v Flight* (1842) 3 WR 529).

11 *York Glass Co Ltd v Jubb* (1925) 134 LT 36 at 41, CA, per Warrington LJ: 'If circumstances are proved which are such that any reasonable man would have inferred from those circumstances that the man was insane, then the man who contracts with him ... would be taken to know that the man was of unsound mind'.

12 *Hart v O'Connor* [1985] AC 1000, [1985] 2 All ER 880, PC (sale of land); *Irvani v Irvani* [2000] 1 Lloyd's Rep 412, CA.

615. Wills and intestacy. In order that a testator may make a valid will it is essential that he should understand the nature of the act and its effect, be able to appreciate the claims to which he ought to give effect and understand the extent of the property of which he is disposing[1]. Thus the intellectual understanding required for testamentary capacity is somewhat different from that required for ordinary contracts, since it includes, for example, appreciation of the claims of possible beneficiaries[2]. A will made during a period of incapacity is void and does not become valid by the testator's subsequent recovery[3]. The burden of establishing testamentary capacity is on the person propounding the will[4].

Where a person lacks capacity in relation to a matter or matters concerning his property and affairs, provision is made under the Mental Capacity Act 2005[5] for the Court of Protection to make decisions on his behalf in relation to such matters[6]. This power includes the execution of a will[7]. In deciding whether or not to execute a will the court must have regard to the person's best interests[8]. The Act lays down a structured decision making process that requires the decision maker to take a number of steps before reaching a decision, including encouraging the vulnerable person to participate in the decision, considering the vulnerable person's past and present wishes (which was always a significant factor to which the court had to pay close regard), his beliefs and values, and taking into account the views of third parties as to what would be in the vulnerable person's best interests[9].

1 *Banks v Goodfellow* (1870) LR 5 QB 549; *Battan Singh v Amirchand* [1948] AC 161, [1948] 1 All ER 152, PC; *Minns v Foster* [2002] All ER (D) 225 (Dec); *Hoff v Atherton* [2004] EWCA Civ 1554, [2004] All ER (D) 314 (Nov). See further WILLS AND INTESTACY vol 102 (2010) PARA 49 et seq.

2 Distinctions are more fully indicated in *Birkin v Wing* (1890) 63 LT 80 at 82. See also *Re Beaney* [1978] 2 All ER 595, [1978] 1 WLR 770; and PARA 617.

3 See WILLS AND INTESTACY vol 102 (2010) PARA 51.

4 *Cleare and Forster v Cleare* (1869) LR 1 P & D 655. See further WILLS AND INTESTACY vol 103 (2010) PARA 899.

5 Guidance given under the Mental Health Acts 1959 and 1983 about making settlements or wills for a person lacking mental capacity can no longer be applied to decisions made under the Mental Capacity Act 2005: see *Re P* [2009] EWHC 163 (Ch), [2010] Ch 33, [2009] 2 All ER 1198; and WILLS AND INTESTACY vol 102 (2010) PARA 47.

6 See the Mental Capacity Act 2005 s 16; and PARA 731. See also *Re D (statutory will)* [2010] EWHC 2159 (Ch), [2012] Ch 57, [2011] 1 All ER 859.

7 See the Mental Capacity Act 2005 s 18(1)(i); and PARA 731.

8 See *Re D (statutory will)* [2010] EWHC 2159 (Ch), [2012] Ch 57, [2011] 1 All ER 859 (it was held to be in the best interests of the testator to order the execution of a statutory will, rather than leaving her estate to be eroded by the costs of litigation after her death, and her memory to be tainted by the bitterness of a contested probate dispute between her children).

9 See *Re M (vulnerable adult) (testamentary capacity)* [2009] EWHC 2525 (Fam), [2010] 3 All ER 682, [2011] 1 WLR 344.

616. Partnership. The Court of Protection has power to make a declaration in relation to a person's property and affairs including in particular the taking of a decision which will have the effect of dissolving a partnership of which that person is a member[1].

A partner's permanent unsoundness of mind has long been a ground on which the High Court[2] might dissolve a partnership, although such unsoundness of mind did not of itself bring the partnership to an end[3]. Before 1959, statutory powers to this effect existed in both the High Court and the Judge in Lunacy. The power of the High Court was removed in 1959[4], while the judge having jurisdiction under the Mental Health Act 1983 retained the power to make an order or give directions or authority for the dissolution of any partnership of which a patient[5] was a member[6]. The court still has power to take a decision which will have the effect of dissolving a partnership of which a person who lacks capacity is a member[7]. However, it seems that the jurisdiction of the High Court to decree a dissolution of partnership whenever circumstances have arisen which, in the court's opinion, render it just and equitable to do so[8] enables the court to dissolve a partnership where a partner suffers from such mental disorder as renders dissolution just. Relief will be given for the preservation of the partnership interest of the mentally disordered partner, if that is needed, pending dissolution[9]; and an injunction restraining a mentally disordered partner from interfering in the conduct of the partnership affairs may be granted in a proper case[10].

1　See the Mental Capacity Act 2005 s 18(1)(e); and PARA 727.
2　As to the High Court see COURTS AND TRIBUNALS vol 24 (2010) PARA 695 et seq.
3　See PARTNERSHIP vol 79 (2008) PARA 184 et seq. See particularly *Sayer v Bennet* (1784) 1 Cox Eq Cas 107, cited in *Jones v Lloyd* (1874) LR 18 Eq 265 at 273–274.
4　Ie on the repeal of the Partnership Act 1890 s 35(a) by the Mental Health Act 1959 s 149(2), Sch 8 Pt I (repealed).
5　As to the meaning of 'patient' see PARA 758 note 4.
6　See the Mental Health Act 1983 s 96(1)(g) (now repealed).
7　See the Mental Capacity Act 1983 s 18(1)(e); and PARA 727.
8　See the Partnership Act 1890 s 35(f); and PARTNERSHIP vol 79 (2008) PARA 190. Alternatively, dissolution may be decreed on the ground of permanent incapacity: see s 35(b); and PARTNERSHIP vol 79 (2008) PARA 186.
9　See *Jones v Lloyd* (1874) LR 18 Eq 265.
10　See *J v S* [1894] 3 Ch 72, where an action for dissolution was pending but the court had not been satisfied that the defendant was permanently of unsound mind and had adjourned the case.

617. Dispositions inter vivos. The Court of Protection[1] has power to make a declaration in relation to a person's property and affairs including in particular the sale, exchange, charging, gift or other disposition of that person's property and the acquisition of property in his name or on his behalf[2]. The definition of mental capacity under the Mental Capacity Act 2005[3] is in line with the existing common law tests and does not replace them, however a judge may adopt the definition under the Act[4].

Under case law the test of capacity to execute a deed is whether the person is capable of understanding what he does by executing the deed in question when its nature and effect are explained to him[5]. A valid deed might be executed during a lucid interval[6] or before mental incapacity supervened[7]. However, the degree or extent of understanding required in respect of any instrument is relative to the particular transaction which it is to effect; if the subject matter and value of a gift are trivial in relation to the donor's other assets a low degree of understanding will suffice; but if its effect is to dispose of the donor's only asset of value and thus for practical purposes to pre-empt the devolution of his estate, then the degree of understanding is as high as that required for a will[8].

A deed executed by a mentally incapacitated person was void in law[9]. However, in deciding whether to set aside such a deed, courts of equity took into consideration the circumstances of the case: rescission would be granted unless it was inequitable to do so[10]. Thus, although a voluntary disposition might be set aside even against subsequent purchasers for value without notice[11], rescission might be refused where there had been delay[12], or where the transaction was prudent and rescission would be inequitable[13]. These cases were all decided before the modern law as to the general effect of contracts made by mentally incapacitated persons became clear[14]. There may be a distinction between dispositions made by deed but for valuable consideration and voluntary dispositions however made[15].

A deed of disposition executed by a person whose property and affairs are under the jurisdiction of the Court of Protection is void[16].

1   As to the Court of Protection see PARA 720 et seq.
2   See the Mental Capacity Act 2005 s 18(1)(b), (c); and PARA 727. See *Re Clarke* [2012] EWHC 2714 (COP), [2012] All ER (D) 19 (Nov) (sale of the home of a person ('P') lacking capacity; court had to balance the consequences of retaining property and leaving P on a low income, or selling the property and maintaining a higher standard of living for P until the funds were exhausted, and having no familiar home and, if P lived long enough, no money either).
3   As to capacity see PARA 601 et seq.
4   See the Department for Constitutional Affairs *Mental Capacity Act 2005 Code of Practice* (2007) para 4.32, 4.33.
5   *Ball v Mannin* (1829) 3 Bli NS 1 at 22, HL; *Leach v Thompson* (1698) Show Parl Cas 150, HL (affg *Thompson v Leach* (1690) 3 Mod Rep 301). See also *Beverley's Case* (1603) 4 Co Rep 123b, as to which see *Re Walker* [1905] 1 Ch 160 at 179, CA (lunatic so found); *Yates v Boen* (1738) 2 Stra 1104 (evidence of insanity admitted on plea of non est factum); *Faulder v Silk* (1811) 3 Camp 126 (evidence similarly admitted); *Daily Telegraph Newspaper Co Ltd v McLaughlin* [1904] AC 776, PC. See further *Price v Berrington* (1849) 7 Hare 394 at 402 (on appeal (1851) 3 Mac & G 486) (legal estate not passed by conveyance of lunatic); *Howard v Earl of Digby* (1834) 2 Cl & Fin 634 at 663, HL (obligation by bond would not bind lunatic).
6   *Towart v Sellars* (1817) 5 Dow 231, HL; *Beverley's Case* (1603) 4 Co Rep 123b.
7   *Affleck v Affleck* (1857) 3 Sm & G 394.
8   *Re Beaney* [1978] 2 All ER 595, [1978] 1 WLR 770. As to capacity to execute a will see PARA 615.
9   *Ball v Mannin* (1829) 3 Bli NS 1 at 22, HL; and see the cases cited in note 1.
10 See generally *Niell v Morley* (1804) 9 Ves 478; *Campbell v Hooper* (1855) 3 Sm & G 153 at 158; *Price v Berrington* (1849) 7 Hare 394 at 402 (on appeal (1851) 3 Mac & G 486). As to rescission generally see CONTRACT vol 22 (2012) PARA 553 et seq.
11 *Clerk v Clerk* (1700) 2 Vern 412 (settlement); *Elliot v Ince* (1857) 7 De G M & G 475 (disentailing deed); *Sentance v Poole* (1827) 3 C & P 1 (promissory note); *Manning v Gill* (1872) LR 13 Eq 485 (voluntary deed). See also GIFTS vol 52 (2009) PARA 212.
12 *Towart v Sellars* (1817) 5 Dow 231 at 236–237, HL, per Lord Eldon (20 or 30 years after disposition, parties best acquainted with circumstances dead).
13 *Selby v Jackson* (1844) 6 Beav 192; *Niell v Morley* (1804) 9 Ves 478. See also *Campbell v Hooper* (1855) 3 Sm & G 153 at 158, cited by Sargant LJ in *York Glass Co Ltd v Jubb* (1925) 134 LT 36 at 44, CA, from which it seems that a deed would not be set aside unless there would be inequity in allowing it to stand.
14 See PARA 614.
15 In *Re Beaney* [1978] 2 All ER 595, [1978] 1 WLR 770, the judge declined to express a view on this matter.
16 *Re Walker* [1905] 1 Ch 160, CA; *Re Marshall, Marshall v Whateley* [1920] 1 Ch 284.

(ii) Lasting Powers of Attorney

618. In general. The Mental Capacity Act 2005[1] introduced a new and expanded statutory form of power of attorney, the 'lasting power of attorney', to replace the enduring power of attorney under the Enduring Powers of Attorney Act 1985[2].

1   See the Mental Capacity Act 2005 ss 9–14, 22–23, Sch 1; PARAs 619–622; and AGENCY vol 1 (2008) PARA 217 et seq.

2 See the Enduring Powers of Attorney Act 1985 (repealed). No enduring power of attorney within the meaning of the Enduring Powers of Attorney 2005 is to be created after the commencement of the Mental Capacity Act 2005 s 66(1)(b): s 66(2). Although the Enduring Powers of Attorney Act 1985 ceases to have effect, the legal effect of an enduring power of attorney already made is preserved and integrated into the scheme of the new legislation: see s 66(1)(b), (3), Sch 4; and AGENCY vol 1 (2008) PARA 194. There are also transitional provisions in connection with the repeal of the Enduring Powers of Attorney Act 1985: see the Mental Capacity Act 2005 s 66(4), Sch 5 Pt 2; the Lasting Powers of Attorney, Enduring Powers of Attorney and Public Guardian Regulations 2007, SI 2007/1253, regs 23–29; and AGENCY vol 1 (2008) PARA 194. A lasting power of attorney may cover personal welfare decisions see PARA 619.

619. Lasting power of attorney and donees. A lasting power of attorney is a power of attorney under which the donor ('P') confers on the donee (or donees) authority to make decisions about all or any of the following:

(1) P's personal welfare or specified matters concerning P's personal welfare[1]; and

(2) P's property and affairs[2] or specified matters concerning P's property and affairs,

and which includes authority to make such decisions[3] in circumstances where P no longer has capacity[4]. The donor must be aged 18 or over and have capacity to execute a lasting power of attorney[5].

A donee of a lasting power of attorney must be an individual who has reached 18, or if the power relates only to P's property and affairs, either such an individual or a trust corporation[6]. An individual who is bankrupt may not be appointed as donee of a lasting power of attorney in relation to P's property and affairs[7]. There are specific provisions applying in relation to an instrument under which two or more persons are to act as donees of a lasting power of attorney[8]. An instrument used to create a lasting power of attorney cannot give the donee (or, if more than one, any of them) power to appoint a substitute or successor, but may itself appoint a person to replace the donee (or, if more than one, any of them) on the occurrence of certain events[9] having the effect of terminating the donee's appointment[10].

There are restrictions placed on the use of restraint by attorneys, matching those applying in relation to 'section 5 acts'[11] and deputies[12]; restraint can only be used to prevent harm to P, and must be proportionate[13].

1 As to lasting powers of attorney relating to personal welfare see the Department for Constitutional Affairs *Mental Capacity Act 2005 Code of Practice* (2007) para 7.21. An attorney cannot act in relation to P's personal welfare where P has capacity, nor where P has made a qualifying advance decision: see the Mental Capacity Act 2005 s 11(7)(a), (b); and AGENCY vol 1 (2008) PARA 217. As to qualifying advance decisions see ss 24–26; and PARA 623 et seq. Although an attorney may give or refuse consent to the carrying out or continuation of health care, this does not extend to refusing life-sustaining treatment unless the lasting power of attorney expressly said so, and is subject to any conditions or restrictions in the lasting power of attorney: see s 11(7)(c), (8); and AGENCY vol 1 (2008) PARA 217. As to issues of capacity see PARA 601 note 3.

2 'Property' includes any thing in action and any interest in real or personal property: Mental Capacity Act 2005 s 64(1). As to decisions relating to property and affairs see the Department for Constitutional Affairs *Mental Capacity Act 2005 Code of Practice* (2007) para 7.36. See also *Re F (mental patient: sterilisation)* [1990] 2 AC 1 sub nom *F v West Berkshire Health Authority and another (Mental Health Act Commission intervening)* [1989] 2 All ER 545.

3 In the Mental Capacity Act 2005, references to making decisions, in relation to a donee of a lasting power of attorney or a deputy appointed by the Court of Protection, include where appropriate, acting on decisions made: s 64(2). As to the meaning of 'deputy' see PARA 606 note 18. As to the Court of Protection see PARA 720. As to decision-making powers of the Court of Protection and court-appointed deputies regarding personal welfare and property and affairs see PARAS 720–739.

4　See the Mental Capacity Act 2005 s 9(1); and AGENCY vol 1 (2008) PARA 217. As to the role of the Public Guardian see PARAS 751–752.

5　See the Mental Capacity Act 2005 s 9(2)(c); AGENCY vol 1 (2008) PARA 217. As to rules that must be complied with, see further s 9. As the formalities in relation to lasting powers of attorney including making instruments, registration, cancellation of registration, notification of severance, and records of alterations in registered powers see Sch 1; the Lasting Powers of Attorney, Enduring Powers of Attorney and Public Guardian Regulations 2007, SI 2007/1253, regs 5–22; and AGENCY vol 1 (2008) PARA 219 et seq. If the rules referred to in s 9(2) are not complied with, the document created will not be a valid lasting power of attorney and cannot lawfully be used to make decisions on behalf of the donor: see s 9(3). The authority conferred is subject to the principles in s 1 (see PARA 601), the best interests requirements in s 4 (see PARA 606), and any conditions or restrictions specified in the instrument: see s 9(4). As to the capacity to make a lasting power of attorney see in particular Sch 1 para 2(e); and *Re K* [1988] Ch 310, [1988] 1 All ER 358, *Re W (enduring power of attorney)* [2001] Ch 609, [2001] 4 All ER 88. See also AGENCY vol 1 (2008) PARA 217.

6　See the Mental Capacity Act 2005 s 10(1); and AGENCY vol 1 (2008) PARA 218. 'Trust corporation' has the meaning given in the Trustee Act 1925 s 68(1) (see TRUSTS vol 48 (2007 Reissue) PARA 798): Mental Capacity Act 2005 s 64(1). See AGENCY vol 1 (2008) PARA 217.

7　See the Mental Capacity Act 2005 s 10(2); and AGENCY vol 1 (2008) PARA 218. As to the bankruptcy of individuals generally see BANKRUPTCY AND INDIVIDUAL INSOLVENCY.

8　See the Mental Capacity Act 2005 s 10(3)–(7); and AGENCY vol 1 (2008) PARA 218. The appointment may specify that they act jointly, jointly and severally, or jointly in respect of some matters and jointly and severally in respect of others (see s 10(4)) but in the absence of specification the assumption is that they act jointly (see s 10(5)). The provisions also cover the implications for breach of any relevant rules, in particular those contained in Sch 1.

9　Ie any events mentioned in the Mental Capacity Act 2005 s 13(6)(a)–(d): see AGENCY vol 1 (2008) PARA 234.

10　See the Mental Capacity Act 2005 s 10(8); and AGENCY vol 1 (2008) PARA 218.

11　See the Mental Capacity Act 2005 s 6; and PARA 611.

12　See the Mental Capacity Act 2005 s 20; and PARA 735.

13　See the Mental Capacity Act 2005 s 11(1)–(5); and AGENCY vol 1 (2008) PARA 217.

620. Scope of lasting powers of attorney in relation to gifts. Provision is made in relation to an attorney's power to make gifts of the donor's property[1].

Where a lasting power of attorney confers authority to make decisions about P's property and affairs, it does not authorise a donee (or, if more than one, any of them) to dispose of the donor's property by making gifts except as permitted by the following provisions[2]. The donee may make gifts: (1) on customary occasions[3] to persons (including himself) who are related to or connected with the donor; or (2) to any charity to whom the donor made or might have been expected to make gifts, if the value of each such gift is not unreasonable having regard to all the circumstances and, in particular, the size of the donor's estate[4].

1　See the Mental Capacity Act 1983 s 12; and AGENCY vol 1 (2008) PARA 217. This provision is similar to the Enduring Powers of Attorney Act 1985 s 3(5) (repealed): see AGENCY vol 1 (2008) PARA 217. As to the meaning of 'property' see PARA 619 note 2.

2　See the Mental Capacity Act 2005 s 12(1); and AGENCY vol 1 (2008) PARA 217.

3　'Customary occasion' means: (1) the occasion or anniversary of a birth, a marriage or the formation of a civil partnership; or (2) any other occasion on which presents are customarily given within families or among friends or associates: Mental Capacity Act 2005 s 12(3).

4　Mental Capacity Act 1983 s 12(2). This is subject to any conditions or restrictions in the instrument: s 12(4). See AGENCY vol 1 (2008) PARA 217.

621. Revocation of lasting powers of attorney. If a donor ('P') has executed an instrument with a view to creating a lasting power of attorney, or a lasting power of attorney is registered as having been conferred by P, P may, at any time when he has capacity[1] to do so, revoke the power[2].

Other events automatically terminate a lasting power of attorney. P's bankruptcy revokes the power so far as it relates to P's property and affairs (although not his personal welfare), although interim bankruptcy restrictions orders do not bring a power of attorney to an end but have the effect of suspending the power[3]. The occurrence of certain events in relation to a donee terminate the appointment and generally revoke the power[4].

Provision is also made for the legal consequences when a registered lasting power of attorney turns out to be invalid or has been revoked, by giving the attorneys and third parties protection from liability if they were unaware that the lasting power of attorney was invalid or had come to an end[5].

1 As to issues of capacity see PARA 601 note 3.
2 See the Mental Capacity Act 2005 s 13(1), (2); and AGENCY vol 1 (2008) PARA 223.
3 See the Mental Capacity Act 2005 s 13(3),(4), (8), (9); and AGENCY vol 1 (2008) PARA 224.
4 See the Mental Capacity Act 2005 s 13(5)–(7), (10), (11); and AGENCY vol 1 (2008) PARA 224. The events include certain disclaimers of the appointment by the donee in accordance with relevant regulations; subject to s 13(8), (9), the death or bankruptcy of the donee or in the case of a trust corporation (see PARA 619 note 6) its winding-up or dissolution; the dissolution or annulment of a marriage or civil partnership (subject to an exception if the instrument provides otherwise); and the donee's lack of capacity. The occurrence of the relevant event does not revoke the power where the donee is replaced under the terms of the instrument, or he is one of two or more persons appointed to act jointly and severally in respect of any matter and after the event there is at least one remaining donee (see also PARA 619). As to regulations providing for the disclaimer of appointment by a done of a lasting power of attorney see the Lasting Powers of Attorney, Enduring Powers of Attorney and Public Guardian Regulations 2007, SI 2007/1253, reg 20; and AGENCY vol 1 (2008) PARA 202 et seq.
5 See the Mental Capacity Act 2005 s 14; and AGENCY vol 1 (2008) PARA 238. Similar provision was made in relation to enduring powers of attorney by the Enduring Powers of Attorney Act 1985 s 9 (repealed): see AGENCY vol 1 (2008) PARA 217.

622. Powers of court in relation to validity and operation of lasting powers of attorney. The Court of Protection[1] has powers in relation to lasting powers of attorney[2]. The court may determine questions about validity and revocation; may direct that an instrument should not be registered or, if it is unregistered, revoke it on the grounds of fraud or undue pressure, or misbehaviour by the attorney[3].

The court also has power to decide questions about the meaning or effect of a lasting power of attorney and to give directions to attorneys where the donor lacks capacity[4]; may give the attorney directions about producing reports, accounts, records and information and about his remuneration and expenses; has power to relieve a donee from some or all of the liabilities arising from a breach of duty; and may authorise gifts beyond the scope of what is permitted[5].

1 As to the Court of Protection under the Mental Capacity Act 2005 see PARA 720.
2 See the Mental Capacity Act 2005 ss 22, 23; and AGENCY vol 1 (2008) PARAS 223, 230, 235, 236. The powers are similar to those under the Enduring Powers of Attorney Act 1985 s 8 (repealed): see AGENCY vol 1 (2008) PARAS 223, 235.
3 See the Mental Capacity Act 2005 s 22. 'Pressure' means to behave in a manner whereby the will of the donor is overborne by the will of another person so that the person is not creating the instrument of his own free will; it can take various forms: physical, psychological, emotional, financial and even pharmacological; 'undue' means excessive; greater than the circumstances warrant: see *Re G* (unreported, 11 October 2001).
4 As to lack of capacity see PARA 603.
5 See the Mental Capacity Act 2005 s 23. As to what is permitted see s 12(2); and PARA 620.

(iii) Advance Decisions to Refuse Treatment

623. In general. The Mental Capacity Act 2005[1] makes provision in relation to advance decisions[2] to refuse treatment. The legal effect of such decisions has been analysed in a number of judgments[3]. The intention of the relevant provisions of the Mental Capacity Act 2005 is to codify and clarify the common law rules[4] and integrate them into the legislation.

1 Ie the Mental Capacity Act 2005 ss 24–26: see PARAS 624–626.
2 As to the meaning of 'advance decision' see PARA 624. 'Best interests' does not apply to the application of an advance decision because the person concerned has identified his best interests when making the advance decision and while capacious. However the Mental Capacity Act 2005 s 4 requires an invalid advance decision to be taken into account when considering a patient's best interests: see s 4(6)(a); and *R (on the application of Burke) v the General Medical Council* [2005] EWCA Civ 1003.
3 Eg see *Re AK (Medical Treatment: Consent)* [2001] 1 FLR 129, [2001] 2 FCR 35; *HE v A NHS Trust* [2003] EWHC 1017 (Fam), [2003] 2 FLR 408, [2003] Fam Law 733; *R (on the application of Burke) v General Medical Council* [2005] EWCA Civ 1003, [2006] QB 273, [2005] 3 WLR 1132; *Knight v Edonya* [2009] EWHC 2181 (Ch), [2009] All ER (D) 207 (Aug). See also PARA 927. As to advance decisions see also Department for Constitutional Affairs *Mental Capacity Act 2005 Code of Practice* (2007) Chapter 9.
4 See PARA 597.

624. Advance decisions to refuse treatment. 'Advance decision' means a decision made by a person ('P'), after he has reached 18 and when he has capacity[1] to do so, that if: (1) at a later time and in such circumstances as he may specify, a specified treatment[2] is proposed to be carried out or continued by a person providing health care for him[3]; and (2) at that time he lacks capacity[4] to consent to the carrying out or continuation of the treatment[5], the specified treatment is not to be carried out or continued[6].

P may withdraw or alter an advance decision at any time when he has capacity to do so[7].

1 As to capacity and lack of capacity see PARA 601 et seq.
2 As to the meaning of 'treatment' see PARA 606 note 9. See *W Healthcare NHS Trust v H* [2004] EWCA Civ 1324, (2004) Times, 9 December (a statement made by the patient that she did not wish to be 'kept alive by machines' was found not sufficiently clear). An advance decision can be overridden if the treatment in question is governed by the Mental Health Act 1983 Pt VI: see the Mental Capacity Act 2005 s 28; and PARA 925. An exception to this is electroconvulsive therapy: see s 28(1A); and Mental Health Act 1983 s 58A; and PARAS 925, 931.
3 Mental Capacity Act 2005 s 24(1)(a). For these purposes, a decision may be regarded as specifying a treatment or circumstances even though expressed in layman's terms: s 24(2).
4 See note 1.
5 Mental Capacity Act 2005 s 24(1)(b).
6 Mental Capacity Act 2005 s 24(1). If a doctor is unable to carry out the wishes of the patient then their duty is to find a doctor who will do so: see the Department for Constitutional Affairs *Mental Capacity Act 2005 Code of Practice* (2007) para 9.61; and *Re B (adult: refusal of medical treatment)* [2002] EWHC 429 (Fam), [2002] 2 All ER 449, [2002] 2 FCR 1 (patient transferred to another hospital to carry out her wishes for treatment to be withdrawn).
7 Mental Capacity Act 2005 s 24(3). A withdrawal (including a partial withdrawal) need not be in writing: s 24(4). An alteration of an advance decision need not be in writing, unless s 25(5) (see PARA 625) applies in relation to the decision resulting from the alteration: s 24(5). There is no formal requirement that an advance decision be made in writing, but see s 25(5); and PARA 625.

625. Validity and applicability of advance decisions. An advance decision[1] does not affect the liability which a person may incur for carrying out or continuing a treatment[2] in relation to a person ('P') unless the decision is at the material time valid, and applicable to the treatment[3].

An advance decision is not valid if P: (1) has withdrawn the decision at a time when he had capacity[4] to do so[5]; (2) has, under a lasting power of attorney[6] created after the advance decision was made, conferred authority on the donee (or, if more than one, any of them) to give or refuse consent to the treatment to which the advance decision relates[7]; or (3) has done anything else clearly inconsistent with the advance decision remaining his fixed decision[8].

An advance decision is not applicable to the treatment in question if at the material time P has capacity to give or refuse consent to it[9]. An advance decision is not applicable to the treatment in question if: (a) that treatment is not the treatment specified in the advance decision[10]; (b) any circumstances specified in the advance decision are absent[11]; or (c) there are reasonable grounds for believing that circumstances exist which P did not anticipate at the time of the advance decision and which would have affected his decision had he anticipated them[12].

An advance decision is not applicable to life-sustaining treatment[13] unless: (i) the decision is verified by a statement by P to the effect that it is to apply to that treatment even if life is at risk[14]; and (ii) the decision and statement comply with the following requirements: (A) they are in writing[15]; (B) they are signed by P or by another person in P's presence and by P's direction[16]; (C) the signature is made or acknowledged by P in the presence of a witness[17]; and (D) the witness signs, or acknowledges his signature, in P's presence[18].

1   As to the meaning of 'advance decision' see PARA 624.
2   As to the meaning of 'treatment' see PARA 606 note 9.
3   Mental Capacity Act 2005 s 25(1). As to withdrawal of a decision see PARA 624. Where life is at stake the validity and applicability of an advance decision must be scrutinised carefully: see *HE v A Hospital NHS Trust* [2003] EWHC 1017 (Fam), [2003] 2 FLR 408, [2003] Fam Law 733.
4   As to capacity see PARA 601 et seq.
5   Mental Capacity Act 2005 s 25(2)(a).
6   As to the meaning of 'lasting power of attorney' see PARA 606 note 16. See also PARA 618 et seq.
7   Mental Capacity Act 2005 s 25(2)(b). The existence of any lasting power of attorney other than one of a description mentioned in s 25(2)(b) does not prevent the advance decision from being regarded as valid and applicable: s 25(7).
8   Mental Capacity Act 2005 s 25(2)(c).
9   Mental Capacity Act 2005 s 25(3).
10 Mental Capacity Act 2005 s 25(4)(a).
11 Mental Capacity Act 2005 s 25(4)(b).
12 Mental Capacity Act 2005 s 25(4)(c).
13 As to the meaning of 'life-sustaining treatment' see PARA 606 note 9. For an advance decision relating to life-sustaining treatment to be valid and applicable, there ought to be clear evidence establishing on the balance of probability that the maker had had capacity at the relevant time and, where the evidence of capacity was doubtful or equivocal, it would not be appropriate to uphold the decision: see *A Local Authority v E (by her litigation friend, the Official Solicitor)* [2012] EWHC 1639 (COP), [2012] 2 FCR 523, 127 BMLR 133.
14 Mental Capacity Act 2005 s 25(5)(a). An advance decision refusing life-sustaining treatment is to be treated as valid and applicable to a treatment, without the requirements in s 25(5)(a), (6)(b)–(d) having to be satisfied, if the following conditions are met: (1) a person providing health care for a person ('P') reasonably believes that (a) P has made the advance decision refusing life-sustaining treatment before 1 October 2007; and (b) P has lacked the capacity to comply with s 25(5)(a), (6)(b)–(d); (2) the advance decision is in writing; (3) P has not withdrawn the decision at a time when he had capacity to do so, or done anything else clearly inconsistent with the advance decision remaining his fixed decision; (4) P does not have the capacity to give or refuse consent to the treatment in question at the material time; (5) the treatment in question is the treatment specified in the advance decision; (6) any circumstances specified in the advance decision are present; (7) there are no reasonable grounds for believing that circumstances exist which P did not anticipate at the time of the advance decision and which would have affected his decision had he anticipated them: Mental Capacity Act 2005 (Transitional and Consequential Provisions) Order 2007, SI 2007/1898, art 5.
15 Mental Capacity Act 2005 s 25(5)(b), (6)(a).
16 Mental Capacity Act 2005 s 25(5)(b), (6)(b). Informal statements may be taken into account by the court see *W (by her litigation friend) v M (by her litigation friend, the Official Solicitor)* [2011] EWHC 2443 (Fam), [2012] 1 All ER 1313, [2012] 1 WLR 1653.

17 Mental Capacity Act 2005 s 25(5)(b), (6)(c).
18 Mental Capacity Act 2005 s 25(5)(b), (6)(d).

626. Effect of advance decisions. If a person ('P') has made an advance decision[1] which is valid and applicable[2] to a treatment[3], the decision has effect as if he had made it, and had had capacity[4] to make it, at the time when the question arises whether the treatment should be carried out or continued[5].

A person does not incur liability for carrying out or continuing the treatment unless, at the time, he is satisfied that an advance decision exists which is valid and applicable to the treatment[6]. A person does not incur liability for the consequences of withholding or withdrawing a treatment from P if, at the time, he reasonably believes that an advance decision exists which is valid and applicable to the treatment[7].

The Court of Protection[8] may make a declaration as to whether an advance decision: (1) exists[9]; (2) is valid[10]; (3) is applicable to a treatment[11]. Nothing in an apparent advance decision stops a person: (a) providing life-sustaining treatment[12]; or (b) doing any act he reasonably believes to be necessary to prevent a serious deterioration in P's condition[13], while a decision as respects any relevant issue is sought from the court[14].

1 As to the meaning of 'advance decision' see PARA 624.
2 As to validity and applicability of advance decisions see PARA 625.
3 As to the meaning of 'treatment' see PARA 606 note 9.
4 As to capacity see PARA 601 et seq.
5 Mental Capacity Act 2005 s 26(1).
6 Mental Capacity Act 2005 s 26(2).
7 Mental Capacity Act 2005 s 26(3).
8 As to the Court of Protection see PARA 720.
9 Mental Capacity Act 2005 s 26(4)(a).
10 Mental Capacity Act 2005 s 26(4)(b).
11 Mental Capacity Act 2005 s 26(4)(c).
12 Mental Capacity Act 2005 s 26(5)(a). As to the meaning of 'life-sustaining treatment' see PARA 606 note 9.
13 Mental Capacity Act 2005 s 26(5)(b).
14 Mental Capacity Act 2005 s 26(5).

(iv) Decisions that Cannot be made on Behalf of a Person

627. Family relationships, etc. Nothing in the Mental Capacity Act 2005 permits a decision on any of the following matters to be made on behalf of a person:

(1)   consenting to marriage or a civil partnership[1];
(2)   consenting to have sexual relations[2];
(3)   consenting to a decree of divorce being granted on the basis of two years' separation[3];
(4)   consenting to a dissolution order being made in relation to a civil partnership on the basis of two years' separation[4];
(5)   consenting to a child's being placed for adoption by an adoption agency[5];
(6)   consenting to the making of an adoption order[6];
(7)   discharging parental responsibilities in matters not relating to a child's property[7];
(8)   giving a consent under the Human Fertilisation and Embryology Act 1990[8];

(9) giving a consent under the Human Fertilisation and Embryology Act 2008[9].

The Court of Protection may, however, make a declaration[10] with regard to a person's capacity to consent to the matters listed above[11].

1 Mental Capacity Act 2005 s 27(1)(a). As to marriage and civil partnerships generally see MATRIMONIAL AND CIVIL PARTNERSHIP LAW.
2 Mental Capacity Act 2005 s 27(1)(b).
3 Mental Capacity Act 2005 s 27(1)(c). As to divorce on the basis of two years' separation see MATRIMONIAL AND CIVIL PARTNERSHIP LAW vol 72 (2009) PARA 363.
4 Mental Capacity Act 2005 s 27(1)(d). As to dissolution in a civil partnership on the basis of two years' separation see MATRIMONIAL AND CIVIL PARTNERSHIP LAW vol 72 (2009) PARA 363.
5 Mental Capacity Act 2005 s 27(1)(e). As to adoption generally see CHILDREN AND YOUNG PERSONS vol 9 (2012) PARA 360 et seq.
6 Mental Capacity Act 2005 s 27(1)(f). 'Adoption order' means: (1) an adoption order within the meaning of the Adoption and Children Act 2002 (including a future adoption order); and (2) an order under s 84 (parental responsibility prior to adoption abroad) (see CHILDREN AND YOUNG PERSONS vol 9 (2012) PARAS 397, 540): Mental Capacity Act 2005 s 27(2).
7 Mental Capacity Act 2005 s 27(1)(g). As to parental responsibilities generally see CHILDREN AND YOUNG PERSONS vol 9 (2012) PARA 150 et seq.
8 Mental Capacity Act 2005 s 27(1)(h). As to the Human Fertilisation and Embryology Act 1990 see CHILDREN AND YOUNG PERSONS vol 9 (2012) PARA 150 et seq; MEDICAL PROFESSIONS vol 74 (2011) PARA 165 et seq.
9 Mental Capacity Act 2005 s 27(1)(i) (added by the Human Fertilisation and Embryology Act 2008 Sch 6 para 40). As to the Human Fertilisation and Embryology Act 2008 see MEDICAL PROFESSIONS.
10 Ie under the Mental Capacity Act 2005 s 15 (see PARA 723).
11 See PARA 603 et seq.

628. Treatment under the Mental Health Act 1983. Nothing in the Mental Capacity Act 2005 authorises anyone to give a patient medical treatment[1] for a mental disorder[2] or to consent to a patient's being given medical treatment for a mental disorder, if at the time when it is proposed to treat the patient, his treatment is regulated by Part 4[3] of the Mental Health Act 1983[4].

1 As to the meaning of 'medical treatment' see the Mental Health Act 1983; and PARA 926 (definition applied by the Mental Capacity Act 2005 s 28(2)).
2 As to the meanings of 'mental disorder' and 'patient' see the Mental Health Act 1983; and PARAS 761, 926 (definitions applied by the Mental Capacity Act 2005 s 28(2)).
3 Ie the Mental Health Act 1983 ss 56–64 (see PARA 924 et seq). There is an exception relating to electroconvulsive therapy given to informal patients under 18 who cannot consent: see the Mental Health Act 2005 s 28(1A); and PARA 925. Community treatment order patients subject to the Mental Health Act 1983 cannot be treated under the authority of the Mental Capacity Act 2005 s 5 (see PARA 611) and must be recalled to hospital for treatment to be administered involuntarily: see s 28(1B); and PARA 611. However treatment could be provided if authorised by a donee of a lasting power of attorney or court deputy. It does not prevent treatment that is regulated under the Mental Health Act 1983 ss 58, 58A (see PARAS 930, 931) being provided under the Mental Capacity Act 2005 to a patient who has not been detained under the Mental Health Act 1983. See further *C (by his litigation friend, the Official Solicitor) v A Borough Council* [2011] EWHC 3321 (COP), [2011] All ER (D) 203 (Dec); *GJ v Foundation Trust* [2009] EWHC 2972 (Fam), [2010] Fam 70, [2010] 3 WLR 840.
4 See the Mental Capacity Act 2005 s 28; and PARA 562.

629. Voting rights. Nothing in the Mental Capacity Act 2005 permits a decision on voting at an election for any public office, or at a referendum[1], to be made on behalf of a person[2].

1 'Referendum' has the same meaning as in the Political Parties, Elections and Referendums Act 2000 s 101 (see ELECTIONS AND REFERENDUMS vol 15(4) (2007 Reissue) PARA 519): Mental Capacity Act 2005 s 29(2).

2   Mental Capacity Act 2005 s 29(1). As to elections generally see ELECTIONS AND REFERENDUMS.
    See also PARA 565.

(v) Restrictions on Intrusive Research

630.   Research. Intrusive research[1] carried out on, or in relation to, a person
who lacks capacity[2] to consent to it is unlawful unless it is carried out: (1) as part
of a research project which is for the time being approved by the appropriate
body[3] for the purposes of the Mental Capacity Act 2005[4]; and (2) in accordance
with the relevant safeguards[5].

A clinical trial which is subject to the provisions of clinical trials regulations[6]
is not to be treated as research for these purposes[7].

Research is not intrusive to the extent that it consists of the use of a person's
human cells to bring about the creation in vitro of an embryo or human admixed
embryo, or the subsequent storage or use of an embryo or human admixed
embryo so created[8].

1   Research is intrusive if it is of a kind that would be unlawful if it was carried out: (1) on or in
    relation to a person who had capacity to consent to it; but (2) without his consent: Mental
    Capacity Act 2005 s 30(2). See note 2. Research is not defined by the Mental Capacity Act 2005
    but see the Department for Constitutional Affairs *Mental Capacity Act 2005 Code of Practice*
    (2007) para 11.2.
2   As to lack of capacity see PARA 603. As to the assumption of capacity in relation to research see
    the Department for Constitutional Affairs *Mental Capacity Act 2005 Code of Practice* (2007)
    para 11.4.
3   Ie for the purposes of the Mental Capacity Act 2005 s 31: see PARA 631. 'Appropriate body', in
    relation to a research project, means the person, committee or other body specified in
    regulations made by the appropriate authority as the appropriate body in relation to a project of
    the kind in question: s 30(4). For the purposes of ss 30, 32, 34, 'appropriate authority' means:
    (1) in relation to the carrying out of research in England, the Secretary of State; and (2) in
    relation to the carrying out of research in Wales, the National Assembly for Wales: s 30(6). As to
    the meaning of 'England' see PARA 557 note 5; and as to the meaning of 'Wales' see PARA 557
    note 5. In relation to a research project referred to in ss 3032, the 'appropriate body' is a
    committee established to advise on, or on matters which include, the ethics of intrusive research
    in relation to people who lack capacity to consent to it, and recognised for that purpose by the
    appropriate authority: Mental Capacity Act 2005 (Appropriate Body) (England)
    Regulations 2006, SI 2006/2810 (amended by SI 2006/3474, SI 2011/2645); Mental Capacity
    Act 2005 (Appropriate Body) (Wales) Regulations 2007, SI 2007/833.
4   Mental Capacity Act 2005 s 30(1)(a). Special provision is made for where a person ('P') has
    consented to take part in a research project before the commencement of s 30, but before the
    conclusion of the project, loses capacity to consent to continue to take part in it: see s 34(1). In
    this situation, the appropriate authority may by regulations provide that, despite P's loss of
    capacity, research of a prescribed kind may be carried out on, or in relation to, P if: (1) the
    project satisfies prescribed requirements; (2) any information or material relating to P which is
    used in the research is of a prescribed description and was obtained before P's loss of capacity;
    and (3) the person conducting the project takes in relation to P such steps as may be prescribed
    for the purpose of protecting him: s 34(2). The regulations may, in particular: (a) make
    provision about when, for the purposes of the regulations, a project is to be treated as having
    begun; (b) include provision similar to any made by s 31 (see PARA 631), s 32 (see PARA 632) or
    s 33 (see PARA 633): s 34(3). 'Prescribed', in relation to regulations made under the Mental
    Capacity Act 2005, means prescribed by those regulations: s 64(1). As to such regulations see
    the Mental Capacity Act 2005 (Loss of Capacity during Research Project) (England)
    Regulations 2007, SI 2007/679; and the Mental Capacity Act 2005 (Loss of Capacity during
    Research Project) (Wales) Regulations 2007, SI 2007/837. As to when an activity is part of
    research or care see the Department for Constitutional Affairs *Mental Capacity Act 2005 Code
    of Practice* (2007) para 11.3.
5   Mental Capacity Act 2005 s 30(1)(b). The safeguards are those in s 32 (see PARA 632) and s 33
    (see PARA 633).
6   'Clinical trials regulations' means: (1) the Medicines for Human Use (Clinical Trials)
    Regulations 2004, SI 2004/1031 (see MEDICINAL PRODUCTS AND DRUGS vol 30(2) (Reissue)

PARA 82 et seq) and any other regulations replacing those regulations or amending them; and (2) any other regulations relating to clinical trials and designated by the Secretary of State as clinical trials regulations for the purposes of the Mental Capacity Act 2005 s 30: s 30(5).

7 Mental Capacity Act 2005 s 30(3). See note 4.

8 Mental Capacity Act 2005 s 30(3A) (s 30(3A), (3B) added by the Human Fertilisation and Embryology Act 2008 Sch 7 para 25). Expressions used in the Mental Capacity Act 2005 s 30(3A) and the Expressions in the Human Fertilisation and Embryology Act 1990 Sch 3 (consents to use or storage of gametes, embryos or human admixed embryos etc) also apply to the Mental Capacity Act 2005 s 30(3A): s 30(3B) (as so added).

631. Requirements for approval. The appropriate body[1] may not approve a research project for the purposes of the Mental Capacity Act 2005[2] unless satisfied that the following requirements will be met in relation to research carried out as part of the project on, or in relation to, a person who lacks capacity[3] to consent to taking part in the project ('P')[4]:

(1) the research must be connected with an impairing condition[5] affecting P, or its treatment[6];

(2) there must be reasonable grounds for believing that research of comparable effectiveness cannot be carried out if the project has to be confined to, or relate only to, persons who have capacity to consent to taking part in it[7];

(3) the research must: (a) have the potential to benefit P without imposing on P a burden that is disproportionate to the potential benefit to P[8]; or (b) be intended to provide knowledge of the causes or treatment of, or of the care of persons affected by, the same or a similar condition[9];

(4) there must be reasonable arrangements in place for ensuring that the relevant safeguard requirements[10] will be met[11].

1 As to the meaning of 'appropriate body' see PARA 630 note 3.

2 As to such research projects see PARA 630. As to when approval is not needed see the Department for Constitutional Affairs *Mental Capacity Act 2005 Code of Practice* (2007) para 11.7.

3 As to lack of capacity see PARA 603.

4 Mental Capacity Act 2005 s 31(1).

5 'Impairing condition' means a condition which is (or may be) attributable to, or which causes or contributes to (or may cause or contribute to), the impairment of, or disturbance in the functioning of, the mind or brain: Mental Capacity Act 2005 s 31(3).

6 Mental Capacity Act 2005 s 31(2). As to the meaning of 'treatment' see PARA 606 note 9.

7 Mental Capacity Act 2005 s 31(4).

8 As to balancing the benefit and burden of research see the Department for Constitutional Affairs *Mental Capacity Act 2005 Code of Practice* (2007) paras 11.14, 11.15.

9 Mental Capacity Act 2005 s 31(5). If the research falls within head (3)(b) in the text but not within head (3)(a) in the text, there must be reasonable grounds for believing: (1) that the risk to P from taking part in the project is likely to be negligible; and (2) that anything done to, or in relation to, P will not interfere with P's freedom of action or privacy in a significant way, or be unduly invasive or restrictive: s 31(6). See further the Department for Constitutional Affairs *Mental Capacity Act 2005 Code of Practice* (2007) paras 11.16–11.19.

10 Ie the requirements of the Mental Capacity Act 2005 s 32 (see PARA 632) and s 33 (see PARA 633).

11 Mental Capacity Act 2005 s 31(7).

632. Consulting carers, etc. If a person ('R') is conducting an approved research project[1], and wishes to carry out research, as part of the project, on or in relation to a person ('P') who lacks capacity[2] to consent to taking part in the project[3], R must take reasonable steps to identify a person who: (1) otherwise than in a professional capacity or for remuneration, is engaged in caring for P or is interested in P's welfare[4]; and (2) is prepared to be consulted by R under these provisions[5].

If R is unable to identify such a person he must, in accordance with guidance issued by the appropriate authority[6], nominate a person who is prepared to be consulted by R under these provisions[7], but who has no connection with the project[8].

R must provide the person identified[9] or nominated[10] with information about the project and ask him: (a) for advice as to whether P should take part in the project[11]; and (b) what, in his opinion, P's wishes and feelings about taking part in the project would be likely to be if P had capacity in relation to the matter[12].

If, at any time, the person consulted advises R that in his opinion P's wishes and feelings would be likely to lead him to decline to take part in the project (or to wish to withdraw from it) if he had capacity in relation to the matter, R must ensure: (i) if P is not already taking part in the project, that he does not take part in it[13]; (ii) if P is taking part in the project, that he is withdrawn from it[14].

If treatment is being, or is about to be, provided for P as a matter of urgency and R considers that, having regard to the nature of the research and of the particular circumstances of the case it is also necessary to take action for the purposes of the research as a matter of urgency[15], but it is not reasonably practicable to consult under the provisions considered above[16], R may take the action if:

(A)   he has the agreement of a registered medical practitioner[17] who is not involved in the organisation or conduct of the research project[18]; or

(B)   where it is not reasonably practicable in the time available to obtain that agreement, he acts in accordance with a procedure approved by the appropriate body at the time when the research project was approved[19].

1   As to research projects see PARA 630. As to the approval requirements see PARA 631.
2   As to lack of capacity see PARA 603.
3   Mental Capacity Act 2005 s 32(1).
4   Mental Capacity Act 2005 s 32(2)(a).
5   Mental Capacity Act 2005 s 32(2)(b). The fact that a person is the donee of a lasting power of attorney given by P, or is P's deputy, does not prevent him from being the person consulted under s 32: s 32(7). As to the meaning of 'lasting power of attorney' see PARA 606 note 16; and see also PARA 618 et seq. As to the meaning of 'deputy' see PARA 606 note 18. See further the Department for Constitutional Affairs *Mental Capacity Act 2005 Code of Practice* (2007) paras 11.22–11.28.
6   As to the meaning of 'appropriate authority' see PARA 630 note 3.
7   Mental Capacity Act 2005 s 32(3)(a).
8   Mental Capacity Act 2005 s 32(3)(b).
9   Ie under the Mental Capacity Act 2005 s 32(2).
10   Ie under the Mental Capacity Act 2005 s 32(3).
11   Mental Capacity Act 2005 s 32(4)(a).
12   Mental Capacity Act 2005 s 32(4)(b).
13   Mental Capacity Act 2005 s 32(5)(a).
14   Mental Capacity Act 2005 s 32(5)(b). However, s 32(5)(b) (see head (ii) in the text) does not require treatment that P has been receiving as part of the project to be discontinued if R has reasonable grounds for believing that there would be a significant risk to P's health if it were discontinued: s 32(6). As to the meaning of 'treatment' see PARA 606 note 9.
15   Mental Capacity Act 2005 s 32(8)(a).
16   Mental Capacity Act 2005 s 32(8)(b).
17   As to registered medical practitioners see MEDICAL PROFESSIONS vol 74 (2011) PARA 176 et seq.
18   Mental Capacity Act 2005 s 32(9)(a). However R may not continue to act in reliance on s 32(9) if he has reasonable grounds for believing that it is no longer necessary to take the action as a matter of urgency: s 32(10).

19 Mental Capacity Act 2005 s 32(9)(b). As to approval of the research project see s 31; and PARA
    631. See note 18.

633. Additional safeguards. Nothing may be done to a person ('P') who is
taking part in an approved research project[1] (even though he lacks capacity[2] to
consent to taking part), or in relation to him in the course of the research[3]:

  (1) to which he appears to object (whether by showing signs of resistance or
       otherwise) except where what is being done is intended to protect him
       from harm or to reduce or prevent pain or discomfort[4]; or

  (2) which would be contrary to an advance decision[5] of his which has
       effect, or any other form of statement made by him and not
       subsequently withdrawn, of which the person conducting the research
       ('R') is aware[6].

The interests of P must be assumed to outweigh those of science and society[7].
If he indicates (in any way) that he wishes to be withdrawn from the project he
must be withdrawn without delay[8]. P must be withdrawn from the project,
without delay, if at any time the person conducting the research has reasonable
grounds for believing that one or more of the requirements for approval[9] is no
longer met in relation to research being carried out on, or in relation to, P[10].
However neither of the above provisions[11] requires treatment[12] that P has been
receiving as part of the project to be discontinued if R has reasonable grounds
for believing that there would be a significant risk to P's health if it were
discontinued[13].

1   As to research projects see PARA 630. As to the approval requirements see PARA 631.
2   As to lack of capacity see PARA 603.
3   See the Mental Capacity Act 2005 s 33(1), (2).
4   Mental Capacity Act 2005 s 33(2)(a). As to taking into consideration the wishes and feelings of
    P see the Department for Constitutional Affairs *Mental Capacity Act 2005 Code of Practice*
    (2007) paras 11.29–11.31.
5   As to the meaning of 'advance decision' see PARA 624.
6   Mental Capacity Act 2005 s 33(2)(b).
7   Mental Capacity Act 2005 s 33(3).
8   Mental Capacity Act 2005 s 33(4).
9   Ie the requirements set out in the Mental Capacity Act 2005 s 31(2)–(7): see PARA 631 heads
    (1)–(4).
10 Mental Capacity Act 2005 s 33(5).
11 Ie neither the Mental Capacity Act 2005 s 33(4) nor s 33(5).
12 As to the meaning of 'treatment' see PARA 606 note 9.
13 Mental Capacity Act 2005 s 33(6).

(vi) Independent Mental Capacity Advocate Service

634. In general. The Mental Capacity Act 2005[1] creates a new scheme for the
input of an independent consultee[2] where certain decisions need to be taken for
particularly vulnerable people who lack capacity[3]. Such decisions would include
serious medical treatment or changes in residence. The independent consultee
works with and supports people who lack capacity, and represents their views to
those who are working out their best interests[4]. The provisions are intended to
supplement the powers and duties conferred elsewhere in the Mental Capacity
Act 2005, and address concerns raised about safeguards for patients with a
mental disorder who lack capacity and are being treated in hospital[5].

1   See the Mental Capacity Act 2005 ss 35–41; and PARA 635 et seq.
2   Ie independent mental capacity advocates: see PARA 635.

3 As to lack of capacity see PARA 603. Such persons may include older people with dementia who have lost contact with friends and family, and people with severe learning difficulties and/or long-term mental health problems who have been in residential institutions for lengthy periods without external contacts.

4 See the Department for Constitutional Affairs *Mental Capacity Act 2005 Code of Practice* (2007) Chapter 10. The independent consultee carries no decision making powers.

5 See *R v Bournewood Community and Mental Health NHS Trust, ex p L* [1999] 1 AC 458, [1998] 3 All ER 289, HL; Application 45508/99 *HL v United Kingdom* (2004) 40 EHRR 761, 81 BMLR 131, ECtHR; and PARA 562 note 9.

635. Appointment of independent mental capacity advocates. The appropriate national authority[1] must make such arrangements as it considers reasonable to enable persons ('independent mental capacity advocates') to be available to represent and support persons to whom certain proposed acts or decisions[2] relate or who fall within certain provisions[3]. In making such arrangements, the appropriate authority must have regard to the principle that a person to whom a proposed act or decision relates should, so far as practicable, be represented and supported by a person who is independent of any person who will be responsible for the act or decision[4].

The appropriate national authority may make regulations as to the appointment of independent mental capacity advocates[5], which may, in particular, provide: (1) that a person may act as an independent mental capacity advocate only in such circumstances, or only subject to such conditions, as may be prescribed[6]; (2) for the appointment of a person as an independent mental capacity advocate to be subject to approval in accordance with the regulations[7].

For the purpose of enabling him to carry out his functions, an independent mental capacity advocate:

(a) may interview in private the person whom he has been instructed to represent[8]; and

(b) may, at all reasonable times, examine and take copies of: (i) any health record[9]; (ii) any record of a local authority[10], or held by it, compiled in connection with a social services function[11]; and

(c) any record held by a person registered under Part II of the Care Standards Act 2000[12] or Chapter 2 of Part 1 of the Health and Social Care Act 2008[13],

which the person holding the record considers may be relevant to the independent mental capacity advocate's investigation[14].

1 As to the meaning of 'appropriate national authority' see the Mental Capacity Act 2005 s 35(7); and PARA 567. As from 1 April 2013 this duty instead falls on the responsible authority and the Mental Capacity Act 2005 s 35(1), (4) are amended accordingly and s 35(6A), (6B) are added by the Health and Social Care Act 2012 Sch 5 para 134: see s 306(4); and the Health and Social Care Act 2012 (Commencement No 4, Transitional, Savings and Transitory Provisions) Order 2013, SI 2013/160, art 2(2). The 'responsible authority' means in relation to the provision of the services of independent mental capacity advocates in the area of a local authority in England, that local authority and, in relation to the provision of the services of independent mental capacity advocates in Wales, the Welsh Ministers: s 35(6A) (as so added). For this purpose 'local authority' has the meaning given in s 64(1) except that it does not include the council of a county or county borough in Wales: s 35(6B) (as so added).

2 Ie acts of decisions proposed under the Mental Capacity Act 2005 ss 37–39: see PARAS 638–640.

3 Mental Capacity Act 2005 s 35(1) (amended by the Mental Health Act 2007 Sch 9 para 3 and prospectively amended (see note 1)). As to the power to adjust the role of the independent mental capacity advocate see PARA 646. The certain provisions mentioned in the text are the Mental Capacity Act 2005 ss 39A, 39C or 39D (see PARAS 642–644). Such circumstances include a review of arrangements as to accommodation see the Mental Capacity Act 2005 (Independent Mental Capacity Advocates) (Expansion of Role) Regulations 2006,

SI 2006/2883, regs 2, 3; and the Mental Capacity Act 2005 (Independent Mental Capacity Advocates) (Wales) Regulations 2007, SI 2007/852, reg 8.

4 Mental Capacity Act 2005 s 35(4) (prospectively amended: see note 1). The arrangements may include provision for payments to be made to, or in relation to, persons carrying out functions in accordance with the arrangements: s 35(5). See note 3.

5 Mental Capacity Act 2005 s 35(2). As to such regulations see the Mental Capacity Act 2005 (Independent Mental Capacity Advocates) (General) Regulations 2006, SI 2006/1832, reg 5; the Mental Capacity Act 2005 (Independent Mental Capacity Advocates) (Wales) Regulations 2007, SI 2007/852, reg 5; and PARA 636.

6 Mental Capacity Act 2005 s 35(3)(a). 'Prescribed', in relation to regulations made under the Mental Capacity Act 2005, means prescribed by those regulations: s 64(1).

7 Mental Capacity Act 2005 s 35(3)(b).

8 Mental Capacity Act 2005 s 35(6)(a).

9 Mental Capacity Act 2005 s 35(6)(b)(i). 'Health record' has the meaning given in the Data Protection Act 1998 s 68, as read with s 69 (see CONFIDENCE AND INFORMATIONAL PRIVACY vol 19 (2011) PARAS 30, 97): Mental Capacity Act 2005 s 64(1).

10 'Local authority' (except in relation to the Mental Capacity Act 2005 Sch A1) means: (1) the council of a county in England in which there are no district councils; (2) the council of a district in England; (3) the council of a county or county borough in Wales; (4) the council of a London borough (see LONDON GOVERNMENT vol 71 (2013) PARAS 15, 20–22, 55 et seq); (5) the Common Council of the City of London (see LONDON GOVERNMENT vol 71 (2013) PARA 34 et seq); or (6) the Council of the Isles of Scilly (see LOCAL GOVERNMENT vol 69 (2009) PARA 36): Mental Capacity Act 2005 s 64(1) (definition amended by the Mental Health Act 2007 Sch 9 para 10(2)). As from 1 April 2013 the definition of 'local authority' is amended by the Health and Social Care Act 2012 Sch 5 para 135 and does not apply to the Mental Capacity Act 2005 s 35(6A)(a) (see note 1): see the Health and Social Care Act 2012 (Commencement No 4, Transitional, Savings and Transitory Provisions) Order 2013, SI 2013/160, art 2(2). As to areas and authorities in England see LOCAL GOVERNMENT vol 69 (2009) PARA 24 et seq; and as to areas and authorities in Wales see LOCAL GOVERNMENT vol 69 (2009) PARA 37 et seq.

11 Mental Capacity Act 2005 s 35(6)(b)(ii). 'Social services function' has the meaning given in the Local Authority Social Services Act 1970 s 1A (see LOCAL GOVERNMENT vol 69 (2009) PARA 588): Mental Capacity Act 2005 s 64(1).

12 Ie the Care Standards Act 2000 Pt II (ss 11–42): see SOCIAL SERVICES AND COMMUNITY CARE.

13 Mental Capacity Act 2005 s 35(6)(b)(iii) (amended by SI 2010/813). The reference in the text is to the Health and Social Care Act 2008 Pt 1 Chapter 2 (ss 8–44): see SOCIAL SERVICES AND COMMUNITY CARE.

14 Mental Capacity Act 2005 s 35(6).

636. Appointment requirements. Persons appointed as independent mental capacity advocates[1] must satisfy the appointment requirements[2]. These are that the person:

(1) has appropriate experience or training or an appropriate combination of experience and training[3];

(2) is a person of integrity and good character[4]; and

(3) is able to act independently of any person who instructs him[5].

1 Ie for the purposes of the Mental Capacity Act 2005 ss 37–39 (see PARAS 638–640) or regulations made by virtue of s 41 (see PARA 646).

2 See the Mental Capacity Act 2005 (Independent Mental Capacity Advocates) (General) Regulations 2006, SI 2006/1832, reg 5; and the Mental Capacity Act 2005 (Independent Mental Capacity Advocates) (Wales) Regulations 2007, SI 2007/852, reg 5 (amended by SI 2009/266). As to the training see further the Department for Constitutional Affairs *Mental Capacity Act 2005 Code of Practice* (2007) para 10.18.

3 See the Mental Capacity Act 2005 (Independent Mental Capacity Advocates) (General) Regulations 2006, SI 2006/1832, reg 5(2)(a); and the Mental Capacity Act 2005 (Independent Mental Capacity Advocates) (Wales) Regulations 2007, SI 2007/852, reg 5(6)(a). In relation to Wales, in determining whether a person meets the appointment requirement in head (1) in the text regard will be had to standards in guidance that may be issued: see reg 5(7). See further the Department for Constitutional Affairs *Mental Capacity Act 2005 Code of Practice* (2007) para 10.18.

4 See the Mental Capacity Act 2005 (Independent Mental Capacity Advocates) (General) Regulations 2006, SI 2006/1832, reg 5(2)(b); and the Mental Capacity Act 2005 (Independent Mental Capacity Advocates) (Wales) Regulations 2007, SI 2007/852, reg 5(6)(b). Before a determination is made in relation to any person for the purposes of head (2) in the text enhanced criminal records must be obtained: see the Mental Capacity Act 2005 (Independent Mental Capacity Advocates) (General) Regulations 2006, SI 2006/1832, reg 5(3) (substituted by SI 2009/2376); and the Mental Capacity Act 2005 (Independent Mental Capacity Advocates) (Wales) Regulations 2007, SI 2007/852, reg 5(8). As to the required independency see further the Department for Constitutional Affairs *Mental Capacity Act 2005 Code of Practice* (2007) para 10.19.
5 See the Mental Capacity Act 2005 (Independent Mental Capacity Advocates) (General) Regulations 2006, SI 2006/1832, reg 5(2)(c); and the Mental Capacity Act 2005 (Independent Mental Capacity Advocates) (Wales) Regulations 2007, SI 2007/852, reg 5(6)(c).

637. Functions of independent mental capacity advocates. The appropriate national authority[1] may make regulations as to the functions of independent mental capacity advocates[2].

The regulations may, in particular, make provision requiring an advocate to take such steps as may be prescribed[3] for the purpose of:

(1) providing support to the person whom he has been instructed to represent ('P') so that P may participate as fully as possible in any relevant decision[4];

(2) obtaining and evaluating relevant information[5];

(3) ascertaining what P's wishes and feelings would be likely to be, and the beliefs and values that would be likely to influence P, if he had capacity[6];

(4) ascertaining what alternative courses of action are available in relation to P[7];

(5) obtaining a further medical opinion where treatment is proposed and the advocate thinks that one should be obtained[8].

The regulations may also make provision as to circumstances in which the advocate may challenge, or provide assistance for the purpose of challenging, any relevant decision[9].

Such regulations provide that the independent mental capacity advocate must determine in all the circumstances how best to represent and support P[10]. In particular, the independent mental capacity advocate must:

(a) verify that the instructions were issued by an authorised person[11];

(b) to the extent that it is practicable and appropriate to do so, interview P and examine the records relevant to P[12] to which the independent mental capacity advocate has access[13];

(c) to the extent that it is practicable and appropriate to do so, consult persons engaged in providing care or treatment for P in a professional capacity or for remuneration and other persons who may be in a position to comment on P's wishes, feelings, beliefs or values[14]; and

(d) take all practicable steps to obtain such other information about P, or the act or decision that is proposed in relation to P, as the independent mental capacity advocate considers necessary[15].

The independent mental capacity advocate must evaluate all the information he has obtained for the purpose of:

(i) ascertaining the extent of the support provided to P to enable him to participate in making any decision about the matter in relation to which the independent mental capacity advocate has been instructed[16];

(ii) ascertaining what P's wishes and feelings would be likely to be, and the beliefs and values that would be likely to influence P, if he had capacity in relation to the proposed act or decision[17];

(iii)   ascertaining what alternative courses of action are available in relation to P[18];

(iv)   where medical treatment is proposed for P, ascertaining whether he would be likely to benefit from a further medical opinion[19].

The independent mental capacity advocate must prepare a report for the authorised person who instructed him and may include in the report such submissions as he considers appropriate in relation to P and the act or decision which is proposed in relation to him[20].

1   As to the meaning of ''appropriate national authority' see the Mental Capacity Act 2005 s 35(7); and PARA 567.
2   Mental Capacity Act 2005 s 36(1). As to independent mental capacity advocates see PARA 634. As to the role of the independent mental capacity advocate see the Department for Constitutional Affairs *Mental Capacity Act 2005 Code of Practice* (2007) para 10.20.
3   Ie prescribed by regulations under the Mental Capacity Act 2005: see s 64(1).
4   Mental Capacity Act 2005 s 36(2)(a).
5   Mental Capacity Act 2005 s 36(2)(b).
6   Mental Capacity Act 2005 s 36(2)(c). As to lack of capacity see PARA 603.
7   Mental Capacity Act 2005 s 36(2)(d).
8   Mental Capacity Act 2005 s 36(2)(e).
9   Mental Capacity Act 2005 s 36(3). Once a decision has been made the independent mental capacity advocate has the same rights to challenge the decision as he would have if he were a person (other than an independent mental capacity advocate) engaged in caring for the person or interested in his welfare: see the Mental Capacity Act 2005 (Independent Mental Capacity Advocates) (General) Regulations 2006, SI 2006/1832, reg 7; and PARA 647.
10   See the Mental Capacity Act 2005 (Independent Mental Capacity Advocates) (General) Regulations 2006, SI 2006/1832, reg 6(3); and the Mental Capacity Act 2005 (Independent Mental Capacity Advocates) (Wales) Regulations 2007, SI 2007/852, reg 6(2).
11   See the Mental Capacity Act 2005 (Independent Mental Capacity Advocates) (General) Regulations 2006, SI 2006/1832, reg 6(4)(a); and the Mental Capacity Act 2005 (Independent Mental Capacity Advocates) (Wales) Regulations 2007, SI 2007/852, reg 6(3)(a). In relation to England an 'authorised person' means a person who is required or enabled to instruct an independent mental capacity advocate under the Mental Capacity Act 2005 ss 37–39 or under regulations made by virtue of s 41 of the Act: Mental Capacity Act 2005 (Independent Mental Capacity Advocates) (General) Regulations 2006, SI 2006/1832, reg 6(2). In relation to Wales, the authorised person is an NHS body or local authority: see the Mental Capacity Act 2005 (Independent Mental Capacity Advocates) (Wales) Regulations 2007, SI 2007/852, reg 6(3)(a).
12   Ie the records to which the independent mental capacity advocate has access under the Mental Capacity Act 2005 s 35(6).
13   See the Mental Capacity Act 2005 (Independent Mental Capacity Advocates) (General) Regulations 2006, SI 2006/1832, reg 6(4)(b); and the Mental Capacity Act 2005 (Independent Mental Capacity Advocates) (Wales) Regulations 2007, SI 2007/852, reg 6(3)(b).
14   See the Mental Capacity Act 2005 (Independent Mental Capacity Advocates) (General) Regulations 2006, SI 2006/1832, reg 6(4)(c); and the Mental Capacity Act 2005 (Independent Mental Capacity Advocates) (Wales) Regulations 2007, SI 2007/852, reg 6(3)(c).
15   See the Mental Capacity Act 2005 (Independent Mental Capacity Advocates) (General) Regulations 2006, SI 2006/1832, reg 6(4)(d); and the Mental Capacity Act 2005 (Independent Mental Capacity Advocates) (Wales) Regulations 2007, SI 2007/852, reg 6(3)(d).
16   See the Mental Capacity Act 2005 (Independent Mental Capacity Advocates) (General) Regulations 2006, SI 2006/1832, reg 6(5)(a); and the Mental Capacity Act 2005 (Independent Mental Capacity Advocates) (Wales) Regulations 2007, SI 2007/852, reg 6(4)(a).
17   See the Mental Capacity Act 2005 (Independent Mental Capacity Advocates) (General) Regulations 2006, SI 2006/1832, reg 6(5)(b); and the Mental Capacity Act 2005 (Independent Mental Capacity Advocates) (Wales) Regulations 2007, SI 2007/852, reg 6(4)(b).
18   See the Mental Capacity Act 2005 (Independent Mental Capacity Advocates) (General) Regulations 2006, SI 2006/1832, reg 6(5)(c); and the Mental Capacity Act 2005 (Independent Mental Capacity Advocates) (Wales) Regulations 2007, SI 2007/852, reg 6(4)(c).
19   See the Mental Capacity Act 2005 (Independent Mental Capacity Advocates) (General) Regulations 2006, SI 2006/1832, reg 6(5)(d); and the Mental Capacity Act 2005 (Independent Mental Capacity Advocates) (Wales) Regulations 2007, SI 2007/852, reg 6(4)(d).

20 See the Mental Capacity Act 2005 (Independent Mental Capacity Advocates) (General) Regulations 2006, SI 2006/1832, reg 6(5), (6); and the Mental Capacity Act 2005 (Independent Mental Capacity Advocates) (Wales) Regulations 2007, SI 2007/852, reg 6(5), (6).

638. Provision of serious medical treatment by an NHS body. If an NHS body[1]: (1) is proposing to provide, or secure the provision of, serious medical treatment[2] for a person ('P') who lacks capacity[3] to consent to the treatment[4]; and (2) is satisfied that there is no person, other than one engaged in providing care or treatment for P in a professional capacity or for remuneration, whom it would be appropriate to consult in determining what would be in P's best interests[5], before such treatment is provided the NHS body must instruct an independent mental capacity advocate[6] to represent P[7]. If the treatment needs to be provided as a matter of urgency, it may be provided even though the NHS body has not been able to comply with this requirement[8].

The NHS body must, in providing or securing the provision of treatment for P, take into account any information given, or submissions made, by the independent mental capacity advocate[9].

1   'NHS body' has such meaning as may be prescribed by regulations made for the purposes of the Mental Capacity Act 2005 s 37 by: (1) the Secretary of State, in relation to bodies in England; or (2) the Welsh Ministers, in relation to bodies in Wales: s 37(7). 'Prescribed', in relation to regulations made under the Mental Capacity Act 2005, means prescribed by those regulations: see s 64(1). As to the meaning of 'England' see PARA 557 note 4; and as to the meaning of 'Wales' see PARA 557 note 5. For the purposes of ss 37 and 38, 'NHS body' means a body in England which is a Strategic Health Authority, an NHS foundation trust, a primary care trust, an NHS Trust or a care trust: Mental Capacity Act 2005 (Independent Mental Capacity Advocates) (General) Regulations 2006, SI 2006/1832, reg 3(1). For this purpose 'care trust' means a body designated as a Care Trust under the Health and Social Care Act 2001 s 45, 'NHS foundation trust' has the meaning given in the Health and Social Care (Community Health and Standards) Act 2003 s 1, 'NHS trust' means a body established under the National Health Service and Community Care Act 1990 s 5, 'primary care trust' means a body established under the National Health Service Act 1977 s 16A and 'strategic health authority' means a Strategic Health Authority established under the National Health Service Act 1977 s 8: Mental Capacity Act 2005 (Independent Mental Capacity Advocates) (General) Regulations 2006, SI 2006/1832, reg 3(2). For the purposes of the Mental Capacity Act 2005 ss 37 and 38 'NHS body' means a local health board, an NHS trust all or most of whose hospitals, establishments and facilities are situated in Wales, a Special Health Authority performing functions only or mainly in respect of Wales: Mental Capacity Act 2005 (Independent Mental Capacity Advocates) (Wales) Regulations 2007, SI 2007/852, reg 3. As from 1 April 2013 primary care trusts and strategic health authorities are abolished: see the Health and Social Care Act 2012 ss 33, 34; and HEALTH SERVICES; SOCIAL SERVICES AND COMMUNITY CARE. As from a day to be appointed, NHS trusts are also abolished: see s 179(1).

2   'Serious medical treatment' means treatment which involves providing, withholding or withdrawing treatment of a kind prescribed by regulations made by the appropriate authority: Mental Capacity Act 2005 s 37(6). As to the meaning of 'treatment' see PARA 606 note 9. As to the meaning of 'appropriate authority' see PARA 630 note 3. See note 1. For this purpose 'serious medical treatment' is treatment which involves providing, withdrawing or withholding treatment in circumstances where in a case where a single treatment is being proposed, there is a fine balance between its benefits to the patient and the burdens and risks it is likely to entail for him, in a case where there is a choice of treatments, a decision as to which one to use is finely balanced or what is proposed would be likely to involve serious consequences for the patient: Mental Capacity Act 2005 (Independent Mental Capacity Advocates) (General) Regulations 2006, SI 2006/1832, reg 4; Mental Capacity Act 2005 (Independent Mental Capacity Advocates) (Wales) Regulations 2007, SI 2007/852, reg 4.

3   As to lack of capacity see PARA 603.

4   Mental Capacity Act 2005 s 37(1)(a).

5   Mental Capacity Act 2005 s 37(1)(b). As to best interests see PARA 606.

6   As to independent mental capacity advocates see PARA 635.

7   Mental Capacity Act 2005 s 37(3). As to exceptions to the application of s 37(3) see PARA 645. Section 37 does not apply if P's treatment is regulated by the Mental Health Act 1983 Pt 4

(ss 56–64) or 4A (see ss 64A–64K): Mental Capacity Act 2005 s 37(2) (amended by the Mental Health Act 1983 s 35(4), (6)). See further the Department for Constitutional Affairs *Mental Capacity Act 2005 Code of Practice* (2007) paras 10.42–10.50.

8   Mental Capacity Act 2005 s 37(4).
9   Mental Capacity Act 2005 s 37(5).

639.   Provision of accommodation by NHS body. If an NHS body[1] proposes to make arrangements: (1) for the provision of accommodation in a hospital[2] or care home[3] for a person ('P') who lacks capacity[4] to agree to the arrangements[5]; or (2) for a change in P's accommodation to another hospital or care home[6], and is satisfied that there is no person (other than one engaged in providing care or treatment[7] for P in a professional capacity or for remuneration)[8] whom it would be appropriate for it to consult in determining what would be in P's best interests[9], then before making such arrangements the NHS body must instruct an independent mental capacity advocate[10] to represent P unless it is satisfied that: (a) the accommodation is likely to be provided for a continuous period which is less than the applicable period[11]; or (b) the arrangements need to be made as a matter of urgency[12].

If the NHS body: (i) did not instruct an independent mental capacity advocate to represent P before making the arrangements because it was satisfied that head (a) or head (b) above applied[13]; but (ii) subsequently has reason to believe that the accommodation is likely to be provided for a continuous period beginning with the day on which accommodation was first provided in accordance with the arrangements, and ending on or after the expiry of the applicable period[14], it must instruct an independent mental capacity advocate to represent P[15].

The NHS body must, in deciding what arrangements to make for P, take into account any information given, or submissions made, by the independent mental capacity advocate[16].

1   As to the meaning of 'NHS body' see: s 38(8); and PARA 638 note 1.
2   As to the meaning of 'hospital' see PARA 577.
3   'Care home' has the meaning given in the Care Standards Act 2000 s 3 (see SOCIAL SERVICES AND COMMUNITY CARE): Mental Capacity Act 2005 s 38(6).
4   As to lack of capacity see PARA 603.
5   Mental Capacity Act 2005 s 38(1)(a).
6   Mental Capacity Act 2005 s 38(1)(b).
7   As to the meaning of 'treatment' see PARA 606 note 9.
8   For the purposes of the Mental Capacity Act 2005 s 38(1), a person appointed under Sch A1 Pt 10 (see PARAS 707–712) to be P's representative is not, by virtue of that appointment, engaged in providing care or treatment for P in a professional capacity or for remuneration: s 38(10) (added by the Mental Health Act 2007 Sch 90 para 4(3)).
9   Mental Capacity Act 2005 s 38(1). Section 38 does not apply if P is accommodated as a result of an obligation imposed on him under the Mental Health Act 1983: Mental Capacity Act 2005 s 38(2). Nor does it apply if an independent mental capacity advocate must be appointed under s 39A or 39C (see PARAS 642, 643) (whether or not by the NHS body) to represent P and the hospital or care home in which P is to be accommodated under the arrangements referred to in s 38 is the relevant hospital or care home under the authorisation referred to that provision: s 38(2A) (added by the Mental Health Act 2007 Sch 9 para 4(2)).
10   As to independent mental capacity advocates see PARA 635. See further the Department for Constitutional Affairs *Mental Capacity Act 2005 Code of Practice* (2007) paras 10.51–10.58.
11   Mental Capacity Act 2005 s 38(3)(a). 'Applicable period' means: (1) in relation to accommodation in a hospital, 28 days; and (2) in relation to accommodation in a care home, eight weeks: s 38(9). As to exceptions to the application of s 38(3) see PARA 645.
12   Mental Capacity Act 2005 s 38(3)(b). See note 11.
13   Mental Capacity Act 2005 s 38(4)(a). As to exceptions to the application of s 38(4) see PARA 645.
14   Mental Capacity Act 2005 s 38(4)(b).

15 Mental Capacity Act 2005 s 38(4).
16 Mental Capacity Act 2005 s 38(5).

640. Provision of accommodation by local authority. If a local authority[1] proposes to make arrangements: (1) for the provision of residential accommodation for a person ('P') who lacks capacity[2] to agree to the arrangements[3]; or (2) for a change in P's residential accommodation[4], and is satisfied that there is no person (other than one engaged in providing care or treatment for P in a professional capacity or for remuneration)[5] whom it would be appropriate for it to consult in determining what would be in P's best interests[6], then before making such arrangements the local authority must instruct an independent mental capacity advocate[7] to represent P unless it is satisfied that: (a) the accommodation is likely to be provided for a continuous period of less than eight weeks[8]; or (b) the arrangements need to be made as a matter of urgency[9].

If the local authority: (i) did not instruct an independent mental capacity advocate to represent P before making the arrangements because it was satisfied that head (a) or head (b) above applied[10]; but (ii) subsequently has reason to believe that the accommodation is likely to be provided for a continuous period that will end eight weeks or more after the day on which accommodation was first provided in accordance with the arrangements[11], it must instruct an independent mental capacity advocate to represent P[12].

The local authority must, in deciding what arrangements to make for P, take into account any information given, or submissions made, by the independent mental capacity advocate[13].

1   As to the meaning of 'local authority' see PARA 635 note 10.
2   As to lack of capacity see PARA 603.
3   Mental Capacity Act 2005 s 39(1)(a).
4   Mental Capacity Act 2005 s 39(1)(b).
5   For the purposes of the Mental Capacity Act 2005 a person appointed under Sch A1 Pt 10 to be P's representative is not, by virtue of that appointment, engaged in providing care or treatment for P in a professional capacity or for remuneration: s 39(7) (added by the Mental Health Act 2007 Sch 9 para 5(3)).
6   Mental Capacity Act 2005 s 39(1).
7   As to independent mental capacity advocates see PARA 635. See further the Department for Constitutional Affairs *Mental Capacity Act 2005 Code of Practice* (2007) paras 10.51–10.58.
8   Mental Capacity Act 2005 s 39(4)(a). As to exceptions to the application of s 39(4) see PARA 645. Section 39 applies only if the accommodation is to be provided in accordance with: (1) the National Assistance Act 1948 s 21 or s 29 (see SOCIAL SERVICES AND COMMUNITY CARE vol 44(2) (Reissue) PARA 1029 et seq); or (2) the Mental Health Act 1983 s 117 (see PARA 574), as the result of a decision taken by the local authority under the National Health Service and Community Care Act 1990 s 47 (see SOCIAL SERVICES AND COMMUNITY CARE vol 44(2) (Reissue) PARA 1015): Mental Capacity Act 2005 s 39(2). In addition, s 39 does not apply if P is accommodated as a result of an obligation imposed on him under the Mental Health Act 1983 (eg a conditional discharge: see PARAS 914, 969): Mental Capacity Act 2005 s 39(3). Nor does s 39 apply if an independent mental capacity advocate must be appointed under s 39A or 39C (whether or not by the local authority) to represent P, and the place in which P is to be accommodated under the arrangements referred to in s 39 is the relevant hospital or care home under the authorisation referred to in that provision: s 39(3A) (added by the Mental Health Act 2007 Sch 9 para 5(2)). See also PARA 787 head (1).
9   Mental Capacity Act 2005 s 39(4)(b). See note 8.
10 Mental Capacity Act 2005 s 39(5)(a). As to exceptions to the application of s 39(5) see PARA 645.
11 Mental Capacity Act 2005 s 39(5)(b). See note 10.
12 Mental Capacity Act 2005 s 39(5). See note 10.
13 Mental Capacity Act 2005 s 39(6).

641. Adult protection cases. The following apply[1] where an NHS body[2] or a local authority[3] proposes to take, or proposes to arrange to be taken, protective measures[4] in relation to a person (P) who lacks capacity to agree to one or more of the measures[5] and the proposal is made, or the measures have been taken, following the receipt of an allegation or evidence that P is being, or has been, abused or neglected by another person or that P is abusing, or has abused, another person[6]. The NHS body or local authority may instruct an independent mental capacity advocate to represent P if it is satisfied that it would be of particular benefit to P to be so represented[7].

An NHS body or local authority which instructs an independent mental capacity advocate must, in making any decision resulting from a review or arrangements as to P's accommodation or in making a decision, or further decision, about protective measures in relation to P, take into account any information given, or submissions made, by the independent mental capacity advocate[8].

1 An independent mental capacity advocate may not be instructed under these provisions where the Mental Capacity Act 2005 ss 37, 38 or 39 (see PARAS 638–640) or, in relation to England, the Mental Capacity Act 2005 (Independent Mental Capacity Advocates) (Expansion of Role) Regulations 2006, SI 2006/2883, reg 3 or, in relation to Wales, the Mental Capacity Act 2005 (Independent Mental Capacity Advocates) (Wales) Regulations 2007, SI 2007/852, reg 8 (see PARA 635), apply: see the Mental Capacity Act 2005 (Independent Mental Capacity Advocates) (Expansion of Role) Regulations 2006, SI 2006/2883, reg 4(1)(c); and the Mental Capacity Act 2005 (Independent Mental Capacity Advocates) (Wales) Regulations 2007, SI 2007/852, reg 9(4).

2 In relation to England, an 'NHS body' means a body in England which is a Strategic Health Authority, an NHS foundation trust, a Primary Care Trust, an NHS Trust or a Care Trust: Mental Capacity Act 2005 (Independent Mental Capacity Advocates) (Expansion of Role) Regulations 2006, SI 2006/2883, reg 1(4). 'Care Trust' means a body designated as a Care Trust under the Health and Social Care Act 2001 s 45; 'NHS foundation trust' has the meaning given in the Health and Social Care (Community Health and Standards) Act 2003 s 1; 'NHS trust' means a body established under the National Health Service and Community Care Act 1990 s 5; 'Primary Care Trust' means a body established under the National Health Service Act 1977 s 16A; and 'Strategic Health Authority' means a Strategic Health Authority established under the National Health Service Act 1977 s 8: Mental Capacity Act 2005 (Independent Mental Capacity Advocates) (Expansion of Role) Regulations 2006, SI 2006/2883, reg 1(5). As to Strategic Health Authorities see HEALTH SERVICES vol 54 (2008) PARAS 94–110. As to NHS foundation trusts see HEALTH SERVICES vol 54 (2008) PARAS 174–187. As to Primary Care Trusts see HEALTH SERVICES vol 54 (2008) PARAS 111–135. As to Care Trusts see HEALTH SERVICES vol 54 (2008) PARA 235. In relation to Wales, an 'NHS body' means a Local Health Board, an NHS trust all or most of whose hospitals, establishments and facilities are situated in Wales, a Special Health Authority performing functions only or mainly in respect of Wales: Mental Capacity Act 2005 (Independent Mental Capacity Advocates) (Wales) Regulations 2007, SI 2007/852, reg 3. As to local health boards see HEALTH SERVICES vol 54 (2008) PARA 74; and as to Special Health Authorities see HEALTH SERVICES vol 54 (2008) PARA 136. As from 1 April 2013 primary care trusts and strategic health authorities are abolished: see the Health and Social Care Act 2012 ss 33, 34; and HEALTH SERVICES; SOCIAL SERVICES AND COMMUNITY CARE. As from a day to be appointed, NHS trusts are also abolished: see s 179(1).

3 In relation to Wales, 'local authority' means a county or county borough council in Wales: Mental Capacity Act 2005 (Independent Mental Capacity Advocates) (Wales) Regulations 2007, SI 2007/852, reg 2(1).

4 'Protective measures' includes measures to minimise the risk that any abuse or neglect of P, or abuse by P, will continue and, in relation to Wales, includes measures taken in pursuance of guidance issued under the Local Authority Social Services Act 1970 s 7 (see SOCIAL SERVICES AND COMMUNITY CARE vol 44(2) (Reissue) PARA 1011): Mental Capacity Act 2005 (Independent Mental Capacity Advocates) (Expansion of Role) Regulations 2006, SI 2006/2883, reg 4(2).

5 Mental Capacity Act 2005 (Independent Mental Capacity Advocates) (Expansion of Role) Regulations 2006, SI 2006/2883, reg 4(1)(a). In relation to England, the proposal must be made

in pursuant to guidance issued under the Local Authority Social Services Act 1970 s 7 (see SOCIAL SERVICES AND COMMUNITY CARE vol 44(2) (Reissue) PARA 1011).

6   Mental Capacity Act 2005 (Independent Mental Capacity Advocates) (Expansion of Role) Regulations 2006, SI 2006/2883, reg 4(1)(b).

7   Mental Capacity Act 2005 (Independent Mental Capacity Advocates) (Expansion of Role) Regulations 2006, SI 2006/2883, reg 5(1). As to the involvement of an independent mental capacity advocate in care reviews and adult protection cases see further the Department for Constitutional Affairs *Mental Capacity Act 2005 Code of Practice* (2007) paras 10.62–10.68.

8   Mental Capacity Act 2005 (Independent Mental Capacity Advocates) (Expansion of Role) Regulations 2006, SI 2006/2883, reg 5(2).

642.   Person is subject to deprivation of liberty provisions. If a person ('P') becomes subject to deprivation of liberty provisions[1] and the managing authority of the relevant hospital or care home[2] is satisfied that there is no person, other than one engaged in providing care or treatment for P in a professional capacity or for remuneration, whom it would be appropriate to consult in determining what would be in P's best interests, the managing authority must notify the supervisory body accordingly[3].

The supervisory body must instruct an independent mental capacity advocate[4] to represent P[5].

1   Ie subject to the Mental Capacity Act 2005 Sch A1 (see PARAS 695–706). P becomes subject to Sch A1 in any of the following cases:
    (1)   where an urgent authorisation is given in relation to P under Sch A1 para 76(2) (urgent authorisation given before request made for standard authorisation: see PARA 713) (s 39B(2), (3) (ss 39A, 39B added by the Mental Health Act 2007 Sch 9 para 6));
    (2)   where the following conditions are met:
        (a)   a request is made under Sch A1 for a standard authorisation to be given in relation to P ('the requested authorisation') (s 39B(4), (5) (as so added)).
        (b)   no urgent authorisation was given under Sch A1 para 76(2) before that request was made (s 39B(6) (as so added));
        (c)   the requested authorisation will not be in force on or before, or immediately after, the expiry of an existing standard authorisation (s 39B(7) (as so added));
        (d)   the expiry of a standard authorisation is the date when the authorisation is expected to cease to be in force (s 39B(8) (as so added));
    (3)   where, under Sch A1 para 69 (see PARA 679), the supervisory body select a person to carry out an assessment of whether or not the relevant person is a detained resident (s 39B(9) (as so added)).
2   As to the meaning of 'managing authority (of hospital, care home and independent hospital)' see PARA 652. As to the meaning of 'relevant hospital or care home' see PARA 663 note 2.
3   Mental Capacity Act 2005 s 39A(1) (as added: see note 1). As to the meaning of 'supervisory body' see PARA 664. For the purposes of the Mental Capacity Act 2005 s 39A(1), a person appointed under Sch A1 Pt 10 to be P's representative is not, by virtue of that appointment, engaged in providing care or treatment for P in a professional capacity or for remuneration: s 39A(6) (as so added).
4   As to independent mental capacity advocates see PARA 635. The Mental Capacity Act 2005 Sch A1 makes provision about the role of an independent mental capacity advocate appointed under s 39A and s 39A is subject to Sch A1 para 161 (see PARA 707): see s 39A(4), (5) (as added: see note 1).
5   Mental Capacity Act 2005 s 39A(2) (as added: see note 1).

643.   Person unrepresented whilst subject to deprivation of liberty provisions. If a deprivation of liberty authorisation[1] is in force in relation to a person ('P'), the appointment of a person as P's representative ends in accordance with regulations[2] and the managing authority of the relevant hospital or care home[3] are satisfied that there is no person, other than one engaged in providing care or treatment for P in a professional capacity or for remuneration, whom it would be appropriate to consult in determining what would be in P's best interests, the managing authority must notify the supervisory body[4] accordingly[5].

The supervisory body must instruct an independent mental capacity advocate[6] to represent P[7].

1   Ie an authorisation under the Mental Capacity Act 2005 Sch A1.
2   Ie regulations made under the Mental Capacity Act 2005 Sch A1 Pt 10.
3   As to the meaning of 'managing authority (of hospital, care home and independent hospital)' see PARA 652. As to the meaning of 'relevant hospital or care home' see PARA 663 note 2.
4   As to the meaning of 'supervisory body' see PARA 664.
5   See the Mental Capacity Act 2005 s 39C(1), (2) (s 39C added by the Mental Health Act 2007 Sch 9 para 6).
6   As to independent mental capacity advocates see PARA 635. The Mental Capacity Act 2005 Sch A1 para 159 (see PARA 683) makes provision about the role of an independent mental capacity advocate appointed under s 39C: s 39C(4) (as added: see note 5). The appointment of an independent mental capacity advocate under s 39C ends when a new appointment of a person as P's representative is made in accordance with Sch A1 Pt 10: s 39C(5) (as so added). For the purposes of s 39C(1), a person appointed under Sch A1 Pt 10 to be P's representative is not, by virtue of that appointment, engaged in providing care or treatment for P in a professional capacity or for remuneration: s 39C(6) (as so added).
7   Mental Capacity Act 2005 s 39C(3) (as added: see note 5).

644. Person subject to deprivation of liberty provisions without paid representation. If a deprivation of liberty authorisation[1] is in force in relation to a person ('P'), P has a representative ('R')[2] and R is not being paid under regulations[3] for acting as P's representative, the supervisory body[4] must instruct an independent mental capacity advocate[5] to represent P in any of the following cases[6]:

(1)   where P makes a request to the supervisory body to instruct an advocate[7];

(2)   where R makes a request to the supervisory body to instruct an advocate[8];

(3)   where the supervisory body have reason to believe one or more of the following:

    (a)   that, without the help of an advocate, P and R would be unable to exercise one or both of the relevant rights[9];

    (b)   that P and R have each failed to exercise a relevant right when it would have been reasonable to exercise it[10];

    (c)   that P and R are each unlikely to exercise a relevant right when it would be reasonable to exercise it[11].

If an advocate is appointed under these provisions, the advocate is, in particular, to take such steps as are practicable to help P and R to understand the effect of the authorisation, the purpose of the authorisation, the duration of the authorisation, any conditions to which the authorisation is subject, the reasons why each assessor who carried out an assessment in connection with the request for the authorisation, or in connection with a review of the authorisation, decided that P met the qualifying requirement in question, the relevant rights and how to exercise the relevant rights[12].

The advocate is, in particular, to take such steps as are practicable to help P or R to exercise the right to apply to court, if it appears to the advocate that P or R wishes to exercise that right, or to exercise the right of review[13], if it appears to the advocate that P or R wishes to exercise that right[14].

1   Ie an authorisation under the Mental Capacity Act 2005 Sch A1.
2   Ie a representative appointed under the Mental Capacity Act 2005 Sch A1 Pt 10.
3   Ie regulations under the Mental Capacity Act 2005 Sch A1 Pt 10.
4   As to the meaning of 'supervisory body' see PARA 664.
5   As to independent mental capacity advocates see PARA 635.

6 Mental Capacity Act 2005 s 39D(1), (2) (ss 39D, 39E added by the Mental Health Act 2007 Sch 9 para 6). If an advocate is already representing P in accordance with an instruction under the Mental Capacity Act 2005 s 39D, s 39D(2) does not require another advocate to be instructed, unless the existing advocate was instructed because of a request by R or because the supervisory body had reason to believe one or more of the things in s 39D(5) and P has requested the other advocated is instructed: see ss 39D(6), 39E (as so added).

7 Mental Capacity Act 2005 s 39D(3) (as added: see note 6).

8 Mental Capacity Act 2005 s 39D(4) (as added: see note 6).

9 Mental Capacity Act 2005 s 39D(5)(a) (as added: see note 6). For these purposes 'relevant rights' means the right to apply to court and the right of review: s 39D(10) (as so added). The 'right to apply to court' means the right to make an application to the court to exercise its jurisdiction under s 21A (see PARA 733) and the 'right of review' means the right under Sch A1 Pt 8: s 39D(10) (as so added).

10 Mental Capacity Act 2005 s 39D(5)(b) (as added: see note 6).

11 Mental Capacity Act 2005 s 39D(5)(c) (as added: see note 6).

12 Mental Capacity Act 2005 s 39D(7) (as added: see note 6).

13 If the advocate helps P or R to exercise the right of review: (1) the advocate may make submissions to the supervisory body on the question of whether a qualifying requirement is reviewable; (2) the advocate may give information, or make submissions, to any assessor carrying out a review assessment: Mental Capacity Act 2005 s 39D(9) (as added: see note 6).

14 Mental Capacity Act 2005 s 39D(9) (as added: see note 6).

645. Exceptions to the involvement of an independent mental capacity advocate. The duty imposed[1] as to the involvement of an independent mental capacity advocate[2] does not apply where there is:

(1) a person nominated by the relevant person lacking capacity ('P') (in whatever manner) as a person to be consulted on matters to which that duty relates[3];

(2) a donee of a lasting power of attorney[4] created by P who is authorised to make decisions in relation to those matters[5];

(3) a deputy appointed by the Court of Protection for P with power to make decisions in relation to those matters[6].

1 Ie the duty imposed by the Mental Capacity Act 2005 s 37(3) (see PARA 638), 38(3) or (4) (see PARA 639), 39(4) or (5) (see PARA 640), 39A(3) (see PARA 642), 39C(3) (see PARA 643)or 39D(2) (see PARA 644).

2 As to independent mental capacity advocates see PARA 635.

3 Mental Capacity Act 2005 s 40(1)(a) (s 40 substituted and s 40(1) numbered as such and amended and s 40(2) added by the Mental Health Act 2007 s 49, Sch 9 para 7). A person appointed under the Mental Capacity Act 2005 Sch A1 (see PARAS 695–706) to be P's representative is not, by virtue of that appointment, a person nominated by P as a person to be consulted in matters to which a duty mentioned in s 40(1) relates: s 40(2) (as so added).

4 As to lasting powers of attorney see PARA 618 et seq.

5 Mental Capacity Act 2005 s 40(1)(b) (as substituted: see note 3).

6 Mental Capacity Act 2005 s 40(1)(c) (as substituted: see note 3). As to the Court of Protection see PARA 720.

646. Power to adjust role of independent mental capacity advocate. The appropriate national authority[1] may make regulations: (1) expanding the role of independent mental capacity advocates[2] in relation to persons who lack capacity[3]; and (2) adjusting the obligation to make arrangements imposed by the provision on the appointment of such advocates[4].

The regulations may, in particular: (a) prescribe certain circumstances[5] in which an independent mental capacity advocate must, or circumstances in which one may, be instructed by a person of a prescribed[6] description to represent a person who lacks capacity[7]; and (b) include provision similar to any made by the provisions in relation to: (i) serious medical treatment by an NHS body; (ii) accommodation by an NHS body; (iii) accommodation by a local authority; or (iv) exceptions[8].

1 As to the meaning of 'appropriate national authority' see the Mental Capacity Act 2005 ss 35(7), 41(3); and PARA 567.
2 As to independent mental capacity advocates see PARA 635.
3 Mental Capacity Act 2005 s 41(1)(a). As to such regulations see the Mental Capacity Act 2005 (Independent Mental Capacity Advocates) (Expansion of Role) Regulations 2006, SI 2006/2883; and the Mental Capacity Act 2005 (Independent Mental Capacity Advocates) (Wales) Regulations 2007, SI 2007/852.
4 Mental Capacity Act 2005 s 41(1)(b). The provision referred to in the text is s 35: see PARA 635.
5 Ie circumstances different to those in the Mental Capacity Act 2005 s 37 (see PARA 638), s 38 (see PARA 639) and s 39 (see PARA 640).
6 Ie prescribed by regulations under the Mental Capacity Act 2005: see s 64(1).
7 Mental Capacity Act 2005 s 41(2)(a). As to lack of capacity see PARA 603.
8 Mental Capacity Act 2005 s 41(2)(b). The provisions referred to in the text are those of s 37 (see PARA 638), s 38 (see PARA 639), s 39 (see PARA 640) or s 40 (see PARA 645).

647. Challenges to decisions affecting persons who lack capacity. In relation to England, where an independent mental capacity advocate has been instructed to represent a person ('P') in relation to any matter and a decision affecting P (including a decision as to his capacity) is made in that matter, the independent mental capacity advocate has the same rights to challenge the decision as he would have if he were a person (other than an independent mental capacity advocate) engaged in caring for P or interested in his welfare[1].

In relation to Wales, where an independent mental capacity advocate has been instructed to act and a decision (including a decision as to P's capacity) is made in relation to P the independent mental capacity advocate has the same rights to challenge the decision as if he were a person (other than an independent mental capacity advocate) who was entitled[2] to be consulted in relation to a matter about which the independent mental capacity advocate is now instructed or it would otherwise be appropriate for an NHS body or a local authority to consult[3].

1 Mental Capacity Act 2005 (Independent Mental Capacity Advocates) (General) Regulations 2006, SI 2006/1832, reg 7.
2 Ie entitled in accordance with the Mental Capacity Act 2005 s 4(7)(b) (see PARA 606).
3 Mental Capacity Act 2005 (Independent Mental Capacity Advocates) (Wales) Regulations 2007, SI 2007/852, reg 7.

(3) DEPRIVATION OF LIBERTY UNDER THE MENTAL CAPACITY ACT 2005

(i) Introduction

648. Deprivation of liberty. The Mental Health Act 1983 provides for the informal admission of a patient suffering from a mental disorder for the treatment of that disorder[1]. However, where a person lacks capacity to consent to his care or treatment, and such care or treatment whether for mental disorder or not amounts to deprivation of liberty[2], there will be a breach of that person's right to liberty if it is not accompanied by certain safeguards[3]. Provision is now made for such circumstances under the Mental Capacity Act 2005.

The Mental Capacity Act 2005 does not authorise any person ('D') to deprive any other person ('P') of his liberty[4]. However D may deprive P of his liberty if, by doing so, D is giving effect to an order of the Court of Protection[5] on a personal welfare issue[6] or if deprivation of liberty is necessary for life-sustaining treatment[7] or if a standard or urgent authorisation[8] is in force[9].

References within the Mental Capacity Act 2005 to deprivation of a person's liberty have the same meaning as in the Convention for the Protection of Human Rights and Fundamental Freedoms article 5[10] and it does not matter whether a person is deprived of his liberty by a public authority or not[11].

Deprivation of liberty has to be distinguished from restraint and restraint by itself is not deprivation of liberty; account must be taken of the individual's whole situation[12]. The difference between deprivation of and restriction upon liberty is one of degree or intensity, and not one of nature or substance[13]. In relation to persons lacking capacity deprivation of liberty has been held to occur where three conditions are established: (1) the objective element of a person's confinement to a certain limited place for a not negligible length of time; (2) the additional subjective element that the person has not validly consented to the confinement in question; and (3) the confinement must be imputable to the State[14]. There is some overlap between these three elements and whether the person objects to the confinement which is imposed is a relevant consideration[15].

1 See the Mental Health Act 1983 s 131; and PARA 764.
2 Ie within the meaning of the Convention for the Protection of Human Rights and Fundamental Freedoms (Rome, 4 November 1950; TS 71 (1953); Cmd 8969) ('the European Convention on Human Rights'), art 5 (see RIGHTS AND FREEDOMS).
3 See Application 45508/99 *HL v United Kingdom* (2004) 40 EHRR 761, 81 BMLR 131, (2004) Times, 19 October, ECtHR.
4 Mental Capacity Act 2005 s 4A(1) (s 4A added by the Mental Health Act 2007 s 50(2)). As to detention under the Mental Health Act 1983 see PARA 766 et seq.
5 Ie an order under the Mental Capacity Act 2005 s 16(2)(a) (see PARA 724). As to the Court of Protection see PARA 720 et seq.
6 See the Mental Capacity Act 2005 s 4A(2)(a), (4) (as added: see note 4).
7 Ie the Mental Capacity Act 2005 s 4B (see PARA 650).
8 Ie an authorisation under the Mental Capacity Act 2005 Sch A1 (see PARAS 695–706).
9 See the Mental Capacity Act 2005 s 4A(2)(b), (5) (as added: see note 4).
10 Ie the Convention for the Protection of Human Rights and Fundamental Freedoms (Rome, 4 November 1950; TS 71 (1953) Cmd 8969), art 5. As to art 5 see RIGHTS AND FREEDOMS. As to when deprivation of liberty of a person with an unsound mind is permissible under art 5 see RIGHTS AND FREEDOMS. As to when there has been a deprivation of liberty under art 5 see RIGHTS AND FREEDOMS.
11 Mental Capacity Act 2005 s 64(5), (6) (added by the Mental Health Act 2007 Sch 9 para 10(4)).
12 See *Cheshire West and Cheshire Council v P* [2011] EWCA Civ 1257, [2012] PTSR 1447, [2012] 1 FLR 693. See also *Re A (a child)(deprivation of liberty) Re C (vulnerable adult) (deprivation of liberty)* [2010] EWHC 978 (Fam), [2010] 2 FLR 1363, [2010] Fam Law 929 (the loving, caring, regime in a family home with a reasonable, proportionate and entirely appropriate regime implemented by devoted parents in the context of a loving family relationship and with the single view to the welfare, happiness and best interests of the child falls significantly short of anything that would engage the European Convention on Human Rights, art 5); *C (by his litigation friend the Official Solicitor) v Blackburn with Darwen Borough Council* [2011] EWHC 3321 COP, [2011] All ER (D) 203 (Dec) (existence of locked doors and a requirement of supervision are not in themselves a deprivation of liberty, where their purpose is to protect a resident from the consequence of an epileptic fit, or harm caused by a lack of awareness of risk, or from self-harm).
   The Code of Practice provides a list of factors relevant to identifying whether steps taken involve more than restraint and amount to a deprivation of liberty: see the Ministry of Justice *Deprivation of Liberty Safeguards – code of practice to supplement the main Mental Capacity Act 2005 code of practice* (2008) Pt 3. As to the Code of Practice see PARA 602.
13 See *Guzzardi v Italy* (1980) 3 EHRR 333; *Ashingdane v United Kingdom* (1985) 7 EHRR 528, ECtHR; and RIGHTS AND FREEDOMS. The notion of deprivation of liberty within the meaning of the European Convention on Human Rights art 5(1) does not only comprise the objective element of a person's confinement to a certain limited place for a not negligible length of time; a

person can only be considered as being deprived of his or her liberty if, as an additional subjective element, he has not validly consented to the confinement in question: see *Storck v Germany* (2005) 43 EHRR 96, [2005] ECHR 61603/00. In order to determine whether there has been a deprivation of liberty, the starting-point is the specific situation of the individual concerned and account must be taken of a whole range of factors arising in a particular case such as the type, duration, effects and manner of implementation of the measure in question: Application 45508/99 *HL v United Kingdom* (2004) 40 EHRR 761, 81 BMLR 131, ECtHR.

14 See *Storck v Germany* (2005) 43 EHRR 96, [2005] ECHR 61603/00 (as discussed in *P (otherwise known as MIG) (by the Official Solicitor, their litigation friend) v Surrey County Council (Equality and Human Rights Commission intervening)* [2011] EWCA Civ 190, [2012] Fam 170, [2012] 2 WLR 1056); and RIGHTS AND FREEDOMS.

15 See *P (otherwise known as MIG) (by the Official Solicitor, their litigation friend) v Surrey County Council (Equality and Human Rights Commission intervening)* [2011] EWCA Civ 190, [2012] Fam 170, [2012] 2 WLR 1056.

649.   Transporting persons lacking capacity.   Transporting a person who lacks capacity from their home, or another location, to a hospital or care home will not usually amount to a deprivation of liberty[1]. However in certain circumstances for example where it is necessary to do more than persuade or restrain the person for the purpose of transportation, or where the journey is exceptionally long, it may be necessary to seek an order from the Court of Protection[2] to ensure that the journey is taken on a lawful basis[3].

Guidance has been drawn up to cover circumstances where someone lacking capacity or under a disability requires to be removed from premises with the help of the police[4].

1 Ministry of *Justice Deprivation of Liberty Safeguards – code of practice to supplement the main Mental Capacity Act 2005 code of practice* (2008) para 2.14. As to what may constitute a deprivation of liberty see PARA 648.

2 As to the Court of Protection see PARA 720. The gap relating to transportation of a person to a hospital or care home can be filled by the Court of Protection: see *GJv Foundation Trust* [2009] EWHC 2972 at [75], [2010] Fam 70 at [75], [2010] 3 WLR 840.

3 Ministry of *Justice Deprivation of Liberty Safeguards – code of practice to supplement the main Mental Capacity Act 2005 code of practice* (2008) para 2.15.

4 See *LBH v GP* (claim no FD08P01058) (8 April 2009, unreported) (such guidance requires an application to the court with the agreement of the police prior to the hearing, if there is no agreement consideration should be given to inviting the police to attend the hearing). See further *DCC v KH* (case no 11729380) (11 September 2009, unreported) (where a standard authorisation is in place this is sufficient protection for the relevant authority).

650.   Life sustaining treatment.   If the following conditions are met, 'D' is authorised to deprive 'P' of his liberty while a decision as respects any relevant issue is sought from the court[1].

The first condition is that there is a question about whether D is authorised to deprive P of his liberty[2].

The second condition is that the deprivation of liberty is:

(1)   wholly or partly for the purpose of giving P life-sustaining treatment or doing any vital act[3]; or

(2)   consists wholly or partly of giving P life-sustaining treatment or doing any vital act[4].

The third condition is that the deprivation of liberty is necessary in order to give the life-sustaining treatment or do the vital act[5].

1 Mental Capacity Act 2005 s 4B(1) (added by the Mental Health Act 2007 s 50(2)).

2 Ie under the Mental Capacity Act 2005 s 4A (see PARA 648): s 4B(2) (as added: see note 1).

3 Mental Capacity Act 2005 s 4B(3)(a) (as added: see note 1). A vital act is any act which the person doing it reasonably believes to be necessary to prevent a serious deterioration in P's condition: s 4B(5) (as so added).

4   Mental Capacity Act 2005 s 4B(3)(b) (as added: see note 1).
5   Mental Capacity Act 2005 s 4B(4) (as added: see note 1). The protection given by s 4B is dependent on the person doing the relevant act having a relevant belief and, in the case of doing a vital act, that person must have reasonably believed the act to be necessary to prevent a serious deterioration in the other person's condition: see *A County Council v MB (by the Official Solicitor as her litigation friend)* [2010] EWHC 2508 (COP), [2011] PTSR 795, [2011] 1 FLR 790.

(ii) Deprivation of Liberty Authorisations under Schedule A1

651.   Schedule A1 authorisations. If the following conditions are met[1]:

(1)   ('P') is detained in a hospital or care home[2] for the purpose of being given care or treatment in circumstances which amount to deprivation of the person's liberty[3];

(2)   a standard or urgent authorisation[4] is in force[5];

(3)   the standard or urgent authorisation relates to P and to the hospital or care home in which P is detained[6],

the managing authority[7] of the hospital or care home may deprive P of his liberty by detaining him as mentioned in head (1) above[8].

A person 'D' does not incur any liability in relation to any act which he does for the purpose of detaining P as mentioned in head (1) above that he would not have incurred if P had had capacity to consent in relation to D's doing the act and had consented to D's doing the act[9].

The above provisions[10] do not exclude a person's civil liability for loss or damage, or his criminal liability, resulting from his negligence in doing any thing[11]. Nor do they authorise a person to do anything otherwise than for the purpose of the standard or urgent authorisation[12] that is in force and, where a standard authorisation is in force, they do not authorise a person to do anything which does not comply with the conditions (if any) included in the authorisation[13].

1   Mental Capacity Act 2005 Sch A1 para 1(1) (Sch A1 added by the Mental Health Act 2007 Sch 7).
2   As to the meaning of 'hospital' see PARA 577. As to the meaning of 'care home' see the Care Standards Act 2000 s 3; and CHILDREN AND YOUNG PERSONS vol 10 (2012) PARA 994 (definition applied by the Mental Capacity Act 2005 Sch A1 para 178 (as added: see note 1)). As to transferring patients see PARA 649.
3   Mental Capacity Act 2005 Sch A1 para 1(2) (as added: see note 1).
4   As to the meaning of 'standard authorisation' see PARA 663 note 1. As to the meaning of 'urgent authorisation' see PARA 713 note 3.
5   Mental Capacity Act 2005 Sch A1 para 1(3) (as added: see note 1). As to standard and urgent authorisations see PARAS 661, 713.
6   Mental Capacity Act 2005 Sch A1 para 1(4) (as added: see note 1).
7   As to the meaning of 'managing authority' see PARA 652.
8   Mental Capacity Act 2005 Sch A1 para 2 (as added: see note 1).
9   Mental Capacity Act 2005 Sch A1 para 3 (as added: see note 1).
10   Ie the Mental Capacity Act 2005 Sch A1 paras 2, 3.
11   Mental Capacity Act 2005 Sch A1 para 4(1) (as added: see note 1).
12   The purpose of a standard authorisation is the purpose which is stated in the authorisation in accordance with the Mental Capacity Act 2005 Sch A1 para 55(1)(d) (see PARA 665) and the purpose of an urgent authorisation is the purpose which is stated in the authorisation in accordance with Sch A1 para 80(d) (see PARA 714): Sch A1 para 11 (as added: see note 1).
13   Mental Capacity Act 2005 Sch A1 para 4(2), (3) (as added: see note 1).

652.   Hospitals, care homes and their managing authorities. For the purposes of deprivation of liberty provisions[1] 'managing authority', in relation to an NHS hospital[2], means:

(1)   if the hospital[3] is vested in the appropriate national authority[4] for the purposes of its functions under the National Health Service Act 2006 or of the National Health Service (Wales) Act 2006, or if the hospital consists of any accommodation provided by a local authority and used as a hospital by or on behalf of the appropriate national authority under either of those Acts, the primary care trust, strategic health authority, local health board or special health authority[5] responsible for the administration of the hospital[6];

(2)   if the hospital is vested in a primary care trust, national health service trust or NHS foundation trust[7], that trust[8];

(3)   if the hospital is vested in a local health board, that Board[9].

'Managing authority', in relation to an independent hospital, means, in relation to England, the person registered, or required to be registered, under the Health and Social Care Act 2008[10] in respect of regulated activities[11] carried on in the hospital, and, in relation to Wales, the person registered, or required to be registered, under the Care Standards Act 2000[12] in respect of the hospital[13].

'Managing authority', in relation to a care home[14], means, in relation to England, the person registered, or required to be registered, under the Health and Social Care Act 2008[15] in respect of the provision of residential accommodation, together with nursing or personal care, in the care home and, in relation to Wales, the person registered, or required to be registered, under the Care Standards Act 2000[16] in respect of the care home[17].

1   Ie for the purposes of the Mental Capacity Act 2005 Sch A1: Sch A1 para 174 (Sch A1 added by the Mental Health Act 2007 Sch 7).
2   As to the meaning of 'NHS hospital' see PARA 577 note 11.
3   As to the meaning of 'hospital' see PARA 577.
4   As to the meaning of 'the appropriate national authority' see PARA 567.
5   As to primary care trusts see HEALTH SERVICES vol 54 (2008) PARA 111 et seq; as to local health boards see HEALTH SERVICES vol 54 (2008) PARA 74 et seq; and as to special health authorities see HEALTH SERVICES vol 54 (2008) PARA 136 et seq. As from 1 April 2013 primary care trusts and strategic health authorities are abolished and the relevant words in the Mental Capacity Act 2005 Sch A1 para 176 are repealed by the Health and Social Care Act 2012 Sch 5 para 136(2): see the Health and Social Care Act 2012 (Commencement No 4, Transitional, Savings and Transitory Provisions) Order 2013, SI 2013/160, art 2(2).
6   Mental Capacity Act 2005 Sch A1 para 176(1)(a) (as added (see note 1); prospectively amended (see note 5)). As from 1 April 2013, in relation to England, if the hospital falls within head (1) in the text and no special health authority has responsibility for its administration, the managing authority is the Secretary of State: Sch A1 para 176(1)(aa) (added by the Health and Social Care Act 2012 Sch 5 para 136(2)(c)): see Health and Social Care Act 2012 (Commencement No 4, Transitional, Savings and Transitory Provisions) Order 2013, SI 2013/160, art 2(2).
7   As to National Health Service Trusts see HEALTH SERVICES vol 54 (2008) PARA 155 et seq and as to NHS foundation trusts see HEALTH SERVICES vol 54 (2008) PARA 174 et seq.
8   Mental Capacity Act 2005 Sch A1 para 176(1)(b) (as added: see note 1).
9   Mental Capacity Act 2005 Sch A1 para 176(1)(c) (as added: see note 1).
10   Ie under the Health and Social Care Act 2008 ss 1–7 (see SOCIAL SERVICES AND COMMUNITY CARE).
11   As to the meaning of 'regulated activities' see the Health and Social Care Act 2008 s 8; and SOCIAL SERVICES AND COMMUNITY CARE.
12   Ie under the Care Standards Act 2000 ss 11–42.
13   Mental Capacity Act 2005 Sch A1 para 177 (as added (see note 1); substituted by SI 2010/813).
14   As to the meaning of 'care home' see the Care Standards Act 2000 s 3; and CHILDREN AND YOUNG PERSONS vol 10 (2012) PARA 994 (definition applied by the Mental Capacity Act 2005 Sch A1 para 178 (as added: see note 1)).
15   Ie under the Health and Social Care Act 2008 ss 1–7 (see SOCIAL SERVICES AND COMMUNITY CARE).
16   Ie under the Care Standards Act 2000 ss 11–42.
17   Mental Capacity Act 2005 Sch A1 para 179 (as added (see note 1); substituted by SI 2010/813).

(iii) Qualifying Requirements

653. The qualifying requirements. The qualifying requirements for the purpose of the deprivation of liberty provisions are[1]:

(1)   the age requirement[2];
(2)   the mental health requirement[3];
(3)   the mental capacity requirement[4];
(4)   the best interests requirement[5];
(5)   the eligibility requirement[6];
(6)   the no refusals requirement[7].

In a case where the question of whether a person meets a particular qualifying requirement arises in relation to the giving of a standard authorisation[8] and any circumstances relevant to determining that question are expected to change between the time when the determination is made and the time when the authorisation is expected to come into force, those circumstances are to be taken into account as they are expected to be at the later time[9].

The qualifying requirements may be subject to review[10].

1   Ie for the purposes of the Mental Capacity Act 2005 Sch A1. Any question of whether a person who is, or is to be, a detained resident meets the qualifying requirements is to be determined in accordance with Sch A1 paras 12–20: Sch A1 para 12(2) (Sch A1 added by the Mental Health Act 2007 Sch 7). As to the situation where there are one or more qualifying requirements see PARA 690. Where a standard authorisation has been given, the court may determine whether the relevant person meets one or more of the qualifying requirements: see the Mental Capacity Act 2005 s 21A(1), (2); and PARA 733.
2   Mental Capacity Act 2005 Sch A1 para 12(1)(a) (as added: see note 1). As to the age requirement see PARA 654.
3   Mental Capacity Act 2005 Sch A1 para 12(1)(b) (as added: see note 1). As to the mental health requirement see PARA 655.
4   Mental Capacity Act 2005 Sch A1 para 12(1)(c) (as added: see note 1). As to the mental capacity requirement see PARA 656.
5   Mental Capacity Act 2005 Sch A1 para 12(1)(d) (as added: see note 1). As to the best interests requirement see PARA 657.
6   Mental Capacity Act 2005 Sch A1 para 12(1)(e) (as added: see note 1). As to the eligibility requirement see PARA 658.
7   Mental Capacity Act 2005 Sch A1 para 12(1)(f) (as added: see note 1). As to the no refusals requirement see PARA 660.
8   As to the meaning of 'standard authorisation' see PARA 663 note 1.
9   Mental Capacity Act 2005 Sch A1 para 12(3) (as added: see note 1).
10   See PARA 683.

654. Age requirement. The relevant person[1] meets the age requirement if he has reached 18[2].

1   As to the meaning of 'relevant person' see PARA 663 note 7.
2   Mental Capacity Act 2005 Sch A1 para 13 (Sch A1 added by the Mental Health Act 2007 Sch 7). As to assessment of the age requirement see PARA 671.

655. Mental health requirement. The relevant person[1] meets the mental health requirement if he is suffering from mental disorder[2], but disregarding any exclusion for persons with learning disability[3].

1   As to the meaning of 'relevant person' see PARA 663 note 7.
2   Ie within the meaning of the Mental Health Act 1983: see s 1; and PARA 761.
3   Mental Capacity Act 2005 Sch A1 para 14(1) (Sch A1 added by the Mental Health Act 2007 Sch 7). An exclusion for persons with learning disability is any provision of the Mental Health Act 1983 which provides for a person with learning disability not to be regarded as suffering from mental disorder for one or more purposes of that Act: Mental Capacity Act 2005 Sch A1 para 14(2) (as so added). As to assessment of the mental health requirement see PARA 672.

656.   Mental capacity requirement.   The relevant person[1] meets the mental capacity requirement if he lacks capacity in relation to the question whether or not he should be accommodated in the relevant hospital or care home[2] for the purpose of being given the relevant care or treatment[3].

1   As to the meaning of 'relevant person' see PARA 663 note 7.
2   As to the meaning of 'relevant hospital or care home' see PARA 663 note 2.

3   Mental Capacity Act 2005 Sch A1 para 15 (Sch A1 added by the Mental Health Act 2007 Sch 7). As to assessment of the mental capacity requirement see PARA 673. 'Relevant care or treatment' means the care or treatment in question: Mental Capacity Act 2005 Sch A1 para 15 (as so added).

657.   The best interests requirement.   The relevant person[1] meets the best interests requirement if all of the following conditions are met[2]. The first condition is that the relevant person is, or is to be, a detained resident[3]. The second condition is that it is in the best interests of the relevant person for him to be a detained resident[4]. The third condition is that, in order to prevent harm to the relevant person, it is necessary for him to be a detained resident[5]. The fourth condition is that it is a proportionate response to the likelihood of the relevant person suffering harm and the seriousness of that harm, for him to be a detained resident[6].

1   As to the meaning of 'relevant person' see PARA 663 note 7.

2   Mental Capacity Act 2005 Sch A1 para 16(1) (Sch A1 added by the Mental Health Act 2007 Sch 7). As to assessment of the best interests requirement see PARA 674.

3   Mental Capacity Act 2005 Sch A1 para 16(2) (as added: see note 2). As to the meaning of 'detained resident' see PARA 661 note 6.

4   Mental Capacity Act 2005 Sch A1 para 16(3) (as added: see note 2).

5   Mental Capacity Act 2005 Sch A1 para 16(4) (as added: see note 2).

6   Mental Capacity Act 2005 Sch A1 para 16(5) (as added: see note 2).

658.   The eligibility requirement.   The relevant person[1] meets the eligibility requirement unless he is ineligible[2] to be deprived of liberty by the Mental Capacity Act 2005[3].

A person ('P') is ineligible to be deprived of liberty by the Mental Capacity Act 2005 ('ineligible') if he falls within one of the following cases[4].

Where P is subject to the hospital treatment regime[5] and is detained in a hospital[6] under that regime, P is ineligible[7].

Where P is subject to the hospital treatment regime but is not detained in a hospital under that regime[8] he is ineligible if the authorised course of action[9] is not in accordance with a requirement[10] which the relevant regime[11] imposes[12] or the relevant care or treatment consists in whole or in part of medical treatment for mental disorder[13] in a hospital[14].

Where P is subject to the community treatment regime[15] he is ineligible if the authorised course of action is not in accordance with a requirement which the relevant regime imposes[16] or the relevant care or treatment consists in whole or in part of medical treatment for mental disorder in a hospital[17].

Where P is subject to the guardianship regime[18] he is ineligible (1) if the authorised course of action is not in accordance with a requirement which the relevant regime imposes[19]; or (2) if the relevant instrument[20] authorises P to be a mental health patient[21], P objects[22] to being a mental health patient or to being given some or all of the mental health treatment; and that a donee[23] or deputy has not made a valid decision to consent to each matter to which P objects[24].

Where P is within the scope of the Mental Health Act 1983[25] but is not subject to any of the mental health regimes[26] he is ineligible if head (2) above applies[27].

1   As to the meaning of 'relevant person' see PARA 663 note 7.

2   The Mental Capacity Act 2005 Sch 1A applies for the purpose of determining whether or not a person is ineligible to be deprived of liberty by the Mental Capacity Act 2005: Sch A1 para 17(2) (Sch A1 added by the Mental Health Act 2007 Sch 7).

3   Mental Capacity Act 2005 Sch A1 para 17(1) (as added: see note 2). As to assessment of the eligibility requirement see PARA 675.

4   See the Mental Capacity Act 2005 Sch 1A paras 1, 2 (Sch 1A added by the Mental Health Act 2007 Sch 8). As to the suspension of a standard authorisation where the eligibility requirement is not met see the Mental Capacity Act 2005 Sch 1A paras 91–97; and PARAS 680–681.

5   P is subject to the hospital treatment regime if he is subject to a hospital treatment obligation under the Mental Health Act 1983 or an obligation under another England and Wales enactment which has the same effect as a hospital treatment obligation: Mental Capacity Act 2005 Sch 1A para 8(1) (as added: see note 4). But where P is subject to any such obligation, he is to be regarded as not subject to the hospital treatment regime during any period when he is subject to the community treatment regime: Sch 1A para 8(2) (as so added). A hospital treatment obligation is an application, order or direction of a kind under the Mental Health Act 1983 s 2 (application for admission for assessment: see PARA 767), s 4 (application for admission for assessment: see PARA 769), s 3 (application for admission for treatment: see PARA 768), s 35 (order for remand to hospital: see PARA 862), s 36 (order for remand to hospital: see PARA 862), s 37 (hospital order: see PARA 864), s 38 (interim hospital order: see PARA 864), 44 (order for detention in hospital: see PARA 873), s 45A (hospital direction: see PARA 863), s 47 (transfer direction: see PARA 892), s 48 (transfer direction: see PARA 893), s 51 (hospital order: see PARA 896): Sch 1A para 8(4) (as so added). As to the meaning of 'medical treatment' see the Mental Health Act 1983 s 145(1); and PARA 926 (definition applied by the Mental Capacity Act 2005 Sch 1A para 17(1) (as so added)).

6   As to the meaning of 'hospital' see the Mental Health Act 1983 and; PARA 577 (definition applied by the Mental Capacity Act 2005 Sch 1A para 17(1) (as added: see note 4)).

7   See the Mental Capacity Act 2005 Sch 1A para 2 Case A (as added: see note 4).

8   See the Mental Capacity Act 2005 Sch 1A para 2 Case B (as added: see note 4).

9   For the purposes of the Mental Capacity Act 2005 Sch A1 para 17 'authorised course of action' means the accommodation of the relevant person in the relevant hospital or care home for the purpose of being given the relevant care or treatment: Sch 1A para 14 (as added: see note 4). As to the meaning of 'relevant care or treatment' see the Mental Capacity Act 2005 Sch A1 para 7; and PARA 663 note 2 (definition applied by Sch 1A para 14 (as added: see note 4)). For the purposes of s 16A (see PARA 726) 'authorised course of action' means any course of action amounting to deprivation of liberty which the order under s 16(2)(a) authorises and 'relevant care or treatment' means any care or treatment which (1) comprises, or forms part of, the authorised course of action; or (2) is to be given in connection with the authorised course of action: Sch 1A para 13 (as so added).

10   This includes any requirement as to where P is, or is not, to reside: Mental Capacity Act 2005 Sch 1A para 3(3) (as added: see note 4).

11   The relevant regime is the mental health regime to which P is subject: Mental Capacity Act 2005 Sch 1A para 3(4) (as added: see note 4). The mental health regimes are the hospital treatment regime, the community treatment regime and the guardianship regime: Sch 1A para 7 (as so added). P is subject to the community treatment regime if he is subject to a community treatment order under the Mental Health Act 1983 s 17A (see PARA 797) or an obligation under another England and Wales enactment which has the same effect as a community treatment order: Sch 1A para 9 (as so added). P is subject to the guardianship regime if he is subject to a guardianship application under the Mental Health Act 1983 s 7 (see PARA 785), a guardianship order under s 37 (see PARA 877) or an obligation under another England and Wales enactment which has the same effect as a guardianship application or guardianship order: Mental Capacity Act 2005 Sch 1A para 10 (as so added). An England and Wales enactment is an enactment which extends to England and Wales (whether or not it also extends elsewhere) and it does not matter if the enactment is in the Mental Health Act 1983 or not: Mental Capacity Act 2005 Sch 1A para 11 (as so added).

12   See the Mental Capacity Act 2005 Sch 1A para 3(1), (2) (as added: see note 4).

13 As to the meaning of 'mental disorder' see the Mental Capacity Act 2005 Sch A1 para 14; and PARA 655 (definition applied by Sch 1A para 17(3) (as added: see note 4)).

14 See the Mental Capacity Act 2005 Sch 1A para 4 (as added: see note 4).

15 See the Mental Capacity Act 2005 Sch 1A para 2 Case C (as added: see note 4).

16 See the Mental Capacity Act 2005 Sch 1A para 3(1), (2) (as added: see note 4).

17 See the Mental Capacity Act 2005 Sch 1A para 4 (as added: see note 4).

18 See the Mental Capacity Act 2005 Sch 1A para 2 Case D (as added: see note 4). See *C (by his litigation friend the Official Solicitor) v Blackburn with Darwen Borough Council* [2011] EWHC 3321 COP, [2011] All ER (D) 203 (Dec).

19 See the Mental Capacity Act 2005 Sch 1A para 3 (as added: see note 4).

20 For the purpose of the Mental Capacity Act 2005 Sch A1 para 17 'relevant instrument' means the standard authorisation under the Sch A1 and for the purposes of s 16A means the order under s 16(2)(a) (see PARA 724): Sch A1 paras, 13 14 (as added: see note 4).

21 For these purposes 'mental health patient' means a person accommodated in a hospital for the purpose of being given medical treatment for mental disorder and 'mental health treatment' means the medical treatment for mental disorder referred to in the definition of 'mental health patient': Mental Capacity Act 2005 Sch 1A para 16(1) (as added: see note 4). A person accommodated at a care home that is registered under the Care Standards Act 2000 (see SOCIAL SERVICES AND COMMUNITY CARE), but is not registered as an independent hospital or part of the NHS, does not fall within the above definition of a mental health patient: see *W Primary Trust v TB* [2009] EWHC 1737 (Fam), [2010] 2 All ER 331, [2010] 1 WLR 2662. In *GJ v The Foundation Trust* [2009] EWHC 2972 (Fam), [2010] Fam 70, [2010] 3 WLR 840 the court concluded that the correct approach for the decision-maker to take when applying Sch 1A para 5(3) is to focus on the reason why P should be deprived of his liberty by applying a 'but for' approach or test, and to do that he should ask himself the following questions, namely: (1) what care and treatment should P (who will usually have a mental disorder within the definition of the Mental Health Act 1983) have if, and so long as, he remains in a hospital: (a) for his physical disorders or illnesses that are unconnected to, and are unlikely to directly affect, his mental disorders (the package of physical treatment); and (b) for his mental disorders, and (c) his physical disorders or illnesses that are connected to them and/or which are likely to directly affect his mental disorders (the package of treatment for mental disorder); and then: (2) if the need for the package of physical treatment did not exist, would he conclude that P should be detained in a hospital, in circumstances that amount to a deprivation of his liberty; and then, on that basis (3) whether the only effective reason why he considers that P should be detained in hospital, in circumstances that amount to a deprivation of liberty, is his need for the package of physical treatment; if he answers part (2) in the negative and part (3) in the affirmative then the relevant instrument does not authorise P to be a mental health patient and the condition in Sch 1A para 5(3) is not satisfied.

22 In determining whether or not P objects to something, regard must be had to all the circumstances (so far as they are reasonably ascertainable), including P's behaviour, P's wishes and feelings and P's views, beliefs and values: Mental Capacity Act 2005 Sch 1A para 5(6) (as added: see note 4). But regard is to be had to circumstances from the past only so far as it is still appropriate to have regard to them: Sch 1A para 5(7) (as so added).

23 For these purposes 'donee' means a donee of a lasting power of attorney granted by P: Mental Capacity Act 2005 Sch 1A para 16(1) (as added: see note 4).

24 See the Mental Capacity Act 2005 Sch 1A para 5 (as added: see note 4).

25 As to when P is within the scope of the Mental Health Act 1983 see PARA 659.

26 See the Mental Capacity Act 2005 Sch 1A para 2 Case E (as added: see note 4).

27 See the Mental Capacity Act 2005 Sch 1A para 5 (as added: see note 4). See further *W Primary Trust v TB* [2009] EWHC 1737 (Fam), [2010] 2 All ER 331, [2010] 1 WLR 2662.

659. Within the scope of the Mental Health Act 1983. A person ('P') is within the scope of the Mental Health Act 1983 if an application in respect of him could be made under the provisions permitting compulsory admission for assessment or treatment[1] and he could be detained in a hospital in pursuance of such an application, were one made[2].

1 Ie under the Mental Health Act 1983 s 2 or 3 (see PARAS 767, 768).

2 Mental Capacity Act 2005 Sch 1A para 12(1) (Sch 1A added by the Mental Health Act 2007 Sch 8). When determining whether an application in respect of P could be made under the Mental Health Act 1983 s 2 or 3 the following provisions apply: Mental Capacity Act 2005 Sch 1A para 12(2) (as so added). If the grounds in the Mental Health Act 1983 s 2(2) are met in

P's case, it is to be assumed that the recommendations referred to in s 2(3) have been given: Mental Capacity Act 2005 Sch 1A para 12(3) (as so added). If the grounds in the Mental Health Act 1983 s 3(2) are met in P's case, it is to be assumed that the recommendations referred to in s 3(3) have been given: Mental Capacity Act 2005 Sch 1A para 12(4) (as so added). In determining whether the ground of the Mental Health Act 1983 s 3(2)(c) is met in P's case, it is to be assumed that the treatment referred to in s 3(2)(c) cannot be provided under the Mental Capacity Act 2005: Sch 1A para 14(5) (as so added). The decision-maker should approach the status test or gateway concerning eligibility in Sch 1A para 12(1) by asking himself whether in his view the criteria set by or the grounds in the Mental Health Act 1983 s 2 or s 3 are met (and if an application was made under them a hospital would detain P). If they are met the Mental Health Act 1983 has primacy and practitioners are not permitted to 'pick and choose' between the Mental Health Act 1983 and the Mental Capacity Act 2005: see *GJ v The Foundation Trust* [2009] EWHC 2972 (Fam), [2010] Fam 70, [2010] 3 WLR 840.

660.   The no refusals requirement.   The relevant person[1] meets the no refusals requirement unless there is a refusal that falls within the following criteria[2]. There is a refusal if the relevant person has made an advance decision[3] which is valid and applicable[4] to some or all of the relevant treatment[5]. There is also a refusal if it would be in conflict with a valid decision of a donee or deputy[6] for the relevant person to be accommodated in the relevant hospital or care home[7] for the purpose of receiving some or all of the relevant care or treatment in circumstances which amount to deprivation of the person's liberty or at all[8].

1   As to the meaning of 'relevant person' see PARA 663 note 7.
2   Mental Capacity Act 2005 Sch 1A para 18 (Sch A1 added by the Mental Health Act 2007 Sch 7). As to assessment of the no refusals requirement see PARA 676.
3   As to the meaning of 'advance decision' see PARA 624.
4   As to when an advance decision is valid and applicable see the Mental Capacity Act 2005 s 25 (applied by Sch 1A para 19(2) (as added: see note 2)).
5   Mental Capacity Act 2005 Sch 1A para 19(1) (as added: see note 2).
6   As to the meaning of 'deputy' see PARA 606 note 18. A donee is a donee of a lasting power of attorney granted by the relevant person: Mental Capacity Act 2005 Sch A1 para 20(2) (as added: see note 2). A decision of a donee or deputy is valid if it is made within the scope of his authority as donee or deputy and in accordance with the Mental Capacity Act 2005 Pt 1 (ss 1–44: see PARA 761 et seq): Sch A1 para 20(3) (as so added).
7   As to the meaning of 'relevant hospital or care home' see PARA 663 note 2.
8   Mental Capacity Act 2005 Sch A1 para 20(1) (as added: see note 2).

(iv)   Standard Authorisations

A.   GIVING A STANDARD AUTHORISATION

661.   Duty to request authorisation: basic cases.   The managing authority[1] must request a standard authorisation[2] in any of the following cases[3].

The first case is where it appears to the managing authority that the relevant person[4] is not yet accommodated in the relevant hospital or care home[5], is likely (at some time within the next 28 days) to be a detained resident[6] in the relevant hospital or care home and is likely, at that time or at some later time within the next 28 days, to meet all of the qualifying requirements[7].

The second case is where it appears to the managing authority that the relevant person is already accommodated in the relevant hospital or care home, is likely, at some time within the next 28 days, to be a detained resident in the relevant hospital or care home and is likely, at that time or at some later time within the next 28 days, to meet all of the qualifying requirements[8].

The third case is where it appears to the managing authority that the relevant person is a detained resident in the relevant hospital or care home and meets all of the qualifying requirements, or is likely to do so at some time within the next 28 days[9].

However, if a decision of the court[10] authorises the relevant person to be a detained resident the above provisions[11] do not require a request for a standard authorisation to be made in relation to that detention unless the following conditions are met[12]. The first condition is that the standard authorisation would be in force at a time immediately after the expiry of the other authority[13]. The second condition is that the standard authorisation would not be in force at any time on or before the expiry of the other authority[14]. The third condition is that it would, in the managing authority's view, be unreasonable to delay making the request until a time nearer the expiry of the other authority[15].

1   As to the meaning of 'managing authority' see PARA 652.
2   As to the meaning of 'standard authorisation' see PARA 663 note 1.
3   Mental Capacity Act 2005 Sch A1 para 24(1) (Sch A1 added by the Mental Health Act 2007 Sch 7). The Mental Capacity Act 2005 Sch A1 para 24 is subject to Sch A1 paras 27–29 (see PARAS 661, 666): Sch A1 para 24(5) (as so added). If a managing authority requests a standard authorisation under Sch A1 para 24 and the supervisory body is prohibited by Sch A1 para 50(2) (see PARA 663) from giving the authorisation, Sch A1 para 24 does not require the managing authority to make a new request for a standard authorisation unless it appears to the managing authority that there has been a change in the relevant person's case and that because of that change, the supervisory body are likely to give a standard authorisation if requested: Sch A1 para 28 (as so added).
4   As to the meaning of 'relevant person' see PARA 663 note 7.
5   As to the meaning of 'relevant hospital or care home' see PARA 663 note 2.
6   'Detained resident' means a person detained in a hospital or care home, for the purpose of being given care or treatment, in circumstances which amount to deprivation of the person's liberty: Mental Capacity Act 2005 Sch A1 para 6 (as added: see note 3).
7   Mental Capacity Act 2005 Sch A1 para 24(2) (as added: see note 3). As to the qualifying requirements see PARAS 653–660.
8   Mental Capacity Act 2005 Sch A1 para 24(3) (as added: see note 3).
9   Mental Capacity Act 2005 Sch A1 para 24(4) (as added: see note 3).
10 Ie under the Mental Capacity Act 2005 s 4A(3) (see PARA 648).
11 Ie the Mental Capacity Act 2005 Sch A1 para 24.
12 Mental Capacity Act 2005 Sch A1 para 27(1), (2) (as added: see note 3).
13 Mental Capacity Act 2005 Sch A1 para 27(3) (as added: see note 3). For these purposes: (1) the other authority is the decision mentioned Sch A1 para 27(1) or any further decision of the court which, by virtue of s 4A(3) (see PARA 648), authorises, or is expected to authorise, the relevant person to be a detained resident; (2) the expiry of the other authority is the time when the other authority is expected to cease to authorise the relevant person to be a detained resident: Sch A1 para 27(6) (as so added).
14 Mental Capacity Act 2005 Sch A1 para 27(4) (as added: see note 3).
15 Mental Capacity Act 2005 Sch A1 para 27(5) (as added: see note 3).

662.   Duty to request authorisation: change in place of detention. The relevant managing authority[1] must request a standard authorisation[2] if it appears to the authority that the following conditions are met[3]. The first condition is that a standard authorisation has been given and has not ceased to be in force[4]. The second condition is that there is, or is to be, a change in the place of detention[5].

Where the managing authority requests a new standard authorisation under the above provisions[6] and it is required[7] to give the new authorisation, the existing authorisation terminates at the time when the new authorisation comes into force[8]. However, if the supervisory body are prohibited[9] from giving the new authorisation, there is no effect on the existing authorisation's continuation in force[10].

1   As to the meaning of 'managing authority' see PARA 652. The 'relevant managing authority' is the managing authority of the new hospital or care home: Mental Capacity Act 2005 Sch A1 para 26(4) (Sch A1 added by the Mental Health Act 2007 Sch 7).

2   As to the meaning of 'standard authorisation' see PARA 663 note 1.

3   Mental Capacity Act 2005 Sch A1 para 25(1) (as added: see note 1). If a managing authority requests a standard authorisation under Sch A1 para 24 and the supervisory body is prohibited by Sch A1 para 50(2) (see PARA 663) from giving the authorisation, Sch A1 para 24 does not require the managing authority to make a new request for a standard authorisation unless it appears to the managing authority that there has been a change in the relevant person's case and that because of that change, the supervisory body are likely to give a standard authorisation if requested: Sch A1 paras 25(4) 28 (as so added).

4   Mental Capacity Act 2005 Sch A1 para 25(2) (as added: see note 1).

5   Mental Capacity Act 2005 Sch A1 para 25(3) (as added: see note 1). There is a change in the place of detention if the relevant person ceases to be a detained resident in the stated hospital or care home and becomes a detained resident in a different hospital or care home ('the new hospital or care home'): Sch A1 para 26(1), (2) (as so added). The stated hospital or care home is the hospital or care home to which the standard authorisation relates: Sch A1 para 26(3) (as so added). As to the meaning of 'hospital' see PARA 577. As to the meaning of 'care home' see the Care Standards Act 2000 s 3; and CHILDREN AND YOUNG PERSONS vol 10 (2012) PARA 994 (definition applied by the Mental Capacity Act 2005 Sch A1 para 178 (as so added)).

6   Ie under the Mental Capacity Act 2005 Sch A1 para 25.

7   Ie required by the Mental Capacity Act 2005 Sch A1 para 50(1) (see PARA 663).

8   Mental Capacity Act 2005 Sch A1 para 62(1)(a), (2) (as added: see note 1).

9   Ie prohibited by the Mental Capacity Act 2005 Sch A1 para 50(2) (see PARA 663).

10 Mental Capacity Act 2005 Sch A1 para 62(3) (as added: see note 1).

663. Supervisory body to give authorisation. Only the supervisory body may give a standard authorisation[1] and it may not do so unless the managing authority of the relevant hospital or care home[2] has requested it[3] or provisions apply[4] that relate to the right of a third party to require consideration of whether authorisation is needed[5].

If the supervisory body is requested to give an authorisation it must secure that certain assessments[6] are carried out in relation to the relevant person[7]. It must then give a standard authorisation if all the assessments are positive[8] and it has written copies of them[9].

1   Mental Capacity Act 2005 Sch A1 para 21 (Sch A1 added by the Mental Health Act 2007 Sch 7). 'Standard authorisation' means an authorisation given under the Mental Capacity Act 2005 paras 21–73: Sch A1 para 8 (as so added). As to the meaning of 'supervisory body' see PARA 664.

2   'Relevant hospital or care home' means the hospital or care home in question: Mental Capacity Act 2005 Sch A1 para 7 (as added: see note 1). As to the meaning of 'hospital' see PARA 577. As to the meaning of 'care home' see the Care Standards Act 2000 s 3; and CHILDREN AND YOUNG PERSONS vol 10 (2012) PARA 994 (definition applied by the Mental Capacity Act 2005 Sch A1 para 178 (as so added)).

3   Mental Capacity Act 2005 Sch A1 para 22(b) (as added: see note 1). The managing authority may not make a request for a standard authorisation unless they are required to do so by Sch A1 para 24 (as read with Sch A1 paras 27–29), they are required to do so by Sch A1 para 25 (as read with Sch A1 para 28) or they are permitted to do so by Sch A1 para 30: Sch A1 para 23 (as so added). As to requests by the managing authority see PARA 661–662.

4   Ie the Mental Capacity Act 2005 Sch A1 para 71 (see PARA 679) applies. See further Sch A1 paras 67–73 (PARA 679) whereby a member of a person's family or a person inspecting the hospital or care home can trigger the assessment process.

5   Mental Capacity Act 2005 Sch A1 para 22(b) (as added: see note 1).

6   As to the assessments see PARA 669.

7   See the Mental Capacity Act 2005 Sch A1 para 33(1), (2); and PARA 669. 'Relevant person' means the person in question: Mental Capacity Act 2005 Sch A1 para 7 (as added: see note 1).

8   All assessments are positive if each assessment carried out under the Mental Capacity Act 2005 Sch A1 para 33 (see PARA 669) has come to the conclusion that the relevant person meets the qualifying requirement to which the assessment relates: Sch A1 para 50(3) (as added: see note 1). The responsibility of the supervisory body is to scrutinise the assessment (best interests)

it receives with independence and a degree of care that is appropriate to the seriousness of the decision and the circumstances of the individual case that are or should be known to it: *Hillingdon London Borough Council v Neary* [2011] EWHC 1377 (COP), [2011] 4 All ER 584, [2011] 3 FCR 448.

9   See the Mental Capacity Act 2005 Sch A1 para 50(1) (as added: see note 1). The supervisory body must not give a standard authorisation except in accordance with Sch A1 para 50(1): Sch A1 para 50(2) (as so added).

664. Supervisory body. In cases where the relevant hospital[1] is situated in England, the identity of the supervisory body is determined as follows[2]. If a primary care trust[3] commissions the relevant care or treatment, that Trust is the supervisory body[4]. If the Welsh Ministers or a local health board[5] commissions the relevant care or treatment, the Welsh Ministers are the supervisory body[6]. In any other case, the supervisory body is the primary care trust for the area in which the relevant hospital is situated[7].

In cases where the relevant hospital is situated in Wales, the identity of the supervisory body is determined as follows[8]. The Welsh Ministers are the supervisory body[9]. But if a primary care trust commissions the relevant care or treatment, that Trust is the supervisory body[10].

In cases where the relevant care home[11] is situated in England or in Wales, the identity of the supervisory body is determined as follows[12]. The supervisory body is the local authority[13] for the area in which the relevant person is ordinarily resident[14]. But if the relevant person is not ordinarily resident in the area of a local authority, the supervisory body is the local authority for the area in which the care home is situated[15].

If, in connection with a particular person's detention as a resident in a hospital or care home, the same body is both the managing authority of the relevant hospital or care home and the supervisory body, the fact that a single body is acting in both capacities does not prevent the body from carrying out functions[16] in each capacity[17].

1   As to the meaning of 'relevant hospital' see PARA 663 note 2 and as to the meaning of 'hospital' see PARA 577.

2   Mental Capacity Act 2005 Sch A1 para 180(1) (Sch A1 added by the Mental Health Act 2007 Sch 7). As to the meaning of 'supervisory body' see PARA 664.

3   As to primary care trusts see HEALTH SERVICES vol 54 (2008) PARA 111 et seq.

4   Mental Capacity Act 2005 Sch A1 para 180(2) (as added: see note 2). As from 1 April 2013 Sch A1 para 180(2) is substituted by the Health and Social Care Act 2012 Sch 5 para 136(3)(a) and if the relevant person is ordinarily resident in the area of a local authority in England, the supervisory body is that local authority: see the Health and Social Care Act 2012 (Commencement No 4, Transitional, Savings and Transitory Provisions) Order 2012, SI 2013/160, art 2(2).

5   As to Local Health Boards see HEALTH SERVICES vol 54 (2008) PARA 74 et seq.

6   Mental Capacity Act 2005 Sch A1 para 180(3) (as added: see note 2). As from 1 April 2013 Sch A1 para 180(3) is amended by the Health and Social Care Act 2012 Sch 5 para 136(3)(b) and will apply where the relevant person is not ordinarily present in England: see the Health and Social Care Act 2012 (Commencement No 4, Transitional, Savings and Transitory Provisions) Order 2012, SI 2013/160, art 2(2).

7   Mental Capacity Act 2005 Sch A1 para 180(4) (as added: see note 2). If a hospital is situated in the areas of two (or more) primary care trusts, it is to be regarded for the purposes of Sch A1 para 180(4) as situated in whichever of the areas the greater (or greatest) part of the hospital is situated: Sch A1 para 180(5) (as so added). As from 1 April 2013 primary care trusts are abolished and accordingly the relevant words are repealed from Sch A1 para 180(4), (5) and replaced by references to a local authority and the following definition of local authority is added by the Health and Social Care Act 2012 Sch 5 para 136(3)(c)–(e): see the Health and Social Care Act 2012 (Commencement No 4, Transitional, Savings and Transitory Provisions) Order 2012, SI 2013/160, art 2(2). 'Local authority' means the council of a county, the council

of a district for which there is no county council, the council of a London borough, the Common Council of the City of London, the Council of the Isles of Scilly: Mental Capacity Act 2005 Sch A1 para 180(4A) (as so added).

8   Mental Capacity Act 2005 Sch A1 para 181(1) (as added: see note 2).

9   Mental Capacity Act 2005 Sch A1 para 181(2) (as added: see note 2).

10 Mental Capacity Act 2005 Sch A1 para 181(3) (as added: see note 2). As from 1 April 2013 Sch A1 para 181(3) is substituted and the definition of 'local authority' in Sch A1 para 181(4) is added by the Health and Social Care Act 2012 Sch 5 para 136(4) and if the relevant person is ordinarily resident in the area of a local authority in England, the supervisory body will be that local authority: see the Health and Social Care Act 2012 (Commencement No 4, Transitional, Savings and Transitory Provisions) Order 2012, SI 2013/160, art 2(2). 'Local authority' means the council of a county, the council of a district for which there is no county council, the council of a London borough, the Common Council of the City of London, the Council of the Isles of Scilly: Mental Capacity Act 2005 Sch A1 para 181(4) (as so added).

11 As to the meaning of 'relevant care home' see PARA 663 note 2.

12 Mental Capacity Act 2005 Sch A1 para 182(1) (as added: see note 2).

13 In relation to England 'local authority' means the council of a county, the council of a district for which there is no county council, the council of a London borough, the Common Council of the City of London, the Council of the Isles of Scilly and, in relation to Wales 'local authority' means the council of a county or county borough: Mental Capacity Act 2005 Sch A1 para 182(4), (5) (as so added).

14 Mental Capacity Act 2005 Sch A1 para 182(2) (as added: see note 2). The National Assistance Act 1948 s 24(5), (6) (deemed place of ordinary residence: see SOCIAL SERVICES AND COMMUNITY CARE vol 44(2) (Reissue) PARA 1032) apply to any determination of where a person is ordinarily resident for the purposes of the Mental Capacity Act 2005 Sch A1 para 182 as those provisions apply to such a determination for the purposes specified in those provisions: Sch A1 para 183(1) (as so added). As from 1 April 2013 Sch A1 para 183(1) is amended and also applies for the purposes of Sch A1 paras 180, 181: see the Health and Social Care Act 2012 Sch 5 para 136(6)(a); and the Health and Social Care Act 2012 (Commencement No 4, Transitional, Savings and Transitory Provisions) Order 2012, SI 2013/160, art 2(2). In the application of the National Assistance Act 1948 s 24(6) that provision is to be read as if it referred to a hospital vested in a Local Health Board as well as to hospitals vested in the Secretary of State and the other bodies mentioned in s 24(6): see the Mental Capacity Act 2005 Sch A1 para 183(2) (as so added). As from 1 April 2013 Sch A1 para 183(2) is amended by the Health and Social Care Act 2012 Sch 5 para 136(6)(b) and the words 'to any determination of where a person is ordinarily resident for the purposes of Sch A1 para 182' are added before the words 'those provisions': : see the Health and Social Care Act 2012 (Commencement No 4, Transitional, Savings and Transitory Provisions) Order 2012, SI 2013/160, art 2(2). Any question arising as to the ordinary residence of a person is to be determined by the appropriate national authority which must make and publish arrangements for determining which cases are to be dealt with by the Secretary of State and which are to be dealt with by the Welsh Ministers: Mental Capacity Act 2005 Sch A1 para 183(3), (4) (as so added). Those arrangements may include provision for the Secretary of State and the Welsh Ministers to agree, in relation to any question that has arisen, which of them is to deal with the case: Sch A1 para 183(5) (as so added). Regulations may make provision about arrangements that are to have effect before, upon, or after the determination of any question as to the ordinary residence of a person: Sch A1 para 183(6) (as so added). The regulations may, in particular, authorise or require a local authority to do any or all of the following things:

(1)   to act as supervisory body even though it may wish to dispute that it is the supervisory body (Sch A1 para 183(7)(a) (as so added));

(2)   to become the supervisory body in place of another local authority (Sch A1 para 183(7)(b) (as so added));

(3)   to recover from another local authority expenditure incurred in exercising functions as the supervisory body (Sch A1 para 183(7)(c) (as so added)).

As to regulations about disputes about the place of ordinary residence see the Mental Capacity (Deprivation of Liberty: Standard Authorisations, Assessments and Ordinary Residence) Regulations 2008, SI 2008/1858, regs 17–19; and the Mental Capacity (Deprivation of Liberty: Assessments, Standard Authorisations and Disputes about Residence) (Wales) Regulations 2009, SI 2009/783, reg 14–16. See also the Ordinary Residence Dispute (Mental Capacity Act 2005) Directions 2010 made pursuant to the Local Authority Social Services Act 1970 s 7A (see SOCIAL SERVICES AND COMMUNITY CARE vol 44(2) (Reissue) PARA 1011).

15 Mental Capacity Act 2005 Sch A1 para 182(3) (as added: see note 2). If a care home is situated in the areas of two (or more) local authorities, it is to be regarded for the purposes of Sch A1 para 182(3) as situated in whichever of the areas the greater (or greatest) part of the care home is situated: Sch A1 para 182(6) (as so added).

16 Ie functions under the Mental Capacity Act 2005 Sch A1.

17 Mental Capacity Act 2005 Sch A1 para 184(1), (2) (as added: see note 2). But, in such a case, Sch A1 has effect subject to any modifications contained in regulations that may be made for this purpose: Sch A1 para 184(3) (as so added).

665. Terms and form of authorisation. If the supervisory body[1] is required to give a standard authorisation[2], it must decide the period[3] during which the authorisation is to be in force[4]. A standard authorisation may provide for the authorisation to come into force at a time after it is given[5].

A standard authorisation may be given subject to conditions[6]. Before deciding whether to give the authorisation subject to conditions, the supervisory body must have regard to any recommendations in the best interests assessment[7] about such conditions[8]. The managing authority of the relevant hospital or care home must ensure that any conditions are complied with[9].

A standard authorisation must be in writing[10] and must state the following things:

(1)   the name of the relevant person[11];
(2)   the name of the relevant hospital or care home[12];
(3)   the period during which the authorisation is to be in force[13];
(4)   the purpose for which the authorisation is given[14];
(5)   any conditions subject to which the authorisation is given[15];
(6)   the reason why each qualifying requirement is met[16].

If the name of the relevant hospital or care home[17] changes, the standard authorisation is to be read as if it stated the current name of the hospital or care home[18].

A supervisory body must keep a written record of all the standard authorisations that it has given, the requests for standard authorisations in response to which they have not given an authorisation and, in relation to each standard authorisation given, the matters stated[19] in the authorisation[20].

If a standard authorisation ceases to be in force the supervisory body must give notice, as soon as practicable, that the authorisation has ceased to be in force to the managing authority[21] of the relevant hospital or care home, the relevant person, the relevant person's representative[22] and every interested person[23] consulted by the best interests assessor[24].

1   As to the meaning of 'supervisory body' see PARA 664.

2   As to the meaning of 'standard authorisation' see PARA 651 note 4.

3   That period must not exceed the maximum authorisation period stated in the best interests assessment: Mental Capacity Act 2005 Sch A1 para 51(2) (Sch A1 added by the Mental Health Act 2007 Sch 7).

4   Mental Capacity Act 2005 Sch A1 para 51(1) (as added: see note 3). A standard authorisation comes into force when it is given: Sch A1 para 63(1) (as so added). But if the authorisation provides for it to come into force at a later time, it comes into force at that time: Sch A1 para 63(2) (as so added). Where a standard authorisation has been given, the court may determine the period during which the standard authorisation is to be in force, the purpose for which it is given and the conditions subject to which it is given: see s 21A(1), (2); and PARA 733. Authorisations do not run from the beginning of (or from an earlier time) the day on which they are given: see *A County Council v MB, JB and a Residential Care Home* [2010] EWHC 2508 (COP), [2011] PTSR 795, [2011] 1 FLR 790 (court recommended that it would be good practice to record the actual time at which an urgent authorisation and a standard authorisation (which did not run from the expiry of, or a specified time before the expiry of, an existing standard authorisation) was given on the form recording its grant).

5   Mental Capacity Act 2005 Sch A1 para 52 (as added: see note 3).

6   Mental Capacity Act 2005 Sch A1 para 53(1) (as added: see note 3). A standard authorisation may not be varied except in accordance with Sch A1 paras 98–100 (see PARA 682) or Sch A1 paras 101–125 (see PARAS 683–689): Sch A1 para 61(1) (as so added). This does not affect the powers of the Court of Protection: Sch A1 para 61(2) (as so added). As to the Court of Protection see PARA 720 et seq.

7   As to the best interests assessment see PARA 674.

8   Mental Capacity Act 2005 Sch A1 para 53(2) (as added: see note 3).

9   Mental Capacity Act 2005 Sch A1 para 53(3) (as added: see note 3).

10   Mental Capacity Act 2005 Sch A1 para 54 (as added: see note 3).

11   Mental Capacity Act 2005 Sch A1 para 55(1)(a) (as added: see note 3). As to the meaning of 'relevant person' see PARA 663 note 7.

12   Mental Capacity Act 2005 Sch A1 para 55(1)(b) (as added: see note 3).

13   Mental Capacity Act 2005 Sch A1 para 55(1)(c) (as added: see note 3). A standard authorisation ceases to be in force at the end of the period stated in the authorisation in accordance with Sch A1 para 55(1)(c): Sch A1 para 64(1) (as so added). But if the authorisation terminates before then in accordance with Sch A1 para 62(2) (see PARAS 662, 667) or any other provision of Sch A1, it ceases to be in force when the termination takes effect: Sch A1 para 64(2) (as so added). Schedule A1 para 64 does not affect the powers of the Court of Protection or of any other court: Sch A1 para 64(3) (as so added).

14   Mental Capacity Act 2005 Sch A1 para 55(1)(d) (as added: see note 3).

15   Mental Capacity Act 2005 Sch A1 para 55(1)(e) (as added: see note 3).

16   Mental Capacity Act 2005 Sch A1 para 55(1)(f) (as added: see note 3). As to the qualifying requirements see PARAS 653–660. The statement of the reason why the eligibility requirement is met must be framed by reference to the cases in Sch 1A para 2 (see PARA 658): Sch A1 para 55(2) (as so added). As to the eligibility requirements see PARA 658.

17   As to the meaning of 'relevant hospital or care home' see PARA 663 note 2. As to the meaning of 'hospital' see PARA 577; and as to the meaning of 'care home' see PARA 652 note 14.

18   Mental Capacity Act 2005 Sch A1 para 56(1) (as added: see note 3). This is subject to any provision relating to the change of name which is made in any enactment or in any instrument made under an enactment: Sch A1 para 56(2) (as so added).

19   Ie the matters stated in the authorisation in accordance with the Mental Capacity Act 2005 Sch A1 para 55 (see PARA 665).

20   Mental Capacity Act 2005 Sch A1 para 60 (as added: see note 3).

21   As to the meaning of 'managing authority' see PARA 652. Any notice under the Mental Capacity Act 2005 Sch A1 must be in writing: Sch A1 para 169 (as added: see note 3).

22   As to the meaning of 'relevant person's representative' see PARA 707 note 2.

23   Each of the following is an interested person:

     (1)   the relevant person's spouse or civil partner (Mental Capacity Act 2005 Sch A1 para 185(a) (as added: see note 3));

     (2)   where the relevant person and another person of the opposite sex are not married to each other but are living together as husband and wife: the other person (Sch A1 para 185(b) (as so added));

     (3)   where the relevant person and another person of the same sex are not civil partners of each other but are living together as if they were civil partners: the other person (Sch A1 para 185(c) (as so added));

     (4)   the relevant person's children and step-children (Sch A1 para 185(d) (as so added));

     (5)   the relevant person's parents and step-parents (Sch A1 para 185(e) (as so added));

     (6)   the relevant person's brothers and sisters, half-brothers and half-sisters, and stepbrothers and stepsisters (Sch A1 para 185(f) (as so added));

     (7)   the relevant person's grandparents (Sch A1 para 185(g) (as so added));

     (8)   a deputy appointed for the relevant person by the court (Sch A1 para 185(h) (as so added));

     (9)   a donee of a lasting power of attorney granted by the relevant person (Sch A1 para 185(i) (as so added)).

An interested person consulted by the best interests assessor is any person whose name is stated in the relevant best interests assessment in accordance with Sch A1 para 40 (interested persons whom the assessor consulted in carrying out the assessment: see PARA 674): Sch A1 para 186(1) (as so added). The relevant best interests assessment is the most recent best interests assessment carried out in connection with the standard authorisation in question (whether the assessment was carried out under Part 4 or Part 8): Sch A1 para 186(2) (as so added). Where Sch A1 imposes on a person a duty towards an interested person, the duty does not apply if the person on whom the duty is imposed is not aware of the interested person's identity or of a way of contacting him and cannot reasonably ascertain it: Sch A1 para 187 (as so added).

24 Mental Capacity Act 2005 Sch A1 para 65 (as added: see note 3). As to the meaning of 'assessor' see PARA 669.

666. Authorisation given: request for further authorisation. If a standard authorisation[1] has been given in relation to the detention of the relevant person[2] and that authorisation ('the existing authorisation') has not ceased to be in force[3], the provisions requiring request for authorisation[4] do not require a new request for a standard authorisation ('the new authorisation') to be made unless the following conditions are met[5].

The first condition is that the new authorisation would be in force at a time immediately after the expiry of the existing authorisation[6].

The second condition is that the new authorisation would not be in force at any time on or before the expiry of the existing authorisation[7].

The third condition is that it would, in the managing authority's[8] view, be unreasonable to delay making the request until a time nearer the expiry of the existing authorisation[9].

1 As to the meaning of 'standard authorisation' see PARA 663 note 1.
2 As to the meaning of 'relevant person' see PARA 663 note 7.
3 Mental Capacity Act 2005 Sch A1 para 29(1) (Sch A1 added by the Mental Health Act 2007 Sch 7).
4 Ie the Mental Capacity Act 2005 Sch A1 para 24 (see PARA 661).
5 Mental Capacity Act 2005 Sch A1 para 29(2) (as added: see note 3).
6 Mental Capacity Act 2005 Sch A1 para 29(3) (as added: see note 3). The expiry of the existing authorisation is the time when it is expected to cease to be in force: Sch A1 para 29(6) (as so added).
7 Mental Capacity Act 2005 Sch A1 para 29(4) (as added: see note 3).
8 As to the managing authority see PARA 652.
9 Mental Capacity Act 2005 Sch A1 para 29(5) (as added: see note 3).

667. Power to request authorisation. The following provisions apply if: (1) a standard authorisation[1] has been given in relation to the detention of the relevant person[2]; (2) that authorisation ('the existing authorisation') has not ceased to be in force[3]; (3) the requirement[4] to make a request for a new standard authorisation does not apply[5]; and (4) a review of the existing authorisation has been requested, or is being carried out[6].

The managing authority[7] may request a new standard authorisation which would be in force on or before the expiry of the existing authorisation[8]; but only if it would also be in force immediately after that expiry[9].

Where the managing authority requests a new standard authorisation under the above provisions[10] and it is required[11] to give the new authorisation, the existing authorisation terminates at the time when the new authorisation comes into force[12]. However, if the supervisory body are prohibited[13] from giving the new authorisation, there is no effect on the existing authorisation's continuation in force[14].

1 As to the meaning of 'standard authorisation' see PARA 663 note 1.
2 Mental Capacity Act 2005 Sch A1 para 30(1)(a) (Sch A1 added by the Mental Health Act 2007 Sch 7). As to the meaning of 'relevant person' see PARA 663 note 7. Further provision relating to cases where a request is made under the Mental Capacity Act 2005 Sch A1 para 30 can be found in Sch A1 para 62 (effect of decision about request: see PARA 662) and Sch A1 para 124 (effect of request on Part 8 review: see PARA 689): Sch A1 para 30(4) (as so added).
3 Mental Capacity Act 2005 Sch A1 para 30(1)(b) (as added: see note 2).
4 Ie the requirement under the Mental Capacity Act 2005 Sch A1 para 24 (see PARA 661).

5 Ie because of the Mental Capacity Act 2005 Sch A1 para 29 (see PARA 666): Sch A1 para 30(1)(c) (as added: see note 2).
6 Ie in accordance with the Mental Capacity Act 2005 Sch A1 Pt 8 (see PARA 689 et seq); Sch A1 para 30(1)(d) (as added: see note 2).
7 As to the managing authority see PARA 652.
8 The expiry of the existing authorisation is the time when it is expected to cease to be in force: Mental Capacity Act 2005 Sch A1 para 30(3) (as added: see note 2).
9 Mental Capacity Act 2005 Sch A1 para 30(2) (as added: see note 2).
10 Ie under the Mental Capacity Act 2005 Sch A1 para 30.
11 Ie required by the Mental Capacity Act 2005 Sch A1 para 50(1) (see PARA 663).
12 Mental Capacity Act 2005 Sch A1 para 62(1)(b), (2) (as added: see note 2).
13 Ie prohibited by the Mental Capacity Act 2005 Sch A1 para 50(2) (see PARA 663).
14 Mental Capacity Act 2005 Sch A1 para 62(3) (as added: see note 2).

668. Information included in request and record of request. A request for a standard authorisation[1] must include the information (if any) required by regulations[2].

The managing authority of a hospital or care home[3] must keep a written record of each request that it makes for a standard authorisation and the reasons for making each request[4].

A supervisory body[5] must keep a written record of each request for a standard authorisation that is made to them[6].

1 As to the meaning of 'standard authorisation' see PARA 663 note 1.
2 Mental Capacity Act 2005 Sch A1 para 31 (Sch A1 added by the Mental Health Act 2007 Sch 7). As to the information to be included see the Mental Capacity (Deprivation of Liberty: Standard Authorisations, Assessments and Ordinary Residence) Regulations 2008, SI 2008/1858, reg 16 and the Mental Capacity (Deprivation of Liberty: Assessments, Standard Authorisations and Disputes about Residence) (Wales) Regulations 2009, SI 2009/783, reg 13.
3 As to the meanings of 'supervisory body' and 'care home' see PARA 652. As to the meaning of 'hospital' see PARA 577.
4 Mental Capacity Act 2005 Sch A1 para 32(1) (as added: see note 2).
5 As to the managing authority see PARA 652.
6 Mental Capacity Act 2005 Sch A1 para 32(2) (as added: see note 2).

669. Assessments. Where the supervisory body[1] is requested to give a standard authorisation[2] it must secure that all of the following assessments are carried out in relation to the relevant person[3]:

  (1)   an age assessment[4];
  (2)   a mental health assessment[5];
  (3)   a mental capacity assessment[6];
  (4)   a best interests assessment[7];
  (5)   an eligibility assessment[8];
  (6)   a no refusals assessment[9].

The person who carries out any such assessment is referred to as the assessor and regulations may be made about the period (or periods) within which assessors must carry out assessments[10].

1 As to the meaning of 'supervisory body' see PARA 652.
2 Mental Capacity Act 2005 Sch A1 para 33(1) (Sch A1 added by the Mental Health Act 2007 Sch 7). As to the meaning of 'standard authorisation' see PARA 663 note 1. The Mental Capacity Act 2005 Sch A1 para 33 is subject to Sch A1 paras 49, 133 (see PARAS 700, 706): Sch A1 para 33(5) (as so added).
3 As to the meaning of 'relevant person' see PARA 663 note 7. As to when the supervisory body are not required to secure that a particular kind of assessment is carried out see the Mental Capacity act 2005 Sch A1 para 49; and PARA 670.
4 Mental Capacity Act 2005 Sch A1 para 33(2)(a) (as added: see note 2). As to the age assessment see PARA 671.

5   Mental Capacity Act 2005 Sch A1 para 33(2)(b) (as added: see note 2). As to the mental health assessment see PARA 672.

6   Mental Capacity Act 2005 Sch A1 para 33(2)(c) (as added: see note 2). As to the mental capacity assessment see PARA 673.

7   Mental Capacity Act 2005 Sch A1 para 33(2)(d) (as added: see note 2). As to the best interests assessment see PARA 674.

8   Mental Capacity Act 2005 Sch A1 para 33(2)(e) (as added: see note 2). As to the eligibility assessment see PARA 675.

9   Mental Capacity Act 2005 Sch A1 para 33(2)(f) (as added: see note 2). As to the no refusals assessment see PARA 676.

10 Mental Capacity Act 2005 Sch A1 para 33(3), (4) (as added: see note 2). As to the time frame for assessments see the Mental Capacity (Deprivation of Liberty: Standard Authorisations, Assessments and Ordinary Residence) Regulations 2008, SI 2008/1858, reg 13 and the Mental Capacity (Deprivation of Liberty: Assessments, Standard Authorisations and Disputes about Residence) (Wales) Regulations 2009, SI 2009/783, reg 9.

670. Equivalent assessment already carried out. The supervisory body[1] is not required[2] to secure that a particular kind of assessment ('the required assessment') is carried out in relation to the relevant person[3] if the following conditions are met[4].

The first condition is that the supervisory body has a written copy of an assessment of the relevant person ('the existing assessment') that has already been carried out[5].

The second condition is that the existing assessment complies with all the requirements[6] with which the required assessment would have to comply if it were carried out[7].

The third condition is that the existing assessment was carried out within the previous 12 months; but this condition need not be met if the required assessment is an age assessment[8].

The fourth condition is that the supervisory body are satisfied that there is no reason why the existing assessment may no longer be accurate[9].

1   As to the meaning of 'supervisory body' see PARA 652.

2   Ie by the Mental Capacity Act 2005 Sch A1 para 33 (see PARA 669).

3   As to the meaning of 'relevant person' see PARA 663 note 7.

4   Mental Capacity Act 2005 Sch A1 para 49(1) (Sch A1 added by the Mental Health Act 2007 Sch 7). As to the no refusals requirement see PARA 676.

5   Mental Capacity Act 2005 Sch A1 para 49(2) (as added: see note 4).

6   Ie the requirements under the Mental Capacity Act 2005 Sch A1.

7   Mental Capacity Act 2005 Sch A1 para 49(3) (as added: see note 4).

8   Mental Capacity Act 2005 Sch A1 para 49(4) (as added: see note 4). As to the age assessment see PARA 671.

9   Mental Capacity Act 2005 Sch A1 para 49(5) (as added: see note 4). If the required assessment is a best interests assessment, in satisfying themselves as mentioned in Sch A1 para 49(5), the supervisory body must take into account any information given, or submissions made, by the relevant person's representative, any section 39C IMCA or any section 39D IMCA: Sch A1 para 49(6) (as so added). A 'section 39C IMCA' is an independent mental capacity advocate appointed under s 39C (see PARA 643) and a 'section 39D IMCA' is an independent mental capacity advocate appointed under s 39D (see PARA 644): see Sch A1 paras 156, 157 (as so added). As to the best interests assessment see PARA 674. It does not matter whether the existing assessment was carried out in connection with a request for a standard authorisation or for some other purpose: Sch A1 para 49(7) (as so added). If, because of Sch A1 para 49, the supervisory body are not required by Sch A1 para 33 (see PARA 669) to secure that the required assessment is carried out, the existing assessment is to be treated for the purposes of Sch A1 as an assessment of the same kind as the required assessment and as having been carried out under Sch A1 para 33 in connection with the request for the standard authorisation: Sch A1 para 49(8) (as so added). As to the meaning of 'standard authorisation' see PARA 663 note 1. As to the meaning of 'relevant person's representative' see PARA 707 note 2.

671. Age assessment. An age assessment is an assessment of whether the relevant person[1] meets the age requirement[2].

1   As to the meaning of 'relevant person' see PARA 663 note 7.

2   Mental Capacity Act 2005 Sch A1 para 34 (Sch A1 added by the Mental Health Act 2007 Sch 7). As to the age requirement see PARA 654.

672. Mental health assessment. A mental health assessment is an assessment of whether the relevant person[1] meets the mental health requirement[2].

When carrying out a mental health assessment, the assessor[3] must also consider how (if at all) the relevant person's mental health is likely to be affected by his being a detained resident[4] and notify the best interests assessor[5] of his conclusions[6].

1   As to the meaning of 'relevant person' see PARA 663 note 7.

2   Mental Capacity Act 2005 Sch A1 para 35 (Sch A1 added by the Mental Health Act 2007 Sch 7). As to the mental health requirement see PARA 655.

3   As to the eligibility to carry out a mental health assessment see PARA 699.

4   As to the meaning of 'detained resident' see PARA 661 note 6.

5   As to the best interests assessor see PARA 669.

6   Mental Capacity Act 2005 Sch A1 para 36 (as added: see note 2).

673. Mental capacity assessment. A mental capacity assessment is an assessment of whether the relevant person[1] meets the mental capacity requirement[2].

1   As to the meaning of 'relevant person' see PARA 663 note 7.

2   Mental Capacity Act 2005 Sch A1 para 37 (Sch A1 added by the Mental Health Act 2007 Sch 7). As to the mental capacity requirement see PARA 656. As to the eligibility to carry out a mental capacity assessment see PARA 699.

674. Best interests assessment. A best interests assessment is an assessment of whether the relevant person[1] meets the best interests requirement[2].

In carrying out a best interests assessment, the assessor[3] must comply with the following duties[4]. The assessor must consult the managing authority[5] of the relevant hospital or care home[6] and must have regard to the conclusions which the mental health assessor has notified to the best interests assessor[7], any relevant needs assessment[8] and any relevant care plan[9].

The managing authority must give the assessor a copy of any relevant needs assessment carried out by them, or on their behalf, or any relevant care plan drawn up by them or on their behalf[10]. The supervisory body[11] must give the assessor a copy of any relevant needs assessment carried out by them or on their behalf or any relevant care plan drawn up by them or on their behalf[12].

Whatever conclusion the best interests assessment comes to the assessor must state in the best interests assessment the name and address of every interested person[13] whom he has consulted in carrying out the assessment[14].

If the best interests assessment comes to the conclusion that the relevant person meets the best interests requirement, the assessor must state in the assessment the maximum authorisation period[15]. The assessor may include in the assessment recommendations about conditions[16] to which the standard authorisation is, or is not, to be subject[17].

The following applies if the best interests assessment comes to the conclusion that the relevant person does not meet the best interests requirement[18].

If, on the basis of the information taken into account in carrying out the assessment, it appears to the assessor that there is an unauthorised deprivation of liberty[19], he must include a statement to that effect in the assessment[20].

1 As to the meaning of 'relevant person' see PARA 663 note 7.
2 Mental Capacity Act 2005 Sch A1 para 38 (Sch A1 added by the Mental Health Act 2007 Sch 7). As to the best interests requirement see PARA 657. The Convention on Human Rights, art 5 does not impose any threshold conditions to be satisfied before a best interests assessment can be carried out: see *G v E (by his litigation friend the Official Solicitor)* [2010] EWCA Civ 822, [2012] Fam 78, [2010] 4 All ER 579. As to the best interests assessment see further the Ministry of *Justice Deprivation of Liberty Safeguards – code of practice to supplement the main Mental Capacity Act 2005 code of practice* (2008) paras 4,58–4.76. The best interests assessment is the cornerstone of the protection that the deprivation of liberty safeguards offer to those facing deprivation of liberty if they are to be effective safeguards at all: *Hillingdon London Borough Council v Neary* [2011] EWHC 1377 (COP), [2011] 4 All ER 584, [2011] 3 FCR 448. If the supervisory body considers that the assessment has been inadequate it is obliged to take all necessary steps to remedy the inadequacy including if necessary to bring the deprivation of liberty to an end, conducting an interview under Sch A1 Pt 8 (see PARA 689 et seq) or applying to the court: *Hillingdon London Borough Council v Neary*.
3 As to the eligibility to carry out a best interests assessment see PARA 700.
4 Mental Capacity Act 2005 Sch A1 para 39(1), (2) (as added: see note 2). The duties with which the best interests assessor must comply are subject to the provision included in appointment regulations under Pt 10 (in particular, provision made under Sch A1 para 146: see PARA 708): Sch A1 para 45 (as so added).
5 As to the managing authority see PARA 652.
6 Mental Capacity Act 2005 Sch A1 para 39(2) (as added: see note 2). As to the meaning of 'relevant hospital or care home' see PARA 663 note 2; and as to the meaning of 'care home' see PARA 652. As to the meaning of 'hospital' see PARA 577. The duty in Sch A1 para 39(2) does not affect any other duty to consult or to take the views of others into account: Sch A1 para 39(8) (as so added).
7 Ie in accordance with the Mental Capacity Act 2005 Sch A1 para 36(b) (see PARA 672).
8 A relevant needs assessment is an assessment of the relevant person's needs which was carried out in connection with the relevant person being accommodated in the relevant hospital or care home and was carried out by or on behalf of the managing authority of the relevant hospital or care home or the supervisory body: Mental Capacity Act 2005 Sch A1 para 39(4) (as added: see note 2).
9 Mental Capacity Act 2005 Sch A1 para 39(3) (as added: see note 2). A relevant care plan is a care plan which sets out how the relevant person's needs are to be met whilst he is accommodated in the relevant hospital or care home and was drawn up by or on behalf of the managing authority of the relevant hospital or care home or the supervisory body: Sch A1 para 39(5) (as so added). The duty in Sch A1 para 39(3) does not affect any other duty to consult or to take the views of others into account: Sch A1 para 39(8) (as so added).
10 Mental Capacity Act 2005 Sch A1 para 39(6) (as added: see note 2).
11 As to the meaning of 'supervisory body' see PARA 652.
12 Mental Capacity Act 2005 Sch A1 para 39(7) (as added: see note 2).
13 As to the meaning of 'interested person' see PARA 665 note 23.
14 Mental Capacity Act 2005 Sch A1 para 40 (as added: see note 2).
15 Mental Capacity Act 2005 Sch A1 paras 41, 42(1) (as added: see note 2). The maximum authorisation period is the shorter of these periods: (1) the period which, in the assessor's opinion, would be the appropriate maximum period for the relevant person to be a detained resident under the standard authorisation that has been requested; (2) 1 year, or such shorter period as may be prescribed in regulations: Sch A1 para 42(2) (as so added). Regulations under head (2) need not provide for a shorter period to apply in relation to all standard authorisations and may provide for different periods to apply in relation to different kinds of standard authorisations: Sch A1 para 42(3) (as so added). Before making regulations under Sch A1 para 42(2)(b) the appropriate national authority is required to consult certain persons and bodies: see Sch A1 para 42(4), (5) (as so added). As to the meaning of 'appropriate national authority' see PARA 567. At the date at which this volume states the law no regulations had been made under Sch 1A para 42(2).
16 Ie conditions to which the standard authorisation is, or is not, to be subject in accordance with the Mental Capacity Act 2005 Sch A1 para 53 (see PARA 665).
17 Mental Capacity Act 2005 Sch A1 para 43 (as added: see note 2).

18 Mental Capacity Act 2005 Sch A1 para 44(1) (as added: see note 2).

19 There is an unauthorised deprivation of liberty if the managing authority of the relevant hospital or care home are already depriving the relevant person of his liberty without authority of the kind mentioned in the Mental Capacity Act 2005 s 4A (see PARA 648): Sch A1 para 44(3) (as added: see note 2).

20 Mental Capacity Act 2005 Sch A1 para 44(2) (as added: see note 2).

675. Eligibility assessment. An eligibility assessment is an assessment of whether the relevant person[1] meets the eligibility requirement[2]. Where an individual is being assessed and the eligibility assessor[3] and the best interests assessor[4] are not the same person the eligibility assessor must request that the best interests assessor provides any relevant eligibility information[5] that the best interests assessor may have and the best interests assessor must comply with such a request[6].

1 As to the meaning of 'relevant person' see PARA 663 note 7.

2 Mental Capacity Act 2005 Sch A1 para 46 (Sch A1 added by the Mental Health Act 2007 Sch 7). As to the eligibility requirement see PARA 658.

3 For these purposes 'eligibility assessor' means a person carrying out an eligibility assessment in relation to the relevant person: Mental Capacity Act 2005 Sch A1 para 47(2) (as added: see note 2); Mental Capacity (Deprivation of Liberty: Standard Authorisations, Assessments and Ordinary Residence) Regulations 2008, SI 2008/1858, reg 15(4); Mental Capacity (Deprivation of Liberty: Assessments, Standard Authorisations and Disputes about Residence) (Wales) Regulations 2009, SI 2009/783, reg 2(1). As to the eligibility to carry out an eligibility assessment see PARA 702.

4 For these purposes 'best interests assessor' means any person who is carrying out, or has carried out, a best interests assessment in relation to the relevant person: Mental Capacity Act 2005 Sch A1 para 47(2) (as added: see note 2); Mental Capacity (Deprivation of Liberty: Standard Authorisations, Assessments and Ordinary Residence) Regulations 2008, SI 2008/1858, reg 2; Mental Capacity (Deprivation of Liberty: Assessments, Standard Authorisations and Disputes about Residence) (Wales) Regulations 2009, SI 2009/783, reg 2.

5 For these purposes 'relevant eligibility information' is information relevant to assessing whether or not the relevant person is ineligible by virtue of the Mental Capacity Act 2005 Sch 1A para 5: Sch A1 para 47(2) (as added: see note 2).

6 See the Mental Capacity Act 2005 Sch A1 para 47(1) (as added: see note 2); Mental Capacity (Deprivation of Liberty: Standard Authorisations, Assessments and Ordinary Residence) Regulations 2008, SI 2008/1858, reg 15(1)–(3); Mental Capacity (Deprivation of Liberty: Assessments, Standard Authorisations and Disputes about Residence) (Wales) Regulations 2009, SI 2009/783, reg 12.

676. No refusals assessment. A no refusals assessment is an assessment of whether the relevant person[1] meets the no refusals requirement[2].

1 As to the meaning of 'relevant person' see PARA 663 note 7.

2 Mental Capacity Act 2005 Sch A1 para 48 (Sch A1 added by the Mental Health Act 2007 Sch 7). As to the no refusals requirement see PARA 660.

677. Duty to give information about decision. If a request is made for a standard authorisation[1] and the supervisory body[2] are required[3] to give the standard authorisation[4], the supervisory body must[5] give a copy of the authorisation to each of the following:

(1) the relevant person's representative[6];

(2) the managing authority of the relevant hospital or care home[7];

(3) the relevant person[8];

(4) any section 39A IMCA[9];

(5) every interested person[10] consulted by the best interests assessor[11].

If a request is made for a standard authorisation and the supervisory body are prohibited[12] from giving the standard authorisation[13], the supervisory body must give notice[14], stating that they are prohibited from giving the authorisation, to each of the following:

(a)   the managing authority of the relevant hospital or care home[15];
(b)   the relevant person[16];
(c)   any section 39A IMCA[17];
(d)   every interested person consulted by the best interests assessor[18].

1   As to the meaning of 'standard authorisation' see PARA 663 note 1.
2   As to the meaning of 'supervisory body' see PARA 664.
3   Ie required by the Mental Capacity Act 2005 Sch A1 para 50(1) (see PARA 663).
4   Mental Capacity Act 2005 Sch A1 para 57(1) (Sch A1 added by the Mental Health Act 2007 Sch 7).
5   The supervisory body must comply with the Mental Capacity Act 2005 Sch A1 para 57 as soon as practicable after they give the standard authorisation: Sch A1 para 57(3) (as added: see note 4).
6   Mental Capacity Act 2005 Sch A1 para 57(2)(a) (as added: see note 4). A request for a standard authorisation is to be regarded for the purposes of Sch A1 as disposed of if the supervisory body have given a copy of the authorisation in accordance with Sch A1 para 57 or notice in accordance with Sch A1 para 58: Sch A1 para 66 (as so added). As to the meaning of 'relevant person's representative' see PARA 707 note 2.
7   Mental Capacity Act 2005 Sch A1 para 57(2)(b) (as added: see note 4). As to the meaning of 'relevant hospital or care home' see PARA 663 note 2.
8   Mental Capacity Act 2005 Sch A1 para 57(2)(c) (as added: see note 4). As to the meaning of 'relevant person' see PARA 663 note 7.
9   Mental Capacity Act 2005 Sch A1 para 57(2)(d) (as added: see note 4). As to the meaning of 'section 39A IMCA' see PARA 705 note 8.
10   As to the meaning of 'interested person' see PARA 665 note 23.
11   Mental Capacity Act 2005 Sch A1 para 57(2)(e) (as added: see note 4). As to the best interests assessor see PARA 665 notes 23, 24.
12   Ie prohibited by the Mental Capacity Act 2005 Sch A1 para 50(2) (see PARA 663).
13   Mental Capacity Act 2005 Sch A1 para 58(1) (as added: see note 4).
14   The supervisory body must comply with this provision as soon as practicable after it becomes apparent to them that they are prohibited from giving the authorisation: Mental Capacity Act 2005 Sch A1 para 58(3) (as added: see note 4). Any notice under Sch A1 must be in writing: Sch A1 para 169 (as so added).
15   Mental Capacity Act 2005 Sch A1 para 58(2)(a) (as added: see note 4).
16   Mental Capacity Act 2005 Sch A1 para 58(2)(b) (as added: see note 4).
17   Mental Capacity Act 2005 Sch A1 para 58(2)(c) (as added: see note 4).
18   Mental Capacity Act 2005 Sch A1 para 58(2)(d) (as added: see note 4).

678.   Duty to give information about effect of authorisation.   If a standard authorisation[1] is given the managing authority[2] of the relevant hospital or care home[3] must take such steps[4] as are practicable to ensure that the relevant person[5] understands all of the following:

(1)   the effect of the authorisation[6];
(2)   the right to make an application to the court to exercise its jurisdiction[7];
(3)   the right[8] to request a review[9];
(4)   the right to have a section 39D IMCA appointed[10];
(5)   how to have a section 39D IMCA appointed[11].

Any written information given to the relevant person must also be given by the managing authority to the relevant person's representative[12] as soon as is practicable after it is given to the relevant person[13]. If the managing authority is notified that a section 39D IMCA has been appointed, as soon as is practicable after being so notified, the managing authority must give the section 39D IMCA a copy of the written information[14].

1 As to the meaning of 'standard authorisation' see PARA 663 note 1.
2 As to the meaning of 'managing authority' see PARA 652.
3 As to the meaning of 'relevant hospital and care home' see PARA 663 note 2.
4 The steps must be taken as soon as is practicable after the authorisation is given and must include the giving of appropriate information both orally and in writing: Mental Capacity Act 2005 Sch A1 para 59(3), (4) (Sch A1 added by the Mental Health Act 2007 Sch 7).
5 As to the meaning of 'relevant person' see PARA 663 note 7.
6 Mental Capacity Act 2005 Sch A1 para 59(1), (2)(a) (as added: see note 4).
7 Ie the jurisdiction of the court under the Mental Capacity Act 2005 s 21A (see PARA 733): Sch A1 para 59(2)(b) (as added: see note 4).
8 Ie the right under the Mental Capacity Act 2005 Sch A1 Pt 8 (paras 101–125).
9 Mental Capacity Act 2005 Sch A1 para 59(2)(c) (as added: see note 4).
10 Mental Capacity Act 2005 Sch A1 para 59(2)(d) (as added: see note 4). As to the meaning of 'section 39D IMCA' see PARA 670 note 9.
11 Mental Capacity Act 2005 Sch A1 para 59(2)(e) (as added: see note 4).
12 As to the meaning of 'relevant person's representative' see PARA 707 note 2.
13 Mental Capacity Act 2005 Sch A1 para 59(5), (6) (as added: see note 4).
14 Mental Capacity Act 2005 Sch A1 para 59(7), (8) (as so added).

679. Right of third party to require consideration of whether authorisation needed. If the following conditions are met, an eligible person[1] may request the supervisory body[2] to decide whether or not there is an unauthorised deprivation of liberty[3]. The first condition is that the eligible person has notified the managing authority[4] of the relevant hospital or care home that it appears to the eligible person that there is an unauthorised deprivation of liberty[5]. The second condition is that the eligible person has asked the managing authority to request a standard authorisation in relation to the detention of the relevant person[6]. The third condition is that the managing authority has not requested a standard authorisation within a reasonable period after the eligible person asks it to do so[7].

If an eligible person requests the supervisory body to decide whether or not there is an unauthorised deprivation of liberty, the supervisory body must select and appoint a person to carry out an assessment[8] of whether or not the relevant person is a detained resident[9]. However, the supervisory body need not select and appoint a person to carry out such an assessment where it appears to the supervisory body that the request by the eligible person is frivolous or vexatious or where it appears to the supervisory body that the question of whether or not there is an unauthorised deprivation of liberty has already been decided and, since that decision, there has been no change of circumstances which would merit the question being decided again[10].

The supervisory body must notify the eligible person who made the request, the person to whom the request relates, the managing authority of the relevant hospital or care home and any section 39A IMCA[11], that the supervisory body have been requested to decide whether or not there is an unauthorised deprivation of liberty, of its decision whether or not to select and appoint a person to carry out an assessment and, if its decision is to select and appoint a person, of the person appointed[12]. If the supervisory body obtains an assessment it must also notify the eligible person who made the request, the person to whom the request relates, the managing authority of the relevant hospital or care home and any section 39A IMCA, of the outcome of the assessment[13].

1 For these purposes 'eligible person' means any person other than the managing authority of the relevant hospital or care home: Mental Capacity Act 2005 Sch A1 para 68(5) (Sch A1 added by the Mental Health Act 2007 Sch 7).
2 As to the meaning of 'supervisory body' see PARA 664.

3 Mental Capacity Act 2005 Sch A1 para 68(1) (as added: see note 1). For these purposes there is an unauthorised deprivation of liberty if a person is already a detained resident in a hospital or care home and the detention of the person is not authorised as mentioned in s 4A (see PARA 648): Sch A1 para 67 (as so added). As to the meaning of 'detained resident' see PARA 661 note 6. As to the meaning of 'care home' see PARA 652. As to the meaning of 'hospital' see PARA 577.

4 As to the meaning of 'managing authority' see PARA 652.

5 Mental Capacity Act 2005 Sch A1 para 68(2) (as added: see note 1).

6 Mental Capacity Act 2005 Sch A1 para 68(3) (as added: see note 1).

7 Mental Capacity Act 2005 Sch A1 para 68(4) (as added: see note 1).

8 The supervisory body must not select and appoint a person to carry out an assessment under this provision unless it appears to the supervisory body that the person would be suitable to carry out a best interests assessment (if one were obtained in connection with a request for a standard authorisation relating to the relevant person) and eligible to carry out such a best interests assessment: Mental Capacity Act 2005 Sch A1 para 69(6) (as added: see note 1). An assessment must be completed, in relation to England, within the period of 7 days beginning with the date that the supervisory body receives the request from an eligible person and, in relation to Wales, within 5 days from the date on which the assessor is instructed by the supervisory body: see the Mental Capacity Act 2005 Sch A1 para 70(1); Mental Capacity (Deprivation of Liberty: Standard Authorisations, Assessments and Ordinary Residence) Regulations 2008, SI 2008/1858, reg 14; Mental Capacity (Deprivation of Liberty: Assessments, Standard Authorisations and Disputes about Residence) (Wales) Regulations 2009, SI 2009/783, reg 10.

9 Mental Capacity Act 2005 Sch A1 para 69(1), (2) (as added: see note 1).

10 Mental Capacity Act 2005 Sch A1 para 69(3) (as added: see note 1).

11 As to the meaning of 'section 39A IMCA' see PARA 705 note 8.

12 Mental Capacity Act 2005 Sch A1 para 69(7), (8) (as added: see note 1). Regulations made under Sch A1 para 129(3) (see PARA 695) apply in relation to the selection and appointment of a person under Sch A1 para 69 as they apply to the selection of a person under Sch A1 para 129 to carry out a best interests assessment: Sch A1 para 70(2) (as so added). The following provisions apply to an assessment under Sch A1 para 69 as they apply to an assessment carried out in connection with a request for a standard authorisation Sch A1 para 131 (examination and copying of records: see PARA 705), Sch A1 para 132 (representations: see PARA 706); Sch A1 paras 134, 135(1) and (2) (duty to keep records and give copies: see PARA 705): Sch A1 para 70(3) (as so added). The copies of the assessment which the supervisory body are required to give under Sch A1 para 135(2) must be given as soon as practicable after the supervisory body are themselves given a copy of the assessment: Sch A1 para 70(4) (as so added).

13 See the Mental Capacity Act 2005 Sch A1 paras 71–73 (as added: see note 1). If the assessment comes to the conclusion that the relevant person is a detained resident and it appears to the supervisory body that the detention of the person is not authorised as mentioned in s 4A (see PARA 648), Sch A1 paras 74–90: see PARA 713 yet seq) apply as if the managing authority of the relevant hospital or care home had, in accordance with Sch A1 Pt 4, requested the supervisory body to give a standard authorisation in relation to the relevant persons mentioned in the text must be notified both that Sch A1 applies and that it appears to the supervisory body that the detention is authorised: see Sch A1 para 71(1)(b), (c), (4)(b), 73(2)(b) (as so added). The managing authority of the relevant hospital or care home must supply the supervisory body with the information (if any) which the managing authority would, by virtue of Sch A1 para 31 (see PARA 668), have had to include in a request for a standard authorisation: Sch A1 para 71(3) (as so added).

B. ELIGIBILITY REQUIREMENT NOT MET: SUSPENSION OF STANDARD AUTHORISATION

680. Suspension of standard authorisation. Where a standard authorisation[1] has been given and has not ceased to be in force and the managing authority[2] of the relevant hospital or care home[3] is satisfied that the relevant person[4] has ceased to meet the eligibility requirement[5] the managing authority of the relevant hospital or care home must give the supervisory body notice[6] that the relevant person has ceased to meet the eligibility requirement[7]. The standard authorisation is subsequently suspended from the time when the notice is given[8] and the supervisory body must give notice of its suspension to the relevant person, the relevant person's representative[9] and the managing authority of the relevant hospital or care home[10].

1 As to the meaning of 'standard authorisation' see PARA 663 note 1.
2 As to the meaning of 'managing authority' see PARA 652.
3 As to the meaning of 'relevant hospital or care home' see PARA 663 note 2.
4 As to the meaning of 'relevant person' see PARA 663 note 7.
5 See the Mental Capacity Act 2005 Sch A1 para 91(1)–(3) (Sch A1 added by the Mental Health Act 2007 Sch 7). As to the eligibility requirement see PARA 658. However the Mental Capacity Act 2005 Sch A1 paras 91–97 do not apply if the relevant person is ineligible by virtue of Sch A1 para 5 (in which case see Sch A1 paras 101–125): Sch A1 para 91(4) (as so added).
6 As to the meaning of 'supervisory body' see PARA 664. Any notice under the Mental Capacity Act 2005 Sch A1 must be in writing: Sch A1 para 169 (as added: see note 5).
7 See the Mental Capacity Act 2005 Sch A1 para 92 (as added: see note 5).
8 See the Mental Capacity Act 2005 Sch A1 para 93(1), (2) (as added: see note 5). The effect of suspending the standard authorisation is that Sch A1 paras 1–4 (see PARA 651) cease to apply for as long as the authorisation is suspended: Sch A1 para 97 (as so added).
9 As to the meaning of 'relevant person's representative' see PARA 707 note 2.
10 See the Mental Capacity Act 2005 Sch A1 para 93(3) (as added: see note 5).

681.   Standard authorisation ceases to be suspended. If, whilst the standard authorisation[1] is suspended, the managing authority[2] is satisfied that the relevant person[3] meets the eligibility requirement[4] again[5] the managing authority must give the supervisory body notice[6] that the relevant person once again meets the eligibility requirement[7]. The standard authorisation ceases to be suspended from the time when the notice is given and the supervisory body must, as soon as practicable after being given such notice, give notice that it has ceased to be suspended to the relevant person, the relevant person's representative[8], any section 39D IMCA[9] and the managing authority of the relevant hospital or care home[10].

1 As to the meaning of 'standard authorisation' see PARA 663 note 1.
2 As to the meaning of 'managing authority' see PARA 652.
3 As to the meaning of 'relevant person' see PARA 663 note 7.
4 As to the eligibility requirement see PARA 658.
5 See the Mental Capacity Act 2005 Sch A1 para 94(1) (Sch A1 added by the Mental Health Act 2007 Sch 7). if no notice is given under the Mental Capacity Act 2005 Sch A1 para 94 before the end of the relevant 28 day period the standard authorisation ceases to have effect at the end of the relevant 28 day period: Sch A1 para 96(1), (2) (as so added). The relevant 28 day period is the period of 28 days beginning with the day on which the standard authorisation is suspended under Sch A1 para 93 (see PARA 680).
6 As to the meaning of 'supervisory body' see PARA 664. Any notice under the Mental Capacity Act 2005 Sch A1 must be in writing: Sch A1 para 169 (as added: see note 5).
7 Mental Capacity Act 2005 Sch A1 para 94(2) (as added: see note 5).
8 As to the meaning of 'relevant person's representative' see PARA 707 note 2.
9 As to the meaning of 'section 39D IMCA' see PARA 670 note 9.
10 See the Mental Capacity Act 2005 Sch A1 para 95 (as added: see note 5). As to the meaning of 'relevant hospital or care home' see PARA 663 note 2.

C. CHANGE IN SUPERVISORY RESPONSIBILITY

682.   Change in supervisory responsibility. If a standard authorisation[1] has been given and has not ceased to be in force and there is a change in supervisory responsibility[2] but no change in the place of detention[3] the new supervisory body becomes the supervisory body in relation to the authorisation[4].

Anything done by or in relation to the old supervisory body in connection with the authorisation has effect, so far as is necessary for continuing its effect after the change, as if done by or in relation to the new supervisory body[5].

Anything which relates to the authorisation and which is in the process of being done by or in relation to the old supervisory body at the time of the change may be continued by or in relation to the new supervisory body[6].

However, the old supervisory body does not, by virtue of these provisions, cease to be liable for anything done by them in connection with the authorisation before the change and the new supervisory body does not, by virtue of these provisions, become liable for any such thing[7].

1   As to the meaning of 'standard authorisation' see PARA 663 note 1.
2   For this purpose there is a change in supervisory responsibility if one body ('the old supervisory body') has ceased to be supervisory body in relation to the standard authorisation and a different body ('the new supervisory body') has become supervisory body in relation to the standard authorisation: Mental Capacity Act 2005 Sch A1 para 99 (Sch A1 added by the Mental Health Act 2007 Sch 7). As to the meaning of 'supervisory body' see PARA 664.
3   As to the meaning of 'place of detention' see the Mental Capacity Act 2005 Sch A1 para 25; and PARA 662.
4   See the Mental Capacity Act 2005 Sch A1 paras 98, 100(1) (as added: see note 2).
5   Mental Capacity Act 2005 Sch A1 para 100(2) (as added: see note 2).
6   Mental Capacity Act 2005 Sch A1 para 100(3) (as added: see note 2).
7   Mental Capacity Act 2005 Sch A1 para 100(4) (as added: see note 2).

D. REVIEW

683.   Review by supervisory body.   If a standard authorisation[1] has been given and has not ceased to be in force the supervisory body[2] may at any time carry out a review[3] of the standard authorisation[4]. It must carry out such a review if requested to do so by an eligible person[5] and an eligible person may, at any time, request the supervisory body to carry out such a review[6]. The managing authority[7] of the relevant hospital or care home[8] must make such a request if one or more of the qualifying requirements[9] appear to them to be reviewable[10].

When a review is complete, the supervisory body must give notice[11] to the managing authority of the relevant hospital or care home, the relevant person, the relevant person's representative[12], of any section 39D IMCA[13].

A supervisory body must keep a written record of each request for a review that is made to it, the outcome of each request, each review which it carries out, the outcome of each review which it carries out and any variation[14] of an authorisation made in consequence of a review[15].

1   As to the meaning of 'standard authorisation' see PARA 663 note 1.
2   As to the meaning of 'supervisory body' see PARA 664.
3   Ie in accordance with the Mental Capacity Act 2005 Sch A1 paras 101–125. As to the powers of the Court of Protection see s 21A; and PARA 733.
4   See the Mental Capacity Act 205 Sch A1 paras 101, 102(1) (Sch A1 added by the Mental Health Act 2007 Sch 7).
5   Mental Capacity Act 2005 Sch A1 para 102(2) (as added: see note 4). Each of the following is an eligible person: (1) the relevant person; (2) the relevant person's representative; (3) the managing authority of the relevant hospital or care home: Sch A1 para 102(3) (as so added). As to the meaning of 'relevant person' see PARA 663 note 7. If, and for so long as, there is a 'section 39C IMCA' head (2) is to be read as a reference to the section 39C IMCA but this does not apply to any function under the relevant provisions for as long as the function is suspended in accordance with provision made under Part 10: see Sch A1 para 159 (as so added). As to the meaning of 'section 39C IMCA' see PARA 670 note 9.
6   Mental Capacity Act 2005 Sch A1 para 103(1) (as added: see note 4).
7   As to the meaning of 'managing authority' see PARA 652.

8   As to the meaning of 'relevant hospital or care home' see PARA 663 note 2.
9   As to the qualifying requirements see PARAS 653–660.
10 Mental Capacity Act 2005 Sch A1 para 103(2) (as added: see note 4).
11 The notice must state the outcome of the review and what variation (if any) has been made to the authorisation under the Mental Capacity Act 2005 Sch A1 paras 101–125: Sch A1 para 120(2) (as added: see note 4). Any notice under Sch A1 must be in writing: Sch A1 para 169 (as so added).
12 As to the meaning of 'relevant person's representative' see PARA 707 note 2. If, and for so long as, there is a 'section 39C IMCA' the reference in the text to relevant person's representative is to be read as a reference to the section 39C IMCA but this does not apply to any function under the relevant provisions for as long as the function is suspended in accordance with provision made under Part 10: see the Mental Capacity Act 2005 Sch A1 para 159 (as added: see note 4).
13 Mental Capacity Act 2005 Sch A1 para 120(1) (as added: see note 4). As to the meaning of 'section 39D IMCA' see PARA 670 note 9.
14 Any variation of the standard authorisation must be in writing: see the Mental Capacity Act 2005 Sch A1 para 119 (as added: see note 4).
15 Mental Capacity Act 2005 Sch A1 para 121 (as added: see note 4).

684.   Grounds for reviewing the qualifying requirements. The only grounds on which the qualifying requirements are reviewable[1] are the non-qualification ground[2], the change of reason ground[3] and the variation of conditions ground[4]. If no qualifying requirements appear to be reviewable the supervisory body[5] is not required to take any action in respect of the standard authorisation[6].

1   See the Mental Capacity Act 2005 Sch A1 para 104 (Sch A1 added by the Mental Health Act 2007 Sch 7).
2   See PARA 685.
3   See PARA 686.
4   See PARA 687.
5   As to the meaning of 'supervisory body' see PARA 664.
6   See the Mental Capacity Act 2005 Sch A1 para 110 (as added: see note 1).

685.   The non-qualification ground. Any of the following qualifying requirements[1] is reviewable on the ground that the relevant person[2] does not meet the requirement: (1) the age requirement[3]; (2) the mental health requirement[4]; (3) the mental capacity requirement[5]; (4) the best interests requirement[6]; (5) the no refusals requirement[7]. The eligibility requirement[8] is reviewable on the ground that the relevant person is ineligible[9].

1   The ground in the Mental Capacity Act 2005 Sch A1 para 105(1) and (2) is referred to as the 'non-qualification' ground: Sch A1 para 105(3) (Sch A1 added by the Mental Health Act 2007 Sch 7).
2   As to the meaning of 'relevant person' see PARA 663 note 7.
3   Mental Capacity Act 2005 Sch A1 para 105(1)(a) (as added: see note 1). As to the age requirement see PARA 654.
4   Mental Capacity Act 2005 Sch A1 para 105(1)(b) (as added: see note 1). As to the mental health requirement see PARA 655.
5   Mental Capacity Act 2005 Sch A1 para 105(1)(c) (as added: see note 1). As to the mental capacity requirement see PARA 656.
6   Mental Capacity Act 2005 Sch A1 para 105(1)(d) (as added: see note 1). As to the best interests requirement see PARA 657.
7   Mental Capacity Act 2005 Sch A1 para 105(1)(e) (as added: see note 1). As to the no refusals requirement see PARA 660.
8   As to the eligibility requirement see PARA 658.
9   Ie ineligible by virtue of the Mental Capacity Act 2005 Sch 1A para 5 (see PARA 658): Sch A1 para 105(2) (as added: see note 1).

686.   Change of reason ground. Any of the following qualifying requirements is reviewable on the ground[1] that the reason why the relevant person[2] meets the requirement is not the reason stated in the standard authorisation[3]: (1) the mental health requirement[4]; (2) the mental capacity requirement[5]; (3) the best interests requirement[6]; (4) the eligibility requirement[7]; (5) the no refusals requirement[8].

1   This ground is referred to as the change of reason ground: Mental Capacity Act 2005 Sch A1 para 106(3) (Sch A1 added by the Mental Health Act 2007 Sch 7).
2   As to the meaning of 'relevant person' see PARA 663 note 7.
3   As to the meaning of 'standard authorisation' see PARA 663 note 1.
4   Mental Capacity Act 2005 Sch A1 para 106(1)(a) (as added: see note 1). As to the mental health requirement see PARA 655.
5   Mental Capacity Act 2005 Sch A1 para 106(1)(b) (as added: see note 1). As to the mental capacity requirement see PARA 656.
6   Mental Capacity Act 2005 Sch A1 para 106(1)(c) (as added: see note 1). As to the best interests requirement see PARA 657.
7   Mental Capacity Act 2005 Sch A1 para 106(1)(d) (as added: see note 1). As to the eligibility requirement see PARA 658.
8   Mental Capacity Act 2005 Sch A1 para 106(1)(e) (as added: see note 1). As to the no refusals requirement see PARA 660.

687.   Variation of conditions ground.   The best interests requirement[1] is reviewable on the ground[2] that there has been a change in the relevant person's case and because of that change, it would be appropriate to vary the conditions[3] to which the standard authorisation[4] is subject[5].

1   As to the best interests requirement see PARA 657.
2   This ground is referred to as the variation of conditions ground: Mental Capacity Act 2005 Sch A1 para 107(2) (Sch A1 added by the Mental Health Act 2007 Sch 7).
3   A reference to varying the conditions to which the standard authorisation is subject is a reference to amendment of an existing condition, omission of an existing condition or inclusion of a new condition (whether or not there are already any existing conditions): Mental Capacity Act 2005 Sch A1 para 107(3) (as added: see note 2). Any variation of the standard authorisation must be in writing: Sch A1 para 119 (as so added).
4   As to the meaning of 'standard authorisation' see PARA 663 note 1.
5   Mental Capacity Act 2005 Sch A1 para 107(1) (as added: see note 2).

688.   Carrying out a review.   To start a review of the standard authorisation[1], the supervisory body[2] must decide which, if any, of the qualifying requirements[3] appear to be reviewable[4].

If the supervisory body is to carry out a review of the standard authorisation, it must give notice[5] of the review to the relevant person[6], the relevant person's representative[7] and the managing authority of the relevant hospital or care home[8].

1   As to the meaning of 'standard authorisation' see PARA 663 note 1.
2   As to the meaning of 'supervisory body' see PARA 664.
3   As to the qualifying requirements see PARAS 653–660.
4   Mental Capacity Act 2005 Sch A1 para 109 (Sch A1 added by the Mental Health Act 2007 Sch 7).
5   The supervisory body must give the notice before they begin the review or, if that is not practicable, as soon as practicable after they have begun it: Mental Capacity Act 2005 Sch A1 para 108(2) (as added: see note 4). Any notice under Sch A1 must be in writing: Sch A1 para 169 (as so added).
6   As to the meaning of 'relevant person' see PARA 663 note 7.
7   As to the meaning of 'relevant person's representative' see PARA 707 note 2. If, and for so long as, there is a 'section 39C IMCA' the reference to relevant person's representative is to be read as a reference to the section 39C IMCA but this does not apply to any function under the relevant provisions for as long as the function is suspended in accordance with provision made under Part 10: see the Mental Capacity Act 2005 Sch A1 para 159 (as added: see note 4). As to the meaning of 'section 39C IMCA' see PARA 670 note 9.

8   Mental Capacity Act 2005 Sch A1 para 108(1) (as added: see note 4). The supervisory body does not have to give notice to any person who has requested the review: see Sch A1 para 108(3) (as so added).

689. Review assessments. A review assessment is an assessment of whether the relevant person[1] meets a qualifying requirement[2]. In relation to a review assessment a negative conclusion is a conclusion that the relevant person does not meet the qualifying requirement to which the assessment relates and a positive conclusion is a conclusion that the relevant person meets the qualifying requirement to which the assessment relates[3].

An age review assessment is a review assessment carried out in relation to the age requirement[4]. A mental health review assessment is a review assessment carried out in relation to the mental health requirement[5]. A mental capacity review assessment is a review assessment carried out in relation to the mental capacity requirement[6]. A best interests review assessment is a review assessment carried out in relation to the best interests requirement[7]. An eligibility review assessment is a review assessment carried out in relation to the eligibility requirement[8]. A no refusals review assessment is a review assessment carried out in relation to the no refusals requirement[9].

In carrying out a review assessment, the assessor[10] must comply with any duties which would be imposed upon him[11] if the assessment were being carried out in connection with a request for a standard authorisation[12].

No review may be requested whilst a standard authorisation is suspended[13] and if a review has already been requested, or is being carried out, when the standard authorisation is suspended, no steps are to be taken in connection with that review whilst the authorisation is suspended[14].

If, the managing authority of the relevant hospital or care home makes a request for a new standard authorisation[15] which would be in force after the expiry of the existing authorisation[16], no review may be requested until the request for the new standard authorisation has been disposed of[17]. If a review has already been requested, or is being carried out, when the new standard authorisation is requested, no steps are to be taken in connection with that review until the request for the new standard authorisation has been disposed of[18].

If a review has been requested, or is being carried out, and the managing authority of the relevant hospital or care home make a request[19] for a new standard authorisation which would be in force on or before, and after, the expiry of the existing authorisation, no steps are to be taken in connection with the review until the request for the new standard authorisation has been disposed of[20].

1   As to the meaning of 'relevant person' see PARA 663 note 7.
2   Mental Capacity Act 2005 Sch A1 para 112(1) (Sch A1 added by the Mental Health Act 2007 Sch 7).
3   Mental Capacity Act 2005 Sch A1 para 112(2) (as added: see note 2). As to positive assessments see PARA 691.
4   Mental Capacity Act 2005 Sch A1 para 112(3) (as added: see note 2). As to the age requirement see PARA 654.
5   Mental Capacity Act 2005 Sch A1 para 112(4) (as added: see note 2). As to the mental health requirement see PARA 655.
6   Mental Capacity Act 2005 Sch A1 para 112(5) (as added: see note 2). As to the mental capacity requirement see PARA 656.
7   Mental Capacity Act 2005 Sch A1 para 112(6) (as added: see note 2). As to the best interests requirement see PARA 657.

8 Mental Capacity Act 2005 Sch A1 para 112(7) (as added: see note 2). As to the eligibility requirement see PARA 658.
9 Mental Capacity Act 2005 Sch A1 para 112(8) (as added: see note 2). As to the no refusals requirement see PARA 660.
10 As to the meaning of 'assessor' see PARA 669.
11 Ie under the Mental Capacity Act 2005 Sch A1 paras 21–73 (see PARAS 663–679). However, in the case of a best interests review assessment, Sch A1 paras 43 and 44 (see PARA 674) do not apply: Mental Capacity Act 2005 Sch A1 para 113(2) (as added: see note 2). Instead of what is required by Sch A1 para 43, the best interests review assessment must include recommendations about whether (and, if so, how) it would be appropriate to vary the conditions to which the standard authorisation is subject: Sch A1 para 113(3) (as so added). Where the best interests requirement appears to be reviewable, but in accordance with Sch A1 para 111(3), the supervisory body are not required to secure that a best interests review assessment is carried out, the supervisory body may vary the conditions to which the standard authorisation is subject in such ways (if any) as the supervisory body think are appropriate in the circumstances: Sch A1 para 114 (as so added). Any variation of the standard authorisation must be in writing: Sch A1 para 119 (as so added).
12 Mental Capacity Act 2005 Sch A1 para 113(1) (as added: see note 2).
13 Ie suspended in accordance with the Mental Capacity Act 2005 Sch A1 paras 91–97 (see PARAS 680–681).
14 See the Mental Capacity Act 2005 Sch A1 para 122 (as added: see note 2).
15 Ie in accordance with the Mental Capacity Act 2005 Sch A1 para 24 (as read with Sch A1 para 29) (see PARA 661).
16 For the purposes of the Mental Capacity Act 2005 Sch A1 paras 123, 124 the existing authorisation is the authorisation referred to in Sch A1 para 101 (see PARA 683) and the expiry of the existing authorisation is the time when it is expected to cease to be in force: Sch A1 para 125 (as added: see note 2).
17 Mental Capacity Act 2005 Sch A1 para 123(1), (2) (as added: see note 2).
18 Mental Capacity Act 2005 Sch A1 para 123(3) (as added: see note 2).
19 Ie a request under the Mental Capacity Act 2005 Sch A1 para 30 (see PARA 667).
20 Mental Capacity Act 2005 Sch A1 para 124 (as added: see note 2).

690. One or more reviewable qualifying requirements. If one or more qualifying requirements[1] appear to be reviewable the supervisory body[2] must secure that a separate review assessment is carried out in relation to each qualifying requirement which appears to be reviewable[3]. However this does not require the supervisory body to secure that a best interests review assessment[4] is carried out in a case where the best interests requirement[5] appears to the supervisory body to be non-assessable[6].

The best interests requirement is non-assessable if the requirement is reviewable only on the variation of conditions ground[7] and the change in the relevant person's case is not significant[8].

In making any decision whether the change in the relevant person's case is significant, regard must be had to the nature of the change and the period that the change is likely to last for[9].

1 As to the qualifying requirements see PARAS 653–660.
2 As to the meaning of 'supervisory body' see PARA 664.
3 Mental Capacity Act 2005 Sch A1 para 111(1), (2) (Sch A1 added by the Mental Health Act 2007 Sch 7).
4 As to best interests assessments see PARA 674.
5 As to the best interest requirement see PARA 657.
6 Mental Capacity Act 2005 Sch A1 para 111(3) (as added: see note 3).
7 As to the variation of conditions ground see PARA 687.
8 Mental Capacity Act 2005 Sch A1 para 111(4) (as added: see note 3).
9 Mental Capacity Act 2005 Sch A1 para 111(5) (as added: see note 3).

691. Positive conclusion of a best interests review assessment. Where a best interests review assessment[1] is carried out and the assessment comes to a positive conclusion[2] the supervisory body[3] must decide the following questions: (1) whether or not the best interests requirement[4] is reviewable on the change of reason ground[5]; (2) whether or not the best interests requirement is reviewable on the variation of conditions ground[6]; (3) if so, whether or not the change in the person's case is significant[7].

If the supervisory body decides that the best interests requirement is reviewable on the change of reason ground, it must vary the standard authorisation[8] so that it states the reason why the relevant person now meets that requirement[9].

If the supervisory body decides that the best interests requirement is reviewable on the variation of conditions ground and the change in the relevant person's case is not significant, it may vary the conditions to which the standard authorisation is subject in such ways (if any) as it thinks appropriate in the circumstances[10].

If the supervisory body decides that the best interests requirement is reviewable on the variation of conditions ground and the change in the relevant person's case is significant, it must vary the conditions to which the standard authorisation is subject in such ways as it thinks are appropriate in the circumstances[11].

If the supervisory body decides that the best interests requirement is not reviewable on the change of reason ground or the variation of conditions ground, it is not required[12] to take any action in respect of the standard authorisation so far as the best interests requirement relates to it[13].

1   As to best interests review assessment see PARA 689.
2   As to the meaning of 'positive conclusion' see PARA 689.
3   As to the meaning of 'supervisory body' see PARA 664.
4   As to the best interests requirement see PARA 657.
5   As to the change of reason ground see PARA 686.
6   As to the variation of conditions ground see PARA 687.
7   Mental Capacity Act 2005 Sch A1 para 115(1), (2) (Sch A1 added by the Mental Health Act 2007 Sch 7).
8   As to the meaning of 'standard authorisation' see PARA 663 note 1. Any variation of the standard authorisation must be in writing: Sch A1 para 119 (as so added).
9   Mental Capacity Act 2005 Sch A1 para 115(3) (as added: see note 7).
10 Mental Capacity Act 2005 Sch A1 para 115(4) (as added: see note 7).
11 Mental Capacity Act 2005 Sch A1 para 115(5) (as added: see note 7).
12 Ie not required under the Mental Capacity Act 2005 Sch A1 paras 101–125.
13 Mental Capacity Act 2005 Sch A1 para 115(6) (as added: see note 7).

692. Positive conclusion of a mental health, mental capacity, eligibility or no refusals review assessment. The following applies if the following conditions are met[1]. The first condition is that one or more of the following are carried out: (1) a mental health review assessment; (2) a mental capacity review assessment; (3) an eligibility review assessment; (4) a no refusals review assessment[2]. The second condition is that each assessment carried out comes to a positive conclusion[3]. The supervisory body[4] must decide whether or not each of the assessed qualifying requirements is reviewable on the change of reason ground[5].

If the supervisory body decides that any of the assessed qualifying requirements is reviewable on the change of reason ground, it must vary the standard authorisation[6] so that it states the reason why the relevant person[7] now meets the requirement or requirements in question[8].

If the supervisory body decides that none of the assessed qualifying requirements[9] are reviewable on the change of reason ground, it is not required[10] to any action in respect of the standard authorisation so far as those requirements relate to it[11].

1 Mental Capacity Act 2005 Sch A1 para 116(1) (Sch A1 added by the Mental Health Act 2007 Sch 7).
2 Mental Capacity Act 2005 Sch A1 para 116(2) (as added: see note 1). As to the review assessments see PARA 689.
3 Mental Capacity Act 2005 Sch A1 para 116(3) (as added: see note 1). As to the meaning of 'positive conclusion' see PARA 689.
4 As to the meaning of 'supervisory body' see PARA 664.
5 Mental Capacity Act 2005 Sch A1 para 116(4) (as added: see note 1). As to the change of reason ground see PARA 686.
6 As to the meaning of 'standard authorisation' see PARA 663 note 1. Any variation of the standard authorisation must be in writing: Sch A1 para 119 (as so added).
7 As to the meaning of 'relevant person' see PARA 663 note 7.
8 Mental Capacity Act 2005 Sch A1 para 116(5) (as added: see note 1).
9 An assessed qualifying requirement is a qualifying requirement in relation to which a review assessment is carried out: Mental Capacity Act 2005 Sch A1 para 116(7) (as added: see note 1).
10 Ie not required under the Mental Capacity Act 2005 Sch A1 paras 101–125.
11 Mental Capacity Act 2005 Sch A1 para 116(6) (as added: see note 1).

693. One or more review assessments negative. If one or more of the review assessments[1] carried out comes to a negative conclusion[2] the supervisory body[3] must terminate the standard authorisation[4] with immediate effect[5].

1 As to the review assessments see PARA 689.
2 As to the meaning of 'negative conclusion' see PARA 689.
3 As to the meaning of 'supervisory body' see PARA 664.
4 As to the meaning of 'standard authorisation' see PARA 663 note 1.
5 Mental Capacity Act 2005 Sch A1 para 117 (Sch A1 added by the Mental Health Act 2007 Sch 7).

694. Completion of a review. The review of the standard authorisation[1] is complete in any of the following cases[2]:
    (1)   where no qualifying requirements appear to be reviewable[3];
    (2)   where one or more qualifying requirements appear to be reviewable[4] and the supervisory body[5] is required to terminate the standard authorisation[6] because one or more of the review assessments carried out comes to a negative conclusion[7].
In such a case, the supervisory body need not comply with any of the other provisions[8] which would be applicable to the review (were it not for the above provisions)[9].
The review of the standard authorisation is also complete where head (1) above applies, the supervisory body is not required[10] to terminate the standard authorisation and the supervisory body has complied with the provisions[11] so far as they are applicable to the review[12].

1 As to the meaning of 'standard authorisation' see PARA 663 note 1.
2 Mental Capacity Act 2005 Sch A1 para 118(1) (Sch A1 added by the Mental Health Act 2007 Sch 7).
3 Ie where the Mental Capacity Act 2005 Sch A1 para 110 (see PARA 684) plies: Sch A1 para 118(2) (as added: see note 2).
4 Ie where the Mental Capacity Act 2005 Sch A1 para 111 (see PARA 690) applies: Sch A1 para 118(3)(a) (as added: see note 2).
5 As to the meaning of 'supervisory body' see PARA 664.
6 Ie under the Mental Capacity Act 2005 Sch A1 para 117 (see PARA 693).

7 Mental Capacity Act 2005 Sch A1 para 118(3)(b) (as added: see note 2). As to the meaning of 'negative conclusion' see PARA 689.

8 Ie the Mental Capacity Act 2005 Sch A1 paras 114–116 (see PARAS 689–692).

9 Mental Capacity Act 2005 Sch A1 para 118(4) (as added: see note 2).

10 Ie where the Mental Capacity Act 2005 Sch A1 para 117 (see PARA 693) does not require the supervisory body to terminate the standard authorisation.

11 Ie has complied with all of the provisions of the Mental Capacity Act 2005 Sch A1 paras 114–116 so far as they are applicable to the review.

12 Mental Capacity Act 2005 Sch A1 para 118(5) (as added: see note 2).

E. ASSESSMENTS

695. Supervisory body to select assessor. It is for the supervisory body[1] to select a person to carry out an assessment[2] but it must not select a person to carry out an assessment unless the person appears to the supervisory body to be suitable to carry out the assessment (having regard, in particular, to the type of assessment and the person to be assessed) and is eligible to carry out the assessment[3]. Regulations may make provision about the selection, and eligibility, of persons to carry out assessments[4].

1 For the purposes of the Mental Capacity Act 2005 Sch A1 paras 126–136 'supervisory body' means the supervisory body responsible for securing that the assessment is carried out: Mental Capacity Act 2005 Sch A1 paras 126, 128 (Sch A1 added by the Mental Health Act 2007 Sch 7). As to the meaning of 'supervisory body' see PARA 664.

2 Mental Capacity Act 2005 Sch A1 para 129(1) (as added: see note 1). For the purposes of Sch A1 paras 126–136 an 'assessment' is either an assessment carried out in connection with a request for a standard authorisation under Sch A1 paras 21–73 (see PARAS 663–679) or a review assessment carried out in connection with a review of a standard authorisation under Sch A1 paras 101–125 (see PARAS 683–689): Sch A1 para 127 (as so added). As to the meaning of 'standard authorisation' see PARA 663 note 1.

3 Mental Capacity Act 2005 Sch A1 para 129(1), (2) (as added: see note 1).

4 Mental Capacity Act 2005 Sch A1 para 129(3) (as added: see note 1). Such regulations may make provision relating to a person's qualifications, skills, training, experience, relationship to, or connection with, the relevant person or any other person, involvement in the care or treatment of the relevant person, connection with the supervisory body or connection with the relevant hospital or care home, or with any other establishment or undertaking: Sch A1 para 130(1), (2) (as so added). The provision that the regulations may make in relation to a person's training may provide for particular training to be specified by the appropriate national authority otherwise than in the regulations: Sch A1 para 130(3), (4) (as so added). The regulations may make provision requiring a person to be insured in respect of liabilities that may arise in connection with the carrying out of an assessment: Sch A1 para 130(4) (as so added). In relation to cases where two or more assessments are to be obtained for the purposes of the relevant procedure, the regulations may limit the number, kind or combination of assessments which a particular person is eligible to carry out: Sch A1 para 130(5) (as so added). These provisions do not limit the generality of the provision that may be made in the regulations: Sch A1 para 130(6) (as so added). As to such regulations see the Mental Capacity (Deprivation of Liberty: Standard Authorisations, Assessments and Ordinary Residence) Regulations 2008, SI 2008/1858, the Mental Capacity (Deprivation of Liberty: Assessments, Standard Authorisations and Disputes about Residence) (Wales) Regulations 2009, SI 2009/783; and PARAS 697–704.

696. Where two or more assessments are required. The following applies if two or more assessments[1] are to be obtained for the purposes of the relevant procedure[2]. Except, in a case where the assessments to be obtained include a mental health assessment and a best interests assessment[3], the supervisory body may select the same person to carry out any number of the assessments which the person appears to be suitable, and is eligible, to carry out[4].

1 As to the meaning of 'assessment' see PARA 695 note 2.

2　Mental Capacity Act 2005 Sch A1 para 129(4) (Sch A1 added by the Mental Health Act 2007 Sch 7). For the purposes of the Mental Capacity Act 2005 Sch A1 paras 126–136 'relevant procedure' means the request for the standard authorisation or the review of the standard authorisation: Sch A1 para 128 (as so added). As to the meaning of 'standard authorisation' see PARA 663 note 1. As to the request for a standard authorisation see PARAS 663–679 and as to the review of a standard authorisation see PARAS 683–689.

3　In such a case the supervisory body must not select the same person to carry out both assessments: Mental Capacity Act 2005 Sch A1 para 129(5) (as added: see note 2). As to the meanings of 'mental health assessment' and 'best interests assessment' see PARAS 672, 674.

4　See the Mental Capacity Act 2005 Sch A1 para 129(6) (as added: see note 2). As to when a person is suitable and eligible see PARAS 697–703.

697. Eligibility: insurance.

For a person to be eligible to carry out an assessment[1] in England, he must satisfy the supervisory body[2] that there is in force in relation to that person an adequate and appropriate indemnity arrangement[3] which provides cover in respect of any liabilities that might arise in connection with carrying out the assessment[4].

In relation to Wales, a person is only eligible to carry out an assessment, other than an age assessment[5], where the supervisory body is satisfied that the person is insured in respect of any liabilities that might arise in connection with carrying out the assessment[6].

1　As to the meaning of 'assessment' see PARA 695 note 2.

2　As to the meaning of 'supervisory body' see PARA 695 note 1.

3　An 'indemnity arrangement' may comprise a policy of insurance, an arrangement made for the purposes of indemnifying a person or a combination of a policy of insurance and an arrangement made for the purposes of indemnifying a person: Mental Capacity (Deprivation of Liberty: Standard Authorisations, Assessments and Ordinary Residence) Regulations 2008, SI 2008/1858, reg 3(2A) (reg 2 substituted and reg 2A added by SI 2009/827);

4　See the Mental Capacity (Deprivation of Liberty: Standard Authorisations, Assessments and Ordinary Residence) Regulations 2008, SI 2008/1858, reg 3(1), (2) (reg 2 as substituted: see note 3).

5　As to the meaning of 'age assessment' see PARA 689.

6　Mental Capacity (Deprivation of Liberty: Assessments, Standard Authorisations and Disputes about Residence) (Wales) Regulations 2009, SI 2009/783, reg 3(1)(a).

698. Eligibility: skills and experience and criminal record check.

For a person to be eligible to carry out an assessment[1] in England, the supervisory body[2] must be satisfied that the person has the skills and experience appropriate to the assessment to be carried out which must include, but are not limited to, an applied knowledge of the Mental Capacity Act 2005 and related Code of Practice and the ability to keep appropriate records[3] and to provide clear and reasoned reports in accordance with legal requirements and good practice[4].

In relation to Wales, a person is only eligible to carry out an assessment, other than an age assessment[5], where the supervisory body is satisfied that the person has the skills and experience appropriate to the assessment he is to carry out which must include, but is not limited to the ability to communicate effectively with a view to identifying characteristics and attributes of a person that are relevant to that person's needs and the ability to act independently of any person who appoints him to carry out an assessment and of any person who is providing care or treatment to the person he is to assess[6].

In relation to both England and Wales, the supervisory body must be satisfied that there is in respect of the person an enhanced criminal record certificate[7] or[8] a criminal record certificate[9].

1　As to the meaning of 'assessment' see PARA 695 note 2.

2　As to the meaning of 'supervisory body' see PARA 695 note 1.

3   As to the keeping of records see PARA 705.

4   See the Mental Capacity (Deprivation of Liberty: Standard Authorisations, Assessments and Ordinary Residence) Regulations 2008, SI 2008/1858, reg 3(3).

5   As to the meaning of 'age assessment' see PARA 689.

6   Mental Capacity (Deprivation of Liberty: Assessments, Standard Authorisations and Disputes about Residence) (Wales) Regulations 2009, SI 2009/783, reg 3(1)(b).

7   Ie an enhanced criminal record certificate issued under the Police Act 1997 s 113B (see SENTENCING AND DISPOSITION OF OFFENDERS vol 92 (2010) PARA 713 et seq).

8   Ie if the purpose for which the certificate is required is not one prescribed under the Police Act 1997 s 113B(2).

9   See the Mental Capacity (Deprivation of Liberty: Standard Authorisations, Assessments and Ordinary Residence) Regulations 2008, SI 2008/1858, reg 3(4); Mental Capacity (Deprivation of Liberty: Assessments, Standard Authorisations and Disputes about Residence) (Wales) Regulations 2009, SI 2009/783, reg 3(2). A criminal record certificate mentioned in the text is a criminal record certificate issued in pursuance of the Police Act 1997 s 113A (see SENTENCING AND DISPOSITION OF OFFENDERS vol 92 (2010) PARA 712).

699.   Eligibility to carry out a mental health assessment.   A person is eligible to carry out a mental health assessment[1] if that person is approved under the Mental Health Act 1983[2] or is a registered medical practitioner[3] who the supervisory body[4] is satisfied has relevant experience[5] in the diagnosis or treatment of mental disorder[6].

1   As to the meaning of mental health assessment see PARA 672.

2   Ie approved under the Mental Health Act 1983 s 12 (see PARA 849).

3   As to the meaning of 'registered medical practitioner' see MEDICAL PROFESSIONS vol 74 (2011) PARA 176.

4   As to the meaning of 'supervisory body' see PARA 695 note 1.

5   In relation to England, such a person must be a registered medical practitioner who the supervisory body is satisfied has at least 3 years post registration experience in the diagnosis or treatment of mental disorder: Mental Capacity (Deprivation of Liberty: Standard Authorisations, Assessments and Ordinary Residence) Regulations 2008, SI 2008/1858, reg 4(2)(b). The supervisory body must also be satisfied that the person has successfully completed the Deprivation of Liberty Safeguards Mental Health Assessors training programme made available by the Royal College of Psychiatrists: reg 4(3). Except in the 12 month period beginning with the date the person has successfully completed the programme referred to in reg 4(3), the supervisory body must be satisfied that the person has, in the 12 months prior to selection, completed further training relevant to their role as a mental health assessor: reg 4(4).

6   Mental Capacity (Deprivation of Liberty: Standard Authorisations, Assessments and Ordinary Residence) Regulations 2008, SI 2008/1858, reg 4(1)(a); Mental Capacity (Deprivation of Liberty: Assessments, Standard Authorisations and Disputes about Residence) (Wales) Regulations 2009, SI 2009/783, reg 4.

700.   Eligibility to carry out a best interests assessment.   A person eligible to carry out a best interests assessment[1] must be one of the following:

(1)   an approved mental health professional[2];

(2)   a first level nurse[3];

(3)   an occupational therapist[4] or a social worker[5];

(4)   a chartered psychologist who is listed in the British Psychological Society's Register of Chartered Psychologists and who holds a relevant practising certificate issued by that Society[6].

However, a supervisory body must not select a person to carry out a best interests assessment if that person is involved in the care, or making decisions about the care, of the relevant person[7].

In relation to England, the supervisory body must be satisfied that the person:

(a)   is not suspended from the register or list relevant to the person's profession mentioned in heads (1) to (4) above[8];

(b)   has at least two years post registration experience in one of the professions mentioned in heads (1) to (4) above[9];

(c)   has successfully completed training that has been approved by the Secretary of State to be a best interests assessor[10];

(d)   except in the 12 month period beginning with the date the person has successfully completed the training referred to in head (c) above, the supervisory body must be satisfied that the person has, in the 12 months prior to selection, completed further training relevant to their role as a best interests assessor[11]; and

(e)   has the skills necessary to obtain, evaluate and analyse complex evidence and differing views and to weigh them appropriately in decision making[12].

In relation to Wales, the supervisory body must be satisfied that a person has the ability to take account of the views of any person who is interested in the welfare of the person to be assessed and the ability to assess the relevance and importance of those views in making an assessment[13].

1   As to the meaning of 'best interests assessment' see PARA 674.

2   Mental Capacity (Deprivation of Liberty: Standard Authorisations, Assessments and Ordinary Residence) Regulations 2008, SI 2008/1858, reg 5(1), (2)(a); Mental Capacity (Deprivation of Liberty: Assessments, Standard Authorisations and Disputes about Residence) (Wales) Regulations 2009, SI 2009/783, reg 5(1)(a). 'Approved mental health professional' means a person approved under section 114(1) of the Mental Health Act 1983 s 114(1) (see PARA 815) to act as an approved mental health professional for the purposes of that Act: see the Mental Capacity (Deprivation of Liberty: Standard Authorisations, Assessments and Ordinary Residence) Regulations 2008, SI 2008/1858, reg 2; and the Mental Capacity (Deprivation of Liberty: Assessments, Standard Authorisations and Disputes about Residence) (Wales) Regulations 2009, SI 2009/783, reg 2.

3   Mental Capacity (Deprivation of Liberty: Standard Authorisations, Assessments and Ordinary Residence) Regulations 2008, SI 2008/1858, reg 5(2)(c); and the Mental Capacity (Deprivation of Liberty: Assessments, Standard Authorisations and Disputes about Residence) (Wales) Regulations 2009, SI 2009/783, reg 5(1)(c). A first level nurse mentioned in the text is one registered in Sub-Part 1 of the Nurses' Part of the Register maintained under the Nursing and Midwifery Order 2001, SI 2002/253, art 5 (see MEDICAL PROFESSIONS vol 74 (2011) PARA 713). As to nurses generally see MEDICAL PROFESSIONS vol 74 (2011) PARA 9.

4   Ie an occupational therapist mentioned in the text is one registered in Part 6 of the register maintained under article 5 of the Health Professions Order 2001, SI 2002/254, art 5 (see MEDICAL PROFESSIONS vol 74 (2011) PARA 928). As to occupational therapists generally see MEDICAL PROFESSIONS vol 74 (2011) PARA 906.

5   Mental Capacity (Deprivation of Liberty: Standard Authorisations, Assessments and Ordinary Residence) Regulations 2008, SI 2008/1858, reg 5(2)(d); and the Mental Capacity (Deprivation of Liberty: Assessments, Standard Authorisations and Disputes about Residence) (Wales) Regulations 2009, SI 2009/783, reg 5(1)(d) (both amended by SI 2012/1479). A social worker mentioned in the text is a social worker registered in Part 16 of the register maintained under the Health and Social Work Professions Order 2001, SI 2002/254, art 5 (see MEDICAL PROFESSIONS).

6   Mental Capacity (Deprivation of Liberty: Standard Authorisations, Assessments and Ordinary Residence) Regulations 2008, SI 2008/1858, reg 5(2)(e); and the Mental Capacity (Deprivation of Liberty: Assessments, Standard Authorisations and Disputes about Residence) (Wales) Regulations 2009, SI 2009/783, reg 5(1)(e).

7   See the Mental Capacity (Deprivation of Liberty: Standard Authorisations, Assessments and Ordinary Residence) Regulations 2008, SI 2008/1858, reg 12(1); and the Mental Capacity (Deprivation of Liberty: Assessments, Standard Authorisations and Disputes about Residence) (Wales) Regulations 2009, SI 2009/783, reg 8. In relation to England, where the managing authority and supervisory body are both the same body, the supervisory body must not select a person to carry out a best interests assessment who is employed by it or who is providing services to it: Mental Capacity (Deprivation of Liberty: Standard Authorisations, Assessments and Ordinary Residence) Regulations 2008, SI 2008/1858, reg 12(2).

8   Mental Capacity (Deprivation of Liberty: Standard Authorisations, Assessments and Ordinary Residence) Regulations 2008, SI 2008/1858, reg 5(3)(a).
9   Mental Capacity (Deprivation of Liberty: Standard Authorisations, Assessments and Ordinary Residence) Regulations 2008, SI 2008/1858, reg 5(3)(b).
10 Mental Capacity (Deprivation of Liberty: Standard Authorisations, Assessments and Ordinary Residence) Regulations 2008, SI 2008/1858, reg 5(3)(c).
11 Mental Capacity (Deprivation of Liberty: Standard Authorisations, Assessments and Ordinary Residence) Regulations 2008, SI 2008/1858, reg 5(3)(d).
12 Mental Capacity (Deprivation of Liberty: Standard Authorisations, Assessments and Ordinary Residence) Regulations 2008, SI 2008/1858, reg 5(3)(e).
13 Mental Capacity (Deprivation of Liberty: Assessments, Standard Authorisations and Disputes about Residence) (Wales) Regulations 2009, SI 2009/783, reg 5(2).

701. Eligibility to carry out a mental capacity assessment. A person is eligible to carry out a mental capacity assessment[1] if that person is eligible to carry out a mental health assessment or a best interests assessment[2].

1   As to the meaning of 'mental capacity assessment' see PARA 673.
2   Mental Capacity (Deprivation of Liberty: Standard Authorisations, Assessments and Ordinary Residence) Regulations 2008, SI 2008/1858, reg 6; Mental Capacity (Deprivation of Liberty: Assessments, Standard Authorisations and Disputes about Residence) (Wales) Regulations 2009, SI 2009/783, reg 6. As to when a person is eligible to carry out a mental health assessment or a best interests assessment see PARAS 699, 700.

702. Eligibility to carry out an eligibility assessment. In relation to England, a person is eligible to carry out an eligibility assessment[1] if that person is approved under the Mental Health Act 1983[2] and is eligible to carry out a mental health assessment[3] or the person is an approved mental health professional[4] and is eligible to carry out a best interests assessment[5].

In relation to Wales, a person is eligible to carry out an eligibility assessment if that person is eligible to carry out a mental health assessment or a best interests assessment[6].

Where an individual is being assessed and the eligibility assessor and the best interests assessor[7] are not the same person, the eligibility assessor must request that the best interests assessor provides any relevant eligibility information that the best interests assessor may have and the best interests assessor must comply with any such request[8].

1   As to the meaning of 'eligibility assessment' see PARA 675.
2   Ie approved under the Mental Health Act 1983 s 12 (see PARA 849).
3   As to when a person is eligible to carry out a mental health assessment see PARA 699.
4   As to the meaning of 'approved mental health professional' see PARA 700 note 2.
5   Mental Capacity (Deprivation of Liberty: Standard Authorisations, Assessments and Ordinary Residence) Regulations 2008, SI 2008/1858, reg 7. As to when a person is eligible to carry out a best interests assessment see PARA 700.
6   Mental Capacity (Deprivation of Liberty: Assessments, Standard Authorisations and Disputes about Residence) (Wales) Regulations 2009, SI 2009/783, reg 6.
7   As to the best interests assessor see PARA 700.
8   See the Mental Capacity (Deprivation of Liberty: Standard Authorisations, Assessments and Ordinary Residence) Regulations 2008, SI 2008/1858, reg 15; and the Mental Capacity (Deprivation of Liberty: Assessments, Standard Authorisations and Disputes about Residence) (Wales) Regulations 2009, SI 2009/783, reg 12.

703. Eligibility to carry out an age assessment and a no refusals assessment. In relation to England, person is eligible to carry out an age assessment and a no refusals assessment[1] if that person is eligible to carry out a best interests assessment[2].

1   As the meanings of 'age assessment' and 'no refusals assessment' see PARAS 671, 676.

2	Mental Capacity (Deprivation of Liberty: Standard Authorisations, Assessments and Ordinary Residence) Regulations 2008, SI 2008/1858, regs 8, 9. As to when a person is eligible to carry out a best interests assessment see PARA 700.

704. Selection of assessors. A supervisory body[1] may only select a person to carry out an assessment in any individual case where the person is:

(1)	not financially interested[2] in the care of the relevant person[3];

(2)	not a relative[4] of the relevant person[5]; and

(3)	not a relative of a person who is financially interested[6] in the care of the relevant person[7].

1	As to the meaning of 'supervisory body' see PARA 695 note 1.

2	A person has a financial interest where that person is a partner, director, other office-holder or major shareholder of the care home or independent hospital that has made the request for a standard authorisation: see the Mental Capacity (Deprivation of Liberty: Standard Authorisations, Assessments and Ordinary Residence) Regulations 2008, SI 2008/1858, reg 11(2); and the Mental Capacity (Deprivation of Liberty: Assessments, Standard Authorisations and Disputes about Residence) (Wales) Regulations 2009, SI 2009/783, reg 7(3)(b). 'Major shareholder' means any person who holds one tenth or more of the issued shares in the care home or independent hospital, where the care home or independent hospital is a company limited by shares and in all other cases, any of the owners of the care home or independent hospital: see the Mental Capacity (Deprivation of Liberty: Standard Authorisations, Assessments and Ordinary Residence) Regulations 2008, SI 2008/1858, reg 11(3); and the Mental Capacity (Deprivation of Liberty: Assessments, Standard Authorisations and Disputes about Residence) (Wales) Regulations 2009, SI 2009/783, reg 7(3)(c).

3	See the Mental Capacity (Deprivation of Liberty: Standard Authorisations, Assessments and Ordinary Residence) Regulations 2008, SI 2008/1858, reg 11(1); and the Mental Capacity (Deprivation of Liberty: Assessments, Standard Authorisations and Disputes about Residence) (Wales) Regulations 2009, SI 2009/783, reg 7(1)(a).

4	As to the meaning of 'relative' see the Mental Capacity (Deprivation of Liberty: Standard Authorisations, Assessments and Ordinary Residence) Regulations 2008, SI 2008/1858, reg 10(2), (3)(a), (b); Mental Capacity (Deprivation of Liberty: Assessments, Standard Authorisations and Disputes about Residence) (Wales) Regulations 2009, SI 2009/783, reg 7(2), (3)(a).

5	See the Mental Capacity (Deprivation of Liberty: Standard Authorisations, Assessments and Ordinary Residence) Regulations 2008, SI 2008/1858, reg 10(1)(a); Mental Capacity (Deprivation of Liberty: Assessments, Standard Authorisations and Disputes about Residence) (Wales) Regulations 2009, SI 2009/783, reg 7(1)(b).

6	See note 2.

7	See the Mental Capacity (Deprivation of Liberty: Standard Authorisations, Assessments and Ordinary Residence) Regulations 2008, SI 2008/1858, reg 10(1)(b), (3)(c); and the Mental Capacity (Deprivation of Liberty: Assessments, Standard Authorisations and Disputes about Residence) (Wales) Regulations 2009, SI 2009/783, reg 7(1)(c).

705. Records and copies of assessment. An assessor[1] may, at all reasonable times, examine and take copies of any health record, any record of, or held by, a local authority and compiled in accordance with a social services function and any record held by a person registered under the Care Standards Act 2000[2] or the Health and Social Care Act 2008[3] which the assessor considers may be relevant to the assessment which is being carried out[4].

If an assessor has carried out an assessment (whatever conclusions the assessment has come to) he must keep a written record of the assessment and, as soon as practicable after carrying out the assessment, give copies of the assessment to the supervisory body[5].

If the supervisory body is given a copy of an assessment it must give copies to the managing authority of the relevant hospital or care home[6], the relevant person[7], any section 39A IMCA[8] and the relevant person's representative[9].

If the assessment is obtained in relation to a request for a standard authorisation[10] and the supervisory body is required[11] to give the standard authorisation, it must give the copies of the assessment when it gives copies[12] of the authorisation[13].

If the assessment is obtained in relation to a request for a standard authorisation, and the supervisory body is prohibited[14] from giving the standard authorisation, the supervisory body must give the copies of the assessment when it gives notice[15] stating that it is prohibited from giving the authorisation[16].

If the assessment is obtained in connection with the review of a standard authorisation, the supervisory body must give the copies of the assessment when it gives notice[17] of the outcome of the review[18].

If the supervisory body is given a copy of a best interests assessment[19] and the assessment includes[20] a statement that it appears to the assessor that there is an unauthorised deprivation of liberty the supervisory body must notify the managing authority of the relevant hospital or care home, the relevant person, any section 39A IMCA and any interested person[21] consulted by the best interests assessor, that the assessment includes such a statement[22].

1 As to the meaning of 'assessor' see PARA 669.
2 Ie under the Care Standards Act 2000 Pt 2 (ss 11–42): see SOCIAL SERVICES AND COMMUNITY CARE.
3 Ie under the Health and Social Care Act 2008 Pt 1 Ch 2 (ss 8–44): see HEALTH SERVICES; SOCIAL SERVICES AND COMMUNITY CARE.
4 Mental Capacity Act 2005 Sch A1 para 131 (Sch A1 added by the Mental Health Act 2007 Sch 7).
5 See the Mental Capacity Act 2005 Sch A1 para 134 (as added: see note 4). As to the meaning of 'supervisory body' see PARA 695 note 1.
6 As to the meaning of 'managing authority' see PARA 652. As to the meaning of 'relevant hospital or care home' see PARA 663 note 2.
7 As to the meaning of 'relevant person' see PARA 663 note 7.
8 A 'section 39A IMCA' is an independent mental capacity advocate appointed under the Mental Capacity Act 2005 s 39A (see PARA 642): Sch A1 para 155 (as added: see note 4).
9 Mental Capacity Act 2005 Sch A1 para 135(1), (2) (as added: see note 4). As to the meaning of 'relevant person's representative' see PARA 707 note 2.
10 As to the meaning of 'standard authorisation' see PARA 663 note 1.
11 Ie required by the Mental Capacity Act 2005 Sch A1 para 50(1) (see PARA 663).
12 Ie when it gives copies of the authorisation in accordance with the Mental Capacity Act 2005 Sch A1 para 57 (see PARA 677).
13 Mental Capacity Act 2005 Sch A1 para 135(3) (as added: see note 4).
14 Ie prohibited by the Mental Capacity Act 2005 Sch A1 para 50(2) (see PARA 663).
15 Ie notice in accordance with the Mental Capacity Act 2005 Sch A1 para 58 (see PARA 677). Any notice under Sch A1 must be in writing: Sch A1 para 169 (as added: see note 4).
16 Mental Capacity Act 2005 Sch A1 para 135(4) (as added: see note 4).
17 Ie notice in accordance with the Mental Capacity Act 2005 Sch A1 para 120 (see PARA 683).
18 Mental Capacity Act 2005 Sch A1 para 135(5) (as added: see note 4).
19 As to the meaning of 'best interests assessment' see PARA 674.
20 Ie in accordance with the Mental Capacity Act 2005 Sch A1 para 44(2) (see PARA 674).
21 As to the meaning of 'interested person' see PARA 665 note 23.
22 Mental Capacity Act 2005 Sch A1 para 136(1)–(3) (as added: see note 4). The supervisory body must comply with Sch A1 para 136 when (or at some time before) they comply with Sch A1 para 135: Sch A1 para 136(4) (as so added).

706. Carrying out and ceasing assessment. In carrying out an assessment[1] the assessor[2] must take into account any information given, or submissions made, by the relevant person's representative[3], any section 39A IMCA[4], any section 39C IMCA[5], and any section 39D IMCA[6].

If an assessment comes to the conclusion that the relevant person[7] does not meet one of the qualifying requirements[8] the supervisory body must give notice[9] to any assessor who is carrying out another assessment in connection with the relevant procedure that they are to cease carrying out that assessment[10].

1 As to the meaning of 'assessment' see PARA 695 note 2.
2 As to the meaning of 'assessor' see PARA 669.
3 As to the meaning of 'relevant person's representative' see PARA 707 note 2.
4 As to the meaning of 'section 39A IMCA' see PARA 705 note 8.
5 As to the meaning of 'section 39C IMCA' see PARA 670 note 9.
6 Mental Capacity Act 2005 Sch A1 para 132 (Sch A1 added by the Mental Health Act 2007 Sch 7). As to the meaning of 'section 39D IMCA' see PARA 670 note 9.
7 As to the meaning of 'relevant person' see PARA 663 note 7.
8 As to the meaning of 'qualifying requirements' see PARA 653.
9 As to the meaning of 'supervisory body' see PARA 695 note 1. If an assessor receives such notice, the Mental Capacity Act 2005 Sch A1 para 133 does not require the assessor to continue carrying out that assessment: Sch A1 para 133(4) (as added: see note 6). Any notice under Sch A1 must be in writing: Sch A1 para 169 (as so added).
10 See the Mental Capacity Act 2005 Sch A1 para 133(1), (3) (as added: see note 6). Schedule A1 does not require the supervisory body to secure that any other assessments under this Schedule are carried out in relation to the relevant procedure: Sch A1 para 133(2) (as so added).

F. RELEVANT PERSON'S REPRESENTATIVE

707. Appointment, termination, suspension etc. The supervisory body[1] must appoint a person to be the relevant person's representative[2] as soon as practicable after a standard authorisation[3] is given[4]. The supervisory body must appoint a person to be the relevant person's representative if a vacancy arises whilst a standard authorisation is in force[5].

The selection of a person for appointment under the above provisions must not be made unless it appears to the person making the selection that the prospective representative would, if appointed, maintain contact with the relevant person[6] and represent and support[7] them[8].

Any appointment of a representative for a relevant person is in addition to, and does not affect, any appointment of a donee or deputy[9]. The functions of any representative are in addition to, and do not affect the authority of any donee, the powers of any deputy or any powers of the court[10].

Regulations may make provision about the appointment of representatives[11], including who may or may not be appointed[12], the circumstances in which the appointment of a person as the relevant person's representative ends or may be ended[13] and the formalities of ending the appointment of a person as a representative[14] and the circumstances in which functions exercisable by, or in relation to, the relevant person's representative may be suspended and, if suspended, revived[15].

1 As to the meaning of 'supervisory body' see PARA 664.
2 The relevant person's representative is a person appointed in accordance with the Mental Capacity Act 2005 Sch A1 paras 137–153: Sch A1 para 137 (Sch A1 added by the Mental Health Act 2007 Sch 7). As to the selection of the representative see PARAS 708–708. The Mental Capacity Act 2005 Sch A1 paras 159 and 160 (see PARAS 683, 707) make provision about the exercise of functions by, or towards, the relevant person's representative during periods when no person is appointed as the relevant person's representative, but a person is appointed as a section 39C IMCA: Sch A1 para 153 (as so added). As to the meaning of 'section 39C IMCA' see PARA 670 note 9. If a person is appointed as the relevant person's representative and a person accordingly ceases to hold an appointment as a section 39C IMCA, where a function under a Sch A1 para 102(3)(b), 108(1)(b) or 120(1)(c) has been exercised by, or towards, the section 39C IMCA, there is no requirement for that function to be exercised again by, or towards, the relevant person's representative: Sch A1 para 160 (as so added). If there is a section 39A IMCA and a person is appointed to be the relevant person's representative (whether or not that person, or any person subsequently appointed, is currently the relevant person's

representative), the duties imposed on, and the powers exercisable by, the section 39A IMCA do not apply and the duties imposed on, and the powers exercisable by, any other person do not apply, so far as they fall to be performed or exercised towards the section 39A IMCA: Sch A1 para 161(1)–(3) (as so added). However this does not apply to any power of challenge exercisable by the section 39A IMCA or any duty or power of any other person so far as it relates to any power of challenge exercisable by the section 39A IMCA: see Sch A1 para 161(4), (5) (as so added). Before exercising any power of challenge, the section 39A IMCA must take the views of the relevant person's representative into account: Sch A1 para 161(6) (as so added) A power of challenge is a power to make an application to the court to exercise its jurisdiction under s 21A (see PARA 733) in connection with the giving of the standard authorisation: Sch A1 para 161(7) (as so added). As to the relevant person's representative see Ministry of Justice *Deprivation of Liberty Safeguards – code of practice to supplement the main Mental Capacity Act 2005 code of practice (2008)* Chapter 7.

3   As to the meaning of 'standard authorisation' 663 note 1.
4   Mental Capacity Act 2005 Sch A1 para 139(1) (as added: see note 2). Regulations may make provision for payments to be made to, or in relation to, persons exercising functions as the relevant person's representative: Sch A1 para 151 (as so added). As to regulations relating to payment see the Mental Capacity (Deprivation of Liberty: Appointment of Relevant Person's Representative) Regulations 2008, SI 2008/1315, reg 15; and the Mental Capacity (Deprivation of Liberty: Appointment of Relevant Person's Representative) (Wales) Regulations 2009, SI 2009/266, reg 17.
5   Mental Capacity Act 2005 Sch A1 para 139(2) (as added: see note 2). Where a vacancy arises, the appointment under Sch A1 para 139 is to be made as soon as practicable after the supervisory body becomes aware of the vacancy: Sch A1 para 139(3) (as so added).
6   As to the meaning of 'relevant person' see PARA 663 note 7.
7   Ie represent and support the relevant person in matters relating to or connected with the Mental Capacity Act 2005 Sch A1.
8   Mental Capacity Act 2005 Sch A1 para 140 (as added: see note 2).
9   Mental Capacity Act 2005 Sch A1 para 141(1) (as added: see note 2). As to the meaning of 'deputy' see s 16(2)(b); and PARA 724: Sch A1 para 188 (as so added).
10 Mental Capacity Act 2005 Sch A1 para 141(2) (as added: see note 2).
11 See the Mental Capacity Act 2005 Sch A1 para 138(1) (as added: see note 2). Such regulations may provide that the procedure for appointing a representative may begin at any time after a request for a standard authorisation is made (including a time before the request has been disposed of): Sch A1 para 142 (as so added). As to the procedure for the appointing and terminating the appointment of a representative see Sch A1 para 145; the Mental Capacity (Deprivation of Liberty: Appointment of Relevant Person's Representative) Regulations 2008, SI 2008/1315, regs 10–15; and the Mental Capacity (Deprivation of Liberty: Appointment of Relevant Person's Representative) (Wales) Regulations 2009, SI 2009/266, regs 4, 5, 12–14, 16, 17. The provisions of the Mental Capacity Act 2005 Pt 10 which specify provision that may be made in regulations under that Part do not affect the generality of the power to make such regulations: see Sch A1 para 152 (as so added).
12 See the Mental Capacity Act 2005 Sch A1 para 144(1)(b) (as so added: see note 2). Such regulations may relate to a person's age, suitability, independence, willingness and qualifications: see Sch A1 para 144(2) (as so added).
13 See the Mental Capacity Act 2005 Sch A1 para 148 (as so added: see note 2). As to such regulations see note 11.
14 See the Mental Capacity Act 2005 Sch A1 para 149 (as so added: see note 2).
15 See the Mental Capacity Act 2005 Sch A1 para 150(1) (as so added: see note 2). The regulations may make provision about the formalities for giving effect to the suspension or revival of a function: see Sch A1 para 150(2) (as so added). The regulations may make provision about the effect of the suspension or revival of a function: see Sch A1 para 150(3) (as so added).

708. Regulations relating to the selection of representatives. Regulations[1] may make provision about the selection of the relevant person's representative[2]. However such regulations may only provide for the following to make a selection:

(1)   the relevant person[3], if he has capacity in relation to the question of which person should be his representative[4];

(2)   a donee of a lasting power of attorney granted by the relevant person, if it is within the scope of his authority to select a person[5];

(3)   a deputy, if it is within the scope of his authority to select a person[6];
(4)   a best interests assessor[7];
(5)   the supervisory body[8],

and the regulations may make provision about who may, or may not, be selected for appointment as a representative[9].

Such regulations may provide that a selection by the relevant person, a donee or a deputy is subject to approval by a best interests assessor[10] or the supervisory body[11]. The regulations may also provide that, if more than one selection is necessary in connection with the appointment of a particular representative (a) the same person may make more than one selection; (b) different persons may make different selections[12].

1 As to such regulations see PARA 709.
2 Mental Capacity Act 2005 Sch A1 paras 138(1), 143(1) (Sch A1 added by the Mental Health Act 2007 Sch 7). As to the meaning of 'relevant person's representative' see PARA 707 note 2.
3 As to the meaning of 'relevant person' see PARA 663 note 7.
4 Mental Capacity Act 2005 Sch A1 para 143(2)(a) (as added: see note 2).
5 Mental Capacity Act 2005 Sch A1 para 143(2)(b) (as added: see note 2).
6 Mental Capacity Act 2005 Sch A1 para 143(2)(c) (as added: see note 2). As to the meaning of 'deputy' see s 16(2)(b); and PARA 724: Sch A1 para 188 (as so added).
7 Mental Capacity Act 2005 Sch A1 para 143(2)(d) (as added: see note 2).
8 Mental Capacity Act 2005 Sch A1 para 143(2)(e) (as added: see note 2). As to the meaning of 'supervisory body' see PARA 664.
9 See the Mental Capacity Act 2005 Sch A1 para 144(1)(a) (as added: see note 2). Such regulations may relate to a person's age, suitability, independence, willingness and qualifications: see Sch A1 para 144(2) (as so added).
10 For these purposes 'a best interests assessor' is a person carrying out a best interests assessment in connection with the standard authorisation in question (including the giving of that authorisation): Mental Capacity Act 2005 Sch A1 para 143(5) (as added: see note 2). In a case where a best interests assessor is to select a person to be appointed as a representative, appointment regulations may provide for the variation of the assessor's duties in relation to the assessment which he is carrying out: Sch A1 para 146 (as so added).
11 Mental Capacity Act 2005 Sch A1 para 143(3) (as added: see note 2).
12 Mental Capacity Act 2005 Sch A1 para 143(4) (as added: see note 2).

709. Eligibility to be a representative. A person can only be selected to be a relevant person's representative[1] if they are:
(1)   18 years of age or over[2];
(2)   able to keep in contact with the relevant person[3];
(3)   in relation to Wales, not prevented by ill-health from carrying out the role of the representative[4];
(4)   willing to be the relevant person's representative[5];
(5)   not financially interested in the care home or independent hospital[6] where the relevant person[7] is, or is to be, detained[8];
(6)   not a relative[9] of a person who is financially interested[10] in the care home or independent hospital where the relevant person is, or is to be, detained[11];
(7)   not providing services to, or not employed to work in, the care home where the relevant person is, or is to be, detained[12];
(8)   not employed to work in the hospital where the relevant person is, or is to be, detained in a role that is, or could be, related to the relevant person's case[13]; and
(9)   not employed to work in the relevant person's supervisory body[14] in a role that is, or could be, related to the relevant person's case[15].

1 As to the meaning of 'relevant person's representative' see PARA 707 note 2.

2 See the Mental Capacity (Deprivation of Liberty: Appointment of Relevant Person's Representative) Regulations 2008, SI 2008/1315, reg 3(1)(a); and the Mental Capacity (Deprivation of Liberty: Appointment of Relevant Person's Representative) (Wales) Regulations 2009, SI 2009/266, reg 6(1)(a).

3 See the Mental Capacity (Deprivation of Liberty: Appointment of Relevant Person's Representative) Regulations 2008, SI 2008/1315, reg 3(1)(b); and the Mental Capacity (Deprivation of Liberty: Appointment of Relevant Person's Representative) (Wales) Regulations 2009, SI 2009/266, reg 6(1)(b). As to monitoring the extent to which the representative is staying in contact with the relevant person see PARA 712.

4 See the Mental Capacity (Deprivation of Liberty: Appointment of Relevant Person's Representative) (Wales) Regulations 2009, SI 2009/266, reg 6(1)(c).

5 See the Mental Capacity (Deprivation of Liberty: Appointment of Relevant Person's Representative) Regulations 2008, SI 2008/1315, reg 3(1)(c); and the Mental Capacity (Deprivation of Liberty: Appointment of Relevant Person's Representative) (Wales) Regulations 2009, SI 2009/266, reg 6(1)(d).

6 As to the meaning of 'care home' and 'independent hospital' see PARA 652.

7 As to the meaning of 'relevant person' see PARA 663 note 7.

8 See the Mental Capacity (Deprivation of Liberty: Appointment of Relevant Person's Representative) Regulations 2008, SI 2008/1315, reg 3(1)(d); and the Mental Capacity (Deprivation of Liberty: Appointment of Relevant Person's Representative) (Wales) Regulations 2009, SI 2009/266, reg 6(1)(e).

9 As to the meaning of 'relative' see the Mental Capacity (Deprivation of Liberty: Appointment of Relevant Person's Representative) Regulations 2008, SI 2008/1315, reg 3(2), (3); and the Mental Capacity (Deprivation of Liberty: Appointment of Relevant Person's Representative) (Wales) Regulations 2009, SI 2009/266, reg 6(2), (3).

10 A person has a financial interest in a care home or independent hospital where that person is a partner, director, other office-holder or major shareholder of the care home or independent hospital that has made the application for a standard authorisation and 'major shareholder' means any person who holds one tenth or more of the issued shares in the care home or independent hospital, where the care home or independent hospital is a company limited by shares and, in all other cases, any of the owners of the care home or independent hospital: see the Mental Capacity (Deprivation of Liberty: Appointment of Relevant Person's Representative) Regulations 2008, SI 2008/1315, reg 3(3)(c), (d); and the Mental Capacity (Deprivation of Liberty: Appointment of Relevant Person's Representative) (Wales) Regulations 2009, SI 2009/266, reg 6(3)(c), (d).

11 See the Mental Capacity (Deprivation of Liberty: Appointment of Relevant Person's Representative) Regulations 2008, SI 2008/1315, reg 3(1)(e); and the Mental Capacity (Deprivation of Liberty: Appointment of Relevant Person's Representative) (Wales) Regulations 2009, SI 2009/266, reg 6(1)(f).

12 See the Mental Capacity (Deprivation of Liberty: Appointment of Relevant Person's Representative) Regulations 2008, SI 2008/1315, reg 3(1)(f); and the Mental Capacity (Deprivation of Liberty: Appointment of Relevant Person's Representative) (Wales) Regulations 2009, SI 2009/266, reg 6(1)(g).

13 See the Mental Capacity (Deprivation of Liberty: Appointment of Relevant Person's Representative) Regulations 2008, SI 2008/1315, reg 3(1)(g); and the Mental Capacity (Deprivation of Liberty: Appointment of Relevant Person's Representative) (Wales) Regulations 2009, SI 2009/266, reg 6(1)(h).

14 As to the meaning of 'supervisory body' see PARA 664. In relation to Wales, 'supervisory body' includes a Local Health Board exercising supervisory functions in accordance with the Mental Capacity (Deprivation of Liberty: Appointment of Relevant Person's Representative) (Wales) Regulations 2009, SI 2009/266, reg 3: reg 2(2).

15 See the Mental Capacity (Deprivation of Liberty: Appointment of Relevant Person's Representative) Regulations 2008, SI 2008/1315, reg 3(1)(h); and the Mental Capacity (Deprivation of Liberty: Appointment of Relevant Person's Representative) (Wales) Regulations 2009, SI 2009/266, reg 6(1)(i).

710. Selection of representative in England. In England, where the best interests assessor[1] determines that the relevant person[2] has capacity in relation to the question of which person should be his representative[3], the relevant person may select a family member, friend or carer[4]. However, where the best interests assessor determines that the relevant person lacks capacity to select a representative and the relevant person has a donee[5] or deputy and it is within the authority of the donee or deputy to do so, the donee or deputy may select a representative[6].

The best interests assessor must confirm that a person selected under the above provisions[7] is eligible to be a representative[8] and, where he confirms eligibility, the assessor must recommend the appointment of that person as a representative to the supervisory body[9]. Where the best interests assessor is unable to confirm the selected person's eligibility, the assessor must advise the person who made the selection of that decision and give the reasons for it and invite them to make a further selection[10].

The best interests assessor may select a family member, friend or carer as representative where:

(1)   the relevant person has the capacity to make a selection[11] but does not wish to do so[12];

(2)   the relevant person's donee or deputy does not wish to make a selection[13]; or

(3)   the relevant person lacks the capacity to make a selection and does not have a donee or deputy or has a donee or deputy but the donee's or deputy's scope of authority does not permit the selection of a representative[14].

Where the best interest assessor selects a person in accordance with heads (1) to (3) above, the assessor must recommend that person for appointment as a representative to the supervisory body[15]. However, the best interests assessor must not select a person under heads (1) to (3) above where the relevant person, donee or deputy objects to that decision[16]. The best interests assessor must notify the supervisory body if he does not select a person who is eligible to be a representative[17].

Where the supervisory body is notified that a person has not been selected to be a representative[18], it may select a person to be the representative[19], who:

(a)   would be performing the role in a professional capacity[20];

(b)   has satisfactory skills and experience to perform the role[21];

(c)   is not a family member, friend or carer of the relevant person[22];

(d)   is not employed by, or providing services to, the relevant person's managing authority[23], where the relevant person's managing authority is a care home[24];

(e)   is not employed to work in the relevant person's managing authority in a role that is, or could be, related to the relevant person's case, where the relevant person's managing authority is a hospital[25]; and

(f)   is not employed by the supervisory body[26].

1   'Best interests assessor' means a person selected to carry out a best interests assessment under the Mental Capacity Act 2005 Sch A1 para 38 (see PARA 674): Mental Capacity (Deprivation of Liberty: Appointment of Relevant Person's Representative) Regulations 2008, SI 2008/1315, reg 2.

2   As to the meaning of 'relevant person' see PARA 663 note 7.

3   As to the meaning of 'relevant person's representative' see PARA 707 note 2.

4   See the Mental Capacity (Deprivation of Liberty: Appointment of Relevant Person's Representative) Regulations 2008, SI 2008/1315, regs 4, 5(1). As to the selection of a representative in relation to Wales see PARA 711.

5   A 'donee' is a person who has a lasting power of attorney conferred on them by the relevant person, and, in relation to England, that power gives that donee the authority to make decisions about the relevant person's personal welfare: see the Mental Capacity (Deprivation of Liberty: Appointment of Relevant Person's Representative) Regulations 2008, SI 2008/1315, reg 2; and

the Mental Capacity (Deprivation of Liberty: Appointment of Relevant Person's Representative) (Wales) Regulations 2009, SI 2009/266, reg 2(1). As to the lasting power of attorney see PARA 618 et seq.

6 See the Mental Capacity (Deprivation of Liberty: Appointment of Relevant Person's Representative) Regulations 2008, SI 2008/1315, reg 6(1). In relation to England, a donee or deputy may select himself to be the relevant person's representative: see the Mental Capacity (Deprivation of Liberty: Appointment of Relevant Person's Representative) Regulations 2008, SI 2008/1315, reg 6(2).

7 Ie a person selected under the Mental Capacity (Deprivation of Liberty: Appointment of Relevant Person's Representative) Regulations 2008, SI 2008/1315, reg 5(1) or 6(1) or (2).

8 Mental Capacity (Deprivation of Liberty: Appointment of Relevant Person's Representative) Regulations 2008, SI 2008/1315, reg 7(1). As to eligibility to be a representative see PARA 709.

9 Mental Capacity (Deprivation of Liberty: Appointment of Relevant Person's Representative) Regulations 2008, SI 2008/1315, reg 7(2). As to the meaning of 'supervisory body' see PARA 664.

10 Mental Capacity (Deprivation of Liberty: Appointment of Relevant Person's Representative) Regulations 2008, SI 2008/1315, reg 7(3).

11 Ie under the Mental Capacity (Deprivation of Liberty: Appointment of Relevant Person's Representative) Regulations 2008, reg 5(1) (see text to notes 1–4).

12 See the Mental Capacity (Deprivation of Liberty: Appointment of Relevant Person's Representative) Regulations 2008, SI 2008/1315, reg 5(2), 8(1), (2).

13 Ie under the Mental Capacity (Deprivation of Liberty: Appointment of Relevant Person's Representative) Regulations 2008, SI 2008/1315, reg 6(1), (2): see reg 8(2)(b).

14 Mental Capacity (Deprivation of Liberty: Appointment of Relevant Person's Representative) Regulations 2008, SI 2008/1315, reg 8(2)(c).

15 Mental Capacity (Deprivation of Liberty: Appointment of Relevant Person's Representative) Regulations 2008, SI 2008/1315, reg 8(3).

16 Mental Capacity (Deprivation of Liberty: Appointment of Relevant Person's Representative) Regulations 2008, SI 2008/1315, reg 8(4).

17 Mental Capacity (Deprivation of Liberty: Appointment of Relevant Person's Representative) Regulations 2008, SI 2008/1315, reg 8(5).

18 Ie given notice under the Mental Capacity (Deprivation of Liberty: Appointment of Relevant Person's Representative) Regulations 2008, SI 2008/1315, reg 8(5).

19 The supervisory body must be satisfied that there is in respect of the person an enhanced criminal record certificate issued pursuant to the Police Act 1997 s 113B (enhanced criminal record certificates: see SENTENCING AND DISPOSITION OF OFFENDERS vol 92 (2010) PARA 713 et seq) or, if the purpose for which the certificate is required is not one prescribed under s 113B(2), a criminal record certificate issued pursuant to s 113A (criminal record certificates: see SENTENCING AND DISPOSITION OF OFFENDERS vol 92 (2010) PARA 712): Mental Capacity (Deprivation of Liberty: Appointment of Relevant Person's Representative) Regulations 2008, SI 2008/1315, reg 9(2).

20 Mental Capacity (Deprivation of Liberty: Appointment of Relevant Person's Representative) Regulations 2008, SI 2008/1315, reg 9(1)(a).

21 Mental Capacity (Deprivation of Liberty: Appointment of Relevant Person's Representative) Regulations 2008, SI 2008/1315, reg 9(1)(b).

22 Mental Capacity (Deprivation of Liberty: Appointment of Relevant Person's Representative) Regulations 2008, SI 2008/1315, reg 9(1)(c).

23 For the purposes of the Mental Capacity (Deprivation of Liberty: Appointment of Relevant Person's Representative) Regulations 2008, SI 2008/1315 'the relevant person's managing authority' means the managing authority that has made the application for a standard authorisation in respect of the relevant person: reg 2. As to the meaning of 'managing authority' see PARA 652.

24 Mental Capacity (Deprivation of Liberty: Appointment of Relevant Person's Representative) Regulations 2008, SI 2008/1315, reg 9(1)(d). As to the meaning of 'care home' see PARA 652 note 14.

25 Mental Capacity (Deprivation of Liberty: Appointment of Relevant Person's Representative) Regulations 2008, SI 2008/1315, reg 9(1)(e). As to the meaning of 'hospital' see PARA 577.

26 Mental Capacity (Deprivation of Liberty: Appointment of Relevant Person's Representative) Regulations 2008, SI 2008/1315, reg 9(1)(f) (substituted by SI 2008/2368).

711. Selection of representative in Wales. In Wales[1], the relevant person[2] may select a person for appointment as his representative[3] where he has the capacity to do so[4]. Where the relevant person does not have capacity in relation to the question of which person should be his representative, and he has a donee[5] or deputy, the donee or deputy may select a person to be appointed as a representative where the donee or deputy has the authority to do so[6].

A person selected in accordance with the above provisions[7] must be approved by the best interests assessor or the supervisory body[8]. Where the best interests assessor or supervisory body does not approve a person selected they may approve another person so selected[9] or the best interests assessor may select a person[10].

Where a person has not been selected for appointment as a representative[11], or the best interests assessor or supervisory body has not approved a person to be a representativer[12], the best interests assessor may select a person to act as a representative for the relevant person[13].

Where a person has not been selected for appointment under the above provisions[14] the supervisory body must select a person to be appointed as a representative for the relevant person[15]. Where a person who is so selected will be acting in a professional capacity[16] that person must have appropriate training and experience and the supervisory body must be satisfied that there is in respect of that person the required criminal record certificate[17].

The managing authority must advise the supervisory body where it becomes aware the representative is not acting in the best interest of, or has not maintained regular contact with, the relevant person[18].

1   As to the selection of a representative in relation to England see PARA 710.

2   As to the meaning of 'relevant person' see PARA 663 note 7.

3   As to the meaning of 'relevant person's representative' see PARA 707 note 2.

4   See the Mental Capacity (Deprivation of Liberty: Appointment of Relevant Person's Representative) (Wales) Regulations 2009, SI 2009/266, reg 7(1), (2). A person selected in accordance with regs 7(2) or 8(2) (see text and note 6) must be approved by the best interests assessor or the supervisory body: reg 9(1). Where the best interests assessor or supervisory body does not approve a person selected, they may approve another person selected in accordance with regs 7(2) or 8(2); or the best interests assessor may select a person in accordance with reg 10 (see text and note 13): reg 9(2).

5   As to the meaning of 'donee' see PARA 710 note 5.

6   See the Mental Capacity (Deprivation of Liberty: Appointment of Relevant Person's Representative) (Wales) Regulations 2009, SI 2009/266, reg 8(1), (2).

7   Ie in accordance with the Mental Capacity (Deprivation of Liberty: Appointment of Relevant Person's Representative) (Wales) Regulations 2009, SI 2009/266, regs 7(2) or 8(2).

8   Mental Capacity (Deprivation of Liberty: Appointment of Relevant Person's Representative) (Wales) Regulations 2009, SI 2009/266, reg 9(1). As to the meaning of 'supervisory body' see PARA 664.

9   Ie another person selected under the Mental Capacity (Deprivation of Liberty: Appointment of Relevant Person's Representative) (Wales) Regulations 2009, SI 2009/266, regs 7(2) or 8(2).

10   See the Mental Capacity (Deprivation of Liberty: Appointment of Relevant Person's Representative) (Wales) Regulations 2009, SI 2009/266, reg 9(2).

11   Ie in accordance with the Mental Capacity (Deprivation of Liberty: Appointment of Relevant Person's Representative) (Wales) Regulations 2009, SI 2009/266, regs 7(2), 8(2).

12   Ie in accordance with the Mental Capacity (Deprivation of Liberty: Appointment of Relevant Person's Representative) (Wales) Regulations 2009, SI 2009/266, reg 9.

13   See the Mental Capacity (Deprivation of Liberty: Appointment of Relevant Person's Representative) (Wales) Regulations 2009, SI 2009/266, reg 10(1), (2).

14   Ie in accordance with the Mental Capacity (Deprivation of Liberty: Appointment of Relevant Person's Representative) (Wales) Regulations 2009, SI 2009/266, regs 7(2), 8(2) or 10(2).

15   See the Mental Capacity (Deprivation of Liberty: Appointment of Relevant Person's Representative) (Wales) Regulations 2009, SI 2009/266, regs 7(3), 8(3), 10(3), 11(1), (2).

16   For this purpose a person acting in a professional capacity is a person selected by the best interests assessor or supervisory body who is not a family member, friend or carer of the relevant

person: Mental Capacity (Deprivation of Liberty: Appointment of Relevant Person's Representative) (Wales) Regulations 2009, SI 2009/266, reg 11(4).

17 Mental Capacity (Deprivation of Liberty: Appointment of Relevant Person's Representative) (Wales) Regulations 2009, SI 2009/266, reg 11(3). The required criminal record certificate mentioned in the text is an enhanced criminal record certificate issued in pursuance to the Police Act 1997 s 113B (see SENTENCING AND DISPOSITION OF OFFENDERS vol 92 (2010) PARA 713 et seq) or, if the purpose for which the certificate is required is not one prescribed under s 113B(2), a criminal record certificate issued pursuant to s 113A (see SENTENCING AND DISPOSITION OF OFFENDERS vol 92 (2010) PARA 712).

18 Mental Capacity (Deprivation of Liberty: Appointment of Relevant Person's Representative) (Wales) Regulations 2009, SI 2009/266, reg 15.

712. Monitoring of representatives. Regulations may make provision requiring the managing authority of the relevant hospital or care home[1] to monitor, and report to the supervisory body[2] on, the extent to which a relevant person's representative[3] is maintaining contact with the relevant person[4].

In relation to Wales[5], such regulations provide that the managing authority must advise the supervisory body where it becomes aware the representative is not acting in the best interest of, or has not maintained regular contact with, the relevant person[6].

1 As to the meaning of 'managing authority' see PARA 652. As to the meaning of 'relevant hospital or care home' see PARA 663 note 2.
2 As to the meaning of 'supervisory body' see PARA 664.
3 As to the meaning of 'relevant person's representative' see PARA 707 note 2.
4 Mental Capacity Act 2005 Sch A1 para 147 (Sch A1 added by the Mental Health Act 2007 Sch 7). As to the meaning of 'relevant person' see PARA 663 note 7.
5 At the date at which this volume states the law no such regulations had been made in relation to England.
6 Mental Capacity (Deprivation of Liberty: Appointment of Relevant Person's Representative) (Wales) Regulations 2009, SI 2009/266, reg 15.

(v) Urgent Authorisations

713. Duty to give urgent authorisation. Only the managing authority[1] of the relevant hospital or care home[2] may give an urgent authorisation[3] and only if required to do so under the following provisions[4].

The managing authority must give an urgent authorisation in either of the following cases[5]. The first case is where the managing authority are required to make a request[6] for a standard authorisation[7] and it believes that the need for the relevant person to be a detained resident is so urgent that it is appropriate for the detention to begin before they make the request[8]. The second case is where the managing authority has made a request[9] for a standard authorisation and it believes that the need for the relevant person to be a detained resident is so urgent that it is appropriate for the detention to begin before the request is disposed of[10].

Where the managing authority has given an urgent authorisation ('the original authorisation') in connection with a case where a person is, or is to be, a detained resident ('the existing detention') no new urgent authorisation is to be given under the above provisions[11] in connection with the existing detention[12]. However, the managing authority may request the supervisory body to extend the duration of the original authorisation[13].

1 As to the meaning of 'managing authority' see PARA 652.
2 As to the meaning of 'relevant hospital or care home' see PARA 663 note 2.

3 Mental Capacity Act 2005 Sch A1 para 74 (Sch A1 added by the Mental Health Act 2007 Sch 7). 'Urgent authorisation' means an authorisation given under the Mental Capacity Act 2005 Sch A1 paras 74–90: Sch A1 para 9 (as so added).
4 See the Mental Capacity Act 2005 Sch A1 para 75 (as added: see note 3).
5 Mental Capacity Act 2005 Sch A1 para 76(1) (as added: see note 3). Schedule A1 para 76 is subject to Sch A1 para 77: Sch A1 para 76(5) (as so added).
6 Ie under the Mental Capacity Act 2005 Sch A1 para 24 or 25 (see PARA 662).
7 As to the meaning of 'standard authorisation' see PARA 663 note 1.
8 Mental Capacity Act 2005 Sch A1 para 76(2) (as added: see note 3). References in Sch A1 para 76 to the detention of the relevant person are references to the detention to which Sch A1 para 24 or 25 relates: Sch A1 para 76(4) (as so added).
9 Ie under the Mental Capacity Act 2005 Sch A1 para 24 or 25 (see PARA 662).
10 Mental Capacity Act 2005 Sch A1 para 76(3) (as added: see note 3).
11 Ie under the Mental Capacity Act 2005 Sch A1 para 76.
12 Mental Capacity Act 2005 Sch A1 para 77(1), (2) (as added: see note 3). See *A County Council v MB, JB and a Residential Care Home* [2010] EWHC 2508 (COP), [2011] PTSR 795, [2011] 1 FLR 790.
13 Mental Capacity Act 2005 Sch A1 para 77(3) (as added: see note 3). Only one request under Sch A1 para 77(3) may be made in relation to the original authorisation: Sch A1 para 77(4) (as so added). Schedule A1 paras 84 to 86 (see PARA 716) apply to any request made under Sch A1 para 77(3): Sch A1 para 77(5) (as so added).

714. Terms and form etc of authorisation. If the managing authority[1] decides to give an urgent authorisation[2], it must decide the period during which the authorisation is to be in force[3]. This must not exceed seven days[4]. The authorisation must be in writing and must state the name of the relevant person[5], the name of the relevant hospital or care home[6], the period during which the authorisation is to be in force[7] and the purpose for which the authorisation is given[8]. If the name of the relevant hospital or care home changes, the urgent authorisation is to be read as if it stated the current name of the hospital or care home[9].

If an urgent authorisation ceases to be in force the supervisory body must, as soon as practicable after the authorisation ceases to be in force, give notice to the relevant person and any section 39A IMCA[10], that the authorisation has ceased to be in force[11].

1 As to the meaning of 'managing authority' see PARA 652.
2 As to the meaning of 'urgent authorisation' see PARA 713 note 3.
3 Mental Capacity Act 2005 Sch A1 para 78(1) (Sch A1 added by the Mental Health Act 2007 Sch 7). Where an urgent authorisation has been given, the court may determine any question relating to whether the urgent authorisation should have been given, the period during which the urgent authorisation is to be in force and the purpose for which the urgent authorisation is given: see the Mental Capacity Act 2005 s 21A(1), (4); and PARA 733. An urgent authorisation comes into force when it is given: Mental Capacity Act 2005 Sch A1 para 88 (as so added). However authorisations do not run from the beginning of (or from an earlier time) the day on which they are given: see *A County Council v MB, JB and a Residential Care Home* [2010] EWHC 2508 (COP), [2011] PTSR 795, [2011] 1 FLR 790 (court recommended that it would be good practice to record the actual time at which an urgent authorisation and a standard authorisation (which did not run from the expiry of, or a specified time before the expiry of, an existing standard authorisation) was given on the form recording its grant).
4 Mental Capacity Act 2005 Sch A1 para 78(2) (as added: see note 3).
5 As to the meaning of the 'relevant person' see PARA 663 note 7.
6 As to the meaning of 'the relevant hospital or care home' see PARA 663 note 2.
7 An urgent authorisation ceases to be in force at the end of this period (subject to any variation in accordance with the Mental Capacity Act 2005 Sch A1 para 85 (see PARA 716): Sch A1 para 89(1) (as so added). But if the required request is disposed of before the end of that period, the urgent authorisation ceases to be in force as follows: Sch A1 para 89(2) (as so added). If the supervisory body are required by Sch A1 para 50(1) (see PARA 663) to give the requested authorisation, the urgent authorisation ceases to be in force when the requested authorisation comes into force: Sch A1 para 89(3) (as so added). If the supervisory body are

prohibited by Sch A1 para 50(2) from giving the requested authorisation, the urgent authorisation ceases to be in force when the managing authority receive notice under Sch A1 para 58: Sch A1 para 89(4) (as so added). For these purposes 'required request' means the request referred to in Sch A1 para 76(2) or (3) and 'requested authorisation' means the standard authorisation to which the required request relates: Sch A1 para 89(5) (as so added). This does not affect the powers of the Court of Protection or of any other court: Sch A1 para 89(6) (as so added).

8   See the Mental Capacity Act 2005 Sch A1 paras 79, 80 (as added: see note 3).
9   Mental Capacity Act 2005 Sch A1 para 81(1) (as added: see note 3). This is subject to any provision relating to the change of name which is made in any enactment or in any instrument made under an enactment: Sch A1 para 81(2) (as so added).
10 As to the meaning of 'section 39A IMCA' see PARA 705 note 8. Any notice under the Mental Capacity Act 2005 Sch A1 must be in writing: Sch A1 para 169 (as added: see note 3).
11 See the Mental Capacity Act 2005 Sch A1 para 90 (as added: see note 3).

715.   Duty to keep records and give copies and information.   The following apply where an urgent authorisation[1] is given[2].

The managing authority[3] must keep a written record of why it has been given and, as soon as practicable after giving the authorisation, the managing authority must give a copy of the authorisation to the relevant person[4] and any section 39A IMCA[5].

The managing authority of the relevant hospital or care home[6] must take such steps as are practicable[7] to ensure that the relevant person understands the effect of the authorisation and the right to make an application to the court to exercise its jurisdiction[8].

1   As to the meaning of 'urgent authorisation' see PARA 713 note 3.
2   See the Mental Capacity Act 2005 Sch A1 paras 82(1), 83(1) (Sch A1 added by the Mental Health Act 2007 Sch 7).
3   As to the meaning of 'managing authority' see PARA 652.
4   As to the meaning of the 'relevant person' see PARA 663 note 7.
5   Mental Capacity Act 2005 Sch A1 para 82(2), (3) (as added: see note 2). As to the meaning of 'section 39A IMCA' see PARA 705 note 8.
6   As to the meaning of 'the relevant hospital or care home' see PARA 663 note 2.
7   Such steps must be taken as soon as is practicable after the authorisation is given and must include the giving of appropriate information both orally and in writing: Mental Capacity Act 2005 Sch A1 para 83(3), (4) (as added: see note 2).
8   Ie its jurisdiction under the Mental Capacity Act 2005 s 21A (see PARA 733): Sch A1 para 83(2) (as added: see note 2).

716.   Request for extension of duration.   If the managing authority[1] makes a request[2] for the supervisory body[3] to extend the duration of the original authorisation[4], the managing authority must keep a written record of why it has made the request and give the relevant person notice[5] that the request has been made[6].

The supervisory body may extend the duration of the original authorisation if it appears to it that the managing authority has made the required request for a standard authorisation[7], there are exceptional reasons why it has not yet been possible for that request to be disposed of and it is essential for the existing detention[8] to continue until the request is disposed of[9].

The supervisory body must keep a written record that the request has been made to it[10].

If, under the above provisions, the supervisory body decides to extend the duration of the original authorisation, the supervisory body must decide the period of the extension[11] and give the managing authority notice stating the period of the extension[12]. The managing authority must then vary the original authorisation so that it states the extended duration[13] and, as soon as practicable after giving the authorisation, give a copy of the authorisation to the relevant person and any section 39A IMCA[14], and take such steps as are practicable to ensure that the relevant person understands the effect of the variation and the right to make an application to the court[15] to exercise its jurisdiction[16]. The supervisory body must keep a written record of the outcome of the request and the period of the extension[17].

If, the supervisory body decides not to extend the duration of the original authorisation it must give the managing authority notice stating the decision and their reasons for making it[18]. The managing authority must give a copy of that notice to the relevant person and any section 39A IMCA[19]. The supervisory body must keep a written record of the outcome of the request[20].

1   As to the meaning of 'managing authority' see PARA 652.
2   Ie under the Mental Capacity Act 2005 Sch A1 para 77 (see PARA 713).
3   As to the meaning of 'supervisory body' see PARA 664.
4   As to the meaning of 'original authorisation' see the Mental Capacity Act 2005 Sch A1 para 77; and PARA 713 (definition applied by Sch A1 para 84(6)(a) (Sch A1 added by the Mental Health Act 2007 Sch 7)).
5   As to the meaning of the 'relevant person' see PARA 663 note 7. Any notice under the Mental Capacity Act 2005 Sch A1 must be in writing: Sch A1 para 169 (as added: see note 4).
6   See the Mental Capacity Act 2005 Sch A1 para 84(1)–(3) (as added: see note 4).
7   The required request for a standard authorisation is the request that is referred to in the Mental Capacity Act 2005 Sch A1 para 76(2) or (3) (see PARA 713): Sch A1 para 84(6)(b) (as added: see note 6). As to the meaning of 'standard authorisation' see PARA 663 note 1.
8   As to the meaning of 'existing detention' see the Mental Capacity Act 2005 Sch A1 para 77; and PARA 713 (definition applied by Sch A1 para 84(6)(a) (as added: see note 4)).
9   Mental Capacity Act 2005 Sch A1 para 84(4) (as added: see note 4).
10 Mental Capacity Act 2005 Sch A1 para 84(5) (as added: see note 4).
11 Mental Capacity Act 2005 Sch A1 para 85(1), (2) (as added: see note 4). The period of extension must not exceed 7 days: Sch A1 para 85(3) (as so added). An urgent authorisation may not be varied except in accordance with Sch A1 para 85 but this does not affect the powers of the Court of Protection or of any other court: Sch A1 para 87 (as so added).
12 Mental Capacity Act 2005 Sch A1 para 85(4) (as added: see note 4).
13 Mental Capacity Act 2005 Sch A1 para 85(5) (as added: see note 4).
14 See the Mental Capacity Act 2005 Sch A1 para 82(3) (applied by Sch A1 para 85(6) (as added: see note 4)). As to the meaning of 'relevant person' see PARA 663 note 7. As to the meaning of 'section 39A IMCA' see PARA 705 note 8.
15 Ie to exercise its jurisdiction under the Mental Capacity Act 2005 s 21A (see PARA 733).
16 See the Mental Capacity Act 2005 Sch A1 para 83 (applied by Sch A1 para 85(6) (as added: see note 4)).
17 Mental Capacity Act 2005 Sch A1 para 85(7) (as added: see note 4).
18 Mental Capacity Act 2005 Sch A1 para 86(1), (2) (as added: see note 4).
19 Mental Capacity Act 2005 Sch A1 para 86(3) (as added: see note 4).
20 Mental Capacity Act 2005 Sch A1 para 86(4) (as added: see note 4).

(vi) Monitoring and Supervisory Powers

717. Power to make regulations to monitor deprivation of liberty provisions.
Regulations may make provision for, and in connection with, requiring one or more prescribed[1] bodies to monitor, and report on, the operation of provisions[2] relating to the deprivation of liberty[3].

In relation to England, the regulations may, in particular, give a prescribed body authority to do one or more of the following things: (1) to visit hospitals and care homes; (2) to visit and interview persons accommodated in hospitals and care homes; (3) to require the production of, and to inspect, records relating to the care or treatment of persons[4].

Regulations may direct a Local Health Board[5] to exercise in relation to its area certain supervisory functions, so far as they are exercisable in relation to hospitals (whether NHS or independent hospitals, and whether in Wales or England), which are specified in the direction[6].

1   'Prescribed' means prescribed in regulations under the Mental Capacity Act 2005 Sch A1 para 162: Sch A1 para 162(3) (Sch A1 added by the Mental Health Act 2007 Sch 7). As to the making of regulations under the Mental Capacity Act 2005 Sch A1 see further Sch A1 paras 170–173 (as so added).

2   Ie the operation of the Mental Capacity Act 2005 Sch A1.

3   See the Mental Capacity Act 2005 Sch A1 para 162(1), 163 (as so added: see note 1). Such regulations may require the disclosure of information, prescribed under the regulations, to supervisory bodies and managing authorities of hospitals or care homes: see Sch A1 para 164 (as so added). As to such regulations see the Mental Capacity (Deprivation of Liberty: Monitoring and Reporting; and Assessments–Amendment) Regulations 2009, SI 2009/827; and PARA 718.

4   See the Mental Capacity Act 2005 Sch A1 para 162(2) (as so added: see note 1).

5   As to Local Health Boards see HEALTH SERVICES vol 54 (2008) PARA 74 et seq. Such functions may be delegated: see the Mental Capacity Act 2005 Sch A1 para 166 (as added: see note 1). As to such regulations see the Mental Capacity (Deprivation of Liberty: Appointment of Relevant Person's Representative) (Wales) Regulations 2009, SI 2009/266, reg 3; and PARA 718.

6   See the Mental Capacity Act 2005 Sch A1 paras 165, 167 (as so added: see note 1). Directions may permit the delegation of such powers: see Sch A1 para 166 (as so added). Regulations under Sch A1 paras 165, 166 include the power to revoke or vary directions so given: see Sch A1 para 168 (as so added).

718. Monitoring by the Care Quality Commission. The Care Quality Commission[1] must monitor the operation of the deprivation of liberty provisions[2] in relation to England[3] and report to the Secretary of State on the operation of such provisions[4]. For the purpose of monitoring, or reporting on, the operation of such provisions the Commission may visit hospitals and care homes[5], visit and interview persons accommodated in hospitals and care homes and require the production of, and inspect, records relating to the care or treatment of persons accommodated in hospitals or care homes who are the subject of an authorisation[6] or whom the Commission has reason to consider ought to have been, or should be, the subject of an assessment[7].

1   Ie the Commission appointed under the Health and Social Care Act 2008 s 1 (see SOCIAL SERVICES AND COMMUNITY CARE): Mental Capacity (Deprivation of Liberty: Monitoring and Reporting; and Assessments–Amendment) Regulations 2009, SI 2009/827, reg 1(3).

2   Ie the operation of the Mental Capacity Act 2005 Sch A1.

3   Mental Capacity (Deprivation of Liberty: Monitoring and Reporting; and Assessments–Amendment) Regulations 2009, SI 2009/827, reg 2.

4   See the Mental Capacity (Deprivation of Liberty: Monitoring and Reporting; and Assessments–Amendment) Regulations 2009, SI 2009/827, reg 3. The Commission may at any time give the Secretary of State advice or information on the operation of the deprivation of liberty provisions in relation to England and, when requested to do so by the Secretary of State, the Commission must give the Secretary of State such advice or information on the operation of such provisions in relation to England as may be specified in the request: see reg 5. As to the Secretary of State see PARA 567 note 1.

5   As to the meaning of 'care home' see PARA 652. As to the meaning of 'hospital' see PARA 577.

6   Ie an authorisation under the Mental Capacity Act 2005 Sch A1.

7   Mental Capacity (Deprivation of Liberty: Monitoring and Reporting; and Assessments–Amendment) Regulations 2009, SI 2009/827, reg 4. An assessment mentioned in the text is one under the Mental Capacity Act 2005 Sch A1 (see PARAS 695–706).

719. Supervisory functions exercisable by Local Health Boards. Each local health board[1] will exercise supervisory functions[2] (1) in relation to any person who is, or is likely to be, accommodated in a hospital (whether NHS or independent hospitals) in its area for the purposes of receiving relevant care or treatment; and (2) where the Local Health Board commissions relevant care or treatment for a person in a hospital (whether a NHS or independent hospital) in England in relation to that hospital[3].

1   As to Local Health Boards see HEALTH SERVICES vol 54 (2008) PARA 74 et seq. Where Welsh Ministers commission relevant care or treatment for a person who is, or is likely to be, accommodated in a hospital (whether a NHS or independent hospital) in England the supervisory body will be the Local Health Board for the area in which that person is usually resident: see the Mental Capacity (Deprivation of Liberty: Appointment of Relevant Person's Representative) (Wales) Regulations 2009, SI 2009/266, reg 3(2).

2   Subject to any directions given by Welsh Ministers, the supervisory functions exercisable by a Local Health Board may, by arrangement with that Board, and subject to such restrictions and conditions as the Board may think fit, be exercised on behalf of that Board by a committee, sub-committee or officer of the Board or jointly with another Local Health Board: see the Mental Capacity (Deprivation of Liberty: Appointment of Relevant Person's Representative) (Wales) Regulations 2009, SI 2009/266, reg 3(3).

3   See the Mental Capacity (Deprivation of Liberty: Appointment of Relevant Person's Representative) (Wales) Regulations 2009, SI 2009/266, reg 3(1).

4. COURT OF PROTECTION

(1) IN GENERAL

720. The Court of Protection. There is to be a superior court of record known as the Court of Protection[1]. The court is to have an official seal[2], and a central office and registry at a place appointed by the Lord Chancellor after consulting the Lord Chief Justice[3].

The court may sit at any place in England and Wales[4], on any day and at any time[5]. The Lord Chancellor, after consulting the Lord Chief Justice, may designate as additional registries of the court any district registry of the High Court and any county court office[6]. The Lord Chief Justice may nominate the President of the Court of Protection[7] or a judicial office holder[8] to exercise his functions under the above provisions[9].

Subject to Court of Protection Rules[10], the jurisdiction of the court is exercisable by a judge nominated for that purpose by the Lord Chief Justice or, where nominated by the Lord Chief Justice to act on his behalf, the President of the Court of Protection or a judicial office holder[11]. To be nominated, a judge must be: (1) the President of the Family Division[12]; (2) the Chancellor[13]; (3) a puisne judge of the High Court[14]; (4) a circuit judge[15]; or (5) a district judge[16].

The Lord Chief Justice, after consulting the Lord Chancellor, must[17]: (a) appoint one of the judges nominated by virtue of heads (1) to (3) above to be President of the Court of Protection[18]; and (b) appoint another of those judges to be Vice-President of the Court of Protection[19]. The Lord Chief Justice, after consulting with the Lord Chancellor, must appoint one of the judges nominated by virtue of head (4) or head (5) above to be Senior Judge of the Court of Protection, having such administrative functions in relation to the court as the Lord Chancellor, after consulting the Lord Chief Justice, may direct[20].

1   Mental Capacity Act 2005 s 45(1). As to the Court of Protection under the Mental Health Act 1983 see PARA 720. The previous Court of Protection (which was in fact an office of the Supreme Court) ceased to exist with the coming into force of the Mental Capacity Act 2005: see s 45(6). As to the Supreme Court generally see COURTS AND TRIBUNALS vol 24 (2010) PARA 640 et seq.

2   Mental Capacity Act 2005 s 45(2).

3   Mental Capacity Act 2005 s 45(4) (amended by SI 2006/1016). As to the Lord Chancellor see COURTS AND TRIBUNALS vol 24 (2010) PARA 603. As to the Lord Chief Justice see COURTS AND TRIBUNALS vol 24 (2010) PARA 604. Certain formal and administrative tasks of the court may be performed by a court officer: see the Court of Protection Rules 2007, SI 2007/1744, rr 7, 7A (r 7A added by SI 2011/2753).

4   As to the meaning of 'England' see PARA 557 note 4. As to the meaning of 'Wales' see PARA 557 note 5.

5   Mental Capacity Act 2005 s 45(3).

6   Mental Capacity Act 2005 s 45(5) (amended by SI 2006/1016). As to the High Court generally see COURTS AND TRIBUNALS vol 24 (2010) PARA 695 et seq. As to county courts generally see COURTS AND TRIBUNALS vol 24 (2010) PARA 758 et seq.

7   As to the President of the Court of Protection see PARA 720.

8   As to the meaning of 'judicial office holder' see the Constitutional Reform Act 2005 s 109(4); and COURTS AND TRIBUNALS vol 24 (2010) PARA 961 (definition applied by the Mental Capacity Act 2005 s 45(5A) (added by SI 2006/1016)).

9   See the Mental Capacity Act 2005 s 45(5A) (as added: see note 8).

10   Ie under the Mental Capacity Act 2005 s 51(2)(d) (see PARA 740).

11   Mental Capacity Act 2005 s 46(1) (amended by SI 2006/1016). As to transitional provisions see the Mental Capacity Act 2005 (Transitional and Consequential Provisions) Order 2007, SI 2007/1898, art 4.

12 Mental Capacity Act 2005 s 46(2)(a). As to the President of the Family Division see COURTS AND TRIBUNALS vol 24 (2010) PARAS 842–843. Where the decision sought to be appealed is a decision of a judge nominated by virtue of s 46(2)(a)–(c), an appeal will lie only to the Court of Appeal: Court of Protection Rules 2007, SI 2007/1744, r 181(1). See also r 181(2).

13 Mental Capacity Act 2005 s 46(2)(b). Section 46(2)(b) refers to the Vice-Chancellor but this is position has been renamed see COURTS AND TRIBUNALS vol 24 (2010) PARA 842.

14 Mental Capacity Act 2005 s 46(2)(c). As to puisne judges of the High Court see COURTS AND TRIBUNALS vol 24 (2010) PARA 695.

15 Mental Capacity Act 2005 s 46(2)(d). As to circuit judges see COURTS AND TRIBUNALS vol 24 (2010) PARAS 850–853.

16 Mental Capacity Act 2005 s 46(2)(e). As to district judges see COURTS AND TRIBUNALS vol 24 (2010) PARA 749.

17 Mental Capacity Act 2005 s 46(3) (amended by SI 2006/1016).

18 Mental Capacity Act 2005 s 46(3)(a).

19 Mental Capacity Act 2005 s 46(3)(b).

20 Mental Capacity Act 2005 s 46(4) (amended by SI 2006/1016).

721. General powers. The Court of Protection[1] has in connection with its jurisdiction the same powers, rights, privileges and authority as the High Court[2]. Office copies of orders made, directions given or other instruments issued by the court and sealed with its official seal[3] are admissible in all legal proceedings as evidence of the originals without any further proof[4].

1 As to the Court of Protection see PARA 720.
2 Mental Capacity Act 2005 s 47(1). As to the High Court see COURTS AND TRIBUNALS vol 24 (2010) PARA 695 et seq. The Law of Property Act 1925 s 204 (orders of High Court conclusive in favour of purchasers: see CONVEYANCING vol 23 (2013) PARA 492) applies in relation to orders and directions of the court as it applies to orders of the High Court: Mental Capacity Act 2005 s 47(2). In exercising its jurisdiction, the Court of Protection has the same powers, rights, privileges and authority as the High Court would have when exercising its jurisdiction under the Human Rights Act 1998 and generally: *YA (F) v A local authority* [2010] EWHC 2770 (Fam), [2011] 1 WLR 1505, [2011] 1 FLR 2007, Ct of Protection (jurisdiction to deal with claim based on breaches of European Convention on Human Rights and to grant declaratory relief in respect of them and to award damages). As to jurisdiction see further PARA 563.
3 As to the official seal see PARA 720.
4 Mental Capacity Act 2005 s 47(3). As to proof generally see CIVIL PROCEDURE vol 11 (2009) PARA 752 et seq.

722. Jurisdiction. The Court of Protection[1] has jurisdiction where an adult (1) is habitually resident in England and Wales; (2) has property in England and Wales; (3) is present in England or Wales or has property there, if the case is urgent; (4) is present in England and Wales if a temporary protective measure is proposed[2]. In certain circumstances the court may also exercise its functions under the Mental Capacity Act 2005 in relation to a British citizen or where the Lord Chancellor has agreed to a request to take protective measures in relation to a person or that person's property[3].

Provision is made in relation to the applicable law in certain situations[4], for the recognition and enforcement of protective measures taken in other countries[5] and for the co-operation between authorities in England and Wales and authorities in other Convention countries[6].

1 As to the Court of Protection see PARA 720.
2 See the Mental Capacity Act 2005 Sch 3 para 7; and CONFLICT OF LAWS vol 19 (2011) PARA 623. As to jurisdiction see PARAS 563, 721. The Court of Protection has jurisdiction and power to award damages under the Human Rights Act 1998: see *YA (F) v A local authority* [2010] EWHC 2770 (Fam), [2011] 1 WLR 1505, [2011] 1 FLR 2007, Ct of Protection.
3 See the Mental Capacity Act 2005 Sch 3 para 8; and CONFLICT OF LAWS vol 19 (2011) PARA 623.

4   Where the court thinks that the matter has a substantial connection with another country, other than England and Wales, it may apply the law of that country: see the Mental Capacity Act 2005 Sch 3 para 11; and CONFLICT OF LAWS vol 19 (2011) PARA 624. As to the applicable law see further Sch 3 paras 12–18; and CONFLICT OF LAWS vol 19 (2011) PARA 624.

5   See the Mental Capacity Act 2005 Sch 3 paras 19–25; and CONFLICT OF LAWS vol 19 (2011) PARA 625.

6   See the Mental Capacity Act 2005 Sch 3 paras 26–29; and CONFLICT OF LAWS vol 19 (2011) PARA 626.

(2) POWERS

(i) Court of Protection

723. Power to make declarations. The Court of Protection[1] may make declarations[2] as to:

(1)   whether a person has or lacks capacity[3] to make a decision specified in the declaration[4];

(2)   whether a person has or lacks capacity to make decisions on such matters as are described in the declaration[5];

(3)   the lawfulness or otherwise of any act[6] done, or yet to be done, in relation to that person[7].

1   As to the Court of Protection see PARA 720.

2   This jurisdiction is founded on the inherent jurisdiction of the High Court: see PARA 721. As to jurisdiction see further PARA 563.

3   As to lack of capacity see PARA 601 et seq.

4   Mental Capacity Act 2005 s 15(1)(a). The Court of Protection has power under the Family Law Reform Act 1969 s 21(4) (see CHILDREN AND YOUNG PERSONS vol 9 (2012) PARA 102) to consent to the taking of a bodily sample from a person lacking capacity notwithstanding the absence of a specific application within the Court of Protection proceedings putting the parentage of an individual in issue: *LG v DK* [2011] EWHC 2453 (COP), [2012] 2 All ER 115, [2012] 1 FCR 476.

5   Mental Capacity Act 2005 s 15(1)(b).

6   'Act' includes an omission and a course of conduct: Mental Capacity Act 2005 s 15(2).

7   Mental Capacity Act 2005 s 15(1)(c).

724. General power to make decisions. If a person ('P') lacks capacity[1] in relation to a matter or matters concerning his personal welfare or his property and affairs[2], the Court of Protection[3] may, by making an order, make the decision or decisions on P's behalf in relation to the matter or matters[4].

1   As to lack of capacity see PARA 603.

2   Mental Capacity Act 2005 s 16(1). As to the powers concerning personal welfare see PARA 726. As to powers concerning property and affairs see PARA 727. As to guidance on s 16 see *Baker v H* [2010] 1 WLR 1103.

3   As to the Court of Protection see PARA 720.

4   Mental Capacity Act 2005 s 16(2)(a). As to matters that cannot be made on behalf of a person see s 27; and PARA 627. As to when an application to the court may be necessary see the Department for Constitutional Affairs *Mental Capacity Act 2005 Code of Practice* (2007) paras 8.3, 8.4. The court must deal with the issue of capacity before it embarks on an enquiry into welfare: *A Local Authority v FG (No 1)* [2011] EWHC 3932 (COP). Significant welfare issues that cannot be resolved by discussion should be placed before the Court of Protection: *Hillingdon London Borough Council v Neary* [2011] EWHC 1377 (COP), [2011] 4 All ER 584, [2011] 3 FCR 448. See further *Sheffield City Council v S (an adult patient)* [2002] EWHC 2278 (Fam); *Re MM (an adult); Local Authority X v MM* [2007] EWHC 2003 (Fam), [2008] 3 FCR 788, [2009] 1 FLR 443; *Re GC* [2008] EWHC 3402 (Fam); *LLBC v TG* [2007] EWHC 2640 (Fam), [2009] 2 FCR 428, [2009] 1 FLR 414; *Re GJ (incapacitated adults)* [2008] EWHC 1097 (Fam), [2008] 2 FLR 1295, [2008] Fam Law 997; *FP v GM and A Health Board* [2011] EWHC 2778 (COP); *K v A local authority* [2012] EWCA Civ 79, [2012] 1 FCR 441; *R (on the*

application of C) v A Local Authority [2011] EWHC 1539 (Admin), [2011] All ER (D) 171 (Jun); *WCC v GS* [2011] EWHC 2244; *A Local Authority v PB* [2011] EWHC 502 (COP); *Re G(TJ)* [2010] EWHC 3005 (COP), [2010] All ER (D) 218 (Nov); *KGS v JDS (by his litigation friend, the Official Solicitor)* [2012] EWHC 302 (COP), [2012] NLJR 1536; *Re D (statutory will)* [2010] EWHC 2159 (Ch), [2012] Ch 57, [2011] 1 All ER 859; *Re P* [2009] EWHC 163 (Ch), [2010] Ch 33, [2009] 2 All ER 1198; *Re M (vulnerable adult) (testamentary capacity)* [2009] EWHC 2525 (Fam), [2010] 3 All ER 682, [2011] 1 WLR 344. Applications are governed by the Court of Protection Rules 2007, SI 2007/1744, r 82A; and Practice Direction 10A–*Applications within proceedings.*

725. Interim jurisdiction. The Court of Protection[1] may, pending the determination of an application to it in relation to a person ('P'), make an order or give directions in respect of any matter if: (1) there is reason to believe that P lacks capacity[2] in relation to the matter[3]; (2) the matter is one to which its powers under the Mental Capacity Act 2005 extend[4]; and (3) it is in P's best interests[5] to make the order, or give the directions, without delay[6].

1 As to the Court of Protection see PARA 720.
2 As to lack of capacity see PARA 603.
3 Mental Capacity Act 2005 s 48(a). For the proper test of engagement of s 48 see *Re F (vulnerable adult) (capacity: jurisdiction to make order on vulnerable adults behalf)* [2009] All ER (D) 257 (Nov).
4 Mental Capacity Act 2005 s 48(b).
5 As to best interests see PARA 606.
6 Mental Capacity Act 2005 s 48(c).

726. Powers relating to personal welfare. The powers of the Court of Protection[1] to make decisions and appoint deputies[2] as respects the personal welfare of a person ('P') lacking capacity[3] extend in particular to:
   (1)   deciding where P is to live[4];
   (2)   deciding what contact, if any, P is to have with any specified persons[5];
   (3)   making an order prohibiting a named person from having contact with P[6];
   (4)   giving or refusing consent to the carrying out or continuation of a treatment[7] by a person providing health care for P[8];
   (5)   giving a direction that a person responsible for P's health care allow a different person to take over that responsibility[9].

If a person is ineligible to be deprived of liberty by the Mental Capacity Act 2005[10], the court may not include in a welfare order[11] provision which authorises the person to be deprived of his liberty[12].

If a welfare order includes provision which authorises a person to be deprived of his liberty and that person becomes ineligible to be deprived of liberty by the Mental Capacity Act 2005, the provision ceases to have effect for as long as the person remains ineligible[13].

1 As to the Court of Protection see PARA 720.
2 Ie the court's powers under the Mental Capacity Act 2005 s 16: see PARA 724.
3 As to lack of capacity see PARA 603.
4 Mental Capacity Act 2005 s 17(1)(a). Section 17(1) is subject to s 20 (restrictions on deputies) (see PARA 737): s 17(2).
5 Mental Capacity Act 2005 s 17(1)(b). See note 4.
6 Mental Capacity Act 2005 s 17(1)(c). See note 4.
7 As to the meaning of 'treatment' see PARA 606 note 9.
8 Mental Capacity Act 2005 s 17(1)(d). See note 4.
9 Mental Capacity Act 2005 s 17(1)(e). See note 4.
10 For these purposes the Mental Capacity Act 2005 Sch 1A (see PARA 658 et seq) applies for determining whether or not P is ineligible to be deprived of liberty by the Mental Capacity Act 2005: s 16A(4)(a) (added by SI 2009/139).

11 For these purposes 'welfare order' means an order under the Mental Capacity Act 2005 s 16(2)(a) (see PARA 724): s 16A(4)(b).

12 Mental Capacity Act 2005 s 16A(1) (as added: see note 10).

13 Mental Capacity Act 2005 s 16A(2) (as added: see note 10). Nothing in s 16A(2) affects the power of the court under s 16(7) (see PARA 734) to vary or discharge the welfare order: s 16A(3) (as so added).

727. Powers relating to property and affairs. The powers of the Court of Protection[1] to make decisions and appoint deputies[2] as respects the property and affairs of a person ('P') lacking capacity[3] extend in particular to:

(1)   the control and management of P's property[4];

(2)   the sale, exchange, charging, gift or other disposition of P's property[5];

(3)   the acquisition of property in P's name or on P's behalf[6];

(4)   the carrying on, on P's behalf, of any profession, trade or business[7];

(5)   the taking of a decision which will have the effect of dissolving a partnership of which P is a member[8];

(6)   the carrying out of any contract entered into by P[9];

(7)   the discharge of P's debts and of any of P's obligations, whether legally enforceable or not[10];

(8)   the settlement of any of P's property, whether for P's benefit or for the benefit of others[11];

(9)   the execution for P of a will[12];

(10)   the exercise of any power (including a power to consent) vested in P whether beneficially or as trustee or otherwise[13];

(11)   the conduct of legal proceedings in P's name or on P's behalf[14].

The powers[15] as respects any other matter relating to P's property and affairs may be exercised even though P has not reached 16, if the court considers it likely that P will still lack capacity to make decisions in respect of that matter when he reaches 18[16].

1 As to the Court of Protection see PARA 720.

2 Ie the court's powers under the Mental Capacity Act 2005 s 16: see PARA 724. As to the meaning of 'deputy' see PARA 606 note 18.

3 As to lack of capacity see PARA 603.

4 Mental Capacity Act 2005 s 18(1)(a). As to the meaning of 'property' see PARA 619 note 2. Section 18(1) is subject to s 20 (restrictions on deputies) (see PARA 737): s 18(6). As to supplementary provisions see PARA 728. See also *Re E (a mental patient)* [1985] 1 All ER 609, [1985] 1 WLR 245, 129 Sol Jo 67.

5 Mental Capacity Act 2005 s 18(1)(b). See note 4. As to supplementary provisions see PARA 729. As to supplementary provisions see *Re G(TJ)* [2010] EWHC 3005 (COP), [2010] All ER (D) 218 (Nov); and *KGS v JDS (by his litigation friend, the Official Solicitor)* [2012] EWHC 302 (COP), [2012] NLJR 1536.

6 Mental Capacity Act 2005 s 18(1)(c). See note 4.

7 Mental Capacity Act 2005 s 18(1)(d). See note 4.

8 Mental Capacity Act 2005 s 18(1)(e). As to partnerships generally see PARTNERSHIP. See note 4.

9 Mental Capacity Act 2005 s 18(1)(f). See note 4.

10 Mental Capacity Act 2005 s 18(1)(g). See note 4.

11 Mental Capacity Act 2005 s 18(1)(h). See note 4. See also PARA 730. The decision must be taken by the court and not a deputy see s 20(3)(a), Sch 2 paras 5, 6; and PARAS 730, 738. See also *Re L (WJG)* [1966] Ch 135, [1965] 3 All ER 865.

12 Mental Capacity Act 2005 s 18(1)(i). As to the power to execute a will see PARA 731. The decision must be taken by the court and not a deputy see s 20(3)(a), Sch 2 paras 2–4; and PARAS 731, 738. The guidance given under the Mental Health Act 1959 and the Mental Health Act 1983 about the making of settlements and wills for a person lacking mental capacity can no longer be applied to a decision being made under the Mental Capacity Act 2005: *Re P* [2009] EWHC 163 (Ch), [2010] Ch 33, [2009] 2 All ER 1198. See also *Re M* [2009] EWHC 2525 (Fam), [2010] 3 All ER 682. As to capacity to make a will see PARA 615.

13 Mental Capacity Act 2005 s 18(1)(j). As to trustees generally see TRUSTS. See note 4.

Supplementary provisions in Sch 2 para 10 concern powers as patron of a benefice. Any functions which P has as patron of a benefice may be discharged only by a person ('R') appointed by the court: Sch 2 para 10(1). R must be an individual capable of appointment under the Patronage (Benefices) Measure 1986 (No 3) s 8(1)(b) (which provides for an individual able to make a declaration of communicant status, a clerk in Holy Orders, etc to be appointed to discharge a registered patron's functions: see ECCLESIASTICAL LAW vol 34 (2011) PARA 561): Mental Capacity Act 2005 Sch 2 para 10(2). The Patronage (Benefices) Measure 1986 (No 3) applies to R as it applies to an individual appointed by the registered patron of the benefice under s 8(1)(b) or s 8(3) to discharge his functions as patron: Mental Capacity Act 2005 Sch 2 para 10(3). As to benefices generally see ECCLESIASTICAL LAW vol 34 (2011) PARA 542 et seq; and as to patronage see ECCLESIASTICAL LAW vol 34 (2011) PARA 550 et seq.

14   Mental Capacity Act 2005 s 18(1)(k). See note 4.
15   Ie the powers under the Mental Capacity Act 2005 s 16: see PARA 724.
16   Mental Capacity Act 2005 s 18(3). See also note 13.

728.   Control and management of property.   The Court of Protection[1] has the power to make decisions and appoint deputies[2] in respect of a person lacking capacity[3] ('P') in relation to the control and management of P's property[4]. If the court is satisfied that: (1) under the law prevailing in a place outside England and Wales[5] a person ('M') has been appointed to exercise powers in respect of the property or affairs of P on the ground (however formulated) that P lacks capacity to make decisions with respect to the management and administration of his property and affairs; and (2) having regard to the nature of the appointment and to the circumstances of the case, it is expedient that the court should exercise its powers under these provisions, the court may direct any stocks[6] standing in the name of P or the right to receive dividends from the stocks, to be transferred into M's name or otherwise dealt with as required by M, and may give such directions as the court thinks fit for dealing with accrued dividends from the stocks[7].

Where P ceases to lack capacity the court may at any time make an order for any relevant property[8] to be transferred to P, or at P's direction, provided that it is satisfied that P has the capacity to make decisions in relation to that property[9].

1   As to the Court of Protection see PARA 720.
2   As to the meaning of 'deputy' see PARA 606 note 18.
3   As to lack of capacity see PARA 603.
4   See the Mental Capacity Act 2005 s 18(1)(a); and PARA 727.
5   As to the meaning of 'England' see PARA 557 note 4; and as to the meaning of 'Wales' see PARA 557 note 5.
6   'Stocks' includes: (1) shares; and (2) any funds, annuity or security transferable in the books kept by any body corporate or unincorporated company or society or by an instrument of transfer either alone or accompanied by other formalities; and 'dividends' is to be construed accordingly: Mental Capacity Act 2005 Sch 2 para 7(3).
7   Mental Capacity Act 2005 Sch 2 para 7(1), (2).
8   For these purposes 'relevant property' means any property belonging to P and forming part of his estate, and which remains under the control of anyone appointed by order of the court or which is held under the direction of the court: Court of Protection Rules 2007, SI 2007/1744, r 202(2).
9   Court of Protection Rules 2007, SI 2007/1744, r 202(1). An application for an order under this rule is to be made in accordance with rr 77–82): r 202(3). See also Practice Direction 23B–*Where P ceases to lack capacity or dies.*

729.   Sale etc of property.   The Court of Protection[1] has the power to make decisions and appoint deputies[2] in respect of a person lacking capacity[3] ('P') in relation to the sale, exchange, charging, gift or other disposition of P's property[4]. Supplementary provisions apply in regard to preservation of interests in property disposed of on behalf of persons lacking capacity[5].

1   As to the Court of Protection see PARA 720.

2   As to the meaning of 'deputy' see PARA 606 note 18.

3   As to lack of capacity see PARA 603.

4   See the Mental Capacity Act 2005 s 18(1)(b); and PARA 727.

5   If: (1) P's property has been disposed of by virtue of the Mental Capacity Act 2005 s 18; (2) under P's will or intestacy, or by a gift perfected or nomination taking effect on his death, any other person would have taken an interest in the property but for the disposal; and (3) on P's death, any property belonging to P's estate represents the property disposed of (Sch 2 para 8(1)), then: (a) the person takes the same interest, if and so far as circumstances allow, in the property representing the property disposed of (Sch 2 para 8(2)); and (b) if the property disposed of was real property, any property representing it is to be treated, so long as it remains part of P's estate, as if it were real property (Sch 2 para 8(3)). The court may direct that, on a disposal of P's property which is made by virtue of s 18 and which would apart from this provision result in the conversion of personal property into real property, property representing the property disposed of is to be treated, so long as it remains P's property or forms part of P's estate, as if it were personal property (Sch 2 para 8(4)). References in Sch 2 para 8(1)–(4) to the disposal of property are references to:

    (i)   the sale, exchange, charging of or other dealing (otherwise than by will) with property other than money;

    (ii)   the removal of property from one place to another;

    (iii)   the application of money in acquiring property;

    (iv)   the transfer of money from one account to another,

and references to property representing property disposed of are to be construed accordingly and as including the result of successive disposals (Sch 2 para 8(5)). The court may give such directions as appear to it necessary or expedient for the purpose of facilitating the operation of Sch 2 para 8(1)–(3), including the carrying of money to a separate account and the transfer of property other than money (Sch 2 para 8(6)).

     If the court has ordered or directed the expenditure of money for carrying out permanent improvements on any of P's property or otherwise for the permanent benefit of any of P's property (Sch 2 para 9(1)), the court may order that: (A) the whole of the money expended or to be expended; or (B) any part of it, is to be a charge on the property either without interest or with interest at a specified rate (Sch 2 para 9(2)). An order under Sch 2 para 9(2) may provide for excluding or restricting the operation of Sch 2 para 8(1)–(3) (Sch 2 para 9(3)). A charge under Sch 2 para 9(2) may be made in favour of such person as may be just and, in particular, where the money charged is paid out of P's general estate, may be made in favour of a person as trustee for P (Sch 2 para 9(4)). No charge under Sch 2 para 9(2) may confer any right of sale or foreclosure during P's lifetime (Sch 2 para 9(5)).

730. Settlement of property.

The Court of Protection[1] has the power to make decisions and appoint deputies[2] in respect of a person lacking capacity[3] ('P') in relation to the settlement of any of P's property, whether for P's benefit or for the benefit of others[4]. If provision is made for the settlement of any property of P or the exercise of a power vested in him of appointing trustees or retiring from a trust, the court may also make as respects the property settled or the trust property such consequential vesting or other orders as the case may require[5]. If a settlement has been made, the court may by order vary or revoke the settlement if: (1) the settlement makes provision for its variation or revocation; (2) the court is satisfied that a material fact was not disclosed when the settlement was made; or (3) the court is satisfied that there has been a substantial change of circumstances[6].

1   As to the Court of Protection see PARA 720.

2   As to the meaning of 'deputy' see PARA 606 note 18.

3   As to lack of capacity see PARA 603.

4   See the Mental Capacity Act 2005 s 18(1)(h); and PARA 727.

5   Mental Capacity Act 2005 Sch 2 para 5(1). The power under Sch 2 para 5(1) includes, in the case of the exercise of such a power, any order which could have been made in such a case under the Trustee Act 1925 Pt IV (ss 41–63A) (see TRUSTS vol 48 (2007 Reissue) PARA 971 et seq): Mental Capacity Act 2005 Sch 2 para 5(2).

6   Mental Capacity Act 2005 Sch 2 para 6(1). Any such order may give such consequential directions as the court thinks fit: Sch 2 para 6(2).

731. Power to execute a will. The Court of Protection[1] has the power to execute a new will[2] in respect of a person lacking capacity[3]. However no will may be made under this power at a time when P has not reached 18[4].

The will may make any provision (whether by disposing of property or exercising a power or otherwise) which could be made by a will executed by P if he had capacity to make it[5]. If the court makes an order or gives directions requiring or authorising a person ('the authorised person') to execute a will on behalf of P[6], any will executed in pursuance of the order or direction: (1) must state that it is signed by P acting by the authorised person; (2) must be signed by the authorised person with the name of P and his own name, in the presence of two or more witnesses present at the same time; (3) must be attested and subscribed by those witnesses in the presence of the authorised person; and (4) must be sealed with the official seal of the court[7].

The Court of Protection should not refrain, as a matter of principle, from directing the execution of a statutory will in a case where the validity of an earlier will is in dispute, however, a previous will is a relevant written statement which falls to be taken into account by the court[8].

In deciding what provision should be made in a will to be executed on a person's behalf (which would only have effect after he was dead) part of the overall picture is that the person's best interests would be served simply by giving effect to his wishes but the decision-maker is entitled to take into account, in assessing what was in the person's best interests, how he would be remembered after death[9].

1   As to the Court of Protection see PARA 720.
2   'Will' includes codicil: Mental Capacity Act 2005 s 64(1). As to wills generally see WILLS AND INTESTACY. See also PARA 615.
3   See the Mental Capacity Act 2005 s 18(1)(i); and PARA 727. Supplementary provisions in Sch 2 paras 2–4 apply in relation to the execution of a will, by virtue of s 18, on behalf of P: Sch 2 para 1.
4   Mental Capacity Act 2005 s 18(2).
5   Mental Capacity Act 2005 Sch 2 para 2.
6   Ie the court makes an order under the Mental Capacity Act 2005 s 16 (see PARA 724).
7   Mental Capacity Act 2005 Sch 2 para 3(1), (2). As to the official seal see PARA 720. The following applies where a will is executed in accordance with Sch 2 para 3: (1) the Wills Act 1837 has effect in relation to the will as if it were signed by P by his own hand, except that: (a) s 9 (requirements as to signing and attestation: see WILLS AND INTESTACY vol 102 (2010) PARA 1 et seq) does not apply; and (b) in the subsequent provisions of the Act any reference to execution in the manner required by the previous provisions is to be read as a reference to execution in accordance with the Mental Capacity Act 2005 Sch 2 para 3 (Sch 2 para 4(1), (2)); (2) the will has the same effect for all purposes as if P had had the capacity to make a valid will, and the will had been executed by him in the manner required by the Wills Act 1837 (Mental Capacity Act 2005 Sch 2 para 4(1), (3)); but (3) the provisions of Sch 2 para 4(3) do not have effect in relation to the will: (a) in so far as it disposes of immovable property outside England and Wales; or (b) in so far as it relates to any other property or matter if, when the will is executed P is domiciled outside England and Wales, and the following condition is met: that, under the law of P's domicile, any question of his testamentary capacity would fall to be determined in accordance with the law of a place outside England and Wales (Sch 2 para 4(1), (4), (5)).
8   See *Re D (statutory will)* [2010] EWHC 2159 (Ch), [2012] Ch 56, [2011] 1 All ER 859.
9   See *Re P* [2009] EWHC 163 (Ch), [2010] Ch 33, [2009] 2 All ER 1198.

732. Lasting powers of attorney. Where a lasting power of attorney has been executed or registered, the Court of Protection[1] may determine any question relating to whether one or more of the requirements for the creation of a lasting power of attorney have been met and whether the power has been revoked or has otherwise come to an end[2]. Under certain circumstances the court may direct that the instrument purporting to create a lasting power of attorney is not to be registered[3] and it may revoke the instrument where the donor lacks capacity to do so[4].

The court may determine any question as to the meaning or effect of a lasting power of attorney or an instrument purporting to create one[5].

1   As to the Court of Protection see PARA 720.
2   See the Mental Capacity Act 2005 s 22; and AGENCY vol 1 (2008) PARA 235.
3   See the Mental Capacity Act 2005 s 22(3), (4); and AGENCY vol 1 (2008) PARA 230.
4   See the Mental Capacity Act 2005 s 22(4)(b); and AGENCY vol 1 (2008) PARA 230. As to the power to cancel a lasting power of attorney see s 22, Sch 1 para 18; and AGENCY vol 1 (2008) PARA 236.
5   See the Mental Capacity Act 2005 s 23(1); and AGENCY vol 1 (2008) PARA 235. As to the directions that may be given see s 23(2)–(4); and AGENCY vol 1 (2008) PARA 235.

733. Powers relating to standard authorisations and urgent authorisations.
The following applies if a standard authorisation or an urgent authorisation[1] has been given[2]. Where a standard authorisation has been given, the Court of Protection[3] may determine any question relating to any of the following matters:

(1)   whether the relevant person[4] meets one or more of the qualifying requirements[5];
(2)   the period during which the standard authorisation is to be in force[6];
(3)   the purpose for which the standard authorisation is given[7];
(4)   the conditions subject to which the standard authorisation is given[8].

If the court determines any question under heads (1) to (4) above the court may make an order varying or terminating the standard authorisation or directing the supervisory body to vary or terminate the standard authorisation[9].

Where an urgent authorisation has been given, the court may determine any question relating to any of the following matters:

(a)   whether the urgent authorisation should have been given[10];
(b)   the period during which the urgent authorisation is to be in force[11];
(c)   the purpose for which the urgent authorisation is given[12].

Where the court determines any question under heads (a) to (c) above the court may make an order varying or terminating the urgent authorisation or directing the managing authority of the relevant hospital or care home to vary or terminate the urgent authorisation[13].

1   Ie as given under the Mental Capacity Act 2005 Sch A1 (see PARAS 651–665). As to the meaning of 'standard authorisation' see PARA 663 note 1. As to the meaning of 'urgent authorisation' see PARA 713 note 3.
2   Mental Capacity Act 2005 s 21A(1) (added by the Mental Health Act 2007 Sch 9 para 2).
3   As to the Court of Protection see PARA 720.
4   As to the meaning of 'relevant person' see PARA 663 note 7.
5   Mental Capacity Act 2005 s 21A(2)(a) (as added: see note 2). As to the meaning of 'qualifying requirements' see PARA 653. An application will be made where an authorisation exists. If no authorisation exists then an application for a court authorisation may be necessary: *A County Council v MB, JB and a Residential Home* [2010] EWHC 2508 (COP), [2011] PTSR 795, [2011] 1 FLR 790. Once an application has been made the court may consider issues of capacity and welfare under the Mental Capacity Act 2005 ss 15, 16 (see PARAS 723–724): *PH v A Local Authority* [2011] EWHC 1704 (Fam). The relevant person's representative under Sch A1 (see PARA 707) may act as a litigation friend: *AB (by his litigation friend NW) v LCC (A Local Authority)* [2011] EWHC 3151 (COP), [2011] NLJR 1744.
6   Mental Capacity Act 2005 s 21A(2)(b) (as added: see note 2).
7   Mental Capacity Act 2005 s 21A(2)(c) (as added: see note 2).
8   Mental Capacity Act 2005 s 21A(2)(d) (as added: see note 2).
9   Mental Capacity Act 2005 s 21A(3) (as added: see note 2). Where the court makes an order under s 21A(3) or (5), the court may make an order about a person's liability for any act done in

connection with the standard or urgent authorisation before its variation or termination: s 21A(6) (as so added). Such an order may, in particular, exclude a person from liability: s 21A(7) (as so added). The court is to make its own decision: *J v The Foundation Trust* [2009] EWHC 2972 (Fam), [2010] Fam 70, [2010] 3 WLR 840.
10 Mental Capacity Act 2005 s 21A(4)(a) (as added: see note 2).
11 Mental Capacity Act 2005 s 21A(4)(b) (as added: see note 2).
12 Mental Capacity Act 2005 s 21A(4)(c) (as added: see note 2).
13 Mental Capacity Act 2005 s 21A(5) (as added: see note 2). See note 9.

(ii) Deputies

734.   General power to appoint deputies.   If a person ('P') lacks capacity[1] in relation to a matter or matters concerning his personal welfare or his property and affairs[2], the Court of Protection[3] may appoint a person (a 'deputy')[4] to make decisions on P's behalf in relation to the matter or matters[5]. This power is subject to the provisions of the Mental Capacity Act 2005[6].

When deciding whether it is in P's best interests to appoint a deputy, the court must have regard[7] to the principles that: (1) a decision by the court is to be preferred to the appointment of a deputy to make a decision[8]; and (2) the powers conferred on a deputy should be as limited in scope and duration as is reasonably practicable in the circumstances[9].

The court may make such further orders or give such directions[10], and confer on a deputy such powers or impose on him such duties, as it thinks necessary or expedient for giving effect to, or otherwise in connection with, an order or appointment made by it under heads (1) and (2) above[11]. The court may make the order, give the directions or make the appointment on such terms as it considers are in P's best interests, even though no application is before the court for an order, directions or an appointment on those terms[12].

An order of the court may be varied or discharged by a subsequent order[13]. The court may, in particular, revoke the appointment of a deputy or vary the powers conferred on him if it is satisfied that the deputy: (a) has behaved, or is behaving, in a way that contravenes the authority conferred on him by the court or is not in P's best interests[14]; or (b) proposes to behave in a way that would contravene that authority or would not be in P's best interests[15].

1 As to lack of capacity see PARA 603.
2 Mental Capacity Act 2005 s 16(1). As to the powers concerning personal welfare see PARA 726. As to powers concerning property and affairs see PARA 727. As to guidance on s 16 see *Baker v H* [2010] 1 WLR 1103.
3 As to the Court of Protection see PARA 720.
4 As to the meaning of 'deputy' see PARA 606 note 18.
5 Mental Capacity Act 2005 s 16(2)(b). As to the appointment of deputies see PARA 735. The following applies where, in accordance with an order made under s 16(2)(a), a person ('T') has been authorised to carry out any transaction for a person who lacks capacity: Lasting Powers of Attorney, Enduring Powers of Attorney and Public Guardian Regulations 2007, SI 2007/1253, reg 45(1). The Public Guardian has the functions of receiving any reports from T which the court may require; dealing with representations (including complaints) about the way in which the transaction has been or is being carried out or any failure to carry it out: reg 45(2). The Lasting Powers of Attorney, Enduring Powers of Attorney and Public Guardian Regulations 2007, SI 2007/1253, regs 38–41 have effect in relation to T as they have effect in relation a deputy: reg 45(3). See *SBC v PBA* [2011] EWHC 2580 (Fam).
6 Mental Capacity Act 2005 s 16(3). The powers of the court are, in particular, subject to s 1 (the principles: see PARA 601) and s 4 (best interests: see PARA 606). The principles laid down by the Court of Protection under the Mental Health Act 1959 and the Mental Health Act 1983 are no longer of direct application to the exercise of the Court's discretion under the Mental Capacity Act 2005 s 16: *Re P* [2009] EWHC 163 (Ch), [2010] Ch 33, [2009] 2 All ER 1198.
7 Ie in addition to the matters mentioned in the Mental Capacity Act 2005 s 4 (see PARA 606).

8 Mental Capacity Act 2005 s 16(4)(a). Section 16(4) is intended to emphasise the principle of least restriction in s 1(6) (see PARA 601 head (5)). As to the role of the Court of Protection and court appointed deputies see the Department for Constitutional Affairs *Mental Capacity Act 2005 Code of Practice* (2007) Chapter 18. See also *G v E* [2010] EWHC 2512 (COP), [2011] 1 FLR 1652, [2011] Fam Law 141; *Re P (vulnerable adult) (capacity: appointment of deputies)* [2010] EWHC 1592 (Fam), [2010] 2 FLR 1712, [2010] Fam Law 1073; *EB v RC* [2011] EWHC 3805 (COP).
9 Mental Capacity Act 2005 s 16(4)(b). See note 8.
10 As to orders and directions see PARA 721.
11 Mental Capacity Act 2005 s 16(5). As to a restriction on or qualification to the power in s 16(5) see s 20(2); and PARA 738.
12 Mental Capacity Act 2005 s 16(6). This is without prejudice to s 4 (see PARA 606).
13 Mental Capacity Act 2005 s 16(7). Section 16(7) is subject to Sch 2 para 6 (see PARA 730): s 18(5). The decision to vary or discharge an order must be made in the patient's best interests: *Long v Rodman* [2012] EWHC 347 (Ch), [2012] All ER (D) 171 (Feb).
14 Mental Capacity Act 2005 s 16(8)(a). See *EB v RC* [2011] EWHC 3805 (COP).
15 Mental Capacity Act 2005 s 16(8)(b).

735. Appointment of deputies. A deputy[1] appointed by the Court of Protection[2] must be an individual who has reached 18[3] or, as respects powers in relation to property and affairs[4], an individual who has reached 18 or a trust corporation[5]. A person may not be appointed as a deputy without his consent[6].

The court may appoint an individual by appointing the holder for the time being of a specified office or position[7]. The court may also appoint two or more deputies to act jointly, jointly and severally, or jointly in respect of some matters and jointly and severally in respect of others[8]. When appointing a deputy or deputies, the court may at the same time appoint one or more other persons to succeed the existing deputy or those deputies in such circumstances, or on the happening of such events, as may be specified by the court[9], for such period as may be so specified[10].

A deputy is to be treated as the agent of the person ('P') lacking capacity[11] in relation to anything done or decided by him within the scope of his appointment and in accordance with Part 1 of the Mental Capacity Act 2005[12]. The deputy is entitled to be reimbursed out of P's property for his reasonable expenses in discharging his functions[13], and if the court so directs when appointing him, to remuneration out of P's property[14] for discharging them[15].

1 As to the meaning of 'deputy' see PARA 606 note 18. See also PARAS 724–727. As to the supervision of deputies by the Public Guardian see PARA 752.
2 As to the Court of Protection see PARA 720.
3 Mental Capacity Act 2005 s 19(1)(a). As to the role of a court appointed deputy see the Department for Constitutional Affairs *Mental Capacity Act 2005 Code of Practice* (2007) Chapter 8.
4 As to the powers in relation to property and affairs see PARA 727.
5 Mental Capacity Act 2005 s 19(1)(b). As to the meaning of 'trust corporation' see PARA 619 note 6. Where the court makes an order, or gives a direction, conferring functions on any person (whether as deputy or otherwise) and requiring him to give security for the discharge of those functions the person on whom functions are conferred must give the security before he undertakes to discharge his functions, unless the court permits it to be given subsequently: Court of Protection Rules 2007, SI 2007/1744, r 200(1), (2). The following apply where the security is required to be given before any action can be taken: r 200(3). Subject to r 200(5), the security must be given in accordance with the requirements of regulation 33(2)(a) of the Lasting Powers of Attorney, Enduring Powers of Attorney and Public Guardian Regulations 2007, SI 2007/1253, reg 33(2)(a) (which makes provision about the giving of security by means of a bond that is endorsed by an authorised insurance company or deposit-taker): Court of Protection Rules 2007, SI 2007/1744, r 200(4). The court may impose such other requirements in relation to the giving of the security as it considers appropriate (whether in addition to, or instead of, those specified in the Court of Protection Rules 2007, SI 2007/1744, r 200(4)): r 200(5). In specifying the date from which the order or directions referred to in r 200(1) are to

take effect, the court will have regard to the need to postpone that date for such reasonable period as would enable the Public Guardian to be satisfied that if r 200(4) applies, the requirements of the Lasting Powers of Attorney, Enduring Powers of Attorney and Public Guardian Regulations 2007, SI 2007/1253, reg 34 have been met in relation to the security and any other requirements imposed by the court under the Court of Protection Rules 2007, SI 2007/1744, r 200(5) have been met: r 200(6).

6   Mental Capacity Act 2005 s 19(3).
7   Mental Capacity Act 2005 s 19(2).
8   Mental Capacity Act 2005 s 19(4). *Re P (vulnerable adult) (capacity: appointment of deputies)* [2010] EWHC 1592 (Fam), [2010] 2 FLR 1712, [2010] Fam Law 1073.
9   Mental Capacity Act 2005 s 19(5)(a).
10 Mental Capacity Act 2005 s 19(5)(b).
11 As to lack of capacity see PARA 603.
12 Mental Capacity Act 2005 s 19(6). The reference in the text is a reference to Pt 1 (ss 1–44) (see PARAS 601–646, 723–727). As to agents generally see AGENCY vol 1 (2008) PARA 1 et seq.
13 Mental Capacity Act 2005 s 19(7)(a).
14 As to the meaning of 'property' see PARA 619 note 2.
15 Mental Capacity Act 2005 s 19(7)(b).

736.   Deputies: powers over property.   The Court of Protection[1] may confer on a deputy[2] power to: (1) take possession or control of all or any specified part of the property of a person ('P') lacking capacity[3]; (2) exercise all or any specified powers in respect of it, including such powers of investment as the court may determine[4]. The court may require a deputy to give to the Public Guardian such security[5] as the court thinks fit for the due discharge of his functions[6], and to submit to the Public Guardian such reports at such times or at such intervals as the court may direct[7].

A deputy may not be given powers with respect to the settlement of any of P's property, whether for P's benefit or for the benefit of others[8], the execution for P of a will[9], or the exercise of any power (including a power to consent) vested in P whether beneficially or as trustee or otherwise[10]. A further restriction is that a deputy may not be given power to make a decision on behalf of P which is inconsistent with a decision made, within the scope of his authority and in accordance with the Mental Capacity Act 2005, by the donee of a lasting power of attorney[11] granted by P (or, if there is more than one donee, by any of them)[12]. A deputy may not refuse consent to the carrying out or continuation of life-sustaining treatment[13] in relation to P[14].

1   As to the Court of Protection see PARA 720.
2   As to the meaning of 'deputy' see PARA 606 note 18.
3   Mental Capacity Act 2005 s 19(8)(a).
4   Mental Capacity Act 2005 s 19(8)(b).
5   As to the meaning of 'Public Guardian' see PARA 744 note 5. See also PARA 751 et seq. As to security see PARA 755.
6   Mental Capacity Act 2005 s 19(9)(a). See *Baker v H* [2010] 1 WLR 1103.
7   Mental Capacity Act 2005 s 19(9)(b). Where the court requires a deputy to submit a report to the Public Guardian and specifies a time or interval for it to be submitted a deputy may apply to the Public Guardian requesting more time for submitting a particular report: Lasting Powers of Attorney, Enduring Powers of Attorney and Public Guardian Regulations 2007, SI 2007/1253, reg 38(1), (2). An application must state the reason for requesting more time and contain or be accompanied by such information as the Public Guardian may reasonably require to determine the application: reg 38(3). In response to an application, the Public Guardian may, if he considers it appropriate to do so, undertake that he will not take steps to secure performance of the deputy's duty to submit the report at the relevant time on the condition that the report is submitted on or before such later date as he may specify: reg 38(4). As to the content of reports to be submitted to the public guardian see the Lasting Powers of Attorney, Enduring Powers of Attorney and Public Guardian Regulations 2007, SI 2007/1253, reg 39. As to the requirement to produce a final report on the termination of appointment see reg 40.
8   Mental Capacity Act 2005 s 20(3)(a).

9   Mental Capacity Act 2005 s 20(3)(b). As to the powers concerning settlement, the execution of a will, and the exercise of any other relevant power see PARAS 724, 727.
10 Mental Capacity Act 2005 s 20(3)(c). See note 9.
11 As to the meaning of 'lasting power of attorney' see PARA 606 note 16. See PARA 618 et seq.
12 Mental Capacity Act 2005 s 20(4).
13 As to the meaning of 'life-sustaining treatment' see PARA 606 note 9.
14 Mental Capacity Act 2005 s 20(5). In particular, his authority is subject to s 1 (the principles: see PARA 601) and s 4 (best interests: see PARA 606): Mental Capacity Act 2005 s 20(6).

737. Deputies: general restriction of power. A deputy[1] does not have power to make a decision on behalf of the person ('P') lacking capacity in relation to a matter if he knows or has reasonable grounds for believing that P has capacity in relation to the matter[2].

1 As to the meaning of 'deputy' see PARA 606 note 18.
2 Mental Capacity Act 2005 s 20(1).

738. Deputies: restriction relating to welfare. Nothing in the provisions relating to powers concerning personal welfare[1] permit a deputy[2] to be given power to prohibit a named person from having contact with P[3], or to direct a person responsible for P's health care to allow a different person to take over that responsibility[4]. A deputy may not be given powers with respect to the settlement of any of P's property, whether for P's benefit or for the benefit of others[5].

A deputy may not do an act that is intended to restrain P unless four conditions are satisfied[6]:

(1)   in doing the act, the deputy is acting within the scope of an authority expressly conferred on him by the court[7];

(2)   P lacks, or the deputy reasonably believes that P lacks, capacity in relation to the matter in question[8];

(3)   the deputy reasonably believes that it is necessary to do the act in order to prevent harm to P[9];

(4)   the act is a proportionate response to the likelihood of P's suffering harm and the seriousness of that harm[10].

1 Ie the Mental Capacity Act 2005 s 16(5) (see PARA 734) or s 17 (see PARA 726).
2 As to the meaning of 'deputy' see PARA 606 note 18.
3 Mental Capacity Act 2005 s 20(2)(a).
4 Mental Capacity Act 2005 s 20(2)(b).
5 Mental Capacity Act 2005 s 20(3)(a). As to the powers concerning settlement, the execution of a will, and the exercise of any other relevant power see PARAS 724, 727.
6 Mental Capacity Act 2005 s 20(7).
7 Mental Capacity Act 2005 s 20(8).
8 Mental Capacity Act 2005 s 20(9).
9 Mental Capacity Act 2005 s 20(10).
10 Mental Capacity Act 2005 s 20(11) (amended by the Mental Health Act 2007 s 51).

739. Conduct of a deputy. The following applies in any case where the Public Guardian[1] has received representations (including complaints) about the way in which a deputy[2] is exercising his powers or any failure to exercise them or, where it appears to the Public Guardian that there are other circumstances which give rise to concerns about, or dissatisfaction with, the conduct of the deputy (including any failure to act) or otherwise constitute good reason to seek information about the deputy's discharge of his functions[3]. The Public Guardian may require the deputy to provide specified information or information of a specified description or to produce specified documents or documents of a specified description[4].

A deputy may require the Public Guardian to reconsider any decision he has made in relation to the deputy[5].

Provision is made for the responsible authority of a person who lacks capacity[6] to make certain direct payments to a deputy appointed by the Court of Protection[7].

1   As to the supervision of deputies by the Public Guardian see PARA 752.
2   As to the meaning of 'deputy' see PARA 606 note 18.
3   Lasting Powers of Attorney, Enduring Powers of Attorney and Public Guardian Regulations 2007, SI 2007/1253, reg 41(1).
4   Lasting Powers of Attorney, Enduring Powers of Attorney and Public Guardian Regulations 2007, SI 2007/1253, reg 41(2). The information or documents must be provided or produced before the end of such reasonable period as may be specified and at such place as may be specified: reg 41(3).
5   Lasting Powers of Attorney, Enduring Powers of Attorney and Public Guardian Regulations 2007, SI 2007/1253, reg 42(1). This is exercisable by giving notice of exercise of the right to the Public Guardian before the end of the period of 14 days beginning with the date on which notice of the decision is given to the deputy: reg 42(2). The notice of exercise of the right must state the grounds on which reconsideration is required and contain or be accompanied by any relevant information or documents: reg 42(3). At any time after receiving the notice and before reconsidering the decision to which it relates, the Public Guardian may require the deputy to provide him with such further information, or to produce such documents, as he reasonably considers necessary to enable him to reconsider the matter: reg 42(4). The Public Guardian must give to the deputy written notice of his decision on reconsideration and if he upholds the previous decision, a statement of his reasons: reg 42(5).
6   Ie within the meaning of the Mental Capacity Act 2005 (see PARA 635).
7   See the Health and Social Care Act 2001 s 57; the Services for Carers and Children's Services (Direct Payments) (England) Regulations 2009, SI 2009/1887; the Community Care, Services for Carers and Children's Services (Direct Payments) (Wales) Regulations 2011, SI 2011/831; the National Health Service (Direct Payments) Regulations 2010, SI 2010/1000; and SOCIAL SERVICES AND COMMUNITY CARE.

(3) PRACTICE AND PROCEDURE

740.   Court of Protection Rules and practice and procedure generally.   No permission is required for an application to the Court of Protection[1] for the exercise of any of its powers under the Mental Capacity Act 2005: (1) by a person who lacks, or is alleged to lack, capacity[2]; (2) if such a person has not reached 18, by anyone with parental responsibility[3] for him[4]; (3) by the donor or a donee of a lasting power of attorney[5] to which the application relates[6]; (4) by a deputy[7] appointed by the court for a person to whom the application relates[8]; or (5) by a person named in an existing order of the court, if the application relates to the order[9]. Nor is permission required for an application to the court by the relevant person's representative[10]. However, permission is required[11] for any other application to the court[12], and in deciding whether to grant permission the court must, in particular, have regard to: (a) the applicant's connection with the person to whom the application relates[13]; (b) the reasons for the application[14]; (c) the benefit to the person to whom the application relates of a proposed order or directions[15]; and (d) whether the benefit can be achieved in any other way[16].

Rules of court with respect to the practice and procedure of the court (to be called 'Court of Protection Rules') may be made[17]. Court of Protection Rules may, in particular, make provision[18]:

(i)   as to the manner and form in which proceedings are to be commenced[19];

(ii)   as to the persons entitled to be notified of, and be made parties to, the proceedings[20];

(iii) for the allocation, in such circumstances as may be specified, of any specified description of proceedings to a specified judge or to specified descriptions of judges[21];

(iv) for the exercise of the jurisdiction of the court, in such circumstances as may be specified, by its officers or other staff[22];

(v) for enabling the court to appoint a suitable person (who may, with his consent, be the Official Solicitor[23]) to act in the name of, or on behalf of, or to represent the person to whom the proceedings relate[24];

(vi) for enabling an application to the court to be disposed of without a hearing[25];

(vii) for enabling the court to proceed with, or with any part of, a hearing in the absence of the person to whom the proceedings relate[26];

(viii) for enabling or requiring the proceedings or any part of them to be conducted in private and for enabling the court to determine who is to be admitted when the court sits in private and to exclude specified persons when it sits in public[27];

(ix) as to what may be received as evidence (whether or not admissible apart from the rules) and the manner in which it is to be presented[28];

(x) for the enforcement of orders made and directions given in the proceedings[29].

Court of Protection Rules may, instead of providing for any matter, refer to provision made or to be made about that matter by directions[30].

Court of Protection Rules may make different provision for different areas[31].

1 As to the Court of Protection see PARA 720. As to practice and procedure under the Mental Health Act 1983 see PARA 740 et seq.
2 Mental Capacity Act 2005 s 50(1)(a). As to lack of capacity see PARA 603.
3 'Parental responsibility' has the same meaning as in the Children Act 1989 (see CHILDREN AND YOUNG PERSONS vol 9 (2012) PARA 151): Mental Capacity Act 2005 s 50(4).
4 Mental Capacity Act 2005 s 50(1)(b).
5 As to the meaning of 'lasting power of attorney' see PARA 606 note 16. See PARA 618 et seq.
6 Mental Capacity Act 2005 s 50(1)(c).
7 As to the meaning of 'deputy' see PARA 606 note 18. See also PARA 724 et seq.
8 Mental Capacity Act 2005 s 50(1)(d).
9 Mental Capacity Act 2005 s 50(1)(e). See also PARA 721.
10 Mental Capacity Act 2005 s 50(1A) (added by the Mental Health Act 2007 Sch 9 para 9). An application to the court mentioned in the text is one under the Mental Capacity Act 2005 s 21A (see PARA 733).
11 Ie subject to Court of Protection Rules (see the text to note 17) and to the Mental Capacity Act 2005 Sch 3 para 20(2) (declarations relating to private international law) (see PARA 561).
12 Mental Capacity Act 2005 s 50(2).
13 Mental Capacity Act 2005 s 50(3)(a).
14 Mental Capacity Act 2005 s 50(3)(b).
15 Mental Capacity Act 2005 s 50(3)(c). As to orders and directions see PARA 721.
16 Mental Capacity Act 2005 s 50(3)(d).
17 Mental Capacity Act 2005 s 51(1) (substituted by SI 2006/1016). Such rules are to be made in accordance with the Constitutional Reform Act 2005 Sch 1 Pt 1: Mental Capacity Act 2005 s 51(1) (as so substituted). 'Court of Protection Rules' has the meaning given in s 51(1): s 64(1). The Court of Protection Rules 2007, SI 2007/1744 make provision for (1) the overriding objective (see rr 3–5; and PARA 742); (2) court documents (see rr 10–24); (3) general case management (see rr 25–28); (4) the service of documents (see rr 29–39); (5) notification (see rr 40–49); (6) permission of the court (see rr 50–60); (7) how to start proceedings (see rr 61–76); (8) applications within proceedings (rr 77–82); (9) procedure for deprivation of liberty applications (see r 82A (added by SI 2009/582)); (10) applications in relation to human rights (see the Court of Protection Rules 2007, SI 2007/1744, r 83); (11) dealing with applications (see rr 84–89); (12) hearings (see rr 90–93); (12) admissions, evidence and depositions (see rr 93–118); (13) experts (see rr 119–131); (14) disclosure (see rr 132–139); (15) litigation friend (see rr 140–149); (16) change of solicitor (see rr 150–154); (17) costs (see rr 155–168; and PARA

747); (18) appeals (see rr 169–182; and PARA 750); (19) enforcement (see rr 183–194); (20) transitory and transitional provisions (see rr 195–199); and (21) miscellaneous matters (see rr 200–203). The court may exercise its powers under its own initiative: see *Havering London Borough Council v LD* [2010] EWHC 3976 (COP). See *Enfield London Borough Council v SA (by her Litigation Friend, the Official Solicitor)* [2010] EWHC 196 (Admin), [2010] 1 FLR 1836, [2010] Fam Law 457; *G v E* [2010] EWHC 621 (Fam), [2010] 2 FLR 294, [2010] Fam Law 703, *AVS v A NHS foundation trust* [2010] EWHC 2746 (COP), [2011] 1 FLR 967, [2011] Fam Law 138. The litigation friend is usually the Official Solicitor (see *G v E* [2010] EWHC 2512 (COP), [2011] 1 FLR 1652, [2011] Fam Law 141) but can be a family member or independent mental health advocate or a representative appointed under the Mental Capacity Act 2005 Sch A1 or a deputy. The litigation friend must confirm they will act in P's best interest: *AB (by his litigation friend NW) v A local authority* [2011] EWHC 3151 (COP), [2011] NLJR 1744. See also note 27. As to practice directions see PARA 741.

18 Mental Capacity Act 2005 s 51(2).
19 Mental Capacity Act 2005 s 51(2)(a).
20 Mental Capacity Act 2005 s 51(2)(b).
21 Mental Capacity Act 2005 s 51(2)(c).
22 Mental Capacity Act 2005 s 51(2)(d).
23 As to the Official Solicitor see COURTS AND TRIBUNALS vol 24 (2010) PARA 755.
24 Mental Capacity Act 2005 s 51(2)(e).
25 Mental Capacity Act 2005 s 51(2)(f).
26 Mental Capacity Act 2005 s 51(2)(g).
27 Mental Capacity Act 2005 s 51(2)(h). As to when the court should allow the media to attend a hearing see *Independent News and Media Ltd v A (by his litigation friend the Official Solicitor)* [2010] EWCA Civ 343, [2010] 3 All ER 32, [2010] 1 WLR 2262; *Hillingdon London Borough Council v Neary* [2011] EWHC 413 (COP), [2011] Fam Law 476, [2011] NLJR 404; and *W (by her litigation friend, B) v M (an adult patient by the Official Solicitor)* [2011] EWHC 1197 (COP), [2011] 4 All ER 1295, [2012] 1 WLR 287; *P (by his litigation friend the Official Solicitor) v Independent Print Ltd* [2011] EWCA Civ 756, [2012] 2 FCR 503, [2012] 1 FLR 212. As to publishing a judgment see *Cheshire West and Chester Council v P* [2011] EWHC 1330 (Fam), [2011] All ER (D) 155 (Jun).
28 Mental Capacity Act 2005 s 51(2)(i). As to evidence generally see CIVIL PROCEDURE vol 11 (2009) PARA 749 et seq.
29 Mental Capacity Act 2005 s 51(2)(j). As to enforcement generally see CIVIL PROCEDURE vol 12 (2009) PARA 1223 et seq.
30 Mental Capacity Act 2005 s 51(3). As to directions see PARA 721.
31 Mental Capacity Act 2005 s 51(4).

741. Practice directions. Directions as to the practice and procedure of the Court of Protection[1] may be made[2]. The Lord Chief Justice may nominate the President of the Court of Protection or a judicial office holder[3] to carry out his functions under these provisions[4].

Practice Directions have been made in relation to the following:

(1)   circumstances in which an authorised court officer is able to exercise the jurisdiction of the court[5];
(2)   general provisions relating to court documents[6];
(3)   documents to be verified by a statement of truth[7];
(4)   service by document exchange[8];
(5)   notification[9];
(6)   permission[10];
(7)   how to start proceedings[11];
(8)   applications within proceedings[12];
(9)   the procedure for deprivation of liberty applications[13];
(10)   human rights[14];
(11)   dealing with applications[15];
(12)   hearings[16];
(13)   the preparation of court bundles[17];
(14)   admissions, evidence and dispositions[18];

(15) experts[19];

(16) litigation friend[20];

(17) change of solicitor[21];

(18) costs[22];

(19) appeals[23];

(20) enforcement[24];

(21) transitory and transitional provisions[25]; and

(22) some miscellaneous circumstances[26].

1   As to the Court of Protection see PARA 720.

2   See the Mental Capacity Act 2005 s 52(1), (2) (substituted by SI 2006/1016). Such directions must be made in accordance with the Constitutional Reform Act 2005 Sch 2 Pt 1. Practice directions given otherwise than under the Mental Capacity Act 2005 s 52(1) may not be given without the approval of the Lord Chancellor and the Lord Chief Justice: s 52(2) (as so substituted).

3   Ie as defined in the Constitutional Reform Act 2005 s 109(4) (see COURTS AND TRIBUNALS vol 24 (2010) PARA 961).

4   See the Mental Capacity Act 2005 s 52(3) (as substituted: see note 2).

5   See Practice Direction 3A–*Authorised Court Officers*.

6   See Practice Direction 4A–*Court documents*.

7   See Practice Direction 4B–*Statements of truth*.

8   See Practice Direction 6A–*Service*.

9   See Practice Direction 7A–*Notifying P*.

10 See Practice Direction 8A–*Permission*.

11 See Practice Direction 9A–*The application procedure*; Practice Direction 9B–*Notification of other persons that an application form has been issued*; Practice Direction 9C–*Responding to an application*; Practice Direction 9D–*Applications by currently appointed Deputies, Attorneys, and Donees in relation to P's property and affairs*; Practice Direction 9E–*Applications relating to serious medical treatment*; Practice Direction 9F–*Applications relating to statutory wills, codicils, settlements and other dealings with P's property*; Practice Direction 9G–*Applications to appoint or discharge a trustee*; and Practice Direction 9H–*Applications relating to the registration of Enduring Powers of Attorney*.

12 See Practice Direction 10A–*Applications within proceedings*; and Practice Direction 10B–*Urgent and interim applications*.

13 See Practice Direction 10AA–*Deprivation of Liberty*.

14 See Practice Direction 11A–*Human rights*.

15 See Practice Direction 12A–*Court's jurisdiction to be exercised by certain judges*; and Practice Direction 12B–*Procedure for disputing the Courts jurisdiction*.

16 See Practice Direction 13A–*Hearings (including reporting restrictions)*.

17 See Practice Direction 13B–*Court Bundles*.

18 See Practice Direction 14A–*Written evidence*; Practice Direction 14B–*Admissions, evidence and depositions*; Practice Direction 14C–*Fee for examiners of the Court*; Practice Direction 14D–*Witness summons*; and Practice Direction 14E–*Section 49 reports*.

19 See Practice Direction 15A–*Expert evidence*.

20 See Practice Direction 17A–*Litigation friend*.

21 See Practice Direction 18A–*Change of solicitor*.

22 See Practice Direction 19A–*Costs*; and Practice Direction 19B–*Fixed costs in the Court of Protection*.

23 See Practice Direction 20A–*Appeals*.

24 See Practice Direction 21A–*Contempt of Court*.

25 See Practice Direction 22A–*Transitional provisions*; Practice Direction 22B–*Transitory provisions*; and Practice Direction 22C–*Appeals against decisions made under Part 7 of the Mental Health Act 1983 or under the Enduring Powers of Attorney Act 1985 which are brought on or after commencement*.

26 See Practice Direction 23A–*Request for directions where notice of objection prevents the Public Guardian from registering an Enduring Power of Attorney*; and Practice Direction 23B–*Where P ceases to lack capacity or dies*.

742. Overriding objective. The Court of Protection Rules 2007[1] have the overriding objective of enabling the court to deal with a case justly, having regard to the principles contained in the Mental Capacity Act 2005[2]. The court will seek to give effect to the overriding objective when it exercises any power under the Court of Protection Rules 2007[3] or interprets any rule or practice direction[4].

Dealing with a case justly includes, so far as is practicable:

(1)   ensuring that it is dealt with expeditiously and fairly[5];
(2)   ensuring that P's interests and position are properly considered[6];
(3)   dealing with the case in ways which are proportionate to the nature, importance and complexity of the issues[7];
(4)   ensuring that the parties are on an equal footing[8];
(5)   saving expense[9]; and
(6)   allotting to it an appropriate share of the court's resources, while taking account of the need to allot resources to other cases[10].

The court will further the overriding objective by actively managing cases[11]. Active case management includes:

(a)   encouraging the parties to co-operate with each other in the conduct of the proceedings[12];
(b)   identifying at an early stage the issues and who should be a party to the proceedings[13];
(c)   deciding promptly which issues need a full investigation and hearing and which do not and the procedure to be followed in the case[14];
(d)   deciding the order in which issues are to be resolved[15];
(e)   encouraging the parties to use an alternative dispute resolution procedure if the court considers that appropriate[16];
(f)   fixing timetables or otherwise controlling the progress of the case[17];
(g)   considering whether the likely benefits of taking a particular step justify the cost of taking it[18];
(h)   dealing with as many aspects of the case as the court can on the same occasion[19];
(i)   dealing with the case without the parties needing to attend at court[20];
(j)   making use of technology[21]; and
(k)   giving directions to ensure that the case proceeds quickly and efficiently[22].

The parties are required to help the court to further the overriding objective[23].

1   Ie the Court of Protection Rules 2007, SI 2007/1744.
2   Court of Protection Rules 2007, SI 2007/1744, r 3(1). In any case not expressly provided for by the Court of Protection Rules 2007, SI 2007/1744 or the practice directions made under them, the Civil Procedure Rules 1998, SI 1998/3132 (including any practice directions made under them) may be applied with any necessary modifications, insofar as is necessary to further the overriding objective: Court of Protection Rules 2007, SI 2007/1744, r 9. See also *KD and LD v Havering London Borough Council* [2010] 1 FLR 1393, [2010] Fam Law 244.
3   See note 1.
4   Court of Protection Rules 2007, SI 2007/1744, r 3(2).
5   Court of Protection Rules 2007, SI 2007/1744, r 3(3)(a).
6   Court of Protection Rules 2007, SI 2007/1744, r 3(3)(b).
7   Court of Protection Rules 2007, SI 2007/1744, r 3(3)(c).
8   Court of Protection Rules 2007, SI 2007/1744, r 3(3)(d).
9   Court of Protection Rules 2007, SI 2007/1744, r 3(3)(e).
10   Court of Protection Rules 2007, SI 2007/1744, r 3(3)(f).
11   Court of Protection Rules 2007, SI 2007/1744, r 5(1).
12   Court of Protection Rules 2007, SI 2007/1744, r 5(2)(a).
13   Court of Protection Rules 2007, SI 2007/1744, r 5(2)(b).
14   Court of Protection Rules 2007, SI 2007/1744, r 5(2)(c).
15   Court of Protection Rules 2007, SI 2007/1744, r 5(2)(d).
16   Court of Protection Rules 2007, SI 2007/1744, r 5(2)(e).
17   Court of Protection Rules 2007, SI 2007/1744, r 5(2)(f).

18 Court of Protection Rules 2007, SI 2007/1744, r 5(2)(g).
19 Court of Protection Rules 2007, SI 2007/1744, r 5(2)(h).
20 Court of Protection Rules 2007, SI 2007/1744, r 5(2)(i).
21 Court of Protection Rules 2007, SI 2007/1744, r 5(2)(j).
22 Court of Protection Rules 2007, SI 2007/1744, r 5(2)(k).
23 Court of Protection Rules 2007, SI 2007/1744, r 4.

743. Parties to the proceedings. Unless the court otherwise directs, the parties to any proceedings are the applicant and any person who is named as a respondent[1] in the application form and who files an acknowledgment of service in respect of the application form[2].

The court may order a person to be joined as a party if it considers that it is desirable to do so for the purpose of dealing with the application[3] and may at any time direct that any person who is a party to the proceedings is to be removed as a party[4].

A party to the proceedings is bound by any order or direction of the court made in the course of those proceedings[5].

Any person with sufficient interest[6] may apply to the court to be joined as a party to the proceedings[7] and the court will consider whether to join such a person as a party to the proceedings and, if it decides to do so, will make an order to that effect[8].

1 Unless the court orders otherwise, P must not be named as a respondent to any proceedings: Court of Protection Rules 2007, SI 2004/1744, r 73(4). P means any person (other than a protected party) who lacks or, so far as consistent with the context, is alleged to lack capacity to make a decision or decisions in relation to any matter that is the subject of an application to the court; and a relevant person as defined by the Mental Capacity Act 2005 Sch A1 para 7 (see PARA 663 note 7), and references to a person who lacks capacity are to be construed in accordance with that Act: Court of Protection Rules 2007, SI 2007/1744, r 6 (definition amended by SI 2009/582). P and any person who has been served with or notified of an application form in accordance with the Court of Protection Rules 2007, SI 2007/1744 is bound by any order made or directions given by the court in the same way that a party to the proceedings is so bound: see r 74.
2 Court of Protection Rules 2007, SI 2007/1744, r 73(1).
3 Court of Protection Rules 2007, SI 2007/1744, r 73(2).
4 Court of Protection Rules 2004, SI 2004/1744, r 73(3). As to the procedure for removing a party see r 76.
5 Court of Protection Rules 2007, SI 2007/1744, r 73(5).
6 An applicant for joinder who does not have an interest in the ascertainment of the incapacitated person's best interests is unlikely to be a 'person with sufficient interest' for the purpose of the Court of Protection Rules 2007, SI 2007/1744, r 75: see *Re SK* [2012] EWHC 1990 (Fam), [2012] All ER (D) 80 (Aug).
7 Court of Protection Rules 2007, SI 2007/1744, r 75(1). As to the application procedure see r 75(2)–(4).
8 Court of Protection Rules 2007, SI 2007/1744, r 75(5).

744. Reports. Where, in proceedings brought in respect of a person ('P') under Part 1 of the Mental Capacity Act 2005[1], the Court of Protection[2] is considering a question relating to P[3], it may require a report[4] to be made to it by the Public Guardian[5] or by a Court of Protection Visitor[6]. The court may require a local authority[7], or an NHS body[8], to arrange for a report to be made: (1) by one of its officers or employees[9]; or (2) by such other person (other than the Public Guardian or a Court of Protection Visitor) as the authority, or the NHS body, considers appropriate[10].

In proceedings brought against a person ('P')[11], the Public Guardian or a Court of Protection Visitor may, at all reasonable times, examine and take copies of: (a) any health record[12]; (b) any record of a local authority, or held by it, compiled in connection with a social services function[13]; and (c) any record held by a person registered under Part II of the Care Standards Act 2000 or Chapter 2 of Part 1 of the Health and Social Care Act 2008[14], so far as the record relates to P[15].

If the Public Guardian or a Court of Protection Visitor is making a visit in the course of complying with a requirement[16], he may interview P in private[17]. If a Court of Protection Visitor who is a Special Visitor[18] is making a visit in the course of complying with a requirement[19], he may if the court so directs carry out in private a medical, psychiatric or psychological examination of P's capacity and condition[20].

1   Ie the Mental Capacity Act 2005 Pt 1 (ss 1–44) (see PARAS 601–646, 723–735).
2   As to the Court of Protection see PARA 720.
3   Mental Capacity Act 2005 s 49(1).
4   The report must deal with such matters relating to P as the court may direct: Mental Capacity Act 2005 s 49(4). Court of Protection Rules may specify matters which, unless the court directs otherwise, must also be dealt with in the report: Mental Capacity Act 2005 s 49(5). The report may be made in writing or orally, as the court may direct: s 49(6). As to Court of Protection Rules see PARA 740.
5   'Public Guardian' has the meaning given in the Mental Capacity Act 2005 s 57 (see PARA 751): s 64(1).
6   Mental Capacity Act 2005 s 49(2). 'Court of Protection Visitor' has the meaning given in s 61 (see PARA 748): s 64(1).
7   As to the meaning of 'local authority' see PARA 635 note 10.
8   'NHS body' has the meaning given in the Health and Social Care (Community Health and Standards) Act 2003 s 148: Mental Capacity Act 2005 s 49(10).
9   Mental Capacity Act 2005 s 49(3)(a).
10 Mental Capacity Act 2005 s 49(3)(b).
11 Ie a requirement imposed under the Mental Capacity Act 2005 s 49(2) or (3): see s 49(11).
12 Mental Capacity Act 2005 s 49(7)(a). As to the meaning of 'health record' see PARA 635 note 9.
13 Mental Capacity Act 2005 s 49(7)(b). As to the meaning of 'social services function' see PARA 635 note 11.
14 Mental Capacity Act 2005 s 49(7)(c) (amended by SI 2010/813). The references in the text are to the Care Standards Act 2000 Pt II (ss 11–42) (see PARA 585; and SOCIAL SERVICES AND COMMUNITY CARE) and the Health and Social Care Act 2008 Pt 1 Chapter 2 (ss 8–44) (see 635 and SOCIAL SERVICES AND COMMUNITY CARE).
15 Mental Capacity Act 2005 s 49(7).
16 See note 11.
17 Mental Capacity Act 2005 s 49(8).
18 As to Special Visitors see PARA 748.
19 See note 11.
20 Mental Capacity Act 2005 s 49(9).

745.   Transfer of proceedings relating to people under 18.   The Lord Chief Justice, with the concurrence of the Lord Chancellor[1], may by order make provision as to the transfer of proceedings relating to a person under 18, in such circumstances as are specified in the order[2] from the Court of Protection to a court having jurisdiction under the Children Act 1989[3].

Accordingly the following apply to any proceedings in the Court of Protection which relate to a person under 18[4]. The Court of Protection may direct the transfer[5] of the whole or part of the proceedings to a court having jurisdiction under the Children Act 1989 where it considers that in all the circumstances, it is just and convenient to transfer the proceedings[6]. It may exercise this power on an application or on its own initiative and, where it orders a transfer, must give reasons for its decision[7].

The Lord Chief Justice, with the concurrence of the Lord Chancellor, may by order make provision as to the transfer of proceedings relating to a person under 18, in such circumstances as are specified in the order from a court having jurisdiction under the Children Act 1989 to the Court of Protection[8].

Accordingly the following apply to any proceedings in a court having jurisdiction under the Children Act 1989 which relate to a person under 18[9]. A court having jurisdiction under the Children Act 1989 may direct the transfer[10] of the whole or part of the proceedings to the Court of Protection where it considers that in all circumstances, it is just and convenient to transfer the proceedings[11]. It may exercise this power on an application or on its own initiative and, where it orders a transfer, must give reasons for its decision[12].

1   As to the Lord Chief Justice see COURTS AND TRIBUNALS vol 24 (2010) PARA 604. As to the Lord Chancellor see CONSTITUTIONAL LAW AND HUMAN RIGHTS vol 8(2) (Reissue) PARA 477 et seq. The Lord Chief Justice may nominate the President of the Court of Protection or a judicial office holder (as defined in the Constitutional Reform Act 2005 s 109(4) (see COURTS AND TRIBUNALS vol 24 (2010) PARA 961)) to exercise any of his functions under the Mental Capacity Act 2005 s 21: see s 21(2) (added by SI 2006/1016).

2   Mental Capacity Act 2005 s 21(1) (renumbered and amended by SI 2006/1016).

3   Mental Capacity Act 2005 s 21(1)(a) (as renumbered: see note 2). As to courts with jurisdiction under the Children Act 1989 see CHILDREN AND YOUNG PERSONS.This provision is to deal with the overlap, as the Mental Capacity Act 2005 deals with people over 16 and the Children Act 1989 with people under 18.

4   Mental Capacity Act 2005 (Transfer of Proceedings) Order 2007, SI 2007/1899, art 2(1). Any fee paid for the purpose of starting any proceedings that are transferred under art 2 or 3 is to be treated as if it were the fee that would have been payable if the proceedings had started in the court to which the transfer is made: art 4.

5   Any proceedings transferred under Mental Capacity Act 2005 (Transfer of Proceedings) Order 2007, SI 2007/1899, art 2 are to be treated for all purposes as if they were proceedings under the Children Act 1989 which had been started in a court having jurisdiction under that Act and are to be dealt with after the transfer in accordance with directions given by a court having jurisdiction under that Act: Mental Capacity Act 2005 (Transfer of Proceedings) Order 2007, SI 2007/1899, art 2(5).

6   Mental Capacity Act 2005 (Transfer of Proceedings) Order 2007, SI 2007/1899, art 2(2). In making a determination, the Court of Protection must have regard to:
   (1)   whether the proceedings should be heard together with other proceedings that are pending in a court having jurisdiction under the Children Act 1989 (Mental Capacity Act 2005 (Transfer of Proceedings) Order 2007, SI 2007/1899, art 2(3)(a));
   (2)   whether any order that may be made by a court having jurisdiction under the Children Act 1989 is likely to be a more appropriate way of dealing with the proceedings (Mental Capacity Act 2005 (Transfer of Proceedings) Order 2007, SI 2007/1899, art 2(3)(b));
   (3)   the need to meet any requirements that would apply if the proceedings had been started in a court having jurisdiction under the Children Act 1989 (Mental Capacity Act 2005 (Transfer of Proceedings) Order 2007, SI 2007/1899, art 2(3)(c)); and
   (4)   any other matter that the court considers relevant (art 2(3)(d)).

7   Mental Capacity Act 2005 (Transfer of Proceedings) Order 2007, SI 2007/1899, art 2(4).

8   Mental Capacity Act 2005 s 21(1)(b) (as renumbered: see note 2). See note 3.

9   Mental Capacity Act 2005 (Transfer of Proceedings) Order 2007, SI 2007/1899, art 3(1).

10   Any proceedings transferred under the Mental Capacity Act 2005 (Transfer of Proceedings) Order 2007, SI 2007/1899, art 3 are to be treated for all purposes as if they were proceedings under the Mental Capacity Act 2005 which had been started in the Court of Protection and are to be dealt with after the transfer in accordance with directions given by the Court of Protection: Mental Capacity Act 2005 (Transfer of Proceedings) Order 2007, SI 2007/1899, art 3(5).

11   Mental Capacity Act 2005 (Transfer of Proceedings) Order 2007, SI 2007/1899, art 3(2). In making a determination, the court having jurisdiction under the Children Act 1989 must have regard to:
   (1)   whether the proceedings should be heard together with other proceedings that are pending in the Court of Protection (Mental Capacity Act 2005 (Transfer of Proceedings) Order 2007, SI 2007/1899, art 3(3)(a));
   (2)   whether any order that may be made by the Court of Protection is likely to be a more appropriate way of dealing with the proceedings (art 3(3)(b));

(3)   the extent to which any order made as respects a person who lacks capacity is likely to continue to have effect when that person reaches 18 (art 3(3)(c)); and

(4)   any other matter that the court considers relevant (art 3(3)(d)).

See *B (a local authority) v RM* [2010] EWHC 3802 (Fam), [2011] 1 FLR 1635, [2011] Fam Law 459 (welfare of 16-year-old who had severe learning disability, autism and tourette syndrome would be better protected in Court of Protection).

12 Mental Capacity Act 2005 (Transfer of Proceedings) Order 2007, SI 2007/1899, art 3(4).

746.   Fees.   The Lord Chancellor[1] may, after consultation[2] and with the consent of the Treasury[3], by order prescribe fees payable in respect of anything dealt with by the Court of Protection[4]. Such an order may in particular contain provision as to: (1) scales or rates of fees[5]; (2) exemptions from and reductions in fees[6]; (3) remission of fees in whole or in part[7].

The Lord Chancellor must take such steps as are reasonably practicable to bring information about fees to the attention of persons likely to have to pay them[8]. Fees payable as above[9] are recoverable summarily as a civil debt[10].

Court of Protection Rules may make provision: (a) as to the way in which, and funds from which, fees are to be paid[11]; (b) for charging fees upon the estate of the person to whom the proceedings relate[12]; (c) for the payment of fees within a specified time of the death of the person to whom the proceedings relate or the conclusion of the proceedings[13].

1   As to the Lord Chancellor see CONSTITUTIONAL LAW AND HUMAN RIGHTS vol 8(2) (Reissue) PARA 477 et seq.

2   Before making an order under the Mental Capacity Act 2005 s 54, the Lord Chancellor must consult: (1) the President of the Court of Protection; (2) the Vice-President of the Court of Protection; and (3) the Senior Judge of the Court of Protection: s 54(3). As to the President, the Vice-President and the Senior Judge of the Court of Protection see PARA 720.

3   As to the Treasury see CONSTITUTIONAL LAW AND HUMAN RIGHTS vol 8(2) (Reissue) PARAS 512–517.

4   Mental Capacity Act 2005 s 54(1). As to the Court of Protection see PARA 720. As to such fees see the Court of Protection Fees Order 2007, SI 2007/1745 (amended by SI 2009/513). See also Practice Direction 14C – *Admissions, Evidence and Depositions*.

5   Mental Capacity Act 2005 s 54(2)(a).

6   Mental Capacity Act 2005 s 54(2)(b).

7   Mental Capacity Act 2005 s 54(2)(c).

8   Mental Capacity Act 2005 s 54(4).

9   Ie fees payable under the Mental Capacity Act 2005 s 54.

10 Mental Capacity Act 2005 s 54(5).

11 Mental Capacity Act 2005 s 56(1)(a).

12 Mental Capacity Act 2005 s 56(1)(b). A charge on the estate of a person created by virtue of s 56(1)(b) does not cause any interest of the person in any property to fail or determine or to be prevented from recommencing: s 56(2).

13 Mental Capacity Act 2005 s 56(1)(c).

747.   Costs.   Subject to Court of Protection Rules[1], the costs of and incidental to all proceedings in the Court of Protection are in its discretion[2]. The rules may in particular make provision for regulating matters relating to the costs of those proceedings, including prescribing scales of costs to be paid to legal or other representatives[3]. The court has full power to determine by whom and to what extent the costs are to be paid[4].

The court may, in any proceedings, disallow, or order the legal or other representatives concerned to meet, the whole of any wasted costs[5] or such part of them as may be determined in accordance with the rules[6].

Court of Protection Rules may make provision: (1) as to the way in which, and funds from which, costs are to be paid[7]; (2) for charging costs upon the estate of the person to whom the proceedings relate[8]; (3) for the payment of costs within a specified time of the death of the person to whom the proceedings relate or the conclusion of the proceedings[9].

Under such rules the following general rules apply:

(a)   where the proceedings concern a person's property and affairs the general rule is that the costs of the proceedings or of that part of the proceedings that concerns the property and affairs, must be paid by that person or charged to his estate[10];

(b)   where the proceedings concern a person's personal welfare the general rule is that there will be no order as to the costs of the proceedings or of that part of the proceedings that concerns his personal welfare[11];

(c)   where the proceedings concern both property and affairs and personal welfare the court, insofar as practicable, will apportion the costs as between the respective issues[12].

The court may depart from heads (a) to (c) above if the circumstances so justify, and in deciding whether departure is justified the court will have regard to all the circumstances, including the conduct of the parties[13], whether a party has succeeded on part of his case, even if he has not been wholly successful, and the role of any public body involved in the proceedings[14].

Where two or more persons having the same interest in relation to a matter act in relation to the proceedings by separate legal representatives, they are not be permitted more than one set of costs of the representation unless and to the extent that the court certifies that the circumstances justify separate representation[15].

Where the court orders a party to pay costs to another party it may either make a summary assessment of the costs or order a detailed assessment of the costs by a costs officer, unless any rule, practice direction or other enactment provides otherwise[16].

An order or direction that costs incurred during a person's ('P's) lifetime be paid out of or charged on his estate may be made within six years after his death[17].

Where the court is considering whether to make a costs order in favour of or against a person who is not a party to proceedings that person must be added as a party to the proceedings for the purposes of costs only and he must be given a reasonable opportunity to attend a hearing at which the court will consider the matter further[18].

Where the court orders that a deputy, donee or attorney is entitled to remuneration out of P's estate for discharging his functions as such, the court may make such order as it thinks fit, including an order that he be paid a fixed amount, he be paid at a specified rate or the amount of the remuneration is determined in accordance with the schedule of fees set out in the relevant practice direction[19].

A practice direction may make further provision in respect of costs in proceedings[20].

1   As to Court of Protection Rules see PARA 740.

2   Mental Capacity Act 2005 s 55(1).

3   Mental Capacity Act 2005 s 55(2). 'Legal or other representative', in relation to a party to proceedings, means any person exercising a right of audience or right to conduct litigation on his behalf: s 55(5). Certain provisions of the CPR (see CIVIL PROCEDURE) apply subject to modifications: see the Court of Protection Rules 2007, SI 2007/1744, r 160.

4   Mental Capacity Act 2005 s 55(3).

5 'Wasted costs' means any costs incurred by a party: (1) as a result of any improper, unreasonable or negligent act or omission on the part of any legal or other representative or any employee of such a representative; or (2) which, in the light of any such act or omission occurring after they were incurred, the court considers it is unreasonable to expect that party to pay: Mental Capacity Act 2005 s 55(6).

6 Mental Capacity Act 2005 s 55(4).

7 Mental Capacity Act 2005 s 56(1)(a).

8 Mental Capacity Act 2005 s 56(1)(b). A charge on the estate of a person created by virtue of s 56(1)(b) does not cause any interest of the person in any property to fail or determine or to be prevented from recommencing: s 56(2).

9 Mental Capacity Act 2005 s 56(1)(c). See *Re RC (dec'd)* [2010] EWHC B29 (COP), [2011] 1 FLR 1447, [2011] Fam Law 345 (Court of Protection had jurisdiction to make costs order after death of person to whom proceedings related).

10 Court of Protection Rules 2007, SI 2007/1744, r 156.

11 Court of Protection Rules 2007, SI 2007/1744, r 157. For a departure from the general rule set out in r 157 see *Manchester City Council v E (by his litigation friend the Official Solicitor)* [2011] EWCA Civ 939, [2011] 2 FLR 1297, [2011] Fam Law 1196 (the authority's behaviour amounted to misconduct which justified departing from the general rule and an order was made apportioning costs). The costs rules do not apply to the Court of Appeal where the general rule is that the unsuccessful party will pay costs: *Cheshire West and Chester Council v P* [2011] EWHC 1330 (Fam), [2011] All ER (D) 155 (Jun). In relation to costs relating to health and welfare issues see *Re RC (dec'd)* [2010] EWHC B29 (COP), [2011] 1 FLR 1447, [2011] Fam Law 345.

12 Court of Protection Rules 2007, SI 2007/1744, r 158.

13 The conduct of the parties includes conduct before, as well as during, the proceedings, whether it was reasonable for a party to raise, pursue or contest a particular issue, the manner in which a party has made or responded to an application or a particular issue and whether a party who has succeeded in his application or response to an application, in whole or in part, exaggerated any matter contained in his application or response: r 159(2).

14 Court of Protection Rules 2007, SI 2007/1744, r 159(1). The court may permit a party to recover their fixed costs in accordance with the relevant practice direction: see r 159(3). *G v E (costs)* [2010] EWHC 3385 (Fam), [2011] 1 FLR 1566, [2011] Fam Law 473 (costs may be awarded against a public body that has acted unlawfully or is guilty of misconduct even where the parties in whose favour the award is made are publicly funded). See also *Hillingdon London Borough Council v Neary* [2011] EWHC 3522 (COP), [2012] All ER (D) 54 (Jan), *SC v London Borough of Hackney* [2010] EWHC B29 (COP), *Manchester City Council v G* [2011] EWCA Civ 939, *D v R (the deputy of S)* [2010] EWHC 3748 (COP), *AH v Hertfordshire Partnership NHS Foundation Trust (including costs)* [2011] EWHC 276 (COP). Rules do not change the long standing practice whereby the court exercises its discretion to share the Official Solicitor's costs across the public bodies in medical treatment cases: *NHS Trust v D (by his litigation friend, the Official Solicitor)* [2012] EWHC 886 (COP), [2012] NLJR 1421.

15 Court of Protection Rules 2007, SI 2007/1744, r 162.

16 Court of Protection Rules 2007, SI 2007/1744, r 164. Where the court orders costs to be assessed by way of detailed assessment, the detailed assessment proceedings must take place in the High Court: Court of Protection Rules 2007, SI 2007/1744, r 161(1). A fee is payable in respect of the detailed assessment of costs and on an appeal against a decision made in a detailed assessment of costs: r 161(2). Where a detailed assessment of costs has taken place, the amount payable is the amount which the court certifies as payable: see r 161(3).

17 Court of Protection Rules 2007, SI 2007/1744, r 165.

18 Court of Protection Rules 2007, SI 2007/1744, r 166(1). This rule does not apply where the court is considering whether to make an order against the Legal Services Commission: r 166(2).

19 Court of Protection Rules 2007, SI 2007/1744, r 167(1). Any amount permitted by the court under r 167(1) constitutes a debt due from P's estate: r 167(2). The court may order a detailed assessment of the remuneration by a costs officer, in accordance with r 164(b) (see text and note 16): r 167(3). Any costs incurred by the Official Solicitor in relation to proceedings under the Court of Protection Rules 2007, SI 2004/1744, or in carrying out any directions given by the court and not provided for by remuneration under r 167 must be paid by such persons or out of such funds as the court may direct: r 163.

20 Court of Protection Rules 2007, SI 2007/1744, r 168. See Court of Protection Practice Direction 19A – *Costs Practice Direction*.

(4) VISITING

748. Court of Protection Visitors. Provision is made in relation to Court of Protection Visitors[1]. A Court of Protection Visitor is a person who is appointed by the Lord Chancellor[2] to a panel of Special Visitors, or a panel of General Visitors[3].

A Court of Protection Visitor may be appointed for such term and subject to such conditions, and may be paid such remuneration and allowances, as the Lord Chancellor may determine[4].

For the purpose of carrying out his functions under the Mental Capacity Act 2005 in relation to a person who lacks capacity ('P'), a Court of Protection Visitor may, at all reasonable times, examine and take copies of: (1) any health record[5]; (2) any record of a local authority[6], or held by it, compiled in connection with a social services function[7]; and (3) any record held by a person registered under Part II of the Care Standards Act 2000 or Chapter 2 of Part 1 of the Health and Social Care Act 2008[8], so far as the record relates to P[9]. A Court of Protection Visitor may also, for the purpose of carrying out his functions, interview P in private[10].

1   See the Mental Capacity Act 2005 s 61.
2   As to the Lord Chancellor see CONSTITUTIONAL LAW AND HUMAN RIGHTS vol 8(2) (Reissue) PARA 477 et seq.
3   Mental Capacity Act 2005 s 61(1). The function and powers of the Court of Protection Visitors are not dissimilar to those of the Lord Chancellor's Visitors under the Mental Health Act 1983 Pt VII (ss 93–113) (repealed).
     A person is not qualified to be a Special Visitor unless he: (1) is a registered medical practitioner or appears to the Lord Chancellor to have other suitable qualifications or training; and (2) appears to the Lord Chancellor to have special knowledge of and experience in cases of impairment of or disturbance in the functioning of the mind or brain: Mental Capacity Act 2005 s 61(2). A General Visitor need not have a medical qualification: s 61(3). As to the meaning of 'registered medical practitioner' see MEDICAL PROFESSIONS vol 74 (2011) PARA 176.
4   Mental Capacity Act 2005 s 61(4).
5   Mental Capacity Act 2005 s 61(5)(a). As to the meaning of 'health record' see PARA 635 note 9.
6   As to the meaning of 'local authority' see PARA 635 note 10.
7   Mental Capacity Act 2005 s 61(5)(b). As to the meaning of 'social services function' see PARA 635 note 11.
8   Mental Capacity Act 2005 s 61(5)(c) (amended by SI 2010/813). The references in the text are references to the Care Standards Act 2000 Pt II (ss 11–42) (see PARA 585; and SOCIAL SERVICES AND COMMUNITY CARE) and the Health and Social Care Act 2008 Pt 1 Chapter 2 (ss 8–44) (see PARA 635 and SOCIAL SERVICES AND COMMUNITY CARE).
9   Mental Capacity Act 2005 s 61(5).
10   Mental Capacity Act 2005 s 61(6).

749. Visits. Where the Public Guardian[1] visits, or directs a Court of Protection Visitor[2] to visit, any person[3] the following provisions apply[4]. The Public Guardian must notify (or make arrangements to notify) the person to be visited of the date or dates on which it is proposed that the visit will take place, to the extent that it is practicable to do so, any specific matters likely to be covered in the course of the visit and any proposal to inform any other person that the visit is to take place[5].

Where the visit is to be carried out by a Court of Protection Visitor the Public Guardian may give such directions to the Visitor and provide him with such information concerning the person to be visited as the Public Guardian considers necessary for the purposes of enabling the visit to take place and the Visitor to prepare any report the Public Guardian may require[6]. The Visitor must seek to carry out the visit and take all reasonable steps to obtain such other information as he considers necessary for the purpose of preparing a report[7].

A Court of Protection Visitor must submit any report requested by the Public Guardian in accordance with any timetable specified by the Public Guardian[8].

If he considers it appropriate to do so, the Public Guardian may, in relation to any person interviewed in the course of preparing a report disclose the report to him and invite him to comment on it[9].

1 As to the Public Guardian see PARA 751.
2 As to Court of Protection Visitors see PARA 748.
3 Ie under any provision of the Mental Capacity Act 2005 or the Lasting Powers of Attorney, Enduring Powers of Attorney and Public Guardian Regulations 2007, SI 2007/1253.
4 Lasting Powers of Attorney, Enduring Powers of Attorney and Public Guardian Regulations 2007, SI 2007/1253, reg 44(1).
5 Lasting Powers of Attorney, Enduring Powers of Attorney and Public Guardian Regulations 2007, SI 2007/1253, reg 44(2).
6 Lasting Powers of Attorney, Enduring Powers of Attorney and Public Guardian Regulations 2007, SI 2007/1253, reg 44(3)(a).
7 Lasting Powers of Attorney, Enduring Powers of Attorney and Public Guardian Regulations 2007, SI 2007/1253, reg 44(3)(b).
8 Lasting Powers of Attorney, Enduring Powers of Attorney and Public Guardian Regulations 2007, SI 2007/1253, reg 44(4).
9 Lasting Powers of Attorney, Enduring Powers of Attorney and Public Guardian Regulations 2007, SI 2007/1253, reg 44(5).

(5) RIGHT OF APPEAL

750. Rights of appeal. An appeal lies to the Court of Appeal[1] from any decision of the Court of Protection[2].

Court of Protection Rules[3] may provide that where a decision of the court is made by: (1) officers or other staff exercising the jurisdiction of the court by virtue of rules made for that purpose[4]; (2) by a district judge[5]; or (3) by a circuit judge[6], an appeal from that decision lies to a prescribed higher judge of the court and not to the Court of Appeal[7]. For these purposes, the higher judges of the court are: (a) in relation to a person mentioned in head (1) above, a circuit judge or a district judge[8]; (b) in relation to a person mentioned in head (2) above, a circuit judge[9]; (c) in relation to any person mentioned above[10], one of the following nominated judges[11]: the President of the Family Division[12], the Chancellor[13], or a puisne judge of the High Court[14].

Court of Protection Rules may make provision:
(i)   that, in such cases as may be specified, an appeal from a decision of the court may not be made without permission[15];
(ii)   as to the person or persons entitled to grant permission to appeal[16];
(iii) as to any requirements to be satisfied before permission is granted[17];
(iv)   that where a higher judge of the court makes a decision on an appeal, no appeal may be made to the Court of Appeal from that decision unless the Court of Appeal considers that the appeal would raise an important point of principle or practice[18], or there is some other compelling reason for the Court of Appeal to hear it[19];
(v)   as to any considerations to be taken into account in relation to granting or refusing permission to appeal[20].

A decision of a judge of the court which was itself made on appeal from a judge of the court may only be appealed further to the Court of Appeal[21]. Permission is required from the Court of Appeal for such an appeal[22] and the Court of Appeal will not give permission unless it considers that the appeal would raise an important point of principle or practice or there is some other compelling reason for the Court of Appeal to hear it[23].

1   As to the Court of Appeal see COURTS AND TRIBUNALS vol 24 (2010) PARA 688 et seq.
2   Mental Capacity Act 2005 s 53(1). This is subject to the other provisions of s 53: see the text to notes 3–20. As to the Court of Protection see PARA 720.
3   As to rules relating to appeals see the Court of Protection Rules 2007, SI 2007/1744, rr 169–182. For further provision as to the procedure on appeal from the Court of Protection see *Practice Direction—Appeals* PD 52 para 21.12; and *Practice Direction–Appeals* 20A. As to the power to make Court of Protection Rules see PARA 740.
4   Mental Capacity Act 2005 s 53(2)(a). The reference in the text is a reference to rules made under s 51(2)(d): see PARA 740 head (iv).
5   Mental Capacity Act 2005 s 53(2)(b). As to district judges see COURTS AND TRIBUNALS vol 24 (2010) PARA 749.
6   Mental Capacity Act 2005 s 53(2)(c). As to circuit judges see COURTS AND TRIBUNALS vol 24 (2010) PARAS 850–853.
7   Mental Capacity Act 2005 s 53(2).
8   Mental Capacity Act 2005 s 53(3)(a).
9   Mental Capacity Act 2005 s 53(3)(b).
10   Ie any person mentioned in the Mental Capacity Act 2005 s 53(2) (see the text and notes 3–7).
11   Ie judges nominated by virtue of the Mental Capacity Act 2005 s 46(2)(a)–(c): see PARA 720 heads (1)–(3).
12   As to the President of the Family Division see COURTS AND TRIBUNALS vol 24 (2010) PARAS 842–843.
13   The Mental Capacity Act 2005 s 53 refers to the Vice-Chancellor but this is position has been renamed see COURTS AND TRIBUNALS vol 24 (2010) PARA 842.
14   Mental Capacity Act 2005 s 53(3)(c). As to puisne judges of the High Court see COURTS AND TRIBUNALS vol 24 (2010) PARA 695.
15   Mental Capacity Act 2005 s 53(4)(a).
16   Mental Capacity Act 2005 s 53(4)(b).
17   Mental Capacity Act 2005 s 53(4)(c).
18   Mental Capacity Act 2005 s 53(4)(d)(i).
19   Mental Capacity Act 2005 s 53(4)(d)(ii).
20   Mental Capacity Act 2005 s 53(4)(e).
21   Court of Protection Rules 2007, SI 2007/1744, r 182(1).
22   Court of Protection Rules 2007, SI 2007/1744, r 182(2).
23   Court of Protection Rules 2007, SI 2007/1744, r 182(3).

5. THE PUBLIC GUARDIAN

751. In general. For the purposes of the Mental Capacity Act 2005, there is an officer known as the Public Guardian[1], who is to be appointed by the Lord Chancellor[2].

The Public Guardian is to be paid out of money provided by Parliament such salary as the Lord Chancellor may determine[3]. The Lord Chancellor may, after consulting the Public Guardian, provide him with such officers and staff or enter into such contracts with other persons for the provision (by them or their sub-contractors) of officers, staff or services, as the Lord Chancellor thinks necessary for the proper discharge of the Public Guardian's functions[4].

1 Mental Capacity Act 2005 s 57(1).
2 Mental Capacity Act 2005 s 57(2). As to the Lord Chancellor see CONSTITUTIONAL LAW AND HUMAN RIGHTS vol 8(2) (Reissue) PARA 477 et seq.
3 Mental Capacity Act 2005 s 57(3). As to Parliament generally see CONSTITUTIONAL LAW AND HUMAN RIGHTS vol 8(2) (Reissue) PARA 201 et seq; PARLIAMENT vol 78 (2010) PARA 801.
4 Mental Capacity Act 2005 s 57(4). Any functions of the Public Guardian may, to the extent authorised by him, be performed by any of his officers: s 57(5). As to the Public Guardian's functions see PARA 752.

752. Functions of the Public Guardian. The Public Guardian has the following functions[1]:

(1) establishing and maintaining a register of lasting powers of attorney[2];

(2) establishing and maintaining a register of orders appointing deputies[3];

(3) supervising deputies appointed by the Court of Protection[4];

(4) directing a Court of Protection Visitor[5] to visit a donee of a lasting power of attorney, a deputy appointed by the court or the person granting the power of attorney or for whom the deputy is appointed ('P'), and to make a report to the Public Guardian on such matters as he may direct[6];

(5) receiving security which the court requires a person to give for the discharge of his functions[7];

(6) receiving reports from donees of lasting powers of attorney and deputies appointed by the court[8];

(7) reporting to the court on such matters relating to proceedings under the Mental Capacity Act 2005 as the court requires[9];

(8) dealing with representations (including complaints) about the way in which a donee of a lasting power of attorney or a deputy appointed by the court is exercising his powers[10];

(9) publishing, in any manner the Public Guardian thinks appropriate, any information he thinks appropriate about the discharge of his functions[11].

The Lord Chancellor may by regulations make provision[12]: (a) conferring on the Public Guardian other functions in connection with the Mental Capacity Act 2005[13]; (b) in connection with the discharge by the Public Guardian of his functions[14].

For the purpose of enabling him to carry out his functions, the Public Guardian may, at all reasonable times, examine and take copies of: (i) any health record[15]; (ii) any record of a local authority[16], or held by it, compiled in connection with a social services function[17]; and (iii) any record held by a person registered under Part II of the Care Standards Act 2000 or Chapter 2 of Part 1 of the Health and Social Care Act 2008[18], so far as the record relates to P[19]. The Public Guardian may also, for the purpose of enabling him to carry out his functions, interview P in private[20].

The Public Guardian must make an annual report to the Lord Chancellor about the discharge of his functions[21].

1　As to the Public Guardian generally see PARA 751. The Public Guardian has the function of making applications to the court in connection with his functions under the Mental Capacity Act 2005 in such circumstances as he considers it necessary or appropriate to do so: Lasting Powers of Attorney, Enduring Powers of Attorney and Public Guardian Regulations 2007, SI 2007/1253, reg 43. As to fees that may be charged see the Public Guardian (Fees, etc) Regulations 2007, SI 2007/2051.

2　Mental Capacity Act 2005 s 58(1)(a). As to the meaning of 'lasting power of attorney' see PARA 606 note 16. See also PARA 618 et seq.

3　Mental Capacity Act 2005 s 58(1)(b). As to the meaning of 'deputy' see PARA 606 note 18; and see also PARA 724. As to the appointment of deputies see PARA 735.

4　Mental Capacity Act 2005 s 58(1)(c). The functions conferred by s 58(1)(c), (h) (see the text and note 10) may be discharged in co-operation with any other person who has functions in relation to the care or treatment of a person granting the power of attorney or for whom the deputy is appointed: see s 58(2). As to the Court of Protection see PARA 720. The Public Guardian must assess whether the level of supervision required is general or minimal: see the Public Guardian (Fees, etc) Regulations 2007, SI 2007/2051, reg 8(2), (3) (reg 8(2) amended by SI 2011/2189; the Public Guardian (Fees, etc) Regulations 2007, SI 2007/2051, reg 8(3) amended by SI 2009/514, SI 2011/2189).

5　As to the meaning of 'Court of Protection Visitor' see PARA 748.

6　Mental Capacity Act 2005 s 58(1)(d). As to visits by the Public Guardian see the Lasting Powers of Attorney, Enduring Powers of Attorney and Public Guardian Regulations 2007, SI 2007/1253, reg 44.

7　Mental Capacity Act 2005 s 58(1)(e). See also PARA 755.

8　Mental Capacity Act 2005 s 58(1)(f). See also PARA 754.

9　Mental Capacity Act 2005 s 58(1)(g).

10　Mental Capacity Act 2005 s 58(1)(h). See note 4. See also the Lasting Powers of Attorney, Enduring Powers of Attorney and Public Guardian Regulations 2007, SI 2007/1253, regs 46, 47.

11　Mental Capacity Act 2005 s 58(1)(i).

12　As to the Lord Chancellor see CONSTITUTIONAL LAW AND HUMAN RIGHTS vol 8(2) (Reissue) PARA 477 et seq.

13　Mental Capacity Act 2005 s 58(3)(a). As to regulations made under s 58(3) see the Lasting Powers of Attorney, Enduring Powers of Attorney and Public Guardian Regulations 2007, SI 2007/1253 (see PARAS 752–756) and the Public Guardian (Fees, etc) Regulations 2007, SI 2007/2051 (amended by SI 2007/2616; SI 2009/514; SI 2010/1062; SI 2011/2189). The Public Guardian (Fees, etc) Regulations 2007, SI 2007/2051 provide for fees to be charged in connection with the functions carried out by the Public Guardian under the Mental Capacity Act 2005.

14　Mental Capacity Act 2005 s 58(3)(b). Regulations made under s 58(3)(b) may in particular make provision as to: (1) the giving of security by deputies appointed by the court and the enforcement and discharge of security so given; (2) the fees which may be charged by the Public Guardian; (3) the way in which, and funds from which, such fees are to be paid; (4) exemptions from and reductions in such fees; (5) remission of such fees in whole or in part; (6) the making of reports to the Public Guardian by deputies appointed by the court and others who are directed by the court to carry out any transaction for a person who lacks capacity: s 58(4).

15　Mental Capacity Act 2005 s 58(5)(a). As to the meaning of 'health record' see PARA 635 note 9.

16　As to the meaning of 'local authority' see PARA 635 note 10.

17　Mental Capacity Act 2005 s 58(5)(b). As to the meaning of 'social services function' see PARA 635 note 11.

18　Mental Capacity Act 2005 s 58(5)(c) (amended by SI 2010/813). The references in the text are references to the Care Standards Act 2000 Pt II (ss 11–42) (see PARA 585; and SOCIAL SERVICES AND COMMUNITY CARE) and the Health and Social Care Act 2008 Pt 1 Chapter 2 (ss 8–44) (see PARA 635; and SOCIAL SERVICES AND COMMUNITY CARE).

19　Mental Capacity Act 2005 s 58(5).

20　Mental Capacity Act 2005 s 58(6).

21 Mental Capacity Act 2005 s 60(1). The Lord Chancellor must, within one month of receiving the report, lay a copy of it before Parliament: s 60(2).

753. Registers. The Public Guardian[1] may include on the register of lasting powers of attorney, the register of enduring powers of attorney and the register of court orders appointing deputies, such descriptions of information about a registered instrument or a registered order as the Public Guardian considers appropriate and entries which relate to an instrument or order for which registration has been cancelled[2].

Any person may, by an application[3], request the Public Guardian to carry out a search of one or more of the registers[4]. As soon as reasonably practicable after receiving the application the Public Guardian must notify the applicant of the result of the search and, in the event that it reveals one or more entries on the register, the Public Guardian must disclose to the applicant all the information appearing on the register in respect of each entry[5].

The following applies where, as a result of a search made under the above provisions, a person has obtained information relating to a registered instrument or a registered order which confers authority to make decisions about matters concerning a person ('P')[6]. On receipt of an application[7] the Public Guardian may, if he considers that there is good reason to do so[8], disclose to the applicant such additional information as he considers appropriate[9].

1 As to the Public Guardian generally see PARA 751.
2 See the Lasting Powers of Attorney, Enduring Powers of Attorney and Public Guardian Regulations 2007, SI 2007/1253, reg 30.
3 An application must state the register or registers to be searched, the name of the person to whom the application relates and such other details about that person as the Public Guardian may require for the purpose of carrying out the search: Lasting Powers of Attorney, Enduring Powers of Attorney and Public Guardian Regulations 2007, SI 2007/1253, reg 31(2). The application must be accompanied by any fee provided for under the Mental Capacity Act 2005 s 58(4)(b) (see PARA 752): Lasting Powers of Attorney, Enduring Powers of Attorney and Public Guardian Regulations 2007, SI 2007/1253, reg 31(1).
4 Lasting Powers of Attorney, Enduring Powers of Attorney and Public Guardian Regulations 2007, SI 2007/1253, reg 31(1). The Public Guardian may require the applicant to provide such further information, or produce such documents, as the Public Guardian reasonably considers necessary to enable him to carry out the search: reg 31(3).
5 Lasting Powers of Attorney, Enduring Powers of Attorney and Public Guardian Regulations 2007, SI 2007/1253, reg 31(4).
6 Lasting Powers of Attorney, Enduring Powers of Attorney and Public Guardian Regulations 2007, SI 2007/1253, reg 32(1).
7 An application must state the name of P, the reasons for making the application and what steps, if any, the applicant has taken to obtain the information from P: Lasting Powers of Attorney, Enduring Powers of Attorney and Public Guardian Regulations 2007, SI 2007/1253, reg 32(4). The Public Guardian may require the applicant to provide such further information, or produce such documents, as the Public Guardian reasonably considers necessary to enable him to determine the application: reg 32(5).
8 In determining whether to disclose any additional information relating to P, the Public Guardian must, in particular, have regard to:
  (1) the connection between P and the applicant (Lasting Powers of Attorney, Enduring Powers of Attorney and Public Guardian Regulations 2007, SI 2007/1253, reg 32(6)(a));
  (2) the reasons for requesting the information (in particular, why the information cannot or should not be obtained directly from P) (reg 32(6)(b));
  (3) the benefit to P, or any detriment he may suffer, if a disclosure is made (reg 32(6)(c)); and
  (4) any detriment that another person may suffer if a disclosure is made (reg 32(6)(d)).
9 Lasting Powers of Attorney, Enduring Powers of Attorney and Public Guardian Regulations 2007, SI 2007/1253, reg 32(2).

754.   Power to require information from donees of lasting power of attorney.
The following applies where it appears to the Public Guardian[1] that there are
circumstances suggesting that the donee of a lasting power of attorney may:

(1)   have behaved, or may be behaving, in a way that contravenes his
       authority or is not in the best interests of the donor of the power[2];

(2)   be proposing to behave in a way that would contravene that authority
       or would not be in the donor's best interests[3]; or

(3)   have failed to comply with the requirements of an order made, or
       directions given, by the court[4].

The Public Guardian may require the donee to provide specified[5] information,
or information of a specified description, or to produce specified documents or
documents of a specified description[6].

The information or documents must be provided or produced before the end
of such reasonable period as may be specified and at such place as may be
specified[7].

The Public Guardian may require any information provided to be verified in
such manner, or any document produced to be authenticated in such manner, as
he may reasonably require[8].

1   As to the Public Guardian generally see PARA 751.
2   Lasting Powers of Attorney, Enduring Powers of Attorney and Public Guardian
     Regulations 2007, SI 2007/1253, reg 46(1)(a). A similar power exists in relation to attorneys
     under enduring powers of attorney: see reg 47. For other functions in relation to enduring
     powers of attorney see reg 48. See further AGENCY vol 1 (2008) PARAS 231, 237.
3   Lasting Powers of Attorney, Enduring Powers of Attorney and Public Guardian
     Regulations 2007, SI 2007/1253, reg 46(1)(b).
4   Lasting Powers of Attorney, Enduring Powers of Attorney and Public Guardian
     Regulations 2007, SI 2007/1253, reg 46(1)(c).
5   'Specified' means specified in a notice in writing given to the donee by the Public Guardian:
     Lasting Powers of Attorney, Enduring Powers of Attorney and Public Guardian
     Regulations 2007, SI 2007/1253, reg 46(5).
6   Lasting Powers of Attorney, Enduring Powers of Attorney and Public Guardian
     Regulations 2007, SI 2007/1253, reg 46(2).
7   Lasting Powers of Attorney, Enduring Powers of Attorney and Public Guardian
     Regulations 2007, SI 2007/1253, reg 46(3).
8   Lasting Powers of Attorney, Enduring Powers of Attorney and Public Guardian
     Regulations 2007, SI 2007/1253, reg 46(4).

755.   Security.   In any case where the court orders a person ('S') to give to the
Public Guardian security[1] for the discharge of his functions the security must be
given by S: (1) by means of a bond[2]; or (2) in such other manner as the court
may direct[3].

Where any security given to the Public Guardian in respect of which an
endorsement has been provided and the court orders the enforcement of the
security, the Public Guardian must notify any person who endorsed the security
of the contents of the order and notify the court when payment has been made of
the amount secured[4].

In relation to any security given by S to the Public Guardian in respect of
which an endorsement has been provided, the security may be discharged if the
court makes an order discharging it[5].

1   As to the Public Guardian generally see PARA 751. As to the requirement to give security see
     PARA 735.
2   Ie a bond entered into in accordance with Lasting Powers of Attorney, Enduring Powers of
     Attorney and Public Guardian Regulations 2007, SI 2007/1253, reg 34: reg 33(2)(a). A bond is
     entered into in accordance with these provisions only if it is endorsed by an authorised insurance

company or an authorised deposit-taker: reg 34(2). A person may enter into the bond under arrangements made by the Public Guardian or other arrangements which are made by the person entering into the bond or on his behalf: reg 34(3). The Public Guardian may make arrangements with any person specified in reg 34(2) with a view to facilitating the provision by them of bonds which persons required to give security to the Public Guardian may enter into: reg 34(4). For these purposes 'authorised insurance company' means (1) a person who has permission under the Financial Services and Markets Act 2000 Pt 4 (ss 40–55: see FINANCIAL SERVICES AND INSTITUTIONS vol 48 (2008) PARA 348) to effect or carry out contracts of insurance; (2) an EEA firm of the kind mentioned in Sch 3 para 5(d) (see FINANCIAL SERVICES AND INSTITUTIONS vol 48 (2008) PARA 315), which has permission under Sch 3 para 15 (see FINANCIAL SERVICES AND INSTITUTIONS vol 48 (2008) PARA 315) to effect or carry out contracts of insurance; (3) a person who carries on insurance market activity (within the meaning given in s 316(3)); and 'authorised deposit-taker' means (a) a person who has permission under the Financial Services and Markets Act 2000 Pt 4 to accept deposits; (b) an EEA firm of the kind mentioned in Sch 3 para 5(d), which has permission under Sch 3 para 15 to accept deposits: Lasting Powers of Attorney, Enduring Powers of Attorney and Public Guardian Regulations 2007, SI 2007/1253, reg 34(5). The definitions of 'authorised insurance company' and 'authorised deposit-taker' must be read with the Financial Services and Markets Act 2000 s 22 (see FINANCIAL SERVICES AND INSTITUTIONS vol 48 (2008) PARA 84), any relevant order under that provision; and Sch 2: Lasting Powers of Attorney, Enduring Powers of Attorney and Public Guardian Regulations 2007, SI 2007/1253, reg 34(6). For the purposes of reg 33(2)(a), S complies with the requirement to give the security only if the endorsement required by reg 34(2) has been provided and the person who provided it has notified the Public Guardian of that fact: reg 33(3). At such times or at such intervals as the Public Guardian may direct by notice in writing, S must satisfy the Public Guardian that any premiums payable in respect of it have been paid: reg 35(2). Where S proposes to replace a security already given by him, the new security is not to be regarded as having been given until the Public Guardian is satisfied that the requirements set out in heads (1) and (2) in the text have been met in relation to it and no payment is due from S in connection with the discharge of his functions: reg 35(3).

3   See the Lasting Powers of Attorney, Enduring Powers of Attorney and Public Guardian Regulations 2007, SI 2007/1253, reg 33(1), (2). For the purposes of head (2) in the text S complies with the requirement to give the security: (1) in any case where the court directs that any other endorsement must be provided, only if that endorsement has been provided and the person who provided it has notified the Public Guardian of that fact; (2) in any case where the court directs that any other requirements must be met in relation to the giving of the security, only if the Public Guardian is satisfied that those other requirements have been met: reg 33(4).

4   See the Lasting Powers of Attorney, Enduring Powers of Attorney and Public Guardian Regulations 2007, SI 2007/1253, reg 36.

5   See the Lasting Powers of Attorney, Enduring Powers of Attorney and Public Guardian Regulations 2007, SI 2007/1253, reg 37(1), (2). Otherwise the security may not be discharged if the person on whose behalf S was appointed to act dies, until the end of the period of two years beginning on the date of his death or, in any other case, until the end of the period of seven years beginning on whichever of the following dates first occurs (1) if S dies, the date of his death; (2) if the court makes an order which discharges S but which does not also discharge the security under reg 37(2) the date of the order; (3) the date when S otherwise ceases to be under a duty to discharge the functions in respect of which he was ordered to give security: reg 37(3) (substituted by SI 2010/1063). For these purposes if a person takes any step with a view to discharging the security before the end of the period specified in the Lasting Powers of Attorney, Enduring Powers of Attorney and Public Guardian Regulations 2007, SI 2007/1253, reg 37(3), the security is to be treated for all purposes as if it were still in place: reg 37(4).

756.   The Public Guardian Board.   There is to be a body, to be known as the Public Guardian Board[1]. Its duty is to scrutinise and review the way in which the Public Guardian[2] discharges his functions and to make such recommendations to the Lord Chancellor[3] about that matter as it thinks appropriate[4]. The Lord Chancellor must, in discharging his functions concerning the Public Guardian[5], give due consideration to recommendations made by the Board[6].

The Board must have: (1) at least one member who is a judge of the Court of Protection[7]; and (2) at least four members who are persons appearing to the Lord Chancellor to have appropriate knowledge or experience of the work of the Public Guardian[8].

The Lord Chancellor may by regulations make provision as to:

(a)   the appointment of members of the Board (and, in particular, the procedures to be followed in connection with appointments)[9];

(b)   the selection of one of the members to be the chairman[10];

(c)   the term of office of the chairman and members[11];

(d)   their resignation, suspension or removal[12];

(e)   the procedure of the Board (including quorum)[13];

(f)   the validation of proceedings in the event of a vacancy among the members or a defect in the appointment of a member[14].

Subject to any provision made in reliance on head (c) or head (d) above, a person is to hold and vacate office as a member of the Board in accordance with the terms of the instrument appointing him[15].

The Lord Chancellor may make such payments to or in respect of members of the Board by way of reimbursement of expenses, allowances and remuneration as he may determine[16].

The Board must make an annual report to the Lord Chancellor about the discharge of its functions[17].

1   Mental Capacity Act 2005 s 59(1).
2   As to the Public Guardian generally see PARA 751.
3   As to the Lord Chancellor see CONSTITUTIONAL LAW AND HUMAN RIGHTS vol 8(2) (Reissue) PARA 477 et seq.
4   Mental Capacity Act 2005 s 59(2).
5   Ie his functions under the Mental Capacity Act 2005 ss 57, 58: see PARAS 761–762.
6   Mental Capacity Act 2005 s 59(3).
7   Mental Capacity Act 2005 s 59(5)(a). As to the Court of Protection and its judges see PARA 720. Where a person to be appointed as a member of the Board is a judge of the court, the appointment is to be made by the Lord Chief Justice after consulting the Lord Chancellor: s 59(5A) (s 59(5A), (5B), (10) added by SI 2006/1016). In any other case, the appointment of a person as a member of the Board is to be made by the Lord Chancellor: Mental Capacity Act 2005 s 59(5B) (as so added). The Lord Chief Justice may nominate any of the following to exercise his functions under s 59: (1) the President of the Court of Protection; (2) a judicial office holder (as defined in the Constitutional Reform Act 2005 s 109(4) (see COURTS AND TRIBUNALS vol 24 (2010) PARA 961)): Mental Capacity Act 2005 s 59(10) (as so added).
8   Mental Capacity Act 2005 s 59(5)(b).
9   Mental Capacity Act 2005 s 59(6)(a).
10   Mental Capacity Act 2005 s 59(6)(b).
11   Mental Capacity Act 2005 s 59(6)(c).
12   Mental Capacity Act 2005 s 59(6)(d).
13   Mental Capacity Act 2005 s 59(6)(e).
14   Mental Capacity Act 2005 s 59(6)(f).
15   Mental Capacity Act 2005 s 59(7).
16   Mental Capacity Act 2005 s 59(8).
17   Mental Capacity Act 2005 s 59(9).

6. PATIENTS WITH MENTAL DISORDER

(1) INTRODUCTION

757. Introduction. The law governing the treatment[1] and care of patients with mental disorder[2] is mainly contained in the Mental Health Act 1983[3]. The Mental Health (Wales) Measure 2010 makes additional provision[4] for mentally disordered patients in Wales[5] including the provision of local primary mental health support services, including a primary mental health assessment[6], the coordination of and care planning for secondary mental health service users[7] the assessment of former users of secondary mental health services[8] and mental health advocacy[9].

The treatment of patients lacking mental capacity is covered by the Mental Capacity Act 2005[10].

1 Seclusion of a patient as a means of lawful medical treatment, if proportionate, will not automatically infringe a patient's rights under the Convention for the Protection of Human Rights and Fundamental Freedoms (Rome, 4 November 1950; TS 71 (1953); Cmd 8969): see *R (on the application of Munjaz) v Mersey Care NHS Trust* [2005] UKHL 58, [2006] 2 AC 148, [2006] 4 All ER 736. As to the Convention see RIGHTS AND FREEDOMS.

2 As to the meaning of 'patient' see PARA 758 note 4.

3 See PARA 758 et seq.

4 At the date at which this volume states the law the Mental Health (Wales) Measure 2010 ss 1, 2, 4, 5, 11–16, 19–40, 44–46, 49–52, 55, 56, Schs 1, 2 were fully in force; ss 17, 18 were in force except in so far as it as they relate to Pt 1; s 7 was in force to the extent that power to make regulations or an order is conferred; ss 41, 42 were in force in so far as they relate to Pts 2, 3; ss 47 was in force to the extent that power to make regulations or an order is conferred and in so far as it relates to Pt 2; and s 43 was in force only in so far as it relates to ss 1, 2, 4, 5, 11 and Pts 2, 3: see s 55; Mental Health (Wales) Measure 2010 (Commencement No 1 and Transitional Provision) Order 2011, SI 2011/3046; Mental Health (Wales) Measure 2010 (Commencement No 2) Order 2012, SI 2012/1397.

5 The Welsh Ministers must review the operation of the Mental Health (Wales) Measure 2010 for the purposes of publishing a report or reports in accordance with s 48(3)–(6) (see notes 6–9): s 48(1). However, before undertaking a review of the operation of any part or provision of the Mental Health (Wales) Measure 2010, the Welsh Ministers must satisfy themselves that there has been sufficient time for that part or provision to have been in operation; but this is subject to s 48(3)–(6): s 48(2). Any two or more reports may be published in the same document: s 48(7).

6 See the Mental Health (Wales) Measure 2010 Pt 1 (ss 1–11). A report on a review of the operation of Pt 1 must be published within 4 years of the commencement of all the duties contained in ss 2(1) (see PARA 586), 3(1) (see PARA 589), 4(1) (see PARA 588), 6(2) (see PARA 881), 7(2) (see PARA 881), 8(2) (see PARA 881), 9(2) (see PARA 883), 10(1)–(3) (see PARA 885): s 48(2). For the purposes of s 48 'commencement' means commencement for any case, class of case, area or purpose: s 48(8).

7 See the Mental Health (Wales) Measure 2010 Pt 2 (ss 12–18): and PARAS 851–858. A report on a review of the operation of Pt 2 must be published within 4 years of the commencement of all the duties contained in ss 13(1) (see PARA 851), 16(1) (see PARA 853), 17(1), (10) (see PARA 854): s 48(3).

8 See the Mental Health (Wales) Measure 2010 Pt 3 (see 19–30); and PARAS 949–954. A report on a review of the operation of Pt 3 must be published within 4 years of the commencement of all the duties contained in ss 18(1), (3) (see PARA 855), 19 (see PARA 950), 23(1), (2) (see PARA 947), 25 (see PARA 949), 26(2) (see PARA 951), 27(1), (2) (see PARA 953): s 48(4).

9 See the Mental Health (Wales) Measure 2010 Pt 4 (ss 31–40) (which add the Mental Health Act 1983 ss 130E–130L and amend s 118, 143); and PARAS 807–814. A report on a review of the operation of the Mental Health (Wales) Measure 2010 Pt 4 must be published within 4 years of the commencement of all the duties contained in the Mental Health Act 1983 s 130E(1) (as added by the Mental Health (Wales) Measure 2010 s 31: see PARA 807): s 48(5).

10 See PARA 597 et seq.

758. Care and treatment of mental disorder generally. In-patient medical treatment[1] may be provided either in hospitals[2] or in registered establishments[3].

Patients[4] may be admitted to hospitals and registered establishments either as informal patients[5] or compulsorily[6]. Patients who do not require care and treatment in hospital but who do require other forms of care under compulsory powers, either in the interests of their own welfare or for the protection of other persons, may be placed under the guardianship of the local social services authority or any other person willing to act as guardian[7]. Patients compulsorily admitted to hospital or received into guardianship may apply or be referred to the appropriate tribunal[8].

Community treatment orders (also referred to as 'supervised community treatment')[9] enable some patients to live in the community but with powers of recall to hospital where necessary[10]. The treatment of such patients while in the community is regulated[11].

Where a person has been detained under the Mental Health Act 1983 there is an implied power for staff to exercise a degree of control over their activities; the common law doctrine of necessity also allows staff to act in such a way as is reasonable, necessary and proportionate to protect the patient from the immediate risk of significant harm[12].

Guidance on the treatment of mental disorder under the Mental Health Act 1983 and more generally is provided by Codes of Practice prepared by the appropriate national authority[13].

The treatment and care generally of patients lacking mental capacity, unless the treatment is for mental disorder under the compulsory powers of the Mental Health Act 1983, is governed by the Mental Capacity Act 2005 together with the relevant Code of Practice[14].

1   As to the meaning of 'medical treatment' see PARA 926.

     Seclusion of a patient as a means of lawful medical treatment, if proportionate, will not automatically infringe a patient's rights under the Convention for the Protection of Human Rights and Fundamental Freedoms (Rome, 4 November 1950; TS 71 (1953); Cmd 8969): see *R (on the application of Munjaz) v Mersey Care NHS Trust* [2005] UKHL 58, [2006] 2 AC 148, [2006] 4 All ER 736. As to the Convention see RIGHTS AND FREEDOMS.

2   As to the meaning of 'hospital' see PARA 577.

3   As to registered establishments see PARAS 578, 585; and SOCIAL SERVICES AND COMMUNITY CARE.

4   'Patient' means a person suffering or appearing to be suffering from mental disorder: Mental Health Act 1983 s 145(1) (amended by the Mental Capacity Act 2005 Sch 6 para 29(7), Sch 7).

5   As to the informal admission of patients see PARA 764.

6   As to the compulsory admission of patients see PARA 767 et seq.

7   As to reception into guardianship see PARA 785 et seq.

8   See the Mental Health Act 1983 ss 66, 67; and PARA 961 et seq. As to the meaning of the 'appropriate tribunal' see PARA 955.

9   See the Mental Health Act 1983 ss 17A–17G; and PARAS 797–803. As to the meaning of 'community treatment order' see PARA 797. These provisions replace the supervised aftercare provisions (ss 25A–25J (repealed)).

10 See the Mental Health Act 1983 s 17E; and PARA 801.

11 See the Mental Health Act 1983 ss 64A–64K; and PARAS 935–941.

12 *R (on the application of Munjaz) v Mersey Care NHS Trust* [2005] UKHL 58, [2006] 2 AC 148, [2006] 4 All ER 736. This applies regardless of the patient's capacity and enables staff to restrain a person with no more force than is reasonably necessary and thereafter to seclude them: see also note 1. As to the common law powers of private individuals to restrain a person of unsound mind see *B v Forsey* 1988 SC (HL) 28, 1988 SLT 572, HL.

13 See the Department of Health *Mental Health Act 1983 Code of Practice* (2008); the Welsh Assembly Government *Mental Health Act 1983 Code of Practice for Wales* (2008) (both

published pursuant to the Mental Health Act 1983 s 118(1), (6)); and PARA 762. As to the code of practice under the Mental Capacity Act 2005 see PARA 602. As to the appropriate national authority see PARA 567.

14 See the Mental Capacity Act 2005 s 28, Sch 1A; and PARA 658.

759. Protection for acts done in pursuance of the Mental Health Act 1983.

No person is to be liable, whether on the ground of want of jurisdiction or on any other ground, to any civil or criminal proceedings to which he otherwise would have been liable in respect of any act purporting to be done in pursuance of the Mental Health Act 1983[1] or any regulations or rules made under that Act, unless the act in question was done in bad faith or without reasonable care[2]. No civil proceedings can be brought[3] against any person in any court in respect of any such act without the leave of the High Court[4], and no criminal proceedings may be brought against any person in any court in respect of any such act except by or with the consent of the Director of Public Prosecutions[5].

The test to be applied by the court is whether the complaint appears to be such that it deserves the further investigation which would only be possible if the case were allowed to proceed[6]. The Court of Appeal has jurisdiction to hear appeals against the granting or refusal of leave by the High Court to the taking of proceedings[7], but no appeal lies to the Supreme Court from the refusal by the Court of Appeal of leave to appeal to that Court[8]. The protection provided does not prevent the High Court from entertaining an application for judicial review in respect of an act done in pursuance of the Mental Health Act 1983, or from granting a writ of habeas corpus[9].

The statutory protection does not apply to proceedings for an offence under the Mental Health Act 1983 to which the consent of the Director of Public Prosecutions is required[10], nor does it apply to proceedings against the appropriate national authority[11] or against a strategic health authority[12], local health board[13], special health authority[14], a primary care trust[15], or a National Health Service Trust[16] or NHS foundation trust[17]. As from 1 April 2013 the statutory protection does not apply to the National Health Service Commissioning Board, a clinical commissioning group[18] or to a person who has functions under an agreement for exercising functions of the Secretary of State[19] in so far as the proceedings relate to the exercise of those functions[20].

1 See eg *Ashingdane v Secretary of State for Social Services* (18 February 1980, unreported) (the decision of a nurses' union not to allow patients who were subject to restriction orders to be transferred to a particular hospital was a policy decision which fell outside the express or implied authority as conferred by the Mental Health Act 1959). However, the provision is not limited to acts done, or purported to be done, in pursuance of functions specifically provided for in the terms of the Act itself: *Pountney v Griffiths* [1976] AC 314, [1975] 2 All ER 881, HL (returning a detained patient to his ward at the end of visiting time was an act in pursuance of the Mental Health Act 1959 and treating patients necessarily involves the exercise of discipline and control). Although there is authority for the proposition that this does not apply to proceedings instituted by informal patients (*R v Runighian* [1977] Crim LR 361) an amendment to exclude informal patients from the operation of this provision was resisted by the government during the passage of the 1982 amendment Act. This position was endorsed in *Lebrooy v Hammersmith and Fulham London Borough Council* [2006] EWHC 1976 QB, [2006] All ER (D) 257 (Apr). See also *R v Broadmoor and Secretary of State for the Home Department, ex p S, H and D* CO/199/98, CA; *R v Mental Health Act Commission, ex p Smith* (1998) 43 BMLR 174; *Broadmoor Hospital Authority v R* [2000] 2 All ER 727, [2000] QB 775, [2000] 1 WLR 1590, CA; *R (on the application of E) v Ashworth Hospital Authority* [2001] EWHC Admin 1089, (2002) Times, 17 January; *R (on the application of A) v Secretary of State for the Home Department* [2003] EWCA Civ 2846; *R (on the application of Munjaz) v Mersey Care NHS Trust* [2005] UKHL 58, [2006] 2 AC 148, [2006] 4 All ER 736.

2 Mental Health Act 1983 s 139(1) (amended by the Mental Capacity Act 2005 Sch 6 para 29(3), Sch 7). See also the text and notes 3–4. This provision extends to Scotland: see the Mental

Health Act 1983 s 146; and PARA 557. Section 139(1) can be read down under the Human Rights Act 1998 so as to permit a claim for damages for unlawful detention without leave of the court: *TTM (by his litigation friend TM) v Hackney London Borough Council* [2011] EWCA Civ 4 at [66]; [2011] 3 All ER 529 at [66], [2011] 1 WLR 2873 at [66].

As to liability for lack of reasonable care see *Everett v Griffiths* [1921] 1 AC 631, HL (action for false imprisonment by reason of negligent certification); *Harnett v Fisher* [1927] AC 573, HL. See also *Harnett v Bond* [1925] AC 669, HL (negligently retaking while on leave of absence); *Re Frost* [1936] 2 All ER 182, CA (leave granted to sue for negligence in improperly taking patient to hospital); *Holgate v Lancashire Mental Hospitals Board, Gill and Robertson* [1937] 4 All ER 19 (negligence in granting licence for absence); *Kynaston v Secretary of State for Home Affairs* (1981) 73 Cr App Rep 281, [1982] Crim LR 117, CA (where the Home Secretary acted on the advice of a board, he had not acted in bad faith or without reasonable care).

A medical practitioner who under the statutes formerly in force undertook the duty of signing a certificate of insanity was under a duty to use reasonable care; if he failed to do so, damages might be recovered against him by the person to whom the certificate related: *Hall v Semple* (1862) 3 F & F 337 (action for assault and false imprisonment by reason of negligent certification); *Everett v Griffiths* (where it was assumed, but not decided, that there was a duty to use reasonable care in certifications); *Harnett v Fisher* (action on similar grounds, where the House of Lords, Lord Blanesburgh dissenting, considered that the duty arose, not under the statute, but at common law); *De Freville v Dill* (1927) 96 LJKB 1056 (action on similar grounds). In *Harnett v Fisher*, the giving of a certificate of insanity under the Lunacy Act 1890 s 4 (repealed) was held to be a direct cause of the subsequent reception order and detention. It would seem that the making of a medical recommendation for the purposes of an application for compulsory admission and detention under the Mental Health Act 1983 Pt 2 (ss 2–34) (see PARA 767 et seq) would be similarly regarded, and that the duty to exercise reasonable care in the making of such a recommendation and the consequences of failure to do so would be as formerly in the case of a certificate: see *Winch v Jones, Winch v Hayward* [1986] QB 296, [1985] 3 All ER 97, CA.

At common law a medical practitioner could not justify the taking charge of and confining an individual whom he had never seen merely upon statements made by relations, unless such statements satisfied him that his intervention was necessary to prevent the individual from doing immediate injury to himself or others (*Anderdon v Burrows* (1830) 4 C & P 210); but restraint of a person dangerous by reason of mental disorder is justifiable both at the moment of the original danger and also until there is reasonable ground for believing that the original danger is over (*Scott v Wakem* (1862) 3 F & F 328; and see *Symm v Fraser* (1863) 3 F & F 859). As to the duty of care owed by medical practitioners and hospital authorities generally see MEDICAL PROFESSIONS vol 74 (2011) PARAS 23–27.

The protection under s 139 applies when patients are being conveyed between Scotland and any place in England, Wales, or Northern Ireland: see the Mental Health (Care and Treatment) (Scotland) Act 2003 (Consequential Provisions) Order 2005, SI 2005/2078, art 12.

3   Proceedings instituted without such leave are a nullity: *Pountney v Griffiths* [1976] AC 314, [1975] 2 All ER 881, HL; *Seal v Chief Constable of South Wales Police* [2007] UKHL 31, [2007] 4 All ER 177, [2007] 1 WLR 1910. As to such applications see CPR Pt 23; and CIVIL PROCEDURE vol 11 (2009) PARA 303 et seq. A successful application under the Mental Health Act 1983 s 139(2) does not prevent a judge, on an application to strike out, concluding on further investigation that the claim should be struck out as disclosing no reasonable cause of action: *X v A, B and C and the Mental Health Act Commission* (1991) 9 BMLR 91. As to leave see *Simpson-Cleghorn v Lancashire County Council* (5 July 1999, unreported), CA; *C v South London and Maudsley Hospital NHS Trust and Lambeth London Borough Council* [2001] 1 MHLR 269 (the overriding objective under the Civil Procedure Rules 1998 has no application here). The words 'no civil proceedings [may] be brought' were introduced with the obvious object of giving mental health professionals greater protection than they had enjoyed before and were re-enacted with knowledge of the effect the courts had given to them; to uphold the decision of the lower courts was not to sanction a departure from the fundamental rule that the subject's recourse to the courts for the determination of his rights was not to be excluded except by clear words: *Seal v Chief Constable of South Wales Police*.

4   Mental Health Act 1983 s 139(2).

5   Mental Health Act 1983 s 139(2). Failure to comply with the necessary consent before the proceedings were begun rendered them a nullity which was incapable of subsequent remedy: *Seal v Chief Constable of South Wales Police* [2007] UKHL 31, [2007] 4 All ER 177, [2007] 1 WLR 1910. In relation to Northern Ireland the reference in the Mental Health Act 1983 s 139 to the Director of Public Prosecutions must be construed as a reference to the Director of Public Prosecutions for Northern Ireland: s 139(5).

6   *Winch v Jones, Winch v Hayward* [1986] QB 296, [1985] 3 All ER 97, CA. See also *Seal v Chief Constable of South Wales Police* [2007] UKHL 31, [2007] 4 All ER 177, [2007] 1 WLR 1910; *Johnstone v Chief Constable of Merseyside Police* [2009] EWHC 2969, (QB), [2009] All ER (D) 226 (Nov). Only if the applicant's affidavits are totally refuted by incontrovertible evidence should leave be denied. See also *Furber v Kratter* (1988) Times, 21 July (leave granted by the High Court for actions in negligence and false imprisonment in relation to the seclusion of the applicant in a special hospital in inadequate conditions); *James v Mayor and Burgesses of the London Borough of Havering* (1992) 15 BMLR 1, CA (application for false imprisonment proceedings rejected as it was unarguable that the social worker or doctor had acted without unreasonable care in regard to the emergency compulsory admission; the Mental Health Act 1983 s 139 is not only a protection against frivolous claims, but also from error in the circumstances set out in that provision). See *DD v Durham City Council* [2012] EWHC 1053 (QB), [2012] PTSR D35 (vicarious liability for approved mental health practitioners).

7   See *Re Shoesmith* [1938] 2 KB 637, [1938] 3 All ER 186, CA; *Richardson v LCC* [1957] 2 All ER 330, [1957] 1 WLR 751, CA.

     Since an order of a judge refusing an application under the Mental Health Act 1983 s 139(2) is an interim, not a final, order, no appeal lies against such an order without the leave of the judge or the Court of Appeal: *Moore v Metropolitan Police Comr* [1968] 1 QB 26, [1967] 2 All ER 827, CA. The onus is on the applicant to satisfy the court that the proceedings should be commenced: *Carter v Metropolitan Police Comr* [1975] 2 All ER 33, [1975] 1 WLR 507, CA.

8   *Whitehouse v Board of Control* [1960] 3 All ER 182n, [1960] 1 WLR 1093, HL.

9   *Ex p Waldron* [1986] QB 824, sub nom *R v Hallstrom, ex p W* [1985] 3 All ER 775, CA. See also *Azam v Secretary of State for the Home Department* [1974] AC 18, [1973] 2 All ER 765, HL.

10 Mental Health Act 1983 s 139(3). The protection is not removed in relation to private hospitals: *TTM v Hackney London Borough Council* [2010] EWHC 1349 (Admin) (first instance, where this is described as 'somewhat anomalous'). The consent of the Director of Public Prosecutions is required for proceedings in respect of offences under s 127 (ill-treatment of patients: see PARA 1010). As to the Sexual Offences Act 2003 ss 30–44 (sexual offences relating to persons with a mental disorder) see PARA 1012. As to the Director of Public Prosecutions see CRIMINAL PROCEDURE vol 27 (2010) PARAS 23, 33 et seq.

11 As to the appropriate national authority see PARA 567.

12 As to the meaning of 'strategic health authority' see PARA 575 note 3. As from 1 April 2013 strategic health authorities are abolished (see PARA 575 note 3) and the words 'strategic health authority' in the Mental Health Act 1983 s 139(4) are repealed by the Health and Social Care Act 2012 Sch 5 para 30(a): see s 306(1)(d); and the Health and Social Care Act 2012 (Commencement No 4, Transitional, Savings and Transitory Provisions) Order 2013, SI 2013/160, art 2(2).

13 As to the meaning of 'local health board' see PARA 575 note 6.

14 As to the meaning of 'special health authority' see PARA 575 note 4.

15 As to the meaning of 'primary care trust' see PARA 575 note 5. As from 1 April 2013 primary care trusts are abolished (see PARA 575 note 5) and the words 'primary care trust' in the Mental Health Act 1983 s 139(4) are repealed by the Health and Social Care Act 2012 Sch 5 para 30(d): see the Health and Social Care Act 2012 (Commencement No 4, Transitional, Savings and Transitory Provisions) Order 2013, SI 2013/160, art 2(2).

16 Ie a National Health Service Trust established under the National Health Service Act 2006 or the National Health Service (Wales) Act 2006. The Mental Health Act 1983 s 139(4) is amended by the Health and Social Care Act 2012 Sch 14 para 50 as from 1 April 2013 and no longer applies to a National Health Service Trust established under the National Health Service Act 2006: see the Health and Social Care Act 2012 (Commencement No 4, Transitional, Savings and Transitory Provisions) Order 2013, SI 2013/160, art 2(2).

17 Mental Health Act 1983 s 139(4) (amended by the National Health Service and Community Care Act 1990 s 66(1), Sch 9 para 24(7); the Health and Social Care (Community Health and Standards) Act 2003 s 34, Sch 4 paras 50, 56; the National Health Service (Consequential Provisions) Act 2006, Sch 1 para 69; SI 2000/90; SI 2002/2469; SI 2007/961 and SI 2010/976).

18 See the Mental Health Act 1983 s 139(4) as further amended by the Health and Social Care Act 2012 Sch 5 para 30(a) as from 1 April 2013: see the Health and Social Care Act 2012 (Commencement No 4, Transitional, Savings and Transitory Provisions) Order 2013, SI 2013/160, art 2(2). As to the National Health Service Commissioning Board and clinical commissioning groups see PARAS 571, 572.

19 Ie functions under the Mental Health Act 1983 by virtue of s 12ZA (see PARA 570).

20 See the Mental Health Act 1983 s 139(4) as further amended by the Health and Social Care
    Act 2012 s 38(3) as from 1 April 2013: see s 306(4); and the Health and Social Care Act 2012
    (Commencement No 4, Transitional, Savings and Transitory Provisions) Order 2013,
    SI 2013/160, art 2(2).

760.   Regulation.   The assessment of, or medical treatment[1] (other than
surgical procedures) for, a mental disorder[2] affecting a person in a hospital[3]
where that person is detained in that hospital[4] or recalled to that hospital[5] are
activities regulated by the Health and Social Care Act 2008[6].

1   As to the meaning of 'medical treatment' see PARA 926: Health and Social Care Act 2008
    (Regulated Activities) Regulations 2010, SI 2010/781, Sch 1 para 6(2)(a).
2   As to the meaning of 'mental disorder' see PARA 761: Health and Social Care Act 2008
    (Regulated Activities) Regulations 2010, SI 2010/781, Sch 1 para 6(2)(b).
3   As to the meaning of 'hospital' see PARA 577: Health and Social Care Act 2008 (Regulated
    Activities) Regulations 2010, SI 2010/781, Sch 1 para 6(2)(c).
4   Ie pursuant to the Mental Health Act 1983 (with the exception of ss 135, 136) or pursuant to an
    order or direction made under another enactment, where that detention takes effect as if the
    order were made pursuant to the provisions of the Mental Health Act 1983.
5   Ie pursuant to the Mental Health Act 1983 s 17E (see PARA 801).
6   Health and Social Care Act 2008 (Regulated Activities) Regulations 2010, SI 2010/781, Sch 1
    para 6(1) (amended by SI 2012/1916). This does not apply to the assessment or treatment by a
    registered medical practitioner appointed for the purposes of the Mental Health Act 1983 Pt 4
    in giving a certificate under s 57, 58 or 58A (see PARAS 928–931): Health and Social Care
    Act 2008 (Regulated Activities) Regulations 2010, SI 2010/781, Sch 1 para 6(1) (added by
    SI 2012/1916).

761.   Mental disorder.   'Mental disorder'[1] is defined by the Mental Health
Act 1983 for the purposes of the statutory provisions for the reception, care and
treatment of mentally disordered persons and the management of their property
and affairs, and related matters[2]. This does not affect the general law relating to
criminal responsibility[3] or to civil capacity, for which the ordinary tests of legal
responsibility apply[4]. However, the statutory definition in the Mental Health
Act 1983 is sometimes applied by other statutes for their own purposes[5]. 'Mental
disorder' is defined in the Mental Health Act 1983 as any disorder or disability
of the mind[6]. Dependence on alcohol or drugs is not considered to be a disorder
or disability of the mind for these purposes[7].

A person with learning disability[8] must not be considered by reason of that
disability to be: (1) suffering from mental disorder for certain purposes[9]; or (2)
requiring treatment in hospital for mental disorder for certain purposes[10], unless
that disability is associated with abnormally aggressive or seriously irresponsible
conduct on his part[11].

1   The adoption of this term was recommended in the *Report of the Royal Commission on the
    Law relating to Mental Illness and Mental Deficiency 1954–1957* (Cmnd 169 (1957)) Pt 3
    paras 146–198. The Commission recommended its use as a general term covering all forms of
    mental ill-health or disability.
2   Mental Health Act 1983 s 1(1). This provision replaces the Mental Health Act 1959 s 4
    (repealed). As to the terms which were superseded by the Mental Health Act 1959 see PARA 559.
    The definition of mental disorder under the Mental Health Act 1983 s 1 has been held to apply
    to the Sexual Offences Act 2003 s 30 (see CRIMINAL LAW vol 25 (2010) PARA 210): see *R v
    Cooper* [2009] UKHL 42, [2009] 4 All ER 1033, [2009] 1 WLR 1786. Since the repeal of the
    Mental Health Act 1983 Part VII by the Mental Capacity Act 2005 the reference to the
    management of property and affairs is otiose. For the purposes of the Mental Health Act 1983
    'mental disorder' has the meaning given in s 1 (subject to ss 86(4) and 141(6B)): s 145(1)
    (definition substituted by the Mental Health Act 2007 Sch 1 para 17). As from 28 April 2013
    the definition of mental disorder in the Mental Health Act 1983 s 145(1) is amended and is no
    longer subject to s 141(6B): see the Mental Health (Discrimination) Act 2013 s 4(2), Schedule
    para 1(1).

3   As to the defence of insanity see CRIMINAL LAW vol 25 (2010) PARAS 30–32.

4   As to civil capacity generally see PARA 993 et seq. As to the effect of mental disorder on the holding of a benefice and as to incapacity to present to an advowson see ECCLESIASTICAL LAW vol 34 (2011) PARA 555. As to incapacity to vote at an election see PARA 565; and ELECTIONS AND REFERENDUMS vol 15(3) (2007 Reissue) PARA 122. As to the change of domicile of a mentally incapacitated person see CONFLICT OF LAWS vol 19 (2011) PARA 357. See also the Mental Capacity Act 2005 at PARA 601 et seq for the test of capacity with respect to decision making for incapacitated persons. If a person who is mentally disordered but who knows the nature and quality of his act commits a tort, it is no defence that he does not know that what he is doing is wrong: *Morriss v Marsden* [1952] 1 All ER 925 (an action for assault and battery; however, it was said at 927 per Stable J that 'if a person in a state of complete automatism inflicted a grievous injury, that would not be actionable'). This seems to have been the old common law view: see *Weaver v Ward* (1616) Hob 134; Bac Abr, Trespass (G 1); and see *Haycraft v Creasy* (1801) 2 East 92 at 104 per Lord Kenyon CJ; *Mordaunt v Mordaunt, Cole and Johnson* (1870) LR 2 P & D 109 at 142 per Kelly CB; *Donaghy v Brennan* (1901) 19 NZLR 289. See also *Hanbury v Hanbury* (1892) 8 TLR 559 at 560, CA, per Lord Esher MR; *Emmens v Pottle* (1885) 16 QBD 354 at 356, CA. However, it remains a question whether the test for liability in negligence is so purely objective that a defendant's lack of understanding or control cannot be a defence: see NEGLIGENCE vol 78 (2010) PARAS 1, 21.

5   Eg, for the purposes of the law of nullity of marriage, by the Matrimonial Causes Act 1973 s 12(d): see MATRIMONIAL AND CIVIL PARTNERSHIP LAW vol 72 (2009) PARA 332.

6   Mental Health Act 1983 s 1(2) (definition substituted by the Mental Health Act 2007 s 1(1), (2)). The expression 'mentally disordered' is construed in accordance with the definition of mental disorder: Mental Health Act 1983 s 1(2) (as so substituted). This definition is consistent with that of 'persons of unsound mind' for the purposes of the European Convention on Human Rights art 5(1)(a): see Application 6301/73 *Winterwerp v Netherlands* (1979) 2 EHRR 387, ECtHR. Mental disorder cannot be identified by reference to diagnostic manuals alone: see *DL-H v Devon Partnership NHS Trust* [2010] UKUT 102 (AAC). See also *R v Dhaliwal (appeal under s 58 of the Criminal Justice Act 2003)* [2006] EWCA Crim 1139, [2006] 2 Cr App Rep 348, [2006] Crim LR 923; *Attia v British Gas plc* [1988] QB 304, [1987] 3 All ER 455; and *St George's Healthcare NHS Trust v S* [1999] Fam 26, [1998] 3 All ER 673 (on the difficulty in drawing a distinction between mental distress and symptoms amounting to a psychiatric illness).

7   Mental Health Act 1983 s 1(3) (substituted by the Mental Health Act 2007 s 3). The inclusion of 'sexual deviancy' has been removed. Psychosis associated with drug or alcohol abuse or dependence falls within the definition: see *CM v Derbyshire Healthcare NHS Foundation Trust* [2011] UKUT 129 (AAC) (detention for the sole purpose of addressing a patient's drug taking and chaotic lifestyle is not lawful). See the Department of Health *Mental Health Act 1983 Code of Practice* (2008), Chapter 3; and the Welsh Assembly Government *Mental Health Act 1983 Code of Practice for Wales* (2008), Chapter 2.

8   For this purpose 'learning disability' means a state of arrested or incomplete development of the mind which includes significant impairment of intelligence and social functioning: Mental Health Act 1983 s 1(4) (added by the Mental Health Act 1983 s 2(3)). Guidance is given in the Department of Health *Mental Health Act 1983 Code of Practice* (2008) paras 4 and 5; and the Welsh Assembly Government *Mental Health Act 1983 Code of Practice for Wales* (2008) paras 2.13–2.16.

9   Ie for the purposes of the Mental Health Act 1983 ss 3, 7, 17A, 20, 20A, 35–38, 45A, 47, 48, 51, 72(1)(b), (c), (4).

10 Ie for the purposes of the Mental Health Act 1983 ss 17E, 50–53.

11 Mental Health Act 1983 s 1(2A), (2B) (added by the Mental Health Act 2007 s 3). See *P v Mental Health Review Tribunal and Rampton Hospital* [2001] EWHC Admin 876; *R v Trent Mental Health Review Tribunal, Ex p Ryan* [1992] COD 157; *Re F (Mental Health Act: Guardianship)* [2000] 1 FCR 11, [2000] 1 FLR 192; *Newham London Borough Council v S (adult: court's jurisdiction)* [2003] EWHC 1909 (Fam), [2003] 2 FLR 1235, [2003] Fam Law 870; *GC v Managers of the Kingswood Centre of Central and North West London NHS Foundation Trust* (CO/7784/2008) (unreported, 3 October 2008); *Lewis v Gibson* [2005] EWCA Civ 587, [2005] 2 FCR 241, 87 BMLR 93 ('abnormally aggressive and seriously irresponsible conduct'). See also the Department of Health *Mental Health Act 1983 Code of Practice* (2008), Chapter 3; and the Welsh Assembly Government *Mental Health Act 1983 Code of Practice for Wales* (2008) Chapter 2.

(2) GUIDANCE

762. Codes of practice under the Mental Health Act 1983. The appropriate national authority[1] must prepare, publish, and from time to time revise, a code of practice[2] for: (1) the guidance of registered medical practitioners[3], approved clinicians[4], managers and staff of hospitals, independent hospitals and care homes[5] and approved mental health professionals[6] in relation to the admission of patients to hospitals and registered establishments[7] and to guardianship and community patients)[8]; (2) the guidance of registered medical practitioners and members of other professions in relation to the medical treatment[9] of patients suffering from mental disorder[10]; and (3) in relation to Wales, the guidance of independent mental health advocates[11]. In performing functions under the Mental Health Act 1983 the persons mentioned in heads (1) to (3) above[12] must have regard to the code[13] and failure to follow the code could be referred to in evidence in legal proceedings[14].

The code must in particular specify additional forms of medical treatment[15] which give rise to special concern and which should accordingly not be given by a medical practitioner unless: the patient has consented to the treatment, or to a plan of treatment including that treatment; and a certificate[16] in writing has been given by another registered medical practitioner, being a practitioner appointed[17] for these purposes by the regulatory authority[18] that the patient is capable of understanding its nature, purpose and likely effects and that having regard to the likelihood of its alleviating or preventing a deterioration of his condition it should be given[19].

The code must include a statement of the principles which the appropriate national authority thinks should inform decisions under the Mental Health Act 1983[20]. In preparing the statement of principles the authority must, in particular, ensure that each of the following matters is addressed:

(a) respect for patients' past and present wishes and feelings[21];

(b) respect for diversity generally including, in particular, diversity of religion, culture and sexual orientation[22];

(c) minimising restrictions on liberty[23];

(d) involvement of patients in planning, developing and delivering care and treatment appropriate to them[24];

(e) avoidance of unlawful discrimination[25];

(f) effectiveness of treatment[26];

(g) views of carers and other interested parties[27];

(h) patient wellbeing and safety[28]; and

(i) public safety[29].

The appropriate national authority must also have regard to the desirability of ensuring the efficient use of resources and the equitable distribution of services[30].

1 As to the appropriate national authority see PARA 567. Before preparing the code or making any alteration in it certain bodies must be consulted: see the Mental Health Act 1983 s 118(3).

2 As to the current codes see the Welsh Assembly Government *Mental Health Act 1983 Code of Practice for Wales* (2008) and the Department of Health *Mental Health Act 1983 Code of Practice* (2008) both of which came into force on 3 November 2008.

3 As to registered medical practitioners see MEDICAL PROFESSIONS vol 74 (2011) PARA 176 et seq.

4 As to the meaning of 'approved clinician' see PARA 831.

5 As to the meaning of 'independent hospital' see PARA 578 note 7; and as to the meaning of 'care home see PARA 583 note 7.

6 As to the meaning of 'approved mental health professional' see the Mental Health Act 1983 s 114; and PARA 815 note 2 (definition applied by s 145(1) (amended by the Mental Health Act 2007 Sch 2 para 11(2))).

7   As to the meaning of 'registered establishment' see the Mental Health Act 1983 s 34; and PARA
    578 (definition applied by s 145(1) (amended by the Care Standards Act 2000 Sch 4
    para 9(10)(d))).
8   Mental Health Act 1983 s 118(1)(a) (amended by the Mental Health (Patients in the
    Community) Act 1995 Sch 1 para 16; the Care Standards Act 2000 Sch 4 para 9(6), the Mental
    Health Act 2007 s 14(2), Sch 2 para 9, Sch 3 para 25). Guardianship and community patients
    mentioned in the text refers to guardianship and community patients under the Mental Health
    Act 1983.
9   As to the meaning of 'medical treatment' see PARA 926.
10 Mental Health Act 1983 s 118(1)(b), (6). This provision brings a severely learning disabled child
    resident in a special school whose condition falls within s 1 within the scope of the Code of
    Practice: see *R(on the application of C) v A Local Authority* [2011] EWHC 1539 (Admin),
    [2011] All ER (D) 171 (Jun) (obiter, the court said that in the absence of statutory control over
    seclusion and restraint in childrens' homes the Codes should be applied as good practice even
    where the children are not suffering from mental disorder within s 1).
11 See the Mental Health Act 1983 s 118(1A) (added by the Mental Health (Wales) Measure 2010
    s 39(2)). As to independent mental health advocates see the independent mental health
    advocates appointed under arrangements made under the Mental Health Act 1983 s 130E (see
    PARA 807).
12 Ie the persons mentioned in the Mental Health Act 1983 s 118(1)(a) or (b) and s 118(1A).
13 Mental Health Act 1983 s 118(2D) (s 118(2A)–(2D) added by the Mental Health Act 2007 s 8).
14 See the Department of Health *Mental Health Act 1983 Code of Practice* (2008) introduction;
    and the Welsh Assemble Government Mental Health Act 1983 *Code of Practice for Wales*
    (2008) introduction. As to the importance of the code see *R (on the application of Munjaz) v
    Mersey Care NHS Trust* [2005] UKHL 58, [2006] 2 AC 148, [2006] 4 All ER 736 (it was held
    that the code has less binding effect than a statutory provision but is more than mere advice;
    there should only be departure from the code where there are cogent reasons for doing so).
15 Ie other than those specified by regulations made for the purposes of the Mental Health
    Act 1983 s 57: see PARA 928. As to the meaning of 'medical treatment' see PARA 926. Certain
    bodies that appear to be concerned must be consulted before the code is prepared or altered: see
    s 118(3).
16 Ie a certificate as to the matters mentioned in the Mental Health Act 1983 s 57(2)(a), (b): see
    PARA 928.
17 As to appointed practitioners see PARA 928 note 10.
18 As to the meaning of 'the regulatory authority' see PARA 573 note 1. The functions of the
    Secretary of State under the Mental Health Act 1983 s 118(2) are transferred to the Care
    Quality Commission: see the Health and Social Care Act 2008 s 52(1)(g); and PARA 573. The
    Care Quality Commission may at any time make proposals relating to the content of the code of
    practice under the Mental Health Act 1983 s 118 in relation to England: see s 118(7) (added by
    the Health and Social Care Act 2008 Sch 3 para 6(3)).
19 Mental Health Act 1983 s 118(2) (amended by the Health and Social Care Act 2008 Sch 3
    para 6(2)). As to care and treatment see also PARA 757 et seq.
20 Mental Health Act 1983 s 118(2A) (as added: see note 13).
21 Mental Health Act 1983 s 118(2B)(a) (as added: see note 13).
22 Mental Health Act 1983 s 118(2B)(b) (as added: see note 13). As to the meaning of 'sexual
    orientation' see the Equality Act 2010 s 12; and DISCRIMINATION (definition applied by the
    Equality Act 2006 s 35 and the Mental Health Act 1983 s 118(2B)(b)).
23 Mental Health Act 1983 s 118(2B)(c) (as added: see note 13).
24 Mental Health Act 1983 s 118(2B)(d) (as added: see note 13).
25 Mental Health Act 1983 s 118(2B)(e) (as added: see note 13).
26 Mental Health Act 1983 s 118(2B)(f) (as added: see note 13).
27 Mental Health Act 1983 s 118(2B)(g) (as added: see note 13).
28 Mental Health Act 1983 s 118(2B)(h) (as added: see note 13).
29 Mental Health Act 1983 s 118(2B)(i) (as added: see note 13).
30 Mental Health Act 1983 s 118(2C) (as added: see note 13).

763.   Codes of practice under the Mental Health (Wales) Measure 2010. The
appropriate national authority[1] may prepare, publish, and from time to time
revise[2], one or more codes of practice for the guidance of: (1) local authorities[3],
local health boards[4], care coordinators[5] or any other persons in relation to their
functions[6] under the Mental Health (Wales) Measure 2010; and (2) for the

guidance of any persons in connection with the operation of the provisions of the Mental Health (Wales) Measure 2010[7]. In performing their functions under the Mental Health (Wales) Measure 2010 the persons mentioned in head (1) must have regard to the code of practice published under these provisions[8].

1   As to the appropriate national authority see PARA 567.
2   Before preparing of revising any such code, the appropriate national authority must consult any persons it considers relevant: Mental Health (Wales) Measure 2010 s 44(4). The appropriate national authority may revoke any code of practice by direction: s 44(8).
3   As to the meaning of 'local authority' see PARA 586 note 1.
4   As to the meaning of 'local health board' see PARA 575 note 6.
5   As to care coordinators see PARA 851.
6   As to the meaning of 'function' see PARA 590 note 2.
7   Mental Health (Wales) Measure 2010 s 44(1), (2). As to the current code of practice see the Welsh Government *Code of Practice to Parts 2 and 3 of the Mental Health (Wales) Measure 2010* (2012).
8   Mental Health (Wales) Measure 2010 s 44(3).

(3) ADMISSION

(i) Voluntary Admission

764. Informal admission. Nothing in the Mental Health Act 1983 is to be construed as preventing a patient[1] who requires treatment for mental disorder[2] from being admitted to any hospital or registered establishment[3] in pursuance of arrangements made in that behalf and without any application[4], order[5] or direction[6] rendering him liable to be detained under that Act, or from remaining in any hospital or registered establishment in pursuance of such arrangements after he has ceased[7] to be so liable to be detained[8].

The use of compulsory powers on a willing and capable patient is not expressly disallowed and can be used, for example, if the patient has a history of changing his mind upon admission[9].

Whilst such provisions allow for the informal admission of patients who are not capable of consenting to admission, where such an admission amounts to a deprivation of liberty this will be in breach of the patients' right to liberty[10]. The deprivation of liberty of a person over the age of 18 who lacks mental capacity is now also provided for under the Mental Capacity Act 2005[11].

Where there is a real and immediate risk of suicide of a voluntary patient there is an operational duty of the right to life under the Human Rights Act 1998 to take reasonable steps to protect such a patient[12].

1   As to the meaning of 'patient' see PARA 758 note 4. As to the informal admission of minors see PARA 765.
2   As to the meaning of 'mental disorder' see PARA 761.
3   As to the meaning of 'hospital' see PARA 577; and as to the meaning of 'registered establishment' see PARA 578. See also PARA 585.
4   Ie an application for admission for assessment or for treatment: see the Mental Health Act 1983 ss 2–4; and PARAS 767–769.
5   Ie a hospital order made by a court for the admission and detention of an offender in hospital: see the Mental Health Act 1983 s 37; and PARA 864.
6   Ie a transfer direction made by the appropriate national authority for the removal of a prisoner to a specified hospital for treatment for mental disorder: see the Mental Health Act 1983 ss 47(1), 48; and PARAS 892–894. As to the appropriate national authority see PARA 567.
7   As to the duration of authority to detain patients admitted for treatment see PARAS 908–912.
8   Mental Health Act 1983 s 131(1) (amended by the Care Standards Act 2000 Sch 4 paras 9(1), (2)). As to when compulsory admission powers should be exercised see the Department of Health *Mental Health Act 1983 Code of Practice* (2008) paras 4.9–4.12; and the

Welsh Assembly Government *Mental Health Act 1983 Code of Practice for Wales* (2008) para 2.27. As to the Codes of Practice see PARA 762. This provision applies to patients who are capable of consenting to their admission and treatment, and also to those patients who are not capable of consenting but do not resist or object to admission to hospital. Capable patients admitted informally under this provision are not subject to the consent to treatment provisions in the Mental Health Act 1983 Pt 4 and can refuse treatment.

9   See the Department of Health *Mental Health Act 1983 Code of Practice* (2008) para 4.11; and the Welsh Assembly Government *Mental Health Act 1983 Code of Practice for Wales* (2008) para 2.28.

10   See *R v Bournewood Community and Mental Health NHS Trust, ex p L* [1999] 1 AC 458, [1998] 3 All ER 289, HL. A patient may be readmitted informally, in accordance with the Mental Health Act 1983 s 131, although unable to consent for lack of capacity: *R v Bournewood Community and Mental Health NHS Trust, ex p L.* But detention in such circumstances will be contrary to the Convention for the Protection of Human Rights and Fundamental Freedoms (Rome, 4 November 1950; TS 71 (1953); Cmd 8969), art 5(1), (4) unless there are procedural safeguards to protect the patient against an assumption by the authority of full control over his liberty and treatment: Application 45508/99 *HL v United Kingdom* (2004) 40 EHRR 461, 81 BMLR 131, (2004) Times, 19 October, ECtHR. This is the so-called 'Bournewood Gap' which was filled by amendments made to the Mental Capacity Act 2005 by the Mental Health Act 2007 and the introduction of the deprivation of liberty safeguards under that Act. See note 11. See the Department of Health *Mental Health Act 1983 Code of Practice* (2008) para 4.16 et seq which offers guidance on when the safeguards under the Mental Capacity Act 2005 may be appropriate in preference to the Mental Health Act 1983. See also PARA 562 on the interaction between the two Acts. For the purposes of the Welsh Assembly Government *Mental Health Act 1983 Code of Practice for Wales* (2008) an informal inpatient is a patient who has come to the ward and who has not acted to resist (verbally or physically) the admission procedure and such a patient remains an inpatient until they have removed themselves (or been removed) from the hospital: see para 8.5. As to the European Convention on Human Rights and Fundamental Freedoms art 5 see RIGHTS AND FREEDOMS.

11   As to the deprivation of liberty under the Mental Capacity Act 2005 of a patient lacking capacity see PARA 603 et seq. Thus the admission to hospital of a person lacking capacity for the assessment or treatment of mental disorder must take place either under the powers of the Mental Health Act 1983 or the Mental Capacity Act 2005 if they are aged over 16 and admission is in their best interests. If no deprivation of liberty is involved then the use of the Mental Capacity Act 2005 s 5 and 6 will permit those caring for the person to use restraint to prevent harm, if the restraint is proportionate to both the likelihood and seriousness of the harm. The Code of Practice offers guidance on the considerations relevant to the use of either the Mental Health Act 1983 or the Mental Capacity Act 2005 in these circumstances: see paras 4.16–4.23.

12   See *Rabone v Pennine Care NHS Foundation Trust* [2012] UKSC 2, [2012] 2 All ER 381 (voluntary patient committed suicide after being permitted to leave the hospital; trust had an operational duty under the Human Rights Act 1998, Sch 1, art 2 (right to life)).

765. Informal admission of minors. In the case of a patient[1] aged 16 or 17 years[2] who has capacity to consent[3] to the making of informal admission[4] arrangements[5], if the patient consents to the making of the arrangements, they may be made, carried out and determined on the basis of that consent even though there are one or more persons who have parental responsibility[6] for him[7]. However, if the patient does not consent to the making of the arrangements, they may not be made, carried out or determined on the basis of the consent of a person who has parental responsibility for him[8].

In respect of any patient who has not attained the age of 18 years and who is admitted to, or remains in, a hospital[9] in pursuance of informal arrangements[10], the managers of the hospital must ensure that the patient's environment in the hospital is suitable having regard to his age (subject to his needs)[11]. For the purpose of deciding how to fulfil this duty, the managers must consult a person who appears to them to have knowledge or experience of cases involving patients who have not attained the age of 18 years which makes him suitable to be consulted[12].

1   As to the meaning of 'patient' see PARA 758 note 4. There is no age below which applications for compulsory admission to hospital under the Mental Health Act 1983 (see PARAS 767–770) cannot be made.

2   A person attains the age expressed in years at the commencement of the relevant anniversary of the date of his birth: see the Family Law Reform Act 1969 s 9(1); and CHILDREN AND YOUNG PERSONS. Regulations may make provision for the determination in accordance with the regulations of the age of any person whose exact age cannot be ascertained by reference to the registers kept under the Births and Deaths Registration Act 1953 (see REGISTRATION CONCERNING THE INDIVIDUAL): Mental Health Act 1983 s 32(1), (2)(d). Provision was formerly made by the Mental Health (Hospital and Guardianship) Regulations 1960, SI 1960/1241, reg 26, but the regulations were revoked without replacement of this provision by the Mental Health (Hospital, Guardianship and Consent to Treatment) Regulations 1983, SI 1983/893, reg 20, Sch 2.

3   For this purpose the reference to a patient who has capacity is to be read in accordance with the Mental Capacity Act 2005 (see PARA 601 et seq): Mental Health Act 1983 s 131(5)(a) (s 131(2) substituted and s 131(3)–(5) added by the Mental Health Act 2007 s 43).

4   Ie under the Mental Health Act 1983 s 131(1) (see PARA 764).

5   Mental Health Act 1983 s 131(2) (as added: see note 3).

6   As to the meaning of 'parental responsibility' see the Children Act 1989 s 3; and CHILDREN AND YOUNG PERSONS vol 9 (2012) PARA 151 et seq (definition applied by the Mental Health Act 1989 s 131(5) (as added: see note 3)).

7   Mental Health Act 1983 s 131(3) (as added: see note 3).

8   Mental Health Act 1983 s 131(4) (as added: see note 3). A parent or other person with parental responsibility may consent to treatment on behalf of a minor who does not have the capacity to do so for himself (see e g *R v Kirklees Metropolitan Borough Council, ex p C* [1992] 2 FCR 321, [1992] 2 FLR 117); but a minor below the age of 16 who has sufficient capacity may consent to treatment on his own behalf, irrespective of parental wishes (*Gillick v West Norfolk and Wisbech Area Health Authority* [1986] AC 112, [1985] 3 All ER 402, HL). It is submitted that these principles apply equally to informal admission to hospital. Quaere whether if a minor of any age has sufficient capacity and does not consent, a parent or other person with parental responsibility can nevertheless consent on his behalf: see *Re R (A Minor) (Wardship: Consent to Treatment)* [1992] Fam 11 at 24–25, [1991] 4 All ER 177 at 186–187, CA, per Lord Donaldson of Lymington MR. The court, in the exercise of its inherent jurisdiction, may certainly do so: *Re J (A Minor) (Inherent Jurisdiction: Consent to Treatment)* (1992) Times, 15 July, CA. See also CHILDREN AND YOUNG PERSONS vol 9 (2012) PARA 4. Guidance on the care and treatment of children and young persons under the age of 18 is given in the Department of Health *Mental Health Act 1983 Code of Practice* (2008) Chapter 36 and the Welsh Assembly Government *Mental Health Act 1983 Code of Practice for Wales* (2008) Chapter 33. As to the Codes of Practice see PARA 762.

9   For this purpose 'hospital' includes a registered establishment: Mental Health Act 1983 s 131A(4) (added by the Mental Health Act 2007 s 31(3)).

10   Ie arrangements under the Mental Health Act 1983 s 131(1) (see PARA 764).

11   Mental Health Act 1983 s 131A(1)(b), (2) (as added: see note 3). See the Department of Health *Mental Health Act 1983 Code of Practice* (2008) paras 36.67–36.74. A locked unit in a psychiatric hospital has been held to be 'accommodation which is provided for the purpose of restricting the liberty' of children to whom the Children Act 1989 s 25 (use of accommodation for restricting liberty) applies: *R v Northampton Juvenile Court, ex p Hammersmith and Fulham London Borough Council* [1985] FLR 193, [1985] Fam Law 124. A locked unit at which staff would endeavour to stop a child from leaving the premises unaccompanied and, where the permission of the court is sought to achieve this was held not to be 'secure accommodation': *South Glamorgan County Council v W and B* [1993] 1 FCR 626, [1993] 1 FLR 574. Secure accommodation is accommodation that is designed for or has as its primary purpose the restriction of liberty: *Re C (a minor) (detention for medical treatment)* [1997] 3 FCR 49, [1997] 2 FLR 180 (a unit for the treatment of anorexia was held not to be 'secure accommodation'). The Children Act 1989 s 25 does not, however, apply to a child who is detained under any provision of the Mental Health Act 1983 or in respect of whom an order has been made under the Powers of the Criminal Courts (Sentencing) Act 2000 s 90 or s 91 (detention at Her Majesty's pleasure or for a specified period) (see SENTENCING AND DISPOSITION OF OFFENDERS vol 92 (2010) PARA 81): Children (Secure Accommodation) Regulations 1991, SI 1991/1505, reg 5 (amended by SI 2002/546; SI 2002/2935). The High Court has power under its inherent jurisdiction to order the detention of a child in a specified unit for the purposes of medical treatment without her agreement (see *Re C* above) and can authorise the use of reasonable force if necessary (*Norfolk and Norwich Healthcare (NHS)*

Trust v W [1997] 1 FCR 269, [1996] 2 FLR 613). A primary aim of the Mental Health Act 1983 s 131A is to ensure that children are not accommodated on adult psychiatric wards (as from 1 December 2003, Department of Health letter to Strategic Health Authority Chief Executives dated 29 June 2007). See also the United Nations Convention on the Rights of the Child art 37(c). The UK has entered a reservation that applies if there is a lack of suitable facilities for a particular individual or where it is deemed to be mutually beneficial to mix adults and children.

12   Mental Health Act 1983 s 131A(3) (as added: see note 3).

(ii) Compulsory Admission

766. Regulations for compulsory admission, reception and removal. The appropriate national authority[1] has power to make regulations[2] prescribing matters which, under the statutory provisions for compulsory admission to hospital[3] are required or authorised to be prescribed, and otherwise for carrying those provisions into effect[4]. The appropriate national authority may[5] also make regulations prescribing the manner in which the functions of hospital managers[6], local social services authorities[7], local health boards[8], special health authorities[9], primary care trusts[10], national health service trusts or NHS foundation trusts[11] are to be exercised[12].

1   As to the appropriate national authority see PARA 567.
2   As to such regulations see the Mental Health (Hospital, Guardianship and Treatment) (England) Regulations 2008, SI 2008/1184; the Mental Health (Hospital, Guardianship, Community Treatment and Consent to Treatment) (Wales) Regulations 2008, SI 2008/2439, and PARAS 886–891.
3   Ie matters under the Mental Health Act 1983 Pt 2 (ss 2–34): see PARA 767 et seq.
4   See the Mental Health Act 1983 s 32(1). The regulations may, in particular, make provision for: (1) prescribing the form of any application, recommendation, report, order, notice or other document to be made or given; (2) prescribing the manner in which such documents may be proved and served; (3) requiring such bodies as may be prescribed by the regulations to keep such registers or other records as may be so prescribed in respect of patients liable to be detained or subject to guardianship under the Mental Health Act 1983 Pt 2 (ss 2–34) or community patients and to furnish or make available to those patients, and their relatives, such written statements of their rights and powers as may be so prescribed; (4) determining the age of patients; and (5) enabling the functions of nearest relatives to be delegated in certain circumstances: see s 32(2) (amended by the Mental Health (Patients in the Community) Act 1995 Sch 1 para 2; and the Mental Health Act 2007 Sch 3 para 15, Sch 11 Pt 5). Regulations made by virtue of the Mental Health Act 1983 s 32(2)(d) apply for the purposes of Pt 4 (ss 56–64) as they apply for the purposes of Pt 2: s 64(1C) (added by the Mental Health Act 2007 s 28(9)).
5   This is subject to the Mental Health Act 1983 s 23(4), (6) (see PARA 913).
6   As to the meaning of 'managers' see PARA 778.
7   As to the meaning of 'local social services authority' see PARA 579.
8   As to the meaning of 'local health board' see PARA 575 note 6.
9   As to the meaning of 'special health authority' see PARA 575 note 4.
10   As to the meaning of 'primary care trust' see PARA 575 note 5. As from 1 April 2013 the words 'primary care trust' are repealed by the Health and Social Care Act 2012 Sch 5 para 27: see the Health and Social Care Act 2012 (Commencement No 4, Transitional, Savings and Transitory Provisions) Order 2013, SI 2013/160, art 2(2).
11   As to national health service trusts and NHS foundation trusts see HEALTH SERVICES vol 54 (2008) PARA 155 et seq.
12   Such regulations may in particular provide for the circumstances and conditions under which functions may be performed by officers or other persons acting on behalf of the managers, boards, authorities and trusts: Mental Health Act 1983 s 32(3) (amended by the National Health Service and Community Care Act 1990 s 66(1), Sch 9 para 24(5); the Health Authorities Act 1995 Sch 1 para 107(4); the Health and Social Care (Community Health and Standards) Act 2003 s 34, Sch 4 paras 50, 55; the Mental Health Act 2007 s 45(2); SI 2000/90; SI 2007/961; and amended (see note 10)). As to the regulations that have been made see the Mental Health (Hospital, Guardianship and Treatment) (England) Regulations 2008,

SI 2008/1184; the Mental Health (Hospital, Guardianship, Community Treatment and Consent to Treatment) (Wales) Regulations 2008, SI 2008/2439; and PARAS 886–891.

767. Compulsory admission for assessment. A patient[1] may be admitted to a hospital[2], and there detained for the period allowed[3], in pursuance of an application for admission for assessment[4]. The patient may apply to the appropriate tribunal[5] within the period of 14 days beginning with the day of his admission[6].

An application for admission for assessment may be made[7] in respect of a patient on the grounds: (1) that he is suffering from mental disorder[8] of a nature or degree which warrants his detention in a hospital[9] for assessment, or assessment followed by medical treatment[10], for at least a limited period[11]; and (2) that he ought to be so detained in the interests of his own health or safety or with a view to the protection of other persons[12]. Every application must be founded on the written recommendations[13] in the prescribed form[14] of two registered medical practitioners[15], including in each case a statement that in the opinion of the practitioner the conditions set out under heads (1) and (2) above are complied with[16].

The maximum period[17] for which a patient so admitted to hospital for assessment may be detained is 28 days, beginning with the day of admission[18]; and he must not be detained after that period unless, before its expiration, he has become liable to be detained by virtue of any subsequent application[19], order[20] or direction[21] which may have been made[22].

1   As to the meaning of 'patient' generally see PARA 758 note 4.

2   As to the meaning of 'hospital', which for this purpose includes a registered establishment, see PARA 577. As to the meaning of 'registered establishment' see PARA 578.

3   As to the maximum duration of detention see the Mental Health Act 1983 s 2(4); and note 18.

4   Mental Health Act 1983 s 2(1).

As to the criteria for detention of persons of unsound mind under the Convention for the Protection of Human Rights and Fundamental Freedoms (Rome, 4 November 1950; TS 71 (1953); Cmd 8969) see *Winterwerp v Netherlands* (1981) 4 EHRR 228, ECtHR generally, and Application 26629/95 *Litwa v Poland* (2000) 33 EHRR 1267, 63 BMLR 199 on the issue of proportionality. See also Application 517/02 *Kolanis v United Kingdom* (2005) 42 EHRR 206, 84 BMLR 102, ECtHR; *Johnson v United Kingdom* (1997) 27 EHRR 296, 40 BMLR 1. As to the proper purpose of detention this includes not only therapy and medication and other clinical treatment to cure or alleviate the condition but also control and supervision to prevent harm to self or others persons: Application 50272/99 *Hutchison Reid v United Kingdom* [2003] ECHR 50272/99, 37 EHRR 211, 14 BHRC 41. As to the appropriate place of detention see *Aerts v Belgium* (1998) 29 EHRR 50, 5 BHRC 382. As to the Convention see RIGHTS AND FREEDOMS. As to the informal detention of patients who are not capable of consenting to detention see *R v Bournewood Community and Mental Health NHS Trust, ex p L* [1999] 1 AC 458, [1998] 3 All ER 289, HL; Application 45508/99 *HL v United Kingdom* (2004) 40 EHRR 761, 81 BMLR 131, ECtHR; and PARA 597. Hospital managers must refer to the appropriate tribunal a patient who is admitted to a hospital in pursuance of an application for admission for assessment: see s 68; and PARA 964.

The Department of Health *Mental Health Act 1983 Code of Practice* (2008) para 4.1 et seq gives general guidance on the making of applications for detention in hospital under the Mental Health Act 1983 Pt 2 (ss 2–34). See also the Welsh Assembly Government *Mental Health Act 1983 Code of Practice for Wales* (2008) para 2.1 et seq. For guidance on the choice between admission for assessment under the Mental Health Act 1983 s 2 or admission for treatment under s 3 (see PARA 768) see the Department of *Health Mental Health Act 1983 Code of Practice* (2008) paras 4.25–4.27; and the Welsh Assembly Government *Mental Health Act 1983 Code of Practice for Wales* (2008) paras 5.1–5.4. For guidance on the choice between detention and reliance on the Mental Capacity Act 2005 see the Department of Health *Mental Health Act 1983 Code of Practice* (2008) paras 4.13–4.24; and the Welsh Assembly Government *Mental Health Act 1983 Code of Practice for Wales* (2008) paras 2.29–2.32. The choice of section should be guided by the principle of least restriction: Department of *Health Mental*

Health Act 1983 Code of Practice (2008) para 1.3; and Welsh Assembly Government *Mental Health Act 1983 Code of Practice for Wales* (2008) para 5.2. As to the Codes of Practice see PARA 762.

5 As to the meaning of 'the appropriate tribunal' see PARA 955.

6 See the Mental Health Act 1983 s 66(1)(a), (i), (2)(a); and PARA 961. The Tribunal Procedure (First-tier Tribunal) (Health, Education and Social Care Chamber) Rules 2008, SI 2008/2699, r 32(1) applies and r 12(2) sets out provisions for the calculation of the time periods. See also *R (on the application of Modaresi) v Secretary of State for Health* [2011] EWCA Civ 1359, [2012] PTSR 999 (application from a 'section 2' patient which was received at the tribunal office on day fifteen was valid because the hospital administrator's office had been closed for the whole of the preceding day and the period before (New Year holidays). As to the criteria for discharge by the tribunal see s 72(1)(a); and PARA 967. Lack of automatic referral does not render the Mental Health Act 1983 s 2 incompatible with the European Convention on Human Rights and Fundamental Freedoms (Rome, 4 November 1950; TS 71 (1953); Cmd 8969, art 5(4): *R (on the application of H) v Secretary of State for Health* [2005] UKHL 60, [2006] 1 AC 441, [2005] 4 All ER 1311. See also PARA 842 note 27.

7 Applications may be made either by the nearest relative of the patient (see PARA 839) or by an approved mental health professional (see PARA 815): see the Mental Health Act 1983 s 11(1); and PARA 847. As to the meaning of 'nearest relative' see PARA 839; and as to the meaning of 'approved mental health professional' see PARA 815 note 2. As to applications by approved mental health professionals see PARA 821. For general requirements for applications for admission see PARA 847. As to the forms for an application for admission for assessment under s 2 see the Mental Health (Hospital, Guardianship and Treatment) (England) Regulations 2008, SI 2008/1184, reg 4(1)(a), Sch 1; and the Mental Health (Hospital, Guardianship, Community Treatment and Consent to Treatment) (Wales) Regulations 2008, SI 2008/2439, reg 4(1)(a), Sch 1.

8 As to the meaning of 'mental disorder' see PARA 761.

9 See *R v Gardner, ex p L, R v Hallstrom, ex p W* [1986] QB 1090, sub nom *R v Hallstrom, ex p W (No 2)* [1986] 2 All ER 306; and PARA 768 note 11.

10 As to the meaning of 'medical treatment' see PARA 926. As to the treatment which may be given to the patient while detained for assessment see PARAS 924, 927 et seq.

The detention must be related to the mental disorder of the person being detained, so where a pregnant woman, who was suffering from depression, was detained in order to carry out an enforced Caesarean section, that detention was unlawful: *St George's Healthcare NHS Trust v S, R v Collins, ex p S* [1998] 3 All ER 673, CA.

11 Mental Health Act 1983 s 2(2)(a). In view of the definition of patient in s 145 (see PARA 758) there is power to admit a patient under s 2 if she appears to be suffering from mental disorder, on the ground that she is so suffering, even though it turns out on assessment that she is not: *R v Kirklees Metropolitan Borough Council, ex p C (a minor)* [1993] 2 FCR 381, [1993] 2 FLR 187, CA; also *St George's Healthcare NHS Trust v S, R v Collins, ex p S* [1999] Fam 26, [1998] 3 All ER 673, [1998] 3 WLR 936.

12 Mental Health Act 1983 s 2(2)(b).

13 As to medical recommendations see PARA 849.

14 As to the forms for any medical recommendations for the purposes of the Mental Health Act 1983 s 2 see the Mental Health (Hospital, Guardianship and Treatment) (England) Regulations 2008, SI 2008/1184, reg 4(1)(b), Sch 1; and the Mental Health (Hospital, Guardianship, Community Treatment and Consent to Treatment) (Wales) Regulations 2008, SI 2008/2439, reg 4(1)(b), Sch 1. The recommendations may be joint in form: Mental Health Act 1983 s 11(7).

15 As to registered medical practitioners see MEDICAL PROFESSIONS vol 74 (2011) PARA 176 et seq.

16 Mental Health Act 1983 s 2(3).

17 As to the power to order a patient's discharge during that time see the Mental Health Act 1983 s 23; and PARA 913.

18 Mental Health Act 1983 s 2(4). However, where immediately before the expiration of that period an application has been made to the county court for an order transferring the functions of the nearest relative, that period must be extended until the application is finally disposed of, and, if the application is granted, for a further seven days: ss 2(4), 29(3)(c), (d), (4). As to the power of the county court to make such orders see PARA 842. See also *R v Wilson ex p Williamson* [1996] COD 42 as to the duration of this order.

19 Ie an application for admission for treatment under the Mental Health Act 1983 s 3(1): see PARA 768. It will, of course, be possible for a patient who is not unwilling to do so to remain in hospital as an informal patient (see PARA 764) after being detained for assessment.

20 Ie a hospital order made by a court having criminal jurisdiction: see the Mental Health Act 1983 ss 37, 40; and PARA 864. It seems unlikely that many patients will, while detained for assessment, become the subject of a hospital order. Cf the power of magistrates to remand to hospital for report under s 35 (see PARA 862) or to remand for medical examination under the Powers of Criminal Courts (Sentencing) Act 2000 s 11 (see MAGISTRATES vol 71 (2013) PARA 558).

21 See the Mental Health Act 1983 ss 47, 48, 51 (empowering the appropriate national authority by warrant to direct the removal of a prisoner to hospital); and PARAS 892–898.

22 Mental Health Act 1983 s 2(4). There is no common law power to detain once the statutory period has expired: *B v Forsey* 1988 SC (HL) 28, 1988 SLT 572, HL. It could in certain circumstances be appropriate to readmit a patient under s 2 subsequent to a discharge to hospital: *R (on the application of Von Brandenburg (aka Hanley)) v East London and the City Mental Health NHS Trust* [2003] UKHL 58, [2004] 2 AC 280, [2004] 1 All ER 400.

768. Compulsory admission for treatment. A patient[1] may be admitted to a hospital[2], and there detained for the period allowed[3], in pursuance of an application for admission for treatment[4]. The patient may apply to the appropriate tribunal[5] within the period of six months beginning with the day of his admission[6].

An application for admission for treatment may be made[7] in respect of a patient on the grounds: (1) that the patient is suffering from mental disorder[8] of a nature or degree which makes it appropriate for him to receive medical treatment[9] in hospital[10]; (2) that it is necessary for the health or safety of the patient or for the protection of other persons that he should receive such treatment[11] and that it cannot be provided unless he is detained[12]; and (3) that appropriate medical treatment is available for him[13].

Every application must be founded on the written recommendations[14] in the prescribed form[15] of two registered medical practitioners[16], including in each case a statement that in the opinion of the practitioner the conditions set out under heads (1) to (3) above are complied with[17]. Each recommendation must include prescribed particulars of the grounds for that opinion so far as it relates to the conditions under heads (1) and (3) above; and also a statement of the reasons for that opinion so far as it relates to the conditions under head (3) above, specifying whether other methods of dealing with the patient are available, and if so why they are not appropriate[18].

1 As to the meaning of 'patient' generally see PARA 758 note 4.

2 As to the meaning of 'hospital', which for this purpose includes a registered establishment, see PARA 577. As to the meaning of 'registered establishment' see PARA 578.

3 The period allowed in the first instance is a period not exceeding six months beginning with the day of admission (see the Mental Health Act 1983 s 20(1)), but the authority for detention may be renewed at the expiration of that period for a further period of six months, and thereafter for one year at a time (see s 20(2)). See PARAS 908, 911. As to the power to order discharge see s 23; and PARA 913.

4 Mental Health Act 1983 s 3(1). As to the forms for an application for treatment under s 3 see the Mental Health (Hospital, Guardianship and Treatment) (England) Regulations 2008, SI 2008/1184, reg 4(1)(c), Sch 1; and the Mental Health (Hospital, Guardianship, Community Treatment and Consent to Treatment) (Wales) Regulations 2008, SI 2008/2439, reg 4(1)(c), Sch 1. An application may be made even though the patient is already in hospital informally or liable to be detained in pursuance of an application for admission for assessment: see the Mental Health Act 1983 s 5(1); and PARA 770. As to the power to make a community treatment order for a patient detained under the Mental Health Act 1983 s 3, see ss 17A–17G; and PARA 797. Hospital managers must refer to the appropriate tribunal a patient who is admitted to a hospital in pursuance of an application for admission for treatment: see s 68; and PARA 964.

For general guidance on the assessment of patients see the Department of Health *Mental Health Act 1983 Code of Practice* (2008) para 4.28 et seq and the Welsh Assembly Government *Mental Health Act 1983 Code of Practice for Wales* (2008) paras 5.1–5.4; and for guidance on the choice between admission for treatment under the Mental Health Act 1983 s 3 and admission for assessment under s 2 (see PARA 767) see the Department of Health *Mental Health Act 1983 Code of Practice* (2008) paras 4.25–4.27 and para 1.3 with regard to the principle of least restriction; and the Welsh Assembly Government *Mental Health Act 1983 Code of Practice for Wales* (2008) para 5.2 and para 5.2 with regard to the principle of least restriction. As to the Codes of Practice see PARA 762. For guidance on the 'appropriate treatment' test see the Department of Health *Mental Health Act 1983 Code of Practice* (2008) Chapter 6; and Welsh Assembly Government *Mental Health Act 1983 Code of Practice for Wales* (2008) Chapter 4 and on personality disorder see the Department of Health *Mental Health Act 1983 Code of Practice* (2008) Chapter 35.

Where a patient has been unlawfully detained as a result of a failure to comply with the relevant statutory requirements, an application for a writ of habeas corpus is an appropriate remedy for the patient: *Re S-C (Mental Patient: Habeas Corpus)* [1996] QB 599, [1996] 1 All ER 532, CA. See also *Barker v Barking, Havering and Brentwood Community Healthcare NHS Trust (Warley Hospital)* [1999] 1 FLR 106, (1998) 47 BMLR 112, CA; *M (by his litigation friend TM) v Hackney London Borough Council* [2011] EWCA Civ 4, [2011] 3 All ER 529, [2011] 1 WLR 2873.

5   As to the meaning of 'the appropriate tribunal' see PARA 955.

6   See the Mental Health Act 1983 s 66(1)(b), (2)(b); and PARA 961. See *R (on the application of Modaresi) v Secretary of State for Health* [2011] EWCA Civ 1359, [2012] PTSR 999.

An order discharging a patient's detention is not a bar to a subsequent detention under s 3: *R v Managers of South Western Hospital, ex p M* [1993] QB 683, [1994] 1 All ER 161; *R v North West London Mental Health NHS Trust, ex p Stewart* [1998] QB 628, [1997] 4 All ER 871, CA. See also *R (on the application of Von Brandenburg (aka Hanley)) v East London and the City Mental Health Trust* [2003] UKHL 58, [2004] 2 AC 280, [2004] 1 All ER 400. And see also *R (on the application of Ashworth Hospital Authority) v Mental Health Review Tribunal for West Midlands and Northwest Region* [2002] EWCA Civ 923, [2003] 1 WLR 127, 70 BMLR 40 and *R (on the application of Care Principles Ltd) v Mental Health Review Tribunal* [2006] EWHC 3194 (Admin), 94 BMLR 145 for decisions on the appropriateness of a stay of a tribunal's decision to discharge a patient as an alternative to re-sectioning in the absence of new information material to the tribunal's decision. If hospital managers are aware of a recent tribunal discharge any application made requires a critical consideration of the justification for the application for re-admission.

7   Applications may be made either by the nearest relative of the patient (see PARA 839) or by an approved mental health professional (see PARA 815): see the Mental Health Act 1983 s 11(1); and PARA 847. As to applications by approved mental health professionals see PARA 821; and for general requirements as to applications for admission see PARA 847.

8   As to the meaning of 'mental disorder' see PARA 761.

9   Patients admitted under the Mental Health Act 1983 s 3 are subject to the consent to treatment provisions under Pt 4: see s 56(3); and PARA 924. As to the meaning of 'medical treatment' see PARA 926. As to the treatment which may be given in hospital see PARAS 924, 927 et seq. As to 'nature' or 'degree' see *R v Mental Health Review Tribunal for the South Thames Region, ex p Smith* (1998) 47 BMLR 104. It may be lawful to detain a patient on the ground of 'nature' in circumstances where they have ceased taking medication and are not showing a current manifestation of symptoms of a 'degree' warranting admission to hospital, if it is assessed on the basis of the patient's history that a relapse in symptoms is likely: see *Smirek v Williamson* [2000] EWCA Civ 3025.

10   Mental Health Act 1983 s 3(2)(a) (amended by the Mental Health Act 2007 Sch 1 para 2).

11   Admission for treatment is restricted to treatment in a hospital as an in-patient: *R v Gardner, ex p L, R v Hallstrom, ex p W* [1986] QB 1090, sub nom *R v Hallstrom, ex p W (No 2)* [1986] 2 All ER 306. This was confirmed in *Barker v Barking, Havering and Brentwood Community Healthcare NHS Trust (Warley Hospital)* [1999] 1 FLR 106, (1998) 47 BMLR 112, CA. See *R (on the application of DR) v Mersey Care NHS Trust* [2002] EWHC 1810 (Admin) which considers the renewal powers under the Mental Health Act 1983 s 20(4)(a) (see PARA 910) holding in that context that a 'significant component' of a treatment plan being 'at' a hospital in contrast to 'in-patient' treatment was sufficient. It is submitted that on the issue of admission criteria under s 3(2)(a) this decision is obiter.

12   See the Mental Health Act 1983 s 3(2)(c). As to the criteria for detention of persons of unsound mind under the Convention for the Protection of Human Rights and Fundamental Freedoms (Rome, 4 November 1950; TS 71 (1953); Cmd 8969) see *Winterwerp v Netherlands* (1981) 4 EHRR 228, ECtHR. See also Application 517/02 *Kolanis v United Kingdom* (2005) 42 EHRR 206, 84 BMLR 102, ECtHR and Application 26629/95 *Litwa v Poland* (2000) 33 EHRR 1267, 63 BMLR 199, ECtHR (on the issue of proportionality). See also *Aerts v Belgium* (1998) 29 EHRR 50, 5 BHRC 382, ECtHR (conditions of detention under the Convention for the

Protection of Human Rights and Fundamental Freedoms art 5 for psychiatrically ill prisoners); *R (on the application of H) v London North and East Region Mental Health Review Tribunal (Secretary of State for Health intervening)* [2001] EWCA Civ 415, [2002] QB 1, [2001] 3 WLR 512 (continued detention of an asymptomatic patient); and PARA 767 note 4.

As to the Mental Health Act 1983 s 3(2)(c) see *Reid v Secretary of State for Scotland* [1999] 2 AC 512, [1999] 1 All ER 481, HL (test is 'necessity' not 'desirability'); *Johnson v United Kingdom* (1997) 27 EHRR 296, 40 BMLR 1. As to the proper purpose of detention this includes not only therapy and medication and other clinical treatment to cure or alleviate the condition but also control and supervision to prevent harm to self or other persons: see *Reid v Secretary of State for Scotland* above. As to the Convention for the Protection of Human Rights and Fundamental Freedoms and the protection of the public see *Ashingdane v United Kingdom* (1985) 7 EHRR 528, ECtHR; Application 26629/95 *Litwa v Poland* (2000) 63 BMLR 199, ECtHR; and RIGHTS AND FREEDOMS.

13   Mental Health Act 1983 s 3(2)(d) (added by the Mental Health Act 2007 s 4(2)(d)). For the purposes of the Mental Health Act 1983 references to appropriate medical treatment, in relation to a person suffering from mental disorder, are references to medical treatment which is appropriate in his case, taking into account the nature and degree of the mental disorder and all other circumstances of his case: s 3(4) (added by the Mental Health Act 2007 s 4(3)). This 'appropriate treatment' provision replaces the previous 'treatability' test whereby the treatment of certain categories of disorder had to be likely to alleviate or prevent a deterioration of the person's condition (now repealed by the Mental Health Act 2007). Under the Mental Health Act 1984 s 145(4) (see PARA 926) the purpose of any medical treatment must now be to alleviate, or prevent a worsening of the disorder or one or more of its manifestations. The European Convention on Human Rights art 5(1)(e) imposes no requirement that there should be efficacious treatment available for the purposes of justifying a detention. Confinement might also be necessary where a person needs control and supervision to prevent them from causing harm to themselves or others: Application 33670/96 *Koniarska v United Kingdom;* Application 50272/99 *Hutchison Reid v United Kingdom* [2003] ECHR 50272/99, 37 EHRR 211, 14 BHRC 41. See the Department of Health *Mental Health Act 1983 Code of Practice* (2008) para 6.16. Treatment need not reduce risk but must be appropriate. Appropriate treatment is available where there is a potential for therapy to benefit the patient (eg milieu therapy): *MD v Nottinghamshire Health Care NHS Trust* [2010] UKUT 59 (AAC). See also *DL-H v Devon Partnership NHS Trust* [2010] UKUT 102 (AAC) (patient with personality disorder refusing treatment).

14   As to medical recommendations see PARA 849.

15   As to the forms for any medical recommendations for the purposes of the Mental Health Act 1983 s 3 see the Mental Health (Hospital, Guardianship and Treatment) (England) Regulations 2008, SI 2008/1184, reg 4(1)(d), Sch 1; and the Mental Health (Hospital, Guardianship, Community Treatment and Consent to Treatment) (Wales) Regulations 2008, SI 2008/2439, reg 4(1)(d), Sch 1. The recommendations may be joint in form: see the Mental Health Act 1983 s 11(7).

16   As to registered medical practitioners see MEDICAL PROFESSIONS vol 74 (2011) PARA 176 et seq.

17   Mental Health Act 1983 s 3(3).

18   Mental Health Act 1983 s 3(3) (amended by the Mental Health Act 2007 s 4(2)(d)).

769. Compulsory admission for assessment in an emergency.   In any case of urgent necessity, an application for admission to hospital[1] for assessment may be made either by an approved mental health professional[2] or by the nearest relative[3] of the patient founded on one only of the two medical recommendations which are required[4] in admission for assessment[5]. This is known as an emergency application[6]. The application must include a statement, to be verified by the medical recommendation, that: (1) it is of urgent necessity for the patient to be admitted and detained for assessment[7]; and (2) compliance with the normal requirements relating to applications for admission for assessment would involve undesirable delay[8]. The medical recommendation for admission for assessment must be given, if practicable, by a practitioner who has previous acquaintance with the patient, and must otherwise comply with the general requirements[9] as to medical recommendations[10].

An emergency application cannot be renewed and ceases to have effect[11] on the expiration of 72 hours from the time when the patient is admitted to hospital unless a second medical recommendation[12] for assessment is given and is received by the managers[13] of the hospital within that period[14].

Patients admitted under these provisions are not subject to the consent to treatment provisions[15].

1 As to the meaning of 'hospital', which for this purpose includes a registered establishment, see PARA 577. As to the meaning of 'registered establishment' see PARA 578.

2 As to the meaning of 'approved mental health professional' see PARA 815 note 2.

3 Mental Health Act 1983 s 4(1) (amended by the Mental Health Act 2007 Sch 2 para 2(a)). As to the meaning of 'nearest relative' see PARA 839.

4 Ie required under the Mental Health Act 1983 s 2(3) (see PARA 767), where the application for admission for assessment is not made in an emergency.

5 Mental Health Act 1983 s 4(1), (3). This is unlikely to be a violation of the Convention for the Protection of Human Rights and Fundamental Freedoms (Rome, 4 November 1950; TS 71 (1953); Cmd 8969) art 5 because the procedural safeguards under the Convention do not apply in emergency situations: see *Winterwerp v Netherlands* (1981) 4 EHRR 228, ECtHR. See PARA 767 note 4. As to the Convention for the Protection of Human Rights and Fundamental Freedoms see RIGHTS AND FREEDOMS.

The Mental Health Act 1983 provides a complete statutory code for the assessment and treatment of patients with mental disorder and common law powers should not be used even on an emergency basis pending the use of emergency powers under this Act. The failure to use this Act may result in an unlawful deprivation of liberty under the Convention for the Protection of Human Rights art 5(1)(e). It is submitted that the use of these provisions may render an unlawful detention lawful: *R (on the application of Sessay) v South London & Maudsley NHS Foundation Trust* [2011] EWHC 2617 (QB), [2012] QB 760, [2012] 2 WLR 1071.

As to the form of the application see the Mental Health (Hospital, Guardianship and Treatment) (England) Regulations 2008, SI 2008/1184, reg 4(1)(e), Sch 1; and the Mental Health (Hospital, Guardianship, Community Treatment and Consent to Treatment) (Wales) Regulations 2008, SI 2008/2439, reg 4(1)(e), Sch 1.

6 Mental Health Act 1983 s 4(1). It is submitted that the general requirements as to applications for admission for assessment apply otherwise than as expressly modified by this provision or elsewhere. As to applications by approved mental health professionals see PARA 821; as to the effect of an application see PARA 771; as to compulsory admission for assessment see PARA 767; as to requirements for applications for hospital admission see PARA 847; and as to requirements for medical recommendations see PARA 849.

The Department of Health *Mental Health Act 1983 Code of Practice* (2008) paras 5.1–5.13 and the Welsh Assembly Government *Mental Health Act 1983 Code of Practice for Wales* (2008) paras 5.5–5.12 give guidance on emergency admission. As to the Codes of Practice see PARA 762.

7 Ie under the Mental Health Act 1983 s 2: see PARA 767.

8 Mental Health Act 1983 s 4(2).

9 Ie the requirements of the Mental Health Act 1983 s 12 (see PARA 849), so far as those requirements are applicable to a single recommendation. As to the required form under which any medical recommendation for the purposes of s 4 must be set out see the Mental Health (Hospital, Guardianship and Treatment) (England) Regulations 2008, SI 2008/1184, reg 4(1)(f), Sch 1; and the Mental Health (Hospital, Guardianship, Community Treatment and Consent to Treatment) (Wales) Regulations 2008, SI 2008/2439, reg 4(1)(f), Sch 1.

10 Mental Health Act 1983 s 4(3).

11 Ie the application will cease to constitute authority for the detention of the patient: see PARA 771. It is submitted that the exercise of this power which is intended to be limited cannot lawfully be renewed: *R v Wilson ex p Williamson* [1996] COD 42.

12 Ie as required under the Mental Health Act 1983 s 2(3) (see PARA 767).

13 As to the meaning of 'managers' see PARA 778.

14 Mental Health Act 1983 s 4(4). As to when it is deemed to be received see PARA 770. A record of the receipt of any recommendation must be made by the managers of the hospital: see the Mental Health (Hospital, Guardianship and Treatment) (England) Regulations 2008, SI 2008/1184, reg 4(4), (5), Sch 1; and the Mental Health (Hospital, Guardianship, Community Treatment and Consent to Treatment) (Wales) Regulations 2008, SI 2008/2439, reg 4(3), Sch 1. There is no common law power to detain once the statutory period has expired: *B v Forsey*

1988 SC (HL) 28, 1988 SLT 572, HL. A patient is able to apply to the tribunal (see the Mental Health Act 1983 s 66(1)(a), (2)(a); and PARA 960) but if the second recommendation is not forthcoming then the provision will lapse.

15 See the Mental Health Act 1983 s 56(3)(a); and PARA 924. If a patient has the capacity to consent, then treatment must be carried out under the common law doctrine of necessity. If a patient lacks capacity then the Mental Capacity Act 2005 ss 5, 6 (see PARA 611) may be used if the proposed treatment is in the patient's best interests.

770. Compulsory admission and temporary detention of in-patients. An application may be made for the admission of a patient[1] to a hospital[2] for assessment or for treatment notwithstanding that the patient is already an in-patient[3] in that hospital and not liable to be detained in pursuance of any application[4] for his compulsory admission[5]. Moreover, an application may be made for admission for treatment notwithstanding that the patient is already liable to be detained in hospital in pursuance of an application for his admission for assessment[6].

Where it appears to the registered medical practitioner or approved clinician[7] in charge of the treatment of a patient who is an in-patient but not liable to be detained[8] that an application ought to be made for the patient's compulsory admission[9], he may furnish to the managers[10] of the hospital a written report to that effect[11]; and in any such case the patient may be detained in the hospital for a period of 72 hours from the time when the report was so furnished[12]. The registered medical practitioner or approved clinician in charge of the treatment of a patient in a hospital may nominate one (but not more than one) person to act for him[13] in his absence[14].

Where it appears to a nurse of a prescribed class[15] that a patient who is receiving treatment for mental disorder as an in-patient but who is not liable to be detained or a community patient[16] is: (1) suffering from mental disorder to such a degree that it is necessary for his health or safety or for the protection of others that he has to be immediately restrained from leaving the hospital; and (2) that it is not practicable to secure the immediate attendance of a practitioner or clinician for the purpose of furnishing a report[17], the nurse may record the fact in writing[18], must deliver the record to the managers of the hospital as soon as possible after it is made[19], and may detain the patient for a period of six hours from the time of recording or until the earlier arrival of a practitioner having power to furnish a report[20].

Patients admitted under these provisions are not subject to the consent to treatment provisions[21].

1 As to the meaning of 'patient' see PARA 758 note 4.
2 As to the meaning of 'hospital' see PARA 577.

3 The term 'in-patient' is not defined. The Department of Health *Mental Health Act 1983 Code of Practice* (2008) para 12.6 states that hospital in-patient for this purpose means any person who is receiving in-patient treatment in a hospital, except a patient who is already liable to be detained under the Mental Health Act 1983 ss 2, 3 or 4 (see PARAS 767–769), or who is a supervised community treatment patient. It includes patients who are in hospital by virtue of a deprivation of liberty authorisation under the Mental Capacity Act 20051 (see Chapter 4). It does not matter whether or not the patient was originally admitted for treatment primarily for a mental disorder. The Welsh Assembly Government *Mental Health Act 1983 Code of Practice for Wales* (2008) states that the Mental Health Act 1983 s 5 should only be used for an informal patient in a hospital and that hospital managers should be able to clearly identify what is meant by informal patient: see para 8.5. See also PARA 764 note 9. See *R (DR) v Mersey Care NHS Trust* [2002] EWHC 1810 (Admin). A patient does not lose in-patient status by expressing a desire to leave: *Re McGee* [2008] MHLR 216 (Northern Ireland). As to the Codes of Practice see PARA 762.

4	Ie under the Mental Health Act 1983 s 2(1) (admission for assessment: see PARA 767), s 3 (admission for treatment: see PARA 768), or s 4 (emergency admission: see PARA 769). As to the application of transfer regulations see s 19(1)(a); and PARA 735.

5	Mental Health Act 1983 s 5(1). This is unlikely to be a violation of the Convention for the Protection of Human Rights and Fundamental Freedoms (Rome, 4 November 1950; TS 71 (1953); Cmd 8969) art 5 because the procedural safeguards under the Convention do not apply in emergency situations: see *Winterwerp v Netherlands* (1981) 4 EHRR 228, ECtHR. As to the Convention for the Protection of Human Rights and Fundamental Freedoms art 5 see RIGHTS AND FREEDOMS.

The Mental Health Act 1983 provides a complete statutory code for the assessment and treatment of patients with mental disorder and common law powers should not be used even on an emergency basis pending the use of emergency powers under that Act. The failure to use the Mental Health Act 1983 may result in an unlawful deprivation of liberty under the Convention on Human Rights art 5(1)(e). It is submitted that the use of these provisions may render an unlawful detention lawful: *R (on the application of Sessay) v South London & Maudsley NHS Foundation Trust* [2011] EWHC 2617 (QB), [2012] QB 760, [2012] 2 WLR 1071.

6	Mental Health Act 1983 s 5(1). Where an application is made by virtue of this provision the patient is treated for the purposes of Pt 2 (ss 2–34) as if he had been admitted to the hospital at the time when the application was received by the managers: s 5(1). Time will therefore run beginning with that date for such purposes as duration of detention (see s 20(1); and PARA 908) and application to the appropriate tribunal (see s 66(1)(b); and PARA 961).

7	As to the meaning of 'approved clinician' see PARA 831. As to registered medical practitioners see MEDICAL PROFESSIONS vol 74 (2011) PARA 176 et seq.

8	Mental Health Act 1983 s 5(6).

9	Ie under the Mental Health Act 1983 Pt 2 (ss 2–34). See note 4.

10	As to the meaning of 'managers' see PARA 778. A report is 'furnished' when it is handed to the officer authorised to receive it or it is committed to the internal mail system operated by the managers: see the Department of Health *Mental Health Act 1983 Code of Practice* (2008) para 12.5; and the Welsh Assembly Government *Mental Health Act 1983 Code of Practice for Wales* (2008) para 8.14.

11	As to the form in which a report made under the Mental Health Act 1984 s 5(2) must be set out: see the Mental Health (Hospital, Guardianship and Treatment) (England) Regulations 2008, SI 2008/1184, reg 4(1)(g), Sch 1; and the Mental Health (Hospital, Guardianship, Community Treatment and Consent to Treatment) (Wales) Regulations 2008, SI 2008/2439, reg 4(1)(g), Sch 1.

12	Mental Health Act 1983 s 5(2) (amended by the Mental Health Act 2007 s 9(2)(a)).

13	Ie under the Mental Health Act 1983 s 5(2).

14	Mental Health Act 1983 s 5(3) (s 5(3) substituted and s 5(3A) added by the Mental Health Act 2007 s 9(2)(b)). For these purposes the registered medical practitioner may nominate another registered medical practitioner, or an approved clinician, on the staff of the hospital and the approved clinician may nominate another approved clinician, or a registered medical practitioner, on the staff of the hospital: Mental Health Act 1983 s 5(3A) (as so added). The Department of Health *Mental Health Act 1983 Code of Practice* (2008) paras 12.2–12.18 and Welsh Assembly Government *Mental Health Act 1983 Code of Practice for Wales* (2008) paras 8.8–8.18 give guidance on the use of the doctor's holding power (ie under the Mental Health Act 1983 s 5(2)). A person who is detained in hospital under s 135 or 136 pending completion of their assessment should not have their detention extended by use of s 5(2) or s 5(4): Department of Health *Mental Health Act 1983 Code of Practice* (2008) para 10.53. It is submitted that the exercise of this power which is intended to be limited cannot be renewed: *R v Wilson ex p Williamson* [1996] COD 42. There is no procedure for discharging a patient from this power which will lapse if it is decided that no application under ss 2 or 3 are needed, or if such an application is made, or if a nominated practitioner decides that no admission is needed. See the Department of Health *Mental Health Act 1983 Code of Practice* (2008) paras 12.19, 12.20 on ending the Mental Health Act 1983 s 5(2) holding power.

15	For the purposes of the Mental Health Act 1983 s 5(4) (power to detain patient in hospital for maximum of 6 hours) a nurse of the prescribed class is a nurse registered in either Sub-Part 1 or 2 of the register maintained under the Nursing and Midwifery Order 2001, SI 2002/253, art 5 (see MEDICAL PROFESSIONS vol 74 (2011) PARA 713), whose registration includes an entry in the register indicating that the nurse's field of practice is either mental health nursing or learning disabilities nursing: see the Mental Health (Nurses) (England) Order 2008, SI 2008/1207, art 2; and Mental Health (Nurses) (Wales) Order 2008, SI 2008/2441, art 2. See also PARA 836.

16	See the Mental Health Act 1983 s 5(6) (amended by the Mental Health Act 2007 Sch 3 para 2).

17	Ie a report under the Mental Health Act 1983 s 5(2).

18　Mental Health Act 1983 s 5(4) (amended by the Mental Health Act 2007 s 9(2)(c)). As to the form to be used for any record made under s 5(4): see the Mental Health (Hospital, Guardianship and Treatment) (England) Regulations 2008, SI 2008/1184, reg 4(1)(h), Sch 1; and the Mental Health (Hospital, Guardianship, Community Treatment and Consent to Treatment) (Wales) Regulations 2008, SI 2008/2439, reg 4(1)(h), Sch 1.

19　Mental Health Act 1983 s 5(5). When a record is made under s 5(4) the period in s 5(2) must, if that power is used, begin when the report was made.

20　Mental Health Act 1983 s 5(4) (as amended: see note 16).

　　　For guidance on the nurse's holding power (ie under the Mental Health Act 1983 s 5(4)) see the Department of Health *Mental Health Act 1983 Code of Practice* (2008) paras 12.21–12.34; and the Welsh Assembly Government *Mental Health Act 1983 Code of Practice for Wales* (2008) paras 8.19–8.30. It is submitted that the exercise of this power which is intended to be limited cannot lawfully be renewed: *R v Wilson ex p Williamson* [1996] COD 42.

21　See the Mental Health Act 1983 s 56(3)(b); and PARA 924. If the patient has capacity to consent, then treatment must be carried out under the common law doctrine of necessity. If a patient lacks capacity then the Mental Capacity Act 2005 ss 5, 6 (see PARA 611) may be used if the proposed treatment is in the patient's best interests.

771.　Effect of applications for admission.　An application for the admission of a patient[1] to hospital[2] for assessment or for treatment duly completed in accordance with the relevant statutory provisions[3] constitutes sufficient authority for the applicant, or any person authorised by the applicant, to take the patient and convey him to the hospital[4]. However, this power must be exercised, except in the case of emergency applications[5], at some time within the period of 14 days beginning with the date on which a medical practitioner last examined the patient before giving a medical recommendation[6] for the purposes of the application[7]; and, in the case of an emergency application, at some time within the period of 24 hours beginning with the date on which the patient was examined by the practitioner giving the first medical recommendation[8] or at the time when the application is made, whichever is the earlier[9].

Where a patient is admitted within these periods to the hospital specified in the application or, being already within that hospital, is treated as if he had been so admitted[10], the application constitutes sufficient authority for the managers[11] of the hospital to detain the patient in the hospital[12].

1　As to the meaning of 'patient' see PARA 758 note 4.

2　As to the meaning of 'hospital', which for this purpose includes a registered establishment, see PARA 577. As to the meaning of 'registered establishment' see PARA 578.

3　Ie the Mental Health Act 1983 ss 2–4 (see PARAS 767–769) and s 11 (see PARAS 821, 847). See the Department of Health *Mental Health Act 1983 Code of Practice* (2008) Chapter 11.

4　Mental Health Act 1983 s 6(1).

　　　As to the position where the requirements of the Mental Health Act 1983 are not fulfilled see *R v Managers of South Western Hospital, ex p M* [1993] QB 683, [1994] 1 All ER 161; *Re S-C (Mental Patient: Habeas Corpus)* [1996] QB 599, [1996] 1 All ER 532, CA. See also *R v Central London County Court, ex p London* [1999] 3 All ER 991, [1999] 2 FLR 161, CA. See further Application 11364/03 *Mooren v Germany* (2009) 50 EHRR 554, [2009] ECHR 11364/03. As to possible damages for false imprisonment see *R v Riverside Mental Health Trust, ex p Huzzey* (1998) 43 BMLR 167. See also PARA 915. If force is required to gain entry after an application has been completed then a warrant under the Mental Health Act 1983 s 135 (see PARA 922) will be necessary. For the use of force see s 137(2); and PARA 776. No move should be carried out unless it is known that the hospital named in the application is willing to accept the patient and consideration has been given to the action to be taken if, on arrival at the named hospital, a bed is no longer available: see the Department of Health *Mental Health Act 1983 Code of Practice* (2008) paras 4.92, 4.99. The Mental Capacity Act 2005 s 5 and s 6 cannot be used to convey a patient to hospital: *R (on the application of Sessay) v South London & Maudsley NHS Foundation Trust* [2011] EWHC 2617 (QB), [2012] QB 760, [2012] 2 WLR 1071.

5　Ie applications for admission for assessment in an emergency: see the Mental Health Act 1983 s 4(1); and PARA 769.

6　See the Mental Health Act 1983 ss 2(3), 3(3); and PARAS 767–768, 849.

7　Mental Health Act 1983 s 6(1)(a).
8　See the Mental Health Act 1983 s 4(3); and PARA 769.
9　Mental Health Act 1983 s 6(1)(b). See also PARA 849.
10　Ie by virtue of the Mental Health Act 1983 s 5(1) (see PARA 770).
11　As to the meaning of 'managers' see PARA 778.
12　Mental Health Act 1983 s 6(2). A patient is thus lawfully detained. If he goes absent without leave he is liable to be taken into custody and returned to hospital: see s 18(1); and PARA 918. For service on an officer of the managers of the hospital who is authorised to receive the application see the Mental Health (Hospital, Guardianship and Treatment) (England) Regulations 2008, SI 2008/1184, reg 3(2).

772.　Proof of form and contents.　Any application for the compulsory admission of a patient[1] to hospital[2] which appears to be duly made and to be founded on the necessary medical recommendations may be acted on without further proof of the signature or qualification of the person by whom the application or medical recommendation is made or given, or of any matter of fact or opinion stated in it[3].

1　As to the meaning of 'patient' see PARA 758 note 4.
2　As to the meaning of 'hospital' see PARA 577.
3　Mental Health Act 1983 s 6(3). The application and recommendations on which it is founded should be carefully examined to see that they do appear to conform with the statutory requirements, but if the documents are in the proper form it seems that they would justify the reception and detention of the person named in them even if that person proves to be not in fact suffering from mental disorder: see *Norris v Seed* (1849) 3 Exch 782; *Mackintosh v Smith and Lowe* (1865) 4 Macq 913, HL. This provision does not make lawful a fundamentally defective application and provides a defence to the managers against an action for acting on an invalid application: *R (on the application of TTM (by his litigation friend)) v Hackney London Borough Council* [2010] EWHC 1349 (Admin), [2010] All ER (D) 88 (Jun). The managers must, depending on the circumstances, scrutinise the application, for example, where they are aware of a recent discharge by the tribunal: see *R (on the application of Care Principles Ltd) v Mental Health Review Tribunal* [2006] EWHC 3194 (Admin), 94 BMLR 145. See also the Department of Health *Mental Health Act 1983 Code of Practice* (2008) Chapter 13.

773.　Cessation of previous applications.　Where a patient is admitted to hospital in pursuance of an application for admission for treatment[1], any previous application[2] by virtue of which he was liable to be detained in hospital[3] or subject to guardianship[4] will cease to have effect[5].

1　See the Mental Health Act 1983 s 3(1); and PARA 768.
2　Ie under the Mental Health Act 1983 Pt 2 (ss 2–34).
3　See the Mental Health Act 1983 ss 2, 4 (detention for assessment), s 3 (detention for treatment); and PARAS 767–769.
4　As to guardianship applications see PARA 785.
5　Mental Health Act 1983 s 6(4). A defective s 3 application that is subsequently found to be unlawful does not invalidate a preceding s 2 application (obiter): see *M v Hospital Managers of Queen Mary's Hospital* [2008] EWHC 1959 (Admin).

774.　Rectification of application or recommendations.　If, within the period of 14 days beginning with the day on which a patient[1] has been admitted to a hospital[2] in pursuance of an application for admission for assessment[3] or for treatment[4], the application or any medical recommendation given for the purposes of the application[5] is found to be in any respect incorrect or defective, the application or recommendation may, within that period and with the consent of the managers[6] of the hospital, be amended by the person by whom it was signed[7]. On the amendment being made the application or recommendation will have effect, and will be deemed to have had effect, as if it had been originally made as so amended[8].

1   As to the meaning of 'patient' see PARA 758 note 4.
2   As to the meaning of 'hospital' see PARA 577.
3   See the Mental Health Act 1983 s 2(1); and PARA 767.
4   See the Mental Health Act 1983 s 3(1); and PARA 768.
5   As to such recommendations see the Mental Health Act 1983 ss 2(3), 3(3), 4(3), (4); and PARAS 767–769. As to the general provisions applying to medical recommendations see PARA 849.
6   As to the meaning of 'managers' see PARA 778. The managers of the hospital or other relevant authorities and trusts may authorise an officer or class of officers or any other person on their behalf to consent to the amendment of an application or recommendation: see the Mental Health Act 1983 s 32(3); and PARA 766.
7   Mental Health Act 1983 s 15(1). As to the meaning of 'beginning with' see *Zoan v Rouamba* [2000] 2 All ER 620, [2000] 1 WLR 1509. Use of an obsolete form would not invalidate an application or recommendation because minor departures from statutory form would be regarded as de minimis: see *Re E (Mental Health: Habeas Corpus)* (10 December 1966, unreported). Rectification cannot be used to retrospectively validate a fundamentally defective application: see *Re S-C (mental patient: habeas corpus)* [1996] QB 599, [1996] 1 All ER 532, [1996] 2 WLR 146. Nor can it cure a defect in the necessary procedural steps. It is intended to cure errors on the face of the document: *R v Managers of South Western Hospital, ex p M* [1993] QB 683, [1994] 1 All ER 161. Steps to be taken in the event of a fundamental flaw in the application include the consideration of the use of powers under s 23 (see PARA 913) by hospital managers or responsible clinicians to discharge the patient, or the use of 'holding' powers under s 5(2), (4) (see PARA 770) pending a fresh application: see the Department of Health *Mental Health Act 1983* Code of Practice (2008) para 13.13; and the Welsh Assembly Government *Mental Health Act 1983 Code of Practice for Wales* (2008) para 10.13.
8   Mental Health Act 1983 s 15(1). This provision applies only to admissions to hospital and so applications for guardianship or community treatment orders are not capable of rectification in this manner. For an application or recommendation to be capable of amendment under this provision, there must, it seems, be a document in existence which can properly be called an application or recommendation for the admission of the patient in question; thus an unsigned application or recommendation, or one referring to another patient, would not be capable of rectification.

775. Procedure on insufficiency of medical recommendations. Without prejudice to the provisions for the rectification of an incorrect or defective application or recommendation[1], if it appears to the managers[2] of the hospital[3] within the period of 14 days[4] that one of the two recommendations on which an application for assessment or for treatment is founded is insufficient to warrant[5] the detention of the patient[6] in pursuance of the application, they may, within that period, give written notice to that effect to the applicant[7]. Where any such notice is given in respect of a recommendation, that recommendation is to be disregarded, but the application will be sufficient[8], and will be deemed always to have been sufficient, if: (1) a fresh medical recommendation complying with the relevant statutory provisions[9] (other than the provisions relating to the time of signature and the interval between examinations[10]) is furnished to the managers within the specified period[11]; and (2) that recommendation and the other recommendation on which the application is founded together comply with those provisions[12]. Where the two medical recommendations on which an application for admission for assessment or for treatment is founded are, taken together, insufficient to warrant the patient's detention in pursuance of the application[13], a notice[14] may be given by the managers in respect of either of those recommendations[15].

The provisions for rectification[16] do not authorise the giving of such a notice in respect of an application made as an emergency application[17]; nor do those provisions authorise the detention of a patient admitted in pursuance of an emergency application after the period of 72 hours authorised by such an application, unless a second medical recommendation has been given and received by the managers within that period and the two recommendations together comply (or would comply apart from any error or defect to which the provisions for rectification apply) with the requirements as to medical recommendations other than those as to the time of signature of the second recommendation[18].

1   Ie the Mental Health Act 1983 s 15(1) (see PARA 774).
2   As to the meaning of 'managers' see PARA 778.
3   As to the meaning of 'hospital' see PARA 577.
4   Ie beginning with the day of admission of the patient: see the Mental Health Act 1983 s 15(1); and PARA 774.
5   The expression 'insufficient to warrant' is used in contrast with the expression 'in any respect incorrect or defective' in the Mental Health Act 1983 s 15(1). It is submitted that the former expression would include eg a medical recommendation which is in the prescribed form but does not contain adequate or convincing reasons for the opinion expressed that the grounds for admission for treatment under s 3(2) exist: see s 3(3); and PARA 768.
6   As to the meaning of 'patient' see PARA 758 note 4.
7   Mental Health Act 1983 s 15(2).
8   Ie sufficient to warrant the patient's detention.
9   Ie the provisions of the Mental Health Act 1983 Pt 2 (ss 2–34). The relevant provisions are s 2(3) (see PARA 767), s 3(3) (see PARA 768) and s 12 (see PARA 849).
10 Ie under the Mental Health Act 1983 s 12(1) (see PARA 849).
11 Mental Health Act 1983 s 15(2)(a). See also the text to note 4. The patient may be detained until the fresh medical recommendation is furnished. The fresh recommendation does not have to comply with the time interval provisions of s 12(1).
12 Mental Health Act 1983 s 15(2)(b).
13 The expression 'taken together, insufficient to warrant the detention' appears to contemplate a contingency in which two medical recommendations, each taken by itself sufficient to warrant the detention of the patient, are, taken together, insufficient to warrant the detention of the patient in pursuance of the application eg because the interval between the two examinations of the patient exceeded the five days prescribed by the Mental Health Act 1983 s 12(1) (see PARA 849) or because neither of the two medical practitioners concerned has been approved by the appropriate national authority as required by s 12(2) (see PARA 849). As to the appropriate national authority see PARA 567.
14 Ie a notice under the Mental Health Act 1983 s 15(2): see the text to note 7.
15 Mental Health Act 1983 s 15(3) (amended by the Mental Health Act 2007 Sch 11 Pt 1).
16 See PARA 774.
17 Ie under the Mental Health Act 1983 s 4 (see PARA 769).
18 Mental Health Act 1983 s 15(4). See also see s 4(4); and PARA 769.

776.   Persons in legal custody.   Any person required or authorised by or by virtue of the Mental Health Act 1983 to be conveyed[1] to any place or to be kept in custody or detained in a place of safety[2], or at any place to which he is taken by direction[3] in the interests of justice or for the purposes of any public inquiry, is, while being so conveyed, detained or kept, as the case may be, deemed to be in legal custody[4].

A constable or any other person required or authorised by or by virtue of that Act to take any person into custody, or to convey or detain any person, has, for the purposes of taking him into custody or conveying or detaining him, all the powers, authorities, protection and privileges which a constable has within the area for which he acts as constable[5].

1   'Convey', for these purposes, includes any other expression denoting removal from one place to another: Mental Health Act 1983 s 137(3). Section 137 extends to Scotland: see s 146; and PARA 557.
2   As to the meaning of 'place of safety' for the purposes of the Mental Health Act 1983 Pt 3 (ss 35–55) see PARA 868 note 4; and for its meaning for the purposes of s 135 and s 136 see s 135(6); and PARA 922 note 10.
3   Ie where he is taken under the Mental Health Act 1983 s 42(6) (see PARA 876).

4   Mental Health Act 1983 s 137(1). As to the equivalent Scottish provisions see the Mental Health (Care and Treatment) (Scotland) Act 2003 (Consequential Provisions) Order 2005, SI 2005/2078 (S 9), art 11. As to escape from custody see PARA 777.

5   Mental Health Act 1983 s 137(2). The effect of these provisions is, inter alia, to enable the authorised person to invoke the assistance of others if necessary. As to the office of constable see POLICE vol 36(1) (2007 Reissue) PARA 101 et seq.

     The power does not include the use of force to enter premises to remove someone believed to be suffering from mental disorder or liable to be taken into custody under the Mental Health Act 1983 (the power under s 135 (see PARA 922) should be used instead): see *R v Rosso* [2003] EWCA Crim 3242, [2003] All ER (D) 381 (Nov). The power cannot be used to detain people in hospital: see *R v Broadmoor Special Hospital Authority, ex p S* [1998] 08 LS Gaz R 32, 142 Sol Jo LB 76, CA.

777. Retaking of persons who escape from legal custody.

A person who escapes from legal custody[1] may be retaken by the person who had his custody immediately before his escape, or by any constable or approved mental health professional[2]. If at the time of the escape the person escaping was liable to be detained in a hospital[3] or under guardianship[4] or a community patient who was recalled to hospital[5] he may also be retaken by any other person who could take him into custody[6] if he were absent without leave[7]; but he may not be retaken by any person after the expiration of the period[8] within which he could have been retaken had he absented himself without leave on the day of his escape[9], unless he is subject to a restriction order or an order or direction having the same effect[10]. Such a patient can be retaken at any time while the restriction is in force[11].

A person who escapes while being taken to or detained in a place of safety[12] may not be retaken after the expiration of a period of 72 hours beginning with the time of escape or the period during which he is liable to be detained, whichever expires first[13].

In computing the period of 28 days during which a hospital order constitutes authority for a person's conveyance and admission to and detention in hospital[14], or during which a court may direct his conveyance to and detention in a place of safety[15], time spent at large by a patient who escapes from legal custody before he is retaken is excluded[16].

Where a patient is absent without leave on the day that he would otherwise cease to be liable to be detained or subject to guardianship, or within the period of one week ending on that day, he does not cease to be so liable or subject[17].

1   Ie legal custody by virtue of the Mental Health Act 1983 s 137 (see PARA 776). This is distinct from absence without leave from hospital (see PARA 918) or guardianship (see PARA 793). It is an offence to induce or knowingly to assist a person to escape (see PARA 1013); but a person detained under the Mental Health Act 1983 who escapes does not thereby commit an offence: see *R v Criminal Injuries Compensation Board, ex p Lawton* [1972] 3 All ER 582 at 584, [1972] 1 WLR 1589 at 1592, DC. The powers of arrest under the Mental Health Act 1983 s 18 and s 138 are specifically preserved by the Police and Criminal Evidence Act 1984 s 26(2), Sch 2: see CRIMINAL LAW, EVIDENCE AND PROCEDURE vol 11(2) (2006 Reissue) PARA 927.

2   Mental Health Act 1983 s 138(1)(a) (amended by the Mental Health Act 2007 Sch 2 para 10(c)). As to the meaning of 'approved mental health professional' see PARA 815 note 2. As to the Scottish provisions relating to persons in legal custody see the Mental Health (Care and Treatment) (Scotland) Act 2003 (Consequential Provisions) Order 2005, SI 2005/2078 (S 9), art 11; and PARA 776. As to patients absent from hospitals in Scotland see art 8; and PARA 919.

3   Ie within the meaning of the Mental Health Act 1983 Pt 2 (ss 2–34) (see PARA 577). As to the application of Pt 2 to patients detained under Pt 3 (ss 35–55) (patients concerned in criminal proceedings or under sentence) see s 145(3); and PARA 860. As to the meaning of 'patient' see PARA 758 note 4.

4   Ie under the Mental Health Act 1983.

5   Ie recalled under the Mental Health Act 1983 s 17E (see PARA 801).

6   Ie under the Mental Health Act 1983 s 18 (see PARA 918). If a person liable to be detained in a
    hospital escapes: (1) while being transferred to or from the hospital under the regulations for the
    transfer of patients (see the Mental Health (Hospital, Guardianship and Treatment) (England)
    Regulations 2008, SI 2008/1184; the Mental Health (Hospital, Guardianship, Community
    Treatment and Consent to Treatment) (Wales) Regulations 2008, SI 2008/2439; and PARAS
    886–891) or in pursuance of any order, direction or authorisation under the Mental Health
    Act 1983 Pt 3 or Pt 6 (other than under s 35, s 36, s 38, s 53, s 83 or s 85) (see PARAS 859 et seq,
    899 et seq); or (2) while being taken to or detained in a place of safety in pursuance of an order
    under Pt 3 (other than under s 35, s 36 or s 38) (see PARAS 862–864, 868) pending his admission
    to that hospital, he is liable to be retaken as if he were liable to be detained in that hospital and,
    if he had not been previously received there, as if he had been so received: s 138(4) (amended by
    the Health and Social Care Act 2012 s 42(3)).
7   Mental Health Act 1983 s 138(1)(b) (amended by the Mental Health Act 2007 Sch 3 para 32).
8   As to such period see the Mental Health Act 1983 s 18(4); and PARA 918. However, a patient
    detained for a short period, whether for assessment (see PARA 767) or as an in-patient (see PARA
    770), cannot be taken into custody if the period for which he was liable to be detained has
    expired: see s 18(5); and PARA 918.
9   This does not apply if he is subject to a restriction order under the Mental Health Act 1983 Pt 3
    (ss 35–55) or an order or direction having the same effect as such an order and s 18(4) applies
    with the necessary modifications.
10 Mental Health Act 1983 s 138(2). As to the retaking of patients absent without leave from
    hospital see PARA 918 et seq.
11 See the Mental Health Act 1983 s 41(3)(d).
12 Ie under the Mental Health Act 1983 s 135 (see PARA 922) or s 136 (see PARA 923). As to the
    meaning of 'place of safety' for this purpose see s 135(6); and PARA 922 note 10.
13 Mental Health Act 1983 s 138(3).
14 Ie for the purposes of the Mental Health Act 1983 s 40(1) (see PARA 867).
15 Ie for the purposes of the Mental Health Act 1983 s 37(4), (5) (see PARA 864).
16 See the Mental Health Act 1983 s 138(5).
17 See the Mental Health Act 1983 ss 20(1), 21, 21A, 21B; and PARAS 908, 911.

778.   Managers of hospitals and registered establishments. Hospitals[1] and
registered establishments[2] are administered by the managers[3]. 'The managers'
means: (1) in relation to a hospital vested in the appropriate national authority[4]
for the purposes of its functions under the National Health Service Act 2006, or
the National Health Service (Wales) Act 2006, and in relation to any
accommodation provided by a local authority and used as a hospital by or on
behalf of the appropriate national authority under those Acts, the primary care
trust[5], strategic health authority[6], local health board[7] or special health authority[8]
responsible for the administration of the hospital; (2) in relation to a hospital
vested in a primary care trust or National Health Service trust[9], the trust; (3) in
relation to a hospital vested in an NHS foundation trust[10], the trust; and (4) in
relation to a registered establishment, if the establishment is in England, the
person or persons registered as a service provider[11] in respect of the regulated
activity[12] relating to the assessment or medical treatment of mental disorder[13]
that is carried out in the establishment, and, if the establishment is in Wales, the
person or persons registered[14] in respect of the establishment[15].

1   As to the meaning of 'hospital' see PARA 577.
2   As to the meaning of 'registered establishment' see PARA 578. See also PARA 585.
3   The functions of managers under the Mental Health Act 1983 include: receiving and deciding
    upon applications for admission to hospital under Pt 2 (ss 2–34) (see s 11(2); and PARAS
    847–848); providing evidence that arrangements have been made for admission to that hospital
    before a court can remand a patient to hospital for reports (see s 35(4); and PARA 862) or for
    treatment (see s 36(3); and PARA 862) or make a hospital order (see s 37(4); and PARAS 864,
    868) or interim hospital order (see s 38(4); and PARAS 864, 868); detaining patients pursuant to
    such applications (see s 6(2); and PARA 771), remands (see ss 35(9)(b), 36(8); and PARA 862),
    and orders (see s 40(1), (3); and PARA 867); receiving reports from the doctor in charge of the
    patient's treatment, or from a nurse, that an informal in-patient ought to be kept in hospital (see

s 5(2), (4), (5); and PARA 770); receiving reports from medical officers to renewal of the authority to detain (see s 20(3); and PARA 910), or preventing discharge by the nearest relative (see s 25(1); and PARA 915) ; discharging patients (see s 23(2)(a); and PARA 913); referring certain patients to tribunals (see s 68(1); and PARA 964); informing the local social services authority of an admission on the application of the patient's nearest relative (see s 14; and PARA 580); informing the nearest relative if a detained patient is discharged (see s 133; and PARA 913) or if the relative is prevented from discharging him (see s 25(2); and PARA 915); informing the patient if his detention is renewed (see s 20(3); and PARA 910); generally giving information to detained patients and their nearest relatives (see s 132; and PARA 779); and censoring certain patients' correspondence (see s 134; and PARA 780). As to the power to make regulations determining the manner in which, inter alia, the managers' functions are to be exercised see PARA 766. Managers are public authorities for the purposes of the Human Rights Act 1998 s 6: *R (on the application of A) v Partnerships in Care Ltd* [2002] EWHC 529 (Admin), [2002] 1 WLR 2610, (2002) Times, 23 April.

  For guidance on the duties of the hospital managers see the Department of Health *Mental Health Act 1983 Code of Practice* (2008) para 30.1 et seq; and the Welsh Assembly Government *Mental Health Act 1983 Code of Practice for Wales* (2008) para 11.1 et seq. As to the Codes of Practice see PARA 762.

4 As to the appropriate national authority see PARA 567.
5 As from 1 April 2013 primary care trusts are abolished and accordingly the words 'primary care trust' in the text are repealed by the Health and Social Care Act 2012 Sch 5 para 31(a): see the Health and Social Care Act 2012 (Commencement No 4, Transitional, Savings and Transitory Provisions) Order 2012, SI 2013/160, art 2.
6 As from 1 April 2013 strategic health authorities are abolished and accordingly the words 'strategic health authority' in the text are repealed by the Health and Social Care Act 2012 Sch 5 para 31(1)(a)(iii)): see the Health and Social Care Act 2012 (Commencement No 4, Transitional, Savings and Transitory Provisions) Order 2012, SI 2013/160, art 2.
7 As to the meaning of 'local health board' see PARA 575 note 6.
8 As to the meaning of 'special health authority' see PARA 575 note 4.
9 As to National Health Service trusts see HEALTH SERVICES vol 54 (2008) PARA 155 et seq.
10 As to NHS foundation trusts see HEALTH SERVICES vol 54 (2008) PARA 174 et seq.
11 Ie registered as a service provider under the Health and Social Care Act 2008 Pt 1 Chapter 2 (ss 1–7) (see SOCIAL SERVICES AND COMMUNITY CARE).
12 Ie a regulated activity within the meaning of the Health and Social Care Act 2008 Pt 1 (ss 1–7: see SOCIAL SERVICES AND COMMUNITY CARE).
13 As to the meaning of 'mental disorder' see PARA 761.
14 Ie registered under the Care Standards Act 2000 Pt 2 (ss 11–42) (see SOCIAL SERVICES AND COMMUNITY CARE).
15 Mental Health Act 1983 s 145(1) (definition amended by the National Health Service and Community Care Act 1990 Sch 9 para 24(9); the Mental Health (Amendment) Act 1994 s 1; the Health Authorities Act 1995 Sch 1 para 107(14); the Health Act 1999 ss 41(2), 65, Sch 5; the National Health Service Reform and Health Care Professions Act 2002 Sch 2 Pt 2 paras 42, 49; the Health and Social Care (Community Health and Standards) Act 2003 Sch 4 paras 50, 57; SI 2000/90; SI 2002/2469; the National Health Service Reform and Health Care Professions Act 2002 Sch 2 para 49; the National Health Service (Consequential Provisions) Act 2006 Sch 1 para 70(d); SI 2007/961; the Mental Health Act 2007 s 46(3)(b); SI 2010/813; and amended as noted to notes 5, 6). As from 1 April 2013 the words 'the Secretary of State where the Secretary is responsible for the administration of the hospital or' are added before the words 'the primary care trust' and the words 'primary care trust' and the words 'strategic health authority' are repealed by the Health and Social Care Act 2012 Sch 5 para 31(1)(a): see the Health and Social Care Act 2012 (Commencement No 4, Transitional, Savings and Transitory Provisions) Order 2012, SI 2013/160, art 2.

779. Duty of managers to give detailed information to detained patients. The

managers[1] of a hospital[2] or registered establishment[3] in which a patient is detained[4] must, as soon as practicable after the commencement of the patient's detention, take such steps as are practicable to ensure that the patient understands: (1) under which of the statutory provisions he is being detained and its effect[5]; (2) his right of application to a tribunal[6]; (3) his right to be discharged[7], to receive and send correspondence[8], and to consent to or refuse treatment[9]; (3) the effect of the Code of Practice[10]; and (4) the protective functions of the regulatory authority[11]. This information must be given orally and in writing[12]. In addition the managers must take such steps as are practicable to inform in writing the patient's nearest relative[13], if any, of the above[14].

1　As to the meaning of 'managers' see PARA 778.
2　As to the meaning of 'hospital' see PARA 577.
3　As to the meaning of 'registered establishment' see PARA 578. See also PARA 585.
4　As to the meaning of 'patient' see PARA 758 note 4. The manager of the responsible hospital has a similar duty to give information to a community patient: see the Mental Health Act 1983 s 132A; and PARA 805.
5　Mental Health Act 1983 s 132(1)(a) (s 132(1), (2), (4) amended by the Care Standards Act 2000 s 116, Sch 4 paras 9(1), (2)).
6　Mental Health Act 1983 s 132(1)(b) (amended by SI 2008/2833). As to those rights see PARA 961. If a patient (nearest relative) fails to make an application to the tribunal or misses the opportunity to do so because information under this provision was not provided, then the Secretary of State should be requested to make a referral to the tribunal under s 67 or s 71 (see PARA 965).
7　Ie under the Mental Health Act 1983 ss 23, 25. As to discharge see PARA 913 et seq.
8　Ie under the Mental Health Act 1983 s 134. As to that right see PARA 780.
9　Ie under the Mental Health Act 1983 ss 56–64. As to consent to treatment see PARA 924 et seq. In *R (on the application of Wooder) v Feggetter* [2002] EWCA Civ 554, [2003] QB 219, [2002] 3 WLR 591 it was held that the patient should be given reasons for the imposition of treatment without consent under s 58 (see PARA 930).
10　Mental Health Act 1983 s 132(2) (as amended: see note 5).
11　Ie under the Mental Health Act 1983 s 120: see PARA 806.
12　Mental Health Act 1983 s 132(3).
13　As to the meaning of 'nearest relative' see PARA 839. This includes a person acting as the nearest relative: see PARA 842.
14　Mental Health Act 1983 s 132(4) (as amended: see note 5). See also the Mental Health (Hospital, Guardianship and Treatment) (England) Regulations 2008, SI 2008/1184, reg 26; and the Department of Health *Mental Health Act 1983 Code of Practice (2008)* Chapter 2. It is submitted that it would not be 'practicable' to provide information to the nearest relative of an incapacitated patient if to do so would cause 'harm' to the patient, such as emotional or psychological distress, and thereby violate the patient's rights under the European Convention on Human Rights and Fundamental Freedoms (Rome, 4 November 1950; TS 71 (1953); Cmd 8969) art 8: see *R (on the application of E) v Bristol City Council* [2005] EWHC 74 (Admin), [2005] All ER (D) 57 (Jan) ; and see RIGHTS AND FREEDOMS.

780. Correspondence of detained patients. A postal packet[1] addressed to any person by a patient[2] detained in a hospital[3] and delivered by the patient for dispatch may be withheld from the postal operator[4] concerned if the addressee has requested[5] that communications addressed to him by that patient should be withheld[6].

Special provisions apply to the post to and from patients detained in hospitals at which high security psychiatric services are provided[7] and a postal packet sent by such a patient may be withheld if the managers consider that it is likely to cause distress to the addressee or any other person[8] or cause danger to anyone[9]. A packet addressed to such a patient may be withheld from that patient if, in the opinion of the managers, it is necessary in the interests of safety of the patient or for the protection of others[10].

The managers of a hospital may inspect and open any postal packet for determining whether the provisions described above apply and may also withhold anything contained in the packet[11]. Where a postal packet or anything in it is withheld[12], the managers must record that fact in writing[13] and, where the withholding is to prevent distress or danger[14], give notice of it in writing within seven days to the patient and, if known, to the person by whom the packet was sent[15]. The functions of the managers may be discharged on their behalf by appointed staff members[16].

However, no postal packet which is delivered for dispatch by a patient may be withheld if the packet is addressed[17] to any of the following[18]: (1) any Minister of the Crown or the Scottish ministers, or member of either House of Parliament or member of the Scottish Parliament or of the Northern Ireland Assembly[19]; (2) any of the Welsh Ministers, the Counsel General to the Welsh Assembly Government or a member of the National Assembly for Wales[20]; (3) any judge or officer of the Court of Protection[21], any of the Court of Protection Visitors[22] or any person asked by that Court for a report[23] concerning the patient[24]; (4) the Parliamentary Commissioner for Administration[25], the Scottish Public Services Ombudsman, the Public Services Ombudsman for Wales[26], the Health Service Commissioner for England, or a local commissioner[27]; (5) the Care Quality Commission[28]; (6) the First-tier Tribunal or the Mental Health Review Tribunal for Wales[29]; (7) a strategic health authority[30], local health board[31], special health authority[32], primary care trust[33], local social services authority[34], community health council[35], local probation board[36] or a provider of probation services[37]; (8) a provider of a patient advocacy and liaison service[38] for the assistance of patients at the hospital and their families and carers[39]; (9) a provider of independent advocacy services[40] for the patient[41]; (10) the managers of the hospital in which the patient is detained[42]; (11) any legally qualified person instructed by the patient to act as his legal adviser[43]; or (12) the European Commission of Human Rights or the European Court of Human Rights[44].

Provision is made for the regulatory authority[45] to review certain decisions to withhold a postal packet (or anything contained in it)[46] if an application for a review of the decision is made[47] within six months of receipt by the applicant of the notice[48] that the postal packet has been withheld[49]. On such an application the regulatory authority may direct that the postal packet (or anything contained in it) is not to be withheld and the managers of the hospital concerned must comply with any such direction[50].

1   As to the meaning of 'postal packet' see the Postal Services Act 2011 s 27; and POSTAL SERVICES vol 85 (2012) PARA 234 (definition applied by the Mental Health Act 1983 s 134(9) (amended by the Postal Service Act 2000 Sch 8 para 19(3), Sch 9; and the Postal Services Act 2011 Sch 12 para 115).

2   As to the meaning of 'patient' see PARA 758 note 4.

3   As to the meaning of 'hospital' see PARA 577 (definition applied by the Mental Health Act 1983 s 134(9)).

4   As to the meaning of 'postal operator' see the Postal Services Act 2011 s 27; and POSTAL SERVICES vol 85 (2012) PARA 234 (definition applied by the Mental Health Act 1983 s 134(9) (as amended: see note 1)).

5   The request must be made in writing by a notice given to the managers of the hospital or the approved clinician with overall responsibility for the patient's case: Mental Health Act 1984 s 134(1) (as amended: see note 6). As to the meaning of 'managers' see PARA 778. As to the meaning of 'approved clinician' see PARA 831.

6   Mental Health Act 1983 s 134(1)(a) (s 134(1) amended by the Postal Services Act 2000 Sch 8 Pt II para 19(2); the Mental Health Act 2007 s 14(4); and the Health and Social Care Act 2012 s 44(1)).

    The Mental Health Act 1983 s 134 does not confer on the management of a hospital the power to require a publisher to return a manuscript that has been written and posted to him by a patient: *Broadmoor Hospital Authority v R* [2000] QB 775, [2000] 2 All ER 727, CA. Any restrictions on correspondence under s 134 will engage the patient's rights under the European Convention on Human Rights and Fundamental Freedoms (Rome, 4 November 1950; TS 71 (1953); Cmd 8969) art 8 and are likely to be justifiable under art 8(2): see Applications 10533/83 *Herczegfalvy v Austria* (1992) 15 EHRR 437, 18 BMLR 48. Such restrictions are also potentially relevant to the rights to freedom of expression under the Convention on Human Rights art 10 (see further RIGHTS AND FREEDOMS). Further provisions relating to items brought for patients into high secure hospitals and access to computers, mobile phones, telephones and post are contained in the High Security Psychiatric Services (Arrangements for Safety and Security at Ashworth, Broadmoor and Rampton Hospitals) Directions 2011.

7	The Department of Health *Mental Health Act 1983 Code of Practice* (2008) para 30.32 and the Welsh Assembly Government *Mental Health Act 1983 Code of Practice for Wales* (2008) para 11.3 advise managers to have a written policy concerning implementation of these powers.

8	Ie not being a person on the staff of the hospital.

9	Mental Health Act 1983 s 134(1)(b) (amended by the Health Act 1999 Sch 4 para 68(a)). This is subject to the Mental Health Act 1983 s 134(3): see heads (1)–(12) in the text.

10	Mental Health Act 1983 s 134(2) (amended by the Health Act 1999 Sch 4 paras 65, 68(b)). This is subject to the Mental Health Act 1983 s 134(3): see heads (1)–(12) in the text. See also the Mental Health (Hospital, Guardianship and Treatment) (England) Regulations 2008, SI 2008/1184, reg 29; and the Mental Health (Hospital, Guardianship, Community Treatment and Consent to Treatment) (Wales) Regulations 2008, SI 2008/2439, reg 41.

11	Mental Health Act 1983 s 134(4).

12	Ie under the Mental Health Act 1983 s 134(1) or s 134(2).

13	Mental Health Act 1983 s 134(5).

14	Ie under the Mental Health Act 1983 s 134(1)(b) or s 134(2).

15	Mental Health Act 1983 s 134(6). The notice must contain a statement of the effect of s 134A(1)–(4) (see PARA 780): s 134(6) (amended by Health and Social Care Act 2008 Sch 3 para 11(3)).

16	Mental Health Act 1983 s 134(7).

17	See, however, the text and notes 1–6.

18	Ie listed in the Mental Health Act 1983 s 134(3): see heads (1)–(12) in the text.

19	Mental Health Act 1983 s 134(3)(a) (amended by the Northern Ireland Act 1998 s 99, Sch 13 para 5(1), (2); and SI 1999/1820).

20	Mental Health Act 1983 s 134(3)(aa) (added by SI 2007/1388).

21	As to the Court of Protection see PARA 720.

22	As to the Court of Protection Visitors see PARA 748.

23	Ie a report under the Mental Capacity Act 2005 s 49 (see PARA 744).

24	Mental Health Act 1983 s 134(3)(b) (substituted by the Mental Capacity Act 2005 Sch 6 para 29(2)).

25	As to the Parliamentary Commissioner for Administration see ADMINISTRATIVE LAW vol 1(1) (2001 Reissue) PARAS 41–43.

26	As to the Public Services Ombudsman for Wales see ADMINISTRATIVE LAW.

27	Mental Health Act 1983 s 134(3)(c) (amended by the Government of Wales Act 1998 s 125, Sch 12 para 22; SI 2004/1823; and the Public Services Ombudsman (Wales) Act 2005 Sch 6 para 21, Sch 7). As to local commissioners see the Local Government Act 1974 Pt III (ss 23–34); and ADMINISTRATIVE LAW vol 1(1) (2001 Reissue) PARAS 44–46; LOCAL GOVERNMENT vol 69 (2009) PARA 839 et seq.

28	Mental Health Act 1983 s 134(3)(ca) (added by the Health and Social Care Act 2008 Sch 3 para 11(2)). As to the Care Quality Commission see PARA 573; and SOCIAL SERVICES AND COMMUNITY CARE.

29	Mental Health Act 1983 s 134(3)(d) (substituted by SI 2008/2833). For the purposes of head (6) in the text the reference to the First-tier Tribunal is a reference to that tribunal so far as it is acting for the purposes of any proceedings under the Mental Health Act 1983 or the Repatriation of Prisoners Act 1984, Schedule para 5(2) (see PRISONS AND PRISONERS vol 85 (2012) PARA 465): Mental Health Act 1983 s 134(3) (amended by SI 2008/2833). As to tribunals see PARA 955 et seq.

30	As to the meaning of 'strategic health authority' see PARA 575 note 3. As from 1 April 2013 strategic health authorities and primary care trusts are abolished (see PARA 575 notes 3, 5) and the Mental Health Act 1983 is amended by the Health and Social Care Act 2012 Sch 5 para 29 and the words 'the National Health Service Commissioning Board, a clinical commissioning group' are inserted and the words 'strategic health authority' and 'primary care trust' are repealed: see the Health and Social Care Act 2012 (Commencement No 4, Transitional, Savings and Transitory Provisions) Order 2013, SI 2013/160, art 2(2). As to the National Health Service Commissioning Board and clinical commissioning groups see PARAS 571, 572.

31	As to the meaning of 'local health board' see PARA 575 note 6.

32	As to the meaning of 'special health authority' see PARA 575 note 4.

33	As to the meaning of 'primary care trust' see PARA 575 note 5. See note 30.

34	As to local social services authorities see PARA 579.

35	As to community health councils see HEALTH SERVICES vol 54 (2008) PARAS 74, 534.

36	As to local probation boards see the Criminal Justice and Court Services Act 2000 s 4; and SENTENCING AND DISPOSITION OF OFFENDERS vol 92 (2010) PARAS 733–760.

37   Mental Health Act 1983 s 134(3)(e) (amended by the Criminal Justice and Court Services Act 2000 s 74, Sch 7 Pt II paras 72, 74; the National Health Service Reform and Health Care Professions Act 2002 s 19(6); SI 2000/90; SI 2002/2469; Local Government and Public Involvement in Health Act 2007 Sch 18 Pt 18; SI 2007/961; and SI 2008/912). As from 1 April 2013 references to the 'national health service commissioner' and 'clinical commissioning group' are added by the Health and Social Care Act 2012 Sch 5 para 29 and the references to 'primary care trust' are repealed by Sch 5 para 29(d): see s 306(1)(d); and the Health and Social Care Act 2012 (Commencement No 4, Transitional, Savings and Transitory Provisions) Order 2013, SI 2013/160, art 2(2). As to clinical commissioning groups see PARA 572.

38   'Patient advocacy and liaison service' means a service of a description prescribed by regulations made by the appropriate national authority: Mental Health Act 1983 s 134(3A)(a) (s 134(3A) added by the Health and Social Care Act 2001 s 67(1), Sch 5 Pt 1 para 6(1), (3)). As to the appropriate national authority see PARA 567.

     See, in relation to England, the Mental Health (Hospital, Guardianship and Treatment) (England) Regulations 2008, SI 2008/1184, reg 31.

39   Mental Health Act 1983 s 134(3)(ea) (s 134(3)(ea), (eb) added by the Health and Social Care Act 2001 s 67(1), Sch 5 Pt 1 para 6(1), (2)).

40   'Independent advocacy services' means services provided under the Mental Health Act 1984 s 130A or s 130E; arrangements under the National Health Service Act 2006 s 248 or the National Health Service (Wales) Act 2006 s 187 (see HEALTH SERVICES vol 54 (2008) PARA 597) or arrangements of a description prescribed: Mental Health Act 1983 s 134(3A)(b) (as added (see note 38); substituted by the Mental Health Act 2007 s 30(3); and amended by the Mental Health (Wales) Measure 2010 s 53(1)). In relation to Wales, for the purposes of the Mental Health Act 1983 s 134(3A)(b)(iii), the prescribed arrangements are arrangements in respect of independent mental capacity advocates made under the Mental Capacity Act 2005 ss 35–41 (independent advocacy service: see PARAS 807–814): see the Mental Health (Hospital, Guardianship, Community Treatment and Consent to Treatment) (Wales) Regulations 2008, SI 2008/2439, reg 42.

41   Mental Health Act 1983 s 134(3)(eb) (as added: see note 39).

42   Mental Health Act 1983 s 134(3)(f).

43   Mental Health Act 1983 s 134(3)(g).

44   Mental Health Act 1983 s 134(3)(h). As to the European Commission of Human Rights and the European Court of Human Rights see RIGHTS AND FREEDOMS.

45   As to the meaning of 'the regulatory authority' see PARA 573 note 1.

46   Ie under the Mental Health Act 1983 s 134(1)(b) or (2).

47   Ie in a case under the Mental Health Act 1983 s 134(1)(b).

48   Mental Health Act 1983 s 134A(1), (2) (added by the Health and Social Care Act 2008 Sch 3 para 2). In case under the Mental Health Act 1983 s 134(1)(b) the application must be made by the patient and in a case under s 134(2) the application must be made by either the patient or by the person by whom the postal packet was sent. The Secretary of State may by regulations make provision in connection with the making to and determination by the Care Quality Commission of applications under s 134(1), including provision for the production to the Commission of any postal packet which is the subject of such an application: s 134A(5). The Welsh Ministers may by regulations make provision in connection with the making to them of applications under s 134A(1), including provision for the production to them of any postal packet which is the subject of such an application: s 134A(6). Accordingly provision has been made in relation to England, that every application for review by the Commission under s 134A(1) must be made in such manner as the Commission may accept as sufficient in the circumstances of any particular case or class of case and may be made otherwise than in writing and made, delivered or sent to an office of the Commission: Mental Health (Hospital, Guardianship and Treatment) (England) Regulations 2008, SI 2008/1184, reg 30(1). Any person making such an application must furnish to the Commission the notice of the withholding of the postal packet or anything contained in it, given under the Mental Health Act 1983 s 134(6), or a copy of that notice: Mental Health (Hospital, Guardianship and Treatment) (England) Regulations 2008, SI 2008/1184, reg 30(2). For the purpose of determining any such application the Commission may direct the production of such documents, information and evidence as it may reasonably require: reg 30(3). At the date at which this volume states the law no such regulations had been made in relation to Wales.

49   Mental Health Act 1983 s 134A(2) (as added: see note 48).

50   Mental Health Act 1983 s 134A(3) (as added: see note 48).

781. Visiting detained patients. Provision is made[1] in relation to the visiting of patients[2] in hospitals[3] or in registered establishments[4]. All detained patients are entitled to maintain contact with and be visited by anyone they wish to see, subject to limited restrictions which are imposed only in exceptional circumstances[5]. The two main grounds justifying exclusion of a visitor are restriction on clinical grounds and restriction on security grounds[6].

While children may visit patients, there should be regularly reviewed written policies on the relevant arrangements which should be drawn up in consultation with local social services authorities[7], and a visit by a child should only take place following a decision that it would be in the child's best interests[8].

The hospital or registered establishment should be sufficiently flexible to enable regular visits to the patient, if the patient so wishes[9]. Every effort must be made to help the patient to make contact with relatives, friends and supporters; and, in particular, patients should have readily accessible and appropriate daytime telephone facilities[10], and no restrictions should be placed upon dispatch and receipt of their mail over and above those referred to in the Mental Health Act 1983[11].

1   See the Department of Health *Mental Health Act 1983 Code of Practice* (2008) Chapter 19; and the Welsh Assembly Government *Mental Health Act 1983 Code of Practice for Wales* (2008) Chapter 20. As to the Codes of Practice see PARA 762.
2   As to the meaning of 'patient' see PARA 758 note 4.
3   As to the meaning of 'hospital' see PARA 577.
4   As to the meaning of 'registered establishment' see PARA 578.
5   See the Department of Health *Mental Health Act 1983 Code of Practice* (2008) para 19.2; and the Welsh Assembly Government *Mental Health Act 1983 Code of Practice for Wales* (2008) para 20.2. The Welsh Assembly Government *Mental Health Act 1983 Code of Practice for Wales* (2008) para 20.5 provides that restricting visitors to informal patients could amount to a deprivation of liberty and may mean an authorisation under the deprivation of liberty safeguards of the Mental Capacity Act 2005 should be considered if the individual lacks mental capacity (see PARA 648).
6   See the Department of Health *Mental Health Act 1983 Code of Practice* (2008) para 19.10; and the Welsh Assembly Government *Mental Health Act 1983 Code of Practice for Wales* (2008) para 20.15.
7   As to the meaning of 'local social services authority' see PARA 579.
8   See the Department of Health *Mental Health Act 1983 Code of Practice* (2008) paras 19.18, 19.17; and the Welsh Assembly Government *Mental Health Act 1983 Code of Practice for Wales* (2008) paras 20.9, 20.12. See the Visits by Children to Ashworth, Broadmoor and Rampton Hospitals Directions 1999 which were held to be lawful in *R (on the application of L) v Secretary of State for Health* [2001] 1 FCR 326, [2001] 1 FLR 406 (child nephews and nieces of patient convicted of murder not permitted to visit).
9   See the Department of Health *Mental Health Act 1983 Code of Practice* (2008) para 19.3; and the Welsh Assembly Government *Mental Health Act 1983 Code of Practice for Wales* (2008) para 20.6.
10 As to telephone monitoring and the European Convention on Human Rights and Fundamental Freedoms (Rome, 4 November 1950; TS 71 (1953); Cmd 8969) art 8 see *R (on the application of N) v Ashworth Special Hospital* (11 May 2001) Lexis; and see RIGHTS AND FREEDOMS.
11 See the Department of Health *Mental Health Act 1983 Code of Practice* (2008) para 19.4; and the Welsh Assembly Government *Mental Health Act 1983 Code of Practice for Wales* (2008) para 20.3. The restrictions are those referred to in the Mental Health Act 1983 s 134 (see PARA 780).

782. Members of Parliament. Until 28 April 2013[1] where a member of the House of Commons or the Welsh Assembly is authorised to be detained[2] under a relevant enactment[3] on the ground, however formulated, that he is suffering from mental disorder[4], it is the duty of the court, authority or person on whose order or application, and of any medical practitioner on whose recommendation or certificate, the detention was authorised, and of the person in charge of the hospital or other place in which the member is authorised to be detained, to notify the Speaker of the House of Commons or the Presiding Officer of the Welsh Assembly[5] that the detention has been authorised[6].

Where the Speaker or Presiding Officer receives a notification under these provisions, or is notified by two members of the House of Commons or the Welsh Assembly that they are credibly informed that such an authorisation has been given, the Speaker or the Presiding Officer must cause the member to whom the notification relates to be visited and examined by two registered medical practitioners[7].

The registered medical practitioners must report to the Speaker or the Presiding Officer whether the member is suffering from mental disorder and is authorised to be detained under the Mental Health Act 1983 as such[8].

If the report is to the effect that the member is suffering from mental disorder and authorised to be detained as aforesaid, the Speaker or the Presiding Officer must at the expiration of six months from the date of the report, if the House or Assembly is then sitting, and otherwise as soon as may be after the House or Assembly next sits, again cause the member to be visited and examined by two such registered medical practitioners as aforesaid, and the registered medical practitioners must report as aforesaid[9].

If the second report is that the member is suffering from mental disorder and authorised to be detained the seat of the member becomes vacant[10].

1 As from 28 April 2013 the Mental Health Act 1983 s 141 is repealed by and any rule of the common law which disqualifies a person from membership of the House of Commons on grounds of mental illness is abolished: see the Mental Health (Discrimination) Act 2013 s 1 s 1(1), (2). Section 1 comes into force at the end of 2 months beginning with the day on which the Mental Health (Discrimination) Act 2013 was passed (ie 28 February 2013): see s 4(1).

2 References in the Mental Health Act 1983 s 141 to a member who is authorised to be detained do not include a member who is a community patient (whether or not he is recalled to hospital under s 17E (see PARA 801): s 141(6C) (added by the Mental Health Act 2007 Sch 3 para 33). As to the House of Commons generally see PARLIAMENT vol 78 (2010) PARA 892 et seq.

3 For this purpose the Mental Health Act 1983, the Criminal Procedure (Scotland) Act 1995, the Mental Health (Care and Treatment) Scotland Act 2003 and the Mental Health (Northern Ireland) Order 1986, SI 1986/596 are relevant enactments: see the Mental Health Act 1983 s 141(6A)(a) (s 141(6A), (6B) added by the Mental Health Act 2007 Sch 1 para 16(5)).

4 This provision does not apply if the Member of Parliament is suffering from any form of mental disorder other than mental illness. Mental disorder is a disqualification at common law for sitting and voting in the House of Commons: see PARLIAMENT vol 78 (2010) PARA 900. As to the meaning of 'mental disorder' see PARA 761.

5 As to the Speaker of the House of Commons see PARLIAMENT vol 78 (2010) PARA 931.

6 Mental Health Act 1983 s 141(1), (9) (s 141(1) amended by the Mental Health Act 2007 Sch 1 para 16(2); the Mental Health Act 1983 s 141(9) added by the Government of Wales Act 1998 Sch 12 para 23 and amended by the Government of Wales Act 2006 Sch 10 para 13). As to the procedure to be followed where the Speaker receives notification under the Mental Health Act 1983 s 141(1) see s 141(2)–(10) (s 141(8)–(10) as added); and PARLIAMENT vol 78 (2010) PARA 1094. Section 141 extends to Scotland: see s 146; and PARA 557.

7 Mental Health Act 1983 s 141(2). The registered medical practitioners to be appointed for this purpose must be appointed by the President of the Royal College of Psychiatrists and must be practitioners appearing to the President to have special experience in the diagnosis or treatment of mental disorders: s 141(3).

8 Mental Health Act 1983 s 141(4), (6A) (s 141(4) amended and s 141(6A), (6C) added by the Mental Health Act 2007 Sch 1 para 16(3)(a), (5)). References in the Mental Health Act 1983 s 141 to a member who is authorised to be detained does not include a member who is a community patient (whether or not he is recalled to hospital under s 17E (see PARA 801)): s 141(6C) (as so added).

9 Mental Health Act 1983 s 141(5) (amended by the Mental Health Act 2007 Sch 1 para 16(4)).

10 See the Mental Health Act 1983 s 141(6) (amended by the Mental Health Act 2007 Sch 1 para 16(4)).

783. Pocket money for in-patients. The appropriate national authority[1] may pay to persons who are receiving treatment as in-patients, whether liable to be detained or not, in hospitals wholly or mainly used for the treatment of persons suffering from mental disorder[2], such amounts as he thinks fit in respect of their occasional personal expenses where it appears to him that they would otherwise be without resources to meet those expenses[3].

1 As to the appropriate national authority see PARA 567. As from 1 April 2013 the Mental Health Act 1983 s 122 is amended by the Health and Social Care Act 2012 s 41(2)(a) to abolish this power in relation to the Secretary of State: see the Health and Social Care Act 2012 (Commencement No 4, Transitional, Savings and Transitory Provisions) Order 2013, SI 2013/160, art 2(2).

2 As to the meaning of 'mental disorder' see PARA 761.

3 Mental Health Act 1983 s 122(1) (amended by the Health Act 1999 Sch 4 paras 65, 66, Sch 5). The making of such payments to persons for whom hospital and specialist services are provided under the National Health Service Act 2006 and the National Health Service (Wales) Act 2006 are to be treated for the purposes of those Acts as included among those services: Mental Health Act 1983 s 122(2) (amended by the National Health Service (Consequential Provisions) Act 2006 Sch 1 para 67).

(4) GUARDIANSHIP

784. Regulations for guardianship. The appropriate national authority[1] has power to make regulations[2] prescribing matters which, under the statutory provisions for guardianship[3] are required or authorised to be prescribed, and otherwise for carrying those provisions into effect[4]. The appropriate national authority may[5] also make regulations prescribing the manner in which the functions of hospital managers[6], local social services authorities[7], local health boards[8], special health authorities[9], primary care trusts[10], national health service trusts or NHS foundation trusts[11] are to be exercised[12].

1 As to the appropriate national authority see PARA 567.

2 See the Mental Health (Hospital, Guardianship and Treatment) (England) Regulations 2008, SI 2008/1184; the Mental Health (Hospital, Guardianship, Community Treatment and Consent to Treatment) (Wales) Regulations 2008, SI 2008/2439, and PARAS 886–891.

3 Ie matters under the Mental Health Act 1983 Pt 2 (ss 2–34): see PARA 767 et seq.

4 See the Mental Health Act 1983 s 32(1). The regulations may, in particular, make provision for: (1) prescribing the form of any application, recommendation, report, order, notice or other document to be made or given; (2) prescribing the manner in which such documents may be proved and served; (3) requiring such bodies as may be prescribed by the regulations to keep such registers or other records as may be so prescribed in respect of patients liable to be detained or subject to guardianship under Pt 2 or community patients and to furnish or make available to those patients, and their relatives, such written statements of their rights and powers under the Mental Health Act 1983 as may be so prescribed; (4) determining the age of patients; and (5) enabling the functions of nearest relatives to be delegated in certain circumstances: see s 32(2) (amended by the Mental Health (Patients in the Community) Act 1995 Sch 1 para 2; and the Mental Health Act 2007 Sch 3 para 15, Sch 11 Pt 5).

5 This is subject to the Mental Health Act 1983 s 23(4), (6) (see PARA 913).

6 As to the meaning of 'managers' see PARA 778.

7 As to the meaning of 'local social services authority' see PARA 579.

8 As to the meaning of 'local health board' see PARA 575 note 6.

9 As to the meaning of 'special health authority' see PARA 575 note 4.

10 As to the meaning of 'primary care trust' see PARA 575 note 5. As from 1 April 2013 the words 'primary care trust' are repealed by the Health and Social Care Act 2012 Sch 5 para 27: see the Health and Social Care Act 2012 (Commencement No 4, Transitional, Savings and Transitory Provisions) Order 2013, SI 2013/160, art 2(2).

11 As to national health service trusts and NHS foundation trusts see HEALTH SERVICES vol 54 (2008) PARA 155 et seq.

12   Such regulations may in particular provide for the circumstances and conditions under which functions may be performed by officers or other persons acting on behalf of the managers, boards, authorities and trusts: Mental Health Act 1983 s 32(3) (amended by the National Health Service and Community Care Act 1990 s 66(1), Sch 9 para 24(5); the Health Authorities Act 1995 Sch 1 para 107(4); the Health and Social Care (Community Health and Standards) Act 2003 s 34, Sch 4 paras 50, 55; the Mental Health Act 2007 s 45(2); SI 2000/90; SI 2007/961; and prospectively amended (see note 10)). As to the regulations that have been made see the Mental Health (Hospital, Guardianship and Treatment) (England) Regulations 2008, SI 2008/1184; Mental Health (Hospital, Guardianship, Community Treatment and Consent to Treatment) (Wales) Regulations 2008, SI 2008/2439: see PARAS 886–891.

785. Guardianship applications.

A patient[1] who has attained the age of 16 years[2] may be received into guardianship for the period allowed[3] in pursuance of an application (referred to as a guardianship application) made in accordance with the Mental Health Act 1983[4]. The patient[5] may apply to the appropriate tribunal within the six months beginning with the day on which the guardianship application is accepted[6].

A guardianship application may be made[7] in respect of a patient on the grounds: (1) that he is suffering from mental disorder[8] of a nature or degree which warrants his reception into guardianship under the Mental Health Act 1983[9]; and (2) that it is necessary in the interests of the welfare of the patient or for the protection of other persons that the patient should be so received[10].

A guardianship application must be founded on the written recommendations in the prescribed form[11] of two registered medical practitioners[12], including in each case a statement that in the opinion of the practitioner the conditions forming the grounds of the application are complied with[13]. Each recommendation must include prescribed particulars[14] of the grounds for that opinion so far as it relates to the first condition and also, so far as it relates to the second condition, a statement of the reasons for that opinion[15].

The purpose of guardianship is to enable patients to receive care outside hospital when it cannot be provided without the use of compulsory powers[16]. It provides an authoritative framework for working with a patient, with a minimum of constraint to achieve as independent a life as possible within the community[17].

The care of an incapacitated person may also be provided for under the Mental Capacity Act 2005 in addition to, or as an alternative to guardianship under the Mental Health Act 1983[18].

1   As to the meaning of 'patient' generally see PARA 758 note 4.

2   Mental Health Act 1983 s 7(1). The application must state the age of the patient if known or, if the exact age is not known, that the patient is believed (if this is true) to have attained the age of 16: s 7(4). As to the appropriateness of wardship as a remedy for a 17 year old see *Re F (Mental Health Act guardianship)* [2000] 1 FCR 11, [2000] 1 FLR 192. As to the Mental Health Act 1983 s 7 see *Re G (An Adult) (Mental Capacity: Court's Jurisdiction)* [2004] EWHC 2222 (Fam), [2004] All ER (D) 33 (Oct).

3   The period allowed in the first instance is a period not exceeding six months beginning with the day on which the guardianship application is accepted (see the Mental Health Act 1983 s 20(1); and PARA 908); the authority for guardianship may be renewed at the expiration of the first period for a further period of six months and thereafter for one year at a time (see s 20(2)). A patient must be informed of any renewal: see s 20(6); and PARA 910. There is no provision for reception into guardianship for assessment or for assessment in an emergency.

4   Mental Health Act 1983 s 7(1). For the forms of application see the Mental Health (Hospital, Guardianship and Treatment) (England) Regulations 2008, SI 2008/1184, reg 5(1)(a), (b), Sch 1; and the Mental Health (Hospital, Guardianship, Community Treatment and Consent to Treatment) (Wales) Regulations 2008, SI 2008/2439, reg 9(1)(a), (b), Sch 1. As to bilingual application forms to be used in Wales see the Mental Health (Hospital and Guardianship)

(Welsh Forms) Regulations 1971, SI 1971/178, reg 3, Schedule. As to the general provisions governing applications for guardianship see PARA 848.

The Department of Health *Mental Health Act 1983 Code of Practice* (2008) Chapter 26; and the Welsh Assembly Government *Mental Health Act 1983 Code of Practice for Wales* (2008) Chapter 6 give general guidance on guardianship and its relationship with supervised community treatment and leave of absence. As to the Codes of Practice see PARA 762.

5 See note 1.

6 As to the acceptance of guardianship applications see PARA 848. The nearest relative must receive notification under the Mental Health (Hospital, Guardianship and Treatment) (England) Regulations 2008, SI 2008/1184, reg 26(3), (4) and the Mental Health (Hospital, Guardianship, Community Treatment and Consent to Treatment) (Wales) Regulations 2008, SI 2008/2439, reg 15. Under the Mental Health Act 1983 s 130D (see PARA 811) notification of the services of an independent mental health advocate must be given to the patient and the nearest relative. As to applications to the appropriate tribunal see the Mental Health Act 1983 s 66(1)(c), (i), (2)(c); and PARA 961. The patient may be discharged by the responsible clinician under s 23(2)(b) (see PARA 913) or the nearest relative. There is no power to make a 'barring order' preventing discharge by a nearest relative and an appropriate application to the county court under s 29 (see PARA 842) will be needed.

7 Applications may be made either by the nearest relative of the patient (see PARA 839) or by an approved mental health professional (see PARA 815 note 2): see the Mental Health Act 1983 s 11(1); and PARA 847. As to applications by approved mental health professionals generally see PARA 821. For general requirements as to applications see PARAS 847–848. As to who can be a guardian see s 7(5); and PARA 787 note 5.

8 As to the meaning of 'mental disorder' see PARA 761. See the restrictive definition given to 'seriously irresponsible conduct' in *Re F (Mental Health Act guardianship)* [2000] 1 FCR 11, [2000] 1 FLR 192 which it is submitted may diminish the use of guardianship for people with learning disabilities.

9 Mental Health Act 1983 s 7(2)(a) (amended by the Mental Health Act 2007 Sch 1 para 3, Sch 11 Pt 1).

10 Mental Health Act 1983 s 7(2)(b).

11 See the Mental Health (Hospital, Guardianship and Treatment) (England) Regulations 2008, SI 2008/1184, reg 5(1)(c), Sch 1; and the Mental Health (Hospital, Guardianship, Community Treatment and Consent to Treatment) (Wales) Regulations 2008, SI 2008/2439, reg 9(1)(c), Sch 1.

12 As to registered medical practitioners see MEDICAL PROFESSIONS vol 74 (2011) PARA 176 et seq. As to the general requirements for medical recommendations see PARA 849 et seq. The medical recommendations should consider whether the proposed application constitutes the least restrictive method of caring for the person: see the Department of Health *Mental Health Act 1983 Code of Practice* (2008) para 26.9; and the Welsh Assembly Government *Mental Health Act 1983 Code of Practice for Wales* (2008) para 6.4.

13 Mental Health Act 1983 s 7(3).

14 As to the prescribed particulars see PARA 768.

15 Mental Health Act 1983 s 7(3)(a), (b). The practitioner is not required, as he is when giving a recommendation for admission for treatment, to specify whether other methods of dealing with the patient are available, and if so why they are not appropriate: cf s 3(3)(b); and PARA 768.

16 Department of Health *Mental Health Act 1983 Code of Practice* (2008) para 26.2; the Welsh Assembly Government *Mental Health Act 1983 Code of Practice for Wales* (2008) para 6.2.

17 Department of Health *Mental Health Act 1983 Code of Practice* (2008) para 26.4.

18 For the interaction between the Mental Capacity Act 2005 and the Mental Health Act 1983 see PARA 562; the Department of Health *Mental Health Act 1983 Code of Practice* (2008) paras 26.10–26.13; and the Department for Constitutional Affairs *Mental Capacity Act 2005 Code of Practice* (2008) paras 13.16–13.21. Guardianship is not intended to be used to authorise a deprivation of liberty but does not prevent an authorisation being granted under the deprivation of liberty safeguards in the Mental Capacity Act 2005 if the person needs to be detained in a hospital in their best interests in order to receive care and treatment so long as it would not be inconsistent with the guardian's decision about where the person should live: Department of Health *Mental Health Act 1983 Code of Practice* (2008) para 26.32. Staff and carers providing general acts of daily care to incapacitated patients under guardianship are protected under the Mental Capacity Act 2005 ss 5, 6 (see PARA 611). This includes acts of restraint falling short of deprivation of liberty see PARA 648. A patient under guardianship is not subject to the consent to treatment provisions of the Mental Health Act 1983 Pt 4 (ss 56–64).

786.   Wards of court.   An application for the admission to hospital of a minor who is a ward of court[1] may be made under the Mental Health Act 1983 Part 2[2] with the leave of the court[3].

Where a minor who is a ward of court is liable to be detained in a hospital by virtue of an application for admission under the Mental Health Act 1983 Part 2[4] or is a community patient, any power exercisable[5] in relation to the patient by his nearest relative[6] is exercisable by or with the leave of the court[7].

A guardianship application may not be made in respect of a minor who is a ward of court, nor may such a minor be transferred into guardianship[8] without the leave of the court[9].

Where a community treatment order has been made in respect of a minor who is a ward of court, the provisions of the Mental Health Act 1983 relating to community treatment orders and community patients[10] have effect in relation to the minor subject to any order which the court makes in the exercise of its wardship jurisdiction; but this does not apply as regards any period when the minor is recalled[11] to hospital[12].

1   As to wards of court see CHILDREN AND YOUNG PERSONS vol 9 (2012) PARA 264 et seq.
2   Ie the Mental Health Act 1983 ss 2–34.
3   Mental Health Act 1893 s 33(1). Section 11(4) (see PARA 847) does not apply to an application made under s 33(1).
4   See note 2.
5   Ie any power exercisable under the Mental Health Act 1983 Pt 2 or under s 66 (see PARA 961).
6   As to the nearest relative see PARA 839.
7   Mental Health Act 1983 s 33(2) (amended by the Mental Health Act 2007 Sch 3 para 16(2)).
8   As to the different consequences of guardianship and wardship see *Re F (Mental Health Act Guardianship)* [2000] 1 FCR 11, [2000] 1 FLR 192, CA.
9   Mental Health Act 1983 s 33(3).
10 Ie the provisions of the Mental Health Act 1983 Pt 2 (ss 2–34).
11 Ie recalled to hospital under the Mental Health Act 1983 s 17E (see PARA 801).
12 Mental Health Act 1983 s 33(4) (added by the Mental Health (Patients in the Community) Act 1995 s 1(2), Sch 1 para 3; and substituted by the Mental Health Act 2007 Sch 3 para 16(3)).

787.   Effect of application.   Where a guardianship application is duly made[1], forwarded to the local social services authority[2] within the period allowed[3], and accepted[4] by that authority, it confers on the authority or person named in the application as guardian[5], the power to: (1) require the patient to reside at a place specified by the authority or person named as guardian[6]; (2) require the patient to attend at places and times so specified for the purpose of medical treatment, occupation, education or training[7]; (3) require access to the patient to be given, at any place where the patient is residing, to any registered medical practitioner, approved social mental health professional[8] or other person so specified[9].

Where a patient is received into guardianship in pursuance of a guardianship application, any previous application[10] by virtue of which he was subject to guardianship or liable to be detained in a hospital[11] ceases to have effect[12].

1   Ie under the provisions of the Mental Health Act 1983 Pt 2 (ss 2–34): see PARA 785. As to guardianship generally see the Department of Health *Mental Health Act 1983 Code of Practice* (2008) Chapter 26 and the Welsh Assembly Government *Mental Health Act 1983 Code of Practice for Wales* (2008) Chapter 6. As to the Codes of Practice see PARA 762.
    As to the purpose of guardianship and its relationship to the Mental Capacity Act 2005 and deprivation of liberty see PARA 785. If a local authority considers that the powers under the Mental Health Act 1983 s 8 are insufficient to manage the case of an incapacitated person then consideration should be given to an application to the Court of Protection under the Mental Capacity Act 2005: see *Lewis v Gibson* [2005] EWCA Civ 587, [2005] 2 FCR 241, 87 BMLR 93. Guardianship does not provide an express power to authorise detention but the powers available to the guardian could have the effect of depriving a person of their liberty: see the

Convention for the Protection of Human Rights and Fundamental Freedoms (Rome, 4 November 1950; TS 71 (1953); Cmd 8969) art 5 (see RIGHTS AND FREEDOMS). Factors such as type, duration and intensity of restrictions are important: see *Guzzardi v Italy* (1980) 3 EHRR 333; *Ashingdane v United Kingdom* (1985) 7 EHRR 528, ECtHR.

2   As to the local social services authority see PARA 579.

3   Ie the period of 14 days beginning with the date on which a registered medical practitioner last examined the patient before giving a medical recommendation for the purpose of the application: Mental Health Act 1983 s 8(2). As to registered medical practitioners see MEDICAL PROFESSIONS vol 74 (2011) PARA 176 et seq. As to the meaning of 'patient' see PARA 758 note 4.

4   As to acceptance see further PARA 848.

5   The guardian named may be either a local social services authority or any other person (including the applicant) but in the latter case the application is of no effect unless accepted on that person's behalf by the local social services authority for the area in which he resides and it must be accompanied by a statement in writing by that person that he is willing to act as guardian: Mental Health Act 1983 s 7(5). See further PARA 848. As to 'the area in which he resides' see *Fox v Stirk; Ricketts v Registration Officer for the City of Cambridge* [1970] 2 QB 463, [1970] 3 All ER 7, CA; and ELECTIONS AND REFERENDUMS vol 15(3) (2007 Reissue) PARA 132.

6   Mental Health Act 1983 s 8(1)(a). The words 'to the exclusion of any other person' excludes decision making under the Mental Capacity Act 2005 and the Court of Protection, so that that court has no jurisdiction to make decisions that conflict with the matters falling within the guardian's powers in the case of an incapacitated person subject to guardianship under this Act; the Mental Health Act 1983 should have primacy over the Mental Capacity Act 2005: see *C (by his litigation friend, the Official Solicitor) v A Borough Council* [2011] EWHC 3321 (COP), [2011] All ER (D) 203 (Dec), *GJ v Foundation Trust* [2009] EWHC 2972 (Fam), [2010] Fam 70, [2010] 3 WLR 840. As to the implied duty to act in the welfare of the patient see *R v Kent County Council, ex parte Marston* CO/1819/96.

As to the power to take the patient to the place of residence see the Mental Health Act 1983 s 18(7); and PARA 920. If the patient absconds he may be taken into custody and returned within a specified period see s 18(4); and PARA 918. The obstruction of a person authorised to return a patient under s 18(3) is a criminal offence under s 129 (see PARA 1015). See also PARA 793.

The local social services authority must arrange for the patient to be visited not less than once every 3 months, and at least one such visit must be made annually by an approved clinician: see the Mental Health (Hospital, Guardianship and Treatment) (England) Regulations 2008, SI 2008/1184, reg 23, and the Mental Health (Hospital, Guardianship, Community Treatment and Consent to Treatment) (Wales) Regulations 2008, SI 2008/2439, reg 10. See PARA 791.

7   Mental Health Act 1983 s 8(1)(b). As to the meaning of 'medical treatment' see PARA 926. The guardian has no power to consent to treatment on behalf of the patient: *T v T* [1988] Fam 52, [1988] 1 All ER 613. The Mental Health Act 1983 Pt 4 does not apply to patients subject to guardianship: see s 56(3); and PARA 924. If a patient has capacity then he may refuse treatment for physical or mental disorder.

8   As to the meaning of 'approved mental health professional' see PARA 815 note 2.

9   Mental Health Act 1983 s 8(1)(c) (amended by the Mental Health Act 2007 Sch 2 para 2(b)).

10   Ie under the Mental Health Act 1983 ss 2(1), 3(1), 4(1), 7(1): see PARAS 767–769, 785.

11   As to the meaning of 'hospital' see PARA 577.

12   Mental Health Act 1983 s 8(5).

788. Proof of form and contents. A guardianship application which appears to be duly made[1] and to be founded on the necessary medical recommendations may be acted on without further proof of the signature or qualification of the person by whom the application or any such medical recommendation is made or given, or of any matter of fact or opinion stated in the application[2].

1   Ie under the provisions of the Mental Health Act 1983 Pt 2 (ss 2–34): see PARA 785.

2   See the Mental Health Act 1983 s 8(3). See also PARA 772.

789. Rectification of guardianship application or recommendation. If, within the period of 14 days beginning with the day on which a guardianship application has been accepted by the local social services authority[1], the guardianship application or any medical recommendation given for the purposes of the application is found to be in any respect incorrect or defective[2], the application or recommendation may, within that period and with the consent of that authority, be amended by the person by whom it was signed; on the amendment being made the application or recommendation has effect, and is deemed to have had effect, as if it had been originally made as so amended[3].

1   See PARA 787 text and note 3. As to the local social services authority see PARA 579.
2   Cf the Mental Health Act 1983 s 15(1); and PARA 774.
3   Mental Health Act 1983 s 8(4). There is no provision in s 8, as there is in s 15(3), (4) (see PARA 775), for the obtaining of a fresh medical recommendation in substitution for one which does not appear to warrant the reception of the patient into guardianship. On an application of the principle de minimis, minor mistakes that are not rectified within the requisite period do not invalidate the application: *Re E (Mental Health: Habeas Corpus)* (10 December 1966, unreported).

790. Power to make regulations as to guardianship. The appropriate national authority[1] may make regulations for regulating the exercise by guardians of their powers[2], and for imposing upon them, and upon local social services authorities[3] in the case of patients[4] under the guardianship of persons other than local social services authorities[5], such duties as he considers necessary or expedient in the interests of the patients[6].

1   As to the appropriate national authority see PARA 567.
2   As to the powers of a guardian see PARA 787.
3   As to local social services authorities see PARA 579.
4   As to the meaning of 'patient' see PARA 758 note 4.
5   See PARA 787.

6   Mental Health Act 1983 s 9(1). The regulations may in particular provide for the visiting of patients on behalf of the local social services authority concerned and must provide for the appointment, in the case of a patient subject to the guardianship of a person other than a local social services authority, of a medical practitioner to act as the nominated medical attendant of the patient: s 9(2). See the Mental Health (Hospital, Guardianship and Treatment) (England) Regulations 2008, SI 2008/1184; and the Mental Health (Hospital, Guardianship, Community Treatment and Consent to Treatment) (Wales) Regulations 2008, SI 2008/2439.

791. Visits on behalf of the responsible local social services authority. The responsible local social services authority[1] must arrange for every patient received into guardianship to be visited at intervals as the authority may decide but, in any case at intervals of not more than three months, and at least one such visit in any year must be made by an approved clinician[2] or approved[3] medical practitioner[4].

1   The responsible local social services authority is: (1) where the patient is subject to the guardianship of a local social services authority, that authority; and (2) where the patient is subject to the guardianship of another person, the local social services authority for the area in which that person resides: Mental Health Act 1983 s 34(3). As to the meaning of 'local social services authority' see PARA 579. As to the meaning of 'patient' see PARA 758 note 4. As to guardianship applications generally see PARA 785.
2   As to the meaning of 'approved clinician' see PARA 831.

3   Ie approved by the appropriate national authority under the Mental Health Act 1983 s 12: see PARA 849.

4   Mental Health (Hospital, Guardianship and Treatment) (England) Regulations 2008, SI 2008/1184, reg 23; Mental Health (Hospital, Guardianship, Community Treatment and Consent to Treatment) (Wales) Regulations 2008, SI 2008/2439, reg 10. For the duty of a local social services authority to visit and to take other steps in relation to a guardianship patient admitted (for any reason) to hospital see PARA 583. As to visits to guardianship patients with a view to ordering discharge or making an application to an appropriate tribunal see PARAS 916, 963. Obstruction of visits to guardianship patients is an offence: see PARA 1015.

792. Duties of private guardians. Where a patient[1] is subject to the guardianship of a private guardian[2], it is the duty of the guardian to:

(1) appoint a registered medical practitioner[3] to act as the nominated medical attendant[4] of the patient[5];

(2) notify the responsible local social services authority[6] of his name and address[7];

(3) in exercising powers and duties conferred or imposed on him by the Mental Health Act 1983 or regulations[8], comply with directions given by the responsible local social services authority, and furnish it with such reports and information with regard to the patient as it may require[9];

(4) notify the responsible local social services authority of his address and that of the patient, on the patient's reception into guardianship[10]; and

(5) notify the responsible local social services authority, in the event of the death of the patient or the termination of the guardianship by discharge, transfer or otherwise, as soon as reasonably practicable[11].

1 As to the meaning of 'patient' see PARA 758 note 4.
2 'Private guardian' in relation to a patient, means a person, other than a local social services authority (see PARA 579), who acts as a guardian under the Mental Health Act 1983: Mental Health (Hospital, Guardianship and Treatment) (England) Regulations 2008, SI 2008/1184, reg 2(1); Mental Health (Hospital, Guardianship, Community Treatment and Consent to Treatment) (Wales) Regulations 2008, SI 2008/2439, reg 2(1). As to guardianship applications generally see PARA 785.
3 As to registered medical practitioners see MEDICAL PROFESSIONS vol 74 (2011) PARA 176 et seq.
4 'Nominated medical attendant', in relation to a patient who is subject to the guardianship of a person other than a local social services authority, means the person appointed in pursuance of regulations made under the Mental Health Act 1983 s 9(2) (see PARA 790 note 6) to act as the medical attendant of the patient: s 34(1).
5 Mental Health (Hospital, Guardianship and Treatment) (England) Regulations 2008, SI 2008/1184, reg 22(1)(a); Mental Health (Hospital, Guardianship, Community Treatment and Consent to Treatment) (Wales) Regulations 2008, SI 2008/2439, reg 11(1)(a).
6 As to the meaning of 'responsible local social services authority' see PARA 791 note 1.
7 Mental Health (Hospital, Guardianship and Treatment) (England) Regulations 2008, SI 2008/1184, reg 22(1)(b); Mental Health (Hospital, Guardianship, Community Treatment and Consent to Treatment) (Wales) Regulations 2008, SI 2008/2439, reg 11(1)(b).
8 Ie the Mental Health (Hospital, Guardianship and Treatment) (England) Regulations 2008, SI 2008/1184; and the Mental Health (Hospital, Guardianship, Community Treatment and Consent to Treatment) (Wales) Regulations 2008, SI 2008/2439.
9 Mental Health (Hospital, Guardianship and Treatment) (England) Regulations 2008, SI 2008/1184, reg 22(1)(c), (d); Mental Health (Hospital, Guardianship, Community Treatment and Consent to Treatment) (Wales) Regulations 2008, SI 2008/2439, reg 11(1)(c), (d).
10 On any permanent change of either address the guardian must notify the authority of the new address either before or not later than 7 days after the change takes place; if the new address is in the area of a different local social services authority, the guardian must notify that authority of his address and that of the patient, and of the name and address of the patient's nominated medical attendant, and a copy of the notification must be sent to the local social services authority which was formerly responsible: see the Mental Health (Hospital, Guardianship and Treatment) (England) Regulations 2008, SI 2008/1184, reg 22(1)(e), (f); and the Mental Health (Hospital, Guardianship, Community Treatment and Consent to Treatment) (Wales) Regulations 2008, SI 2008/2439, reg 11(1)(e), (f).
11 See the Mental Health (Hospital, Guardianship and Treatment) (England) Regulations 2008, SI 2008/1184, reg 22(1)(g); and the Mental Health (Hospital, Guardianship, Community Treatment and Consent to Treatment) (Wales) Regulations 2008, SI 2008/2439, reg 11(1)(g).

793. Absence without leave of patients subject to guardianship. Where a patient[1] subject to guardianship[2] absents himself without the leave[3] of the guardian from the place at which he is required by the guardian to reside[4], he may, within the period permitted[5], be taken into custody[6] and returned to that place by any officer on the staff of a local social services authority[7], by any constable[8], or by any person authorised in writing by the guardian or a local social services authority[9]. A patient must not be so taken into custody after the later of the end of six months beginning with the first day of his absence without leave and the end of the period for which he is liable to be detained or subject to guardianship[10].

1 As to the meaning of 'patient' see PARA 758 note 4.
2 As to guardianship applications generally see PARA 785.
3 As to the meaning of 'absent without leave' see PARA 918 note 4.
4 See PARA 787.
5 Ie by the Mental Health Act 1983 s 18(4): see the text and note 10.
6 As to the meaning of 'legal custody' see PARA 777.
7 As to the local social services authority see PARA 579.
8 As to the office of constable see POLICE vol 36(1) (2007 Reissue) PARA 101 et seq.
9 Mental Health Act 1983 s 18(3). The power of arrest under s 18 was preserved by the Police and Criminal Evidence Act 1984 s 26(2), Sch 2: see CRIMINAL LAW, EVIDENCE AND PROCEDURE vol 11(2) (2006 Reissue) PARA 927.
10 See the Mental Health Act 1983 s 18(4); and PARA 918.

794. Death or resignation of the guardian. If any person (other than a local social services authority[1]) who is the guardian of a patient[2] received into guardianship[3] dies or gives notice in writing to the local social services authority that he desires to relinquish the functions of guardian, the guardianship of the patient then vests in the local social services authority[4]. The authority may either continue to act as guardian, or guardianship may subsequently be transferred in pursuance of the appropriate regulations[5] to another person who is willing to act[6].

1 For the purposes of the Mental Health Act 1984 s 10 'the local social services authority', in relation to a person (other than a local social services authority) who is the guardian of a patient, means the local social services authority for the area in which that person resides (or resided immediately before his death): s 10(5) (added by the Mental Health Act 2007 Sch 2 para 3(3)). As to the local social services authority see PARA 579.
2 As to the meaning of 'patient' see PARA 758 note 4.
3 Ie under the Mental Health Act 1983 Pt 2 (ss 2–34), in pursuance of a guardianship application under s 7(1) (see PARA 785) or a guardianship order (see PARA 877), since a patient subject to such an order is to be treated for this purpose as if he had been received into guardianship in pursuance of such an application under Pt 2: see s 40(2).
4 Mental Health Act 1983 s 10(1).
5 See the Mental Health (Hospital, Guardianship and Treatment) (England) Regulations 2008, SI 2008/1184, reg 8; and the Mental Health (Hospital, Guardianship, Community Treatment and Consent to Treatment) (Wales) Regulations 2008, SI 2008/2439, reg 24.
6 Mental Health Act 1983 s 10(1). If the guardian has performed his functions negligently or in a manner contrary to the interests of the welfare of the patient, a court may order that the guardianship be transferred to the local social services authority or to any person approved for the purpose by that authority: see s 10(3); and PARA 796. If the guardian becomes ill and has not relinquished his functions, the authority may perform them on his behalf: see s 10(2); and PARA 795.

795. Illness of the guardian. If any person is incapacitated by illness or any other cause from performing the functions of a guardian[1], and has not given written notice to the local social services authority[2] that he desires to relinquish those functions, the authority may during his incapacity perform them on his behalf or any other person approved by the authority for that purpose may do so[3].

1   Ie under the Mental Health Act 1983 Pt 2 (ss 2–34), in pursuance of a guardianship application
    under s 7(1) (see PARA 785) or a guardianship order (see PARA 877), since a patient subject to
    such an order is to be treated for this purpose as if he had been received into guardianship in
    pursuance of such an application under Pt 2: see s 40(2).
2   Ie notice under the Mental Health Act 1983 s 10(1)(b) (see PARA 794). As to the meaning of
    'local social services authority' see PARA 794 note 1.
3   Mental Health Act 1983 s 10(2).

796.   Transfer of guardianship by order of the county court.   If it appears to
the county court[1] on application made by an approved mental health
professional[2] acting on behalf of the local social services authority[3] that any
person other than a local social services authority having the guardianship of a
patient[4] received into guardianship[5] has performed his functions negligently or in
a manner contrary to the interests of the welfare of the patient, the court may
order that the guardianship of the patient be transferred to the local social
services authority or to any other person approved for the purpose by that
authority[6].

1   As to county courts generally see COURTS AND TRIBUNALS vol 24 (2010) PARA 758 et seq.
2   As to the meaning of 'approved mental health professional' see PARA 815 note 2.
3   As to the meaning of 'local social services authority' see PARA 794 note 1.
4   As to the meaning of 'patient' see PARA 758 note 4.
5   Ie under the Mental Health Act 1983 Pt 2 (ss 2–34): see PARA 794 note 3.
6   Mental Health Act 1983 s 10(3) (amended by the Mental Health Act 2007 Sch 2 para 3(2)).

(5) COMMUNITY TREATMENT ORDERS

797.   Making a community treatment order.   The responsible clinician[1] may
by order in writing discharge a detained patient[2] from hospital subject to his
being liable to recall[3]. Such an order is known as a community treatment order[4].
The responsible clinician may not make a community treatment order unless in
his opinion, the relevant criteria are met and an approved mental health
professional[5] states in writing that he agrees with that opinion and that it is
appropriate to make the order[6].
The relevant criteria are that:

(1)   the patient is suffering from mental disorder[7] of a nature or degree
       which makes it appropriate for him to receive medical treatment[8];
(2)   it is necessary for his health or safety or for the protection of other
       persons that he should receive such treatment[9];
(3)   subject to his being liable to be recalled as mentioned in head (5) below,
       such treatment can be provided without his continuing to be detained in
       a hospital[10];
(4)   it is necessary that the responsible clinician should be able to exercise
       the power[11] to recall the patient to hospital[12]; and
(5)   appropriate medical treatment is available for him[13].

The patient may apply to the appropriate tribunal in respect of a community
treatment order within six months beginning with the day on which the
community treatment order is made[14].

1   As to the meaning of 'responsible clinician' see PARA 834.
2   A detained patient is a patient who is liable to be detained in a hospital in pursuance of an
    application for admission for treatment: Mental Health Act 1983 s 17A(2) (added by the Mental
    Health Act 2007 s 32(2)). As to the meaning of 'patient' see PARA 758 note 4. This includes a
    patient on s 17 leave (see PARA 917) and a patient under a s 37 (see PARA 864) hospital order
    without restrictions (see s 47(3), Sch 1 para 1). As to the forms see the Mental Health (Hospital,
    Guardianship and Treatment) (England) Regulations 2008, SI 2008/1184, reg 6(1); and the

Mental Health (Hospital, Guardianship, Community Treatment and Consent to Treatment) (Wales) Regulations 2008, SI 2008/2439, reg 16.

3   Mental Health Act 1983 s 17A(1) (as added: see note 2). Recall is in accordance with s 17E (see PARA 801). As to the relevant forms for the purpose of making a community treatment order see the Mental Health (Hospital, Guardianship and Treatment) (England) Regulations 2008, SI 2008/1184, reg 6(1); and the Mental Health (Hospital, Guardianship, Community Treatment and Consent to Treatment) (Wales) Regulations 2008, SI 2008/2439, reg 16.

4   Mental Health Act 1983 s 17A(3) (as added: see note 2). For the purposes of the Mental Health Act 1983 'the community treatment order', in relation to a community patient, means the community treatment order in force in respect of him: Mental Health Act 1983 s 17A(7) (as so added). 'Community patient' means a patient in respect of whom a community treatment order is in force: s 17A(7) (as so added). A community treatment order is also referred to as supervised community treatment: see the Department of Health *Mental Health Act 1983 Code of Practice* (2008) Chapters 25, 28, 29. A community treatment order suspends the effect of an admission under the Mental Health Act 1983 s 3 (or other relevant admission power) which is revived if the patient is recalled to hospital (see PARAS 798, 801). The introduction of community treatment orders was one of the key changes introduced by the Mental Health Act 2007. The purpose of such an order is to allow suitable patients to be safely treated in the community rather than under detention in hospital: see the Department of Health *Mental Health Act 1983 Code of Practice* (2008) para 25.2; and the Welsh Assembly Government *Mental Health Act 1983 Code of Practice for Wales* (2008) para 30.3. It is aimed at treating certain patients under compulsory powers in the community. These patients are largely so-called 'revolving door' patients who have a demonstrable history of stopping medication once discharged from hospital, relapsing and being readmitted. However, under these provisions a patient in the community cannot be medicated compulsorily (see PARA 798). A community treatment order is an alternative to guardianship and long term leave under the Mental Health Act 1983 s 17 (see PARA 917) and the relevant guidance for the use of s 17 leave and community treatment orders is provided in the Department of Health *Mental Health Act 1983 Code of Practice* (2008) Chapter 28 and the Welsh Assembly Government *Mental Health Act 1983 Code of Practice for Wales* (2008) Chapter 30.

     It is submitted that a community treatment order is not intended to apply to a patient who remains under detention in a hospital so that the conditions applied must not amount to a deprivation of liberty in a hospital (see PARA 800).

     The care of an incapacitated person may also be provided for under the Mental Capacity Act 2005 in addition to or as an alternative to a community treatment order under the Mental Health Act 1983. The Mental Capacity Act 2005 deprivation of liberty safeguards are available if appropriate: see the Department of Health *Mental Health Act 1983 Code of Practice* (2008) paras 28.7–28.10. For the interaction between the Mental Health Act 1983 and the Mental Capacity Act 2005 see PARA 562; the Department of Health *Mental Health Act 1983 Code of Practice* (2008) paras 26.10–26.13; and the Department for Constitutional Affairs *Mental Capacity Act 2005 Code of Practice* (2007) paras 13.16–13.21.

5   As to the meaning of 'approved mental health professional' see PARA 815 note 2.

6   Mental Health Act 1983 s 17A(4) (as added: see note 2). As to which approved mental health professional should carry out this role see the Department of Health *Mental Health Act 1983 Code of Practice* (2008) para 25.26.

7   As to the meaning of 'mental disorder' see PARA 761.

8   Mental Health Act 1983 s 17A(5)(a) (as added: see note 2).

9   Mental Health Act 1983 s 17A(5)(b) (as added: see note 2).

10   Mental Health Act 1983 s 17A(5)(c) (as added: see note 2).

11   Ie the power under the Mental Health Act 1983 s 17E(1) (see PARA 801).

12   Mental Health Act 1983 s 17A(5)(d) (as added: see note 2). In determining whether the criterion in s 17A(5)(d) is met, the responsible clinician must, in particular, consider, having regard to the patient's history of mental disorder and any other relevant factors, what risk there would be of a deterioration of the patient's condition if he were not detained in a hospital (as a result, for example, of his refusing or neglecting to receive the medical treatment he requires for his mental disorder): s 17A(6) (as so added). A responsible clinician must inform the hospital managers if he is considering making a community treatment order with regard to patients under unrestricted hospital orders, hospital directions or transfer directions so that obligations under the Domestic Violence, Crime and Violence Act 2004 may be satisfied with regard to representations from victims. See also the Department of Health; Ministry of Justice; National Offender Management Service *Mental Health Act 2007: guidance on the extension of victims' rights under the Domestic Violence, Crime and Victims Act 2004* (17 October 2008).

13   Mental Health Act 1983 s 17A(5)(e) (as added: see note 2).

14 See the Mental Health Act 1983 s 66(1)(ca), (i), (2)(ca); and PARA 961. A nearest relative may also apply to the tribunal if a barring order is issued by the responsible clinician against a discharge. Hospital managers must refer a patient to the appropriate tribunal if the community treatment order is revoked: see s 68; and PARA 964.

798. Effect of community treatment order. The application for admission for treatment in respect of a patient[1] does not cease to have effect by virtue of his becoming a community patient[2]. However, while he remains a community patient the authority of the managers[3] to detain him[4] in pursuance of that application is suspended[5] and certain provisions in the Mental Health Act 1983 do not apply to him[6].

1 As to the meaning of 'patient' see PARA 758 note 4.
2 Mental Health Act 1983 s 17D(1) (added by the Mental Health Act 2007 s 32(2)). As to the meaning of 'community treatment patient' see PARA 797 note 4.
3 As to the meaning of 'the managers' see PARA 778.
4 Ie the authority to detain him under the Mental Health Act 1983 s 6(2) (see PARA 771).
5 Mental Health Act 1983 s 17D(2)(a) (as added: see note 2).
6 Reference (however expressed) in the Mental Health Act 1983 or any other Act, or in any subordinate legislation (within the meaning of the Interpretation Act 1978), to patients liable to be detained, or detained, under the Mental Health Act 1983 does not include such a patient referred to in the text: see s 17D(2)(b) (as added: see note 2). Section 20 does not apply to him while he remains a community patient and accordingly authority for his detention does not expire during any period in which that authority is suspended by virtue of s 20(2)(a) (see PARA 909): s 17D(3) (as so added). Under Pt 4A (ss 64A–64K) a mentally capable or incapable patient under a community treatment order and who has not been recalled to hospital may be treated only with his or her consent, or if they lack capacity to consent, if they do not actively object. The medical treatment of a community patient who has been recalled is governed by s 62A (see PARA 934).

799. Duration of community treatment order. A community treatment order[1] remains in force until it expires[2], the patient is discharged[3], the application for admission for treatment in respect of the patient otherwise ceases to have effect[4] or the order is revoked[5].

A community treatment order ceases to be in force on expiry of the period of six months beginning with the day on which it was made ('the community treatment period')[6]. The community treatment period may, unless the order has previously ceased to be in force, be extended from its expiration for a period of six months, and from that period of extension for a further period of one year, and so on for periods of one year at a time[7].

Within the period of two months ending on the day on which the order would cease to be in force in default of an extension under these provisions, it is the duty of the responsible clinician[8] to examine the patient[9]. If it appears to that clinician that certain conditions are satisfied, and if a statement is made by an approved mental health professional[10] that it appears to him that those conditions are satisfied and that it is appropriate to extend the community treatment period, the clinician must furnish to the managers of the responsible hospital[11] a report to that effect in the prescribed form[12].

The conditions referred to above are that:

(1) the patient is suffering from mental disorder[13] of a nature or degree which makes it appropriate for him to receive medical treatment[14];

(2) it is necessary for his health or safety or for the protection of other persons that he should receive such treatment[15];

(3) subject to his continuing to be liable to be recalled as mentioned in head (4) below, such treatment can be provided without his being detained in a hospital[16];

(4)   it is necessary that the responsible clinician should continue to be able to exercise the power[17] to recall the patient to hospital[18]; and

(5)   appropriate medical treatment is available for him[19].

Where a report is duly furnished under the above provisions, the community treatment period must be thereby extended for the period prescribed[20] in that case[21].

On expiry of the community treatment order[22], and if the order has not previously ceased to be in force, a community patient is deemed to be discharged absolutely from liability to recall under Part 2 of the Mental Health Act 1983[23], and the application for admission for treatment ceases to have effect[24].

1   As to the meaning of 'community treatment order' see PARA 797.

2   Ie until the period mentioned in the Mental Health Act 1983 s 20A(1) (as extended under any provision of the Mental Health Act 1983) expires, but this is subject to ss 21 and 22 (see PARA 912): s 17C(a) (added by the Mental Health Act 2007 s 32(2)). See also the Mental Health Act 1983 ss 21A, 21B; and PARA 911.

3   Ie in pursuance of an order under the Mental Health Act 1983 s 23 (see PARA 913) or a direction under s 72 (see PARA 967): s 17C(b) (as added: see note 2).

4   Mental Health Act 1983 s 17C(c) (as added: see note 2).

5   Ie under the Mental Health Act 1983 s 17F (see PARA 802): s 17C(d) (as added: see note 2).

6   See the Mental Health Act 1983 s 20A(1), (2) (ss 20A, 20B added by the Mental Health Act 2007 s 32(3)). This is subject to the Mental Health Act 1983 Pt 2 (ss 2–34).

7   See the Mental Health Act 1983 s 20A(3) (as added: see note 2).

8   As to the meaning of 'responsible clinician' see PARA 834.

9   Mental Health Act 1983 s 20A(4)(a) (as added: see note 6). If the responsible clinician decides not to review the community treatment order he must inform the hospital managers if the patient comes within the scope of the Domestic Violence, Crime and Victims Act 2004: see PARA 797 note 12.

10   As to the meaning of 'approved mental health professional' see PARA 815 note 2.

11   'The responsible hospital', in relation to a community patient, means the hospital in which he was liable to be detained immediately before the community treatment order was made, subject to the Mental Health Act 1983 s 19A (see PARA 804): s 17A(7) (added by the Mental Health Act 2007 s 32(2)).

12   See the Mental Health Act 1983 s 20A(4)(b), (8) (as added: see note 6). Where such a report is furnished in respect of the patient, the managers must, unless they discharge him under s 23 (see PARA 913), cause him to be informed: s 20A(5) (as so added). Before furnishing a report under s 24A(4) the responsible clinician must consult one or more other persons who have been professionally concerned with the patient's medical treatment: s 20A(9) (as so added). As to the issue of such a report see the Mental Health (Hospital, Guardianship and Treatment) (England) Regulations 2008, SI 2008/1184, reg 13(6), (7). There is a duty to inform the patient's nearest relative if an order has been extended: see the Mental Health (Hospital, Guardianship and Treatment) (England) Regulations 2008, SI 2008/1184, reg 26(1)(e); and the Mental Health (Hospital, Guardianship. Community Treatment and Consent to Treatment) (Wales) Regulations 2008, SI 2008/2439, reg 22(1)(a). As to the duty to provide information see PARA 805.

13   As to the meaning of 'mental disorder' see PARA 761.

14   Mental Health Act 1983 s 20A(6)(a) (as added: see note 6).

15   Mental Health Act 1983 s 20A(6)(b) (as added: see note 6).

16   Mental Health Act 1983 s 20A(6)(c) (as added: see note 6).

17   Ie the power under the Mental Health Act 1983 s 17E(1) (see PARA 801).

18   Mental Health Act 1983 s 20A(6)(d) (as added: see note 6). In determining whether the criterion in head (4) in the text is met, the responsible clinician must, in particular, consider, having regard to the patient's history of mental disorder and any other relevant factors, what risk there would be of a deterioration of the patient's condition if he were to continue not to be detained in a hospital (as a result, for example, of his refusing or neglecting to receive the medical treatment he requires for his mental disorder): s 20A(7) (as so added).

19   Mental Health Act 1983 s 20A(6)(e) (as added: see note 6).

20   Ie as prescribed under the Mental Health Act 1983 s 20A(3) (see the text and note 7).

21   Mental Health Act 1983 s 20A(10) (as added: see note 6).

22 For the purposes of the Mental Health Act 1983 s 20B(1), a community treatment order expires on expiry of the community treatment period as extended under Pt 2, but this is subject to ss 21 and 22 (see PARAS 911, 912): s 20B(1) (as added: see note 6).

23 Ie the Mental Health Act 1983 Pt 2 (ss 2–34).

24 See the Mental Health Act 1983 s 20B(2) (as added: see note 6). There are special provisions that apply to patients who have been absent without leave on the day on which the community treatment order would cease to have effect or within one week of that day whereby the order will be extended until a period of one week from the time the patient is returned under s 18 or returns to hospital, or the order will cease at the end of the period during which he could be taken into custody under s 18: see s 21(1), (2), (4); and PARA 911.

800. Conditions. A community treatment order[1] must specify conditions to which the patient[2] is to be subject while the order remains in force[3]. The order must specify a condition that the patient make himself available for examination[4] and a condition that, if it is proposed to give a certificate in respect of treatment[5] in his case, he make himself available for examination so as to enable the certificate to be given[6]. Subject to this[7], the order may specify conditions only if the responsible clinician[8], with the agreement of the approved mental health professional[9], thinks them necessary or appropriate for one or more of the following purposes:

(1) ensuring that the patient receives medical treatment[10];

(2) preventing risk of harm to the patient's health or safety[11];

(3) protecting other persons[12].

The responsible clinician may from time to time by order in writing vary the conditions specified in a community treatment order[13]. He may also suspend any conditions specified in a community treatment order[14].

The responsible clinician may recall a patient to hospital if he fails to comply with a condition under the above provisions[15].

1 As to the meaning of 'community treatment order' see PARA 797.

2 As to the meaning of 'patient' see PARA 758 note 4.

3 Mental Health Act 1983 s 17B(1) (added by the Mental Health Act 2007 s 32(2)). As to the relevant forms for the purpose of the Mental Health Act 1983 s 17B see the Mental Health (Hospital, Guardianship and Treatment) (England) Regulations 2008, SI 2008/1184, reg 6(2); and the Mental Health (Hospital, Guardianship. Community Treatment and Consent to Treatment) (Wales) Regulations 2008, SI 2008/2439, reg 16. A patient should agree to keep the conditions or to try to do so and to have access to the help they need to comply: see the Department of Health *Mental Health Act 1983 Code of Practice* (2008) para 25.35. It is submitted that an incapacitated patient may be subject to a community treatment order so long as they are compliant with conditions. The Mental Health Act 1983 s 18(7) (see PARA 918) does not apply to a patient under a community treatment order and there is no power to take an objecting patient to the place of where they are required to be as a condition of a community treatment order.

It is submitted that it would be unlawful to impose conditions that would amount to a deprivation of liberty within the meaning of the European Convention on Human Rights and Fundamental Freedoms (Rome, 4 November 1950; TS 71 (1953); Cmd 8969) art 5 (see RIGHTS AND FREEDOMS). If a deprivation of liberty arises as a result of the patient's wider care needs as opposed to the need for medical treatment for mental disorder then the Mental Capacity Act 2005 deprivation of liberty safeguards are available in addition to the community treatment order. By a similar token discharge under the community treatment order from a hospital to a hospital is unlikely to be lawful because a hospital is a place of treatment and not residence.

4 Ie under the Mental Health Act 1983 s 20A (see PARA 799).

5 Ie a certificate under the Mental Health Act 1983 Pt 4A (ss 64A–64K) that falls within s 64C(4) (see PARA 936).

6 Mental Health Act 1983 s 17B(3)(b) (as added: see note 3). Conditions under s 17A(3) are mandatory and enforceable by recall under s 17E(2). See the Department of Health *Mental Health Act 1983 Code of Practice* (2008) paras 25.29–25.34 and the Welsh Assembly Government *Mental Health Act 1983 Code of Practice* (2008) para 30.16 et seq for guidance on

community treatment order conditions generally. The tribunal has no power to amend or vary conditions for which an application for judicial review would be necessary.

7   Ie subject to the Mental Health Act 1983 s 20A(3).

8   As to the meaning of 'responsible clinician' see PARA 834.

9   Ie the approved mental health professional mentioned in the Mental Health Act 1983 s 17A(4)(b) (see PARA 799). As to the meaning of 'approved mental health professional' see PARA 815 note 2.

10   Mental Health Act 1983 s 17B(2)(a) (as added: see note 3). If a community patient fails to comply with a condition specified in the community treatment order by virtue of s 20A(2), that fact may be taken into account for the purposes of exercising the power of recall under s 17E(1) (see PARA 801): s17B(6) (as so added).

11   Mental Health Act 1983 s 17B(2)(b) (as added (see note 3); amended by the Health and Social Care Act 2012 s 299(6)).

12   Mental Health Act 1983 s 17B(2)(c) (as added: see note 3). Before an approved mental health professional agrees to the imposition of a condition he must consider any representations from victims if the patient is within the scope of the Domestic Violence, Crime and Victims Act 2004. See PARA 797 note 12.

13   Mental Health Act 1983 s 17B(4) (as added: see note 3).

14   Mental Health Act 1983 s 17B(5) (as added: see note 3).

15   See the Mental Health Act 1983 s 17E(2); and PARA 801.

801. Power to recall to hospital.

The responsible clinician[1] may recall a community patient to hospital[2] if in his opinion the patient requires medical treatment[3] in hospital for his mental disorder[4] and there would be a risk of harm to the health or safety of the patient or to other persons if the patient were not recalled to hospital for that purpose[5]. This power of recall[6] is exercisable by notice in writing to the patient and such a notice is sufficient authority for the managers[7] of that hospital to detain the patient there in accordance with provisions of the Mental Health Act 1983[8].

The responsible clinician may also recall a community patient to hospital (which need not be the responsible hospital)[9] if the patient fails to comply with a condition[10] of his community treatment order[11].

The above provisions do not prevent a patient from being recalled to a hospital even though he is already in the hospital at the time when the power of recall is exercised[12].

1   As to the meaning of 'responsible clinician' see PARA 834.

2   As to the meaning of 'community patient' see PARA 797 note 4. As to the meaning of 'hospital' see PARA 577. As to the meaning of 'patient' see PARA 758 note 4.

3   As to the meaning of 'medical treatment' see PARA 926.

4   Mental Health Act 1983 s 17E(1)(a) (added by the Mental Health Act 2007 s 32(2)). As to the meaning of 'mental disorder' see PARA 761.

5   Mental Health Act 1983 s 17E(1)(b) (as added: see note 4). As to the authority to treat community patients who are not recalled to hospital under s 17E see Pt 4A (ss 64A–64K); and PARAS 935–941.

6   Ie the power of recall under the Mental Health Act 1983 s 17E(1), (2).

7   As to the meaning of 'the managers' see PARA 778.

8   Mental Health Act 1983 s 17E(5), (6) (as added: see note 4). Where a patient refuses to accept the notice or cannot be found see the Department of Health *Mental Health Act 1983 Code of Practice* (2008) paras 25.55, 25.58; and the Welsh Assembly Government *Mental Health Act 1983 Code of Practice for Wales* (2008) paras 30.54–30.62. The notice should be delivered to the patient's last known or usual address. If a patient fails to respond to a recall notice ss 18, 21, 21A and 21B (see PARAS 918, 911) will apply. If access is denied to a recalled patient see s 135(2); and PARA 922. As regards a child community patient who is a ward of court see s 33(4); and PARA 786. The Mental Health (Hospital, Guardianship and Treatment) (England) Regulations 2008, SI 2008/1184, reg 6(7); and the Mental Health (Hospital, Guardianship. Community Treatment and Consent to Treatment) (Wales) Regulations 2008, SI 2008/2439, reg 22(1) require hospital managers to take steps to inform a patient of the effect of recall.

Recall could be to a hospital out-patient department: see *R (On the Application of DR) v Mersey Care NHS Trust* (2002) MHLR 386, QB (Admin); the Department of Health *Mental*

Health Act 1983 Code of Practice (2008) para 25.61; and the Welsh Assembly Government *Mental Health Act 1983 Code of Practice for Wales* (2008) para 30.71. The recalled patient is not liable to be detained so is not eligible for leave under s 17 (see PARA 917).

9   'The responsible hospital', in relation to such a patient, means the hospital in which he was liable to be detained immediately before the community treatment order was made, subject to the Mental Health Act 1983 s 19A (see PARA 804): s 17A(7) (added by the Mental Health Act 2007 s 32(2)).

10   Ie a condition specified under the Mental Health Act 1983 s 17B(3) (see PARA 800).

11   See the Mental Health Act 1983 s 17E(2), (3) (as added: see note 4).

12   Mental Health Act 1983 s 17E(4) (as added: see note 4). References to recalling the patient are be construed accordingly. Such a patient may be recalled as an informal patient. There is nothing to prevent recall even though the patient is complying with conditions imposed under s 17B (see PARA 800). There is no requirement for the responsible clinician to examine the patient before recall and he may act on reports received about the patient's behaviour and situation.

802. Powers in respect of recalled patients. The following applies to a community patient[1] who is detained in a hospital[2] by virtue of a notice[3] recalling him there[4].

The patient may be transferred to another hospital[5] in such circumstances and subject to such conditions as may be prescribed in regulations made by the appropriate national authority[6].

The responsible clinician[7] may by order in writing revoke the community treatment order if, in his opinion, the conditions for admission[8] are satisfied in respect of the patient and an approved mental health professional[9] states in writing that he agrees with that opinion and that it is appropriate to revoke the order[10].

The responsible clinician may at any time release the patient under these provisions, but not after the community treatment order has been revoked[11].

If the patient has not been released, nor the community treatment order revoked, by the end of the period of 72 hours[12], he must then be released[13]. But a patient who is released under these provisions remains subject to the community treatment order[14].

1   As to the meaning of 'community patient' see PARA 797 note 4. As to the meaning of 'patient' see PARA 758 note 4.

2   As to the meaning of 'hospital' see PARA 577.

3   Ie a notice recalling him there under the Mental Health Act 1983 s 17E (see PARA 801).

4   Mental Health Act 1983 s 17F(1) (added by the Mental Health Act 2007 s 32(2)).

5   If he is so transferred to another hospital, he must be treated for the purposes of the Mental Health Act 1983 s 17F (and s 17E (see PARA 801)) as if the notice under that provision were a notice recalling him to that other hospital and as if he had been detained there from the time when his detention in hospital by virtue of the notice first began: s 17F(3) (as added: see note 4).

6   Mental Health Act 1983 s 17F(2) (as added: see note 4). For these purposes the appropriate national authority is the Secretary of State, if the hospital in which the patient is detained is in England, or the Welsh Ministers, if that hospital is in Wales. As to the transfer of a recalled patient to hospital and the relevant forms see the Mental Health (Hospital, Guardianship and Treatment) (England) Regulations 2008, SI 2008/1184, reg 9; and the Mental Health (Hospital, Guardianship. Community Treatment and Consent to Treatment) (Wales) Regulations 2008, SI 2008/2439, reg 26.

7   As to the meaning of 'responsible clinician' see PARA 834.

8   Ie the conditions under the Mental Health Act 1983 s 3(2) (see PARA 768).

9   As to the meaning of 'approved mental health professional' see PARA 815 note 2.

10   Mental Health Act 1983 s 17F(4) (as added: see note 4). The responsible clinician must notify the hospital managers if the patient is within the scope of the Domestic Violence, Crime and Victims Act 2004. See PARA 797 note 12.

11   Mental Health Act 1983 s 17F(5) (as added: see note 4).

12   'The period of 72 hours' means the period of 72 hours beginning with the time when the patient's detention in hospital by virtue of the notice under the Mental Health Act 1983 s 17E

(see PARA 801) begins and references to being released must be construed as references to being released from that detention (and accordingly from being recalled to hospital): s 17F(8) (as added: see note 4).

13 Mental Health Act 1983 s 17F(6) (as added: see note 4).

14 Mental Health Act 1983 s 17F(7) (as added: see note 4).

803. Effect of revoking community treatment order. The following provisions apply if a community treatment order[1] is revoked[2] in respect of a patient[3].

The provisions of the Mental Health Act 1983 or any other Act relating to patients liable to be detained (or detained) in pursuance of an application for admission for treatment apply to the patient as they did before the community treatment order was made, unless otherwise provided[4].

If, when the order is revoked, the patient is being detained in a hospital other than the responsible hospital, the provisions of Part 2 of Mental Health Act 1983 have effect as if the application for admission for treatment in respect of him were an application for admission to that other hospital and he had been admitted to that other hospital at the time when he was originally admitted in pursuance of the application[5].

A patient can appeal to the appropriate tribunal where a community treatment order is revoked under the above provisions, within six months beginning with the day on which the community treatment order was revoked[6]. Where a patient has not exercised this right the managers of the hospital must refer the patient's case to the appropriate tribunal, on expiry of the period of six months beginning with the applicable day[7].

1 As to the meaning of 'community treatment order' see PARA 797.

2 Ie revoked under the Mental Health Act 1983 s 17F (see PARA 802). See the Department of Health *Mental Health Act 1983 Code of Practice* (2008) paras 25.65–25.70; and the Welsh Assembly Government *Mental Health Act 1983 Code of Practice for Wales* (2008) paras 30.78–30.82.

3 Mental Health Act 1983 s 17G(1) (added by the Mental Health Act 2007 s 32(2)). The Mental Health Act 1983 s 6(2) (see PARA 771) has effect as if the patient had never been discharged from hospital by virtue of the community treatment order: s 17G(2) (as so added).

4 Mental Health Act 1983 s 17G(3) (as added: see note 3).

5 Mental Health Act 1983 s 17G(4) (as added: see note 3). But, in any case, s 20 (see PARA 768) has effect as if the patient had been admitted to hospital in pursuance of the application for admission for treatment on the day on which the order is revoked: s 17G(5) (as so added).

6 See the Mental Health Act 1983 s 66(1)(cb), (i), (2)(cb); and PARA 960.

7 See the Mental Health Act 1983 s 68(1)(d), (2); and PARA 964. The managers must not refer the patient's case if a reference has been made under s 68(7) (see PARA 964) which provides for the hospital managers to refer the case to the tribunal as soon as practicable after the order is revoked.

804. Assignment of responsibility of community patient. Responsibility for a community patient[1] may be assigned to another hospital[2] in such circumstances and subject to such conditions as may be prescribed by regulations made by the appropriate national authority[3].

If responsibility for a community patient is assigned to another hospital the application for admission for treatment in respect of the patient has effect[4] as if it had always specified that other hospital, the patient is treated as if he had been admitted to that other hospital at the time when he was originally admitted in pursuance of the application[5] and that other hospital becomes 'the responsible hospital' in relation to the patient for the purposes of the Mental Health Act 1983[6].

In relation to England, the following applies to a community patient[7]. Responsibility for the community patient may be assigned by the managers of the responsible hospital to any other hospital whether or not that other hospital is under the same management as the responsible hospital[8]. However, responsibility for a patient must not be assigned to a hospital which is not under the same management as the responsible hospital unless an authority for the assignment is given by the managers of the assigning responsible hospital[9], that assignment has been agreed by the managers of the hospital which will be the responsible hospital if the proposed assignment takes effect, the managers of the hospital have specified the date on which the assignment will take place and the managers of the assigning responsible hospital record[10] the agreement of the managers of the new responsible hospital to the assignment and the date on which the assignment is to take place[11].

The managers of the receiving hospital must notify the patient in writing of the assignment, either before it takes place or as soon as reasonably practicable thereafter; and their name and address (irrespective of whether or not there are any changes in the managers)[12].

In relation to Wales, the following applies in respect of any patient who is for the time being a community patient[13]. Responsibility for a community patient may be assigned to another hospital under different management from the responsible hospital ('other hospital') where an authority for assignment[14] is given by the managers[15] of the assigning responsible hospital prior to assignment[16], those managers are satisfied that arrangements have been made for the assignment of responsibility of the patient to the other hospital within a period of 28 days beginning with the date of the authority for assignment[17], on assignment, the managers of the other hospital must record[18] the assignment[19].

In relation to England and Wales, where responsibility for a patient is assigned from a responsible registered establishment to another hospital which is not under the same management and the patient is maintained under a contract with a Strategic Health Authority[20], local health board[21], Primary Care Trust[22], National Health Service trust[23], National Health Service foundation trust[24], a Special Health Authority[25] or the Welsh Ministers, the authority for assignment under the above provisions may be given by an officer of that authority, board or trust authorised by it in that behalf, or by those Ministers, instead of by the managers[26].

1   As to the meaning of 'community patient' see PARA 797 note 4.
2   As to the meaning of 'hospital' see PARA 577.
3   Mental Health Act 1983 s 19A(1) (added by the Mental Health Act 2007 Sch 3 para 4). For these purposes the appropriate national authority is the Secretary of State, if the responsible hospital is in England, or the Welsh Ministers, if that hospital is in Wales.
4   This is subject to the Mental Health Act 1983 s 17D (see PARA 798).
5   And as if he had subsequently been discharged under the Mental Health Act 1983 s 17A (see PARA 797).
6   Mental Health Act 1983 s 19A(2) (as added: see note 3).
7   See the Mental Health (Hospital, Guardianship and Treatment) (England) Regulations 2008, SI 2008/1184, reg 17(1). This applies whether or not the patient has been recalled to hospital in accordance with the Mental Health Act 1983 s 17E (see PARA 801).
8   See the Mental Health (Hospital, Guardianship and Treatment) (England) Regulations 2008, SI 2008/1184, reg 17(2). Any hospital to which a patient has been assigned may, in accordance with the provisions of this regulation, assign the patient to another hospital: reg 17(6).
9   Ie in the specified form see the Mental Health (Hospital, Guardianship and Treatment) (England) Regulations 2008, SI 2008/1184, reg 17(3)(a). The functions of the managers may be performed by an officer authorised by them in that behalf: reg 17(7).
10   Ie in the specified form see the Mental Health (Hospital, Guardianship and Treatment) (England) Regulations 2008, SI 2008/1184, reg 17(3)(d).
11   Mental Health (Hospital, Guardianship and Treatment) (England) Regulations 2008, SI 2008/1184, reg 17(3) (amended by SI 2008/2560).

12 Mental Health (Hospital, Guardianship and Treatment) (England) Regulations 2008, SI 2008/1184, reg 17(4).
13 Mental Health (Hospital, Guardianship, Community Treatment and Consent to Treatment) (Wales) Regulations 2008, SI 2008/2439, reg 25(1).
14 As to the form for the authority see the Mental Health (Hospital, Guardianship, Community Treatment and Consent to Treatment) (Wales) Regulations 2008, SI 2008/2439, reg 25(2)(a).
15 The functions of the managers referred to in the Mental Health (Hospital, Guardianship, Community Treatment and Consent to Treatment) (Wales) Regulations 2008, SI 2008/2439, reg 25 may be performed by an officer authorised by them in that behalf: reg 25(6).
16 Mental Health (Hospital, Guardianship, Community Treatment and Consent to Treatment) (Wales) Regulations 2008, SI 2008/2439, reg 25(2)(a).
17 Mental Health (Hospital, Guardianship, Community Treatment and Consent to Treatment) (Wales) Regulations 2008, SI 2008/2439, reg 25(2)(b). Where such conditions of reg 25(2) are satisfied, the assignment of responsibility must be effected within 28 days of the date of the authority as provided under reg 25(2)(a), failing which responsibility for the community treatment order will remain with the hospital so responsible prior to assignment: reg 25(3).
18 As to the form for the assignment see the Mental Health (Hospital, Guardianship, Community Treatment and Consent to Treatment) (Wales) Regulations 2008, SI 2008/2439, reg 25(2)(c).
19 Mental Health (Hospital, Guardianship, Community Treatment and Consent to Treatment) (Wales) Regulations 2008, SI 2008/2439, reg 25(2)(c). Responsibility for a community patient to whom this regulation applies may be assigned to another hospital managed by the same hospital managers, in which event the provisions of reg 25(2), (3) and reg 32(b) will not apply: reg 25(4).
20 'Strategic health authority' means a strategic health authority established under the National Health Service Act 2006 s 13 (see HEALTH SERVICES vol 54 (2008) PARA 94): Mental Health Act 1983 s 145(1) (definition added by SI 2002/2469). As from 1 April 2013 strategic health authorities and primary care trusts are abolished and the definition of strategic health authority is repealed by the Health and Social Care Act 2012 Sch 5 para 31(1)(a): see the Health and Social Care Act 2012 (Commencement No 4, Transitional, Savings and Transitory Provisions) Order 2013, SI 2013/160, art 2(2).
21 As to the meaning of 'local health board' see PARA 575 note 7.
22 As to the meaning of 'primary care trust' see PARA 575 note 5. See note 20.
23 As to National Health Service trusts see HEALTH SERVICES vol 54 (2008) PARA 155 et seq.
24 As to NHS foundation trusts see HEALTH SERVICES vol 54 (2008) PARA 174 et seq.
25 As to the meaning of 'special health authority' see PARA 575 note 4.
26 See the Mental Health (Hospital, Guardianship and Treatment) (England) Regulations 2008, SI 2008/1184, reg 17(5); and the Mental Health (Hospital, Guardianship, Community Treatment and Consent to Treatment) (Wales) Regulations 2008, SI 2008/2439, reg 25(5).

805. Duty of managers to give information to community patients. The managers of the responsible hospital[1] must take such steps[2] as are practicable to ensure that a community patient[3] understands the effect of the provisions of the Mental Health Act 1983 applying to community patients and what rights of applying to a tribunal are available to him in that capacity[4]. Such steps must be taken as soon as practicable after the patient becomes a community patient[5].

The managers of the responsible hospital must, except where the community patient otherwise requests, take such steps as are practicable to furnish the person (if any) appearing to them to be his nearest relative with a copy of any information given to him[6]; and those steps must be taken when the information is given to the patient or within a reasonable time thereafter[7].

1 As to the meaning of 'managers' see PARA 778. As to the meaning of 'responsible hospital' see PARA 801 note 9.
2 The steps to be taken must include giving the requisite information both orally and in writing: Mental Health Act 1983 s 132A(2) (s 132A added by the Mental Health Act 2007 Sch 3 para 30).
3 As to the meaning of 'community patient' see PARA 797 note 4.
4 Mental Health Act 1983 s 132A(1) (as added (see note 2); s 132A(1) amended by SI 2008/2833).
5 Mental Health Act 1983 s 132A(1) (as added: see note 2).

6 Ie given to him in writing under the Mental Health Act 1983 s 132A(2).
7 Mental Health Act 1983 s 132A(3) (as added: see note 2).

(6) PROTECTION OF RELEVANT PATIENTS

806. General protection of relevant patients. The regulatory authority[1] must keep under review and, where appropriate, investigate the exercise of the powers and the discharge of the duties conferred or imposed by the Mental Health Act 1983 so far as relating to the detention of patients or their reception into guardianship or to relevant patients[2]. Relevant patients are patients liable to be detained under Mental Health Act 1983[3], community patients[4] and patients subject to guardianship[5].

The regulatory authority must make arrangements for persons authorised by it to visit and interview relevant patients in private, in the case of relevant patients detained under the Mental Health Act 1983, in the place where they are detained and, in the case of other relevant patients, in hospitals and regulated establishments[6] and, if access is granted, other places[7].

The regulatory authority must also make arrangements for persons authorised by it to investigate any complaint[8] as to the exercise of the powers or the discharge of the duties conferred or imposed by the Mental Health Act 1983 in respect of a patient who is or has been detained under that Act or who is or has been a relevant patient[9].

Such arrangements may exclude matters from investigation in specified circumstances and do not require any person exercising functions under the arrangements to undertake or continue with any investigation where the person does not consider it appropriate to do so[10].

For the purposes of a review or investigation under the above provisions or the exercise of functions under arrangements made under the above provisions, a person authorised by the regulatory authority may at any reasonable time:

(1) visit and interview in private any patient in a hospital or regulated establishment[11];

(2) if the authorised person is a registered medical practitioner or approved clinician, examine the patient in private there[12]; and

(3) require the production of and inspect any records relating to the detention or treatment of any person who is or has been detained under the Mental Health Act 1983 or who is or has been a community patient or a patient subject to guardianship[13].

The regulatory authority may direct certain persons[14] to publish a statement as to the action the person proposes to take as a result of a review or investigation under the above provisions[15].

1 As to the meaning of 'regulatory authority' see PARA 573 note 1.
2 Mental Health Act 1983 s 120(1) (s 120 substituted and ss 120A, 120B added by the Health and Social Care Act 2008 Sch 3 paras 8, 9). The regulatory authority may make provision for the payment of remuneration, allowances, pensions or gratuities to or in respect of persons exercising functions in relation to any review or investigation for which it is responsible under the Mental Health Act 1983 s 120(1) or functions under arrangements made by it under s 120: s 120(8) (as so substituted). The regulatory authority may publish a report of a review or investigation carried out by it under s 120(1): s 120A(1) (as so added). The Secretary of State may by regulations make provision as to the procedure to be followed in respect of the making of representations to the Care Quality Commission before the publication of a report by the Commission under s 120A(1) but must consult the Care Quality Commission before making any such regulations: s 120A(2), (3) (as so added). The Welsh Ministers may by regulations make provision as to the procedure to be followed in respect of the making of representations to them

before the publication of a report by them under s 120A(1): s 120A(4) (as so added). This following applies to the following persons: (1) the managers of a hospital (within the meaning of Pt 2 (see PARA 778)); (2) a local social services authority; and (3) the persons of any other description prescribed in regulations: s 120C(1) (as so added). A person to whom s 120C applies must provide the regulatory authority with such information as the authority may reasonably request for or in connection with the exercise of its functions under s 120: s 120C(2) (as so added). A person to whom s 120C applies must provide a person authorised under s 120 with such information as the person so authorised may reasonably request for or in connection with the exercise of functions under arrangements made under that provision: s 120C(3) (as so added). Section 120C is in addition to the requirements of s 120(7)(c) (as so added). 'Information' includes documents and records and 'regulations' means regulations made by the Secretary of State, in relation to England and, by the Welsh Ministers, in relation to Wales: s 120C(5), (6) (as so added). At the date at which this volume states the law no such regulations had been made under these provisions. As soon as possible at the end of each financial year the regulatory authority must publish an annual report on its activities in the exercise of its functions under the Mental Health Act 1983: s 120D(1), (2) (as so added). For this purpose 'financial year' means the period beginning with the date on which the Health and Social Care Act 2008 s 52 (see SOCIAL SERVICES AND COMMUNITY CARE) comes into force and ending with the next 31 March following that date and each successive period of 12 months ending with 31 March: Mental Health Act 1983 s 120D(5) (as so added). As to the meaning of local social services authority see PARA 579.

3　As to patients detained under the Mental Health Act 1983 see PARA 766 et seq.

4　As to community patients see PARA 797 et seq.

5　Mental Health Act 1983 s 120(2) (as substituted: see note 2). As to guardianship see PARA 784 et seq.

6　For this purpose 'registered establishment' means an establishment in respect of which a person is registered under the Care Standards Act 2000 Pt 2 (see PARA 585) or premises used for the carrying on of a regulated activity (within the meaning of the Health and Social Care Act 2008 Pt 1 (ss 1–7): see SOCIAL SERVICES AND COMMUNITY CARE) in respect of which a person is registered under Chapter 2 of that Part: Mental Health Act 1983 s 120(9) (as substituted: see note 2).

7　Mental Health Act 1983 s 120(3) (as substituted: see note 2).

8　As to where any such complaint as is mentioned in the Mental Health Act 1983 s 120(4) is made by an appropriate national authority see s 120(6) (as substituted: see note 2). As to the appropriate national authority see PARA 567.

9　Mental Health Act 1983 s 120(4) (as substituted: see note 2).

10　Mental Health Act 1983 s 120(5) (as substituted: see note 2).

11　Mental Health Act 1983 s 120(7)(a) (as substituted: see note 2).

12　Mental Health Act 1983 s 120(7)(b) (as substituted: see note 2).

13　Mental Health Act 1983 s 120(7)(c) (as substituted: see note 2).

14　The persons are: (1) the managers of a hospital; (2) a local social services authority; (3) persons of any other description prescribed in regulations made by the appropriate national authority: see the Mental Health Act 1983 s 120B(2), (4) (as added: see note 2). Regulations may make further provision about the content and publication of statements under s 120B: s 120B(3) (as so added). At the date at which this volume states the law no regulations had been made under s 120B.

15　Mental Health Act 1983 s 120B(1) (as added: see note 2).

(7) INDEPENDENT MENTAL HEALTH ADVOCATES

807. Arrangements for independent mental health advocates. The appropriate national authority[1] must make such arrangements[2] as it considers reasonable to enable persons ('independent mental health advocates') to be available to help qualifying patients[3] or, in relation to Wales, Welsh qualifying compulsory patients[4] and Welsh qualifying informal patients[5]. The appropriate national authority may by regulations make provision as to the appointment of persons as independent mental health advocates[6] and such regulations may, in particular, provide:

(1)   that a person may act as an independent mental health advocate only in such circumstances, or only subject to such conditions, as may be specified in the regulations[7];

(2)   for the appointment of a person as an independent mental health advocate to be subject to approval in accordance with the regulations[8].

In making arrangements under these provisions, the appropriate national authority must have regard to the principle that any help available to a patient under the arrangements should, so far as practicable, be provided by a person who is independent of any person who is professionally concerned[9] with the patient's medical treatment or, in relation to Wales, falls within a description specified in regulations[10].

1   In relation to Wales, the Mental Health Act 1983 ss 130A(1), (2), (4) are amended, s 130C(2) is substituted and s 130C(5), (6) repealed by the Mental Health (Wales) Measure 2010 Sch 1, paras 1–7, Sch 2 to effectively apply those provisions in relation to England only.
      In relation to England, references to the appropriate national authority are, in relation to a qualifying patient in England, to the Secretary of State and, in relation to a qualifying patient in Wales, to the Welsh Ministers: see the Mental Health Act 1983 s 130C(5) (ss 130A–130D added by the Mental Health Act 2007 s 30(2); and the Mental Health Act 1983 s 130C(5), (6) repealed in relation to Wales). For these purposes:
      (1)   a qualifying patient falling within s 130C(2)(a) (see note 3) is to be regarded as being in the territory in which the hospital or registered establishment in which he is liable to be detained is situated (s 130C(6)(a) (as so added and repealed in part));
      (2)   a qualifying patient falling within s 103C(2)(b) (see note 3) is to be regarded as being in the territory in which the area of the responsible local social services authority within the meaning of s 34(3) (see PARA 791 note 1) is situated (s 130C(6)(b) (as so added and repealed in part));
      (3)   a qualifying patient falling within s 130C(2)(c) (see note 3) is to be regarded as being in the territory in which the responsible hospital is situated (s 130C(2)(c) (as so added and repealed in part));
      (4)   a qualifying patient falling within s 103C(3) (see note 3) is to be regarded as being in the territory determined in accordance with arrangements made for the purposes of this provision, and published, by the Secretary of State and the Welsh Ministers (s 130C(2)(d) (as so added; and repealed in part)).
      In relation to Wales the reference to the appropriate national authority refers to the Welsh Ministers see PARA 567.
      In relation to England, the duty to arrange independent mental health advocates is transferred from the Secretary of State to the local social services authority and accordingly the Mental Health Act 1983 s 130A is amended and s 130C(4A), (4B) are added by the Health and Social Care Act 2012 s 43(1)–(3) as follows:
      (a)   the words 'Secretary of State' in the Mental Health Act 1983 s 130A(1) are substituted by the words 'A local social services authority whose area is in England' and the words 'for whom the authority is responsible for the purposes of s 130A' are added at the end of s 130A; and
      (b)   in s 130A(4) the words 'Secretary of State' are replaced by the words 'a local social services authority'.
      A local social services authority is responsible for a qualifying patient if:
      (i)   in the case of a qualifying patient falling within s 130C(2)(a) (see note 3), the hospital or registered establishment in which he is liable to be detained is situated in that authority's area (s 130C(4A)(a) (as so added));
      (ii)   in the case of a qualifying patient falling within s 130C(2)(b) (see note 3), that authority is the responsible local social services authority within the meaning of s 34(3) (see PARA 791 note 1) (s 130C(4A)(b) (as so added));
      (iii)   in the case of a qualifying patient falling within s 130C(2)(c) (see note 3), the responsible hospital is situated in that authority's area (s 130C(4A)(c) (as so added));
      (iv)   in the case of a qualifying patient falling within s 130C(3) (see note 3), in a case where the patient has capacity or is competent to do so, he nominates that authority as responsible for him for the purposes of s 130A or, in any other case, a donee or deputy or the Court of Protection, or a person engaged in caring for the patient or interested in his welfare, nominates that authority on his behalf as responsible for him for the purposes of that provision (s 130C(4A)(d) (as so added)).

In head (iv) above the reference to a patient who has capacity is to be read in accordance with the Mental Capacity Act 2005, the reference to a donee is to a donee of a lasting power of attorney (within the meaning of s 9) created by the patient, where the donee is acting within the scope of his authority and in accordance with that Act and the reference to a deputy is to a deputy appointed for the patient by the Court of Protection under s 16, where the deputy is acting within the scope of his authority and in accordance with that Act: s 130C(4B) (as so added).

The above amendments made by the Health and Social Care Act 2012 are in force in so far as it is necessary for enabling the exercise of any power to make an order or regulations or to give directions and otherwise as from 1 April 2003: see s 306(1)(d); and the Health and Social Care Act 2012 (Commencement No 4, Transitional, Savings and Transitory Provisions) Order 2013, SI 2013/160, art 2(2).

2   Such arrangements may include provision for payments to be made to, or in relation to, persons carrying out functions in accordance with the arrangements: see the Mental Health Act 1983 ss 130A(6), 130E(6) (s 130A as added (see note 1); s 130E added by the Mental Health (Wales) Measure 2010 s 31).

3   For the purposes of the Mental Health Act 1983 s 130A a patient is a qualifying patient if he is liable to be detained under the Mental Health Act 1983 (otherwise than by virtue of s 4 or s 5(2) or (4) or s 135 or s 136), or he is subject to a guardianship under the Mental Health Act 1983 or he is a community patient: s 130C(1), (2) (as added (see note 1)). An informal patient is also a qualifying patient if:

     (1)   not being a qualifying patient falling within s 130C(2), he discusses with a registered medical practitioner or approved clinician the possibility of being given a form of treatment to which s 57 above applies (s 130C(3)(a) (as so added)); or

     (2)   not having attained the age of 18 years and not being a qualifying patient falling within s 130C(2), he discusses with a registered medical practitioner or approved clinician the possibility of being given a form of treatment to which s 58A above applies (s 130C(3)(b) (as so added)).

Where a patient who is a qualifying patient falling within s 130C(3) is informed that the treatment concerned is proposed in his case, he remains a qualifying patient falling within that provision until the proposal is withdrawn or the treatment is completed or discontinued: s 130C(4) (as so added). As to the help available to a qualifying patient see PARA 807.

In relation to Wales, for the purposes of the Mental Health Act 2010 s 130C(3) a patient is a qualifying patient if he is to be regarded as being in England as determined in accordance with arrangements made for the purposes of s 130C(3) and s 130I(4) and published by the Secretary of State and the Welsh Ministers: see s 130C(3A) (added by the Mental Health (Wales) Measure 2010 Sch 1 para 6).

4   For the purposes of the Mental Health Act 1983 s 130E a patient is a Welsh qualifying compulsory patient if he is liable to be detained under the Mental Health Act 1983 (other than under s 135 or s 136) and the hospital or registered establishment in which he is liable to be detained is situated in Wales, or he is subject to guardianship under the Mental Health Act 1983 and the area of the responsible local social services authority within the meaning of s 34(3) is situated in Wales, or he is a community patient and the responsible hospital is situated in Wales: s 130I(1), (2) (added by the Mental Health (Wales) Measure 2010 s 35). A patient is also a Welsh qualifying compulsory patient if the patient is to be regarded as being in Wales for the purposes of s 130I and:

     (1)   not being a qualifying patient falling within s 130I(2), he discusses with a registered medical practitioner or approved clinician the possibility of being given a form of treatment to which s 57 above applies (s 130I(3)(a) (as so added)); or

     (2)   not having attained the age of 18 years and not being a qualifying patient falling within s 130I(2), he discusses with a registered medical practitioner or approved clinician the possibility of being given a form of treatment to which s 58A applies (s 130I(3)(b) (as so added).

For the purposes of s 130I(3), a patient is to be regarded as being in Wales if that has been determined in accordance with arrangements made for the purposes of that provision and s 130C(3), and published, by the Secretary of State and the Welsh Ministers: s 130I(4) (as so added). For the help available to a Welsh qualifying compulsory patient see PARA 809.

Where a patient who is a Welsh qualifying compulsory patient falling within s 130I(3) is informed that the treatment concerned is proposed in his case, he remains a qualifying patient falling within that subsection until the proposal is withdrawn or the treatment is completed or discontinued: s 130I(5) (as so added).

5	Mental Health Act 1983 ss 130A(1), 130E(1) (s 130A as added, amended and prospectively amended (see note 1); s 130E as added (see note 2)). For the purposes of the Mental Health Act 1983 s 130E a patient is a Welsh qualifying informal patient if:
   (1)	the patient is an in-patient at a hospital or registered establishment situated in Wales (s 130J(1), (2)(a)) (s 130J added by the Mental Health (Wales) Measure 2010 s 36));
   (2)	the patient is receiving treatment for, or assessment in relation to, mental disorder at the hospital or registered establishment (s 130J(1), (2)(b) (as so added)); and
   (3)	no application, order, direction or report renders the patient liable to be detained under the Mental Health Act 1983 (s 130J(1), (2)(c) (as so added)).
   As to independent mental health advocates see the Department of Health *Mental Health Act 1983 Code of Practice* (2008) Chapter 20; and the Welsh Assembly Government *Mental Health Act 1983 Code of Practice for Wales* (2008) Chapter 25.

6	Mental Health Act 1983 s 130A(2), 130E(2) (ss 130A as added and amended (see note 1); s 130E as added (see note 2)). Regulations under ss 130A, 130E–130H may make different provisions for different cases, may make provision which applies subject to specified exceptions and may include transitional, consequential, incidental or supplemental provision: ss 130A(7), 130E(7) (as so added). As to regulations made under ss 130A, 130E see the Mental Health (Independent Mental Health Advocates) (Wales) Regulations 2011, SI 2011/2501; and PARA 814.

7	Mental Health Act 1983 ss 130A(3)(a), 130E(3)(a) (as added: see notes 1, 2).

8	Mental Health Act 1983 ss 130A(3)(b), 130E(3)(b) (as added: see notes 1, 2).

9	For the purposes of the Mental Health Act 1983 ss 130A(4), 130E(4) a person is not to be regarded as professionally concerned with a patient's medical treatment merely because he is representing him in accordance with arrangements under s 35 (see PARA 862) or of a description specified in regulations under s 130A or s 130E as appropriate: ss 130A(5), 130E(5) (as added: see note 2). For the purposes of s 130A(5) a person is not to be regarded as professionally concerned with a qualifying patient's medical treatment if that person is (1) representing the patient in accordance with arrangements made for the purposes of s 130A functions and arrangements made other than for the purposes of that provision; (2) has in the past represented the qualifying patient in accordance with arrangements referred to in head (1) and in doing so was not otherwise professionally concerned in that patient's treatment: Mental Health Act 1983 (Independent Mental Health Advocates) (England) Regulations 2008, SI 2008/3166, reg 7.

10	Mental Health Act 1983 ss 130A(4), 130E(4) (s 130A as added and amended (see note 1); s 130E as added (see note 2)).

808. Help available to a qualifying patient. The help available to a qualifying patient[1] includes help in obtaining information about and understanding:

(1)	the provisions of the Mental Health Act 1983 by virtue of which he is a qualifying patient[2];

(2)	any conditions or restrictions to which he is subject by virtue of the Mental Health Act 1983[3];

(3)	what (if any) medical treatment is given to him or is proposed or discussed in his case[4];

(4)	why it is given, proposed or discussed[5];

(5)	the authority under which it is, or would be, given[6]; and

(6)	the requirements of the Mental Health Act 1983 which apply, or would apply, in connection with the giving of the treatment to him[7].

The help available under the arrangements to a qualifying patient also includes help in obtaining information about and understanding any rights which may be exercised under the Mental Health Act 1983 by or in relation to him and help (by way of representation or otherwise) in exercising those rights[8].

For the purpose of providing help to a patient in accordance with the arrangements, an independent mental health advocate[9] may:

(a)	visit and interview the patient in private[10];

(b)	visit and interview any person who is professionally concerned with his medical treatment[11];

(c)	require the production of and inspect any records relating to his detention or treatment in any hospital or registered establishment or to any aftercare services[12] provided for him[13];

(d) require the production of and inspect any records of, or held by, a local social services authority which relate to him[14].

But an independent mental health advocate is not entitled to the production of, or to inspect, records in reliance on head (c) or (d) above unless, in a case where the patient has capacity[15] or is competent to consent, he does consent or, in any other case, the production or inspection would not conflict with a decision made by a donee[16] or deputy[17] or the Court of Protection and the person holding the records, having regard to such matters as may be prescribed in regulations[18] considers that the records may be relevant to the help to be provided by the advocate and the production or inspection is appropriate[19].

For the purpose of providing help to a patient in accordance with the arrangements, an independent mental health advocate must comply with any reasonable request for him to visit and interview the patient made to him by the person (if any) appearing to the advocate to be the patient's nearest relative, the responsible clinician[20] for the purposes of the Mental Health Act 1983 or an approved mental health professional[21].

Nothing in the Mental Health Act 1983 prevents the patient from declining to be provided with help under the arrangements[22].

1   Ie the help available to a qualifying patient under the Mental Health Act 1983 s 130A (see PARA 807. As to the meaning of 'qualifying patient' see PARA 807 note 3.
2   Mental Health Act 1983 s 130B(1)(a) (s 130B added by the Mental Health Act 2007 s 30(1), (2)).
3   Mental Health Act 1983 s 130B(1)(b) (as added: see note 2).
4   Mental Health Act 1983 s 130B(1)(c) (as added: see note 2).
5   Mental Health Act 1983 s 130B(1)(d) (as added: see note 2).
6   Mental Health Act 1983 s 130B(1)(e) (as added: see note 2).
7   Mental Health Act 1983 s 130B(1)(f) (as added: see note 2).
8   Mental Health Act 1983 s 130B(2) (as added: see note 2).
9   As to the appointment of an independent mental health advocate see PARA 807.
10   Mental Health Act 1983 s 130B(3)(a) (as added: see note 2).
11   Mental Health Act 1983 s 130B(3)(b) (as added: see note 2).
12   Ie aftercare services provided for him under the Mental Health Act 1983 s 117 (see PARA 945).
13   Mental Health Act 1983 s 130B(3)(c) (as added: see note 2).
14   Mental Health Act 1983 s 130B(3)(d) (as added: see note 2).
15   Access to the patient's records is covered by the Department of Health *Mental Health Act 1983 Code of Practice* (2008) paras 20.25–20.33; and the Welsh Assembly Government *Mental Health Act 1983 Code of Practice for Wales* (2008) paras 25.31–25.34. The reference in the text to a patient who has capacity is to be read in accordance with the Mental Capacity Act 2005: Mental Health Act 1983 s 130B(7)(a) (as added: see note 2). As to when a person has capacity see PARA 603.
16   The reference in the text to a donee is to a donee of a lasting power of attorney (within the meaning of the Mental Capacity Act 2005 s 9 (see PARA 619)) created by the patient, where the donee is acting within the scope of his authority and in accordance with that Act: Mental Health Act 1983 s 130B(7)(b) (as added: see note 2).
17   The reference in the text to a deputy is to a deputy appointed for the patient by the Court of Protection under the Mental Capacity Act 2005 s 16 (see PARA 724), where the deputy is acting within the scope of his authority and in accordance with that Act: Mental Health Act 1983 s 130B(7)(c) (as added: see note 2).
18   Ie regulations under the Mental Health Act 1983 s 130A (see PARA 807).
19   Mental Health Act 1983 s 130B(4) (as added: see note 2).
20   As to the meaning of 'responsible clinician' see PARA 834.
21   See the Mental Health Act 1983 s 130B(5) (as added: see note 2).
22   Mental Health Act 1983 s 130B(6) (as added: see note 2).

809. Help available to a Welsh qualifying compulsory patient. The help available to a Welsh qualifying compulsory patient[1] includes help in obtaining information about and understanding:

(1) the provisions of the Mental Health Act 1983 by virtue of which he is a qualifying compulsory patient[2];

(2) any conditions or restrictions to which he is subject by virtue of the Mental Health Act 1983[3];

(3) what (if any) medical treatment is given to him or is proposed or discussed in his case[4];

(4) why it is given, proposed or discussed[5];

(5) the authority under which it is, or would be, given[6]; and

(6) the requirements of the Mental Health Act 1983 which apply, or would apply, in connection with the giving of the treatment to him[7].

The help available under the arrangements to a Welsh qualifying compulsory patient also includes:

(a) help in obtaining information about and understanding any rights which may be exercised under the Mental Health Act 1983 by or in relation to him[8];

(b) help (by way of representation or otherwise) (i) in exercising the rights referred to in head (a); (ii) for patients who wish to become involved, or more involved, in decisions made about their care or treatment, or care or treatment generally; (iii) for patients who wish to complain about their care or treatment[9];

(c) the provision of information about other services which are or may be available to the patient[10];

(d) other help specified in regulations made by the Welsh Ministers[11].

In the case of a Welsh qualifying compulsory patient who has been admitted for assessment[12], the independent mental health advocate may visit and interview the approved mental health professional or nearest relative who made the application for admission[13] and the doctor who provided the medical recommendation[14], where such persons are not also professionally concerned with the medical treatment of the Welsh qualifying compulsory patient[15].

1 Ie the help available to a Welsh qualifying compulsory patient under arrangements under the Mental Health Act 1983 s 130E (see PARA 807). As to the meaning of Welsh qualifying compulsory patient see PARA 807 note 4.
2 Mental Health Act 1983 s 130F(1)(a) (added by the Mental Health (Wales) Measure 2010 s 32).
3 Mental Health Act 1983 s 130F(1)(b) (as added: see note 2).
4 Mental Health Act 1983 s 130F(1)(c) (as added: see note 2).
5 Mental Health Act 1983 s 130F(1)(d) (as added: see note 2).
6 Mental Health Act 1983 s 130F(1)(e) (as added: see note 2).
7 Mental Health Act 1983 s 130F(1)(f) (as added: see note 2).
8 Mental Health Act 1983 s 130F(2)(a) (as added: see note 2).
9 Mental Health Act 1983 s 130F(2)(b) (as added: see note 2).
10 Mental Health Act 1983 s 130F(2)(c) (as added: see note 2).
11 Mental Health Act 1983 s 130F(2)(d) (as added: see note 2).
12 Ie under the Mental Health Act 1983 s 4 (see PARA 769).
13 Ie in accordance with the Mental Health Act 1983 s 4(2) (see PARA 769).
14 Ie in accordance with the Mental Health Act 1983 s 4(3) (see PARA 769).
15 Mental Health (Independent Mental Health Advocates) (Wales) Regulations 2011, SI 2011/2501, reg 6.

810. Help available to a Welsh informal patient. The help available to a Welsh qualifying informal patient[1] includes help in obtaining information about and understanding:

(1)   what (if any) medical treatment is given to him or is proposed or discussed in his case[2];
(2)   why it is given, proposed or discussed[3];
(3)   the authority under which it is, or would be, given[4].

The help available under the arrangements to a Welsh qualifying informal patient also includes:

(a)   help (by way of representation or otherwise) for patients who wish to become involved, or more involved, in decisions made about their care or treatment, or care or treatment generally and help for patients who wish to complain about their care or treatment[5];
(b)   the provision of information about other services which are or may be available to the patient[6];
(c)   other help specified in regulations made by the Welsh Ministers[7].

1   Ie the help available to a Welsh qualifying informal patient under the Mental Health Act 1983 s 130E (see PARA 807).
2   Mental Health Act 1983 s 130G(1)(a) (added by the Mental Health (Wales) Measure 2010 s 33).
3   Mental Health Act 1983 s 130G(1)(b) (as added: see note 2).
4   Mental Health Act 1983 s 130G(1)(c) (as added: see note 2).
5   Mental Health Act 1983 s 130G(2)(a) (as added: see note 2).
6   Mental Health Act 1983 s 130G(2)(b) (as added: see note 2).
7   Mental Health Act 1983 s 130G(2)(c) (as added: see note 2).

811.   Duty to give information about independent mental health advocates.
The responsible person[1] in relation to a qualifying patient[2], a Welsh qualifying compulsory patient[3] or Welsh informal patient[4] must take such steps[5] as are practicable to ensure that the patient understands that help is available to him from an independent mental health advocate and how he can obtain that help[6].

The steps to be taken must include giving the requisite information both orally and in writing[7].

1   The 'responsible person' in relation to a qualifying patient means:
    (1)   in relation to a qualifying patient falling within the Mental Health Act 1983 s 130C(2)(a) (see PARA 807) (other than one also falling within head (2)), the managers of the hospital or registered establishment in which he is liable to be detained (s 130D(2)(a) (added by the Mental Health Act 2007 s 30(2));
    (2)   in relation to a qualifying patient falling within the Mental Health Act 1983 s 130C(2)(a) and conditionally discharged by virtue of s 42(2), 73 or 74 (see PARAS 876, 969, 970), the responsible clinician (s 130D(2)(b) (as so added));
    (3)   in relation to a qualifying patient falling within s 130C(2)(b) (see PARA 807), the responsible local social services authority within the meaning of s 34(3) (see PARA 791 note 1) (s 130D(2)(c) (as so added));
    (4)   in relation to a qualifying patient falling within s 130C(2)(c) (see PARA 807), the managers of the responsible hospital (s 130D(2)(d) (as so added));
    (5)   in relation to a qualifying patient falling within section 130C(3) (see PARA 807), the registered medical practitioner or approved clinician with whom the patient first discusses the possibility of being given the treatment concerned (s 130D(2)(e) (as so added)).
    The 'responsible person' in relation to a Welsh qualifying compulsory patient means:
    (a)   in relation to a Welsh qualifying compulsory patient falling within s 130I(2)(a) (see PARA 807) (other than one also falling within head (b) below), the managers of the hospital or registered establishment in which he is liable to be detained (s 130K(2)(a) (s 130K added by the Mental Health (Wales) Measure 2010 s 37)); or
    (b)   in relation to a Welsh qualifying compulsory patient falling within the Mental Health Act 1983 s 130I(2)(a) (see PARA 807) and conditionally discharged by virtue of s 42(2), 73 or 74 (see PARAS 876, 969, 970), the responsible clinician (s 130K(2)(b) (as so added));
    (c)   in relation to a Welsh qualifying compulsory patient falling within s 130I(2)(b) (see

PARA 807), the responsible local social services authority within the meaning of s 34(3) (see PARA 791 note 1) (s 130K(2)(c) (as so added));

(d)   in relation to a Welsh qualifying compulsory patient falling within s 130I(2)(c) (see PARA 807), the managers of the responsible hospital (s 130K(2)(d) (as so added));

(e)   in relation to a Welsh qualifying compulsory patient falling within s 130I(3) (see PARA 807), the registered medical practitioner or approved clinician with whom the patient first discusses the possibility of being given the treatment concerned (s 130K(2)(e) (as so added)).

The 'responsible person' in relation to a Welsh informal patient means the managers of the hospital or registered establishment to which the patient is admitted as an in-patient: s 130L(2) (s 130L added by the Mental Health (Wales) Measure 2010 s 38). As to the meaning of 'responsible clinician' see PARA 834.

2   Ie within the meaning of the Mental Health Act 1983 s 130C (see PARA 807).

3   Ie within the meaning of the Mental Health Act 1983 s 130I (see PARA 807).

4   Ie within the meaning of the Mental Health Act 1983 s 130J (see PARA 807).

5   The steps under the Mental Health Act 1983 ss 130D(1), 130K(1) must be taken:

(1)   where the responsible person falls within s 130D(2)(a) or s 130K(2)(a), as soon as practicable after the patient becomes liable to be detained (ss 130D(3)(a), 130K(3)(a) (as added: see note 1));

(2)   where the responsible person falls within s 130D(2)(b) or s 130K(2)(b), as soon as practicable after the conditional discharge (ss 130D(3)(b), 130K(3)(b) (as so added));

(3)   where the responsible person falls within s 130D(2)(c) or s 130K(2)(c), as soon as practicable after the patient becomes subject to guardianship (ss 130D(3)(c), 130K(3)(c) (as so added));

(4)   where the responsible person falls within s 130D(2)(d) or s 130K(2)(d), as soon as practicable after the patient becomes a community patient (ss 130D(3)(d), 130K(3)(d) (as so added));

(5)   where the responsible person falls within s 130D(2)(e) or s 130K(2)(e), while the discussion with the patient is taking place or as soon as practicable thereafter (ss 130D(3)(e), 130K(3)(e) (as so added)).

The steps to be taken under s 130I(1) must be taken as soon as practicable after the patient becomes an in-patient: s 130I(3) (as added: see note 1).

6   Mental Health Act 1983 ss 130D(1), 130K(1), 130L(1) (as added: see note 1).

7   Mental Health Act 1983 ss 130D(4), 130K(4), 130L(4) (as added: see note 1).

The responsible person in relation to a qualifying patient falling within s 130C(2) (other than a patient liable to be detained by virtue of the Mental Health Act 1983 Pt 3) must, except where the patient otherwise requests, take such steps as are practicable to furnish the person (if any) appearing to the responsible person to be the patient's nearest relative with a copy of any information given to the patient in writing under s 130C(1): s 130D(5) (as added: see note 1). Such steps must be taken when the information concerned is given to the patient or within a reasonable time thereafter: s 130D(6) (as so added).

The responsible person in relation to a Welsh qualifying compulsory patient falling within s 130I(2) (other than a patient liable to be detained by virtue of Pt 3) must, except where the patient otherwise requests, take such steps as are practicable to furnish any person falling within s 130K(6) with a copy of any information given to the patient in writing under s 130K(1): s 130K(5) (as added: see note 1). Such steps must be taken when the information concerned is given to the patient or within a reasonable time thereafter: s 130K(7) (as so added).

A person falls within this provision if:

(1)   the person appears to the responsible person to be the patient's nearest relative (s 130K(6)(a) (as so added));

(2)   the person is a donee of a lasting power of attorney (within the meaning of the Mental Capacity Act 2005 s 9 (see PARA 619)) created by the patient and the scope of the donee's authority includes matters related to the care and treatment of the patient (Mental Health Act 1983 s 130K(6)(b) (as so added));

(3)   the person is a deputy appointed for the patient by the Court of Protection under the Mental Capacity Act 2005 s 16 and the scope of the deputy's authority includes matters related to the care and treatment of the patient (Mental Health Act 1984 s 130K(6)(c) (as so added)).

The responsible person in relation to a Welsh qualifying informal patient must, except where the patient otherwise requests, take such steps as are practicable to furnish any person falling within s 130L(6) with a copy of any information given to the patient in writing under s 130L(1): s 130L(5) (as added: see note 1).

A person falls within this provision if:

(a)   the person appears to the responsible person to be a carer of the patient (s 130L(6)(a) (as so added));

(b)   the person is a donee of a lasting power of attorney (within the meaning of the Mental Capacity Act 2005 s 9 (see PARA 619)) created by the patient and the scope of the donee's authority includes matters related to the care and treatment of the patient (Mental Health Act 1984 s 130L(6)(b) (as so added));

(c)   the person is a deputy appointed for the patient by the Court of Protection under the Mental Capacity Act 2005 s 16 (see PARA 724) and the scope of the deputy's authority includes matters related to the care and treatment of the patient (Mental Health Act 1984 s 130L(6)(c) (as so added)).

Such steps must be taken when the information concerned is given to the patient or within a reasonable time thereafter: s 130L(8) (as so added). In s 130L(6), 'carer', in relation to a Welsh qualifying informal patient, means an individual who provides or intends to provide a substantial amount of care on a regular basis for the patient, but does not include any individual who provides, or intends to provide, care by virtue of a contract of employment or other contract with any person or as a volunteer for a body (whether or not incorporated): s 130L(7) (as so added).

812. Independent mental health advocates Wales. For the purpose of providing help to a patient in accordance with arrangements made in relation to independent mental health advocates in Wales[1], an independent mental health advocate may:

(1)   visit and interview the patient in private[2];

(2)   visit and interview: (a) any person who is professionally concerned with his medical treatment; (b) any other person who falls within a description specified in regulations made by the appropriate national authority[3];

(3)   require the production of and inspect any records relating to his detention, treatment or assessment in any hospital or registered establishment or to any aftercare services[4] provided for him[5];

(4)   require the production of and inspect any records of, or held by, a local social services authority which relate to him[6].

But an independent mental health advocate is not entitled to the production of, or to inspect, records in reliance on head (3) or (4) above unless, in a case where the patient has capacity[7] or is competent to consent, he does consent or, in any other case, the production or inspection would not conflict with a decision made by a donee[8] or deputy[9] or the Court of Protection[10] and the person holding the records, having regard to such matters as may be prescribed in regulations[11] considers that the records may be relevant to the help to be provided by the advocate or that the production or inspection is appropriate[12].

For the purpose of providing help to a Welsh qualifying compulsory patient in accordance with the arrangements, an independent mental health advocate must comply with any reasonable request made to him by any of the following for him to visit and interview the patient:

(a)   the patient[13];

(b)   the person (if any) appearing to the advocate to be the patient's nearest relative[14];

(c)   the responsible clinician for the purposes of the Mental Health Act 1983[15];

(d)   an approved mental health professional[16];

(e)   a registered social worker who is professionally concerned with the patient's care, treatment or assessment[17];

(f)   where the patient is liable to be detained in a hospital or registered establishment, the managers of the hospital or establishment or a person duly authorised on their behalf[18];

(g)   the patient's donee or deputy[19].

For the purpose of providing help to a Welsh qualifying informal patient in accordance with the arrangements, an independent mental health advocate must comply with any reasonable request made to him by any of the following for him to visit and interview the patient:

(i)   the patient[20];

(ii)   the managers of the hospital or establishment in which the patient is an in-patient or a person duly authorised on their behalf[21];

(iii)   any person appearing to the advocate to whom the request is made to be the patient's carer[22];

(iv)   the patient's donee or deputy[23];

(v)   a registered social worker[24] who is professionally concerned with the patient's care, treatment or assessment[25].

Nothing in the Mental Health Act 1983 prevents the patient from declining to be provided with help under the arrangements[26].

1   Ie under the Mental Health Act 1983 s 130E (see PARA 807).
2   Mental Health Act 1983 s 130H(1)(a) (added by the Mental Health (Wales) Measure 2010 s 34).
3   Mental Health Act 1983 s 130H(1)(b) (as added: see note 2). As to the appropriate national authority see PARA 567.
4   Ie aftercare services provided for him under the Mental Health Act 1983 s 117 (see PARA 945).
5   Mental Health Act 1983 s 130H(1)(c) (as added: see note 2).
6   Mental Health Act 1983 s 130H(1)(d) (as added: see note 2).
7   The reference to a patient who has capacity is to be read in accordance with the Mental Capacity Act 2005: Mental Health Act 1983 s 130H(6) (as added: see note 2).
8   In the Mental Health Act 1983 s 130H(2)–(4) the reference to a donee is to a donee of a lasting power of attorney (within the meaning of the Mental Capacity Act 2005 s 9 (see PARA 619)) created by the patient, where the donee, in making the decision referred to in the Mental Health Act 1983 s 130H(2) or the request referred to in s 130H(3) or (4), is acting within the scope of his authority and in accordance with the Mental Capacity Act 2005: Mental Health Act 1983 s 130H(8)(a) (as added: see note 2).
9   In the Mental Health Act 1983 s 130H(2)–(4) the reference to a deputy is to a deputy appointed for the patient by the Court of Protection under the Mental Capacity Act 2005 s 16 (see PARA 724), where the deputy, in making the decision referred to in the Mental Health Act 1983 s 130H(2) or the request referred to in s 130H(3) or (4), is acting within the scope of his authority and in accordance with the Mental Capacity Act 2005: s 130H(8)(b) (as added: see note 2).
10 As to the Court of Protection see PARA 720.
11 Ie regulations under the Mental Health Act 1983 s130E (see PARA 807).
12 Mental Health Act 1983 s 130H(2) (as added: see note 2).
13 Mental Health Act 1983 s 130H(3)(a) (as added: see note 2).
14 Mental Health Act 1983 s 130H(3)(b) (as added: see note 2).
15 Mental Health Act 1983 s 130H(3)(c) (as added: see note 2). As to the meaning of 'responsible clinician' see PARA 834.
16 Mental Health Act 1983 s 130H(3)(d) (as added: see note 2).
17 Mental Health Act 1983 s 130H(3)(e) (as added: see note 2).
18 Mental Health Act 1983 s 130H(3)(f) (as added: see note 2).
19 Mental Health Act 1983 s 130H(3)(g) (as added: see note 2).
20 Mental Health Act 1983 s 130H(4)(a) (as added: see note 2).
21 Mental Health Act 1983 s 130H(4)(b) (as added: see note 2).
22 Mental Health Act 1983 s 130H(4)(c) (as added: see note 2). For this purpose 'carer', in relation to a Welsh qualifying informal patient, means an individual who provides or intends to provide a substantial amount of care on a regular basis for the patient, but does not include any

individual who provides, or intends to provide care by virtue of a contract of employment or other contract with any person or as a volunteer for a body (whether or not incorporated): s 130H(7)(a) (as so added).

23 Mental Health Act 1983 s 130H(4)(d) (as added: see note 2).

24 For this purpose 'registered social worker' means a person included in the principal part or the visiting European part of a register maintained under the Care Standards Act 2000 s 56(1) (see SOCIAL SERVICES AND COMMUNITY CARE): Mental Health Act 1984 s 130H(8)(b) (as added: see note 2).

25 Mental Health Act 1983 s 130H(4)(e) (as added: see note 2).

26 Mental Health Act 1983 s 130H(5) (as added: see note 2).

813. Independent mental health advocates in England: conditions. Where a commissioning body[1], in exercising its functions[2], enters into arrangements with an individual who may be made available to act as an independent mental health advocate certain conditions must be satisfied[3]. Those conditions are that the person:

(1) has appropriate experience or training or an appropriate combination of experience and training[4];

(2) is a person of integrity and good character[5];

(3) is able to act independently of any person who is professionally concerned with the qualifying patient's medical treatment[6]; and

(4) is able to act independently of any person who requests that person to visit or interview the qualifying patient[7].

1 'Commissioning body' means a local social services authority whose area is in England: Mental Health Act 1983 (Independent Mental Health Advocates) (England) Regulations 2008, SI 2008/3166, reg 2 (amended by SI 2013/261).

2 Ie its functions under the Mental Health Act 1983 s 130A (see PARA 807).

3 See the Mental Health Act 1983 (Independent Mental Health Advocates) (England) Regulations 2008, SI 2008/3166, regs 3(1), 6(1) (reg 3 substituted by SI 2013/261).

4 Mental Health Act 1983 (Independent Mental Health Advocates) (England) Regulations 2008, SI 2008/3166, reg 6(2)(a). For the purposes of the condition referred to in head (1) in the text regard must be had to standards in guidance that may be issued from time to time by the Secretary of State which may include any qualification that the Secretary of State may determine as appropriate: see reg 6(3), (4).

5 Mental Health Act 1983 (Independent Mental Health Advocates) (England) Regulations 2008, SI 2008/3166, reg 6(2)(b). For the purposes of the condition referred to in head (2) in the text there must be obtained, in respect of that person, an enhanced criminal record certificate issued pursuant to the Police Act 1997 s 113B (see SENTENCING AND DISPOSITION OF OFFENDERS vol 92 (2010) PARA 713 et seq) which includes:

(1) where the qualifying patient has not attained the age of 18, suitability information relating to children (within the meaning of the Police Act 1997 s 113BA (see SENTENCING AND DISPOSITION OF OFFENDERS vol 92 (2010) PARA 713) (Mental Health Act 1983 (Independent Mental Health Advocates) (England) Regulations 2008, SI 2008/3166, reg 6(5)(a) (substituted by SI 2009/2376));

(2) where the qualifying patient has attained the age of 18, suitability information relating to vulnerable adults (within the meaning of the Police Act 1997 s 113BB (see SENTENCING AND DISPOSITION OF OFFENDERS vol 92 (2010) PARA 713) (Mental Health Act 1983 (Independent Mental Health Advocates) (England) Regulations 2008, SI 2008/3166, reg6(5)(b) (as so substituted)).

6 Mental Health Act 1983 (Independent Mental Health Advocates) (England) Regulations 2008, SI 2008/3166, reg 6(2)(c).

7 Mental Health Act 1983 (Independent Mental Health Advocates) (England) Regulations 2008, SI 2008/3166, reg 6(2)(d).

814. Independent mental health advocates in Wales: conditions. Subject to directions that may be given by the appropriate national authority[1], a local health board[2] must make such arrangements[3] as it considers reasonable to enable independent mental health advocates[4] to be available to act in respect of a Welsh qualifying compulsory patient who:

(1)   is liable to be detained in a hospital or registered establishment, whether or not in a hospital or registered establishment located within the area of the local health board, and is present in the area of the local health board at the time when the independent mental health advocacy service is to be provided[5];

(2)   is subject to guardianship under the Mental Health Act 1983 or is a community patient and is present in the area of the local health board at the time when the independent mental health advocacy service is to be provided[6]; or

(3)   qualifies as a Welsh qualifying compulsory patient[7] and is present in the area of the local health board at the time when the independent mental health advocacy service is to be provided[8].

Subject to directions that may be given by the appropriate national authority, a local health board must make such arrangements as it considers reasonable to enable independent mental health advocates to be available to act in respect of a Welsh qualifying informal patient who is present in a hospital or registered establishment located within the area of the local health board at the time when the independent mental health advocacy service is to be provided[9].

In making arrangements under the above provisions[10] a local health board may make arrangements with a provider of advocacy services[11] and no person may act as an independent mental health advocate unless that person is approved[12] by the local health board or is employed to act as such by a provider of advocacy services[13] with which a local health board has made such arrangements[14].

1   As to the appropriate national authority see PARA 567.
2   As to the meaning of 'local health board' see PARA 575 note 6.
3   In making arrangements under the Mental Health (Independent Mental Health Advocates) (Wales) Regulations 2011, SI 2011/2501, reg 3(1), (2) a local health board must, as far as reasonably practicable, have regard to the diverse circumstances (including but not limited to the ethnic, linguistic, cultural and demographic needs) of Welsh qualifying compulsory patients and Welsh qualifying informal patients in respect of whom the local health board may exercise those functions: reg 3(4). As to the meaning of Welsh qualifying compulsory patient see PARA 807 note 4.
4   As to independent mental health advocates see the Mental Health Act 1983 s 130E; and PARA 807.
5   Mental Health (Independent Mental Health Advocates) (Wales) Regulations 2011, SI 2011/2501, reg 3(1)(a).
6   Mental Health (Independent Mental Health Advocates) (Wales) Regulations 2011, SI 2011/2501, reg 3(1)(b).
7   Ie qualifies as a Welsh qualifying compulsory patient under the Mental Health Act 1983 s 130I(3) (see PARA 807).
8   Mental Health (Independent Mental Health Advocates) (Wales) Regulations 2011, SI 2011/2501, reg 3(1)(c).
9   Mental Health (Independent Mental Health Advocates) (Wales) Regulations 2011, SI 2011/2501, reg 3(2).
10   Ie under the Mental Health (Independent Mental Health Advocates) (Wales) Regulations 2011, SI 2011/2501, reg 3(1), (2).
11   Mental Health (Independent Mental Health Advocates) (Wales) Regulations 2011, SI 2011/2501, reg 3(3). A local health board must ensure that any provider of advocacy services with whom it makes arrangements under reg 3 is required, in accordance with the terms of that arrangement, to ensure that any person who is employed by that provider of advocacy services and is made available to act as an independent mental health advocate, satisfies the appointment requirements in reg 4 and the independence requirements in reg 5: reg 3(7).

12 Before approving any person under the Mental Health (Independent Mental Health Advocates) (Wales) Regulations 2011, SI 2011/2501, reg 3(5) a local health board must be satisfied that the person satisfies the appointment requirements in reg 4 and the independence requirements in reg 5: reg 3(6).

13 In the Mental Health (Independent Mental Health Advocates) (Wales) Regulations 2011, SI 2011/2501 a person is employed by the provider of advocacy services if that person is employed by the provider of advocacy services under a contract of service or engaged by the provider of advocacy services under a contract for services: reg 3(8).

14 Mental Health (Independent Mental Health Advocates) (Wales) Regulations 2011, SI 2011/2501, reg 3(5).

(8) MENTAL HEALTH PROFESSIONALS

(i) Approved Mental Health Professionals

815. Approval of approved mental health professionals. A local social services authority[1] may approve a person to act as an approved mental health professional[2] for the purposes of the Mental Health Act 1983[3]. However, a local social services authority may not approve a registered medical practitioner[4] to act as an approved mental health professional[5]. The local social services authority must keep a record of all persons that it approves as approved mental health professionals[6].

Before approving a person under these provisions, a local social services authority must be satisfied that the person has appropriate competence[7] in dealing with persons who are suffering from mental disorder[8].

In relation to Wales the following apply. A local social services authority may only grant approval to a person to be an approved mental health professional, where that person is not already approved as such[9], or has not been so approved within the previous five years, if that person fulfils the professional requirements[10], is able to demonstrate that he possesses the relevant competencies[11] and has completed within the last two years a course for the initial training of approved mental health professionals approved by the Care Council for Wales[12]. A local social services authority may only approve a person to be an approved mental health professional, where the person is not already approved as such[13], but is approved to act in relation to England, or has been so approved within the previous five years if that person fulfils the professional requirements and he is able to demonstrate that he possesses the relevant competencies such as will enable that person to act within Wales, or if not, completes such course as the approving local social services authority deems necessary to enable him to do so[14]. A local social services authority may grant approval of a person who has previously been approved within Wales, such approval having been in force within the previous five years prior to the proposed date of reapproval, where that person fulfils the professional requirements and is able to demonstrate that he or she possesses the relevant competencies[15].

1 As to the meaning of 'local social services authority' see PARA 579.

2 For the purposes of the Mental Health Act 1983 'approved mental health professional' means, in relation to acting on behalf of a local social services authority whose area is in England, a person approved under s 114(1) by any local social services authority whose area is in England, and, in relation to acting on behalf of a local social services authority whose area is in Wales, a person approved under that provision by any local social services authority whose area is in Wales: ss 114(10), 145(1) (s 114 substituted by the Mental Health Act 2007 s 18; and definition in s 145(1) added by the Mental Health Act 2007 s 14(5)). A local social services authority may approve an approved mental health professional for a period of five years: Mental Health

(Approved Mental Health Professionals) (Approval) (England) Regulations 2008, SI 2008/1206, ~~reg 4; Mental Health (Approval of Persons~~ to be Approved Mental Health Professionals) (Wales) Regulations 2008, SI 2008/2436, reg 4.

3   Mental Health Act 1983 s 114(1) (s 114 substituted by the Mental Health Act 2007 s 18). A local authority should ensure that there are sufficient approved mental health professionals to carry out the functions under the Mental Health Act 1983: see the Department of Health *Mental Health Act 1983 Code of Practice* (2008) para 4.33; and the Welsh Assembly Government *Mental Health Act 1983 Code of Practice for Wales* (2008) para 2.74. The appropriate national authority may by regulations make provision in connection with the giving of approvals under the Mental Health Act 1983 s 114(1): s 114(4) (as so substituted). The provision which may be made by regulations under s 114(4) includes, in particular, provision as to:

   (1)   the period for which approvals under s 114(1) have effect (s 114(5)(a) (as so substituted));

   (2)   the courses to be undertaken by persons before such approvals are to be given and during the period for which such approvals have effect (s 114(5)(b) (as so substituted));

   (3)   the conditions subject to which such approvals are to be given (s 114(5)(c) (as so substituted)); and

   (4)   the factors to be taken into account in determining whether persons have appropriate competence as mentioned in s 114(3) (s 114(5)(d) (as so substituted)).

   Provision made by virtue of head (2) above may relate to courses approved or provided by such person as may be specified in the regulations (as well as to courses approved under s 114ZA or s 114A): s 114(6) (as so substituted; amended by the Health and Social Care Act 2012 s 217(3). An approval by virtue of the Mental Health Act 1984 s 114(6) may be in respect of a course in general or in respect of a course in relation to a particular person: s 114(7) (as so substituted). The power to make regulations under s 114(4) includes power to make different provision for different cases or areas: s 114(8) (as so substituted). For these purposes 'the appropriate national authority' means, in relation to persons who are or wish to become approved to act as approved mental health professionals by a local social services authority whose area is in England, the Secretary of State and, in relation to persons who are or wish to become approved to act as approved mental health professionals by a local social services authority whose area is in Wales, the Welsh Ministers: s 114(9) (as so substituted).

4   As to registered medical practitioners see MEDICAL PROFESSIONS vol 74 (2011) PARA 176 et seq.

5   Mental Health Act 1983 s 114(2) (as substituted: see note 3).

6   See the Mental Health (Approved Mental Health Professionals) (Approval) (England) Regulations 2008, SI 2008/1206, reg 8(1); and the Mental Health (Approval of Persons to be Approved Mental Health Professionals) (Wales) Regulations 2008, SI 2008/2436, reg 9(1). As to the information to be kept see the Mental Health (Approved Mental Health Professionals) (Approval) (England) Regulations 2008, SI 2008/1206, reg 8(1)(a)–(h); and the Mental Health (Approval of Persons to be Approved Mental Health Professionals) (Wales) Regulations 2008, SI 2008/2436, reg 9(1)(a)–(h). Such records must be kept, in relation to England, for a period of five years commencing with the day on which the approved mental health professional's approval ended, and in relation to Wales, for three years following the ending of such persons' approval: see the Mental Health (Approved Mental Health Professionals) (Approval) (England) Regulations 2008, SI 2008/1206, reg 8(2); and the Mental Health (Approval of Persons to be Approved Mental Health Professionals) (Wales) Regulations 2008, SI 2008/2436, reg 9(2).

7   As to when a person has appropriate competence see PARA 816 et seq.

8   See the Mental Health Act 1983 s 114(3) (as substituted: see note 3); the Mental Health (Approved Mental Health Professionals) (Approval) (England) Regulations 2008, SI 2008/1206, reg 3(1); and the Mental Health (Approval of Persons to be Approved Mental Health Professionals) (Wales) Regulations 2008, SI 2008/2436, reg 3(1)(b), (2)(a). As to the meaning of 'mental disorder' see PARA 761. As to the appropriate competency in relation to England see PARA 816.

9   Ie under the Mental Health (Approval of Persons to be Approved Mental Health Professionals) (Wales) Regulations 2008, SI 2008/2436.

10 As to the professional requirements see PARA 818.

11 As to the relevant competencies see PARA 817. In determining whether a person seeking approval as an approved mental health professional possesses the relevant competencies as required under the Mental Health (Approval of Persons to be Approved Mental Health Professionals) (Wales) Regulations 2008, SI 2008/2436, reg 3(1)(b) or (2)(b), the local social services authority must have regard to the references of that person: reg 3(3).

12 Mental Health (Approval of Persons to be Approved Mental Health Professionals) (Wales) Regulations 2008, SI 2008/2436, reg 3(1). As to the Care Council for Wales see the Care Standards Act 2000 s 54; and SOCIAL SERVICES AND COMMUNITY CARE vol 44(2) (Reissue) PARA 1003.

13 Ie under the Mental Health (Approval of Persons to be Approved Mental Health Professionals) (Wales) Regulations 2008, SI 2008/2436.

14 Mental Health (Approval of Persons to be Approved Mental Health Professionals) (Wales) Regulations 2008, SI 2008/2436, reg 3(2).

15 Mental Health (Approval of Persons to be Approved Mental Health Professionals) (Wales) Regulations 2008, SI 2008/2436, reg 8(1). In determining whether the person seeking approval as an approved mental health professional possesses the relevant competencies as required under reg 8(1), the local social services authority must have regard to the references of that person: reg 8(2).

816. Appropriate competence in England. In relation to England, in determining whether a person has appropriate competence in dealing with persons suffering from a mental disorder[1], a local service social services authority[2] must take into account the following factors[3]:

(1)   that the person fulfils at least one of the professional requirements[4]; and

(2)   the following key competency areas[5]:

    (a)   the application of values to the role of approved mental health professional[6];

    (b)   the application of knowledge relating to the legal and policy framework[7];

    (c)   the application of knowledge relating to mental disorder[8];

    (d)   the application of skills in relation to working in partnership[9]; and

    (e)   the application of skills in relation to the making and communicating of informed decisions[10].

Before a local social services authority may approve a person to act as an approved mental health professional who has not been approved, or been treated as approved, before in England and Wales, the person must have completed within the last five years a course approved by the Health and Care Professions Council or the Care Council for Wales[11].

1   As to the meaning of 'mental disorder' see PARA 761.

2   As to the meaning of 'local social services authority' see PARA 579.

3   See the Mental Health (Approved Mental Health Professionals) (Approval) (England) Regulations 2008, SI 2008/1206, reg 3(2).

4   For the professional requirements see PARA 818.

5   See the Mental Health (Approved Mental Health Professionals) (Approval) (England) Regulations 2008, SI 2008/1206, reg 3(2), Sch 2.

6   Ie whether the applicant has:

    (1)   the ability to identify, challenge and, where possible, redress discrimination and inequality in all its forms in relation to approved mental health professional practice (Mental Health (Approved Mental Health Professionals) (Approval) (England) Regulations 2008, SI 2008/1206, Sch 2 para 1(a));

    (2)   an understanding of and respect for individuals' qualities, abilities and diverse backgrounds, and is able to identify and counter any decision which may be based on unlawful discrimination (Sch 2 para 1(b));

    (3)   the ability to promote the rights, dignity and self-determination of patients consistent with their own needs and wishes, to enable them to contribute to the decisions made affecting their quality of life and liberty (Sch 2 para 1(c)); and

    (4)   a sensitivity to individuals' needs for personal respect, confidentiality, choice, dignity and privacy while exercising the approved mental health professional role (Sch 2 para 1(d)).

7   Ie whether the applicant has:

    (1)   an appropriate knowledge of and ability to apply in practice the mental health

legislation, related codes of practice and national and local policy guidance, and relevant parts of other legislation, codes of practice, national and local policy guidance, in particular the Children Act 1989, the Children Act 2004, the Human Rights Act 1998 and the Mental Capacity Act 2005 (Mental Health (Approved Mental Health Professionals) (Approval) (England) Regulations 2008, SI 2008/1206 Sch 2 para 2(1)(a));

(2) a knowledge and understanding of the particular needs of children and young people and their families, and an ability to apply approved mental health professional practice in the context of those particular needs (Sch 2 para 2(1)(b));

(3) an understanding of, and sensitivity to, race and culture in the application of knowledge of mental health legislation (Sch 2 para 2(1)(c));

(4) an explicit awareness of the legal position and accountability of approved mental health professionals in relation to the Mental Health Act 1983, any employing organisation and the authority on whose behalf they are acting (Mental Health (Approved Mental Health Professionals) (Approval) (England) Regulations 2008, SI 2008/1206, Sch 2 para 2(1)(d));

(5) the ability to evaluate critically local and national policy to inform approved mental health professional practice and to base that practice on a critical evaluation of a range of research relevant to evidence-based practice, including that on the impact on persons who experience discrimination because of mental health (Sch 2 para 2(1)(e)).

In head (1) above, 'relevant' means relevant to the decisions that an approved mental health professional is likely to take when acting as such: Sch 2 para 2(2).

8 Ie whether the applicant has a critical understanding of, and is able to apply in practice:

(1) a range of models of mental disorder, including the contribution of social, physical and development factors (Mental Health (Approved Mental Health Professionals) (Approval) (England) Regulations 2008, SI 2008/1206, Sch 2 para 3(a));

(2) the social perspective on mental disorder and mental health needs, in working with patients, their relatives, carers and other professionals (Sch 2 para 3(b));

(3) the implications of mental disorder for patients, their relatives and carers (Sch 2 para 3(c)); and

(4) the implications of a range of treatments and interventions for patients, their relatives and carers (Sch 2 para 3(d)).

9 Ie whether the applicant has the ability to:

(1) articulate, and demonstrate in practice, the social perspective on mental disorder and mental health needs (Mental Health (Approved Mental Health Professionals) (Approval) (England) Regulations 2008, SI 2008/1206, Sch 2 para 4(a));

(2) communicate appropriately with and establish effective relationships with patients, relatives, and carers in undertaking the approved mental health professional role (Sch 2 para 4(b));

(3) articulate the role of the approved mental health professional in the course of contributing to effective inter-agency and inter-professional working (Sch 2 para 4(c));

(4) use networks and community groups to influence collaborative working with a range of individuals, agencies and advocates (Sch 2 para 4(d));

(5) consider the feasibility of and contribute effectively to planning and implementing options for care such as alternatives to compulsory admission, discharge and aftercare (Sch 2 para 4(e));

(6) recognise, assess and manage risk effectively in the context of the approved mental health professional role (Sch 2 para 4(f));

(7) effectively manage difficult situations of anxiety, risk and conflict, and an understanding of how this affects the approved mental health professional and other people concerned with the patient's care (Sch 2 para 4(g));

(8) discharge the approved mental health professional role in such a way as to empower the patient as much as practicable (Sch 2 para 4(h));

(9) plan, negotiate and manage compulsory admission to hospital or arrangements for supervised community treatment (Sch 2 para 4(i));

(10) manage and co-ordinate effectively the relevant legal and practical processes including the involvement of other professionals as well as patients, relatives and carers (Sch 2 para 4(j)); and

(11) balance and manage the competing requirements of confidentiality and effective information sharing to the benefit of the patient and other persons concerned with the patient's care (Sch 2 para 4(k)).

10 Ie whether the applicant has the ability to:

(1) assert a social perspective and to make properly informed independent decisions

(Mental Health (Approved Mental Health Professionals) (Approval) (England) Regulations 2008, SI 2008/1206, Sch 2 para 5(a)).;

(2) obtain, analyse and share appropriate information having due regard to confidentiality in order to manage the decision-making process including decisions about supervised community treatment (Sch 2 para 5(b));

(3) compile and complete statutory documentation, including an application for admission (Sch 2 para 5(c));

(4) provide reasoned and clear verbal and written reports to promote effective, accountable and independent approved mental health professional decision making (Sch 2 para 5(d));

(5) present a case at a legal hearing (Sch 2 para 5(e));

(6) exercise the appropriate use of independence, authority and autonomy and use it to inform their future practice as an approved mental health professional, together with consultation and supervision (Sch 2 para 5(f));

(7) evaluate the outcomes of interventions with patients, carers and others, including the identification of where a need has not been met (Sch 2 para 5(g));

(8) make and communicate decisions that are sensitive to the needs of the individual patient (Sch 2 para 5(h)); and

(9) keep appropriate records with an awareness of legal requirements with respect to record keeping and the use and transfer of information (Sch 2 para 5(i)).

11 Mental Health (Approved Mental Health Professionals) (Approval) (England) Regulations 2008, SI 2008/1206, reg 3(3) (amended by SI 2012/1479). As to the Care Council for Wales see the Care Standards Act 2000 s 54; and SOCIAL SERVICES AND COMMUNITY CARE vol 44(2) (Reissue) PARA 1003.

817. Appropriate competence in Wales. In relation to Wales, the following key competency areas are to be taken into consideration to determine the relevant competence of a person for the role of approved mental health professional:

(1)   values-based practice[1];

(2)   the application of knowledge relating to legislation and policy[2];

(3)   the application of knowledge relating to mental disorder[3];

(4)   the application of skills relating to effective working partnerships[4]; and

(5)   the application of skills relating to professional decision making[5].

1 Ie:

(1) the ability to identify what constitutes least restrictive health and social care for those dealt with or who may be dealt with under the Mental Health Act 1983 (Mental Health (Approval of Persons to be Approved Mental Health Professionals) (Wales) Regulations 2008, SI 2008/2436, reg 2, Sch 2 para 1.1);

(2) the ability to identify, challenge and, where practicable, redress discrimination and inequality in all its forms in relation to approved mental health professional practice (Sch 2 para 1.2);

(3) understanding and respect for diversity and the ability to identify and counter any decision which may be based upon oppressive practice (Sch 2 para 1.3);

(4) understanding and respect for individuals' qualities, abilities and diverse backgrounds (Sch 2 para 1.4);

(5) race and culturally-sensitive understanding in the application of knowledge of mental health legislation (Sch 2 para 1.5);

(6) consideration of the needs of individuals for whom Welsh is their language of choice (Sch 2 para 1.6);

(7) the ability to promote the rights, dignity and self-determination of patients consistent with their own needs and wishes, to enable them to contribute to the decisions made affecting their quality of life and liberty (Sch 2 para 1.7).

2 Ie:

(1) appropriate knowledge of and ability to apply in practice mental health legislation, related codes of practice and national and local policy guidance and relevant parts of other legislation, codes of practice, national and local policy guidance, in particular the Children Act 1989, the Children Act 2004, the Human Rights Act 1998 and the Mental Capacity Act 2005 (Mental Health (Approval of Persons to be Approved Mental Health Professionals) (Wales) Regulations 2008, SI 2008/2436, reg 2, Sch 2 para 2.1);

(2)   application of knowledge of Welsh language legislation and policy (Sch 2 para 2.2);

(3)   an explicit awareness of the legal position and accountability of approved mental health professionals in relation to the Mental Health Act 1983, any employing organisation and the authority on whose behalf they are acting (Mental Health (Approval of Persons to be Approved Mental Health Professionals) (Wales) Regulations 2008, SI 2008/2436, Sch 2 para 2.3);

(4)   the ability to evaluate critically local and national policy and relevant case law to inform approved mental health professional practice (Sch 2 para 2.4);

(5)   the ability to base approved mental health professional practice on a critical evaluation of a range of research relevant to evidence based practice, including that on the impact of the experience of discrimination on mental health (Sch 2 para 2.5).

3   Ie:

(1)   critical and applied understanding of a range of models of mental health and mental disorder, including the contribution of social, physical and development factors (Mental Health (Approval of Persons to be Approved Mental Health Professionals) (Wales) Regulations 2008, SI 2008/2436, Sch 2 para 3.1);

(2)   critical and applied understanding of the social perspective on mental disorder and mental health needs in working with patients, relatives, carers and other professionals (Sch 2 para 3.2);

(3)   critical and applied understanding of the implications of mental disorder for patients, children, families and carers (Sch 2 para 3.3);

(4)   critical and applied understanding of the implications of a range of relevant treatments and interventions for patients, children, families and carers (Sch 2 para 3.4);

(5)   critical understanding of the resources that might be available to provide an alternative to admission to hospital (Sch 2 para 3.5).

4   Ie:

(1)   the ability to articulate, and demonstrate in practice, the social perspective on mental disorder and mental health needs (Mental Health (Approval of Persons to be Approved Mental Health Professionals) (Wales) Regulations 2008, SI 2008/2436, reg 2, Sch 2 para 4.1);

(2)   the ability to communicate appropriately with, and to establish effective relationships with, patients, relatives and carers (Sch 2 para 4.2);

(3)   the ability to articulate the role of the approved mental health professional in the course of contributing to effective inter-agency and inter-professional working (Sch 2 para 4.3);

(4)   the ability to use networks and community groups to influence collaborative working with a range of individuals, agencies and advocates (Sch 2 para 4.4);

(5)   the ability to contribute effectively to planning and implementing options for care, such as alternatives to compulsory admission, discharge and aftercare (Sch 2 para 4.5);

(6)   the ability to recognise, assess and manage effectively risk in the context of the approved mental health professional role (Sch 2 para 4.6);

(7)   the ability to manage effectively difficult situations of anxiety, risk and conflict, reflecting on the potential impact of such situations on patients and others (Sch 2 para 4.7);

(8)   the ability to balance the inherent power in the approved mental health professional role with the objectives of empowering patients (Sch 2 para 4.8);

(9)   the ability to plan, negotiate and, manage, compulsory admission to hospital, reception into guardianship or arrangements for supervised community treatment (Sch 2 para 4.9);

(10)   the ability to manage and co-ordinate effectively the relevant legal and practical processes including the involvement of other professionals as well as patients, relatives and carers (Sch 2 para 4.10);

(11)   the ability to balance and manage the competing requirements of confidentiality and effective information sharing to the benefit of patients and other stakeholders (Sch 2 para 4.11).

5   Ie:

(1)   the ability to assert a social perspective in decision making and to make properly informed, independent decisions (Mental Health (Approval of Persons to be Approved Mental Health Professionals) (Wales) Regulations 2008, SI 2008/2436, Sch 2 para 5.1);

(2)   the ability to obtain, analyse and share appropriate information from individuals and other resources in order to manage the decision-making process (Sch 2 para 5.2);

(3) the ability to provide reasoned and clear oral and written reports to promote effective, accountable and independent approved mental health professional decision making (Sch 2 para 5.3);
(4) the ability to present a case at a legal hearing (Sch 2 para 5.4);
(5) the ability to exercise their functions as an approved mental health professional independently, and with authority and autonomy (Sch 2 para 5.5);
(6) the ability to evaluate the outcomes of interventions with patients, carers and others, including the identification of any unmet need (Sch 2 para 5.6).

818. Professional requirements. In order to be an approved mental health professional a person must fulfil one of the following professional requirements:
(2) a first level nurse, registered in sub-part 1 of the nurses' part of the register[1], with the inclusion of an entry indicating their field of practice is mental health or learning disabilities' nursing[2];
(3) an occupational health therapist registered in Part 6[3] of the health professions register or a social worker registered in Part 16[4];
(4) a chartered psychologist who is listed in the British Psychological Society's Register of Chartered Psychologists and who holds a relevant practising certificate issued by that Society[5].

1 Ie under the Nursing and Midwifery Order 2001, SI 2002/253, art 5 (see MEDICAL PROFESSIONS vol 74 (2011) PARA 713).
2 Mental Health (Approved Mental Health Professionals) (Approval) (England) Regulations 2008, SI 2008/1206, Sch 1(b); Mental Health (Approval of Persons to be Approved Mental Health Professionals) (Wales) Regulations 2008, SI 2008/2436, Sch 1(b).
3 Ie the register maintained under the Health Professions Order 2001, SI 2002/254, art 5 (see MEDICAL PROFESSIONS vol 74 (2011) PARAS 906, 928).
4 Mental Health (Approved Mental Health Professionals) (Approval) (England) Regulations 2008, SI 2008/1206, Sch 1(c); Mental Health (Approval of Persons to be Approved Mental Health Professionals) (Wales) Regulations 2008, SI 2008/2436, Sch 1(c) (both amended by SI 2012/1479).
5 Mental Health (Approved Mental Health Professionals) (Approval) (England) Regulations 2008, SI 2008/1206, Sch 1(d); Mental Health (Approval of Persons to be Approved Mental Health Professionals) (Wales) Regulations 2008, SI 2008/2436, Sch 1(d).

819. Training. The Health and Care Professions Council[1] may approve courses for persons who are, or wish to become, approved to act as approved mental health professionals[2] by a local social services authority[3] whose area is in England[4]. The Council must publish a list of the courses which it has approved and the courses which it has, but no longer, approves and the periods for which they were so approved[5].

The Care Council for Wales[6] may, in accordance with rules made by it, approve courses for persons who are, or wish to become, approved to act as approved mental health professionals by a local social services authority whose area is in Wales[7]. The Care Council for Wales may also carry out, or assist other persons in carrying out, research into matters relevant to training for approved mental health professionals[8].

The Welsh Ministers may by regulations make provision modifying the functions[9] of the Care Council for Wales in relation to the education and training of persons who are or wish to become approved mental health professionals[10].

1 As to the Health and Care Professions Council see MEDICAL PROFESSIONS vol 74 (2011) PARA 916.
2 As to the meaning of 'approved mental health professional' see PARA 815 note 2.
3 As to the meaning of 'local social services authority' see PARA 579.
4 Mental Health Act 1983 s 114ZA(1) (added by the Health and Social Care Act 2012 s 217(2)). Where the function under the Mental Health Act 1983 s 114ZA(1) is, in accordance with the Health and Social Work Professions Order 2001, SI 2002/254 (see MEDICAL PROFESSIONS),

exercisable by a committee of the Council, the committee may arrange for another person to exercise the function on the Council's behalf: Mental Health Act 1983 s 114ZA(4) (as so added).

5   Mental Health Act 1983 s 114ZA(2) (as added: see note 4).

6   As to the Care Council for Wales see the Care Standards Act 2000 s 54; and SOCIAL SERVICES AND COMMUNITY CARE vol 44(2) (Reissue) PARA 1003.

7   Mental Health Act 1983 s 114A(1) (added by the Mental Health Act 2007 s 19). For this purpose the Care Standards Act 2000 s 63(2)–(4)(a), (7) (see SOCIAL SERVICES AND COMMUNITY CARE) apply as they apply to approvals given, rules made and courses approved under that provision and ss 66 and 71 apply accordingly: Mental Health Act 1983 s 114A(2) (as so added).

8   Mental Health Act 1983 s 114A(5) (as added (see note 7); and amended by the Health and Social Care Act 2012 s 217(4), (7)).

9   'Functions' includes powers and duties: Health and Social Care Act 2008 s 126(4).

10 Health and Social Care Act 2008 s 126(1) (amended by the Health and Social Care Act 2012 Sch 15 para 47(2)(a)). 'Approved mental health professional' has the same meaning as in the Mental Health Act 1983 s 114 (see PARA 815 note 2): Health and Social Care Act 2008 s 126(4). The power to make regulations under s 126(1) may be exercised by amending, repealing or applying (with or without modifications) any provision of any enactment and any other instrument or document: s 126(2). Schedule 9 paras 4–6, 9, 10 apply to the making of regulations under s 126(1) as they apply to the making of regulations under s 124 but as if the references in Sch 9 and 10 to social care workers were references to approved mental health professionals: reg 126(3).

820. Functions of approved mental health professionals. The functions of approved mental health professionals include making applications[1] for compulsory admission to hospital for assessment[2] (including emergency applications[3]) or for treatment[4] or for reception into guardianship[5], gaining access to patients under guardianship[6], applying to a county court for guardianship to be transferred[7], returning detained patients who are absent without leave[8], applying to a county court for the appointment of an acting nearest relative for a patient[9] or for the variation of such an order[10], conveying to hospital patients subject to hospital orders[11], retaking patients who are absent without leave from hospitals in Northern Ireland, the Channel Islands or Isle of Man[12], entering and inspecting certain premises where mentally disordered persons are living[13], laying information to obtain a warrant to search for and remove certain persons believed to be suffering from mental disorder[14], interviewing persons found in public places[15], and retaking persons who escape from legal custody[16].

The functions of an approved mental health professional are not considered relevant social work for the purposes of Part 4[17] of the Care Standards Act 2000[18].

An approved mental health professional may at all reasonable times enter and inspect any premises (other than a hospital) in which a mentally disordered patient is living, if he has reasonable cause to believe that the patient is not under proper care[19].

1   See the Mental Health Act 1983 s 11(1) (see PARA 847). As to the meaning of 'approved mental health professional' see PARA 815 note 2. An approved mental health professional is exercising functions of a public nature and is a 'public authority' for the purposes of the Human Rights Act 1998 and must act compatibly with the patient's human rights under the European Convention on Human Rights and Fundamental Freedoms (Rome, 4 November 1950; TS 71 (1953); Cmd 8969) art 8 (see RIGHTS AND FREEDOMS): see s 6(3)(b); and R *(on the application of Wilkinson) v Responsible Medical Officer Broadmoor Hospital* [2001] EWCA Civ 1545, [2002] 1 WLR 419, 65 BMLR 15).

2   Ie under the Mental Health Act 1983 s 2 (see PARA 767).

3   See the Mental Health Act 1983 s 4(2); and PARA 769.

4   See the Mental Health Act 1983 s 3; and PARA 768.

5   See the Mental Health Act 1983 s 7; and PARA 785.

6   See the Mental Health Act 1983 s 8(1)(c); and PARA 787.

7   See the Mental Health Act 1983 s 10(3); and PARA 796.
8   See the Mental Health Act 1983 s 18(1); and PARA 918.
9   See the Mental Health Act 1983 s 29(2); and PARA 842.
10   See the Mental Health Act 1983 s 30(2); and PARA 843.
11   See the Mental Health Act 1983 s 40(1)(a); and PARA 867.
12   See the Mental Health Act 1983 ss 87, 89; and PARA 920.
13   See the Mental Health Act 1983 s 115; and PARA 820.
14   See the Mental Health Act 1983 s 135(1), (4); and PARA 922.
15   See the Mental Health Act 1983 s 136(2); and PARA 923.
16   See the Mental Health Act 1983 s 138(1); and PARA 777. As to the meaning of 'legal custody' see s 137(1); and PARA 776. An approved mental health professional acts on behalf of' a local authority: see ss 114(10), 145(1AC) (s 145(1AC) added by the Mental Health Act 2007 Sch 2 para 11(3)). This is intended to underline the independence of the approved mental health professional from the trust that may employ the doctors who also examine a patient's case for admission. It emphasises that the responsibility for providing an approved mental health professional is placed with the local social services authority. An approved mental health professional is an independent statutory decision maker but the local authority will be liable for any lack of care or bad faith on the part of an approved mental health professional: see *R (on the application of TTM (by his litigation friend TM)) v Hackney London Borough Council* [2010] EWHC 1349 (Admin), [2011] 1 WLR 2873 (approved on this point in [2011] EWCA Civ 4, [2011] 3 All ER 529, [2011] 1 WLR 2873). There is no reason in principle why an approved mental health professional should not owe a patient a duty of care: see *R (on the application of TTM (by his litigation friend TM)) v Hackney London Borough Council* [2010] EWHC 1349 (Admin), [2011] 1 WLR 2873.
17   Ie for the purposes of the Care Standards Act 2000 ss 54–71 (see SOCIAL SERVICES AND COMMUNITY CARE).
18   Mental Health Act 1983 ss 114ZA(3), 114A(4) (s 114ZA added by the Health and Social Care Act 2012 s 217(2); and the Mental Health Act 1983 s 114A added by the Mental Health Act 2007 s 19).
19   Mental Health Act 1983 s 115(1) (substituted by the Mental Health Act 2007 Sch 2 para 8). This power is exercisable only after the professional has produced, if asked to do so, some duly authenticated document showing that he is an approved mental health professional: Mental Health Act 1983 s 115(2) (as so substituted).

821. Applications by approved mental health professionals. If a local social services authority[1] has reason to think that an application for admission to hospital[2] or a guardianship application[3] may need to be made in respect of a patient[4] within its area, it must make arrangements for an approved mental health professional[5] to consider the patient's case on their behalf[6]. If that professional is satisfied that such an application ought to be made in respect of the patient and he is of the opinion, having regard to any wishes expressed by relatives of the patient or any other relevant circumstances, that it is necessary or proper for the application to be made by him, he must make the application[7].

Before making an application for the admission of a patient to hospital an approved mental health professional must interview the patient in a suitable manner and satisfy himself that detention in a hospital is in all the circumstances of the case the most appropriate way of providing the care and medical treatment of which the patient stands in need[8].

An approved mental health professional may not make an application for admission for treatment or for guardianship if the patient's nearest relative[9] has notified him, or the local social services authority on whose behalf the professional is acting, that the relative objects to the application being made; nor can he make such an application without consulting the person, if any, who appears to be the patient's nearest relative, unless it appears to the approved mental health professional that such consultation is not reasonably practicable or would involve unreasonable delay[10]. Further, if an approved mental health professional applies for a patient to be admitted for assessment, he must, before or within a reasonable time after such application, take such steps as are practicable to inform the person who appears to be the patient's nearest relative both of the application and of the relative's power to discharge the patient[11]. However, it is the duty of a local social services authority, if so required by the nearest relative of a patient[12], to direct an approved mental health professional to consider the case with a view to making an application for admission to hospital, and if the approved mental health professional decides not to apply he must inform the relative of his reasons in writing[13].

1   As to the meaning of 'local social services authority' see PARA 579.
2   As to such applications see PARAS 767–769. As to the meaning of 'hospital' see PARA 577.
3   As to guardianship applications see PARA 785.
4   As to the meaning of 'patient' see PARA 758 note 4.
5   As to the meaning of 'approved mental health professional' see PARA 815 note 2.
6   Mental Health Act 1983 s 13(1) (s 13(1) substituted and s 13(1A)–(1C) added by the Mental Health Act 2007 Sch 2 para 5(2)). Nothing in the Mental Health Act 1983 s 13 is to be construed as authorising or requiring an application to be made by an approved mental health professional in contravention of the provisions of s 11(4) or of regulations under s 12A (see PARA 825), or as restricting the power of a local social services authority to make arrangements with an approved mental health professional to consider a patient's case or of an approved mental health professional to make any application under the Mental Health Act 1983: s 13(5) (amended by the Mental Health Act 2007 Sch 2 para 6). As to the role of the approved mental health professional see the Department of Health *Mental Health Act 1983 Code of Practice* (2008) paras 4.48–4.70; and the Welsh Assembly Government *Mental Health Act 1983 Code of Practice for Wales* (2008) paras 2.33–2.51.
7   Mental Health Act 1983 s 13(1A) (as added: see note 6). The words 'that professional' indicate that the responsibilities under this provision are placed on the approved mental health professional and not on the employing authority: see *Nottingham City Council v Unison* [2004] EWHC 893. As to the vicarious liability of the employing authority see PARA 820. An approved mental health professional must exercise his or her own independent judgment and personally make the appropriate decision: see *St George's Healthcare NHS Trust v S, R v Collins, ex p S* [1999] Fam 26, [1998] 3 All ER 673, CA. As to 'necessary or proper' see *St George's Healthcare NHS Trust* at 695. Where: (1) a local social services authority makes the arrangements under s 13(1) in respect of a patient; (2) an application for admission for assessment is made under s 13(1A) in respect of the patient; (3) while the patient is liable to be detained in pursuance of that application, the authority have reason to think that an application for admission for treatment may need to be made in respect of the patient; and (4) the patient is not within the area of the authority, s 13(1) is construed as requiring the authority to make arrangements under that provision in place of the authority mentioned there: s 13(1B), (1C) (as so added). An application under s 13(1A) may be made outside the area of the local social services authority on whose behalf the approved mental health professional is considering the patient's case: s 13(3) (substituted by the Mental Health Act 2007 Sch 2 para 5(4)). An application for admission to hospital may not lawfully be made if the patient has been discharged from detention in hospital by a decision of a tribunal unless the approved mental health professional has formed a reasonable and bona fide opinion that he has information that was not known to the tribunal and which changes the nature of the case presented before the tribunal: *R v East London and City Mental Health NHS Trust ex p Von Brandenburg (aka Hanley)* [2003] UKHL 58, [2004] 2 AC 280, [2004] 1 All ER 400. If an approved mental health professional makes a decision that is contrary to that of a recent tribunal then he or she is obliged to give the patient reasons: *R v East London and City Mental Health NHS Trust ex p Von Brandenburg (aka Hanley)*.
8   Mental Health Act 1983 s 13(2) (amended by the Mental Health Act 2007 Sch 2 para 5(3)). An interview under the Mental Health Act 1983 s 4(2) (see PARA 769) may also be also used for s 3 purposes (see PARA 768): *Re GM (Patient: Consultation)* [2000] 1 MHLR 41. The interview required under this provision may take place more than 14 days before the application provided s 11(5) (see PARA 847) is complied with and the patient is told 'face to face' with that an application is necessary within 14 days: *Re Whitbread (Mental Patient: Habeas Corpus)* (1997) 39 BMLR 94, CA. An attempt to communicate with a patient who is either unwilling or unable to respond is likely to be sufficient: *M v South West London and St George's Mental Health NHS Trust* [2008] EWCA Civ 1112, [2008] All ER (D) 63 (Aug). 'In all the circumstances of the case' includes medical considerations: see *GJ v Foundation Trust* [2009] EWHC 2972 (Fam), [2010] 3 WLR 840. 'Care and medical treatment' must be for the mental disorder and not an

unconnected medical disorder: see *St George's Healthcare NHS Trust v S, R v Collins, ex p S* [1999] Fam 26, [1998] 3 All ER 673, [1998] 3 WLR 936.

Before or within a reasonable time after an application the impact of contact with the patient's nearest relative on the patient's health and well-being must be considered in the context of private and family life rights and may mean that it is not practicable for a nearest relative to be consulted: see the Mental Health Act 1983 s 11(3); PARA 847; and *R(E) v Bristol City Council* [2005] EWHC 74 (Admin).

9   As to the meaning of 'nearest relative' see PARA 839.

10 Mental Health Act 1983 s 11(4) (substituted by the Mental Health Act 2007 Sch 2 para 1(4)). This provision does not apply to an application for admission of a minor who is a ward of court: see the Mental Health Act 1983 s 33(1); and PARA 847. Such applications can only be made with leave of the court: see s 33(1); and PARA 847. See generally CHILDREN AND YOUNG PERSONS. For the circumstances in which an approved mental health professional application should not be made due to conflict of interest see PARAS 825–830. If a nearest relative objects to an application under s 3 (see PARA 768) for a patient already admitted under s 2 (see PARA 767), the 28 day period is extended if an approved mental health professional applies to the county court for the nearest relative to be displaced under s 29(2)(c) or (d): see s 29(4); and PARA 842.

Applications were previously made by an approved social worker (see ss 13, 11 (as originally enacted)) and the following cases may remain of interest. If an approved mental health professional makes an application where the nearest relative has objected the patient's detention will be unlawful from the outset. The remedy will lie against the local authority as having 'directly caused' the detention even though it is not the detaining authority. Lawfulness rests on whether there is in fact an objection and not the approved mental health professional's reasonable belief as to the same: *M (by his litigation friend TM) v Hackney London Borough Council* [2011] EWCA Civ 4, [2011] 3 All ER 529, [2011] 1 WLR 2873. As to previous objections see *R v East London NHS Foundation Trust & Hackney London Borough Council, ex p M* [2009] MHLR 154. Although it was desirable for consultation under s 11(4) to be conducted by the approved social worker, consultation could be delegated if it was full and effective; the person appearing to be the nearest relative must at least be legally capable of being the nearest relative: *R v Managers of South Western Hospital, ex p M* [1993] QB 683, [1994] 1 All ER 161. The approved mental health professional does not need to turn into a sleuth to discover the identity of the nearest relative: *Re D (Mental Patient: Habeas Corpus)* [2000] 2 FLR 848, CA; *R (C) v South London and Maudsley NHS Trust* [2001] EWHC Admin 1025. Consultation of the nearest relative prior to seeing and interviewing the patient satisfies the requirements of the Mental Health Act 1983 s 11(4). The nearest relative must be given sufficient information to enable him to form an opinion: *Re Whitbread, Whitbread v Kingston and District NHS Trust* (1997) 39 BMLR 94, CA. Lack of objection by the nearest relative is sufficient for the purposes of the Mental Health Act 1983 s 11(4), positive consent is not necessary and, if left till the last minute, is unlikely to be effective: *R (on the application of Ganatra) v Ealing London Borough Council* [2002] EWHC 1112 (Admin), [2002] All ER (D) 294 (Apr). The approved mental health professional does not need to ask a specific question about any objection: *Re GM (Patient: Consultation)* [2000] MHLR 41. The objection does not have to be reasonable or sensible: *GD v Hospital Managers of the Edgware Community Hospital* [2008] EWHC 3572 (Admin), [2008] All ER (D) 439 (Jun). Consultation may not be appropriate if it would cause harm to the patient: see *Re P (Adoption: Natural Father's Rights)* [1995] 2 FCR 58, [1994] 1 FLR 771. 'Practicable' in the Mental Health Act 1983 s 11(4) does not mean 'possible': *R (on the application of WC) v South London and Maudsley NHS Trust and Orekeye* [2001] 1 MHLR 187; *R(E) v Bristol City Council* [2005] EWHC 74 (Admin). See also Application 26494/95 *JT v United Kingdom* [2000] 30 EHRR CD 77, [2000] 1 FLR 909, ECtHR; *Re D (Mental Patient: Habeas Corpus)* [2001] 1 FCR 218, CA. For an unreasonable delay and an assumption by an approved social worker that a patient's nearest relative would consent meant that proper approach under s 11(4) had not been followed: see *V v South London and Maudsley NHS Foundation Trust* [2010] All ER (D) 76 (Feb). Where there is no pressing need for admission there could be no argument that no consultation with the nearest relative was undertaken so as to avoid an unreasonable delay: *R(GP) v Derby City Council and Derbyshire Mental Health NHS Foundation Trust* [2012] EWHC 1451. As to the use of the word 'practicable' in a different context see PARA 849.

The duty of the approved social worker to inform the nearest relative under the Mental Health Act 1983 s 11(3), (4) could interfere with the patient's rights under the European Convention on Human Rights and Fundamental Freedoms (Rome, 4 November 1950; TS 71 (1953); Cmd 8969) art 8 (see RIGHTS AND FREEDOMS): see *R (on the application of E) v Bristol City Council* [2005] EWHC 74 (Admin), [2005] All ER (D) 57 (Jan) (where it was held that contacting the nearest relative would infringe the patient's Convention rights in circumstances where the patient had a poor relationship with the relative).

11 Mental Health Act 1983 s 11(3) (amended by the Mental Health Act 2007 Sch 2 para 4(3)). It is submitted that this provision applies to emergency applications, as these are applications for admission for assessment (see the Mental Health Act 1983 s 4(1)), and provision is made (in s 4(5)) for the modification of s 11 in respect of them: see PARA 847. As to the nearest relative's power to order discharge see s 23; and PARA 913.

12 Ie a patient residing in its area.

13 Mental Health Act 1983 s 13(4) (amended by the Mental Health Act 2007 Sch 2 para 5).

822. Approval conditions. In relation to England, an approval to be an approved mental health professional[1] is subject to the following conditions:

(1) in each year that the approved mental health professional is approved, he must complete at least 18 hours of training agreed with the approving local social services authority[2] as being relevant to his role as an approved mental health professional[3];

(2) the approved mental health professional must undertake to notify the approving local social services authority in writing as soon as reasonably practicable if he agrees to act as an approved mental health professional on behalf of another local social services authority, and when such agreement ends[4];

(3) the approved mental health professional must undertake to cease to act as an approved mental health professional and to notify the approving local social services authority immediately if he is suspended from any of the registers or listings referred to in the professional competencies, or if any such suspension ends[5]; and

(4) the approved mental health professional must undertake to cease to act as an approved mental health professional and to notify the approving local social services authority immediately if he no longer meets at least one of the professional requirements[6].

In relation to Wales, an approval to be an approved mental health professional is subject to the following conditions:

(a) the approved mental health professional must complete whilst he remains approved such training as required by the approving local social services authority, at such intervals as determined by the local social services authority as being necessary[7];

(b) the approved mental health professional must provide evidence to the reasonable satisfaction of the approving local social services authority, at no less than annual intervals of the date of his approval, that he continues to have appropriate competence to carry out functions as an approved mental health professional[8];

(c) the approved mental health professional must notify the approving local social services authority in writing as soon as reasonably practicable if he agrees to carry out duties as an approved mental health professional on behalf of another local social services authority, and when such agreement ends[9];

(d) the approved mental health professional must notify the approving local social services authority, in writing as soon as reasonably practicable, if he is approved by a different local social services authority[10];

(e) the approved mental health professional must notify the approving local social services authority immediately if he no longer meets any of the requirements set out in provisions relating to the granting of approval[11] or reapproval[12] as the case may be[13];

(f)   the approved mental health professional must notify the approving local social services authority immediately in the event of him being suspended from registration or listing, as the case may be, or having conditions attached to the same[14].

1   As to the meaning of 'approved mental health professional' see PARA 815 note 2.
2   As to the meaning of 'local social services authority' see PARA 579.
3   Mental Health (Approved Mental Health Professionals) (Approval) (England) Regulations 2008, SI 2008/1206, reg 5(a).
4   Mental Health (Approved Mental Health Professionals) (Approval) (England) Regulations 2008, SI 2008/1206, reg 5(b).
5   Mental Health (Approved Mental Health Professionals) (Approval) (England) Regulations 2008, SI 2008/1206, reg 5(c). As to the professional competencies see PARAS 816, 817.
6   Mental Health (Approved Mental Health Professionals) (Approval) (England) Regulations 2008, SI 2008/1206, reg 5(d). As to the professional requirements see PARA 818.
7   Mental Health (Approval of Persons to be Approved Mental Health Professionals) (Wales) Regulations 2008, SI 2008/2436, reg 7(a).
8   Mental Health (Approval of Persons to be Approved Mental Health Professionals) (Wales) Regulations 2008, SI 2008/2436, reg 7(b). As to the appropriate competence see PARA 817.
9   Mental Health (Approval of Persons to be Approved Mental Health Professionals) (Wales) Regulations 2008, SI 2008/2436, reg 7(c).
10 Mental Health (Approval of Persons to be Approved Mental Health Professionals) (Wales) Regulations 2008, SI 2008/2436, reg 7(d).
11 Ie as set out in the Mental Health (Approval of Persons to be Approved Mental Health Professionals) (Wales) Regulations 2008, SI 2008/2436, reg 3 (see PARA 815).
12 Ie as set out in the Mental Health (Approval of Persons to be Approved Mental Health Professionals) (Wales) Regulations 2008, SI 2008/2436, reg 8 (see PARA 815).
13 Mental Health (Approval of Persons to be Approved Mental Health Professionals) (Wales) Regulations 2008, SI 2008/2436, reg 7(e).
14 Mental Health (Approval of Persons to be Approved Mental Health Professionals) (Wales) Regulations 2008, SI 2008/2436, reg 7(f).

823.   Suspension of approval.   If at any time after being approved, the registration or listing required by the professional requirements[1] of a person approved to act as an approved mental health professional[2] is suspended, the approving local social services authority[3] must suspend that approved mental health professional's approval for as long as that registration or listing is suspended[4].

In relation to England, where an approved mental health professional's approval is suspended, that person may not act as an approved mental health professional unless and until the suspension of approval is ended by the approving local social services authority in accordance with the following[5]. Where the approving local social services authority is notified that the suspension of the approved mental health professional's registration or listing has ended, the approving local social services authority must, unless it is not satisfied the approved mental health professional has appropriate competence in dealing with persons suffering from mental disorder[6], end the suspension of approval[7]. Where the suspension of approval has ended, the approval continues to run for any unexpired period of approval, unless the approving local social services authority ends it earlier[8] in accordance with the relevant provisions[9].

In relation to Wales, in the event of conditions being attached to an approved mental health professional's registration or listing, as the case may be, the local social services authority may attach such conditions to the approval as it may deem necessary, or it may suspend the approval[10]. Where the suspension of approval has ended, the approval will continue to run for any unexpired period of approval, unless the approving local social services authority ends it[11] earlier in accordance with the relevant provisions[12].

1 As to the professional requirements see PARA 818.
2 As to the meaning of 'approved mental health professional' see PARA 815 note 2.
3 As to the meaning of 'local social services authority' see PARA 579.
4 See the Mental Health (Approved Mental Health Professionals) (Approval) (England) Regulations 2008, SI 2008/1206, reg 6(1); and the Mental Health (Approval of Persons to be Approved Mental Health Professionals) (Wales) Regulations 2008, SI 2008/2436, reg 6(1).
5 Mental Health (Approved Mental Health Professionals) (Approval) (England) Regulations 2008, SI 2008/1206, reg 6(2).
6 As to when the approved mental health professional has competence in dealing with persons suffering from mental disorder see PARAS 816–818.
7 Mental Health (Approved Mental Health Professionals) (Approval) (England) Regulations 2008, SI 2008/1206, reg 6(3).
8 Ie ends it earlier in accordance with the Mental Health (Approved Mental Health Professionals) (Approval) (England) Regulations 2008, SI 2008/1206, reg 7.
9 Mental Health (Approved Mental Health Professionals) (Approval) (England) Regulations 2008, SI 2008/1206, reg 6(4).
10 Mental Health (Approval of Persons to be Approved Mental Health Professionals) (Wales) Regulations 2008, SI 2008/2436, reg 6(2).
11 Ie ends it earlier in accordance with the Mental Health (Approval of Persons to be Approved Mental Health Professionals) (Wales) Regulations 2008, SI 2008/2436, reg 5.
12 Mental Health (Approval of Persons to be Approved Mental Health Professionals) (Wales) Regulations 2008, SI 2008/2436, reg 6(3).

824. End of approval. A person ceases to be approved to act as an approved mental health professional[1] at the end of the day on which his period of approval[2] expires[3]. However, the approval of a person as an approved mental health professional will cease before the period of approval has expired[4] in certain circumstances[5].

1 As to the meaning of 'approved mental health professional' see PARA 815 note 2.
2 As to the period of approval see PARA 815 note 2.
3 See the Mental Health (Approved Mental Health Professionals) (Approval) (England) Regulations 2008, SI 2008/1206, reg 5(1); and the Mental Health (Approval of Persons to be Approved Mental Health Professionals) (Wales) Regulations 2008, SI 2008/2436, reg 7(1). When an approval ends, the approving local social services authority must notify the approved mental health professional immediately that the approval has ended and give reasons for ending the approval: see the Mental Health (Approved Mental Health Professionals) (Approval) (England) Regulations 2008, SI 2008/1206, reg 5(3); and the Mental Health (Approval of Persons to be Approved Mental Health Professionals) (Wales) Regulations 2008, SI 2008/2436, reg 7(3). When an approval ends, the approving local social services authority must notify that fact to any other local social services authority for whom it knows the approved mental health professional has agreed to act: see the Mental Health (Approved Mental Health Professionals) (Approval) (England) Regulations 2008, SI 2008/1206, reg 5(4); and the Mental Health (Approval of Persons to be Approved Mental Health Professionals) (Wales) Regulations 2008, SI 2008/2436, reg 7(4). As to the meaning of 'local social services authority' see PARA 579.
4 In relation to Wales, where an approving local social services authority ends the approval of an approved mental health professional under the Mental Health (Approval of Persons to be Approved Mental Health Professionals) (Wales) Regulations 2008, SI 2008/2436, reg 7(2), that local social services authority must immediately notify that person in writing of the date of the ending of and the reasons for ending that approval: reg 7(5).
5 In relation to England, except where the Mental Health (Approved Mental Health Professionals) (Approval) (England) Regulations 2008, SI 2008/1206, reg 6 applies (see PARA 823), the approving local social services authority must end the approval of a person it has approved to act as an approved mental health professional before their period of approval expires:
    (1)   in accordance with a request in writing to do so from that approved mental health professional (s 7(2)(a));
    (2)   if it is no longer satisfied that the approved mental health professional has appropriate competence taking into account the matters set out in Sch 2 (see PARA 816) (s 7(2)(b));
    (3)   immediately upon becoming aware that the approved mental health professional is no

longer a person who meets at least one of the professional requirements, or he is in breach of any of the conditions set out in reg 5 (see PARA 822) or he has been approved to act as an approved mental health professional by another local social services authority (s 7(2)(c)).

If a local social services authority approves a person as an approved mental health professional knowing that that approved mental health professional is already approved by another local social services authority, it must notify the previous approving local social services authority: reg 7(5).

In relation to Wales, the approval of a person as an approved mental health professional will cease before the period of approval has expired in the following circumstances:

(a)   if that person ceases to carry out functions as an approved mental health professional on behalf of the approving local social services authority (Mental Health (Approval of Persons to be Approved Mental Health Professionals) (Wales) Regulations 2008, SI 2008/2436, reg 5(2)(a));

(b)   if that person fails to meet any of the conditions attached to his approval in accordance with reg 7 (reg 5(2)(b));

(c)   if, in the opinion of the approving local social services authority, that person no longer possesses the relevant competencies (reg 5(2)(c));

(d)   if that person no longer fulfils the professional requirements (reg 5(2)(d));

(e)   if that person becomes approved as an approved mental health professional by another local social services authority (reg 5(2)(e));

(f)   if that person makes a written request for cessation of approval (reg 5(2)(f)).

(ii) Conflict of Interest

825. Power to make regulations. The appropriate national authority[1] may make regulations[2] as to the circumstances in which there would be a potential conflict of interest such that (1) an approved mental health professional[3] may not make an application for admission for assessment, an application for admission for treatment or a guardianship application[4]; (2) a registered medical practitioner[5] may not give a recommendation[6] for the purposes of an application for the admission of a patient or a guardianship application[7].

1   For these purposes 'the appropriate national authority' means in relation to applications in which admission is sought to a hospital in England or to guardianship applications in respect of which the area of the relevant local social services authority is in England, the Secretary of State; and, in relation to applications in which admission is sought to a hospital in Wales or to guardianship applications in respect of which the area of the relevant local social services authority is in Wales, the Welsh Ministers: Mental Health Act 1983 s 12A(3) (s 12A added by the Mental Health Act 2007 s 22(5)). References in the Mental Health Act 1983 s 12A to the relevant local social services authority, in relation to a guardianship application, are references to the local social services authority named in the application as guardian or (as the case may be) the local social services authority for the area in which the person so named resides: s 12A(4) (as so added). As to the meaning of 'local social services authority' see PARA 579.

2   Such regulations may make provision for the prohibitions in the Mental Health Act 1983 s 12A(1) to be subject to specified exceptions, different provision for different cases and transitional, consequential, incidental or supplemental provision: s 12A(2) (as added: see note 1). As to such regulations see the Mental Health (Conflicts of Interest) (England) Regulations 2008, SI 2008/1205; the Mental Health (Conflicts of Interest) (Wales) Regulations 2008, SI 2008/2440; and PARA 831 et seq.

3   As to the meaning of 'approved mental health professional' see PARA 815 note 2.

4   Ie an application mentioned in the Mental Health Act 1983 s 11(1) (see PARA 847).

5   As to registered medical practitioners see MEDICAL PROFESSIONS vol 74 (2011) PARA 176 et seq.

6   Ie a recommendation for the purposes of an application mentioned in the Mental Health Act 1983 s 12(1) (see PARA 849).

7   Mental Health Act 1983 s 12A(1) (as added: see note 1). As to conflict of interest see the Department of Health *Mental Health Act 1983 Code of Practice* (2008) Chapter 7 and the Welsh Assembly Government *Mental Health Act 1983 Code of Practice for Wales* (2008) Chapter 3.

826. Potential conflict for financial reasons. An assessor[1] has a potential conflict of interest for financial reasons if he has a financial interest, or in relation to Wales, financial gain[2], in the outcome of a decision whether or not to make an application or give a medical recommendation[3].

In relation to England, where an application for the admission of the patient to a hospital which is a registered establishment is being considered, a registered medical practitioner who is on the staff of that hospital has a potential conflict of interest for financial reasons where the other medical recommendation is given by a registered medical practitioner who is also on the staff of that hospital[4].

In relation to Wales, where the application is for the admission of the patient to a hospital which is not a registered establishment, one (but not more than one) of the medical recommendations may be given by a registered medical practitioner who is on the staff of that hospital or who receives or has an interest in the receipt of any payments made on account of the maintenance of the patient[5]. However, where the application is for the admission of the patient to a hospital which is a registered establishment, neither of the medical recommendations may be given by a registered medical practitioner who is on the staff of that hospital or who receives or has an interest in the receipt of any payments made on account of the maintenance of the patient[6].

1 In relation to England an 'assessor' means an approved mental health professional or a registered medical practitioner (Mental Health (Conflicts of Interest) (England) Regulations 2008, SI 2008/1205, reg 2) and, in relation to Wales, means an approved mental health professional considering making an application or a registered medical practitioner considering giving a medical recommendation (see the Mental Health (Conflicts of Interest) (Wales) Regulations 2008, SI 2008/2440, reg 2). As to registered medical practitioners see MEDICAL PROFESSIONS vol 74 (2011) PARA 176 et seq.
2 For this purpose 'financial gain' does not include any fee paid to a practitioner in respect of the examination of a patient pursuant to the Mental Health Act 1983 s 12 (see PARA 849) or the provision of any recommendation as a result of such examination: Mental Health (Conflicts of Interest) (Wales) Regulations 2008, SI 2008/2440, reg 4(4).
3 See the Mental Health (Conflicts of Interest) (England) Regulations 2008, SI 2008/1205, reg 4(1); and the Mental Health (Conflicts of Interest) (Wales) Regulations 2008, SI 2008/2440, reg 4(1).
4 Mental Health (Conflicts of Interest) (England) Regulations 2008, SI 2008/1205, reg 4(2).
5 Mental Health (Conflicts of Interest) (Wales) Regulations 2008, SI 2008/2440, reg 4(2).
6 Mental Health (Conflicts of Interest) (Wales) Regulations 2008, SI 2008/2440, reg 4(3).

827. Potential conflict for business reasons. When considering making an application or considering giving a medical recommendation in respect of a patient, an assessor[1] will have a potential conflict of interest for business reasons if both the assessor and the patient or another assessor are closely involved in the same business venture, including being a partner, director, other office-holder or major shareholder of that venture[2].

Where the patient's nearest relative is making an application, a registered medical practitioner[3] or, in relation to Wales, an assessor, who is considering giving a medical recommendation in respect of that patient has a potential conflict of interest for business reasons if that registered medical practitioner and the nearest relative are both closely involved in the same business venture, including being a partner, director, other office-holder or major shareholder of that venture[4].

1 As to the meaning of 'assessor' see PARA 826 note 1.
2 See the Mental Health (Conflicts of Interest) (England) Regulations 2008, SI 2008/1205, reg 5(1); and the Mental Health (Conflicts of Interest) (Wales) Regulations 2008, SI 2008/2440,

reg 5(1). In relation to Wales there is also a conflict of interest where an assessor is closely involved in the same business venture as the patient's nearest relative: see reg 5(1). As to the nearest relative see PARA 839.

3   As to registered medical practitioners see MEDICAL PROFESSIONS vol 74 (2011) PARA 176 et seq.

4   See the Mental Health (Conflicts of Interest) (England) Regulations 2008, SI 2008/1205, reg 5(2); and the Mental Health (Conflicts of Interest) (Wales) Regulations 2008, SI 2008/2440, reg 5(2).

828.   Potential conflict for professional reasons.   In relation to England, when considering making an application or considering giving a medical recommendation in respect of a patient, an assessor[1] has a potential conflict of interest for professional reasons if the assessor:

(1)   directs the work of, or employs, the patient or one of the other assessors making that consideration[2]; or

(2)   is a member of a team organised to work together for clinical purposes on a routine basis and the patient is a member of the same team or the other two assessors are members of the same team[3].

Where the patient's nearest relative is making an application, a registered medical practitioner who is considering giving a medical recommendation in respect of that patient has a potential conflict of interest for professional reasons if that registered medical practitioner directs the work of, or employs, the nearest relative or works under the direction of, or is employed by, the patient's nearest relative[4].

In relation to Wales, when considering a patient, an assessor will have a potential conflict of interest if he works under the direction of, or is employed by, one of the other assessors considering the patient or he is a member of a team organised to work together for clinical purposes on a routine basis of which the other two assessors are also members[5].

Where the patient's nearest relative is making an application, an assessor will have a potential conflict of interest if he works under the direction of, or is employed by, that patient's nearest relative or he employs the patient's nearest relative or the nearest relative works under his direction or he is a member of a team organised to work together for clinical purposes on a routine basis of which the nearest relative is also a member[6].

When considering a patient, an assessor will have a potential conflict of interest if he works under the direction of, or is employed by, the patient or he employs the patient or the patient works under his direction or he is a member of a team organised to work together for clinical purposes on a routine basis of which the patient is also a member[7].

1   As to the meaning of 'assessor' see PARA 826 note 1.

2   Mental Health (Conflicts of Interest) (England) Regulations 2008, SI 2008/1205, reg 6(1)(a).

3   Mental Health (Conflicts of Interest) (England) Regulations 2008, SI 2008/1205, reg 6(1)(b). This does not prevent a registered medical practitioner giving a medical recommendation or an approved mental health professional making an application if, in their opinion, it is of urgent necessity for an application to be made and a delay would involve serious risk to the health or safety of the patient or others: reg 6(3). As to registered medical practitioners see MEDICAL PROFESSIONS vol 74 (2011) PARA 176 et seq.

4   Mental Health (Conflicts of Interest) (England) Regulations 2008, SI 2008/1205, reg 6(2).

5   Mental Health (Conflicts of Interest) (Wales) Regulations 2008, SI 2008/2440, reg 3(1).

6   Mental Health (Conflicts of Interest) (Wales) Regulations 2008, SI 2008/2440, reg 3(2).

7   Mental Health (Conflicts of Interest) (Wales) Regulations 2008, SI 2008/2440, reg 3(3).

829.   Potential conflict on the basis of a personal relationship.   An assessor[1] who is considering making an application or considering giving a medical recommendation in respect of a patient, has a potential conflict of interest on the basis of a personal relationship if that assessor is:

   (1)   related to a relevant person[2] in the first degree[3];

   (2)   related to a relevant person in the second degree[4];

   (3)   related to a relevant person as a half-sister or half brother[5];

   (4)   the spouse, ex-spouse, civil partner or ex civil partner of a relevant person[6]; or

   (5)   living with a relevant person as if he was a spouse or a civil partner[7].

1   As to the meaning of 'assessor' see PARA 826 note 1.
2   'Relevant person' means another assessor, the patient, or if the patient's nearest relative is making the application, the nearest relative: Mental Health (Conflicts of Interest) (England) Regulations 2008, SI 2008/1205, reg 7(2)(a); Mental Health (Conflicts of Interest) (Wales) Regulations 2008, SI 2008/2440, reg 6(2)(a). As to the nearest relative see PARA 839.
3   Mental Health (Conflicts of Interest) (England) Regulations 2008, SI 2008/1205, reg 7(1)(a); Mental Health (Conflicts of Interest) (Wales) Regulations 2008, SI 2008/2440, reg 6(1)(a). 'Related in the first degree' means as a parent, sister, brother, daughter or son; and includes step relationships: Mental Health (Conflicts of Interest) (England) Regulations 2008, SI 2008/1205, reg 7(2)(b); Mental Health (Conflicts of Interest) (Wales) Regulations 2008, SI 2008/2440, reg 6(2)(b). References to step relationships are to be read in accordance with the Civil Partnership Act 2004 s 246 (see MATRIMONIAL AND CIVIL PARTNERSHIP LAW vol 72 (2009) PARA 129): Mental Health (Conflicts of Interest) (England) Regulations 2008, SI 2008/1205, reg 7(2)(d); Mental Health (Conflicts of Interest) (Wales) Regulations 2008, SI 2008/2440, reg 6(2)(d).
4   Mental Health (Conflicts of Interest) (England) Regulations 2008, SI 2008/1205, reg 7(1)(b); Mental Health (Conflicts of Interest) (Wales) Regulations 2008, SI 2008/2440, reg 6(1)(b). 'Related in the second degree' means as an uncle, aunt, grandparent, grandchild, first cousin, niece, nephew, parent-in-law, grandparent-in-law, grandchild-in-law, sister-in-law, brother-in-law, daughter-in-law or son-in-law and includes step relationships: Mental Health (Conflicts of Interest) (England) Regulations 2008, SI 2008/1205, reg 7(2)(c); Mental Health (Conflicts of Interest) (Wales) Regulations 2008, SI 2008/2440, reg 6(2)(c). References to in-laws are to be read in accordance with the Civil Partnership Act 2004 s 246 (see MATRIMONIAL AND CIVIL PARTNERSHIP LAW vol 72 (2009) PARA 129): Mental Health (Conflicts of Interest) (England) Regulations 2008, SI 2008/1205, reg 7(2)(d); Mental Health (Conflicts of Interest) (Wales) Regulations 2008, SI 2008/2440, reg 6(2)(d).
5   Mental Health (Conflicts of Interest) (England) Regulations 2008, SI 2008/1205, reg 7(1)(c); Mental Health (Conflicts of Interest) (Wales) Regulations 2008, SI 2008/2440, reg 6(1)(c).
6   Mental Health (Conflicts of Interest) (England) Regulations 2008, SI 2008/1205, reg 7(1)(d); Mental Health (Conflicts of Interest) (Wales) Regulations 2008, SI 2008/2440, reg 6(1)(d).
7   Mental Health (Conflicts of Interest) (England) Regulations 2008, SI 2008/1205, reg 7(1)(d); Mental Health (Conflicts of Interest) (Wales) Regulations 2008, SI 2008/2440, reg 6(1)(d).

830. Emergency provision: Wales. The potential conflict provisions[1] do not prevent an approved mental health professional[2] making an application or a registered medical practitioner[3] giving a medical recommendation if there would otherwise be delay involving serious risk to the health or safety of the patient or others[4].

1   Ie provisions under the Mental Health (Conflicts of Interest) (Wales) Regulations 2008, SI 2008/2440.
2   As to the meaning of 'approved mental health professional' see PARA 815 note 2.
3   As to registered medical practitioners see MEDICAL PROFESSIONS vol 74 (2011) PARA 176 et seq.
4   Mental Health (Conflicts of Interest) (Wales) Regulations 2008, SI 2008/2440, reg 7.

(iii) Approved Clinician and Responsible Clinician

831. Approved clinician. 'Approved clinician' means a person approved by the appropriate national authority[1] to act as an approved clinician[2] for the purposes of the Mental Health Act 1983[3].

1   Ie the Secretary of State (in relation to England) and the Welsh Ministers (in relation to Wales). As to the delegation of this power see PARA 570.

2   Professionals who may act as approved clinicians are registered medical practitioners, chartered psychologists who are listed in the British Psychological Society's Register of Chartered Psychologists and hold a relevant practising certificate issued by that Society, first level nurses, registered in Sub-Part 1 of the Nurses' Part of the register maintained under the Nursing and Midwifery Order 2001, SI 2002/253, art 5 (see MEDICAL PROFESSIONS vol 74 (2011) PARA 713), with the inclusion of an entry indicating their field of practice is mental health or learning disabilities nursing, occupational therapists registered in Part 6 of the Register maintained under the Health Professions Order 2001, SI 2002/254, art 5 (see MEDICAL PROFESSIONS vol 74 (2011) PARA 928) and social workers registered as such with the General Social Care Council: see the Mental Health Act 1983 Approved Clinician (General) Directions 2008, Sch 1. References in the Mental Health Act 1983 Pt 4 (ss 56–64) to the approved clinician in charge of a patient's treatment are, where the treatment in question is a form of treatment to which s 57 (see PARA 928) applies, construed as references to the person in charge of the treatment: s 64(1A) (added by the Mental Health Act 2007 s 12(7)(b)). References in the Mental Health Act 1984 Pt 4 to the approved clinician in charge of a patient's treatment are, where the treatment in question is a form of treatment to which s 58A (see PARA 931) applies and the patient falls within s 56(5) (see PARA 924), be construed as references to the person in charge of the treatment: s 64(1B) (added by the Mental Health Act 2007 s 28(9)).

3   Mental Health Act 1983 s 145(1). As from 1 April 2013 the Secretary of State may delegate the power to approve an approved clinician and accordingly the words 'or another person by virtue of s 12ZA or 12ZB' are added by the Health and Social Care Act 2012 s 38(1): see the Health and Social Care Act 2012 (Commencement No 4, Transitional, Savings and Transitory Provisions) Order 2013, SI 2013/160, art 2(2).

832.   Functions of approved clinician.   The functions of an approved clinician[1] include applying for the admission in respect of a patient already in hospital[2] and the right to visit and examine patients[3]. A registered medical practitioner[4] who is an approved clinician[5] may recommend admission of a patient or guardianship[6].

1   As to the meaning of 'approved clinician' see PARA 831.
2   Ie under the Mental Health Act 1983 s 5; and PARA 770.
3   Ie under the Mental Health Act 1983 s 24; and PARA 916.
4   As to registered medical practitioners see MEDICAL PROFESSIONS vol 74 (2011) PARA 176 et seq.
5   Such approval is automatic under the Mental Health Act 1983 s 12 (see PARA 849).
6   See the Mental Health Act 1983 s 12; and PARA 849. Any person who is approved in relation to England for the purposes of s 12(2), or treated as approved by virtue of s 12(2A) is, in all circumstances relevant to the purposes of s 12(2), treated as approved in relation to Wales: Mental Health (Mutual Recognition) Regulations 2008, SI 2008/1204, reg 2(1). Any person who is approved in relation to Wales for the purposes of the Mental Health Act 1983 s 12(2), or treated as approved by virtue of s 12(2A) is, in all circumstances relevant to the purposes of s 12(2), treated as approved in relation to England: Mental Health (Mutual Recognition) Regulations 2008, SI 2008/1204, reg 2(1).

833.   Mutual recognition.   The Secretary of State jointly with the Welsh Ministers[1] may by regulations make provision as to the circumstances in which a practitioner approved for the purposes of making a medical recommendation for the admission of a patient or a guardianship application[2] or a person approved to act as an approved clinician[3] for the purposes of the Mental Health Act 1983, approved in relation to England is to be treated, by virtue of his approval, as approved in relation to Wales too, and vice versa[4].

The circumstances in which a person who is approved to act as an approved clinician in relation to England is treated, by virtue of his approval, as approved in relation to Wales too are where the approved clinician is acting in respect of a patient who is liable to be detained in accordance with the provisions of the Mental Health Act 1983 or is subject to a community treatment order[5], the patient is in Wales[6] and the patient's relevant hospital[7] is in England[8].

The circumstances in which a person who is approved to act as an approved clinician in relation to Wales is treated, by virtue of his approval, as approved in relation to England too are where the approved clinician is acting in respect of a patient who is liable to be detained in accordance with the provisions of the Mental Health Act 1983 or is subject to a community treatment order[9], the patient is in England[10] and the patient's relevant hospital is in Wales[11].

In relation to a patient subject to guardianship, the circumstances in which a responsible local social services authority in England[12] may treat a person who is approved to act as an approved clinician in relation to Wales as approved in relation to England in order to authorise that person to be the patient's responsible clinician are where the patient is in Wales or the patient receives medical treatment for mental disorder in Wales[13].

In relation to a patient subject to guardianship, the circumstances in which a responsible local social services authority in Wales may treat a person who is approved to act as an approved clinician in relation to England as approved in relation to Wales in order to authorise that person to be the patient's responsible clinician are where the patient is in England or the patient receives medical treatment for mental disorder in England[14].

In relation to a patient subject to guardianship, the circumstances in which a person approved to act as an approved clinician in England is treated as approved to act as an approved clinician in relation to Wales are where that approved clinician has been authorised to act as the patient's responsible clinician by the patient's responsible local social services authority in England and that approved clinician is acting in respect of a patient who is in Wales[15].

In relation to a patient subject to guardianship, the circumstances in which a person approved to act as an approved clinician in Wales is treated as approved to act as an approved clinician in relation to England are where that approved clinician has been authorised to act as the patient's responsible clinician by the patient's responsible local social services authority in Wales and that approved clinician is acting in respect of a patient who is in England[16].

1   As to the Secretary of State and the Welsh Ministers see PARAS 567.
2   Ie for the purposes of the Mental Health Act 1983 s 12 (see PARA 849).
3   As to the meaning of 'approved clinician' see PARA 831.
4   Mental Health Act 1983 s 142A (added by the Mental Health Act 2007 s 17).
5   Mental Health (Mutual Recognition) Regulations 2008, SI 2008/1204, reg 3(1)(a).
6   Mental Health (Mutual Recognition) Regulations 2008, SI 2008/1204, reg 3(1)(b).
7   For these purposes 'relevant hospital', in respect of a patient liable to be detained, means the hospital in which the patient is liable to be detained in accordance with the provisions of the Mental Health Act 1983 and, in respect of a patient subject to a community treatment order, has the same meaning as 'the responsible hospital': Mental Health (Mutual Recognition) Regulations 2008, SI 2008/1204, reg 3(3). As to the meaning of 'responsible hospital' see PARA 801 note 9.
8   Mental Health (Mutual Recognition) Regulations 2008, SI 2008/1204, reg 3(1)(c).
9   Mental Health (Mutual Recognition) Regulations 2008, SI 2008/1204, reg 3(2)(a).
10 Mental Health (Mutual Recognition) Regulations 2008, SI 2008/1204, reg 3(2)(b).
11 Mental Health (Mutual Recognition) Regulations 2008, SI 2008/1204, reg 3(2)(c).
12 For these purposes 'responsible local social services authority' has the same meaning as in the Mental Health Act 1983 s 34(3) (see PARA 791 note 1): Mental Health (Mutual Recognition) Regulations 2008, SI 2008/1204, reg 4(5).
13 Mental Health (Mutual Recognition) Regulations 2008, SI 2008/1204, reg 4(1). As to the meaning of 'mental disorder' see PARA 761.
14 Mental Health (Mutual Recognition) Regulations 2008, SI 2008/1204, reg 4(2).
15 Mental Health (Mutual Recognition) Regulations 2008, SI 2008/1204, reg 4(3).
16 Mental Health (Mutual Recognition) Regulations 2008, SI 2008/1204, reg 4(4).

834. Responsible clinician. The responsible clinician is the approved clinician[1] who has overall responsibility for a patient's[2] case[3].

The functions of the responsible clinician include granting a detained patient leave of absence[4], making and revoking community treatment orders[5], recalling a community patient to hospital[6], examining[7] and discharging patients[8].

1   As to the meaning of 'approved clinician' see PARA 831. Protocols should be in place for the allocation of a responsible clinician: see the Department of Health *Mental Health Act 1983 Code of Practice* (2008) para 14.3; and the Welsh Assembly Government *Mental Health Act 1983 Code of Practice for Wales* (2008) para 12.3.

2   As to the meaning of 'patient' see PARA 758 note 4.

3   See the Department of Health *Mental Health Act 1983 Code of Practice* (2008) para 14.2; and the Welsh Assembly Government *Mental Health Act 1983 Code of Practice for Wales* (2008) para 12.2. For the purposes of the Mental Health Act 1983 Pt 2 (ie ss 2–34) 'the responsible clinician' means:

     (1)   in relation to a patient liable to be detained by virtue of an application for admission for assessment or an application for admission for treatment, or a community patient, the approved clinician with overall responsibility for the patient's case;

     (2)   in relation to a patient subject to guardianship, the approved clinician authorised by the responsible local social services authority to act (either generally or in any particular case or for any particular purpose) as the responsible clinician: s 34(1) (definition substituted by Mental Health Act 2007 s 9(10)).

   For the purposes of the Mental Health Act 1983 Pt 3 (ie ss 35–55), in relation to a person liable to be detained in a hospital within the meaning of Pt 2, 'the responsible clinician' means the approved clinician with overall responsibility for the patient's case: s 55(1) (definition substituted by the Mental Health Act 2007 s 11(7)). The Mental Health Act 1983 s 34 applies to patients on s 37 hospital or guardianship orders, see Schedule 1 Pt 1 para 1, and to those on restriction orders (with some modifications), see Schedule 1 Pt 2 para 2.

   In the Mental Health Act 1983 Pt 4 (ie ss 56–64) 'the responsible clinician' means the approved clinician with overall responsibility for the case of the patient in question: s 64(1) (amended by Mental Health Act 2007 s 12(7) and the Care Standards Act 2000 Sch 4). As to the meaning of 'responsible local services authority' see PARA 791 note 1.

   Decisions relating to patients detained in private hospitals are of a public nature: *R (on the application of A) v Partnerships in Care Ltd* [2002] EWHC 529 (Admin), [2002] 1 WLR 2610, (2002) Times, 23 April.

   A responsible clinician cannot require a health authority to give priority care to a detained patient: *R (on the application of F) v Oxfordshire Mental Healthcare NHS Trust* [2001] EWHC Admin 535, [2001] All ER (D) 19 (Jul); *R (on the application of K) v West London Mental Health NHS Trust* [2006] EWCA Civ 118, [2006] 1 WLR 1865, 90 BMLR 214.

4   See the Mental Health Act 1983 s 17(1); and PARA 917.

5   See the Mental Health Act 1983 s 17A; and PARA 797.

6   See the Mental Health Act 1983 s 17E; and PARA 801.

7   See the Mental Health Act 1983 ss 20(3), 20A(4); and PARA 799.

8   See the Mental Health Act 1983 s 23(3); and PARA 913.

(iv) Medical Practitioners and Mental Health Nurses

835. Remuneration of medical practitioners. A registered medical practitioner[1] who carries out a medical examination of any person with a view to an application for his admission to hospital for assessment or treatment under the Mental Health Act 1983[2] is entitled to reasonable remuneration in respect of that examination and in respect of any recommendation or report made by him with regard to the person examined, and the amount of any expenses reasonably incurred by him in connection with the examination or the making of any such recommendation or report[3].

1   As to registered medical practitioners see MEDICAL PROFESSIONS vol 74 (2011) PARA 176 et seq.

2   Ie under the Mental Health Act 1983 Pt 2 (ss 2–34): see PARA 767 et seq.

3   See the National Health Services Act 2006 s 236; the National Health Services (Wales) Act 2006 s 181; and HEALTH SERVICES vol 54 (2008) PARA 524.

836.   Mental health nurses.   The Nursing and Midwifery Council prepares and maintains a register of qualified nurses, midwives and specialist public health nurses[1]. The part of the register relating to nurses is divided into two sub-parts, sub-part 1 and sub-part 2[2]. The entries in the register are to include such entry as the Council considers appropriate to indicate a qualification held by, or field of practice of, a registrant; and these include in the case of a nurse registered in the nurses register sub-part 1 a recordable qualification in mental health nursing and the field of practice of mental health nursing, and in the case of a nurse registered in the nurses register sub-part 2 the field of practice of mental health nursing[3].

Under certain circumstances a nurse registered in either sub-part 1 or sub-part 2 of the register with an entry indicating that the nurse's field of practice is either mental health nursing or learning disabilities nursing may detain for six hours an in-patient who is receiving medical treatment for mental disorder[4].

1   See the Nurses and Midwives (Parts of and Entries in the Register) Order of Council 2004, SI 2004/1765, art 2; and MEDICAL PROFESSIONS vol 74 (2011) PARA 715. As to the Nursing and Midwifery Council see MEDICAL PROFESSIONS vol 74 (2011) PARA 691 et seq.
2   See the Nurses and Midwives (Parts of and Entries in the Register) Order of Council 2004, SI 2004/1765, Sch 1; and MEDICAL PROFESSIONS vol 74 (2011) PARA 715.
3   See the Nurses and Midwives (Parts of and Entries in the Register) Order of Council 2004, SI 2004/1765, art 7(1), (3), (5), (6); and MEDICAL PROFESSIONS vol 74 (2011) PARA 715.
4   See the Mental Health Act 1983 s 5(4); the Mental Health (Nurses) (England) Order 2008, SI 2008/1207, art 2; the Mental Health (Nurses) (Wales) Order 2008, SI 2008/2441, art 2; and PARA 770.

(v) Pensions

837.   Pensions.   Statutory authority for the payment of pension benefits to persons employed in the mental health services is the same as that for other employees of the national health service[1], although special provision is made for mental health officers[2].

1   Ie the National Health Service Pension Scheme Regulations 1995, SI 1995/300: see HEALTH SERVICES vol 54 (2008) PARA 717 et seq.
2   See the National Health Service Pension Scheme Regulations 1995, SI 1995/300, reg R3 (amended by SI 2005/3074, SI 2009/2919, SI 2008/654, SI 2009/2446). See also HEALTH SERVICES vol 54 (2008) PARA 737.

(9) RELATIVES

838.   Meaning of 'relative'.   For the purposes of the statutory provisions relating to compulsory admission to hospital and reception into guardianship[1], a 'relative' of a patient[2] means any of the following: (1) husband or wife or civil partner[3]; (2) son or daughter; (3) father or mother; (5) brother or sister; (6) grandparent; (7) grandchild; (8) uncle or aunt; (9) nephew or niece[4]; and (10) a person other than a relative, with whom the patient ordinarily resides (or, if the patient is an in-patient in hospital, last ordinarily resided before admittance) and with whom he has or had been ordinarily residing for a period of not less than five years[5]. Any relationship of the half-blood is treated as a relationship of the whole blood[6]. An illegitimate person is treated as the legitimate child of his mother and, if his father has parental responsibility for him[7], his father[8].

1   Ie the Mental Health Act 1983 Pt 2 (ss 2–34), and such provisions of that Part as are applied to patients admitted under Pt 3 (ss 35–55) by s 40(4), s 41(3) and Sch 1: see PARAS 767 et seq, 860–862, 867, 869.
2   As to the meaning of 'patient' generally see PARA 758 note 4.

3   'Husband' or 'wife' or 'civil partner' includes a person who is living with the patient as the
    patient's husband or wife or as if they were civil partners, as the case may be (or, if the patient is
    for the time being an in-patient in a hospital, was so living until the patient was admitted), and
    has been or had been so living for a period of not less than six months: Mental Health Act 1983
    s 26(6) (amended by the Mental Health Act 2007 s 26(4)). See, however, PARA 839 note 12. The
    factors relevant to determining whether a man and woman are living together as husband and
    wife were considered in *Kimber v Kimber* [2000] 1 FLR 383, [2000] Fam Law 317. For a
    consideration of the six month period of co-habitation see *R(Robinson) v The Hospital
    Managers of Park Royal Hospital* (26 November 2007 (unreported)).
4   Mental Health Act 1983 s 26(1) (amended by the Mental Health Act 2007 s 26(2)). An adopted
    person is treated as the child of the adoptive parent: see CHILDREN AND YOUNG PERSONS vol 9
    (2012) PARA 360.
5   Mental Health Act 1983 s 26(7). However, such a person cannot be treated as the nearest
    relative of a married person or person in a civil partnership unless the husband or wife or civil
    partner is disregarded under s 26(5)(b) (see PARA 839): s 26(7) (amended by the Mental Health
    Act 2007 s 26(5)).
6   Mental Health Act 1983 s 26(2). However, in ascertaining the person who is for these purposes
    to be treated as the nearest relative of the patient, relatives of the whole blood are preferred to
    relatives of the same description of the half-blood and the elder or eldest of two or more
    relatives preferred to the other or others of those relatives, regardless of sex: see s 26(3); and
    PARA 839. As to the meaning of 'nearest relative' see PARA 839.
7   Ie within the meaning of the Children Act 1989 s 3: see CHILDREN AND YOUNG PERSONS vol 9
    (2012) PARA 151.
8   Mental Health Act 1983 s 26(2) (amended by SI 1991/1881). The result is that the child is
    treated for these purposes not only as the legitimate child of his mother and of his father if the
    father has parental responsibility, but also as a relative of their relatives.

839.   Meaning of 'nearest relative'.   For the purposes of the statutory
provisions relating to compulsory admission and reception into guardianship[1],
the 'nearest relative' of a patient[2] means, subject to certain exceptions[3], the
person first described in the list of relatives[4] who is for the time being surviving[5].
Where a patient ordinarily resides with or is cared for by one or more of his
relatives (or, if in hospital[6], he last ordinarily resided with a relative or relatives),
preference must be given to that relative or relatives over the other or others; as
between two or more of such relatives, preference is given according to the list of
relatives[7]. Where more than one relative of the same description is surviving,
relatives of the whole blood must be preferred to relatives of the half-blood and
the elder or eldest of two or more relatives must be preferred to the other or
others, regardless of sex, in ascertaining who is the nearest relative[8].

However, where the person so ascertained as the nearest relative: (1) is not
ordinarily resident[9] within the United Kingdom[10], the Channel Islands or the Isle
of Man[11]; or (2) being the husband or wife or civil partner[12] of the patient, is
permanently separated from the patient, either by agreement or under a court
order, or has deserted or been deserted by the patient for a period which has not
come to an end[13]; or (3) not being the husband, wife, civil partner, father or
mother of the patient, is for the time being under 18 years of age[14], then the
nearest relative of the patient must be ascertained as if that person were dead[15].

Where the patient is a child or young person and is in the care of a local
authority by virtue of a care order within the meaning of the Children
Act 1989[16], that authority is deemed to be the nearest relative of the patient in
preference to any other person except the patient's husband or wife or civil
partner, if any[17].

Where a patient has not attained the age of 18 years[18] and a guardian[19] has
been appointed for him or a residence order[20] is in force in relation to him, the
guardian (or guardians) or person named in the residence order is deemed to be
his nearest relative[21] to the exclusion of any other person[22].

1   Ie for the purposes of the Mental Health Act 1983 Pt 2 (ss 2–34) and such provisions of that Part as are applied to patients admitted under Pt 3 (ss 35–55) by s 40(4), s 41(3) and Sch 1: see PARAS 767 et seq, 860–862, 867, 869.

2   As to the meaning of 'patient' see PARA 758 note 4.

3   Ie subject to the Mental Health Act 1983 ss 26(4), 27–29: see notes 7–22; and PARAS 841–842.

4   See PARA 838.

5   Mental Health Act 1983 s 26(3). The nearest relative plays an important role in the scheme of the Act: see PARA 840; and *R (on the application of M) v Secretary of State for Health* [2003] EWHC 1094 (Admin), [2003] 3 All ER 672n, (2003) Times, 25 April.

        A person defined as the nearest relative is not obliged to so act and may authorise another (apart from someone under s 26(5)) to act in their stead: see the Mental Health (Hospital, Guardianship and Consent to Treatment) (England) Regulations 2008, SI 2008/1184, reg 24; and PARA 841.

        A 'next of kin' has no powers under the Mental Health Act 1983 unless they are also the nearest relative. For the nearest relative's rights of access to confidential information relating to the patient see *R (on the application of Stevens) v Plymouth City Council* [2002] EWCA Civ 388, [2002] 1 WLR 2583, [2002] LGR 565.

        If a patient has no nearest relative or it is not reasonably practicable to ascertain whether he has a nearest relative, an application may be made to the county court to appoint an acting nearest relative under s 29(3)(a) (see PARA 842). For the grounds for removing a nearest relative see s 29(3)(b)–(e); and PARA 842.

        A donee of a lasting power of attorney or court appointed deputy under the Mental Capacity Act 2005 do not have power to override a nearest relative under the Mental Health Act 1983 unless they are the patient's nearest relative as defined, or have otherwise been nominated or appointed to fulfil that role: see the Mental Health (Hospital, Guardianship and Consent to Treatment) (England) Regulations 2008, SI 2008/1184, regs 24, 29, 33.

        As to the compatibility of these provisions with the requirements of the Convention for the Protection of Human Rights and Fundamental Freedoms (Rome, 4 November 1950; TS 71 (1953); Cmd 8969) and the possible amendment of the Mental Health Act 1983 so as to allow a patient detained under the Act to apply to have the designated nearest relative replaced see Application 26494/95 *JT v United Kingdom* [2000] 30 EHRR CD 77, [2000] 1 FLR 909, ECtHR; *R (on the application of M) v Secretary of State for Health* [2003] EWHC 1094 (Admin), [2003] 3 All ER 672n (declaration of incompatibility made in relation to a patient's inability to have the designated nearest relative replaced). See also *R (on the application of E) v Bristol City Council* [2005] EWHC 74 (Admin), [2005] All ER (D) 57 (Jan); and PARA 821 note 10. As to the Convention for the Protection of Human Rights and Fundamental Freedoms and declarations of incompatibility see RIGHTS AND FREEDOMS.

6   As to the meaning of 'hospital' see PARA 577.

7   Mental Health Act 1983 s 26(4). As to 'cared for' see *Re D (Mental Patient: Habeas Corpus)* [2001] 1 FCR 218, [2000] 2 FLR 848, CA (the relative must provide more than minimal services and not necessarily over the long term).

8   Mental Health Act 1983 s 26(3).

9   For a consideration of the meaning of the words 'ordinarily resident' see *Akbarali v Brent London Borough Council* [1983] 2 AC 309 at 342, sub nom *Shah v Barnet London Borough Council* [1983] 1 All ER 226 at 235, HL, per Lord Scarman (the phrase refers to a man's abode in a particular place or country which he has adopted voluntarily and for settled purposes); *Mohamed v Hammersmith and Fulham London Borough Council* [2001] UKHL 57, [2002] 1 AC 547, [2002] 1 All ER 176; *R (on the application of Greenwich London Borough Council) v Secretary of State for Health* [2006] EWHC 2576 (Admin), [2006] All ER (D) 178 (Jul). For a consideration of 'voluntariness' see *Al-Ameri v Kensington and Chelsea Royal London Borough Council, Osmani v Harrow London Borough Council* [2003] EWCA Civ 235, [2003] 2 All ER 1, [2003] 1 WLR 1289. The fact that a person has left his home does not necessarily mean that he has changed his ordinary residence: *R v Liverpool CC ex p F* (CO/2744/96) 16 April 1997. See also CONFLICT OF LAWS vol 19 (2011) PARA 359.

10 As to the meaning of 'United Kingdom' see PARA 560 note 14.

11 Mental Health Act 1983 s 26(5)(a).

12 'Husband', 'wife' and 'civil partner' include a person who is living with the patient as the patient's husband or wife or as if they were civil partners, as the case may be (or, if the patient is for the time being an in-patient in a hospital, was so living until the patient was admitted), and has been or had been so living for a period of not less than six months; but a person is not to be treated as a nearest relative for these purposes unless the husband, wife or civil partner of the patient is disregarded by virtue of permanent separation, court order or desertion under the Mental Health Act 1983 s 26(5)(b): s 26(6) (amended by the Mental Health Act 2007 s 26(4)).

13 Mental Health Act 2007 s 26(5)(b) (amended by the Mental Health Act 2007 s 26(3)). As to the elements necessary to constitute desertion see MATRIMONIAL AND CIVIL PARTNERSHIP LAW vol 72 (2009) PARA 362 et seq. If desertion is clearly established, it seems that the fact that it had commenced recently and that the period was consequently short would not matter for the purposes of displacing the deserting husband or wife as the nearest relative of the deserted spouse.

14 Mental Health Act 2007 s 26(5)(c). Thus a husband, wife, civil partner, father or mother, notwithstanding that they are under 18, may exercise the functions of the nearest relative in respect of a spouse or child. 'Under 18 years of age' means before the commencement of a person's eighteenth birthday: see the Family Law Reform Act 1969 s 9(1).

15 Mental Health Act 1983 s 26(5) (amended by the Children Act 1989 s 108(7), Sch 15).

16 'Care order' means an order under the Children Act 1989 s 31(1)(a) placing the child in the care of a designated local authority and includes (except where express provision to the contrary is made) an interim care order made under s 38: ss 31(11), 105(1). It also includes any order which by or under any enactment has the effect of or is deemed to be a care order for the purposes of the Children Act 1989: s 105(1). For the orders deemed to be care orders see s 108(6), Sch 14 paras 15, 16 (amended by the Courts and Legal Services Act 1990 ss 116, 125(7), Sch 16 para 33, Sch 20; the Armed Forces Act 1991 s 26(2), Sch 3; and SI 1991/828).

17 Mental Health Act 1983 s 27 (substituted by the Children Act 1989 s 108(5), Sch 13 para 48(1); and amended by the Mental Health Act 2007 s 26(6)).

18 The age of 18 is attained at the commencement of a person's eighteenth birthday: see the Family Law Reform Act 1969 s 9(1).

19 Ie including a special guardian (within the meaning of the Children Act 1989) (see CHILDREN AND YOUNG PERSONS vol 9 (2012) PARA 305) but not including a guardian under the Mental Health Act 1983 Pt 2: s 28(3) (substituted by the Children Act 1989 Sch 13 para 48(2), (4); and amended by the Adoption and Children Act 2002 s 139(1), Sch 3 para 41).

20 'Residence order' means an order settling the arrangements to be made as to the person with whom a child is to live: Children Act 1989 s 8(1). See CHILDREN AND YOUNG PERSONS vol 9 (2012) PARA 282 et seq.

21 However, the exclusions listed in the Mental Health Act 1983 s 26(5) (see the text and notes 9–15) apply to such a person: s 28(2). For example, if he was not ordinarily resident within the United Kingdom, he would not be deemed to be the nearest relative.

22 Mental Health Act 1983 s 28(1) (substituted by the Children Act 1989 Sch 13 para 48(2), (3)).

840. Powers of the nearest relative. An application for admission for assessment[1], an application for admission for treatment[2] and a guardianship application[3] may be made either by the patient's[4] nearest relative[5] or by an approved mental health professional[6]. In any case of urgent necessity, an emergency application for admission for assessment[7] may also be made either by the patient's nearest relative or by an approved mental health professional[8]. A nearest relative must be consulted by an approved mental health professional before making an application for admission for treatment and may object to the same[9]. An approved mental health professional must also inform the nearest relative if a patient is to be or has been admitted for assessment and of their power to discharge the patient[10].

The nearest relative (amongst others) may apply to a county court[11] for an order that the statutory functions of the nearest relative be exercisable by the applicant or by a person specified in the application[12]. If the person having the functions of the nearest relative by virtue of such an order dies, any relative, including the nearest relative, has the right to apply for discharge or variation of the order[13].

The nearest relative of a patient who is for the time being liable to be detained or subject to guardianship[14] may, by an order in writing[15], discharge such a patient[16]. The nearest relative must give 72 hours' notice in writing to the managers[17] of the hospital[18] of his intention to order discharge[19]. The nearest relative also has the right, in prescribed circumstances[20], to apply to a tribunal[21]. Where a minor who is a ward of court is liable to be detained[22] or is a community patient[23], any power exercisable[24] in relation to the patient by his nearest relative is exercisable by or with the leave of the court[25].

1 Ie under the Mental Health Act 1983 s 2: see PARA 767. 'Application for admission for assessment' has the meaning given in s 2 (see PARA 767): s 145(1).
2 Ie under the Mental Health Act 1983 s 3: see PARA 768. 'Application for admission for treatment' has the meaning given in s 3 (see PARA 768): s 145(1).
3 Ie under the Mental Health Act 1983 s 7(2): see PARA 785.
4 As to the meaning of 'patient' see PARA 758 note 4.
5 As to the meaning of 'nearest relative' see PARA 839.
6 See the Mental Health Act 1983 s 11(1); and PARA 847. As to the meaning of 'approved mental health professional' see PARA 815 note 2. As to the duties of an approved mental health professional in making such applications (including the duty to consult the patient's nearest relative), the nearest relative's power to object to an application for admission for treatment, and the nearest relative's right to request consideration of a case by an approved mental health professional see PARA 821.
7 Ie under the Mental Health Act 1983 s 4(1): see PARA 769.
8 See the Mental Health Act 1983 s 4(2); and PARA 769.
9 See the Mental Health Act 1983 s 11(3); and PARA 821.
10 See the Mental Health Act 1983 s 11(4); and PARA 821.
11 As to county courts generally see COURTS AND TRIBUNALS vol 24 (2010) PARA 758 et seq.
12 See the Mental Health Act 1983 s 29(1)–(3); and PARA 842.
13 See the Mental Health Act 1983 s 30(3); and PARA 843. The functions of the nearest relative are meanwhile in abeyance: see s 30(3)(b); and PARA 843.
14 Ie under the Mental Health Act 1983 Pt 2 (ss 2–34): s 23(1). This provision does not apply to patients liable to be detained or under guardianship by virtue of orders or directions under Pt 3 (ss 35–55): cf s 40(4), s 41(3), Sch 1.
15 There are forms which may be used by the nearest relative: see the Mental Health (Hospital, Guardianship and Treatment) (England) Regulations 2008, SI 2008/1184, reg 25(1), Sch 1; and the Mental Health (Hospital, Guardianship, Community Treatment and Consent to Treatment) (Wales) Regulations 2008, SI 2008/2439, reg 34(1), Sch 1. As to the manner in which the order must be served see the Mental Health (Hospital, Guardianship and Treatment) (England) Regulations 2008, SI 2008/1184, reg 25(1); and the Mental Health (Hospital, Guardianship, Community Treatment and Consent to Treatment) (Wales) Regulations 2008, SI 2008/2439, reg 34(2); and PARA 850.
16 See the Mental Health Act 1983 s 23(2); and PARA 913.
17 As to the meaning of 'managers' see PARA 778.
18 As to the meaning of 'hospital' see PARA 577.
19 See the Mental Health Act 1983 s 25(1); and PARA 915. The order will have no effect if in the meantime the responsible medical officer has reported to the managers that, in his opinion, the patient, if discharged, would be likely to act in manner dangerous to other persons or himself: s 25(1); see PARA 915.
20 These include a case where he has been debarred from discharging the patient in the circumstances set out in note 19: See the Mental Health Act 1984 s 66(1)(g); and PARA 961.
21 See PARA 961.
22 Ie by virtue of an application for admission under the Mental Health Act 1983 Pt 2. As to wards of court generally see CHILDREN AND YOUNG PERSONS vol 9 (2012) PARA 218 et seq.
23 As to community patients see PARA 264 et seq.
24 Ie under the Mental Health Act 1984 Pt 3 or s 66 (see PARA 961).
25 See the Mental Health Act 1983 s 33(2); and PARA 786.

841. Delegation of functions by nearest relative. The nearest relative[1] of a patient[2] may authorise in writing any other person to perform in respect of the patient the statutory functions conferred on the nearest relative[3], and may revoke any such authority[4]. However, such functions may not be delegated to the patient himself, a person disqualified from being the nearest relative[5] or a person in respect of whom, in relation to England an order has been made by[6], or in relation to Wales an application has been made to[7], the court for displacement of that nearest relative[8]. On making or revoking such an authority, the nearest relative must forthwith give the authority[9] or written notice of the revocation[10] to the person authorised and must notify the patient, the managers[11] of the hospital in the case of a patient liable to be detained there, and the responsible local social services authority[12] and the private guardian, if any, and, in the case of a case of a community patient, the managers of the responsible hospital[13].

1   As to the meaning of 'nearest relative' see PARA 839.
2   As to the meaning of 'patient' see PARA 758 note 4.
3   Ie by or under the Mental Health Act 1983 Pt 2 (ss 2–34) (see PARA 840) and s 66 (see PARA 960).
4   See the Mental Health Act 1983 s 32(2)(e); the Mental Health (Hospital, Guardianship and Treatment) (England) Regulations 2008, SI 2008/1184, reg 24(1)–(3), (5); and the Mental Health (Hospital, Guardianship, Community Treatment and Consent to Treatment) (Wales) Regulations 2008, SI 2008/2439, reg 33(1), (2), (5). In relation to Wales, the patient to be authorised must give his consent and confers upon the person authorised all the rights of the nearest relative that are reasonably necessary for and incidental to the performance of the functions referred to in reg 33(2) or are reasonably necessary to carry those functions into full effect: see reg 33(3), (7)(a).
5   Ie a person mentioned in the Mental Health Act 1983 s 26(5) (see PARA 839).
6   Ie a person in respect of whom the court has made an order on the grounds set out in the Mental Health Act 1983 s 29(3)(b)–(e) (see PARA 842) (which sets out the grounds on which an application to the court for the appointment of a person to exercise the functions of a nearest relative may be made) for so long as an order under that provision is in effect.
7   Ie any person having made an application to the court for displacement of that nearest relative under the Mental Health Act 1983 s 29 on the grounds listed in s 29(3)(b)–(e).
8   See the Mental Health Act 1983 s 32(2)(e); the Mental Health (Hospital, Guardianship and Treatment) (England) Regulations 2008, SI 2008/1184, reg 24(1); and the Mental Health (Hospital, Guardianship, Community Treatment and Consent to Treatment) (Wales) Regulations 2008, SI 2008/2439, reg 33(1), (8).
9   The authority so given takes effect on receipt of it by the person authorised: Mental Health (Hospital, Guardianship and Treatment) (England) Regulations 2008, SI 2008/1184, reg 24(4); Mental Health (Hospital, Guardianship, Community Treatment and Consent to Treatment) (Wales) Regulations 2008, SI 2008/2439, reg 33(4). An authorisation or notification may be transmitted by means of electronic communication if the recipient agrees: Mental Health (Hospital, Guardianship and Treatment) (England) Regulations 2008, SI 2008/1184, reg 24(8); Mental Health (Hospital, Guardianship, Community Treatment and Consent to Treatment) (Wales) Regulations 2008, SI 2008/2439, reg 33(9).
10   The revocation takes effect on receipt of a notice of revocation by the person authorised: see the Mental Health (Hospital, Guardianship and Treatment) (England) Regulations 2008, SI 2008/1184, reg 24(6); and the Mental Health (Hospital, Guardianship, Community Treatment and Consent to Treatment) (Wales) Regulations 2008, SI 2008/2439, reg 33(6).
11   As to the meaning of 'managers' see PARA 778.
12   As to the meaning of 'local social services authority' see PARA 579.
13   Mental Health (Hospital, Guardianship and Treatment) (England) Regulations 2008, SI 2008/1184, reg 24(7); Mental Health (Hospital, Guardianship, Community Treatment and Consent to Treatment) (Wales) Regulations 2008, SI 2008/2439, reg 33(7)(b).

842. Appointment by the county court of an acting nearest relative. On application[1] by the patient[2], any relative of the patient[3], any other person with whom the patient is residing (or, if the patient is then an in-patient in a hospital, was last residing before he was admitted) or an approved mental health professional[4], the county court[5] may by order[6] direct that the statutory functions of the nearest relative of a patient[7] are to be exercisable, during the continuance in force of the order[8], by the person specified in the order[9].

The order may be made upon any of the following grounds: (1) that the patient has no nearest relative[10], or that it is not reasonably practicable to ascertain whether he has such a relative, or who that relative is[11]; (2) that the patient's nearest relative is incapable of acting as such by reason of mental disorder or other illness[12]; (3) that the patient's nearest relative unreasonably objects[13] to the making of an application for admission for treatment[14] or a guardianship application[15] in respect of the patient[16]; (4) that the patient's nearest relative has exercised, without due regard[17] to the patient's welfare or the interests of the public, his power to discharge the patient[18] or is likely to do so[19]; or (5) that the nearest relative of a patient is otherwise not a suitable person to act as such[20].

If the court decides to make an order on an application under the above provisions, the following rules have effect for the purposes of specifying a person in the order:

(a)   if a person is nominated in the application to act as the patient's nearest relative and that person is, in the opinion of the court, a suitable person to act as such and is willing to do so, the court must specify that person (or, if there are two or more such persons, such one of them as the court thinks fit)[21];

(b)   otherwise, the court must specify such person as is, in its opinion, a suitable person to act as the patient's nearest relative and is willing to do so[22].

An order made under head (1), (2) or (5) above may specify a period for which it is to continue in force unless previously discharged[23].

If, immediately before the expiration of the 28 day period during which a patient may be detained for assessment[24], an application to the county court is pending[25] on any of the grounds set out in head (3) or head (4) above, that period must be extended in any case until the application has been finally disposed of[26], and, if an order is made by the county court, for a further seven days[27].

Where the functions of the nearest relative are exercisable by another person by virtue of head (3) or (4) above, the nearest relative has the right, if the patient is or subsequently becomes liable to be detained or subject to guardianship or who is a community patient[28], to apply to the appropriate tribunal[29] in respect of the patient within the period of 12 months beginning with the date of the order and in any subsequent period of 12 months during which the order continues in force[30].

1   As to the procedure on such applications see PARA 846.

2   As to the meaning of 'patient' see PARA 758 note 4.

3   As to the meaning of 'relative' see PARA 838.

4   As to the meaning of 'approved mental health professional' see PARA 815 note 2.

5   As to county courts generally see COURTS AND TRIBUNALS vol 24 (2010) PARA 758 et seq. For procedure see the Mental Health Act 1983 s 31; PARA 846; CPR 8.1(6), Practice Direction 8A; CIVIL PROCEDURE vol 11 (2009) PARA 127. The court may sit in private. Jurisdiction can only be exercised by a circuit judge. Applications must be dealt with quickly: *R (on the application of Stevens) v Plymouth City Council* [2002] EWCA Civ 388, [2002] 1 WLR 2583, [2002] LGR 565. Applications may be made without giving notice to the nearest relative if it is necessary to act urgently: *R v Uxbridge County Court ex p Binns* [2000] MHLR 179; *R (on the application of Holloway) v Oxfordshire County Council* [2007] EWHC 776 (Admin), [2007] LGR 891. Generally there is a duty to make full and fair disclosure of important points for and against the application when it is made without notice: *B Borough Council v S* [2006] EWHC 2584 (Fam), [2007] 1 FCR 574, [2007] 1 FLR 1600. For the applicable rules see CPR 23.9, 23.10; and CIVIL PROCEDURE vol 11 (2009) PARAS 311, 312.

6   Although the county court has jurisdiction to make an interim order under the Mental Health Act 1983 s 29, in general a final order ought to be made before the making of an application under s 3 (see PARA 768): *R v Central London County Court, ex p London* [1999] QB 1260, [1999] 3 All ER 991, CA.

7   Ie under the Mental Health Act 1983 Pt 2 (ss 2–34) and ss 66, 69: see PARAS 840, 961. As to the meaning of 'nearest relative' see PARA 839.

8   While such an order is in force, the provisions of the Mental Health Act 1983 Pt 2 (other than the power to appoint an acting nearest relative and the power to discharge and vary such orders

(see ss 29, 30; and PARAS 842–845) apply in relation to the patient as if for any reference to the nearest relative there were substituted a reference to the person having the functions of that relative and, without prejudice to the power to discharge and vary such orders, so apply notwithstanding that the person who was the patient's nearest relative when the order was made is no longer his nearest relative: s 29(6). As to the duration of such orders see PARA 845.

9   Mental Health Act 1983 s 29(1), (2) (s 29(1), (2) amended by the Mental Health Act 2007 s 23(2), (4), Sch 2 para 7(c), Sch 11 Pt 4). The judge has a discretion whether or not to make an order notwithstanding that one of the grounds in the Mental Health Act 1983 s 29(3) is made out: *Barnet LBC v Robin* (1999) 2 CCLR 454, CA. See *Lewis v Gibson* [2005] EWCA Civ 587, [2005] 2 FCR 241, 87 BMLR 93 (in all the circumstances the judge had been entitled to confirm an interim order displacing the claimant as nearest relative to her daughter, who suffered from Down's syndrome). The judge should at the earliest opportunity make enquiries as to whether the patient's rights under the Convention for the Protection of Human Rights and Fundamental Freedoms (Rome, 4 November 1950; TS 71 (1953); Cmd 8969) have been protected. See *R (on the application of M) v Secretary of State for Health* [2003] EWHC 1094 (Admin), [2003] 3 All ER 672n, (2003) Times, 25 April (declaration of incompatibility made in relation to a patient's inability to have the designated nearest relative replaced). As to the Convention for the Protection of Human Rights and Fundamental Freedoms and declarations of incompatibility see RIGHTS AND FREEDOMS. See also PARA 839 note 5.

10   Ie within the meaning of the Mental Health Act 1983: see PARA 839.

11   Mental Health Act 1983 s 29(3)(a).

12   Mental Health Act 1983 s 29(3)(b). As to the meaning of 'mental disorder' see PARA 761.

13   The objection must be unreasonable at the time of the application and at the time of the hearing: see *Lewis v Gibson* [2005] EWCA Civ 587, [2005] 2 FCR 241. The test is not what the relative subjectively considers reasonable but what a reasonable relative would do in the particular circumstances, akin to that laid down for dispensing with parental agreement to adoption on the ground that it is unreasonably withheld in *Re W (An Infant)* [1971] AC 682, [1971] 2 All ER 49, HL: see *W v L* [1974] QB 711, [1973] 3 All ER 884, CA. See also *Smirek v Williams* [2000] MHLR 38 and *B(A) v B(L) (Mental Health Patient)* [1979] 3 All ER 494, [1980] 1 WLR 116, CA in which it was suggested that the court should consider the merits of the admission application before considering the reasonableness of the objection.

14   The objection of the nearest relative to an application for the admission of the patient to hospital for treatment (but not for assessment) or a guardianship application will prevent an approved mental health professional from making such an application: see the Mental Health Act 1983 s 11(4); and PARA 821.

15   See note 13.

16   Mental Health Act 1983 s 29(3)(c). See *Lewis v Gibson* [2005] EWCA Civ 587, [2005] 2 FCR 241; and note 9.

17   As to the objective test in relation to 'without due regard' see *Surrey County Council Social Services v McMurray* (11 November 1994) Lexis, CA.

18   Ie under the Mental Health Act 1983 Pt 2 (ss 2–34). As to such orders for discharge see PARA 913.

19   Mental Health Act 1983 s 29(3)(d). However, such an order will be of no effect if the responsible clinician (see PARA 834) is prepared to certify to the managers (see PARA 778) that the patient would be likely, if discharged, to act in a manner dangerous to other persons or to himself: see s 25; and PARA 915.

20   Mental Health Act 1983 s 29(3)(e) (added by the Mental Health Act 2007 s 23(5)). As to the suitability of a nearest relative see the Department of Health *Mental Health Act 1983 Code of Practice* (2008) para 8.13. An approved mental health professional is not under a duty to consult with a nearest relative upon making an application for admission for treatment if such consultation would be detrimental to the patient and breach his rights under the Convention for the Protection of Human Rights and Fundamental Freedoms (Rome, 4 November 1950; TS 71 (1953) Cmd 8969) art 8 (see RIGHTS AND FREEDOMS): *R (on the application of E) v Bristol City Council* [2005] EWHC 74 (Admin), [2005] All ER (D) 57 (Jan). In order to succeed an applicant must show that the statutory criteria for admission are satisfied at the date of the application and the date of the hearing: see *Lewis v Gibson* [2005] EWCA Civ 587, [2005] 2 FCR 241. The displacement of a nearest relative does not remove their legitimate interest in the welfare of the patient which should be paid proper respect by the local social services authority when making arrangements for care: *Surrey County Council Social Services v McMurray* (11 November 1994) Lexis, CA. For the nearest relative's rights of access to confidential information relating to the patient in preparation for an application under the Mental Health Act 1983 s 29 see *R (on the application of Stevens) v Plymouth City Council* [2002] EWCA Civ 388, [2002] 1 WLR 2583.

21   Mental Health Act 1983 s 29(1A)(a) (s 29(1A) added by the Mental Health Act 2007 s 23(3)).

22 Mental Health Act 1983 s 29(1A)(b) (as added: see note 21).

23 ~~Ie under the~~ Mental Health Act 1983 s 30 (see PARA 843): s 29(5) (amended by the Mental Health Act 2007 s 23(6)).

24 As to detention for assessment see PARA 767.

25 See note 26.

26 An application will be deemed to have been finally disposed of at the expiration of the time allowed for appealing from the decision of the county court or, if notice of appeal has been given within that time, when the appeal has been heard or withdrawn; and 'pending' must be construed accordingly: Mental Health Act 1983 s 29(4). As to the time within which notice of appeal must be served see CIVIL PROCEDURE vol 12 (2009) PARA 1684.

27 Mental Health Act 1983 s 29(4). An application under s 3 (see PARA 768) can made be made before proceedings under s 29 have been resolved: see *R(M) v Homertone University Hospital* [2008] EWCA Civ 197.

 See *R (on the application of MH) v Secretary of State for Health* [2005] UKHL 60, [2005] All ER (D) 218 (Oct) sub nom *R (on the application of H) v Secretary of State for Health* [2005] UKHL 60, [2006] 1 AC 441, [2005] 4 All ER 1311, where the House of Lords overruled the Court of Appeal (see [2004] EWCA Civ 1609, [2005] 3 All ER 468, [2005] 1 WLR 1209) and maintained that the Mental Health Act 1983 ss 2, 29(4) are not incompatible with the Convention for the Protection of Human Rights and Fundamental Freedoms (Rome, 4 November 1950; TS 71 (1953) Cmd 8969) art 5(4) (which states that detained persons are entitled to take proceedings by which the lawfulness of their detention will be decided speedily by a court and their release ordered if the detention is not lawful) (see RIGHTS AND FREEDOMS). The Mental Health Act 1983 s 2 (see PARA 767) was held not to be incompatible as the Convention art 5(4) did not require that every case be considered by a court, rather that the person detained should have the right to 'take proceedings': although the argument that such a right was ineffective if the patient lacked the ability to bring the proceedings was powerful it did not lead to the conclusion that the Mental Health Act 1983 s 2 was itself incompatible with the Convention or that the solution was to require a reference in every case, rather that every sensible effort should be made to enable the patient to exercise that right if there was reason to think that he would wish to do so. The Mental Health Act 1983 s 29(4) was held not to be incompatible although the inaction or inaction of the authorities under it might be so.

28 As to compulsory admission to hospital or guardianship see PARA 767 et seq. As to the meaning of 'community patient' see PARA 797 note 4.

29 As to the meaning of 'appropriate tribunal' see PARA 955.

30 See the Mental Health Act 1983 s 66(1)(h), (ii), (2)(g); and PARA 961.

843. Variation of county court orders. An order appointing an acting nearest relative[1] made in respect of a patient[2] by the county court[3] may be varied by that court, on the application[4] of the patient or of the person having the functions of the nearest relative by virtue of the order or on the application of an approved mental health professional[5], by substituting another person for the person having those functions[6].

If the court decides to vary an order on such an application, the following rules have effect for the purposes of substituting another person:

(1)   if a person is nominated in the application to act as the patient's nearest relative and that person is, in the opinion of the court, a suitable person to act as such and is willing to do so, the court must specify that person (or, if there are two or more such persons, such one of them as the court thinks fit)[7];

(2)   otherwise, the court must specify such person as is, in its opinion, a suitable person to act as the patient's nearest relative and is willing to do so[8].

In the event of the death of the person having the functions of the nearest relative by virtue of the order, the order may be discharged or varied on the application of any relative[9] of the patient and not only of the nearest relative[10]. Until an order is discharged or varied in these circumstances, the functions of the nearest relative are not exercisable by any person[11].

The variation of an order does not affect the validity of anything previously done in pursuance of the order[12].

1   Ie under the Mental Health Act 1983 s 29: see PARA 842. As to the meaning of 'nearest relative' see PARA 839.
2   As to the meaning of 'patient' see PARA 758 note 4.
3   As to county courts generally see COURTS AND TRIBUNALS vol 24 (2010) PARA 758 et seq.
4   For the procedure on such applications see PARA 846.
5   As to the meaning of 'approved mental health professional' see PARA 815 note 2.
6   Mental Health Act 1983 s 30(2) (amended by the Mental Health Act 2007 s 24(4), Sch 2 para 7(d)).
7   Mental Health Act 1983 s 30(2A)(a) (s 30(2A) added by the Mental Health Act 2007 s 24(5)).
8   Mental Health Act 1983 s 30(2A)(b) (as added: see note 7).
9   As to the meaning of 'relative' see PARA 838.
10 Mental Health Act 1983 s 30(3).
11 Mental Health Act 1983 s 30(3). The nearest relative will not therefore be able to resume the functions transferred from him when the acting nearest relative dies; he can only do so if the order is discharged on the application of himself or any other relative.
12 Mental Health Act 1983 s 30(5).

844. Discharge of county court orders. An order appointing an acting nearest relative made[1] in respect of a patient[2] by the county court[3] may be discharged by that court on the application[4] of (1) the patient or the person having the functions of the nearest relative by virtue of the order[5]; (2) where the order was made on the ground that the patient had no nearest relative or that it was not reasonably practicable to ascertain whether he had such a relative, or who that relative was[6], or that the nearest relative of the patient is incapable of acting as such by reason of mental disorder or other illness[7] or that the nearest relative of the patient is otherwise not a suitable person to act as such[8] or where the person who was the nearest relative of the patient when the order was made has ceased to be his nearest relative, on the application of the nearest relative of the patient[9]. Where an order is made on these grounds it may specify a period during which it is to remain in force unless previously discharged[10].

In the event of the death of the person having the functions of the nearest relative by virtue of the order, the order may be discharged on the application of any relative[11] of the patient and not only of the nearest relative[12]. Until an order is discharged or varied in these circumstances, the functions of the nearest relative are not exercisable by any person[13].

The discharge of an order does not affect the validity of anything previously done in pursuance of the order[14].

1   Ie under the Mental Health Act 1983 s 29: see PARA 842. As to the meaning of 'nearest relative' see PARA 839.
2   As to the meaning of 'patient' see PARA 758 note 4.
3   As to county courts generally see COURTS AND TRIBUNALS vol 24 (2010) PARA 758 et seq.
4   For the procedure on such applications see PARA 846.
5   Mental Health Act 1983 s 30(1)(a) (amended by the Mental Health Act 2007 s 24(2)). If the order is discharged, the nearest relative from whom his functions were transferred by the order will again be able to exercise them.
6   Ie on the ground specified in the Mental Health Act 1983 s 29(3)(a): see PARA 842.
7   Ie on the ground specified in the Mental Health Act 1983 s 29(3)(b): see PARA 842.
8   Ie on the ground specified in the Mental Health Act 1983 s 29(3)(e): see PARA 842. But, in the case of an order made on the ground specified in s 29(3)(e) of s 29(3), an application may not be made under s 30(1)(b) by the person who was the nearest relative of the patient when the order was made except with leave of the county court: s 30(1A) (added by the Mental Health Act 2007 s 24(3)).
9   Mental Health Act 1983 s 30(1)(b) (amended by the Mental Health Act 2007 s 24(2)(b)).
10 See PARA 842.

11 As to the meaning of 'relative' see PARA 838.

12 Mental Health Act 1983 s 30(3).

13 Mental Health Act 1983 s 30(3). The nearest relative will not therefore be able to resume the functions transferred from him when the acting nearest relative dies; he can only do so if the order is discharged on the application of himself or any other relative.

14 Mental Health Act 1983 s 30(5).

845. Duration of county court orders. An order made on the ground that the nearest relative of the patient[1] unreasonably objects to the making of an application for admission for treatment or a guardianship application in respect of the patient[2], or that the nearest relative of the patient has exercised without due regard to the welfare of the patient or the interests of the public his power to discharge the patient under Part 2 of the Mental Health Act 1983, or is likely to do so[3], must unless previously discharged[4] cease to have effect under the following circumstances[5].

If on the date of the order the patient was liable to be detained or subject to guardianship by virtue of a relevant application, order or direction[6] or he becomes so liable or subject within the period of three months beginning with that date or he was a community patient on the date of the order, the order ceases to have effect when he is discharged[7] or the relevant application, order or direction otherwise ceases to have effect (except as a result of his being transferred in pursuance of regulations[8] as to the transfer of patients)[9]. Otherwise, the order ceases to have effect at the end of the period of three months beginning with the date of the order[10].

An order made on the ground that the patient has no nearest relative, or that it is not reasonably practicable to ascertain whether he has such a relative, or who that relative is[11], or that the nearest relative of the patient is incapable of acting as such by reason of mental disorder or other illness[12], or that the nearest relative of the patient is otherwise not a suitable person to act as such[13], ceases to have effect on the expiry of any period specified[14] for that purpose[15]. However, if no such period is specified, the order remains in force until it is discharged[16] by the court[17].

1 As to the meaning of 'nearest relative' see PARA 838. As to the meaning of 'patient' see PARA 758 note 4.
2 Ie on the ground specified in the Mental Health Act 1983 s 29(3)(c): see PARA 842.
3 Ie on the ground specified in the Mental Health Act 1983 s 29(3)(d): see PARA 842.
4 Ie under the Mental Health Act 1983 s 30(1) (see PARA 844).
5 Mental Health Act 1983 s 30(4) (amended by the Mental Health Act 2007 s 24(6)).
6 For these purposes, reference to a relevant application, order or direction is to an application for admission for treatment, a guardianship application or an order or direction under the Mental Health Act 1983 Pt 3 (other than under s 35, 36 or 38): s 30(4A) (added by the Mental Health Act 2007 Sch 3 para 14(3)).
7 Ie under the Mental Health Act 1983 s 23 (see PARA 913) or s 72 (see PARA 967).
8 Ie regulations under the Mental Health Act 1983 s 19 (see PARAS 886–889).
9 Mental Health Act 1983 s 30(4)(a) (s 30(4)(a), (b) substituted by the Mental Health Act 2007 Sch 3 para 14(2)).
10 Mental Health Act 1983 s 30(4)(b) (as substituted: see note 9).
11 Ie on the ground specified in the Mental Health Act 1983 s 29(3)(a): see PARA 842.
12 Ie on the ground specified in the Mental Health Act 1983 s 29(3)(b): see PARA 842.
13 Ie on the ground specified in the Mental Health Act 1983 s 29(3)(e): see PARA 842.
14 Ie a period specified under the Mental Health Act 1983 s 29(5) (see PARA 842).
15 Mental Health Act 1983 s 30(4B)(a) (s 30(4B) added by the Mental Health Act 2007 s 24(7)).
16 Ie discharged under the Mental Health Act 1983 s 30(1) (see PARA 844).
17 Mental Health Act 1983 s 30(4B)(b) (as added: see note 15).

846. Procedure on applications to the county court. County court rules which relate to applications authorised by Part 2 of Mental Health Act 1984[1] to be made to a county court may make provision:

(1) for the hearing and determination of such applications otherwise than in open court[2];

(2) for the admission on the hearing of such applications of evidence of such descriptions as may be specified in the rules notwithstanding anything to the contrary in any enactment or rule of law relating to the admissibility of evidence[3];

(3) for the visiting and interviewing of patients in private by or under the directions of the court[4].

1 Ie the Mental Health Act 1983 ss 2–34.
2 Mental Health Act 1983 s 31(a).
3 Mental Health Act 1983 s 31(b).
4 Mental Health Act 1983 s 31(c).

(10) APPLICATIONS PROCEDURES

847. Requirements for applications for hospital admission. An application for the admission of a patient[1] for assessment[2] or for treatment[3] may generally[4] be made either by the patient's nearest relative[5] or by an approved mental health professional[6]. However, no application may be made by an approved mental health professional if the circumstances are such that there would be a potential conflict of interest[7]. Nor may an approved mental health professional make an application for admission for treatment or a guardianship application in respect of a patient in either of the following cases:

(1) the nearest relative of the patient has notified that professional, or the local social services authority[8] on whose behalf the professional is acting, that he objects to the application being made[9]; or

(2) that professional has not consulted the person (if any) appearing to be the nearest relative[10] of the patient, but the requirement to consult that person does not apply if it appears to the professional that in the circumstances such consultation is not reasonably practicable[11] or would involve unreasonable delay[12].

No application for the admission of a patient may be made by any person unless that person has personally seen[13] the patient within the period of 14 days ending with the date of the application[14], but an emergency application cannot be made unless the applicant has personally seen the patient within the previous 24 hours[15].

Every application must be addressed to the managers[16] of the hospital[17] to which admission is sought and must specify the applicant's qualification[18] to make the application[19].

An application for the admission of a patient will be sufficient if the recommendations[20] on which it is founded are given either as separate recommendations, each signed by a medical practitioner, or as a joint recommendation signed by two such practitioners[21].

If the patient is a minor who is a ward of court[22], an application for admission may only be made with the leave of the court[23].

1 As to the meaning of 'patient' see PARA 758 note 4.
2 Ie under the Mental Health Act 1983 s 2(1) or, in an emergency, under s 4(1): see PARAS 767, 769. As to the procedure for and record of admissions under ss 2(1), 4(1) see the Mental Health

(Hospital, Guardianship and Consent to Treatment) (England) Regulations 2008, SI 2008/1184, reg 4(1)(a), (b), (e), (2), (4), (5), Sch 1; and the Mental Health (Hospital, Guardianship, Community Treatment and Consent to Treatment) (Wales) Regulations 2008, SI 2008/2439, reg 4(1)(a), (b), (e), (3), (5), Sch 1.

3   Ie under the Mental Health Act 1983 s 3(1): see PARA 768. As to the procedure for and record of admissions under s 3(1) see the Mental Health (Hospital, Guardianship and Consent to Treatment) (England) Regulations 2008, SI 2008/1184, reg 4(1)(d), (2), (4), Sch 1; and the Mental Health (Hospital, Guardianship, Community Treatment and Consent to Treatment) (Wales) Regulations 2008, SI 2008/2439, reg 4(1)(d), (3), (4), Sch 1.

4   Ie the provisions of the Mental Health Act 1983 s 11: see notes 6–21; and PARA 821.

5   As to the meaning of 'nearest relative' see PARA 839.

6   Mental Health Act 1983 s 11(1) (amended by the Mental Health Act 2007 Sch 2 para 4(2)). As to the meaning of 'approved mental health professional' see PARA 815 note 2. For the duties and powers of approved mental health professionals in relation to the making of applications under the Mental Health Act 1983 see PARA 821. Before or within a reasonable time after an application for the admission of a patient for assessment is made by an approved mental health professional, that professional must take such steps as are practicable to inform the person (if any) appearing to be the nearest relative of the patient that the application is to be or has been made and of the power of the nearest relative under s 23(2)(a): s 11(3) (amended by the Mental Health Act 2007 Sch 2 para 4(3)). See *Re GM* [2000] MHLR 41. If an approved mental health practitioner makes a genuine mistake and informs a person who is not in fact the nearest relative the application under s 2 is not invalidated: *R v Birmingham MH Trust ex p Phillips* (CO/1501/95) (May 1995 unreported)

7   Mental Health Act 1983 s 11(1A) (added by the Mental Health Act 2007 s 22(2)). As to where there is a conflict of interest see regulations made under the Mental Health Act 1983 s 12A: see the Mental Health (Conflicts of Interest) (England) Regulations 2008, SI 2008/1205; the Mental Health (Conflict of Interest) (Wales) Regulations 2008, SI 2008/2440; and PARAS 825–834.

8   As to the meaning of 'local social services authority' see PARA 579.

9   Mental Health Act 1983 s 11(4)(a) (substituted by the Mental Health Act 2007 Sch 2 para 4(4)). If an approved mental health practitioner acts in contravention of this provision the patient's detention will be unlawful as a matter of domestic law and under the Convention for the Protection of Human Rights and Fundamental Freedoms (Rome, 4 November 1950; TS 71 (1953); Cmd 8969): see *M (by his litigation friend TM) v Hackney London Borough Council* [2011] EWCA Civ 4 at [54], [2011] 3 All ER 529 at [54]. The Convention for the Protection of Human Rights and Fundamental Freedoms art 5(5) provides an enforceable right to compensation. The local authority will have 'directly caused' the false imprisonment and can be sued: *M (by his litigation friend TM) v Hackney London Borough Council*. See also *GD v Edgware Community Hospital* [2008] MHLR 282; *R (on the application of Ganatra) v Ealing London Borough Council* [2002] EWHC 1112 (Admin), [2002] All ER (D) 294 (Apr); *Re GM (patient consultation)* [2000] MHLR 41. As to the Convention see RIGHTS AND FREEDOMS.

10 This does not include the situation where the person is not legally capable of being the nearest relative having regard to the terms of the Mental Health Act 1983 s 26 (see PARA 838): *R v Managers of South Western Hospital, ex p M* [1993] QB 683, [1994] 1 All ER 161.

11 It is possible to interpret the words 'not reasonably practicable' in the Mental Health Act 1983 s 11 so as to take account of the claimant's wishes and health and wellbeing: *R (on the application of E) v Bristol City Council* [2005] EWHC 74 (Admin), [2005] All ER (D) 57 (Jan).

12 Mental Health Act 1983 s 11(4)(b) (as substituted: see note 9). Burden of showing proper consultation is on the approved mental health practitioner: *B v Cygnet Healthcare* [2008] EWHC 1259 (Admin), [2008] All ER (D) 35 (Mar). See also *R (on the application of V) v South London & Maudsley NHS Foundation Trust* [2010] EWHC 742 (Admin); *Re D (Mental Patient: Habeas Corpus)* [2001] 1 FCR 218, [2000] 2 FLR 848, CA; *R (WC) v South London and Maudsley NHS Trust* [2001] EWHC 1025 (Admin); *GD v Edgware Community Hospital* [2008] MHLR 282.

13 'Personally seen' means without an intermediary: see *R v Managers of South Western Hospital, ex p M* [1993] QB 683, [1994] 1 All ER 161; *Re Whitbread (Mental Patient: Habeas Corpus)* (1997) 141 Sol Jo LB 152, CA.

14 Mental Health Act 1983 s 11(5).

15 Mental Health Act 1983 s 11(5) (modified by s 4(5)). It is submitted that the provisions of s 11 otherwise apply to emergency applications as they apply to applications for admission for assessment. As to emergency applications see generally PARA 769.

16 As to the meaning of 'managers' see PARA 778. The managers are the detaining authority: *R v Managers of South Western Hospital, ex p M* [1993] QB 683, [1994] 1 All ER 161.

17 As to the meaning of 'hospital' see PARA 577.

18　Ie as nearest relative or as approved mental health professional.
19　Mental Health Act 1983 s 11(1), (2) (s 11(1) as amended: see note 6).
20　As to recommendations see PARA 849.
21　Mental Health Act 1983 s 11(7).
22　As to wards of court generally see CHILDREN AND YOUNG PERSONS vol 9 (2012) PARA 264 et seq.
23　Mental Health Act 1983 s 33(1). After admission, the power of the nearest relative under s 23 (see PARA 913) to discharge a patient who is a ward of court may only be exercised with the leave of the court: s 33(2).

848.　Requirements for guardianship applications. The general provisions relating to applications for admission to hospital for treatment[1] apply also to guardianship applications[2]. The person named as guardian in such an application may be either a local social services authority[3] or any other person, including the applicant himself[4]. The application must be addressed and forwarded[5] to the local social services authority which is named as guardian in the application, or, if a local social services authority is not so named, to the local social services authority for the area in which the person named as guardian resides[6]. If such an authority is not named as guardian, the application must be accompanied by a statement in writing by the person so named that he is willing to act as guardian[7]. Such an application is of no effect unless it is accepted on behalf of that person by the local social services authority for the area in which he resides[8].

1　See the Mental Health Act 1983 s 11(1), (1A), (2), (4), (5), (7); note 6; and PARAS 821, 847.
2　For the form for guardianship application and acceptance by the local social services authority see the Mental Health (Hospital, Guardianship and Treatment) (England) Regulations 2008, SI 2008/1184, reg 5, Sch 1; and the Mental Health (Hospital, Guardianship, Community Treatment and Consent to Treatment) (Wales) Regulations 2008, SI 2008/2439, reg 9, Sch 1. As to the grounds on which an application may be founded see the Mental Health Act 1983 s 7(2); and PARA 785. As to the general provisions relating to medical recommendations for guardianship see PARA 849. As to the form and rectification of guardianship applications see PARAS 788–789.
3　As to the local social services authority see PARA 579.
4　Mental Health Act 1983 s 7(5).
5　As to the service of documents on a local social services authority see PARA 850.
6　Mental Health Act 1983 s 11(2).
7　Mental Health Act 1983 s 7(5).
8　Mental Health Act 1983 s 7(5). See note 2.

849.　Requirements for medical recommendations. The medical recommendations required[1] for the admission of a patient[2] to hospital[3] under the Mental Health Act 1983[4] or for a guardianship application must be signed on or before the date of the application which they support[5]. They must be given by medical practitioners who have personally examined[6] the patient either together or separately, but in the latter case not more than five days may elapse between the days on which the separate examinations take place[7]. The application itself will be effective[8] for a period of 14 days beginning with the date on which the patient was last examined by one of the practitioners giving the recommendations[9], except in the case of an emergency application, which will be effective for 24 hours only, beginning from the time when the patient was examined by the practitioner giving the medical recommendation or when the application is made, whichever is the earlier[10].

One of the two medical recommendations must be given by a practitioner approved for the purpose by the appropriate national authority[11] as having special experience in the diagnosis or treatment of mental disorder[12]; unless that

practitioner has previous acquaintance with the patient, the other
recommendation must, if practicable, be given by a medical practitioner who has
such acquaintance[13].

No medical recommendation may be given for the above purposes if the
circumstances are such that there would be a potential conflict of interest[14].

1   Ie required by the Mental Health Act 1983 s 2(3) (see PARA 767), s 3(3) (see PARA 768), s 4(3)
     (see PARA 769).
2   As to the meaning of 'patient' see PARA 758 note 4.
3   As to the meaning of 'hospital' see PARA 577.
4   Ie under the Mental Health Act 1983 Pt 2 (ss 2–34), for assessment under s 2(1) (see PARA 767),
     for treatment under s 3(1) (see PARA 768), or for assessment in an emergency under s 4(1) (see
     PARA 769).
5   Mental Health Act 1983 s 12(1) (amended by the Mental Health Act 2007 s 22(3)). Where two
     recommendations are required, they may be separate or joint: Mental Health Act 1983 s 11(7).
     Any person who before the 31 October 2012 (ie the day on which the Mental Health (Approval
     Functions) Act 2012 was passed) has done anything in the purported exercise of an approval
     function is to be treated for all purposes as having had the power to do so: s 1(1). 'Approval
     function' means (1) the function of giving an approval for the purposes of the Mental Health
     Act 1983 s 12 (practitioners approved to give medical recommendations); or (2) the function of
     approving a person as an approved clinician for the purposes of that Act: Mental Health
     (Approval Functions) Act 2012 s 1(2).
        For the form of joint or individual medical recommendations for hospital admissions see the
     Mental Health (Hospital, Guardianship and Treatment) (England) Regulations 2008,
     SI 2008/1184, reg 4(1)(b), (d), (f), (2), Sch 1; and the Mental Health (Hospital, Guardianship,
     Community Treatment and Consent to Treatment) (Wales) Regulations 2008, SI 2008/2439,
     reg 4(1)(b), (d), (f), (3), (4), Sch 1; for the form of joint or individual recommendations for
     guardianship see the Mental Health (Hospital, Guardianship and Treatment) (England)
     Regulations 2008, SI 2008/1184, reg 5(1)(c), (5) Sch 1; and the Mental Health (Hospital,
     Guardianship, Community Treatment and Consent to Treatment) (Wales) Regulations 2008,
     SI 2008/2439, reg 9(1)(c), (2), (3), Sch 1.
        The Department of Health *Mental Health Act 1983 Code of Practice* (2008) para 4.28 et seq
     and the Welsh Assembly Government *Mental Health Act 1983 Code of Practice for Wales*
     (2008) para 2.33 et seq give general guidance about the assessment process, where it may lead to
     an application for admission under the Mental Health Act 1983. As to the Codes of Practice see
     PARA 762.
        A doctor who completes a medical recommendation form is acting in his clinical capacity
     and is not providing a reasoned determination in the manner of a mental health review tribunal
     (now the appropriate tribunal): *R (on the application of H) v Oxfordshire Mental Healthcare
     NHS Trust* [2002] EWHC 465 (Admin), [2002] All ER (D) 63 (Mar). A doctor making
     recommendations under the Mental Health Act 1983 is exercising the functions of a public
     authority under the Human Rights Act 1998 s 6(3)(b) (see RIGHTS AND FREEDOMS): *R (on the
     application of Wilkinson) v Responsible Officer of Broadmoor Hospital* [2002] EWCA Civ
     1545, [2002] 1 WLR 419, 65 BMLR 15. Assessment must be on the basis of actual mental
     health and not past events: Application 31365/96 *Varbanov v Bulgaria* (5 October 2000,
     unreported), ECtHR. As to the recommending doctor's liability in tort to the patient for
     negligence or unlawful imprisonment see *Everett v Griffiths* [1921] 1 AC 631, HL; *Harnett v
     Fisher* [1927] AC 573, HL. A person responsible for making the decision to detain a patient may
     be liable for his unlawful imprisonment, even though it is another person who acts on that
     decision by detaining the patient; if one doctor is of the opinion that the statutory criteria for
     detention are not satisfied the approved mental health practitioner can go to another: see *TTM
     (by his litigation friend TM) v Hackney London Borough* [2011] EWCA Civ 4 sub nom *M (by
     his litigation friend TM) v Hackney London Borough Council* [2011] 3 All ER 529.
6   The Department of Health *Mental Health Act 1983 Code of Practice* (2008) para 4.71 et seq
     and the Welsh Assembly Government *Mental Health Act 1983 Code of Practice for Wales*
     (2008) para 2.54 et seq give guidance on the requirements of a proper medical examination. As
     to the expression 'personally examined' see also *Routley v Worthing Health Authority*
     (14 January 1983) Lexis, CA. A doctor can 'examine' a patient for the purpose of reaching an
     opinion as to her mental health by observing her conduct over a sufficient period of time, even
     if she refuses, for example, to answer questions or to submit to a physical examination: *R (on
     the application of M) v The hospital managers of Queen Mary's Hospital* [2008] EWHC 1959
     (Admin).

7   Mental Health Act 1983 s 12(1).

8   Ie it will constitute authority for the patient's conveyance to hospital and his detention there: see the Mental Health Act 1983 s 6(1), (2).

9   See the Mental Health Act 1983 s 6(1)(a); and PARA 771.

10 See the Mental Health Act 1983 s 6(1)(b); and PARAS 769, 771. However, it seems that an effective application, even if signed at a time before the examination, could never be made earlier than the date of examination, because the medical recommendation must be signed on or before the date of the application: see ss 4(3), 12(1).

11 As to the appropriate national authority see PARA 567. As to the delegation of this power see PARA 570.

12 Mental Health Act 1983 s 12(2). See *R v Trent Health Authority, ex p Somaratne* (1996) 31 BMLR 140, CA (the matters which a health authority can consider when deciding whether to grant or refuse approval are limited to the matters of special experience stipulated in the Mental Health Act 1983 s 12(2)). A registered medical practitioner who is an approved clinician is treated as also approved for the purposes of s 12(2) as having special experience as mentioned there: s 12(2A) (added by the Mental Health Act 2007 s 16). As to the meaning of 'approved clinician' see PARA 831.

13 Mental Health Act 1983 s 12(2). It is submitted that 'acquaintance' must mean a doctor and patient relationship.
    As to the meanings of 'practicable' and 'previous acquaintance' see *Reed v Bronglais Hospital Pembrokeshire and Derwen NHS Trust* [2001] EWHC 792 (Admin); *R (on the application of C) v London Maudsley NHS Trust and the Mental Health Review Tribunal* [2003] EWHC 3467 (Admin). There was criticism in both cases of the wording of the *Mental Health Act 1983 Code of Practice* (1999) para 2.29, and the suggestion that the test is one of 'exceptional circumstances' instead of 'practicability' was considered wrong.

14 Mental Health Act 1983 s 12(3) (substituted by the Mental Health Act 2007 s 22(4)). As to a potential conflict of interest see regulations made under the Mental Health Act 1983 s 12A; and PARAS 825–830.

850.   Service of documents.   Any document required or authorised[1] to be served upon any authority, body or person in relation to the compulsory admission to hospital[2], guardianship or community treatment orders[3] may be served by delivering it to: (1) the authority, body or person upon whom it is to be served[4]; (2) any person authorised by that authority, body or person to receive it[5]; (3) by sending it pre-paid post[6] addressed to the authority or body at their registered or principal office or the person upon whom it is to be served at that person's usual or last known residence[7]; or (4) by delivering it using an internal mail system operated by the authority, body or person[8].

Any application for the admission of a patient to a hospital[9] must be served by delivering the application to an officer of the managers of the hospital[10] to which it is proposed that the patient will be admitted, who is authorised by them to receive it[11].

Where a patient is liable to be detained in hospital[12] any order by the nearest relative of the patient[13] for the patient's discharge[14] and the notice of such order[15], or notice at that hospital, must be served to an officer of the managers authorised to receive it or by sending it pre-paid post to those managers at that hospital or by delivering it using an internal mail system operated by the managers upon whom it is to be served, if those managers agree[16].

Where a patient is a community patient any order by the nearest relative of the patient[17] for the patient's discharge[18] and the notice of such order given[19] must be served by delivery of the order or notice at the patient's responsible hospital to an officer of the managers authorised by the managers to receive it, or sending it by pre-paid post to the managers at that hospital or by delivering it using an internal mail system operated by the managers whom is to be served if those managers agree[20].

Any report for the detention of a patient already in hospital for 72 hours[21] must be served by:

(A)   delivery of the report to an officer of the managers of the hospital authorised by those managers to receive it[22]; or

(B)   delivering it using an internal mail system operated by the managers upon whom it is to be served if those managers agree[23].

1   Subject to the Mental Health Act 1983 s 6(3) and 8(3) (see PARAS 771, 788), any document required or authorised by or under Pt 2 (ss 2–34) or under the Mental Health (Hospital, Guardianship and Treatment) (England) Regulations 2008, SI 2008/1184 or the Mental Health (Hospital, Guardianship, Community Treatment and Consent to Treatment) (Wales) Regulations 2008, SI 2008/2439, and purporting to be signed by a person required or authorised by or under that Part or those regulations, may be received in evidence and deemed to be such a document without further proof: Mental Health (Hospital, Guardianship and Treatment) (England) Regulations 2008, SI 2008/1184, reg 3(8); Mental Health (Hospital, Guardianship, Community Treatment and Consent to Treatment) (Wales) Regulations 2008, SI 2008/2439, reg 3(8).

2   As to the meaning of 'hospital' see PARA 577.

3   Ie under the Mental Health Act 1983 Pt 2 (ss 2–34) or the Mental Health (Hospital, Guardianship and Treatment) (England) Regulations 2008, SI 2008/1184 or the Mental Health (Hospital, Guardianship, Community Treatment and Consent to Treatment) (Wales) Regulations 2008, SI 2008/2439.

4   Mental Health (Hospital, Guardianship and Treatment) (England) Regulations 2008, SI 2008/1184, reg 3(1)(a); Mental Health (Hospital, Guardianship, Community Treatment and Consent to Treatment) (Wales) Regulations 2008, SI 2008/2439, reg 3(1)(a).

5   Mental Health (Hospital, Guardianship and Treatment) (England) Regulations 2008, SI 2008/1184, reg 3(1)(b); Mental Health (Hospital, Guardianship, Community Treatment and Consent to Treatment) (Wales) Regulations 2008, SI 2008/2439, reg 3(1)(b).

6   Where a document is sent by pre-paid first class post, service is deemed to have taken place on the second business day following the day of posting and where it is sent by second class post service is deemed to have taken place on the fourth business day following posting, unless the contrary is shown: Mental Health (Hospital, Guardianship and Treatment) (England) Regulations 2008, SI 2008/1184, reg 3(6); Mental Health (Hospital, Guardianship, Community Treatment and Consent to Treatment) (Wales) Regulations 2008, SI 2008/2439, reg 3(6).

7   Mental Health (Hospital, Guardianship and Treatment) (England) Regulations 2008, SI 2008/1184, reg 3(1)(c); Mental Health (Hospital, Guardianship, Community Treatment and Consent to Treatment) (Wales) Regulations 2008, SI 2008/2439, reg 3(1)(c).

8   See the Mental Health (Hospital, Guardianship and Treatment) (England) Regulations 2008, SI 2008/1184, reg 3(1)(d); and the Mental Health (Hospital, Guardianship, Community Treatment and Consent to Treatment) (Wales) Regulations 2008, SI 2008/2439, reg 3(1)(d). In relation to England, the authority, body or person must agree: see Mental Health (Hospital, Guardianship and Treatment) (England) Regulations 2008, SI 2008/1184, reg 3(1)(d). Where a document is delivered using an internal mail system, service is considered to have taken place immediately it is delivered into the internal mail system: Mental Health (Hospital, Guardianship and Treatment) (England) Regulations 2008, SI 2008/1184, reg 3(7); Mental Health (Hospital, Guardianship, Community Treatment and Consent to Treatment) (Wales) Regulations 2008, SI 2008/2439, reg 3(7).

9   Ie under the Mental Health Act 1983 Pt 2 (ss 2–34).

10 Where under the Mental Health Act 1983 Pt 2 (ss 2–34) or under the Mental Health (Hospital, Guardianship and Treatment) (England) Regulations 2008, SI 2008/1184 or the Mental Health (Hospital, Guardianship, Community Treatment and Consent to Treatment) (Wales) Regulations 2008, SI 2008/2439, the managers of a hospital are required to make any record or report, that function may be performed by an officer authorised by those managers in that behalf and where the agreement to accept service by a particular method requires the agreement of the managers of a hospital, that agreement may be given by an officer authorised by those managers in that behalf: Mental Health (Hospital, Guardianship and Treatment) (England) Regulations 2008, SI 2008/1184, reg 3(9), (10); Mental Health (Hospital, Guardianship, Community Treatment and Consent to Treatment) (Wales) Regulations 2008, SI 2008/2439, reg 3(10), (11). In relation to Wales, any document required to be addressed to the managers of a hospital is deemed to be properly addressed to such managers if addressed to the administrator of that hospital: Mental Health (Hospital, Guardianship, Community Treatment and Consent to Treatment) (Wales) Regulations 2008, SI 2008/2439, reg 3(9).

11 See the Mental Health (Hospital, Guardianship and Treatment) (England) Regulations 2008, SI 2008/1184, reg 3(2); and the Mental Health (Hospital, Guardianship, Community Treatment and Consent to Treatment) (Wales) Regulations 2008, SI 2008/2439, reg 3(2). The meaning of the word 'officer' would depend upon the context in which it was used. In the present context it was natural to exclude from a tribunal those who managed the affairs of the authority in question: *R (on the application of D) v West Midlands and North West Mental Health Review Tribunal* [2004] EWCA Civ 311, 148 Sol Jo LB 384.

12 Ie under the Mental Health Act 1983 Pt 2 (ss 2–34).

13 Ie under the Mental Health Act 1983 s 23 (see PARA 913).

14 Mental Health (Hospital, Guardianship and Treatment) (England) Regulations 2008, SI 2008/1184, reg 3(3)(a); Mental Health (Hospital, Guardianship, Community Treatment and Consent to Treatment) (Wales) Regulations 2008, SI 2008/2439, reg 3(3)(a).

15 Ie under the Mental Health Act 1983 s 25(1) (see PARA 915).

16 Mental Health (Hospital, Guardianship and Treatment) (England) Regulations 2008, SI 2008/1184, reg 3(3)(b); Mental Health (Hospital, Guardianship, Community Treatment and Consent to Treatment) (Wales) Regulations 2008, SI 2008/2439, reg 3(3)(b). See *Re GK (Patient: Habeas Corpus)* (1999) MHLR 128.

17 Ie under the Mental Health Act 1983 s 23 (see PARA 913).

18 Mental Health (Hospital, Guardianship and Treatment) (England) Regulations 2008, SI 2008/1184, reg 3(4)(a); Mental Health (Hospital, Guardianship, Community Treatment and Consent to Treatment) (Wales) Regulations 2008, SI 2008/2439, reg 3(4)(a).

19 Ie given under the Mental Health Act 1983 s 25(1A) (see PARA 915).

20 Mental Health (Hospital, Guardianship and Treatment) (England) Regulations 2008, SI 2008/1184, reg 3(4)(b); Mental Health (Hospital, Guardianship, Community Treatment and Consent to Treatment) (Wales) Regulations 2008, SI 2008/2439, reg 3(4)(b).

21 Ie a report made under the Mental Health Act 1983 s 5(2) (see PARA 770).

22 Mental Health (Hospital, Guardianship and Treatment) (England) Regulations 2008, SI 2008/1184, reg 3(5)(a); Mental Health (Hospital, Guardianship, Community Treatment and Consent to Treatment) (Wales) Regulations 2008, SI 2008/2439, reg 3(5)(a).

23 Mental Health (Hospital, Guardianship and Treatment) (England) Regulations 2008, SI 2008/1184, reg 3(5)(b); Mental Health (Hospital, Guardianship, Community Treatment and Consent to Treatment) (Wales) Regulations 2008, SI 2008/2439, reg 3(5)(b).

(11) CARE COORDINATORS: WALES

851.   Duty to appoint care coordinator.   The relevant mental health service provider[1] for a relevant patient[2] must appoint an individual as care coordinator for the patient to perform in relation to the patient the functions conferred on care coordinators by and under Part 2[3] of the Mental Health (Wales) Act 2010[4]. This duty is to be performed as soon as is reasonably practicable after an individual becomes a relevant patient or, in a case where an individual permanently ceases to be appointed as a relevant patient's care coordinator, that permanent cessation[5].

Where the relevant mental health service provider considers that a patient's care coordinator is for whatever reason temporarily unable to act as such, the provider may appoint an individual to be the patient's temporary care coordinator to perform in relation to the patient the above functions[6].

1 For the purposes of the Mental Health (Wales) Measure 2010 Pt 2 (ss 12–18), 'mental health service providers' are the Welsh Ministers, a local health board and a local authority in Wales: s 13(1). But the Welsh Ministers are not to be treated as being responsible for providing any service that is provided in the exercise of a function to which a direction given under the National Health Service (Wales) Act 2006 s 12(1) relates: s 13(2). As to the meaning of 'local health board' see PARA 575 note 7. As to the meaning of 'local authority' see PARA 586 note 1.

2 For the purposes of the Mental Health (Wales) Measure 2010 Pt 2 (ss 12–18), an individual is a relevant patient if a mental health service provider is responsible for providing a secondary mental health service for the individual: s 12(1). An individual who does not fall within s 12(1) is also a relevant patient if the individual is under the guardianship of a local authority in Wales or a mental health service provider has decided that the individual would be provided with a

secondary mental health service if the individual cooperated with its provision: s 12(2). As to the meaning of 'secondary mental health service' see PARA 586 note 6.

3   Ie the Mental Health (Wales) Act 2010 Pt 2 (ss 12–18).
4   Mental Health (Wales) Act 2010 s 14(1).
5   Mental Health (Wales) Act 2010 s 14(2).
6   Mental Health (Wales) Act 2010 s 14(3). A temporary appointment under s 14(3) ceases when the relevant mental health service provider considers that the individual previously appointed as care coordinator has regained the ability to act as such, in which case that individual's appointment revives: s 14(4). Arrangements may be made between two local health boards for the functions of one of them under s 14(1) or (3) to be exercised by the other: s 14(5). Any such arrangements do not affect the responsibility of a local health board as relevant mental health service provider under s 14(1) or (3): s 14(6). Section 15 (see PARA 852) makes provision about the identification of the relevant mental health service provider for a relevant patient: s 14(7).

852. Identification of the relevant mental health service provider for a relevant patient.

Where a local health board[1] is responsible for providing a secondary mental health service[2] for a relevant patient[3] and a local authority[4] is not responsible for providing such a service, the board is the relevant mental health service provider[5].

Where a local health board is responsible for providing a secondary mental health service for a relevant patient and a local authority is also responsible for providing such a service, the identification of one of them as the relevant mental health service provider is to be made in accordance with provision in regulations made by the Welsh Ministers[6].

Where neither of the above provisions[7] apply, the relevant mental health service provider is:

(1)   if a local authority is responsible for providing the patient with a secondary mental health service, the authority[8];

(2)   if the patient is under the guardianship of a local authority, the authority[9];

(3)   where neither head (1) or (2) above apply but the appropriate national authority[10] is responsible for providing a secondary mental health service for the patient, the appropriate national authority[11].

1   As to the meaning of 'local health board' see PARA 575 note 7.
2   As to the meaning of 'secondary mental health service' see PARA 586 note 6.
3   As to the meaning of 'relevant patient' see PARA 851 note 2.
4   As to the meaning of 'local authority' see PARA 586 note 1.
5   Mental Health (Wales) Measure 2010 s 15(1), (2). For the purposes of the Mental Health (Care Co-ordination and Care and Treatment Planning) (Wales) Regulations 2011, SI 2011/2942 'relevant mental health service provider' means the secondary mental health service provider who is identified as a relevant patient's relevant mental health service provider in accordance with the Mental Health (Wales) Measure 2010 s 15 (identification of the relevant mental health service provider for a relevant patient: see PARA 852) or the Mental Health (Care Co-ordination and Care and Treatment Planning) (Wales) Regulations 2011, SI 2011/2942, reg 3: reg 2(1).
6   Mental Health (Wales) Measure 2010 s 15(3), (4). Regulations under s 15(4) may:
   (1)   provide for disputes as to the operation of the regulations to be determined by the Welsh Ministers (s 15(5)(a));
   (2)   provide for the Welsh Ministers to make such determination as they think fit requiring payments to be made by one of the persons referred to in s 15(3) to the other person in the light of a determination referred to in head (1) above (s 15(5)(b));
   (3)   identify a provider as the relevant mental health service provider pending a determination under head (1) above (s 15(5)(c)).
   Where a local health board is responsible for providing a secondary mental health service to a relevant patient and a local authority is also responsible for providing such a service, then the following provisions apply: Mental Health (Care Co-ordination and Care and Treatment Planning) (Wales) Regulations 2011, SI 2011/2942, reg 3(1). The local health board is the relevant mental health service provider for a relevant patient unless reg 3(3) or (4) apply: reg 3(2). A local authority is the relevant mental health service provider for a relevant patient if

that patient is the subject of a guardianship application made under the Mental Health Act 1983 s 7 (see PARA 785) or a guardianship order made under s 37 (see PARA 877): Mental Health (Care Co-ordination and Care and Treatment Planning) (Wales) Regulations 2011, SI 2011/2942, reg 3(3). A local authority is the relevant mental health service provider for a relevant patient if that patient is:

    (a)   under the age of 18 years and is looked after by a local authority within the meaning of the Children Act 1989 s 22(1) (general duty of local authority in relation to children looked after by them: see CHILDREN AND YOUNG PERSONS vol 10 (2012) PARA 843) (Mental Health (Care Co-ordination and Care and Treatment Planning) (Wales) Regulations 2011, SI 2011/2942, reg 3(4)(a));

    (b)   is a relevant child within the meaning of the Children Act 1989 s 23A (the responsible authority and relevant children: see CHILDREN AND YOUNG PERSONS vol 10 (2012) PARA 931) (Mental Health (Care Co-ordination and Care and Treatment Planning) (Wales) Regulations 2011, SI 2011/2942, reg 3(4)(b));

    (c)   qualifies for advice and assistance under the Children Act 1989 s 24(1A) (persons qualifying for advice or assistance: CHILDREN AND YOUNG PERSONS vol 10 (2012) PARA 926) or s 24(1B) (Mental Health (Care Co-ordination and Care and Treatment Planning) (Wales) Regulations 2011, SI 2011/2942, reg 3(4)(c));

    (d)   is admitted to a school in accordance with a statement of special educational needs made under the Education Act 1996 s 324 (statement of special educational needs: see EDUCATION vol 36 (2011) PARA 1192) of the Education Act 1996 that names the school (Mental Health (Care Co-ordination and Care and Treatment Planning) (Wales) Regulations 2011, SI 2011/2942, reg 3(4)(d)).

7   Ie where neither the Mental Health (Wales) Measure 2010 s 15(1) or (3) apply.
8   Mental Health (Wales) Measure 2010 s 15(6)(a).
9   Mental Health (Wales) Measure 2010 s 15(6)(b).
10 As to the 'appropriate national authority' see PARA 567.
11 Mental Health (Wales) Measure 2010 s 15(6)(c).

853. Further provisions about the appointment of care coordinators. A provider[1] must not appoint an individual as a care coordinator[2] unless the individual is eligible to be appointed[3] as a care coordinator[4]. The appropriate national authority[5] may by regulations make provision about the eligibility of individuals to be appointed as a care coordinator which may make provision relating to a person's qualifications, skills, training or experience[6]. Such regulations provide that a person is eligible to be appointed as a care coordinator if that person fulfils one or more of the professional requirements[7] and has demonstrated to the satisfaction of the relevant mental health service provider that he has appropriate experience, skills or training, or an appropriate combination of experience, skills and training[8].

A provider must not appoint an individual as a care coordinator[9] from amongst the staff of another person without that person's consent[10].

1   As to the mental health service provider see PARA 852.
2   Ie under the Mental Health (Wales) Measure 2010 s 14(1) (see PARA 851).
3   Ie eligible to be appointed as a care coordinator under regulations made under the Mental Health (Wales) Measure 2010 s 47 (see PARA 851).
4   Mental Health (Wales) Measure 2010 s 16(1). Unless regulations made by the Welsh Ministers provide otherwise, an individual's appointment as a care coordinator does not come to an end as a result of a change in a relevant patient's relevant mental health service provider as identified under s 15 (see PARA 852): s 16(3). A relevant mental health service provider may terminate the appointment of an individual appointed as a care coordinator under s 14(1) (see PARA 851): s 16(4).
5   As to the appropriate national authority see PARA 567.
6   Mental Health (Wales) Measure 2010 s 47(1)(b), (2). The regulations may make different provision in relation to the eligibility of individuals to carry out a primary mental health assessment compared to that which is made in relation to the eligibility of individuals to be appointed as care coordinators: s 47(3).
7   The professional requirements are that a person must be:
    (1)   a qualified social worker registered with the Care Council for Wales or in Part 16 of the

register maintained under the Health and Social Work Professions Order 2001, ~~SI 2002/254, art 5 (see~~ MEDICAL PROFESSIONS) (Mental Health (Care Co-ordination and Care and Treatment Planning) (Wales) Regulations 2011, SI 2011/2942, Sch 1 para 1(a) (amended by SI 2012/1479));

(2) a first or second level nurse, registered in Sub-Part 1 or Sub-Part 2 of the register maintained under the Nursing and Midwifery Order 2001, SI 2002/253, art 5 (see MEDICAL PROFESSIONS vol 74 (2011) PARA 713), with the inclusion of an entry indicating that his or her field of practice is mental health or learning disabilities nursing (Mental Health (Care Co-ordination and Care and Treatment Planning) (Wales) Regulations 2011, SI 2011/2942, Sch 1 para 1(b));

(3) an occupational therapist who is registered in Part 6 of the register maintained under the Health and Social Work Professions Order 2001, SI 2002/254, art 5 (see MEDICAL PROFESSIONS vol 74 (2011) PARA 906) (Mental Health (Care Co-ordination and Care and Treatment Planning) (Wales) Regulations 2011, SI 2011/2942, Sch 1 para 1(c) (amended by SI 2012/1479));

(4) a practitioner psychologist who is registered in Part 14 of the register maintained under the Health and Social Work Professions Order 2001, SI 2002/254, art 5 (see MEDICAL PROFESSIONS vol 74 (2011) PARA 911) (Mental Health (Care Co-ordination and Care and Treatment Planning) (Wales) Regulations 2011, SI 2011/2942, Sch 1 para 1(d) (amended by SI 2012/1479));

(5) a registered medical practitioner (see MEDICAL PROFESSIONS vol 74 (2011) PARA 176) (Mental Health (Care Co-ordination and Care and Treatment Planning) (Wales) Regulations 2011, SI 2011/2942, Sch 1 para 1(e));

(6) a dietician who is registered in Part 4 of the register maintained under the Health and Social Work Professions Order 2001, SI 2002/254, art 5 (see MEDICAL PROFESSIONS vol 74 (2011) PARA 904) (Mental Health (Care Co-ordination and Care and Treatment Planning) (Wales) Regulations 2011, SI 2011/2942, Sch 1 para 1(f) (amended by SI 2012/1479));

(7) a physiotherapist who is registered in Part 9 of the register maintained under the Health and Social Work Professions Order 2001, SI 2002/254, art 5 (see MEDICAL PROFESSIONS vol 74 (2011) PARA 910) (Mental Health (Care Co-ordination and Care and Treatment Planning) (Wales) Regulations 2011, SI 2011/2942, Sch 1 para 1(g) (amended by SI 2012/1479)); or

(8) a speech and language therapist who is registered in Part 12 of the Register maintained under the Health and Social Work Professions Order 2001, SI 2002/254, art 5 (see MEDICAL PROFESSIONS vol 74 (2011) PARA 915) (Mental Health (Care Co-ordination and Care and Treatment Planning) (Wales) Regulations 2011, SI 2011/2942, Sch 1 para 1(h) (amended by SI 2012/1479)).

As to the Care Council for Wales see the Care Standards Act 2000 s 54; and SOCIAL SERVICES AND COMMUNITY CARE vol 44(2) (Reissue) PARA 1003. As to registered medical practitioners see MEDICAL PROFESSIONS vol 74 (2011) PARA 176 et seq.

8　Mental Health (Care Co-ordination and Care and Treatment Planning) (Wales) Regulations 2011, SI 2011/2942, reg 4(1). When determining whether a person satisfies the appointment requirement in reg 4(1)(b) (demonstrated appropriate skills etc) regard must be had to standards in any Codes of Practice issued under the Mental Health (Wales) Measure 2010 s 44 (codes of practice: see PARA 763) and any guidance that may be from time to time issued by the Welsh Ministers: Mental Health (Care Co-ordination and Care and Treatment Planning) (Wales) Regulations 2011, SI 2011/2942, reg 4(2).

9　Ie under the Mental Health (Wales) Measure 2010 s 14(1) (see PARA 851).

10　Mental Health (Wales) Measure 2010 s 16(2).

854. Duty to coordinate provision of mental health services. For the purpose of improving the effectiveness of the mental health services provided to a relevant patient[1], a mental health service provider[2] must take all reasonable steps to ensure that:

(1)　different mental health services which it is responsible for providing for the patient are coordinated with each other[3];

(2)　the mental health services which it is responsible for providing for the patient are coordinated with any other such services the provision of which is the responsibility of any other mental health service provider[4];

(3)   the mental health services which it is responsible for providing are coordinated with any services related to mental health provided for the patient by a voluntary organisation[5].

A mental health service provider may seek the advice of a patient's care coordinator as to how the provider should discharge its duty under the above provisions and a care coordinator may at any time give such advice to a mental health service provider[6].

1   As to the meaning of 'relevant patient' see PARA 851 note 2. For these purposes mental health services are secondary mental health services, services under the Mental Health (Wales) Measure 2010 Pt 1 (ss 1–11) and things done in the exercise of a local authority's powers in the Mental Health Act 1983 s 8 (see PARA 787) in respect of a person who is subject to the authority's guardianship: Mental Health (Wales) Measure 2010 s 17(5). As to the meaning of 'secondary mental health services' see PARA 586 note 6.
2   As to the meaning of 'mental health service provider' see PARA 851 note 1.
3   Mental Health (Wales) Measure 2010 s 17(1)(a).
4   Mental Health (Wales) Measure 2010 s 17(1)(b).
5   Mental Health (Wales) Measure 2010 s 17(1)(c). For these purposes 'voluntary organisation' means a body whose activities are carried on otherwise than for profit: s 17(6).
6   Mental Health (Wales) Measure 2010 s 17(2), (3). A mental health service provider must have regard to any advice given under s 17(2) and (3) in discharging its duty under s 17(1): s 17(4).

855. Functions of the care coordinator. A relevant patient's care coordinator[1] must work with the relevant patient and the patient's mental health service providers[2]:

(1)   with a view to agreeing the outcomes which the provision of mental health services[3] for the patient are designed to achieve, including (but not limited to) achievements in one or more of the following areas:
       (a)   finance and money[4];
       (b)   accommodation[5];
       (c)   personal care and physical well-being[6];
       (d)   education and training[7];
       (e)   work and occupation[8];
       (f)   parenting or caring relationships[9];
       (g)   social, cultural or spiritual[10];
       (h)   medical and other forms of treatment including psychological interventions[11];
(2)   with a view to agreeing a plan ('a care and treatment plan') for achieving those outcomes[12];
(3)   in connection with the review and revision of a care and treatment plan in accordance with provision in regulations made by the Welsh Ministers[13].

The following apply if the outcomes referred to in head (1) above or the plan referred to in head (2) above cannot be agreed between the relevant patient's care coordinator, the relevant patient and the patient's mental health service providers[14].

If the relevant patient has a sole mental health service provider, the provider must, having regard to any views expressed by the relevant patient, determine the outcomes which the provision of mental health services for the patient are designed to achieve and determine a plan for achieving those outcomes[15].

If the relevant patient has more than one mental health service provider, each provider must, having regard to any views expressed by the patient, determine the outcomes which the provision of mental health services by the provider are designed to achieve and determine a plan for achieving those outcomes[16].

The Welsh Ministers may by regulations make provision as to:

(i)   the form and content of care and treatment plans[17];

(ii)   any persons whom the care coordinator is to consult in connection with the exercise of the coordinator's functions under head (1) or (2) above[18];

(iii) the obligations of persons specified in the regulations in connection with the agreement or determination of care and treatment plans[19];

(iv)   the persons to whom written copies of a care and treatment plan are to be provided (including in specified cases the provision of copies without the consent of the relevant patient to whom the plan relates)[20];

(v)   the information to be provided by mental health service providers to an individual who has ceased to be a relevant patient[21].

So far as it is reasonably practicable to do so, a mental health service provider must ensure that mental health services for a relevant patient are provided in accordance with the patient's current care and treatment plan[22].

1   As to the meaning of 'relevant patient' see PARA 851 note 2.
2   As to the meaning of 'mental health service providers' see PARA 851 note 1.
3   As to the meaning of 'mental health services' see the Mental Health (Wales) Measure 2010 s 17(5); and PARA 854 (definition applied by s 18(11)).
4   Mental Health (Wales) Measure 2010 s 18(1)(a)(i). As to the provision of copies where a relevant patient's care coordinator has agreed a care and treatment plan for a relevant patient and recorded the plan in writing as provided by s 18(1), (2) see the Mental Health (Care Co-ordination and Care and Treatment Planning) (Wales) Regulations 2011, SI 2011/2942, reg 8. As to the delivery of such copies see reg 9.
5   Mental Health (Wales) Measure 2010 s 18(1)(a)(ii).
6   Mental Health (Wales) Measure 2010 s 18(1)(a)(iii).
7   Mental Health (Wales) Measure 2010 s 18(1)(a)(iv).
8   Mental Health (Wales) Measure 2010 s 18(1)(a)(v).
9   Mental Health (Wales) Measure 2010 s 18(1)(a)(vi).
10 Mental Health (Wales) Measure 2010 s 18(1)(a)(vii).
11 Mental Health (Wales) Measure 2010 s 18(1)(a)(viii).
12 Mental Health (Wales) Measure 2010 s 18(1)(b). Where a care and treatment plan has been agreed, the care coordinator must record the plan in writing: s 18(2).
13 Mental Health (Wales) Measure 2010 s 18(1)(c). The provision that may be made by regulations under s 18(1)(c) includes (but is not limited to) provision:
    (1)   for care and treatment plans to be reviewed and revised in specified circumstances (s 18(9)(a));
    (2)   conferring a discretion upon the care coordinator as to whether a review or revision is to be carried out (s 18(9)(b));
    (3)   as to any persons whom the care coordinator is to consult in connection with a review or revision (s 18(9)(c));
    (4)   imposing obligations upon persons specified in the regulations in connection with a review or revision (s 18(9)(d));
    (5)   as to the provision of copies of revised plans to specified persons (including in specified cases the provision of copies without the consent of the relevant patient to whom the plan relates) (s 18(9)(e)).
    As to the review and revision of care and treatment plans see PARA 857.
14 Mental Health (Wales) Measure 2010 s 18(3).
15 Mental Health (Wales) Measure 2010 s 18(4). Where a plan has been determined under s 18(4) the care coordinator must record the plan in writing: see s 18(6)(a). The records made under s 18(6) are care and treatment plans for the purposes of s 18(1)(c) and 18(8)–(10): s 18(7). As to the provision of copies where a relevant patient's care coordinator has recorded the plan or plans determined under the provisions of s 18(4) or (5) in writing as provided by s 18(6) see the Mental Health (Care Co-ordination and Care and Treatment Planning) (Wales) Regulations 2011, SI 2011/2942, reg 8. As to delivery of such copies see reg 9.
16 Mental Health (Wales) Measure 2010 s 18(5). Where plans are determined under s 18(5) the care coordinator must record all of them in writing in a single document: see s 18(6)(b).
17 Mental Health (Wales) Measure 2010 s 18(8)(a). A care coordinator must ensure that a care and treatment plan which records all of the outcomes which the provision of mental health services are designed to achieve for a relevant patient is completed in writing in the form set out in the

Mental Health (Care Co-ordination and Care and Treatment Planning) (Wales) Regulations 2011, SI 2011/2942, Sch 2: reg 5(1). The outcomes must include (but are not limited to) achievements in at least one of the areas provided in the Mental Health (Wales) Measure 2010 s 18(1)(a) (functions of the care coordinator): Mental Health (Care Co-ordination and Care and Treatment Planning) (Wales) Regulations 2011, SI 2011/2942, reg 5(2). 'Care and treatment plan' means a plan prepared for the purpose of achieving the outcomes which the provision of mental health services for a relevant patient is designed to achieve, as provided in the Mental Health (Wales) Measure 2010 s 18(1)(b) (functions of the care coordinator): Mental Health (Care Co-ordination and Care and Treatment Planning) (Wales) Regulations 2011, SI 2011/2942, reg 2(1).

18 Mental Health (Wales) Measure 2010 s 18(8)(b). As to the persons to be consulted by a care coordinator see PARA 856.
19 Mental Health (Wales) Measure 2010 s 18(8)(c).
20 Mental Health (Wales) Measure 2010 s 18(8)(d).
21 Mental Health (Wales) Measure 2010 s 18(8)(e).
22 Mental Health (Wales) Measure 2010 s 18(10).

856. Persons to be consulted by care coordinator. Where a relevant patient's[1] care coordinator must work with a relevant patient and that patient's mental health service providers[2] to agree the outcomes which the provision of mental health services for that patient are designed to achieve[3], agree a care and treatment plan for that patient[4] or review and revise a care and treatment plan for that patient[5], then the following provisions apply[6].

The care coordinator is to take all practicable steps to consult the following persons[7] where those persons are identified in relation to a relevant patient:

(1)   all persons with parental responsibility for that patient[8];
(2)   all carers and adult placement carers[9] of that patient[10];
(3)   that patient's responsible clinician[11];
(4)   where a guardian has been appointed for that patient as a result of a guardianship application[12] or a guardianship order[13], that patient's guardian[14];
(5)   a donee of that patient's lasting power of attorney[15] or a deputy of that patient who has been appointed by the Court of Protection[16], provided that in the case of a donee, the matters which are to be considered in the consultation fall within the scope of the lasting power of attorney or, in the case of a deputy, the matters which are to be considered in the consultation fall within the scope of the order, directions or terms of appointment of the deputy which have been specified by the Court of Protection[17];
(6)   where there are acts or decisions proposed in relation to that patient[18], an Independent Mental Capacity Advocate who has been appointed[19] to represent that patient[20];
(7)   where that patient is subject to a standard authorisation[21], the managing authority[22], the supervisory body[23] and the relevant person's representative[24] who has been appointed for that patient[25]; and
(8)   where that patient is subject to an urgent authorisation[26], the managing authority and the supervisory body[27].

Where the following persons are identified in relation to a relevant patient, they may be consulted by the care coordinator[28]:

(a)   any person who the care coordinator wishes to consult, in order to facilitate the carrying out of the care coordinator's functions[29]; and
(b)   any person who that patient wishes to be consulted in connection with the care coordinator carrying out his or her functions[30].

1   As to the meaning of 'relevant patient' see PARA 851 note 2.

2 As to the meaning of 'mental health service provider' see PARA 851 note 1.

3 ~~Ie as provided by the Mental Health (Wales) Measure 2010 s 18(1)(a) (see PARA 855).~~

4 Ie as provided by the Mental Health (Wales) Measure 2010 s 18(1)(b) ~~(see PARA 855).~~

5 Ie as provided by the Mental Health (Wales) Measure 2010 s 18(1)(c) (see PARA 855).

6 Mental Health (Care Co-ordination and Care and Treatment Planning) (Wales) Regulations 2011, SI 2011/2942, reg 6(1).

7 This is subject to the Mental Health (Care Co-ordination and Care and Treatment Planning) (Wales) Regulations 2011, SI 2011/2942, reg 6(4). Before consulting any of the persons mentioned in reg 6(2) and reg 6(3)(a) the care coordinator is to take account of the views of a relevant patient regarding whether such persons ought to be consulted: reg 6(4). But the care coordinator may consult any of the persons mentioned in reg 6(2) and 6(3)(a) against the wishes of a relevant patient provided that the care coordinator has given due consideration to the views of that patient: reg 6(5). Where the same person is to be consulted in more than one capacity under reg 6(2) and 6(3), only one consultation need take place: reg 6(6). Where the person consulted is not an individual, consultation may take place with an individual acting on behalf of, or employed by, the person: reg 6(7).

8 Mental Health (Care Co-ordination and Care and Treatment Planning) (Wales) Regulations 2011, SI 2011/2942, reg 6(2)(a). As to the meaning of 'parental responsibility' see the Children Act 1989 s 3; and CHILDREN AND YOUNG PERSONS vol 9 (2012) PARA 151 (definition applied by the Mental Health (Care Co-ordination and Care and Treatment Planning) (Wales) Regulations 2011, SI 2011/2942, reg 2(1)).

9 'Carer' means, in relation to a relevant patient, an individual who provides or intends to provide a substantial amount of care on a regular basis for that patient, but does not include an individual who provides, or intends to provide care for that patient by virtue of a contract of employment or other contract with any person or as a volunteer for a body (whether incorporated or not incorporated): Mental Health (Care Co-ordination and Care and Treatment Planning) (Wales) Regulations 2011, SI 2011/2942, reg 2(1). 'Adult placement carer' means a person in whose home an adult is or may be accommodated and provided with personal care under an adult placement agreement entered into or proposed to be entered into by the carer: reg 2(1).

10 Mental Health (Care Co-ordination and Care and Treatment Planning) (Wales) Regulations 2011, SI 2011/2942, reg 6(2)(b).

11 Mental Health (Care Co-ordination and Care and Treatment Planning) (Wales) Regulations 2011, SI 2011/2942, reg 6(2)(c). As to the meaning of 'responsible clinician' see the Mental Health Act 1983 s 34(1); and PARA 834 (definition applied by the Mental Health (Care Co-ordination and Care and Treatment Planning) (Wales) Regulations 2011, SI 2011/2942, reg 2(1)).

12 Ie an application made under the Mental Health Act 1983 s 7 (see PARA 785).

13 Ie an order made under the Mental Health Act 1983 s 37 (see PARA 864).

14 Mental Health (Care Co-ordination and Care and Treatment Planning) (Wales) Regulations 2011, SI 2011/2942, reg 6(2)(d).

15 Ie a donee who has been appointed in accordance with the Mental Capacity Act 2005 s 10 (appointment of donees: see AGENCY vol 1 (2008) PARA 218).

16 Ie a deputy who has been appointed by the Court of Protection in accordance with the Mental Capacity Act 2005 s 16 (powers to make decisions and appoint deputies: see PARA 607). As to the Court of Protection see PARA 720.

17 Mental Health (Care Co-ordination and Care and Treatment Planning) (Wales) Regulations 2011, SI 2011/2942, reg 6(2)(e).

18 Ie under the Mental Capacity Act 2005 ss 37 (provision of serious medical treatment by NHS body: see PARA 638), 38 (provision of accommodation by NHS body: see PARA 639), 39 (provision of accommodation by local authority: see PARA 640), 39A (person becomes subject to Sch A1: see PARA 642), 39C (person unrepresented whilst subject to Sch A1: see PARA 643) or 39D (person subject to Sch A1 without paid representative: see PARA 644).

19 Ie in accordance with the Mental Capacity Act 2005 s 35 (appointment of independent mental capacity advocates: see PARA 635).

20 Mental Health (Care Co-ordination and Care and Treatment Planning) (Wales) Regulations 2011, SI 2011/2942, reg 6(2)(f).

21 Ie a standard authorisation given under the Mental Capacity Act 2005 Sch A1 Pt 4 (see PARA 661 et seq).

22 As to the meaning of 'managing authority', in relation to a National Health Service hospital, see the Mental Capacity Act 2005 Sch A1 para 176 (hospitals and their managing authorities: see PARA 652), in relation to an independent hospital, see Sch A1 para 177(b) (hospitals and their managing authorities) and, in relation to a care home, see Sch A1 para 179(b) (care homes and

their managing authorities): Mental Health (Care Co-ordination and Care and Treatment Planning) (Wales) Regulations 2011, SI 2011/2942, reg 2(1).

23 'Supervisory body' in relation to a hospital has the identity given by the Mental Capacity Act 2005 Sch A1 para 181 (supervisory bodies: hospitals: see PARA 664), and in relation to a care home has the identity given by Sch A1 para 182 (supervisory bodies: care homes): Mental Health (Care Co-ordination and Care and Treatment Planning) (Wales) Regulations 2011, SI 2011/2942, reg 2(1).

24 Ie who has been appointed for that patient under the Mental Capacity Act 2005 Sch A1 para 139 (see PARA 707).

25 Mental Health (Care Co-ordination and Care and Treatment Planning) (Wales) Regulations 2011, SI 2011/2942, reg 6(2)(g).

26 Ie an urgent authorisation given under the Mental Capacity Act 2005 Sch A1 Pt 5 (see PARA 713 et seq).

27 Mental Health (Care Co-ordination and Care and Treatment Planning) (Wales) Regulations 2011, SI 2011/2942, reg 6(2)(h).

28 This is subject to the Mental Health (Care Co-ordination and Care and Treatment Planning) (Wales) Regulations 2011, SI 2011/2942, reg 6(4) (see note 6).

29 Mental Health (Care Co-ordination and Care and Treatment Planning) (Wales) Regulations 2011, SI 2011/2942, reg 6(3)(a).

30 Mental Health (Care Co-ordination and Care and Treatment Planning) (Wales) Regulations 2011, SI 2011/2942, reg 6(3)(b).

857. Review and revision of care plans. A care and treatment plan[1] may be reviewed or revised by the care coordinator at any time provided that the care coordinator agrees to that review or revision[2].

A care coordinator must review and, if necessary revise, a care and treatment plan[3] when:

(1)   a period of no more than twelve calendar months has elapsed since the initial preparation or the last review of that plan[4];

(2)   a relevant patient[5] requests a review of his or her plan before the twelve calendar month period has elapsed[6];

(3)   a relevant patient's carer or adult placement carer[7] requests a review of that patient's plan before the twelve calendar month period has elapsed[8]; or

(d)   a mental health service provider for the purposes of provisions relating to the coordination of and care planning for secondary mental health service users[9] requests a review of a relevant patient's plan[10].

But a care coordinator need not review a care and treatment plan at the request of a relevant patient, that patient's carer or that patient's adult placement carer if, in his or her opinion, the request for a review is frivolous or vexatious or since the last review there has been no change in circumstances which merit the holding of another review before the twelve month period in head (1) above has passed[11].

With the exception of the requirement to have a review and, if necessary, a revision of a care and treatment plan as provided in head (1) above, a care coordinator need not review a care and treatment plan under any of the above provisions if minor amendments are required to the plan which, in the care coordinator's opinion, it is appropriate to make without a review being carried out[12].

1 As to the meaning of 'care and treatment plan' see PARA 855 note 17.

2 Mental Health (Care Co-ordination and Care and Treatment Planning) (Wales) Regulations 2011, SI 2011/2942, reg 7(1). As to the provision of copies where a relevant patient's care coordinator reviewed or revised a care and treatment plan for a relevant patient as provided by reg 7 or 11 see reg 8. As to the delivery of copies see reg 9.

3 This is subject to the Mental Health (Care Co-ordination and Care and Treatment Planning) (Wales) Regulations 2011, SI 2011/2942, reg 11 (transitional provisions).

4 Mental Health (Care Co-ordination and Care and Treatment Planning) (Wales) Regulations 2011, SI 2011/2942, reg 7(2)(a).

5 As to the meaning of 'relevant patient' see PARA 851 note 2.

6 Mental Health (Care Co-ordination and Care and Treatment Planning) (Wales) Regulations 2011, SI 2011/2942, reg 7(2)(b).

7 As to the meanings of 'carer' and 'adult placement carer' see PARA 859 note 9.

8 Mental Health (Care Co-ordination and Care and Treatment Planning) (Wales) Regulations 2011, SI 2011/2942, reg 7(2)(c).

9 Ie for the purposes of the Mental Health (Wales) Measure 2010 Pt 2 (ss 12–18).

10 Mental Health (Care Co-ordination and Care and Treatment Planning) (Wales) Regulations 2011, SI 2011/2942, reg 7(2)(d).

11 Mental Health (Care Co-ordination and Care and Treatment Planning) (Wales) Regulations 2011, SI 2011/2942, reg 7(3).

12 Mental Health (Care Co-ordination and Care and Treatment Planning) (Wales) Regulations 2011, SI 2011/2942, reg 7(4).

858. Information for persons ceasing to be relevant patients. An individual who is discharged from secondary mental health services must be provided in writing with the reason for his discharge and, if that individual considers that further support and advice in relation to his mental health is required following discharge, the action which may be taken, and by whom[1].

An adult must be provided with information in writing regarding his entitlement to an assessment[2] of former users of secondary mental health services[3].

Where an individual is discharged from secondary mental health services as a child but becomes an adult during the relevant discharge period the following information must be provided in writing:

(1)   information on his entitlement on reaching the age of eighteen years to an assessment[4];

(2)   an explanation of how his or her eighteenth birthday is relevant for the purposes entitlement to such an assessment[5]; and

(3)   the length of the relevant discharge period which is unexpired at the individual's eighteenth birthday[6].

1 See the Mental Health (Care Co-ordination and Care and Treatment Planning) (Wales) Regulations 2011, SI 2011/2942, reg 10(1). Information other than that which must be provided in accordance with reg 10(1), (2) and (3) may be given to the individual on his or her discharge from secondary mental health services: reg 10(4). Where a local health board discharges an individual from secondary mental health services, the Board must provide that individual with information in accordance with reg 10(1), (2), (3) and (4) if, at the date of discharge, no local authority is providing that individual with a secondary mental health service: reg 10(5). Where a local authority discharges an individual from secondary mental health services, the authority must provide that individual with information in accordance with reg 10(1), (2), (3) and (4) if, at the date of discharge, no local health board is providing that individual with a secondary mental health service: reg 10(6).

2 Ie an assessment under the Mental Health (Wales) Measure 2010 Pt 3 (ss 19–30).

3 Mental Health (Care Co-ordination and Care and Treatment Planning) (Wales) Regulations 2011, SI 2011/2942, reg 10(2).

4 Mental Health (Care Co-ordination and Care and Treatment Planning) (Wales) Regulations 2011, SI 2011/2942, reg 10(3)(a). The assessment mentioned in the text is an assessment under the Mental Health (Wales) Measure 2010 Pt 3 (ss 19–30).

5 Mental Health (Care Co-ordination and Care and Treatment Planning) (Wales) Regulations 2011, SI 2011/2942, reg 10(3)(b).

6 Mental Health (Care Co-ordination and Care and Treatment Planning) (Wales) Regulations 2011, SI 2011/2942, reg 10(3)(c).

(12) HOSPITAL AND GUARDIANSHIP ORDERS BY CRIMINAL COURTS

859. General effect of the legislation. The criminal courts[1] have powers under the Mental Health Act 1983[2] to order that an offender be admitted to hospital or placed under guardianship. If the Crown Court[3] finds upon the appropriate medical evidence[4] that an offender is suffering from mental disorder[5] of a nature or degree which warrants hospital treatment and appropriate medical treatment is available for him, it may authorise by order his admission to and detention in hospital for that purpose[6], either with or without a restriction order[7]. On appropriate medical evidence that an offender is suffering from mental disorder and that there is reason to suppose that a hospital order may be appropriate in his case, the court may make an interim hospital order[8]. The Crown Court also has power, upon medical evidence, to remand an accused person to hospital either for a report upon his medical condition[9] or for medical treatment[10].

A magistrates' court may remand an accused person to hospital for a report, and may make a hospital order[11] or interim hospital order on similar evidence[12], but may not remand an accused person for medical treatment or make a restriction order; an offender may, however, be committed to the Crown Court with a view to that court's making a hospital order accompanied by a restriction order if that court thinks proper[13]. In addition, if a magistrates' court is satisfied that the accused did the act or made the omission charged but considers that there ought to be an inquiry into his mental condition, it must adjourn the case for an examination and report to be made and remand him in custody or on bail and in the latter case require the accused to undergo medical examination by two registered medical practitioners[14] and for that purpose attend any relevant institution or place and comply with relevant directions[15].

Both the Crown Court and a magistrates' court may, on the appropriate medical evidence, make an order placing an offender under the guardianship of a local social services authority[16] or person approved by that authority[17].

Alternatively, the court may deal with the offender in any other suitable manner[18], leaving the local social services authority to make arrangements for his informal or compulsory admission to hospital, reception into guardianship or informal care in the community[19].

1   As to criminal courts see COURTS AND TRIBUNALS; CRIMINAL PROCEDURE; SENTENCING AND DISPOSITION OF OFFENDERS. See also MAGISTRATES.
2   Ie the Mental Health Act 1983 Pt 3 (ss 35–55): see the text and PARA 860 et seq.
3   As to the Crown Court see COURTS AND TRIBUNALS vol 24 (2010) PARA 716 et seq.
4   As to the general requirements for medical evidence see PARA 865.
5   As to the meaning of mental disorder see PARA 761.
6   See the Mental Health Act 1983 s 37(1), (2); and PARA 877. These orders are referred to as 'hospital orders': see ss 37(4), 145(1); and PARA 864. As to hospital orders see PARA 864 et seq; and SENTENCING AND DISPOSITION OF OFFENDERS vol 92 (2010) PARA 332.
    A conditionally discharged patient may be lawfully detained under the Mental Health Act 1983 s 3, notwithstanding that he remains liable to detention under s 37: *R v North West London Mental Health NHS Trust, ex p Stewart* [1998] QB 628, [1997] 4 All ER 871, CA.
7   Ie under the Mental Health Act 1983 s 41(1). As to restriction orders see PARA 869 et seq; and SENTENCING AND DISPOSITION OF OFFENDERS vol 92 (2010) PARA 337. See further *R v Welsh* [2011] EWCA Crim 73[2011] 2 Cr App Rep (S) 399, [2011] Crim LR 421; and PARA 864 note 13. As to sentencing see also *R v Sweeney* [2010] EWCA Crim 2355; *R v Wood* [2009] EWCA Crim 651, [2010] 1 Cr App Rep (S) 6, [2009] Crim LR 543; and SENTENCING AND DISPOSITION OF OFFENDERS.
8   See the Mental Health Act 1983 s 38(1); and PARA 864. As to interim hospital orders see PARA 864; and SENTENCING AND DISPOSITION OF OFFENDERS vol 92 (2010) PARA 334.

9　See the Mental Health Act 1983 s 35(1); and PARA 862. As to the meaning of 'medical treatment' see PARA 926. As to remand to hospital for report see PARA 862; and SENTENCING AND DISPOSITION OF OFFENDERS vol 92 (2010) PARA 335.

10　See the Mental Health Act 1983 s 36(1); and PARA 862. As to remand to hospital for treatment see PARA 862; and SENTENCING AND DISPOSITION OF OFFENDERS vol 92 (2010) PARA 336.

11　Where the court is satisfied that the defendant is suffering from mental disorder and did the act or made the omission charged it may make a hospital order without convicting him: see the Mental Health Act 1983 s 37(3); and PARA 871.

12　This order can only be made following a conviction: see the Mental Health Act 1983 s 38(1); and PARA 864.

13　See the Mental Health Act 1983 ss 37(1), 43(1); and PARA 877. As to committal to the Crown Court for a restriction order see PARA 873.

14　As to registered medical practitioners see MEDICAL PROFESSIONS vol 74 (2011) PARA 176 et seq.

15　See the Powers of Criminal Courts (Sentencing) Act 2000 s 11; and CRIMINAL PROCEDURE vol 27 (2010) PARA 261.

16　As to the local social services authority see PARA 579.

17　See the Mental Health Act 1983 s 37(1); and PARA 877. Such orders are referred to as 'guardianship orders': see ss 37(6), 145(1). As to guardianship orders see PARAS 877–878; and SENTENCING AND DISPOSITION OF OFFENDERS vol 92 (2010) PARA 332.

18　In any other case where an offender is or appears to be mentally disordered, depending on the circumstances the court has duties to consider a medical report, any other relevant information relating to his mental condition and the likely effect of any sentence on any condition or treatment before passing a custodial sentence other than one fixed by law: see the Criminal Justice Act 2003 s 157; and SENTENCING AND DISPOSITION OF OFFENDERS vol 92 (2010) PARA 627. See also s 156.

19　Guidance on provision for mentally disordered offenders is given in Home Office Circular 66/90. Its purpose is to draw the attention of the courts and those services responsible for dealing with mentally disordered persons who commit, or are suspected of committing, criminal offences to: (1) the legal powers which exist; and (2) the desirability of ensuring effective co-operation between agencies to ensure that the best use is made of resources and that mentally disordered persons are not prosecuted where this is not required by the public interest. See also Home Office Circular 12/95 Inter Agency Working. See also the Code for Crown Prosecutors (2010) which sets out factors for and against the prosecution of mentally disordered offenders and the circumstances in which the Crown Prosecution Service will consider diversion out of the criminal justice system. As to the prosecution of mentally disordered offenders who threaten or use acts of violence or abuse towards NHS staff see the Memorandum of Understanding between the NHS Counter Fraud and Security Management Service and the Crown Prosecution Service (taking effect July 2008). See also the Ministry of Justice *Legal Guidance: Mentally Disordered Offenders* and the Crown Prosecution Service *Victims and Witnesses who have Mental Health Issues and/or Learning Disabilities – Prosecution Guidance*.

860. Effect of hospital orders, guardianship orders and interim hospital orders. Where an offender is admitted to hospital[1] or placed under guardianship by virtue of a hospital order, a guardianship order or an order or direction having the same effect as such orders[2], he must be treated for the purpose of the general statutory provisions relating to compulsory admission or guardianship[3] as if on the date of the order he had been admitted or placed in pursuance of an application for admission for treatment or a guardianship application[4], but with some exceptions and modifications[5]. These exceptions and modifications are different in the case of hospital orders without restriction orders[6], guardianship orders[7] and orders or directions[8] having the same effect[9], from those in the case of hospital orders with restriction orders[10] and orders or directions[11] having the same effect[12]. This provision[13] does not apply[14] to offenders who are admitted to hospital pursuant to a remand for report[15] or for treatment[16] or an interim hospital order[17].

1　As to the meaning of 'hospital' see PARA 577.
2　As to such orders and directions see PARA 861.
3　Ie the provisions set out in the Mental Health Act 1983 Sch 1.
4　Ie under the Mental Health Act 1983 Pt 2 (ss 2–34).

5   See the Mental Health Act 1983 ss 40(4), 41(3), (5), 55(4), Sch 1; and notes 9, 12. Further, in relation to a person who is liable to be detained or subject to guardianship or a community patient by virtue of an order or direction under Pt 3 (ss 35–55) (other than under s 35 (remand to hospital for report: see PARA 862), s 36 (remand to hospital for treatment: see PARA 862) or s 38 (interim hospital orders: see PARA 864)), any reference in the Act to any enactment contained in Pt II or in s 66 or s 67 (see PARA 961 et seq) is to be construed as a reference to that enactment as it applies to that person by virtue of Pt 3: s 145(3) (amended by the Mental Health Act 2007 Sch 3 para 34(4)).

6   Ie orders having effect under the Mental Health Act 1983 ss 37, 40: see PARAS 877–878.

7   Ie orders having effect under the Mental Health Act 1983 ss 37, 40: see PARAS 877–878.

8   As to such orders and directions generally see PARA 861.

9   In these cases: (1) the following provisions of the Mental Health Act 1983 apply without modification: s 9 (regulations as to guardianship: see PARA 790); s 10 (transfer of guardianship: see PARAS 794–796); s 17 (leave of absence from hospital: see PARA 917); s 17A (community treatment orders: see PARA 797); s 17B (conditions: see PARA 800); s 17C (duration of community treatment orders: see PARA 799), 17E (power to recall to hospital: see PARA 801); s 17F (powers in respect of recalled patients: see PARA 802), 20A (community treatment period: see PARA 799) and ss 21A, 21B (special provisions as to patients absent without leave: see PARA 911); s 26 (definition of 'relative': see PARA 838); s 27 (children and young persons in care: see PARA 839); s 28 (nearest relative of a minor under guardianship: see PARA 839); s 31 (procedure on application to a county court: see PARA 846); s 32 (power to make regulations: see PARA 766); s 34 (interpretation); s 67 (power to refer to the appropriate tribunal: see PARA 965); s 76 (visiting and examination of patients: see PARA 963); (2) the following provisions apply with modification: s 17D (effect of community treatment order: see PARA 798); s 17G (effect of revoking community treatment order: see PARA 803); s 18 (return and readmission of patients absent without leave: see PARA 918); s 19 (regulations as to transfer of patients: see PARAS 886–889); s 20 (duration of authority: see PARAS 908–910); s 22 (special provisions as to patients sentenced etc: see PARA 912); s 23 (discharge of patients: see PARA 913); s 66 (applications to tribunals: see PARA 961); s 68 (duty of managers of hospitals to refer cases to tribunals: see PARA 964); (3) the remaining provisions of Pt 2 do not apply: see the Mental Health Act 1983 s 40(4), Sch 1 Pt I (amended by the Mental Health (Patients in the Community) Act 1995 ss 1(2), 2(8), Sch 1 paras 6, 14; the Mental Health Act 2007 ss 36(4), 37(6), Sch 3 para 36(2), (3), Sch 11 Pts 1, 5; and the Health and Social Care Act 2012 s 39(3)(a)).

10   Ie orders having effect under the Mental Health Act 1983 s 41: see PARA 869.

11   As to such orders and directions generally see PARA 861.

12   In these cases: (1) the following provisions apply without modification: s 32 (regulations: see PARA 766); s 76 (visiting and examination of patients and inspection of records: see PARAS 916, 963); (2) the following provisions apply with modification: s 17 (leave of absence: see PARA 917); s 18 (return and readmission of patients absent without leave: see PARA 918); s 19 (regulations as to transfer of patients: see PARAS 886–889); s 22 (special provisions as to patients sentenced to imprisonment etc: see PARA 912); s 23 (discharge of patients: see PARA 913); s 34 (definitions); and (3) the remaining provisions of Pt II do not apply: see the Mental Health Act 1983 ss 40(4), 41(3), (5) (s 41(3) amended by the Mental Health (Patients in the Community) Act 1995 s 1(2), Sch 1 para 5; and the Crime (Sentences) Act 1997 s 49(2)); and the Mental Health Act 1983 Sch 1 Pt II (amended by the Mental Health (Patients in the Community) Act 1995 s 3(2); the Crime (Sentences) Act 1997 ss 49(4), 56(2), Sch 6; and the Health and Social Care Act 2012 s 39(3)(b)).

13   Ie the Mental Health Act 1983 s 40(4).

14   Ie because the provisions listed do not provide that remands and orders made under them are to have the same effect as a hospital order; they are not, therefore, included in the Mental Health Act 1983 s 40(4) by virtue of s 55(4). See also note 5.

15   Ie under the Mental Health Act 1983 s 35: see PARA 862.

16   Ie under the Mental Health Act 1983 s 36: see PARA 862.

17   Ie under the Mental Health Act 1983 s 38: see PARA 864.

861. Effect of transfer and restriction directions. Transfer directions by the appropriate national authority[1] for the removal to hospital[2] of persons serving sentences, or other prisoners[3], have the same effect as hospital orders[4] made in such cases[5]. Restriction directions by the appropriate national authority restricting the discharge of prisoners removed to hospital[6] have the same effect as restriction orders[7] made in such cases[8]. Orders by magistrates' courts directing persons to be admitted to and detained in hospital instead of committing them in custody with a view to a restriction order being made[9] have the same effect as hospital orders together with restriction orders[10], made without limitation of time[11].

Any reference to a hospital order, guardianship order or a restriction order in the provisions of the Mental Health Act 1983 dealing with:

(1)   the effects of hospital orders (but not interim hospital orders) and guardianship orders, other than the provision conferring initial authority to convey the patient and admit him to hospital[12];

(2)   the effects of restriction orders[13];

(3)   the powers of the appropriate national authority in respect of patients subject to restriction orders[14]; and

(4)   rights of application to tribunals[15],

must be construed as including references to any order or direction[16] having the same effect as such orders[17].

Patients detained pursuant to orders or directions in other parts of the United Kingdom[18] who are removed and admitted to hospitals in England and Wales[19] are to be treated as if admitted in pursuance of an order or direction made on the date of their admission under the corresponding enactment in England and Wales[20].

1   As to the appropriate national authority see PARA 567.
2   As to the meaning of 'hospital' see PARA 577.
3   Ie directions under the Mental Health Act 1983 ss 47, 48: see PARAS 892–893.
4   See the Mental Health Act 1983 s 55(4); and note 17.
5   See the Mental Health Act 1983 ss 47(3), 48(3); and PARAS 892–893.
6   Ie directions under the Mental Health Act 1983 s 49(1): see PARA 894.
7   Ie orders made under the Mental Health Act 1983 s 41: see PARA 869.
8   Mental Health Act 1983 s 49(2).
9   Ie orders under the Mental Health Act 1983 s 44: see PARA 873.
10 Ie orders made under the Mental Health Act 1983 s 41: see PARA 869.
11 Mental Health Act 1983 s 44(3). See notes 9–10. Where there is no space immediately available, the court can make directions to convey the person to a place of safety: see s 37(5); and PARA 868.
12 Ie under the Mental Health Act 1983 s 40(2), (4), (5): see PARAS 867, 878.
13 Ie under the Mental Health Act 1983 s 41(3)–(5): see PARAS 869–870.
14 Ie under the Mental Health Act 1983 s 42: see PARAS 876, 914.
15 Ie under the Mental Health Act 1983 s 69(1): see PARA 961.
16 Ie under the Mental Health Act 1983 Pt 3 (ss 35–55).
17 Mental Health Act 1983 s 55(4). The exceptions and modifications set out in Sch 1 (see PARA 860 text and notes 9, 12) accordingly include those which are consequential on this provision: s 55(4).
18 As to the meaning of 'United Kingdom' see PARA 560 note 14.
19 As to the meanings of 'England' and 'Wales' see PARA 557 notes 4, 5.
20 See the Mental Health Act 1983 ss 82, 85(2); the Mental Health (Care and Treatment) (Scotland) Act 2003 ss 289, 290; the Mental Health (Care and Treatment) (Scotland) Act 2003 (Consequential Provisions) Order 2005, SI 2005/2078 (S 9); and PARAS 904–905.

862.   Remand to hospital for report or for treatment. The Crown Court[1] or a magistrates' court[2] may remand an accused person[3] to a hospital[4] specified by the court for a report on his mental condition if: (1) the court is satisfied, on the evidence of a registered medical practitioner[5], that there is reason to suspect that the accused is suffering from mental disorder[6]; and (2) the court is of the opinion that it would be impracticable for a report on his mental condition to be made if he were remanded on bail[7].

The Crown Court may, instead of remanding an accused person[8] in custody, remand him to a hospital specified by the court if satisfied, on the written or oral evidence of two registered medical practitioners[9], that he is suffering from mental disorder of a nature or degree which makes it appropriate for him to be detained in a hospital for medical treatment and appropriate medical treatment is available for him[10].

The court must not remand an accused person to hospital for report[11] or for treatment[12] unless it is satisfied, on the written or oral evidence of the approved clinician[13] who would have overall responsibility for his case, or of some other person representing the managers[14] of the hospital, that arrangements have been made for his admission to that hospital within the period of seven days beginning with the date of the remand[15]. If the court is so satisfied, it may give directions for his conveyance to and detention in a place of safety[16] pending his admission to hospital[17].

Where a court has remanded an accused person to hospital for report or for treatment, it may further remand him[18] if it appears to the court: (a) on the written or oral evidence of the registered medical practitioner responsible for making the report, that a further remand is necessary for the purpose of completing the assessment of the accused person's mental condition[19]; or (b) on the written or oral evidence of the responsible clinician[20], that a further remand is warranted[21].

An accused person may not be remanded for report or for treatment for more than 28 days at a time or for more than 12 weeks in all and the court may at any time terminate the remand if it appears to the court appropriate to do so[22]. A person remanded to hospital is entitled to obtain at his own expense an independent report on his mental condition from a registered medical practitioner or approved clinician chosen by him and to apply on the basis of that report for his remand to be terminated[23].

If an accused person remanded for report or for treatment absconds from the hospital to which he has been remanded, or while being conveyed to or from that hospital, he may be arrested without warrant by any constable[24] and must as soon as practicable thereafter be brought before the court which remanded him, which may thereupon terminate the remand and deal with him in any way in which it could have dealt with him had he not been remanded to hospital under these provisions[25].

Remands to hospital under these provisions do not have the same effect as hospital orders[26], nor are the persons remanded to be treated as if a hospital order had been made[27]. Accordingly, the other provisions of the Mental Health Act 1983 which apply to hospital order patients do not apply to them[28]. The provisions of the Act concerning consent to treatment apply to persons remanded for treatment, but not to those remanded for report[29].

1   As to the Crown Court see COURTS AND TRIBUNALS vol 24 (2010) PARA 716 et seq.
2   As to magistrates' courts see MAGISTRATES vol 71 (2013) PARA 470 et seq.

3   For these purposes, 'accused person' means: (1) in relation to the Crown Court, any person who is awaiting trial before the court for an offence punishable with imprisonment or who has been arraigned before the court for such an offence and has not yet been sentenced or otherwise dealt with for that offence, but not a person who has been convicted before the court if the sentence for the offence for which he has been convicted is fixed by law; and (2) in relation to a magistrates' court, any person who has been convicted by the court of an offence punishable on summary conviction with imprisonment and any person charged with such an offence if the court is satisfied that he did the act or made the omission charged or has consented to the exercise by the court of the powers conferred by the Mental Health Act 1983 s 35: s 35(2), (3) (amended by the Mental Health Act 2007 Sch 1 para 5).

4 As to the meaning of 'hospital', which does not include a prison hospital, see PARA 577.

5 The registered medical practitioner must be approved for the purposes of the Mental Health Act 1983 s 12 (see PARA 849): see s 54(1); and PARA 865. As to registered medical practitioners see MEDICAL PROFESSIONS vol 74 (2011) PARA 176 et seq.

6 As to the meaning of 'mental disorder' see PARA 761.

7 Mental Health Act 1983 s 35(1), (3) (s 35(3) amended by the Mental Health Act 2007 Sch 7 para 5). As to bail generally see CRIMINAL PROCEDURE vol 27 (2010) PARA 66–109. As to the corresponding powers in the Criminal Courts (Sentencing) Act 2000 s 11 and the Criminal Justice Act 2003 s 157 see PARA 859.

8 For these purposes, 'accused person' means any person who is in custody awaiting trial before the Crown Court for an offence punishable with imprisonment (other than an offence the sentence for which is fixed by law) or who at any time before sentence is in custody in the course of a trial before that court for such an offence: Mental Health Act 1983 s 36(2).

9 One of those practitioners must be approved for the purposes of the Mental Health Act 1983 s 12 (see PARA 849): see s 54(1); and PARA 865.

10 Mental Health Act 1983 s 36(1) (amended by the Mental Health Act 2007 s 5(2), Sch 1 para 6). As to the meaning of 'medical treatment' see PARA 926. The alternative of a remand in custody during which the appropriate national authority may exercise the power to direct a transfer to hospital under s 48 (see PARA 893) may in certain circumstances (eg if the trial is to be long delayed) be more appropriate. Section 36 is an alternative to the 'unfit to plead' procedure under the Criminal Procedure (Insanity) Act 1964 (see CRIMINAL PROCEDURE). In some circumstances a remand for treatment under section 36 can render the defendant fit to plead and stand trial: see Home Office Circular 71/1984.

11 Ie under the Mental Health Act 1983 s 35(1): see the text and note 7.

12 Ie under the Mental Health Act 1983 s 36(1): see the text and note 10.

13 As to the 'approved clinician' see PARA 831.

14 As to the meaning of 'managers' see PARA 778.

15 Mental Health Act 1983 ss 35(4), 36(3) (both amended by the Mental Health Act 2007 s 10). See *R (on the application of Bitcon) v West Allderdale Magistrates' Court* [2003] EWHC 2460 (Admin), 147 Sol Jo LB 1028 (confirmation that the court was correct to revoke its own order under the Mental Health Act 1983 s 35 as being ultra vires when funding fell through and arrangements for admission could not be fulfilled; advice given on the procedure to be undertaken before an order is made under s 35).

16 As to the meaning of 'place of safety' for this purpose see PARA 868 note 4.

17 Mental Health Act 1983 ss 35(4), 36(3). Where a person is remanded under s 35 or s 36, a constable or other person directed to do so by the court must convey the person to the hospital within the seven day period and the managers must admit him within that period and thereafter detain him in accordance with the relevant provision: ss 35(9), 36(8). Ensuring production of the patient at subsequent court appearances is the responsibility of hospital managers: see Home Office Circular 71/84.

18 The power of further remand may be exercised without bringing the accused before the court if he is represented by an authorised person who is given an opportunity to be heard: Mental Health Act 1983 ss 35(6), 36(5) (both amended by the Mental Health Act 2007 Sch 21 paras 54, 55). 'Authorised person' means a person who, for the purposes of the Legal Services Act 2007, is an authorised person in relation to an activity which constitutes the exercise of a right of audience (within the meaning of that Act) (see LEGAL PROFESSIONS vol 65 (2008) PARA 412): Mental Health Act 1983 s 55(1) (definition added by Legal Services Act 2007 Sch 21 para 59).

19 Mental Health Act 1983 s 35(5).

20 As to the meaning of 'responsible clinician' see PARA 834.

21 Mental Health Act 1983 s 36(4) (amended by the Mental Health Act 2007 s 10(2)).

22 Mental Health Act 1983 ss 35(7), 36(6). As to the powers of the relevant judicial authority (following breach of orders) to remand in custody under the Family Law Act 1996 for medical reports where there is reason to suspect mental illness or severe mental impairment see s 48; and MATRIMONIAL AND CIVIL PARTNERSHIP LAW vol 73 (2009) PARA 994.

23 Mental Health Act 1983 ss 35(8), 36(7) (both amended by the Mental Health Act 2007 s 10(2), (3)).

24 As to the office of constable see POLICE vol 36(1) (2007 Reissue) PARA 101 et seq.

25 Mental Health Act 1983 ss 35(10), 36(8).

26 As to hospital orders see PARA 864 et seq.

27 Cf the provisions discussed in PARA 861.

28 Cf PARA 860.

29 See PARA 924.

863. Hospital and limitation directions. Where, in the case of a person convicted before the Crown Court[1] of an offence the sentence for which is not fixed by law: (1) the court is satisfied, on the written or oral evidence of two registered medical practitioners[2], that: (a) the offender is suffering from mental disorder[3]; (b) the mental disorder from which the offender is suffering is of a nature or degree which makes it appropriate for him to be detained in a hospital[4] for medical treatment; and (c) that appropriate medical treatment is available for him[5]; and (2) the court considers making a hospital order in respect of him before deciding to impose a sentence of imprisonment ('the relevant sentence') in respect of the offence[6], the court may give both of the following directions[7]. It may give a direction that, instead of being removed to and detained in a prison, the offender be removed to and detained in such hospital as may be specified in the direction (a 'hospital direction')[8], and a direction that the offender be subject to special restrictions (a 'limitation direction')[9].

A hospital direction and a limitation direction must not be given in relation to an offender unless at least one of the medical practitioners whose evidence is taken into account by the court has given evidence orally before the court[10]. A hospital direction and a limitation direction must not be given in relation to an offender unless the court is satisfied on the written or oral evidence of the approved clinician[11] who would have overall responsibility for his case, or of some other person representing the managers[12] of the hospital that arrangements have been made for his admission to that hospital, and for his admission to it within the period of 28 days beginning with the day of the giving of such directions[13]. Pending his admission within that period, the court may give such directions as it thinks fit for his conveyance to and detention in a place of safety[14]. If within that period of 28 days it appears to the Secretary of State that by reason of an emergency or other special circumstances it is not practicable for the patient[15] to be received into the hospital specified in the hospital direction, he may give instructions for the admission of the patient to such other hospital as appears to be appropriate instead of the hospital so specified[16]. Where such instructions are given, the appropriate national authority[17] must cause the person having the custody of the patient to be informed, and the hospital direction has effect as if the hospital specified in the instructions were substituted for the hospital specified in the hospital direction[18].

A hospital direction and a limitation direction given in relation to an offender have effect not only as regards the relevant sentence but also (so far as applicable) as regards any other sentence of imprisonment imposed on the same or a previous occasion[19].

A hospital direction and a limitation direction are sufficient authority for a constable[20] or any other person directed to do so by the court to convey the patient to the hospital specified in the hospital direction within a period of 28 days, and for the managers of the hospital to admit him at any time within that period and thereafter detain him under the Mental Health Act 1983[21].

With respect to any person, a hospital direction has effect as a transfer direction[22], and a limitation direction has effect as a restriction direction[23]. While a person is subject to a hospital direction and a limitation direction, the responsible clinician must, at such intervals (not exceeding one year) as the appropriate national authority may direct, examine and report to the authority on that person; and every report must contain such particulars as the authority may require[24].

1   As to the Crown Court see COURTS AND TRIBUNALS vol 24 (2010) PARA 716 et seq.

2 As to registered medical practitioners see MEDICAL PROFESSIONS vol 74 (2011) PARA 176 et seq.

3 As to the meaning of 'mental disorder' see PARA 761. The purpose of the power in the Mental Health Act 1983 s 45A is explained in Home Office Circular 52/97. The power to impose the 'hybrid' sentence under s 45A is justified where although the defendant was suffering from a mental disorder criminal culpability had clearly not been wholly absent: see *R v Fox (Wayne Anthony)* [2011] EWCA 3299. Note that this power cannot be used for defendants under the age of 21 as it is a sentence of imprisonment: *AG's ref (no 54 of 2011)* [2011] EWCA Crim 2276.

4 As to the meaning of 'hospital' see PARA 577.

5 Mental Health Act 1983 s 45A(1)(a), (2) (s 45A added by the Crime (Sentences) Act 1997 s 4; the Mental Health Act 1983 s 45A(2) amended by the Mental Health Act 2007 s 4(6), Sch 1 para 9). As to the meaning of 'medical treatment' see PARA 926.

6 Mental Health Act 1983 s 45A(1)(b) (as added (see note 5); and amended by the Criminal Justice Act 2003 ss 304, 332, Sch 32 Pt I paras 37, 39, Sch 37 Pt 7).

7 Mental Health Act 1983 s 45A(3) (as added: see note 5).

8 Mental Health Act 1983 s 45A(3)(a) (as added: see note 5); s 145(1) (definition added by the Crime (Sentences) Act 1997 s 56, Sch 4 para 12(19)(a)). Any power to specify a hospital conferred by the Mental Health Act 1983 s 45A includes power to specify a hospital unit; and where such a unit is specified in relation to any person in the exercise of such a power, any reference in any enactment (including one contained in the Crime (Sentences) Act 1997) to him being, or being liable to be, detained in a hospital must be construed accordingly: s 47(1)(b).

9 Mental Health Act 1983 s 45A(3)(b) (as added: see note 5); s 145(1) (definition added by the Crime (Sentences) Act 1997 Sch 4 para 12(19)(b)). Reference is made in the Mental Health Act 1983 s 45A(3)(b) to the special restrictions set out in s 41 (see PARA 869).

10 Mental Health Act 1983 s 45A(4) (as added: see note 5).

11 As to the meaning of 'approved clinician' see PARA 831.

12 As to the meaning of 'managers' see PARA 778.

13 Mental Health Act 1983 s 45A(5) (as added (see note 5); amended by the Mental Health Act 2007 s 10(8)).

14 See note 13.

15 As to the meaning of 'patient' see PARA 758 note 4.

16 Mental Health Act 1983 s 45A(6) (as added: see note 5).

17 As to the 'appropriate national authority' see PARA 567.

18 Mental Health Act 1983 s 45A(7) (as added: see note 5).

19 Mental Health Act 1983 s 45A(9) (as added: see note 5).

20 As to the office of constable see POLICE vol 36(1) (2007 Reissue) PARA 101 et seq.

21 Mental Health Act 1983 s 45B(1) (s 45B added by the Crime (Sentences) Act 1997 s 46).

22 As to transfers see PARA 892 et seq.

23 Mental Health Act 1983 s 45B(2) (as added: see note 21). As to restriction directions see PARA 894.

24 Mental Health Act 1983 s 45B(3) (as added (see note 21); amended by the Mental Health Act 2007 s 10(9)(a)).

864. Hospital orders and interim hospital orders. Where a person is convicted before the Crown Court[1] of an offence punishable with imprisonment[2], or is convicted by a magistrates' court[3] of an offence punishable on summary conviction with imprisonment[4], the court may make an order (a 'hospital order')[5] authorising his admission to and detention in a hospital[6] specified[7] in the order, if the following conditions are fulfilled[8]:

(1) the court is satisfied on the written or oral evidence of two registered medical practitioners[9] that the offender is suffering from mental disorder[10], and that the mental disorder is of a nature or degree which warrants the detention of the patient in a hospital for medical treatment[11]; and appropriate medical treatment is available for him[12]; and

(2) the court is of the opinion, having regard to all the circumstances, including the nature of the offence and the character antecedents of the

offender and to the other available methods of dealing with him, that the most suitable method of disposing of the case is by means of a hospital order[13].

The object of the order, where punishment is not intended, is that the defendant should receive treatment and be at large as soon as he can safely be discharged[14] and the matter should not be left to be dealt with by the appropriate national authority[15] under powers of removal to a hospital of a person under sentence[16].

Where a person is so convicted[17], the court may, before making a hospital order or dealing with him in some other way, make an order (an 'interim hospital order')[18] authorising his admission to and detention in a hospital specified by the court, if the court is satisfied[19] that the offender is suffering from mental disorder and that there is reason to suppose that the mental disorder from which the offender is suffering is such that it may be appropriate for a hospital order to be made in his case[20]. An interim hospital order is in force for the period, not exceeding 12 weeks, which is specified by the court when making the order, but may be renewed[21], on the written or oral evidence of the approved clinician who would have overall responsibility for the offender's case[22], that its continuation is warranted, for further periods of not more than 28 days at a time[23]. However, no such order can be in force for more than 12 months in all and the court must terminate the order if it makes a hospital order[24] or decides[25] to deal with the offender in some other way[26].

No hospital order or interim hospital order may be made unless the court is satisfied, on the written or oral evidence of the approved clinician who has overall responsibility for the offender's case or of some other person representing the managers of the hospital[27], that arrangements have been made for the admission of the offender to that hospital, and for that admission to take place within a period of 28 days beginning with the date of the making of the order[28].

Where a court is minded to make a hospital order[29] or an interim hospital order, it may request the primary care trust[30] or local health board[31] for the area in which the person concerned resides or last resided, or the National Assembly for Wales or any other primary care trust or local health board that appears to it to be appropriate, to furnish the court with information[32] with respect to the hospital or hospitals, if any, in its area or elsewhere at which arrangements could be made for the admission of that person in pursuance of the order; the primary care trust or health authority must comply with such a request[33].

1   As to the Crown Court see COURTS AND TRIBUNALS vol 24 (2010) PARA 716 et seq.

2   Ie other than an offence the sentence for which is fixed by law.

    In the case of an offence the sentence for which would otherwise fall to be imposed:

(1)   under the Firearms Act 1968 s 51A(2) (see CRIMINAL LAW vol 26 (2010) PARA 616);

(2)   under the Powers of Criminal Courts (Sentencing) Act 2000 s 110(2) or s 111(2) (see CRIMINAL LAW vol 25 (2010) PARA 290; CRIMINAL LAW vol 26 (2010) PARA 725);

(3)   under any of the Criminal Justice Act 2003 ss 225–228 (see SENTENCING AND DISPOSITION OF OFFENDERS vol 92 (2010) PARAS 73–75, 82, 84); or

(4)   under the Violent Crime Reduction Act 2006 s 29(4) or (6) (see CRIMINAL LAW vol 26 (2010) PARA 656),

nothing in those provisions prevents a court from making an order under the Mental Health Act 1983 s 37(1) for the admission of the offender to a hospital: s 37(1A) (s 37(1A), (1B) added by the Criminal Justice Act 2003 Sch 32 Pt 1 paras 37, 38(b); and the Violent Crime Reduction Act 2006 Sch 1 para 2). As from a day to be appointed head (3) above is amended by to apply to the Criminal Justice Act 2003 ss 225(2)–226(2) by the Criminal Justice and Immigration Act 2008 Sch 26 para 8 and the Mental Health Act 1983 s 37(1A) is amended by the Legal Aid, Sentencing and Punishment of Offenders 2012 Sch 19 para 1, Sch 26 para 2(2), (3) and in the case of an offence the sentence for which would also fall to be imposed, (a) under the Prevention of Crime Act 1953 s 1A(5); (b) under the Criminal Justice Act 1988 s 139AA(7); (c) under the Criminal Justice Act 2003 s 224A, nothing in those provisions prevents a court from making an order under the Mental Health Act 1983 s 37(1) for the admission of the offender to a hospital. At the date at which this volume states the law no such days had been appointed.

References in the Mental Health Act 1983 s 37(1A) to a sentence falling to be imposed under any of the provisions there mentioned are to be read in accordance with the Criminal Justice Act 2003 s 305(4) (see SENTENCING AND DISPOSITION OF OFFENDERS vol 92 (2010) PARA 19): Mental Health Act 1983 s 37(1B) (as so added).

For guidance on the Secretary of State's jurisdiction to decide whether to treat a prisoner as if he had been made the subject of a hospital order under the Mental Health Act 1983 s 37 and as to the possible effects of 'technical lifer' status see *R (on the application of R) v Shetty (Responsible Medical Officer)* [2003] EWHC 3152 (Admin), (2004) Times, 9 January. As to 'technical lifer' status see PARA 894 note 8.

3 As to the making of a hospital order by a magistrates' court see the Mental Health Act 1983 s 37(3); and PARA 871.

4 The reference to an offence punishable on summary conviction with imprisonment must be construed without regard to any prohibition or restriction imposed by or under any enactment on the imprisonment of young offenders: Mental Health Act 1983 s 55(2).

5 Mental Health Act 1983 s 37(4). 'Hospital order' has the meaning given in s 37 (see ss 37(4), 145(1)), and includes a reference to any order or direction having the same effect (see s 55(4)). The order constitutes the authority for the patient's admission to and detention in hospital: see s 40(1); and PARA 867. A hospital order may be made for admission to a hospital in any part of the country where a vacancy exists: *R v Marsden* [1968] 2 All ER 341, [1968] 1 WLR 785, CA.

6 In the Mental Health Act 1983 Pt 3 (ss 35–55), 'hospital' includes a registered establishment unless the contrary is stated (eg as in s 47(1): see PARA 892 et seq): see PARA 577.

7 Any power to specify a hospital conferred by the Mental Health Act 1983 s 37 includes power to specify a hospital unit; and where such a unit is specified in relation to any person in the exercise of such a power, any reference in any enactment (including one contained in the Crime (Sentences) Act 1997) to him being, or being liable to be, detained in a hospital is to be construed accordingly but this does not apply unless the court also makes an order under the Mental Health Act 1983 s 41 (see PARA 869): Crime (Sentences) Act 1997 s 47(1)(a), (2)(a).

8 Mental Health Act 1983 s 37(1) (amended by the Crime (Sentences) Act 1997 s 55, Sch 4 para 12(1); and the Criminal Justice Act 2003 Sch 32 Pt 1 paras 37, 38(a)).

As to the power of the courts to make hospital orders in the case of persons committed for trial or sentence who have been transferred to hospital by direction under the Mental Health Act 1983 s 48(2)(a) (see PARA 893) where it is impracticable or inappropriate to bring them before the court see s 51(5)(b), (6); and PARA 896. As to the duty of the court to make appropriate orders after a special verdict or findings of disability see the Criminal Procedure (Insanity) Act 1964 ss 5, 5A; PARA 874; and SENTENCING AND DISPOSITION OF OFFENDERS vol 92 (2010) PARAS 332 et seq. As to the power of civil courts to make hospital orders in committal proceedings for contempt of court see the Contempt of Court Act 1981 s 14(4); and CONTEMPT OF COURT vol 22 (2012) PARA 111.

See *A v Harrow Crown Court* [2003] EWHC 2020 (Admin), [2003] All ER (D) 78 (Aug); *R (on the application of G) v Mental Health Review Tribunal* [2004] EWHC 2193 (Admin), [2004] All ER (D) 86 (Oct); *R (on the application of the Secretary of State for the Home Department) v Mental Health Review Tribunal* [2004] EWHC 2194 (Admin), [2004] All ER (D) 87 (Oct). See also *R v Galfetti* [2002] EWCA Crim 1916, [2002] All ER (D) 521 (Jul) (judge not wrong in principle to impose an order nine months after conviction after excessive delay by the health authorities in providing a hospital place).

9 One of the registered medical practitioners must be approved for the purposes of the Mental Health Act 1983 s 12: see s 54(1); and PARA 865.

The preconditions for s 37 are up-to-date medical assessments so that the court is satisfied as to the offender's current medical condition and susceptibility to treatment: *R v Preston* [2003] EWCA Crim 2086.

10 As to the meaning of 'mental disorder' see PARA 761. See *R (on the application of MM) v Secretary of State for the Home Department* [2007] EWCA Civ 687, (2007) 98 BMLR 130.

11 Mental Health Act 1983 s 37(2)(a) (amended by the Mental Health Act 2007 Sch 1 para 7). As to the meaning of 'medical treatment' see PARA 926. For the treatment which may be given see PARAS 924, 927–933.

12 Mental Health Act 1983 s 37(2)(a)(i) (amended by the Mental Health Act 2007 s 4(5)). As to guardianship orders see s 37(2)(a)(ii); and PARA 877.

13 Mental Health Act 1983 s 37(2)(b). A hospital order may be substituted on appeal for a sentence of imprisonment and it is not to be regarded as an increase of sentence, even though its

result may be to subject the appellant to a longer period of detention: *R v Bennett* [1968] 2 All ER 753, [1968] 1 WLR 988, CA. When deciding whether to impose a hospital order the court must bear in mind that defendants made subject to such orders, whether restricted or not, are entitled to be released when the medical conditions justifying their original admissions ceases to be met, and, further, that they are liable to recall only on medical grounds: see *R v Welsh* [2011] EWCA Crim 73, [2011] 2 Cr App Rep (D) 521, [2006] Crim LR 79; and PARA 859 note 7 (hospital order would not adequately protect public from risk posed by schizophrenic defendant in light of previous propensity for violence and gravity of offence). As to applications to the appropriate tribunal by or in respect of persons subject to hospital orders see the Mental Health Act 1983 s 69; and PARA 961.

14 See *R v Morris* [1961] 2 QB 237, [1961] 2 All ER 672, CCA; *R v Cox* [1968] 1 All ER 386, [1968] 1 WLR 308, CA; and cf *R v Gunnell* (1966) 50 Cr App Rep 242, 110 Sol Jo 706, CCA (where, as punishment was intended, a hospital order was refused). See also *Kiernan v Harrow Crown Court* [2003] EWCA Crim 1052 (where it was held that a judge who faced conflicting medical evidence erred in not giving reasons why he preferred the evidence in favour of mental illness, and thus the order was quashed as there was insufficient evidence to justify it; and it was said per curiam that doctors who had interviewed the victims had acted inappropriately as they were not investigators).

15 As to the appropriate national authority see PARA 567.

16 Ie the powers under the Mental Health Act 1983 s 47 (see PARA 892). See *R v A* [2005] EWCA Crim 2077, [2006] 1 Cr App Rep (S) 521, [2006] Crim LR 79 (importance of the safety issue).

17 Ie as set out in the text and notes 2–4.

18 'Interim hospital order' has the meaning given in the Mental Health Act 1983 s 38: ss 38(1), 145(1).

19 Ie on the same medical evidence as is required for a hospital order: see the text and notes 9–12. However, at least one of the medical practitioners whose evidence is taken into account must be employed by the hospital to be specified in the order: Mental Health Act 1983 s 38(3). There are no provisions preventing the medical practitioners from coming from the same hospital.

20 Mental Health Act 1983 s 38(1) (amended by the Mental Health Act 2007 Sch 1 para 8). The provisions of the Mental Health Act 1983 s 38(1), (5) have effect as if any reference to the making of a hospital order included a reference to the giving of a hospital direction and a limitation direction (see PARA 863): Mental Health Act 1983 s 45A(8) (added by the Crime (Sentences) Act 1997 s 46).

21 The power of renewing an interim hospital order may be exercised without the offender's being brought before the court if he is represented by counsel or a solicitor and his counsel or solicitor is given an opportunity of being heard: Mental Health Act 1983 s 38(6).

22 As to the meaning of 'approved clinician' see PARA 831.

23 Mental Health Act 1983 s 38(5) (amended by the Mental Health Act 2007 s 10(5)).

24 The court may make a hospital order in the case of an offender who is subject to an interim hospital order without his being brought before the court if he is represented by an authorised person who is given an opportunity of being heard: Mental Health Act 1983 s 38(2) (amended by the Legal Services Act 2007 Sch 21 para 56). As to the meaning of 'authorised person' see PARA 862 note 18.

25 Ie after considering the written or oral evidence of the responsible clinician: Mental Health Act 1983 s 38(5) (amended by the Mental Health Act 2007 s 10(5)(b)).

26 Mental Health Act 1983 s 38(5) (amended by the Crime (Sentences) Act 1997 s 49(1)).

27 Mental Health Act 1983 ss 37(4), 38(4) (both amended by the Mental Health Act 2007 s 10(4), (5)). As to the meaning of 'managers' see PARA 778.

28 Mental Health Act 1983 ss 37(4), 38(4) (s 37(4) amended by the Crime (Sentences) Act 1997 ss 55, 56(2), Sch 4 para 12(3), Sch 6). The 28 day period is that within which a hospital order or an interim hospital order may be acted on (see the Mental Health Act 1983 s 40(1), (3); and PARA 867), unless the time is enlarged by reason of the offender's escaping (see s 138(5); and PARAS 777, 867). The appropriate national authority may by order reduce the length of the periods mentioned in ss 37(4), (5), 38(4) which may include such consequential amendments of ss 40(1), 44(3) (see PARA 861, 867) as appear necessary or expedient: see s 54A (added by the Criminal Justice Act 1991 s 27(2)). As to the retaking of patients escaped from custody see PARA 777. As to the power to reduce the prescribed period of 28 days see PARA 868 note 5.

Where s 37(4) has not been complied with, justices have a power to rescind the order under the Magistrates' Courts Act 1980 s 142 (see **MAGISTRATES** vol 71 (2013) PARA 596): *R v Thames Magistrates' Court, ex p Ramadan* [1999] 1 Cr App Rep 386, 163 JP 428, DC.

29 In relation to a person who has not attained the age of 18 years, the Mental Health Act 1983 s 39(1) has effect as if the reference to the making of a hospital order includes a reference to a

remand under s 35 or 36 (see PARA 862) or the making of an order under s 44 (see PARA 873): s 39(1A) (s 39(1A), (1B) (added by the Mental Health Act 2007 s 31(2)).

30 As to the meaning of 'primary care trust' see PARA 575 note 5. As from 1 April 2013, the words 'primary care trust' are repealed from s 39 in both places they appear by the Health and Social Care Act 2012 Sch 5 para 28(2) and the Mental Health Act 1983 s 39 is amended so that a court may also request such information as mentioned in the text from the clinical commissioning group for the area in which the person concerned resides or last resided or the National Health Service Commissioning board or any other clinical commissioning group that appears to the court to be appropriate. A request under the Mental Health Act 1983 to the National Health Service Commissioning Board may relate only to services or facilities the provision of which the Board arranges: s 39(1ZA) (added by the Health and Social Care Act 2012 Sch 5 para 28(3): see the Health and Social Care Act 2012 (Commencement No 4, Transitional, Savings and Transitory Provisions) Order 2013, SI 2013/160, art 2(2). As to clinical commissioning groups see PARA 572.

31 As to the meaning of 'local health board' see PARA 575 note 6.

32 Where the person concerned has not attained the age of 18 years, the information which may be requested under the Mental Health Act 1983 s 39(1) includes, in particular, information about the availability of accommodation or facilities designed so as to be specially suitable for patients who have not attained the age of 18 years: s 39(1B) (as added: see note 29).

33 Mental Health Act 1983 s 39(1) (amended by the Health Authorities Act 1995 s 2(1), Sch 1 para 107(1), (5); the National Health Service Reform and Health Care Professions Act 2002 s 2(5), Sch 2 Pt 2 paras 42, 46; SI 2007/961; and prospectively amended (see note 30)).

865. Requirements as to medical evidence. Of the two registered medical practitioners[1] whose written or oral evidence is taken into account[2] by the court in deciding whether to remand to hospital for treatment or make a hospital order or interim hospital order, at least one must be a practitioner approved[3] by the appropriate national authority[4] as having special experience in the diagnosis or treatment of mental disorders[5]. The registered medical practitioner whose evidence is taken into account[6] in deciding whether to remand to hospital for a report[7] must be such a practitioner[8]. Where[9] the court may act on the written evidence of any person, a report in writing purporting to be signed by that person may be received in evidence without proof of signature, qualifications, approval or authority or being of the requisite description to give the report, but the court may require the signatory to give oral evidence[10]. Where, in pursuance of directions of the court, any such report is tendered in evidence otherwise than by or on behalf of the accused a copy must be given to an authorised person representing that person[11], or, if he is not so represented, its substance must be disclosed to him or, where he is a child or young person, to his parent or guardian if present in court[12]; and, except where the evidence relates only to arrangements for admission to hospital, that person may require that the signatory be called to give oral evidence, and evidence to rebut the evidence contained in the report may be called by or on behalf of the accused[13].

1 As to registered medical practitioners see MEDICAL PROFESSIONS vol 74 (2011) PARA 176 et seq.
2 Ie under the Mental Health Act 1983 ss 36(1), 37(2)(a), 38(1), 45A(2), 51(6)(a): see PARAS 862–864.
3 Ie approved for the purposes of the Mental Health Act 1983 s 12: see PARA 849.
4 As to the appropriate national authority see PARA 567. As from 1 April 2013 the Secretary of State may delegate the power to approve an approved clinician and accordingly the words 'or by another person by virtue of s 12ZA or 12ZB' are added by the Health and Social Care Act 2012 s 38(2): see the Health and Social Care Act 2012 (Commencement No 4, Transitional, Savings and Transitory Provisions) Order 2013, SI 2013/160, art 2(2).
5 Mental Health Act 1983 s 54(1) (amended by the Crime (Sentences) Act 1997 s 55, Sch 4 para 12(6); and prospectively amended (see note 4)).
6 Ie under the Mental Health Act 1983 s 35(3)(a): see PARA 862.
7 As to such reports see the Mental Health Act 1983 s 47(1), s 48(1); and PARAS 892–893.
8 Mental Health Act 1983 s 54(1).

9   Ie for the purpose of any provision of the Mental Health Act 1983 Pt 3 (ss 35–55).
10   Mental Health Act 1983 s 54(2), (2A) (s 54(2) substituted and s 54(2A) added by the Mental Health Act 2007 s 11(6)).
11   Mental Health Act 1983 s 54(3)(a) (amended by the Legal Services Act 2007 Sch 21 para 58). As to the meaning of 'authorised person' see PARA 862 note 18.
12   Mental Health Act 1983 s 54(3)(b).
13   Mental Health Act 1983 s 54(3)(c).

866. Restriction on making of other orders.

866. Restriction on making of other orders. Where the court makes a hospital order[1], it must not pass a sentence of imprisonment[2] or impose a fine or make a community order[3] or a youth rehabilitation order[4], in respect of the offence[5], nor[6] may it make a referral order[7] in respect of the offence[8], nor make in respect of the offender an order relating to the binding over of a parent or guardian[9], although it may make any other order[10] which it has power to make[11].

1   Or a guardianship order: see PARA 877. The reference in the text is a reference to orders under the Mental Health Act 1983 s 37: see PARA 864. As to the meaning of 'hospital order' see PARA 864 note 5.
2   For this purpose, a sentence of imprisonment includes any sentence or order for detention: Mental Health Act 1983 s 37(8).
3   Ie a community order within the Criminal Justice Act 2003 Pt 12 (ss 142–305): see SENTENCING AND DISPOSITION OF OFFENDERS vol 92 (2010) PARA 163.
4   Ie a youth rehabilitation order within the meaning of the Criminal Justice and Immigration Act 2008 Pt 1 (ss 1–8): see SENTENCING AND DISPOSITION OF OFFENDERS vol 92 (2010) PARA 202 et seq.
5   Mental Health Act 1983 s 37(8)(a) (amended by the Criminal Justice Act 2003 s 304, Sch 32 Pt 1 paras 37, 38(c); and the Criminal Justice and Immigration Act 2008 Sch 4 para 30(a)).
6   Ie if the order is a hospital order.
7   Ie within the meaning of the Powers of Criminal Courts (Sentencing) Act 2000: see SENTENCING AND DISPOSITION OF OFFENDERS vol 92 (2010) PARA 344 et seq.
8   Mental Health Act 1983 s 37(8)(b) (amended by the Powers of Criminal Courts (Sentencing) Act 2000 s 165(1), Sch 9 para 90(1), (6)(a)).
9   Mental Health Act 1983 s 37(8)(c) (amended by the Powers of Criminal Courts (Sentencing) Act 2000 Sch 9 paras 90(1), (6)(b); and the Criminal Justice and Immigration Act 2008 Sch 4 para 30(b), Sch 28, Pt 1). As to orders relating to the binding over of a parent or guardian see the Powers of Criminal Courts (Sentencing) Act 2000 s 150; and CHILDREN AND YOUNG PERSONS vol 10 (2012) PARA 1299; SENTENCING AND DISPOSITION OF OFFENDERS vol 92 (2010) PARA 312.
10   Ie any other order which it has power to make apart from the Mental Health Act 1983 s 37, such as confiscation or forfeiture orders.
11   Mental Health Act 1983 s 37(8) (amended by the Youth Justice and Criminal Evidence Act 1999 s 67, Sch 4 para 11).

867. Effect of hospital order and interim hospital order.

867. Effect of hospital order and interim hospital order. A hospital order[1] is sufficient authority for a constable[2], approved mental health professional[3] or other person directed to do so by the court to convey the patient[4] to the hospital[5] specified in the order within a period of 28 days[6], and for the managers[7] of the hospital to admit him at any time within that period and detain him afterwards[8].

Where an interim hospital order[9] is made, a constable or other person directed to do so by the court must convey the offender to the specified hospital within 28 days[10] and the managers must admit him within that period and detain him afterwards in accordance with the relevant statutory provision[11]. If an offender absconds from a hospital in which he is detained in pursuance of an interim hospital order, or while being conveyed to or from such a hospital, he may be arrested without warrant by a constable; after being arrested, he must as soon as practicable be brought before the court that made the order and the court may thereupon terminate the order and deal with him in any way in which it could have dealt with him[12].

Once the patient is admitted to a hospital in pursuance of a hospital order, any previous application, hospital order (without a restriction order[13]) or guardianship order ceases to have effect[14]. A patient so admitted must be treated for the purposes of the general statutory provisions relating to compulsory admission to hospital[15] as if he had been so admitted on the date of the order in pursuance of an application for admission for treatment[16], with certain modifications and exceptions[17]. The most important distinctions are that the power to order his discharge will not be exercisable by his nearest relative[18] and the patient does not have the right to apply to an appropriate tribunal within the first six months after the order[19].

The statutory provisions relating to consent to treatment apply to patients liable to be detained under either hospital orders or interim hospital orders[20].

1   As to the meaning of 'hospital order' see PARA 864 note 5.
2   As to the office of constable see POLICE vol 36(1) (2007 Reissue) PARA 101 et seq.
3   As to the meaning of 'approved mental health professional' see PARA 815 note 2.
4   As to the meaning of 'patient' see PARA 758 note 4.
5   As to the meaning of 'hospital' see PARA 577.
6   Mental Health Act 1983 s 40(1)(a) (amended by the Mental Health Act 2007 Sch 2 para 7(e)). In computing this period no account is to be taken of any time during which the patient is at large: Mental Health Act 1983 s 138(5). As to the power to reduce the period prescribed by this provision see PARA 868. An order ceases to have effect if the offender is not admitted to the hospital named in the order within the period of 28 days from the date of the making of the order, as stipulated by it: see *R (on the application of DB) v Nottinghamshire Healthcare NHS Trust; R (on the application of X) v An NHS Trust* [2008] EWCA Civ 1354, [2009] 2 All ER 792, [2009] PTSR 547 (transfer of patient outside 28-day period was unlawful).
7   As to the meaning of 'managers' see PARA 778.
8   Mental Health Act 1983 s 40(1)(b).
9   As to the meaning of 'interim hospital order' see PARA 864 note 18.
10 Ie the period specified in the Mental Health Act 1983 s 38(4): see PARA 864. As to the power to reduce the period prescribed by this provision see PARA 868. See also *R v Chowdhury* [2011] EWCA Crim 936.
11 Mental Health Act 1983 s 40(3). Such detention must be in accordance with s 38 (see PARA 864). As to the duration of interim hospital orders see PARA 864.
12 Mental Health Act 1983 s 38(7).
13 A hospital order does not cease to have effect under this provision if a restriction order is in force at the material time: Mental Health Act 1983 s 41(4).
14 Mental Health Act 1983 s 40(5). However, if the order or the conviction on which it was made (or the special verdict of not guilty by reason of insanity, or findings that the accused did the act or made the omission charged against him but was under a disability) is quashed on appeal, this does not apply. Instead s 22 (see PARA 912) applies as if the patient had been detained in custody during the period for which he was liable to be detained under the quashed order: s 40(5).
    In addition, where a patient admitted to a hospital in pursuance of a hospital order is absent without leave and a warrant to arrest him has been issued under the Criminal Justice Act 1967 s 72 (see PARA 921) and he is held pursuant to the warrant in any country or territory other than the United Kingdom, any of the Channel Islands and the Isle of Man, he is to be treated as having been taken into custody under the Mental Health Act 1983 s 18 on first being so held: s 40(6) (added by the Mental Health (Patients in the Community) Act 1995 s 2(4)).
    As to appeals generally see PARAS 879–880. As to the return and readmission of patients absent without leave etc see the Mental Health Act 1983 ss 18, 21, 21A, 21B, 22; and PARAS 918, 911–912. As to the meaning of 'United Kingdom' see PARA 560 note 14.
15 Ie those applied by the Mental Health Act 1983 Sch 1 Pt I: see PARA 860 note 9.
16 Ie under the Mental Health Act 1983 s 3: see PARA 768.
17 See the Mental Health Act 1983 s 40(4). As to the modifications and exceptions referred to in the text see Sch 1 Pt I; and PARA 860 note 9. This provision does not apply to interim hospital orders.
18 Mental Health Act 1983 Sch 1 Pt I paras 2, 8 (amended by the Mental Health Act 2007 Sch 3 para 36(7)). As to the power to order discharge see PARA 913. As to the meaning of 'nearest relative' see PARA 839.

19 Mental Health Act 1983 Sch 1 Pt I paras 2, 9 (amended by the Mental Health (Patients in the Community) Act 1995 s 1(2), Sch 1 para 14).

20 See the Mental Health Act 1983 s 56(1); and PARAS 924–934.

868. Detention of patient in place of safety pending admission to hospital.
The court by which a hospital order[1] or an interim hospital order[2] is made may give such directions as it thinks fit for the conveyance of the patient[3] to a place of safety[4] and his detention there pending admission to hospital within the prescribed period[5] of 28 days[6].

If, within the period of 28 days beginning with the day on which a hospital order[7] is made, it appears to the Secretary of State that by reason of an emergency or other special circumstances it is not practicable for the patient to be received into the hospital specified in the order, he may give directions for the admission of the patient to such other hospital as appears to be appropriate[8].

1 As to the meaning of 'hospital order' see PARA 864 note 5.
2 As to the meaning of 'interim hospital order' see PARA 864 note 18.
3 As to the meaning of 'patient' see PARA 758 note 4.
4 'Place of safety', in relation to a person not being a child or young person, means any police station, prison or remand centre, or any hospital the managers of which are willing temporarily to receive him; and in relation to a child or young person it means a place of safety within the meaning of the Children and Young Persons Act 1933 (see CHILDREN AND YOUNG PERSONS vol 9 (2012) PARA 632): Mental Health Act 1983 s 55(1). 'Child' and 'young person' have the same meanings as in the Children and Young Persons Act 1933 (see CHILDREN AND YOUNG PERSONS vol 9 (2012) PARA 3): Mental Health Act 1983 s 55(1). As to the meaning of 'hospital' see PARA 577. As to the meaning of 'managers' see PARA 778.
5 Ie the period prescribed by the Mental Health Act 1983 s 37(4) (see the text and note 6), s 38(4) (see PARA 864). The appropriate national authority has the power to make an order reducing the length of the periods prescribed by ss 37(4), (5) and s 38(4), and to make consequential amendments to s 40(1) (see PARA 867) and s 44(3) (see PARA 873): see s 54A (added by the Criminal Justice Act 1991 s 27(2)). As to the appropriate national authority see PARA 567.
6 See the Mental Health Act 1983 s 37(4), s 38(4); and PARA 864.
7 Similar provision for interim hospital orders is not made by the Mental Health Act 1983 s 38 (see PARA 364).
8 Mental Health Act 1983 s 37(5). Where such directions are given, the appropriate national authority must cause the person having the custody of the patient to be informed, and the hospital order will have effect as if the hospital specified in the direction of the appropriate national authority were substituted for the hospital specified in the order: s 37(5). As to the power to reduce the period prescribed under this provision see note 5.

869. The Crown Court's power to make a restriction order. Where a hospital order[1] is made in respect of an offender by the Crown Court[2] and it appears to the court, having regard to the nature of the offence, antecedents of the offender and the risk of his committing further offences if set at large, that it is necessary for the protection of the public from serious harm to do so, the court may, subject to the requirement of oral evidence[3], further order that the offender is to be subject to special restrictions[4], known as a restriction order[5].

A restriction order may not be made unless at least one of the two medical practitioners whose evidence must be taken into account by the court when making the hospital order[6] has given evidence orally before the court[7].

So long as a restriction order is in force, the following special restrictions apply:

(1) the general statutory provisions relating to the duration, renewal and expiration of the authority for detention[8] do not apply and the patient[9] continues to be liable to be detained until duly discharged[10] or absolutely discharged[11] by the Secretary of State[12];

(2)	the statutory provisions relating to community treatment orders and community patients do not apply[13];

(3)	the ordinary provisions[14] relating to application to the appropriate tribunal either by the patient or by his nearest relative do not apply[15];

(4)	the consent of the Secretary of State must be obtained to: (a) any grant of leave of absence to the patient[16]; (b) any transfer of the patient to another hospital or to guardianship[17]; and (c) any order for the discharge[18] of the patient[19];

(5)	if leave of absence is granted, the Secretary of State as well as the responsible clinician[20] has power to recall the patient[21] to hospital and may do so at any time[22]; and

(6)	if the patient is absent without leave, the Secretary of State has power to take the patient into custody and return him to hospital[23] at any time, irrespective of the length of his absence[24].

In relation to any such patient the general provisions as to compulsory admission and guardianship have effect subject to certain exceptions and modifications[25].

Patients subject to restriction orders have a specific right of application to a tribunal[26].

1	As to hospital orders see PARA 864 et seq.
2	As to the Crown Court see COURTS AND TRIBUNALS vol 24 (2010) PARA 716 et seq.
3	Ie subject to the Mental Health Act 1983 s 41(2): see the text and notes 6–7.
4	Ie those set out in the Mental Health Act 1983 s 41(3): see the text and notes 8–24.
5	Mental Health Act 1983 s 41(1) (amended by the Mental Health Act 2007 s 40(1), Sch 11 Pt 8). It is the seriousness of the harm which the public might suffer rather than the seriousness of the risk of re-offending that is in question: *R v Birch* (1989) 90 Cr App Rep 78, 11 Cr App Rep (S) 202, CA (where the Court of Appeal considered the general principles to be observed in deciding whether a restriction order is appropriate, when quashing a restriction order imposed upon a woman who had shot and killed her husband). A restriction order should be considered in cases where the protection of the public is involved, particularly in cases of violence or the more serious sexual offences: *R v Gardiner* [1967] 1 All ER 895, [1967] 1 WLR 464, CA. See also *R (on the application of Jones) v Isleworth Crown Court* [2005] EWHC 662 (Admin), [2005] All ER (D) 33 (Mar) (in assessing the risk of serious harm the judge is not bound to determine future risk solely by reference to the nature of violence in the past). There must be a risk of serious harm to the public at large: *R v Courtney* (1987) 9 Cr App Rep (S) 404, [1988] Crim LR 130, CA (where the Court of Appeal quashed a restriction order imposed upon a man of good character who had killed his wife while undergoing treatment for depression). See also *R v Macrow* [2004] EWCA Crim 1159, [2004] All ER (D) 277 (Apr). There must be a proportionate relationship between the offence and the history of offending, together with an assessment of risk based on medical opinion, before an order is made: *R v Martin* (6 November 1998, unreported), CA. Possible early release by the tribunal is not a ground for passing a life sentence as an alternative (although release procedures under a life sentence and a hospital order with restrictions are similar in practice): *R v Mitchell* [1997] 1 Cr App Rep (S) 90, [1996] Crim LR 604. As to what constitutes 'serious harm' see *R v Melbourne* [2000] 1 MHLR 2, CA; *R v Kamara* [2000] 1 MHLR 9, CA; *R v Czarnota* [2002] EWCA Crim 785, [2002] 1 MHLR 144. In a case where the 20-year old defendant had pleaded guilty to one count of rape, eight counts of indecent assault and three counts of possession of an offensive weapon and was sentenced to life imprisonment, the appropriate sentence was a hospital order with indefinite restriction under the Mental Health Act 1983 s 41; while judges give appropriate weight to the differences between the regimes of custody for life and a hospital order with an indefinite restriction, the latter regime would not in this case afford significantly less protection to the public than the former: see *R v A* [2005] EWCA Crim 2077, [2006] 1 Cr App Rep (S) 521, [2006] Crim LR 79. Before making a restriction order the court should inquire whether the hospital has facilities for keeping patients in safe custody: see *R v Higginbotham* [1961] 3 All ER 616, [1961] 1 WLR 1277, CCA; *R v Cox* [1968] 1 All ER 386, [1968] 1 WLR 308, CA. See also *R v Nwohia* [1996] 1 Cr App Rep (S) 170, (1995) 26 BMLR 157, CA (where a restriction order was imposed on a man who committed an unprovoked, violent offence against an unsuspecting member of the

public). The power to direct that such an order is to cease to have effect is vested in the Secretary of State: see the Mental Health Act 1983 s 42(1); and PARA 876. As to the Secretary of State see PARA 567.

See also *A v Harrow Crown Court* [2003] EWHC 2020 (Admin), [2003] All ER (D) 78 (Aug); *R (on the application of G) v Mental Health Review Tribunal* [2004] EWHC 2193 (Admin), [2004] All ER (D) 86 (Oct); *R (on the application of the Secretary of State for the Home Department) v Mental Health Review Tribunal* [2004] EWHC 2194 (Admin), [2004] All ER (D) 87 (Oct).

For the purposes of the Mental Health Act 1983 'restriction order' has the meaning given by s 41: s 145(1). As to visiting patients subject to a restriction order and the power to withhold their correspondence see PARAS 780, 781.

A conditionally discharged patient may be lawfully detained under the Mental Health Act 1983 s 3, notwithstanding that he remains liable to detention under s 41: *R v North West London Mental Health NHS Trust, ex p Stewart* [1998] QB 628, [1997] 4 All ER 871, CA. A restriction order remains in force even if the patient who is conditionally discharged is subsequently imprisoned for an offence; the patient may be recalled to hospital at the end of the prison sentence: *R v Merseyside Mental Health Review Tribunal, ex p K* [1990] 1 All ER 694; *R v Secretary of State for the Home Department, ex p K* [1991] 1 QB 270, [1990] 3 All ER 562.

6 Ie the medical practitioners upon whose written or oral evidence the court must act when making a hospital order: see the Mental Health Act 1983 s 37(2)(a); and PARA 864.

7 Mental Health Act 1983 s 41(2). It is not necessary for this to be the medical practitioner who would be in charge of the patient's treatment in hospital, nor is it necessary for either medical practitioner to recommend the making of a restriction order: *R v Blackwood* (1974) 59 Cr App Rep 170, [1974] Crim LR 437, CA; *R v Royse* (1981) 3 Cr App Rep (S) 58, CA. The court cannot make an order, based on its own previous experience in the courts, unsupported by medical evidence: *R v Reynolds* [2000] All ER (D) 1313, CA; and see *R v Ristic* [2002] EWCA Crim 165, [2002] All ER (D) 341 (Jan) (although the doctors were not suggesting a restriction order, a judge could impose one after consideration of the evidence and the legislative requirements). See further *R v Hurst* [2007] EWCA Crim 3436; *R v Mahmood* [2002] MHLR 416; *R v Osker* [2010] EWCA Crim 955. As to the evidence of the medical practitioners see *R v Birch* (1989) 90 Cr App Rep 78, 11 Cr App Rep (S) 202, CA; *R v Crookes* [1999] 1 MHLR 45, CA; *R v Chalk* [2002] EWCA Crim 2434, [2002] All ER (D) 509 (Oct); *R (on the application of Jones) v Isleworth Crown Court* [2005] EWHC 662 (Admin), [2005] All ER (D) 33 (Mar). See also *R v Ancharya* [2005] EWCA Crim 772, [2005] All ER (D) 225 (Mar) (judges should balance the risks, e g the risk of relapse from failure to comply with treatment, against the disadvantages of imposing the order).

8 Ie the provisions contained in the Mental Health Act 1983 Pt 2 (ss 2–34). See, in particular, ss 20–22; and PARAS 908–912.

9 As to the meaning of 'patient' see PARA 758 note 4.

10 Ie under the Mental Health Act 1983 Pt 2: see s 23; and PARA 913. His nearest relative has no power to discharge him since he is detained under a hospital order (see PARA 867) and the consent of the appropriate national authority is necessary for others to do so: see the text and notes 20–22.

11 Ie under the Mental Health Act 1983 s 42(2): see PARA 914.

12 Mental Health Act 1983 s 41(3)(a).

13 Mental Health Act 1983 s 41(3)(aa) (added by the Mental Health (Patients in the Community) Act 1995 s 1(2), Sch 1 para 5; and amended by the Mental Health Act 2007 Sch 3 para 17). The provisions referred to in the text are those of the Mental Health Act 1983 Pt 2 (ss 2–34).

14 Ie the Mental Health Act 1983 ss 66, 69(1): see PARA 961.

15 Mental Health Act 1983 s 41(3)(b) (amended by SI 2008/2833). However, the patient has the right to apply to a tribunal under the Mental Health Act 1983 s 70: see PARA 962.

16 Mental Health Act 1983 s 41(3)(c)(i). This power is under s 17: see PARA 917. The Secretary of State can attach conditions to the grant of leave of absence: *R (on the application of A) v Secretary of State for the Home Department* [2002] EWHC 1618 (Admin), [2003] 1 WLR 330, (2002) Times, 5 September. The Mental Health Act 1983 s 17 and s 41(3)(c) should operate to ensure that there is no unreasonable delay in the implementation of a tribunal decision: see *Johnson v United Kingdom* (1997) 27 EHRR 296, 40 BMLR 1, ECtHR. There is no obligation to grant a patient unescorted leave as an alternative to a conditional discharge by a tribunal where conditions are fulfilled: *R (on the application of Hurlock) v Page and Secretary of State for the Home Department* [2001] EWHC 380 (Admin).

17 Mental Health Act 1983 s 41(3)(c)(ii) (amended by the Crime (Sentences) Act 1997 s 49(2)). See *R (on the application of the Secretary of State for the Home Department) v Mental Health Review Tribunal* [2004] EWHC 2194 (Admin), [2004] All ER (D) 87 (Oct).

18 Ie under the Mental Health Act 1983 s 23: see PARA 913 et seq.
19 Mental Health Act 1983 s 41(3)(c)(iii).
20 As to the meaning of 'responsible clinician' see PARA 834.
21 The responsible medical officer may not recall a patient after he has ceased to be liable to be detained under the Mental Health Act 1983 Pt 2: see the Mental Health Act 1983 s 17(5); and PARA 917.
22 Mental Health Act 1983 s 41(3)(c), (d).
23 Ie under the Mental Health Act 1983 s 18: see PARA 918. These powers of arrest are specifically preserved by the Police and Criminal Evidence Act 1984 s 26(2), Sch 2: see CRIMINAL LAW, EVIDENCE AND PROCEDURE vol 11(2) (2006 Reissue) PARA 927.
24 Mental Health Act 1983 s 41(3)(d).
25 See the Mental Health Act 1983 ss 40(4), 41(3), Sch 1 Pt 2; and PARA 860 note 12.
26 Mental Health Act 1983 ss 70, 79(1). See PARA 962.

870. Effect of cessation of order restricting discharge. Where a restriction order[1] ceases to have effect[2] while the relevant hospital order[3] remains in force, the patient[4] must be treated as if he had been admitted to the hospital[5] concerned in pursuance of a hospital order, without an order restricting his discharge, made on the date when the restriction order ceased to have effect[6].

1 See the Mental Health Act 1983 s 41(1); and PARA 869.
2 Ie either because the order was for a limited duration (see the Mental Health Act 1983 s 41(1); and PARA 869) which has expired or because the Secretary of State has so directed (see s 42(1); and PARA 876). As to the Secretary of State see PARA 568.
3 As to the meaning of 'hospital order' see PARA 864 note 5.
4 As to the meaning of 'patient' see PARA 758 note 4.
5 As to the meaning of 'hospital' see PARA 577.
6 Mental Health Act 1983 ss 40(4), 41(5), Sch 1 Pt I (amended by the Mental Health (Patients in the Community) Act 1995 ss 1(2), 2(8), Sch 1 paras 6, 14; the Mental Health Act 2007 s 36, Sch 3 para 36, Sch 11 Pt 1; and the Health and Social Care Act 2012 s 39(3)(a)). As to the right of such a patient to apply to the appropriate tribunal see the Mental Health Act 1983 s 69(2)(a); and PARA 961. If a patient has been conditionally discharged before restrictions end, he will cease to be liable to be detained: see s 42(5); and PARA 914.

871. Magistrates' court power to make a hospital order. Where a magistrates' court[1] would have power, on convicting a person charged with any act or omission as an offence, to make a hospital order[2] in his case then it may, if satisfied that he did the act or made the omission charged, make a hospital order without convicting him[3].

Where the court is of the opinion that an inquiry ought to be made into the mental condition of the accused before determining the method of dealing with him, it must adjourn the case and remand[4] the accused for a medical examination[5].

1 As to magistrates' courts see MAGISTRATES vol 71 (2013) PARA 470 et seq.
2 As to the meaning of 'hospital order' see PARA 864 note 5.
3 Mental Health Act 1983 s 37(3) (amended by the Mental Health Act 2007 Sch 1 para 7(b), Sch 11 Pt 1). See *R v Lincolnshire (Kesteven) Justices, ex p O'Connor* [1983] 1 All ER 901, [1983] 1 WLR 335, DC; *R v Ramsgate Justices, ex p Kazmarek* (1984) 80 Cr App Rep 366, 149 JP 16, DC; *R v Chippenham Magistrates' Court, ex p Thompson* (1996) 32 BMLR 69, 160 JP 207. As to appeals against such orders see PARA 880. There is no power to make an interim hospital order without a conviction and therefore it is not available where there has been a finding that the accused did the act or made the omission charged: see *R (on the application of Bartram) v Southend Magistrates' Court* [2004] EWHC 2691 (Admin), [2004] All ER (D) 326 (Oct).
The Mental Health Act 1983 s 37(3) provides the magistrates' court with the power to abstain from either convicting or acquitting but instead make a hospital order; although there is no entitlement to a trial if no order can be made under s 37(3) the case should proceed to trial: see *R (on the application of Singh) v Stratford Magistrates' Court* [2007] EWHC 1582 (Admin), [2007] 4 All ER 407, [2007] 1 WLR 3119.

4   The magistrates court may remand the accused to a hospital for a report on his medical
     condition: see the Mental Health Act 1983 s 35(1); and PARA 862.
5   See the Powers of Criminal Courts (Sentencing) Act 2000 s 11(1), (3); and MAGISTRATES vol 71
     (2013) PARA 558. Where the defendant was or might be mentally ill or suffering from severe
     mental impairment, the appropriate procedure is a combination of the Mental Health Act 1983
     s 37(3) and the Powers of Criminal Courts (Sentencing) Act 2000 s 11(1): *R (on the application
     of P) v Barking Youth Court* [2002] EWHC 734 (Admin), [2002] 2 Cr App Rep 294, 166 JP
     641; *R (on the application of Singh) v Stratford Magistrates' Court* [2007] EWHC 1582
     (Admin), [2007] 4 All ER 407, [2007] 1 WLR 3119. See further *Blouet v Bath and Wansdyke
     Magistrates Court* [2009] EWHC 759 Admin.

872.   Power of a youth court to make a hospital order.   The youth court[1] is a
magistrates' court[2] and as such the statutory framework for dealing with
defendants suffering from a mental disorder in a magistrates' court[3] also applies
to youth courts[4]. Consequently a youth court may consider making a hospital
order without convicting a defendant[5].

1   As to youth courts see CHILDREN AND YOUNG PERSONS vol 10 (2012) PARA 1225 et seq.
2   As to magistrates' courts see MAGISTRATES vol 71 (2013) PARA 470 et seq.
3   As to the framework for dealing with defendants suffering from a mental disorder in a
     magistrates' court see PARA 871.
4   See *R (on the application of P) v Barking Youth Court* [2002] EWHC 734 (Admin), [2002] 2 Cr
     App Rep 294, 166 JP 641. As to the procedure in determining the capacity of a defendant in a
     youth court see *DPP v P* [2007] EWHC 946 (Admin), [2007] 4 All ER 628, [2008] 1 WLR
     1005. Note however that the defence of doli incapax has been abolished by the Crime and
     Disorder Act 1998 s 34: see *R v T* [2008] EWCA Crim 815, [2008] 3 WLR 923, [2008] 2 Cr
     App Rep 235.
5   See CrimPR 37.3; and CRIMINAL PROCEDURE vol 27 (2010) PARA 249.

873.   Committal by magistrates' court to Crown Court for restriction order.
When a magistrates' court[1] is dealing with an offender of 14 years or over, where
the conditions[2] for making a hospital order[3] are satisfied but it appears to the
court, having regard to the nature of the offence, the antecedents of the offender
and the risk of his committing further offences if set at large, that if a hospital
order is made then a restriction order should also be made, the court may,
instead of making a hospital order or dealing with the offender in any other
manner, commit him in custody[4] to the Crown Court to be dealt with in respect
of his offence[5]. The Crown Court may then[6] either make a hospital order[7], with
or without a restriction order, or deal with the offender in any other manner in
which the magistrates' court might have done[8].

1   As to magistrates' courts see MAGISTRATES vol 71 (2013) PARA 470 et seq.
2   See the Mental Health Act 1983 s 37(1); and PARA 864.
3   As to the meaning of 'hospital order' see PARA 864 note 5.
4   Instead of committing the offender in custody, the court, if satisfied on written or oral evidence
     (given by the approved clinician who would have overall responsibility for the offender's case)
     that arrangements have been made for the admission of the offender to a hospital, may direct
     that he be admitted to that hospital and detained there until the case is disposed of by the
     Crown Court, giving such directions as it thinks fit for his production by the hospital to the
     Crown Court: Mental Health Act 1983 s 44(1), (2) (amended by the Mental Health Act 2007
     s 10(7)). The provisions of the Mental Health Act 1983 s 37(4), (5) and s 40(1) (see PARA 868)
     apply as if to a hospital order but omitting reference to the period of 28 days; until the case is
     disposed of by the Crown Court the order has the effect of a hospital order with a restriction
     order: s 44(3) (amended by the Mental Health Act 2007 s 40(3)(a), Sch 11 Pt 8). The power of
     the Crown Court in certain circumstances to make a hospital order where it is impracticable or
     inappropriate to bring the person before the court (ie under the Mental Health Act 1983
     s 51(5), (6): see PARA 896) applies to persons admitted to hospital under this provision: s 51(7).
     As to the meaning of the 'approved clinician' PARA 831. As to the Crown Court see COURTS AND
     TRIBUNALS vol 24 (2010) PARA 716 et seq.

5 See the Mental Health Act 1983 s 43(1). The power of a magistrates' court under the Powers of ~~Criminal Courts (Sentencing) Act 2000 s 3~~ (which enables such a court to commit an offender to the Crown Court where the court is of the opinion that greater ~~punishment should be inflicted~~ for the offence than the court has power to inflict: see CRIMINAL PROCEDURE vol 27 (2010) PARAS 276–277) may also be exercised where the magistrates' court is of the opinion that such greater punishment should be inflicted unless a hospital order with a restriction order is made in his case: Mental Health Act 1983 s 43(4) (amended by the Powers of Criminal Courts (Sentencing) Act 2000 s 165(1), Sch 9 para 91). As to these powers see MAGISTRATES vol 71 (2013) PARA 561.

Partly as from a day to be appointed, the Mental Health Act 1983 s 43(4) is substituted so as to refer also to the Powers of Criminal Courts (Sentencing) Act 2000 s 3B: Mental Health Act 1983 s 43(4) (prospectively substituted by the Criminal Justice Act 2003 s 41, Sch 3 Pt 2 para 55(1), (2)). At the date at which this volume states the law this substitution was in force in relation to certain local justice areas (namely Bath and Wansdyke; Berkshire; Bristol; Liverpool and Knowsley; North Avon; North Hampshire; North Somerset; Ormskirk; Sefton; St Helens; Wigan and Leigh; and Wirral) and where a Crown Court deals with a person sent for trial by a magistrates' court in one of the above named local justice areas or where a person is committed for sentence by a magistrates' court in one of the above named local justice areas: see the Criminal Justice Act 2003 (Commencement No 28 and Saving Provisions) Order 2012, SI 2012/1320, art 4(1)(c), (2), (3).

The power of the Crown Court to make a hospital order with or without a restriction order in the case of a person convicted before that court of an offence may, in the same circumstances and subject to the same conditions, be exercised by such a court in the case of a person committed to the court under the Vagrancy Act 1824 s 5 (which provides for the committal to the Crown Court of persons who are incorrigible rogues within the meaning of that provision: see CRIMINAL LAW vol 26 (2010) PARA 774): Mental Health Act 1983 s 43(5). This provision is prospectively repealed by the Criminal Justice Act 2003 s 332, Sch 37 Pt 9 as from a day to be appointed under s 336(3). At the date at which this volume states the law no such day had been appointed.

6 Ie after inquiring into the circumstances of the case: see the Mental Health Act 1983 s 43(2).

7 Ie if it would have power to do so on conviction before it of such an offence as is mentioned in the Mental Health Act 1983 s 37(1): see PARA 864.

8 Mental Health Act 1983 s 43(2). The Crown Court has the same power under ss 35, 36, 38 to remand such a person to hospital for report or medical treatment as it has in the case of an accused person (see PARA 861) and to make an interim hospital order as it has in the case of a person convicted before it (see PARA 864): s 43(3). As to the meaning of 'medical treatment' see PARA 926.

874. Duty of court to make orders after special verdict or findings of disability. Where a special verdict is returned that the accused is not guilty by reason of insanity[1] or findings have been made that an accused is under a disability and that he did the act or made the omission charged against him[2], the court must make in respect of the accused: (1) a hospital order[3] (with or without a restriction order)[4]; (2) a supervision order[5]; or (3) an order for his absolute discharge[6]. Where the offence to which the special verdict or the findings relate is an offence the sentence for which is fixed by law and the court has power to make a hospital order, the court must make a hospital order with a restriction order (whether or not it would[7] have power to make a restriction order)[8]. There are similar powers[9] on an appeal[10] where the Court of Appeal is of the opinion that there should have been such a verdict or findings[11].

There are corresponding provisions in regard to persons on trial before a court-martial under the Courts-Martial (Appeals) Act 1968[12] and the Armed Forces Act 2006[13].

1 See the Trial of Lunatics Act 1883 s 2(1) (amended by the Criminal Procedure (Insanity) Act 1964 s 1). Except for persons arraigned before 1 January 1992, such a verdict cannot be returned except on written or oral evidence (to which the provisions of the Mental Health Act 1983 s 54(2), (3) (see PARA 865) apply) of two or more registered medical practitioners (at least one of whom is approved for the purpose of the Mental Health Act 1983 s 12 (see PARA

849)): see the Criminal Procedure (Insanity and Unfitness to Plead) Act 1991 ss 1(1), (2), 6(1), 8(1); and the Criminal Procedure (Insanity and Unfitness to Plead) Act 1991 (Commencement) Order 1991, SI 1991/2488. As to question of whether a defendant is fit to be tried see CRIMINAL PROCEDURE vol 27 (2010) PARA 370.

2 Criminal Procedure (Insanity) Act 1964 s 5(1) (s 5 substituted by the Domestic Violence, Crime and Victims Act 2004 s 24(1)). As to findings of unfitness to plead and that the accused did the act or made the omission charged against him see also the Criminal Procedure (Insanity) Act 1964 ss 4, 4A; and CRIMINAL PROCEDURE vol 27 (2010) PARA 370.

3 'Hospital order' has the meaning given in the Mental Health Act 1983 s 37 (see PARA 864 note 5): Criminal Procedure (Insanity) Act 1964 s 5(4) (as substituted: see note 2). Previously compliance with the Mental Health Act 1983 s 37 (see PARA 864) as to medical evidence was technically not required although in practice it was followed, but now such compliance is legally required. See note 4.

4 Criminal Procedure (Insanity) Act 1964 s 5(2)(a) (as substituted: see note 2). 'Restriction order' has the meaning given in the Mental Health Act 1983 s 41 (see PARA 869): Criminal Procedure (Insanity) Act 1964 s 5(4) (as so substituted). Note that unlike the procedure under the Mental Health Act 1983 s 41 (see PARA 869) there is no requirement for oral medical evidence at this stage.
   As to the application of the Mental Health Act 1983 ss 35–38 (see PARA 864) see the Criminal Procedure (Insanity) Act 1964 s 5A(1)–(4); and SENTENCING AND DISPOSITION OF OFFENDERS vol 92 (2010) PARAS 332 et seq. Under s 5A, where the court has not yet made one of the disposals referred to in s 5(2) (see heads (1)–(3) in text), there are powers for the court to make orders under the Mental Health Act 1983 s 35 (remand to hospital for report on the accused's medical condition: see PARA 862), s 36 (remand of the accused to hospital for treatment: see PARA 862) and s 38 (interim hospital order: see PARA 864).

5 Criminal Procedure (Insanity) Act 1964 s 5(2)(b) (as substituted: see note 2). 'Supervision order' has the meaning given in Sch 1A Pt 1 (see SENTENCING AND DISPOSITION OF OFFENDERS vol 92 (2010) PARA 368): s 5(4) (as so substituted). See also s 5A(5), Sch 1A. See note 4.

6 Criminal Procedure (Insanity) Act 1964 s 5(2)(c) (as substituted: see note 2). See also s 5A(6); and SENTENCING AND DISPOSITION OF OFFENDERS vol 92 (2010) PARA 40. See note 4.

7 Ie apart from the Criminal Procedure (Insanity) Act 1964 s 5.

8 Criminal Procedure (Insanity) Act 1964 s 5(3) (as substituted: see note 2).

9 Depending on the circumstances, there may be power to make a hospital order (with or without a restriction order), a supervision order, an order for absolute discharge, an order for remand to hospital for report or treatment or an interim hospital order.

10 Ie an appeal against conviction under the Criminal Appeal Act 1968 s 1(1) or against a finding of not guilty by reason of insanity under s 12.

11 See the Criminal Appeal Act 1968 ss 6, 14 (both substituted by the Criminal Procedure (Insanity and Unfitness to Plead) Act 1991 s 4; and amended by the Domestic Violence, Crime and Victims Act 2004 s 24(3) and the Criminal Justice and Immigration Act 2008 Sch 8 para 7, Sch 28, Pt 3). The powers under the Criminal Appeal Act 1968 s 6 are available on any appeal against conviction. The powers under s 14 are available on an appeal under s 12: see further PARA 875. As to the Court of Appeal see COURTS AND TRIBUNALS vol 24 (2010) PARA 688 et seq.

12 Ie under the Courts-Martial (Appeals) Act 1968 s 16: see ARMED FORCES vol 3 (2011) PARA 668.

13 Ie under the Armed Forces Act 2006 ss 169, 170: see ARMED FORCES vol 3 (2011) PARA 650.

875. Substitution of findings on unfitness. Where on an appeal against a verdict of 'not guilty by reason of insanity'[1] the Court of Appeal[2], on the written or oral evidence of two or more registered medical practitioners[3], is of the opinion that the case is not one where there should have been a verdict of acquittal, but there should have been findings that the accused was under a disability and that he did the act or made the omission charged against him[4], the Court of Appeal must make in respect of the accused: (1) a hospital order[5] (with or without a restriction order)[6]; (2) a supervision order[7]; or (3) an order for his absolute discharge[8].

Where the offence to which the appeal relates is an offence the sentence for which is fixed by law and the court has power to make a hospital order, the court must make a hospital order with a restriction order (whether or not it would otherwise[9] have power to make a restriction order)[10]. Where the Court of Appeal makes a supervision order[11], any power of revoking or amending it is exercisable as if the order had been made by the court below[12].

1   As to such appeals see the Criminal Appeal Act 1968 s 12; and CRIMINAL PROCEDURE vol 28 (2010) PARA 766.
2   As to the Court of Appeal see COURTS AND TRIBUNALS vol 24 (2010) PARA 688 et seq.
3   Ie at least one of whom is duly approved. As to such approval see PARA 849. As to registered medical practitioners see MEDICAL PROFESSIONS vol 74 (2011) PARA 176 et seq.
4   Criminal Appeal Act 1968 s 14(1) (s 14 substituted by the Criminal Procedure (Insanity and Unfitness to Plead) Act 1991 s 4(2)). There are identical powers of disposal to those under the Criminal Appeal Act 1968 s 14 in s 6 although the latter are on any appeal against conviction: see PARA 874 note 11; and CRIMINAL PROCEDURE vol 28 (2010) PARA 798.
5   For these purposes, 'hospital order' has the meaning given in the Mental Health Act 1983 s 37 (see PARA 864 note 5): Criminal Appeal Act 1968 s 14(7) (s 14(2)–(7) substituted by the Domestic Violence, Crime and Victims Act 2004 s 24(3)).
6   Criminal Appeal Act 1968 s 14(2)(a) (as substituted: see note 4). For these purposes, 'restriction order' has the meaning given in the Mental Health Act 1983 s 41 (see PARA 869): Criminal Appeal Act 1968 s 14(7) (as so substituted). See note 10.
7   Criminal Appeal Act 1968 s 14(2)(b) (as substituted: see note 4). For these purposes, 'supervision order' has the meaning given in the Criminal Procedure (Insanity) Act 1964 Sch 1A Pt 1 (see SENTENCING AND DISPOSITION OF OFFENDERS vol 92 (2010) PARA 250): Criminal Appeal Act 1968 s 14(7) (as so substituted). See note 10.
8   Criminal Appeal Act 1968 s 14(2)(c) (as substituted: see note 4). See note 10. As to appeal against a finding of disability see the Criminal Justice Act 1968 s 15; and CRIMINAL PROCEDURE vol 28 (2010) PARA 767. As to disposal of appeal against a finding of disability see the Criminal Justice Act 1968 s 16; and CRIMINAL PROCEDURE vol 28 (2010) PARA 801.
9   Ie apart from the Criminal Appeal Act 1968 s 14(3).
10 Criminal Appeal Act 1968 s 14(3) (as substituted: see note 4). The Criminal Procedure (Insanity) Act 1964 s 5A applies in relation to the Criminal Appeal Act 1968 s 14 as it applies in relation to the Criminal Procedure (Insanity) Act 1964 s 5 (see PARA 874): Criminal Appeal Act 1968 s 14(4) (as so substituted). Where the court has not yet made one of the disposals referred to in s 14(2) (see heads (1)–(3) in the text) there are powers for the court to make orders for remand to hospital for report or treatment or an interim hospital order (see note 11).
11 Ie by virtue of the Criminal Appeal Act 1968 s 14.
12 Criminal Appeal Act 1968 s 14(6) (as substituted: see note 4).

876.   Additional powers of Secretary of State in respect of patients subject to restriction orders.   Where a person is subject to either a restriction order[1] or a restriction direction[2], the responsible clinician[3] must at such intervals (not exceeding one year) as the appropriate authority[4] may direct, examine and report to the Secretary of State on that person: every report must contain such particulars as he may require[5]. If the Secretary of State is satisfied that a restriction order[6] is no longer required for the protection of the public from serious harm, he may direct that the patient[7] cease to be subject to the special restrictions applicable where such an order is in force[8], and where he does so that order ceases to have effect[9].

If satisfied that the attendance at any place in Great Britain[10] of a patient who is subject to a restriction order is desirable in the interests of justice or for the purposes of any public inquiry, the Secretary of State may direct him to be taken to that place; and where a patient is so directed to be taken to any place he must, unless the Secretary of State directs otherwise, be kept in custody while being so taken, while at that place and while being taken back to the hospital in which he is liable to be detained[11].

The Secretary of State also has power to discharge a restricted patient either absolutely or conditionally[12], to recall a conditionally discharged patient to hospital[13], and to refer the case of a restricted patient to the appropriate tribunal[14].

1   Ie under the Mental Health Act 1983 s 41(1): see PARA 869. For these purposes, a restriction order includes orders or directions having the same effect: see s 55(4); and PARA 861.

2   Ie under the Mental Health Act 1983 s 49: see PARA 894.

3   As to the meaning of 'responsible clinician' see PARA 834.

4   As to the appropriate national authority see PARA 567.

5   Mental Health Act 1983 ss 41(6), 49(3) (both amended by the Mental Health Act 2007 s 10(6), (9)(b)).

6   See note 1. This power applies whether the restriction order was made without limit of time or for a specified period.

7   As to the meaning of 'patient' see PARA 758 note 4.

8   Ie the special restrictions set out in the Mental Health Act 1983 s 41(3) (which inter alia require the consent of the Secretary of State to the exercise of the power to grant leave of absence, transfer or discharge the patient, and give the Secretary of State power to recall a patient from leave and retake a patient who is absent without leave at any time): see PARAS 869, 918.

9   Mental Health Act 1983 s 42(1). As to the effect of such a direction where the hospital order does not cease to have effect see PARA 870.

10 As to the meaning of 'Great Britain' see PARA 560 note 14.

11 Mental Health Act 1983 s 42(6). This provision extends to Scotland: see s 146; and PARA 557. As to the provisions for taking such persons into custody see PARAS 776–777.

12 Mental Health Act 1983 s 42(2), (5). See PARA 914.

13 Mental Health Act 1983 s 42(3), (4). See PARA 914.

14 Mental Health Act 1983 s 71(1) (amended by SI 2008/2833). See also PARA 965. As to the meaning of 'the appropriate tribunal' see PARA 955.

877. Guardianship orders. Where a person is convicted before the Crown Court[1] or a magistrates' court[2] of an offence in respect of which the court would have power to make a hospital order[3], the court may make an order placing him under the guardianship of a local social services authority[4] or of a specified person approved by such authority[5], if the following conditions are fulfilled:

(1)   the court is satisfied on the written or oral evidence of two registered medical practitioners[6] that the offender is suffering from mental disorder[7] and that, in the case of an offender who has attained the age of 16 years, his mental disorder is of a nature or degree which warrants his reception into guardianship[8]; and

(2)   the court is of the opinion, having regard to all the circumstances including the nature of the offence and the character antecedents of the offender, and to the other available methods of dealing with him, that the most suitable method of disposing of the case is by means of such an order[9].

A guardianship order may not be made unless the court is satisfied that the local social services authority or person concerned is willing to receive the offender into guardianship[10]. Where a court is minded to make a guardianship order, it may request a local social services authority[11] to inform the court whether it or any other person approved by it is willing to receive the offender into guardianship, and if so to give such information as it reasonably can about how it or the other person could be expected to exercise the powers of a guardian[12] in relation to him, and the authority must comply with the request[13].

1   As to the Crown Court see COURTS AND TRIBUNALS vol 24 (2010) PARA 716 et seq.

2   As to magistrates' courts see MAGISTRATES vol 71 (2013) PARA 470 et seq.

3   See the Mental Health Act 1983 s 37(1); and PARA 864. As to the meaning of 'hospital order' see PARA 864 note 5.

4   As to the meaning of 'local social services authority' see PARA 579.

5   Mental Health Act 1983 s 37(1). Such an order is referred to in the Mental Health Act 1983 as a 'guardianship order': see s 37(6); and PARA 859 note 17. As to the application of the general provisions of the Act to guardianship orders see ss 40(4), 55(4), Sch 1 Pt I; and PARA 860. For the documents to be sent by the court to the local social services authority see the Criminal Procedure Rules 2011, SI 2011/1709, r 42.9.

6   As to the requirements for such evidence see PARA 865. As to registered medical practitioners see MEDICAL PROFESSIONS vol 74 (2011) PARA 176 et seq.
7   As to the meaning of 'mental disorder' see PARA 761.
8   Mental Health Act 1983 s 37(2)(a)(ii) (amended by the Mental Health Act 2007 Sch 1 para 7(a)). As to hospital orders see the Mental Health Act 1983 s 37(2)(a)(i); and PARA 864. As to the other orders which can and cannot be combined with a guardianship order see PARA 866.
9   Mental Health Act 1983 s 37(2)(b).
10 Mental Health Act 1983 s 37(6).
11 Ie the local social services authority (see PARA 579) for the area in which the offender resides or last resided, or any other such authority that appears to the court to be appropriate.
12 Ie the powers conferred by the Mental Health Act 1983 s 40(2).
13 Mental Health Act 1983 s 39A (added by the Criminal Justice Act 1991 s 27).

878. Effect of guardianship orders. A guardianship order[1] confers on the authority or person named in it as guardian the same powers as a guardianship application[2] and the patient[3] is to be treated[4] as if he had been placed under guardianship on the date of the order in pursuance of such an application[5]. The most important distinction is that the patient's nearest relative has no power to order his discharge from guardianship[6]. A patient subject to a guardianship order and his nearest relative have the right to apply to the appropriate tribunal[7].

When a person is placed under guardianship by a guardianship order, any previous application[8], hospital order without a restriction order[9], or guardianship order ceases to have effect[10].

1   As to the meaning of 'guardianship order' see PARA 859 note 17. See also PARA 877.
2   Ie made and accepted under the Mental Health Act 1983 Pt 2 (ss 2–34): s 40(2). As to those powers see s 8(1); and PARAS 787, 790–796.
3   As to the meaning of 'patient' see PARA 758 note 4.
4   Ie subject to the modification of certain provisions. The modifications are the same as those in relation to hospital orders without restrictions: see PARA 860 note 9. As to the meaning of 'hospital order' see PARA 864 note 5.
5   See the Mental Health Act 1983 s 40(4), Sch 1 Pt I (amended by the Mental Health (Patients in the Community) Act 1995 s 1(2), Sch 1 paras 6, 14; the Mental Health Act 2007 ss 36(4), 37(6), Sch 3 para 36, Sch 11, Pts 1, 5; and the Health and Social Care Act 2012 s 39(3)).
6   Mental Health Act 1983 Sch 1 paras 2, 8 (Sch 1 Pt 1 para 2 amended by the Mental Health (Patients in the Community) Act 1995 s 1(2), Sch 1 para 6(b); the Mental Health Act 2007 s 37(6), Sch 3 para 36(3), Sch 11 Pt 5; and the Mental Health Act 1983 Sch 1 para 8 amended by the Mental Health Act 2007 Sch 3 para 36(7)). As to orders for discharge see PARA 913.
7   See the Mental Health Act 1983 s 69(1)(b); and PARA 961. The nearest relative's right is different from that of the nearest relative of a detained patient or a community patient: cf s 69(1)(a) (see PARA 961).
8   Ie an application for admission or for guardianship under the Mental Health Act 1983 Pt 2: see PARA 767 et seq.
9   A hospital order does not cease to have effect so long as a restriction order is in force: Mental Health Act 1983 s 41(4).
10 Mental Health Act 1983 s 40(5). As to the position where the order is quashed on appeal see PARA 867 note 14.

879. Appeals from the Crown Court. An appeal lies to the Court of Appeal[1] in respect of any hospital order[2], with or without a restriction order[3], or any interim hospital order[4] or any hospital direction and limitation direction[5] made by the Crown Court[6] following conviction on indictment[7]. An appeal will also lie in respect of such orders made by the Crown Court following a summary conviction[8]. Where there is a special verdict that the accused is not guilty by reason of insanity, or there are findings that he is under a disability and that he did the act or made the omission charged against him[9], the accused may appeal from the Crown Court to the Court of Appeal against the verdict or any of those findings[10].

1   As to the Court of Appeal see COURTS AND TRIBUNALS vol 24 (2010) PARA 688 et seq.
2   Ie made under the Mental Health Act 1983 s 37(1): see PARA 864.
3   Ie made under the Mental Health Act 1983 s 41(1): see PARA 869.
4   Ie made under the Mental Health Act 1983 s 38: see PARA 864.
5   Ie made under the Mental Health Act 1983 ss 45A, 45B: see PARA 863.
6   As to the Crown Court see COURTS AND TRIBUNALS vol 24 (2010) PARA 716 et seq.
7   See the Criminal Appeal Act 1968 ss 9(1), 50(1)(a), (b) (bb); and SENTENCING AND DISPOSITION OF OFFENDERS vol 92 (2010) PARA 46.
8   See the Criminal Appeal Act 1968 s 10(1), (2)(a); and SENTENCING AND DISPOSITION OF OFFENDERS vol 92 (2010) PARA 47. There is no appeal to the Court of Appeal from proceedings in the Crown Court on appeal from magistrates' courts: see CRIMINAL LAW vol 26 (2010) PARA 765. See also *Kiernan v Harrow Crown Court* [2003] EWCA Crim 1052.
9   As to the orders which may be made upon such verdict or findings see PARA 874.
10   See the Criminal Appeal Act 1968 ss 12, 15; and CRIMINAL PROCEDURE vol 28 (2010) PARAS 766, 767. Where the Court of Appeal allows an appeal against a finding that the appellant is under a disability (ie an appeal under the Criminal Appeal Act 1968 s 15 (see CRIMINAL PROCEDURE vol 28 (2010) PARA 767)) the appellant may be tried accordingly for the offence with which he was charged; and the Court may (subject to the Criminal Justice and Public Order Act 1994 s 25 (see CRIMINAL PROCEDURE vol 27 (2010) PARA 72)) make such orders as appear to them necessary or expedient pending any such trial for his custody, release on bail or continued detention under the Mental Health Act 1983 and the Criminal Appeal Act 1968 Sch 3 has effect for applying provisions in Pt 3 to persons in whose case an order is made by the Court under s 16(3): see s 16(3) (substituted by the Criminal Procedure (Insanity and Unfitness to Plead) Act 1991 Sch 3 para 3; and amended by the Criminal Justice and Public Order Act 1994 s 168(2), Sch 10 para 21).

880. Appeals from magistrates' courts. Where on the trial of an information charging a person with an offence a magistrates' court[1] makes a hospital order[2] or guardianship order[3] in respect of him without convicting him, he has the same right of appeal to the Crown Court[4] against the order as if it had been made on his conviction[5]. On such an appeal, the Crown Court has the same powers as if the appeal had been against both conviction and sentence[6].

1   As to magistrates' courts see MAGISTRATES vol 71 (2013) PARA 470 et seq.
2   As to the meaning of 'hospital order' see PARA 864 note 5.
3   As to the meaning of 'guardianship order' see PARA 859 note 17.
4   As to the Crown Court see COURTS AND TRIBUNALS vol 24 (2010) PARA 716 et seq.
5   Mental Health Act 1983 s 45(1). As to rights of appeal to the Crown Court on conviction by a magistrates' court generally see CRIMINAL PROCEDURE vol 28 (2010) PARA 695.
6   Mental Health Act 1983 s 45(1). As to when a designated officer must send notice to the appropriate officer of the Crown Court of written evidence considered when the magistrates' court made the order appealed against see the Magistrates' Courts Rules 1981, SI 1981/552, r 74; and CRIMINAL PROCEDURE vol 28 (2010) PARA 704. As to appeals from magistrates' courts to the Crown Court generally see CRIMINAL PROCEDURE vol 28 (2010) PARA 695; MAGISTRATES.

(13) PRIMARY MENTAL HEALTH ASSESSMENTS: WALES

881. Duty to carry out mental health assessments. The following applies to an individual who is liable to be detained under the Mental Health Act 1983 or is subject to a guardianship order under the Mental Health Act 1983 or is a community patient[1] or who is receiving secondary mental health services[2]. A primary mental health assessment must be carried out in respect of the individual[3] if:

    (1)   the relevant scheme provides[4] that primary mental health assessments are to be made available in respect of all or specified categories of the individuals referred to above[5];

(2)　the individual falls within the scheme's description of those individuals in respect of whom primary mental health assessments are to be made available[6]; and

(3)　a relevant referral for the purposes of these provisions is made[7].

Where an individual does not fall into any of the above descriptions[8] but a request, that meets certain conditions[9], has been made that the individual has a primary mental health assessment, a primary mental health assessment must be carried out[10] in respect of that individual[11].

1　Ie within the meaning of the Mental Health Act 1983 s 17A (see PARA 797 note 4).

2　Mental Health (Wales) Measure 2010 s 8(1). As to the meaning of 'secondary mental health services' see PARA 586 note 6.

3　Ie in accordance with the Mental Health (Wales) Measure 2010 s 9 (see PARA 883).

4　Ie provides under the Mental Health (Wales) Measure 2010 s 2(4)(b) (see PARA 586).

5　Mental Health (Wales) Measure 2010 s 8(2)(a).

6　Mental Health (Wales) Measure 2010 s 8(2)(b).

7　Mental Health (Wales) Measure 2010 s 8(2)(c). A relevant referral for the purposes of s 8 means a request that an individual has a primary mental health assessment which meets the following conditions: (1) that the request is made to a local mental health partner for the local authority area in which the individual is usually resident; (2) that the request is made by a member of staff who falls within a category specified in the scheme for that local authority area under s 2(5) (see PARA 586): s 8(3)–(5).

8　Ie any of the descriptions in the Mental Health (Wales) Measure 2010 s 8(1).

9　For the purposes of the Mental Health (Wales) Measure 2010 s 6 the conditions are that:
　　(1)　the request is made by:
　　　　(a)　a contractor with whom a general medical services contract has been entered into under the National Health Service (Wales) Act 2006 s 42 (see HEALTH SERVICES vol 54 (2008) PARA 242) by the local health board to which the request is made or, where the request is made to a local authority, the local health board which is the authority's local mental health partner (Mental Health (Wales) Measure 2010 s 6(4)(a));
　　　　(b)　a person with whom arrangements have been made under the National Health Service (Wales) Act 2006 s 50 (see HEALTH SERVICES vol 54 (2008) PARA 267) by the local health board to which the request is made or, where the request is made to a local authority, the local health board which is the authority's local mental health partner (Mental Health (Wales) Measure 2010 s 6(4)(b)); or
　　　　(c)　a registered medical practitioner employed for the purposes of the National Health Service (Wales) Act 2006 s 41 (see HEALTH SERVICES vol 54 (2008) PARA 74) by the local health board to which the request is made or, where the request is made to a local authority, the local health board which is the authority's local mental health partner (Mental Health (Wales) Measure 2010 s 6(4)(c));
　　(2)　the individual in respect of whom the request is made is a registered patient of the contractor, person or practitioner making the referral (s 6(5)); and
　　(3)　the request is made to a local mental health partner for the local authority area in which the individual is usually resident (s 6(6)).

For the purposes of s 7 the conditions are that:
　　(i)　the request is made by:
　　　　(A)　a contractor with whom a general medical services contract has been entered into under the National Health Service (Wales) Act 2006 s 42 by the local health board to which the request is made or, where the request is made to a local authority, the local health board which is the authority's local mental health partner (Mental Health (Wales) Measure 2010 s 7(4)(a));
　　　　(B)　a person with whom arrangements have been made under the National Health Service (Wales) Act 2006 s 50 by the local health board to which the request is made or, where the request is made to a local authority, the local health board which is the authority's local mental health partner (Mental Health (Wales) Measure 2010 s 7(4)(b));
　　　　(C)　a registered medical practitioner employed for the purposes of the National Health Service (Wales) Act 2006 s 41 by the local health board to which the

request is made or, where the request is made to a local authority, the local health board which is the authority's local mental health partner (Mental Health (Wales) Measure 2010 s 7(4)(c)); or

(D) a registered medical practitioner providing services to prisoners under arrangements made between the registered medical practitioner and a person responsible for the provision or running of a contracted out prison (within the meaning of the Criminal Justice Act 1991 s 84(4)) in Wales (Mental Health (Wales) Measure 2010 s 7(4)(d));

(ii) the request is made to a local mental health partner for the local authority area in which the contractor, person or practitioner carries on the majority of the contractor's, person's or practitioner's business or activities (s 7(5));

(iii) the individual in respect of whom the request is made falls within a category specified in regulations made by the Welsh Ministers or the scheme for that local authority area under s 2(4)(c) (s 7(6)).

For the purposes of ss 6–8 a request is to be treated as made by a contractor under a general medical services contract entered into under the National Health Service (Wales) Act 2006 s 42, a person with whom arrangements have been made under s 50, or a practitioner employed for the purposes of s 41, if it is made with the contractor's, person's or practitioner's authority: Mental Health (Wales) Measure 2010 s 6(7). As to regulations made under s 7(6)(a) see the Mental Health (Primary Care Referrals and Eligibility to Conduct Primary Mental Health Assessments) (Wales) Regulations 2012, SI 2012/1305, reg 3; and PARA 882.

10 Ie carried out in accordance with the Mental Health (Wales) Measure 2010 s 9 (see PARA 883).
11 See the Mental Health (Wales) Measure 2010 ss 6(1)–(3), 7(1)–(3).

882. Persons whom a primary care provider may refer to local primary mental health support services. A primary care provider[1] may refer[2] any person who is entitled to receive primary medical services[3] and who appears to be in need of a primary mental health assessment[4], for a primary mental health assessment[5].

1 As to the meaning of 'primary care provider' see the Mental Health (Wales) Measure 2010 s 51(1); and PARA 587 note 7 (definition applied by the Mental Health (Primary Care Referrals and Eligibility to Conduct Primary Mental Health Assessments) (Wales) Regulations 2012, SI 2012/1305, reg 2).

2 In accordance with the Mental Health (Wales) Measure 2010 s 7(5) (see PARA 881), the primary care provider must, if it determines to make a referral for a primary mental health assessment, make such a referral to the local mental health partner for the local authority area in which the primary care provider carries on the majority of its business or activities: Mental Health (Primary Care Referrals and Eligibility to Conduct Primary Mental Health Assessments) (Wales) Regulations 2012, SI 2012/1305, reg 3(2). As to the meaning of 'local mental health partners' see the Mental Health (Wales) Measure 2010 s 1; and PARA 586 note 1 (definition applied by the Mental Health (Primary Care Referrals and Eligibility to Conduct Primary Mental Health Assessments) (Wales) Regulations 2012, SI 2012/1305, reg 2).

3 'Primary medical services' means:
   (1) medical services provided under the National Health Service (Wales) Act 2006 Pt 4 whether by (a) a contractor with whom a general medical services contract has been entered into with a local health board under s 42 (see HEALTH SERVICES vol 54 (2008) PARA 242); (b) a person with whom arrangements have been made under s 50 of that Act by a local health board; (c) a registered medical practitioner employed for the purposes of s 41(2)(a) by a local health board; or (d) a registered medical practitioner with whom a local health board has made arrangements under s 41(2)(b) (Mental Health (Primary Care Referrals and Eligibility to Conduct Primary Mental Health Assessments) (Wales) Regulations 2012, SI 2012/1305, reg 2); or
   (2) medical services provided by (a) a registered medical practitioner under arrangements made between a registered medical practitioner and a person responsible for the provision or running of a contracted out prison (within the meaning of the Criminal Justice Act 1991 s 84(4) (see PRISONS AND PRISONERS vol 85 (2012) PARA 521) in Wales; or (b) a registered medical practitioner employed by Her Majesty's Prison Service in Wales (Mental Health (Primary Care Referrals and Eligibility to Conduct Primary Mental Health Assessments) (Wales) Regulations 2012, SI 2012/1305, reg 2).
As to registered medical practitioners see MEDICAL PROFESSIONS vol 74 (2011) PARA 176 et seq.

4   As to the meaning of 'primary mental health assessment' see the Mental Health (Wales) Measure 2010 s 51(1); PARA 586 note 6 (definition applied by the Mental Health (Primary Care Referrals and Eligibility to Conduct Primary Mental Health Assessments) (Wales) Regulations 2012, SI 2012/1305, reg 2).

5   Mental Health (Primary Care Referrals and Eligibility to Conduct Primary Mental Health Assessments) (Wales) Regulations 2012, SI 2012/1305, reg 3(1). This is subject to the Mental Health (Wales) Measure 2010 s 8(1) (see PARA 881): see the Mental Health (Primary Care Referrals and Eligibility to Conduct Primary Mental Health Assessments) (Wales) Regulations 2012, SI 2012/1305, reg 3(1).

883.   Conduct of primary mental health assessments.   A primary mental health assessment is an analysis of an individual's mental health which identifies the local primary mental health treatment (if any) which might improve or prevent a deterioration in the individual's mental health[1] and other services[2] (if any) which might improve or prevent a deterioration in the individual's mental health[3].

The local mental health partners must ensure that the assessment is carried out by an individual who is eligible[4] to carry out primary mental health assessments[5]. The Welsh Ministers[6] may by regulations make provision about the eligibility of individuals to exercise the function of a local mental health partner to carry out primary mental health assessments which may make provision relating to a person's qualifications, skills, training or experience[7].

1   Any treatment so identified must be provided: see the Mental Health (Wales) Measure 2010 ss 3 and 5.

2   This reference to other services is a reference to:
    (1)   secondary mental health services (Mental Health (Wales) Measure 2010 s 9(3)(a));
    (2)   services of a type that are normally provided by primary care providers (s 9(3)(b));
    (3)   community care services (not being secondary mental health services) (s 9(3)(c));
    (4)   services provided under the Children Act 1989 Pt III (not being secondary mental health services) (Mental Health (Wales) Measure 2010 s 9(3)(d));
    (5)   housing or well-being services (s 9(3)(e)); and
    (6)   education or training which may be beneficial to an individual's mental health (s 9(3)(f)).
    As to the meaning of 'secondary mental health services' see PARA 586 note 6. As to the meaning of 'primary care provider' see PARA 587 note 7. As to the meaning of 'community care services' see the National Health Service and Community Care Act 1990 s 46; and SOCIAL SERVICES AND COMMUNITY CARE vol 44(2) (Reissue) PARA 1012 (definition applied by the Mental Health (Wales) Measure 2010 s 51(1)). As to the meaning of 'housing or well-being services' see s 50; and PARA 587 note 10.

3   Mental Health (Wales) Measure 2010 s 9(2).

4   Ie eligible under the Mental Health (Wales) Measure 2010 s 47.

5   Mental Health (Wales) Measure 2010 s 9(3).

6   As to the Welsh Ministers see PARA 567.

7   Mental Health (Wales) Measure 2010 s 47(1)(a), (2). The regulations may make different provision in relation to the eligibility of individuals to carry out a primary mental health assessment compared to that which is made in relation to the eligibility of individuals to be appointed as care coordinators: s 47(3). As to such regulations see the Mental Health (Primary Care Referrals and Eligibility to Conduct Primary Mental Health Assessments) (Wales) Regulations 2012, SI 2012/1305, reg 4; and PARA 884.

884.   Eligibility requirements for persons who may conduct primary mental health assessments.   A person is eligible to perform the functions of a local mental health partner to carry out a primary mental health assessment[1] if that person fulfils one or more of the professional requirements[2] and has demonstrated to the satisfaction of the relevant local mental health partner[3] that he has appropriate experience, skills or training, or an appropriate combination of experience, skills and training[4].

1   As to the meaning of 'primary mental health assessment' see the Mental Health (Wales) Measure 2010 s 51(1); PARA 586 note 6 (definition applied by the Mental Health (Primary Care Referrals and Eligibility to Conduct Primary Mental Health Assessments) (Wales) Regulations 2012, SI 2012/1305, reg 2).

2   Ie the following professional requirements as set out in the Mental Health (Primary Care Referrals and Eligibility to Conduct Primary Mental Health Assessments) (Wales) Regulations 2012, SI 2012/1305, Schedule (amended by SI 2012/1479):
    (1)   a qualified social worker registered with the Care Council for Wales or in Part 16 of the register maintained under the Health and Social Work Professions Order 2001, SI 2002/254, art 5;
    (2)   a first or second level nurse, registered in Sub-Part 1 or Sub-Part 2 of the register maintained under the Nursing and Midwifery Order 2001, SI 2002/253, art 5 (see MEDICAL PROFESSIONS vol 74 (2011) PARA 713) with the inclusion of an entry indicating that his or her field of practice is mental health or learning disabilities nursing;
    (3)   an occupational therapist who is registered in Part 6 of the register maintained under the Health and Social Work Professions Order 2001, SI 2002/254, art 5 (scc MEDICAL PROFESSIONS vol 74 (2011) PARA 906);
    (4)   a practitioner psychologist who is registered in Part 14 of the register maintained under the Health and Social Work Professions Order 2001, SI 2002/254, art 5 (see MEDICAL PROFESSIONS vol 74 (2011) PARA 911); or
    (5)   a registered medical practitioner.
    As to registered medical practitioners see MEDICAL PROFESSIONS vol 74 (2011) PARA 176 et seq. As to the Care Council for Wales see the Care Standards Act 2000 s 54; and SOCIAL SERVICES AND COMMUNITY CARE vol 44(2) (Reissue) PARA 1003.

3   'Relevant local mental health partner' means the local mental health partner that is responsible for providing the majority of the local primary mental health support services under the Scheme agreed under the Mental Health (Wales) Measures 2010 s 2 (see PARA 586) or, if a Scheme is not agreed under those provisions, the relevant local mental health partner is the local health board for the local authority area in question: see the Mental Health (Primary Care Referrals and Eligibility to Conduct Primary Mental Health Assessments) (Wales) Regulations 2012, SI 2012/1305, reg 2. 'Scheme' means a scheme that local mental health partners must take all reasonable steps to agree in accordance with the Mental Health (Wales) Measure 2010 s 2 (see PARA 586): Mental Health (Primary Care Referrals and Eligibility to Conduct Primary Mental Health Assessments) (Wales) Regulations 2012, SI 2012/1305, reg 2.

4   Mental Health (Primary Care Referrals and Eligibility to Conduct Primary Mental Health Assessments) (Wales) Regulations 2012, SI 2012/1305, reg 4(1). When determining whether a person he has appropriate experience, skills or training, or an appropriate combination of experience, skills and training regard must be had to standards in any Codes of Practice issued under the Mental Health (Wales) Measure 2010 s 44 (see PARA 763), and any guidance that may from time to time be issued by the Welsh Ministers: Mental Health (Primary Care Referrals and Eligibility to Conduct Primary Mental Health Assessments) (Wales) Regulations 2012, SI 2012/1305, reg 4(2).

885.   Action following a primary mental health assessment.   Where a primary mental health assessment identifies[1] services which might improve, or prevent a deterioration in, an individual's mental health, the local mental health partner[2] which carried out the assessment must, if the partner considers that it would be the responsible authority[3] for providing any of the services, decide whether or not the provision of any of those services is called for and, if the partner considers that it would not be the responsible authority for providing any of the services, make a referral[4] to the person whom the partner considers would be the responsible authority for providing those services[5].

A person to whom a referral has been made must decide whether the provision of any of the services to which the referral relates is called for[6].

1   Ie under the Mental Health (Wales) Measure 2010 s 9(1)(b) (see PARA 883). As to the meaning of 'primary mental health assessment' see PARA 883.
2   As to the meaning of 'local mental health partner' see PARA 586 note 1.

3 For these purposes 'responsible authority' means the person who would be responsible for providing services if a decision were made to provide the services: Mental Health (Wales) Measure 2010 s 10(4).

4 The referral must inform the recipient that the local mental health partner making the referral has identified services which it considers might improve, or prevent a deterioration in, the individual's mental health and that the partner considers that the recipient would be the responsible authority for providing those services: Mental Health (Wales) Measure 2010 s 10(2). Nothing in this section requires or authorises a referral to be made to a responsible authority constituted, or acting exclusively, for an area wholly within England: s 10(5).

5 Mental Health (Wales) Measure 2010 s 10(1).

6 Mental Health (Wales) Measure 2010 s 10(3).

(14) TRANSFER OF PATIENTS

(i) Transfer from Hospital to Hospital or Guardianship

886.   Regulations as to the transfer of patients.   The appropriate national authority[1] may make regulations[2] prescribing the circumstances in which, and the conditions subject to which, patients[3] who are liable to be detained[4] or subject to guardianship under the general provisions as to compulsory admission to hospital and guardianship[5] may be transferred from one hospital[6] to another or from the guardianship of one authority or person to that of another, or from hospital to guardianship or vice versa[7].

1 As to the appropriate national authority see PARA 567.

2 See the Mental Health (Hospital, Guardianship and Treatment) (England) Regulations 2008, SI 2008/1184; the Mental Health (Hospital, Guardianship, Community Treatment and Consent to Treatment) (Wales) Regulations 2008, SI 2008/2439; and PARAS 887–891.

3 As to the meaning of 'patient' see PARA 758 note 4.

4 Ie whether for assessment or for treatment.

5 Ie under the Mental Health Act 1983 Pt 2 (ss 2–34). See, in particular, ss 2–4, 7; and PARAS 767–769, 785.

6 In this context, 'hospital' includes a registered establishment: see PARA 577. As to the meaning of 'registered establishment' see PARA 578.

7 Mental Health Act 1983 s 19(1). For patients subject to hospital orders but not subject to special restrictions, s 19(1) applies without modification: see ss 40(4), 55(4), Sch 1 Pt I paras 2, 5; and see PARAS 860–861. For patients who are subject to special restrictions, whether under restriction orders (PARA 869), orders for committal to hospital (see PARA 873), admission orders with restrictions (see PARA 874), directions for detention in hospital (see PARA 874) or transfer directions with restrictions (see PARA 894), s 19(1) is modified so that the consent of the Secretary of State is required before a patient can be transferred from one hospital to another and references to transfers to and from guardianship are omitted: see ss 40(1), 41(3), 55(4), Sch 1 Pt II paras 2, 5; and see PARAS 860–861.

887.   Authority for transfer from hospital to hospital or guardianship.   The authority for transfer from hospital[1] to hospital or guardianship must be given in the prescribed form[2] by the managers[3] of the hospital in which the patient[4] is liable to be detained or by an officer of the managers authorised by them in that behalf[5]. In the case of a patient liable to be detained in a registered establishment[6] the patient may be transferred from that establishment to another registered establishment where both are under the same management and the above provisions[7] do not apply[8]. Where such a patient is maintained under a contract with a strategic health authority, local health board, primary care trust, National Health Service trust, National Health Service foundation trust, a special health authority or Welsh Ministers[9], authority for transfer may be given by an officer of that authority, board or trust authorised by it in that behalf[10].

In the case of a transfer from hospital to hospital, the authority for transfer must not be given unless the person giving it is satisfied that arrangements have been made for the admission of the patient to the receiving hospital[11].

A hospital patient may be transferred into the guardianship of a local social services authority, or a person approved by a local social services authority, where authority for transfer is given by the managers of the hospital in which the patient is detained[12], the transfer has been agreed by the local social services authority which will be the responsible one if the proposed transfer takes effect[13], that local social services authority has specified the date on which the transfer will take place[14]; and where the person named in the authority for transfer as guardian will be a private guardian, the agreement of that person has been obtained[15].

No authority for transfer is required if the patient is to be transferred from one hospital to another hospital[16] under the same management[17] or from one registered establishment to another under the same management[18]. Nor is any such authority required in relation to transfer between and from special hospitals[19].

1   As to the meaning of 'hospital' see PARA 577.
2   As to the prescribed form for transfer to a hospital see the Mental Health (Hospital, Guardianship and Treatment) (England) Regulations 2008, SI 2008/1184, reg 7(2)(a); and the Mental Health (Hospital, Guardianship, Community Treatment and Consent to Treatment) (Wales) Regulations 2008, SI 2008/2439, reg 23(2)(a).
3   As to the meaning of 'managers' see PARA 778.
4   As to the meaning of 'patient' see PARA 758 note 4.
5   See the Mental Health Act 1983 s 19(1)(a); the Mental Health (Hospital, Guardianship and Treatment) (England) Regulations 2008, SI 2008/1184, reg 7(2), (6); and the Mental Health (Hospital, Guardianship, Community Treatment and Consent to Treatment) (Wales) Regulations 2008, SI 2008/2439, reg 23(2), (7)
6   As to the meaning of 'registered establishment' see PARA 578.
7   Ie the Mental Health (Hospital, Guardianship and Treatment) (England) Regulations 2008, SI 2008/1184, reg 7(2) or the Mental Health (Hospital, Guardianship, Community Treatment and Consent to Treatment) (Wales) Regulations 2008, SI 2008/2439, reg 23(2), as appropriate, do not apply.
8   See the Mental Health (Hospital, Guardianship and Treatment) (England) Regulations 2008, SI 2008/1184, reg 7(5)(a); and the Mental Health (Hospital, Guardianship, Community Treatment and Consent to Treatment) (Wales) Regulations 2008, SI 2008/2439, reg 23(6)(a).
9   As to the meaning of 'strategic health authority' see PARA 575 note 3. As to the meaning 'primary care trust' see PARA 575 note 5. As to the meaning of 'special health authority' see PARA 575 note 4. As to the meaning of 'local health board' see PARA 575 note 6. As from 1 April 2013 strategic health authorities and primary care trusts are abolished: see the Health and Social Care Act 2012 ss 33, 34; and the Health and Social Care Act 2012 (Commencement No 4, Transitional, Savings and Transitory Provisions) Order 2013, SI 2013/160, art 2(2).
10 See the Mental Health (Hospital, Guardianship and Treatment) (England) Regulations 2008, SI 2008/1184, reg 7(5)(b); and the Mental Health (Hospital, Guardianship, Community Treatment and Consent to Treatment) (Wales) Regulations 2008, SI 2008/2439, reg 23(6)(b).
11 See the Mental Health (Hospital, Guardianship and Treatment) (England) Regulations 2008, SI 2008/1184, reg 7(2)(b); and the Mental Health (Hospital, Guardianship, Community Treatment and Consent to Treatment) (Wales) Regulations 2008, SI 2008/2439, reg 23(2)(b). In relation to England this must be within a period of 28 days: see the Mental Health (Hospital, Guardianship and Treatment) (England) Regulations 2008, SI 2008/1184, reg 7(2)(b). Upon completion of the transfer the managers of the receiving hospital must record the patient's admission in the prescribed form: see the Mental Health (Hospital, Guardianship and Treatment) (England) Regulations 2008, SI 2008/1184, reg 7(3); and the Mental Health (Hospital, Guardianship, Community Treatment and Consent to Treatment) (Wales) Regulations 2008, SI 2008/2439, reg 23(3). See also PARA 886 note 7.
12 See the Mental Health (Hospital, Guardianship and Treatment) (England) Regulations 2008, SI 2008/1184, reg 7(4)(a); and the Mental Health (Hospital, Guardianship, Community Treatment and Consent to Treatment) (Wales) Regulations 2008, SI 2008/2439, reg 23(4)(a). As

to the prescribed form see the Mental Health (Hospital, Guardianship and Treatment) (England) Regulations 2008, SI 2008/1184, reg 7(4)(a); and the Mental Health (Hospital, Guardianship, Community Treatment and Consent to Treatment) (Wales) Regulations 2008, SI 2008/2439, reg 23(4)(a).

13 See the Mental Health (Hospital, Guardianship and Treatment) (England) Regulations 2008, SI 2008/1184, reg 7(4)(b); and the Mental Health (Hospital, Guardianship, Community Treatment and Consent to Treatment) (Wales) Regulations 2008, SI 2008/2439, reg 23(4)(b). In relation to England the managers of the transferring hospital must record the agreement of the local social services authority referred to in the Mental Health (Hospital, Guardianship and Treatment) (England) Regulations 2008, SI 2008/1184, reg 7(4)(b) and the date for transfer referred to in reg 7(4)(c), in the form set out in Sch 1: reg 7(7)(d).

14 See the Mental Health (Hospital, Guardianship and Treatment) (England) Regulations 2008, SI 2008/1184, reg 7(4)(c); and the Mental Health (Hospital, Guardianship, Community Treatment and Consent to Treatment) (Wales) Regulations 2008, SI 2008/2439, reg 23(4)(c).

15 See the Mental Health (Hospital, Guardianship and Treatment) (England) Regulations 2008, SI 2008/1184, reg 7(4)(e); and the Mental Health (Hospital, Guardianship, Community Treatment and Consent to Treatment) (Wales) Regulations 2008, SI 2008/2439, reg 23(4)(d).

16 Ie in a hospital vested in the Secretary of State for the purposes of his functions under the National Health Act 2006, the Welsh Ministers for their purposes under the National Health (Wales) Act 2006, in any accommodation used under either of those Acts by the managers of such a hospital or in a hospital vested in a National Health Service trust, NHS foundation trust, local health board or primary care trust: Mental Health Act 1983 19(3) (amended by the National Health Service and Community Care Act 1990 s 66(1), Sch 9 para 24(2); the Health and Social Care (Community Health and Standards) Act 2003 s 34, Sch 4 paras 50, 52; the National Health Service (Consequential Provisions) Act 2006 Sch 1 para 64; the Mental Health Act 2007 s 46(2); and SI 2000/90). As from 1 April 2013 the Mental Health Act 1983 s 19(3) is amended by the Health and Social Care Act 2012 Sch 5 para 25 and the words 'primary care trust' and 'NHS foundation trust' are omitted: see s 306(1)(d); and the Health and Social Care Act 2012 (Commencement No 4, Transitional, Savings and Transitory Provisions) Order 2013, SI 2013/160, art 2(2).

17 See the Mental Health Act 1983 s 19(3) (as amended: see note 16).
    The Mental Health Act 1983 s 19(3) is modified in relation to patients who are subject to special restrictions: see Sch 1 Pt II para 5(c); and PARA 860 note 12.

18 Ie under the Mental Health Act 1983 s 19(3): see the Mental Health (Hospital, Guardianship and Treatment) (England) Regulations 2008, SI 2008/1184, reg 7(1)(a); and the Mental Health (Hospital, Guardianship, Community Treatment and Consent to Treatment) (Wales) Regulations 2008, SI 2008/2439, reg 23(1)(a).

19 Ie under the Mental Health Act 1983 s 123(1), (2) (repealed): see the Mental Health (Hospital, Guardianship and Treatment) (England) Regulations 2008, SI 2008/1184, reg 7(1)(b); and the Mental Health (Hospital, Guardianship, Community Treatment and Consent to Treatment) (Wales) Regulations 2008, SI 2008/2439, reg 23(1)(b).

888.   Authority for transfer from guardianship to guardianship. A patient[1] ('a guardianship patient') who is for the time being subject to the guardianship of a local social services authority[2] or other person by virtue of an application under the Mental Health Act 1983 Part 2[3] may be transferred into the guardianship of another local social services authority or person under the following conditions[4].

A guardianship patient may be transferred into the guardianship of another local social services authority or another person where an authority for transfer has been given by the guardian[5], the transfer has been agreed by the local social services authority, which will be the responsible one if the proposed transfer takes effect[6], the local social services authority has specified the date on which the transfer will take place[7] and where the person named in the authority for transfer as proposed guardian will be a private guardian, the agreement of that person has been obtained and recorded in the prescribed form[8].

1 As to the meaning of 'patient' see PARA 758 note 4.
2 As to the meaning of 'local social services authority' see PARA 579. As to the form to be used by the authority to transfer to hospital a guardianship patient see the Mental Health (Hospital, Guardianship and Treatment) (England) Regulations 2008, SI 2008/1184, reg 8(2); and the

Mental Health (Hospital, Guardianship, Community Treatment and Consent to Treatment) (Wales) Regulations 2008, SI 2008/2439, reg 24(3), (4).

3 Ie the Mental Health Act 1983 Pt 2 (ss 2–34).

4 See the Mental Health Act 1983 s 19(1)(b).

5 See the Mental Health (Hospital, Guardianship and Treatment) (England) Regulations 2008, SI 2008/1184, reg 8(2)(a); and the Mental Health (Hospital, Guardianship, Community Treatment and Consent to Treatment) (Wales) Regulations 2008, SI 2008/2439, reg 24(2)(a). As to the prescribed form see the Mental Health (Hospital, Guardianship and Treatment) (England) Regulations 2008, SI 2008/1184, reg 8(1)(a); and the Mental Health (Hospital, Guardianship, Community Treatment and Consent to Treatment) (Wales) Regulations 2008, SI 2008/2439, reg 24(2)(a).

6 See the Mental Health (Hospital, Guardianship and Treatment) (England) Regulations 2008, SI 2008/1184, reg 8(1)(b); and the Mental Health (Hospital, Guardianship, Community Treatment and Consent to Treatment) (Wales) Regulations 2008, SI 2008/2439, reg 24(2)(b). In relation to England the guardian must record the agreement of the receiving local social services authority mentioned in the Mental Health (Hospital, Guardianship and Treatment) (England) Regulations 2008, SI 2008/1184, reg 8(1)(b) and the date for transfer mentioned in reg 8(1)(c): see reg 8(1)(d).

7 See the Mental Health (Hospital, Guardianship and Treatment) (England) Regulations 2008, SI 2008/1184, reg 8(1)(c); and the Mental Health (Hospital, Guardianship, Community Treatment and Consent to Treatment) (Wales) Regulations 2008, SI 2008/2439, reg 24(2)(c).

8 See the Mental Health (Hospital, Guardianship and Treatment) (England) Regulations 2008, SI 2008/1184, reg 8(1)(e); and the Mental Health (Hospital, Guardianship, Community Treatment and Consent to Treatment) (Wales) Regulations 2008, SI 2008/2439, reg 24(2)(d). As to the prescribed form see the Mental Health (Hospital, Guardianship and Treatment) (England) Regulations 2008, SI 2008/1184, reg 8(1)(e); and the Mental Health (Hospital, Guardianship, Community Treatment and Consent to Treatment) (Wales) Regulations 2008, SI 2008/2439, reg 24(2)(d).

889. Authority for transfer from guardianship to hospital. The authority for transfer from guardianship to hospital[1] must be given in the prescribed form[2] by the responsible local social services authority[3]. No such authority may be given unless: (1) an application for admission for treatment[4] has been made by an approved mental health professional[5] in the prescribed form[6]; (2) that application is founded upon two medical recommendations or a joint medical recommendation in the prescribed forms[7]; (3) the responsible local social service authority is satisfied that arrangements have been made for the admission of the patient to that hospital[8]; (4) in relation to Wales, an application for admission for treatment has been made by the nearest relative[9]. Where these conditions are satisfied the transfer of the patient must be effective, in relation to England, within 14 days of the date on which the patient was last examined, and in relation to Wales, within 28 days of the date of authority, failing which the patient remains in the guardianship of the initial guardian[10].

On the transfer of the patient to hospital, a record of admission must be made by the managers[11] of the hospital to which the patient is transferred[12].

A patient who is thus transferred has the right to apply to a tribunal[13] once[14] within the period of six months beginning with the day on which he is so transferred[15]. If he does not exercise this right, the hospital managers must, at the expiration of such period, automatically refer his case to the tribunal[16].

1 As to the meaning of 'hospital' see PARA 577.

2 Mental Health Act 1983 s 19(1)(b). As to the prescribed from see the Mental Health (Hospital, Guardianship and Treatment) (England) Regulations 2008, SI 2008/1184, reg 8(2); and the Mental Health (Hospital, Guardianship, Community Treatment and Consent to Treatment) (Wales) Regulations 2008, SI 2008/2439, reg 24(4).

3 Mental Health (Hospital, Guardianship and Treatment) (England) Regulations 2008, SI 2008/1184, reg 8(2); the Mental Health (Hospital, Guardianship, Community Treatment and Consent to Treatment) (Wales) Regulations 2008, SI 2008/2439, reg 24(4). As to the meaning of

'responsible local social services authority' see PARA 791 note 1. Hospital managers must refer to the appropriate tribunal a patient who is transferred from guardianship to a hospital in pursuance of regulations made under the Mental Health Act 1983 s 19: see s 68; and PARA 964.

4   As to admission for treatment see PARA 768.

5   As to the meaning of 'approved mental health professional' see PARA 815 note 2.

6   Mental Health (Hospital, Guardianship and Treatment) (England) Regulations 2008, SI 2008/1184, reg 8(2)(a); the Mental Health (Hospital, Guardianship, Community Treatment and Consent to Treatment) (Wales) Regulations 2008, SI 2008/2439, reg 24(4)(a). For this purpose, the provisions of the Mental Health Act 1983 s 11(4) (consultation with nearest relative) and s 13 (duty of approved mental health professional) (see PARA 821) apply as if the proposed transfer were an application for admission for treatment: Mental Health (Hospital, Guardianship and Treatment) (England) Regulations 2008, SI 2008/1184, reg 8(3); the Mental Health (Hospital, Guardianship, Community Treatment and Consent to Treatment) (Wales) Regulations 2008, SI 2008/2439, reg 24(4)(b).

7   See the Mental Health (Hospital, Guardianship and Treatment) (England) Regulations 2008, SI 2008/1184, reg 8(2)(b); the Mental Health (Hospital, Guardianship, Community Treatment and Consent to Treatment) (Wales) Regulations 2008, SI 2008/2439, reg 24(4)(c). The transfer must be effected within 14 days of the date on which the patient was last examined: see the Mental Health (Hospital, Guardianship and Treatment) (England) Regulations 2008, SI 2008/1184, reg 8(8); the Mental Health (Hospital, Guardianship, Community Treatment and Consent to Treatment) (Wales) Regulations 2008, SI 2008/2439, reg 24(4)(c).

8   Mental Health (Hospital, Guardianship and Treatment) (England) Regulations 2008, SI 2008/1184, reg 8(2)(c); Mental Health (Hospital, Guardianship, Community Treatment and Consent to Treatment) (Wales) Regulations 2008, SI 2008/2439, reg 24(4)(d).

9   Mental Health (Hospital, Guardianship, Community Treatment and Consent to Treatment) (Wales) Regulations 2008, SI 2008/2439, reg 24(4)(b).

10 See the Mental Health (Hospital, Guardianship and Treatment) (England) Regulations 2008, SI 2008/1184, reg 8(5); the Mental Health (Hospital, Guardianship, Community Treatment and Consent to Treatment) (Wales) Regulations 2008, SI 2008/2439, reg 24(7).

11 The functions of managers under these provisions may be performed by an officer authorised by them in that behalf: see the Mental Health (Hospital, Guardianship and Treatment) (England) Regulations 2008, SI 2008/1184, reg 8(6); and the Mental Health (Hospital, Guardianship, Community Treatment and Consent to Treatment) (Wales) Regulations 2008, SI 2008/2439, reg 24(6). As to the form for recording the admission see the Mental Health (Hospital, Guardianship and Treatment) (England) Regulations 2008, SI 2008/1184, reg 8(4); the Mental Health (Hospital, Guardianship, Community Treatment and Consent to Treatment) (Wales) Regulations 2008, SI 2008/2439, reg 24(5).

12 See the Mental Health (Hospital, Guardianship and Treatment) (England) Regulations 2008, SI 2008/1184, reg 8(4); the Mental Health (Hospital, Guardianship, Community Treatment and Consent to Treatment) (Wales) Regulations 2008, SI 2008/2439, reg 24(5).

13 As to applications to a tribunal see PARA 961.

14 Any withdrawn application is disregarded: see the Mental Health Act 1983 s 77(2) (see PARA 959).

15 Mental Health Act 1983 s 66(1)(e), (2)(e).

16 See the Mental Health Act 1983 s 68(1); and PARA 964.

890. Effect of transfer. Where a patient[1] is transferred in pursuance of the regulations for that purpose[2], the effect is that in the case of transfer from hospital[3] to hospital the patient is treated as if he had been admitted to the receiving hospital on the same day as that on which he was originally admitted to the sending hospital and by virtue of the same application as that which authorised his admission to the sending hospital[4]. If he is transferred from hospital to guardianship he is treated as if received into guardianship when originally admitted to hospital, the application for admission to hospital being treated as if it had been a guardianship application[5]. If he is transferred from guardianship to hospital he is similarly treated as if admitted to hospital at the time when the guardianship application was accepted and as if that application had been an application for admission to hospital for treatment[6]. In the case of transfer from guardianship to guardianship, he is treated as if his reception into the later guardianship had been authorised by the same guardianship application as authorised the earlier guardianship and on the same date[7].

These provisions[8] are modified in relation to patients who are subject to hospital orders[9] or to special restrictions[10].

1   As to the meaning of 'patient' see PARA 758 note 4.
2   As to the regulations see PARAS 886–889.
3   As to the meaning of 'hospital' see PARA 577.
4   Mental Health Act 1983 s 19(2)(a). The dates at which the authority for detention (or guardianship) will expire under s 20 unless renewed continues to be calculated from the date of the original admission, notwithstanding any transfer: see PARAS 908–909.
5   Mental Health Act 1983 s 19(2)(b).
6   Mental Health Act 1983 s 19(2)(d). He is so treated notwithstanding the fact that the transfer itself involves medical recommendations additional to those on which the original application was founded.
7   Mental Health Act 1983 s 19(2)(c). Where guardianship is transferred to the local social services authority (see PARA 579) or other person by reason of the death, resignation or incapacity of the guardian or by the county court on the ground that the guardian has performed his functions negligently or in a manner contrary to the patient's interests, this provision applies to the patient as if he had been transferred into the later guardianship in pursuance of the regulations for that purpose: s 10(4); and see PARAS 794–796.
8   Ie the provisions of the Mental Health Act 1983 s 19(2): see the text and notes 2–7.
9   In relation to a patient in respect of whom a hospital order without restrictions (see PARA 864), a transfer direction without restrictions (see PARAS 892–893) or a guardianship order (see PARA 877) has been made, the provisions of the Mental Health Act 1983 s 19(2) have effect as if the order or direction by which he was liable to be detained or subject to guardianship before being transferred were an order or direction for his admission or removal to the hospital to which he is transferred or placing him under the guardianship of the authority or person into whose guardianship he is transferred, as the case may be: see ss 40(4), 55(4), Sch 1 Pt I paras 2, 5; and PARAS 860–861.
10 In relation to a patient in respect of whom a restriction order (see PARA 869), an order for committal to hospital (see PARA 873), an admission order with a restriction direction (see PARA 874), a direction for detention in hospital (see PARA 874) or a transfer direction with restrictions (see PARA 894) has been made or given, the provisions of the Mental Health Act 1983 s 19(2) have effect as if the order or direction by which he was liable to be detained before being transferred were an order or direction for his admission or removal to the hospital to which he is transferred: see ss 40(4), 41(3), 55(4), Sch 1 Pt II paras 2, 5(b); and PARAS 860–861.

891.   Conveyance to hospital.   Where the following conditions[1] are met the authority for transfer given in accordance with those conditions[2] is sufficient authority for the following persons to take the patient and convey him to the hospital[3] to which the patient[4] is being transferred within the periods specified:

(1)   in a case where a hospital patient is being transferred to another hospital[5] an officer of the managers[6] of either hospital or any authorised person[7] within the period of 28 days beginning with the date of the authority for transfer[8];

(2)   in a case where a guardianship patient is transferred to hospital[9], an officer of, or any person authorised by, the responsible local social services authority, within the period of 14 days beginning with the date on which the patient was last examined by a medical practitioner for that purpose[10];

(3)   in the case of the transfer of a community patient recalled to hospital[11], an officer of (in relation England either hospital), or any other person authorised by the managers of the hospital to which the patient is being transferred, within the period of 72 hours beginning with the time of the patient's detention pursuant to the patient's recall[12].

In a case to which a hospital patient who is detained in a registered establishment[13] is transferred from that registered establishment to another registered establishment under the same management[14], an officer or any other person authorised by the managers of the registered establishment may take and convey the patient to the registered establishment to which he is being transferred[15].

1 Ie in relation to England, the conditions under the Mental Health (Hospital, Guardianship and Treatment) (England) Regulations 2008, SI 2008/1184, reg 7(2) or 8(2) (see PARAS 887, 888), or in relation to Wales, the conditions under the Mental Health (Hospital, Guardianship, Community Treatment and Consent to Treatment) (Wales) Regulations 2008, SI 2008/2439, reg 23(2), 24(4) or 26(2) (see PARAS 887, 889).
2 Ie the authority for transfer given in accordance with the provisions in note 1.
3 As to the meaning of 'hospital' see PARA 577.
4 As to the meaning of 'patient' see PARA 758 note 4.
5 Ie in a case to which the Mental Health (Hospital, Guardianship and Treatment) (England) Regulations 2008, SI 2008/1184, reg 7(2) and the Mental Health (Hospital, Guardianship, Community Treatment and Consent to Treatment) (Wales) Regulations 2008, SI 2008/2439, reg 23(2) apply.
6 As to the meaning of 'managers' see PARA 778.
7 In relation to England this is a person authorised by the managers of the hospital to which the patient is being transferred and, in relation to Wales, this is a person authorised by the managers of both hospitals.
8 Mental Health (Hospital, Guardianship and Treatment) (England) Regulations 2008, SI 2008/1184, reg 11(1)(a); Mental Health (Hospital, Guardianship, Community Treatment and Consent to Treatment) (Wales) Regulations 2008, SI 2008/2439, reg 27(1)(a).
9 Ie in a case to which the Mental Health (Hospital, Guardianship and Treatment) (England) Regulations 2008, SI 2008/1184, reg 8(2) (see PARA 889) and the Mental Health (Hospital, Guardianship, Community Treatment and Consent to Treatment) (Wales) Regulations 2008, SI 2008/2439, reg 24(4) (see PARA 889) apply.
10 See the Mental Health (Hospital, Guardianship and Treatment) (England) Regulations 2008, SI 2008/1184, reg 11(1)(b); and the Mental Health (Hospital, Guardianship, Community Treatment and Consent to Treatment) (Wales) Regulations 2008, SI 2008/2439, reg 27(1)(b).
11 Ie a case to which the Mental Health (Hospital, Guardianship, Community Treatment and Consent to Treatment) (Wales) Regulations 2008, SI 2008/2439, reg 26 (see PARA 802) applies.
12 Ie pursuant to the patient's recall under the Mental Health Act 1983 s 17E (see PARA 801): see the Mental Health (Hospital, Guardianship and Treatment) (England) Regulations 2008, SI 2008/1184, reg 12; and the Mental Health (Hospital, Guardianship, Community Treatment and Consent to Treatment) (Wales) Regulations 2008, SI 2008/2439, reg 27(1)(c).
13 As to the meaning of 'registered establishment' see PARA 578.
14 Ie a case to which the Mental Health (Hospital, Guardianship and Treatment) (England) Regulations 2008, SI 2008/1184, reg 7(5)(a) (see PARA 887) or the Mental Health (Hospital, Guardianship, Community Treatment and Consent to Treatment) (Wales) Regulations 2008, SI 2008/2439, reg 23(6)(a) (see PARA 887) applies.
15 Mental Health (Hospital, Guardianship and Treatment) (England) Regulations 2008, SI 2008/1184, reg 11(3); Mental Health (Hospital, Guardianship, Community Treatment and Consent to Treatment) (Wales) Regulations 2008, SI 2008/2439, reg 27(3).

(ii) Transfer and Removal of Prisoners to Hospital

892. Removal to hospital of persons serving sentences of imprisonment. If a person is serving a sentence of imprisonment[1], and the Secretary of State[2] is satisfied, by reports[3] from at least two registered medical practitioners[4]: (1) that that person is suffering from mental disorder[5]; and (2) that the mental disorder[6] from which the person is suffering is of a nature or degree which makes it appropriate for him to be detained in a hospital[7] for medical treatment[8]; and (3) such appropriate medical treatment is available for him[9], then if the Secretary of State is of the opinion having regard to the public interest and all the circumstances that it is expedient to do so, he may by warrant direct that that person be removed to and detained in such hospital as may be specified in the direction[10]. Such a direction, which is referred to as a 'transfer direction'[11], ceases to be effective if the prisoner is not received into the hospital specified within a period of 14 days beginning with the date on which it is given[12].

A transfer direction with respect to any person has the same effect as a hospital order[13] made in his case[14].

1   References in this provision to a person serving a sentence of imprisonment include references: (1) to a person detained in pursuance of any sentence or order for detention made by a court in criminal proceedings or service disciplinary proceedings (other than an order made in consequence of a finding of insanity or unfitness to stand trial or a sentence of service detention within the meaning of the Armed Forces Act 2006: see PARA 874); (2) to a person committed to custody under the Magistrates' Courts Act 1980 s 115(3) (which relates to persons who fail to comply with an order to enter into recognisances to keep the peace or be of good behaviour: see SENTENCING AND DISPOSITION OF OFFENDERS vol 92 (2010) PARA 152); and (3) to a person committed by a court to a prison or other institution to which the Prison Act 1952 applies (see PRISONS AND PRISONERS) in default of payment of any sum adjudged to be paid on his conviction: Mental Health Act 1983 s 47(5)(a)–(c) (amended by the Domestic Violence, Crime and Victims Act 2004 s 58(1), Sch 10 para 18; the Armed Forces Act 2006 Sch 16 para 97(2)); Mental Health Act 1983 s 55(6).

2   As to the Secretary of State PARA 568.

3   The reports must comply with the provisions of the Mental Health Act 1983 ss 12, 54(1): see PARAS 849, 865. As to reliable reports see *R v Secretary of State for the Home Department, ex p Gilkes* (1999) 1 MHLR 6 (approved in *R (on the application of TF) v Secretary of State for Justice* [2008] EWCA Civ 1457, 106 BMLR 54.

4   As to registered medical practitioners see MEDICAL PROFESSIONS vol 74 (2011) PARA 176 et seq.
      In practice, the Home Secretary is likely to want one of the two doctors to be practising at the hospital named in the proposed transfer direction so as to ensure agreement as to the patient's reception by the hospital and his diagnosis, treatability and detention: see *R (on the application of D) v Secretary of State for the Home Department* [2004] EWHC 2857 (Admin), [2004] All ER (D) 250 (Dec).

5   Mental Health Act 1983 s 47(1)(a) (amended by the Mental Health Act 2007 Sch 1 Pt 1 para 10).

6   As to the meaning of 'mental disorder' see PARA 761.

7   As to the meaning of 'hospital' see PARA 577.

8   As to the meaning of 'medical treatment' see PARA 926.

9   Mental Health Act 1983 s 47(1)(b).

10   Mental Health Act 1983 s 47(1)(c) (substituted by the Mental Health Act 2007 s 4(7)). Any power to specify a hospital conferred by the Mental Health Act 1983 s 47 includes power to specify a hospital unit; and, where such a unit is specified in relation to any person in the exercise of such a power, any reference in any enactment (including one contained in the Crime (Sentences) Act 1997) to him being, or being liable to be, detained in a hospital is to be construed accordingly (although this does not apply unless the court also gives a direction under the Mental Health Act 1983 s 49 (see PARA 894)): Crime (Sentences) Act 1997 s 47(1)(c), (2)(b).
      The prisoner's sentence and any licence period and conditions, including prospect of recall to prison, continue to run notwithstanding transfer to hospital: *R (on the application of Miah) v Secretary of State for the Home Department* [2004] EWHC 2569 (Admin), (2004) Times, 10 September. See also the Prison Act 1952 s 22(2)(b); and SENTENCING AND DISPOSITION OF OFFENDERS. See further PARA 895.
      Delay in a transfer is not an infringement of the Convention for the Protection of Human Rights and Fundamental Freedoms (Rome, 4 November 1950; TS 71 (1953); Cmd 8969) art 8 (see RIGHTS AND FREEDOMS) where the delay was due to difficulties in satisfying conditions for the exercise of the statutory power, especially if the diagnosis was uncertain and there were few places available: *R (on the application of D) v Secretary of State for the Home Department* [2004] EWHC 2857 (Admin), [2004] All ER (D) 250 (Dec) (in this case it was held that the Home Secretary has a duty to act expeditiously on receipt of information as to the possible need for a transfer and on receipt of medical reports; and suggestions were made as to the setting-up of a central database of hospitals for placement finding).
      Failure to transfer is judicially reviewable if the mentally disordered prisoner demonstrates that he is denied medical treatment: *R v Drew* [2003] UKHL 25, [2003] 4 All ER 557, [2003] 1 WLR 1213. As to the High Court's jurisdiction to direct the Secretary of State to order transfer see *R (on the application of D) v Secretary of State for the Home Department*. As to appropriate conditions of detention see *Aerts v Belgium* (1998) 29 EHRR 50, 5 BHRC 382, ECtHR.

See also *R (on the application of TF) v Secretary of State for Justice* [2008] EWCA Civ 1457, (2009) 106 BMLR 54 (judge had no power to render lawful detention in a hospital where he found transfer of patient was unlawful).

11 Mental Health Act 1983 ss 47(1), 145(1) (s 47(1) amended by the Crime (Sentences) Act 1997 ss 49(3), 56(2), Sch 6).

12 Mental Health Act 1983 s 47(2).

13 See the Mental Health Act 1983 s 37(1); and PARA 864. Consequently, the provisions of Pt 2 (ss 2–34) apply to a patient detained in pursuance of a transfer direction without restrictions as they do to a patient detained in pursuance of a hospital order without restrictions: see ss 40(4), 55(4); and PARA 867. Where the Secretary of State, when giving a transfer direction, also gives a restriction direction (see PARA 894), the provisions of Pt 2 apply as they apply to a patient detained in pursuance of a hospital order with an order restricting discharge: see ss 40(4), 41(3), 55(4) (s 41(3)); and PARA 860. As to the meaning of 'hospital order' see PARA 864 note 5.

14 Mental Health Act 1983 s 47(3).

893. Removal to hospital of other prisoners. If the Secretary of State[1] is satisfied by the same reports as are required in the case of persons serving sentences of imprisonment[2], that a person is suffering from mental disorder[3] of a nature or degree which makes it appropriate for him to be detained in a hospital[4] for medical treatment[5], he is in urgent need of such treatment[6] and appropriate medical treatment is available for him[7], the Secretary of State has the same power of giving a transfer direction[8] as if he were a person serving such a sentence[9]. These provisions apply to: (1) persons detained in a prison or remand centre, not being persons serving a sentence of imprisonment or falling within heads (2) to (4) below[10]; (2) persons remanded in custody by a magistrates' court[11]; (3) civil prisoners, that is to say persons committed by a court to prison for a limited term[12], but not being persons falling to be dealt with under the provisions[13] relating to the removal to hospital of persons serving prison sentences[14]; and (4) persons detained under the Immigration Act 1971 or the Nationality, Immigration and Asylum Act 2002[15].

1 As to the Secretary of State see PARA 568.

2 Ie the same reports as are required for the purposes of the Mental Health Act 1983 s 47 (see PARA 892).

3 As to the meaning of 'mental disorder' see PARA 761.

4 As to the meaning of 'hospital' see PARA 577.

5 Mental Health Act 1983 s 48(1)(a) (s 48(1)(a), (b) substituted by the Mental Health Act 2007 Sch 1 Pt 1 para 11(a)). As to the meaning of 'medical treatment' see PARA 926.

6 Mental Health Act 1983 s 48(1)(b) (as substituted: see note 5).

7 Mental Health Act 1983 s 48(1)(c) (added by the Mental Health Act 2007 s 5(3)).

8 As to the meaning of 'transfer direction' see PARA 892.

9 Mental Health Act 1983 s 48(1). The provisions of s 47(2), (3) (see PARA 892) apply for the purposes of s 48 and of any transfer direction given by virtue of s 48 as they apply for the purposes of s 47 and of any transfer direction under s 47: s 48(3) (amended by the Mental Health Act 1983 Sch 1 Pt 1 para 11(b)). As to the application of s 48 to a person detained under the Immigration Act 1971 see *R (on the application of AS (Lebanon) v Secretary of State for Home Department* [2012] EWHC 1349 (Admin), [2012] All ER (D) 198 (May).

10 Mental Health Act 1983 s 48(2)(a). As from a day to be appointed, this provision is amended so as to omit the reference to a remand centre: see s 48(2)(a) (prospectively amended by the Criminal Justice and Court Services Act 2000 ss 74, 75, Sch 7 Pt II paras 72, 73, Sch 8). At the date at which this volume states the law no such day had been appointed.

  Where the Secretary of State gives a transfer direction in respect of any such person he must also give a restriction direction: see the Mental Health Act 1983 s 49(1); and PARA 894. As to restriction directions see PARA 894.

11 Mental Health Act 1983 s 48(2)(b). Where the Secretary of State gives a transfer direction in respect of any such person he must also give a restriction direction: see s 49(1); and PARA 894. As to magistrates' courts see MAGISTRATES vol 71 (2013) PARA 470 et seq.

12 Persons committed to prison for contempt of court must now be committed for a fixed term and are therefore included: see the Contempt of Court Act 1981 s 14(1). The court also has power to

make a hospital order as if a person committed for contempt had been convicted: see s 14(4); and PARA 864. As to committal for contempt of court see CONTEMPT OF COURT vol 22 (2012) PARA 95.
13 Ie under the Mental Health Act 1983 s 47: see PARA 892.
14 Mental Health Act 1983 s 48(2)(c) (amended by the Statute Law (Repeals) Act 2004).
15 Mental Health Act 1983 s 48(2)(d) (amended by the Nationality, Immigration and Asylum Act 2002 s 62(10)(a)). The reference in the text is a reference to persons detained under the Immigration Act 1971 or the Nationality, Immigration and Asylum Act 2002 s 62: see IMMIGRATION AND ASYLUM vol 57 (2012) PARA 191 et seq. See also *R (on the application of HA (Nigeria)) v Secretary of State for the Home Department* [2012] EWHC 979 (Admin), [2012] All ER (D) 76 (Apr) (the court decided obiter that the power to transfer a detained person to hospital under the Mental Health Act 1983 s 48 did not apply to those detained under the UK Borders Act 2007.

894. Direction restricting discharge of prisoner removed to hospital. Where the Secretary of State[1] gives a transfer direction in respect of any person[2], he may, if he thinks fit[3], by warrant further direct that that person is to be subject to the same special restrictions on discharge as would be imposed by a restriction order made by a court[4]; and, where the Secretary of State gives a transfer direction in respect of a person committed or remanded in custody awaiting trial or sentence[5] or in respect of a person ordered by the Court of Appeal[6] to be kept in continued detention pending trial after a successful appeal against findings that he is under a disability and did the acts or made the omission charged[7], he must give a restriction direction[8]. A restriction direction has the same effect as a restriction order[9].

1 As to the Secretary of State PARA 568.
2 As to the giving of transfer directions see PARAS 892–893.
3 The Secretary of State is not bound to give a restriction direction in all cases in which he gives a transfer direction but he must give a restriction direction in respect of persons falling within the Mental Health Act 1983 s 48(2)(a) or s 48(2)(b): see PARA 893.
4 Ie a restriction order under the Mental Health Act 1983 s 41 (see PARA 869): s 49(1). A court must hear oral evidence from at least one of the registered medical practitioners whose evidence is taken into account when making the relevant hospital order: see s 41(2); and PARA 869. There is no corresponding requirement in the case of the Secretary of State, although he would no doubt rely on medical advice. The effect of the special restrictions on discharge imposed by a restriction order or restriction direction is that the authority for the detention of the patient continues irrespective of the provisions relating to duration, renewal and expiration (see ss 20, 21; and PARAS 908–911), and he may not be discharged, transferred to another hospital or granted leave of absence without the consent of the Secretary of State; if absent without leave he may be taken into custody and returned to hospital at any time without limitation of period (see s 41(3); and PARA 869). An application may be made by the patient or his nearest relative to a tribunal: see s 70; and PARA 962.
5 Ie the persons described in the Mental Health Act 1983 s 48(2)(a) (which applies to persons detained in prison or in a remand centre and not serving a prison sentence) and s 48(2)(b) (which applies to persons remanded in custody by magistrates' courts).
6 As to the Court of Appeal see COURTS AND TRIBUNALS vol 24 (2010) PARA 688 et seq.
7 Ie an appeal under the Criminal Appeal Act 1968 s 15 against a determination under the Criminal Procedure (Insanity) Act 1964 (see PARA 874): see the Criminal Appeal Act 1968 s 16(3), Sch 3 para 2 (s 16(3) substituted by the Criminal Procedure (Insanity and Unfitness to Plead) Act 1991 s 7, Sch 3 para 3; and amended by the Criminal Justice and Public Order Act 1994 s 168(2), Sch 10 para 21; and the Criminal Appeal Act 1968 Sch 3 para 2 substituted by the Mental Health Act 1983 s 148(1), Sch 4 para 23(n)). This applies the Mental Health Act 1983 Pt 3 (ss 35–55) to such a person as if he had been ordered to be kept in custody pending trial and were detained in pursuance of a transfer direction together with a restriction direction. See also CRIMINAL PROCEDURE vol 28 (2010) PARA 767.
8 Mental Health Act 1983 s 49(1). 'Restriction direction' has the meaning given by s 49: s 145(1). While a person is subject to a restriction direction, the responsible clinician must make a regular report on him: s 49(3) (amended by the Mental Health Act 2007 s 10(9)(b)). See PARA 876. As to the meaning of 'responsible clinician' see PARA 834.

The policy is to impose a restriction direction unless it is proposed to transfer the prisoner within days of the release date and the nature of the offence raises no issue regarding the protection of the public from serious harm: see *R (on the application of T) v Secretary of State for the Home Department* [2003] EWHC 538 (Admin).

As to 'technical lifers' and the possible violation of the Convention for the Protection of Human Rights and Fundamental Freedoms (Rome, 4 November 1950; TS 71 (1953); Cmd 8969) art 5(4) see Application 28212/95 *Benjamin v United Kingdom* (2002) 36 EHRR 1, 13 BHRC 287, ECtHR; *R (on the application of D) v Secretary of State for the Home Department* [2002] EWHC 2805 (Admin), [2003] 1 WLR 1315, (2002) Times, 31 December; *R (on the application of R) v Shetty (Responsible Medical Officer)* [2003] EWHC 3152 (Admin), (2004) Times, 9 January; and see RIGHTS AND FREEDOMS. 'Technical lifers' are those sentenced to life imprisonment (discretionary or mandatory) and treated as though originally made subject to the Mental Health Act 1983 s 37 (see PARA 864) and s 41 (see PARA 869) by the court on transfer to hospital; this is a desirable status for such a prisoner because he cannot be returned to prison, becomes entitled to access to an appropriate tribunal under the Convention for the Protection of Human Rights and Fundamental Freedoms art 5(4) even before his tariff has expired and is entitled to be discharged if the tribunal so recommends (see PARA 969). Technical lifer is status no longer awarded since April 2005.

9   Mental Health Act 1983 s 49(2). Consequently the Secretary of State, if satisfied that a restriction direction is no longer required for the protection of the public from serious harm, may direct that the patient is to cease to be subject to the restrictions which it imposed: see s 42(1); and PARA 876. A restriction direction in the case of a person serving a sentence of imprisonment ceases to have effect, if it has not previously done so, on his release date: s 50(2) (substituted by the Criminal Justice Act 2003 s 294(1), (3)). When a restriction direction ceases to have effect while the relevant transfer direction continues in force, the patient must be treated as if he had been admitted to hospital in pursuance of a hospital order made on the date when the restriction direction ceased to have effect (see the Mental Health Act 1983 s 41(5); and PARA 870), and the general provisions relating to compulsory admission will apply to him from that time, subject to exceptions and modifications (see PARA 860).

895.   Further provisions as to transferred prisoners under sentence.

Where a transfer direction[1] and a restriction direction[2] have been given in respect of a person serving a sentence of imprisonment[3] and before his release date[4] the appropriate national authority[5] is notified by a responsible clinician[6] or any other approved clinician[7] or the appropriate tribunal[8] that that person no longer requires treatment for mental disorder or that no effective treatment for his disorder can be given in the hospital[9] to which he has been removed[10], the Secretary of State may: (1) by warrant direct that he be remitted to any prison or other institution in which he might have been detained if he had not been removed to hospital, there to be dealt with as if he had not been so removed[11]; or (2) exercise any power of releasing him on licence or discharging him under supervision[12] which would have been exercisable if he had been remitted to such a prison or institution[13]. In such an event, on the arrival of the person concerned in the prison or other institution or, as the case may be, on his release on licence or discharge under supervision, the transfer direction and the restriction direction cease to have effect[14].

A restriction direction in the case of a person serving a sentence of imprisonment ceases to have effect, if it has not previously done so, on his release date[15].

1   As to transfer directions see PARA 892 et seq.
2   As to restriction directions see PARA 894.
3   As to persons serving a sentence of imprisonment see PARA 892 note 1.
4   For these purposes, references to a person's release date are references to the day (if any) on which he would be entitled to be released (whether unconditionally or on licence) from any prison or other institution in which he might have been detained if the transfer direction had not been given; and in determining that day there is to be disregarded: (1) any powers that would be exercisable by the Parole Board if he were detained in such a prison or other institution; and (2) any practice of the Secretary of State in relation to the early release under discretionary powers

of persons detained in such a prison or other institution: Mental Health Act 1983 s 50(3) (substituted by the Criminal Justice Act 2003 s 294(1), (3)).

For the purposes of the Prison Act 1952 s 49(2) (which provides for discounting from the sentences of certain prisoners periods while they are unlawfully at large: see PRISONS AND PRISONERS vol 85 (2012) PARA 429), a patient who, having been transferred in pursuance of a transfer direction from any such institution as is referred to in that provision, is at large in circumstances in which he is liable to be taken into custody under any provision of the Mental Health Act 1983, is to be treated as unlawfully at large and absent from that institution: s 50(4). As to the meaning of 'patient' see PARA 758 note 4.

The provisions of s 50(1)–(4) have effect as if references in s 50(3)–(4) to a transfer direction included references to a hospital direction: s 50(5)(c) (s 50(5) added by the Crime (Sentences) Act 1997 s 55, Sch 4 para 12(5)).

5   As to the appropriate national authority see PARA 567.
6   As to the meaning of 'responsible clinician' see PARA 834.
7   As to the meaning of 'approved clinician' see PARA 831.
8   As to the meaning of 'appropriate tribunal' see PARA 955.
9   As to the meaning of 'hospital' see PARA 577.
10 Mental Health Act 1983 s 50(1) (amended by the Criminal Justice Act 2003 s 294(1), (2); the Mental Health Act 2007 s 11(2); and SI 2008/2833).

The provisions of the Mental Health Act 1983 s 50(1)–(4) have effect as if the reference in s 50(1) to a transfer direction and a restriction direction having been given in respect of a person serving a sentence of imprisonment included a reference to a hospital direction and a limitation direction having been given in respect of a person sentenced to imprisonment: see s 50(5)(a) (as added: see note 4). As to hospital and limitation directions see ss 45A, 45B; and PARA 863.

When considering whether to notify the Secretary of State that a prisoner who has been removed to a hospital is not treatable, the responsible medical officer (now the responsible clinician) must take an overall view and is not necessarily under a duty to disclose dissenting views: *R (on the application of Morley) v Nottinghamshire Health Care NHS Trust* [2002] EWCA Civ 1728, [2003] 1 All ER 784. Any challenge under the Convention for the Protection of Human Rights and Fundamental Freedoms (Rome, 4 November 1950; TS 71 (1953); Cmd 8969) (see RIGHTS AND FREEDOMS) lies against the Home Secretary, not the responsible medical officer (now the responsible clinician) who is exercising clinical judgment: *R (on the application of R) v Shetty (Responsible Medical Officer)* [2003] EWHC 3152 (Admin), (2004) Times, 9 January.

See also *R v Secretary of State for the Home Department, ex p Hickey* [1995] QB 43, [1995] 1 All ER 479, CA; *R (on the application of D) v Secretary of State for the Home Department* [2002] EWHC 2805 (Admin), [2003] 1 WLR 1315, (2002) Times, 31 December.
11 Mental Health Act 1983 s 50(1)(a).
12 As to release on licence from prison and discharge under supervision see PRISONS vol 36(2) (Reissue) PARA 612 et seq.
13 Mental Health Act 1983 s 50(1)(b). A life prisoner who becomes a mental patient while under detention is not entitled to seek a recommendation of the Parole Board while he is in hospital: *R v Secretary of State for the Home Department, ex p T* (1994) Times, 29 July, CA. The use of a policy under the Mental Health Act 1983 s 50(1)(b) is not unlawful: *R v Secretary of State for the Home Department, ex p S* (1992) Times 19 August.
14 Mental Health Act 1983 s 50(1).
15 Mental Health Act 1983 s 50(2) (substituted by the Criminal Justice Act 2003 s 294(1), (3)). The provisions of the Mental Health Act 1983 s 50(1)–(4) have effect as if the reference in s 50(2) to a restriction direction included a reference to a limitation direction: s 50(5)(b) (as added: see note 4). As to the release date see note 4.

896. Expiry of transfer direction in case of person committed in custody for trial or sentence. Any transfer direction[1] given in respect of any mentally disordered[2] person detained in a prison or a remand centre, not being a person serving a sentence of imprisonment[3], ceases to have effect when his case is disposed of by the court having jurisdiction to try or otherwise deal with him; but without prejudice to any power of that court to make a hospital order[4] or other order[5] under Part 3 of the Mental Health Act 1983[6] in his case[7].

Where a transfer direction has been given in respect of such a person ('the detainee'[8]), then if the appropriate national authority[9] is notified by the responsible clinician[10] or any other approved clinician[11] or the appropriate tribunal[12], at any time before the detainee's case is disposed of, that he no longer requires treatment in hospital[13] for mental disorder[14] or that no effective treatment for his disorder can be given at the hospital to which he has been removed, the appropriate national authority may by warrant direct that he be remitted to any place where he might have been detained if he had not been removed to hospital, there to be dealt with as if he had not been so removed[15]. If, no such direction having been given, the court is satisfied, on the written or oral evidence of the responsible clinician, that that detainee no longer requires treatment in hospital for mental disorder, or that no effective treatment for his disorder can be given at the hospital to which he has been removed, the court may order him to be remitted to any such place as is mentioned above[16], or released on bail[17]. On his arrival at such place, or on his release on bail, the transfer direction ceases to have effect[18].

If, however, in a case where the appropriate national authority has not given a direction for remission, it appears to that court that it is impracticable or inappropriate[19] to bring the detainee in question before the court, the court may, subject to the following conditions, make a hospital order (with or without a restriction order) in his absence; and, in the case of a detainee awaiting trial, may do so without convicting him[20]. Before making such an order, the court must be satisfied on the oral or written evidence of at least two registered medical practitioners[21] that the detainee in question is suffering from mental disorder of a nature or degree which makes it appropriate for him to be detained in a hospital for medical treatment[22] and that appropriate medical treatment is available for him; it must also be of the opinion, after considering any depositions or other documents required to be sent to the proper officer of the court, that it is proper to make the order[23].

1   As to transfer directions see PARA 892 et seq.
2   As to the meaning of mental disorder see PARA 761.
3   Ie the persons described in the Mental Health Act 1983 s 48(2)(a) (see PARA 893): s 51(1). The provisions of s 51 also apply to persons remanded in custody by a magistrates' court who are sent in custody to the Crown Court for trial or to be otherwise dealt with while a transfer direction is still in effect in their case: see s 52(2), (5), (6); and PARA 897.
4   As to hospital orders see PARA 864.
5   Ie an interim hospital order (see PARA 864), a guardianship order (see PARA 877) or, in conjunction with a hospital order, a restriction order (see PARA 869). As to hospital and limitation directions see PARA 863.
6   Ie the Mental Health Act 1983 Pt 3 (ss 35–55).
7   Mental Health Act 1983 s 51(2).
8   Mental Health Act 1983 s 51(1).
9   As to the appropriate national authority see PARA 567.
10 As to the meaning of 'responsible clinician' see PARA 834. See *R (on the application of R) v Shetty (Responsible Medical Officer)* [2003] EWHC 3152 (Admin), (2004) Times, 9 January.
11 As to the meaning of 'approved clinician' see PARA 831.
12 As to the meaning of 'the appropriate tribunal' see PARA 955.
13 As to the meaning of 'hospital' see PARA 577.
14 As to the meaning of 'mental disorder' see PARA 761.
15 Mental Health Act 1983 s 51(3) (amended by the Mental Health Act 2007 s 11(3)(a), Sch 3 para 43).
16 Ie any such place as is mentioned in the Mental Health Act 1983 s 51(3).
17 Mental Health Act 1983 s 51(4) (amended by the Criminal Justice and Public Order Act 1994 s 168(2), Sch 10 para 51; and the Mental Health Act 2007 s 11(3)). Such release is subject to the Criminal Justice and Public Order Act 1994 s 25 (no bail for defendants charged with or convicted of homicide or rape after previous convictions for such offences: see CRIMINAL PROCEDURE vol 27 (2010) PARA 72).
18 See the Mental Health Act 1983 s 51(3), (4) (s 51(4) as amended: see note 17).

19 The word 'inappropriate' is to be restrictively construed and the provision should not be used as a way of avoiding a potentially troublesome trial: *R (on the application of Kenneally) v Snaresbrook Crown Court, R (on the application of Kenneally) v Rampton Health Authority* [2001] EWHC 968 (Admin), [2002] QB 1169.

20 Mental Health Act 1983 s 51(5). The court should exercise its power under s 51(5) to make a hospital order without first convicting a detainee only in exceptional circumstances: *R (on the application of Kenneally) v Snaresbrook Crown Court, R (on the application of Kenneally) v Rampton Health Authority* [2001] EWHC 968 (Admin), [2002] QB 1169. Once the trial has commenced, mental fitness must be determined under the Criminal Procedure (Insanity) Act 1964 s 4 (see PARA 874; and CRIMINAL PROCEDURE vol 27 (2010) PARA 370): see *R v Griffiths* [2002] EWCA Crim 1762.

21 One of the practitioners must have been approved as having special experience in the diagnosis or treatment of mental disorders: see the Mental Health Act 1983 ss 12, 54(1); and PARAS 849, 865.

22 As to the meaning of 'medical treatment' see PARA 926; and as to the treatment which may be given in hospital see PARAS 924, 927–934.

23 Mental Health Act 1983 s 51(6) (amended by the Mental Health Act 2007 s 5(4), Sch 1 para 12). The provisions of the Mental Health Act 1983 s 51(5), (6) apply also to a person who is admitted to a hospital in pursuance of an order under s 44 after being committed under s 43 (see PARA 873) to the Crown Court for a restriction order, as if he were a person subject to a transfer direction: s 51(7).

897.   Expiry of transfer direction in case of person remanded in custody by magistrates' court.   A transfer direction[1] given in respect of a person suffering from a mental disorder[2] remanded in custody by a magistrates' court ('the accused')[3] ceases to have effect on the expiration of the period of remand[4] unless, on being brought before the magistrates' court, he is committed in custody for trial at the Crown Court[5]. However, if the magistrates' court is satisfied, on the written or oral evidence of the responsible clinician[6], that the accused no longer requires treatment in hospital for mental disorder or that no effective treatment can be given in the hospital to which he has been removed, it may direct that the transfer direction is to cease to have effect notwithstanding that the period of remand has not expired or the accused has been committed to the Crown Court[7].

The magistrates' court may, in the absence of the accused, send him to the Crown Court for trial[8] if the court is satisfied, on the written or oral evidence of the responsible clinician, that the accused is unfit to take part in the proceedings and the accused is represented by an authorised person[9].

1 As to transfer directions see PARA 892 et seq.

2 As to the meaning of 'mental disorder' see PARA 761.

3 Ie a person described in the Mental Health Act 1983 s 48(2)(b) (see PARA 893): s 52(1). As to remand by a magistrates' court see CRIMINAL PROCEDURE vol 27 (2010) PARA 224; MAGISTRATES vol 71 (2013) PARA 548 et seq.

4 Where a transfer direction has been given in respect of a person so remanded, the power of further remanding him under the Magistrates' Courts Act 1980 s 128 (see MAGISTRATES vol 71 (2013) PARAS 551–552) may be exercised by the court without his being brought before the court; and, if the court further remands such a person in custody, the period of remand is to be deemed for these purposes not to have expired: Mental Health Act 1983 s 52(3). Notice in writing of any further remand must be given to the managers (see PARA 778) of the hospital where the person is detained: see the Criminal Procedure Rules 2012, SI 2012/1726, r 11.3. The magistrates' court must not further remand the person in his absence unless he has appeared before the court within the previous six months: Mental Health Act 1983 s 52(4).

5 Mental Health Act 1983 s 52(2). Where he is so committed for trial, the transfer direction given in his case is treated as if it were a direction given in respect of a person falling within s 51 (see PARA 896): s 52(6); and see PARA 896.

As from a day to be appointed, the provisions of s 52(2), (5), (6) are amended so as to refer to a person being 'sent' instead of 'committed': s 52(2), (5), (6) (prospectively amended by the Criminal Justice Act 2003 s 41, Sch 3 Pt 2 para 55(1), (3)(a)–(c)). At the date at which this volume states the law, this amendment was in force for certain purposes only: see s 51A(3)(d);

Criminal Justice Act 2003 (Commencement No 9) Order 2005, SI 2005/1267, Schedule, Pt 1, ~~para 1(1)(k);~~ ~~Criminal Justice Act 2003~~ (Commencement No 28 and Saving Provisions) Order 2012, SI 2012/1320, art 4(1)(a), (c)(iii)–(iv).

6   As to the meaning of 'responsible clinician' see PARA 834.
7   Mental Health Act 1983 s 52(5) (amended by the Mental Health Act 2007 s 11(4)). See note 5.
8   Ie under the Crime and Disorder Act 1998 s 51 or s 51A: see CRIMINAL PROCEDURE vol 27 (2010) PARAS 206, 287–285.
9   Mental Health Act 1983 s 52(7) (amended by the Criminal Justice Act 2003 ss 41, 332, Sch 3 Pt 2 para 55, Sch 37 Pt 4; the Legal Services Act 2007 Sch 21 para 57; and the Mental Health Act 2007 s 11(4)). As to the meaning of 'authorised person' see PARA 862 note 18.

898. Expiry of transfer direction in case of civil prisoner. Any transfer direction[1] given in respect of a civil prisoner[2] ceases to have effect on the expiration of the period during which he would, but for his removal to hospital[3], be liable to be detained in the place from which he was removed[4].

Where a transfer direction and a restriction direction[5] have been given in respect of any such person then, if the appropriate national authority[6] is notified by the responsible clinician[7], any other approved clinician[8] or the appropriate tribunal[9] at any time before the expiration of the period that[10]: (1) that person no longer requires treatment in hospital for mental disorder[11]; or (2) that no effective treatment for his disorder can be given in the hospital to which he has been removed[12], the appropriate national authority may by warrant direct that he be remitted to any place where he might have been detained if he had not been removed to hospital and, on his arrival at such a place, the directions cease to have effect[13].

1   As to transfer directions see PARA 892 et seq.
2   Ie a person described in the Mental Health Act 1983 s 48(2)(c) or (d) (see PARA 893): s 53(1).
3   As to the meaning of 'hospital' see PARA 577.
4   Mental Health Act 1983 s 53(1).
5   As to restriction directions see PARA 894.
6   As to the appropriate national authority see PARA 567.
7   As to the meaning of 'responsible clinician' see PARA 834.
8   As to the meaning of 'approved clinician' see PARA 831.
9   As to meaning of 'appropriate tribunal' see PARA 955.
10 Mental Health Act 1983 s 53(2) (amended by the Mental Health Act 2007 s 11(5); and SI 2008/2833).
11 Mental Health Act 1983 s 53(2)(a). As to the meaning of 'mental disorder' see PARA 761.
12 Mental Health Act 1983 s 53(2)(b).
13 Mental Health Act 1983 s 53(2).

(iii) Transfer within United Kingdom etc

899. Removal of patients from England and Wales to Scotland. If it appears to the appropriate national authority[1], in the case of a patient[2] who is for the time being liable to be detained[3], that it is in the interests of the patient to remove him to Scotland, and that arrangements have been made for admitting him to hospital[4] or, as the case may be, for receiving him into guardianship there, or, where he is not to be admitted to a hospital, for his detention in hospital to be authorised[5], the Secretary of State may authorise his removal to Scotland and may give any necessary directions for his conveyance to his destination[6].

If it appears to the appropriate national authority, in the case of a patient who is subject to a restriction order[7] and has been conditionally discharged[8], that a transfer[9] would be in the interests of the patient, the appropriate national authority may, with the consent of the minister exercising corresponding functions in Scotland, transfer responsibility for the patient to that minister[10].

If it appears to the appropriate national authority[11], in the case of a community patient, that the following conditions are met, the authority may authorise the transfer of responsibility for him to Scotland[12]. The conditions are a transfer under this section is in the patient's interests and arrangements have been made for dealing with him under enactments in force in Scotland corresponding or similar to those relating to community patients in the Mental Health Act 1983[13].

1   As to the appropriate national authority see PARA 567.
2   As to the meaning of 'patient' see PARA 758 note 4.
3   Ie under the Mental Health Act 1983, but otherwise than by virtue of s 35 (remand to hospital for report: see PARA 862), s 36 (remand to hospital for treatment: see PARA 862), or s 38 (interim hospital order: see PARA 864): s 80(1). Section 80 extends to Scotland: see s 146; and PARA 557.
4   For these purposes, 'hospital' has the same meaning as in the Mental Health (Care and Treatment) (Scotland) Act 2003: Mental Health Act 1983 s 80(7) (amended by SI 2005/2078; and SSI 2005/465).
5   Ie authorised by virtue of the Mental Health (Care and Treatment) (Scotland) Act 2003 or the Criminal Procedure (Scotland) Act 1995. Reference in the Mental Health Act 1983 s 80 to a patient's detention in hospital being authorised by virtue of the Mental Health (Care and Treatment) (Scotland) Act 2003 or the Criminal Procedure (Scotland) Act 1995 are to be read as including references to a patient in respect of whom a certificate under one of the provisions listed in the Mental Health (Care and Treatment) (Scotland) Act 2003 s 290(7)(a) is in operation: Mental Health Act 1983 s 80(8) (added by SI 2005/2078).
6   Mental Health Act 1983 s 80(1) (amended by SI 2005/2078; SSI 2005/465; and the Mental Health Act 2007 Sch 5, Pt 1, para 2, Sch 11, Pt 7). The Mental Health Act 1983 ss 80, 80A have effect as if any hospital direction under s 45A (see PARA 863) were a transfer direction under s 47 (see PARA 892), and as if any limitation direction under s 45A were a restriction direction under s 49 (see PARA 894): s 92(4) (added by the Crime (Sentences) Act 1997 s 55, Sch 4 para 12(16)).
7   Ie under the Mental Health Act 1983 s 41: see PARA 869.
8   Ie under the Mental Health Act 1983 s 42 (see PARA 914) or s 73 (see PARA 969).
9   Ie under the Mental Health Act 1983 s 80A.
10   Mental Health Act 1983 s 80A(1) (s 80A added by the Crime (Sentences) Act 1997 s 48, Sch 3 para 1; and amended by SI 2005/2078; SSI 2005/465; and the Mental Health Act 2007 Sch 5, Pt 1, para 4).
11   For this purpose, 'the appropriate national authority' means, in relation to a community patient in respect of whom the responsible hospital is in England, the Secretary of State, and, in relation to a community patient in respect of whom the responsible hospital is in Wales, the Welsh Ministers: Mental Health Act 1983 s 80ZA(4) (added by the Mental Health Act 2007 Sch 5 para 3). The appropriate national authority may not act under the Mental Health Act 1983 s 80ZA(1) while the patient is recalled to hospital under s 17E (see PARA 801): s 80ZA(3).
12   Mental Health Act 1983 s 80ZA(1) (as added: see note 11).
13   Mental Health Act 1983 s 80ZA(2) (as added: see note 11).

900. Removal of detained patients to England and Wales from Scotland. The following applies to a patient[1] if he is removed to England and Wales under the relevant regulations[2] and immediately before his removal, his detention in hospital was authorised[3], and, on his removal, he is admitted to a hospital in England or Wales[4].

He is treated as if, on the date of his admission to the hospital, he had been so admitted in pursuance of an application made, or an order or direction made or given, on that date under the enactment in force in England and Wales which most closely corresponds to the enactment by virtue of which his detention in hospital was authorised immediately before his removal[5].

If, immediately before his removal, he was subject to a measure under any enactment in force in Scotland restricting his discharge, he is treated as if he were subject to an order or direction under the enactment in force in England and Wales which most closely corresponds to that enactment[6].

If, immediately before his removal, the patient was liable to be detained[7] by virtue of a transfer for treatment direction[8], given while he was serving a sentence of imprisonment[9] imposed by a court in Scotland, he is treated as if the sentence had been imposed by a court in England and Wales[10].

If, immediately before his removal, the patient was subject to a hospital direction[11] or transfer for treatment direction[12], the restriction direction to which he is subject[13] expires on the date on which that hospital direction or transfer for treatment direction (as the case may be) would have expired if he had not been so removed[14].

If, immediately before his removal, the patient was liable to be detained[15] by virtue of a hospital direction, he is treated as if any sentence of imprisonment passed at the time when that hospital direction was made had been imposed by a court in England and Wales[16].

1   As to the meaning of 'patient' see PARA 758 note 4.
2   Ie under regulations made under the Mental Health (Care and Treatment) (Scotland) Act 2003 s 290(1)(a). Any directions given by the Scottish Ministers under regulations made under s 290 as to the removal of a patient to which the Mental Health Act 1983 s 80B applies have effect as if they were given under the Mental Health Act 1983: s 80B(7) (added by the Mental Health Act 2007 Sch 5 para 4).
3   Ie authorised by virtue of the Criminal Procedure (Scotland) Act 1995. The Mental Health Act 1983 s 80(8) applies to a reference in s 80B as it applies to one in s 80: s 80B(8) (as added: see note 2).
4   Mental Health Act 1983 s 80B(1) (as added: see note 2).
5   Mental Health Act 1983 s 80B(2) (as added: see note 2).
6   Mental Health Act 1983 s 80B(3) (as added: see note 2).
7   Ie under the Mental Health (Care and Treatment) (Scotland) Act 2003.
8   Mental Health Act 1983 s 80B(4) (as added: see note 2).
9   Ie within the meaning of the Mental Health (Care and Treatment) (Scotland) Act 2003 s 136(9).
10 Mental Health Act 1983 s 80B(5) (as added: see note 2).
11 For these purposes 'hospital direction' means a direction made under the Criminal Procedure (Scotland) Act 1995 s 59A: Mental Health Act 1983 s 80B(9) (as added: see note 2).
12 As to the meaning of 'transfer for treatment direction' for these purposes see the Mental Health (Care and Treatment) (Scotland) Act 2003 s 136.
13 Ie by virtue of the Mental Health Act 1983 s 80B(3).
14 Mental Health Act 1983 s 80B(5) (as added: see note 2).
15 Ie under the Mental Health (Care and Treatment) (Scotland) Act 2003.
16 Mental Health Act 1983 s 80B(6) (as added: see note 2).

901.   Removal of patients subject to compulsion in the community from Scotland.   Where a patient[1] is subject to provisions relating to a requirement other than detention[2], and he is removed to England and Wales[3] under those provisions, he is treated as if on the date of his arrival at the place where he is to reside in England or Wales as if he had been admitted to a hospital in England or Wales in pursuance of an application or order made on that date under the corresponding enactment[4] and a community treatment order[5] had then been made discharging him from the hospital[6].

As soon as practicable after the patient's arrival at the place where he is to reside in England or Wales, the responsible clinician[7] must specify the conditions[8] to which he is to be subject[9] and the conditions are deemed to be specified in the community treatment order[10].

1   As to the meaning of 'patient' see PARA 758 note 4.
2   Ie he is subject to an enactment in force in Scotland by virtue of which regulations under the Mental Health (Care and Treatment) (Scotland) Act 2003 s 289(1) apply.
3   As to the meanings of 'England' and 'Wales' see PARA 557 notes 4, 5.
4   For these purposes:
    (1)   if the enactment to which the patient was subject in Scotland was an enactment

contained in the Mental Health (Care and Treatment) (Scotland) Act 2003, the corresponding enactment is the Mental Health Act 1983 s 3 (see PARA 768) (s 80C(3)(a) (added by the Mental Health Act 2007 Sch 5 para 4)).

(2) if the enactment to which he was subject in Scotland was an enactment contained in the Criminal Procedure (Scotland) Act 1995, the corresponding enactment is the Mental Health Act 1983 s 37 (s 80C(3)(b) (as so added)).

5 As to the meaning of 'community treatment order' see PARA 797 note 4.
6 Mental Health Act 1983 s 80C(1), (2) (as added: see note 4). 'The responsible hospital', in the case of a patient in respect of whom a community treatment order is in force by virtue of s 80C(2), means the hospital to which he is treated as having been admitted by virtue of that subsection, subject to s 19A (see PARA 804): s 80C(4) (as so added).
7 As to the meaning of 'responsible clinician' see PARA 834.
8 The responsible clinician may only specify conditions under the Mental Health Act 1983 s 80C(5) which an approved mental health professional agrees should be specified: s 80C(6) (as added: see note 4). As to the meaning of 'approved mental health professional' see PARA 815 note 2.
9 Ie for the purposes of the Mental Health Act 1983 s 17B(1) (see PARA 800).
10 Mental Health Act 1983 s 80C(5) (as added: see note 4).

902. Transfer of conditionally discharged patients from Scotland. The transfer of a patient[1], who is subject to (1) a restriction order[2] and (2) a conditional discharge[3], to England and Wales under specified regulations[4] has effect only if the Secretary of State[5] has consented to the transfer[6].

If a transfer under those regulations has effect, the patient is treated as if on the date of the transfer he had been conditionally discharged[7] and he were subject to a hospital order[8] and a restriction order[9].

If the restriction order to which the patient was subject immediately before the transfer was of limited duration, the restriction order to which he is subject[10] expires on the date on which the first-mentioned order would have expired if the transfer had not been made[11].

1 As to the meaning of 'patient' see PARA 758 note 4.
2 Ie under the Criminal Procedure (Scotland) Act 1995 s 59.
3 Ie under the Mental Health (Care and Treatment) (Scotland) Act 2003 s 193(7).
4 Ie made under the Mental Health (Care and Treatment) (Scotland) Act 2003 s 290. As to the meanings of 'England' and 'Wales' see PARA 557 notes 4, 5.
5 As to the Secretary of State see PARA 567.
6 Mental Health Act 1983 s 80D(1), (2) (added by the Mental Health Act 2007 Sch 5 para 4).
7 Ie under the Mental Health Act 1983 s 42 (see PARA 876) or s 73 (see PARA 969).
8 Ie under the Mental Health Act 1983 s 37 (see PARA 864).
9 Ie under the Mental Health Act 1983 s 41 (see PARA 869): s 80D(3) (as added: see note 6).
10 Ie by virtue of the Mental Health Act 1983 s 80D(3).
11 Mental Health Act 1983 s 80D(4) (as added: see note 6).

903. Removal of patients to Northern Ireland. If it appears to the Secretary of State[1], in the case of a patient[2] who is for the time being liable to be detained or subject to guardianship[3], that it is in the patient's interest to remove him to Northern Ireland and that arrangements have been made for admitting him to a hospital[4] or for receiving him into guardianship there, the Secretary of State may authorise the removal of the patient to Northern Ireland and give any necessary directions for his conveyance to his destination[5].

Where such a patient is liable to be detained by virtue of an application, order or direction under any enactment in force in England and Wales[6], he must, on admission to a hospital in Northern Ireland, be treated as if, on the date of his admission, he had been so admitted in pursuance of an application made, or an order or direction made or given, on that date under the corresponding enactment in force in Northern Ireland, and, where he is subject to a hospital order and a restriction order or a transfer direction and a restriction direction under any enactment in the Mental Health Act 1983, as if he were subject to a hospital order and a restriction order or a transfer direction and a restriction direction under the corresponding enactment in force in Northern Ireland[7].

Where such a patient is subject to guardianship by virtue of an application, order or direction under any enactment in force in England and Wales, he must be treated as if, on the date on which he arrives at the place where he is to reside, he had been received into guardianship in pursuance of an application, order or direction under the corresponding enactment in force in Northern Ireland, accepted, made or given on that date[8].

Where a person so removed was immediately before his removal liable to be detained by virtue of an application for admission for assessment under the Mental Health Act 1983[9], he must be treated, on admission to a hospital in Northern Ireland, as if he had been admitted in pursuance of an application for admission for assessment under the Mental Health (Northern Ireland) Order 1986[10] made on the date of his admission[11].

Where a person so removed was immediately before his removal liable to be detained by virtue of an application for admission for treatment[12], he must be treated, on admission to a hospital in Northern Ireland, as if he were detained for treatment[13] by virtue of a report[14] made on the date of his admission[15].

Where a person so removed was immediately before his removal liable to be detained by virtue of a transfer direction[16] given while he was serving a sentence of imprisonment[17] imposed by a court in England and Wales, he must be treated as if the sentence had been imposed by a court in Northern Ireland[18].

If it appears to the Secretary of State, in the case of a patient who is subject to a hospital order and a restriction order[19] or to a transfer direction and a restriction direction[20] and has been conditionally discharged[21], that a transfer[22] would be in the interests of the patient, the Secretary of State may, with the consent of the minister exercising corresponding functions in Northern Ireland, transfer responsibility for the patient to that minister[23].

The above provisions[24] apply in the case of a community patient as they apply in the case of a patient who is for the time being liable to be detained under the Mental Health Act 1983, as if the community patient were so liable[25].

Where responsibility for such a patient is so transferred, the patient must be treated as if on the date of the transfer he had been conditionally discharged under the corresponding enactment in force in Northern Ireland, and as if he were subject to a hospital order and a restriction order or to a transfer order and a restriction direction under the corresponding enactment in force in Northern Ireland[26]. Where a patient responsibility for whom is so transferred was immediately before the transfer subject to a restriction direction of limited duration, the restriction direction to which he is subject[27] expires on the date on which the first-mentioned direction would have expired if the transfer had not been made[28].

1   As to the Secretary of State see PARA 567.
2   As to the meaning of 'patient' see PARA 758 note 4.
3   Ie under the Mental Health Act 1983, otherwise than by virtue of s 35, s 36 or s 38 (see PARA 899 note 3): s 81(1).
    The Mental Health Act 1983 ss 80–85A have effect as if any hospital direction under s 45A (see PARA 863) were a transfer direction under s 47 (see PARA 892), and as if any limitation direction under s 45A were a restriction direction under s 49 (see PARA 894): s 92(4) (added by the Crime (Sentences) Act 1997 s 55, Sch 4 para 12(16)).

4   For these purposes, 'hospital' has the same meaning as in the Mental Health (Northern Ireland) Order 1986, SI 1986/595 (NI 4): Mental Health Act 1983 s 81(8) (s 81(2), (4), (5), (7), (8) amended by SI 1986/596).

5   Mental Health Act 1983 s 81(1). The authority under which the patient was detained or subject to guardianship ceases to have effect on his reception into a hospital or into guardianship in Northern Ireland: s 91(1). Where responsibility for a community patient is transferred to a jurisdiction outside England and Wales (or such a patient is removed outside England and Wales) in pursuance of arrangements under the Mental Health Act 1983 Pt 6, the application, order or direction mentioned in s 91(1) in force in respect of him ceases to have effect on the date on which responsibility is so transferred (or he is so removed) in pursuance of those arrangements: s 91(2A) (added by the Mental Health Act 2007 Sch 5 para 16).

6   As to the meaning of 'England' see PARA 557 note 6. As to the meaning of 'Wales' see PARA 557 note 7.

7   Mental Health Act 1983 s 81(2) (as amended (see note 4); further amended by the Mental Health Act 2007 Sch 5 para 5). Where a person so removed was subject to a restriction direction of limited duration, the restriction direction expires on the date on which the first mentioned restriction direction would have expired if he had not been so removed: Mental Health Act 1983 s 81(7) (as amended (see note 4); further amended by the Mental Health Act 2007 Sch 11 Pt 8). As to restriction orders see PARA 869; and as to restriction directions see PARA 894.

8   Mental Health Act 1983 s 81(3).

9   Ie under the Mental Health Act 1983 s 2(1): see PARA 767.

10 Ie under the Mental Health (Northern Ireland) Order 1986, SI 1986/595 (NI 4), art 4.

11 Mental Health Act 1983 s 81(4) (as amended: see note 4).

12 Ie under the Mental Health Act 1983 s 3(1): see PARA 768.

13 Ie under the Mental Health (Northern Ireland) Order 1986, SI 1986/595 (NI 4), Pt II, (arts 4–41).

14 Ie under the Mental Health (Northern Ireland) Order 1986, SI 1986/595 (NI 4), art 12(1).

15 Mental Health Act 1983 s 81(5) (as amended: see note 4).

16 As to transfer directions see PARA 892.

17 Ie a sentence of imprisonment within the meaning of the Mental Health Act 1983 s 47(5) (see PARA 892 note 1).

18 Mental Health Act 1983 s 81(6). Section 81(6) has effect as if any reference to a transfer direction given while a patient was serving a sentence of imprisonment imposed by a court included a reference to a hospital direction given by a court after imposing a sentence of imprisonment on a patient: s 92(5) (added by the Crime (Sentences) Act 1997 Sch 4 para 12(16)).

19 Ie under the Mental Health Act 1983 s 37 (see PARA 864) and s 41 (see PARA 869).

20 Ie under the Mental Health Act 1983 s 47 (see PARA 892) and s 49 (see PARA 894).

21 Ie under the Mental Health Act 1983 s 42 (see PARA 914) or s 73 (see PARA 969).

22 Ie under the Mental Health Act 1983 s 81A.

23 Mental Health Act 1983 s 81A(1) (s 81A added by the Crime (Sentences) Act 1997 s 48, Sch 3 para 2; amended by the Mental Health Act 2007 Sch 5 para 7(2)). See note 3.

24 Ie where the Mental Health Act 1983 s 81 applies. Any reference in s 81 to the application, order or direction by virtue of which a patient is liable to be detained under the Mental Health Act 1983 is construed, for these purposes, as a reference to the application, order or direction under the Mental Health Act 1983 in respect of the patient: s 81ZA(2) (added by the Mental Health Act 2007 Sch 5 para 6).

25 Mental Health Act 1983 s 81ZA(1) (as added: see note 24).

26 Mental Health Act 1983 s 81A(2) (as added (see note 23); amended by the Mental Health Act 2007 Sch 5 para 7(3)). See note 3.

27 Ie by virtue of the Mental Health Act 1983 s 81A(2) (see the text and note 23).

28 Mental Health Act 1983 s 81A(3) (as added (see note 23); amended by the Mental Health Act 2007 Sch 11 Pt 8). See note 3.

904.   Removal of patients to England and Wales from Northern Ireland.   If it appears to the responsible authority[1], in the case of a patient[2] who is liable to be detained or subject to guardianship under the Mental Health (Northern Ireland) Order 1986[3], that it is in the patient's interests to remove him to England and Wales[4], and that arrangements have been made for admitting him to a hospital[5] or for receiving him into guardianship there, the responsible authority may authorise his removal to England and Wales and may give any necessary directions for his conveyance to his destination[6].

Where such a patient is liable to be detained by virtue of an application, order or direction under the Mental Health (Northern Ireland) Order 1986, he must, on admission to a hospital in England and Wales, be treated as if on the date of his admission he had been so admitted in pursuance of an application made, or an order or direction made or given, on that date under the corresponding enactment in force in England and Wales[7]. Where such a patient is subject to a hospital order and a restriction order or a transfer direction and a restriction direction under any enactment in that Order, he must be treated as if he were subject to a hospital order and a restriction order or a transfer direction and a restriction direction under the corresponding enactment in force in England and Wales[8].

Where such a patient is subject to guardianship by virtue of an application, order or direction under any enactment in force in Northern Ireland, he must be treated as if, on the date on which he arrives at the place where he is to reside, he had been received into guardianship in pursuance of an application, order or direction under the corresponding enactment in force in England and Wales, accepted, made or given on that date[9].

Where such a patient was immediately before his removal liable to be detained by virtue of an application for admission for assessment under the Mental Health (Northern Ireland) Order 1986[10], he must be treated on his admission to hospital in England and Wales as if he had been admitted in pursuance of an application for admission for assessment under the Mental Health Act 1983[11] made on the date of his admission[12]. Where such a patient was immediately before removal liable to be detained for treatment[13], he must be treated on his admission to a hospital in England and Wales as if he had been admitted in pursuance of an application for admission for treatment[14] made on the date of his admission[15].

Where such a patient was immediately before removal liable to be detained[16] by virtue of a transfer direction given while he was serving a sentence of imprisonment[17] imposed by a court in Northern Ireland, he must be treated as if the sentence had been imposed by a court in England and Wales[18].

If it appears to the Department of Justice in Northern Ireland, in the case of a patient who is subject to a restriction order or restriction direction[19] and has been conditionally discharged[20], that a transfer[21] would be in the interests of the patient, the Department of Justice for Northern Ireland may, with the consent of the Secretary of State, transfer responsibility for the patient to the Secretary of State[22]. Where responsibility for such a patient is so transferred, the patient must be treated as if on the date of the transfer he had been conditionally discharged[23] and as if he were subject to a hospital order and a restriction order[24] or to a transfer direction and a restriction direction[25]. Where a patient responsibility for whom is so transferred was immediately before the transfer subject to a restriction order or restriction direction of limited duration, the restriction order or restriction direction to which he is subject[26] expires on the date on which the first-mentioned order or direction would have expired if the transfer had not been made[27].

1   As to the responsible authority see the Mental Health Act 1983 s 82(7) (s 82(1)–(3), (5)–(7) amended by SI 1986/596; SI 2010/976).
     The Mental Health Act 1983 s 82, s 82A have effect as if any hospital direction under s 45A (see PARA 863) were a transfer direction under s 47 (see PARA 892), and as if any limitation direction under s 45A were a restriction direction under s 49 (see PARA 894): s 92(4) (added by the Crime (Sentences) Act 1997 s 55, Sch 4 para 12(16)).

2   As to the meaning of 'patient' see PARA 758 note 4.
3   Ie otherwise than by virtue of the Mental Health (Northern Ireland) Order 1986, SI 1986/595 (NI 4), art 42, 43 or 45 (cf the Mental Health Act 1983 ss 80(1), 81(1); and see PARAS 899 note 3, 903 note 3): s 82(1) (as amended: see note 1).
4   As to the meanings of 'England' and 'Wales' see PARA 557 notes 4, 5.
5   Ie a hospital within the meaning of the Mental Health Act 1983 Pt II (ss 2–34) (scc PARA 577): s 92(1).
6   Mental Health Act 1983 s 82(1) (as amended: see note 1).
7   Mental Health Act 1983 s 82(2) (as amended: see note 1). A patient transferred under this provision has a right to apply to a tribunal: see s 66(1), s 69(2)(a), s 70, s 79(1)(c); and PARAS 961–962.
8   Mental Health Act 1983 s 82(2) (as amended (see note 1); further amended by the Mental Health Act 2007 Sch 5 para 8). Where a person removed under s 82 was immediately before removal subject to a restriction order or restriction direction of limited duration, it expires on the date on which such an order or direction would have expired if he had not been so removed: s 82(6) (as so amended). As to restriction orders see PARA 869; and as to restriction directions see PARA 894.
9   Mental Health Act 1983 s 82(3) (as amended: see note 1).
10 Ie under the Mental Health (Northern Ireland) Order 1986, SI 1986/595 (NI 4), art 4.
11 See the Mental Health Act 1983 s 2(1); and PARA 767.
12 Mental Health Act 1983 s 82(4A) (added by SI 1986/596).
13 Ie by virtue of a report under the Mental Health (Northern Ireland) Order 1986, SI 1986/595 (NI 4), art 12(1) or art 13.
14 See the Mental Health Act 1983 s 3(1); and PARA 768.
15 Mental Health Act 1983 s 82(4) (substituted by SI 1986/596).
16 Ie under the Mental Health (Northern Ireland) Order 1986, SI 1986/595 (NI 4).
17 Ie within the meaning of the Mental Health (Northern Ireland) Order 1986, SI 1986/595 (NI 4), art 53(5).
18 Mental Health Act 1983 s 82(5) (as amended: see note 1).
19 Ie under the Mental Health (Northern Ireland) Order 1986, SI 1986/595 (NI 4), art 47(1) or art 55.
20 Ie under the Mental Health (Northern Ireland) Order 1986, SI 1986/595 (NI 4), art 48(2) or art 78(2).
21 Ie under the Mental Health Act 1983 s 82A.
22 Mental Health Act 1983 s 82A(1) (added by the Crime (Sentences) Act 1997 Sch 3 para 3). See note 1.
23 Ie under the Mental Health Act 1983 s 42 (see PARA 914) or s 73 (see PARA 969).
24 Ie under the Mental Health Act 1983 s 37 (see PARA 864) and under s 41 (see PARA 869).
25 Mental Health Act 1983 s 82A(2) (as added (see note 22); amended by the Mental Health Act 2007 Sch 5 para 9). The reference in the text is a reference to a transfer direction under the Mental Health Act 1983 s 47 (see PARA 892) and a restriction direction under s 49 (see PARA 894). See note 1.
26 Ie by virtue of the Mental Health Act 1983 s 82A(2).
27 Mental Health Act 1983 s 82A(3) (as added: see note 22). See note 1.

905.   Removal of patients from the Channel Islands and the Isle of Man to England and Wales.   The appropriate national authority[1] may by warrant direct that any offender found by a court in any of the Channel Islands or in the Isle of Man to be insane or to have been insane at the time of the alleged offence and ordered to be detained during Her Majesty's pleasure, be removed to a hospital[2] in England and Wales[3]. The Secretary of State may by warrant direct that any patient[4] so removed to England and Wales be returned to the island from which he was so removed, there to be dealt with according to law in all respects as if he had not been so removed[5].

Where a patient is detained or subject to guardianship in the Channel Islands or the Isle of Man[6] and removed to England and Wales[7], that patient is treated as if he had been admitted to hospital or received into guardianship under the provision of the Mental Health Act 1983 corresponding to the Channel Islands or Isle of Man enactment[8].

Where a patient admitted to hospital in England and Wales is subject to an order or direction restricting his discharge, he is to be treated on admission as if he were subject to a hospital order and a restriction order or to a hospital direction and a limitation direction or to a transfer direction and a restriction direction[9]. Where such a patient was immediately before removal liable to be detained by virtue of a transfer direction given while he was serving a sentence of imprisonment imposed by a court in the island in question he must be treated as if the sentence had been imposed by a court in England and Wales[10].

Any patient responsibility for whom is transferred to the Secretary of State by the authority exercising corresponding functions in any of the Channel Islands or the Isle of Man[11], must be treated as if on the date of the transfer he had been conditionally discharged[12] and as if he were subject to a hospital order and a restriction order[13] or a hospital direction and a limitation direction order[14] a transfer direction and a restriction direction[15]. Where the patient was immediately before the transfer subject to an order or direction restricting his discharge, being an order or direction of limited duration, the restriction order, limitation direction or restriction direction to which he is subject[16] expires on the date on which the first-mentioned order or direction would have expired if the transfer had not been made[17].

1   As to the appropriate national authority see PARA 567.
2   Ie a hospital within the meaning of the Mental Health Act 1983 Pt 2 (ss 2–34): s 92(1).
3   Mental Health Act 1983 s 84(1). As to the meanings of 'England' and 'Wales' see PARA 557 notes 4, 5.
     There are no suitable facilities on the islands mentioned for treatment and care of the patients to whom s 84 relates, and they are normally transferred to a hospital in England which provides high security psychiatric services. As to such hospitals see PARA 569. A patient so removed must be treated as if he were subject to a hospital order with a restriction order: s 84(2) (amended by the Domestic Violence, Crime and Victims Act 2004 s 58(1), Sch 10 para 22; and the Mental Health Act 2007 Sch 11 Pt 8).
     The Mental Health Act 1983 ss 80–85A have effect as if any hospital direction under s 45A (see PARA 863) were a transfer direction under s 47 (see PARA 892), and as if any limitation direction under s 45A were a restriction direction under s 49 (see PARA 894): s 92(4) (added by the Crime (Sentences) Act 1997 s 55, Sch 4 para 12(16)).
4   As to the meaning of 'patient' see PARA 758 note 4.
5   Mental Health Act 1983 s 84(3).
6   Ie under a provision corresponding to an enactment contained in the Mental Health Act 1983 other than s 35, s 36 or s 38 (see PARA 899 note 3): s 85(1).
7   Ie under a provision corresponding to the Mental Health Act 1983 s 83 (see PARA 906).
8   Mental Health Act 1983 s 85(1)–(3). The patient transferred also has the right to apply to a tribunal: see PARA 961 et seq. While being conveyed to hospital or to the place where he is to reside, a patient under guardianship is deemed to be in legal custody (see PARA 776), and s 138 (see PARA 777) applies: s 85(6). See also note 3.
9   Mental Health Act 1983 s 85(2) (amended by the Mental Health Act 2007 Sch 5 para 11). Where he was immediately before removal subject to an order or direction of limited duration restricting his discharge, the restriction order or restriction direction to which he is subject on admission to a hospital in England and Wales expires on the date on which such an order or direction would have expired if he had not been removed: Mental Health Act 1983 s 85(5). As to restriction orders see PARA 869 and as to restriction directions see PARA 894. See note 3.
10   Mental Health Act 1983 s 85(4), (7). See note 3.
11   Mental Health Act 1983 s 85A(1) (s 85A added by the Crime (Sentences) Act 1997 s 48, Sch 3 para 5). The text refers to the exercise of functions under a provision corresponding to the Mental Health Act 1983 s 83A: see PARA 906. See note 3.
12   Ie under the Mental Health Act 1983 s 42 (see PARA 914) or s 73 (see PARA 969).
13   Ie under the Mental Health Act 1983 s 37 (see PARA 864) or s 41 (see PARA 869).
14   Ie under the Mental Health Act 1983 s 45A (see PARA 863).
15   Mental Health Act 1983 s 85A(2) (as added (see note 11); amended by the Mental Health Act 2007 Sch 5 para 13(2)). As to a transfer direction and a restriction direction see s 47 (see PARA 892) and s 49 (see PARA 894). See note 3.

16 Ie by virtue of the Mental Health Act 1983 s 85A(2) (see the text and note 15).
17 Mental Health Act 1983 s 85A(3) (as added (see note 11); amended by the Mental Health Act 2007 Sch 5 para 13(3)). See note 3.

906. Removal of patients to the Channel Islands and the Isle of Man from England and Wales. If it appears to the appropriate national authority[1], in the case of a patient[2] who is liable to be detained or subject to guardianship[3], that it is in the patient's interests to remove him to any of the Channel Islands or the Isle of Man, he may authorise the patient's removal to the island in question and give any necessary directions for his conveyance to his destination; proper arrangements must have been made for admitting him into a hospital or guardianship there[4].

The above provisions apply in the case of a community patient as it applies in the case of a patient who is for the time being liable to be detained under the Mental Health Act 1983, as if the community patient were so liable[5]. However where there are in force in any of the Channel Islands or the Isle of Man enactments ('relevant enactments') corresponding or similar to those relating to community patients in the Mental Health Act 1983 the above provisions do not apply as regards that island and the following provisions apply instead[6].

If it appears to the appropriate national authority[7], in the case of a community patient, that certain conditions are met, the authority may authorise the transfer of responsibility for him to the island in question[8]. The conditions are that such a transfer is in the patient's interests and arrangements have been made for dealing with him under the relevant enactments[9].

If it appears to the appropriate national authority, in the case of a patient who is subject to a restriction order or restriction direction[10] and has been conditionally discharged[11], that a transfer[12] would be in the interests of the patient, the appropriate national authority may, with the consent of the authority exercising corresponding functions in any of the Channel Islands or in the Isle of Man, transfer responsibility for the patient to that authority[13].

1 As to the appropriate national authority see PARA 567.
2 As to the meaning of 'patient' see PARA 758 note 4.
3 Ie under the Mental Health Act 1983 otherwise than by virtue of s 35, s 36, or s 38 (see PARA 899 note 3): s 83.
    The Mental Health Act 1983 ss 80–85A have effect as if any hospital direction under s 45A (see PARA 863) were a transfer direction under s 47 (see PARA 892), and as if any limitation direction under s 45A were a restriction direction under s 49 (see PARA 894): s 92(4) (added by the Crime (Sentences) Act 1997 s 55, Sch 4 para 12(16)).
4 Mental Health Act 1983 s 83.
5 Mental Health Act 1983 s 83ZA(1) (added by the Mental Health Act 2007 Sch 5 para 10).
6 Mental Health Act 1983 s 83ZA(2) (as added: see note 5).
7 For this purpose 'the appropriate national authority' means, in relation to a community patient in respect of whom the responsible hospital is in England, the Secretary of State and, in relation to a community patient in respect of whom the responsible hospital is in Wales, the Welsh Ministers: Mental Health Act 1983 s 83ZA(6) (as added: see note 5).
8 Mental Health Act 1983 s 83ZA(3) (as added: see note 5). However the authority may not act under s 83ZA(3) while the patient is recalled to hospital under s 17E: s 83ZE(5) (as so added).
9 Mental Health Act 1983 s 83ZA(4) (as added: see note 5).
10 Ie under the Mental Health Act 1983 s 41 (see PARA 869) or s 49 (see PARA 894).
11 Ie under the Mental Health Act 1983 s 42 (see PARA 914) or s 73 (see PARA 969).
12 Ie under the Mental Health Act 1983 s 83 (see the text and notes 1–4).
13 Mental Health Act 1983 s 83A (added by the Crime (Sentences) Act 1997 s 48, Sch 3 para 4). See note 3.

907. Removal of alien patients. If it appears to the appropriate national authority[1], in the case of any patient[2] who is neither a British citizen nor a

Commonwealth citizen having a right of abode in the United Kingdom[3] and who is receiving treatment for mental disorder[4] as an in-patient in a hospital in England and Wales[5] or in Northern Ireland[6] and who is detained for treatment[7], that proper arrangements have been made for the removal of the patient to a country or territory outside the United Kingdom, the Isle of Man and the Channel Islands and for his care and treatment there, the appropriate national authority may by warrant authorise the removal of the patient from the place where he is receiving treatment and may give such directions as it thinks fit for the conveyance of the patient to his destination and for his detention in any place or on board any ship or aircraft until his arrival at any specified port or place in any such country or territory[8]. However, such removal may only be authorised if it is in the patient's interests[9]. Further, the appropriate national authority's powers in respect of any patient may not be exercised except with the approval of the appropriate tribunal[10]. Where the patient is removed, any restriction order still in force continues to apply to him if he returns to England and Wales[11].

1   The appropriate national authority decides after appropriate consultation whether authority should be given under the Mental Health Act 1983 s 86 or whether the patient should be repatriated under other powers: see the memorandum issued by the Department of Health and Social Security, 'Mental Health Act 1983: Memorandum on Parts I to VI, VIII and X' (2008). See also note 8. As to the appropriate national authority see PARA 567. In relation to a patient receiving treatment in a hospital within the meaning of the Mental Health (Northern Ireland) Order 1986, SI 1986/595 (NI 4) any reference to the appropriate national authority in the Mental Health Act 1983 s 86(2) or (3) is construed as a reference to the Department of Justice in Northern Ireland: s 86(4) (added by the Mental Health Act 2007 Sch 1 para 15(3)).

2   As to the meaning of 'patient' see PARA 758 note 4.

3   Ie by virtue of the Immigration Act 1971 s 2(1)(b): see BRITISH NATIONALITY vol 4 (2011) PARAS 412, 420. As to the meaning of 'United Kingdom' see PARA 560 note 14.

4   Ie mental illness as distinguished from other forms of mental disorder mentioned in the Mental Health Act 1983 s 1(2): see PARA 761. In relation to a patient receiving treatment in a hospital within the meaning of the Mental Health (Northern Ireland) Order 1986, SI 1986/595 (NI 4), the reference in the Mental Health Act 1983 s 86(1) to mental disorder is construed in accordance with that Order: Mental Health Act 1983 s 86(4) (as added: see note 1).

5   Ie a hospital within the meaning of the Mental Health Act 1983 Pt 2 (ss 2–34) (see PARA 577): s 92(1). As to the meaning of 'England' see PARA 557 note 4; and as to the meaning of 'Wales' see PARA 557 note 5.

6   Ie a hospital within the meaning of the Mental Health (Northern Ireland) Order 1986, SI 1986/595 (NI 4).

7   Ie pursuant to an application for admission for treatment (under the Mental Health Act 1983 s 3 (see PARA 768)) or a report (under the Mental Health (Northern Ireland) Order 1986, SI 1986/595 (NI 4), art 12(1) or art 13), or a hospital order (under the Mental Health Act 1983 s 37 (see PARA 864) or the Mental Health (Northern Ireland) Order 1986, SI 1986/595 (NI 4), art 44), or an order or direction (under the Mental Health Act 1983, other than s 35, s 36, or s 38 (see PARAS 862, 864) or the Mental Health (Northern Ireland) Order 1986, SI 1986/595 (NI 4), other than art 42, art 43 or art 45) having the same effect as such a hospital order: Mental Health Act 1983 s 86(1)(a)–(c) (amended by SI 1986/596).

8   Mental Health Act 1983 s 86(1), (2) (as amended (see note 7); further amended by the Mental Health Act 2007 Sch 1 para 15(2)). The Mental Health Act 1983 86 does not override the Secretary of State's power to issue removal directions under the Immigration Act 1971: *R (on the application of X) v Secretary of State for the Home Department* [2001] 1 WLR 740, CA. See also the Convention for the Protection of Human Rights and Fundamental Freedoms (Rome, 4 November 1950; TS 71 (1953); Cmd 8969) art 3; Application 30240/96 *D v United Kingdom* (1997) 24 EHRR 423, [1997] 24 LS Gaz R 33, ECtHR; *Bensaid v United Kingdom* (2001) 33 EHRR 205, ECtHR; *R v Secretary of State for the Home Department, ex p Turgut* [2001] 1 All ER 719, [2000] Imm AR 306, CA; and RIGHTS AND FREEDOMS.

9   Mental Health Act 1983 s 86(2). See *R v Secretary of State for the Home Department, ex p Talmasani* [1987] Imm AR 32, CA, and *R v Immigration Appeal Tribunal and Secretary of State for the Home Department, ex p Alghali* [1986] Imm AR 376, where submissions that the Secretary of State should have proceeded under the Mental Health Act 1983 s 86 rather than deporting the patient under the Immigration Act 1971 were rejected. In the former case,

however, it was said, obiter, that the result might have been different had the patient been so severely ill that it would have been inhumane to deport him without making arrangements for his care and treatment in the country of destination.

10   Mental Health Act 1983 s 86(3) (amended by SI 2008/2833). As to tribunals generally see PARA 955 et seq.

11   Mental Health Act 1983 s 91(2) (amended by the Mental Health Act 2007 s 40(6), Sch 11 Pt 8). Otherwise, the application, order or direction by virtue of which he is liable to be detained ceases to have effect when he is duly received into a hospital or other institution in pursuance of the arrangements made under the Mental Health Act 1983 s 86(2): s 91(1). As to restriction orders see PARA 869. See also PARA 908.

(15) DURATION, DISCHARGE (OTHER THAN BY TRIBUNAL) AND RECLASSIFICATION

908.   Duration of authority for detention or guardianship.   Subject to certain exceptions, a patient[1] admitted to hospital[2] in pursuance of an application for admission for treatment[3], a hospital order without restrictions[4], an admission order without restrictions[5] or a transfer direction without restrictions[6] and a patient placed under guardianship in pursuance of a guardianship application[7] or order[8] may be detained in a hospital or kept under guardianship for a period not exceeding six months beginning with the day of admission or of acceptance of the guardianship application or of the order or direction[9], as the case may be, but not for any longer period unless the authority for his detention or guardianship is renewed[10]. The exceptions relate to patients absent without leave[11] or in prison[12].

Where a patient liable to be detained or subject to guardianship by virtue of an application, order or direction[13] is removed from England and Wales[14] in pursuance of the arrangements for the removal of patients[15], the application, order or direction ceases to have effect when he is duly received into a hospital or other institution, or placed under guardianship or, where he is not received into a hospital but his detention in hospital is authorised[16], in pursuance of those arrangements[17].

1   As to the meaning of 'patient' see PARA 758 note 4.
2   As to the meaning of 'hospital' see PARA 577.
3   As to compulsory admission for treatment see PARA 768. As to the duration of authority for detention in the case of admission for assessment or assessment in an emergency see the Mental Health Act 1983 ss 2(4), 4(4); and PARAS 767, 769.
4   As to hospital orders see PARA 864; and as to restriction orders see PARA 869. For the duration of remands to hospital for report or treatment and of interim hospital orders see the Mental Health Act 1983 ss 35(7), 36(6), 38(5); and PARAS 862–864.
5   As to admission orders see PARA 874.
6   As to transfer directions see PARAS 892–893.
7   As to compulsory guardianship see PARA 785.
8   As to guardianship orders see PARA 877.

9   In the application of the Mental Health Act 1983 s 20(1) to patients with respect to whom a hospital order without restrictions (see PARA 864), an admission order without restrictions (see PARA 874), a transfer direction without restrictions (see PARAS 892–893) or a guardianship order (see PARA 877) has been made, for the reference to the days of admission or of acceptance of guardianship there is to be substituted a reference to the date of the relevant order or direction under Pt 3 (ss 35–55): see ss 40(4), 55(4), Sch 1 Pt I paras 2, 6; and PARAS 860–861.

10   Mental Health Act 1983 s 20(1). The authority for detention of a patient also ceases to be effective after he has ceased to be liable for detention under Pt 2 (ss 2–34) (see s 17(5); and PARA 917); and the authority for detention or for guardianship of a patient (except in the case of a patient subject to restrictions: see s 41(3)(a), (d); and PARA 869) ceases to be effective if he is absent without leave for the later of six months or the period he is liable to be detained or

subject to guardianship (see s 18(4), ss 40(4), 55(4), Sch 1 Pt I paras 2, 4; and PARAS 793, 918). There is no common law power to detain once the statutory period has expired: *B v Forsey* 1988 SLT 572, HL.

11 Ie subject to the rule in the Mental Health Act 1983 s 18(4): see note 10. See ss 21, 21A–21B; and PARA 911.
12 See the Mental Health Act 1983 s 22; and PARA 912.
13 Ie under the Mental Health Act 1983 Pt 2, Pt 3 or Pt 4 (ss 80–92).
14 As to the meanings of 'England' and 'Wales' see PARA 557 notes 4, 5.
15 Ie arrangements made under the Mental Health Act 1983 Pt 4: see PARA 899 et seq.
16 Ie authorised by virtue of the Mental Health (Care and Treatment) (Scotland) Act 2003 or the Criminal Procedure (Scotland) Act 1995. Reference in the Mental Health Act 1983 s 91 to a patient's detention in hospital being authorised by virtue of the Mental Health (Care and Treatment) (Scotland) Act 2003 or the Criminal Procedure (Scotland) Act 1995 is to be read as including references to a patient in respect of whom a certificate under one of the provisions listed in the Mental Health (Care and Treatment) (Scotland) Act 2003 s 290(7)(a) is in operation: Mental Health Act 1983 s 91(3) (added by SI 2005/2078).
17 Mental Health Act 1983 s 91(1) (amended by SI 2005/2078).

909. Renewal of authority for detention or guardianship. Unless the patient[1] has previously been discharged[2], the authority for detention or guardianship may be renewed: (1) from the expiration of the period of six months[3] for a further period of six months[4]; and (2) from the expiration of any such period of renewal for a further period of one year, and so on for periods of one year at a time[5].

1 As to the meaning of 'patient' see PARA 758 note 4.
2 Ie under the Mental Health Act 1983 s 23 (see PARA 913).
3 Ie the period referred to in the Mental Health Act 1983 s 20(1): see PARA 908.
4 The decision that to renew while the patient was on leave of absence was unlawful in *R v Gardner, ex p L, R v Hallstrom, ex p W* [1986] QB 1090, sub nom *R v Hallstrom, ex p W (No 2)* [1986] 2 All ER 306 (see PARA 917) was overruled by *Barker v Barking, Havering and Brentwood Community Healthcare NHS Trust (Warley Hospital)* [1999] 1 FLR 106, (1998) 47 BMLR 112, CA (see PARA 910).
5 Mental Health Act 1983 s 20(2) (amended by the Mental Health Act 2007 Sch 3 para 5(a)).

910. Procedure and criteria for renewal. Where a patient[1] is liable to be detained for treatment[2], it is the duty of the responsible clinician[3], within the period of two months ending on the day on which the patient would cease to be so liable in default of the renewal of the authority for his detention[4], to examine the patient and, if certain conditions are fulfilled, to furnish a report to the managers[5]. A report[6] must be furnished if: (1) the patient is suffering from mental disorder[7] and his mental disorder is of a nature or degree which makes it appropriate for him to receive medical treatment in a hospital[8]; and (2) it is necessary for the health or safety of the patient or for the protection of others that he should receive such treatment and it cannot be provided unless he continues to be detained[9]; and (3) appropriate medical treatment is available for him[10]. The responsible clinician may not furnish such a report unless a person who has been professionally concerned with the patient's medical treatment; but who belongs to a profession other than that to which the responsible clinician belongs, states in writing that he agrees that the conditions set out in heads (1) to (3) above are satisfied[11]. Before furnishing a report, the responsible clinician must consult one or more persons who have been professionally concerned with the patient's medical treatment[12]. These provisions may only be used to renew authority to detain a patient whose condition requires detention as an in-patient[13].

Where the patient is subject to guardianship[14] it is the duty of the appropriate practitioner to examine the patient within the period of two months ending on the day on which the patient would cease to be so subject in default of the renewal of the authority for guardianship[15]. If the original grounds for guardianship apply, the appropriate practitioner must furnish to the guardian and, if the guardian is a person other than a local social services authority, to the responsible local social services authority[16], a report to that effect in the prescribed form[17].

Where a report is so furnished, the authority for detention or for guardianship, as the case may be, is thereby renewed for the prescribed[18] period[19]. On receiving the report, the managers or the local social services authority must, unless they discharge the patient[20], cause him to be informed of the renewal[21], and the patient may within the period for which the authority for detention or guardianship is renewed by virtue of the report apply[22] to the appropriate tribunal[23].

1   As to the meaning of 'patient' see PARA 758 note 4.
2   Ie in pursuance of an application for admission for treatment, or in pursuance of a hospital order, admission order or transfer direction without restrictions: see PARA 908. See the Mental Health Act 1983 s 40(4), Sch 1 Pt I paras 2, 6; and PARAS 860–861.
3   As to the meaning of 'responsible clinician' see PARA 834.
4   The period is varied as regards patients absent without leave: see the Mental Health Act 1983 s 21; and PARA 911.
5   Mental Health Act 1983 s 20(3) (amended by the Mental Health Act 2007 s 9(4)). As to the hospital managers see PARA 778.
6   Where the form of mental disorder specified in a report under the Mental Health Act 1983 s 20(3) or (6) is different from that specified in the application, order or direction, then that application, order or direction has effect as if the other form of mental disorder were specified in it; there is no need to furnish a report of reclassification: ss 20(9), 40(4), Sch 1 Pt I paras 2, 6. See also PARAS 860–861.
7   As to the meaning of 'mental disorder' see PARA 761.
8   Mental Health Act 1983 s 20(4)(a) (amended by the Mental Health Act 2007 Sch 1 para 4(a)). As to the meaning of 'medical treatment' see PARA 926. As to the meaning of 'hospital' see PARA 577. 'Treatment in hospital' can include monitoring and assessing the patient's condition, and need not be treatment as an in-patient: see *Barker v Barking, Havering and Brentwood Community Healthcare NHS Trust (Warley Hospital)* [1999] 1 FLR 106, (1998) 47 BMLR 112, CA; *R (on the application of DR) v Merseycare NHS Trust* (2002) Times, 11 October, [2002] All ER (D) 28 (Aug).
9   Mental Health Act 1983 s 20(4)(c). Absence from hospital on leave does not mean that a patient is no longer detained: *Barker v Barking, Havering and Brentwood Community Healthcare NHS Trust (Warley Hospital)* [1999] 1 FLR 106, (1998) 47 BMLR 112, CA. See also *R (on the application of CS) v Mental Health Review Tribunal* [2004] EWHC 2958 (Admin); *R (on the application of Epsom and St Helier NHS Trust) v Mental Health Review Tribunal* [2001] EWHC 101 (Admin), [2001] 1 MHLR 8.
10 Mental Health Act 1983 s 20(4)(d) (added by the Mental Health Act 2007 s 4(4)(b)).
11 Mental Health Act 1983 s 20(5A) (added by the Mental Health Act 2007 s 9(4)(b)).
12 Mental Health Act 1983 s 20(5) (amended by the Mental Health Act 2007 s 9(4)(a)).
13 See *R v Gardner, ex p L, R v Hallstrom, ex p W* [1986] QB 1090, sub nom *R v Hallstrom, ex p W (No 2)* [1986] 2 All ER 306.
    A renewal of detention under the Mental Health Act 1983 s 20 is possible if the patient has been granted absence of leave, provided the course of treatment requires an in-patient element: *Barker v Barking, Havering and Brentwood Community Healthcare NHS Trust (Warley Hospital)* [1999] 1 FLR 106, (1998) 47 BMLR 112, CA. In renewing detention, the essential question is whether hospital treatment is a significant element of the proposed treatment plan and not whether it is planned for the patient to be an in-patient: *R (on the application of DR) v Merseycare NHS Trust* (2002) Times, 11 October, [2002] All ER (D) 28 (Aug).
14 Ie under the Mental Health Act 1983 Pt 2 (ss 2–34) (see PARA 785 et seq) or under a guardianship order (see PARA 877): see s 40(4), Sch 1 Pt I paras 2, 6; and PARAS 860–861.
15 Mental Health Act 1983 s 20(6) (amended by the Mental Health Act 2007 s 9(4)(c)).
16 Ie the local social services authority (see PARA 579) for the area in which the guardian resides: Mental Health Act 1983 s 34(3)(b).
17 Mental Health Act 1983 s 20(6), (7) (s 20(7) amended by the Mental Health Act 2007 Sch 1 para 4(b)).

18 Ie the period prescribed by the Mental Health Act 1983 s 20(2): see PARA 909.
19 Mental Health Act 1983 s 20(8). The authority is renewed without any action on the part of the
    managers or the local social services authority, as the case may be; however, there is power to
    discharge the patient at any time (see s 23; and PARA 913) and the forms provide space for
    recording the fact that they have considered the report and their decision whether or not to
    discharge the patient. There is no common law power to detain once the statutory period has
    expired: *B v Forsey* 1988 SC (HL) 28, 1988 SLT 572, HL.
20 Ie under the Mental Health Act 1983 s 23 (see PARA 913).
21 Mental Health Act 1983 s 20(3), (6) (both amended by the Mental Health Act 2007 Sch 3
    para 5(b)). The power of the managers to discharge is under the Mental Health Act 1983
    s 23(2)(a) (see PARA 913) and they must consider the conditions of renewal under s 20(4) in
    exercising this power: *R (on the application of DR) v Merseycare NHS Trust* (2002) Times,
    11 October, [2002] All ER (D) 28 (Aug). Even if they find that conditions for renewal are met,
    the managers can exercise their discretion under the Mental Health Act 1983 s 23(2) to order
    discharge: *R v Riverside Mental Health Trust, ex p Huzzey* (1998) 43 BMLR 167.
22 He may apply only once during that period: see the Mental Health Act 1983 s 77(2); and PARA
    959. A withdrawn application is to be disregarded: see s 77(2); and PARA 959.
23 See the Mental Health Act 1983 s 66(1)(f), (i), 2(f); and PARA 961.

911. Effect on duration of absence without leave. Where a patient[1] is absent
without leave on the day on which, apart from this provision, he would
otherwise cease to be liable to be detained or subject to guardianship[2], or, in the
case of a community patient, the community treatment order would cease[3] to be
in force, or within the period of one week ending with that day, he does not cease
to be so liable or subject, or the order does not cease to be in force, until the
relevant time[4]. The relevant time: (1) where the patient is taken into custody[5], is
the end of the period of one week beginning with the day on which he is returned
to the hospital or place where he ought to be[6]; (2) where the patient returns
himself to the hospital or place where he ought to be within the period during
which he can be taken into custody[7], is the end of the period of one week
beginning with the day on which he so returns himself[8]; and (3) otherwise, is the
end of the period during which he can be taken into custody[9].

Where a patient is absent without leave on the day on which the managers
would be required[10] to refer the patient's case to the appropriate tribunal[11], that
requirement does not apply unless and until the patient is taken into custody[12]
and returned to the hospital where he ought to be or the patient returns himself
to the hospital where he ought to be within the period during which he can be
taken into custody[13].

Where a community patient is absent without leave on the day on which the
72-hour period applicable to recalled patients[14] would expire, that period does
not expire until the end of the period of 72 hours beginning with the time when
the patient is taken into custody[15] and returned to the hospital where he ought to
be or the patient returns himself to the hospital where he ought to be within the
period during which he can be taken into custody[16].

Where a patient who is absent without leave is taken into custody[17], or
returns himself to the hospital or place where he ought to be, not later than the
end of the period of 28 days beginning with the first day of his absence without
leave[18]: (a) where the period for which the patient is liable to be detained or
subject to guardianship is extended[19], any examination and report[20] to be made
and furnished in respect of the patient may be made and furnished within the
period as so extended[21]; (b) where the authority for the detention or
guardianship of the patient is renewed by virtue of head (a) above after the day
on which that authority would have expired, the renewal takes effect as from
that day[22]. In the case of a community patient, where the period for which the
community treatment order is in force is extended[23], any examination and report

to be made and furnished in respect of the patient[24] may be made and furnished within the period as so extended[25]. Where the community treatment period is so extended after the day on which the order would have ceased to be in force, the extension takes effect as from that day[26].

The following applies where a patient who is absent without leave is taken into custody[27], or returns himself to the hospital or place where he ought to be, later than the end of the period of 28 days beginning with the first day of his absence without leave[28]. It is the duty of the appropriate practitioner, within the period of one week beginning with the day on which the patient is returned or returns himself to the hospital or place where he ought to be (his 'return day'), to examine the patient and, if it appears to him that the relevant conditions[29] are satisfied, to furnish to the appropriate body[30] a report to that effect in the prescribed form; and, where such a report is furnished in respect of the patient, the appropriate body must cause him to be informed[31]. Where the patient is liable to be detained or is a community patient, rather than subject to guardianship, the appropriate practitioner must, before furnishing a report, consult one or more other persons who have been professionally concerned with the patient's medical treatment, and an approved mental health professional[32]. Where the patient would, apart from any renewal of the authority for his detention or guardianship on or after his return be liable to be detained or subject to guardianship after the end of the period of one week beginning with that day, or, in the case of a community patient, the community treatment order would (apart from any extension of the community treatment period on or after that day) be in force after the end of that period, he ceases to be so liable or subject, or the community treatment period shall be deemed to expire, at the end of that period unless a report is duly furnished in respect of him[33]. Where the patient would have ceased to be liable to be detained or subject to guardianship on or before the day on which a report is duly furnished in respect of him, the report must renew the authority for his detention or guardianship for the period prescribed in that case[34]. Where the authority for the detention or guardianship of the patient is renewed, the renewal takes effect as from the day on which the authority would have expired, and if the renewed authority would expire on or before the day on which the report is furnished, the report must further renew the authority as from the day on which it would expire, for the period prescribed in that case[35].

In the case of a community patient, where the community treatment order ceases to be in force on or before the day on which a report is duly furnished in respect of him, the report must extend the community treatment period for the period prescribed[36] in that case[37]. Where the community treatment period is so extended the extension takes effect as from the day on which the order would have ceased to be in force and, if the period as so extended would expire on or before the day on which the report is furnished, the report must further extend that period, as from the day on which it would expire, for the period prescribed[38] in that case[39].

1   As to the meaning of 'patient' see PARA 758 note 4.

2   Ie under the Mental Health Act 1983 Pt 2 (ss 2–34).

3   For the purposes of the Mental Health Act 1983 ss 21, 21A–22, to the time when a community treatment order would cease, or would have ceased, to be in force are construed as a reference to the time when it would cease, or would have ceased, to be in force by reason only of the passage of time: s 21(5) (s 21(4), (5) added by the Mental Health Act 2007 Sch 3 para 6(3)).

4   Mental Health Act 1983 s 21(1) (s 21 substituted by the Mental Health (Patients in the Community) Act 1995 s 2(2); amended by the Mental Health Act 2007 Sch 3 para 6(2)).

The Mental Health Act 1983 s 21 applies with any necessary modifications to a patient who ~~is at large and liable to be retaken~~ by virtue of s 138 (see PARA 777) as it applies to a patient who is absent without leave within the meaning of s 18 (see PARA 918); ~~and references in s 21 to s 18~~ are to be construed accordingly: s 138(6).

5 Ie under the Mental Health Act 1983 s 18 (see PARA 918).

6 Mental Health Act 1983 s 21(2)(a) (as substituted: see note 4). As to the meaning of 'hospital' see PARA 577.

7 Ie under the Mental Health Act 1983 s 18 (see PARA 918).

8 Mental Health Act 1983 s 21(2)(b) (as substituted: see note 4).

9 Mental Health Act 1983 s 21(2)(c) (as substituted: see note 4).

10 Ie required under the Mental Health Act 1983 s 68 (see PARA 964).

11 As to the meaning of 'appropriate tribunal' see PARA 955.

12 Ie under the Mental Health Act 1983 s 18 (see PARA 918).

13 Mental Health Act 1983 s 21(3) (added by the Mental Health Act 2007 s 37(2)).

14 Ie the period mentioned in the Mental Health Act 1983 s 17F (see PARA 802).

15 Ie under the Mental Health Act 1983 s 18 (see PARA 918).

16 Mental Health Act 1983 s 21(4) (as added: see note 4).

17 Ie under the Mental Health Act 1983 s 18 (see PARA 918).

18 Mental Health Act 1983 s 21A(1) (ss 21A, 21B added by the Mental Health (Patients in the Community) Act 1995 s 2(2)).

19 Ie by the Mental Health Act 1983 s 21.

20 Ie under the Mental Health Act 1983 s 20(3) or (6) (see PARA 910).

21 Mental Health Act 1983 s 21A(2) (as added: see note 18).

22 Mental Health Act 1983 s 21A(3) (as added: see note 18).

23 Ie extended by the Mental Health Act 1983 s 21.

24 Ie under the Mental Health Act 1983 s 20A(4) (see PARA 799).

25 Mental Health Act 1983 s 21A(4) (s 21A(4), (5) added by the Mental Health Act 2007 Sch 3 para 7).

26 Mental Health Act 1983 s 21A(5) (as added: see note 25).

27 Ie under the Mental Health Act 1983 s 18.

28 Mental Health Act 1983 s 21B(1) (as added: see note 18).

29 'Relevant conditions' means, in relation to a patient who is liable to be detained in a hospital, the conditions set out in the Mental Health Act 1983 s 20(4), and, in relation to a patient who is subject to guardianship, the conditions set out in s 20(7): s 21B(10) (as added: see note 10). As to the conditions see PARA 910.

30 'Appropriate body' means, in relation to a patient who is liable to be detained in a hospital, the managers of the hospital, in relation to a patient who is subject to guardianship, the responsible local social services authority, and, in relation to a community patient, the managers of the responsible hospital: Mental Health Act 1983 s 21B(10) (as added (see note 18); substituted by the Mental Health Act 2007 Sch 3 para 8(8)(a)). As to the meaning of 'managers' see PARA 778.

31 Mental Health Act 1983 s 21B(2) (as added (see note 18); amended by the Mental Health Act 2007 s 9(5)(a), Sch 3 para 8(2)).

32 Mental Health Act 1983 s 21B(3) (as added (see note 18); amended by the Mental Health Act 2007 s 9(5)(a), Sch 2 para 7(b), Sch 3 para 8(3). As to the meaning of 'medical treatment' see PARA 926.

33 Mental Health Act 1983 s 21B(4) (as added (see note 18); substituted by the Mental Health Act 2007 Sch 3 para 8(4)). If, in the case of a community patient, the community treatment order is revoked under the Mental Health Act 1983 s 17F (see PARA 802) during the period of one week beginning with his return day s 21B(2), (4) do not apply and any report already furnished in respect of him under s 21B(2) is of no effect: s 21B(4A) (added by the Mental Health Act 2007 Sch 3 para 8(5)).

34 Mental Health Act 1983 s 21B(5) (as added: see note 18). As to the period prescribed see s 20(2); and PARA 909.

35 Mental Health Act 1983 s 21B(6) (as added: see note 18). As to the period prescribed see s 20(2); and PARA 909. Where the authority for the detention or guardianship of the patient would expire within the period of two months beginning on the day on which a report is duly furnished in respect of him under s 21B(2) (see the text and notes 29–31), the report also, if it so provides, has effect as a report duly furnished under s 20(3) or (6) (see PARA 910): s 21B(7) (as so added). 'Authority' includes any authority renewed under s 21B(5) (see the text and note 34) by the report: s 21B(7) (as so added).

36 Ie the period prescribed by the Mental Health Act 1983 s 20A(3) (see PARA 799).

37 Mental Health Act 1983 s 21B(6A) (s 21B(6A), (6B) added by the Mental Health Act 2007 Sch 3 para 8(6)).

38 Ie prescribed by the Mental Health Act 1983 s 20A(3) (see PARA 799).
39 Mental Health Act 1983 s 21B(6B) (as added: see note 37).

912.   Patients detained in custody by sentence or court order. If: (1) a qualifying patient[1] is detained in custody in pursuance of any sentence or order passed or made by a court in the United Kingdom (including an order committing or remanding him in custody); and (2) he is so detained for a period exceeding, or for successive periods exceeding in the aggregate, six months, the relevant application[2] ceases to have effect on expiry of that period[3].

The remaining provisions apply if a qualifying patient is detained in custody as mentioned in head (1) above but for a period not exceeding, or for successive periods not exceeding in the aggregate, six months[4]. If, apart from this provision, the patient would have ceased to be liable to be detained or subject to guardianship by virtue of the relevant application on or before the day on which he is discharged from custody or, in the case of a community patient, the community treatment order would have ceased to be in force on or before that day, he does not cease and is deemed not to have ceased to be so liable or subject, or the order does not cease and is deemed not to have ceased to be in force, until the end of that day[5]. In any case (except as otherwise provided)[6], certain provisions relating to patients absent without leave[7] and patients who are taken into custody or return within 28 days[8] apply in relation to the patient as if he had absented himself without leave on that day[9].

1 A patient is a qualifying patient for these purposes if he is liable to be detained by virtue of an application for admission for treatment; he is subject to guardianship by virtue of a guardianship application; or he is a community patient: Mental Health Act 1983 s 22(1) (substituted by the Mental Health Act 2007 Sch 3 para 9).
2 'The relevant application', in relation to a qualifying patient, means, in the case of a patient who is subject to guardianship, the guardianship application in respect of him and, in any other case, the application for admission for treatment in respect of him: Mental Health Act 1983 s 22(3) (as substituted: see note 1).
3 Mental Health Act 1983 s 22(2) (as substituted: see note 1).
4 Mental Health Act 1983 s 22(4) (as substituted: see note 1).
5 Mental Health Act 1983 s 22(5) (as substituted: see note 1).
6 Ie except as provided by the Mental Health Act 1983 s 22(8) (see note 7).
7 Ie the Mental Health Act 1983 s 18 (see PARA 727) and s 21 (see PARA 911). In its application by virtue of s 22(6), s 18 has effect as if in s 18(4) for the words from 'later of' to the end there were substituted 'end of the period of 28 days beginning with the first day of his absence without leave' and s 22(4A), (4B) were omitted: s 22(7) (as substituted: see note 1). In relation to a community patient who was not recalled to hospital under s 17E (see PARA 801) at the time when his detention in custody began s 18 does not apply but ss 21 and 21A (see PARA 911) apply as if he had absented himself without leave on the day on which he is discharged from custody and had returned himself as provided in those sections on the last day of the period of 28 days beginning with that day: s 22(8) (as so substituted).
8 Ie the Mental Health Act 1983 s 21A (see PARA 911).
9 Mental Health Act 1983 s 22(6) (as substituted: see note 1).

913.   Orders for discharge. A patient[1] who is for the time being liable to be detained or subject to guardianship[2] ceases to be so liable or subject if an order in writing discharging him absolutely from detention or guardianship (an 'order for discharge') is duly[3] made[4]. A community patient ceases to be liable to recall, and the application for admission for treatment ceases to have effect, if an order for discharge is made[5].

An order for discharge may be made in respect of a patient: (1) where the patient is liable to be detained in a hospital[6] in pursuance of an application for admission for assessment[7] or of an application for admission to treatment[8], by the responsible clinician[9] or by the managers[10] of the hospital or the nearest relative of the patient[11]; (2) where the patient is subject to guardianship[12], by the responsible clinician, by the responsible local social services authority[13] or by the patient's nearest relative[14].

Where an order for discharge is made otherwise than by virtue of an application made by the nearest relative of the patient to be discharged, the managers of the hospital or registered establishment[15] have a duty to take such steps as are practicable to inform the person, if any, appearing to them to be the patient's nearest relative, at least seven days before the date of discharge[16].

1   As to the meaning of 'patient' see PARA 758 note 4.
2   Ie under the Mental Health Act 1983 Pt 2 (ss 2–34).
3   Ie in accordance with the Mental Health Act 1983 s 23. An order for discharge granted by a panel constituted under this provision may only be made if a unanimous decision of all three members is made: *R (on the application of Tagoe-Thompson) v Central and North West London Mental Health NHS Trust* [2003] EWCA Civ 330, [2003] 1 WLR 1272, (2003) Times, 18 April. As to discharge by the tribunal see PARA 967 et seq.
4   Mental Health Act 1983 s 23(1), (1B) (s 23(1) amended and s 23(1A), (1B) added by the Mental Health Act 2007 Sch 3 para 10(2), (3)). In the application of the Mental Health Act 1983 s 23(1) to patients with respect to whom a hospital order with a restriction order (see PARA 869), an order for committal to hospital (see PARA 873), an admission order with restrictions (see PARA 874), a direction for detention in hospital (see PARA 874) or a transfer direction with restrictions (see PARA 894) has been made, references to guardianship must be omitted and the consent of the Secretary of State is required for the making of an order for discharge: see ss 40(4), 41(3), 55(4), Sch 1 Pt II paras 2, 7 (s 41(3); and PARAS 860–861. See also PARA 869. As to the additional power to discharge restricted patients see PARA 914.
5   Mental Health Act 1983 s 23(1A) (as added: see note 4).
6   As to the meaning of 'hospital', which for this purpose includes a registered establishment, see PARA 577.
7   As to admissions for assessment see the Mental Health Act 1983 s 2; and PARA 767.
8   As to applications for admission for treatment see the Mental Health Act 1983 s 3; and PARA 768.
9   As to the meaning of 'responsible clinician' see PARA 834. In relation to England, for the purposes of the Mental Health Act 1983 s 23 (discharge of patients) a responsible clinician's order for the discharge of: (1) a patient liable to be detained under the Mental Health Act 1983, or a community patient, must be sent to the managers of the hospital in which the patient is liable to be detained or the responsible hospital (as applicable) as soon as practicable after it is made; (2) a guardianship patient, must be sent to the guardian as soon as practicable after it is made: Mental Health (Hospital, Guardianship and Treatment) (England) Regulations 2008, SI 2008/1184, reg 18.
10 As to the meaning of 'managers' see PARA 778. The powers conferred by the Mental Health Act 1983 s 23 on any authority, trust (other than an NHS foundation trust), board or body of persons may be exercised (subject to s 23(3)) by any three or more members of that authority, trust, board or body authorised in that behalf or by three or more members of a committee or sub-committee of that authority, trust, board or body which has been authorised in that behalf: s 23(4) (amended by the National Health Service and Community Care Act 1990 s 66(1), Sch 9 para 24(3)(b); the Health and Social Care (Community Health and Standards) Act 2003 s 34, Sch 4 paras 50, 53(b); and SI 2007/961). The reference in the Mental Health Act 1983 s 23(4) to the members of an authority, trust, board or body or the members of a committee or sub-committee of an authority, trust, board or body: (1) in the case of a local health board, special health authority or primary care trust or a committee or sub-committee of a local health board, special health authority or primary care trust, is a reference only to the chairman of the authority, board or trust and such members of the authority, trust, board, committee or sub-committee, as the case may be, as are not also officers of the authority or trust, within the meaning of the National Health Service Act 2006 or the National Health Service (Wales) Act 2006; and (2) in the case of an NHS trust or a committee or sub-committee of such a trust, is a reference only to the chairman of the trust and such directors or (in the case of a committee or sub-committee) members as are not also employees of the trust: Mental Health Act 1983 s 23(5) (added by the National Health Service and Community Care Act 1990 Sch 9 para 24(3)(c); and amended by the Health Authorities Act 1995 s 2(1), Sch 1 para 107(2); SI 2000/90; and SI 2007/961). The powers conferred by the Mental Health Act 1983 s 23 on

any NHS foundation trust may be exercised by any three or more persons authorised by the board of the trust in that behalf each of whom is neither an executive director of the board nor an employee of the trusts: s 23(6) (added by the Health and Social Care (Community Health and Standards) Act 2003 Sch 4 paras 50, 53(c); amended by the Mental Health Act 2007 s 45(1)). As from1 April 2013 the words 'primary care trust' are repealed in the Mental Health Act 1983 s 23(4) by the Health and Social Care Act 2012 Sch 5 para 26: see the Health and Social Care Act 2012 (Commencement No 4, Transitional, Savings and Transitory Provisions) Order 2013, SI 2013/160, art 2(2). As to the meaning of 'special health authority' see PARA 575 note 4. As to the meaning of 'primary care trust' see PARA 574 note 5. As to NHS trusts and NHS foundation trusts see HEALTH SERVICES vol 54 (2008) PARA 155 et seq. See also *R (on the application of Tagoe-Thompson) v Central and North West London Mental Health NHS Trust* [2003] EWCA Civ 330, [2003] 1 WLR 1272; and note 3.

As to guidance to hospital managers on the exercise of their power under the Mental Health Act 1983 s 23 see Department of Health *Mental Health Act 1983 Code of Practice* (2008) Chapter 30 and the Welsh Assembly Government *Mental Health Act 1983 Code of Practice for Wales* (2008) Chapter 11. There is no requirement to hold a meeting but in practice one is normally held which must accord with the rules of natural justice, and a patient can apply to the managers as frequently as he wishes. See PARA 910 note 21. As to the Codes of Practice see PARA 762.

11 Mental Health Act 1983 s 23(2)(a) (amended by the Mental Health Act 2007 s 9(6)). As to the meaning of 'nearest relative' see PARA 839. For restrictions on discharge by the nearest relative see PARA 915. As to the criteria for use by hospital managers when considering the continued detention of a s 3 patient where the application for discharge had been subject to a 'barring report' under s 25 (see PARA 915) see *R v Riverside Mental Health Trust, ex p Huzzey* (1998) 43 BMLR 167. See also *R (on the application of SR by her Litigation Friend the Official Solicitor) v Huntercombe Maidenhead Hospital* [2005] EWHC 2361 (Admin), [2005] All ER (D) 115 (Sep) (under the Mental Health Act 1983 s 23 the managers have a wide discretion to discharge a patient but there is no inflexible rule that if the resident medical officer's view as to dangerousness is overruled discharge is inevitable). As to the exercise of the power under the Mental Health Act 1983 s 23(2) see PARA 910 note 21. See also *R (on the application of South West London and St George's Mental Health NHS Trust) v W* [2002] All ER (D) 62 (Aug). As to the form to be used for an order made by the responsible clinician or hospital managers under the Mental Health Act 1983 s 23(2)(a) (discharge of patients) for the discharge of a patient who is liable to be detained see the Mental Health (Hospital, Guardianship. Community Treatment and Consent to Treatment) (Wales) Regulations 2008, SI 2008/2439, reg 7.

12 As to applications for guardianship see the Mental Health Act 1983 s 7; and PARA 785 et seq.

13 As to the meaning of 'responsible local social services authority' see PARA 791 note 1. As to the members of the authority who may exercise this power see note 9.

14 Mental Health Act 1983 s 23(2)(b) (amended by the Mental Health Act 2007 s 9(6)). In the application of the Mental Health Act 1983 s 23(2) to patients with respect to whom a hospital order without restrictions (see PARA 864), an admission order without restrictions (see PARA 874), a transfer direction without restrictions (see PARAS 892–893) or a guardianship order (see PARA 877) has been made, the words 'for assessment or' in s 23(2)(a) and the reference in s 23(2)(a), (b) to the nearest relative of the patient must be omitted: see ss 40(4), 55(4), Sch 1 Pt I paras 2, 8. In the application of s 23(2) to patients with respect to whom a hospital order with restrictions (see PARA 869), an order for committal to hospital (see PARA 873), an admission order with restrictions (see PARA 874), a direction for detention in hospital (see PARA 874) or a transfer direction with restrictions (see PARA 894) has been made, the words 'for assessment or' and the reference to the nearest relative of the patient in s 23(2)(a), and the whole of s 23(2)(b), must be omitted: see ss 40(4), 41(4), 44(3), 49(2), 55(4), Sch 1 Pt II paras 2, 7; and PARAS 860, 861. The Secretary of State may himself discharge a patient who is subject to restrictions: see s 42(2); and PARA 914. As to the form to be used for an order made by the responsible clinician or responsible local social services authority of the patient under s 23(2)(b) for discharge of a patient subject to guardianship see the Mental Health (Hospital, Guardianship, Community Treatment and Consent to Treatment) (Wales) Regulations 2008, SI 2008/2439, reg 14.

15 As to the meaning of 'registered establishment' see PARA 578.

16 Mental Health Act 1983 s 133(1) (amended by the Care Standards Act 2000 s 116, Sch 4 para 9(1), (2)). The reference in the Mental Health Act 1983 s 133(1) to a patient who is to be discharged includes a patient who is to be discharged from hospital under s 17A (see PARA 797): 133(1A) (s 133(1A), (1B) added by the Mental Health Act 2007 Sch 3 para 31). The Mental Health Act 1983 s 133(1) also applies in a case where a community patient is discharged under s 23 or 72 (otherwise than by virtue of an order for discharge made by his nearest relative), but with the reference in that provision to the managers of the hospital or registered establishment

being read as a reference to the managers of the responsible hospital: s 133(1B) (as so added). This does not apply where the patient or nearest relative has requested that such information should not be given: Mental Health Act 1983 s 133(2). As to discharge of restricted patients see PARA 914.

914. Discharge of restricted patients by appropriate national authority. At any time while a restriction order[1] (or an order or direction having the same effect[2]) is in force in respect of a patient[3], the appropriate national authority[4] may, if he thinks fit, discharge the patient either absolutely or subject to conditions[5]. Where a person is absolutely discharged in this manner he then ceases to be liable to be detained by virtue of the relevant hospital order (or direction) and the restriction order (or direction) ceases to have effect accordingly[6].

Where a patient has been conditionally discharged in this manner, the Secretary of State may, at any time during the continuance in force of a restriction order, by warrant recall the patient to such hospital[7] as may be specified in the warrant[8]; and then: (1) if the hospital so specified is not the hospital from which the patient was conditionally discharged, the hospital order and restriction order have effect as if the hospital specified in the warrant were substituted for the hospital specified in the hospital order[9]; and (2) in any case, the patient must be treated[10] as if he had absented himself without leave from the hospital specified in the warrant[11].

If a restriction order ceases to have effect after the patient has been conditionally discharged[12] the patient is, unless previously recalled to hospital, deemed to be absolutely discharged on the date when the order ceases to have effect, and ceases to be liable to be detained under the relevant hospital order accordingly[13].

1 As to restriction orders see PARA 869.
2 Eg a direction for detention in hospital (see PARA 874), or a transfer direction with restrictions (see PARAS 892–894). Patients admitted under admission orders with restriction directions are treated as if admitted under a hospital order and a restriction order: see PARA 874.
   A restriction order cannot cease to have effect by inference or implication, eg by merely allowing the conditions under which the patient was discharged to lapse: *R v Secretary of State for the Home Department, ex p Didlick* [1993] 16 BMLR 71, (1993) Times, 30 March.
3 As to the meaning of 'patient' see PARA 758 note 4.
4 As to the appropriate national authority see PARA 567. This consent is necessary to any discharge of the patient by the responsible medical officer or the hospital managers: see PARA 913. As to his other functions in relation to restricted patients see PARAS 869, 876.

5 Mental Health Act 1983 s 42(2). The Convention for the Protection of Human Rights and Fundamental Freedoms (Rome, 4 November 1950; TS 71 (1953); Cmd 8969) art 8 (see RIGHTS AND FREEDOMS) applies to conditions imposed on a patient discharged under the Mental Health Act 1983 s 42(2): see *R (on the application of Craven) v Secretary of State for the Home Department* [2001] EWHC 850 (Admin), [2001] All ER (D) 74 (Oct). A conditionally discharged patient can be detained under the Mental Health Act 1983 s 2, 3 (see PARA 767 et seq): see *R v North West London Mental Health NHS Trust, ex p S* [1998] QB 628, [1997] 4 All ER 871.
   A condition requiring a patient to remain in hospital is inconsistent with the duty to discharge conditionally: *Secretary of State for the Home Department v Mental Health Review Tribunal for the Mersey Regional Health Authority, Secretary of State for the Home Department v Mental Health Review Tribunal for Wales* [1986] 3 All ER 233, [1986] 1 WLR 1170. However, see *R (on the application of the Secretary of State for the Home Department) v Mental Health Review Tribunal* [2004] EWHC 2194 (Admin). See also *R (on the application of G) v Mental Health Review Tribunal* [2004] EWHC 2193 (Admin), [2004] All ER (D) 86 (Oct), where the degree and intensity of the restrictions imposed by the conditions was considered; followed in *R (on the application of the Secretary of State for the Home Department) v Mental Health Review Tribunal* [2004] EWHC 2194 (Admin), [2004] All ER (D) 87 (Oct).

A patient who is conditionally discharged under the Mental Health Act 1983 s 42(2) or ss 72–73 (see PARAS 969–970) is not subject to the consent to treatment provisions in Pt 4 (ss 56–64): see s 56(1); and PARA 924. See also PARA 640 note 8.

6   Mental Health Act 1983 s 42(3).

7   As to the meaning of 'hospital' see PARA 577. Recall may be to a hospital in which the Mental Health Act 1983 s 3 (see PARA 768) is implemented: see *Dlodlo v Mental Health Review Tribunal for the South Thames Region* (1996) 36 BMLR 145, CA. A patient recalled to hospital must have his case referred to the appropriate tribunal within one month: see the Mental Health Act 1983 s 75(1)(a); and PARA 965. Judicial review would not be an appropriate challenge to such recalls: see *R (on the application of Biggs) v Secretary of State for the Home Department* [2002] EWHC 1012 (Admin), [2002] All ER (D) 292 (May). As to recall and reclassification see *R (on the application of AL) v Secretary of State for the Home Department* [2005] EWCA Civ 02, [2005] All ER (D) 142 (Jan); and note 8.

8   The Secretary of State may issue such a warrant without medical evidence that the person in respect of whom the restriction order is in force is suffering from mental disorder: *R v Secretary of State for the Home Department, ex p K* [1991] 1 QB 270, [1990] 3 All ER 562, CA. See also *R (on the application of Von Brandenburg (aka Hanley)) v East London and the City Mental Health NHS Trust* [2003] UKHL 58, [2004] 2 AC 280, [2004] 1 All ER 400.

Except in emergency cases, the exercise of this power of recall is a violation of the Convention for the Protection of Human Rights and Fundamental Freedoms (Rome, 4 November 1950; TS 71 (1953); Cmd 8969) art 5: *Winterwerp v Netherlands* (1981) 4 EHRR 228, ECtHR; and see RIGHTS AND FREEDOMS.

The exercise of the power under the Mental Health Act 1983 s 42(3) (see PARA 876) where there has been a special verdict finding by a jury (see PARA 874) is not limited to the same form of mental disorder as founded the original detention in hospital: see *R (on the application of AL) v Secretary of State for the Home Department* [2005] EWCA Civ 02, [2006] 1 WLR 88, [2005] NLJR 140. Recall is only justified where there has been a change in circumstances since discharge: *R (on the application of T) v Secretary of State for Justice* [2008] EWHC 1707 (Admin), [2008] All ER (D) 259 (Jul).

9   Mental Health Act 1983 s 42(4)(a).

10 Ie for the purposes of the Mental Health Act 1983 s 18: see PARA 918.

11 Mental Health Act 1983 s 42(4)(b) (amended by the Mental Health Act 2007 Sch 11 Pt 8).

12 Eg because the restrictions are lifted by the Secretary of State under the Mental Health Act 1983 s 42(1) (see PARA 876), or because the order was of limited duration under s 41(1) and the period of its duration has expired (see PARA 869), or under s 50(2) at the expiration of the sentence of a transferred prisoner (see PARA 895).

13 Mental Health Act 1983 s 42(5).

915.   Restrictions on discharge by nearest relative.   An order for the discharge[1] of a community patient, or a patient[2] who is liable to be detained in a hospital[3], may not be made[4] by his nearest relative[5], except after giving not less than 72 hours' notice in writing to the managers[6] of the hospital[7]. If, within 72 hours after such notice has been given, the responsible clinician[8] furnishes to the managers a report[9] certifying that in that clinician's opinion the patient, if discharged, would be likely to act in a manner dangerous to other persons or to himself, any order made by the nearest relative in pursuance of the notice is of no effect; and no further order may be made by that relative during the period of six months beginning with the date of the report[10].

Where such a report is furnished, it is the duty of the managers to cause the patient's nearest relative to be informed[11], and the relevant application may be made to the appropriate tribunal in respect of the patient[12].

1   As to orders for discharge generally see PARA 913. The nearest relative has no power to order the discharge of patients subject to hospital or guardianship orders or orders or directions having the same effect. As to hospital and guardianship orders see PARA 859 et seq.

2   As to the meaning of 'patient' see PARA 758 note 4.

3   As to the meaning of 'hospital' see PARA 577. The restrictions in the Mental Health Act 1983 s 25 do not apply to the discharge of patients subject to guardianship applications.

4   Ie under the Mental Health Act 1983 s 23 (see PARA 913).

5   As to the meaning of 'nearest relative' see PARA 839.

6   As to the meaning of 'managers' see PARA 778. The Mental Health Act 1983 s 25(1) applies to an order for the discharge of a community patient as it applies to an order for the discharge of a patient who is liable to be detained in a hospital, but with the reference to the managers of the hospital being read as a reference to the managers of the responsible hospital: s 25(1A) (as added: see note 7).

7   Mental Health Act 1983 s 25(1), (1A) (s 25(1) amended and s 25(1A) added by the Mental Health Act 2007 Sch 3 para 12(2), (3)). The effect of this requirement is to prevent the nearest relative from discharging a patient admitted for assessment in an emergency under the Mental Health Act 1983 s 4 (see PARA 769) unless the period is extended beyond the initial 72 hours by the giving of a second medical recommendation under s 4(4) (see PARA 769). See *Kinsey v North Mersey Community NHS Trust* (21 June 1999, unreported). As to the managers' criteria see *R v Riverside Mental Health Trust, ex p Huzzey* (1998) 43 BMLR 167; *R (on the application of SR by her Litigation Friend the Official Solicitor) v Huntercombe Maidenhead Hospital* [2005] EWHC 2361 (Admin), [2005] All ER (D) 115 (Sep); and PARA 913.

8   As to the meaning of 'responsible clinician' see PARA 834.

9   If the hospital managers are not persuaded by the report, the nearest relative is entitled to an order for discharge: *R v Riverside Mental Health Trust, ex p Huzzey* (1998) 43 BMLR 167. See also *R (on the application of SR by her Litigation Friend the Official Solicitor) v Huntercombe Maidenhead Hospital* [2005] All ER (D) 115 (Sep).

10 Mental Health Act 1983 s 25(1) (amended by the Mental Health Act 2007 s 9(8)(a)). The furnishing of such a report by the responsible medical officer does not prevent the managers themselves from discharging the patient at any time if they think fit.

11 Mental Health Act 1983 s 25(2) (amended by the Mental Health Act 2007 Sch 3 para 12(4)). The obligation to inform the nearest relative applies only in the case of a patient detained in pursuance of an application for admission for treatment, or in respect of a community patient.

12 See the Mental Health Act 1983 s 66(1)(g), (i), (ii), (2)(a), (d); and PARA 961. As to the meaning of 'appropriate tribunal' see PARA 955.

916.   Visiting and examination of patients with a view to discharge.   For the purpose of advising as to the exercise by the nearest relative[1] of a patient[2] who is liable to be detained or subject to guardianship[3] or is a community patient of any power to order his discharge[4], any registered medical practitioner or approved clinician[5] authorised by or on behalf of the nearest relative may, at any reasonable time, visit the patient and examine him in private[6] and require the production of and inspect any records relating to the detention or treatment of the patient in any hospital[7] or to any aftercare services provided for the patient[8].

1   As to the meaning of 'nearest relative' see PARA 839.

2   As to the meaning of 'patient' see PARA 758 note 4.

3   Ie under the Mental Health Act 1983 Pt 2 (ss 2–34). For the application of this provision to persons liable to be detained or subject to guardianship by virtue of an order or direction under Pt 3 (ss 35–55) see PARA 860.

4   As to such powers see PARAS 913, 915. The nearest relative has no power to order the discharge of a patient liable to be detained or subject to guardianship under the Mental Health Act 1983 Pt 3.

5   As to registered medical practitioners see MEDICAL PROFESSIONS vol 74 (2011) PARA 176 et seq. As to the meaning of 'approved clinician' see PARA 831.

6   Mental Health Act 1983 s 24(1) (amended by the Mental Health Act 2007 Sch 3 para 11(2)). Obstruction of a medical practitioner authorised to visit and examine a patient under the Mental Health Act 1983 s 24 would, if established, constitute an offence under s 129: see PARA 1015. For equivalent provision as to visits and examination for the purposes of applying to the appropriate tribunal see s 76; and PARA 963. As to the power to visit a patient in hospital for purposes connected with legal proceedings see *Re Petition for Judicial Separation, ex p Beecham* [1901] P 65.

7   As to the meaning of 'hospital' see PARA 577.

8   Mental Health Act 1983 s 24(2) (amended by the Mental Health (Patients in the Community) Act 1995 s 1(2), Sch 1 para 1; and the Mental Health Act 2007 s 9(7)). Such aftercare services are provided under the Mental Health Act 1983 s 117: see PARAS 580, 945.

(16) ABSENCE AND ESCAPE

917. Leave of absence from hospital. The responsible clinician[1] may grant any patient[2] who is for the time being liable to be detained in a hospital[3] under the Mental Health Act 1983[4] leave to be absent from the hospital subject to such conditions, if any, as he considers necessary in the interests of the patient or for the protection of other persons[5]. Leave may be granted indefinitely[6], or on specified occasions, or for any specified period; and where it is granted for a specified period, the period may be extended by further leave granted in the absence of the patient[7]. But longer-term leave may not be granted[8] to a patient unless the responsible clinician first considers whether the patient should be dealt with by a community treatment order[9]. Where it appears to the responsible clinician that it is necessary to do so in the interests of the patient or for the protection of other persons, he may, on granting leave of absence, direct that the patient must remain in custody[10] during absence[11]. In this event the patient may be kept in the custody of any officer on the staff of the hospital concerned or of any other person authorised in writing by the managers of the hospital[12].

Where it appears to the responsible clinician that it is necessary to do so in the interests of the patient's health or safety or for the protection of other persons, he may revoke any leave of absence which has been granted and recall the patient to hospital by notice in writing given to the patient or to the person for the time being in charge of the patient[13]. However, a patient must not be so recalled after he has ceased to be liable to be detained[14] under the Mental Health Act 1983[15].

1   As to the meaning of 'responsible clinician' see PARA 834.
2   As to the meaning of 'patient' see PARA 758 note 4.
3   As to the meaning of 'hospital' see PARA 577.
4   Ie under the Mental Health Act 1983 Pt 2 (ss 2–34). The provisions of s 17 as to the grant etc of leave of absence also apply without modifications to hospital order patients who are not subject to special restrictions and with modifications to patients who are subject to special restrictions: see ss 40(4), 41(3), 55(4), Sch 1 Pt I para 1, Sch 1 Pt II paras 2, 3; and PARAS 860–861.
5   Mental Health Act 1983 s 17(1) (amended by the Mental Health Act 2007 s 9(3)(a)). As to where the patient is subject to special restrictions, the responsible medical officer may only grant leave of absence with the consent of the Secretary of State: Mental Health Act 1983 see ss 40(4), 55(4), Sch 1 Pt II paras 2, 3(a); and PARA 869.
    The Secretary of State's consent should be given or refused in accordance with s 17 and not by virtue of s 42 (see PARA 876): see *R (on the application of A) v Secretary of State for the Home Department* [2002] EWHC 1618 (Admin), [2003] 1 WLR 330, (2002) Times, 5 September. The tribunal is not bound to discharge a patient on leave of absence under the Mental Health Act 1983 s 17; and periods of absence from hospital are not inconsistent with continuing detention under the Mental Health Act 1983: see *R (on the application of S) v Mental Health Review Tribunal* [2004] EWHC 2958 (Admin), [2004] All ER (D) 87 (Dec). The grant of a leave of absence under the Mental Health Act 1983 s 17 of a patient requiring a stay in another hospital does not trigger an obligation on the part of the authority to fund the cost of the residence of the patient in the other institution during such period: see *R (on the application of K) v West London Mental Health NHS Trust* [2006] EWCA Civ 118, [2006] 1 WLR 1865, 90 BMLR 214.
6   However, a patient absent on leave is not normally liable to recall to hospital after he has ceased to be liable to be detained under the Mental Health Act 1983 s 17: see s 17(5); and the text and note 13. See also *R (on the application of S) v Mental Health Review Tribunal* [2004] EWHC 2958 (Admin), [2004] All ER (D) 87 (Dec).
7   Mental Health Act 1983 s 17(2).
8   For these purposes, longer-term leave is granted to a patient if leave of absence is granted to him under the Mental Health Act 1983 s 17 either indefinitely or for a specified period of more than seven consecutive days or a specified period is extended under s 17 such that the total period for which leave of absence will have been granted to him under this section exceeds seven consecutive days: s 17(2B) (s 17(2A), (2B) added by the Mental Health Act 2007 s 33(2)).

9   Ie an order under the Mental Health Act 1983 s 17A (see PARA 797): s 17(2A) (as added: see note 8).

10   For the purpose of giving effect to a direction or condition imposed by virtue of a provision corresponding to the Mental Health Act 1983 s 17(3), the person may be conveyed to a place in, or kept in custody or detained at a place of safety in, England and Wales by a person authorised in that behalf by the direction or condition: s 17(7) (s 17(6), (7) added by the Mental Health Act 1983 s 39(1)). This applies to a person who is granted leave by or by virtue of a provision in force in Scotland, Northern Ireland, any of the Channel Islands or the Isle of Man and corresponding to the Mental Health Act 1983 s 17(1): s 17(6) (as so added). The custody will be legal custody, and any person authorised to keep the patient in custody will have all the powers, authorities, protection and privileges which a constable has in the area for which he acts as constable: see Mental Health Act 1983 s 137(1), (2); and PARA 776. It is an offence to induce or knowingly to assist a patient to escape from legal custody: see s 128(2); and PARA 1013.

11   Mental Health Act 1983 s 17(3) (amended by the Mental Health Act 2007 s 9(3)(b)).

12   Mental Health Act 1983 s 17(3). Where a patient is required as a condition imposed on the grant of leave of absence to reside in another hospital, the person having custody includes any officer on the staff of that other hospital: s 17(3). As to the meaning of 'managers' see PARA 778.

13   Mental Health Act 1983 s 17(4) (amended by the Mental Health Act 2007 s 9(3)(c)). Where the patient is subject to special restrictions, the Secretary of State as well as the responsible medical officer may recall him to hospital: see ss 40(4), 41(3), 55(4), Sch 1 Pt II paras 2, 3(b). Leave of absence can only be revoked and the patient recalled to hospital if he needs to become an in-patient once again in the interests of his health or safety or for the protection of other persons; it is unlawful to recall a patient on leave simply to renew his detention under s 20 (see PARAS 908–910): *R v Gardner, ex p L, R v Hallstrom, ex p W* [1986] QB 1090, sub nom *R v Hallstrom, ex p W (No 2)* [1986] 2 All ER 306. The Convention for the Protection of Human Rights and Fundamental Freedoms (Rome, 4 November 1950; TS 71 (1953); Cmd 8969) art 5 (see RIGHTS AND FREEDOMS) requires up-to-date medical evidence of mental disorder to justify revocation of leave of absence: *K v United Kingdom* (1998) 40 BMLR 20.

14   Ie under the Mental Health Act 1983 Pt 2. References to the provisions of Pt 2 in the case of patients detained under Pt 3 (ss 35–55) include those provisions to the extent that Pt 2 applies to such patients: s 145(3).

15   Mental Health Act 1983 s 17(5) (amended by the Mental Health (Patients in the Community) Act 1995 s 3(1)). Patients subject to special restrictions do not cease to be liable to be detained under these provisions: Mental Health Act 1983 s 41(3)(a), (d). As to the recall of such patients see ss 40(4), 41(3), 55(4), Sch 1 Pt II paras 2, 3(c); and PARA 869. The provisions of the Mental Health Act 1983 Pt 2 relating to aftercare under supervision do not apply to a patient who is subject to special restrictions: see s 41(3)(aa); and PARA 869.

918.   Return and readmission of patients absent without leave.   Where a patient[1] for the time being liable to be detained under the Mental Health Act 1983[2] in a hospital[3]: (1) absents himself from the hospital without leave[4]; or (2) fails to return to the hospital on any occasion on which, or at the expiration of any period for which, leave of absence was granted to him, or on being recalled to hospital[5]; or (3) absents himself without permission from any place where he is required to reside in accordance with conditions imposed on the grant of leave of absence[6], he may, within certain limits of time[7], be taken into custody[8] and returned to the hospital or place[9] by any approved mental health professional[10], by any officer on the staff of the hospital[11], by any constable[12], or by any person authorised in writing by the managers of the hospital[13]. Where a community patient is at any time absent from a hospital to which he is recalled[14], he may be taken into custody and returned to the hospital by any approved mental health professional, by any officer on the staff of the hospital, by any constable, or by any person authorised in writing by the responsible clinician or the managers of the hospital[15].

A patient must not be taken into custody[16] after the later of: (a) the end of the period of six months beginning with the first day of his absence without leave[17]; and (b) the end of the period for which[18] he is liable to be detained or subject to guardianship or, in the case of a community patient, the community treatment order is in force[19]. In determining for the purpose of head (b) above or any other provision of the Mental Health Act 1983 whether a person who is or has been absent without leave is at any time liable to be detained or subject to guardianship, a report furnished[20] before the first day of his absence without leave is not to be taken to have renewed the authority for his detention or guardianship unless the period of renewal began before that day[21]. Similarly, in determining for those purposes whether a community treatment order is at any time in force in respect of a person who is or has been absent without leave, a report[22] furnished before the first day of his absence without leave must not be taken to have extended the community treatment period unless the extension began before that day[23].

Patients liable to be detained for assessment[24] or as informal in-patients[25] cannot be taken into custody[26] once the maximum period for which they can be detained has expired[27].

1   As to the meaning of 'patient' see PARA 758 note 4.
2   Ie under the Mental Health Act 1983 Pt 2 (ss 2–34). For patients who are subject to hospital orders but not subject to special restrictions, the provisions of s 18 as to the return and readmission of patients absent without leave apply with the omission of s 18(5): see ss 40(4), 55(4), Sch 1 Pt I paras 2, 4. For patients who are subject to special restrictions, the provisions of s 18(1), (2), (6) apply, but s 18(3)–(5) are omitted: see ss 40(4), 41(3), 55(4), Sch 1 Pt II paras 2, 4; and PARAS 860–861.
3   As to the meaning of 'hospital' see PARA 577.
4   Mental Health Act 1983 s 18(1)(a). 'Absent without leave' means absent from any hospital or other place and liable to be taken into custody and returned under s 18(6); and related expressions must be construed accordingly: ss 18(6), 145(1). Section 18 should be read in conjunction with s 21 and ss 21A–21B (see PARA 911). As to absence without leave from guardianship see PARA 793. As to absconding from hospital during remand for report or for treatment see PARA 862. As to absconding from hospital during an interim hospital order see PARA 867. For the power to issue warrants for the arrest of convicted mental patients liable to be retaken under s 18 see the Criminal Justice Act 1967 s 72; and PARA 921. See *R (on the application of Ashworth Hospital Authority) v Mental Health Review Tribunal for West Midlands and Northwest Region* [2002] EWCA Civ 923, [2003] 1 WLR 127, 70 BMLR 40 (return of a patient to hospital granted following a stay on the discharge by the tribunal).
5   Mental Health Act 1983 s 18(1)(b). As to the power of recall see PARA 917.
6   Mental Health Act 1983 s 18(1)(c).
7   Ie the time limits laid down by the Mental Health Act 1983 s 18(4), (5): see the text and notes 14–27.
8   As to legal custody see PARAS 776–777, 917.
9   Ie the place where he is required to reside in accordance with conditions imposed upon a grant of leave of absence: see the Mental Health Act 1983 s 18(1)(c). In relation to a patient who has yet to comply with a requirement imposed by virtue of the Mental Health Act 1983 to be in a hospital or place, references in that Act to his liability to be returned to the hospital or place include his liability to be taken to that hospital or place; and related expressions are construed accordingly: s 18(7) (added by the Mental Health Act 2007 Sch 3 para 3(5)).
10 As to the meaning of 'approved mental health professional' see PARA 815 note 2.
11 This refers to the hospital at which the patient is liable to be detained; but see note 13.
12 As to the office of constable see POLICE vol 36(1) (2007 Reissue) PARA 101 et seq.
13 Mental Health Act 1983 s 18(1) (amended by the Mental Health Act 2007 Sch 2 para 7(a)). As to the meaning of 'managers' see PARA 778. If the place where a patient is required to reside in accordance with conditions imposed upon his leave of absence is another hospital, references to an officer on the staff of the hospital and to the managers of the hospital include an officer and the managers of that hospital, in addition to the hospital at which he is liable to be detained: see the Mental Health Act 1983 s 18(2).
     Section 18 applies to hospital (and guardianship) order patients who are not subject to special restrictions as it applies to patients admitted under Pt 2 (see s 40(4), Sch 1 Pt I paras 2, 4; and PARAS 860–861); it does not apply to patients subject to special restrictions (see the Mental Health Act 1983 ss 40(4), 41(3), Sch 1 Pt II paras 2, 4; and PARAS 860–861).
14 Ie under the Mental Health Act 1983 s 17E (see PARA 801).
15 Mental Health Act 1983 s 18(2A) (added by the Mental Health Act 2007 Sch 3 para 3(2)).

16 Ie under the Mental Health Act 1983 s 18.

17 Mental Health Act 1983 s 18(4)(a) (s 18(4) substituted by the Mental Health (Patients in the Community) Act 1995 s 2(1)).

18 Ie apart from the Mental Health Act 1983 s 21 (see PARA 911), which extends the authority for detention or guardianship.

19 Mental Health Act 1983 s 18(4)(b) (as substituted (see note 17); amended by the Mental Health Act 2007 Sch 3 para 3(3)(b), Sch 11 Pt 5).

20 Ie furnished under the Mental Health Act 1983 s 21 or 21B: see PARA 911.

21 Mental Health Act 1983 s 18(4A) (s 18(4A), (4B) added by the Mental Health Act 2007 Sch 3 para 3(4)).

22 Ie a report furnished under the Mental Health Act 1983 s 20A (see PARA 799) or 21B (see PARA 911).

23 Mental Health Act 1983 s 18(4B) (as added: see note 21).

24 Ie for the periods specified in the Mental Health Act 1983 ss 2(4), 4(4): see PARAS 767, 769.

25 Ie for the periods specified in the Mental Health Act 1983 s 5(2), (4): see PARA 770.

26 Ie under the Mental Health Act 1983 s 18.

27 Mental Health Act 1983 s 18(5).

919. Patients absent from hospitals in Scotland. Any person who may be taken into custody in Scotland under certain provisions of the Mental Health (Care and Treatment) (Scotland) Act 2003[1], may be taken into custody in, and returned to Scotland from, any other part of the United Kingdom[2].

1 Ie under the Mental Health (Care and Treatment) (Scotland) Act 2003 ss 301–303 or under regulations made under ss 289, 290, 309 or s 310.

2 Mental Health (Care and Treatment) (Scotland) Act 2003 (Consequential Provisions) Order 2005, SI 2005/2078 (S 9), art 8(1) (amended by the Mental Health Act 2007 Sch 5 para 21(3)). As to the meaning of 'United Kingdom' see PARA 560 note 14. For the purposes of the provisions referred to in note 1 in their application to England and Wales, 'constable' includes a constable in England and Wales, and 'mental health officer' includes any approved mental health professional within the meaning of the Mental Health Act 1983 (see PARA 815 note 2): Mental Health (Care and Treatment) (Scotland) Act 2003 (Consequential Provisions) Order 2005, SI 2005/2078 (S 9), art 8(2) (amended by SI 2008/2828). As to the meanings of 'England' and 'Wales' see PARA 557 notes 4, 5.

920. Persons absent from institutions in Northern Ireland, the Channel Islands or the Isle of Man. Any person who may be taken into custody in Northern Ireland, under the provisions for retaking patients absent without leave[1] or patients escaping from custody[2] or under the special provisions as to persons sentenced to imprisonment[3], may be taken into custody in, and returned to Northern Ireland from, England and Wales[4] by an approved mental health professional[5], by any constable or by any person authorised by or by virtue of the Mental Health (Northern Ireland) Order 1986[6].

Any person who may be taken into custody in any of the Channel Islands or the Isle of Man, under any provision corresponding to those in the Mental Health Act 1983 for retaking patients absent without leave[7] or patients escaping from legal custody[8], may be taken into custody in, and returned to the island in question from, England and Wales by an approved mental health professional or a constable[9].

1 Ie under the Mental Health (Northern Ireland) Order 1986, SI 1986/595 (NI 4), art 29.

2 Ie under the Mental Health (Northern Ireland) Order 1986, SI 1986/595 (NI 4), art 132.

3 Ie under the Mental Health (Northern Ireland) Order 1986, SI 1986/595 (NI 4), art 29 as applied by art 31.

4 As to the meanings of 'England' and 'Wales' see PARA 557 notes 4, 5.

5 As to the meaning of 'approved mental health professional' see PARA 815 note 2.

6 Mental Health Act 1983 s 87(1) (amended by SI 1986/596; and the Mental Health Act 2007 Sch 2 para 7(f)). This provision does not apply to persons subject to guardianship: Mental Health Act 1983 s 87(2).

7   Ie the Mental Health Act 1983 s 18: see PARA 918.
8   Ie the Mental Health Act 1983 s 138: see PARA 777.
9   Mental Health Act 1983 s 89(1) (amended by the Mental Health Act 2007 Sch 2 para 7(h)).
     This provision does not apply to any person who is subject to guardianship: Mental Health
     Act 1983 s 89(2).

921. Warrants for the arrest of escaped convicted mental patients. On an
information in writing being laid before a justice of the peace for any area and
substantiated on oath, alleging that any person is a convicted mental patient[1]
liable to be retaken under the statutory provisions relating to the retaking of
mental patients who are absent without leave or have escaped from custody[2], the
justice may issue a warrant to arrest him and bring him before a magistrates'
court for that area[3]. Where a person is brought before a magistrates' court in
pursuance of a warrant for his arrest under this provision, the court must, if
satisfied that he is the person named in the warrant and that he is such a
convicted mental patient, order him to be returned to the institution where he is
required or liable to be detained or order him to be kept in custody or detained
in a place of safety[4] pending his admission to hospital[5].

1   'Convicted mental patient' means a person liable after being convicted of an offence to be
     detained under the Mental Health Act 1983 Pt 3 (ss 35–55) (see PARAS 864 et seq, 892 et seq) or
     the equivalent Scottish or Northern Ireland provisions, in pursuance of a hospital order or
     transfer direction together with an order or direction restricting his discharge, or in pursuance of
     a hospital direction and a limitation direction (see PARA 863), or a person liable to be detained
     under s 38 (see PARA 864) or the equivalent Northern Ireland provision: see the Criminal Justice
     Act 1967 s 72(4) (definition amended by the Mental Health (Amendment) Act 1982 s 65(1),
     Sch 3 Pt I para 35; the Mental Health Act 1983 s 148(1), (2), Sch 4 para 21; the Mental Health
     (Scotland) Act 1984 s 127(1), Sch 3 para 9; the Crime (Sentences) Act 1997 s 55, Sch 4
     para 5(2); and SI 1986/596).
2   Ie under the Mental Health Act 1983 ss 18, 38(7), 138 or the equivalent Scottish or Northern
     Ireland provisions (see PARAS 777, 918–920).
3   See the Criminal Justice Act 1967 s 72(1) (s 72(1), (3) amended by the Mental Health Act 1983
     Sch 4 para 21; the Mental Health (Scotland) Act 1984 Sch 3 para 9; and SI 1985/596). The main
     purpose of this provision is to facilitate the recovery of prisoners and convicted mental patients
     who have absconded to the Republic of Ireland, where extradition may be sought provided that
     an arrest warrant has been obtained from a judicial authority: see 283 HL Official Report (5th
     series) col 778 (12 June 1967).
4   'Place of safety' has the same meaning as in the Mental Health Act 1983 Pt 3 (see PARA 868
     note 4): Criminal Justice Act 1967 s 72(4) (definition amended by the Mental Health Act 1983
     Sch 4 para 21).
5   Criminal Justice Act 1967 s 72(2). The provisions relating to the custody, conveyance and
     detention of certain mental patients (ie the Mental Health Act 1983 s 137 and the equivalent
     Scottish and Northern Ireland provisions: see PARA 776) apply to a convicted mental patient
     required by this provision to be conveyed to any place or to be kept in custody or detained in a
     place of safety: see the Criminal Justice Act 1967 s 72(3) (as amended: see note 3).

(17) PLACE OF SAFETY POWERS

922. Warrants to search for and remove patients. If it appears to a justice of
the peace[1], on information[2] on oath laid by an approved mental health
professional[3], that there is reasonable cause to suspect that a person believed to
be suffering from mental disorder[4] has been or is being ill-treated, neglected[5] or
kept otherwise than under proper control[6], in any place within the jurisdiction of
the justice[7], or, being unable to care for himself, is living alone in any such place,
the justice may issue a warrant[8] authorising any constable[9] to enter, if need be by
force, any premises specified in the warrant in which that person is believed to be
and, if thought fit, to remove him to a place of safety[10] with a view to the

making of an application for his compulsory admission to hospital and guardianship[11] or other arrangements[12] for his treatment or care[13].

Furthermore, if it appears to a justice of the peace, on information on oath[14] laid by any constable or other person who is authorised[15] to take a patient to any place[16], or to take into custody or retake a patient who is liable under the Mental Health Act 1983 to be so taken or retaken[17], that there is reasonable cause to believe that the patient is to be found on premises within the jurisdiction of the justice, and that admission to the premises has been refused or that a refusal of such admission is apprehended, the justice may issue a warrant authorising any constable[18] to enter the premises, if need be by reasonable force, and remove the patient[19].

A patient who is removed to a place of safety under these provisions[20] may be detained there for a period not exceeding 72 hours[21]. A constable, an approved mental health professional or a person authorised by either of them for these purposes may, before the end of the period of 72 hours, take a person detained in a place of safety to one or more other places of safety[22].

A person who escapes while being taken to or detained in a place of safety cannot be retaken[23] after the expiration of 72 hours beginning with the time of his escape or the period for which he is liable to be so detained, whichever expires first[24].

1   As to justices of the peace see MAGISTRATES vol 71 (2013) PARA 404 et seq.
2   The information need not name the patient: Mental Health Act 1983 s 135(5). As to the meaning of 'patient' see PARA 758 note 4.
3   As to the meaning of 'approved mental health professional' see PARA 815 note 2.
4   It seems that an approved mental health worker should satisfy himself as to the sufficiency of the grounds for belief that the person is suffering from mental disorder: see *Buxton v Jayne* [1960] 2 All ER 688 at 695–696, [1960] 1 WLR 783 at 792–793, CA (construction of analogous provisions in the Lunacy Act 1890 ss 14, 20 (repealed)). As to the meaning of 'mental disorder' see PARA 761.
5   It seems that a justice might hesitate to issue a warrant upon the ground of neglect unless there was reasonable cause to suspect that neglect was causing the patient some degree of physical distress: see *R v Board of Control, ex p Rutty* [1956] 2 QB 109, [1956] 1 All ER 769, DC (construing the words 'found neglected' in the (now repealed) Mental Deficiency Act 1913 s 2(1)(b)(i)). However, a person might have been 'found neglected' within that enactment if, although living in a comfortable home, he was not receiving the training he ought to have been receiving: *Re Wilkinson* (1919) 83 JP Jo 422.
6   Cf *Richardson v LCC* [1957] 2 All ER 330, [1957] 1 WLR 751, CA, where it was held that a person could be 'found neglected' within the meaning of the Mental Deficiency Act 1913 s 2(1)(b)(i) (repealed) if he was not under the control which he ought to be under. There is no need for a warrant if the person has no right to exclusive occupation (eg a room in a hotel where members of the public can reside): see *R v Rosso* [2003] EWCA Crim 3242, [2003] All ER (D) 381 (Nov).
7   As to the areas of jurisdiction see MAGISTRATES vol 71 (2013) PARA 428.
8   The warrant need not name the patient concerned: Mental Health Act 1983 s 135(5).
9   When executing the warrant, the constable must be accompanied by an approved mental health professional (not necessarily the approved mental health professional who laid the information under the Mental Health Act 1983 s 135(1)) and a registered medical practitioner: s 135(4) (amended by the Police and Criminal Evidence Act 1984 s 119(1), Sch 6 Pt I para 26; and the Mental Health Act 2007 Sch 2 para 10(a)). As to registered medical practitioners see MEDICAL PROFESSIONS vol 74 (2011) PARA 176 et seq. As to the office of constable see POLICE vol 36(1) (2007 Reissue) PARA 101 et seq.

    There is no power enabling the naming of professionals in the warrant. Accordingly, names on a warrant are surplus to requirements and thus have no effect on the legality of the warrant or of its execution: see *Ward v Metropolitan Police Comr* [2005] UKHL 32, [2006] 1 AC 23, [2005] 3 All ER 1013.
10 'Place of safety' means residential accommodation provided by a local social services authority under the National Assistance Act 1948 Pt III (ss 21–35) (see PARA 580; and SOCIAL SERVICES AND COMMUNITY CARE), a hospital (see PARA 577), a police station, an independent hospital or

care home for mentally disordered persons (see PARAS 578, 583, 585; and SOCIAL SERVICES AND COMMUNITY CARE), or any other suitable place the occupier of which is willing temporarily to receive the patient: Mental Health Act 1983 s 135(6) (amended by the National Health Service and Community Care Act 1990 s 66(2), Sch 10; and the Care Standards Act 2000 s 116, Sch 4 para 9(1), (9)).

11 Ie an application under the Mental Health Act 1983 Pt 2 (ss 2–34): see PARA 767 et seq.

12 Eg arrangements for the informal admission of the patient to hospital (see PARA 764) or for him to be cared for in the community (see PARA 579 et seq).

13 Mental Health Act 1983 s 135(1) (amended by the Police and Criminal Evidence Act 1984 Sch 7 Pt 1; and the Mental Health Act 2007 Sch 2 para 10(a)). The alternative power to remove remains the Police and Criminal Evidence Act 1984 s 17(1)(d): see *D'Souza v DPP* [1992] 4 All ER 545, [1992] 1 WLR 1073; and CRIMINAL LAW, EVIDENCE AND PROCEDURE vol 11(2) (2006 Reissue) PARA 884. As to the common law power see *McLeod v Metropolitan Police Comr* [1994] 4 All ER 553, CA. For the purposes of the Convention for the Protection of Human Rights and Fundamental Freedoms (Rome, 4 November 1950; TS 71 (1953); Cmd 8969) art 8 (see RIGHTS AND FREEDOMS), entry into a person's home must be proportionate. In relation to the Mental Health Act 1983 ss 135, 136 see also the Department of Health *Mental Health Act 1983 Code of Practice* (2008) Chapter 10; and the Welsh Assembly Government *Mental Health Act 1983 Code of Practice for Wales* (2008) Chapter 7.

14 In this case the information must name the patient: cf the position under the Mental Health Act 1983 s 135 (see note 2).

15 Ie under the Mental Health Act 1983 or the Mental Health (Care and Treatment) (Scotland) Act 2003 (Consequential Provisions) Order 2005, SI 2005/2078 (S 9), art 8.

16 Eg an approved social worker who has authority to convey a patient to hospital for the purpose of compulsory admission under the Mental Health Act 1983 s 6(1): see PARA 771.

17 Eg a person authorised in writing by the managers (see PARA 778) of a hospital to retake and return a patient liable to be detained who is absent without leave under the Mental Health Act 1983 s 18(1): see PARA 918.

18 When executing the warrant, the constable may (but need not) be accompanied by a registered medical practitioner and by a person authorised under the Mental Health Act 1983 or the Mental Health (Care and Treatment) (Scotland) Act 2003 (Consequential Provisions) Order 2005, SI 2005/2078 (S 9), art 8 to take or retake the patient: Mental Health Act 1983 s 135(4) (amended by the Mental Health (Scotland) Act 1984 s 127(1), Sch 3 para 56; the Police and Criminal Evidence Act 1984 Sch 6 Pt I para 26; and the Mental Health (Care and Treatment) (Scotland) Act 2003 (Consequential Provisions) Order 2005, SI 2005/2078 (S 9), art 15, Sch 1 para 2(1), (9)(a)). Cf the requirements when executing a warrant under the Mental Health Act 1983 s 135(1): see note 9.

19 Mental Health Act 1983 s 135(2) (amended by the Mental Health (Scotland) Act 1984 Sch 3 para 56; the Police and Criminal Evidence Act 1984 Sch 7 Pt I; and SI 2005/2078 (S 9)).

20 Ie under the Mental Health Act 1983 s 135(1), (2) (see the text and notes 1–19).

21 Mental Health Act 1983 s 135(3).

22 Mental Health Act 1983 s 135(3A) (s 135(3A), (3B) added by the Mental Health Act 2007 s 44(2)). A person who is so taken to a place of safety may be detained there for a period ending no later than the end of the period of 72 hours mentioned in the Mental Health Act 1983 s 135(3): s 135(3B) (as so added).

23 Ie under the Mental Health Act 1983 s 138 (see PARA 777).

24 See the Mental Health Act 1983 s 138(3); and PARA 777.

923. Removal of mentally disordered persons found in public places. If a constable[1] finds in a place to which the public has access[2] a person who appears to him to be suffering from mental disorder[3] and to be in immediate need of care or control, then, if he thinks it necessary to do so in the interests of that person or for the protection of other persons, the constable may remove him to a place of safety[4]. A person so removed to a place of safety may be detained there for a period not exceeding 72 hours[5] for the purpose of examination by a registered medical practitioner[6], interview by an approved mental health professional[7] and the making of any necessary arrangements[8] for his treatment or care[9]. A constable, an approved mental health professional or a person authorised by either of them for these purposes, may, before the end of the 72 hour period, take a person so detained in a place of safety to one or more other places of safety[10].

1 As to the office of constable see POLICE vol 36(1) (2007 Reissue) PARA 101 et seq.
2 A public place is a place to which the public can and do have access; it does not matter whether they came at the invitation of the occupier or merely with his permission, or whether some payment or the performance of some formality is required before access can be had: *R v Kane* [1965] 1 All ER 705, 129 JP 170. See also *R v Edwards* (1978) 67 Cr App Rep 228, [1978] Crim LR 564, CA; *Carter v Metropolitan Police Comr* [1975] 2 All ER 33, [1975] 1 WLR 507; *Knox v Anderton* (1982) 76 Cr App Rep 156, 147 JP 340, DC.
3 As to the meaning of 'mental disorder' see PARA 761.
4 Mental Health Act 1983 s 136(1). As to the meaning of 'place of safety' see PARA 922 note 10. This power of arrest is specifically preserved by the Police and Criminal Evidence Act 1984 s 26(2), Sch 2: see CRIMINAL LAW, EVIDENCE AND PROCEDURE vol 11(2) (2006 Reissue) PARA 927. Delay in admitting a person who is detained in a police cell during a period of severe mental illness with no access to psychiatric treatment has been held to be an affront to human dignity and violated the European Convention on Human Rights, art 3 (see RIGHTS AND FREEDOMS): see Application 24527/08 *MS v United Kingdom* (2012) 126 BMLR 168, (2012) Times, 14 May, ECtHR (held that there was no attempt to humiliate a person detained by police after failed attempts to find a psychiatric placement for him).

   For an illustration of the use of the Mental Health Act 1983 s 136 see *R (on the application of Anderson) v HM Coroner for Inner North Greater London* [2004] EWHC 2729 (Admin), [2004] All ER (D) 410 (Nov). In relation to the Mental Health Act 1983 ss 135, 136 see also the Department of Health *Mental Health Act 1983 Code of Practice* (2008) Chapter 10; and the Welsh Assembly Government *Mental Health Act 1983 Code of Practice for Wales* (2008) Chapter 7. As to the powers of the police to arrest persons who may or may not be mentally disordered if they have reasonable cause to believe they may cause physical injury to themselves or another, or to be suffering physical injury or about to commit an offence against public decency see the Police and Criminal Evidence Act 1984 s 24; and CRIMINAL LAW, EVIDENCE AND PROCEDURE vol 11(1) (2006 Reissue) PARA 924.
5 As to the power to retake persons who escape while being taken to or detained in a place of safety under this provision see PARA 922. See also PARA 777.
6 As to registered medical practitioners see MEDICAL PROFESSIONS vol 74 (2011) PARA 176 et seq.
7 As to the meaning of 'approved mental health professional', and as to his functions, see PARAS 815 note 2, 820.
8 Eg for his compulsory (see PARA 767 et seq) or informal (see PARA 764) admission to hospital or for his care in the community (see PARA 579 et seq). If suitable arrangements can be made, these may be regarded as an alternative to prosecuting him for an offence he may be alleged to have committed (see PARA 859).
9 Mental Health Act 1983 s 136(2) (amended by the Mental Health Act 2007 Sch 2 para 10(b)).
10 Mental Health Act 1983 s 136(3) (s 136(3), (4) added by the Mental Health Act 2007 s 44(3)). A person taken to a place of a safety under the Mental Health Act 1983 s 136(3) may be detained there for a purpose mentioned in s 136(2) for a period ending no later than the end of the period of 72 hours mentioned in that provision: s 136(4) (as so added).

(18) MEDICAL TREATMENT

(i) Consent to Treatment

924. Patients to whom consent to treatment provisions apply. Part 4 of the Mental Health Act 1983[1] makes provision as to a patient's[2] consent to treatment. It applies to any patient liable to be detained[3] except where he is detained[4];

(1) under the provisions relating to an emergency application for assessment[5];

(2) under the provisions relating to temporary detention of an in-patient following a report by either the registered medical practitioner[6] or approved clinician[7] in charge of the patient's treatment or by a nurse of the prescribed class[8];

(3) under the provisions relating to a remand to hospital for report[9];

(4) under the provisions relating to a removal by warrant to a place of safety[10];

(5)   under the provisions relating to a removal to a place of safety by a constable[11];

(6)   under the provisions relating to a direction for detention pending admission to hospital under a hospital order[12];

(7)   under the provisions relating to the direction for his detention in a place of safety by the court[13];

(8)   following a conditional discharge[14] and he has not been recalled[15] to hospital.

Part 4 also applies to a patient who is a community patient and is recalled[16] to hospital[17].

However, certain provisions[18] apply to patients who are not liable to be detained[19], and are not community patients[20].

Where a patient lacks capacity to consent, legal protection may be provided by the Mental Capacity Act 2005[21] but this does not apply to treatment given for a mental disorder under Part 4 of the Mental Health Act 1983[22].

1   Ie the Mental Health Act 1983 Pt 4 (ss 56–64). Where a patient is being regulated under Pt 4 the Mental Capacity Act 2005 does not apply (see note 22). As to medical treatment and second opinions generally see the Department of Health *Mental Health Act 1983 Code of Practice* (2008) Chapters 23, 24; and the Welsh Assembly Government *Mental Health Act 1983 Code of Practice for Wales* (2008) Chapters 17, 18. As to the importance of the code see *R (on the application of Munjaz) v Mersey Care NHS Trust* [2005] UKHL 58, [2006] 2 AC 148, [2006] 4 All ER 736. As to the Codes of Practice see PARA 762. For the treatment of patients in the community who have not been recalled see the Mental Health Act 1983 Pt 4A (ss 64A–64K) and PARAS 935–941.
2   As to the meaning of 'patient' see PARA 758 note 4.
3   Ie detained under the Mental Health Act 1983 Pt 2 (ss 2–34) or Pt 3 (ss 35–55). Guardianship and informal hospital patients are not liable to be detained; but see the text and note 10.
4   Mental Health Act 1983 s 56(1) (substituted by the Mental Health Act 2007 s 34(2)).
5   Ie under the Mental Health Act 1983 s 4(1), where a second medical recommendation as required under s 4(4)(a) has not been given and received. See PARA 769.
6   As to registered medical practitioners see MEDICAL PROFESSIONS vol 74 (2011) PARA 176 et seq.
7   As to the meaning of 'approved clinician' see PARA 831.
8   Ie under the Mental Health Act 1983 s 5(2), (4): see PARA 770.
9   Ie under the Mental Health Act 1983 s 35: see PARA 862.
10   Ie under the Mental Health Act 1983 s 135: see PARA 922.
11   Ie under the Mental Health Act 1983 s 136: see PARA 923.
12   Ie under the Mental Health Act 1983 s 37(4): see PARA 868.
13   Ie under the Mental Health Act 1983 s 45A(5): see PARA 863.
14   Ie the conditional discharge of a restricted patient under the Mental Health Act 1983 s 42(2) by the Secretary of State (see PARA 914) or under s 73 or s 74 by a tribunal (see PARAS 969–970).
15   Mental Health Act 1983 s 56(2), (3) (as substituted: see note 4).
16   Ie recalled to hospital under the Mental Health Act 1983 s 17E (see PARA 801).
17   Mental Health Act 1983 s 56(4) (as substituted: see note 4).
18   Ie the Mental Health Act 1983 ss 57, 58A and, so far as relevant to those provisions, ss 59–62.
19   Ie informal patients including children under the age of 18.
20   Mental Health Act 1983 s 56(1), (5) (as substituted: see note 4).
21   See the Mental Capacity Act 2005 s 5; and PARA 611.
22   See the Mental Capacity Act 2005 s 28(1); and PARA 925. The Mental Capacity Act 2005 cannot be used to authorise giving an incapacitated patient medical treatment for a mental disorder or consent on behalf of a patient being given medical treatment for a mental disorder. Except for electro-convulsive therapy under the Mental Health Act 1983 s 58A, see s 58A(5)(c), this means that neither the donee of a health and welfare lasting power of attorney, nor a court appointed deputy under the Mental Capacity Act 2005 may grant consent for treatment that is being authorised under Part 4. Again except for electro-convulsive therapy under s 58A, an advance decision made by the patient under the Mental Capacity Act 2005 s 24 cannot be used to refuse treatment for mental disorder under the Mental Health Act 1983 Part 4. However, a clinician should take account of the advance decision as expressing the patient's wishes and feelings.

925. Effect of the Mental Capacity Act 2005. The Mental Capacity Act 2005 does not authorise anyone to give a patient medical treatment for mental disorder[1] or to consent to a patient's being given medical treatment for mental disorder, if, at the time when it is proposed to treat the patient, his treatment is regulated by Part 4 of the Mental Health Act 1983[2]. However, this exemption does not apply in relation to certain forms of treatment[3] and there is special provision in relation to an informal patient under 18 who cannot give consent[4].

1 As to the meaning of 'medical treatment' see PARA 926; as to the meaning of 'mental disorder' see PARA 761; and as to the meaning of 'patient' see PARA 758 note 4 (definitions applied by the Mental Capacity Act 1983 s 28(2)).

2 Mental Capacity Act 2005 s 28(1). The reference in the text is a reference to the Mental Health Act 1983 Pt 4 (ss 56–64) (see PARAS 924–934). As to the treatment of incapacitated adults under the Mental Capacity Act 2005 see PARA 601 et seq. Thus there is a separate regime for the treatment of incapacitated adults subject to the Mental Health Act 1983 Pt 4: see PARA 924 et seq. The common law relating to consent to treatment and a patient's best interests is codified by the Mental Capacity Act 2005: see PARA 597.

3 Ie treatment to which the Mental Health Act 1983 s 58A (see PARA 931) applies if the patient comes within s 58A(7).

4 Mental Capacity Act 2005 s 28(1A) (added by the Mental Health Act 2007 s 28(10)). The Mental Capacity Act 2005 s 58A does not by itself confer the authority to treat such patients. See s 5 (see PARA 611) for children over the age of 16 and parental consent for younger children. The Department of Health *Mental Health Act 1983 Code of Practice* (2008) para 36.60 states that it would not be prudent to rely on parental consent with respect to a child under the age of 16 and court authorisation should be sought unless it is an emergency. For the treatment of young people under 18 generally see the Department of Health *Mental Health Act 1983 Code of Practice* (2008) Chapter 36 and the Welsh Assembly Government *Mental Health Act 1983 Code of Practice for Wales* (2008) Chapter 33.

926. Meaning of 'medical treatment'. In the Mental Health Act 1983, 'medical treatment' includes nursing, psychological intervention and specialist mental health habilitation, rehabilitation and care; and any reference in the Mental Health Act 1983 to medical treatment, in relation to mental disorder[1], is to be construed as a reference to medical treatment the purpose of which is to alleviate, or prevent a worsening of, the disorder or one or more of its symptoms or manifestations[2].

1 As to the meaning of 'mental disorder' see PARA 761.

2 Mental Health Act 1983 s 145(1), (4) (s 145(1) amended, s 145(4) added, by the Mental Health Act 2007 s 7).

927. Treatment without consent. The consent of a patient[1] to whom Part 4 of the Mental Health Act 1983[2] applies[3] is not required for any medical treatment[4] given to him for the mental disorder[5] from which he is suffering, not being one of the specific treatments requiring consent and/or a second opinion under the Act[6], provided that the treatment is given by or under the direction of the approved clinician in charge of the treatment[7].

1 As to the meaning of 'patient' see PARA 758 note 4.

2 Ie the Mental Health Act 1983 Pt 4 (ss 56–64). As to the effect of the Mental Capacity Act 2005 on the Mental Health Act 1983 Pt 4 see PARA 925.

3 As to such patients see PARA 924.

4 As to the meaning of 'medical treatment' see PARA 926.

5 As to the meaning of 'mental disorder' see PARA 761. As to 'medical treatment for the mental disorder' see *B v Croydon Health Authority* [1995] Fam 133, [1995] 1 All ER 683, CA. Medical treatment may cover nursing and caring for a patient in seclusion, even though seclusion does not properly form part of a treatment programme: see *R (on the application of Munjaz) v Mersey Care NHS Trust* [2005] UKHL 58, [2006] 2 AC 148, [2006] 4 All ER 736. See also *Tameside and Glossop Acute Services Trust v CH* [1996] 1 FCR 753, [1996] 1 FLR 762,

31 BMLR 93 (where the treatment amounted to dealing with danger to an unborn child); but distinguish *Re C (Adult: Refusal of Medical Treatment)* [1994] 1 All ER 819, [1994] 2 FCR 151. See also *GJ v Foundation Trust* [2009] EWHC 2972 (Fam), [2010] Fam 70, [2010] 3 WLR 840.

In *T v T* [1988] Fam 52, [1988] 1 All ER 613, it was held that termination of pregnancy and sterilisation of a mentally handicapped woman were not treatment for her mental disorder. See also *Re F (Mental Patient: Sterilisation)* [1990] 2 AC 1, sub nom *F v West Berkshire Health Authority (Mental Health Act Commission intervening)* [1989] 2 All ER 545, HL; *St George's Healthcare NHS Trust v S, R v Collins, ex p S* [1999] Fam 26, [1998] 3 All ER 673, CA. However, in *R v Mental Health Act Commission, ex p W* (1988) Times, 27 May, it was said by Stuart-Smith LJ that, where a patient was both mentally disordered and sexually deviant, 'it seems likely that the sexual problem will be inextricably linked with mental disorder, so that treatment for one is treatment for the other'. See also *South West Hertfordshire Health Authority v KB* [1994] 2 FCR 1051 (anorexia nervosa amounts to mental disorder; no consent required for naso-gastric feeding as integral part of treatment).

6   Ie treatment falling within the Mental Health Act 1983 ss 57, 58, 58A: see PARAS 928, 930, 931.

7   Mental Health Act 1983 s 63 (amended by the Mental Health Act 2007 ss 12(6), 28(8)). As to the meaning of 'approved clinician' see PARA 831.

     See *B v Croydon Health Authority* [1995] Fam 133, [1995] 1 All ER 683, CA (feeding by tube in the circumstances part of medical treatment); *R (on the application of Munjaz) v Mersey Care NHS Trust* [2005] UKHL 58, [2006] 2 AC 148, [2006] 4 All ER 736 (seclusion capable of being within 'medical treatment'). See *Tameside and Glossop Acute Services Trust v CH* [1996] 1 FCR 753, [1996] 1 FLR 762, 37 BMLR 93 (where the schizophrenic patient lacked the ability to give meaningful consent due to her mental disorder, treatment could in the circumstances be administered without consent); but see *Re C (Adult: Refusal of Treatment)* [1994] 1 All ER 819, [1994] 2 FCR 151 (where it was held that the schizophrenic patient was not so mentally ill as not to be capable of giving or withholding meaningful consent). See *R v Collins, ex p Brady* (2000) 58 BMLR 173, 58 MHLR 17 (patient's hunger strike was a symptom of his personality disorder so that force feeding was permitted under the Mental Health Act 1983 s 63). The forcible treatment of mental disorder according to the principle generally accepted at the time and which is a medical necessity justifying treatment is not contrary to the Convention for the Protection of Human Rights and Fundamental Freedoms (Rome, 4 November 1950; TS 71 (1953); Cmd 8969), art 8: Application 10533/83 *Herczegfalvy v Austria* (1992) 15 EHRR 437, 18 BMLR 48. The provision is sufficiently precise in its application to the treatment of a symptom of a disorder so that there is no violation of art 8: *B v Croydon Health Authority* [1995] Fam 133, [1995] 1 All ER 683, CA.

928. Treatment requiring consent and a second opinion. The provisions of the Mental Health Act 1983 requiring consent and a second opinion[1] apply to all patients whether detained or not or subject to a community treatment order[2], and concern the following forms of treatment[3] for mental disorder[4]: (1) surgical operations for destroying brain tissue or for destroying the functioning of brain tissue[5]; and (2) the surgical implantation of hormones for the purpose of reducing male sexual drive[6].

Except in cases of urgency[7], a patient[8] must not be given such treatment unless: (a) he has consented to it[9]; (b) an appointed registered medical practitioner[10] (not being the responsible clinician[11] if there is one or the person in charge of the treatment in question) and two other persons[12] (not being registered medical practitioners) have certified[13] in writing that the patient is capable of understanding the nature, purpose and likely effects of the treatment and has consented to it[14]; (c) the registered medical practitioner[15] has certified[16] in writing that, having regard to the likelihood of the treatment's alleviating or preventing a deterioration of the patient's condition, the treatment should be given[17].

1   Ie the Mental Health Act 1983 s 57. As to the effect of the Mental Capacity Act 2005 on the Mental Health Act 1983 Pt 4 (ss 56–64) see PARA 925. The combined effect of s 57 and the Mental Capacity Act 2005 s 28 means that an incapacitated person may never receive treatment under the Mental Health Act 1983 s 57: Ministry of *Justice Deprivation of Liberty Safeguards – code of practice to supplement the main Mental Capacity Act 2005 code of practice* (2008)

para 13.51. See also the Department of Health *Mental Health Act 1983 Code of Practice* (2008) paras 24.6–24.9; and the Welsh Assembly Government *Mental Health Act 1983 Code of Practice for Wales (*2008) Chapter 17. In relation to treatments under the Mental Health Act 1983 s 57 the approved clinician is a reference to the person in charge of the treatment: see s 64(1); and PARA 831.

2   See the Mental Health Act 1983 s 56(1); and PARA 942 et seq.

3   Any consent or certificate under the Mental Health Act 1983 s 57 may relate to a plan of treatment under which the patient is to be given one or more of the forms of treatment to which s 57 applies: s 59. Any certificate for the purposes of Pt 4 must be in such form as may be prescribed by regulations made by the appropriate national authority: s 64(2). As to the appropriate national authority see PARA 567.

4   As to the meaning of 'mental disorder' see PARA 761.

5   Mental Health Act 1983 s 57(1)(a).

6   Ie such other form of treatment as may be specified for the purpose of the Mental Health Act 1983 s 57 by regulations made (after consulting such bodies as appear to him to be concerned) by the appropriate national authority: ss 57(1)(b), (4), 143(1); Mental Health (Hospital, Guardianship and Consent to Treatment) (England) Regulations 2008, SI 2008/1184, reg 27(1)(a); and the Mental Health (Hospital, Guardianship, Community Treatment and Consent to Treatment) (Wales) Regulations 2008, SI 2008/2439, reg 38(1). A course of treatment with a drug which is not a hormone and not surgically implanted does not fall within this provision: *R v Mental Health Act Commission, ex p W* (1988) Times, 27 May, DC. See also *R v Mental Health Act Commission, ex p X* (1988) 9 BMLR 77.

7   As to urgent treatment see the Mental Health Act 1983 s 62; and PARA 932.

8   As to the patients to whom this provision applies see PARA 924.

9   Mental Health Act 1983 s 57(2)(a). As to withdrawal of consent see s 60; and note 17.

10   Ie a medical practitioner appointed for these purposes by the Mental Health Act Commission acting on behalf of the regulatory authority: Mental Health Act 1983 ss 57(2)(a) (amended by the Health and Social Care Act 2008 Sch 3 para 2). As to the meaning of 'regulatory authority' see PARA 573 note 1. The regulatory authority may make provision for payment of remuneration, allowances, pensions or gratuities in respect of appointed medical practitioners: Mental Health Act 1983 s 119(1) (amended by the Health and Social Care Act 2008 Sch 3 para 7(2)(a)). An appointed practitioner may, for the purpose of exercising his functions, at any reasonable time visit and interview and examine in private any patient detained in a hospital or registered establishment or any community patient in a hospital or regulated establishment (other than a hospital) or (if access is granted) other place and require the production of and inspect any records relating to the treatment of the patient there: Mental Health Act 1983 s 119(2) (amended by the Health and Social Care Act 2008 Sch 3 para 7(3), Sch 15, Pt 1; and the Mental Health Act 2007 s 35(2); SI 2010/813). For this purpose the 'regulated establishment' means an establishment in respect of which a person is registered under the Care Standards Act 2000 or premises used for the carrying on of a regulated activity within the meaning of the Health and Social Care Act 2008 Pt 1 (ss 1–7: see SOCIAL SERVICES AND COMMUNITY CARE), in respect of which a person is registered under Pt 1 Chapter 2: Mental Health Act 1983 s 119(3) (substituted by SI 2010/813). The appointed doctor must form an independent view of the desirability of the approved clinician's proposals: *R (on the application of Wilkinson) v Responsible Officer of Broadmoor Hospital* [2001] EWCA Civ 1545, [2002] 1 WLR 419, 65 BMLR 15; *X v A, B and C and Mental Health Act Commission* (1991) 9 BMLR 91. A second opinion doctor is a 'public authority' for the purposes of the Human Rights Act 1998 s 6 because he is exercising functions of a public nature: *R (on the application of Wilkinson) v Responsible Officer of Broadmoor Hospital*. As to when a second opinion should be requested see the Department of Health *Mental Health Act 1983 Code of Practice* (2008) para 24.39; and the Welsh Assembly Government *Mental Health Act 1983 Code of Practice for Wales* (2008) para 18.9. It is for the clinician in charge of the treatment to personally request a second opinion see the Department of Health *Mental Health Act 1983 Code of Practice* (2008) para 24.38; and the Welsh Assembly Government *Mental Health Act 1983 Code of Practice for Wales* (2008) para 18.8.

11   For meaning of 'responsible clinician' see PARA 834.

12   Ie appointed by the regulatory authority.

13   Ie in the form prescribed by the Mental Health (Hospital, Guardianship and Consent to Treatment) (England) Regulations 2008, SI 2008/1184, reg 27(1)(b), Sch 1; and the Mental Health (Hospital, Guardianship, Community Treatment and Consent to Treatment) (Wales) Regulations 2008, SI 2008/2439, reg 40(1), Sch 1.

14   Mental Health Act 1983 s 57(2)(a) (amended by the Mental Health Act 2007 s 12(2)(a)). It is submitted that the test of capacity in the Mental Capacity Act 2005 ss 2, 3 should now be used

to determine whether a patient is capable of understanding the treatment: see the Department of Health *Mental Health Act 1983 Code of Practice* (2008) para 23.28. In *Re C (Adult: Refusal of Medical Treatment)* [1994] 1 All ER 819, [1994] 2 FCR 151 it was held that the phrase 'nature, purpose and likely effects' is declaratory of the common law position relating to the information that must be given to a patient before a valid consent can be obtained. See also *R (on the application of Wilkinson) v Responsible Officer of Broadmoor Hospital* [2001] EWCA Civ 1545, [2002] 1 WLR 419, 65 BMLR 15; *R (on the application of B) v S* [2006] EWCA Civ 28, [2006] 1 WLR 810, 90 BMLR 1. The appointed persons are 'public authorities' within the Human Rights Act 1998 s 6 (see RIGHTS AND FREEDOMS): *R (on the application of Wilkinson) v Responsible Officer of Broadmoor Hospital.*

15   See note 9.

16   See note 12.

17   Mental Health Act 1983 s 57(2)(b) (amended by the Mental Health Act 2007 s 6(2)(a)). 'Appropriate' means taking into account the nature and degree of the mental disorder from which the patient is suffering and all the circumstances: Department of Health Reference Guide to the Mental Health Act 1983 (2008) para 16.14. See also the Mental Health Act 1983 s 64(3); and PARA 931. As to the role of 'best interests' see *R (on the application of B) v S* [2006] EWCA Civ 28, [2006] 1 WLR 810, 90 BMLR 1; *R (on the application of B) v Haddock* [2005] EWHC 921 (Admin), 85 BMLR 57. Before giving such a certificate, the practitioner must consult two other persons (one of whom must be a nurse and the other neither a nurse nor a medical practitioner) who have been professionally concerned with the patient's treatment but of those persons one must be a nurse and the other neither a nurse nor a registered medical practitioner, and neither must be the responsible clinician (if there is one) or the person in charge of the treatment in question: Mental Health Act 1983 s 57(3) (amended by the Mental Health Act 2007 s 12(2)(b)). The consultation can take place with a person who has no current involvement with the patient if it is reasonable to do so in the context of the non-availability of a person with current involvement: *R (on the application of Wooder) v Feggetter* [2002] EWCA Civ 554, [2003] QB 219, [2002] 3 WLR 591. See also *R v Mental Health Act Commission, ex p X* (1988) 9 BMLR 77. See also Department of Health Reference Guide to the Mental Health Act 1983 (2008) para 16.20.

As to the private duty of care of the appointed doctors see *X v A, B and C and the Mental Health Act Commission* (1991) 9 BMLR 91. As to the independence of the appointed doctor, fairness, and the need for written reasons see *R (on the application of Wilkinson) v Responsible Officer of Broadmoor Hospital* [2002] EWCA Civ 1545, [2002] 1 WLR 419, 65 BMLR 15.

929. Withdrawal of consent. Where the consent of a patient[1] to any treatment has been given[2], the patient may[3] at any time before completion of the treatment withdraw his consent; the statutory provisions then apply to the remainder of the treatment as if it were a separate form of treatment[4].

Where the consent of a patient to any treatment has been given[5] but before the completion of the treatment the patient ceases to be capable of understanding its nature, purpose and likely effects[6], the patient must[7] be treated as having withdrawn his consent, and the statutory provisions then apply as if the remainder of the treatment were a separate form of treatment[8].

1   As to the meaning of 'patient' see PARA 758 note 4.

2   Ie for the purposes of the Mental Health Act 1983 ss 57, 58, 58A (see PARAS 928, 930, 931).

3   Subject to the Mental Health Act 1983 s 62 (see PARA 932).

4   Mental Health Act 1983 s 60(1) (amended by the Mental Health Act 2007 s 28(4)). Without prejudice to the Mental Health Act 1983 s 60(1)–(1D), a patient may withdraw his consent to further treatment under a plan of treatment or to further treatment of any description under the plan: s 60(2) (amended by the Mental Health Act 2007 s 29(3)).

5   See note 2.

6   Where a certificate has been given under the Mental Health Act 1983 s 58 or 58A that a patient is not capable of understanding the nature, purpose and likely effects of the treatment to which the certificate applies, but before the completion of the treatment, the patient becomes capable of understanding its nature, purpose and likely effects, the certificate, subject to s 62, ceases to apply to the treatment and the statutory provisions then apply as if the remainder of the treatment were a separate form of treatment: s 60(1C), (1D) (s 60(1A)–(1D) added by the Mental Health Act 2007 s 29(2)).

7　This is subject to the Mental Health Act 1983 s 62 (see PARA 932).
8　Mental Health Act 1983 s 60(1A), (1B) (as added: see note 6).

930. Treatment requiring consent or a second opinion. The provisions of the Mental Health Act 1983 requiring consent or a second opinion[1] apply to the following forms of treatment[2] for mental disorder[3]: (1) such forms of treatment as may be specified for this purpose by regulations[4]; and (2) the administration of medicine by any means[5] if three months or more have elapsed since the first occasion during the patient's period of detention when medicine was administered to him by any means for his mental disorder[6].

Except in the case of urgency[7], a patient[8] may not be given such treatment unless either: (a) he has consented to it and either the approved clinician in charge of it[9] or an appointed registered medical practitioner[10] has certified[11] in writing that the patient is capable of understanding its nature, purpose and likely effects and has consented to it[12]; or (b) the appointed medical practitioner[13] has certified[14] in writing that the patient is not capable of understanding the nature, purpose and likely effects of that treatment or being so capable has not consented to it but that it is appropriate for the treatment to be given[15].

Consent to treatment may be withdrawn[16].

1　Ie the Mental Health Act 1983 s 58. As to the effect of the Mental Capacity Act 2005 on the Mental Health Act 1983 Pt 4 (ss 56–64) see PARA 925.
2　Any consent or certificate under the Mental Health Act 1983 s 58 may relate to a plan of treatment under which the patient is to be given one or more of the forms of treatment referred to in s 58: s 59.
3　As to the meaning of 'mental disorder' see PARA 761.
4　Ie such form of treatment as may be specified for the purpose of the Mental Health Act 1983 s 58 by regulations made (after consultation with such bodies as appear to be concerned) by the appropriate national authority: ss 58(1)(a), (5), 143(1). As to the appropriate national authority see PARA 567. At the time of writing no treatments have been specified in regulations and so only medication after 3 months is covered by s 58. If in due course any type of medication were to be specified in regulations, then s 58 would apply to that medication from first prescription and there would be no exception for the first 3 months: see the Department of Health *Reference Guide to the Mental Health Act 1983* (2008) para 16.30.
5　Not being a treatment specified under the Mental Health Act 1983 s 58(1)(a) or s 57 or s 58A(1)(b). See the Department of Health *Mental Health Act 1983 Code of Practice* (2008) paras 24.10–24.17. Only medication for mental disorder is covered and includes medication aimed at relieving symptoms of the mental disorder see s 145(4); PARA 926; and *B v Croydon Health Authority* [1995] Fam 133, [1995] 1 All ER 683, CA.
6　Mental Health Act 1983 s 58(1)(b) (amended by the Mental Health Act 2007 s 28(2)(a)). The period mentioned in the text may be varied by order: see the Mental Health Act 1983 ss 58(2), 143(1). 'Month' means calendar month: Interpretation Act 1978 s 5, Sch 1. The period must be continuous and is broken by the patient's discharge from detention. The 3 month period does not violate the Convention for the Protection of Human Rights and Fundamental Freedoms (Rome, 4 November 1950; TS 71 (1953), art 8: *Petition of WM* [2002] MHLR 367.
7　As to urgent treatment see the Mental Health Act 1983 s 62; and PARA 932.
8　As to the patients to whom this provision applies see PARA 924.
9　As to the meaning of 'approved clinician' see PARA 831.
10　Ie a practitioner appointed by the regulatory authority see PARA 928 note 10.
11　Ie in the form prescribed by the Mental Health (Hospital, Guardianship and Consent to Treatment) (England) Regulations 2008, SI 2008/1184, reg 27(2), Sch 1. See also the Mental Health Act 1983 s 64(2); and PARA 928. A doctor certifying that a restricted patient should be given treatment without consent should give reasons in writing for his opinion; those reasons may be disclosed to the patient unless to do so is likely to cause serious harm to the physical or mental health of the patient or another person: *R (on the application of Wooder) v Feggetter* [2002] EWCA Civ 554, [2003] QB 219. [2002] 3 WLR 591. There is a question mark over the accuracy of the Department of Health *Mental Health Act 1983 Code of Practice* (2008) para 24.79. It is submitted that the form provides authority for the treatment until the patient withdraws consent, becomes mentally incapable or the form of treatment changes, or there is a permanent change in approved clinician.

12 Mental Health Act 1983 s 58(3)(a) (amended by the Mental Health Act 2007 s 12(3)(a), Sch 3 para 3). See the Department of Health *Reference Guide to the Mental Health Act 1983* (2008) para 16.35.

13 Ie the practitioner as appointed by the regulatory authority (not being the responsible clinician in charge of the treatment in question).

14 See note 11.

15 Mental Health Act 1983 s 58(3)(b). Before giving such a certificate, the practitioner must consult two other persons who have been professionally concerned with the patient's treatment but, of those persons one must be a nurse and the other must be neither a nurse nor a registered medical practitioner; and neither may be the responsible clinician or the approved clinician in charge of the treatment in question: s 58(4) (amended by the Mental Health Act 2007 s 12(3)(b)). For the purposes of the Mental Health Act 1983 Pt 4 (ss 56–64), it is appropriate for treatment to be given to a patient if the treatment is appropriate in his case, taking into account the nature and degree of the mental disorder from which he is suffering and all other circumstances of his case: s 64(3) (added by the Mental Health Act 2007 s 6(3)).

'Mental disorder' is to be construed widely and beyond formal classification: see *R (on the application of B) v Ashworth Hospital Authority* [2005] UKHL 20, [2005] 2 AC 278, [2005] 2 All ER 289; *R (on the application of B) v Haddock* [2005] EWHC 921 (Admin), 85 BMLR 57.

The second opinion doctor is under a duty to provide reasons for providing a certificate under the Mental Health Act 1983 s 58 that a mentally competent patient should be given treatment against his will. The grant of a certificate may be challenged by way of judicial review: *R (on the application of Wooder) v Feggetter* [2002] EWCA Civ 554, [2003] QB 219, [2002] 3 WLR 591. See also the Department of Health *Mental Health Act 1983 Code of Practice* (2008) para 24.59; and the Welsh Assembly Government *Mental Health Act 1983 Code of Practice for Wales* (2008) para 18.27. On an application for judicial review of a decision under s 58(3)(b), the court is entitled to reach its own view as to the merits of the decision and whether it infringes the patient's human rights, and the patient is entitled to require the attendance of medical experts for cross-examination: *R (on the application of Wilkinson) v Broadmoor Hospital* [2001] EWCA Civ 1545, [2002] 1 WLR 419, 65 BMLR 15. This case was decided on the basis that the certification process by the appointed doctor is one that engages the Convention for the Protection of Human Rights and Fundamental Freedoms (Rome, 4 November 1950; TS 71 (1953); Cmd 8969) art 6. Procedure on such applications has been further refined so that oral evidence is not always necessary: *R (on the application of B) v Haddock* [2006] EWCA Civ 961, 93 BMLR 52; *R (on the application of Taylor) v Dr Haydn-Smith* [2005] EWHC 1668 (Admin), [2005] All ER (D) 460 (May); *M v South West London and St George's Mental Health NHS Trust* [2008] EWCA Civ 1112, [2008] All ER (D) 63 (Aug). As to the appropriate standard of proof to be applied by the court see *R (on the application of N) v M* [2002] EWCA Civ 1789, [2003] 1 WLR 562, [2003] 1 FCR 124. The court must decide also whether the proposed treatment would infringe the Convention on Human Rights and Fundamental Freedoms arts 2, 3 or 8: see *R (on the application of Wilkinson) v Broadmoor Hospital* [2001] EWCA Civ 1545, [2002] 1 WLR 419, 65 BMLR 15; *R (on the application of PS) v Responsible Medical Officer* [2003] EWHC 2335 (Admin), [2003] All ER (D) 178 (Oct). See also *R (on the application of B) v S* [2005] EWHC 1936 (Admin), [2005] All ER (D) 38 (Sep) (upheld in [2006] EWCA Civ 28, [2006] 1 WLR 810, 90 BMLR 1) on the relevance of the patient's capacity to consent to lawfulness of treatment under the Convention for the Protection of Human Rights and Fundamental Freedoms (Rome, 4 November 1950; TS 71 (1953); Cmd 8969), arts 3, 8. As to the Convention see RIGHTS AND FREEDOMS. See also PARA 554.

16 See the Mental Health Act 1983 s 60; and PARA 929.

931.   Consent for particular forms of treatment. Except in the case of urgency[1], a patient must not be given as a medical treatment for mental disorder[2], electro-convulsive therapy, or the administration of medicine as part of that therapy[3], unless[4]:

   (1)   he has attained the age of 18 years, he has consented to the treatment in question[5] and, either the approved clinician[6] in charge of it or an appointed registered medical practitioner[7] has certified in writing[8] that the patient is capable of understanding the nature, purpose and likely effects of the treatment and has consented to it[9];

(2)   he has not attained the age of 18 years, but he has consented to the treatment in question and an appointed registered medical practitioner[10] (not being the approved clinician[11] in charge of the treatment) has certified in writing[12] that the patient is capable of understanding the nature, purpose and likely effects of the treatment and has consented to it and that it is appropriate for the treatment to be given[13];

(3)   an appointed registered medical practitioner[14] (not being the responsible clinician[15] (if there is one) or the approved clinician in charge of the treatment in question) has certified in writing[16] that the patient is not capable of understanding the nature, purpose and likely effects of the treatment, but that it is appropriate for the treatment to be given and that giving him the treatment would not conflict with an advance decision[17] which the registered medical practitioner concerned is satisfied is valid and applicable[18] or a decision made by a donee[19] or deputy[20] or by the Court of Protection[21].

Before giving a certificate under head (3) above the registered medical practitioner concerned must consult two other persons who have been professionally concerned with the patient's medical treatment but, of those persons one must be a nurse and the other must be neither a nurse nor a registered medical practitioner and neither may be the responsible clinician (if there is one) or the approved clinician in charge of the treatment in question[22].

1   As to urgent treatment see the Mental Health Act 1983 s 62; and PARA 932.
2   As to the meaning of 'mental disorder' see PARA 761.
3   Ie such other forms of treatment as may be specified for this purpose by regulations made by the appropriate national authority unless such treatment falls within the Mental Health Act 1983 s 62(1)(a) or (b) (treatment immediately necessary to save the patient's life or to prevent a serious deterioration in the patient's condition: see PARA 932): Mental Health Act 1983 s 58A(1)(b); Mental Health (Hospital, Guardianship and Treatment) (England) Regulations 2008, SI 2008/1184, reg 27(3)(a), (4); and the Mental Health (Hospital, Guardianship, Community Treatment and Consent to Treatment) (Wales) Regulations 2008, SI 2008/2439, reg 38. In the Mental Health Act 1983 s 58A, 'the appropriate national authority' means, in a case where the treatment in question would, if given, be given in England, the Secretary of State and, in a case where the treatment in question would, if given, be given in Wales, the Welsh Ministers: s 58A(10) (added by the Mental Health Act 2007 s 27). Before making any regulations for the purposes of the Mental Health Act 1983 s 58A, the appropriate national authority must consult such bodies as appear to it to be concerned: s 58A(8) (as so added).
4   See the Mental Health Act 1983 s 58A(1), (2) (as added: see note 3).
5   Any consent or certificate under the Mental Health Act 1983 s 58A may relate to a plan of treatment under which the patient is to be given (whether within a specified period or otherwise) one or more of the forms of treatment to which that section applies: s 59 (amended by the Mental Health Act 2007 28(3)).
6   As to the meaning of 'approved clinician' see PARA 831.
7   Ie appointed as mentioned in the Mental Health Act 1983 s 58(3) (see PARA 930). As to registered medical practitioners see MEDICAL PROFESSIONS vol 74 (2011) PARA 176 et seq.
8   As to the certificates required for the purposes of the Mental Health Act 1983 s 58(3), (4) and (5) see the Mental Health (Hospital, Guardianship and Treatment) (England) Regulations 2008, SI 2008/1184, reg 27(3)(b); and the Mental Health (Hospital, Guardianship, Community Treatment and Consent to Treatment) (Wales) Regulations 2008, SI 2008/2439, reg 40(2), (3).
9   Mental Health Act 1983 s 58A(3) (as added: see note 3). Section 58A does not by itself confer sufficient authority for a patient who falls within s 56(5) (see PARA 924) to be given a form of treatment to which s 58A applies if he is not capable of understanding the nature, purpose and likely effects of the treatment (and cannot therefore consent to it): s 58A(7) (as so added).
10   See note 7.
11   As to the meaning of 'approved clinician' see PARA 831.
12   See note 8.

13 Mental Health Act 1983 s 58A(4) (as added: see note 3). For the purposes of Pt 4 (ss 56–64), it is appropriate for treatment to be given to a patient if the treatment is appropriate in his case, taking into account the nature and degree of the mental disorder from which he is suffering and all other circumstances of his case: s 64(3) (added by the Mental Health Act 2007 s 6(3)).

14 See note 7.

15 As to the meaning of 'responsible clinician' see PARA 834.

16 See note 8.

17 For this purpose the reference to an advance decision is to an advance decision (within the meaning of the Mental Capacity Act 2005 (see PARA 624)) made by the patient: Mental Health Act 1983 s 58A(9)(a) (as added: see note 3).

18 'Valid and applicable', in relation to such a decision, means valid and applicable to the treatment in question in accordance with the Mental Capacity Act 2005 s 25 (see PARA 625): Mental Health Act 1983 s 58A(9)(b) (as added: see note 3).

19 For this purpose a reference to a donee is to a donee of a lasting power of attorney (within the meaning of the Mental Capacity Act 2005 s 9 (see PARA 619)) created by the patient, where the donee is acting within the scope of his authority and in accordance with the Mental Capacity Act 2005: Mental Health Act 1983 s 58A(9)(c) (as added: see note 3).

20 For this purpose the reference to a deputy is to a deputy appointed for the patient by the Court of Protection under the Mental Capacity Act 2005 s 16 (see PARA 724), where the deputy is acting within the scope of his authority and in accordance with the Mental Capacity Act 2005: Mental Health Act 1983 s 58A(9)(d) (as added: see note 3).

21 Mental Health Act 1983 s 58A(5) (as added: see note 3). As to the Court of Protection see PARA 720.

22 Mental Health Act 1983 s 58A(6) (as added: see note 3).

932. Urgent treatment. The special requirements for certain treatments[1] do not apply[2] to any treatment which: (1) is immediately necessary to save the patient's life[3]; (2) not being irreversible[4], is immediately necessary to prevent a serious deterioration of his condition[5]; or (3) not being irreversible[6] or hazardous[7] is immediately necessary to alleviate serious suffering by the patient or is immediately necessary and represents the minimum interference necessary to prevent the patient from behaving violently or being a danger to himself or others[8].

The requirements for electro-convulsive therapy[9] do not apply to any treatment which falls within heads (1) or (2) above[10] and the requirements for the administration of medicine as part of that therapy[11] do not apply to any treatment which falls within heads (1) to (3) above as may be specified in regulations[12].

1 Ie the Mental Health Act 1983 ss 57–58: see PARAS 928, 930.

2 Treatment may accordingly be given without consent under the Mental Health Act 1983 s 63 to the patients to whom that provision applies (see PARAS 924, 927) or in certain circumstances under the common law (see PARA 927).

3 Mental Health Act 1983 s 62(1)(a). As to the meaning of 'patient' see PARA 758 note 4. As to the effect of the Mental Capacity Act 2005 on the Mental Health Act 1983 Pt 4 (ss 56–64) see PARA 925.

4 Treatment is irreversible if it has unfavourable irreversible physical or psychological consequences: the Mental Health Act 1983 s 62(3).

5 Mental Health Act 1983 s 62(1)(b).

6 See note 4.

7 Treatment is hazardous if it entails significant physical hazard: Mental Health Act 1983 s 62(3).

8 Mental Health Act 1983 s 62(1)(c), (d). A withdrawal of consent or a notice of discontinuance of treatment under s 60 and 61(3) (see PARA 933) does not preclude the continuation of any treatment or plan pending compliance with ss 57, 58, 58A (see PARAS 928, 930, 931) if the approved clinician in charge of treatment considers that the discontinuance of the treatment or of treatment under the plan would cause serious suffering to the patient: s 62(2) (amended by the Mental Health Act 2007 ss 12(5), 28(7)). As to the meaning of 'approved clinician' see PARA 831.

See *B v Croydon Health Authority* [1995] Fam 133, [1995] 1 All ER 683, CA (tube feeding, ~~to alleviate symptoms of mental~~ disorder in the form of refusal to eat in order to inflict self-harm, was held to be as much part of ~~the treatment for the disorder as the treatment to~~ remedy its underlying cause).

9   Ie the Mental Health Act 1983 s 58A, in so far as it relates to electro-convulsive therapy by virtue of s 58A(1)(a) (see PARA 931).

10 Mental Health Act 1983 s 62(1A) (s 62(1A)–(1C) added by the Mental Health Act 2007 s 68(6), (7)).

11 Ie the Mental Health Act 1983 s 58A, in so far as it relates to a form of treatment specified by virtue of s 58A(1)(b) (see PARA 931).

12 See the Mental Health Act 1983 s 62(1B) (as added: see note 10). For the purposes of s 62(1B), the regulations may make different provision for different cases (and may, in particular, make different provision for different forms of treatment), may make provision which applies subject to specified exceptions and may include transitional, consequential, incidental or supplemental provision: s 62(1C) (as so added).

933.   Review of treatment. Where a patient[1] is given treatment[2], a report on it and the patient's condition must be given by the approved clinician in charge of treatment[3] to the regulatory authority[4] on the next occasion on which he furnishes a report for renewal of authority for detention[5] and at any other time if so required by the regulatory authority[6]. Special provision is made in respect of restricted patients[7]. The regulatory authority may at any time give notice to the approved clinician in charge of the treatment directing that, except in cases of urgent treatment[8], a certificate[9] in respect of a patient does not apply to treatment given to him (whether in England or Wales) after a date specified in the notice and the treatment provisions[10] apply to such treatment as if that certificate had not been given[11].

1   As to the meaning of 'patient' see PARA 758 note 4.
2   Ie treatment in accordance with the Mental Health Act 1983 s 57(2) (see PARA 928) or s 58(3)(b) (see PARA 930) or 58A(4) or (5) (see PARA 931) or by virtue of s 62A (see PARA 934) in accordance with a Pt 4A certificate (within the meaning of s 62A) that falls within s 64C(4) (see PARA 936): s 61(1) (amended by the Mental Health Act 2007 ss 28(4), 34(3)(a); and the Health and Social Care Act 2012 s 299(7))
3   As to the meaning of 'approved clinician' see PARA 831.
4   Mental Health Act 1983 s 61(1) (amended by the Mental Health Act 2007 s 12(4)(a)(i) and the Health and Social Care Act 2008 Sch 3 para 4(2)). As to the meaning of 'regulatory authority' see PARA 573 note 1.
5   Ie a report under the Mental Health Act 1983 s 20(3) (see PARA 910), 20A(4) (see PARA 799) or s 21B(2) (see PARA 911) in respect of the patient: s 61(1)(a) (amended by the Mental Health (Patients in the Community) Act 1995 s 2(5); and the Mental Health Act 2007 s 34(3)(b)). As to the effect of the Mental Capacity Act 2005 on the Mental Health Act 1983 Pt 4 (ss 56–64) see PARA 925.
6   Mental Health Act 1983 s 61(1)(b) (amended by the Health and Social Care Act 2008 Sch 3 para 4(2)).
7   In relation to a patient subject to a restriction order or direction (see PARA 869) or a limitation direction (see PARA 863), a report must be made: (1) in the case of treatment in the period of six months beginning with the date of the restriction order or direction or limitation direction, at the end of that period; (2) in the case of treatment at any subsequent time, on the next occasion on which the responsible clinician furnishes a report under the Mental Health Act 1983 s 41(6), s 45B(3) or s 49(3) (see PARAS 863, 876): s 61(2) (amended by the Crime (Sentences) Act 1997 s 55, Sch 4 para 12(7) and the Mental Health Act 2007 s 12(4)(b)).
8   See the Mental Health Act 1983 s 62; and PARA 932.
9   Ie a certificate under the Mental Health Act 1983 s 57(2), s 58(3)(b) or s 58A(4), (5): see PARAS 928, 930, 931.
10 Ie the Mental Health Act 1983 s 57, 58, 58A (see PARAS 928, 930, 931).
11 Mental Health Act 1983 s 61(3), (3A) (s 61(3) amended by the Mental Health Act 2007 s 28(5)(b); the Health and Social Care Act 2008 Sch 3 para 4(3); and the Mental Health Act 1983 s 61(3A) added by the Mental Health Act 2007 s 12(4)(d)).

934. Treatment on recall of community patient or revocation of order. The following provisions apply where a community patient[1] is recalled to hospital[2] or a patient is liable to be detained under the Mental Health Act 1983 following the revocation of a community treatment order[3] in respect of him[4].

For the purposes of the administration of medicine where consent or a second opinion is required[5], the patient is to be treated as if he had remained liable to be detained since the making of the community treatment order[6]. However the provisions requiring consent or a second opinion for treatment to be given[7] do not apply to treatment given to the patient if the certificate requirement is met[8] or the certificate requirement would not apply[9].

The provision relating to electro-convulsive therapy or the administration of medicine as part of that therapy[10] does not apply to treatment given to the patient if there is authority to give the treatment, and the certificate requirement is met[11], for certain purposes[12].

1   As to the meaning of 'patient' see PARA 797 note 4.
2   Ie under the Mental Health Act 1983 s 17E (see PARA 801): s 62A(1)(a) (added by the Mental Health Act 2007 s 34(4)).
3   Ie under the Mental Health Act 1983 s 17F (see PARA 802).
4   Mental Health Act 1983 s 62A(1)(b) (as added: see note 2). In a case where s 62A(1)(b) applies, s 62A(3) only applies pending compliance with s 58 (see PARA 930): s 62A(7) (as so added).
5   Ie for the purposes of the Mental Health Act 1983 s 58(1)(b) (see PARA 930).
6   Mental Health Act 1983 s 62A(2) (as added: see note 4).
7   Ie the Mental Health Act 1983 s 58 (see PARA 930).
8   Ie the certificate requirement for the purposes of the Mental Health Act 1983 s 64C (see PARA 936) or s 64E (see PARA 940). In a case where s 62A applies and the Part 4A certificate falls within s 64C(4), the certificate requirement is met only in so far as the Part 4A certificate expressly provides that it is appropriate for one or more specified forms of treatment to be given to the patient in that case (subject to such conditions as may be specified) or a notice having been given under s 64H(5), treatment is authorised by virtue of s 64H(8): 62A(5) (as added (see note 2); amended by the Health and Social Care Act 2012 s 299(8)). This does not preclude the continuation of any treatment, or of treatment under any plan, pending compliance with the Mental Health Act 1983 s 58 or 58A or 64B or 64E if the approved clinician in charge of the treatment considers that the discontinuance of the treatment, or of the treatment under the plan, would cause serious suffering to the patient: s 62A(6) (as so added; amended by the Health and Social Care Act 2012 s 299(9)). In a case where the Mental Health Act 1983 s 62A applies and the certificate requirement is no longer met for the purposes of s 64C(4A), the continuation of any treatment, or of treatment under any plan, pending compliance with s 58 or 58A above or 64B or 64E is not precluded if the approved clinician in charge of the treatment considers that the discontinuance of the treatment, or of treatment under the plan, would cause serious suffering to the patient: s 62A(6A) (s 62A as so added; s 62A(6A) added by the Health and Social Care Act 2012 s 299(10)). As to the meaning of 'Part 4A certificate' for the purposes of the Mental Health Act 1983 s 62(5) see s 64H; PARA 944 (definition applied by s 62A(8) (as so added)). 'Specified' in relation to a Part 4A certificate means specified in the certificate: see s 62A(8) (as so added).
9   Ie as a result of the Mental Health Act 1983 s 64B(4) or 64E(4) (see PARA 940): s 62A(3) (as added: see note 2).
10   Ie the Mental Health Act 1983 s 58A (see PARA 931).
11   See note 8.
12   Mental Health Act 1983 s 62A(4) (as added: see note 2). The certain purposes referred to in the text are s 64C or s 64E (see PARA 940).

(ii) Treatment of Community Patients not Recalled to Hospital

935. Adult community patients. Relevant treatment[1] cannot be given to a community patient[2] who is not recalled to hospital[3] and has attained the age of 16 years[4] unless there is authority to give it to him[5] and, if it is section 58 type treatment or section 58A type treatment[6], the certificate requirement is met[7].

However, the certificate requirement does not apply if giving the treatment to the patient is authorised[8], or the treatment is immediately necessary and the patient has capacity to consent to it[9] and does consent to it, or a donee[10] or deputy[11] or the Court of Protection[12] consents to the treatment on the patient's behalf[13].

Nor does the certificate requirement apply in so far as the administration of medicine[14] to the patient at any time during the period of one month beginning with the day on which the community treatment order[15] is made is section 58 type treatment[16].

1 For the purposes of the Mental Health Act 1986 Pt 4A (ss 64A–64K) 'relevant treatment', in relation to a patient, means treatment which is for the mental disorder from which the patient is suffering and is a not form of treatment to which s 57 (see PARA 928) applies: s 64A (ss 64A–64K added by the Mental Health Act 2007 s 35(1)).

2 As to the meaning of 'patient' see PARA 758 note 4.

3 Ie recalled to hospital under the Mental Health Act 1983 s 17E (see PARA 801). As to the meaning of 'hospital' see PARA 577.

4 As to patients under 16 see PARA 940.

5 As to when there is authority to give treatment to a patient see PARAS 938–941.

6 Relevant treatment is section 58 type treatment or section 58A type treatment if, at the time when it is given to the patient, the Mental Health Act 1983 s 58 or 58A (see PARAS 930, 931) (respectively) would have applied to it, had the patient remained liable to be detained at that time (rather than being a community patient): s 64C(3) (as added: see note 1).

7 Mental Health Act 1983 s 64B(1), (2) (as added: see note 1). As to when the certificate requirement is met see PARA 936.

8 Ie in accordance with the Mental Health Act 1983 s 64G (see PARAS 937, 943): s 63B(3)(a) (as added: see note 1).

9 For the purposes of the Mental Health Act 1983 Pt 4A (ss 64A–64K) references to a patient who lacks capacity are to a patient who lacks capacity within the meaning of the Mental Capacity Act 2005 (see PARA 601 et seq) and references to a patient who has capacity are to be read accordingly: Mental Health Act 1983 s 64K(1)–(3) (as added: see note 1). As to when treatment is immediately necessary see PARA 937.

10 For the purposes of the Mental Health Act 1983 Pt 4A references to a donee are to a donee of a lasting power of attorney (within the meaning of the Mental Capacity Act 2005 s 9 (see PARA 619)) created by the patient, where the donee is acting within the scope of his authority and in accordance with that Act: Mental Health Act 1983 s 64K(1), (4) (as added: see note 1).

11 For the purposes of the Mental Health Act 1983 Pt 4A references to a deputy are to a deputy appointed for the patient by the Court of Protection under the Mental Capacity Act 2005 s 16 (see PARA 724), where the deputy is acting within the scope of his authority and in accordance with that Act: Mental Health Act 1983 s 64K(1), (5) (as added: see note 1).

12 As to the Court of Protection see PARA 720.

13 Mental Health Act 1983 s 64B(3)(b) (as added: see note 1). Treatment of a patient to whom s 64B(3)(b) applies may include treatment by way of the administration of medicines as part of electro-convulsive therapy but only where that treatment falls within s 64C(5)(a) or (b): Mental Health (Hospital, Guardianship and Treatment) (England) Regulations 2008, SI 2008/1184, reg 28(2); Mental Health (Hospital, Guardianship, Community Treatment and Consent to Treatment) (Wales) Regulations 2008, SI 2008/2439, reg 39(a).

14 This reference to the administration of medicine does not include any form of treatment specified under the Mental Health Act 1983 s 58(1)(a) (see PARA 930): s 64B(5) (as added: see note 1).

15 As to the meaning of 'community treatment order' see PARA 797.

16 Mental Health Act 1983 s 64B(4) (as added: see note 1).

936. When certificate requirement is met. The certificate requirement is met in respect of treatment to be given to a patient[1] if an appointed registered medical practitioner[2] (not being the responsible clinician[3] or the person in charge of the treatment) has certified in writing that it is appropriate for the treatment to be given[4] or for the treatment to be given subject to such conditions as may be specified in the certificate and, if conditions are so specified, the conditions are satisfied[5].

Where there is authority to give treatment because the patient has capacity to consent to the treatment and does consent[6], the certificate requirement is also met in respect of the treatment if the approved clinician[7] in charge of the treatment has certified in writing that the patient has capacity to consent to the treatment and has consented to it[8]. However, this does not apply to section 58A type treatment[9] if the patient has not attained the age of 18[10].

1   As to the meaning of 'patient' see PARA 758 note 4.
2   Ie appointed for the purposes of the Mental Health Act 1983 Pt 4 (ss 56–64). As to registered medical practitioners see MEDICAL PROFESSIONS vol 74 (2011) PARA 176 et seq.
3   As to the meaning of 'responsible clinician' see the Mental Health Act 1983 s 34(1); and PARA 834 (definition applied by s 64K(6) (ss 64C, 64K added by the Mental Health Act 2007 s 35(1))).
4   As to when it is appropriate for treatment to be given see the Mental Health Act 1983 s 64(3); and PARA 930 note 15 (definition applied by s 64K(8) (as added: see note 3)). The patient should be interviewed in private if possible: Department of Health *Mental Health Act 1983 Code of Practice* (2008) para 24.27; Welsh Assembly Government *Mental Health Act 1983 Code of Practice for Wales* (2008) para 18.16.
5   Mental Health Act 1983 s 64C(1), (4) (as added: see note 3).
6   Ie where there is authority to give treatment by virtue of the Mental Health Act 1983 s 64C(2)(a) (see PARA 938).
7   As to the meaning of 'approved clinician' see PARA 831.
8   Mental Health Act 1983 s 64C(4A) (s 64C as added (see note 3); s 64C(4A), (4B) added by the Health and Social Care Act 2012 s 299(2)).
9   As to the meaning of 'section 58A type treatment' see PARA 935 note 6.
10   Mental Health Act 1983 s 64C(4B) (s 64C as added (see note 3); s 64C (4B) as added (see note 8)).

937. When treatment is immediately necessary. In a case where the treatment is section 58 type treatment[1], treatment is immediately necessary if:

(1)   it is immediately necessary to save the patient's life[2]; or

(2)   it is immediately necessary to prevent a serious deterioration of the patient's condition and is not irreversible[3]; or

(3)   it is immediately necessary to alleviate serious suffering by the patient and is not irreversible or hazardous[4]; or

(4)   it is immediately necessary, represents the minimum interference necessary to prevent the patient from behaving violently or being a danger to himself or others and is not irreversible or hazardous[5].

In a case where the treatment is electro-convulsive therapy[6], treatment is immediately necessary if it falls within head (1) or (2) above[7].

In a case where the treatment is the administration of medicine as part of electro-convulsive therapy[8], treatment is immediately necessary if it falls within such of heads (1) to (4) above as may be specified[9] in regulations[10].

1   As to the meaning of 'section 58 type treatment' see PARA 935 note 6.
2   Mental Health Act 1983 ss 64C(5)(a), 64G(5)(a) (ss 64C, 64G added by the Mental Health Act 2007 s 35(1)). As to the meaning of 'patient' see PARA 758 note 4.
3   Mental Health Act 1983 ss 64C(5)(b), 64G(5)(b) (as added: see note 2).
4   Mental Health Act 1983 ss 64C(5)(c), 64G(5)(c) (as added: see note 2). For this purpose treatment is irreversible if it has unfavourable irreversible physical or psychological consequences and hazardous if it entails significant physical hazard: s 62(3) (applied by s 64C(9) (as so added)).
5   Mental Health Act 1983 ss 64C(5)(d), 64G(5)(d) (as added: see note 2).
6   Ie section 58A type treatment by virtue of the Mental Health Act 1983 s 58A(1)(a) (see PARA 931). As to the meaning of 'section 58A type treatment' see PARA 935 note 6.
7   Mental Health Act 1983 ss 64C(6), 64G(6) (as added: see note 2).
8   Ie section 58A type treatment by virtue of the Mental Health Act 1983 s 58A(1)(b) (see PARA 931).
9   Ie as specified in regulations made under the Mental Health Act 1983 s 58A (see PARA 931).

10 Mental Health Act 1983 ss 64C(7), 64G(7) (as added: see note 2). For the purposes of ss 64C(7), 64G(7) the regulations may make different provision for different cases (and may, in particular, make different provision for different forms of treatment), may make provision which applies subject to specified exceptions and may include transitional, consequential, incidental or supplemental provision: ss 64C(8), 64G(8) (as so added). Such regulations provide that treatment of a patient to whom s 64G (emergency treatment for patients lacking capacity or competence) applies may include treatment by way of the administration of medicine as part of electro-convulsive therapy but only where that treatment falls within s 64G(5)(a) or (b) (treatment immediately necessary to save the patient's life or to prevent a serious deterioration in the patient's condition): see the Mental Health (Hospital, Guardianship and Treatment) (England) Regulations 2008, SI 2008/1184, reg 28(3); and the Mental Health (Hospital, Guardianship, Community Treatment and Consent to Treatment) (Wales) Regulations 2008, SI 2008/2439, reg 39(b).

938. Authority to give treatment. There is authority to give treatment to an adult community patient[1] if: (1) he has capacity to consent[2] to it and does consent to it[3]; (2) a donee[4] or deputy[5] or the Court of Protection[6] consents to it on his behalf[7]; or (3) giving it to him is authorised[8].

1 Ie a patient under the Mental Health Act 1983 s 64A (see PARA 935). As to the meaning of 'patient' see PARA 758 note 4.
2 As to when a patient has capacity see PARA 935 note 9.
3 Mental Health Act 1983 s 64C(1), (2)(a) (added by the Mental Health Act 2005 s 35(1)).
4 As to the meaning of 'donee' see PARA 935 note 10.
5 As to the meaning of 'deputy' see PARA 935 note 11.
6 As to the Court of Protection see PARA 720.
7 Mental Health Act 1983 s 64C(2)(b) (as added: see note 3).
8 Mental Health Act 1983 s 64C(2)(c) (as added: see note 3). As to when it is authorised see ss 64D–64G; and PARAS 939–943.

939. Adult community patient lacking capacity. A person is authorised to give relevant treatment[1] to a patient[2] if the following conditions are met[3].

The first condition is that, before giving the treatment, the person takes reasonable steps to establish whether the patient lacks capacity[4] to consent to the treatment[5].

The second condition is that, when giving the treatment, he reasonably believes that the patient lacks capacity to consent to it[6].

The third condition is that he has no reason to believe that the patient objects[7] to being given the treatment or, he does have reason to believe that the patient so objects, but it is not necessary to use force against the patient in order to give the treatment[8].

The fourth condition is that he is the person in charge of the treatment and an approved clinician[9] or the treatment is given under the direction of that clinician[10].

The fifth condition is that giving the treatment does not conflict with an advance decision[11] which he is satisfied is valid and applicable[12] or a decision made by a donee or deputy[13] or the Court of Protection[14].

1 As to the meaning of 'relevant treatment' see PARA 935 note 1.
2 Ie as mentioned in the Mental Health Act 1986 s 64C(2)(c) (see PARA 938). As to the meaning of 'patient' see PARA 758 note 4.
3 Mental Health Act 1983 s 64D(1) (ss 64D, 64I, 64J added by the Mental Health Act 2007 s 35(1)). Nothing in the Mental Health Act 1983 s 64D excludes a person's civil liability for loss or damage, or his criminal liability, resulting from his negligence in doing anything authorised to be done by that provision: s 64I (as so added).
4 As to when a patient lacks capacity see PARA 935 note 9.
5 Mental Health Act 1983 s 64D(2) (as added: see note 3).
6 Mental Health Act 1983 s 64D(3) (as added: see note 3).

7   In assessing for the purposes of the Mental Health Act 1983 Pt 4A (ss 64A–64K) whether he has reason to believe that a patient objects to treatment, a person must consider all the circumstances so far as they are reasonably ascertainable, including the patient's behaviour, wishes, feelings, views, beliefs and values: s 64J(1) (as added: see note 3). However, circumstances from the past can be considered only so far as it is still appropriate to consider them: s 64J(2) (as so added).

8   Mental Health Act 1983 s 64D(4) (as added: see note 3).

9   As to the meaning of 'approved clinician' see PARA 831.

10 Mental Health Act 1983 s 64D(5) (as added: see note 3).

11 For this purpose reference to an advance decision is to an advance decision (within the meaning of the Mental Capacity Act 2005 (see PARA 624)) made by the patient: Mental Health Act 1983 s 64D(6)(a) (as added: see note 3).

12 For this purpose 'valid and applicable', in relation to such a decision, means valid and applicable to the treatment in question in accordance with the Mental Capacity Act 2005 s 25 (see PARA 625): Mental Health Act 1983 s 64D(6)(b) (as added: see note 3).

13 As to the meanings of 'donee' and 'deputy' see PARA 935 notes 10, 11.

14 Mental Health Act 1983 s 64D(6) (as added: see note 3). As to the Court of Protection see PARA 720.

940. Child community patients. Relevant treatment[1] may not be given to a community patient who is not recalled to hospital[2] and has not attained the age of 16 years[3] unless there is authority to give it to him[4] and, if it is section 58 type treatment or section 58A type treatment[5], the certificate requirement is met[6]. However, the certificate requirement does not apply if giving the treatment to the patient is authorised[7] or in a case where the patient is competent to consent to the treatment and does consent to it, the treatment is immediately necessary[8].

Nor does the certificate requirement apply in so far as the administration of medicine[9] to the patient at any time during the period of one month beginning with the day on which the community treatment order is made is section 58 type treatment[10].

1   As to the meaning of 'relevant treatment' see PARA 935 note 1.

2   Ie is not recalled to hospital under the Mental Health Act 1983 s 17E (see PARA 801). As to the meaning of 'hospital' see PARA 577.

3   See the Mental Health Act 1983 s 64E(1) (s 64E added by the Mental Health Act 2007 s 35(1)). As to patients who have attained the age of 16 years see PARA 935. As to when a person has attained 16 see the regulations under s 32(2)(d) as applied by s 64E(8) (as so added).

4   For this purpose there is authority to give treatment to a patient if he is competent to consent to it and he does consent to it or giving it to him is authorised in accordance with the Mental Health Act 1983 s 64F (see PARA 941) or s 64G (see PARA 943): s 64E(6) (as added: see note 3).

5   As to the meaning of 'section 58 type treatment' and 'section 58A type treatment' see the Mental Health Act 1983 s 64C(3); and PARA 935 note 6 (applied by s 64E(7) (s 64E as so added; s 64E(7) amended by the Health and Social Care Act 2012 s 299(3))).

6   Mental Health Act 1983 s 64E(2) (as added: see note 3). As to when the certificate requirement is met see s 64C(4), (4A); and PARA 936 (applied and modified by s 64E(7) (as so added and as amended (see note 4))).

7   Ie in authorised in accordance with the Mental Health Act 1983 s 64G (see PARA 943): s 64E(3)(a) (as added: see note 3).

8   Mental Health Act 1983 s 64E(3)(b) (as added: see note 3). As to when treatment is immediately necessary see s 64C(5)–(9); and PARA 937 (applied by s 64E(7) (as so added and as amended (see note 4))). Treatment of a patient to whom s 64E(3)(b) applies may include treatment by way of the administration of medicines as part of electro-convulsive therapy but only where that treatment falls within s 64C(5)(a) or (b): Mental Health (Hospital, Guardianship and Treatment) (England) Regulations 2008, SI 2008/1184, reg 28(2); Mental Health (Hospital, Guardianship, Community Treatment and Consent to Treatment) (Wales) Regulations 2008, SI 2008/2439, reg 39(a).

9   This does not include any form of treatment specified under the Mental Health Act 1983 s 58(1)(a) (see PARA 930): s 64E(5) (as added: see note 3).

10 Mental Health Act 1983 s 64E(4) (as added: see note 3).

941. Child community patients lacking competence. A person is authorised to give relevant treatment[1] to a child community patient[2] if the following conditions are met[3].

The first condition is that, before giving the treatment, the person takes reasonable steps to establish whether the patient is competent to consent to the treatment[4].

The second condition is that, when giving the treatment, he reasonably believes that the patient is not competent to consent to it[5].

The third condition is that he has no reason to believe that the patient objects[6] to being given the treatment or he does have reason to believe that the patient so objects, but it is not necessary to use force against the patient in order to give the treatment[7].

The fourth condition is that he is the person in charge of the treatment and an approved clinician[8] or the treatment is given under the direction of that clinician[9].

1 As to the meaning of 'relevant treatment' see PARA 935 note 1.
2 Ie a patient as mentioned in the Mental Health Act 1983 s 64E(6)(b) (see PARA 940). As to the meaning of 'patient' see PARA 758 note 4.
3 See the Mental Health Act 1983 s 64F(1) (ss 64F, 64I, 64J added by the Mental Health Act 2007 s 35(1)). Nothing in the Mental Health Act 1983 s 64F excludes a person's civil liability for loss or damage, or his criminal liability, resulting from his negligence in doing anything authorised to be done by that provision: s 64I (as so added).
4 Mental Health Act 1983 s 64F(2) (as added: see note 3).
5 Mental Health Act 1983 s 64F(3) (as added: see note 3).
6 In assessing for the purposes of the Mental Health Act 1983 Pt 4A (ss 64A–64K) whether he has reason to believe that a patient objects to treatment, a person must consider all the circumstances so far as they are reasonably ascertainable, including the patient's behaviour, wishes, feelings, views, beliefs and values: s 64J(1) (as added: see note 3). However, circumstances from the past can be considered only so far as it is still appropriate to consider them: s 64J(2) (as so added).
7 Mental Health Act 1983 s 64F(4) (as added: see note 3).
8 As to the meaning of 'approved clinician' see PARA 831.
9 Mental Health Act 1983 s 64F(5) (as added: see note 3).

942. Withdrawal of consent. Where the consent of a patient[1] to any treatment has been given[2] the patient may at any time before the completion of the treatment withdraw his consent; the statutory provisions then apply to the remainder of the treatment as if it were a separate form of treatment[3].

Where the consent of a patient to any treatment has been given[4] but before the completion of the treatment, the patient loses capacity or (as the case may be) competence to consent to the treatment, the patient is treated as having withdrawn his consent and the statutory provisions then apply as if the remainder of the treatment were a separate form of treatment[5].

Without prejudice to the application of the above provisions to any treatment given under the plan of treatment to which a patient has consented, a patient who has consented to such a plan may at any time withdraw his consent to further treatment, or to further treatment of any description, under the plan[6].

1 As to the meaning of 'patient' see PARA 758 note 4.
2 Ie as mentioned in the Mental Health Act 1983 s 64C(2)(a) (see PARA 938) for the purposes of s 64B or 64E (see PARAS 935, 940).
3 Mental Health Act 1983 s 64FA(1) (added by the Health and Social Care Act 2012 s 299(4)).
4 Ie as mentioned in the Mental Health Act 1983 s 64C(2)(a) above for the purposes of s 64B or 64E.
5 See the Mental Health Act 1983 s 64FA(2), (3) (as added: see note 3).

6   Mental Health Act 1983 s 64FA(4) (as added: see note 3). Section 64FA does not preclude the continuation of any treatment, or of treatment under any plan, pending compliance with s 58, 58A, 64B or 64E if the approved clinician in charge of the treatment considers that the discontinuance of the treatment, or of treatment under the plan, would cause serious suffering to the patient: s 64FA(5) (as so added).

943. Emergency treatment for patients lacking capacity or competence. A person is also authorised to give relevant treatment[1] to a patient[2] if the following conditions are met[3].

The first condition is that, when giving the treatment, the person reasonably believes that the patient lacks capacity to consent to it or, as the case may be, is not competent to consent to it[4].

The second condition is that the treatment is immediately necessary[5].

The third condition is that if it is necessary to use force against the patient in order to give the treatment the treatment needs to be given in order to prevent harm to the patient; and the use of such force is a proportionate response to the likelihood of the patient's suffering harm, and to the seriousness of that harm[6].

1   As to the meaning of 'relevant treatment' see PARA 935 note 1.
2   Ie as mentioned in the Mental Health Act 1983 s 64C(2) or 64E(6)(b) (see PARAS 938, 940). As to the meaning of 'patient' see PARA 758 note 4.
3   See the Mental Health Act 1983 s 64G(1) (ss 64G, 64I added by the Mental Health Act 2007 s 35(1)). Nothing in the Mental Health Act 1983 s 64G excludes a person's civil liability for loss or damage, or his criminal liability, resulting from his negligence in doing anything authorised to be done by that provision: s 64I (as so added).
4   Mental Health Act 1983 s 64G(2) (as added: see note 3). As to when a patient lacks capacity see PARA 935 note 9. As to when a community patient lacks capacity see s 64D; and PARA 939. As to when a child lacks competence see s 64F; and PARA 941.
5   Mental Health Act 1983 s 64G(3) (as added: see note 3). As to when treatment is immediately necessary see PARA 937.
6   Mental Health Act 1983 s 64G(4) (as added: see note 3).

944. Part 4A certificates. A 'Part 4A certificate'[1] may relate to a plan of treatment under which the patient is to be given (whether within a specified period or otherwise) one or more forms of section 58 type treatment or section 58A type treatment[2]. A Part 4A certificate must be in such form as may be prescribed by regulations made by the appropriate national authority[3]; and the regulations may make different provision for the different descriptions of Part 4A certificate[4].

Before giving a Part 4A certificate that it is appropriate for treatment to be given[5], the registered medical practitioner[6] concerned must consult two other persons who have been professionally concerned with the patient's medical treatment but, of those persons at least one must be a person who is not a registered medical practitioner and neither may be the patient's responsible clinician[7] or the person in charge of the treatment in question[8].

Where a patient is given treatment in accordance with a Part 4A certificate that it is appropriate for treatment to be given[9], a report on the treatment and the patient's condition must be given by the person in charge of the treatment to the regulatory authority[10] if required by that authority[11].

The regulatory authority may at any time give notice[12] directing that a Part 4A certificate that it is appropriate for treatment to be given[13] does not apply to treatment given to a patient after a date specified in the notice, and the relevant statutory provisions[14] then apply to any such treatment as if that certificate had not been given[15]. This does not preclude the continuation of any treatment or of treatment under any plan pending compliance with the relevant section if the person in charge of the treatment considers that the discontinuance of the treatment or of treatment under the plan would cause serious suffering to the patient[16].

1   Ie a certificate under the Mental Health Act 1983 s 64B(2)(a) (see PARA 935) or s 64E(2)(b) (see PARA 940).
2   Mental Health Act 1983 s 64H(1) (ss 64H, 64K added by the Mental Health Act 2007 s 35(1); the Mental Health Act 1983 s 64H(2)–(5) amended by the Health and Social Care Act 2012 s 299(5), Sch 3 para 5). As to the meaning of 'section 58 type treatment' and 'section 58A type treatment' see PARA 935 note 6.
3   For these purposes 'the appropriate national authority' means, in relation to community patients in respect of whom the responsible hospital is in England, the Secretary of State and, in relation to community patients in respect of whom the responsible hospital is in Wales, the Welsh Ministers: Mental Health Act 1983 s 64H(9) (as added: see note 2). As to the meaning of 'hospital' see PARA 577. As to the form in which the certificates must be set out see the Mental Health (Hospital, Guardianship and Treatment) (England) Regulations 2008, SI 2008/1184, reg 28(1), (1A) (reg 28(1) amended and reg 28(1A) added by SI 2012/1118); and the Mental Health (Hospital, Guardianship, Community Treatment and Consent to Treatment) (Wales) Regulations 2008, SI 2008/2439, reg 40(4), (5) (reg 40(4) amended and reg 40(5) added by SI 2012/1265).
4   Mental Health Act 1983 s 64H(2) (as added and amended: see note 2).
5   Ie a Part 4A certificate that falls within the Mental Health Act 1983 s 64C(4) (see PARA 936).
6   As to registered medical practitioners see MEDICAL PROFESSIONS vol 74 (2011) PARA 176 et seq.
7   As to the meaning of 'responsible clinician' see the Mental Health Act 1983 s 34(1); and PARA 834 (definition applied by s 64K(6) (as added: see note 2)).
8   Mental Health Act 1983 s 64H(3) (as added and amended: see note 2).
9   See note 5.
10 As to the meaning of 'regulatory authority' see PARA 573 note 1.
11 Mental Health Act 1983 s 64H(4) (as added and amended: see note 2).
12 This notice must be given to the person in charge of the treatment in question: Mental Health Act 1983 s 64H(7) (as added and amended: see note 2).
13 See note 5.
14 The relevant statutory provisions are: (1) if the patient is not recalled to hospital in accordance with the Mental Health Act 1983 s 17E (see PARA 801), s 64B (see PARA 935) or s 64E (see PARA 940); (2) if the patient is so recalled or is liable to be detained under the Mental Health Act 1983 following revocation of the community treatment order under s 17F (see PARA 802), s 58 (see PARA 930), in the case of section 58 type treatment, and s 58A (see PARA 931), in the case of section 58A type treatment (subject to s 62A(2) (see PARA 934)): s 64H(6) (as added and amended: see note 2).
15 Mental Health Act 1983 s 64H(5) (as added and amended: see note 2).
16 Mental Health Act 1983 s 64H(8) (as added and amended: see note 2).

(19) AFTERCARE AND ASSESSMENTS

(i) Aftercare

945. Provision of aftercare. The primary care trust or local health board[1] and the local social services authority[2] have a duty[3] to provide, in co-operation with the relevant voluntary agencies, aftercare services[4] for certain detained patients who cease to be detained and then leave hospital[5]. Such duty continues until such time as those authorities are satisfied that the person concerned is no longer in need of such services, except in the case of a community patient who remains such a patient[6].

1   As to the meanings of 'primary care trust' and 'local health board' see PARA 575 notes 5, 6. See also the Mental Health Act 1983 s 117(3); and PARA 574. As from 1 April 2013, the duty of the primary care trust under these provisions is transferred to the clinical commissioning group and accordingly s 117(2) is amended by the Health and Social Care Act 2012 s 40(2) and the following provisions, as added by s 40(3), apply: see s 306(1)(d)l and the Health and Social Care Act 2012 (Commencement No 2, Transitional, Savings and Transitory Provisions) Order 2013,

SI 2013/160, art 2(2). The Mental Health Act 1983 s 117(2), in its application to the clinical commissioning group, has effect as if for 'to provide' there were substituted 'to arrange for the provision of': s 117(2D) (as so added). The appropriate national authority may by regulations provide that the duty imposed on the clinical commissioning group by s 117(2) is, in the circumstances or to the extent prescribed by the regulations, to be imposed instead on another clinical commissioning group or the National Health Service Commissioning Board: s 117(2E) (as so added). Where such regulations provide that the duty imposed by s 117(2) is to be imposed on the National Health Service Commissioning Board, s 117(2D) has effect as if the reference to the clinical commissioning group were a reference to the National Health Service Commissioning Board: s 117(2F) (as so added). The National Health Service Act 2006 s 272(7), (8) (see HEALTH SERVICES vol 54 (2008) PARA 9) applies to the power to make regulations under the Mental Health Act 1983 s 117(2E) as it applies to a power to make regulations under the National Health Service Act 2006: Mental Health Act 1983 s 117(2G) (as so added). As to clinical commissioning groups see PARA 572. As to the appropriate national authority see PARA 567. As to the duty to comply with the Human Rights Act 1998 see the Health and Social Care Act 2008 s 145 (SOCIAL SERVICES AND COMMUNITY CARE); *YL v Birmingham City Council* [2007] UKHL 27, [2008] 1 AC 95, [2007] 3 All ER 957; and RIGHTS AND FREEDOMS. See also *R (on the application of A) v Partnerships in Care Ltd* [2002] EWHC 529 (Admin), [2002] 1 WLR 2610, (2002) Times, 23 April; and *R (on the application of IH) v Secretary of State for the Home Department* [2002] EWCA Civ 646, [2003] QB 320, [2002] 3 WLR 967; *Johnson v United Kingdom* (1997) 27 EHRR 296, 40 BMLR 1; *Kolanis v United Kingdom* (2005) 42 EHRR 206, 84 BMLR 102; Application 45049/98 *Clunis v UK* (unreported).

2   Ie the local social services authority for the area in which the person concerned is resident or to which he is sent on discharge by the hospital in which he was detained: see the Mental Health Act 1983 s 117(3) (amended by the Health Authorities Act 1995 s 2(1), Sch 1 para 107(1), (8)(b)). If a patient is sent to a different area from which he was resident on admission, then the area in which he was resident remains responsible for his aftercare services. If a patient has no place of residence then the relevant bodies are those for the area he is sent on discharge: *R v Mental Health Review Tribunal, ex p Hall* [1999] 4 All ER 883, [2000] 1 WLR 1323, CA. As to the meaning of 'hospital' see PARA 577. As to a discussion of the meaning of the word 'resident' in the Mental Health Act 1983 s 117 see *R (on the application of M) v Hammersmith and Fulham London Borough Council* [2010] EWHC 562 (Admin), [2010] LGR 678, 116 BMLR 46 (confirmed *R (on the application of Hertfordshire County Council) v London Borough of Hammersmith & Fulham* [2011] EWCA Civ 77, [2011] LGR 536, 119 BMLR 27); and *R (on the application of Sunderland City Council) v South Tyneside Council* [2012] EWCA Civ 1232, [2012] NLJR 1323.

3   The duty is not absolute, and the nature and extent of the services provided is at the discretion of the authority: *R (on the application of K) v Camden and Islington Health Authority* [2001] EWCA Civ 240, [2002] QB 198, [2001] 3 WLR 553. See also *R (on the application of H) v Secretary of State for the Home Department* [2003] UKHL 59, [2004] 2 AC 253, [2004] 1 All ER 412 ('best endeavour principle' with regard to conditions of a discharge confirmed); *W v Doncaster Metropolitan Borough Council* [2004] EWCA Civ 378, [2004] LGR 743, 148 Sol Jo LB 572(authority not in breach of its duty under the Mental Health Act 1983 s 117); *R (on the application of B) v Camden London Borough Council* [2005] EWHC 1366 (Admin), [2006] LGR 19, 85 BMLR 28 (authority under no duty to monitor patients while detained). See also *R v Ealing District Health Authority, ex p Fox* [1993] 3 All ER 170, [1993] 1 WLR 373, 11 BMLR 59; *R v Mental Health Review Tribunal, ex p Hall* [1999] 4 All ER 883, [2000] 1 WLR 1323, 51 BMLR 117.

As to the extent of the duty see *Clunis v Camden and Islington Health Authority* [1998] QB 978, [1998] 3 All ER 180, CA (health authority not liable to a discharged patient for deterioration of his condition consequent upon his killing a stranger once at large; statutory obligations of the health authority to provide him with aftercare did not give rise to a common law duty of care); *W v Doncaster Metropolitan Borough Council* [2004] EWCA Civ 378, [2004] LGR 743 (provided that a local authority used its best endeavours to fulfil any conditions imposed by a mental health review tribunal (see now the appropriate tribunal) in respect of the conditional discharge from a secure hospital of a restricted patient, it will meet its obligations both under the Mental Health Act 1983 s 117 in regard to its duty to provide aftercare to the patient, and under the European Convention on Human Rights and Fundamental Freedoms (Rome, 4 November 1950; TS 71 (1953); Cmd 8969) (see RIGHTS AND FREEDOMS)); *R (on the application of B) v Camden London Borough Council* [2005] EWHC 1366 (Admin), [2005] All ER (D) 43 (Jul) (the Mental Health Act 1983 s 117 does not impose an obligation on authorities to monitor patients whilst detained with a view to the provision of aftercare services; such a duty is only imposed once a person has ceased to be detained and has left hospital). No charge may be made for the services required under the Mental Health Act 1983 s 117: *R (on the application of Stennett) v Manchester City Council, R (on the application of Armstrong) v Redcar and Cleveland Borough Council, R (on the application of Cobham) v Harrow London Borough Council* [2002] UKHL 34, [2002] 2 AC 1127, [2002] 4 All ER 124. A patient is not prevented from paying for their own care as a matter of public policy if they choose to do so: *Coombs v Dorset NHS Primary Care Trust* [2012] EWHC 521 (QB), [2012] NLJR 543.

4   References in the Mental Health Act 1983 to aftercare services provided for a patient under s 117 include references to services provided for the patient in respect of which direct payments are made under regulations under the Health and Social Care Act 2001 s 57 (see SOCIAL SERVICES AND COMMUNITY CARE) or the National Health Service Act 2006 s 12A(4) (see SOCIAL SERVICES AND COMMUNITY CARE) and which would be provided under the Mental Health Act 1983 s 117 apart from the regulations: s 117(2C) (added by the Health Act 2009 Sch 1 para 3). See also *R (on the application of K) v Camden and Islington Health Authority* [2001] EWCA Civ 240, [2002] QB 198, 61 BMLR 173; *R (on the application of Mwanza) v Greenwich London Borough Council* [2010] EWHC 1462 (Admin), [2010] LGR 868, [2011] PTSR 965; *R (on the application of B) v Lambeth London Borough Council* [2006] EWHC 2362 (Admin).

5   See the Mental Health Act 1983 s 117(2) (amended by the National Health Service Reform and Health Care Professions Act 2002 Sch 2 para 47; SI 2007/961). The Mental Health Act 1983 s 117 applies to persons who are detained under s 3 (see PARA 768), or admitted to a hospital in pursuance of a hospital order made under s 37 (see PARAS 864, 866, 868), or transferred to a hospital in pursuance of a hospital direction made under s 45A (see PARA 863) or a transfer direction made under s 47 or 48 (see PARAS 892, 893), and then cease to be detained and (whether or not immediately after so ceasing) leave hospital: s 117(1) (amended by the Mental Health (Patients in the Community) Act 1995 Sch 1 para 15(2); and the Crime (Sentences) Act 1997 Sch 4 para 12(17)). The Mental Health Act 1983 s 32 (see PARA 766) applies for the purposes of s 21 as it applies for the purposes of Pt 2 (ss 2–34): s 117(2B) (added by the Mental Health (Patients in the Community) Act 1995 Sch 1 para 15(4)).

    The local authority also has a duty to carry out an assessment of needs for community care services: see the National Health Service and Community Care Act 1990 s 47; PARA 574 note 2; and SOCIAL SERVICES AND COMMUNITY CARE vol 44(2) (Reissue) PARA 1015 et seq. As to the entitlement to community care assessment see *R (on the application of HP) v Islington London Borough Council* [2004] EWHC 7 (Admin), 82 BMLR 113. See also *R (on the application of B) v Camden London Borough Council* [2005] EWHC 1366 (Admin), [2005] All ER (D) 43 (Jul).

6   See the Mental Health Act 1983 s 117(2) (amended by the Health Authorities Act 1995 s 2(1), Sch 1 para 107(1), (8)(a); the Mental Health (Patients in the Community) Act 1995 s 1(2), Sch 1 para 15(1), (3); the National Health Service Reform and Health Care Professions Act 2002 s 2(5), Sch 2 Pt 2 paras 42, 47; the Mental Health Act 2007 Sch 3 para 24; and SI 2007/961). As to the meaning of 'patient' see PARA 758 note 4. As to the assessment of needs for community care services see the National Health Service and Community Care Act 1990 s 47; and SOCIAL SERVICES AND COMMUNITY CARE vol 44(2) (Reissue) PARA 1015. See also the Nationality, Immigration and Asylum Act 2002 s 54, Sch 3; and IMMIGRATION AND ASYLUM vol 57 (2012) PARA 347.

946.   Payments for aftercare.   For the purpose of securing the provision for a patient of aftercare services[1], payments ('direct payments')[2], may be made, with the patient's consent, to the patient or to a person nominated by the patient, where a pilot scheme is in place[3].

Provision is also made for direct payments in respect of a person securing the provision of certain social care services[4].

1   Ie for the purpose of securing the provision for a patient of services that must be provided under the Mental Health Act 1983 s 117 (see PARA 945).

2   As to the regulations that may be made about direct payments see the National Health Service Act 2006 s 12B; and HEALTH SERVICES.

3   See the National Health Service Act 2006 s 12A(4), (5); and the National Health Service (Direct Payments) Regulations 2010, SI 2010/1000, reg 2. See also HEALTH SERVICES. As to direct payments see further the National Health Service (Direct Payments) Regulations 2010, SI 2010/1000.

4   See the Community Care, Services for Carers and Children's Services (Direct Payments) (England) Regulations 2009, SI 2009/1887; the Community Care, Services for Carers and

Children's Services (Direct Payments) (Wales) Regulations 2011, SI 2011/831; and SOCIAL SERVICES AND COMMUNITY CARE vol 44(2) (Reissue) PARA 1018.

(ii) Assessment of Former Users of Secondary Mental Health Services: Wales

947. Assessment entitlement. An adult[1] is entitled to an assessment[2] if:

(1)   the adult requests either of the local mental health partners for the local authority area[3] in which the adult is usually resident to carry out such an assessment[4];

(2)   the adult has been discharged from secondary mental health services[5] (whether or not the services were the responsibility of the local mental health partner to whom the request for an assessment is made)[6];

(3)   the request is made within the relevant discharge period[7]; and

(4)   the local mental health partner to whom the request is made does not consider the request to be frivolous or vexatious[8].

The assessment must be carried out as soon as reasonably possible after the request referred to above is made[9].

1   As to the meaning of 'adult' see PARA 591 note 4.
2   Ie an assessment as described in the Mental Health (Wales) Measure 2010 s 25 (see PARA 949).
3   As to the meaning of 'local mental health partners' see PARA 586 note 1. As to the meaning of 'local authority area' see PARA 586 note 1.
4   Mental Health (Wales) Measure 2010 s 22(1)(a).
5   As to the meaning of 'secondary mental health services' see PARA 586 note 6. For these purposes an adult has been discharged from secondary mental health services if the adult was being provided with a secondary mental health service or services but is no longer, for whatever reason, being provided with any secondary mental health service: Mental Health (Wales) Measure 2010 s 22(2). The reference to an adult being discharged from secondary mental health services includes a discharge that occurred when the adult was a child: s 22(3). An individual who has ceased to be under the guardianship of a local authority and, upon so ceasing, was not being provided with any secondary mental health service, is to be treated as having been discharged from secondary mental health services on the date on which the individual ceased to be under the guardianship of the local authority: Mental Health (Wales) Measure 2010 s 30.
6   Mental Health (Wales) Measure 2010 s 22(1)(b).
7   Mental Health (Wales) Measure 2010 s 22(1)(c). The relevant discharge period begins on the date on which an adult is discharged from secondary mental health services and ends upon the expiry of a period of three years from that date: s 23(1); Mental Health (Assessment of Former Users of Secondary Mental Health Services) (Wales) Regulations 2011, SI 2011/2500, reg 3(1). The relevant discharge period also ends if, before the expiry of the period of time referred above an event specified in regulations made by the Welsh Ministers occurs: Mental Health (Wales) Measure 2010 s 23(2). But if an adult was discharged from secondary mental health services prior to the date of the coming into force of the Mental Health (Assessment of Former Users of Secondary Mental Health Services) (Wales) Regulations 2011, SI 2011/2500, the relevant discharge period for that adult is as provided in reg 6 (which is the period of time beginning on the coming into force of the Mental Health (Assessment of Former Users of Secondary Mental Health Services) (Wales) Regulations 2011, SI 2011/2500 and ending on the expiry of three years from that adult's date of discharge): see regs 3(2), 6.
8   Mental Health (Wales) Measure 2010 s 22(1)(d).
9   Mental Health (Wales) Measure 2010 s 26(1).

948. Provision of information about assessment entitlement. Where a local health board[1] discharges an adult[2] from secondary mental health services[3], the board must provide the adult with information in writing about entitlement to assessment[4] if, at the date of discharge, no local authority is providing the adult with a secondary mental health service[5].

Where a local authority discharges an adult from secondary mental health services, the authority must provide the adult with information in writing about entitlement to assessment[6] if, at the date of discharge, no local health board is providing the adult with a secondary mental health service[7].

1 As to the meaning of 'local health board' see PARA 575 note 7.
2 As to the meaning of 'adult' see PARA 591 note 4.
3 As to the meaning of 'secondary mental health services' see PARA 586 note 6.
4 Ie entitlement under the Mental Health (Wales) Measure 2010 Pt 3 (ss 19–30).
5 Mental Health (Wales) Measure 2010 s 24(1). Where the relevant discharge period begins when an individual is a child and ends when that individual becomes an adult, the board or authority has the same duty to provide that individual with information about their entitlement to an assessment as it has to provide an adult with such information under s 24(1) and (2): s 24(3). For the purposes of s 24, a Board or authority discharges an individual from secondary mental health services when it implements a decision that the Board or authority no longer needs to provide the individual with any such service: s 24(4).
6 Ie entitlement under the Mental Health (Wales) Measure 2010 Pt 3 (ss 19–30).
7 Mental Health (Wales) Measure 2010 s 24(2). See note 5.

949. Purpose of assessment. An assessment under Part 3[1] of the Mental Health (Wales) Measure 2010 is an analysis of an adult's[2] mental health which identifies:

(1) the secondary mental health services[3] (if any) which might improve or prevent a deterioration in the mental health of the person being assessed[4];

(2) the community care services[5], not being secondary mental health services, (if any) which might improve or prevent a deterioration in the mental health of the person being assessed[6]; and

(3) the housing or well-being services[7] (if any) which might improve or prevent a deterioration in the mental health of the person being assessed[8].

1 Ie under the Mental Health (Wales) Measure 2010 ss 19–30.
2 As to the meaning of 'adult' see PARA 591 note 4.
3 As to the meaning of 'secondary mental health services' see PARA 586 note 6.
4 Mental Health (Wales) Measure 2010 s 25(a).
5 As to the meaning of 'community care services' see the National Health Service and Community Care Act 1990 s 46; and SOCIAL SERVICES AND COMMUNITY CARE vol 44(2) (Reissue) PARA 1012 (definition applied by the Mental Health (Wales) Measure 2010 s 51(1)).
6 Mental Health (Wales) Measure 2010 s 25(b).
7 As to the meaning of 'housing or well-being services' see PARA 587 note 10. As to referrals where housing or well-being have been identified see PARA 954.
8 Mental Health (Wales) Measure 2010 s 25(c). As to referrals relating to housing or well-being services see PARA 954.

950. Assessment arrangements. The local mental health partners for a local authority area[1] must take all reasonable steps to agree arrangements[2]: (1) for the carrying out of assessments[3] for adults[4] who are usually resident in that area and are entitled[5] to such assessments[6]; and (2) the making of referrals[7] following such assessments[8].

The arrangements must identify the extent to which each of the partners is to carry out those assessments and make those referrals[9].

The arrangements may provide that one of the partners is to provide all the assessments and make all the referrals and that different aspects of an assessment, and different referrals following an assessment, will be undertaken by different partners[10].

If the partners cannot agree arrangements under the above provisions: (a) for so long as there is no agreement, the local health board[11] must carry out the assessments[12] and make the referrals[13]; (b) inform the Welsh Ministers that agreement cannot be reached[14]; and (c) the Welsh Ministers may determine arrangements[15].

If one partner wishes to alter the arrangements, but the other does not, the arrangements may, upon a request being made to the Welsh Ministers by either partner, be altered by the Welsh Ministers to such extent as the Welsh Ministers think fit[16].

Unless head (a) above applies, the local mental health partners for a local authority area must carry out assessments and make referrals in accordance with the arrangements for their area[17] or the arrangements for their area determined[18] by the Welsh Ministers[19].

1   As to the meaning of 'local mental health partners' see PARA 586 note 1. As to the meaning of 'local authority area' see PARA 586 note 1. As to the determination of an adult's usual residence see PARA 952. The Welsh Ministers may, by regulations, modify the operation of the Mental Health (Wales) Measure 2010 Pt 3 (ss 19–30) so that schemes can be made for an area wider than a local authority area: see s 46. As to regulations made under s 46 see the Mental Health (Regional Provision) (Wales) Regulations 2012, SI 2012/1244.

2   If arrangements have been agreed, the partners must ensure that the arrangements are recorded in writing: Mental Health (Wales) Measure 2010 s 19(2).

3   Ie in accordance with the Mental Health (Wales) Measure 2010 ss 25, 26 (see PARAS 947, 949, 951).

4   As to the meaning of 'adult' see PARA 591 note 4.

5   Ie entitled under the Mental Health (Wales) Measure 2010 s 22 (see PARA 947).

6   Mental Health (Wales) Measure 2010 s 19(1)(a).

7   Ie referrals described in the Mental Health (Wales) Measure 2010 s 28(1) (see PARA 954).

8   Mental Health (Wales) Measure 2010 s 19(1)(b).

9   Mental Health (Wales) Measure 2010 s 19(3). The partners may alter their arrangements (including arrangements determined by the Welsh Ministers under s 21 and arrangements which have already been altered) if they agree the alterations: s 19(5). If arrangements are altered under s 19(5), the partners must ensure that the alterations are recorded in writing: s 19(6).

10   Mental Health (Wales) Measure 2010 s 19(4).

11   As to the meaning of 'local health board' see PARA 575 note 6.

12   Ie the assessments referred to in the Mental Health (Wales) Measure 2010 s 19(1)(a).

13   Ie the referrals referred to in the Mental Health (Wales) Measure 2010 s 19(1)(b).

14   Mental Health (Wales) Measure 2010 s 21(1)(a), (b).

15   Mental Health (Wales) Measure 2010 s 21(1)(c). If the Welsh Ministers determine arrangements they must record them in writing: s 21(1)(c).

16   Mental Health (Wales) Measure 2010 s 21(2). If the Welsh Ministers alter arrangements under s 21(2), they must record the alterations in writing: s 21(3).

17   Ie as agreed under the Mental Health (Wales) Measure 2010 s 19.

18   Ie determined by the Welsh Ministers under the Mental Health (Wales) Measure 2010 s 21.

19   Mental Health (Wales) Measure 2010 s 20(1). If arrangements have been altered under s 19(5) or 21(2), assessments must be carried out and referrals made in accordance with the altered arrangements: s 20(2).

951. Assessment report. The local mental health partners[1] must ensure that (1) an assessment results in a single report in writing which records whether the assessment has identified any services[2]; and (2) a copy of that report is provided to the adult[3] who has been assessed within such period following completion of the assessment as is specified in regulations made by the Welsh Ministers[4]. Such regulations provide that a copy of an assessment report is to be provided to an adult who has had a mental health assessment no later than ten working days following the completion of the assessment[5].

Where a sole local mental health partner has carried out an assessment[6] the partner must, if it considers it appropriate to do so, provide a copy of the report to the other partner as soon as it is reasonably practicable to do so[7].

1 As to the meaning of 'local mental health partners' see PARA 586 note 1.
2 Ie in accordance with the Mental Health (Wales) Measure 2010 s 25 (see PARA 949).
3 As to the meaning of 'adult' see PARA 591 note 4.
4 Mental Health (Wales) Measure 2010 s 26(2).
5 Mental Health (Assessment of Former Uses of Secondary Mental Health Services) (Wales) Regulations 2011, SI 2011/2500, reg 4(1). For these purposes the copy of the assessment report is provided on the day when it is delivered by hand to an adult or sent by prepaid post addressed to an adult at that adult's usual or last known residence: reg 4(2). As to the determination of that adult's usual residence see PARA 952.
6 Ie an assessment under the Mental Health (Wales) Measure 2010 Pt 3 (ss 19–30).
7 Mental Health (Wales) Measure 2010 s 26(3).

952. Determination of usual residence. For the purposes of the assessment of former users of secondary mental health services[1], any question as to the local authority area[2] in which an adult[3] usually resides is to be determined in accordance with provision in regulations made by the Welsh Ministers[4].

Such regulations provide that where there is a question as to whether an adult's usual residence lies within a local authority area ('local authority area A'), then the local authority for local authority area A ('local authority A') is responsible for determining within which local authority area that adult usually resides in accordance with the following[5]:

(1)   an adult is to be deemed as usually resident at the address given by that adult to local authority A as being the address at which he usually resides[6];

(2)   where an adult gives no such address that adult is to be deemed as usually resident at the address which he gives to local authority A as being his most recent address[7];

(3)   where an adult's usual residence cannot be determined under heads (1) or (2) above, that adult is to be deemed as usually resident in the area in which he is present[8].

Until such time as a determination of an adult's usual residence is made under the above provisions that adult is deemed to be usually resident within local authority area A[9]. However, where the local mental health partners[10] for another local authority area ('local authority area B') agree to act as the local mental health partners for an adult, then that adult is deemed to be usually resident within local authority area B[11].

1   Ie for the purposes of the Mental Health (Wales) Measure 2010 Pt 3 (ss 19–30).
2   As to the meaning of 'local authority area' see PARA 586 note 1.
3   As to the meaning of 'adult' see PARA 591 note 4.
4   Mental Health (Wales) Measure 2010 s 29(1). As to the Welsh Ministers see PARA 567. The provision that may be made in regulations under s 29 (1) includes (but is not limited to) provision conferring power to determine the local authority area in which an adult usually resides and for deeming an adult to be usually resident in an area: s 29(2).
5   Mental Health (Assessment of Former Uses of Secondary Mental Health Services) (Wales) Regulations 2011, SI 2011/2500, reg 5(1).
6   Mental Health (Assessment of Former Uses of Secondary Mental Health Services) (Wales) Regulations 2011, SI 2011/2500, reg 5(2)(a).
7   Mental Health (Assessment of Former Uses of Secondary Mental Health Services) (Wales) Regulations 2011, SI 2011/2500, reg 5(2)(b).
8   Mental Health (Assessment of Former Uses of Secondary Mental Health Services) (Wales) Regulations 2011, SI 2011/2500, reg 5(2)(c).
9   Mental Health (Assessment of Former Uses of Secondary Mental Health Services) (Wales) Regulations 2011, SI 2011/2500, reg 5(3).
10 As to the meaning of 'local mental health partners' see PARA 586 note 1.
11 Mental Health (Assessment of Former Uses of Secondary Mental Health Services) (Wales) Regulations 2011, SI 2011/2500, reg 5(4).

953.   Action following assessment.   Where an assessment[1] has identified secondary mental health services or community care services[2] (not being secondary mental health services) which might help to improve, or prevent a deterioration in, an adult's[3] mental health[4] and one of the local mental health partners[5] would be the responsible authority[6] in relation to any such service, that partner must decide whether the provision of the service is called for[7].

1   Ie an assessment under the Mental Health (Wales) Measure 2010 s 25(a) or (b) (see PARA 949).
2   As to the meaning of 'secondary mental health services' see PARA 586 note 6. As to the meaning of 'community care services' see the National Health Service and Community Care Act 1990 s 46; and SOCIAL SERVICES AND COMMUNITY CARE vol 44(2) (Reissue) PARA 1012 (definition applied by the Mental Health (Wales) Measure 2010 s 51(1)).
3   As to the meaning of 'adult' see PARA 591 note 4.
4   Mental Health (Wales) Measure 2010 s 27(1).
5   As to the meaning of 'local mental health partners' see PARA 586 note 1.
6   For this purpose 'responsible authority' means the authority which would be responsible for providing services if a decision were made to do so: Mental Health (Wales) Measure 2010 s 27(3).
7   Mental Health (Wales) Measure 2010 s 27(2).

954.   Referrals relating to housing or well-being services.   Where a secondary mental health assessment[1] has identified a housing or well-being service[2] which might help to improve, or prevent a deterioration in, an adult's[3] mental health, the partner must ask the responsible service provider[4] to consider whether to provide the service to the adult or, if that is not appropriate, whether to invite the adult to apply for the service[5].

However, where the local authority mental health partner would be the responsible service provider in relation to such a housing or well-being service, the authority must decide whether the provision of the service is called for or, if that is not appropriate, whether to invite the adult to apply for the service[6].

1   Ie under the Mental Health (Wales) Measure 2010 s 25(c) (see PARA 949). As to the meaning of 'secondary mental health services' see PARA 586 note 6.
2   As to the meaning of 'housing or well-being services' see the Mental Health (Wales) Measure 2010 s 50; and PARA 587 note 10.
3   As to the meaning of 'adult' see PARA 591 note 4.
4   For the purposes of the Mental Health (Wales) Measure 2010 s 28(1) and (2), 'responsible service provider' means a person carrying out activities in Wales who would provide the service if a decision were made to do so: s 28(3).
5   Mental Health (Wales) Measure 2010 s 28(1).
6   Mental Health (Wales) Measure 2010 s 28(2).

7. APPLICATIONS TO TRIBUNALS

(1) THE TRIBUNALS

(i) The Appropriate Tribunal

955. The appropriate tribunal: the First-tier Tribunal or the Mental Health Review Tribunal for Wales. Certain matters under the Mental Health Act 1983 may be referred to the appropriate tribunal[1]. The appropriate tribunal is, in relation to England, the First-tier Tribunal[2] or, in relation to Wales, the Mental Health Review Tribunal for Wales[3].

1   As to the matters which may be referred to the appropriate tribunal see the Mental Health Act 1983 s 66; and PARA 960.
2   See PARA 956. The Mental Health Review Tribunal has been abolished in relation to England and its functions transferred to the First-tier Tribunal: see the Tribunals, Courts and Enforcement Act 2007 s 30(1); the Transfer of Functions Order 2008, SI 2008/2833, art 4, Sch 1; and COURTS AND TRIBUNALS vol 24 (2010) PARA 866. As to the First-tier Tribunal see PARA 956.
3   See the Mental Health Act 1983 ss 66(4), 145(1) (s 66(4) and the definition of 'appropriate tribunal' in s 145(1) both added by SI 2008/2833). As to the Mental Health Review Tribunal for Wales see PARA 957.

(ii) First-tier Tribunal

956. The First-tier Tribunal (Health, Education and Social Care Chamber). In relation to England, the Health, Education and Social Care chamber of the First-tier Tribunal[1] has jurisdiction over appeals formerly heard by the Mental Health Review Tribunal[2] and deals with applications and references by and in respect of patients under the provisions of the Mental Health Act 1983[3]. However, at any point during proceedings the Chamber President[4] may allocate the matter to another chamber within the same tribunal[5].

1   See the First-tier Tribunal and Upper Tribunal (Chambers) Order 2010, SI 2010/2655, art 4; see COURTS AND TRIBUNALS vol 24 (2010) PARA 874.
2   See COURTS AND TRIBUNALS vol 24 (2010) PARA 876.
3   See the First-tier Tribunal and Upper Tribunal (Chambers) Order 2010, SI 2010/2655, art 4(i); and COURTS AND TRIBUNALS vol 24 (2010) PARA 879.
4   As to the Senior President of the Tribunals see COURTS AND TRIBUNALS vol 24 (2010) PARA 867.
5   See the First-tier Tribunal and Upper Tribunal (Chambers) Order 2010, SI 2010/2655, art 15; and COURTS AND TRIBUNALS.

(iii) Mental Health Review Tribunal for Wales

957. Mental Health Review Tribunal for Wales. The Mental Health Review Tribunal for Wales[1], has the purpose of dealing with applications and references by and in respect of patients under the provisions of the Mental Health Act 1983[2].

1   See the Mental Health Act 1983 s 65(1) (s 65(1) substituted and s 65(1A)–(1C) added by the Health Authorities Act 1995 Sch 1 para 107(6); the Mental Health Act 1983 s 65(1), (1A), (2), (3) amended and s 65(4) added by SI 2008/2833). As to the constitution of the tribunal see the Mental Health Act 1983 s 65(3), Sch 2 (amended by the Judicial Pensions and Retirement Act 1993 Sch 6 para 40, the Constitutional Reform Act 2005 Sch 4 para 158, Sch 18 Pt 2, the Mental Health Act 2007 s 38(5)–(8), SI 2008/2833, SI 2009/1307). As to the remuneration of

members of the tribunal see the Mental Health Act 1983 s 65(4) (as substituted). As to the appointment of the tribunal see the Mental Health Review Tribunal for Wales Rules 2008, SI 2008/2705, r 11.

2   Mental Health Act 1983 s 65(2) (as amended: see note 1). As appeals against a decision of the Mental Health Review Tribunal for Wales see PARA 958.

(iv) Further Appeals

958.   Further appeals to Upper Tribunal.   An appeal against a decision of the Mental Health Review Tribunal for Wales[1] lies to the Upper Tribunal[2]. A party to any proceedings before the Mental Health Review Tribunal for Wales may appeal to the Upper Tribunal on any point of law arising from a decision made by the Mental Health Review Tribunal for Wales in those proceedings[3].

Such an appeal may be brought only if, on an application made by the party concerned, the Mental Health Review Tribunal for Wales or the Upper Tribunal has given its permission for the appeal to be brought[4].

The Upper Tribunal also has jurisdiction to hear appeals from the First-tier Tribunal[5].

1   As to the Mental Health Review Tribunal for Wales see PARA 957.
2   See the Transfer of Functions Order 2008, SI 2008/2833, art 6(1), (2)(a).
3   Mental Health Act 1983 s 78A(1) (s 78A added by SI 2008/2833).
4   Mental Health Act 1983 s 78A(2) (as added: see note 3). As to proceedings on appeal to the Upper Tribunal see the Tribunals, Courts and Enforcement Act 2007 s 12 (see COURTS AND TRIBUNALS vol 24 (2010) PARA 928) which applies in relation to appeals to the Upper Tribunal under the Mental Health Act 1983 s 78A as it applies to appeals under the Tribunals, Courts and Enforcement Act 2007 s 11, but as if references to the First-tier Tribunal were references to the Mental Health Review Tribunal for Wales: see s 78A(3) (as so added).
5   See COURTS AND TRIBUNALS vol 24 (2010) PARA 883.

(2) APPLICATIONS AND REFERENCES

959.   Right to make applications.   Applications to the appropriate tribunal[1] by or on behalf of a patient under the Mental Health Act 1983 may only be made in such cases and at such times as are expressly authorised[2]; and, where an application is so authorised to be made within a specified period, only one such application may be made within that period[3], but disregarding any application which is withdrawn in accordance with rules[4].

1   As to the meaning of 'appropriate tribunal' see PARA 955.
2   Mental Health Act 1983 s 77(1) (amended by SI 2008/2833). See PARA 961 et seq.
3   Mental Health Act 1983 s 77(1), (2) (amended by SI 2008/2833).
4   Mental Health Act 1983 s 77(2) (amended by SI 2009/1307). The rules referred to in the text are the Tribunal Procedure Rules or rules made under the Mental Health Act 1983 s 78 (see PARAS 980 et seq). For rules as to withdrawal of applications see PARAS 964, 988.

960.   Applications to tribunals concerning Part 2 Patients.   In regard to Part 2 Mental Health Act 1983[1] patients[2], an application to the appropriate tribunal[3] may be made by the following persons ('applicants') within the specified periods:

(1)   by a patient who is admitted to hospital[4] in pursuance of an application for admission for assessment[5], within 14 days of admission[6];

(2)   by a patient who is admitted to hospital in pursuance of an application for treatment[7], within six months of admission[8];

(3)   by a patient received into guardianship in pursuance of a guardianship application[9], within six months of acceptance of the application[10];

(4)		by a patient in respect of whom a community treatment order is made[11], within six months beginning with the day on which the community treatment order was made[12];

(5)		by a patient in respect of whom a community treatment order is revoked[13], within six months beginning on the day on which the community treatment order is revoked[14];

(6)		by a patient having been transferred from guardianship to hospital[15], within six months of the transfer[16];

(7)		by a patient where a report has been furnished for renewal of his detention or guardianship[17] and he has not been discharged[18], within the period or periods for which authority for detention or guardianship has been renewed by virtue of the report[19];

(8)		by a patient where a report has been furnished for extending the community treatment period of his community treatment order[20] and the patient is not discharged[21], within the period or periods for which the community treatment period for which the community treatment period is extended by virtue of the report[22];

(9)		by a patient where a report is furnished when the patient returns to hospital or the place where he should be[23] and he would have ceased to be liable to be detained or subject to guardianship on or before the day on which the report is furnished[24] or where he would have ceased to be liable to be detained or subject to guardianship on or before the day on which the report is furnished and renewed authority for his detention or guardianship expires on or before the day on which the report is furnished[25], within the period for which authority for detention or guardianship has been renewed by virtue of the report[26];

(10)	by a patient where a report is furnished when the patient returns to hospital or the place where he should be[27] and where a community treatment order ceases to be in force on or before the day on which a report is duly furnished in respect of him[28] or where a community treatment order ceases to be in force on or before the day on which a report is duly furnished in respect of him and the extended period would expire on or before the day on which the report is furnished[29], the period or periods for which the community treatment period is extended by virtue of the report[30];

(11)	by a patient's nearest relative[31] where a report barring discharge by the nearest relative has been furnished[32] in respect of a patient detained in pursuance of an application for admission for treatment or a community patient[33], within 28 days of the applicant's being informed that the report has been furnished[34];

(12)	by a patient's nearest relative[35] where an order has been made[36] appointing an acting nearest relative in respect of a patient who is, or who subsequently becomes, liable to be detained or subject to guardianship or who is a community patient, within 12 months beginning with the date of the order and in any subsequent 12 months during which the order continues in force[37].

1	Ie the Mental Health Act 1983 Pt 2 (ss 2–34).
2	As to the meaning of 'patient' see PARA 758 note 4.
3	As to the meaning of 'appropriate tribunal' see PARA 955.
4	For the purposes of the Mental Health Act 1983 Pt 5 (ss 65–79), unless the context otherwise requires, 'hospital' means a hospital as defined in PARA 577: s 79(6).

5 Ie under the Mental Health Act 1983 s 2: see PARA 767. See *R (on the application of MH) v Secretary of State for Health* [2005] UKHL 60, [2006] 1 AC 441, [2005] 4 All ER 1311; and PARA 842 note 27.

6 Mental Health Act 1983 s 66(1)(a), (i), (2)(a). If the patient's status changes to s 3 (admission for treatment: see PARA 768) before an application under s 2 (admission for assessment: see PARA 767) is heard he does not lose his right to a hearing using the discharge criteria for s 3 under s 72(1)(b) (see PARA 967); he can still make an application to a mental health review tribunal under s 66(1)(b), (i), (2)(b) (see head (2) in the text) if unsuccessful: see *R v Mental Health Review Tribunal for the South Thames Region, ex p Smith* (1998) 47 BMLR 104. The Mental Health Act 1983 s 32 (see PARA 765) applies for the purposes of s 66 as it applies for the purposes of Pt 2 (ss 2–34): s 66(3). For provision determining to which of those tribunals applications by or in respect of a patient under the Mental Health Act 1983 must be made, see s 77(3), (4): s 66(5) (added by SI 2008/2833).

7 Ie under the Mental Health Act 1983 s 3: see PARA 768.

8 Mental Health Act 1983 s 66(1)(b), (i), (2)(b). See note 6. Nothing in s 66(1)(b) entitles a community patient to make an application by virtue of that provision even if he is admitted to a hospital on being recalled there under s 17E (see PARA 801): s 66(2A) (added by the Mental Health Act 2007 Sch 3 para 18(4)).

9 Ie under the Mental Health Act 1983 s 7: see PARA 785.

10 Mental Health Act 1983 s 66(1)(c), (i), (2)(c) (amended by the Mental Health Act 2007 s 36(3)).

11 Ie under the Mental Health Act1983 s 17A: see PARA 797.

12 Mental Health Act 1983 s 66(1)(ca), (i), (2)(ca) (s 66(1)(ca), (cb), (2)(ca), (cb) added by the Mental Health Act 2007 Sch 3 para 18(2)(a), (3)(a)).

13 Mental Health Act 1983 s 17F: see PARA 802.

14 Mental Health Act 1983 s 66(1)(cb), (i), (2)(cb) (as added: see note 12).

15 Ie in pursuance of regulations made under the Mental Health Act 1983 s 19: see PARA 889.

16 Mental Health Act 1983 s 66(1)(e), (i), (2)(e).

17 Ie pursuant to the Mental Health Act 1983 s 20: see PARAS 908–910.

18 Ie discharged under the Mental Health Act 1983 s 23 (see PARA 913).

19 Mental Health Act 1983 s 66(1)(f), (i), (2)(f) (s 66(1)(f) amended by the Mental Health Act 2007 Sch 3 para 18(2)(b); and the Mental Health Act 1983 s 66(2)(f) amended by the Mental Health (Patients in the Community) Act 1995 ss 1(2), 2(6)(b), Sch 1 para 7(4)).

20 Ie a report is furnished under the Mental Health Act 1983 s 20A: see PARA 799.

21 Ie discharged under the Mental Health Act 1983 s 23 (see PARA 913).

22 Mental Health Act 1983 s 66(1)(fza), (i), (2)(fza) (s 66(1)(fza), (faa), (2)(fza) added by the Mental Health Act 2007 Sch 3 para 18(2)(c), (d), (3)(b)).

23 Ie under the Mental Health Act 1983 s 21B(2): see PARA 911.

24 Ie the Mental Health Act 1983 s 21B(5) applies: see PARA 911.

25 Ie under the Mental Health Act 1983 s 21B(5), (6)(b): see PARA 911.

26 Mental Health Act 1983 s 66(1)(fa), (i), (2)(f) (amended by the Mental Health (Patients in the Community) Act 1995 s 2(6)).

27 Ie under the Mental Health Act 1983 s 21B(2): see PARA 911.

28 Ie under the Mental Health Act 1983 s 21B(6A): see PARA 911.

29 Ie under the Mental Health Act 1983 s 21B(6A) and (6B)(b): see PARA 911.

30 Mental Health Act 1983 s 66(1)(faa), (i), (2)(fza) (as added: see note 22).

31 As to the meaning of 'nearest relative' see PARA 839.

32 Ie pursuant to the Mental Health Act 1983 s 25: see PARA 915.

33 As to the meaning of 'community patient' see PARA 797 note 4.

34 Mental Health Act 1983 s 66(1)(g), (ii), (2)(d) (amended by the Mental Health (Patients in the Community) Act 1995 s 2(6)).

35 See note 31.

36 Ie pursuant to the Mental Health Act 1983 s 29 on a ground specified under s 29(3)(c) or (d): see PARA 842.

37 Mental Health Act 1983 s 66(1)(h), (ii), (2)(g) (s 66(1)(h) amended by the Mental Health Act 2007 Sch 3 para 18(2)(f)).

961. Applications to tribunals concerning Part 3 patients. A patient[1] who is subject to Part 3 of the Mental Health Act 1983[2] (that is, provisions relating to criminal offenders) who is admitted to hospital[3] in pursuance of a hospital order or who is placed under guardianship by a guardianship order, and who thus falls to be treated as a patient under Part 2 of the Mental Health Act 1983 for certain purposes[4], has the same rights of application to an appropriate tribunal[5] as Part 2 patients under certain[6] provisions[7].

In regard to patients under the Mental Health Act 1983 Part 3, an application to an appropriate tribunal may also be made by the following persons ('applicants') within the specified periods[8]:

(1)　　by a patient liable to be detained in pursuance of a hospital order or a community patient[9] who was so liable immediately before he became a community patient, by the nearest relative[10] of the patient in any period in which an application may be made by the patient under any such provision as so applied[11];

(2)　　by a patient placed under guardianship by a guardianship order[12], within six months beginning with the date of the order[13];

(3)　　by the nearest relative of a patient placed under guardianship by a guardianship order[14], within 12 months beginning with the date of the order, and in any subsequent period of 12 months[15];

(4)　　by a patient who is treated as subject to a hospital order, hospital direction or transfer direction, either when a restriction order ceases to have effect while a hospital order remains in force, or when he is transferred to a hospital in England and Wales[16] from Northern Ireland, the Channel Islands, the Isle of Man or Scotland, or when an order for his admission to hospital is made following a special verdict or findings that he is under a disability[17], within six months beginning with the date of the order or direction[18];

(5)　　by a patient who is subject to a direction transferring him to hospital[19], within six months beginning with the date of the direction[20].

1　　As to the meaning of 'patient' see PARA 758 note 4.
2　　Ie the Mental Health Act 1983 ss 35–55.
3　　For the purposes of the Mental Health Act 1983 Pt 5 (ss 65–79), unless the context otherwise requires, 'hospital' means a hospital as defined in PARA 577: s 79(6).
4　　See the Mental Health Act 1983 s 40(4).
5　　Ie under the Mental Health Act 1983 s 66(1)(ca), (cb), (e), (f), (fa), (fza), (faa), (i), (2)(ca), (cb), (e), (f), (fza) (see PARA 960) (as applied by s 40(4) and modified by Sch 1 para 9 (see note 7)). The provisions of s 66 as applied by s 40(4) are subject to s 69(4): s 69(3) (s 69(3)–(5) added by the Mental Health Act 2007 Sch 3 para 20(c)). If the initial detention period has not elapsed when the relevant application period begins, the right of a hospital order patient to make an application by virtue of the Mental Health Act 1983 s 66(1)(ca) or (cb) is exercisable only during whatever remains of the relevant application period after the initial detention period has elapsed: s 69(4) (as so added). For these purposes 'hospital order patient' means a patient who is subject to a hospital order, excluding a patient of a kind mentioned in s 69(2)(a) or (b) (see text to notes 16–20); 'the initial detention period', in relation to a hospital order patient, means the period of 6 months beginning with the date of the hospital order; and 'the relevant application period' means the relevant period mentioned in s 66(2)(ca) or (cb), as the case may be: s 69(5)
6　　As to the meaning of 'appropriate tribunal' see PARA 955.
7　　See the Mental Health Act 1983 s 40(4), Sch 1 Pt I para 9 (amended by the Mental Health (Patients in the Community) Act 1995 Sch 1 para 14).
8　　Mental Health Act 1983 s 69(1) (amended by SI 2008/2833).
9　　As to the meaning of 'community patient' see PARA 797 note 4.
10　As to the meaning of 'nearest relative' see PARA 839.
11　Mental Health Act 1983 s 69(1)(a) (substituted by the Mental Health Act 2007 Sch 3 para 20(a)).
12　Ie under the Mental Health Act 1983 s 37: see PARA 877.
13　Mental Health Act 1983 s 69(1)(b)(i).
14　Ie under the Mental Health Act 1983 s 37: see PARA 877.
15　Mental Health Act 1983 s 69(1)(b)(ii).
16　As to the meaning of 'England' see PARA 557 note 4. As to the meaning of 'Wales' see PARA 557 note 5.

17 Ie by virtue of the Mental Health Act 1983 s 41(5) (see PARA 870), s 80B(2) (see PARA 900), s 82(2) (see PARA 904) or s 85(2) (see PARA 905).
18 Mental Health Act 1983 s 69(2)(a) (amended by the Mental Health Act 2007 Sch 5 para 18(b)).
19 Ie by virtue of the Mental Health Act 1983 s 47(3) (see PARA 892), s 48(3) (see PARA 893).
20 Mental Health Act 1983 s 69(2)(b).

962. Applications to tribunals concerning restricted patients. A patient[1] who is a restricted patient[2] and is detained in a hospital[3] may apply to the appropriate tribunal[4] in the period between the expiration of six months and the expiration of 12 months beginning with the date of the relevant hospital order, hospital direction or transfer direction[5] and in any subsequent period of 12 months[6]. Where a restricted patient has been conditionally discharged[7] but has not been recalled to hospital he may apply to the appropriate tribunal in the period between the expiry of 12 months and the expiry of two years beginning with the date on which he was conditionally discharged, and in any subsequent period of two years[8].

1 As to the meaning of 'patient' see PARA 758 note 4. For the purposes of the Mental Health Act 1983 Pt 5 (ss 65–79), 'restricted patient' means a patient who is subject to a restriction order, limitation direction or restriction direction (see PARA 869) and Pt 5, subject to the provisions of s 79, has effect in relation to any person who is treated by virtue of any enactment as subject to a hospital order and a restriction order or who is treated as subject to a hospital order and a restriction order, or to a hospital direction and a limitation direction, or to a transfer direction and a restriction direction, by virtue of any provision of Pt 6 (ss 80–92) (except s 80D(3), 82A(2) or 85A(2) (see PARAS 902, 904, 905)), as it has effect in relation to a restricted patient: s 79(1) (amended by the Crime (Sentences) Act 1997 s 55, Sch 4 para 12(14); the Domestic Violence, Crime and Victims Act 2004 Sch 10 para 21, Sch 11; and the Mental Health Act 2007 Sch 5 para 19(2)). The Mental Health Act 1983 s 75 also have effect in relation to a qualifying patient subject to modifications: see s 79(5A)–(5C) (added by the Mental Health Act 2007 Sch 5 para 19(4)). For these purposes 'a qualifying patient' is a patient who is treated by virtue of the Mental Health Act 1983 ss 80D(3), 82A(2) or 85A(2) (see PARAS 902, 904, 905) as if he had been conditionally discharged and were subject to a hospital order and a restriction order, or to a hospital direction and a limitation direction, or to a transfer direction and a restriction direction: s 79(5B) (as so added).
2 Ie within the meaning of the Mental Health Act 1983 s 79 (see note 1).
3 As to the meaning of 'hospital' for these purposes see PARA 961 note 3; and see also PARA 577.
4 As to the meaning of 'appropriate tribunal' see PARA 955.
5 Subject to the Mental Health Act 1983 s 77(3)–(6) 'the relevant hospital order', 'the relevant hospital direction' and 'the relevant transfer direction', in relation to a restricted patient, mean the hospital order, the hospital direction or transfer direction by virtue of which he is liable to be detained in a hospital: s 79(2) (amended by the Crime (Sentences) Act 1997 Sch 4 para 12(15)).
6 Mental Health Act 1983 s 70 (amended by the Crime (Sentences) Act 1997 Sch 4 para 12(9); and SI 2008/2833). Where a conditionally discharged restricted patient is recalled to hospital, this applies to him as if the relevant hospital order, hospital direction or transfer direction had been made on the day on which he returned or was returned to hospital: Mental Health Act 1983 s 75(1)(b) (amended by the Crime (Sentences) Act 1997 Sch 4 para 12(13)).
7 As to conditional discharge of restricted patients see PARA 914.
8 Mental Health Act 1983 s 75(2) (amended by SI 2008/2833). Any application under the Mental Health Act 1983 s 75(2) must be made to the First-tier Tribunal where the patient resides in England and to the Mental Health Review Tribunal for Wales where the patient resides in Wales: s 77(4) (amended by SI 2008/2833).

963. Visiting and examination of patients. For the purpose of advising whether an application to the appropriate tribunal[1] should be made by or in respect of a patient[2] who is liable to be detained or subject to guardianship[3], or a community patient[4] or of furnishing information for the purposes of such an application[5], any registered medical practitioner[6] or approved clinician[7] authorised by or on behalf of the patient or other person who is entitled to make, or has made, the application may at any reasonable time visit the patient and examine him in private, and may require production of and inspect any records relating to the detention and treatment of the patient in any hospital[8] or relating to any after-care services provided for the patient[9]. Equivalent provision is made for the purpose of furnishing information for the purpose of any reference to a tribunal by the hospital managers[10] or by the appropriate national authority[11].

1   As to the meaning of 'appropriate tribunal' see PARA 955.
2   For the meaning of 'patient' see PARA 758 note 4.
3   Ie under the Mental Health Act 1983 Pt 2 (ss 2–34).
4   As to the meaning of 'community patient' see PARA 797 note 4.
5   Although the doctor is instructed by or on behalf of the patient, the public and private interest in maintaining the confidentiality of communications between them must be balanced against the public interest in limited disclosure of information vital to the protection of the public; hence an independent psychiatrist instructed to prepare a report with a view to a tribunal application by a restricted patient who had shot and killed five people and wounded two others was justified in sending his report to the responsible authority: *W v Egdell* [1990] Ch 359, [1990] 1 All ER 835, CA.
6   As to registered medical practitioners see MEDICAL PROFESSIONS vol 74 (2011) PARA 176 et seq.
7   As to the meaning of 'approved clinician' see PARA 831.
8   For the purposes of the Mental Health Act 1983 Pt 5 (ss 65–79), unless the context otherwise requires, 'hospital' means a hospital as defined in PARA 577: s 79(6).
9   Mental Health Act 1983 s 76(1) (amended by the Mental Health (Patients in the Community) Act 1995 s 1(2), Sch 1 para 11; the Mental Health Act 2007 s 13(2)(b), Sch 3 para 22, Sch 11 Pt 5; SI 2008/2833). The Mental Health Act 1983 s 32 (making of regulations: see PARA 766) applies for the purposes of s 76 as it applies for the purposes of Pt 2: s 76(2).
10 Mental Health Act 1983 s 68(8) (substituted by the Mental Health Act 2007 37(3)). As to such references see PARA 964. As to the meaning of 'managers' see PARA 778.
11 Mental Health Act 1983 s 67(2) (amended by the Mental Health (Patients in the Community) Act 1995 Sch 1 para 8; and the Mental Health Act 2007 s 13(2)(a)). As to such references see PARA 965. There is no such provision in respect of references relating to restricted patients under the Mental Health Act 1983 s 71 (see PARA 965). As to the appropriate national authority see PARA 567.

964.   Duty of hospital managers to refer cases to tribunals.   Where a patient[1] who is admitted to hospital[2] in pursuance of an application for admission or for treatment[3] or a community patient[4], or a patient whose community treatment order is revoked[5] or a patient who is transferred from guardianship to hospital[6], the managers[7] of the hospital must refer the patient's case[8] to the appropriate tribunal on expiry of the period of six months[9] beginning with the applicable day[10]. The managers of the hospital must also refer the patient's case to the appropriate tribunal if a period of more than three years[11] (or, if the patient has not attained the age of 18 years, one year) has elapsed since his case was last considered by such a tribunal, whether on his own application or otherwise[12].

A person who applies to a tribunal but subsequently withdraws his application is treated for these purposes as not having exercised his right to apply, and if he withdraws his application on a date after expiry of the period[13], the managers must refer the patient's case as soon as possible after that date[14].

1   As to the meaning of 'patient' see PARA 758 note 4.
2   As to the meaning of 'hospital' for these purposes see PARA 961 note 3; and see also PARA 577.
3   Ie under the Mental Health Act 1983 s 3 (see PARA 768).
4   As to the meaning of 'community patient' see PARA 797 note 4.
5   Ie revoked under the Mental Health Act 1983 s 17F (see PARA 802). If, in the case of a community patient, the community treatment order is revoked under s 17F, the managers of the hospital must also refer the patient's case to the appropriate tribunal as soon as possible after the order is revoked: s 68(7) (s 68 substituted and s 68A added by the Mental Health Act 2007 s 37(3)). As to the meaning of 'the appropriate tribunal' see PARA 955.
6   Ie in pursuance of regulations made under the Mental Health Act 1983 s 19 (see PARA 886 et seq).

7   As to the meaning of 'managers' see PARA 778. Reference in the Mental Health Act 1983 s 68 to the managers of the hospital, in relation to a community patient, is to the managers of the responsible hospital and, in relation to any other patient, is to the managers of the hospital in which he is liable to be detained: s 68(9) (as substituted: see note 5).

8   No such reference may be made, however, if during that period: (1) any right has been exercised by or in respect of the patient by virtue of any of the Mental Health Act 1983 s 66(1)(b), (ca), (cb), (e), (g) or (h) (see PARA 960); (2) a reference has been made in respect of the patient under s 67(1) (see PARA 965), not being a reference made while the patient is or was liable to be detained in pursuance of an application for admission for assessment; or (3) a reference has been made in respect of the patient under s 68(7): s 68(3) (as substituted: see note 5). As to the furnishing of information for the purposes of a reference under s 68 see s 68(8); and PARA 963.

9   The appropriate national authority may from time to time by order amend the Mental Health Act 1983 s 68(2) or (6) so as to substitute for a period mentioned there such shorter period as is specified in the order: s 68A(1) (as added: see note 5). Such an order may include such transitional, consequential, incidental or supplemental provision as the appropriate national authority thinks fit and may, in particular, make provision for a case where a patient in respect of whom s 68(1) applies is, or is about to be, transferred from England to Wales or from Wales to England; and the period by reference to which s 68(2) or (6) operates for the purposes of the patient's case is not the same in one territory as it is in the other: s 68A(2) (as so added). A patient is transferred from one territory to the other if:

    (1)   he is transferred from a hospital, or from guardianship, in one territory to a hospital in the other in pursuance of regulations made under s 19 (see PARA 886 et seq) (s 68A(3)(a) (as so added));

    (2)   he is removed under s 19(3) (see PARA 887) from a hospital or accommodation in one territory to a hospital or accommodation in the other (s 68A(3)(b) (as so added));

    (3)   he is a community patient responsibility for whom is assigned from a hospital in one territory to a hospital in the other in pursuance of regulations made under s 19A (see PARA 804) (s 68A(3)(c) (as so added)); or

    (4)   on the revocation of a community treatment order in respect of him under s 17F (see PARA 802) he is detained in a hospital in the territory other than the one in which the responsible hospital was situated (s 68A(3)(d) (as so added)).

Provision made by virtue of heads (1)–(4) above may require or authorise the managers of a hospital determined in accordance with the order to refer the patient's case to the appropriate tribunal: s 68A(5) (as so added; amended by SI 2008/2833).

In so far as making provision by virtue of heads (1)–(4) above, the order may make different provision for different cases and may make provision which applies subject to specified exceptions: Mental Health Act 1983 s 68A(6) (as so added). Where the appropriate national authority for one territory makes an order under s 68A(1), the appropriate national authority for the other territory may by order make such provision in consequence of the order as it thinks fit and such an order may, in particular, make provision for a case within s 68A(3) (and s 68A(4)–(6) apply accordingly): s 68A(7), (8) (as so added). For the purposes of s 68A 'the appropriate national authority' means, in relation to a hospital in England, the Secretary of State and, in relation to a hospital in Wales, the Welsh Ministers: s 68A(9) (as so added).

10   See the Mental Health Act 1983 s 68(1), (2) (as substituted (see note 5); s 68(2) amended by SI 2008/2833. For the purposes of the Mental Health Act 1983 s 68(2) 'the applicable day' means:

    (1)   in the case of a patient who is admitted to a hospital in pursuance of an application for admission for assessment, the day on which the patient was so admitted (s 68(5)(a) (as so substituted));

    (2)   in the case of a patient who is admitted to a hospital in pursuance of an application for admission for treatment: (a) the day on which the patient was so admitted; or (b) if, when he was so admitted, he was already liable to be detained in pursuance of an application for admission for assessment, the day on which he was originally admitted in pursuance of the application for admission for assessment (s 68(5)(b) (as so substituted));

    (3)   in the case of a community patient or a patient whose community treatment order is revoked under s 17F (see PARA 802), the day mentioned in head (2)(a) or (b) above as the case may be (s 68(5)(c) (as so substituted));

    (4)   in the case of a patient who is transferred from guardianship to a hospital, the day on which he was so transferred (s 68(5)(d) (as so substituted)).

11   See note 9.

12   Mental Health Act 1983 68(6) (as substituted (see note 5); amended by SI 2008/2833.

13 Ie the date mentioned in the Mental Health Act 1983 s 68(2).
~~14 Mental Health Act 1983 s 68(4) (as substituted: see note 5).~~

965. Powers and duties of the appropriate national authority to refer cases to tribunals. The appropriate national authority[1] may, if it thinks fit, at any time refer to the appropriate tribunal[2] the case of a patient[3] who is liable[4] to be detained or subject to guardianship or of any community patient[5].

The appropriate national authority may at any time refer the case of a restricted patient[6] to the appropriate tribunal[7]. However, it must refer to a tribunal: (1) any restricted patient detained in a hospital[8] whose case has not been considered by a tribunal, whether on his own application or otherwise, within the last three years[9]; and (2) any conditionally discharged[10] restricted patient who is recalled to hospital[11], within one month of the day of which he returns or is returned to hospital[12].

1   As to the appropriate national authority see PARA 567.
2   As to the meaning of 'appropriate tribunal' see PARA 955.
3   For the meaning of 'patient' see PARA 758 note 4.
4   Such liability is under the Mental Health Act 1983 Pt 2 (ss 2–34).
5   Mental Health Act 1983 s 67(1) (amended by the Mental Health (Patients in the Community) Act 1995 s 1(2), Sch 1 para 8; Mental Health Act 2007 Sch 3 para 19, Sch 11 Pt 5; SI 2008/2833). This provision also applies to patients subject to hospital orders without restrictions, guardianship orders, and orders having the same effect: Mental Health Act 1983 ss 40(4), 55(4), Sch 1 Pt I para 1; and see PARAS 860–861. As to independent visiting and examination of the patient see PARA 963. As to the meaning of 'community patient' see PARA 797 note 4.
6   As to the meaning of 'restricted patient' see PARA 962 note 1.
7   Mental Health Act 1983 s 71(1) (amended by SI 2008/2833). Any such reference relating to a conditionally discharged patient who has not been recalled to hospital must be made to the tribunal for the area in which he resides: Mental Health Act 1983 s 71(4). See note 8.
8   As to the meaning of 'hospital' for these purposes see PARA 961 note 3; and see also PARA 577.
9   Mental Health Act 1983 s 71(2) (amended by SI 2008/2833). This period may be varied by order which may include transitional, consequential, incidental or supplemental provisions: see the Mental Health Act 1983 s 71(3), (3A) (s 71(3A) added by the Mental Health Act 2007 s 37(4)).
10 Ie under the Mental Health Act 1983 s 42(2) (see PARA 914) or ss 73, 74 (see PARAS 969–970).
11 As to the power to recall conditionally discharged patients to hospital see PARA 914.
12 Mental Health Act 1983 s 75(1)(a) (amended by SI 2008/2833). This provision was enacted as a direct result of the decision of the European Court of Human Rights in the case of *X v United Kingdom* (1981) 4 EHRR 188, that a person detained following recall to hospital is entitled, under the Convention for the Protection of Human Rights and Fundamental Freedoms (Rome, 4 November 1950; TS 71 (1953) Cmd 8969) art 5(4) (see RIGHTS AND FREEDOMS), to take proceedings whereby the lawfulness of his detention may be decided speedily by a court and his release ordered if the detention is not lawful. The provision was examined in *R (on the application of C) v Secretary of State for the Home Department* [2001] EWHC 501 (Admin) (at first instance). In the event of a change of circumstances of a patient given a conditional discharge by a mental health review tribunal, the correct procedure is to invite the tribunal to reconsider its decision: see *R (on the application of C) v Secretary of State for the Home Department* [2002] EWCA Civ 647, (2002) Times, 24 May; *R (on the application of IH) v Secretary of State for the Home Department* [2002] EWCA Civ 646, [2003] QB 320, [2002] 3 WLR 967; *R (on the application of Rayner) v Secretary of State for the Home Department* [2008] EWCA Civ 176, [2009] 1 WLR 310, 101 BMLR 83.

966. Practice directions. A practice direction has been made in relation to proceedings brought under the Mental Health Act 1983[1]. If the patient is an in-patient[2] the responsible authority must send or deliver to the tribunal a statement of information about the patient[3], a responsible clinician's report[4], an in-patient nursing report[5] and a social circumstances report[6]. If the patient is a community patient[7] the responsible authority must send or deliver to the tribunal a statement of information about the patient[8], a responsible clinician's report[9] and a social circumstances report[10]. If the patient has been received into guardianship[11] the responsible authority must send or deliver to the tribunal a statement of information about the patient[12], a responsible clinician's report[13] and a social circumstances report[14].

On being notified by the tribunal of an application or reference in relation to a conditionally discharged patient[15], the responsible clinician must send or deliver a responsible clinician's report[16] and any social supervisor must send or deliver a social circumstances report[17].

All the above requirements apply, as appropriate, to patients under 18[18].

1   Ie *Practice Direction (First-tier Tribunal: mental health cases)* (6 April 2012).
2   For these purposes a patient is an in-patient if they are in hospital to be assessed or treated for a mental disorder, even if treatment is being provided informally, or under a provision other than that to which the application or reference to the tribunal relates: *Practice Direction (First-tier Tribunal: mental health cases)* (6 April 2012, unreported) Part A para 3. A patient is also an in-patient if he is detained in hospital through the criminal justice system, or if he has been transferred to hospital from a custodial establishment. This includes patients detained under a hospital order or removed to hospital from prison, whether or not the patient is also a restricted patient: Part A para 4. In the case of a restricted patient detained in hospital, the tribunal may make a provisional decision to order a conditional discharge, but before it finally grants a conditional discharge, the tribunal may defer its decision so that arrangements to its satisfaction can be put in place. Unless and until the tribunal finally grants a conditional discharge, the patient remains an in-patient, and so Part A of the Practice Direction applies: Part A para 5.
3   As to the information to be contained in the statement of information about the patient see *Practice Direction (First-tier Tribunal: mental health cases)* (6 April 2012, unreported) Part A para 9.
4   As to the responsible clinician's report see *Practice Direction (First-tier Tribunal: mental health cases)* (6 April 2012, unreported) Part A para 10.
5   As to the in-patient nursing report see *Practice Direction (First-tier Tribunal: mental health cases)* (6 April 2012, unreported) Part A para 11.
6   See *Practice Direction (First-tier Tribunal: mental health cases)* (6 April 2012, unreported) Part A para 6. As to the social circumstances report see Part A para 12.
7   Ie a patient under the Mental Health Act 1983 s 17E (see PARA 801).
8   As to the statement of information see *Practice Direction (First-tier Tribunal: mental health cases)* (6 April 2012, unreported) Part B para 14.
9   As to the responsible clinician's report see *Practice Direction (First-tier Tribunal: mental health cases)* (6 April 2012, unreported) Part B para 15.
10 *Practice Direction (First-tier Tribunal: mental health cases)* (6 April 2012, unreported) Part B para 13. As to the social circumstances report see Part B para 16.
11 Ie under the Mental Health Act 1983 s 7 (see PARA 785).
12 As to the statement of information see *Practice Direction (First-tier Tribunal: mental health cases)* (6 April 2012, unreported) Part C para 18.
13 As to the responsible clinician's report see *Practice Direction (First-tier Tribunal: mental health cases)* (6 April 2012, unreported) Part C para 19.
14 *Practice Direction (First-tier Tribunal: mental health cases)* (6 April 2012, unreported) Part C para 17. As to the social circumstances report see Part C para 20.
15 A conditionally discharged patient is a restricted patient who has been discharged from hospital into the community, subject to a condition that the patient will remain liable to be recalled to hospital for further treatment, should it become necessary: *Practice Direction (First-tier Tribunal: mental health cases)* (6 April 2012, unreported) Part D para 21. In the case of a restricted patient in hospital, the tribunal may make a provisional decision to order a conditional discharge: see Part D para 22.
16 As to the responsible clinician's report see *Practice Direction (First-tier Tribunal: mental health cases)* (6 April 2012, unreported) Part D para 25.
17 *Practice Direction (First-tier Tribunal: mental health cases)* (6 April 2012, unreported) Part D para 23.
18 *Practice Direction (First-tier Tribunal: mental health cases)* (6 April 2012, unreported) Part E para 27. Additional information is required in the social circumstances report: see Part E para 28.

(3) POWERS OF TRIBUNALS

967. Powers to direct discharge of non-restricted patients. Where an application[1] is made to the appropriate tribunal by or in respect of a patient[2] liable to be detained[3] under the Mental Health Act 1983 or is a community patient[4], the tribunal may in any case direct that the patient be discharged[5].

The tribunal must direct the discharge of a patient liable to be detained for assessment[6] if it is not satisfied: (1) that he is then[7] suffering from mental disorder[8] or from mental disorder of a nature or degree which warrants his detention in hospital[9] for assessment (or for assessment followed by medical treatment[10]) for at least a limited period[11]; or (2) that his detention is justified in the interests of his own health or safety or with a view to the protection of other persons[12]. In any other case[13], the tribunal must direct the discharge of a patient if not satisfied: (a) that he is then suffering from mental disorder[14] or from mental disorder which makes it appropriate for him to be liable to be detained in a hospital for medical treatment[15]; or (b) that it is necessary for the health or safety of the patient or for the protection of other persons that he should receive such treatment[16]; (c) that appropriate medical treatment is available for him[17]; or (d) in the case of applications made by the nearest relative following the barring of a discharge order[18], that the patient, if released, would be likely to act in a manner dangerous to other persons or to himself[19].

The tribunal must direct the discharge of a community patient if it is not satisfied[20]: (i) that he is then suffering from mental disorder or mental disorder of a nature or degree which makes it appropriate for him to receive medical treatment[21]; or (ii) that it is necessary for his health or safety or for the protection of other persons that he should receive such treatment[22]; or (iii) that it is necessary that the responsible clinician should be able to exercise the power[23] to recall the patient to hospital[24]; or (iv) that appropriate medical treatment is available for him[25]; or (v) in the case of an application in respect of a patient who is detained in pursuance of an application for admission for treatment or a community patient[26] that the patient, if discharged, would be likely to act in a manner dangerous to other persons or to himself[27].

In addition, where, in the case of an application to the appropriate tribunal by or in respect of a patient who is subject to guardianship under the Mental Health Act 1983, the tribunal may in any case direct that the patient be discharged and must so direct if it is satisfied that he is not suffering from a mental disorder or that it is not necessary in the interests of the welfare of the patient, or for the protection of other persons, that the patient should remain under guardianship[28].

1   See PARA 961. The Mental Health Act 1983 s 72(1)–(4) applies in relation to references to the appropriate tribunal (see text to notes 2–28) as it applies in relation to an application made by or on behalf of a patient: s 72(6) (amended by the Mental Health Act 2007 Sch 1 para 14(c); SI 2008/2833). As to the meaning of 'appropriate tribunal' see PARA 955.

2   As to the meaning of 'patient' see PARA 758 note 4.

3   The Mental Health Act 1983 s 72(1) does not apply to a restricted patient, except as provided in ss 73, 74 (see PARAS 969–970): s 72(7). For the meaning of 'restricted patient' see PARA 962 note 1. As to the powers of tribunals in relation to restricted patients see PARAS 969–970. The expression 'liable to be detained' includes those on leave of absence under s 17 (see PARA 917): *Ex p Waldron* [1986] QB 824, sub nom *R v Hallstrom, ex p W* [1985] 3 All ER 775; *R (on the application of Epsom and St Helier NHS Trust) v Mental Health Review Tribunal* [2001] EWHC 101 (Admin), [2001] 1 MHLR 8.

4   As to the meaning of 'community patient' see PARA 797 note 4.

5   Mental Health Act 1983 s 72(1) (substituted by SI 2001/3712; and amended by SI 2008/2833). Thus the patient may be discharged even though the legal grounds for compulsory detention still

subsist. 'Discharge' means release from hospital: *Secretary of State for the Home Department v Mental Health Review Tribunal for Mersey Regional Health Authority* [1986] 3 All ER 233, [1986] 1 WLR 1170.

The Mental Health Act 1983 does not empower a tribunal to determine whether the circumstances of a case were such as to render unlawful the detention of a patient: *Ex p Waldron* [1986] QB 824 at 846, sub nom *R v Hallstrom, ex p W* [1985] 3 All ER 775 at 784, CA, per Ackner LJ. The remedy of a patient who by himself or by others alleges that he is unlawfully detained is by way of application to the Queen's Bench Division for a writ of habeas corpus: see *R v Board of Control, ex p Rutty* [1956] 2 QB 109, [1956] 1 All ER 796, DC; *R v Board of Control, ex p Winterflood* [1938] 1 KB 420, [1937] 4 All ER 163, DC (revsd on other grounds [1938] 2 KB 366, [1938] 2 All ER 463, CA). Alternatively, such a patient may apply for judicial review: see *R v Gardner, ex p L, R v Hallstrom, ex p W* [1986] QB 1090, sub nom *R v Hallstrom, ex p W (No 2)* [1986] 2 All ER 306. See also *R v Wessex Mental Health Review Tribunal, ex p Wiltshire County Council* (1989) Times, 29 August, CA.

6 Ie under the Mental Health Act 1983 s 2: see PARA 767.

7 Ie at the time of the tribunal hearing. The tribunal is not required to make a decision that will remain accurate indefinitely or for any given period of time: *R (on the application of Von Brandenburg (aka Hanley)) v East London and the City Mental Health NHS Trust* [2003] UKHL 58, [2004] 2 AC 280, [2004] 1 All ER 400. See also *R (on the application of S) v Mental Health Review Tribunal* [2004] EWHC 2958 (Admin), [2004] All ER (D) 87 (Dec); and PARA 917.

8 As to the meaning of 'mental disorder' see PARA 761.

9 As to the meaning of 'hospital' for these purposes see PARA 961 note 3; and see also PARA 577. As to 'nature' and 'degree' see the general admission criteria; and PARAS 768, 864.

10 As to the meaning of 'medical treatment' see PARA 926. For these purposes, 'medical treatment' is to be construed widely: see *Reid v Secretary of State for Scotland* [1999] 2 AC 512, [1999] 1 All ER 481, HL.

11 Mental Health Act 1983 s 72(1)(a)(i) (as substituted (see note 5); amended by SI 2008/2833). For the duty to discharge to apply, the tribunal must be satisfied that the patient is not so suffering, which is 'not the same thing as saying the tribunal is not satisfied that he is so suffering': *R v Wessex Mental Health Review Tribunal, ex p Wiltshire County Council* (1989) Times, 29 August, CA, per Lord Donaldson of Lymington MR.

As to the burden of proof under the Mental Health Act 1983 s 72(1) and under s 73(1) (see PARA 969) see *R (on the application of H) v London North and East Region Mental Health Review Tribunal (Secretary of State for Health intervening)* [2001] EWCA Civ 415, [2002] QB 1, [2001] 3 WLR 512 (in which a declaration of incompatibility under the Human Rights Act 1998 s 4 (see RIGHTS AND FREEDOMS) was made in relation to the Mental Health Act 1983 ss 72–73). The burden of proof justifying the continued detention of a patient in hospital is now on the detaining authority, i e the hospital. The tribunal must direct the discharge of a patient if it is not satisfied that the Mental Health Act 1983 criteria continue to be fulfilled.

12 Mental Health Act 1983 s 72(1)(a)(ii) (as substituted: see note 5). See note 11.

13 Ie in the case of patients liable to be detained otherwise than under the Mental Health Act 1983 s 2 (see PARA 767). This includes patients admitted in pursuance of applications for admission for treatment under s 3 (see PARA 768), hospital orders (see PARA 864), transfer directions without restriction (see PARAS 892–893), and orders or directions having the same effect (see PARA 861).

14 As to the meaning of 'mental disorder' see PARA 761.

15 Mental Health Act 1983 s 72(1)(b)(i) (as substituted (see note 5); amended by the Mental Health Act 2007 Sch 1 para 14(a); SI 2008/2833). See *R v Canons Park Mental Health Review Tribunal, ex p A* [1995] QB 60, [1994] 2 All ER 659, CA (when exercising its mandatory power to discharge a patient, a tribunal does not have to have regard to the treatability test but only to the appropriateness and safety tests contained in the Mental Health Act 1983 s 72(1)(b)); *R (on the application of the Secretary of State for the Home Department) v Mental Health Review Tribunal* [2004] EWHC 1029 (Admin), [2004] All ER (D) 127 (Apr); *Reid v Secretary of State for Scotland* [1999] 2 AC 512, [1999] 1 All ER 481, HL (consideration of appropriateness test; it was held that the same criteria are to be applied on discharge as on admission, effectively overruling *R v Canons Park Mental Health Review Tribunal, ex p A* on this point).

As to the relevant standard of proof under the Mental Health Act 1983 s 72 and s 73 (see PARA 969) see *R (on the application of N) v Mental Health Review Tribunal (Northern Region)* [2005] EWCA Civ 1605, [2006] QB 468, [2006] All ER 194. See also *R v London South and West Region Mental Health Review Tribunal, ex p Moyle* (2000) Times, 10 February (criteria for discharge mirror criteria for admission but burden of proof reversed). See note 11. As to the meaning of 'hospital' for these purposes see PARA 961 note 3; and see also PARA 577.

16 Mental Health Act 1983 s 72(1)(b)(ii) (as substituted: see note 5). When giving reasons, the tribunal should indicate to which issue in either head (a) or head (b) in text the reasons are directed: *R v Mental Health Review Tribunal, ex p Pickering* [1986] 1 All ER 99 at 104 per Forbes J. See also *Reid v Secretary of State for Scotland* [1999] 2 AC 512, [1999] 1 All ER 481, HL. As to the protection of other persons see *R (on the application of Li) v Mental Health Review Tribunal* [2004] EWHC 51 (Admin), [2004] All ER (D) 173 (Jan). See note 11.

17 Mental Health Act 1983 s 72(1)(b)(iia) (s 72 as substituted (see note 5); s 72(1)(b)(iia) added by the Mental Health Act 2007 s 8(8)(a)).

18 See PARAS 915, 961 head (3).

19 Mental Health Act 1983 s 72(1)(b)(iii) (as substituted: see note 5). 'If released' does not necessarily refer to immediate release: see *R (on the application of B) v Mental Health Review Tribunal* [2003] EWHC 815 (Admin). See note 11.

20 Mental Health Act 1983 s 72(1)(c) (added by the Mental Health Act 2007 Sch 3 para 21(2)(b); and amended by SI 2008/2833).

21 Mental Health Act 1983 s 72(1)(c)(i) (as added: see note 20).

22 Mental Health Act 1983 s 72(1)(c)(ii) (as added: see note 20).

23 Ie under the Mental Health Act 1983 s 17E (see PARA 801).

24 Mental Health Act 1983 s 72(1)(c)(iii) (as added: see note 20). In determining whether the criterion in s 72(1)(c)(iii) is met, the tribunal must, in particular, consider, having regard to the patient's history of mental disorder and any other relevant factors, what risk there would be of a deterioration of the patient's condition if he were to continue not to be detained in a hospital (as a result, for example, of his refusing or neglecting to receive the medical treatment he requires for his mental disorder: s 72(1A) (added by the Mental Health Act 2007 Sch 3 para 21(3)).

25 Mental Health Act 1983 s 72(1)(c)(iv) (as added: see note 20).

26 Ie an application under the Mental Health Act 1983 s 66(1)(g) (see PARA 960).

27 Mental Health Act 1983 s 72(c)(1)(v) (as added: see note 20).

28 Mental Health Act 1983 s 72(4) (amended by the Mental Health Act 2007 Sch 1 para 14(b); SI 2008/2833)

968. Powers to direct discharge of non-restricted patients at a future date. A tribunal may direct[1] the discharge of a patient[2] on a future date specified in the direction[3]. Where a tribunal does not direct the discharge of a patient[4] the tribunal may, with a view to facilitating his future discharge[5], recommend that he be granted leave of absence or transferred to another hospital[6] or into guardianship and further consider his case[7] in the event of such a recommendation not being complied with[8].

1 Ie under the Mental Health Act 1983 s 72(1) (see PARA 967).

2 As to the meaning of 'patient' see PARA 758 note 4.

3 See the Mental Health Act 1983 s 72(3). The power to delay discharge applies whether the tribunal exercises its discretion to discharge under s 72(1) or its mandatory powers: see *R v Mental Health Review Tribunal, ex p P* CO/467/96. The Mental Health Act 1983 s 72(3) does not apply to restricted patients: see *R (on the application of the Secretary of State for the Home Department) v Mental Health Review Tribunal for the North East Thames Region* (2000) 63 BMLR 181. However, see the Mental Health Act 1983 s 73(7); and PARA 969.

4 Ie where it does not direct the discharge of a patient under the Mental Health Act 1983 s 72(1) (see PARA 967).

5 As to the meaning of 'with a view to facilitating future discharge' see *R (on the application of H) v Mental Health Review Tribunal and the Secretary of State for the Home Department* [2002] EWHC 1522 (Admin), [2002] All ER (D) 542 (Jul). If future discharge is delayed unreasonably, it could give rise to violation of the Convention for the Protection of Human Rights and Fundamental Freedoms (Rome, 4 November 1950; TS 71 (1953) Cmd 8969) art 5 (see RIGHTS AND FREEDOMS): see *Johnson v United Kingdom* (1997) 27 EHRR 296, 40 BMLR 1, ECtHR. See also Application 517/02 *Kolanis v United Kingdom* (2005) 42 EHRR 206, 84 BMLR 102, ECtHR (in which there was held to be a violation of the Convention for the Protection of Human Rights and Fundamental Freedoms art 5(4), as detention in hospital was no longer necessary).

6 As to the meaning of 'hospital' for these purposes see PARA 961 note 3; and see also PARA 577.

7 A reconvened tribunal at the time of further consideration has all of the powers of the original tribunal: *Mental Health Review Tribunal v Hempstock* (1997) 39 BMLR 123. The phrase 'his

case' referred to the patient's application to the tribunal, and so the patient may withdraw the application after the tribunal has made its recommendation: *R (on the application of O) v Mental Health Review Tribunal* [2006] EWHC 2659 (Admin), (2006) 93 BMLR 110.

8   Mental Health Act 1983 s 72(3) (amended by SI 2008/2833). As to the power of tribunals to discharge restricted patients see PARAS 969–971.

969.   Powers to direct discharge of restriction order patients. Where an application to the appropriate tribunal[1] is made by a restricted patient[2] who is subject to a restriction order[3], or where the case of such a patient is referred to the appropriate tribunal[4], the tribunal must direct the patient's absolute discharge[5] if: (1) it is not satisfied either: (a) that the patient is then suffering from mental disorder or from a mental disorder of a nature or degree which makes it appropriate for him to be liable to be detained in a hospital for medical treatment; or (b) that it is necessary for the health or safety of the patient or for the protection of other persons that he should receive such treatment; or (c) that appropriate medical treatment is available for him[6]; and (2) it is satisfied that it is not appropriate for the patient to remain liable to be recalled to hospital for further treatment[7]. Where a patient is absolutely discharged, he thereupon ceases to be liable to be detained by virtue of the hospital order[8] and the restriction order[9] ceases to have effect[10].

In the case of such patients, where the situation set out in head (1) above applies but not that set out in head (2) above, the tribunal must direct the conditional discharge of the patient[11]. The patient must then comply with such conditions as are imposed at the time by the tribunal[12] or at any subsequent time by the appropriate national authority[13] and may be recalled to hospital by the appropriate national authority[14] as if he had been conditionally discharged by that Authority[15]. If the restriction order ceases to have effect after the patient has been conditionally discharged by a tribunal he is, unless previously recalled to hospital, deemed to be absolutely discharged on the date when the order ceases to have effect[16]. The tribunal may defer a direction for conditional discharge until the arrangements which appear to it necessary for the purpose[17] have been made to its satisfaction[18].

Unlike in the case of unrestricted patients, the tribunal has no power to make recommendations in regard to restricted patients[19]. There is also no power to adjourn to allow the patient's condition to improve or to allow for sustained development[20]. The tribunal may now, when considering making a deferred conditional discharge order, adjourn for the necessary arrangements to be made and reconvene to reconsider the case in the event that it does not prove possible to fulfil the proposed conditions[21].

1   As to the 'appropriate tribunal' see PARA 955. Tribunals were given powers to direct the discharge of restriction order patients following the decision of the European Court of Human Rights in *X v United Kingdom* (1981) 4 EHRR 188, ECtHR, that all persons detained because they are 'of unsound mind' are entitled to a periodic judicial consideration of the merits of their continued detention, under the Convention for the Protection of Human Rights and Fundamental Freedoms (Rome, 4 November 1950; TS 71 (1953); Cmd 8969)) art 5(4) (see RIGHTS AND FREEDOMS). The system in the United Kingdom whereby the decision to order a patient's discharge could only be taken by the Secretary of State was held to contravene the European Convention on Human Rights art 5(4): Application 28212/95 *Benjamin v United Kingdom* (2002) 36 EHRR 1, 13 BHRC 287, ECtHR. See also *R (on the application of P) v Secretary of State for the Home Department* [2003] EWHC 2953 (Admin), (2003) Times, 29 December (the right to review the lawfulness of detention does not mean that the mental health review tribunal and the discretionary lifer panel of the Parole Board have to be convened simultaneously). See also Application 517/02 *Kolanis v United Kingdom* (2005) 42 EHRR 206, 84 BMLR 102, ECtHR (in which there was held to be a violation of the Convention for the

Protection of Human Rights and Fundamental Freedoms art 5(4) as the patient's detention in hospital was in the circumstances longer than necessary).

2   As to the meaning of 'restricted patient' see PARA 962 note 1.

3   As to restriction orders see PARA 869. Cf the tribunal's powers in relation to restriction directions: see PARA 970.

4   As to such references see PARA 965.

5   There is no general discretion to discharge as with unrestricted patients: see PARA 967.

6   Ie as to the matters mentioned in the Mental Health Act 1983 s 72(1)(b)(i) or (ii) or (iia): see PARA 967. For the meaning of 'hospital' for these purposes see PARA 961 note 3; and see also PARA 577.

    The liability to be recalled is not simply to address the danger to others but may also be for therapeutic reasons: *R v North West Thames Mental Health Review Tribunal, ex p Cooper* (1990) 5 BMLR 7. See also *R v Mental Health Review Tribunal for South Thames Region, ex p Smith* (1998) 47 BMLR 104 (degree of illness irrelevant; nature of illness considered to determine whether discharge was appropriate); *R v London South and West Region Mental Health Review Tribunal, ex p Moyle* (2000) Times, 10 February (criteria for discharge mirror criteria for admission but burden of proof reversed).

    As to the relevant standard of proof under the Mental Health Act 1983 s 72 (see PARA 967) and s 73 see *R (on the application of DJ) v Mental Health Review Tribunal, R (on the application of AN) v Mental Health Review Tribunal (Northern Region)* [2005] EWHC 587 (Admin), (2005) Times, 18 April (affd *R (on the application of AN)*, cited, affirmed sub nom *R (on the application of N) v Mental Health Review Tribunal (Northern Region)* [2005] EWCA Civ 1605, [2006] QB 468, [2006] 4 All ER 194). See also *R (on the application of East London and the City Mental Health NHS Trust) v Mental Health Review Tribunal* [2005] EWHC 2329 (Admin), [2005] All ER (D) 107 (Aug).

7   Mental Health Act 1983 s 73(1) (s 73(1), (2) substituted by SI 2001/3712; amended by SI 2008/2833). The mental health review tribunal must address this provision: *R (on the application of the Secretary of State for the Home Department) v Mental Health Review Tribunal* [2001] EWHC 849 (Admin). The liability to recall is not simply to address danger to others but could also be for therapeutic reasons: *R v North West Thames Mental Health Review Tribunal, ex p Cooper* (1990) 5 BMLR 7. Under this provision, the tribunal has to focus on the existence or potential risk of recurrence of any mental impairment making detention in hospital for appropriate treatment necessary for the patient's health and safety or for the protection of other persons; the judge also has to consider the defendant's psychiatric problems and the benefit medical evidence might suggest that the defendant is likely to receive from treatment: see *R v A* [2005] EWCA Crim 2077, [2006] 1 Cr App Rep (S) 521, [2006] Crim LR 79. See also *R (on the application of DJ) v Mental Health Review Tribunal; R (on the application of AN) v Mental Health Review Tribunal (Northern Region)* [2005] EWHC 587 (Admin), (2005) Times, 18 April; and note 6.

    As to the burden of proof under the Mental Health Act 1983 s 73(1) see PARA 967 note 11.

8   As to the meaning of 'hospital order' see PARA 864 note 5.

9   As to the meaning of 'restriction order' see PARA 869.

10 Mental Health Act 1983 s 73(3). Where a patient's discharge has been ordered, an approved social worker can only lawfully apply for the patient's readmission if he reasonably considers in good faith that there is fresh information not known to the tribunal but altering the complexion of the case: *R (on the application of Von Brandenburg (aka Hanley)) v East London and the City Mental Health NHS Trust)* [2003] UKHL 58, [2004] 2 AC 280, [2004] 1 All ER 400. Note that an application by an approved social worker can relate only to a civil detention under the Mental Health Act 1983 Pt II (ss 2–34). As to the link between s 73(3) and s 75(3) (see PARA 971) see *R (on the application of SC) v Mental Health Review Tribunal* [2005] EWHC 17 (Admin), (2005) Times, 24 January.

11 Mental Health Act 1983 s 73(2) (as substituted: see note 7). Even though the tribunal finds as a fact that the patient is not then suffering from mental disorder, it must direct a conditional discharge unless satisfied that it is not appropriate for him to remain liable to recall to hospital. He remains a 'patient' for this purpose until discharged absolutely, although s 145(1) provides that a 'patient' means a person suffering or appearing to be suffering from mental disorder: *R v Merseyside Mental Health Review Tribunal, ex p K* [1990] 1 All ER 694, CA; *R v North West Thames Mental Health Review Tribunal, ex p Cooper* (1990) 5 BMLR 7. The mental health review tribunal has no power to order a local authority or a health authority to produce a care plan for a patient who has been given a conditional discharge: *R v Mental Health Review Tribunal, ex p Hall* [1999] 4 All ER 883, [2000] 1 WLR 1323, CA. See also *R (on the application of the Secretary of State for the Home Department) v Mental Health Review Tribunal* [2004] EWHC 1029 (Admin), [2004] All ER (D) 127 (Apr) (the failure of the tribunal

to consider the question of conditional discharge as required by the Mental Health Act 1983 s 73(2), having concluded that the interested party who had been detained was not suffering from a psychopathic disorder for the purposes of s 72(1)(b) (see PARA 967), vitiated its decision).

In so far as the Mental Health Act 1983 s 73 places the burden of proof on a restricted patient to show that he is no longer suffering from a mental disorder warranting detention, it is incompatible with the Convention for the Protection of Human Rights and Fundamental Freedoms (Rome, 4 November 1950; TS 71 (1953); Cmd 8969) art 5: *R (on the application of H) v Secretary of State for the Home Department* [2003] UKHL 59, [2004] 2 AC 253, [2004] 1 All ER 412. See also note 6. A patient assessed as no longer suffering from mental illness need not inevitably be immediately given an absolute discharge, and a conditional discharge is a lawful alternative. It is important, however, that once a conditional discharge is made and deferred (ie under the Mental Health Act 1983 s 73(7): see note 18), arrangements are made so that the patient's actual discharge is not unreasonably delayed: see *Johnson v United Kingdom* (1997) 27 EHRR 296, 40 BMLR 1, ECtHR. Unless a patient is assessed as no longer suffering from mental disorder at all, a finding that he is entitled to a conditional discharge is not necessarily a finding that the criteria for compulsory detention under *Winterwerp v Netherlands* (1981) 4 EHRR 228, ECtHR, are no longer fulfilled: see *Johnson v United Kingdom* above; Application 517/02 *Kolanis v United Kingdom* [2005] All ER (D) 227 (Jun), ECtHR. See also note 17. A conditional discharge may require residence and strict conditions in another hospital so long as the patient is not actually detained or deprived from his liberty as such: *R (on the application of the Secretary of State for the Home Department) v Mental Health Review Tribunal* [2002] EWCA Civ 1868, [2002] All ER (D) 307 (Dec); but see *R (on the application of the Secretary of State for the Home Department) v Mental Health Review Tribunal* [2004] EWHC 2194 (Admin), [2004] All ER (D) 87 (Oct); Application 7367/76 *Guzzardi v Italy* (1980) 3 EHRR 333, ECtHR; *Ashingdane v United Kingdom* (1985) 7 EHRR 528, ECtHR. As to the relevant conditions of a conditional discharge see *R v Mental Review Tribunal, ex p Hall* [1999] 4 All ER 883, [2000] 1 WLR 1323, (1999) 51 BMLR 117; *R (on the application of H) v Secretary of State for the Home Department* [2003] UKHL 59, [2004] 2 AC 253, [2004] 1 All ER 412; *W v Doncaster Metropolitan Borough Council* [2004] EWCA Civ 378, [2004] LGR 378, sub nom *R (on the application of W) v Doncaster Metropolitan Borough Council* (2004) Times, 13 May. A conditional discharge that amounts to a deprivation of liberty cannot be made even if it is in the best interests of the patient: see *Secretary of State for Justice v RB* [2011] EWCA Civ 1608, [2012] 1 WLR 2043, 124 BMLR 13. See also PARAS 914 note 5, 640.

12 The tribunal cannot impose a condition that the patient remain in a hospital, since discharge for this purpose must mean release from hospital: see *Secretary of State for the Home Department v Mental Health Review Tribunal for the Mersey Regional Health Authority, Secretary of State for the Home Department v Mental Health Review Tribunal for Wales* [1986] 3 All ER 233, [1986] 1 WLR 1170; and PARA 914 note 5. As to residence in hospital as opposed to detention there see also note 11.

13 Mental Health Act 1983 s 73(4)(b). The appropriate national authority may from time to time vary any condition so imposed: s 73(5). As to the appropriate national authority see PARA 567.

14 Ie under the Mental Health Act 1983 s 42(3): see PARA 876.

15 Mental Health Act 1983 s 73(4)(a). As to conditional discharge (and recall) see s 42(2); and PARA 914. Section 73 is without prejudice to s 42: s 73(8). As to the additional powers in respect of restriction order patients see PARAS 869, 876.

16 Mental Health Act 1983 s 73(6).

17 The necessary arrangements must be made for the purpose of the conditional discharge. Any unreasonable delay in achieving a deferred conditional discharge (eg due to a failure to implement any of the conditions proposed by the tribunal) may result in a violation of the Convention for the Protection of Human Rights and Fundamental Freedoms (Rome, 4 November 1950; TS 71 (1953); Cmd 8969) art 5: *Johnson v United Kingdom* (1997) 27 EHRR 296, 40 BMLR 1, ECtHR; *R (on the application of K) v Camden and Islington Health Authority* [2001] EWCA Civ 240, [2002] QB 198, (2001) 61 BMLR 173; Application 517/02 *Kolanis v United Kingdom* [2005] All ER (D) 227 (Jun), ECtHR. This has been remedied by allowing a tribunal to reconsider its decision and conditions in the light of any such difficulties. The ruling in *Campbell v Secretary of State for the Home Department* [1988] AC 120, sub nom *Secretary of State for the Home Department v Oxford Regional Mental Health Review Tribunal* [1987] 3 All ER 8, HL, has been overruled on this point to ensure compatibility with the Convention for the Protection of Human Rights and Fundamental Freedoms art 5: see *R (on the application of H) v Secretary of State for the Home Department* [2003] UKHL 59, [2004] 2 AC 253, [2004] 1 All ER 412, endorsing the ruling of the Court of Appeal. Thus a deferred conditional discharge direction is no longer a final decision of the tribunal, but provisional upon realisation of appropriate conditions. See also *R (on the*

application of C) v Secretary of State for the Home Department [2002] EWCA Civ 647, (2002) Times, 24 May. Leave of absence or a transfer may be used to facilitate a conditional discharge. In *R (on the application of H) v Mental Health Review Tribunal*, the court identified 'categorical differences' between patients no longer suffering from mental disorder (see e g *Johnson v United Kingdom* above), and those whose mental disorder was simply no longer of a sufficient 'nature or degree'. See also *W v Doncaster Metropolitan Borough Council* [2004] EWCA Civ 378, (2004) Times, 13 May. This approach has been confirmed in Application 517/02 *Kolanis v United Kingdom* above. In that case, the court also found that a finding of entitlement to conditional discharge in a case, other than that falling into the *Johnson v United Kingdom* above category, did not necessarily mean that a person was unlawfully detained under the Convention for the Protection of Human Rights and Fundamental Freedoms article 5 (see *Winterwerp v Netherlands* (1981) 4 EHRR 228, ECtHR); the court noted the difference in wording between the criteria in *Winterwerp v Netherlands* above and the criteria for admission or discharge under the Mental Health Act 1983.

There may be a damages claim under the Convention for the Protection of Human Rights and Fundamental Freedoms art 5(5); and for the relevant procedure see *Anufrijeva v Southwark London Borough Council, R (on the application of N) v Secretary of State for the Home Department, R (on the application of M) v Secretary of State for the Home Department* [2003] EWCA Civ 1406, [2004] QB 1124, [2004] 1 All ER 833.

18 Mental Health Act 1983 s 73(7) (amended by SI 2008/2833). Further, if because of such deferment no direction has been given before the patient's case comes before the tribunal on a subsequent application or reference, the previous application or reference must be treated as one on which no direction can be given: Mental Health Act 1983 s 73(7). See notes 11, 17.

19 *Grant v Mental Health Review Tribunal* (1986) Times, 28 April.

20 *R v Nottingham Mental Health Review Tribunal, ex p Secretary of State for the Home Department, R v Trent Mental Health Review Tribunal, ex p Secretary of State for the Home Department* (1988) Times, 12 October, CA.

21 See note 17. As to the burden of proof etc see PARA 967.

970. Powers in relation to transferred prisoners. Where an application to the appropriate tribunal is made by a restricted patient[1] who is subject to a limitation direction or restriction direction[2], or the case of such a patient is referred to the appropriate tribunal[3], the tribunal[4] must notify the appropriate national authority[5] whether, in its opinion, the patient would be entitled to be absolutely or conditionally discharged[6]; and, if the latter, it may recommend that he continue to be detained in hospital[7] if not discharged[8]. If the patient is subject to a transfer direction[9] under the powers relating to remand or civil prisoners[10] and the tribunal notifies the appropriate national authority that he would be entitled to be discharged, the appropriate national authority must, unless the tribunal has made a recommendation that he should continue to be detained in hospital[11], by warrant direct that he be remitted to prison or another institution[12], there to be dealt with as if he had not been removed to hospital[13]. In the case of other patients, if the tribunal notifies the appropriate national authority that the patient would be entitled to be discharged, and within the period of 90 days beginning with the date of that notification the Secretary of State gives notice to the tribunal that the patient may be discharged, the tribunal must direct his absolute or conditional discharge[14]. If the appropriate national authority does not give such notice, the hospital managers[15] must, unless the tribunal has also recommended that the patient should continue to be detained in hospital[16], transfer him to a prison or another institution[17], there to be dealt with as if he had not been removed to hospital[18].

1 As to the meaning of 'appropriate tribunal' see PARA 955. As to the meaning of 'restricted patient' see PARA 962 note 1.

2 As to limitation directions see PARA 863. As to restriction directions see PARA 894. See also PARA 894 note 8.

3 See PARA 965.

4 Mental Health Act 1983 s 74(1) (amended by the b Crime (Sentences) Act 1997 s 55, Sch 4 para 12(10)). See *R (on the application of A) v Mental Health Review Tribunal* [2004] EWHC 1999 (Admin), [2004] All ER (D) 78 (Aug) (discharge of an ill foreign national detained also under the Immigration Act 1971 and the Anti-Terrorism, Crime and Security Act 2001 s 21 (now repealed)).

5 As to the appropriate national authority see PARA 567.

6 Ie under the Mental Health Act 1983 s 73: see PARA 969.

7 For the meaning of 'hospital' for these purposes see PARA 961 note 3; and see also PARA 577.

8 Mental Health Act 1983 s 74(1)(a), (b) (amended by SI 2008/2833). This advisory power of the tribunal to recommend discharge has been found to be incompatible with the Convention for the Protection of Human Rights and Fundamental Freedoms (Rome, 4 November 1950; TS 71 (1953) Cmd 8969) art 5(4) (see RIGHTS AND FREEDOMS): see *R (on the application of D) v Secretary of State for the Home Department* [2002] EWHC 2805 (Admin), [2003] 1 WLR 1315, (2002) Times, 31 December; Application 28212/95 *Benjamin v United Kingdom* (2003) 36 EHRR 1, 13 BHRC 287, ECtHR. See also *R (on the application of P) v Secretary of State for the Home Department* [2003] EWHC 2953 (Admin), (2003) Times, 29 December. This incompatibility has been cured by amending the Mental Health Act 1983 so that it provides that where the tribunal has made a recommendation as in s 74(1)(b) in the case of a patient who is subject to a restriction direction or a limitation direction: (1) the fact that the restriction direction or limitation direction remains in force does not prevent the making of any application or reference to the Parole Board by or in respect of him or the exercise by him of any power to require the Secretary of State to refer his case to the Parole Board; and (2) if the Parole Board makes a direction or recommendation by virtue of which the patient would become entitled to be released (whether unconditionally or on licence) from any prison or other institution in which he might have been detained if he had not been removed to hospital, the restriction direction or limitation direction ceases to have effect at the time when he would become entitled to be so released: s 74(5A) (added by the Criminal Justice Act 2003 s 295; amended by SI 2008/2833).

9 As to transfer directions see PARA 892.

10 Ie under the Mental Health Act 1983 s 48: see PARA 893.

11 Ie a recommendation under the Mental Health Act 1983 s 74(1)(b) (see the text and note 8).

12 Ie in which he might have been detained had he not been removed to hospital.

13 Mental Health Act 1983 s 74(4) (amended by SI 2008/2833). On his arrival in the prison or other institution, the relevant hospital direction and the limitation direction or, as the case may be, the relevant transfer direction and restriction direction cease to have effect: s 74(5) (amended by the Crime (Sentences) Act 1997 Sch 4 para 12(11)). As to hospital directions see PARA 863.

14 Mental Health Act 1983 s 74(2) (amended by SI 2008/2833). The provisions of the Mental Health Act 1983 s 73(3)–(8) apply in relation to absolute or conditional discharge under s 74 as they apply to absolute or conditional discharge under s 73 (see PARA 969), taking references to the relevant hospital order and the restriction order as references to hospital direction and the limitation direction or, as the case may be, to the transfer direction and the restriction direction: s 74(6) (amended by the Crime (Sentences) Act 1997 Sch 4 para 12(12)).

15 As to the meaning of 'managers' see PARA 778.

16 See note 13.

17 See note 14.

18 Mental Health Act 1983 s 74(3) (amended by SI 2008/2833). On his arrival in the prison or other institution, the relevant hospital direction and the limitation direction or, as the case may be, the relevant transfer direction and restriction direction cease to have effect: Mental Health Act 1983 s 74(5) (as amended: see note 13).

971. Powers in relation to conditionally discharged restricted patients. Where an application to a tribunal is made by a conditionally discharged restricted patient who is subject to a limitation direction, restriction direction or restriction order[1], the tribunal may vary any condition to which the patient is subject or impose any condition which might have been imposed, or may direct that the restriction order, limitation direction or restriction direction to which he is subject is to cease to have effect[2]. If the latter, the patient ceases to be liable to be detained by virtue of the relevant hospital order, hospital direction or transfer direction[3].

1 Ie where the Mental Health Act 1983 s 73, 74 apply.

2   Mental Health Act 1983 s 75(3). See *R (on the application of SC) v Mental Health Review Tribunal* [2005] EWHC 17 (Admin), (2005) Times, 24 January.
3   Mental Health Act 1983 s 75(3) (amended by the Mental Health Act 1983 s 41; and SI 2008/2833). As to hospital orders see PARA 864. As to transfer directions see PARA 892. Subject to the Mental Health Act 1983 s 75(3)–(6), in ss 65–79 'the relevant hospital order', 'the relevant hospital direction' and 'the relevant transfer direction', in relation to a restricted patient, mean the hospital order, the hospital direction or transfer direction by virtue of which he is liable to be detained in a hospital: s 79(2) (amended by the Crime (Sentences) Act 1997 Sch 4 para 12(15)).

(4) PROCEDURE

(i) General Provisions

972.   Procedure for making applications.   The application to a tribunal must be made in writing addressed[1]:

(1)   in the case of a patient[2] who is liable to be detained in a hospital, to the First-tier Tribunal where that hospital is in England and to the Mental Health Review Tribunal for Wales where that hospital is in Wales[3];

(2)   in the case of a community patient[4], to the First-tier Tribunal where the responsible hospital is in England and to the Mental Health Review Tribunal for Wales where that hospital is in Wales[5];

(3)   in the case of a patient subject to guardianship, to the First-tier Tribunal where the patient resides in England and to the Mental Health Review Tribunal for Wales where the patient resides in Wales[6].

1   The manager at a hospital at which high security services are provided may not prevent patients detained there from sending communications so addressed: see the Mental Health Act 1983 s 134(2), (3)(d); and PARA 780. As to such hospitals see PARA 569.
2   As to the meaning of 'patient' see PARA 758 note 4.
3   Mental Health Act 1983 s 77(3)(a) (s 77(3)(a)–(c) substituted by the Mental Health Act 2007 Sch 3 para 23).
4   As to the meaning of 'community patient' see PARA 797 note 4.
5   Mental Health Act 1983 s 77(3)(b) (as substituted: see note 3).
6   Mental Health Act 1983 s 77(3)(c) (as substituted: see note 3).

(ii) First-tier Tribunal (Health, Education and Social Care Chamber)

973.   Procedure in mental health cases.   The following apply in relation to mental health cases[1]. An application or reference must be made in writing, signed (in the case of an application, by the applicant or any person authorised by the applicant to do so); and sent or delivered to the tribunal[2] so that it is received within the specified[3] time[4]. Subject to the provisions relating to withholding evidence likely to cause harm[5], when the tribunal receives a document from any party it must send a copy of that document to each other party[6].

If the patient[7] is a conditionally discharged patient, upon being notified by the tribunal of an application, the appropriate national authority[8] must immediately provide to the tribunal the names and addresses of the responsible clinician[9] and any social supervisor in relation to the patient; and, upon being notified by the tribunal of an application or reference, the responsible clinician and any social supervisor named by the appropriate national authority under these provisions must send or deliver the documents specified in the relevant practice direction to the tribunal so that they are received by the tribunal as soon as practicable and in any event within three weeks after the notification[10].

Where an application is made in respect of an admission for assessment[11], on the earlier of receipt of the copy of the application or a request from the tribunal, the responsible authority[12] must immediately send or deliver to the tribunal a copy of the application for admission and the written medical recommendations on which that application was founded, and must as soon as practicable send or deliver to the tribunal the documents specified in the relevant practice direction[13].

If the above provisions do not apply[14], the responsible authority must send or deliver the documents specified in the relevant practice direction to the tribunal so that they are received by the tribunal as soon as practicable and in any event within three weeks after the responsible authority made the reference or received a copy of the application or reference[15].

Where a conditionally discharged restricted patient who has been recalled to hospital is referred to the appropriate tribunal[16] the appropriate national authority must send[17] to the tribunal any observations the appropriate national authority wishes to make and the following information:

(1)   a summary of the offence or alleged offence that resulted in the patient being detained in hospital subject to a restriction order or, in the case of a patient subject to a restriction or limitation direction, that resulted in the patient being remanded in custody, kept in custody or sentenced to imprisonment[18];

(2)   a record of any other criminal convictions or findings recorded against the patient[19];

(3)   full details of the history of the patient's liability to detention under the Mental Health Act 1983 since the restrictions were imposed[20];

(4)   any further information in the possession of the appropriate national authority that it considers relevant to the proceedings[21].

If the appropriate national authority wishes to seek the approval of the tribunal to remove a patient to a country or territory outside the United Kingdom, Isle of Man and Channel Islands[22], it must refer the patient's case to the tribunal and the provisions of the Tribunal Procedure (First-tier Tribunal) (Health, Education and Social Care Chamber) Rules 2008[23] applicable to references under the Mental Health Act 1983 apply to the proceedings[24].

1   Tribunal Procedure (First-tier Tribunal) (Health, Education and Social Care Chamber) Rules 2008, SI 2008/2699, r 31. A mental health case is a case started under the Mental Health Act 1983 or the Repatriation of Prisoners Act 1984 Schedule para 5(2) (see PRISONS AND PRISONERS vol 85 (2012) PARA 465): Tribunal Procedure (First-tier Tribunal) (Health, Education and Social Care Chamber) Rules 2008, SI 2008/2699, r 1(3). As to the overriding objective of the tribunal see r 2, as to general powers and provisions relating to the tribunal see rr 4–17 and as to correcting, setting aside and appealing against a decision of the tribunal see rr 44–50. See also COURTS AND TRIBUNALS.

2   For the purposes of the Tribunal Procedure (First-tier Tribunal) (Health, Education and Social Care Chamber) Rules 2008, SI 2008/2699 'tribunal' means First-tier Tribunal: r 1(3).

3   Ie the time specified in the Mental Health Act 1983 or the Repatriation of Prisoners Act 1984 (see PRISONS AND PRISONERS).

4   Tribunal Procedure (First-tier Tribunal) (Health, Education and Social Care Chamber) Rules 2008, SI 2008/2699, r 32(1). As to the information to be contained within an application see r 32(2), (2A) (r 32(2) amended and r 32(2A) added by SI 2012/500).

5   Ie subject to the Tribunal Procedure (First-tier Tribunal) (Health, Education and Social Care Chamber) Rules 2008, SI 2008/2699, r 14(2) (see COURTS AND TRIBUNALS vol 24 (2010) PARA 879). Although full disclosure of records is generally to be given, as to the procedure where medical records contain information the responsible authority considers too sensitive for disclosure see *Dorset Healthcare NHS Foundation Trust v MH* [2009] UKUT 4 (AAC), [2009] PTSR 1112, 111 BMLR 1.

6 Tribunal Procedure (First-tier Tribunal) (Health, Education and Social Care Chamber) Rules 2008, SI 2008/2699, r 32(3).

7 For the purposes of the Tribunal Procedure (First-tier Tribunal) (Health, Education and Social Care Chamber) Rules 2008, SI 2008/2699 'patient' means the person who is the subject of a mental health case: r 1(3).

8 As to the appropriate national authority see PARA 567.

9 As to the responsible clinician see PARA 834.

10 Tribunal Procedure (First-tier Tribunal) (Health, Education and Social Care Chamber) Rules 2008, SI 2008/2699, r 32(4) (r 32(4)–(7) substituted and r 32(7A), (7B) by SI 2012/500). If the patient is a restricted patient, a person or body providing a document to the tribunal in accordance with the Tribunal Procedure (First-tier Tribunal) (Health, Education and Social Care Chamber) Rules 2008, SI 2008/2699, r 32(4)(b) or (6) must also send or deliver a copy of the document to the appropriate national authority: r 32(7) (as so substituted). When the tribunal receives the information required by r 32(4), (5) or (6) it must give notice of the proceedings, where the patient is subject to the guardianship of a private guardian, to the guardian; where there is an extant order of the Court of Protection, to that court; subject to a patient with capacity to do so requesting otherwise, where any person other than the applicant is named by the authority as exercising the functions of the nearest relative, to that person; where a health authority, primary care trust, National Health Service trust or NHS foundation trust has a right to discharge the patient under the Mental Health Act 1983 s 23(3) (see PARA 913), to that authority or trust; and to any other person who, in the opinion of the tribunal, should have an opportunity of being heard: Tribunal Procedure (First-tier Tribunal) (Health, Education and Social Care Chamber) Rules 2008, SI 2008/2699, r 33. As to the meaning of 'restricted patient' see the Mental Health Act 1983 s 79(1); and PARA 962 note 1 (definition applied by the Tribunal Procedure (First-tier Tribunal) (Health, Education and Social Care Chamber) Rules 2008, SI 2008/2699, r 1(3)).

11 Ie in proceedings under the Mental Health Act 1983 s 66(1)(a) (see PARA 960).

12 For the purposes of the Tribunal Procedure (First-tier Tribunal) (Health, Education and Social Care Chamber) Rules 2008, SI 2008/2699 'responsible authority' means:

   (1) in relation to a patient detained under the Mental Health Act 1983 in a hospital within the meaning of Pt 2 (ss 2–34), the managers (as defined in s 145 (see PARA 778)) (Tribunal Procedure (First-tier Tribunal) (Health, Education and Social Care Chamber) Rules 2008, SI 2008/2699, r 1(3));

   (2) in relation to a patient subject to guardianship, the responsible local social services authority (as defined in the Mental Health Act 1983 s 34(3) (see PARA 579)) (Tribunal Procedure (First-tier Tribunal) (Health, Education and Social Care Chamber) Rules 2008, SI 2008/2699, r 1(3));

   (3) in relation to a community patient, the managers of the responsible hospital (as defined in the Mental Health Act 1983 s 145 (see PARAS 778, 799 NOTE 11)) (Tribunal Procedure (First-tier Tribunal) (Health, Education and Social Care Chamber) Rules 2008, SI 2008/2699, r 1(3));

   (4) in relation to a patient subject to after-care under supervision, the primary care trust or local health board which has the duty to provide after-care for the patient (r 1(3)).

13 Tribunal Procedure (First-tier Tribunal) (Health, Education and Social Care Chamber) Rules 2008, SI 2008/2699, r 32(5) (as substituted: see note 10).

14 Ie if neither the Tribunal Procedure (First-tier Tribunal) (Health, Education and Social Care Chamber) Rules 2008, SI 2008/2699, r 32(4) or (5) applies.

15 Tribunal Procedure (First-tier Tribunal) (Health, Education and Social Care Chamber) Rules 2008, SI 2008/2699, r 32(6) (as substituted: see note 10). See note 10.

16 Ie in proceedings under the Mental Health Act 1983 s 75(1) (see PARAS 962, 965).

17 Such information must be sent as soon as practicable and in any event, in relation to proceedings under the Mental Health Act 1983 s 75(1), within 2 weeks after the appropriate national authority received the documents sent or delivered in accordance with the Tribunal Procedure (First-tier Tribunal) (Health, Education and Social Care Chamber) Rules 2008, SI 2008/2699, r 32(7): s 32(7A)(a) (as added: see note 10). Otherwise within 3 weeks after the appropriate national authority received the documents sent or delivered in accordance with r 32(7): r 32(7A)(b) (as so added).

18 Tribunal Procedure (First-tier Tribunal) (Health, Education and Social Care Chamber) Rules 2008, SI 2008/2699, r 32(7B)(a) (as added: see note 10).

19 Tribunal Procedure (First-tier Tribunal) (Health, Education and Social Care Chamber) Rules 2008, SI 2008/2699, r 32(7B)(b) (as added: see note 10).

20 Tribunal Procedure (First-tier Tribunal) (Health, Education and Social Care Chamber) Rules 2008, SI 2008/2699, r 32(7B)(c) (as added: see note 10).

21 Tribunal Procedure (First-tier Tribunal) (Health, Education and Social Care Chamber) Rules 2008, SI 2008/2699, r 32(7B)(d) (as added: see note 10).
22 Ie seek approval under the Mental Health Act 1983 s 86(3) (see PARA 907).
23 Ie the Tribunal Procedure (First-tier Tribunal) (Health, Education and Social Care Chamber) Rules 2008, SI 2008/2699.
24 Tribunal Procedure (First-tier Tribunal) (Health, Education and Social Care Chamber) Rules 2008, SI 2008/2699, r 32(8) (amended by SI 2012/500).

974.   Medical examination of the patient.   Before a hearing to consider the disposal of a mental health case[1], an appropriate member of the tribunal[2] must, so far as practicable examine the patient[3] and take such other steps as that member considers necessary to form an opinion of the patient's mental condition[4].

That member may examine the patient in private, examine records relating to the detention or treatment of the patient and any after-care services and take notes and copies of records for use in connection with the proceedings[5].

1   As to the meaning of 'mental health case' see PARA 973 note 1.
2   As to the meaning of 'tribunal' see PARA 973 note 2.
3   As to the meaning of 'patient' see PARA 973 note 7.
4   Tribunal Procedure (First-tier Tribunal) (Health, Education and Social Care Chamber) Rules 2008, SI 2008/2699, r 34(1).
5   Tribunal Procedure (First-tier Tribunal) (Health, Education and Social Care Chamber) Rules 2008, SI 2008/2699, r 34(2).

975.   Hearings.   The tribunal[1] must hold a hearing before making a decision which disposes of proceedings[2]. The tribunal may make a decision on a reference by the manager of a hospital[3] without a hearing if the patient is a community patient aged 18 or over and either:

(1)   the patient has stated in writing that he does not wish to attend or be represented at a hearing of the reference and the tribunal is satisfied that the patient has the capacity to decide whether or not to make that decision[4]; or

(2)   the patient's representative has stated in writing that the patient does not wish to attend or be represented at a hearing of the reference[5].

Each party to proceedings is entitled to attend a hearing[6] and any person notified of the proceedings[7] may attend and take part in a hearing to such extent as the tribunal considers proper, or provide written submissions to the tribunal[8].

The tribunal must give reasonable notice[9] of the time and place[10] of the hearing (including any adjourned or postponed hearing), and any changes to the time and place of the hearing, to each party entitled to attend a hearing and any interested person who has been notified[11] of the proceedings[12].

1   As to the meaning of 'tribunal' see PARA 973 note 2.
2   Tribunal Procedure (First-tier Tribunal) (Health, Education and Social Care Chamber) Rules 2008, SI 2008/2699, r 35(1) (substituted by SI 2012/500). This does not apply to a decision under Pt 5 (rr 43–50: see COURTS AND TRIBUNALS): r 35(2). The tribunal may dispose of proceedings without a hearing under r 8(3) (striking out a party's case: see r 35(4) (r 35(3), (4) added by SI 2012/500).
3   Ie a reference under the Mental Health Act 1983 s 68 (see PARA 964).
4   Tribunal Procedure (First-tier Tribunal) (Health, Education and Social Care Chamber) Rules 2008, SI 2008/2699, r 35(3)(a) (as added: see note 2).
5   Tribunal Procedure (First-tier Tribunal) (Health, Education and Social Care Chamber) Rules 2008, SI 2008/2699, r 35(4)(b) (as added: see note 2).
6   Tribunal Procedure (First-tier Tribunal) (Health, Education and Social Care Chamber) Rules 2008, SI 2008/2699, r 36(1). This is subject to r 38(4) (see PARA 976).
7   Ie under the Tribunal Procedure (First-tier Tribunal) (Health, Education and Social Care Chamber) Rules 2008, SI 2008/2699, r 33 (see PARA 973).

8   Tribunal Procedure (First-tier Tribunal) (Health, Education and Social Care Chamber) Rules 2008, SI 2008/2699, r 36.
9   The period of notice under the Tribunal Procedure (First-tier Tribunal) (Health, Education and Social Care Chamber) Rules 2008, SI 2008/2699, r 37(3) must be at least 14 days, except that in proceedings under the Mental Health Act 1983 s 66(1)(a) (see PARA 960) the period must be at least 3 working days; and the tribunal may give shorter notice with the parties' consent or in urgent or exceptional circumstances: Tribunal Procedure (First-tier Tribunal) (Health, Education and Social Care Chamber) Rules 2008, SI 2008/2699, r 37(4).
10 In proceedings under the Mental Health Act 1983s 66(1)(a) (see PARA 960) the hearing of the case must start within 7 days after the date on which the Tribunal received the application notice and in proceedings under s 75(1) (see PARAS 962, 965), the hearing of the case must start at least 5 weeks but no more than 8 weeks after the date on which the Tribunal received the reference: Tribunal Procedure (First-tier Tribunal) (Health, Education and Social Care Chamber) Rules 2008, SI 2008/2699, r 37(1), (2).
11 Ie notified under the Tribunal Procedure (First-tier Tribunal) (Health, Education and Social Care Chamber) Rules 2008, SI 2008/2699, r 33 (see PARA 973).
12 Tribunal Procedure (First-tier Tribunal) (Health, Education and Social Care Chamber) Rules 2008, SI 2008/2699, r 37(3).

976. Public and private hearings. All hearings must be held in private unless the tribunal[1] considers that it is in the interests of justice for the hearing to be held in public[2].

If a hearing is held in public, the tribunal may give a direction that part of the hearing is to be held in private[3].

Where a hearing, or part of it, is to be held in private, the tribunal may determine who is permitted to attend the hearing or part of it[4].

The tribunal may give a direction excluding from any hearing, or part of it:

(1)   any person whose conduct the tribunal considers is disrupting or is likely to disrupt the hearing[5];

(2)   any person whose presence the tribunal considers is likely to prevent another person from giving evidence or making submissions freely[6];

(3)   any person who the tribunal considers should be excluded in order to give effect to a direction[7] relating to the withholding of information likely to cause harm[8]; or

(4)   any person where the purpose of the hearing would be defeated by the attendance of that person[9].

The tribunal may give a direction excluding a witness from a hearing until that witness gives evidence[10].

1   As to the meaning of 'tribunal' see PARA 973 note 2.
2   Tribunal Procedure (First-tier Tribunal) (Health, Education and Social Care Chamber) Rules 2008, SI 2008/2699, r 38(1). As to the relevant factors in deciding whether to direct a hearing in public see *AH v West London MH Trust* (2010) UKUT 264 (AAC).
3   Tribunal Procedure (First-tier Tribunal) (Health, Education and Social Care Chamber) Rules 2008, SI 2008/2699, r 38(2).
4   Tribunal Procedure (First-tier Tribunal) (Health, Education and Social Care Chamber) Rules 2008, SI 2008/2699, r 38(3).
5   Tribunal Procedure (First-tier Tribunal) (Health, Education and Social Care Chamber) Rules 2008, SI 2008/2699, r 38(4)(a).
6   Tribunal Procedure (First-tier Tribunal) (Health, Education and Social Care Chamber) Rules 2008, SI 2008/2699, r 38(4)(b).
7   Ie a direction under the Tribunal Procedure (First-tier Tribunal) (Health, Education and Social Care Chamber) Rules 2008, SI 2008/2699, r 14(2) (see COURTS AND TRIBUNALS vol 24 (2010) PARA 879).
8   Tribunal Procedure (First-tier Tribunal) (Health, Education and Social Care Chamber) Rules 2008, SI 2008/2699, r 38(4)(c).
9   Tribunal Procedure (First-tier Tribunal) (Health, Education and Social Care Chamber) Rules 2008, SI 2008/2699, r 38(4)(d).

10 Tribunal Procedure (First-tier Tribunal) (Health, Education and Social Care Chamber) Rules 2008, SI 2008/2699, r 38(5).

977. Hearing's in a party's absence. If a party fails to attend a hearing the tribunal[1] may proceed with the hearing if the tribunal is satisfied that the party has been notified of the hearing[2] or that reasonable steps have been taken to notify the party of the hearing; and it considers that it is in the interests of justice to proceed with the hearing[3].

However, the tribunal may not proceed with a hearing in the absence of the patient[4] unless the patient has been medically examined[5] and the tribunal is satisfied that the patient has decided not to attend the hearing or the patient is unable to attend the hearing for reasons of ill health[6].

1 As to the meaning of 'tribunal' see PARA 973 note 2.
2 As to notification of the hearing see PARA 973.
3 Tribunal Procedure (First-tier Tribunal) (Health, Education and Social Care Chamber) Rules 2008, SI 2008/2699, r 39(1).
4 As to the meaning of 'patient' see PARA 973 note 7.
5 Ie unless the requirements of the Tribunal Procedure (First-tier Tribunal) (Health, Education and Social Care Chamber) Rules 2008, SI 2008/2699, r 34 (see PARA 974) have been satisfied.
6 Tribunal Procedure (First-tier Tribunal) (Health, Education and Social Care Chamber) Rules 2008, SI 2008/2699, r 39(2).

978. Power to pay allowances. The tribunal[1] may pay allowances in respect of travelling expenses, subsistence and loss of earnings to any person who attends a hearing as an applicant or a witness, a patient[2] who attends a hearing otherwise than as the applicant or a witness and any person (other than a legal representative) who attends as the representative of an applicant[3].

1 As to the meaning of 'tribunal' see PARA 973 note 2.
2 As to the meaning of 'patient' see PARA 973 note 7.
3 Tribunal Procedure (First-tier Tribunal) (Health, Education and Social Care Chamber) Rules 2008, SI 2008/2699, r 40.

979. Decisions. The tribunal[1] may give a decision orally at a hearing[2] and must provide[3] to each party as soon as reasonably practicable after making a decision which finally disposes of all issues in the proceedings[4] a decision notice stating the tribunal's decision, written reasons for the decision; and notification of any right of appeal against the decision and the time within which, and the manner in which, such right of appeal may be exercised[5].

1 As to the meaning of 'tribunal' see PARA 973 note 2.
2 Tribunal Procedure (First-tier Tribunal) (Health, Education and Social Care Chamber) Rules 2008, SI 2008/2699, r 41(1).
3 This is subject to the Tribunal Procedure (First-tier Tribunal) (Health, Education and Social Care Chamber) Rules 2008, SI 2008/2699, r 14(2) (withholding information likely to cause harm: see COURTS AND TRIBUNALS vol 24 (2010) PARA 879).
4 Except a decision under the Tribunal Procedure (First-tier Tribunal) (Health, Education and Social Care Chamber) Rules 2008, SI 2008/2699, Pt 5 (see COURTS AND TRIBUNALS).
5 Tribunal Procedure (First-tier Tribunal) (Health, Education and Social Care Chamber) Rules 2008, SI 2008/2699, r 41(2). The documents and information referred to in r41(2) must in proceedings under the Mental Health Act 1983 s 66(1)(a) (see PARA 960), be provided at the hearing or sent within 3 working days after the hearing and, in other cases, be provided at the hearing or sent within 7 days after the hearing: Tribunal Procedure (First-tier Tribunal) (Health, Education and Social Care Chamber) Rules 2008, SI 2008/2699, r 41(3). The Tribunal may provide written reasons for any decision to which r 41(2) does not apply: r 41(4).

(iii) Mental Health Review Tribunal for Wales

980.   Regulation of procedure. The Lord Chancellor[1] has power to make rules[2] with respect to the making of applications[3] to the Mental Health Review Tribunal for Wales, and with respect to the proceedings of that tribunal and matters incidental to or consequential on such proceedings[4]. Any such rules may in particular make provision enabling a tribunal to postpone consideration of an application[5]; for the transfer of proceedings to or from the Mental Health Review Tribunal for Wales in any case where, after the making of the application, the patient is moved into or out of Wales[6]; to dispose of an application without a formal hearing where this is not requested by the patient or it appears that such a hearing would be detrimental to his health[7]; to exclude members of the public or to prohibit publication of reports of the proceedings or the names of those concerned in them[8]; to regulate the representation of applicants[9]; and to regulate the methods by which relevant information may be obtained[10]. The rules may also restrict the persons qualified to serve on tribunals[11]; confer ancillary powers on tribunals[12]; require tribunals to make available to applicants and patients copies of documents, and statements of the substance of oral information, furnished or received in connection with the proceedings[13]; and require tribunals to state the reasons for their decisions[14].

In addition rules may be made for enabling any functions of a tribunal which relate to preliminary or incidental matters to be performed by the chairman of the tribunal[15]. If the chairman is unable to act, any functions conferred by the Mental Health Act 1983 on the chairman may be exercised by another tribunal member appointed for that purpose[16].

1   As to the Lord Chancellor see CONSTITUTIONAL LAW AND HUMAN RIGHTS vol 8(2) (Reissue) PARA 477 et seq. The Lord Chancellor's function under the Mental Health Act 1983 s 78 is a protected function for the purposes of the Constitutional Reform Act 2005 s 19: see s 19(5), Sch 7 para 4; and CONSTITUTIONAL LAW AND HUMAN RIGHTS.

2   Mental Health Review Tribunal for Wales Rules 2008, SI 2008/2705 (see PARAS 981–992). The overriding objective of the rules is to enable the tribunal to deal with cases fairly, justly, efficiently and expeditiously: r 3(1). Dealing with a case in accordance with r 3(1) includes avoiding unnecessary formality and seeking flexibility in the proceedings, ensuring, so far as practicable, that the parties are able to participate fully in the proceedings, using any special expertise of the tribunal effectively and avoiding delay, so far as compatible with proper consideration of the issues: r 3(2). The tribunal must seek to give effect to the overriding objective when it exercises any power under the rules or interprets any rule: r 3(3). An irregularity resulting from a failure to comply with any provision of the rules or a direction does not of itself render void the proceedings or any step taken in the proceedings: r 7(1). If a party has failed to comply with a requirement in the rules or a direction, the tribunal may take such action the tribunal considers just, which may include waiving the requirement or requiring the failure to be remedied: r 7(2).

3   The Mental Health Act 1983 s 78(1), (2) apply in relation to references to the Mental Health Review Tribunal for Wales as they apply in relation to applications to that tribunal by or in respect of patients: 78(3) (amended by SI 2008/2833).

4   Mental Health Act 1983 s 78(1)–(5) (s 78(1)–(4), (6)–(9) amended by SI 2008/2833). This includes provisions relating to assessment applications. Any rules under this power may be so framed as to apply to all applications or references or to applications or references of any specified class, and may make different provision in relation to different cases: s 78(5). The Mental Health Act 1983 s 78(2), (4), (6) prospectively amended by the Mental Health Act 2007 s 38(3) so that the word 'chairman' wherever it appears is replaced by the word 'president'. At the date at which this volume states the law no such day had been appointed.

5   See the Mental Health Act 1983 s 78(2)(a) (as amended and prospectively amended (see note 4)); the Mental Health Review Tribunal for Wales Rules 2008, SI 2008/2705, r 21; and PARA 985.

6   See the Mental Health Act 1983 s 78(2)(b) (substituted by SI 2008/2833). Rules may also be made concerning the transfer of references concerning restricted patients: see the Mental Health Act 1983 s 78(4)(b) (substituted by SI 2008/2833).
7   See the Mental Health Act 1983 s 78(2)(d) (as amended: see note 4).
8   See the Mental Health Act 1983 s 78(2)(e) (as amended: see note 4).
9   See the Mental Health Act 1983 s 78(2)(f) (as amended: see note 4).
10 See the Mental Health Act 1983 s 78(2)(g) (as amended: see note 4).
11 See the Mental Health Act 1983 s 78(2)(c) (as amended : see note 4). Rules may also be made restricting the persons qualified to serve as president of a tribunal when considering an application or reference relating to a restricted patient: s 78(4)(a) (prospectively amended: see note 4).
12 See the Mental Health Act 1983 s 78(2)(j) (as amended : see note 4).
13 See the Mental Health Act 1983 s 78(2)(h) (as amended: see note 4).
14 See the Mental Health Act 1983 s 78(2)(i) (as amended: see note 4).
15 Mental Health Act 1983 s 78(2)(k) (as amended (see note 4).
16 Mental Health Act 1983 s 78(6).

981.   Directions. The Mental Health Review Tribunal for Wales may give directions at any time in relation to the conduct or disposal of proceedings[1], including a direction amending or suspending an earlier direction[2]. The tribunal may give a direction on the application of one or more of the parties or on its own initiative[3]. An application for directions[4] must include the reason for making that application[5].

Unless the tribunal considers that there is a good reason not to do so, it must send written notice of any direction to every party and any other person affected by the direction[6].

1   Mental Health Review Tribunal for Wales Rules 2008, SI 2008/2705, r 5(1). As to power to extend time see r 5(2).
2   Mental Health Review Tribunal for Wales Rules 2008, SI 2008/2705, r 6(1).
3   Mental Health Review Tribunal for Wales Rules 2008, SI 2008/2705, r 6(2).
4   An application for directions may be made either by sending or delivering a written application to the tribunal or orally during the course of a hearing: Mental Health Review Tribunal for Wales Rules 2008, SI 2008/2705, r 6(4).
5   Mental Health Review Tribunal for Wales Rules 2008, SI 2008/2705, r 6(3).
6   Mental Health Review Tribunal for Wales Rules 2008, SI 2008/2705, r 6(5).

982.   Sending and delivery of documents. Any document to be sent or delivered to the Mental Health Review Tribunal for Wales under the Mental Health Review Tribunal for Wales Rules 2008[1] must be sent by prepaid post or delivered by hand, sent by facsimile transmission[2] to the number specified by the tribunal or sent or delivered by such other method as the tribunal may permit or direct[3].

A party may inform the tribunal and all other parties that a particular form of communication (other than pre-paid post or delivery by hand) should not be used to send documents to that party[4].

1   Ie under the Mental Health Review Tribunal for Wales Rules 2008, SI 2008/2705. Where any document is required or authorised by these Rules to be sent to any person it may be sent by prepaid post or delivered to the last known address of the person to whom the document is directed: r 9(4). This is subject to r 9(3).
2   If a party provides a facsimile transmission number, email address or other details for the electronic transmission of documents to them, that party must accept delivery of documents by that method: Mental Health Review Tribunal for Wales Rules 2008, SI 2008/2705, r 9(3).
3   Mental Health Review Tribunal for Wales Rules 2008, SI 2008/2705, r 9(1).
4   Mental Health Review Tribunal for Wales Rules 2008, SI 2008/2705, r 9(2). This is subject to r 9(3).

983.   Prohibitions on disclosure or publication.   Unless the Mental Health Review Tribunal for Wales gives a direction to the contrary, information about proceedings before it and the names of any persons concerned in such proceedings must not be made public[1].

The tribunal may make an order prohibiting the disclosure or publication of specified documents or information relating to the proceedings or any matter likely to lead members of the public to identify any person who the tribunal considers should not be identified[2].

1   Mental Health Review Tribunal for Wales Rules 2008, SI 2008/2705, r 10(1).

2   Mental Health Review Tribunal for Wales Rules 2008, SI 2008/2705, r 10(2). The tribunal may use the power in r 10(2) in order to take action under r 17 (withholding documents or information likely to cause harm: see PARA 984) and in such other circumstances as it considers just: r 10(3).

984.   Withholding information or documents likely to cause harm..   The Mental Health Review Tribunal for Wales must give a direction prohibiting the disclosure of a document or information to a person if it is satisfied that such disclosure would be likely to cause that person or some other person serious harm and having regard to the interests of justice that it is proportionate to give such a direction[1].

If a party ('the first party') considers that the tribunal should give such a direction prohibiting the disclosure of part or all of a document or of information to another party ('the second party'), the first party must exclude that part of the relevant document or that information from any document that will be provided to the second party and provide to the tribunal the excluded part of document or information and the reason for its exclusion, in order that the tribunal may decide whether the document or information should be disclosed to the second party or should be the subject of such a direction[2].

If the tribunal gives such a direction preventing disclosure to a party who has a representative, the tribunal may give a direction that the document or information be disclosed to that representative if it is satisfied that disclosure to the representative would be in the interests of the party and the representative would not be likely to act contrary to the following provision[3].

Documents or information disclosed to a representative in accordance with such a direction must not be disclosed either directly or indirectly to any other person without the tribunal's consent or be used otherwise than in connection with the proceedings[4].

1   Mental Health Review Tribunal for Wales Rules 2008, SI 2008/2705, r 17(1). The tribunal must conduct proceedings as appropriate in order to avoid undermining a direction given under r 17(1): r 17(3). See also *Dorset Healthcare NHS Foundation Trust v MH* [2009] UKUT 4 (AAC), [2009] PTSR 1112, 111 BMLR 1.

2   Mental Health Review Tribunal for Wales Rules 2008, SI 2008/2705, r 17(2).

3   Mental Health Review Tribunal for Wales Rules 2008, SI 2008/2705, r 17(4).

4   Mental Health Review Tribunal for Wales Rules 2008, SI 2008/2705, r 17(5).

985.   Postponement.   The Mental Health Review Tribunal for Wales may at any time postpone or adjourn a hearing for the purpose of obtaining further information or for such other purposes as it may think appropriate[1]. However, before postponing or adjourning any hearing, the tribunal may give such direction as it thinks fit for ensuring the prompt consideration of the application at a postponed or adjourned hearing[2].

Where a party requests that a hearing postponed or adjourned in accordance with these provisions be reconvened[3], the hearing must be reconvened if the tribunal is satisfied that reconvening would be in the interests of the patient[4].

1 Mental Health Review Tribunal for Wales Rules 2008, SI 2008/2705, r 21(1).
2 Mental Health Review Tribunal for Wales Rules 2008, SI 2008/2705, r 21(2).
3 Save in respect of an application under the Mental Health Act 1983 s 66(1)(a) (see PARA 960), before the tribunal reconvenes any hearing which has been adjourned without a further hearing date being fixed, it must give to all parties not less than 14 days' notice (or such shorter notice as all parties may consent to) of the date, time and place of the reconvened hearing: Mental Health Review Tribunal for Wales Rules 2008, SI 2008/2705, r 21(4)
4 Mental Health Review Tribunal for Wales Rules 2008, SI 2008/2705, r 21(3).

986. Substitution and addition of parties. The Mental Health Review Tribunal for Wales may give a direction substituting a party if the wrong person has been named as a party or the substitution has become necessary because of a change in circumstances since the start of proceedings[1]. The tribunal may give a direction adding a person to the proceedings as an interested party[2].

1 Mental Health Review Tribunal for Wales Rules 2008, SI 2008/2705, r 12(1). If the Tribunal gives a direction under r 12(1) or (2) it may give such consequential directions as it considers appropriate: r 12(3).
2 Mental Health Review Tribunal for Wales Rules 2008, SI 2008/2705, r 12(2).

987. Representatives. A party may appoint a representative[1] (whether legally qualified or not) to represent that party in the proceedings, not being a person liable to be detained or subject to guardianship or after-care under supervision or a community patient under the Mental Health Act 1983, or a person receiving treatment for mental disorder at the same hospital or registered establishment as the patient[2].

Anything permitted or required to be done by or provided to a party under these provisions or a direction, other than signing a witness statement, may be done by or provided to the representative of that party[3].

In the event of a representative being duly appointed the tribunal and other parties may assume that the representative is and remains authorised until receiving written notification to the contrary from the representative or the represented party and the tribunal must provide to the representative any document which is required to be sent to the represented party, and need not provide that document to the represented party[4].

Where the patient has not appointed a representative, the tribunal may appoint one if the patient has stated that they do not wish to conduct their own case or that they wish to be represented or the patient lacks the capacity to appoint a representative but the tribunal believes that it is in the patient's best interests for the patient to be represented[5].

Unless the tribunal otherwise directs, a patient or any other party may be accompanied by such other person as the patient or party wishes, in addition to any representative that may have been appointed under these provisions, provided that such person does not act as the representative of the patient or other party[6].

1 Mental Health Review Tribunal for Wales Rules 2008, SI 2008/2705, r 13(2).
2 Mental Health Review Tribunal for Wales Rules 2008, SI 2008/2705, r 13(1).
3 Mental Health Review Tribunal for Wales Rules 2008, SI 2008/2705, r 13(3).
4 Mental Health Review Tribunal for Wales Rules 2008, SI 2008/2705, r 13(4).
5 See the Mental Health Review Tribunal for Wales Rules 2008, SI 2008/2705, r 13(5).
6 Mental Health Review Tribunal for Wales Rules 2008, SI 2008/2705, r 13(6).

988. Before the final determination. An application or reference must be made in writing[1], be signed (in the case of an application, by the applicant or any person authorised by the applicant to do so) and be provided to the Mental Health Review Tribunal for Wales so that it is received within the specified[2] time[3].

When the tribunal receives a document from any party it must send a copy of that document to each other party and when it receives an application or reference it must send to the responsible authority or the Secretary of State, as the case may be, a request for certain documents and information[4]. On receipt of such information the tribunal must give notice of the proceedings:

(1)   where the patient is subject to the guardianship of a private guardian, to the guardian[5];

(2)   where there is an extant order of the superior court of record[6] to that court[7];

(3)   unless the patient requests otherwise, where any person other than the applicant is named in the responsible authority's statement as exercising the functions of the nearest relative[8], to that person[9];

(4)   where a local health board, a National Health Service trust, a primary care trust, a NHS Foundation Trust, a Strategic Health Authority, the Welsh Ministers or the Secretary of State has or have a right to discharge the patient[10], to such board, trust, authority, person or persons[11]; and

(5)   to any other person the tribunal may consider should have an opportunity of being heard[12].

Without restriction on the general power of giving directions[13] the tribunal may give further directions regarding certain matters[14]. The tribunal may admit evidence[15] whether or not the evidence would be admissible in a civil trial in the United Kingdom or whether or not the evidence was available to a previous decision maker[16]. It may also exclude evidence that would otherwise be admissible where the evidence was not provided within the time allowed by a direction, the evidence was otherwise provided in a manner that did not comply with a direction or it would otherwise be unfair to admit the evidence[17].

An applicant may withdraw an application by writing at any time with the consent of the tribunal[18].

1   As to the information to be included if possible see the Mental Health Review Tribunal for Wales Rules 2008, SI 2008/2705, r 14(2).
2   Ie the time specified in the Mental Health Act 1983 or the Repatriation of Prisoners Act 1984 (see PRISONS AND PRISONERS).
3   Mental Health Review Tribunal for Wales Rules 2008, SI 2008/2705, r 14(1). On receipt of an application or reference the tribunal must send a notice of the same to the responsible authority, the patient (where the patient is not the applicant) and, if the patient is a restricted patient, the Secretary of State: r 14(3). As to the transfer of proceedings see r 23.
4   See the Mental Health Review Tribunal for Wales Rules 2008, SI 2008/2705, r 15(1)–(5).
5   Mental Health Review Tribunal for Wales Rules 2008, SI 2008/2705, r 16(a). As to guardianship see PARA 784 et seq.
6   Ie established under the Mental Capacity Act 2005 s 45(1) (see PARA 720).
7   Mental Health Review Tribunal for Wales Rules 2008, SI 2008/2705, r 16(b).
8   As to the nearest relative see PARA 839.
9   Mental Health Review Tribunal for Wales Rules 2008, SI 2008/2705, r 16(c).
10 Ie under the Mental Health Act 1983 s 23(3) (see PARA 913).
11 Mental Health Review Tribunal for Wales Rules 2008, SI 2008/2705, r 16(d).
12 Mental Health Review Tribunal for Wales Rules 2008, SI 2008/2705, r 16(e).
13 Ie the general power under the Mental Health Review Tribunal for Wales Rules 2008, SI 2008/2705, r 5 (see PARA 981).

14   Mental Health Review Tribunal for Wales Rules 2008, SI 2008/2705, r 18(1).

15   The Tribunal may require any witness to give evidence on oath or affirmation, and may administer an oath or affirmation for that purpose: Mental Health Review Tribunal for Wales Rules 2008, SI 2008/2705, r 18(3). As to the summoning of witnesses see r 19.

16   Mental Health Review Tribunal for Wales Rules 2008, SI 2008/2705, r 18(2)(a).

17   Mental Health Review Tribunal for Wales Rules 2008, SI 2008/2705, r 18(2)(b).

18   See the Mental Health Review Tribunal for Wales Rules 2008, SI 2008/2705, r 22.

989.   Medical examination. Before the hearing to consider the final determination, a medical member of the Mental Health Review Tribunal for Wales must, so far as practicable examine the patient and take such other steps as that member considers necessary to form an opinion of the patient's mental condition[1]. For this purpose that member may examine the patient in private, examine records relating to the detention or treatment of the patient and any after-care services and take notes and copies of records for use in connection with the proceedings[2].

At any time before the tribunal makes the final determination, the tribunal or any one or more of its members may interview the patient, which interview may take place in the absence of any other person[3].

1   Mental Health Review Tribunal for Wales Rules 2008, SI 2008/2705, r 20(1).

2   Mental Health Review Tribunal for Wales Rules 2008, SI 2008/2705, r 20(2).

3   Mental Health Review Tribunal for Wales Rules 2008, SI 2008/2705, r 20(3).

990.   Hearings. The Mental Health Review Tribunal for Wales may give a direction permitting or requesting any person to attend and take part in a hearing[1] to such extent as the tribunal considers appropriate or make written submissions in relation to a particular issue[2].

Except where a patient requests a hearing in public[3] and the tribunal is satisfied that that would be in the interests of the patient, all hearings must be held in private[4]. Where a hearing is held in private, the tribunal may exclude particular individuals from the hearing or part of it or permit particular individuals to attend the hearing or part of it on such terms as it considers appropriate[5].

The tribunal may give a direction excluding from the hearing, or part of it:

(1)   any person whose conduct, in the opinion of the tribunal, is disrupting or is likely to disrupt the hearing[6];

(2)   any person whose presence the tribunal considers is likely to prevent another person from giving evidence or making submissions freely[7]; or

(3)   any person who the tribunal considers should be excluded in order to give effect to a direction[8] regarding the withholding information likely to cause harm[9].

The tribunal may give a direction excluding a witness from a hearing until that witness gives evidence[10].

If a party fails to attend a hearing, the tribunal may proceed with the hearing if it is satisfied that the party has been notified of the hearing or that reasonable steps have been taken to notify the party of the hearing and the tribunal is not aware of any good reason for the failure to attend or the tribunal otherwise considers that it is in the interests of the patient to proceed with the hearing[11].

1   As to the time and place of hearings see the Mental Health Review Tribunal for Wales Rules 2008, SI 2008/2705, r 24.

2   Mental Health Review Tribunal for Wales Rules 2008, SI 2008/2705, r 26.

3 Where the tribunal refuses a request for a public hearing or directs that a hearing which has begun in public continues in private, the tribunal must record in writing its reasons for holding the hearing in private and inform the patient of those reasons: Mental Health Review Tribunal for Wales Rules 2008, SI 2008/2705, r 25(2).
4 Mental Health Review Tribunal for Wales Rules 2008, SI 2008/2705, r 25(1).
5 Mental Health Review Tribunal for Wales Rules 2008, SI 2008/2705, r 25(3).
6 Mental Health Review Tribunal for Wales Rules 2008, SI 2008/2705, r 25(4)(a).
7 Mental Health Review Tribunal for Wales Rules 2008, SI 2008/2705, r 25(4)(b).
8 Ie a direction under the Mental Health Review Tribunal for Wales Rules 2008, SI 2008/2705, r 17 (see PARA 984).
9 Mental Health Review Tribunal for Wales Rules 2008, SI 2008/2705, r 25(4)(c).
10 Mental Health Review Tribunal for Wales Rules 2008, SI 2008/2705, r 25(5).
11 Mental Health Review Tribunal for Wales Rules 2008, SI 2008/2705, r 27.

991. Decisions. The Mental Health Review Tribunal for Wales may give a decision orally at a hearing or may reserve its decision[1] but it must send[2] to each party as soon as reasonably practicable following a final determination a notice stating the tribunal's decision and written reasons for the decision[3].

Where the tribunal considers that the full disclosure of the recorded reasons for its decision to the patient would cause the patient or any other person serious harm, the tribunal may instead communicate its decision to him in such manner as it thinks appropriate and may communicate its decision to the other parties subject to any conditions it may think appropriate as to the disclosure thereof to the patient[4].

Where the tribunal makes a decision with recommendations, the decision may specify any period at the expiration of which the tribunal will consider the case further in the event of those recommendations not being complied with[5].

1 Mental Health Review Tribunal for Wales Rules 2008, SI 2008/2705, r 28(1).
2 Such documents must be sent in proceedings under the Mental Health Act 1983 s 66(1)(a) (see PARA 960), within 3 working days of the hearing and, in other proceedings, within 7 days of the hearing: Mental Health Review Tribunal for Wales Rules 2008, SI 2008/2705, r 28(3). Subject to r 10 (prohibitions on disclosure or publication: see PARA 983) the tribunal may, where appropriate, send notice of a decision or the reasons for it to any person: r 28(6).
3 Mental Health Review Tribunal for Wales Rules 2008, SI 2008/2705, r 28(2).
4 Mental Health Review Tribunal for Wales Rules 2008, SI 2008/2705, r 28(4).
5 Mental Health Review Tribunal for Wales Rules 2008, SI 2008/2705, r 28(5).

992. Permission to appeal. A party seeking permission to appeal on a point of law[1] from the Mental Health Review Tribunal for Wales to the Upper Tribunal must send or deliver to the tribunal a written application for permission to appeal so that it is received no later[2] than 28 days after the date that the tribunal sent written reasons for the decision to the party making the application[3].

The application must identify the decision of the tribunal to which it relates, identify the alleged error or errors of law in the decision and state the result the party making the application seeks[4].

Upon considering the application for permission to appeal, the tribunal must send to the parties as soon as practicable a record of its decision and, if the tribunal has refused to grant permission[5], reasons for such refusal and notification of the right to make an application to the Upper Tribunal for permission to appeal and the time within which, and the method by which, such application must be made[6].

1 Ie under the Mental Health Act 1983 s 78A (see PARA 958).
2 If the party sends or delivers the application to the tribunal later than the time required by the Mental Health Review Tribunal for Wales Rules 2008, SI 2008/2705, r 30(2) or by any extension of time under r 5(2)(a) (power to extend time: see PARA 981) the application must

include a request for an extension of time and the reason why the application was not provided in time and unless the tribunal extends time for the application under r 5(2)(a), the tribunal must not admit the application: r 30(3).

3   Mental Health Review Tribunal for Wales Rules 2008, SI 2008/2705, r 30(1), (2).

4   Mental Health Review Tribunal for Wales Rules 2008, SI 2008/2705, r 30(4).

5   The tribunal may grant permission to appeal on limited grounds, but must comply with these provisions in relation to any grounds on which it has refused permission Mental Health Review Tribunal for Wales Rules 2008, SI 2008/2705, r 30(6).

6   Mental Health Review Tribunal for Wales Rules 2008, SI 2008/2705, r 30(5).

8. LITIGATION

(1) CIVIL

993.   Limitation.   A person who lacks capacity to conduct legal proceedings[1] is to be treated as under a disability for the purpose of the Limitation Act 1980[2]. Where a right of action accrues to a person under a disability the period within which the claim must be brought generally begins to run only from the time when he ceases to be under a disability[3].

1   Ie within the meaning of the Mental Capacity Act 2005 (see PARA 597).
2   See the Limitation Act 1980 s 38(2); and LIMITATION PERIODS vol 68 (2008) PARA 1170.
3   See the Limitation Act 1980 s 28; and LIMITATION PERIODS vol 68 (2008) PARAS 1171–1179. However, the Court of Protection has power in relation to litigation on behalf of a patient: see PARAS 724, 727. As to the extension of time in latent damage cases see s 28A; and LIMITATION PERIODS vol 68 (2008) PARA 1173.

994.   Solicitor's authority.   The authority of a solicitor under a retainer[1] given by a client not mentally disordered at the time of giving it ceases[2] as soon as the client becomes mentally disordered[3]. It is immaterial whether or not the solicitor was aware that the client had become mentally disordered, and if he continues to appear for him after the mental disorder has supervened he is liable in damages[4] to the other party to the claim[5]. However, the question whether a claimant is mentally disordered is not an issue which it is competent to the defendant to raise in his defence, since, in effect, it challenges the authority of the claimant's solicitor to institute proceedings, and that is a matter which must be dealt with by an application to stay the claim[6]. A defence which sets up, or attempts to set up, such an issue may be struck out or treated as irrelevant[7].

1   As to the principles governing the retainer of a solicitor by a client see LEGAL PROFESSIONS vol 66 (2009) PARA 763 et seq; as to retainer by mentally disordered persons see LEGAL PROFESSIONS vol 66 (2009) PARA 771.
2   As to the determination of agency on the person who has appointed an agent becoming incapacitated see PARA 600. In a proper case where a solicitor has acted in litigation for a claimant, an inquiry will be directed as to the competency of the claimant at the date of the claim form to retain a solicitor: *Pomery v Pomery* [1909] WN 158.
3   *Yonge v Toynbee* [1910] 1 KB 215, CA. However, it seems that the solicitor is under a duty to furnish the person proposing to be litigation friend (formerly 'next friend' or 'guardian ad litem') with the necessary order, certificate or other document (see PARA 996) required under CPR 21; c f *Fore Street Warehouse Co Ltd v Durrant & Co* (1883) 10 QBD 471 at 474. As to the position where the claimant becomes a patient after a claim is begun see PARA 997. As to representation at a tribunal see PARA 955.
4   The measure of damages is the amount of costs thrown away by the other party to the claim: *Yonge v Toynbee* [1910] 1 KB 215, CA.
5   *Yonge v Toynbee* [1910] 1 KB 215, CA. As to a solicitor's continued authority to act despite his client's incapacity see *Practice Direction* (1995) 145 NLJ 1403.
6   *Richmond v Branson & Son* [1914] 1 Ch 968 at 974; *J (otherwise B) v J* [1953] P 186 at 190, [1952] 2 All ER 1129 at 1132.
7   *Richmond v Branson & Son* [1914] 1 Ch 968.

995.   Necessity for litigation friend.   A protected party[1] must have a litigation friend[2] to conduct proceedings on his behalf[3].

A person may not, without the permission of the court, make an application against a protected person before proceedings have started or take any step in proceedings (except issuing and serving a claim form or applying for the appointment of a litigation friend[4]) until the protected party has a litigation friend[5]. If during proceedings a party lacks capacity to continue to conduct proceedings, no party may take any further step in the proceedings without the permission of the court until the protected party has a litigation friend[6].

Where a protected party regains or acquires capacity to conduct the proceedings, the litigation friend's appointment continues until it is ended by court order[7].

1   A 'protected party' means a party, or an intended party, who lacks capacity to conduct the proceedings: CPR 21.1(2)(d). As to the meaning of 'lacks capacity' see the Mental Capacity Act 2005; and PARA 603 (definition applied by CPR 21.1(2)(c)).The Mental Capacity Act 2005 principles are thus introduced into civil litigation so that all practicable steps must be taken to assist the person to litigate: see *Saulle v Nouvet* [2007] EWHC 2902 (QB), [2007] All ER (D) 08 (Dec). The test of mental capacity is issue specific: see *Bailey v Warren* [2006] EWCA Civ 51, (2006) Times, 20 February. See also *Masterman-Lister v Brutton & Co* [2003] EWCA Civ 70, [2003] 1 WLR 1511. The court must investigate the issue of capacity at the first convenient opportunity when it is suspected it may be absent: see *Saulle v Nouvet*; and *Masterman-Lister v Brutton and Co*.

2   A person may become a litigation friend without a court order under CPR 21.5 (see PARA 996) or by a court order under CPR 21.6 (see PARA 997). See also *Practice Direction—Children and Patients* PD 21 paras 2.1–2.4.

3   See CPR 21.2(1); and CIVIL PROCEDURE vol 11 (2009) PARA 222. See also *Practice Direction—Children and Patients* PD 21. Failure to have a litigation friend may result in a settlement agreement being void: see *Dunhill (by her litigation friend, Paul Tasker) v Burgin* [2012] EWCA Civ 397, [2012] All ER (D) 32 (Apr) (compromise agreement held void where claimant lacked capacity).

     Case law decided under the former rules of court held that if a plaintiff was not in fact a patient, he could apply to have the action dismissed and the next friend ordered to pay the costs (*Palmer v Walesby* (1868) 3 Ch App 732; *Didisheim v London and Westminster Bank* [1900] 2 Ch 15, CA); in this connection an inquiry could be directed whether the plaintiff was mentally disordered and whether the action was for his benefit (*Howell v Lewis* (1891) 65 LT 672; *Pomery v Pomery* [1909] WN 158), and when it was shown that an action was not for the plaintiff's benefit the court would stay it (*Didisheim v London and Westminster Bank* above; *New York Security and Trust Co v Keyser* [1901] 1 Ch 666 at 670; *Beall v Smith* (1873) 9 Ch App 85; *Porter v Porter* (1888) 37 ChD 420, CA; *Waterhouse v Worsnop* (1888) 59 LT 140).

     The requirement for a litigation friend is unlikely to breach the Convention for the Protection of Human Rights and Fundamental Freedoms (Rome, 4 November 1950; TS 71 (1953); Cmd 8969) art 6(1) (see RIGHTS AND FREEDOMS): *Stewart-Brady v United Kingdom* (1997) 24 EHRR CD 38. See also *Ashingdane v United Kingdom* (1985) 7 EHRR 528, ECtHR.

4   Ie under CPR 21.6 (see PARA 997).

5   CPR 21.3(2). It has been decided in the past that the litigation friend (formerly 'next friend') is not a party as such: see *Pink v JA Sharwood & Co Ltd* [1913] 2 Ch 286.

6   CPR 21.3(3). Any step taken before a protected party has a litigation friend is of no effect unless the court otherwise orders: CPR 21.3(4). Pending appointment of a litigation friend, further steps in the proceedings may be taken with the permission of the court. The court is likely to regularise the position if the parties have acted in good faith and there is no manifest disadvantage to the party subsequently found to be a protected party: see *Masterman-Lister v Brutton & Co* [2003] EWCA Civ 70, [2003] 1 WLR 1511.

7   CPR 21.9(2). An application for such an order may be made by the former protected party, the litigation friend or a party: CPR 21.9(3). As to relevant procedure see CPR 21.9(4)–(6).

996. Appointment otherwise than by court order. A deputy appointed by the Court of Protection[1] under the Mental Capacity Act 2005 with power to conduct legal proceedings on the protection party's[2] behalf is entitled to be the litigation friend[3] of the protected party in any proceedings to which his power extends[4]. If nobody has been appointed by the court or, in the case of a protected party, is so authorised as a deputy, a person may act as a litigation friend if he: (1) can fairly and competently conduct proceedings on behalf of the protected party; (2) has no interest adverse to that of the protected party; and (3) where the protected party is a claimant, undertakes to pay any costs which the protected party may be ordered to pay in relation to the proceedings, subject to any right he may have to be repaid from the assets of the protected party[5].

If the court has not appointed a litigation friend, a person who wishes to act as a litigation friend must follow the following procedure[6]. A deputy appointed by the Court of Protection under the Mental Capacity Act 2005 must file an official copy of the order of the Court of Protection which confers his power to act either, where the deputy is to act as a litigation friend for a claimant, at the time the claim is made or, where the deputy is to act as a litigation friend for a defendant, at the time when he first takes a step in the proceedings on behalf of the defendant[7]. Any other person must file a certificate of suitability stating that he satisfies the conditions specified in heads (1) to (3) above either, where the person is to act as a litigation friend for a claimant, at the time when the claim is made or, where the person is to act as a litigation friend for a defendant, at the time when he first takes a step in the proceedings on behalf of the defendant[8]. The litigation friend must serve the certificate of suitability on every person on whom[11] the claim form should be served and also file a certificate of service[12] when filing the certificate of suitability[13].

1   As to the Court of Protection see PARA 720.
2   As to the meaning of 'protected party' see PARA 995 note 1.
3   As to the litigation friend see PARA 995.
4   CPR 21.4(2). CPR 21.4 does not apply if the court has appointed a person to be litigation friend (see PARA 997): see CPR 21.4(1).
5   CPR 21.4(3).
6   CPR 21.5(1).
7   CPR 21.5(2).
8   CPR 21.5(3).
11 Ie in accordance with CPR 6.13: see PARA 999.
12 As to the details to be contained such a certificate see CPR 6.17 and 6.29; and CIVIL PROCEDURE vol 11 (2009) PARAS 154, 179.
13 CPR 21.5(4).

997.   Appointment by court order.   The court may make an order appointing a litigation friend[1] and an application for such an order may be made by a person who wishes to be the litigation friend or a party[2]. Where a person makes a claim against a protected party[3], the protected party has no litigation friend, and either someone who is entitled to be a litigation friend files a defence or the claimant wishes to take some step in the proceedings, the claimant must apply to the court for an order appointing a litigation friend for the protected party[4].

The court may make an order: (1) directing that a person may not act as a litigation friend; (2) terminating a litigation friend's appointment; or (3) appointing a new litigation friend in substitution for an existing one[5].

An application for such an order[6] must be served on every person on whom[7] the claim form should be served[8]. Where an application for a court order[9] is in respect of a patient, the application must also be served on the patient unless the court orders otherwise[10]. An application to change a litigation friend[11] must also be served on the person who is the litigation friend, or who is purporting to act as the litigation friend, when the application is made, and the person who it is proposed should be the litigation friend, if he is not the applicant[12]. On an application for either order[13], the court may appoint the person proposed or any other person complying with the relevant conditions[14].

1   As to the litigation friend see PARA 995.
2   CPR 21.6(1), (2).
3   As to the meaning of 'protected party' see PARA 995 note 1.

4   CPR 21.6(3). Such an application must be supported by evidence, including consents to act, and
    the court may not appoint a litigation friend unless there is compliance with the conditions in
    CPR 21.4(3) (see PARA 996): CPR 21.6(4), (5). See further *Folks v Faizey* [2006] EWCA Civ
    381, [2006] All ER (D) 83 (Apr).
5   CPR 21.7(1). Such an application must be supported by evidence and there must be compliance
    with the conditions in CPR 21.4(3) (see PARA 996): CPR 21.7(2), (3).
6   Ie an order under CPR 21.6 or CPR 21.7.
7   Ie in accordance with CPR 6.13: see PARA 999.
8   CPR 21.8(1).
9   Ie an application under CPR 21.6.
10 CPR 21.8(2).
11 Ie an application under CPR 21.7.
12 CPR 21.8(3).
13 Ie an order under CPR 21.6 or CPR 21.7.
14 CPR 21.8(4). The conditions referred to in the text are those specified in CPR 21.4(3) (see PARA
    996).

998.   Proceedings by foreign curator.   A foreign curator or other authorised
person duly appointed by a foreign court may sue in his own name and that of
the patient for the recovery of the patient's property[1], but the court has
discretion as to directing the property to be handed over to the curator or other
authorised person, although an order will generally be made[2]. Appointment of a
foreign curator does not displace the jurisdiction of the English court to
determine what course of action is in the best interests of the person concerned[3].

1   *Didisheim v London and Westminster Bank* [1900] 2 Ch 15 at 43–44, CA; *Thiery v Chalmers,
    Guthrie & Co* [1900] 1 Ch 80. A Scottish curator may sue and give discharges for the patient's
    personal estate in England: *Scott v Bentley* (1855) 1 Jur NS 394.
        In *Pélégrin v Coutts & Co, Pélégrin v L Messel & Co* [1915] 1 Ch 696, the plaintiff who
    was the provisional administrator of the property of a foreign lunatic, was empowered by the
    Civil Tribunal of the Seine to receive all money, securities and deeds deposited by the lunatic
    with the defendants, who refused to deliver up the securities and money, but required the
    plaintiff to bring an action in this country for their protection. It was held that, the order by the
    French court being substantially the same as the order made in *Didisheim v London and
    Westminster Bank*, the defendants, in refusing to act on the order of the French court, had
    exercised undue caution and were not entitled to costs against the plaintiff.
2   *Re Knight* [1898] 1 Ch 257, CA; *New York Security and Trust Co v Keyser* [1901] 1 Ch 666; *Re
    Hill* [1900] 1 IR 349; *Re Barlow's Will* (1887) 36 ChD 287, CA (distinguished in *Re De Linden,
    Re Spurrier's Settlement, De Hayn v Garland* [1897] 1 Ch 453).
3   *Re S (Hospital Patient: Foreign Curator)* [1996] Fam 23, [1995] 4 All ER 30, [1996] 1 FCR
    128.

999.   Procedure.   Where a defendant is a protected person[1] the claim form
must be served on the attorney under a registered enduring power of attorney,
the donee of a lasting power of attorney or the deputy appointed by the Court of
Protection[2] or, where there is no such person, an adult with whom the protected
party resides or in whose care the protected party is[3]. In the case of an
application for an order appointing a litigation friend[4] where a patient has no
litigation friend[5], service must be on every person on whom the claim form
should be served, namely the above named persons[6]. In the case of any other
document, service must be made on the litigation friend who is conducting
proceedings on behalf of the protected person[7]. The court may make an order
permitting a claim form to be served on the protected person, or some person
other than the person specified above[8]. The court may also order that, although
a document has been served on someone other than the person specified above,
the document is to be treated as if it had been properly served[9].

Where the defendant makes certain admissions[10], the claimant has a right to enter judgment except where the defendant is a protected party or, in the case of some of those admissions[11], where the claimant is a protected party[12].

1 As to the meaning of 'protected person' see PARA 995 note 1.
2 As to the Court of Protection see PARA 720.
3 CPR 6.13(2). Service on the medical officer of the institution in which the defendant was resident was allowed in relation to a corresponding previous rule (*Raine v Wilson* (1873) LR 16 Eq 576); and that was the proper practice where the defendant was detained in an institution (*Fore Street Warehouse Co Ltd v Durrant & Co* (1883) 10 QBD 471, DC; *Robinson v Galland* (1889) 5 TLR 504 at 505), and the keeper of an institution who refuses to allow service is liable to committal (*Denison v Hardings* [1867] WN 17). Service on the defendant's business manager is insufficient: *Fore Street Warehouse Co Ltd v Durrant & Co.*
4 As to the litigation friend see PARA 995.
5 Ie an application under CPR 21.8: see PARA 997.
6 CPR 6.25(1), CPR 21.8(1).
7 CPR 6.25(2).
8 CPR 6.13(4); CPR 6.25(3). Such an application may be made without notice: CPR 6.13(5) CPR 6.25(4).
9 CPR 6.13(6); CPR 6.25(5). If documents are served on the patient as if he were not a patient the proceedings against him are technically invalid: *Cutbush v Cutbush* (1893) 37 Sol Jo 685 (a decision in regard to an earlier version of the rules).
10 The admissions are: admission of the whole of a claim for a specified amount of money (under CPR 14.4); admission of part of a claim for a specified amount of money (under CPR 14.5); admission of liability to pay the whole of a claim for an unspecified amount of money (under CPR 14.6); and admission of liability to pay a claim for an unspecified amount of money where the defendant offers a sum in satisfaction of the claim (under CPR 14.7).
11 Ie the admissions under CPR 14.5 and CPR 14.7.
12 CPR 14.1(4).

1000. Recovery on behalf of a patient. Where a claim is made by or on behalf of a protected party[1] or against a protected party, no settlement, compromise or payment, and no acceptance of money paid into court is valid, so far as it relates to the claim by, on behalf of or against the patient, without the approval of the court[2].

In any proceedings where: (1) money is recovered by or on behalf of or for the benefit of, a protected party[3]; or (2) money paid into court is accepted by or on behalf of a protected party[4], the money must be dealt with in accordance with directions given by the court and not otherwise[5], which may provide that the money be wholly or partly paid into court and invested or otherwise dealt with there[6]. Where money is recovered by or on behalf of a protected party or money paid into court is accepted by or on behalf of a protected party, before giving such directions, the court will first consider whether the protected party is a protected beneficiary[7].

A litigation friend who incurs expenses[8] on behalf of a protected party in any proceedings is entitled to recover the amount paid or payable out of any money recovered or paid into court to the extent that it has been reasonably incurred and is reasonable in amount[9].

1 As to the meaning of 'protected party' see PARA 995 note 1.
2 CPR 21.10(1). Where before proceedings in which a claim is made by or on behalf of, or against a protected party (whether alone or with any other person) are begun, an agreement is reached for the settlement of the claim and the sole purpose of the proceedings on that claim is to obtain the approval of the court to a settlement or compromise of the claim, the claim must be made using the alternative procedure for claims (see CPR Pt 8) and must include a request to the court for approval of the settlement or compromise: CPR 21.10(2). In proceedings relating to fixed recoverable costs in road traffic accidents (see CPR Pt 45 Section II or VI), the court must not make an order for detailed assessment of costs payable to the protected party but must assess the

costs in the manner set out in CPR Pt 45 Section II or VI: CPR 21.10(3). For provisions where money is payable to a patient see CPR 48.5. Hearings under CPR 21.10 must be held in public, however the hearing, or part of it, may be held in private if necessary to protect the interests of any protected party: see CPR 39.2(1), (3)(d); and CIVIL PROCEDURE vol 11 (2009) PARA 6. See further *JXF (a child, by his mother and litigation friend) v York Hospitals NHS Foundation Trust* [2010] EWHC 2800 (QB), 117 BMLR 1; *Re Guardian News and Media Ltd* [2010] UKSC 1, [2010] 2 AC 697, [2010] 2 All ER 799; *JIH v News Group Newspapers Ltd* [2011] EWCA Civ 42, [2011] 2 All ER 324, [2011] 1 WLR 1645; *CVB v MGN Ltd* [2012] EWHC 1148 (QB), [2012] All ER (D) 82 (May); *ETK v News Group Newspapers Ltd* [2011] EWCA Civ 439, [2011] 1 WLR 1827, [2011] 18 LS Gaz R 18; *Re (a child) (publication of report of proceedings: restrictions)* [2011] EWHC 454 (QB), 120 BMLR 59, [2011] EMLR 338.

A compromise agreement may be withdrawn prior to formal approval by the court even if made or accepted by reference to CPR Pt 36: *Drinkall v Whitwood* [2003] EWCA Civ 1547, [2004] 4 All ER 378 [2004] 1 WLR 462. As to the need for any hearing to be in private and the provision of counsel's opinion in advance see *Beatham v Carlisle Hospitals NHS Trusts* (1999) Times, 20 May. See also CPR 39.2(3)(d). The aim is to ensure that there is adequate compensation for the claimant and that his interests are properly protected: see *Black v Yates* [1992] QB 526, [1991] 4 All ER 722. As to costs where money is payable to a protected party see CPR 48.5. As to expert reports see *IB v CV* [2010] EWHC 3815 (QB).

3   CPR 21.11(1)(a).

4   CPR 21.11(1)(b).

5   CPR 21.11(1). See CPR 21.11; and CIVIL PROCEDURE vol 11 (2009) PARA 73. As to the apportionment between entitled persons of money recovered under the Fatal Accidents Act 1976 see *Practice Direction—Children and Patients* PD 21 paras 7.1–7.4.

6   CPR 21.11(2). Such directions may include: that the money be paid into the High Court for investment; that certain sums be paid direct to the protected person, his litigation friend (see PARA 995) or his legal representative for the immediate benefit of the protected person or for expenses incurred on his behalf; and that the applications in respect of the investment of the money be transferred to a local district registry: see *Practice Direction—Children and Patients* PD 21 paras 8.1–8.4.

Where the sum to be administered is over £30,000, unless a person with authority as the attorney under a registered enduring power of attorney, the donee of a lasting power of attorney or the deputy appointed by the Court of Protection, the order approving the settlement will contain a direction to the litigation friend to apply to the Court of Protection for the appointment of a deputy, after which the fund will be transferred to the Court of Protection; where the sum to be administered is under £30,000, it may be retained in court and dealt with as if the protected person were a child: *Practice Direction—Children and Patients* PD 21 para 10.2.

7   CPR 21.11(3).

8   Expenses may include all or part of an insurance premium, as defined by CPR 43.2(1)(m) or interest on a loan taken out to pay an insurance premium or other recoverable disbursement: CPR 21.12(2).

9   CPR 21.12(1). No application may be made under the rule for expenses that are of a type that may be recoverable on an assessment of costs payable by or out of money belonging to a child or protected party; but are disallowed in whole or in part on such an assessment: CPR 21.12(3). In deciding whether the expenses were reasonably incurred and reasonable in amount, the court will have regard to all the circumstances of the case including the factors set out in rule 44.5(3). When the court is considering the factors to be taken into account in assessing the reasonableness of the expenses, it will have regard to the facts and circumstances as they reasonably appeared to the litigation friend or to the protected party's legal representative when the expense was incurred: CPR 21.12(4). Where the claim is settled or compromised, or judgment is given, on terms that an amount not exceeding £5,000 is paid to the protected party, the total amount the litigation friend may recover under these provisions must not exceed 25% of the sum so agreed or awarded, unless the court directs otherwise. Such total amount must not exceed 50% of the sum so agreed or awarded: CPR 21.12(6).

1001. Costs where money is payable by a protected person. Where a party is a protected party[1] and money is ordered or agreed to be paid to, or for the benefit of, that party or money is ordered to be paid by him or on his behalf, the general rule is that the court must order a detailed assessment of the costs[2] payable by, or out of money belonging to, any party who is a protected party[3].

On such an assessment the court must also assess any costs payable to that party in the proceedings, unless the court has issued a default costs certificate in relation to those costs[4] or the costs are payable in proceedings[5] to which fixed recoverable costs in road traffic accidents apply[6].

Where a claimant is a protected party and a detailed assessment has taken place under the above provisions, the only amount payable by the protected party is the amount which the court certifies as payable[7].

1 As to the meaning of 'protected party' see CPR 48.5(1); and PARA 995 note 1.
2 The court need not order detailed assessment of costs in the circumstances set out in the Costs Practice Direction: CPR 48.5(3).
3 CPR 48.5(1), (2)(a). This applies to a counterclaim by or on behalf of a protected party by virtue of CPR 20.3: see CIVIL PROCEDURE vol 11 (2009) PARA 619.
4 Ie under CPR 47.11 (see CIVIL PROCEDURE vol 12 (2009) PARA 1789).
5 Ie proceedings to which CPR Pt 45 section II or section VI applies.
6 CPR 48.5(2)(b).
7 CPR 48.5(4).

1002. Enforcement against a patient. If judgment is obtained against a defendant under a mental disability, a stay of execution may be granted[1] to enable an application to be made by the receiver of the income to the Court of Protection for leave to pay the amount of the judgment debt out of the protected person's estate[2].

When a charging order is obtained under the general enactments relating to execution[3] against the property of a mentally disordered person, the court has no power to make an order providing that the amount to be charged is to be determined by the master of the Court of Protection, for the judgment creditor is entitled to an unconditional order[4].

Although disability is in itself not a bar to the granting of an injunction or the enforcing of an order made, if a person against whom an injunction is being sought is incapable of understanding what he is doing or that it is wrong, an injunction ought not to be granted against him, because he would not be capable of complying with it, it would have no deterrent effect, and he would have a clear defence to an application for committal for contempt[5].

1 *Burt v Blackburn* (1887) 3 TLR 356, CA.
2 *Ames v Parkinson* (1847) 2 Ph 388. As to the meaning of 'protected person' see PARA 995 note 1.
3 See generally CIVIL PROCEDURE vol 12 (2009) PARAS 1242, 1467 et seq.
4 See *Horne v Pountain* (1889) 23 QBD 264; but see note 1.
5 See *Wookey v Wookey, Re S (A Minor)* [1991] Fam 121, [1991] 3 All ER 365, CA (non-molestation injunction under the Domestic Violence and Matrimonial Proceedings Act 1976). See also *P v P (Contempt of Court: Mental Capacity)* [1999] 2 FLR 897, CA; *Harris v Harris* (22 April 1999) Lexis, CA. As to non-molestation orders see now the Family Law Act 1996 s 42; and MATRIMONIAL AND CIVIL PARTNERSHIP LAW vol 73 (2009) PARA 716 et seq.

1003. Competence. In civil proceedings a person is not competent to give evidence if, at the time of being tendered as a witness he is mentally incapable of testifying, he was for the time being incapable of understanding questions and of giving a rational account of events due to illness; or he does not appreciate the nature and obligation of an oath or affirmation[1].

Questions as to the competence or incompetence of a witness are decided by the court[2]. In civil proceedings the court has a general discretionary power to control evidence[3].

1 See CIVIL PROCEDURE vol 11 (2009) PARA 966.

2   See CIVIL PROCEDURE vol 11 (2009) PARA 967.
3   See CIVIL PROCEDURE vol 11 (2009) PARAS 791, 967.

(2) CRIMINAL

1004.   Criminal responsibility.   Where, on a criminal charge, it appears that, at the time of the act or omission giving rise to the offence alleged, the defendant was labouring under a defect of reason owing to a disease of the mind so as not to know the nature and quality of his act, or, if he knew this, so as not to know that what he was doing was wrong, he is not regarded in law as responsible for his act[1]. Under such circumstances the defendant is entitled to an acquittal, and the proper verdict in the Crown Court is one of not guilty by reason of insanity[2].

It may be necessary for the court to obtain and consider a medical report where the offender is or appears to be mentally disordered[3].

1   See CRIMINAL LAW vol 25 (2010) PARA 30. The question whether, owing to a defect of reason due to disease of the mind, the defendant was not responsible for his act is a question of fact and is therefore to be determined by the jury in a case tried in the Crown Court: CRIMINAL LAW vol 25 (2010) PARA 30. See also CRIMINAL LAW vol 25 (2010) PARA 31. As to the burden and mode of proof of insanity see CRIMINAL LAW vol 25 (2010) PARA 32.
2   See CRIMINAL LAW vol 25 (2010) PARA 35. As to the powers to deal with persons not guilty by reason of insanity or unfit to plead see the Criminal Procedure (Insanity) Act 1964 s 5; and SENTENCING AND DISPOSITION OF OFFENDERS.
3   See SENTENCING AND DISPOSITION OF OFFENDERS vol 92 (2010) PARA 627.

1005.   Competence.   A person is not competent to give evidence in criminal proceedings if it appears to the court that he is unable to understand questions put to him as a witness, and give answers to them which can be understood[1]. The competence of a witness must be determined by the court and it is for the party calling the witness to satisfy the court that, on a balance of probabilities, the witness is competent to give evidence in the proceedings[2].

Special measures may be taken where the court considers that the quality of evidence given by a witness is likely to be diminished because the witness suffers from mental disorder within the meaning of the Mental Health Act 1983, or otherwise has a significant impairment of intelligence and social functioning[3].

A statement not made in oral evidence in the proceedings is admissible as evidence of any matter stated where a person is unfit to be a witness because of his mental condition[4].

For such evidence to be admissible the person making the statement must have the required capability at the time he made the statement[5].

In criminal cases, it may be necessary to warn the jury in clear terms of the danger of convicting on the unsupported evidence of patients from hospitals providing high security psychiatric services[6].

1   See the Youth and Criminal Evidence Act 1999 s 53(3); and CRIMINAL PROCEDURE vol 28 (2010) PARA 508.
2   See the Youth and Criminal Evidence Act 1999 s 54(1), (2); and CRIMINAL PROCEDURE vol 28 (2010) PARA 508.
3   See the Youth and Criminal Evidence Act 1999 ss 16, 18; and CRIMINAL PROCEDURE vol 28 (2010) PARA 537. As to the special measures see ss 23–30; and CRIMINAL PROCEDURE vol 28 (2010) PARA 541–548. As to the status of evidence given in accordance with the special measures see s 31; and CRIMINAL PROCEDURE vol 28 (2010) PARA 549.
4   See the Criminal Justice Act 2003 s 116; and CRIMINAL PROCEDURE vol 28 (2010) PARA 643.
5   See the Criminal Justice Act 2003 s 123; and CRIMINAL PROCEDURE vol 28 (2010) PARAS 514, 651.

6   See *R v Spencer* [1987] AC 128, [1986] 3 All ER 928, HL; and CRIMINAL PROCEDURE vol 28
     (2010) PARAS 577, 578. As to patients from hospitals providing high security psychiatric services
     (formerly special hospitals) see PARA 569 et seq.

1006. Confessions. Where the prosecution case relies wholly or mainly on the
confession of a mentally handicapped person made without an independent
person present, the judge is required to warn the jury that there is a special need
for caution before convicting in reliance upon it[1]. Where the trial is one without
a jury the court must treat the case as one in which there is a special need for
caution before convicting the accused on his confession[2]. The Code of Practice
for the detention, treatment and questioning of persons by police officers[3] makes
special provision for the questioning of people who are suspected of being
mentally disordered, mentally vulnerable or unable to understand the
significance of questions put to them[4].

1   See the Police and Criminal Evidence Act 1984 s 77(1), (2); and CRIMINAL PROCEDURE vol 28
     (2010) PARA 666. As to confessions generally see CRIMINAL PROCEDURE vol 28 (2010) PARAS
     659–671.
2   See the Police and Criminal Evidence Act 1984 s 77(2A); and CRIMINAL PROCEDURE vol 28
     (2010) PARA 666.
3   Ie made in pursuance of the Police and Criminal Evidence Act 1984 ss 66, 67(7); see CRIMINAL
     PROCEDURE vol 28 (2010) PARA 666.
4   See Code C: Code of Practice for the Detention, Treatment and Questioning of Persons by Police
     Officers; and CRIMINAL PROCEDURE vol 28 (2010) PARA 662.

1007. Fitness to plead. Where on the trial of a person the question arises as to
whether that person is under a disability that would constitute a bar to his being
tried, the question of fitness to be tried is determined by the court, without a
jury, on the written recommendation of two or more registered medical
practitioners[1].

The question of fitness to be tried must be determined as soon as it arises[2].
However, the question may be postponed until any time up to the opening of the
case for the defence where the court is of the opinion that, having regard to the
disability, it is expedient to do so and in the interests of the accused[3].

If, before the question of fitness to be tried falls to be determined, the jury
return a verdict of acquittal on the count or each of the counts on which the
accused is being tried, that question must not be determined[4].

1   See the Criminal Procedure (Insanity) Act 1964 s 4(1), (5), (6); and CRIMINAL PROCEDURE
     vol 27 (2010) PARA 370.
2   See the Criminal Procedure (Insanity) Act 1964 s 4(4); and CRIMINAL PROCEDURE vol 27 (2010)
     PARA 370.
3   See the Criminal Procedure (Insanity) Act 1964 s 4(2); and CRIMINAL PROCEDURE vol 27 (2010)
     PARA 370.
4   See the Criminal Procedure (Insanity) Act 1964 s 4(3); and CRIMINAL PROCEDURE vol 27 (2010)
     PARA 370.

9. OFFENCES

1008. Forgery of statutory documents with intent to deceive. Any person who without lawful authority or excuse has in his custody or under his control any specified document which is, and which he knows or believes to be, false within the meaning of Part 1 of the Forgery and Counterfeiting Act 1981[1] is guilty of an offence[2].

Also guilty of an offence is any person who without lawful authority or excuse makes, or has in his custody or under his control, any document so closely resembling a specified document as to be calculated to deceive[3].

The specified documents are any document purporting to be: (1) an application under Part 2 of the Mental Health Act 1983[4]; (2) a medical or other recommendation or report under that Act[5]; and (3) any other document[6] required or authorised to be made for any of the purposes of that Act[7].

1   Ie the Forgery and Counterfeiting Act 1981 Pt I (ss 1–13). As to the meaning of 'false' see s 9; and CRIMINAL LAW vol 25 (2010) PARA 339.

2   Mental Health Act 1983 s 126(1). Proceedings under the Mental Health Act 1983 s 126 may be instituted by a local social services authority: see s 130; and PARA 584. As to the offence of false descriptions of establishments and agencies under the Care Standards Act 2000 see s 26; and SOCIAL SERVICES AND COMMUNITY CARE. As to registered establishments under the Care Standards Act 2000 see PARA 578.

3   Mental Health Act 1983 s 126(2). To deceive is to induce a man to believe a thing to be true which is false and which the person practising the deceit knows or believes to be false: *Re London and Globe Finance Corpn Ltd* [1903] 1 Ch 728 at 732 per Buckley J. It also includes the inducing of a person to believe a thing to be false which is true: *Welham v DPP* [1961] AC 103, [1960] 1 All ER 805, HL, per Lord Radcliffe.

4   Ie the Mental Health Act 1983 Pt 2 (ss 2–34). As to such applications see PARAS 767–769, 785.

5   As to medical recommendations see PARAS 767–769, 785. As to medical reports see eg PARAS 770, 910, 915.

6   Eg a report by a nurse (see PARA 770), a record of admission (see PARA 771), or an order for discharge (see PARA 913).

7   Mental Health Act 1983 s 126(3) (amended by the Mental Health (Patients in the Community) Act 1995 s 1(2), Sch 1 para 17). Any person guilty of an offence is liable on summary conviction to imprisonment for a term not exceeding six months or a fine not exceeding the statutory maximum or both, or on conviction on indictment to imprisonment for a term not exceeding two years or a fine of any amount or both: Mental Health Act 1983 s 126(5). As to the statutory maximum see SENTENCING AND DISPOSITION OF OFFENDERS vol 92 (2010) PARA 140.

1009. Wilfully making a false entry or statement. Any person who wilfully makes a false entry or statement in any application, recommendation, report, record or other document required or authorised to be made for any of the purposes of the Mental Health Act 1983[1] or, with intent to deceive, makes use of any such entry or statement which he knows to be false, commits an offence[2].

1   As to such documents see PARA 1008 text to notes 4–7.

2   Mental Health Act 1983 s 126(4). A local social services authority may institute proceedings for an offence under this provision: see s 130; and PARA 584. As to the penalties see PARA 1008 note 7. As to the offence of false descriptions in registration applications under the Care Standards Act 2000 see s 27; and SOCIAL SERVICES AND COMMUNITY CARE. As to registered establishments under the Care Standards Act 2000 see PARA 578.

1010. Ill-treatment or wilful neglect under the Mental Health Act 1983. It is an offence for any person who is a manager[1] or officer on the staff of or otherwise employed in, a hospital[2] or independent hospital[3] or care home[4]: (1) to ill-treat[5] or wilfully to neglect[6] a patient for the time being receiving treatment for mental disorder[7] as an in-patient in that hospital or home; or (2) to ill-treat or wilfully to neglect, on the premises of which the hospital or home forms part, an out-patient for the time being receiving such treatment there[8].

Any individual who ill-treats[9] or wilfully neglects[10] a mentally disordered patient who is subject to his guardianship[11] or otherwise in his custody or care, whether by virtue of any legal or moral obligation or otherwise, commits an offence[12].

1 As to the meaning of 'manager' see PARA 778.
2 As to the meaning of 'hospital' see PARA 577.
3 As to the meaning of 'independent hospital' see PARA 578 note 7.
4 As to the meaning of 'care home' see PARA 583 note 7.
5 A single act (eg one slap to the patient's face) is sufficient to show ill-treatment: *R v Holmes* (1979) 1 Cr App Rep (S) 233, [1979] Crim LR 52. Ill-treatment is any deliberate conduct which could properly be described as ill-treatment, whether or not it had caused or was likely to cause harm. The accused must either realise that he is inexcusably ill-treating the patient or be reckless as to whether he is doing so: *R v Newington* (1990) 91 Cr App Rep 247, [1990] Crim LR 593, CA.
6 Ill-treatment and wilful neglect are two separate offences: *R v Newington* (1990) 91 Cr App Rep 247, CA. In the context of the offence of wilfully neglecting a child in a manner likely to cause unnecessary suffering or injury to health under the Children and Young Persons Act 1933 s 1, it has been held that neglect cannot be described as 'wilful' unless the person either: (1) had directed his mind to whether there was some risk (though it might fall far short of a probability) that the child's health might suffer from the neglect and had made a conscious decision to refrain from acting; or (2) had so refrained because he did not care whether the child might be at risk or not: *R v Sheppard* [1981] AC 394, [1980] 3 All ER 899, HL. See also CHILDREN AND YOUNG PERSONS vol 9 (2012) PARA 635. As to genuine mistake in failing to treat a patient rather than wilful neglect see *R v Morrell* [2002] EWCA Crim 2547, [2002] All ER (D) 372 (Nov).
7 As to the meaning of 'mental disorder' see PARA 761.
8 Mental Health Act 1983 s 127(1) (amended by the Care Standards Act 2000 s 116, Sch 4 para 9(1), (8)). A person guilty of an offence under the Mental Health Act 1983 s 127 is liable on summary conviction to imprisonment for a term not exceeding six months or a fine not exceeding the statutory maximum or both, or on conviction on indictment to imprisonment for a term not exceeding five years or a fine or both: s 127(3) (amended by the Mental Health Act 2007 s 42). As from a day to be appointed this maximum term of imprisonment is increased to a maximum term of 12 months (see the Magistrates' Courts Act 1980 s 32(1), Sch 1 (s 32(1) as prospectively amended)), although this does not affect the penalty for any offence committed before that day (see the Criminal Justice Act 2003 s 282(4) (not yet in force)). At the date at which this volume states the law no such day had been appointed. As to the statutory maximum see SENTENCING AND DISPOSITION OF OFFENDERS vol 92 (2010) PARA 140. Proceedings for an offence under the Mental Health Act 1983 s 127 must not be instituted except by or with the consent of the Director of Public Prosecutions: s 127(4). Subject to this provision, proceedings may be instituted by a local social services authority: see s 130; and PARA 584. As to the Director of Public Prosecutions see CRIMINAL PROCEDURE vol 27 (2010) PARAS 23, 33 et seq. As to the status of a hospital where there is a charge under the Mental Health Act 1983 s 127 see *R v Davies* [1999] All ER (D) 1450, CA. As to ill-treatment or wilful neglect under the Mental Capacity Act 2005 see PARA 1011.
9 See note 5.
10 See note 6.
11 Ie under the Mental Health Act 1983. As to such guardianship see PARAS 785, 877.
12 Mental Health Act 1983 s 127(2). As to the penalties, and as to the institution of proceedings, see note 8.

1011. Ill-treatment or wilful neglect under the Mental Capacity Act 2005. A person ('D') who:

(1) has the care of a person ('P') who lacks, or whom D reasonably believes to lack, capacity[1];

(2) is the donee of a lasting power of attorney[2], or an enduring power of attorney[3], created by P[4]; or

(3) is a deputy[5] appointed by the Court of Protection[6] for P[7],

is guilty of an offence if he ill-treats or wilfully neglects P[8].

1   Mental Capacity Act 2005 s 44(1)(a). As to lacking capacity see PARA 601 et seq. Any question as to whether a person lacks capacity is to be decided on a balance of probabilities but the burden of proving of the offence remains with the prosecution to prove to the criminal standard: see *R v Hopkins; R v Priest* [2011] EWCA Crim 1513, 123 BMLR 1. The matter in respect of which capacity is required to be lacking for the purposes of the Mental Capacity Act 2005 s 44 is the person's ability to make decisions concerning his or her own care: see *R v Dunn* [2010] EWCA Crim 2935, [2011] 1 Cr App Rep 425, 174 CL&J 766. The court also held that the Mental Capacity Act 2005 s 2(4) (see PARA 603) should be construed as applicable to proof of the criminal offence. See however *R v Hopkins* where the court stated that unconstrained by authority, it would have been minded to accept the appellants' submission that s 44(1)(a), read together with s 2(1), was so vague that it failed the test of sufficient certainty at common law and the European Convention for the Protection of Human Rights and Fundamental Freedoms (1950) (Rome, 4 November 1950; TS 71 (1953); Cmd 8969) art 7(1). See RIGHTS AND FREEDOMS.
2   As to the meaning of 'lasting power of attorney' see PARA 606 note 16. See also PARA 618 et seq.
3   Ie within the meaning of the Mental Capacity Act 2005 Sch 4: see PARA 618; and AGENCY vol 1 (2008) PARA 195 et seq.
4   Mental Capacity Act 2005 s 44(1)(b).
5   As to the meaning of 'deputy' see PARA 606 note 18. See also PARA 724.
6   As to the Court of Protection see PARA 720.
7   Mental Capacity Act 2005 s 44(1)(c).
8   Mental Capacity Act 2005 s 44(2). A person guilty of an offence under s 44 is liable: (1) on summary conviction, to imprisonment for a term not exceeding 12 months or a fine not exceeding the statutory maximum or both; (2) on conviction on indictment, to imprisonment for a term not exceeding five years or a fine or both: s 44(3). As to the statutory maximum see PARA 1008 note 7. As to ill-treatment or wilful neglect under the Mental Health Act 1983 see PARA 1010. As to the statutory maximum see SENTENCING AND DISPOSITION OF OFFENDERS vol 92 (2010) PARA 140.

1012. Unlawful sexual activity with persons with a mental disorder. Under the Sexual Offences Act 2003[1], there are various offences involving sexual activity with persons with a mental disorder[2], which are dealt with elsewhere in this work. These offences include:

(1)   sexual activity with a person with a mental disorder impeding choice[3];

(2)   causing or inciting a person, with a mental disorder impeding choice, to engage in sexual activity[4];

(3)   engaging in sexual activity in the presence of a person with a mental disorder impeding choice[5];

(4)   causing a person, with a mental disorder impeding choice, to watch a sexual act[6];

(5)   inducement, threat or deception to procure sexual activity with a person with a mental disorder[7];

(6)   causing a person with a mental disorder to engage in or agree to engage in sexual activity by inducement, threat or deception[8];

(7)   engaging in sexual activity in the presence, procured by inducement, threat or deception, of a person with a mental disorder[9];

(8)   causing a person with a mental disorder to watch a sexual act by inducement, threat or deception[10].

There are also offences relating specifically to care workers, namely:

(a)   sexual activity with a person with a mental disorder[11];

(b)   causing or inciting sexual activity[12];

(c)   sexual activity in the presence of a person with a mental disorder[13]; and

(d)   causing a person with a mental disorder to watch a sexual act[14].

1   Ie the Sexual Offences Act 2003 ss 30–44: see the text and notes 3–14; and CRIMINAL LAW vol 25 (2010) PARA 209 et seq. As to the penalties for offences under these provisions see CRIMINAL LAW vol 25 (2010) PARAS 214, 219, 227.

2   For the purposes of the Sexual Offences Act 2003 Pt 1 (ss 1–79), 'mental disorder' has the same meaning as in the Mental Health Act 1983 s 1 (see PARA 761): Sexual Offences Act 2003 s 79(6).

3   A person ('A') commits an offence if: (1) he intentionally touches another person ('B'); (2) the touching is sexual; (3) B is unable to refuse because of or for a reason related to a mental disorder; and (4) A knows or could reasonably be expected to know that B has a mental disorder and that because of it or for a reason related to it B is likely to be unable to refuse: see the Sexual Offences Act 2003 s 30; and CRIMINAL LAW vol 25 (2010) PARA 210.

4   A person ('A') commits an offence if: (1) he intentionally causes or incites another person ('B') to engage in an activity; (2) the activity is sexual; (3) B is unable to refuse because of or for a reason related to a mental disorder; and (4) A knows or could reasonably be expected to know that B has a mental disorder and that because of it or for a reason related to it B is likely to be unable to refuse: see the Sexual Offences Act 2003 s 31; and CRIMINAL LAW vol 25 (2010) PARA 211.

5   A person ('A') commits an offence if: (1) he intentionally engages in an activity; (2) the activity is sexual; (3) for the purpose of obtaining sexual gratification, he engages in it: (a) when another person ('B') is present or is in a place from which A can be observed; and (b) knowing or believing that B is aware, or intending that B should be aware, that he is engaging in it; (4) B is unable to refuse because of or for a reason related to a mental disorder; and (5) A knows or could reasonably be expected to know that B has a mental disorder and that because of it or for a reason related to it B is likely to be unable to refuse: see the Sexual Offences Act 2003 s 32; and CRIMINAL LAW vol 25 (2010) PARA 212.

6   A person ('A') commits an offence if: (1) for the purpose of obtaining sexual gratification, he intentionally causes another person ('B') to watch a third person engaging in an activity, or to look at an image of any person engaging in an activity; (2) the activity is sexual; (3) B is unable to refuse because of or for a reason related to a mental disorder; and (4) A knows or could reasonably be expected to know that B has a mental disorder and that because of it or for a reason related to it B is likely to be unable to refuse: see the Sexual Offences Act 2003 s 33; and CRIMINAL LAW vol 25 (2010) PARA 213.

7   A person ('A')' commits an offence if: (1) with the agreement of another person ('B') he intentionally touches that person; (2) the touching is sexual; (3) A obtains B's agreement by means of an inducement offered or given, a threat made or a deception practised by A for that purpose; (4) B has a mental disorder; and (5) A knows or could reasonably be expected to know that B has a mental disorder: see the Sexual Offences Act 2003 s 34; and CRIMINAL LAW vol 25 (2010) PARA 215.

8   A person ('A') commits an offence if: (1) by means of an inducement offered or given, a threat made or a deception practised by him for this purpose, he intentionally causes another person ('B') to engage in, or to agree to engage in, an activity; (2) the activity is sexual; (3) B has a mental disorder; and (4) A knows or could reasonably be expected to know that B has a mental disorder: see the Sexual Offences Act 2003 s 35; and CRIMINAL LAW vol 25 (2010) PARA 216.

9   A person ('A') commits an offence if: (1) he intentionally engages in an activity; (2) the activity is sexual; (3) for the purpose of obtaining sexual gratification, he engages in it: (a) when another person ('B') is present or is in a place from which A can be observed; and (b) knowing or believing that B is aware, or intending that B should be aware, that he is engaging in it; (4) B agrees to be present or in the place referred to in head (3)(a) because of an inducement offered or given, a threat made or a deception practised by A for the purpose of obtaining that agreement; (5) B has a mental disorder; and (6) A knows or could reasonably be expected to know that B has a mental disorder: see the Sexual Offences Act 2003 s 36; and CRIMINAL LAW vol 25 (2010) PARA 217.

10   A person ('A') commits an offence if: (1) for the purpose of obtaining sexual gratification, he intentionally causes another person ('B') to watch a third person engaging in an activity, or to look at an image of any person engaging in an activity; (2) the activity is sexual; (3) B agrees to watch or look because of an inducement offered or given, a threat made or a deception practised by A for the purpose of obtaining that agreement; (4) B has a mental disorder; and (5) A knows or could reasonably be expected to know that B has a mental disorder: see the Sexual Offences Act 2003 s 37; and CRIMINAL LAW vol 25 (2010) PARA 218.

11   A person ('A') commits an offence if: (1) he intentionally touches another person ('B'); (2) the touching is sexual; (3) B has a mental disorder; (4) A knows or could reasonably be expected to know that B has a mental disorder; and (5) A is involved in B's care in a way that falls within the Sexual Offences Act 2003 s 42: see s 38; and CRIMINAL LAW vol 25 (2010) PARA 220.

For the purposes of ss 38–41, a person ('A') is involved in the care of another person ('B') in a way that falls within s 42 if any of the following applies:

(a)   B is accommodated and cared for in a care home, community home, voluntary home or children's home, and A has functions to perform in the home in the course of employment which have brought him or are likely to bring him into regular face to face contact with B (see s 42(1), (2));

(b)   if B is a patient for whom services are provided by a National Health Service body or an independent medical agency, or in an independent clinic or an independent hospital, and A has functions to perform for the body or agency or in the clinic or hospital in the course of employment which have brought him or are likely to bring him into regular face to face contact with B (see s 42(1), (3));

(c)   if A is, whether or not in the course of employment, a provider of care, assistance or services to B in connection with B's mental disorder, and as such, has had or is likely to have regular face to face contact with B (see s 42(1), (4)).

For the purposes of s 42, 'care home' means an establishment which is a care home for the purposes of the Care Standards Act 2000 (see PARA 583 note 7); 'children's home' has the meaning given by s 1 (see CHILDREN AND YOUNG PERSONS vol 10 (2012) PARA 992; SOCIAL SERVICES AND COMMUNITY CARE); 'community home' has the meaning given by the Children Act 1989 s 53 (see CHILDREN AND YOUNG PERSONS vol 10 (2012) PARA 976); 'employment' means any employment, whether paid or unpaid and whether under a contract of service or apprenticeship, under a contract for services, or otherwise than under a contract; 'independent clinic' has the meaning given by the Care Standards Act 2000 s 2 (see SOCIAL SERVICES AND COMMUNITY CARE); 'independent hospital', in England, means a hospital as defined by the National Health Service Act 2006 s 275 that is not a health service hospital as defined by that provision or any other establishment in which any of the services listed in s 22(6) are provided and which is not a health service hospital as so defined; and, in Wales, has the meaning given by the Care Standards Act 2000 s 2; 'independent medical agency' means an undertaking (not being an independent hospital, or in Wales an independent clinic) which consists of or includes the provision of services by medical practitioners; 'National Health Service body' means a local health board, a National Health Service trust (see HEALTH SERVICES vol 54 (2008) PARA 155 et seq), a primary care trust, or a special health authority; and 'voluntary home' has the meaning given by the Children Act 1989 s 60(3) (see CHILDREN AND YOUNG PERSONS vol 10 (2012) PARA 985): see the Sexual Offences Act 2003 s 42(5) (amended by SI 2007/961). As from 1 April 2013, the definition 'National Health Service Body' is further amended by the Health and Social Care Act 2012 Sch 5 para 117 and no longer applies to a primary care trust but to the Secretary of State in relation to the exercise of functions under the National Health Service Act 2006 s 2A or 2B or Sch 1 para 7C, 8 or 12 and a local authority in relation to the exercise of functions under s 2B or 111 or Sch 1 para 1–7B (see HEALTH SERVICES): see the Health and Social Care Act 2012 (Commencement No 4, Transitional, Savings and Transitory Provisions) Order 2013, SI 2013/160, art 2.

Conduct by a person ('A') which would otherwise be an offence under any of ss 38–41 against another person ('B') is not an offence under that provision if at the time B is 16 or over, and A and B are lawfully married or civil partners of each other and in proceedings for such an offence, it is for the defendant to prove that A and B were at the time lawfully married or civil partners of each other: Sexual Offences Act 2003 s 43 (amended by the Civil Partnerships Act 2004 s 261(1), Sch 27 para 175).

Conduct by a person ('A') which would otherwise be an offence under any of ss 38–41 against another person ('B') is not an offence under that provision if, immediately before A became involved in B's care in a way that falls within the Sexual Offences Act 2003 s 42, a sexual relationship existed between A and B: s 44(1). Section 44(1) does not apply if at that time sexual intercourse between A and B would have been unlawful: s 44(2). In proceedings for an offence under any of ss 38–41, it is for the defendant to prove that such a relationship existed at that time: s 44(3).

12   A person ('A') commits an offence if: (1) he intentionally causes or incites another person ('B') to engage in an activity; (2) the activity is sexual; (3) B has a mental disorder; (4) A knows or could reasonably be expected to know that B has a mental disorder; and (5) A is involved in B's care in a way that falls within the Sexual Offences Act 2003 s 42 (see note 11): see s 39; and CRIMINAL LAW vol 25 (2010) PARA 221.

13   A person ('A') commits an offence if: (1) he intentionally engages in an activity; (2) the activity is sexual; (3) for the purpose of obtaining sexual gratification, he engages in it: (a) when another person ('B') is present or is in a place from which A can be observed; and (b) knowing or believing that B is aware, or intending that B should be aware, that he is engaging in it; (4) B has a mental disorder; (5) A knows or could reasonably be expected to know that B has a mental disorder; and (6) A is involved in B's care in a way that falls within the Sexual Offences Act 2003 s 42 (see note 11): see s 40; and CRIMINAL LAW vol 25 (2010) PARA 222.

14 A person ('A') commits an offence if: (1) for the purpose of obtaining sexual gratification, he
intentionally causes another person ('B') to watch a third person engaging in an activity, or to
look at an image of any person engaging in an activity; (2) the activity is sexual; (3) B has a
mental disorder; (4) A knows or could reasonably be expected to know that B has a mental
disorder; and (5) A is involved in B's care in a way that falls within the Sexual Offences
Act 2003 s 42 (see note 11): see s 41; and CRIMINAL LAW vol 25 (2010) PARA 223.

1013. Assisting patients to absent themselves without leave or to escape. Any
person who induces or knowingly[1] assists any other person who is liable to be
detained in a hospital[2] or is subject to guardianship under the Mental Health
Act 1983[3] or is a community patient to absent himself without leave[4] commits
an offence[5]. Any person who induces or knowingly assists any other person
being in legal custody by virtue of the Mental Health Act 1983[6] to escape from
such custody commits an offence[7].

Any person who in England and Wales or Northern Ireland does anything in
relation to a person whose detention in hospital[8] is authorised by the Mental
Health (Care and Treatment) (Scotland) Act 2003 which, if done in Scotland,
would make him guilty of an offence[9] is guilty of an offence[10].

1   Knowledge is an essential ingredient of the offence. As to what constitutes knowledge see
    Gaumont British Distributors Ltd v Henry [1939] 2 KB 711, [1939] 2 All ER 808, DC; *R v
    Hallam* [1957] 1 QB 569, [1957] 1 All ER 665, CCA. Neglect to make reasonable inquiries is
    not knowledge, but where a person deliberately refrains from making inquiries the results of
    which he might not care to have, this constitutes in law actual knowledge of the facts in
    question: see *Taylor's Central Garages (Exeter) Ltd v Roper* (1951) 115 JP 445 at 449–450, DC,
    per Devlin J.
2   Ie within the meaning of the Mental Health Act 1983 Pt II (ss 2–34), which includes registered
    establishments: see PARA 577. As to registered establishments see PARA 578.
3   As to such guardianship see PARAS 785, 877.
4   As to the meaning of 'absence without leave' see PARA 918.
5   Mental Health Act 1983 s 128(1) (amended by the Mental Health Act 2007 Sch 3 para 28). Any
    person guilty of such an offence is liable on summary conviction to imprisonment for a term not
    exceeding six months or to a fine not exceeding the statutory maximum, or to both, and on
    conviction on indictment to imprisonment not exceeding two years or to a fine of any amount,
    or to both: Mental Health Act 1983 s 128(4). As to the statutory maximum see SENTENCING
    AND DISPOSITION OF OFFENDERS vol 92 (2010) PARA 140. A local social services authority may
    institute proceedings for an offence under the Mental Health Act 1983 s 128: see s 130; and
    PARA 584. Section 128 (except so far as it relates to patients subject to guardianship) extends to
    Scotland: see s 146; and PARA 557.
6   Ie under the Mental Health Act 1983 s 137: see PARA 776.
7   Mental Health Act 1983 s 128(2). For the penalty and institution of proceedings see note 5. As
    to the meaning of 'knowingly' see note 1. A person detained under the Mental Health Act 1983
    who escapes from custody does not thereby commit an offence: see *R v Criminal Injuries
    Compensation Board, ex p Lawton* [1972] 3 All ER 582 at 584, [1972] 1 WLR 1589 at
    1592, DC, per Lord Widgery CJ.
8   Ie within the meaning of the Mental Health (Care and Treatment) (Scotland) Act 2003 s 329(1):
    see the Mental Health (Care and Treatment) (Scotland) Act 2003 (Consequential Provisions)
    Order 2005, SI 2005/2078 (S 9), art 1(3).
9   Ie under the Mental Health (Care and Treatment) (Scotland) Act 2003 s 316 (inducing and
    assisting absconding etc).
10 Mental Health (Care and Treatment) (Scotland) Act 2003 (Consequential Provisions)
    Order 2005, SI 2005/2078 (S 9), art 10(1). Any person guilty of such an offence is liable on
    summary conviction to imprisonment for a term not exceeding three months or to a fine not
    exceeding level 5 on the standard scale and on conviction on indictment, to imprisonment for a
    term not exceeding two years or to a fine, or both: art 10(3). As to the standard scale see
    SENTENCING AND DISPOSITION OF OFFENDERS vol 92 (2010) PARA 142.
        Where a person is charged with an offence under art 10(1) as it applies to the Mental Health
    (Care and Treatment) (Scotland) Act 2003 s 316(1)(b) (harbouring a patient), it is a defence for
    such person to prove that the doing of that with which the person is charged: (1) did not
    obstruct the discharge by any person of a function conferred or imposed on that person by

virtue of the Mental Health (Care and Treatment) (Scotland) Act 2003 or the Mental Health (Care and Treatment) (Scotland) Act 2003 (Consequential Provisions) Order 2005, SI 2005/2078 (S 9); and (2) was intended to protect the interests of the patient: art 10(2).

1014.   Harbouring a patient absent without leave. Any person who knowingly[1] harbours a patient who is absent without leave[2] or otherwise at large and liable to be retaken under the Mental Health Act 1983[3], or gives him any assistance with intent to prevent, hinder or interfere with his being taken into custody or returned to the hospital or other place where he ought to be, commits an offence[4].

Any person who in England and Wales or Northern Ireland does anything in relation to a person whose detention in hospital[5] is authorised by the Mental Health (Care and Treatment) (Scotland) Act 2003 which, if done in Scotland, would make him guilty of an offence[6] is guilty of an offence[7].

1   As to the meaning of 'knowingly' see PARA 1013 note 1.
2   As to the meaning of 'absence without leave' see PARA 918.
3   Ie under the Mental Health Act 1983 s 128(3): see PARAS 777, 918.
4   Mental Health Act 1983 s 128(3). Section 128 (except so far as it relates to patients subject to guardianship) extends to Scotland: see s 146; and PARA 557. As to the penalty and institution of proceedings see PARA 1013 note 5.
5   See PARA 1013 note 8.
6   Ie under the Mental Health (Care and Treatment) (Scotland) Act 2003 s 316 (inducing and assisting absconding etc). Section 316(1)(b) specifically includes harbouring a patient who has, with that result, done or failed to do anything.
7   Mental Health (Care and Treatment) (Scotland) Act 2003 (Consequential Provisions) Order 2005, SI 2005/2078 (S 9), art 10(1). As to the penalty and defence see art 10(2), (3).

1015.   Obstruction. Any person who without reasonable cause: (1) refuses to allow the inspection of any premises[1]; or (2) refuses to allow the visiting, interviewing or examination of any person by a person authorised in that behalf by or under the Mental Health Act 1983 or to give access to any person to a person so authorised[2]; or (3) refuses to produce for the inspection of any person so authorised any document or record the production of which is duly required by him[3]; (4) fails to comply with a request[4] to provide information[5]; or (5) otherwise obstructs any such person in the exercise of his functions[6], commits an offence[7].

1   Mental Health Act 1983 s 129(1)(a). As to the power to enter and inspect premises under the Mental Health Act 1983 see s 115; and PARA 820. As to the power to enter and inspect the relevant premises of registered establishments under the Care Standards Act 2000 see ss 31–32; SOCIAL SERVICES AND COMMUNITY CARE.
2   Mental Health Act 1983 s 129(1)(b) (amended by the Mental Health (Patients in the Community) Act 1995 s 1(2), Sch 1 para 19). As to rights of visiting, interviewing and examination see the Mental Health Act 1983 s 9(2) (see PARA 790), s 24 (see PARA 916), s 31(c) (see PARA 846), s 76 (see PARA 963), s 78(2)(g) (see PARA 980), s 116 (see PARA 583). Any person who insists on being present when requested to withdraw by a person authorised to interview or examine a patient in private commits the offence of obstruction: s 129(2). An approved social worker is not authorised to interview a patient in private before making an application under Part 2 (ss 2–34): see s 13(2); and PARA 821. However, a person who disrupts an approved social worker's interview with a patient is guilty of an offence under s 129(1)(d): see the text and note 6.
3   Mental Health Act 1983 s 129(1)(c). As to requirements to produce documents and records see s 24(2), (4) (see PARA 916), s 76(1)(b) (see PARA 963), s 78(2)(g) (see PARA 980).
4   Ie a request under the Mental Health Act 1983 s 120C (see PARA 806 note 2).
5   Mental Health Act 1983 s 129(1)(ca) (added by the Health and Social Care Act 2008 Sch 3 para 10).
6   Mental Health Act 1983 s 129(1)(d). Obstruction does not necessarily connote physical force; anything which makes it more difficult for a person to carry out his duty may amount to

obstruction: see *Borrow v Howland* (1896) 74 LT 787, DC; *Hinchliffe v Sheldon* [1955] 3 All ER 406, [1955] 1 WLR 1207, DC; *Lewis v Cox* [1985] QB 509, [1984] 3 All ER 672, DC. However, standing by and doing nothing does not amount to obstruction unless there is a legal duty to act (see *Swallow v LCC* [1916] 1 KB 224, DC; *Baker v Ellison* [1914] 2 KB 762, DC); nor is a mere refusal to answer questions obstruction (see *Rice v Connolly* [1966] 2 QB 414, [1966] 2 All ER 649, DC). It is an offence to remain if there has been a request to withdraw: see note 2. Giving a verbal warning of an impending inspection may amount to obstruction: see *Green v Moore* [1982] QB 1044, [1982] 1 All ER 428, DC.

7 Mental Health Act 1983 s 129(1). The penalty for these offences, on summary conviction, is imprisonment for a term not exceeding 3 months or a fine not exceeding level 4 on the standard scale or both: s 129(3). As from a day to be appointed, s 129(3) is amended so that the only penalty for these offences is a fine not exceeding level 4 on the standard scale: s 129(3) (prospectively amended by the Criminal Justice Act 2003 s 332, Sch 37 Pt 9). At the date at which this volume states the law no such day had been appointed. As to the standard scale see SENTENCING AND DISPOSITION OF OFFENDERS vol 92 (2010) PARA 142.

A local social services authority may institute proceedings for these offences: see the Mental Health Act 1983 s 130; and PARA 584.

1016. Sale of firearm to mentally disordered person. It is an offence for any person to sell or transfer any firearm or ammunition to, or repair, prove or test any firearm or ammunition for, any other person whom he knows or has reasonable cause for believing to be of unsound mind[1].

1 See the Firearms Act 1968 s 25; and CRIMINAL LAW vol 26 (2010) PARA 624. The penalty for this offence, on summary conviction, is imprisonment for three months or a fine of level 3 on the standard scale or both: s 51(1), Sch 6 Pt I (amended by virtue of the Criminal Justice Act 1982 s 38, 46). As to the standard scale see SENTENCING AND DISPOSITION OF OFFENDERS vol 92 (2010) PARA 142.

INDEX

Medical Products and Drugs

ADVERTISEMENT
  meaning, 333
  authorisation holder, duties of, 335
  complaints—
    ministers' duty to consider, 348
    OFCOM, consideration by, 350
    power to refer, 349
  generally, 333, 334
  herbal medicinal products, traditional,
    345
  homoeopathic medicinal products,
    registered, 344
  injunction—
    accuracy of factual claim, evidence as
      to, 352
    application for, 351
    publication of court's decision, 353
    scope of, 351
  ministers, scrutiny by. *See* scrutiny by
    ministers *below*
  persons qualified to prescribe or supply
    medicinal products—
    abbreviated advertisement, 339
    free samples, 341
    general provisions, 338
    inducements and hospitality, 343
    medical sales representatives,
      promotion by, 342
    written material accompanying
      promotions, 340
  promotional purposes, sale or supply
    for, 337
  public, to the—
    general restrictions, 336
    promotional purposes, sale or supply
      of product for, 337
  registration holder, duties of, 335
  reminder of product, intended as,
    336n21
  restrictions on publishing—
    generally, 334
    public, advertising to, 336
  scrutiny by ministers—
    advertisement incompatible with
      regulations, 347

ADVERTISEMENT—*continued*
  scrutiny by ministers—*continued*
    complaints. *See* complaints *above*
    copy of advertisement, right to see,
      346
    injunction, power to apply for. *See*
      injunction *above*
    powers to prohibit or determine
      advertisement, 347
    veterinary medicinal product, as to. *See*
      under VETERINARY MEDICINAL
      PRODUCT
ANIMAL
  meaning, 387n2, 473n6
  food-producing animal—
    keeper's duty to maintain records,
      433
    medicinal product administered to,
      387, 423n4
    medicated animal feeding stuff, 547n1
    poisons, destroyed by, 387
    veterinary medicinal product,
      administration to. *See under*
      VETERINARY MEDICINAL PRODUCT
APPEAL
  clinical trial, ethics committee opinion,
    116
  vaccine damage payment, as to, 385
  veterinary products committee, to, 442
AUTHORISATION
  advanced therapy medicinal product—
    meaning, 146n2
    exemption for, 146
  Article 126a authorisation—
    meaning, 141n6
    assessment report, member state
      requesting copy, 233
    conditions for grant, 232
    duration, 232
    member state requesting copy of
      authorisation, 233
  borderline products—
    challenge to provisional
      determination, 152
    contents of notice, 151

AUTHORISATION—*continued*
  borderline products—*continued*
    effect of final determination, 154
    final determination without
      representation, 153
    offence following final
      determination, 154
    provisional determination, 151
    written representations, 152n^2
  clinical trial. *See under* CLINICAL TRIAL
  defence to contravention of provisions,
    141
  enforcement authority, 142n^{13}
  EU marketing authorisation—
    meaning, 141n^3
    offences—
      advanced therapy medicinal
        products, 180
      generally, 179
      See also under marketing
        authorisation *below*
  European systems for. *See under*
    MEDICINAL PRODUCT
  general sale medicinal products, mixing
    of, 144
  homoeopathic medicinal products,
    certification. *See under*
    HOMOEOPATHIC MEDICINAL
    PRODUCT
  manufacture and assembly etc, 141
  marketing authorisation—
    meaning, 141n^3
    offences—
      application for grant, renewal or
        variation, 183
      defence, 141, 186
      European Medicines Authority,
        failure to inform, 177
      false or misleading information,
        provision of, 184
      general defence, 186
      general offence, 186
      paediatric regulation, as to, 181
      penalties, 141n^{16}, 142n^{29}, 145n^{14}
      pharmacovigilance condition,
        breach of, 185
      sponsor of UK paediatric trial, by,
        182
      urgent safety restrictions, as to,
        178
    relevant medicinal product, 155
    UK authorisation. *See* UK marketing
      authorisation *below*
  non-prescription medicines in course of
    business, use of, 143

AUTHORISATION—*continued*
  offence. *See under* marketing
    authorisation *above*
  parallel import licence, 147
  pharmacists—
    meaning, 52n^5
    exemption for, 150
  radiopharmaceuticals, 148
  record-keeping requirements, 145
  requirement for—
    exemptions—
      advanced therapy medicinal
        products, 146
      general sale medicinal products,
        mixing of, 144
      non-prescription medicines in
        course of business, use of, 143
      pharmacists, 150
      radiopharmaceuticals, 148
      special patient needs, 142
      supply in response to certain
        pathogenic agents etc, 149
    generally, 141
    offence, 142
  special patient needs, 142
  supply in response to certain pathogenic
    agents etc, 149
  traditional herbal registration. *See under*
    HERBAL MEDICINAL PRODUCT
  UK marketing authorisation—
    meaning, 141n^3
    application for grant—
      accompanying material, 157
      active substances used in products
        previously authorised, 157n^{14}
      active substances in well-established
        use, 157n^{13}
      biological medicinal product,
        157n^{12}
      consideration of application, 158
      generally, 156
      generic medicinal product, 157n^{10}
      information, duty to update, 157n^3
      procedure, 156
      product by reference to another
        product, 157n^{11}
      radionuclide generator, 157n^3
      renewal of application, 159
      time limit for determining, 158
    assessment report, 164
    cessation, 166
    conditions attached to grant—
      classification of authorisations, 163
      deadlines for fulfilment of, 160
      European Medicines Agency,
        notification to, 162n^{11}

AUTHORISATION—*continued*
  UK marketing authorisation—*continued*
    conditions attached to
      grant—*continued*
        examples, 160
        exceptional circumstances, in, 161
        failure to comply with, 160, 161,
          162
        generally, 160
        new obligations
          post-authorisation, 162
        safety study, 162n[4]
        written observations, holder's right
          to submit, 162n[7]
    duration, 165
    exemption from cessation,
      circumstances for grant, 166n[2]
    further application for renewal, 165
    holder's obligations—
      appropriate and continued supplies,
        ensuring, 176
      information relating to safety etc,
        information as to, 173
      placing on market etc, notification
        as to, 171
      product information, keeping up to
        date, 174
      record-keeping, 175
      scientific and technical progress,
        taking account of, 172
    licensing authority's duties, 164
    obligations of holder. *See* holder's
      obligations *above*
    offences. *See under* marketing
      authorisation *above*
    relevant medicinal product,
      suspension of use etc, 168
    revocation, suspension or variation,
      167
    sale etc of suspended product, 170
    validity, 165
    withdrawal of product from market,
      169
  veterinary medicinal product. *See under*
    VETERINARY MEDICINAL PRODUCT

BLOOD QUALITY AND SAFETY
  blood—
    meaning, 449n[2]
    import, 450
  blood and blood components—
    imported from outside EU, 457
    labelling, 457
    management of supply, 468
    requirements, 456
    traceability—
      meaning, 458n[8]

BLOOD QUALITY AND
  SAFETY—*continued*
  blood and blood
    components—*continued*
    traceability—*continued*
      need for, 457
  blood bank—
    assessment by Secretary of State of
      events etc, 452
    fees payable by, 452
    inspection, 452
  blood component—
    meaning, 25n[7], 449n[3]
    import, 450
    See also blood and blood components
      above
  blood donations—
    deferral, 451n[3]
    donor: meaning, 468n[1]
    donor carer: meaning, 456[20]
    requirements, 456
    specific epidemiological situations,
      451
    specified information, need to
      record, 456n[30]
  blood establishment—
    meaning, 453n[4]
    authorisation—
      activities not subject to restriction
        following, 453n[2]
      annual fee, 453n[12]
      generally, 453
      grant, 453
      need for, 453
      removal or variation of conditions,
        453
      specified activities, restriction on,
        453
      suspension or revocation—
        objections to, 460
        Secretary of State's powers as
          to, 454
    blood and blood components. *See*
      blood and blood components
      above
    blood bank. *See* hospital blood bank
      below
    blood donations. *See* blood donations
      above
    blood products etc, management of,
      468
    change to activities—
      application, fee and procedure,
        453n[15]
      examples, 453n[14]
      restrictions on, 453

BLOOD QUALITY AND
   SAFETY—*continued*
blood establishment—*continued*
  contract laboratory, 452n^{12}
  disclosure of information—
    circumstances, permissible, 463
    compliance with requirements, to
      ensure, 464
    inspector's powers to ensure, 465
    restriction on, 463
    security, need for, 463
    serious adverse events or reactions,
      where, 464
    specified requirements, in
      accordance with, 463n^6
  discrepancies as to data, procedures
    for resolving, 463
  duties, 456
  entry powers for inspection etc, 465
  fees payable by, 452
  hospital blood bank. *See* hospital
    blood bank *below*
  inspection—
    meaning, 464n^2
    appointment of inspectors, 464
    duty to secure premises where
      unoccupied etc, 465
    fees payable for, 452, 464n$^{5,\ 10}$
    inspector's powers, 465
    power to conduct, 464
    Secretary of State, by, 452
    seizure , power of, 465
    warrant, issue of, 465
  labelling of blood and blood
    components, 457
  person responsible for—
    delegation of tasks, notification
      procedure, 455n^{10}
    disclosure of information. *See*
      disclosure of information
      above
    need to designate, 455
    qualifications, necessary, 455n^2
    replacement, 455
    responsible person: meaning, 455n^2
    retention of data, 461
    Secretary of State's scrutiny of, 455
    serious adverse reactions and
      events, duty to report, 462
    tasks for which responsible, 455
  record-keeping, 456
  reporting year: meaning, 456n^{31}
  requirements, 456
  Secretary of State—
    inspection by, 452
    records to be kept by, 466

BLOOD QUALITY AND
   SAFETY—*continued*
blood establishment—*continued*
  Secretary of State—*continued*
    report to, 456
    serious adverse reactions and
      events, provision of
      information as to, 467
    serious adverse reactions and events,
      duty to report, 462
    specific epidemiological situations,
      response to, 451
    specified activities at—
      fee for application to carry on,
        453n^{10}
      restriction on, 453
    validation of testing and processes,
      456n^7
  blood product—
    meaning, 449n^4
    management, 468
  Care Quality Commission, 449
  competent authority, 449
  contract laboratory—
    meaning, 452n^{12}
    fees payable by, 452
    inspection, 452
  distribution: meaning, 449n^4
  generally, 17
  hospital blood bank—
    meaning, 458n^1
    compliance with requirements, report
      as to, 458
    inspection, 464
    person responsible for management
      of—
      meaning, 458n^1
      disclosure of information. *See under*
        blood establishment *above*
    discrepancies as to data, procedures
      for resolving, 463
    failures etc, procedure in case of,
      459
    objection to notice served on, 460
    retention of data, 461
    service of notice on, by Secretary of
      State, 459
    requirements, 458
    serious adverse reactions and events,
      duty to report, 462
    traceability of blood, 458
  import of blood and blood
    components, 450
  non-food producing animals, blood
    banks for, 449

References are to paragraph numbers; superior figures refer to notes

BLOOD QUALITY AND
  SAFETY—*continued*
  offences—
    body corporate, by, 470
    defence of due diligence, 471
    generally, 469
  scope of regulation, 449
BRITISH PHARMACOPOEIA
  COMMISSION
  annual report, duty to give, 32
  British Pharmacopoeia—
    contents, 237
    editions of, duty to prepare, 237
    list of names of substances and
      articles, duty to prepare, 238
  compendia, duty to prepare, 237
  current edition of publications,
    presumptions as to, 240
  documents relating to substances etc,
    duty to prepare, 239
  functions, 32
  specified publication: meaning, 240n^2
CE MARKING
  medical device. *See* MEDICAL DEVICE
    (CE marking)
CLINICAL TRIAL
  meaning, 18n^1, 107
  adverse event: meaning, 132n^3
  authorisation—
    amendments to—
      meaning, 122n^2
      licensing authority, by, 122
      rejected proposal for, modification
        or adaptation, 124
      sponsor, by, 123
      substantial amendment: meaning,
        123n^4
      valid notice of: meaning, 123n^{11}
    Commission on Human Medicines,
      reference to, 125
    gene therapy, medicinal products for,
      119
    general medicinal products, in case
      of, 118
    need for, 112
    reference to appropriate committee,
      125
    request for, procedure, 117
    special characteristics, medicinal
      products with, 120
    third country, trial in, 121
    valid request for: meaning, 118n^6
  chief investigator: meaning, 114n^3
  competent authority, 109
  conclusion, 135
  conditions for, 18, 112

CLINICAL TRIAL—*continued*
  conduct of—
    adverse events, notification, 132
    clinical trial authorisation, in
      accordance with, 127
    good clinical practice, need for, 126
    protection of subjects, 126, 129
    serious breaches, notification of, 128
    suspension or termination of trial,
      130
    trial master file, need for. *See* trial
      master file *below*
    urgent safety measures, 129
  due diligence, defence of, 139
  early termination, 135
  enforcement provisions, 137
  essential documents relating to, 131n^5
  ethics committee. *See* ETHICS
    COMMITTEE
  examples, 112n^4
  false or misleading information,
    provision of, 138
  incapable adult taking part in, 115n^{24}
  informed consent to take part in,
    115n^{21}
  infringement notice, service of, 137
  investigational medicinal product—
    meaning, 107n^1
    supply of products for trial, 113
  investigator: meaning, 113n^4
  investigator's brochure—
    meaning, 108n^2, 115n^{19}
    sponsor's responsibility for, 108
  labelling of investigational medical
    products, 136
  marketing authorisation: meaning,
    107n^1
  minor taking part in, 115n^{24}
  non-interventional trial: meaning, 107n^2
  notice suspending or terminating trial—
    issue, licensing authority's duties on,
      130n^{11}
    service, 130n^{10}
  penalties for contravention of
    regulations, 140
  pharmaceutical form of an active
    substance: meaning, 107n^1
  regulation, 18
  regulations, penalties for contravention
    of, 140
  safety report, duty to furnish, 134
  serious adverse event: meaning, 132n^3
  serious adverse reaction—
    meaning, 132n^3
    annual list of suspected reactions,
      134

CLINICAL TRIAL—*continued*
  sponsor—
    meaning, 107
    investigator's brochure, responsibility
      for, 108
    trial master file, duty to keep, 131
  subject—
    meaning, 107n[1]
    recruitment of, conditions to be
      satisfied, 112
  suspected unexpected serious adverse
    reaction, notification, 133
  trial master file—
    archiving documents in, 131n[2]
    duty to keep, 131
    essential documents, 131n[5]
    retention and availability, 131n[8]
    transfer of ownership of data etc,
      131n[8]
  trial site: meaning, 113n[4]
  unexpected serious adverse reaction,
    132n[3]
CODE OF PRACTICE
  Qualified Persons in the Pharmaceutical
    Industry, 104
COMMISSION ON HUMAN
    MEDICINES
  advice to licensing authority, 31
  advice to ministers, 31
  functions, 31
  generally, 31
  reference to, 125
  report, duty to give, 31
CONTROLLED DRUG
  meaning, 481
  activities otherwise unlawful,
    authorisation, 502
  addiction regulations—
    Crown, application to, 513
    drug: meaning, 513n[3]
    generally, 513
    person addicted to drugs, 513n[2]
    specified substances, 513n[4]
  Advisory Council on the Misuse of
    Drugs—
    duties, 490
    establishment, 490
    Secretary of State consulting with,
      502n[24]
  amphetamine, 484n[3]
  articles for administration, supply of,
    501
  cannabinol derivatives, 484n[4]
  cannabis—
    meaning, 484n[5]
    cultivation of cannabis plants, 497

CONTROLLED DRUG—*continued*
  cannabis resin, 484n[6]
  Class A drug—
    meaning, 481
    coca leaf, 483n[3]
    cocaine, establishing possession of,
      483n[4]
    concentrate of poppy-straw, 483n[8]
    list, 483
    medicinal opium, 483n[6]
    poppy-straw, 483n[7]
    raw opium, 483n[5]
  Class B drug—
    meaning, 481
    amphetamine, 484n[3]
    cannabinol derivatives, 484n[4]
    cannabis, 484n[5]
    cannabis resin, 484n[6]
    list, 484
  Class C drug—
    meaning, 481
    list, 485
  closure of premises, 499
  coca leaf: meaning, 483n[3]
  cocaine, establishing possession of,
    483n[4]
  concentrate of poppy-straw, 483n[8]
  Crown, application of legislation to,
    513, 518
  destruction, 506
  directions to practitioner or pharmacist.
    See prohibition direction *below*
  enforcement—
    entry and inspection powers, 516,
      523
    search and seizure powers, 524
  entry powers—
    generally, 516, 523
    offences in connection with, 527
  excepting drugs from restrictions, 502
  export restrictions, 491
  financial provisions, 480
  forfeiture, 526
  generally, 480, 481
  guidance, power to issue, 517
  import restrictions, 491
  information, power to require, 510
  inspection powers—
    generally, 516, 523
    offences in connection with, 527
  legislation—
    Crown, application to, 518
    generally, 480
    Misuse of Drugs Act. *See* Misuse of
      Drugs Act 1971 *below*
    regulations. *See* regulations *below*

CONTROLLED DRUG—*continued*
  legislation—*continued*
    scope, 480
  licence or authority, 488
  marking of bottles etc, 511
  medicinal opium, 483n[6]
  misuse, prevention of—
    addiction regulations. *See* addiction
        regulations *above*
    documents to be obtained by
        supplier, 508
    information, power to require, 510
    marking of bottles etc, 511
    registers and records, 509
    regulations, power to make, 505
    safe custody of drugs. *See* safe
        custody of drugs *below*
    social problems caused by drugs,
        dealing with, 510
    supply on prescription, 512
  Misuse of Drugs Act 1971—
    generally, 480
    regulations varying, 487
    scope, 480
    service under, 489
  occupier or manager of premises,
      offences by, 498
  offences—
    authorisation of activities otherwise
        unlawful, 502
    cultivation of cannabis plants, 497
    entry and inspection powers, in
        connection with, 527
    forfeiture, 526
    generally, 504, 525
    import and export, 491
    magistrates' court's power to try
        information for, 525
    obstruction, 523, 527
    occupier or manager of premises, by,
        498
    opium, smoking etc, 500
    possession, 495
    production and supply, 492
    supply of articles for the
        administration of drugs, 501
  opium—
    medicinal opium, 483n[6]
    offences relating to, 500
    raw opium, 483n[5]
  poppy-straw, 483n[7]
  possession—
    authorised persons, 496
    excluded drugs, 495n[1]
    offence, 495
    restrictions on, 495

CONTROLLED DRUG—*continued*
  premises—
    closure of, 499
    entry and inspection powers, 516
  prescription, supply on, 512
  production—
    authorised persons, 493
    offence, 492
    records, duty to keep, 509
    restrictions, 492
  prohibition direction—
    addiction regulations, contravention
        of, 520
    advisory body, reference to, 521
    convicted practitioner or pharmacist,
        519
    effective date, 520n[8]
    practitioner acting irresponsibly, 520
    temporary direction in urgent case,
        522
    tribunal, reference to, 521
  public interest, acting in, 502
  raw opium, 483n[5]
  registers and records—
    duty to keep, 509
    power to request, 510
  regulations—
    generally, 486
    misuse, for preventing, 505
    Misuse of Drugs Act 1971, varying,
        487
    power to make, 480, 486, 505
  safe custody of drugs—
    generally, 506
    notices directing special precautions,
        507
    occupier or manager's duty, 506
    prescribed structural requirements,
        506
  search and seizure powers, 524
  Secretary of State's powers, 480
  service of notices or documents, 489
  supervision of management and use—
    accountable officers, 514
    co-operation between health bodies
        and other organisations, 515
    cross-border body: meaning, 514n[1]
    Crown, application to, 518
    entry and inspection powers, 516
    guidance, 517
    responsibilities, 514
  supply—
    authorised persons, 494
    documents to be obtained by
        supplier—
      duty to obtain, 508

CONTROLLED DRUG—*continued*
  supply—*continued*
    documents to be obtained by
      supplier—*continued*
      retention of documents in
        dispensary, 508n[13]
      signed requisition, 508n[9]
      specified drugs exemption, 508n[14]
      specified persons, supply to, 508n[8]
      urgency, undertaking in case of,
        508n[10]
      veterinary requisition, 508n[9]
    offence, 492
    permitted, where, 492
    prescription, on, 512
    register, duty to keep, 509
    restrictions, 492
  temporary class drug order—
    conditions for making, 482
    duration, 482n[9]
    generally, 482
    provisions in, 503
    temporary class drug: meaning, 481
    urgency condition, 482n[4]
  veterinary prescription, retention of
    records, 509
  wholesale dealer—
    meaning, 509n[24]
    duty to keep records, 509

DRUG
  meaning, 513n[3]
  controlled. *See* CONTROLLED DRUG
  homoeopathic. *See* HOMOEOPATHIC
    MEDICINAL PRODUCT
  medicinal. *See* MEDICINAL PRODUCT
  veterinary. *See* VETERINARY MEDICINAL
    PRODUCT

ENFORCEMENT
  medicinal products, as to. *See under*
    MEDICINAL PRODUCT
  poisons, as to. *See under* POISON
  veterinary medicinal product, as to. *See*
    under VETERINARY MEDICINAL
    PRODUCT

ETHICS COMMITTEE
  meaning, 111n[2]
  appointing authority: meaning, 111n[27]
  disclosure of information, 110
  establishment, 111
  gene therapy advisory committee, 111n[2]
  opinion—
    appeal against, 116
    application for, 114
    conditions, subject to, 115
    false or misleading information,
      offence, 114

ETHICS COMMITTEE—*continued*
  opinion—*continued*
    favourable opinion, need for, 112
    generally, 115
    Gene Therapy Advisory Committee,
      notification from, 115
    matters for consideration, 115
    review as to, 116
    specified period for giving, 115n[2]
    summary, publication of, 115
    time for giving, 115
    valid application: meaning, 115n[3]
  recognition, 111
  revocation etc of recognition, 111
  UK Ethics Committees Authority's
    monitoring role, 110

EUROPEAN MEDICINES AGENCY
  Eudravigilance database, 14
  European medicines web-portal, 14
  failure to provide information to,
    offence, 14
  functions, 14

EXPORT
  advanced therapy products,
    prohibition, 75
  controlled drug, restrictions, 491
  pancuronium bromide, restrictions, 543
  veterinary medicinal product, 436

HERBAL MEDICINAL PRODUCT
  meaning, 51n[2]
  advertisements for, 345
  application for registration—
    accompanying material, 209
    applicable products, 206
    circumstances for granting, 208, 211
    consideration of, 211
    generally, 208
    obligation to update information in
      connection with, 210
    offences, 229
    oral or written explanation, 211
    procedure, 208
    refusal, 211
    relevant herbal monograph, need to
      take account of, 211
    renewal of registration, 212
    time limit for determining, 211
    vitamins or minerals, addition of, 207
  registration—
    application for. *See* application for
      registration *above*
    cessation, 215
    classification of, 213
    conditions attached to, 213
    duration of certificate, 214

HERBAL MEDICINAL
   PRODUCT—*continued*
  registration—*continued*
   failure to place on market etc, effect,
    215
   holder's obligations—
    appropriate and continued supplies,
     ensuring, 227
    new herbal monograph, following,
     223
    placing on market etc, notification
     as to, 221
    product information, keeping up to
     date, 225
    record-keeping, 226
    safety etc, information as to, 224
    scientific and technical progress,
     taking account of, 222
   offences—
    applications, as to, 229
    false or misleading information,
     provision of, 230
    general defence, 231
    general offence, 231
    urgent safety restrictions, 228
   renewal of registration, 214
   revocation, 216, 217
   suspension, 216
   validity of certificate, 214
   variation, 216
  sale etc of suspended product, 220
  suspension of use etc, 218
  withdrawal from market, licensing
   authority requiring, 219

HOMOEOPATHIC MEDICINAL
   PRODUCT
  meaning, 187n[1]
  advertisements for, 344
  application for certification—
   applicable products, 187
   consideration of application, 189
   offence, 203
   procedure, 188
   renewal of applications, 190
  certificate of registration—
   application. *See* application for
    certification *above*
   cessation, 194
   classification, 192
   conditions attached to, 191, 192
   duration, 193
   holder's obligations—
    appropriate and continued supplies,
     ensuring, 202
    information requirements, 197

HOMOEOPATHIC MEDICINAL
   PRODUCT—*continued*
  certificate of registration—*continued*
   holder's obligations—*continued*
    placing on market etc, notification
     as to, 197
    product information, 200
    record-keeping, as to, 201
    safety etc, information as to, 199
    scientific and technical progress,
     taking account of, 198
    volume of sales, provision of
     information, 197
    withdrawal of product, notification
     as to, 197
   revocation, variation or suspension,
    195
   validity, 193
  failure to place on market etc, effect on
   certificate, 194
  offences—
   application, in connection with, 203
   defence, 205
   false and misleading information,
    provision of, 204
   general offence, 205
  packaging etc, 325
  withdrawal of product from market,
   196

HOSPITAL BLOOD BANK. *See under*
  BLOOD QUALITY AND SAFETY

HUMAN MEDICINE
  authorisation. *See* AUTHORISATION
  British Pharmacopoeia Commission. *See*
   BRITISH PHARMACOPOEIA
   COMMISSION
  clinical trial. *See* CLINICAL TRIAL
  Commission on Human Medicines, 31
  expert advisory groups, 33
  fees, payment and recovery etc, 30
  generally, 25
  investigational medicinal product. *See*
   INVESTIGATIONAL MEDICINAL
   PRODUCT
  legislation—
   Medicines Act 1968, operation and
    effect, 29
   orders and regulations, power to
    make, 27
   review by Secretary of State, 34
  licensing—
   licensing authority. *See* licensing
    authority *below*
   manufacturer's licence. *See*
    manufacturer's licence *below*

HUMAN MEDICINE—*continued*
  licensing—*continued*
    wholesale dealer's licence. *See*
      wholesale dealer's licence *below*
  licensing authority—
    meaning, 35n[1]
    civil liability, immunity from, 36
    clinical trial, request for
      authorisation. *See* CLINICAL TRIAL
      (authorisation)
    failure to comply with notice,
      offence, 38n[4]
    false information, offence of giving,
      38n[3]
    grant or refusal of licence by, 37
    information, power to request, 38
    manufacturer's licence, grounds for
      suspension etc of, 41
    power to suspend, revoke or vary
      licences, 40
    reasons for decision, duty to give, 39
    responsibilities, 35
    urgency, procedure in cases of, 43
    variation of licence on holder's
      application, 44
    wholesale dealer's licence, grounds for
      suspension etc of, 42
  manufacturer's licence—
    application for, 53
    certification, 55
    conditions—
      exempt advanced therapy products.
        See exempt advanced therapy
        products *below*
      general conditions, 56
      manufacture etc. *See* manufacture
        or assembly of products *below*
      non-EEA state, import of products
        from—
        good manufacturing practice, 67
        standard provisions, inclusion
          of, 66
      qualified persons, as to. *See*
        qualified person *below*
    determination of application for,
      relevant factors, 54
    doctors and dentists, exemption as
      to, 49
    exempt advanced therapy products—
      adverse reaction, details of, 70
      blood or blood products, import
        and use, 72
      human cells or tissues, use of, 71
      import and export, prohibition on,
        75
      offence as to data provisions, 76

HUMAN MEDICINE—*continued*
  manufacturer's licence—*continued*
    exempt advanced therapy
      products—*continued*
      packaging, 68
      risk management system, 74
      tracing data, 69
      wholesale dealing, distribution by
        way of, 73
    herbal medicines, exemption as to, 51
    import exemptions, 46
    investigational medicinal products,
      exemption as to, 47
    manufacture or assembly of
      products—
      good manufacturing practice, 62
      imported blood or blood products,
        65
      limited to products covered by
        licence, 64
      staff and premises conditions, 63
      standard provisions in licence, 61
    mixing of medicines, exemption as
      to, 50
    pharmacists, exemptions for, 52
    qualified person—
      meaning, 57n[5]
      long experience, with, 60
      obligations of, 58
      qualification requirements, 59
      requirements as to, 57
    registered nurses and midwives,
      exemption as to, 48
    requirement for, 45
  medicinal product—
    meaning, 25
    classification, 26
    subject to general sale: meaning, 26
  non-medicinal products, application of
    provisions to, 28
  pharmacovigilance. *See*
    PHARMACOVIGILANCE
  pharmacy medicine, 26
  prescription only medicine, 26
  quality and standards. *See under*
    MEDICINAL PRODUCT
  sale or supply, prohibited. *See*
    MEDICINAL PRODUCT (prohibited
    sales etc)
  wholesale dealer's licence—
    adverse reactions, provision of
      details, 93
    advertising, 96
    application for, 80
    authorisation requirement, 85

HUMAN MEDICINE—*continued*
  wholesale dealer's licence—*continued*
    continued supply to pharmacies etc,
      need to ensure, 83
    determination of application, relevant
      factors, 81
    documents, keeping of, 86
    due diligence, need for, 95
    exemption from requirement for, 78
    exporting products, 94
    good distribution practice, compliance
      with, 82
    grounds for suspension etc, 42
    importing products, 87, 94
    inspections, 88
    obtaining and distributing products,
      91
    requirement for, 77
    responsible persons, need for, 90
    restrictions on persons to be supplied
      with products, 79
    specified persons only, requirement to
      deal with, 89
    staff, premises and equipment,
      maintenance etc, 84
    tracing data, 92
IMPORT
  meaning, 97n^5
  advanced therapy products,
    prohibition, 75
  blood and blood components, 450
  controlled drug, restrictions, 491
  veterinary medicinal products—
    authorised products, 434
    unauthorised products, 435
IN VITRO DIAGNOSTIC DEVICE. *See
  under* MEDICAL DEVICE
INVESTIGATIONAL MEDICINAL
  PRODUCT
  meaning, 18n^6, 107n^1
  assembling, 97n^4
  clinical trial, supply of products for,
    113
  dossier, 106n^{22}
  labelling, 97n^4, 136
  manufacture and import—
    assemble: meaning, 97n^4
    authorisation. *See* manufacturing
      authorisation *below*
    container: meaning, 97n^4
    exemption from provisions, 98
    import: meaning, 97n^5
    labelling: meaning, 97n^4
    manufacture: meaning, 97n^3
  manufacturing authorisation—
    application for, 99

INVESTIGATIONAL MEDICINAL
  PRODUCT—*continued*
  manufacturing authorisation—*continued*
    application of, 103
    consideration of application, 100
    effect, 103
    grant or refusal, 101
    hearing to consider application, 102
    procedural provisions, 102
    qualified persons, need for, 104
    requirement for, 97
    revocation or suspension, 106
    variation, 105
  market authorisation, 47n^3
LABELLING
  blood and blood components, 457
  investigational medical product, 97n^4,
    136
  poison, 544
  radionuclides, 323
  veterinary medicinal product. *See under*
    VETERINARY MEDICINAL PRODUCT
LICENCE
  medicinal product. *See under* HUMAN
    MEDICINE; MEDICINAL PRODUCT
LOCAL AUTHORITY
  meaning, 535
  poisons, enforcement powers and
    duties, 549, 550, 551
MANUFACTURE
  meaning, 97n^3, 141n^7, 410
  human medicine, licence. *See* HUMAN
    MEDICINE (manufacturer's licence)
  investigational medicinal product. *See*
    INVESTIGATIONAL MEDICINAL
    PRODUCT (manufacture and import)
MARKETING
  authorisation. *See under*
    AUTHORISATION
  veterinary marketing authorisation. *See*
    VETERINARY MARKETING
    AUTHORISATION (marketing
    authorisation)
MEDICAL DEVICE
  meaning, 472
  accessory, 473n^4, 475n^4
  active implantable device—
    meaning, 474n^4
    criteria for, 474
    custom-made device, 474n^{15}
    excluded, where, 474n^6
    hazard existing, where, 474n^4
    relevant device, 474n^4
    restrictions, 474
  animal tissues, use of, 473n^6

MEDICAL DEVICE—*continued*
  CE marking—
    meaning, 473n[4]
    active implantable medical device,
      474n[4]
    conformity assessment bodies, 476
    general medical device, 473
    in vitro diagnostic device, 475
  conformity assessment bodies, 476
  criteria for placing on market, 473
  custom-made device, 473n[15], 474n[15]
  diagnostic and screening procedures—
    excluded from regulation, where, 478
    regulated activities, as, 478
  enforcement procedures, 477
  general medical devices—
    criteria for, 473
    excluded, where, 473n[6]
    relevant device, 473n[4]
    restrictions, 473
  generally, 472
  hazard existing, requirements to be met
    where, 473
  in vitro diagnostic device—
    meaning, 475n[4]
    accessory, 475n[4]
    criteria for, 475
    device for performance evaluation,
      475n[16]
    excluded, where, 475n[6]
    relevant device, 475n[4]
    restrictions, 475
    specimen receptacle, 475n[4]
  intended for clinical investigation,
    472n[1]
  intended purpose: meaning, 472n[1]
  intrauterine contraceptive device,
    insertion or removal as regulated
    activity, 479
  manufacturer: meaning, 472n[1]
  markings, restrictions on, placing of,
    476
  notified bodies, 476
  placing on the market—
    meaning, 472n[1]
    active implantable device. *See* active
      implantable device *above*
    general medical devices. *See* general
      medical devices *above*
    in vitro diagnostic device. *See* in vitro
      diagnostic device *above*
  putting into service—
    meaning, 473n[3]
    active implantable device. *See* active
      implantable device *above*
    criteria for, 473, 474

MEDICAL DEVICE—*continued*
  putting into service—*continued*
    excluded, where, 473n[6]
    general medical devices. *See* general
      medical devices *above*
    in vitro diagnostic device. *See* in vitro
      diagnostic device *above*
    relevant device, 473n[4]
    restrictions, 473, 474
  regulations, exemptions from, 472
  single-use combination product, 473n[4]
  stable derivatives device, 472n[8]
  supply, 473n[7]

MEDICAL SUPPLIES
  meaning, 2n[2]
  control of maximum price for, 2

MEDICINAL PRODUCT
  meaning, 6n[1], 12n[2], 25, 30n[8]
  adulteration, 234
  advanced therapy medicinal product—
    meaning, 5n[4], 23, 146n[2], 180n[2],
      378n[1]
    Committee for Advanced Therapies,
      22
    European regulation, 22
    prohibitions as to traceability of
      treatment with, 378
    UK regulation, 24
  advertisement. *See* ADVERTISEMENT
  authorisation—
    animal diseases, products for, 5
    European systems for. *See* European
      systems for authorisation *below*
    See also AUTHORISATION
  blood and blood products. *See* BLOOD
    QUALITY AND SAFETY
  British Pharmacopoeia Commission. *See*
    BRITISH PHARMACOPOEIA
    COMMISSION
  classification, 26
  clinical trial. *See* CLINICAL TRIAL
  colouring—
    children, aspirin and paracetamol
      for, 332
    power to make regulations, 331
  container—
    child resistant—
      exemptions, 316
      not reclosable, but still child
        resistant, 315n[3]
      regulated medicinal products to be
        sold or supplied in, 315
    compliance with requirements, 314
    purposes for which regulations
      made, 314n[5]
    regulations, power to make, 314

MEDICINAL PRODUCT—*continued*
  enforcement—
    advanced therapy medicinal products,
      prohibitions in connection with,
      378
    Human Medicines Regulations 2012,
      under—
      body corporate, offences by, 375
      certificate, offence relating to, 374
      contravention due to another's
        fault, 372
      disclosure of information,
        restrictions on, 369
      enforcement authorities, 362
      entry powers—
        application for warrant, 364
        identification, need for, 363
        inspector's right to enter, 363
        powers on entry, 364
        restriction on powers, 363
        trespass, need to secure premises
          against. 364
      inspection powers—
        findings and reports, 368
        generally, 365
        indemnity, inspector's right to,
          370
        inspector: meaning, 363n[1]
        liability, protection from, 370
      legal proceedings—
        licences, authorisations etc,
          validity of, 361
        validity of licensing authority's
          decisions, 361
      offences relating to, 371, 374, 375
      presumptions, 377
      prosecutions, 376
      remedying failures, 368
      samples. *See under* sample *below*
      seizure of goods and documents,
        powers of, 365
      warranty—
        defence, as, 373
        offence relating to, 374
    Medicines Act 1968, under—
      analysis of samples, 357
      body corporate, offences by, 375
      contravention due to another's
        fault, 372
      enforcement authorities, 354
      entry powers, 355
      indemnity, right to, 360
      information, disclosure of, 359
      inspection powers, 356
      liability, protection from, 360
      offences related to, 358, 375

MEDICINAL PRODUCT—*continued*
  enforcement—*continued*
    Medicines Act 1968,
      under—*continued*
      presumptions, 377
      prosecutions, 376
      samples. *See* sample *below*
      seizure of goods and documents,
        powers of, 356
      self-incrimination, right to avoid,
        358n[4]
      warranty as defence, 373
  European law—
    authorisation, European systems for.
      See European systems for
      authorisation *below*
    blood and blood products, 17
    clinical trials, 18
    falsified medicines, 21
    generally, 1
    herbal medicinal products for humans
      use, 19
    manufacturing of products, 12
    medical devices, 20
    pharmacovigilance. *See*
      PHARMACOVIGILANCE
    traceability, 13
    Variations Regulation, 11
  European systems for authorisation—
    Article 126a authorisation, 10
    centralised procedure, 5, 11
    compassionate use exemption, 8
    decentralised procedure, 7
    European Medicines Agency,
      application to, 5
    marketing authorisation, 6
    mutual recognition procedure, 7, 11
    products for which authorisation
      required, 5
    requirement for authorisation, 4
    routes for authorisation, 4
    temporary use exemption, 9
    variation of licences, 11
    veterinary medicinal product, 6
  falsified medicines, 21
  free samples, restrictions on supplying,
    341
  health service medicines, limiting prices
    or profits, 2
  herbal medicinal products for humans
    use, 19
  human medicines. *See* HUMAN MEDICINE
  labelling requirements for
    radionuclides, 323
  leaflet. *See* package leaflet *below*

MEDICINAL PRODUCT—*continued*
legislation—
  European law. *See* European law
    above
  Human Medicines
    Regulations 2012—
      enforcement under. *See under*
        enforcement *above*
      scope of control, 1
      sample under. *See under* sample
        below
  Medicines Act 1968—
    enforcement under. *See under*
      enforcement *above*
    operation and effect, 29
    sample under. *See under* sample
      below
licensing—
  authority—
    ministers acting as, 1
    packaging etc, submission of
      mock-ups to, 328
    UK marketing authorisation
      duties, 164
    See also under HUMAN MEDICINE
  generally, 1
  See also under HUMAN MEDICINE
marking etc, power to make
  regulations, 331
medical devices, 20
offences—
  body corporate, by, 375
  contravention due to another's fault,
    372
  enforcement provisions. *See*
    enforcement *above*
  prescribing medicinal products, 379
  presumptions, 377
  prohibitions medicinal products, 379
  prosecutions, 376
  warranties and certificates, relating
    to, 374
package leaflet—
  meaning, 68n[5]
  generally, 321
  homoeopathic medicines, 325
  language requirements, 327
  mock-ups, submission to licensing
    authority, 328
  offences relating to, 329
  pharmacies, special provision for, 318
  pictures and symbols, use of, 322
  radionuclides, for, 324
  regulations, non-compliance with,
    330
  requirements, 321

MEDICINAL PRODUCT—*continued*
package leaflet—*continued*
  scope of provisions, 317
  target groups, need to consult, 321
packaging—
  blind people, information for, 320
  general requirements, 319
  homoeopathic medicines, 325
  language requirements, 327
  leaflets. *See* package leaflet *above*
  mock-ups, submission to licensing
    authority, 328
  offences relating to, 329
  partially sighted people, information
    for, 320
  pharmacies, special provision for, 318
  pictures and symbols, use of, 322
  radionuclides, labelling requirements,
    323
  regulations, non-compliance with,
    330
  scope of provisions, 317
  specific requirements, 319
  traditional herbal medicinal
    products, 326
pharmaceutical services. *See under*
  PRIMARY CARE TRUST
pharmacovigilance. *See*
  PHARMACOVIGILANCE
pharmacy, products available from,
  26n[16]
prescription only medicine—
  meaning, 26
  appropriate practitioners in relation
    to, 271
  conditions on practitioners, power to
    impose, 272
  examples, 26n[11]
  exemptions—
    doctors and dentists etc, 280
    power to apply, 272
  generally, 272
  power to specify products as, 272,
    273
  requirements for—
    EEA health professionals, 276
    generally, 275
  restrictions on sale or supply, 271
  supplementary prescribers,
    prescription and administration
    by, 274
price control, 2
prohibited sales etc—
  automatic machines, sale from, 279
  Bal Jivan Chamcho, 308
  chloroform, 310

MEDICINAL PRODUCT—*continued*
prohibited sales etc—*continued*
exemptions—
administration of certain medicines
in emergency, 296
aloxiprin, products containing, 294
aspirin products containing, 294
cases involving another's default,
302
certain collection and delivery
arrangements, 306
doctors and dentists etc, 280
emergency sale by pharmacist—
pandemic, in, 283
patient's request, at, 282
prescriber unable to prescribe,
281
ephedrine base or salts, products
containing, 295
exempted products, 280n14
forged prescription, in case of, 303
generally, 292, 293
health centre, 280
health professionals, 285
herbal remedies, 299
high dilution, medicinal products
at, 300
homoeopathic medicinal products,
301
hospital, 280, 284
medicinal products not subject to
general sale, 293
national health service bodies, 286
pandemic disease, supply in event
or anticipation of, 305
paracetamol, products containing,
294
patient group direction. *See* patient
group direction, supply under
below
pseudoephedrine salts, products
containing, 295
radioactive medicinal products, 298
registered midwife, 280
requirement for prescription not
met, 304
smallpox vaccine, administration
of, 297
kava-kava, products containing, 312
non-medicinal antimicrobial
substances, 309
patient group direction, supply
under—
dental practices and clinics, by, 289
doctors or dentists, to assist, 287
independent hospitals, by, 288

MEDICINAL PRODUCT—*continued*
prohibited sales etc—*continued*
patient group direction, supply
under—*continued*
police, to assist, 291
retail pharmacy business, by person
conducting, 290
plants, products containing certain,
311
power to prohibit, 307
prescription only medicine. *See*
prescription only medicine *above*
products not subject to general sale,
277
products subject to general sale, 278
Senecio, products containing, 313
specified medicinal products, 307
starting materials, 270
quality and standards—
adulteration, 234
protection of purchasers, 235
published monograph, compliance
with standards in, 236
warranty as defence, 234n6, 373
radioactive materials. *See* RADIOACTIVE
SUBSTANCE
radionuclide—
meaning, 25n9
labelling requirements, 323
leaflets for, 324
restrictions, legislative, 1
sale or supply, prohibited. *See*
prohibited sales etc *above*
sample—
Human Medicines Regulations 2012,
under—
analysis of, procedure for, 367
application of sampling procedure,
366
power to take or purchase, 365
Medicines Act 1968, under—
analysis of, procedure for, 357
automatic machine, purchased
from, 357n11
facilities for examination of drugs,
provision of, 357
power to take, 356
purchased otherwise than from an
automatic machine, 357n10
retention where seller or owner
unknown, 357n13
unopened containers, dividing,
357n9
shape of products, power to make
regulations, 331
traceability, 13

MEDICINAL PRODUCT—*continued*
  unauthorised, 141
    vaccine damage payment. *See* VACCINE
      DAMAGE PAYMENT
    veterinary medicines. *See* VETERINARY
      MEDICINAL PRODUCT

MEDICINE
  human use, for. *See* HUMAN MEDICINE

PHARMACIST
  meaning, $52n^5$, $539n^8$
  authorisation, exemption from, 150
  controlled drugs, prohibition direction,
    519
  medicinal product, emergency sales—
    pandemic, in, 283
    patient's request, at, 282
    prescriber unable to prescribe, 281

PHARMACOVIGILANCE
  application of provisions, 241
  duty to operate system, 15
  enforcement, 268
  European Medicines Agency, 14
  holder's duties—
    holder: meaning, $246n^1$
    medical literature, monitoring, 251
    periodic safety update reports. *See*
      periodic safety update reports
      below
    pharmacovigilance system—
      meaning, $15n^1$
      audit of system, 248
      operation of, 243
      risk management system. *See* risk
        management system *below*
    public announcements, as to, 267
    recording obligations, 249
    reporting obligations, 251
    risk management system—
      duty to operate, 246
      exception from duty to operate,
        247
      imposition of obligation,
        circumstances for, 247
    signal detection, 252
  infringement notice, 268
  licensing authority's duties—
    audit duties, 244
    delegation of duties, 245
    evaluation of information, 243
    general obligations, 242
    national web-portal, as to, 265
    periodic safety update reports,
      submission of. *See* periodic safety
      update reports *below*
    pharmacovigilance system, operation
      of, 243

PHARMACOVIGILANCE—*continued*
  licensing authority's duties—*continued*
    public announcements, as to, 266
    recording obligations, 249
    reporting obligations, 250
    risk management system, imposition
      on holder, 247
    signal detection, 252
  marketing authorisation holder, duty
    on, 16
  offences, 269
  periodic safety update reports—
    assessment where EU single
      assessment procedure
      inapplicable, 257
    contents, 253, 254
    derogation from general
      requirements, 254
    duty to submit, 253
    electronic submission, 253
    frequency, $253n^9$
    harmonisation of frequency or date of
      submission, 255
    responding to single assessment of,
      256
  post-authorisation safety study—
    draft study protocol for required
      study—
      amendment, 262
      commencement, $261n^{10}$
      submission, 261
      time limit for responding to, 261
    final study report—
      follow-up, 264
      implementation of measures
        following, 264
      submission and evaluation, 263
    general provisions, 260
    holder's duties, 260
    inapplicable, where, 260
    protocol and progress reports,
      submission, 260
    relevant post-authorisation safety
      study: meaning, $260n^1$
  system—
    meaning, 15
    audit of, 244
    duty to operate, 243, 246
    failure to comply with, enforcement
      procedure, 368
    master file: meaning, $246n^3$
    purpose, 243, 246
  transparency and communications—
    national medicines web-portal, 265
    public announcements, 266, 267

References are to paragraph numbers; superior figures refer to notes

PHARMACOVIGILANCE—*continued*
  urgent action—
    EU urgent action procedure, 259
    generally, 258
    information requirements, 258
    relevant circumstances for, 258
  veterinary medicines. *See under*
    VETERINARY MEDICINAL PRODUCT

POISON
  meaning, 528n[1]
  analyst's certificate as evidence, 555
  compressed hydrogen cyanide, sake or
    supply, 544
  control, 528
  cruel poisons, 529
  employee's default, proceedings for, 553
  enforcement—
    information, failure to provide, 551
    local authority, by—
      enforcement duties, 549
      inspectors, powers of, 550
      obstruction of inspectors, 551
      penalties, 552
    Pharmaceutical Society inspectors—
      obstruction, 551
      powers of, 548
  exemption from restrictions—
    articles and substances, 547
    sales, 546
  labelling, 544
  legislation, 528
  non-medicinal poison, 532n[2]
  offences—
    analyst's certificate as evidence, 555
    employee's default, proceedings for,
      553
    fails to comply: meaning, 552n[2]
    penalties, 552
    time limit for prosecutions, 554
  packaging, 544
  pancuronium bromide, export of, 543
  penalties for offences, 552
  Poisons Act 1972, poisons included in,
    539n[14]
  Poisons Board—
    directions from Secretary of State to,
      534
    nature of, 530
  Poisons List—
    generally, 531
    Part I poisons, 532
    Part II poisons, 533
    power to amend or vary, 531
  Poisons Rules, power to make, 534
  sale—
    agreement to sell, 539n[3]

POISON—*continued*
  sale—*continued*
    compressed hydrogen cyanide, 544
    cyanides, 542
    effective time of, 539n[3]
    emergency, in case of, 541n[16]
    householder not known to seller,
      certificate from, 541n[9]
    listed seller—
      listing. *See* local authority's list
        below
      Part II poisons, of, 540n[12]
      sale by, 535, 540
      use of titles, 537
    local authority's list—
      duty to keep, 535
      fees payable in respect of, 535
      local authority: meaning, 535n[1]
      refusal of entry in, 536
      removal from, 536
      sale by listed seller, 535, 540
      use of titles, 537
    pancuronium bromide, 543
    persons to whom may be sold, 541
    record-keeping, 541n[13]
    restrictions—
      exempted sale, 539n[12]
      generally, 538
      listed sellers, by, 540
      retail pharmacy business, through,
        539
    signed record, exemption from need
      for, 541n[16]
    strychnine, 542
    unlawful sale of certain poisons, 542
    wholesale dealing, by way of, 541n[21]
  storage, 545
  transport, 545

PRESCRIPTION (MEDICAL)
  controlled drug, 512
  medicinal product. *See* MEDICINAL
    PRODUCT (prescription only
    medicine)

PRICE
  health service medicines, limiting price
    for, 2
  medical supplies, control of maximum
    price for, 2

PRIMARY CARE TRUST
  pharmaceutical services—
    meaning, 3
    assessment of needs, 3
    list of those providing, preparation etc
      of, 3

PROFIT
　health service medicines, limiting profits
　　from, 2

RADIOACTIVE SUBSTANCE
　administration of, 382
　application of provisions to, 381
　ionising radiation—
　　meaning, 382n^1
　　administration of, 382
　　protection against exposure to, 383
　medical exposure, conditions for, 382n^9
　protection against radiation, 383
　radioactive medicinal product:
　　meaning, 298n^2, 382n^4
　regulations applicable to, 381

SALE
　medicinal product. *See* MEDICINAL
　　PRODUCT (prohibited sales etc)
　poison. *See under* POISON

SAMPLE
　medicinal product—
　　free sample, 341
　　See also under MEDICINAL PRODUCT
　power to take, under Medicines
　　Act 1968, 356

SECRETARY OF STATE
　meaning, 2n^1
　blood establishment, and. *See under*
　　BLOOD QUALITY AND SAFETY
　health service medicines, limiting price
　　or profits for, 2
　human medicine legislation, review of,
　　34
　veterinary products committee—
　　appeal against Secretary of State's
　　　decision, 442, 443
　　power to appoint members of, 442n^1

SERVICE (DOCUMENTS)
　Misuse of Drugs Act 1971, under, 489

SUPPLY
　controlled drug. *See under* CONTROLLED
　　DRUG
　medicinal product. *See under* MEDICINAL
　　PRODUCT (prohibited sales etc)

TRADITIONAL HERBAL MEDICINAL
　PRODUCT. *See generally* HERBAL
　MEDICINAL PRODUCT
　meaning, 155n^6
　enforcement provisions. *See* MEDICINAL
　　PRODUCT (enforcement)(Medicines
　　Act 1968)
　packaging requirements, 326
　registration. *See under* HERBAL
　　MEDICINAL PRODUCT

VACCINE DAMAGE PAYMENT
　after 9 May 1978 and before 22 March
　　1979, made, 386
　appeal procedure, 385
　balance of probability, in determining
　　cause of disability, 385n^{10}
　claimant aged 18 or over, payment to,
　　386
　diseases causing damage, list of, 384n^4
　circumstances giving rise to right to,
　　384n^8
　conditions of entitlement to, 384
　determination of claims, procedure, 385
　medical examination, claimant
　　submitting to, 385n^{10}
　personal representatives, payment to,
　　386
　persons severely damaged by
　　vaccination, 384
　proceedings, payment not prejudicing
　　right to institute etc, 386
　relevant statutory sum: meaning, 384n^6
　repayment, in case of fraud etc, 385
　right to, 384
　severe disability, determining, 384n^3
　trustees, payment to, 386
　vaccination given outside UK and Isle of
　　Man, 384n^{11}
　vaccination not compulsory, where,
　　384n^7
　writing, need for claim in, 385n^4

VENDING MACHINE
　power to order opening of, 356n^{18}, 365
　seizure of medicinal product from,
　　356n^{19}, 365

VETERINARY MEDICINAL PRODUCT
　meaning, 6n^2, 387
　administration to animals—
　　animal test certificate, under, 428
　　exemption from authorisation. *See*
　　　under authorisation *below*
　　food chain, where animal put into,
　　　387, 423n^4
　　offence, where, 422
　　surgeons from other member states,
　　　by, 425
　advertisement—
　　defence of publication in course of
　　　business, 441
　　human medicines for animal use, 439
　　misleading or otherwise inaccurate,
　　　439
　　narcotics, product containing, 440
　　prescription only products, offences as
　　　to, 440

VETERINARY MEDICINAL
   PRODUCT—*continued*
advertisement—*continued*
  psychotropic drugs, product
    containing, 440
animals destroyed by poisons, 387
animals put into food chain,
   administered to, 387, 423n[4]
annual audit, need for, 431
authorisation—
  exemptions—
    administration outside terms of
      authorisation, 423
    animal test certificate,
      administration under, 428
    aquarium animals, 429n[2]
    exceptional circumstances,
      treatment in, 426
    generally, 422
    homoeopathic remedy, use of, 427
    immunological products, 424
    small pets, 422, 429
    surgeons from other member states,
      administration by, 425
    unnecessary suffering, to avoid,
      423
  manufacturing. *See* manufacturing
    authorisation *below*
  marketing. *See* marketing
    authorisation *below*
  wholesale dealer authorisation. *See*
    wholesale dealer authorisation
    below
bulk package, labelling, 414
certificate of good manufacturing
   practice, 413, 414
classification, 431
control tests—
  need to carry out, 415
  proof of, 414
enforcement—
  appeals procedure, 443
  improvement notice, 447
  inspector's entry powers, 444
  obstruction, offence, 446
  pharmacies, inspection of, 445
  seizure of products, 444n[20]
  veterinary products committee, by.
    See veterinary products
    committee *below*
export, 436
food-producing animal, keeper's duty to
   maintain records, 433
generally, 387
immunological product, whether
   possible to prohibit supply, 407

VETERINARY MEDICINAL
   PRODUCT—*continued*
imports—
  authorised products, 434
  unauthorised products, 435
inspection of premises—
  inspector's entry powers, 444
  obstruction, 446
  pharmacies, 445
labelling—
  at time of retail supply, 438
  contents, 437, 438
  information not visible, 438
licensed procedure, product
   administered in course of, 387
manufacturing authorisation—
  application for, 411
  certificate of good manufacturing
    practice, 413, 414
  control tests—
    need to carry out, 415
    proof of, 414
  grant, 411
  holder's duties, 414, 433
  inspection of premises, 413
  material alterations, notification or
    variation in case of, 411
  manufacture: meaning, 410
  need for, 410
  qualified persons—
    appointment and role, 415
    register of, 416
  quality assurance and quality
    control, 414
  record-keeping, 433
  register of holders, 416
  revocation, 412
  suspension, 412
  test sites, 417
  variation, 412
  written report from Secretary of State
    following inspection, 413
marketing authorisation—
  administration of product outside
    terms of, 423
  application for—
    additional information required,
      where, 391
    assessment report, 393
    derogation from requirement to
      provide information, 389n[3]
    food-producing animals, time limits
      in case of, 389n[2]
    generally, 389
    more than one member state, in,
      408

References are to paragraph numbers; superior figures refer to notes

VETERINARY MEDICINAL PRODUCT—*continued*
marketing authorisation—*continued*
  application for—*continued*
    mutual recognition procedure, 7, 11, 408
    products authorised in another member state, effect, 392
    time limit for determining, 390, 393n[2]
  cessation of validity, 403
  control tests, duty to carry out, 401
  decentralised procedure, 7, 11
  duration, 403
  expertise in analysing samples, holder's duty to provide, 398
  failure to place product on market, effect, 403
  grant—
    exceptional circumstances, in, 397
    generally, 394
    publication procedures following, 396
  homoeopathic remedy, 409
  immunological product, holder's duties relating to, 400
  information, holder's duty to provide, 399
  limited authorisation, reassessment, 397
  manufacturing authorisation, need for. *See* manufacturing authorisation *above*
  minor change in, application for, 404
  mutual recognition procedure, 7, 11, 408
  need for, 6, 388
  offence in absence of, 388
  pharmacovigilance system, need for. *See* pharmacovigilance system *below*
  placing product on the market, notification duty, 402
  prohibition on supply of products, 407
  provisional authorisation, reassessment, 397
  recall of products, 407
  refusal, 395
  removal of product from the market, notification duty, 402
  renewal—
    time limit for application, 403n[1]
    validity following, 403
  revocation, 406, 430
  samples, power to request, 398

VETERINARY MEDICINAL PRODUCT—*continued*
marketing authorisation—*continued*
  scientific and technical progress, need to take account of, 404
  suspension, 405, 430
  validity, 403
  variation of authorisation, 404, 430
  variation of licences, 11
  volume of sales, provision of information as to, 402
offences—
  absence of marketing authorisation, 388
  advertising, as to, 439, 440
  exports, as to, 436
  finished product, as to, 448
  generally, 448
  imports, as to, 434, 435
  penalties, 448n[2]
  records, failure to keep, 433
package leaflets, 437
pharmacovigilance system—
  adverse reactions and other problems, duty to report, 430
  duty to operate, 15
  generally, 430
  information, provision of, 430
  marketing authorisation holder—
    duty on, 16
    suspension etc of authorisation, 430
  periodic safety update reports, submission of, 430
  qualified person, need for, 430
  responsibilities under, 430
  restrictions on alerting public to concerns, 430
prohibition on supply of products, 407
qualified persons—
  appointment and role, 415
  register of, 416
quality assurance and quality control, 414
radioactive isotopes, product based on, 387
recall of products, 407
record-keeping, 433
regulations, scope, 387
retail supply, 431
samples, need to keep, 414
test sites, 417
veterinary products committee—
  appeal to, right of, 442
  members, Secretary of State's power to appoint, 442n[1]

References are to paragraph numbers; superior figures refer to notes

VETERINARY MEDICINAL
    PRODUCT—*continued*
veterinary products
    committee—*continued*
    role, 442
    Secretary of State's decision—
        appeal to appointed person
            against, 443
        power to make, 442
veterinary surgeon's duty to keep
    records, 433
wholesale dealer authorisation—
    application for, 419
    breaking open of packages, 432
    duration, 419

VETERINARY MEDICINAL
    PRODUCT—*continued*
wholesale dealer
    authorisation—*continued*
    generally, 432
    grant, 419
    holder's duties, 421
    material alterations, notification or
        variation in case of, 419
    more than one site, covering, 419
    need for, 418
    record-keeping, 433
    suspension, variation or revocation,
        420
wholesale supply, 432

Mental Health and Capacity

ABSENCE WITHOUT LEAVE
hospital, from. *See under* MENTALLY
    DISORDERED PERSON OR PATIENT
    (absence from hospital)
ACCUSED
mental disorder. *See* MENTALLY
    DISORDERED PERSON OR PATIENT
    (accused person)
ADMINISTRATION OF DECEASED'S
    ESTATE
mental disorder of person entitled to
    grant, 564
ADOPTION
mentally disordered person's consent,
    627
ADVOWSON
incapacity to present to, $761n^4$
AFTER-CARE
duty to provide services—
    discretionary nature of duty, $945n^3$
    extent, $945n^3$
    generally, 945
    payments for, $945n^4$, 946
AGENT
mental disorder—
    breach of warranty of authority
        following, 600
    effect on ability to appoint, 600
ALIEN
mentally disordered patient, removal
    from UK, 907

APPEAL
Court of Appeal. *See* COURT OF APPEAL
Upper Tribunal, to. *See under* UPPER
    TRIBUNAL
BANKRUPTCY
donor of lasting power of attorney, 621
BENEFICE
mental disorder, effect on holding,
    $761n^4$
BROADMOOR
patients, 556
statutory management, 556
CARE AND TREATMENT PLAN
meaning, $855n^{17}$
completion in writing etc, $855n^{17}$
form and content, regulations as to,
    855
outcomes in, $855n^{17}$
CARE COORDINATOR
adult placement carer: meaning, $856n^9$
appointment—
    Codes of Practice and guidance as
        to, $853n^8$
    duty to appoint, 851
    professional requirements, $853n^7$
    regulations as to eligibility, 853
    restrictions on, 853
care and treatment plan. *See* CARE AND
    TREATMENT PLAN
carer: meaning, $856n^9$
consultation provisions, 856
functions, 855

CARE COORDINATOR—*continued*
information, patient's right to, 858
mental health service provider—
  meaning, 851n[1]
identifying relevant provider, 852
provision of mental health services, duty
  to coordinate, 854
regulations, power to make, 855
relevant patient—
  meaning, 851n[2]
identifying relevant provider for, 852
information for persons ceasing to
  be, 858
review and revision of care plans, 857
temporary appointment, cessation,
  851n[6]

CARE COUNCIL FOR WALES
approval of training courses, 819

CARE QUALITY COMMISSION
deprivation of liberty provisions, duty to
  monitor, 718
establishment, 573
functions, 573
purpose, 573

CHANNEL ISLANDS
mentally disordered patient. *See under*
  MENTALLY DISORDERED PERSON OR
  PATIENT

CHILD
informal admission to hospital. *See*
  MENTALLY DISORDERED PERSON OR
  PATIENT (child, informal admission)
special educational needs, with, 592

CIVIL PARTNERSHIP
capacity to consent to, 609

CODE OF PRACTICE
care coordinator, appointment of,
  853n[8]
guidance in, 758
mental capacity, as to persons lacking,
  602
Mental Health Act 1983, under, 568,
  762
Mental Health (Wales) Measure 2010,
  under, 763
order for discharge, guidance for
  hospital managers, 913n[10]
police questioning of mentally
  vulnerable persons, 1006

COMMUNITY PATIENT
meaning, 797n[4]
absence without leave—
  assisting absence, offence, 1013
  custody, taking into, 918
  effect on duration, 911
  examination of patient following, 911

COMMUNITY PATIENT—*continued*
absence without leave—*continued*
  harbouring a patient absent without
    leave, 1014
assignment of responsibility for, 804
child community patient. *See under*
  MENTALLY DISORDERED PERSON OR
  PATIENT
consent to treatment provisions. *See*
  MENTALLY DISORDERED PERSON OR
  PATIENT (consent to treatment)
discharge by tribunal, 967
managers' duty to give information to,
  805
not recalled to hospital, treatment
  where. *See* MENTALLY DISORDERED
  PERSON OR PATIENT (community
  patient not recalled to hospital)
order for discharge—
  nearest relative making, restriction
    on, 915
  to whom sent, 913n[9]
tribunals, application or reference to.
  See under FIRST-TIER TRIBUNAL;
  MENTAL HEALTH REVIEW TRIBUNAL
  FOR WALES

COMMUNITY TREATMENT ORDER
meaning, 797
absence without leave—
  assisting absence, offence, 1013
  effect on duration, 911
  harbouring a patient absent without
    leave, 1014
assignment of responsibility for patient,
  804
clinician's duty to examine patient, 799
community patient. *See* COMMUNITY
  PATIENT
conditions, patient subject to, 800
criteria for making, 797
detained patient, 797n[2]
duration, 799
effect, 797n[4], 798
extension, grounds for, 799
generally, 758, 797
information, patient's right to, 805
purpose, 797n[4]
recalling patient to hospital—
  power to recall, 801
  recalled patients, powers in respect
    of, 802
  subsequent release of patient, 802
  transfer to another hospital, 802n[5]
responsible clinician's duties, 797n[12]
responsible hospital, 799n[11]

COMMUNITY TREATMENT
ORDER—*continued*
revocation—
generally, 802, 803
reference to tribunal on, 964n5
service of documents, 850
tribunal—
nearest relative's power to apply to,
797n14
patient's power to apply to, 797, 803
COMPROMISE OF CLAIM
mentally disordered patient, on behalf
of, 1000
CONFESSION
mentally disordered person, by, 1006
CONTEMPT OF COURT
hospital order made in committal
proceedings for, 864n8
CONTRACT
capacity of mentally disordered person.
See MENTALLY DISORDERED PERSON
OR PATIENT (contractual capacity)
COSTS
Court of Protection proceedings, in. *See*
under COURT OF PROTECTION
COUNTY COURT
acting nearest relative, power to
appoint—
discharge of court order, 844
disposal of application, 842n26
duration of order, 842, 845
generally, 839n5, 842
grounds for making, 842
human rights provisions, and, 842n27
interim order, 842n6
nearest relative objecting to hospital
admission, 842n13, 14
procedure on application to, 846
relative's functions exercisable by
another person, where, 842
rules for specifying person, 842
variation of court order, 843
guardianship order, power to transfer,
796
COURT OF APPEAL
absolute discharge, on appeal against
'not guilty by reason of insanity'
verdict, 875
appeal to—
Crown Court, from, 879
Court of Protection, from, 750
hospital order, power to make, 875
supervision order, power to make, 875
unfitness, substitution of findings on,
875

COURT OF PROTECTION
active case management, 742
advance decision as to medical,
declaration as to, 626
appeal, rights of, 750
application to—
permission not required, where, 740
permission required, where, 740
rules of court, 740
authorisations, determining questions as
to, 733
benefice, acting as patron of, 727n13
care or treatment, protection of those
providing, 611
civil partnership, questions of capacity,
609
contractual capacity, deciding on, 614
costs—
conduct of parties, 747n13
court's powers as to payment etc, 747
deceased's estate, payment from, 747
deputy, donee or attorney, payment
to, 747
detailed assessment, 747
fixed costs, recovery, 747n14
health and welfare issues, 747n11
legal or other representative:
meaning, 747n3
local authority's misbehaviour,
747n11
more than one party, separate
representation, 747
person not a party to proceedings,
747
public body acting unlawfully etc,
747n14
summary assessment, 747
wasted costs, 747n5
Court of Protection Visitor. *See* COURT
OF PROTECTION VISITOR
decisions, power to make, 724
declarations, power to make, 723
deputies—
appointment, 735
conduct, 739
general power to appoint, 734
powers—
property, over, 736
Public Guardian, submission of
report to, 736
restriction on. *See* restriction on
powers *below*
Public Guardian's supervision of
conduct, 739
restriction on powers—
capacity, where person has, 737

COURT OF PROTECTION—*continued*
  deputies—*continued*
    restriction on powers—*continued*
      property, as to, 736
      restraint, where necessary, 738
      welfare, as to, 738
    rights, 735
    role, 734
    variation or discharge of order, 734
  divorce and dissolution of marriage,
    610
  fees, 746
  general powers, 721
  General Visitor. *See* COURT OF
    PROTECTION VISITOR
  generally, 720
  jurisdiction—
    by whom exercisable, 720
    conflict of laws, 722
    extent, 722
    generally, 722
    interim, 725
  lasting power of attorney, powers as
    to, 622, 732
  Lord Chief Justice, appointments by,
    720
  marriage, questions of capacity, 609
  overriding objective, court's duty to
    further, 742
  parties to proceedings—
    application to be joined as, 743
    bound by order or direction, 743
    generally, 743
    overriding objective of rules, duty to
      help further, 742
    person joined as party, 743
  personal welfare, person's—
    court deputies, power to appoint,
      607, 726
    general powers to make decisions,
      607, 726
  powers—
    benefice, as patron of, 727n[13]
    business matters, as to, 727
    decisions, to make, 724
    declarations, to make, 723
    deputies. *See* deputies *above*
    interim jurisdiction, 725
    lasting power of attorney, 732
    personal welfare, as to, 726
    property, as to. *See* property, dealing
      with *below*
    standard and urgent authorisations, as
      to, 733
    will, execution of, 731

COURT OF PROTECTION—*continued*
  practice and procedure—
    active case management, 742
    application. *See* application to *above*
    costs. *See* costs *above*
    fees, 746
    generally, 740
    overriding objective of rules, court's
      duty to further, 742
    parties. *See* parties to proceedings
      above
    practice directions, 741
    reports, power to request, 744
    transfer of proceedings where person
      under 18, 745
  property, dealing with—
    control and management, 728
    disposal of various interests, 729n[5]
    generally, 727
    permanent improvements to
      property, 729n[5]
    sale etc, 729
    settlement, 730
    stocks: meaning, 728n[6]
  protector of settlement, taking place of,
    564
  Public Guardian, and. *See under* PUBLIC
    GUARDIAN
  reports, power to request, 744
  rules of court, power to make, 740
  sexual relations, person's capacity to
    consent to. 608
  Special Visitor. *See* COURT OF
    PROTECTION VISITOR
  transfer of proceedings where person
    under 18, 745
  transport of persons, power to order,
    649
  visiting—
    Court of Protection Visitor. *See*
      COURT OF PROTECTION VISITOR
    Public Guardian, by. *See under* PUBLIC
      GUARDIAN
  will, power to execute, 731

COURT OF PROTECTION VISITOR
  meaning, 748
  appointment, 748
  directions from Public Guardian, 749
  information, provision of, 749
  interviewing powers, 748
  provisions applicable to visit, 749
  qualification requirements, 748n[3]
  record, examination etc, 748
  remuneration and allowances, 748
  report by, 744, 749
  term etc, 748

CROWN COURT
  guardianship order. *See* MENTALLY
    DISORDERED PERSON OR PATIENT
    (guardianship order)
  hospital order. *See* MENTALLY
    DISORDERED PERSON OR PATIENT
    (hospital order)
  restriction order. *See* MENTALLY
    DISORDERED PERSON OR PATIENT
    (restriction order)
DEATH
  mentally disordered patient's guardian,
    of, 794
DEED
  mentally incapacitated person, executed
    by, 617
DETENTION
  mentally disordered patient. *See under*
    MENTALLY DISORDERED PERSON OR
    PATIENT
DIVORCE
  mentally disordered patient, of, 610
EDUCATION
  child with special educational needs,
    592
ENDURING POWER OF ATTORNEY
  replacement by lasting power of
    attorney, 618
FIREARM
  sale to mentally disordered person,
    1016
FIRST-TIER TRIBUNAL
  allocation of matter to another
    chamber, 956
  application—
    Part 2 Mental Health Act 1983
      patients, by, 960
    Part 3 Mental Health Act 1983
      patients, by, 961
    practice direction, 966
    procedure. *See* procedure for making
      application *below*
    report prior to, confidentiality and,
      963n[5]
    restricted patients, by, 962
    right to make, 959
    visiting and examination of patients
      prior to, 963
  generally, 955
  Health, Education and Social Care
    Chamber, jurisdiction, 956
  hearing—
    absence of patient at, 977
    appeal, notification of right of, 979
    attendance at, 975, 976
    change to time and place, 975

FIRST-TIER TRIBUNAL—*continued*
  hearing—*continued*
    decision notice, 979
    decision without, 975
    earnings, payment for loss of, 978
    excluding parties from, 976
    failure of party to attend, tribunal
      proceeding where, 977
    need for, 975
    notice requirements, 975
    private hearing, 976
    public hearing, 976
    travelling expenses, subsistence etc,
      payment, 978
    witness excluded from, 976
  mental health case, procedure in. *See*
    procedure for making application
    below
  powers—
    conditionally discharged restricted
      patients, as to, 971
    discharge of non-restricted patient,
      directing—
      appropriateness and safety tests,
        reference to, 967n[15]
      future date, at, 968
      generally, 967
      legal grounds for detention still
        subsisting, 967n[5]
      mental disorder, patient nor
        suffering from, 967n[11]
      reconvened tribunal, scope of
        powers, 968n[7]
      treatability test, no need to have
        regard to, 967n[15]
    discharge of restriction order patient,
      directing—
      adjournment of proceedings, 969
      application for patient's
        readmission, 969n[10]
      burden of proof, 969n[11]
      condition that patient remain in
        hospital, 969n[12]
      conditional discharge, 969
      deferment resulting in no direction
        being given, 969n[18]
      delay in achieving deferred
        conditional discharge, 969n[17]
      generally, 969
      grounds for, 969
      human rights, infringement of,
        969n[17]
      no power to make
        recommendations, 969
      recall for therapeutic reasons,
        969n[6, 7]

FIRST-TIER TRIBUNAL—*continued*
  powers—*continued*
    discharge of restriction order patient,
      directing—*continued*
      standard of proof, 969n[6]
    transferred prisoners, as to, 970
  procedure for making application—
    allowances, power to pay, 978
    appeal, right of, 979
    decision notice, 979
    generally, 972, 973
    hearing. *See* hearing *above*
    information requirements, 973
    medical examination, need for, 974
    removal of patient from UK, 973
    written application, need for, 972
  reference to—
    hospital managers' duty to refer
      cases, 964
    information and report requirements,
      966
    practice direction, 966
    Secretary of State's powers and
      duties, 965
    time limit for making, 964
    transfer of patient from one territory
      to another, 964n[9]
    withdrawal of application, following,
      964
  Upper Tribunal, appeal to, 958
FORGERY
  Mental Health Act 1983, statutory
    documents, 1008
GIFT
  lasting power of attorney, under, 620
GUARDIANSHIP
  mentally disordered patient. *See under*
    MENTALLY DISORDERED PERSON OR
    PATIENT
GUARDIANSHIP ORDER
  offender suffering from mental disorder.
    See MENTALLY DISORDERED PERSON
    OR PATIENT (guardianship order)
HEALTH AND CARE PROFESSIONS
  COUNCIL
  approval of training courses, 819
HIGH COURT OF JUSTICE
  inherent jurisdiction—
    mental capacity, in cases of, 563
    undue influence, in son's dealings
      with elderly parents, 563n[2]
HOSPITAL
  mental health services. *See under*
    MENTALLY DISORDERED PERSON OR
    PATIENT

HOSPITAL ORDER
  offender suffering from mental disorder.
    See MENTALLY DISORDERED PERSON
    OR PATIENT (hospital order)
HOUSE OF COMMONS
  mental disorder, vacation of seat due
    to, 564
HOUSE OF LORDS
  mental disorder, whether justifying
    vacation of seat, 564
ILL-TREATMENT
  Mental Capacity Act 2005, under, 1011
  Mental Health Act 1983, under, 1010
INCOME TAX
  mentally disordered person's liability
    to, 595
INDEPENDENT MENTAL CAPACITY
  ADVOCATE
  appointment, 635
  challenging decisions, 637, 647
  creation of scheme, under Mental
    Capacity Act 2005, 634
  deprivation of liberty provisions, where
    person subject to, 642, 643, 644
  duties, 637
  examples of persons to be supported
    etc, 634n[3]
  exceptions to involvement of, 645
  functions, 637
  generally, 634
  information, evaluation of, 637
  local authority's duty to instruct—
    adult protection cases, in, 641
    residential accommodation, prior to
      provision of, 640
  NHS body's duty to instruct—
    accommodation, prior to provision
      of, 639
    adult protection cases, in, 641
    NHS body: meaning, 638n[1]
    serious medical treatment, prior to
      provision of, 638
  power to adjust role of, 646
  powers, 635
  regulations in respect of, power to
    make, 646
  report, duty to prepare, 637
  requirements for appointment, 636
INDEPENDENT MENTAL HEALTH
  ADVOCATE
  appointment, 807
  arrangements for, 807
  commissioning body, 813n[1]
  England, in, conditions to be satisfied,
    813
  generally, 807

INDEPENDENT MENTAL HEALTH
    ADVOCATE—*continued*
information about, duty to give—
    generally, 811
    responsible person's duty, 811n[1, 7]
qualifying compulsory patient—
    proposal for treatment, effect on
        status, 807n[4]
    Wales, in—
        help available to, 809
        qualification as, 807n[4]
qualifying informal patient—
    generally, 807n[3]
    Wales, in—
        carer in relation to, 811n[7]
        help available to, 810
        qualification as, 807n[5]
qualifying patient—
    meaning, 807n[3]
    compulsory patient. *See* qualifying
        compulsory patient *above*
    help available to, 808
    informal patient. *See* qualifying
        informal patient *above*
    person professionally concerned with
        treatment, 807n[9]
    proposal for treatment, effect on
        status, 807n[3, 4]
    Wales, in, 807n[3]
Wales, in—
    arrangements, power to make, 814
    conditions to be satisfied, 814
    generally, 812
    patient's right to refuse help, 812
    powers, 812
    right to request records, 812
    visits and interviews, 812
INQUIRY
mental health services, 596
INTESTACY
mentally disordered person, 615
ISLE OF MAN
mentally disordered patient. *See under*
    MENTALLY DISORDERED PERSON OR
    PATIENT
JURISDICTION
Court of Protection. *See under* COURT
    OF PROTECTION
JUROR
mental disorder, 564
LASTING POWER OF ATTORNEY
bankruptcy of donor, effect, 621
court's powers as to validity and
    operation, 622
customary occasions, gifts made on,
    620n[3]

LASTING POWER OF
    ATTORNEY—*continued*
donee—
    information from, Public Guardian's
        power to require, 754
    nearest relative, whether able to
        override decisions of, 839n[5]
    replacement, 619
    requirements, 619
donor's personal welfare, restriction on
    donee's acts, 619
generally, 618
gifts, scope in relation to, 620
invalidity, effect, 621
mental disorder of donor, effect, 600
more than one donee, 619n[8]
nature of, 619
restraint by attorney, to prevent harm
    etc, 619
revocation, 621
validity—
    court's powers, 622
    protection in case of invalidity, 621
LIBERTY
deprivation, under Mental Capacity
    Act 2005. *See under* MENTALLY
    DISORDERED PERSON OR PATIENT
LIMITATION OF ACTIONS
mental incapacity, in case of, 993
LITIGATION FRIEND
appointment—
    application to terminate, 995n[7]
    court order, by, 997
    duration, 995
    other than by court order, 996
certificate of suitability, filing and
    service, 996
Court of Protection deputy as, 996
expenses, recovery of, 1000
human rights, whether infringement of,
    995n[3]
need for, 995
protected party—
    meaning, 995n[1]
    application against, restriction on
        making, 995
    capacity, regaining or acquiring, 995
    steps taken before appointment of
        litigation friend, 995n[6]
LOCAL HEALTH BOARD
after-care services, duty to provide, 945
secondary mental health services,
    provision of information on
    discharge from, 948
supervisory functions, 719

LOCAL SOCIAL SERVICES AUTHORITY
meaning, 579
after-care services, duty to provide, 945
approved mental health professional, instructing, 821
Care Standards Act 2000, registration requirements under, 585
default in provision of mental health services, 568
functions—
　care and after-care, 581
　generally, 580
　prevention of illness, 581
guardianship, patient received into—
　generally, 758
　visiting arrangements, 791
mental health professional—
　application by, 821
　approval, 815
　cessation of approval, 824
　competence, duty to ensure, 816
　See generally under MENTAL HEALTH PROFESSIONAL
prosecution of offences, 584
residential accommodation, no duty to provide, 581n[4]
secondary mental health services, provision of information on discharge from, 948
social circumstances reports, 582
supervision and direction of, 568
visiting patients in hospital, 583

LORD CHANCELLOR
Court of Protection proceedings, power to prescribe fees, 746

MAGISTRATES' COURT
guardianship order. *See* MENTALLY DISORDERED PERSON OR PATIENT (guardianship order)
hospital order. *See* MENTALLY DISORDERED PERSON OR PATIENT (hospital order)

MARRIAGE
capacity to consent to, 609

MEDICAL PRACTITIONER
allowances or gratuities, 928n[10]
mental health professional. *See* MENTAL HEALTH PROFESSIONAL
mentally disordered patient, visiting to interview and examine, 928n[10]
pension, 928n[10]
remuneration, 835, 928n[10]

MEDICAL TREATMENT
meaning, 926

MEDICAL TREATMENT—*continued*
admission to hospital for, application procedure, 847
advance decision to refuse—
　advance decision: meaning, 624
　applicability, 625
　duty to find doctor to carry out patients' wishes, 624n[6]
　effect, 626
　generally, 623, 624
　lasting power of attorney, effect, 625n[7]
　liability in case of, 626
　life-sustaining treatment, whether applicable to, 625
　Mental Capacity Act 2005, under, 623
　no wish to be 'kept alive by machines', 624n[2]
　overriding, 624n[2]
　validity, 625
　withdrawal or alteration of, 624
consent to—
　anticipatory refusal of consent, binding nature of, 612n[5]
　capacity—
　　adult, 612
　　bone marrow transplant, 612n[4]
　　consent needed, where, 612
　　duty to give advice and information, 612
　　emergency, in, 612n[4]
　　independent mental capacity advocate, appointment, 612
　　medical opinion not reasonable etc, doctor's liability where, 612n[8]
　　necessity, doctrine of, 612n[2]
　　presumption of, 612n[11]
　　real nature of consent, 612
　　sterilisation, in case of, 612n[4, 10]
　　unconscious person, 612n[4]
　child, on behalf of, 612
　court's consent, in case of sterilisation, 612n[10]
mentally disordered patient. *See* MENTALLY DISORDERED PERSON OR PATIENT (treatment)

MEMBER OF PARLIAMENT
mental disorder, detention following, 782

MENTAL CAPACITY
agency, effect on, 600
approved research project. *See* intrusive research *below*

MENTAL CAPACITY—*continued*
best interests—
'balance sheet' or pros and cons, 606n[2]
care or treatment, 611
checklist of factors, 606n[1, 4]
determining, 606
examples, 606n[1]
expert advice, taking account of, 606n[15]
life-sustaining treatment: meaning, 606n[9]
medical treatment, consent to. *See under* MEDICAL TREATMENT
relevant circumstances: meaning, 606n[3]
restraint, examples of, 611n[8]
civil partnership, consent to, 609
codes of practice, power to issue, 602
common law, under—
generally, 597
necessity, doctrine of, 611n[3]
presumption of capacity, 598
contractual capacity. *See under* MENTALLY DISORDERED PERSON OR PATIENT
deprivation of liberty. *See under* MENTALLY DISORDERED PERSON
family relationships etc, decisions as to, 627
generally, 597
independent mental capacity advocate service. *See* INDEPENDENT MENTAL CAPACITY ADVOCATE
inter vivos dispositions, 617
intestacy, 615
intrusive research—
meaning, 630n[1]
appropriate body: meaning, 630n[3]
carers etc, need to consult, 632
clinical trial, whether treated as research, 630
impairing condition, 631n[5]
lawful, where, 630
not intrusive, where, 630
requirements for approval of research project, 631
safeguards, 633
unlawful, where, 630
lasting power of attorney. *See under* LASTING POWER OF ATTORNEY
life-saving treatment, in respect of, 601n[3]
long time elapsing, since act complained of, 598
marriage, consent to, 609

MENTAL CAPACITY—*continued*
medical treatment, consent to. *See under* MEDICAL TREATMENT
Mental Capacity Act 2005—
deprivation of liberty under. *See under* MENTALLY DISORDERED PERSON
generally, 597
independent consultee, input of, 597n[9]
Mental Health Act 1983, and regulation of treatment under, 628
person lacking capacity. *See* person lacking capacity *below*
mental disorder, and, 599
partnership, dissolution, 616
person lacking capacity—
ability to weigh up information, 605n[7]
best interests. *See* best interests *above*
children, 604
circumstances, relevant, 603
civil partnership, consent to, 609
common law approach, importance of, 600n[1]
compulsive disorder or phobia, effect, 605n[7]
conditions leading to, examples, 603
Court of Protection. *See* COURT OF PROTECTION
credible evidence, need for, 605n[4]
decisions that cannot be made on behalf of, 627
different times and for different reasons, at, 601n[1]
divorce or dissolution of marriage, consent to, 610
general principles, 601
inability to make decisions, 605
inter vivos dispositions, 617
locked-in syndrome, 605n[8]
matters to be considered in determining, 603n[4]
necessary goods and services, payment for, 613
partnership, dissolution, 616
rational and practicable wish, expressing, 606n[11]
relevant information, problems of identifying, 605n[5]
retention of relevant information for short period, 605n[6]
sexual relations, consent to, 608
testamentary capacity, 615
vegetative state, person in, 606n[12]

References are to paragraph numbers; superior figures refer to notes

MENTAL CAPACITY—*continued*
  person lacking capacity—*continued*
    will overborne, where, 605n[7]
  power of attorney, effect on, 600
  presumption of—
    civil cases, in, 598
    common law, at, 598
    criminal cases, in, 598n[1]
  sexual relations, consent to, 608
  statutory framework for dealing with.
    See Mental Capacity Act 2005
    above
  testamentary capacity, 615
  vegetative state, person in, 606n[12]
  voting rights, 629

MENTAL DISORDER. *See also* MENTALLY
  DISORDERED PERSON
  meaning, 559[10, 12], 761
  advowson, incapacity to present to,
    761n[4]
  alcohol or drugs, dependence on, 761
  benefice, effect on holding of, 761n[4]
  capacity, effect on. *See* MENTAL
    CAPACITY
  categories—
    abolition, 559
    introduction, 559
  generally, 761
  jury service, ineligibility due to, 564
  learning disability, person with, 761
  positions of responsibility, effect on
    those in, 564
  voting, effect on rights, 565

MENTAL HEALTH
  Broadmoor patients, 556n[2]
  High Court's inherent jurisdiction, 563
  idiot and lunatic, distinction between,
    559
  legislation—
    current, general overview, 560
    former statutory law, 556
    human rights legislation, and, 560
    interaction between Acts, 562
    Mental Capacity Act 2005—
      common law developments,
        incorporating, 560n[20]
      generally, 560, 561
      interaction with other Acts, 562
      origins, 560n[19]
      private international law, and, 561
      purpose, 562
      scope, 559
      See also under MENTAL CAPACITY
    Mental Health Act 1959—
      amendments to, 557
      former jurisdiction in lunacy, 558

MENTAL HEALTH—*continued*
  legislation—*continued*
    Mental Health Act 1959—*continued*
      origin and scope, 557
    Mental Health Act 1983—
      amendments to, 559
      false entry or statement in
        connection with, wilfully
        making, 1009
      generally, 560
      scope, 557
    Mental Health Act 2007, 559
    private international law, 561
    Wales, in general, 560
  lunatic—
    meaning, 559n[2]
    former jurisdiction in lunacy, 558
    generally, 559n[2]
    idiot, distinguished from, 559
    lunacy: meaning, 559n[3]
  offences—
    assisting absence without leave or
      escape, 1013
    false entry or statement, wilfully
      making, 1009
    forgery of statutory document with
      intent to deceive, 1008
    harbouring a patient absent without
      leave, 1014
    ill-treatment or wilful neglect, 1010,
      1011
    obstruction, 1015
    sale of firearm, 1016
    unlawful sexual activity, 1012
  professionals. *See* MENTAL HEALTH
    PROFESSIONAL
  services. *See* MENTAL HEALTH SERVICES
  terminology—
    dementia, types, 559n[3]
    historical development, 559
    idiot and lunatic distinguished, 559
    lunatic. *See* lunatic *above*
    madness, 559n[3]
    mental defectiveness, 559n[7]
    mental disorder. *See* MENTAL
      DISORDER
    mental impairment, 559n[13]
    non compos mentis, 559
    psychopathic disorder, 559n[14]
    severe mental impairment, 559n[15]
  tribunals. *See* FIRST-TIER TRIBUNAL;
    MENTAL HEALTH REVIEW TRIBUNAL
    FOR WALES

MENTAL HEALTH NURSE
  detention, powers of, 836
  register, 836

MENTAL HEALTH PROFESSIONAL
approved—
  meaning, 815n^2
  application by—
    emergency applications, 821n^{11}
    generally, 821
    interview, need for, 821n^8
    nearest relative, consultation and
      contact with, 821n$^{8, 10}$
    outside a particular local social
      services authority area, 821n^7
    procedure, 821
    restrictions on making, 821
    unlawful, where, 821n^7
  approval—
    cessation, 824
    conditions, 822
    procedure, 815
    suspension, 823
    Wales, in. *See* Wales, approval in
      below
  competence, appropriate—
    England, in—
      abilities and knowledge
        required, 816n$^{6-10}$
      courses, need to have
        completed, 816
      generally, 816
      key competency areas, 816
    Wales, in—
      abilities and knowledge
        required, 817n$^{1-3}$
      key competency areas, 817
  entry and inspection powers, 820
  functions, 820
  independent nature of, 820n^{16}
  professional requirements, 818
  regulations as to approval, power to
    make, 815n^3
  restrictions on approval, 815
  sufficient numbers, need to ensure,
    815n^3
  training courses, 819
  Wales, approval in—
    appropriate competence, need for.
      See under competence,
      appropriate *above*
    approved clinician, 833
    cessation, 824n^4
    conditions, 822
    procedure, 815, 822
  who may approve, 815
approved clinician—
  meaning, 831
  England and Wales, mutual
    recognition, 833

MENTAL HEALTH
    PROFESSIONAL—*continued*
approved clinician—*continued*
    functions, 832
    guardianship, patient subject to, 833
    persons who may act as, 831n^2
  clinician—
    approved. *See* approved clinician
      above
    responsible clinician—
      meaning, 834
      functions, 834
      priority to detained patient, no
        power to require, 834n^3
  conflict of interest—
    assessor: meaning, 826
    business reasons, for, 827
    emergency provision in Wales, 830
    financial reasons, for, 826
    personal relationship, on basis of,
      829
    professional reasons, for, 828
    regulations as to, power to make,
      825
  mental health nurse, powers of
    detention, 836
  pensions, 837
  remuneration of medical practitioner,
    835

MENTAL HEALTH REVIEW TRIBUNAL
    FOR WALES
application—
    Part 2 Mental Health Act 1983
      patients, by, 960
    Part 3 Mental Health Act 1983
      patients, by, 961
    procedure. *See* procedure for making
      application *below*
    report prior to, confidentiality and,
      963n^5
    restricted patients, by, 962
    right to make, 959
    visiting and examination of patients
      prior to, 963
    withdrawal, 988
  hearing—
    adjournment, 985
    appeal, right of, 992
    attendance of parties at, 990
    decision, 991
    excluding parties from, 990
    failure to attend, tribunal proceeding
      where, 990
    generally, 990
    postponement, 985
    private nature of, 990

References are to paragraph numbers; superior figures refer to notes

MENTAL HEALTH REVIEW TRIBUNAL
FOR WALES—*continued*
hearing—*continued*
  public hearing, refusal of request for,
    990n[3]
  public hearing continuing in private,
    990n[3]
  reconvening, 985
  witness excluded from, 990
powers—
  conditionally discharged restricted
    patients, as to, 971
  discharge of non-restricted patient,
    directing—
    appropriateness and safety tests,
      reference to, 967n[15]
    future date, at, 968
    generally, 967
    legal grounds for detention still
      subsisting, 967n[5]
    mental disorder, patient nor
      suffering from, 967n[11]
    reconvened tribunal, scope of
      powers, 968n[7]
    treatability test, no need to have
      regard to, 967n[15]
  discharge of restriction order patient,
    directing—
    adjournment of proceedings, 969
    application for patient's
      readmission, 969n[10]
    burden of proof, 969n[11]
    condition that patient remain in
      hospital, 969n[12]
    conditional discharge, 969
    deferment resulting in no direction
      being given, 969n[18]
    delay in achieving deferred
      conditional discharge, 969n[17]
    generally, 969
    grounds for, 969
    human rights, infringement of,
      969n[17]
    no power to make
      recommendations, 969
    recall for therapeutic reasons,
      969n[6, 7]
    standard of proof, 969n[6]
  transferred prisoners, as to, 970
procedure for making application—
  addition of parties, 986
  directions, power to give, 981, 988
  disclosure of details, prohibition, 983
  documents, sending and delivery, 982
  evidence, admissibility and exclusion,
    988

MENTAL HEALTH REVIEW TRIBUNAL
FOR WALES—*continued*
procedure for making
  application—*continued*
  final determination, procedure prior
    to, 988
  generally, 972, 988
  hearing. *See* hearing *above*
  information and documents, power to
    request, 988
  interview before final determination,
    989
  medical examination prior to
    hearing, 989
  notice requirements, 988
  publication of details, prohibition,
    983
  regulation of, 980
  representatives—
    appointment, 987
    powers, 987
  rules as to, power to make, 980
  substitution of parties, 986
  withholding information or
    documents likely to cause harm,
    984
  written application, need for, 972,
    988
purpose, 957
reference to—
  hospital managers' duty to refer
    cases, 964
  information and report requirements,
    966
  practice direction, 966
  procedural requirements, 988
  time limit for making, 964
  transfer of patient from one territory
    to another, 964n[9]
  Welsh Ministers' powers and duties,
    965
  withdrawal of application, following,
    964
Upper Tribunal, appeal to, 958

MENTAL HEALTH SERVICES
approval of medical practitioners, 568
Care Quality Commission, 573
central government functions—
  appropriate national authority—
    duties, 568
    generally, 567
  generally, 568
  high security psychiatric services,
    duties as to, 569
  Secretary of State—
    delegation of functions, 570

MENTAL HEALTH
  SERVICES—*continued*
central government
  functions—*continued*
  Secretary of State—*continued*
    generally, 567
    Welsh Ministers, 567
clinical commissioning groups, 572
code of practice, duty to prepare, 568
convention rights, need for compatibility
  with, 566
coordination, provider's duty, 854
education, training and employment,
  592
finances—
  income tax, liability to, 595
  pocket money for in-patients, 594
  social security benefits, receipt of,
    593
generally, 566
health and hospital services—
  arrangements for special cases,
    notification procedure, 576
  general NHS responsibilities, 574
  hospital: meaning, 577
  hospital and specialist services, 575
high security psychiatric services, duties
  as to, 569
hospital patients—
  alien patients, removal abroad, 568
  pocket money, provision of, 568
  transfer of, 568
  travelling expenses of visitors,
    payment of, 568
inquiries and investigations, 596
local primary mental health support
  services in Wales. *See under* WALES
local social services authority. *See*
  LOCAL SOCIAL SERVICES AUTHORITY
mental health professional. *See* MENTAL
  HEALTH PROFESSIONAL
National Health Service Commissioning
  Board, 571
prisoners, powers in relation to, 568
registered establishment: meaning, 578
social services. *See* LOCAL SOCIAL
  SERVICES AUTHORITY
special educational needs, child with,
  592
special restrictions, patients subject to,
  568
travelling expenses, payment of—
  high security psychiatric services, in
    connection with, 569
  hospital visitors, 568

MENTAL HOSPITAL
  meaning, 565n[3]
  duty to provide accommodation in, 568

MENTALLY DISORDERED PERSON
  OR PATIENT
absence from hospital—
  assisting absence, offence, 1013
  conditions attached to grant of leave,
    917
  grant of leave, 917
  harbouring a patient absent without
    leave, 1014
  longer-term leave, 917n[8]
  recall, restriction on, 917
  revocation of leave, 917
  warrant for arrest of escaped
    convicted mental patient, 921
  without leave—
    absent without leave: meaning,
      918n[4]
    Channel Islands, from hospital in,
      920
    custody, taking patient into, 918
    effect on duration of detention,
      911
    hospital order, patient subject to,
      918n[2]
    interim hospital order, while subject
      to, 867
    Isle of Man, from hospital in, 920
    Northern Ireland, from hospital
      in, 920
    readmission of patients, 918
    remand for report or for treatment,
      while on, 862
    renewal of authority for detention
      in case of, 910
    return of patients, 918
    Scotland, from hospital in, 919
absolute discharge—
  acquittal on criminal appeal, on, 875
  special verdict or finding of disability,
    on, 874
accused person—
  meaning, 862n[3, 8]
  remand to hospital for report or
    treatment—
    absconding, 862
    court's powers, 862
    duration of remand, 862
    further remand, exercise of power,
      862n[18]
    medical evidence, requirements as
      to, 865
    time limit for conveyance and
      admission, 862n[17]

MENTALLY DISORDERED PERSON OR PATIENT—*continued*

admission to hospital or registered establishment—
application procedure, 847
approved mental health professional's power to apply for, 840
child, informal admission. *See* child, informal admission *below*
compulsory admission. *See* compulsory admission to hospital etc *below*
detention in place of safety pending admission to hospital, 868
nearest relative's power to apply for, 840
reception and removal, power to make regulations as to, 766
requirements for, 847
service of documents, 850
voluntary admission—
assessment, for, 764n[11]
informal nature of, 764, 765
minor. *See* child, informal admission *below*
patient with history of changing her mind, 764
suicide, where danger of, 764
ward of court, 786
after-care services. *See* AFTER-CARE
alien patient, removal, 907
arrest of escaped convicted mental patient, warrant for, 921
assessment—
compulsory admission for. *See* assessment, compulsory admission for *below*
former user of secondary mental health services. *See* former user of secondary mental health services, assessment of *below*
primary. *See* primary mental health assessment *below*
assessment, compulsory admission for—
application procedure, 847
appropriate place of detention, 767n[4]
consent, patient unable to give, 767n[4]
grounds for admission, 767
human rights, and, 767n[4]
maximum period of detention, 767
mental disorder proving to be non-existent, 767n[11]
pregnant woman suffering from depression, 767n[10]
proper purpose of detention, 767n[4]
tribunal, patient's application to, 767

MENTALLY DISORDERED PERSON OR PATIENT—*continued*

assessment, compulsory admission for—*continued*
unlawful detention, where, 767n[10]
who may apply for admission, 767n[7]
care and treatment, 758
care coordinator. *See* CARE COORDINATOR
Channel Islands—
removal of patient from, 905
removal of patient to, 906
return of absent patient, 920
child, informal admission—
adult wards, avoidance of use of, 765n[11]
capacity to consent, patient having, 765
generally, 765
High Court's power to order child's detention, 765n[11]
locked unit, 765n[11]
minor below the age of 16, 765n[8]
parent etc consenting to treatment, 765n[8]
suitable environment, need for, 765
child community patient—
authorised treatment, 940
certification requirement, inapplicability, 940
competence, lacking, 941
objection to treatment, 941n[6]
restriction on treatment, 940
treatment immediately necessary, 937
civil litigation—
claim form, service, 999
competence of witness, 1003
costs where money payable by protected person, 1001
enforcement against patient, 1002
foreign curator etc, proceedings by, 998
judgment, claimant's right to enter, 999
limitation of actions, 993
litigation friend. *See* LITIGATION FRIEND
procedure, 999
recovery on patient's behalf—
agreement reached prior to proceedings, 1000n[2]
apportionment, 1000n[5]
compromise agreement, withdrawal, 1000n[2]
court directions, 1000n[6]

MENTALLY DISORDERED PERSON
OR PATIENT—*continued*
civil litigation—*continued*
recovery on patient's
behalf—*continued*
fixed recoverable costs in road
traffic accidents, 1000n[2]
generally, 1000
private hearing, 1000n[2]
solicitor's authority, 994
Code of Practice, guidance in, 758
community patient not recalled to
hospital—
adult community patient—
conditions for giving treatment to,
939
lacking capacity, where, 939
restrictions on giving treatment to,
935
authorised treatment, 935
authority to give treatment, 938
certificate requirement—
inapplicable, where, 935
met, where, 936
relevant treatment, 935n[1]
treatment necessary—
certification unnecessary, 935
consent given, and, 935
examples, 937
community treatment order. *See*
COMMUNITY TREATMENT ORDER
compulsory admission to hospital etc—
absent without leave, patient going,
771n[12]
application—
acting on, where apparently duly
made etc, 772
careful examination, need for,
772n[3]
cessation of previous applications,
773
proof of form and contents, 772
recommendation, founded on. *See*
recommendations *below*
rectification, 774
assessment, for. *See* assessment,
compulsory admission for *above*
assessment in emergency, for. *See*
emergency application *below*
child visiting a patient, 781
correspondence of detained patients,
dealing with. *See* postal packet
sent by *below*
effect of applications for admission,
771
false imprisonment, 771n[4]

MENTALLY DISORDERED PERSON
OR PATIENT—*continued*
compulsory admission to hospital
etc—*continued*
force to detain and convey patient to
hospital, use of, 771n[4]
legal custody—
constables etc, powers of, 776
conveying a person: meaning,
776n[1]
escape from. *See* escape from legal
custody *below*
persons deemed to be in, 776
retaking of persons who escape
from, 777
use of force to enter premises,
and, 776n[5]
managers—
meaning, 778
functions, 778n[3]
information to detained patients,
duty to give, 779
registered establishment: meaning,
578
Member of Parliament detained, 782
nurse's holding power, 770n[18]
pocket money for in-patient, 783
recommendations—
application founded on, 772
procedure on insufficiency of, 775
rectification, 774
requirements for, 849
tort, recommending doctor's
liability in, 849n[5]
two required, where, 849n[5]
regulations—
contents, 766n[4]
functions of boards, trusts etc, as
to, 766n[12]
power to make, 766
temporary detention of in-patients,
and, 770
treatment, for. *See* treatment,
compulsory admission for *below*
tribunal, patient's right to apply to,
767, 768, 769n[14]
visiting detained patients, 781
consent to treatment—
advance decision, whether valid and
applicable, 931n[18]
appropriate treatment, whether,
930n[15], 931n[13]
capacity, protection for patient
lacking, 924

MENTALLY DISORDERED PERSON OR PATIENT—*continued*

consent to treatment—*continued*
  certificate advising treatment—
    consultation requirement, 928n[17], 930n[15]
    electro-convulsive therapy, for, 931
    form of, 928n[3], 930n[11]
    patient subsequently becoming capable, 929n[6]
    visit etc, prior to giving, 928n[10]
  community patient, treatment of—
    certificate requirements, 934n[8]
    recall of, on, 934
    revocation of order, on, 934
  electro-convulsive therapy, 931, 932, 934
  hazardous treatment, 932n[7]
  human rights, whether treatment infringing, 930n[15]
  medical treatment: meaning, 926
  Mental Capacity Act 2005, effect, 925
  mental disorder, wide construction of meaning, 930n[15]
  not necessary, where, 927
  patients to whom provisions apply, 924
  review of treatment, 933
  second opinion, 928, 930, 934
  tube feeding, 932n[8]
  types of treatment requiring, 928, 930, 931
  urgency, treatment in case of, 928, 930, 931, 932
  withdrawal—
    continuation of treatment despite withdrawal, 932n[8]
    generally, 929, 942
contractual capacity—
  common law rules, effect, 614
  Court of Protection's powers, 614
  effect of mental disorder on, 600
  judicial approach, 614
  test of capacity, 614
convicted mental patient—
  meaning, 921n[1]
  warrant for arrest of, 921
county court applications—
  acting relative, appointment. *See under* COUNTY COURT
  procedure, 846
criminal litigation—
  competence of witness, 1005
  confessions, 1006
  criminal responsibility, 1004

MENTALLY DISORDERED PERSON OR PATIENT—*continued*

criminal litigation—*continued*
  fitness to plead, 1007
deprivation of liberty—
  age requirement, 654
  authorised course of action, 658n[9]
  best interests requirement, 657
  eligibility requirement, 658
  generally, 648
  hospital treatment regime, person subject to, 658n[5]
  life-sustaining treatment, for, 650
  mental capacity requirement, 656
  Mental Health Act 1983, person within scope of, 659
  mental health patient: meaning, 658n[21]
  mental health regimes, 658n[11]
  mental health requirement, 655
  monitoring—
    Care Quality Commission, by, 718
    power to make regulations as to, 717
  no refusals requirement, 660
  objections from patient, 658n[22]
  occurring, where, 648
  qualifying requirements, 653
  restraint, distinguished from, 648
  Sch A1, under—
    conditions to be met, 651
    generally, 651
    hospitals and care homes, provisions as to, 652
    liability, whether arising, 651
    managing authority: meaning, 652
    negligence, effect, 651
  standard authorisation. *See* standard authorisation *below*
  supervision by local health boards, 719
  transport of persons—
    police, with help of, 649
    whether amounting to deprivation, 649
  treatment, for purposes of, 648
  unauthorised—
    meaning, 679n[3]
    arising, where, 674n[19]
    assessment as to, time limit for carrying out, 679n[8]
    third party's right to question possibility of, 679
  urgent authorisation—
    meaning, 713n[3]
    cessation, 714

References are to paragraph numbers; superior figures refer to notes

MENTALLY DISORDERED PERSON
  OR PATIENT—*continued*
 deprivation of liberty—*continued*
  urgent authorisation—*continued*
   commencement, 714n^3
   copies, duty to provide, 715
   court's powers in relation to,
    714n^3, 733
   duration, 714
   duty to give, 713
   extension of duration, request for,
    716
   form of, 714
   information about, duty to give,
    715
   records, duty to keep, 715
   relevant cases, 713
   terms, 714
 detention—
  authority for—
   absence of leave—
    effect on duration, 911
    examination of patient
     following, 911
    renewal in case of, 910n^{13}, 911
   duration of, 908
   duty to examine patient, 910, 911
   procedure and criteria for renewal,
    910
   renewal, 909, 910
  burden of proof justifying, 967n^{11}
  clinician's duty to prepare report, 910
  court order, by, 912
  expiry of statutory period, effect on
   legality of, 910n^{19}
  failed attempts to find psychiatric
   placement, 923n^4
  Member of Parliament, 782
  order for discharge. *See* order for
   discharge *below*
  place of safety, in. *See under* place of
   safety *below*
  sentence, by, 912
 discharge—
  absolute discharge. *See* absolute
   discharge *above*
  conditional—
   condition at odds with, 914n^5
   consent to treatment provisions,
    patient not subject to, 914n^5
   recall following, 914
  examination of patients with view
   to, 916
  order for. *See* order for discharge
   below
  visiting with view to, 916

MENTALLY DISORDERED PERSON
  OR PATIENT—*continued*
 emergency application—
  meaning, 769
  cessation, 769
  common law doctrine of necessity,
   treatment under, 769n^{15}
  consent to treatment provisions,
   inapplicability, 769
  false entry or statement, wilfully
   making, 1009
  form of application, 769n^5
  generally, 769
  human rights, and, 769n^5
  Mental Health Act 1983, effect of
   failure to use, 769n^5
  procedure, 769
  tribunal, patient's right to apply to,
   769n^{14}
  who may apply, 769, 840
 escape—
  hospital, from. *See* absence from
   hospital *above*
  legal custody, from. *See* legal custody,
   escape from *below*
  warrant for arrest of escaped
   convicted mental patient, 921
 former user of secondary mental health
  services, assessment of—
  action following, 953
  adult discharged from services, 947n^5
  arrangements for carrying out, 950
  assessment report—
   copies, provision of, 951
   duty to prepare, 951
   time for providing copy, 951n^5
  discharge period—
   child becoming adult during, 948n^5
   duration, 947n^7
  entitlement to, 947
  housing or well-being services, referral
   relating to, 954
  information about entitlement,
   provision of, 948
  purpose, 949
  secondary mental health services:
   meaning, 586n^6
  usual residence, determination of,
   952
 general protection, 806
 generally, 757
 guardianship—
  absence without leave of person
   subject to—
   assisting absence, offence, 1013
   effect on duration, 911

MENTALLY DISORDERED PERSON OR PATIENT—*continued*

guardianship—*continued*

absence without leave of person subject to—*continued*

harbouring a patient absent without leave, 1014

power to take into custody, 793

application—

age, need to state, $785n^2$

effect, 787

false entry or statement, wilfully making, 1009

forms of, $785n^4$

grounds for, 785

notification, right to, $785n^6$

procedure, 785

proof of form and contents, 788

recommendations in support of—

generally, 788

rectification, 789

requirements for, 849

tort, recommending doctor's liability in, $849n^5$

two required, where, $849n^5$

rectification, 789

requirements for, 848

who may apply, 785

approved clinician, 833

authority for—

duration of, 908

duty to examine patient, 910

procedure and criteria for renewal, 910

renewal, 909, 910

change of address, need to notify, $792n^{10}$

clinician's duty to prepare report, 910

death of guardian, 794

discharge. *See* order for discharge *below*

guardian, examples of, $787n^5$

illness of guardian, 795

nominated medical attendant, $792n^4$

place of residence, taking patient to, $787n^6$

private guardian—

meaning, $792n^2$

duties of, 792

purpose, 785

regulations—

contents, $784n^4$

power to make, 784, 790

resignation of guardian, 794

service of documents, 850

MENTALLY DISORDERED PERSON OR PATIENT—*continued*

guardianship—*continued*

transfer by order of county court, 796

transfer of patient. *See* transfer of patient *below*

transfer to local social services authority, $890n^7$

visiting arrangements, $787n^6$, 791

ward of court, 786

who may be received into, 785

guardianship order—

conditions for making, 877

Crown Court—

magistrates' court, appeal from, 880

powers in respect of, 859, 877

effect, 860, 878

generally, 859, 877

information requirements, 877

local social services authority arrangements, 859

magistrates' court—

appeal from, to Crown Court, 880

powers in respect of, 859

orders and directions having same effect, 861

restriction on making, 877

tribunal, right to appeal to, 961

guidance. *See* CODE OF PRACTICE

hospital—

meaning, 577

absconding from, during remand for report or for treatment, 862

admission to, 758

community patient not recalled to. *See* community patient not recalled to hospital *above*

conveyance to, 891

detention in, while case disposed of by Crown Court, $873n^4$

detention in place of safety pending admission to, 868

duty to provide accommodation in, 568

remand to, for report or treatment, 862, 865

hospital accommodation, duty to provide, 568

hospital direction—

appeal from Crown Court, 879

provisions generally, 863

transfer direction, effect as, 863

hospital order—

meaning, 864

MENTALLY DISORDERED PERSON
    OR PATIENT—*continued*
hospital order—*continued*
    appeal from Crown Court, 879
    committal proceedings for contempt
        of court, made in, 864n[8]
    conditions for making, 864
    conflicting medical evidence,
        consideration of, 864n[14]
    Court of Appeal—
        appeal to, from Crown Court, 879
        power to make order, 875
    Crown Court—
        appeal from, 879
        magistrates' court, appeal from,
            880
        powers in respect of, 859, 862, 873
    delay in imposing, 864n[8]
    direction, as to persons transferred
        by, 864n[8]
    effect, 860, 867
    finding of disability, on, 874
    generally, 859
    imprisonment, substituted for
        sentence of, 864n[13]
    information requirements, 864
    interim hospital order—
        meaning, 864
        absconding from hospital, 867
        conditions for making, 864
        conviction, need for, 871n[3]
        duration, 864
        effect, 860, 867
        information requirements, 864
        medical evidence, requirements as
            to, 865
        power to make, 864
        renewal, 864
    local social services authority
        arrangements, 859
    magistrates' court's powers, 859, 862,
        871
    matters for court to bear in mind,
        864n[13]
    medical evidence, requirements as to,
        865
    orders and directions having same
        effect, 861
    power to specify hospital, 864n[7]
    purpose of order, 864
    restriction directions, effect, 861
    restriction on making other orders,
        866
    restriction order. *See* restriction order
        below

MENTALLY DISORDERED PERSON
    OR PATIENT—*continued*
hospital order—*continued*
    return etc of patient absent without
        leave, 918n[2]
    special verdict, on, 874
    transfer directions, effect, 861
    tribunal, right to appeal to, 961
    youth court, power to make, 872
House of Commons, vacation of seat,
    564
House of Lords, vacation of seat, 564
ill-treatment or wilful neglect—
    burden of proof, 1011n[1]
    ill-treatment, what constitutes,
        1010n[5]
    Mental Capacity Act 2005, under,
        1011
    Mental Health Act 1983, under,
        1010
    penalties, 1010n[8], 1011n[8]
    separate nature of offences, 1010n[6]
implied powers for staff, 758
independent mental health advocate. *See*
    INDEPENDENT MENTAL HEALTH
    ADVOCATE
in-patient medical treatment, provision
    of, 758
Isle of Man—
    removal of patient from, 905
    removal of patient to, 906
    return of absent patient, 920
jury service, ineligible for, 564
knowledge of nature and quality of act,
    having, 761n[4]
learning disability: meaning, 761n[8]
legal custody, escape from—
    inducement to escape, 777n[1]
    knowingly to assist escape, offence
        of, 777n[1]
    retaking escapee, 777
    time limit for retaking person, 777
legislation—
    Health and Social Care Act 2008,
        760
    Mental Health Act 1983, 757
    Mental Health (Wales)
        Measure 2010, 757
liability, protection from—
    bad faith, 759
    discipline and control, need for,
        759n[1]
    generally, 759
    lack of reasonable care, 759n[2]
    patient returned to ward at end of
        visiting time, 759n[1]

MENTALLY DISORDERED PERSON
OR PATIENT—*continued*

liability, protection from—*continued*
proceedings brought without leave, 759n[3]
transfer of patients, refusal to allow, 759n[1]
limitation direction—
appeal from Crown Court, 879
provisions generally, 863
restriction direction, effect as, 863
litigation—
civil. *See* civil litigation *above*
criminal. *See* criminal litigation *above*
local social services authority. *See*
LOCAL SOCIAL SERVICES AUTHORITY
medical treatment. *See* treatment *below*
mental capacity. *See* MENTAL CAPACITY
mental disorder. *See* MENTAL DISORDER
Mental Health Act 1983, protection for acts done in pursuance of, 759
mental health assessment. *See* primary mental health assessment *below*
mental health professional. *See* MENTAL HEALTH PROFESSIONAL
nearest relative—
meaning, 839
confidential information, access to, 839n[5]
county court's power to appoint acting relative. *See under* COUNTY COURT
dead, where treated as, 839
delegation of functions by, 841
guardian as, 839
human rights provisions, and, 839n[5]
local authority as, 839
not obliged to act, 839n[5]
objection to admission to hospital etc—
effect, 842n[14]
unreasonable nature of, 842n[13]
order for discharge, restriction on making, 915
overriding decisions of, 839n[5]
powers—
authorising others to act, 839n[5]
generally, 840
preference given to, 839
replacement, 839n[5]
residence order in force, where, 839n[20]
necessity, common law doctrine of, 758
next of kin, restriction on powers, 839n[5]

MENTALLY DISORDERED PERSON
OR PATIENT—*continued*

Northern Ireland—
removal of patient from, 904
removal of patient to, 903
return of absent patient, 920
offender—
court's duties in general, 859n[18]
guardianship order. *See* guardianship order *above*
guidance, 859n[19]
hospital order. *See* hospital order *above*
order for discharge—
barring report, application for discharge subject to, 913n[11]
nearest relative making, restriction on, 915
other than by mental health review tribunal, 913
restricted patients by appropriate national authority, 914
to whom sent, 913n[9]
place of safety—
meaning, 868n[4], 922n[10]
delay in admitting person, whether affront to human dignity, 923n[4]
detention in—
duration, 922, 923
pending admission to hospital, 868
escape while in or being taken to, 922
failed attempts to find psychiatric placement, 923n[4]
public place—
meaning, 923n[2]
mentally disordered persons found in, 923
other places of safety, subsequent removal to, 922, 923
removal to—
mentally disordered persons found in public places, of, 923
warrant for, 922
warrants to search for and remove patients, 922
postal packet sent by—
excluded addressees, 780
humans rights, whether infringed, 780n[6]
hospital with high security psychiatric services, 780
manuscript sent to publisher, 780n[6]
review of decisions to withhold, 780
withheld from patient, 780
withheld from postal operator, 780

MENTALLY DISORDERED PERSON
  OR PATIENT—*continued*
primary mental health assessment—
  meaning, 586n[6], 883
  action following, 885
  availability, 586n[6]
  circumstances for carrying out, 881
  conditions, necessary, 881n[10]
  conduct, 883
  duty to carry out, 881
  eligibility to carry out—
    generally, 883, 884
    professional requirements, 884n[2]
  persons referred for, 882
  primary medical services—
    meaning, 882n[3]
    entitlement to, 882
  relevant local mental health partner,
    884n[3]
  relevant referral, 881n[7]
private hospital, detention in, 834n[3]
proportionate seclusion of patient,
  legality of, 757n[1]
protection, 806
recall—
  by warrant, without medical
    evidence, 914
  conditional discharge, following, 914
  following end of detention, 869n[21]
  human rights, whether violation of,
    914n[8]
registered establishment etc, compulsory
  admission. *See* compulsory
  admission to hospital etc *above*
relative—
  meaning, 838
  acting relative, county court's power
    to appoint. *See under* COUNTY
    COURT
  nearest relative. *See* nearest relative
    above
restriction order—
  meaning, 869
  cessation—
    after patient's conditional
      discharge, 914
    but hospital order still in force,
      870
    inference or implication, not by,
      914n[3]
  committal to magistrates' court to
    Crown Court for, 873
  conditionally discharged patient
    subsequently imprisoned, 869n[5]
  conditions for making, 869
  Crown Court's power to make, 869

MENTALLY DISORDERED PERSON
  OR PATIENT—*continued*
restriction order—*continued*
  discharge of patient subject to, 914
  examples of danger to public, 869n[5]
  leave of absence, conditions attached
    to, 869n[16]
  restrictions applicable under, 869
  Secretary of State's powers, 876
review of standard authorisation—
  best interests requirement, review of,
    687, 690, 691
  carrying out a review, 688
  change of reason ground, 686
  commencement, 688
  completion, 694
  duties in carrying out, compliance
    with, 689
  eligible person's right to request,
    683n[5]
  grounds for review of qualifying
    requirements, 684
  more than one reviewable
    requirement, procedure where,
    690
  non-qualification ground, 685
  notice of completion of, 683
  one or more review assessments
    negative, 693
  positive conclusion—
    best interests review assessment,
      of, 691
    eligibility review assessment, of,
      692
    mental capacity review assessment,
      of, 692
    mental health review assessment,
      of, 692
    no refusals review assessment, of,
      692
  request for, 683
  restrictions on carrying out, 689
  review assessments, 689
  reviewable requirements, 685, 686
  supervisory body, by, 683
  variation of conditions ground, 687
Scotland—
  removal of patient from, 900, 901,
    902
  removal of patient to, 899
  return of absent patient, 919
service of documents, 850
standard authorisation—
  assessment—
    age assessment, 671, 703

MENTALLY DISORDERED PERSON
  OR PATIENT—*continued*
  standard authorisation—*continued*
    assessment—*continued*
      best interests assessment. *See* best
        interests assessment *below*
      ceasing to carry out, 706
      copies, right to examine and take,
        705
      duty to ensure, 663
      eligibility assessment. *See* eligibility
        assessment *below*
      eligibility to carry out. *See*
        eligibility to carry out
        assessment *below*
      equivalent assessment already
        carried out, 670
      information and submissions,
        taking into account, 706
      mental capacity assessment, 673,
        701
      mental health assessment, 672, 699
      no refusals assessment, 676, 703
      not required, where, 670
      record-keeping, 705
      regulations, power to make, 669
      relevant needs assessment, 674n[8]
      selection of assessor, 695, 704
      two or more required, where, 696
      types, 669
    best interests assessment—
      meaning, 674
      best interests assessor: meaning,
        675n[4], 708n[10], 710n[1]
      continuing accuracy of assessment,
        670n[9]
      duties in carrying out, 674
      eligibility to carry out, 700
      generally, 674
      maximum authorisation period,
        674n[15]
      relevant care plan, and, 674n[9]
      unauthorised deprivation of
        liberty, 674n[19]
      relevant needs assessment, and,
        674n[8]
    cessation—
      time of, 665n[13]
      notification procedure, 665
    change in supervisory responsibility,
      682
    conditions, given subject to, 665
    copies of, duty to provide, 677
    Court of Protection's power to
      determine questions, 733
    detained resident: meaning, 662n[6]

MENTALLY DISORDERED PERSON
  OR PATIENT—*continued*
  standard authorisation—*continued*
    duration, 665n[4]
    duty to request—
      basic cases, 661
      change in place of detention, 662
    effect of authorisation, duty to give
      information about, 678
    eligibility assessment—
      meaning, 675
      best interests assessor, 675n[4]
      eligibility assessor, 675n[3]
      eligibility to carry out, 702
      relevant eligibility information,
        675n[5]
    eligibility to carry out assessment—
      age assessment, 703
      best interests assessment, 700
      criminal record check, need for,
        698
      eligibility assessment, 702
      indemnity arrangement, need for,
        697
      mental capacity assessment, 701
      mental health assessment, 699
      no refusals assessment, 703
      skills and experience, need for, 698
    entry into force, 665n[4]
    form of, 665
    further authorisation—
      conditions to be met, 666
      power to request, 667
    information included in request for,
      668
    interested person: meaning, 665n[23]
    need for, third party rights as to
      whether, 679
    power to request further
      authorisation, 667
    record of request, 668
    relevant person's representative—
      meaning, 707n[2]
      appointment, 707
      donee or deputy, effect of
        appointment on, 707
      eligibility, 709
      England, selection in, 710
      financial interest in care home etc,
        person having, 709n[10]
      monitoring, 712
      regulations as to selection of, 708
      suspension, 707
      termination, 707
      Wales, selection in, 711

References are to paragraph numbers; superior figures refer to notes

MENTALLY DISORDERED PERSON
    OR PATIENT—*continued*
standard authorisation—*continued*
    review. *See* review of standard
        authorisation *above*
    supervisory body—
        meaning, 664
        assessments. *See* assessments *above*
        duty to provide copies of
            authorisation, 677
        power to give authorisation, 663
        power to select assessor, 695
        prohibited from giving
            authorisation, notice where,
            677
    suspension—
        cessation of suspension, 681
        conditions for, 680
    terms of, 665
    third party rights as to whether
        authorisation needed, 679
    writing, need for, 665
supervision order—
    meaning, 874n^5
    acquittal on criminal appeal, on, 875
    Court of Appeal making, 875
    special verdict or finding of disability,
        on, 874
tort—
    mentally disordered person, by,
        761n^4
    recommending doctor's liability in,
        849n^5
transfer direction—
    meaning, 892
    cessation—
        civil prisoner, in case of, 898
        person committed in custody for
            trial or sentence, 896
        person remanded in custody by
            magistrates' court, 897
        person serving sentence of
            imprisonment, 892
    circumstances for, 892
    delay, whether infringement of human
        rights, 892n^{10}
    effect, 892
    expiry. *See* cessation *above*
    judicial review of failure to transfer,
        892n^{10}
    life prisoner becoming mental
        patient, 895n^{13}
    person no longer requiring
        treatment, 895
    person serving sentence of
        imprisonment, 892n^1

MENTALLY DISORDERED PERSON
    OR PATIENT—*continued*
transfer direction—*continued*
    power to specify hospital, 892n^{10}
    prisoner—
        generally, 893
        not treatable, where, 895n^{10}
        removal of restriction, 894n^9
        serving sentence of imprisonment,
            892n^1
        tariff expiring, no reference to
            Parole Board, 895n^{10}
        under sentence, 895
    restricting discharge of prisoner
        removed from hospital, 894
    restriction direction—
        meaning, 894n^8
        cessation, 894n^9
        person no longer requiring
            treatment, 895
        removal, 894n^9
    sentence etc continuing to run,
        892n^{10}
    'technical lifers', human rights
        consideration, 894n^8
transfer of patient—
    alien patients, removal, 907
    Channel Islands and Isle of Man—
        from, 905
        to, 906
    conveyance to hospital, necessary
        conditions, 891
    effect, 890
    guardianship to guardianship,
        authority for transfer, 888
    guardianship to hospital—
        authority for transfer, 889
        reference to tribunal, 964
    hospital to guardianship, authority for
        transfer, 887
    hospital to hospital, authority for
        transfer, 887
    Northern Ireland—
        from, 904
        to, 903
    prisoner, removal to hospital. *See*
        transfer direction *above*
    regulations, power to make, 886
    Scotland—
        from—
            conditionally discharged
                patients, 902
            detained patients, 900
            subject to compulsion in the
                community, where, 901
        to, 899

MENTALLY DISORDERED PERSON
    OR PATIENT—*continued*
  treatment—
    advance decision—
      not conflicting with, 939
      valid and applicable, 939n[12]
    child community patient. *See* child
      community patient *above*
    community patient not recalled to
      hospital. *See* community patient
      not recalled to hospital *above*
    compulsory admission for. *See*
      treatment, compulsory admission
      for *below*
    consent to. *See* consent to treatment
      above
    emergency treatment where patient
      lacking capacity or competence,
      943
    objection to, 941n[6]
    Part 4A certificate, 944
  treatment, compulsory admission for—
    application for, procedure, 768
    appropriate medical treatment,
      768n[13]
    consent to treatment provisions,
      applicability, 768n[9]
    false entry or statement, wilfully
      making, 1009
    general guidance on assessment,
      768n[4]
    generally, 768
    grounds for admission, 768
    'nature', detention on ground of,
      768n[9]
    proper purpose of detention, 768n[12]
    subsequent detention, following
      earlier discharge, 768n[6]
    tribunal, patient's application to, 768
    unlawful detention, remedy, 768n[4]
    who may apply for admission, 767n[7]
  trustee, replacement, 564
  unlawful sexual activity with, 1012
  Wales in—
    former user of secondary mental
      health services, assessment of. *See*
      former user of secondary mental
      health services, assessment of
      above
    legislation, 757
    review of legislation by Welsh
      Ministers, 757n[5]

NATIONAL ASSEMBLY FOR WALES
  mentally disordered member, detention,
    782

NATIONAL HEALTH SERVICE
  mental health services, 574
NEAREST RELATIVE
  meaning, 839
  mentally disordered patient, of—
    acting, country court's power to
      appoint. *See under* COUNTY
      COURT
    See also under MENTALLY DISORDERED
      PERSON OR PATIENT
NECESSARIES
  mentally disordered person's contract
    for, 613
  necessary: meaning, 613n[1]
NORTHERN IRELAND
  mentally disordered patient. *See under*
    MENTALLY DISORDERED PERSON OR
    PATIENT
NURSE
  mental health services. *See* MENTAL
    HEALTH NURSE
OFFENDER
  mental disorder, suffering from. *See*
    under MENTALLY DISORDERED
    PERSON OR PATIENT
PAROLE BOARD
  life prisoner becoming mental patient,
    895n[13]
  tariff expiring in case of mentally
    disordered patient, 895n[10]
PARTNER
  mental disorder, 616
PATIENT
  mentally disordered. *See* MENTALLY
    DISORDERED PERSON OR PATIENT
PATRONAGE (ECCLESIASTICAL)
  mentally disordered person, 727n[13]
PENSION
  mental health services, employment in,
    837
PLACE OF SAFETY
  mentally disordered person, for. *See*
    under MENTALLY DISORDERED
    PERSON OR PATIENT
POCKET MONEY
  mentally disordered in-patent, for, 568,
    594, 783
POSTAL PACKET
  mentally disordered patient, sent by,
    780
POWER OF ATTORNEY
  lunatic, granted by, 600n[1]
  mental disorder, effect, 600
PRACTICE DIRECTION
  Court of Protection, 741
  First-tier Tribunal, 966

PRESUMPTION
  mental capacity, 598
PRIMARY CARE TRUST
  meaning, 575n^6
  after-care services, duty to provide, 945
  arrangements for special cases,
    notification procedure, 576
  hospital and specialist services,
    administration of, 575
PRIMARY MENTAL HEALTH
  ASSESSMENT. *See under* MENTALLY
  DISORDERED PERSON OR PATIENT
PRISONER
  mental disorder, removal to hospital. *See*
    MENTALLY DISORDERED PERSON OR
    PATIENT (transfer direction)
PRIVATE INTERNATIONAL LAW
  Mental Capacity Act 2005, provisions
    under, 561
PROPERTY
  Court of Protection dealing with. *See*
    under COURT OF PROTECTION
PUBLIC GUARDIAN
  annual report by, 752
  applications to court, power to make,
    752n^1
  co-operative nature of functions, 752n^4
  Court of Protection, and—
    Court of Protection Visitor, directions
      to, 749
    court's power to require report from,
      744
    deputy's provision of security to, 736
    submission of report to, 736
    supervisory powers, 739
    visits. *See* visit by *below*
  functions—
    generally, 752
    information, power to request, 754
    registers, as to. *See* registers *below*
    security for discharge of, 755
  generally, 751
  lasting power of attorney, information
    from donees of, 754
  officers and staff etc, provision of, 751
  powers, 752
  Public Guardian Board, establishment
    and functions etc, 756
  registers—
    disclosure of information, 753
    functions as to, 753
    search of, duties in connection with,
      753
  remuneration, 751
  security for discharge of functions—
    bond, given by way of, 755n^2

PUBLIC GUARDIAN—*continued*
  security for discharge of
    functions—*continued*
      compliance with requirement to give,
        755n^3
      discharge of security, 755
      generally, 755
  visit by—
    interview during, 744, 752
    notification requirements, 749
    provisions, applicable, 749
    report, disclosure, 749
REMAND
  hospital, to, for report or treatment in
    case of mental illness, 862, 865
REMUNERATION
  Court of Protection Visitor, 748
  medical practitioner, of, 835, 928n^{10}
  Public Guardian, 751
RESTRICTION ORDER
  offender suffering from mental illness
    etc. *See* MENTALLY DISORDERED
    PERSON OR PATIENT (restriction
    order)
SALE
  mentally disordered person's property,
    of, 729
SCOTLAND
  mentally disordered patient. *See under*
    MENTALLY DISORDERED PERSON OR
    PATIENT
SECRETARY OF STATE
  meaning, 567n^1
  delegation of functions, 570
  generally, 567
  restriction order, powers where patient
    subject to, 876
SERVICE (DOCUMENTS)
  mentally disordered patient—
    admission to hospital, 850
    community treatment order, 850
    guardianship order, 850
    pre-paid first class post, sent by, 850n^6
SETTLEMENT OF PROPERTY
  mentally disordered person's property,
    of, 730
SEXUAL OFFENCE
  mentally disordered person, unlawful
    sexual activity with, 1012
SOCIAL SECURITY BENEFIT
  mentally disordered person, receipt on
    behalf of, 593
SOCIAL SERVICES
  mentally disordered person. *See*
    AFTER-CARE; LOCAL SOCIAL
    SERVICES AUTHORITY

References are to paragraph numbers; superior figures refer to notes

SOLICITOR
mentally disordered client, 994

SPECIAL EDUCATIONAL NEEDS
child with, local authority's duty to
identify and assist, 592

SPECIAL HEALTH AUTHORITY
meaning, 575n[5]
hospital and specialist services,
administration of, 575

STOCK TRANSFER
mentally disordered person, 728

STRATEGIC HEALTH AUTHORITY
meaning, 575n[4]
hospital and specialist services,
administration of, 575

SUPERVISED COMMUNITY
TREATMENT. *See* COMMUNITY
TREATMENT ORDER

TORT
mentally disordered person, by, 761n[4]
recommending doctor's liability in,
849n[5]

TRANSFER DIRECTION. *See under*
MENTALLY DISORDERED PERSON OR
PATIENT

TRIBUNAL
England, for. *See* FIRST-TIER TRIBUNAL
Wales, for. *See* MENTAL HEALTH REVIEW
TRIBUNAL FOR WALES

TRUSTEE
mental disorder, replacement due to,
564

UPPER TRIBUNAL
appeal to—
First-tier Tribunal, from, 958
Mental Health Review Tribunal for
Wales, from, 958

VISITOR
Court of Protection Visitor. *See* COURT
OF PROTECTION VISITOR
hospital visitor, payment of travelling
expenses, 568

VOTING
mentally disordered person, 565, 629

WALES
care coordinator in. *See* CARE
COORDINATOR
deprivation of liberty provisions,
supervision of, 719
independent mental health advocate. *See*
under INDEPENDENT MENTAL
HEALTH ADVOCATE
local primary mental health treatment:
meaning, 586n[4]

WALES—*continued*
local primary mental health support
services—
meaning, 587
agreement as to, 586
alteration, 586
cooperation and joint working
between various bodies, 590
duty to provide, 589
failure to agree schemes, 588
housing or well-being services,
587n[10]
information sharing, 591
joint schemes for provision of, 586
local mental health partners, 586n[1]
primary care provider, 587n[7]
primary mental health assessment. *See*
under MENTALLY DISORDERED
PERSON OR PATIENT
scope of services provided in scheme,
586n[6]
services: meaning, 587n[10]
Welsh Ministers' powers, 586n[1]
writing, scheme recorded in, 586n[2]
Mental Capacity Act 2005,
representative appointed under,
711
secondary mental health service, 586n[6]
Welsh Ministers, mental health
functions, 567

WARD OF COURT
admission to hospital for mental
disorder, 786
community treatment order in respect
of, 786
guardianship application, prohibition on
making, 786

WELSH MINISTERS
legislation, power to review, 757n[5]
mental health functions, 567
regulations, power to make, 586n[1],
806n[2], 855
tribunal, powers and duties to refer
cases to, 965

WILFUL NEGLECT
Mental Capacity Act 2005, under, 1011
Mental Health Act 1983, under, 1010

WILL (TESTAMENT)
Court of Protection's power to execute,
615, 731
mentally disordered person's capacity,
615
statutory will—
drafting, 731
execution, 731

References are to paragraph numbers; superior figures refer to notes

WITNESS
  First-tier Tribunal, exclusion from
    hearing, 976
  mental competence—
    civil litigation, 1003
    criminal litigation, 1005

WITNESS—*continued*
  Mental Health Review Tribunal for
    Wales, exclusion from hearing, 990

YOUTH COURT
  hospital order, power to make, 872

Words and Phrases

Words in parentheses indicate the context in which the word or phrase is used

abbreviated advertisement, 339n[1]

absent without leave (from hospital), 918n[4]

accessory (medical device), 473n[4], 475n[4]

accused person, 862n[3, 8]

active implantable medical device, 474n[4]

additional supply optometrist, 79n[20]

administer (medicinal product), 25n[4]

adult placement carer, 856n[9]

advanced electronic signature, 275n[18]

advanced therapy medicinal product, 23

adverse event, 132n[3]

adverse reaction, 70n[6], 132n[3]

advertisement, 333

advisory body (human medicines), 33n[1]

aerosol (medicinal product), 282n[9]

age assessment, 671

allopathic medicinal product, 187n[5]

amphetamine, 484n[3]

animal—
  (medical devices), 473n[6]
  (veterinary medicines), 387n[2]

approval function, 570n[3]

approved clinician, 831

approved mental health professional, 815n[2]

Article 126a authorisation, 141n[6]

assemble—
  (investigational medicinal product), 97n[4]
  (medicinal product), 141n[8]

association agreement, 475n[4]

authorisation (human medicines), 26n[3, 8]

authorised representative, 475n[4]

best interests assessment, 674

best interests assessor, 675n[4], 708n[10], 710n[1]

biomedical research institution, 464n[8]

blood, 449n[2]

blood component, 13n[2], 25n[7], 449n[3]

blood establishment, 453n[4]

blood product, 449n[4]

board (body corporate), 536n[5]

British approved name, 66n[21], 94n[15]

business (medicinal products), 52n[10], 113n[2]

cannabinol derivatives, 484n[4]

cannabis, 484n[5]

cannabis resin, 484n[6]

care and treatment plan, 855n[17]

care order, 839n[16]

care trust, 638n[1]

cared for, 839n[7]

carer, 856n[9]

CE marking, 473n[4]

cell (human), 13n[1]

certificate of registration, 141n[4]

chief investigator (clinical trial), 114n[3]

civil partner, 838n[3], 839n[12]

Class A drug, 481

Class B drug, 481

Class C drug, 481

clinical management plan, 274n[6], 493n[15]

clinical trial, 18n[1], 107

coastal voyage, 355n[8]

coca leaf, 483n[3]

collection and delivery arrangement, 306n[4]

commissioning body, 813n[1]

community patient, 797n[4]

community practitioner nurse prescriber, 271n[11]

concentrate of poppy-straw, 483n[8]

conditionally discharged patient, 966n[15]

consumer goods, 477n[9]

contact lens specialist, 79n[25]

container, 97n[4]

contract laboratory, 452n[12]

controlled drug, 481

convey (person in legal custody), 776n[1]

convicted mental patient, 921n[1]

Court of Protection Visitor, 748

cross-border body, 514n[1]

current scientific knowledge, 174n[4], 179n[17], 225n[5]

custom-made device, 473n[15], 474n[15]

customary occasion (gifts made on), 620n[3]

cyanogenic substances, 26n[11]

deferral (blood donation), 451n[3]

dentist, 48n[6], 487n[9], 534n[14]

detained resident, 662n[6]

device for performance evaluation, 475n[16]

director (Veterinary Medicines Regulations 2012), 448n[2]

disease, 25n[3]

distribution, 449n[4]

doctor, 48n[6], 487n[9], 534n[14]

donor (blood), 468n[1]

donor carer (blood safety and quality), 456n[20]

References are to paragraph numbers; superior figures refer to notes

drug (controlled), 513n[3]
EEA health professional, 271n[16]
EEA state (clinical trial), 107n[1]
electronic signature, 114n[11]
eligibility assessment, 675
enforcement authority (clinical trials), 137n[4]
engineered (cells or tissues), 23n[4]
ethics committee (clinical trial), 111n[2]
EU marketing authorisation, 141n[3]
EU single assessment procedure, 256n[2]
European Pharmacopoeia, 66n[21]
excluded product (Human Medicines Regulations 2012), 301n[3]
export (human medicines), 55n[5], 106n[20]
extension of marketing authorisation, 11n[6]
external use (medicinal product), 300n[5], 312n[3], 313n[2]
facility (blood safety and quality), 464n[8]
financial interest (
food (Poisons Rules 1982), 545n[4]
free circulation in member states, 311n[10], 312n[8], 313n[8]
gene therapy advisory committee, 111n[2]
gene therapy medicinal product, 23n[1]
good manufacturing practice, 12n[5]
health and social services board, 111n[9]
health board, 111n[9]
health care, 113n[7], 514n[6]
health care professional, 36n[8], 113n[5]
health centre, 52n[4]
health prescription, 275n[14], 509n[25]
hearing aid dispenser, 478n[16]
herbal medicinal product, 51n[2]
home-going ship, 355n[8]
homoeopathic medicinal product, 187n[1]
homoeopathic remedy, 409n[1]
hospital, 52n[3], 113n[23], 458n[1], 577
hospital blood bank, 458n[1]
hospital premises, 569n[3]
housing or well-being services, 587n[10]
human adverse reaction, 430n[9]
husband, 838n[3], 839n[12]
idiot, 559
immediate packaging, 278n[5]
impairing condition, 631n[5]
import, 55[5], 97n[5]
in vitro diagnostic medical device, 475n[4]
indemnity arrangement, 697n[3]
independent advocacy services, 780n[40]
independent clinic, 288n[7], 458n[1]
independent hospital, 578n[7]
independent medical agency, 288n[8]
information period, 38n[3]
inland waters, 355n[8]

in-patient, 770n[3], 966n[2]
inspection (blood banks and facilities), 464n[2]
insurance or indemnity, 115n[26]
intended for clinical investigation, 472n[1]
intended purpose (medical device), 472n[1]
international non-proprietary name, 66n[21], 94n[14]
investigational medicinal product, 18n[6], 107n[1]
investigational medicinal product dossier, 106n[22]
investigator (clinical trial), 113n[4]
investigator's brochure (clinical trial), 108n[2], 115n[19]
ionising radiation, 382n[1]
labelling, 97n[4]
learning disability, 761n[8]
letter (Human Medicines Regulations 2012), 261n[9]
licensed service (OFCOM), 350n[4]
licensing authority, 35n[1]
life-sustaining treatment, 606n[9]
listed seller of Part II poisons, 540n[12]
local authority—
  (deprivation of liberty provisions), 664n[7, 10, 13]
  (independent mental capacity advocates), 635n[10]
  (listed sellers of poisons), 535
  (local primary mental health support services), 586n[1]
local authority area (Wales), 586n[1]
local primary mental health support services, 587
local social services authority, 579
lunatic, 559n[2]
madness, 559n[3]
major variation of type II, 11n[4]
managers (hospitals and registered establishments), 778
manufacture—
  (investigational medicinal product), 97n[3]
  (medicinal product), 141n[7]
  (veterinary medicinal product), 410
manufacturer—
  (medical device), 472n[1]
  (medicinal product), 449n[4]
manufacturing authorisation (clinical trial) 98
manufacturer's licence, 45
marketing authorisation—
  (clinical trial), 107n[1]
  (investigational medicinal product), 47n[3]

References are to paragraph numbers; superior figures refer to notes

marketing authorisation—*continued*
  (requirement for), 141n[3]
  (wholesaler dealer's licence), 77n[6], 85n[6], 86n[8]
medical device, 472
medical exposure (radioactive medicinal product), 298n[3]
medical supplies, 2n[2]
medical treatment, 926
medicated animal feeding stuff, 547n[1]
medicinal opium, 483n[6]
medicinal product—
  (for human use), 25
  (United Kingdom turnover), 30n[8]
mental capacity assessment, 673
mental defectiveness, 559n[7]
mental disorder, 559[10, 12], 761
mental health assessment, 672
mental health patient, 658n[21]
mental health service providers, 851n[1]
mental hospital, 565n[3]
mental impairment, 559n[13]
minor variation of type 1A, 11n[3]
minor variation of type 1B, 11n[5]
mixing of medicines, 50n[2]
monitored publication, 251n[13]
monograph name, 66n[21], 94n[15]
mutual recognition agreements, 476n[3]
nearest relative, 839
NHS body, 638n[1]
no refusals assessment, 676
nominated medical attendant, 792n[4]
non-interventional trial (clinical trial), 107n[2]
non-medicinal poison, 532n[2]
non-viable, 472n[12]
notified body, 476n[3]
nurse (blood safety and quality), 456n[20]
nurse independent prescriber, 50n[3], 492n[8]
operating department practitioner, 494n[8]
optometrist independent prescriber, 271n[13]
outer packaging, 278n[5]
package (medicinal product), 51n[48]
package leaflet (medicinal product), 68n[5]
paediatric indication, 181n[11]
parallel import licence, 147n[2]
parenteral administration, 274n[4]
patient, 758n[4]
patient (blood etc administered to), 468n[1]
patient group direction, 286n[20]
person, 151n[8]
person lawfully conducting a retail pharmacy business, 493n[6]
person qualified to prescribe or supply medicinal products, 333

person responsible for management of a hospital blood bank, 458n[1]
personal records, 510n[6]
personally examined, 849n[6]
pharmaceutical form of an active substance, 107n[1]
pharmaceutical list, 3
pharmaceutical quality assurance, 12n[7]
pharmaceutical services, 3
pharmacist, 52n[5], 98n[9]
pharmacist independent prescriber, 50n[4], 492n[7]
pharmacovigilance system, 15n[1], 243n[2]
pharmacovigilance system master file, 246n[3]
pharmacy medicine, 26
place of safety, 868n[4], 922n[10]
placing on the market (medical device), 472n[1]
poison, 528n[1], 539n[11]
poppy-straw, 483n[7]
port health authority (sale of poisons), 542n[14]
post-authorisation efficacy study, 162n[6]
practitioner, 487n[9]
premises—
  (controlled drugs, closure of premises), 499n[1]
  (Veterinary Medicines Regulations 2011), 444n[2]
preparation (controlled drug), 483n[19], 508n[3]
prescription only medicine, 26
presentation (medicines), 2n[6]
pressure (undue pressure), 622n[3]
primary care provider, 587n[7]
primary care trust, 575n[6]
primary medical services, 882n[3]
primary mental health assessment, 883
prison service, 290n[7]
private guardian, 792n[2]
product information, 174n[3]
professional register (nursing and midwifery), 50n[3], 492n[6]
property, 619n[2]
protected party, 995n[1]
protective measures, 641n[4]
psychopathic disorder, 559n[14]
public place (removal of mentally disordered persons in), 923n[2]
publication (advertisement), 334n[5]
publish (advertisement), 334n[5]
putting into service (medical device), 473n[3]
qualified health professional (blood safety and quality), 456n[20]

qualified person (manufacturing authorisation), 104n[2]

radioactive medicinal product, 298n[2], 382n[4]

radionuclide, 25n[9]

radionuclide generator, 148n[5]

radionuclide kit, 148n[6]

radionuclide precursor, 148n[7]

radiopharmaceutical, 148n[2]

reasonably calculated, 537n[3]

registered dispensing optician, 79n[22]

registered establishment, 578

registered midwife, 48n[3]

registered nurse, 48n[3]

registered optometrist, 36n[8]

registered pharmacy, 52n[2]

registered provider, 288n[10]

regulated medicinal product (child resistant container), 315n[1]

relating to him personally, 536n[5]

relative, 838

relevant allopathic substance, 187n[5]

relevant manager, 288n[22]

relevant needs assessment, 674n[8]

relevant post-authorisation safety study, 260n[1]

relevant prescriber (Human Medicines Regulations 2012), 281n[5]

reporting year—
 (blood establishment), 456n[31]
 (clinical trial), 134n[1]

residence order, 839n[20]

responsible clinician, 834

responsible deputy (Poisons Rules 1982), 540n[15]

responsible person (blood establishment), 455n[2]

restriction direction, 894n[8]

restriction order, 869, 875n[6]

retail dealer (supply of drugs), 506n[1], 509n[29]

risk management plan, 16n[7], 160n[5]

risk management system, 16n[5], 74n[6]

risk-benefit balance, 395n[4]

sale by way of wholesale dealing (poisons), 541n[21]

secondary mental health service, 586n[6]

serious adverse event—
 (blood safety and quality), 452n[7]
 (clinical trials), 132n[3]

serious adverse reaction, 71n[8], 132n[3], 430n[8], 452n[7]

serious breach (good clinical practice), 128n[4]

serious medical treatment, 638n[2]

severe mental impairment, 559n[15]

single-use combination product, 473n[4]

site (blood establishment), 453n[8]

somatic cell therapy medicinal product, 23n[2]

special health authority, 575n[5]

special medicinal product, 269n[6]

specialist group or committee, 115n[2]

specimen receptacle, 475n[4]

sponsor (clinical trial), 107

stable derivatives device, 472n[8]

stocks, 728n[6]

strategic health authority, 111n[9], 575n[4]

subject (clinical trial), 107n[1]

substance (medicinal product), 25n[2]

summary of the product characteristics (medicinal product), 55n[11]

supervision order, 874n[5], 875n[7]

supplementary prescriber, 50n[5]

supply (medical product), 473n[7]

suspected (in relation to adverse reaction), 70n[7]

S4C Digital, 350n[5]

technical lifer, 894n[8]

temporary class drug, 481

third country—
 (clinical trial), 121n[5]
 (sale or supply of medicinal products), 311n[11], 312n[9], 313n[9]

tissue—
 (human), 13n[1]
 (Medical Devices Regulations 2002), 472n[10]

tissue engineered product, 23

traceability (blood or blood component), 458n[8]

traditional herbal medicinal product, 155n[6]

traditional herbal registration, 141n[5]

transfer direction, 892

treatment, 606n[9]

trial site (clinical trial), 113n[4]

UK marketing authorisation, 141n[3]

unexpected adverse reaction, 132n[3]

unexpected serious adverse reaction, 132n[3]

United Kingdom turnover (medicinal products), 30n[7]

vaccine, 297n[2]

valid application (variation of manufacturing authorisation), 105n[5]

validation (blood establishment's testing and processes), 456n[7]

veterinary medicinal product, 387

veterinary practitioner, 487n[9], 534n[14]

veterinary surgeon, 487n[9], 534n[14]

wasted costs, 747n[5]

References are to paragraph numbers; superior figures refer to notes

wholesale dealer, $509n^{24}$

wholesale dealer's licence, 77

wife, $838n^3$, $839n^{12}$

wilfully, $551n^1$

writing, $507n^2$

year, $535n^9$

ML

**Books are to be returned on or before
the last date below.**